Proceedings of

EuroCogSci07

The European Cognitive Science Conference 2007

European Cultural Center of Delphi
Delphi/Greece
May 23–27, 2007

University of Athens

Jointly organized by
the **Cognitive Science Society,**
the **Hellenic Cognitive Science Society,** and
the **Graduate Program in Basic and Applied Cognitive Science**
National and Kapodistrian University of Athens.

Edited by:
Stella Vosniadou, Daniel Kayser & Athanassios Protopapas

Routledge
Taylor & Francis Group
LONDON AND NEW YORK

First published 2007 by Lawrence Erlbaum Associates

Published 2017 by Routledge
2 Park Square, Milton Park, Abingdon, Oxon OX14 4RN
711 Third Avenue, New York, NY 10017, USA

First issued in hardback 2017

Routledge Press is an imprint of the Taylor & Francis Group, an informa business

British Library Cataloguing in Publication Data
A catalogue record for this book is available from the British Library

Library of Congress Cataloging in Publication Data
A catalogue record for this book has been requested

ISBN 13: 978-1-138-41161-6 (hbk)
ISBN 13: 978-1-84169-696-6 (pbk)

Table of contents

Papers presented as posters

Posters

Preface

This volume contains the invited lectures, invited symposia, symposia, papers and posters presented at the 2nd European Cognitive Science Conference, in Delphi, Greece, May 23–27. The 2007 European Cognitive Science Conference – EuroCogSci07 – is the second European Conference in Cognitive Science to be held under the auspices of the Cognitive Science Society. The first such Conference – EuroCogSci03 – took place in Osnabrück, Germany in 2003 and was organized by Franz Schmalhofer and Richard Young.

EuroCogSci07 follows a long tradition of European Meetings in Cognitive Science including a series of biennial meetings with the title "European Conference on Cognitive Science" (E.C.C.S.). The first E.C.C.S. was held in 1995 in St. Malo (France), the second in Manchester (U.K.), and the third in Sienna (Italy). In 2001, the Cognitive Science Society held its first non-North American Conference in Edinburgh (U.K.), organized by Keith Stenning and Johanna Moore. The success of the meeting prompted European researchers to propose that the Cognitive Science Society holds its meeting in Europe once every three years and also that it sponsors a series of regional European Conferences to be held every four years. The University of Osnabrück was the selected site for the first of these meetings.

The papers presented in this volume range from empirical psychological studies and computational models to philosophical arguments, meta-analyses and even to neuroscientific experimentation. The quality of the work shows that the Cognitive Science Society community in Europe is an exciting and vibrant one. There are 210 contributions by cognitive scientists from 27 different countries, including USA (33), France (29), UK (23), Germany (21), Greece (19), Italy (12), Belgium (11), Japan (6), Spain (5), Bulgaria (5), the Netherlands (5), Australia (4), Canada (4), Cyprus (4), Finland (4), Ireland (4), Switzerland (4), Russia (3), Sweden (3), Norway (2), Poland (2), Singapore (2), Argentina, Austria, Brazil, Israel, and South Korea.

An international program committee with members from 12 European countries, Australia, and the United States, and a panel of 321 reviewers from around the world, helped us in the selection of the best papers. A total of 211 six-page papers and 96 one-page "poster abstracts" were submitted for review. From these, 85 papers were accepted for oral presentation and for publication in this volume. An additional 68 six-page papers and 68 one-page submissions were accepted for poster presentation and publication.

We would like to acknowledge help from the following sources who contributed to the success of the conference: The Cognitive Science Society Board, for inviting us to host the EuroCogSci07 and for providing the framework, expertise, and support; the Program Committee, who assigned submissions to referees, read their resulting reviews and made final recommendations to the chairs; the reviewers, who reviewed the submissions and gave feedback to the committee and to the authors; the Local Organizing Committee, and the Students of the Local Organizing Committee, who helped with the myriad local arrangements for the meeting; and the many volunteers, who contributed to the success of the Conference. Our special thanks go especially to Svetlana-Lito Gerakakis for providing extremely helpful administrative support. We are also thankful to the University of Athens Cognitive Science Lab secretary, S. Efthymiou for secretarial support.

We would also like to thank the Invited Speakers: Margaret Boden, Cristiano Castelfranchi, Jerry Fodor, Catherine Fuchs, Randy Gallistel, Rochel Gelman, Gerd Gigerenzer, and Nancy Nersessian; the Organizers of the Invited Symposia: Tatiana Chernigovskaya, Erik De Corte, Stefan Frank, Peter Gärdenfors, Dedre Gentner, Kenneth Hugdahl, Boicho Kokinov, Konstantinos Moutoussis, and Hedderik van Rijn; all those who submitted proposals, for their considerable effort and for their interest in the conference; the authors and symposium participants, for the preparation and presentation of their work; and all those who attended the conference and made it what it was.

Finally, we wish to acknowledge the following for their financial contributions to the conference, and to thank them for their support: European Office of Aerospace Research and Development – Air Force Office of Scientific Research – United States Air Force Research Laboratory, Association pour la Recherche Cognitive, British Council of Greece, Cognitive Science Society, Education Research Center of Greece, Endolysi-Medical Technologies, French Embassy of Greece, Info-Quest, Institut Français d'Athènes, Istituto Italiano di Cultura di Atene, Laboratoire d'Informatique de Paris-Nord, Greek Ministry of National Education and Religious Affairs, Office of Naval Research, Olympic Airlines, Plus Orthopedics Hellas SA, University of Athens, University of Paris-Nord.

Stella Vosniadou, Daniel Kayser, and Athanassios Protopapas

May 2007

EuroCogSci07

May 23-27, 2007

European Cultural Center of Delphi

Program Chairs

Stella Vosniadou (National and Kapodistrian
  University of Athens, Greece)
Daniel Kayser (Université Paris Nord, France)

International Program Committee

Maria Teresa Bajo Molina (Spain)
Bruno Bara (Italy)
Cristiano Castelfranchi (Italy)
Fintan Costello (Ireland)
Michel Denis (France)
Robert French (CNRS, France)
Peter Gärdenfors (Sweden)
Dedre Gentner (USA)
Gerd Gigerenzer (Germany)
Christopher Habel (Germany)
Boicho Nikolov Kokinov (Bulgaria)
Jesus M. Larrazabal (Spain)
Daniel Navarro (Australia)
Nancy Nersessian (USA)
Jean – Luc Nespoulous (France)
Mike Oaksford (UK)
Fabio Paglieri (Italy)
Massimo Poesio (UK)
Emmanuel M. Pothos (UK)
Athanassios Raftopoulos (Cyprus)
Franz Schmalhofer (Germany)
Gale Sinatra (USA)
Matti Sintonen (Finland)
Peter Slezak (Australia)
Gerhard Strube (Germany)
John Taplin (Australia)
Maarten Van Someren (Netherlands)
Bernard Victorri (France)
Richard M Young (UK)

Conference Secretariat

Svetlana Lito Gerakakis

Electronic Submission and Review Site Administration

Athanassios Protopapas

Local Organizing Committee

Georgios Giftodimos
Maria Grigoriadou
Georgios Kouroupetroglou
Alexandra Oikonomou
Stathis Psillos
Petros Roussos
Stavroula Samartzi
Fotini Stilianopoulou
Petros Tzelepidis

Graduate students of the Local Organising Committee

Constantinos Christou
Rania Gikopoulou
Kalliopi Ikospentaki
Philippos Katsoulis
Maria Koulianou
Katerina Ligovanli
Georgia Rovatsou
Irini Skopeliti
Stergios Tegos
Xenia Vamvakoussi

Student Volunteers

Panajotis Blitsas
Giorgos Briskolas
Aspasia Kanelou
Thanos Kremizis
Eleftheria-Maria Pattakou
Despina Sakoulogeorga
Maria Stournara
Amalia Syrgounioti

Reviewers

Brandon Abbs
Marianne Abramson
Afra Alishahi
Jedediah Allen
Janet Andrews
Christa S.C. Asterhan
Dilip Athreya
Roger Azevedo
Joscha Bach
Teresa Bajo
Benjamin Balas
Gianluca Baldassarre
Jerry Ball
Bruno G. Bara
Luke Barrington
Lawrence Barsalou
William Bechtel
Giovanni Bennardo
Bettina Berendt
Nadia Berthouze
Lisa Best
Maryse Bianco
Zafer Bilda
Nik Nailah Binti Abdullah
Henrike Blumenfeld
Tibor Bosse
Lewis Bott
Ken Brown
Duncan Brumby
Raff Calitri
Thomas Capo
Laura Carlson
Cristiano Castelfranchi
Stephanie Chambaron
Christine Chan
Franklin Chang
Tatiana Chernigovskaya
Seth Chin-Parker
Key-Sun Choi
Georgios Christou
Evangelia Chrysikou
Adam Chuderski
Bill Clancey
Catherine Clement
Charles Clifton
James Close
Cheryl Cohen
Louise Connell
Fofi Constantinidou
Rick Cooper
Adam Corner
James Corter
Rui Costa

Fintan Costello
Rick Dale
Moritz M. Daum
Eddy Davelaar
Jim Davies
Michel Denis
Natacha Deroost
Cathy Desoto
Barry Devereux
Denise Dillon
Mike Dowman
Kevin Dunbar
Nicholas Duran
Lisa Durrance
Karine Duvignau
Simon Dymond
Jeronimo Dzaack
Inge-Marie Eigsti
Michelle Ellefson
Shira Elqayam
Stephanie Elzer
Tanja Engelmann (née Keller)
Susan Epstein
Martha Evens
Michele Feist
Anne Fernald
Roland Fernandez
Philip Fernbach
Mark Finlayson
Brian Fisher
Robin Flanagan
Kristine Flood
Stephani Foraker
Tim Fosker
Stefan Frank
Bob French
Daniel Freudenthal
Caren Frosch
Danilo Fum
Francesco Gagliardi
David Galbraith
Joao Gama
Peter Gardenfors
Margarida Garrido
Dedre Gentner
Claudia Gianelli
Marco Giunti
Fernand Gobet
Winston Goh
Ariel Goldberg
Laura Gonnerman
Arthur Graesser
Floriana Grasso
Ann Grbavec
Collin Green

Michelle Greene
Thomas Griffiths
Maurice Grinberg
Martin Groen
Joshua Gross
Amal Guha
Michelle Gumbrecht
Glenn Gunzelmann
Christopher Habel
James Hampton
Oliver Hardt
K. David Harrison
Sebastien Helie
Tatjana S. Hilbert
Paul Hodgson
John Hoeks
Elena Hoicka
Jessica Horst
Penka Hristova
Evgenia Hristova
Janet Hui-Wen Hsiao
Sylvie Huet
Markus Huff
Almut Hupbach
Fumihito Ikeda
Armina Janyan
Tiffany Jastrzembski
Melander Johns
Jeffrey Johnson
Linda Kaastra
Daniel Kayser
John Kearns
Frank Keller
William Kennedy
Tim Kenyon
Laura Kertz
Julian Kiverstein
Sachiko Kiyokawa
Alexander Klippel
Harumi Kobayashi
Boicho Kokinov
Lars Konieczny
Anna Koop
Kepa Korta
Alexander Kranjec
Josef Krems
Ben Krose
Sven Kuehne
Kai-Uwe Kühnberger
David Lagnado
David Landy
Jesus Maria Larrazabal
Jorge Larreamendy-Joerns
Sangmok Lee
Hye-Won Lee

Louis Lee
Benoit Lemaire
Margarita Limon
Craig Lindley
Alexandre Linhares
Daniel Little
Manuel Liz
Marcio Lobo Netto
Jeffrey Loewenstein
Deryle Lonsdale
Emiliano Lorini
Max Louwerse
Christopher Lucas
Dermot Lynott
Franŋois Livy
Matt Macmahon
Carol J. Madden
Joe Magliano
Lorenzo Magnani
Klara Marton
Fulvio Mastrogiovanni
Michael Matessa
Rachel McCloy
Alastair Mckenzie-Kerr
Sean McLennan
David Mendonca
Arron Metcalfe
Kelly Mix
Naomi Miyake
Sergio Moreira
Francesca Morganti
Bradley Morris
Arthi Murugesan
Shahin Nabavian
Mitchell Nathan
Daniel Navarro
Nancy Nersessian
Jean-Luc Nespoulous
Yuk Han Priscilla Ngan
Eric Nichols
Shusaku Nomura
Laura Novick
Padraig O'Seaghdha
Mike Oaksford
Philipp Otto
Bernard Pachoud
Fabio Paglieri
Thomas Palmeri
Sangho Park
Neal Pearlmutter
Bo Pedersen
David Peebles
Amotz Perlman

Georgi Petkov
Giovanni Pezzulo
Raedy Ping
Massimo Poesio
Thierry Poibeau
Fenna Poletiek
Ferran Pons
Emmanuel Pothos
Athanassios Protopapas
Jennifer Queen
Athanassios Raftopoulos
Christopher Ramey
Tânia Ramos
David Reitter
Irene Reppa
Antonio Rizzo
Hannah Rohde
Michael Romano
C. Anton Rytting
Kayo Sakamoto
Ron Salden
Franco Salvetti
Ava Santos
Megan Saylor
Franz Schmalhofer
Ute Schmid
Michael Schneider
Mike Schoelles
Jonathan Schooler
Wolfgang Schoppek
Holger Schultheis
Gerhard Schurz
Roger Schvaneveldt
Angela Schwering
Christopher Schwint
Yasuhiro Shirai
Gale Sinatra
Matti Sintonen
Peter Slezak
Vladimir Sloutsky
Asha Smith
Derek John Smith
Melanie Soderstrom
Hans Spada
David Spurrett
Narayanan Srinivasan
Edward Stabler
Jim Staszewski
Georgia Stephanou
James Stewart
Terry Stewart
Ted Strauss
Gerhard Strube

Tarja Susi
Biswanath Swain
Emmanuel Sylvestre
Niels Taatgen
Hermina J.M. Tabachneck-Schijf
Vanessa Taler
Andrzej Tarlowski
Eric Taylor
Paul Thagard
Jean-Pierre Thibaut
Scott Thomas
Susan Thompson
Robert Thomson
Andree Tiberghien
Maurizio Tirassa
Marc Tomlinson
Jan Treur
Manos Tsakiris
Paolo Turrini
Ryan Tweney
M. Afzal Upal
Frederic Vallee-Tourangeau
Maurits Van Den Noort
Han Van Der Maas
Frank Van Der Velde
Mija Van Der Wege
Tamara Van Gog
Hedderik Van Rijn
Iris Van Rooij
Maarten Van Someren
Argiro Vatakis
Marga Vazquez
Tom Verguts
Bernard Victorri
Stella Vosniadou
Edward Vul
Samuel Waldron
Paul Ward
Daniel Weiss
Markus Werning
Kathryn Wheeler
Jörg Wittwer
Fei Xu
Jie Yan
Ya-Ting Yang
Sule Yildirim
Michael Yip
Richard Young
Johannes Ziegler
Tom Ziemke
Elena Ziori
Iraide Zipitria

Invited Lectures

Using Information Theory to Better Understand Associative Learning

Randy Gallistel (galliste@ruccs.rutgers.edu)
Rutgers Center for Cognitive Science (RuCCS), Psych Bldg Addition, Busch Campus,
152 Frelinghuysen Road, Rutgers University - New Brunswick, Piscataway, NJ 08854-8020 USA

Abstract

Using Shannon's theory of information to quantify the information that a conditioned stimulus (CS) conveys regarding the timing of the next unconditioned stimulus (US) gives a parameter-free, quantitatively rigorous account of background conditioning, blocking, overshadowing and relative validity, while also giving for the first time an empirically valid specification and quantification of the notion of temporal pairing. These results strengthen the idea, dating back to the 1970s, that what drives the learning that occurs in paradigms designed to establish the laws of association formation is not temporal contiguity but rather the learning of the temporal intervals themselves. Learning those intervals is essential to extracting from a protocol the mutual information between two events. The learning that occurs should be conceptualized as the extraction of that mutual information, not the formation of a conductive connection.

Model-based Reasoning in Distributed Cognitive-Cultural Systems: Studies of interdisciplinary research labs

Nancy J. Nersessian (nancyn@cc.gatech.edu)
School of Interactive Computing, Georgia Institute of Technology
Atlanta, GA 30332-0280, USA

Abstract

This paper will examine "model-based reasoning" in the interplay of representation and experiment in the context of two biomedical engineering research laboratories, where problem solving is by means of constructing, manipulating, and revising physical models. Designing, re-designing, and experimenting with *in vitro* simulation models ("devices") is a signature cognitive practice. These physical models are technological devices that either simulate well-understood mechanisms, such as the forces on arterial vessels from the flow of blood through them, or hypothesized mechanisms, such as how learning takes place among neurons. The devices provide sites of experimentation where *in vitro* models are used to screen and control specific aspects of *in vivo* phenomena that the researchers want to examine. They are constructed and modified in the course of research with respect to problems encountered and changes in understanding. Simulation is an epistemic activity involving exploration, testing, and generation of hypotheses, explanation, prediction, and inference.

In this analysis, I draw on and contribute to research in contemporary cognitive science that construes cognition as a complex system in which cognitive processes are "embodied, "situated" in environments, and "distributed" across people and artifacts. Model-based reasoning in the complex systems of the laboratory is argued to involve simulation processes in which mental and physical models of both the phenomena under investigation and the simulation device are co-constructed, manipulated, and revised. That is, the devices act as 'hubs' for interlocking mental models and experimentation. The design and redesign of a device is thus both driven by changes in the mental models and experimental results and lead to changes in mental models and experimental designs. The discovery processes thus run on a hybrid of internal and external structures. Further devices are hubs of interdisciplinary *melding* of cultural, social, material, and cognitive practices. In particular, the mental models are hybrids of various disciplines, and the structure of the device concretely instantiates this hybrid nature. Modelbased reasoning, thus, needs to be understood as being performed within complex cognitive-cultural systems, distributed in space and time.

Gut Feelings: The Intelligence of the Unconscious

Gerd Gigerenzer (sekgigerenzer@mpib-berlin.mpg.de)
Center for Adaptive Behavior and Cognition, Max Planck Institute for Human Development
Lentzeallee 94, 14195 Berlin, German

Abstract

We think of intelligence as a deliberate, conscious activity guided by the laws of logic. Yet much of our mental life is unconscious, based on processes alien to logic: gut feelings, or intuitions. We have intuitions about sports, friends, the toothpaste to buy, and other dangerous things. We fall in love, and we sense that the Dow Jones will go up. How do these feelings work? I define an intuition as a judgment that (i) appears quickly in consciousness, (ii) whose underlying process we are not aware of, yet (iii) is strong enough to act upon. I argue that the underlying process can often be described by fast and frugal heuristics, which take advantage of evolved capacities of the brain. Good intuitions behave differently from logical systems: more information or more time does not always lead to better decisions. Moreover, in a moderately unpredictable world, simple heuristics can lead to better judgments than can "optimal" models of decision making. The science of intuition studies the processes underlying snap judgments, and the environmental structures in which they fail and succeed.

References

Gigerenzer, G. (2007). *Gut feelings: The intelligence of the unconscious*. New York: Viking Press.

Early Cognitive Development and Beyond

Rochel Gelman (rgelman@ruccs.rutgers.edu)
Rutgers Center for Cognitive Science (RuCCS), Psych Bldg Addition, Busch Campus, 152 Frelinghuysen Road,
Rutgers University - New Brunswick, Piscataway, NJ 08854-8020, USA

Abstract

Any account cognitive development must handle two general facts about knowledge acquisition. Young children, living in reasonably healthy and normal environments of their culture, learn a great deal without formal instruction and often "on the fly".   Indeed, they acquire the language of their community, and develop a set of intuitive understandings of natural number arithmetic, the difference between animate and inanimate objects and the role of causality regarding the transformation and movements of different kinds of objects. In the case of early learnings, children benefit from the existence of skeletal, domain-specific structures. They use these to identify examples of data in the environment that are structural maps. In this sense, some early kinds of learning are privileged. Although some of these structures can foster the accumulation of yet more knowledge in a domain, there are clear cases where this is not the case. Indeed, evidence indicates that early learnings can stand in the way of the mastery of new knowledge with understanding. For example, children's knowledge of natural numbers is inconsistent with the task of learning, with understanding about rational numbers and therefore a conceptual change about the nature of natural numbers. The learning problem is tied to the fact that the mathematical structure for rational numbers does not map readily to that for natural numbers. For example, whereas every natural number has an unique next, this is not so for the rational numbers. Additionally when two natural numbers that are >1 are multiplied, the answer is always greater. However, multiplication of two fractions yields a smaller value. The learning task then becomes one of mounting both a new structure with new entities and the rules of combination. We know that the acquisition of new conceptual structures takes work on the part of the learner and a great deal of time. The question then becomes: what fosters the acquisition of new domains of knowledge. I will propose that a variety of learning tools are called upon to help in the creation of new organized domains of understanding.

The History of Cognitive Science: Seven Key Dates

Margaret A. Boden (maggieb@cogs.susx.ac.uk)
Cognitive and Computing Sciences, University of Sussex
Falmer, Brighton, BN1 9QN, UK

Abstract

Cognitive science has seen seven key dates. The first four were 1943, 1956, 1958, and 1960. Important things happened later, too: in 1969, 1986, and 1987. Those seven years (with 1947 and 1979 as runners-up) all saw seminal publications and/or influential interdisciplinary meetings, in which different methodologies and research opportunities were introduced or highlighted--or, in one case, trenchantly attacked. The current profile of the field has been shaped accordingly.

Introduction

Cognitive science has been studied for some seventy years, and covers six different disciplines: AI/A-Life, psychology, neuroscience, linguistics, anthropology, and philosophy. So distilling its history into just seven dates is highly artificial. The thumbnail sketch that follows is based on the book I've recently written on the topic, where everything mentioned here is explored in greater detail (Boden 2006).

The thematic heart of cognitive science is psychology, and its intellectual heart is AI/A-Life. In other words, it's the study of *mind as machine,* its core assumption being that the same scientific concepts apply to minds and mindlike artefacts.

Since the machines in question are of two main types, there are two major theoretical pathways across the field. One is grounded in logical-symbolic computation, or GOFAI (Good Old-Fashioned AI). The other features adaptive, self-organizing, and/or feedback devices--including certain sorts of connectionist system. We may call them the cybernetic/connectionist and the symbolic--but they both arose out of the cybernetics movement of the 1940s, as we'll see. The field's history has been shaped by the contrasts and competition between these two approaches.

Wartime Thoughts

The first key date within cognitive science is 1943. That wartime year saw three influential publications. The most important was Warren McCulloch and Walter Pitts' essay 'A Logical Calculus of the Ideas Immanent in Nervous Activity'.

This combined three hugely exciting, but *prima facie* highly diverse, ideas of the early twentieth century: neurone theory, the Turing machine, and the Russell-Whitehead propositional calculus. The authors argued that these were formally equivalent. That is: every expression of the propositional calculus could be computed by some Turing machine, which in turn could be physically implemented in some definable neural net. Logic, computation, and the brain were all of a piece.

In seeing the mind/brain as a Turing machine, McCulloch and Pitts weren't thinking only of cognition: for *all* psychological processes, they said, "the fundamental relations are those of two valued logic". Even in psychiatry, they added, "Mind no longer goes 'more ghostly than a ghost'". Formal networks should be the psychologist's goal: "specification of the net would contribute all that could be achieved in [psychology, however defined]".

These ideas inspired John von Neumann immediately, leading him to design his computer as a machine grounded in binary (true/false) logic instead of decimal arithmetic. But their influence on theoretical psychology was delayed, for three reasons. First, the paper appeared in an obscure journal which few psychologists saw. Second, it used a rebarbative logical formalism (borrowed from Rudolf Carnap), guaranteed to repel most readers. And last, it had no connection with the various wartime problems dominating psychologists' minds in 1943. Its significance would be widely realized only later.

McCulloch and Pitts here initiated *both* theoretical pathways of cognitive science. On the one hand, their paper led to the psychologically oriented connectionism of the 1940s/1950s, initially implemented in wire-and-solder contraptions, not in general purpose computers. On the other hand, once digital computers arrived a few years later, their paper was seen to imply that language-based meanings and reasoning could be modelled by them. (McCulloch, in fact, had long been a follower of the logical atomists' philosophy of language). That is, it seemed reasonable to hope both that symbolic AI was possible and that it could be seen as theoretical psychology.

(Four years later, these two authors would admit that their precisely structured logical networks, and unvarying neural thresholds, didn't reflect the noisy, error-prone, and damageable nature of the brain: Pitts and McCulloch 1947. So they now outlined a statistical form of connectionism--and even suggested which parts of the brain perform which types of computation. As the pioneering paper in computational neuroscience, and in distributed computing and probabilistic networks too, this might tempt one to add an *eighth* key date to the list. However, their later paper didn't attract many followers. Moreover, they saw it as an "extension" of the earlier one, whose core claim--that neural networks can be *theoretically* mapped onto binary logic--was specifically repeated. Let's mark 1947, then, as an honourable runner-up.)

While McCulloch and Pitts had been writing their ground-breaking paper, three other members of the cybernetic community--including Norbert Wiener himself--had been analysing "purpose and teleology" in terms of negative feedback (Rosenblueth et al. 1943).

This, they said, could be used so as to reduce the differences between the current state and the goal--an idea that was mentioned in the 'Logical Calculus' paper, too. As they put it, "The signals from the goal are used to restrict outputs which would otherwise go beyond the goal" (p. 19). The examples they listed included heat-seeking missiles, and the muscular overshoot seen (in grasping a glass, for instance) in Parkinsonism. In general, adaptive 'goal-seeking' behaviour of humans and animals was assumed to be controlled in this way.

However, these authors thought of the "goal" as a target, rather than a goal. (In their most persuasive example, heat-seeking missiles, it was exactly that.) The key was perception, not intention. Goals (and sub-goals) considered as imaginary, and intended, future states weren't in question. Nor could they be. For there was no mention of internal models, or representations, of the goal--or of current states of the world.

In the very same year, those very matters were being highlighted across the Atlantic in Kenneth Craik's little book *The Nature of Explanation* (1943). This introduced the notion of cerebral models, borrowed from the neurologist Henry Head, into cognitive psychology and the philosophy of mind (Craik described his book as a work of *philosophy*). And it glossed them, for the first time, in terms of the functioning of man-made machines.

The machines Craik had in mind were analogue devices, such as the tidal predictor and the differential analyser. The representational power of cerebral models, he said, lay in the fact that--like the machines just mentioned--each one was "a physical working model which works in the same way as the process it parallels, in the aspects under consideration at any moment" (1943: 51). And he offered some specific hypotheses about the neurophysiology of various analogue "models" for perception.

Although Craik called his approach "a symbolic theory of thought" and referred to "symbolism" in the brain, he seemed to be thinking of representation in general (including language) rather than the logical-computational variety. He died (in an accident) in 1945, so didn't see the rise of GOFAI. Probably, he would have accepted formal-symbolic representations as alternative types of cerebral model. Certainly, many of his followers did. Two early cognitive scientists who acknowledged Craik's inspiration were Richard Gregory (e.g. 1966) and Jerome Bruner (who'd visited Craik's group in England in 1955-56).

Largely as a result of these three publications of 1943, the next quarter-century saw pioneers working on both types of AI and/or computational psychology.

It would be misleading to say that they were working on both sides of the theoretical *divide*, because the unpleasantly antagonistic schism between connectionism and GOFAI, or (more broadly) between bottom-up and top-down approaches, hadn't yet developed. At that time, there was still one intellectual community ("cybernetics"), with shared aims and interests. To be sure, some people were focussing more on adaptation and self-organization, others more on logic and meaning--although a few, such as McCulloch, tackled both. Indeed, the rapid rise of GOFAI was mainly due to its promise, not matched by the adaptationists, to deal with inference and linguistic meaning. In general, however, the two sides communicated freely and agreed to differ on what might be the most promising theoretical approach. Only much later did the community separate into distinct sociological camps, with little love lost between them (see Section V).

The 1950s

The key dates of the following decade were 1956 and 1958. Indeed, 1956 was the *annus mirabilis* of cognitive science. It saw no fewer than six events that raised the spirits of the nascent cognitive scientists, convincing them that something exciting was happening. Four were publications, and two were meetings aimed at consciousness raising in the emerging interdisciplinary community.

The publications included a book reporting an imaginative series of psychological experiments: Bruner's *A Study of Thinking* (Bruner et al. 1956). (The title alone was a provocation, in those behaviourist days.) Bruner posited several information-processing strategies for concept learning, each more or less appropriate depending on the circumstances--and all defined in broadly computational terms. His ideas would be reflected in much early AI and computational psychology.

In addition, there were three papers. The most influential was George Miller's (1956) information-theoretic 'The Magical Number Seven'--which by the mid-1970s had become the most-cited paper in the whole of cognitive psychology. Another described the first computer model of Donald Hebb's "connectionism" (the word was his coinage). This showed that Hebbian theory could be implemented, but only if his 'ft/wt' learning rule was expressed more precisely (Rochester et al. 1956). And--across the ocean--the last was Ullin Place's 'Is Consciousness a Brain Process?' (Place 1956).

Place's paper is the outlier here, for his mind-brain identity theory wasn't a contribution to cognitive science as such: it said nothing about mind as machine. But it was eagerly welcomed by scientifically-minded readers, and its materialist spirit--though not its reductionist letter—was retained when philosophical functionalism replaced it four years later (see Section IV).

As for the two consciousness-raising meetings of 1956, the first was the "Summer Research Project on Artificial Intelligence", at Dartmouth College. Organized by the youngsters Marvin Minsky and John McCarthy, this introduced AI to a wider audience. (It also launched the discipline's name, which has been a philosophical millstone around its neck ever since.)

For instance, Minsky handed out the draft of an insightful review of early AI (Minsky 1956). Published a few years later as 'Steps Toward Artificial Intelligence', this was widely seen as AI's manifesto. Or perhaps one should rather say "as GOFAI's manifesto", for it argued that connectionist AI had fundamental limitations not shared by symbolic AI. It did, however, suggest that a *combination* of neural networks and GOFAI would be needed to emulate human thought—a suggestion that went largely unheeded. (Minsky himself seemed to forget it in the 1960s, as we'll see, but he eventually followed it up in his "society" theory of mind.)

The Summer Project wasn't a meeting in the usual sense, but a two-month period during which about a dozen AI pioneers were located at Dartmouth, and anyone who was interested could drop in. The core group included Arthur Samuel and Oliver Selfridge--and, for the .final week, Allen Newell and Herbert Simon. In the earlier weeks they'd played truant, trying to finish programming their Logic Theorist. This proved theorems (in propositional logic) from the Russell-Whitehead *Principia Mathematica,* and even found a more elegant proof for one of them (Newell et al. 1957).

The Logic Theorist wasn't the first AI program, though it's often described that way. Quite apart from 'toy' programs written by Alan Turing and others, Samuel had implemented a heuristic program for playing checkers (draughts) in 1949, and a learning version was up-and-running early in 1955 (Samuel 1959: 72). It had even featured on American TV in February 1956, six months before the Dartmouth event. Unlike Newell and Simon, however, Samuel attended that meeting without bringing along printout evidence. That's partly why the participants were more enthused by the Logic Theorist. In addition, logic struck most people as more impressive--more 'human'--than draughts.

But the main reason why more interest was aroused by Newell and Simon's program was that it was explicitly intended as a model of human thinking, guided by Gestalt psychology and by their own experiments. In their view, computers and psychology should be seen as equal partners: "artificial intelligence was to borrow ideas from psychology and psychology from artificial intelligence" (Newell and Simon 1972: 883). Buffs on both sides of this disciplinary fence were excited accordingly.

The second 1956 meeting was the IEEE's three-day Symposium on Information Theory, convened at MIT in mid-September--almost back-to-back with the Dartmouth event. This had more direct influence in bringing psychologists into cognitive science. For among the papers given there were Miller's 'Magical Number Seven', Newell and Simon on the Logic Theorist, and Noam Chomsky on formal grammars--which showed that language, considered as structured sentences not just as word strings, can be formally described.

Miller himself instantly put those other two talks together: "I went away from the Symposium with a strong conviction, more intuitive than rational, that human experimental psychology, theoretical linguistics, and computer simulation of cognitive processes were all pieces of a larger whole, and that the future would see progressive elaboration and coordination of their shared concerns" (quoted in Gardner 1985: 29). This epiphany soon led him to play a crucial role in establishing cognitive science as such (see Section IV).

So 1956 was a good year for the field--but it was soon followed by another. In November 1958, a four-day interdisciplinary seminar took place at the National Physical Laboratory (NPL) in London--a resonant venue, given its post-war connection with Turing. Hosted by the psychophysiologist Albert Uttley, this brought other leading neurophysiologists--Horace Barlow, for example-- into the discussion.

About two dozen people, almost all now important names in cognitive science, gathered there. Most had experience of interdisciplinary thinking, having done war-work on the design and use of various novel machines. And Craik was a highly respected name--and, for several attendees, an inspiring personal memory. Recognized intellectual leaders such as McCulloch, Frederic Bartlett, and the anatomist J. Z. Young were joined by youngsters who today are at least as famous. And the youngsters served up some very rich fare.

The atmosphere was electric: it was clear that something exciting was happening. The importance of this meeting for both "sides" of cognitive science--and for AI, A-Life, psychology, and neuroscience--can be indicated by listing a few of the talks (see Blake and Uttley 1959). Among NPL's many memorable moments were these: Selfridge on *Pandemonium;* Frank Rosenblatt on perceptrons; Barlow on his 'coding' theory of perception; Gregory on the misuse of brain-ablation studies; Donald MacKay on the need for hybrid (analogue-digital) machines; McCarthy on giving programs "common sense" *via* predicate calculus (and Yehoshua Bar- Hillel's critical reply on what's now called the frame problem); Gordon Pask on his electrochemical model of a developing concept; and, not least, Minsky on heuristic programming--who summarized the AI manifesto circulated at Dartmouth two years earlier.

The NPL meeting was only one of three events which made 1958 special. The others were two highly contrasting papers, both published in the same volume of *Psychological Review* and both--at least for a while-- hugely influential.

The first to appear was a theory of human problem solving, based on the Logic Theorist and its successor the General Problem Solver, or GPS (Newell et al. 1958). Even more powerful than the Logic Theorist, GPS whetted the appetite of psychologists who hadn't heard of the Logic Theorist, and enthused those who had still further. They were attracted, too, by the programme of ongoing psychological experimentation initiated by the authors.

The second seminal paper was Rosenblatt's (1958) account of "perceptrons", also featured at NPL but here reaching a much wider audience. This described a class of connectionist computer models based on Hebbian theory, and focused not on problem solving but on pattern recognition. They could learn to distinguish an A from a B, for example.

Although perceptrons excited many people, including youngsters entering AI, they didn't convince everyone whom one might have expected to be sympathetic. Indeed, when cognitive science's manifesto appeared two years later (see Section IV), they were near-invisible: even in those hope-filled pages, parallel processing would be mentioned only in two footnotes. Rosenblatt's hopes were more robust. He saw perceptrons as prefiguring a general theory of human psychology, and was even more daring-- some would soon say even more preposterous--than Newell and Simon in his predictions concerning future versions of his machine.

It's noteworthy that these two papers were published in the same Journal. That might have happened ten years later--but not ten years after that. For by then the schism mentioned in Section II had emerged: the field's two pathways had diverged not only theoretically but sociologically too.

Meeting-House, Manifesto, and Mind

Most of the influences mentioned so far were drawn together in two ground-breaking projects of 1960. One was cognitive science's first research institute, the other its manifesto.

Harvard's provocatively named Center for Cognitive Studies was co-founded by Bruner and Miller. Bruner had been running a seminar on these matters for some years, attended (for instance) by the young Chomsky and Jerry Fodor. That had sown important seeds in the local community, for Chomsky later acknowledged Bruner's (neo-Craikian) influence on his positing inner representations of syntactic structure. But in 1960 the new Center put interdisciplinary cognitive science publicly on the academic map.

The name was provocative because it was rejecting behaviourism, then dominant in US psychology. But the word "Cognitive" carried less weight than is often thought, being used simply as an anti-behaviourist shorthand. As Miller later put it: "[We] were setting ourselves off from behaviorism. We wanted something that was *mental* --but "mental psychology" seemed terribly redundant" (Miller 1986: 210). In speaking of "cognition", he said, they weren't intentionally excluding "volition" or "conation", but "just reaching back for common sense". In short, even though in practice most cognitive scientists have focused on cognition, the field has always been concerned in principle with *all* aspects of the mind--as McCulloch and Pitts had urged in 1943.

Besides co-founding the Center, Miller offered another spur to cognitive science in 1960. This was his remarkable book *Plans and the Structure of Behavior,* written with Eugene Galanter and Karl Pribram (MGP for short). The book was (unavoidably) simplistic, and careless to boot. Nevertheless, it was a work of vision. Its declared goal was to discover "whether the cybernetic ideas have any relevance for psychology" (p. 3), and its answer was a confident "Yes".

MGP used the notion of a Plan--simply defined as a TOTE unit (Test-Operate-Test-Exit), or as TOTEs made up of lower-level TOTEs--to sketch mental processes. Their discussion ranged over the whole of psychology. Animals and humans; instinct and learning; language and memory; habit and motor skill; chess and choice; values and facts; self image and social role; knowledge and affect; intention and desire; hope and morality; personality and hypnosis; normal life and psychopathology ... *everything* was included.

Plans was the first book to apply computational ideas so widely. Thanks to the recent work of Newell and Simon and of Chomsky, all of whom were repeatedly cited, the most persuasive parts of the book concerned cognition. But the promises reached beyond the persuasion. Miller and Bruner's intention that the "Cognitive" in "Cognitive Studies" should really be read

as "mental"-- *anything* mental--was reflected in this volume.

Even sympathetic readers were almost deafened by the sound of handwaving. However, they were excited too. For some years, the book would function as a manifesto for the new science of the mind. (A good way of judging progress in cognitive science is to compare today's achievements with the hopes and promises expressed therein.)

Meanwhile, a mile or so away from the new Center, another 1960 landmark had been constructed: Hilary Putnam's functionalism (Putnam 1960). For budding cognitive scientists, this new philosophy offered relief, revelation, and promise. It escaped various dilemmas that had plagued the philosophy of mind--including Place's identity theory--through the 1950s. More to the point, it saw Turing computation as the causal process at the core of mental life, and the mind as the 'program' of the brain. By implication, it underwrote the AI-based theoretical psychology that was already emerging.

There were naysayers, of course. Indeed, competing varieties of functionalism would later develop within cognitive science. And there would be plenty of objections from philosophers outside the field. (Putnam himself rejected it, eventually.) Nevertheless, this paper had given sharp philosophical teeth to those who wished to chew the mind in computational terms.

By 1960, then, the field had visibly got off the ground.

A Temporary Glitch

The fifth key date, 1969, marks a publication seen by some people as a step backwards rather than forwards. On that view, the damage caused in 1969 wasn't mended until some twenty years later.

MGP weren't the only ones to be under-impressed by perceptrons: Minsky, with Seymour Papert, had a low opinion of them too. He'd already expressed doubts in his 'Steps' paper. But in the 1960s, when Rosenblatt's ideas were threatening to grab the graduate students, and the funding, he (and others at MIT) felt that sterner measures were called for. The result was an explosive little book called *Perceptrons: An Introduction to Computational Geometry* (Minsky and Papert 1969).

As the sub-title implied, this was a mathematical critique. Minsky and Papert showed that simple parallel processors couldn't do certain things, such as recognizing connectedness, which one might have expected them to do--and which the then-current GOFAI programs could do. And they predicted that more complex versions wouldn't be much better. Admittedly, in 1959-60 Rosenblatt had proved that perceptrons could learn to do whatever they could be programmed to do. His proof was allowed to be both valid and "seductive" (p. 14), but-- Minsky and Papert argued--it had little practical relevance in face of the combinatorial explosion. What the widely hailed perceptrons could actually do was highly limited. In short, they were fool's gold.

After this publication, funding for connectionism virtually stopped. In the USA it had started to dry up already, thanks to the circulation of the (even more vitriolic) draft of *Perceptrons* during the early-mid 1960s, and to Minsky's close friendship with the key funder at DARPA (Joseph Licklider).

Carver Mead later spoke of "the twenty-year famine" in connectionism (Anderson and Rosenfeld 1998: 141). But, rightly, he didn't put all of the blame onto Minsky and Papert's shoulders. Rather, he blamed the early-1960s "overhype" about perceptrons--to which they'd been responding.

A Double Renaissance

Both of our last two key dates mark a new visibility, not a new activity. Namely, the public renaissance of connectionism--more precisely, of parallel distributed processing (PDP)--in 1986, and of A-Life a year later. In each case, the new visibility prompted an explosion of further activity that's still expanding.

Connectionism hadn't stopped dead in its tracks in 1969. Throughout the 1970s, important work was done on associative memories and distributed representation. However, it was seen as maverick, and largely ignored. A consciousness-raising meeting was held in La Jolla in 1979 (Hinton and Anderson 1981), but it was highly technical: few newcomers were enticed to join the band.

What mended the damage done to connectionism's reputation by Minsky and Papert's attack was the publication in 1986 of the PDP 'bible' (Rumelhart and McClelland 1986; McClelland and Rumelhart 1986). This was deliberately written, priced, and targetted to attract graduate students away from GOFAI and into the PDP stable. So it did--and it attracted many philosophers too. They valued it because it offered a more plausible account of concepts and conceptual similarity.

Crucially, the bible (alongside some lectures by Stephen Grossberg) also attracted the funding authorities. DARPA organized an urgent five-month review of their past funding policy, which had near-ignored connectionism for two decades. Although Minsky, one of the first invited speakers, refused to withdraw his 1969 criticisms (see Minsky and Papert 1988), the outcome was that DARPA changed their mind. They initiated "a major new program in neural networks beginning in 1989" (DARPA 1988: xxv), and gave Minsky and Papert a coded rebuke: "Neural network research is not new--it is, rather, newly revived from an obscurity and even disrepute which is now understood to have been undeserved" (DARPA 1988: 23). The twenty-year famine was over.

Here, we should note another runner-up for an eighth key date. To do that we have to backtrack seven years, to a masterpiece that paved the way for the connectionist renaissance: Douglas Hofstadter's *Gödel, Escher, Bach* (1979). This was an intoxicating document. It wove music, logic, biology, and Alice in Wonderland into a song of praise for AI/A-Life in general, and parallel distributed processing in particular. It became a cult book, winning the Pulitzer prize and appearing in many languages. (It's still much admired: in 1999 the *New Scientist* invited a dozen people to choose a science book from the last quarter-century to take to a desert island, and three chose this one.)

So why not add 1979 to our list without further ado? Well, for all its brilliance, *GEB* didn't outline a research programme that others could take up. However, it did raise the profile, and indicate the breadth, of cognitive science for the general public. Without its insightful flamboyance to ease the way, acceptance of the much dryer PDP bible would have been less immediate--and much less wide.

The last key date marks a further intellectual renaissance. In 1987 Christopher Langton organized the first conference on "artificial life", at Los Alamos. A-Life, he said, concerned "life as it could be", not just "life as we know it": abstract, preferably formal, descriptions of life were the goal. More generally, the focus was on self-organization and bottom-up processing, in various domains.

He circulated the invitation widely. In the event, a wide spectrum turned up: biologists, biochemists, physicists, mathematicians, AI researchers, neuroscientists, and philosophers (and the journalists turned up too). They discovered--as Langton had hoped--that, despite the superficial differences, they'd been working on closely related issues.

The interdisciplinarity and excitement rivalled the NPL meeting of 1958--and the 1950s Macy meetings of the cybernetics community, too. Indeed, that community was much in people's minds. Ross Ashby, Grey Walter, and Pask were honoured by their A-Life descendants after being near-forgotten for a generation. Now, they're familiar names in cognitive science.

Conclusion

And that, for a while, was that. It's not that nothing went on: cognitive science has continued to advance since 1987. And, increasingly, neuroscientific detail has been brought into formerly abiological zones. But nothing of comparable historical importance has occurred in the last twenty years.

Or rather, nothing that can be recognized *today* as having equal weight. There's plenty of new work out there that's promising, of course--including some which is truly fascinating, not run-of the- mill (see Boden 2006: ch. 17). A few of these examples may turn out to be historical high points. As yet, however, it's too early to tell.

References

Blake, D. V., and Uttley, A. M. (eds.) (1959), *The Mechanization of Thought Processes,* 2 vols. Proceedings of a Symposium held at NPL on 24-27 November 1958. (London: Her Majesty's Stationery Office).

Boden, M. A. (2006), *Mind as Machine: A History of Cognitive Science,* 2 vols. (Oxford: Oxford University Press).

Bruner, J. S., Goodnow, J., and Austin, G. (1956), *A Study of Thinking* (New York: Wiley).

Craik, K. J. W. (1943), *The Nature of Explanation* (Cambridge: Cambridge University Press).

DARPA (1988), *DARPA Neural Network Study: October 1987-February 1988* (Fairfax, Virginia: AFCEA International Press).

Gardner, H. (1985), *The Mind's New Science: A History of the Cognitive Revolution* (New York: Harper Collins).

Gregory, R. L. (1966), *Eye and Brain: The Psychology of Seeing* (London: Weidenfeld and Nicolson).

Hinton, G. E., and Anderson, J. A. (1981), *Parallel Models of Associative Memory* (Hillsdale, N.J.: Lawrence Erlbaum).

Hofstadter, D. R. (1979), *Godel, Escher, Bach: An Eternal Golden Braid* (New York: Basic Books).

McClelland, J. L., Rumelhart, D. E., and the PDP Research Group (1986), *Parallel Distributed Processing: Explorations in the Microstructure of Cognition,* Vol. 2, *Psychological and Biological Models* (Cambridge, Mass.: MIT Press).

McCulloch, W. S., and Pitts, W. H. (1943), 'A Logical Calculus of the Ideas Immanent in Nervous Activity', *Bulletin of Mathematical Biophysics,* 5: 115-133.

Miller, G. A. (1956), 'The Magical Number Seven, Plus or Minus Two: Some Limits on Our Capacity for Processing Information', *Psychological Review,* 63: 81-97.

Miller, G. A. (1986), 'Interview with George A. Miller', in B. J. Baars (ed.), *The Cognitive Revolution in Psychology* (London: Guilford Press), 200-223.

Miller, G. A., Galanter, E., and Pribram, K. H. (1960), *Plans and the Structure of Behavior* (New York: Holt).

Minsky, M. L. (1956), *Heuristic Aspects of the Artificial Intelligence Problem.* Group Report 34-55 (Lexington, Mass.: MIT Lincoln Laboratories, December). Revised as 'Steps Toward

Arti.cial Intelligence', *Proceedings of the Institute of Radio Engineers,* 49 (1961): 8-30. -9-

Minsky, M. L., and Papert, S. A. (1969), *Perceptrons: An Introduction to Computational Geometry* (Cambridge, Mass.: MIT Press).

Minsky, M. L., and Papert, S. A. (1988), 'Prologue: A View From 1988' and 'Epilogue: The New Connectionism', in *Perceptrons: An Introduction to Computational Geometry,* 2nd edn.(Cambridge, Mass.: MIT Press), viii-xv & 247-280.

Newell, A., Shaw, J. C., and Simon, H. A. (1957), 'Empirical Explorations with the Logic Theory Machine', *Proceedings of the Western Joint Computer Conference,* 15: 218-239.

Newell, A., Shaw, J. C., and Simon, H. A. (1958), 'Elements of a Theory of Human Problem- Solving', *Psychological Review,* 65: 151-166.

Newell, A., and Simon, H. A. (1972), *Human Problem Solving* (Englewood Cliffs, N.J.: Prentice- Hall).

O'Reilly, R. C., and Munakata, Y. (2000), *Computational Explorations in Cognitive Neuroscience: Understanding the Mind by Simulating the Brain* (Cambridge, Mass.: MIT Press).

Pitts, W. H., and McCulloch, W. S. (1947), 'How We Know Universals: The Perception of Auditory and Visual Forms', *Bulletin of Mathematical Biophysics,* 9 (1947), 127-147.

Place, U. T. (1956), 'Is Consciousness a Brain Process?', *British Journal of Psychology,* 47: 44-50.

Putnam, H. (1960), 'Minds and Machines', in S. Hook (ed.), *Dimensions of Mind: A Symposium* (New York: New York University Press), 148-179.

Rochester, N., Holland, J. H., Haibt, L. H., and Duda, W. L. (1956), 'Tests on a Cell Assembly Theory of the Action of the Brain, Using a Large Digital Computer', *Institute of Radio Engineers Transactions on Information Theory,* 2: 80-93.

Rosenblatt, F. (1958), 'The Perceptron: A Probabilistic Model for Information Storage and Organization in the Brain', *Psychological Review,* 65: 386-408.

Rosenblatt, F. (1962), *Principles of Neurodynamics: Perceptrons and the Theory of Brain Mechanisms* (Washington, DC: Spartan).

Rosenblueth, A., Wiener, N., and Bigelow, J. (1943), 'Behavior, Purpose, and Teleology', *Philosophy of Science,* 10: 18-24.

Rumelhart, D. E., McClelland, J. L., and the PDP Research Group (1986), *Parallel Distributed Processing: Explorations in the Microstructure of Cognition,* Vol.1, *Foundations* (Cambridge, Mass.: MIT Press).

Samuel, A. L. (1959), 'Some Studies in Machine Learning Using the Game of Checkers', *IBM Journal of Research and Development,* 3: 211-229. -10-

For a Systematic Theory of Expectations

Cristiano Castelfranchi (cristiano.castalfranchi@istc.cnr.it)
Institute for Cognitive Sciences and Technologies - CNR Rome, Italy

'More geometrico demonstrata'
Spinoza

Abstract

I analyze 'Expectation' as an amalgam of more elementary cognitive components (beliefs and goals). I claim that this produces a unitary 'mental states' with its specific functions. I explain the crucial role of expectations in choices, intentions, attempts, and as the background for several emotions like hope, fear, disappointment, relief. The fundamental role of mental 'anticipation' in the origin and nature of mind is stressed.

Cognitive Anatomy of Expectations

'Expectations' are not just 'Predictions'; they are not fully synonyms. And we do not want to use 'expectations' (like in the literature) just to mean 'predictions', that is, epistemic representations about the future. We consider, in particular, a 'forecast' [3] [4] as a mere belief about a future state of the world and we distinguish it from a simple 'hypothesis'. The difference is in terms of degree of certainty: a hypothesis may involve the belief that future p is possible while in a forecast the belief that future p is probable. A forecast implies that the chance threshold has been exceeded (domain of probability).

Putting aside the degree of confidence (we need a general term covering weak and strong predictions), for us 'expectations' have a more restricted meaning (and this is why computer can produce weather 'predictions' or 'forecasts' but do not have 'expectations'). In 'expectations'

- (i) the prediction is *relevant* for the predictor; he is *concerned*, *interested*, and that is why
- (ii) he is 'expecting', that is the prediction is aimed at being verified; he is *waiting* in order to know whether the prediction is true or not.[1]

---

[1] Notice that the first two meanings of 'to expect' in an English dictionary are the following ones:

1 to believe with confidence, or think it likely, that an event will happen in the future

2. to wait for, or look forward to, something that you believe is going to happen or arrive

While the definition of 'to forecast' is as follows:

1. to predict or work out something that is likely to happen, for example, the weather conditions for the days ahead

(Encarta® World English Dictionary © 1999 Microsoft Corporation).

Notice, the second component of 'expecting' meaning (absent in 'forecasting'): *wait for, or look forward to*. But also the idea that there is some 'confidence' in expectation: the agent *counts on* that.

Expectation is a suspended state *after* the formulation of a prediction[2]. If there is an expectation then there is a prediction, but not the other way around.

Epistemic Goals and Activity.

First of all, X has the Goal of knowing whether the predicted event or state really happens (epistemic goal). She is 'waiting for' this; at least for curiosity. This concept of 'waiting for' and of 'looking for' is necessarily related to the notion of expecting and expectation, but not to the notion of prediction.

Either X is actively monitoring what is happening and comparing the incoming information (for example perception) to the internal mental representation; or X is doing this cyclically and regularly; or X will in any case at the moment of the future event or state compare what happens with her prediction (epistemic actions) [14] [15]. Because in any case she has the Goal to know whether the world actually is as anticipated, and if the prediction was correct. Schematically [3]:

Expectation x p => Bel x at t' that p at t" (where t" > t') & Goal x from t' to t"' KnowWhether x p or Not p at t" (t"' ≥ t"). This really is 'expecting' and the true 'expectation'.

Content Goals.

This Epistemic/monitoring Goal is combined with *Goal that p*: the agent's need, desire, or 'intention that' the agent should realize [5] [6]. The Goal that p is true (that is the Goal that p) or the Goal that Not p. This is really why and in which sense X is 'concerned' and not indifferent, and also why she is monitoring the world. She is an agent with interests, desires, needs, objectives on the world, not just a predictor. This is also why computers, that already make predictions, do not have expectations.

When the agent has a goal opposite to her prediction, she has a 'negative expectation'; when the agent has a

---

[2] 'Prediction' is the result of the action of predicting; but 'expectation' is not the result of the action of expecting; it is that action or the outcome of a prediction relevant to goals, basis of such an action.

[3] We will not use here a logical formalization; we will just use a self-explanatory and synthetic notation, useful for a schematic characterization of different combinations of beliefs and goals. For a real formalization of some of these mental attitudes see [4].

goal equal to her prediction she has a 'positive expectation' (see § 3.1).[4]

In sum, Expectations (Exp) are axiological anticipatory mental representations, endowed with *Valence*: they are positive or negative or ambivalent or neutral; but in any case they are *evaluated against some concern, drive, motive, goal of the agent*. In Exp we have to distinguish two components:

- On the one side, there is a mental anticipatory representation, the belief about a future state or event, the "mental anticipation" of the fact, what we might also call the pre-vision (to for-see).

The format of this belief or pre-vision can be either propositional or imagery (or mental model of); this does not matter. Here just the function is pertinent.

- On the other side, as we just argued, there is a co-referent Goal (wish, desire, intention, or any other motivational explicit representation).

Given the resulting *amalgam* these representations of the future are charged of value, their intention or content has a 'valence': it is positive, or negative.[5] More precisely, Exp s can be:

- **positive** (goal conformable): $(\text{Bel } x \; p^{t'})^{t < t'} \; \& \; (\text{Goal } x \; p^{t'})$ [or $(\text{Bel } x \; \neg p^{t'})^{t < t'} \; \& \; (\text{Goal } x \; \neg p^{t'})$]

- **negative** (goal opposite): $(\text{Bel } x \; p^{t'})^{t < t'} \; \& \; (\text{Goal } x \; \neg p^{t'})$ [or $(\text{Bel } x \; \neg p^{t'})^{t < t'} \; \& \; (\text{Goal } x \; p^{t'})$]

- **neutral**: $(\text{Bel } x \; p^{t'})^{t < t'} \; \& \; \neg(\text{Goal } x \; p^{t'}) \; \& \; \neg(\text{Goal } x \; \neg p^{t'})$ [or $(\text{Bel } x \; \neg p^{t'})^{t < t'} \; \& \; \neg(\text{Goal } x \; p^{t'}) \; \& \; \neg(\text{Goal } x \; \neg p^{t'})$]

- **ambivalent**: $(\text{Bel } x \; p^{t'})^{t < t'} \; \& \; (\text{Goal } x \; p^{t'}) \; \& \; (\text{Goal } x \; \neg p^{t'})$ [or $(\text{Bel } x \; \neg p^{t'})^{t < t'} \; \& \; (\text{Goal } x \; p^{t'}) \; \& \; (\text{Goal } x \; \neg p^{t'})$]

The quantitative aspects of mental attitudes

Decomposing in terms of beliefs and goals is not enough. We need 'quantitative' parameters. Frustration and pain have an *intensity*, can be more or less severe; the same holds for surprise, disappointment, relief, hope, joy, ... Since they are clearly related with what the agent believes, expects, likes, pursues, can we account for those dimensions on the basis of our (de)composition of those mental states, and of the basic epistemic and motivational representations? We claim so.

Given the two basic ingredients of any Exp (defined as different from simple forecast or prediction) Beliefs + Goals, we postulate that:

P1: Beliefs & Goals have specific quantitative dimensions; which are basically independent from each other.

Beliefs have strength, a degree of subjective certainty; the subject is more or less sure and committed about their content [25]. *Goals have a value, a subjective importance for the agent*.

To simplify, we may have very important goals combined with uncertain predictions; pretty sure forecasts for not very relevant objectives; etc.

Thus, we should explicitly represent these dimensions of Goals and Beliefs: $\text{Bel}^{\%} \; x \; p^{t}$; $\text{Goal}^{\%} \; x \; p^{t}$

Where % in Goals represents their subjective importance or value; while in Beliefs % represents their subjective credibility, their certainty.

An Exp (putting aside the Epistemic Goal) will be like this:

$$\text{Bel}^{\%} \; x \; p^{t} \; \& \; \text{Goal}^{\%} \; x \; [\neg] \; p^{t}$$

The subjective *quality* of those "configurations" or macro-attitudes will be very different precisely depending on those parameters. Also the effects of the invalidation of an Exp are very different depending on: (i) the positive or negative character of the Exp ; (ii) the strengths of the components. (See § 6.)

We also postulate that:

P2: The dynamics and the degree of the emergent configuration, of the Macro-attitude are strictly a function of the dynamics and strength of its micro-components.

For example anxiety will probably be greater when the goal is very important and the uncertainty high, than when the

---

[4] To be true a Goal equal to the prediction in Expectation is always there, although frequently quite weak and secondary relatively to the main concern. In fact, when X predicts that p and monitors the world to know whether actually p, she has also the Goal that p, just in order to not disconfirm her prediction, and to confirm to be a good predictor, to feel that the world is predictable and have a sense of 'control'. (see § 3.2). We are referring to *predictability*, that is, the cognitive component of self-efficacy [16]: the need to anticipate future events and the consequent need to find such an anticipation validated by facts. This need for prediction is functional in humans in order to avoid anxiety, disorientation and distress. Cooper and Fazio [17] have experimentally proved that people act in order to find their forecasts (predictions) validated by facts and feel distressed by invalidation.

[5] • Either, the expectation entails a cognitive evaluation [18]. In fact, since the realization of p is coinciding with a goal, it is "good"; while if the belief is the opposite of the goal, it implies a belief that the outcome of the world will be 'bad'.
• Or the expectation produces an implicit, intuitive appraisal, simply by activating associated affective responses or somatic markers [18]; or both;
• Or the expected result will produce a *reward* for the agent, and – although not strictly driving its behavior, it is positive for it since it will satisfy a drive and reinforce the behavior.
We analyze here only the Expectations in a strong sense, with an explicit Goal; but we mentioned Expectations in those forms of reactive, rule-based behaviors, first in order to stress how the notion of Expectation always involves the idea of a *valence* and of the agent being concerned and monitoring the world; second, to give an idea of more elementary and forerunner forms of this construct. It is in fact the case of proto-expectations or expectations in 'Anticipatory-Classifiers' based behaviors, strictly conceived as reactive (not really goal-driven) behaviors, but based on anticipatory representation of the outcomes [1] [2] [7] [13].

goal is not so crucial or the certainty is high.. Let us characterize a bit some of these emergent macro-attitudes.

Hope and Fear.

'Hope' is in our account [3] [4] a peculiar kind of 'positive Exp' where the goal is rather relevant for the subject while the Exp (more precisely the prediction) is not sure at all but rather weak and uncertain.[6]

$$\text{Bel}^{\textbf{low}} x \, p^t \, \& \, \text{Goal}^{\textbf{high}} x \, p^t$$

Correspondingly one might characterize being afraid, 'fear', as an Exp of something bad, i.e. against our wishes:

$$\text{Bel}^{\%} x \, p^t \, \& \, \text{Goal}^{\%} x \, \neg p^t$$

but it seems that there can be 'fear' at any degree of certainty and of importance.[7]

Of course, these representations are seriously incomplete. We are ignoring their 'affective' and 'felt' component, which is definitely crucial. We are just providing their cognitive skeleton [26].

The Implicit Counterpart of Expectations

Since we introduce a quantification of the degree of subjective certainty and reliability of Belief about the future (the forecast) we get a hidden, strange but nice consequence. There are other implicit opposite beliefs and thus implicit Exp s. For "implicit" belief we mean here a belief that is not 'written', is not contained in any 'data base' (short term, working, or long term memory) but is only potentially known by the subject since it can be simply derived from actual beliefs. For example, while my knowledge that Buenos Aires is the capital of Argentina is an explicit belief that I have in some memory and I have just to retrieve it, on the contrary my knowledge that Buenos Aires is not the capital of Greece (or of Italy, or of India, or of ...) is not in any memory, but can just be derived (when needed) from what I explicitly know. Until it remains implicit, merely potential, until is not derived, it has *no effect* in my mind; for example, I cannot perceive possible contradictions: my mind is only potentially

---

[6] We may also have – it is true - 'strong hope' but we explicitly call it 'strong' precisely because usually 'hope' implies *low* confidence and some anxiety and worry. In any case, 'hope' (like explicit 'trust') can never really be subjectively 'certain' and absolutely confident. Hope implies uncertainty.

[7] To characterize *fear* another component would be very relevant: the goal of avoiding the foreseen danger; that is, the goal of *doing* something such that Not p. This is a goal activated while feeling fear; fear 'conative' and 'impulsive' aspect. But it is also a component of a complete fear mental state, not just a follower or a consequence of fear. This goal can be a quite specified action (motor reaction) (a cry; the impulse to escape; etc.); or a generic goal 'doing something' ("my God!! What can I do?!") [27]. The more intense the felt fear, the more important the activate goal of avoidance [26].

contradictory if I believe that p, I believe that q, and p implies Not q, but I didn't derive that Not q.

Now, a belief that "70% it is the case that p", implies a belief that "30% it is the case that Not p"[8]. This has interesting consequences on Exps and related emotions. The Positive Exp that p, entails an implicit (but sometime even explicit and compatible) Negative Exp:

$$
\begin{array}{c}
\text{Bel}^{\%} x \, p^t \\
\& \\
\text{Goal}^{\%} x \, p^t
\end{array}
\;\rightarrow\;
\begin{array}{c}
\text{Bel}^{\%} x \, \neg p^t \\
\& \\
\text{Goal}^{\%} x \, p^t
\end{array}
$$

This means that a hope implicitly contains some fear, and that any worry implicitly preserves some hope. But also means that when one gets a 'relief' because a serious threat strongly expected is not arrived and the world is conforming to her desires, she also gets (or can get) some exultance. It depends on her focus of attention and framing: is she focused on her worry and evanished threat, or on the unexpected achievement? Vice versa when one is satisfied for the actual expected realization of an important goal, she also can get some measure of relief while focusing on the implicit previous worry. Not necessarily at the very moment that one feels a given emotion (for example fear) she also feels the complementary emotion (hope) in a sort of oscillation or ambivalence and affective mixture. Only when the belief is explicitly represented and one can focus – at least for a moment – her attention on it, it can generate the corresponding emotion.

Analytical Decomposition and the Gestalt Character of Mental Attitudes

Moreover, a hard problem for symbolic (and analytic) cognitive science deserves to be underlined: *the mental Gestalt problem*. Disappointment, expectation, relief, etc. seem to be unitary subjective experiences, typical and recognizable "mental states"; they have a global character; although made up of (more) atomic components, they form a *gestalt*. To use again the metaphor of molecules vs. atoms, the molecule (like 'water') has emergent and specific properties that its atoms (H & O) do not have. How can we account for this gestalt property in our analytic, symbolic, (de)composition framework? We have implicitly pointed out some possible solutions to this problem. For example:

- A higher-level predicate exists (like 'EXPECT') and one can assume that although decomposable in and implying specific beliefs and goals, this molecular predicate is used by mental operations and rules.
- Or one might assume that the left part of a given rule for the activation of a specific goal is just the combined pattern: belief + goal; for example, an avoidance goal and behavior would be

---

[8] We are simplifying the argument. In fact it is possible that there is an interval of ignorance, some lack of evidences; that is that I estimate with a probability of 45% that p and with a probability of 30% Not p, while having a gap of 25% neither in favor of p nor of Not p [29] [30].

elicited by a serious negative *Exp* (and the associated 'fear'), not by the simple prediction of an event.

- One might assume that we "recognize" - or better "individuate" (and "construct")- our own mental state (thanks to this complex predicate or some complex rule) and that this "awareness" is part of the mental state: since we have a complex category or pattern of "expectation" or of "disappointment" we recognize and *have* (and feel) this complex mental state.

This would create some sort of "molecular" causal level. However, this might seem not enough in order to account for the gestaltic subjective experience, and reasonably something additional should be found in the direction of some typical "feeling" related to those cognitive configurations. Here we deal with the limits of any disembodied mind (and model).

Expectation: An 'Emergent' Mental Object and its Functions

Exps are new mental entities; they play a role as such, as global representations, as a gestalt, not just on the basis of their atomic components: beliefs and goals. Since in fact what matters is also the specific <u>structure</u> or <u>relation</u> (between Bel and G) which makes an Exp, makes it 'positive', 'negative', 'ambivalent', or 'indifferent', and makes its 'strength' which is neither reducible to the value of the goal, nor reducible to the certainty of the prediction.

Let us consider some of the main functions of Exp as a unitary mental representation:

Choices are Expectation-Based

A goal has a 'motivating force', which predicts the probability of its being pursued against costs and efforts, or chosen against other possible attractive goals (its 'priority'). However, the priority of the goal, its *motivating force* is not only due the subjective *'value'* of the goal: how important it is for us, how much it promises to us.

The *'value'* of a goal (desire, intention, objective, purpose, ...) either

- is not derived but just given if it is a 'terminal' (non instrumental) goal, an aim/end, the 'motive', ('given' of course for a given person in a given moment on the basis of its age, condition, personality, gender, culture, experience,..; or

- is derived from the value of the higher goals (to whom it is instrumental), and from the value of the goals that one has to sacrifice for achieving it: *costs* (invested resources) and *renounces*.

The motivating force and the priority of a goal is due both to its 'value' and to its estimated possibility. In other terms, what really matters in deliberation, what really prevails in choice, is not merely the goal with its 'value', but the 'Exp', with its new emergent metrics, which is the resultant of the goal-value and of the certainty of the prediction. It would be stupid (irrational) to give priority, to choose always the most valuable goal independently from

its low possibility to be achieved; or - vice versa - to choose always the most probable result, independently from its marginal value. The right strategy is choosing the most valuable goal among the most probable goals; or the most probable goal among the most valuable ones.

Economic theory has proposed the SEU (the multiplication of Utility per Probability). This is a good mathematical solution for economics; but both the notion of 'utility' and the notion of 'probability' have serious problems for psychological theories.

Independently from the precise mathematical function (one might also think of several possible context-dependent heuristics for the choice) what matters here is the idea that the objects of a choice/deliberation, what is taken into account, are not Goals but complex and global Exps. We compare two Exps (not just two goals), and we are motivated in our intentional action by the Exp (the value and the likelihood).

This makes also more integrated and homogeneous the background of the candidate (or chosen) 'intention': the beliefs supporting and justifying on the one side the 'value' ascribed to the goal, and on the other side, the credibility/strength of the belief (prediction). Also because some beliefs might affect both of them. For example, the belief that the achievement of the goal is very close, on the one side increases the *certainty* of the Exp, but - on the other side - increases its importance (the *value* of the goal).

There are – of course - other situations or processes where not the Exp but just the *value* of the goal counts. This is the case, for example, in the degree of the 'frustration' (and consequent 'suffering'): the greater the value of the frustrated goal, the greater the pain. There might even be no Exp at all but just a (inactive) goal. (This of course does not mean that Exps do not play their own role in suffering; see later). In general, Goals have their specific and separated functions. For example goals, (mere goals not joined with any prediction) are used for *evaluating* the current state of the world (the match/mismatch step in cybernetic regulation of purposive behavior). The goal can be realized, not to be pursue, and thus without any anticipatory character, but it remains a goal (what one wishes, likes, wants, desires, …) while evaluating the world as 'good', as 'satisfying'; or while evaluating a 'success' (on the action). In that very moment only the goal counts; there is no probability estimation about its future achievement.

Analogously, mere predictions (beliefs about future states or events) can have their own specific functions, without any combination with motivational stuff, 'duties' or 'desires'. Like forecasts that we make for the others, even ignoring their specific goal.

Intentions are Expectation Driven

Decisions about future actions and the resulting 'intentions', and intentional actions presuppose an explicit Exp about the result. In order to decide to pursue and to pursue an intention the agent has to believe a lot of things

[8] [9] [20] [24] that the goal is not yet realized, that it is not impossible (it can be realized), that it is not self-realizing (by a natural process or by the forthcoming action of another agent), thus that it should be realized by the agent itself (it depends on the agent). Moreover, he has to believe that he knows the right action (plan), that is, that there is an action/plan producing that specific outcome, that he is able to correctly perform that action, and that there are the external conditions for a successful execution of that action. Only when/if the agent believes so he decides to pursue the goal by doing that action. But this obviously means that he *believes that the goal will be realized by his performing the action*; that is, the subject while intentionally acting (not just subjectively 'attempting') has *positive Exps* about the performance of the action and the realization of the goal. He is not intentionally 'trying', he is intentionally 'doing'.

We can formulate intentions only because we are able to build predictions relevant for and related to our desires.

Attempting

Another function of Exp (not of a mere goal) is the subjective 'attempt'. While, from the point of view of the observer, any intentional (or at least purposive) action actually is an 'attempt', since and until it cannot be sure that it will succeed, not any intentional action is an 'attempt' from the subjective point of view of its agent. Subjectively speaking one 'does' something, doesn't 'attempt to do' something. Or better, it is different when one 'does' something and when one just 'attempts' to do something [31]. It is different if one subjectively is 'paying' or 'closing the door' and when he is subjectively 'attempting to pay or to close the door'.

In order to subjectively just 'attempting to do' it is necessary that the agent explicitly conceives and takes into account the possibility of failure. He is not sure about the achievement of the goal of the action.

As we know (§3) any positive Exp (since is about the future and cannot really be 100% certain) logically/necessarily implies a negative one; and vice versa. However, we know that such complementary Exp can be merely 'implicit', 'potential', not really mentally formulated. In other terms, the subject can find satisfactory a belief that P with 80% of certainty, and fill fully certain, without considering (generating) at all the fact that there is a 20% possibility that Not p. Failure remains in his mind just a potential knowledge. Moreover, the subject can formulate for a moment the idea of a possible Not P (20%), but nevertheless he can put this aside, and do not take into account at all this eventuality in his reasoning and decision. This is why subjectively speaking not all our actions are 'attempts' and when we intentionally do something we are not 'trying'.

However, sometimes we really subjectively 'attempt' to do something. In this case, our mental representation is precisely the idea of the possibility of a failure. We have both a positive and a negative Exp; we are explicitly

uncertain about the result. Thus, an attempt necessarily entails an Exp in the agent: an Exp not so sure about the positive result, implying some represented Exp of failure [9].

There also are attempts or better trials not really aimed at succeeding (but with some doubt), but just or mainly aimed at learning. The agent acts in order to see whether (the door is open or not) or to discover how (the door opens). The epistemic function, which is present in any action and especially (consciously) in any attempted action, here is dominant or is the only real goal.

Sustaining Persistence (Waiting for Rewards)

Another interesting function of the Exp as such, as a whole, is the fact that entertaining an Exp in mind (especially a sensory-motor representation of a desirable, pleasant state) seems to be useful for our capacity of *delaying* the realization of our the desires (Freud), although *persisting* in a prolonged activity, and paying costs, or persisting just in waiting for something, without receiving rewards (except from our imagination) (DESIRES). Long term planning is a fundamental capacity of humans, and the needed persistence and coherence [23] is neither due simply to 'predictions' (belief) per se', nor just to the goal. The goal without the Exp cannot *sustain* and *support* the effort toward the future; the belief per se' has no motivational power.

This is also why one of the worst forms (and causes) of suffering [28] is not just that our goal is frustrated but that this is 'forever'. That is when we do not only see our goal destroyed, but also wasted any possible 'hope'. We cannot have any (although weak) Exp about a future realization of our goal; the world doesn't simply answer "No!", it answers "Never!".

We can cope with a failure or a loss also thanks to the 'consolation' that at least one day it will be possible (again)

Expectations and Suffering

Expect can make suffering worst. If not only a given goal is frustrated, but there also was a joined prediction which is invalidated (was wrong), in other words, if there was not simply a goal but a full Expt, then the sufferance is worst (given the same value of the goal). To the frustration it is added the 'disappointment' (see later), which is an additional dimension of sufferance; either because you were already enjoying the desired result (it was already 'yours'), and you perceive this failure more as a loss than as a simple missed gain; or because also the meta-goal of being a good predictor is frustrated; or because not only you do not get the price, but you also get *less than* expected.

Emotional Response to Expectation is Specific: the Strength of Disappointment

As we said, also the effects of the *invalidation* of an expectation are very different depending on: a) the positive or negative character of the expectation; b) the strengths of the components. Given the fact that X has previous expectations, how this changes her evaluation of and reaction to a given event?

Invalidated Expectations

We call invalidated expectation, an expectation that results to be wrong: i.e. while expecting that p at time t', X now beliefs that NOT p at time t'.

$$(Bel \; x \; p^{t'})^{t<t'} <==> (Bel \; x \; \neg p^{t'})^{t''>t}$$

This crucial belief is *the 'invalidating' belief.*

- Relative to the goal component it represents "frustration", "goal-failure" (is the *frustrating* belief): I desire, wish, want that p but I know that not p.

FRUSTRATION: $(Goal \; x \; p^{t'}) \& (Bel \; x \; \neg p^{t'})$

- Relative to the prediction belief, it represents 'falsification', 'prediction-failure':

INVALIDATION: $(Bel \; x \; p^{t'})^{t<t'} \& (Bel \; x \; \neg p^{t'})^{t''>t}$

$(Bel \; x \; p^{t'})^{t<t'}$ represents the former illusion or delusion (X illusorily believed at time t that at t' p would be true).

This configuration provides also the cognitive basis and the components of "**surprise**": *the more certain the prediction the more intense the surprise.* [10] [11] Given positive and negative Expectations and the answer of the world, that is the *frustrating* or *gratifying* belief, we have:

	P	¬P
Bel x p & Goal x p	No surprise + achievement	*surprise* + *frustration* **disappointment**
Bel x ¬p & Goal x p	*surprise* + *non-frustration* **relief**	no surprise + frustration

Disappointment. Relative to the whole mental state of "positively expecting" that p, the *invalidating&frustrating* belief produces "disappointment" that is based on this basic configuration (plus the affective and cognitive reaction to it):

DISAPPOINTMENT: $(Goal^{\%} \; x \; p^{t'})^{t \; \&t'} \&$

$(Bel^{\%} \; x \; p^{t'})^t \& (Bel^{\%} \; x \; \neg p^{t'})^{t'}$

At t X believes that at t' (later) p will be true; but now – at t' – she knows that Not p, while she continues to want that p. Disappointment contains goal-frustration and forecast failure, surprise. It entails a greater *sufferance* than simple frustration [28] for several reasons: (i) for the additional failure; (ii) for the fact that this impact also on the self-esteem as epistemic agent (Badura's "predictability" and related "controllability") and is disorienting; (iii) for the fact that losses of a pre-existing fortune are worst than missed gains (see below), and long expected and surely expected desired situation are so familiar and "sure" that we feel a sense of loss.

The stronger and well-grounded the belief the more disorienting and restructuring is the *surprise* (and the stronger the consequences on our sense of predictability). The more important the goal the more *frustrated* the subject.

In Disappointment these effects are combined: *the more sure the subject is about the outcome & the more important the outcome is for her, the more disappointed the subject will be.*

- Te degree of disappointment seems to be a function of both dimensions and components [9]. It seems to be felt as a unitary effect.

"How much are you disappointed?" "I'm very disappointed: I was <u>sure</u> to succeed"

"How much are you disappointed?" "I'm very disappointed: it was very <u>important</u> for me"

"How much are you disappointed?" "Not at all: it was not <u>important</u> for me"

"How much are you disappointed?" "Not at all: I have just tried; I was <u>expecting</u> a failure".

Obviously, worst disappointments are those with great value of the goal and high degree of certainty. However, the *surprise* component and the *frustration* component remain perceivable and a function of their specific variables.

Relief. Relief is based on a 'negative' expectation that results to be wrong. The prediction is invalidated but the goal is realized. There is no frustration but surprise. In a sense relief is the opposite of disappointment: the subject was "down" while expecting something bad, and now feel much better because this expectation is invalidated.

RELIEF: $(Goal \; x \; \neg p^{t'}) \& (Bel \; x \; p^{t'}) \& (Bel \; x \; \neg p^{t'})$ [10]

- *The harder the expected harm and the more sure the expectation (i.e. the more serious the subjective threat) the more intense the 'relief'.*

More precisely: the higher the worry, the threat, and the stronger the relief. The worry is already a function of the value of the harm and its certainty.

Analogously, **joy** seems to be more intense depending on the value of the goal, but also on how *unexpected* it is.

A more systematic analysis should distinguish between different kinds of surprise (based on different monitoring activities and on explicit vs. implicit beliefs), and different kinds of disappointment and relief due to the distinction between 'maintenance' situations and 'change/achievement' situations.

More precisely (making constant the value of the Goal) the case of loss is usually worst than simple non-achievement. This is coherent with the theory of psychic suffering [28] that claims that pain is greater when there is not only frustration but disappointment (that is a previous Exp), and

---

[9] As a first approximation of the degree of Disappointment one might assume some sort of multiplication of the two factors: Goal-value * Belief-certainty. Similarly to 'Subjective Expected Utility': the greater the SEU the more intense the Disappointment.

[10] Or – obviously - (Goal x pt') & (Bel x ¬pt') & (Bel x pt').

when there is 'loss', not just 'missed gains', that is when the frustrated goal is a maintenance goal not an achievement goal. However, the presence of Exps makes this even more complicated.

Level of expectation: how to be unhappy with positive results

The *level of Exp* also plays a very important role. In fact after having Exps (with a given expected *value*) the appreciation of the outcome is no longer *absolute*: good or bad, achieved goal vs. frustrated goal, failure (or at most the evaluation of the degree of the achievement/frustration: fully vs. partially achieved). The appreciation of the outcome becomes *relative* to the expected outcome.[11] This also has not so nice consequences, like the possibility to find unsatisfactory even good results (if inferior to the Exps).

What matters in fact is not only if the outcome is positive or negative, but if it better or worst of the desired and predicted level. Suppose a polarity of good (pleasant)/bad (unpleasant) results; and suppose now that we have a given positive Exp (Expected positive value – ExPV) or a given negative Exp (Expected negative value – ExNV). Given this and given the positive result of Event 1 (Ev1) or the negative result of Event 2 (Ev2), we get both an absolute Actual positive (APV) or Actual negative value (ANV) of Ev1 and Ev2 (relative to the 0 point), but also a relative value of Ev1 or Ev2 relatively to their Exp levels.

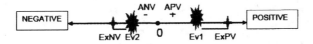

The interval (ExPV – APV) gives us the measure of the 'disappointment', 'discontent' even with a positive result. The APV can give us the measure of a possible 'consolation' ("nevertheless the result is quite good").

On the negative side, the interval (ExNV – ANV) gives us the level of the 'relief,' even with a negative event. The APV gives us the level of absolute frustration, but (ExNV – ANV) (if ANV is less than ExNV) can give a sort of 'consolation': "It might have been much worst!").

Of course, the APV can be greater/better than the ExPV; and in this case there is surprise and joy; while the ANV can be greater/worst than the ExNV; and in this case we get a higher degree of frustration than just due to ANV; the ANV is made worst by the fact that it is even worst than expected. Pessimistic Exps in part protect us from frustration and disappointment; while too optimistic Exps can expose to frustration even with good results.

In other words, we have to cross two dimensions of evaluation of the results: on the one side if they are good or

bad (realized goals or frustrated goals), on the other side if they are better or worst than expected.

RESULTS	GOOD	BAD
< Expectation	Disappointment	Relief
> Expectation	?? "Whoow!"	?? "Not so bad"

Relief: less bad than expected; *Disappointment*: less good than expected; *Consolation*: Although bad, at least something good. [12]

All this is due not just to our goals and their values, but to the fact that we *expect* certain outcomes

Concluding remarks

In conclusion, Exps are composite and hybrid mental representations with an epistemic component or attitude and a motivational component and attitude about the same content. But in fact this mental representation is a new unitary mental object with its own specific uses and functions, and gives rise to typical and new psychic phenomena. Like the activity of 'expecting for', the possibility of complex rational decisions based on the comparison not simply between two goals with their importance, or specific emotional states (hope, trust, fear, worries, …) and emotional reactions due to the pre-existence of such a state (relief, disappointment,..).

Expectations play a major role in the pressure for the origin of mind with its crucial anticipatory nature (cit), and primitive expectations - related to actions as anticipated rewarding perceptual inputs for monitoring and learning - are a fundamental step towards the evolution of true goal-directed (purposive) systems.

One of the aims of this contribution is to show that there is room for some sort of 'theoretical psychology', where an analytical and formal modeling is supposed to provide important insights and predictions, and produces indications and interpretations for empirical research. In other terms, we attempt to modestly follow the old arrogant program of

---

[11] We might call the Goal within a positive Exp 'aspiration' and 'aspiration level' its expected degree of realization combined with its subjective Value.

[12] The theory of 'relief' and of 'disappointment' is even more complicated. They are in fact 'counterfactual' emotions. They are based on the idea (imagination) of what *might have been/happen*. Relief is when what actually is now (what has happened) is better of what could have been; Disappointment is when the actual situation is worst than the possible one. Relief and disappointment due to a previous (bad/good) Exp are just sub-cases of this. In fact, if X expects/forecasts that P, this implies that he was considering P possible, probable; also after that P didn't in fact become true. Moreover, at least 'relief' is also possible simply at the end of an actual and present pain or sufferance. This is coherent with this analysis; since a current experienced sufferance – when finished – entails the (implicit) belief, the a-posteriori Exp, that it could have continued, and the relief is due to this possible but falsified continuation.

Spinoza about emotions (and mind) "more geometrico demostrata".

Acknowledgments

European Project *MindRaces* N°511931- EC's 6th Framework Programme - Unit: Cognitive Systems; & European HUMAINE network. I would like to tank Maria Miceli, Emiliano Lorini which have developed with me the general theory of expectations and of related emotional states, and their formalization; Giovanni Pezzulo for our view of anticipation and mind; Luca Tummolini with whom I have developed the social and normative aspects of expectations; Michele Piunti which has developed a computational model of this and of surprise and cautiousness.

References

Bandura A., (1990). Self-efficacy mechanism in human agency. *American Psychologist*, 37, pp. 122-147, 1990.

Bratman M. E., (1988). Intentions, plans, and practical reason, Cambridge, MA: Harvard University Press, 1988.

Butz, M.V. & Hoffman, J. (2002) Anticipations control behavior: Animal behavior in an anticipatory learning classifier system. *Adaptive Behavior*, 10, 75-96.

Butz, M.V. (2002) *Anticipatory learning classifier system* Boston, MA: Kluwer Academic Publisher.

Castelfranchi C., (1996). Reasons: Belief Support and Goal Dynamics. *Mathware & Soft Computing, 3.* pp. 233-47, 1996.

Castelfranchi, C. (2005) Mind as an Anticipatory Device: For a Theory of Expectations, *Brain, Vision and Artificial Intelligence, 1st International Symposium* (BV&AI 2005), eds. M. De Gregorio, V. Di Maio, M. Frucci and C. Musio, Springer-Verlag, Berlin, 2005, pp. 258-276.

Castelfranchi, C., Lorini E., (2003). Cognitive Anatomy and Functions of Expectations. In *Proceedings of IJCAI'03 Workshop on Cognitive Modeling of Agents and Multi-Agent Interactions*, Acapulco, Mexico, August 9-11, 2003.

Castelfranchi, C., Paglieri, F. (2007). "The role of beliefs in goal dynamics: Prolegomena to a constructive theory of intentions". *Synthese*, in press. (DOI: 10.1007/s11229-006-9156-3).

Castelfranchi, C., Tummolini, L. and Pezzulo, G. (2005) From Reaction to Goals – AAAI Ws on From Reaction to Anticipation,. 2005

Cohen, P. R., Levesque H. J., (1990). Intention is choice with commitment. *Artificial Intelligence, 42*, pp. 213-261, 1990.

Cooper, J., Fazio R. H., (1984). A new look at dissonance theory. In L. Berkovitz (Ed.), *Advances in experimental social psychology, Vol. 17*, pp. 229-266, San Diego, CA: Academic Press, 1984.

Corrêa, M., Coelho, E., Agent´s programming from a mental states framework. In Proceedings of the 14th Brazilian Symposium on Artificial Intelligence (SBIA98), Lecture Notes in AI 1515, pp. 31-39, Springer-Verlag, 1998.

Drescher, G. (1991) *Made-up minds: A constructivist approach to artificial intelligence.* MIT Pres.

Galliers, J.R. (1991). Modelling Autonomous Belief Revision in Dialogue, In *Decentralized AI-2*, Y. Demazeau, J.P. Mueller (eds), 231-43. Armsterdam: Elsevier.

Jones, O. R. (1983). Trying. *Mind*, XCII(367):368-385.

Kahneman, D., Miller D. T., (1986). Norm Theory: Comparing reality to its alternatives. *Psychological Review*, 93, pag. 136-153, 1986.

Kirsh, D., Maglio. P., On distinguishing epistemic from pragmatic action. *Cognitive Science, 18*, pp. 513-549, 1994.

Lorini, E. and Castelfranchi, C. (2007). The cognitive structure of surprise: looking for basic principles. *Topoi: an International Review of Philosophy*, (forthcoming).

Lorini, E., Castelfranchi C., (2004). The role of epistemic actions in expectations. In *Proceedings of Second Workshop of Anticipatory Behavior in Adaptive Learning Systems 2004 (ABIALS 2004)*, Los Angeles, 17 July 2004.

Lorini, E., Herzig, A., and Castelfranchi, C. (2006). Introducing Attempt in a modal logic of intentional action. Michael Fisher, Wiebe van der Hoek (Eds.), 10th European Conference on Logics in AI (JELIA06), Springer-Verlag, LNAI, p. 280-292.

Miceli, M. & Castelfranchi, C. (1997). Basic principles of psychic suffering: A preliminary account. *Theory & Psychology*, 7, 769-798.

Miceli, M. & Castelfranchi, C. (2005). Anxiety as an "epistemic" emotion: An unceraity theory of anxiety. *Anxiety, Stress, and Coping, 18*, 291-319.

Miceli, M. & Castelfranchi, C. (2006) Hope: The power of wish and possibility. (Submitted).

Miceli, M. & Castelfranchi, C. (2000). The role of evaluation in cognition and social interaction. In K. Dautenhahn (Ed.), *Human cognition and agent technology.* Amsterdam: Benjamins, 225-61.

Miceli, M., Castelfranchi. C., (2002) The Mind and the Future. The (Negative) Power of Expectations. *Theory & Psychology*, 12(3), pp. 335-366, 2002.

Miller, G., Galanter E., and Pribram. K. H., (1960) Plans and the structure of the behavior. Rinehart & Winston, New York.

Ortony, A., Partridge. O., (1987) Surprisingness and expectation failure: What's the difference? In *Proceedings of the 10th International Joint Conference on Artificial Intelligence*, pp. 106-108, Los Altos, CA: Morgan Kaufmann, 1987.

Pezzulo, G., Lorini, E., Calvi G. (2004). How do I know how much I don't know? A cognitive approach about Uncertainty and Ignorance. In *Proceedings of 26th Annual Meeting of the Cognitive Science Society (CogSci 2004)*, Chicago, USA, 5-7 August, 2004

Rao, A.S., Georgeff M.P., (1992). An abstract architecture for rational agents. In Proceedings of the Third International Conference on Principles of Knowledge Representation and Reasoning, C. Rich, W. Swartout, and B. Nebel (Eds.), pp. 439-449, Morgan Kaufmann Publishers, San Mateo, CA, 1992.

Rosenblueth, A., Wiener N., and Bigelow. J., (1960) Behavior, Purpose, and Teleology. In W. Buckley (Ed.), Modern Systems Research for the Behavioral Scientist, Aldine, Chicago.

Shafer G., (1976). *A mathematical theory of evidence.* Princeton University Press, Cambridge, 1976.

Language Activity as a Representational Activity: Typological Approaches to Comparison

Catherine Fuchs (catherine.fuchs@ens.fr)
Lattice, ENS, 1 rue Maurice Arnoux, 92120 Montrouge, France

Abstract

Within the field of cognitive science, linguistics has to account both for the diversity of semantic representations construed by various languages and for their unity (as regards their mapping into universal conceptual representations). This issue is illustrated here by examples from typological studies on the diversity of linguistic expressions of comparison.

Introduction

Language ability is part of the human nature; being somehow rooted in the human brain, it is an object of science for neurobiologists and experimental psychologists. Linguists for their part are interested in languages: by analyzing languages (*"les langues"*), they try to enlighten general properties of language (*"le langage"*). In other words, the universal faculty of language is, no doubt, an innate property of human species, but linguists are faced with language diversity, not with language universality.

Now, if we assume that *(a)* natural language is a mechanism that connects mental or conceptual representations to syntactic (and ultimately phonetic) forms, and *(b)* the conceptual representations that underlie non-linguistic thinking are universal, being part of our biological endowment, how then can we describe the connection between universality and diversity? Various answers have been put forward, ranging from Chomsky's 'universal grammar' (focusing on syntactic structures) and Fodor's 'language of mind', to different types of 'cognitive grammars' (mainly concerned with semantic structures).

Different Levels of Representation

The notion of 'representation' can be misleading: different levels of representation must be distinguished (Culioli, 1995).

Conceptual Representations. The conceptualization of reality (objects and events) deriving from our perceptions, tastes, dislikes, collective representations, *etc.*, is part of human cognitive activity: it is the level of conceptual representations (CRs), to which we have no direct access other than through our actions, including our language activity.

Semantic Representations. Through language activity, utterances (the only observable language phenomena) are produced in communication acts. Utterances are concatenations of 'markers' (signs) - the relationship between the *signifiants* and the *signifiés* being specific to each particular language. Consequently, utterances give birth to linguistic (semantic) representations (SRs) that stand for mental representations, but do not code them univocally in term for term relationships: SRs and CRs are not isomorphic (see also Levinson, 1997).

Thus the task of linguistics is to elaborate metalinguistic representations of the SRs of particular languages; such metalinguistic representations consist of rules and operations, which should be subject to generalization. For simplicity's sake, I will not concern myself with the formal aspect of metalinguistic representations, which will be accounted for in terms of simple glosses.

Linguistics within the Field of Cognitive Science

In my view (Fuchs, 1999), the main task of linguistics within the field of cognitive science is to provide a description of semantic representations that underlie linguistic meaning in various languages, and to account both for their diversity (since they make different choices among various conceptualizations of situations) and for their unity (since they are supposed to correspond ultimately to unique mental structures). For, if languages were direct codes of non-linguistic thinking, they would all be similar: language diversity implies the existence of an intermediate level of variable (semantic) representations between the level of mental representations and that of superficial structures.

Such investigations have been carried out at large in a number of lexical domains (colours, numbers, …) and grammatical domains (space, temporality, possession, actancy, …). But other domains, which obviously do not fall within the scope of elementary categories, may also be of interest: such is the case of 'comparison', which I will take as an illustration of the methodological and theoretical problems faced by linguistics in *(1)* studying the representational activity at work in SRs of particular languages (*i.e.* looking for linguistic operations with cognitive impact), and *(2)* trying to pinpoint similarities (as well as differences) between SRs of various languages (*i.e.* looking for cross-linguistic invariants), in order to *(3)* discover some general properties of language itself, concerning the link between SRs and CRs.

Looking for Linguistic Operations in Particular Languages

As regards the grammatical category of comparison, cognitively significant observations made on single instances of language, like English or French (but undoubtedly subject to further generalizations) may be summarized as follows.

Prototypical Representation and Basic Structures

Quantification vs. Qualification. Two main types of comparison are to be distinguished, namely 'quantitative' and 'qualitative' comparison. The former implies grading (two items being graded against each other, regarding a given property, ex: *The tower is higher than the house*), as opposed to the latter (two items being compared as to their manner of performing a given action, or of verifying a given property, ex: *He swims like a duck*).

The Prototypical Representation (Stassen, 1985) is concerned with comparison between two objects or individuals (typically expressed in the form of NPs) — named the 'comparee' and the 'standard' — with respect to a given 'parameter' (typically expressed in the form of a verbal or adjectival predicate). This representation presumably reflects some kind of cognitively-based process: assigning a graded position on a predicative scale (for instance, the scale of *heaviness*) respectively to two objects (for instance, two *stones*), in order to make a relevant choice before performing a given action; or evaluating the similarity of two objects (*e.g.* two *stones*) with respect to a given capacity (*e.g.* their capacity of *hurting*) or quality (*e.g.* their *roundness*).

Identity vs. Non-Identity. There appear to be only two types of relations (Rivara, 1975, 1995): either identity (=) or non-identity (≠). Equality (*i.e.* quantitative identity) and inequality (*i.e.* quantitative non-identity) operate on subjectively oriented scales: either on the scale of great quantities (as = 'as much, as many'; more / -er = 'more much, more many') or on the scale of small quantities (as little, as few; less = 'less little, less few') — which means that, contrary to logical relations, semantic relations of quantitative comparison are not symmetrical: *John is more friendly than Peter* = 'John surpasses Peter in friendliness on the scale of great quantities' ≠ *Peter is less friendly than John* = 'Peter surpasses John in friendliness on the scale of small quantities'.

Basic Structures. All possible constructions are not equally frequent: inequalities and equalities operating on the 'great quantities' scale are more frequently expressed than those operating on the opposite scale; and, concerning qualitative comparison, similarity (*i.e.* qualitative identity, expressing sameness of manner) is more frequent than dissimilarity (*i.e.* qualitative non-identity, expressing difference of manner).

Consequently, the three basic structures — probably the most cognitively salient — are the following:
(i) inequality on the scale of great quantities (known as 'superiority'): *Mary is prettier than Jane*
(ii) equality on the scale of great quantities: *Mary is as pretty as Jane*
(iii) similarity: *Mary sings like a nightingale.*

Non-Basic Structures

Now, if one looks more closely into the system of widely described languages like English (or French), one can easily notice various extensions of these basic structures, leading to more abstract and complex types of representations that could hardly be conceivable without the help of language.

The Parameter can be extended to a 'secondary quality' — e.g. an adverb qualifying the main predicate (*Mary sings louder than Jane; Mary sings as loudly as Jane*) or to a 'secondary predicate' (*Being prettier than Jane, Mary won; Being as expensive as John's, Peter's car is likely to be stolen*).

The Compared Items can be other than two objects or individuals. Comparison markers are also used to express comparisons between two circumstances (*It's colder today than yesterday; The weather is as cold in Paris as it is in London*), two properties (*Mary is more cunning than intelligent; Jane is as pretty as she is intelligent*), two modalities (*Mary is prettier than I thought; The sky is as sunny as I hoped*), two events (*Jane loves her son, more than you do yours; Mary bought a flat, as you did a house*), or even two 'enunciations' (*"P", as they say*).

Marker-Operation Relationships

Just like any detailed study of a given grammatical category, the study of comparison must take into account the non-univocal relationships between markers and operations: that is, polysemy on one side, and paraphrase on the other. Let's take the example of the French marker *comme*. It is a polysemous item, which covers a large range of meanings (Fuchs & Le Goffic, 2005): similarity (*chanter comme un rossignol*: "to sing like a nightingale"), temporal simultaneity (*Il arriva comme je partais*: "He arrived just as I was leaving"), a kind of inference (*Comme je ne suis pas pressé, je vais attendre*: "Since I am in no hurry, I will wait"), exclamation (*Comme elle est jolie!*: "How pretty she is!"), etc. And as a marker of comparison, it has a number of 'quasi-synonyms' (Fuchs, 2007): *ainsi que, de même que, à la façon de, à la manière de*, etc. Such multiple correlations, which are specific to a given language, speak for the relative autonomy of SRs as procedures of meaning construction.

Looking for Cross-Linguistic Invariants

This is where typologists come in. Working on data from extensive samples of historically unrelated languages, they classify languages (on a structural basis, not on a genetic one) and formulate generalizations supplementing the regularities discovered in the study of single instances of language. The pioneering research in linguistic typology was devoted to word-order and morpho-syntax.

For many years, comparison was considered so central that the word order patterning of a specific language was supposed to be determined by the order of elements in a comparative construction — cf. the so-called 'implicational' (or relational) 'universal 22' in Greenberg (1966); see also Lehmann (1972). Although the validity of that claim has been questioned later on (Andersen, 1983), it seems that the prototypical inequality comparative is "the most secure of constructions" regarding word-order, since "it is never changed for poetic effect" (Lehmann, 1973). This stability in word-order within each particular language gives evidence that the comparative SRs – and especially the SRs of inequality - are deeply rooted in languages, and meant to express some fundamental cognitive processes.

More recent typological studies have been concerned with the semantics of comparison. Most of them confine themselves to describing the basic structures where two objects or individuals are being compared, for the grammars of their sample languages generally do not provide sufficiently reliable data on other more complex constructions.

Semantic Variations

The methodology consists, first in observing the cross-linguistic variations (lexical, syntactic and semantic variations) from a 'semasiological' point of view (i.e. from forms to meanings), and gathering the various representations into several 'types'; and only then in trying to recover invariants: "*In order to understand the grammar of comparative constructions, not much is gained in looking for one uniform universal structure; rather what is required is that the entire pool of possible conceptual sources be considered*" (Heine, 1997). Actually, there are numerous surface constructions available across languages, which can be reduced to a small number of representation types. The markers involved in these representations are generally used for a number of different grammatical categories and not exclusively for expressing comparison – which indicates that they represent an inventory of the possible sources to choose from.

The three main typological works I am referring to are: Stassen (1985) - who studied inequality in 110 different languages, Haspelmath & Buchholz (1998) - who examined equative and similative constructions in 47 European plus several non-European languages, and Henkelmann (2006) – who studied equative constructions in 25 languages all over the world. To summarize briefly the results of these works: comparatives turn out not to be independent, autonomous construction types, but to derive from more basic representations. For instance, it should be noticed

that many languages do not resort to relative degree words (such as French *plus* or English *more*) to encode quantitative comparison – in these languages, the notion of grading results from other types of semantic operations.

Main Types of Inequality SRs. A limited number of types (underlying SRs) can be determined, which correspond to various semantic 'strategies', *i.e.* to different choices made by languages among elementary conceptual sources. The main 'schemas' that happen to be used for encoding inequality – equivalent to English *A is bigger than B* (Stassen, 1985; Heine, 1997) – are the following:

(a) 'Action Schema', glossed: *A big EXCEEDS B* (surface variants: *A is big surpasses B / A is big to surpass B / B is big (but) A exceeds / A surpasses B (at) bigness*)

(b) 'Spatial Schemas', which can be subdivided into three subtypes:

- 'source (or separative) schema', glossed: *A big FROM B* (by far the most common spatial schema expressing comparison in the languages of the world; surface variants: ablative or genitive adverbial phrases)
- 'locative schema', glossed: *A big AT B* (second best spatial schema expressing comparison; surface variants: *A is big on / above / in / by / ... B*)
- 'allative (or goal) schema', glossed: *A big TO B* (rather rare; surface variants: allative / benefactive / dative / ... adverbial phrases)

(c) 'Conjoined Schemas', which can be subdivided into two subtypes:

- 'polarity schema', glossed: *A big (AND) B not big* (either positive/negative polarity: *A is big and/but/while B is not big* – variant *B is not big and/but/while A is big* - or antonymy: *A is big and/but/while B is small* – variant *B is small and/but/while A is big*)
- 'sequence (temporal) schema', glossed: *A big THEN B* (surface variants: *A is big and/and then/thereafter/... B*)

It should be noted, incidentally, that from a typological point of view, French constructions (*A est plus grand que B*) and English ones (*A is bigger than B*), are difficult to classify, for they "*have been grammaticalized to such an extent that the cognitive schema underlying them is not readily reconstructible*" (Heine, 1997). Some typologists consider that such constructions correspond to a specific 'particle schema'; other tentatively analyze them as resulting from a process of syntactization, which could have led to the transformation of a coordinate clause (corresponding to a 'conjoined schema' – whether a 'polarity' or a 'sequence' one) into a subordinate clause.

Main Types of Equality SRs. A limited number of underlying schemas has also been listed for the encoding of equality (Henkelmann, 2006):

(a)'Extents Schema', glossed: *A (as) big (as/like) B* (equality relation is established between the relative extents of the quality that is being attributed to the entities being compared)

(b) 'Entities Schema', glossed: *A big EQUALS B* (equality relation is established between the entities directly by means of an equative predicate; *cf.* inequality 'action schema' *supra*)

(c) 'Possessive Schema', glossed: *A's bigness is B's bigness* (the extent of the quality that is said to be equal is represented as a possession of the entities being compared)

(d) 'Representative Schema', glossed: *A is (of) B's bigness* (the entities being compared are represented as instances or representatives of an equal quality appearing as an entity)

(e) 'Implicit Schema', glossed: *A big, B big* (two predications in the positive degree are juxtaposed without any explicit encoding of the notion equality; *cf.* inequality 'conjoined schema' *supra*).

Invariants

The first observation to be made is that underlying comparative SRs are neither indefinite nor random: they are in a relatively small number and seem to derive from cognitively motivated basic schemas. The different ways of encoding quantitative comparison thus illustrate different choices made by languages within a limited 'repertoire' of possible conceptual sources.

From SRs to CRs. As has been pointed out by Levinson (1997), the relation between SRs and CRs is a matter for empirical investigation. There seem to be good psycholinguistic and neurolinguistic reasons to assume that on the CRs level, the cognitive structure of comparison is in the form of a spatial global configuration: the parameter being pictured as an axis, marked for positive-negative polarity; the two objects being positioned on the axis so that their positions define extents, which represent the degree to which the compared objects possess the quality at issue - in other words, relative degrees of intensity with respect to a certain quality being represented in terms of relative distance on the axis. According to Stassen, the mapping of this CR into various SRs could be seen as a transition of such a spatially modelled configuration into a configuration which is modelled on 'temporal chaining' (*i.e.* temporal ordering between two events): strategies 'read off' various bits of information from the CR and codify them in the form of a sequence of two propositions. Thus, the three types of cognitive strategies distinguished by Stassen could fit inequality as well as equality schemas :

(a) The 'Independent Strategy', where the axis is taken as the salient feature of the CR, so that the compared items A and B are associated with the opposite sides of the axis – thus leading to the 'polarity schema' of inequality and to the 'implicit schema' of equality.

(b) The 'Ordered Strategy', where the salient feature is provided by the extents demarcated on the axis, so that A and B are both associated with the positive side

of the axis – thus leading to the 'action schema' for inequality and to the 'extents schema' and 'entities

(c) the 'Relative Strategy', where the spatial relation between A and B is the salient feature, so that only one of them is associated with the axis – thus leading to the 'spatial schemas' and 'sequence schema' for inequality and to the 'possessive schema' and 'representative schema' for equality.

General Grammar. The aim of linguistic typology is precisely to sketch out a 'general grammar' (or 'typological universal grammar'), at the intermediate level between the universal level of mental representations – conceptualization of the world - and that of particular languages, *i.e.* to discover the 'menu' of techniques and grammatical categories where individual languages make their choice (Seiler, 2000; Lazard, 2000).

While some typologists balk at the idea of semantic 'universals', they all agree to pinpoint 'invariants', *i.e.* general regularities which impose limits to the variations and govern the possible relationships between markers and underlying operations.

Besides, it should be noted that typological investigations have showed the role of areal forces that are largely responsible for the choice of SRs types made by languages (Heine, 1997; Haspelmath & Buchholz, 1998).

Looking for General Properties of Language

Within the field of cognitive science, linguistics – defined as the science of language apprehended through the diversity of languages (Culioli, 1995) – has a specific role to play, by proposing metalinguistic representations of SRs in various languages, and relating them both to CRs and to surface structures. From that cross-linguistic point of view, only local theories can be constructed for the time being. Several local theories, which are more or less disjoined, are being produced on limited domains of grammatical systems or lexical fields, but only 'local maps' (so to speak) are available, and we still lack a general overview model.

Linguistic Relativity

Limited though they may be, 'local maps' drawn by typologists cannot but contribute to throw light on representational activity at work in languages. In the first place, they give evidence against any assimilation of SRs to CRs., and tend to favor some kind of 'constructivist' approach to linguistic meaning: language activity means producing and recognizing significant configurations (or 'forms' in the abstract sense of the term).

This, in turn, could contribute to the question of 'linguistic relativity', which has been widely debated for years. The clear-cut opposition between so-called 'Whorfian' positions (*i.e.* variant SRs mapping into variant CRs) and 'anti-Whorfian' positions (*i.e.* SRs mapping directly into universal CRs) has probably been overestimated. As advocated by cognitive grammars, semantic variability manifested in SRs does not involve conceptual variability in non-linguistic thinking and does not go against psychic unity of mankind. But, as far as it concerns 'thinking for speaking' (Slobin, 1996), it illustrates the relative autonomy of languages towards mental representations.

Cognitive Impact of SRs. Languages enforce obligatory grammatical and semantic distinctions, which reorganize mental representations; cross-linguistic studies thus shed a light on the specific ways in which small sectors of cognition are being structured in order to be represented by languages: they allow us to discover, so to speak, the topography of those sectors. Regularities can be observed in the 'grammatical slicing' operated by languages (Lazard, 2004): there seems to be invariant notions around which the grammatical categories of individual languages tend to take form. Some regions of what may be called the 'conceptual space' are such that most languages construct grammatical tools there: for instance temporality, space, or possession. In turn, these grammatical tools serve to express more complex notions (such as comparison for instance).

Language activity also contributes to reorganizing mental representations by forcing a linearization of thought and the taking of perspective (Levinson, 1997). Furthermore, while some SRs, which are prototypical, clearly derive from cognitively based conceptualizations, other SRs turn out to be secondary complexes that seem to be made possible by language activity itself (for instance comparisons where the compared items are no longer objects or individuals, but abstract constructs – such as events, modal or propositional contents). In other words, language activity has probably been a facilitating factor for the development of reflexive thinking.

A unified Approach to Language? Neurobiology has recently made great progress in the exploration of the brain, offering very precise insights into normal and pathological functioning of language. So has experimental psychology concerning language acquisition and linguistic performances of humans. But mutual contributions with linguistics (which is concerned with the very nature of linguistic systems and their variability) remain somewhat limited. Since linguistic phenomena are far from being known as they should, the gap between neuropsychological research on language faculty and linguistic studies on invariants is not likely to be filled in the near future. For only when linguistic invariants have been discovered at large and confirmed by adequate investigations, time will come to look for their possible psychological and neurological roots.

References

Andersen, P. K. (1983). *Word order typology and comparative constructions.* Amsterdam/Philadelphia: John Benjamins.

Culioli, A. (1995). *Cognition and representation in linguistic theory.* Amsterdam/Philadelphia: John Benjamins.

Fuchs, C. (1999). Diversity in linguistic representations: a challenge for cognition. In C. Fuchs & S. Robert (Eds.), *Language diversity and cognitive representations.* Amsterdam/Philadelphia: John Benjamins.

Fuchs, C. (2007). Relations de synonymie entre polysèmes: le réseau 'comme-manière-façon'. *Le Français moderne, LXXV:1.*

Fuchs, C., & Le Goffic, P. (2005). La polysémie de 'comme'. In O. Soutet (Ed.), *La polysémie.* Paris: Presses de l'Université de Paris-Sorbonne.

Greenberg, J. (1966). *Language universals.* The Hague: Mouton.

Haspelmath, M., & O. Buchholz (1998). Equative and similative constructions in the languages of Europe. In J. van der Auwera (Ed.), *Adverbial constructions in the languages of Europe.* Berlin/New-York: Mouton-de Gruyter.

Heine, B. (1997). *Cognitive foundations of grammar.* Oxford/New-York: Oxford University Press.

Henkelmann, P. (2006). Constructions of equative comparison. *Sprachtypol. Univ. Forsch., 59:4,* 370-398.

Lazard, G. (2000). Two-level relationships between language typology and cognitive linguistics. *Proceedings of the international conference on Cognitive Typology (Antwerpen).*

Lazard, G. (2004). On the status of linguistics with particular regard to typology. *The Linguistic Review, 21,* 389-411.

Lehmann, W. (1972). Contemporary linguistics and IE studies. *Publications of the Modern Language Association of America, 87,* 976-993.

Lehmann, W. (1973). *Historical linguistics: an introduction.* 2nd ed. New-York: Holt, Rinehart & Winston.

Levinson, S. (1997). From outer to inner space: categories and non-linguistic thinking. In E. Pederson & J. Nuyts (Eds.). *Language and conceptualization* Cambridge: Cambridge University Press.

Rivara, R. (1975). How many comparatives are there?. *Linguistics, 163,* 35-51.

Rivara, R. (1995). Pourquoi il n'y a que deux relations de comparaison. *Faits de langues, 5,* 19-39.

Seiler, H-J. (2000). *Language universals research: a synthesis.* Tübingen: Gunter Narr Verlag.

Slobin, D. (1996). From 'thought and language' to 'thinking for speaking'. In J. Gumperz & S. Levinson (Eds.). *Rethinking language relativity.* Cambridge: Cambridge University Press.

Stassen, L. (1985). *Comparison and universal grammar.* Oxford: Basil Blackwell.

Against Darwinism

Jerry Fodor (fodor@ruccs.rutgers.edu)
Department of Philosophy – Rutgers University, Davison Hall, Douglass Campus
New Brunswick, NJ 08903, New Jersey, USA

This started out to be a paper about why I don't like EP (i.e. the evolutionary theory of prepositional attitudes, hence of intentional states). But then it occurred to me that what the paper was really about wasn't the tension between Darwinism and theories that are intentional (with a 't'), but the tension between Darwinism and theories that are intensional (with an 's') [1]. The latter is more worrying since Darwinism, or anyhow adaptationism, is itself committed to intensionally individuated processes like 'selection for.' So the claim turned out to be that there is something seriously wrong with adaptationism per se. Having arrived at that, I could have rewritten this as straight-forwardly a paper about adaptationism, but I decided not to do so. It seems to me of interest to chart a route from being suspicious of Evolutionary Psychology to having one's doubts about the whole adaptationist enterprise. Hence what follows.

The central claim of Evolutionary Psychology (EP) is that heritable properties of psychological phenotypes are typically adaptations; which is to say that they are typically explained by their histories of selection. In particular, this is claimed on behalf of heritable phenotypic properties that involve intentional states like believing, desiring, and acting (or being disposed to act) in one way or another. It is reasonable to hold that the evidence for this claim, so far at least, is underwhelming. Be that as it may; in the first part of this paper I want to argue for something much stronger: that the whole idea of an evolutionary psychology is very likely ill-conceived. Much of the main line of argument I'll pursue is already to be found in the philosophical literature, especially the literature on evolutionary semantics. So my strategy is to start by reminding you of some of the morals of that discussion and to contend that they apply quite generally to selectionist accounts of the cognitive psychological phenotype.

The Edifying Fable of the Frogs and the Flies

Frogs snap at flies; having caught one, they then ingest it. It is in the interest of frogs to do so since, all else equal, the fitness of a frog that eats flies (and hence the likelihood of its contributing to the local gene pool) exceeds the fitness of a frog that doesn't. It is likewise plausible that the frogs' penchant for catching flies is an adaptation; which is to say that it was established in their behavioral phenotype by a process of natural selection. If so, then perhaps it follows that the function of the behavior (and/or of the physiological mechanisms by which the behavior is implemented), is precisely to mediate the catching of the flies by the frogs. Maybe, that's to say, some selectionist story about the phylogeny of fly-snapping can provide, at the same time, an account of the teleology of that response. I don't believe much of that, but never mind; let's assume for now that it's all true.

I suppose it is likewise plausible that frogs catch flies with the intention of doing so. (If you are unprepared to swallow the attribution of intentions to frogs, please feel free to proceed up the phylogenetic ladder until you find a kind of creature to which such attributions are, in your view, permissible.) Now, intentions-to-act have intentional objects, which may serve to distinguish among them. A frog's intention to catch a fly, for example, is an intention to catch a fly, and is ipso facto distinct from, say, the frog's intention to sun itself on the leaf of a lily. This consideration may encourage the following speculation: the fact about the teleology of the frog's fly catching mechanisms and the fact about the intentional object of its snaps both reduce to the fact that the frog's behavior is an evolutionary adaptation selected for catching and eating flies; which is, in turn, a fact that a selectionist account of the behavior's phylogeny may be supposed to entail. If that's right, then the transition from an adaptationist theory that explains the frog's behavior in terms of its effects on fitness, to a functional theory that explains the frog's behavior in terms of its teleology, to a psychological theory that explains the frog's behavior in terms of the content of its propositional attitudes amounts, in effect, to a reduction of intentionality to selection. This line of thought is not without its partisans, either in philosophy or in cognitive science at large.

But for every ointment there is a fly. The problem is that nothing about content or about teleology appears to follow directly from the assumption that fly-catching is an evolutionary adaptation in frogs. At a minimum, such inferences require the further, stronger, assumption that fly-catching behavior is an adaptation for catching flies; (i.e that catching flies is what the behavior was selected for). But 'adaptation for…', 'selection for…' and the like are themselves intensional contexts (just like 'belief that…' and 'intention to…'.). A mechanism that's selected for catching flies is not ipso facto a mechanism that's selected for catching ambient black nuisances; not even if, either in this part of the woods or in general, all and only the ambient black nuisances are flies. This logical quirk distinguishes 'selection for' from mere selection. If you select a mechanism that catches Xs, and if the Xs are Ys, then you thereby, select a mechanism that catches Ys. Selection is an extensional process, so it can't, as it were, 'see' the difference between intentional states that are extensionally equivalent. But the analogous point doesn't hold if the topic is 'selection for…' If you are selecting for Bs and Bs are Cs, it doesn't follow (and it needn't be true) that you are selecting for Cs. 'Select' doesn't distinguish among extensionally identical states, but 'select for...' does.

So the situation is this: either natural selection is a species of 'selection for...', and is thus itself a kind of intensional process; or natural selection is a species of selection tout court, and therefore cannot distinguish between coextensive mental states. In the former case it may, but in the latter case it doesn't, provide an explanation either of the teleology or of the intentional content of the frogs' snapping.

In the literature on philosophical semantics, the present point is often formulated as the 'disjunction problem'. In the actual world, where ambient black dots are flies, it is in a frog's interest to snap at flies. But, in such a world, it is equally in the frog's interest to snap at flies-or-ambient-black-dots. Snap for snap, snaps at the one will net you exactly as many flies to eat as snaps at the other. Snaps of which the intentional objects are flies and snaps whose intentional objects are black dots both affect a frog's fitness in exactly the same way and to exactly the same extent. Hence the disjunction problem: what is a frog snapping at when it snaps at a fly?

Thus far: It's plausible that natural selection can account for (heritable) intentional properties of a creature's phenotype only if it can distinguish selection of creatures that have such properties from selection of creatures for having such properties. If that's right, we can take the line of thought a step further. It would seem that the relevant difference between mere selection and selection for has to do with the status of certain counterfactuals. For example, according to this suggestion, to claim that frogs were selected for snapping at flies is to say (first) that in this world, where the ambient black- dots-or-flies are generally flies, frogs that snap at them are selected; and (second) that such frogs would not be selected in (nearby) counterfactual worlds where the ambient flies-or-black dots generally aren't flies (perhaps they're bee bees) So, now: can natural selection settle the issue between these counterfactuals?

I can think of two ways in which it might be supposed to do so. Both crop up, more or less explicitly, in the adaptationist literature, but I'm going to argue that neither of them has a prayer of working. I haven't heard of other alternatives and I can't prove that there are none. But I do rather think that these two exhaust the options. I am even prepared to wager moderate sums that they do.

First Option: Mother Nature

There's a sort of analogy between what natural selection does when it culls a population and what breeders do when they select from a population those members that they encourage to reproduce. This analogy was noticed by Darwin himself, and it has been influential in the popularizing adaptationist literature ever since. Suppose Granny breeds zinnias, with the intention of selling them on Market Day. Then Granny is selecting zinnias for their value on the market, and not, say, for the elaboration of their root-systems. This is so even if, as a matter of fact, it's precisely zinnias with elaborate root-systems that sell at the best prices. Likewise, the fact about her intentional psychology that explains which zinnias Granny chooses

when she sorts them is that she is interested in selling them, and not that she is interested in their having lots of roots. (Granny may not even know about the connection between market values and root systems. Or, if she knows, she may not care.) In short, since Granny is in it for the money and not for the roots, there is a matter of fact about what she selects for when she selects some of the zinnias and rejects the others. What Granny selects for is: whatever it is that she has in mind when she does her selecting.

So, then, perhaps we should take the analogy between natural selection and selective breeding at its face value. Perhaps we should say of natural selection just what we said of Granny: that what it selects for is whatever it has in mind in selecting? The counterfactuals fall out accordingly: If Granny is interested in high market value rather than big roots, that decides what she would do in a world where the salable zinnias are the ones with short roots, or no roots, or green roots with yellow polka dots, or whatever. Likewise, if natural selection has it in mind that there should be lots of frogs that eat flies, then, in the actual world, where the flies or bee bees are mostly flies, it favors both frogs that snap at flies and frogs that snap at bee bees. But in the counterfactual world where the flies-or-bee-bees are mostly bee bees, natural selection will favor only the frogs that snap at flies.

That, surely, is the thought that explains the prominence of anthropomorphized avatars of natural selection in the EP literature: Mother Nature, The Blind Watchmaker, The Selfish Gene or, for that matter, God. All of these are supposed to be (as one says); 'intentional systems': they have intentions in light of which they act. So, if one construes natural selection on the model of selection by an intentional system, one thereby makes room for a distinction between selection that has it in mind to propagate frogs that snap at flies and selection that has it in mind to propagate frogs that snap at flies-or-bee-bees; which is, I'm supposing, precisely the sort of distinction that you need to make room for if you are going to make sense of selection for beliefs, desires, goals and the like.

When it's put that baldly, however, it's perfectly obvious what's wrong with this line of thought: natural selection doesn't have a mind; a fortiori, it has nothing in mind when it selects among frogs. Likewise, if genes were intentional systems, there would be an answer to, for example, the question whether natural selection favors creatures that really do care about the flourishing of their children or creatures that really care only for the propagation of their genotypes. All you have to do, if you want to know, is find out which phenotype their genes prefer.

So, if genes are themselves intentional systems, or if there is a Mother Nature who selects with ends in view, then which creatures are selected can after all determine which traits they are selected for. That's the good news. The bad news is that, unlike natural selection, Mother Nature is a fiction, and fictions can't select things, however hard they try. Nothing cramps one's causal powers like not existing. Likewise, mutatis mutandis, the genes that make you cause your children to flourish (if, indeed, there are such genes) couldn't care less about why you want your children to do so. They couldn't care less about that because they don't care at all about anything.

Only agents have minds, and only agents act out of their intentions, and natural selection isn't an agent. To the contrary, it's an important part of the advertising for adaptationism that its way of explaining why the selection of phenotypes generally tends towards increasing fitness doesn't require attributions of agency. Because that's so (and assuming that it's true), adaptationism can legitimately claim to advance the scientific program of naturalizing nature.

You may think the preceding speaks without charity; that I am, in fact, shooting in a barrel that contains no fish. Surely, you may say, nobody could really hold that genes are literally concerned to replicate themselves? Or that natural selection literally has goals in mind when it selects? Or that it's literally run by an intentional system? Maybe.[2] But, before you deny that anybody could claim any of that, please do have an unprejudiced read through the EP literature. Meanwhile, I propose to consider a different way of arguing that adaptationism, because it can support the counterfactuals that distinguish mere selection from selection for, can likewise distinguish fly-snapping frogs from fly-or-bee-bee snapping frogs; thereby providing a paradigm for selectionist accounts of the content (and the teleology) of intentional states.

Second Option: Laws of Selection

Laws can support counterfactuals. Arguably, that's what makes laws different from mere true empirical generalizations. So, then, suppose there is a law from which it follows that t1s are selected in competitions with t2s. It's truistic that, if there is such a law, then it holds in all nomologically possible situations; which is to say that it determines the outcome of any nomologically possible t1 v. t2 competition. That includes competitions that are merely counterfactual, so long as they are nomologically possible. So then, if there's a law that connects the property of being a t1 and the property of competing successfully with t2s, and if the distinction between selection of t1s and selection for being t1s turns on the corresponding counterfactuals, then laws of selection might vindicate the selection/selection for distinction.

Well, are there such laws? I think it's most unlikely.

It's a thing about laws that they aspire to generality. In the paradigm cases, a law about Fs is supposed to apply to instances of F per se. Conversely, to the extent that a generalization applies not to Fs per se, but only to Fs-in-such-and-such circumstances, it's correspondingly unlikely that the generalization is a law (or, if it is a law, it's correspondingly unlikely that it's a law about Fs per se.) I take that to be common ground; but if it's right, then quite likely there aren't laws of selection. That's because who wins a t1 v. t2 competition is massively context sensitive. (Equivalently, it's massively context sensitive whether a certain phenotypic trait is conducive to a creature's fitness.) There are a number of respects in which this is true, some obvious some less so.

For example, it's obvious that no trait could be adaptive across the board. Rather, the adaptivity of a trait depends on the ecology in which its bearer is embedded. In

principle, if a trait is maladaptive in a certain context, you can fix that either by changing the trait or by changing the context. Is a creature's being green good for its fitness? That depends on whether the creature's background is green too. Is being the same color as its background good for a creature's fitness? That depends on whether camouflage that makes the creature hard for predators to find also makes it hard for the creature to find a mate. Is it good for a creature's fitness to be big? Well, being big can make it hard to flee from predators. Is it good for a creature to be small? Perhaps not if its predators are big. Is it good for a creature to be smart? Ask Hamlet (and bear in mind that, when it's all over and evolution has finished doing its thing, it's more than likely, that the cockroach will inherit the earth). Whether a trait militates for a creature's fitness is the same question as whether there's an `ecological niche' for creatures that have the trait to occupy; and that always depends on what else is going on in the neighborhood. Is it good to be a square peg? Not if the local holes are mostly round.

I want to emphasize that my point isn't just that, if there are laws about which traits win which competitions, they must be `ceteris paribus' laws. To the contrary, I take it to be true quite generally that special science laws hold only `all else equal'. If that's so, it's not a complaint against the putative laws of selection that they do too. I think, however, that the present considerations go much deeper.

To a first approximation, the claim that, ceteris paribus Fs cause Gs says something like: `given independently justified idealizations, Fs cause Gs.'[3] The intuition is that, underlying the observed variance, there is a bona fide, reliable, counterfactual-supporting connection between being F and causing Gs, the operation of which is obscured by the effects of unsystematic, interacting variables; the underlying generalization comes into view when the appropriate idealizations are enforced. By contrast (so I claim) there just aren't any reliable generalizations about which traits win competitions with which others. It simply isn't true, for example, that being big is in general better for fitness than being small except when there are effects of interacting variables; or that flying slow and high is in general better for fitness than flying fast and low except when there are effects of interacting variables; or that being monogamous is in general better for fitness than being polygamous except when there are effects of interacting variables etc. It's not that the underlying generalizations are there but imperceptible in the ambient noise. It's rather that there's just nothing to choose between (e.g.) the generalization that being small is better for fitness than being big and the generalization that being big is better for fitness than being small. Witness the fact that the world contains vastly many creatures of both kinds. I don't doubt that there are explanations of why competitions between creatures with different traits come out the way they do; but such explanations don't work by subsuming the facts they explain under general laws about the relative fitness of the traits. (I'll say something, pretty soon now, about how I think they actually do work.)

Nor is that by any means the whole story about the context dependence of being a trait that's selected for. In fact, strictly speaking, traits don't get selected at all; traits don't either win competitions or loose them. What wins or looses competitions are the creatures that have the traits. That's to say that what's selected is whole phenotypes; and, quite possibly, whether a certain trait is fitness-enhancing depends a lot on what phenotype it's embedded in. That too is practically a truism; but it's one that game-theoretic models of evolution (for example) have a bad habit of ignoring. 'What would happen if a population of ts were to invade a population of not-ts?' That depends a lot on what other differences distinguish the ts from the not-ts. 'Yes, but all else equal what will happen if a population of ts invades a population of not-ts?' Since 'all else' never is equal, the question doesn't seriously arise. Unlike a scientist in a laboratory, natural selection can't control for confounding variables; it has no access to the method of differences.

As we're about to see, these sorts of considerations apply to adaptationist explanations across-the-board; but they apply in spades when what's at issue is selection for intentional states. That's because, unlike any others, intentional states invariably have unintended consequences, and natural selection can't see the difference between a consequence that is intended and a consequence that isn't. 'Jack and Jill/ Went up the hill/ To fetch a pail of water/ Jack fell down/ And broke his crown/ And thus decreased his fitness.' We can see that what was detrimental to Jack's fitness was neither his intention to fetch water, nor his intention to climb a hill in order to do so. It was the falling down that was bad for him, and that wasn't part of the intention on which he acted. Since we can see all that, we're prepared to conclude that, although Jack's action brought him to grief, evolution shouldn't count its having done so as a reason for selecting against mental states whose intentional objects are climbings of hills or fetchings of water. Jack's climbing the hill eventuated in damage to his crown; but it wasn't, as one says, 'intentional under that description.'

To suppose that the processes of evolution can see that the actual outcome of Jack's action was incidental to its intentional object is precisely to beg the questions that are now at issue. We can understand what went wrong with Jack because we have the concept of 'the maxim of an act' (the description under which the act was intended), and it's clear to us that the maxim of Jack's act was something like 'when thirsty, fetch water' and nothing at all like 'when thirsty, fall down/ and break your crown'. But, recall that (putting aside the loose talk about what evolution can 'see') the adaptationist's aim was to explain how the fitness of an intentional state varies as a function of its content. So, if he's to avoid circularity, he can't take for granted either that intentional states with distinct effects on fitness are ipso facto distinct in content or that intentional states that are distinct in content are ipso facto distinct in their effects on fitness. Jack's crown got broken and Jill's didn't. It remains entirely possible that they both acted with the very same end in view.

I hope it's clear that I've thus far been running two kinds of arguments in tandem; two kinds of arguments that happen to converge in the case of issues about evolutionary psychology. The first concerns the goals of evolutionary psychology in particular; it's that data about effects on fitness can't, even in principle, distinguish the selection of any given intentional state from the selection of any other intentional state with the same actual outcomes. What's making the trouble here is the intensionality of the mental: Beliefs, desires and the like are individuated not by the consequences of having them but by their contents, and these two come apart whenever (or to the extent that) the actual effects of being in such a state are not the effects intended. But while the kind of worry we've just been discussing arises because of the intensionality of mental traits, there is another and independent kind of worry that derives from the intensionality of the notion of selecting for a trait, mental or otherwise. Once again, which trait a phenotype was actually selected for depends on which phenotype would have been selected-tout-court in appropriate counterfactual situations. And, once again, natural selection has no access to the counterfactuals; it can only 'see' the actual outcomes of phenotypic variations.

Because 'selection for' is intensional, so too are a galaxy of other adaptationist concepts that are defined in terms of it including, notably, that of a 'problem of adaptation' (aka an 'ecological problem'); the very same configuration of the environment may present a problem of adaptation to one kind of creature but not to another even though the creatures live side by side. And, just as one would expect, the intensionality of ecological problems makes their individuation deeply obscure.

In familiar cases, solutions are defined by the problems that they solve. Thus the order of metaphysical dependence is that keys solve the problem of finding something to open locks, not that locks solve the problem of finding something for keys to open. In adaptationist theory, by contrast, there's a sort of topsy-turvy: Which problem a creature had depends on which of its traits were selected for solving it. But that there are spiders, who would have guessed that how to spin webs to catch flies is an ecological problem? Or that there are creatures whose fitness is a consequence of their having solved it? Because selection for is intentional, a range of questions to which a theory of adaptation ought to be responsive are, in fact, answered entirely post hoc.

The long and short is that the intensionality of the attitudes and the intensionality of selection for both raise problems of individuation, but the first kind of problem is much less of a worry than the second. A reasonable biologist might be willing to live without a selectionist evolutionary psychology so long as there's no implied threat to adaptationism per se. So, when the weather gets rough, there's an entirely understandable temptation to lighten the ship by throwing the psychologists overboard. But, in fact, to do so wouldn't help; the intentionality of selection for makes trouble for adaptationism as such, and it would continue to do so even if, in our panic, we were to adopt some sort of behaviorism or neurological reductionism, thereby making intentional psychology disappear.

Exasperation may now urge the following response. 'Why shouldn't I think that that was all just epistemology pretending to be metaphysics? 'What you've offered isn't grounds for claiming that there are no laws of selection. At most it's grounds for claiming that, if there are such laws, then, because of their context dependence, they must be very complicated; perhaps, even, they're not within our capacity to formulate. But nothing of metaphysical interest follows from that. In particular, nothing follows as to the status of counterfactuals about which phenotypes would, and which ones wouldn't, be selected in possible worlds other than our own. Laws that are too complex for us to formulate can support counterfactuals all the same.

"After all, do you really want to say that adaptationist explanations aren't ever any good; that selection histories never explain phenotypic traits, psychological or otherwise? Surely you're aware that the textbooks simply team with examples to the contrary. These textbook explanations purport to, and often clearly do, give reasons why phenotypes are the way they are; why there are lots of populations of T1s, but few or no populations of T2s. Well, there can't be such explanations unless there are laws about the relative fitness of various traits. Since you can't have the explanations without the laws, and since the illumination that the explanations often provide isn't subject to serious doubt, it would seem that if you don't like laws of selection, you will have to learn to lump them."

Thus the voice of exasperation, and I think there's a lot in what it says. Certainly I have no objection to the form of its argument: If there are few or no examples of laws of selection on offer, that could be either because there are few or no such laws; or because there are many such but we aren't smart enough to find them out. And I, for one, disapprove, vehemently, of arguments that purport to draw metaphysical conclusions from epistemological premises. Still more vehemently do I disapprove of ignoring what otherwise seems to be successful science on the grounds of merely philosophical scruples.

On the other hand, it's crucial in the present case not just that there are bona fide successful adaptationist explanations, but also that such explanations invoke laws of selection. If they don't, then the success of the explanations is not a reason to think that there are such laws. In fact, I'm inclined to think that the premises invoked in explaining phenotypes by reference to selection histories generally aren't nomological, and that they don't claim or even aspire to be. What they are is precisely what they look like on the face of them; they're historical explanations. Very roughly, historical explanations offer not covering laws but plausible narratives; narratives which (purport to) articulate the causal chain of events leading to the event that is to be explained. Whereas covering law explanations are about (necessary) relations among properties, historical narratives are about (causal) relations among events. That's why the former support counterfactuals, but the latter don't.

Historical explanations are as far as I know, often perfectly ok. Certainly they are sometimes thoroughly persuasive, so perhaps they are sometimes true. But, prima facie at least, historical explanations don't seek to subsume events under laws. 'She fell because she slipped on a banana peel.' Very likely she did; but there's no law ---there's not even a statistical law--- that has 'banana peel'

in its antecedent and 'slipped and fell' in its consequent. Likewise, Napoleon lost at Waterloo because it had been raining for days, and the ground was too muddy for cavalry to charge. So, anyhow, I'm told; and who am I to say otherwise? But it doesn't begin to follow that there are laws that connect the amount of mud on the ground with the outcomes of battles.

Metaphysical naturalists have to say, I suppose, that the effect of the mud on the outcome of the battle at Waterloo must have fallen under some covering laws or other. No doubt, for example, it instantiated laws of the mechanics of middle-sized objects. But it doesn't follow that there are laws about mud so described, or about battles so described, still less about causal connections between them so described; which is what would be required if 'he lost because of the mud' is to be an instance of a covering-law explanation. It likewise doesn't follow, and it isn't remotely plausible, that whatever explains why Napoleon lost at Waterloo likewise explains why Nelson won at Trafalgar; i.e. that there are laws about battles as such, of which Nelson's victory and Wellington's are both instances. 'Is a battle' doesn't pick out a natural kind; it's not (in Nelson Goodman's illuminating term) 'projectible'.

It's of a piece with their not appealing to covering laws that historical-narrative explanations so often seem to be post hoc. The reason they so often seem to be is that they usually are. Given that we already know who won, we can tell a pretty plausible story (of the too-much-mud-on-the-ground variety) about why it wasn't Napoleon. But, what with their being no covering law to cite, I doubt that Napoleon or Wellington or anybody else could have predicted the outcome prior to the event. The trouble is that there would have been a plausible story to explain the outcome whoever had won; prediction and retrodiction are famous for exhibiting this asymmetry. That being so, there are generally lots of reasonable historical accounts of the same event, and there need be nothing much to choose between them. Did Wellington really win because of the mud? Or was it because the Prussian mercenaries turned up just in the nick of time? Or was it simply that Napoleon had lost his touch? (And while you're at it, what, exactly, caused the Reformation?)

It's not in dispute that competitions between creatures with different phenotypes often differ in their outcomes; and, of course, there must be, in each case, some explanation or other of why the winner won and the looser didn't. But there's no reason at all to suppose that such explanations typically invoke laws that apply to the creatures in virtue of their phenotypic traits. That being so, there need be nothing to choose between claims about the corresponding counterfactuals. Small mammals won their competition with large dinosaurs. But did they do so because of their smallness? That depends (inter alia) on whether they would have won even if there hadn't been a meteor. I can tell you a plausible story about why they might have won: Small animals are able to snitch dinosaur eggs to eat when the dinosaurs aren't looking, (which is bad for the dinosaurs' fitness.) On the other hand, I can tell you a plausible story about why they might not have won: lacking the meteor, there wouldn't have been selection for tolerance to climate change, which mammals had but dinosaurs didn't. (Notice that, according to the latter story, it wasn't the smallness or quickness of the mammals that was selected for, but the range of temperatures they were able to tolerate.) So which of the counterfactuals do our evolutionary narratives about the extinction of dinosaurs support? Neither? Both? And, likewise, what intentional content did evolution select for when it selected creatures that protect their young? Was it an altruistic interest in their offspring or a selfish interest in their genes?

The moral, so far, is that a phenotype's having been selected doesn't determine which (if any) of its traits a creature was selected for. Quite generally, if you want to infer from the one to the other, you have two choices (and, as far as I can see, only two.) You can try attributing intentions to the agent of selection (hence Mother Nature); or you can try to find a covering law that connects its having some phenotypic trait with a creature's having been selected. The former tactic is hopeless; there simply isn't any Mother Nature, and natural selection has nothing in mind when it prefers some creatures to others; natural selection has nothing in mind at all. But the second tactic seems hopeless too, given the extreme context sensitivity of selection processes. Whether a trait is conducive to fitness appears to be just about arbitrarily dependent on which sort of creature it's a trait of and what sort of ecology the creature inhabits. If that's so, then there can't be laws of selection, and `selected for' can't be a projectible predicate.

There is, however, a model of adaptationist explanation that seems to fit the facts pretty well. If it's otherwise viable, it suggests that such explanations, though they aren't nomic, have perfectly respectable precedents. Adaptationist explanations are species of historical narratives. If so, then everything can be saved from the wreckage except the notion of selection for: Since historical narratives don't support counterfactuals, it seems selection for very likely can't be salvaged. That's all right; much spilled ink to the contrary notwithstanding, there very likely isn't any such thing.

I want to close by suggesting an analogy; it is, I think, a very close analogy. For each rich person, there must be something or other that explains his being so: heredity, inheritance, cupidity, acuity, mendacity, grinding the faces of the poor, being in the right place at the right time, having friends in high places, sheer brute luck, highway robbery or whatever. Which things conduce to getting rich is, of course, highly context dependent: It's because of differences in context that none of us now has a chance of getting rich in (for example) the way that Genghis Khan did; or in the (not dissimilar) way that Andrew Carnegie did; or in the (quite different) way that Andrew Carnegie's heirs did; or in the (again quite different) way that Liberacie did; and so forth. Likewise (and not withstanding all those how-to-get-rich books) the extreme context sensitivity of the traits that eventuate in getting rich make it most unlikely that there could be a theory of getting rich per se. In particular, it's most unlikely that there are generalizations that are lawful (hence counterfactual supporting, not ad hoc, and not vacuous) that specify the various situations in which it is possible to get rich and the properties in virtue of which, if one had

them, one would get rich in those situations. This is, please notice, fully compatible with there being convincing stories that explain, case by case, what it was about a guy in virtue of which he got as rich as he did in the circumstances that prevailed when and where he did so.

Well, I think adaptationist explanations of the evolution of heritable traits are sort of like that. When they work it's because they provide plausible historical narratives, not because they cite covering laws. In particular, pace Darwinists, adaptionism doesn't articulate the mechanisms of the selection of heritable phenotypic traits; that's because there aren't any mechanisms of the selection of heritable phenotypic traits as such. All there are is the many, many different kinds of ways in which various kinds of creatures manage to flourish in the many, many environmental situations in which the do so.

None of this should lighten the heart of anybody in Kansas; not even a little. In particular, I've provided not the slightest reason to doubt the central Darwinist thesis of the mutability of species. Nor have I offered the slightest reason to doubt that we and chimpanzees had (relatively) recent common ancestors. Nor do I suppose that the intentions of a designer, intelligent or otherwise, are among the causally sufficient conditions that good historical narratives would appeal to in order to explain why a kind of creature has the phenotypic traits it does (saving, of course, cases like Granny and her zinnias.) It is, in short, one thing to wonder whether evolution happens; it's quite another thing to wonder whether adaptation is the mechanism by which evolution happens. Well, evolution happens; the evidence that it does is overwhelming. I blush to have to say that so late in the day; but these are bitter times.

Footnotes

[1] It's hard to imagine a less fortunate terminology than the philosopher's `intention/intension' distinction. But I suppose there's nothing can be done at this late date. In what follows, an intensional context is one in which the substitution of coextensive expressions isn't valid. Intentional states are just the familiar beliefs, desires, intentions and so forth that populate theories of cognition and the integration of behavior. I assume, following the tradition, that expressions that refer to propositional attitudes typically establish intensional contexts, so that one can believe that Venus is the Morning Star and yet not believe that Venus is the Evening star, despite the fact that… etc.

[2] Admittedly, the tactic of resorting to scare quotes when push comes to shove (as in `what natural selection `prefers,'' `what Mother Nature `designs,'' `what the selfish genes `want'' and so forth) can make it hard to tell just what is being claimed in some of the canonical texts. Still, there are plenty of apparently unequivocal passages. Thus Pinker (1997, p.93): "Was the human mind ultimately designed to create beauty? To discover truth? To love and to work? To harmonize with other human beings and with nature? The logic of natural selection gives the answer. The ultimate goal that the mind was designed to attain is maximizing the number of copies of the genes that created it. Natural selection cares only about the long-term fate of entities that replicate…" Fiddlesticks. The human mind wasn't created, and it wasn't designed and there is nothing that natural selection cares about; it just happens. This isn't Kansas, Toto.

[3] It's crucial that the idealizations are independently justified; otherwise `ceteris paribus Fs cause Gs' collapses into `Fs cause Gs except when they don't.'

Invited Symposia

Analogy-Making: Resolved and Unresolved Mysteries

Boicho Kokinov (bkokinov@nbu.bg)
Central and East European Center for Cognitive Science, Department of Cognitive Science and Psychology,
New Bulgarian University, 21, Montevideo Str., Sofia 1635, Bulgaria

Dedre Gentner (gentner@northwestern.edu)
Department of Psychology, School of Education and Social Policy Northwestern University
2029 Sheridan Road; Evanston, IL 60208, USA

Researchers agree that analogy-making is about relational processing, and that the main components of analogy-making are representation building, memory retrieval, mapping, transfer, evaluation, and learning. There is also agreement in that analogy is a major contributor to human learning and reasoning. In this symposium, we would like to explore the extent of this agreement and understand where disagreements start. The contributors are researchers from various theoretical traditions, all engaged in original studies in various directions exploring new and still unresolved issues. They will explore the degree of convergence (or divergence) as to which territory to explore and how to best approach the issues.

Learning New Relations

Dedre Gentner & Stella Christie, Northwestern University

A hallmark of human cognition is the use of relational concepts—concepts like *monotonicity* and *reciprocity*. How do such concepts get formed? This is a challenging question, especially given that young children tend to focus on objects rather than relations. Our studies show that aligning two examples during learning dramatically increase children's relational insight, as compared to seeing the examples sequentially. A model of this phenomenon using SME (the structure-mapping Engine) suggests that comparison promotes relational insight: (1) by promoting a focus on connected relational structure; and (2) by inviting relational re-representation. Implications for purely Bayesian accounts of learning are discussed.

A Theory of Relation Discovery and Predication

Leonidas A. A. Doumas, Indiana University

The ability to think and reason about relations is a central component of human cognition. While we understand much about the mechanisms of relational thinking and analogy, little is known about how children and adults acquire relational concepts and represent them in a form that is useful for the purposes of relational thought (i.e., as structures that can be dynamically bound to arguments). We present DORA, a computational theory of relation discovery. DORA is a neurally-plausible cognitive architecture that learns relational concepts from examples and represents these concepts as explicit structures (predicates) that can take arguments.

Categories Based on Analogies

Kenneth Kurtz, State University of New York at Binghamton

The discovery of commonalities among the representational elements used to encode examples is critical to schema abstraction and category formation. In the categorization literature, similarity-based abstraction is traditionally understood in terms of overlapping or intercorrelated sets of features. In the comparison literature, similarity-based abstraction is based on alignable sets of explicitly-coded relations between objects/features. As part of an effort to bring these two views of learning and abstraction into closer contact, my talk will focus on behavioral data and theoretical claims addressing the acquisition, structure, and function of categories that cohere (like analogies) around relational content.

Analogy Programs that Learn

Robert French, CNRS and University of Burgundy

In this presentation we will concentrate on what we believe to be the challenges facing the new generation of analogy-making programs. These will focus on developing analogy-programs that learn and some of the challenges in developing these programs. In particular, we will discuss what will be required to break free from tradition of doing analogy-making with hand-coded problems. We will present a list of criteria for determining the success (or failure) of these new programs.

Modular or Interactive, Sequential or Parallel Processing in Analogy-Making

Boicho Kokinov, New Bulgarian University

The interactions between perception (representation building), memory retrieval (memory construction), mapping, transfer, and re-representation will be explored. Various theoretical possibilities, such as encapsulated modules vs. fully interactionist systems, sequential vs. parallel processing views, will be discussed together with their ability to generate testable predictions. Experimental designs to test some of these predictions will be suggested and the results of some initial experiments will be presented.

Language and Brain

Tatiana Chernigovskaya (Tatiana@TC3839.spb.edu)
Department of General Linguistics, Philological Faculty, St. Petersburg State University,
University Åmb.11, 199034 St. Petersburg, Russia

The cerebral basis for language is a central problem within cognitive science and can be studied only in a multidisciplinary anthropological perspective. Among other questions this symposium considers the importance of cross-language results, the diversity of behavioral, neuro-imaging and clinical data, and their interpretation. It also discusses the role of attention and error detection, the importance of species specific factors and input characteristics for language acquisition and processing. The results are observed in the framework of neurobiological localisation vs. network models and in connection with the debate on single vs. dual mechanism of mental lexicon organization.

On the Relationship between Functional and Structural Differences in the Brain

Kenneth Hugdahl University of Bergen

Brain asymmetry relates to both functional and structural differences between the two cerebral hemispheres. Despite all research devoted to functional asymmetry, very little is known of corresponding structural, or anatomical, differences. One notable exception is the larger left planum temporale area in the upper posterior part of the temporal lobe, and the relation of this to functional differences for speech perception. In my talk I will review recent data on asymmetry of speech sound perception, from both a basic and clinical perspective. In particular I will make an argument that auditory hallucinations in schizophrenia may be instances of speech sound mis-perceptions, caused by pathology at the neuronal level in the left planum temporale area. I will review data using both behavioural and psychophysiological measures, focusing on fMRI studies of neuronal activation during dichotic listening to simple speech sound syllables.

Speech Perception and Linguistic Experience

Inger Moen University of Oslo

Speech perception involves the identification of different types of structural information such as the identification of particular phonemes, lexical items, suprasegmentals, or the various phonetic properties associated with syntactic boundaries or discourse units. This is an ability which develops on the basis of linguistic experience. The details of this process are not fully understood. What is clear is that for continuous speech, perception does not depend solely on cues present in the acoustic waveform. The paper will present data from two Norwegian investigations which indicate that frequency of use is an important feature in speech perception.

Brain Mechanisms of Error Detection

Svyatoslav Medvedev Institute of the Human Brain, Russian Academy of Sciences

The brain mechanisms of error detection (ED), was firstly described by Bechtereva and Gretchin in 1968, as a physiological reaction to erroneous performance. The error detection system is a stabilizing mechanism of brain functioning. The basic functional principle of ED is the dissociation between the reality and the model in relevant memory matrix. Malfunctioning of ED is a physiological basis of some mental and language disorders. The data to be presented show that ED is functioning even when error (deception) is profitable for the performed task. There is a special mechanism that activates even in an intention to make the wrong action. ED forms a brain basis of conscience and language acquisition.

Normal and Deviant Processing of Inflected Nouns

Jussi Niemi University of Joensuu

Psycholinguistic studies of Finnish morphology show that in this language – excluding the very high frequent end of the continuum – inflected nouns like sauna-ssa 'sauna'-inessive, i.e. 'in a/the sauna' are morphologically parsed into their components in perception. In our presentation we will discuss the normal ontogenetic path of processing of these types of lexical items and especially deviant processing by speakers exhibiting Specific/Familial Language Impairment (SLI/FLI). Our extensive analysis of surface and lemma frequencies of Finnish noun paradigms and the expected use of frequency by normals and the unexpected insignificance of frequency in SLI/FLI are – we claim – in line with our previous findings regarding the present SLI/FLI individuals in fMRI and in dichotic listening, in which it was shown that these speakers have abnormal attentional patterns

Computational Psycholinguistics beyond Words

Hedderik van Rijn (D.H.van.Rijn@rug.nl)
Artificial Intelligence, University of Groningen, The Netherlands

Stefan L. Frank (S.Frank@nici.ru.nl)
NICI, Radboud University Nijmegen, The Netherlands

Research on language production and perception aims for the precise description and quantification of the cognitive processing steps involved in language use. While numerous detailed computational models have been presented that involve single word production and perception, only recently has research become more prominent that focusses specifically on modeling language above the level of single words. This symposium highlights this development by presenting four lines of research from different fields all involved in "Computational Psycholinguistics beyond Words".

A Probabilistic, Corpus-based Model of Syntactic Parallelism

Amit Dubey, University of Edinburgh
Although most research on sentence processing involves modeling ambiguity resolution, certain processes actually work to remove ambiguity from language. Two such phenomena are syntactic priming (Bock, 1986), a general process, and the parallelism effect, which Frazier et al. (2000) claim is due to a mechanism distinct from priming. After describing these two effects, we then introduce a sentence processing model which helps answer a basic theoretical question: is parallelism really distinct, or an instance of the more general priming effect? The model accounts for syntactic priming by making the novel assumption that a probabilistic sentence processor (Jurafsky, 1996) operates within the ACT-R cognitive architecture. Overall, we find that evidence against a general mechanism is not as strong as previously thought.

Modelling Sentence Comprehension as Situation Construction

Stefan Frank, Radboud University Nijmegen
There is increasing consensus among discourse-comprehension researchers that understanding a text involves the construction of a mental representation of the described situation, which depends more on the reader's world knowledge and experience than on the text's linguistic and propositional form (Zwaan, 1999). Yet, nearly all computational models of sentence comprehension represent meaning propositionally, that is, as a combination of arbitrary symbols forming predicate and arguments (e.g., Mayberry et al., 2006). In contrast, I present a connectionist model that constructs non-propositional and non-symbolic 'situational representations' (Frank et al., 2003) given sentences describing situations in a simple microworld. Also, its ability to account for experimental data is discussed.

Connectionist Models of Sentence Comprehension in Context

Marshall R. Mayberry, III, Saarland University
According to the coordinated interplay account (CIA), there is a dynamic interaction between language and visual context, in which comprehension of a situated utterance rapidly guides attention to objects and events in a scene and, in turn, the attended region of the scene tightly constrains and influences comprehension (Knoeferle & Crocker, 2006). We present an architecture, CIANet, that directly models the CIA by means of an explicit attentional mechanism to select the event in the scene most relevant to the utterance (Mayberry et al., 2006). We show how this mechanism enables predictions of how people resolve conflicting information, as well as how argument information from the scene can be used in the face of initial structural ambiguity.

Producing Time

Hedderik van Rijn, University of Groningen
Simone Sprenger, Radboud University Nijmegen
Performance in relative clock time naming (e.g., pronouncing 3:50 as "ten to four") has been described as depending on three factors: reference hour determination, minute transformation, and an additional distance component (Meeuwissen et al., 2003). However, this account does not specify the cognitive operations that are responsible for the distance effect. We present a computational model that explicates these cognitive operations, and provide support for this model by sets of regression models of speech onset latencies.

References

Bock, J.K. (1986). Syntactic persistence in language production. *Cognitive Psychology, 18*, 355–387.

Frank, S.L., Koppen, M., Noordman, L.G.M., & Vonk, W. (2003). Modeling knowledge-based inference in story comprehension. *Cognitive Science, 27*, 875–910.

Frazier, L., Munn, A., & Clifton, C. (2000). Processing coordinate structures. *J. of Psycholinguistic Res., 29*, 343–370.

Jurafsky, D. (1996). A probabilistic model of lexical and syntactic access and disambiguation. *Cognitive Science, 20*, 137–194.

Knoeferle, P., & Crocker, M.W. (2006). The coordinated interplay of scene, utterance, and world knowledge: evidence from eye-tracking. *Cognitive Science, 30*, 481–529.

Mayberry, M.R., Crocker, M.W, & Knoeferle, P. (2006). A connectionist model of the coordinated interplay of scene, utterance, and world knowledge. *Proc. of CogSci Conf.*

Meeuwissen, M., Roelofs, A., Levelt, W.J.M. (2003). Planning levels in naming and reading complex numerals. *Memory & Cognition, 31*, 1238–1248.

Zwaan, R.A. (1999). Embodied cognition, perceptual symbols, and situation models. *Discourse Processes, 28*, 81–88.

Cooperation and the Evolution of Cognition

Peter Gardenfors (Peter.Gardenfors@lucs.lu.se)
Cognitive Science, Lund University, Kunghuset, Lundagård, S-222 22
Lund Sweden

In the debate concerning the evolution of cognition, much focus has been put on deception, in term of so called Machiavellian intelligence. The symposium will instead focus on the role of cooperation as a selective force for primate and hominid cognition. Different forms of cooperation will be related to the role of a theory of mind (intersubjectivity) and different communication systems.

On why Humans are the Only Animals who Have Developed A Symbolic Communication System

Peter Gardenfors, Cognitive Science, Lund University

This talk proposes an ecologically based answer to why humans are the only animals who have developed a symbolic communication system. The overall thesis is that there has been a co-evolution of anticipation, co-operation and communication. The first part of the argument claims that the Oldowan culture generated selective forces that lead to the evolution of anticipatory cognition, that is, the ability to mentally represent future needs and events. It is argued that anticipatory planning opened up for new forms of cooperation about future goals that were beneficial for hominid societies. Symbolic communication then emerged as the most efficient way of solving problems concerning cooperation about future non-existent goals. For example, the evolution of indirect reciprocity, which seems to be a uniquely human form of co-operation, depends on a symbolic communicative system and shared beliefs concerning the "reputation" of individuals.

An Embodied and Distributed Approach to Primate Cognitive Evolution.

Louise Barrett, University of Lethbridge, Alberta, Canada

Living in a group is a cooperative act, which requires a delicate balance between individual and group level costs and benefits. Among primates, the social intelligence hypothesis has tended to focus attention on the means by which (Machiavellian) individuals cope with, and overcome, the costs that group-living imposes so that they may reap the associated benefits. These have been argued to involve highly cognitive strategies designed to track, monitor, cooperate with, and potentially outwit, other individuals. This, in turn, stems from a Cartesian view of the mind and cognition, and also from the kinds of evolutionary models used to predict and explain cooperative behaviour. This is problematic, however, as it has created a view of primate social complexity that is congenial to our view of ourselves, rather than one that is representative of primate social worlds. Here, drawing on work in cognitive science, including robotics, as well as neurobiology, I argue for a more embodied and distributed approach to primate cognitive evolution. Such an approach, when incorporated into evolutionary theories of multi-level selection and niche construction, presents us with the opportunity to explore primate cooperation and social complexity in ways that allow the animals to speak with their own voice, and not merely echo our own anthropocentric concerns.

The Cooperative Problem-Solving Abilities of Chimpanzees and Bonobos.

Brian Hare, Max Planck Institute for Evolutionary Anthropology

We compared the cooperative problem-solving abilities of chimpanzees and bonobos. When two subjects were confronted with a tray of out-of-reach, sharable food, both species were skillful at spontaneously pulling a rope simultaneously to obtain the food. When two subjects were again placed in the same situation, except the food was no longer sharable, bonobos showed more skill at solving the task. These results support the hypothesis that flexibility in cooperative problem solving is relative to different levels of emotional reactivity and suggests that the flexibility seen in our own species cooperative skills may have only evolved after the evolution of our unique human temperament.

Discussant

Cristiano Castelfranchi, CNR Rome, Italy

Consciousness and the Brain

Konstantinos Moutoussis (k.moutoussis@ucl.ac.uk)
Department of Philosophy and History of Science, University of Athens
Panepistimioupolis, GR. 157 71, Athens, Greece

One of the most exciting questions in Philosophy, Psychology & Neuroscience is that of consciousness and its relation to matter. The symposium will focus on a very basic form of consciousness, that of sensory awareness, present in both humans and animals. How can brain activation result in a subjective experience of the world, through the senses? Three invited speakers will give their own account with respect to visual perception.

The Many Consciousnesses of the Brain

Semir Zeki, Wellcome Laboratory of Neurobiology, University College London

The visual brain is now known to consist of many distinct visual areas, specialized to process and perceive different attributes of the visual scene. Contrary to common assumption, we do not perceive different attributes simultaneously. Instead we perceive some attributes before others; for example we perceive colour by about 100ms before we perceive motion, and we perceive simple forms after we perceive colour. Since perceiving an attribute is being conscious of it, and the perception of these different attributes is the result of activity in geographically distinct visual areas, it follows that visual consciousness is distributed in space. Equally, since we become conscious of different attributes at different times, visual consciousness is also distributed in time. It follows therefore that there is not a single unified visual consciousness, but there are instead many visual micro-consciousnesses. Moreover, binding of activity in these different areas occurs post-consciously.

Investigation of Subjective Motion Perception

Lars Muckli, Max-Planck Institute for Brain Research, & Department of Psychology, University of Glasgow

Bistable perception is ideally suited for the investigation of the cortical correlates of conscious perception. We used various apparent motion illusions (apparent motion breakdown, motion quartet) to induce bistable perception, and we investigated the cortical activation as a function of these subjectively perceived switches in perception. Cortical activation was measured by using functional magnetic resonance imaging (fMRI), and electroencephalography (EEG) and revealed how a cortical network comprising of motion specialized regions (including V5) interacts with retinotopic visual areas (including V1). We found fMRI activation and perceptual interference along the path of the apparent motion illusion. I like to speculate, that the perceived gist of a visual scene is the most important content of visual consciousness and, moreover, that the visual system uses the perceived gist to predict the near future and to provide effective filters for expected information – affecting also primary sensory areas.

How are Conscious and Unconscious Mental States Encoded in the Human Brain?

John-Dylan Haynes, Bernstein Center for Computational Neuroscience Berlin and Charité - Universitätsmedizin, Berlin & Max-Planck Institute for Human Cognitive and Brain Sciences

Accurate prediction of the conscious experience of an individual based only on measurements of their brain activity would provide strong evidence for a close link between brain and mind. Recent empirical and methodological advances in such 'brain reading' have yielded promising findings, particularly in the domain of visual perception. Here we show that conscious awareness of both simple features and complex object categories can be predicted from characteristic, distributed activity patterns in human visual cortex. Furthermore, feature-selective processing can also be demonstrated for stimuli of which the subject is completely unaware. Such an approach can also extend to decoding of other types of mental states, such as a subject's current focus of attention, their current intentions and even unconscious determinants of their behaviour. Taken together, this novel line of research helps reveal the way in which individual experiences are encoded in the human brain, and how they may be practically decoded.

Discussant

Fotini Stylianopoulou, University of Athens, Greece

Can Design Research Contribute to Bridge the Gap between Theory and Educational Practice?

Erik De Corte (erik.decorte@ped.kuleuven.be)
Centr. Instructiepsychol.&technologie, University of Leuven,
Andreas Vesaliusstraat 2, bus 3770, 3000 Leuven, Belgium

Stella Vosniadou (svosniad@phs.uoa.gr)
Department of Philosophy and History of Science, University of Athens
University Town, 157 71, Athens, Greece

Applied cognitive science research in education has a dual goal: (1) to develop theories and the impact of instructional interventions on learning and development, and (2) to contribute to the improvement of educational/classroom practices. The history of the field shows that there has always been a tension between these two goals. The aim of this symposium is to unravel and discuss from different perspectives the promises, the potential, but also the possible pitfalls of design-based research in the light of the dual goal mentioned above.

Design Experiments for Improving Thinking Skills through the Content of Learning

Benő Csapó, University of Szeged, Hungary

The most promising methods for developing general thinking skills are those that use the content of teaching itself for composing specific training exercises (often called enrichment, infusion or embedding). Experimenting with these methods is especially difficult. Furthermore, the limitations and the specific settings that are determined by the nature of the teaching materials challenge the generalizability of the results. This paper presents examples from the teaching of a variety of reasoning skills (e.g. operational, analogical and inductive reasoning) and school subjects in order to demonstrate how such difficulties may be overcome by further increasing the complexity of the design.

The Potential of Design-Based Research for Bridging the Theory – Practice Gap Relating to Education

Erik De Corte, University of Leuven, Belgium

Design-based research aims at the simultaneous pursuit of the advancement of our understanding of the processes of learning and instruction, on the one hand, and at the improvement of classroom practices, on the other hand. However, recently some authors (e.g., Phillips & Dolle, 2006) have disputed the potential of design experiments to achieve both goals simultaneously. Moreover, design experiments are criticized from a methodological perspective for lack of control and randomization resulting in confounding of variables. It will be argued, and illustrated, in this presentation that under certain conditions design-based research can accommodate both of these objections.

Bridging the Gap between Basic and Applied Research by an Integrative Research Approach (IRA)

Heinz Mandl & Robin Stark, University of Munich & Saarland University, Germany

The main goal of IRA is to bridge the methodological gap between basic and applied research on learning environments. IRA was developed and realized in the context of a special priority program of Deutsche Forschungsgemeinschaft (DFG) to investigate and foster processes of learning and teaching in the context of initial training in business administration. IRA combines laboratory with field methodology in a special way. Theory-based lab experiments are conducted with use questions in mind: Results of the experiments should be applied later on in practice. Field studies on the other side are conducted as "controlled" as possible. All characteristics of IRA will be exemplified by our research projects in the domain of economics and medicine.

The Problem of Knowledge in the Design of Learning Environments

Stella Vosniadou, University of Athens, Greece

The *cognitive apprenticeship* metaphor has played an important role in guiding the engineering approach to the design of learning environments. I will argue that the cognitive apprenticeship metaphor has provided important guidelines for teaching cognitive skills but that it has downgraded the problem of knowledge. Learning and the development of expertise in curricular domains require the construction of significant domain knowledge. Furthermore, the acquisition of *learning how to learn* skills cannot be divorced from substantial knowledge building.

Discussant

Naomi Miyake, Chukyo University, Japan

Symposia

NEUROCOGNITION OF HUMAN SPATIAL MEMORY: NEW APPROACHES, TESTS AND TECHNOLOGIES

Panagiota Panagiotaki (panagiota.panagiotaki@college-de-france.fr)

LPPA, Collège de France, Paris, France
Laboratory of Physiology of Perception and Action, CNRS- Collège de France,
11, place Marcelin Berthelot, 75005, Paris, France

Introduction

Spatial memory is a necessary cognitive property for human life. Previous studies mainly focused on static aspects of spatial encoding, such as object-location binding, or Euclidean positional memory. Nevertheless, the study of spatial tasks like navigation and reorientation into the 3-dimensional space demands to take under serious consideration their dynamic properties.

The purpose of this symposium is to present and discuss novel methodological approaches that contribute to the exploration of the cognitive mechanisms involved in the dynamic aspects of spatial encoding and of the neural networks underlying this processing. New paradigms focusing on this problematic are described: new neuropsychological tests administered in healthy controls and different categories of neurological patients, assessing different components of spatial memory; novel experiments of cognitive psychology investigating distinct cognitive strategies of encoding and storing spatial information; and finally studies on immersive virtual reality that test the function of cognitive strategies in humans that are present in lower levels of the phylogenetic continuum.

Cecilia Guariglia (cecilia.guariglia@uniroma1.it)

Università di Roma "La Sapienza"-IRCCS Fondazione Santa Lucia, Rome, Italy

Visuo-spatial exploration and memory for object arrays in the peripersonal space and for environmental information are often been considered equivalent in the neuropsychology. Nevertheless, there are some evidences that inability in coding and memorizing visuo-spatial information in the peripersonal space not ever corresponds to an inability in coding and memorizing information for environmental navigational purposes. A set of data showing that the system coding environmental information for building mental maps of the environment to be stored in long term memory could be double dissociated from the process involved in coding visuo-spatial information in the peripersonal space. In each experiment two tests were used: Corsi test and an experimental version of Corsi test on large scale. Two neuropsychological studies on neurological impaired subjects are also presented. The results of both studies underline the presence of dissociations in the two kinds of tests strongly supporting the hypothesis of separate memory systems for different types of visuo-spatial information.

Jan Wiener (jan.wiener@college-de-france.fr)
MPI for Biological Cybernetics, Tübingen, Germany & LPPA, Collège de France, Paris, France

A series of three experiments is presented that studied human path planning performance as well as the cognitive strategies and processes involved. 25 places were arranged on a regular grid in a large room. Each place was marked by a unique colored symbol. Subjects were repeatedly asked to solve traveling salesman problems (TSP), i.e. to find the shortest closed loop connecting a given start place with a number of target places. To specifically test for the relevance of spatial working memory (SWM) and spatial long-term memory (LTM) for path planning, the number of target places (ranging from 4 to 9 targets) as well as the mode of presenting targets was varied. Path planning performance systematically decreased with increasing TSP size. Furthermore, performance between the three experiments differed systematically. The results suggest the usage of different path planning strategies according to the specific memory demands.

Panagiota Panagiotaki

We present a study, where we explore the accuracy of human visual path integration (vPI) in complex and long paths (significantly longer than the simple triangle tasks) to the encoding and recalling of navigated paths. During this experiment, participants navigated semi-actively in an immersive virtual environment, performing an outbound searching trajectory in order to reach a specific goal. Once their goal reached, participants had to return immediately to their base (inbound journey), either based on visual cues or by performing vPI. Our results indicate that human vPI appears very deteriorated and it cannot be a reliable strategy for homing after complex and long trajectories.

Discussant: Alain Berthoz (alain.berthoz@college-de-france.fr)
Laboratory of Physiology of Perception and Action, CNRS-Collège de France,11, place Marcelin Berthelot, 75005, Paris, France

Causal Reasoning in Practice – How Causal Assumptions affect Explanations, Inferences and Decision Making

York Hagmayer (yhagmay@gwdg.de)
Department of Psychology, University of Göttingen,
Gosslerstr. 14
37073 Göttingen, Germany

Denis Hilton (hilton@univ-tlse2.fr)
Laboratoire Dynamiques Sociocognitives et Vie Politique,
Universite de Toulouse II - le Mirail,
Allees Antonio Machado 5
31058 Toulouse Cedex 9, France

Motivation

Causal learning and reasoning has been investigated intensively in the last decade, crucial insights were made and new theories were developed to explain both the acquisition and the use of causal knowledge. However, this research mostly focused on causal reasoning itself. Only recently researchers on causality became interested in how causal reasoning affects other areas of thought. This symposium aims to show that causal learning and reasoning is not distinct from other areas but permeates reasoning, judgment and decision making throughout. Examples from cognitive, social, clinical and applied psychology will be presented. In addition, it will be shown how theories of causal reasoning provide new insights and offer new theoretical accounts.

York Hagmayer – Decision Making

Causal considerations must be relevant to making good decisions. Nevertheless, most current decision making theories do not explicitly take causality into account. Experimental evidence will be presented showing that people are sensitive to the causal structure underlying a given decision problem. They tend to prefer the option that has the causal power to increase the probability of the desired outcome the most. A descriptive model of decision making integrating causal considerations will be introduced.

Dave Lagnado – Legal Decision Making

Causal models are critical to the evaluation of evidence in legal contexts, both from a normative and descriptive perspective. A series of experiments investigates how mock jurors combine several items of evidence to make judgments of guilt or innocence. The main findings are that people's reasoning is well-captured by qualitative Bayesian network models, but they are susceptible to biases due to the integrative encoding of information. A game-theoretic approach to modelling the informational interactions in the legal process is also proposed.

Clare Walsh – Judgments of Responsibility

People tend to ascribe more responsibility for actions and failures to act when both lead to the same unwanted outcome. We consider two alternative explanations for this difference. Counterfactual theorists propose that it is easier to imagine an alternative to an action than a failure to act. Other theorists propose that an action involves a process of transmission from cause to effect whereas failures to act do not. We tested these theories by examining judgments of responsibility for actions that change the outcome but do not involve a process of transmission.

Denis Hilton – Selection of Explanations

Causal explanations are often selected from complex causal chains. I examine what principles govern selections from *unfolding causal chains* and present data that suggest that: a) the proximal abnormal condition is selected, unless b) a voluntary deliberate action precedes it, and c) these selections are in part predicted by surprise value, i.e.: perceived (un)predictability of consequents given antecedents.

John McClure – Causal Attributions for Brain Injuries

I report studies that show how attributions about brain injuries are shaped by the visibility of markers of the injury and information about the normality of the behaviour for the individual and for the culture. Causal assumptions on these two parameters shape judgments about treatment and interventions for the persons, as well as court decisions about liability for the outcomes of the injury.

JF Bonnefon, R Da Silva Neves, D Dubois, & H Prade – Causal Transitivity

If A caused B, and if B in turn caused C, is it true that A caused C? Despite its critical importance, the issue of transitivity has been neglected in experimental research. Drawing onto a formal qualitative model from AI, we identify a key condition for accepting the transitivity property: A will be perceived to have caused C when B is generally diagnostic of A, that is, when there are few conceivable ways for B to occur in the absence of A. We present results supporting that prediction, and discuss them in relation to other theories of causation.

Discussant Fintan Costello
University College Dublin

Thinking With and Without Language

Does the language we speak shape the thoughts we think? We observe children who have not been exposed to an accessible model of language and ask whether they can perform spatial and number tasks previously hypothesized to depend on language. Two papers examine deaf children who have not acquired spoken language and who have not been exposed to sign language. While these children invent homesigns to communicate, their systems lack signs for many of the notions central to understanding spatial and numerical relations. Can these children perform non-linguistic tasks involving these relations? The third paper examines spatial tasks in four closely related genera, humans and three non-human primates who do not possess language. The symposium thus examines which tasks can – and cannot – be performed without human language.

Language and Numerical Cognition: The Case of Nicaraguan Homesigners

Elizabet Spaepen (liesje@uchicago.edu), Marie Coppola
Dept. of Psychology, University of Chicago, Chicago IL
Susan Carey, Elizabeth Spelke
Dept. of Psychology, Harvard University, Cambridge, MA
Susan Goldin-Meadow
Dept. of Psychology, University of Chicago, Chicago IL

Evidence from animals and pre-linguistic infants suggests that exact representations of small sets and approximate representations of the cardinal values of large sets can be developed without linguistic input. By contrast, cross-linguistic and cross-cultural evidence suggests that representations of large exact numbers may require access to a conventional count list. We tested six child and two adult homesigners, who do not have access to a conventional count list, on a variety of verbal (gestural) and nonverbal numerical cognition tasks. Some, but not all, of the homesigners created and used gestures for number. The results supported the hypothesis that learning a conventionalized count list is critical to representing the natural number system. Further research is needed to determine the nature of the homesigners' representations of numbers.

Spatial Language Potentiates Spatial Cognition: Turkish Homesigners

Dedre Gentner (gentner@northwestern.edu),
Dept. of Psychology, Northwestern University, Evanston, IL
Asli Ozyürek
Max Planck Institute for Psycholinguistics, Nijmegen, NL
Susan Goldin-Meadow
Dept. of Psychology, University of Chicago, Chicago IL
Ozge Gurcanli
Dept. of Psychology, Johns Hopkins University, MD

Previous work suggests that spatial language aids in spatial cognition, based on findings that preschool children performed better on a spatial mapping task when spatial relational terms (such as *top, middle, bottom*) were used. However, these children were learning English, and may have internally invoked spatial terms. Here we present more definitive evidence, by giving the same task to two groups in Turkey: homesigners, deaf children who are *not* learning a conventional language, and whose homesigns did not include gestures for spatial relations, and hearing children. The homesigners performed far worse than the hearing children. These findings suggest that spatial relational language may play a central role in promoting spatial reasoning.

Cognitive Inheritance and Cultural Override in Human Spatial Cognition

Daniel B.M. Haun (haun@eva.mpg.de)
Max Planck Inst. for Evolutionary Anthropology, Leipzig
Christian J. Rapold
Max Planck Institute for Psycholinguistics, Nijmegen, NL
Josep Call
Max Planck Inst. for Evolutionary Anthropology, Leipzig
Gabriele Janzen
Donders Centre for Cognitive Neuroimaging, Nijmegen, NL
Stephen C. Levinson
Max Planck Institute for Psycholinguistics, Nijmegen, NL

In order to investigate language impact on non-linguistic cognition we first need to know the structure of non-linguistic cognition. The present study systematically extends prior work with non-human animals by investigating the spatial relations of our closest phylogenetic relatives (*Pongo, Gorilla,* and *Pan)*. If all great ape genera share a particular cognitive preference, it has most likely been passed on from the common ancestor, and is therefore part of the inherited defaults of human cognition. We found that all three non-human great ape genera prefer to process spatial relations based on environmental cues and not self. We also compared human children and adults from two linguistic communities with different dominant spatial relation representations. The data show a correlation between the linguistic representation and the preferred cognitive strategy both children and adults used to process spatial relations. The model for human cognition that we propose then, has a rich, inherited primate basis, which may be overlaid by language and culture.

Acknowledgments

Funding and support provided by NSF-ROLE grant #REC-0196471; NIH grant #5 R01 DC0049; NSF-ROLE grant # 21002/REC-0087516; and the Max Planck Institutes in Nijmegen and Leipzig.

The body: from experience to representation

Andrea Serino (serino@cnc.psice.unibo.it)
Faculty of Psychology, Centro studi e ricerche in
Neuroscienze Cognitive, University of Bologna, Italy

Manos Tsakiris (e.tsakiris@ucl.ac.uk)
Department of Psychology
University College London, UK. (Symposium Organiser)

Katerina Fotopoulou (a.fotopoulou@iop.kcl.ac.uk)
Institute of Psychiatry, King's College, UK

Frederique de Vignemont (fvignemont@isc.cnrs.fr)
Institut des Sciences Cognitives, Lyon, France

Much of our mental life relates to our physical body. Despite the pervasive role of the body-representation concept in almost every aspect of psychology, it is yet unclear how the versatile nature of body-experiences, from multisensory perception and body-ownership to voluntary control of the body and tool-use, is represented in the brain. The symposium will focus on the behavioral, functional and neural correlates of body-specific processing from the perspectives of cognitive neurosciences cognitive sciences, clinical neuropsychology, and philosophy of mind.

A. Serino: "Extending the body space by long term tool-use experience"

Representation of body space extends to the space that is reachable by an arm movement. However, in everyday life we use tools to interact with objects placed in far space, suggesting that tool-use experience might extend the representation of space surrounding the body. Audio-tactile integration was studied in the space around the hand and in far space in blind and sighted subjects who used a cane to navigate, before and after a short training with the cane. In sighted subjects, before tool-use, auditory peripersonal space was limited around the hand, then it expanded after tool-use and contracted backwards after a resting period. On the contrary, in blind subjects, peri-hand space was immediately expanded when holding the cane but limited around the hand when holding a short handle.

K. Fotopoulou: "Is this My Hand is I see before me? Body Representation and Ownership in Anosognosia for Hemiplegia"

Anosognosia for hemiplegia (AHP) refers to the apparent unawareness of paralysis in neurological patients. The neurological and neuropsychological profile of six patients with severe AHP following right-hemisphere (RH) stroke will be compared to control patients showing similar RH lesions, hemiparesis, visuospatial neglect but no AHP. The experimental investigations addressed two main questions: a. Does motor intention influence the awareness of movement? b. Are there implicit emotional biases in AHP? The results suggest that motor intention has a profound influence on the on-line representation of one's actions, and emotional factors may have a top-down influence on one's body-representation. The relation of these findings to critical determinants of bodily representation and awareness will be discussed.

M. Tsakiris: "The bodily self: signatures of body-ownership in the brain"

We constantly feel, see and move our body, and have no doubt that it is our own. This sense of 'body-ownership' is a basic form of self-consciousness. Consistent psychophysical results suggest that body-ownership arises as an interaction between multisensory perception and representations of the body's permanent structure: current sensory integration is modulated by top-down processes reflecting a pre-existing reference of the postural and visual features of one's body. This functional interaction has identifiable neural signatures in the right hemisphere. The right temporo-parietal junction modulates the assimilation of sensory signals to a body-reference, while the subjective experience of body-ownership is correlated to activity in the right posterior insula. These structures may form a network that plays a fundamental role in self-consciousness

F. de Vignemont: "How many representations of the body?"

The body can be viewed from many different perspectives (e.g. semantic, emotional, spatial, motor, tactile, visual, proprioceptive, etc.) and described with many pairs of opposing properties: conscious/unconscious, conceptual/non-conceptual, dynamic/stable, innate/acquired, personal/generic, spatial/non-spatial. How many body representations do we really have? One representation, integrating all the different types of information into a unified neuromatrix? Two representations, based on the model of visual perception, distinguishing the body image for recognition and the body schema for action? Three representations, for a more fine-grained distinction within the body image, disentangling the visuo-spatial bodily map and the body semantics?

Discussion:

"Somatognosia: scientific and philosophical perspectives" (Coordinator: K Fotopoulou)

Metacognition, Mindreading and Self-consciousness

Cristiano Castelfranchi
ISTC-CNR, Roma
cristiano.castelfranchi@istc.cnr.it

Joëlle Proust
Institut Jean Nicod, Paris
jproust@ehess.fr

Tjeerd Jellema
University of Hull
t.jellema@hull.ac.uk

Fabio Paglieri
ISTC-CNR, Roma
fabio.paglieri@istc.cnr.it

This symposium will bring together leading scholars from four large-scale ongoing research projects on the study of metacognition and consciousness, to discuss the following research challenges:

- *continuity between mindreading, metacognition and self-consciousness* in evolution and development;
- conceptual differences between *metacognition* and *metarepresentation*;
- the role of *sensory-motor capacities* in enabling both mindreading and metacognition.

Each of the three speakers will have a commentator and will reply to his critical remarks on the presentation. The three invited discussants for this event will be dr. Julian Kiverstein (University of Edinburgh), prof. Andreas Roepstorff (University of Aarhus), and prof. Jerome Dokic (Institut Jean Nicod, Paris).

In order to allow for in depth debate on each of the presentations, the symposium will have a duration of 3 hours, with a 15-minutes break after the first relation.

The *European Science Foundation* is financing the event, and a representative of the ESF, dr. Eva Hoogland, will open the symposium by briefly outlining the new EuroCORES Program "CNCC – Consciousness in a Natural and Cultural Context" (http://www.esf.org/cncc).

Joëlle Proust

Metacognition without metarepresentation

Commentator: Julian Kiverstein, University of Edinburgh

Metacognition is often defined as thinking about thinking. It is exemplified in all the activities through which one tries to predict and evaluate one's own mental dispositions, states and properties for their cognitive adequacy. This talk will discuss the view that metacognition has metarepresentational structure. Properties such as causal contiguity, epistemic transparency and procedural reflexivity are present in metacognition but missing in metarepresentation, while open-ended recursivity and inferential promiscuity only occur in metarepresentation. It is concluded that, although metarepresentations can redescribe metacognitive contents, metacognition and metarepresentation are functionally distinct.

Tjeerd Jellema

Developmental and neuroscientific perspectives on mindreading and action understanding

Commentator: Andreas Roepstorff, University of Aarhus

My talk will be on the neural basis of social cognition and ToM from an evolutionary perspective. A basic question is what are the neural structures and computational/cognitive processes that enable us to infer an individual's goal or intention, or to attribute a mental state (ToM), when all we see are their bodily postures, implied and actual articulated actions, gaze direction and facial expression. A working hypothesis is that differential but overlapping neural substrates exist for the forming of descriptions of social behaviour: (a) in terms of the 'mechanics', i.e. the physical causes, action sequences and consequences of actions allowing prediction of the most likely next behaviour ('behaviour reading'), and (b) in terms of the 'mentalistic' underpinnings of the behaviour ('mind reading'). Specific questions that will be looked at are: What are the necessary building blocks, or precursors, that lead to the forming of ToM, to what extent are they already present in non-human primates, how can we 'measure' their operations in humans, and to what extent is the automation of social cue evaluation compromised in autism?

Fabio Paglieri

From mindreading to mindchanging: Metacognition, social influence, and self-consciousness

Commentator: Jerome Dokic, Institut Jean Nicod, Paris

Regardless heated debate on the proper format of our capacities for understanding each other mental states, proponents of both simulationist and theoretical accounts of mindreading tend to agree on what are the main adaptive functions that are served by such alleged capacities: *interpreting*, *predicting*, and *coordinating* with the behaviour of others. In contrast, *influencing* the conduct of other agents through an adequate appreciation of their inner states does not usually figure among the main functions of mindreading. In this talk, I will argue that, on the contrary, influencing each other conduct is one of the most relevant powers engendered by sophisticated mindreading skills, and that this crucial capacity is intertwined with other functions of mindreading.

In particular, the presentation will aim to:

- outline a more fine-grained *theory of interference*;
- define *influence* as a specific type of interference;
- relate *types of interference with different cognitive capacities*, in particular influence and mindreading;
- show the *mutual interactions between different functions of mindreading*: explanation, prediction, coordination, and interference;
- discuss the import of the influence function of mindreading for a theory of *self-consciousness* and *strength of will*.

Papers

Elementary student nascent abilities for scientific argumentation

Loucas Louca (Louca.L@cytanet.com.cy)
Learning in Science Group, University of Cyprus
P.O. Box 20537, Nicosia 1678, Cyprus

David Hammer (davidham@umd.edu)
Department of Physics & Department of Curriculum and Instruction, University of Maryland
2226 Benjamin Building, College Park, MD 20742 USA

Abstract

We analyze a 5-6th grade class conversation about what will happen to a pendulum if it is released at the highest point of its swing. Using two frameworks for analyzing the quality of argumentation, we argue that prior to any formal instruction the students showed abilities for scientific argumentation. This and other evidence in the literature supports the contention that children have resources for argumentation from their everyday experience, which suggests a shift in orientation for instruction and research: Rather than work to instruct students in scientific argumentation, educators should focus first on recognizing and cultivating the abilities they already have.

Introduction

There has been substantial growth of research in science education on student argumentation (Kelly, et al., 1998; Newton et al., 1999; Driver, et al., 2000; Jimenez-Aleixandre, Rodriguez & Duschl, 2000; Felton & Kuhn, 2001; Kelly & Takao 2002; Kuhn & Udell, 2003; Erduran et al., 2004). This work is motivated by old and widely subscribed views of a need for increased emphasis on students learning to engage in scientific inquiry (NSES, 1996; CSMEE, 2000; Minstrell & van Zee, 2000).

Although researchers have not formalized a single definition of argumentation, all share a basic view of it as the advancement and supporting of claims with logic and evidence, and of sophisticated argumentation as involving attention and response to others' reasoning (Erduran et al., 2004; Kuhn, 1993; Toulmin, 1958, Osborne et al., 2004; Jimenez-Aleixander et al., 2000; Driver et al., 2000). The literature is not so consistent, however, with respect to what educators should *expect* to see in students. By large, it either argues or assumes that prior to explicit instruction, students lack abilities for argumentation.

Our purpose in this paper is to argue for this interpretation, that children bring resources for argumentation with them to the classroom from their everyday experience, and that the central role of instruction at the outset should be to elicit, recognize, and promote those abilities (Hammer & Elby, 2003; Hammer, 2004). We make this case by using data from a 45-minute conversation in a combined 5th-6th grade science class of student who had never had formal instruction in scientific argumentation. We show that, analyzed using existing coding schemes (Erduran et al., 2004; Felton & Kuhn, 2001), there is ample evidence of students' nascent abilities.

Views about student abilities for argumentation

A large body of the recent literature on argumentation (Kelly et al., 1998; Jimenez-Aleixandre et al, 2000; Erduran et al., 2004; Osborne et al., 2004) draws on Toulmin's (1958) "argument pattern" (TAP), defining argumentation in terms of *claims*, *data* that support the claim, *warrants* for linking the data to the claim, *backings* for the warrants in the form of generalizations from a body of experience, and *rebuttals* that attempt to "undermine the force of the supporting arguments" (Toulmin, in Erduran el al., p. 918).

Erduran et al. discussed methodological challenges in applying TAP to analyzing student argumentation, such as the ambiguity of distinguishing between data and warrants or between warrants and backings. Following earlier work (Kelly et al., 1998), they simplified the scheme to focus on *claims*, *justifications*, and *rebuttals*, where justifications may be any use of data, warrants or backings to support the claim, and rebuttals are attempts to identify flaws in the justifications for an opposing view.

Kuhn and her colleagues (Felton & Kuhn, 2001; Kuhn & Udell, 2003) draw on Walton's (1989) work, rather than Toulmin's (1958), but their scheme has similar features. They quote Walton's description of skilled argumentation as having two goals, one to "secure commitments from the opponent that can be used to support one's own argument," and the other "to undermine the opponent's position by identifying and challenging weaknesses in his or her argument." This supports Kuhn and her colleagues to see sophisticated argumentation as involving recognizing and responding to the opinions, reasons, and evidence of an opponent's position. Felton & Kuhn (2001) identify "challenge type" discourse including "Counter-A" and "Counter-C," defined as disagreements accompanied by an alternative argument (A) or a critique (C).

The two schemes both depict sophisticated argumentation to involve not only supporting one's own views with reasoning but also attending and responding to others' reasoning. In this way, they represent a consensus in the literature for what educators should hope to see in students' argumentation.

Expectations for student abilities

The literature is not so consistent, however, with respect to student abilities for scientific argumentation. Kuhn and her colleagues have pursued a developmental view, documenting limitations of abilities for coordinating theory and evidence in children and scientifically naïve adults (Kuhn, 1989, 1993; Felton & Kuhn, 2001; Kuhn & Udell, 2003; Kuhn et al., 2004). Kuhn & Udell suggest that there are serious weaknesses in the skills of adolescent and young adults. Although children encounter evidence from early ages, the coordination of evidence does not take place at a level of conscious awareness or control until much later.

Kuhn's findings of developmental limitations has been the subject of much debate. Metz (1995) argued that developmental accounts have systematically underestimated children's abilities in science. Koslowski (1996) criticized Kuhn's work for placing too much emphasis during the interviews on covariation of evidence and not enough on mechanism. When presented with simpler tasks, even first and second graders can distinguish between theory and evidence (i.e., Samarapungavan, 1992).

A number of studies give evidence of students' abilities for a "natural form of argumentation" (Jimenez-Aleixandre et al., 2000). Given appropriate opportunities, these studies suggest, students will draw on these abilities (Gallas, 1995; Hammer, 2004). In fact, this view of student abilities has some support in the findings of most studies. Erduran et al.'s (2004) analysis records instances of high-level argumentation in 12-14 year old students pre-instruction, almost as many as it records for the students post-instruction. Kuhn & Udell (2003) report increases in "challenge type" codings of argumentation as a result of instruction, but there are instances at the outset. Similarly, McNeill et al.'s (2006) analysis identified pre-instructional instances of students using evidence to support claims.

There is evidence of argumentation in many case studies of children's reasoning (Gallas, 1995; Hammer and van Zee, 2006). But it is not always easy to discern, which raises an important possibility: Educators may think that abilities for argumentation do not come naturally because the abilities are difficult to recognize in their natural forms. If so, it is a crucial agenda for research to learn better to identify nascent abilities, to identify circumstances in which they tend to appear, and to make progress in understanding how they develop into expert abilities. As well, if the developmental issue involves meta-level awareness and control, as Kuhn and her colleagues suggested, it is important to identify the "inchoate forms" of argumentation such that children recognize them as well.

Methodology

Like other recent efforts, we are studying argumentation as it occurs in a classroom setting rather than in clinical interviews, because we expect that children's abilities depend on context. In particular, we examine a 45-minute conversation among students in a combined fifth and sixth-grade class (17 fifth and 11 sixth grade, ages 10-12) at a public elementary school in Prince George's County, Maryland. It was a racially diverse class, reflecting the school population, with African Americans the majority.

Our purpose in this paper is to document children's pre-instructional abilities for scientific argumentation, as defined in the literature. To that end, we base our main analysis on the coding scheme presented in Erduran et al. (2004) focused on identifying rebuttals. Erduran et al.'s. (2004) scheme consists of a five-level framework, summarized in Table 1, for coding episodes of opposition they identified in student conversations.

We present the results of our analyses at two levels of explication. Our main analysis consists of coding 16 minutes of continuous conversation (120 utterances) using Erdurna's at al (2004) coding scheme. Second, we apply a narrative analysis, to examine five minutes from the conversation in detail. We present the transcript of these five minutes, providing the results from (i) the Erduran et al. (2004) coding scheme, along with (ii) Felton & Kuhn's (2001) coding scheme, accompanied by further insights from the narrative analysis.

Adapting and applying an existing coding scheme

The units for analysis in Erduran et al.'s (2004) coding were *episodes* of opposition they identified in the data as a first step. We have modified their framework slightly to take *conversational turns* as the units of analysis, because we found it difficult to segment the transcript into episodes. That change obviated the difference between levels 4 and 5 in their framework. Rather than identify oppositional episodes, we coded 16 uninterrupted minutes of the conversation, coding each conversational turn in the transcript by the first 4 levels of Erduran et al.'s scheme.

Conducting the analysis below, we worked principally from the transcript of the conversation, consulting the video only in particular moments. Each of us coded 16 minutes of transcript (120 utterances) independently by our adaptation of Erduran et al.'s (2004) scheme. Our agreement was 80% (Cohen's Kappa: 71%), and we resolved disagreement through discussion.

To provide further support for our claim of nascent abilities, we chose a five-minute segment of the conversation for additional coding by a second scheme by Felton & Kuhn (2001). Because we were studying a conversation among more than two students, we adapted their codings to substitute "another student" for "partner." We also allowed that the preceding utterance might not be immediately preceding in the transcript, such as when a student waits several conversational turns for the chance to respond to a particular statement.

Narrative analysis of student discourse

For our second analysis we used narrative analysis seeking to examine the details and to make explicit our assessment of student argumentation. Like Kelly et al. (1998), we expect that the substantive details and context of the conversation are critical and need to be examined; unlike those authors we work from the whole of the conversation rather than try to isolate and code only specific utterances. This difference in approach stems in part from a difference in theoretical perspective: We expect that student abilities for argumentation may be activated or not in different contexts, including within the conversation itself (Louca, Hammer & Bell, 2002). In this analysis, then we attend closely to the conversational context.

Level 1 argumentation consists of arguments that are a simple claim vs. a counter-claim or a claim vs. a claim.
Level 2 argumentation has arguments consisting of a claim vs. a claim with either data, warrants, or backings but do not contain any rebuttals.
Level 3 argumentation has arguments with a series of claims or counter-claims with either data, warrants, or backings with the occasional weak rebuttal.
Level 4 argumentation shows arguments with a claim with a clearly identifiable rebuttal.
Level 5 argumentation displays an extended argument with more than one rebuttal.

Table 1: Analytical framework used for assessing the quality of argumentation (from Erduran et al., 2004)

Data synopsis

We begin with a brief description of the conversation as a whole, and in the next section provide findings.

The teacher started the conversation by showing students a pendulum made of a metal washer and a string, and asked the class to explain how the washer would move if the string were cut just when the pendulum had swung to its highest point. As we recount elsewhere (Louca et al., 2002), for the first several minutes of the conversation the students' contributions consisted almost entirely of claims for what would happen, with little or no justification, even with the teacher prompting. Two students sketched their answers on the board, as shown in Figure 1: Chris[1] drew answer 1; Ike answer 2.

Victoria (49)[2] then provided answer 3, in sharp contrast with Chris's and Ike's, that the washer would fall straight down, explaining that "the string is gonna kind of curve," but "gravity is gonna push it [the washer] down" (56).

Victoria's idea sparked a new level of energy in the class —with students competing for the floor. Jeff (60) seconded her answer; Brandon (61) disagreed, and Shadawn (62) said that "it depends on how fast it's going," that "if it's going really fast and you cut it, it's gonna fly somewhere," but if it's "going really slow" then "it's just gonna go straight down." Mathew (64) offered an analogy in support of Shadawn's idea, comparing the pendulum question to what happens when someone swings from a rope into a lake. Vanice (65) objected to that comparison, because "the

---

[1] We have obtained permission to use students' real first names.
[2] Numbers in parentheses refer to the conversational turn in the transcript. The portion we analyzed begins at with Victoria's comment, the 49th turn in the transcript.

washer is tied to the string" but the person who swings from the rope lets go of it.

The conversation continued, lasting about 30 minutes in all. Much of it concerned the students discussing how the motion of the bob may depend on its weight, how quickly it is moving when it is released, and where it is released in the swing. In many instances, they explain their reasoning using comparisons to other situations or objects, including swinging keys, heavy weights on cranes, or a pencil.

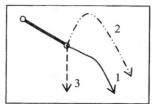

Figure 1: Summary of the three different ideas

Analysis and findings

A segment of conversation

64. Mathew: Can I say something? I, I agree with, um, Shadawn because it's kind of like, you, you have a little, like you know how some times on movies and things and real life, they have lakes or swimming pools and you have a little rope and you run and grab on to the rope and then fly and then let go and you go flying over to the side? That's just like that, the washer. It depends on how much force is on it.

65. Vanice: Not exactly Mathew, because the pendulum is, I mean the washer is tied to the string so it won't go to the other side.

66. Mathew: But she is cutting it, or she'll let it go.

67. Vanice: I know but it still not going to go to the other side because it's hooked together, if it wasn't hooked together then yeah it might go to the other side, like the str, the string would still be in your hand but the pendulum, I mean the washer will go somewhere else.

68. Mathew: I know that. It's kind like, it's kind like, um, the person flying off of it letting go and then going into the water.

69. Vanice: I know but it's not connected I mean it's connected so that wouldn't work.

70. Grace: Well um, I agree with Chris because um it can't really go up more because like gravity doesn't go up. And like I don't think it can just go straight down because I think you're swinging it.

71. Mathew: I disagree with, I disagree with Grace because, because it's kind of like you throw a bucket or a ball up in the air, gravity is coming down forcing it to come down, but you still, it still going up.

Mathew and Vanice – Coding & narrative analysis

The segment starts with Mathew agreeing (64) with Shadawn that the answer to the question depends on "how fast it's going" (62), justifying his agreement with a comparison to the experience of swinging from a rope into water. Vanice took issue with that comparison (65), pointing out a difference: The string stays attached to the washer, but the rope does not stay attached to the swimmer.

Mathew's initial contribution (64) was a clear example of a level 2, since there was a justification but no rebuttal. We coded Vanice's response (65) as level 4, because she provided data against the comparison, undermining Mathew's justification for his claim.

Mathew's responses (66 & 68) to Vanice were more difficult to code. One of us originally coded them each as level 1, on the rationale that it was simply a claim; the other coded them as level 4, on the rationale that Mathew was taking issue with Vanice's reasoning in her rebuttal: She had said the washer is tied to the string, and here Mathew was countering that the string would be cut or released (66) and arguing that her reasoning actually supports his position (68). We coded them each as level 2, treating his statements as justifications for why the two situations are comparable.

Analyzing by Felton and Kuhn's (2001) scheme, we saw most of the students' contributions as Counter-C, because the speaker's strategy was to disagree with the preceding remark while providing a critique. For example, Vanice's objection to Mathew's comparison criticized it (65), and Mathew's response to that criticism (66) was a counter in itself. Mathew's argument (64) showed another strategy (Advance) in his elaboration of Shadawn's previous argument. We coded Vanice's elaboration of her concern (67) as Counter-A, because there she provided further argumentation for her position, and Mathew's response (68) to that as a Coopt, because his approach was to try to incorporate her explanation into his own view.

Assessed by either coding scheme, the students were showing the beginnings of abilities for argumentation. We see further strengths to what Mathew and Vanice were doing, beyond what the coding schemes recognize.

First, Mathew's argument (64) was the first reference in the conversation to another situation, articulating the connection between the pendulum question and familiar experiences. That is a strength in his justification: It invokes knowledge he expected others would share and find compelling. Second, Vanice's response (65) attended to the details of the comparison he offered, noticing a specific difference that was likely connected to her sense of the mechanism by which the washer would move: With the string attached, she seemed to be thinking, the washer would still be tethered, "so it won't go to the other side." We noted further that her critique focused specifically on the relevance of the experience that Mathew provided as grounds to his claim. She did not challenge Mathew's reasoning about what happens on rope swings; she challenged whether what happens on rope swings can be compared to the washer on the string.

We also note a weakness. Part of the reason for our ambivalence in coding Mathew's responses to Vanice's argument (66,68) was that he did not understand her point. He probably intended to be undermining the force of her argument (Counter-C), and he was providing justification to support the comparison he was making (level 2), but it is clear he missed her meaning.

Grace and Mathew - Coding & narrative analysis

When Grace agreed (70) with Chris, she supported his answer by arguing against the competing possibilities: "it can't really go up more because gravity doesn't go up," and it cannot "just go straight because … you were swinging it." Mathew (71) responded to her first argument, again comparing the situation of the washer to other, more familiar situations: Grace's first point cannot be correct, he argued, because it is clearly possible to "throw a bucket or a ball up in the air," even with "gravity coming down."

We coded Grace's contribution (70) as level 2, because she provided a claim, in her agreement with Chris, and she supported it with two lines of justification. Someone might argue that her respective reasons for supporting Chris were rebuttals of the alternative answers, but we did not see evidence that she was attending to the reasoning that supported those claims. We coded Mathew's contribution as level 4, since he provided a rebuttal to the justification Grace had provided. Had we isolated this pair of statements as an episode to code as a unit we would have counted it as level 4, rather than coding one turn at level 2 and the other at level 4. According to Felton and Kuhn's scheme, Grace was advancing Chris's prior claim, and Mathew's strategy was Counter-A, to disagree with Grace and provide an argument in support of his disagreement.

Again, Mathew was referring to a shared, everyday experience to make his counter-argument, and in the process he was drawing a clear distinction between the motion of an object and the influence of another causal agent. Part of what is impressive about his argument is its clarity in that distinction, which is generally considered to be a difficult one for students to make.

We suspect, however, that Grace did not fully explain her reasoning: She was probably arguing that the washer cannot go up more once it has reached the apex of its swing, without articulating a sense that, at that point, the washer's own upward motion had run out. For it go up higher, something would have to push it higher, but "gravity doesn't go up." Here, then, Mathew may have again misunderstood the reasoning on the other side.

Coding levels of rebuttals

Figure 2 shows the total number of conversational turns we coded at each level: 18 at level 1 (34%), 17 at level 2 (32%), 8 at level 3 (15%) and 10 at level 4 (19%). The codes at level 4 involved turns by five different students; the codes at level 3 involved 4 additional students. Thus nine different students showed they were capable of some level of rebuttal over the course of the 16 minute excerpt.

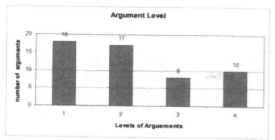

Figure 2: Summary of coding findings over 16 minutes of conversation

Our results are qualitatively comparable to Erduran et al.'s (2004): Across 43 discussion groups, pre-instruction they coded 28 episodes at level 3 or above (40% of coded arguments), post-instruction 36 (55%). In our case, analyzing a single 16-minute excerpt, we coded 18 utterances (34%) at level 3 or above. This supports our claim that children arrive pre-instruction with nascent abilities, including for generating rebuttals to others' arguments. We found further support to this claim from applying the Felton & Kuhn's (2001) scheme to the brief segment of data, which resulted in several codes of challenge-type discourse.

Quantitative comparison would not be meaningful for several reasons. First, as we noted above, we chose to code conversational turns rather than oppositional episodes, which resulted in many more codes than Erduran et al. (2004). Second, we understand the activation of student abilities for argumentation as sensitive to context, including fine-grained contexts within the course of a conversation. Different situations will trigger different argumentation.

Figure 3 includes coding results from the whole conversation. It displays the shift that followed Victoria's contribution (49), making apparent the increase of level 3 and the appearance of level 4 arguments. Students in the 16 minutes that followed Victoria's contribution do not engage in upper-level argumentation all the time, but they shift from level 1 through level 4 and vice versa. A topic for further study will be to understand what prompts these shifts during the conversation.

Conclusions and implications

Children's abilities for argumentation

In this paper we have documented 5th and 6th graders' making claims, supporting those claims with reasoning, and attending and responding to each others' claims and reasoning. The students had had no formal instruction in argumentation, and there was no particular teaching agenda for this discussion that they engage in argumentation. Still, they showed levels of argumentation comparable to the pre- or post-instructional levels reported in Erduran et al.'s (2004) study.

Of course, we do not claim that the students are already experts. There are several respects in which it is evident they are not, such as students misunderstanding each other's

ideas, varying levels of articulateness, as well as the time it took the class to move past the initial phase of simply stating claims. That is, while there is evidence of students' abilities for argumentation, there is also evidence that they do not always use those abilities, as displayed in Figure 3.

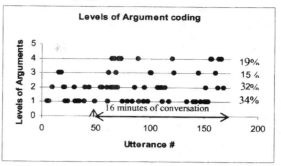

Figure 3: Tracking levels of argument coding over the course of the conversation

Our conclusion then is that children come to science instruction with nascent abilities for argumentation, that they may invoke spontaneously directly in line with the abilities educators have described as important to impart. In this we support the arguments in the literature that students have "natural" abilities (Jimenez-Aleixandre et al., 2000) for argumentation, as well as evidence from elsewhere, including Erduran et al.'s (2004) findings of high level episodes pre-instruction, Kuhn and Udell's (2003) of pre-instructional instances of counter-arguments. However, students' use of those abilities seems to be sensitive to context. That sensitivity provides an explanation for evidence in some studies (Kuhn, 1991, 1993) that show limitations: Depending on their design the contexts in different studies may not tap students' productive resources. This also provides an alternative account of the gains documented in various instructional studies (Erduran et al., 2004; Kuhn et al, 2006; Kuhn & Udell, 2003; McNeil et al., 2006): Improved performance may arise mainly from the activation of students' existing abilities, rather than from the acquisition of new abilities.

Implications for instruction

The first implication of this view for instruction is that the initial focus of attention should shift to children's current abilities, and the second is that teachers should be cautious in ascribing developmental limitations. That expectation should guide both the setting of objectives and the assessment of what takes place in class.

Rather than expect that "the use of valid argument does not come naturally" (Osborne et al, 2004, p. 996), educators should expect abilities for argumentation exist in "natural form" (Jimenez-Aleixandre et al. 2000), and that what comes naturally depends on the context. And so, rather than expect that argumentation must be "explicitly taught through suitable instruction, task structuring, and modelling" (Osborne et al, 2004, p. 997), educators should see the first step as helping children tap the resources they already have (Hammer and Elby, 2003). In other words, the initial emphasis should be on *eliciting and supporting* argumentation rather than on *instructing* students in it.

If the first step for instruction is to create contexts in which students are inclined to draw on their resources for argumentation, a subsequent step must involve helping them become aware of what they are doing, toward "enhanced metalevel awareness" (Kuhn and Udell, 2003). As the case study we presented illustrated, children may enter or leave productive argumentation, and so part of their development toward expertise should involve their developing more reliable access to those abilities.

Rather than suppose students lack abilities for argumentation pre-instruction, researchers might suppose they have abilities but do not use them reliably. On this view, some of the improvement documented in instructional studies (Kuhn & Udell, 2003; McNeill et al., 2006; Osborne et al., 2004) reflects increased use of abilities that students had already developed. This difference in interpretation would have substantial implications for research and instruction. Understanding children as lacking abilities, educators design instruction to help children form those abilities, and research focuses on assessing progress in that formation to identify factors that lead to the greatest improvement. In contrast, on the view that children already have abilities for argumentation, educators would design instruction to help children draw on those abilities, and the objective for research would be to understand their nature.

Acknowledgments

This study was supported by the NSF Award ESI-9986846.

References

Center for Science, Mathematics, & Engineering Education [CSMEE] (2000). *Inquiry and the National Science Education Standards a guide for teaching and learning*. Washington, DC: National Academy Press.

Driver, R., Newton, P. & Osborne, J. (2000). Establishing the norms of scientific argumentation in classrooms. *Science Education*, 84(3): 287-312.

Erduran, S., Simon, S. & Osborne J. (2004). TAPping into argumentation: Developments in the application of Toulmin's argument pattern for studying science discourse. *Science Education*, 88(6): 915-933.

Felton, M. & Kuhn D. (2001). The development of argumentive discourse skill. *Discourse Processes*, 32(2-3): 135-153.

Gallas, K. (1995). *Talking their way into science: hearing children's questions and theories, responding with curricula*. NY: Teachers College Press.

Hammer, D. & van Zee, E. H. (2006). *Seeing the science in children's thinking: Case studies of student inquiry in physical science*. Portsmouth, NH: Heinemann.

Hammer, D. & Elby, A. (2003). Tapping students' epistemological resources. *The Journal of the Learning Sciences*, 12 (1): 53-91.

Hammer, D. (2004). The variability of student reasoning, lectures 1-3. In E. Redish and M. Vicentini (Eds.), *Proceedings of the Enrico Fermi Summer School, Course CLVI* (pp. 279-340): Italian Physical Society.

Jimenez-Aleixandre, M. P., Rodriguez, A. B. & Duschl, R. A. (2000). "Doing the lesson" or "doing science": Argument in high school genetics. *Science Education* 84(6): 757-792.

Kelly, G. J. & Takao, A. (2002). Epistemic levels in argument: An analysis of university oceanography students' use of evidence. *Science Education* 86(3): 314-342.

Kelly, G. J., Druker, S. & Chen, C. (1998). Students' reasoning about electricity: combining performance assessments with argumentation analysis. *International Journal of Science Education*, 20(7): 849-871.

Koslowski, B. (1996). *Theory and evidence: the development of scientific reasoning*. Cambridge, Mass: MIT Press.

Kuhn, D. & Udell, W. (2003). The development of argument skills. *Child Development*, 74(5): 1245-1260.

Kuhn, D., Katz, J. B. & Drean Jr, D. (2004). Developing reason. *Thinking & Reasoning*, 10(2):197-219.

Kuhn, D. (1989). Children and adults as intuitive scientists. *Psychological Review*, 96(4): 674-689.

Kuhn, D. (1993). Science as Argument: Implications for Teaching and Learning Scientific Thinking. *Science Education*, 77(3): 319-337.

McNeill, K. L., Lizotte, D. J., Krajcik, J., & Marx, R. W. (2006). Supporting Students' Construction of Scientific Explanations by Fading Scaffolds in Instructional Materials. *The Journal of the Learning Sciences*, 15(2): 153-191.

Metz, K. (1995). Reassessment of developmental constraints on children's science instruction. Review of Educational Research, 65(2): 93-127.

Minstrell, J. A. & Van Zee, E. H. (2000). *Inquiring into inquiry: learning and teaching in science*. Washington, D.C., American Association for the Advancement of Science.

Newton, P., Driver, R and Osborne, J. (1999). The place of argumentation in the pedagogy of school science. *International J. of Science Education*, 21(5): 553-576.

National Research Council [NRC]. (1996). National Science Education Standards. Washington DC: National Academy Press.

Osborne, J., Erduran, S. and Simon, S. (2004). Enhancing the quality of argumentation in school science. *J. of Research in Science Teaching*, 41(10): 994-1020.

Samarapungavan, A. (1992). Children's judgments in theory choice tasks: Scientific rationality in childhood. *Cognition*, 45: 1-32.

Toulmin, S. (1958). *The uses of argument*. Cambridge: Cambridge University Press.

Walton, D. N. (1989). Dialogue theory for critical thinking. *Argumentation*, 3: 169–184.

Nascent abilities for scientific inquiry in elementary science

Loucas Louca (Louca.L@cytanet.com.cy)
Learning in Science Group, Department of Educational Sciences, University of Cyprus
P.O. Box 20537, Nicosia 1678, Cyprus

Zacharia C. Zacharia (zach@ucy.ac.cy)
Learning in Science Group, Department of Educational Sciences, University of Cyprus
P.O. Box 20537, Nicosia 1678, Cyprus

Abstract

In this case study we analyze a series of student conversations about projectiles and relative motion in a combined 5th-6th grade science afternoon club to provide detailed descriptions of student inquiry, seeking to contribute to the development of a better understanding of nascent student inquiry in classroom settings. Prior to any formal instruction, we contend these students "have" a repertoire of abilities, e.g. for mechanistic or analogical reasoning and argumentation. With ambiguities regarding productive science inquiry, findings from this study reveal new insights with respect to the challenge of diagnosing student progress in the classroom. We also suggest that the role of instruction should be less on the direct teaching of elements of student inquiry and more on helping students develop reliable access to those abilities.

Introduction

Despite decades of calls for promoting inquiry in elementary grades, the agenda has yet to establish in instructional practice (Hawkins, 1974; NSES, 1996; Minstrell & van Zee, 2000; Osborne et al., 2004; Louca et al., 2002) for a number of reasons. First, while there is a consensus for the importance of inquiry in science learning, the education community has yet to agree on precisely what is important. For many, inquiry is a method for learning science "content," and it is important because it is more effective than other methods. Others consider it as part of science, and as an objective of itself. Second, there is not a consensus regarding what "productive" inquiry entails, especially in the early grades. For example, what should teachers be looking for and trying to cultivate? Answers have varied from Hawkins's (1974) general appeal for "messing about" to more specific targets for developing "concrete" abilities of observation and controlling variables in experiments (see Metz, 1995).

With these ambiguities, in contrast to tangible and seemingly straightforward objectives of traditional content, it is difficult to sustain instructional attention to student inquiry (Hammer, 1995). Regardless of any particular account of children's inquiry, there is the challenge of diagnosing student progress in any classroom situation.

To make progress in promoting student inquiry, science education needs to develop better understanding of student abilities for nascent inquiry in classroom settings. The purpose of this case study is to provide detailed descriptions of nascent student inquiry from the authentic learning context of the science classroom. We analyze a series of student conversations in science, identifying instances of productive student inquiry and looking for different elements of scientific inquiry that include mechanistic and analogical reasoning and argumentation. At the same time, we seek to speak to the debate about the development of student abilities for scientific inquiry, pointing to data that suggest that students without any formal instruction "have" the beginnings of those abilities. Our motivation comes from two directions. First, we seek to contribute to research aiming to help teachers understand how student inquiry looks in the science classroom and what they should be looking for to evaluate student progress regarding inquiry. Second, we seek to contribute to a growing body of research (e.g., Koslowski, 1996; Metz, 1995), suggesting that it is more productive to view students as "having" abilities for scientific inquiry and need to develop reliable access to.

Following current emphasis in science education for studying classroom-based scientific discourse, in this paper we adopt an analytic framework of recent research in science education about what constitutes student inquiry in the elementary science classroom, focusing on a number of different elements of student inquiry in science that have been highlighted in recent literature as central elements of scientific inquiry (Louca & Hammer, submitted).

Elements of scientific inquiry

Working from a variety of perspectives and intellectual traditions, the literature about elements of student abilities for scientific inquiry shows a general consensus with respect to the sorts of things we should value and try to promote in children's inquiry. That consensus, however, does not extend to the definition of what scientific inquiry looks like in the science classroom. It competes in particular with a widely-shared, if mostly tacit, sense of inquiry as a pedagogical strategy, a method for teaching the traditionally construed "content" of science. By this view, assessing the quality of children's inquiry is equivalent to assessing their progress toward the correct answers in the canon of accepted knowledge. Indeed, science educators have a much clearer sense of the canon of accepted knowledge than of what constitutes "good inquiry." Thus, while it is comparably straightforward to determine whether they are *correct*, inquiry-oriented objectives remain ambiguous.

To offer a working definition, we take inquiry to mean *the pursuit of causal, coherent explanations of natural phenomena* (Hammer, 2004). That pursuit may take many forms, both experimental and theoretical; in whatever form, the instructional agenda is to help students learn to engage in that pursuit for themselves. In this paper we suggest that evidence from classroom discourse shows that scientific inquiry includes a number of different elements that have been offered through recent literature about student inquiry in science. These elements may abilities for argumentation, mechanistic reasoning, and analogical reasoning and the list can go on to include abilities for modeling discourse, design and implement experiments and controlling variables. For the case study that we present below, students did not engaged in any experimentation, and thus we do not address issues related with those abilities. By this we do not suggest that these are the only elements of scientific inquiry nor do we believe that science education research community is anywhere close to a consensus about what student inquiry looks like in the science classroom.

Mechanistic reasoning

One area of research is calling attention to the scientific discourse that involves causal mechanism (Russ et al., submitted), following a number of studies that partly focused on student use of causation in science (i.e., Schauble, 1996; Koslowski, 1996). This suggests that "assessing when and how students seek causal mechanism in their understanding should be part of assessing their reasoning as inquiry" (Russ et al., submitted, p.1)

Using a framework derived from the philosophy of science, Russ et al. (submitted) propose a coding scheme of 7 major components of mechanistic reasoning that can be used to identify and assess student use of mechanistic reasoning. Those components include (i) descriptions of the target phenomenon (what we see happening), (ii) identification of the set-up conditions that are necessary for the phenomenon to happen, (iii) identification of entities (conceptual or real objects that play a particular role in the phenomenon, (iv) identification of (iv) the entities activities that cause changes in the surrounding entities, (v) the entities properties, and (vi) the entity organization (how entities are located, structured or oriented within the phenomenon), and (vii) chaining, that is using knowledge about causal structure to make claims about what has happened prior to a phenomenon and what will happen.

Analogical reasoning

Expert scientific inquiry also involves the generation, use and evaluation of analogies (May et al., 2006) because analogies can be valuable tools for constructing one's own understanding in a variety of contexts. Unlike most of the research about analogies (focused almost exclusively on their pedagogical value in curriculum materials and teacher explanations for promoting conceptual change in students (May et al., 2006)), we are interested in student abilities for analogical reasoning that includes (i) the generation of

analogies (that includes a target case (unknown), a base case (known) and a relation that maps elements from one case to the other), (ii) the evaluation of the validity of an analogy and subsequent refinement (that includes identification of the key features of an analogy and its limitations), (iii) the use of analogies to create new knowledge by making new inferences about the target case and creating abstract generalizations and (iv) the use of analogies to communicate ideas in science to others (Clement, 1998; May et al., 2006).

Argumentation

Argumentation is one of the areas that research has made significant progress in understanding and defining it. Kuhn (1989; 1993) was the first to call attention to inquiry as an essential objective for science education, focusing specifically on abilities for coordinating theory and evidence. A number of recent efforts have focused on analyzing the sophistication of student arguments in science. Louca and Hammer (submitted) propose a framework for studying argumentation discourse in the science classroom, specifically focusing on students abilities to generate, use and evaluate arguments. Their framework consists of a modified coding scheme adopted from Erduran et al. (2004) looking for components of arguments that include (i) claims, (ii) grounds, (iii) counterclaims, and (iv) rebuttals.

Views about the development of student abilities for scientific inquiry

The disagreement about what educators should *expect* to see in children's inquiry in the science classroom also includes ongoing differences with respect to the development of abilities of scientific inquiry.

One view follows a developmental approach, focusing on the development of student abilities. Evidence from a number of studies (Kuhn, 1989; 1993) suggests that abilities for i.e. scientific argumentation increased with the subjects' age, suggesting that this ability may be part of general cognitive development providing evidence for a developmental trend in particular in argumentation (Kuhn & Udell 2003).

A second view has argued that developmental perspectives have systematically underestimated children's abilities providing differences in findings that reflect the contexts of the interviews and framing of the questions (Metz, 1995). These concerns are supported by evidence from psychology and education research regarding the universality of abilities and developmental stages (Feldman, 1994; Karmiloff-Smith, 1992; Koslwoski, 1996; Samarapungavan, 1992). On these accounts, human knowledge and reasoning is far more variable than traditional developmental schemes have indicated. Dunbar and Blanchette (2001) describe dramatic differences in the phenomenology of analogical reasoning between *in vitro* studies and their in *vivo* observations: Uses of analogy that are difficult to produce in the laboratory occur easily and spontaneously in naturalistic settings.

A third approach has argued that abilities for i.e. argumentation can and should be explicitly taught as early as in elementary school, including abilities for scientific argumentation (e.g., Erduran et al., 2004; Osborne et al., 2004). This view has motivated research to develop pedagogical practices that specifically support aspects of scientific inquiry (Osborne, Erduran et al., 2004), also suggesting that prior to any intervention students' skills are poor (Bugallo Rondriguez & Jimenez-Aleixandre, 1996).

We, on the other hand, suggest that children come to class already with abilities in engaging in scientific inquiry, and that teachers need to help them refine those abilities (not teach or develop) and most importantly to help them develop reliable access to those abilities for using them in the right context and time. We feel that the literature over-emphasizes the need to actually teach students how to construct, evaluate and respond to causal mechanism, analogies and arguments. Most of research in classroom-based argumentation discourse (Erduran et al, 2004; Kuhn & Udell, 2003) provide some evidence that children have at least *the beginnings* of abilities regarding argumentation. In this view, we will use our analysis below to suggest that we need to reconsider the fact that children may have already appropriated the beginnings of inquiry practices.

Methodology

This interpretive case study illustrates young children's nascent abilities for scientific inquiry. Data originate from a larger research study funded by the Cyprus Research Promotion Foundation aiming to develop case studies of student inquiry as professional development materials for science teachers.

This case study involves a group of 15 fifth and sixth grade students who volunteer for participating in an afternoon science club at their school. Data originate from 4 90-minute whole-class conversations about a combined projectile and relative motion that were facilitated by the club teacher. For the purpose of this paper, we focus on discourse-based data looking for different aspects of scientific inquiry that students use in the conversations. The conversations took place during March 2005, in the context of developing models of the phenomenon. Students had no prior formal instruction about any of the 3 elements of student inquiry that we are investigating.

We analyzed transcripts of student discussions using analysis of student conversation, following a current trend in research in science education focusing on classroom discourse in science and mathematics (e.g., Ball, 1993; Gallas, 1995) and shares the interest of the science education community in classroom discourse. In doing this we seek to describe the variability in students' scientific inquiry, as well as contextual possibilities that might have lead to different uses of different elements of scientific inquiry. This analysis uses transcribed conversations as a gateway to student thinking (Edwards & Mercer, 1995).

After transcribing all videos of whole-class conversations of this case, we skimmed the transcripts independently,

identifying episodes in the conversations that fall under the three elements of scientific inquiry. After agreeing on 46 episodes, we characterized them independently identifying the components of each element based on the literature that we presented above. Our inter-coder agreement was 89% and we resolve disagreements over discussion. Below, we briefly present 5 short analyzed excerpts that are representative of the findings to support our claims.

The conversation that we present below started by the teacher by stating the question: "There is a boy standing on a moving hallway at a local airport. The boy is holding a ball in his hand. Suppose he throws the ball up in the air, where would the ball land?"

Findings

The presentation of findings below is structured following the temporal sequence of how things happened over time.

Asserting answers

At the outset, students simply described what they think would happen, disagreeing over two possibilities (the ball would fall in the boy's hand, or behind the boy) but doing little to justify their answers, without making any progress as to what causes the ball to fall either back to the boy's hand or behind it.

> 17. Myriani: Since his hand is open like that, when he'll throw the ball up this way, he'll move a little, and thus the ball will come back down and hit him on his head[1]. [...]
> 27. Dioni: It will fall behind the student.
> 28. Teacher: Why do you think that?
> 29. Sabina: As soon as he throws the ball, he moves. But the ball is going to fall back to the same point that was thrown initially. Therefore, it is going to fall behind him. [...]
> 32. Dioni: Well, the... the student is..., well, he is moving with the moving hallway, but the ball is going to fall back to the same point [that was initially thrown from], and therefore the ball will fall behind him[...]
> 61. Teacher: Ok. If you think the right answer is this [it will fall back in his hand], why do you think that the other answer [will fall back in his hand] is wrong?
> 62. Nasia: Well, if he's throwing it while he is moving, it [the ball] cannot fall back to his hand.

At the beginning of the conversation, students described the story of the physical system under study, by describing what would happen eventually, without providing any explanations as to why all these happen or how they happen. Although their answers seemed to have an underlying mechanism that could explain what they describe (17, 29, 32)[2], students neither articulated it nor addressed it, even when they disagreed with each other. In terms of mechanistic reasoning (Russ et al., submitted) the students

---

[1] Student conversations are translations from greek.
[2] Numbers represent utterance number from the transcript.

described the target phenomenon without any references to entities, their properties and their organization, which are more sophisticated elements of mechanistic reasoning. Even when the teacher prompted them to explain their ideas (28, 61), their answers were simply re-statements of their ideas (29, 62). In terms of argumentation students were simply constructing and providing claims without any justifications or grounds whatsoever.

As the conversation continued several students offered ideas about dependencies that affect the phenomenon.

> 37. Myriani: I think it depends on whether he would move a little or more. I mean, if he throws it and moves a little, then the ball might fall just in front of him. But if he moves a lot, then the ball would fall behind him.
> 38. Teacher: So, are you saying that it depends on the speed of the hallway?
> 39. Panayiotis: Can you tell us how much is the speed of the hallway? […]
> 45. Erini: Well, it also depends on how high he throws the ball.
> 46. Kyrilos: That's exactly right! If he throws it high, he will move much further, but if he doesn't throw it high, the ball can even land on his head!

According to Russ et al.'s (submitted) scheme, in this mode of work students identified a number of possible set-up conditions that could affect the mechanism that produced the phenomenon. Myriani (37) was the first to suggest that the speed of the moving hallway can affect where the ball would land, indicating that if the boy moves only a little, the ball would fall in front of the boy, but if he moves a lot, then the ball would fall behind him. Myriani's idea may had sparked Erini's idea (45) that the higher the ball would thrown, the further back from the boy it would fall.

Beginnings of student inquiry

In line 131, the teacher decided to prompt students to bring in the conversation any relevant experiences to support their answers. Thus far, the use of experiences from everyday life was completely absent from the conversation, and the teacher thought that this could help students to make progress in the conversation. Students immediately started describing experiences, evaluating at the same time their relevance with the phenomenon under study.

> 138. Dioni: This is the same with throwing a ball in a moving car – but it has to have on open ceiling. Because there are some cars that have no ceiling.
> 139. Teacher: ok. […]
> 146. Erini: Be in an airplane.
> 147. Teacher: So, when you are in an airplane or a car, like Dioni said, and you throw the ball up in the air what is going to happen to the ball?
> 148. Dioni: It is going to fall behind you.
> 149. Teacher: ok, it will fall behind you.

> 150. Panayiotis: It is going to fall in your hand! […]
> 153. Merriam: It is going to fall behind you.
> 154. Sabine: Does the car have a ceiling or not?
> 155. Teacher: Does it matter?
> 156. Sabine: Of course! If it has a ceiling, then the ball is going to hit the ceiling and then return to the point that it was thrown in the first place.
> 157. Teacher: You mean in your hand? […]
> 161. Sabine: Yea. [it will fall] In your hand, because it is going to hit the car's ceiling and then fall back down.

As soon as the teacher prompted for related experiences a couple of students provided some, related with cars and airplanes traveling with people sitting inside them, suggesting their similarities with the phenomenon. Dioni (138) suggested that the phenomenon under study was similar to throwing a ball within a car, highlighting at the same time that for the two situations to be comparable, the car should not have a ceiling, possibly thinking that if the ball touches the ceiling then the phenomenon would have different set-up conditions. Erini (143) talked about the example of a flying airplane, and for the first time Panayiotis introduced the idea that the ball would fall back in the boy's hand.

The teacher's prompt (131) sparked a new dynamic in the conversation. Students not only offered experiences as a justification of their ideas, but they also attempted to evaluate the relevance of these experiences with the phenomenon under study. At the same time, when Sabina (156, 161) for instance described what would happen to the ball when you throw it from within a moving car, she becomes quite specific, talking about the ball's motion "…the ball is going to hit the ceiling and then return to the point that it was thrown in the first place" making some references to a mechanism that could provide a partial explanation of the phenomenon.

In terms of analogical reasoning (May et al., 2006), the same conversational data suggest that students can generate analogies (by identifying a target (the phenomenon under discussion) and a base case (the car or the airplane example) and their relation), and they can also validate and evaluate the relevance those analogies by identifying their key features and their limitations (i.e., the car has to be without a ceiling). In terms of argumentation (Louca & Hammer, submitted), students' statements were now accompanied by some grounds, although they were doing much more (i.e. evaluating the relevance of experiences) that the argumentation coding scheme cannot capture.

> 204. Panayiotis: If the car has a ceiling, then the ball will fall back in his hand, but if the car's ceiling is open, then the ball will fall back.
> 205. Teacher: And why is that?
> 206. Panayiotis: Because when the ball gets outside the car, then it becomes a separate object from the car

which moves forward, whereas the ball falls straight down, after the car moved forward.

When Panayiotis re-iterated the car idea and its relationship with the phenomenon under study, he proposed the idea of independent systems. In an open-ceiling car, if the ball gets outside the car, then the ball becomes independent from the car and acts as a different object, whereas when the ball is within the car it acts like one object with the car. In this contribution, Panayiotis talked about set-up conditions (if the car has a ceiling... and if the car does not have a ceiling, if the ball gets outside of the car ... and if the ball does not get outside of the car), different entities that play different roles in the phenomenon (the ball and the car), about the properties of these entities (the ball becomes a different object as soon as it gets outside the car), and those entities' activities (the ball would stay at the same stop, whereas the car will keep moving forward). Despite the wrong application of the idea of independent systems, all these suggest more sophisticated student inquiry in terms of mechanistic reasoning that was not evident thus far.

Hidden assumptions

Despite that progress, students did not seem to move towards analyzing the "story" of the physical system into smaller conceptual entities (Russ et al., submitted), their characteristics and their behavior, which is required to make progress in terms developing a mechanistic explanation about how the phenomenon happens. Apart for talking about physical entities, it is also important that students address conceptual entities (such as velocity in this case) that play important roles in the phenomenon. We are not suggesting that student do not have any ideas or cannot conceptualize those conceptual entities. In fact, the discourse suggests that their ideas had two underlying "hidden assumptions" (Hammer, personal communication) concerning the ball's horizontal velocity, which prevented them for making any progress: they thought that the ball had either no horizontal velocity or the horizontal velocity became 0 after leaving the boy's hand. For instance, when Dioni (32) stated her idea, she indicated that "...when the ball leaves the boy's hand, and because the hallway is moving forward, the ball is going to fall behind." Whereas Panayioitis indicated that starting from the point that the ball is released from the boy's hand "... the ball's velocity is slowly decreasing."

Analyze the story into conceptual entities

The problem was that although these ideas underlie their contributions about what would happen in the phenomenon, students did not address them directly. The teacher decided to help students realize and evaluate those hidden assumptions by prompting them to talk about the different velocities during the ball's motion. He decided to provide students with a video of the phenomenon and have a discussion specifically about the ball's motion. This happened over the next two meetings and students had the opportunity to watch a video about the phenomenon, and talk about why the ball falls back into the boy's hand. After

that, students could clearly distinguish between the two velocities (the horizontal and the vertical one), and could talk about the result of the combination of those two velocities.

> 1013. Panayiotis: So, when the ball moves like that..., there is one velocity like that [his left hand shows the upwards velocity's direction] and there is another velocity that moves like that [his right hand shows the direction of the velocity due to the hallway's motion]. When you put these two [velocities] together, then they form this shape [shows the oval trajectory of the ball with his hand].
>
> 1014. Teacher: ok. Let's take them one-by-one. What do we know about the vertical velocity?
>
> 1015. Costas: When the ball leaves the hand, that velocity starts decreasing, until one point where it will become zero. Then, the ball will start falling down and its velocity will start increasing.
>
> 1016. Teacher: What about the other velocity?
>
> 1017. Myriani: That velocity is steady, and is the same with the hallway's velocity.

By analyzing the video about the phenomenon under study, students broke down the ball's story into smaller conceptual entities, sketching their relationships. They had now a more analytic understanding of the phenomenon, being able to describe the phenomenon both in small conceptual entities (i.e., the horizontal (1013) and vertical velocity (1015)) and as a whole (the result of the two velocities) (1013). In terms of mechanistic reasoning, students were able to talk about entities, their properties and organization and activities of these entities that produce change in the phenomenon, showing more sophisticated abilities for mechanistic reasoning.

Discussion

This case study is a demonstration of nascent student inquiry in classroom settings. Although we do not claim that our analysis covers the complete spectrum of classroom-based student inquiry, findings from this and other studies (Feldman, 1994; Karmiloff-Smith, 1992; Koslowski, 1996; Louca & Hammer, submitted; Metz, 1995), contend these students come in the classroom "having" some abilities for i.e., argumentation, mechanistic reasoning, and analogical reasoning. With ambiguities regarding productive science inquiry, findings from this study reveal insights with respect to the challenge of defining what student inquiry can look like in the classroom and what teachers should expect to see, speaking to the debate regarding what "productive" inquiry entails, especially in early grades.

Students in this class were able to use a number of different components of the 3 elements of student inquiry – some more sophisticated than others. We do not suggest that these students are experts in scientific inquiry, but rather that they have the beginnings of abilities for scientific inquiry. At the same time, these students seem not to use and apply those abilities in a systematic way. The use of those abilities seemed to vary probably due to a number of factors, possibly including the teacher's specific prompts and the micro-context of the conversation – in many cases, when a student entered a new "mode" of conversation that consisted of more sophisticated reasoning than before, other students followed this new mode of sophisticated inquiry.

Still, if we were to make an assessment of the students' abilities for scientific discourse from those first 46 conversational turns, we would have a very different sense than from what followed. Of course, the students have not developed new abilities in the five minutes since the beginning of the conversation. Rather, they are applying different abilities from their repertoire showing some sophistication in those abilities.

All these suggest that the emphasis of instruction should be on identifying the beginnings of abilities for scientific inquiry in children, focusing on abilities that they already have and possibly use in different contexts. We feel that the literature over-emphasizes the need to actually teach students about how to use arguments, analogies or even mechanistic reasoning. For instance, most of research in classroom-based argumentation discourse (Erduran et al., 2004; Kuhn & Udell, 2003) provide some evidence that children have at least *the beginnings* of abilities regarding argumentation. Instead of seeing children as capable of learning i.e. how to use and evaluate arguments, use analogies, or develop scientific explanations, we suggest that science educators need to help students refine (not teach or develop) abilities for scientific inquiry that they already have. Since is seems to be a matter of ability activation in the appropriate context, by refining we mean helping students develop reliable access to those abilities for using them in the right context and time.

Acknowledgments

This study was supported by the Cyprus Research Foundation Awards #ENIΣX/0603/09 & ENIΣX/0505/44.

We thank Dr. Michalis P. Michaelides for his comments and suggestions during the manuscript preparation.

References

Ball, D. L., (1993). With an eye on the mathematical horizon: dilemmas of teaching elementary school. *The Elementary School Journal*, 93 (4): 373-397.

Blanchette, I., & Dunbar, K. (2001). Analogy use in naturalistic settings: The influence of audience, emotion, and goals. *Memory and Cognition*, 29(5): 730-735.

Bugallo Rodrıguez, A., & Jimenez-Aleixandre, M. P. (1996, August). Using Toulmin's argument pattern to analyze genetics questions. *Paper presented at the Third European Science Education Research Association (ESERA) Summer school*, Barcelona.

Clement, J. (1998). Expert novice similarities and instruction using analogies. *International Journal of Science Education*, 20, 1271– 1286.

Driver, R., Newton, P. & Osborne, J. (2000). Establishing the norms of scientific argumentation in classrooms. *Science Education*, 84(3): 287-312.

Erduran, S., Simon, S. & Osborne J. (2004). TAPping into argumentation: Developments in the application of Toulmin's argument pattern for studying science discourse. *Science Education*, 88(6): 915-933.

Feldman, D. H. (1994). *Beyond Universals in Cognitive Development*. Norwood, NJ: Ablex.

Gallas, K. (1995). *Talking their way into science: hearing children's questions and theories, responding with curricula*. NY: Teachers College Press.

Hammer, D. (1995). Student Inquiry in a physics class discussion. *Cognition and Instruction*, 13(3): 401-430.

Hawkins, D. (1974). *The Informed Vision: Essays on Learning and Human Nature*. New York: Agathon Press.

Karmiloff-Smith, A. (1992). *Beyond Modularity*. Cambridge, MA: MIT Press.

Koslowski, B. (1996). *Theory and evidence: the development of scientific reasoning*. Cambridge, Mass: MIT Press.

Kuhn, D. (1989). Children and adults as intuitive scientists. *Psychological Review*, 96(4): 674-689.

Kuhn, D. (1993). Science as argument: Implications for teaching and learning scientific thinking. *Science Education*, 77(3): 319-337

Kuhn, D. & Udell, W. (2003). The development of argument skills. *Child Development*, 74(5): 1245-1260.

Louca, L. & Hammer, D. Student Nascent Abilities for Scientific Argumentation: The Case of a 5th-6th-Grade Conversation about a Dropped Pendulum. Paper submitted to *Cognition & Instruction*.

Louca, L., Elby, A., Hammer, D., & Kagey, T. (2004). Epistemological resources: Applying a new epistemological framework to science instruction. *Educational Psychologist*, 39(1): 57-68.

May, D. B., Hammer, D., & Roy, P. (2006). Children's analogical reasoning in a 3rd-grade science discussion. *Science Education*, 90(2): 316-330.

Metz, K. (1995). Reassessment of developmental constraints on children's science instruction. *Review of Educational Research*, 65(2): 93-127.

Minstrell, J. A. & Van Zee, E. H. (2000). *Inquiring into inquiry: learning and teaching in science*. Washington, D.C., AAAS.

National Research Council [NRC]. (1996). *National Science Education Standards*. Washington DC: National Academy Press.

Osborne, J., Erduran, S. & Simon, S. (2004). Enhancing the quality of argumentation in school science. *J. of Research in Science Teaching*, 41(10): 994-1020.

Russ, R., Scherr, E., R., Hammer, D., & Mikeska, J. Recognizing mechanistic reasoning in scientific inquiry. Paper submitted in *Science Education*.

Samarapungavan, A. (1992). Children's judgments in theory choice tasks: Scientific rationality in childhood. *Cognition*, 45: 1-32.

Schauble, L. (1996). The development of scientific reasoning in knowledge-rich contexts. *Developmental Psychology*, 32 (1): 102-119.

Can Tutored Problem Solving Benefit From Faded Worked-Out Examples?

Rolf Schwonke (rolf.schwonke@psychologie.uni-freiburg.de)
Department of Psychology, University of Freiburg
Engelbergerstr. 41, D-79085 Freiburg, Germany

Jörg Wittwer (wittwer@ipn.uni-kiel.de)
Leibniz Institute for Science Education at the University of Kiel
Olshausenstr. 62, D-24098 Kiel, Germany

Vincent Aleven (aleven@cs.cmu.edu)
Human-Computer Interaction Institute, School of Computer Science, Carnegie Mellon University
5000 Forbes Ave, Pittsburgh, PA 15213 USA

Ron Salden (rons@cs.cmu.edu)
Human-Computer Interaction Institute, School of Computer Science, Carnegie Mellon University
5000 Forbes Ave, Pittsburgh, PA 15213 USA

Carmen Krieg (krieg@ psychologie.uni-freiburg.de)
Department of Psychology, University of Freiburg
Engelbergerstr. 41, D-79085 Freiburg, Germany

Alexander Renkl (renkl@psychologie.uni-freiburg.de)
Department of Psychology, University of Freiburg
Engelbergerstr. 41, D-79085 Freiburg, Germany

Abstract

Although problem solving supported by Cognitive Tutors has been shown to be successful in fostering initial acquisition of cognitive skills, this approach does not seem to be optimal with respect to focusing the learner on the domain principles to be learned. In order to foster a deep understanding of domain principles, we developed a Cognitive Tutor that contained, on the basis of the theoretical rational of example-based learning, faded worked-out examples. We conducted two experiments in which we compared the example-enriched Cognitive Tutor with a standard Cognitive Tutor. In Experiment 1, we found no significant differences in the effectiveness of the two tutor versions. However, the example-enriched Cognitive Tutor was more efficient (i.e., students needed less learning time). A problem that was observed is that students had great problems in appropriately using the example-enriched tutor. In Experiment 2, we, therefore, provided students with additional instructions on how to use the tutor. Results showed that students in fact acquired a deeper conceptual understanding when they worked with the example-enriched tutor and they needed less learning time than in the standard tutor. The results are suggestive of ways in which instructional models of problem-solving and example-based learning can be fruitfully combined.

Introduction

Cognitive Tutors® (a trademark of Carnegie Learning, Inc.) an intelligent tutoring system – have been proven to be very effective in supporting students' learning in a variety of domains, including mathematics, computer programming, and genetics (for an overview, see Anderson, Corbett, Koedinger, & Pelletier, 1995; Koedinger & Corbett, 2006). On the basis of an online assessment of the student's learning, they provide individualized support for guided learning by doing. Specifically, the tutor selects appropriate problems, gives just-in-time feedback, and presents hints. Despite their effectiveness, a shortcoming of these tutors is that they primarily focus on students' problem solving and do not necessarily support a conceptual understanding about the domain to be learned.

Previous research has attempted to address this limitation by introducing self-explanation prompts to the students who work with the tutor. The prompts require students to provide an explanation for each of their solution steps, by making an explicit reference to the underlying principle. Empirical findings show that this instructional approach makes the cognitive tutor indeed more effective (Aleven & Koedinger, 2002). However, from a cognitive load perspective (e.g., Sweller, van Merriënboer, & Paas, 1998), it might be objected that the technique is nevertheless suboptimal because the induction of self-explanation activities in addition to problem solving places fairly high demands on students' limited cognitive capacity, particularly in the early stages of skill acquisition. Therefore, the tutor's effectiveness might be further improved by reducing cognitive load (e.g., van Merriënboer, Kirschner, & Kester, 2003), allowing students to spend more attentional capacity to engage in meaningful learning activities.

Against this background, it might be sensible to provide students with worked-out examples. The instructional model of example-based learning developed by Renkl and Atkinson (in press) suggests that learners gain a deep understanding of a skill domain when they receive worked-out examples at the beginning of cognitive skill acquisition. A worked-out example consists of a problem formulation, solution steps, and the final solution. When studying worked-out examples instead of solving problems, the learners are freed from performance demands and they can concentrate on achieving a deep understanding. Assuring that learners have a basic understanding before they start to solve problems should help them to deal with the problem-solving demands by referring to already acquired principles, which should prevent them from using only shallow strategies, such as means-end analysis or copy-and-adapt strategies (e.g., using the solution of a previously solved problem that is adapted with respect to the specific numbers). The use of principles enables learners to deepen their knowledge by applying the principles to new problems and, in addition, will cause them to notice gaps in their principle-related understanding when they reach an impasse (cf. VanLehn et al., 2005).

There is ample empirical evidence showing that learning from worked-out examples leads to superior learning outcomes as compared to the traditional method of problem solving (for an overview, see Atkinson, Derry, Renkl, & Wortham, 2000). However, it is important to note that studying worked-out examples loses its effectiveness with increasing expertise. In later stages of skill acquisition, the skillful execution of problem-solving activities plays a more important role because emphasis is put on increasing speed and accuracy of performance (Renkl & Atkinson, 2003). For example, Kalyuga, Chandler, Tuovinen, and Sweller (2001) found that learning from worked-out examples was superior in the initial phase of cognitive skill acquisition. However, when learners already had a basic understanding of the domain, solving problems proved to be more effective than studying examples (*expertise reversal effect*; Kalyuga, Ayres, Chandler, & Sweller, 2003). Therefore, Renkl and Atkinson (2003) proposed a fading procedure in which problem-solving elements are successively integrated into example study until the learners are expected to solve problems on their own. First, a complete example is presented. Second, a structurally identical incomplete example is provided in which one single step is omitted. In the subsequent isomorphic examples, the number of blanks is increased step by step until just the problem formulation is left, that is, a problem to be solved. Hence, by gradually increasing problem-solving demands, the learners should retain sufficient cognitive capacity to successfully cope with these demands and, thereby, to focus on domain principles and on gaining understanding. In a number of experiments, Renkl and colleagues provided empirical evidence for the effectiveness of a smooth transition from example study to problem solving (e.g., Atkinson, Renkl, & Merrill, 2003; Renkl, Atkinson, & Große, 2004).

Against this background, we expected that a Cognitive Tutor that not only prompts students to engage in self-explaining but also provides them with gradually faded worked-out examples should foster students' learning, particularly with respect to their conceptual understanding. In addition, the empirical results on the *worked-example effect* (positive effect of studying examples) also leads to the expectation that the learners need less study time (cf. e.g., Sweller & Cooper, 1985) when they use an example-enriched Cognitive Tutor as compared to the standard version. Accordingly, we hypothesized that a combination of example study and tutored problem solving would be more effective and more efficient than tutored problem solving alone. To test this hypothesis, we modified a Cognitive Tutor to achieve a state-of-the-art implementation of example-based learning with a gradual transition into problem solving .

In this article, we present two experiments in which we investigated the question whether an 'example-enriched' Cognitive Tutor would lead to superior learning when compared with a standard version of a Cognitive Tutor. For this purpose, we used the Cognitive Tutor Geometry. Students were asked to work on geometry problems that required them to apply different geometry principles.

Experiment 1

Method

Sample and Design

Fifty students from a German high school, 22 eighth-grade students and 28 ninth-grade students, participated in the experiment (average age: 14.3 years; 22 female, 28 male). The students were randomly assigned to one of the two experimental conditions. In the experimental condition (*example condition*; $n = 25$), students worked with a Cognitive Tutor that presented faded worked-out examples. In the control condition (*problem condition*; $n = 25$), the students worked with a standard version of the tutor in which students received no faded worked-out examples.

Learning Environment – The Cognitive Tutor

The students used two versions of the Geometry Cognitive Tutor, which differed by a single factor: whether or not worked-out examples were presented. In both versions, self-explanation prompts were employed (Aleven & Koedinger, 2002). In addition, information such as text and diagrams was presented in a single worksheet (i.e., in an integrated format). For the purpose of comparing worked-out examples with problem solving, the integrated format of the tutor was important because example-based learning might be more effective than problem solving only when a 'split source format' is avoided (i.e., the advantages of examples may not materialize when related information such as text and schematics or diagrams is presented separately, cf. Tarmizi & Sweller, 1988). Thus, this Cognitive Tutor version allowed a fair and a state-of-the-art implementation of worked-out examples. The Cognitive Tutor itself is a state-of-the-art intelligent tutoring system, in regular use in about 350 schools across the United States as part of the regular geometry curriculum.

In general, Cognitive Tutors employ two algorithms to support learners. These algorithms are called 'model tracing' and 'knowledge tracing'.

Model Tracing In order to provide appropriate just-in-time feedback and hints, the Cognitive Tutor relies on a computational model that represents the domain-specific knowledge that is necessary to solve problems. The model may also include problem-solving knowledge and skills that are typical for novices (Koedinger & Corbett, 2006). In addition, the model may include incorrect problem-solving approaches that are common for novices. The problem-solving skills (so-called *knowledge components*) are represented as production rules (i.e., if-then rules that link internal goals or external cues with new goals or actions). All user interactions with the tutor are interpreted relative to this model. Student answers that correspond to production rules are marked as correct. If an answer relates to a rule that represents an incorrect strategy, an error feedback message is presented to the student. Answers that do not correspond to any production rule are marked as incorrect. At any point in time, the student can request a hint from the tutor. The tutor will use its cognitive model to decide what a good next problem-solving step will be, and it will present hints using text templates attached to the relevant production rule(s).

Knowledge Tracing The full-scale Cognitive Tutors also implement a cognitive mastery learning criterion (Corbett & Anderson, 1995) but this capability was turned off during the experiment to keep the number and order of problems constant across participants.

Learning material In total, students were asked to work on seven problems. The first three problems required the application of only one geometry principle. In order to solve the last four more complex problems, it was necessary to apply these geometry principles in combination. In the *problem condition*, solving a problem required students (a) to enter a numerical value (such as the measure of an angle) in an entry field that was embedded in a graphical representation of the problem (in a worksheet), and (b) to justify each given numerical answer. This justification could be entered either by typing the name of a relevant principle into a text entry field (next to the numerical value entry field), or by selecting a principle from a glossary that contained a list of all principles used in the unit (i.e., explanation by reference). The combination of entering a value and providing a justification is called a learning event. For example, given the measure of an angle $m\angle ABC = 145°$, a student may be asked to figure out the measure of the supplementary angle $\angle ABD$. The correct entry would be $m\angle ABD = 35°$, because $m\angle ABD = 180° - m\angle ABC$. After entering the value (or an artihmetic expression, leaving the computation

to the tutor) the student has to justify (i.e., to explain) this numerical answer in a second step. In this case, a valid explanation would be 'supplementary angles'.

In the *example condition*, students were asked to study a sequence of worked-out examples that corresponded exactly to the problems that students in the problem condition were asked to solve. A worked-out example provided the students with the numerical value (to be figured out in the problem condition) together with the necessary solution steps. The examples were gradually faded out according to the fading scheme displayed in Table 1. The table shows that the application of the principle in each of the first three problems was illustrated by a worked-out example. Also, worked-out examples were used for the fourth problem that required the application of the three principles in combination. In the subsequent problems, however, each of the principles was gradually faded out until just the problem formulation was left (problem 7).

Table 1: The sequencing of problems and fading of worked-out steps.

| | Examples | | | Problem solving | | |
| | Principles | | | | | |
Problems	P1	P2	P3	P1	P2	P3
P1	W			S		
P2		W			S	
P3			W			S
P4	W	W	W	S	S	S
P5	W	W	S	S	S	S
P6	W	S	S	S	S	S
P7	S	S	S	S	S	S

Note. W stands for worked-out examples and *S* for problem solving.

In order to hold the self-explanation activities across the two experimental conditions constant, students in both versions of the Cognitive Tutor were asked to provide justifications for all solution steps and worked-out steps. Hence, when working on the first four problems, students in the example condition had to enter justifications for the numerical answers that were provided in the worked-out examples by the tutor. Like in the problem condition, the justifications could be typed in or selected from the glossary. From problem five to problem seven, problem-solving demands in the example condition were gradually increased. Hence, students were required not only to give justifications but also to solve the problem on their own.

Instruments

Pretest A short pretest on circles geometry containing 4 problems examined the topic-specific prior knowledge of the students. The maximum score to be obtained in the pretest was 12 points (3 points for each problem that was solved correctly).

Post-test The post-test that measured students' learning consisted of 13 questions. Two questions required the students to solve problems that were isomorphic to the problems previously presented by the Cognitive Tutor (near transfer items). In addition, 2 questions were devised to test students' ability to apply their knowledge about the geometry principles to new geometry problems (far transfer items). As both transfer scores correlated with .69 ($p < .001$), we aggregated them to an overall transfer score. Finally, 9 questions assessed the conceptual understanding that students acquired with the help of the tutor. Students were asked to explain the geometry principles (a maximum of 22 points could be obtained).

Procedure

The experimental sessions lasted, on average, 90 minutes and were divided into three parts: pretest and introduction, tutoring, and post-test. In the pretest and introduction part, students were asked to complete the pretest measuring their prior knowledge. Afterwards, they read an instructional text that provided them with information about the rules and principles that were later addressed by the Cognitive Tutor. In addition, they received a brief introduction on how to use the tutor. In the tutoring part, students worked either with the standard Cognitive Tutor Geometry or with the example-enriched version. In the post-test part, all students answered the transfer questions and the questions assessing their conceptual knowledge.

Results

First, we analyzed students' prior knowledge in order to assure that the experimental conditions did not differ with respect to this important learning prerequisite. There were no significant differences between the experimental groups, $t(48) = -0.75$, $p > .05$, $d = -0.21$. The low test scores obtained in the pretest (cf. Table 2) indicate that students in both experimental conditions were in fact in the initial phase of skill acquisition.

In a second step, we analyzed whether learning with a combination of example study and tutored problem solving was better than tutored problem solving alone. We found, however, no significant differences in students' learning outcomes, neither for conceptual knowledge, $t(48) = -0.11$, $p > .05$, $d < 0.01$, nor for transfer, $t(48) = 0.22$, $p > .05$ $d = 0.08$. Hence, both versions of the cognitive tutor were similarly effective.

In a last step, we examined how efficiently students worked with the tutor. For this purpose, we compared the time that students spent working on the problems or examples provided by the tutor. The analysis revealed significant time on task differences, $t(48) = -3.11$, $p < .001$ (one-tailed), $d = -0.88$. Students in the problem condition spent more time for learning than students in the example condition (cf. Table 2).

In order to quantify the differences in efficiency, we adopted the efficiency measure developed by Paas and colleagues (Paas, Tuovinen, Tabbers, & Van Gerven, 2003;

Paas & Van Merriënboer, 1993). This measure relates performance in terms of learning outcomes to mental effort in terms of cognitive load as measured, for example, by questionnaires.

Table 2: Means and standard deviations of pretest and post-test scores, learning time, and learning efficiency for the experimental conditions in Experiment 1.

	Example		Problem	
Variable	M	SD	M	SD
Pretest[a]	.13	.11	.15	.11
Learning time[b]	30.0	6.56	35.4	5.72
Conceptual knowledge[a]	.54	.21	.54	.21
Transfer[a]	.12	.12	.11	.13
Conceptual knowledge acquisition efficiency[c]	0.28	1.13	-0.28	1.13
Transfer acquisition efficiency[c]	0.31	1.28	-0.31	1.11

Note. [b]Solution probability. [a]Learning time in minutes. [c]Efficiency = $(z_{Post-test} - z_{Learning\ time})/SQRT(2)$.

More specifically, the efficiency score equals to the difference of z-scores of mean performance and effort measures (i.e., $z_{performance} - z_{effort}$) divided by the square root of two. For our purposes, we related performance in terms of the acquisition of conceptual knowledge and of transferable knowledge respectively to effort in terms of time on task (i.e., the time spent working on the problems). This relationship is depicted in the following formula:

$$\text{learning efficiency} = (z_{Post-test} - z_{TimeOnTask})/\sqrt{2}$$

Applying this efficiency formula to our data, we found significant differences between the experimental conditions for both the efficiency of conceptual knowledge acquisition, $t(48) = 1.73$, $p < .05$ (one-tailed), $d = 0.50$, and the efficiency of the acquisition of transferable knowledge, $t(48) = 1.82$, $p < .05$ (one-tailed), $d = 0.52$, which both represent medium sized effects (see Table 2).

Discussion

Both tutored problem-solving and learning with a smooth transition from worked-out examples to problem solving led to comparable levels of conceptual and procedural knowledge (in terms of near and far transfer). However, about the same learning outcomes were achieved in shorter learning times in the example-enriched Cognitive Tutor. Accordingly, the efficiency of learning was superior in this latter learning condition.

Contrary to our expectation, there was no difference in the effectiveness of the two conditions. The lack of difference might be explained by the fact that even the standard version of the Cognitive Tutor is very supportive. Thus, there might not have been much room for improvement (cf. Koedinger & Aleven, in press). Both versions of the tutor provided corrective feedback on errors and induced students to engage in self-explaining activities. Both versions provided on-demand hints (even if students did not use them very frequently). However, students in both experimental conditions achieved relatively low post-test scores making this explanation not very likely.

Informal observations and analyses of the log-file data suggested that students had difficulties in working with the Cognitive Tutor. These problems were clearly more pronounced in the example condition than in the problem condition. Although students received instructions on how to use the tutor, students in the example condition in particular had trouble in understanding the purpose of the worked-out examples. One severe and persistent misunderstanding related, for example, to the justifications that students had to give for a solution step. In the majority of cases, the students assumed that they had to enter the justification 'given' (because the numerical value had been provided by the tutor) instead of the mathematical principle relevant to the task at hand.

In order to examine whether students' problems in using the Cognitive Tutor, especially working on the worked-out geometry tasks, diminished possible differences between the two experimental conditions, we conducted another experiment. In this experiment, we gave the students more detailed and specific instructions on how to use the tutor.

Experiment 2

In the second experiment, we provided the students in both experimental conditions with more specific instructions prior to using the tutor. In addition, when students worked on the two warm-up examples provided by the tutor, they received, in case of problems in understanding, scaffolding from the experimenter.

Method

Experiment 2 was identical to Experiment 1 with respect to the experimental set up, the learning environment, and the instruments (e.g., pretest and post-test). Yet, the experiment was different with respect to the level of detail of the instruction and scaffolding provided in advance, as explained before. In addition, students in experiment 2 participated in individual sessions in the study, whereas Experiment 1 took place in a group session format.

Sample and Design

In Experiment 2, 16 ninth-grade students and 14 tenth-grade students of a German high school (average age: 15.7 years; 17 female, 13 male) took part. As in experiment 1, one half of the students were assigned to the example condition ($n = 15$) and the other half to the problem condition ($n = 15$). The procedure was similar to the procedure of Experiment 1.

Results and Discussion

In a first step, we analyzed students' prior knowledge. Again, there were no significant differences between the experimental conditions, $t(28) = 0.27$, $p > .05$, $d = 0.1$ (cf.

Table 3). We then examined whether students in the example condition benefited more from the example-enriched Cognitive Tutor than students in the problem-solving condition. With regard to students' conceptual understanding, we indeed found an advantage of the example condition over the problem condition, $t(28) = 1.85$, $p < .05$ (one-tailed), $d = 0.73$ (medium sized effect). However, again there were no significant differences in students' transfer knowledge, $t(28) = -0.61$, $p > .05$, $d = -0.21$.

Table 3: Means and standard deviations of pretest and post-test scores, learning time, and learning efficiency for the experimental conditions in Experiment 2.

Variable	Example		Problem	
	M	SD	M	SD
Pretest[a]	.14	.16	.13.	.12
Learning time[b]	30.0	6.48	39.2	9,31
Conceptual knowledge.[a]	.61	.14	.50	.16
Transfer[a]	.19	.22	.24	.25
Conceptual knowledge acquisition efficiency[b]	0.58	0.90	-0.58	0.94
Transfer acquisition efficiency[c]	0.31	1.28	-0.31	1.11

Note. [a]Solution probability. [b]Learning time in minutes. [c]Efficiency = $(z_{Post-test} - z_{Learning\ time})/SQRT(2)$.

In a last step, we computed the efficiency of students' using the Cognitive Tutor. The differences found in experiment 1 could be replicated. This time, the differences were even more pronounced. Again, students in the problem condition spent more time working with the tutor than students in the example condition, $t(28) = -3.14$, $p < .001$ (one-tailed), $d = -1.17$ (large sized effect). Hence, when we related performance in terms of the acquisition of conceptual knowledge to the effort in terms of time on task, we obtained a large effect, $t(28) = 3.48$, $p < .001$ (one-tailed), $d = 1.26$. The efficiency of transferable knowledge acquisiton failed to reach the level of significance, $t(28) = 1.44$, $p = .08$ (one-tailed), $d = 0.52$.

General Discussion

In the two experiments, we compared a standard Cognitive Tutor with an example-enriched Cognitive Tutor. Both versions of the tutor offered corrective feedback and self-explanation prompts. The present research extends previous research in important ways. First, we found evidence, that a state-of-the-art implementation of a faded worked-out steps procedure can lead to a deeper conceptual understanding than intelligently tutored problem solving. In contrast to previous studies that usually compared example-based learning with largely unsupported problem solving (cf. Atkinson et al., 2000), in the present study, the Cognitive Tutor (as used in the control condition) provided students with a substantial amount of support by hints and corrective feedback. Therefore, it was comparatively difficult to find incremental effects on students' performance by adding worked-examples (cf. the results of McLaren, Lim, Gagnon, Yaron, & Koedinger, 2006). This probably accounts for the fact that we did not find differences in procedural knowledge (as did previous studies). Nevertheless, the results on learning time and hence on efficiency clearly show that example-based learning can be less time consuming without a loss or even a gain in conceptual knowledge. This result is also of practical relevance as it offers an alternative for the allocation of the precious resource 'learning time'. Second, and on a more general level, the present research is an example of how different instructional approaches (i.e. tutored problem solving and worked-out examples) can be productively combined to the benefits of learners.

Finally, some remarks on potentially fruitful future research directions It can be speculated that faded examples could be even more beneficial to learning if they take into account the individual prerequisites of the students. It is plausible to assume that students might differ considerably in the speed and accuracy with which they learn domain principles. Therefore, it should be sensible to adapt the speed of fading worked-out steps to the students' individual learning progress. We will conduct an experiment in which we examine the surplus value of a fading procedure that dovetails with the students' specific needs.

Acknowledgments

This research was supported by the National Science Foundation (NSF).

References

Aleven, V., & Koedinger, K. R. (2002). An effective metacognitive strategy: Learning by doing and explaining with a computer-based cognitive tutor. *Cognitive Science, 26*, 147-179.

Anderson, J. R., Corbett, A. T., Koedinger, K. R., & Pelletier, R. (1995). Cognitive tutors: Lessons learned. *The Journal of the Learning Sciences, 4*, 167-207.

Atkinson, R. K., Derry, S. J., Renkl, A., & Wortham, D. W. (2000). Learning from examples: Instructional principles from the worked examples research. *Review of Educational Research, 70*, 181-214.

Atkinson, R. K., Renkl, A., & Merrill, M. M. (2003). Transitioning from studying examples to solving problems: Combining fading with prompting fosters learning. *Journal of Educational Psychology, 95*, 774-783.

Corbett, A. T., & Anderson, J. R. (1995). Knowledge tracing: Modeling the acquisition of procedural knowledge. *User Modeling and User-Adapted Interaction, 4*, 253-278.

Kalyuga, S., Ayres, P., Chandler, P., & Sweller, J. (2003). The expertise reversal effect. *Educational Psychologist, 38*, 23-31.

Kalyuga, S., Chandler, P., Tuovinen, J., & Sweller, J. (2001). When problem solving is superior to studying worked examples. *Journal of Educational Psychology, 93*, 579-588.

Koedinger, K. R. & Aleven, V. (in press). Exploring the assistance dilemma in experiments with cognitive tutors. *Educational Psychology Review.*

Koedinger, K. R., & Corbett, A. T. (2006). Cognitive tutors: Technology bringing learning sciences to the classroom. In R. K. Sawyer (Ed.), *The Cambridge handbook of the learning sciences.* New York, NY: Cambridge University Press.

McLaren, B. M., Lim, S., Gagnon, F., Yaron, D., & Koedinger, K. R. (2006, June, 26-30). *Studying the effects of personalized language and worked examples in the context of a web-based intelligent tutor.* Paper presented at the 8th International Conference on Intelligent Tutoring Systems (ITS-2006), Jhongli, Taiwan.

Renkl, A. & Atkinson, R. K. (2003). Structuring the transition from example study to problem solving in cognitive skills acquisition: A cognitive load perspective. *Educational Psychologist, 38*, 15-22.

Renkl, A., & Atkinson, R. K. (in press). Cognitive skill acquisition: Ordering instructional events in example-based learning. F. E. Ritter, J. Nerb, E. Lehtinen, T. O'Shea (Eds.), *In order to learn: How ordering effect in machine learning illuminate human learning and vice versa.* Oxford, UK: Oxford University Press.

Renkl, A., Atkinson, R. K., & Große, C. S. (2004) How fading worked solution steps works – A cognitive load perspective. *Instructional Science, 32*, 59-82.

Paas, F., & van Merriënboer, J. J. G. (1993). The efficiency of instructional conditions: An approach to combine mental effort and performance measures. *Human Factors, 35*, 737-743.

Paas, F., Tuovinen, J. E., Tabbers, H., & Van Gerven, P. W. M. (2003). Cognitive load measurement as a means to advance cognitive load theory. *Educational Psychologist, 38*, 63-71.

Sweller, J., & Cooper, G. A. (1985). The use of worked examples as a substitute for problem solving in learning algebra. *Cognition & Instruction, 2*, 59-89.

Sweller, J., van Merriënboer, J. J. G., & Paas, F. (1998). Cognitive architecture and instructional design. *Educational Psychology Review, 10*, 251-296.

Tarmizi, R. A., & Sweller, J. (1988). Guidance during mathematical problem solving. *Journal of Educational Psychology, 80*, 424-436.

van Merriënboer, J. J. G., Kirschner, P. A., & Kester, L. (2003). Taking the load off a learner's mind: Instructional design for complex learning. *Educational Psychologist, 38*, 5-13.

VanLehn, K., Lynch, C., Schulze, K., Shapiro, J., Shelby, R., Taylor, L. et al. (2005). The Andes physics tutoring system: Lessons learned. *International Journal of Artificial Intelligence in Education, 15*, 147-204.

Effects of Feedback on the Strategic Competence of Gifted Children

Ageliki Foustana (afousta@primedu.uoa.gr)
Department of Primary Education, University of Athens
Harilaou Trikoupi 24, 106 79 Athens, Greece

Koen Luwel (Koen.Luwel@ped.kuleuven.be)
Department of Educational Sciences, University of Leuven
Vesaliusstraat 2, B-3000 Leuven, Belgium

Lieven Verschaffel (Lieven.Verschaffel@ped.kuleuven.be)
Department of Educational Sciences, University of Leuven
Vesaliusstraat 2, B-3000 Leuven, Belgium

Abstract

The effect of two types of feedback on the strategic competence of high and average intelligent children was examined in the context of a numerosity judgment task. We used a pretest-intervention-posttest design in which children's strategic competence in the pre- and the posttest session was assessed by means of the choice/no-choice method (Siegler & Lemaire, 1997). The intervention session involved the administration of solely a choice condition to two different feedback groups: half of the participants in each intelligence group received strategy-related feedback and the other half got outcome-related feedback. Results show differential effects of feedback type and intelligence level on several aspects of strategic competence.

Theoretical Background

The last 20 years have witnessed a great progress in the research on strategy choice and strategy use in many domains of human cognition (Siegler, 1996, 2005). This has resulted in new theoretical insights and formal (computer) models regarding the (development of) choice and use of strategies, in important methodological innovations (such as the microgenetic method and the choice/no-choice paradigm), and in educational applications aimed at supporting a varied and flexible use of strategies (see Torbeyns et al., 2004, for a critical review).

A powerful theoretical framework to analyse individuals' strategic competence has been proposed by Lemaire and Siegler (1995). In this framework, a distinction is made between four dimensions of strategic competence: (a) the strategic *repertoire* (i.e., which strategies an individual uses to solve a specific task), (b) the relative *frequency* of strategy use (i.e., how often each of the different strategies are applied), (c) the *efficiency* of strategy execution (i.e., how fast and accurate each strategy is executed), and (d) the *adaptiveness* of strategy choices (i.e., the extent to which strategy choices are calibrated towards problem characteristics as well as towards the one's own strategy efficiency). According to Lemaire and Siegler, improvements in overall task performance can be the result of changes in any of these dimensions.

The different aspects of strategic competence can be assessed by means of the choice/no-choice method devised by Siegler and Lemaire (1997). This method involves testing each participant under two types of conditions: (a) a choice condition in which participants can freely choose which strategy to use, and (b) a number of no-choice conditions in which participants are required to use one specific strategy on all problems. In principle, the number of no-choice conditions equals the number of strategies occurring in the choice condition. Data from the choice condition provide information about participants' strategic repertoire as well as about their frequency of strategy use. Since all participants are required to apply a given strategy on all items of the task in each no-choice condition, confounds between strategy selection and execution are excluded. As a result, data from the no-choice conditions can offer unbiased measures of strategy efficiency. Finally, the adaptiveness of strategy choices can be assessed by comparing the performance in the choice and no-choice conditions.

Although Lemaire and Siegler's (1995) framework in combination with the choice/no-choice method was originally used to study the development of strategy performance by comparing different age groups on the four parameters of strategic competence (e.g., Siegler & Lemaire, 1997; Luwel, Lemaire, & Verschaffel, 2005), it has recently also been used to examine the effect of situational variables on strategic performance by comparing different experimental conditions on these four dimensions (e.g., Imbo & Vandierendonck, in press,), or to study differences in strategic competence of different mathematical ability groups (e.g., Torbeyns, Verschaffel, & Ghesquière, 2004). Although intelligence has proven to play a major role in many cognitive tasks (Hong, 1999), this theoretical framework has, to the best of our knowledge, never been used to assess the contribution of intelligence to the different aspects of strategic performance.

Of course, some studies have already examined the effect of intelligence on strategic competence, but all these studies focussed on only one or two parameters of strategic competence and never on all four of them. As far as the repertoire of strategies is concerned, previous studies have shown that gifted children seem to use qualitatively different strategies to solve problems than did average intelligent children (e.g., Larkin, et al, 1980; Priest, & Lindsay, 1992), whereas other researchers found that the strategy repertoire is similar for gifted children and their average peers (e.g., Bouffard-Bouchard, Parent & Larivee, 1993; Gaultney, Bjorklund, & Goldstein, 1996).

Studies that examined the efficiency of strategy execution suggested that gifted children show more efficient strategy processes compared to children of a lower intellectual ability (e.g., Geary & Brown, 1991; Saccuzzo, Johnson, & Guertin, 1994). The speed and the accuracy of the responses were greater for the gifted groups.

With respect to strategy selection, it has been reported that the source of gifted children's generally superior cognitive performance is in their more frequent and more adaptive use of particular strategies and in the subsequent generalization of these strategies to new tasks (e.g., Ippel & Beem, 1987; Scruggs & Cohn, 1983; Wong, 1982). In sum, there are individual differences in strategy choices when solving problems. The nature and quality of these strategy shifts seems to be aptitude-dependent, meaning that individuals who are particularly adept at making optimal strategy selections tend to have higher (fluid) intelligence scores.

As mentioned earlier, previous research on the contribution of intelligence to strategic performance only lead to partial conclusions due to the limited number of dimensions of strategic performance addressed in these studies. Moreover, they yielded contradictory findings with respect to some of these dimensions. With the present study we wanted to investigate the role of intelligence in strategic competence by contrasting a group of gifted children with a group of average intelligent children on all four parameters of strategic performance. Moreover, we wanted to examine the extent to which different types of feedback would lead to improvements in one or more of these parameters (Kluger & De Nisi, 1996) and to test the assumption whether gifted children would benefit less from this feedback than average intelligent children (Rohwer, 1973).

The Present Study

In the present study, participants were asked to judge different numerosities of green blocks that were presented in a 7 x 7 grid. This task allows for two strategies: (a) an addition strategy through which the given quantity of blocks is divided into a number of subgroups and the judged numerosities of the different subgroups are added, and (b) a smart subtraction strategy in which the number of empty squares is subtracted from the total number of squares in the grid.

The experiment consisted of three sessions: a pretest, an intervention and a posttest session. In the pre- and the posttest session, the same set of experimental trials was administered under three different conditions: one choice condition and two no-choice conditions. In the choice

condition participants were allowed to choose freely between the two strategies (addition or subtraction) on all trials of the task. In the no-choice/addition condition participants were required to determine all the numerosities by means of the addition strategy, whereas in the no-choice/subtraction condition only the use of the subtraction strategy was allowed.

The intervention only involved a choice condition in which half of the participants in each intelligence group received outcome feedback (OFB), in which they were informed about the accuracy of their numerosity judgment in each trial, while the other half received strategy feedback (SFB), with information about the appropriateness of their strategy choice in each trial.

The predictions we formulated concern intelligence-related differences and the effect of feedback in each of the four strategic dimensions. First, more gifted than average children will use the subtraction strategy in the pretest and the frequency of the subtraction use will increase with intelligence in the pretest. Second, there will be an intelligence-related increase in the efficiency of both strategies. Third, gifted children will select their strategies more adaptively than average children. These differences are assumed to decrease in the course of the study, since it is expected that average will benefit more than gifted from the intervention. Finally, the effects of strategy feedback are expected to be more beneficial than those of the outcome feedback.

Method

Participants

Participants were 40 intellectually gifted and 40 average intelligent first-grade students from several private and public secondary schools in the county of Attica (Greece). The mean chronological age was 12.54 yrs., ranging from 11.41 to 13.67 yrs. ($SD = 0.36$). In each group boys and girls were almost equally represented. The mean WISC- III full scale IQ of the gifted sample was 128.67 (range: 123-145, $SD = 5.98$), whereas that of the average intelligent sample was 103.57 (range: 90-110, $SD = 6.88$).

Materials

The numerosity judgment task was presented to the participants using an Acer personal computer and a 17-inch monitor with a resolution set to 1024 X 768 pixels. Stimuli were square grids consisting of 7 X 7 little square units that were intersected by red lines. The outline of the grid was visible and colored red. Each square unit in the grid had a size of 1 X 1 cm. These squares units could either be "on" (i.e., being filled with a green colored block) or "off" (remaining empty, i.e., having the same black color as the background of the whole of the screen). In all experimental sessions (pretest, intervention, posttest) and conditions (choice and no-choice conditions), participants ran 26 trials whereby all numerosities of blocks between 20 and 45 were presented. For each participant, the sequence of the stimuli as well as the placement of the blocks in the grid was randomized by the computer. We chose the relatively small 7 X 7 grid to ensure that all participants could solve all trials relatively easily by solely using the addition or the subtraction strategy (Luwel et al., 2005).

Design

As explained above, each participant was examined in three different sessions: a pretest, an intervention and a posttest session. The pretest and the posttest sessions consisted of three conditions: one choice condition and two no-choice conditions. The presentation order of the different conditions in both test sessions was counterbalanced across participants with the important restriction that the choice condition was always presented first, so that strategy choices could not be affected by recency effects. After the choice condition half of the participants in each intelligence and feedback group were enrolled in the no-choice/addition condition followed by the no-choice/subtraction condition, whereas the other half went through both no-conditions in the opposite order. At posttest participants received both no-choice conditions in the opposite order as in the pretest.

Procedure

All participants were tested individually and were seated at about 50 cm from the computer screen. Before the start of the actual experiment they were given five example trials that were representative for the whole continuum of numerosities in the grid (i.e., 7, 15, 25, 40, 46). Participants were instructed to determine each of the numerosities as accurately and fast as possible. After each example trial, participants were asked to explain briefly how they had handled the task.

At the beginning of the choice condition from both the pretest and the posttest, participants were told that they had to determine each numerosity by using either the addition or the subtraction strategy. For each trial, participants were instructed to indicate with their finger the units (i.e., green blocks/empty squares) they were counting. This instruction allowed the experimenter to determine whether participants were applying the addition strategy (i.e., when pointing to the green blocks) or the subtraction strategy (i.e., when pointing to the empty squares).

In the two no-choice conditions from the pretest and the posttest participants were told that they had to determine all numerosities of blocks by using only one strategy, either the addition strategy (no-choice/addition) or the subtraction strategy (no-choice/subtraction). Participants were again asked to indicate the blocks/empty squares that they were counting in order to guarantee that participants always used the required strategy.

The stimulus remained on the screen until the participants had made their numerosity judgment. They were asked to verbally state their answer as soon as they knew it. The experimenter then immediately pressed a key that stopped the computer timer and at the same time emptied the grid. After the response was typed in by the experimenter, a new

stimulus appeared on the screen. After each trial, the computer recorded participants' response (entered by the experimenter) and response time (with an exactitude of 0.1 s). A brief pause was given between the different choice and no-choice conditions.

In the intervention session, participants were presented all numerosities between 20 and 45 in a choice condition only. The procedure and instructions were exactly the same as for the choice condition from the pretest and posttest session, except for the feedback that was given after each trial. Half of the participants in each intelligence group received outcome feedback (OFB) whereby the students were informed about the accuracy of their numerosity judgment in each trial (i.e., the number of blocks that their answer deviated from the actual numerosity)., whereas the other half received strategy feedback (SFB), which informed students about the adaptiveness of their strategy choice on each trial as indicated by the no-choice data from the pre-test session (see further).[1]

Results

Strategy Repertoire

Figure 1 presents the number of children in each intelligence and feedback group that uses both the addition and subtraction strategy in the choice condition of the different sessions.

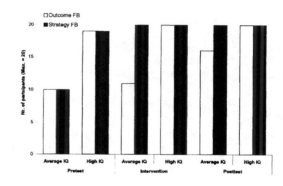

Figure 1: Number of participants in both intelligence and feedback groups that used the addition and subtraction strategy in the choice condition of the pretest, intervention, and posttest session.

As can be derived from the figure, there were more gifted than average intelligent children who applied both strategies in the pretest session and, as expected, there was no difference between both feedback groups in the pretest session. In the intervention session, there was a large increase in the number of average intelligent children with

---

[1] For each subject, the trials appeared in a predetermined random order so that the experimenter knew in advance which feedback to provide.

both strategies in their repertoire in the SFB group but only a minor increase in the OFB group. In the posttest session, the number of average intelligent children in the OFB group that used both strategies further increased, however, without reaching the maximum. In the high intelligence group, this maximum was already reached for both feedback groups in the intervention session.

Frequency of Strategy Use

A 2 (intelligence: average vs. high) X 2 (feedback type: OFB vs. SFB) X 3 (session: pretest, intervention, and posttest) ANOVA with repeated measures on the last factor was conducted on the percentage use of subtraction in each of the three choice conditions.

The analysis showed a significant main effect of intelligence, $F(1, 76) = 24.62$, $p < .0001$, indicating that the gifted children used the subtraction strategy more often ($M = 61\%$) than the average intelligent children ($M = 41\%$). We also observed a significant main effect of feedback, $F(1, 76) = 8.77$, $p = .004$, demonstrating that children in the SFB condition ($M = 57\%$) used the subtraction strategy more frequently than children in the OFB condition ($M = 45\%$) There was also a significant main effect of session, $F(2, 152) = 32.00$, $p < .0001$, showing an increase in the frequency of the subtraction strategy during the course of the study (Ms: 40%, 54%, and 58% for pretest, intervention and posttest, respectively). We also observed a significant intelligence X session interaction, $F(2, 152) = 10.96$, $p < .0001$, which showed that the significant increase in the use of the subtraction strategy from the pretest to the intervention session was restricted to the average intelligence group. Finally, we observed a significant feedback X session interaction, $F(2, 152) = 3.58$, $p = .03$, revealing that the more frequent use of the subtraction strategy in the SFB group than compared to the OFB group occurred in the intervention and posttest session but not in the pretest session.

Strategy Efficiency

Strategy efficiency was examined in terms of solution times (i.e., RTs) and of error rates (i.e., absolute deviations between the given response and the actual numerosity). Since only the no-choice conditions provide unbiased measures of strategy performance (Siegler & Lemaire, 1997), we will only discuss the strategy efficiency as measured under no-choice conditions.

Solution times Solution times were only analysed for items that were solved correctly. A 2 (intelligence: average vs. high) X 2 (type of feedback: OFB vs. SFB) X 2 (session: pretest vs. posttest) X 2 (strategy: addition vs. subtraction) ANOVA with repeated measures on the last two factors revealed a significant main effect of intelligence, $F(1, 76) = 11.58$, $p = .001$, indicating that gifted children ($M = 11.68$ s) were faster in their strategy execution than average intelligent children ($M = 13.53$ s). We also found a significant main effect of session, $F(1, 76) = 21.27$, $p <$

.0001, showing that children were faster in the posttest ($M = 12.10$ s) than in the pretest session ($M = 13.98$ s). Moreover, there was a significant main effect of strategy, $F(1, 76) = 335.76$, $p < .0001$, indicating that the subtraction strategy ($M = 10,85$ s) was executed faster than the addition strategy ($M = 14.36$ s)[2]. Furthermore, we observed a significant intelligence X strategy interaction, $F(1, 76) = 22.74$, $p < .0001$ and a significant session X strategy interaction, $F(1, 76) = 35.81$, $p < .0001$. Both interactions were involved in a significant intelligence X strategy X session interaction, $F(1. 76) = 20.26$, $p < .0001$. This interaction showed that, notwithstanding that the average intelligent children showed a dramatic increase in subtraction strategy speed from the pre- to the posttest session, this group remained significantly slower in the execution of that strategy compared to the gifted children. There were no significant differences in the speed of the addition strategy, neither between intelligence groups nor between sessions.

Error Rates A similar analysis as for the solution times was conducted on the error rates. This analysis revealed a significant main effect of intelligence, $F(1, 76) = 10.24$, $p = .002$, indicating that gifted children ($M = 0.22$) were more accurate in their responses than the average intelligent children ($M = 0.43$). A significant main effect of strategy was also observed, $F(1, 76) = 10.27$, $p = .002$, showing that the addition strategy ($M = 0.24$) was more accurate than the subtraction strategy ($M = 0.42$). We also found a significant main effect of session, $F(1, 76) = 12.56$, $p = .0007$, revealing an increase in overall accuracy between the pre- ($M = 0.41$) and the posttest session ($M = 0.24$). We observed an intelligence X strategy interaction, $F(1, 76) = 6.04$, $p = .02$, showing that the subtraction strategy was less accurate than the addition strategy in the average intelligence group but not in the gifted group. Furthermore, it showed that the gifted children applied the subtraction strategy more accurately than the average intelligent children, but not the addition strategy. Finally, there was a session X strategy interaction, $F(1, 76) = 4.11$, $p < .05$, showing that the initial difference between the addition and subtraction strategy in the pretest session disappeared in the posttest session due to a significant increase in the accuracy of the subtraction strategy from pre- to posttest.

Adaptiveness of Strategy Choices

Adaptiveness of strategy choices was analyzed by means of an analytical technique devised by Luwel et al. (2003). With this technique, one can compare the location of the actual change point (i.e., the trial on which participants switched from the addition towards the subtraction strategy in the

---

[2] Given that previous findings (e.g., Luwel, et al., 2005) have shown that the addition strategy is faster than the subtraction strategy, this finding seems to be counter-intuitive. However, it is important to note that 76% of the items included a grid that was more than half filled with green blocks. It is especially on these large-numerosity items that the subtraction strategy becomes faster than the addition strategy.

choice condition) with the location of the optimal change point as estimated by the no-choice data.

Since the actual change point cannot always be determined unambiguously, we applied the same criterion as Luwel, et al (2005): the first numerosity on which participants started to use the subtraction strategy and did so for at least three consecutive numerosities. The optimal change point was determined by fitting a linear regression on the individual response time patterns of the correctly solved trials of both no-choice/addition and no-choice/subtraction conditions (see Figure 2). The numerosity on which both regression lines intersect each other is considered as the optimal change point, since from this trial on, the subtraction strategy becomes faster than the addition strategy without a loss of accuracy. Since the projected change point indicates for each individual the trial on which it would be most efficient to switch from the addition strategy towards the subtraction strategy, the absolute difference in location between the actual and the optimal change point can be conceived as a measure of adaptiveness: the smaller this difference, the better an individual's strategy choices are calibrated to his/her unbiased estimates of strategy performance.

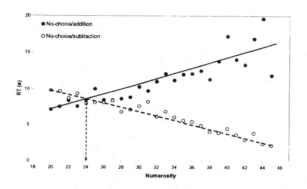

Figure 2: Example of two individual response-time patterns from respectively a no choice/addition and no-choice/subtraction session with their corresponding linear regression lines.

A 2 (intelligence: average vs. high) x 2 (session: pretest vs. posttest) x 2 (type of feedback: outcome feedback vs. strategy feedback) ANOVA was run on the difference scores between the actual and the optimal change point. First, we found a main effect of intelligence, $F(1, 76) = 18.14$, $p < .0001$, indicating that the gifted children ($M = 4.34$) were more adaptive than the average intelligent children ($M = 7.74$). A significant main effect of feedback type was also observed, $F(1, 76) = 6.44$, $p = .01$, showing that children in the SFB group ($M = 5.03$) were more adaptive than children in the OFB group ($M = 7.05$). We also found a significant main effect of session, $F(1, 76) = 36.16$, $p < .0001$, indicating that the adaptiveness increased drastically from the pre- ($M = 7.71$) to the posttest session

($M = 4.36$). Furthermore, we observed a feedback X session interaction, $F(1, 76) = 6.77$, $p = .01$ and an intelligence X session interaction, $F(1, 76) = 9.04$, $p = .004$. Both interactions were involved in an intelligence X feedback X session interaction, $F(1, 76) = 4.44$, $p = .04$. Additional testing showed that, in the pretest session, there was no difference between both feedback groups and that the gifted children were more adaptive than the average intelligent children. In the posttest session, we found that the average intelligent students in the SFB group had made a significantly greater improvement in adaptiveness than the average intelligent children from the OFB group. Actually, the increase in adaptiveness in the SFB group was so large that the initial difference with the gifted children disappeared. The gifted children only showed a slight (non-significant) increase in adaptiveness from the pre- to posttest and within the gifted children there was also no difference in adaptiveness between both feedback groups.

Discussion

The present study demonstrated the effect of intelligence on each of the four parameters of strategic competence. Gifted children used the smart subtraction strategy (next to the addition strategy) in each session and with a greater frequency compared to the average intelligent children. Almost all gifted students' repertoire included both strategies right from the beginning of the task showing an inclination to invent and use more advanced strategies than average intelligent children. The measures of the strategy efficiency and the adaptiveness of strategy choices showed a superiority of the gifted children, as well. Of interest is the finding that gifted children didn't improve in each of the four parameters of the strategic competence as a result of the intervention. The type of feedback played a crucial role: on almost all strategic parameters, except for strategy efficiency, it was found that strategy feedback lead to greater improvements than outcome feedback. In general, one can conclude that the gifted children were already performing at an almost optimal strategic level and, therefore, there was little or no room for further strategic improvement in this group.

The present research showed qualitative differences of the gifted children compared to the average ones in their learning, since they revealed a different cognitive profile in their strategy use and execution. This finding has very important implications in relation to the Education of gifted students since strategic competence is apparent in almost all school lessons. The present study suggests that educating gifted children in learning and applying strategies that they already know has little effect on them. A more appropriate approach would be to teach them by their own learning pace and/or cognitive style. There have already been developed a number of instructional systems and techniques that take such a differentiated approach into account, such as providing differentiated curriculums (VanTassel-Baska, 1997; Ward, 1961), the Problem-Based Learning System (Gallagher, 1997) and the Self-Directed Learning System

(Treffinger, 1986) and teaching methods like the problem solving and the independent study method (Coleman & Cross, 2001).

To conclude, the present study demonstrated the value of the theoretical framework of Lemaire and Siegler (1995) in combination with the choice/no-choice method to unravel the contribution of intelligence on different aspects of strategic performance. These findings, in conjunction with the findings from the Educational research, could help orientating Gifted Education.

Acknowledgments

Koen Luwel is Postdoctoral Fellow of the Fund for Scientific Research-Flanders (Belgium). This study is co-financed within Op. Education by the ESF (European Social Fund), National Greek Resources, and the GOA grant 2006/1 from the Research Fund K.U. Leuven, Belgium to the CIP&T.

References

Bouffard-Bouchard, T., Parent, S., & Larivee, S. (1993).Self-regulation on a concept–formation task among average and *gifted* students. *Journal of Experimental Child Psychology, 56,* 115-134.

Coleman, L., & Cross, T. (2001).*Being gifted in school.* Prufrock Press, Inc.

Gallagher, S. (1997).Problem-based learning: Where did it come from, what does it do, and where is it going? *Journal for the Education of the Gifted, 20,* 332-362.

Gaultney, J.F., Bjorklund, D.F., Goldstein, D. (1996).To be young, gifted and strategic: Advantages for memory performance. *Journal of Experimental Child Psychology, 61,* 43-66.

Geary, D.C., & Brown, S.C. (1991). Cognitive addition: Strategy choice and speed-of-processing differences in gifted, normal, and mathematically disabled children. *Developmental Psychology, 27,* 398-406.

Hong, E. (1999). Studying the Mind of the Gifted. *Roeper Review, 21 (4),* 244-52.

Imbo, I., & Vandierendonck, A. (in press). The role of phonological and executive working-memory resources in simple arithmetic strategies. *European Journal of Cognitive Psychology.*

Ippel, M.J., & Beem, A.L. (1987). A theory of antagonistic strategies. In E.D. Corte, H.Lodewijks, R.Parmentier, & P. Span (Eds.), *Learning and instruction* (Vol. 1). New York: Pergamon.

Kluger, A. N., & DeNisi, A. (1996). The effects of feedback interventions on performance. *Psychological Bulletin, 119,* 254-84.

Larkin, J. H., McDermott, J., Simon, D. P., & Simon, H. A. (1980). Models of competence in solving physics problems. *Cognitive* Science, *4,* 317-345.

Lemaire, P., & Siegler, R. S. (1995). Four aspects of strategic change: Contributions to children's learning of multiplication. *Journal of Experimental Psychology: General, 124,* 83-97.

Luwel, K., Lemaire, P., & Verschaffel, L. (2005). Children's strategies in numerosity judgement. *Cognitive Development, 20,* 448-471.

Luwel, K., Verschaffel, L., Onghena, P., & De Corte, E. (2003). Analysing the adaptiveness of strategy choices using the choice/no-choice method: The case of numerosity judgement. *European Journal of Cognitive Psychology, 15(4),* 511-537.

Priest, A. G., & Lindsay, R. O. (1992). New light on novice-expert differences in physics problem solving. *British-Journal-of-Psychology, 83,* 389-405.

Rohwer, W. D., Jr. (1973). Elaboration and learning in childhood and adolescence. In H. W. Reese (Ed.), *Advances in child development and behaviour.* New York: Academic Press.

Saccuzzo, D. P., Johnson, N. E., & Guertin, T. L. (1994). Information processing in gifted versus nongifted African American, Latino, Filipino, and white children: Speeded versus nonspeeded paradigms. *Intelligence, 19,* 219-243.

Scruggs, T. E., & Cohn, S. J. (1983). Learning characteristics of verbally gifted students. *Gifted Child Quarterly, 27,* 169-172.

Siegler, R. S. (1996). *Emerging minds: The process of change in children's thinking.* New York: Oxford University Press.

Siegler, R. S. (2005). Children's learning. *American Psychologist, 60,* 769-778.

Siegler, R.S., & Lemaire, P. (1997).Older and younger adult's strategy choices in multiplication: Testing predictions of ASCM using the choice/no choice method. *Journal of Experimental Psychology: General, 126,* 71-92.

Torbeyns, J., Arnaud, L., Lemaire, P., & Verschaffel, L. (2004). Cognitive change as strategy change. In A. Demetriou & A. Raftopoulos (Eds.), *Cognitive Developmental Change: Theories, models and measurement.* Cambridge: Cambridge University Press.

Torbeyns, J., Verschaffel, L. & Ghesquière, P.(2004). Strategy development in children with mathematical disabilities: insights from the choice/no-choice method and the chronological-age/ability-level-match design. *Journal of Learning Disabilities, 37,* 119-131.

Treffinger, D. (1986).*Blending gifted education with the total school program.* Buffalo, NY: D.O.K.

VanTassel-Baska, J. (1997).What matters in curriculum for gifted learners: Reflections on theory, research, and practice. In N. Colangelo & G. Davis (Eds.), *Handbook of gifted education* (2nd ed., pp. 113-125). Boston: Allyn and Bacon.

Ward, V. S. (1961).*Educating the gifted: An axiomatic approach.* Columbus, OH: Charles E. Merrill.

Wong, B. (1982). Strategic behaviors in selecting retrieval cues in gifted, normal achieving and learning-disabled children. *Journal of Learning Disabilities, 15,* 33-37.

"Knowledge and Information Awareness" for Enhancing Computer-Supported Collaborative Problem Solving by Spatially Distributed Group Members

Tanja Engelmann (née Keller) (**t.engelmann@iwm-kmrc.de**)
Knowledge Media Research Center, Konrad-Adenauer-Str. 40
72072 Tuebingen, Germany

Sigmar-Olaf Tergan (s.tergan@iwm-kmrc.de)
Knowledge Media Research Center, Konrad-Adenauer-Str. 40
72072 Tuebingen, Germany

Abstract

Computer-supported collaboration via the Internet becomes increasingly important in many educational and workplace settings. However, there are still problems regarding computer-supported collaboration, especially interaction problems within groups. In this paper, we suggest enhancing "knowledge and information awareness" (KIA) to solve these problems. KIA is defined as awareness of a group member with regard to task-relevant domain knowledge and information underlying this knowledge of her/his collaborators. In this paper, an empirical study is presented, which investigates whether KIA is an efficient means to foster computer-supported collaborative problem solving. In this study, an experimental condition, in which the group members of a triad are provided with an environment for enhancing "knowledge and information awareness", is compared to a control condition, in which the group members are not provided with this environment. Results showed that groups with a KIA environment performed better in their problem-solving tasks than groups without one.

Introduction

Today's information society involves significant changes in the world of learning and working. Given the complexity of modern problems and the ill-structuredness of subject matter, combined with the impossibility of everyone meeting at the same location, computer-supported collaboration between individuals becomes necessary. In order to collaborate effectively, there is a need to be aware of the subject-matter knowledge of the collaborators and the information their knowledge is based upon. However, fostering awareness of the individual group members' task-relevant knowledge and information is still a major problem in virtual collaboration settings.

In this paper, the potential and the problems associated with computer-supported collaboration are first outlined. Afterwards, an innovative solution for problems in computer-supported collaboration is described. This solution is built upon an approach for making individual group members aware of the knowledge and information resources of other members, which are necessary for coping effectively with a task. In order to confirm the efficiency of the suggested approach, an empirical study is presented and its results are discussed. The paper ends with conclusions.

Potential and Problems Associated with Computer-Supported Collaboration

Computer-supported collaboration becomes increasingly important when learners have to construct a shared knowledge and information basis in order to cooperatively solve problems by using the Internet as a communication medium. According to Koschmann (2002), computer-supported learning (CSCL) could be characterized as "practices of meaning-making in the context of joint activity, and the ways in which these practices are mediated through designed artifacts" (p. 18). Following this often cited definition, there are two important features that characterize CSCL: First, the collaboration aspect implies that a group, not only an individual, is involved. Stahl, Koschmann, and Suthers (2006) explain that this group learning is not merely accomplished interactionally, but is actually constituted of the interactions between participants. This statement points out that, in such situations, the interaction between the group members is essential for group efficiency. Second, Koschmann's definition highlights the aspect of mediation through designed artifacts. This aspect refers to the computer support of the group interaction, i.e., the technology should be designed to mediate and encourage social acts that lead to efficient group work. It is important to mention that the research area of CSCL does not only include learning settings, but also settings that are learning relevant, such as computer-supported collaborative decision making or problem solving (e.g., Fjermestad, 2004). In this paper, computer-supported collaborative problem solving is the focus.

Results of empirical research suggest that learners in computer-supported collaboration may provide more complete reports, may make decisions with higher quality, and may be better in idea generation (Fjermestad, 2004). However, research results also show that efficient computer-supported collaboration is not easy to achieve (Dewiyanti, Brand-Gruwel, & Jochems, 2005). According to Janssen, Erkens, Jaspers, and Broeken (2005), groups who are collaborating with computer support often have communication and interaction problems. They may perceive their discussion as confused (Thompson & Coovert, 2003), they may need more time to arrive at a consensus and for making decisions (Fjermestad, 2004), and they may need more time for solving tasks (Baltes, Dickson, Sherman, Bauer, & LaGanke, 2002). Following the conclusions of Carroll, Neale, Isenhour, Rosson, and McCrickard (2003), in CSCL settings, the group task is often not perceived as a group task; i.e., the group members work individually instead of collaboratively, and coordination is missing. In addition, the individual group members often do not trust in the fact that the others are doing their part of the work.

In the CSCL research community, there are different strands of research addressing such problems of CSCL. On the one hand, there are approaches that foster computer-supported collaboration by explicit methods like scripting (e.g., Kollar, Fischer, & Slotta, 2005), i.e., the learners are instructed how they should behave to be efficient. On the other hand, there are approaches that seek to support computer-supported collaboration by using implicit methods focused on enhancing different kinds of *group awareness* (e.g., Gross, Stary, & Totter, 2005). These implicit approaches provide no instructions, but inform learners about relevant information. They assume that the group members have the ability to collaborate efficiently if they are informed regarding relevant information, i.e., if they are aware regarding this information.

"Knowledge and Information Awareness" as an Innovative Solution for Enhancing Computer-Supported Collaboration

Group awareness according to Gross et al. (2005) is defined as "consciousness and information of various aspects of the group and its members" (p. 327). However, in the literature, there is no consensus about the definition of the term group awareness. Some authors try to differentiate it according to several dimensions. Carroll et al. (2003), for example, differentiate three different types of group awareness on the working processes level: While social awareness is defined as awareness regarding who is currently available for collaboration, action awareness additionally provides information regarding who is doing what at the moment, as well as who did what recently. This last type of awareness refers to feedback on single occurrences. However, Carroll et al. (2003) point out the importance of activity awareness for computer-supported collaborative scenarios. They defined activity awareness as awareness regarding not only who is currently available and is doing what, but also awareness regarding the relevance of an activity with regard to the group goal.

In most papers, the meaning of awareness refers to both social awareness and action awareness. However, in specific situations, social and action awareness may not be enough to support effective collaboration, but rather knowledge is needed about the mental representations regarding the task domain of each of the group members, the concepts and information resources they use and share, as well as the knowledge gaps that are responsible for misunderstandings, ineffective shared knowledge construction, and deficient problem solving. In such situations, "*knowledge and*

information awareness" (*KIA*) is needed. KIA is defined as awareness of a group member regarding both the knowledge and the information underlying this knowledge of her/his collaborators (Keller, Tergan, & Coffey, 2006).

A situation in which KIA is necessary arises, for example, when spatially distributed group members with different domain expertise have to solve a task together that requires not only the expertise of the group members, but also knowledge about a large amount of task-relevant information resources that is distributed among the experts. The need for KIA results from the explosive increase in information and information resources. This information flood requires a changed handling of information, namely a self-regulated, resource-based activity (Rakes, 1996). The handling of complex contents or a large amount of information or information resources can lead to cognitive overload, which may hinder the efficiency of an individual or a group (Chandler & Sweller, 1991).

Visualizations are suggested to reduce cognitive load while interacting with large and complex amounts of information, because they could be used as cognitive tools for overcoming limits of cognitive capacity (Ware, 2005). Concept maps, developed by J. D. Novak (e.g., Novak & Gowin, 1984), are a type of knowledge visualization for representing the knowledge of an individual by means of nodes displaying concepts and labeled links between the nodes representing the relations between the concepts. While traditional concept maps were created using paper and pencil, computer-based concept mapping tools allow for the creation of digital concept maps. An example is CmapTools developed by the Florida Institute of Human Machine and Cognition in Pensacola, (USA). Traditional concept maps have been criticized for some shortcomings in representing knowledge. For example, they only visualize abstract concept knowledge, leaving the information underlying the concepts (e.g., examples and images of a concept) unconsidered (e.g., Tergan, Keller, & Burkhard, 2006). By contrast, advanced digital concept mapping tools allow the representation of information underlying the conceptual knowledge. These types of visualizations combine the advantages of both traditional knowledge visualizations and information visualizations (Tergan et al., 2006). Information visualizations, with their origin in computer science, are interactive, spatial-visual representations of abstract data (Card, Mackinlay, & Shneiderman, 1999). In Tergan and Keller (2005), as well as in Tergan et al. (2006), the potential of synergistic approaches between information visualizations and knowledge visualizations is presented and discussed. KIA could be enhanced by means of such knowledge and information visualizations by using CmapTools.

When using an environment based on knowledge and information visualizations, users are not only able to check visually which concept is based on an information resource, but can also access information relevant for an explanation of a concept and its relation to other concepts. It is suggested that being aware of one's own knowledge and the knowledge of others, as well as the information resources linked to the concepts, may help cooperative problem solvers in shared knowledge-construction and problem-solving tasks. This assumption is based on the theory of transactive memory (Wegner, 1986). According to this theory, a transactive memory system is a set of individual memory systems combined with communication between the group members. This enhances the expertise of each group member, because everyone has access to the knowledge and information of the others.

It is assumed that KIA is helpful in a computer-supported, collaborative problem-solving scenario, because it can be expected that KIA will have a positive impact on interaction, especially on the processes and the effectiveness of communication, coordination, and collaborative problem solving. On the one hand, according to Clark and Brennan (1993), shared understanding in communication is crucial for individuals working in a group. Making visual representations of the knowledge structures and the underlying information of each group member available to the group should facilitate shared understanding and knowledge construction. On the other hand, the exchange of unshared information is very important (e.g., Stasser, Vaughan, & Stewart, 2000). It has been shown that information that is shared by all group members is often mentioned in group discussion, while unshared information that is known, e.g., by only one group member, mostly remains unmentioned. Such unshared information could be important for problem solving. Therefore, it is important to recognize unshared information. By comparing the external representations of the knowledge structures of the collaborators and the information resources linked to the knowledge elements, group members can easily recognize which knowledge and information is shared and which is not. This should have a positive effect on group coordination. In addition, it is assumed that the capability to view the knowledge and underlying information of the others in the group provides a kind of affordance to make use of these representations (Suthers, 2005).

Experimental Study

This experiment investigated whether an environment for fostering awareness regarding the knowledge and underlying information of the collaborators leads to more efficient collaboration (in the sense of coordination and communication) of a group and, as a result, to more efficient problem solving compared to a condition with groups in which the group members do not have a KIA environment.

Method

Participants Participants were 90 students (58 female, 32 male) of the University of Tuebingen, Germany. Average age was 24.47 ($SD = 3.83$). The students were randomly assigned to the experimental condition or to the control condition. Each group consisted of three participants, resulting in 15 control groups and 15 experimental groups.

Materials and Procedures The participants worked in groups of three students in a room that was divided by partition walls into three separate sections. Each of the sections was equipped with a desk and a computer. The participants could not see each other, but could speak with each other. The experimental environment used in this study provided information elements that are necessary to care for a fictitious kind of spruce forest. These information elements consisted of 13 concepts, 30 relations between these concepts, and 13 background resources, i.e., information underlying a concept, and were evenly distributed among the three group members. Each participant had access to several concepts, relations, and background resources that were unshared, shared with one collaborator, or shared with both collaborators. The experimental environment consisted of two software components. The first was an information space that contained the different information units the group members needed for solving the problems. This information space was based on a Zope3-based groupware that was developed by the Knowledge Media Research Center in Tuebingen, Germany. The other was CmapTools (described above).

Procedure: (1) At the start of the study, the participants took a pencil-paper diagnostic test aimed at assessing the *control variables*, i.e., their experience with computers, mapping techniques, and group work. (2) Afterwards, they received an introduction and *practice using CmapTools* (without time limit). (3) After ensuring that all participants could use CmapTools without problems, they started with *individual phase 1* of the experiment: At the outset of this phase, participants were told that they are experts who have to protect a spruce forest and that they first have to refresh their domain expertise before they start to collaborate and find a common solution for the problems. During this phase, which lasted 23 minutes, the group members worked separately, accessing the information elements in their own information window located at the left side of their screen and structuring their information and knowledge in their own working window located at the right side of their screen. (4) In the *individual phase 2*, each participant of the control group had 5 minutes to examine her/his own map (see Figure 1, left side). Each participant of the experimental group, however, had 5 minutes to view her/his own map, as well as the maps of her/his collaborators (see Figure 1, right side). The 23-minutes and 5-minutes time slots were based on experience from a pilot study. (5) After this activity, all participants had to fill out a 15-items questionnaire used as a *manipulation check* to measure the amount of knowledge the participants acquired from the maps. (6) Subsequently, the three group members had to *collaborate to solve two problems*, i.e., which pesticide and which fertilizer they would use to protect the spruce forest. To solve these problems, the participants needed to compile the knowledge and information they had structured and visualized in the individual phase 1 in the form of a digital concept map.

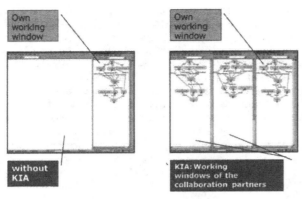

Figure 1: Individual phase 2
(left: control group; right: experimental group).

To do this, they used a shared working space to create a common digital concept map containing all the knowledge and information they acquired in the individual phase. Based on experience from a pilot study, they had 40 minutes for collaboration. During this phase, they could speak with one another. They were told that they were using a kind of hands-free speaking system. In the control condition, the participants could only see their own working window and the shared working window (see Figure 2, above). In the experimental condition, the participants also saw the individual maps of their collaborators, i.e., they were also aware of the knowledge and information their collaborators had (see Figure 2, below). The individuals' interactions were recorded as log files and audio data.

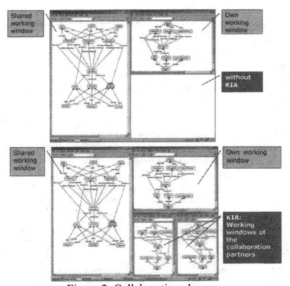

Figure 2: Collaborative phase
(above: control group; below: experimental group).

(7) After this collaborative phase, the participants were given another *test* containing 30 items *to measure the knowledge* they had acquired regarding taking care of the spruce forest. In this test phase, the experimental environment was no longer available. There were no time limits on this test. (8) At the end of the study, participants had to fill out a *questionnaire* asking about difficulties regarding communication and collaboration, the use of CmapTools, and the helpfulness of the KIA environment.

Design and Dependent Measures The analysis was based on a comparison of the control and the experimental condition. In the experimental condition, the participants were provided with a KIA environment, i.e., they could see the individual concept maps of their collaboration partners and, therefore, could become aware of the knowledge and information their collaborators had. In the control condition, the participants were not provided with a KIA environment.

With regard to the dependent measures, the distinction was made between product-related measures and process-related measures. The *product-related measures* could be divided into three categories:

First, the *domain knowledge* measured with 30 multiple-choice test items: Several sub-variables could be differentiated, for example, knowledge regarding relations and contents underlying a concept, as well as knowledge pertaining to whether it is unshared, shared with one other member, or shared with both members.

Second, the *quality of the common concept map* that the group created in the collaboration phase: Several sub-variables were used, for example, the number of correct nodes and relations.

Third, the *quality of the group answers to the two problem-solving tasks,* measured by means of the number of correct solutions and correct reasons.

Regarding the *process-related measures*, the communication and collaboration aspects were of interest: In the collaboration phase, the development of the group map was recorded in a *log file* and the verbal communications were recorded in an *audio file* for later analysis. In addition, *subjective items* were captured through a questionnaire.

Results and Discussion

Several ANCOVAs were performed. In all analyses of variance reported in this paper, the control measure item "experience in creating computer-based graphics" was used as a covariate. The reason is that with regard to this item, a significant difference existed between the control condition and the experimental condition, with a higher value in the sense of more experience in the control condition. In addition, this item was strongly associated with dependent measures. With regard to other control items, there were no significant differences between the control and the experimental condition. All analyses presented here are based on group level, that is, the group values are calculated as means of the values of the individuals of a group.

Analysis on the group level was necessary, due to the fact that the group members were not independent of each other.

The first analysis determined whether the KIA environment was used by the participants in the experimental condition. For this purpose, the questionnaire items were analyzed through the use of a five-point rating scale, with the number one for "no agreement", the number three for "partial agreement", and the number five for "complete agreement". The experimental groups agreed on average that it was helpful to have an overview of the maps of the collaborators ($M_E = 4.27$; $SD_E = 0.75$) and that seeing the maps of the others was useful ($M_E = 3.58$; $SD_E = 0.58$).

The second analysis explored whether the use of the KIA environment had an effect on the dependent measures: The questionnaire at the end of the study showed that the study was more stressful for participants in the control condition ($M_C = 3.2$; $M_E = 2.7$; $F(1,27) = 4.66$; $MSE = 0.28$; $p < .05$), although the experimental condition had more problems regarding the use of the different windows on the desktop ($M_C = 1.8$; $M_E = 2.2$; $F(1,27) = 6.25$; $MSE = 0.25$; $p < .05$) compared to the control groups. This last result was not unexpected, due to the fact that, in the experimental condition, the participants had to work with two more windows than in the control condition. The previous result showed that the cognitive load in the control condition was higher than in the experimental condition. In addition, in the experimental condition, the participants stated that the collaboration with each other led to a better overview regarding the relations of the domain compared to the control groups ($M_C = 4.0$; $M_E = 4.3$; $F(1,27) = 5.89$; $MSE = 0.22$; $p < .05$). This could be confirmed by the analysis of the domain knowledge measures: The analysis revealed marginally better performance for the experimental groups regarding the knowledge on domain relations compared to the control groups ($M_C = 3.4$; $M_E = 3.7$; $F(1,27) = 3.43$; $MSE = 0.21$; $p = .075$). Regarding the domain knowledge performance, the experimental condition gained a higher performance on domain relations that were shared by a participant collaborator dyad as compared to the control groups ($M_C = 2.1$; $M_E = 2.4$; $F(1,27) = 4.2$; $MSE = 0.14$; $p < .05$). This result constitutes evidence for the helpfulness of the KIA environment, because the participants were aware of which other collaborator had the same relation knowledge that they had. In addition, the analyses revealed higher performance by the experimental groups with regard to knowledge about information that is linked to concepts: In this context, the experimental groups gained higher values in knowledge regarding information that is only shared by the other collaborators; that is, the participant himself did not have this information ($M_C = 2.6$; $M_E = 2.9$; $F(1,27) = 4.17$; $MSE = 0.41$; $p = .05$). This result *also* provides evidence of the efficiency of the KIA environment: Considering information underlying a concept, participants in the experimental condition did remember more often items that both other collaborators had. In respect of the quality of the group maps there were no significant differences between the conditions with regard to the included correct relations ($M_C = 23.3$; $M_E = 21.5$; $F(1,27) = 1.81$; $MSE = 22.21$; $p = .19$) or correct nodes ($M_C = 12.9$; $M_E = 12.6$; $F(1,27) = 1.71$; $MSE = 0.46$; $p = .20$). With regard to the problem-solving tasks, the experimental groups tended to be more confident that they had solved the two tasks correctly as compared to the control group (w.r.t. the pesticide problem: $M_C = 3.8$; $M_E = 4.2$; $F(1,27) = 3.38$; $MSE = 0.47$; $p = .077$; w.r.t. the fertilizer problem: $M_C = 3.8$; $M_E = 4.2$; $F(1,27) = 3.17$; $MSE = 0.57$; $p = .086$). This subjective estimation is partly mirrored in objective results, namely in the group answers given: Regarding the number of correct answers to the pesticide problem, the data did not show a significant difference between the conditions ($Pearson\text{-}\chi2 (2) = 3.20$; $p = .20$). However, with regard to the reasons given as to why they chose the correct pesticide, the experimental condition was marginally superior to the control condition ($M_C = 0.2$; $M_E = 0.8$; $F(1,27) = 3.36$; $MSE = 0.7$; $p < .1$). By contrast, regarding the number of correct answers to the fertilizer problem, the experimental condition achieved a marginally higher performance compared to the control condition ($Pearson\text{-}\chi^2 (2) = 4.9$; $p < .1$). But with regard to the reasons given as to why they chose the correct fertilizer, there was no significant difference between the groups ($M_C = 0.7$; $M_E = 1.3$; $F(1,27) = 0.79$; $MSE = 1.01$; $p = .38$).

Conclusions

The presented study demonstrated that computer-supported collaborative problem solving can be supported by enhancing KIA, i.e., awareness of a group member with regard to the knowledge and the underlying information of the other collaborators. In this study, an experimental condition using an environment for enhancing KIA was compared to a control condition that worked without it. Results of the analysis showed that the participants of the experimental condition evaluated the use of the KIA environment as helpful. Comparing the two conditions, it could be shown that the study was more stressful under the control condition, although the experimental condition had more difficulties in using the windows. Therefore, the benefit of using a KIA environment seems to be great enough to compensate for the higher cognitive load caused by the need to use more windows on the screen. The analyses also showed that the experimental groups achieved higher performance in both knowledge regarding content information that was only shared by the other collaborators and in knowledge regarding relation information that both an individual and another collaborator had. In addition, the study demonstrated that using a KIA environment was helpful for problem-solving performances. The results support hypotheses concerning the support of computer-supported collaborative problem solving by enhancing KIA. Further research activities will investigate in greater detail the factors that are causative for the efficiency of the KIA environment.

Acknowledgements

This project was supported by the KMRC (Tuebingen, Germany). We thank Dr. J. Coffey of the IHMC (Pensacola, USA) who adjusted CmapTools for us and the technical group of the KMRC for the technical assistance.

References

Baltes, B. B., Dickson, M. W., Sherman, M. P., Bauer, C. C., & LaGanke, J. (2002). Computer-mediated communication and group decision making: A meta-analysis. *Organizational Behavior and Human Decision Processes, 87*(1), 156-179.

Card, S. K., Mackinlay, J. D. & Shneiderman, B. (1999). Information visualization. In S. K. Card, J. D. Mackinlay & B. Shneiderman (Eds.), *Information visualization. Using vision to think* (pp. 1-34). San Francisco: Morgan Kaufmann.

Carroll, J. M., Neale, D. C., Isenhour, P. L., Rosson, M. B., & McCrickard, D. S. (2003). Notification and awareness: Synchronizing task-oriented collaborative activity. *International Journal of Human-Computer Studies, 58*(5), 605-632.

Chandler P., & Sweller J. (1991). Cognitive load theory and the format of instruction. *Cognition and Instruction, 8,* 293-332.

Clark, H. H., & Brennan S. E. (1993). Grounding in communication. In R. E. Baecker (Ed.), *Readings in groupware and computer-supported cooperative work assisting human collaboration* (pp. 222-233). San Mateo, CA.: Morgan Kaufman

Dewiyanti, S., Brand-Gruwel, S., & Jochems, W. (2005). Learning together in an asynchronous computer-supported collaborative learning environment: The effect of reflection on group processes in distance education. *Paper presented at Earli*, 2005, Nicosia, Cyprus.

Fjermestad, J. (2004). An analysis of communication mode in group support systems research. *Decision Support Systems, 37*(2), 239-263.

Gross, T., Stary, C., & Totter, A. (2005). User-Centered Awareness in Computer-Supported Cooperative Work-Systems: Structured Embedding of Findings from Social Sciences. *International Journal of Human-Computer Interaction, 18,* 323-360.

Janssen, J., Erkens, G., Jaspers, J., & Broeken, M. (2005). Effects of visualizing participation in computer-supported collaborative learning. *Paper presented at Earli*, 2005, Nicosia, Cyprus.

Keller, T., Tergan, S.-O., & Coffey, J. (2006). Concept maps used as a "knowledge and information awareness" tool for supporting collaborative problem solving in distributed groups. In A. J. Cañas, & J. D. Novak (Eds.), *Concept Maps: Theories, Methodology, Technology* (pp. 128-135). San José: Sección de Impresión del SIEDIN.

Kollar, I., Fischer, F., & Slotta, J. D. (2005). Internal and external collaboration scripts in webbased science learning at schools. In T. Koschmann, D. Suthers, & T. W. Chan (Eds.), *Computer Supported Collaborative Learning 2005: The Next 10 Years* (pp. 331-340). Mahwah, NJ: Lawrence Erlbaum.

Koschmann, T. (2002). Dewey's contribution to the foundations of CSCL research. In G. Stahl (Ed.), *Computer support for collaborative learning: Foundations for a CSCL community* (pp. 17-22). Boulder, CO: Lawrence Erlbaum.

Novak, J. D., & Gowin, D. B. (1984). *Learning how to learn.* New York: Cambridge University Press.

Rakes, G. C. (1996). Using the internet as a tool in a resource-based learning environment. *Educational Technology, 36*(5), 52-56.

Stahl, G., Koschmann, T., & Suthers, D. (2006). Computer-supported collaborative learning. In R. K. Sawyer (Ed.), *Cambridge Handbook of the Learning Sciences* (pp. 409-426). Cambridge: University Press.

Stasser, G., Vaughan, S. I., & Stewart, D. D. (2000). Pooling unshared information: The benefits of knowing how access to information is distributed among members. *Organizational Behavior and Human Decision Processes, 82,* 102-116.

Suthers, D. D. (2005). Technology affordances for intersubjective learning: A thematic agenda for CSCL. In T. Koschmann, D. D. Suthers & T. W. Chan (Eds.), *Computer Supported Collaborative Learning 2005: The Next 10 Years!* (pp. 662-672). Mahwah, NJ: Lawrence Erlbaum.

Tergan, S.-O., & Keller, T. (Eds.) (2005). *Knowledge and information visualization: Searching for synergies.* LNCS 3426. Berlin:. Springer.

Tergan, S.-O., Keller, T., & Burkhard, R. (2006). Integrating Knowledge and Information: Digital Concept Maps as a Bridging Technology. *Information Visualization, 5* (3), 167-174.

Thompson, L. F., & Coovert, M. D. (2003). Teamwork online: The effects of computer conferencing on perceived confusion, satisfaction and post-discussion accuracy. *Group Dynamics, 7*(2), 135-151.

Ware, C. (2005). Visual queries: The foundations of visual thinking. In S.-O. Tergan & T. Keller (Eds). *Knowledge and information visualization: Searching for synergies* (pp. 27-35). LNCS 3426. Berlin: Springer.

Wegner, D. M. (1986). Transactive memory: A contemporary analysis of the group mind. In B. Mullen & G. R. Goethals (Eds.), *Theories of group behaviour* (pp. 185-208). New York: Springer.

Computational Evidence for Two-Stage Categorization as a Process of Adjective Metaphor Comprehension

Akira Utsumi (utsumi@se.uec.ac.jp)
Department of Systems Engineering
The University of Electro-Communications
1-5-1, Chofugaoka, Chofushi, Tokyo 182-8585, Japan

Maki Sakamoto (sakamoto@hc.uec.ac.jp)
Department of Human Communication
The University of Electro-Communications
1-5-1, Chofugaoka, Chofushi, Tokyo 182-8585, Japan

Abstract

Most of existing metaphor studies address comprehension of nominal metaphors like "My job is a jail" and predicative metaphors like "He shot down all of my arguments". However, little attention has been given to how people comprehend adjective metaphors such as "red voice". In this paper, we address adjective metaphors and argue that adjective metaphors are comprehended via a two-stage categorization process. In a two-stage categorization process, the adjective of an adjective metaphor evokes an intermediate category, which in turn evokes an abstract category of property to be mapped onto the target noun, rather than directly creating a category of property as predicted by the categorization theory. We then test our argument by means of computer simulation in which the meanings of adjective metaphors are computed from the representations of the adjective and the noun in a multidimensional semantic space constructed by latent semantic analysis. In the simulation, three algorithms for adjective metaphor comprehension, i.e., two-stage categorization, categorization and comparison, were compared in terms of how well they mimic human interpretation of adjective metaphors. The simulation result was that the two-stage categorization algorithm best mimicked human interpretation of adjective metaphors, thus suggesting that the two-stage categorization theory is a more plausible theory of adjective metaphor comprehension than the categorization theory and the comparison theory.

Keywords: Metaphor comprehension; Computational modeling; Latent semantic analysis (LSA); Adjective metaphor; Two-stage categorization

Introduction

Many studies in the domain of cognitive science have been made on the mechanism of metaphor comprehension. Although they have paid much attention to nominal metaphors such as "*My job is a jail*" (e.g., Bowdle & Gentner, 2005; Gentner, Bowdle, Wolff, & Boronat, 2001; Glucksberg, 2001; Jones & Estes, 2006; Utsumi & Kuwabara, 2005) and predicative metaphors such as "He *shot down* all of my arguments" (e.g., Lakoff & Johnson, 1980; Martin, 1992), little attention has been given to adjective metaphors such as "argumentative melody" and how they are comprehended. Some studies (e.g., Shen & Cohen, 1998; Werning, Fleischhauer, & Beşeoğlu, 2006; Yu, 2003) have focused on a synesthetic metaphor, a kind of adjective metaphor in which an adjective denoting the perception of one sense modality modifies a noun denoting a different modality. However these studies only examine how the acceptability of synesthetic metaphors can be explained by the pairing of adjective's and noun's modalities, rather than exploring the mechanism of adjective metaphor comprehension.

In this paper, we address the problem of how adjective metaphors are comprehended and argue that adjective meta-phors are comprehended via a *two-stage categorization* process, which is an extended view of Glucksberg's categorization theory (Glucksberg, 2001; Glucksberg & Keysar, 1990). We then test our argument by means of computer simulation of adjective metaphor comprehension. For this purpose, we use a semantic space constructed by latent semantic analysis (LSA) (Landauer & Dumais, 1997) and provide a computational model of the two-stage categorization process, together with computational models of other possible processes for adjective metaphor comprehension such as categorization and comparison. In the computer simulation, we examine how well a computational model embodying each metaphor theory mimics human comprehension by comparing the interpretations of metaphors obtained by the computer simulation with human interpretations of the same metaphors obtained in a psychological experiment (Sakamoto & Sano, 2004). The metaphor theory that achieves the best simulation performance can be seen as the most plausible theory of adjective metaphor.

Adjective Metaphor Comprehension

Metaphor comprehension can be viewed as the process of finding relevant features (or predicates) that constitute the metaphorical meaning from the interaction between a source concept and a target concept, i.e., the process of generating the modified target concept in which some features or properties are highlighted and some other features are downplayed. In the case of adjective metaphors, the target concept is expressed by the head noun and modified by the source concept expressed by or associated with the adjective. The problem is how people determine which features of the target concept are highlighted or downplayed by the source concept.

One probable theory that can explain the mechanism of adjective metaphor comprehension would be the categorization theory of metaphor proposed by Glucksberg and his colleagues (Glucksberg, 2001; Glucksberg & Keysar, 1990). The categorization theory addresses mainly nominal metaphors and argues that people understand nominal metaphors by seeing the target concept as belonging to the superordinate metaphorical category exemplified by the source concept. Glucksberg (2001) has also argued that predicative metaphors function very much as do nominal metaphors; just as nominal metaphors use vehicles that epitomize certain categories of objects or situations, predicative metaphors use verbs that epitomize certain categories of actions. Some empirical evidence in favor of this view of predicative metaphors was also provided by Torreano, Cacciari, and Glucksberg (2005). Therefore, although they do not explicitly mention adjective metaphors in their works, it is likely that the same argument can be applied to adjective metaphors, that is, adjective metaphors use adjectives that epitomize certain categories of properties. According to this view, an adjective metaphor "red voice", for example, is comprehended so that the source concept *red* evokes an ad hoc category of property like "scary, screaming and dangerous" and such metaphorical property is mapped onto the target concept.

Against the categorization theory of adjective metaphors, we propose a two-stage categorization theory. The intuitive idea behind two-stage categorization is that correspondences between the properties literally expressed by the adjective and the properties to be mapped onto the target concept would be indirect, mediated by an intermediate category, rather than direct as predicted by the categorization theory. In the case of "red voice" metaphor, for example, the adjective *red* first evokes an intermediate category "red things", to which blood, fire, passion, apple, danger typically belong. Then exemplars relevant to the target concept *voice* such as blood, passion and danger are selected and they evoke a final abstract category of property like "scary, screaming and dangerous". [1]

An alternative, but probably less likely, explanation of adjective metaphor comprehension is given by the comparison theory of metaphor (Gentner, 1983; Gentner et al., 2001). This theory argues that metaphors are processed via a comparison process consisting of an initial alignment process between the source and the target concepts followed by a process of projection of aligned features into the target concept. According to the comparison theory, the "red voice" metaphor is comprehended in such a way that two concepts *red (or redness)* and *voice* are aligned, some features such as ones about scariness, scream or danger are found, and they are mapped onto the target noun.

In the rest of this paper, we examine which of these three theories best explains the mechanism of adjective metaphor comprehension by comparing them in terms of how accurately computational models embodying these theories simulate human behavior.

Computational Model

Vector Space Model

A vector space model is the most commonly used geometric model for the meanings of words. The basic idea of a vector space model is that words x are represented by high-dimensional vectors $v(x)$, i.e., *word vectors*, and the degree of semantic similarity $sim(x, y)$ between any two words x and y can be easily computed as the cosine $\cos(v(x), v(y))$ of the angle formed by their vectors.

Word vectors are constructed from the statistical analysis of a huge corpus of written texts in the following way. First, all content words in a corpus are represented as m-dimensional feature vectors, and a matrix A is constructed using n feature vectors as rows. Then the dimension of M's rows is reduced from m to l. A number of methods have been

---

[1] Our preliminary experiment demonstrated that figurative meanings of adjectival metaphors with color adjectives were not directly associated with adjectives, but could be explained more appropriately by considering intermediate concepts associated with both adjectives and target nouns. This finding may lend support to our view based on two-stage categorization.

proposed for computing feature vectors and for reducing dimensions (Utsumi & Suzuki, 2006). In this paper, we used an LSA technique (Landauer & Dumais, 1997) for constructing word vectors. LSA uses the term frequency in a paragraph as an element of feature vectors, and singular value decomposition as a method for dimensionality reduction. LSA was originally proposed as a document indexing technique for information retrieval, but several studies (e.g., Kintsch, 2001; Landauer & Dumais, 1997) have shown that LSA successfully mimics many human behaviors associated with semantic processing.

For example, using a semantic space derived from a corpus of Japanese newspaper used in this paper, similarity between *computer* ("konpyuta" in Japanese) and *Windows* ("uindouzu" in Japanese; Microsoft's OS) is computed as .63, while similarity between *computer* and *window* ("mado" in Japanese; glass in the wall) is computed as –.02.

Metaphor Comprehension Algorithms

In the vector space model, a vector representation $v(s)$ of a piece of text s (e.g., phrase, clause, sentence, paragraph) consisting of constituent words $w_1, \cdots, w_n$ can be defined as a function $f(v(w_1), \cdots, v(w_n))$. Therefore, adjective metaphor comprehension is modeled as computation of a vector $v(M) = f(v(w_T), v(w_S))$ which represents the meaning of an adjective metaphor M with the noun w_T (target) and the adjective w_S (source). In the rest of this paper, I use the phrase "n neighbors of a word (or a category) x" to refer to words with n highest cosine similarity to x, and denote a set of n neighbors of x by $N_n(x)$.

Categorization The algorithm of computing a metaphor vector $v(M)$ by the process of categorization is as follows.

1. Compute $N_{m_1}(w_S)$, i.e., m_1 neighbors of the source w_S.

2. Selects k words with the highest similarity to the target noun w_T from $N_{m_1}(w_S)$.

3. Compute a vector $v(M)$ as the centroid of $v(w_T)$, $v(w_S)$ and k vectors of the words selected at Step 2.

This algorithm is identical to Kintsch's (2000) predication algorithm and it is also used as a computational model of the categorization process in Utsumi's (2006) simulation experiment. As Kintsch suggests, this algorithm embodies the categorization view in that a set of k words characterizes an abstract superordinate category exemplified by the vehicle.

Two-stage categorization We propose the algorithm of two-stage categorization as follows.

1. Compute $N_{m_1}(w_S)$, i.e., m_1 neighbors of the source w_S.

2. Selects k words with the highest similarity to the target noun w_T from $N_{m_1}(w_S)$.

3. Compute a vector $v(C)$ of an intermediate category C as the centroid of $v(w_T)$, $v(w_S)$ and the vectors of k words selected at Step 2.

4. Compute $N_{m_2}(C)$, i.e., m_2 neighbors of the intermediate category C.

5. Compute a metaphor vector $v(M)$ as the centroid of $v(w_T)$, $v(w_S)$ and m_2 vectors selected at Step 4.

The first three steps, which are identical to the original categorization algorithm, correspond to the process of generating an intermediate category. Steps 4 and 5 correspond to the second categorization process.

Comparison The algorithm of computing a metaphor vector $v(M)$ by the process of comparison is as follows.

1. Compute a set of k words (i.e., alignments between the target w_T and the source w_S) by finding the smallest i that satisfies $|N_i(w_T) \cap N_i(w_S)| = k$.
2. Compute a metaphor vector $v(M)$ as the centroid of $v(w_T)$ and k vectors computed at Step 1.

This algorithm is proposed by Utsumi (2006). Step 1 corresponds to the initial alignment process, while Step 2 corresponds to the later projection process.

Besides these three models, for comparison purposes, we also consider a simple combination algorithm by which a metaphor vector $v(M)$ is computed as the centroid of the target vector $v(w_T)$ and the source vector $v(w_S)$.

Simulation Experiment

Method

Human experiment For human interpretation of adjective metaphors, we used the result of the psychological experiment reported in Sakamoto and Sano (2004). The materials used in the experiment were 50 Japanese adjective metaphors. They were created from all possible adjective-noun combinations of five adjectives (red ["akai"], blue ["aoi"], yellow ["kiioi"], white ["shiroi"], black ["kuroi"]) with 10 nouns (voice ["koe"], sound ["oto"], mind ["kokoro"], feeling ["kimochi"], words ["kotoba"], atmosphere ["funiki"], character ["seikaku"], past ["kako"], future ["mirai"], taste ["aji"]).

Thirty-eight undergraduate students of the University of Electro-Communications, who were all native speakers of Japanese, were assigned to all the 50 metaphors. They were asked to choose among 24 perceptual adjectives (i.e., features) appropriate ones for the meaning of each adjective metaphor. For each chosen feature w_i of an adjective metaphor M, the degree of salience $sal(w_i, M)$ is then assessed as the number of participants who chose that adjective. These features were used as landmarks with respect to which model's interpretation and human interpretation were compared for evaluation. Note that any adjective chosen by only one participant was not included in the analysis. For example, as shown in the bar graph of Figure 1, seven adjectives were chosen for the metaphor "black future", and the adjective *dark* had the highest salience, i.e., the number of participants (26 participants) who listed it was largest.

Computer simulation The semantic space used in the simulation experiment was constructed from a Japanese corpus of 251,287 paragraphs containing 53,512 different words, which came from a CD-ROM of Mainichi newspaper articles (4 months) published in 1999. The dimension l of the semantic space was set to 300, and thus all words were represented as 300-dimensional vectors.

In the computer simulation, for each of the 50 adjective metaphors, four kinds of metaphor vectors were computed using the four comprehension algorithms presented in the preceding section, i.e., categorization, two-stage categorization,

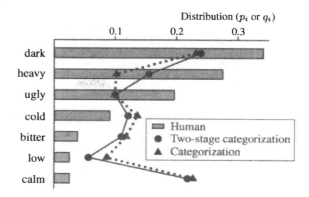

Figure 1: "Black future" metaphor

comparison and simple combination. In computing the metaphor vectors, we varied the parameter m_1 in steps of 50 between 50 and 500, and the parameters k and m_2 from 1 to 10. After that, for all the features $w_i, \cdots, w_n$ chosen for a metaphor M in the human experiment, similarity to the metaphorical meaning $sim(w_i, M)$ was computed separately using the four metaphor vectors. Features with higher similarity to the metaphorical meaning can be seen as more relevant to the interpretation of the metaphor. In Figure 1, for example, the word *dark* has the highest similarity to both the metaphor vectors computed by the categorization algorithm and by the two-stage categorization algorithm, but a least salient word *calm* is also highly similar to the metaphor vectors.

Evaluation measures To evaluate the ability of the model to mimic human interpretations, we use the following measures, which were also used in Utsumi's (2006) simulation experiment for nominal metaphors.

- *Kullback-Leibler divergence (KL-divergence)*:

$$D = \sum_{i=1}^{n} p_i \log \frac{p_i}{q_i} \tag{1}$$

$$p_i = \frac{sal(w_i, M)}{\sum_{j=1}^{n} sal(w_j, M)} \tag{2}$$

$$q_i = \frac{sim(w_i, M) - \min_x sim(x, M)}{\sum_{j=1}^{n} \{sim(w_j, M) - \min_x sim(x, M)\}} \tag{3}$$

It measures how well a model simulates the salience distribution of features relevant to human interpretation, or in other words, the degree of dissimilarity between human interpretation p_i and computer's interpretation q_i. Hence, *lower divergence means that the model achieves better performance*. In Figure 1, for example, KL-divergence between the salience distribution of human interpretation and the similarity distribution of computer interpretation is 0.546 for the categorization model ($m_1 = 50$, $k = 1$) and 0.396 for the two-stage categorization model ($m_1 = 50$, $k = 1$, $m_2 = 1$). This result suggests that, in this case, the two-stage categorization model better mimics human interpretation than the original categorization model.

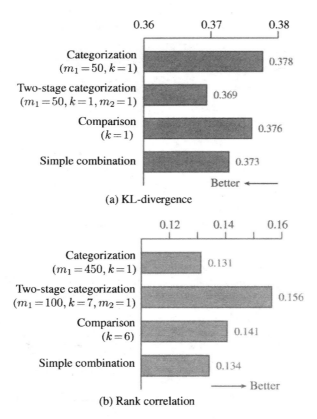

(a) KL-divergence

(b) Rank correlation

Figure 2: Simulation results: Comparison among the four comprehension models for adjective metaphors

- *Spearman's rank correlation*:

$$r = 1 - \frac{6 \sum_{i=1}^{n} d_i^2}{n^3 - n} \qquad (4)$$

$$d_i = rank(sim(w_i, M)) - rank(sal(w_i, M)) \qquad (5)$$

It measures how strongly the computed similarity of relevant features is correlated with the degree of salience of those features. *A higher correlation means that the model yields better performance*. In Figure 1 the two-stage categorization yields a higher correlation ($r = .46$) than the categorization model ($r = .28$), which again indicates that the two-stage categorization model is superior to the categorization model.

Result

For each of the 50 metaphors, KL-divergences and rank correlations were computed using the four metaphor vectors. These values were then averaged across metaphors. Concerning KL-divergence, the categorization algorithm achieved the best performance when $m_1 = 50$ and $k = 1$, the two-stage categorization model did the best performance when $m_1 = 50$, $k = 1$ and $m_2 = 1$, and the comparison model did the best performance when $k = 1$. Concerning rank correlation, the combination of $m_1 = 450$ and $k = 1$ was optimal for the

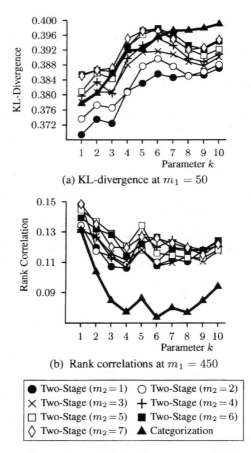

(a) KL-divergence at $m_1 = 50$

(b) Rank correlations at $m_1 = 450$

● Two-Stage ($m_2 = 1$)	○ Two-Stage ($m_2 = 2$)
✕ Two-Stage ($m_2 = 3$)	+ Two-Stage ($m_2 = 4$)
□ Two-Stage ($m_2 = 5$)	■ Two-Stage ($m_2 = 6$)
◇ Two-Stage ($m_2 = 7$)	▲ Categorization

Figure 3: Simulation results of the two-stage categorization model and the categorization model obtained with various values of parameters k and m_2

categorization model, while the combination of $m_1 = 100$, $k = 7$ and $m_2 = 1$ was optimal for the two-stage categorization model. For the comparison model, $k = 6$ was optimal.

Figure 2 shows mean divergences and correlations calculated using these optimal parameters. The two-stage categorization model outperformed the other three models on both measures. It suggests that *the two-stage categorization theory is the most plausible theory of adjective metaphor comprehension*. Furthermore, in order to demonstrate that this simulation result in favor of the two-stage categorization theory is general, not specific to the particular value of the parameters, we show the simulation results obtained with various values of parameters in Figure 3. Figure 3(a) shows that, when they were compared at the same value of k, the two-stage categorization algorithm had lower divergence (i.e., better performance) than the categorization algorithm at almost all the values of m_2, although it had worse performance at some higher values of m_2 and lower values of k. Similarly, as shown in Figure 3(b), the two-stage categorization algorithm achieved a higher correlation (i.e., better performance) regardless of values of m_2. These results clearly indicate the plausibility of the two-stage categorization model as a cognitive theory of adjective metaphor comprehension.

Discussion

Related Work

Until now there have been some computational studies on metaphor comprehension. For nominal metaphors, Thomas and Mareschal (2001) proposed a connectionist implementation of comprehending nominal metaphors on the basis of the categorization theory, but they did not test the validity of their models in a systematic way, nor did they make a new contribution to the psychological or cognitive theory of metaphor. Kintsch (2000) proposes an LSA-based computational model of metaphor comprehension. His predication algorithm is also used in this study as a model of categorization, but he did not test its psychological validity as a model of metaphor comprehension. In addition, his study does not allow for the fact that some metaphors are comprehended as comparisons. Lemaire and Bianco (2003) also employ LSA to develop a computational model of referential metaphor comprehension. However, they do not address how well it mimics human interpretations; they only showed that it mimics processing time difference between when supporting context is provided and when it is not provided. Moreover, their model is theoretically less well motivated. For adjectival metaphors, Weber (1991) proposed a connectionist model of adjectival metaphors, which can be seen as one computational implementation of the categorization theory. This model uses two methods (direct value transference and scalar correspondence) for establishing semantic correspondences between the properties literally expressed by the adjective and the properties to be mapped onto the target concept. However, her model was not tested in a systematic way, either.

In contrast, our LSA-based computational methodology used in this study tests the validity of competing metaphor theories and predicts which is most plausible. Utsumi (2006) has applied this methodology to nominal metaphors and demonstrated that the interpretive diversity view of metaphor (Utsumi, 2007; Utsumi & Kuwabara, 2005) best explains the mechanism of nominal metaphor comprehension.

Does Two-Stage Categorization Better Explain Nominal Metaphor Comprehension?

In this paper, we have shown that adjective metaphors are comprehended via a two-stage categorization process, rather than via a categorization process or a comparison process. This raises a new interesting question whether or not people also comprehend other types of metaphors, especially nominal metaphors, via a two-stage categorization process.

Recent studies have claimed that people comprehend nominal metaphors as categorizations or comparisons depending on a metaphor property such as vehicle conventionality (Bowdle & Gentner, 2005), metaphor aptness (Jones & Estes, 2006) or interpretive diversity (Utsumi, 2007; Utsumi & Kuwabara, 2005). Especially Utsumi (2007) has demonstrated through a psychological experiment that interpretively diverse metaphors are processed as categorizations but less diverse metaphors are processed as comparisons. Utsumi (2006) also confirmed this finding by means of computer simulation. Therefore, the question mentioned above can be

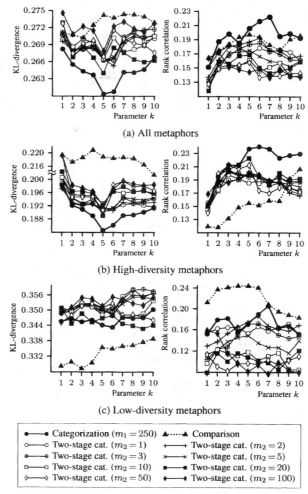

(a) All metaphors

(b) High-diversity metaphors

(c) Low-diversity metaphors

Figure 4: Simulation results of nominal metaphor comprehension ($m_1 = 250$)

refined as follows: Does the two-stage categorization process better explain comprehension of high-diversity metaphors than the categorization process, and comprehension of low-diversity metaphors than the comparison process?

In order to tackle this question, we conducted an additional simulation experiment in which the metaphorical meanings of 40 nominal metaphors such as "Life is a game" were computed by the two-stage categorization algorithm, and the results were compared with the results of the categorization algorithm and the comparison algorithm obtained in our preceding study (Utsumi, 2006). The simulation method and evaluation measures used in this additional experiment were identical to those used in the main simulation experiment of this study. For human interpretation of the nominal metaphors, the result obtained in a psychological experiment (Utsumi, 2005) was used. (For further details of the simulation experiment of nominal metaphors, see Utsumi, 2006).

The overall result was that the two-stage categorization algorithm did not achieve better performance than the categorization algorithm and the comparison algorithm. As shown in Figure 4(a), when the scores of all metaphors were averaged, the categorization algorithm had lower divergence and higher correlation (and thus better mimics human interpretation) than the two-stage categorization algorithm at the same value of the parameter k, regardless of value of m_2. Furthermore, Figure 4(b) also shows that the categorization algorithm outperformed the two-stage categorization model even when metaphors were highly diverse, and Figure 4(c) shows that, when metaphors were less diverse, the comparison algorithm outperformed the two-stage categorization model. These findings clearly indicate that people do not comprehend nominal metaphors via the process of two-stage categorization, and the interpretive diversity view (Utsumi, 2007; Utsumi & Kuwabara, 2005) is still the most plausible theory of nominal metaphor comprehension. In other words, the process of adjective metaphor comprehension essentially differs from the process of nominal metaphor comprehension.

Concluding Remarks

Our simulation experiment has shown that adjective metaphors are likely to be comprehended via a two-stage categorization process. We are now trying to confirm this finding by a psychological experiment. It would also be interesting for further work to investigate, both psychologically and computationally, whether people comprehend predicative metaphors via a two-stage categorization process.

Acknowledgments

This research was supported by Grant-in-Aid for Scientific Research(C) (No.17500171) from Japan Society for the Promotion of Science.

References

Bowdle, B., & Gentner, D. (2005). The career of metaphor. *Psychological Review*, *112*(1), 193–216.

Gentner, D. (1983). Structure mapping: A theoretical framework for analogy. *Cognitive Science*, *7*, 155–170.

Gentner, D., Bowdle, B., Wolff, P., & Boronat, C. (2001). Metaphor is like analogy. In D. Gentner, K. Holyoak, & B. Kokinov (Eds.), *Analogical mind: Perspectives from cognitive science* (pp. 199–253). MIT Press.

Glucksberg, S. (2001). *Understanding figurative language: From metaphors to idioms*. Oxford University Press.

Glucksberg, S., & Keysar, B. (1990). Understanding metaphorical comparisons: Beyond similarity. *Psychological Review*, *97*, 3–18.

Jones, L., & Estes, Z. (2006). Roosters, robins, and alarm clocks: Aptness and conventionality in metaphor comprehension. *Journal of Memory and Language*, *55*, 18–32.

Kintsch, W. (2000). Metaphor comprehension: A computational theory. *Psychonomic Bulletin & Review*, *7*(2), 257–266.

Kintsch, W. (2001). Predication. *Cognitive Science*, *25*(2), 173–202.

Lakoff, G., & Johnson, M. (1980). *Metaphors we live by*. The University of Chicago Press.

Landauer, T. K., & Dumais, S. T. (1997). A solution to Plato's problem: The latent semantic analysis theory of the acquisition, induction, and representation of knowledge. *Psychological Review*, *104*, 211–240.

Lemaire, B., & Bianco, M. (2003). Contextual effects on metaphor comprehension: Experiment and simulation. In *Proceedings of the 5th International Conference on Cognitive Modeling (ICCM'2003)*.

Martin, J. (1992). Computer understanding of conventional metaphoric language. *Cognitive Science*, *16*, 233–270.

Sakamoto, M., & Sano, M. (2004). Emergent features of color metaphors viewed as a combination of color terms and nouns. In *Proceedings of the 21st Annual Meeting of the Japanese Cognitive Science Society* (pp. 188–189). (in Japanese)

Shen, Y., & Cohen, M. (1998). How come silence is sweet but sweetness is not silent: A cognitive account of directionality in poetic synaesthesia. *Language and Literature*, *7*(2), 123–140.

Thomas, M., & Mareschal, D. (2001). Metaphor as categorization: A connectionist implementation. *Metaphor and Symbol*, *16*(1 & 2), 5–27.

Torreano, L., Cacciari, C., & Glucksberg, S. (2005). When dogs can fly: Level of abstraction as a cue to metaphorical use of verbs. *Metaphor and Symbol*, *20*(4), 259–274.

Utsumi, A. (2005). The role of feature emergence in metaphor appreciation. *Metaphor and Symbol*, *20*(3), 151–172.

Utsumi, A. (2006). Computational exploration of metaphor comprehension processes. In *Proceedings of the 28th Annual Meeting of the Cognitive Science Society* (pp. 2281–2286).

Utsumi, A. (2007). *Interpretive diversity explains metaphor-simile distinction*. (submitted for publication)

Utsumi, A., & Kuwabara, Y. (2005). Interpretive diversity as a source of metaphor-simile distinction. In *Proceedings of the 27th Annual Meeting of the Cognitive Science Society* (pp. 2230–2235).

Utsumi, A., & Suzuki, D. (2006). Word vectors and two kinds of similarity. In *Proceedings of the 21st International Conference on Computational Linguistics and the 44th Annual Meeting of the Association for Computational Linguistics (COLING-ACL 2006) Main Conference Poster Sessions* (pp. 858–865).

Weber, S. (1991). A connectionist model of literal and figurative adjective noun combinations. In D. Fass, E. Hinkelman, & J. Martin (Eds.), *Proceedings of the IJCAI Workshop on Computational Approaches to Non-Literal Language: Metaphor, Metonymy, Idioms, Speech Acts, Implicature* (pp. 151–160).

Werning, M., Fleischhauer, J., & Beşeoğlu, H. (2006). The cognitive accessibility of synaesthetic metaphors. In *Proceedings of the 28th Annual Conference of the Cognitive Science Society* (pp. 2365–2370).

Yu, N. (2003). Synesthetic metaphor: A cognitive perspective. *Journal of Literary Semantics*, *32*(1), 19–34.

Is a small apple more like an apple or more like a cherry?
A study with real and modified sized objects.

Valentina Bazzarin (valentina.bazzarin@unibo.it)
Department of Psychology, 5 Viale Berti Pichat 5
Bologna, 40135 Italy

Anna M. Borghi (annamaria.borghi@unibo.it)
Department of Psychology, 5 Viale Berti Pichat 5
Bologna, 40135 Italy

Alessia Tessari (alessia.tessari@unibo.it)
Department of Psychology, 5 Viale Berti Pichat 5
Bologna, 40135 Italy

Roberto Nicoletti (nicoletti@dsc.unibo.it)
Department of Communication Disciplines, Via Azzo Gardino 23
Bologna, 40122 Italy

Abstract

In a categorization experiment we assessed whether seeing objects automatically activates information on how to manipulate them. The experiment also aims at investigating the role played in a categorization task by online, visual information (i.e., of information mediated by the dorsal system), and by information stored in memory (i.e., information mediated by the ventral system). Participants categorized photographs of objects manipulable either with a power or a precision grip into artifacts or natural kinds. Target-objects were preceded by primes consisting of photographs of hands in either grasping postures (precision or power grip) or in a neutral posture (grip). Target-objects could be presented either in their real size or in modified size, so that they activated a different kind of grip. For example, a strawberry was presented both in its real size and with the size of an apple, so that it activated a power grip. Results confirm that visual stimuli activate motor information. More importantly, they suggest a crucial role of online, visual information even in a categorization task. Results are discussed in the framework of theories on the role of online and offline memory features.

Introduction

In the last years many studies have highlighted the importance of action for knowledge. Recent evidence has shown that manipulable objects directly activate motor information. Neuroimaging studies have shown that specific *brain areas* are activated for manipulable compared to non manipulable objects. Martin, Wiggs, Ungerleider, and Haxby (1996) found that naming tools, compared to naming animals, differentially activated the left middle temporal gyrus – an area nearly identical to the area activated by action generation tasks - and the left premotor cortex, an area generally activated when participants imagine themselves grasping objects with their dominant hand. Grafton, Fadiga, Arbib and Rizzolatti (1997) found that retrieval of actions associated with tools produced activation in the left premotor cortex. More recently, Chao & Martin (2000) carried out a fMRI study showing that the left premotor cortex responds selectively to photographs of tools but not to other objects such as animals, faces, and houses. Consider that this different activation pattern cannot be due to the difference between artifacts and natural kinds, but it is probably due to the fact that tools are manipulable objects. This is confirmed by a PET study by Gerlach, Law and Paulson, (2002) who showed in a categorization task that the left ventral premotor cortex was activated with both artifact and natural manipulable objects – more specifically, it was activated during categorization of fruit/vegetables and clothing, relative to animals and non-manipulable artifacts. In line with these results, Kellenbach, Brett and Patterson (2003) found that the response of the left ventral premotor cortex and the left middle temporal gyrus was stronger for manipulable than for non-manipulable objects in action judgements, whereas no specific cortical region was more activated by function relative to action judgements.

On the behavioral side, different studies have demonstrated the close relationships between perceptual and motor information. Behavioral studies with compatibility paradigms, i.e. paradigms implying some kind of correspondence between stimuli and responses, indicate that the vision of objects elicits motor information – more specifically, information related to reaching and grasping movements. Ellis and Tucker (2001) asked participants to categorize objects graspable either with a precision or with a power grip into artifacts or natural kinds by pressing a device. Participants responded faster to object graspable with a power grip by mimicking a power grip, and to objects graspable with a precision grip by mimicking a precision grip. Thus they found a compatibility effect between the object size and the grip used to respond, even if the object size was not relevant to the task. Borghi, Bonfiglioli, Lugli, Ricciardelli, Rubichi and Nicoletti (2006) asked participants to categorize photographs of objects graspable with a power or a precision grip into artifacts or natural kinds. Target objects were preceded by a prime consisting of photographs of hands in either grasping posture (precision or power grip) or in a neutral posture (open hand). Participants were required to decide, by pressing a different key, whether the target objects were artefacts or natural kinds. Borghi et al. (2006) found a compatibility effect between the hand posture (power, precision) and the kind of grip required by the object, provided that the experiment was preceded by a motor training phase in which participants repeated the postures they saw in the photographs. This study showed that visual hand stimuli activate a motor resonance phenomenon and that seeing objects evokes a specific motor program also in absence of a motor response relevant to the task. Namely, participants simply had to press a different key in order to categorize objects.

The reported studies on prehension clearly suggest that visual stimuli activate motor information, both when the object size is not relevant to the task (Ellis & Tucker, 2000 and Borghi et al. 2006) and when the motor response is not relevant to the task. Moreover, the study by Borghi et al. (2006) suggests that seeing hand postures and using the body to reproduce the seen postures might induce a motor resonance behavior, mediated by the mirror neuron system (Di Pellegrino et al., 1992). This motor resonance explains the prime-target compatibility effect.

However, these studies providing evidence for compatibility effects leave a question open. Namely, it is unclear whether the compatibility effect are due to the processing of online, visual information, or if they are due to the influence of conceptual information stored in long term memory. In order to explain the relationships between vision and action, an influential model (Milner & Goodale, 1995) proposes that visual information is processed in the brain in two different streams: the ventral and the dorsal route. Whereas the main role of the ventral stream pertains object recognition, the dorsal stream has primarily a pragmatic role. Accordingly, there would be two different routes to action: one mediated by object recognition (ventral stream), the other one implying a direct vision-action mapping (dorsal stream) (Rumiati & Humphreys, 1998). However, recent evidence suggests that the distinction implied by this model between an "acting" and a "knowing" brain might be too sharp (see for a first comment Gallese, Craighero, Fadiga & Fogassi, 1999) and that different kinds of action-related information might be subserved by different neural pathways (Gentilucci, 2003).

Aim of our study was to assess whether the compatibility effect found are due to online information or to information related to past visuomotor experiences stored in memory. We used a paradigm similar to the one used by Borghi et al. (2006), with some slight variations and a more important variation. We presented three hand primes, two prehensile postures (precision, power) and a catch-trial (fist). Compared to the study by Borghi et al. (2006), we used more dynamical primes, so that they could more directly elicit motor information even without a motor preparation phase. As in the previous study, the hand primes were followed by target-objects, half artefacts and half natural kinds. All objects were manipulable, half were graspable with a power grip (e.g., apple), and half with a precision grip (e.g., strawberry). The most important variation we introduced consisted of the fact that the targets could represent objects either in their real size or in a modified size. Thus, the objects typically affording a precision grip were zoomed out (for example a nut was enlarged to an orange size) and the object usually affording a power grasp were zoomed in (for example an apple was resized to became as small as a cherry). In this way we were able to disentangle the contribution played by online, visual information, and the contribution of off-line information stored in memory, in explaining the effects.

The main predictions of our work are the following. First, we predict to replicate with different stimuli the results found by Borghi et al (2006). Thus, we predict a processing advantage of natural kind objects over artefacts, as the first activate only action and the latter both action and functional information. In addition, if seeing an object activate motor information, we predict an advantage of objects graspable with a power grip in their real size (e.g., of apples and tins over strawberries and rubbers, independent of whether apples and tins were presented in their real or modified dimensions) over objects graspable with a precision grip. This should happen because, in real life, the power grip is less complex than the precision grip. The crucial prediction, however, concerns the role played by online and offline information. If the role of online visual information overcomes that the information stored in memory, then we should find an interaction between the object size (real, modified) and the grip the object typically elicits (power, precision). More specifically, if online information is more important than information stored in memory, then there should be a different response pattern when the object size is the same as the typical one (for example, when an apple is presented in its standard size) as well as when it is modified (for example, when an apple is presented with the same size as a cherry). Namely, with modified size objects participants should respond on the basis of what they SEE (i.e., on the basis of the modified object size) rather than of what they KNOW (i.e. of the real object size). On the contrary, if memory information plays a more important role than online visual information, then we should find the same effect with real and modified size objects.

Finally, if the compatibility effects found in previous studies (Ellis & Tucker, 2001; Borghi et al., 2006) depend on online information, then we should find a compatibility effect between the prime and the target presented in its modified dimension. Otherwise, if long term visuomotor memories are responsible of the effect, then faster responses should be expected in case of compatibility between the postures of the hand primes and the real dimension of the objects.

Method

Participants

Twenty students (12 women and 8 men) of the Department of Communication Sciences of Bologna's University took part in the experiment. All were right handed, they all had normal or corrected to normal vision and they don't receive any payment or credits for the time spent doing this experiment.

Materials and design

The stimulus set was made of coloured digital photos of a human hand displaying one of three different postures (precision, power, or fist) (see fig. 1) and by 24 pictures showing a common object closed to a 50cent coin (see fig. 2, as example). Then a new set of photos was created using the previous set of 24 pictures and manipulating them with Acrobat Photoshop program in order to modify the objects' size. The objects normally affording a precision grip were zoomed out, between 7 and 10 cm height (for example the nut was enlarged to the orange size) and the object usually affording a power grasp were zoomed in, approximately 2 cm height (for example the apple was resized to became small as a cherry). The 50cent coin size was the same in each picture. The presence of the coin allowed to understand whether the objects was presented in its real or modified size. A special care was taken in selecting everyday and common objects.

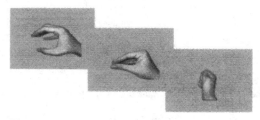

Figure 1: The three hand primes. The first two primes display a precision and a power grip. The third prime, that worked as a catch-trial, displays a fist. Both left and right hand primes were presented.

Twelve of the objects were natural (fruit, vegetables, flowers or animals) and the other twelve were man-made (tools or utensils). Within each category half of the objects required a precision grip and half a power grip. Each slide

was presented two times with the objects in their real size and two times with the objects in their modified size.

Procedure

Participant sat in front of a computer monitor. Each trial began with a fixation point (+) displayed on the monitor for 500 ms. When the fixation cross disappeared, one of the three hand photographs was displayed. In half of the trials, the hand on the screen was a right hand and in half of the trials, it was a left hand. The prime was followed after 250 ms by the target consisting of the picture of an object (e.g., a tin, an orange) closed to the 50cent coin. The sequence is showed in fig. 3. All stimuli were displayed centrally on the monitor ad randomised. When the prime was a hand mimicking a precision or a power grip, half of the participants were required to make a right-hand key press response if the target object was natural and a left-hand key press response if it was an artefact. Half were randomly assigned to the opposite hand-to-category arrangement. When the prime was a fist (catch trial), participants had to refrain from responding to the target and had to wait for the next trial. The target object was displayed on the screen for 2000 ms or until the participant responded. All participants were informed that their response times would be recorded and invited to respond as quickly as possible while still maintaining accuracy.

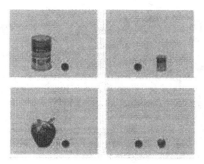

Figure 2: An example of the stimuli: an artefact (tin) graspable with a power grip in its real and modified size and a natural object (strawberry) graspable with a precision grip in its real and modified size.

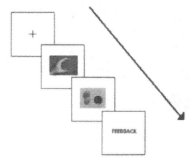

Figure 3: The experimental sequence.

Results

3,5% of the trials were removed as errors. Reaction times (RTs) more or less than 2 standard deviations from each participant's mean, as well as RTs for incorrect responses, were excluded from this analysis. This trimming method lead to remove 2% of the data. The mean RTs for correct response for each participant were submitted to a repeated measures 2x2x2x2 ANOVA with the within subjects factors of Object Kind (artefact, natural object), Grip (precision, power), Hand Prime (precision, power), and Object Size (real, modified). Two participants were eliminated as they made more than 14% of errors. Given that the analysis on errors (excluding time-outs and errors with the catch-trials) revealed that there was no evidence of a speed accuracy trade-off, we focused on the RT analysis.

Among the main effects, the Grip was significant due to the fact that, as predicted, objects graspable with a power grip (e.g., orange, tin) were processed faster than objects graspable with a precision grip (e.g., strawberry, match), F $(1,17) = 4.7$, $MSe = 1208.22$, $p < .045$. Also the difference between artefacts and natural kinds was marginally significant, $F(1,17) = 4.25$, $MSe = 2130,26$ $p < .055$, due to the advantage of natural kinds over artefacts, probably caused by the activation of functional information with the latter.

The most important result was the interaction between and Object Size and Grip, $F(1,17) = 22.36$, $MSe = 823.49$, $p < .001$. Newman-Keuls post-hoc analyses showed that this was due to the fact that, whereas real size objects graspable with a power grip were processed faster than real size objects graspable with a precision grip (e.g., apples were processed faster than nuts), this was not the case for objects presented in their modified size. Namely, with modified size objects the pattern was reversed, as the objects typically graspable with a precision grip but presented with enlarged dimensions (e.g., a nut as large as an apple) were processed faster than objects graspable with a power grip presented with reduced size (e.g., an apple as large as a nut). However, the last difference did not reach significance (see Fig, 4).

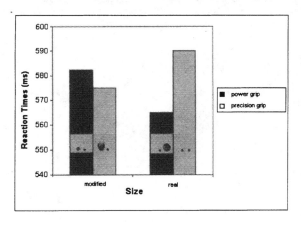

Figure 4: Interaction between Object Size and Grip.

The result suggests an important role played by online, visual information, and thus of the dorsal system, even in a task, a categorization one, in which the ventral system is necessary involved. As it can be in the figure (see Fig 5), the pattern we found is much more similar to the pattern that could be elicited by the activation of online information (dorsal system) than to the pattern that could be elicited by the activation of offline memory features (ventral system). Namely, if results depended only on online information, then objects larger in size should be processed faster than small objects, independently from their original size. For example, the results should be the same for large strawberries as well as for standard apples.

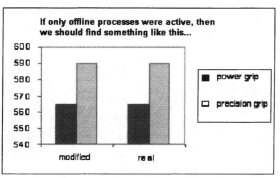

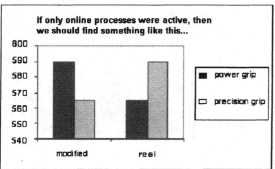

Figure 5: Possible results.

On the contrary, if results depended only on information in memory, then we should find that responses to objects in their real and modified dimension do not vary (Figure 5b).
We also found a significant interaction between the Prime, the Kind of Object and the Object size, $F(1,17) = 4.34$, $MSe = 468.03$, $p < .053$, (see Fig 6).

Newman-Keuls post-hoc analyses showed that this was due to the fact that for real size objects artefacts preceded by a power grip were slower than natural kinds preceded by both power and precision grip (593 vs. 565 and 571ms). This interaction suggests that visual hand primes have an influence on real size but not on modified size objects. The faster RTs obtained with the precision compared with the power prime, confirm that artefacts evoke functional information, as the precision posture is typically more linked to fine prehension, and thus to function.

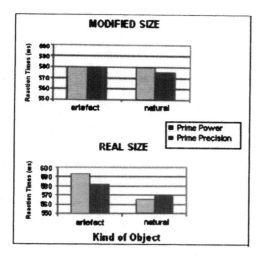

Figure 6: Interaction between Object Size and Grip.

Discussion

Our results clearly confirm previous studies showing that visual stimuli activate motor information. More importantly, this study suggests an important role of the online information also in a categorization task.

The advantage of objects typically graspable with a power grip over objects graspable with a precision grip suggests that visual stimuli automatically activate motor information and lead to internally "simulate" a grasping action. Namely, the longer RTs with the precision grip is due to the fact that, in real life, grasping an object with a precision grip is more complex than grasping an object with a power grip (Ehrsson, Fagergren, Jonsson, Westling, Johansson, Forssberg, 2000). The difference between artefacts and natural kinds can be explained by the fact that the first evoke both action and functional information, while the second activate only action information (Warrington & Shallice, 1984). The activation of functional information with artefacts might have lead to the longer processing times with the latter.

The most important result, however, concerns the role of online and offline memory features in explaining the effects. Even though a categorization task was used, the role of on-line information, mediated by the dorsal system, was clearly very relevant, as shown by the interaction between Grip and Object Size. The results indicate that categorization is *mainly based* on online processed information. This suggests a major role of the dorsal system in explaining our results. This is particularly striking as it occurs in a categorization task, that is in a task that implies the involvement of the ventral system (semantic knowledge).

However, we also found that information stored in memory (off-line information) influences the recognition process. Namely, the 3-way interaction we found between Prime, Object Kind and Grip showed that the prime was effective only with objects presented in their real dimension and not with objects presented in their modified dimension. The absence of a congruency effect between the prime and the target can be due to the fact that, as in Experiment 1 by Borghi et al. (2006), no motor training phase preceded the experiment. Even though the prime stimuli were more dynamical than in the previous experiment, no motor resonance effect was triggered by the prime, thus no compatibility effect was found. However, the 3-way interaction revealed that participants were sensitive to the prime influence.

Overall, our results are in line with various recent studies that suggest that the distinction between the dorsal and the ventral stream as proposed by Milner and Goodale (1995) is probably too rigid and dichotomic (Gallese et. al. ; 1999; Derbishire, Ellis & Tucker, 2006). For example, it has been proposed that the dorsal route can be distinguished into a pure dorsal-dorsal route and a ventral-dorsal one, and that some kind of object representation is encoded in the dorsal route as well (Gentilucci, 2003). In addition, recent studies with language suggest that motor and pragmatic information is crucial for conceptual information (Barsalou et al, 2003; Glenberg, 1997; Buxbaum et al, 2003). In order to better disentangle the role played by the two systems, further experiments are planned. Namely, we aim at increasing the influence of prime on the categorization task and to verify whether we find a compatibility effect between the prime and the stimuli presented in their real or in their modified size.

Acknowledgments

Thanks to Giulia Baroni, Claudia Bonfiglioli, Giovanni Buccino, Laura Freina, Claudia Gianelli, Cristina Iani, Luisa Lugli, Antonello Pellicano, Paola Ricciardelli, Lucia Riggio and Sandro Rubichi for comments and useful suggestions on this work.

References

Barsalou, L.W., Simmons, W. K., Barbey, A.K., & Wilson, C.D. (2003). Grounding conceptual knowledge in modalityspecific systems. *Trends in Cognitive Science, 7*, 84-91.

Borghi, A., Bonfiglioli, C., Lugli, L., Ricciardelli, P., Rubichi, S., Nicoletti, R. (in press). Are visual stimuli sufficient to evoke motor information? Studies with hand primes. *Neuroscience Letters*.

Buxbaum, L. J., Sirigu, A., Schwartz, M., & Klatzky, R. (2003). Cognitve representations of hand posture in ideomotor apraxia. *Neuropsychologia, 41*, 1091–1113.

Chao, L.L., Martin, A. (2000). Representation of manipulable man-made objects in the dorsal stream. *NeuroImage, 12*, 478-484.

Derbyshire, N., Ellis, R. & Tucker, M. (2006). The potentiation of two components of the reach-to-grasp action during object categorisation in visual memory. *Acta Psychologica, 122*, 74-98.

Ehrsson, H.H., Fagergren, A., Jonsson, T. , Westling, G., Johansson, R.S., Forssberg, H. (2000). Cortical activity in precision- versus power-grip tasks: An fMRI study. *Journal of Neurophysiology, 83,* 528-536.

Ellis, R. & Tucker, M. (2000). Micro-affordance: The potentiation of components of action by seen objects. *British Journal of Psychology, 91*, 451-471.

Gallese, V., Craighero. L., Fadiga, L., & Fogassi, L. (1999). Perception through action. *Psyche, 5*, 5-21.

Gentilucci, M. (2003). Object motor representation and language. *Experimental Brain Research, 153*, 260-265.

Gerlach, C., Law, I., & Paulson, O. B. (2002). When action turns into words. Activation of motor-based knowledge during categorization of manipulable objects. *Journal of Cognitive Neuroscience, 14*, 1230-1239.

Glenberg, A.M. (1997). What memory is for. *Behavioral and Brain Sciences, 20*, 1-55.

Grafton, S.T., Fadiga, L., Arbib, M.A., & Rizzolatti, G. (1997). Premotor cortex activation during observation and naming of familiar tools. *Neuroimage, 6*, 231-236.

Kellenbach, M.L., Brett, M. and Patterson, K., 2003. Actions speak louder than functions: the importance of manipulability and action in tool representation. *J. Cogn. Neurosci. 15*, pp. 30–46.

Martin, A., Wiggs, C.L., Ungerleider, L.G., Haxby, G.V. (1996). Neural correlates of category specific knowledge. *Nature, 379*, 649-652.

Milner, A. D. & Goodale, M. A. (1995) The visual brain in action. *Oxford University Press.*

di Pellegrino, G., Fadiga, L., Fogassi, L., Gallese, V. & Rizzolatti, G. (1992) Understanding motor events: A neurophysiological study. *Experimental Brain Research 91,*176.80.

Rumiati, R.I., Humphreys, G.W. (1998). Recognition by action: Dissociating visual and semantic routes to action in normal observer. *Journal of Experimental Psychology: Human Perception and Performance, 24*, 631-647.

Tucker, M. & Ellis, R. (2001) The potientation of grasp types during visual objects categorization, *Visual Cognition, 8*, 769-800

Warrington, E.K. & Shallice, T. (1984). Category-specific semantic impairment. *Brain, 107,* 829-854.

False Memory for Analogical Inferences: An Indicator of Representational Change of the Target Text but not an Indicator of Conceptual Change of the Target Issue

Ricardo A. Minervino (rminervino@ciudad.com.ar)
Consejo Nacional de Investigaciones Científicas y Técnicas; Department of Psychology, University of Buenos Aires,
Calle Independencia 3065, 3° Piso, Oficina 8
1225, Buenos Aires, Argentina

Nicolás Oberholzer (oberholzer@fibertel.com.ar)
Humanities Faculty, Research Department, University of Belgrano, Zabala 1837, 12° Piso
1426, Buenos Aires, Argentina

Oscar A. López Alonso (alalonso@ciudad.com.ar)
Consejo Nacional de Investigaciones Científicas y Técnicas; Institute of Psychologycal Research, University of Salvador,
Marcelo T. De Alvear 1314, 1° Piso
1428, Buenos Aires, Argentina

Abstract

An experiment was performed to investigate whether false memory for analogical inferences implies a conceptual change of the issue described by the *target analogue* (TA), as suggested by Blanchette and Dunbar (2002) and Perrott, Gentner and Bodenhausen (2005), or only a representational change of the target text. A group of participants who received a *source analogue* (SA) after having read a TA, produced more false recognitions for analogical inferences than a group without a SA. However, there was no difference between the participants who misrecognized analogical inferences and those who did not misrecognize them on the level of agreement with those inferences in the analogy group. These results show that false memory for analogical inferences is an indicator of representational change of the target text, but it is not an indicator of conceptual change of the target issue described by the target text.

Introduction

An important feature of human cognition is people's ability to use analogical reasoning (de la Fuente & Minervino, 2004; Holyoak & Morrison, 2005). Analogy involves applying knowledge from one relatively well-known domain (the *source analogue:* SA) to another unfamiliar domain (the *target analogue:* TA) on which the reasoner is working. Analogical thinking is involved in tasks such as problem solving, learning with examples, scientific discovery, persuasion and many others (for an overview of the role of analogy in a wide range of cognitive tasks, see Gentner, Holyoak & Kokinov, 2001).

Mapping and inference generation has been considered the central components of analogical thinking (Gentner, 1983; Holyoak & Thagard, 1989; Keane, Ledgeway & Duff, 1994). Mapping is the mechanism of aligning elements (e.g., predicates and entities) that are present in the initial representations of the analogues being compared. Inference generation entails the transfer of source elements that are not initially presented in the target, but can be hypothetically postulated in accordance with the correspondences provided by the mapping and the structure of the analogy (Gentner, 1989; Holyoak, Novick & Melz, 1994). For most models of analogy, inference generation consists in creating new propositions by substituting the corresponding target elements for their source counterparts in initially unmapped source propositions. For example, when an analogy is formed between the solar system and the atom (Gentner, 1983), a reasoner might first notice that the nucleus corresponds to the sun, that the planets correspond to the electrons, and that the planets revolve around the sun. Using these mappings, the reasoner may then copy the relation "revolve around" and substitute the target elements ("nucleus" and "planets") for the source ones ("sun" and "planets", respectively) to infer that "the electrons revolve around the nucleus" (for computational implementations of this mechanism, see Falkenhainer, Forbus & Gentner, 1989; Holyoak et al., 1994; Hummel & Holyoak, 2002).

Inference generation is controlled in people by syntactic constraints such as *systematicity* (Clement & Gentner, 1991; Markman, 1997; Yanowitz, 2001) and *one-to-one* mapping (Krawczyk, Holyoak & Hummel, 2005), and also by pragmatic (Spellman & Holyoak, 1996) and semantic restrictions (Holyoak & Thagard, 1995). However, these principles do not guarantee the validity of the projected inferences for the TA. Inference generation propose plausible inferences about the target, but these inferences must still be evaluated, and could be accepted, adapted or rejected considering particular aspects of the target (Gentner & Markman, 1997; Holyoak et al., 1994).

Analogy is thought to be a powerful device for altering the mental representation of knowledge (Dietrich, 2000; Hosftadter & Fluid Analogical Research Group [FARG], 1995). However, the relation between analogy and knowledge change has received little empirical and computational attention (Minervino, Adrover & de la Fuente, 2006). Inference generation is considered one of the mechanisms of knowledge change (e.g., Gentner & Wolff, 2000). In order to produce conceptual change, analogical inferences must be accepted as valid for the TA (Gentner, Brem, Ferguson, Wolff, Markman & Forbus, 1995; Holyoak & Thagard, 1995). The aim of this study was to investigate the relation between generation and misrecognitions of analogical inferences and conceptual changes in the TA.

Blanchette and Dunbar (2002) demonstrated in a serie of experiments that analogical inferences are integrated into the representation of the target text. They asked participants to read a text about a target issue (e.g., the legalization of marijuana). In the experimental condition, the text ended with the description of a SA (e.g., lifting the period of the prohibition of alcohol). Participants in the control condition read the same target text without the description of the SA at the end. On a subsequent recognition test, the participants in the analogy group often misidentified analogical inferences as sentences actually presented in the target text. Furthermore, this effect was robust across variations in passage length, types of analogy (intra or interdomain), familiarity of the target issue, and delay between the reading phase and the test recognition (one week or 15 min).

Perrott, Gentner and Bodenhausen (2005) demonstrated that analogical inferences can be integrated into mental representations of the target text even when these inferences contradict previous attitudes toward the target issue or when participants do not find the analogy to be accurate. Participants read a target passage on the role and status of gay people in society. In the experimental condition the text presented at the end was an analogue describing historical persecution of left-handers. This analogue was not present in the control condition. On a subsequent recognition test, participants who read the analogy were more likely than control participants to misrecognize analogical inferences as statements explicitly presented in the text they had read. Previous negative attitudes toward gays and participants' negative evaluation of the soundness of the analogy did not moderate these findings.

Blanchette and Dunbar (2002) suggest that the incorporation of analogical inferences in the TA could imply an important change in the representation of the target issue: "Our results are consistent with the hypothesis that participants … drew inferences and that these inferences alter the initial target representation … they appear to have engaged in analogical reasoning, and this led *to alterations in their representation of the target issue*" (p. 676; italics added). This insertion of inferences could result, according to these authors, in conceptual change: "Our results show that this process can have profound influences on the representation of the target. … The research reported here indicates that analogy is one potential way that underlying representations of complex knowledge can be changed" (p. 682).

In the same vein, Perrot et al. (2005) considered the incorporation of counter attitudinal analogical inferences as

a possible means of representational change: "This [incorporation] would suggest that the analogical insertion effect might be a means of knowledge accretion, and even conceptual change, against the learner's will. Such a mechanism might help explain some of the shifts from one mental model to another in the course of domain learning" (p. 696).

Although Blanchette and Dunbar's (2002) research demonstrated that analogical thinking can result in an alteration of the representation of a target text by the influence of a SA, and Perrot et al.'s (2005) study showed that this effect can occur even when the inferences contradict previous attitudes or the analogy itself is not convincing, it remains to be investigated if this change in the representation of the target text implies a conceptual change with respect to the target issue treated by the target text. An example could clarify why these two levels of analysis should be differentiated.

After the invasion of Kuwait, President George Bush tried to persuade people that the Gulf situation could be compared to the events that had led to World War II (Spellman & Holyoak, 1992). This analogy promotes the matching of Irak with Germany, Saddam Hussein with Hitler, Kuwait with Poland, and so on. Suppose the audience hear this analogy in a speech given by Bush and make the required mappings to understand it. Suppose now that the last sentence of Bush's speech was "In World War II it was necessary to put together a multinational coalition to win the war". Probably, the audience would infer that Bush is trying to convey that in the Gulf situation "it is necessary to put together a multinational coalition to win the war", a sentence not explicitly asserted by Bush. Probably, in a recognition test presented later, the audience would tend to misrecognize this last sentence as having being explicitly pronounced by Bush. Does this memory error imply that people accepted the inference? People might have been able to understand the analogy proposed by Bush and to draw the intended analogical inference suggested by him, but still refused its validity, considering, for example, the differences between the situations under comparison. In short, misidentification of analogical inferences as if they were initially in the target text can be taken perhaps as an indicator of inference generation and inference attribution to the provider of the analogy, but cannot be taken without further proof as evidence that the receiver of the analogy is accepting the inferences for the TA. The point is that this acceptance is, as we said, a necessary condition to consider that conceptual change has taken place. If misrecognitions for analogical inferences are not associated with the acceptance of these inferences, these misrecognitions cannot be taken as an indicator of conceptual change and must be simply considered as a memory phenomenon.

There is some evidence (Blanchette & Dunbar, 2002, Exp. 4; Day & Gentner, in press, Exp. 3) that in experimental settings like those employed by these authors, people generate the expected analogical inferences, and that they do it during the processing of the analogy. It can be postulated, considering this evidence, that the difference between people who produce false memory for analogical inferences and those who do not consists in that the former erroneously attribute the inferences to the provider of the analogy, while the later believe themselves to be the source of these inferences. We believe that, at least for situations in which the receiver of the analogy has considerable knowledge about the TA, the evaluation of the inferences will be made independently from any belief about the source of the inferences under consideration.

Experiment

The goal of the present experiment was to investigate whether the misrecognition of analogical inferences in the representation of a target text supposes the acceptance of the validity of these inferences for the target issue. Participants read a descriptive text about an ambiguous car accident where it was difficult to determine if the car driver was responsible for the damage caused to a pedestrian. We manipulated the presence of a SA. The participants in the experimental group read the text about the car accident and then the description of a potential SA that intended to promote the ascription of the responsibility of the accident to the car driver. In this analogue, the car accident was compared to a pistol accident in which the responsible was clearly the owner of the pistol. Participants in the control condition read the same target text without the description of the SA at the end. After a distractor task, participants of both groups completed a recognition test that evaluated the representation of the TA. This test intended to find out whether participants of the experimental group, in contrast to those of the control group, falsely recognized as present in the target text sentences that were analogical inferences. Afterwards, participants of both groups were tested on their level of agreement with those analogical inferences. The purpose of this test was to determine if people who incorporated the analogical inferences for the TA (i.e., participants who produce false alarms for the analogical inferences) tended to consider them more valid than participants that did not incorporate them in their representation of the target text (i.e., they did not produce false alarms). Since only the analogy group could derive analogical inferences, we were interested in the relation between false alarms to analogical inferences and the level of agreement with them in this group.

Our hypothesis was that the incorporation of analogical inferences (representational change of the target text) does not imply the acceptance of these inferences for the target issue treated by the target text. We predicted that those participants in the analogy group who committed false alarms for an analogical inference would not agree with that inference more than those participants of the same group that did not produce these memory errors. Our prediction was based on the assumption that participants would evaluate the analogical inferences considering their previous knowledge and attitudes with respect to responsibility in car accidents like the one described in the text, and that this evaluation would not depend on the belief that the inferences were stated by the provider of the analogy or generated by the receiver of it.

Participants Participants were 120 psychology students at the University of Buenos Aires, with a mean age of 20.9 (range 19-43; 91 females and 29 males).

Design A 2 x 3 mixed factor design was employed, with condition (*analogy* or *no-analogy*) as a between-subjects factor, and the recognition test item type (*text item, novel item, analogical inference*) as a within-subject factor. The dependent variables were the number of "yes" answers to the items in the recognition test, and the level of agreement with the analogical inferences.

Procedure Half of the participants were randomly assigned to the analogy group and half to the no-analogy group. Participants in both groups read the text describing the car accident, followed by a SA in the experimental group and by a filler text in the no-analogy group. They were asked to carefully read the texts since they would have to answer some questions about them afterwards. After 5 min, the reading material was removed and they received a booklet with all the following tasks to complete in writing. As Blanchette and Dunbar (2002, Exp. 2), we presented then a 15 min distractor activity (an inductive reasoning task). These authors found that a 15 min distractor task produce similar memory intrusions as the ones produces by a 1-week delay. Following this task, the participants completed, with no time limit, the recognition task and, after that, the task where they had to express their level of agreement with the analogical inferences.

Materials The target text (204 words) described a car accident where a person was driving under the speed limit and was about to pass a green light. On the sidewalk there was an old lady waiting to cross the street when a person unintentionally pushed her and made her fall on the street. Although he tried, the car driver could not help hitting the old lady. The TA should satisfy two conditions. First, it should describe a familiar situation so participants would have some kind of previous opinion about the topic. Second, the specific situation should be ambiguous enough so that an analogy could produce some change in their opinions. A previous informal test showed that when a driver does everything according to the law and pedestrians do not people tend to blame pedestrians if an accident takes place. In the situation described in the TA the pedestrian falls on the street by accident (somebody pushes her). As a result there were some chances to influence the opinion of the participants by providing them with a SA. In any case, it is important to bear in mind that our experimental goal was to test if the misrecognition of the analogical inferences was related to the evaluation of the validity of those inferences and that, for that purpose, the chosen analogy or its persuasive power is not relevant. The SA (407 words) read by participants in the analogy group, described another person's unintentional accident with his pistol. The man erroneously interpreted that a young man wanted to hurt him with a gun. He tried to warn the young man by shooting to the ground, but the bullet hit the youngster. The aim of the analogy was to promote the idea that the car driver is a holder of a dangerous object, similar to a gun, and therefore responsible for the accident unintentionally caused by another person. After the target text, participants in the control group read a filler text (412 words) which described a situation that had no resemblance to the TA.

In the analogy condition, three statements of the source text did not have a match in the target text but could be transformed into three analogical inferences. The filler text in the no-analogy condition also included those statements although they were about situations that were not analogous to the ones described in the target text (it was not possible to derive true analogical inferences from the filler text).

In the recognition test, participants had to indicate, for each of a series of statements, whether the statement was or was not in the text they had read in the first part of the experiment. Three different types of items were included: three text items (statements that were actually in the text), three analogical inferences (statements that were not in the text but could be inferred from the SA in the analogy condition), and three novel items (statements that were not in the text and could not be generated via analogy). The order of presentation of the nine items was counterbalanced. To derive the analogical inferences, some words from the three statements of the SA that had no match in the target text, were replaced by their corresponding words in the TA. For example, the statement "*Lorenzo* [the pistol owner] is responsible for the accident and must pay for the injuries caused to the *young man*" became the following analogical inference: "*Bruno* [the car driver] is responsible for the accident and must pay for the injuries caused to the *old lady*". In the no-analogy condition the same source statements were used to derive statements equivalent to the analogical inferences. The substituted and substituting words were the same as in the analogy condition but they did not match up within any analogy. In this way, the analogical inferences were familiar to both groups (i.e., both groups had read the statements from where the analogical inferences were derived). The text items were statements taken from the target text and were the same in both conditions. The novel items differed from one condition to the other. They were constructed following the same procedure used to derive the analogical inferences: one or two words of three statements from the source text (analogy condition) or the filler text (control condition), were changed with words from the target text. Hence, the familiarity of the novel items and the analogical inferences was the same in both groups. In the analogy condition the selected statements were not part of the structure of the SA implicated in the analogy. By including the text and novel items, we will be able to compare the general memory performance of the groups, separately from their memory

performance for analogical inferences. There were no differences between the mean number of words of the different types of items in the analogy condition, $F(2, 6) = .06$, $p > .05$, $MSE = 15.667$; and in the no-analogy condition either, $F(2, 6) = .08$, $p > .05$, $MSE = 17.889$.

In a separate sheet of paper, participants in both conditions had to express to what extent they agree with the three analogical inferences, in a 5-points Likert scale (1 = very much in disagreement, and 5 = very much in agreement). The order in which the analogical inferences were presented was counterbalanced.

Results and Discussion

Three participants (one participant in the analogy condition and two in the no-analogy condition) were not considered in the analysis because they did not complete all of the tasks. A 3 x 2 mixed analysis of variance (ANOVA) was performed on the proportion of "yes" answers to the recognition test items, with item type (text item, novel item, analogical inferences) as a within-subject factor, and condition (analogy, no-analogy) as between-subjects factor. The means of both groups are presented in Table 1. This analysis revealed a significant interaction between condition and item type, $F(2, 230) = 12.67$, $p < .001$, $MSE = .728$.

Table 1: Answers to the recognition test items

Condition	Proportion of "yes" answers to text items		Proportion of "yes" answers to novel items		Proportion of "yes" answers to analogical inferences	
	M	DE	M	DE	M	DE
Analogy	.91	.15	.09	.23	.43	.35
No-Analogy	.89	.23	.03	.10	.11	.24

Tests of simple effects revealed that there was a significant difference between the analogy and no-analogy groups in the average proportion of "yes" answers to analogical inferences, $t(115) = 5.67$, $p < .001$. Participants in the analogy condition answered "yes" more frequently than those in the no-analogy group. In contrast, there were no significant difference in the proportion of "yes" answers to text items, $t(115) = .69$, $p > .05$, and novel items, $t(115) = 1.85$, $p > .05$. Thus, we reproduced the results obtained by Blanchette and Dunbar (2002) and Perrot et al. (2005): Participants who read the SA erroneously recognized as present in the text the analogical inferences more often than participants in the no-analogy condition. This difference can not be explained by a poorer general memory performance of the analogy group, since there were no performance differences between the two conditions in the other types of items (text items and novel items). It is particularly remarkable that we found differences in the analogical inferences but not in the novel items, since these two type of items were constructed using the same procedure and therefore demand the same memory skills (i.e., realizing that an item was not present in the text although having read the same statement applied to other concepts). Neither can the difference in false alarms in analogical inferences be explained by familiarity with those items because both groups read the sentences from which the inferences were derived.

A non parametric analysis was performed employing Mann-Whitney's U test on the level of agreement with the analogical inferences to determine if the presence of the SA increases the level of agreement with those inferences. There were no differences between the analogy condition and the no-analogy condition on the level of agreement with analogical inferences, $U(351) = 14680$, $z = -.785$, $p > .05$. The presence of a SA did not increase the agreement with the idea that the car driver, like the owner of the pistol, was responsible for the accident and other related statements. It should be remembered that our intention was not to test the efficacy of analogies as persuasive means. Our objective was to determine whether the false recognition of analogical inferences, an indicator of representational change of the target text, is also an indicator of representational change of the target issue.

Accordingly, the most relevant data analysis for our experimental goals was to determine whether participants in the analogy group who produced false alarms to analogical inferences would agree with these inferences more than participants from the same group that did not produce false alarms. It is important to bear in mind that only in this group the items analogical inferences were really such since they could be derived from the analogy, something that could not be done in the no-analogy condition. Participants in the analogy condition who produced false alarms did not agree with these inferences more than those who did not produce these errors, $U(177) = 3550.5$, $z = -.887$, $p > .05$ (Figure 1 shows the distribution of the responses of agreement with the analogical inferences in the analogy group). We neither found differences in the level of agreement with analogical inferences between participants who produced false alarms and those that produced hits in the no-analogy group, $U(174) = 1515$, $z = -.122$, $p > .05$, nor in general (i.e., considering both groups together), $U(351) = 11401$, $z = -1.028$, $p > .05$.

In summary, on the one hand the results replicated the findings of Blanchette and Dunbar (2002) and Perrot et al. (2005) regarding the fact that people erroneously recognize analogical inferences when they are given to read a SA for a target text, and those false alarms are specific to those items. On the other hand, as we predicted and in contrast to what Blanchette and Dunbar (2002) and Perrot et al. (2005) suggested, the results showed that although an analogy can promote a change in the representation of the target text, this change does not imply that the analogy is able to promote conceptual changes regarding the issue addressed by the target text. Participants who produced memory errors to analogical inferences in the analogy group did not have a greater tendency to accept them than participants of the same group who did not misrecognize them. The fact that a

person derives the inference "Bruno is responsible for the accident and must pay for the injuries caused to the old lady" from the source statement "Lorenzo is responsible for the accident and must pay for the injuries caused to the young man", and later erroneously beliefs that the inference was present in the text, does not seem to be related to the evaluation of the validity of the inference that the person does. It seems that people tend to evaluate the inferences separately from their beliefs about who produced them.

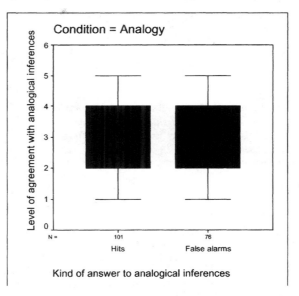

Figure 1. Distribution of responses of agreement with the analogical inferences in the analogy group

False memory for analogy inferences seems to be simply an indicator of representational change of the target text but not an indicator of conceptual change of the target issue presented by this text. Our findings do not exclude the possibility that misrecognitions of analogical inferences and conceptual change may be associated in other circumstances. It is possible that for situations in which the receiver of the analogy has little or no knowledge about the target, her or his acceptance of analogical inferences will depend on the localization of the source of the inferences. Since the only criterion for evaluating inferences was authority, inferences would be accepted to the extent that they were attributed to the provider of the analogy. In such circumstances, false memory for analogical inferences could be associated with a greater acceptance of them. In any case, false memory for analogical inferences doesn't seem to be the most valid and direct instrument for measuring conceptual change.

Acknowledgments

This paper was made possible by a grant (P030) from the University of Buenos Aires to the first author, and a grant

(PIP5526) from Consejo Nacional de Investigaciones Científicas y Técnicas (Argentina) to the third author.

References

Blanchette, I., & Dunbar K. (2002). Representational change and analogy: How analogical inferences alter target representations. *Journal of Experimental Psychology: Learning, Memory, and Cognition, 4,* 672-685.

Clement, C. A., & Gentner, D. (1991). Systematicity as a selection constraint in analogical mapping. *Cognitive Science, 15,* 89-132.

Day, S. B. & Gentner, D. (in press). Nonintentional analogical inference in text comprehension. *Memory & Cognition.*

Dietrich, E. (2000). Analogy and conceptual change. In E. Dietrich & A. B. Markman (Eds.), *Cognitive dynamics: Conceptual and representational change in humans and machines.* Mahwah, NJ: Erlbaum.

de la Fuente Arnanz, J., & Minervino, R. A. (2004). Pensamiento analógico. In M. Carretero & M. Asensio (Coords.), *Psicología del pensamiento.* Alianza: Madrid.

Falkenhainer, B., Forbus, K. D., & Gentner, D. (1989). The structure-mapping engine: Algorithm and examples. *Artificial Intelligence, 41,* 1-63.

Gentner, D. (1983). Structure-mapping: A theoretical framework for analogy. *Cognitive Science, 7,* 155-170.

Gentner, D. (1989). The mechanisms of analogical learning. In S. Vosniadou & A. Ortony (Comps.), *Similarity and analogical reasoning.* New York: Cambridge University Press.

Gentner, D., Brem, S., Ferguson, R. W., Wolff, P., Markman, A. B., & Forbus, K. D. (1997). Analogy and creativity in the works of Johannes Kepler. In T. B. Ward, S. M. Smith & J. Vaid (Eds.), *Creative thought: An investigation of conceptual structures and processes.* Washington, DC: American Psychological Association.

Gentner, D., Holyoak, K. J., & Kokinov, B. N. (Eds.) (2001). *The analogical mind.* Cambridge: MIT Press.

Gentner, D., & Markman, A. B. (1997). Structure mapping in analogy and similarity. *American Psychologist, 52,* 45-56.

Gentner, D., & Wolff, P. (2000). Metaphor and knowledge change. In E. Dietrich & A. B. Markman (Eds.), *Cognitive dynamics: Conceptual and representational change in humans and machines.* Mahwah, NJ: Erlbaum.

Hofstadter D. R., & FARG (1995). *Fluid concepts and creative analogies: Computer models of the fundamental mechanisms of thought.* New York: Basic Books.

Holyoak, K. J., & Morrison, R. G. (2005). Analogy. *The Cambridge handbook of thinking and reasoning.* Cambridge: Cambridge University Press.

Holyoak, K, J., Novick, L. R., & Melz, E. R. (1994). Component processes in analogical transfer: Mapping, pattern completion, and adaptation. In K. J. Holyoak & J. A. Barden (Eds.), *Advances in connectionist and neural computation theory, Vol. 2: Analogical connections.* Norwood, NJ: Ablex.

Holyoak, K. J., & Thagard, P. R. (1989). Analogical mapping by constraint satisfaction. *Cognitive Science, 13,* 295-355.

Holyoak, K. J., & Thagard, P. R. (1995). *Mental leaps: Analogy in creative thought.* Cambridge, MA: MIT Press.

Hummel, J. E., & Holyoak, K. J. (2002). Analogy and creativity: Schema induction in a structure-sensitive connectionist model. In T. Dartnall (Ed.), *Creativity, cognition, and knowledge: An interaction.* Wesport, CT: Praeger.

Keane, M. T., Ledgeway, T., & Duff, S. (1994). Constraints on analogical mapping: A comparison of three models. *Cognitive Science, 18,* 387-438.

Krawczyk, D. C., Holyoak, K. J., & Hummel J. E. (2005). The one-to-one constraint in analogical mapping and inference. *Cognitive Science, 29,* 797-806.

Markman, A. B. (1997). Constraints on analogical inference. *Cognitive Science, 21,* 373-418.

Minervino, R. A., Adrover, J. F., & de la Fuente J. (2006). Los límites del modelo estándar acerca del componente semántico en el establecimiento de correspondencias analógicas. *Anales de Psicología, 1,* 120-131.

Perrot, D. A., Gentner, D., & Bodenhausen, G. V. (2005). Resistance is futile: The unwitting insertion of analogical inferences in memory. *Psychonomic Bulletin & Review, 4,* 696-702.

Spellman, B. A. y Holyoak, K. J. (1996). Pragmatics in analogical mapping. *Cognitive Psychology, 31,* 307-346.

Yanowitz, K. L. (2001). Transfer of structure-related and arbitrary information in analogical reasoning. *The Pychological Record, 51,* 357-379.

Adults differently process taxonomic and thematic semantic relations according to object kinds

Solène Kalénine (solene.kalenine@upmf-grenoble.fr)
Laboratoire de Psychologie et Neurocognition, UMR 5105, UPMF,
Grenoble, France

Françoise Bonthoux (francoise.bonthoux@upmf-grenoble.fr)
Laboratoire de Psychologie et Neurocognition, UMR 5105, UPMF,
Grenoble, France

Abstract

Researches in cognitive psychology, developmental psychology and neuroimagery suggest that taxonomic and thematic relations between objects might be differently relevant according to object kinds. To test this hypothesis, adults were asked to select among 2 pictures the one that was semantically linked to a target picture. The semantic relation proposed was either taxonomic at the superordinate level or thematic. Target pictures represented various natural and artefact concepts. Reaction times and errors were recorded. Results revealed an interaction between the type of semantic relation and the type of objects. Participants were faster to evaluate taxonomic relations for natural concepts than for artefacts but they were faster to recognize thematic relations for artefacts than for natural concepts.

Introduction

Classical theories assume that amodal semantic representations organized in semantic networks represent conceptual knowledge about the world. Alternatively another conception is that information is distributed over visual, tactile, auditory, motor and verbal-declarative features as a function of their activation level when the knowledge is acquired (Allport, 1985). Recent researches suggest that particular aspects of this distributed information, e.g., sensori-motor, emotional; that arise during perception and action are re-activated as a function of the requirement of the semantic task (Buxbaum & Saffran, 2002; Myung, Blumstein, & Sedivy, 2006; Simmons & Barsalou, 2003). The modalities involved in previous experiences with an object seem to be recruited again when processing this concept. Pecher, Zeelenberg and Barsalou (2003; 2004) and Marques (2006) have investigated whether representations are affected by recent experiences with a concept in a property verification task. In one experiment (Pecher et al., 2004), concept names were presented twice with a different property on each occasion, either from the same or different motor-perceptual modalities. Participants were faster to check a particular property for a concept when they had previously responded to a property of the same than a different motor-perceptual modality. Behavioural evidence for the involvement of sensori-motor representations in language has also been obtained. For example, when a text involves an object in a particular orientation, visual recognition of this object is faster when it

is presented in the same than in the different orientation (Stanfield & Zwaan, 2001), suggesting that readers simulate the object in this orientation. A similar effect has been observed with congruent shapes (Zwaan, Stanfield, & Yaxley, 2002). In fact, it seems that concepts are at least partially grounded in our sensori-motor experiences (Barsalou, 1999, 2005; Rakison, 2005; Smith, 2005). Conceptual knowledge would be the productive activation of remembered aspects of perceptual, motor and internal experiences (Deák, 2003).

This hypothesis is consistent with data from neuroimagery. In a recent review, Martin (2007) investigated the neural correlates of concept processing. Retrieving object properties, particularly sensori-motor properties, elicits activity in the corresponding sensory and motor processing neural systems (Chao & Martin, 2000; Gerlach, Law, & Paulson, 2002). In addition, the regions associated with the representation of object properties appear to be differentially engaged as a function of object category membership. The evidence put forward the possibility of dedicated neural networks for perceiving and knowing about animate objects and common tools. For animate objects, two regions in the posterior temporal cortex, namely the lateral portion of the fusiform gyrus and the posterior superior temporal sulcus would be particularly involved in the representation of visual form and motion that are central in the understanding of these objects. For tools, a neural circuitry including the medial portion of the fusiform gyrus, the posterior middle temporal gyrus, the intraparietal sulcus and the left ventral premotor cortex would represent their visual form and action properties (motion and manipulation). If we consider that sensori-motor experiences underlie conceptual representations, these experiences would be quite different according to the kind of objects, animate objects or artefacts. The visual system would be specifically linked to the processing of natural concepts. Visual experience seems indeed particularly relevant to the understanding of natural kinds. Behavioral studies in adults support this idea since visual properties appear predominant when participants generate or judge properties of natural kinds (Cree & McRae, 2003; Devlin, Gonnerman, Andersen, & Seidenberg, 1998; Garrard, Lambon Ralph, Hodges, & Patterson, 2001; Marques, 2002). On the contrary, regions implicated in object use and manipulation would be mainly recruited to access artefacts' knowledge. This seems consistent with a central role of contextual and functional information in the understanding of artefacts. Even if visual attributes usually outnumber functional ones in generation tasks for both natural kinds and artefacts, functional properties appear more important in artefacts (Cree & McRae, 2003; Farah & McClelland, 1991; McRae & Cree, 2002).

The implication of perception and action in concept processing might also be observed in categorization behaviours. In this domain, two kinds of conceptual organizations have been intensively studied, i.e., thematic and taxonomic relations. Taxonomic relations refer to groupings of objects of the same kind belonging to a semantic category (i.e. dog and cat as animals). Taxonomic related objects share similarity links, perceptual (e.g., birds have a beak) and non perceptual (e.g., birds can fly). On the contrary, thematic relations correspond to an organization of knowledge in terms of familiar scenes or events. Thematic related objects share contextual relations (i.e. dog and bone since the dog usually eats bones). Until recently, thematic organization was thought to be the preferential mode of both young and elderly adults (Smiley & Brown, 1979). On the contrary, taxonomic systems of organization have been related to adults' categorization (Davidoff & Roberson, 2004). When taxonomic and thematic relations are contrasted in sorting and matching tasks, adults generally choose to group objects of the same kind. They would therefore rely on the similarity (perceptual and non perceptual) between taxonomically related objects to determine their choices. However, more recent studies have shown that thematic relations based on contextual links (e.g. a hammer and a nail) appear to be still meaningful and salient in adulthood depending on the presented stimuli (Lin & Murphy, 2001; Murphy, 2001; Osborne & Heath, 2003). Thus both taxonomic and thematic links seem to be involved in adults' conceptual organization. An assumption is that each relation is more or less relevant according to object kinds. This varying sensibility to taxonomic and thematic relations could be linked to the different sensori-motor experiences underlying objects' processing. More precisely, perceptual experiences would direct attention toward perceptual similarity relations among objects that are frequently linked to more abstract similarity relations (e.g., birds have wings and can fly). Similarly, experiences of use and action would allow the extraction of common context and common functions between objects. Moreover, according to norms about visual/functional attributes collected in adults and data from neuroimagery, perceptual experiences seem to be particularly salient for natural kinds (e.g., animals) whereas experiences of use and action are more specific for artefacts (e.g., tools). Therefore, taxonomic categorization based on similarity relations would be more accessible for natural kinds than for artefacts. On the contrary, thematic relations based on contextual and functional relations between objects would be more easily available for manufactured than for natural objects. When asking adults to sort objects into their appropriate superordinate taxonomic categories, Gale, Laws and Foley (2006) already observed faster categorization for living than for non living things. Using a matching task assessing taxonomic and thematic categorization, we also expected faster taxonomic superordinate categorization for natural kinds than for artefacts. We further assume that for thematic relations the reverse pattern should be observed, with faster categorization for artefacts than natural kinds. Previous research in children has demonstrated that contextual cues facilitate artefacts' categorization (Scheuner & Bonthoux, 2004). The present experiment aims at testing the consequences of a differential development of natural and artefacts' concepts through sensori-motor experiences on adults' conceptual organization.

Method

Participants
Forty-eight undergraduate psychology students participated in the present experiment. Participants ranged in age from 17 to 50 years (mean =22 years). Ten additional adults rated the associative strength between pictures.

Materials
Stimuli were 240 black-and-white drawings selected from several picture data bases. Forty-eight items were target pictures, 96 were semantically related to target pictures and 96 were neither semantically nor perceptually related to target pictures.

Table 1: Design used for controlling domain and manipulability across items

Semantic relation	Target domain	Associate domain	Foil domain	Target manipulability
Taxonomic	Artifacts	Artifacts	Artifacts	No
				Yes
	Natural	Natural	Natural	No
				Yes
Thematic	Artifacts	Artifacts	Artifacts	No
				Yes
			Natural	No
				Yes
	Artifacts	Natural	Artifacts	No
				Yes
			Natural	No
				Yes
	Natural	Natural	Natural	No
				Yes
			Artifacts	No
				Yes
	Natural	Artifacts	Natural	No
				yes
			Artifacts	No
				Yes

Half of the target pictures represented natural concepts and half were artefacts concepts. Eleven semantic categories were used: animals, plants, fruit/vegetables, body parts for natural kinds and tools, kitchen utensils, clothes, vehicles, furniture, habitat for artefacts. Domain and manipulability of target pictures, related pictures and non-related pictures were controlled (Table 1). Among the 96 related pictures, 48 were taxonomically related (e.g., squirrel - goat) and 48 were thematically related (e.g., squirrel – hazelnuts). For each target picture, a taxonomic and a thematic associate were selected. Ninety-six triads including a target picture, a related picture (either thematically, Figure 1, or taxonomically related, Figure 2) and a non-related picture were constructed for test trials. Eight additional triads of the same kind involving different semantic categories were elaborated for practice trials. The associative strength between target and related pictures on the one hand, and between target and non-related pictures on the other hand was rated by 10 additional adults on a 10-points scale since several studies have demonstrated that thematic relations are generally more strongly associated than superordinate taxonomic relations (Osborne & Heath, 2003; Pennequin, Fontaine, Bontoux, Scheuner, & Blaye, 2006; Scheuner & Bonthoux, 2004). Moreover, items' difficulty also depends on the difference of associative strength between related and non-related pictures. Therefore a measure of this contrast was obtained for each triad by subtracting the associative strength between the target and the unrelated picture to the associative strength between the target and the related picture. This measure was introduced in the by-items analysis as a covariate. Two lists of 48 triads were elaborated. Each target picture appeared twice, with a taxonomic associate in one list and with a thematic associate in the other.

pictures appeared in the top center of the screen. Related and non-related pictures were presented either in the bottom left or bottom right of the screen, their relative position being counterbalanced across trials. Participants were asked to decide which one of the two bottom pictures was semantically related to the target picture. They were instructed to press either 1 or 2 on the keyboard with their right index and middle finger, 1 for the bottom left picture and 2 for the bottom right picture. They were told to respond as quickly and accurately as possible. The triad was presented until participant's response. Each participant performed 8 practice trials and then underwent the two lists of 48 trials each. The order of lists presentation was counterbalanced between subjects. Reaction times and accuracy were recorded for the 96 experimental trials.

Figure 2: Example of a taxonomic triad with a target picture (a squirrel), a taxonomically related picture (a goat) and a non-related picture (a tyre).

Results

Preliminary analysis

First, mean reaction times and number of errors were calculated for each participant. Three participants who made more than ten errors were removed from the analysis because they were above two standard deviations from the mean number of errors (m = 4,42; SD = 2,52) . Moreover, for each participant, reaction times which were above three standard deviations from the mean reaction time of the participant were removed. With this criterion, from 0.8 to 1.,6 percent of measures were removed from each condition. Finally, 3 items which were globally failed (more than 3 SD from the mean number of errors of the whole set) were also removed. This was not foreseeable since the items' associative strength was relatively high. Thus, the final analysis concerned 45 participants on 93 experimental trials.

Figure 1: Example of a thematic triad with a target picture (a squirrel), a thematically related picture (hazelnuts) and a non-related picture (a cactus).

Procedure

Each participant was tested individually in a darkened quiet room. Triads were displayed on a computer monitor using E-prime software (E-prime Psychology Software Tools Inc., Pittsburgh, USA). Each trial began with a fixation point for 500 ms immediately followed by a picture triad. Target

Main analysis

Participants were correct on most trials (Table 2); analysis of the mean number of errors did not reveal any effect. Anova with semantic relation (taxonomic vs. thematic) and domain (natural things vs. artefacts) as within-subjects factors conducted on mean reaction times indicated a main effect of the kind of semantic relation [$F_1(1,44) = 12,15$; $p< .005$] with faster reaction times for taxonomic relations than for thematic relations. A main effect of domain was also observed [$F_1(1,44) = 5,03$; $p< .05$] with faster reaction times for natural concepts than for artefacts.

Table 2: Means and Standard Deviations for RT and Errors measures as a function of Semantic Relation and Object kinds

Semantic relation	Object kinds	RTs (ms)		% Errors	
		Mean	*SD*	*Mean*	*SD*
Taxonomic	Natural kinds	1343.3	271.6	3.1	4.3
	Artefacts	1455.8	303.2	2.5	3.0
Thematic	Natural kinds	1480.9	289.1	4.1	4.2
	Artefacts	1431.9	262.6	3.0	3.9

More important, the expected interaction between kind of semantic relation and domain was significant in the by-subject analysis [$F_1(1,44) = 52,82$; $p< .001$] as in the by-item analysis [$F_2(1,88) = 7,95$; $p< .01$]. These results are illustrated on Figure 3.

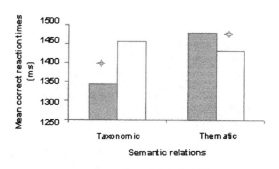

♦ Differences are significant at p< .05

Figure 3 : Mean correct reaction times according to the kind of semantic relation (taxonomic vs. thematic) and the domain (natural kinds vs. artefacts).

Planned comparisons revealed that participants were faster to evaluate taxonomic relations for natural concepts than for artefacts [$F_1(1,44) = 39,51$; $p< .001$ and $F_2(1,88) = 7,35$; $p< .01$]. On the contrary, the by-subject comparison showed that they were faster to recognize thematic relations for artefacts than for natural concepts [$F_1(1,44) = 7,39$; $p< .01$] although this difference did not reach significance in the by-item comparison [$F_2(1,88) = 1,67$; $p = .20$]. Note however that no significant difference was observed between taxonomic and thematic relations for artefacts [$F(1,44)= 1,55$; $p = .22$].

Discussion

Overall, results show a different involvement of taxonomic and thematic semantic relations according to object kinds in adults' conceptual organization. Superordinate taxonomic relations appear more rapidly processed when they concern natural kinds than artefacts whereas thematic relations are more rapidly processed in the case of artefacts.

This pattern can be linked to the differential weighting of visual and functional/contextual features as a function of domain observed in adults' concept studies. Results from property verification tasks using a wide definition of functional properties (functional and associative attributes) indicate that functional/associative attributes are judged more rapidly for artefacts than for natural kinds (Laws, Humber, Ramsey, & McCarthy, 1995; Roll-Carpentier, Bonthoux, & Kalénine, 2006; Ventura, Morais, Brito-Mendes, & Kolinsky, 2005). On the contrary, adults seem to verify more rapidly the visual attributes of natural kinds than the visual attributes of artefacts. This difference regarding the access to visual and functional properties could be due to the predominance of visual or action experiences with natural objects and artefacts. Moreover, as taxonomic relations appear more easily accessible for natural kinds for than for artefacts, our data support the idea that taxonomic organization probably originates from visual similarity relations. Similarly, as thematic relations are more easily accessible for artefacts, our results suggest that thematic organization would be based on functional and contextual relations. Note however that participants were not faster to identify thematic relations for artefacts than for natural kinds. This result is not surprising given that when a wide definition of functional attributes is used, it is frequent that artefacts are not better characterized by functional/associative properties than visual properties (Cree & McRae, 2003; Garrard et al., 2001; Marques, 2002)

Our results are also consistent with previous data from studies in children as young as 3 that demonstrate a various implication of similarity and contextual relations in the formation of natural and artefacts concepts (Bonthoux, Scheuner, & Roll, 2003; Kalénine & Bonthoux, 2006; Scheuner & Bonthoux, 2004). In a longitudinal study between 3 and 4-year-olds (Scheuner & Bonthoux, 2004), children were asked to sort objects of the same kind. Taxonomically related objects proposed could share a perceptual link, a contextual link, both links or neither a perceptual nor a contextual link. Results showed that children relied more on perceptual cues to sort natural kinds in comparison to artefacts, this tendency increasing with age. On the contrary, children as they grow up appeared to rely more on contextual information in the case of artefacts than natural kinds. In addition, superordinate taxonomic categorization of natural and artefacts concepts appear to vary according to children's sensibility to similarity vs. contextual relations. In one study in 3-year-olds (Kalénine & Bonthoux, 2006) a first session was designed to evaluate children's sensitivity to perceptual similarity vs. contextual relations. In this session, children were asked to choose between 3 pictures (a basic-level taxonomic match, e.g., a poodle; a thematic match, e.g., a bone and a foil, e.g., a lamp) the one that "goes best" with a target picture (e.g., a German shepherd). Following this session, children were divided in two groups according to their greater sensitivity to perceptual similarity or contextual relations. A superordinate taxonomic matching task was proposed in a second session. Performance in this task according to object kinds was modulated by children's sensitivity. The advantage observed for natural concepts' categorization was greater for children most sensitive to perceptual similarity relations than for children most sensitive to contextual relations. Our results are consistent with the idea that adults' conceptual organization may result from the way they used to interact and process objects since their younger age. Conceptual development should be therefore considered in a pluralistic perspective (Lautrey, 2003) with several pathways leading to the construction of categories, their implication varying according to individuals, situations and particularly object kinds. Specifically, natural concepts would principally emerge from perceptual relations between objects in relation to the preponderance of perceptual experiences with natural kinds. On the contrary, artefacts' concepts would derive from contextual and functional relations between objects as action and use dominate our experiences with artefacts. The assumption that previous sensori-motor experiences play a role in the semantic of objects could enlighten several cases of atypical category-specific deficits in neuropsychology. Categories such as instruments, body parts or monuments appear altered with either living things or non-livings things. Thus it would be relevant to focus on the way these particular objects are experienced and which sensori-motor modalities are mainly involved in their processing to more precisely understand such deficits. Data from neuroimagery also support this interpretation. For example, when adults see artefacts (Chao & Martin, 2000; Creem-Regehr & Lee, 2005) or recall semantic information about artefacts (Boronat et al., 2005), neural regions classically involved in the real use of objects are recruited. In this perspective, the neural correlates of taxonomic and thematic relations processing according to domains would need further investigations. Even if a broad semantic network should be commonly activated in any case, sensori-motor regions implicated in object action and perception may differently be involved as a function of the kind of semantic relation, i.e., taxonomic and thematic, and the kind of objects.

Acknowledgments

This research was supported by grants from the University Pierre Mendes France of Grenoble and the Centre National de la Recherche Scientifique, Authors thank the students who participated in these studies.

References

Allport, D. A. (1985). Distributed memory, modular subsystems and dysphagia. In S. K. Newman & R. Epstein (Eds.), *Current perspectives in dysphagia*. Edinburgh: Churchill Livingstone.

Barsalou, L. W. (1999). Perceptual symbol systems. *Behavioral and Brain Sciences, 22*(4), 577-609.

Barsalou, L. W. (2005). Abstraction as dynamic interpretation in perceptual symbol systems. In L. Gershkoff-Stowe & D. Rakison (Eds.), *Building object categories in developmental time*. Majwah, NJ: Erlbaum.

Bonthoux, F., Scheuner, N., & Roll, N. (2003). Des modes de construction des catégories différenciés selon le domaine. Eléments de réponse chez l'enfant et l'adulte âgé. *Cogntion, Brain, Behavior, 7*, 91-109.

Boronat, C. B., Buxbaum, L. J., Coslett, H. B., Tang, K., Saffran, E. M., Kimberg, D. Y., et al. (2005). Distinctions between manipulation and function knowledge of objects: evidence from functional magnetic resonance imaging. *Cognitive Brain Research, 23*(2-3), 361-373.

Buxbaum, L. J., & Saffran, E. M. (2002). Knowledge of object manipulation and object function: dissociations in apraxic and nonapraxic subjects. *Brain and Language, 82*(2), 179-199.

Chao, L. L., & Martin, A. (2000). Representation of manipulable man-made objects in the dorsal stream. *Neuroimage, 12*(4), 478-484.

Cree, G. S., & McRae, K. (2003). Analyzing the factors underlying the structure and computation of the meaning of chipmunk, cherry, chisel, cheese, and cello (and many other such concrete nouns). *Journal of Experimental Psychology: General, 132*(2), 163-201.

Creem-Regehr, S. H., & Lee, J. N. (2005). Neural representations of graspable objects: are tools special? *Cognitive Brain Research, 22*(3), 457-469.

Davidoff, J., & Roberson, D. (2004). Preserved thematic and impaired taxonomic categorisation: a case study. *Language and cognitive processes, 19*(1), 137-174.

Deák, G. O. (2003). Categorization and concept learning. In J. W. Guthrie (Ed.), *Encyclopedia of Education, 2nd Ed.* New York: Macmillan.

Devlin, J. T., Gonnerman, L. M., Andersen, E. S., & Seidenberg, M. S. (1998). Category-specific semantic deficits in focal and widespread brain damage: a computational account. *Journal of Cognitive Neuroscience, 10*(1), 77-94.

Farah, M. J., & McClelland, J. L. (1991). A computational model of semantic memory impairment: modality specificity and emergent category specificity. *Journal of Expérimental Psychology: General, 120*(4), 339-357.

Gale, T. M., Laws, K. R., & Foley, K. (2006). Crowded and sparse domains in object recognition: Consequences for categorization and naming. *Brain and Cognition, 60*(2), 139-145.

Garrard, P., Lambon Ralph, M. A., Hodges, J. R., & Patterson, K. (2001). Prototypicality, distinctiveness and intercorrelation: Analyses of the semantic attributes of living and non living concepts. *Cognitive Neuropsychology, 18*(2), 125-174.

Gerlach, C., Law, I., & Paulson, O. B. (2002). When action turns into words. Activation of motor-based knowledge during categorization of manipulable objects. *Journal of Cognitive Neuroscience, 14*(8), 1230-1239.

Kalénine, S., & Bonthoux, F. (2006). The formation of living and non-living superordinate concepts as a function of individual differences. *Current Psychology Letters, 19*(2).

Lautrey, J. (2003). A pluralistic approach to cognitive differenciation and development. In R. Sternberg (Ed.), *Models of intelligence: International perspectives* (pp. 117-131). Washington, DC: A.P.A. Press.

Laws, K. R., Humber, S. A., Ramsey, D. J. C., & McCarthy, R. A. (1995). Probing sensory and associative semantics for animals and objects in normal subjects. *Memory, 3*(3/4), 397-408.

Lin, E. L., & Murphy, G. L. (2001). Thematic relations in adults' concepts. *Journal of Experimental Psychology General, 130*(1), 3-28.

Marques, J. F. (2002). Names, concepts, features and the living/nonliving things dissociation. *Cognition, 85*(3), 251-275.

Marques, J. F. (2006). Specialization and semantic organization: evidence for multiple semantics linked to sensory modalities. *Memory and Cognition, 34*(1), 60-67.

Martin, A. (2007). The representation of object concepts in brain. *Annual Review of Psychology, 58*.

McRae, K., & Cree, G. S. (2002). Factors underlying category-specific semantic deficits. In E. M. E. Forde & G. W. Humphreys (Eds.), *Category-Specificity in Brain and Mind* (pp. pp. 211-249). East Sussex: UK: Psychology Press.

Murphy, G. L. (2001). Causes of taxonomic sorting by adults: a test of the thematic-to-taxonomic shift. *Psychonomic Bulletin and Review, 8*(4), 834-839.

Myung, J.-Y., Blumstein, S. E., & Sedivy, J. C. (2006). Playing on the typewriter, typing on the panio: Manipulation knowledge of objects. *Cognition, 98*(3), 223-243.

Osborne, J. G., & Heath, J. (2003). Predicting taxonomic and thematic relational responding. *The Analysis of Verbal Behavior, 19*, 55-89.

Pecher, D., Zeelenberg, R., & Barsalou, L. W. (2003). Verifying different-modality properties for concepts produces switching costs. *Psychol Sci, 14*(2), 119-124.

Pecher, D., Zeelenberg, R., & Barsalou, L. W. (2004). Sensorimotor simulations underlie conceptual representations: modality-specific effects of prior activation. *Psychon Bull Rev, 11*(1), 164-167.

Pennequin, V., Fontaine, R., Bontoux, F., Scheuner, N., & Blaye, A. (2006). Categorization deficit in old age, reality or artefact ? *Journal of Adult Development, 13*, 1-9.

Rakison, D. (2005). The perceptual to conceptual shift in infancy and early childhood: a surface or deep distinction. In L. Gershkoff-Stowe & D. Rakison (Eds.), *Building object categories in developmental time*. Mahwah, NJ: Erlbaum.

Roll-Carpentier, N., Bonthoux, F., & Kalénine, S. (2006). Vieillissement de l'organisation conceptuelle : accès aux propriétés des objets naturels et fabriqués. *L'année Psychologique, 106*, 27-47.

Scheuner, N., & Bonthoux, F. (2004). La construction des catégories surordonnées chez l'enfant : utilisation différentielle des indices perceptifs et contextuels selon le domaine. *Bulletin de Psychologie, 57*(469), 99-103.

Simmons, K., & Barsalou, L. W. (2003). The similarity-in-topography principle: Reconciling theories on conceptual deficits. *Cognitive Neuropsychology, 20*, 451-486.

Smiley, S. S., & Brown, A. L. (1979). Conceptual preference fot thematic ot taxonomic relations : A nonmonotonic age trend from preschool to old age. *Journal of Experimental Child Psychology, 28*, 249-257.

Smith, L. B. (2005). Emerging ideas about categories. In L. Gershkoff-Stowe & D. Rakison (Eds.), *Building object categories in developmental time*. Majwah, NJ: Erlbaum.

Stanfield, R. A., & Zwaan, R. A. (2001). The effect of implied orientation derived from verbal context on picture recognition. *Psychological Science, 12*(2), 153-156.

Ventura, P., Morais, J., Brito-Mendes, C., & Kolinsky, R. (2005). The mental representation of living and nonliving things: differential weighting and interactivity of sensorial and non-sensorial features. *Memory, 13*(2), 124-147.

Zwaan, R. A., Stanfield, R. A., & Yaxley, R. H. (2002). Language comprehenders mentally represent the shapes of objects. *Psychological Science, 13*(2), 168-171.

'Emeralds are expensive because they are rare': Plausibility of Property Explanations

Daniel Heussen (D.Heussen@city.ac.uk)
James A. Hampton (J.A.Hampton@city.ac.uk)
Department of Psychology, Northampton Square
London, EC1V 0HB UK

Abstract

Research on explanation has primarily focused on event explanations, overlooking how we explain properties. A qualitative study revealed that when people explained a property of an entity, they regularly referred to another property to provide an explanation. Why axes are dangerous was explained by their property of being sharp. The present study looked at what affects the relative plausibility of such explanations. A set of 224 explanations of the form 'x has p because it has q' were judged for plausibility. Measures of counterfactual relations between the two properties (i.e. likelihood of having p without q), co-occurrence and mutability of each property, as well as a measure of conceptual coherence based on network diagrams (Sloman, Love & Ahn, 1998) were used in a regression analysis to predict plausibility. Conceptual coherence followed by counterfactuals were the strongest predictors of plausibility in a model explaining almost 56% of the variance in plausibility of property explanations.

Introduction

Explanations come in a range of different forms and guises. They answer why-questions about people's behavior, provide accounts of physical processes and shed light on the occurrence of events. The diversity of explanation has led some to suggest that explanations might not constitute a uniform phenomenon (Keil & Wilson, 2000).

Despite this diversity of explanations, theoretical and empirical research on explanation has focused on events, i.e. explanations of why a particular event occurred. For instance, Hempel's deductive nomological model was only intended to cover singular events as remarked in a footnote in Hempel and Oppenheim's original paper:

> "Our analysis will be restricted to the explanation of particular events, i.e. to the case where the explanandum, E, is a singular sentence." (Hempel & Oppenheim, 1948, p.159)

Similarly Salmon's (1998) and Lewis's (1986) causal theories of explanation refer to the causal history of an event in terms of a succession of events that constitute its explanation.

Theories in psychology like attribution theory (Ajzen & Fishbein, 1975; Heider, 1958, Hilton & Slugoski, 1986) and its modern derivatives in the form of Bayes Nets (Glymour, 2000) and Causal Power Theory (Cheng, 1997) mirrored this emphasis on events in theorizing about explanations.

This preoccupation with events has left a gap in the literature on how we understand, judge and generate explanations of properties.

Property Explanations

Properties are attributes, features and characteristics of things. In Philosophy there is an ongoing debate about the nature of properties, whether they exist without being instantiated and whether they can do any explanatory work at all (Swoyer, 1996). However, here the focus was on how people understand and judge explanations of properties. We take properties to be any descriptive phrase that people consider to apply generally to an object or natural kind. In fact, the properties used here were all sampled from a database based on a feature generation task for a range of different concepts (Cree & McRae, 2003). As a consequence, these properties are mostly enduring characteristics that generally apply to the class of things in question. In addition superordinate category membership was also considered a property of the entities.

Explanations of properties are ubiquitous in everyday life. We wonder why structurally complex organisms are mostly diploid, why flat pack assembly instructions have to be so complicated and why most leading conservative politicians are so badly dressed. Questions about properties sometimes seem more fundamental than questions about events. They are about the characteristics of things that endure and sometimes define or make the entity what it is. They ask about the system of the entity, the underlying nature and the interplay of properties and therefore seem less likely to be explicable circumstantially. As the focus of research on explanation has so far been on events, it is of considerable interest to explore how we understand and judge explanations of properties.

In this paper the focus was on a particular type of explanation of properties. In an exploratory study we found that when people were asked to generate an explanation for a property of an object they regularly referred to another property of that object to provide the explanation. For instance, participants consistently refer to the rarity of emeralds when asked to explain why they are expensive. Property explanations commonly took the following form:

Xs have p because they have q

where 'p' and 'q' are two properties of the concept 'X'. The natural question that arose was what determines whether 'q' is a good explanans for 'p' in any given X. That is the question that we address in this paper.

Study

The overall aim of our study was to investigate the determinants of plausibility in property explanations. Regression analysis was used to establish the relative contribution of a range of predictors to the plausibility of property explanations. The predictors consisted of measures of causal, statistical and local coherence relations between properties and a global measure of feature centrality for individual properties. Pairs of properties were selected and each property pair was tested in both directions for each measure. This enabled us to test whether property explanations exhibit symmetry; i.e. where two properties are equally able to explain one another. For instance, do people judge 'Emeralds are expensive because they are rare' as equally plausible as 'Emeralds are rare because they are expensive'. Similarly the causal, statistical and dependence relations were measured in both directions.

Method

Materials A sample of 28 natural kind and 28 artifact concepts was randomly drawn from Cree and McRae's (2003) database. Using the same database two properties for each concept were drawn at random and two additional properties were selected so that roughly equal numbers of property types (see Wu & Barsalou's, 2002 classification) were present in each of the two domains.

The four properties per concept were paired up to create two pairs such that at least one of the resulting explanations seemed plausible to the experimenter. For instance the four properties 'having a siren', 'being a vehicle', 'being large' and 'being used for emergency' for the concept 'Ambulance' could be paired up in three different ways. The relation between 'having a siren' and 'being used for emergency' seemed most likely to produce a plausible explanation, and consequently this pairing was adopted.

Each pair of properties was used to generate two explanations (e.g. "Axes are dangerous because they are sharp." vs. "Axes are sharp because they are dangerous.") resulting in four explanations per concept. The exact same principal applied to co-occurrence judgments (e.g. "Of all man-made things that are dangerous, what percentage is also sharp?" vs. "Of all man-made things that are sharp, what percentage is also dangerous?") and counterfactuals (e.g. "If axes were not dangerous, would they be sharp?" vs. "If axes were not sharp, would they be dangerous?").

Mutability was judged for each property individually (e.g. "How difficult is it to imagine axes that are not dangerous?" vs. "How difficult is it to imagine axes that are not sharp?"). Dependence was measured by network diagrams consisting of the concept with all four properties displayed. Participants saw all 56 concepts and were asked to draw arrows between the properties of a concept indicating the strength of the dependence by using different colors. Based on pilot work, participants were asked to consider carefully the direction of the dependence, and only to draw bidirectional arrows if they were convinced that they applied. (see Figure 1; a solid line represents the strongest dependence relation, a dotted line represents weakest dependence). Arrows are drawn from one property to a

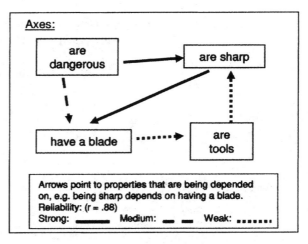

Figure 1. Dependence Net Diagrams

property that it depends on. The full set of measures is illustrated in Figure 2.

Participants A total of 386 participants were recruited for the five different measures. The three paper-based measures were collected at City University London with a total of 80 participants each for co-occurrence and plausibility judgments and 21 for the dependence measure. The sample size was 109 and 96 for counterfactuals and mutability respectively. The whole sample consisted of University undergraduate and postgraduate students with an average age of 22 years. The majority (88%) were native English speakers with the remainder having a high command of English as their second language.

Procedure & Design The complete set of 224 items was divided into four subsets, each of which contained one of the four explanations per concept. Each questionnaire therefore contained 56 target items with an additional four warm-up items at the beginning of each questionnaire. Two different random orders of items were used for each questionnaire. Each subset and each measure was completed by different groups of participants. Counterfactuals and mutability were collected online using a website and recruitment took place via email. The paper-based questionnaires were collected in classrooms. For each measure, participants had the chance to win a £20 voucher from Amazon as an incentive to participate.

Results

All measures had a Cronbach Alpha between .88 and .94 (see figure 2). The data were averaged across participants for each of the measures and the analyses were carried out on the individual items. All variables apart from the dependence measure were roughly normally distributed. Dependence was consequently transformed by taking the square root of its values. In the analyses that follow the transformed version of both dependence measures were used.

```
                Concept: Axes
        Property p: dangerous  Property q: sharp
Plausibility Judgments (p > q): X has p because it has q
   How plausible is the explanation?        {r = .88 - .92}*
   Axes are dangerous because they are sharp.
Dependence (p>q)          p depends on q        {r = .88}
   For axes being dangerous depends on being sharp.
Dependence (q>p)          q depends on p
   For axes being sharp depends on being dangerous.
Counterfactuals (¬ p):       If not p then q?    {r = .90 - .95}
   If axes were not dangerous would they be sharp?
Counterfactuals (¬ q):       If not q then p?
   If axes were not sharp would they be dangerous?
Co-occurrence (%q in p):    Percentage of q in p  {r = .90 - .93}
   Of all man-made things that are dangerous,
   what percentage is sharp?
Co-occurrence (%p in q):    Percentage of p in q
   Of all man-made things that are sharp,
   what percentage is dangerous?
Mutability (mu - p):        Mutability of p       {r = .93 - .94}
   How difficult is it to imagine axes that are not dangerous?
Mutability (mu - q):        Mutability of q
   How difficult is it to imagine axes that are not sharp?
(*Numbers in brackets indicate reliability range for each measure across four stimuli sets)
```

Figure 2. Summary of all Measures

First we compared the average scores across domains (artifact vs. natural kind) on each of the measures using a one-way multivariate analysis of variance. Results of evaluation of assumptions of normality, homogeneity of variance-covariance matrices, linearity and multi-collinearity were satisfactory.

The combined dependent measures were significantly affected by domain, $F(5, 218) = 6.63$, $p < .001$. Although significant, the results only showed a small association between domain and the combined dependent variables, partial $^2 = .13$, reflecting the small effective difference between the two domains across the different measures.

In univariate ANOVAs of each measure only plausibility ($F(1, 222) = 20.03$, $p < .001$) and counterfactuals ($F(1, 222) = 12.75$, $p < .001$) showed significant differences between the two domains. Pairs of artifact properties produced both more plausible explanations and were more counterfactually dependent on each other than those of natural kinds (see Table 1).

Property Explanations across Property Types. Table 2 provides frequencies of plausible explanations (items that were rated above 5 on a 10-point scale for plausibility) broken down by the different property types for the two positions in the explanation and the two domains.

Table 1: Domain Differences with Mean and (Standard Deviation) for each Measure.

	Natural Kind		Artifact	
Plausibility	4.11	(1.40)	5.09	(1.80)
Dependence	0.64	(0.64)	0.74	(0.65)
Counterfactuals	2.17	(0.75)	2.58	(0.94)
Mutability	5.76	(1.80)	5.58	(2.00)
Co-occurrence	48.61	(18.0)	49.93	(21.0)

Starting with natural kinds we can see that out of the 24 plausible explanations 10 (42%) had a superordinate property in the 'q'-position. A further 6 explanations consisted of a superordinate property in the 'p'-position resulting in two thirds of all plausible property explanations for natural kinds containing a superordinate in either the 'p' or the 'q'-position.

For artifacts, the 52 plausible explanations were more evenly distributed across the different property types with components (44.2%) and functions (25%) being the most strongly represented property types in 'q'-position with a similar distribution for the 'p'-position.

However, taking the base rate of the different property types into account revealed a different picture. Figure 3 represents the proportion of plausible explanations over the total number of explanations for each property type. Of all explanations that contained a function in 'q'-position 86% were plausible, compared with only 47% of property explanations containing a component in q position. Thus despite the range of property types in plausible explanations for artifacts, taking the base rate of the different property types into account there was a clear dominance of functional properties as explanations for artifacts.

Correlation and Regression The pattern of correlations was virtually the same in each domain in terms of rank order and absolute strengths. Regression models including all predictors for the two domains were compared by calculating the difference in regression coefficients across domain. Comparing all significant predictors in either domain with their counterpart in the other domain showed no differences greater than two standard errors. In addition, a principle components analysis showed the same pattern of loadings for the two domains. Both domains produced a two factor solution with artifacts showing smaller cross-loadings than natural kinds. Thus, in what follows the items were collapsed across domains.

Table 2: Distribution of property type pairing across domains and position.

Natural Kind

'p' – position	Component	Function	Superordinate	Other	Total 'p'
Component	0	0	6	2	33%
Functional	3	0	0	2	21%
Superordinate	3	0	0	3	25%
Other	1	0	4	0	21%
Total 'q':	29%	0%	42%	29%	24

Artifact

'p' - position	Component	Function	Superordinate	Other	Total 'p'
Component	10	7	3	4	46%
Functional	8	0	1	3	23%
Superordinate	4	1	0	0	10%
Other	1	5	3	2	21%
Total 'q':	44%	25%	13%	17%	52

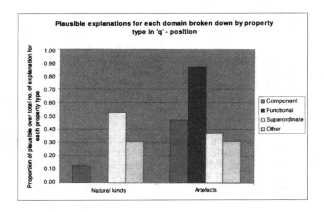

Figure 3. Plausible explanation over total no. of explanations by domain and property type

Table 3 shows the correlations between plausibility and the significant predictors. In line with our predictions both dependence (p>q) (r = .625) and counterfactual (¬q) (r = .567) were strongly correlated with plausibility (p>q). Mutability (mu-q) (r = .319) and co-occurrence (%p in q) (r = .305) were only moderately correlated with plausibility. Interestingly the other co-occurrence measure (%q in p) (r = .372) had just as strong a correlation with plausibility as its converse. For example, "axes are dangerous because they are sharp" is rendered more plausible as an explanation if a high percentage of dangerous things tend to be sharp (%q in p), as well as if a high percentage of sharp things tend to be dangerous (%p in q)

In the instructions for the dependence diagrams participants were asked to choose and only draw the stronger direction of the two dependence relations. As a result the two complement dependence measures showed a small but significant negative correlation (r = -.132, p < .05). For all the other predictors there were no significant correlations between the two complements. The only other correlation among complements that was significant

was for plausibility (r = .441, p < .001) indicating that many property explanations work in both directions.

Suprisingly we found that a number of explanations were equally plausible in both directions. For instance, 'Whistles are used for alerting because they are loud' was as plausible as 'Whistles are loud because they are used for alerting.' This symmetry was more prominent for artifacts. Nevertheless some natural kind explanations also showed symmetry; (e.g.) 'Carrots are roots because they are found underground' and 'Carrots are found underground because they are roots.'

The overall aim of the study was to establish a model to predict plausibility judgments of these property explanations. A regression using backwards elimination with plausibility (p>q) as dependent variable and each of the two variables for counterfactuals, co-occurrence, mutability and dependence as predictors was carried out.

Dependence (p>q) turned out to be the strongest predictor of plausibility (p>q) followed by the equally strong counterfactuals (¬q) and (¬p) and then mutability-q. Table 3 provides the results for the final regression model. Overall the model predicted 56% of variance in plausibility judgments. Neither of the two co-occurrence measures entered the model despite their moderate positive correlations with plausibility. Interestingly despite the weak correlations with plausibility both complement measures of dependence (q>p) and counterfactuals (¬p) entered the model. Dependence (p>q) turned out to be the strongest predictor of plausibility (p>q) followed by the equally strong counterfactuals (¬q) and (¬p) and then mutability-q. Table 3 provides the results for the final regression model arrived at by backwards elimination. Overall the model predicted 56% of variance in plausibility judgments. Neither of the two co-occurrence measures entered the model despite their moderate positive correlations with plausibility. Interestingly despite the weak correlations with plausibility both complement measures of dependence (q>p) and counterfactuals (¬p) entered the model.

Table 3: Regression Table for the final model with plausibility as dependent variable.

	Plausibility (p>q)	Dependence (p>q)	Counterfactual (¬p)	Counterfactual (¬q)	Dependence (q>p)	Mutability -q	B	Beta
Dependence (p>q)	0.625**						2.010	.478
Counterfactual (¬p)	0.299**	-0.004					.474	.241
Counterfactual (¬q)	0.567**	0.546**	0.094				.441	.224
Dependence (q>p)	0.182**	-0.132*	0.546**	-0.004			.522	.124
Mutability-q	-0.319**	-0.281**	0.194**	-0.396**	0.065		-.133	-.151
Mean	4.59	.69	2.37	2.37	.69	5.67	R²	**.569**
StD.	1.70	.64	.41	.41	.64	1.94	Adj. R²	**.559**

**. Correlation is significant at the 0.01 level (2-tailed).

*. Correlation is significant at the 0.05 level (2-tailed).

A further point to note was that, despite dependence having the lowest Cronbach alpha with .88, it turned out to have the greatest influence on plausibility. In theory two equally strong predictors would show differential influence on the dependent variable as a result of their reliability with the variable with higher reliability showing a stronger influence. Thus, despite the slight underestimation of the influence of dependence (p>q) on plausibility, it turned out to be the strongest predictor in this model. However the correlation between dependence (p>q) and plausibility (p>q) (r = .625) was not significantly different from the correlation between counterfactual (¬q) and plausibility (p>q) (r = .567), which means that counterfactual (¬q) could have equally turned out to be the strongest predictor. Thus no strong claims can be made here about the dominance of one of the two measures over the other.

Discussion

Property explanations were found to be more plausible for artifacts than for natural kinds. For natural kinds, plausible property explanations contained mostly superordinates in either the 'p' or the 'q'-position of the explanation. In contrast for artifacts the dominant property type in plausible explanations was function. Plausibility judgments of some property explanations in both domains showed symmetry, i.e. 'p' and 'q' were equally capable of explaining one another. In the regression, dependence (p>q) followed by both counterfactual measures turned out to be the strongest predictor of plausibility. However, as the correlations of dependence (p>q) with plausibility did not significantly differ from the correlation of counterfactual (¬q) with plausibility, no strong claims can be made about the superiority of dependence over counterfactuals as predictors of plausibility.

The domain difference for plausibility and for counterfactuals between living natural kinds and man-made artifacts was significant. Despite the effect being rather small, artifacts had twice as many property explanations with high plausibility ratings as did natural kinds. One attempt to explain the domain difference might be by reference to the predominant property types in plausible explanations. Most of the plausible explanations for natural kinds contained a superordinate in either the 'p' or the 'q'-position of the explanation, whereas for artifacts a range of property types were explanatory. Thus, if natural kind property explanations were constrained by having to contain a superordinate in order to be plausible and only a fifth of all the explanations in our item pool contained a superordinate then the proportion of plausible explanations for natural kinds is inevitably smaller than that for artifacts.

This raises the question of why superordinates are the only explanatory property for natural kinds. Intuitively one might say that the reason why living natural kinds have the properties they have, is because of some evolutionary processes that brought them about.[1] Only superordinates might be considered to be associated with evolutionary processes and thus have explanatory value. Apart from that,

properties in and of themselves don't refer to or instantiate evolutionary processes that could be explanatory, therefore property explanations for natural kinds were less plausible overall.

Furthermore, comparing the two domains, functions play a large explanatory role for artifacts, whereas for natural kinds, they are not explanatory at all (McLaughlin, 2000). The only functional properties generated for natural kinds in Cree and McRae's (2003) database were functions that the entity had for humans, e.g. 'horses are used for pulling things.' But these kinds of functional properties do not readily explain why for instance the horse has certain features. Thus in the present study, functions of natural kinds were not explanatory.

One might object that a human heart is a natural kind and that it clearly has a function that has explanatory power for its features. However this objection only holds if the natural kind is part of a self-reproducing system, where the function provides an evolutionary advantage and thereby explains its existence (McLaughlin, 2000). In the present case all natural kinds were complete entities, for which participants did not generate functions as their properties (Cree & McRae, 2003).

Artifacts conversely do have functions. Their existence seems to be based on the functions they are or were meant to perform. Most of their properties can be explained by reference to their intended function. Thus, for artifacts, having both superordinates and functions as explanatory properties resulted in the overall observed domain difference.

But why are functions so explanatory for artifacts and superordinates so explanatory for natural kinds? Psychological essentialism (Medin & Ortony, 1989) may provide an account for both. Psychological essentialism is the view that we represent things in the world as having essences which bring about their properties and make the entities what they are. For natural kinds, superordinate properties are the most likely candidates to stand in for essential properties and therefore are most able to explain surface features of natural kinds.

One view argues that for artifacts that intended functions constitute their essences (Bloom, 1996). The essential features bring about the non-essential properties in an entity and as a result are explanatory for them.

Another view might simply be that functions in artifacts and superordinates in natural kinds constitute a common cause structure for their properties, which doesn't rely on the idea of essences. The present study though was not equipped to distinguish between these two possibilities. Whether or not we hold the stronger view of psychological essentialism, what we found was that some kind of common cause structure underlies plausibility judgments for property explanations. The most likely candidates for these common causes were superordinates for natural kinds and functions for artifacts.

A surprising finding made in this study was the symmetry that some of the explanations exhibited. If property explanations are predominantly based on causal relations as is thought to be the case for event explanations, then these explanations should not exhibit symmetry because causal

---

[1] Our sample of items only contained living natural kinds.

relations are asymmetrical (Salmon, 1998). One view might be that property explanations are not based on causal relations between the two properties and therefore are able to exhibit symmetry, which would undermine any account that mainly relies on causal relations (Sloman, 2005). However correlations between the symmetry of plausibility and the symmetry of counterfactuals were not significant, suggesting that for some items that were equally plausible in both directions, counterfactual judgments were only high in one direction.

Another account of the symmetry might be that one of the directions is plausible in a diagnostic rather than explanatory way. "Flamingos are birds because they have wings" might be understood as 'I can tell that flamingos are birds because they have wings.' This may be a plausible account for natural kinds involving superordinates, however it would not explain the symmetry of artifact items like: "Sofas have cushions because they are used for relaxing." Future studies will have to address this distinctive feature of property explanations.

The regression suggested that the best way to model plausibility of property explanations was in the form of dependence net diagrams that capture the local aspect of conceptual coherence. Mutability in contrast captures the more global aspect of coherence by measuring the centrality of a property to its concept. The combined finding of the strong influence of dependence and the lack of influence of mutability on plausibility suggests that the local aspect of conceptual coherence is more important for plausibility judgments than the global.

The present results are mostly in line with Thagard and Verbeurgt's (1998) view of coherence as a constraint satisfaction model. In their view concepts are coherent sets of properties. Coherence depends on the relations between these properties. Certain relations might then be seen to provide stronger constraints than others. As in Quine's (1960) idea of a coherent net of knowledge, certain properties are more difficult to remove from our conception of a concept because a number of other properties stand in strong constraint relations to them. They constitute local coherence constraints. Other properties of the same concept might not depend on any of these properties and may be part of their own local coherence net. Coherence under this view is a net of pair-wise constraint relations with some parts that are more tightly connected and others more loosely.

This view provides an explanation for why conceptual coherence was so much more influential when measured as pair-wise dependence rather than as mutability. According to Sloman et al. (1998) dependence is a very general and basic notion. "Every directional, semantic relation between features can be treated as a generic dependency relation." (Sloman et al., 1998, p. 204). Thus, when judging dependence, people are able to form a general impression that encompasses causal, logical or any other type of relation between the properties. With this view of dependence in place, we can see that judgments of dependence would incorporate the other measure of counterfactuals, co-occurrence and mutability, so that the dominance of dependence as a predictor of plausibility would follow directly. Future study will have to address

both the symmetry and the domain difference in plausibility of property explanations.

References

Ajzen, I., & Fishbein, M. (1975). A bayesian analysis of attribution processes. *Psychological Bulletin, 82*, 261–277.

Bloom, P. (1996). Intention, history, and artifact concepts. *Cognition, 60*, 1–29.

Cheng, P. W. (1997). From covariation to causation: A causal power theory. *Psychological Review, 104 (2)*, 367–405.

Cree, G., & McRae, K. (2003). Analyzing the factors underlying the structure and computation of the meaning of chipmunk, cherry, chisel, cheese, and cello (and many other such concrete nouns). *Journal of Experimental Psychology: General, 132*, 163–201.

Glymour, C. (2000). Bayes nets as psychological models. In F. Keil & R. Wilson (Eds.), *Explanation and Cognition*. MIT Press.

Heider, F. (1958, reprinted 1983). *The psychology of interpersonal relations*. NJ, US: Lawrence Erlbaum Associates.

Hempel, C., & Oppenheim, P. (1948). Studies in the logic of explanation. *Philosophy of Science, 15*, 135–175.

Hilton, D. J., & Slugoski, B. R. (1986). Knowledge-based causal attribution - The abnormal conditions focus model. *Psychological Review, 93 (1)*, 75–88.

Keil, F., & Wilson, R. (2000). Explaining explanation. In F. Keil & R. Wilson (Eds.), *Explanation and Cognition*. MIT Press.

Lewis, D. (1986a). Causal explanation. In D.-H. Ruben (Ed.), *Explanation*. Oxford, UK: Oxford University Press.

McLaughlin, P. (2000). *What functions explain: Functional explanations and self-reproducing systems*. Cambridge University Press.

Medin, D., & Ortony, A. (1989). Psychological essentialism. In S. Vosniadou and A. Ortony (Eds.), *Similarity and analogical reasoning*. Cambridge University Press.

Quine, W. (1960). *Word and object*. MIT Press.

Salmon, W. C. (1998). *Causality and explanation*. Oxford University Press.

Sloman, S. A. (2005). *Causal Models*. MIT Press.

Sloman, S. A., Love, B. C., & Ahn, W.-k. (1998). Feature centrality and conceptual coherence. *Cognitive Science, 22 (2)*, 189–228.

Swoyer, C. (1996). Theories of Properties: From Plenitude to Paucity, *Philosophical Perspectives, 10*; 243-264.

Thagard, P., & Verbeurgt, K. (1998). Coherence as constraint satisfaction. *Cognitive Science, 22 (1)*, 1–24.

Wu, L. L., & Barsalou, L. W. (2002). Grounding concepts in perceptual simulation: Evidence from property generation. Manuscript submitted for publication.

A flow-of-conversation plays a role: Examining line-of-regard of young children and adults in a discrepant labeling situation

Harumi Kobayashi (h-koba@i.dendai.ac.jp)
Social Informatics, Graduate School, Tokyo Denki University
Saitama, 350-0394 JPN

Tetsuya Yasuda
Department of General Education, School of Science and Engineering, Tokyo Denki University
Saitama, 350-0394 JPN

Abstract

Previous studies demonstrated that young children are sensitive to the referential intentions of others and readily relate a novel label to an intended novel object. However, the movement of child's line-of-regard in establishing joint attention has rarely been closely examined. In the present study, 15 2- and 14 4-year-olds and 35 adults were videotaped in a discrepant labeling paradigm, or the experimenter looked at an object and said the novel label, "Oh, muta!" when the participant was concentrated on playing with a different object for more than 10 seconds. The participants' line-of-regards were examined in a frame-by-frame method. The results showed that a substantial ratio of 2-year-olds (40%) looked at the other object immediately after hearing the novel word without checking the experimenter's line-of-regard. More than half (55%) of the 4-year-olds and many of the adults (69%) similarly looked at the other object without checking the experimenter's line-of-regard. We interpreted this result that those children and adults who directly looked at the other object made a correct inference of the intended object considering the flow of conversation. They might have thought that when the experimenter said "Oh, muta!" she must be focusing on the other object rather than the object the participant was already focused on for more than 10 seconds.

Introduction

Infants properly follow adults' gaze direction (Brooks & Meltzoff, 2002; Moll & Tomasello, 2004). Infants also have an ability to actively consult cues that speakers provide to know the reference of their utterances (Golinkoff, & Hirsh-Pasek, 1999; Hirsh-Pasek, Golinkoff, & Hollich, 2000). Among different cues for word learning, cues of adults' social intent seem to be well established. For example, Hollich, Hirsh-Pasek, and Golinkoff (2000) examined the effects of competing perceptual and social cues on word learning in 12-, 19-, and 24-month-olds. Children were presented with novel objects, one interesting and one boring, and given the opportunity to explore each one. Then the objects were placed on the board and the experimenter enthusiastically looked at, pointed to, and labeled either the interesting (coincident) or boring (conflict) object. Children were later tested to choose the referent of the novel object. The object-looking time of each child in each condition was examined. The results were that 19- and 24-month-olds looked at and chose the socially intended object as a referent even when the object was boring, but 12-month-olds tended to look at and choose the interesting object as a referent regardless of the existence of the social cue. Hollich, et al. interpreted this result that children make a shift in word learning from relying on perceptual cues to relying on social intent cues. In a discrepant labeling situation that Baldwin (1991, 1993) examined, infants would establish an incorrect word-object mapping if they failed to recognize the significance of cues such as line-of-regard for determining the speaker's reference. In this paradigm, an experimenter showed infants two equally attractive novel toys and gave one to the child to play with while the experimenter retained the other. When the infants' attention was focused on the toy, the experimenter looked at and labeled her own toy, the situation being a discrepancy between the infants' focus and that of the speaker at the time the label was uttered. Without the ability to consult the speaker for cues to reference, infants should fall prey to a mapping error—time contingency would lead them to link the new label with the toy of their own focus. On the other hand, if infants appreciated the relevance of the speaker's non-verbal cues such as line-of-regard and body orientation directed toward the speaker's toy, they could use these cues and establish the correct word-to-object link. According to Baldwin, infants readily glanced up at the experimenter when discrepant labeling occurred and followed her gaze to the object of her focus. In a comprehension test. Infants of 18 months or older did not link the new label with the toy they were actually focused on when they heard the new label. Eighteen- to nineteen-month-olds seems to have established a stable mapping between the label and the object of the speaker's focus. These results suggest that infants have the ability to appreciate that speakers provide cues that are relevant to interpreting new words and consult these cues when faced with discrepant labeling. Baldwin's studies successfully showed infants' sensitivity to know the others' direction of attention by confirming the nonverbal cues of eye gaze and face or body direction of others, but children seem to have abilities to use relevant cues that are beyond such physical cues.

In our pilot study, we tested two-year-olds in this discrepant labeling paradigm and were surprised with an unexpected result. We expected that 2-year-olds would have little difficulty to check the experimenter's face in the experiment of the discrepant labeling paradigm. However, despite of our expectation, close to half of the children immediately changed their focus of attention and took the Out-of-Attention Object WITHOUT looking at the experimenter. Why these children did not look at the experimenter's face? We speculated that they are likely aware that adults may not necessarily say the name of the object the child is attending. Young children may think from the excitement of the voice that the label must be the referent of the other object which is not the present focus of the child. If this is the case, young children certainly rely on social pragmatic cues in a sense, in a more sophisticated way than simply checking the adults' line-of-regard. That is, there may be another state of development that can be measured in the discrepant labeling situation. We tested this hypothesis by a modified discrepant paradigm with participants of 2-, 4-year-olds and adults.

In our study, an experimenter placed down two unfamiliar objects, then asked the child to choose one of the objects and play with it for a while rather than the experimenter simply giving one of the objects to the child, a procedure used in the usual discrepant labeling paradigm. We thought that our slightly older children might be capable of changing their focus of attention in this more difficult situation in which the child could play with the object that she thought more attractive than the other. After the experimenter confirmed that the child was concentrated on manipulating the chosen object for more than 10 seconds, then the experimenter said "Oh, muta!" and looked at the other object that the child had not manipulated.

Method

Pariticipants

Fifteen 2-year-olds (range 1;7~2;5), 14 4-year-olds (3;2~4;10), and 35 university students participated in the study. Children were tested at their preschool rooms in Saitama Prefecture in Japan that was a part of a greater Tokyo area. University students were tested at a university experimental room in the same prefecture.

Material

Each participant saw four pairs of objects that were all unfamiliar to young children. One pair included a brass hanger and a toilet tank ball, the other pair included a wood honey roller and a cloth holder made of stainless steel. The Criteria for selection of the objects were that the objects be novel, visually distinct from one another, balanced in salience within a pair, and manipulable for two-year-olds. The novel labels used were muta, heku, ruto, and omi that were used in Kobayashi (1998)'s study.

Procedure

Figure 1 shows the experimental situation for children. A child and an experimenter sat on a table face-to-face. An assistant videotaped the experiment. On the table, the experimenter placed the two novel objects in front of the child. The two objects were at an equal distance from the child. The experimenter said to the child, "Which do you like? You can play with the one you like." Then the child took one of the objects and manipulated it. When it was confirmed that the child was focused on the chosen object for more than 10 seconds, the experimenter looked at the other object that the child did not choose and said, "Oh, (child's name), muta, muta!" The child's response was noted. Immediately after each trial of labeling, the experimenter presented the two previously shown objects and asked the child, "Which is muta?" The child's responses, both verbal and nonverbal were noted. The experimenter accepted any kind of response from the child, saying "I see!" without feedback of right or wrong. If the child took both objects when asked to choose one, the experimenter waited until the child's attention was focused on only one of these and said the novel label. For adults, the procedure was mostly the same, but they were instructed to think the word "muta" was a foreign word. This change was made because adults have much more knowledge including the labels of experimental objects.

The video data were analyzed with a frame-by-frame method at the rate of 30 frames per second. First, the frame of the video data in which the first sound of "Oh, muta!" occurred was specified. Then an experienced coder coded the object of the child's line-of-regard immediately before and after hearing the novel label. Two additional moves of the line-of regard following the immediately-after-move were coded to provide more information about the movements of line-of-regard. The looked object was coded to four categories; Experimenter, In-Attention Object, Out-of-Attention Object, and Other. The participant's line-of-regard was coded Experimenter when the child looked at the experimenter's face or body. The participant's line-of-regard was coded In-Attention Object when the child looked at the object that the child chose and was focused on. It was coded Out-of-Attention Object when the child looked at the other object that the experimenter looked at. It was coded Other when the child looked at anything that were not included to the already defined three categories, such as looking at other objects in the room or any part of the room such as the floor. Another coder independently coded 25% of the video data. The agreement between the two coding results was more than 90%. The first coder's coded data was taken for further analysis.

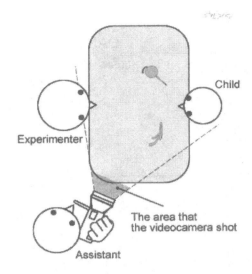

Figure 1: The experimental situation

Figure 2: An example of a set of experimental objects

Result

The mean ratio of change of line-of-regard was calculated for each movement. Figure 2 shows the data of two-year-olds. The moves that occurred in less than 5% of the all moves from one category to the other category were omitted as infrequent moves. Immediately before hearing of the novel label, 15% of 2-year-olds looked at the experimenter, 76% of them looked at the In-Attention Object, and only 9% looked at the other thing. After hearing the label, 88% of the children who looked at the experimenter then looked at the Out-of-Attention Object. But children who looked at the In-Attention Object were divided into two types. 57% of the children then looked at the experimenter and 88% of those children then looked at

the Out-of-Attention Object. Whereas 40% of the children who previously looked at the In-Attention Object directly looked at the Out-of-Attention Object without checking the experimenter's line-of-regard.

As for 4-year-olds, immediately before hearing the novel label, 17% of 4-year-olds looked at the experimenter and 80% of them looked at the In-Attention Object. Only less than 3% of the 4-year-olds looked at the other thing (In Figure 4, the movement is omitted.) After hearing the label, 100% of the children who looked at the experimenter then looked at the Out-of-Attention. But children who looked at the In-Attention Object were again divided into two types. 43% of the children then looked at the experimenter and 95% of those children then looked at the Out-of-Attention Object. Whereas 55% of the children who previously looked at the In-Attention Object directly looked at the Out-of-Attention Object without checking the experimenter's line-of-regard.

Finally, 97% of the adults looked at the In-Attention Object immediately before hearing the label. Less than 3% of the adults looked at other things and the movement is omitted in Figure 5. The adults who looked at the In-Attention Object were divided into two types. 31% of the adults then looked at the experimenter and 94 of those adults then looked at the Out-of-Attention Object. Whereas 69% of the adults who previously looked at the In-Attention Object directly looked at the Out-of-Attention Object without checking the experimenter's line-of-regard.

The mean frequency of choosing the Out-of-Attention Object was computed for each age. There were 4 trials so the maximum score was 4. The mean frequency of choosing the Out-of-Attention Object in 2-year-olds was 2.7. The mean frequency of choosing the Out-of-Attention Object in 4-year-olds was 3.4 and that in adults was 4.0.

In order to further clarify the movement from the In-Attention Object to the Out-of-Attention Object, we pulled out only the result of the first trial. If the participant only "learned" to pay attention to the Out-of-Attention Object as they repeated the task, then they may not directly look at the Out-of-Attention Object in the first trial after looking at the In-Attention Object. Figure 6 shows the result of those participants who looked at the In-Attention Object immediately before hearing the novel label. The results were roughly the same with the mean frequency data that are shown in Figure 3, 4, and 5. Many 4-year-olds and adults directly moved their line-of-regard from the In-Attention Object to the Out-of-Attention Object without checking the experimenter at the first trial already. Many of those children who did not look at the Out-of-Attention Object without checking the experimenter quickly looked at the experimenter and then looked at the Out-of-Attention Object and touched the object. Some children then went back to the In-Attention Object and continued manipulation, other children started to manipulate the Out-of-Attention Object.

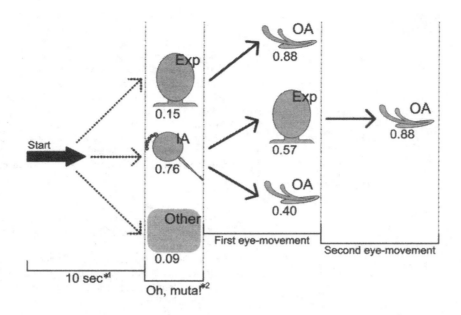

Figure 3: Movement of line-of-regard of 2-year-olds when the novel label was heard after 10 seconds of concentration on a participant-chosen object

Notes. Exp means the experimenter. IA means the In-Attention Object or the object the participant attended. OA means the Out-of-Attention Object that the experimenter looked at and said "Oh, muta!" *1 The participant manipulates the chosen object. *2 means the object that the participant looked at immediately before hearing the label. The numbers mean the ratio of movement from one object to the other object. Movements occurred less than 0.05 were omitted.

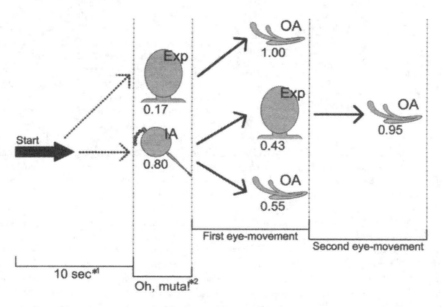

Figure 4: Movement of line-of-regard of 4-year-olds when the novel label was heard after 10 seconds of concentration on a participant-chosen object

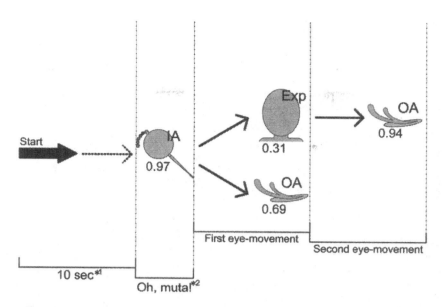

Start

IA
0.97

Exp
0.31

OA
0.94

OA
0.69

First eye-movement

Second eye-movement

10 sec*1

Oh, muta!*2

Figure 5: Movement of line-of-regard of adults when the novel label was heard after 10 seconds of concentration on a participant-chosen object

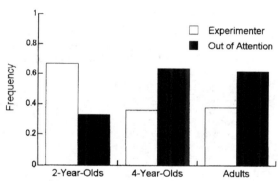

Figure 6: Direction of movement of line-of-regard in the first trial of those participants who previously looked at the In-Attention Object

Note. White bars represent the percent frequency of Experimenter. Colored bars represent that of the Out-of-Attention Object (the object to which experimenter looked at and provided a novel label).

Discussion

This study examined movement of line-of-regard of 2-, 4-year-olds and adults in a discrepant labelling situation. Unlike the usual discrepant labelling paradigm, participants chose the first object on their own choice so that she can concentrate more on the first object. The experimental situation was videotaped and the movement of the participant's line-of-regard was recorded with a frame-by-frame method. We think the most interesting result of this study was the fact that both children and adults do not always check the direction of the line-of-regard when they heard a novel label. 40% of the 2-year-olds, 55% of the 4-year-olds, and about 70% of the adults who looked at the object that they chose and manipulated it DIRECTLY moved their line-of-regard to the object the experimenter looked at immediately after hearing a novel label WITHOUT checking the experimenter's eyes, face or body. They did so even in the first trial. Because most of the 4-year-olds and the adults correctly associated the intended object and the novel word in the test, they certainly knew that the object they were not focus on was the object to learn the name of it.

Then why the substantial number of the 2-year-olds and many of the 4-year-olds and the adults were able to know the correct referential intentions of the other person? There are several possibilities. The first possibility is that the child may detect the direction of the experimenter's voice. But the voice direction seems too ambiguous to detect and cannot explain the very quick movement of the children's line-of-regard. The second possibility is that the child may see the direction of the experimenter's body by one's peripheral vision even when the eye gaze is directed to something other than the experimenter. However, peripheral vision seems too ambiguous to explain the quick and correct action. Our interpretation of the phenomenon of the absence of direct look at the speaker is that the child had knowledge of the flow of conversation. If the speaker wanted to comment on the object that the child chose and manipulated, she should have commented earlier. Because she commented after 10 seconds had passed since the child had started to manipulate the object, she must have intended to make an inference about the object which had not been the already chosen object. A stronger test of this hypothesis might be to contrast children's responses in two alternative situations: modifying the amount of time elapsing between when the child began playing with object, and when the experimenter labelled the other novel object. Thus, in one situation, the child hears the novel word immediately after she touches the object she chose, and in another situation, the child hears the novel word after 10 seconds elapsing after her touching the object. If children look at the Out-of-Attention Object immediately after their touching the chosen object only when in the 10 second-elapsing condition, the social pragmatic explanation can be more strongly validated. We are currently planning to conduct more stringent tests in a more improved method to carefully examine our hypothesis.

The result of this study supports the recent contention of the importance of the flow of conversation proposed by Tomasello and colleagues (Tomasello, & Akhtar, 1995; Tomasello, & Haberl, 2001. In several studies Tomasello and Akhtar demonstrated that young children have the ability to know the referential intentions of adults even when seeing an object and hearing the label of it do not occur simultaneously. One of the most important thing for children to know in learning object names is knowing the adult's desire and hopes and how such internal information may appear in facial expressions and tone of the voice. We think the present study added a new insight to this concept of the flow of conversation. Even the consecutive manipulation of only 10 seconds may be enough for children to conclude that the already manipulated object must not the object that the adult commented on with a nuance of excitement. The result of this study also partly supports the recent contention of a social shift in word learning proposed by Golinkoff, Hirsh-Pasek, and colleagues (Golinkoff, & Hirsh-Pasek, 1999; Hirsh-Pasek, Golinkoff, & Hennon, 2000). They state that children come to rely on social intent as a more reliable cue than other cues such as perceptual saliency in word learning after around 18 months of age. This study provides evidence that as children get older, this kind of sensitivity to adult intent are sharpened and used for further word learning. Thus, we don't have to look at the face of another to know the direction of their attention when the flow of conversation provides sufficient cues. Here, looking at an others' face may give some additional information such as the emotional states or exchanging emotional information, other than just knowing the direction of others' attention.

Conclusion

Young children are equipped with the ability to know others' referential intentions without looking at their line-of-regard. They seem to use the flow of conversation as an important cue to know the referent in the given situation. They may develop this ability from early on and through childhood to quickly and correctly learn the meaning of words.

Acknowledgement

This study was partly supported by the Grant-in-Aid for Scientific Research (C), Ministry of Education, Culture, Sports, Science and Technology (MEXT), Japan.

References

Baldwin, D. (1991). Infants' contribution to the achievement of joint reference. *Child Development, 62,* 875-890.

Baldwin, D. (1993). Early referential understanding: Infants' ability to recognize referential acts for what they are. *Developmental Psychology, 29,* 832-843.

Brooks, R. & Meltzoff, A. N. (2002). The importance of eyes: How infants interpret adult looking behaviour. *Developmental Psychology, 38,* 958-966.

Golinkoff, R. M. & Hirsh-Pasek, K. (1999). *How babies talk: The magic and mystery of language development in the first three years of life.* New York: Penguin, Dutton.

Hirsh-Pasek, K., Golinkoff, R. M., & Hollich, G. (2000). An emergentist coalition model for word learning: Mapping words to objects is a product of the interation of multiple cues. In R. M. Golinkoff, K. Hirsh-Pasek, L. Bloom, L. B. Smith, A. L. Woodard, N. Akhtar, M. Tomasello, & G. Hollich (Eds.), *Becoming a word learner: A debate of lexical acquisition* (pp.179-186). New York: Oxford University Press.

Hollich, G., Hirsh-Pasek, K., & Golinkoff R. M. With Hennon, E., Chung, H. L., Rocroi, C., Brand, R. J., & Brown, E. (2000). Breaking the language barrier: An emergentist coalition model for the origins of word learning. *Monographs of the Society for Research in Child Development, 65,* (3, Serial No. 262).

Kobayashi, H. (1998). How 2-year-old children learn novel part names of unfamiliar objects. *Cognition, 68,* B41-51.

Moll, H., & Tomasello, M. (2004). 12- and 18-month-old infants follow gaze to spaces behind barriers. Developmental Science, 7, F1-F9.

Tomasello, M., & Akhtar, N. (1995). Two-year-olds use pragmatic cues to differentiate reference to objects and actions. *Cognitive Development, 10,* 201-224.

Tomasello, M. & Haberl, K. (2001). Understanding Attention: 12- and 18-Month-Olds Know What Is New for Other Persons. *Developmental Psychology, 39(5),* 906-912

Pruden, S. M., Hirsh-Pasek, K., Golinkoff, R. M., & Hennon, E. A.(2006). The birth of words: Ten-month-olds learn words through perceptual salience. *Child Development, 77,* 266-280.

Post-Interpretive Processes Influence Interpretive Processing During Reading: Evidence from Eye Movements

Christiane Bohn (cbohn@uni-potsdam.de)
Department of Psychology, University of Potsdam,
PO Box 601553, 14415 Potsdam, Germany

Reinhold Kliegl (kliegl@uni-potsdam.de)
Department of Psychology, University of Potsdam,
PO Box 601553, 14415 Potsdam, Germany

Abstract

Sentence reading is the prototype of automatic language processing. As a challenge to this account, we show how the frequency and difficulty of comprehension questions (i.e., the amount of verbatim overlap between words in the sentence and words in the question) affects word recognition during sentence reading. We had two groups of young and old adults read the same sentences followed by easy or difficult questions. Difficult questions led to slower reading, more regressions, and less skipping, especially in older adults. Very difficult questions caused an additional spillover effect on the subsequent sentence. In contrast to Caplan and Waters' (1999) idea of resource independence of interpretive processes, we present evidence demonstrating that highly automated 1st pass reading is dynamically modulated by high-level processing, such as reading intention and depth of comprehension, parameters specified during post-interpretive processing.

Reading Processes, Age and Strategy

For skilled readers, reading a sentence for comprehension is a highly automated and efficient process. From a modular point of view, Caplan and Waters (1999) call the processes of lexical access, construction of syntactic representations, assigning thematic roles, focus and other aspect of semantics *interpretive processes*. Interpretive processes are obligatory, highly specialized, and independent of working memory (wm) and effects of aging. In contrast, *post-interpretive processes* such as using the sentence's meaning for other tasks, reasoning and planning are supposed to be mediated through verbal working memory and are therefore sensitive to age because wm capacity is found to decline with age (Salthouse, Babcock, & Shaw, 1991).

In agreement with Caplan and Waters, several studies report relatively small effects of age in reading fixations (Kliegl et al., 2004; Rayner et al., 2006; Smiler, Gagne, & Stine-Morrow, 2003) suggesting that reading is a highly automated skill acquired over age and that it is primarily influenced by changes in visual acuity, not by changes related to language processing. On the one hand, reading times of older adults show the same effects of word variables as those of young adults, but durations are somewhat prolonged. On the other hand, there is clear age-related decline in language tasks when they tax the efficiency of working-memory or executive control, processes subsumed under the label of post-interpretive processes (Caplan & Waters, 1999). For example, age

differences related to syntactic complexity were found in tasks such as answering questions on sentences (Davis & Ball, 1989), oral recall of sentences (Norman et al., 1991), oral imitation of prompts (Kemper, 1988) or grammatical acceptability judgments (Kemper, 1997), all tasks involving post-interpretive processes.

From a different perspective, Stine-Morrow and colleagues (Stine-Morrow, Loveless, & Soederberg, 1996; Stine-Morrow, Ryan, & Leonard, 2000) discuss their results of age effects in studies examining online measures during text reading, e.g. reading times, as differences in the strategy of resource allocation during sentence comprehension. They claim that old readers, who are limited in their wm capacity and may have processing deficiencies, allocate their processing resources in sentence reading differently from younger adults in order to optimize subsequent memory performance. This conclusion is inconsistent with a modularity view postulating that interpretive processes are preserved with age (Caplan & Waters, 1999) because it posits that there might be a strategic component in reading that is sensitive to age effects and modulates individual reading behavior during interpretive processing. Other studies clearly report strategy effects in online reading time measures, indicating that reading intention does play a role in sentence processing. For example, Rayner and Raney (1996) found word frequency effects on fixation durations in reading for comprehension, but not in a lexical search task.

As far as we know, there is no experimental evidence that post-interpretive processes dynamically modulate interpretive processes, because by definition, the latter are automatic and not accessible to conscious control. Applying tasks on the propositional representation of a sentence usually involves conscious, controlled processes, and further, readers become aware of the difficulty of the task and how well they perform. We propose that the difficulty of the task following a sentence, e.g. comprehension questions, and the reader's performance on these questions will consciously or unconsciously define the reader's intention and thus, modulate his reading strategy. Regardless of differences in syntactic complexity or other sentence or word variables, we expect that a conscious parameter specification at the reader level as a result of resource demands during post-interpretive processes will in turn influence the operations of the interpretive processes. Thus, in contrast to Caplan and Waters (1999), we propose that differences in reading strategy, modulated by demands on post-interpretive processing, are correlated with performance in online-measures during sentence processing.

The goal of the current study is to examine the effect of difficulty of reading task on the eye movement pattern in single-sentence reading. Keeping the reading material and the general reading task (reading for comprehension) constant, the difficulty of the task is manipulated by the difficulty and the frequency of the comprehension questions after the trials. We hypothesize that the fixational eye-movement behavior on sentences followed by difficult questions will differ from eye movement patterns on the identical sentence material followed by easy questions. We expect that comprehension questions, that engender high-level language processes, will tax the reader's semantic system and working memory and cause an adaptation of their reading strategy, at least to a certain degree. This might be reflected in an increase in the number of fixations and fixation durations. We further expect that due to wm limitations old readers will be more affected by task demands. Consequently, old readers should show more changes in their eye movements as well in accuracy of answers and response latencies during reading with difficult questions.

Method

Participants

Data of four samples are compared in this study. A group of 24 high-school students (in the following labeled as 'easy young'; mean age 17.6 years) and a group of 32 older readers ('easy old'; mean age 70.6 years) read the sentences with easy questions [1]. An age matched group of 30 high-school students ('hard young'; mean age 18.5 years) and 23 old readers ('hard old'; mean age 68.0 years) read the same material with difficult questions. In comparison to young readers, old readers scored significantly higher on Lehrl's (Lehrl, 1977) multiple-choice measure of vocabulary ($F_{(1,107)} = 45.25$, MSe = 4.83, p < 0.001) and lower on Wechsler's (Wechsler, 1964) Digit-Symbol-Test ($F_{(1,107)} = 53.04$, MSe = 90.4, p < 0.001). Comparisons within age levels revealed no significant differences between the easy and hard group in age, vocabulary or attention indices. A reading-span test as reported in Oberauer et al. (2003) was administered for the hard groups. Reading span was reliably reduced with age ($F_{(1,51)} = 93.03$, MSe = 0.01488, p < 0.001).

Apparatus

Single sentences were presented on the center-line of a 21-in. EYE-Q 650 Monitor (832 pixels x 632 pixels resolution; frame rate 75 Hz; font: regular, New Courier, 12 point) controlled by an Apple Power Macintosh G3 computer. Participants were seated in front of the monitor with the head positioned on a chin rest. Eye movements

of three samples were recorded with an EyeLink II system (SR Research, Osgoode, ON, Canada) with a 500-Hz-sampling rate. The sample 'easy old' was recorded with an EyeLink I system with a 250-Hz-sampling rate. All recordings and calibrations were binocular.

The Potsdam Sentence Corpus (PSC)

The PSC comprises 144 German single sentences (1,138 words), which represent a large variety of grammatical structure (Kliegl et al., 2004). Sentences range from 5 to 11 words (M = 7.9, SD = 1.4). Norms on various psycholinguistic variables such as word length, word frequency (Geyken et al., 2006) and predictability norms from an independent study are available for each word in the PSC.

Comprehension Questions for the PSC

In the easy condition, easy multiple-choice comprehension questions were asked after 27% of all sentences. Questions used identical wording of the previous sentence and three alternative choices were provided. These questions were similar to single word probe tasks and therefore correct responses were possible solely by visual word recognition of the answering options. For example, after the sentence

Martins gebrochener Zeh schwoll rasch an.

(Martin's broken toe swelled quickly.)

the following comprehension question was asked:

Was schwoll an?

(What was swelling?)

and the choices given were the following:

Fuss   Ferse   Zeh

(foot   heel   toe)

In the difficult condition, a three alternative multiple-choice comprehension question was asked after each sentence. Six different questions types were used that occurred in equal proportions: (1) subject-questions, (2) object-questions, questions asking for (3) verbal information, (4) time and location information, and (5) other adverbial information given in the sentence. Verification questions (6) maintained a statement about the sentence the subject had to respond to with 'yes/ no/ maybe'-type of answer. The combination of questions and the multiple choice answers was designed to reduce the verbatim overlap with the original sentence, in order to rule out solution by simple word form recognition. For the example given above, the difficult question was:

Was passierte mit Martins Zeh?

(What happened to Martin's toe?)

and the choices provided were:

wurde blau   wurde steiff   wurde dick

(became blue   became stiff   became thick)

The content of all questions aimed at checking a complete and detailed propositional representation of the sentence.

---

[1]Data of these two samples were included in the analyses in Kliegl, Nuthmann, & Engbert (2006), labeled sample 4 and sample 9 respectively.

Procedure

In both experimental conditions, participants were calibrated with a standard nine-point grid for both eyes. They were instructed to read the sentence for comprehension and to fixate on a dot in the lower right corner of the monitor to signal the completion of a trial. After validation of calibration accuracy, a fixation dot appeared on the left side of the centerline on the monitor. If the eye tracker identified a fixation on the fixation spot, a sentence was presented so that the midpoint between the beginning and the center of the first word was positioned at the location of the fixation spot. Sentences were shown until participants looked at the lower right corner of the screen. Then in 27% (easy condition) or 100% (hard condition) respectively, the sentence was replaced by a three-alternative multiple-choice question, that the participant answered via a mouse click. After every 15 sentences, a complete recalibration with the nine-point grid was presented. The task was initiated with 10 training trials.

Analysis and Data Selection

To investigate effects of experimental manipulation and effects of age, we analyze fixation probabilities and fixation durations in the two reading conditions in both age groups, as listed in Table 1. Eye movement data were screened for loss of measurement and blinks. Data of sentences without problems were reduced to a fixation format after detecting saccades as rapid binocular eye movements by using a binocular velocity-based detection algorithm (Engbert & Kliegl, 2003). Fixations were assigned to letters. For detailed analysis of question type effects, we look at response accuracy and latency in the hard reading condition. Logarithmic response latencies (in ms) were corrected for length (in letters) of questions and answering options via linear regression.

Results

Global Summary Statistics

ANOVAs on global summary statistics (see Table 1) revealed several main effects of age and of reading condition. Old readers made significantly more skippings ($F_{(1,105)} = 27.22$, MSe = 0.005, $p < 0.001$), had a lower probability of fixating a word once ($F_{(1,105)} = 18.07$, MSe = 0.005, $p < 0.001$) or twice ($F_{(1,105)} = 8.95$, MSe = 0.0022, $p < 0.01$), and made significantly more regressions ($F_{(1,105)} = 6.51$, MSe = 0.012, $p < 0.05$). First fixation duration was longer in old adults than young adults ($F_{(1,105)} = 6.15$, MSe = 724, $p < 0.05$).

Effects of experimental condition primarily appeared in differences in fixation durations. In comparison to the easy groups, the hard group showed prolonged single fixation durations ($F_{(1,105)} = 7.02$, MSe = 853, $p < 0.01$), 2nd fixation durations ($F_{(1,105)} = 11.71$, MSe = 703, $p < 0.001$), gaze durations ($F_{(1,105)} = 10.91$, MSe = 1655, $p < 0.01$), as well as total reading times ($F_{(1,105)} = 49.36$, MSe = 4479, $p < 0.001$). The overall reading speed decreased more than 50 words per minute in the young readers, and more than 80 words per minute

in the old readers in the hard condition. In both age groups the number of regressions increases about 100% in the difficult condition ($F_{(1,105)} = 27.76$, MSe = 0.012, $p < 0.001$). One interaction term of age and condition reached significance: The proportion of multiple fixations on a word was tripled in the hard old condition compared to the easy old condition, whereas young adult's behavior remained stable across reading conditions ($F_{(1,105)} = 4.07$, MSe = 0.0003, $p < 0.05$).

Response Accuracy, Latency and Spillover Effects in the Hard Condition

For the hard groups, accuracy profiles and profiles of mean residual log. latency for response per question type are illustrated in Figure 1. Old adults were less accurate ($F_{(1,51)} = 14.76$, MSe = 0.00687, $p < 0.001$) and slower ($F_{(1,51)} = 47.59$, MSe = 0.1734, $p < 0.001$) than young readers in answering the hard questions. More interestingly, verification questions seemed to be most troublesome for both age groups, reflected by significantly lower accuracies ($F_{(1,51)} = 85.66$, MSe = 0.00664, $p < 0.001$) and higher response latencies ($F_{(1,51)} = 128.34$, MSe = 0.006, $p < 0.001$) for verification questions in contrast to all other question types. The interaction with age was significant for accuracy ($F_{(1,51)} = 21.63$, $p < 0.001$) and log. residual latency ($F_{(1,51)} = 29.98$, $p < 0.001$).

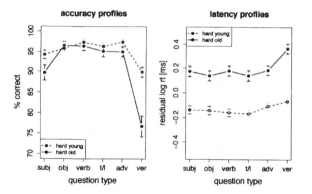

Figure 1: Accuracy and latency profiles for hard young and hard old; residual log. latencies are plotted; question types: subj = subject, obj = object, verb = verbal, t/l = time/ location, adv = adverbial, ver = verification

Verification questions were designed to test the integrated, complete meaning of a sentence. Thus, this type of question makes large demands on wm because a full-integrated model needs to be represented for chosing the correct answer. If verification was the hardest question type, the query arises whether the obvious struggle over this question during post-interpretive processing is reflected in the eye movement data during interpretive processing of the subsequent trial. Since our experimental manipulation occurred after the sentence was read and after eye movements were recorded, we tested for the existence of spillover effects of question type on reading

Table 1: Global statistics for easy and hard groups

Variable		Easy young	Easy old	Hard young	Hard old
N of readers		24	32	30	23
N of fixations/ sentence	M	9.2	8.9	11.5	12.0
	SD	1.8	2.1	2.8	3.5
N of sentences	M	122	133	108	100
	SD	23	10	24	28
Fixation probabilities					
skipping	M	.16	.25	.17	.21
	SD	.07	.09	.07	.06
single fixation	M	.64	.57	.60	.56
	SD	.07	.08	.06	.06
double fixation	M	.13	.10	.14	.12
	SD	.05	.05	.04	.04
three-plus fixation	M	.02	.01	.02	.03
	SD	.02	.01	.02	.03
regression	M	.08	.14	.18	.26
	SD	.05	.10	.08	.18
Fixation duration (ms)					
single fixation	M	221	218	230	238
	SD	23	29	31	33
1st of multiple	M	209	216	210	231
	SD	19	28	27	32
2nd of multiple	M	181	179	194	202
	SD	22	28	25	30
gaze duration	M	261	250	275	289
	SD	38	37	40	48
total reading time	M	281	280	356	386
	SD	46	51	76	89
reading rate (words/ min)		241	256	186	172

times in the hard groups. We contrasted two conditions: the first condition included sentence trials that followed a verification question, the second condition included all remaining sentence trials following the other five question types. In an ANOVA, we compared total reading times (trt) per sentence in the two conditions of both age groups. There was a main effect of question type ($F_{(1,51)}$ = 4.52, MSe = 0.00597, p < 0.05) in the order of 87 ms longer trts in trials following a verification question in contrast to the other trials. The interaction of condition and age was not significant ($F_{(1,51)}$ = 1.11, p > 0.05). We controlled whether the same sentences occurred in both conditions and found no differences. However, the number of data points in the four cells are not balanced, because verification questions occurred in only 1/6 of the trials.

Discussion

In the present study, we tested the effects of comprehensive processing depth on eye movement behavior in isolated sentence reading. Keeping the reading material constant (PSC), we manipulated the frequency and difficulty of the comprehension questions following each sentence trial. There are two major results that are of high value for the interpretation of eye movement data in reading research. First, difficulty of comprehension questions dynamically influences reading strategies in young as well as in old readers. Second, first pass reading is not simply a reflection of automatic and fast sentence processing but can be influenced by reading intention and general working memory load.

We have demonstrated that intrinsic demands of comprehension questions lead to different eye movements in reading of isolated sentences. Both young and old readers read slower and showed an increased number of regressive eye movements when frequent and more demanding questions were asked. A similar change in reading strategy has been observed when difficult text was given to subjects (Rayner & Pollatsek, 1989). In the present study, stimulus material as well as reading instruction was identical and the change in reading strategy was indirectly induced by the demands of the comprehension questions. Our results can be described as the inverse effect of the eye movement behavior during skimming. Readers who skim a text make fewer and shorter fixations on the stimulus material than normal readers but are disadvantaged in both answering high-level questions as well as low-level questions about specific details in the text (Masson, 1985). In our study, subjects needed to build a detailed representation of the sentence content in order to select the correct response alternative and thus, slowed down and made more fixations. This result raises the methodological issue of how we control for the reader's intention in our reading experiment (Radach & Kennedy, 2004). Obviously, differences in design of the reading studies across laboratories may yield differences in mean fixation durations. Here we demonstrate, that not the variation in instruction and material, but the internal processing depth and thus differences at parameter specification on the reader's side suffices to induce a change in eye movements. We successfully changed the reading behavior to a 'mindful' reading by demanding higher linguistic processing, specifically deeper semantic processing from the readers.

In our study, the recorded eye movements all reflect interpretive processes of on-line sentence comprehension, whereas response latencies and accuracy scores for the different question types in the hard reading condition reflect post-interpretive processes. Looking at post-interpretive prosessing, we found large age differences in accuracies and response latencies in the hard group. A reading span and attention test, two measures related to working memory capacity, showed age effects in the same direction. In line with Caplan and Waters (1999), we asssume a correlation between wm tests and performance on the comprehension questions, indicating that answering questions uses resources that strongly depend on verbal working memory and age. Note that even though old readers with lower reading spans spent considerably more time processing the sentences in 1st and 2nd pass reading, they showed poorer comprehension compared to young readers.

The story about eye movements is not as straight forward. In the easy condition, there were differences between age groups concerning number of regressions and skipping, typical of results reported before (Kliegl et al. 2004, Rayner et al. 2006). At the same time, single fixation durations, gaze and total reading time were almost equal in the two easy groups, indicating that sentence reading is an automated process preserved with aging. In the difficult reading condition, however, we found pronounced differences between age groups in the distribution of fixations as well as in fixation durations. This finding of individual differences contradicts the modularity hypothesis claimed by Caplan and Waters and rather supports a "single processing resource hypothesis" (Just & Carpenter, 1992), that argues for a general verbal working memory system used for all verbally mediated cognitive functions. Moreover, a working memory load induced by the demands of the comprehension questions impacts subsequent eye movement dynamics while reading a relatively simple sentence. This interpretation is supported by the spillover effects we found for the most difficult questions, the verification questions. Both young and old readers in the hard group had lower accuracy scores and longer response latencies for verification questions. Total reading times for sentences following verification question were significantly longer than subsequent total reading times after other question types, though this result needs to be replicated in a balanced design. In the framework of a 'separate language processing resource' theory, these spillover effects cannot be explained by troubles of recovering from the demands induced by the manipulation of questions. According to this theory, reading the subsequent sentence would tap separate wm resources than answering questions and thus, no effect of question type should be observable in online-measures.

Therefore, our results provide initial evidence that there are resources used during offline processing tasks, such as answering questions, that are shared with online processing tasks during sentence reading. Or in other words: Post-interpretive processes influence interpretive processes during reading for comprehension. Indicated by differences in reading span, the effects of condition and age are plausibly related to wm resources declining with age. We argue that, in the difficult condition, reading intention was changed by task demands that increased memory load. Old readers allocated more time to accomplish sentence comprehension, an effect that has been discussed in the context of self-regulatory processes in language understanding in old adults (Smiler, Gagne, & Stine-Morrow, 2003). In summary, on-line processes in reading seem to be more prone to reading intention, reading strategy and individual differences such as age and wm capacities than previously assumed.

References

Caplan, D., & Waters, G. S. (1999). Verbal working memory and sentence comprehension. *Behavioral and Brain Science, 22*(1), 77-94; discussion 95-126.

Davis, G. A., & Ball, H. E. (1989). Effects of age on comprehension of complex sentences in adulthood. *Journal of Speech and Hearing Research, 32*(1), 143-150.

Engbert, R., & Kliegl, R. (2003). Microsaccades uncover the orientation of covert attention. *Vision Research, 43*(9), 1035-1045.

Geyken, A., Hanneforth, T., Würzner, K., & Kliegl, R. (2006). The DWDS-Cropus: A reference corpus for the German language of the 20th century. In C. Fellbaum (Ed.), *Collocations and Idioms: Linguistic, Lexicographic, and Computational Aspects*. London: Continuum Press.

Just, M.A. & Carpenter, P.A. (1992). A capacity theory of comprehension: Individual differences in working memory. *Psychological Review, 99*(1), 122-149.

Kemper, S. (1988). Geriatric psycholinguistics: Syntactic limitations of oral and written language. In L. L. L. D. M. Burke (Ed.), *Language, memory, and aging*. Cambridge: University Press.

Kemper, S. (1997). Metalinguistic judgments in normal aging and Alzheimer's disease. *Journal of Gerontology Series B: Psychological Sciences and Social Sciences, 52*(3), 147-155.

Kliegl, R., Grabner, E., Rolfs, M., & Engbert, R. (2004). Length, frequency, and predictability effects of words on eye movements in reading. *European Journal of Cognitive Psychology, 16*(1-2), 262-284.

Kliegl, R., Nuthmann, A., & Engbert, R. (2006). Tracking the mind during reading: the influence of past, present, and future words on fixation durations. *Journal of Experimental Psychology: General,135*(1), 12-35.

Lehrl, S. (1977). *Mehrfach-Wortschatz-Test Form B [multiple choice vocabulary test]*. Erlangen, Germany: Perimed.

Masson, M. E. J. (1985). Rapid reading processes and skills. *Reading Research: Advances in Theory and Practice, 4*, 183-230.

Norman, S., Kemper, S., Kynette, D., Cheung, H. T., & Anagnopoulos, C. (1991). Syntactic complexity and adults' running memory span.*Journal of Gerontology, 46*(6), 1356-351.

Oberauer, K., Süß, H.-M., Wilhelm, O., & Wittman, W.W. (2003). The multiple faces of working memory: Storage, processing, supervision, and coordination. *Intelligence, 31*, 167-193.

Radach, R., & Kennedy, A. (2004). Theoretical perspectives on eye movements in reading: Past controversies, current issues, and an agenda for future research.*European Journal of Cognitive Psychology, 16*(1-2), 3-26.

Rayner, K., & Pollatsek, A. (1989).*The psychology of reading.* Englewood Cliffs, NJ: Prentice Hall.

Rayner, K., & Raney, G. E. (1996). Eye movement control in reading and visual search: Effects of word frequency. *Psychonomic Bulletin & Review, 3*(2), 245-248.

Rayner, K., Reichle, E. D., Stroud, M. J., Williams, C. C., & Pollatsek, A. (2006). The effect of word frequency, word predictability, and font difficulty on the eye movements of young and older readers.*Psychology and Aging, 21*(3), 448-465.

Salthouse, T. A., Babcock, R. L., & Shaw, R. J. (1991). Effects of adult age on structural and operational capacities in working memory. *Psychology and Aging, 6*(1), 118-127.

Smiler, A. P., Gagne, D. D., & Stine-Morrow, E. A. (2003). Aging, memory load, and resource allocation during reading. *Psychology and Aging, 18*(2), 203-209.

Stine-Morrow, E. A., Loveless, M. K., & Soederberg, L. M. (1996). Resource allocation in on-line reading by younger and older adults. *Psychology and Aging, 11*(3), 475-486.

Stine-Morrow, E. A., E. A., Ryan, S., & Leonard, J. S. (2000). Age differences in on-line syntactic processing. *Experimental Aging Research, 26*(4), 315-322.

Wechsler, D. (1964). *Der Hamburger Wechsler Intelligenztest für Erwachsene (HAWIE)*. Bern, Switzerland: Huber.

Learned Attention in Language Acquisition:
Blocking, Salience, and Cue Competition

Nick C. Ellis (NCELLIS@Umich.Edu)
Department of Psychology and English Language Institute, University of Michigan
401 E. Liberty St., Ste. 350, Ann Arbor, MI 48104 USA

Abstract

Adult language acquisition typically falls far short of nativelike competence. Various explanations have been proposed for this limited attainment of adults compared to children, including critical periods for language acquisition, sociocultural differences, motivational differences, and restricted input. This paper considers alternative explanations in terms of the associative learning phenomena of salience, overshadowing, and the attentional blocking of later experienced cues by earlier learned ones. It illustrates these phenomena in investigations of learned attention in the acquisition of temporal reference in a small subset of Latin under experimental conditions. Within the experiment, early experience of adverbial cues blocked the acquisition of verbal tense morphology, and, contrariwise, early experience of tense blocked later learning of adverbs. There were also long-term language transfer effects: first language speakers of Chinese languages, which do not exhibit verb tense morphology, failed to acquire inflectional cues when adverbial and verbal cues were equally available. These demonstrations support explanations of limited adult language attainment that are grounded in cognitive and perceptual learning, in usage and transfer, rather than in age or biology per se.

Cues in First and Second Language Acquisition

Languages allow the same idea to be expressed in a variety of ways. Consider time, a concept fundamental to human cognition and action. All languages have rich means to express the position of events in a time line; they variously utilize tense (verbal inflectional morphology, e.g. *walked* vs. *walk*), lexical adverbs (e.g. *now, next, yesterday, tomorrow*), prepositional phrases (*in the morning, in the future*), serialization (presenting events in their order of occurrence), and calendric reference (*May 12, Monday*). Any stretch of discourse typically uses a variety of these cues in combination (e.g. *yesterday I walked to the university but next Tuesday I'll ride the bus*).

Children acquiring their first language (L1) eventually learn all of these constructions for expressing time. Adults learning a second language (L2) typically do not. Usage-based L2A is limited in its end-state, with naturalistic or communicatively-based L2A stabilizing at levels far short of nativelike ability at a 'Basic Variety' of interlanguage which, although sufficient for everyday communicative purposes, predominantly comprises just nouns, verbs and adverbs, with closed-class items, in particular grammatical morphemes and prepositions, being rare, if present at all. There is typically no functional inflection: no tense, no aspect, no mood, no agreement, no casemarking, no gender assignment. L2 temporal reference is initially made exclusively by use of devices such as temporal adverbials, prepositional phrases, serialization, and calendric reference,

with the grammatical expression of tense and aspect emerging only slowly thereafter, if at all.

One likely explanation for this is the salience of the formal cues. Prepositional phrases, temporal adverbs, and other lexical cues to time are quite pronounced in the speech stream. Verbal inflections are not (consider *yesterday I walked*). Zipf's (1949) principle of least effort describes how frequent words become shorter with use. Speakers want to minimize articulatory effort and hence encourage brevity and phonological reduction. The more they use the more frequent words, automatization of production causes shortening. The most frequent items of language are the closed class words and grammatical morphemes, hence it is these items that are the least salient in the speech stream and, because shorter words tend to be more homophonous, they are also more ambiguous in their interpretations. The low salience and low reliability of grammatical cues tends to make them less learnable (Ellis, 2006).

But salience and reliability affect L1A and L2A alike. There has to be something else which explains the limited endstate of L2A. The classic explanations center upon a critical period for language acquisition, with adult brains being less capable of language learning (perhaps because they no longer have access to universal grammar), or upon social interactional factors (adults are less immersed in the L2, their language development is less scaffolded by their interlocutors). This paper describes experiments exploring a competing line of explanation in terms of standard associative learning effects of 'learned attention': blocking, overshadowing, and other effects of transfer and inhibition that shift learners' attention to language as a result of language experience.

Kruschke and Blair (2000) describe the associative learning phenomenon of blocking. Learning that a particular stimulus (A) is associated with a particular outcome (X), makes it harder to learn that another cue (B), subsequently paired with that same outcome, is also a good predictor of it, as schematized in Figure 1. Thus, for example, someone who knows that the rooster's crowing signals dawn may be less likely to notice that increasing traffic noise can reliably be used as a sign of wake-up-time than is someone who hasn't been exposed to the animal's alarm.

Blocking is an effect of learned attention. For those who previously learned that "A" predicts "X", "B" is merely distracting them from a perfectly predictive symptom. To avoid this error-inducing distraction, they shift their attention away from cue "B" to cue "A", and consequently learn only a weak association from "B" to "X". They also learn that when symptoms "B" and "A" appear together, "B" should be ignored and "A" should be attended to, i.e., symptom "B" should be attentionally blocked.

Learning Phase	Cue⇒Outcome
Early training	A⇒X
Late training	A&B⇒X
	C&D⇒Y
Test	B&D⇒?
	(preferred response is Y)

Figure 1: Blocking

When children are learning their native language they are at the same time learning about the world and about various discourse strategies. Young children do not yet know about the custom of recounting events in their usual script order of occurrence nor do they clearly understand the meaning of temporal adverbs. Adults however, as a result of their L1 experience, do know these things; they know there are reliable and salient means of expressing past time (e.g. *yesterday*) that are far simpler than the non-salient and ambiguous morphological means which vary in complex ways by person and number, etc. Perhaps these already known cues block the acquisition of temporal morphology. On hearing *yesterday I walked*, the morphological tense marker is redundant; successful interpretation of the message does not require its processing, and lack of processing entails lack of acquisition. Similarly, if a learner knows the French word for yesterday, then in the utterance *Hier nous sommes allés au cinéma* (Yesterday we went to the movies) both the auxiliary and past participle are redundant past markers.

It is not just tense that is subject to such effects. Inflexions for number are often overshadowed by the more obvious plurality of the clear subject of the verb (*seven cats run0 down the road, the black cat0 runs down the road*. Naturalistic L2 learners, but not instructed learners, tend to omit plural –*s* endings on nouns that are premodified by quantifiers. This nonredundant marking of plurality is characteristic of L2 learners and pidgin speakers alike. There are many such examples. Thus second language acquisition seems a problem space that is particularly susceptible to effects of blocking and overshadowing. This paper explores these phenomena in two language learning experiments. The first investigates short-term instructional sequence effects in adults learning temporal reference in Latin. The second explores long term language transfer effects whereby the nature of the learners' L1 (+/- verb tense morphology) biases the acquisition of verbal inflectional vs. lexical cues to temporal reference in Latin.

Experiment 1

Experiment 1 involves the learning of a small number of Latin expressions and their English translations. It investigates the effects of successive learning of different types of cue for temporal reference, adverbs (*hodie*, today; *heri*, yesterday; *cras*; tomorrow) and verbal inflections (*cogito*, I think; *cogitavi*, I thought; *cogitabo*, I will think). It determines if the acquisition of one set of cues is impaired if another is already known as a reliable indicator of event time.

Participants

Participants were students from the University of Michigan. They were volunteers and were paid $10 for their participation in the experiment. None had learned Latin before. They were randomly allocated to one of three conditions. The Adverb Pretraining group comprised 10 males and 12 females of age range 19-35 (mean 21.7 years), native languages 19 English, 2 Chinese, 1 Korean. The Verb Pretraining group comprised 8 males and 13 females of age range 18-33 (mean 21.8 years), native languages 18 English, 3 Chinese, 1 Russian. The No Pretraining control group comprised 10 males and 12 females of age range 18-33 (mean 21.0 years), native languages 18 English, 4 Chinese.

Procedure

The experiment was programmed in E-Prime. It took less than one hour. It comprised three phases, Phase 1 – Pretraining, Phase 2 – Sentence decoding, Phase 3 – Reception testing. The procedure is schematized in Figure 2.

Participants in the Adverb Pretraining condition in Phase 1 had 36 randomized trials where they saw either the adverb *hodie* or the adverb *heri*. Note that Phase 1 involved only present and past temporal reference, no future. The participants had to choose whether *today* or *yesterday* was the correct translation by clicking the appropriate alternative with the mouse. These alternatives appeared in counterbalanced positions on the screen. A correct choice returned the feedback 'Correct', an incorrect one 'Wrong – the meaning of [Latin] is [English]' with these slots filled appropriately. After this, in Phase 2 they were exposed to 6 sentences which appropriately combined the adverb with a verb, three in adverb-verb word order and three in verb-adverb, and had to choose whether these sentences referred to the present, the past, or the future. There were six blocks of these trials to consolidate learning. Again, they were given feedback if incorrect. Following the lead of Competition Model studies of cue use (MacWhinney, 1987), in the Reception test, Phase 3, all combinations of adverb (*hodie*, *heri*, *cras*) and verb tense marking (*cogito*, *cogitavi*, *cogitabo*) were combined and the participants were asked to judge whether each sentence referred to the past, present, or future on a 5 point scale ranging from extreme past 1, through present 3, to extreme future 5. The ideal responses which averaged over the cues present in the sentence are shown on the right hand side of the Phase 3 panel of Figure 2.

There was no feedback in Phase 3. Both permissible word orders were tested and the block was repeated twice to allow reliable assessment of the relative weight that learners put on interpreting adverbial and inflectional cues to temporal

CONDITION	PHASE 1 Pretraining (+ feedback)	PHASE 2 Sentence Decoding (+ feedback)	PHASE 3 Reception testing (- feedback)		
ntrials	36 randomised	36 (these x 6 = 3 x 12) randomised in blocks	48 (24 x 2) randomised in blocks		
Adverb Pretraining condition	hodie today heri yesterday		**Test with** Past....Present....Future 1....2.....3.....4.....5	**Test with** Past....Present....Future 1....2....3.....4.....5	
		hodie cogito present	hodie	3	cras cogito	4
		cogito hodie present	heri	1	cras cogitavi	3
Verb Pretraining condition	cogito I think cogitavi I thought	heri cogitavi past	cras	5	cras cogitabo	5
		cogitavi heri past	cogito	3	cogito hodie	3
			cogitavi	1	cogitavi hodie	2
		cras cogitabo future	cogitabo	5	cogitabo hodie	4
		cogitabo cras future	hodie cogito	3	cogito heri	2
Control	No phase 1		hodie cogitavi	2	cogitavi heri	1
			hodie cogitabo	4	cogitabo heri	3
			heri cogito	2	cogito cras	4
			heri cogitavi	1	cogitavi cras	3
			heri cogitabo	3	cogitabo cras	5

Figure 2: The design of Experiment 1

reference. The accuracy of learner responses on the adverbs and verbs reflected the relative degree of their learning of these temporal reference cues from their language experiences in the earlier phases. In this Adverb Pretraining condition, any blocking would evidence itself as a detrimental effect of prior learning of lexical cues to time upon later learning of inflectional cues.

Participants in the Verb Pretraining condition underwent identical Phase 2 – Sentence decoding, Phase 3 – Reception testing to the above. The only difference concerned Phase 1 where instead of the adverbial cues to tense, they were exposed to the inflectional cues. For these participants, blocking would show itself as detrimental effects of early exposure to the inflectional cues reducing learning from later experience of the adverbial cues.

Participants in the No Pretraining condition had no Phase 1, and so they first met the adverbial and inflectional cues to tense simultaneously in Phase 2 and had to induce their meanings. They underwent identical Phase 3 – Reception testing to the above.

The dependent variables were accuracy and latency of responding. Comparisons between and across the learners in the three conditions illustrate whether first learned cues block those experienced subsequently and also the degree to which more salient lexical cues overshadow less obvious morphological ones.

Results

Despite having no pretraining, Control condition learning of the temporal reference of the sentences as a whole in Phase 2 was much the same as it was in the Adverb and Verb Pretraining groups. By the second half of Phase 2, Control performance was 87% correct compared to 97% for both the Adverb and Verb Pretraining conditions.

However, participants in these three groups were very different in the particular cues they used in understanding the sentences of Phase 2, and from this usage, learned to attend subsequently as important communicators of temporal information. The key to their cue use is their performance in Phase 3. Figure 3 illustrates the average group understanding of the time referred to by each of the constructions of Phase 3 in terms of the deviations from ideal interpretation shown in the right column of Phase 3 Figure 2. The sentences are ordered from extreme past on the left to extreme future on the right. It can be seen in Figure 3 that the three groups react to the cues present in the sentences of Phase 3 in very different ways. In two word sentences, where there is temporal information cued by both an adverb and a verbal inflection, when these cues deviate, the Verb pretraining group follows the verbal cue and the Adverb pretraining group follows the adverbial cue, so that these two groups move in opposite directions, as one leans to the future so the other leans to the past. In these cases of cue conflict, the Control group lies in between, seemingly attending to both cues equally.

These impressions are confirmed by three multiple regression analyses, one for each group, where the dependent variable is group mean temporal interpretation for each of the 24 sentences and the independent variables are the interpretation cued by the adverbial cue and that predicted by the verbal inflection. The differential cue use by each of the three groups, in standardized β coefficients, are as follows:

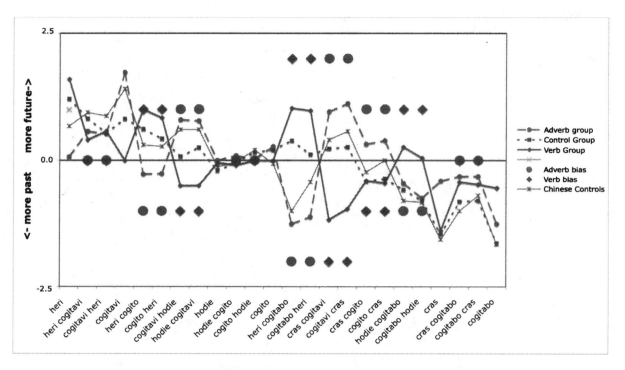

Figure 3: Group mean deviations from ideal temporal interpretations in Phase 3. The solid bias symbols mark the interpretation that would be made for the Adverbial cues only (circles) and Verb inflection cues only (diamonds)

Adverb Group:
Time = 0.98 Adverb + 0.19 Verb $R^2 = 0.99$
         responses explain 66% of ideal
Verb Group:
Time = 0.97 Verb + 0.21 Adverb $R^2 = 0.98$
         responses explain 67% of ideal
Control Group:
Time = 0.69 Verb + 0.67 Adverb $R^2 = 0.91$
         responses explain 85% of ideal

Participants who first learned adverbial cues to temporal reference continued to use those cues to the exclusion of others. In subsequent sentences that contained both adverbial and inflectional cues to event time, verbal morphology accounted for less than 4% of their performance, whilst adverbial cues determined 96%.

Likewise, participants who first learned inflectional cues to temporal reference continued to use those cues to the exclusion of others. In subsequent sentences that contained both adverbial and inflectional cues to event time, adverbial cues accounted for 4.4% of their performance, whereas verbal morphology determined 94%.

Control participants, however, who had no prior experience of Latin adverbial morphological cues to time before they were exposed to sentences containing both cues learned to attend to both cues, with 48% of the variance in their judgments being accounted for by the verbal cues and 45% by the adverbs. The control group's performance is thus much closer to the ideal, explaining 85% of the correct averaged interpretations, compared to just 66% for the Adverb Pretraining and 67% for the Verb Pretraining groups respectively.

The matched attention to verbal and adverbial cues in the control participants here, however clearly it differentiates them from those pretrained with verbal or adverbial cues, is unlikely reflective of natural language learning. The stimuli in the present experiment were a meager subset of Latin, a minilanguage which by chance allowed the three adverbs to differ from each other in relatively slight ways (*hodie, heri, cras*) approximating the similarity in here of the verbal inflections (*cogito, cogitavi, cogitabo*). In natural languages this is not the typical case. Verbal morphology, due to its high frequency, is typically of low salience in its surface manifestations compared to lexical cues (*yesterday, today, tomorrow* vs. I walk*ed*, I walk∅, I*'ll* walk), and hence inflections are typically overshadowed and adumbrated by more salient lexical and discourse cues.

These quantitative results illustrate large and significant effects of blocking in the early acquisition of language. Note that these effects reflect attentional biases to particular dimensions of cue (adverb vs. verbal inflection) rather than to particular words. These are not merely proactive interference effects where, in paired associate learning experiments, memory for association A-B is worse after prior learning of A-C in comparison with a control condition involving prior learning of unrelated material D-E (Baddeley, 1976, chapter 5). That this is the case is clearly demonstrated by the participants' performance on judging future time reference in Phase 3. In Phase 1, participants in the Adverb and Verb pretraining conditions learned particular constructions relating to the present and the past. There was no reference to future at this stage. Thus, while subsequent responses relating to past and present judgments could reflect interference from these specific prior-learned associations, responses relating to future judgments could not. Any bias in interpretation of adverb or inflectional cues to future time must have come from generalized attention to these cues, not from particular memories of specific items. Figure 3 demonstrates that the Adverb and Verb Pretraining groups are as unalike and dissociated in their performance on *cras* and *cogitabo* items referring to the future as they are on the other past and present reference ones.

As with all learning experiments, it is appropriate to ask whether the group performance means are truly reflective of the individuals within that group or whether they provide a central tendency that blurs individual within-group differences. As in the multiple regression analyses reported for each group above, it is possible to take each individual's responses in Phase 3 and assess the degree to which their temporal rating on each construction reflected the information provided by the verb cue and that separately provided by the adverbial cue. Figure 4, which plots each individual in the space defined in this way, shows the large majority of Verb Pretrained individuals heavily influenced by the verb cue and hardly at all by the adverbs, and, conversely, the large majority of the Adverb pretraining participants strongly influenced by the adverbial cues to the exclusion of any information provided by the verb inflections. The control group participants, in contrast, do not lie along the 45% diagonal, equally affected by these two cues as the group mean suggests. Instead their distribution is rather more bimodal, with some individuals picking up more on the adverbial cues and others on the inflections. This finding is in line with others demonstrating that in the early stages of acquisition from a problem space comprising multiple cues to interpretation, participants typically focus upon one cue at a time, exploring its utility and only introducing others later, one-by-one, as they reduce error of estimation (Cheng & Holyoak, 1995; MacWhinney, 1987; Matessa & Anderson, 2000).

Thus, as in the case of associative learning of other cue-outcome interpretations in medical diagnosis or in stock market prediction (Kruschke & Blair, 2000; Shanks, 1995), these data demonstrate that for linguistic constructions too, early learning of one cue blocks the later acquisition of other cues, however reliable they are as predictors in their own right.

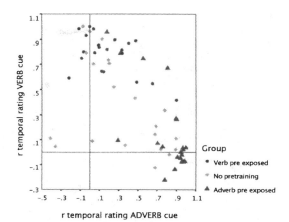

Figure 4: Individual participants from the three training groups as they are affected by adverbial and verbal inflectional cues to temporal reference in Phase 3

Experiment 2

Usage-based views of language acquisition hold that short-term effects sum to long-term effects (Barlow & Kemmer, 2000), as the individual increments of learning integrate over time to form the processes, representations, and attentional biases that fill our minds. Thus experience of how our native language maps on to experience colors our expectations and learning of second language – there are large effects of cross-linguistic transfer upon L2A (MacWhinney, 1997; Robinson & Ellis, to appear). By these accounts, limited adult language attainment is grounded in L1 entrenchment and transfer, rather than in age or biology per se.

Experiment 2 investigated whether long-term learned attention affects that stem from L1 experience also bias cue acquisition in this experimental paradigm. The impetus for assessing this came from observations of the few Chinese first language participants who participated in Experiment 1 and who, especially in the Control condition, seems more to behave like those from the Adverb pretraining group. There are no tenses in Chinese languages and instead temporal information is typically conveyed using direct time reference in the form of temporal adverbs or prepositional phrases. One would expect, therefore, that L1 experience would sum to long-term biases towards these types of cue, with consequent blocking of verbal inflectional cues.

Participants

Participants were 15 Chinese native-language students from the University of Michigan. All students were, of course, bilingual with quite an advanced English language proficiency sufficient – one assessed to be sufficient to allow their study through the medium of English. They were volunteers and were paid $10 for their participation in the experiment.

Procedure

The participants partook in an exact replication of the No Pretraining control group condition of Experiment 1. It comprised Phase 2 – Sentence decoding, Phase 3 – Reception testing.

Results

The performance of the Chinese native individuals in terms of deviation from ideal judgment in Phase 3 of the experiment is shown in Figure 3 as the starred line. It can be seen that their performance lies to the Adverb side of the prior Control group line, tracking the information given by the adverbial cue much more than by that from the verbal morphology. This is confirmed by the results of the multiple regression analyses for the whole group:

Control Group (Native Chinese)
Time = 0.93 Adverb + 0.30 Verb $\quad R^2 = 0.96$
responses explain 72% of ideal

Comparing these results with those from Experiment 1, it can be seen that they lie closer to those of the original Adverb group rather than the original Control group:

Control Group (Expt. 1. Predominantly L1 English):
Time = 0.69 Verb + 0.67 Adverb $\quad R^2 = 0.91$
Adverb Group:
Time = 0.98 Adverb + 0.19 Verb $\quad R^2 = 0.99$

These findings confirm a long-term influence of attention to language, a processing bias and subsequent blocking of cue learning that comes from a lifetime of prior L1 usage. It is perhaps especially compelling in that these participants had been exposed to a subsequent second language prior to the Latin learning experiment, the English in which they had become quite proficient and which, as a second language learning experience, must have brought to their awareness the potential productivity of inflectional cues in tense marking.

Conclusions

These experiments demonstrate clear effects of attentional bias and subsequent blocking of cue acquisition that stem from both short-term and long-term learning sequence effects. Early learned language cues block the acquisition of later ones. It is possible then that L2 learners' use of adverbs and other devices for expressing time blocks their acquisition of less salient and less reliable verb morphology, thus resulting in the 'Basic Variety' of limited L2 endstate (Ellis, 2006).

There are many questions still to be answered. Can these effects be shown in the classroom learning of a more naturalistic sample of language where a wide range of cues conspire and compete for attention? To what extent are these attentional biases overt or covert – there is scope for extending these experiments using eye movements (Kruschke, Kappenman, & Hetrick, 2005). Given that proficient language users do use cues in combination, and that multiple cues in interaction provide highly constraining solutions unattainable from individual cues alone, how do other cues become integrated into the learner's inference (MacWhinney, 1987)? How does the relative salience of these cues play in the equation of their use?

Meanwhile, the findings of these experiments reinforce the possibility that understanding the limited attainment of adult second and foreign language learning needs posit no critical periods or language acquisition devices, but instead falls within the remit of the cognitive science of the associative learning of linguistic constructions.

Acknowledgments

I thank Nina Wickens and Emily Cahill for help designing, piloting, and administering these experiments.

References

Baddeley, A. D. (1976). *The psychology of memory*. New York: Harper and Row.

Barlow, M., & Kemmer, S. (Eds.). (2000). *Usage based models of language*. Stanford, CA: CSLI Publications.

Cheng, P. W., & Holyoak, K. J. (1995). Adaptive systems as intuitive statisticians: causality, contingency, and prediction. In J.-A. Meyer & H. Roitblat (Eds.), *Comparative approaches to cognition* (pp. 271-302). Cambridge MA: MIT Press.

Ellis, N. C. (2006). Selective attention and transfer phenomena in SLA: Contingency, cue competition, salience, interference, overshadowing, blocking, and perceptual learning. *Applied Linguistics, 27*(2), 1-31.

Kruschke, J. K., & Blair, N. J. (2000). Blocking and backward blocking involve learned inattention. *Psychonomic Bulletin & Review, 7*, 636-645.

Kruschke, J. K., Kappenman, E. S., & Hetrick, W. P. (2005). Eye gaze and individual differences consistent with learned attention in associative blocking and highlighting. *Journal of Experimental Psychology: Learning, Memory & Cognition, 31*(5), 830-845.

MacWhinney, B. (1987). The Competition Model. In B. MacWhinney (Ed.), *Mechanisms of language acquisition* (pp. 249-308).

MacWhinney, B. (1997). Second language acquisition and the Competition Model. In A. M. B. De Groot & J. F. Kroll (Eds.), *Tutorials in bilingualism: Psycholinguistic perspectives* (pp. 113-142). Mahwah, NJ: Lawrence Erlbaum Associates.

Matessa, M., & Anderson, J. R. (2000). Modeling focused learning in role assignment. *Language & Cognitive Processes, 15*(3), 263-292.

Robinson, P., & Ellis, N. C. (Eds.). (to appear). *A handbook of cognitive linguistics and SLA*. Mahwah, NJ: Lawrence Erlbaum.

Shanks, D. R. (1995). *The psychology of associative learning*. New York: Cambridge University Press.

Zipf, G. K. (1949). *Human behaviour and the principle of least effort: An introduction to human ecology*. Cambridge, MA: Addison-Wesley.

Processing Parallel Structure: Evidence from Eye-Tracking and a Computational Model

Jens Apel (j.apel@sms.ed.ac.uk)
Department of Psychology, University of Edinburgh
7 George Square, Edinburgh, EH8 9JZ, UK

Pia Knoeferle (knoferle@coli.uni-sb.de)
Department of Computational Linguistics
Saarland University, 66041 Saarbrücken, Germany

Matthew W. Crocker (crocker@coli.uni-sb.de)
Department of Computational Linguistics
Saarland University, 66041 Saarbrücken, Germany

Abstract

The parallelism effect in human parsing is a phenomenon in which the second constituent of a coordinate structure is processed faster when it parallels the first constituent in comparison with when it does not parallel the first constituent. The main aim of this paper is to investigate whether the parallelism effect, which was first discovered in ambiguous coordinate structures, also occurs in non-coordinate constructions, and in structurally unambiguous sentences. The motivation for investigating these two issues was to determine the extent of, and the mechanisms underlying parallelism effects, with the goal of informing the development of a computational model. Two eye-tracking studies of German showed that parallelism effects are obtained in unambiguous sentences, and strongly suggest that the effect is restricted to coordinate structures. Additionally, the parallelism effect is shown to be sensitive to the fine-grained parts-of-speech of the parallel constituents. Based on these findings, we present a computational system that is able to model our effects, and is consistent with other prevailing results.

Introduction

The Parallelism Effect

The parallelism effect in human parsing is a phenomenon in which the second constituent of a coordinate structure is processed faster when it parallels the first constituent in comparison with when it does not parallel the first constituent. In the first study of this phenomena, Frazier, Taft, Roeper, & Clifton (1984) conducted a series of five self-paced reading experiments which examined the parallelism effect for a range of clause types. The conjoined clauses of their sentences were either parallel or non-parallel. For example, in Sentence (1) the first and second clause are both active and thus, parallel, whereas in Sentence (2) the two coordinated clauses are non-parallel: the first clause is passive, and the second clause active.

(1) The tall gangster hit John and the short thug hit Sam.

(2) John was hit by the tall gangster and the short thug hit Sam.

The most interesting finding in this study was that the parallelism effect (i.e. faster processing of *the short thug hit Sam* in (1) than in (2)) was detected in all tested sentence constructions and seems to be very stable among different syntactic structures.

Frazier, Munn, & Clifton (2000) further investigated the scope of the parallelism effect by testing whether it also occurs in non-coordinate structures. If the effect is not restricted to structures within coordination, then a priming effect that occurs in both coordinate and non-coordinate constructions might be the cause of the facilitation of the second constituent. Frazier et al. (2000) tested this question by first replicating the parallelism effect in sentences containing coordinated noun phrases (NP). In a second study they then restructured the sentences such that the NPs were in subject and object position. In the parallel condition both NPs consisted of a determiner, an adjective and a noun. In the non-parallel condition the first NP consisted of a determiner and a noun and the second NP of determiner, adjective and noun.

Frazier et al. (2000) found parallelism effects in the sentences containing a coordinate structure. However, the results from the second experiment revealed that the noun phrase in object position was not faster processed when its syntactic structure paralleled that of the noun phrase in subject position. Frazier et al. (2000) concluded that the parallelism effect does not affect structures (e.g. NPs) that are not coordinated with each other. To explain their findings, Frazier et al. (2000) argue that parallel structures are most predictable in coordinated environments, and suggest that the parallelism effect might be an instance of this predictability. That is, facilitation of the second constituent might be processed more quickly when its structure can be predicted by the first conjunct.

However, reading times in the first experiment (coordinated NPs) were measured by using eye-tracking, whereas self-paced reading was used in the second experiment (non-coordinated NPs). As a result of the differences in methods, it is difficult to directly compare findings from the two experiments. Furthermore, with self-paced, moving window presentation, the reader is prevented from looking back at earlier regions once they have pressed a button to move to the next part of the sentence. It may be that important re-reading times, which would be observed using eye-tracking, were therefore crucially missing from the reported total times.

Furthermore, the sentences including a coordinate structure in Frazier et al.'s (2000) study contained a local ambiguity, despite the intention of examining parallelism in unambiguous sentences. Specifically, the second noun phrase of the coordinate structure (as e.g. in *Hilda noticed a strange man and a tall woman...*) could also be attached as the subject of a coordinated sentence resulting in sentences like *Hilda noticed a strange man and a tall woman entered the house.*

In this paper we present two eye-tracking studies of German, to clarify (a) whether or not parallelism is limited to coordinate constructions, (b) whether it can be observed in completely unambiguous sentences, and (c) the level of granularity in lexico-syntactic structure which is required for constituents to be considered parallel. By using eye-tracking for both studies, we are able to more directly compare our findings, and ensure that any possible null-effect in the no-coordination study could not be an artifact of the self-paced reading method used. Based on the evidence from the two experiments presented here, as well as the proposals of Frazier and colleagues, we develop a computational model in which the likelihood that the parser initially interprets a coordinate structure as being parallel is higher than interpreting it as non-parallel.

Experiment 1

Experiment 1 was conducted in order to investigate the parallelism effect in fully unambiguous coordinate structures. In addition to contrasting noun phrases containing an adjective or no noun modifier at all, we added a third condition in which the noun modifier consists of a participle. This enabled us to investigate whether the parallelism effect still occurs when the number of words in the noun phrase stays the same and only the parts of speech (POS) of the noun modifiers differ.

Method

Participants Thirty-six participants from Saarland University took part in Experiment 1. The average age of participants was 23.9 (range 19-50). All participants were native speakers of German and showed no visual impairments. Each participant was paid 7,50 Euro for participation.

Materials Twenty-four sentences were used as experimental items. Examples of the sentences are illustrated below:

(3) **Der Esel** und **der melkende Bauer** sind vor dem Gewitter geflüchtet.
The donkey and the milking farmer fled from the thunderstorm.

(4) **Der dämliche Esel** und **der melkende Bauer** sind vor dem Gewitter geflüchtet.
The dim-witted donkey and the milking farmer fled...

(5) **Der stampfende Esel** und **der melkende Bauer** sind vor dem Gewitter geflüchtet.
The stomping donkey and the milking farmer fled...

The second noun phrase of the coordinate structure always consisted of a determiner, a participle and a noun. The first constituent differed in the type of noun modifier. In the first condition (Sentence 3), no noun modifier was present (Empty-Part) and thus, the constituents

were non-parallel concerning number of words and consequently also differed in the parts of speech of the words. In the second condition (Sentence 4) the noun modifier consisted of an adjective (Adj-Part). Thus, the constituents differed only in the part of speech of the noun modifier. In the third condition (Sentence 5) the noun modifier was a participle (Part-Part) and the two constituents of the coordinate structure were parallel concerning number of words and the part of speech of the noun modifier.

The length of the corresponding words (i.e. determiner, noun modifier and noun) within the coordinated noun phrases varied by at most two characters in the three conditions of an item (mean lengths in characters: adjective: 9.11, participle first NP: 9.59, participle second NP: 9.63, first NP: 7.67, second NP: 7.89). Furthermore, the corresponding words in the three conditions of an item possessed the same number of syllables, and had the same stress pattern. The frequency of the word pairs was also kept similar (i.e. the difference of frequency is not more than 0.3 log frequency for the corresponding words in the three conditions of an item; mean frequency obtained from the celex database: adjective: 0.02, participle first NP: 0.01, participle second NP: 0.02, first NP: 0.45, second NP: 0.54). To ensure that the plausibility of the sentences in the three different conditions was similar, a pre-test was conducted. Twenty-one participants rated the 24 sentences on a scale between 7 (very plausible) and 1 (very implausible). A one-way repeated measure analysis of variance (ANOVA; 1 factor, 3 levels), by subjects (F_1) and by items (F_2), was conducted yielding no significant difference between the three conditions [$F_1(2,19)=0.20$, $p > .10$, and $F_2(2,22)=0.23$, $p > .10$].

If the parallelism effect extends to non-ambiguous sentences, we expect faster reading times on the second noun phrase of the coordinate structure when it parallels the first constituent in comparison to when it does not. The experimental design of this study allows us to further determine how a parallel structure is defined. If the second noun phrase is read faster in both the Adj-Part and Part-Part conditions than in the Empty-Part condition, this would suggest that parallelism does not depend on exact parallel parts of speech. If a parallelism effect only occurs in the Part-Part condition, parallel parts of speech are necessary to trigger the parallelism effect.

Design and Procedure One factor [Type of Parallelism (Par-Type)] with three levels (Empty-Part, Adj-Part, Part-Part) was used in the experiment. Par-Type was a within-subject variable, meaning that each participant saw repeated instances of every condition but only one sentence of each item.

The 24 experimental items were mixed with 72 filler items. Yes-no questions on the content were asked for 36 filler items to ensure that participants remained concentrated. The items were pseudo randomized such that all experimental items were separated by at least one filler item. Each participant received an individually randomized list.

An SMI EyeLink head-mounted eye-tracker with a sampling rate of 250 Hz was used to track the eye movements of the participants. This system consists of a headset with two cameras to enable eye-movement recording. Only the dominant eye was recorded.

Data Analysis Fixation duration times and locations were recorded for every word of the sentences. However, we were especially interested in the second conjunct (the second noun phrase) of the coordinate structure since previous studies have found parallelism effects in the second conjunct of coordinate structures. In case we replicate the parallelism effect, faster reading times are expected in this region.

A one-way repeated measure ANOVA analysis was conducted on reading times for all of the regions. The subjects' performance in answering the questions was also analyzed. Participants who deviated more than 2SD from the mean response accuracy across all conditions were excluded from the analysis. The mean of incorrectly answered questions was 34 %. The relatively high error rate presumably resulted from including difficult questions, a choice made to ensure thorough reading. One participant, who answered 44% of the questions wrong, was excluded. Therefore, 35 participants were included in the analysis.

Results and Discussion

As a main observation of this experiment, we replicated the finding from Frazier et al. (2000). We found significant differences between parallel and non-parallel conditions in regression path time (RPD) of the noun in the second noun phrase. RPD is defined as the sum of all fixations beginning with the first fixation in the region and ending when the eye moves rightward to the next region (this includes all regressive fixations). The RPD reading time of the noun in the second constituent of the coordinate structure differed significantly between the conditions $F_1(2, 33) = 3.56$, $p < .05$; $F_2(2, 22) = 3.98$, $p < .05$] [1]. The descriptive data is illustrated in Figure 1.

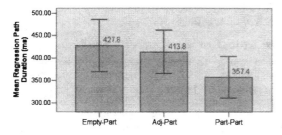

Figure 1: Mean RPD of the Noun of the Second Noun Phrase in Experiment 1.

Post hoc analyses revealed that in both the subjects and items analyses, the RPD fixation durations were significantly shorter in the Part-Part condition (357.8 ms) than in the Empty-Part condition (427.8 ms; p<.05). Furthermore, RPD fixation durations were shorter in

[1]Since the raw data was not normally distributed, the data was transformed using a log_{10} transformation in both Experiments 1 and 2.

the Part-Part condition than in the Adj-Part condition (413.8 ms). However, this difference was only marginally significant in the per subjects analysis and not significant in the per items analysis.

Experiment 2

In Experiment 2 we tested whether a parallelism effect can be observed in non-coordinated structures.

Method

Participants Twenty-one further participants from the same population in Experiment 1 took part in Experiment 2. The average age of participants was 29.2 (range 17-51).

Materials Twenty-four sentences were used as experimental items. Examples of the sentences are illustrated below:

(6) **Der Esel beißt den melkenden Bauern** ohne jede Vorwarnung.
The donkey bites the milking farmer without any warning.

(7) **Der dämliche Esel beißt den melkenden Bauern** ohne jede Vorwarnung.
The dim-witted donkey bites the milking farmer...

(8) **Der stampfende Esel beißt den melkenden Bauern** ohne jede Vorwarnung.
The stomping donkey bites the milking farmer...

The sentences were based on the items of Experiment 1. The first noun phrase from the coordination in Experiment 1 served as the subject. The second noun phrase took the place of the object. The same conditions as in Experiment 1 were used: Empty-Part, Adj-Part and Part-Part.

A plausibility rating test was also conducted for Experiment 2, yielding no significant difference between the three conditions [$F_1(2, 19) = 1.14$, $p > .10$, and $F_2(2,22)=1.85$, $p > .10$.].

Design and Procedure Design and procedure were the same as in Experiment 1.

Data Analysis The data analysis was the same as in Experiment 1. Response accuracy on the questions was high (15% error rate), and no participant mean deviated more than 2SD from the mean response accuracy.

Results and Discussion

Since the parallelism effect in Experiment 1 did only appear at the noun of the second noun phrase, we also expected the effect to appear on this region (i.e. the noun of the object noun phrase) in Experiment 2 if the parallelism effect extends to non-coordinate structures. Furthermore, as in Experiment 1, we expected an effect in the RPD measure. As a main result, however, we could not find any differences in reading time between the three conditions at this region.

Figure 2 illustrates the RPD-data at the noun of the noun phrase in object position. The main effect was not

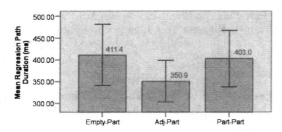

Figure 2: Mean RPD of the Noun of the Second Noun Phrase in Experiment 2.

reliable [$F_1(1, 19) = 1.87, p = .18; F_2(2, 22) = 1.22, p = .31$].

In order to test the possibility that the effect might occur earlier or later than in Experiment 1, we examined reading times for regions adjacent to the second noun, and also other measures than RPD. However, we could not find any significant effects in support of a parallelism effect.

Discussion of Results

The two experiments replicated the results from the study by Frazier et al. (2000). A significant parallelism effect was found in Experiment 1 but not in Experiment 2. Thus, the parallelism effect seems to be restricted to coordinate structures and does not come to play when the noun phrases take a subject and object position. A general priming approach as the origin of the parallelism effect can be rejected. It is more likely that a mechanism specific to coordinate structures is responsible for the effect. Furthermore, since in Experiment 1 a parallelism effect was only found in parallel syntactic structures, the parallelism effect seems to depend on parallel parts of speech. Keeping the surface structure of the constituents the same is not sufficient. Finally, since the sentences in Experiment 1 do not exhibit any ambiguity, it can be concluded that the parallelism effect does not only occur in ambiguous sentences but extends to unambiguous structures.

In the next section, we introduce the computational model of the study.

A Computational Model

Several proposals have been made to explain parallelism effects. Frazier and Clifton (2001) postulated a copy α mechanism, which copies the syntactic structure of the first constituent of a coordinate structure to the second constituent and therefore, saves processing costs if the first constituent parallels the second one. This mechanism only applies to coordinate constructions. When the model encounters a conjunction, a pointer is set at the beginning of the first constituent of a coordinate structure. The whole syntactic structure is then copied to the second constituent and if this constituent parallels the first one, no extra cost for building the structure of the second constituent is spent.

Steiner (2003) proposes an alternative mechanism. The distinctive feature of this model is that the syntactic tree can be three-dimensional. Whenever a coordinate structure is encountered (triggered by a conjunction), the parser jumps back to the beginning of the first constituent and opens a third dimension. The terminal nodes of the second constituent are attached to the existing syntactic structure of the first constituent if the two constituents are parallel. If the coordinate structure is not parallel a new structure has to be built. Steiner (2003) argues that reusing structure saves time, and therefore, a parallel second constituent is processed faster than a non-parallel one.

Neither of these two models is very clear concerning how the first constituent of a parallel coordinate structure is to be identified. In the model by Frazier and Clifton (2001), a pointer is moved to the antecedent constituent to copy the structure of this constituent to the second one. However, Frazier and Clifton (2001) do not make explicit how the beginning of the antecedent constituent is found. The conjunction in sentences like *The man saw the boy and...* could coordinate the noun phrase, the verb phrase or the sentential phrase of the sentence. Thus, the beginning of the antecedent constituent is ambiguously defined. Furthermore, how does the parser recognize that the first clause parallels the second one in order to copy the syntactic structure of the first to the second constituent? Parsing the whole sentence again after a conjunction was found, to detect and analyze the antecedent clause, would probably nullify the advantages of the copy α mechanism. Steiner (2003) integrated a connectionist component with a spreading activation principle into her model in order to solve the problem of comparing the first constituent with the second one to use the same structure when they are parallel.

In the model of the current study, an alternative two-dimensional parsing mechanism is introduced. We further describe a method that is able to deal with the problem of detecting the beginning of the first constituent in a parallel structure. The validity of the model will be evaluated by testing it with sentences from the current study and with sentences from another study by Knoeferle & Crocker (2006).

The Model of the Current Study

The system is divided into two main processing modules. The first module is an incremental serial arc-eager left-corner chart parser. The second module which is termed coordination-module (C-Module[2]) is specifically designed to handle coordinate structures. The Parser works entirely independent from the C-Module.

The structure of the whole system is illustrated in Figure 3. It was implemented using the computational modeling environment COGENT (Cooper, 2002). The Parser and the C-Module are processing modules and both have reading (indicated by arrows with a triangle) and writing (indicated by normal arrows) capability to various modules such as Potential Operators, Oracle, Choice Points, Chart and the C-Chart. The Parser is only able to read from the Grammar Rules

---

[2]The components of the model are kept in a different font in order to better recognize them.

while the C-Module both reads from and writes to the Grammar Rules. In addition, the Parser alone is able to read from the Lexicon and read from and write to the Edge Labeling. In the next section, the components of the model will be briefly described before explaining the C-Module in more detail.

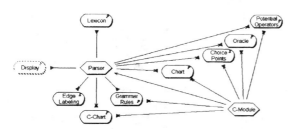

Figure 3: The structure of the system.

In the Lexicon and the Grammar Rules the lexicon and grammar rules are stored. The grammar rules consist of phrase structure rules that each exhibit a resting activation (RA). In the parser, the RAs are all set to a value of 10. To represent a lower frequency of object-verb-subject sentences and to process the sentences from the Knoeferle & Crocker (2006) study (see Evaluation section), the corresponding rule received a lower RA of 2. If the parser processes an ambiguous structure, the grammar rule with the higher RA is more likely to be applied. In the Potential Operators module, all possible parsing routes are stored. Possible parsing routes are: Inserting a new word into the parse tree (1), allocating a POS to a word (2), applying a grammar rule to a POS (3) and merging two edges with each other (4). The numbers (1) - (4) indicate the priority of each of the parsing routes. If more than on route could be applied the one with the higher priority wins the race. This approach is similar to the "race model" proposed by Traxler, Pickering, and Clifton (1998). The remaining routes are stored in the Choice Points module, for potential later access, in case a pursued route fails (see Cooper (2002) for a similar system). The parser uses a so-called oracle, that identifies a wrong parsing route early, without unnecessary backtracking, improving the performance of the parser. In the Chart the chart of the whole parse tree is stored and can be illustrated. The usage of the C-Chart is explained in the following section. Finally the Parser reads the linguistic information (i.e. words from the sentences) word-by-word from the Display.

We used a left-corner parser, because in comparison to the top-down and bottom-up parser it performs similar as the human parser concerning memory load while processing embedded sentences (Resnik, 1992). Furthermore, by using the arc-eager version of the left-corner parser we were able to model the preference of most languages to attach a new phrase at the last constructed one (Late-closure principle; Frazier, 1978).

The C-Module consists of four main processing steps. These steps are activated when the parser encounters the coordinating conjunction ("and").

Step 1) Add possible candidates to C-chart
Possible candidates are all phrases that might become the first constituent of a coordinate structure. For example in the sentence *The boy saw the dog and*, possible candidates would be *the dog* (NP), *saw the dog* (VP), *The boy saw the dog* (S).

Step 2) Select a candidate from the C-chart
Since the parser follows the late-closure principle (Frazier, 1978), this would be the lowest attached phrase (*the dog* in the example above).

Step 3) Increase the resting activation of the grammar rule, which built the selected candidate in the C-Chart
This procedure has the effect that when more than one grammar rule could be applied, the probability that the parser chooses the one applied earlier in coordination is increased.[3]

Step 4) IF the coordinate structure was completely explored
THEN delete all entries in the C-chart and set the resting activations of the grammar rules to their initial state
ELSE select another candidate in the C-chart and continue at Step 3.

As outlined above, the basic functionality of the model is that the probability of applying the grammar rule, which was applied for the first constituent of a coordinate structure to the second constituent rises when a conjunction is encountered. Thus, the probability that the parser initially applies the grammar rule which postulates a parallel structure, is higher than a rule postulating a non-parallel structure. This approach is not unlike Frazier et al.'s (2000) proposal that a parallel coordinate structure is more predictable and therefore, faster processed. The problem of the existing approache (Frazier and Clifton, 2001) to select the appropriate syntactic structure of the antecedent phrase in an ambiguous coordinate construction to copy it to the second constituent does not occur in the current approach. The RAs of the grammar rules of all possible phrases are boosted and due to the inherent properties of the arc-eager left-corner parser, the model selects independently from this procedure the lowest-attached phrase.

Evaluation

To evaluate the model, we used the sentences from the two experiments of the present paper, as well as sentences from the Knoeferle & Crocker (2006) study.

Processing steps in COGENT are counted in cycles. To evaluate the system, we directly compared these processing steps with the RPD fixation times of the experiments. Specifically, the RPDs of the whole second

---

[3]A reviewer correctly pointed out that the resting activation of the grammar rules of all candidates could be raised instead of only the one from the selected candidate. This would not change the results but probably speed up the performance of the parser. In a possible next version of the system this change will be implemented.

constituent are compared with the number of cycles the parser needed to parse this section of the sentences. In order to compare the two values and present them in the same charts, the numbers of cycles were multiplied by 27. This number seems to be a good approximation to align the processing cycles of COGENT with the RPD times of an eye-tracking study. Figure 4 illustrates the results of the evaluation.

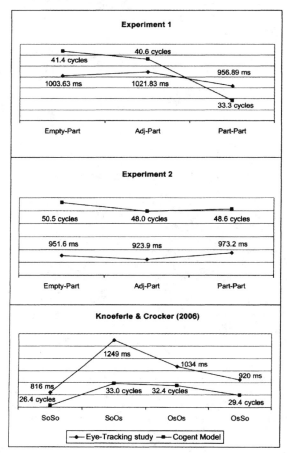

Figure 4: Evaluation of the model using results from Experiment 1 and 2 and the Knoeferle & Crocker (2006) study

As can be seen, the proportions of the cycles and the fixation duration times were approximately the same in all three experiments.

Conclusion

The results of the two experiments conducted in this study confirmed the findings by Frazier et al. (2000). The parallelism effect seems to be restricted to coordinate structures. Our findings strongly suggest that the origin of the parallelism effect is not a general priming effect but that it only applies in coordinate structures. Since we tested sentences that did not exhibit syntactic ambiguities we also conclude that the parallelism effect is not restricted to ambiguous structures. Furthermore, the absence of a parallelism effect between the Empty-Part and the Adj-Part conditions suggests that the parallelism effect depends crucially on the specific parts of speech being parallel in both constituents rather than just a parallel surface structure. Based on these findings, we constructed a computational model, which is able to account for the results found in the experiments of this thesis and the results of experiments conducted by Knoeferle and Crocker (2006). In this model, the parser increases the resting activation of grammar rules which where applied in the first constituent of a coordinate structure. When selecting grammar rules for the second constituent, the rules applied in the first constituent are preferred. In comparison with existing models, our mechanism further eschews the problem of finding the beginning of the antecedent constituent, and qualitatively fits the reading time behavior observed in three experiments.

Acknowledgments

This research was supported by a German Research Foundation grant (CR 135/1-2) awarded to MWC.

References

Cooper, R. P. (2002). *Model ling high-level cognitive processes*. Mahwah, New Jersey: Lawrence Erlbaum Associates.

Frazier, L. (1978). *On comprehending sentences: Syntactic parsing strategies*.. Doctoral dissertation, University of Connecticut.

Frazier, L., & Clifton, C. (2001). Parsing coordination and ellipsis: Copy α. *Syntax, 4(1)*, 1–22.

Frazier, L., Munn, A., & Clifton, C. (2000). Processing coordinate structures. *Journal of Psycholinguistic Research, 29*, 345–370.

Frazier, L., Taft, L., Roeper, T., & Clifton, C. (1984). Parallel structure: A source of facilitation in sentence comprehension. *Memory & Cognition, 12(5)*, 421–430.

Knoeferle, P., & Crocker, M. (2006). The mechanism(s) underlying parallelism: eye tracking coordinate structures in german. *Proceedings of the CUNY Sentence Processing Conference*, CUNY, New York City.

Resnik, P. (1992). Left-corner parsing and psychological plausibility. *In Proceedings of the 14th Conference on Computational Linguistics - Volume 1*, Nantes, France.

Steiner, I. (2003). Parsing syntactic redundancies in coordinate structures. *Proceedings of EuroCogSci 03 The European Cognitive Science Conference 2003* (pp. 443). Osnabrueck, Germany: Lawrence Erlbaum.

Traxler, M., Pickering, M., & Clifton, J., C. (1998). Adjunct attachment is not a form of lexical ambiguity resolution. *Journal of Memory and Language, 39*, 558–592.

The Effect of Phonological Parallelism in Coordination: Evidence from Eye-tracking

Amit Dubey and Frank Keller and Patrick Sturt
Human Communication Research Centre, University of Edinburgh
2 Buccleuch Place, Edinburgh EH8 9LW, UK
{amit.dubey,patrick.sturt,frank.keller}@ed.ac.uk

Abstract

In this paper we report an eye-tracking experiment designed to investigate syntactic and phonological parallelism effects in comprehension. Eye-movements were recorded while participants read sentences that contained particle verb constructions. Each experimental item included a coordinated verb phrase (VP), whose two conjuncts either exhibited parallel syntactic forms in terms of particle placement (e.g., *The lawyer won over the jury and fought off the developers*), or did not (e.g., *The lawyer won the jury over and fought off the developers*). In addition to the manipulation of syntactic form, the number of syllables intervening between the verb and the particle ranged from zero to five across the item set. Linear regression analysis revealed a reading time advantage for VPs that were parallel in terms of the number of intervening syllables. However, processing was not speeded by parallelism of syntactic form per se. We argue that theories that seek to explain syntactic parallelism need to take account of phonological length.

Introduction

Research in psycholinguistics has shown evidence for a general facilitation for the processing of structure that is structurally similar to recently processed material. For example, work on *syntactic priming* in production (Bock, 1986; Pickering & Branigan, 1998) shows that people prefer to produce sentences using syntactic structures that have recently been produced. Although most of the work in syntactic priming concerns language production, there are some studies that show a similar facilitation in comprehension. For example, Branigan et al. (1995) showed that whole-sentence reading times for garden path sentences were reduced when a similar garden path sentence had been read in an immediately preceding trial, while Branigan et al. (2005) showed that picture-matching latencies were facilitated when the relevant picture matched the syntactic structure of the preceding trial.

A phenomenon that is closely related to syntactic priming in comprehension is the *parallelism effect*. In an eye-tracking experiment investigating noun phrase coordination, Frazier et al. (2000) showed that the second conjunct *a short poem* was read more quickly in (1-a), when it matched the form of the first conjunct, than in (1-b), when it did not.

(1) a. Terry wrote a long novel and *a short poem* during her sabbatical
    b. Terry wrote a novel and *a short poem* during her sabbatical

Frazier et al. interpreted the parallelism effect as a syntactic phenomenon—in other words, the relative facilitation in (1-a)

was due to the fact that both noun phrase conjuncts had the form DETERMINER ADJECTIVE NOUN. However, there are other possible interpretations of the effect. One possible contributing factor is the relative lengths of the two noun phrase conjuncts. For example, the two conjuncts in (1-a) have the same number of syllables, while those in (1-b) do not (henceforth, we will assume that the syllable is the appropriate measure for length effects, and we will refer to such effects in terms of phonology). Another potentially relevant difference is that the determiner and the head noun are separated by one intervening syllable for both conjuncts in (1-a), while this is not the case in (1-b).

Parallelism has also been studied in corpus-based investigations. Dubey et al. (2005) show that the frequencies of various noun phrase structures are increased when the same structure has already appeared in the preceding text. Dubey et al. (2005) also show that the effect can be found whether or not the noun phrases in question are coordinated, although the effect is stronger in coordinated environments. Recent corpus work (Gries, 2005; Szmrecsanyi, 2005; Reitter et al., 2006) has shown that the phenomenon is general across a range of construction types in corpora.

The experiment which we report here investigates the parallelism phenomenon in English particle verbs (also known as phrasal verbs). Particle verbs are of particular interest for the investigation of parallelism, because they allow for a syntactic alternation which has only a minimal effect on meaning. Consider (2-a) and (2-b), for example:

(2) a. The lawyer won over the jury.
    b. The lawyer won the jury over.

Besides information structure differences, these two sentences have identical meanings, while they differ in syntactic form.

A second reason for using particle verbs in our study is that the alternation allows us to compare a purely syntactic view of parallelism with a view that takes account of phonological factors. Consider the following:

(3) a. The lawyer won over the jury.
    b. The campaigner paid bribes out.
    c. Graham knocked the shed down.
    d. The lawyer won the jury over.
    e. The politician handed the estimate in.
    f. The lawyer fought the developers off.

In the sequence of sentences in (3), the number of syllables intervening between the particle and the verb increases from zero in (3-a) to five in (3-f). Thus, from a phonological point of view, the degree of separation can be seen as varying quasi-continuously from (3-a) to (3-f). This contrasts with a syntactic view. In terms of the syntactic rules (3-a) differs from all the other sentences, because (3-a) uses a VERB NP PARTICLE template, while all the other examples use a VERB PARTICLE NP template.

In the theoretical linguistics and psycholinguistics literature, it has been noted that particle verb sentences become intuitively more difficult as the degree of separation between the verb and particle increases (Hawkins, 1995; Frazier & Fodor, 1978).[1] More recently, Gries (1999) has argued that this effect of constituent length can be subsumed under a more general theory in which processing difficulty is explained by semantic, pragmatic and discourse-level factors. However, to our knowledge, this phenomenon has not been studied using on-line techniques. Therefore, a third objective of our paper is to examine how processing difficulty is affected by the degree of separation between verb and particle. This in turn allows us to consider the question of whether the degree of the parallelism preference is affected by the degree of processing difficulty involved in the relevant structure.

Experiment

This experiment had a dual purpose: Firstly, we wanted to test whether the parallelism effect demonstrated by Frazier et al. (2000) for NP coordination generalizes to VP coordination. The second aim was to determine whether phonological factor influence parallelism, such as the number of syllables intervening between a verb and its particle in particle verb constructions such as the ones in (2).

We follow previous work on parallelism in terms of methodology: experimental participants had to read written stimuli while their eye-movements were recorded using an eye-tracker. The eye-tracking record allows us to measure the predicted speedup effects in the second conjunct with great accuracy.

Method

Participants   Thirty-two native English speakers (students from the University of Edinburgh) took part in this study, receiving £4 subject payment. Participants were tested in individual sessions, each of which took about 25 minutes to complete.

Materials   We designed 28 different materials, each consisting of a sentence with VP coordination involving particle verbs in both conjuncts (no particle verb was used in more than one material). Four different conditions were generated for each of the materials by varying whether the particle was adjacent to the verb or moved in either the first or the second VP. An example material in all four conditions is as follows:

(4) a. Before the lawyer won over the jury and fought off the developers, the project was stalled.

b. Before the lawyer won the jury over and fought off the developers, the project was stalled.

c. Before the lawyer won over the jury and fought the developers off, the project was stalled.

d. Before the lawyer won the jury over and fought the developers off, the project was stalled.

The items were allocated to four lists. Each list contained each of the 28 material in one of the four conditions (according to a Latin square). A list of 90 filler sentences was also generated. Eight participants each read one of the lists (assigned at random), as well as all of the fillers. Items and fillers were presented in random sequence generated for each participant, preceded by five practice items.

Procedure   Participants were seated approximately 65 cm from a 21" color monitor with 1024×768 pixel resolution; twenty-four pixels equaled about one degree of visual angle. Participants wore an SR Research Eyelink II head-mounted eye-tracker running at 500 Hz sampling rate. Viewing was binocular, but only the participant's dominant eye was tracked (the right eye for about 68% of the participants, as determined by a simple parallax test prior to the experiment). Participants were instructed to avoid strong head movements throughout the experiment. A USB gamepad was used to record button responses. Stimulus presentation and data recording were controlled by two PCs running EyeTrack, experimental software developed at the University of Massachusetts.

At the start of the experiment, the experimenter performed the standard Eyelink calibration routine, which involves participants looking at a grid of nine fixation targets in random succession. Then a validation phase followed to test the accuracy of the calibration against the same targets. Calibration and validation was repeated at least twice throughout the experiment, or if the experimenter noticed that measurement accuracy was poor (e.g., after strong head movements or a change in the participant's posture).

Each trial was structured as follows: first a gaze trigger was displayed on the left of the screen. Once the participants had fixated the gaze trigger, the trial began, with the trigger being replaced by the first letter of the sentence. Once the participant had finished reading the sentences, he/she pressed a button to signal the end of the trial. Participants were instructed to read the sentences attentively, so that they were able to answer subsequent questions. In 25% of the cases, the trial was followed by a question on the screen, replacing the sentences. Whenever such a question appeared, subjects had to answer it by pressing either the "yes" button or the "no" button on the gamepad.

Results

Data Analysis   The raw eye-tracking data was processed with EyeDoctor, part of the UMass suite of eye-tracking tools. EyeDoctor was used to correct cases of vertical drift of the tracker, and to delete abandoned trials, fillers, and practice items. Fixations shorter than 80 ms (approximately 2–3% of all fixations) were pooled with preceding or following fixations. Times for blinks were added to the immediately preceding fixations (assuming that processing does not pause during a blink) and fixations outside the screen area (less than 1% of all fixations) were deleted.

---

[1] Although we know of no result applying Gibson's Locality Theory (Gibson, 1998) to processing particle verb constructions, it is nonetheless interesting to note this theory may provide some explanation as to why non-adjacent particle verb constructions are more difficult to process.

The data was then analyzed with UMass EyeDry, which computes a range of eye-tracking measures based on a region definition provided by the experimenter. We defined four regions as follows:

- Region r_1: all material up to end of the subject NP (*Before the lawyer* in (4-a));

- Region r_2: first VP (*won over the jury* in (4-a));

- Region r_3: conjunction *and*;

- Region r_4: second VP (*fought the developers off* in (4-a));

- Region r_5: all remaining material (*the project was stalled* in (4-a)).

Region r_4 is the critical region on which we expect to see the parallelism effect. Region r_5 is the spillover region, and might also show an effect. On for these regions, we computed the following reading measures: first-pass time, number of regressions in, number of regressions out, regression path time, second pass time, and total time.

The *first-pass reading times* are the sum of the durations of all initial fixations, from the time that the eye gaze first enters the region from the left until the gaze moves outside the region, either to left or right. *Regression path times* are the sum of all fixations that are made (including to the left of the region) before the eye gaze first moves to the right of the word. *Second pass reading times time* are the sum of all fixations that are made on the region after the region has been fixated and exited for the first time. Finally, *Total time* is the sum of all fixations on the region, and equates to the sum of first-pass and second-pass reading times.

We calculated two measures based on the frequency of regressive saccades: *regressions out* refers to the percentage of trials in which the reader makes a regressive saccade to the left of the region, before any fixations are made to the right of the region. Finally *regressions in* refers to the percentage of trials in which the region was re-fixated following a regressive saccade from the right.

We also coded the experimental stimuli as follows. A categorical variable was introduced that indicates whether the verb and its particle are contiguous (cont) or non-contiguous (non) in both VPs. We will refer to these as vp1 and vp2, respectively. To enable more fine-grained analysis of particle movement effects, we coded also the number of syllables intervening between verb and particle in the first VP and the second VP. We will refer to these variables as syl1 and syl2. Both variables ranges from 0 to 5.

Phonological Parallelism As noted above, we measure the parallelism effect using two variables, syl1, which indicates the number of syllables between the verb and the particle in the first VP, and syl2, which is the same measure for VP_2.

To analyze the data, we regress reading time against the syl1 and syl2 variables. Noting that a verb and particle are more likely to be adjacent when the phrasal verb takes a non-pronominal NP object, we would expect a local minimum when syl2 = 0. Under the hypothesis that syllabic parallelism influences reading times, we would further expect a local minimum as the difference between syl1 and syl2

increase. This will be encoded in a new variable absdiff = $abs(\text{syl1} - \text{syl2})$. As we expect these variables to affect reading times linearly, we use linear regression. The regression model used was

$$r_4 \sim \text{syl1} * \text{syl2} + \text{absdiff}$$

Note that the $*$ represents all possible interactions and main effects between the 'multiplied' variables. Regressing syl1, syl2 and absdiff against reading times produced no statistically significant results ($P > .1$ for all coefficients) for first pass, regression path, regressions in, regressions out, and second path reading times.

This regression model, though, is unable to capture an interesting property of particle verbs. In corpora, some verbs more likely to appear non-adjacent to their particle than other verbs. As the human comprehension system has been hypothesized to be *tuned* to the frequencies of its environment (Mitchell et al., 1996), these corpus preferences could influence reading times. We therefore predict these frequencies affect reading times. Unfortunately, it is difficult to calculate these preferences as many of the verbs used in the experiment too infrequently in even a large corpus such as the 100 million word British National Corpus (BNC). Therefore, we estimated this tendency using counts derived from the world wide web, which have proven to be a reliable method for overcoming sparse bigram statistics (Keller et al., 2002). Keller et al. (2002) observe that web counts *decrease* data sparseness at the expense of *increased* variance. Google searches were used to determine how often the word pairs were seen together or apart. For example, the pair of queries (both in quotes), "prop up" and "prop * up" were submitted, resulting in an estimate of 1.59 million and 301,000 documents. We then calculate

$$P_{together} = \frac{1.59}{1.59 + 0.301} = .841$$

A limitation of Google counts is that they do not take word class into consideration. For example, a search may well return pages with the target words which nonetheless are not in a particle verb construction, for example a sentence such as 'he won victory over himself'[2]. It is therefore necessary to verify that the Google counts are reasonable estimates for actual verb particle frequencies. To determine if this was they case, we used a version of the BNC which was parsed by a highly accurate automatic parser (Charniak, 2000). This parsed BNC was then used to derive accurate word counts for the subset of particle verbs which did appear in the BNC. Computing the Pearson correlation of the log of these BNC counts against the log of the Google counts, we found a significant Pearson correlation for the numerators, $r = .71, n = 13, P < 0.01$, and the correct trend for the denominators $r = .42, n = 13, P = 0.15$

The probability $P_{together}$ is calculated for both verbs in each item. These probabilities are referred to as vp1pref and vp2pref for the first and second verb, respectively. Including these two quantities in the regression, we get the following equation:

$$
\begin{aligned}
r_4 \sim\ & \text{syl1} * \text{syl2} * \text{vp1pref} * \text{vp2pref} \\
& + \text{absdiff} * \text{vp1pref} * \text{vp2pref}
\end{aligned}
$$

---

[2]This example was provided by an anonymous reviewer.

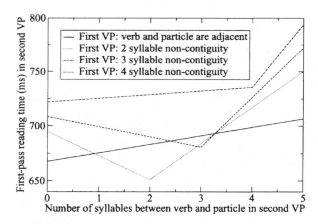

Figure 1: The predicted effect of syl2 on VP_2 first-pass reading time, when vp1pref and vp2pref take their median values. The lines show various values of syl1. There is a local minimum/inflection point at syl2 = 0 and when syl1 = syl2.

With the verb-particle preferences included, the regression now yields statistically significant estimates for nearly all coefficients in first-pass reading times. Of particular interest, the syllabic interactions syl1:syl2:vp1pref:vp2pref and absdiff:vp1pref:vp2pref were both statistically significant ($P <$ 0.05). A summary of the co-efficients is shown in Table 1. No other reading time measure produced significant results.

The regression predicts ease of processing in a manner consistent with the phonological parallelism effect. While difficult to assess directly, it is possible to interpret the regression graphically. Figure 1 shows a two-dimensional characterization of the results. Choosing the median values for vp1pref and vp2pref, this figure shows reading times as a function of syl2. Each line represents a different value for syl1. As expected, there is a minimum when syl2 = 0, when the verb and particle are adjacent. Reading times increase as the number of syllables increase, validating earlier research showing long NPs between a verb and particle are harder to process. However, this increase in processing load is mitigated at a local minimum/inflection point when syl1 = syl2, denoting syllabic parallelism. This interaction can be seen more clearly in Figure 2, which plots the relationship between syl1, syl2 and reading times in a three dimensional plot. As in Figure 1, vp1pref and vp2pref are set to their median values.

Alternative Encoding   There is another explanation for the results. For both syl1 and syl2 (let us refer to them collectively as syl), the difference between keeping the verb and particle adjacent (i.e. syl = 0) and non-adjacent (i.e. syl > 0) is more noticeable than adding one syllable to the object noun phrase in the non-adjacent condition (e.g. changing syl = 3 to syl = 4). Therefore, it is possible that a categorical variable encoding adjacency vs non-adjacency can explain all the variance, and the ordinal variables syl and absdiff are not required. If we encode these variables as vp1 and vp2, it is possible to regress these against reading times to test this hypothesis.

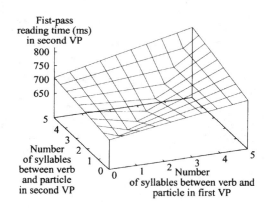

Figure 2: The predicted joint effect of syl1 and syl2 on VP_2 first-pass reading times, when vp1pref and vp2pref take their median values.

1	1st person singular pronoun
2	2nd person singular pronoun
3	3rd person singular pronoun
4	Proper names
5	Kin terms
6	Animate beings
7	Concrete objects
8	Containers
9	Locations
10	Sensual Entities
11	Abstract Entities

Table 2: Silverstein Hierarchy (SH), shown by Gries (1999) to influence particle placement

However, the regression

$$r_4 \sim vp1 * vp2 * vp1pref * vp2pref$$

yielded no significant effects for any coefficient in any reading time measure. In particular all the interaction terms vp1:vp2 and vp1:vp2:vp1pref:vp2pref were not significant ($P > .1$ in all measures).

Removing the vp1pref and vp2pref variables, it is possible to perform a traditional ANOVA analysis on the data. This also produced no statistically significant results ($P > .05$ for all measures).

Discussion

Our main result is that the reading times of particle verbs do exhibit the parallelism effect. Surprisingly, we found no evidence for pure syntactic parallelism. In other words, there was no evidence that one use of the rule VP→V NP Part predicted another use of VP→V NP Part. Rather, the parallelism effect here appears to operate on the phonological level: we found evidence for more parallelism when the number of syllables in the first NP were closer to the number of syllables in the second.

	Estimate	t value	$Pr(>|t|)$	
(Intercept)	-11850	-2.396	0.0168	*
syl1	-13097	-1.697	0.0901	.
syl2	-15831	-2.008	0.0449	*
vp1pref	12789	2.534	0.0115	*
vp2pref	13469	2.542	0.0112	*
absdiff	14981	1.960	0.0503	.
syl1:syl2	9745	2.339	0.0196	*
syl1:vp1pref	13468	1.703	0.0890	.
syl2:vp1pref	16380	2.027	0.0430	*
syl1:vp2pref	15084	1.822	0.0688	.
syl2:vp2pref	18079	2.137	0.0329	*
vp1pref:vp2pref	-13777	-2.549	0.0110	*
vp1pref:absdiff	-15511	-1.980	0.0481	*
vp2pref:absdiff	-17171	-2.095	0.0364	*
syl1:syl2:vp1pref	-10053	-2.352	0.0189	*
syl1:syl2:vp2pref	-11099	-2.466	0.0139	*
syl1:vp1pref:vp2pref	-15515	-1.828	0.0679	.
syl2:vp1pref:vp2pref	-18705	-2.156	0.0313	*
vp1pref:vp2pref:absdiff	17785	2.117	0.0345	*
syl1:syl2:vp1pref:vp2pref	11453	2.480	0.0133	*

Table 1: Regression coefficients and their significance. Significance codes: '*': 0.05 '.': 0.1

Moreover, it appears as if the parallelism effect is influenced by the tendencies of particle verbs to appear adjacent or not adjacent to their particles. It is possible that these preferences are due to some latent factors which have no other effects. However, another explanation is that these adjacency preferences are due to the selectional preference the verbs place upon their NP objects. In turn, characteristics of the selected NPs influence particle placement. In particular, it is known that the preference for a non-adjacent placement of a particle is influenced by the accessibility of the non-adjacent construction, which is in turn influenced by what is known as the *entrenchment* of the noun phrase (Gries, 1999). This is encoded in the Silverstein hierarchy (SH), which posits a scale of entrenchment from abstract entities down to the 1st person singular pronoun. Following Gries (1999), we utilize Deane's (1987) modified version of the SH, shown in Table 2.

Using only corpus studies, it would be tedious to directly ascertain how a verb's selectional preferences (as encoded using the SH) influence its preference for preferring an adjacent particle. However, it is possible to indirectly measure this – by encoding each object noun phrase in VP_2 with its level on the SH, and correlating this with vp2pref. We found a statistically significant Pearson correlation ($r = .53, n = 28, P < 0.01$). Although this indicates some interaction is present, it is difficult to draw firm conclusions about the nature of the interactions because this is only an indirect measure. However, it is suggestive of a semantic influence on parallelism, in addition to the phonological effect shown above.

Theoretical Implications

There has been some debate concerning the mechanism responsible for the parallelism effect. Some (Dubey et al., 2005, 2006) have argued that the parallelism effect is an instance of comprehension-comprehension syntactic priming. Others

(Frazier et al., 2000) have argued for a distinct mechanism, separate from syntactic priming. Frazier et al. (2000) base their argument upon an experiment showing a null effect for priming in non-coordinate contexts whereas similar items do in fact show a parallelism effect in coordinated contexts. Dubey et al. (2005) counter this with corpus studies showing that, at least in corpora, effects can be seen both in co-ordinated and non-coordinated context, although the effect is weaker in the latter. As this experiment found the presence of a parallelism effect only after taking phonology and latent preference into account, a full test of a similar effect in a non-coordinated context may also depend upon taking these factors into account, in order to overcome the much smaller effect size in such contexts.

Regardless of the cause of the parallelism effect, this study does have implications upon whatever mechanism is responsible for it: parallelism does not operate on the level of syntax alone (as depicted in Figure 3(a)). In fact, Figure 3(b) gives a more accurate picture: the parallelism effect must at least operate on both the level of syntax and phonology. Moreover, there must be some interaction between the two: a change in syl1 or syl2 from 0 to a non-zero value indicates a syntactic difference, whereas other changes in syl1 and syl2 are due to phonological differences. Therefore, the parallelism effect is not purely syntactic, but operates on several distinct modules of the human sentence processor, and requires interactions between these modules.

References

Bock, J. K. (1986). Syntactic persistence in language production. *Cognitive Psychology*, *18*, 355–387.

Branigan, H. P., Pickering, M. J., Liversedge, S. P., Stewart, A. J., & Urbach, T. P. (1995). Syntactic priming - inves-

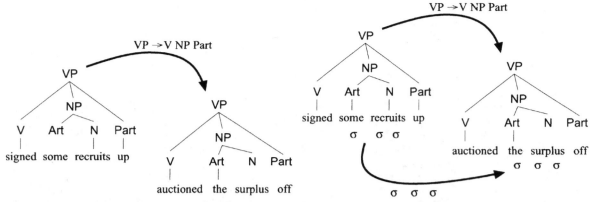

(a) The Parallelism Effect has previously been associated with syntactic structures.

(b) The present work finds evidence that the Parallelism Effect operates *simultaneously* on syntax and phonology.

Figure 3: Parallelism may operate on more than one level.

tigating the mental representation of languge. *Journal of Psycholinguistic Research*, *24*, 489–506.

Branigan, H. P., Pickering, M. J., & McLean, J. F. (2005). Priming prepositional-phrase attachment during comprehension. *Journal of Experimental Psychology: Learning, Memory and Cognition*, *31*, 468–481.

Charniak, E. (2000). A Maximum-Entropy-Inspired Parser. In *Proceedings of the 1st Conference of North American Chapter of the Association for Computational Linguistics*, (pp. 132–139), Seattle, WA.

Deane, P. D. (1987). English possessives, topicality, and the SH. In *Proceedings of the 13th Annual Meeting of the Berkeley Linguistics Society*, (pp. 64–76), Berkeley, CA. Berkeley Linguistics Society.

Dubey, A., Keller, F., & Sturt, P. (2006). Integrating syntactic priming into an incremental probabilisti parser, with an application to psycholinguistic modeling. In *Proceedings of the 21st International Conference on Computational Linguistics and 44th Annual Meeting of the Association for Computational Linguistics*, (pp. 417–424), Sydney. The Association for Computational Linguistics.

Dubey, A., Sturt, P., & Keller, F. (2005). Parallelism in coordination as an instance of syntactic priming: Evidence from corpus-based modeling. In *Proceedings of the Human Language Technology Conference and the Conference on Empirical Methods in Natural Language Processing*, (pp. 827–834), Vancouver. The Association for Computational Linguistics.

Frazier, L., & Fodor, J. D. (1978). The sausage machine: A new two-stage parsing model. *Cognition*, *6*, 291–325.

Frazier, L., Munn, A., & Clifton, C. (2000). Processing coordinate structure. *Journal of Psycholinguistic Research*, *29*, 343–368.

Gibson, E. A. F. (1998). Linguistic complexity: Locality of syntactic dependencies. *Cognition*, *68*, 1–76.

Gries, S. T. (1999). Particle movement: A cognitive and functional approach. *Cognitive Linguistics*, *10*, 105–145.

Gries, S. T. (2005). Syntactic priming: a corpus-based approach. *Journal of Psycholinguistic Research*, *34*, 365–399.

Hawkins, J. A. (1995). *A performance theory of order and constituency*. Cambridge, UK: Cambridge University Press.

Keller, F., Lapata, M., & Uryupyna, O. (2002). Using the web to obtain frequencies for unseen bigrams. In *Proceedings of EMNLP 2002*, Philadelphia, PA.

Mitchell, D. C., Cuetos, F., Corley, M. M. B., & Brysbaert, M. (1996). Exposure-based models of human parsing: Evidence for the use of coarse-grained (non-lexical) statistical records. *Journal of Psycholinguistic Research*, *24*, 469–488.

Pickering, M. J., & Branigan, H. P. (1998). The representation of verbs: Evidence from syntactic priming in language production. *Journal of Memory and Language*, *39*, 633–651.

Reitter, D., Moore, J., & Keller, F. (2006). Priming of syntactic rules in task-oriented dialogue and spontaneous conversation. In R. Sun (ed.), *Proceedings of the 28th Annual Conference of the Cognitive Science Society*, (pp. 685–690), Vancouver.

Szmrecsanyi, B. (2005). Language users as creatures of habit: A corpus-linguistic analysis of persistence in spoken english. *Corpus Linguistics and Linguistic Theory*, *1*, 113–150.

Conceptual Changes in the Acquisition of Fractional Number Understanding

Judi Humberstone (judih@unimelb.edu.au)
Department of Psychology, University of Melbourne, Vic 3010, Australia

Robert A Reeve (r.reeve@unimelb.edu.au)
Department of Psychology, University of Melbourne, Vic 3010, Australia

Abstract

To explore the conceptual bases of different mental models of fraction competence, 223 Grades 4 to 8 students completed fraction equivalence (*produce a different, numerically equal fraction*), fraction ordering (*which fraction is bigger?*), and fraction addition problem-solving tasks. Each task comprised five instances of eight different types of fraction problems, ranging in difficulty from common fractions to mixed-number fractions. Hierarchical cluster analyses revealed five, well-ordered (based on error and correctness patterns) competency profiles (mental models) for each of the fraction tasks. Surprisingly, students from all grades were represented in each of the competency profiles. To investigate the degree to which fraction addition competence could be predicted from the fraction equivalence and ordering profiles, a multinomial logistic regression was performed. This analysis, in conjunction with a multilevel correspondence analysis, showed that both common across-task and unique within-task knowledge factors in the fraction equivalence and ordering profiles were associated with the fraction addition competency profiles. These results are discussed in terms of the factors associated with transitions in mental models of fractional number competence.

Keywords: Conceptual change; Mental Models; Fraction competence

Introduction

Researchers interested in mathematical cognition have often noted substantial variability in the ways students acquire new concepts (Siegler, 2006). For example, similar aged students tend to exhibit different kinds of problem-solving competencies (indicated by their successes, errors and strategies) as they solve fractional number problems—patterns of competencies that likely reflect different forms of understanding. Can these forms of understanding be differentiated and characterised; and, if so, what do they imply about the acquisition of fractional number concepts? Surprisingly little research has addressed these questions directly. Although some researchers have presented evidence for the impact of natural number knowledge on fractional number problem solving (Smith, 1995; Ni & Zhou, 2005), few have analysed the nature of changes that occur as students acquire fractional number competence.

Different experimental methods have been used to study fraction knowledge as if each method elicited similar information. For example, performance on fraction equivalence (*which fractions are the same?*), fraction ordering (*which fraction is bigger?*) and fraction addition tasks have been treated as if they depend on similar competencies. Although this assumption is likely to be, in part, correct, it is also possible that some different competencies underlie successful performance on these tasks, a more complete understanding of which would provide information about the acquisition of fractional number competence. The research reported herein was designed to (1) determine whether separate mental models of fraction equivalence, ordering and addition could be identified, (2) whether they reflect similar or different forms of fractional number competencies, and (3) whether both fraction equivalence and ordering competency profiles are required to predict fraction addition problem-solving ability.

Much of the research examining fraction understanding has focussed on the difficulties students experience in making the transition from whole to fractional number competence. On the basis of error analyses it is evident that many students erroneously apply whole number principles in solving fractional number problems (Hartnett & Gelman, 1998; Ni & Zhou, 2005). For example, in solving fraction addition problems, a student may add the numerators and/or denominators, as if the separate components of the fractional number were equivalent to whole numbers. Moreover, researchers have most often examined the difficulties experienced by younger students in understanding simple fractions (e.g., proper fractions) and have paid far less attention to the broader class of fraction problems (e.g., improper fractions and mixed numbers) that older students encounter, the solving of which may depend on different kinds of conceptual knowledge from that of proper fractions. This limited research focus is problematic in that it constrains knowledge of the acquisition of fraction understanding. It is important to identify patterns of fractional number competence across a range of problems and students in order to examine fraction understanding more broadly, and to characterise differences in mental models of fractional number knowledge. Similar to Stafylidou and Vosniadou (2004), we use the term *mental model* to refer to a form of coherent mental organisation that provides a mechanism for interpreting, as well as solving, problems. Of interest is whether different mental models of fraction understanding can be identified, and whether these models are well-ordered in the sense that they reflect transitions in the acquisition of fractional number competence.

Researchers have used fraction equivalence, ordering and addition tasks to study the nature of students' fraction competence as if they elicited similar competencies (*cf.* Behr, Wachsmuth, Post, & Lesh, 1984; Smith, 1995). (Fraction equivalence typically involves identifying a numerically equal fraction or inserting a missing numerator into an equivalent fraction; fraction ordering involves indicating which of two fractional numbers is larger). Although performance on such tasks may reflect common overlapping competence (general fraction knowledge), it is also possible that each task requires a unique task-specific form of competence. (Indeed, some researchers (e.g., Post, Wachsmuth, Lesh, & Behr, 1985) have described the different characteristics of order and equivalence tasks, but they do not discuss the implications of these differences for fraction problem-solving competence more generally.) This issue is important because it suggests that a better understanding of students' fraction knowledge may be gained by exploring both the separate and overlapping competencies on fraction equivalence, ordering and addition tasks.

Fraction equivalence and ordering tasks are potentially useful in revealing important differences between natural number and fraction understanding. Equivalence and ordering appear straightforward for natural numbers. A natural number is only equivalent to itself, and each number has a unique *successor* which allows natural numbers to be ordered by counting. Some properties of natural number arithmetic depend on these properties (e.g., addition). However, equivalence and ordering of fractions is very different and more complex. Although the fractions 2/3 and 8/12 appear different, they represent the same rational number, two-thirds. Each rational number can be represented by an infinite set of equivalent fractions and this many-to-one relation between fraction numerals and the rational numbers complicates judgments of order.

A brief analysis shows that both common fraction knowledge and unique task-dependent skills are involved in solving equivalence and ordering tasks, and that fraction addition problem-solving involves both equivalence and ordering competencies. Both tasks demand an understanding of the mathematical relationship between the numerator and denominator embodied in symbolic fractions, and, in the case of mixed number fractions, knowledge of the relationship between the unit concept and the fractional aspects is required. However, different skills are necessary to generate an equivalent fraction from those involved in determining which of two fractions is larger. Specifically, equivalent fractions result from applying identical operations to the numerator and denominator of the given fraction and rely on the knowledge that the relative ratio between numerator and denominator must remain constant. In contrast, in order to identify the larger of two fractions, the fractions must be compared. Knowledge that larger denominators relate to smaller entities and that the numerator determines the number of designated fractional parts is essential (but not sufficient) to complete the task. When the denominators are different, additional abilities are required to assess which combination of numerator and denominator represents a larger quantity. In some cases, the only way to accurately assess the larger of two fractions is to convert both to equivalent fractions with a common denominator. It should be noted that both the similar and the

different aspects of fraction equivalence and ordering knowledge are required to successfully solve fraction addition problems. The two fraction addends must be compared in order to determine the common denominator (as for ordering tasks), and, when the two addends have different denominators, equivalent fractions must be generated with the same denominator.

The different skills required for different fraction problem-solving tasks can result in different error patterns being produced which provide important information about the acquisition of fractional number understanding (Reeve & Pattison, 1996). Although the nature of the errors in ordering tasks is unknown, in fraction equivalence tasks, for example, the error of inverting fractions suggests a whole number interpretation of fractions as being represented by two unrelated numbers. Converting mixed number fractions to improper fractions in equivalence tasks is indicative of knowledge of the bi-directional relationship between the two fraction types, and reveals an understanding of the mathematical relationships between the unit, numerator and denominator in fractions, even though a different equivalent fraction is not produced.

On the basis of the similarities and differences in the competencies required for fraction equivalence, ordering and addition, it seems reasonable to claim that a more complete characterisation of children's successes and error patterns on equivalence, ordering and addition tasks may reveal important information about mental models of understanding associated with the acquisition of fractional number understanding. The current research is therefore designed to characterise different patterns of fraction ability that reflect transitions in students' mental models of fractional number. Students' understanding is assessed in terms of their ability to produce an equivalent fraction, to determine which of two fractions is larger, and to add two fractions. Four fraction types, proper (e.g. 5/6), improper (e.g. 9/7), mixed number (e.g., 1 3/5) and whole number (e.g., 3/1), are each presented in reduced and non-reduced forms. We are interested in (1) characterising within-task fractional number competence profiles; (2) examining across-task competency profiles, and (3) investigating the contribution of fraction equivalence and ordering profiles to the prediction of fraction addition competence. We suggest that this analysis will provide an account of different mental models associated with the acquisition of fractional number competence. It is anticipated that distinct profiles of understanding can be determined within each task and that a cross-task comparison will reveal both common and unique competencies that provide important predictive information about transitions in fractional number understanding.

Method

Participants

Two-hundred-twenty-three Grades 4 to 8 students, ($n = 47, 46, 48, 42, 40$ respectively) comprising approximately equal numbers of males and females, participated. Students attended one of six schools in a large Australian city and came from diverse ethnic and socio-economic backgrounds. None of them possessed any known learning difficulty, and all were proficient in English.

Materials and Procedure.

Students completed a *Fraction Equivalence*, a *Fraction Ordering*, and a *Fraction Addition Task*. The three tasks (on A4 sheets) were presented in random order to small groups of students ($n \leq 5$) with no completion time restrictions.

The *Fraction Equivalence Task* and the *Fraction Ordering Task* each comprised five representative instances of eight fractions types (i.e., each task comprised 40 problems). Fraction types expressed in both reduced and non-reduced form were: proper (e.g., 5/8; 3/9), improper (e.g., 8/5; 12/8), mixed numbers (e.g., 1 3/5; 1 6/8) and whole numbers (e.g., 3/1; 15/3). The more complex fraction types (improper fractions and mixed numbers) were included to elicit a broad range of information about children's fractional number competence. For the *Ordering* task, the pairs of fractions all featured different denominators. The reason for this was based on research showing that ordering fractions with different denominators requires more advanced fraction skills (Post et al., 1985) and will therefore elicit more complete information about fraction ordering knowledge.

The *Fraction Addition Task* comprised five instances of two types of fractions, proper and improper, and four problem types (i.e., $n = 40$ problems). The four problem types were: (1) the Lowest Common Denominator (LCD) was the denominator of both fractions (e.g., 1/7 + 3/7); (2) the LCD was the denominator of one of the fractions (e.g., 9/7 +17/14); (3) the LCD was the product of the denominators (e.g., 3/7 + 5/8) and (4) the LCD was one of the denominators, but there was a missing addend (e.g., 3/7 + __ = 9/14). Problems for all three tasks were presented in booklet form.

For the *Equivalence* task, students were required to produce a different fraction equivalent to the one presented (e.g. *Write a different fraction equivalent to:* 9/6). The *Fraction Ordering Task* required students to circle the larger fraction of a pair of fractions (e.g., *Circle the larger fraction:* 7/4 : 6/5) and for the *Fraction Addition Task*, students were required to either add the fractions together or to find the missing addend (i.e. subtraction of fractions is required to determine the solution).

Responses were coded as (1) incorrect, (2) correct for the *Ordering* task and according to correctness and type of error produced for *Equivalence* and *Addition*. *Equivalence* response codes were: (1) no apparent strategy; (2) inverted fraction; (3) numerator or denominator halved or doubled; or whole number doubled together with correct equivalent fraction; (4) alternative version of same fraction (e.g. 3/1 as 3 or 8/5 as 1 3/5); (5) correct. The different error categories reflect increasing sophistication of fraction understanding. For example, inverted fractions reflect an understanding of fractions from the whole number perspective of a fraction being comprised of two unrelated numbers. The error of doubling the whole number in mixed numbers or doubling

or halving either the numerator or the denominator also reveals a whole number understanding of fractions, and likely results from an incorrectly applied procedure for generating equivalent fractions, the conceptual basis for which is evidently not understood. Converting mixed number fractions to whole numbers and vice versa represents more advanced fraction understanding in that the relationship between two fraction types is understood, but students have failed to produce a different equivalent fraction. *Addition* task responses were coded according to increasing sophistication of fraction knowledge: (1) no apparent strategy; (2) add or multiply numerators/no strategy for denominators; (3) add numerators/add denominators or multiply numerators/add denominators; (4) correct. The error of adding numerators and adding denominators indicates a lack of understanding of the importance of the mathematical relationship between the numerator and denominator within each attend.

Results

Conventional analyses revealed significant effects for *Grade* and *Fraction Problem* type for the three tasks (*Equivalence:* $F (7, 212) = 68.41$, $p < .001$; *Ordering:* $F (7, 212) = 25.53$, $p < .001$; *Fraction Addition:* $F (7, 212) = 21.14$, $p < .001$ which mirror previous findings[1]. However, significant *Grade*-related variations were observed on most fraction measures. To understand the conceptual implications of this variability, separate hierarchical cluster analyses were conducted on the correct responses to the eight fraction types for the *Equivalence, Ordering and Addition* fraction tasks, each of which yielded five-cluster solutions accounting for 78%, 56% and 90% of variance respectively. To confirm that cluster membership added interpretive meaning over and above that provided by *Grade*, separate regression analyses for the *Equivalence* and *Ordering* tasks were conducted in which success on *Addition* was predicted by entering *Grade* (Step 1) and cluster membership (Step 2) in the equation. These analyses confirmed that cluster membership added significantly to the overall regression equations ($p < .001$) in both cases. Indeed, inspection of *Grade × Cluster Membership* cross-classification showed that students from all grades were represented in each of the clusters (See Figure 1 for the *Equivalence Task*).

To further investigate the meaning of cluster membership for the three tasks, we examined the association between cluster membership and performance (both correct and error responses for the *Equivalence* and the *Addition* task and correct responses for the *Ordering* task). For the *Equivalence* task the error of inverting the fraction was associated uniquely with Cluster 1. The error of doubling the whole number for mixed numbers or doubling or halving either the denominator or the numerator tended to be

---

[1] Reliability analyses for *Equivalence, Ordering and Addition* fraction tasks revealed alpha values of 0.93, 0.79 and 0.98 respectively, as a consequence of which scores were summed within each test.

associated with Clusters 2 and 3 (Cluster 2 was differentiated from Cluster 3 on the basis of overall success). The error of converting an improper fraction to an identical mixed number (or vice versa) was common in Clusters 4 and 5. However, Cluster 5 only made this error in response to fractions in their reduced form. A similar sequence of conceptual models could be adduced from the *Addition* cluster analysis. Specifically, in Cluster 1 the error of adding numerators and denominators was common for all fraction types. For Clusters 2 to 4, this error was progressively associated with more difficult fraction addition problems. Students in Cluster 5 made few errors. For the *Ordering* task, cluster membership was associated with distinct patterns of correctness across the different problem types. Specifically, Cluster 1 performed poorly on all problems, Clusters 2 and 3 successfully judged pairs of fractions in reduced form (e.g., *Circle the larger fraction: 7/4 6/5*), but performed poorly on fractions presented in non-reduced form (e.g., *Circle the larger fraction: 8/6 10/8*). Cluster 3 was differentiated from Cluster 2 both on the basis of overall success across all fraction types and on being unsuccessful on only improper and whole-number fractions in non-reduced form. Clusters 4 and 5 were successful across all fraction types, although students in Cluster 5 experienced greater success across all fraction types. Overall, the error/success patterns from the three tasks strongly suggest sequences of conceptual models of fraction understanding[2].

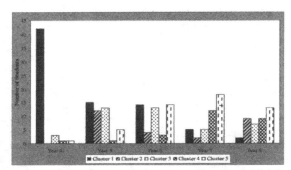

Figure.1. Equivalence Task clusters as a function of Grade.

The pattern of findings presented thus far support the claims that (1) cluster groups for the three tasks reflect distinct fraction competence models, as indicated by the correct and error profiles, and (2) students' models of the fraction domain are somewhat independent of *Grade*. Of interest is whether cluster membership in the three tasks reflects common or somewhat different fractional number understanding. Any differences in the profiles from the separate tasks will provide important additional information about students' mental models of fractional number over and above that provided by the common fraction knowledge revealed by the task profiles.

---

[2] For all three tasks the clusters were ordered on the basis of increasing competence outlined above.

To examine the potentially differential importance of cluster membership, a multinomial logistic regression analysis was conducted in which *Addition* cluster membership was predicted from cluster membership on the *Equivalence* and *Ordering* tasks. The results showed the goodness of fit for the overall model was very good (Pearson χ^2 (56) = 63.91 p = .48; r^2 (Cox and Snell) = .604). Table 1 reports the percentages of each of the addition clusters correctly classified on the basis of fraction equivalence and ordering competency profiles and shows that overall, 61% of the students were correctly allocated to fraction addition competency groups. Specifically, over 80% of individuals in each of Clusters 1, and 5 were correctly classified. However, only 40% of individuals in *Addition* Cluster 4 and 24% in *Addition* Cluster 2 were allocated correctly. The high percentages correctly classified in *Addition* Clusters 1 and 5 likely reflect common fraction abilities required across the tasks. The lower percentages correctly allocated to *Addition* Clusters 2 – 4 are indicative of differences in the progressive acquisition of fraction knowledge in the *Equivalence* and *Ordering* profiles and suggest specific abilities involved in the separate tasks with differential predictive information about addition competence.

The differential contribution of fraction equivalence and ordering ability to the prediction of fraction addition success is confirmed from the results of the multinomial logistic regression equation: *Equivalence* (Likelihood Ratio χ^2 (16) = 76.33 p = < .001); and *Ordering* (Likelihood Ratio χ^2 (16) = 71.44 p = < .001). This result shows that each of the *Equivalence* and *Ordering* competency profiles made a significant contribution to the prediction of *Addition* competence.

Table 1
Multinomial Regression Classification Table Predicting Percentage Membership of Addition Cluster from Equivalence and Ordering Clusters

Observed	Predicted					
	1	2	3	4	5	Correct
1	66	6	0	2.	2	87
2	23	10	0	2	6	24
3	8	2	0	2	5	0
4	5	2	0	11	9	41
5	4	1	0	7	50	80
Overall	47	10	0	11	32	61

Finally, a multilevel correspondence analysis (see Figure 2) was conducted to visually represent the relationship between cluster memberships on the three tasks. As can be seen from Figure 2 there is a substantial overlap in cluster membership across the three tasks. Specifically, Clusters 1 and 5 are strongly associated across all tasks. Patterns of association for the other three clusters are less distinct and reflect specific task-related differences in fraction understanding. This result supports the findings from the multinomial logistic regression that the competency profiles from the three tasks reflect both overlapping and unique fraction understanding. The unique contribution of fraction equivalence and ordering abilities to the prediction of fraction addition competence is revealed in the asynchrony in the progression of fraction competence on the three tasks.

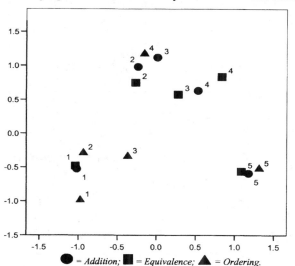

Figure.2. Multilevel correspondence analysis between *Equivalence, Ordering* and *Addition* cluster memberships (numbers 1 to 5 indicate cluster group number).

Together, the results from the multinomial logistic regression and the multilevel correspondence analyses indicate that both common and importantly different competencies involved in fraction equivalence and ordering contribute to fractional number problem-solving abilities.

Discussion and Conclusion

The results demonstrated that: (1) the substantial variance in the three fraction competence measures (equivalence, ordering and addition) could be meaningfully partitioned to yield fraction competency profiles for each task that were somewhat independent of grade; (2) there was substantial overlap, but some notable differences, in the competency profiles between the three measures, and (3) both common across-task and unique within-task knowledge factors from the fraction equivalence and ordering profiles differentially predicted fraction addition competencies. What are the implications of different fraction competency profiles in terms of different mental models of fraction understanding?

On the basis of problem solving successes, it was evident that different competency profiles could be identified. Importantly, these profiles were associated with distinct error patterns that revealed different fractional number understanding within the cluster groupings in each task. We suggest that the competency profiles depict different, but related, mental models associated with conceptual changes

involved in the acquisition of fraction understanding. Specifically, fraction competencies ranged from students who had little understanding of the meaning of fractional representations to those who exhibited an understanding of fractions grounded in the specific mathematical relationship between by the numerator and denominator.

In the *Fraction Equivalence Task*, models of understanding ranged from those students in *Cluster 1* who tended to invert the fraction – revealing a whole-number approach to fractions as if the fraction is represented by two independent natural numbers – to students in *Cluster 5* who exhibited competence across most fraction types. Students in *Clusters 2, 3* and *4* made progressively fewer errors and the specific nature of their errors reflected increased fraction knowledge. Nevertheless, it is worth noting that even students in *Cluster 5* tended to convert mixed numbers to improper fractions and vice versa when the fraction was presented in reduced form (i.e., *Write a different fraction equivalent to 11/8*), indicating that they had incomplete advanced knowledge of fractions. It was evident that students in Cluster 5 had acquired an understanding of the bi-directional relationship between improper fractions and mixed numbers; however, they were not able to generate a different equivalent fraction maintaining the constant ratio between the numerator and denominator for some problem types.

Although the *Fraction Ordering Task* only required students to identify the larger of two fractions, the cluster groups based on fraction ordering correctness revealed a progression towards success on harder fraction types. Similarly, the profiles for the *Fraction Addition Task* revealed progressive competence across the groups in response to the harder problems. Specifically, in the *Fraction Addition Task*, the error of adding the numerators and adding the denominators which is associated with a whole number understanding of fractions was confined to the most difficult problem types in *Clusters 3* and *4* and was not evident at all in *Cluster 5*.

In sum, the results of the initial classification analyses showed that ordered competency profiles could be established on the basis of correctness and associated error patterns for the three different fraction tasks and that these profiles revealed distinctly different mental models of fraction understanding for each task. It is important to note that the classification analyses highlighted a potential interpretive difficulty associated with using aggregated data as an index of a group's competence (see Granott, 1998). Although overall grade was associated with fraction competence, students from all grades were represented in all clusters in each of the tasks.

Consistent with previous research (Smith, 1995; Ni & Zhou, 2005), we found that some of the difficulties students experienced resulted from a lack of understanding of the mathematical relationships expressed in fractions and a tendency to apply whole number procedures to fraction problem-solving. However, whereas prior research had tacitly assumed that the competencies from different tasks could be used interchangeably, the current research demonstrated that different competencies are required for solving fraction equivalence, ordering and addition problems. Nevertheless, there was significant overlap between the three profiles in common fraction understanding. In particular, students who had limited fraction understanding and who approached fraction problem-solving from a whole number perspective were represented in *Cluster 1* in the equivalence, ordering and addition competence profiles. Similarly, students in *Cluster 5* for all three tasks had an advanced representation of fractions based on knowledge of the mathematical relationship between the numerator and denominator. Important differences were exhibited by the asynchronous associations between *Clusters 2, 3* and *4* on the three tasks. The asynchrony between the three profiles of fraction competence suggests that the acquisition of fraction knowledge necessary for each of the tasks is based on different competencies from those involved in the other two tasks. More specifically, the present findings highlighted the fact that neither fraction equivalence nor fraction ordering competencies alone were sufficient to account for fraction addition problem-solving ability.

It is apparent from the current research that important knowledge about the acquisition of fraction understanding can be gained from the fraction equivalence, ordering and addition competency profiles. However, it should be noted that although the mental models of fraction understanding for each of the tasks were well-ordered, there may not be a common measurement metric associated with cluster profiles either within or between tasks. Further research is necessary in order to determine more precisely the relative contribution of competencies from each of the tasks to the acquisition of fraction knowledge. For example, the degree of close association between *Ordering* clusters 1 – 3 suggests that they were not be as well defined as the *Equivalence* and *Addition* clusters. It may be possible to obtain additional information about the profiles of understanding involved in fraction ordering from a more heterogeneous range of problem types including comparisons in which one of the denominators is the common denominator of the pair (as in the *Fraction Addition Task*) or by including a record of individual strategy-use in solving fraction ordering problems.

An extension of the current research might investigate how students move from one knowledge state to another in acquiring fractional number understanding. Conceptual changes involved in the acquisition of fraction knowledge may be revealed by a *prompted assessment* procedure. *Prompted assessment* has been proposed as a way of analysing difficulties, and revealing the status of individuals' understanding, during the learning process (Sternberg & Grigorenko, 2002). In *prompted assessment*, individual differences in learning potential are assessed by determining the amount and nature of assistance students require to solve problems within a specified domain (e.g., fractional numbers), and the information gained provides different profiles of understanding involved in the acquisition of mathematical competence.

The present research was designed to determine the degree to which mental models of fraction equivalence, ordering and addition reflected both common and unique fraction competencies and to investigate whether equivalence and ordering knowledge differentially predicted different fraction addition competencies. It has been demonstrated that meaningful, ordered profiles of fraction understanding were revealed that reflected increasing competence within each task and which were more informative than grade competence profiles. Significantly though, the profiles based on fraction equivalence, ordering and addition performance were shown to comprise both overlapping and unique competencies. Specifically, a differential contribution of fraction equivalence and ordering abilities predicted fraction addition problem-solving ability and neither task was individually sufficient to account for the fraction addition competence profiles. These findings have significant implications for future research into the acquisition of fractional number understanding. On the basis of the current study, it is evident that a number of different competencies are involved in the acquisition of fractional number understanding and that a range of different tasks and problem types are required in order to determine the precise nature of the conceptual changes involved the acquisition of fractional number competence.

References

Behr, M. J., Wachsmuth, I., Post, T. R., & Lesh, R. (1984). Order and equivalence of rational numbers: A clinical teaching experiment. *Journal for Research in Mathematics Education*, 15, 323-341.

Granott, N. (1998). A paradigm shift in the study of development: Essay review of *Emerging minds* by R. S. Siegler. *Human Development*, 41, 360–365.

Hartnett, P., & Gelman, R. (1998). Early understandings of numbers: paths or barriers to the construction of new understanding? *Learning and Instruction*, 8(4), 341–374.

Ni, Y., & Zhou, Y-D., (2005). Teaching and learning fraction and rational numbers: The origins and implications of whole number bias. *Educational Psychologist*, 40 (1), 27-52.

Post, T. R., Wachsmuth, I., Lesh, R., & Behr, M. J. (1985). Order and equivalence of rational numbers: A cognitive analysis. *Journal for Research in Mathematics Education*, 16(1), 18-36.

Reeve, R. A., & Pattison, P. E. (1996). The referential adequacy of students' visual analogies of fractions. *Mathematical Cognition*, 2(2), 137-169.

Siegler, R.S. (2006). Microgenetic analyses of learning. In W. Damon & R. M. Lerner (Series Eds.) & D. Kuhn & R. S. Siegler (Vol. Eds.), *Handbook of Child Psychology: Volume 2: Cognition, Perception, and Language* (6th ed., pp. 464-510). Hoboken, NJ: Wiley.

Smith, J. P. (1995). Competent reasoning with rational numbers. *Cognition and Instruction*, 13(1), 3-50.

Stafylidou, S. & Vosniadou, S. (2004). The development of students' understanding of the numerical value of fractions. Conceptual Change in Mathematics Learning and Teaching, Special Issue o*f Learning and Instruction*, 14, pp.503-518.

Sternberg, R. J., & Grigorenko, E. L. (2002). *Dynamic testing. The nature and measurement of learning potential.* Cambridge, UK: Cambridge University Press.

Conceptual Change in Evolutionary Theory: The Effects of Scripted Argumentative Monologue in Peer Settings

Christa S.C Asterhan (kooij@mscc.huji.ac.il)
Baruch B. Schwarz (msschwar@mscc.huji.ac.il)
School of Education, Hebrew University of Jerusalem, Mt. Scopus
Jerusalem, 91905 Israel

Abstract

In this study we investigated the potentially beneficial role of argumentation on conceptual change in learning tasks that are based on the socio-cognitive conflict paradigm. Forty-two undergraduates participated in one of two conditions: Experimental students engaged in monological argumentation on their own and an equal-status peer confederate's explanation of an evolutionary phenomenon in response to prompts read by the confederate, whereas in the control condition subjects and the confederate merely read aloud their respective explanations. Students in the argumentative conditions were found to outperform control students on two different measures of conceptual understanding. The advantage of the argumentative conditions also held for the stricter criterion of conceptual change. The particular patterns of change are discussed. In addition, many students were found to be inconsistent in the explanatory schemas they applied at a given test occasion. We discuss the implications of this finding for the conceptualization and assessment of conceptual change.

Humans primarily construct personal conceptions about scientific phenomena on the basis of their personal experience in the world. These naïve ideas are often incompatible with the scientific explanations pupils are confronted with in classroom settings. They may be replaced or restructured hopefully, but by no way inexorably, leading to the acquisition of correct scientific concepts. Such a process has traditionally been referred to as *conceptual change* (Vosniadou 1999).

Research on inducing conceptual change among students has traditionally been conducted in the Piaget-inspired cognitive conflict paradigm in which students' naïve conceptualizations are confronted with anomalous data or contradicting views or are paired with peers who have different views (socio-cognitive conflict). Inducing conceptual change has been extensively shown to be a hard goal to achieve, especially in individual settings (Limon, 2001): Students have to become aware of their initial (mis)conceptions, understand the new information presented to them, become aware of the contradictions, compare and evaluate the different ideas, and adapt their misconceptions.

In this paper, we present results from a study on the effects of engagement in dialectical argumentative reasoning on conceptual understanding in evolutionary theory. Specifically, we propose that the engagement in dialectical argumentation on one's own and another person's views by producing reasoned arguments in favour and against these ideas will facilitate conceptual change

processes. We base this claim on the fact that dialectical argumentation intertwines a number of social and cognitive processes that are considered to promote concept learning:

First of all, similar to the 'self-explanation effect', the epistemic examination of one's personal theories and the reasons behind them, has been known to promote understanding and knowledge construction processes (Chi, deLeeuw, Chiu & Lavancher, 1994; Kuhn, 1991). Furthermore, in dialectical argumentation participants are exposed to a multiplicity of ideas and encouraged to explore each other's validity. This implies that they have to consider objections to their personal theories and assumptions, to attempt to understand alternative positions and to formulate objections and/or counter-objections. The unique structure of argumentation that links premises, conclusions, conditions, rebuttals and so forth is, in addition, thought to considerably improve and extend the organization of knowledge, leading to better recall and understanding on subsequent test occasions (Means & Voss, 1996).

In theory, the engagement in solitary argumentative reasoning may be expected to yield similar results. However, argumentation is basically a social process that presupposes the presence of an audience (Leitao, 2000). Solitary argumentation on scientific concepts is cognitively very demanding. The presence of a dialog partner may promote reflection and awareness to one's own beliefs (Amigues, 1988), cause learners to engage in explanatory activities (Okada & Simon, 1997) and reduce cognitive load through the personification of different alternatives.

In a recent study we investigated the effects of argumentative dialog on concept learning in evolutionary theory (Asterhan & Schwarz, 2005). Undergraduates were assigned to dyads and collaboratively tried to solve an evolutionary phenomenon (i.e. the evolution of webbed feet of ducks). Half of these dyads were instructed to engage in dialectical argumentative dialog on their respective solutions and received examples of argumentative moves within a dialog; the other half was merely instructed to collaborate. Individual evolutionary understanding was assessed on three test occasions: Prior to, immediately after and a week following the intervention. Delayed posttest explanations in the argumentative condition were found to be of a higher quality than in the control condition, when controlled for pretest performance. Furthermore, the pattern through of change revealed that students in both conditions improved their conceptual understanding immediately following the intervention; however, while students who were merely instructed to collaborate lost this temporary gain, students in the argumentative condition retained the same level of performance. Whereas manipulation check analyses were successful, not all experimental dyads engaged in *dialectical* argumentation, whereas a small number of control dyads spontaneously did. Post-hoc analyses on natural differences revealed that only dyads who engaged in dialectical argumentation showed conceptual gains; those that engaged in mere one-sided argumentation or no argumentation did not gain at all.

In the present study, we attempted to extent these findings by further isolating the element thought to be responsible for the difference in cognitive gains, namely *dialectical* argumentation. Instead of being instructed to conduct an argumentative dialog with an assigned peer, students were prompted to engage in scripted *monological dialectical* argumentation on their own and a confederate's solution of an evolutionary phenomenon in response to structural prompts read aloud by the confederate. In the control condition, subjects and the same confederate merely read aloud their solutions to each other, without discussing them further. Thus, students in both conditions were withheld from conducting a dialogical discussion with each other and were exposed to the same misconception in the intervention phase. The conditions were identical on factors such as, social facilitation, exposure to content matter and personification of viewpoints, and only differed in the elicitation of monological dialectical argumentation.

Method

Participants

Forty-four university students from the Education (10%), Social Sciences (56%) and Humanities (34%) departments were recruited through publication of announcements on note boards around campus (mean age = 27.14). The data of two Ss were omitted from analyses since they did not manage to finish the pre-test questionnaires within the 25 minutes time-limit. Most Ss (76%) reported not to have received any formal education on the subject of evolution in either high school or academic courses. Forty participants were financially rewarded, two received course credit.

Design

A pre-test, intervention, and post-test experimental design was used. All students received instruction on Darwinist evolutionary theory and shared their answers with a peer confederate. The two conditions differed on whether Ss were instructed to engage in monological argumentation on their own and the confederate's explanation of evolutionary processes or not (see Procedure section). Individual conceptual understanding in evolution was assessed on three separate test occasions (pretest, immediate posttest and delayed posttest).

Coding Evolutionary understanding

The dependent measure of conceptual understanding concerning evolutionary change processes was assessed according to a coding scheme we developed in a previous study (Asterhan & Schwarz, 2005), which comprises two separate but complementary means of scoring:

Explanatory schema score. Based on and inspired by previous works we identified ten qualitatively different *explanatory schemas*[1] in students' explanations of evolutionary change. These different schemas were then quantitatively assessed on four different dimensions: Whether evolutionary change was considered at all, whether this change was explained, whether some sort of selection mechanism was used and whether existing intra-species variation was considered. Based on the appearance of each of these four dimensions, the ten qualitatively different explanatory schemas were assigned to one of five different categories. The score for each schema category was based on the number of dimensions that featured in the schema in that category. An additional null-category was added to distinguish between explanations that did not consider change (the lowest category) and those responses that simply did not answer the question at all (by stating that they did not know the answer or by repeating the data given in the item without providing additional information). This procedure yielded the following explanatory schema categories and their corresponding scores.

Non-answers (score 0): Responses that indicated absolute ignorance on the subject or responses that merely repeated the data that was given in the question item.

No change considered (score 1): Responses that simply denied that species evolve over time, responses that refer to a disaster scenario according to which everything will go extinct, and responses that refer to species intentionally moving away to other (better) areas to protect themselves.

Unexplained change (score: 2): This category includes responses that refer to species changing over time without providing a reason for it or describing how it occurs. Typically, they refer to evolution as a process according to which everything changes for the better and species keep on perfecting themselves.

Typological change: (score: 3) None of the four schemas in this category consider intra-species variation and selection, but they all acknowledge and explain change, Their accounts on <u>why</u> or <u>how</u> this change occurs is what distinguishes between them: Lamarckian (individual members acquire a trait which is then passed on to offspring), Mutations after (as a result of the change in the environment, individual members "undergo mutations"

---

[1] Even though the term 'mental models' is the commonly used term in the concept learning literature, we prefer the term *explanatory schemas* (Ohlsson, 2002). While explanations are content-specific generative descriptions, explanatory schemas encode the structure shared by a set of explanations, that is defined by the set of generative relations and the way they are combined (Ohlsson, 2002).

which are then passed on to off-spring); Mating outside species (individual members will search to mate with members of other species that have an advantageous trait); and Dormant genes (the trait was always present in the species' genetic make-up, but was dormant until it was "needed" and activated).

Hybrid explanations (score: 4) This category includes responses that integrate features of both natural selection as well as typological change mechanisms. They are similar to the former category in that they do not consider existing intra-species variation, but instead refer to variation that is created in reaction to environmental change and needs. However, they do consider selection: The transformed individual members of the species manage to survive and reproduce, whereas the others go extinct. Two different types of hybrid models were identified, differing in their accounts on how variation is created: (a) Some individual members of the species underwent genetic mutations in reaction to the change in the environment; and (b) Some individual members acquired the trait and this acquired trait is passed on.

Darwinian (score: 5) Responses that explain change in terms of natural selection and existing intra-species variation.

Darwinist principles score. The complementary coding scheme is adapted from Ohlsson (1992) who proposed a summary of modern evolution theory in the form of a number of key principles. It assesses the appearance of the following Darwinist principles: Intra-species variability, Source of intra-species variability (i.e., random changes in genetic material), Differential survival rates, Differential reproduction rates, Accumulation of changes (i.e, the process is repeated many times), Changes within the population (i.e., proportion of individuals carrying the advantageous trait(s) will increase within the population).

The appearance of each principle in each target item was assessed according to the following grading key: The principle is mentioned and used correctly (2 points), only a part of the principle is mentioned and used correctly (1 point), or the principle is not mentioned at all (0 points).

Inter-rater agreement was $r = .97$ for the explanatory schema score and $r = .95$ for the Darwinian principles score.

Coding argumentative reasoning

Protocols of student conversations during the intervention phase were transcribed and coded according to the following criteria: Number of reasons participants proposed in favor of their own solution (strengths of their solution), number of objections they proposed against their solution (weaknesses in their solution), and number of supporting and objecting arguments for and against the confederate's solution. Supports or objections that did not relate to content, but were of a pure evaluative nature without providing further reasons (e.g., "Your solution is better than mine") or that related to superficial features of the solution

only (e.g., "It is formulated very well") were discarded. Any support or objection that did relate to content was coded, whether it was objectively correct or not. All twenty-two transcripts were coded by two independent human coders. Pearson correlations between their assessments were $r = .81$ (support own), $r = .97$ (objections own), $r = .78$ (support other) and $r = .84$ (objections other). Disagreements were resolved through discussion.

Materials and procedure

All students participated in the following sequence of activities: (1) Individual pretest (T1) to assess prior evolutionary understanding; (2) Instructional intervention: screening of instructional movie excerpt on Darwinist evolutionary theory; (3) Individual administration of a single transfer test item; (4) Experimental intervention with confederate in which they read each others' responses to the single test item according to different conditions; (5) Immediate posttest (T2): Re-administration of the single transfer item immediately following the experimental intervention (T2); (6) Delayed posttest (T3): Individual delayed post-test administered a week later. The total length of an experimental session was approximately one and a half hour.

All tests were administered to individuals as paper-and-pencil tests. The pre- and delayed posttest consisted of three open format test items (one warming-up item and two target items). Target test item templates were similar, but their content related to different evolutionary phenomena (i.e., running speed of cheetahs, mosquito insecticide immunity, webbed feet of ducks, pigmentation of moths and iguanas' swimming ability). Test item difficulty was assessed on a separate sample and was not found to differ among target items.

All students were shown a twenty-minute excerpt of an instructional movie that presented the Darwinian explanation of evolutionary processes. It mentioned a number of evolutionary changes in different Galapagos species, without providing any explanation of the process of change. Changes in a population of Galapagos finches, however, were discussed in detail and explained in terms of the Darwinian account, including a step-by-step graphical presentation.

Immediately after watching the movie excerpt, Ss were asked to solve a single test item on a novel evolutionary phenomenon (the webbed feet of Ducks) and hand in their answer sheets. They were then introduced to the confederate who, they were told, had just completed the same stages of the experiment as they had. The confederate was a female undergraduate of the same age group as participants. Great efforts were made to ensure that her physical appearance and behavior did not reveal her being a confederate,.

Ss in the experimental conditions were told that they would participate in a short collaborative task with pre-defined roles (reader and respondent) and instructions. The confederate chose a piece of paper from an urn and invariantly picked up the role of the 'reader'. All interactions were audio-taped.

The confederate then read aloud the general instructions that shortly described the task at hand and stated that the goal of the activity was to reach a better understanding of evolutionary change processes, rather than to 'win' a certain argument. The task itself consisted of nine steps that were read aloud by the collaborator. Six of these steps prompted the participant to engage in dialectical argumentative reasoning on their own and the confederate's explanation of the Ducks item; three of these steps contained procedural instructions:

First, participants were requested to read aloud their answer to the Ducks item from the previously filled out answer sheet. They were then asked to discuss the strengths of that solution, asked to criticize it and discuss whether it explained the change that occurred to the Ducks' feet, in that sequence. Following, the confederate was requested to read aloud "her" solution, after which participants were asked to discuss that solution according to the previous steps. Finally, they were requested to evaluate the two solutions and their personal conceptual understanding of evolution. At each of the six argumentative steps the collaborator read the question aloud and waited for participants to complete their response, after which she then encouraged them to elaborate some more according to fixed prompts. At the end of the collaborative task, confederate and participant separately answered the Ducks item one more time on a clean answer sheet (T2).

The confederate's behavior was limited to reading the written prompts and reacting neutrally, but friendly, to the content of participants' responses. She was instructed to refrain from reacting to efforts from the participants to elicit comments or develop a dialogue.

So as to ensure uniformity concerning the exposure to another misconception (i.e., the confederate's solution), while, on the other hand, preserving a minimum difference between that and the S's explanatory schema, two different answer sheets were prepared for the confederate: One containing a typical Lamarckian answer and the other a typical explanatory schema of the same schema category, namely 'mutations after'. Both provided a typological explanation of evolutionary change, but differed in their description of the way the change occurred (see Coding section).

While the dyad started reading the instructions the S's explanatory schema was quickly assessed based on his/her answer sheet filled out immediately following the movie. The confederate's response was then chosen according to the following principle: If the S's response represented a Lamarckian schema, the confederate was given the 'mutations after' response. In any other case, she was given the Lamarckian response. The experimenter then re-entered the room and "returned" the dyad's answer sheets in time for the S to read aloud his/her answer, with the excuse that the experimenter forgot to return them. The average length of

scripted dialog was 8:05 minutes (ranging from 5:50 to 13:40).

In the control condition, Ss were also seated with the confederate. They were first given a short, neutral task (eight open questions on which animal is the fastest, strongest, heaviest, etceteras alive today). So as to control for time-on-task in both conditions, they were given seven minutes to complete this task. During this task the experimenter assessed the participant's mental model. Their sheets were then "returned" to them and they were requested to read their respective answers to each other while refraining from any further verbal communication, before answering the Ducks item once more on a new answer sheet (T2).

The confederate was given the Lamarckian response in 46% of the experimental interventions and in 50% of the control cases.

Results

Manipulation check
Nineteen of the twenty-two experimental subjects proposed at least one supporting reason for their own solution and an identical number of students proposed at least one objection. The number of subjects that mentioned at least one supporting argument for or at least one objecting argument against the confederate's solution was smaller (12 and 16, respectively). Two subjects only provided support for their own solution without further criticizing their own or the confederate's solution. The mean number of supporting arguments for own argument ($M = 1.22$, $SD = .75$), objections to own ($M = 1.27$, $SD = .83$), supporting arguments for other ($M = .59$, $SD = .59$) and objections against other ($M = .91$, $SD = .87$) were all significantly larger than zero ($p < .001$).

Conceptual gains
Mean explanatory schema scores and mean Darwinist principle scores were calculated for pretest, immediate posttest and delayed posttest occasions and are presented by condition in Figures 1 and 2.

Effect of condition Two separate, one-way analyses of variance (ANCOVA) were conducted on the delayed posttest variables of mean explanatory schema score and mean Darwinist principles score, while controlling for subjects' pretest scores on these respective variables and formal biology education as covariates. The experimental subjects showed superior conceptual understanding, both on the mean explanatory schema score, $F(1, 38) = 8.87$, $p = .005$, $\eta^2 = .19$, as well as on the Darwinist principles score, $F(1, 38) = 9.81$, $p = .003$, $\eta^2 = .21$. Previous biology education was not found to have an effect in either one of the analyses ($F(1, 38) = 1.13$, ns and $F(1, 38) = 8.41$, ns, respectively), whereas pretest scores were a significant predictor of delayed posttest performance in both ($F(1, 38) = 35.30$, $p < .001$ and $F(1, 38) = 50.42$, $p < .001$, respectively).

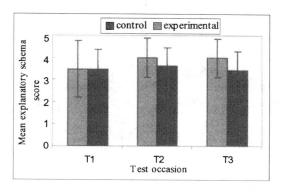

Figure 1. Mean explanatory schema scores by test occasion and experimental condition.

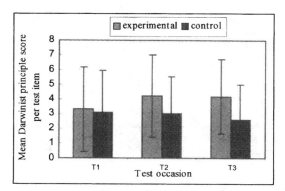

Figure 2. Mean Darwinian principles score by test occasion and experimental condition

Patterns of change So as to uncover the patterns of change over the three tests in each of the conditions, the two dependent variables were subsequently analyzed in two separate analyses of variance (2X3) with time of assessment (pretest vs. immediate posttest vs. delayed posttest) as a within-subject factor, condition as a between-subject factor and formal schooling in Biology as a covariate. Huyn-Feldt corrections were applied when necessary. Previous biology education was not found to have an effect in either one of the analyses ($F < 1$ and $F (2, 78) = 1.96$, ns, respectively).

On the explanatory schema score a main effect for test occasion was found, $F (1.70, 66.42) = 5.1$, $p = .012$, $\eta^2 = .116$. More importantly, the effect of test occasion was found to be dependent on condition, $F (1.70, 66.42) = 3.70$, $p = .037$, $\eta^2 = .087$. Planned comparisons were conducted between the mean scores of each two consecutive tests (from T1 to T2 and from T2 to T3) within each condition: Cognitive gains of experimental Ss were obtained immediately following the intervention ($F (1, 20) = 4.60$, $p = .044$, $\eta^2 = .19$) and a similar level of performance was maintained on the delayed post test ($F < 1$). However, control subjects in this study showed a mere small and non-significant improvement at the immediate posttest ($F (1, 18)$

= 1.89, ns), followed by a small and non-significant decrease at the delayed posttest ($F (1, 18) = 2.00$, ns). In other words, the explanatory schema score of control subjects did not significantly change from assessment to assessment.

With regards to number of Darwinist principles that were integrated in Ss' responses, time was not found to effect, $F (2, 78) = 2.18$, ns. However, condition was found to interact with time, $F (1.70, 66.32) = 3.63$, $p = .039$, $\eta^2 = .09$. The data in Figure 2 seem to suggest that the pattern of change over the three test occasions resembles the trends found on the explanatory schema score. However, none of the four planned comparisons reached significance.

Conceptual change
Our hypothesis that the engagement in monological argumentation improves conceptual understanding was confirmed at the explanatory schema level as well as the number of Darwinist principles. The question remains, however, whether this advantage will also hold under the stricter criterion of *conceptual change*. Whereas the mean increase for the argumentative condition was .36, the intra-group variance was relatively large: Some radically changed their explanatory schemas, whereas others did not gain at all, or even slightly deteriorated. How many students did actually attain conceptual change? To answer such questions we first have to define what is considered conceptual change in evolutionary theory and what would account for a 'mere' amelioration of existing conceptions?

Whereas the surface features of two explanatory schemas from the same category are different, the underlying explanatory mechanism is the same. An intra-categorical shift from one schema to another would, therefore, not account for conceptual change. We therefore argue that only shifts from one explanatory schema category to another involve the substantive re-organization that is described in conceptual change theory and research (e.g., Vosniadou, 1999).

However, the student responses to the two target items on both the pre- and the posttests reveal that students were not necessarily consistent in the explanatory schemas they applied on a given test occasion: Only seventy percent of the total number of pretest and posttest questionnaires revealed consistent use of explanatory schema categories on a given test (76% and 64% on the pre- and delayed posttest, respectively). The mean difference between two test item responses on 'inconsistent' questionnaires was similar on pre- and delayed post-test ($M = 1.00$, $SD = .58$ and $M = 1.01$, $SD = .49$, respectively).

A definition of conceptual change has to take this instability into account. Whereas a student who applied an explanatory schema of a one-point higher category on only one of the two test items (i.e., a mean pre- to posttest increase of .5 points) has indeed shown improved conceptual understanding, we argue that this does not provide *sufficient proof* for a substantive change. We therefore defined an increase of at least one point from mean pretest to mean posttest score as sufficient proof for a more profound change in conceptual understanding, that is: conceptual change. Table 1 presents the number of students for which sufficient evidence for conceptual change from pre- to delayed posttest was found. Students with pretest scores above 4.0 were excluded from this analysis.

Table 1: Number of students for which evidence of conceptual change was found, by condition.

	No conceptual change (d < 1)	Conceptual change (d >= 1)
Experimental	9	6
Control	15	0

* d = difference between mean pre- and delayed post-test scores

The data in Table 1 show that among those students that could achieve conceptual change (i.e., pre-test scores below or equal to 4.0), forty percent of experimental students and none of the control subjects substantively changed the explanatory schemas they used to explain evolutionary phenomena. The occurrence of conceptual change was found to be dependent on experimental condition, Fisher's exact test, $\chi^2 (1, N = 30) = 7.50, p = .017$.

Discussion

The results presented here provide further support for the assertion that argumentation promotes conceptual understanding in a cognitive conflict learning paradigm. Students that were engaged in scripted dialectical argumentation by providing justifications, counterarguments and evaluations on their own and another person's solution, showed superior conceptual understanding in evolution and were more likely to have attained conceptual change, than control students. This study also replicated the pattern of change in argumentative condition which was characterized by immediate conceptual gains that were preserved until the delayed posttest (Asterhan & Schwarz, 2005). Students in the control condition, however, did not show improvement on any of the test occasions. When they were refrained from engagement in dialog and were exposed to the same misconception, the pattern of temporary gains found in the previous study disappeared.

The finding that at least a third of students in our sample applied substantively different explanatory schemas at the same test occasion is especially noteworthy. It, first of all, stresses the importance of multiple assessments. Secondly, this finding seems to corroborate with current theoretical models and empirical findings that regard explanatory schemas (mental models) as temporary mental representations that are constructed in working memory according to specific demands of the task at hand and based on schema configurations stored in LTM (Schnotz & Preuss, 1999; Ohlsson, 2002). At any given time, different schema configurations compete with each other and have different likelihoods of being activated. As a result, a student may construct different mental models to explain different phenomena that relate to the same scientific concept. Accordingly, conceptual change should not be conceptualized as a shift from one particular conception to

the other. Like Siegler's overlapping waves theory (1996), it should be regarded as a change in the probability according to which more advanced schema configurations are activated and used to construct explanations.

Acknowledgments
This work was partially funded by a grant from the Israel Foundations Trustee (No. 27/35) to Christa Asterhan.

References

Amigues, R. (1988). Peer interaction in solving physics problems: Socio-cognitive confrontation and meta-cognitive aspects. *Journal of Experimental Child Psychology, 45,* 141-158.

Asterhan, C. S. C., & Schwarz, B. B. (2005). Argumentation in dyadic talk and conceptual change in evolutionary theory. Paper presented at a Festschrift Conference in the honor of Lauren Resnick. Pittsburgh, PA: University of Pittsburgh, The Learning Research and Development Center.

Chi, M. T. H., DeLeeuw, N., Chiu, M., & Lavancher, C. (1994). Eliciting self-explanations improves understanding. *Cognitive Science, 18,* 439-477.

Driver, R., Newton, P., & Osborne, J. (2000). Establishing the norms of scientific argumentation in classrooms. *Science Education, 84,* 287-312.

Kuhn, D. (1991). *The skills of argument.* Cambridge: Cambridge University Press.

Leitao, S. (2000). The potential of argument in knowledge building. *Human Development, 43,* 332-360.

Limon, M. (2001). On the cognitive conflict as an instructional strategy for conceptual change: A critical appraisal. *Learning & Instruction, 11,* 357-380.

Means, M. L. & Voss, J. F. (1996). Who reasons well? Two studies of informal reasoning among children of different grade, ability, and knowledge levels. *Cognition & Instruction, 14,* 139-179.

Ohlsson, S. (1992). Young adults' understanding of evolutionary explanations: Preliminary observations (Tech Rep). Pittsburgh, PA: Learning Research and Development Center.

Ohlsson, S. (2002). Generating and understanding qualitative explanations. In: J. Otero, J.A. Leon, & A.C. Graesser (Eds), *The psychology of science text comprehension.* Mahwah, NJ, US: Lawrence Erlbaum.

Okada, T. & Simon, H.A. (1997). Collaborative discovery in a scientific domain. *Cognitive Science, 21,* 109-146.

Schnotz, W., & Preuss, A. (1999). Task-dependent construction of mental models as a basis for conceptual change. In: W. Schnotz, S. Vosniadou & M. Carretero (Eds), *New perspectives on conceptual change.* Amsterdam: Pergamon Press.

Siegler, R.S. (1996). *Emerging Minds: The process of change in children's thinking.* Oxford: Oxford University Press.

Vosniadou, S. (1999). Conceptual change research: State of the art and future directions. In: W. Schnotz, S. Vosniadou & M. Carretero (Eds), *New perspectives on conceptual change.* Amsterdam: Pergamon Press.

Conceptual Change in Cognitive Science Education - towards Understanding and Supporting Multidisciplinary Learning

Otto Lappi (otto.lappi@helsinki.fi)
Cognitive Science Unit, Department of Psychology,
PO BOX 9, 00014 University of Helsinki, Finland

Abstract

Entering into higher education, students' conceptions undergo a restructuring process. When this reorganization is comprehensive, it is called "conceptual change". In this paper, a framework for discipline-based research into student conceptions and learning in cognitive science education is presented, in which a process of abstraction, leading to conceptual differentiation, is taken to be the key to conceptual change in learning cognitive science. From this perspective, commonsense concepts are seen as loosely organized clusters of features without unified, coherent logical structure, yet already containing, in embryonic form, the basic denoting elements and thought patterns out of which the scientific conceptions are constructed. This construction process requires that the student first differentiates or abstracts the appropriate conceptual elements (both in terms of contexts of application, terminology associated with them, and the inferential patterns they enter into), and then organizes them into definite schemata in which conceptual relations are based on theoretical definitions, rather than situational cues or associations. The special requirements of a multidisciplinary science and empirical, and educational implications of the focus on differentiation are discussed.

Introduction

When students enter university education, their conceptions of various phenomena in a domain undergo (or at least are hoped to undergo) a restructuring process that leads from commonsense belief (naive physics, folk biology, folk psychology...) to scientific conceptions. When this reorganization is comprehensive enough to constitute a wholesale reworking of one's ontological commitments, inferential practices, or the domain and standards of explanation - even the individuation of core concepts in the domain - it is called conceptual change (Carey, 1985; Hewson, 1984; Strike & Posner, 1982).

Conceptual change does not occur spontaneously. Nor is it generally enough that the scientific conceptual framework and patterns of thought are made available to students in clearly presented form. This is because students enter higher education with a rich and robust array of preconceptions - some of them misconceptions creatively concocted on the basis of previous education - a commonsense conceptual framework within which they make sense of the world and interpret instruction (Caramazza et al., 1981; McCloskey, 1983). These students' alternative conceptions are sometimes a source of resilience to influence by instruction and confusion. But they are also the seeds of scientific conceptions. (Indeed, if the basic thought patterns of the expert were not already present in some rudimentary and undisciplined form in the novice, then concept acquisition and the development of expertise in the discipline would appear altogether mysterious).

From a theoretical point of view, acquisition of expertise must be seen as a transformation of the initial state of the novice to the final state of the expert. Characterization of the initial state of this process is a necessary prerequisite. From a practical point of view, instruction must be adapted to what the student is able and willing to digest (where they are on the novice-to-expert trajectory), and what they are more likely to reject. We ignore student preconceptions at our peril.

In this paper, a framework for understanding student conceptions and learning in cognitive science education is presented. Some practical implications and the special requirements the multidisciplinarity of cognitive science places on the student and instructor are discussed briefly.

Cognitive Science Education

The outlook in this paper is that of discipline-based research. This differs from traditional research in higher education in that the focus is on (development of) student understanding of specific concepts, rather than learning in general, or individual differences in students that affect learning outcome. The approach is by far most developed in the context of physics education (see McDermott & Redish, 1999).

Such research is most naturally carried out by researchers and teachers working within the field in question. As McDermott (1991) notes, "Physicists are much more likely than science educators or cognitive psychologists to be able to explore student understanding of physics in depth". But in this regard, cognitive science is in a unique position. Since cognitive science is the discipline within whose domain the empirical study of concepts (and hence conceptual change) most naturally falls, cognitive scientists should have the best of both worlds, i.e. theoretical understanding of concept development *and* an in depth understanding of the theories cognitive science students are expected to master.

Therefore, it is somewhat surprising that to date very little discipline-based research into student conceptions and conceptual change in learning cognitive science has been carried out. By far the greatest bulk of discipline based research to date has been carried out within the discipline of physics. Also most of cognitive science on conceptual change centers on learning and problem solving in physics. On the other hand, the fragmented theoretical landscape -

compared to that of basic physics - and the controversy even among experts of the appropriate definition of key concepts such as representation, information or language - makes this perhaps less surprising.

Much of the research on learning physics should generalize into other disciplines, including Cognitive Science. However, as a discipline Cognitive Science probably has some unique features as well. These stem from the multi-disciplinary nature of the discipline, and the fact that as sciences go, Cognitive Science is a relative newcomer.

In established sciences, most notably basic physics, the underlying logic of the theories - basic concepts and the dependence of more specialized fields on a common core - is thoroughly worked out and agreed upon. In cognitive science, even the appropriate definition of its (arguably) most fundamental concepts are matters of philosophical debate (concepts such as knowledge, learning, innateness, computation, information, mind, concept...). There are also few established "first principles" in cognitive science proper. Neighboring disciplines (computer science and AI, linguistics, to a lesser extent neuroscience, psychology and philosophy) do have fundamental concepts and basic principles to bring unity beyond specific cases; but this immediately creates its own difficulties for the students who face a bewildering array of technical and semi-technical terminology stemming, historically, from various sources in different disciplines. Often the underlying concept for a given term is subtly different in meaning and application, depending on which discipline a particular theory or foundational approach is most closely associated with. All too often interpreting a term used in one context from the point of view of another leads to inconsistency and confusion, as the student struggles to piece together a consistent overall perspective from what must initially be a fragmented patchwork of conceptions. (For example, who would ever come to think of a computational explanation of color perception based on our everyday experience of computers and color phenomenology?)

Instructors involved in curriculum design face the complementary problem of depth and breadth of coverage. Given that cognitive science majors cannot be expected to acquire all the same competences as computer science majors, linguistics majors, neuroscience majors and so on, what are the appropriate standards of student assessment? What level of theoretical understanding and thought processes (problem solving, experimental design...) in information theory, psychophysics, or logic and linguistics should we expect from students of cognitive science, for example? The answer one gives to these questions depends in part on one's theoretical understanding of what kind of learning is involved in acquiring competence in problem solving and mastering the concepts of these disciplines, and their integration into a coherent cognitive science framework.

Differentiation by Abstraction as Key to Conceptual Change

"Conceptual change" is a somewhat blurry cover term, often used to denote global change in a conceptual framework

(Chi & Roscoe, 2002; Duit, 1999). When applied to individual learning it is taken to entail some kind of wholesale reconstruction of one's theoretical outlook on a domain (Carey 1985, 1991). In this paper, "conceptual change" refers the process off overcoming the divide between commonsense conceptions and scientific theories. (This is taken to be a different form of conceptual change from conceptual development in childhood and adolescence, i.e. the spontaneous emergence of commonsense conceptions and intuitive theories, including our naïve theory of mind). A change in concepts is involved insofar as the (literal) meaning associated with words used to describe the domain changes.

There are differences between acquisition of commonsense and scientific theories in both process and outcome. As for process, acquisition of commonsense conceptions occurs relatively spontaneously and uniformly, based on everyday experience and relatively little explicit instruction – whereas conceptual change in higher education requires considerable conscious effort, external support, and ingenuity on the part of the instruction. Indeed, research on student conceptions in physics education has shown time and time again how a relatively small percentage of students acquires a deep conceptual understanding of the scientific theories they are exposed to. In terms of outcome, scientific knowledge differs from commonsense conceptions and folk "theories" in terms of both the systematicity of its organization and the disciplined manner it is applied to specific instances.

As the student undergoes the cognitive transformation associated with learning a new scientific theory, theoretical terms acquire new, sharp, "technical" meanings where there previously were just undisciplined connotations. And where the interpretation of phenomena was previously performed in terms of loosely organized associations cued by surface features and specific contexts, interpretation now becomes based on basic concepts.

The view of conceptual change in science students, especially cognitive science students developed here builds on research on conceptual change in physics (e.g. Chi, 1981; DiSessa, 1988, 1993; Larkin, 1983; Larkin et al., 1980; Wiser & Carey, 1983). Especially germane is Carey's idea of differentiation (Carey, 1985, 1991; Wiser & Carey, 1983). Carey suggests conceptual change to come about by way of three processes of reorganization, which can be characterized by analogy from examples in the history of science: replacement (which like the replacement of the concept of phlogiston by the concept oxygen in theories of combustion), coalescence (as in Galileo's reinterpretation of the aristotelian distinction between natural and violent motions as a distinction without a difference in his development of a unified concept of motion), and differentiation (as in Black's differentiation of hotness/coldness into temperature and heat, See Wiser & Carey, 1983). It seems plausible that some movement toward more "analytic" mode of thought and ability to make finer distinctions is part of the competences that lead from unscientific to scientific conceptions.

What kind of cognitive operations might best characterize this relation of conceptual change between the initial state and the outcome in learning science? Differentiation results not just in several categories where there previously were one: instead, a more qualitative shift in the organization of knowledge from commonsense into theoretical must also be involved. This task faced by the individual university student is different from conceptual change in childhood, where the outcome is a commonsense theory, but also from conceptual change (paradigm shift) in science, where the initial state is also a scientific theory. (To the extent the original theory is much cruder, qualitative than the successor, "pre-paradigmatic", the historical case gives better and better approximation of the individual case.

It is crucial is that the student abstract from their intuitive commonsense concepts the (few) features which will come to form basic concepts around which the emerging scientific schema will be built. By "features" I mean basic conceptual elements which can be identified or recognized in different contexts, and patterns of inference related to them. They can be "cued" by the situation or "recognized" by the individual as recurring patterns in surface features of situations, and are used in categorizing, reasoning about, and making sense of everyday experience and interpreting claims about it made by other people (including scientific claims made by instructors). However, in distinction to the respective scientific concepts, they have no clear definitions, no definite operational criteria of application, and, most of all, the way that they are organized together into commonsense concepts lacks the systematicity of formal theories in the sciences. They cohere, but only weakly and haphazardly.

A commonsense concept can be thought of as a loosely organized cluster of such features, connotations of the corresponding term, if you will. (Though there generally won't be a single word, but many, the more "technical" terms merely being used in more "scientific" registers). These features may be organized into rudimentary schemata that fit specific phenomena for interpretation, but this organization is loose and sensitive to specific context. It is not "deep" in the sense of being governed by an understanding of first principles.

What I have in mind is something along the lines of DiSessa's (1988, 1993) "knowledge in pieces" account of the incoherent and superficial nature of commonsense conceptions (see also Wilson & Keil, 1998). DiSessa (ibid.) has attempted to define and tabulate some of the elements involved in our intuitive understanding of mechanics and mechanisms generally, which form the core of later scientific theories (though his "p-prims" are probably meant to be lower level elements than what is meant here by "features").

The features themselves need not be full-blown concepts. At least they are generally not, individually, the full meanings of the terms used to describe a domain - typically, the student would not have easy access to a verbal expression of them - either via name or definite description. Not all commonsense concepts or features have a term associated with them, either. For example, the commonsense concept IMPETUS seems to underlie many patterns of misinterpretation and misconception in learning mechanics (Caramazza et al., 1981; McCloskey, 1983), and therefore it is inferred to "be there", in the form of an ontological assumption on the part of the student (of *something* – not always the same something - being given to a projectile when "impelled", where this something is not force, momentum or kinetic energy in the scientific sense). Yet "impetus" is not so denoted in most subjects' vocabulary. Instead they may speak of "push", "force", or "speed" given to a projectile and gradually dying away - these terms are equivocally used for other concepts as well, e.g. "speed" is used for SPEED as well as IMPETUS.

Differentiation then leads from IMPETUS-based theory to a scientific conception which schematizes phenomena in terms of SPEED, VELOCITY, FRAMES OF REFERENCE, ACCELERATION, FORCE, MOMENTUM, KINETIC ENERGY, WORK etc. What is involved is not a wholesale *rejection* of the features and relations that make up the commonsense (mis)conception, but abstraction of certain features and relations as the "legitimate" ones, and construction of a scientific conception.

The operation of abstraction involves somehow becoming aware of the relevant features all at once (and becoming aware of their relevance), and relating them into a robust enough pattern to be applied in learning and problem solving. In learning a theory, some of the features associated with the commonsense concepts will be compatible with the scientific theory, and will be reorganized to form scientific concepts. Others will not. What is more, when a scientific conception is constructed, the elements will receive the status of full concepts. In effect, they will come to constitute the "technical" meaning of terms in the theory.

Also, the patterns of inference will then be governed by the formal structure of the theory. What I mean by their being governed by the theory is that - unlike commonsense misconceptions - the paths of qualitative reasoning lead to legitimate conclusions, sometimes via sustained logical argument, and can be refined or articulated in terms of more formal representations. This does not entail that the expert would always work formally and from first principles, instead, expert performance seems to depend on powerful qualitative schemata of representation and reasoning (Chi et al., 1981, 1982; Larkin et al., 1980; Larkin, 1983; VanHeuvelen, 1991).

To summarize, here is what is meant by differentiation *by abstraction*: the right features must be differentiated or abstracted from their host commonsense concept clusters (bound by loose association based on experience), and reorganized into a new scientific concept (or a systematic cluster of interdefined concepts), so that after completion all the inferential licences afforded by the theory are recognized - and only those. The intuitive plausibility jumping to theoretically unwarranted conclusions will carry no weight after conceptual change has occurred (whereas untutored common sense trades almost exclusively on intuitive plausibility, which in turn depends on "interpretation" of the concept in question (this can in turn be considered to be salience, in context, of particular features).

Some Implications for Cognitive Science Education

Having characterized in broad outline the general framework for understanding conceptual change, I now turn to the implications of this framework to instruction and assessment in cognitive science, and discipline-based research in cognitive science.

The first implication is that instruction and assessment should be sensitive to students' ability to differentiate concepts. This is especially important in a multidisciplinary science, where many of the basic concepts are borrowed from established theories in already established disciplines. The student should at the outset be made sensitive to the fact that terms such as "learning" or "inference", even "computation", have both various connotations (not all of which will apply in any particular context), and different technical meanings for computer scientists, neuroscientists and philosophers. What is more, students' ability to differentiate should be emphasized in instruction and assessment. If student conceptions, especially the inferential licences they take specific concepts to invoke, are not explicitly probed, major confusion may go unnoticed (as the instructor interprets students' use of terms from the point of view of their own conceptual framework, rather than the student's).

Care should be taken to ensure students recognize homonymous use of terms, and are able to "keep track" of the interpretation and inferential role of a concept within the framework of a specific theory. If confusion in these basic issues is not diagnosed and addressed from the beginning, confusion is bound to result. This means, that instructional materials should be designed so that they explicitly address the need of the student to be able to differentiate between different interpretations of terms (and their relation to commonsense conceptions).

Take, for example, the concept INNATENESS. The commonsense term "innate" has a variety of biological and psychological connotations. For example, Mameli and Bateson's (2006) philosophical analysis reveals twenty-six different and sometimes mutually incompatible definitions for the commonsense concept. (They conclude that the commonsense concept probably does not have a unique scientific counterpart concept, a conclusion which under the present assumption makes sense). In neuroscience, philosophy, developmental psychology and behavioral genetics the term is used in decidedly differing meanings. However, if neuroscientists in neuroscience textbooks generally present one interpretation, philosophers another and geneticists yet a third, it is left to the student to figure out the interrelations (either that or decide to stick within the confines of a single discipline). The lesson here is that, if indeed differentiation by abstraction is crucial to learning cognitive science concepts, multidisciplinary study materials explicitly contrasting these and forcing the student to do so as well are needed (it will not do to expect most students to perform this feat of abstraction themselves).

Second, since the claim is that the misconception is the father of the science (as the child is said to be the father to the man), then the implication is that instruction ought not to strive directly at the *replacement* of student conceptions – which runs the risk of creating parallel systems of commonsense conceptions and superficial, inert, scientific knowledge – but restructuring of them. This can be done by building up knowledge in a way that it is "anchored" to preconceptions (Clement et al., 1989), or by providing "ontology training" (Slotta & Chi, 2006) to make salient the features to be differentiated and the inferential licences that are associated (and, crucially, which inferences are *not* licenced).

A third implication is that we should find concepts that need to be differentiated in order to be acquired generally difficult for students to master, and certainly not expect the appropriate differentiations to be abstracted spontaneously from everyday experience or just clear and ambiguous presentation of material. It necessary for students to realize that not all - in fact very few - of the connotations associated with commonsense terms (or similar terms in related theories) carry over. Luckily, most students pick this up themselves - which is not to say that explicit practice and guidance is not called for, especially for the more difficult-to-learn concepts.

In this regard, the present hypothesis would predict the "accessibility" of the abstracted elements to affect learnability. This can be understood roughly as how far removed from experience, in terms of the process of abstraction, the concepts are. For example, it would make sense that the concept of chromatic color should be relatively easier to differentiate than innateness (should an unambiguous formal concept of innateness exist). This is because the to-be-abstracted features - hue, saturation, and brightness that define color concepts in the chromatic color space - find interpretation in intuitive experience relatively straightforwardly. The definition of innateness, on the other hand, as "information acquired by mechanisms other than learning" refers to unobservable properties and depends on *other* differentiated concepts – viz. "information" and "learning". It can only be interpreted correctly in light of already abstracted concepts. Instruction should then be designed so that students can work their way from common sense, bootstrapped by differentiated conceptions of theories of nearby disciplines on both sides.

Finally, when it comes to selecting topics for discipline-based research into conceptual change in cognitive science students, what are the important topics to start out with? On the present suggestion the natural starting point is the differentiated (or not) nature of student conceptions, especially, concerning concepts such as innateness, learning, or modularity, spanning multiple disciplines.

Conclusion

I have presented an outline for a framework for discipline-based research on intellectual development and conceptual change in acquisition of cognitive science concepts.

The proposal is that what gives scientific knowledge its abstract character is that you are not allowed to read into a concept all the features or attributes which intuitively "go together" (connotation), and that you are not allowed to make inferences beyond those that are licenced by formal definitions and the logical structure of a theory. This kind of knowledge is a product of differentiation by abstraction, where some few features belonging to the connotation of a commonsense concept are abstracted away from it, and used as the core of a new, scientific, conceptual framework. In this framework, merely connoted inferential licence does not apply. You can only infer what is explicitly licenced by the theory. This is in contrast to untutored common sense where connotational licence governs (reducing in the limiting case to undisciplined free association and rhetoric conclusion-drawing cued by key terms and phrases in the truly naïve subject).

This concept of differentiation by abstraction draws on discipline-based and cognitive science research into conceptual development in physics students. To what extent does research on learning physics carry over to cognitive science? If the logical structure of theories or the modes of explanation applied differ significantly, then one would expect to find differences in learning as well. (For example, in cognitive science there is less reduction to known first principles than in physics, and cognitive science employs teleological and rational explanation not recognized in physics). Also, the multidisciplinary nature of cognitive science means that there is perhaps less global coherence and more equivocal use of terminology (even among experts) than there is in physics, creating unique challenges for the learner. Thus the transfer of physics education theories and approaches might not turn out to be entirely smooth.

Another critical point to consider is the domain of application of the differentiation of concepts framework. I would expect it to best characterize the initial state of undergraduate training (with its characteristic confusion and disorientation), and be less applicable to (or less explanatory with respect to) acquisition of higher levels of expertise. In other words, ability to differentiate by abstraction in intermediate between conceptual change in childhood (acquisition of commonsense picture of the world) and high-level expertise in a field. I.e. the first major hurdle in university education.

Some implications for teaching and research were presented. In discipline-based research the application of general principles is very much dependent on the specific content to be studied. Therefore, the same kinds of paradigmatic "test cases" where reproducible and robust differences in student conceptions, patterns of inference, judgments of similarity etc. can be diagnosed, as are found in physics education literature, are called for.

Cumulative work on devising and refining such diagnostic test cases will enable contrasting interpretations (e.g. differentiation vs. category shift based explanations) to be evaluated and developed further. From a practical standpoint, such diagnostic tools can be used for the purpose of student assessment and gauging the effectiveness of teaching.

Overall, such research should contribute to both our theoretical understanding of learning in general and in our students in particular, which should also be reflected in the quality of teaching and thereby the outcome of learning.

Acknowledgments

Thanks to Dr. Marjaana Lindeman and Dr. Anne Nevgi for encouragement and useful discussions, and to Ms. Anna-Mari Rusanen for valuable comments on a draft of this paper.

References

Caramazza, A., McCloskey, M., & Green, B. (1981). Naive Beliefs in 'Sophisticated' Subjects: Misconceptions about Trajectories of Objects. *Cognition, 9*(2), 117-123.

Carey, S. (1985). *Conceptual Change in Childhood.* Cambridge, MA: MIT Press.

Carey, S. (1991). Knowledge acquisition: enrichment or conceptual change? In S. Carey & R. Gelman (eds.), *The Epigenesis of Mind: Essays in Biology and Cognition.* Hillsdale, NJ: Erlbaum, 257-291.

Chi, M., T.H., Feltovich, P., & Glaser, R. (1981). Categorization and Representation of Physics Problems by Experts and Novices. *Cognitive Science, 5,* 121-152.

Chi, M., T.H., Glaser, R., & Rees, E. (1982). Expertise in Problem Solving. In R. J. Sternberg (Ed.), *Advances in the Psychology of Human Intelligence.* Hillsdale, NJ: Erlbaum.

Chi, M., T.H., & Roscoe, R. D. (2002). The Process and Challenges of Conceptual Change. In M. Limon & L. Mason (Eds.), R*econsidering Conceptual Change. Issues in Theory and Practice* (pp. 3-27). Dordrecht: Kluwer Academic Publishers.

Clement, J., Brown, D. E., & Zietsman, A. (1989). Not All Preconceptions Are Misconceptions: Finding anchoring conceptions for grounding instruction on students' intuitions.. *International Journal of Science Education, 11*(Special Issue), 554-565.

DiSessa, A. A. (1988). Knowledge In Pieces. In G. Forman & P. Pufall (Eds.), *Constructivism in the Computer Age* (pp. 49-70). Hillsdale, NJ: Erlbaum.

DiSessa, A. A. (1993). Toward an Epistemology of Physics. *Cognition and Instruction, 10*(2 & 3), 105-225.

Duit, R. (1999). Conceptual Change Approaches in Science Education. In W. Schnotz, S. Vosniadou & M. Carretero (Eds.), *New Perspectives on Conceptual Change* (pp. 263-282). Amsterdam: Pergamon.

Hewson, P. (1984). A Conceptual Change Approach to Learning Science. European *Journal of Science Education, 3,* 383-396.

Larkin, J., McDermott, J., Simon, D. P., & Simon, H. A. (1980). Expert and Novice Performance in Solving Physics Problems. *Science, 208,* 1335-1342.

Larkin, J. H. (1983). The Role of Problem Representation in Physics. In D. Gentner & A. N. Stevens (Eds.), *Mental Models* (pp. 75-98). Hillsdale, NJ: Erlbaum.

Mameli, M. & Bateson, P. (2006). Innateness and the Sciences. *Biology and Philosophy, 21,* 155-188.

McCloskey, M. (1983). Naive Theories of Motion. In D. Gentner & A. N. Stevens (Eds.), *Mental Models* (pp. 299-324). Hillsdale, NJ: Erlbaum.

McDermott, L. C. (1991). What We Teach and What is Learned - Closing the Gap. *American Journal of Physics, 59*(4), 301-315.

McDermott, L. C., & Redish, E. F. (1999). Resource Letter: PER-1: Physics Education Research. *American Journal of Physics, 67*(9), 755-767.

Slotta, J. D., & Chi, M., T.H. (2006). Helping Students Understand Challenging Topics in Science Through Ontology Training. *Cognition & Instruction, 24*(2), 261-289.

Strike, K. A., & Posner, G. J. (1982). Conceptual Change and Science Teaching. *European Journal of Science Education, 4*(3), 231-240.

VanHeuvelen. (1991). Learning to Think like a Physicist: A review of Research-Based Instructional Strategies. *American Journal of Physics, 59*(10), 891-896.

Wilson, R. A., & Keil, F. (1998). The Shadows and Shallows of Explanation. *Minds and Machines,* 8, 137-159.

Wiser, M., & Carey, S. (1983). When Heat and Temperature were One. In D. Gentner & A. N. Stevens (Eds.), *Mental Models* (pp. 267-297). Hillsdale, NJ: Erlbaum.

A Role for Personal Epistemology in Conceptual Change in Physics

Christina Stathopoulou (cstath@phs.uoa.gr)
Department of Philosophy and History of Science, University of Athens
University Town, Ilisia, 15771, Athens, Greece

Stella Vosniadou (svosniad@phs.uoa.gr)
Department of Philosophy and History of Science, University of Athens
University Town, Ilisia, 15771, Athens, Greece

Abstract

Results from three studies are summed up in this paper. The studies were designed to test hypotheses emerging from a theoretical framework which is proposed for conceptualizing the role of personal epistemology in conceptual change in physics. Results support the hypotheses that physics-related personal epistemology may either facilitate or constrain the process of conceptual change not only directly, but also indirectly through certain mediating cognitive, metacognitive, and also motivational and affective factors.

The Nature of Personal Epistemology

Two mainstream theoretical approaches to the nature of personal epistemology can be roughly distinguished. The first approach, the *developmental approach,* considers a rather coherent, developmental structure that does not allow for horizontal (within-stage of development) variation (Perry, 1998; King & Kitchener 1994; Baxter Magolda, 1992; Belenky et al., 1986; Kuhn, 1991), whereas the second, *the multidimensional approach*, refers to a system of rather orthogonal (uncoordinated) dimensions, that are more or less independent, developing not necessarily in synchrony. (Schommer, 1990, 1993; Schommer et al., 1992).

Our theoretical approach, the *theory approach* can be seen as a bridge between the developmental and the multidimensional approach. We consider personal epistemology as an individually held *theory-like construct*, namely, *a* system of beliefs that are nonetheless, interconnected (see also Hofer & Pintrich, 1997). According to our theoretical position which is in line with the conceptual change approach that we adopt, personal epistemology forms initially a narrow but relatively coherent set of beliefs regarding the nature of knowledge and the process of knowing, which is based on the limited range of children's initial experiences and information that they receive from social-cultural environment. As experience and/or cultural information accumulates, this set of beliefs becomes gradually more differentiated, gradually changing some beliefs, but not others, and connecting them to different contexts of use. By the term *theory-like* we describe a structure that can generate explanations and predictions, which however, lacks many features of a scientific theory, since it is not explicit, well formed or socially shared. Also we assume that most individuals are not metaconceptually aware of this set of their beliefs.

Conceptualizing personal epistemology as a theory-like construct, which allows for general- and domain-specific beliefs to co-exist in an interconnected network, helps us understand better how it can be acquired and change, how it is related to individuals' learning in areas such as physics and how it is possible to have different personal epistemologies in different disciplines (Hofer & Pintrich, 1997; Hofer, 2000, Buehl, Alexander, & Murphy, 2002).

How May Conceptual Change in Physics Proceed?

The conceptual change approach adopted in this study attempts to provide a framework about how students learn physics. According to this approach it is assumed that human beings are prepared through evolution to learn some things more easily, by picking up certain information from the physical world and by gradually organizing their perceptual experiences in conceptual structures, such as the concept of the physical object. For example, young infants are by evolution predisposed to organize experience in terms of rigid objects that move as wholes on continuous paths, they do not penetrate one another and they interact only when they come into contact (Spelke, 1990). Consequent ontological and epistemological presuppositions are also attached to these conceptual structures. For example, physical objects are considered as solid and stable entities, in a space organized in terms of upward and downward directions, where unsupported objects fall downwards. On the other hand, epistemological presuppositions, such as that rest is the natural state of inanimate objects and motion needs to be explained, or that entities such as force, and weight are properties of physical objects, are the outcome of children's early attempts to understand motion. Both ontological and epistemological presuppositions are continuously corroborated by everyday sensory experience. In this way, a substantial knowledge about the physical world, in the form of naive physics, based on everyday sensory experience and information from the cultural context, develops early in infancy and allows children to make sense of and operate in their physical environment. However, naive physics can stand in the way of learning school physics in the sense that they can constrain the process of further knowledge acquisition about the physical world. This is so, because naïve physics provide narrow but nonetheless relatively coherent explanatory frameworks ('framework theories') for conceptualising the physical world that are usually at odds with scientific theories. Therefore, the learning of physics often requires that students construct differentiated/incommensurable theories about the workings of the physical world compared with the existing ones. (Vosniadou, 1994, 1999, 2002, in press; Vosniadou & Brewer 1994; Carey, 1985)

Conceptual change described as substantial reorganization and restructuring of existing conceptual structures, can efficiently explain the phenomena of 'misconceptions' observed in physics classrooms at all levels of education. What is called 'misconceptions' is the result of students' attempts to reconcile information from incompatible explanatory frameworks such as their initial explanatory frameworks about the workings of the physical world and the counter-intuitive scientifically accepted theories. More specifically 'misconceptions' can be produced as students attempt to assimilate certain aspects of scientifically accepted knowledge to which they are exposed through instruction into their existing knowledge structures. (Vosniadou, 1999, 2002, Ioannides & Vosniadou 2002).

In dynamics for instance, secondary students favor the meaning of force as an acquired property of moving inanimate objects, also known as the 'impetus misconception' (McCloskey, 1983). Instruction, at least at the secondary education level, does not appear to substantially change the 'acquired force' meaning, since it cannot easily influence the entrenched in the initial explanatory framework presuppositions that motion is a process that needs to be explained in terms of a causal (pushing/pulling) agent. Therefore, under the influence of instruction, students appear to simply assimilate in the existing notion of 'acquired force' the notion of force as push or pull and also the force of gravity. Vosniadou, 2002, in press).

In their influential model of conceptual change as a rational process, mentioned earlier, Posner et al. (1982), suggested four conditions (i.e., dissatisfaction with the current concept and also ineligibility, plausibility and fruitfulness of the new concept) for a successful conceptual change to take place in the learner's conceptual context ('conceptual ecology'). The metaphor of conceptual ecology was used to describe the learner's existing interrelated networks of concepts that influence the selection of a new concept playing a central and organizing role in thought. Among them, personally held 'epistemological commitments' namely, assumptions or views concerning the nature of knowledge and knowing were considered as playing an important role. Furthermore, in a 'revisionist' approach of the initial overtly rational model of conceptual change, Strike and Posner suggested that "motives and goals and the institutional and social sources of them need to be considered" as well, in attempting to describe a learner's evolving 'conceptual ecology' and understand the construct's impact on conceptual understanding (Strike & Posner, 1992, p.162). The need to incorporate variables of motivational and affective character such as personal beliefs and attitudes (e.g., beliefs about the nature of knowledge, and knowing, beliefs about learning, about the role of self as learner, goal orientation, motivation to engage in academic tasks, interest/value) into models of conceptual change is stressed by cognitive psychologists who also go beyond an approach that emphasizes the overtly rational nature of conceptual change (e.g., Pintrich, 1993, 1999, Dole & Sinatra, 1998, Gregoire, 2003; Sinatra, 2005).

Relating Personal Epistemology to Conceptual Change in Physics

There is evidence in the literature to suggest that aspects of personal epistemology are related to comprehension and metacompehension, strategy use, and learning. (e.g., Schommer, 1990, 1993; Schommer et al., 1992; Kardash & Scholes, 1996; Windschitl and Andre, 1998; Southerland and Sinatra, 2003; Mason, 2000, 2001; Mason & Gava, in press). More specifically, there is also evidence that aspects of personal epistemology are related to physics learning (e.g., Songer & Linn, 1991; Hammer, 1994; Qian & Alverman, 1995, Qian & Pan, 2002). The question is what is the nature of this relationship between personal epistemology and learning, particularly physics learning?

Hofer and Pintrich suggest that personal epistemologies functioning as implicit theory-like structures, which strongly interact with the cultural environment, can influence academic achievement indirectly, by affecting goal orientation. More precisely, personal epistemology is suggested to give rise to certain types of learning goals, such as mastery, performance, and completion goals, which can guide the selection of cognitive and metacognitive strategies in information processing (Hofer & Pintrich, 1997). In a more recent approach Hofer (2004) suggests that personal epistemology, in the form of a theory-like set of beliefs, may be seen as an aspect of metacognition. Thus, personal epistemology mostly operates at the metacognitive level, but also has a motivational function in the learning process.

Our position is that personal epistemology may influence conceptual change in a variety of different ways. Understanding the role of personal epistemology in conceptual change, involves, as mentioned earlier, more that considering conceptual change as an overtly rational process. The conflict between prior and the new -to be acquired- knowledge generates learning situations which involve not only cognitive and metacognitive factors but also variables of motivational and affective character. Among them are beliefs about the nature of knowledge and the process of knowing, as well as beliefs about the role of the self as learner, goal orientation, values, interest, etc (see also Pintrich, 1999; Gregoire, 2003; Sinatra, 2005).

According to our theoretical framework, personal presuppositions and beliefs about the nature of physics knowledge and knowing (what we thereafter call *physics-related personal epistemology*) can constrain or facilitate the knowledge acquisition process, in a direct or indirect way, just like ontological presuppositions and other beliefs and commitments of motivational and affective character can do. This is so because they may influence both the kind of new information that is picked up from the physical and social-cultural environment, and the way in which this information is interpreted (Vosniadou, 1994, 2003, in press; Vosniadou & Brewer, 1994). Thus, beliefs in piecemeal-factual and/or certain-unchanging physics knowledge, may directly guide students' attention to factual information, while, in contrast, beliefs in complex and/or evolving physics knowledge may guide students to focus more on patterns of relationships and their changes over time. Physics-related personal epistemologies, like ontological and motivational beliefs and commitments, may also affect the knowledge acquisition process indirectly, by influencing goal orientation, strategy use, metaconceptual awareness and, in general, the process of engaging in *metalearning,* or *deep learning* (Entwistle, in press, Entwistle, Tait, & McCune, 2000; Stathopoulou and Vosniadou, in press b). For example, the belief in piecemeal-factual knowledge may lead to the selection of rehearsal strategies to strengthen memorization and recall of piecemeal factual information.

In the following pages we will present some empirical evidence, regarding the nature of the relationship between personal epistemology and conceptual change (in physics), from a number of studies that we have conducted to investigate this relationship.

Assessing Personal Epistemology

A review of the literature, concerning measurement of personal epistemology, reveals that students' epistemologies have been investigated through interviews, production-type tasks and various paper and pencil instruments, depending mainly on the underlying theory about the construct under measurement (e.g., Duell & Schommer-Aikins, 2001). It is quite clear that researchers, who adopt unidimensional, developmental theoretical approaches, prefer qualitative measures that are compatible with their more holistic perspective on personal epistemology. In contrast, researchers that are interested in capturing the hypothetical multiple dimensions of the construct and focus on their relation to other cognitive constructs such as learning, tend to flavor quantitative, easy to administer and score and appropriate for correlational investigations, measuring instruments. The use of standardized, regardless the context, quantitative instruments is rejected by researchers who view personal epistemology as situated in context. Therefore, it is assumed that in order for a study to tap students' epistemologies, e.g., in introductory physics, it should be conducted in the closest possible context as that of an ongoing introductory physics course (Hammer, 1994).

It is clear in the literature (e.g. Pintrich, 2002), that the developmental approach considers epistemological beliefs as essentially domain-general, whereas, in contrast, the multidimensional approach allows for domain-specificity in epistemological beliefs (Hofer, 2000; Buehl, Alexander, & Murphy, 2002), and the contextualist approach suggests a within a domain, and largely context-specific consideration of the construct. According to our position, some aspects of personal epistemology may be domain-specific but others may not. This is in line, as mentioned, with our conceptualization of personal epistemology as a theory-like set of interconnected beliefs. Thus, consideration of domain-specificity and context-sensitivity of personal epistemology is very important in designing instruments for the assessment of the construct.

A number of the existing quantitative measures of personal epistemology, however, (e.g., those reported by Schommer, 1990; Jehng, Johnson, & Anderson, 1993; Schraw, Bendixen, & Dunkle, 2002), investigate general and not physics-specific personal epistemologies.

There are a few physics-specific quantitative instruments, such as the Epistemological Beliefs Assessment for Physical Science (EBAPS) (Elby, Frederiksen, Schwarz, & White, 2001) and the Maryland Physics Expectation Survey (MPEX) (Redish, Saul, & Steinberg, 1998). These instruments however, do not focus on the particular aspects of personal epistemology which are, in our opinion, more important, i.e., structure and stability of knowledge, source and justification of knowing (the 'core' as opposed to the 'peripheral' dimensions of personal epistemology, according to Hofer & Pintrich, 1997). Thus, for the purpose of assessing secondary students' physics-related personal epistemologies we have constructed and validated a physics-specific and, as possible, contextualized quantitative instrument, the Greek Epistemological Belief Evaluation instrument for Physics (GEBEP) (Stathopoulou & Vosniadou, in press a). The design of GEBEP was influenced by some existing qualitative instruments and research materials, particularly those reported by Driver and her colleagues (Driver, Leach, Millar, & Scott, 1996) and by Carey and her colleagues (Carey, Evans Honda, Jay, & Unger, 1989; Carey & Smith, 1993; Smith et al., 2000). It should be mentioned that the validation of the GEBEP involved also comparing results received through the GEBEP with results received through students' interviews and think-alouds.

Assessing Conceptual Change in Physics

Assessing conceptual change in physics is not an easy task, since conceptual change is a gradual and time consuming process. Attempts to assess such a process, may involve the design of (long-term) interventions and the use of appropriate diagnostic and/or achievement tests. In our studies so far, we measured conceptual understanding in Newtonian dynamics, instead of conceptual change in this area. For this purpose we used the Force and Motion Conceptual Evaluation instrument (FMCE), which is a research-based, multiple-choice assessment instrument designed by Thornton and Sokoloff (1998) at Tufts University to probe high school, college, and university students' understanding of Newton's three laws of motion.

We had also extensively used in our lab the FMCE, to assess physics understanding in 10th graders and 1st year university physics students in Greece. The results showed superficial understanding of Newton's Laws of motion even for university physics students after they had been exposed to traditional instruction. For example, only 3.3% of the 10th graders and 45.4% of the physics students answered in the scientifically accepted way all the items assessing Newton's first law. Moreover, none of the 10th graders and only 33.0% of the university physics students gave scientifically accepted responses to all the items assessing Newton's second Law (Mol, Stathopoulou, & Vosniadou, 2004; Mol, Stathopoulou, Vosniadou, & Karabarbounis, 2004). Information about the difficulty level for each item was also obtained. Thus it was found that some items were easier to answer than others, particularly those that did not require counterintuitive responses. In contrast, a number of other items, and particular combinations of items, were answered in the scientifically accepted way by very few, if any, students. In short, we had enough information to be able to know when a student could be said to have understood Newton's three laws on the basis of their performance on the FMCE. There is no doubt that understanding in-depth Newton's three laws is a rather difficult task that requires conceptual change, thus, the administration of the FMCE made it possible to determine the students who had achieved what might be called conceptual change in the area of Newtonian dynamics.

Along with the use of FMCE we collected data from interviews, think-alouds, and observations of students as they were involved in specially designed tasks such as answering questions and solving problems concerning certain situations in Newtonian dynamics. We selected the particular problems because they targeted some well known students' 'misconceptions' such as the 'impetus misconception'. We re-examined this way the depth of students' conceptual understanding in the area of Newtonian dynamics and found comparable results with those received through the use of FMCE.

In parallel, we also examined, through interviews, think-aloud and observation of students, in a context-sensitive way, their adopted approaches to learning and studying (deep vs. superficial), in the context of a problem-solving task.

Empirical Evidence on the Role of Personal Epistemology in Conceptual Change in Physics

Results from a study that we conducted, which targeted secondary students (10th-graders) in two extreme groups, i.e., 38 students with constructivist[1] personal epistemologies and 38 students with less-constructivist personal epistemologies respectively (as measured through the GEBEP), showed statistically significant difference in the FMCE scores achieved by students in the two groups ($t = 5.209$, df $= 47$, $p<.001$). Furthermore, results indicated that a constructivist physics-related epistemology may be a necessary (although not sufficient) condition for conceptual change in physics. This was our interpretation or the finding that only 11 students, all with constructivist personal epistemologies, showed evidence of having achieved conceptual change in Newtonian dynamics, as indicated by their high scores in the FMCE. The finding that there were students with constructivist personal epistemologies who achieved low scores in the FMCE shows that a constructivist personal epistemology is not sufficient for conceptual change. There is no doubt that it takes more than a constructivist physics-related personal epistemology to achieve conceptual change in physics.

Results of the aforementioned study also showed that students' beliefs concerning the *Structure* as well as the *Construction and Stability of physics knowledge*[2] were

---

[1] We use the term *constructivist personal epistemology* to refer to a set of contextual, constructivist, and evaluative beliefs about knowledge and knowing (Hofer & Pintrich, 1997; Hofer, 2002; Pintrich, 2002).

[2] Thus were named the two of the four dimensions of personal epistemology extracted through the use of GEBEP. The other two were *Source of Knowledge* and *Attainability of Absolute/Objective Truth* (Stathopoulou & Vosniadou, in press, a).

found to predict the score in the FMCE, [$R =.441$, $F(2,73) = 8.827$, $p <.001$], and conceptual change in Newtonian dynamics accordingly (Stathopoulou & Vosniadou, in press, a).

Beliefs concerning the *Construction and Stability of Knowledge* were also found a good predictor of physics understanding by another study that we conducted which targeted a new group of 98 secondary students (10th-graders) and did not focus on the two extreme groups [$R =.226$, $F(1,95) = 5.037$, $p<.01$] (Stathopoulou & Vosniadou, in press, a)

The overall results of the above-mentioned two studies support our suggestion that there is a strong relationship between physics-related personal epistemology and conceptual change in physics. It is essential however, to investigate the nature of this relationship further, through well designed experimental studies. We must also have in mind that his relationship is likely to be a reciprocal one (Pintrich 2002). As students develop a deeper understanding in physics their personal physics-related epistemologies would be likely to change. As noted earlier, conceptualizing personal epistemologies as theory-like structures can help us understand better the mechanisms of their change, however, the exact processes thereby which personal epistemologies change is an issue that needs thorough investigation.

Another study that we conducted, investigated further the nature of the relationship between personal epistemology and conceptual change (Stathopoulou and Vosniadou, in press, b). It was hypothesized, according to the theoretical position presented earlier, that the approach to learning and studying that students adopt, i.e., deep vs. superficial (e.g., Entwistle, in press; Entwistle et al., 2000), may intervene in the relationship between personal physics-related personal epistemology and conceptual change in physics.

More specifically, we hypothesized that a constructivist physics-related personal epistemology is more likely to guide students to the adoption of a deep approach to learning and studying, facilitating thus, physics understanding and conceptual change in physics, than a less-constructivist epistemology. We considered as *deep* an approach to learning and studying that involves goals of personal making of meaning, and accordingly, deep strategy use, such as integration of ideas. It also involves metaconceptual awareness, i.e., awareness of one's own beliefs. In contrast a *superficial* approach is characterized by performance orientation, or lack of purpose, and involves superficial strategy use, such as memorization of facts. It is also characterized by lack of metaconceptual awareness.

To examine this hypothesis ten students were selected to participate in the study. Five of them were found to score high on both the GEBEP and the FMCE. These students were expected to show evidence of adopting a deep approach to learning and studying, as opposed to the remaining five students, who had low scores on both the GEBEP and the FMCE and were expected to adopt a superficial approach to learning and studying. The adopted approach to learning and studying was investigated in a context-sensitive way, through interviews, think-alouds and observation of students, as they were involved in problem-solving tasks.

Results showed that all the five students, who held constructivist physics-related epistemologies and had achieved conceptual change in dynamics, adopted indeed a deep approach to learning and studying. In contrast, the remaining five students who had less-constructivist physics-related epistemologies and were far from having achieved deep conceptual understanding of dynamics, showed evidence of what may be considered a superficial approach to learning and studying.

Conclusions

The results from a number of inter-related studies that we conducted, which are summed up in this paper, support the suggestion that there is an important role for personal epistemology in the study of conceptual change in physics. The results are in line, but also extent findings reported in the literature (e.g., Songer & Linn, 1991; Qian & Alvermann, 1995; Qian & Pan, 2002; Hammer, 1994). They also agree with the hypotheses emerging from our theoretical framework, according to which personal epistemology may either facilitate or constrain the knowledge acquisition process both directly, through guiding attention to certain information and through influencing intentions regarding knowledge construction and revision, but also indirectly through certain mediating cognitive, metacognitive, and also motivational and affective factors (e.g., Vosniadou, 1994, 2003, in press; Sinatra & Pintrich, 2003; Mason, 2003; Pintrich, 1999; Dole & Sinatra, 1998; Gregoire, 2003; Sinatra, 2005).

References

Baxter Magolda, M.B. (1992). *Knowing and reasoning in college: Gender-related patterns in students' intellectual development*. San Francisco: Jossey-Bass.

Buehl, M.M., Alexander, P.A., & Murphy, P.K. (2002). Beliefs about schooled knowledge: Domain specific or domain general? *Contemporary Educational Psychology, 27,* 415-449.

Carey, S., & Smith, C. (1993). On understanding the nature of scientific knowledge. *Educational Psychologist, 28* (3), 235-251.

Dole, J., & Sinatra, G. (1998). Reconceptualizing change in the cognitive construction of knowledge. *Educational Psychologist, 33,* 109-128.

Driver, R., Leach, J., Millar, R., & Scott, P. (1996). *Young people's images of science*. Buckingham: Open University Press.

Duell, O.K., & Schommer-Aikins, M. (2001). Measures of people's beliefs about knowledge and learning. *Educational Psychology Review, 13* (4), 419-449.

Entwistle, N. (in press). Conceptions of learning and the experience of understanding: Thresholds, contextual influences, and knowledge objects. In S. Vosniadou, A. Baltas & X. Vamvakoussi (Eds.) *Reframing the conceptual change research in learning and instruction*. Oxford: Elsevier.

Entwistle, N, Tait, H., & McCune, V. (2000). Patterns of response to an approaches to studying inventory across contrasting groups and contexts. *European Journal of Psychology of Education, XV* (1), 33-38.

Gregoire, M. (2003). Is it a challenge or a threat? A dual-process model of teachers' cognition and appraisal processes during conceptual change. *Educational Psychology Review, 15* (2), 147-179.

Hammer, D. (1994). Epistemological beliefs in introductory physics. *Cognition and Instruction, 12* (2), 151-183

Hofer, B.K. (2000). Dimensionality and disciplinary differences in personal epistemology. *Contemporary Educational Psychology, 25,* 378-405.

Hofer, B.K. (2002). Personal epistemology as a psychological and educational construct: An introduction. In B.K. Hofer & P.R. Pintrich (Eds.), *Personal epistemology: The psychology of beliefs about knowledge and knowing* (pp. 3-14). Mahwah, N.J.: Lawrence Erlbaum Associates.

Hofer, B.K. (2004). Epistemological understanding as a metacognitive process: Thinking aloud during online searching. *Educational Psychologist, 39* (1), 43-55.

Hofer, B.K., & Pintrich, P.R. (1997). The development of epistemological theories: Beliefs about knowledge and knowing and their relation to learning. *Review of Educational Research, 67*(1), 88-140.

Jehng, J.C., Johnson, S.D., & Anderson, R.C. (1993). Schooling and students' epistemological beliefs about learning. *Contemporary Educational Psychology, 18,* 23-35.

Kardash, C.M., & Scholes, R.J. (1996). Effects of pre-existing beliefs, epistemological beliefs and need for cognition on interpretation of controversial issues. *Journal of Educational Psychology, 88,* 260-271.

King, P.M., & Kitchener, K.S. (1994). *Developing reflective judgement: Understanding and promoting intellectual growth and critical thinking in adolescents and adults*. San Francisco: Jossey-Bass.

Kuhn, D. (1991). *The skills of argument*. Cambridge: Cambridge University Press.

Leach, J. Millar, R. Ryder, J., & Sere, M.G. (2000). Epistemological understanding in science learning: The consistency of representations across contexts. *Learning and Instruction, 10,* 497-527.

Mason, L. (2000). Role of anomalous data and epistemological beliefs in middle students' theory change on two controversial topics. *European Journal of Psychology of Education, 15,* 329-346.

Mason, L. (2001). Responses to anomalous data on controversial topics and theory change. *Learning and Instruction 11,* 453-483.

Mason, L. (2003). Personal epistemologies and intentional conceptual change. In G.M. Sinatra & P.R. Pintrich (Eds.) (2003). *Intentional conceptual change*. Mahwah, NJ: Lawrence Erlbaum Associates.

Mason, L., & Gava, M. (in press). Effects of epistemological beliefs and learning text structure on conceptual change. In S. Vosniadou, A. Baltas & X. Vamvakoussi (Eds.) *Reframing the conceptual change research in learning and instruction*. Oxford: Elsevier.

Mol, A., Stathopoulou, C., & Vosniadou, S. (2004, May). Consistency versus fragmentation in Mechanics. Paper presented at the 4th European Symposium of the European Association for Research on Learning and Instruction on 'Conceptual Change: Philosophical, Historical, Psychological and Educational Approaches', Delphi, Greece.

Mol. A., Stathopoulou, C. Vosniadou, S., & Karabarbounis, A. (2004, January/February). High school students' problems in understanding Newton's first and second law. Paper presented at the 10th conference of the Hellenic Physical Society, Loutraki, Greece.

Perry, W.C. Jr. (1998). *Forms of intellectual and ethical*

development in the college years: A scheme. San Francisco: Jossey-Bass (Originally published in 1970. New York: Holt, Rinehart & Winston).

Pintrich, P.R. (1999). Motivational beliefs as resources for and constrains on conceptual change. In W. Schnotz, S. Vosniadou, & M. Carretero (Eds.), *New perspectives on conceptual change* (pp. 33-50). Oxford: Elsevier.

Pintrich, P.R. (2002). Future challenges and directions for theory and research on personal epistemologies. In B. K. Hofer & P. R. Pintrich (Eds.), *Personal epistemology: The psychology of beliefs about knowledge and knowing* (pp. 103-118). Mahwah, N.J.: Lawrence Erlbaum Associates.

Posner, G.J., Strike, K.A., Hewson, P.W., & Gertzog, W.A. (1982). Accommodation of a scientific conception. Toward a theory of conceptual change. *Science Education, 66*(2), 211-227.

Qian, G., & Alvermann, D. (1995). Role of epistemological beliefs and learned helplessness in secondary school students' learning science concepts from text. *Journal of Educational Psychology, 87*(2) 282-292.

Qian, G., & Pan, J. (2002). A comparison of epistemological beliefs and learning from science text between American and Chinese high school students. In B.K. Hofer & P.R. Pintrich (Eds.) *Personal Epistemology: The Psychology of Beliefs about Knowledge and Knowing.* Mahwah, NJ: Lawrence Erlbaum Associates.

Schommer, M. (1990). Effects of beliefs about the nature of knowledge on comprehension. *Journal of Educational Psychology, 82*, 498-504.

Schommer, M. (1993). Epistemological development and academic performance among secondary students. *Journal of Educational Psychology, 85* (3), 406-411.

Schommer-Aikins, M. (2002). An evolving theoretical framework for an epistemological belief system. In B. K. Hofer & P. R. Pintrich (Eds.) *Personal Epistemology: The psychology of beliefs about knowledge and knowing* (pp. 103-118). Mahwah, N.J.: Lawrence Erlbaum Associates.

Schommer, M., Crouse, A., & Rhodes, N. (1992). Epistemological beliefs and mathematical text comprehension: Believing it is simple does not make it so. *Journal of Educational Psychology, 84*(4) 435-443.

Smith, C.L., Maclin, D., Houghton, C., & Hennessey, M.G. (2000). Sixth-grade students' epistemologies of science: The impact of school science experiences on epistemological development. *Cognition and Instruction, 18*(3), 349-422.

Sinatra, G.M. (2005). The "warming trend" in conceptual change research: The legacy of Paul Pintrich. *Educational Psychologist, 40*(2), 107-115.

Sinatra, G.M. & Pintrich, P.R. (2003). The role of intentions in conceptual change learning. In G.M. Sinatra & P.R. Pintrich (Eds.) *Intentional conceptual change* (pp. 1-18). Mahwah, NJ: Lawrence Erlbaum Associates, Inc.

Southerland, S. A., & Sinatra, G. M. (2003). Learning about biological evolution: A special case of intentional conceptual change. In G. M. Sinatra & P. R. Pintrich (Eds.), *Intentional conceptual change* (pp. 317-345). Mahwah, NJ: Lawrence Erlbaum Associates.

Songer, N.B., & Linn, M.C. (1991). How do students' views of science influence knowledge integration? *Journal of Research in Science Teaching, 28* (9), 761-784.

Strike, K.A., & Posner, G.J. (1992). A Revisionist Theory of Conceptual Change. In R.A. Duschl & R.J. Hamilton (Eds.), *Philosophy of Science, Cognitive Psychology and Educational Theory and Practise* (pp 147-176). New York: State University of New York Press.

Stathopoulou, C., & Vosniadou, S. (in press a). Exploring the relationship between physics-related epistemological beliefs and physics understanding. *Contemporary Educational Psychology.*

Stathopoulou, C., & Vosniadou, S. (in press, b). Conceptual change in physics and physics-related epistemological beliefs: A relationship under scrutiny. In S. Vosniadou, A. Baltas & X. Vamvakoussi (Eds.) *Reframing the conceptual change research in learning and instruction.* Oxford: Elsevier.

Thornton, R.K., & Sokoloff, D.R. (1998). Assessing student learning of Newton's laws: The Force and Motion Conceptual Evaluation and the evaluation of active learning laboratory and lecture curricula. *American Journal of Physics, 66*(4), 338-352.

Vosniadou, S. (1994). Capturing and modeling the process of conceptual change. *Learning and Instruction, 4*, 45-69.

Vosniadou, S. (1999). Conceptual change research: State of the art and future directions. In W. Schnotz, S. Vosniadou, & M. Carretero (Eds.), *New perspectives on conceptual change.* Oxford: Elsevier.

Vosniadou, S. (2002). On the nature of naive physics. In M. Limon & L. Mason (Eds.), *Reconsidering conceptual change: Issues in theory and practice* (pp. 61-76). Dordrecht: Kluwer

Vosniadou, S. (2003). Is intentional learning necessary for conceptual change? In G. Sinatra and P. Pintrich (Eds.), *Intentional conceptual change.* Hillsdale, NJ: Erlbaum.

Vosniadou, S. (in press). The Conceptual Change Approach and its Re-framing. In S. Vosniadou, A. Baltas & X. Vamvakoussi (Eds.) *Reframing the conceptual change research in learning and instruction.* Oxford: Elsevier.

Vosniadou, S., & Brewer, W.F. (1994). Mental models of the day/night cycle. *Cognitive Science, 18*, 123-183.

Windschitl, M., & Andre, T. (1998). Using computer simulations to enhance conceptual change: The roles of constructivist instruction and student epistemological beliefs. *Journal of Research in Science Teaching, 35*, 145-160.

Implementing the Subset Principle in Syntax Acquisition: Lattice-Based Models

Janet Dean Fodor (jfodor@gc.cuny.edu)
Ph.D. Program in Linguistics, The Graduate Center, City University of New York
365 Fifth Avenue, New York, NY 10016

William Gregory Sakas (sakas@hunter.cuny.edu)
Department of Computer Science, Ph.D. Programs in Linguistics and Computer Science
Hunter College and The Graduate Center, City University of New York
North Building 1008; 695 Park Avenue, New York, NY 10021

Arthur Hoskey (ahoskey1@gc.cuny.edu)
Ph.D. Program in Computer Science, The Graduate Center, City University of New York
365 Fifth Avenue, New York, NY 10016

Abstract

Language learners with insufficient access to negative evidence about what is not in their target language must rely on the Subset Principle (SP), or some other similar conservative learning strategy, in order to avoid overgeneration. Recent attempts to incorporate such a strategy into psychologically realistic models of syntax acquisition have revealed two severe problems: SP application appears to demand computational resources that exceed those of children; and SP causes *under*generation failures if learning is incremental. We present a representational scheme for the domain of grammars which can alleviate both problems, and we report simulation data showing how it can best be employed in a learning model.

Implementation Challenges

Because language learners receive little information about non-sentences of their target language (Marcus, 1993), any model of natural language syntax acquisition must have some means of avoiding or minimizing overgeneration. The learning mechanism (LM) must be conservative: other things being equal, the grammar hypothesis it adopts must be the one that fits the positive input most snugly. This general principle has been cast as the *Subset Principle* in studies of syntax acquisition grounded in generative linguistics (Berwick, 1985; Manzini & Wexler, 1987). It is also a close relation of the domain-general *size principle* of Bayesian learning theory (Tenenbaum & Griffiths, 2001). For convenience here we will refer to this conservative tendency as the Subset Principle (SP) but leaving open the existence of many varied implementations of it. Our concern is a duo of recently uncovered practical problems that must be addressed by *any* such implementation if it is intended as a contribution to a psychological model of how children acquire syntax.

As noted in Fodor & Sakas (2005), one problem is that rigorous application of SP appears to demand an undue share of the on-line computational resources that can reasonably be ascribed to a pre-school child. The second problem is that under some familiar learning regimes, SP becomes over-zealous and prevents convergence on the target grammar: without SP, learners are at risk of *over*generation errors, but with SP they are at risk of *under*generation errors. Thus despite its central importance, it is unclear whether SP (and/or its close relations in other frameworks, including statistical learning models) can be successfully incorporated into psychologically faithful models of language acquisition.

We illustrate these problems below in a specific modeling framework that has served in the past as our basis for simulation experiments comparing the efficiency of various acquisition tactics (Fodor & Sakas, 2004). The targets for learning are parameter-based grammars (Chomsky, 1981 et seq.). In parameter setting ('triggering') models, it is commonly assumed that LM has no memory for prior input sentences or for which grammars it entertained previously. It retains from its past experience only the knowledge that is encapsulated in its current grammar. Thus, in contrast to models that accumulate data and seek regularities in it, parameter setting is *incremental*, in the sense that LM receives target language sentences one at a time and decides, on the basis of each one, either to retain its current grammar hypothesis or to switch to a different one.

Despite these specific properties, we believe that the points we raise here have bearing on a broad range of approaches to syntax acquisition. The implementation of SP is equally challenging, or more so, for other current learning models, and any advances that can be made may therefore benefit those other approaches as well. In this paper we argue that it is essential to augment in some way the severely restricted memory of incremental models, and we propose a novel representational scheme that allows LM to keep track of the domain of grammar hypotheses, and thereby alleviates both the problem of on-line computational resources and the undergeneralization problem.

The Computational Resources Problem

SP is a *comparative* criterion for grammar selection: whether it permits a grammar hypothesis to be adopted depends on what alternative hypotheses are available. Given input sentence *i*, LM should ideally adopt a grammar G such that the language L(G) includes *i* and has no proper subset L(G') that includes *i*, where G' is a possible grammar that has not been disconfirmed by prior input (if the model has knowledge of that; see below). But how can LM know which grammar satisfies these criteria? It appears that LM must have the ability to identify grammars that license an arbitrary sentence *i*, and moreover that it must have exhaustive knowledge of *all* (non-disconfirmed) grammars that license *i*, so that it can compare them against each other to ensure that it does not unwittingly adopt one that is prohibited by the existence of a less inclusive one. Thus, when LM's current grammar fails on an input *i* and a new grammar must be adopted, LM has three tasks to do. Task A: Find a new grammar hypothesis G which does license *i*. Task B: Identify all other grammars that license *i* (in order to be able to check for subset relations as in Task C). Task C: Check whether any other grammar that licenses *i* generates a subset of L(G).

Task A has proved to be a cumbersome problem for syntax acquisition models. It is not always obvious by inspection of an input word string what grammar might have generated it. Various strategies which start from the current grammar and amend it (e.g., reset one parameter at a time; reset only incorrect parameters) have been found to be inadequate because, for example, it is often unclear which parameters are incorrect. Recent models typically undertake extensive trial and error, selecting a grammar and then testing to see whether it will parse *i* (e.g., Gibson & Wexler, 1994; Clark, 1992; Yang, 2002). The models that we have developed use the parsing routines instead to identify needed changes to the current grammar (Sakas & Fodor, 2001). However, this technique has its limits. It can reliably identify *one* grammar that generates *i*, but not more than one without exceeding standardly accepted limits on the capacity of the human parsing mechanism.

Task B (identifying *all* grammars compatible with *i*) is a challenge of a higher order. The natural language domain is highly ambiguous, with most sentence types compatible with multiple grammars (Clark, 1989). It is also a very large search space, possibly on the order of billions of grammars (2^n for *n* independent binary parameters), so the workload would be prohibitive if indeed every grammar must be checked whenever LM is considering adopting a new one. It is clearly beyond the bounds of psychological plausibility to suppose that a child runs a billion parse tests, each with a different grammar, on a single input sentence to see which grammars succeed. To solve this problem, a completely different approach to SP is required which does *not* require exhaustive knowledge of all grammars that license *i*, as we discuss below.

Task C (discovering subset relations between grammars that license *i*) might be achieved by comparing languages (sets of sentences) on-line, but this too would exceed plausible computational resources. An alternative approach would be to assume that LM is equipped with prior information as to which languages are subsets of which others. Ideally, these subset relations between languages would be transparently reflected in formal relations between their grammars, so that LM could simply inspect two grammars to find out whether one generates a subset of the other.

This was proposed by Manzini & Wexler (1987), who suggested that each parameter has a default value and a marked value (notated 0 and 1 respectively) and that subset relations between grammars are due exclusively to these values: for any pair of grammars differing with respect to the value of a parameter P, the language with value 0 for P is a proper subset of the language with value 1 for P; and no other subset-superset relations hold between any grammars in the domain. We have called this the *Simple Defaults Model* (Fodor & Sakas, 2005). If it were true of natural languages, it would strongly limit the number of subset relations in the domain, thus reducing the scale of Task C. And it would provide LM with a trivially easy way to identify all the subsets of a language L(G): they would be all and only those languages whose grammars differ from G by having value 0 for one or more parameters for which G has value 1.

Unfortunately, it seems that this optimal situation does not obtain in the case of natural languages. For our parameter-setting simulation experiments we have created a domain of 3,072 artificial languages, defined by 13 syntactic parameters and designed to be as much like real natural languages as possible despite necessary simplifications. In this domain the Simple Defaults Model fails. A high proportion (over 42%) of the subset relations that hold between grammars are *not* predictable from the subset values of individual parameters; they are due instead to interactions, often quite unruly, among two or more parameters. Therefore, any SP-implementation based on the Simple Defaults Model would under-report the subsets a language has, and would fail to protect LM against overgeneration errors. Simulation data confirm this expectation; we observe 64% failures for a model that performs without error when supplied with full information about subset relations.

Perhaps other linguistic theories might offer better ways of predicting subset relations between languages based on their grammars, but none is known at present and in fact there are good reasons to suspect that the relationship between grammars and the languages they generate is bound to be disorderly: a small change in a grammar can completely change the set of sentences (word strings) it generates, and word strings generated by quite different grammars may happen to coincide. It therefore becomes important to consider what theoretical options there are, if it does turn out that subset relations cannot be projected on-line by LM. It seems unavoidable to suppose, in that case, that LM has access to an innate database of some kind which provides subset-superset information. The biological origin of such a knowledge structure may be a mystery in the present state of understanding, and remains to be explored, but a first step is to find out whether, if it *did* exist, it would permit Task C to be achieved without incurring an unreasonable computational workload.

From Enumeration to Lattice

Formal learnability studies in the tradition of Gold (1967)

assumed that the learning algorithm was provided with subset-superset information in the form of an *enumeration* of grammars: a total ordering of all the possible grammars, in which any subset grammar precedes all of its superset grammars. (Note that for convenience from now on we refer to subset relations between *grammars*, as a shorthand for subset relations between the languages that the grammars generate.) Because of its foundational status in formal learning theory, it is worthwhile to see whether an enumeration can be adapted for psychological purposes.

The enumeration could serve as the innate database about subset-superset relations that LM would consult for Task C. It could also provide dynamic guidance for LM in its on-line process of grammar hypothesization. If LM hypothesizes grammars strictly in accord with the enumeration ordering, moving on to the next one only when the previous one has proven incompatible with the input, it will have obeyed SP without explicitly applying it. In particular, an enumeration-based LM obeys SP without exhaustively identifying and comparing all candidate grammars; thus, the enumeration does away with Task B. It does so by rendering illicit grammars (i.e., superset grammars) *inaccessible* to LM; LM has access to a grammar only after all its subsets, prior to it in the ordering, have been disconfirmed. Also inaccessible are all previously disconfirmed grammars, since they are necessarily prior in the enumeration to LM's current grammar; so those hypotheses are not revisited and convergence is thereby speeded.

Thus a classic Gold-type enumeration makes short work of Tasks B and C. It falters, however, on Task A: selecting a new grammar compatible with the current input sentence. The enumeration gives LM no choice with respect to its next grammar hypothesis: when its current grammar fails to license input *i*, LM must try out the immediately next grammar in the enumeration. This has the obvious disadvantage that a grammar late in the ordering can be attained only after eliminating all billion-or-so grammars prior to it in the enumeration. As described so far, the model has no way to use the properties of the input sentence to move *directly* to an appropriate grammar, skipping over irrelevant ones in between. More importantly, we cannot *introduce* any devices that would do this, because once intervening grammars are allowed to be passed over, the role of the enumeration as the enforcer of SP is lost. The danger of LM passing over an intervening *subset* grammar would obviate the whole purpose of the grammar ordering. However, without the ability to move faster through the sequence by skipping grammars along the way, enumeration-based learning is generally regarded as being unredeemably slow and has not been embraced by psychological models of language acquisition (Pinker, 1979).

The excessive rigidity of the classic enumeration can be remediated, however, by shifting to a *partial* ordering of grammars, which places all subset grammars prior to their superset grammars but does not impose a fixed order otherwise. The partial ordering is sufficient to ensure compliance with SP, but in other respects it leaves LM free to move around the grammar search space, from less profitable to more profitable regions, using whatever skills it

may possess for identifying a likely grammar to license *i*. On this proposal the database of grammars takes the form of a *lattice* (or strictly, a *poset*), as illustrated in Figure 1.

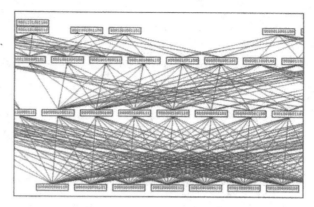

Figure 1: A small fragment (less than 1%) of a lattice representation of the domain of 3,072 parameterized languages used in the simulation experiments described below. Supersets are above subsets.

Observe that the classic one-dimensional enumeration has been reshaped here. The smallest subset grammars in the domain are presented at the lower edge of the lattice, with their supersets above them. The lowest grammars are all and only those that constitute legitimate hypotheses for LM at the initial stage of learning prior to any input. A grammar that is higher in the lattice may be adopted only after all the grammars it dominates have been tested and disconfirmed by the input. This means that higher grammars will be attained more slowly on average than lower grammars, but the disparity is far less than between the earliest and latest grammars in a classic enumeration: the maximum depth of the lattice for our natural-language-like domain of grammars is 7; the mean depth is 3.4. It can be supposed that as lower grammars are disconfirmed they are deleted from the lattice, so that the set of grammars accessible to LM, at the lower edge of the lattice, gradually changes over time. A grammar that has many subsets will start out high in the lattice but will work its way down if and when the subset grammars beneath it are erased.

As far as SP is concerned, LM may choose freely from among the accessible grammars at the bottom of the lattice. It might do so by random trial and error if no better mechanism is available. But the lattice has a considerable advantage over a total enumeration in that it leaves LM some elbowroom to apply useful grammar-guessing strategies. Any linguistic knowledge that LM may have can be put to work to extract relevant properties of input sentences to guide its grammar choices. The family of learning models that we have proposed, known as *Structural Triggers Learners* (*STLs*; Fodor & Sakas, 2004), can do this. STLs use the technique noted above, of employing the parsing routines for on-line detection of how the current grammar can be supplemented to accommodate input *i*. It works as follows. The parser applies LM's current grammar, $G_{current}$, to the input sentence. If the parse succeeds, LM retains G_current. If the parse fails, then at the specific locus of that failure in the word string, the parser is permitted to draw on other linguistic resources (specifically, previously unused parameter values) as necessary in order to complete the parse. LM then adopts whichever new parameter values contributed to rescuing the parse.

We call this *decoding* the input sentence. The parser does not merely register *whether* a given grammar licenses *i* or not, but actively *finds* a grammar that licenses *i*. As noted above, it cannot realistically be assumed that for an ambiguous input the human parser computes *every* grammar that could license it. Moreover, the one grammar it does find may not be the correct grammar for *i* in the target language, but it is at least a genuine candidate hypothesis, one that might be correct or could lead LM in the direction of one that is. The consequence of combining this decoding strategy with the lattice representation of possible grammars is that LM does not waste effort checking grammars that have no relation to the current input. Instead, the work of testing and discarding grammars in the lattice is highly focused on grammars that do license sentences in the learner's input sample. In many regions of the lattice there may be no activity at all, because the grammars there are unable to parse target language sentences (e.g., they generate head-final constructions while the target language is head-initial). The lattice representation combined with input decoding thus may be a step towards an optimal grammar search strategy.

To summarize: Like an enumeration, the partial ordering of grammars in a lattice encodes essential information about the subset-superset relations in the domain. Also like an enumeration, it blocks LM's access to unsafe (superset) grammars, so that LM can avoid them without engaging in resource-heavy comparisons between grammars. Unlike an enumeration, it does not insist on a single fixed sequence of grammar hypotheses. Subset-superset grammars must be ordered because of SP, but other grammars are freely accessible. This decreases the learning time discrepancy between the least and most accessible grammars in the domain, and also permits LM to take advantage of linguistic information (cues, triggers) in the input to *guide* its search through the lattice for the target grammar. The simulation data we present below show that while there are better and worse ways for a learner to make use of a lattice, a lattice-based model can indeed reliably prevent overgeneration without exceeding reasonable computation loads.

The Undergeneralization Problem

The erasure of disconfirmed grammars from the lattice offers a straightforward solution to the problem of undergeneralization that can afflict incremental learners. Incremental learning is widely favored over batch learning from a psychological point of view, because it presupposes neither memory for the entire input sample, nor methods for fitting a grammar to a large corpus. However, there is a fundamental incompatibility between incremental learning and the conservative learning that is needed for avoiding overgeneration. SP is often cast informally as the requirement that LM should select the least inclusive grammar compatible with the input. But if the only input

accessible to LM is the current sentence, the least inclusive grammar compatible with it will generate a very small language indeed; it is likely to lack many language phenomena that were acquired from previous inputs no longer in memory. For instance, all long-distance movement would be lost if the current sentence has none. The fact that the previously acquired phenomena are generated by LM's current grammar does not protect them from loss. Conservative learning requires that all contents of the current grammar be given up when a new grammar is about to be adopted, *except those that are known to be correct*. Otherwise LM's grammar would just keep growing as the sum of all its previous false hypotheses, and overgeneration would be rife. However, since most learning models hypothesize grammars on the basis of ambiguous input (and most cannot even tell which inputs are ambiguous and which are not), LM can rarely be certain that some phenomenon it previously 'acquired' is veridical. Hence SP (or comparable conservative learning principles) would repeatedly force the learner to regress to very limited languages compatible with just the current input. (See Fodor & Sakas, 2005, for additional discussion of this problem of *excessive retrenchment*.)

Since there is no evidence that child learners are afflicted with this problem, it should not occur in our learning models either. A simple solution would be to abandon incremental learning entirely. If it were assumed instead that LM holds in memory all or many of its prior input sentences, it could not be forced by SP to adopt a language smaller than the minimal one that contains all of those sentences. Psychological models of parameter setting that base each grammar hypothesis on a collection of many sentences (unlike 'triggering') may well be of interest but no standard implementation currently exists (though see Kapur, 1994). An alternative approach, which avoids giving up the psychologically desirable aspects of incremental learning, is to eliminate languages from the hypothesis space as and when they are found to be too limited to include the input. As learning proceeds, languages that are excessively small will be ruled out; the smallest languages in the pool will be larger and larger, and LM can now adopt them even in response to a single input sentence. E.g., once languages without long-distance movement have been eliminated by previous input exhibiting long-distance movement, LM will necessarily adopt a grammar that licenses long-distance movement even if the current sentence exhibits no movement at all. Elimination of disconfirmed grammars is very natural in a lattice-based model, as sketched above. Note that this antidote to excessive retrenchment adds memory to the incremental model in order to solve the undergeneration problem, but it does so in an economical way. A lattice model with erasure retains the fruits of past learning not by accumulating memory traces of prior events, but by unburdening long-term memory as the innate lattice representation is progressively simplified.

Computational Evaluation of Lattice Models

Our simulation studies are conducted on the domain of constructed languages described above, defined by familiar syntactic parameters that govern word order, null subjects, wh-movement and so forth. To isolate syntactic parameter setting from the acquisition of lexical items, the sentences are pre-coded as strings of part-of-speech labels (cf. Gibson & Wexler, 1994). A detailed description and examples of the languages can be found in Sakas (2003). The sentences of a target language are fed to a learning model which guesses a grammar after each one. In the simulations reported below, each learning model was run 100 times on each language in the domain, with a ceiling of 10,000 input sentences on any trial. We record the percent of successful convergence on the target grammar, and the average number of input sentences consumed before convergence. These measures allow us to quantify the reliability and efficiency of a wide variety of alternative models.

Six variants of the lattice-based model outlined above have been tested in this environment. They differ from each other as indicated below. Some make use of the lattice but do not decode the input; some do decoding but do not make full use of the lattice. Our purpose in comparing this range of models was to assess the relative contributions of these two components, and to identify limits on the usefulness of the lattice concept. The results are shown in Table 1. Note that *SL* denotes the set of 'smallest languages' at the lower edge of the lattice. The descriptions indicate what the learning model does on receiving a novel input *i* which Gcurrent does not license; its task is to find and adopt an SP-compatible grammar that parses *i*. Unless otherwise specified, a grammar that has failed on *i* is erased from the lattice before the next input is processed.

M1: No Decoding, SL: If Gcurrent fails, select any grammar G in SL; run parse-test; if G fails erase it from the lattice and retain Gcurrent; if G succeeds, adopt it as Gcurrent.

M2: No Decoding, SL, Activation: Like M1 except that every grammar has an activation score. If Gcurrent fails, select the grammar G in SL with the highest activation; run parse-test; if G fails, erase it from the lattice and select the grammar with the next highest activation as the new Gcurrent; if G succeeds, adopt it as Gcurrent and add one activation unit to all grammars that dominate it in the lattice (since these all also license *i*).

M3: Decoding and SL: Decode *i* (i.e., use Gcurrent to initiate a parse of *i*; if it succeeds, retain Gcurrent; if it fails, patch the parse tree with new parameter values as necessary and adopt them into Gcurrent), but subject to the condition that only values in the grammars in SL are available for adoption. If decoding fails, as it may due to this restriction, select a grammar at random from SL to be the next Gcurrent.

M4: Decoding (Defaults), SL as Filter: Decode *i* (see above), favoring subset (i.e., default) values of parameters if there are alternative parses of *i*; if the decoded grammar is in SL, adopt it; else retain Gcurrent.

M5: Decoding (Random), SL as Filter: Decode *i* (see above), making a random choice if there are alternative

parses of *i*; if the decoded grammar is in SL, adopt it; else retain Gcurrent.

M6: Decoding (Random), Track Downward: Like M5, but if the decoded grammar G' is not in SL, run parse tests on daughters of G' until a grammar is found that parses *i*; repeat recursively on its daughters until a grammar is found with no daughters that parse *i*; adopt that grammar. (See discussion of this strategy below.)

Table 1: Measures of reliability and efficiency for some lattice-based learning models

Model	% success	Average sentences	Average for 99%	# parses per sentence
M1	100	858	1,454	1
M2	100	900	968	1
M3	100	140	286	1
M4	12	23	71	1
M5	31	2,631	6,032	1
M6	96	190	694	mean 4.8

Note that the fourth column of Table 1 shows how many input sentences were required, averaged across languages, for 99 of the 100 trials of the learning model on a given language to attain the target grammar. Since the vast majority of children do acquire their target language, this is an appropriate and rigorous estimate of a model's performance.

Discussion of Results

The data make it evident that not every way of incorporating a lattice representation into a learning model is helpful, but at least one of the designs we tested is both reliable and speedy. Not unexpectedly this is version M3, which is the only one that fully integrates partial decoding and the lattice representation. It required fewer than 300 input sentences for 99% convergence on grammars in this domain. This compares favorably with the performance of decoding learning models that we have tested in the past which lacked any machinery for applying SP (so that it had to be externally imposed by an oracle that blocked adoption of overgenerating grammars).

Other noteworthy outcomes include the fact that model M1, which employs the lattice without taking advantage of the opportunity to do decoding, is very slow, as is characteristic of models that rely on trial and error in selecting which grammars to test. Models M4 and M5 use the lattice not to help *select* their hypotheses but only to *filter* them after selection, and they are both extremely slow, with many 'time-out' failures (88% and 69% respectively). M4 is speedy only for a handful of target languages near the bottom of the lattice, for which it does succeed; M5 is a generally slow trial-and-error system.

Despite a few time-outs, model M6 mostly works fast in terms of number of input sentences, but it does extra work in processing each one, to make up for the fact that it does not restrict its hypotheses to the 'safe' grammars at the bottom of the lattice. This gives LM the freedom to focus on a preferred grammar, but the cost is that multiple parse tests are then needed to identify any SP-compatible grammars beneath it in the lattice, since they must take precedence. The average of approximately 5 parse-tests per sentence is less than we had anticipated but is still an implausible amount of computation to be performed every time a child hears a sentence.

A promising finding for future work is that M2's activation levels for grammars confers some advantage compared with M1, at least in the 99% convergence score. This activation strengthens grammars in proportion to how many target language sentences they have been observed to license, and thus helps to attract the learner toward profitable areas of the lattice. It may be that incorporating activation into model M3, which already successfully combines SL and decoding, will yield the best performance of all but we have not yet investigated this.

The Source of the Lattice

What may be hard to swallow about the subset-superset lattice is why it should exist at all in the minds of language learners. Perhaps the best that can be said in its defense is that it is not an impossibility if the domain of grammars is finite. But it is likely to be very large, and it serves no other apparent purpose than SP. The principles-and-parameters theory assumes that the set of all possible grammars is determined by the innately-given parameters and their values. So why should each grammar also be individually specified in a lattice? Clearly, the lattice-based model for SP-implementation would be more palatable if, as we considered above, there were general principles for projecting not just the set of grammars but all the subset relations between them. However, the facts of our constructed language domain do not encourage confidence in this. In Figure 1, which is quite typical of the domain as a whole, it can be seen that there are pairs of grammars for which one of the subset-superset parameters (P4-P7, P10-P13) has value 0 in the superset grammar and value 1 in the subset grammar, contrary to the Simple Defaults Model. For instance, there are over 50 such reversals just for parameter P13 (Question Inversion). We are currently exploring richer predictive schemas for identifying subset relations between languages by inspection of their parameter values, in hope that the subset relations in the lattice will ultimately prove to be fully projectible on-line rather than needing to be hardwired. But in the meantime we hope to have shown here that a lattice representation of subset relations – or some projectible version of it – is worthy of study since it offers solutions to two thorny problems in modeling conservative learning from text.

Acknowledgements

This research was supported in part by grants 67827-00 36 and 67560-00 36 to the first two authors, from the Professional Staff Congress of the City University of New York.

References

Berwick, R. C. (1985). *The acquisition of syntactic knowledge.* Cambridge, MA: MIT Press.

Chomsky, N. (1981). *Lectures on government and binding.* Dordrecht: Foris Publications.

Clark, R. (1989). On the relationship between the input data and parameter setting. *Proceedings of the 19th Annual Meeting of the North East Linguistic Society* (pp. 48–62).

Clark, R. (1992). The selection of syntactic knowledge. *Language Acquisition, 2,* 83-149.

Fodor, J. D. & Sakas, W. G. (2004). Evaluating models of parameter setting. *Proceedings of the 28th Annual Boston University Conference on Language Development* (pp. 1-27). Boston: Cascadilla Press.

Fodor, J. D. & Sakas, W. G. (2005). The Subset Principle in syntax: Costs of compliance. *Journal of Linguistics, 41,* 513-569.

Gibson, E. A .F. & Wexler, K. (1994). Triggers. *Linguistic Inquiry, 25,* 407-454.

Gold, E. M. (1967). Language identification in the limit. *Information and Control, 10,* 447-474.

Kapur, S. (1994). Some applications of formal learning theory results to natural language acquisition. In B. Lust, G. Hermon & J. Kornfilt (eds.) *Binding, dependencies, and learnability,* Vol. 2 of *Syntactic theory and first language acquisition: Cross-linguistic perspectives.* Hillsdale, NJ: Lawrence Erlbaum Associates.

Manzini, R. & Wexler, K. (1987). Parameters, binding theory, and learnability. *Linguistic Inquiry, 18,* 413-444.

Marcus, G. F. (1993). Negative evidence in language acquisition. *Cognition, 46,* 53-85.

Pinker, S. (1979). Formal models of language learning. *Cognition, 7,* 217-283.

Sakas, W. G. (2003). A word-order database for testing computational models of language acquisition. *Proceedings of the 41st Annual Meeting of The Association for Computational Linguistics* (pp. 415-422). East Strasburg, PA: Association of Computational Linguistics.

Sakas, W. G. & Fodor, J. D. (2001). The Structural Triggers Learner. In S. Bertolo (ed.), *Language acquisition and learnability.* Cambridge: Cambridge University Press.

Tenenbaum, J. B. & Griffiths, T. L. (2001). Generalization, similarity, and Bayesian inference. *Behavioral and Brain Sciences, 24,* 629-641.

Yang, C. D. (2002). *Knowledge and learning in natural language.* New York: Oxford University Press.

Bottom-Up Learning of Phonemes: A Computational Study

Rozenn Le Calvez (rozenn.le.calvez@ens.fr)
Laboratoire de Sciences Cognitives et Psycholinguistique (EHESS, DEC-ENS, CNRS) & Université de Paris 6
46 rue d'Ulm, 75005 Paris, France

Sharon Peperkamp (sharon.peperkamp@ens.fr)
Laboratoire de Sciences Cognitives et Psycholinguistique (EHESS, DEC-ENS, CNRS) & Université de Paris 8
46 rue d'Ulm, 75005 Paris, France

Emmanuel Dupoux (dupoux@lscp.ehess.fr)
Laboratoire de Sciences Cognitives et Psycholinguistique (EHESS, DEC-ENS, CNRS)
46 rue d'Ulm, 75005 Paris, France

Abstract

We present a computational evaluation of a hypothesis according to which distributional information is sufficient to acquire allophonic rules (and hence phonemes) in a bottom-up fashion. The hypothesis was tested using a measure based on information theory that compares distributions. The test was conducted on several artificial language corpora and on two natural corpora containing transcriptions of speech directed to infants from two typologically distant languages (French and Japanese). The measure was complemented with three filters, one concerning the statistical reliability due to sample size and two concerning the following universal properties of allophonic rules: constituents of an allophonic rule should be phonetically similar, and allophonic rules should be assimilatory in nature.

Acquisition of Allophonic Rules

During their first year of life, infants learn many aspects of the phonology of their native language. At birth, they all discriminate speech segments (atomic units corresponding to consonants and vowels) in a language-universal way. Their perception then becomes attuned to their native language: at 6-8 months (Kuhl et al. 1992), infants learn the vowel categories of their native language and at 10-12 months the consonant categories (Werker & Tees 1984). These remarkable steps are reached before infants have a lexicon and before they can talk. Infants' learning mechanisms include extracting statistical regularities present in the speech signal such as frequency distributions of segments and transitional probabilities between segments (Jusczyk 1997; Maye, Werker & Gerken 2002). One aspect of early phonological acquisition that remains to be studied is how children go beyond the segmental representation and acquire the phonemes of their language.

Phonemes and Allophonic Rules

Languages represent speech sounds at two levels. At the abstract (underlying) level, word forms are made up of a combination of a finite set of phonemes. At the surface level, the pronunciation of a word is specified in terms of a larger set of context-dependent segments. For instance in Mexican Spanish, the word /felis/ ("feliz", happy) is pronounced as [feliz] when it is followed by a voiced consonant and [felis] otherwise.

Allophonic rules express the phonetic realizations of a given phoneme according to its context. For instance, the allophonic rule of voicing in Mexican Spanish is written as follows:

$$/s/ \rightarrow \left\{ \begin{array}{ll} [z] & \text{before voiced consonants} \\ [s] & \text{elsewhere} \end{array} \right. \tag{1}$$

[z] is called the allophone and [s] the default segment. These two segments never occur in the same contexts: they are in "complementary distributions".

Whether a given pair of segments is in an allophonic relationship or not is language-specific: unlike in Mexican Spanish, /s/ and /z/ are two distinct phonemes in French so that /felis/ and /feliz/ could be two different French words. Therefore, phonemes (and allophonic rules) must be learned at some point in the course of language acquisition.

A Bottom-Up Hypothesis

When and how phonemes are learned is controversial. Phonemes might be learned in a top-down fashion with the help of the lexicon or the orthography: knowing the abstract form of a word, children would learn to match phonemes with their phonetic realizations (Kazanina, Phillips & Idsardi 2006). Alternatively, phonemes might be learned very early in life *before* infants have a lexicon, based on complementary distributions of segments (Peperkamp & Dupoux 2002). This is the hypothesis we endorse here.

A Computational Evaluation

We present a computational study of the bottom-up learning of phonemes. Our approach is that a significant number of allophonic pairs can be acquired without the help of lexical information. We suppose that, prior to this acquisition, infants can extract phonetic segments from the speech they hear, use statistical learning mechanisms, and that they have a similarity metrics allowing them to compare the segments of their native language (Liberman & Mattingly 1985). We investigate to what extent statistical information is sufficient or to what extent other information (in the form of linguistic biases) might be necessary.

Related Work

Phonological rule induction models have been studied within various frameworks. Structural linguists have formulated procedures to discover phonemes from a set of language data by hand (Harris 1951 and references therein). Johnson (1984) presented a formal procedure in a generative linguistics approach for the learning of ordered phonological rules. Neither of these approaches, though, were robust to noise.

Gildea & Jurafsky (1996) introduced a stochastic algorithm using finite-state transducers. They included three learning biases often implicit in linguistic theories: faithfulness (surface forms are close to underlying forms), community (similar segments tend to behave similarly) and context (phonological rules are accessed in their context). While in this machine learning approach the algorithm was robust to noise, it had the disadvantage of being supervised by a virtual teacher.

In order to understand how children might learn their language, we develop a statistical algorithm that is unsupervised. It tracks complementary distributions of segments using a measure from information theory. This algorithm was shown to efficiently detect allophonic pairs in a French corpus provided two linguistic filters restricting learning to universally possible allophonic rules were added (Peperkamp et al. 2006). This first study had a number of limitations: the measure was not shown to scale up according to the number of rules and rule complexity; it did not take into account spurious complementary distributions due to small sample size ; it was only tested in one language and the artificial corpora only used very unrealistic languages with equiprobable "phonemes". In the present study, we add a reliability filter to remove statistically unreliable rules due to small sample size. Tests were performed on a wider range of languages: more realistic artificial languages were used to study the influence of corpus size and number of rules; finally two natural languages (French and Japanese) were studied.

The paper is structured as follows: in the next section, we present the algorithm. We then evaluate it on several artificial language corpora. Finally, the algorithm is tested on natural language corpora of speech transcriptions from two typologically distant languages, namely French and Japanese.

Algorithm

Looking for Complementary Distributions

The algorithm looks for near-complementary distributions of segments using the symmetric Kullback-Leibler divergence (henceforth *KL-measure*) that compares two probability distributions (Kullback & Leibler 1951).

Specifically we compared the probability distributions of two segments s_1 and s_2 as follows:

$$m_{KL}(s_1, s_2) = \sum_c \left(P_1 \, \log \left(\frac{P_1}{P_2} \right) + P_2 \, \log \left(\frac{P_2}{P_1} \right) \right) \quad (2)$$

where s_1 and s_2 are two segments,
c are the contexts (right segment, left segment or both) occuring in a corpus,
$P_1 = P(c|s_1)$, $P_2 = P(c|s_2)$,
$P(c|s) = \frac{n(c,s)+1}{n(s)+N}$ with $n(c,s)$ the number of occurences of segment s in context c, $n(s)$ the number of occurences of segment s and N the number of different contexts[1].

The measure is high for segment pairs that have complementary distributions. All segment pairs above a certain threshold (Z-score > 1, corresponding to the mean of measures plus one standard deviation) are selected as candidate allophonic pairs.

Default Phone or Allophone?

A relative entropy criterion then determines the roles of the two segments of the pair, either default segment (that globally appears more often and in more contexts) or allophone. The default segment s_d has the smallest relative entropy:

$$s_d = \arg \min_s \left[\sum_c P(c|s) \log \frac{P(c|s)}{P(c)} \right] \quad (3)$$

where s are the two segments s_1 and s_2 of the phoneme,
and c are the contexts of the segments.

Reliability Filter

The statistical reliability of probability estimations depends on the sample size of corpora. We use a reliability filter to discard unreliable pairs that were selected as candidate allophonic pairs by the KL-measure. The Ψ-criterion (Jaynes 2003) compares observed frequency counts to a theoretical probability distribution. It is similar to a χ^2-test but it is also valid for small samples. It is defined as follows:

$$\Psi(s_1, s_2) = n(s_1) \sum_c f_c(s_1) \, \log \left(\frac{f_c(s_1)}{P(c|s_2)} \right) \quad (4)$$

where $n(s_1)$ is the number of occurences of segment s_1,
$f_c(s) = \frac{n(c,s)}{n(s)}$ with $n(c,s)$ the number of occurences of segment s in context c,
$P(c|s_2)$ is the conditional probability estimation of c given s_2 defined as in Equation 2.

The criterion thus evaluates whether the frequency counts of a segment s_1 are different from the theoretical probability distribution of a segment s_2. If they are

---

[1] We add one occurence of each segment to the corpus to avoid null probabilities that may arise in limited size corpora.

not considered sufficiently different, the pair of segments is discarded. We use a conservative level of confidence of 10^{-3} (one learner in 1,000 fails): pairs with $\Psi < 3$ are discarded as unreliable.

When we calculate this criterion, we compare the distributions of segments pairwise. To correct for the number of comparisons, we divide the Ψ criterion by the number of comparisons (Bonferroni correction)[2].

Linguistic Filters In Peperkamp et al. (2006), we found that the KL-measure selected spurious allophonic pairs due to phonotactic (i.e. distributional) constraints in natural languages. Two linguistic filters were added to discard them based on linguistic properties of possible allophonic rules. First, allophonic pairs consist of phonetically close segments. In particular, there should not be any intermediate segment between them:

$$\nexists\, s, \quad \forall i \in \{1\ldots 6\}, d_i(s_a) \leq d_i(s) \leq d_i(s_d) \\ \text{or } \forall i \in \{1\ldots 6\}, d_i(s_d) \leq d_i(s) \leq d_i(s_a) \quad (5)$$

where s is a segment appearing in at least one context of the allophone,
s_d the default segment and s_a the allophone,
$d_i(s)$ is the ith component of the distance representation.

Second, allophonic rules are assimilatory in nature. That is, the allophone should be closer to its contexts than the default segment:

$$\forall i, \; |\sum_{C_{s_a}} \left(d_i(s_a) - d_i(C_{s_a}) \right)| \leq \; |\sum_{C_{s_a}} \left(d_i(s_d) - d_i(C_{s_a}) \right)|$$
$$(6)$$

where s, s_d, s_a, d_i are defined as above,
C_{s_a} are the contexts of the allophone.

To apply the filters, segments are defined along a numerical articulatory-phonetic distance. The six dimensions used were: *place of articulation* from 1 (bilabial) to 13 (uvular), *sonority* from 1 (voiceless stops) to 12 (low vowels), *voicing* (0 or 1), *nasality* (0 or 1), *rounding* (0 or 1) and *length* (0 for simple segments, 1 for geminates and long vowels).

Linguistic filters were not used for tests on artificial language corpora in which segments are arbitrary symbols rather than segments with phonetic properties. The complete algorithm is summarized in Figure 1.

Simulations with Artificial Languages

Two series of simulations were performed to evaluate the performance of the algorithm. We used artificial languages in order to examine the efficiency of the reliability filter and precisely characterise the sensitivity of the algorithm. We studied the influence of two parameters

---

[2]For instance, for 100 ($= 10 \times 10$) comparisons (about 10 segments in the language), the corrected criterion will be $\Psi = -\log(\frac{10^{-3}}{10^2}) = 5$.

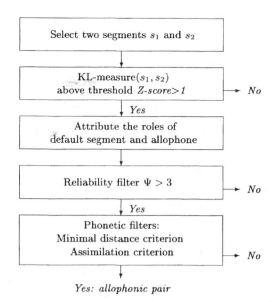

Figure 1: Summary of the algorithm. Is the current segment pair an allophonic pair?

that are important for our problem: corpus size and the number of allophonic rules.

Corpus Size

Methods We generated artificial language corpora having the following characteristics: the language has 60 segments (similar to the natural corpora used in the next section) with a frequency ratio of 1.000 between the most frequent and least frequent segments and a logarithmic distribution of the frequencies. In this language, ten allophonic rules triggered by randomly determined right contexts were implemented. We chose six corpus sizes varying from 100 to 10^7 segments and drew 20 random corpora of each.

Performance was measured as follows: segment pairs were ranked according to their KL-measure with the pair with the highest KL-measure having rank one. The optimal performance would result in the ten allophonic pairs being ranked from 1 to 10. Hence, the higher the median rank, the worse the performance.

Results Results are shown in Figure 2: box-and-whiskers plots include minimum rank, quartiles and maximum rank.

Median ranks and quartiles decrease with the application of the filter: the reliability filter considerably improves the performance although some outliers remain. The filter is especially efficient on small and middle size corpora. Curves are bell-shaped whether the reliability filter is applied or not (with a maximum around 10^5 segments).

Further analyses (not shown here) revealed that the bell shape is due to two factors: segment frequency and

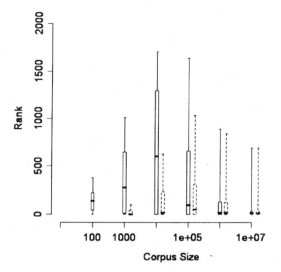

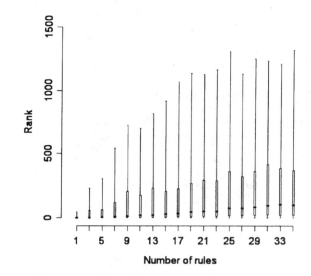

Figure 2: Influence of corpus size with corpora ranging from 100 segments to 10^7 segments. Box-and-whiskers plots show the results of 20 random corpora of each corpus size. Plain (left): Ranks of allophonic pairs before the application of the reliability filter. Dashed (right): Ranks of allophonic pairs after the application of the reliability filter.

interactions among allophonic pairs. Concerning segment frequency, allophonic pairs comprising a rare segment are not present in small corpora; in middle size corpora they are present but mostly unreliably so, leading to a rank increase; in large corpora, rare phonemes are reliably found and ranked well. Concerning interactions, allophonic pairs can for instance share the same allophone. The effect of these interactions is to increase the ranks of allophonic rules in middle size corpora (10^5 segments). Both effects are reduced with the application of the filter.

Number of Rules

Methods The artificial language has 60 segments with a frequency ratio of 1.000 between the most frequent and least frequent segments and a logarithmic distribution of the frequencies. Corpus size was set at a reliable sample size of 10^7 segments, the number of rules varied within a reasonable range for the natural language corpora we use: 1 to 35 rules were triggered by randomly determined right contexts. Twenty corpora were drawn randomly for each number of rules. Simulations were performed with the application of the reliability filter.

Results Results are shown in Figure 3: box-and-whiskers plots include minimum rank, quartiles and maximum rank.

Figure 3: Influence of the number of rules (1 to 35) implemented in a random corpus. Box-and-whiskers plots show the results of 20 random corpora for each number of rules.

Quartiles increase with the number of rules. A few outliers are always badly ranked. The worst rank augments gradually as the number of rules gets bigger, until there are around 25 of them. The median rank is always worse than its optimal value, indicating that some non-allophonic pairs are ranked better than allophonic pairs. These pairs mainly consist of one allophone and another segment (allophone or not) and are thus the result of "allophonic confusion".

Overall, simulations on artificial languages suggest that the algorithm is quite robust to corpus size variation and to variation in the number of rules. The algorithm is particularly sensitive to three characteristics: segment frequency (frequent segments tend to be better ranked), interactions among allophonic pairs in middle size corpora, and allophonic confusion. In natural language corpora, linguistic filters reduce (or remove) the negative effects of these latter two characteristics.

Simulations with Natural Languages

Finally, the algorithm was evaluated on transcribed corpora of child-directed speech in order to examine the performance of the algorithm on two phonologically diverse languages: French and Japanese.

French

The corpus consists of child-directed speech from the CHILDES corpus (MacWhinney 2000). This corpus contains dialogs between parents and children that were orthographically transcribed. Only utterances from adults were kept. We used the VoCoLex dictionary (Dufour et al. submitted) to get a phonemic transcription of the corpus and implemented 11 allophonic rules of French (Dell 1973):

- Sonorants /ʁ,l,m,n,ɲ,ŋ,ɥ,j,w/ are devoiced when followed or preceded by a voiceless consonant /p,t,k,f,s,ʃ/.

- Velars /k,g/ are palatalized when followed by front vowels and semi-vowels /i,y,e,ɛ,ø,œ,j,ɥ,ɛ̃/.

The resulting semi-phonetic corpus included 45 distinct segments of which 11 were allophones. It was 43.000 utterances long (for a total of about 200.000 segments). We ran the algorithm on the corpus. 432 pairs were selected by the KL-measure as candidate allophonic pairs, none of which was discarded by the reliability filter. Among the 432, 8 were correct allophonic pairs. The rest were spurious pairs due to phonotactics (distributional restrictions of phonemes in the language) and allophonic confusion.

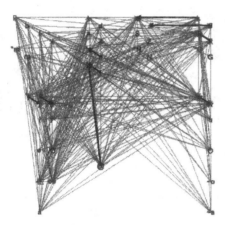

Figure 4: Representation of the results obtained with the CHILDES French corpus. Black lines: pairs kept after the application of the linguistic filters. Gray lines: spurious pairs removed by the filters.

The application of the linguistic filters removed 422 of the 424 spurious pairs. The remaining spurious pairs were [w̥]-[ɥ] (two segments belonging to two different allophonic pairs) and [ə]-[l̥] (due to phonotactic constraints). The action of the linguistic filters is shown in Figure 4 on a 2-dimensional representation of our 6-dimensional distance, roughly showing place of articulation on the horizontal axis and sonority on the vertical axis. Without the filters, all the segment pairs on the figure were selected as candidate allophonic pairs. The filters removed all the gray pairs and kept only the black ones. Notice that most of the spurious pairs (in gray) are distant on the figure.
The three allophonic pairs that were not found by the algorithm were [m]-[m̥], [ŋ]-[ŋ̥] and [ɲ]-[ɲ̥]. Allophones of

these pairs were rare in the corpus, hence had a small KL-measure and were not selected.

Japanese

The corpus consists of child-directed speech from the CHILDES corpus of Japanese (MacWhinney 2000). We introduced a number of well-known phonological rules of Japanese (palatalization, affrication, nasal assimilation). The resulting corpus contained 15 allophonic pairs, due to the following allophonic rules:

- /t,d,z/ and their geminates turn into affricates before [u].

- /h/ turns into [f] before [u].

- the moraic nasal /N/ is velarized when followed by velar consonants /k,g/.

- /a,i,u,e,o,aː,iː,uː,eː,oː/ are nasalized when followed by the moraic nasal /N/.

The corpus included 53 distinct segments and was 81.000 utterances long (for a total of about 800.000 segments).

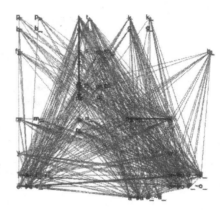

Figure 5: Representation of the results obtained with the CHILDES Japanese corpus. Black lines: pairs kept after the application of the linguistic filters. Gray lines: spurious pairs removed by the filters.

The KL-measure selected 725 candidate allophonic pairs, five of which were removed by the reliability filter. Of the resulting 720 pairs, 8 were allophonic pairs and the remaining were spurious. After the application of the two linguistic filters, only 9 pairs were left: 8 allophonic pairs and 1 spurious pair involving [h] and [N] (due to phonotactic constraints). The action of the filters is represented in Figure 5. As for French, all candidate allophonic pairs selected by the KL-measure are pictured. Pairs discarded by the linguistic filters are pictured in gray, pairs passing the filters in black. The 7 allophonic pairs that were not found (nasalisation of the 5 long vowels, affrication of geminate /t/, [h]-[f]) contained rare allophones.

Discussion

The algorithm with linguistic filters performed very well: it discovered 8/11 and 7/15 of the allophonic pairs in French and Japanese respectively. It should be noted that in both languages there were interactions between rules. For instance in French, several rules applied in the same contexts, leading to complementary distributions between default segments and allophones of different allophonic pairs (such as [m] and [j]). These interactions didn't impede the performance of the algorithm, due to the fact that the linguistic filters removed most of these spurious complementary distributions.

Very few spurious pairs were kept: two for French and one for Japanese. They were due to phonotactic constraints and confusion between elements of different allophonic pairs. Adding constraints on the participation of a segment to several allophonic pairs might help to discard them. For instance, we may not allow to keep two allophonic pairs and a third pair consisting of one segment of each of the other two pairs. Such constraints would act on the set of allophonic pairs instead of on individual allophonic pairs. They would thus constrain the phonological system as a whole.

In Japanese, the reliability filter removes several allophonic pairs, thus indicating that the corpus is too small to get reliable information on all pairs. A bigger corpus would be needed to improve the performance.

Conclusion

We presented an algorithm for the bottom-up learning of phoneme categories. Simulations on artificial languages studied the influence of corpus size and number of allophonic rules. The algorithm was applied on data from two languages: French and Japanese. We obtained a good performance provided the algorithm is complemented with three filters: a reliability filter removing unreliable pairs due to insufficient sample size, and two linguistic filters constraining the nature of allophonic rules. The statistical part of our algorithm yielded a very large number of false alarms, most of which are due to phonotactic constraints in these languages. As in Peperkamp et al. (2006), we showed that these false alarms can be pruned down using linguistic filters based on a phonetic representation of the segments that introduce constraints on the universal properties of allophonic rules. Yet, it is unclear as to whether such a phonetic representation is available or not to infants during their first year of life. Further work using an acoustic representation instead of a handmade phonetic one is needed. Another line of research would be to independently acquire phonotactic constraints and use this knowledge to prune spurious allophonic pairs. In brief, in agreement with current language acquisition theories, this study suggests that infants may gain considerable knowledge without a lexicon using a few computational principles and appropriate learning biases.

Acknowledgments

We would like to thank Jean-Pierre Nadal for his help in conceiving the algorithm for the detection of complementary distributions. Research for this work was supported by a graduate student research grant from the French Ministery of Research to R. Le Calvez, as well as by a grant from the Agence Nationale de la Recherche n° ANR-05-BLAN-0065-01.

References

Dell, F. (1973). *Les règles et les sons*. Paris: Hermann.

Dufour, S., Peereman, R., Pallier, C., & Radeau, M. (2002). VoCoLex: Une base de données lexicales sur les similarités phonologiques entre les mots français. *L'Année Psychologique, 102*, 725–746.

Gildea, D. & Jurafsky, D. (1996). Learning bias and phonological rule induction. *Computational Linguistics, 22*, 497–530.

Harris, Z. (1951). *Methods in Structural Linguistics*. Chicago: University of Chicago Press.

Jaynes, E.T. (2003). *Probability theory: The logic of science*. Cambridge University Press.

Johnson, M. (1984). A discovery procedure for certain phonological rules. *Proceedings of the 10th International Conference on Computational Linguistics and 22nd Annual Meeting of the Association for Computational Linguistics*.

Jusczyk, P. (1997). *The discovery of spoken language*. Cambridge, MA: MIT Press.

Kazanina, N., Phillips C. and W. Idsardi (2006). The influence of meaning on the perception of speech sounds. *PNAS, 103(30)*, 11381–11386.

Kuhl, P., Williams, K., Lacerda, F., Stevens, K. & Lindblom, B. (1992). Linguistic experience alters phonetic perception in infants by six months of age. *Science, 255*, 606–608.

Liberman, A. M. & Mattingly, I. (1985). The motor theory of speech perception revised. *Cognition, 21*, 1–36.

MacWhinney, B. (2000). *The CHILDES Project: Tools for Analyzing Talk*. 3rd Edition. Mahwah, NJ: Lawrence Erlbaum Associates.

Maye, J., Werker, J. F., & Gerken, L. (2002). Infant sensitivity to distributional information can affect phonetic discrimination. *Cognition, 82 (3)*, B101–B111.

Peperkamp, S. & Dupoux, E. (2002). Coping with phonological variation in early lexical acquisition. In: I. Lasser (ed.) *The Process of Language Acquisition*. Frankfurt: Peter Lang, 359–385.

Peperkamp, S., Le Calvez, R., Nadal, J.-P. & Dupoux, E. (2006). The acquisition of allophonic rules: statistical learning with linguistic constraints. *Cognition, 101 (3)*, B31–B41.

Werker, J. & Tees, R. (1984). Cross language speech perception: Evidence for perceptual reorganization during the first year of life. *Infant Behavior and Development, 7*, 49–63.

The Bilingual Phono-Translation Effect:
Facilitation or Inhibition Depends on Second-Language Proficiency

Winston D. Goh (psygohw@nus.edu.sg)
Meijie Chen (meijie.chen@gmail.com)
Department of Psychology, National University of Singapore
11 Law Link, Singapore 117570, Singapore

Abstract

A picture-word interference experiment was conducted to investigate whether the phono-translation effect depends on the second-language proficiency level of bilingual speakers. English-Chinese bilinguals of varying L2 proficiency were asked to name pictures in their L1 (English) and L2 (Chinese), while being primed with auditory distracters in the other language. Highly-proficient bilinguals took longer to name pictures in L2 (e.g. *qiao2*, 'bridge' in English) when it was presented together with a distracter that was phonologically-related to its L1 translation-equivalent (e.g. *breech*), than when it was presented with a phonologically-unrelated distractor (e.g. *flat*), which replicates the phono-translation interference effect. However, an opposite *facilitation* effect was found with less-proficient bilinguals. No evidence of phono-translation effects on L1-picture naming was found. The pattern of opposing effects is consistent with a lexical-mediation account of L2 word retrieval in less proficient bilinguals.

Keywords: Phono-translation effect; picture-word interference; bilingualism; speech production.

Introduction

Do the two languages of bilingual speakers interfere with each other in the course of lexical selection during speech production? This is a fundamental question that has received much attention from investigators in bilingual research for many years. The accumulated evidence indicates that first-language (L1) and second-language (L2) translation equivalents are often simultaneously activated during a bilingual's speech production (e.g. Costa, 2005; Poulisse, 1993, 1999).

Variants of the picture naming paradigm have often been used in such studies, where the pattern of results suggest that there is evidence for both facilitative and inhibitory effects, depending on the experimental manipulations. An example of facilitative effects was demonstrated by Caramazza and Costa (2000), who found that Spanish-Catalan bilinguals were able to name pictures with cognate names (i.e. translation equivalents with similar phonology, e.g. *gat/gato*) faster than pictures with non-cognate names (i.e. translation equivalents with dissimilar phonology, e.g. *taula/mesa*). This is because cognate names receive converging phonological activation from both its L1 and L2 lexical nodes, compared to non-cognates which receive relevant activation from only one lexical node (see also Costa, Caramazza, & Sebastián-Gallés, 2000). Evidence of

inhibitory effects have been found with the picture-word interference paradigm (Costa, Colomé, Gómez & Sebastián-Gallés, 2003; Hermans, Bongaerts, De Bot & Schreuder, 1998). The present experiment will focus on the latter set of findings, specifically the *phono-translation effect*.

The condition of interest in the picture-word interference paradigm is the *phono-translation condition*, in which participants were asked to name pictures in their L2, while being primed with auditory distracters that were phonologically-similar to its L1 translations. For example, Hermans *et al.* (1998) asked Dutch-English bilinguals to name the picture of a *mountain* in English (L2) while they were presented with an auditory Dutch (L1) distracter *berm* (Dutch for the English word 'verge'), which was phonologically related to the Dutch translation of 'mountain', *berg*. This is contrasted with a condition in which the auditory distractor is phonologically unrelated to *berg* (e.g. *kaars*, Dutch for 'candle'). The authors argued that the activation level of the target's Dutch-translation node (*berg*) would be higher when presented with the phonologically-related distracter (*berm*), than with the unrelated distracter (*kaars*). This is because in the former case, it would receive activation from two sources (i.e. the picture's semantic representation and the distracter), whereas in the latter case it would receive activation only from one source (i.e. the picture's semantic representation). Results from the experiment showed that naming latencies were indeed slower when the pictures were presented with related than with unrelated distracters, a finding that has come to be known as the *phono-translation interference* effect. This finding has been replicated in another recent study (Costa *et al.*, 2003) with highly-proficient Spanish-Catalan bilinguals, hence increasing confidence in the reliability of this effect, and its generalisability to other language-pairs, as well as to highly-proficient bilinguals. Taken together, these results suggest that there is cross-language competition during speech production in bilingual participants.

Several researchers (Costa *et al.*, 2003; Kiyak, 1982; Poulisse & Bongaerts, 1994) have suggested that the level of L2 proficiency may modulate the amount of cross-language interference faced by the bilingual. However, this issue has yet to be tested experimentally and is the primary motivation of the present study. One hypothesis is that a larger degree of *phono-translation interference* should be expected in bilinguals who are less proficient in their L2 (cf.

Costa *et al.*, 2003), as manifested in the form of a larger difference in naming latencies between the phonologically related and unrelated distracter conditions, compared to more proficient bilinguals. The present study sets out to test this prediction, by directly comparing between two English-Chinese bilingual groups of differing L2 (Chinese[1]) proficiencies with the same picture-naming task.

However, an alternative hypothesis is that there may be a facilitative, rather than inhibitory phono-translation effect for bilinguals who are less proficient in their L2. According to the revised hierarchical bilingual lexical model proposed by Kroll and Stewart (1994) and shown in Figure 1, the semantic concept of the image can access L2 words in two ways, either *directly* (as shown by the bold line), or *indirectly* via its translation equivalent in L1 (as shown by the dashed lines). Many empirical studies (e.g. Chen & Ho, 1986; Chen & Ng, 1989; Cheung & Chen, 1998; Kroll, 1993; Kroll & Stewart, 1994; Tzelgov & Eben-Ezra, 1992) have found that L2 production for less proficient bilinguals is often lexically-mediated via L1, but directly conceptually-mediated in proficient bilinguals.

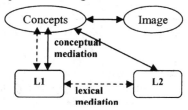

Figure 1. Schematic adaptation of Kroll and Stewart's (1994) revised hierarchical model.

One interesting prediction from this account is that participants with low L2 proficiency may actually benefit from being primed with a related phonological distracter in their stronger L1. The image of the picture will lead to an activation of the semantic concept. This would then activate the L1 equivalent of the target L2 word and thus facilitate the L1-to-L2 translation pathway. On the other hand, priming with an unrelated L1 phonological distracter would not facilitate the translation process as the wrong L1 word would be activated. If this account is correct, there phono-translation interference effect should be reversed for bilinguals with low L2 proficiency.

A secondary objective of the present study is more exploratory in nature. We included trials in the experimental design to determine if there is any evidence of phono-translation effects in L1 speech production, i.e., when the target language is English and the auditory distractors are in Chinese. This has not been tested experimentally, although it is has been assumed that because L1 lexical nodes are used more frequently, they

should be more highly activated than the corresponding L2 nodes, and are hence easier to select (De Bot & Schreuder, 1993; Green, 1986; Roelofs, 1992) and therefore should be less susceptible to interference. In addition, although L1 intrusions are common in L2 speech production, L2 intrusions in L1 speech are few and far between (Poulisse & Bongaerts, 1994), and usually only under conditions of constant code-switching (Grosjean 1982, 1997, 1998; Hermans *et al.*, 1998). Nevertheless, it is possible that differential patterns of interference in L1 may be also observed depending on the proficiency level of L2.

Method

Participants

An initial 135 psychology undergraduates from the National University of Singapore, who received course credit for their participation, were recruited for screening of their language background. All were Singaporean English-Chinese bilinguals who had obtained at least a 'B' grade in the GCE 'Ordinary' level English and Chinese examinations, as well as at least a 'C' grade in the GCE 'Advanced' level English (General Paper) and Chinese examinations[2].

Each participant completed a questionnaire adapted from Rickard Liow and Poon (1998) that assessed their self-reported proficiency as well as approximate age of acquisition of the two languages. The ratings were done on 5-point scales for how well participants felt they speak, read, and write the language, and also how often they use the language at home and with friends. The self-report scores were summed together to get a composite estimate of the subjective proficiency ratings. Participants were also asked to report their English and Chinese grades for the above examinations and completed separate English and Chinese lexical decision tests adapted from Tham (2003), in which they were to decide if each item was a real word or a nonword. The self-report ratings, grades, and lexical decision scores were used to rank order participants for proficiency in each language.

Participants who had acquired either language after age 5[3] were eliminated. Since the goal of the study is to examine differences due to L2 proficiency while ensuring that L1 proficiency was high, 58 participants who were from the top half of the rank-ordering for English background were selected for the main experiment. These participants were then rank ordered on their Chinese background and a

---

[1] The dialect of Chinese used in Singapore in education and the media (and also in the majority of conversational settings) is Mandarin. Chinese will be used throughout this paper to refer to this particular dialect.

[2] The Singapore-Cambridge General Certificate of Education Examination is a standardised examination taken across the cohort by most students in Singapore, typically at age 16 for the 'Ordinary' level and age 18 for the 'Advanced' level. 'A', 'B' and 'C' are pass grades.

[3] Formal teaching of English as a first language and Chinese as a second language for all Chinese Singaporeans starts from kindergarten at age 5. The language of education in Singapore is English for all subjects including Math and Science. Ethnic languages such as Chinese, Malay, and Tamil are taught as a second language.

---

median split was used to categorise them into the high and low L2 proficiency groups.

Design

A 2 (L2 Proficiency: high, low) x 2 (Naming Language: L1, L2) x 2 (Distractor Type: related, unrelated) mixed factorial design was used in this experiment. All independent variables were run within subjects while L2 proficiency was a subject variable.

Materials

48 black-and-white line drawings (300 x 300 pixels in size, .bmp format) with at least 80% target name agreement were obtained from the online International Picture Naming Project (2005) database. All the pictures were of common objects, and had non-cognate, monosyllabic target names in both English and Chinese.

Each English target name (e.g. *bridge*) was matched with two monosyllabic English distracters: one that was phonologically-related (but semantically-unrelated) to the English target name (e.g. *breech*), and one that was unrelated (e.g. *flat*). The corresponding Chinese target name (e.g. *qiao2*[4]) was similarly matched with two monosyllabic Chinese distracters that were phonologically-related (but semantically-unrelated) to the Chinese target name (e.g. *qiao1*, for the example of *qiao2*), and one that was unrelated (e.g. *suo1*). Table 1 shows how the stimuli associated with the picture of a bridge relate to the various conditions in the study. The onset consonant phonemes of all related monosyllabic distractors were identical to the onsets of the cross-language target translation, and 90% of these distractors also had nucleus vowels that were identical to the cross-language target translation.

Table 1: Examples of manipulations across the within-subjects experimental conditions for the bridge picture

Naming Language	Target Word	Distractor Type	
		Related	Unrelated
L1 (English)	bridge	qiao1	suo1
L2 (Chinese)	qiao2	breech	flat

The English and Chinese distracter words were spoken by a native Singaporean female speaker who was highly proficient in both languages, and digitally recorded in 16-bit mono, 11 kHz, .wav format. The overall root-mean-square amplitude levels of the sound files were digitally leveled. In a separate study, 20 undergraduates (from the same population as the sample in this experiment but who did not take part in the study) identified the auditory stimuli and tokens that did not achieve at least 80% accuracy were re-recorded and re-tested.

---

[4] For ease of understanding, the Chinese words reported in this study are shown in their *Hanyu Pinyin* (Romanized phonemic notation) form, instead of in Chinese characters. The numbers 1-4 denote the four different tones which are contrastive in Chinese.

Procedure

Participants were tested individually in a cubicle, seated approximately 40 cm away from the computer screen, and 5 cm away from the head of a microphone connected to a voicekey. The monitor resolution was set to 800 x 600. Pictures were presented in the centre of the computer screen, and the auditory stimuli were played through headphones at approximately 70 db SPL. A tape recorder also recorded all participant responses.

The 48 pictures were divided into 4 separate lists of 12 pictures each. A 4 x 4 balanced latin square was used to rotate the lists across the 4 within-subjects conditions. Each picture was therefore only seen once by each participant and was never repeated. The latin-square counterbalanced picture-lists with conditions across participants.

The trials for the English and Chinese naming language conditions were blocked, with the related and unrelated trials presented in a randomised order within each block. The order in which the blocks were presented was counterbalanced, such that half the participants were first presented with the English-naming block followed by the Chinese-naming block, and vice-versa for the other half.

Each naming language block consisted of a picture-familiarisation phase, followed by a picture-naming phase, which approximately followed the procedure of previous studies using the picture-word interference paradigm (Costa *et al.*, 2003; Hermans *et al.*, 1998). In the picture-familiarisation phase, participants were shown each picture with its corresponding English or Chinese target name printed at the bottom, and were instructed to familiarise themselves with the target name for that picture. This continued for all 24 pictures in the block. This phase was self-paced, and participants were told to take as long as necessary to familiarise themselves with the pictures and names.

In the picture-naming phase, participants were instructed to name the pictures as quickly as possible with the target name they had been familiarised with, and to ignore whatever was played over the headphones. The pictures used in this phase were exactly the same as those in the picture-familiarisation phase, except without the target name at the bottom. Each trial began when the participant pressed a key to indicate that they were ready to begin. A fixation point appeared on the screen for 500 ms, following which the auditory stimulus began playing. The picture appeared on the screen 150 ms after the onset of the auditory stimulus, and remained on-screen for 3000 ms or until the voicekey was triggered. Participants then pressed a key to begin the next trial. Naming latencies were measured from the onset of the picture's appearance. The entire experiment lasted approximately 15 minutes.

Results

Trials in which participants produced verbal dysfluencies (i.e. stuttering, utterance repairs, non-verbal sounds that triggered the voicekey), incorrect responses, or no response within the 3000ms time limit, were scored as invalid. Naming latencies which deviated more than two standard deviations from the participant mean in the relevant conditions were also considered invalid. Five participants whose total valid trials fell two standard deviations below the mean were excluded from the subsequent analyses. For the remaining 53 participants, 14.6% of the trials were classified as invalid and discarded.

Language background analyses

The English and Chinese background scores of the high and low L2 proficiency groups were compared to determine if the two groups were in fact equated on English proficiency and differed on Chinese proficiency. These scores are shown in Table 2.

Table 2: Mean language background scores.

L2 Proficiency	Background Scores		
	Self-report	Grades	Lexical Decision
English (L1)			
High	19.88 (2.75)	2.98 (0.84)	217.35 (11.80)
Low	21.15 (2.82)	2.67 (1.01)	222.63 (14.47)
Chinese (L2)			
High	20.00 (1.72)	1.75 (0.64)	144.08 (14.70)
Low	13.67 (2.77)	2.52 (1.12)	136.22 (12.67)

Notes. *SD*s in parentheses; higher self-report and lexical decision scores indicate greater proficiency, lower grade scores indicate better examination results[5].

For the English background scores, there was no difference between the two L2 proficiency groups among all measures, all $ts(51) < 1.7$. For the Chinese background scores, the high proficiency group had significantly higher scores for the self-report, $t(51) = 9.94, p < .001$, and lexical decision measures, $t(51) = 2.09, p < .05$, and significantly better (lower) grade scores, $t(51) = 3.05, p < .01$. These analyses indicate that the categorisation of participants was successful in creating two groups that were equated on L1 proficiency but differed in L2 proficiency.

Naming latency analyses

The average naming latencies across the 8 conditions are summarized in Table 3. The data were subjected to a three-way mixed design analysis of variance, which yielded a main effect of naming language, $F(1,51) = 74.94, MSe = 19115.49, p < .001$, in which latencies in English naming ($M = 719.69, SD = 105.34$) were significantly faster than in Chinese naming ($M = 884.16, SD = 176.35$). This is not surprising as English is the L1 for all participants. No other main effects were significant, $Fs < 1$.

The two-way interaction between L2 Proficiency and Distractor Type was significant, $F(1,51) = 10.56, MSe = 2494.07, p < .01$, as was the three-way interaction, $F(1,51) = 11.24, MSe = 2525.00, p < .01$. No other interactions were reliable. As the higher order interaction takes precedence,

---

[5] Letter grades in the 'O' and "A" level examinations are accompanied by a numerical score, e.g. A1, A2, B3, B4. The average of the numerical scores for both examinations were used as the grade score.

the rest of the analyses will focus on the nature of this three-way interaction.

Table 3: Mean naming latency in ms across distractor type, L2 proficiency, and naming language.

L2 Proficiency	Related Distractors		Unrelated Distractors	
	M	SD	M	SD
L1 (English) naming				
High	751.15	113.66	751.05	129.82
Low	689.19	84.83	687.38	87.20
L2 (Chinese) naming				
High	908.96	183.79	855.73	166.92
Low	867.09	198.54	904.74	180.24

To probe the three-way interaction, the L2 Proficiency x Distractor Type simple interaction was tested at each level of the Naming Language factor. In L1 naming, the interaction was not reliable, $F < 1$, indicating that there was no evidence of a phono-translation effect in L1 speech production. Figure 2 shows the pattern of results for L1 naming.

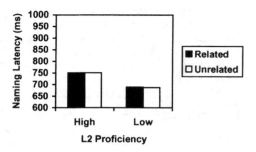

Figure 2. No evidence of a phono-translation effect in L1 naming.

In L2 naming, the simple interaction was significant, $F(1,51) = 15.80, MSe = 3460.70, p < .001$. This is due to a reliable phono-translation interference effect for the group with high L2 proficiency, where naming latency for related distractor trials were significantly *slower* than unrelated distractor trials, $F(1,51) = 10.64, MSe = 3460.70, p < .01$, and an opposite phono-translation facilitation effect for the group with low L2 proficiency, where naming latency for related distractor trials were significantly *faster* than unrelated distractor trials, $F(1,51) = 5.53, MSe = 3460.70, p < .05$. Figure 3 shows the pattern of results for L2 naming.

Discussion

Do the two languages of bilingual speakers interfere with each other in the course of lexical selection during speech production? Does the nature or magnitude of the interference depend on the proficiency level of the bilingual speakers and what is the extent of the interference for L1 and L2 speech production? These were the questions the present study set out to investigate, focusing on the phono-translation effect found in the picture-word interference paradigm.

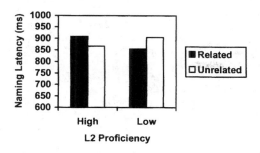

Figure 3. Phono-translation interference and facilitation effects in L2 naming, depending on L2 proficiency.

Previous research (Costa *et al.*, 2003; Hermans *et al.*, 1998) has shown that auditory phono-translation distracters in L1 that were phonologically similar to the L1 translations of the target word slowed down naming latencies more than unrelated distracters during L2 naming, an effect that has been demonstrated with highly proficient Spanish-Catalan bilinguals, as well as less fluent Dutch-English bilinguals. This interference effect has been interpreted to mean that the lexical nodes of the non-response language compete during lexical selection.

Costa *et al.* (2003) suggested that the degree to which lexical competition is present in bilingual speakers could depend on their proficiency level, and that the magnitude and extent of cross-language interference may increase with less proficient bilinguals. In the present study, the exact opposite effect was found!

The high-L2 proficiency group replicated the phono-translation *interference* effect as found in Hermans *et al.*'s (1998) and Costa *et al.*'s (2003) studies, and hence increased confidence in the reliability of the effect and its generalisability even to very different language pairs such as English and Chinese. This pattern of results suggests that words from L1 are entered into the lexical selection process for L2 naming.

However, the low-L2 proficiency group did not demonstrate the phono-translation *interference* effect, and indeed, appeared to show an opposite *facilitation* effect. When primed with an auditory distracter that was phonologically similar (e.g. *breech*) to the English (L1) translation of the target word (e.g. *bridge*), low-L2 participants were able to name the picture (*qiao2*) in Chinese (L2) faster than when primed with an unrelated English distracter (e.g. *flat*).

This result is compatible with an account that incorporates lexical mediation from L1-to-L2 for the less proficient bilinguals (cf. Kroll & Stewart, 1994). For highly proficient bilinguals, direct links between the concept for both the L1 words *and* the L2 words may be well established. The semantic concept can therefore directly access L2 words. When primed with phonologically-similar L1 words (e.g. *breech*), this increases the activation of the L1 word (*bridge*) beyond its usual suppressed state (as the language not-in-use), such that the L1 word now acts as a competitor against the L2 word (*qiao2*) for lexical selection, leading to the interference effect. For less proficient bilinguals, they may not have attained the level of L2 proficiency required for direct access yet as the conceptually mediated link may be less developed. Hence, L2 words are instead accessed via the L1 words. As such, priming them with phonologically-similar L1 words (e.g. *breech*) increased the activation of the L1 word (*bridge*), and hence facilitated the L1-to-L2 translation from *bridge* to *qiao2*. This resulted in faster naming speeds than when they were primed with unrelated L1 words (e.g. *flat*) that did not facilitate the translation process in any way (and may indeed have interfered with it) since it would have activated the wrong L1 word.

Kiyak (1982) and Chen and Leung (1989) reported that less-proficient bilinguals had often acquired L2 by using their L1 words, whereas highly-proficient bilinguals had usually acquired L2 through directly associating L2 words with underlying conceptual representations. This difference in learning strategy is consistent with the claim of stronger direct concept-to-L2 links in proficient bilinguals. However, it remains nonetheless possible for less proficient bilinguals, as proficiency in L2 increases, to undergo a developmental shift from indirect to direct concept-to-L2 access (Chen & Leung, 1989; Hong & Silver, 2001).

It is interesting to note that the bilingual participants in Hermans *et al.*'s (1998) study showed an interference effect, despite having a later age of acquisition and fewer years of study in L2 than the low-L2 group in the present study. This somewhat contradictory finding can perhaps be explained by the larger language distance between L1 and L2 for the bilinguals in this study (English and Chinese[6]) compared to Hermans' study (Dutch and English). It is widely acknowledged that the larger the language distance between L1 and L2 (i.e. the less L2 resembles L1), the harder it will be to acquire the L2 (Weltens & Grendel, 1993). As such, a much higher level of L2 proficiency is probably required for English-Chinese bilinguals to make the developmental shift, compared to Dutch-English bilinguals.

The present findings also indicate that there is no empirical evidence for phono-translation effects in L1 naming. This is consistent with the argument that L1 nodes are more easily selected compared to L2 nodes and would therefore be less susceptible to interference from L2 (De Bot & Schreuder, 1993; Green, 1986; Roelofs, 1992) and the observation that L2 intrusions in L1 speech are rare (Poulisse & Bongaerts, 1994).

In summary, the main goal of the present study was to test previous suggestions that the magnitude of the phono-translation interference effect could depend on the L2 proficiency levels of the participants. The interference

---

[6] English and Chinese are very dissimilar in orthography and phonology; whereas Dutch and English are related alphabetic languages from the same Germanic language family (see Smith, 1997).

effect was replicated for English-Chinese bilinguals that were highly-proficient in Chinese. However, we found that the nature of the effect actually reverses and appears facilitative for low-proficiency participants. This underscores the need to consider L2 proficiency levels as a factor in future experiments and theoretical explanations of bilingual speech production.

Acknowledgments

This work was supported by Research Grant R-581-000-048-112 to WDG.

References

Caramazza, A., & Costa, A. (2000). The semantic interference effect in the picture-word interference paradigm: Does the response set matter? *Cognition, 75,* B51-64.

Chen, H-C., & Leung Y-S. (1989). Patterns of lexical processing in a nonnative language. *Journal of Experimental Psychology: Learning, Memory and Cognition, 15,* 316-325.

Chen, H-C., & Ng, M-L. (1989). Semantic facilitation and translation priming effects in Chinese-English bilinguals. *Memory and Cognition, 17,* 454-462.

Chen, H-C., & Ho, C. (1986). Development of Stroop interference in Chinese-English bilinguals. *Journal of Experimental Psychology: Learning, Memory and Cognition, 12,* 397-401.

Cheung, H., & Chen, H-C. (1998). Lexical and conceptual processing in Chinese-English bilinguals: Further evidence for asymmetry. *Memory and Cognition, 26,* 1002-1013.

Costa, A. (2005). Lexical access in bilingual production. In J. F. Kroll & A. De Groot (Eds.), *Handbook of bilingualism: psycholinguistics approaches* (pp. 308-325). New York: Oxford University Press.

Costa, A., Caramazza, A., & Sebastián-Gallés, N. (2003). The cognate facilitation effect: Implications for the models of lexical access. *Journal of Experimental Psychology: Learning, Memory, and Cognition, 26,* 1283-1296.

Costa, A., Colomé, À., Gómez, O., & Sebastián-Gallés, N. (2003). Another look at cross-language competition in bilingual speech production: Lexical and phonological factors. *Bilingualism: Language and Cognition, 6,* 167-179.

De Bot, K., & Schreuder, R. (1993). Word production and the bilingual lexicon. In R. Schreuder & B. Weltens (Eds.), *The bilingual lexicon* (pp. 191-214). Amsterdam: John Benjamins Publishing Company.

Green, D. W. (1986). Control, activation and resource. *Brain and Language, 27,* 210-223.

Grosjean, F. (1982). *Life with two languages: An introduction to bilingualism.* Cambridge: Harvard University Press.

Grosjean, F. (1997). Processing mixed language: issues, findings and models. In A. De Groot & J. Kroll (Eds). *Tutorials in bilingualism: Psycholinguistic perspectives* (pp. 225-254). Mahwah: Erlbaum.

Grosjean, F. (1998). Transfer and language mode. *Bilingualism: Language and Cognition, 1,* 175-176.

Hermans, D., Bongaerts T., De Bot, K., & Schreuder, R. (1998). Producing words in a foreign language: Can speakers prevent interference from their first language? *Bilingualism: Language and Cognition, 1,* 213-229.

Hong, E-L., & Silver, R. E. (2001). The psychology of bilingual language acquisition: Its importance and implications for the Singaporean society. In A-G. Tan & M. Goh (Eds.), *Psychology in Singapore: Issues of an emerging discipline* (pp. 149-176). Singapore: McGraw Hill.

International Picture Naming Project, (2005). Center for Research in Language, University of California, San Diego. http://crl.ucsd.edu/~aszekely/ipnp/

Kiyak, H. A. (1982). Interlingual interference in naming color words. *Journal of Cross-cultural Psychology, 13,* 125-135.

Kroll, J. F. (1993). Accessing conceptual representations for words in a second language. In R. Schreuder & B. Weltens (Eds.), *The bilingual lexicon* (pp. 53-82). Amsterdam: John Benjamins Publishing Company.

Kroll, J. F., & Stewart, E. (1994). Category interference in translation and picture naming: Evidence for asymmetric connections between bilingual memory representations. *Journal of Memory and Language, 33,* 149-174.

Poulisse, N. (1993). A theoretical account of lexical communication strategies. In R. Schreuder & B. Weltens (Eds.), *The bilingual lexicon* (pp. 157-190). Amsterdam: John Benjamins Publishing Company.

Poulisse, N. (1999). Slips of the tongue: Speech errors in first and second language production. Amsterdam: John Benjamins Publishing Company.

Poulisse, N. & Bongaerts, T. (1994). First language use in second language production. *Applied Linguistics, 15,* 36-57.

Rickard Liow, S. J., & Poon, K. (1998). Phonological awareness in Chinese-English biscriptal children. *Applied Psycholinguistics, 19,* 339-362.

Roelofs, A. (1992). A spreading-activation theory of lemma retrieval in speaking. *Cognition, 42,* 107-142.

Tham, W. (2003). *Neuroanatomical representation of language in English-Chinese bilingual biscriptals: An fMRI study.* Masters thesis, National University of Singapore.

Tzelgov, J., & Eben-Ezra, S. (1992). Components of between-language semantic priming effect. *European Journal of Cognitive Psychology, 4.*

Weltens, B., & Grendel, M. (1993). Attrition of vocabulary knowledge. In R. Schreuder & B. Weltens (Eds.), *The bilingual lexicon* (pp. 135-157). Amsterdam: John Benjamins Publishing Company.

Frequency and Lexical Marking of Different Types of Conditionals by Children and Adults in an Elicitation Task

Sara Verbrugge (Sara.Verbrugge@psy.kuleuven.be)
Laboratory of Experimental Psychology, University of Leuven
Tiensestraat 102, Leuven, Belgium
Department of Linguistics, University of Leuven,
Blijde-Inkomststraat 21, Leuven, Belgium

Abstract

This study investigates the types of conditionals adults and children come up with when they are given the antecedent of a conditional and have to complete the consequent. Conditionals can be interpreted in different domains: the content, the epistemic, and the speech act domain (Dancygier, 1998; Sweetser, 1990). The experiment showed that children give many more conditionals that are a direct reflection of the course of events as they happen in reality (content conditionals). Adults express more variety. In many cases they also complete the conditionals to content conditionals, but their completions comprise nearly twice as many epistemic consequents. Moreover, the number of completions to epistemic conditionals can be manipulated along all age groups by suggesting particular lexical markers that have to be used in the consequent of the conditional. We will discuss these findings in the light of the linguistic skills required to understand relations in the content and the epistemic domain.

Introduction

Different types of classifications have been used to categorize coherence relations and their lexical expressions (by means of connectives). Below we will discuss the distinction between semantic – pragmatic relations and the distinction between content – epistemic – speech act relations. These two systems of classification partially overlap. Semantic relations coincide with content relations. Pragmatic relations cover epistemic and speech act relations. We will deal with the emergence and order of acquisition of these cognitive domains. We will also give special attention to the role modal elements can play as a facilitating tool to express relations in the epistemic domain.

Semantic - Pragmatic

Spooren, Tates and Sanders (1996) claim that, in general, less complex relations are acquired before more complex situations. For example, additive relations are acquired before causal relations.

Spooren et al. (1996) distinguish between semantic and pragmatic relations. Semantic relations hold between the propositional content of the sentences of a text. E.g. *He had been working late yesterday. So he was tired.* Pragmatic relations hold between the utterances of the text or the

beliefs the text is based on (Knott, 2001). E.g. *He was yawning. So he was tired.*

Spooren et al. (1996) conducted an experiment with six – seven year olds and eleven – twelve years olds. It included two tasks, one that biased the production of semantic relations (description of images with causal relations) and one that biased the production of pragmatic relations (formulating own ideas about controversial topics such as homework, television programmes). Overall, children produced more semantic than pragmatic relations. Young children produced proportionally fewer pragmatic relations than older children. Spooren et al. (1996) explain this by referring to the fact that pragmatic relations are more complex. Semantic relations are cognitively less complicated than pragmatic relations.

Also, children used more linguistic markers for semantic than for pragmatic relations. In line with Bloom and Capatides (1987), they explain this by referring to the cognitive load needed to process sentences. Semantic relations require less cognitive load and leave therefore enough capacity/energy to spend on picking the correct connectives. With pragmatic relations, cognitive load is already relatively high, and because of the (over)load children will not bother with the connectives anymore. As soon as children have acquired a particular relation, they find the energy to use connectives to make their discourse more comprehensible for the hearer.

Content – Epistemic – Speech Act

Kryatzis, Gua and Ervin-Tripp (1990) make a distinction between three types of causal expressions: Speech Act-Level Causals, Content-Level Causals and Epistemic Causals (see also Dancygier 1998, Sweetser 1990).

In Speech Act-Level Causals "the reason clause (i.e., the clause with "because" or "so") justifies why something is said, and why the hearer should comply with what is said, rather than explaining the event that is referred to in the matrix clause" (Kryatzis et al., 1990, p. 205). E.g. *Is everything allright? Because you look really sad today.* In Content-Level Causals "the event being explained is the event actually referred to in the main clause, and a real-world causality connects the two events described in the two clauses" (1990, p. 206). E.g. *The water boils because Mum put the kettle on.* In Epistemic Causals "the event being explained is not the event referred to propositionally in the main clause. Rather, it is a conclusion arrived upon by the speaker, and the event described in the subordinate clause is the speaker's evidence for the conclusion" (1990, p. 207). E.g. *He must have arrived because his car is outside.*

The purpose of the study of Kryatzis et al. (1990) was to examine the relative frequency of these three types of causals in child discourse. For the data-analysis, children were divided in three age groups; Group 1= 2;4 – 3;6. Group 2= 3;7 – 6;6   Group 3= 6;7 – 12;0.

Kryatzis et al. (1990) observed that children produced more speech act level causals than content or epistemic causals. The youngest children only formulated speech act causals[1]. The number of content causals increased between the second and third age groups. Epistemic causals were very infrequent for all age groups. They relate this to the finding that epistemic meanings as a rule emerge later than deontic ones. "These findings suggest that epistemic meanings are more cognitively complex for young children." (1990, p. 209-210)

Evers-Vermeul (2005) conducted an experiment among Dutch children of four and five years old. The goal was to investigate whether young children can already produce epistemic relations. Therefore, the context was manipulated to favour epistemic utterances. She shows that "children as young as four are capable of producing epistemic relations when they have the communicative goal of persuading someone, which is the case in an argumentative context" (2005, p. 235). Moreover, the 5 year old children produced more epistemic relations than the 4 year old children. This shows that the ability to produce epistemic relations increases with age.

In a longitudinal study investigating the acquisition order of the domains by observing emergence and use of connectives such as *omdat (because), want (since), daarom (therefore), dus (so)* in the different domains, Evers-Vermeul shows that "the epistemic domain seems to be acquired last" (2005, p. 243). However, she also claims that the context in which the sentences are uttered plays a crucial role.

Modal elements

The following studies are only concerned with experiments involving adults.

Westerbos (2004) conducted an elicitation experiment in Dutch in which participants were asked to complete the second part of causal sentences. They were given the first part which ended with *dus (so)*. Half of the first part of the sentences comprised a modal verb (*zal wel, 'may well'*), e.g. *The trains may well have been delayed, so....* The other half did not, e.g. *The baby started crying, so....*

For the condition without modal verb in the first part, Westerbos looked at the pragmatic markers participants inserted spontaneously into their completions of the sentences. When participants disrupted the order of events as they happen in reality, they were more inclined to use a pragmatic marker than when they did not disrupt the order. This means that when sentences become more complex and diverge more from what is observed in reality, people will use markers to make their utterances more comprehensible.

Traxler, Sanford, Aked and Moxey (1997) showed that the use of modal constructions or expressions like '*says that* [sentence]' or '*thinks that* [sentence]' can help the reader in the direction of a particular interpretation. They conducted a reading time experiment with causal and diagnostic (i.e., epistemic) sentences involving 'because' (e.g., causal sentence: *Tina had to walk five miles because her engine stalled on the motorway*; diagnostic sentence: *Tina ran out of gas because her engine stalled on the motorway*). Overall, the processing of the second clauses of diagnostic sentences took longer than the processing of the second clauses of causal sentences. Yet, in their second experiment they report that when a particular modal construction (e.g., *perhaps, maybe, might*) was added (e.g., causal: *Perhaps Jeff got angry at his neighbours because they played their stereo too loud.* Diagnostic: *Perhaps Jeff had inconsiderate neighbours because they played their stereo too loud*), reading times decreased considerably for the second clauses of the diagnostic sentences. They were then as easily processed as causal sentences. Apparently, these modal constructions create a mental space more compatible with a diagnostic interpretation. Diagnostic interpretations become more readily available and are consequently more easily processed.

Hypotheses

On the basis of the literature discussed above, we can conclude that children are apparently able to produce epistemic relations from the age of four (or maybe even earlier). However, when children are not prompted to do so, they produce fewer epistemic relations than older children and adults.

The experiment that will be discussed below investigates the number of epistemic relations that children and adults utter in an elicitation task. Contrary to the previous studies, this task focuses particularly on *conditional* sentences and the epistemic relations they can express. To the best of our knowledge, this kind of elicitation task has not been conducted with content and epistemic conditionals.

Experiment

The experiment was set up in order to elicit content or epistemic conditionals. Speech act conditionals will most probably not be produced by the participants because these conditionals need a conversational context. Our focus is on

---

[1] There is discussion whether content conditionals or speech act conditionals are the first to emerge. For an overview of the literature on this topic, see Evers-Vermeul (2005).

epistemic conditionals, because they are supposed to be the less frequent category.

For the children participating, we have chosen age groups of 9-10 and 11-12, because the children needed to have a relatively fluent command of the written language in order to fill in the paper-and-pencil task.

We can formulate the following hypotheses:

1. Adults will generate more epistemic conditionals than children.

2. Adults will use more epistemic markers spontaneously than children. Since adults have fully mastered the epistemic relations, they will be better able to insert epistemic markers to clarify their discourse (cf. Bloom & Capatides, 1987).

3. When participants have to incorporate a particular epistemic marker into their sentences, they will produce more epistemic conditionals. In line with Traxler et al. (1997) we predict that particular modal constructions will create a mental space more compatible with an epistemic interpretation.

Method

Participants. 253 children and adults in total participated in the experiment. 76 children of 9-10 years and 69 children of 11-12 years old took part in the study. 108 first year psychology students participated as part of a course requirement.

Materials and Design. The items were presented to the participants in Dutch. The experiment consisted of a paper and pencil task. Two age groups of children (9-10 and 11-12) and one group of adults were asked to complete 10 conditional sentences. They were each time given the antecedent and could complete the conditional with a consequent of their liking. No context was provided. An example of an item is: *If John is tired, then ... .* This sentence can be completed to a content conditional, e.g. *... then he must go to bed early.* It can also be completed to become an epistemic conditional, e.g. *... then has been working hard today.* For full examples of the materials, see Appendix.

There were three conditions: In one condition they were asked to complete the conditional. In the second condition they were asked to complete the conditional making use of the marker '*zal wel*' (combination of future tense and adverb of modality; a bit stronger than '*may well*'). In the third condition they were asked to complete the conditional making use of the marker '*waarschijnlijk*' (adverb of modality, '*probably*'). This variable was manipulated between subjects.

Results

Firstly, we will discuss the results for the frequency of the different types of conditionals. Secondly, we will deal with

the cases in which participants spontaneously came up with a lexical marking of the epistemic conditionals.

Frequency of Different types of Conditionals. Per participant we checked how many epistemic conditionals were given out of the possible ten. This number was used in the analysis. An analysis of variance (ANOVA) was conducted with age and suggested markers (none – 'may well' - 'probably') as between subjects variables. The analysis revealed a main effect of markers ($F(2,244)=11.49$; $p<.0001$) and a main effect of age ($F(2,244)=26.53$; $p<.00001$). No interaction was observed.

As for suggested markers, planned comparisons revealed that the condition without marker differed significantly from the condition 'may well' ($F(1,244)=9.86$; $p<.01$) and from the condition 'probably' ($F(1,244)=21.74$; $p<.0001$). The conditions 'may well' and 'probably' did not differ significantly from one another. See Figure 1.

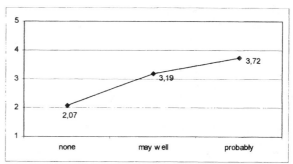

Figure 1: Average number of epistemic conditionals given per condition.

As for age, planned comparisons revealed that the adult group differed significantly from 9-10 ($F(1,244)=40.99$; $p<.00001$) and 11-12 ($F(1,244)=32.92$; $p<.00001$). Age groups 9-10 and 11-12 did not differ significantly from one another. See Figure 2.

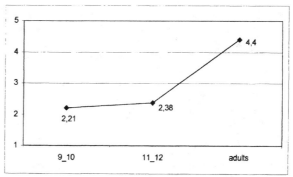

Figure 2: Average number of epistemic conditionals given per age group.

Lexical Marking of Epistemic Conditionals. For the condition that asked the participants to complete the sentence without a particular marker that had to be used, participants sometimes inserted markers spontaneously. Children of the youngest age group (9-10) did not do this. Children of age group 11-12 did this in only 4.76% of the possible cases (two cases out of 42 epistemic conditionals that were produced). Adults used many more markers without being asked to use them. They did so in 21.74% of the possible cases (25 cases out of 115 epistemic conditionals that were produced). A chi-square test showed that this distribution differed from chance ($\chi^2 = 7.2$, $df=2$, $p<.05$). Table 1 gives an overview of the types of markers that adults used.

Table 1: Markers used spontaneously by adults

Marker	Translation	Count
Waarschijnlijk	Probably	11
Zal wel	May well	6
Moet	Must	2
Vast	Definitely	2
Zeker	Certainly	2
Wil dat zeggen dat	It means that	1
Komt het omdat	It is because	1

The first group 'waarschijnlijk' (probably), 'zal wel' (may well), 'moet' (must), 'vast' (definitely), 'zeker' (certainly) refers to the certainty with which conclusions are drawn (see also Smessaert & Verbrugge, 2006). The first two are more tentative, the latter three refer to relative certain conclusions. The other two markers 'wil dat zeggen dat' (it means that) and 'komt het omdat' (it is because) make explicit the relation of inferring between antecedent and consequent.

Discussion

Frequency of Different types of Conditionals. There is a clear age trend in the number of epistemic conditionals participants generate. The younger children produced fewest, the 11-12 year old a few more. There is a significant gap with the adults. It has been stated in the literature (Bloom, Lahey, Hood, Lifter, & Fiess, 1980; Evers-Vermeul, 2005; Kryatzis et al., 1990; Spooren et al., 1996) that epistemic relations are the latest to emerge. The experiment discussed above only handles with content and epistemic conditionals and not with speech act conditionals (due to the set up of the experiment speech act relations were not elicited), but again it is shown that children will generate more content relations spontaneously than epistemic relations. Children may well understand epistemic conditionals, but will not very often use them spontaneously. This probably relates to the child's

occupation with the present and the future rather than the past.

The manipulation with modal elements such as 'waarschijnlijk' (probably) and 'zal wel' (may well) proved worthwhile. The number of epistemic conditionals increases considerably when participants have to incorporate these modal elements into their sentences. Apparently, when participants are prompted to use a particular modal construction that is highly compatible with an epistemic interpretation, they will be more inclined to generate epistemic relations. In line with Traxler et al. (1997) we can say that the modal elements that participants have to use, set up a mental space in which participants will more easily understand (and apparently also generate) epistemic utterances. 'Zal wel' (may well) is a lexical construction used to venture a conclusion about something that has been said or observed. The insertion of 'waarschijnlijk' (probably) gave rise to a slightly (but not significantly) higher number of epistemic conditionals than 'may well'. This may be because 'probably' conveys a greater level of plausibility than 'may well'.

Lexical Marking of Epistemic Conditionals. Close observation of the participants' completions shows that even when participants are not explicitly asked to do so, they still insert epistemic lexical markers into the consequent of the conditionals. The tendency to use lexical markers increases with age. The youngest group in our study did not insert any markers spontaneously. The middle group only did so in two cases. The adult group already did so in almost 22% of the possible cases.

Bloom and Capatides (1987) observe that children will mark objective relations before subjective relations. In their opinion this is because objective relations are less complex. The more complex relations require all the children's cognitive capacity (Bates, 1976) and no extra capacity remains to mark the utterances with extra lexical elements. It seems that children first have to fully acquire the relations before they can add elements to make their utterances more insightful to the hearer.

The implications for our experiment are as follows: For the content conditionals (the default type), the general conditional markers if-then and the future tense mark the predictive conditionals sufficiently. For epistemic conditionals, however, which are more complex (e.g. because of their divergence of the order of events as they happen in reality), it will take children longer to be able to mark them. But as soon as the two types are fully mastered (as is definitely the case for the adults in our study), people will make freely use of modal elements to make their utterances more comprehensible whenever they think it necessary.

The exact instances in which adults deem it necessary to add modal elements to elucidate their discourse is an interesting topic for future research.

General Discussion

The elicitation experiment proved to be an interesting method to observe different types of conditional sentences. It made sure participants only used conditional utterances, while they were still free to complete the sentences in whatever manner that best suited their purposes.

The analysis of the frequencies of different types of conditionals shows that the tendency to use epistemic conditionals instead of content conditionals increases with age. The adults produced nearly twice as many epistemic conditionals as the children.

Another factor that played an important role for producing epistemic conditionals was the insertion of the lexical elements 'may well' and 'probably'. When participants were asked to use one of these markers in the consequent, they produced a significantly higher number of epistemic conditionals. This may well have to do with the mental space that is set up (cf. Traxler et al., 1997). These lexical markers set up an epistemic mental space.

The experiment also showed that, even when participants were not explicitly asked to use the markers, they sometimes came up with their own markers. The fact that the markers that participants came up with most frequently coincide with the ones we selected ('may well' and 'probably') is a good confirmation of our lexical marker manipulation.

Overall, we can conclude that content relations are easier to produce for children than epistemic relations. This complements with previous studies that have shown that content relations require less reading time than epistemic relations (for conditionals, see Verbrugge, Smessaert & Dieussaert, submitted; for other connectives, see Noordman & de Blijzer, 2000). As can be expected, production and reception are on the same line.

Acknowledgments

The research was carried out thanks to a grant for the author (Research Assistant of the Research Foundation Flanders). Special thanks to Els Mampay for collecting the children's data.

References

Bates, E. (1976). *Language and Context: the Acquisition of Pragmatics*. London: Academic Press.

Bloom, L., & Capatides, J. B. (1987). Expression of affect and the emergence of language. *Child Development, 58*, 1513–1522.

Bloom, L., Lahey, M., Hood, L., Lifter, K., & Fiess, K. (1980). Complex sentences: acquisition of syntactic connectives and the semantic relations they encode. *Journal of Child Language 7*, 235-261.

Dancygier, B. (1998). *Conditionals and Prediction. Time, Knowledge and Causation in Conditional Constructions*. Cambridge: Cambridge University Press.

Evers-Vermeul, J. (2005). *The development of Dutch connectives. Change and acquisition as windows on form-function relations*. Doctoral dissertation, Utrecht Institute of Linguistics, The Netherlands.

Knott, A. (2001). Semantic and pragmatic relations and their intended effects. In T. Sanders, J. Schilperoord, and W. Spooren (Eds.), *Text representation: linguistic and psycholinguistic aspects*. Amsterdam: Benjamins.

Kryatzis, A., Gua, J., & Ervin-Tripp, S. (1990). Pragmatic Conventions Influencing Children's Use of Causal Constructions in Natural Discourse. *Proceedings of the sixteenth annual meeting of the Berkeley Linguistics Society* (pp. 205-214). Berkeley: Berkeley Linguistics Society.

Noordman, L. & de Blijzer, F. (2000). On the Processing of Causal Relations. In: Couper Kuhlen, E., & Kortmann, B. (Eds.), *Cause-Condition-Concession-Contrast: Cognitive and Discourse Perspectives*. Berlin: Mouton de Gruyter.

Spooren, W., Tates & Sanders, T. (1996). Taalverwerving en de classificatie van coherentierelaties. *Nederlandse Taalkunde 1*, 26-51.

Smessaert, H. & Verbrugge, S. (2006). *De lexicalisatie van inferentiële versus meta-inferentiële conditionele zinnen*. In P. J. Schellens, B. Hendriks en H. Hoeken (Eds.), Studies in taalbeheersing 2 (pp. 309-319). Assen: Van Gorcum.

Sweetser, E. (1990). *From Etymology to Pragmatics: Metaphorical and Cultural Aspects of Semantic Structure*. Cambridge: Cambridge University Press.

Traxler, M.J., Sanford, A.J., Aked, J.P., & Moxey, L.M. (1997). Processing causal and diagnostic statements in discourse. *Journal of Experimental Psychology: Learning, Memory, and Cognition, 23* (1), 88-101.

Verbrugge, Smessaert & Dieussaert (submitted). Syntactic and semantic differences between content and inferential conditionals: compatibility tasks and reading time studies.

Westerbos, A. (2004). *De complexiteit van epistemische relaties: de rol van volgorde*, dus en zal wel. Unpublished Masters Thesis. University of Tilburg.

Appendix

The 10 sentences to be completed:
1. If that prisoner is guarded well, then ...
2. If John is tired, then ...
3. If Ann got presents from Santa Claus, then ...
4. If that girl is covered with mud, then ...
5. If Paul suffers from wind, then ...
6. If Mum is angry with Koen, then ...
7. If Mark is ill, then ...
8. If that man has lost his legs, then ...
9. If Anke kicks her friend, then ...
10. If the lights are out in that house, then ...

Effects of Other-generated Hypothesis on Hypothesis Revision

Sachiko Kiyokawa (kiyo@p.u-tokyo.ac.jp)
Center for Research of Core Academic Competences, Graduate school of Education, University of Tokyo,
7-3-1 Hongo Bunkyo-ku Tokyo 113-0033 Japan

Kazuhiro Ueda (ueda@gregorio.c.u-tokyo.ac.jp)
Graduate School of Arts and Sciences, University of Tokyo,
3-8-1 Komaba Meguro-ku Tokyo, 153-8902, Japan

Takeshi Okada (okadatak@p.u-tokyo.ac.jp)
Graduate school of Education, University of Tokyo,
7-3-1 Hongo Bunkyo-ku Tokyo 113-0033 Japan

Abstract

In the present study, we experimentally clarified whether other-generated hypotheses can facilitate inductive reasoning using a rule-discovery task. In two experiments, participants were randomly assigned to one of two conditions: self-generated hypothesis or other-generated hypothesis. In Experiment 1, the participants in the other-generated hypothesis condition were presented with a sequence of hypotheses which was disconfirmed twice. The result showed that those who were asked to evaluate other-generated hypotheses produced better performance than those who generated their own hypotheses and assess them. In addition, while plausibility rating of hypotheses was likely to be higher in the self-generated hypothesis condition after the participants saw counterevidence to their hypotheses, those in the other-generated hypothesis condition became lower. In Experiment 2, a sequence of other-generated hypothesis was substitute for one that was disconfirmed once. The results showed that there was no effect of other-generated hypothesis. It is interpreted that whether other-generated hypothesis facilitate hypothesis revision depends on how often one can see the other-generated hypothesis be revised.

Introduction

Previous studies have shown that people tend to persist in a particular hypothesis people entertain at that time, even though there are simpler hypotheses than those under consideration. Garst et al. (2002) showed that people are less likely to generate plausible alternative hypotheses when they already have a hypothesis which accounts for the data in hand. Nakashima (1997) found that people tend to partially, rather than drastically, revise their hypotheses when confronted with counterevidence. Moreover, it has been shown that people tend to consider only positive data to their own hypotheses (Wason, 1960). In sum, it can be said that we have difficulty in revising hypotheses appropriately on the basis of observed data. Therefore, it is important to identify how to facilitate hypotheses revision in order for us to reasoning appropriately.

In this study, we will clarify the effects of source of hypotheses, that is, the effects of other-generated hypothesis on hypothesis revision. Although there are several studies on them, the effects are still controversial. On the one hand, several studies have suggested that other-generated hypothesis has facilitative effects on inductive reasoning. Schunn and Klahr (1993) investigated the effects of other-generated hypotheses on inductive reasoning. They used complex microworld called Milktruck (Schunn & Klahr, 1992). The results showed that giving the other-generated hypothesis led participants to investigate the plausibility of hypotheses more thoroughly and less false terminations with incorrect solutions.

Adsit and London (1997) examined the extent to which hypothesis generation affects hypothesis-testing performance using a rule-discovery task. Participants were randomly assigned to one of four conditions: self-generated, other-generated, experimenter-supplied, or control. Hypothesis-testing performance in the experimenter-supplied condition was significantly higher than in the other conditions, suggesting that other-generated hypothesis has positive effects on inductive reasoning only if it is correct one.

On the other hand, there are also some studies showing the negative effects of other-generated hypothesis on hypothesis revision. Koelher (1994) showed that the participants who were asked to generate their own hypotheses expressed less confidence on them than those who were presented with the same hypotheses for evaluation. Furthermore, the participants who generated their own hypotheses appeared to be more sensitive to their accuracy than were those who evaluated the hypotheses. Koelher (1994) interpreted the results as evidence that the hypothesis generation task leads the participants to consider more alternative hypotheses than those who are asked to evaluate a prespecified hypothesis.

The purpose of this study is to determine what effects other-generated hypotheses have on inductive reasoning, especially on hypothesis revision in a rule-discovery task and when other-generated hypothesis can facilitate inductive reasoning.

Experiment 1

Method

Participants Sixty-seven undergraduates participated in the experiment for course credit.

Task We used a modified version of the rule discovery task proposed by Nakashima (1997). In the task, 30 pairs of figures with results derived from a predetermined rule were presented in a booklet, one per page. Each pair incorporated three dimensions: frame (a triangle or a square), number (a whole number from 1 to 9), and side dimensions (left or right) (See Figure 1). Each time they viewed a pair of figures, the participants were asked to search for the rule by which the winner of the figure pair could be decided and to evaluate their plausibility on an 11-point scale (0: not certain at all to 10: very certain).

Conditions and Procedures Participants were randomly assigned to one of two conditions: *self-generated hypothesis or other-generated hypothesis.*

In the self-generated hypothesis condition, the participants (N=31) were asked to generate their own hypotheses and to evaluate their plausibility each time they viewed a pair of figures.

In the other-generated hypothesis condition, the participants (N=36) were presented with a series of other-generated hypotheses as well as pairs of figures (See Table 1) and were required to evaluate plausibility on them until 14th pair of figures. After 15th instance was presented, the participants were asked to generate their own hypotheses and to assess their plausibility in the same way as those in the self-generated hypothesis condition.

The series of hypotheses presented in the other-generated hypothesis condition was typical one generated by most participants in the previous study (Kiyokawa et al., 2003). As shown in Table 1, from 1st to 5th instance, hypothesis was related only to number dimension. Because the hypothesis was disconfirmed at 6th instance, the hypothesis was revised to new hypothesis which involves number and frame dimensions. Because the hypothesis also turned out to be inconsistent with the 11th instance, the hypothesis was revised again. Note that these presented hypotheses were different from the correct rule.

Figure 1: An example of instance presented to the participants. A circle represents that the figure above it is the "winner."

Table 1: The sequence of hypotheses presented in the other-generated hypothesis condition in Experiment 1.

# of instance	Other-generated hypothesis
1 to 5	The figure with the larger number is the "winner."
6 to 10	If the numbers in the figures are different from each other, then the one with larger number is the "winner". Otherwise, square is the "winner."
11 to 14	Suppose that a square means 4 and a triangle means 3 and add these numbers to each number in the figures. Then the larger is the "winner."

Results

Effects of other-generated hypotheses on performance In order to determine whether the other-generated hypotheses could facilitate hypotheses revision, we examined the participants' final rules in the task.

The correct rule was, "Add one to the number in the right figure and compare that with the number in the left figure; the larger is the winner." This rule involved just two dimensions: the numbers in the figures (number dimension) and the side on which the figures were located (side dimension). The frame dimension was irrelevant to the rule; but if the participants considered frame, they might either generate more complicated rules than the correct one or be unable to discover the correct rule at all. Despite its irrelevance, the frame dimension tended to be related to the rule by participants more often than the side dimension. We were able to examine whether the participants could revise their hypotheses appropriately by evaluating their final rules, because they could make rules consistent with all the evidence (in terms of the combination of the number and frame dimensions) by the 15th pair of figures.

The rules were evaluated in terms of consistency with the results and parsimony, and were classified into the following four categories: *Inconsistent, Redundant, Branching-off,* and *Correct.* Inconsistent rules were inconsistent with any of the evidence provided. The inconsistent rules violated the instruction that the rule should be able to explain all the results, and thus this category of rules was considered to represent the lowest level of performance. The Redundant rules included an unnecessary dimension. As the correct rule involved only two dimensions, the frame dimension was unnecessary. All rules that were consistent with all the evidence but that included the frame dimension were, therefore, classified as

Redundant rules. The Branching-off rules were consistent with all the evidence provided and did not include an unnecessary dimension, but were subdivided. As the correct rule had no subdivisions, the Branching-off rules were more complicated than necessary. The Correct rule was the simplest rule among all the rules that was consistent with all the evidence provided. The proportion of each rule category is shown in Figure 2.

We compared the proportion of each category in the self-generated hypothesis condition with that in the other-generated hypothesis condition and found that the proportion of each rule category was significantly different among conditions (p<0.05; Fisher's exact test). Residual analyses revealed that there were more Inconsistent rules in the self-generated hypothesis condition (z=2.28, p<0.05), and fewer Inconsistent rules in the other-generated hypothesis condition (z=-2.28, p< 0.05) than the expected value.

These results support the hypothesis that other-generated hypothesis can facilitate hypothesis revision and produce higher performance in inductive reasoning.

Effects of other-generated hypotheses on plausibility judgment Figure 3 shows the means of plausibility ratings in each condition as function of time of plausibility judgment. Until the 11th instance was presented, plausibility ratings were higher in the other-generated hypotheses condition than in the self-generated hypotheses condition. After the 12th instance, however, the pattern of plausibility ratings reversed.

In order to examine significance of the observation, we conducted a 2 X 3 (Condition X Timing of plausibility judgment) mixed analysis of variance (ANOVA). The ANOVA revealed significant interaction (F(1,53)=7.61, p<0.01). A simple main effect of timing of plausibility judgment in the self-generated hypothesis condition was marginally significant (F(1,53)=3.03, p=0.09), suggesting the plausibility ratings after the 11th instance were higher than those before it.

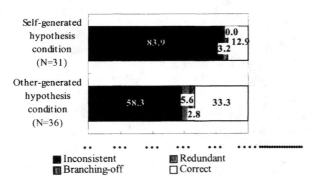

Figure 2: The proportion of each rule category in each condition in Experiment 1.

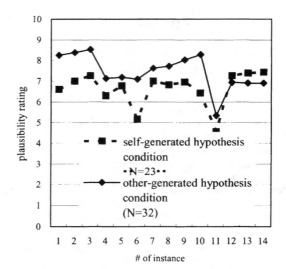

Figure 3: Means of plausibility rating in each condition in Experiment 1.

In contrast, a simple main effect of timing of plausibility judgment in the other-generated hypothesis condition was significant (F(1,53)=4.67, p<0.05), showing that the plausibility ratings before the 11th instance were higher than those after it.

In sum, plausibility ratings increase in the self-generated hypotheses condition after 11th instance, they decrease in the other-generated hypotheses condition.

Discussion

The results of Experiment 1 suggested that other-generated hypothesis can facilitate hypothesis revision and produce higher performance in inductive reasoning. In addition, significant interaction between condition and timing on plausibility judgment was observed. Specifically, while the plausibility ratings increased after the 11th instance in the self-generated hypothesis condition, those decreased in the other-generated hypothesis condition. It may be that direction of change in plausibility ratings is related to the possibility of hypothesis revision.

Why did the plausibility ratings change between before and after the 11th instance? One possible interpretation is that the effects of other-generated hypothesis depend on whether people can observe disconfirmation of hypothesis or not. In the other-generated hypothesis condition, the first hypothesis was disconfirmed at the 6th instance and the second one was disconfirmed at the 11th instance. In short, the participants in the other-generated hypothesis condition were able to experience disconfirmation of hypothesis twice. It is possible that the experience prevents the participants from being overconfident of a particular hypothesis in the other-generated hypothesis condition.

Experiment 2

The purpose of Experiment 2 is to examine the effects of other-generated hypothesis on inductive reasoning when the hypothesis is disconfirmed once. If disconfirmation is important for the facilitative effect of other-generated hypothesis, it is expected that the same effect as that in Experiment 1will not be obtained in Experiment 2. However, If disconfirmation is not so important, it is expected that the same effect as that in Experiment 1 will be observed in Experiment 2.

Method

Participants Sixty-two undergraduates participated in the experiment for course credit.

Task The task was the same as in Experiment 1.

Conditions and Procedures Conditions were identical to those in Experiment 1, except that a series of hypotheses presented in the other-generated hypothesis condition was changed. As shown in Table 2, the other-generated hypothesis presented in Experiment 2was disconfirmed and revised at once. Because the hypothesis at 14th instance in the other-generated hypothesis condition of Experiment 2 was same as that in the condition of Experiment 1, the difference between both other-generated hypothesis conditions was only in the times of disconfirming and revising hypothesis.

Results

Effects of other-generated hypotheses on performance The participants' final rules were evaluated in the same way as in Experiment 1; the proportion of each rule category is shown in Figure 4.

Table 2: The sequence of hypotheses presented in the other-generated hypothesis condition in Experiment 2.

# of instance	Other-generated hypothesis
1 to 5	The figure with the larger number is the "winner."
6 to 14	Suppose that a square means 4 and a triangle means 3 and add these numbers to each number in the figures. Then the larger is the "winner."

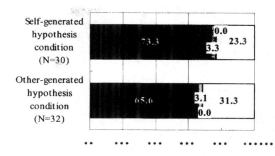

■ Inconsistent ▨ Redundant
▨ Branching-off □ Correct

Figure 4: The proportion of each rule category in each condition in Experiment 2.

The results showed that the proportion of each rule category was not significantly different among conditions (p>0.10; Fisher's exact test). In conclusion, the facilitative effect of other-generated hypothesis was not obtained in Experiment 2.

Effects of other-generated hypotheses on plausibility judgment Figure 5 shows the means of plausibility ratings in each condition as function of time of plausibility judgment. As shown in Figure 5, contrary to the results of Experiment 1, there was no change between before and after the 11th instance.

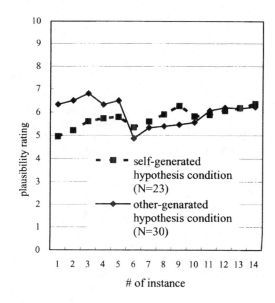

Figure 5: Means of plausibility rating in each condition in Experiment 2.

Instead, there was change between before and after the 6th instance. Specifically, until the 5th instance was presented, plausibility ratings were higher in the other-generated hypotheses condition than in the self-generated hypotheses condition. After the 6th instance, however, the pattern of plausibility ratings reversed. Finally, the ratings in both conditions became nearly equal.

Discussion

In Experiment 2, the facilitative effect of other-generated hypothesis on inductive reasoning was not obtained. The difference between Experiment 1 and 2 lies only in the sequence of other-generated hypothesis. In other words, the participants in Experiment 1 experienced more disconfirmation than those in Experiment 2. It can be said that disconfirmation is important for the facilitative effect of other-generated hypothesis on inductive reasoning to emerge.

General Discussion

In this study, we experimentally examined the effects of source of hypotheses on inductive reasoning in terms of the performance of a rule discovery task and in terms of plausibility ratings. In Experiment 1, it was revealed that the other-generated hypotheses were more likely to revise than the self-generated ones. In addition, the results showed that the plausibility ratings became higher in the self-generated hypotheses condition after 11th instance, while it decreased in the other-generated hypotheses condition. In Experiment 2, on the other hand, the facilitative effects were not obtained even though other-generated hypothesis similar to that in Experiment 1 was presented.

What can account for the dissociation between these results? These results can be interpreted in terms of experience of disconfirmation. As shown in Experiment 1 and 2, other-generated hypothesis is evaluated as more plausible than self-generated one as long as they are confirmed. However the more often hypothesis is disconfirmed; the more likely it is that plausibility rating on other-generated hypothesis decreases. Therefore, other-generated hypothesis can facilitate hypothesis revision and produce better performance in inductive reasoning when disconfirmation is possible. The dissociation among previous studies mentioned earlier can be interpreted in terms of disconfirmation.

In Koelher's (1994) experiment, the participants were asked to generate their own hypotheses or to evaluate other-generated hypotheses only at a time. Therefore, they were not able to experience disconfirmation of these hypotheses. As a result, other-generated hypotheses were evaluated as more plausible than self-generated ones.

In Schunn and Klahr's (1993) experiment, on the other hand, the participants were asked to test their own or other-generated hypotheses, therefore, they were able to experience disconfirmation. As a consequence, the plausibility ratings decreased in the other-generated hypothesis condition. Schunn and Klahr (1993) have suggested that skepticism increased when people evaluate other-generated hypotheses. Because an increase in skepticism could prevent participants from persisting particular hypotheses, the participants in the other-generated hypothesis condition revised the hypotheses more easily than those in the self-generated hypothesis condition. Taken together, it could be interpreted that the participants in the other-generated hypothesis condition revised their hypotheses more easily than those in the self-generated hypothesis condition; in consequence, other-generated hypotheses produced better performance.

In sum, it may be interpreted that plausibility ratings depends on whether there are opportunity of facing counterevidence to the hypotheses under consideration. In other words, under condition when one can encounter counterevidence, the other-generated hypotheses may be evaluated more accurately than the self-generated ones.

This study can contribute to uncover one of the processes of collaborative problem solving. Several researches have showed that collaboration is effective in solving scientific problems (e. g. Kiyokawa, Ueda & Okada, 2003; Okada & Simon, 1997). Since, in collaborative problem solving, members exchange their own ideas and evaluate them with each other, there are many opportunities assessing the other-generated hypotheses. It may be interpreted that the effects of the other-generated hypotheses is responsible for the effects of collaboration on scientific reasoning. Shirouzu, Miyake, and Masukawa (2002) have suggested that frequent role exchange between a Task-Doer and a Monitor in collaborative problem solving involved shift in strategies and produced better performance. In addition, they pointed out that a Monitor can have wider point of view that a Task-Doer.

It is necessary to examine the effects of types of hypotheses presented to participants as other-generated ones on hypotheses revision in more detail. In addition, it should be investigated whether the other-generated hypotheses affects the way of experimentation using a more realistic and complex task such as Milktruck (Schunn & Klahr, 1992)

Conclusion

In the present study, we experimentally clarified whether assessing other-generated hypotheses could facilitate later hypotheses revision using a rule-discovery task. At first, participants were asked either to generate their own hypotheses and assess them or to evaluate the hypotheses presented as other-generated hypotheses. After that, all participants were required to generate their own hypotheses and evaluate their plausibility.

The results showed that participants who assessed the other-generated hypotheses produced better performance than those who generated their own hypotheses and assess them. In addition, while plausibility on their own hypotheses became higher as the participants saw instances in the self-generated hypothesis condition, plausibility on the hypotheses became lower in the other-generated hypothesis condition.

It was concluded that the source of hypotheses affected the plausibility on the hypothesis, especially after the participants were faced with the counterevidence to their hypotheses. In other words, other-generated hypotheses were evaluated as less confident than self-generated ones after the data inconsistent with the hypotheses was presented, which enabled the participants to revise hypotheses more easily in the other-generated hypothesis condition than in the self-generated hypothesis condition.

References

Adsit, D. J. & London, M. (1997). Effects of hypothesis generation on hypothesis testing in rule-discovery tasks. *The Journal of General Psychology, 124*, 35-47.

Freedman, E. G. (1992). Scientific induction: Individual versus group processes and multiple hypotheses. *Proceedings of the 14th Annual Conference of the Cognitive Science Society* (pp. 183-188). Hillsdale, NJ: Erlbaum Abstract.

Garst, J., Kerr, N. L., Harris, S. E., & Sheppard, L. A(2002). •• Satisfying in hypothesis generation. *American Journal of* ••*Psychology, 115*, 475-500.

Kiyokawa, S., Ueda, K., & Okada, T. (2003). The effect of metacognitive suggestions on viewpoint change in collaborative problem solving. *Proceedings of the 4th International Conference on Cognitive Science and the Annual Meeting of the 7th Australian Cognitive Science Society Joint Conference.* [In CD-ROM]

Koehler, D. J. (1994). Hypothesis generation and confidence in judgment. *Journal of Experimental Psychology: Learning, Memory and Cognition, 20*, 461-469.

Miyake, N. (1986). Constructive interaction and the iterative process of understanding. *Cognitive Science, 10*, 151-177.

Nakashima, N. (1997). The role of counterevidence in rule revision; The effects of instructing metaknowledge concerning non adhocness of theory. *Japanese Journal of Educational Psychology, 45*, 263-273. [in Japanese]

Okada, T. & Simon, H. A. (1997). Collaborative discovery in a scientific domain. *Cognitive Science, 21*, 109-146.

Schunn, C. D., & Klahr, D. (1992). Complexity management in a discovery task. *Proceedings of the 14th Annual Conference of the Cognitive Science Society* (pp.177-182). Hillsdale, NJ: Erlbaum.Abstract.

Schunn, C. D., & Klahr, D. (1993). Self- vs. other-generated hypothesis in scientific discovery. *Proceedings of the 15th Annual Conference of the Cognitive Science Society* (pp. 900-905). Hillsdale, NJ: Erlbaum.

Shirouzu, H., Miyake, N., & Masukawa, H. (2002). Cognitively active externalization for situated reflection. *Cognitive Science, 26*, 469-501.

Cooperation through communication: Reciprocal exchange of relevant information among humans involved in strategic interaction

Francesca Giardini (francesca.giardini@istc.cnr.it),
Gennaro Di Tosto (gennaro.ditosto@istc.cnr.it)
Institute of Cognitive Sciences and Technologies, Via San Martino della Battaglia 44
Roma, 00185 ITALY

Abstract

In this preliminary study we examine whether and how people cooperate in a special kind of memory game where exchange of messages containing relevant information about the game was allowed. We explore the role of communication not as an external device of the game, but as the mean of coordination. We hypothesize that people cooperate until their partners in the game do cooperate, we expect that cooperation is mediated by a norm of reciprocity. Deviations from the norm are found to be sanctioned with exclusion from the communication. This means that non cooperative behavior is not imitated, but more subtle forms of punishment are applied.

Introduction

Humans often adopt cooperative behaviors, and this tendency toward cooperation represents one of the most debated human features in a wide variety of disciplines. Cooperation is usually termed as a puzzling phenomenon (Boyd & Richerson, 2006; Noe, 2006), whose motives and mechanisms are still obscure. This is partially due to the lack of agreement on the definition of cooperation *per se*, which leads to a terminological and conceptual confusion between altruism, reciprocity and cooperation (Croson, *forthcoming*).

Noe (2006) identifies in the experimental literature three main uses of the term: cooperation as a certain type of interaction with a specific form or outcome, as a strategy used by members in an interaction, or even as a characteristic of a long-term relationship. Here, we focus on the meaning of cooperation as a strategy people adopt in a coordination game, and we will investigate how normative reasoning can pave the way for the emergence and the maintenance of cooperation.

The positive effects of communication on rates of cooperation is a robust experimental finding. When individuals can talk to one other, cooperation increases significantly. Proposed explanations to this phenomenon consider the formation of group identity (Kollock, 1998), as well as the chance to make explicit commitments (Kritikos & Meran, 1998)—where reputational and moral factors come into play (Milinski et al., 2002)—as fundamental causes. This research, however, looks at communication as a way of establishing and enforcing cooperation among people; to our knowledge, no attempt has been made to analyze communication strategies, when

communication processes are actually the place where cooperation evolve.

We developed a novel experimental setting in which participants playing a memory game (with numbers instead of images) could either play alone, or exchange messages containing the position and the value of the cards, so that those who received a truthful message could more easily get a match. This setting was conceptually modeled after the *stag hunt game* (Boyd & Richerson, 2006; Skyrms, 2001), a coordination game in which players do better if they coordinate their behavior with the behavior of others. In our setting, playing alone is like hunting hare, a solitary activity that leads to small payoffs, whereas exchanging relevant information is analogous to hunting stag. In the latter case, players engage in a mutually beneficial activity whose results are faster exploration of the game board and the resulting higher probability of getting a match. In our experiment, playing alone is faster than sending messages, but it leads to a quicker depletion of the available moves (for further details see Experiment section). On the contrary, sending messages is more time consuming, but it allows players to know the position of cards, provided the information is correct, without wasting moves in trying to guess. Moreover, participants can decide how many addressees their message can have, choosing from three alternatives: group message, private message and sub-group message. Whether one or many receivers are selected depends upon the preferred strategy, which is conditional to the expected contribution of other players.

In this framework, the exchange of valuable information is a costly action, analogous to other costly behaviors normally considered inside the game-theoretic literature. We are thus concerned with whether and how cooperative behavior gives rise to the emergence of a norm which sustains and promotes cooperation, including the punishment of those who do not cooperate. Our hypothesis is that cooperative behavior is mediated by normative reasoning that leads people to cooperate, in our case by sending group messages, and to expect cooperation in return. When this expectation is not fulfilled, subjects punish those who do not cooperate, by excluding them from communication. More specifically:

- Communication through group messages is a mutually beneficial activity, allowing participants to jointly discover the game board, to score higher and more

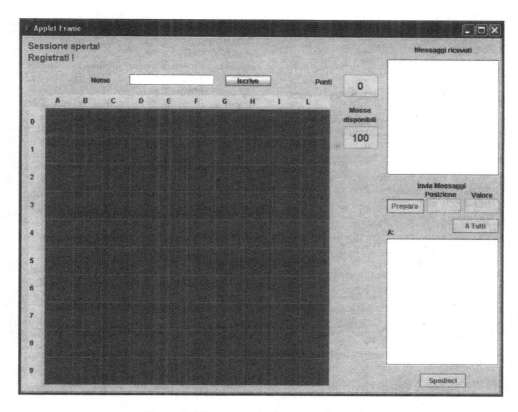

Figure 1: The customized graphical interface

efficiently.

- Cooperation through communication is conditional to receiving messages from other participants. This strategic behavior could be explained according to two alternative frameworks (Conte & Castelfranchi, 1995):

  1. game-theoretical interpretation of reciprocity, analyzed as an imitation strategy (Tit-For-Tat).
  2. a cognitive view in which cooperative behavior is regarded as a socially prescribed activity, and every deviation from the norm is punished according to the interpretation of the violation.

Following these two alternative hypotheses, we expect subjects to show different reactions to non-cooperative use of the communication process. If the Tit-For-Tat interpretation holds, then we should observe subjects reciprocating by means of imitation (i.e. returning false information to sender of false information, and refraining from cooperation with people who do not communicate). In the other case, the cognitive interpretation of the normative prescription predicts a different behavior: non-cooperators are excluded from the benefits of cooperation.

The experiment was conducted using a customized computer graphical interface featuring a mechanism to send and receive messages to and from other participants (see Figure 1). Computer mediated communication is known to be less effective than face-to-face communication in the establishment of cooperation (Brosig et al., 2003), even though, in the present study, it offered the possibility to control and monitor the information flow, to reduce the complexity and ambiguity of natural language and to clearly distinguish between false and truthful communication.

We acknowledge from the start that our study is exploratory and that further studies are needed to put forward firm conclusions about the effect of normative reasoning on cooperation in a coordination game setting. This is a critical issue which deserves a deeper theoretical analysis as well as more experimentally grounded results.

Experiment

To test whether and how people cooperate by exchanging relevant information, we designed a novel experimental setting using the well-known memory cards game. Players had to find the greatest number of matching pairs among all cards placed face-down on the game board. We modified the game, adding two constraints:

Moves limit the subjects were allowed 100 moves to play the game; two cards selected equaled one move. Once the available moves were exhausted, the game ended.

Time limit each session lasts a maximum of 10 minutes. Players are not informed about the exact length of the experiment.

Card selection and communication processes were concurrent activities; participants decided autonomously whether to communicate with other subjects or to play alone. The game and the communication platform were implemented on a client-server software architecture. On the client side, the user interface is composed of:

- A board of 50 pairs of cards, numbered form 0 to 49, placed in a 10 x 10 matrix and identified by their coordinates (LETTER; number).

- The message preparation form, composed of a list of the other participants, from whom the user could select the receiver(s); two boxes comprising the content of the communication (that is, the card's coordinates and value); and a button to send the messages.

- The incoming message frame, displaying a list of the messages received by the subject, each message being a pair of *card's coordinates* and *card's value*, plus the *nickname* of the sender.

- A display of the score —the number of matching cards discovered in the board.

- A display of the number of moves remaining. When the player(s) use up those 100 moves, the computer program automatically blocked that player's session, and the subject was prevented from continuing the game and also from sending messages.

Participants

Twenty-four students from the University of Siena, Italy (11 male, 13 female), mean age 22.71 ($SD = 2.19$), volunteered to participate in the experiment and were paid a 5 euro show-up fee, along with their earnings for participation in the experiment for one hour of experimental time (mean earnings = 7.90 Euros, plus the show-up fee). Subjects were assigned randomly to one of 4 groups of six subjects. Each subjects participated in 3 sessions of the game. They were naïve with respect to the nature and aims of the experiment.

Procedure

The game The subjects were assigned to one of four groups; each group was tested separately along three 10 minute sessions (with a 5 minutes interval between them and a short training session at the very beginning, lasting 3 minutes). The participants, registered in the system using nicknames to preserve anonymity, played a memory card game together, on different computers but with the same game board. At the beginning of the game, all cards were laid face-down, and subjects were provided with 100 moves to explore the board: one mouse-click revealed the value of the chosen card. Each time they uncovered a pair of cards with the same value, one point was added to their score and the matching cards remained face-up on that player's board.

Communication During the exploration of the board, subjects could send information about uncovered cards through the interface. No other forms of communication were allowed. The designed procedure required them to activate the message preparation phase, then select the coordinates of a card by mouse-clicking on it and entering its value. The system did not check the content of the communication, so participants had the possibility of sending false messages, as either an intentional lie or an unintentional typing error. To send the message, subjects should select one, more than one, or even all of the possible recipients from the list of active participants, and then press the "send" button, generating a *Private*, *Sub-group* or *Group* message, respectively. All messages then appeared in the incoming message frame of the receiver(s), in chronological order and until the end of the session.

Questionnaires

After the three experimental sessions, participants responded to a questionnaire designed to assess the utility, from the standpoint of participants' perception, of the messages and highlight the emergence of communicative strategies. The questionnaire comprised 4 questions (1. "Did you send at least 5 messages to the other participants? Yes or No"; 2. "Provided you sent messages, they were: a. mostly true; b. mostly false; c. always true; d. always false"; 3. "Provided you sent messages, these were addressed: a. to everybody; b. to someone on purpose; c. to someone by chance; d. to those who already sent me a message."; 4. "Do you believe that receiving messages affected your final score? Yes or No"), plus a blank space where subjects were required to briefly explain why they exchanged messages with other players.

Results

The results showed that subjects' mean score (see Figure 2) significantly increased between the first and second session for each group of subjects (Wilcoxon rank sum test, $Z = 402$, $p = 0.009$), and between first and third session ($Z = 452$, $p < .001$); we found no significant differences between the second and third session ($Z = 342$, $p = 0.134$).

The average number of sent messages (see Figure 3) increased all along the experiment. On the contrary, no significant difference was observed in the number of moves used by subjects over the different sections (J-T test[1], *trend p − value = 0.984, rank correlation = −0.002*).

Figure 4 shows a significant change in the communicative strategy of subjects. In the first session they almost equally used single ($M = 1.37; SD = 2.93$), group ($M = 1.41; SD = 2.63$) and subgroup messages ($M = 2.41; SD = 2.60$), whereas they decisively turned to the group message in the second (Single $M = 0.87$ with $SD = 1.96$; SubGroup $M = 0.91$ with $SD = 1.66$; Group $M = 5.83$ with $SD = 2.83$) and in the third session (Single $M = 0.91$ with $SD = 2.82$; SubGroup

---

[1]performed using the R package SAGx

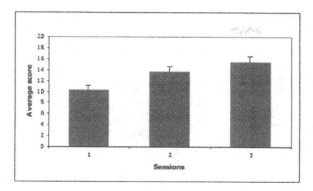

Figure 2: Average score of each session among all the groups of subjects ($N = 24$). Average scores in the second and third sessions are significantly higher than the one of the first session.

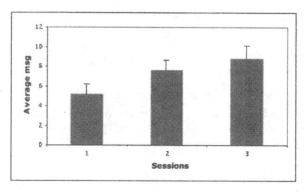

Figure 3: Average number of sent messages along the three sessions, $N = 24$.

$M = 0.58$ with $SD = 1.10$; Group $M = 7.29$ with $SD = 6.81$).

The percentage of false messages was extremely low, as showed in Figure 5(a). The highest number of false messages was observed in Group 3. In the same group we found the greatest number of Sub-group messages (see Figure 5(b)).

A chi-squared test of independence was performed to examine the relationship between score and received messages. The relation between these variables was significant, $\chi^2 (2, N = 24) = 18.95, p = 0.025$. There was a positive relationship between score and number of received messages. A second chi-squared test of independence was performed to examine the relationship between received messages and sent messages. The relation between these variables was significant, $\chi^2 (2, N = 24) = 28.79, p < .001$.

The analysis of the responses to the questionnaire showed that all subjects sent at least 5 messages. The great majority (90%) responded they used "always true" messages, whereas some (10%) responded "mostly true" messages. Group messages prevailed (90%) and all sub-

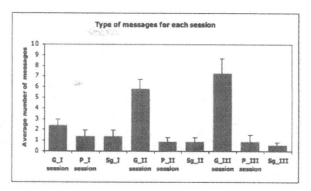

Figure 4: Group, Sub-group and Private messages' average number in each session.

jects agreed about the existence of a correlation between received messages and their score. We grouped the responses about personal motives for communication into two classes: conditional and unconditional cooperation. The 70% of participants responded they sent messages "in order to receive messages from other players", whereas the remaining 30% reported that they "communicated with the aim to help other people in getting matches".

Discussion

Our results, although preliminary, seem to show that cooperation through communication emerged and evolved in a coordination game. In the memory game, the possibility to exchange relevant information with other players puts the participants in front of a social dilemma: to cooperate or to play alone? Sending messages was a useful tool for saving moves and, at the same time, quickly uncovering the game board, provided all cooperate. On the contrary, playing alone was less time consuming, and it was a better strategy when others did not cooperate. Participants to our experiment solved the social dilemma in a cooperative way: they sent messages to other players expecting messages in return. This choice was rewarding, as demonstrated by the positive dependence between average score and received messages; communication seems at least equally important in the interpretation of the observed behavior. The preference for cooperation emerged also in responding to the questionnaires, since people recognized the importance of cooperation, and the great majority of them explicitly declared that they sent messages "in order to receive messages from other players" (as written by many subjects).

However, we are not able to rule out the possibility of an increase in the subjects' score due to a learning effect: participants' mnemonic skills improved during the experiment as an effect of the stimulus exposure. Also, an alternative explanation can be put forward: participants do not only improved their memory, they also learned that sending messages will be repaid with other messages, and these two combined effects can explain the constant increase in the number of exchanged messages

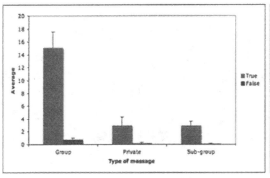

(a) Average messages per type.

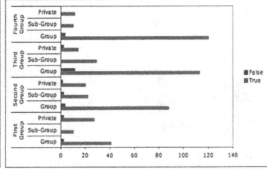

(b) Types of messages per group.

Figure 5: Distribution of true and false messages: (a) Average number of true and false Group, Sub-Group and Private messages (b) Absolute number of true and false messages divided by group of subjects.

and in the score. Moreover, the prevalence of truthful communication can be interpreted as further evidence of cooperative behavior, since participants did not try to negatively interfere with others by sending false messages, but mostly sent true messages. In this setting, cooperation is an equilibrium whose emergence is favored by cooperative behavior, and whose maintenance requires a cognitively mediated form of reciprocation.

Game-theoretic approaches predict a Tit-for-Tat strategy in these cases, but in the third group of subjects we found a different behavior. Non-cooperators (liars or people avoiding communication) were not directly retaliated against, but they were excluded from communication: subjects who spread false information were excluded from further communication—but were not the addressee of following false messages—as well as subjects who refused to share their information; that is the reason why we observed the formation of subgroups, where cooperative participants coordinate playing the game. This is further confirmation of the importance of cooperation, which was actively pursued but also withheld from noncooperators. These exploratory findings support the hypothesis that, to preserve cooperation from the exploitation of non-cooperative people, strategic interaction does not rely upon a mere mirroring behavior, but it requires a fully cognitive means-ends reasoning. Unfortunately, we observed this behavior in only one group, thus new investigations and a greater number of subjects are required to fully validate this hypothesis.

Beacuse this is an exploratory study that utilizes a novel setting, some adjustments are needed. For instance, the computer interface might be a bit tricky. To send a message subjects had to activate the message preparation phase in order to select coordinates and value of a card and, finally, to select one or more (even all) recipients from the list of active participants. Another potentially influential point was the difference between the time and the effort required to select one or more participants, compared to the ease of sending a message to "all addressees". In fact, in the latter case, subjects had an *All* button that automatically selected all other players. Moreover, the number of participants to this study is actually too scarce, and an enlargement of the set of subjects is required.

Acknowledgements

We would like to thank Rosaria Conte for her helpful comments, Daniele Denaro for his fundamental contribution in the experimental software development, and Antonietta di Salvatore for her help with the statistical analysis of results. This work was partially supported by the European Community under the FP6 programme (eRep project, contract number CIT5-028575) and by the Italian Ministry of University and Scientific Research under the Firb programme (Socrate project, contract number RBNE03Y338).

References

Boyd, R. & Richerson, P. J. (2006). *Culture and the Evolution of the Human Social Instincts.* Berg, Oxford.

Brosig, J., Weimann, J., & Ockenfels, A. (2003). The effect of communication media on cooperation. *German Economic Review*, 4(2):217–241.

Conte, R. & Castelfranchi, C. (1995). *Cognitive and Social Acition.* UCL Press, London.

Croson, R. T. A. (forthcoming). *Differentiating Altruism and Reciprocity.* Elsevier, Amsterdam.

Kollock, P. (1998). Social dilemmas: The anatomy of cooperation. *Annual Reviews of Sociology*, 24:183–214.

Kritikos, A. & Meran, G. (1998). Social norms, moral commitment, and cooperation. *Homo Oeconomicus*, 15:71–92.

Milinski, M., Semmann, D., & Krambeck, H.-J. (2002). Reputation helps solve the 'tragedy of the commons'. *Nature*, 415(6870):424–426.

Noe, R. (2006). Cooperation experiments: coordination through communication versus acting apart together. *Animal Behaviour*, 71(1):1–18.

Skyrms, B. (2001). The stag hunt. *Proceedings and Addresses of the American Philosophical Association*, 75(2):31–41.

Is Cooperation in the Iterated Prisoner's Dilemma Game Due to Social Interaction?

Maurice Grinberg (mgrinberg@nbu.bg)
Central and Eastern European Center for Cognitive Science,
New Bulgarian University, 21 Montevideo Street, 1618 Sofia, Bulgaria

Evgenia Hristova (ehristova@cogs.nbu.bg)
Central and Eastern European Center for Cognitive Science,
New Bulgarian University, 21 Montevideo Street, 1618 Sofia, Bulgaria

Abstract

The comparison of four forms of presentation of the same sequence of Prisoner's Dilemma games reveals considerable differences in the way people play the game and cooperate. Cooperation was the smallest when participants had full information about the game's payoffs and about the presence of an opponent. Surprisingly, in the simple reinforcement condition – no explicit game, two choices, and a received payoff given – the largest cooperation was observed. This result seems to contradict the explanations of cooperation in PD games which attribute cooperation to social interactions involving altruism, reputation and reciprocity. In order to investigate this phenomenon in detail two other intermediate situations were tested: no game context but four possible payoffs and two choices and full PD game with no information about the specific payoffs but just about their relative magnitude and information about the opponent's moves. The results from the comparisons show that more information about the game leads to lower cooperation and thus in a 'social interaction' condition (game with an opponent) the cooperation and the received payoffs are much lower than in a reinforcement condition (two choices and payoffs).

Introduction

Prisoner's Dilemma (PD) Game

The PD game is a two-person game. It is widely used as a model of social interaction. The interest in studying PD game arises from the idea that many social situations and problems such as overpopulation, pollution, energy savings, participation in a battle, etc. have such a dilemma structure (Dawes, 1980). It is especially used as a tool for studying cooperative behavior. There are thousands of studies exploring various factors influencing the players' behavior. Such factors range from changing the payoffs to changing the description of the game and the way it is presented to the subjects (Colman, 1995).

The payoff table for this game is presented in Figure 1. The players simultaneously choose their move – C (cooperate) or D (defect), without knowing their opponent's choice. R is the payoff if both cooperate (play C), P is the payoff if both "defect" (play D), T is the payoff if one defects and the other cooperates, S is the payoff if one cooperates by playing C and the other defects by playing D. An important characteristic of the payoff matrix is that payoffs satisfy the inequalities $T > R > P > S$ and $2R > T + S$.

		Player II	
		C	*D*
Player I	*C*	R, R	S, T
	D	T, S	P, P

Figure 1: Payoff table for the PD game. In each cell the comma separated payoffs are the Player I's and Player II's ones, respectively.

In the Prisoner's dilemma game each player gets higher payoff for a defecting choice no matter what the other player does. So D is the dominant strategy. On the other hand, each player is better if all cooperate than if all defect. However, even if for some reason both players manage to cooperate, and the outcome is CC, still it is not a Nash equilibrium because it is unstable due to the temptation to defect (and get the largest payoff T, see Figure 1). So, standard game theory predicts that players should always chose D. However, people quite often cooperate in real life and in laboratory conditions. There are a lot of examples in real life in which people cooperate. There are also hundreds of experiments in which participants play PD games. Sally (1995) provides a meta-review of the experiments involving PD games published between 1958 and 1995 and shows that in its iterated version (the game is played many times), cooperation choices are made in 20-50 % of the games (mean 47.4 %) and even in one-shot games many players cooperate although much less than in the iterated version.

There are many theories that try to account for the contradiction between the normative predictions and the experimental results. The most influential ones are presented below.

Theories of cooperation in the PD game

A lot of theories try to explain cooperative behaviour in PD games in terms of socially established values and stress the importance of social interaction and relationships as tools for achieving cooperation. Among them are theories that explain cooperation by altruism, reciprocity or reputation building.

One of the main theories aimed to explain cooperation in iterated PD game is the *reputation building theory* (Kreps et al., 1982). The reputation building theory assumes that players are self-interested (not altruists) but the repeated nature of the game creates incentives to cooperate. In this model, the player is building himself a reputation of a cooperative player and expects that the other player will also cooperate. According to this model, cooperation should be greater in the beginning and will decline with time (because at the end of the game there is little sense in building reputation). This prediction is experimentally proven (e.g. Andreoni & Miller, 1993). However, the reputation building model applies only to repeated play of PD games and fails to explain the cooperation in one-shot games.

Reputation building is closely related to the concept of *reciprocity*. Many researchers point to the fact that the norm of reciprocity is widespread and is the basis of many relationships and societies (Trivers, 1972). People reciprocate cooperation with cooperation. One of the most studied strategies that are based on reciprocity is the tit-for-tat (TFT) strategy. A player using the TFT strategy cooperates initially, and then plays the same as his/her opponent did in the previous game. If previously the opponent was cooperative, the player is also cooperative. It is demonstrated analytically and in computer tournaments that the TFT strategy receives higher payoffs compared to other strategies in the long run (Axelrod, 1984; Komorita, 1991).

Another influential theory about cooperation in PD game is based on the concept of *altruism*. In contrast to reputation building theory, this theory assumes that some players are not strictly self-interested and benefit from cooperation and from other's payoffs (Cooper et al., 1996). For altruistic players the actual payoffs in the game are not equal to the payoffs presented in the payoff matrix. Such a player receives an additional payoff (a) when cooperating and it may happen that cooperation is no longer a dominated strategy. This is the case when $a > T - R$ and larger than $a > P - S$. Then cooperation yields higher payoffs than defection.

A different approach aimed at explaining cooperation is based on reinforcement learning models. In contrast to the theories that rely on social relations and concepts of cooperation, reinforcement learning models try to demonstrate that even in the absence of social interactions cooperation can occur as it leads to higher payoffs.

Several computational reinforcement learning models were applied in an attempt to capture players' behaviour in experimental games (see e.g. Erev & Roth, 1998; Erev & Roth, 1999; Erev & Roth, 2001; Flache & Macy, 2002; Macy & Flache, 2002; Camerer, Ho, & Chong, 2002). In the reinforcement learning models positive outcomes increase the probability that the corresponding behaviour will be repeated whereas negative outcomes reduce the probability that the associated behavior will be repeated. Usually the evaluation of the outcome as positive or negative is performed relative to an aspiration level or a reference point. Schematically a reinforcement learning model with aspiration level can be described as follows (e.g. Macy & Flache, 2002): the choices as made using a probabilistic decision rule, then the received payoffs are evaluated relative to an aspiration level, and next choice propensities are updated. Reinforcement learning models are found to be

successful in explaining important aspects of players' behavior in many repeated games (including PD). However, these models have some drawbacks. For instance the reinforcement learning models, used so far for PD game playing modeling, are 'backward looking'. Choices are modeled as depending on previous experience rather than on forward looking calculations. This presumption is doing well when the repeated game modeled consists of hundreds of repetitions of one and the same payoff matrix. However, it is not well justified in the cases when the payoff values are changing in each game and the goal is to investigate how players play a particular game. A second drawback of the reinforcement learning models is that they completely ignore the choices and payoffs of the other player (or players).

These two types approaches – the 'social interaction' and the reinforcement approach – are quite different and it is quite challenging to understand how they interact in actual choice making. It is the main goal of this paper to investigate this problem by comparing experimental data to model predictions. This is part of a larger effort of clarifying the cognitive processes underlying PD game playing (e.g. Hristova & Grinberg, 2004, 2005a, and 2005b), which displayed its context sensitivity and dependence on the acquired part of information. These experiments showed that people use different strategies. Part of the players use essentially information about the payoffs, others pay more attention to the opponent's moves. This was demonstrated both by eye-tracking and by behavioural data.

Experimental design

Four experimental conditions were designed in an attempt to separate different factors and to explore different theories. The main idea is to make different groups of participant play one and the same sequence of PD games against the same computer opponent but using different interfaces and instructions. The different interfaces ranged from a simple interface giving two choices for the player and the received payoff to a complete PD game interface with the game matrix and information about the moves, the received payoff and the total amount of points. In the former case the participants had just to make a choice and try to maximize the received payoffs without being in a game context (they ignored completely the participation of a computer player and the structure of the game). In the latter they were put in typical PD game playing condition. Two additional interfaces were included. The first is similar to the 'reinforcement' condition but with information about the possible payoffs (without specifying the correspondence between moves and payoffs) and the second representing a PD game but with information only about the moves of the opponent and the structure of the game matrix without the actual payoffs. Thus the experiment consisted of four experimental conditions enforcing different framing of the same situation and different type of available information.

In all four conditions participants played against one and the same computer player which used a modified version of TFT strategy. The computer player takes into account the last two moves of the participant and plays the same move, if both previous moves were the same, with probability 0.8

or makes a move (*C* or *D*) with probability 0.5, if the previous moves were different.

In all four instructions it was emphasized that the subject should aim at receiving maximum points and not compete with the computer player. Cooperation or defection was mentioned neither in the game interface nor in the instructions. The possible moves were labeled '1' and '2'. Each participant played 300 PD games with randomly generated payoffs. The lowest payoff S was always taken to be zero. The payoffs were hold within some limits in order to avoid difference-in-magnitude effects. All subjects were paid for the participation according to points they got during the experiment. Throughout the game, participants could monitor the cumulative number of received points and its money equivalent (except for the *Move-PD* condition, see the explanation below).

A total of 89 participants took part in the experiment: 18 in the *Blind-PD* condition, 26 in the *Row-PD* condition, 22 in the *Move-PD* condition, and 23 in the *Full-PD* condition. Each subject participated in only one experimental condition. The differences between the four conditions are outlined below.

The *Blind-PD* condition

Participants in this condition saw only two possible moves labeled '1' and '2'. After choosing a move, they received a certain payoff. They didn't get any other information, e.g. that they were playing against the computer or that their payoff depends not only on their choice but also on the computer's choice. Participants didn't even see the payoff matrix. This condition was supposed to lead to a simple backward reinforcement learning type of behaviour taken to be a kind of baseline as compared to the other three conditions.

The *Row-PD* condition

Here, we tried to eliminate the influence of the opponent. Participants had information about only about their own possible payoffs. The values of the possible payoffs were displayed ordered from highest to lowest (T, R, P, and S). The moves were labeled '1' and '2'. Moreover, the subjects didn't know they were playing against an opponent. In the beginning they didn't even know the correspondence between moves and payoffs. They were supposed to discover this relation in the course of the game. After choosing a move, the subject received one of the payoffs.

It was interesting to check what would be the cooperativeness in the behavior in this condition (and representation of the PD game). In particular, would one find the influence of the ratio between the payoffs (i.e. the cooperation index). Or, alternatively, would the behaviour be reinforcement based (depending on previous received payoffs) like the expected in the Blind PD condition?

The *Move-PD* condition

This condition was actually a normal presentation of the game (see below the description of the *Full-PD* condition) except for the lack of information about the specific game payoffs which were presented only symbolically. Participants were trained with 100 PD games in which they

saw the actual payoffs in the game matrix in order to get accustomed to the structure of the payoffs and understand well the game. During the 300 'actual' PD games they saw an abstract payoff matrix with a symbolic denotation of the payoffs – R, S, P, and T and their relative magnitude T > R > P > S. On the other hand participants had information about the computer's move and the type of outcome of the game. So, the received payoff was symbolically presented as the payoffs in the matrix and the total amount of point was directly transformed in its money equivalent, preventing to easily infer the amount of the received payoff (the ratio points to money was very small). The idea behind this condition was to make participants concentrate on the moves of the computer opponent and ellicit move oriented strategies (e.g. like tit-for-tat).

The *Full-PD* condition

In this condition the participants had complete information about the game. They knew what were their and the computer's possible payoffs. After choosing a move, participants saw what the computer's choice was, the points they received form the game and the points received by the computer player.

This is in a sense the other extreme with respect to the *Blind-PD* condition, with maximum information provided.

Experimental Goals and Hypotheses

The main question we tried to answer is how strategies change depending on the different information people had about the game. We want to explore several factors that might affect playing (cooperation) in iterated PD games. Performing this series of experiments, we expected to be able to separate the socially determined factors (interaction with the other player) from factors related only to payoffs. We explored the following factors:

- The influence of the availability and structure of the payoff matrix, and the access the actual payoffs (relationship between payoffs);
- The influence of the participation of an opponent;
- Reinforcement learning effects due to received payoffs.

Schematically the characteristics of the different conditions are presented in Table 1.

Table 1: Characteristics of the four condition with respect to the information about the PD game available to the participants. (Note: for *Move-PD*, 'R, S, P, T' means that this information was available only symbolically and not numerically; see the text for details.)

Condition	Opponent	Payoff matrix	Received payoff
Blind-PD	–	–	+
Row-PD	–	+	+
Move-PD	+	R, S, P, T	R, S, P, T
Full-PD	+	+	+

The best way to proceed was to run models based on the theories described in the beginning and to generate predictions about a set of outcomes and then compare them to the experimental results presented below. Here, we will compare only the general qualitative predictions of the different theories described above. The four conditions cover quite general situations which can arise in the playing of any player in different moments of the game. As mentioned already, people attend to different part of the information at different times (see Hristova & Grinberg, 2005b).

As discussed in the beginning, D is the dominant strategy although mutual cooperation is better than mutual defection in the iterated PD because $R > P$. By choosing C the player can try to establish mutual cooperation with the other player in the course of the play. If this is true, then one could expect that this mechanism will work in the *Move-PD* and the *Full-PD* condition and missing in the other two conditions. Thus it will be an additional source of cooperation and could lead to higher cooperation in the 'social interaction' conditions *Move-PD* and *Full-PD* and to lower cooperation in *Blind-PD* and *Row-PD* in which participants don't know they have an opponent. In the *Blind-PD* condition participants don't even see what the possible payoffs are. So, for this case one could hypothesize that given that the average payoff after a C move is lower than the average after a D move ($R < T$, $S < P$), participants will be reinforced to some extent to avoid C and this will lead to a decrease in cooperation.

Comparing these two types of conditions – the reinforcement and the 'social interaction' one – it is possible to study the influence of knowledge about the dependence of the received payoff on the social interaction with another player. In such a way we hope to able to differentiate between theories taking into account altruism and theories relying more on reinforcement mechanisms in move choice making.

It might be also the case that these theories give similar results and cannot be experimentally distinguished.

Experimental results

Cooperation

First we analyzed the number of games in which players cooperated. The results are given in Figure 2. Players in the *Full-PD* and *Move-PD* conditions cooperated less (28% and 32%, respectively) than those in *Blind-PD* and the *Row-PD* conditions (40% and 36%, respectively). It is interesting to note (see Figure 2) the tendency of decrease of the cooperation rate from *Blind-PD* to *Full-PD*, in other words with increasing information about the game.

However, the analysis shows that only the difference in cooperation between participants in *Blind-PD* and *Full-PD* conditions is statistically significant (2-tailed independent samples t-test, p=0.047)[1]. All other comparisons yielded non-significant differences. Although there is no statistical

---

[1] Comparisons were made using the number of games in which players cooperated. However, we present data in percentages in the sake of clarity.

significance, the difference between cooperation in the *Row-PD* and the *Full-PD* conditions is about 8%.

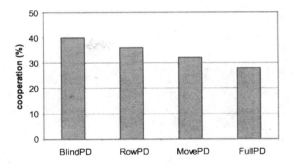

Figure 2: Mean cooperation (%) in each experimental condition.

Thus, it turns out that contrary to our expectations the cooperation was greatest in the *Blind-PD* condition. In this condition players don't have any information about the game – they have only to choose a move and receive a payoff. This result is in contradiction with the predictions of the theories that would state a strong social basis for cooperation (such as altruism or reciprocity). It might be the case that counter effects like temptation to get the highest payoff or fear of defection lead to lower cooperation.

Game outcomes (*CC, CD, DC, DD*)

The second analysis was performed using the number of different game types that resulted in the course of the game. The game type is determined by both opponents in a game. So, there are four possible game types – *CC, CD, DC,* and *DD*. Each game type is bound to a certain payoff – *CC* to R, *CD* to S, *DC* to T, and *DD* to P. Thus, the game type incorporates a lot of information about the game – the choices of the two players and the payoffs – and captures the interplay between the players. Statistics about the number of games of each type complement data about average cooperation and have to be reproduced/predicted by any model together with mean cooperation and other characteristics.

As mentioned already, all four groups of participants played against the same computer opponent. It is interesting to check to what extent the difference in the conditions lead to differences in the game outcome distributions. And more interestingly, in which condition subjects were more successful in achieving mutual cooperation (that results in *CC* games). The results are shown in Figure 3.

The mean number of *CC* games is significantly different between the conditions (F(3, 83)=4.56, p=0.005). Post-hoc comparisons show that the number of *CC* games in the *Full-PD* condition is less than the number of *CC* games in the *Row-PD* condition (p=0.049) and less than the number of *CC* games in the *Blind-PD* condition (p=0.002). They also show that there are more *CC* games in the *Blind-PD* condition compared to the *Move-PD* condition (p=0.004).

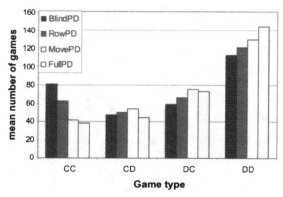

Figure 3: Mean number of game types (*CC*, *CD*, *DC*, and *DD*) in each experimental condition.

This analysis demonstrates that players in the *Blind-PD* condition were more successful in promoting mutual cooperation than the players in the *Full-PD* and in the *Move-PD* conditions. Participants in the *Row-PD* condition also provoked more mutual cooperation than the players in *Full-PD* condition. When players don't know that they have an opponent, they play in a way that is more successful in getting the other player to cooperate (at least in this case of a probabilistic tit-for-tat player).

Payoffs received

The previous analyses demonstrate that there are differences in the way participants play in these four different forms of the PD game. The question that arises is in which experimental condition players got larger payoffs as a result of the differences in their playing. In order to answer this question we compared the mean number of points (per game) that players received.

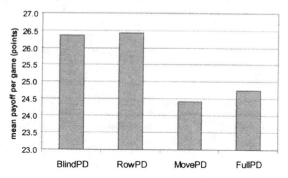

Figure 4: Mean payoff (points) per game in each of the four conditions.

As seen from Figure 4, the mean payoff per game is 24.7 points in the *Full-PD* condition, 24.4 points in *Move-PD* condition and 26.4 points in the *Row-PD* and *Blind-PD* conditions. The main effect of the experimental condition is significant ($F_{(3, 85)}=3.78$, p=0.0013). Post-hoc analysis revealws that the mean payoff in the *Full-PD* condition is

less than the payoff in the *Row-PD* condition (p=0.023) and less than the payoff in the *Blind-PD* condition (p=0.049). Also the mean payoff in the *Move-PD* condition is less than payoff in *Row-PD* condition (p=0.008) and less than the payoff in *Blind-PD* condition (p=0.02).

In other words, players in the *Row-PD* and the *Blind-PD* conditions got higher payoffs than the players in the 'social interaction' conditions.

In fact, the participants in the *Full-PD* and the *Move-PD* conditions got at the end of the sessions noticeably less money than the subjects participating in the *Row-PD* and the *Blind-PD* conditions.

Cooperation after various game outcomes

Next we analyzed what is the cooperation after each possible game outcome (*CC*, *CD*, *DC*, or *DD*). The question investigated is how the move choice depends on the previous game.

As mentioned above, each game outcome is related to a specfic payoff - R , S, T, or P. In PD games the inequality T>R>P>S holds. What is more, in the current experiment S was set to 0. So we investigated what happens after each of these game outcomes. For example, are players satisfied with the payoff R after a *CC* game or are they trying to get the higher T payoff? Or are the players switching to defection, after a *CD* outcome (payoff = S = 0), because by defecting the player always gets a payoff larger than 0.

In order to be able to answer these questions, we analyzed the players' moves after each possible game outcome – *CC*, *CD*, *DC*, and *DD*. Using chi-square, we analyzed if there is a different distribution of choices between the experimental conditions after each game type. All four analyses yield a chi-square statistics with significance smaller than 0.001. Here we present the analysis of the cooperation after *CC* and *CD* outcomes.

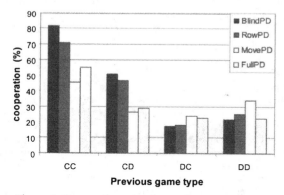

Figure 5: Cooperation rate after each game outcome.

After a *CC* game outcome (received payoff = R) the players in the *Blind-PD* and *Row-PD* conditions were choosing more often the cooperative choice (in 82% and 71% of the cases, respectively) than the players in the *Move-PD* and the *Full- PD* conditions (choosing after a *CC* game to cooperate in 46% and 55% of the games, respectively). It seems that after achieving mutual cooperation, players in the

Move-PD and the *Full-PD* conditions tried to exploit this by choosing defection (and get the highest payoff).

The result was similar after a *CD* outcome (received payoff = 0). Players in the *Blind-PD* and the *Row-PD* conditions were choosing more often to cooperate (in 51% and 47% of cases, respectively) after getting 0 points than the players in the *Move-PD* and the *Full-PD* conditions (choosing to cooperate in 27% and 29% of the games, respectively after a *CD* game). After choosing to cooperate and getting a 0 payoff, the players in the *Move-PD* and the *Full-PD* conditions usually switched to defection. One interpretation is that in such a way they are trying to punish the other player.

Conclusion

In this paper, the results from an experiment with four experimental conditions were discussed. The performed comparisons show that given identical series of PD games people cooperate more and receive larger payoffs what the games are presented as a reinforcement learning situation than in the usual terms as a social interaction situation. This result is supported by the larger number of mutual cooperative game outcome (*CC* outcome).

It seems that having access only to partial information about the game (like in the *Row-PD* and the *Blind-PD* conditions) leads not only to more cooperative behavior but also to greater payoffs. Simple reliance on received payoffs brings the subjects to better results than interaction with the other players and rich information about the game.

Decrease in cooperation in *Full-PD* might be explained by temptation to get the highest payoff, or by trying to compete with the other player. Another possibility might be that these results are due to cognitive limitations of the player. In *Full-PD* condition subjects have to deal with a larger amount of information before and after each game (compared to the *Row-PD* condition and especially to the *Blind-PD* condition).

When we compare cooperation when the previous game type was *CC*, it turns out that it is greatest in *Blind-PD* and smallest in *Ful- PD*. It might be the case that subjects in the *Full-PD* condition were trying to exploit the cooperation of the computer in order to get the T payoff in the next game by playing *D*. On the contrary, subjects in the *Blind-PD* condition were satisfied with the R payoff (they didn't see the possible payoffs and they didn't know that there is a larger payoff that they could get). Again we got a relatively unexpected result: having information about the possible payoffs does not promote cooperation but tempted the subjects and they were not satisfied with the R payoffs and wanted the highest T payoff. As a consequence, this strategy led to worse results in terms of received money.

At the end, we want to note that all results might depend very strongly on the strategy of the computer opponent. In the current experiment it was a probabilistic tit-for-tat strategy. The computer opponent is the same in all conditions and its effect shouldn't influence the comparisons. However, repetition of the experiment using different opponents might lead to different results. In general, exploring the role of the opponent is a very important line of research to be carried on in the future.

References

Andreoni, J. & Miller, J. (1993). Rational cooperation in finitely repeated Prisoner's Dilemma: Experimental evidence. *Economic Journal, 103*, 570-585.

Axelrod, R. (1984). *The evolution of cooperation.* New York: Basic Books.

Colman, A. (1995). *Game theory and its applications in the social and biological sciences.* Oxford: Butterworth-Heinemann Ltd.

Cooper, R., DeJong, D., Forsythe, R., & Ross, T. (1996). Cooperation without reputation: experimental evidence from Prisoner's dilemma games. *Games and Economic Behavior, 12*, 187-218.

Dawes, R. (1980). Social dilemmas. *Annual Review of Psychology, 31*, 169-193.

Erev, I., & Roth, A. (1998). Predicting how people play games: reinforcement learning in experimental games with unique, mixed strategy equilibria. *The American Economic Review, 88*, 848-881.

Erev, I., & Roth, A. (1999). On the role of reinforcement learning in experimental games: the cognitive game-theoretic approach. In: D. Budescue, I. Erev, & R. Zwick (Eds.), *Games and human behavior: Essays in honor of Amnon Rapoport.* Mahwah, NJ: Lawrence Erlbaum.

Erev, I. & Roth, A. (2001). Simple reinforcement learning models and reciprocation in the prisoner's dilemma game. In G. Gigerenzer and R. Selten (Eds.) *Bounded rationality: the adaptive toolbox,* Cambridge, Mass.: MIT Press.

Flache, A., & Macy, W. (2002). The power law of learning. *Journal of Conflict Resolution, 46*, 629-653.

Hristova, E. & Grinberg M. (2004). Context Effects On Judgment Scales in the Prisoner's Dilemma Game. Proceedings of the 1st European Conference on Cognitive Economics. ECCE1, Gif-sur-Yvette, France

Hristova, E & Grinberg, M. (2005a). Investigation of Context Effects in Iterated Prisoner's Dilemma Game. In: Dey, A., Kokinov, B., Leake, D. Turner, R. (eds.): Modeling and Using Context, LNAI 3554, Springer Verlag, 183-196

Hristova, E., Grinberg, M. (2005b). Information Acquisition in the Iterated Prisoner's Dilemma Game: An Eye-tracking Study. Proceedings of the 27th Annual Conference of the Cognitive Science Society. Elbraum, Hillsdale, NJ

Komorita, S. S. (1965). Cooperative choice in a Prisoner's Dilemma Game. *Journal of personality and social psychology, 2*, 741-745.

Kreps, D., Milgrom, P., Roberts, J., & Wilson, R. (1982). Rational cooperation in the finitely repeated Prisoner's dilemma'. *Journal of Economic Theory, 27*, 245-252.

Macy, M., & Flache, A. (2002). Learning dynamics in social dilemmas. *Proceedings of the National Academy of Sciences of the USA, 99*, 7229-7236.

Trivers, R. (1972). The evolution of reciprocal altruism. *Quarterly Review of Biology, 46*, 35-37.

Sally, D. (1995). Conversation and cooperation in social dilemmas. A meta-analysis of experiments from 1958 to 1992. *Rationality and Society, 7*, 58-92.

Computational Model of Cooperative Behavior: Adaptive Regulation of Goals and Behavior

Yugo Nagata (yugo@complex.eng.hokudai.ac.jp)
Graduate School of Information Science and Technology, Hokkaido University
Kita 14, Nishi 9, Kita, Sapporo, 060-0814, JAPAN

Satoru Ishikawa (ishi_s@hokusei.ac.jp)
School of Humanities, Hokusei Gakuen University
2-3-1, Ohyachi-Nishi, Atsubetsu-ku, Sapporo, 004-8631, JAPAN

Takashi Omori (omori@lab.tamagawa.ac.jp)
Tamagawa University Research Institute
6-1-1, Tamagawa Gakuen, Machida, Tokyo, 194-8610 JAPAN

Koji Morikawa (morikawa.koji@jp.panasonic.com)
Advanced Technology Research Laboratory, Matsushita Electric Industrial Co., Ltd.
3-4 Hikaridai, Seika, Soraku, Kyoto, 619-0237, JAPAN

Abstract

We are not living alone, but in society based on interaction with others. The ability to smoothly cooperate with others by estimating their intentions is a fundamental social tenet. What mechanism underlies it? To clarify this mechanism, we developed a computational model of cooperation in which an action decision process is dynamically controlled based on an estimation of another's goal. To analyze the model, we simulated tasks in which two hunters cooperatively chased two preys and showed that this model achieved smooth cooperative work. Computer simulation revealed that an action decision process that only reflected estimates of another's goal (Level-1 estimation) was insufficient for achieving smooth cooperative work; action decision processes based on the estimation of one's goal by another (Level-2 estimation) and one that didn't change one's goal were effective for achieving smooth cooperative work in some circumstances. This suggests that one way to smoothly achieve cooperative tasks is switching multiple action decision processes depending on circumstances and others.

Introduction

We are not living alone, but living and interacting with others in society. Our ability to smoothly cooperate with others facilitates making and maintaining large groups in society. Actually, we can cooperate smoothly with a stranger we are meeting for the first time. For example, imagine two persons cooperatively picking up garbage scattered in a room. In this situation, we can smoothly pick up the garbage by predicting the other's behavior without long-term learning.

Understanding the ability of cooperative behavior with someone new is important for understanding the nature of human social intelligence. To obtain insight into this ability, we constructed a computational model of the cognitive process in cooperative behavior. The purpose of this paper is to find sufficient functions for smooth cooperation with others and its computational modeling.

Cooperation accomplished between agents has been studied in game theory. In game theory, a player's behavior is decided rationally based on a payoff matrix that shows the payoff each player receives, and cooperation is usually evaluated by the outcome with the highest payoff for both players (Pareto efficiency). Some studies have tried to realize cooperation in iterated prisoner's games by multi-agent learning (e.g., Makino and Aihara 2006, Moriyama and Numano 2002).

However, in iterated games, observable information of the other's behavior is limited to the results of strategy. On the other hand, in daily cooperative behavior, we can observe more detailed behavior of the other on an action time scale. We can actually regulate our own behavior in the middle of actions using information on detailed time scales. Nevertheless, game theory only treats incentive to decide a strategy without explaining such action regulations during strategy execution. For understanding daily "face-to-face" cooperative behavior, a model must consider mutual observation in action time scale.

Some studies addressed the realization of cooperative behavior by multi-agent systems and robots in mutual-observation situations (e.g., Ikenoue, Asada, and Hosoda 2002, Nagayuki, Ishi, and Doya 2000). In these systems, agents learned cooperative behavior by trial and error through interaction with other agents. However, the method requires a long learning time, and acquired action rules depend on specific task situations. It cannot explain our ability to cooperate with strangers.

To smoothly cooperate with others, agents must react to others in novel situations. To realize this, we believe that estimating the intentions and behavior of others by observing their actions are effective.

In this paper we propose a computational model of the cognitive process that enables smooth cooperative behavior with common others, not only a specific other. In our model, an agent decides its own actions based on the observation and prediction of other's actions, not using rules acquired for specific others. In our model, the other's behavior is predicted based on estimation of his/her intention. The other's intention that is directly unobservable is estimated using knowledge about one's own action decision.

In this paper, we show that predicting other's behavior is unstable in mutual-prediction situations and that such prediction recursion as "prediction of prediction" can resolve the problem. However, the proper depth of prediction recursion cannot be decided *a priori* because the other's recursion level is generally unknown. To solve this problem, we determined prediction level online based on the condition of the other and one's self.

Model

Cooperation

Allwood (1976) defined cooperation as a "type of interaction involving two or more normal rational agents who were (1) considering each other and (2) trying to achieve one or more common purposes." Namatame (2004) defined it as trying to modulate behaviors each other to achieve a shared purpose efficiently. Although these definitions of cooperation embrace trying for common purposes, our definition includes accomplishment of cooperation to evaluate our model's ability to cooperate. In this paper, accomplishment of cooperation is defined as "accomplishing a relation desirable for each other by regulating each other's behavior." We address cooperation involving two participants.

We used a cooperative task equivalent to cooperation as defined above to evaluate cooperation ability in our proposed model. In the cooperative task, two agents (hunters) cooperatively chase two preys. A desirable relation to be accomplished in the task is a condition where each hunter catches a different prey. Therefore, a hunter must decide which prey to chase depending on which prey the other will chase. Details of the task are described below.

Estimation of Other's Intention

The self's behavior should be decided depending on the other's state to achieve a relation between the self and the other. However, when the other's state is changing with time, the self's behavior cannot be decided properly from the current states of the other and the environment.

In such conditions, the self's proper behavior must be decided depending on the other's future behavior, which is predicted from current and past states. Prediction facilitates smooth (efficient) accomplishment of cooperation.

The other's behavior can be predicted by estimating the other's intention and assuming that behaviors originate from intentions. Premack and Woodruff (1978) called the ability to impute mental states to oneself and others "theory of mind," which healthy human beings have. So to some extent we can estimate the intention and predict the behavior of someone new. However, others' intentions are internal states that cannot be observed immediately from outside. What is the mechanism for estimating others' intentions? In the following section, two probable mechanisms are considered.

First, the other's intention is learned as a pattern of behavior by observing the other's behaviors. Actually, our experience shows that we can make predictions about a person with whom we have a long association. As a model of the mechanism, Tohyama et al. (2003) proposed a computational model of identification and learning of other's intention. However, this mechanism requires long learning time before being able to predict the other's action; it cannot explain our ability to predict the behavior of someone new.

Second, the other's internal state is estimated using one's own internal state. Based on 'simulation theory,' other people's mental states are represented by adopting their perspective: by tracking or matching their states with one's own resonant states (Gallese and Goldman 1998). This theory is supported by mirror neurons discovered in the premotor cortex of monkeys (Gallese et al. 1996) that respond both when a particular action is performed by the recorded monkey and when the same action is performed by another individual. An equivalent mirror system is thought to exist in humans (Gallese et al. 1998).

Based on these considerations, we hypothesize that the other's intention is estimated using the knowledge of one's own action decision. When one internally has knowledge of behavior (B) based on intention (I) and observes the other's behavior that resembles B, one estimates the other's intention as I. This mechanism doesn't require long observing time and learning the other's behavior. What we assume is just that one can access one's own knowledge on one's own behaviors.

Mutual-prediction Problem

In face-to-face cooperation of two agents, they make predictions about each other. In such mutual prediction situations, estimation of the other's intention is unstable since an agent might predict that the other will make a prediction about the agent self and change the intention. Here we explain this situation by introducing a 'level' of action strategies.

We defined *level* as follows. An agent of *level-0* decides actions based on one's intention independently of the other. An agent of *level-1* considers the other level-0 and acts based on this estimation of the other's intention. An agent of *level-2* considers the other of level-1 and acts based on this estimation of the contents of the other's estimation, or in other words, what the self's intention is estimated by the other.

For stable accomplishment of cooperation by the two agents, at least one must be level-1 that estimates the other's intention, because level-0 and level-2 don't estimate other's intention; in other words, they ignore the other's behaviors. However, when both agents are level-1, they cannot accomplish cooperation efficiently. Some simulations show that level-1 cannot accurately predict the behavior of level-1 because level-1 thinks the other is level-0 (Nagata et al. 2006, Makino et al. 2006, Takano, Kato, and Arita 2006). Here, we call this the *mutual-prediction problem*.

Despite the mutual-prediction problem, human beings seem to be able to cooperate smoothly with each other in such mutual-prediction situations. Perhaps a problem-solving mechanism exists in human cognitive processes. In the following section, we propose a model of the mechanism.

Level Selection Model

Although level-1 cannot accurately predict another level-1, based on the definition of level, the prediction should function well when the difference of levels is one: level-1 can predict level-0, and level-2 can predict level-1. However, one's own proper level depends on the other's level, which is generally unknown. Next we propose a model that can properly select one's own level when the other's level is unknown.

Considering that estimation of the other's intention (level-1) is required to accomplish cooperation, we base our model on level-1. In the following, the mutual-prediction problem is analyzed into two causes, and mechanisms to avoid them are added to level-1.

Selection of Level 0 Based on Certainty Factor One cause of inaccurate prediction in mutual-prediction situations is the frequent changing of intention. When an agent tries to identify the other's intention before being certain, estimation errors tend to occur frequently that require repeated re-estimation. Changing of its intention also occurs frequently. Furthermore, such frequent changing of its intention increases the uncertainty of its intention estimation by the other, leading to other's estimation error and frequent changing of the other's intention.

To avoid this vicious cycle, our model uses the 'certainty factor,' which is an index of the certainty with which the other's intention is estimated at the present moment. When certainty factor C is low, the model doesn't estimate the other's intention and or change its intention; that is, it selects level-0 instead of level-1 for its own behavior level to avoid mistakes of its own intention decisions and simplifies the estimates of its own intention by the other.

Selection between Levels-1 and -2 Another cause for inaccurate prediction in mutual-prediction situations is the simultaneous changing of intention by both agents. When the certainty factors of both agents are high, both may change their intentions simultaneously; nevertheless, since neither expects the other to change intention, the predictions fail.

To avoid the simultaneous changing of intentions, the agent must properly select its own intention depending on either the estimation of the other's intention (level-1) or the prediction that the other will change intention (level-2). For proper selection, we consider the effectiveness of level-1 or level-2. Level-1 is effective when the other's intention is manifest from the other's behavior because it decides its own intention that reflects the estimation of the other's intention. By contrast, level-2 is effective when its intention is manifest because level-2 assumes that the other decides its intention by reflecting the estimation of 'the self's intention estimated by the other.' Therefore, the model must select its level between level-1 and level-2 based on which intention is more manifest, the other's or its own.

Computational Model

In this section, the scheme proposed above is implemented as a computational model.

Estimation of Other's Intention

In our model, an agent estimates the other's intention using its own knowledge of action decision. Here, *intention* means a goal possessed by each agent, and estimation of the other's intention means an estimation of the other's goal.

We assume that each agent has knowledge about "which action a should be selected at current state s for goal G." This knowledge is represented as probability function $\Pr(a|s,G)$, which is the probability of selecting action a when current state and goal are s and G, respectively. We assume that the knowledge is acquired by *a priori* learning. In this paper, we used reinforcement learning (RL) (Sutton and Barto 1998).

The other's goal G is estimated from $h_o(t)$, the other's history of state s, and action a at time t:

$$h_o(t) = \{s_o(t), a_o(t), \ldots, s_o(t-T+1), a_o(t-T+1)\} \quad (1).$$

Subscript o means it has another origin. T is the length of the history.

The other's goal G is estimated using accumulated log likelihood $L(G|h_o(t))$. The higher the likelihood of goal G is, the higher the probability is that the other's goal is G. Likelihood is computed using one's own knowledge of action decision $\Pr(a|s,G)$ and the following equation:

$$L(G \mid h_o(t)) = \sum_{(s,a) \in h_o(t)} \log \Pr(a \mid s, G). \quad (2)$$

The other's goal at time t is estimated by the following probability function:

$$f(G \mid h_o(t)) = \frac{\exp(\beta L(G \mid h_o(t)))}{\sum_{G'} \exp(\beta L(G' \mid h_o(t)))} \quad (3)$$

β is a parameter greater than or equal to zero.

Behavior of Each Level

The computational model of the action decision process for each level is as follows.

Level-0 acts to reach its own goal G_s and disregards the other. When the current self's state is s_s, the action decision is based on probability function $\Pr(a|s_s, G_s)$.

Level-1 estimates the other's goal $\hat{G}_o(t-1)$ at time $t-1$ based on the other's history $h_o(t-1)$ and the probability function of Eq. (3). The other's goal at time t is predicted as $\hat{G}_o(t) = \hat{G}_o(t-1)$. Its own goal at time t, $G_s(t)$ is decided

Compute certainty factor C.
If $C < \theta$,
  Don't change its own goal (select **level-0**)
If $C \geq \theta$,
  Estimate $\hat{G}_o$, the other's intention.
  If changing of its own goal isn't necessary:
    Don't change its own goal (select **level-0**).
  If changing its own goal is necessary:
    1. Estimate $\hat{G}_s^o$, the other's estimation about the self's intention.
    2. Select either **level-1** or **level-2** based on the probability function of Eq. (5).

Figure 1: Process of level selection

based on the prediction, and action at time t is decided similar to level-0.

Level-2 estimates the contents of the other's estimation $\hat{G}_s^o(t-1)$, that is, what the self's intention is estimated by the other. The estimation is based on one's own history $h_s(t-1)$ and the probability function $f(G \mid h_s(t-1))$. The other's goal at time t, $\hat{G}_o(t)$, is predicted using $\hat{G}_s^o(t-1)$ based on the assumption that the other is level-1. Its own goal and action at time t are decided similar to level-1.

Level Selection

The computational model of the level selection process for each level is as follows.

Selection of Level-0 Based on Certainty Factor The certainty factor is computed using the accumulated log likelihood of Eq. (2). Certainty factor C is defined as the difference of the largest accumulated log likelihood $L(G_{1st} \mid h_o)$ and the second-largest accumulated log likelihood $L(G_{2nd} \mid h_o)$:

$$C = L(G_{1st} \mid h_o) - L(G_{2nd} \mid h_o)$$
$$G_{1st} = \arg\max_G L(G \mid h_o) \qquad (4)$$
$$G_{2nd} = \arg\max_{G \neq G_{1st}} L(G \mid h_o).$$

If the likelihood of a goal is sufficiently higher than the likelihoods of the other goals, the goal is certainly the other's goal, and certainty factor C is high. If certainty factor C is less than threshold θ, the agent doesn't estimate the other's goal and decides the action based on level-0.

Selection between Level-1 and Level-2 If certainty factor C is greater than the threshold, the agent estimates the other's goal. If the agent needs to change its own intention due to the estimation, the agent selects either level-1 or level-2 based on which intention is more manifest: the other's or its own.

In our model, the manifestness of other's intention is defined as the likelihood of the estimation of the other's goal, $L(\hat{G}_o \mid h_o)$. The manifestness of the self's intention is defined as the likelihood of the estimation of the contents of the other's estimation of the self's goal, $L(\hat{G}_s^o \mid h_s)$.

If $L(\hat{G}_o \mid h_o)$ is relatively large, then the agent selects level-1 based on the estimation of the other's intention; otherwise, the agent selects level-2 based on the estimation of its intention by the other. In the model, the agent selects level-i based on the following probability function:

$$\Pr(i) = \frac{\alpha_i \exp(\beta' L_i)}{\sum_{j=1,2} \alpha_j \exp(\beta' L_j)} \quad (i = 1,2) \qquad , \quad (5)$$
$$L_1 = L(\hat{G}_o \mid h_o), \quad L_2 = L(\hat{G}_s^o \mid h_s)$$

where $\beta' \geq 0$ is a parameter and $\alpha_i \geq 0$ is a weighting parameter for level-i such that $\alpha_1 + \alpha_2 = 1$. The level selection process is summarized in Figure 1.

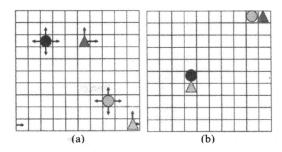

Figure 2: (a) simulation environment (in actual simulation, grid is 20×20). Triangles represent hunters and circles represent preys; (b) example task accomplishment.

Computer Simulation

Setup

We evaluated the effectiveness of our model in a cooperative task by computer simulation. The task is a hunter task in which two agents (hunters) cooperatively chase two preys.

The simulation environment is shown in Figure 2a. In a 20×20 toroidal grid world, the two hunter agents are represented by circles and the two preys by triangles. The hunters perform one of five actions: staying, moving up, down, left, or right from their current position at discrete time steps. The preys' actions are probabilistic and independent of the hunters' positions. The probability of moving up is 1/5 and moving right or staying is 2/5.

We defined the accomplishment cooperation condition as when each agent catches a different prey: one agent catches a prey and the other agent catches the other prey. A prey is considered captured when an agent is adjacent to it. An example of task accomplishment is shown in Figure 2b.

We regard this task as a simple model of a dynamic environment where estimations of partners' intentions are required for cooperation. Therefore, we don't aim to reproduce predator and prey behaviors in the natural world.

In the task, each agent's goal is to choose to catch one of the two preys. To accomplish the task smoothly, the agent estimates the other's goal (which prey the other agent will chase) and decides to catch the other prey as its own goal. Knowledge $\Pr(a|s,G)$ used for both the estimation and its

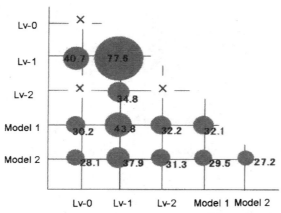

Figure 3: Average time steps to accomplish cooperation

own action decision was learned by reinforcement learning (Sutton et al. 1998) independently of each other. Actions a and goals G were defined as noted above. We represented states s by relative positions between the self agent and the target prey in the grid world.

At the beginning of an episode, agents and preys are placed randomly in the grid world. Each agent and prey performs its action simultaneously at time steps. When the accomplishment cooperation condition is satisfied (when each agent is adjacent to a different prey), the episode ends and a new episode begins. When only one agent is adjacent to a prey, the episode continues. Depending on the circumstances, the agent can leave its chosen prey and catch the other prey.

We prepared five types of hunter agents: Lv-0, Lv-1, Lv-2, Model 1, and Model 2. The Lv-x agent's behavior depends on level-x. The Model 1 agent uses the selection of level-0 based on certainty factor, but not selection between level-1 and level-2: when $C \geq \theta$, it always selects level-1. The Model 2 agent depends on the proposed model summarized in Figure 1.

We used the following parameters: T=5, β=1.0, θ=5 (for Model 1), θ=1.5 (for Model 2), β'=1.0, α_1=0.6, and α_2=0.4.

Results

Figure 3 shows average time steps to accomplish cooperation between different agent pairs. The circle size represents average time steps from 1000 episode results. The × mark indicates the pairs removed from the analysis because neither agent estimated the other's intention, so they couldn't accomplish cooperation in the time-step limits with high probability. The Lv-1 agent showed different performance depending on its cooperator type ($F_{[4,4995]}$=175.7, p<.001: one-way ANOVA). In the Lv-1/Lv-1 pair, accomplishing cooperation needs longer time steps than the other pairs especially the estimation agents (Lv-2, Model 1, and Model 2). On the other hand, the Model 2 agent showed fewer average time steps through all cooperator types compared to the Lv-1 agent. However, there is still a main effect of cooperator type

($F_{[4,4995]}$=41.6, p<.001: one-way ANOVA) when the Model 2:Model 2 pair showed lower average time steps than the pairs with other estimating agents (Model 2:Model 1, and Model 2/Lv-2). These results show the effectiveness of the proposed model in the cooperative task for both selection of level-0 based on certainty factor and selection between level-1 and level-2.

Discussion

The long time steps in the Lv-1/Lv-1 pair show that cooperation cannot be accomplished smoothly in the mutual-prediction situation. In contrast, cooperation between pairs Lv-0/Lv-1 and Lv-1/Lv-2 was accomplished smoothly. This shows that prediction works well when the level difference is one.

The result shows that Model 1 agents can smoothly cooperate with Lv-1. This means that the selection of level-0 based on the certainty factor is effective in cooperative tasks. It is likely that Model 1 agent can be accurately predicted by Lv-1 by inhibiting unnecessary changing of its own goal, that is, by selecting level-0. In the Model 1/Model 1 pair, a similar process likely occurs.

A comparison between Models 1 and 2 in Figure 3 shows that Model 2 outperforms Model 1, particularly when paired with Lv-1. This reflects the effectiveness of the selection of level-1 or level-2 in the cooperative task. In pairs Lv-1/Model 1 and Model 1/Model 1, the agent sometimes makes prediction errors and changes its own goal simultaneously with the other. In contrast, the Model 2 agent likely reduced error by predicting the changes of the other's goal, that is, by selecting level-2.

The contribution of estimating the other's intention for cooperation has been suggested empirically. However, our results suggest that estimation of the other's intention is inadequate for smooth cooperation and that estimation of the content of the other's estimation about itself is effective for smooth cooperation. By using both the estimation of the other's intention (level-1) and estimation of the other's estimation of its intention (level-2), agents can consider the intentions of both itself and the other. This enables agents to recognize cooperation situations from a "bird's eye view" (Tomasello et al. 2005) and to take proper actions based on complete information. In addition to the ability to estimate the other's intention (level-1), the ability to estimate the other's estimation (level-2) and adaptively select proper levels might be the ability that enables human beings to cooperate with others smoothly.

Conclusion

In this paper we proposed a computational model of cooperative behavior that accomplishes cooperation effectively by regulating personal goals adaptively based on the estimation of intention. We showed the difficulty of prediction in a 'mutual-prediction' situation. Computer simulation of the cooperative task showed that the proposed model solved it by selecting a proper level of estimation, and that not only the estimation of other's intention but also estimation of the contents of other's estimation about its own intention and the restriction of needless changing of its own intention are effective for smooth cooperation with the other. This result suggests that our proposed model is a possible candidate of our ability to cooperate smoothly with others.

Future work will evaluate the model in different tasks. Since it was only evaluated by one kind of task, it must be evaluated by other more complex and realistic tasks. For example, tasks must be considered that include three or more agents, agents that possess different knowledge, and in competitions as well as cooperation.

Furthermore, although the model was evaluated by computer simulation, there is no evidence that the model reflects the actual human cognitive process. Hence, additional future works must verify our model by behavioral experiences. In interactions between humans and humans or machines, the effect of the estimation of other's intention and the estimation of the contents of other's estimation about its intention should be identified. The products of this study should encourage understanding of human social cognition and the realization of smooth human-machine-interaction.

References

Allwood, J. (1976). Linguistic Communication as Action and Cooperation: A study in Pragmatics. *Gothenburg Monographs in Linguistics 2, University of Gothenburg, Dept. of Linguistics*.

Gallese, V., Fadiga, L., Fogassi, L., and Rizzolatti, G. (1996). Action recognition in the premotor cortex. *Brain.* 119, pp. 593-609.

Gallese, V., and Goldman, A. (1998). Mirror neurons and the simulation theory of mind-reading. *Trends in Cognitive Sciences*, 2, pp. 493-501.

Ikenoue, S., Asada, M., and Hosoda, K. (2002). Cooperative behavior acquisition by asynchronous policy renewal that enables simultaneous learning in multiagent environment. *Proceedings of the 2002 IEEE/RSJ Intl. Conference on Intelligent Robots and Systems*, pp. 2728-2734.

Makino, T. and Aihara, K. (2006). Multi-agent reinforcement learning algorithm to handle beliefs of other agents' policies and embedded beliefs. *In Proceedings of the 5th International Joint Conference on Autonomus Agents and Multiagent Systems (AAMAS'06)*, pp. 789-791.

Moriyama, K. and Numano, M. (2002). Construction of a Learning Agent Handling Its Rewards According to Environmental Situation, *Transaction of the Japanese Society of Artificial Intelligence* Vol. 17, No. 6, pp. 676-683. (in Japanese)

Nagata, Y., Ishikawa, S., Omori, T., and Morikawa, K. (2006). Computational Modeling of Cooperative Behavior Based on Estimation of Other's Intention. *Proceedings of the 20th Annual Conference of JSAI, 2006*, IB4-2. (in Japanese)

Nagayuki, Y., Ishii, S., and Doya, K. (2000). Multi-agent reinforcement learning: an approach based on the other agent's internal model. *Fourth International Conference on Multi-Agent Systems*, pp. 215-221.

Namatame, A. (2004). *Game Theory and Evolutionary Dynamics*. Morikita Publisher. (in Japanese)

Premack, D. and Woodruff, G. (1978). Does the chimpanzee have a theory of mind? *Behavioral and Brain Sciences*, 1, pp. 515-526.

Sutton, R. S. and Barto, A. G. (1998). *Reinforcement Learning: An Introduction*. MIT Press

Takano, M., Kato, M., and Arita, T. (2005). A Constructive Approach to the Evolution of the Recursion Level in a Theory of Mind, *Cognitive Studies*, Vol. 12, No. 3, pp. 221-233 (in Japanese)

Tomasello, M., Carpenter, M., Call, J., Behne, T., and Moll, H. (2005). Understanding and sharing intentions: The origins of cultural cognition. *Behavioral and Brain Sciences*, 28, pp. 675 – 691.

Tohyama, S., Omori, T., Oka, N., and Morikawa, K. (2003). Identification and learning of other's action strategies in cooperative task. *Proc. of 8-th International Conference on Artificial Life and Robotics (AROB8th'03)*, pp. 40-43

Conscious and Unconscious Processing of Emotional Words

Maurits van den Noort (Maurits.Noort@psybp.uib.no)
Department of Biological and Medical Psychology, Jonas Lies vei 91
Bergen, N-5009 Norway

Peggy Bosch (Pbosch@online.no)
Department of Psychiatry and Clinical Medicine, Sandviksleitet 1
Bergen, N-5035 Norway

Kenneth Hugdahl (Hugdahl@psybp.uib.no)
Department of Biological and Medical Psychology, Jonas Lies vei 91
Bergen, N-5009 Norway

Abstract

Attitudes can vary in valence and in strength. There are two main theories on how they are processed in the brain (Hellige, 1993). The right hemisphere theory (Borod, Kent, Koff, Martin, & Alpert, 1988) posits that the right hemisphere is dominant over the left hemisphere for all attitudes. The valence theory (Lee, Loring, Dahl, & Meador, 1993), on the other hand, states that the right hemisphere is dominant for negative attitudes and the left hemisphere is dominant for positive attitudes. In this study, a divided visual field technique was used to further investigate this with emotional words. We were particularly interested in the question if the language aspect of word processing is more dominant than the processing of its emotional content. We found that at the conscious level, normal language processing was the most dominant process. At the unconscious level, this was not the case, but no strong support for one of the two attitude theories could be found.

Introduction

Humans evaluate objects every day, but do not always have the same opinion on these objects. It is, for instance, possible that you like a person, but that at the same time someone else does not like this person at all. In psychology this is called a difference in attitude. Eagly and Chaiken (1993) define an attitude as "an evaluative state that intervenes between certain classes of stimuli and certain classes of evaluative responses, which express approval or disapproval, favor or disfavor, liking or disliking, approach or avoidance, attraction or aversion towards the attitude object".

Attitudes can vary on several aspects. They can differ with respect to valence. If we have positive memories of an object; we will have a positive attitude towards that object. On the other hand, if we have negative memories of an object; we will have a negative attitude towards that object. Moreover, attitudes can differ with respect to strength. If you work in a sports school your whole life; you will have a strong attitude towards that sports school. Whereas if you have never worked in a sports school; you will have a weak attitude towards it.

An indicator of attitude strength is accessibility. Attitude strength is defined as the probability that an attitude will be remembered automatically when the object is presented (Fazio, 1995). Attitude accessibility can change over time. It can increase if one object has been evaluated more often (Fabrigar, Priester, Petty, & Wegener, 1998). It depends on the association between the attitude object and its evaluation. This association is stronger for the strong attitudes compared to the weak attitudes (Holland, Verplanken, & Knippenberg, 2002). The higher the accessibility of the attitude, the more stable it will be over time (Fabrigar et al., 1998). Strong attitudes are stable over a long period and are resistant against influence, whereas weak attitudes are instable and easy to influence (Petty & Krosnick, 1995).

Previous social cognition studies have shown that a great deal of human object evaluation is rooted in unconscious processes (Bargh, Chaiken, Raymond, & Hymes, 1996; Van den Noort, 2003; Van den Noort, Bosch, & Hugdahl, 2005a; Van den Noort, Hugdahl, & Bosch, 2005b). During the last two decades, several studies were conducted, showing that humans evaluate objects (as for example "good" or "bad") at an unconscious level (Bargh, Chaiken, Govender, & Pratto, 1992; Bargh et al., 1996).

From cognitive neuroscience it is known that attitude objects are first processed via an automatically engaged neural mechanism, which occurs outside conscious awareness. This mechanism operates in conjunction with a slower and more comprehensive process that allows a detailed evaluation of the potentially harmful stimulus (LeDoux, 1996; Liddell, Williams, Rathjen, Shevrin, & Gordon, 2004; Williams et al., 2006).

Not much research has been conducted on the question where attitudes are located in the brain. So far, there are two main theories (Hellige, 1993). The right hemisphere theory (Borod et al., 1988) posits that the right hemisphere is dominant over the left hemisphere for all attitudes. In line with this theory, Cacioppo, Crites, and Gardner (1996) conducted an event-related potentials (ERP)-study on positive, negative and neutral attitude objects. They found a larger activation in the right hemisphere if people had to evaluate negative and positive attitude objects. For the neutral attitude objects, no significant differences were found between the right and the left hemisphere. These results are in line with previous neuropsychology studies on affective information (e.g. Borod, 1992; Dowling, 1992; Kolb & Taylor, 1981).

The valence theory, on the other hand, states that hemispheric asymmetry for expression and perception of emotions depends on emotional valence; the right hemisphere is dominant for negative attitudes and the left hemisphere is dominant for positive attitudes (Lee et al., 1993). It has been proposed that the origin of hemispheric asymmetry for emotions is based on the distinction between approach and withdrawal. A number of researchers (e.g. Davidson, 1995, 2004; Davidson, Ekman, Saron, Senulis, & Friesen, 1990) have suggested that the left hemisphere is intimately tied to approach behaviors and the right hemisphere is tied to withdrawal. There is interplay between the medial regions of the prefrontal cortex in the right- and the left hemisphere (Davidson, 1995; Sutton & Davidson, 1997; 2000).

In this paper, the focus will be on how humans process emotional words and two studies will be discussed. We are particularly interested in the question as to what process is more dominant; the language processing of words or the emotional content of these words? From cognitive neuroscience it is known that in 95% of right handed individuals the left hemisphere is dominant for language function (Vikingstad, George, Johnson, & Cao, 2000). If this is the most dominant process one would hypothesize that all emotional words are processed better and faster when they are presented in the right visual field (and processed in the left hemisphere). However, when the emotional content of the words is the most dominant process there would be two possibilities; 1) According to the right hemisphere theory (Borod et al., 1988) all attitudes are processed better and faster in the right hemisphere. In that case, the hypothesis would be that all emotional words are processed better and faster when they are presented in the left visual field (and processed in the right hemisphere). 2) Whereas according to valence theory (Lee et al., 1993) the right hemisphere is dominant for negative attitudes and the left hemisphere is dominant for positive attitudes. In line with the valence theory, the hypothesis would be that the negative emotional words are processed better and faster when they are presented in the left visual field and the positive words are processed better and faster when they are presented in the right visual field.

In addition to the question what theory (the language theory or one of the two attitude theories) can best explain our behavioral data; we are interested in the question if the results are the same at different presentation times. Perhaps humans process emotional words at the conscious level differently compared to the unconscious level? This will be investigated further in the second study.

Study 1

Participants

Fifty-nine students from the Radboud University Nijmegen (the Netherlands) participated in this study following written informed consent according to institutional guidelines. All participants were consistent right-handed as measured by the Edinburgh Handedness Inventory (laterality index: mean +/- SD, 97% +/- 5%; range 87%-100%) (Oldfield, 1971). There were 29 males and 30 females with an average age of 22 years and they were all native speakers of Dutch. An honorarium was given for participation.

Experimental Design

A 2 (Visual field: left vs. right) x 2 (Attitude strength: weak vs. strong) x 2 (Valence: positive vs. negative) x 2 (Response button: positive-left/negative-right vs. positive-right/negative-left), within subject design was used (with the last factor as a between subjects factor).

Pilot-Study

A pilot-study was conducted with sixty-seven participants (31 males and 36 females) to investigate the strong and weak attitudes and the positive and negative attitudes. Hundred attitudes were presented in a questionnaire and the participants had to indicate on a 11-pointsscale, from -5 extremely negative to +5 extremely positive, what their attitude was with respect to that object. Neutral attitudes were removed and finally 84 attitude objects were used for the experiment. Care was taken that there were no differences in word length between the negative words and the positive words. Moreover, the frequency of the emotional words was controlled for between the negative and the positive words (Van den Noort, Bosch, & Hugdahl, 2006). The CELEX lexical database (Baayen, Piepenbrock, & Van Rijn, 1993) was used to determine the frequency of the emotional words.

Procedure

The study consisted of two different sessions; a pre-measure and the experimental session. The pre-measure was important to make a selection per person of the positive and negative emotional words and consisted of two different parts.

In the first part of the pre-measure, all participants conducted an attitude accessibility task (Fazio, Sanbonmatsu, Powell, & Kardes, 1986). First, a fixation cross was presented at the center of the computer screen for 2 seconds. Then the fixation-cross disappeared and a word appeared at the center of the screen. Participants had to evaluate the word as positive or negative by pressing on the 'positive' or the 'negative' button as soon as possible, after which the word disappeared (Bargh et al., 1992; Fazio et al., 1986). After 1 second, the fixation-cross appeared and a new trial started. In total, eighty-four words were randomly presented. The location of the 'positive' and 'negative' button was varied between participants. For half of the participants, the 'positive' button was on the left and the 'negative' button on the right and for the other half of the participants it was vice versa. Participants were randomly divided into two groups. The positive and negative evaluations and the reaction times were collected.

In the second part of the pre-measure, all participants received a questionnaire on the computer screen where they had to evaluate all words on a 11-pointsscale (-5 extremely negative to +5 extremely positive). This task was necessary to make sure that the participants had made no mistakes in the previous task. The words that were evaluated as positive in the attitude accessibility task and were evaluated as negative in the questionnaire (or vice versa) were removed (3.3% of the attitude words).

Based on the accessibility task and the questionnaire, a selection of the emotional words was made per person. Forty-eight words were selected; 12 strong positive, 12 weak positive, 12 strong negative, and 12 weak negative.

After one week, the experimental session took place. This one week delay is important since the accessibility of the weak emotional words would otherwise be too high and as a result they would not be representative. All participants were instructed to sit calmly behind the computer screen. All participants were positioned at a distance of 60 cm. from the computer screen (see Hellige & Yamauchi, 1999). The experimental set-up was generally the same as in the accessibility task, but there were a few differences. Contrary to the accessibility task, a divided visual field technique (see Nicholls, Wood, & Hayes, 2001) was used, and as a result, the attitude words were presented in the left- or in the right visual field. Here, it is important to note that there were no significant differences in average word length between the positive and the negative words. In addition, all words (both short and long words) were presented such that the middle for the long and short words was the same. In the first study, all emotional words were presented for 180 ms. Forty-eight (12 strong positive, 12 weak positive, 12 strong negative and 12 weak negative) emotional words were used. As mentioned before, these words differ per participant and were selected based on the pre-measure tasks. Again, the participants task was to evaluate the words as positive or negative by pressing on the 'positive' and the 'negative' button as soon as possible and the location of the 'positive' and 'negative' button (left vs. right) was varied between participants. Both the positive and negative responses and the reaction times were measured.

After the experiment, all participants were asked if they knew the goal of the experiment after which they received feedback about the experiment.

Results

Reaction times under 300ms (1.9%) and above 3000ms (0.2%) were excluded from further analysis. Moreover, all responses in which the participant responded differently compared to the pre-measures were excluded (15.6%).

A 2 (Visual field: left vs. right) x 2 (Attitude strength: strong vs. weak) x 2 (Valence: positive vs. negative) x 2 (Response button: positive-left/negative-right vs. positive-right/negative-left), within subject multivariate analysis of variance (MANOVA) was conducted (with the last factor as a between subjects factor).

As can be seen in Table 1, a significant main effect for attitude strength was found, $F(1,57) = 69.2$, $p < .001$. As expected, the reaction times for the strong attitudes were faster than for the weak attitudes. No significant main effects for lateralization and valence were found. Finally, a significant difference between the weak negative attitudes that were presented in the left visual field and those that were presented in the right visual field was found, $F(1,58) = 8.34$, $p < .005$ (see Table 1).

Table 1: Mean reaction time for the positive and negative words; specified for visual field (left vs. right) and attitude strength (strong vs. weak).

	Left	Right
Strong positive	563ac	565ac
Strong negative	625ac	612ac
Weak positive	705bc	672bc
Weak negative	656bc	722bd

*Note: Means (across rows and colons) with different subscripts are significantly different ($p < .05$).

As can be seen in Table 2, participants process strong attitudes significantly better than weak attitudes, $F(1,57) = 48.77$, $p < .01$.

Table 2: Mean number of inconsistent responses for the strong and weak emotional words; specified for visual field (left vs. right).

	Left	Right
Strong	.81ac	.73ac
Weak	1.48bd	1.36bd

*Note: Means (across rows and colons) with different subscripts are significantly different ($p < .05$).

Discussion

In the first study, no significant main effects for lateralization and valence were found. At 180ms, the language aspect of word processing was not more dominant than the processing of its emotional content. At the same time, no strong support for one of the two attitude theories was found. Only a significant difference between the weak negative attitudes that were presented in the left visual field and those that were presented in the right visual field was found. Participants processed weak negative words significantly faster when they were presented in the left visual field than when they were presented in the right visual field. Note that this is what both attitude theories would predict. Finally, as expected, the reaction times for the strong attitudes were faster and more accurate than for the weak attitudes.

To get a more complete picture, we decided to vary the presentation times in the second study. In the first study, all emotional words were presented for 180ms, but what would happen at a much longer or shorter presentation time?

Study 2

Participants

Thirty-five students from the University of Bergen (Norway) participated in this study following written informed consent according to institutional guidelines. All participants were consistent right-handed as measured by the Edinburgh Handedness Inventory (laterality index: mean +/- SD, 98% +/- 5%; range 87%-100%) (Oldfield, 1971). There were 15 males and 20 females with an average age of 23 years and they were all native speakers of Norwegian. An honorarium was given for participation.

Experimental Design

A 3 (Visual field: left, right, center) x 3 (Presentation time: 10ms, 120ms, 1000ms) x 2 (Valence: positive vs. negative) x 2 (Response button: positive-left/negative-right vs. positive-right/negative-left), within subject design was used (with the last factor as a between subjects factor).

Procedure

In general, the same procedure as in the first study was used, but there were two differences. Contrary to the first study, the emotional words were presented at different presentation times (10ms, 120ms, 1000ms) in order to investigate what happens at a completely unconscious and at a completely conscious level. In addition, the emotional words were presented in the left and right visual field and at the center of the screen in order to make comparisons between the left and right visual field data and the control data (center) possible. Again, the participants task was to evaluate the words as positive or negative by pressing on the 'positive' and the 'negative' button as soon as possible and the location of the 'positive' and 'negative' button (left vs. right) was varied between participants. Both the positive and negative responses and the reaction times were measured. The most common frequency book for Norwegian was used to determine the frequency of the emotional words in Norwegian (Heggestad, 1982).

Results

A 3 (Visual field: left, right, center) x 3 (Presentation-time: 10ms, 120ms, 1000ms) x 2 (Valence: positive vs. negative) x 2 (Response button: positive-left/negative-right vs. positive-right/negative-left), within subject MANOVA was conducted (with the last factor as a between subjects factor).

As can be seen in Table 3, a significant main effect for valence was found, $F(1,34) = 29.2$, $p < .001$. Participants process positive words faster than negative words both at the subliminal and at the supraliminal level. Moreover, a significant main effect for valence was found on evaluation

accuracy, $F(1,34) = 9.2$, $p < .05$. Participants process negative words more accurately both at the subliminal and at the supraliminal level. No significant main effect for lateralization was found.

Table 3: Mean reaction time for the positive and negative words; specified for visual field (left vs. right) and presentation time (1000ms, 120ms, 10ms).

	Duration	Left	Right
Positive	1000ms	1474ac	1228bc
Negative	1000ms	1340ad	1334ad
Positive	120ms	1216ac	1202ac
Negative	120ms	1373ad	1291bd
Positive	10ms	1559ac	1591ac
Negative	10ms	2147ad	1701bd

*Note: Means (across rows and colons) with different subscripts are significantly different ($p < .05$).

Discussion

In this study, it was found that at the conscious level, emotional words that were presented in the right visual field were processed faster than words that were presented in the left visual field. At the conscious level, normal language processing is more dominant than the emotional content of the words. In addition, it was found that participants process positive words faster than negative words, but negative words better than positive words at the subliminal, supraliminal, and conscious level.

To get a more complete understanding of the results, we also conducted a divided visual field study with sixty emotional pictures (30 positive and 30 negative) and a presentation time of 120ms. The pictures were taken from the International Affective Picture System (Ito, Cacioppo, & Lang, 1998) and from the internet. There were no significant differences in size and brightness between the 30 positive and 30 negative pictures. The results of this study showed evidence in favor of the valence theory (Lee et al., 1993).

General Discussion

In this study, the focus was on how humans process emotional words. To investigate this, two studies were conducted; one with a presentation time of 180ms and one with different presentation times (10ms, 120ms and 1000ms). We were particularly interested in the question what process is more dominant; the language processing of words or the emotional content of these words? If the language processing of words is the most dominant process, one would hypothesize that all emotional words are processed better and faster when they are presented in the right visual field (and processed in the left hemisphere) (Vikingstad et al., 2000). However, when the emotional content of the words is the most dominant process, there would be two possibilities; 1) According to the right hemisphere theory (Borod et al., 1988) all attitudes are processed better and faster in the right hemisphere. In that case the hypothesis would be that all emotional words are processed better and faster when they are presented in the left visual field (and processed in the right hemisphere). 2) Whereas according to valence theory (Lee et al., 1993) the right hemisphere is dominant for negative attitudes and the left hemisphere is dominant for positive attitudes. In line with the valence theory, the hypothesis would be that the negative emotional words are processed better and faster when they are presented in the left visual field and the positive words are processed better and faster when they are presented in the right visual field.

In addition to the question what theory (the language theory or one of the two attitude theories) can best explain our behavioral data; we were interested in the question if the results are the same at different presentation times?

In this study, it was found that at the conscious level, emotional words that were presented in the right visual field were processed faster than words that were presented in the left visual field. At the conscious level, normal language processing is indeed the most dominant process. At the unconscious level, this was not the case, but no strong support for one of the two attitude theories could be found. Note that our study with the emotional pictures showed evidence in favor of the valence theory (Lee et al., 1993) when pictures instead of emotional words were used.

So far, previous studies with ERP have shown evidence in favor of both the right hemisphere theory (Borod et al., 1988) and the valence theory (Lee et al., 1993). Cacioppo et al. (1996) found a larger activation in the right hemisphere if people had to evaluate negative and positive attitude objects. For the neutral attitude objects, no significant differences were found between the right and the left hemisphere. However, Sutton and Davidson (1997; 2000) found evidence in favor of the valence theory or more precisely: the approach-withdrawal theory. There is interplay between the medial regions of the prefrontal cortex in the right- and the left hemisphere. The left hemisphere is responsible for approach behavior while the right hemisphere is responsible for withdrawal behavior (Davidson, 2004). Recently, Cunningham, Espinet, DeYoung, and Zelazo (2005) used dense-array ERP to examine the time course and neural bases of evaluative processing. Their results were consistent with a model in which discrete regions of prefrontal cortex are specialized for the evaluative processing of positive and negative stimuli.

In a functional Magnetic Resonance (fMRI)-study with positive and negative emotional words, Fossati et al. (2003) found that a widely distributed network of brain areas contributes to emotional processing. In other fMRI-studies, evidence for right lateralized processing of negative information has been found (e.g. Anderson et al., 2003; Cunningham, Raye, & Johnson, 2004). Specifically, areas of right inferior frontal cortex and anterior insula consistently appear to be involved more in processing negative than positive stimuli. Other studies have found that particular areas of orbitofrontal cortex (e.g. Anderson et al., 2003) and basal ganglia (Tanaka, Doya, Okada, Ueda, Okamoto, &

Yamawaki, 2004) are involved more in the processing of positive affect than negative effect (Wager, Phan, Liberzon, & Taylor, 2003 for a meta-analysis). Although such findings do not necessarily imply that the processing of positive and negative stimuli is fully dissociated, they suggest the presence of at least partially separable circuits.

In future research it would be particularly interesting to use the same stimuli in a combined ERP-fMRI study (Eichele et al., 2005).

Acknowledgments

The authors would like to thank the Max Planck Institute for Psycholinguistics in Nijmegen, the Netherlands for allowing the use of the CELEX lexical database.

References

Anderson, A. K. Christoff, K., Stappen, I., Panitz, D., Ghahremani, D. G., Glover, G., Gabrieli, J. D., & Sobel, N. (2003). Dissociated neural representations of intensity and valence in human olfaction, *Nature Neuroscience, 6*, 196-202.

Baayen, R. H., Piepenbrock, R., & Van Rijn, H. (1993). *The CELEX Lexical Database.* Philadelphia: Linguistic Data Consortium.

Bargh, J. A., Chaiken, S., Govender, R., & Pratto, F. (1992). The generality of the automatic attitude activation effect. *Journal of Personality and Social Psychology, 62*, 893-912.

Bargh, J. A., Chaiken, S., Raymond, P., & Hymes, C. (1996). The automatic evaluation effect: Unconditionally automatic attitude activation with a pronunciation task. *Journal of Experimental Social Psychology, 32*, 104-128.

Borod, J. C. (1992). Interhemispheric and intrahemispheric control of emotion: A focus on unilateral brain damage. *Journal of Consulting and Clinical Psychology, 60*, 339-348.

Borod, J. C., Kent, J., Koff, E., Martin, C., & Alpert, M. (1988). Facial asymmetry while posing positive and negative emotions: Support for the right hemisphere hypothesis. *Neuropsychologia, 26*, 759-764.

Cacioppo, J. T., Crites, S. L., & Gardner, W. L. (1996). Attitudes to the right: evaluative processing is associated with lateralized late positive event-related brain potentials. *Personality and Social Psychology Bulletin, 22*, 1205-1219.

Cunningham, W. A., Espinet, S. D., DeYoung, C. G., & Zelazo, P. D. (2005). Attitudes to the right- and left: Frontal ERP asymmetries associated with stimulus valence and processing goals. *NeuroImage, 28*, 827-834.

Cunningham, W. A., Raye, C. L., & Johnson, M. K. (2004). Implicit and explicit evaluation: fMRI correlates of valence, emotional intensity, and control in the processing of attitudes, *Journal of Cognitive Neuroscience, 16*, 1717-1729.

Davidson, R. J. (1995). Cerebral Asymmetry, Emotion, and Affective Style. In R. J. Davidson & K. Hugdahl (Eds.), *Brain Asymmetry* (pp. 361-387). Cambridge, MA: MIT Press.

Davidson, R. J. (2004). What does the prefrontal cortex "do" in affect: perspectives on frontal EEG asymmetry research. *Biological Psychology, 67,* 219-233.

Davidson, R. J., Ekman, P., Saron, C. D., Senulis, J. A., & Friesen, W. V. (1990). Approach-withdrawal and cerebral asymmetry. *Journal Personality, Social Psychology, 58,* 330-341.

Dowling, J. E. (1992). *Neurons and Networks: An Introduction to Neuroscience.* Cambridge, MA: Harvard University Press.

Eagly, A. H., & Chaiken, S. (1993). *The psychology of attitudes.* New York: Harcourt Brace Jovanovich.

Eichele, T., Specht, K., Moosmann, M., Jongsma, M. L., Quiroga, R. Q., Nordby, H., & Hugdahl, K. (2005). Assessing the spatiotemporal evolution of neuronal activation with single-trial event-related potentials and functional MRI. *Proceedings of the National Academy of Sciences (PNAS), 49,* 17798-17803.

Fabrigar, L. R., Priester, J. R., Petty, R. E., & Wegener, D. T. (1998). The impact of attitude accessibility on elaboration of persuasive message. *Personality and Social Psychology Bulletin, 24,* 339-352.

Fazio, R. H. (1995). Attitudes as object-evaluation associations: Determinants, consequences, and correlates of attitude accessibility. In R. E. Petty & J. A. Krosnick (Eds.), *Attitude strength: Antecedents and consequences.* Mahwah, NJ: Lawrence Erlbaum Associates.

Fazio, R. H., Sanbonmatsu, D. M., Powell, M. C., & Kardes, F. R. (1986). On the automatic activation of attitudes. *Journal of Personality and Social Psychology, 50,* 229-238.

Fossati, P., Hevenor, S. J., Graham, S. J., Grady, C., Keightley, M. L., Craik, F., & Mayberg, H. (2003). In Search of the Emotional Self: An fMRI Study Using Positive and Negative Emotional Words. *American Journal of Psychiatry, 160,* 1938-1945.

Heggestad, K. (1982). *Norsk frekvensordbok.* Bergen: Universitetsforlaget.

Hellige, J. B. (1993). *Hemispheric Asymmetry.* Cambridge, MA: Harvard University Press.

Hellige, J. B., & Yamauchi, M. (1999). Quantitative and Qualitative Hemispheric Asymmetry for Processing Japanese Kana. *Brain and Cognition, 40,* 453-463.

Holland, R. W., Verplanken, B., & Van Knippenberg, A. (2002). On the nature of attitude-behavior relations: the strong guide, the weak follow. *European Journal of Social Psychology, 32,* 869-876.

Ito, T. A., Cacioppo, J. T., & Lang, P. J. (1998). Eliciting affect using the Internacional Affective Picture System: Bivariate evaluation and ambivalente. *Personality and Social Psychology Bulletin, 24,* 855-879.

Kolb, B., & Taylor, L. (1981). Affective behaviour in patients with localized cortical excisions: Role of lesion site and side. *Science, 214,* 89-91.

LeDoux, J. E. (1996). *The emotional brain.* New York: Simon & Schuster.

Lee, G. P., Loring, D. W., Dahl, J. L., & Meador, K. J. (1993). Hemispheric specialization for emotional expression. *Neuropsychiatry, neuropsychology, and Behavioral Neurology, 6,* 143-148.

Liddell, B. J., Williams, L. M., Rathjen, J., Shevrin, H., & Gordon, E. (2004). A Temporal Dissociation of Subliminal versus Supraliminal Fear Perception: An Event-related Potential Study. *Journal of Cognitive Neuroscience, 16,* 479-486.

Nicholls, M. E. R., Wood, A. G., & Hayes, L. (2001). Cerebral asymmetries in the level of attention required for word recognition. *Laterality, 6,* 97-110.

Oldfield, R. C. (1971). The assessment and analysis of handedness: the Edinburgh Inventory. *Neuropsychologia, 9,* 97-113.

Petty, R. E., & Krosnick, J. A. (1995). *Attitude strength: Antecedents and consequences.* Hillsdale, NJ: Erlbaum.

Sutton, S. K., & Davidson, R. J. (1997). Prefrontal brain asymmetry: A biological substrate of the behavioural approach and inhibition systems. *Psychological Science, 8,* 204-210.

Sutton, S. K., & Davidson, R. J. (2000). Prefrontal brain electrical asymmetry predicts the evaluation of affective stimuli. *Neuropsychologia, 38,* 1723-1733.

Tanaka, S. C., Doya, K., Okada, G., Ueda, K., Okamoto, Y., & Yamawaki, S. (2004). Prediction of immediate and future rewards differentially recruits cortico-basal ganglia loops, *Nature Neuroscience, 7,* 887–893.

Van den Noort, M. W. M. L. (2003). *The Unconscious Brain: The Relative Time and Information Theory of Emotions.* Oegstgeest, NL: Citadel.

Van den Noort, M. W. M. L., Bosch, M. P. C., & Hugdahl, K. (2005a). Understanding the Unconscious Brain: Evidence for Non-Linear Information Processing. In B.G. Bara, L. Barsalou, & M. Bucciarelli (Eds.), Paper published in the *Proceedings of the 27th Annual Meeting of the Cognitive Science Society* (pp. 2254-2258). Mahwah, NJ: Lawrence Erlbaum Associates.

Van den Noort, M. W. M. L., Hugdahl, K., & Bosch, M. P. C. (2005b). Human Machine Interaction: The Special Role for Human Unconscious Emotional Information Processing. *Lecture Notes in Computer Science, 3784,* 598-605.

Van den Noort, M. W. M. L., Bosch, M. P. C., & Hugdahl, K. (2006). Foreign language proficiency and working memory capacity. *European Psychologist, 11,* 289-296.

Vikingstad, E. M., George, K. P., Johnson, A. F., & Cao, Y. (2000). Cortical language lateralization in right handed normal subjects using functional magnetic resonance imaging. *Journal of the Neurological Sciences, 175,* 17-27.

Wager, T. D., Phan, K. L., Liberzon, I., & Taylor, S. F. (2003). Valence, gender, and lateralization of functional brain anatomy in emotion: a meta-analysis of findings from neuroimaging, *NeuroImage, 19,* 513-531.

Williams, L. M., Liddell, B. J., Kemp, A. H., Bryant, R. A., Meares, R. A., Peduto, A. S., & Gordon, E. (2006). Amygdala-Prefrontal Dissociation of Subliminal and Supraliminal Fear. *Human Brain Mapping, 27,* 652-661.

Differential Effect of Spectral Detail in Perceiving Identity, Emotion and Intelligible Speech from Voice: Exploring the Face Analogy

Alexandros Kafkas (Alexandros.Kafkas@postgrad.manchester.ac.uk)
School of Psychological Sciences
The University of Manchester
Manchester M13 9PL

Sophie Scott (sophie.scott@ucl.ac.uk)
Institute of Cognitive Neuroscience, UCL, 17 Queen square
London WC1N 3AR

Abstract

Voice is an important carrier of linguistic and paralinguistic information (e.g. affective and identity cues) that facilitate human interaction and communication. The way that this information is extracted and processed remains to a great extent elusive. A recent neurocognitive model (Belin et al., 2004) has proposed separate functional and anatomical systems responsible for processing affective, identity and linguistic clues from vocal signals, as is the case for face perception. In the present study it is attempted to acoustically separate these three kinds of information by systematically varying the spectral detail of the vocal signal. It is illustrated that speech intelligibility, emotion recognition and speaker identification are differentially affected by the manipulation of the amount of spectral information. This differential reliance on the same acoustic parameters constitutes an important indication for the parallel processing of affective, identity and linguistic information from voice.

Introduction

The understanding of vocal signals constitutes an important human ability, essential for social interaction and communication. Perhaps we dedicate more time hearing voices than attending any other stimulus in our environment. In animals conspecific vocalizations represent an essential way of communicating danger, commencing forage-related behaviour and transmitting procreation signals (Arcadi, 2005). Likewise, human communication is crucially based on vocal signals not only due to their linguistic function, constituting the vehicle of speech, but also owing to the transmission of social significant speaker-related information (identity, emotional mood, age, gender; Lattner, Meyer & Friederici, 2005). In the present study, drawing on previous observations concerning the distinct processing of linguistic and paralinguistic vocal information, is investigated whether linguistic, identity-related and affective elements are differentially modulated by the spectral manipulation of the vocal signal. The differential reliance of these three kinds of voice information on the same acoustic parameters has important implications for models proposing parallel stages for extracting linguistic and paralinguistic references from voice.

The "Auditory Face"

In analogy to faces, voices carry substantial paralinguistic information more prominently concerning speaker identification and his/her emotional state. For this reason Belin, et al. (2004) describe voice as an "auditory face".

According to the influential model proposed by Bruce and Young (1986) face perception contains several independent sub-stages that act in parallel and are responsible for extracting different classes of information from face. According to this model after a common structural representation of face, the visual analysis of emotional expression and face recognition follow independent and parallel processing pathways.

This model is supported by studies indicating lack of behavioural or electrophysiological interaction between face familiarity and the emotion expressed (e.g. Caharel, et al., 2005; Calder, et al., 2000); by neuropsychological dissociations with some prosopagnosic patients retaining the ability to recognize emotional expressions and other patients showing the reverse pattern (e.g. Duchaine, Parker & Nakayama, 2003); and by neuroimaging studies that have identified separable neural networks responsible for processing identity and expression from faces (e.g. Winston, et al., 2004). Nevertheless, these dissociations as Calder and Young (2005) suggest should not be interpreted in a strict manner, but as revealing that recognition of facial identity and perception of facial expressions are only partially independent.

In a similar vein, voice perception has been proposed to incorporate three types of information embedded within vocal signal: speech content, affective information and speaker's identity clues. These types of information might be processed by partially independent functional pathways similar to those described for face perception (Belin, et al., 2004). The different levels of voice processing are thought to work in unison with the similar stages found in face perception, integrating information from both modalities. This assumption is in accordance with contemporary studies of cross-modal communication (de Gelder & Vroomen, 2000; Pourtois, et al., 2005).

More analytically, vocal signals are important carriers of speech which entails access to low level acoustic properties, phonetic cues, syntactic structure and finally higher level conceptual-semantic information (Price, Thierry & Griffiths, 2005). In particular, speech intelligibility refers to the successful decoding of the vocal signal and it is commonly measured as a function of the accurate reception of speech content.

Nevertheless, in our daily life the ability to understand vocal signals is based not only on verbal cues but also on paralinguistic expressions conveyed by suprasegmental aspects of speech such as pitch (fundament frequency/F0), intensity, duration and voice quality (Berckmoes & Vingergoets, 2004; Friederici & Alter, 2004). These acoustic properties are generally referred to as prosody and may serve linguistic (e.g. emphasizing, questioning) and affective functions. According to Banse & Scherer (1996) affective prosody induced by physiological changes related to respiration, phonation and articulation, reflects the emotional state of the speaker and is transmitted as part of the speech signal. Finally, voice is an important perceptual tool, which actively interacts with facial perceptual clues (von Kriegstein, et al., 2005), for recognizing familiar and discriminating unfamiliar people.

The idea of partially distributed mechanisms responsible for processing linguistic (speech content) and paralinguistic (affective elements, identity) information from vocal stimuli has not yet been systematically investigated, but some evidence exists for their independent processing.

The distinct processing of the three kinds of vocal information, as has been proposed by Belin et al (2004), is supported not only by sparse neuroimaging and neuropsychological data (see e.g. Imaizumi et al., 1997; Kittredge, Davis & Blumstein, 2006), but also by observations concerning their reliance on acoustic parameters of the vocal signal. Speech intelligibility relies mostly on phonemic analysis and rapidly changing temporal signals, whereas speaker identification is transmitted by spectral properties with vocal tract features (voice timber) playing a crucial role in determining talker's identity (Lavner, Gath & Roesenhouse, 2000). Furthermore, many studies (e.g. Bänziger & Scherer, 2005) have underlined the significance of intonational cues and especially the role of fundamental frequency (F0/pitch) in perceiving the emotional state of the speaker (Scherer, 2003). In an early study Scherer, Ladd and Silverman (1984) indicated that voice quality and F0 contour are the strongest transmitters of vocal affect independently of the verbal context. In particular, regarding the independent processing of emotional prosody from linguistic content, has been reported that participants from different countries are able to extract emotional cues from speech signals even when the language is completely unknown to them (Scherer, Banse & Wallbott, 2001); thus, relying exclusively on prosodic cues.

The aim of the present study is to offer behavioural observations that empirically evaluate a model of voice processing consisting of distinct processing systems for accesing linguistic, affective and speaker's identity-related information. The empirical confirmation of such a model of human voice perception is essential to enhance research within the different processing stages (linguistic and paralinguistic), as well as to successfully integrate observed cross-modal interactions with the corresponding systems of face processing (see e.g. de Gelder & Vroomen, 2000). Thus, in the current study it is attempted to acoustically segregate the three mechanisms responsible for extracting linguistic and paralinguistic (speaker identity, emotion recognition) vocal information by modulating the spectral detail of the vocal signals.

To this aim noise-vocoded speech sounds were used with gradually increasing spectral detail and their impact on performing the three tasks (intelligibility, emotion recognition and speaker identification) were measured. It is hypothesized that the addition of more spectral detail (frequency channels) would result in greater performance for all the three tasks, but within this general pattern a diverse performance in recognizing the three kinds of information is expected. More specifically, intelligibility of speech sounds due to its reliance on fast temporal signals (Boemio, et al., 2005) should be affected less than speaker identification and emotion recognition. Moreover, the way that emotion recognition and speaker identification progress with the addition of more channels constitutes an important exploration relevant to the separation of these two types of paralinguistic information.

Methods

Participants

Thirty native British English speakers with no history of hearing problem were included in the study. The participants' mean age was 25.47 years (SD=7.96).

Design and Material

The experiment consisted of three blocks with a total of 290 trials. A within-groups design was employed across all tasks. Stimuli for all the three blocks contained three-digit numbers that were delivered by two female and two male speakers with standard British accent. Speech samples were recorded, digitized and then converted into noise-vocoded sounds. Noise-vocoded sound-distortion technique has been described by Shannon, et al. (1995) as a method that alters the spectral detail of speech, preserving at the same time the temporal and amplitude cues of each band. Specifically, each acoustic signal was divided into 1, 4, 6, 8, 12, 16, 20, 24, 28, or 32 frequency bands. The amplitude envelope of each band was extracted and a spectrally limited noise of the same frequency range was modulated. Thus, the produced noise was characterized by the same amplitude fluctuations of the original band. Finally, the modulated bands were recombined to compose the distorted stimuli. The same process was conducted for each of the 10 frequency band conditions.

The first block of stimuli measured intelligibility of noise-vocoded speech sounds depending on the number of the active frequency channels. To avoid repetition of the same three-digit number every stimulus was heard once and has a different number of frequency bands available.

The second part of the experiment consisted of 200 trials and was devised to measure recognition of different emotions with varying available spectral information. The same three-digit numbers were used delivered in ten different emotional tones. Positive and negative emotions with characteristic acoustic properties were used: achievement, amusement, anger, contentment, disgust, fear, pleasure, relief, sadness and surprise.

Finally, in the third block participants were asked to identify if two speakers are "same" or "different" across 10 noise-vocoded band conditions. All trials within each block were randomly presented to the participants.

Procedure and Analysis

The participants were individually tested in a quiet testing room insulated from external noise. The subjects were seated comfortably and the stimuli were binaurally presented over headphones (*Technics*, model RP-F200) at a constant volume level. The entire testing session for all tasks lasted approximately 35-40 minutes and the participants received £5 for their participation.

Three repeated measures analyses of variance (ANOVAs) were employed to analyze the data for intelligibility, emotion recognition and identification tasks. Also, a one-way ANOVA was carried out to compare *β-values* for intelligibility, identification and emotion recognition. *Post-hoc* comparisons were conducted using Bonferroni's correction for multiple comparisons. Eta-squared (η^2) effect size was calculated for each main effect and interaction. Regression analysis was also employed to introduce models of the observed data and linear and logarithmic lines were fitted.

Results

To score intelligibility performance participants received one point for each correctly reported digit (in the right order) in each of the 10 spectral conditions. A one-way repeated measures ANOVA was then conducted to compare the differences in intelligibility across the ten levels of the independent variable.

The results showed that speech intelligibility was significantly affected by the number of the available modified frequency bands, $F(9, 261)=42.10$, $p<0.001$, $\eta^2=0.59$. Regression analysis of the effect of spectral detail on intelligibility produced a significant logarithmic model $F(1,8)=20.48$, $p<0.01$ with $R^2=0.72$. As shown in Figure 1, this model denotes that high performance is observed with little spectral detail (as little as 4-6 frequency channels) with the subsequent increase in the amount of spectral information contributing less to speech comprehension.

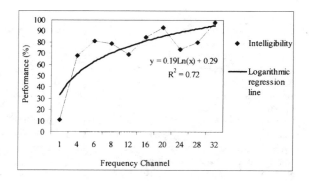

Figure 1: Effect of spectral detail on intelligibility of the vocal signal.

Performance for emotion recognition was well above chance for most emotions with sufficient spectral detail. However, emotional categories like disgust and emotions expressed with less frequency channels were recognized with greater difficulty. The proportional scores of emotion recognition were analysed in an ANOVA with the number of channels and emotion category as the within-subject factors (10 × 10 repeated measures design). There was a significant main effect of the amount of spectral information (channel) on emotion recognition performance, $F(9, 261)=16.69$, $p<0.001$, $\eta^2=0.37$. Regression analysis produced a significant linear effect ($R^2=0.70$, $F(1, 8)=18.27$, $p<0.01$) nevertheless, a logarithmic effect of the amount of spectral information on emotion recognition constitutes a better explanation for the observed data ($R^2= 0.88$, $F(1, 8)=58.71$, $p<0.001$). This means that a more significant increase in performance is observable for the first few levels of the independent variable, accompanied by a less profound influence of later additions of frequency channels (Figure 2).

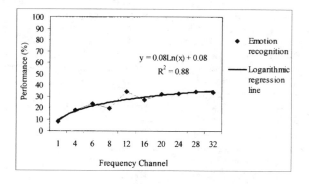

Figure 2: Effect of the amount of spectral detail on emotion recognition.

There was also a significant main effect of emotion category ($F(9, 261)=16.23$, $p<0.001$, $\eta^2=0.36$), implying that emotion recognition reaches different levels for the various emotions expressed. Finally, the significant interaction effect between emotion category and number of available frequency channels ($F(81, 2349)=1.92$, $p<0.001$, $\eta^2=0.06$) denotes that recognition of the various emotions progressed differently as more spectral detail was added to the vocal signal. Indeed, the analysis of the effect of spectral information separately for each emotion revealed that for some emotions recognition progresses very little with performance remaining at low levels across the ten frequency channels (e.g. disgust, pleasure, contentment, and relief). On the contrary, most of the other emotions achieved highest recognition with 12 available frequency channels, with performance being stabilized for later additions of frequency bands.

Speaker's identification task consisted of "same/different" responses. Proportional scores for each subject were extracted by subtracting the proportion of false alarms (i.e. different speakers falsely recognised as same) from the proportion of hits (i.e. correctly recognised speakers as same). This measure resembles d-prime values (d′) but allows expressing performance in this task on the same scale as the other two measures (intelligibility, emotion recognition). The adjusted for response-bias scores were analyzed in a one-way repeated-measures ANOVA to assess the differences in speaker identification performance across the ten frequency channels. The ANOVA yielded a significant effect of spectral information on speaker identification ($F(9, 252)=30.58$, $p<0.001$, $\eta^2=0.52$). Regression analysis demonstrated a significant logarithmic effect of spectral detail on performing speaker discrimination ($R^2=0.69$, $F(1, 8)=18.10$, $p<0.01$) denoting that performance increase is greater for the first few levels of the independent variable (Figure 3). A closer inspection of the data reveals that this pattern seems to be more robust in trials with different speakers than for items spoken by the same speaker. In fact, examination of false alarm rates suggests that participants tended to choose the "same" label as a default choice when the spectral detail was insufficient to provide a clear percept.

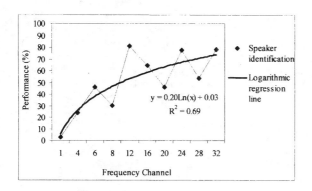

Figure 3: Effect of the amount of spectral detail on speaker identification.

Speech perception, recognition of affective prosody and speaker identification seem to advance differently as more spectral detail is added. This implies that the three types of vocal information relate differently to the amount of the available spectral information in the vocal stimuli. To statistically assess this difference in performance for the three kinds of information embedded in vocal signal a separate analysis of variance (ANOVA) was performed on the β-values generated by the different regression analyses of spectral detail on performance in the three tasks.

The results showed that performance in each of these tasks was differentially affected by the amount of spectral information, $F(2, 56)=23.11$, $p<0.001$, $\eta^2=0.45$. Post-hoc pairwise comparisons indicated, as shown in figure 4, that speaker identification ($t(28)=7.03$, $p<0.001$) and speech recognition ($t(28)=5.60$, $p<0.001$) increases more than emotion recognition as more spectral information is added. Furthermore, speaker identification performance advances more than speech recognition ($t(28)=2.1$, $p<0.05$) as spectral information becomes more detailed.

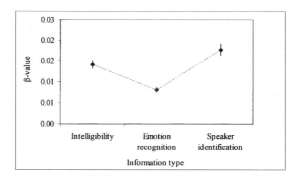

Figure 4: Differential effect of the addition of spectral information in performing intelligibility, emotion recognition and speaker identification tasks.

Discussion

In the present study the recognition of linguistic, affective and identity information was explored under conditions of modulated spectral detail of speech sounds. Specifically, the amount of frequency channels available in speech stimuli was systematically varied, and the impact of this modulation on recognizing the three kinds of information, transmitted by the vocal signal, was tested. The main hypothesis was that if the three kinds of vocal information are processed by partially separable systems (that are responsible for processing different vocal cues), then the systematic modulation of acoustic parameters like spectral information, would have different effect on performing the three tasks of the experiment. To achieve that, noise-vocoded speech sounds were used that preserve the temporal characteristics of the signal, allowing the manipulation of the available spectral detail.

Indeed, consistent with this hypothesis the results indicate that as the number of frequency bands increased, performance in the three tasks of the present experiment was differentiated. This means that participants relied differently on the various acoustic properties of the signaled sounds to extract the relevant, for each task, information (linguistic, affective or identity-related).

Analytically, in accordance with previous studies (see e.g. Shannon et al., 1995; Smith et al., 2002) the current results indicate that noise-vocoded speech with as little as 4 available frequency channels provides sufficient information to be reliably understood by the listener. Later additions of spectral detail enhance speech comprehension less. This illustrates that the temporal content of the original speech sound, with very little spectral detail, includes enough information for the speech to be linguistically accessible to the receiver.

Furthermore, this is the first study that explores the impact of noise-vocoded speech on perceiving affective prosody. Emotion recognition increased with the addition of more frequency channels, but the overall recognition remained at lower levels, as compared to speech intelligibility or speaker identity recognition, even in conditions where 32 noise-modulated bands were available. This result signifies that despite the increase of spectral detail, participants needed additional acoustic cues to fully decode the emotional significance of the vocal signal. Previous studies (e.g. Bänziger & Scherer, 2005; Friederici & Alter, 2004) have illustrated that emotion recognition relies predominantly on intonational aspects of voice. These acoustic parameters are less accessible from noise-vocoded modulated speech that excludes voice quality information. Also of note, the overall recognition was different for the various emotional categories. Earlier studies have suggested the relative difficulty in recognizing emotions like disgust or pleasure from voice (Scherer, 2003). Indeed, the results of the present study indicate that disgust and pleasure along with contentment and relief are less recognizable, whereas achievement, amusement, anger, sadness and surprise are decoded better from the voice. It is possible that the reason for this pattern is communicative and human interaction relies differently on the various channels (voice, face, body stance etc) to extract affective information.

Finally, the increase of the number of frequency channels led to better discrimination of same or different speakers. This is in accordance with previous observations (Fu, et al., 2005; Warren, et al., in press) that have demonstrated that increased spectral detail of a speech sound facilitates better reception of speaker personal information, such as his/her gender, his/her familiarity or unfamiliarity. More importantly for the present study, these results underline an essential difference between emotion recognition and speaker identification. Although both kinds of paralinguistic information are sensitive to signal's spectral detail and voice quality, emotion recognition seems to rely more on voice quality, which is degraded even when 32 noise modulated bands are presented. On the contrary, spectral detail as expressed by the existence of more frequency channels, permits full access on vocal cues that allow speaker

discrimination. This is in accordance with an earlier study by Remez, Fellowes and Rubin (1997) who presented evidence that talker's information remained accessible in vocal sounds despite the discarding of intonation and vocal timbre elements.

Also of note is the clear tendency of the participants to better discriminate different speakers and especially speakers with different gender, even with less spectral detail. This result signifies that perceivers of the vocal signal are based more on differences between the speakers in order to discriminate their identity, rather than on absolute vocal acoustic features. This finding is well in accordance with Lavner, Gath & Rosenhouse's (2000) observation that even though vocal tract characteristics constitute important cues for identifying a person, each speaker has a different personal combination of acoustic features that facilitate his/her identity recognition. Therefore, it is possibly through this different combination of vocal features that participants discriminate same or different speakers. Nevertheless, further research is needed to elucidate the mechanisms behind speaker discrimination.

Overall, the results are in accordance with a model of voice processing consisting of three distinguishable systems that act independently to extract linguistic and paralinguistic information. It is important to note that even though the data support the separate processing of these three kinds of vocal information, the proposed model should not be interpreted as excluding any interaction between the different streams. As has been suggested for the domain of face perception (Calder & Young, 2005), even though these functional streams may be dedicated for processing distinct characteristics of vocal signal, they dynamically interact to give a concrete perception of the transmitted object. Therefore, the current results should be seen as an indication of partially separate stages, under a common system, for processing linguistic, affective and identity-related clues.

Thus, a common level of processing is expected that codes all the three kinds of vocal information (or integrates perception from the three streams), but the current data are inadequate to illuminate its location. An important direction for future work is to investigate, both experimentally and by using functional neuroimaging techniques, the relation between the different processing streams, the way they independently extract information from a given vocal signal, and the way they interact to give rise to the integrated perception. Future work can bring to light further functional dissociations, as well as commonalities, in the processing of different kinds of vocal information by systematically manipulating variables that may affect the decoding of the vocal signal. The unveiling of variables that influence one process greater than the other would further support the proposal that the three processes operate separately up to a level. Moreover, considering that human communication draws on various modalities it is essential to understand the mechanisms of information integration from various sources (e.g. face and voice). Finally, these results may have important implications for understanding voice perception and especially the recognition of paralinguistic aspects of speech in cochlear implant users.

From the present data there is a clear indication for the distinct processing of these three kinds of vocal information, on the basis of differential reliance on specific acoustic parameters. Nevertheless, the confirmation of such a model requires further convergent cognitive and neurocognitive evidence to support the idea of partially separate systems within voice perception.

In summary, the present work elucidates the different reliance of each of the three kinds of voice information on the spectral detail of the vocal signal. This difference in accessing linguistic content, speaker's affective state and his/her identity is concordant with a parallel processing of linguistic and paralinguistic aspects of speech. The implications of these results can be proved valuable in further exploring the organization of human voice perception.

References

Arcadi, A. C. (2005). Language Evolution: What Do Chimpanzees Have to Say? *Current Biology, 15,* 884-886.

Banse, R., & Scherer, K. R. (1996). Acoustic profiles in vocal emotion expression. *Journal of Personality and Social Psychology, 70,* 614-636.

Bänziger, T., & Scherer, K. R. (2005). The role of intonation in emotional expressions. *Speech Communication, 46,* 252-267.

Belin, P., Fecteau S., & Bédard, C. (2004). Thinking the voice: neural correlates of voice perception. *Trends in Cognitive Sciences, 8,* 129-135.

Berckmoes, C., & Vingergoets, G., (2004). Neural foundations of emotional speech processing. *Current Directions in Psychological Science, 13,* 182-185.

Boemio, A., Fromm, S., Braun, A., & Poeppel, D. (2005). Hierarchal and asymmetric temporal sensitivity in human auditory cortices. *Nature Neuroscience, 8,* 389-395.

Bruce, V. & Young, A. W. (1986). Understanding face recognition. *British Journal of Psychology, 77,* 305-327.

Caharel, S., Courtay, N., Bernard, C., Lalonde, R. & Rebaï, M. (2005). Familiarity and emotional expression influence an early stage of face processing: An electrophysiological study. *Brain and Cognition, 59,* 96-100.

Calder, A.J. & Young, A.W. (2005). Understanding the recognition of facial identity and facial expression. *Nature Reviews Neuroscience, 6,* 641- 651.

Calder, A. J., Young, A. W., Keane, J., & Dean, M. (2000). Configural information in facial expression perception. *Journal of Experimental Psychology: Human Perception and Performance, 26,* 527-551.

de Gelder, B., & Vroomen, J. (2000). The perception of emotions by ear and by eye. *Cognition and Emotion, 14,* 289-311.

Duchaine, B.C., Parker, H. & Nakayama, K. (2003). Normal recognition of emotion in a prosopagnosic. *Perception, 32,* 827-838.

Friederici, A. D., & Alter, K. (2004). Lateralization of auditory language functions: A dynamic dual pathway model. *Brain and Language, 89,* 267-276.

Fu, Q.-J., Chinchilla, S., Nogaki, G., & Galvin, J. J. (2005). Voice gender discrimination: the role of periodicity and spectral profile. *Journal of the Acoustical Society of America, 118,* 1711-1718.

Imaizumi, S., Mori, K., Kiritani, S., Kawashima, R., Suigiura, M., Fukuda, H., Itoh, K., Kato, T., Nakamura, A., Hatano, K., Kojima, S., Nakamura, K. (1997). Vocal identification of speaker and emotion activates different brain regions. *Cognitive Neuroscience and Neuropsychology, 8,* 2809-2812.

Kittredge, A., Davis, L., & Blumstein, S. E. (2006). Effects of non-linguistic auditory variations on lexical processing in Broca's aphasics. *Brain and Language, 97,* 25-40.

Lattner, S., Meyer, M. E., & Friederici, A. D. (2005). Voice perception: Sex, pitch and the right hemisphere. *Human Brain Mapping, 24,* 11-20.

Lavner, Y., Gath, I., & Rosenhouse, J. (2000). The effects of acoustic modifications on the identification of familiar voices speaking isolated vowels. *Speech Communication, 30,* 9-26.

Pourtois, G., de Gelder, B., Bol, A., & Commelinck, M. (2005). Perception of facial expressions and voices and of their combination in the human brain. *Cortex, 41,* 49-59.

Price, C., Thierry, G., & Griffiths, T. (2005). Speech-specific auditory processing: where is it? *Trends in Cognitive Sciences, 9,* 271-276.

Remez, R. E., Fellowes, J. M., & Rubin, P. E. (1997). Talker identification based on phonetic information. *Journal of Experimental Psychology: Human Perception and Performance, 23,* 651-666.

Scherer, K. R. (2003). Vocal communication of emotion: A review of research paradigms. *Speech communication, 40,* 227-256.

Scherer, K., Banse, R., & Wallbott, H. G. (2001). Emotion inferences from vocal expression correlate across languages and cultures. *Journal of Cross-cultural Psychology, 32,* 76-92.

Scherer, K. R., Ladd, D. R., & Silverman, K. E. A. (1984). Vocal cues to speaker affect: Testing two models. *Journal of the Acoustical Society of America, 76,* 1346-1356.

von Kriegstein, K., Kleinschmidt, A., Sterzer, P., & Giraud, A.-L. (2005). Interaction of face and voice areas during speaker recognition. *Journal of Cognitive Neuroscience, 17,* 367-376.

Winston, J.S., Henson, R.N., Fine-Goulden, M.R. & Dolan, R.J. (2004). fMRI-adaptation reveals dissociable neural representations of identity and expression in face perception. *Journal of Neurophysiology, 92,* 1830-1839.

Shannon, R. V., Zeng, F-G., Kamath, V., Wygonski, J., & Ekelid, M. (1995). Speech recognition with primary temporal cues. *Science, 270,* 303-304.

Smith, Z. M., Delgutte, B., & Oxenham, A. J. (2002). Chimaeric sounds reveal dichotomies in auditory perception. *Nature, 416,* 87-90.

Warren, J. D., Scott, S. K., Price, C. J., & Griffiths, T. D. (2006). Human brain mechanisms for the early analysis of voices. *Neuroimage, 31,* 1389-1397.

Recognizing emotions from faces:
Do we look for specific facial features?

Paolo Viviani (Paolo.Viviani@pse.unige.ch)
Faculty of Psychology and Educational Sciences, University of Geneva,
Switzerland, and Laboratory of Action, Perception and Cognition, Faculty of
Psychology, UHSR University, Milan, Italy

Chiara Fiorentini (Chiara.Fiorentini@pse.unige.ch)
Faculty of Psychology and Educational Sciences, University of Geneva,
Switzerland

Abstract

Two identification experiments investigated the recognition of the facial expressions of four basic emotions (Anger, Fear, Happiness, and Disgust). The novelty of the study is the adoption of an advanced morphing manipulation, for generating controlled transitions between expressions. In Experiment 1 morphs were equally spaced. Identification accuracy was highest (lower JND) when contrasting positive and negative emotions (Happiness and Disgust). In Experiment 2 we generated "chimerical morphs", in which the upper and lower parts of the face were morphed at different rates. The position of the PSE along the morphing sequence was sensitive to the rate of change, suggesting that specific facial features play a differential role in the recognition of different emotions. Key cues appear to be the shape of the mouth for Happiness, and the shape of the eyes for Fear, Anger, and Disgust.

Introduction

Inferring emotional states of other people from their facial expressions plays a major role in shaping our everyday social interactions, but a detailed cognitive account of how we recognize emotions from faces is still missing (Calder, Burton, Miller, Young, & Akamatsu, 2001). Neuropsychological and imaging studies have shown that facial affect recognition is subserved by a distributed neural network of interacting areas. It has also been suggested that different strategies concur to achieve recognition (Adolphs, 2002; Haxby, Hoffmann, & Gobbini, 2002). However, it is still actively debated (see Massaro, 1998 for an overview) whether a single holistic cue, or multiple cues are involved in extracting the relevant emotional information from facial expressions.

According to the configural encoding hypothesis, the spatial relations between the parts of the face provide a vital source of information when processing a facial expression. Instead, single-feature models claim that information concerning specific features might be sufficient, in principle, to make reliable inference about emotional states, or to associate facial expressions to emotion categories. Supporting evidence exists for both these views (see e.g., Calder, Young, Keane, & Dean, 2000 for a configural

processing account, and Cottrell, Dailey, Padgett, & Adolphs, 2001 for a feature-based account). It is also possible that feature-based and configuration-based processing play differential roles according to the emotion that is involved. For example, whereas it seems quite straightforward to infer happiness by detecting a single feature, namely the smile (Adolphs, 2002), discriminating between emotions with negative valence might require additional information about the configuration of the face. Because prototypical facial expressions of basic emotions, such as happiness or fear, naturally preserve the spatial relations between upper and lower halves of the face, the configural hypothesis can be evaluated by testing the interaction between upper and lower facial halves of the face (Meulders, De Boeck, Van Mechelen, & Gelman, 2005). The typical experimental strategy along these lines is to compare identification accuracy with facial expressions that either preserve or disrupt the spatial relations between the upper and lower halves of the face. In previous studies, this has been generally obtained by using chimeras, i.e. facial expressions in which the upper and lower halves of the face correspond to different basic emotions (see de Bonis, de Boeck, Pérez-Diaz, & Nahas, 1999).

The goal of this study is to investigate further the relative weight of holistic and local cues by using a more sophisticated set of stimuli. Generating realistic facial expressions has long proved to be challenging. Recent advances in the techniques for processing of digital images have made it possible to generate controlled blends (morphs) of two or more facial expressions. Although the same basic principles are embodied in most morphing algorithms, technical differences may have significant effects on the quality of the stimuli. A number of previous studies of facial expressions recognition has used morphed stimuli generated by commercially available software, mainly to address the issue of categorical perception (e.g., Calder, Young, Perret, Etcoff, & Rowland, 1996; Campanella, Quinet, Bruyer, Crommelinck, & Guerit, 2002; Etcoff & Magee, 1992; Young, Rowland, Calder, Etcoff, Seth, & Perrett, 1997). Instead, we designed a new, more advanced software (LOKI) that can produce highly controlled, "natural" transformations with an unlimited number of intermediate steps (for a more detailed description of the software, see Viviani et al. (2006)). More importantly, LOKI is capable of imposing different, user-defined, profiles of morphing rates to different parts of the face.

The study involves two experiments performed on the same population of participants. In Experiment 1, using fine-grained blends of pairs of expressions of basic emotions, we estimate the individual points of subjective equality (PSE), i.e. the point along the morphing sequence that in a forced-choice task is identified at chance level. Moreover, for each participant we also estimate the accuracy with which pairs of facial expressions are identified (JND). In Experiment 1, the rate of morphing being uniform, all parts of the face changed *pari passu*.

Experiment 1 provides the baseline for Experiment 2 in which we exploit the new feature of LOKI by using as stimuli morphing sequences in which either the lower of or the upper part of the face changes faster than the other one. The logic of the experiment is simple. If indeed the presence of a single feature is instrumental for identifying certain expressions, we expect that the individual PSEs are shifted systematically. For example, suppose that the smile is both necessary and sufficient for identifying Happiness. Then using a morphing sequence between Happiness and Disgust in which the lower part of the face changes faster than the upper face, one should observe a leftward shift of the PSE with respect to the value measured in Experiment 1.

Experiment 1

Experiment 1 estimates the accuracy with which people can identify the facial expressions of four basic emotions (Anger, Fear, Happiness, and Disgust). Three expressions pairs were chosen for examination: Anger-Fear (A/F); Anger-Disgust (A/D); Happiness-Disgust (H/D). We chose the H/D pairs as an example of clear opposition along a hypothetical positive-negative dimension of the emotion space. The other two pairs (A/F and A/D) were chosen for their intrinsic "confusability", demonstrated by several cross cultural studies (see Ekman, 1994 for a review). For each pair the stimuli to be used in a classical forced-choice identification task were sampled from a continuous morphing transformation between the selected prototypes. The distance between stimuli along the morphing sequence was constant, and the entire face underwent the same transformation. As mentioned in the Introduction, the main aim of the experiment is to provide a baseline for comparison with the results of Experiment 2 in which the upper and lower part of the face are transformed at different rates.

Methods

Participants: 15 undergraduates from UHSR University in Milan (age-range 20-35), in exchange of course credit.
Stimuli: The prototypes were facial expressions associated to four basic emotions: Anger, Fear, Happiness, and Disgust. The four expressions were posed by a professional mime, photographed against a dark background in full-frontal view with a high-resolution digital camera (EOS-1Ds), and processed with Photoshop CS2 to equalize overall luminance, contrast, and chromatic spectrum. For each expression pair the morphing software LOKI (Viviani, Binda, & Borsato, 2006) generated a sequence of 51 intermediated samples from a continuous linear transformation between prototypes.

For each continuum (A/F, A/D, H/D), the actual stimuli used in the experiment were 21 contiguous pictures, (rank order 15 to 35), within the corresponding sequence. The generation of each morphing sequence involved different steps. First, we identified the same set of salient facial features in both faces (landmarks). Then, a unique topological correspondence between templates was established by calculating the Delaunay triangulations (Okabe, Boots, Sugihara, & Chiu, 2000) of the two sets of landmarks. In the linear mode, the rate of morphing is constant, and so is the spacing between successive blends.

Experimental procedure: We adopted a forced-choice identification task, testing each pair of emotions in separate sessions (with session order counterbalanced between participants). In each trial, one expression morph from a given continuum was displayed on a computer screen and participants had to decide which prototype of the pair the stimulus was more similar to (e.g., "Is it more Anger or more Fear?"). Each stimulus was presented 40 times. The order of presentation was randomized across participants, with the constraint that successive stimuli had to be at least three steps away in the morphing sequence. In each session were presented $21 \times 40 = 840$ stimuli. At the beginning of each session, participants were shown the prototypes of the tested pair, and also performed a few practice trials. The stimulus remained visible for 3 sec., and we encouraged participants to respond as quickly and as accurately as possible, by pressing two keys on the keyboard. We recorded both the response and the response latency (RT) measured from the onset of the stimuli. The experiment was self-paced, each trial starting 500 ms after recording the previous response. There was no time-limit for responding and no feedback was given.

Results and discussion

Figures 1 summarizes the results. The lower plot in each panel reports the psychometric function relating the rank order of the stimuli within the morphing sequence to the relative frequency F_B of identifying the stimulus as template B (e.g., for the A/F pair, we reported the response frequency of identifying the stimulus as Fear). Bars are the 95% confidence intervals of the observed frequencies computed with the exact binomial theory (Sachs, 1984). Psychometric functions are characterized qualitatively by the median ($F_B = .5$) and the JND, both computed from the best-fitting Gaussian interpolation of the data points (continuous black lines). A comparison of these estimators across pairs of templates showed that: 1) for both the A/D and H/D pairs the point of indifference is roughly in the middle of the ran-

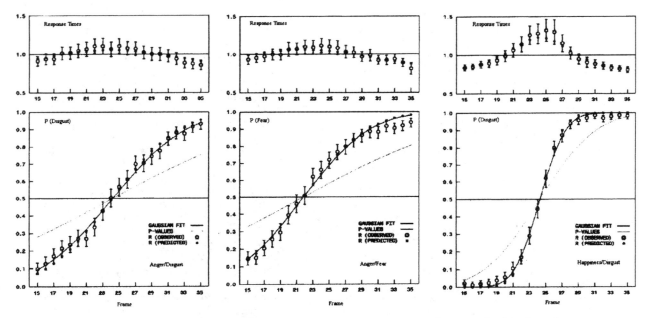

Figure 1: Exp.1. Response probabilities and response times (RTs) for the three tested pairs of emotions.

ge of variation of the stimuli. For the A/F pair the PSE indicated an earlier recognition of Fear with respect to the objective equilibrium between the two prototypes; 2) the discriminating power depends on the templates, being much higher (lower JND) for the pair H/D than for the other two pairs. Note that this is in line with the findings of past research showing a higher inter-rater agreement for facial expressions of happiness than for negative emotions. Statistical analysis (ANOVA, 3[face pair] × 21[rank], repeated measures; Greenhouse-Geisser correction; arcsin transformation) detected a highly significant main effect of the stimulus rank ($F(20,260)=281.676$, $p<.0001$), as well as a significant interaction between face pair and stimulus rank.

The upper plots in Figure 1 summarize the response time data. Data points are mean RTs over all participants, normalized to the general mean for all stimuli. Bars are 95% confidence intervals of the means (normal approximation). Mean RTs for the pair H/D were significantly lower than those for the other two pairs, especially for stimuli falling near each prototype on the physical continuum. More importantly, for all pairs of templates RTs were symmetrically bell-shaped with a maximum close to the point of indifference.

To sum up, the most salient result of Experiment 1 was that discrimination power is much higher (lower JND) for the pair H/D than for the other two pairs, implying that perceptual identification is easier along a positive-negative axis (H/D), than for the two negative pairs (A/F and A/D). Lower response time for the pair H/D than for both A/F or A/D confirms further the suggestion that participants were more confident and found the identification task easier when a positive and a negative emotion are involved than when two negative ones are in the pair. These findings are fully consistent with the conclusions of previous studies on facial expression perception.

Experiment 2

Our aim with Experiment 2 was to evaluate whether some key facial features present in different parts of the face (e.g., the presence/absence of the smile in the lower face; the appearance of the eyes in the upper face) can play a differential role in the identification of the same emotion expressions.

To this end, we created "chimerical" expressions blends, generated by making different parts of the face change at different rates during the morphing transformation. For example, in the Happiness → Disgust morphing sequence, in some trials the upper face began and completed the transition before the lower one, while in other trials the opposite occurred. We used these chimerical morphs in an identification task analogous to that in Experiment 1.

Assuming that the PSE location along the physical continuum is a reliable indicator of where the two emotions in a pair are perceived as contributing equally to a given morph, we predicted a shift toward the left side of the continuum when the transition occurs first in that part of the face that is more crucial for the recognition of the expression whose prototype is at the left of the continuum.

Methods

Participants: The same as in Experiment 1.
Stimuli: Chimerical morphs for Experiment 2 were created by applying a non-linear (logistic) transition function to the same pairs used in Experiment 1 (A/F, A/D, H/D). For each continuum, we generated two different sequences of 51 morphs, labelled "Bottom first" and "Top first", respectively, depending on the part of the face that was affected first by the morphing transformation.

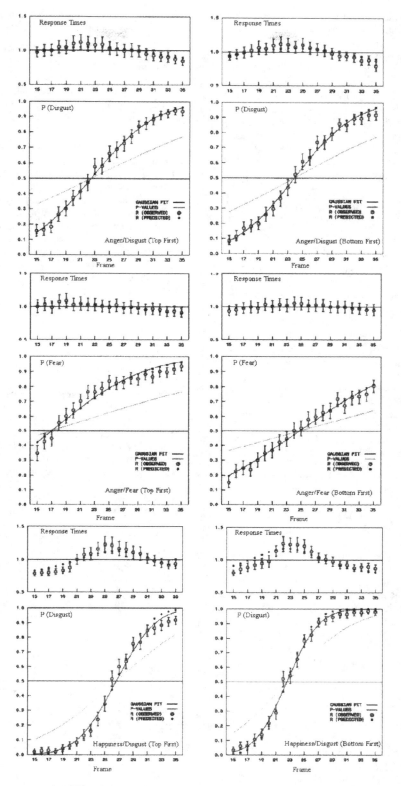

Figure 2: Exp.2. Response probabilities and RTs for A/D, A/F and H/D pairs: Top first and Bottom first sequences.

Thus, for instance, in the "Bottom first" transition the lower part of the face underwent a 50% change at 20% of the morphing sequence. The opposite was true in the "Top first" transition, so that the two sequences were in fact complementary. In either case, all the landmarks relative to each half of the face moved together. We created a total of 6 (3 emotions × 2 "Bottom first"/"Top first") sequences. For each continuum, the range of the actual stimuli, the number of repetitions, as well as the task and the procedure were the same as in Experiment 1. Each sequence was tested in a separate session.

Results and discussion

The three panels of Figure 2 (Top: A/D; centre: A/F; bottom: H/D) summarize the results of Experiment 2, with the same conventions of Experiment 1. The main findings were as follows.

First, consistently with our prediction, the part of the face that was affected first by the morphing transformation had a profound effect on the psychometric functions. The PSE tended to shift to either side of the physical continuum in opposite directions in the two sequences ("Bottom first" versus "Top first") of each pair (A/F, A/D, H/D). Moreover, for each face pair, manipulating the rate of morphing induced a shift of the PSE in either direction with respect to the median estimated from Experiment 1. Thus, both transformations produced a detectable, complementary effect.

Second, the JND also varied with the rate of change of the morphs, and, with the exception of the A/D pair, tended to be lower for the sequence that facilitates more the differentiation between the two prototype expressions.

Third, and more important, different effects are produced for the different pairs, according to which half of the face is more relevant for the recognition: 1) for the A/F and the A/D pairs the "Top first" sequence produced a shift of the PSE toward the left side of the continuum, reflecting an earlier recognition of the Fear and the Disgust expressions, respectively. Instead, an earlier identification of Happiness in the (H/D) pair occurred with the "Bottom first" sequence. 2) The discriminating power still depended on the pair of templates, being higher (lower JND) for the pair H/D than for the other two pairs, but was also affected by the non-linear transformation. This suggests that, independently of how early along the sequence a particular expression can be recognized, desynchronizing the physical morphing of the two halves of the face affects the discriminating power more for this couple of expressions than for the H/D or A/D pairs. Statistical analysis of the response probabilities (ANOVA, 3[face pair] × 2[face part] × 21[rank], repeated measure; arcsin transformation; Greenhouse-Geisser correction) detected a significant main effect of stimulus rank ($F_{(20,280)}$ =137.562, p < .0001) and face pair ($F_{(2,28)}$ =8.556, p < .005). The absence of any significant main effect of face part is explained by the fact that the same face part did not produce similar effects for all pairs. As expected, the interaction between face part and face pair was highly significant ($F_{(2,28)}$ =37.180, p < .0001), supporting further the claim of a differential contribution of specific facial features in the

recognition of different emotions. Moreover, also the interactions involving stimulus rank, such as face part × rank ($F_{(20,280)}$ =3.089, p < .05), and face pair × rank (F40,560) =29.945, p < .0001), were significant. In particular, the high degree of significance of the triple interaction face part × face-pair × rank (F(40,560) =5.368, p < .0001) suggests that our non-linear manipulations are effective in enhancing or attenuating the other effects (face pair, rank) already detected in Experiment 1.

General discussion

Data from Experiment 1 represent a "baseline" estimate of the accuracy with which observers identify facial expressions of basic emotions when the stimulus space results from a simple linear transformation, and equal incremental changes affect simultaneously all the elements of the configuration. In this condition, we demonstrated that the accuracy with which we identify facial expressions as belonging to a specific emotion category vary as a function of the prototype pair to be distinguished, being higher when a positive-negative opposition (H/D) is involved.

With Experiment 2 we introduced a novel technique for investigating whether specific facial features can play a differential role in the recognition of specific emotions. We addressed the issue of configural- versus feature-based processing by using non-linear morphing functions to change different parts of the face at different times along the transformation.

The main result of Experiment 2 was the demonstration of a differential involvement of the two halves of the face in the PSE shift, depending on which half contains the facial feature that is crucial for detecting a given expression. In fact, in the H/D pair the "Bottom first" sequence produced an earlier recognition of the Disgust expression, whereas recognition of the same expression was delayed in "Top first" sequence, suggesting that the mere presence/absence of the smile is the most important element to identify confidently a facial expression as happiness. This is likely to hold true for any other face pair having Happiness as a member.

Conversely, in the A/F, and A/D pairs, the emotions Fear and Disgust are recognized earlier when the upper part of the face is transformed first, as revealed by the shift of the PSE toward the left part of the continuum in the correspondent "Top first" sequences of each pair. This seems to imply that both Fear and Disgust, which share a negative connotation, are mostly identified on the basis of the appearance of the eyes. These findings replicate previous demonstrations that some facial expressions of basic emotions are more recognizable from the top half of the face, whereas others are more easily recognized from the bottom half (e.g., Bassili, 1979; Calder et al., 2000). Moreover, they seem also in line with recent evidence suggesting that the eye region of the face is heavily involved in the recognition of complex mental states such as the so-called "social emotions", (e.g. guilt, admiration, flirtatiousness; Baron-Cohen, Wheelwright, & Joliffe, 1997; Baron-Cohen, Wheelwright, Hill, Raste, & Plumb, 2001). This ability seems to be severely impaired in autistic patients (Baron-Cohen, Ring, Wheelwright, Bullmore,

Brammer, Simmons, & Williams, 1999), as well as in subjects with unilateral or bilateral amygdala damage, who are not able to recognize those emotions from the region of the eye of the face alone (Adolphs, Baron-Cohen, & Tranel, 2002). Interestingly, Adolphs, Gosselin, Buchanan, Tranel, Schyns, & Damasio (2005) reported a patient with a selective impairment in recognizing fear, and demonstrated that her impairment stems from an inability to make normal use of visual information from the eye region of the face only when judging emotions. Note that also the discrimination of two other emotions, sadness and anger, has been consistently reported to be impaired after amygdale damage, suggesting a role of this structure in the resolution of ambiguity in facial expressions through attentional modulation (Adolphs et al., 2005).

In summary, our results suggest that the recognition of facial expressions can rely to a great extent on the processing of single facial features, and that the key role is played by different facial features depending on the specific emotion. In particular, the eyes appear to be essential for differentiating between negative-valence emotions that cannot be discriminated by the presence/absence of the smile. However, it should be stressed that our results do not rule out the possibility of a significant role of configural information. They only suggest that the feature-based mode of processing is sufficient for identification whenever configural information is somehow ambiguous or inconsistent as in our experiments.

References

Adolphs, R. (2002). Recognizing emotion from facial expressions: psychological and neurological mechanisms. *Behavioral and Cognitive Neuroscience Reviews*, 1, 21-61.

Adolphs, R., Baron-Cohen, S., & Tranel, D. (2002). Impaired recognition of social emotions following amygdala damage. *Journal of Cognitive Neuroscience*, 14, 1264-1274.

Adolphs, R., Gosselin, F., Buchanan, T. W., Tranel, D., Schyns, P., & Damasio, A. R. (2005). A mechanism for impaired fear recognition after amygdala damage. *Nature*, 433, 68-72.

Baron-Cohen, S., Ring, H. A., Wheelwright, S., Bullmore, E. T., Brammer, M. J., Simmons, A., & Williams, S. C. R. (1999). Social intelligence in the normal autistic brain: An fMRI study. *European Journal of Neuroscience*, 11, 1981-1898.

Baron-Cohen, S., Wheelwright, S., & Joliffe, T. (1997). Is there a "Language of the Eyes"? Evidence from normal adults with Autism or Asperger Syndrome, *Visual Cognition*. 4, 311-331.

Baron-Cohen, S., Wheelwright, S., Hill, J., Raste, Y., & Plumb, I. (2001). The "reading the mind in the eyes" test revised version: A study with normal adults, and adults with Asperger syndrome or high-functioning autism. *Journal of Child Psychology and Psychiatry*, 42, 241-251.

Bassili, J. N. (1979). Emotion recognition: The role of facial movement and the relative importance of upper and lower areas of the face. *Journal of Personality and Social Psychology*, 37, 2049-2058.

Calder, A. J., Burton, A. M., Miller, P., Young, A. W., & Akamatsu, S. (2001). A principal component analysis of facial expressions. *Vision Research*, 41, 1179-1208.

Calder, A. J., Young, A. W., Keane, J., & Dean, M. (2000). Configural information in facial expression perception. *Journal of Experimental Psychology: Human Perception and Performance*, 26, 527-551.

Calder, A. J., Young, A. W., Perrett, D. I., Etcoff, N. L., & Rowland, D. (1996). Categorical perception of morphed facial expressions. Visual Cognition, 3, 81-117.

Campanella, S., Quinet, P., Bruyer, R., Crommelinck, M., & Guerit, J. M. (2002). Categorical perception of happiness and fear facial expressions: an ERP study. *Journal of Cognitive Neuroscience*, 14, 210-227.

Cottrell, G. W., Dailey, M. N., Padgett, C., & Adolphs, R. (2001). Is all face processing holistic? In M. J. Wenger & J. T. Towsend (Eds.), *Computational, geometric, and process perspectives on facial cognition*. Mahwah, NJ: Lawrence Erlbaum.

de Bonis, M., de Boeck, P., Pérez-Diaz, F., & Nahas, M. (1999). A two-process theory of facial perception of emotions. *Comptes Rendus de l'Académie des Sciences, Série III*, 322, 669-675.

Ekman, P. (1994). All emotions are basic. In P. Ekman & R. J. Davidson (Eds.), *The nature of emotion: Fundamental questions*. New York: Oxford University Press.

Etcoff, N. L., & Magee, J. J. (1992). Categorical perception of facial expressions. *Cognition*, 44, 227-240.

Haxby, J. V., Hoffman, E. A., & Gobbini, M. I. (2002). Human neural systems for face recognition and social communication. *Biological Psychiatry*, 51, 59-67.

Massaro, D. W. (1998). *Perceiving talking faces: from Speech Perception to a Behavioral principle*. London: MIT Press.

Meulders, M., De Boeck, P., Van Mechelen, I., & Gelman, A. (2005). *Applied Statistics*, 54, 781-793.

Okabe, A., Boots, B., Sugihara, K., & Chiu, S. N. (2000). *Spatial tessellation: Concepts and application of Voronoi diagrams*. Chichester, UK: John Wiley.

Sachs, L. (1984). *Applied statistics*. New York/Berlin: Springer-Verlag.

Viviani, P., Binda, P., & Borsato, T. (2006). Categorical perception of newly learned faces. *Visual Cognition*, 00, 000-000.

Young, A. W., Rowland, D., Calder, A. J., Etcoff, N. L., Seth, A., Perrett, D. I. (1997). Facial expression megamix: tests of dimensional and category accounts of emotion recognition. *Cognition*, 63, 271-313.

Human Recognition of Faces and PCA based Machine Recognition: The Effect of Distinctiveness

Naiwala P. Chandrasiri ††, Ryuta Suzuki†,
Nobuyuki Watanabe†, Hiroyuki Yoshida†, Hiroshi Yamada†, Hiroshi Harashima‡

Email: chandxp@gmail.com

†College of Humanities and Sciences, Nihon University, Japan.
‡Graduate School of Interfaculty Initiative in Information Studies, The University of Tokyo, Japan.

Abstract

Face recognition by machines has attracted more attention recently mainly for its potential in applications such as security. Although, it's not essential for machines to recognize faces in the same way humans recognize, there are interesting findings that computer based algorithms like Principal Component Analysis (PCA) have some similarity to human recognition of faces. In this paper, we attempt to further investigate some of the results of psychological experiments and computer analysis results of face recognition using face images. Two psychological experiments, 1) Classical experiment of distinctiveness rating and, 2) Novel experiment of recognition of an average face were carried out. In the later experiment, we examined on how average face of two face images was recognized by a human in a similarity test respect to the original images which were utilized for the calculation of the average face. To explain results of these psychological experiments, eigenface spaces were constructed based on PCA. High correlations were found between human and PCA based computer recognitions. Enhancing the rate of machine recognition of faces and emulating of human recognition by machines are two of the expected applications of this research.

Introduction

Psychologists and computer scientists/engineers have addressed the face recognition problem from different perspectives for decades. Psychologists have mainly concentrated to reveal cognitive process following perception and to develop information models or to investigate perceptual processing of face patterns (Hancock et al., 1996). On the other hand, computer scientists/engineers have been interested in finding solutions to the face recognition task for potential applications in such as security and customized services.

However, from a broader perspective, there are works that show similarities in characteristics of face recognition in humans and computer based algorithms (Hancock et al., 1996; O'Toole et al., 1994). In these works, they consider Principal Component Analysis (PCA) belongs to the right class of image analysis techniques with psychological plausibility.

In this paper, we attempt to further investigate some of the results of psychological experiments and computer analysis results of face recognition based on two psychological experiments. 1) Classical experiment of distinctiveness rating of face images and, 2) Novel experiment of recognition of an average face were carried out. PCA based eigenfaces were calculated using stimuli images which were utilized in the psychological experiments. Results of psychological experiments were interpreted by PCA based computer analysis results. As results, high correlations were found between human and PCA based (face spaces) computer recognitions.

Face recognition: Psychological background

In recognizing a face by a human, there are three known factors that mainly influence the ability of an observer to carry out the task. They are the perceived distinctiveness, orientation and race of the target face. Although, each of these factors had been investigated in isolation based on different theoretical explanations earlier, Valentine proposed a single framework for dealing with all of them (Valentine, 1991). According to his model, individual faces are assumed to be encoded as a point in a multidimensional space defined by dimensions that serve to discriminate faces. The main assumption of their framework is that a location in a Euclidean multidimensional space provides an appropriate metaphor for the mental representation of a face.

The process on how faces are represented in the brain, there are mainly two hypotheses, exemplars and axes. In the exemplar model, faces are represented by matching to a set of stored exemplars. On the other hand, in the axis model (face space) faces are represented by measuring the distances from a standard prototype along a set of different axes (Johnston et al., 1997; Valentine, 1991). However, most of the findings can be explained using both models.

In this paper we use face space model in describing results of the experiments. In the literature there are only few attempts have been made to number or label the dimensions of this space (Hancock et al., 1996; Johnston et al., 1997). We utilize concrete dimensions; eigen faces to discriminate faces.

Computer synthesis and analysis of images

In this section, we explain how average faces are synthesized and how face images are analyzed based on eigenfaces (PCA) respectively.

Average face

We synthesize average face images in terms of the average shape and texture (Nagata et al., 1999). In this technique, to avoid blurring of the resulting image, we have to make correspondences between facial feature points such as eyes, eyebrows, mouth, nose etc. of original images. This can be done by using a wireframe model. First, face modeling is carried out. Figure 1 shows an example of constructing a 3D face model by using Face-Fit [1]. A 3D generic wireframe model is shown in Figure

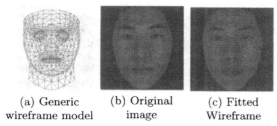

| (a) Generic wireframe model | (b) Original image | (c) Fitted Wireframe |

Figure 1: Face modeling using FaceFit software.

1(a). Building a person specific model by fitting the 3D generic wireframe model on to an original frontal face image (Figure 1(b)) is illustrated in Figure 1(c). This is done manually by clicking and dragging some feature vertexes of the generic face wireframe model to fit on the original image. We manually do it to make fitting error-free. Some points of the head, face outline, eyes, brows, nose, mouth, and neck (The neck model is eliminated in the calculation of the average face) are utilized as feature points. Other vertexes of the wireframe model are adjusted automatically. Note that the depth values (z) are set to defaults and only x,y coordinates are adopted for further calculations. We can save fitted data to a pnt file [2]. 3D face model with texture is built using texture mapping techniques that are based on triangular patches. Average face is constructed by calculating average vertex values and then mapping average textures of triangular patches on to the average wireframe model. Average face of all of the twelve stimuli images is shown in Figure 2.

Figure 2: Average face of twelve face stimuli.

[1] Face tools including FaceFit were developed under IPA (face Image Processing system for human like "kansei" Agent) project and, free software download is available under software download service in Harashima & Naemura lab home page http://www.hc.ic.i.u-tokyo.ac.jp

[2] A pnt file contains face shape in terms of x,y,z coordinates of the facial vertexes of the face wireframe model. Once we have a bitmap file and a pnt file of a face image, we can reconstruct the 3D face model

Eigenface

Principal component analysis is one of the frequently used methods for representing face images effectively. Sirovich et al. have proposed an orthogonal basis; eigenpicture for this purpose (Sirovich & Kirby, 1987). Eigenface which was proposed later by Turk et al. is one of the most famous methods for recognition of face images based on the above orthogonal basis (Turk & Pentland, 1991). Later, eigenface methods have been extended by morphing the faces to an average shape prior to PCA (Harashima et al., 1991). This enables the dealing of shape and shape-free texture separately. In eigenface method, eigenfaces (principal components of the distribution of faces: eigen vectors) of a set of images are calculated first. Example of top six (with higher eigen values) full face and shape-free eigenfaces calculated from our stimuli set (twelve images) are shown in Figure 3 and Figure 4 respectively. Each face in the stimuli set can be represented exactly in terms of weighted sum of the eigenfaces. These weights are the coordinates of the face images on the face space. We use these face spaces for calculating computer recognitions. In this paper, we use 60 key feature points of a face to represent its shape. These points are extracted based on the fitted wireframe model on to the face images. Eigenface spaces are calculated for full face, shape and shape-free textures.

Artifacts can be seen on the contours of full face eigenfaces in Figure 3 in comparison to shape-free eigenfaces (Figure 4). Prior to synthesizing full face eigenfaces, only three reference points are utilized for normalization of the images. The reasons for the artifacts are variations of contours across original face images.

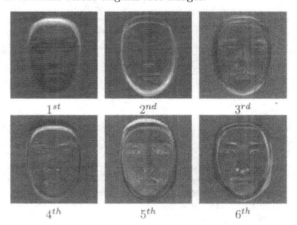

Figure 3: Eigenfaces with higher eigen values (Affine transformed full faces, reference points: centers of eyes and center of mouth).

Experiment 1

Faces were rated for perceived distinctiveness in this experiment.

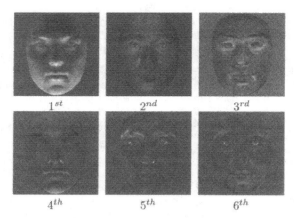

Figure 4: Shape-free eigenfaces with higher eigen values.

Participants

Fifty seven (17 females and 40 males) university students (19 years old in average) made the distinctiveness ratings. They were not familiar with any of the people shown to them on the screen. All the participants had normal or corrected-to-normal vision.

Stimuli

Twelve face images were randomly selected from a pool of grayscale images (512 × 512 pixels, 256 gray levels) of twenty young Japanese male faces[3]. All were images in full face pose with a neutral expression. Moles and facial hair on the original images were removed manually. Face area was extracted using the wireframe model eliminating hair, neck and the background. Background is set to black color. Since user responses to a displayed image on a computer screen may differ with face image size and brightness, height of a face image was kept to 7 cms on the screen and the brightness of the image on the computer screen was set to $20cd/m^2$.

Procedure

In a class room, face images were displayed on computer screens (TEKGEMS, AS-1503SG, 15 inch, TFT) of individual students. The procedure for rating the faces was that used by Valentine & Bruce (1986). Participants were asked to rate each face on a 1-7 scale. They were instructed to imagine that they had to meet each person for the first time at a railway station and to rate each face for how easy it would be to spot in a crowd. A face that was very distinctive and so would be easy to spot in a crowd should be rated 7, on the other hand a typical face that would be difficult to identify in a crowd should be rated 1. To make ratings, images were selected by a student from a list on a webpage and, each student was provided with a unique random order of a face list. participants were allowed to select and rate face images in their own pace.

---

[3]Twenty images were chosen from facial information database (Watanabe et al., in press; Yamaguchi et al., 2003)

Results and discussion

Mean distinctiveness ratings of faces are shown in Table 1 and Figure 5. Mean distinctiveness ratings varies from 2.8 to 6.1 and, overall average is 3.9.

In the conventional face space model, it is assumed that storing representations of faces in memory involves the abstraction of a face norm (Johnston et al., 1997; Valentine, 1991). Each individual face is stored in memory according to its deviation from a single general face norm which is located at the origin of the face space. Based on this hypothesis, we used the Euclidean distances from the origin in eigenface space as a measure in calculating computer recognitions. Note that as an approximation of the face norm, the average face of twelve face stimuli (Figure 2) is used in this work.

The striking finding in the data presented here is that the rated mean distinctiveness of face images and the Euclidean distances from a prototype face (average face) in PCA based face spaces have high correlations (Table 2). It can be seen that both texture and shape of face images have affected the correlation coefficients. Significant correlation is found in full face eigenface space ($r = 0.63$).

In face recognition, these results support the Valentine's framework of face space model whose axes are defined by eigenfaces.

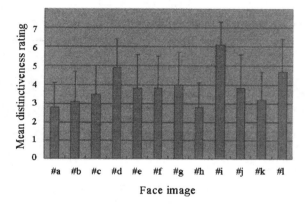

Figure 5: Mean distinctiveness ratings of face images.

Experiment 2

We conducted psychological experiments on how average face of two face images was recognized by a human in a similarity test respect to the original images which were utilized for the calculation of the average face. PCA based algorithms were utilized to investigate the results of the psychological experiments and computer analysis results.

Participants

Thirty Japanese university students (14 females and 16 males) participated voluntary in the experiment. Their average age was 21.9 years and they did not overlap with the participants of the experiment 1. Also, they were not

Face image	# a	# b	# c	# d	# e	# f	# g	# h	# i	# j	# k	# l
Mean distinctiveness rating	2.8	3.1	3.5	4.9	3.8	3.8	4.0	2.8	6.1	3.8	3.2	4.7

Table 2:

Correlation coefficients (r) between mean distinctiveness ratings of face images and their Euclidean distances from the origin in face space,

Dimensions	1D	2D	3D	4D	5D	6D	7D	8D	9D	10D	11D
Full Face	0.37	0.57	0.62	0.58	0.57	0.52	0.55	0.55	0.58	**0.63**	0.60
Shape	0.43	0.43	0.48	0.48	0.48	0.48	0.49	**0.50**	0.50	0.49	0.49
Shape free texture	0.36	0.39	0.33	0.43	0.39	0.42	0.43	0.45	0.45	**0.46**	0.45

Note: $r = 0.58$ is significant at 0.05, two-tailed test.

familiar with any of the people shown to them on the screen. All the participants had normal or corrected-to-normal vision. One participant took part in the experiment at a time.

Stimuli

The main stimuli were twelve face images that were the same as used in the experiment 1. In addition to that, sixty-six ($12 \times 11/2 = 66$) average faces were synthesized based on the procedure given in the subsection of **Average face** for each of the image pairs of twelve images. As moles and facial hair on the original images had been removed, the resulting average face did not contain obtrusive objects.

Procedure

As shown in the Figure 6, three images were displayed on the middle of a computer display. The average face image was shown on the upper part and, the two original images that were used for the calculation were shown on the lower part of the display. To avoid position effect, positions of the stimuli were counter-balanced. One set of the experiment consisted of 132 trials (66×2) and, stimuli were presented in random order. A participant was seated on a chair 90 cm away from the display (Dell E152FPC, 15 inch, TFT). She was instructed to compare the average face with two of its original images carefully and select which was more similar to the average face by pressing a key out of two marked keys on a keypad (ELE-COM, TK-UYLG). In the judgements, she was asked to focus on the 'face as a whole' not on specific facial parts. She was also asked to judge as quickly as possible.

Results and discussion

First, Kendall's coefficient of concordance was computed for all participants' responses ($\chi^2(70) = 655$, $p < .001$) and, there was a significant agreement among participants. Also, average responses of the participants were distributed nonuniformly across original images (see the row of the average participant responses in the Table 4). In 35 cases among 66 average faces used in the experiment, significant number of responses have been acquired by one of the original images ($\chi^2(1) = 6.63$, $p = .01$). If

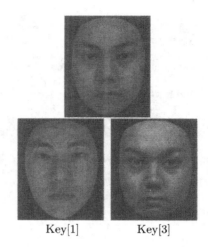

Key[1]   Key[3]

Figure 6: Average face (on the upper part) was compared with two of the face images that were utilized for its calculation (on the lower part) for similarity as a whole.

there is no bias towards original face images ($\#a \sim \#l$) which are utilized for calculating average face images, it's expected that there is no significant differences of participant responses to original face images. As the responses are nonuniformly-distributed across original face images with a significant agreement among participants, it is suggested that there is a bias of recognizing an average face image.

For comparison of human and computer recognitions, full face, shape-free and shape eigenface spaces are constructed. The highest correlation between average participant responses and Euclidean distances of the original face images from the origin is found in the shape-free eigen space(Figure 8, Table 4).

As it is explained in the results and discussion of the experiment 1, our results supported the Valentine's frame work of face space model whose axes are defined by eigenfaces. In this face recognition model, each individual face is stored in memory according to its deviation from a single general face norm which is located at the origin of the face space. Based on this assumption we used the Euclidean distances from the origin in eigenface space as a measure in calculating computer recognitions. Typical faces are generally located near the center of the space while distinctive faces will tend to be present in the outer region in a face space (Johnston et al., 1997; Valentine, 1991). According to our experiment, farther away an original face is situated from the origin, the more number of responses it tend to acquire. According to the Table 4, #c and #i images have received higher number of responses in average from the participants and, they are placed rather away from the origin (See also Figure 7). On the other hand #a, #f, #k and #l images have received lower number of responses and, they are situated nearer in the distance to the origin. In the Table 3, correlation coefficients (r) between average participant responses and Euclidean distances from the origin are shown for 1 to 11 dimensions in fullface, shape and shape-free eigenface space. Significant correlation is found even using a single dimension. The maximum correlation of 0.94 ($p < .001$) is seen using 8 dimensions.

In shape and full face eigenface space, only correlations of 0.35 and 0.51 in maximum ($r = 0.58$ is significant at 0.05, two-tailed test) can be seen between average participant responses and Euclidean distances from the origin.

In memory experiments, analysis based upon PCA of shape-free faces has given the highest predictions of false positives; those faces easy to reject as being unseen (Hancock et al., 1996), even though it's difficult to make a clear relation with our experiment.

Although face shape is very important in discriminating individuals, the texture might be the dominant factor due to the characteristics of our experiment with instructions to compare images as a whole under the direct comparison of face images. It is arguable that comparing images 'as a whole' might have directed the participants to neglect the shape and focus on the texture.

Further psychological experiments will be needed for searching on the effects of the shape and texture in recognizing an average face. However, there is a significant bias in comparison of faces in terms of texture is evident in our results of the experiments.

Conclusions and future directions

We have conducted one classical and one novel psychological experiments of face recognition, and then explored their correlations with PCA based computer recognitions.

Significant correlations were found between mean distinctiveness ratings of face images and their Euclidean distances from the origin in a PCA based face space (for full faces). This result supported the Valentine's face space model in which eigenfaces served as concrete dimensions in discriminating individual faces.

Also, we found that there was a bias in recognition of an average face. This bias can be explained using the same framework of the face space model which was utilized in explanations of the results of experiment 1.

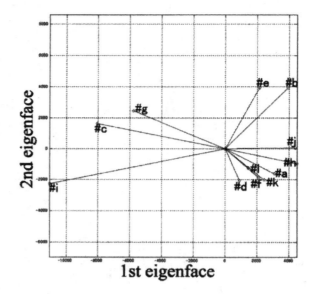

Figure 7: A face space: Twelve face stimuli on shape-free eigenface space.

When an average face is synthesized from two original face images, there is a tendency that humans recognize it as more similar to the original face image which is placed further away from the origin (distinctive face) of a shape-free eigenface space.

According to the results of the experiments, significant correlations were found between human and PCA based computer recognitions.

Valentine's face space model suggests that the distribution of face images around it becomes more dense when a face becomes less distinctive (typical face). Therefore, the more typical a faces is, the more easier to be wrongly recognized by a human as there are larger number of neighboring faces in the face space. If this is true for PCA based face spaces, the rate of machine recognition can be enhanced and the computation cost can be reduced by changing the level of attention to details of face information along the dimension of distinctiveness. Emulating of human recognition of faces by machine is an another expected application of this research.

Acknowledgments

The first author, N.P. Chandrasiri is a Research Fellow of the Japan Society for the Promotion of Science (JSPS), and he is also a Guest Researcher at the Intelligent Modelling Laboratory (IML), University of Tokyo.

Special thanks goes to Tatsuo Yotsukura of Advanced Telecommunications Research Institute International (ATR), Japan for his technical support.

Table 3:

Correlation coefficients (r) between average participant responses and Euclidean distances from the origin in face space

Dimensions	1D	2D	3D	4D	5D	6D	7D	8D	9D	10D	11D
Full Face	0.51	0.50	0.47	0.43	0.35	0.33	0.39	0.37	0.44	0.42	0.44
Shape	0.35	0.20	0.22	0.18	0.20	0.20	0.20	0.20	0.20	0.20	0.20
Shape free texture	0.85	0.87	0.87	0.89	0.91	0.92	0.93	0.94	0.93	0.92	0.91

Note: $r = 0.58$ is significant at 0.05, two-tailed test.

Table 4:

Average participant responses and Euclidean distance ($\times 10^3$ (8D)) from the origin on the shape-free eigenface space

Face image	# a	# b	# c	# d	# e	# f	# g	# h	# i	# j	# k	# l
Average participant responses	7.5	11.7	**15.5**	10.8	10.3	6.4	11.5	11.6	**16.9**	12.9	8.6	8.3
Euclidean distance from origin	4.2	6.6	**9.0**	4.8	5.9	3.8	7.5	6.9	**11.8**	6.5	4.0	4.2

Note: Chance level of average participant responses = 11.

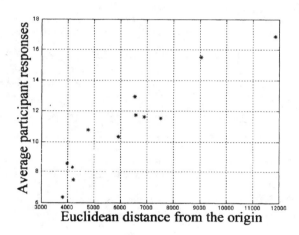

Figure 8: Correlation between average participant responses and distances from the origin on the shape-free eigenface space (8D).

References

Calder, A. J., Burton, A. M., Miller, P., Young, A. W., & Akamatsu, S. (2001). A principal component analysis of facial expressions. *Vision Research, 41,* 1179-1208.

Chandrasiri, N.P., Suzuki, R., Watanabe, N., Yoshida H., Yamada, H., & Harashima, H., (2007). Is average face recognized as the average?. *Proc.(CD-ROM) IEEE Int'l Symposium on Signal Processing and its Applications (ISSPA 2007), U.A.E.,* 4 pages.

Hancock, P. J. B., Burton, A., & Bruce, V. (1996). Face processing: Human perception and principal components analysis. *Memory and Cognition, 24,* 26-40.

Harashima, H., Okazaki, T., Choi, C., & Takebe, T. (1991). Principal-component analysis of facial images and its applications. *IEICE Technical Report, HC90-28,* 25-33. (in Japanese with English abstract)

Johnston, R. A., Milne, A. B., & Williams, C. (1997). Do distinctive faces come from outer space? An investigation of the status of a multi-dimensional face-space. *Visual Cognition, 4,* 59-67.

Nagata, A., Kaneko, M., & Harashima, H. (1999). Analysis of facial impressions using average faces. *Electronics and Communications in Japan, 81,* 29-35. (in Japanese with English abstract)

O'Toole, A., Deffenbacher, K., Valentin, D., & Abdi, H. (1994). Structural aspects of face recognition and the other race effect. *Memory and Cognition, 22,* 208-224.

Sirovich, L., & Kirby, M. (1987). Low-dimensional procedure of characterization of human faces. *Journal of the Optical Society of America A, 4,* 519-524.

Turk, M., & Pentland, A. P. (1991). Eigenfaces for recognition. *Journal of Cognitive Neuroscience, 3,* 71-86.

Valentine, T. (1991). A unified account of the effects of distinctiveness, inversion and race of face recognition. *Quarterly Journal of Experimental Psychology, 43A,* 161-204.

Valentine, T., & Bruce, V. (1986). The effect of distinctiveness in recognizing and classifying faces. *Perception, 15,* 525-535.

Watanabe, N., Suzuki, R., Yoshida, H., Tsuzuki, D., Bamba, A., Tokita, G. et al. (in press). Facial Information Norm Database (FIND): Constructing the database of Japanese facial images. *The Japanese Journal of Research on Emotions.* (in Japanese with English abstract)

Yamaguchi, T., Watanabe, N., Suzuki, R., Amano, Y., Mizunuma, M., & Yamada, H. (2003). A fundamental examination of constructing the facial information database. *Technical Report of IEICE, HCS2002-51,* 25-30. (in Japanese with English abstract)

How material culture extends the mind: mental time-travel and the invention of the calendar

Helen De Cruz (hdecruz@vub.ac.be)
Centre for Logic and Philosophy of Science – Free University of Brussels; Pleinlaan 2
1050 Brussels, Belgium

Johan De Smedt (Johan.DeSmedt@UGent.be)
Department of Philosophy and Moral Science – Ghent University; Blandijnberg 2
9000 Ghent, Belgium

Abstract

The extended mind thesis proposes that humans are capable of advanced cognition, not mainly through radical structural changes in the brain, but through their ability to delegate cognitive tasks to the external world. It views material culture as an important causal factor in human cognitive evolution. Here, we explore this hypothesis through an analysis of Upper Palaeolithic forms of material culture which have been interpreted as artificial memory systems. We argue that material calendrical systems complement evolved internal time representations, because they enable humans to project past events into the future more accurately than is possible with episodic memory alone, which greatly improves foraging strategies. Thus, the earliest calendars can be seen as a material extension of the human mind's evolved cognitive abilities.

Introduction

Ever since Darwin, comparative psychologists have considered the problem of the apparent mental discontinuity between humans and other animals. Why are humans, more so than other animals, capable of advanced, representation-hungry cognition? The extended mind thesis (e.g., Clark & Chalmers, 1998) suggests that what is distinctive about the human brain is how its structure is supplemented by material culture. Humans rely heavily on environmental support such as books, electronically stored documents, nautical slide rulers, or simply pen and paper to delegate computational problems to the external world. These instances are a two-way interaction, in which humans and external aids constitute a coupled cognitive system. It is this system as a whole that produces the cognitive output. Therefore, when the external part is removed, behavioural competence will drop. For instance, when a Scrabble player is allowed to physically re-arrange the tiles on her tray, performance is significantly better than when she is forced to re-arrange the tiles mentally. In a very real sense then, this re-arranging of tiles is an integral part of problem solving itself.

There have been several attempts to characterize the role of external media in human cognitive evolution. Donald (1991) views the evolution of human cognition as stages in which new memory representations emerged; the final stage is marked by the use of material culture as external memory system. According to Mithen (2000), the Upper Palaeolithic symbolic revolution, the sudden appearance of art, symbolic storage and a wide variety of specialized technologies starting 45,000 BP (before present), marks the extension of the mind beyond the brain. Material culture can serve as an anchor for counterintuitive concepts like religious ideas that have 'no natural home within the mind' (Mithen, 2000, 214). Gods typically behave according to a belief-desire psychology, which should enable us to interact with them using our theory of mind. However, because gods are not really there, interaction with them is difficult. Only when gods are made tangible and visible, in the shape of masks or icons, it becomes possible to use basic social cognitive skills in this domain (Day, 2004). Because of its endurance, material culture can extend cognition in several ways, the most obvious as a non-biological memory. Visual art and written documents enable us to store information beyond the scope of the individual memory and to reliably transmit it across generations. Furthermore, material culture can improve cognitive performance by enhancing conceptual stability. The cultural evolution of positive integers, for example, requires material anchors such as body-parts or tallies to develop a one-to-one correspondence between countable objects and a stably ordered counting list (De Cruz, 2006). Extending the mind through material culture constitutes an epistemic action (Kirsh, 1996): it makes the world more cognitively congenial without actually altering it physically.

By exclusively focusing on art and religion, cognitive archaeologists have not yet probed how material culture was used in epistemic contexts where it causes effects in the real world, such as improving foraging success. Calendars provide an interesting case-study as they do not physically alter the environment (e.g., increasing the number of potential prey in the territory), but render it more cognitively congenial (e.g., enhancing hunting success by predicting migration events). This paper's aim is to examine the epistemic role of material culture by specifying how it can supplement evolved human cognitive abilities. We take the invention of calendrical notation-systems in the Upper Palaeolithic as a case-study, arguing that calendars extend evolved cognitive abilities by allowing humans to accurately predict cyclically occurring events. Human time processing abilities are unable to recognize cyclicity in the environment whereas a coupled cognitive system, consisting of a calendar and an interpreting human can. First, we look at evolved cognitive mechanisms for keeping track of time, focusing on mental time-travel. Next, anthropological examples will illustrate how humans supplement these evolved mechanisms with material anchors. We then argue that the extension of episodic memory by material culture dates back to the Upper Palaeolithic, and illustrate this with examples of material culture interpreted by archaeologists as calendars. We conclude with a general discussion of the role of material culture in human cognitive evolution, evaluating the extended mind thesis in the light of these results.

Cognitive processes underlying the perception of time

Salient systems of time-processing

The natural world is filled with temporal regularities, which animal brains are adapted to exploit. Timing enables animals to anticipate opportunities and risks, which greatly improves their chances of survival. Two timing mechanisms are salient in a wide variety of species. To learn associations to events with particular times of day, organisms use their circadian clock, internally generated 24-hour oscillations in the suprachiasmatic nucleus (Antle & Silver, 2005). For shorter durations ranging from a few seconds to a few hours, animals rely on interval timing, which enables them to optimize their foraging behaviour in terms of time and energy costs (Bateson, 2003).

Circadian and interval timing are not the only timing mechanisms available to animals. Some species have highly specialized abilities that keep track of longer spans of time. For example, male house mice kill any neonate in their territory, except when they have mated 18 to 22 days before. During this period, where the possibility exists that the neonate is their offspring, they switch to nurturing behaviour. This hormonal mechanism enables house mice to detect relationships between events widely distributed in space and time, which could never be detected through associative learning alone (Kummer, 1995). Given that animals keep track of time through both widespread and specialized mechanisms, it seems useful to investigate whether humans possess derived cognitive mechanisms for dealing with time.

Episodic memory and mental time-travel

Within neuropsychology Tulving's hypothesis that human memory is composed of at least two functionally distinct systems, semantic and episodic memory (see Tulving, 2002, for an overview) has gained a firm foothold. Semantic memory can be broadly defined as our factual knowledge of the world (e.g., the Parthenon is in Athens). It does not refer in any way to personal experience. Episodic memory, on the other hand, allows us to remember personally experienced events and to travel back in time to re-experience those events (e.g., last summer I went to Athens and visited the Parthenon). It is oriented towards the past, whereas semantic memories are oriented towards the present. A rat using its semantic memory to avoid a food-type it remembers as

noxious need not think back to earlier experiences involving this food. Indeed, learning as a rule does not require episodic memory. This was demonstrated by a case study of three amnesiac patients with early focal pathology in the hippocampus (Vargha-Khadem et al., 1997). Remarkably, despite their inability to remember personal experiences, all three achieved near normal levels of language competence and factual knowledge, and even attended mainstream schools.

The ability for mental time-travel and episodic memory develop *in tandem* during cognitive development, suggesting that it is episodic memory which allows us to simulate future experiences. Episodic future thinking (Atance & O'Neill, 2001) enables humans to foresee possible future consequences of their current behaviour, or to make preparations in anticipation of a planned activity. Episodic memory arises gradually in human development, long after semantic memory is in place, as is illustrated by infantile amnesia, which persists until three to five years of age (Perner & Ruffman, 1995). The ability to travel mentally into the future follows a similar developmental trajectory: given the choice between a small immediate reward and a larger delayed reward, only children of four years and older forego immediate gratification and choose the delayed one (Thompson, Barresi & Moore, 1997).

Mental time-travel in an evolutionary context

Since Suddendorf and Corballis (1997) have suggested that only humans travel mentally in time, comparative psychologists have investigated whether nonhuman animals are able to remember consciously experienced events and imagine the future. To date, the strongest candidate for episodic-like memory in nonhuman animals is the food-caching scrub jay, *Aphelocoma californica* (Clayton & Dickinson, 1998): the birds' recoveries of previously stored food-items show sensitivity to what was cached where and when. For most other studies of episodic recall in animals, including primates, alternative non-episodic accounts such as familiarity can be offered (Roberts, 2002). Why is evidence for mental time-travel in nonhuman animals mostly lacking, seen its apparent benefits in food-caching and foraging? As most animal learning does not require episodic memory, its benefits must outweigh the costs of altering pre-existing neural structures to accommodate it. Episodic memory, however, tends to be less accurate than semantic memory. Numerous laboratory experiments (e.g., Marsh & Tversky, 2004) show that episodic memories, however vivid and confident, are vulnerable to distortion. Retelling personal recollections involves exaggerations, omissions, and simplifications to entertain or help the audience better understand. Under controlled experimental conditions, biased retellings of events alter the memories one has of the event (Tversky & Marsh, 2000); they routinely become part of one's own episodic recall, replacing more accurate memories. These shortcomings make episodic memory particularly unfit to recognize cyclical seasonal events. How can a hunter-gatherer remember when to return to a specific berry-tree in the groups' territory where she has fortuitously encountered an abundant supply of berries some months ago? Farmers need even more precise information on when to plant or harvest what type of crop. As distorted retellings corrode episodic memories, sharing these reminiscences with a wider audience clearly does not increase their reliability. This experimental evidence speaks against Caspari and Lee (2004), who explain the Upper Palaeolithic symbolic revolution as a consequence of increased human longevity. They argue that intensified oral intergenerational transmission of complex cultural information may have contributed to the innovations associated with behavioural modernity. Seeing that episodic memories are susceptible to distortion through retelling, distributing cognition through communication does not increase conceptual stability. On the other hand, extending the mind by means of material objects may prove more fruitful, as it protects episodic memories from misrepresentation.

Material anchors and epistemic artefacts

In disparate cultures, people keep track of cyclical events by extending their evolved internal timing mechanisms into the world by using cyclical natural events as material anchors. Horticulturalists from the Torres Islands, Vanuatu (Melanesia) traditionally calibrate their lunar calendar to seasonal events. The appearance of a ubiquitous sea-worm, *palolo*, in October, marks the planting of yam and other garden crops. The metamorphosis of a local species of ant into its winged phase, *vühoro*, in January serves as a marker for the end of the planting cycle (Mondragón, 2004). Material anchors need not be restricted to the visual modality. The Andaman Islanders knew a calendar of scents: the distinct succession of odours in the densely covered jungles was used to mark different periods of the year (Radcliffe-Brown, 1922). In both cases, a mental representation of cyclic activities (e.g., yearly cycle of planting, weeding and harvesting) is rendered more stable and reliable by tying it to seasonal occurrences in nature.

Elsewhere, humans draw on calendars, especially designed artefacts to keep track of cyclical events. The Mandan (a Native American Great Plains culture) recorded lunar phases as rows of crescents onto sheets of paper. Some of these are accompanied by plant symbols, indicating a record of planting and harvesting (Thornton, 2003). Artefacts have the advantage that they are less constrained by processes in nature, thereby further enhancing the stability of the representation of cyclical events. In Chankillo, Peru, a calendar (2300 BP) consisting of 13 aligned towers was calibrated to the winter and summer solstices. The towers and gaps in between enabled tracking the progress of the Sun to within an accuracy of 2 or 3 days, which was vital for agriculture in this arid region (Ghezzi & Ruggles, 2007). Sterelny (2004) has termed artefacts exclusively made to serve epistemic purposes *epistemic artefacts*. They are a distinctive feature of human cognition. Nonhuman animals sometimes use objects for purely epistemic purposes, such as the female gorilla observed by Breuer, Ndoundou-Hockembal

and Fishlock (2005), which probed the depth of a pool with a stick before deciding to cross it. To our knowledge, however, no animal has been observed to make tools exclusively for epistemic purposes.

Evidence for the extended mind in the archaeological record

The earliest archaeological evidence for epistemic artefacts in the form of art and incised bones dates back to the early Upper Palaeolithic at around 45,000 BP. Here, we discuss both direct and indirect evidence that strongly suggests that calendars were invented during this period, and that they had a significant impact on human foraging success.

Incised bone and antler objects

Upper Palaeolithic bone and antler objects with regular incisions have been recovered since the 1860s. The fact that they have ordered sets of notches or incisions indicates that these artefacts were used to represent numerical information. Marshack (1972) proposed the influential hypothesis that many of these objects were lunar calendars. His conclusion that notched bones represent the first human notation systems has gained general acceptance in the cognitive archaeological community. Based on microscopic analysis, d'Errico (1998) has subsequently developed both a theoretical framework and an explicit methodology for evaluating the use of incised bone objects. When morphologically resembling stone points were used and abandoned subsequently, the accumulation of the engravings was probably gradual, similar to a tally-stick. If, in contrast, morphologically distinct burins were used simultaneously, we can infer that the artefact was conceived as a whole, representing different items with different symbols, like a calendar. The code for the symbols is lost, as we do not have enough information about these prehistoric societies to find out what they mean. From ethnographic parallels however plausible functions of these objects can be inferred.

To take but one example: the Taï plaque from the Taï cave (Aquitaine, France) dates to the end of the last Ice Age (about 10,000 BP). It is engraved with long horizontal lines, each marked with hundreds of small, vertical notches. According to Marshack (1991), this plaque represents a lunar calendar—an interpretation supported by its resemblance to ethnographic examples, such as the stick-calendar (Figure 1) used by the Yakut, a subarctic Siberian culture subsisting on hunting, gathering and herding reindeer. The latter shows two months along each edge, incised with day units. Several days bear signs to mark seasonal events (e.g., the flowering of certain plants), astronomical observations (e.g., the appearance of the Pleiades, important in their shamanistic rituals), as well as Christian (Orthodox) holidays.

Rock art

Many scholars (e.g., Mithen, 1988) agree that Palaeolithic art has served as artificial memory system for ecologically relevant information. Rock art often emphasizes information useful to hunters, such as the ex-

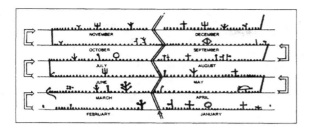

Figure 1: Schematic representation of Yakut stick calendar. Reprinted, with permission, from Marshack (1991), p. 32, Fig. 6.

aggerated representation of fat deposits on horses and aurochs, or the depiction of footprints of prey species in lieu of hoofs. Water birds and sea-mammals are often depicted in prehistoric art. The rarity of these animals in the Palaeolithic diet and their use as temporal cues by contemporary hunter-gatherers suggest that their representation served as an external storage of cues for seasonal changes. In historical times, the mating behaviour of geese, ducks and sea mammals served as cues for seasonal changes to Northwest Coast Native Americans and Inuit.

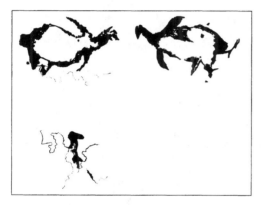

Figure 2: Scene depicting three auks at the Cosquer cave (Bouches-du-Rhône, France).

D'Errico's (1994) detailed analysis of a scene depicting three birds identified as great auks (*Pinguinus impennis*) at the Cosquer cave (Figure 2), dated at about 27,000 years ago, supports this interpretation. These large, flightless, now-extinct birds seasonally flocked to form large breeding colonies on offshore islands. This behaviour was seasonally restricted to May-June, when mating occurred, eggs were hatched and chicks raised. The conspicuousness of large breeding colonies on nearby islands may have been useful for prehistoric hunter-gatherers as a material anchor for seasonal events related to the beginning of summer. The scene shows three individuals, two facing each other with wings outspread, and a third, lying down with wings folded. As in all *Alcidae*, the great auk's wings were useless for flight; they were only

used during swimming or in combat for mates, when they were vigorously flapped. This opposing pair could be interpreted as males in combat, the third as a female they are disputing. Paintings depicting this mating behaviour may have served as artificial memory systems to remember and communicate their significance as a temporal marker.

Improved foraging techniques

How does the use of epistemic artefacts extend human cognition? Middle Palaeolithic (MP) hominids hunted and gathered less efficiently than Upper Palaeolithic (UP) hominids. Take the transition from MP to UP in the Southern Russian plains. In marked contrast to the earlier (MP) occupations, later (UP) sites show fewer species of prey and less variability in the concentration of fossil bones across seasons. This is taken as evidence for higher selectivity in the choice of prey and time of occupation, indicating specialized hunting and seasonal occupation of sites tuned to animal migrations (Soffer, 1989). The failure of earlier humans to recognize or record cyclicity in their environment could explain this difference. Material culture allowed the recording of cyclical patterns, enabling hunter-gatherers to time their visits to sites according to patterns in animal migration and plant growth.

The capture of Cape fur seals (*Arctocephalus pusillus*) in south-western African coastal sites presents a pertinent case-study (Klein, Cruz-Uribe & Skinner, 1999). Fur seals breed on offshore islands, the majority of births occurring during late November and early December. About nine months later, adult seals force their young from the rocks into sea. Large numbers of these young seals wash ashore, exhausted or dead—an ideal time for mobile hunter-gatherers to visit these sites. Fossil remains from seals in UP sites indeed mostly represent individuals of about nine months old, implying that UP people timed their visits to the coast to fall within the August-October peak in juvenile seal availability. In contrast, MP sites do not show such a fixed pattern. The bones of seals recovered from these sites are commonly older, ranging from sub-adults to adults, not showing any cyclicity at all, a pattern similar to that in dens of fossil hyenas.

Recognizing cyclicity not only had an impact on hunting success, but also probably resulted in a substantial broadening of the human diet. Fish bones are mostly absent in the MP archaeological record. In contrast, numerous archaeological sites indicate that UP people relied heavily on fish for their diet. They show patterns of seasonal and specialized fish exploitation. At Ishango, Congo, along the Upper Semliki River, dense concentrations of fish remains, together with hundreds of barbed points used to spear the fish, dated at about 25 000 BP have been recovered (Stewart, 1994). More than 30 % of these remains belong to the genus *Barbus*, a large minnow-like fish. Their size range represents primarily mature populations, probably caught on their spawning migration. This implies that the fishermen at Ishango timed their capture to the rainy season, when large quantities of *Barbus* congregate in river mouths on their yearly spawning migration. The repeated rainy season occupations at Ishango indicate the predictability of these. Interestingly, two incised bones dating to the same period have been recovered at Ishango (Figure 3). The spatial distribution of their notches almost certainly indicates that they are artificial memory systems.

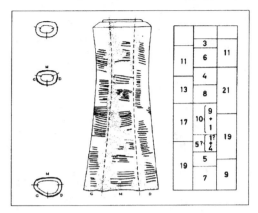

Figure 3: Notched bone from Ishango. Reprinted with permission of the Belgian Royal Museum for Natural History.

One reason why MP people neglected such a stable and abundant food source may be that the systematic exploitation of fish requires recognizing cyclical patterns of spawning and migration. In historic times, the Northwest Coast Native Americans planned and prepared for the capture of salmon months in advance. There is no reliable evidence for epistemic artefacts in the form of art or notched bones prior to the UP. Older findings are usually ambiguous. The co-occurrence of the earliest epistemic artefacts with improved foraging techniques and increased dietary breadth suggests that recognizing cyclicity in the environment requires an extended mind.

Discussion and concluding remarks

We have presented a cognitive archaeological perspective on the extended mind. Since the symbolic revolution, humans have created epistemic artefacts that make them part of distributed cognitive systems with computational capacities extending their evolved cognitive abilities. Calendars and interpreting humans constitute a coupled cognitive system that enables humans to predict cyclic events far more accurately than evolved cognitive abilities for keeping track of time allow. The archaeological evidence discussed above suggests that hominids prior to the UP were incapable of recognizing cyclicity, despite some indication of an episodic-like memory in early *Homo* starting 2.5 million years ago with the appearance of the first stone tools. The caching of these Oldowan tools for future use (Potts, 1994) can be tentatively taken as evidence for episodic future thinking. Apparently, this was not enough to allow them to predict cyclical events. Why did epistemic artefacts appear relatively late in the archaeological record at about 45,000 years ago? Possibly, new cognitive capacities such as metarepresentation enabled hominids to externally represent ideas. In the broadest sense of the term, a metarepresentation is a representation of a representation. A cave painting of a horse is the material representation of the painter's mental representation of horses. To date, there is no convincing evidence for metarepresentation in nonhuman animals, including great apes (Call & Tomasello, 1999), suggesting that it is a human cognitive specialization. Art and notched artefacts are representations that are deliberately manipulated (e.g., the exaggeration of some body parts, the grouping of notches into spatially distinct clusters), suggesting that Upper Palaeolithic people who made them possessed the ability to manipulate representations. Such manipulations require metarepresentation (see also Dennett, 2000 and Leslie, 1987).

In conclusion, the invention of calendars and other epistemic artefacts at about 45,000 years ago enabled humans to accurately time cyclical events, which greatly increased their foraging success. Some philosophers of mind (e.g., Giere, 2004) have raised criticisms against an interpretation of the extended mind where cognition actually takes place outside the brain. Calendars don't plan, humans who use them do. Therefore, the extended mind can only be properly understood in terms of a coupled system in which the brain holds a privileged position. Without our ability to mentally travel in time, we could not foresee future imagined events, and calendars would be useless. Likewise, without metarepresentation the extended mind would not be possible as symbolic storage requires second-order representations. To date, the extended mind hypothesis has mainly been a philosophical construct that has hardly been empirically investigated (but, see e.g., Kirsh, 1996). This has made it difficult to assess how far-reaching the influence of epistemic artefacts on human cognition is. Cognitive science, firmly embedded in archaeology can provide an explanatory framework for elucidating the adaptive advantages of an extended mind.

References

Antle, M. C., & Silver, R. (2005). Orchestrating time: arrangements of the brain circadian clock. *Trends in Neuroscience, 28*, 145–151.

Atance, C. M., & O'Neill, D. K. (2001). Episodic future thinking. *Trends in Cognitive Science, 5*, 533–539.

Bateson, M. (2003). Interval timing and optimal foraging. In W.H. Meck (Ed.), *Functional and neural mechanisms of interval timing*. Broca Raton: CRC Press.

Breuer, T., Ndoundou-Hockembal, M., & Fishlock, V. (2005). First observation of tool use in wild gorillas. *PLoS Biology, 3*, e380.S.

Call, J., & Tomasello, M. (1999). A nonverbal false belief task: the performance of children and great apes. *Child Development, 70*, 381–395.

Caspari, R., & Lee, S.-H. (2004). Older age becomes common late in human evolution. *Proceedings of the National Academy of Sciences USA, 101,* 10895–10900.

Clark, A., & Chalmers, D. (1998). The extended mind. *Analysis, 58,* 7–19.

Clayton, N. S., & Dickinson, A. (1998). Episodic-like memory during cache recovery by scrub jays. *Nature, 395,* 272–274.

Day, M. (2004). Religion, off-line cognition and the extended mind. *Journal of Cognition and Culture, 4,* 101–121.

De Cruz, H. (2006). Why are some numerical concepts more successful than others? An evolutionary perspective on the history of number concepts. *Evolution and Human Behavior, 27,* 306–323.

Dennett, D. (2000). Making tools for thinking. In D. Sperber (Ed.), *Metarepresentation. A multidisciplinary perspective.* New York: Oxford University Press.

d'Errico, F. (1994). Birds of Cosquer cave. The great auk (*Pinguinus impennis*) and its significance during the Upper Palaeolithic. *Rock Art Research, 11,* 45–57.

d'Errico, F. (1998). Palaeolithic origins of artificial memory systems: an evolutionary perspective. In C. Renfrew & C. Scarre (Eds.), *Cognition and material culture: the archaeology of symbolic storage.* Cambridge: McDonald Institute for Archaeological Research.

Donald, M. (1991). *Origins of the modern mind: three stages in the evolution of culture and cognition.* Cambridge, Ma.: Harvard University Press.

Ghezzi, I. & Ruggles, C. (2007). Chankillo: a 2300-year-old solar observatory in coastal Peru. *Science, 315,* 1239–1243.

Giere, R.N. (2004). The problem of agency in scientific distributed cognitive systems. *Journal of Cognition and Culture, 4,* 759–774.

Kirsh, D. (1996). Adapting the environment instead of oneself. *Adaptive Behavior, 4,* 415–452.

Klein, R. G., Cruz-Uribe, K., & Skinner, J. (1999). Fur seal bones reveal variability in prehistoric human seasonal movements on the southwest African coast. *Archaeozoologia, 10,* 181–188.

Kummer, H. (1995). Causal knowledge in animals. In D. Sperber, D. Premack & A. J. Premack (Eds.), *Causal cognition. A multidisciplinary debate.* Oxford: Clarendon Press.

Leslie, A.M. (1987). Pretense and representation: the origins of "theory of mind". *Psychological Review, 94,* 412–426.

Marsh, E.J., & Tversky, B. (2004). Spinning the stories of our lives. *Applied Cognitive Psychology, 18,* 491–503.

Marshack, A. (1972). Cognitive aspects of Upper Paleolithic engraving. *Current Anthropology, 13,* 445–461.

Marshack, A. (1991). The Taï plaque and calendrical notation in the Upper Palaeolithic. *Cambridge Archaeological Journal, 1,* 25–61.

Mithen, S. (1988). Looking and learning: Upper Palaeolithic art and information gathering. *World Archaeology, 19,* 297–327.

Mithen, S. (2000). Mind, brain and material culture: an archaeological perspective. In P. Carruthers & A. Chamberlain (Eds.), *Evolution and the human mind. Modularity, language and meta-cognition.* Cambridge: Cambridge University Press.

Mondragón, C. (2004). Of winds, worms and mana: the traditional calendar of the Torres Islands, Vanuatu. *Oceania, 74,* 289–308.

Perner, J., & Ruffman, T. (1995). Episodic memory and autonoetic consciousness: developmental evidence and a theory of childhood amnesia. *Journal of Experimental Child Psychology, 59,* 516–546.

Potts, R. (1994). Variables versus models of early Pleistocene hominid land use. *Journal of Human Evolution, 27,* 7–24.

Radcliffe-Brown, A. R. (1922). *The Andaman islanders.* New York: The Free Press of Glencoe.

Roberts, W. A. (2002). Are animals stuck in time? *Psychological Bulletin, 128,* 473–489.

Soffer, O. (1989). The Middle to Upper Palaeolithic transition on the Russian plain. In P. Mellars & C. Stringer (Eds.), *The human revolution. Behavioural and biological perspectives in the origins of modern humans.* Edinburgh: Edinburgh University Press.

Sterelny K. (2004). Externalism, epistemic artefacts and the extended mind. In R. Schantz (Ed.), *The externalist challenge.* Berlin & New York: Walter de Gruyter.

Stewart, K.M. (1994). Early hominid utilisation of fish resources and implications for seasonality and behaviour. *Journal of Human Evolution, 27,* 229–245.

Suddendorf, T., & Corballis, M. C. (1997). Mental time travel and the evolution of the human mind. *Genetic, Social and General Psychology Monographs, 123,* 133–167.

Thompson, C., Barresi, J., & Moore, C. (1997). The development of future-oriented prudence and altruism in preschoolers. *Cognitive Development, 12,* 199–212.

Thornton, R. (2003). A report of a new Mandan calendric chart. *Ethnohistory, 50,* 697–705.

Tulving, E. (2002). Episodic memory: from mind to brain. *Annual Review of Psychology, 53,* 1–25.

Tversky, B., & Marsh, E.J. (2000). Biased retellings of events yield biased memories. *Cognitive Psychology, 40,* 1–38.

Vargha-Khadem, F., Gadian, D. G., Watkins, K. E., Connelly, A., Van Paesschen, W., & Mishkin, M. (1997). Differential effects of early hippocampal pathology on episodic and semantic memory. *Science, 277,* 376–380.

Knowledge Construction with Multiple External Representations: What Eye Movements Can Tell Us

Rolf Schwonke (rolf.schwonke@psychologie.uni-freiburg.de)
Alexander Renkl (renkl@psychologie.uni-freiburg.de)
Department of Psychology, University of Freiburg
Engelbergerstr. 41, D-79085 Freiburg, Germany

Kirsten Berthold (kirsten.berthold@ifv.gess.ethz.ch)
Institute for Behavioural Sciences, ETH Zurich,
Turnerstr. 1, 8092 Zurich, Switzerland

Abstract

Although multiple external representations can have benefits, especially for learning new and complex ideas, they are often not as effective as expected. The present study employed eye tracking and retrospective stimulated recall in order to analyze how learners use different external representations in learning from worked-out examples, how these activities are related to learning outcomes, and how well the intended cognitive functions of the multiple representation match with the functions perceived by the learners. 16 psychology students studied worked-out examples from probability. Each worked-out example consisted of a problem formulation, an equation, and a tree diagram. The function of the diagrams was to mediate between the text and the high abstract equation. During the learning phase the gazes of the participant were recorded. After the learning phase, participants were exposed to a gaze replay of their viewing behavior and were asked to think aloud. The distribution of fixation durations on the representations and transitions between them indicated that no single representation was neglected or processed in isolation. However, transitions between representations were of value only for learners with better learning prerequisites. In the case of poorer learning prerequisites, these transition indicated unsystematic search processes. For all learners, frequent direct transitions between equations and text were dysfunctional, pointing to the mediating function of the diagrams. Verbal reports revealed a mismatch between the intended and the perceived cognitive functions of the multiple representations. The results suggest to inform learners more fully of the intended functions and/or to make intended functions more salient.

Introduction

When confronted with new and complex ideas, it is beneficial to have multiple external representations available such as, for example, text, tables, pictures or graphs. According to Ainsworth (2006), using more than one representation can aid learning in different ways. First, multiple representations can complement each other in that each representation provides different information or stimulates different cognitive processes (e.g., different strategies). Second, representations can also help to disambiguate each others meaning. This may either be achieved by familiarity with one type of representation that helps to interpret a less familiar type of representation or by certain properties inherent to the type of representation (e.g., pictures are inherently more specific than texts). Finally, providing learners with more than one external representation can help to construct a deeper understanding of the learning contents. Gaining understanding may either be facilitated by extending knowledge gained from one (type of) representation (e.g., a graph) to another (type of) representation (e.g., a table), or by relating aspects of different representation to one another (e.g., relating the contents of a graph to the contents of a corresponding equation). A last and probably the most demanding cognitive function is abstraction. In this context, abstraction means that learners construct new concepts on a higher level of organization by integrating aspects from different external representations and their prior knowledge. Whereas the functions of constraining and complementing do not rely that much on integrating different representations, integration is essential, if multiple representations are intended to foster the construction of deeper understanding.

It is important to note that the functions of multiple representation that we discussed are those intended, for example, by a teacher or an instructional designer. They do not necessarily correspond to the functions as perceived by the learners. In addition, many studies have shown that integration poses a major problem for learners (e.g. Anzai, 1991; Hegarty, Narayanan, & Freitas, 2002; Schoenfeld, Smith, & Arcavi, 1993). In Ainsworth, Bibby, and Wood, (2002), for example, students that learned estimation in mathematics profited from either a mathematical or a pictorial representation, but not from a combined representation (i.e., providing a pictorial and a mathematical representation at the same time). The learners were able to understand each single representation as well as their respective relations to the domain. The detrimental effect of the combined version was attributed to a failure to integrate the single representations.

Berthold and Renkl (2005) found in a study on learning probability with multi-representational worked-out examples that some of the participants acquired substantial conceptual knowledge, but acquired little procedural knowledge whereas other participants acquired substantial procedural knowledge, but little conceptual knowledge. Yet, there was no student that acquired both, conceptual and procedural knowledge to a substantial degree. As it is known that people often cope with complexity by focusing their attention on specific aspects of the learning material (Ainsworth, 2006), it might be hypothesized that participants neglected certain aspects of the environment (e.g., focusing only on text and equations, while neglecting the tree diagrams). .

In this study, we were looking for indicators of dysfunctional, but also of beneficial uses of the multiple representations. We recorded learners' eye-movements while they were studying a set of multi-representational worked-out examples (adapted materials from Berthold & Renkl, 2005). As already mentioned, a critical factor that moderates the effectiveness of multiple representations should be that the intended functions of multiple representation are not necessarily perceived and hence used by the learners. Therefore, after the learning phase, we presented learners their own eye-movement data, recorded during learning, to stimulate verbal reports. The reports should provide us with information on the cognitive functions actually perceived by the learners. The main intended cognitive function of the worked-out examples used in this study was to help learners to acquire a deeper understanding of probability principles (construction function). Therefore, we were particularly interested whether learners used the provided representations accordingly. More specifically, this explorative study was conducted in order to get a better understanding of

(a) how learners actually use different external representations in learning,

(b) how viewing behavior is related to learning outcomes, and

(c) how well cognitive functions (as intended by the instructional designers) match with the functions perceived by the learners.

Methods

Design

As we were interested in the spontaneous use of multiple representations, there was no experimental variation. Rather, all participants run through the same computer-based learning environment. Eye-movement parameters recorded during learning were correlated with learning outcomes measured by a post-test on procedural and conceptual knowledge (7 items each). In addition, verbal data from the stimulated recall procedure were used to assess the degree of correspondence of theoretically postulated and actually perceived cognitive functions of multiple representations.

Participants

16 psychology students (9 female, 7 male) participated in this study. Their mean age was $M = 24.21$ ($SD = 4.76$). Most of the participants were studying in their second or third year (number of semesters: $M = 4.77$, $SD = 2.98$). Although all participants were aware that their gazes were recorded during the learning phase, they were blind to the purpose of

the study (i.e., the identification of beneficial and detrimental uses of multiple representations). The study was framed as an experiment on computer-based learning that should help the participants to improve their knowledge of probability. Participants were paid 10 € for participating.

Materials

Learning Environment The computer-based learning environment consisted of a set of 15 static slides presented on the 17" screen of the eye tracker. In order to be able to obtain spontaneous behavior, time-on-task was not held constant. Thus, participants were free to spend as much time as they needed on each worked-out example. Participants were informed, that the learning environment would not allow them to return to previous slides.

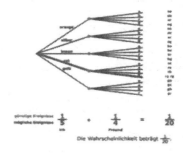

Figure 1. A worked-out example as presented in the computer-based learning environment.

Probability theory was chosen as the learning domain for two reasons. First, it is a domain, where the use of different representational codes (pictorial and arithmetic) is appropriate and common. In text books, for example, probability principles are often explained with pictures of a ballot box. Second, probability theory is a relatively difficult subject matter for students.

The first seven slides were an introduction into the basics of probability theory (specifically: complex events). We introduced two principles and their combined use: *relevance of order* and *replacement*. After the introduction, a number of worked-out examples were presented.

Each combination of probability principles (e.g., order relevance with replacement) was illustrated by two isomorphic worked-out examples. That means that each of these two examples had the same mathematical structure, but a different cover story. For example, the combination of order relevance and replacement was presented within a story problem on the distribution of bicycle helmets on a mountain-bike tour and, in addition, with a cover story on winning a medal in a sports event. Combining the two probability principles and using two cover stories for each problem type led to eight worked-out examples.

Each example consisted of the problem formulation (presented in the upper part of the screen), a tree diagram illustrating quantitative and qualitative aspects of the story problem in a graphical form (in the middle of the screen), and an equation providing a numerical representation of the story problem (in the lower part of the screen; see Figure 1). In addition, at the right side of each branch of the tree diagram, there were combinations of single letters corresponding to the combination depicted by the single branches of the tree diagram (e.g., in a tree diagram on bicycle helmets, a combination of the letters 'o' and 'g' indicated the combination of an orange and a green helmet).

In order to control for position effects, the worked-out examples were presented in a balanced order. Thus, with 16 participants, four learner went through the same order of examples.

During the learning phase, we used a Tobii 1750® Eye Tracker to record the learners' gazes (the system has a temporal resolution of 50 Hz and a spatial resolution of 0.5°). This equipment allows for a lot of freedom of head movements, making it ideal for research on complex learning tasks and/or tasks that extend over longer periods of time.

Stimulated Recall Procedure Directly after the learning phase, participants were exposed to a *gaze replay* of their viewing behavior during learning. A gaze replay is an animation showing the learning materials with the participants' eye fixations superimposed. As we did not want the participants to get tired before the post-test, we decided not to expose them to all eight examples, but only to the first and the last worked-out example. The first and last examples were presented in order to analyze potential changes in the perception and/or the uses of the multiple representations as an effect of practice.

While viewing the gaze replay, participants were asked to describe their activities during the learning phase. This kind of stimulated retrospective recall procedure has been found to be a valuable method (van Gog, Paas, Merriënboer, and Witte, 2005) making it a promising method to produce a broad range of useful information.

Post-Test The post-test consisted of 7 items on procedural and 7 items of conceptual knowledge. Procedural knowledge can be defined as knowledge of actions and manipulations in a domain (de Jong & Ferguson-Hessler, 1996). The post-test on procedural knowledge comprised four near transfer items (i.e., items with the same structure as the worked-out examples but with different surface features such as the cover story) and three far transfer items (i.e., different structure and different surface features). Here is an example of a near-transfer item: "Number-locks for bicycles often use a code that consists of four digits (zero to nine each). What is the probability of guessing the correct code at your first guess?" The solution to this problem would look like this: $1/10 * 1/10 * 1/10 * 1/10 = 1/10000$.

We awarded the correct solution of each item on procedural knowledge by one point. Thus, a maximum score of seven points could be achieved.

Conceptual knowledge refers to static knowledge about facts, concepts, principles, and their interrelation within a domain (de Jong & Ferguson-Hessler, 1996). Thus, the post-test on conceptual knowledge assessed students (deeper) understanding of the probability principles. Some of the conceptual items presented worked-out examples (similar the one in figure 1). Here, students were required to answer a set of open questions. They should, for example, explain why the fractions were multiplied and not added. On other items, students were asked to draw lines between corresponding entities of the equation and the diagram. Where applicable, two trained research assistants rated the responses on 6-point rating scales (1 = *no conceptual understanding; 6 = very clear conceptual understanding*). A very clear conceptual understanding was indicated by a correct answer with a high degree of reasoning and elaboration. An inter-rater reliability of 89 % was obtained.

Procedure

The study was conducted in individual sessions. First, all participants completed a questionnaire on demographic data. Then, all participants ran through a calibration procedure, necessary for the eye tracker to work properly. Then all participants entered the learning environment. On average, they spent 13 to 14 minutes ($M = 13.67$; $SD = 5.02$) in this environment. During learning the participants' gazes were recorded. Directly after the learning phase, the participants were shown a gaze replay on the first and last worked-out example. The focus of the participants' fixations was represented by a moving spot and a tail representing the direction; both were superimposed on the learning material. While observing their gazes, participants were asked to verbalize their thoughts. Finally, all participants completed the post-test, which took them 36 minutes on average ($M = 35.86$; $SD = 10.90$). The individual sessions lasted approximately 1 ½ hours ($M = 85.07$; $SD = 19.95$).

Data Analysis

Eye Movement Data have proved to be a valuable source of information for the study of cognitive processes (Radach & Kennedy, 2004). Moreover, the collection of eye-movement data provides a non-intrusive way to gather rich data on the spatial and temporal distribution of visual attention during the interaction of learners with complex learning environments. Temporal measures as fixation and gaze durations, for example, have been found to be valid indicators of processing load; spatial parameters as the position of fixations provide information on the direction and sequence of processing.

In preparation of the eye-movement data analysis, each worked-out example was divided in three rectangular areas of interest (AOI): *text* (i.e., the story problem), *diagram* (i.e., the tree diagram), and equation (i.e., the arithmetical representation). These AOIs superimposed on the materials facilitate the data analysis in that they function as units of aggregation. This way it was, for example, possible to compute a sum of single fixation durations (see below) on each representation, telling us how long participants spent on each type of representation. Four different eye movement parameters have been analyzed: *fixation duration*, *cumulative fixation duration*, *gaze duration*, and *transition frequency*.

Fixation Duration can be defined as a time (in ms) of relative stability of the eye between two rapid movements (i.e., saccades; for an overview of eye-movement parameters, see Rötting, 2001). In this study, durations of at least 100 ms within a circular area with a diameter of 30 pixels were recorded as single fixations. It is known, that the minimum fixation duration, necessary for cognitive processing is about 100 – 150 ms. Typical fixation durations for text last about 225 ms. For pictorial representations, mean fixation durations tend to be longer (about 330 ms). However, fixation duration seems strongly to depend on the difficulty of the material, and hence, on the knowledge learners bring to the task.

Differences in fixation durations are related to qualitative differences of cognitive processes (Sintschenko, Vdovina, & Gordon, 1979; Velichkovsky, Sprenger, & Unema, 1997). Sintschenko et al., for example, found that longer fixation durations are associated with cognitive and meta-cognitive processing, and shorter fixation durations are associated with perceptive processing of figures. Velichkovsky et al. relate fixation duration to the depth of processing. Similar to the results of Sintschenko et al., they found higher cognitive processes, as for example, deep semantic processing and communicating knowledge, to be associated with longer fixation durations.

Based on these results, we interpreted fixation duration not merely as a measure of processing load, but as an indicator of depth of processing. Specifically, longer mean fixation durations should be associated with better learning outcomes in terms of conceptual understanding.

Cumulative Fixation Duration is defined as the total sum of all fixations within an AOI (Rötting, 2001). It indicates the relative amount of visual attention on an object. It is assumed that more important objects, but also objects or areas with a higher information density, are processed more extensively. Here, it is interpreted as the relative amount of visual attention on an area of interest (i.e., an AOI-specific time-on-task). This measure should provide us with information on whether single external representations are neglected, as it has been suggested in the literature (e.g., Ainsworth, 2006).

Gaze Duration was calculated by adding up all subsequent fixation durations on an AOI between two transitions. Gaze duration has been reported as a measure of the difficulty of encoding. However, this interpretation applies mainly to materials with unstructured layouts, to materials of low readability, and to materials with high information density.

In our study, none of these aspects applied. The worked-out examples were highly structured (and the layout remained constant over the course of the learning phase); they were of good readability and of moderate information density (each example comprises three to four sentences, a diagram, and an equation). Therefore, in this context, gaze duration may be better seen as an indicator of attempts to relate entities within a specific external representation (i.e., attempts of intra-representational integration). Other things being equal, longer gaze durations should therefore be associated with a better understanding of single external representations.

Transition Frequencies are defined as the number of eye shifts between AOIs. In visual search tasks frequent transitions indicate inefficient scanning with extensive search (Rötting, 2001). Again, this might not apply in our context, for the same reasons as mentioned with respect to the interpretation of gaze duration. The materials used in this study are well structured so that no intensive search processes should occur. Therefore, we interpret transitions between external representations as attempts to relate entities of different external representations. Thus, transition frequencies might be called a measure of attempts of inter-representational integration. Higher frequencies should therefore be associated with the acquisition of conceptual knowledge, because deeper understanding requires successful integration of information that is distributed over different but related external representations.

Verbal Protocols The think-aloud data collected in the retrospective stimulated recall procedure were transcribed and analyzed with reference to the taxonomy of cognitive functions of multiple representations by Ainsworth (2006). The scheme was constructed to assess the cognitive functions as perceived by the learners. It consisted of the three main categories *complementary roles*, *constrain interpretation*, and *construct deeper understanding*, each with two to three sub-categories (not detailed here).

Due to technical difficulties, only 12 protocols could be finally included in the analysis. As it was not possible to relate specific and coherent semantic protocol units to specific categories of the coding scheme, we opted for a holistic rating of the protocols. Two trained research assistants rated the transcribed protocols on six-point rating scales (1 = *category hardly discernable*; 6 = *category highly discernable*). An inter-rater reliability of 91% could be obtained. If, for instance, a learner would focus mainly on equations while ignoring the diagrams, this would indicate a complementary use of diagrams and equations (allowing for individual preferences or processes).

Results

Due to the explorative character of the study, for all analyses, the level of significance was set to .10. Two subjects had to be excluded from data analysis because of erroneous eye-movement data. Thus, we could finally included the data of 14 participants.

Learning Outcomes

As the learning outcomes were not at the heart of this study, only some main results are reported. Post-test results on procedural knowledge showed that participants were descriptively better at near transfer items (mean solution probability: $M = .55$, $SD = .24$) than on far transfer items ($M = .33$, $SD = .26$). Near and far transfer items correlated significantly with one another ($r = .50$, $p < .10$). Moreover, correlations between eye movement parameters on the one hand and near and far transfer on the other hand yielded highly comparable patterns. Therefore, we aggregated near and far transfer scores to a score of procedural knowledge.

The post-test on conceptual knowledge revealed that participants had acquired relatively little conceptual knowledge (ratings transformed to solution probability: $M = .25$, $SD = .12$). These moderate levels of knowledge have to be taken into account, when interpreting the associations between learning outcomes and learning activities as assessed by eye tracking.

Use of Multiple Representations

Cumulative Fixation Duration The cumulative fixation duration (as the time maximally available for encoding) was distributed unevenly over the single representations. As could have been expected, participants spent most of the time on the text (53 %). 27 % of the time was spent on the diagrams, and 16 % on the equations.

Fixation Duration We found lowest mean fixation durations for the text (in milliseconds: $M = 216.6$; $SD = 28.4$) and longer mean fixations for equations ($M = 241.0$; $SD = 57.2$). Longest fixation durations were determined for diagrams ($M = 278.3$; $SD = 90.4$).

Gaze Duration (in seconds) were longest for text ($M = 4.40$; $SD = 2.02$) and much shorter for equations ($M = 1.04$; $SD = 0.34$) or diagrams ($M = 1.14$; $SD = 0.38$). This means that the students spent relatively extended periods of time on the text, but visited equations and diagrams only briefly before shifting attention to another representation.

Transitions Unidirectional transitions, for example from diagrams to equations and from equations to diagrams, were aggregated to bidirectional transitions. The largest number of such bidirectional transitions per worked-out example occurred between diagrams and equations ($M = 7.96$; $SD = 3.70$). Fewer transitions occurred between text and diagram ($M = 5.83$; $SD = 3.99$). The transitions between text and equation were least frequent ($M = 1.14$; $SD = 0.38$).

Eye-Movements and Learning Outcomes

All correlations reported in the following are partial correlations with time-on-task serving as a control variable. The rationale for reporting partial correlations is that time-on-task is an easily obtainable but rather coarse process measure. It is coarse, because it does not provide us with information on how the time was actually spent on parts of the visual display. Hence, we determined what eye-movement data can tell us beyond time-on-task.

Cumulative Fixation Duration The total time spent on diagrams correlated substantially and positively with procedural knowledge ($r = .56$; $p < .05$) as well as with conceptual knowledge ($r = .50$; $p < .10$).

Gaze Duration Gaze durations on diagrams were positively associated with post-test scores on conceptual knowledge ($r = .53$; $p < .05$).

Transitions between representations Transitions between diagrams and combinations were positively correlated with procedural knowledge ($r = .46$; $p < .10$), whereas (direct) transitions between text and equations were negatively correlated with conceptual knowledge ($r = .46$; $p < .10$). Against our expectations, transitions between diagrams and equations were not significantly related to learning outcomes. As we expected that interactions between these two supportive representations would foster conceptual learning, we decided post-hoc to compute separate correlations for low and high prior knowledge students. The analysis revealed that for high prior knowledge students, transitions between diagrams and equations were positively correlated with conceptual knowledge ($r = .62$; $p < .10$). The opposite was true for students with low prior knowledge ($r = -.74$; $p < .10$).

Reported Use of Cognitive Functions Rather low ratings were obtained for all of the postulated cognitive functions. If at all, students seemed to use mainly the complementing function ($M = 2.18$; $SD = 1.03$). The mean rating for the construction function ($M = 1.33$; $SD = 0.44$) and the constraining function ($M = 1.29$; $SD = 0.19$) were very low.

Discussion

The main results of this study can be summarized as follows: First, as indicated by the distribution of cumulative fixation duration, the learners did not neglect single the representations. Second, we found support for associations between viewing behavior and learning outcomes; especially the inclusion of the diagrams (e.g., in terms of longer mean fixation durations and gaze durations) was positively related to the acquisition of conceptual knowledge. Third, transitions between representations were found to be an indicator of successful attempts to integrate different representations, but only for learners with higher prior knowledge. For low prior knowledge learners, frequent transitions seemed to indicate unsystematic search processes (even within this highly structured learning material) rather than attempts to relate representations in any meaningful way. Finally, the verbal data suggest that learners were not aware of the intended cognitive functions of the multiple representation in the worked-out examples (i.e., the construction function), and hence, did not use the examples in an optimal way.

In the literature on multiple representations it is hypothesized that single representations might be neglected (e.g., Ainsworth, 2006). Our data do no support this claim. Rather, the data suggest that learners actually try to relate different representations. Relatively short gaze durations on diagrams and equations together with frequent transitions between these representations indicate that these representations are not processed independently from one another. However, the differential results for high and low knowledge students suggest that frequent transitions per se are not crucial. Frequent transitions between equations and text were even detrimental. An explanation for this latter finding is that a neglect of the mediating function of the tree diagrams (between text and equation) leads to a more shallow understanding of the principles to be learned. In conclusion, it can be stated that the function of transitions seem to depend on characteristics of the learners as well as on characteristics of the representations involved.

It is also important to note that eye-movement data provided us with more fine-grained information on the learning process than simple time-on-task measures. It was, for example, found that more time spent specifically on diagrams (but not on equations or text) was positively associated with performance in the post-test, indicating that time-on-task per se was not the crucial factor.

The verbal protocols revealed that the learners were not really aware of any of the cognitive functions of multiple representations. The learner show a rather unsystematic or even unintentional use of external representations. This mismatch suggests to inform learners more fully of the intended functions (e.g., by an informed training), and/or by making the intended functions more salient (e.g., by prompting).

It can be argued that some of our interpretations of the eye-movement parameters might overstretch their meaning. For instance, instead of interpreting gaze durations as attempts to relate elements within a representation, subsequent gazes might indicate quite different things (e.g., search processes as a consequence of confusion). However, the substantial correlations with learning outcomes in terms of conceptual knowledge provided at least some support for our interpretation. Experimental studies that systematically instruct participants to adopt certain visual strategies might help to disambiguate eye-movement parameters. In an experiment, we are planning to use eye-movement data (in real time) to generate automated just-in-time feedback in either a visual form (e.g., with a map that illustrates the distribution of visual attention on and transitions between different representations) or in form of conceptual prompts. By such procedures, we expect to foster a more productive use of multiple representations.

References

Ainsworth, S. (2006). DeFT: A conceptual framework for considering learning with multiple representations. *Learning and Instruction, 16*, 183-198.

Anzai, Y. (1991). Learning and use of representations for physics expertise. In K. Anders-Ericsson & J. Smith (Eds.), *Towards a general theory of expertise: Prospects and limits.* Cambridge: Cambridge University Press.

Berthold, K., & Renkl, A. (2005). Fostering the understanding of multi-representational examples by self-explanation prompts. In B. G. Bara, L. Barsalou, & M. Bucciarelli (Eds.), *Proceedings of the 27th Annual Conference of the Cognitive Science Society* (pp. 250-255). Mahwah, NJ: Erlbaum.

Conati, C., Merten, C., Muldner, K., & Ternes, D. (2005). Exploring eye tracking to increase bandwidth in user modeling. *Proceedings of the UM 2005 User Modeling: Tenth international Conference. Edinburgh, UK, July 26-30.*

de Jong, T., & Ferguson-Hessler, M. G. M. (1996). Types and qualities of knowledge. *Educational Psychologist, 31*, 105–113.

Hegarty, M., Narayanan, N. H., & Freitas, P. (2002). Understanding Machines from Multimedia and Hypermedia Presentations. In J. Otero, A. C. Graesser, & J. Leon (Eds.), *The Psychology of Science Text Comprehension* (pp. 357-384). Mahwah, NJ: Erlbaum.

Radach, R., & Kennedy, A. (2004). Theoretical perspectives on eye movements in reading: Past controversies, current issues, and an agenda for future research. *European Journal of Cognitive Psychology, 16*, 3-26.

Rötting, M. (2001). *Parametersystematik der Augen- und Blickbewegungen für arbeitswissenschaftliche Untersuchungen [Systematics of eye-movement parameters for studies in work science]*. Aachen: Shaker.

Schoenfeld, A. H., Smith, J. P., & Arcavi, A. (1993). Learning: The microgenetic analysis of one student's evolving understanding of a complex subject matter domain. In R. Glaser (Ed.), *Advances in Instructional Psychology* (Vol. volume 4). Hillsdale, NJ: LEA.

Sintschenko, W.P., Vdowina, L.I., & Gordon, W.M. (1979). Die Untersuchung der funktionalen Struktur des Lösungsprozesses von Kombinationsaufgaben [The analysis of functional structures of the solution process of combination tasks]. In B.F. Lomow & N.J. Vergiles (Hrsg.). *Motorische Komponenten des Sehens* (167-184). Berlin: VEB Deutscher Verlag der Wissenschaften.

van Gog, T., Paas, F., Van Merriënboer, J. J. G., & Witte, P. (2005). Uncovering the problem-solving process: Cued retrospective reporting versus concurrent and retrospective reporting. *Journal of Experimental Psychology: Applied, 11*, 237-244.

Velichkovsky, B., Sprenger, A., & Unema. P. (1997). Towards gaze-mediated interaction: Collecting solutions of the „Midas touch problem". In S. Howard, J. Hammond & G. Lingard (Eds.). *Human-Computer Interaction: INTERACT'97* (Sydney, July 14-19th), London: Chapman & Hall.

Reasoning with External Representations in Elementary Astronomy

Irini Skopeliti (eskopel@phs.uoa.gr) &
Stella Vosniadou (svosniad@phs.uoa.gr)
Cognitive Science Lab
Department of Philosophy and History of Science
National and Kapodistrian University of Athens
Ano Ilissia, 157 71, Greece

Abstract

This experiment investigated the effect of the presentation of two culturally accepted external representations of the earth -a map and a globe- on children's reasoning in elementary astronomy. Eighty four children from grades 1 and 3 were interviewed individually. First, the children were given a pre-test which determined their internal representations by asking them to make drawings and play-dough models of the earth and indicate where people live. The children were then divided in two experimental groups: Half of the children were presented with a globe, and half with a map. In both groups the children were asked to answer another set of questions about the earth, in order to determine how the external representations influenced their responses. In the pre-test children constructed relatively consistent models of the earth. However, when an external model was presented the children used this model to reason with. This often resulted in internally consistent responses as students relied on their incompatible prior knowledge to answer questions the answers to which could not be provided directly from the external model. We concluded that the use of an external representation is not an act of 'direct cultural transmission', but a constructive process during which the information that comes from the culture is interpreted and influenced by what is already known.

Introduction

The purpose of the experiment presented in this paper is to examine how two different external representations of the earth –a map and a globe– influence the way children reason in elementary astronomy. Previous studies investigating elementary school children's reasoning about the earth, showed that young children had sophisticated knowledge of the physical tools provided and could accomplish complex reasoning about the earth and gravity using them (Schoultz, Saljo, & Wyndhamn, 2001; Ivarsson, Schoultz & Saljo, 2002). It was thus concluded that in the presence of cultural artifacts and appropriate questionnaires children do not have any problems understanding the scientific information about the earth. (Nobes, Moore, Martin, Clifford, Butterworth, Panagiotaki & Siegal, 2003; Siegal, Butterworth, Newcombe, 2004).

The results of these studies have challenged the argument by Vosniadou and her colleagues (Vosniadou & Brewer, 1992, 1994; Vosniadou, Archontidou, Kalogiannidou, & Ioannides, 1996; Diakidoy, Vosniadou, & Hawks, 1997) that elementary school children have difficulty understanding scientific information about the earth.

We agree with Schoultz et al. (2001) that the presence of a globe can facilitate children's reasoning about the earth because it can, in fact, be used as a prosthetic device to help children think, fulfilling in this way its role as a cultural tool. However, we claim that the process of appropriation or internalization of an external representation is not a passive act involving simple and direct transmission, but a constructive process during which information coming from the outside is interpreted in the light of prior knowledge. Therefore this process is likely to be characterized by distortions or misinterpretations.

The purpose of the present study was to investigate this hypothesis. In the first part of the experiment, the children were asked to indicate verbally, in drawing, and in play-dough models, the shape of the earth and where people live. In the second part of the experiment the children were presented either with a map or with a globe and were asked a second series of questions about the earth and where people live. We hypothesized that: (1) the children would construct relatively internally consistent models of the earth in the 1st part of the experiment, (2) they would use the externally provided models in the 2nd part of the experiment, and (3) intrusions from incompatible prior knowledge would create internal inconsistency in their responses to the inferential questions in the 2nd part of the experiment.

Method

Subjects

The sample consisted of 84 children, students in two middle-class schools of central Athens. Forty children attended 1st grade and their age ranged from 5 years and 6 months to 7 years (M= 6 years and 1 month) and 44 attended 3rd grade and ranged in age from 7 years and 6 months to 10 years (M= 8 years and 5 months).

Materials

A two-part earth shape questionnaire was used, based on the original Vosniadou & Brewer (1992) study. It consisted of a total of 22 questions. In Questionnaire Part I (QPI), each child was asked to indicate the shape of the earth and where people live on the earth both verbally, in drawings, and in play-dough models. In Questionnaire Part II (QPII), the child's own drawings and play-dough models were removed and s/he was presented either with a globe (diameter 30cm) or with a map (94cm x 63cm). Both parts of the questionnaire are shown in Table 1 that follows.

Table 1: Earth Shape Questionnaire

Earth Shape Questionnaire: Part I

1. What is the shape of the earth?
2. *(If child says round, then ask :)* If the earth is round, does it look like a circle or like a ball?
3. How do you know that the earth is ...... *(Use child's word)*?
4. *(If the child said round, then ask:)* Here is a picture of a house. The house is on the earth. How come here the earth is flat but before you said it is round?
5. Please make a drawing of the earth.
6. Draw where you think people live on the earth.
7. Draw where you think the sky and the stars are located.
8. Please make the shape of the earth using this play-dough?
9. Show me where people live on your play-dough model.
10. Show me where you think the sky and stars are located.

Earth Shape Questionnaire: Part II

1. Here is a globe. *(If the child before said that the earth is not round, ask:)* You said that the earth is…. But here the earth is shown to be round. Can you explain that?

OR

1. Here is a map. *(If the child before said that the earth is not flat, ask:)* You said that the earth is…. But here the earth is shown to be flat. Can you explain that?
2. If you walked for many days in a straight line, where would you end up? Is there an end to the earth? Would you ever reach the end of the earth?
3. Would you fall off that end? Why/Why not?
4. Can people live down here? Why? / Why not?
5. If a little girl lived down here and she had a ball and the ball fell from her hands, show me where it would fall.
6. Is there something that holds the earth up?
7. Finally, what do you think is the real shape of the earth?

(If the child changes his/her response, then we ask the following questions)

8. Take this play-dough and make the model of the earth as you finally think it really is.
9. If the earth is as you have now made it, then why did you made it differently before?

(If the child made a spherical earth then ask 10.)

10. Here is a picture of a house. This house is on the earth, isn't it? How come here the earth is flat but before you said it is round? Can you explain this a little more?
11. Where do you think people live on the earth?
12. Can people live down here? Why? / Why not?

Procedure

The children were assigned to an experimental group on the basis of their responses in QPI. Most of the children who gave responses consistent with a flat, rectangular or disk model of the earth in QPI were assigned to Experimental Group 1 (EG1), and where shown the globe as the external representation of the earth. Most of the children who gave spherical earth responses in QPI, were assigned to Experimental Group 2 (EG2), and where shown the map. We did this in order to be able to investigate how the presence of an external representation would affect children's responses in situations where the external representation came in conflict with the child's internal representation of the earth.

The children were interviewed individually in a separate classroom in their school by two experimenters. One experimenter posed the questions and the other kept detailed notes of children's responses during the interview. In case children's responses were not clear the experimenter asked the child to clarify his/her response. Testing took place in two parts. QPI was administered first, followed by QPII. Children's own representations of the earth were removed and an external representation (map or globe) was provided in QPII. The interviews were audio-recorded and video-taped and children's play-dough models were photographed. Each interview lasted approximately 20 – 25 minutes.

Scoring

Children's responses were scored for both QPI and QPII in ways that made it possible to retain information that could be diagnostic of alternative representations of the earth. The authors of the paper scored half of the data independently. Then they met and agreed on a scoring key. All responses that were consistent with the spherical model of the earth were marked as scientific. The responses that were consistent with a flat model of earth were marked as initial. The remaining responses were marked as alternative responses. Using the scoring key, the remaining half of the data was scored independently. Then, the scorers met again, discussed the scoring and revised the scoring key as needed until agreement was achieved. The agreement between the two scorers at this point was very high (98%). Subsequently, an independent researcher used the scoring key to independently score the same data. At the end the whole team met to discuss disagreements. The agreement between the initial scoring of the two researchers and that of the independent scoring of the third researcher was high (96%). All disagreements were discussed until resolved.

Results

Questionnaire Part I (QPI): For a quantitative analysis of QPI all scientifically correct responses were scored as 2, alternative earth responses as 1, and flat earth responses as 0. The sum of the total scores for each child was then subjected to a 2 (grade) x 2 (experimental group) ANOVA. The data followed a normal distribution and the homogeneity tests showed that the dependent variables were equal across groups. The analysis showed significant main effects for grade [$F(3,80)=7,880, p<.01$], which was due to the fact that the older children gave more scientifically correct responses than the younger children.

Our next step was to see if the children could be assigned to a qualitative earth model on the basis of their responses. We distinguished 9 questions which were found in previous studies to critically differentiate among the different possible representations of the earth. Based on the findings of previous research, we defined the expected pattern of responses to these questions for six common models of the earth, independently of children's obtained responses. (For a more detailed description of this process, please refer to Vosniadou, Skopeliti, Ikospentaki, 2005.) The criteria for placement in a model category were as follows: For the spherical model we expected children to say that the earth is round, that it does not have an end/edge, to construct a sphere, and to say that the people can live at the bottom of the earth. For the sphere without gravity, we expected children to give responses similar to the sphere model, for all the questions except the last. In the hollow sphere model we expected children to say that the earth is round and that it does not have an end, to construct a sphere, a vertical ring, or a cylinder and to clearly say that people live inside the earth, and to also say that people cannot live at the bottom of the earth. For the dual earth model we expected children to say that the earth is round and construct two earth models: a spherical one and a flat earth on which people live. We also expected these children to say that there is an end/edge to the earth and that people cannot live at the bottom of the earth. For the disc earth we expected the children to construct a flat disc model say that there is an end/edge to the earth and that people cannot live at the bottom of the earth. For the flat models we expected children to say that the earth is flat and construct a flat rectangle or square. These children were also expected to say that there is an end/edge to the earth and that people cannot live at the bottom of the earth.

In order to be assigned to a model category a child should provide responses consistent one of the above mentioned patterns of responses. As can be seen, in Table 2, most of the children constructed relatively consistent models of the earth and were placed in a well defined model category in QPI. Only 15% of the 1st graders and 14% of the 3rd graders were not assigned to a model category.

Table 2: Frequency/Percent of Children in the EGI & II Placed in Model Categories as a function of Grade

Model Categories	1st Grade	3rd Grade
1. Sphere	8 (20%)	13 (31%)
2. Sphere without gravity	2 (5%)	4 (10%)
3. Hollow sphere	10 (25%)	10 (24%)
4. Dual Earth	-	-
5. Flattened Sphere	1 (2,5%)	1 (2%)
6. Disk	10 (25%)	8 (19%)
7. Flat Earth	3 (7,5%)	-
8. Mixed	6 (15%)	6 (14%)

Questionnaire Part II: First we analyzed responses to Question 1 which asked children to explain discrepancies between their representations of the earth and those provided by the external model. Tables 3 and 4 show the categories of responses for Q1 for the two experimental groups. In the case of the globe, 85% of the 1st graders and 46% of the 3rd graders were asked Q1 because only these children had not constructed a spherical model. In the case of the map, 95% of the 1st graders and 91% of the 3rd graders were asked to explain the inconsistency between their model and the model presented because only these children had not constructed a flat model of the earth.

Table 3: Frequency/Percent of Responses to Q1 of QPII in EGI (Globe) as a function of Grade

Q.1: Here is a globe. *(If the child before said that the earth is not round, ask:)* You said that the earth is…. But here the earth is shown to be round. Can you explain that?		
Response	**Gr.1 N=17 (85% asked)**	**Gr.3 N=10 (46% asked)**
1) Not asked. The child had made a spherical earth model.	**3/20 (15%)**	**12/22 (54%)**
2) I've made a mistake The earth is round (change).	5/17 (30%)	1/10 (10%)
3) I wanted to make it like that, but I couldn't (change).	4/17 (23%)	5/10 (50%)
4) People make the earth round to represent all countries (no change).	2/17 (12%)	1/10 (10%)
5) There is another earth, where people live and looks like my model (no change).	-	1/10 (10%)
6) The earth looks like the one I made (no change).	2/17 (12%)	-
7) Don't know (no change).	4/17 (23%)	2/10 (20%)

A chi-square analysis showed that the difference in children's responses about the shape of the earth before and after the presentation of the external representation reached statistical significance in EG1 (globe) [$x^2(2)=7,845$, $p<.05$], but not in the case of EG2 (map).

Table 4: Frequency/Percent of Responses to Q1 of QPII in EGII (Map) as a function of Grade

Here is a map. *(If the child before said that the earth is not flat, ask:)* You said that the earth is…. But here the earth is shown to be flat. Can you explain that?		
Response	**Gr.1 N=19 (95% asked)**	**Gr.3 N=20 (91% asked)**
1) Not asked. The child had made a flat earth model.	**1/20 (5%)**	**2/22 (9%)**
2) People make the earth flat in order to represent all countries (no change).	6/19 (32%)	13/20 (65%)
3) The map is a piece of paper; it can't be round (no change).	5/19 (26%)	2/20 (10%)
4) The map shows us the inside part of the earth (no change).	-	1/20 (5%)
5) The earth looks like the one I made (no change).	2/19 (10%)	-
6) Don't know (no change).	6/19 (32%)	4/20 (20%)

In EG1 (globe) most of the children changed their initial non-spherical earth answer and accepted the globe as a better model of the earth, while in the case of EG2 (map) most of the children retained their initial answer of a spherical earth. This result shows that different external representations can have different effects on children's responses. Children filter the external representations presented and do not accept them regardless of their content.

Children's responses to the remaining questions of QPII were scored as 2 for each scientifically correct response, as 1 for each alternative earth response, and as 0 for each flat earth response. The sum of the total scores was then subjected to a 2 (grade) x 2 (experimental group) ANOVA. The analysis showed a significant main effect for grade [$F(3,80)=8,429$, $p<.005$] only, with third graders doing significantly better than first graders. There was no statistically significant difference between the two experimental groups.

In a second analysis, we examined how each external representation (globe vs. map) separately affected children's responses by comparing pre and post scores within experimental group. A 2 (grade) x 2 (pre/post test score) mixed ANOVA was used. In the case of EG1 (globe), the analysis showed main effects for the pre/post test score [$F(1,40) = 11,575$, $p<.005$] which was due to the fact that more scientifically accepted responses were produced in the post-test, after the presentation of the globe, compared to the pre-test. There were also main effects for grade, [$F(1,40) = 8,304$, $p<.01$] due to the fact that the third graders systematically outperformed the first graders.

As can be seen in Figure 1, before the presentation of the globe, the mean total score was 6,7 for the first graders and 9,4 for the third graders, while after the presentation of the globe the mean total score was 8,7 for the first graders and 11,05 for the third graders.

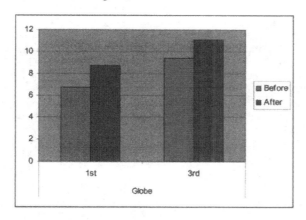

Figure 1: Children's Mean Total Score in EG1 (Globe) Before & After the Presentation of the Globe as a function of Grade

In the case of the EG2 (map), the ANOVA did not show main effects neither for the pre/post test score, nor for grade. As shown in Figure 2, the first graders before the presentation of the map had a high mean total score of 9,6 and after the presentation of the map had a slightly lower score of 9,2. The third graders before the presentation of

the map had a mean total score 10,1 and after the use of the map they had a mean total score of 11.

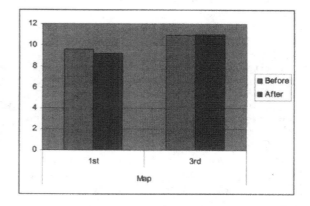

Figure 2: Children's Mean Scores in EG2 (Map) Before & After the Presentation of the Map as a function of Grade

Our next step was to see if the children could be assigned to well-defined model category on the basis of their responses in QPII. We used the pattern of responses described earlier. As can be seen in Tables 4 and 5, while most of the children were placed in a well defined model category in QPI, in QPII the number of children placed in the mixed category increased remarkably. More specifically, in QPI, before the use of the globe, 90% of the children (38/42) from both age groups gave internally consistent responses and were assigned to a model category. On the contrary, in QPII, after the use of the globe, the frequency of the internally consistent models decreased with only 35% of the 1st graders and 55% of the 3rd graders being assigned to a model category (see Table 5).

Table 5: Frequency/Frequency of Subjects in the Scientific, Alternative & Mixed Model Categories in EG1 Before & After the Use of the Globe

Model Categories	Before the Use of the Globe		After the Use of the Globe	
	1st Grade	3rd Grade	1st Grade	3rd Grade
Scientific	3 (15%)	6 (27%)	5 (25%)	11 (50%)
Alternative	15 (75%)	14 (64%)	2 (10%)	1 (5%)
Mixed	2 (10%)	2 (9%)	13 (65%)	10 (45%)

Similarly, before the use of the map 80% of the 1st graders and 90% of the 3rd graders in EG2, gave internally consistent responses and were assigned to a model category, while, after the use of the map, the frequency of the internally consistent models decreased with only 30% of the 1st graders and 40% of the 3rd graders being assigned to a model category (see Table 6). The use of the globe (EG1) resulted in an increase in the number of sphere models and also of mixed models and a dramatic decrease in the number of alternative models. In EG2 (map) the number of scientific models remained the same, while the number of mixed models increased remarkably and alternative models almost disappeared. A close look revealed that the use of the map did not result in an increase of the flat representations of the earth. However the presentation of the map influenced children's responses to some of the questions as it will be later shown in the discussion section.

A chi-square comparing the frequency of sphere, alternative, initial, and mixed model categories before and after the use of the external models gave statistically significant results for both cases, (for the globe: $[x^2(2)=36,455, p<.001]$, for the map: $[x^2(2)=31,004, p<.001]$).

Table 6: Frequency of Subjects in the Scientific, Alternative and Mixed Model Categories in EG2 Before and After the Use of the Map

Model Categories	Before the Use of the Map		After the Use of the Map	
	1st Grade	3rd Grade	1st Grade	3rd Grade
Scientific	5 (25%)	8 (36%)	5 (25%)	8 (36%)
Alternative	11 (55%)	12 (54%)	1 (5%)	1 (5%)
Mixed	4 (20%)	2 (9%)	14 (70%)	13 (59%)

Discussion

The results of the present study replicated previous findings by Vosniadou and colleagues (Vosniadou & Brewer, 1992; 1994; Vosniadou, Archontidou, Kalogiannidou, & Ioannides, 1996; Diakidoy, Vosniadou, & Hawks, 1997; Vosniadou, Skopeliti & Ikospentaki, 2004; 2005) that in the absence of an external representation, children construct relatively consistent models of the earth, which they can externalize through drawings and play-dough models and which they use to reason with.

The results also showed that the external representations provided (globe and map) influenced children's responses differently. The presentation of the globe caused a dramatic change in children's responses regarding the shape of the earth, with most children abandoning their previous representation of the earth and adopting the culturally accepted representation. On the contrary, in the case of the map, none of the children who had previously constructed a spherical model of the earth changed their original responses regarding the shape of the earth to construct a flat representation of the earth. Also children who initially constructed alternative models of the earth and changed their responses in QPII mostly gave responses that were not consistent to a certain representation of the earth and were grouped in the mixed model category.

The finding that the globe influenced children's responses in a different way from the map shows that the children were not just accepting the external representation passively, but were interpreting it on the basis of what they already knew. This finding is consistent with a constructivist approach and does not agree with a radical socio/cultural perspective that denies the usefulness of prior knowledge (Vosniadou, in press).

The non-spherical earthers who changed their responses in the presence of the globe possible did so because the external model reminded them of the scientifically correct and culturally accepted model to which they had probably been exposed. This interpretation is consistent with the results of other studies that show increase in scientific responses regarding the shape of the earth when a globe is provided (Schoultz et al., 2001; Ivarsson et al., 2002; Vosniadou et al., 2005), or when a forced-choice questionnaire is used (Nobes et al., 2003; Siegal et al., 2004; Vosniadou et al. 2004). These results have been interpreted to show that the recognition of scientifically correct responses is easier than their recall (Vosniadou et al., 2004).

Results such as these have led us to argue that there are different modes of knowing a scientific fact or an explanation, ranging from their simple repetition to their generative use. It appears that there is not a clear cut dichotomy between 'knowing' and 'not knowing', but rather a long process of learning science which often results in the creation of synthetic models and misconceptions (Vosniadou et al., 2004). The above agree with a view of concepts not as fixed and unchanging structures, but rather as malleable and flexible entities greatly affected by context.

Finally, our results showed that when an external representation is present, the frequency of internally inconsistent responses increases. It appears that the children used the external representation to answer questions the responses to which could be derived directly from the model provided. However, when the responses could not be derived directly from the external model, the children filled the gaps using their prior knowledge. This reduced the internal consistency in children's responses in the 2nd part of the questionnaire, when the external models were present.

This argument is supported by evidence derived from a more detailed examination of children's responses to some specific questions. For example, in Q4 the children were asked "can people live down here" showing the location of the South Pole. Both in the case of the map, and in the case of the globe, the scientific response is encouraged by the external representation and this was the response given by the majority of the children in QPII, although not in QPI. In the case of the map the flat representation of the earth poses no problem as far as the location of the South Pole is concerned. In the case of the globe, most of the children gave their responses only after bending to look if there is a country indicated at the place where the South Pole should be. Seeing that there is something like a country there, they answered in the affirmative.

However, interesting differences between the two groups emerged in Q5 ("If a little girl lived and she had a ball and the ball fell from her hands, where would it fall? Show me."). Almost all the children (90% of the 1st graders and 95% of the 3rd graders) in the EG2 (map) said that the ball would fall toward the earth. On the contrary, in case of the EG1 (globe), only 60% of the 1st graders and 64% of the 3rd graders said that the ball would fall towards the earth, even though 80% and 85% respectively had said that the people could live "down here" in the South Pole in Q4. These differences suggest that both in the case of the globe and in the case of the map, the children are reasoning closely on the basis of the external representation to provide their responses. However, when the scientific response is not immediately obvious and can not be derived directly from the external model, incompatible prior knowledge might be used. Thus, the children relying on their previous knowledge that gravity operates in an up/down fashion causing people to fall from the 'bottom of the earth', they responded negatively in Q5, contradicting their positive response to Q4, and thus creating internal inconsistencies in their responses.

These findings are consistent with our previous arguments that the use of an external representation is not an act of 'direct cultural transmission' (e.g., Nobes et al., 2003; Siegal et al, 2004), but rather a constructive process during which the information that comes from the cultural artifacts is interpreted and sometimes actively distorted in the process of being made consistent with what the child already knows (Vosniadou et al., 2004, 2005).

The above also agree with the view that external representations can play a direct role in cognitive processing without the mediation of an internal representation (Zhang & Norman, 1994; Zhang, 1997) and that different representations differentially constrain or facilitate reasoning.

Acknowledgements

The project is co-financed within Op. Education by the ESF (European Social Fund) and National Resources.

References

Diakidoy, I.A., Vosniadou, S., & Hawks, J. (1997). Conceptual change in astronomy: Models of the earth and of the day/night cycle in American-Indian children. *European Journal of Education, XII*, pp. 159-184.

Ivarsson, J., Schoultz, J., & Säljö, R.(2002). Map Reading versus Mind Reading: Revisiting Children's Understanding of the Shape of the Earth. In Limon, M. & Mason (Eds), L. *Reconsidering Conceptual Change: Issues in Theory and Practice*. Kluwer Academic Publishers.

Nobes, G., Moore, D., Martin, A., Clifford, B., Butterworth, G. Panayiotaki, G. & Siegal, M (2003). Children's understanding of the earth in a multicultural community: mental models or fragments of knowledge? *Developmental Science* 6(1), 72-85.

Schoultz, J., Säljö, R., & Wyndhamn, J. (2001). Heavenly talk: discourse, artifacts, and children's understanding of elementary astronomy. *Human Development, 44*, 103-118.

Siegal, M., Butterworth, G., & Newcombe, P.A. (2004). Culture and children's cosmology, *Developmental Science, 7*:3, pp. 308-324.

Vosniadou, S. (in press). The Cognitive-Situative Divide and the Problem of Conceptual Change. *Educational Psychologist*.

Vosniadou, S., & Brewer, W.F. (1992). Mental models of the earth: A study of conceptual change in childhood. *Cognitive Psychology, 24*, pp. 535-585.

Vosniadou, S., & Brewer, W.F. (1994). Mental models of the day/night cycle. *Cognitive Science, 18*, pp. 123-183.

Vosniadou, S., Archontidou, A., Kalogiannidou, A., & Ioannides, C., (1996). How Greek children understand the shape of the earth: A study of conceptual change in childhood. *Psychological Issues, 7*(1), pp. 30-51 (in Greek).

Vosniadou, S., Skopeliti, I., & Ikospentaki, K. (2004). Modes of knowing and ways of reasoning in elementary astronomy, *Cognitive Development, 19*, pp. 203-222.

Vosniadou, S., Skopeliti, I., & Ikospentaki, K. (2005). Reconsidering the role of Artifacts in Reasoning: Children's Understanding of the Globe as a Model of the Earth. *Learning and Instruction, 15*, pp. 333-351.

Zhang, J. (1997). The nature of external representations in problem solving. *Cognitive Science, 21*, pp. 179-217.

Zhang, J. & Norman, D. A., (1994). Representations in distributed cognitive tasks. *Cognitive Science, 18*(1), pp. 87-122.

Adaptive Expertise as Knowledge Building in Science Teachers' Problem Solving

Valerie M. Crawford (valerie.crawford@sri.com)
SRI International, 333 Ravenswood Ave., BN362
Menlo Park, CA 94025 USA

Abstract

Research on expert/expert differences has lead to a differentiation of adaptive expertise and routine expertise. Adaptive expertise was investigated as a knowledge-building orientation to problem solving in high school science teachers' instructional problem solving. An authentic task was administered to adaptive and routine experts as well as novices. Adaptive experts were found to show a higher orientation to knowledge-building during problem solving than routine experts.

Adaptive Expertise

Across many professions and domains of expertise, research has documented that self-directed, effortful problem solving in the context of everyday practice enables practitioners to learn and develop expertise (Chi, Glaser, & Farr, 1988; Eraut, 1994; Ericsson, 1996). Not all veteran practitioners attain excellence or become innovative in their practice. Increasingly, *adaptive expertise* is a construct used to explain the different developmental trajectories leading to excellence versus mere efficiency in problem solving (Hatano & Inagaki, 1986; Patel, Glaser & Arocha, 2000; Schwartz, Bransford, & Sears, 2005) as well as the superior performance of some experts over other experts (Raufaste, Eyerolle, & Marine, 1998; Wineburg, 1998).

The concept of adaptive expertise is rooted in findings from expert/expert studies, from which the contrast of adaptive experts and routine expertise arose (e.g., Bereiter & Scardamalia, 1993; Feltovich, Spiro, & Coulson, 1997; Gott, Hall, Pokorny, Dibble & Glaser, 1992; Hatano & Inagaki, 1986; Raufaste et al., 1998; Wineburg, 1998) . Among various distinguishing characteristics noted by experts, a key distinction is that *routine* experts excel in the application of skill and knowledge to familiar problems, and *adaptive* experts are able to *construct new knowledge* as they solve problems, are more accurate in problem solving, and handle new problems more successfully. During problem solving, the cognitive processes of adaptive experts are distinguished by a greater attention to available evidence; closer analysis of data; a dialectical working back and forth from data to knowledge base; and deliberate, explicit thinking-through of questions posed to the self and conclusions. It is likely through these cognitive processes that adaptive experts *build* their existing knowledge base rather than merely apply it (Chi, 2006; Feltovich et al., 1997; Raufaste et al., 1998; Wineburg, 1998).

Adaptive Expertise in the Practice of Teaching

Adaptive expertise has been described in a range of practices and contexts, including medical diagnosis (Feltovich et al., 1997; Patel et al., 2000), analysis of historical texts (Wineburg, 1998), business management (Barnett & Koslowski, 2002), and avionics device troubleshooting (Gott et al., 1992). Similarly, theoretical accounts of teacher learning and the development of teaching expertise have drawn the distinction between learning processes that make teaching more efficient or routine and those that lead to the progressive development of what has been termed flexible, transferable, or adaptive expertise (Ball & Bass, 2000; Bereiter & Scardamalia, 1993; Darling-Hammond & Bransford, 2005; Hatano & Inagaki, 1986; Wineburg, 1998). Not every problem of daily practice requires *adaptive* expertise to be solved adequately, but the processes of adaptive expertise are thought to enable professionals to build greater knowledge and skill through their practice—to *learn more* from experience (Bereiter & Scardamalia, 1993; Feltovich et al., 1997; Gott et al., 1992).

Adaptive expertise entails learning through problem-solving as opposed to simply applying knowledge and familiar heuristics to problems. Informal learning through practice of this nature is increasingly recognized as important in teachers' professional growth (Ball & Cohen, 1999; Bereiter & Scardamalia, 1993). Research has shown that instructional decision-making, lesson planning, and other aspects of teachers' everyday practice can be important loci for the development of expertise (Ball & Cohen, 1999; Shulman, 1986). Yet not all teachers learn and build expertise through practice in the same way or progress to the same level of expertise.

The aim of this theory-elaboration study was elaborate an analytical description of adaptive expertise in teaching. With this, one can understand how adaptive expertise contributes to teachers' development, link characteristics of adaptive practice to instructional performance, construct reliable measures of adaptiveness in instructional practice, and develop interventions that foster adaptive expertise. I do not view adaptiveness as a fixed or intrinsic attribute of individuals, but rather as a set of cognitive, metacognitive, social, and affective strategies and dispositions triggered in particular situations that merit abandonment of routine problem-solving strategies in favor of a learning-oriented approach to problem solving. Nor is adaptiveness viewed as characteristic of experts alone. Adaptiveness can occur, and can contribute to the development of expertise, at any point in a teacher's professional trajectory (Crawford & Brophy, 2006; Hatano & Oura, 2003).

The analysis reported in this paper stems from a larger study that used a laboratory-based research protocol to develop a theoretical description of adaptive expertise in a key aspect of teaching: instructional decision making. The goal of the analysis was to determine how veteran biology teachers with routine and adaptive profiles, as well as novice teachers, differ in their knowledge-building orientation in an instructional decision-making task that we devised.

The objective of this study was to examine expert/expert differences in problem solving orientation. Adaptive expertise entails a propensity to see problems as an opportunity for constructing new knowledge, rather than just applying existing knowledge, so that knowledge is more likely to be constructed through problem solving. This is akin to "general expertise" (Wineburg, 1998) that enables successful application of knowledge to moderately novel domains. With adaptive expertise, a knowledge-building orientation is balanced with considerations of efficiency and the use of efficient heuristics in problem solving (Schwartz, Bransford, & Sears, 2005). We examined differences between adaptive and routine experts in knowledge building during problem solving.

Hypotheses

Knowledge-building and detailed examination of empirical evidence are described in the literature as characteristics of adaptive expertise in problem solving (Bereiter & Scardamalia, 1993; Feltovich et al., 1997; Hatano & Inagaki, 1986; Wineburg, 1998), and as core characteristics of effective teacher learning (Ball, 2003; Ball & Bass, 2000; Ball & Cohen, 1999). For example, Ball and her colleagues have described analysis of student work and errors as fertile ground for the development of teachers' pedagogical content knowledge and knowledge of students. Thus, thoughtful analysis of student work has great potential to develop teachers' skill in instructional diagnosis.

To validate our theoretical framework, which views these characteristics of adaptive expertise as applicable to instructional diagnosis and decision making in high school science teachers, we examined the occurrence of knowledge building and use of evidence in problem solving among the high school biology teachers in our study who were selected to represent three profiles: adaptive veterans, routine veterans, and novices (two of whom we identified as having strong potential to show adaptiveness). The coding and analysis were intended to test several hypotheses. Some hypotheses relate to differences between adaptive veterans and routine veterans; other hypotheses relate to differences between veterans as a group and novices.

Regarding knowledge-building and efficiency in problem solving, we hypothesized the following:

1. Teachers identified *a priori* as adaptive veterans will show a greater proportion of knowledge-building utterances (text units) than routine veterans.
2. Veterans as a group will show a higher proportion of efficiency utterances (text units) than novices, who, we speculated, are likely not yet to have mastered the analytical heuristics that support efficient problem solving.
3. Novice teachers will show a higher proportion of knowledge building overall than both groups of veteran teachers. We reasoned that because novice teachers have less relevant knowledge (e.g., pedagogical content expertise; knowledge of students; curriculum knowledge), they would spend more time constructing knowledge through the task than would veteran teachers.

Research Design and Methods

An authentic instructional problem-solving task was administered to research participants, using a think-aloud approach. Our study protocol was a variation of the traditional laboratory-based problem-solving task used in the study of expert-novice problem solving (Chi, Glaser, & Farr, 1988; Ericsson & Simon, 1993; Ericsson & Smith, 1991; Gott et al., 1992). We adapted the method in several ways to approximate the complexity of an authentic instructional decision-making task in high school biology teaching.

Participant Recruitment and Selection

We sought to recruit high school biology teachers whose backgrounds and other characteristics conformed to one of three profiles: routine veteran teacher (we defined veteran as 7 or more years teaching high school biology), adaptive veteran teacher, and novice teacher (we defined novice as 2 or 3 years' teaching high school biology). We selected participants through questionnaires on their background, experience, professional activities, and beliefs; in some cases, we also used professional recommendations from local experts and two of the researchers involved in the study.

Criteria for the adaptive expert profile were derived from the literature on adaptive expertise and from approaches used in other studies of adaptiveness in problem solving, primarily Barnett and Koslowski (2002), Gott et al. (1992), and Wineburg (1998). Specifically, we sought individuals with some advanced training in education theory and/or research methods, or with a prior career that involved rich experience with problem solving and/or research. The rationale was that teachers with this profile would be likely to address problem solving in a more flexible, hypothesis-testing way, would evince a knowledge-building orientation, and would show less concern for efficiency in problem solving. Candidates with 7 or more years of experience teaching biology, but having none of the background criteria listed above, were considered routine veterans. We selected novice teachers who had come to teaching from another career that involved some form of research, hypothesizing that such experience might confer Wineburg's "general expertise" (Wineburg, 1998) or a form of problem-solving expertise that would be applied in our instructional reasoning task.

Thirteen high school biology teachers participated (all names used in this article are pseudonyms). Nine were veteran and four were novice teachers (2 to 3 years of experience). Based on the background information we collected at the time of recruitment, four of the nine veteran teachers were categorized as belonging to the "adaptive" profile and five to the "routine" profile, before they performed on our laboratory-based task. Two of the 4 novices selected had come to teaching from another career that involved some form of research. All participants but one were current high school biology teachers.

Instructional Decision-Making Task

The task and all accompanying materials were developed in consultation with a master high school biology teacher and a nationally recognized expert on genetics teaching and learning. Study participants were presented with a scenario in which the participant is taking over a 10th-grade biology class of 22 students for a teacher going on maternity leave. The fictional class has almost completed a 5-week genetics unit (encompassing Mendelian genetics, DNA, genes, and protein synthesis). The main task statement for the participant reads: "Your task is to understand, as best you can, what your students have and have not learned in the genetics unit so far." To accomplish the task, the following task materials were available to the teacher participant:

- A set of 22 student scored practice tests and the practice test answer key.
- The class grade book (a printout from a grade book software program) containing information about students' cumulative course points, homework points.
- A table summarizing individual students' scores on each practice test question, along with average points scored on each item and average practice test scores. This artifact was given participants on request or after participants had examined the student practice tests for 10 minutes, whichever came first.
- The genetics unit lesson plans, including many activity materials, handouts, and assignments, and the course textbook.
-

The task was extensively pilot-tested with biology teachers and science teacher educators with biology backgrounds, and refined through several iterations throughout the pilot-testing process. Participants and experts in teacher learning deemed the task authentically representative of tasks that teachers perform in their practice.

Embedded Features of the Task Structure. The design of the practice test questions and the design of the student responses on multiple-choice and constructed-response items embedded patterns of correct and incorrect responses, which indicated misconceptions well researched in the literature on genetics learning (Heim, 1999; Stewart 1982; 1983). Two patterns of erroneous responses indicated specific student misconceptions in genetics: one on genetics reasoning (reasoning from effect (phenotype) to cause (genotype) and cause to effect), the other related to concept of dominance of an allele. We embedded these patterns to provide opportunities for teachers to engage in instructional diagnosis and to trigger episodes of reasoning in which teachers could display adaptive constructs (e.g., forward and backward reasoning processes; knowledge-constructive analysis of the case materials) during problem solving.

Procedures

Informed consent was obtained. Participants were trained in the think-aloud process, using standard training procedures (Ericsson & Simon, 1993). After the think-aloud training, participants were reminded that their task was to determine what students had learned from the unit so far, and they were encouraged to ask the experimenter for any information or artifacts they felt they needed, in addition to those in front of them.

The task was administered in two phases: The first phase, the "initial scenario," had participants perform the task with minimum interruptions from the experimenter (other than reminding them to continue to think aloud, and providing them with the spreadsheet on request or after 10 minutes of examining student tests). This phase ended when the participant indicated that he or she had completed the task of determining what students had learned from the unit so far. The second phase, "prompt administration," was initiated immediately after the participant had completed the task on his or her own. The experimenter gave conditional prompts to orient the participant to examine (or re-examine) key parts of the materials to determine whether prompting to examine task materials more closely would help the participant to discern data patterns not detected in their "initial phase."

Upon completion of the prompt section, a cognitive interview was conducted with the participant to clarify, where necessary, participants' strategies and thinking during and resulting from the first two phases of the task. Finally, the participant was debriefed about the research study. The whole session, including the think-aloud training, took up to 2 hours, and was audio- and video-recorded.

Data Coding and Analysis

Coding of Verbal Protocols. The resulting think-aloud protocols were transcribed verbatim. Transcripts were prepared to indicate length of pauses and were annotated, based on the videotape, with information on the research participant's use of the task materials. The primary unit of analysis for the transcribed text was a *text unit* of the verbal protocol transcript. Adapting Gee's (1996) approach to the treatment of transcribed text for discourse analysis, we defined a "text unit" as a complete idea, including main clause, any subordinate clauses, and any associated false starts, (Gee, 1996). Utterances that were participants' reading of text contained in the task materials were group the specific text unit related to the that material.

The transcripts were coded for *task orientation*. Task orientation was coded in terms of two mutually exclusive categories: *knowledge-building* and *efficiency*. Our goal with task orientation coding was to capture "meta" statements that indicate participants' orientation to the task at a given moment. We want to identify where the participant was opening up the problem space (indicating a knowledge-building orientation) and where the participant was closing down or reducing the problem space, for example, to finish up the task (indicating an efficiency-orientation). We assumed that all participants would exhibit some degree of both of these, and that some participants would show an orientation to the task that privileged one over the other, and that some participants would show a balance of the two.

This analysis examined the degree to which participants demonstrated an effortful attempt to construct knowledge related to analysis of the data to draw conclusions, and the degree to which participants attempted to simplify the task, think about the effective use of time while doing the task, and finish up the task. We defined **knowledge-building orientation** as ways that participants approached the task such that she or he is oriented to "opening up" the problem space and exploring the available artifacts in the service of sense-making and knowledge construction. We used a single code to capture this orientation. Types of utterances coded as "knowledge-building" included:

- Questions or statements to self about what one would like to know or to find out. Example: "I wonder how pedigree is taught."
- Drawing conclusions based on examination of the artifacts
- Examination of artifacts
- Indications of interest, curiosity. Example: "I am curious why students did not get this."
- Metacognitive or self-regulative statements about the participant's own knowledge state or understanding with respect to understanding what students know and don't know. Example: "Okay, I have some idea about what students know"; "As I look at this, I am a little confused about student thinking."

Excluded were utterances that indicated an *intention* to find out something for the purpose of planning a lesson for the remaining days before the final test, or completing the task. Example: "I think I am done with the task, but let me double-check the task scenario."

An **efficiency orientation** was defined as involving simplification of the task or the problem space, monitoring time spent on or remaining for the task, considering trade-offs in time required to accomplish a sub-goal versus time available or value of the results, and thinking about what remained to do to finish the task. In our pilot-testing, we noted that nearly all teachers spend time describing how they would approach instruction related to topic, and nearly all teachers did planning related to how the last one or more lessons would be implemented to help the students learn content identified as still needing to learn. Such lesson planning was categorized as efficiency because all teachers felt that this was the last step of the task, to plan the lesson; piloting showed us that many teachers "rushed" into lesson planning to complete the task, foreclosing on analysis of data. Thus, lesson planning was identified as an orientation to task completion rather than problem or data exploration or sense making.

Two researchers were trained with this coding scheme, coded half of one transcript and compared the coding results. The reliability for both the efficiency code and the knowledge-building code was above .95. The researchers discussed the disagreements and refined the decision rules, and recoded the disagreements. After this reliability was established, all the transcripts were single-coded by one the analyst. Questionable cases were flagged in the course of coding, discussed by the two analysts, and resolved.

Findings and Discussion

For this analysis, we examined only participants' performance in the initial task scenario (the participants' initial completion of the task, prior to the experimenters' prompts to the participants to examine or re-examine specific aspects of the task). We compared groups (adaptive veteran, routine veteran, and novice) on the mean percentages of text units coded as knowledge building and efficiency. As expected, routine and adaptive veterans were highly similar in the proportion of *efficiency-oriented* utterances they displayed (adaptive-veteran mean = 11.52%; routine-veteran profile = 13.55%) (see Figure 1). However, the two groups differ markedly in knowledge-building orientation exhibited during the task. The adaptive-veteran group had a mean of 17.37% of all text units coded as knowledge building, whereas the routine-veteran group showed a mean of only 7.68% of all text units. Novices were similar to the adaptive-veteran group, with a mean of 16.35%.

Next experience-level groups (veteran and novice) were compared on knowledge building and efficiency. As expected, the veteran teachers as a group and the novice teachers differed markedly in their degree of efficiency demonstrated during the completion of the task. Novices showed much less orientation to efficiency in their completion of the task. Veteran teachers had a mean of 12.65% text units coded as related to efficiency in task performance, whereas novice teachers had a mean of 2.6% of text units coded as related to efficiency. Although the samples are very small, this difference is statistically significant at the .05 probability level. ($t = 2.34$; df = 11, $p = .039$). The novice teachers also showed somewhat more knowledge building during the initial task than the veterans as a group. Veterans had a mean of 12% of all text units coded as knowledge building; novices as a group had a mean of 16.36%. The difference is not statistically significant.

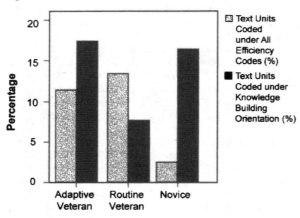

Figure 1. Mean percentage of efficiency and knowledge-building text units, by profile.

We speculate that novice teachers' comparative lack of efficiency during problem solving reflected that they had yet to develop the efficient heuristics and routines associated with expertise coping with domain-specific problem. The level of knowledge building displayed by novices, which was about equal to that of adaptive veterans, is difficult to interpret. Their sense-making efforts could reflect their relatively lower levels of domain knowledge. Alternatively, because we purposely selected novices who had previously engaged professional in some form conceptual problem solving, these novices may have been exhibited adaptiveness in problem solving. A general-knowledge task would be required to disentangle knowledge from adaptiveness. Indeed, such a line of research is critical to further elaborating the construct of adaptive expertise (Crawford & Brophy, 2006).

The finding that adaptive and routine veterans exhibited equal amounts of efficiency during problem solving supports Schwartz, Bransford and Sears's (2005) formulation of adaptive expertise as an optimal balance of innovation (or knowledge building, in my terms) and efficiency in problem solving (see Figure 2). Adaptive and routine experts differed only in the level of knowledge building they exhibited, not in the level of efficiency. Adaptive experts were as efficient in problem solving as routine experts, but they explored the task more deeply.

Overall, adaptive experts created a more complex functional problem space for themselves than did routine experts. Qualitative analysis of utterances coded as knowledge building indicated that adaptive veterans differed most from routine veterans in the nature of their high-level sense-making during analysis of student understandings as exhibited on the test. Adaptive veterans closely analyzed the test questions to better interpret the student responses; routine veterans almost never analyzed the test questions. Adaptive veterans much more frequently posed questions or

wondered to themselves about many of their observations, directing their review of the materials to answer these various questions. In sharp contrast, the routine veterans took a satisficing approach to the task; generating a simple list of "topics to review" seem to be the functional task for most routine veterans.

This analysis of knowledge building and efficiency in problem solving demonstrated that as postulated, teachers tended to show three basic patterns or orientations in the approach the task: and tendency toward knowledge building with a lack of efficiency in the process (the novice profile); a tendency toward extreme efficiency at the expense of knowledge building through the task (the routine-veteran profile); or a balance of knowledge building with efficiency (the adaptive-veteran profile). In addition to these three predicted patterns, some participants showed low levels of both variables such that an overriding pattern or tendency could not be discerned.

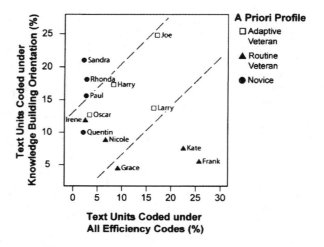

Figure 2. Knowledge building plotted against efficiency in problem solving: Adaptiveness as optimal balance of the two dimensions.

We maintain that adaptiveness can be exhibited at any time in the development of a teacher's practice. I further view adaptiveness not as an intrinsic trait but as a set of cognitive and self-regulative skills and abilities, as well as habits of mind and dispositions. Adaptiveness in our theoretical framework comprises dispositions and habits of mind that enable one to jump out of the ruts of habit (highly automated heuristics), set aside routines, and selectively give up efficiency in order to "go deep"—and to recognize and pursue the promising problems that reward "going deep." Doing so creates rich opportunities for knowledge building and innovation of new procedures. In addition, adaptiveness requires proficiency with some skills and abilities, such as specific problem-solving heuristics, so that one is not unable to sort out minutiae to discern the important patterns in a set of data, unable to formulate worthwhile overarching goals for the analysis, or unable to identify, develop, and pursue a productive line of analysis to arrive at a solution or understanding of a problem.

Acknowledgments

I thank Yukie Toyama, Mark Schlager, Phil Vahey, Cathy Kliegel for their valuable contributions to this research project. This research was supported by a grant from the National Science Foundation under Grant No. ESI-0353451. Any findings, opinions, conclusions, or recommendations in this paper are mine alone and do not necessarily represent the views of the National Science Foundation.

References

Ball, D. L., & Cohen, D. K. (1999). Developing practice, developing practitioners: Toward a practice-based theory of professional education. In L. Darling-Hammond & G. Sykes (Eds)., *Teaching as the learning profession: Handbook of policy and practice*. San Francisco, CA: Jossey-Bass.

Barnett, S., & Koslowski, B. (2002). Adaptive expertise: Effects of type of experience and the level of theoretical understanding it generates. *Thinking and Reasoning, 8*(4), 237-267.

Bereiter, C., & Scardamalia, M. (1993). *Surpassing ourselves: An inquiry into the nature and implications of expertise*. Chicago, IL: Open Court.

Bransford, J. D., Brown, A., & Cocking, R. (Eds).. (2000). *How people learn: Brain, mind, experience, and school (Expanded Edition)*. Washington, DC: National Academy Press.

Bransford, J. D. & Schwartz, D. L. (1999). Rethinking transfer: A simple proposal with multiple implications. In A. Iran-Nejad and P. D. Pearson (Eds)., *Review of Research in Education, 24* (pp. 61-100). Washington, D.C.: American Educational Research Association.

Chi, M. T. H. (2006). Two approaches to the study of expert' characteristics. In K. A. Ericsson, N. Charness, P. Feltovich, & R. Hoffman (Eds.), *The Cambridge handbook of expertise and expert performance* (pp. 21-30), New York: Cambridge University Press.

Chi, M. T. H., Glaser, R., & Farr, M. (1988). *The nature of expertise*. Hillsdale, NJ: Erlbaum.

Darling-Hammond, L. & Bransford, J. (2005). (Editors) *Preparing teachers for a changing world: What teachers should learn and be able to do*. Jossey-Bass: San Francisco, CA.

Eraut, M. (1994). *Developing Professional Knowledge and Competence*. London: Falmer.

Ericsson, K. A. (1996). *The road to excellence*. Mahawah, NJ: Erlbaum.

Ericsson, K. A., & Simon, H. A. (1993). P*rotocol analysis: Verbal reports as data* (revised edition). Cambridge, MA: MIT Press.

Ericsson, K. A., & Smith, J. (1991). *Toward a general theory of expertise: Prospects and limits*. New York: Cambridge University Press.

Feltovich, P. J., Spiro, R. J., & Coulson, R. L. (1997). Issues of expert flexibility in contexts characterized by complexity and change. In P. J. Feltovich, K. M. Ford, & R. R. Hoffman, (Eds)., *Expertise in context* (pp.126-146). Menlo Park, New Jersey: AAAI Press/MIT Press.

Gee, J. P. (1996). *Social linguistics and literacies: Ideology in discourses* (second edition). Taylor & Frances: Bristol, PA.

Gott, S., Hall, P., Pokorny, A., Dibble, E., & Glaser, R. (1992). A naturalistic study of transfer: Adaptive expertise in technical domains. In D. Detterman & R. Sternberg (Eds)., *Transfer on trial: Intelligence, cognition, and instruction* (pp. 258-288). Norwood, NJ: Ablex.

Hatano, G., & Oura, Y. (2003). Commentary: Reconceptualizing school learning using insight from expertise research. *Educational Researcher, 32*(8), 26-29.

Hatano, G., & Inagaki, K. (1986). Two courses of expertise. In H. Stevenson, H. Azuma, & K. Hakuta (Eds)., *Child development and education in Japan* (pp. 262-272). New York: W. H. Freeman and Company.

Heim, W. G. (1991). What is a recessive allele? *The American Biology Teacher, 53*(2), 94-97.

Patel, V. L., Glaser, R., & Arocha, J. F. (2000). Cognition and expertise: Acquisition of medical competence. *Clinical Investigation and Medicine, 23*(4), 256-260.

Patel, V. L., & Groen, G. J., (1986). Knowledge-based solutions in medical reasoning. *Cognitive Science,10,* 91–116.

Raufaste, E., Eyrolle, H., & Marine, C. (1998). Pertinence generation in radiological diagnosis: Spreading activation and the nature of expertise. Cognitive Science 22(4), 517-546.

Schwartz, D. L., Bransford, J. D., & Sears, D. A. (2005). Efficiency and innovation in transfer. In J. Mestre (Ed)., *Transfer of learning from a modern multidisciplinary perspective* (pp. 1-52). Greenwich, CT: Information Age Publishing.

Shulman, L. (1986). Those who understand: Knowledge growth in teaching. *Educational Researcher, 15*(2), 4-14.

Stewart, J. (1982). Difficulties experienced by high school students when learning basic Mendelian genetics. *The American Biology Teacher, 44*, 80-84.

Stewart, J. (1983). Student problem solving in high school genetics. *Science Education*, 67, 523-540.

Wineburg, S. (1998). Reading Abraham Lincoln: An expert/expert study in the interpretation of historical texts. *Cognitive Science, 22*(3), 319-346.

Modeling Human Expertise for Instructional Design:
Applications to Landmine Detection

James J. Staszewski (jjs@cmu.edu)
Department of Psychology, Carnegie Mellon University
5000 Forbes Avenue, Pittsburgh, PA 15213 USA

Abstract

Landmines pose a major military threat as well as a serious humanitarian problem. The difficulty and cost of detecting buried landmines, especially those with minimal metallic content, aggravates the problem. The two projects described here used cognitive science's understanding of human expertise and its acquisition to improve detection capability via development and implementation of training based on experts' skills. Field testing of the landmine detection skills of expert users of two different handheld detection systems, the PSS-12[1], the U.S. Army standard equipment, and the PSS-14, an advanced technology system under development at the time of this work, yielded rich multi-media data for analysis and modeling. The resulting models served as blueprints for designing training programs whose efficacy was tested. Both proved highly effective for developing detection skills, producing the greatest increases in detection rates against the most difficult to find mines. The US Army has adopted both programs and uses them to train troops. The outcomes demonstrate the practical utility of information-processing models of expertise for designing instruction and developing important human skills. Some implications of this work for cognitive science are discussed.

Introduction

Chase and Simon's (1973a, b) seminal studies of chess expertise introduced the revolutionary idea that experts' extraordinary performance is based mainly on knowledge acquired through experience, rather than rare immutable abilities or innate talents. The generality of this claim and the phenomena on which it was based have been tested and confirmed by many subsequent studies (Chase, 1986; Chi, Glaser, & Farr, 1988; Ericsson & Staszewski, 1989; Ericsson & Charness, 1994).

Instructional theorists quickly grasped the implications of this discovery for the field of education, arguing that an understanding of how experts achieved success in their domains could inform instructional design (Bransford, Brown, & Cocking, 1999; Glaser, 1989; Glaser & Bassok, 1989). Despite the promise of using domain-specific process accounts of expertise for improving teaching and learning and studies showing that information-processing models of expertise are useful resources for designing instruction (Biederman & Schiffrar, 1987; Chase & Ericsson, 1982; Wenger & Payne, 1995; Staszewski, 1988, 1990), the absence of evidence for the practical utility of using models of expertise for instructional design has justified questions about

---

[1] The official names for the equipment discussed here is Army-Navy/Portable Special Search-12 (PSS-12) and Army-Navy/Portable Special Search-14.

the viability of using such models for pedagogical purposes (Alexander, 2003; Patel, Kaufman, & Magder, 1996).

This report addresses this issue by summarizing the results and impacts of two use-inspired (Stokes, 1997) projects. Their common goal was to develop training for operators of specific handheld landmine detection systems that would improve upon existing training and increase landmine detection capability. Both projects employed a cognitive engineering approach, which used equipment-specific models of expert skill to guide the design of the respective training programs.

This paper will first describe the approach to training development called Cognitive Engineering Based on Expert Skill (CEBES). The problem-domain in which its practical utility was tested is then discussed. Sketches of the goals, methods, and results of each of two projects follow, along with the practical impact of each. The utility of the CEBES approach is discussed along with some implications of this work for cognitive science.

General Approach

Cognitive engineering applies the theory, principles, and methods of cognitive science to solve applied problems in which human performance depends upon the quality of participants' thinking and skills. Cognitive engineering based on expert skill (CEBES) is a specialized case of cognitive engineering that uses domain-specific models of human expertise as the foundation for designing instruction. This approach first analyzes the knowledge and skills used by experts to perform tasks with high proficiency and then uses the findings to develop cognitive models of expert skill. These models are then used as blueprints for designing instruction. Just as microbiology's models of the genome support cloning of organisms with desirable properties, the CEBES approach uses models of expertise as templates for replicating the knowledge and skills that are the foundation of exemplary human performance.

The advantage of the CEBES approach over conventional training design has been demonstrated in two recent landmine detection training projects. Both used the CEBES approach to design training programs for operators of the currently fielded PSS-12 and recently developed and deployed PSS-14 handheld landmine detectors.

The first step of each project identified experts by empirical testing of operators who had extensive experience with specific handheld landmine detection equipment. Information-processing analyses of the most proficient operators were performed and findings were used to develop cognitive process models of the experts' skills. The content and structure of the models then guided the design of equipment-specific training programs for novices. Each training program was administered and trainees' performance was tested on multiple occasions.

The Landmine Problem

Landmines are a major threat to both military and civilian personnel. A recent military assessment (Hambric and Schneck, 1996) stated "Mines are a major threat in all types of combat and will be the major threat in Operations Other than War...The widespread employment of landmines threatens to neutralize advantages in firepower and mobility by severely limiting ability to maneuver and disrupting tactical synchronization." Later reports from Bosnia (Schneck & Green, 1997), Afghanistan (LaMoe & Read, 2002), and Iraq confirmed this assessment and suggested that the threat's severity may have been underestimated. Subsequent events have confirmed LaMoe & Reed's (2002) prediction that the countermine problem in contemporary operational environments would worsen (Kern, 2005).

Landmines also jeopardize civilians, whose lands have been mined during conflict and remain so for years afterward -- unless the ordnance is either removed or neutralized -- due to this weapon's longevity. A United Nations report has described landmines as "one of the most widespread, lethal, and long lasting forms of pollution" (Geneva International Centre for Humanitarian Demining, 2003). An estimated 45-50 million mines remain to be cleared in 90 countries. Mines claim an estimated 15-20,000 victims per year, one third of whom die. Survivors typically lose limbs, although blindness and shrapnel wounds also occur. Beyond this physical toll, mine warfare imposes serious psychological and economic hardships on affected societies as well.

Landmine Detection: Skilled PSS-12 Operation

Removing and/or neutralizing buried mines involves first detecting their locations. Detection typically relies on human operators of hand-held equipment working in close proximity to live ordnance. Few tasks punish human error more suddenly and brutally.

After-action reports from combat and peacekeeping operations as well as controlled testing showed that U.S. soldiers' performance with the standard issue PSS-12 equipment was substandard and that detection rates for low metal mines were dangerously low.

Two heavily experienced PSS-12 operators, however, produced 90%+ detection rates against high- and low-metal anti-tank (AT) and anti-personnel (AP) mines in field tests. Analysis of the experts' detection activities also showed that their techniques and strategies differed from conventionally taught operating procedures (Staszewski, 1999).

The most important differences were in the techniques experts used to enhance the sensitivity of their equipment and in their strategies for information search and decision. Whereas soldiers made mine declarations on the basis of auditory outputs signalling the location of conductive material, experts used the onset and offset of auditory outputs that occurred during sweeping motions of the detector to synthesize spatial patterns that they would then compare to the patterns they had learned mines produced. (See Staszewski, 2006 for illustrations of the empirically derived patterns for as well as the macrostructure of the model of PSS-12 expertise).

The differences between more- and less-experienced operators in performance and process motivated development of training that based instruction on experts' techniques and strategies. Studies then tested whether instruction based on a cognitive model of PSS-12 expertise could close the observed expert-novice performance gap.

CEBES Training for the PSS-12 Detector[2]

Four general principles guided the design of training. First, training content and organization reflected the expert model. Second, detection rate was made the focal measure of performance and learning, reasoning that improvements in discrimination and rate of area coverage would follow. Third, instruction and tasks were organized hierarchically, based on the expert's goal structure, to minimize information/working memory overload; instruction and drills started on part-tasks, and, when proficiency was achieved, instruction and drills focused on integration of the acquired subskills. The fourth principle involved providing individual trainees with ample practice and timely feedback on performance in each drill.

Initial instruction and drills focused on three basic skills: (1) proper equipment preparation, (2) sweep/area coverage techniques that maximized the PSS-12's sensitivity and ensured thorough area coverage for identifying and localizing potential threats, and (3) development of pattern acquisition and target recognition skills. After the basics, soldiers proceeded to blind search drills, which called for integration of basic skills in a simulated mine detection activity. Details on the training program, its component tasks, procedures, and training materials, can be found in Staszewski & Davison (2000), Davison & Staszewski (2002), or Davison, Staszewski, & Boxley (2001).

In the initial test of the program, 22 U. S. Army combat engineers who had recently completed standard mine detection training participated as operators/trainees. This experiment used a pretest-posttest design. Mine simulants served as targets in testing and training. Targets included 5 different mine types and represented high- (M) and low-metal (LM) AT and AP mine types.

Pretest performance failed to distinguish the treatment and control groups. Both achieved very low detection rates (15-17%) on low metal anti-personnel (AP-LM) mines. Treatment-group soldiers then received approximately 15 hours of experimental, hands-on training. Posttest results showed that the treatment group achieved an overall

[2] Development and testing of the PSS-12 training program were performed in collaboration with Dr. Alan Davison, Chief, Army Research Laboratory, Human Research and Engineering Directorate U.S. Army Maneuver Support Center Field Element.

detection rate of 0.94. This rate exceeded the control group's by a factor of 3. The treatment group's detection rate on the smallest, low metal targets (M14 simulants) was more than 6 times that of the control group. Treatment-control results by target type are shown in Figure 1.

A second study intended both to confirm the reliability of the initial study's treatment effects and explore their generality retested a subset of the treated soldiers in the same setting, now wearing body armor. Results replicated those of Study 1.

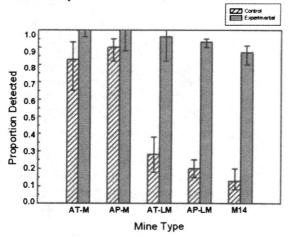

Figure 1. Detection rate as a function of target class. Error bars show 95% confidence intervals. M14 results are a subset of the displayed AP-LM data.

A third study tested treatment group soldiers on real, deactivated mine targets in a different location. Multiple mines of each mine type were used. The surface of the test lanes was expected to increase detection difficulty. Soldiers nonetheless achieved an aggregate detection rate of 0.97 and showed significant improvement in finding 100% of the M14s.

Subsequent practical training efforts using (a) older non-commissioned officers as trainees and (b) military instructors have generalized these findings. Despite unanticipated reductions in training times per man to 3-4 hrs and 1 hr in these studies, respectively, the pattern of robust pre-test post-test gains found in the initial study resulted, although detection rates dropped roughly 10%.

Following these tests a committee of high-ranking officers at the U.S. Army Engineer School (USAES) reviewed and evaluated the content and test results of the CEBES training program and recommended its adoption. The USAES commandant subsequently ordered its adoption. A Safety of Use Message was broadcast to all U.S. Army units to cease use of the old techniques due to the hazard involved and mandated training on the techniques of the CEBES program. Troops so trained use the PSS-12 for countermine operations in current theaters of conflict. The Colombian Army has also adopted the training program and its countermine personnel use the techniques it teaches.

CEBES Training for the PSS-14 Detector

A second project tested whether the CEBES approach could improve performance of an advanced, dual-sensor handheld detection technology (PSS-14) while it was in development. Like the PSS-12, the PSS-14 used electro-magnetic induction (EMI) to sense conductive material, specifically the metallic components found in mines. Along with the EMI sensor, the PSS-14 incorporated ground-penetrating radar and related signal processing algorithms to locate buried objects. Different auditory output tones for each sensor, which could occur simultaneously, alerted the operator to the presence and location of buried objects with the appropriate properties.

After nine-years and $38M had been invested in system development, the prototype's performance in initial testing was disappointing. As shown by the solid black bars in Figure 2, detection rates against small, low-metal AP mines were worse than those for the PSS-12, the system the prototype was designed to replace. A subsequent performance review conducted by a panel of military, government, academic, and private sector personnel concluded that weak operator training contributed substantially to the poor showing and made it difficult to assess the system's potential.

The program was granted a reprieve and, in hope of improving performance, funding for an additional year of development was approved. This funding included support for application of the CEBES approach to develop new operator training. An information-processing analysis of the skills of the most experienced and highest-performing operator was carried out and a model of his skill was developed. Although skilled operation of the PSS-14 demanded greater precision in the movement of the sensor head over the ground surface than was required for the PSS-12 and the outputs of two independent sensor channels produced patterns of substantially greater complexity, the expert models for the two systems were surprisingly similar in terms of mechanisms and their organization (Staszewski, 2006).

A training program for novice operators was designed using the expert model as a blueprint. The surprisingly strong similarities between the models of PSS-12 and PSS-14 expertise made it possible to employ many of the components of the PSS-12 training program in the PSS-14 training. Like the PSS-12 program, it incorporated drills designed to facilitate acquisition of sweep/area coverage techniques that maximized the equipment's sensitivity as well as exercises to support development of pattern acquisition and recognition subskills.

The greater complexity of the PSS-14 system, however, meant that achieving these goals required additional training steps. For example, maximizing the sensitivity of the metal detection and ground-penetrating radar sensors required maintaining the sensor head movements within narrow ranges of velocity and height above the ground surface. Because effective coverage also required that these movement parameter values be maintained over cross-lane sweeps (perpendicular to the path of the operator) 1.5 m long, with sufficient forward overlap on successive sweeps as the operator moved forward, while simultaneously listening for the output of either sensor, just remembering all the requirements, let alone meeting them, threatened to overload novices. To reduce complexity and information overload, the sweep/coverage task was divided into simpler components, with each component being trained and learned individually and progressively combined. To give trainers needed measures of sweep dynamics and trainees feedback, an automated computer-based optical senor-head tracking system was developed (Herman, McMahill, & Kantor, 2000) that captured a trainee's movements of the sensor head in various drills and displayed performance on selected dimensions against the specified standard via a graphical interface.

Also, because the PSS-14's two sensors responded to different properties of mines and pattern/signature acquisition techniques differed for each sensor, these techniques were trained and executed separately, with trainees receiving instruction and practice on how to integrate the distinct metal and GPR signatures into a whole, complex pattern and interpret them.

These factors, plus the requirement that operators be trained to detect mines in two environments (gravel roadway and fields with vegetation) increased training time beyond that for the PSS-12 training to 32-35 hours per operator.

Two field tests of the PSS-14 training program were performed, the first using two U.S. Army NCOs and three civilians as trainees. Since all had been exposed to earlier versions of the PSS-14, a second test was performed with active duty personnel who had no prior knowledge of the system. Participating in the second test were two enlisted U.S. Army paratroopers and two U.S. Marine Corps enlistees.

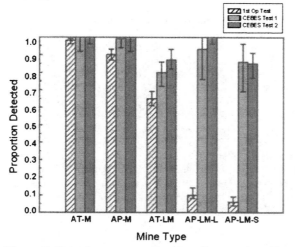

Figure 2. Detection rate as a function of target class. Error bars show 95% confidence intervals. -L and -S suffixes in abscissa labels signify AP-LM targets with large (3.5-4.1") and small (2.2-3.1") diameters, respectively.

Results from both CEBES training tests are shown with the results from the initial prototype test in Figure 2. CEBES-trained operators produced substantial detection gains overall relative to initial test results and achieved manifold improvement against the greatest threat: small, low-metal AP mines.

The results of these two tests cast the potential of the PSS-14 in a considerably better light than the results of the initial operational field test. In addition, consistencies in performance among operators against specific AT-LMs and AP-LMs identified limitations in the system's design that guided re-engineering efforts. Most importantly, the observed performance improvements justified continuation of funding for PSS-14 development.

Subsequent refinements raised detection rates into the 97-100% range (Santiago, Locke, & Reidy, 2004). Recognizing the critical contribution that operator training makes to the PSS-14's mine detection capability, the U. S. Army has adopted the policy of distributing the CEBES training program with the PSS-14 equipment only as an integrated package. U.S. forces trained in this program now use the PSS-14 in countermine operations in current theatres of conflict. Reports from the field indicate that the PSS-14's performance in the hands of a well-trained soldier represents a leap forward in mine detection capability. The U.S. Humanitarian Demining Research and Development Program is now developing the system further for humanitarian demining applications.

Discussion

The results of the training studies and the subsequent large-scale institutional adoption of the expertise-based landmine detection training programs demonstrate the practical utility of cognitive models of human expertise for instructional design. Some implications of this work for applied cognitive science, expertise research, theory testing, and broader disciplinary concerns merit discussion.

As Anderson et al (1995) and McNamara (2006) have pointed out, educational environments are natural contexts for application of cognitive science. The results of these two mine detection training projects illustrate the performance gains producible with well designed training for both fielded and emerging technologies. They also show how a reasonably detailed and coherent understanding of how experts perform at levels that make them experts can effectively guide instructional design, validating claims about the promise of expertise research (Glaser, 1984, 1989).

Sound, general conclusions about the effectiveness of the CEBES approach will require investigation in other tasks and domains. Nonetheless, the successes achieved with this approach should be sufficient to motivate future evaluative studies of CEBES and revive enthusiasm for investigating expertise in other domains that can advance basic understanding of expert skill as well as support new instructional applications.

This work offers a clear and concrete response to the question: "Once you have done a cognitive task analysis, how do you make use of the products?" (Schraagen, Chipman, & Shalin, 2000, p. 9). Given the resource-intensive nature of analyzing whole tasks at a fine temporal grain and synthesizing a coherent process model from the observations (Newell, 1973; Simon, 1980) -- even in a controlled laboratory environment --, the value of such investments is a non-trivial question. A substantial return is needed to justify the investment and motivate others to take the risk of applying this approach.

Regarding the practical utility of CEBES, the outcomes of the training studies illustrate the effectiveness of this approach. Another important dimension of practicality in engineering involves economics. Because cognitive task analyses require non-trivial time and resources, it is reasonable to ask 'Is the CEBES approach cost-effective?' For the PSS-14 effort (for which cost information is available), the answer is affirmative. The total cost of analyzing and modeling its expert's skill, developing the training program, and testing it represented roughly 0.3% of the prototype system's development cost.

How does this work inform basic understanding in cognitive science? First, regarding expertise research, pattern recognition was put forth as a key explanatory mechanism for expert performance in Chase and Simon's (1973a, b) chess studies. Much of the experimental evidence supporting and generalizing this claim came from laboratory studies examining expertise in games (Chase, 1986), leading some critics to question its relevance to expertise in natural environments. The finding that visuo-spatial pattern recognition is the foundation of expert landmine detection performance testifies to the ability of principles and theories established in controlled laboratory environments to generalize to considerably different tasks performed in natural environments.

This work also illustrates the utility of training studies as a way of testing theories of expertise that complements computer simulation. A fundamental tenet of information-processing psychology holds that a cognitive process explanation of human performance should be validated by postulating a theory/model that will reproduce the performance (Simon, 1980). Computer simulation has served traditionally in cognitive science as a medium for expressing theories and a vehicle for theory testing; the empirical results produced by running the simulation are assessed for their ability to match human performance (Newell and Simon, 1972; Simon & Kaplan, 1990). If a theory of expertise claims to reflect the knowledge and processes that produce expert performance, an instructional program whose content purportedly reflects the model's mechanisms represents an analogous expression of the theory, and the performance of the novices to whom the program is administered can be examined for the fidelity which with it reproduces expert performance. Although neither approach to theory testing is without limitations, both offer clear and complementary benefits. A noteworthy benefit of using instructional contexts to test cognitive

theories is that it can inform basic understanding *and* address applied needs.

From a broad disciplinary perspective, the emerging body of applied contributions to which this work adds (Allen, 2006; Anderson et al, 1995; Schaafstal & Schraggen, 2000) shows that the principles, theory, and methods accumulated in the relatively brief lifetimes of cognitive science and cognitive psychology are sufficiently mature to support engineering applications of national and social value. If, as Stokes (1997) has argued, the implicit "quid pro quo" compact between government and scientists has frayed enough to threaten funding streams for basic research, and this assessment applies to our traditionally basic research-oriented field, contributions of transparent significance to those outside of our field are needed to encourage policy makers to sustain programmatic investment in research aimed at understanding thinking and learning and whose products can be effectively applied to address significant practical problems.

References

82nd Airborne Division Public Affairs Office. (2003). Media release #03-018 Fort Bragg, NC: 82nd Airborne Division.

Alexander, P. A. (2003). Can we get there from here? *Educational Researcher, 32(8)*, 3-4.

Allen, G. A. (Ed.) (2006). *Applied spatial cognition: From research to cognitive technology.* Mahwah, NJ: Erlbaum Associates.

Anderson, J. R., Corbett, A. T., Koedinger, K. R., & Pelletier, R. (1995). Cognitive tutors: Lessons learned. *The Journal of the Learning Sciences, 4* (2), 167-207.

Biederman, I., & Shiffrar, M. M. (1987). Sexing day-old chicks: A case study and expert systems analysis of a difficult perceptual-learning task. *Journal of Experimental Psychology Learning, Memory, and Cognition, 13*, 640-645.

Bransford, J. R., Brown, A. L., & Cocking, R. R. (1999). *How people learn: Brain, mind, experience, and school.* Washington, D.C. National Academy Press.

Chase, W. G. (1986). Visual information processing. In K. R. Boff, L. Kaufman, & J. P. Thomas (Eds.), *Handbook of perception and human performance, Vol. 2* (pp. 28-1 - 28-71). New York: Wiley.

Chase, W. G., & Ericsson, K. A. (1982). Skill and working memory. In G. H. Bower (Ed.), *The psychology of learning and motivation*, Vol. *16*, pp. 1-58). New York, NY: Academic Press.

Chase, W. G., & Simon, H. A. (1973a). The mind's eye in chess. In W. G. Chase (Ed.), Visual information processing (pp. 215-281). New York, NY: Academic Press.

Chase, W. G., & Simon, H. A. (1973b). Perception in chess. Cognitive Psychology, 4, 55-81.

Chi, M. T. H., Glaser, R., and Farr, M. J. (Eds.). (1988). *The nature of expertise*. Hillsdale, NJ: Erlbaum Associates.

Davison, A., & Staszewski, J. (2002). *Handheld mine detection based on expert skill: Reference guide for training plan design and training site development.*

Aberdeen Proving Ground, MD: Army Research Laboratory Human Research and Engineering Directorate.

Davison, A., Staszewski, J., & Boxley, G. (2001). Improving soldier performance with the AN/PSS12. *Engineer, 31*, 2001, 17-21.

Ericsson, K. A., & Charness, N. (1994). Expert performance: Its structure and acquisition. American Psychologist, 49(8), 725-747.

Ericsson, K. A., & Staszewski, J, J. (1989). In D. Klahr & K. Kotovsky (Eds.), *Complex information processing: The impact of Herbert A. Simon* (pp. 235-267). Hillsdale, NJ: Erlbaum.

Geneva International Center for Humanitarian Demining (GICHD) ((2003). A guide to mine action. Geneva ,Switzerland: GICHD.

Glaser, R. (1984). Education and thinking: The role of knowledge. *American Psychologist, 39*, 93-104.

Glaser, R. (1989). Expertise and learning: How do we think about instructional processes now that we have discovered knowledge structures? In D. Klahr and K. Kotovsky (Eds.), *Complex information processing: The impact of Herbert A. Simon* (pp. 269-282). Hillsdale, NJ: Erlbaum.

Glaser, R., & Bassok, M. (1989). Learning theory and the study of instruction. Annual Review of Psychology, 40 631-666.

Hambric, H. H., & Schneck, W. C. (1996). The antipersonnel mine threat. Proceedings of the Technology and the Mine Problem Symposium, *1*, Naval Postgraduate School, 18-21 November 1996, 3-11 – 3-45.

Herman, H., McMahill, J., & Kantor, G. (2000). Training and performance assessment of landmine detector operator using motion tracking and virtual mine lane. In A. C. Dubey & J. F. Harvey & J. T. Broach & R. E. Dugan (Eds.), Detection and remediation technologies for mines and minelike targets V, Proceedings of the Society for Photo-Optical Instrumentation Engineers 13th Annual Meeting, Vol. 4038. Orlando: SPIE.110-121.

Kern, P. (2005). Clearing the roads in Iraq and Afghanistan. In A. M. Bottoms and C. Scandrett (Eds.). *Applications of technology to demining, Part 1, Vol. 1: Landmine countermeasures*, Monterey, CA: The Society for Counter-Ordnance technology.

LaMoe, J. P., & Read, T. (2002). Countermine operations in the contemporary operational environment. *Engineeer, 32*, April 2002, 21-23.

McNamara, D. S. (2006). Bringing cognitive science into education and back again" The value of interdisciplinary research. Cognitive Science, 30, 605-608.

Newell, A., & Simon, H. A. (1972). *Human problem solving.* Englewood Cliffs, NJ: Prentice-Hall.

Patel, V. L., Kaufman, D. R., & Magder, S. A. (1996). The acquisition of medical expertise in complex dynamic environments. In K. A. Ericsson (Ed.), The road to excellence. Hillsdale, NJ: Erlbaum.

Santiago, A., Locke, M., & Reidy, D. (2004). Operational test results for the AN/PSS-14 (HSTAMIDS). *Proceedings of the UXO/Countermine Forum*, 9-12 March 2004, St. Louis, MO.

Schneck, W. C., & Green, B. M. (1997). A road fraught with danger: Lessons in mine clearance. *Janes's International Defense Review, 11*, 66-69.

Schafstaal, A., & Schraggen, J. M. (2000). Training of troubleshooting: A structured task analytical approach. In J. M. Schraagen, S. Chipman, and V. L. Shalin (Eds.), *Cognitive task analysis* (pp. 57-70). Mahwah, NJ: Erlbaum.

Schraagen, J.M., Chipman, S., & Shalin, V. L. (2000). Introduction to cognitive task analysis. In S. Chipman, J. M. Schraagen, and V. L. Shalin (Eds.), *Cognitive task analysis* (pp. 3-23). Mahwah, NJ: Erlbaum.

Simon, H. A. (1980). How to win at twenty questions with nature. In R. A. Cole (Ed.), *Perception and production in fluent speech*, (pp. 535-548). Hillsdale, NJ: Erlbaum.

Simon, H. A., & Kaplan, C. A. (1990). Foundations of cognitive science. In M. I. Posner (Ed.), Foundations of cognitive science (pp. 1-47). Cambridge, MA: The MIT Press.

Staszewski, J. (1988). Skilled memory in expert mental calculation, In M. T. H. Chi, R. Glaser, & M. J. Farr (Eds.), *The nature of expertise* (pp. 71-128). Hillsdale, NJ: Erlbaum.

Staszewski, J. (1990). Exceptional memory: The influence of practice and knowledge on the development of elaborative encoding strategies. In W. Schneider & F. E. Weinert (Eds.) *Interactions among aptitudes, strategies, and knowledge in cognitive performance* (pp. 252-285). New York: Springer-Verlag.

Staszewski, J. (1999). Information processing analysis of human land mine detection skill. In T. Broach, A. C. Dubey, R. E. Dugan, and J. Harvey, (Eds.), Detection and Remediation Technologies for Mines and Minelike Targets IV, Proceedings of the Society for Photo-Optical Instrumentation Engineers 13th Annual Meeting, SPIE *Vol. 3710*, 766-777.

Staszewski, J. (2001a). Expert analysis and training: Using cognitive engineering to develop mine detection skill. *Demining Technology Information Forum Journal, 1*, http://www.maic.jmu.edu/dtif/toc_dtif.html.

Staszewski, J. (2001b). Training for Operators of Handheld *Detection Equipment: A Cognitive Engineering Approach. Proceedings of the UXO/Countermine Forum*, 9-11 April 2001, New Orleans, LA.

Staszewski, J. (2006). Spatial thinking and the design of landmine detection training. In G. A. Allen, (Ed.), *Applied spatial cognition: From research to cognitive technology* (pp. 231-265). Mahwah, NJ: Erlbaum Associates.

Staszewski, J., & Davison, A. (2000). Mine detection training based on expert skill. In A. C. Dubey J. F. Harvey, J. T. Broach, and R. E. Dugan, (Eds.), Detection and Remediation Technologies for Mines and Mine-like Targets V, Proceedings of Society of Photo-Optical Instrumentation Engineers 14th Annual Meeting, SPIE *Vol. 4038*, 90-101.

Stokes, D.E. (1997). Pasteur's Quadrant: Basic science and technical innovation. Washington D. C.: The Brookings Institution Press

Wenger, M., & Payne, D. (1995). On the acquisition of mnemonic skill: Application of skilled memory theory. *Journal of Experimental Psychology: Applied, 1*, 195-215.

Are Long Words Holistically Processed?
De-individuation Effects of Embedded CVC Clusters

Lile Jia (U0300857@nus.edu.sg)
Winston D. Goh (psygohw@nus.edu.sg)
Department of Psychology, National University of Singapore, 11 Law Link,
Singapore 117570, Singapore

Abstract

Previous literature has shown that long words provide a stronger lexical context in speech perception. We investigated whether this was because long words are processed in a more holistic way. Vitevitch and Luce (1998) demonstrated that when processing consonant–vowel–consonant (CVC) clusters, sub-lexical phonotactic probability has a facilitatory effect on the processing of nonwords, whereas lexical neighbourhood density has an inhibitory effect on the processing of words. In the current study, we replicated these findings when the CVCs were embedded in disyllabic nonwords. However, when the CVCs were processed as part of disyllabic words, both effects disappeared. These results indicate that the constituent components within long words were "de-individuated" and lost some of their respective characteristics, suggesting that long words were holistically processed. This finding favours the interactive account of speech perception such as TRACE, which has built-in inter-level positive feedback loops.

Introduction

A key factor that contributes to speech perception is our ability to rely on word contexts to deal with phonetic ambiguities and imperfections. Various aspects of this ability have been examined using different paradigms such as phoneme categorization (Connie, Titone, & Wang, 1993; Ganong, 1980), phoneme monitoring (Cutler, Mehler, Norris, & Seguí, 1987), and phoneme restoration (Samuel, 1981), and the importance of lexical effects on phonetic perception is now a widely acknowledged fact (see Norris, McQueen, & Cutler, 2000 for a review). As the general literature on the lexical effect expands, however, surprisingly little research has been carried out to systematically investigate factors that interact with it. One such factor, word length, has been recently studied by Samuel and Pitt (2003).

Samuel and Pitt (2003) investigated the influence of word context on the effect of compensation for coarticlulation, which was first discovered by Mann and Repp (1981), who found that when two words are processed consecutively, the fricative end of the first word can create a shift in the perception of the stop-initial consonant of the following word. For example, a pair of such words could be "Spanish [t/k]apes", in which [t/k] is an ambiguous intermediate phoneme on the /t—k/ continuum and either end of the continuum, /t/ or /k/, makes the second word a real word ("tapes" or "capes"). In this case, the ambiguous stop-initial [t/k] is more likely to be categorized as /t/ because the preceding fricative is /ʃ/. On the other hand, if the first word is "Christmas", the second word would be perceived more as "capes". Mann and Repp argued that this phenomenon is the consequence of our perceptual system attempting to compensate for the effect of coarticulation of phonemes. Samuel and Pitt (2003), together with previous findings (Elman & McClelland, 1988), showed that this presumably sub-lexical process can be influenced by word context. For example, even when the fricative end of the first word (Spanish) was replaced by an ambiguous phoneme [s/ʃ], it shifted the perception of the following ambiguous stop-initial [t/k] in the same way (more [t] was percieved) as in the presentation of an unambiguous fricative (/ʃ/). The word context biased the perception of the ambiguous fricative, which in turn biased the perception of the following stop-initial. More important, Samuel and Pitt's study varied the word length of the first words and demonstrated that when other factors were held equal, shorter words did not provide an adequate lexical effect for compensation for coarticulation to be observed. On the other hand, longer words produced a much more pronounced compensation effect and were concluded as being a stronger lexical context.

The theoretical implications of the results aside, an intriguing question arises from Samuel and Pitt's (2003) study: what property(ies) do long words possess that make them such a better lexical context? One obvious answer is that long words are more unique than short words, an attribute widely operationalised as a lower neighbourhood density. The effect of this trait has been carefully incorporated in various models of speech perception. For example, the intra-level inhibitions at the lexical processing level in both TRACE (McClelland & Elman, 1986) and Merge (Norris et al., 2000) architectures allow for higher and easier activations of long words than short words, due to the comparatively lower extent of lexical competition. Put it in another way, the observed strength of lexical contexts of long words for compensation effects could be due to the higher "predictive power" of the context in identifying the ambiguous phoneme, as there are fewer alternatives than in the case of short words.

However, another key variable studied by Samuel and Pitt (2003) raised the possibility that long words have another special characteristic in addition to their low neighbourhood density. They studied the effects of long words on perceptual grouping – the extent to which the word-final fricative is bound to the previous phonemes. They presented word or nonword stimuli with fricative endings (e.g. /bʊʃ/) repeatedly and asked participants to report what they heard. Evidence for the perceived cleavage of the fricative from the preceding phoneme was found in cases when participants reported hearing /bʊ/, indicating a loss of the fricative, or /ʃbʊʃ/, indicating that the final fricative was assigned as the beginning of the following stimuli. The finding relevant to the present study was that the perceived cleavage of word-final fricatives from the preceding vowel was reported much less frequently in the context of long words than in short words; and in words than in pseudowords. Apparently the bonding among phonemes in long words is more entrenched. This characteristic of long words cannot be clearly attributed as an emerging property of their uniqueness without considering how different theories conceptualize the nature of lexical influences on phonetic perception. As a result, empirical evidence of this sort can shed light on the nature of lexical influences.

Particularly, the observed relation between perceptual grouping and word length seems to be in keeping with the interactive models of phoneme perception such as that of TRACE. In TRACE, longer words enjoy a greater number of positive feedback loops due to the involvement of a larger number of phoneme nodes compared to short words. This leads to a much quicker and heightened activation of both the word nodes and the constituent phoneme nodes (McClelland & Elman, 1986). The high activation at both the sub-lexical and lexical levels of processing may contribute to a more holistic processing of the long words. In other words, components of long words may tend to be processed as a whole, losing some of their individual elements. Perhaps, it is this "de-individuation" that endows long words with a stronger perceptual grouping. In view of this, the motivation of the current study was to provide additional and more convincing empirical support to the idea of more holistic processing of long words, and subsequently to the interactive model that has a built-in system of positive feedback circuits.

If long words were processed in a more holistic way, it follows that some of the properties initially possessed by the components of long words may be lost, or at least attenuated. Also, if the same notion is supported by mechanisms akin to the positive feedback loops proposed in TRACE, the effect of components of long words losing some of their individual characteristics should occur both sub-lexically and at the word level.

To investigate these possibilities, we capitalised on the findings of Vitevitch and Luce (1998), who demonstrated a dissociation of sub-lexical and lexical effects on the processing of consonant-vowel-consonant (CVC) clusters. Prior to their study, a strong correlation between two inherent properties of English words had been identified: phonological neighbourhood density – the number of words that sound similar to the target word, and phonotactic probability – a general measure of how probable the constituent phonemes occur in a particular sequence or position (Landauer & Streeter, 1973). This high correlation made Vitevitch and Luce wonder if phonotactic probability is an independent measure at the sub-lexical level or, as suggested in TRACE, an emerging property of the 'conspiracy' of all the word nodes at the lexical level (McClelland & Elman, 1986). In their study, they found a

dissociable effect of phonotactic probability from that of neighbourhood density. High-probability-density CVC *nonwords* were processed faster than low-probability-density CVC *nonwords*. On the other hand, high-probability-density CVC *words* were processed slower compared with words low in neighbourhood density and phonotactic probability. This effectively demonstrated that phonotactic probability has a facilitatory effect on the processing of CVC nonwords at the sub-lexical level; while neighbourhood density has an inhibitory effect at the lexical level of processing when the CVCs are words, presumably due to a greater number of competing words.

We propose the following novel question: what if these CVCs are part of long words? In accordance with the notion of the de-individuation of long word components, both the facilitatory effect of high phonotactic probabilities in CVC nonwords and the inhibitory effect of high neighbourhood densities in CVC words would disappear or be at least significantly weakened.

In the current study, auditory stimuli of disyllabic words and nonwords with CVC endings (e.g. /faɪnaɪt/ or "finite") were presented to participants, who were asked to focus on and repeat only the second syllables (/naɪt/ or "night") – the CVC clusters. The reason for selecting words with CVC endings, but not CVC initials, was to maximize any possible effect of the feedback loops. As demonstrated in the original simulation of TRACE, positive feedback loops have stronger effects on word-final phonemes (McClelland & Elman, 1986). This general construct allowed for the investigation of possible differential responses of participants to the same CVC clusters in either the dysillabic word or nonword contexts. In particular, it was expected that participants would produce the same pattern of responses to CVC endings as observed in Vitevitch and Luce (1998) when the CVCs were embedded in disyllabic *nonword* contexts. However, when these CVCs are embedded in disyllabic *words*, the holistic processing of the long words would nullify or mitigate the effects of phonotactic probabilities or neighbourhood densities on the processing of CVC clusters.

Method

Participants

Forty psychology students from the National University of Singapore participated in the study. All participants reported no history of speech or hearing disorders.

Design

The current study employed the 4 CVC conditions used in Vitevitch and Luce (1998), but in which the CVCs are embedded in both long word contexts and long nonword contexts. The design was a 2 (CVC Lexicality: word, nonword) x 2 (Probability-density: high, low) x 2 (Disyllabic Lexicality: word, nonword) completely within-subjects design (see Table 1 for examples of the manipulations).

Table 1. Examples of disyllabic stimuli with the corresponding target CVC endings

CVC Lexicality	Disyllabic Lexicality	CVC Probability-Density	Disyllabic Phonetic Transcription	Disyllabic Word	Target CVC Phonetic Transcription	Target CVC Word
Word	Word	Low	faɪnaɪt	finite	naɪt	night
		High	pəreɪd	parade	reɪd	raid
	Nonword	Low	ɪnaɪt	-	naɪt	night
		High	dɪreɪd	-	reɪd	raid
Nonword	Word	Low	frɪdʒɪd	frigid	dʒɪd	-
		High	kəmbaɪn	combine	baɪn	-
	Nonword	Low	mɜ:dʒɪd	-	dʒɪd	-
		High	kʊbaɪn	-	baɪn	-

Materials

Selection of Disyllabic Words In the current study, all words were selected from the online Neighbourhood University Database, hosted by the Speech & Hearing Lab at Washington. A total of 160 disyllabic words with CVC endings were selected such that all the CVC endings were different with no repetition. Half of the CVC endings were words while the other half were nonwords. Within the set of CVC words or nonwords respectively, half of them were high in phonotactic probability and neighbourhood density while the other half were low in phonotactic probability and neighbourhood density. As a result, the 160 CVC endings were divided into the four experimental conditions studied by Vitevitch and Luce (1998): high-probability, high-density words and nonwords, and low-probability, low-density words and nonwords. All the disyllabic words were equated on log KF written frequency (Kucera & Francis, 1967) and familiarity (as it is used in Neighborhood Database) across the four conditions ($F < 1$ for both measures).

Manipulation of CVC Endings Due to the importance of phonotactic probability and neighbourhood density of the CVC endings to our hypotheses, these two measures were carefully manipulated. Phonotactic probabilities of the CVC endings were calculated with the online Phonotactic Probability Calculator developed by Vitevitch and Luce (2004). They adopted the definition of phonotactic probability from a previous study (Jusczyk, Luce, & Charles-Luce, 1994) that comprises positional segment frequency (i.e. how often a particular phoneme occurs in a given position in a word) and biphone frequency (i.e. the frequency of the co-occurrence of two consecutive phonemes). Because all CVC clusters had three phonemes, the phonotactic probabilities were calculated by summing up three positional segment frequencies and two biphone frequencies. For the low-probability-density CVC words, the mean phonotactic probability was 0.1478, whereas for the high-probability-density CVC words, the mean phonotactic probability was 0.1799, $t(78) = 3.51$, $p < .001$. For the low-probability-density CVC nonwords, the mean phonotactic probability was 0.0983, whereas for the high-probability-density CVC nonwords, the mean

phonotactic probability was 0.1792, $t(78) = 14.64$, $p < .0001$.

In operationalising the neighbourhood density, frequency-weighted similarity neighbourhood measure was adopted (Vitevitch & Luce, 1998). For all CVC clusters, their respective phonological neighbours were first identified using the online database. Phonological neighbours were defined as all the words that could be obtained from the target word or nonword by addition, deletion, or substitution of any phoneme in any position. The summation of the log KF-written frequencies (Kucera & Francis, 1967) of these neighbours gave us the frequency-weighted neighbourhood density. For the low-probability-density CVC words, the mean frequency-weighted neighbourhood density was 33.84, whereas the mean value of their high-probability-density counterparts was 62.02, $t(78) = 10.36$, $p < .0001$. The low-probability-density nonwords had a mean frequency-weighted neighbourhood density of 17.31, whereas the high-probability-density nonwords had a mean value of 30.52, $t(78) = 3.50$, $p < .001$.

In addition, for CVC words, log frequency (Kucera & Francis, 1967) and familiarity (Neighborhood Database) were equated for both probability-density conditions, all Fs < 1. Since it was possible that the contrast between the phonotactic probability of the first syllables of the disyllabic stimuli and that of CVC endings would have a subtle influence on the naming task, we have also equated the phonotactic probability of word-initial segments across all four CVC conditions, $F < 1$.

Creation of Disyllabic Nonwords Disyllabic nonwords were created from the disyllabic words. Each disyllabic word was first divided into the word-initial segment and the word-final CVC ending. As the disyllabic words were previously divided into four experimental conditions according to their CVC endings, within each condition, the word-initial segments and word-final CVC endings were randomly reshuffled to form disyllabic nonwords with CV endings identical to those of disyllabic words. This created a total of 160 disyllabic words and 160 disyllabic nonwords.

Analysis of the disyllabic words and nonwords showed that phonotactic probability and frequency-weighted neighbourhood density were matched in all 4 crucial pairs of conditions (all $ps > .2$). Previous studies have also demonstrated an effect of stress patterns of multi-syllabic stimuli on the activation of embedded words (Vroomen & de Gelder, 1997). Though this was not conscientiously equated during the preparation of stimuli, as we strived to maintain a naturalness of recording, a post-hoc analysis showed a matched stress pattern in all crucial pairs of conditions (all $ps > .2$). Finally, since the naming task required the participants to repeat only the CVC endings, how closely the first phoneme of CVC endings is bound to the last phoneme of the first syllable could possibly affect the processing time of CVC clusters. Across all 8 conditions, the sequential probabilities of phonemes at these two positions were equated $F(7,312) = 1.40$, $MS_e = 0.000012, p > .2$.

The disyllabic stimuli were spoken by a trained female phonetician and digitally recorded in 16-bit mono, 11 kHz .wav format. The overall root-mean-square amplitude levels were digitally equated. A pilot test was run to assess the clarity of the stimuli. Five raters were presented with all the stimuli independently. They were instructed to type down what they have heard to the best of their ability, followed by confidence ratings on a 9-point Likert scale. All stimuli that received one or more incorrect answers out of the five responses or scored an average confidence rating below 6 were recorded again and retested for clarity.

Procedure

The main experimental task was a naming repetition task in which participants, upon hearing the stimuli, were to vocally respond by repeating the target CVC clusters. Participants were tested individually in a booth equipped with a computer. The disyllabic stimuli were presented through headphones at approximately 70 db SPL and participants spoke into a microphone that triggered a voice key which recorded the response time. Participants were instructed to repeat only the second syllable of all stimuli as quickly and as accurately as possible. The response time was measured from the onset of the stimuli to the onset of participants' response by the computer. A digital recorder was used to record all responses for accuracy analysis.

In each trial, participants were presented with a visual "Ready" prompt on the monitor followed by an auditory stimulus. After participants have made a response, their response time was presented on screen and participants pressed a key to proceed to the next trial. Due to the way nonword stimuli were generated, the 320 disyllabic stimuli were divided into 2 sets, with each set containing 80 disyllabic words and 80 disyllabic nonwords without any repetitions of the CVC endings. Half the participants were assigned to each set of 160 disyllabic stimuli, which comprised trials from the 8 experimental conditions of the study. Half the subjects had the disyllabic words presented first, and the other half had the disyllabic nonwords presented. Stimuli were presented randomly across conditions within the blocks of words and nonwords. In addition to the task trials, each participant also received 10 practice trials to familiarize themselves with the task. All participants indicated a good sense of familiarity with the task after the practice trials. At the end of the experiment, participants' grades in GCE 'A' Level General Paper were recorded as a general measure of English proficiency.

Since what interested us was the time participants spent on processing the second syllable, the time for the first syllable was subtracted from the participants' response time. We first determined the onset time of the CVC endings in all stimuli with the aid of a spectrogram. The response times obtained during the experimental trials were subtracted with the onset time of the second syllable to result in participants' processing time, the measure that was used for data analysis. A response was scored as correct if it matched the CVC endings on all three phonemes.

Results

All incorrect responses and those responses that failed to activate the voice key were discarded. In addition, we eliminated any potentially outlier data (6%) by discarding responses that had a processing time more than two standard deviations away from the mean for any particular participant in any particular condition. When conducting accuracy checks, it was found that nearly half of the participants responded with 'stake' instead of 'take' for the stimulus 'mistake'. Therefore, all responses for the stimulus 'mistake' were taken out from data analysis.

Effects of the two counter-balancing variables (i.e. sequence of the blocking of words and nonwords, and the two sets of lists) and participants' general English proficiency did not have an effect on the data analysis in a way that would interfere with the investigation of our hypotheses. Thus, they are discussed no further in this paper. Error analysis was also excluded because the average accuracy rate for all participants was 97%.

Mean processing times and standard deviations (in parentheses) for all 8 conditions are reported in Table 2. A 2 (CVC Lexicality) x 2 (Probability-Density) x 2 (Disyllabic Lexicality) analysis of variance was performed. A significant three-way interaction was found both by items $F_1(1,311) = 5.89$, $MS_e = 3941$, $p < .05$ and by subjects $F_2(1,39) = 25.65$, $MS_e = 795.8$, $p < .0001$. To probe the nature of this interaction, the Probability-Density x Disyllabic Lexicality simple interactions at each level of the CVC Lexicality factor were examined.

When CVC endings were nonwords, the simple interaction was marginally significant by items $F_1(1,156) = 2.868$, $MS_e = 4457$, $p < .10$, but significant by subjects $F_2(1,39) = 10.56$, $MS_e = 1218$, $p < .01$. The nature of the interaction was that while high-probability-density nonword CVC endings ($M = 688$ msec) were processed significantly faster than low-probability-density nonword CVC endings ($M = 726$ msec) when they were embedded in disyllabic nonwords, $t_1(78) = 2.45$, $p < .02$ by items, $t_2(39) = 6.96$, $p < .0001$ by subjects, there was no significant difference between the two sets of nonword CVC endings in terms of processing time when they were part of disyllabic words, all $ts < 1$.

When CVC endings were words, the simple interaction was marginally significant by items $F_1(1,311) = 3.06$, $MS_e = 3420$, $p < .09$ and significant by subjects $F_2(1,39) = 9.23$,

Table 2. Mean processing times (+SDs) for all 8
conditions

CVC Lexicality	Disyllabic Lexicality	CVC Probability-Density	Mean Processing Time (msec)
Words	Words	Low	672 (61.1)
		High	664 (49.4)
	Nonword	Low	724 (60.5)
		High	749 (61.7)
Nonword	Words	Low	650 (74.7)
		High	648 (51.3)
	Nonword	Low	726 (77.8)
		High	688 (59.7)

MS_e = 851.0, $p < .005$. Low-probability-density word CVC endings (M = 749 msec) were processed significantly slower than high-probability-density word CVC endings (M = 724 msec) when they were embedded in disyllabic nonwords, $t_1(78) = 1.75$, $p < .09$ by items, $t_2(39) = 2.86$, $p < .001$ by subjects; the difference between these two conditions were not significant when they are in disyllabic words, both $ts < 1$.

General Discussion

In the current study, we reviewed the moderating effect of word length on lexical context effects found in earlier studies and speculated that one of the reasons could be that long words may be more holistically processed. We hypothesized that there may be differential processing of CVC clusters within longer sequences depending on whether the clusters were embedded in words or nonwords The overall pattern of results were in line with our hypotheses. First, our novel experimental manipulation of embedding CVC clusters in long nonwords did not eliminate participants' sensitivity to either the effect of phonotactic probability or neighbourhood density on the shorter CVC clusters. The combined pattern of results of CVC endings at the disyllabic nonword conditions mirrored the findings of Vitevitch and Luce (1998). Specifically, high phonotactic probability had a facilitatory effect on the processing of CVC nonwords, whereas high neighbourhood density had an inhibitory effect when CVC words were processed. However, when the same set of CVC clusters were embedded in long words, neither the sub-lexical nor the lexical effects of probability-density was observable. This is strong evidence that components of long words, embedded CVC clusters in this case, have lost some of their individual characteristics, and this de-individuation effect occurs at both the sub-lexical and the lexical levels.

The immediate implication of this finding concerns the nature of lexical effects on phoneme perception. The notion of a more holistic processing of longer words cannot be directly predicted from their higher uniqueness. Thus, how uniqueness of long words is related to the current finding can only be conceived in the context of specific theorizations of lexical involvement in phoneme processing. In general, the finding of holistic processing of long words is more in keeping with interactive models such as TRACE. In TRACE, the processing of words is characterized by a constant looping of excitatory inputs between word nodes

and constituent phoneme nodes (McClelland & Elman, 1986). This system of positive feedback loops is a suitable candidate for the mechanism behind the holistic processing of long words. As long words are more unique and have more exchanges of information with phoneme levels by virtue of the larger number of phonemes, they have a greater number of feedback loops that favour the simultaneously high activation of the word nodes and constituent phonemes – components of long words tend to be processed together. On the other hand, the strength of this concurrent activation of words and their components is much weaker for the processing of short words, because of the fewer number of feedback loops and the high activation of competing nodes due to other similar feedback circuits. In other words, the system of positive feedback loops is the possible means by which the uniqueness of long words is translated to a more holistic processing. Admittedly, the current TRACE model in particular and interactive accounts in general offer no direct provision for the lexical influence on inter-phoneme bonding, but the system of bidirectional feedback endows this kind of model with such a potential. One piece of good evidence is that while the system of feedback loops implies a much enhanced activation of both the phoneme and word nodes, the current results have shown that the de-individuation effect of the components of long words indeed occur both sub-lexically and lexically.

Conversely, the general lack of top-down influence on the perception of phonemes makes autonomous models, such as Merge, inadequate in explaining the current findings. Though the Merge architecture, with bottom-up activations of word nodes and lateral inhibitions at the lexical level in place (Norris et al., 2000), may have a conceivable means to account for the de-individuation effect at the word level of processing, it cannot eschew the awkwardness in accounting for the nullifying effects of long words on sub-lexical phonotactic dynamics in CVC nonwords. A possible explanation could be that as the participants were making conscious phonetic judgment, the phonetic decision stage in Merge did not code for the sub-lexical effect of phonotactic probability on CVC processing. This line of argument flies immediately in the face of the retained effect of phonotactics when participants were performing phonetic identification in the disyllabic nonword condition. In sum, the current finding supports the interactive account of speech perception, but further research is needed to incorporate more specific features into the existing models to fully explicate the "de-individuation" effects.

Another discussion raised by this study pertains to the strength of the holistic processing of long words, or the strength of de-individuation of their components. Though the current finding is suggestive of a strong effect, the whole body of literature on the activation of embedded short words in carrier words (e.g. Shillock, 1990; Luce & Cluff, 1998; Vroomen & de Gelder, 1997) strongly indicates that the de-individuation effect is far from being absolute. The experimental paradigms used in these studies often involved the processing of the entire long word carriers, a condition whereby holistic processing of long words was more favoured than in the current design.

Nonetheless, activations of semantic meanings of embedded words were successfully detected using indirect measures such as semantic priming. In addition, Samuel and Pitt (2003) have also found a reliable effect of sequential probability of the word-final vowel-consonant cluster on the perceived cleavage of the final fricative on top of the effect of word length. Therefore, it seems that even though words are processed in a more holistic way, some of the effects of their individual components, be it semantic or perceptual, can persist and interact with the processing in a complex manner. The issue regarding the strength of the de-individuation effect, thus, calls for more extensive research.

In conclusion, our results provide a possible candidate for explaining the previously observed effect of word length on the strength of lexical context. The more holistic processing of long words is probably an emerging property of their uniqueness, mediated by a mechanism akin to the system of positive feedback loops suggested in TRACE. Thus, the current finding is more consistent with the interactive account of speech perception. The absence of provision for top-down lexical effects on phoneme perception in autonomous models renders them less competent in explaining the de-individuation effects that have occurred both sub-lexically and lexically. Further research is in need to study the extent to which holistic processing of the words affects the individual components of the words. On a final note, the current study is not surprising considering the tradition of Gestalt psychology. The claim that people tend to perceive stimuli and events as a whole seems to be mirrored in word processing and the system of positive feedbacks between lower and higher levels of processing may be at the root of this early wisdom.

Acknowledgements

This research was supported by Research Grant R-581-000-048-112 to WDG. We thank Seok Hui Tan for her assistance in recording the auditory stimuli.

References

Cairns, P., Shillock, R., Chater, N., & Levy, J. (1995). Bottom-up connectionist modelling of speech. In J. P. Levy, D. Bairaktaris, J. A. Bullinaria & P. Cairns (Eds.), *Connectionist models of memory and language*, University College London Press.

Connine, C. M., Titone, D., & Wang, J. (1993). Auditory word recognition: Extrinsic and Intrinsic effects of word frequency. *Journal of Experimental Psychology: Learning, Memory, and Cognition, 19,* 81-94

Cutler, A., Mehler, J., Norris, D., & Seguí, J. (1987). Phoneme identification and the lexicon. *Cognitive Psychology, 19,* 141–77.

Elman, J. L., & McClelland, J. L. (1988). Cognitive penetration of the mechanisms of perception: Compensation for coarticulation of lexically restored phonemes. *Journal of Memory and Language, 27,* 143–65.

Ganong, W. F. (1980). Phonetic categorization in auditory word perception. *Journal of Experimental Psychology: Human Perception and Performance, 6,* 110-125.

Jusczyk, P. W., Luce, P. A., & Charles-Luce, J. (1994). Infants' sensitivity to phonotactic patterns in the native language. *Journal of Memory and Language, 33,* 630-645.

Kucera, H., & Francis, W. N. (1967). *Computational Analysis of Present-Day American English.* Providence: Brown University Press.

Luce, P. A., & Cluff, M. S. (1998). Delayed commitment in spoken word recognition: Evidence from cross-modal priming. *Perception & Psyhophysics, 60,* 484-490.

Mann, V. A., & Repp, B. H. (1981). Influence of preceding fricative on stop consonant perception. *Journal of the Acoustical Society of America, 69,* 546–58.

McClelland, J. L., & Elman, J. L. (1986). The TRACE model of speech perception. *Cognitive Psychology, 18,* 1–86.

Norris, D., McQueen, J. M., & Cutler, A. (2000). Merging information in speech recognition: Feedback is never necessary. *Behavioral and Brain Sciences, 23,* 299-370.

Samuel, A. G., & Pitt, M. A. (2003). Lexical activation (and other factors) can mediate compensation for coarticulation. *Journal of Memory and Language, 48,* 416–34.

Shillock, R. (1990). Lexical hypotheses in continuous speech. In G. T. Altmann (Ed.), *Cognitive models of speech processing* (pp. 24-49). Cambridge, MA:MIT Press.

Shillcock, R., Lindsey, G., Levy, J., & Chater, N. (1992). A phonologically motivated input representation for the modeling of auditory word perception in continuous speech. *In Proceedings of the 14th Annual Cognitive Science Society Conference, Bloomington* (pp. 408–413).

Vitevitch, M. S., & Luce, P. A. (1998). When words compete: Levels of processing in spoken word recognition. *Psychological Science, 9,* 325–29.

Vitevitch, M. S. & Luce, P. A. (2004). A web-based interface to calculate phonotactic probability for words and nonwords in English. *Behavior Research Methods, Instruments, & Computers, 36,* 481-487.

Vroomen, J. & de Gelder, B. (1997). Activation of embedded words in spoken word recognition. *Journal of Experimental Psychology: Human Perception and Performance, 21,* 98-198.

Washington University Speech & Hearing Lab Neighbourhood Database, http://128.252.27.56/ Neighborhood/GettingStarted.asp

The Development of Lexical Knowledge:
Toward a Model of the Acquisition of Lexical Gender in French

Harmony Marchal (Harmony.Marchal@upmf-grenoble.fr)
L.S.E., University of Grenoble-2 & IUFM
38040 Grenoble Cedex 9 FRANCE

Maryse Bianco (Maryse.Bianco@upmf-grenoble.fr)
L.S.E., University of Grenoble-2 & IUFM
38040 Grenoble Cedex 9 FRANCE

Philippe Dessus (Philippe.Dessus@upmf-grenoble.fr)
L.S.E., University of Grenoble-2 & IUFM
38040 Grenoble Cedex 9 FRANCE

Benoît Lemaire (Benoit.Lemaire@imag.fr)
Laboratoire TIMC-IMAG (CNRS UMR 5525), Faculté de Médecine
38706 La Tronche Cedex FRANCE

Abstract

This paper attempts to answer a threefold question: from what kind of cues gender can reliably be assigned to French nouns? How the usage of these sublexical cues is acquired by children? What kind of computational models could account for the human data? We conducted an experiment with 73 1st and 2nd grade children to assess their knowledge about gender information associated with suffixes using a gender decision task. Children had to assign gender to pseudo-words whose endings correspond to French suffixes (-*ture*, -*ment*...). Results show that French children implicitly acquire this knowledge, even before learning to read. Simulation results fit experimental data and show that the word ending represented by suffixes is one of the main cues to assign gender to French words.

Introduction

The aim of this paper is to study how lexical information about words (in our case, gender) is acquired by children, and then to propose a computational model of this acquisition. Very broadly, research aimed at modeling gender assignment in adult speakers is twofold. Some models consider that gender is coded as part of the lexical form of each noun (Schriefers & Jescheniak, 1999), while others consider that sublexical and formal properties of nouns (e.g., phonological, morphological, orthographical) can be related to their gender (Lyster, 2006). These two lines of models are not contradictory, however: the way words are processed in order to be assigned to a given gender remains far from clear. Native speakers are able to assign gender to unknown words (i.e., not represented as lemmas), while L2 French speakers have difficulties to perform this task even for real words.

In French, many word-endings reliably predict gender. For instance, 70% of words respect the following rule: vocalic ending for masculine nouns, consonantal ending for feminine ones (Prodeau & Carlo, 2002). This paper attempts to answer a threefold question: from what kind of cues gender can reliably be assigned to French nouns? How the usage of these sublexical cues is acquired by children? What kind of computational models could account for the human data?

The remainder of this paper is as follows. First, we review literature about the cues by which gender can be inferred, as well as about the development of such abilities. Second, we report an experiment designed to explore whether 6 to 7 year-old children rely on suffixes to build knowledge about gender. Third, we present computational models and how well they fit our experimental data.

Morphological Cues in French Grammatical Gender Assignment

Gender assignment in French can be performed using two main kinds of information. Firstly, *lexical information*, related to the co-occurring words (e.g., articles, adjectives) which most of times marks gender unambiguously. Secondly, *sublexical information*, especially noun-endings are pretty good predictors of their grammatical gender (e.g., almost all nouns endings in –*age* are masculine). Research shows that phonological (Starreveld & La Heij, 2004), orthographic (Terriault, 2006), or both cues (Holmes & Segui, 2004) are used in such a task.

Taft and Meunier (1998, experiment 1) manipulated two factors: the regularity of the word-ending and the noun frequency. They showed effects of regularity and frequency on students' decision time: regular nouns and high-frequency words were more rapidly assigned than irregular and low-frequency ones, and with less errors. However, no interaction between these two factors was found. This finding is along the same line as Monaghan et al. (2005) claim: "[...] distributional information is most useful for high frequency words, and the artificial language learning experiment indicates that phonological information is compensatory for learning of low frequency words" (p. 178).

In sum, there is a large consensus to consider that "word endings" are powerful cues to gender assignment in French, even if the definition of "word ending" is rather vague and variable across authors. We will nevertheless concentrate on these sublexical cues and especially on morphological suffixes.

Morphological Development and Gender Assignment

Gender information attached to sublexical units is for a large part implicit in nature. This can be illustrated by some recent grammarian's conceptions arguing that word endings are of no use in determining nouns' gender in French (see Lyster 2006). Such a misconception rests undoubtedly on the distributional features of the gender information carried on by word endings. This kind of information can easily be captured by an implicit learning mechanism rather than by a rule-based explicit one. Several linguists have however noticed these regularities. In particular, they described gender information attached to derivational French suffixes (for example words ending in *–age* and *–oir* are masculine whereas those ending in *–elle* and *–ture* are feminine, Riegel, Pellat & Rioul, 2005). The question we address here is to study how and when French native children acquire this knowledge in the course of their lexical development. As gender information attached to derivational suffixes is never explicitly taught in the beginning classes of the primary school, our goal is to study how this information is learned in the course of oral language acquisition and what is the impact of written language learning at the beginning of primary school on this development.

Derivational morphology is largely recognized as a powerful tool for vocabulary growth, at least in later and literate lexicon development. Ravid (2004) argues that before formal written language learning, children have few occasions to be confronted to morphosyntactic forms such as derived nouns, which are rare in oral and everyday language. However, research on morphological awareness has shown that 5-year-old children possess morphological knowledge about words (Colé et al., 2004), especially when this awareness is evaluated through implicit tasks. For example, Casalis and Louis-Alexandre (2000) showed that 5-year-old children succeed at 63.8% in matching a picture to a morphological complex word ("*enrouler*", to roll up), with pictures representing "*enrouler*", "*dérouler*", to unroll, "*rouler*", to roll, "*rouleau*", a roll) spoken by the experimenter. Likewise, when first-grade children read a complex morphological word (e.g., "*laitier*", milkman), reading is easier when children were primed with a morphological associate ("*lait*", milk) rather than with an orthographical associate ("*laitue*", lettuce). These results show that children early acquire some knowledge related to the morphological structure of words and that they can use it in linguistic activities. At least when implicit tasks are used, semantic information attached to affixes seems to be available to young children. Results are less clear when more explicit tasks of morphological awareness, such as word segmentation (to segment the word

"*pommade*", ointment, in its morphemes "*pomm–*" and "*–ade*") are involved. In such tasks, children's performance does not exceed 50%. We can conclude that young children have developed morphological knowledge about words before formal learning of written language and that they are especially able to use semantic information captured in morphological units.

It is therefore worth to ask what other kind of information–e.g., grammatical gender–is also early learned by children. Few developmental studies focused on gender acquisition. Tucker et al. (1968) carried out a seminal experiment studying the influence of word-ending on gender assignment. Participants (grade 4 to 7 French native speakers pupils) were asked to assign gender to French words and nonwords (endings were derivational suffixes such as *–aie*, *–ée*, *–é*, *–eur*, *–oir*). Results showed that word-endings are reliably correlated to gender assignment.

Karmiloff-Smith (1979) also carried out a study about the development of grammatical gender. She investigated the ability of children (from 3 to 12 years old) to assign a correct definite article to non-words (the "correct" gender being previously mentioned by means of an indefinite article). She showed that three-year-old children were less able to infer the right definite article without the help of phonological cues (e.g., 100% 4-year-old children assigned correct gender to words like "*une plichette*" compared to 78% to more opaque words, like "*une dilare*"). A complementary experiment showed that when confronted to a discordant information concerning gender (i.e., a masculine article followed by a noun with a feminine-marked suffix), children up to 5 privileged phonological cues over the article.

As in adult experiments, the notion of "word ending" is rather vague and often mixes up phonological, derivational and even orthographic cues. In the Karmiloff-Smith study for example, it is not clear if word-endings such as *–ette* or *–are* are derivational or phonological cues. Early morphological development likely lies on phonological cues and derivational morphology more generally may emerge from the convergence of phonological, orthographical and semantic codes (Seidenberg & Gonnermann, 2000). We will not address this complex issue here but we will rather adopt a classical perspective in isolating derivational units and exploring their impact on gender assignment by grade-1 and 2 children.

Experiment

Our purpose is to examine to what extent 6 to 7 year-old children can rely on derivational suffix to assign gender to nouns. In other words, is gender information encoded with word-endings (potentially suffixes) at the beginning of primary school, before formal learning to read and to spell? To answer this question, we used pseudo-words whose endings represented derivational suffixes (replicating Tucker et al. paradigm with younger children). Using pseudo-words enables to disentangle sublexical processing in gender assignment from lexical processing.

We controlled and manipulated two factors that are not taken into account in the studies reviewed above. The first one concerns the frequency of pseudo-suffixed words, which are non-suffixed words sharing the same word-ending as the suffixed words (e.g., the ending –*ment* of *aliment*, food, is not a suffix). Indeed, in the studies reviewed (e.g., Taft & Meunier, 1998), the frequency of word-endings is computed irrespectively of whether they are suffixed or non-suffixed. This variable, called "frequency of non-suffixed nouns" may have an effect on gender assignment. We suppose that if gender information is associated with suffixes this information will be facilitated (built earlier and easier to access) when there are fewer confusing exemplars. In other words, a high frequency of non-suffixed nouns would disturb suffix gender assignment.

The second variable manipulated concerns the "gender exception frequency" of suffixes. We took into account the frequency of suffix gender relative to the total number of nouns sharing the same word-ending but differing in gender (e.g., "*jument*", mare, is feminine while –*ment* is a mostly masculine ending). As Taft and Meunier (1998) showed, low-frequency irregular forms take longer to be assigned a gender than low-frequency regular ones. This variable can predict that when no exception is encountered gender information is acquired earlier.

Furthermore, we controlled the gender of suffixes and a third factor was added to the design: the participants' school level (grades 1 and 2).

Method

Participants Participants were 73 pupils from two schools: 31 children in grade 1 (16 boys and 15 girls) and 42 in grade 2 (25 boys and 17 girls). The experiment was conducted at the beginning of the school year. All children were French native speakers and had no speech or hearing deficiencies.

Material Design First, in order to have an idea about the common nouns known by our participants, we used the *Manulex Infra* database (Peereman, Lété & Sprenger-Charolles, in press). This database is derived from *Manulex*, a web-accessible database listing the word-frequency values for 48,886 lexical entries encountered in 54 French elementary school books, concerning grades 1 and 2. This database presents, for each word, several infralexical variables (syllable, grapheme-to-phoneme mappings, bigrams) and lexical variables (lexical neighborhood, homophony and homography). Second, we selected ten suffixes (5 masculine: –*age*, –*ment*, –*oir*, –*o*, –*ot*; 5 feminine: –*ade*, –*ation*, –*elle*, –*otte*, –*ture*) from a list of thirty French nominal suffixes (available on http://www.etudes-litteraires.com).

The non-suffixed nouns variable had 3 conditions: few [0-400 per million words], medium [401–1000] or high [1001–2000] non-suffixed, while the "gender exception frequency" variable had two: no exception and with exceptions. These values as well as the frequency of non-suffixed nouns were computed from two separate databases (*Manulex Infra* Grades 1 and 2) corresponding to the two school levels.

Material and Procedure For each suffix, 6 pseudo-words were built, using *WordGen* (Duyck et al., 2004). This software generates pseudo-words that are likely to resemble real words while controlling several characteristics–taken from *Manulex Infra*–such as their number of letters or syllables, their number of orthographic neighbors, the frequency of their bigrams. Thus, two lists of 30 pseudo-words were elaborated, 3 words per suffix. The pseudo-words created were five to eleven letters long depending on the suffix and were composed of two or three syllables. Each participant was given a list composed of 15 pseudo-words whose expected gender is masculine (3 words*5 masculine suffixes, such as "*brido*" or "*rinloir*") and 15 pseudo-words whose expected gender is feminine (3 words*5 feminine suffixes, such as "*surbelle*", or "*marniture*"). The experiment was conducted in the children's regular classrooms as part of their school day.

Each participant was presented with the following material, through a computer-based interface. First, pupils were introduced with the task of the experiment, which was to listen to different pseudo-words and to determine their gender. Second, after a five-item practice, each pseudo-word was simultaneously spoken and displayed in the center of the screen, when the articles "*le*" (masculine article in French) and "*la*" (feminine article) were displayed at the bottom of the screen (their position was counterbalanced). Participants then had to press on the corresponding key of the keyboard. The order of word presentation was randomized. Answers and reaction times were recorded.

Data Analysis Each participant's answer was coded 1 (when answer is the expected gender) or 0 (otherwise), then an overall score by suffix was calculated for each participant. We had two dependent variables: the reaction time and the score of correct answers. Analyses of variance were carried out on these two dependent variables. Effects on frequency of non-suffixed nouns, gender exception frequency and school level were tested.

Results

We first looked at gender rate attributed by children for each suffix and tested if the distribution between masculine and feminine attribution differed from chance.

Table 1 shows two interesting results. First, 6 to 7 year-old children have acquired some implicit knowledge regarding gender information associated with suffix. Indeed, children responses are compatible with the expected gender of the majority of suffixes. Gender attribution was above chance level, at first grade for six out of the ten suffixes (–*elle*, –*otte*, –*ture*, –*age*, –*o*, –*oir*), and for eight out of ten at second grade (the same as in first grade plus –*ation* and –*ot*). Second, there is a clear developmental trend since gender attribution in the expected direction is stronger at grade 2 and two more suffixes are determined for the older children. The exposure to written language during the first school year probably reinforces the implicit knowledge developed by children before primary school.

We then computed analyses of variance, using participants (F_1) and items (F_2) as random variables. Table 2 shows the mean scores observed for gender exception frequency, frequency of non-suffixed nouns and school level.

Table 1: Gender attribution rate as a function of suffix, gender exception frequency and grade level.

Suff.	Gd.	GEF	Grade 1			Grade 2		
			%M	%F	χ^2	%M	%F	χ^2
ade	f	Med.	43.0	57.0	2.67	42.9	57.1	2.57
ation	f	Few	41.9	58.1	2.67	34.9	65.1	11.46***
elle	f	Few	37.6	62.4	6*	35.7	64.3	10.29**
otte	f	Few	31.2	68.8	13.5***	27.8	72.2	24.89***
ture	f	Few	32.3	67.7	13.5***	31.7	68.3	16.79***
age	m	High	64.5	35.5	7.04**	61.1	38.9	6.22*
ment	m	Med.	54.8	45.2	0.67	50.0	50.0	0.00
o	m	High	63.4	36.6	7.04**	78.6	21.4	41.14***
oir	m	Few	62.4	37.6	5.04*	68.3	31.7	16.79***
ot	m	Few	55.9	44.1	0.67	72.2	27.8	24.89***

Legend: Gd.: Gender; Suff.: Suffixes; GEF: Gender Exception Frequency; Med: Medium
* $p < .05$, ** $p < .01$, *** $p < .001$

Table 2: Mean scores and standard deviations on reaction times (s) and correct answers (CA).

	GEF	FnSN	Grade 1				Grade 2			
			CA	SD	RT	SD	CA	SD	RT	SD
		Few	1.65	1.05	4.63	3.37	1.50	0.97	6.99	3.67
	With	Med	1.71	0.90	3.90	2.30	1.71	1.04	5.86	3.27
Grade 1		High	1.92	0.84	4.05	2.31	2.10	0.72	5.92	3.50
DB		Few	1.90	0.80	4.05	2.13	2.06	0.70	5.61	3.05
	No	Med	1.87	0.66	4.05	2.13	1.99	0.59	5.54	2.77
		High	1.85	0.65	3.83	2.14	2.11	0.65	5.36	2.38

Legend: GEF: Gender Exception Frequency; FnSN: Frequency of non-Suffixed Nouns; DB: Database; Med: Medium

Separate analyses of variance were carried out using the two lexical databases. We observed comparable effects with the two databases, but reaching more often significance with the first grade database. We will only describe these effects.

First, the developmental trend observed on raw data is confirmed. Grade 1 pupils answered more rapidly than grade 2 pupils [$F1(1, 71) = 8.97$, $p = .0038$; $F2(1, 4) = 115.10$, $p < .001$], but no effect of the school level was obtained on correct answers scores.

Second, gender exception has a significant effect by participant not by item, on pupils reaction time [$F1(1, 71) = 11.31$, $p = .0012$] and on correct answers scores [$F1(1, 71) = 6.55$, $p = .0126$]. Mean reaction time is shorter and correct answers scores are higher in the "no exception" condition than in the "with exception" condition, as expected.

Third, we observed that a low frequency of non-suffixed nouns increases the mean reaction times [$F1(2, 142) = 7.21$, $p = .001$] and a high level of non-suffixed nouns increases the correct answers scores [$F1(2, 142) = 4.38$, $p = .0143$]. This result is surprising but can be further explained by the interaction between the gender exception factor and the non-suffixed nouns factor that approaches significance in the participant analysis, on reaction time [$F1(2, 142) = 2.88$, $p =$

.0593] and on correct answers scores [$F1(2, 142) = 2.82$, $p = .0628$]. It shows that in the "no exception" condition, pupils' reaction time and correct answers scores vary little according to the modalities of the "non-suffixed" variable, while pupils' reaction time is higher and correct answers scores are weaker in the "few non-suffixed nouns" and "with exceptions" conditions.

Computational Cognitive Models of Gender Assignment

We also performed computer simulations to account for these results. Computational models of gender assignment have already been presented and compared to human data in the literature (Eddington, 2002), even for the French language (Matthews, 2005) but, as opposed to our approach, they aim at modelling the adult behavior. Therefore, the input of these models is generally a set of words representative of all words in the language. In our developmental approach, we need to identify the words children are supposed to know in first and second grade. Consequently, we relied on the same database we used for designing the experimental material in order to get an estimate of the words children know in 1st and 2nd grade. We tested three models of growing complexity.

Occurrence-Based Modeling

The first model we built was quite simple. It only relies on suffixes to predict gender. Basically, children would associate a probability of being masculine or feminine to each suffix, according to the words they were exposed to. In this simple model, the probability of a suffix being masculine is just the proportion of masculine words in the set of all words of that suffix the child knows. The probabilities of a given suffix S being masculine or feminine are:

$$p_{masculine}(S) = \text{number of masculine words ending in } S \, / \text{ number of words ending in } S$$
$$p_{feminine}(S) = 1 - p_{masculine}(S)$$

For each of the suffixes of our experiment, we computed its probability of being masculine. We then calculated correlations with children data. We found interesting significant correlations of .65 for 1st grade and .77 for 2nd grade. This result means that children heavily rely on suffixes to predict gender at least in 2nd grade. This is coherent with the fact that the ending of the word is the best predictor of gender in French (Tucker et al., 1968). However, the ending of a word that children would store in memory might not be the last suffix but rather its last phoneme, its last syllable, etc. Which of these children rely on?

In order to answer that question, we modified the model for taking into account the last phoneme or the last syllable instead. Correlations with children data were not higher: when the model relied on the last syllable, correlations were .64 for 1st grade and .75 for 2nd grade whereas results were .52 for the 1st grade and .63 for the 2nd grade when the model relied on the last phoneme. We need to obtain more data to investigate this important issue that we will discuss in the conclusion part.

Frequency-Based Modeling

Word frequency should also play a role in gender assignment. Let us present the case of the suffix –age. In French, most of the words ending in –age are masculine. There are a few exceptions, but their frequencies are quite high in particular in the children lexicon (image, cage, etc.). These high frequencies should interfere with the normal assignment of a non-word ending in /age/ as masculine. How could we account for that in order to test that hypothesis? We modified the previous model in order to take into account word frequencies. This second model is more coherent with the analysis of children data in which variables also relied on frequencies. These frequencies were also obtained from the Manulex database. We normalized by taking the log of these frequencies and summed up for all words.

$$p_{masculine}(S) = \text{sum of frequency of masculine words ending in } S \text{ / sum of frequency of words ending in } S$$
$$p_{feminine}(S) = 1 - p_{masculine}(S)$$

Correlations with human data were almost the same as in model 1. Although some suffixes got different probabilities, the difference was quite small. For instance, the probability of a word ending in –age being masculine only decreased from .94 in model 1 to .87 in that model. It might be the case that word-endings frequency does not play the role we expected it to do. Word frequency has a main role in many cognitive processes, but is it the same with word-ending frequency?

Analogical Modeling

We previously showed the importance of the word ending in the gender assignment. However, it is likely that the rest of the word would somehow play a role. In order to investigate that issue, we implemented and tested a cognitive model of gender assignment that would take into account all parts of the word. The analogical model (AM, (Skousen, 1989) is an exemplar-based model which has been used to predict several psycholinguistic processes, in particular gender assignment (Eddington, 2002). AM is based on the idea that the gender of a new word can be identified from a set of words that are analogous to it. This analogy is drawn by considering each letter (or each phoneme) of the new word as a variable. By considering some of these variables as placeholders (or empty slots), AM progressively generalizes the new word in order to get examples that match it. A generalization is interesting if all examples that it matches belong to the same category. Let us take an example.

Suppose we want to assign a gender to the non-word "prage". We first put only one placeholder at a time, which gives us 5 generalizations: /*rage/, /p*age/, /pr*ge/, /pra*e/ and /prag*/. The first one matches with 9 examples that are all masculine (barrage, courage, etc.). This first generalization is therefore called deterministic; its examples will be

kept as analogical examples in what is called an analogical set. The second generalization matches two conflicting examples, one masculine (péage) and one feminine (plage), which is not good for considering it for analogy. However, AM makes an exception in this case and keeps generalizations that are not deterministic but whose ancestors do not match any example. Once all generalizations with only one placeholder have been considered, AM attempts to generalize a bit more by putting two placeholders to all generalizations that have been successful. For instance, the generalizations /**age/, /*r*ge/, /*ra*e/ and /*rag*/ will be constructed from /*rage/. In our 1st grade database, 63 examples match /**age/, only two of them being feminine. This generalization will however not be kept for further generalization because it is not homogeneous. The next generalization, /*r*ge/, matches 9 examples (orage, naufrage, etc.) that are all masculine. This generalization is therefore interesting and will be kept for further generalization, leading to /***ge/, /*r**e/ and /*r*g*/. Once no more generalization can be found, the prediction is made according to the analogical examples found. In our case, the probability is the proportion of analogical examples of the corresponding gender:

$$p_{masculine}(S) = \text{number of masculine examples analogous to } S \text{ / number of examples analogous to } S$$
$$p_{feminine}(S) = 1 - p_{masculine}(S)$$

This method is interesting in that examples that seem far from the given word can contribute to the prediction, because what distinguish them from the given word are variables that do not change the gender. This is not the case with a nearest neighbor algorithm which only relies on examples that resembles the given word. We implemented the model in Perl, ran it on the 1st and 2nd grade lexicon and obtained the following significant correlations with the children data: .60 for the 1st grade and .66 for the 2nd grade. These results are not better than those obtained with the model 1.

We then realized that the AM algorithm was too rigid from the sake of cognitive plausibility. In the previous example, the generalization /**age/ will be ruled out because the examples it matches (61 masculine and 2 feminine) do not belong to the same gender. However, it is possible that this generalization would be used by children for predicting a masculine word because 97% of the examples are masculine. We then modified the AM algorithm and considered a generalization as homogeneous if more than 95% of the examples it matches belong to the same gender. We also changed the matching algorithm of the initial AM model. The idea is that a word like "bousculade" (rush) might serve as an example for predicting the gender of the non-word "boucade", which is not the case in the AM algorithm since the matching is done variable per variable. In our new algorithm, a letter of the given word can be replaced by several letters in the examples. Correlations with children data did not change for the 1st grade and were slightly higher for the 2nd grade: .72 but the difference is not significant. Although we could not conclude anything from this result, we believe the scientific community would benefit from this idea of a fuzzy matching in the AM model.

Last but not least, we also applied the algorithm on the phonetic form of the data. Matthews (2005) did not obtained better results in applying the AM model on phonetic data, but it was worth trying it on children data. All examples and test items were considered as sequences of phonemes. We obtained correlations of .57 for 1st grade and .74 for the 2nd grade, which is always in the same range of values.

Conclusion

Our experiment showed that French children implicitly acquire knowledge to predict gender, even before learning to read. There was an increase of performance during the 1st grade, while no knowledge about cues was taught at school, possible as an effect of the exposition to written material. Our simulations showed that the word ending represented by suffixes is likely the main information from which gender can be predicted in French: more complicated models, as well as models using other types of units (syllable, phoneme) did not succeed in better accounting for children data. However, the nature of word ending remains to be more precisely defined. For example, one might ask why children would rely on predefined endings like syllables, bigrams or morphemes as we researchers would expect. They could instead use the most efficient ending depending on its prediction power. If the last letter or the last phoneme is enough to predict gender, then why would we store more information? However, in some cases, a longer string of letters is necessary to predict gender. For instance, the ending –on is obviously not enough to predict the gender since, in our 1st-grade data, there are 116 feminine and 131 masculine nouns with the same ending. The trigram /ion/ is much better: 98 feminine and 9 masculine nouns. /tion/ is really a good unit to code: no masculine nouns at all. Therefore, why would we store a specific information for /ation/?

Acknowledgments

We are grateful to Laurent Lima for his statistical help. We also would like to thank teachers from Barraux and Domène who kindly allowed us to experiment in their classrooms.

References

Casalis, S., Louis Alexandre, M.-F. (2000). Morphological analysis, phonological analysis and learning to read French. *Reading and Writing, 12,* 303-335.

Colé, P., Royer, C., Leuwers, C. & Casalis, S. (2004). Les connaissances morphologiques dérivationnelles et l'apprentissage de la lecture chez l'apprenti-lecteur du C.P. au C.E.2. *L'Année Psychologique, 104,* 701-750.

Duyck, W., Desmet, T., Verbeke, L., & Brysbaert, M. (2004). A tool for word selection and non-word generation in Dutch, German, English, and French. *Behavior Research Methods, Instruments & Computers, 36*(3), 488-499.

Eddington, D. (2002). Spanish gender assignment in an analogical framework. *Journal of Quantitative Linguistics, 9,* 49-75.

Holmes, V. M., & Segui, J. (2004). Sublexical and lexical influences on gender assignment in French. *Journal of Psycholinguistic Research, 33*(6), 425-457.

Karmiloff-Smith, A. (1979). *A Functional Approach to Child Language.* Cambridge: Cambridge University Press.

Lyster, R. (2006). Predictability in French gender attribution: A corpus analysis. *French Language Studies,* 16, 69-92.

Matthews, C. A. (2005). French gender attribution on the basis of similarity: A comparison between AM and connectionist models. *Journal of Quantitative Linguistics, 12*(2-3), 262-296.

Monaghan, P., Chater, N., & Christiansen, M. H. (2005). The differential role of phonological and distributional cues in grammatical categorisation. *Cognition, 96,* 143-182.

Peereman, R., Lété, B., & Sprenger-Charolles, L. (in press). Manulex-Infra: Distributional characteristics of grapheme-phoneme mappings, infra-lexical and lexical units in child-directed written material. *Behavior Research Methods, Instruments and Computers.*

Prodeau, M., & Carlo, C. (2002). Le genre et le nombre dans des tâches verbales complexes en français L2: grammaire et discours. *Marges Linguistiques, 4,* 165-174.

Ravid, D. (2004). Later lexical development in Hebrew: derivational morphology revisited. In R.A. Berman (Ed.), *Language development across childhood and adolescence* (pp. 53-82). Amsterdam: John Benjamins.

Riegel, M., Pellat, J.C., & Rioul, R. (2005). *Grammaire méthodique du français.* Paris: PUF.

Schriefers, H., & Jescheniak, J. D. (1999). Representations and processing of grammatical gender in language production: A review. *Journal of Psycholinguistic Research, 28*(6), 575-599.

Seidenberg, M.S. & Gonnermann, L.M. (2000). Explaininng derivational morphology as the convergence of codes. *Trends in Cognitive Science, 4*(9), 353-361.

Skousen, R. (1989). *Analogical Modeling of Language.* Dordrecht: Kluwer.

Starreveld, P. A. & La Heij, W. (2004). Phonological facilitation of grammatical gender retrieval. *Language and Cognitive Processes, 19*(6), 677-711.

Taft, M., & Meunier, F. (1998). Lexical representation of gender: A quasiregular domain. *Journal of Psycholinguistic Research, 27*(1), 23-45.

Terriault, L. (2006). L'attribution passive et l'acquisition du genre grammatical en français langue seconde. *Proc. Conf. CeSLa '06.* Montreal.

Tucker, G. R., Lambert, W. E., Rigault, A., & Segalowitz, N. (1968). A psychological investigation of French speakers' skill with grammatical gender. *Journal of Verbal Learning and Verbal Behavior, 7*(2), 312-316.

Role of surface frequency on morphological family organization

Delphine Fabre (delphine.fabre@univ-lyon2.fr)
Institut des Science de l'Homme, 14 av Berthelot
69363 Lyon cedex 07, France

Fanny Meunier (fanny.meunier@ish-lyon.cnrs.fr)
Institut des Science de l'Homme, 14 av Berthelot
69363 Lyon cedex 07, France

Michel Hoen (michel.hoen@phonak.ch)
Institut des Science de l'Homme, 14 av Berthelot
69363 Lyon cedex 07, France

Abstract

Three lexical decision experiments using different priming paradigms tested the format of derived words' lexical representations. In Experiment 1, a visual masked priming paradigm is used, and data analysis reveals that stems are activated during the early processing of derived words. Experiment 2 and 3 address then the question of later stage processing with extra-time allocated to process prime words, either with a non-masked visual priming paradigm or an inter-modal one (with spoken primes and visual targets). In the visual modality, data analysis shows that not only morphemic representations but also whole-form representations are activated during derived word processing, whereas only morphemic components receive activation in the auditory modality. To account for these results, we proposed a distinct organization of the visual and auditory lexicons regarding polymorphemic words.

Introduction

The purpose of our work is to provide information about the lexical representation of morphologically complex words. In the experiments reported, we focused on the role of surface frequency in processing derived words, and on the way these words are lexically represented. Two extreme views of how morphological complex words are processed and represented have been initially proposed. The first posits a prelexical decomposition of each word into its constituent morphemes with morphemic lexical representations (e.g. Taft & Forster, 1975). The other extreme claims that morphologically complex words are processed and represented as monomorphemic words using their full form (e.g. Butterworth, 1983). The majority of recent theoretical propositions make compromise as they assume two different formats of processing or representation of complex words: a decomposed one and a direct or full form one (see McQueen & Cutler, 1998, for a review). Important components of these models are the lexical factors that determine which representations, morphemic or full-form, will lead to word identification. Several factors have been proposed: semantic transparency, cumulative frequency, productivity of the affix and surface frequency (Frauenfelder & Schreuder, 1992; Laudanna, Badecker & Caramazza, 1989; Laudanna & Burani, 1985; Schreuder & Baayen, 1995). It is on the latter component that we are going to focus. Although it has been proposed as determining, few experiments have been conducted to define the role of the surface frequency of a derived word on the kind of relationship that this word has with its stem and how it is stored and processed. Moreover results observed are hard to interpret conjointly.

Using a masked priming experiment, a priming technique that allows to investigate early stages of word processing, Giraudo and Grainger (2000) showed that only high frequency derived words prime their stem. A lack of priming is reported for low frequency derived words. These authors interpreted this pattern of results in the framework of the supralexical model of morphological representation, where effects of morphology necessarily depend on processing of a whole-word form that gives rise to effects of surface frequency. However, using a cross-modal priming paradigm in which the prime is consciously perceived, Meunier and Segui (1999) reported that low surface frequency derived words prime their stem more efficiently than high surface frequency derived words. These authors interpreted their results as supporting dual-route model in which a decomposed representation would be shared by all members of a morphological family would with in addition whole-word representations for free stem and high frequency derived words. The idea is that low surface frequency words are always identified through decomposition, while high frequency derived words are recognized through their own representations, so the subsequent recognition of the stem just profits from a spreading activation between the different representations of a given morphological family. When a low frequency suffixed word is heard as a prime, however, the morphemic representation is activated and the stem is recognized faster because the recognition is made through the morphemic representation. This representation would correspond to the stem with all the different stem + affix combinations. Within this morphemic representation, the different affixed combinations would be organized on the basis of their surface frequency (Meunier & Segui, 1999).

Clearly these two studies, both done in French, lead to different interpretations; however it is difficult to compare them as different linguistic material, different type of base lines and different priming paradigms were used. One aim of the experiments presented in this article is to investigate the role of the surface frequency of derived words on the relationship they have with their stem using 3 different priming paradigms with the same linguistic material. We ran 3 priming experiments: one using a visual masked priming paradigm, one a conscious visual priming paradigm and one a cross-modal priming paradigm.

Masked intra-modality priming

The aim of this first experiment is to investigate the role of the prime derived word surface frequency on their stem recognition and during the early stage of processing. We used the masked priming paradigm that consists of presenting a prime on a screen for a very short duration (typically for less than 50 ms) and to mask it by the subsequent presentation of the target. Masked priming was first used to avoid episodic effects associated with the unmasked priming paradigm, and to avoid strategies in the lexical decision process (see Forster & Davis, 1984; Forster, 1998). It is assumed that the observed masked priming effects reflect the early stages of word processing, and reveal what properties of words are extracted before they are consciously perceived. In our experiment we compared the priming between a high surface frequency suffixed word and its stem, and the priming between low surface frequency suffixed word and its stem, to the priming obtained on the stem when preceded by an unrelated word.

Furthermore, the experiment also investigate the effect of orthographic and semantic prime words on the recognition of related target words in order to check the reliability of the paradigm, namely if the effects observed for these two conditions corroborate with previous findings (e.g., Rastle Davis, Marslen-Wilson & Tyler, 2000).

Method

Participants Thirty students of the Institut des Sciences Politiques at the Université Lyon 2 participated in the experiment. They were all native speakers of French with no language disturbance and had normal or corrected-to-normal vision. They were between 20 and 25 year old.

Stimuli We selected 60 French target words, and for each of them we selected 3 different primes: a high frequency derived prime word (HF), a low frequency derived prime word (LF) and an unrelated prime (Un). Examples are given in Table 1.

Table 1: Sample of stimuli.

	Prime	Target
Derived HF	pureté 'purity'	PUR 'pure'
Derived LF	puriste 'purist'	PUR 'pure'
Unrelated	garage 'garage'	PUR 'pure'

On average HF derived word have a frequency of 26.3 per million, LF ones of 2.1 and unrelated prime 17.9. The three types of primes are comparable in length, respectively 8.3, 8.5 and 8.4 letter lengths.

Moreover, sixty other French target words have been selected with again for each of them 3 type of primes: a word that started orthographically and phonologically as the target, a word that is semantically linked with the target and an unrelated word (see Table 2). We called these conditions, the orthographic condition (Ortho), the semantic condition (Sem) and the unrelated 2 condition (Un2).

Table 2: Sample of stimuli.

	Prime	Target
Ortho	canevas 'tapestry'	CANNE 'stick'
Sem	Béquille 'crutch'	CANNE 'stick'
Un 2	missive 'document'	CANNE 'stick'

On average Orthographic prime words had a frequency of 4.3 per million, Semantic ones of 22.7 and unrelated primes 21.7. The three prime types were in average long of respectively 8.0, 6.3 and 6.7 letters.

Design Three experimental lists have been constructed. Each list is made of 20 pairs of words from each condition (HF, LF, Un, Ortho, Sem, Un2). A given target word is display only once in each of the 3 lists and with one of the 3 possible primes. When a prime is presented in one list, it is not used a second time in another list. So each participant sees each target once, but all prime-target combinations are tested over the 3 lists.

Regarding the experimental conditions, there is in each list 80 prime-target pairs sharing a link and 40 unrelated ones. In order to reduce the proportion of related words to 30 %, further 147 unrelated prime-target pairs have been constructed. This procedure aims to reduce the chance that participants use strategy during the experiment (Andrew, 1986). Moreover, because each list contained 267 prime-word-targets, an equal number of prime-nonword-targets have been added. Hence the number of 'word' and 'nonword' answers is balanced.

Trials have been arranged in a quasi-random order such that (a) there is no more than 3 target words or nonword targets in a row, (b) there is at least 4 unrelated prime-target pairs between 2 prime-target pairs sharing the same link.

Procedure We used a masked priming procedure as in Forster and Davis (1984). Each trial began with a mask of hashmarks (######) which appeared in the middle of the screen for 500 ms, immediately followed by the prime, in lower case, displayed for 47 ms and then immediately masked by the target, in upper case. The stimulus remained on the screen until the participant responded or when a 2000 ms deadline was reached, whichever came first. The experiment was run on PC-computer using DMDX software (Foster & Foster, 2000).

Participants had to decide as quickly and accurately as possible whether the item presented in upper case on the screen is a French word or not. We did not mention the presence of the prime. The manual 'word' and 'nonword' responses were recorded with a game-pad joystick. Prior to the experiment proper, participants completed a series of 10 warm-up trials that were similar to the experimental trials.

Results

Only reaction times for correct 'word' responses shorter than 1500 ms and longer than 300 ms are retained for reaction time (RT) analyses (outliers corresponded to 3.8 % of the data). There is an error rate of 4.16 %; regarding this low rate, no analysis has been conducted on errors.

HF derived words vs. LF derived words (Figure 1)
Overall, the analysis of variance (ANOVA) on RTs indicated a main effect of the prime type [F1(2,29)=7.32, p<.001; F2(2,59)=3.85, p=.02]. Planned comparison indicated that response times are faster when they appeared after high frequency derived primes than unrelated primes, with a difference of 27 ms (SD=42), significant by subject and item [F1(1,29)=12.57, p=.001; F2(1,59)=7.94, p<.01]. RTs are also faster when targets are preceded by a low frequency derived prime than an unrelated one, with a difference of 17 ms (SD=28), significant by subject only [F1(1,29)=10.84, p<.01; F2(1,59)=1.69, n.s.]. The 10 ms difference (SD=45) observed between the priming effect produced by the high and the low derived words is not significant [F1(1,29)=1.50, n.s.; F2(1,59)=2.26, n.s.].

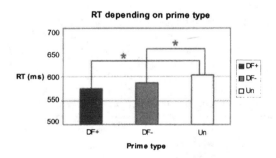

Figure 1: Response times observed for morphological conditions.

Orthographic vs. Semantic prime conditions On average Ortho show RTs of 647 ms, Sem of 643 ms and Un2 of 650 ms. Overall, the analysis of variance (ANOVA) on RTs indicated no effect of the prime type [F_1(2,29)=1, n.s.; F_2<1].

Discussion

This first experiment shows that derived words prime their stem independently of their surface frequency. Indeed, both high and low derived words prime their stem regarding to the unrelated control condition, and no difference between the priming effects produce by high and low frequency derived words is observed. Orthographic and semantic prime words

do not prime their related target word. This observation is consistent with the used of a masked priming paradigm (see Rastle & al., 2000) and the lack of semantic priming points out that the meaning of the derived prime words is not activated at that stage.

If we compared our results with those of Giraudo and Grainger (2000), it appears that different effects are observed between the two studies, especially for the low frequency derived word condition. Giraudo and Grainger (2000) observed a lack of priming effect in the low frequency derived word condition, which differed significantly with the priming effect they obtained with high frequency derived primes. However, the prime duration in their study (57 ms) is longer than ours (47 ms) and they used two base line conditions: an orthographic and unrelated one matched on surface frequency with the derived conditions. Moreover it can be notice that these authors observed that low frequency unrelated primes produce shorter RTs on stem targets recognition than high frequency unrelated primes. This result appears unusual regarding the classic frequency effect (Cattell, 1886).

In a second experiment we investigated the same set of stimuli but using a non-masked priming paradigm. The aim is to look at the role of derived word surface frequency when extra-time is given to process them.

Unmasked intra-modality priming

The aim of this second experiment is to investigate the role of the prime derived word surface frequency on their stem recognition when extra-time is allocated to process prime derived words.

Method

Participants Thirty students of the Institut des Sciences Politiques at the Université Lyon 2 who have not participated to the previous experiment participated in this one. They were all native speakers of French with no language disturbance and had normal or corrected-to-normal vision. They were between 20 and 25 year old.

Stimuli and Design The stimuli and design were the same as in Experiment 1, only the paradigm is differing.

Procedure The procedure is the same as in the previous experiment, excepting the time presentation of the prime. In this experiment the prime duration is 230 ms. In this situation the prime is consciously processed (Rastle et al., 2000).

Results

Only reaction times for correct 'words' responses shorter than 1500 ms and longer than 300 ms were retained for RT analyses (outliers corresponded to 4 % of the data). The error rate data is 3 %, regarding this low rate, we did not analyzed errors further.

HF derived words vs. LF derived words (Figure 2)
Overall, the analysis of variance (ANOVA) on RTs indicated a main effect of the prime type [$F_1(2,29)=10.57$, $p<.001$; $F_2(2,59)=7.56$, $p<.001$]. Planned comparison indicated that response times to targets were significantly faster by subject and item when they appeared after derived primes than unrelated primes, for the HF condition [$F_1(1,29)=20.17$, $p<.001$; $F_2(1,59)=15.38$, $p<.001$] and for the LF condition: [$F_1(1,29)=4.96$, $p<.05$, $F_2(1,59)=3.40$, $p=.07$]. Moreover, a significant difference by participant and item is observed between the 2 priming effects produced by HF and LF derived primes [$F_1(1,29)=5.81$, $p=.02$; $F_2(1,59)=4.11$, $p<.05$], with HF derived primes generating response times 26 ms (SD=56) faster than LF derived prime.

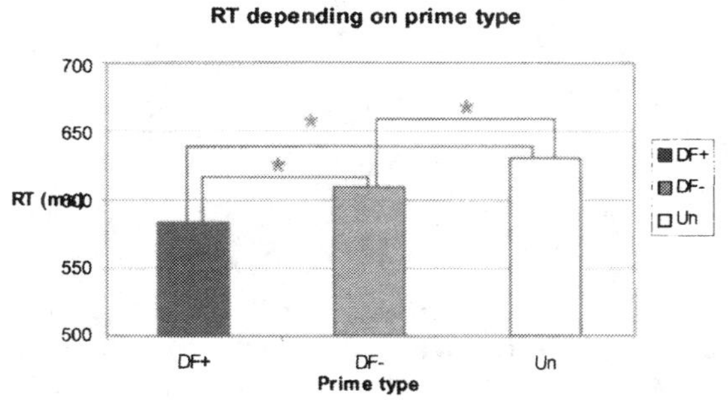

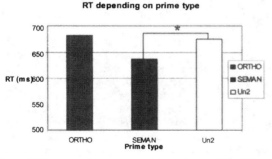

Figure 2: Response times observed for morphological conditions.

Orthographic vs. Semantic prime conditions (Figure 3)
Overall, the analysis of variance (ANOVA) on RTs indicated an effect of the prime type by subject only and a trend by item [$F_1(2,29)=9.18$, $p<.001$; $F_2(2,59)=2.60$, $p=.07$]. Planned comparison indicated that response times to targets were significantly faster by subject and item when they appeared after semantically related primes than unrelated primes [$F_1(1,29)=12.26$, $p=.001$; $F_2(1,59)=5.12$, $p=.02$]. No effect is observed for the orthographic condition [$Fs < 1$].

RT depending on prime type

Figure 3: Response times observed for orthographic and semantic conditions.

Discussion

This experiment shows that extra-time to process derived prime words influence the subsequent stem recognition depending on their surface frequency. High derived words prime their stem better than low frequency derived words do.

Moreover in this experiment we observed a semantic priming effect while it was not the case in the first experiment. This is in accordance with the paradigm used, and it indicates that participant might have activated the whole derived word meaning.

In the study presented by Meunier and Segui (1999), extra-time is also allocated to process the prime word regarding a masked priming procedure, however, these authors observed a significant difference between the priming produce by HF and LF derived words but with response time being faster when the prime word is a LF derived word. Nevertheless, their experimental procedure was a cross-modal one. The following experiment investigates whether the influence of the derived word surface frequency on their stem recognition depends on the time allowed to process the prime or to the modality of presentation. Thus, we tested the same set of stimuli with a cross-modal priming paradigm.

Cross-modal priming

In the cross-modal priming, participants hear a prime word and, at its acoustic offset, see a target item. Participants have to make a lexical decision to the word or nonword visually presented. The advantage of this paradigm is that it taps directly onto the level of the central representation. Cross-modal priming effects are supposed to reflect repeated access to a lexical representation shared by prime and target (Marslen-Wilson, Tyler, Waksler & Older, 1994).The aim of this third experiment is to investigate the role of the prime derived word surface frequency on their stem recognition when prime derived words are auditorily presented and stems visually presented.

Method

Participants Thirty students of the Institut des Sciences Politiques at the Université Lyon 2 which had not participated to the 2 previous experiments participated to this one. They were all native French speakers with no language disturbance and had normal or corrected-to-normal vision. They were between 20 and 25 year old.

Stimuli and Design The stimuli and design were the same as in Experiments 1 and 2, only the paradigm is differing.

Procedure The procedure is the same that in the previous experiment, excepting the modality of the prime presentation. Primes were recorded by a French female native speaker. We used an ISI of 0 ms. The prime was binaurally presented after an auditory warning signal, and then immediately followed by the visual target. The target remains on the screen until response was given or for 2000 ms. Participants had to decide as quickly and accurately as possible whether the visual item is a French word or not.

Results

Only reaction times for correct 'word' responses shorter than 1500 ms and longer than 300 ms were retained for RT analyses (outliers corresponded to 2.7 % of the data). There were 5.08 % of errors; regarding this low rate, we did not analyse errors further.

HF derived words vs. LF derived words (Figure 4)

Overall, the analysis of variance (ANOVA) on RTs indicated a main effect of the prime type [$F_1(2,29)=9.09$, $p<.001$; $F_2(2,59)=6.24$, $p=.002$]. Planned comparison show that derived words prime their stem regarding to the unrelated condition, for HF derived condition [$F_1(1,29)=15.20$, $p<.001$; $F_2(1,59)=11.99$, $p=.001$] with an amount of priming of 34 ms (SD=48) and for the LF derived words condition [$F_1(1,29)=9.30$, $p=.004$; $F_2(1,59)=8.74$, $p<.01$] with an amount of priming of 29 ms (SD=52). No significant difference is obtained between the priming generated by HF derived words and LF derived words [both $Fs <1$].

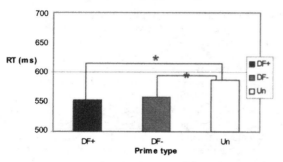

Figure 4: Response times observed for morphological conditions.

Orthographic vs. Semantic prime conditions (Figure 5)

Overall, the analysis of variance (ANOVA) on RTs indicated an effect of the prime type by subject only [$F_1(2,29)=3.57$, $p<.03$; $F_2(2,59)=1.39$, n.s.]. Planned comparison indicated that response times to targets were 27 ms faster when target words were preceded by semantically related words regarding the unrelated condition. This effect is significant by subject only [$F_1(1,29)=6.59$, $p=.01$; $F_2(1,59)=2.19$, n.s]. There is no effect for the orthographic condition [$Fs<1$].

Discussion

This experiment shows that derived words prime their stem, independently of their surface frequency. No significant difference between the priming generated by HF derived words and LF derived words is observed. This result is different from those observed by Meunier and Segui (1999). These authors reported that low frequency words prime their stem more than high frequency words. But once again, the procedure used is different between our study and their study. Indeed, Meunier and Segui (1999) have used an identity control condition, i.e. when prime and target are the same word (e.g., *pur-PUR*). We will discuss these differences in the general discussion. Before that, we tested whether the level of processing reach in the Experiments 2 and 3 is identical or not. Indeed, even if in both experiments

primes are presented enough to reach consciousness, in the visual paradigm the word-prime is available for 230 ms precisely; while in the cross-modal procedure, it is less clear given the temporality nature of spoken words. In order to compare lexical activations reached in both experiments, we contrasted semantic priming effects obtained in Experiments 2 and 3.

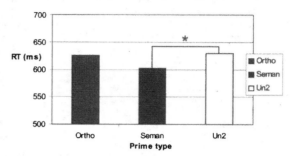

Figure 5: Response times observed for orthographic and semantic conditions.

Comparison between Experiments 2 & 3 Analysis of variance on RTs obtained in Experiments 2 and 3 have been run, including the factor Type of experiment. Regarding effects to which we are interested in, we observed a significant effect of the Type of experiment by item [$F_1(2,58)=2.78$, $p=.12$; $F_2(2,116)=21.27$, $p<.0001$], a significant semantic priming effect [$F_1(2,58)=11.88$, $p <.001$; $F_2(2,116)=3.91$, $p=.02$], and no interaction between these two factors [$Fs<1$]. Indeed planned comparison do not show different semantic priming effects between the 2 experiments [$Fs <1$].

General discussion

This study attempts to identify how derived words are processed during lexical recognition, depending on their surface frequency, presentation's modality and duration of the prime.

First, the result of Experiment 1 indicates that briefly presented masked derived primes facilitate the related stem processing in a lexical decision task, regardless of the derived prime word surface frequencies. Additionally, and according to the paradigm used, no semantic and orthographic priming effect is observed. This finding is taken as support for a prelexical morphological decomposition model which predicts no difference in the amount of priming generated by derived primes with high or low surface frequencies, since stems must be rapidly extracted from polymorphemic stimuli before whole-word representations are activated.

Second, the unmasked visual experiment demonstrated that high surface frequency derived words prime their stem more than low frequency derived words do. In addition, we also observed that the recognition of a target word is facilitated when preceded by a semantically related prime. As the only difference between this experiment and the first one regards the prime duration, we must emphasize that the distinct results between Experiments 1 and 2 regarding the derived words priming effect is driven by the extra-time allocated to process prime words in the second experiment. One possible explanation is that the lexical processing is completed, allowing the semantic representation of the whole derived word surface form to be activated. This representation would then spread back activation to their stem representation, with stronger activation from high derived words than low one. This is through this latter procedure that stem target words would be more pre-activated when preceded by high derived words than low derived one, and then recognized more rapidly in a lexical decision task.

Another interpretation, which is not exclusive with the first one, would be to explain the difference of priming effect between high and low derived prime words as reflecting the examination processing through morphological family member from the more frequent to the less frequent (Colé, Beauvillain & Segui, 1989). This procedure would allow whole word representation to be checked first for high frequency word, and then activated before low frequency derived words. Consequently, more cognitive resources are available when recognizing the target word.

Finally, in the cross-modal priming experiment, extra-time to process the prime word is available regarding the masked priming experiment and logically, we observed a semantic priming effect. However, contrary to the unmasked intra-visual priming experiment, in which extra-time to process the prime word compared to the masked priming experiment is also available, the morphological condition shows no significant difference between the priming generated by high frequency derived primes and low derived primes. Moreover, a further analysis indicates that the semantic priming effect observed in the cross-modal experiment is not significantly different to the one observed in the unmasked priming experiment. Hence it suggests that a full activation of the prime is reached in both experiments. However, in the cross-modal experiment the target appears as soon as the prime ended, so it is not the same as 230 ms processing in parallel of the whole-word. Therefore it could be that the effect observed in the unmasked priming experiment is a late effect. Further experiments in visual modality should be designed in order to test exactly the running time of this frequency effect. Another possible interpretation would be to attribute the difference observed to the modality of the prime presentation. In that case two different organisations for each of the two access files of the lexicon, the orthographic and the phonologic ones[1], must be envisaged. Again further experiments should be run to deepen this point.

References

Andrews, S. (1986). Morphological in uences on lexical access : Lexical or non lexical effects ? *Journal of Memory an Language, 256*, 726-740.

Butterworth, B. (1983). Lexical representation. In B. Butterworth (Ed.) *Language Production,* (pp. 257-294). London: Academic Press.

Caramazza, A. & Hillis, A. E. (1990). Where do semantic errors come from. Cortex, 26, 95122.

Catell, J. (1886). The time taken up by cerebral operation. *Mind, 11*, 277-282, 524-538.

Colé, P., Beauvillain, C. & Segui, J. (1989). On the representation and processing of prefixed and suffixed derived words : a differential frequency effect. *Journal of Memory and Language, 28,* 1-13.

McQueen, J.M. & Cutler, A. (1998). Morphology in word recognition. In A. Spencer & A.M. Zwicky (Eds.), *The Handbook of Morphology* (pp. 406--427). Oxford: Blackwell.

Frauenfelder, U. H. & Schreuder, R. (1992). Constraining psycholinguistic models of morpho-logical processing and representation : The role of productivity. In G. E. Booij et J. Van Marle (Eds.), *Yearbook of Morphology 1991* (pp. 165-183). The Netherlands : Kluwer Academic Publi-shers.

Forster, K. & Davis, C. (1984). Repetition priming and frequency attenuation in lexical access. *Journal of Experimental Psychology: Learning, Memory, and Cognition, 10,* 680-698.

Forster, K. & Forster, J. (2003). DMDX : a windows display program with millisecond ac-curacy. *Behavior Research Methods, Instruments Computers : a journal of the Psychonomic society, 35(1),* 116-24.

Giraudo. H., & Grainger, J. (2000). Effects of prime word frequency and cumulative root frequency in masked morphological priming. *Language and Cognitive Process, 15, (4/5),* 421-444.

Laudanna, A., Badecker, W. & Caramazza, A. (1989). Priming homographic stems. *Journal of memory and language, 28 (5),* 531-546.

Laudanna, A. & Burani, C. (1985). Address mechanisms to decomposed lexical entries. *Linguistics, 23,* 775-792.

Marslen-Wilson, W. D., Tyler, L. K., Waksler, R. & Older, L. (1994). Morphology and meaning in the English mental lexicon. *Psychological review, 101,* 3-33.

Meunier, F. & Segui, J. (1999). Morphological priming effect: The role of surface frequency. *Brain & Language, 68,* 54-60.

Rastle, K., Davis, M. H., Marslen-Wilson, W. D. & Tyler, L. K. (2000). Morphological and semantic effects in visual word recognition : A time course study. *Language and Cognitive Processes, 15(4-5),* 507-537.

Schreuder, R. &. Baayen, R. H. (1995). Modeling morphological processing, in L.B. Feldman, *Morphological Aspects of Language Processing,* Hillsdale (New-Jersey), Lawrence Erlbaum, p. 131-154

Taft, M. & Forster, K. I. (1975). Lexical storage and retrieval of prefixed words. *Journal of Verbal Learning and Verbal Behavior, 14,* 638-647.

---

[1] See for instance Caramazza & Hillis, 1990 for evidence of two distinct orthographic and phonological sub-lexicon.

Implicit Cues to Grammatical Category in the Orthography of English

Joanne Arciuli (jarciuli@csu.edu.au)
Department of Psychology, Charles Sturt University
Panorama Ave, Bathurst 2795

Padraic Monaghan (p.monaghan@psych.york.ac.uk)
Department of Psychology, University of York
York, YO105DD, UK

Abstract

We report the results of corpus analyses demonstrating that there is a rich source of non-morphological probabilistic cues to grammatical category (noun vs. verb) in the spelling of English trisyllables. The cues are located in the beginnings and endings of individual words. Follow-up behavioural testing revealed that participants are sensitive to these cues. Trisyllabic words with consistent cues to grammatical category in their beginning and ending elicited faster responses during a speeded grammatical classification task than trisyllabic words without any orthographic cues to grammatical category. These findings have important consequences for cognitive and computational models of language processing.

Introduction

Grammatical category distinctions, in particular the distinction between nouns and verbs, are found in all of the world's languages (Baker, 2001). The possibility that there is a rich source of *non-morphological* and *probabilistic* cues to grammatical category operating at the single word level is attracting growing interest in cognitive science. This possibility represents a significant shift in the way we think about the representation and processing of grammatical category. Importantly, the existence of such cues does not fit easily with the traditional Saussurian assumption of arbitrariness between word-form and function. Certainly, cases of onomatopoeia and the like suggest there are *sometimes* links between form and function but there is growing interest in the possibility of a number of more *systematic* associations between form and function within languages (Gasser, Sethuraman, & Hockema, 2005).

In addition, grammatical category distinctions are often (and occasionally *only*) resolved at the phrasal level, for example, comprehension is facilitated when an ambiguous word is preceded by a syntactically constraining context – "Laurie took the *prune* out of the fruit bowl and ate it" (Folk & Morris 2003). While we acknowledge that there are effective cues to grammatical category operating at the phrasal level we argue that this does not preclude the presence and use of additional cues that operate at the single word level. Such an hypothesis is in line with a broader view of language processing as an example of statistical learning which is optimised through the use of multiple probabilistic cues (Monaghan, Chater, & Christiansen, 2005; Morgan, Meier, & Newport, 1987; Newport & Aslin, 2004; Onnis, Monaghan, Richmond, & Chater, 2005).

Interestingly, in spite of the challenges posed to notions of arbitrariness and the privileged role of phrasal-level constraints it is clear that grammatical category information is sometimes reflected in individual words. However, discussion of this topic has generally been limited to the role of morphological processes. In particular, derivational morphology marks grammatical category (e.g., addition of the derivational suffix 'ful' turns the noun root 'bliss' into an adjective). However, morphemes are sometimes very difficult to identify in English (the transparency between stem and affix can be lost over time). Moreover, some words are clearly monomorphemic. For these reasons it is worth considering the (perhaps more parsimonious) possibility that there may be probabilistic cues to grammatical category that extend beyond derivational and inflectional morphology and operate in a fairly straightforward manner.

Importantly, a number of studies have examined the role of non-morphological probabilistic cues to grammatical category in the phonology of English (e.g., Arciuli & Cupples, 2004; 2003; Farmer et al., 2006; Onnis et al., 2005). This research adds to an earlier review of the contributions of phonological and prosodic properties to grammatical categorisation (Kelly, 1992). In fact, phonological cues to grammatical category have now been identified in languages as diverse as French, Dutch, Turkish, Japanese, and Mandarin (Durieux & Gillis, 2001; Monaghan et al., 2005; Shi, Morgan, & Allopenna, 1998). Theses studies demonstrate that there is a rich source of probabilistic phonological information pertaining to grammatical category that includes stress patterns and manner and place of articulation amongst other cues.

A smaller number of studies have focussed on non-morphological cues to grammatical category in *orthography*. Arciuli and Cupples (in press) examined cues in the beginnings of disyllables (onset plus first vowel: e.g., 'tu-', 'sta-', 'li-'), and Arciuli and Cupples (2006) examined cues in the endings of disyllables (rime of final syllable: e.g., '-ip', '-ibe', '-oin'). Each study also tested participants' sensitivity to these cues using nonsense words containing either biasing beginnings or endings. Results showed clear sensitivity when participants were asked to use these nonsense words during an off-line sentence construction task (i.e., noun-like nonsense words tended to be used as nouns in sentences whereas verb-like nonsense words tended to be used as verbs).

In the current study, we focus on non-morphological probabilistic orthographic cues, however, we extended previous research in two important ways. First, we investigated the importance of consistent probabilistic cues to grammatical category across *both* the beginning and ending of a word. While previous studies have examined probabilistic orthographic cues in either beginnings or endings no previous work has examined the influence of beginnings and endings simultaneously.

Second, we examined the processing of these cues during the reading of *trisyllables*. While previous studies have examined the reading of disyllables, trisyllables have not yet been investigated. Of particular relevance here, it has been reported that syllable number is a strong cue to grammatical category with verbs tending to have fewer syllables than nouns. Kelly (1992) reported that, in child-directed language, most monosyllables tend to be verbs and there are fairly even numbers of disyllabic verbs and nouns but only 8% of trisyllabic words in child-directed language are verbs. As mentioned, we subscribe to the view that there are likely to be multiple cues to grammatical category in language (including a number of phonological/orthographic markers in addition to morphological and phrasal cues), however, it is beneficial to gain some perspective on the relative contributions of these cues and to ascertain whether non-morphological orthographic cues to *verb* status, in particular, are strong enough to override length cues when processing trisyllables. Cassidy and Kelly (2001), for instance, tested children's classification of monosyllabic and trisyllabic nonsense words as either nouns or verbs in the absence of information other than length of the nonwords. They found that monosyllabic nonwords were more likely to be classified as verbs and trisyllabic nonwords as nouns. What would happen, however, if all the stimuli were the same length, and more subtle cues distinguished nouns from verbs. Would the classification of trisyllabic stimuli as nouns override these other probabilistic contributors to grammatical category, or would a combination of cues determine processing?

Corpus Analyses

We conducted a corpus analysis in order to ascertain whether trisyllables, like disyllables, contain reliable probabilistic cues to grammatical category. We limited our focus to the categories of noun and verb. Using CELEX (Baayen, Pipenbrock & Gulikers, 1995) we selected all trisyllabic nouns and verbs that were unambiguous with regard to grammatical category (i.e., they could only be used as either a noun or a verb). We excluded any words with hyphens, stops or apostrophes. There were 14638 words in total – 9680 nouns and 4958 verbs. This represents a significantly larger proportion of verbs than reported by

Kelly (1992), however, it is clear that there is a striking difference in the ratio of nouns to verbs (2:1).

We then created a script that automatically segmented the letters in the word that reflected the word's beginning (onset and first vowel) and the letters that corresponded to the word's ending (rime of final syllable). This definition of beginnings and endings is taken from the earlier work of Arciuli and Cupples (2006; in press). So, for a word like 'elephant' the beginning was 'e' and the ending was 'ant'. There were 581 distinct beginnings and 946 distinct endings. Clearly, the number of beginnings and endings extends well beyond the known set of prefixes and suffixes (Fudge, 1984, lists around 250 prefixes and around 50 suffixes). In a discriminant analysis (variables that failed the tolerance test – too little variance – were omitted from the discriminant analyses), the beginnings correctly classified 73.5% of nouns and 56.4% of verbs. Overall, beginnings correctly classified 67.7% of the words correctly which was significant (Wilks' lambda = .871, df = 580, p < .001). The endings correctly classified 97.5% of nouns and 83.1% of verbs – 92.6% of all words. Once again, this was significant (Wilks' lambda = .254, df = 945, p < .001).

Another way to determine more clearly the influence of non-morphological beginnings and endings (as opposed to prefixes and suffixes) is to analyse just the monomorphemic trisyllables in the CELEX database. Our analysis revealed 604 monomorphemic unambiguous trisyllabic nouns and verbs. This word set revealed 144 different beginnings and 162 different endings. Discriminant analysis of the beginnings resulted in correct classification of 91.7% of nouns and 73.9% of verbs, which is 91.1% of all words (Wilks' lambda = .765, df = 144, p < .001). For the discriminant analysis for endings, 99.0% of nouns and 69.6% of verbs were correctly classified, 97.8% overall accuracy (Wilks' lambda = .398, df = 161, p < .001). These results support our assertion that there are non-morphological cues to grammatical category in English trisyllables. These results also suggest a more even contribution of beginnings and endings than our initial analysis which included morphologically complex words.

Importantly, the results point to a very clear behavioural test: sensitivity to words with consistent cues in their beginning and ending vs. words that have no cues in either their beginning or ending.

Behavioural Testing

The speeded grammatical classification task allows us to tap processing of grammatical category at the single word level. The task has been used in several previous studies (e.g., Arciuli & Cupples, 2003; Davis & Kelly, 1997).

Method

Thirty-two native speakers of English from the Charles Sturt University first-year Psychology program participated in exchange for course credit.

Experimental items consisted of 40 trisyllabic words. Of these, 20 words had consistent cues to grammatical category in beginnings and endings (10 nouns with noun-like beginnings and endings and 10 verbs with verb-like beginnings and endings – noun-like and verb-like orthographic patterns were determined from our corpus analyses) and 20 had no cues that were in line with their actual grammatical status (10 nouns with verb-like orthography and 10 verbs with noun-like orthography). Hereafter, we refer to these two conditions as CC (consistent cues) and NC (no cues). Every effort was made to select words that did not contain *beginnings that are known prefixes* or *endings that are known suffixes*, however, due to the constraints imposed in the use of real words that must be matched on a number of different variables (listed below) a very small percentage did contain a such a string (e.g., 're' in 'redirect' is both a 'beginning' by our definition and a prefix as listed by Fudge, 1984). Importantly, there were an even number of these kinds of items across conditions. In addition to the experimental items another 40 words (which had cues in either beginnings or endings) were used as fillers. Experimental stimuli are listed in Appendix A.

CC and NC words did not differ significantly in terms of length (syllable length or number of letters), written frequency and orthographic neighbourhood size (determined from the CELEX database). Imageability values were not available for our stimuli so we collected ratings using a separate group of 30 participants who judged a random ordering of the words on a 7-point scale from 1 (not at all imageable) to 7 (highly imageable). Statistical tests demonstrated that the stimuli were group-wise matched on imageability.

Participants were told they would see one word at a time on the computer screen. Their task was to classify each word as being either a noun or a verb. They were given a brief reminder of what 'noun' and 'verb' refer to and examples of several nouns and verbs. Half of the participants pressed the right response button if the word was a noun (and the left response button if the word was a verb) and the order of responses was reversed for the other half. Item presentation and data collection was controlled using E-prime (Schneider, Eschman & Zuccolotto, 2002).

Each trial consisted of the presentation of a fixation cross (+) positioned in centre of the computer monitor for 500 ms. Immediately following this, the participant saw the target and responded. Participants were encouraged to respond as quickly and accurately as possible.

The dependent variables were response time and error rate. The independent variable was presence/absence of orthographic cues to grammatical category (CC vs NC).

Results

Errors were excluded from analyses of response times. Words with consistent cues in both beginnings and endings (CC) elicited a mean response time of 1049 ms (sd 174.38). This was considerably faster than the response time elicited by words with no cues to grammatical category (NC) of 1107 ms (sd 184.21).

A paired samples t-test showed that this 58 ms difference was significant by subjects ($t(31)$ = -2.99, p = .005). Similarly, an independent samples t-test showed a significant effect by items ($t(38)$ = -2.85, p = .007). We ran an additional analysis of item means after removing the small number words with known prefixes/suffixes and the significant difference remained t(32) = -.2.71, p = .011.

An analysis of errors confirmed there was no speed-accuracy trade-off.

General Discussion

The aim of this study was to extend previous studies in two important ways. First, whereas previous studies have examined *either* beginnings or endings, we sought to examine the importance of consistent cues in beginnings *and* endings. Indeed, our corpus analysis of monomorphemic trisyllables revealed strong evidence that non-morphological probabilistic cues to grammatical category operate across both beginnings and endings. Follow-up behavioural testing showed that participants are clearly sensitive to these cues. Words with biasing and consistent beginnings and endings elicited faster responses than words that have no cues to grammatical category in their beginnings or endings.

Second, we extended investigation to the reading of trisyllables. Clearly, it is important to address this significant gap in the literature and generalise findings to trisyllables (previous studies of orthographic beginnings and endings have concentrated on disyllables). However, investigation of trisyllables also presented a unique opportunity to investigate the competing influence of syllable number vs. orthographic cues in the processing of verbs, in particular. Even though studies differ somewhat in their reporting of the number of trisyllabic verbs in English (partly dependent on whether one looks at child-directed speech or databases that more closely resemble adult language) the clear majority of English trisyllables are nouns (our corpus analysis reported here revealed a noun to verb ratio of 2:1). Importantly, it has been shown that participants are sensitive to syllable number as a cue to grammatical category when processing nonsense words (Cassidy & Kelly, 2001). In view of this, it could be argued that, when processing *real words*, trisyllabic verbs with particularly verb-like spellings may not elicit advantaged processing compared to trisyllabic verbs with noun-like spellings – because syllable number tends to indicate noun status and this cue may compromise the competing orthographic cue. The results of the current study make an important contribution by demonstrating that, in fact, orthographic cues to grammatical category over-ride length cues (at least, in the tasks employed here).

This study adds to the growing body of research indicating that there are cues to grammatical category in single words - cues that extend beyond inflectional and derivational morphology. Such findings challenge traditional notions of arbitrariness between word form and function and point to the mutli-faceted nature of grammatical category representation. As such, they have important consequences for cognitive models of language processing. Where modellers may have incorporated grammatical category information only at the phrasal level or via morphological processes it is timely to consider that grammatical category information is also reflected probabilistically in word-forms (in both phonology and orthography).

Appendix A

Consistent Cues	No Cues
capsicum	canoodle
decorate	carburet
entertain	circumvent
evanesce	dialect
fuselage	diatribe
fusillade	disrepute
holograph	dividend
intercede	domineer
interject	electrode
introduce	emirate
iodise	gallivant
marathon	intellect
novella	jettison
pedantry	malinger
polygon	millipede
redirect	pettifog
reminisce	retrospect
semester	sequester
stalagmite	sultanate
supervise	terrify

Acknowledgments

This research was funded by a CSU Grant to Dr Joanne Arciuli. We thank Lauren Terrill and Rachael Diacono for their assistance with data collection.

References

Arciuli, J., & Cupples, L. (in press). Would you rather 'embert a cudsert' or 'cudsert an embert'? How spelling patterns at the beginning of English disyllables can cue grammatical category. To appear in: *Mental States: Language and Cognitive Structure*. Schalley, A. & Khlentzos, D. (Eds.). Accepted 2007.

Arciuli, J., & Cupples, L. (2006). The processing of lexical stress during visual word recognition: Typicality effects and orthographic correlates. *Quarterly Journal of Experimental Psychology, 59*, 920-948.

Arciuli, J., & Cupples, L. (2004). The effects of stress typicality during spoken word recognition by native and non-native speakers: Evidence from onset-gating. *Memory and Cognition, 32:1*, 21-30.

Arciuli, J., & Cupples, L. (2003). Effects of stress typicality during speeded grammatical classification. Language and Speech, 46:4, 353-374.

Baayen, R.H., Pipenbrock, R., & Gulikers, L. (1995). *The CELEX Lexical Database*. (CD-ROM). Linguistic Data Consortium, University of Pennsylvania, Philadelphia, PA.

Baker, M.C. (2001). *The atoms of language: The mind's hidden rules of grammar*. New York: Basic Books.

Cassidy, K. W. & Kelly, M. (2001). Children's use of phonology to infer grammatical class in vocabulary learning. *Psychonomic Bulletin & Review Journal, 8:3,* 519-523.

Davis, S. M, & Kelly, M. (1997). Knowledge of the English noun-verb stress difference by native and nonnative speakers. *Journal of Memory and Language 36:3*, 445-460.

Durieux, G. & Gillis, S. (2001). Predicting grammatical classes from phonological cues: An empirical test. In J. Weissenborn & B. Höhle (Eds.) *Approaches to bootstrapping: Phonological, lexical, syntactic and neurophysiological aspects of early language acquisition Volume 1* (pp.189-229). Amsterdam: John Benjamins.

Farmer, T.A., Christiansen, M.H., & Monaghan, P. (2006). Phonological typicality influences lexical processing. *Proceedings of the National Academy of Sciences, 103,* 12203-12208.

Folk, J. & Morris, R. (2003). Effects of syntactic category assignment on lexical ambiguity resolution in reading: An eye movement analysis. *Memory & Cognition, 31:1,* 87-99.

Fudge, E. (1984). *English Word Stress*. London: Allen & Unwin.

Gasser, M., Sethuraman, N., & Hockema, S. (2005). Iconicity in expressives: An empirical investigation. In S. Rice and J. Newman (Eds.), *Experimental and empirical methods*. Stanford, CA: CSLI Publications.

Kelly, M.H. (1992). Using sound to solve syntactic problems: The role of phonology in grammatical category assignments. *Psychological Review, 99,* 349-364.

Monaghan, P., Chater, N., & Christiansen, M.H. (2005). The differential contribution of phonological and distributional cues in grammatical categorization. *Cognition, 96,* 143-182.

Morgan, J.L., Meier, R.P., & Newport, E.L. (1987). Structural packaging in the input to language learning: Contributions of prosodic and morphological marking of phrases to the acquisition of language. *Cognitive Psychology, 19,* 498-550.

Newport, E.L., & Aslin, R.N. (2004). Learning at a distance I. Statistical learning of nonadjacent dependencies. *Cognitive Psychology, 48,* 127-162.

Onnis, L., Monaghan, P., Richmond, K., & Chater, N. (2005). Phonology impacts segmentation in speech processing. *Journal of Memory and Language, 53,* 225-237.

Shi, R., Morgan, J., & Allopenna, P. (1998). Phonological and acoustic bases for earliest grammatical category assignment: A cross-linguistic perspective. *Journal of Child Language, 25,* 169-201.

Schneider, W., Eschman, A., & Zuccolotto, A. (2002). *E-prime Reference Guide*. Pittsburgh: psychology Software Tools, Inc.

The Limits of Mechanistic Explanation in Neurocognitive Sciences

Anna-Mari Rusanen (anna-mari.rusanen@helsinki.fi)
Department of Philosophy, PO Box 9
00014 University of Helsinki, Finland

Otto Lappi (otto.lappi@helsinki.fi)
Cognitive Science Unit, Department of Psychology
PO Box 9, 00014 University of Helsinki, Finland

Abstract

In this paper we discuss the nature of computational explanation in the neurocognitive sciences. We ask whether current models of mechanistic explanation can do justice to some important charasteristics of computational explanation. What we argue is that if one considers neurocognitive systems at a genuinely cognitive level, where explanations refer to the level of description that Marr called computational, then the mechanistic approach, as it stands, does not offer the appropriate model of computational explanation in these sciences.

Introduction

Many philosophers have proposed that the mechanistic model of explanation offers a satisfactory model of explanation for the neurosciences (Bechtel and Richardson, 1993; Bechtel and Abrahamsen, 2005; Craver, 2005; Craver and Darden, 2005; Glennan, 2005; Machamer, Darden and Craver, 2000). Recently, Piccinini has argued that the mechanistic model could be extended to cover computational explanations as well (Piccinini, 2004; Piccinini, 2006a; Piccinini, 2006b). Might this model of explanation extend all the way to the neuro*cognitive* sciences?

By neurocognitive sciences we mean the branches of theoretical and computational neuroscience that are concerned with cognitive capacities of organisms, i.e. the representation and processing of information. These sciences include, for example, traditional cognitive neuroscience and those strands of computational neuroscience that model brain function at the cognitive level, as opposed to computational modeling of noncognitive processes (for the distinction, see Grush, 2001).

We are not concerned with those varieties of computational and systems neuroscience that are not in the business of computational explanation of *cognition*. These fields of inquiry are trying to discover and model computationally principles of brain organization operating at levels of explanation "below" that which is required to account for cognitive organization. These principles of organization may be about "low level" small scale organization – e.g. molecular or cellular – or "high-level" large scale organization - i.e. systems level or behavioral.

Overall, we agree with the mechanists that the mechanistic model of explanation is useful in the neurosciences on levels of description higher than physiology, at least up to

some "functional" level of molecular and systems neuroscience. We will even be prepared to assume with the mechanists that up to the "syntactic" or "algorithmic" levels, it is possible to describe and explain computational processes mechanistically (cf. Piccinini, 2004; Piccinini 2006a; Piccinini, 2006b).

However, if one considers the neurocognitive systems at a genuinely cognitive level, and specifically when one considers neurocognitive explanations which refer to the level of explanation that Marr (1982) called computational, then the mechanistic approach, as it stands, does not offer an appropriate model of computational explanation.

This "marrian" form of explanation has an important role in cognitive sciences, and it has no direct analogy in the non-cognitive and non-representational branches of bio-, computer- or neurosciences for which the current mechanistic model of explanation was mainly developed. There is interesting work being done in theoretical neuroscience and cognitive modeling within this framework in the domains of vision, language, and the probabilistic approach to cognition (for overviews, see Anderson, 1991a; Anderson 1991b; Chater, 1996; Chater et al., 2006). This approach to neurocognitive explanation certainly merits philosophical attention. What we are concerned with is the question: Can this marrian approach to "computational mechanisms" be satisfactorily subsumed within the framework of *mechanistic* explanation?

What we suggest is that the current mechanistic model of explanation fails to capture that which is special in explanations in neurocognitive (and, generally, cognitive) sciences.

The Mechanistic Model of Explanation

The most recent discussion of mechanistic explanation has emerged in the context of philosophy of the life sciences (Bechtel & Abrahamsen, 2005; Bechtel & Richardson, 1993; Craver, 2005; Craver & Darden, 2005; Glennan, 2005; Machamer, Darden & Craver, 2000). In those sciences explanations usually involve presenting a model of a mechanism that is taken to be responsible for a given phenomenon (Bechtel & Richardson, 1993; Craver, 2005; Glennan, 2005).

In Craver's account of mechanistic explanation (2001, 2005, 2006), a mechanism is a structure performing a function in virtue of its component parts, component operations performed by those parts, and the organization of the parts into a functional whole (the "system"). For example, the heart's function is to maintain blood pressure and circulation which is achieved by an intricate system contractile fibers and a neural mechanism to synchronize their contractions.

Craver distinguishes etiological, contextual and constitutive mechanistic explanations (Craver, 2001; Craver, 2005). We focus here only on constitutive explanations. We take it that computational explanation is not a form of etiological explanation. Perhaps computational explanations could be seen as some sort of contextual explanations. But since it seems to us that this would require precisely the same sort of revision to the mechanistic model of explanation that we are suggest for constitutive explanation, we do not offer a separate treatment of contextual explanations.

Constitutive mechanistic explanations are explanations where the explanandum is always at a higher level of organization than the explanans. In the case of the heart, for example, the pumping action and ensuing circulation of the blood are the phenomena to be explained.

The explanandum of a constitutive mechanistic explanation is some overall behavior of the mechanism, some output caused by or organized by the mechanism; the activity or behavior exhibited by a system. The explanans of is a model of the mechanism that describes the causal agents responsible for carrying out the component operations that produce the phenomenon (Craver, 2006). It is a description of the internal organization or structure of the system in terms of the lower level entities, activities and their relations which together constitute the system and are causally responsible for its behavior, and its capacity to function in some causal role in the system (Craver, 2001; Craver, 2005; Craver, 2006; Machamer, Darden & Craver, 2000).

Two Notions of Computational Explanation

From a broadly cognitive science perspective, *computational mechanisms* are clearly mechanisms in the above sense, but mechanisms of a very special kind. They are mechanisms that can be made to perform information processing tasks in a rational and semantics-sensitive manner. In other words, computational mechanisms are devices where the design allows one to set initial conditions so that when some piece of information from a domain is encoded in them, they will operate on that information so that when the mechanism is done, one ends up with another, semantically related, piece of information from the same domain. Assuming this sort of characterization of computation, is *computational explanation* mechanistic, and if so in what sense?

Piccinini has recently proposed in a series of papers (2006a, 2006b, 2006c) that computational explanation in neuroscience is (or should be) a form of mechanistic explanation as described in the previous section. Piccinini also holds the mechanistic view of computational individuation, i.e. that computational states are individuated by their mechanistic properties without appealing to any "higher level" semantic properties (such as the fact that they can be assigned interpretations that make overall sense of their behavior as instances of rational inference). The individuating properties are instead supposed to be picked out by the mechanistic explanation (Piccinini, 2006a). Piccinini himself argues for this mechanistic and syntactic view of computation by appealing to the purely formal way computer science and computability theory individuate computation (Piccinini, 2004a, 2004b, 2006a, 2006b).

Piccinini suggests that computing mechanisms - such as brains or the microprocessors of desktop computers - are analyzed in terms of their component parts, their functions, and their organization. Computational explanation is then "a mechanistic explanation that characterizes the inputs, outputs, and sometimes internal states of a mechanism as strings of symbols, and it provides a rule, defined over the inputs (and possibly the internal states), for generating the outputs" (Piccinini, 2006b).

Likewise, in order to isolate the explanatory relevant properties of computational mechanisms it is required that one is able to describe "which of a computing mechanism's properties are relevant to its computational inputs and outputs and how they are relevant" (Piccinini, 2006a).

Piccinini suggests that the relevance for computing of a certain mechanism would be evaluated by knowing how the mechanism's inputs and outputs interact with their context i.e. by knowing its causal (as opposed to say, intentional relations) with the environment (Piccinini, 2006a, 2007, see also Burge, 1986; Egan; 1999; Shapiro, 1997; Shagrir, 2001).

We disagree. In the neurocognitive sciences, properties of a computational mechanism are evaluated *for explanatory relevance* at least partially by describing the *task* of the computing mechanism. The theories which specify the nature of neurocognitive tasks, or functions, are theories of neurocognitive competences, or "computational level theories" in Marr's sense of computation (as opposed to representations and algorithmic mechanisms). The computational level is invoked to explain and to assess the explanatory relevance of the mechanisms at the algorithmic and implementation levels (though not necessarily to individuate them). Seen from the marrian perspective, we doubt very much whether the evaluation of explanatory relevance could - in the context of cognitive (neuro)sciences - be done mechanistically in the sense Piccinini envisions.

However, even if it could be, there would still be another problem, the direction of interlevel exaplanation, for extending mechanistic models to marrian computational explanations. In the mechanistic approach interlevel explanations are always bottom-up explanations, in that the relevant mechanistic organization explains the computation/competence. In the next section we will take a look at the marrian approach, where explanations characteristically are "top-down".

Marr and top-down computational explanation

In Marr's taxonomy the computational level is the level that gives an account of the tasks that the neurocognitive system performs, or problems that the cognitive system in question is though to have the capacity to solve, as well as the information requirements of the tasks (Marr, 1982). This level is also the level, whereby the appropriateness and adequacy (for the task) of mappings from representations to others are assessed (cf. Marr, 1982).

In the case of human vision, one such task might be to faithfully construct 3D descriptions of the environment from two 2D projections. The task is specified by giving the abstract set of rules that tells us what the system does and when it performs a computation. This abstract computational theory characterizes the tasks as mappings, functions from one kind of information to another. It constitutes, in other words, a theory of competence for a specific cognitive capacity - vision, language, decision making etc.

Descriptions of performances corresponding to particular competences are given at the algorithmic or implementation levels; in the case of neurocognitive sciences these might go all the way down to functional or neurological (systemic, cellular or molecular) level mechanisms. In a nutshell, cognitive *competences* are specified at the higher computational level in Marr's taxonomy and *performances* at the lower, algorithmic and implementation levels.

In this model of explanation the higher levels are considered largely autonomous with respect to the levels below, and thus the computational problems of the highest level may be formulated independently of assumptions about the algorithmic or neural mechanisms which perform the computation (Marr, 1982; see also Shapiro, 1997; Shagrir, 2001). The level where the cognitive capacities in question are specified is not logically dependent on the ways the causal mechanisms sustain them (Marr, 1982; Shapiro, 1997).

It is important that at the computational or competence level theories one does not yet commit to anything specific concerning the mechanisms carrying out the required information processing at the algorithmic or implementation levels. The specification of a competence is abstract in the sense that nothing specific in terms of entities or activities causally related to each other is yet assumed.

The computational theory answers "what"- questions and "why" questions (Marr, 1982). These questions and answer are typically formulated along the following lines: "What is the goal of the computation performed by this system/algorithm?" Answer: to add natural numbers. "Why is the algorithm employed appropriate?" Answer: given the representational convention of the arabic numerals, the algorithm is faithful to the rules governing the operation of addition, which is defined at the level of computation. Similarly, as Marr himself showed, the computational theory helps us to understand why the receptive fields of retinal ganglion cells or lateral geniculate neurons are circularly symmetrical or why their excitatory and inhibitory regions have their characteristic shapes and distributions,

one must have a theory of the computational tasks these cells are solving (Marr, 1982).

With a computational theory we can answer many questions about mechanisms. For example, if one considers, *why* this synaptic change is such-and-such, one can answer *because it serves to store the value of x needed in order to compute y*. Or, *why* is the wiring in this ganglion such-and-such? *Because it computes, or approximates computation of x.* In other words we are able to *explain* many phenomena at the lower levels by their representational character and the appropriateness of the mechanism for the computational task.

The level of algorithms and representations, on the other hand, gives a description of the mechanisms that fulfill tasks that are described at the computational level. This level answers "how"-questions. For example, if one considers how the number representations - numerals – are meant to be manipulated, the answer will be given by describing the syntactic or formal means of that manipulation. Whereas the computational level specifies the information represented and operated on, the level of representations and algorithms describes the syntactic or formal means of explicitly representing some of the information needed, and operating upon it "mechanically".

As Marr stressed, although the algorithms and mechanisms are perhaps empirically easier to access, the computational level is an equally important level from an information-processing theory point of view (Marr, 1982). If we are to explain the workings of a neurocognitive system, the explanation requires as one component a precise understanding of the information extraction problem the system solves. Without the computational level in our theory we can't make head or tails of the neural processes. We probably would not even in principle be able to identify the relevant functional properties of the neural systems except by reference to this higher level.

Anderson (1991b, p.471) characterizes the issue thus:
"A rational theory [...] provides an explanation at a level of abstraction above specific mechanistic proposals. [...] One might take the view [...] that we do not need a mechanistic theory, that a rational theory offers a more appropriate explanatory level for behavioral data. This creates an unnecessary dichotomy between alternative levels of explanation, however.–It is more reasonable to adopt Marr's view that a rational theory (which he called 'the computational level') helps define the issues in developing a mechanistic theory (which he called the level of 'algorithm and representation'). In particular, a rational theory provides a precise characterization and justification the mechanistic theory should achieve."

The competence level theories are not only idealizations of causal processes or mechanisms at the performance level. Thus unlike, for example, in the case of the heart, the theory of cognitive competence cannot be simply equated with the theory of totality of (counterfactual) patterns of behavior as a behavioral capacity of the system. Individual performances always occur in causal interaction with systems that are not part of the neural basis of "the system" as characterized at the level of competence. For example, in the case of a singular visual perception, other neurocognitive mechanisms such as memory mechanisms, attention mechanisms, motivational mechanisms and auditory mechanisms plausibly have an effect on the behavior of the visual system and the outcomes (percepts) produced.

It makes sense to consider the behavioral capacity as a phenomenon to be explained (cf. Craver, 2006). Indeed, being the set of all possible performances, it is something that needs to be explained. However, the explanation can proceed bottom up (from implementing mechanisms) or top-down (from the computational theory). This latter form of explanation is a distinctly different sort of interlevel explanation from the standard mechanistic explanation in terms of lower-level implementing causal mechanisms.

In neurocognitive explanation, thus, there are *two* angles of attack, two modes of explanation, only one of which is conforms to the explanatory strategy of constitutive mechanistic explanation. One approach is to study the mechanism sustaining the cognitive activity and develop more abstract functional level accounts that enable to state more powerful generalizations about the (counterfactual) behavior of that mechanism. The other is to identify the information extracting problems (such as generation of veridical three-dimensional descriptions from two-dimensional retinal images) as computational tasks, and then *explain the behaviors* in terms of their interpretations. However, in neurocognitive explanations the higher level of organization – viz. computational competence - can be an explanans as well as an explanandum:

"[A] correct explanation of some psychophysical observation must be formulated at the appropriate level. ... To be sure, part of the explanation of [the Necker cube's] perceptual reversal must have to do with a bistable neural network (that is, one with two distinct stable states) somewhere inside the brain, but few would feel satisfied by an account that failed to mention the existence of two different but perfectly plausible three dimensional interpretations of this two dimensional image." (Marr, 1982; p.25-26)

It is the interpretations which *explain* what the bistable networks inside the brain are all about. What this also means is that the phenomenon of (mechanisms for) bistable representational states may be explained with reference to the computational task of deriving three-dimensional descriptions of objects from two-dimensional data (and the ensuing ambiguity). Then the object of explanation, the phenomenon, the bistable behavior of the neural mechanism, is at a *lower* level explanation than the interpretation which is doing the explaining.

To take another example, Marr's analysis of the problem of matching parts in two figures which together constitute a random dot stereogram (ibid. pp.111ff) establishes a small set of rules that a stereovision algorithm should respect (and their appropriateness and adequacy, i.e. "rational" grounds for opting to implement them). This analysis then enables the evaluation of the adequacy of presented al-gorithms (and the inadequacy of some other prima facie plausible algorithms), and therefore a kind of explanation of the behavior of a system running such algorithms (why it uses these particular algorithms in contrast to the others).

Generally, only with this twofold explanatory capacity is it possible to develop and evaluate an algorithmic theory, since the purpose of algorithmic level is to define algorithms that are used to solve a given task. This two-pronged approach is, furthermore, characteristic of neuro*cognitive* explanation.

Computational explanation is not (constitutive) mechanistic explanation

Suppose we wanted mechanistic explanations that would include all of Marr's levels, including the computational level. The level of computation is understood here as a *higher* level of abstraction than that of representation and algorithms. For example, given a computational task, the realization can based on various different representations and various appropriate algorithms might be acceptable for any given representation (Shagrir, 2001). These algorithms may then be multiply realized in terms of physical implementation.

Therefore explanation where both the computational and algorithmic level are explicitly presented is *multilevel* explanation, since the explanation-relation spans distinct levels of analysis. The computational level entities and principles would have to be either the *explananda* or *explanantia* of this interlevel explanation.

According to constitutive mechanistic explanations phenomena at a higher level (in both the sense of level of abstraction as well as the level of organization) are explained by their lower-level constitutive causal mechanisms but not *vice versa* (Bechtel and Richardson, 1993; Craver, 2001; Craver, 2005; Craver, 2006; Machamer, Darden and Craver, 2000).

For example Craver (2001, p. 70) notes that "Constitutive explanations are inward and downward looking, looking within the boundaries of X to determine the lower level mechanisms by which the lower level mechanisms by which it can Φ. The explanandum... is the Φ-ing of an X, and the explanans is a description of the organized σ-ing (activities) of Ps (still lower level mechanisms)."

According to such models competences would always be explained by causal mechanisms operating at the lower level of performances giving answers to how-questions. Indeed, this is what many philosophers seem to have in mind when they talk of mechanistic explanation of the mind.

However, if the explanandum is a performance and the explanation calls for *causal power* for both the mechanism and its constituent elements, then the abstract competence level just cannot serve as a source of explanations. The computational/information structure ("interpretations") clearly are not characterized in terms of causal organization. It is abstract structure governing logically, but not causally or imposed upon, the mechanism.

For this reason any talk of "generative mechanisms" operating at the computational level cannot be referring to constitutive mechanisms in the sense the term is used in current mechanistic explanation. So, insofar as these generative mechanisms are explanatory, they are explanatory in some other sense of interlevel explanation. It would be a confusion to interpret any talk of "generative mechanisms" as specifications of the computational mechanisms involved in the perfomances, where "computational mechanisms" are understood as causal, algorithm-level, mechanisms - as discussed for example by Piccinini (Piccinini, 2006a; Piccinini 2006b.)

Thus, the problem for extending the current mechanistic explanation to computational explanation is the direction of interlevel explanation. In the mechanistic approach the interlevel constitutive explanations are always "bottom-up"-explanations, but in the marrian model they are genuinely top-down.

Conclusions

A representational system (as opposed to most biological systems) needs to be explained in terms of both the implementing causal mechanisms (or the functional causal organization of the system's performances), as well as an analysis of the representational requirements of the problem solving task or the function represented (the "interpretations" of the functional states qua representational).

The analysis of the competence, i.e. the specification of the system of representation for representing what needs to be represented to get the job done, explains observed performances, i.e. the relevant causal organization. In computational explanation the abstract competence can serve as explanans, the performances (or behavioral capacities of the mechanism) being the explanandum.

It is not easy to see how neurocognitive explanation could be accommodated into the constitutive mechanistic model of explanation. In the mechanistic model of explanation the phenomenon to be explained is always at a higher level of explanation, and the explaining is done by giving a description of the lower level mechanism that "sustains" or "produces" the phenomenon. It seems downright impossible to construe such a version of mechanistic model, where the explananda of constitutive explanation *could* lie at lower level.

The problem for extending constitutive mechanistic explanations to computational explanations is that it only recognizes "bottom-up" interlevel explanation – explanation of computation by realizing mechanisms – and thus can't be reconciled with scientific explanations where the competence level serves as explanans, the performance as the explanandum. If it is the case that in the cognitive sciences theories of competences are used to explain performances, then this mode of explanation is not a case of mechanistic computational explanation of the mind/brain, i.e. a case of explaining the workings of the mind/brain mechanistically. What is explained mechanistically is *how* minds are physically/functionally realized by mechanisms –

how it is in principle possible for a physical system to "be a mind". This, however, does not exhaust the notion of computational explanation in neurocognitive sciences.

Based on the fact that in neurocognitive explanations the higher level of organization – viz. computational competence - can be an explanans as well as an explanandum, the character of computational explanation is not captured by the standard forms of mechanistic model of explanation. We concluded that there are two different roles for competences (explanans and explanandum) corresponding to two different modes of explanation in the neurocognitive sciences. Only one of them is covered by the current mechanistic models where explanantia (mechanisms) are located at a lower level of organization than the explananda (phenomena).

Extending the mechanistic model of explanation to cover neurocognitive explanation would mean several major revisions. In current mechanistic models the computational level - a higher level of abstraction - can be seen exclusively as phenomena in need of explanation. This is not in accordance with Marr's original motivation of emphasizing the explanatory relevance of the computational level, where answers to what and why questions are equal in explanatory importance to answers to how-questions.

Thus, there are characteristic and special features of neurocognitive explanation that are not captured by any current version of mechanistic model. This is not to say that the mechanistic model could not conceivably be extended to handle computational competences as explanantia as well as explananda. We are in principle sympathetic to the idea that although the notion of generative mechanisms differs in important explanatory respects from the constitutive causal mechanisms that are explicated in the philosophy of mechanistic explanation, computational-representational explanation could still be interpreted as some kind of mechanistic explanation.

Intuitively, it is tempting to think of computations in terms of algorithmic mechanisms, and the computational hypothesis as a mechanical explanation of the mind. But what is explained mechanically by "the computational hypothesis" is *how* it is possible for a mechanical system (such as the brain) to be a mind, and exhibit intelligence without causal (mechanical) intervention by an immaterial soul. What is *not* explained mechanically is why a brain with a (specific kind of) mind should be organized thus and so at the lower levels. These explanations are top-down rational explanations, and hence are not constitutive mechanistic explanations.

Acknowledgments

We would like to thank especially Petri Ylikoski for his insightful comments on several versions of this paper. We´d also like to thank Professor Matti Sintonen, the members of Philosophy of Science Research Group (Department of Philosophy, University of Helsinki), and Gualtiero Piccinini for comments on an earlier draft.

References

Anderson, J. R. (1991a). The Adaptive Nature of Human Categorization. *Psychological Review*, 98, 409-429.

Anderson, J. R. (1991b). Is Human Cognition Adaptive? *Behavioral and Brain Sciences*, 14, 471-457.

Bechtel, W., & Abrahamsen, A. (2005). Explanation: A Mechanistic Alternative. *Studies in the History and Philosophy of Biomedical Sciences*, 36, 421-441.

Bechtel, W., & Richardson, R. (1993). *Discovering Complexity, Decomposition and Localization as Strategies in Scientific Research*. New Jersey: Princeton University Press.

Burge, T. (1986). Individualism and the Nature of Syntactic States. *British Journal for the Philosophy of Science*, 49, 557-574.

Chater, N. (1996). Reconciling Simplicity and Likelihood Principles in Perceptual Organization. *Psychological Review*, 103, 566-581.

Chater, N., Tenenbaum, J. B., & Yuille, A. (2006). Probabilistic Models of Cognition: Conceptual Foundations. *Trends in Cognitive Sciences*, 10, 287-291.

Churchland, P., & Sejnowski, T. (1992). *The Computational Brain*. Cambridge, MA.: MIT Press.

Craver, C. (2001). Role functions, Mechanisms and Hierarchy. *Philosophy of Science*, 68, 53-74.

Craver, C. (2005). Beyond Reductionism: Mechanisms, Multifield Integration and the Unity of Neuroscience. *Studies in the History and Philosophy of Biomedical Sciences*, 36, 373-395.

Craver, C. (2006). When Mechanistic Models Explain. Synthese, forthcoming.

Egan, F. (1999). In Defense of Narrow Mindedness. Mind and Language, 14 (2), 177-194.

Friston, K. (2002). Functional Integration and Inference in the Brain. *Progress in Neurobiology*, 68, 113-143.

Friston, K. (2005). A Theory of Cortical Responses. *Philosophical Transactions of the Royal Society B*, 360, 815-836.

Glennan, S. (2005). Modeling Mechanisms. *Studies in the History and Philosophy of Biomedical Sciences*, 443-464.

Grush, R. (2001). The Semantic Challenge to Computational Neuroscience. In P. K. Machamer, R. Grush & P. McLaughlin (Eds.), *Theory and Method in the Neurosciences* (pp. 155-172). Pittsburgh: University of Pittsburgh Press.

Machamer, P. K., Darden, L., & Craver, C. (2000). Thinking About Mechanisms. *Philosophy of Science*, 67, 1-25.

Marr, D. (1982). *Vision: A Computational Investigation into the Human Representation of Visual Information*. San Francisco: W.H. Freeman.

Piccinini, G. (2004a). Functionalism, Computationalism and Mental Contents. *Canadian Journal of Philosophy*, 34, 375-410.

Piccinini, G. (2004b). Functionalism, Computationalism, and Mental States. *Studies in the History and Philosophy of Science*, 35, 811-833.

Piccinini, G. (2006a). Computational Explanation and Mechanistic Explanation of Mind. In M. DeCaro, F. Ferretti & M. Marraffa (Eds.), *Cartographies of the Mind: The Interface Between Philosophy and Cognitive Science*. Dordrecht: Kluwer.

Piccinini, G. (2006b). Computational Explanation in Neuroscience. *Synthese*, 153, 343-353.

Piccinini, G. (2006c). Computational Modeling vs. Computational Explanation: Is Everything a Turing Machine and Does It Matter for the Philosophy of Mind? *Australasian Journal of Philosophy*, forthcoming.

Piccinini, G. (2007). Computation without Representation. forthcoming in *Philosophical Studies*.

Shagrir, O. (2001). Content, Computation and Externalism. *Mind* 110, 369-400.

Shapiro, L. A. (1997). A Clearer Vision. *Philosophy of Science*, 64, 131-153.

Free will and the power of veto: convergent evidence from decision-making

Alexandre Linhares (linhares@clubofrome.org.br)
Getulio Vargas Foundation, EBAPE/FGV, Praia de Botafogo 190
Rio de Janeiro, RJ 22250-900 Brazil

Abstract

There is immense controversy over Libet's "power of veto" interpretation of free will. This theory states that humans have free will by an indirect way: by the ability to discard, or veto, actions that are automatically provided by one's brain (independently of one's conscious thought or will). Libet's theory stems from powerful, robust, experiments, which show that one's brain prepares for an action before one is conscious of the action. These experiments have been robustly replicated, so there is not much to argue scientifically, besides its interpretations and the philosophical implications for free will. In this article, we present convergent evidence to the "power of veto" doctrine. Surprisingly, this convergent evidence arises from a field which has hitherto ignored Libet's findings: the field of decision-making.

Introduction

The traditional view of free will places responsibility for actions at one's conscious acts. Acts have to be conscious in order for one to be "accountable" for them, in many religious doctrines. The current doctrine of free will is not merely an abstraction for the fancy of philosophers or theologians. It molds modern society. Jurisdiction is considered under a doctrine of consciousness concerning acts: violent prisoners in Western societies usually attempt to, sometimes successfully, claim "mental illnesses", which enables their transfer to mental institutions. The crucial point is that the philosophical doctrine holds that people have free will over the acts *they choose* to commit.

Implicit in this view is the idea that, at any given point in time, one has a number of choices, or branchpoints, and one consciously selects a course of action from these alternatives. This, in a few words, is the essence of the traditional view of free will. Aside from the debate between determinism or indeterminism of the universe (see Dennett, 1991, 2003; however, the arguments brought here apply in either case), there has been a serious attack over the traditional view of free will. The traditional philosophical view has been, over the last decades, put into question by the experiments of neuroscientist Benjamin Libet and colleagues, with a host of ensuing controversy over its implications and interpretation. In this paper we present, for the first time, evidence from the field of decision-making which support's Libet's controversial theory of the "veto".

We may start the discussion by reviewing Libet's original findings.

Libet's findings and the consequent veto theory of free will

Libet and colleagues made fundamental discoveries concerning two related, but different phenomenon:

- Timing factors for a conscious experience to arise, and
- The cerebral production of a voluntary, conscious, act.

The first experiments are not the subject of this paper (for recent references, see (Libet 2002, Klein 2002, and Gomes 2002). We will, however, be involved with Libet's experiments concerning the timing of three events: A button that is pressed (which can be accurately timed), the moment when one decides to press the button, and the moment when one's brain starts to operate. Let us start with the latter.

Experimental setting

The readiness potential (from the German *Bereitschaftspotential*) is a pre-motor manifestation of cortical activity, first reported by Kornhuber & Deecke (1965). This first report placed the cerebral activity of the readiness potential occurring prior to volitional acts (such as pressing a button), and thus a first attack on the idea of the passive brain. The potential showed the brain prepared an action before it was carried out. The strange problem with the results seemed to be the long times involved: The potential would start to gather momentum one second before the act. Since humans do not take one second to respond to a stimulus, there seemed to be a problem to be explained. But that was just an illusion, as the readiness potential was being measured on experiments with volitional acts, in which no stimulus-response applied.

Thus, one second before a volitional act, the brain started to prepare for the act. This was one of the major conclusions from Kornhuber & Deecke (1965).

What Libet questioned was the timing of the conscious decision to act. If the brain took one second before the act, when should one's personal, subjective, conscious decision set in? Libet used Wundt's complexity clock (an oscilloscope timer) to precisely capture a subject's timing of a conscious decision to execute an act. This timer consisted of a rapidly moving dot, which performs each cycle at 2.56 seconds; and has been considered a very robust method for the timing of conscious events.

What was found out, in summary, was that the timing of conscious events follows this sequence: (i) first, the readiness potential starts to prepare for an act; then (ii) the subject reports conscious desire to conduct the act, and finally (iii) the act is executed. This sequence has been replicated in many experiments, and is puzzling for two reasons: first, the timing involved: subjects reported the conscious urges to act sometimes half a second after their brains had been operating on such acts; the other reason was that the timing was robustly measured, and these results had to be interpreted as accurate.

In Libet's words: "the brain evidently 'decides' to initiate or, at least, to prepare to initiate an act before there is any reportable subjective awareness that such a decision has taken place"; "it is concluded that cerebral initiation even of a spontaneous voluntary act of the kind studied here can and usually does begin unconsciously" (Libet et al., 1983).

Libet's interpretation and theory of free will

How can free will arise, if the brain decides to act before a person's conscious urge?

Tough there has been a number of criticisms about his interpretations, as one would expect in such a case, Libet proposed the following theory: one does not have control over the brain's activity, and the brain is responsible for bringing to consciousness sudden urges to act. However, according to Libet and colleagues, free will still exists, as consciousness can decide to 'veto' an impulse, instead of simply following it through. While this has been, for understandable reasons, called the theory of "free won't", it remains an important position in a crucial philosophical debate (Libet et al, 1979, Libet, 1985).

We provide arguments towards this view, stemming from an unlikely source: a new theory of decision-making.

Recognition-primed decision model

Naturalistic decision-making

The recent field of naturalistic decision making stands as a new, alternative model of study of decision-making. It bears contrast to both the classical model of rational choice and to the program of heuristics and biases.

The classical model of rational choice and optimization which has been the basis of studies in economics (for instance, in game theory), management science and operations research (in for example mathematical programming models), and in artificial intelligence (the symbols and search paradigm), proposes a set of standard, quantitative, methods in order to 'rationally' select a choice. Under this theory, the decision-maker (i) identifies a set of options, (ii) identifies ways of evaluating these options, (iii) weighs each evaluation dimension, (iv) calculates a rating of each option, and, finally, (v) selects one with the maximum

score. Note that this model implies that, in order to have a number of choices to choose from, one must first have (i) perceived a problem, and (ii) perceived a set of alternative choices. The rational model will deal only with the phase of (iii) selecting one choice from the set.

Despite its widespread use in a number of distinct areas, the rational choice model has not found to be psychologically plausible, for a number of reasons (Plous, 1993). One of the reasons is that the chosen alternative depends on how decision-makers initially frame a problem (Kahneman and Tversky, 1979). There has been strong criticism of the rational choice model from the heuristics and biases research program, in which problems are carefully devised to show that one's intuitions generally depart from the expected optima, and are generally inconsistent. A large number of biases which depart from the 'rational choice' have been found (see, for instance, Plous, 1993), placing great strain on the traditional rational actor doctrine.

Yet the heuristics and biases studies are concentrated on carefully devised questionnaires applied mostly to undergraduate students. Thus a new field of naturalistic decision-making emerged, in which the focus is centered around real life settings, decisions being made under rapidly changing circumstances. A number of studies have been conducted, from firefighters to nurses to chess players to military personnel. One of the most interesting theories to emerge from naturalistic decision-making, the recognition-primed decision model, was devised by Gary Klein and his colleagues (Klein, 1999).

Recognition-primed decision

Consider the following cases:

EXAMPLE #1. The Cuban World Chess Champion José Raoul Capablanca once remarked about his personal, subjective, experience: "I know at sight what a position contains. What could happen? What is going to happen? You figure it out, I know it!" In another occasion, talking about the numerous possibilities that less-skilled players usually consider on each board position, he bluntly remarked: "I see only one move: The best one." Perhaps the reader may think that Capablanca was quite simply being arrogant. But there is evidence to the contrary, that expert decision-makers actually are biased towards very high quality choices. We believe that, in fact, Capablanca was telling us an important fact about expert human psychology and decision-making, which would later be documented in recognition-primed decision studies.

EXAMPLE #2. A baby at an infirmary suddenly turns blue. Within seconds, a nurse has a diagnosis and a potential action. In this case, the nurse thinks the baby has a pneumopericardium, which means the sac surrounding the baby's heart is inflated with air, and the resulting pressure detracts from the heart's pumping of blood. There is a problem with this diagnosis, though. The electrocardiogram is showing a healthy 80 beats per minute. If nothing is done, the baby will die within a few minutes. The doctor walks into the room to find the nurse screaming for silence and listening to the baby's heart with an stethoscope. She is now sure of her diagnosis, and she gives the doctor a syringe: "stick the heart, it's a pneumopericardium, I know it". Given the electrocardiogram, other nurses are skeptical, until the x-ray operator screams out: "she's right!" Her intuitive diagnosis saves the baby's life.

Klein (1999) conducted a series of studies with decision-makers under rapidly changing scenarios. During interviews, when questioned how a specific decision (or course of action) was adopted, decision-makers such as the nurse would proclaim, to Klein's frustration, that they "did not make decisions". One experienced firefighter proclaimed "I don't make decisions--I don't remember when I've ever made a decision" (Klein, 1999, p.10). Decision-makers did not seem to be comparing alternative courses of actions, as classical models would predict. "It is usually obvious what to do in any given situation" (p.11). Repeated statements of the sort by different decision-makers led Klein to propose a psychologically plausible model of decision-making which radically departed from the established view of "comparing alternatives and selecting the optimum".

Klein (1999) proposed a model of recognition-primed decision, in which experienced decision-makers would find themselves immersed in complex situations and rapidly take adequate courses of action. Decision-makers would rapidly perceive cues from any situation and retrieve from episodic memory similar situations (Tulving 1983), which would bring assessments and diagnoses and plausible courses of action. Because priming mechanisms are automatic and unconscious (Bargh and Chartrand 1999, Bargh et al. 2001), these decision-makers reported doing "the obvious" action in different situations. This "obvious" course of action, Klein proposes, is brought from long-term episodic memory by priming mechanisms. Hence, decision-makers would not be selecting among distinct alternatives, but rather simply performing the automatically-provided action.

Even if the "obvious" action seemed plausible for a theory, another problem remained: if decision-makers did not compare alternatives, then how could they know that a course of action was good? In subsequent interviews, evidence emerged that decision-makers would be using the simulation heuristic, proposed by Kahneman and Tversky (1982). That is, facing a particular situation, experienced decision-makers would be primed towards a particular course of action, to the detriment of most alternative courses of action. This primed alternative would be 'simulated', or 'run through', one's mind, and, if found acceptable during the simulation processing, would be acted upon without further deliberation. If problems emerged during mental simulation, another different course of action would be primed. Thus was born a theory of intuitive decision-making, in which experienced people would not be selecting choices from a vast set of alternatives, but instead 'testing'

their initially primed predispositions with a simulation heuristic.

This model, of course, applied only to expert decision-makers with years of experience. It involves access to a large episodic memory in order to rapidly retrieve a suitable course of action. This was initially found surprising by Klein: "Before we did this study, we believed the novices impulsively jumped at the first option they could think of, whereas experts carefully deliberated about the merits of different courses of action. Now it seemed that it was the experts who could generate a single course of action, while novices needed to compare different approaches." (1999, p.21)

Because priming mechanisms that brought plausible actions to mind are unconscious, people would report having "done the obvious thing to do". Decision-makers would be unable to visualize the cognitive processes underlying their decisions, and would in many cases even believe that they had skills of the "fantastic" variety: One firefighter demands that his whole crew abandon operations inside a house, just to see it collapse seconds afterward. A radar operator would 'chill' after spotting a new track, and would fire counter missiles against it, based on the 'feeling' that it was a hostile missile. It took over a year for this radar operator, after being interviewed by Klein, to understand the incredibly subtle cues that he was responding to whenever he perceived the new radar track. Unable to reasonably explain their life-saving, rapid, decisions, both the firefighter and the radar operator thought that they had ESP or other fantastic abilities. Careful probing would show that they were able to unconsciously perceive subtle cues, which primed them towards adequate responses.

Discussion

How does the recognition-primed decision model support Libet's theory of the "veto"?

As one is immersed into a situation, preceding episodes are retrieved from memory, and one feels "primed to act" in a particular way—in detriment of all other potential actions. This is an unconscious, automatic response, obtained after years of practice. This "primed action", however, is just a tentative action, it is not executed without being mentally simulated. It is at this point that one may veto an initial urge to respond in a certain manner, and retrieve another episode from memory in order to look for a suitable alternative action.

While classical rational choice theory postulates that people hold many actions in mind for comparison and selection of a choice, recognition-primed decision postulates a very different view: people are biased towards an act (or decision) as they perceive a situation. After this automatic bias, people simulate the consequences of executing such acts in their minds, and, if problems or difficulties arise, the possibility is discarded. This theory of intuitive decision-making therefore proposes the following sequence of events:

i) One faces a situation and is automatically biased to act

ii) One simulates the act mentally

iii) The act is either discarded or executed. If discarded, another act will eventually be primed.

How can these correspond to someone's conscious perception? As Klein (1999) observes, experts (such as firefighters, nurses, chess players, or jet pilots) respond that "they do not make decisions", "that it was the obvious thing to do", and so forth. This corresponds to step (i), in which a certain predisposition to act is automatically primed. This part of the sequence obviously requires brain effort with the associated rise in readiness potential. It is also reported to be unconscious.

Part (ii) of the sequence, or mental simulation of the act, is reported to be conscious. Decision-makers see themselves responding to the situation, mentally carrying out acts, before they actually execute them. Since the act can be stopped prior to execution (if anything feels wrong during its simulation), this corresponds directly to what Libet calls the power of veto. Hence, the veto on one's impulses seems to be conscious, according to Klein's (1999) proposition of a simulation heuristic prior to acting.

Whenever an act is vetoed, according to Klein (1999), a new action will be primed as an alternative. Thus, if this model is correct, while we may not have a large number of potential acts to choose from at any point in time, we may have a "good hunch" (in the sense of being a high-quality response, such as those from section 2) given the primed option. Moreover, new choices may come subsequently, should that particular one turn out to be insufficient or undesirable. This new model of free will has, thus, for the first time, been provided with a convergent explanation from decision-making, an area which has not yet taken Libet's profound results into full consideration.

References

Bargh, J. A., & Chartrand, T. L. (1999) The unbearable automaticity of being. *American Psychologist*, 54, 462 - 479.

Bargh, J. A., Gollwitzer, P. M., Lee-Chai, A. Y., Barndollar, K., & Troetschel, R. (2001) The automated will: Nonconscious activation and pursuit of behavioral goals. *Journal of Personality and Social Psychology*, 81, 1014 - 1027.

Dennett, D.C. (1991) *Consciousness Explained*, Little Brown.

Dennett, D.C. (2003) *Freedom Evolves*, Viking Adult.

Gomes, G. (2002) Problems in the timing of conscious experience, *Consciousness and Cognition*, 11, 191—197.

Kahneman, D. & Tversky, A. (1982) *The simulation heuristic*. In D. Kahneman, P. Slovic & A. Tversky (eds.). Judgment under uncertainty: Heuristics and biases. Cambridge, UK: Cambridge University Press. pp. 201-210.

Kahneman, D. and Tversky, A. (1979) Prospect theory: an analysis of decision under risk. *Econometrica* 47, 263-291.

Klein, G., (1999) *Sources of power: how people make decisions*. Cambridge: MIT Press.

Klein, S.A. (2002) Libet's temporal anomalies: a reassessment of the data, Consciousness and Cognition, 11, 198—214.

Kornhuber, HH and L. Deecke (1965) Hirnpotentialänderungen bei Willkürbewegungen und passiven Bewegungen des Menschen: Bereitschaftspotential und reafferente Potentiale. *Pflügers Arch* 284: 1-17

Libet, B. (1985) Unconscious cerebral initiative and the role of conscious will in voluntary action. *Behavioral and Brain Sciences* 8 (4): 529-539.

Libet, B. (1999) Do we have free will?, *Journal of consciousness studies* 6, no 8—9, 47—57.

Libet, B., (2002) The timing of mental events: Libet's experimental findings and their implications, *Consciousness and Cognition*, 11, 291—299.

Libet, B., Wright, E.W., Feinstein, B., and Pearl, D. K.(1979) Subjective referral of the timing for a conscious sensory experience, *Brain*, 102, pp.193-224

Libet, B, C.A. Gleason, E.W. Wright and D.K. Pearl, (1983) Time of conscious intention to act in relation to onset of cerebral activity (readiness-potential): the unconscious initiation of a fully voluntary act, *Brain* 106, 3, 623-642, 1983

Plous, S. (1993) The psychology of judgment and decision-making. New York: McGraw-Hill.

Normative Rationality and the Is-ought Fallacy

Shira Elqayam (selqayam@dmu.ac.uk)
School of Applied Social Sciences, De Montfort University
Leicester LE1 9BH, UK

Abstract

I argue against the notion of normative rationality. I propose that normative rationality is commonly conflated with a computational level analysis, and that this muddle gives rise to the 'is-ought' fallacy. Hence, while one can empirically arbitrate between competing computational accounts, there is no way to do so for competing normative ones. After proposing a typology of relations between norm and an empirical corpus of work, I proceed to examine two prominent rationality agendas, rational analysis of Oaksford and Chater and the use of the understanding / acceptance principle in Stanovich's individual differences programme. Each of these programmes commits the is-ought fallacy in some part of its arguments. I conclude that psychological theory would be better off concentrating on computational rather than normative issues.

Keywords: reasoning; normative rationality; computational vs. normative; is-ought fallacy

Introduction

A critical football match is about to start and Jack speeds along the deserted highway. One normative system says he shouldn't do that – British traffic law. Another system says he's quite justified – his chances of being caught are small enough and his longing to see the game strong enough to justify risking the fine, so by Subjective Expected Utility he is being rational. And of course, he's being adaptively rational because he acts towards satisfying his personal goal of seeing the match. Is Jack, then, being rational? There, in a nutshell, we have a classic rationality dilemma.

The psychological literature on rationality can be broadly divided into two types of conceptions (Evans, 1993). On the one hand, there is the notion of adaptation and attainment of personal goals (e.g., Anderson, 1990; Gigerenzer, 1996), variably called 'personal rationality', 'adaptive rationality' or 'rationality$_1$' (Evans, 1993; Evans & Over, 1996; Evans, Over, & Manktelow, 1993). On the other, the concept of conforming to a formal norm (e.g., Inhelder & Piaget, 1958; Stanovich, 1999), called 'impersonal rationality', 'normative rationality' or 'rationality$_2$' (Evans & Over, 1996). Early conceptions of this duality have linked it to dual process approach to thinking (Evans & Over, 1996), but the link is not all that obvious and is explicitly abandoned in later work (Evans, 2006; Evans, 2007). My concern in this paper, however, is specifically with normative rationality rather than its link with dual processing.

One special case of normative rationality which has come under major criticisms in the literature (Evans, 1993; 2002; Oaksford & Chater, 1998) is logicism, the idea that textbook extensional logic is the appropriate normative system for human thinking. However, the problems with normative rationality go deeper than the problems with logicism, and pertain to any sort of norm, be it extensional logic, Bayesian probability, or Subjective Expected Utility.

I will try to demonstrate that normative rationality as a psychological conception involves a deep-seated muddle. I will try to dig out the roots of the confusion and show that it is still with us today, and in the writing of influential theorists. My assertion is that the source of the confusion is conflating normative theory with computational-level analysis. Once the confusion is disentangled, I aim to liberate psychological theory from normative consideration.

First, we should distinguish between normative theory and computational or competence theory. The distinction is much clearer in linguistics, so this is where we now turn to. For a classical example, consider the sentence 'I don't know nothing'. Although in Standard English the use of double negation is non-grammatical, this sentence is nonetheless a grammatically correct expression in non-standard varieties of English, e.g. African American Vernacular English (AAVE). A normative theory of language will condemn double negation as 'wrong' (doubtless numerous teachers in primary education do so to this very day). A competence theory, though, is a very different matter. A competence theory of AAVE would strive to describe the rules governing these expressions in AAVE that its native speakers consider correct, and would hence include double negation as a grammatical rule, although it is non-normative in Standard English, describing rather than judging. The accepted wisdom in linguistics – and one that goes back to Ferdinand de Saussure's seminal 'Course in General Linguistics' (1959) – is that an adequate linguistic theory would be far more interested in a description of grammar rules in AAVE than in condemning it as 'irrational' or 'ungrammatical' (e.g., Trudgill, 2000). This example makes quite clear the difference between a normative theory and a competence-level theory. It is the latter that, I will argue, constitutes a hard-core scientific question, whereas the former is at best a matter for educational policy.

The difference between the normative and the computational becomes crucial when theoretical accounts compete – either competing normative accounts or competing competence accounts. When one has to arbitrate between different competence / computational theories, one can do so with the aid of empirical data to support or undermine one or the other. I will show that using the same strategy to arbitrate between competing normative accounts is logically unsound.

I will first examine the various ways in which normative systems can relate to a specific empirical database. I will then go on to examine two prominent theoretical proposals, each with its own arbitration mechanism: Oaksford and Chater's rational analysis, and Stanovich's individual differences agenda. I will demonstrate how both proposals suffer from the same fallacy, and suggest that the fallacy is inherent, and no amount of empirical evidence can arbitrate between competing normative accounts. I conclude by suggesting that research in reasoning and decision making would be better off liberated from rationality concerns and concentrating instead on computational level analysis.

A NORMATIVE CONFLICT TYPOLOGY

What Evans (1993) calls the 'normative system problem' and Stanovich (1999) calls 'the inappropriate norm argument' means that deciding on an appropriate normative system for any set of experimental findings is more often than not far from obvious. Indeed, one is hard put to find an experimental paradigm that has just one obvious norm to compare against and no competing alternative norms. Such cases though do exist, as well as more radical cases of normative conflict. In the following I suggest a typology of four normative situations, based on the nature and number of competing normative accounts of a particular experimental paradigm. Of the four types, two involve normative conflict and two involve no conflict.

Type A. Perhaps the simplest (and quite rare), in this one-norm no-conflict situation there is just one applicable norm, typically the one that the originators of the paradigm had in mind.

Type B. Far more common state of affairs, this is the standard-alternative conflict situation, with a standard norm competing with alternative accounts. It is so common that it has become the only acknowledged type in, for instance, Stanovich's account (1999).

Type C. The existence of a standard norm is not universally the case – there is also type C, the multiple norm conflict type, in which there are several alternative norms, none of which has any claim for ascendancy.

Type D. Finally, type D is the no-norm no-conflict condition: where no norm exists there is obviously no conflict. This condition makes the idea of normative rationality even more difficult to maintain. I will now examine some typical examples to illustrate each case.

Table 1 summarizes the four types.

Table 1: The four types of normative conflict

Type	Conflict / No conflict	No. / type of norms involved	Example
A	No Conflict	1	Disjunction effect 1992-2006
B	Conflict	1 Standard + at least 1 Alternative	Disjunction effect post-2006
C	Conflict	Multiple	Meta-deduction
D	No Conflict	0	Metadeductive conditionals

Type A one-norm no-conflict situations seem to offer the prototypical normative condition, but after half a century of contentious reasoning and decision making research, such cases have become all but extinct. One has to look for relatively recent experimental paradigms to find some in which the norm that first motivated the authors has remained unchallenged. One such type A paradigm has been Tversky and Shafir's disjunction effect (1992), and the norm in question is Savage's Sure Thing Principle (1954): if one prefers X to Y when condition C obtains, and one also prefers X to Y when condition C does not obtain, then one should prefer X to Y regardless of C. Tversky and Shafir's (1992) classic paper demonstrates that, when faced with disjunctive possibilities, naïve reasoners repeatedly violate STP by failing to choose a favoured option. Although the disjunction effect itself has been challenged (e.g., Kühberger, Komunska, & Perner, 2001), for years no one has challenged the assumption that STP is the appropriate norm against which to judge it. However, this state of affairs ended in a recent CogSci conference, when an alternative construal was offered in terms of quantum probability which makes the disjunction effect perfectly normative (Busemeyer, Matthew, & Wang, 2006).

A far more prevalent type is B, the standard-alternative conflict situation so extensively covered in Stanovich (1999). In a typical debate of this type, a standard account of a particular observation competes with another, alternative account (or accounts), making an observed behaviour rational[2] according to the latter but not according to the former (and vice versa). With the Busemeyer et al. paper, the disjunction effect has become a type B situation.

What makes one account 'standard' and the other 'alternative' is less than clear in Stanovich's account. Perhaps the simplest criterion is that the 'standard' norm is the one that originally motivated the paradigm. Or one could perhaps propose that the 'standard' norm is a sort of Kuhnian paradigm. Or simply choose the norm that has been around longer. The problem, of course, is that while some criteria may coincide at times, others may give rise to different answers. Once one considers this question, some type B cases may actually be type C cases in disguise.

To fully appreciate this, we now turn to examine this type. The type C multiple-norm conflict is a more radical case, in which there is no normative standard whatsoever and many systems compete for the same observation. For example, take the reasoning literature on metadeduction (Byrne & Handley, 1997; e.g., Byrne, Handley, & Johnson-Laird, 1995; Elqayam, 2006; Rips, 1989; Schroyens, Schaeken, & d'Ydewalle, 1999). Here reasoners are presented with the Island of Knights and Knaves, in which all the inhabitants are either knights, who only tell the truth, or knaves, who only lie. Participants are given statements and asked to identify whether the speakers are knights or knaves. Consider the following statement:

I am a knave and snow is black

Since conjunctions are false whenever one of the conjuncts is false, it seems that the sentence is false and the speaker is a knave. This is the stock answer in metadeductive literature, and answers that deviate from it are typically considered erroneous by most authors regardless of theoretical persuasion (e.g. Rips, 1989; Johnson-Laird & Byrne, 1990). However, this is not the only possible answer. On the Island of Knights and Knaves, 'I am a knave' is paradoxical – a knave cannot utter it because it would be true and knaves lie, and a knight cannot utter it because it would be false and knights don't lie. In fact, it is a version of the Liar paradox (e.g., Martin, 1984). The question now shifts to how we treat sentences with paradoxical constituents, which brings us to many-valued truth systems. Elqayam (2003) has argued that the plethora of such systems (for reviews see Gottwald, 2001; Rescher, 1969) does not allow for one type of solution to be preferred over the other.

Notice the difference between this type C multiple-norm conflict to a type B standard-alternative norm conflict. In the latter there exists a 'normative standard' response (e.g., preferring X whether C obtains or not in the disjunction effect) and a 'normative alternative' one (e.g. rejecting X until C is known). In a type C conflict, however, there is no standard, no alternative; there are many systems, each equally standard and equally alternative, each sanctioning a different response patterns (and often suggested by the same authors in the same work!). Hence, the argument cannot be that reasoners should conform to some normative system X, or normative system Y rather than X: one should first convince why any system should have any sort of precedence.

Let us now turn to the last type, D, the no-norm no-conflict type. As the name implies, this is where no pre-existing normative theory exists at all. One such case is conditional inference with meta-deductive constituents (Elqayam, Handley, & Evans, 2005). In this study participants were presented with various conditional statements made on the Island of Knights and Knaves, such as 'If I am a knight then I live in Emerald City', and with distributions of knights and knaves in the Island's various cities, e.g.:

50 knaves in Emerald City
150 knaves in Diamond City
500 knights in Emerald city
500 knights in Diamond city

When the Liar paradox is not involved, the suppositional theory of conditionals (Edgington, 1995; Edgington, 2003; Evans & Over, 2004) has a clear norm. Consider the following conditional: 'If Pete is a knave then he lives in Emerald City', with the same distribution as above. In this case, the famous Ramsey test (Ramsey, 1931) is applicable: reasoners mentally simulate the antecedent (in this case, that Pete is a knave) and asses their belief in the consequent in that context. The normative solution according to the suppositional theory of the conditionals is therefore the conditional probability, $P(q|p)$. This is also the response pattern that the majority of intelligent adults come up with when object-language level conditionals (i.e., conditionals that refer to anything but semantic concepts) are involved (Evans, Handley, & Over, 2003; Evans & Over, 2004).

However, when the antecedent is the Liar paradox, things get complicated. Can one even mentally simulate a paradox? To the best of my knowledge, there is no discussion in the philosophical literature on suppositional conditionals with indeterminate antecedents. We could fall back on the material conditional, and find numerous multi-valued systems with various material conditional solutions, but this would only put us in a type C condition, with a multiple-norm conflict – hardly helpful.

Out of these four types, there is just one in which the relation between the experimental paradigm and the potential normative system(s) is not strained, and that is type A, where there is just one normative system. However, most type B and type C paradigms started off as type A paradigms, with alternative norms added on by subsequent critics. The Busemeyer et al. paper is a case in point. It seems a safe bet that for the few type A paradigms still around, it is just a matter of time until someone finds an alternative norm.

The case for type D paradigms is even more tenuous. When there is no formal system to conform to, how can one be rational$_2$? Type D paradigms by themselves are enough to throw serious doubt on normative rationality.

Finally, for the conflict cases B and C, it is clear that we need a guide for the perplexed. How does one choose a normative system? Is there any failsafe principle to select and distinguish between normative alternatives? My answer is that any arbitration criterion that involves empirical evidence would be inherently fallacious, because a normative theory is not a competence theory. To understand this, let us examine in detail two of the major rationality programmes in the field: Oaksford and Chater's (1998), and Stanovich's (1999).

IS-OUGHT FALLACY I: RATIONAL ANALYSIS

The first proposal I will examine is rational analysis, Oaksford and Chater's (1998) prominent rationality programme. They suggest (ibid, p. 7) that a rational norm is one that is computationally adequate. The distinction is based on Marr's (1982) definition of three levels of theoretical explanation: the computational level – *what* is computed; the algorithmic – *how* it is computed; and the implementational – the 'hardware' / 'wetware' physical level. Oaksford an Chater propose that a computational system would be psychologically complete if it can generate all 'intuitively correct' answers (just as Chomsky (1957) proposed that a linguistic theory would be descriptively adequate if it can generate all grammatical utterance).

I see various difficulties with this. First, there may be cases in which none of the alternative norms are complete in the sense that Oaksford and Chater propose. Moreover, the concept 'intuitively correct' itself begs the question. It seems far removed from Chomsky's notion of intuitive grammaticality. We are all capable of judging grammaticality in our own native language or dialect, but different people can have very different logical 'intuitions'. Stanovich's individual differences programme (e.g., 1999) – the next I will explore – demonstrates how different we can be in terms of logicality intuitions. For instance, different response patterns sometimes tend to be associated with different ability scores. Do higher ability reasoners speak a different logical native language?

Suppose, then, we take away the intuition part of the equation, and maintain that a theory is computationally complete if it creates all correct answers (rather than all intuitively correct answers). Unfortunately, this will not remedy the situation. 'All correct answers' necessitates one to define a norm to judge if answers are correct or not. Thus, we are left with a circular definition.

But the major problem I have with this proposal is that, while adopting a similar strategy to the linguistics agenda, it does not keep to the linguistics distinctions. It fails to separate the normative from the computational, a separation that is, as we have seen, very clear in linguistics. Another way to put it is that Oaksford and Chater conflate the normative / descriptive distinction with the computational / algorithmic distinction. However, a computational theory – or a competence theory, in Chomsky's terms – is not conceived as a normative theory; it does not endeavour to dictate 'good' language. In other words, a computational level theory is just as descriptive as an algorithmic level theory.

The lack of clear boundaries between computational theory and normative analysis in Oaksford and Chater is not a problem in itself, but unfortunately maintaining such boundaries is essential if one is to avoid the is-ought fallacy. The is-ought fallacy, first identified by Hume (Hume, 2000) (also see Cohon, 2004), means that whenever the premises in an argument are merely descriptive ('is'), it is logically invalid to derive from them a normative conclusion ('ought') (although cf. Searle, 1964). For instance, the following argument contains an is-ought fallacy:

Human beings have natural fear of heights. (is)
Therefore, we should not fly in aeroplanes. (ought)

The conclusion that we should not fly in aeroplanes only follows if we add the implicit 'ought' premise that we should avoid anything that we have a natural fear of.

Confusing a competence theory with a normative theory inevitably triggers the same sort of fallacy. A competence / computational theory is an 'is' type of theory, and empirical evidence is an 'is' type of argument. Supporting the former with the latter involves, therefore, no is-ought fallacy. However, a normative theory is an 'ought' type of theory – how we should reason rather than how we do reason. One should not derive the 'ought' from the 'is'.

A simplified account of rational analysis arguments for normative rationality can be presented as:
Some behaviours approximate Bayesian rules. (is)
These behaviours are successfully adaptive. (is)
Therefore, Bayesian rules are the appropriate normative system. (ought)

Note, however, that, the argument is made valid if we add the 'ought' premise:

We should follow whatever normative system makes our behaviour adaptive. (ought)

Oaksford and Chater follow this route by explicitly stating that any adaptively rational behaviour should be justified in terms of some normative system (1998, pp 291-297); otherwise, they maintain, its rationality is meaningless. Thus, one can maintain that rational analysis avoids the is-ought fallacy. However, this strategy depends on a circular argument: the premise that we should follow the normative system that makes behaviour adaptive. Oaksford and Chater compound the problem by proposing that the answer should be addressed empirically, by looking to see whether adaptive behaviours actually conform to some normative standard. This is, of course, an is-ought fallacy. So at best, the rationally analysis treatment of normative rationality is circular; at worst, it commits the is-ought fallacy.

IS-OUGHT FALLACY II: THE UNDERSTANDING / ACCEPTANCE PRINCIPLE

Another highly influential research programme that falls prey to the is-ought fallacy is that of Stanovich (1999; Stanovich & West, 1998; Stanovich & West, 2000), who adopts the understanding / acceptance principle suggested by Slovic and Tversky (1974): the more one understands the normative principles involved in an inference task, the more likely one is to endorse these principles. Hence, the more cognitively gifted reasoners are more likely to respond in congruence with the 'appropriate' normative model – such as it is – for a particular problem set. Stanovich reverses the principle and maintains that we should accept as normative whatever is congruent with responses given by higher ability reasoners. In other words: if the participants who respond according to a specific pattern P1 are more intelligent than participants who respond according to another pattern P2, P1 should be considered normative and the system it conforms to should be considered appropriate.

However, the understanding / acceptance principle in Stanovich's writing suffers from a host of minor problems and one major one. First, even if one accepts the rule, the converse may not necessarily be the case – even if we agree that understanding triggers acceptance, it does not necessarily mean that acceptance is diagnostic of understanding. Participants may behave in a way that seems congruent with the rule but for their own reasons. Secondly, like many normative arguments, this one is at least partially circular: we know a normative system is 'right' because the brighter participants comply with it, but we know they are brighter because they comply with these same normative systems, whose assumptions are often incorporated into general intelligence tests.

Finally, if participants with higher ability are our standard to what should be considered right or wrong, what would we do when these bright kids reject inferences that are generally considered valid? For instance, higher-ability participants tend to draw fewer Modus Tollens inferences (Evans, Handley, Neilens, & Over, 2005; Newstead, Handley, Harley, Wright, & Farelly, 2004). Modus Tollens is non-controversial as a valid argument under any conditional theory (Evans & Over, 2004), but if norms should be established according to whatever smarter participants prefer, than Modus Tollens should be rejected on the basis of these data.

However, all these are rather trivial problems compared to the biggest hitch in the understanding / acceptance principle: it involves the is-ought fallacy since it derives normative, 'ought' conclusion from descriptive, 'is' data, the data concerning performance of higher ability participants. It says, in effect: X is the way smart people do respond (is); therefore, X is the way we should respond (ought).

The is-ought fallacy is akin to the naturalistic fallacy (but see also Frankena, 1939; Moore, 1903), which derives moral norms from natural phenomena (recall our aeroplane example: that was a typical case of naturalistic fallacy). Stanovich (1999) acknowledges the naturalistic fallacy in the understanding / acceptance argument, but goes on to argue that 'if the theorists discussed so far are actually committing the naturalistic fallacy, then many of the best minds in cognitive science seem to be doing so' (p. 60). This answer is no help: it merely replaces the naturalistic fallacy with an appeal to authority one. One could even consider it another case of the is-ought fallacy, as ideas are again judged valid due to their source. Regrettably, we would have to reject the understanding / acceptance principle as guide for the perplexed.

CAN NORMATIVE RATIONALITY BE EXPERIMENTALLY ARBITRATED?

A clarifying aside seems to be in order, as there seems to be a superficial resemblance between the arguments presented here and some of Cohen's (1981). In a highly controversial paper, Cohen (1981) argued that human rationality should be considered as a given, and that no amount of empirical evidence can demonstrate that humans are irrational. This is a variation of what Stanovich (1999) calls a 'Panglossian' position, the position that humans are a-priori rational. The position seems to be similar to the one presented in this paper because my argument, too, denies the applicability of empirical evidence to human rationality. However, the resemblance ends there. The aims and conclusions of this paper are diametrically opposed to Cohen's. Cohen wants to save human rationality from psychological theory; I want to save psychological theory from rationality considerations. I have no Panglossian axe to grind.

Concluding comments

Can we, then, have a psychological account of normative rationality? And do we really want it? My answer is no, and no. The way I see it, asking whether participants in a particular experiment are conforming to a set of normative rules (whether textbook logic or Bayesian makes no difference), is analogous to a linguist trying to ask whether speakers of AAVE conform to rules of 'good English'. At best, the question is relatively uninteresting; at worst, it does not make any sense. It is much more productive to concentrate on a computational level analysis.

What, then, about instrumental or adaptive rationality? Prima facie, instrumental rationality involves no norms, no 'ought', and therefore no is-ought or naturalistic fallacy. Insofar as we can keep the normative question out of the game, insofar as we can regard instrumental rationality at a purely descriptive level (whether computational or algorithmic), I have no problem with it. However, the question is far from obvious: for instance, Stanovich (1999, p. 243-244) maintains that by his framework, both rationality$_1$ and rationality$_2$ are cases of normative rationality, since they both relate to personal goals. Whether instrumental rationality should be considered normative is beyond the scope of this paper. However, this does not alter the main conclusion of this paper: normative rationality is not amenable to empirical investigation.

To clarify: rejecting normative rationality does not mean that research programmes in reasoning and decision making are meaningless. On the contrary, my aim is to liberate these programmes from normative considerations. We should be much more wary of using normative nomenclature: too often, authors in the reasoning and decision making literature resort to normative terms when computational or competence language would do just as well and better. For example, it makes sense to ask which is a better *competence* theory for the disjunctions effect, STP or quantum mechanics. When researchers are liberated from the constant hunt for 'errors' they can start looking for response patterns – a more psychologically productive strategy.

Linguistics only came of age when it discarded its historical obsession with norms. The obsessive back-and-forth dialogue with normative theory is a peculiarity of reasoning and decision making theories (Evans, 1993). Let us leave the 'ought', then, to clergymen and politicians, and concentrate on the 'is' instead.

Acknowledgments

I thank Jonathan Evans and four anonymous reviewers for comments on an earlier draft; Vinod Goel, Helen Neilens, Keith Stanovich, Valerie Thompson, and Rich West for helpful comments.

REFERENCES

Anderson, J. R. (1990). *The Adaptive Character of Thought*. Hillsdale, N.J.: Erlbaum.

Busemeyer, J. R., Matthew, M. R., & Wang, Z. (2006). A quantum information processing explanation of disjunction effects. In *Proceedings of the 28th Annual Conference of the Cognitive Science Society* (Hillsdale, NJ: Lawrence Erlbaum.

Byrne, R. M. J. & Handley, S. H. (1997). Reasoning strategies for suppositional deductions. *Cognition, 62*, 49.

Byrne, R. M. J., Handley, S. J., & Johnson-Laird, P. N. (1995). Reasoning from suppositions. *The Quarterly Journal of Experimental Psychology, 48A*, 915-944.

Chomsky, N. (1957). *Syntactic Structures*. The Hague: Mouton.

Cohen, L. J. (1981). Can human irrationality be experimentally demonstrated? *Behavioral and Brain Sciences, 4*, 317-370.

Cohon, R. (2004). Hume's moral philosophy. In E.N.Zalta (Ed.), *The Stanford Encyclopedia of Philosophy (Winter 2004 Edition)*, URL: <*http://plato.stanford.edu/archives/win2004/entries/hume-moral/*>. (.

Edgington, D. (1995). On conditionals. *Mind, 104*, 235-329.

Edgington, D. (2003). What if? Questions about conditionals. *Mind & Language, 18*, 380-401.

Elqayam, S. (2003). Norm, error and the structure of rationality: The case study of the knight-knave paradigm. *Semiotica, 147*, 265-289.

Elqayam, S. (2006). The collapse illusion effect: a pragmatic-semantic illusion of truth and paradox. *Thinking and Reasoning, 12*, 180.

Elqayam, S., Handley, S. J., & Evans, J. St. B. T. (2005). The limits of supposing: Semantic illusions and conditional probability. In *Proceedings of the 27th Annual Conference of the Cognitive Science Society* (Hillsdale, NJ: Lawrence Erlbaum.

Evans, J. St. B. T. (1993). Bias and rationality. In K.I.Manktelow & D. E. Over (Eds.), *Rationality: Psychological and Philosophical Perspectives* (pp. 6-30). London: Routledge.

Evans, J. St. B. T. (2002). Logic and human reasoning: An assessment of the deduction paradigm. *Psychological Bulletin, 128*, 978-996.

Evans, J. St. B. T. (2006). The heuristic-analytic theory of reasoning: Extension and evaluation. *Psychonomic Bulletin & Review, 13*, 378-395.

Evans, J. St. B. T. (2007). *Hypothetical thinking: Dual processes in reasoning and judgement*. Psychology Press.

Evans, J. St. B. T., Handley, S. H., & Over, D. E. (2003). Conditionals and conditional probability. *Journal of Experimental Psychology: Learning, Memory and Cognition, 29*, 321-355.

Evans, J. St. B. T., Handley, S. J., Neilens, H., & Over, D. E. (2005). The mental representation of abstract conditional sentences: A study of qualitative individual differences. *Unpublished manuscript, University of Plymouth*.

Evans, J. St. B. T. & Over, D. E. (1996). *Rationality and Reasoning*. Hove: Psychology Press.

Evans, J. St. B. T. & Over, D. E. (2004). *If*. Oxford: Oxford University Press.

Evans, J. St. B. T., Over, D. E., & Manktelow, K. I. (1993). Reasoning, decision making and rationality. *Cognition, 49*, 165-187.

Frankena, W. (1939). The naturalistic fallacy. *Mind, 48*, 464-477.

Gigerenzer, G. (1996). Reasoning the fast and frugal way: models of bounded rationality. *Psychological Review, 103*, 650-669.

Gottwald, S. (2001). *A Treatise on Many-Valued Logics (Studies in Logic and Computation, vol. 9)*. Baldock: Research Studies Press Ltd.

Hume, D. (2000). *A treatise on human nature (Original publication date 1739-1740)*. Oxford: Clarendon Press.

Inhelder, B. & Piaget, J. (1958). *The Growth of Logical Thinking*. New York: Basic Books.

Kühberger, A., Komunska, D., & Perner, J. (2001). The disjunction effect: Does it exist for two-step gambles? *Organizational Behavior and Human Decision Processes, 85*, 264.

Marr, D. (1982). *Vision: A Computational Investigation into the Human Representation and Processing of Visual Information*. San Francisco: Freeman.

Martin, R. L. (1984). *(Ed.) Recent essays on truth and the Liar paradox*. Oxford, UK: Oxford Univerity Press.

Moore, G. E. (1903). *Principia ethica*. New York, NY: Cambridge University Press.

Newstead, S. E., Handley, S. H., Harley, C., Wright, H., & Farelly, D. (2004). Individual differences in deductive reasoning. *Quarterly Journal of Experimental Psychology, 57A*, 33-60.

Oaksford, M. & Chater, N. (1998). *Rationality in an Uncertain World*. Hove, UK: Psychology Press.

Ramsey, F. P. (1931). *The foundations of mathematics and other logical essays*. London: Routledge and Kegan Paul.

Rescher, N. (1969). *Many-valued logics*. New York, NY: McGraw-Hill.

Rips, L. J. (1989). The psychology of knights and knaves. *Cognition, 31*, 85-116.

Saussure, F. d. (1959). *Course in General Linguistics (Original publication 1916)*. New York, NY: McGraw Hill.

Savage, L. J. (1954). *The Foundations of Statistics*. New York: Wiley.

Schroyens, W., Schaeken, W., & d'Ydewalle, G. (1999). Error and bias in meta-propositional reasoning: A case of the mental model theory. *Thinking and Reasoning, 5*, 65.

Searle, J. R. (1964). How to derive 'ought' from 'is'. *Philosophical Review, 73*, 43-58.

Stanovich, K. E. (1999). *Who is Rational? Studies of Individual Differences in Reasoning*. Mahway, NJ: Lawrence Elrbaum Associates.

Stanovich, K. E. & West, R. F. (1998). Cognitive ability and variation in selection task performance. *Thinking and Reasoning, 4*, 193-230.

Stanovich, K. E. & West, R. F. (2000). Individual differences in reasoning: Implications for the rationality debate. *Behavioral and Brain Sciences, 23*, 645-726.

Trudgill, P. (2000). *Sociolinguistics : An introduction to language and society*. (4th ed.) London, UK: Penguin.

Tversky, A. & Shafir, E. (1992). The disjunction effect in choice under uncertainty. *Psychological Science, 3*, 305-309.

The Case of Hyper-intensionality in Two-Dimensional Modal Semantics:

A false problem due to a misunderstanding

Alexandra Arapinis

IHPST / University Paris I

Department of Philosophy

alexandra.arapinis@wanadoo.fr

Introduction

Two-dimensional Modal Semantics (2DMS) has received increasing attention in the past years in the area of natural language semantics. Indeed, a lot of people tend to see in 2DMS a bridge between Kripkean intuitions concerning the semantics of proper names and Fregean ones, therefore reducing the uncomfortable gap between the behavior of proper names in propositional attitude contexts on the one hand, and their modal behavior on the other. The central notion of 'diagonal proposition' has thus been interpreted as a way of reintroducing the Fregean notion of 'Sense' [Fre92] in natural language semantics, while maintaining the Kripkean thesis according to which proper names are rigid designators[1]. Based on such a neo-Fregean interpretation of this semantic apparatus, some philosophers have raised the question of hyper-intensionality, seeking for a solution to the problem of substitutivity of synonymous expressions in propositional attitude contexts.

The main aim of this paper is to show that such a neo-Fregean interpretation of the apparatus is a mistaken one, and consequently to show that the problem of hyper-intensionality as defined in 2DMS is inaccurate. In what follows I will argue that, far from being a revival of the Fregean 'Sinn', two-dimensionalism should be seen as an argument against it. If it can be interpreted as "neo-Fregean" it is only in a wide sense; in what 2DMS considers as a semantic task, and not in the way semantics must take up such a task. Indeed, the development of 2DMS originates in the need to find a semantic solution to what is generally called 'Frege's puzzle'- as opposed to theories leaving aside the problem by considering it as a pragmatic one. But, in doing so it is led to considering the meaning of words-as-tokens and not, as Frege did, of words-as-types. In fact, the intuition behind the development of 2DMS is quite similarly to the one put forward by the Reichenbachian theories of indexicals and proper names recently developed by people like Perry [Per97, Per01b] and Carpintero [Car98b]. This similarity has already been noted, but unfortunately never fully explored.

Furthermore, I will argue that, not only is the problem of hyper-intensionality wrongly put in terms of the diagonal proposition, but it is a false problem *tout court*. Indeed, a number of linguistic theories of nominal polysemy largely ignored by philosophers of language, have convincingly shown that questions of synonymy could only be addressed at the level of tokens. It appears that, in order to adequately address questions of meaning and reference, and to avoid such misleading problems, philosophy of language should find the means to integrate such linguistic insights. I will thus conclude by arguing that 2DMS has the means to do so. Namely, considering the phenomenon of nominal polysemy as accounted for in terms of facets [Cru86, Cru95], I will sketch the way two-dimensionalism could extend to nominal expressions.

In order to defend this position, I will proceed as follows: in the first section I will briefly present 2DMS and define its main notions. In the second section I will present the core theses of the Reichenbachian theories of proper names and indexicals developed recently and show how they can provide a better understanding of what is at stake in 2DMS. In the third section I will present the arguments against the assimilation of the diagonal proposition to some kind of Fregean notion of 'Sense' and show that to raise the question of hyper-intensionality in terms of the diagonal proposition is simply to misunderstand the framework itself. Finally, in the last section, I will argue that two-dimensionalism has the means to take into account the essentially polysemic nature of nominal expressions, and that in doing so it will support the linguistic evidence for the inaccuracy of the problem of hyper-intensionality.

2DMS: The core ideas

Initially, 2DMS appears to be a simple extension of the framework developed by Kaplan in the 1980's in order to provide a semantic analysis of indexicals and demonstratives [Kap89]. Stalnaker himself, who is considered as the father of 2DMS, has acknowledged a strong relation between his work and Kaplan's on many occasions. On the very first page of his seminal article "Assertion" [Sta99a] , he specifies in a footnote that "The development of the ideas in this paper was stimulated by David Kaplan's lectures [...] on the logic of demonstratives". In his "Assertion Revisited" [Sta04] he mentions the parallel between them once again, and makes clear that "The two theories are not competing theories for

---

[1]For an example of such a neo-Fregean interpretation of 2DMS see [Cha04]. In the very first pages of his article he argues that 2DMS will restor the "golden triangle" that linked the Fregean notion of 'sense', the Kantian notion of 'a priory' and the Carnapian notion of 'intension', a triangle broken by Kripke's criticism of descriptivism.

explaining the same phenomena, or competing interpretations of the abstract framework, but complementary theories that use formally similar tools to answer different questions".

Indeed, this framework is based on the idea that, like demonstratives and indexicals, our sentences express propositions only when taken in a particular context. Thus, assertions as such, taken independently of their context of interpretation, should rather be associated with what Stalnaker calls a 'propositional concept', this notion being very similar to what Kaplan considers to be the character of an expression. Similarly to the Kaplanian characters, propositional concepts are defined as functions mapping possible contexts of interpretation, represented as a set of possible worlds, onto propositions as defined in classical modal semantics. Hence, since propositions are considered as functions from possible world states to truth-values, propositional concepts can equivalently by defined as functions from ordered pairs of possible worlds to truth-values. Graphically, propositional concepts correspond to two-dimensional matrixes of the following form:

	w_0	w_1	w_2	...
w_0	V	F	F	...
w_1	V	F	V	...
w_2	F	F	V	...

The possible worlds represented on the horizontal line are possible circumstances of evaluation, i.e. possible world states considered as counterfactual; while on the vertical axis the worlds represented correspond to possible contexts of interpretation.

Intuitively, the introduction of a second dimension in the semantical analysis corresponds to the idea that facts play two distinct roles in determining what is expressed by an assertion. On the one hand, our sentences say something about the world, something that can be either true or false according to the state of the world. In that sense, what is said by a sentence can be considered as providing a partition of the possible ways the world might have been, a partition between the set of counterfactual situations satisfying the sentence and the set of situations falsifying it. On the other hand, facts determine what is said by our sentences. A clear example of this second kind of interaction between facts and the content of our sentences can be found in every sentence containing indexicals. What is said by the sentence "I am trying to make a clear presentation of 2DMS" will differ from one context to another, according to the person uttering it. If I utter this sentence it will mean that I am trying to make a clear presentation of 2DMS, and it will be true in exactly those worlds were I am doing so. While, if another person utters the same sentence it will mean that that person is trying to make the presentation, and it will be true in the worlds where that person is doing so.

If 2DMS had stopped at that point, confining its analysis to the sole observation of the interaction between the two dimensions mentioned, it would in effect have been a simple extension of Kaplan's framework to the whole language. But, what is innovative in such an analysis, isn't a mere matter of extension. The key notion of this formal apparatus, the one it was meant to grasp, is that of diagonal proposition. Formally, it corresponds to the diagonalization of two-dimensional matrixes. In terms of function, it thus corresponds to the function which maps the possible contexts of interpretation onto the truth-values of the sentence in those contexts, the sentence being interpreted in them, formally $f(w_i, w_i)$. In fact, this notion of diagonal proposition, which has no analogue in Kaplan's work, plays a central role, not only as a technicality that allows two-dimensionalists to solve Frege's puzzle by what could seem an *had oc* postulation of some kind of mysterious proposition. Most of all, it is a notion that will provide the foundation of what I take to be an adequate theory of meaning, in favor of which I will argue in the next sections.

But before getting to the philosophical foundation of the notion of diagonal proposition, let's take a look at a concrete example in order to see how it works. Take, for instance, the famous Fregean example of Hesperus and Phosphorus. The question goes as follows: the statement "Hesperus is Phosphorus" expresses a necessary truth, since, following the Kripkean theory of proper names, both 'Hesperus' and 'Phosphorus' rigidly name the planet Venus, and since this planet is necessarily identical to itself. But this statement appears to convey much more than simple information on the identity of an object with itself. So, what is the informational content conveyed? In other words, how is it that such a sentence can say something necessarily true and yet knowable only a posteriori?

In terms of 2DMS, the puzzle can be reformulated in the following way. Let's begin by simplifying the situation a little by supposing that there are only three possible situations; one which corresponds to the actual situation in which 'Hesperus' and 'Phosphorus' both name the planet Venus, one in which 'Hesperus' names the planet Venus and 'Phosphorus' the planet Mars, and one in which they both name the planet Mars. Lets furthermore respectively call w_0, w_1 and w_2 each of the situations mentioned. The propositional concept associated with the sentence "Hesperus is Phosphorus" would then be the following:

M

	w_0	w_1	w_2	...
w_0	V	V	V	...
w_1	F	F	F	...
w_2	V	V	V	...

In matrix M, the proposition represented on the first horizontal line corresponds to the proposition actually expressed by the sentence, that is that Venus is identical to Venus, which is necessarily true. The next two horizontal lines represent the propositions that would have been expressed if the worlds w_1 and w_2 had respectively turned out to be actual. The second horizontal line thus represents the fact that if w_1 hade turned out to be actual, then the sentence would have said that Venus is identical to Mars, and would have thus expressed a necessarily false proposition. And so on for w_2.

The fact that the sentence "Hesperus is Phosphorus" expresses an a posteriori truth is then represented by the fact that the diagonal proposition isn't a necessarily true proposition. In other words, the fact that a proposition is necessary a posteriori amounts to the fact that, though the proposition actually expressed by a sentence is necessarily true, the sentence doesn't necessarily express the proposition it does. The point in Frege's Puzzle is not, as many people put it, to understand how what is said by the sentence is necessarily true but could have been false. Rather, it is to understand that the same sentence, while expressing something true, could have expressed something false, which is exactly what the diagonal proposition says.

Diagonal proposition: A neo-Reichenbachian approach

In the previous section I briefly sketched the way the formal apparatus works and the way in which the diagonal proposition was meant to solve Frege's puzzle as well as questions raised by sentences expressing necessary a posteriori truths. But this still doesn't explain how to interpret the diagonal proposition. An important question thus remains: assuming that what is conveyed by the sentences we're interested in is actually the diagonal proposition, what does this proposition really say?

Indeed, though many semanticists of natural language have explored the different possibilities offered by 2DMS and have argued in favor of different interpretations of this theory, we still don't have a clear idea of what the diagonal proposition really is! The main defenders of 2DMS, that is Stalnaker and Chalmers, have themselves made attempts to provide such an answer but only in a very allusive way. In [Sta99a] Stalnaker explains what is said by the diagonal proposition associated with the sentence "You are a fool" [2]in the following way:

"What the [diagonal proposition] says is roughly this: *What is said in S's utterance of* **You are a fool** *is true*, where the definite description, *What is said in S's utterance of* **You are a fool** may be a non-rigid designator - a description that refers to different propositions in different worlds."

Chalmers, on the other hand, takes a very different path in order to elucidate the status of the diagonal proposition. Unfortunately he does so in a very indirect and metaphorical manner. In [Cha06] he explains that:

"Although the primary intension of an expression [which is equivalent to Stalnaker's diagonal proposition] may not be equivalent to that of a description, one can often at least approximately characterize an expression's primary intension using a description. For example, one might roughly characterize the primary intension of a typical use of 'water' by saying that in a centered world w, it picks up the dominant clear, drinkable liquid with which the individual at the center of w is acquainted. [...] But these characterizations will usually be imperfect, and it will be possible to find Kripke-style counterexamples to them. Ultimately a primary intension is not grounded in any description, but rather is grounded in an expressions inferential role."

But none of these explanations is satisfactory enough, at least from my point of view. Moreover, I think that, for a better understanding of what is at stake in the notion of diagonal proposition, one should look in the recently developed Reichenbachian theories of reference, in particular the ones proposed by Perry and Carpintero. It appears that, though these theories don't deal with 2DMS directly , they provide a solid foundation for the notion of diagonal proposition.

In effect, their starting point is the idea, cherished by Reichenbach, that the main semantic properties should be attributed to expressions-as-tokens instead of expressions-as-types. This means that, an expression's contribution to the truth-value of the sentences containing it - in the case of referential expressions like indexicals, demonstratives and proper names, the contribution is their referent - should be determined at the level of tokens[3]. This is a central point, since it signs the divergence from the classical Kaplanian theory of reference, in the same way 2DMS diverges from it. As Carpintero puts it, Kaplan only dealt with "types in context". In Kaplan's view, the character of an expression-as-type was enough, when completed by features of the context, to determine the content of the expression. But once

---

[2]The full scenario imagined by Stalnaker is roughly this: a person a says to b that he is a fool. b understands that a is speaking to him but thinks he isn't a fool. A third person c goes by an hears what a is saying but wrongly thinks that a is talking to him, and furthermore agrees on the fact that b is a fool. Considering as possible contexts of interpretation the ways a, b and c respectively imagine the actual situation is, Stalnaker sketches the propositional context associated with the sentence "You are a fool" and tries to define what is commonly understood by a, b, and c, though they interpret a's utterance differently.

[3]Actually, designating Reichenbach's, Perry's and Carpintero's theories under the common label of 'token-reflexive theories of reference' is a little oversimplified. In fact, Reichenbach as well as Carpintero put the semantical analysis at the level of the token. Perry, on the other hand attributes semantic properties to utterances. In [Per97] Perry distinguishes these levels very well, and makes it clear that the difference between them isn't merely a difference of formulation. An utterance is an act of language, while a token is the physical concretization of such an act either written, oral or other. This could seem like a minor difference, but it isn't if we assume that semantic conditions are defined in terms of possible worlds. What it means for an utterance to be the same across possible worlds is not exactly the same as the question of what it is for one and the same token to be identifiable across possible worlds. In other terms, it raises the question of what the essential properties of a token are on the one hand, tokens being physical objects, and, on the other, what the essential properties of an utterance are, utterances being acts of language. For a discussion on that topic see [Cha04]. But since this debate isn't of great importance for the purpose of this article, I will equally use the term of token-reflexive theory in each case, since it was the term originally used by Reichenbach, to which the authors mentioned attribute the paternity of their theory.

we acknowledge the central role of the context in determining the meaning of an expression, it seems natural to take the semantic analysis to the level of tokens produced on the occasion of particular utterances. It is precisely those particular utterances that are made in context and it seems quite awkward to take something as general as a type and to saturate it with something as particular as a context.

This leads us to the second core idea of the Reichenbachian theories of reference, that is token-reflexivity. In brief, it consists in defining the meaning of tokens in terms of the tokens themselves. For instance, if someone says:

(1)   "I am very tired"

what is expressed by (1) is something about the particular token of 'I' in (1). That is:

(1')   That the speaker of the token of 'I' in (1) is tired

The picture is then essentially the same in the case of the content of proper names. But one must be careful here in order to avoid any confusion on the linguistic status of proper names: proper names aren't disguised indexicals! To be more precise, here's how things work. A person or an object is "tagged" with a name according to certain conventions, conventions grossly corresponding to the process of baptism described by Kripke in [Kri80], and which Perry calls "permissive conventions" (see [Per01b]). It is then in terms of those conventions that the reflexive content of proper names is defined. Similarly, Carpintero invokes "acts of calling", which he defines as a "specific linguistic act, whose conventional purpose is to define a term, to explain its meaning", in order to define the content of names (see [Car98b])[4]. Consider for example an utterance of the following sentence:

(2)   "John is very tired"

What is it that a competent speaker of English understands when he hears this, assuming he doesn't know who the person named 'John' is? On the token-reflexive account what he understands is something like:

(2')   That the person, the permissive conventions exploited by (2) permits one to designate with 'John', is tired

Of course, one could equally formulate such a content in the terms adopted by Carpintero, but I leave this transposition to the reader.

For a more detailed discussion on the adequacy of token-reflexive theories of reference one can refer to all

---

[4]The main difference between the token-reflexive content of indexicals and that of names is the fact that, in appealing to "permissive conventions" or "acts of calling", we insure a certain stability to the content of names. Their referent won't vary radically from one context to another, since the conventions used to fix the referent of names won't themselves vary much from one context of utterance to another.

of Perry's and Carpintero's works cited so far. But since the goal of this paper isn't to discuss the soundness of these theories, something which has already been done, but to link them with 2DMS arguments, I will now turn to the connections between the two. For that purpose let's turn back to Stalnaker's explanation of what is said by the diagonal proposition of the assertion "You are a fool", cited in the beginning of this section. In fact, Stalnaker makes an explicit reference to the utterance itself in his explanation. It thus seems very natural to define

"*What is said in S's utterance of* **You are a fool** *is true*"

as

That the addressee of 'You' as it occurs in S's utterance of **You are a fool** is a fool

The transition from the two-dimensional account of meaning to token-reflexive accounts thus seems very natural, these theories mutually supporting one another. From now on and based on this observation, I will equally use the notion of token-reflexive content and that of diagonal proposition in answering questions addressed to 2DMS, and in particular the issue of hyper-intensionality.

The case of hyper-intensionality

In order to understand what people try to grasp when they talk about the phenomenon of **hyper-intensionality**, one must first understand what a phenomenon of **intensionality** is. Indeed, people generally conceive of hyper-intensionality as an "isomorphic" phenomenon to that of intensionality, the only difference between them being a difference of level at which such phenomena appear.

When talking of phenomena of intensionality what is aimed at is the following: in certain contexts, like propositional attitude contexts or modal contexts, it appears that terms having the same referent can't always mutually be substituted without affecting the truth-value of the sentence in which they appear. Here is one famous example of such a phenomenon. Imagine someone says:

I believe that Cicero killed Catalina

and truly believes that. Since Cicero and Tully are in fact the same person then, and in virtue of Leibnitz's principle of substitutivity of identicals, this should entail that the speaker could have equally said:

I believe that Tully killed Catalina

But this is obviously not a valid inference, since the speaker may ignore that Cicero and Tully are in fact the same person. The difficulty is then to find out what leads to the failure of such a substitution.

Frege tried to solve this problem by invoking the notion of Sense. The names 'Cicero' and 'Tully' do share the same referent, but each of them is associated with different modes of presentation of the individual they name. Frege then conceived these modes of presentation, the senses, as objets pertaining to some kind of Platonic world of thoughts; platonic objects to which words are associated, and by ways of which words are related to their denotation.

Such an objectivist conception of sense, then raised the question of the substitutivity of synonymous expressions. Indeed, Leibnitz's principle that proved to fail in certain contexts can be reformulated in this way:

> If, following the principle of semantic compositionality, the semantic value of a sentence is a function of the semantic value of its parts, and if the contribution of referring terms to the truth-value of sentences containing them is just their referent, then it is possible to mutually substitute two co-referring terms in a sentence *salva veritate*.

The idea was then to extend this principle to the level of meaning and to see if the same kind of failure occured at that level too. The extended principle could then be formulated in this way:

> If, following the principle of compositionality of meaning, the meaning of a sentence is a function of the meaning of its parts, then it is possible to mutually substitute synonymous expressions in a sentence *salva significatione*.

Moreover, some people argued that this is obviously not the case, since substituting an expression by a synonymous one often radically changes the meaning of the whole sentence. Once again we have to deal with the same kind of phenomenon: expressions associated with the same object, in this case the same sense, appear to have different values when embedded in a wider context. This is why such phenomena are generally called phenomena of hyper-intensionality.

Now, let's reformulate the difficulty in terms of 2DMS. If we take up a neo-Fregean interpretation of 2DMS, according to which we interpret the diagonal proposition as a reformulation in modal terms of the Fregean notion of sense, then the question of hyper-intensionality can be reformulated in 2DMS terms in the following way: it is clear that the substitution of an expression by a synonymous one in a sentence won't change the diagonal proposition associated to the sentence. Hence, one could think the diagonal proposition captures what is common to the meaning of synonymous expressions, but isn't enough fine-grained to provide an account of the way the meaning of a sentence can be modified by such a substitution.

I argue that this is a false difficulty since the diagonal proposition isn't some kind of a disguised Fregean sense. As I tried to show in the last section, the diagonal proposition is more like some sort of token-reflexive content. Unlike Fregean senses, it doesn't correspond to a general property, expressed by type-expressions, that should be grasped in order to provide access to their referent. The diagonal content expressed only gives us a rule that determines the way particular tokens of a type-expression relate to their reference, this rules being formulated in terms of the token itself.

Even more, Frege explicitly said that the cognitive value of a term couldn't just be a matter of signs and their use. As Perry puts it in [Per01a], what is behind the Fregean notion of sense is the idea that:

> "The real knowledge, which determines the cognitive value, is what we learn in addition to what is fixed by our knowledge of language; that is what the truth of the sentence requires beyond what is required by the truth of the conventions of language."

But if the diagonal proposition doesn't provide us with Fregean senses, if what is expressed is information about the linguistic conventions governing the particular uses of words, then why should we expect it to provide us with an account of hyper-intentionality? The question of hyper-intensionality can only be raised within the context of a theory that deals with the kind of cognitive value of words and sentences aimed by Frege.

Against hyper-intensionality: the case of nominal polysemy

Until now, I have argued that 2DMS doesn't deal with the kind of meaning aimed at in raising the problem of hyper-intensionality. But this raises a new question: Does this mean that 2DMS misses or ignores a semantically crucial part of the meaning expressed by type-expressions? Or should we conclude that their is no such meaning as the one that is supposed to be shared by type-expressions generally considered as synonymous?

I believe the answer to this question is to be found in cognitive linguistics, and more precisely in the theory of facets developed by Cruse [Cru86, Cru95]. Indeed, this theory is built on two central claims that prove to be very enlightening in the debate concerning hyper-intensionality: (1) It defends a referential theory of meaning, claiming that natural language is fundamentally turned on the outside, and that the meaning of words and sentences is to be considered as saying something about the world. This is an important feature, since natural language semantics as developed by philosophers of language is based on the intuition that meaning is essentially linked to reference and truth-conditions. (2) It accounts for the fact that one and the same object can be apprehended from different perspectives. Based on the idea that objects are always referred to under a given perspective, nominal expressions are then defined as having different semantic facets, as it is the case for example with the word *book* which sometimes denotes a physical object: a [tome], and other times an abstract object: a [text].

The notion of facet accounts for the fact that, while having a unitary global semantic content, nominal expressions can be used in context to denote only part of their facets, therefore accounting for the variation of meaning observed across contexts. Moreover, the different facets of a nominal expression prove to support different semantic relations. Depending on the facet that appears to be the most salient, a word will thus support different relations of hyponymy and synonymy across contexts. As Cruse argued, in some contexts, the word *book* will be used as a synonym for *tome* and as a hyperonym for *hardback*. While in others, it will be used as a synonym for *text* and as a hyperonym for *novel*.

Now, if we turn back to the question raised in the beginning of this section, it appears that, when substitution of nominal expressions, generally considered as synonymous, significantly affects the meaning of the hole sentence, it indicates that there was no real synonymy in the first place. The difficulty isn't a matter of defining a sufficiently fine-grained notion of meaning that would account for the impossibility to substitute synonymous expression, as it is generally assumed by people seeking for a solution to the problem of hyper-intensionality. What one should aim at, is a framework that accounts for the inaccuracy of the notion of synonymy as applied to type-expressions.

I believe that, if extended to nominal expressions, two-dimentionalism can provide such an account. Indeed, in defining his two-dimensional framework, Stalnaker [Sta99b] himself argued for an extension of his contextual analysis to what he considers to be "less obvious" cases of context-sensitivity. He assumed that

> "The semantic rules which determine the content of a sentence may do so only relative to the context in which it is uttered. This is obviously the case with sentences using personal pronouns, demonstratives, quantifiers, definite descriptions, or proper names. I suspect it happens in less obvious cases as well".

It appears that Stalnaker's intuition can be carried out successfully once we consider nominal polysemy in terms of facets. Namely, we could define the diagonal content of a nominal expression X as expressing something like X *with respect to its most salient facet in the context of utterance*. Of course, the two-dimensional reformulation of the notion of facet sketched here needs to be developed in grater detail, and a choice between the actually available theories that raise the question of reference under perspective should be made and appropriately justified [5]. There is much left to be done. But as I have argued throughout this paper (convincingly enough I hope) such a project is philosophically well motivated, and supported by important linguistic evidence.

References

[Car98a] Manuel García Carpintero. Fregean versus kripkean reference. *Teorema*, XVII:21–44, 1998.

[Car98b] Manuel García Carpintero. Indexicals as token-reflexives. *Mind*, 107:529–564, 1998.

[Cha04] David Chalmers. The foundations of two-dimensional semantics. In M. García Carpintero and J. Macia, editors, *The Two-dimensional Framework: Foundations and Applications*. Oxford University Press, 2004.

[Cha06] David Chalmers. Two-dimensional semantics. In Ernest LePore and Barry Smith, editors, *Oxford Handbook of Philosophy of Language*. Oxford University Press, forthcoming 2006.

[Cru86] D. A. Cruse. *Lexical Semantics*. Cambridge University Press, Cambridge, 1986.

[Cru95] D. A. Cruse. Polysemy and related phenomena from a cognitive linguistic viewpoint. In Patrick Saint-Dizier and Evelyne Viegas, editors, *Computational Lexical Semantics*, pages 33–49. Cambridge University Press, Cambridge, England, 1995.

[Fre92] Gottlob Frege. Über Sinn und Bedeutung. *Zeitschrift für Philosophie und Philosophische Kritik*, 100:25–50, 1892. (Translated by M. Black under the title "On Sense and Reference", in P. Geach and M. Black, Translations from the Philosophical Writings of Gottlob Frege, Oxford, 1952.).

[Kap89] David Kaplan. Demonstratives. In Joseph Almog, John Perry, and Howard Wettstein, editors, *Themes From Kaplan*, pages 481–563. Oxford University Press, Oxford, 1989.

[Kle99] Georges Kleiber. *Problèmes de Sémantique: La Polysémie en Question*. d'Ascq: Presse Universitaire du Séptentrion, Villeneuve, 1999.

[Kri80] Saul Kripke. *Naming and Necessity*. Harvard University Press, 1980.

[Per97] John Perry. Indexicals and demonstratives. In Robert Hale and Crispin Wright, editors, *A Companion to the Philosophy of Language*. Oxford: Blackwells Publishers Inc., 1997.

[Per01a] John Perry. Frege on identity, cognitive value, and subject matter. In Nortmann Newen and Stuhlmann-Laeisz, editors, *Building on Frege. New Essays about Sense, Content, and Concept*. CSLI Publications, 2001.

[Per01b] John Perry. *Reference and Reflexivity*. CSLI Publications, Stanford, CA, 2001.

[Sta99a] Robert C. Stalnaker. Assertion. In *Context and Content: Essays on Intentionality in Speech and Thought*, Oxford Cognitive Science Series, pages 78–95. Oxford University Press, 1999.

[Sta99b] Robert C. Stalnaker. Pragmatic presuppositions. In *Context and Content: Essays on Intentionality in Speech and Thought*, Oxford Cognitive Science Series, pages 47–62. Oxford University Press, 1999.

[Sta04] Robert C. Stalnaker. Assertion revisited: On the interpretation of two-dimensional modal semantics. *Philosophical Studies*, pages 299–322, 2004.

---

[5] For a good overview of the different actually available theories based on the idea of reference under perspective see [Kle99].

A Model of Flexible Control in Task Switching

Adam Chuderski (achud@emapa.pl)
Institute of Psychology, Jagiellonian University
3 Al. Mickiewicza, 31-120 Cracow, Poland

Abstract

The paper presents an ACT-R model of task switching, which implements flexible mechanism of control over task rules, that adapts to the level of task change predictability. In predictable task switching situations, the model loads relevant task rules into an easily accessible focus of attention (simulated with an ACT-R goal buffer). However, when tasks change randomly, such strategy would lead to long recovery from incorrect rules already loaded into the focus. So, during unpredictable task changes the model always retrieves relevant task rules from its declarative memory. Two experiments were administered to test assumptions of the model: one required predictable switching while the other imposed some level of unpredictability. The model aptly simulated the pattern of switch trial RTs from both studies, and it also replicated constant RTs of repeat trials in fully predictable conditions, as well as decreasing RTs of repeat trials in less predictable conditions.

Introduction

Due to the processes of cognitive control humans are able to behave in a goal-driven and not in stimulus-driven way. When the control fails, as in some neuropsychological deficits, people produce numerous lapses and errors (Shallice, 1988). Especially, mechanisms of control seem to be crucial for correct processing in new or highly distracting situations. Several experimental paradigms are used for examination of the nature of executive control processes. For example, task switching is believed to strongly engage cognitive control (Monsell, 2003).

Most of psychological research on task switching is focused on factors influencing *switch costs*: longer latencies (and, often, higher error rates) in trials following changes of a task (*switch trials*) in comparision to trials when a task was repeated (*repeat trials*). Although some researchers (Allport & Wylie, 2000) believe that switch costs do not reflect involvement of cognitive control, and some others even doubt if the control is needed for switching at all (Logan & Bundesen, 2003), analysis of patterns of task switching costs remains one of the main methods for examination of control processes. Thus, the proper estimation of switch cost values seems to be crucial.

However, such an estimation depends strongly on whether a switch was completed during switch trial (i.e., after switch trial a subject is fully prepared for executing a new task) or was not completed (i.e., a subject requires one or more repeat trials to complete the preparation process). In the former case, a difference in RT between a switch trial and a first repeat trial should capture all latency of a switching

process and thus RTs of all the consecutive repeat trials should reflect only time (constant on average) needed to execute the very task. In the latter case, the first repeat trial RT reflects in some part a switching process latency as well, so responses in consecutive repeat trials may get shorter. Then, the switch cost may not reflect the full duration of control process.

Closer examination of task switching studies shows that there are significant differences between some studies in respect to how complete a switching process is. These differences strongly depend on experimental paradigms used. When a sequence of tasks is predictable (for example, AABB or AAAABBBB; as in alternating-runs paradigm, Rogers & Monsell, 1995) reactions for all repeat trials following the switch trial usually do not differ in latency. In random task sequences, when each stimulus is cued with information indicating the proper task, second repeat trial is usually faster than the first repeat trial (Milán, Sanabria, Tornay, & González, 2005). This indicates that when tasks change on random, the involvement of control processes in switching may not be limited to switch trials only.

Monsell, Sumner, and Waters (2002), in order to compare task switching paradigms, used in a single experiment both predictable and random task sequences. RTs in consecutive repeat trials were constant in predictable task sequence condition, but they were decreasing in random sequences. Authors explained the observed effect in terms of attenuation of cognitive control in random switching. According to them, "if the next switch is likely, participants to some degree voluntarily attenuate or restrain the increment in readiness that would otherwise result from one performance of a task" (ibidem, p. 340). The attenuation of control is fragile: after two or three task repeat trials in random sequence, even if a subjective probability of switch is high, subjects' endogenous control of readiness is overwhelmed and they quickly reach its maximal level.

Above mentioned explanation sounds reasonable, but it does not propose any precise mechanism of cognitive control responsible for changing the level of readiness. The aim of this paper is to describe a computational model of task switching, which specifies in detail the operation of cognitive processes in both low and highly predictable task switching situations. The model will be successfully fitted to data gathered from two experiments.

Computational Models of Task Switching

Several mathematical models of task switching have been proposed in literature (e.g., De Jong, 2000; Logan & Bundesen, 2003; Meiran, 2000; Yeung & Monsell, 2003).

Among computational models, which seem to be an especially promising method for understanding cognitive processes involved in task switching (Monsell, 2003), there exist both connectionist (Gilbert & Shallice, 2002) and symbolic models. The latter are mainly implemented within two leading cognitive architectures (EPIC: Kieras, Meyer, Ballas, & Lauber, 2000; ACT-R: Altmann & Gray, 1999; Sohn & Anderson, 2001).

EPIC architecture (Kieras et. al., 2000) is a modular production system that simulates cognition in parallel process of matching productions (representing well-learned knowledge about a task) with contents of working memory (WM, representing knowledge on a current state of the task). Productions change contents of WM, so in a next cycle new productions can be matched to WM. When more than one production may be fired, cognitive control has to be involved: executive productions are run to schedule task-specific productions and/or resolve conflicts among them.

Based on EPIC assumptions, Rubinstein, Meyer, and Evans (2001) proposed two-stage executive control process that appropriately configures contents of WM for an incoming task. First stage consists on goal shifting, i.e. putting into WM the information which task is the proper one. Usually, when a cue precisely indicates the task, the goal shifting process may be fully completed before stimulus identification. Switch costs can be significantly reduced with long cue-stimulus intervals (CSI), because with more time it is easier to switch to the proper goal. Second stage – rule activation process – can be run exogenously only, i.e. after stimulus appearance. It is assumed, that in order to avoid interference caused by the same stimuli used for all tasks, subjects activate proper rules by adding or activating them in WM, while deleting or deactivating incorrect ones. In the first trial of a task, after stimulus identification, adequate rule is activated in time reflected in additional latency of this switch trial. In repeat trials, as there is no change in a task, no rule activation is needed. Therefore, latency of all repeat trials is similar, reflecting only time needed for rule application and movement production. The rule activation process may be responsible for a common observation that although with long CSIs the switch cost is reduced, it is not eliminated (the cost that cannot be further reduced is called *residual*).

Following Rubinstein at al.'s (2001) theoretical proposal, Kieras et al. (2000) implemented an EPIC model of task switching that removed irrelevant and loaded relevant goals and rules from/into WM. Although authors do not present simulation data on repeat trials beyond the first one, it can be deduced that simulated response latencies would be constant for succesive task repetitions, as task rules are loaded into WM and can be accessed in constant time.

ACT-R cognitive architecture is also implemented as a production system (Anderson et al., 2004). It differs from EPIC in two major attributes. First, resolution of conflicts is not based on strategic productions, but on built-in rule selection mechanism, that runs only one (usually optimal) production at a time. Second, ACT-R includes numerical parameters assigned to all symbolic structures, which modulate cognitive processing. For example, in ACT-R declarative memory, an activation level is assigned to each memory chunk. The higher chunk's activation value is, the greater probability and shorter latency of its retrieval are.

Sohn and Anderson (2001) proposed an ACT-R model of task switching. The model can prepare for the task (if it is known in advance) by loading into system's focus of attention (the goal buffer) a representation indicating the task. This is a similar operation to goal shifting in EPIC model. The main difference between both proposals is that ACT-R model does not load any task rules into the goal buffer. At each trial, the proper rule is retrieved from declarative memory. After each retrieval, a level of a rule's activation rises and on the next trial this rule can be retrieved faster. Although the autors did not present data on repeat trials beyond the first one, it may be deduced that latencies would be shorter for successive task repetitions.

A Model of Flexible Control in Task Switching

The model proposed in this paper integrates both presented mechanisms of task rules activation. We assume that, when a task sequence is predictable, it is optimal to load task rules into the focus of attention of WM, i.e. the most active and easily accessible part of WM (Cowan, 1995; Oberauer, 2002). If rules are already in the focus, they become the most active representations within cognitive system and they can be applied very fast. No effects of facilitation will be observed, as their activation is at ceiling. So, if task switches are predictable, the model loads proper rules into its focus of attention, like the model by Kieras et al. (2000).

However, in random task sequence situation, loading rules into the focus of attention may not be the optimal strategy. If the task suddenly changed while inproper rules are in the focus, the cognitive system would not be prepared for a new task. Highly active but inproper rules would probably lead to a slower access to less activated proper rules. So, during unpredictable task changes it is probably better to hold in the focus only information that identifies which task to perform, while keeping all task rules in working memory area outside the focus, at similar activation levels (Meiran, 2000). Although access to these rules will be slower, and they will be subject to decay and interference to a greater extend, the cognitive system will not suffer from unpredictable task changes so much as when focusing on inproper rules. So, if task switches are unpredictable, the model keeps all rules in active part of memory outside a focus, like model by Sohn and Anderson (2001).

Thus, our model, which is implemented in ACT-R architecture, assumes that *the control mechanism over task rules may be flexibly adapted to the level of predictability of a task switching situation by changing the mode of access to task rules*. This novel assumption is implemented with two mechanisms:

(1) a monitoring process estimating the level of task change predictability on a basis of both cues and stimuli,

(2) a rule loading process which, if the monitoring process allows (i.e. when the task to come has been identified), loads the proper task rule into the goal buffer and turns off the monitoring process.

Description of the Model

The model is able to switch between two tasks, one that requires responding to two-digit numbers greater than 50 (and witholding responses to numbers less than 50), and the other that requires responding to even numbers (and witholding responses to odd numbers). We used go/no-go methodology in order to keep the model very simple. For example, we did not have to model response choice process.

The representation of both tasks in declarative memory consists of four chunks: two reflecting task names: (task even) and (task greater), and two reflecting the pattern of stimuli that requires manual reaction: (even X0 X2 X4 X6 X8) and (greater 5X 6X 7X 8X 9X), where X stands for any digit. Task names and task rules for the same task are mutually associated (this association is probably acquired by subjects during training). When a task name chunk is loaded into the goal buffer, ACT-R propagates some source activation from the goal to a respective task rule chunk. In a foreknowledge condition (when a cue that identifies an incoming task is being presented before presentation of a first stimulus in a new task), the proper task name chunk may be loaded into the goal buffer, and all source activation is being spread to the associated rule. In a no-foreknowledge condition (when there is no cue), both task names are loaded into the goal buffer, as both tasks are equally probable. Source activation is divided between both task rules. Due to activation decay and noise, in a proportion of trials task rules may not be properly retrieved, causing errors of omission. The model includes also eight productions:

(1) *Encode Stimulus*: if a stimulus is being presented this production makes a memory trace for each of its digits.

(2) *Retrieve Rules*: if the task name(s) is(are) in the goal buffer, it retrieves associated task rule(s). If monitoring production (6) allows, it loads the task rule into the goal buffer and blocks production (6). So, after loading, production (2) does not need to access declarative memory. When the rule is loaded, production (4) is run in a next ACT-R cycle.

(3) *Retrieval Failure*: if no rule can be retrieved it hands control over to the production (1).

(4) *Categorize*: it applies currently retrieved task rule to a stimulus chunk and runs production (5).

(5) *Compare*: it compares in parallel all patterns in task rule to a stimulus chunk, and runs production (7), if a stimulus fills any pattern.

(6) *Monitor*: on a stimulus categorization, it checks whether any task rule may be loaded into the goal buffer and may replace a task name. To allow for loading the proper rule into the goal buffer, it requires any stimulus if there is one task name in the buffer (i.e., in a foreknowledge condition), and it requires a target if there are two task names (i.e., no-foreknowledge).

(7) *Press Button*: it just stores reaction time for a trial.

(8) *Wait*: if there is no stimulus on a screen or a stimulus is already categorized, the model waits for 100 ms.

Productions (2) and (6) are control processes regulating in a feedback loop access to task rules, and blocking each other depending on a perceived level of predictability. Switch cost values generated with the model depend on whether and for how long production (2) accesses declarative memory.

Experiment 1

Experiment was designed to test whether subjects' behavior in predictable task switching situation would be consistent with the model's predictions. Three hypotheses were tested. Most important, a position of a repeat trial in a sequence was manipulated (1 to 3). We expected that RTs in repeat trials on all positions should not differ significantly. Of course, we expected longer RTs for switch trials.

Second, we tested if the switch cost can be reduced or even eliminated. In Gonzáles, Milán, Pereda, and Hochel (2005) if subjects emitted an extra response just before a switch trial the residual switch costs were eliminated. We expected similar effect when presenting to subjects, just before a switch trial, a neutral stimulus that does not require any response, but requires a categorization process. In such a case the model assumes a boost in task rules activation, which should lead to reduction in relevant chunk retrieval latency, and in consequence, in reduced RT.

Third, we manipulated foreknowledge on an incoming task. In a foreknowledge condition, a cue indicated the proper task. In a no-foreknowledge condition there was no cue and the first target stimulus indicated the proper task. The model predicts that in the latter condition switch costs will be higher, as subjects will not load the goal of processing ('task name') before the first target presentation.

Method

Subjects 35 college students (25 men, one excluded due to low accuracy) were examined (subjects were 18-31 yrs old).

Tasks Two-digit numbers were used as stimuli for both tasks. Two tasks were used: "greater than 50" and "even". Odd numbers above 52 were used as targets for the former, while even numbers below 50 were used as targets for the latter. Odd numbers below 50 were non-targets for both tasks. Even numbers above 50 were not used at all. In a single sequence of stimuli, all targets belonged to the same category. Subjects were to press a button if they identified a target, and withhold it when a non-target was presented.

Design A position of a target in the sequence was the first manipulated variable: always four targets were presented in the sequence. The first target trial was considered as a switch trial, next target trials were repeat trials. In one half of the trials, fifth target was also shown, but responses to it were not analysed. It was only aimed to keep subjects vigilant during the fourth target trial. Between each pair of targets, one or two (on random) non-targets were presented.

Priming with a neutral stimulus constituted the second independent variable: in one half of sequences a non-target number was presented before the first target. The non-target did not carry any information on the proper task, and thus served as a neutral prime.

A foreknowledge on an incoming task was the third manipulated variable. In one half of sequences a cue informed which task is the proper one for an incoming sequence of stimuli ("EVEN" or "GREATER", in Polish). In the other half of sequences (i.e., in no-foreknowledge condition), the cue just reminded that one of two tasks may occur ("EVEN or GREATER" or "GREATER or EVEN", on random, in Polish). Subjects were informed that in no-foreknowledge condition the first target indicates the proper task to be performed (i.e., three or four targets following the first one would belong to the same number category).

Apparatus and Stimuli Stimuli (37 × 50 mm in size) were presented on a screen of a laptop computer. Each sequence started with a cue presented for 500 ms. After the cue, "**" stimulus was presented for 2000 ms in no-priming condition. In the priming condition, "**" was presented for 1000 ms, and then a non-target prime was presented for 900 ms, followed by the mask ("##") shown for 100 ms. Then the first target was presented, followed by non-targets and repeat trial targets, each one presented for 900 ms + 100 ms for the mask (see Fig.1). Subjects switched on random to one of two tasks from another task: "greater than 50 and even", that inluded even numbers above 50 as targets.

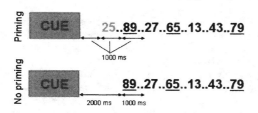

Figure 1: Sample sequences of stimuli in both priming and no-priming conditions. Targets underlined, prime in gray.

Procedure Subjects were examined in groups of two or three. Several training and 80 experimental sequences were presented to each subject (conditions randomly intermixed).

Data Collection Subjects responded with an index finger, pressing a mouse button. Not pressing the button during a target or a mask presentation was recorded as an error of omission. Responding during non-target presentation was taken as a false alarm error and signaled with a beep. We were mainly interested in mean latency of correct responses dependent variable. With task requirement to respond within presentation time of a target and a mask (1000 ms on total) very long responses (outliers) were naturally eliminated.

Results and Discussion

Foreknowledge and priming influenced accuracy only for switch trials: $F(3,32) = 20.74$, $p < 0.001$; $F(3,32) = 6.95$,

$p < 0.001$, respectively (Figure 2, dashed lines). Mean false alarms rate was low (6.92%) and is not analysed here.

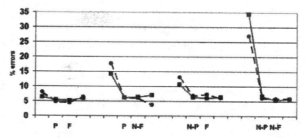

Figure 2: Observed (black dashed lines) and simulated (grey solid lines) error rates (%) in four experimental conditions (P stands for priming, F – for foreknowledge, N- for "no-").

Response latency data are presented in Figure 3 (dashed lines). There is switch versus repeat trial main effect, $F(3,31) = 69.19$, $p < 0.001$, but no significant difference in latency of consecutive repetitions ($p > 0.1$; 453, 451, 457 ms, respectively). Thus, at least within the paradigm used here, no effect of speeding up repeat trials was observed.

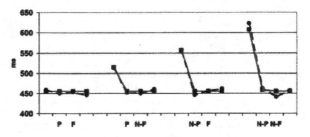

Figure 3: Observed (black dashed lines) and simulated (grey solid lines) latencies (ms) in four experimental conditions.

Both factors of foreknowledge and priming interacted with target position: informative cues as well as primes decreased response latency exclusively in the first trial, $F(3,32) = 20.74$, $p < 0.001$; $F(3,32) = 6.95$, $p < 0.001$, respectively. These two factors additively influenced switch cost: no significant three-way interaction was observed ($p = 0.090$). Priming facilitated cognitive processing, no matter whether subjects did or did not know which task to perform. In foreknowledge-priming condition, the switch cost was practically eliminated (9 ms), switch and repeat trial latencies did not differ significantly ($p > 0.1$). Lack of priming added ~100 ms to the switch cost, lack of foreknowledge added another ~50 ms. Mean latencies in each experimental condition, compared to average repeat trial RT (each compared difference constitutes a respective switch cost), are presented in Figure 4.

All hypotheses were confirmed: we observed switch cost, but limited only to the first trial in a sequence. This cost was eliminated with priming, but only in foreknowledge condition. Lack of foreknowledge on an incoming task made switch costs significantly longer.

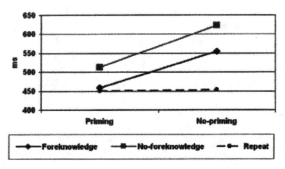

Figure 4: Response latency (ms) in switch trials in four experimental conditions compared to repeat trials.

Data Simulation

To test the model, data from the experiment presented above were simulated in 2000 Monte Carlo runs for each condition. Five parameters influencing model's simulated accuracy were set. Two were optimized to get the best fit: declarative memory activation noise (0.12) and chunk retrieval threshold (0.15). Three parameters were set to arbitrary but reasonable values: strength of associations between task names and task rules (0.5), probability of failed loading of a task rule into the goal buffer (0.12), and a probability of failed categorization of a stimulus (0.12). The fit (presented in Figure 2) was good, R^2 equaled to 0.897.

The crucial test of the model was fitting of response latencies. Values of two additional parameters that are used by ACT-R to translate chunk activation units into latency of chunk retrieval were optimized: latency factor (0.38) and latency exponent (2.8). Standard ACT-R value of productions latency was used (50 ms). Summary duration of perception processes and motor response, not influencing R^2, was set to a reasonable value of 300 ms. The fit of observed and simulated latency patterns was very good (R^2 = 0.983). The model replicated non-trivial effect of error-latency asymmetry in no-priming-foreknowledge, and priming-no-foreknowledge conditions: error rate in switch trials was higher in the former than in the latter condition, but the reverse is true for latencies (see: Fig. 3).

Experiment 2

In the simulation presented above, the model always produced answers for repeat trials with the proper task rule loaded into the goal buffer, as always task sequence became predictable after presentation of the first target. It is interesting to test the model against data acquired in less predictable conditions, when we may expect faster consecutive repeat trials. The computerized switching test from Experiment 1 was used, but only in the no-foreknowledge condition, and with several alterations. The main change consisted on not informing subjects that the first target indicated the task in the whole sequence (although the first and consecutive targets indeed belonged to the same task). As the change made the test more difficult, both stimulus' and mask's presentation times were prolonged, as well as a cue presentation time. In

consequence of longer stimulus presentation time, the cue-stimulus interval was made longer. Trial's length was shortened, now each trial included three targets. All other experimental conditions were the same as in Experiment 1.

Method

Subjects 73 college students were examined (their demographic data are lost, unfortunately).

Tasks The same tasks and response rules were used as in Experiment 1.

Design A position of the target in a sequence was the first manipulated variable: this time three targets were presented in each sequence. Priming was the second independent variable: in one half of sequences a non-target stimulus was presented before the first target.

Apparatus and Stimuli They were identical as in Experiment 1, except for the following. Each sequence started with a cue ("EVEN or GREATER"/"GREATER or EVEN", in Polish) presented for 3000 ms. After the cue, stimulus "**" was presented for 2400 ms in no-priming condition, and for 1200 ms in priming condition. Stimuli were presented in 1000 ms pace (and each one was followed by a 200 ms mask).

Procedure and Data Collection They were indentical as in Experiment 1.

Results and Discussion

Due to very low error rates, only latency data are presented. Again, an interactive effect of priming and target position occured: a non-target reduced a mean latency only for the switch trial, $F(2,71) = 167.97; p < 0.001$, but it did not eliminate residual switch cost. The main hypothesis was confirmed: response latency for the third target position in a sequence was significantly shorter (22 ms) than for the second one, $F(1,72) = 47.92; p < 0.001$.

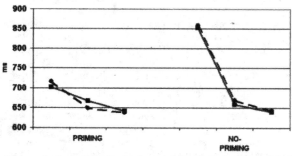

Figure 5: Latencies (ms) observed in Experiment 2 (black dashed lines) and simulated (grey solid lines).

Data Simulation

Because neither cues nor targets yielded any information on a task, the monitoring process never allowed for loading task rules into the goal buffer. In comparision to

Experiment 1 data simulation, we changed two parameters: latency factor (0.55) and the intercept value (480 ms). This was nessesary due to longer cue and stimuli presentation times used in Experiment 2. The simulated data fitted observed data very well ($R^2 = 0.982$). Most important, an effect of repetition facilitation was replicated, as shown in solid lines in Figure 5.

Summary and Conclusions

The presented model is a preliminary proposal of the cognitive control mechanism responsible for different behavior in task switching situations with low and high levels of task changes predictability. The model integrates assumptions of two leading (ACT-R and EPIC) task switching models. It is based on the hypothesis, that the control mechanism over task rules may be flexibly adapted to the level of predictability of a task switching situation by changing the mode of access to task rules. If the task changes are predictable, the model loads relevant task rules into its easily accessible focus of attention. When the changes are less predictable, it always retrieves these rules from declarative memory outside the focus. Although such an access mode is slower, it grants that rules for all (equally possible) tasks are available to the same extend. With nine free parameters set, the model aptly predicted 38 data points (16 for accuracy + 22 for latency), that were gathered in two experiments, which probably differed in subjects' perception of task changes predictability level (in case of latency $R^2 = .982$ and .983, respectively).

The hypothesis on flexible nature of cognitive control engaged in task switching allows for integration of data observed in two most popular task switching experimental paradigms (namely, alternating-runs and explicit cueing), and sheds light on cognitive mechanisms of control processes involved in switching. However, the model is still very simple, and it certainly has to be developed and tested in more complex task switching situations than those presented in this paper, especially in the experimental situations involving two or more possible reactions, univalent stimuli, and tasks more mutually differing than the ones exploited in this research.

Acknowledgments

The presented work is a part of the author's doctoral dissertation supervised by Edward Nęcka. The author thanks also Kamila Śmigasiewicz and Zbigniew Stettner for comments on an earlier draft of this paper.

References

Altmann, E. M., Gray, W. D. (1999). An integrated model of set shifting and maintenance. [in:] N. Taatgen, J. Aasman (ed.), *Proceedings of the 3rd International Conference on Cognitive Modelling*. Veenendaal: Universal Press, 17-24.

Anderson, J. R., Bothell, D., Byrne, M. D., Douglass, S., Lebiere, C., & Qin, Y. (2004). An integrated theory of the mind. *Psychological Review, 111*, 1036-1060.

Cowan, N. (1995*). Attention and memory: An integrated framework.* New York: Oxford University Press.

De Jong, R. (2000). An intention-activation account of residual switch costs. [in:] J. Driver., & S. Monsell. (eds.) *Control of Cognitive Processes, Attention, and Performance XVIII*. Cambridge, MA: MIT Press, 357-375.

Gilbert, S., Shallice, T. (2002). Task switching: A PDP model. *Cognitive Psychology, 44*, 297-337.

Gonzáles, A., Milán, E. G., Pereda A., & Hochel M. (2005). The response-cued completion hypothesis and the nature of residual cost in regular switch. *Acta Psychologica, 120*, 327-341.

Kieras, D. E., Meyer, D. E., Ballas, J. A., Lauber, E. J. (2000). Modern computational perspectives on executive mental processes and cognitive control: Where to from here?. [in:] Monsell S., Driver J. (ed.) *Control of Cognitive Processes. Attention and Performance XVIII*. Cambridge MA, MIT Press, 681-712

Logan, G. D., Bundesen, C. (2003). Clever homunculus: Is there an endogenous act of control in the explicit task-cuing procedure? *Journal of Experimental Psychology: Human Perception and Performance, 29*, 575-599.

Meiran, N. (2000). Modeling cognitive control in task-switching. *Psychological Research 63*, 234-249.

Milán, E. G., Sanabria, D., Tornay, F., González, A. (2005). Exploring task-set reconfiguration with random task sequences. *Acta Psychologica, 118*, 319-331.

Monsell, S. (2003). Task switching. *Trends in Cognitive Sciences, 7*, 134-140.

Monsell, S., Sumner, P., Waters, H. (2003). Task-set reconfiguration with predictable and unpredictable task switches. *Memory & Cognition, 31*, 327-342.

Oberauer, K. (2002). Access to information in working memory: Exploring the focus of attention. *Journal of Experimental Psychology: Learning, Memory, and Cognition, 28*, 411-421.

Rogers, R. D., Monsell, S. (1995). Costs of a predictable switch between simple cognitive tasks. *Journal of Experimental Psychology: General, 124*, 207-231.

Rubinstein, J. S., Meyer, D. E., Evans, J. E. (2001). Executive control of cognitive processes in task switching. *Journal of Experimental Psychology: Human Perception, and Performance, 27*, 763-797.

Shallice, T. (1988). *From neuropsychology to mental structure*. Cambridge: Cambridge University Press.

Sohn, M., Anderson, J. R. (2001). Task preparation and task repetition: Two component model of task switching. *Journal of Experimental Psychology: General 130*, 764-778.

Yeung, N., Monsell, S. (2003). Switching between task of unequal familiarity: The role of stimulus-attribute and response-set selection. *Journal of Experimental Psychology: Human Perception and Performance, 29*, 455-465.

A Generalization of Hebbian Learning in Perceptual and Conceptual Categorization

Harry E. Foundalis (harry@cogsci.indiana.edu)
Center for Research on Concepts and Cognition, Indiana University
Bloomington, IN 47408, USA

Maricarmen Martínez (m.martinez97@uniandes.edu.co)
Department of Mathematics, Universidad de los Andes
Bogotá, Colombia

Abstract

An algorithm for unsupervised competitive learning is presented that, at first sight, appears as a straightforward implementation of Hebbian learning. The algorithm is then generalized in a way that preserves its basic properties but facilitates its use in completely different domains, thus rendering Hebbian learning a special case of its range of applications. The algorithm is not a neural network application: it works not at the neural but at the conceptual level, although it borrows ideas from neural networks. Its performance and effectiveness are briefly examined.

Introduction

Traditionally, learning has been considered to be one of the foundational pillars of cognition. In 1949, Donald Hebb expressed the basic idea of *association learning* as follows: when two neurons are physically close and are repeatedly activated together, some chemical changes must occur in their structures that signify the fact that the two neurons fired together (Hebb, 1949). Neuroscientists and cognitive science researchers dubbed this idea "Hebbian learning", and took it to mean that whenever two percepts appear together, we (or animals in general) learn an association between them. The "how" is usually left to algorithms in artificial neural networks (ANN's). James McClelland points out in a recent study that the potential of Hebbian learning has been largely underestimated (McClelland, 2006). McClelland focuses on the neuronal level, but refers also to work at the conceptual level (the focus of the present article); specifically, in *categorization* (e.g., Schyns, 1991) and in self-organizing topological maps (Kohonen, 1982).

In what follows, an algorithm that uses Hebbian learning at the conceptual level is introduced through an example that appears in human cognition. It is then generalized in a way that, while retaining its basic properties, makes it applicable to problems that involve the detection (and hence the learning) of sets of entities that are most closely related to each other.

The Basic Algorithm

Suppose we are given input consisting of a pair of elements, i.e., a drawing depicting some familiar objects, and a phrase with identifiable words, the meaning of which is unknown (Figure 1). The phrase is supposed to be "about" the objects, their properties, and/or relations. The problem is to find the correct associations between words and percepts; or, stated otherwise, to learn the *meaning* of the words (in some rudimentary sense of the word "meaning"[1]).

nae triogon aems es nae cycol

Figure 1: A drawing, and its associated phrase

The drawing in Figure 1 shows two familiar geometric objects, and the phrase is given underneath the objects in italics. The learner is not expected to know any words for these objects or their properties in some other language; indeed, the phrase might originate from what will turn out to be the learner's native language.[2] The learner will receive a number of such examples, pairing visual and linguistic data, and the algorithm described below will discover the correct associations between words and visual percepts. This problem has been examined also by Deb Roy (Roy, 2002), but Roy's learning succeeds by batch processing, whereas the learning described in the present article is incremental.

Suppose the learner is capable of perceiving some objects, features, and/or relations — collectively called *percepts* — by looking at the visual input, which activate corresponding *concepts* in long-term memory (LTM). Also, the learner can identify (i.e., separate from each other) the words in the given phrase.[3] In reality, an infant learning a language will not identify all the words in a phrase, but it does not harm the generality of our algorithm to assume so.

As a first — perhaps naïve — step in our effort to discover which word corresponds to which percept, let us adopt the following simplistic strategy: associate every concept with every word. Figure 2 depicts this idea. LTM concepts that were activated by percepts in the input are listed on the top row, and the words of the given phrase are added to LTM and shown on the bottom row. Notice that

---

[1] Contrary to our simplifying assumption, in reality words and percepts are not associated according to a 1–1 correspondence.
[2] However, infants do not become native speakers by hearing phrases that refer to geometric objects. What is described here is an abstraction of a real-world situation.
[3] Thus, suppose the "word-segmentation problem" is solved.

each word is shown only once (for instance, *"nae"*, which is repeated in the input, is not repeated in Figure 2).

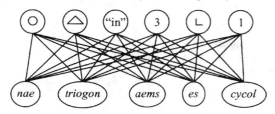

Figure 2: First uninformed step in the algorithm

The top row of nodes in Figure 2 shows only *some* of the LTM concepts that could be activated by the input; specifically, "circle", "triangle", "in", "three-ness", "right angle", and "one-ness". A look by a different agent (or by the same agent at a different time) might activate different concepts, such as "round", "surrounds", "slanted line", etc. Those shown in Figure 2 are the ones that happened to be activated most strongly in the given learning session.

Next, the learning session continues with a second pair of visual and linguistic input.

doy triagon, ot nae ainei scelisoes

Figure 3: A second pair of visual and linguistic input

The image in Figure 3 activates again some concepts in LTM, some of which were activated also by the input of Figure 1 (e.g., "triangle"). Linguistically, there are some old and new words. Also, one word looks very much like an old one (*"triagon"* vs. *"triogon"*). A suitable word-identification algorithm would not only see the similarity, but also analyze their morphological difference, which would later allow the agent to make an association between this morphological change and the visual percept that was responsible for the change. But at this stage no handling of morphology is required by the algorithm; suffice it to assume that the two words, *"triagon"* and *"triogon"*, are treated as "the same".

The algorithm now adds the new concepts to the list at the top (that is, it forms the union of the sets of the old and new concepts) and the new words to the list at the bottom.

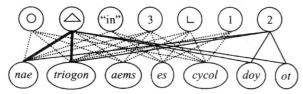

Figure 4: Some associations are reinforced

For lack of horizontal space, only a few of the new words and concepts are shown in Figure 4. The important development in Figure 4 is that those concept–word pairs that are repeated in inputs 1 and 2 (such as △ – *"triogon"*

and △ – *"nae"*) have their associations *reinforced* (shown in Figure 4 with bold lines), whereas the associations of those pairs of input 1 that did not co-occur in input 2 have *faded* slightly (shown in Figure 4 with dotted lines). At the same time, as before, the added words and concepts form all possible associations (lines of normal thickness).

The expectation is now clear: given more instances of paired visual and linguistic input (not too many — at most a few dozen) the "correct" associations (i.e., those intended by the input provider) should prevail, while those that are "noise" (unintended) should be eliminated, having faded beyond some detection threshold.

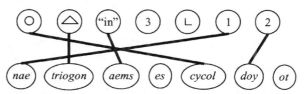

Figure 5: Desired (final) set of associations

Figure 5 shows an approximation of the desired result of this procedure. (There will be many more concepts and words introduced on the two rows of nodes, and most, but not all associations will be "correct": there will be spurious associations that did not fade to the point of elimination.)

Activations of Associations

For the above-outlined algorithm to converge to the desired associations, a precise mechanism of association fading and reinforcement must be established. If the associations fade too fast, for example, they will all be eliminated before additional evidence arrives making them strong enough to survive to the end of the process; if they fade too slow, all associations (including "noise") will eventually survive; finally, if a minute degree of fading is allowed even after the system receives no further input (waiting, doing nothing), then given enough time all associations will drop back to zero and the system will become amnesic. To counter these problems, the "strength" of each association, which we call *activation,* is expected to have the following properties.

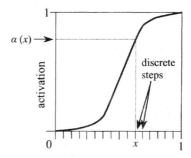

Figure 6: How activation changes over time

The activation of an association is the quantity $\alpha(x)$ on the y-axis of Figure 6. Suppose that, at any point in time, there is a quantity x on the x-axis ranging between 0 and 1, but that can take on values only along one of the discrete points shown on the x-axis. (The total number of these points is an important parameter, to be discussed soon.) Thus, x makes only discrete steps along the x-axis. Then the quantity $\alpha(x)$ is given by the sigmoid-like function α, also ranging between 0 and 1. Below, we explain how and when x moves along the x-axis, and why α must be sigmoid-like.

Activations *fade* automatically, as time goes by. This means that if a sufficient amount of time elapses, x makes one discrete step backwards in its range. Consequently, $\alpha(x)$ is decreased, since α is monotonic. "Time" is usually simulated in computational implementations, but in a real-time learning system it is assumed to be the familiar temporal dimension (of physics).

Activations are *reinforced* by the learning system by letting x make a discrete step forward in its range. Again, the monotonicity of α implies that $\alpha(x)$ is increased. However, when x exceeds a threshold that is just before the maximum value 1, the number of discrete steps along the x-axis is increased somewhat (the resolution of segmenting the x-axis grows). This implies that the subsequent fading of the activation will become slower, because x will have more backward steps to traverse along the x-axis. The meaning of this change is that associations that are well established should become progressively harder to fade, after repeated confirmations of their correctness. The amount by which the number of steps is increased is a parameter of the system.

Finally, an explanation must be given for why α must be sigmoid-like. First, observe that α must be increasing strictly monotonically, otherwise the motion of x along the x-axis would not move $\alpha(x)$ in the proper direction. Now, of all the monotonically increasing curves that connect the lower-left and upper-right corners of the square in Figure 6, the sigmoid is the most appropriate shape for the following reasons: the curve must be initially increasing *slowly,* so that an initial number of reinforcements starting from $x = 0$ does not result in an abrupt increase in $\alpha(x)$. This is necessary because if a wrong association is made, we do not want a small number of initial reinforcements to result in a significant $\alpha(x)$ — we do not wish "noise" to be taken seriously. Conversely, if x has approached 1, and thus $\alpha(x)$ is also close to 1, we do not want $\alpha(x)$ to suddenly drop to lower values; α must be *conservative,* meaning that once a significant $\alpha(x)$ has been established it should not be too easy to "forget" it. This explains the slow increase in the final part of the curve in Figure 6. Having established that the initial and final parts must be increasing slowly, there are only few possibilities for the middle part of a monotonic curve, hence the sigmoid shape of curve α.

Implementation

The above-described principles were implemented as part of *Phaeaco,* a visual pattern-recognition system (Foundalis, 2006), in which the visual input consisted of a 200 × 200 rectangle of black-and-white dots. A "training set" consisted of 50 pairs of the form [image, phrase], where the images were similar to those shown earlier in Figure 1 and Figure 3 (they contained geometric figures), and phrases (in English) were likewise relevant to the content of their paired images. Phaeaco is capable of perceiving the geometric structure of such figures, building an internal representation of the structure in its "working memory" according to its

architectural principles, and letting the parts of this representation activate the corresponding concepts in its long-term memory (LTM). Thus, if a square is drawn in the input, the following concepts might be activated in Phaeaco's LTM: *square, four, four lines, parallel lines, equal lengths, interior, four vertices, right angle, equal angles,* etc. (listed in no particular order). Some of these concepts will be more strongly activated than others, due to the principles in Phaeaco's architecture (e.g., *square* is more "important" than *vertex,* because a vertex is only a part of the representation of a square). Normally, Phaeaco starts with some "primitives", or *a priori* known concepts (such as *point, line, angle, interior,* etc.), and is capable of learning other concepts (such as *square*) based on the primitives.[4] However, for the purposes of the described experiment we suppressed Phaeaco's mechanism of learning new concepts, so as to avoid interference with the learning of associations between words and concepts. Thus, we worked with an LTM that already included composite concepts such as *square, triangle,* etc. — i.e., anything that might appear in the visual input of a training set.

An additional simplifying assumption was that the rudimentary morphology of English was ignored. Thus, words such as "triangle" and "triangles" were treated as identical; so were all forms of the verb "to be", etc.

The entire training set can be found in Martínez (2006).

Performance

The following graph (Figure 7) presents the progress of the learning of correct associations over time.

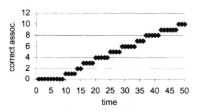

Figure 7: Progress of learning over time

The graph in Figure 7 shows that the average number of correctly learned associations (y-axis) is a generally increasing function with respect to the number of input pairs presented (x-axis). Since the input pairs were presented at regular intervals in our implementation, the x-axis can also be seen as representing time. The y-values are averages of a large number (100) of random presentation orderings of the training set. The gradient of the slope of the curve (the "speed of learning") depends on a variety of factors, including the settings of the activation parameters and the content of the visual and linguistic input. Under most reasonable settings, however, the learning curve appears to slowly increase with respect to time, and this was the main objective of our implementation. In addition, notice that our algorithm requires only one presentation of the training set, as opposed to multiple epochs typically required in ANN's.

---

[4] This learning ability is completely unrelated to the algorithm of learning associations, discussed in the present text.

A Seemingly Different Application

The above-described process can be generalized in an obvious — and rather trivial — way, to any case in which data from two different sets can be paired, and associations between their members can be discerned and learned. For example, consider discovering the cause for an allergy. One set is "the set of all possible pathogens that could cause me this allergy", and the second set has a single member, the event (or fact) "I have this allergy". What is needed is an association of the form "pathogen X causes this allergy to me". We might observe the candidate causes during a long period of time, and *subconsciously* only, without actively trying to discover the cause. Over time, some candidates are reinforced due to repetition, whereas others fade. Given the right conditions (sufficient number of repetitions and not too long an interval of observation time forcing all associations to fade back to zero), we might reach an "Aha!" moment, in which one of the associations becomes strong enough to be noticed consciously.[5] Similarly, some examples of scientific discovery ("what could be the cause of phenomenon X?") can be implemented algorithmically by means of the same process. However, the generalization discussed in what follows goes beyond the pairing of elements of two sets.

Suppose that the input is in the visual modality only, and consists of the shapes shown in Figure 8 (a).

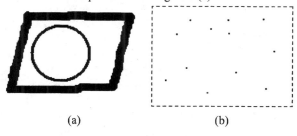

(a)   (b)

Figure 8 (a): Sample visual input; (b): a few pixels seen

Suppose also that a visual processing system examines the black pixels of this input, not in some systematic, top-to-bottom, left-to-right fashion, but randomly. Indeed, this is the way in which Phaeaco examines its input (Foundalis, 2006). After some fast initial processing, Phaeaco has seen a few pixels that belong to the central ("median") region of the parallelogram and/or the circle, as shown in Figure 8 (b).

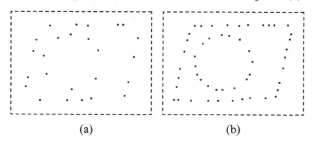

(a)   (b)

Figure 9 (a) – (b): More pixels seen

---

[5] It might be incorrect to make this association, thus concluding the wrong cause, but it is the process that concerns us here.

Shortly afterwards, a few more pixels become known, as shown in Figure 9 (a), where the outlines of the figures are barely discernible (to the human eye). Within similarly short time, enough pixels have been seen — as in Figure 9 (b) — for the outlines to become quite clear, at least to the human eye. What is needed is an algorithm that, when employed by the visual processing system, will make it as capable and fast in discerning shapes from a few pixels as the human visual system. To achieve this, Phaeaco employs the following algorithm.

As soon as the first pixels become known (Figure 8 (b)), Phaeaco starts forming hypotheses about the line segments on which the so-far known pixels might lie (Figure 10).

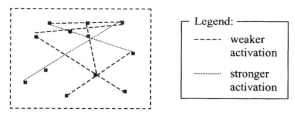

Figure 10: First attempts to "connect the dots" with lines

Most of these hypotheses will turn out to be wrong ("false positives"). But it does not matter. Any of these initial hypotheses that are mere "noise" will not be reinforced, so their activations will fade over time; whereas the correct hypotheses for line segments will endure. Thus, Phaeaco entertains *line-segment detectors,* which are line segments equipped with an activation value. The method of least squares is used to fit points to line segments, and the activation value of each detector depends both on how many points (pixels) participate in it, and how well the points fit. Note that only one of the detectors in Figure 10 is a "real" one, i.e., one that will become stronger and survive until the end (the nearly horizontal one at the top); but Phaeaco does not know this yet.

Subsequently more points arrive, as in Figure 9 (a). Some of the early detectors of Figure 10 will receive one or two more spurious points, but their activations will fade more than they will be reinforced. Also, a few more spurious detectors might form. But, simultaneously, the "real" ones will start emerging (Figure 11).

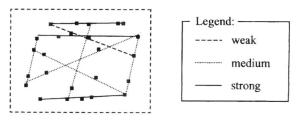

Figure 11: More points keep the detectors evolving

Note that several of the early detectors in Figure 10 have disappeared in Figure 11, because they were not fed with more data points and "died". Thus, the fittest detectors survive at the expense of other detectors that do not explain the data sufficiently well. The last (but not final) stage in this series is shown in Figure 12, below.

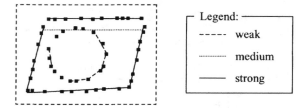

Figure 12: Most of the surviving detectors are "real"

In Figure 12, the desired detectors that form the sides of the parallelogram are among the survivors. Also, the tiny detectors that will be used later to identify the circle have started appearing. In the end, all "true" detectors will be reinforced with more points and deemed *the* line segments of the image, whereas all false detectors will fade and die.

The particular reasons why Phaeaco employs this rather unconventional (randomized) processing of its visual input are explained in Foundalis (2006). For the purposes of the present article it is important to point out that the above procedure is extendible to any case where the detection of the most salient among a group of entities (objects, features, etc.) is required. The reason why this process is similar to the Hebbian association-building will be discussed soon.

Generalizing to Categorization

The process described in the previous section is a specific application of the more general and fundamental process of *categorization*. An example will suffice to make this clear.

Suppose we are visitors at a new location on Earth where we observe the inhabitants' faces. Initially all faces appear unfamiliar, and, having seen only a few of them, we can do no better than place them all in one large category, "inhabitant of this new place", as abstracted in Figure 13.

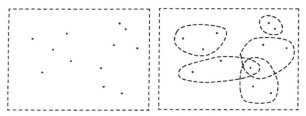

Figure 13: Categorization in abstract space of facial types

Note that the face-space on the left side of Figure 13 includes only two facial dimensions, x and y, since each dot represents a face. In reality the space is multidimensional, and we become capable of perceiving more dimensions as our experience is enriched with examples. An initial stage at categorization is shown on the right side of Figure 13. The dashed outlined regions are detectors of categories, almost identical in nature with the detectors of lines of the previous section. As before, new examples are assigned to the group in which they best fit, statistically. Over time, as more examples become available, the categories that are "noise"

fade, and we end up with a clearer view of the correct categories in this space, as shown in Figure 14. (The space dimensionality has been kept constant, equal to 2, for purposes of illustration.)

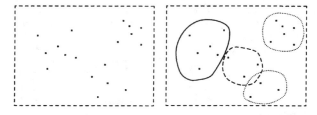

Figure 14: More points help to better discern the categories

The algorithm is described in detail in Foundalis (2006, pp. 228–235). In Phaeaco, categories formed in this way (see Figure 15) are defined by the barycenter ("centroid") of the set, its standard deviation, and a few more statistics. They also include a few of the initially encountered data points. Thus, they are an amalgam of the prototype (Rosch, 1975; Rosch and Mervis, 1975) and exemplar (Medin and Schaffer, 1978; Nosofsky, 1992) theories of category representation, following the principles of the FARG family of cognitive architectures (Hofstadter, 1995).

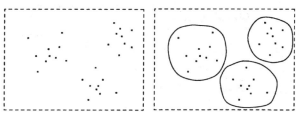

Figure 15: The categories finally become clear

The connection with the earlier discussion of line segment detection should now be clear: the same mechanism can be employed in both cases for the gradual emergence and discerning of the categories, or *concepts,* in the given space. The two cases, perceptual detection of lines and conceptual detection of categories, are very nearly *isomorphic* in nature. In general, the discerning of concepts (of any kind, whether concrete objects or abstract categories), might be thought to rely on a process similar to the one described here. For concrete objects, this process has been completely automated and has been hardwired by evolution, so that very few parameters of it need be learned; for other, more abstract and gradually discerned categories, it might look more like the mechanism outlined above.

Discussion

Two seemingly different case-studies were discussed in the previous sections: a Hebbian-like "association-building by co-occurrences" process, and one of gradual discerning of categories in a multidimensional space. What is the deeper commonality between the two?

Both are about *discerning* entities. In the case of Hebbian learning the entities are the associations, whereas in the other examples mentioned the entities are categories that appear as clusters of objects. The discerning is gradual, and initially there is a lot of "noise" in the form of wrongly detected entities. But over time the "noise" fades away and the correct entities emerge highly activated.

This is an unsupervised learning algorithm, the success of which depends on the appropriate settings of the parameters of the *activations* of entities. Activations (illustrated in Figure 6) must have the following properties:

- The initial increase in activation must be *conservative,* to avoid an early commitment to "noise".
- The activation strength must be fading automatically as time goes by, to avoid having all activations of associations or categories eventually reach the value 1.
- Those associations or categories that appear to stand consistently above others in strength must curb the fading speed of their activations, to avoid forgetting even the most important ones among them over time.

It might be thought that our choice of setting the starting value of an activation to 0 results in a strictly deterministic process. However, this criticism is superficial. Although our model is indeed deterministic, in a real-world situation the order in which the input is encountered is practically never predetermined. Indeterminism arises from the real world. Thus, what is required is that any (random) order allows our algorithm to run, and indeed, in our measurements we varied the input presentation order randomly, observing no dependence of the algorithm on any particular input order.

Although ideas similar to the above have traditionally been viewed as belonging to the neural level that inspired ANN's, our work supports the idea that it is possible that the same principles have been utilized by human cognition at a higher conceptual level. This is not without precedent in material evolution and has been noted also in other scientific disciplines (e.g., physics, chemistry, biology). For example:

- The structure of a nucleus with surrounding material is found in atoms at the quantum level, and in planetary systems and galaxies at the macroscopic level. It is also found in biology in eukaryotic cells, and in animal societies organized around a leading group, with "distances" of individuals from the leader, or leaders, varying according to their social status.
- The notion of "force": in the quantum world, forces are interactions of fermions through the exchange of bosons (e.g., Ford, 2004). Chemically, forces are responsible for molecular structure. In biology, a force is exerted usually by a muscular structure. By analogy, a "force" can be of psychological or social nature.
- The notion of "wave": in the microworld there are waves of matter, or waves of probability; in the macroworld there are waves of sound, fluids, gravity, etc. More abstractly, there are "waves" of fashion, cultural ideas, economic crises, etc.

In a similar manner, we suggest that, through evolutionary mechanisms, cognition abstracted from what was initially employed as a simple association-building mechanism in creatures that appeared early on in evolutionary history to a conceptual categorization method, which finds its most versatile expression and application in human cognition.

References

Ford, Kenneth W. (2004). *The Quantum World*: Harvard University Press.

Foundalis, Harry E. (2006). "Phaeaco: A Cognitive Architecture Inspired by Bongard's Problems". Ph.D. dissertation, Computer Science and Cognitive Science, Indiana University, Bloomington, Indiana.

Hebb, Donald O. (1949). *The Organization of Behavior*. New York: Wiley.

Hofstadter, Douglas, R. (1995). *Fluid Concepts and Creative Analogies: Computer Models of the Fundamental Mechanisms of Thought*. New York: Basic Books.

Kohonen, Teuvo (1982). "Self-organized formation of topologically correct feature maps". *Biological Cybernetics*, no. 43, pp. 59–69.

Martínez, Maricarmen (2006). "Implementation and performance results of the learning algorithm presented at the 2007 European Cognitive Science Conference, Delphi, Greece": http://pentagono.uniandes.edu.co/~mmartinez97/EuroCogSci07

McClelland, James L. (2006). "How Far Can You Go with Hebbian Learning, and When Does it Lead you Astray?". In Y. Munakata and M. H. Johnson (ed.), *Processes of Change in Brain and Cognitive Development: Attention and Performance XXI*, pp. 33–69. Oxford: Oxford University Press.

Medin, D. L. and M. M. Schaffer (1978). "Context theory of classification learning". *Psychological Review*, no. 85, pp. 207-238.

Nosofsky, Robert M. (1992). "Exemplars, prototypes, and similarity rules". In A. Healy, S. Kosslyn and R. Shiffrin (ed.), *From Learning Theory to Connectionist Theory: Essays in Honor of W. K. Estes*, vol. 1 pp. 149-168. Hillsdale, NJ: Erlbaum.

Rosch, Eleanor (1975). "Cognitive representations of semantic categories". *Journal of Experimental Psychology: General*, no. 104, pp. 192-233.

Rosch, Eleanor and C. B. Mervis (1975). "Family resemblance: Studies in the internal structure of categories". *Cognitive Psychology*, no. 7, pp. 573-605.

Roy, Deb K. (2002). "Learning Words and Syntax for a Visual Description Task". *Computer Speech and Language*, vol. 16, no. 3.

Schyns, Philippe G. (1991). "A Modular Neural Network Model of Concept Acquisition". *Cognitive Science*, vol. 15, no. 4, pp. 461–508.

An Unsupervised, Dual-Network Connectionist Model
of Rule Emergence in Category Learning

Rosemary A. Cowell and Robert M. French
LEAD-CNRS, UMR5022, Université de Bourgogne, 21000 Dijon, France
{Rosemary.Cowell, Robert.French}@u-bourgogne.fr

Abstract

We develop an unsupervised "dual-network" connectionist model of category learning in which rules gradually emerge from a standard Kohonen network. The architecture is based on the interaction of a statistical-learning (Kohonen) network and a competitive-learning rule network. The rules that emerge in the rule network are weightings of individual features according to their importance for categorisation. Once the combined system has learned a particular rule, it de-emphasizes those features that are not sufficient for categorisation, thus allowing correct classification of novel, but atypical, stimuli, for which a standard Kohonen network fails. We explain the principles and architectural details of the model and show how it works correctly for stimuli that are misclassified by a standard Kohonen network.

Introduction

The categorisation of objects on the basis of their visual attributes is a cognitive capacity fundamental to our survival. The mechanisms underlying categorisation behavior in humans have been the subject of much theoretical and empirical work, both in adults and infants. Human adults, as well as infants above the age of around a year, are able to categorise objects based not only on the statistical structure of categories of observed objects, but also by making use of rules derived from that structure. Rules have the intrinsic advantage of radically reducing cognitive load: if an object can be categorised by paying attention to only a few of its features, instead of a great many, cognitive resources can be freed up for other tasks.

The ontological status of rules in a connectionist modeling framework has from the outset been a hotly debated topic (Seidenberg & McClelland, 1989; Pinker & Prince, 1988; Chalmers, 1990; Marcus et al., 1999; etc.). In this paper we have chosen a conciliatory point of view — namely, that rules do, indeed, have a distinct ontological status compared to purely statistical-learning mechanisms, but these rules, in general, must *emerge* from the "statistical" learning substrate.

A number of current models of category learning incorporate both a module for statistical learning of category structure and a rule module. The former gradually learns the statistical distributions of the perceptual attributes of objects in the world and uses this knowledge to determine the category membership of newly encountered objects. The rule module, on the other hand, has built-in rules capable of categorising these same objects directly. These models currently include, notably, ATRIUM (Erickson & Kruschke, 1998) and COVIS (Ashby et al., 1998). This distinction between statistical learning and rule-based learning parallels the distinction between exemplar models (Nosofsky, 1988; Kruschke, 1992; etc.) and prototype models (Rosch, 1978; Posner,

1986; etc.) of categorisation, as well as the distinction between implicit and explicit (i.e., verbal) categorisation strategies (Reber, 1967; Ashby et al., 1998, etc.).

It seems reasonable to assume that the acquisition of the rules underlying category structure should be possible through experience with stimuli from those categories. In other words, *it should be possible to extract knowledge of the rule automatically from knowledge about the statistical distribution of the perceptual characteristics of items in each category.* Current connectionist models of category learning that incorporate rule modules typically assume the *a priori* existence of these rules and model their application to the problem of object categorisation. These models do not, however, synthesize the rules themselves. For example, in ATRIUM (Erickson & Kruschke, 1998), the rule module contains an "off-the-shelf" rule for category membership; the stimulus dimension on which the rule is based is hard-wired, and the network must learn which values along that dimension are associated with each category. Similarly, in COVIS (Ashby et al., 1998), several pre-existing rules are hard-wired into the model's rule component and learning of the rule consists of selecting between available rules to find the one most appropriate to the current category structure.

Overview of the model

In what follows we will present a connectionist model of unsupervised category learning. This model consists of two interacting networks: a "statistical" network that learns the distributions of perceptual properties of the stimuli in each category and a "rule" network that derives its rules by continually monitoring the statistical network.

The statistical part of the network is a Kohonen network (Kohonen, 1982, 1993) and the rules emerge from a competitive network that monitors the Kohonen network. The Kohonen network self-organizes the inputs into a map in which representations of stimuli from the same category are clustered together. The competitive network monitors the Kohonen network as category learning proceeds and determines which input features are the most important in — in fact, *sufficient for* — determining category membership. This determination of a feature, or set of features, that is sufficient to determine category membership is what we mean by rule extraction.

We have chosen to implement our Kohonen network in a neurobiologically plausible manner, using leaky integrators, similar to an implementation described by Kohonen (1993). We suggest that processing of this type could occur in visual cortex and that a plausible candidate for the site of the competitive-learning algorithm used to model rule extraction could be pre-frontal cortex.

We will present a simulation that demonstrates the operation of the model. In particular, we will provide an example of an instance in which the statistical-learning component of the model (i.e., the Kohonen network) alone fails to generalise correctly from the learned category structure to a novel, atypical stimulus, whereas the combination of the statistical and rule-learning components of the model (i.e., the Kohonen and competitive learning networks, respectively) succeeds in correctly categorising the same stimulus.

Extraction of a rule

In the everyday categorisation of most commonly encountered classes of objects, the classifier can exploit the fact that the items belonging to a given category are likely to share a number of visual attributes: birds possess feathers, wings and a beak; tables almost always have legs and a flat surface; trees have a trunk, as well as leaves (or needles) during summertime.

A "rule" for category membership has traditionally been defined, in formal logic, as a necessary and sufficient condition — in this case, the presence of certain features in a particular combination — that unequivocally determines category membership. However, it has been recognised at least as far back as Wittgenstein (1951) that very few, if any, real-world categories have membership rules that meet this lofty standard. Therefore we can, in practice, use a "quasi-sufficient" condition for category membership as a "rule" for determining whether a given object is or is not a member of a real-world category. This simply means that, in general, the presence or absence of a particular feature (or set of features) is sufficient for determining category membership.

Rules of this nature might include: animals with feathers or beaks are birds; animals with gills are fish; land animals that weigh more than 5 tons are elephants; animals with opposable thumbs are primates; and so on. And while it is true that opossums, koalas and giant pandas also have opposable thumbs, and that the rule: "If X has a beak, X is a bird" caused early 19th century zoologists to think that duck-billed platypus specimens were a hoax, these rules are generally reliable and, most importantly, can be extracted from the feature statistics of primates and birds. This is precisely what our model does: *it identifies, for each category, the feature(s) whose presence is diagnostic of membership in that category.*

Further, it may well be that no single feature is sufficient for determining category membership, but a unique combination of features, each of which may be shared with other categories, will be sufficient to ensure correct category identification. For example, elephants live on land, as do lots of other animals, and weigh more than five tons, a property possessed by many species of whales. However, the combination of living on land AND weighing more than five tons is sufficient for correct category identification. Our model is also capable of extracting this type of conjunctive combination of features for category identification.

We argue that the emergence of a rule of the above kind is accompanied by a decrease in attention to the non-diagnostic features. And this is why a purely statistical approach to categorisation falls short: it has no ability to weight various features according to their importance to the categorisation task. The rule-network, on the other hand, constantly monitors the statistical network and provides a means of achieving that weighting.

Our model is designed only to learn positive diagnostic rules, e.g. "if X has a beak, X is a bird". One way to teach the system negative diagnostic rules, such as "if X is under 18 X can't vote", would simply be to define explicitly negative categories (in this case, "can't vote"). One potentially more serious limitation is that the model can verify only the conditional statements (if p, then q), and not their contrapositive (if $\sim q$, then $\sim p$). In other words, the system will learn, "If it has trunk, it is an elephant", but cannot check that "if it is not an elephant, it does not have a trunk". Since, technically speaking, verifying the rule requires checking the validity not only of the conditional, but of its contrapositive, our system is not doing traditional rule-learning. However, in terms of the evolution of human cognition, the type of rule learned by the present system, however incomplete from the standpoint of Aristolean logic, would still have provided animals with a significant adaptive advantage over those lacking this mechanism. We therefore suggest that our mechanism is a plausible account of the way in which humans attain at least a subset of the rules they acquire.

The importance of rules

There is evidence that young infants perform categorisation of cats and dogs in a purely bottom-up manner, basing their category discrimination on the statistical distributions of the perceptual characteristics of the two categories (Mareschal, Quinn, & French, 2002; French, Mareschal, Mermillod, & Quinn, 2004). On the basis of this research, it seems likely that, under the age of 3-4 months, infants do not learn rules underlying category structure. Rather, the data seem to indicate that they perform categorisation using a strategy that does not differentiate between features that are simply correlated with category membership and features whose presence or absence can be used to diagnose category membership.

There are at least two ways in which such a strategy might be disadvantageous. First, attending to all perceptual features of stimuli, when the application of a simple rule would suffice for categorization, squanders cognitive resources. Second, and more importantly, a purely bottom-up strategy can lead to misclassification of certain types of novel stimuli.

Consider a person who wishes to sort shirts according to brand. Many features can be used for this sorting, including the quality of the fabric, the quality of the sewing, the number and type of buttons, the presence/absence of a collar, etc. But one day he realizes that if there is a little green crocodile anywhere on the shirt, it is a "Lacoste" shirt. Henceforth, he can identify Lacoste shirts without paying any attention whatsoever to the other features. He has extracted a rule: IF *green crocodile*, THEN *Lacoste*. One day he sees a shirt that unlike any he has seen before: it is made of leather, has pearl buttons and leaves the wearer's navel exposed. But it has a little green crocodile over the left breast. His rule allows him to ignore the other features of the shirt and conclude, albeit with some surprise, that it is a Lacoste shirt.

In short, to go from attending to all features to attending to only a small subset of category-specific diagnostic features, one must learn which features to ignore. During the acquisition of the rule, features associated with several categories must "drop out" of the representation in the rule network. This elimination of features as diagnostic for categorisation signals the emergence of a rule.

Operation of the model

The essence of the present model is the tandem operation of a statistical-learning (Kohonen) network and a rule-extracting network (driven by competitive learning) that continuously monitors the state of the statistical-learning network. The overarching principle of the rule-extracting network is as follows. If a particular input (i.e., feature) unit in the Kohonen network has a high-valued weight connecting it to only one category output node, and small weights to all other category output nodes, then that feature is a defining feature for that category, one which we will refer to as a "diagnostic" feature. For example, in Figure 1 the weight between *beak* and *bird* will become large during training, while the weights between *beak* and any other category node will remain small (because only birds have beaks).

The rule-network consists of a copy of the original Kohonen network in which competition between the weights emanating from each feature node determines which feature nodes are important for categorisation. When a particular feature (e.g., *eyes* in Fig. 1) is shared by a number of categories, the competitive-learning process pushes down the values of all of the weights emanating from the *eyes* feature unit in the rule network, so that *eyes* is not a diagnostic feature for any particular category.

The category response of the network to a given novel stimulus is a linear combination of the output of the statistical (Kohonen) network and the rule network.

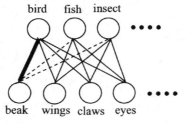

Figure 1. Any animal for which the first feature (*beak*) is active is a *bird*. In the Kohonen weights, the weight between *beak* and *bird* is large, while the *beak-fish*, *beak-insect*, *beak-automobile*, etc. weights are small. This is what the rule-network notices.

Implementation details of the model

The Kohonen network used in our model is a two-layered network with perceptual feature nodes on input and category nodes on output. During learning, neighbouring regions of the output layer are trained to represent stimuli with similar perceptual features, so that representations of similar stimuli cluster together. Thus, if stimuli within a category share many perceptual features, they are "classified" by the Kohonen network as belonging to the same category. The network is implemented using leaky integrators and interneurons to provide neurobiological plausibility, since it has been argued that this type of network exists in visual cortex Kohonen (1993).

Statistical-Learning Network

Kohonen networks are designed to model the type of

neural processing that occurs in mammalian cortex. The Kohonen network in the present model comprises a one-dimensional array of processing units that receives stimulus inputs from the input layer and implements lateral excitation and inhibition between neighbouring units (Figure 2). The weights from input units (feature units) to output units (or category units) are trained by the successive presentation of a number of stimulus inputs; units' weights are incrementally adapted on each presentation via a Hebb-type learning rule. This results in an automatic mapping of stimulus inputs onto a set of representations that possess the same topological order as the stimuli, that is, similar stimuli are represented in neighbouring locations on the output layer.

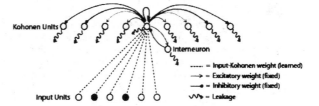

Figure 2: Statistical Learning Component of the Model. For clarity, only 6 units are shown in the input layer; there are 10 input units in the model. All output units are coupled with an interneuron and have lateral connections to all other output nodes. All input units are connected to all output units.

We have attempted to implement the Kohonen network of the present model in a biologically plausible manner; many of the neuron-like properties are illustrated in Figure 2. Lateral interactions are implemented directly between individual output units. Each unit in the output layer receives input from the input layer, from an inhibitory interneuron, and from other collateral units. The activations of units in the output layer are then calculated iteratively and simultaneously, so that each unit's activation evolves according to the input it receives from other units, whose activations are simultaneously being adjusted. Both output units and interneurons are subject to a degree of activation leakage. This was implemented as a set of non-linear differential equations similar to those described in Kohonen (1993).

Rule Network

While other algorithms have been developed (e.g., Thomas, van Hulle, & Vogels, 2000) for determining the relative importance of the weights in a Kohonen network, one of the aims of our model was to implement the rule-network with structures and mechanisms that could conceivably arise in the cortex. Thus, the overarching idea of this network — comparison of (by means of competition between) the synaptic weights in a copy of the statistical-learning network — was implemented by introducing a set of rule units whose activations could be used to implement this competition (see Figure 3). The rule network consists of a copy of the weights of the Kohonen network that lead, not to the category nodes of the Kohonen network, but to a set of rule units. (We acknowledge that there is currently little biological evidence suggesting a precise mechanism by which this copy might be made). The copied weights and rule units are organized so that for each input feature of the Kohonen network there is a "column" of nodes in the rule network, i.e. one node for each Kohonen weight emanating from that feature. The competition between weights emanating from a feature of the Kohonen network is thereafter implemented as competition between the activation levels of units in the corresponding column of nodes in the rule network.

The detailed operation of the rule network is illustrated in Figures 3 and 4. In Figure 3, the manner in which the rule network monitors the Kohonen network is shown. Each weight emanating from an input feature of the Kohonen network to the Category (output) layer corresponds to a node in a column of "rule units" in the rule network. This column can be said to contain the set of rules pertaining to that input feature, e.g. "if feature F, then Category Y". As shown in Figure 3, competition is implemented among units in a given column via lateral weights. The activity of the rule units allows the rule network to determine which weights of the Kohonen network – and therefore which of the input features – are influential in activating the various category units.

Crucially, the mechanism of competition within each column is what causes activation levels of non-diagnostic features to be depressed in the rule network. Assume that a given feature in the Kohonen network sends high-valued weights to numerous category nodes (e.g., the *eyes* feature node in Figure 1). This will result in a high level of activation of the numerous nodes in the column of rule nodes associated with that feature in the rule network. Mutual inhibition within this column will then depress the activations of *all* of the nodes in that feature column. The result will be that this feature will not be perceived by the rule network as diagnostic for any particular category.

The competition between the activated rule units is implemented on every trial, thus the system gradually determines which feature(s) are diagnostic for membership of each category. This diagnostic information must not only be averaged over trials and stored, but must also be available for retrieval by the network. Both of these aims are achieved by developing a set of "rule weights" that link the original feature inputs of the Kohonen network to the rule units. The rule network's stored knowledge can thus be retrieved by passing the input activation through these weights. The input features now feed into two networks: the statistical Kohonen network, as before, and the rule network.

The connectivity shown in Figure 3 (the copy of the Kohonen weights providing input to the rule units) is used to determine the activity of the rule units *during training*. The connectivity shown in Figure 4 – the set of 'rule weights' – is used to determine the activity of the rule units *after training*, and hence to determine the output of the rule extracting component of the model when confronted with novel stimuli. The rule weights are learned by a Hebb-type algorithm that depends on both the input unit activations and the rule unit activations.

The competition for activation within each column of rule units is implemented by each rule unit having a recurrent, excitatory link to itself and inhibitory links to all other units in the column. The activation of rule units is determined first by passing activation from input units to rule units, then by iterating the activations of all rule units in the column through the mutually inhibitory lateral weights for a fixed number of cycles.

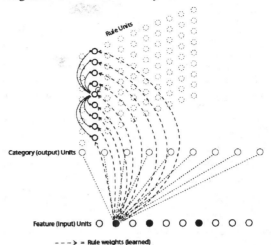

Figure 3: The statistical-learning component of the model is shown at the bottom of the figure and the rule-extracting network is shown above it. The two components share a set of input units. Note the arrangement of the rule units and the connections providing their input (the 'copy' of the Kohonen weights). These connections are employed in determining the activation of the rule units during training, and are instrumental in monitoring the 'knowledge' in the Kohonen network.

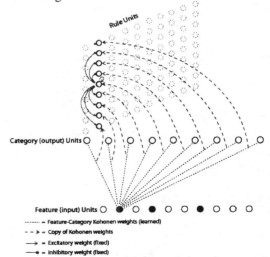

Figure 4: The "rule weights" of the rule network connect the feature units to the rule units. The rule weights are learned via a Hebbian process, which depends on the rule unit activations, which are determined by the connectivity shown in Figure 3.

Input and output

The model is trained with stimuli from three categories of objects. Many exemplars from each category are presented to the Kohonen network. Since, after training, each category becomes associated with a particular region of the Kohonen network output layer, any output unit in this region will be said to "represent" the associated category. (The units in the center of the region are, in general, better representatives of the category than those on the periphery of the region.) The model output can therefore be interpreted as a "choice of category".

During the test phase, the model is presented with a novel stimulus and we consider three different outputs from the system: the response of the statistical learning component alone, the response of the rule network alone, and the linear sum of the responses from both components of the model. For the response of the statistical learning component, we take the most active unit in the output layer of the Kohonen network. To determine the rule-network response, we send the input stimulus activation through the rule weights and sum the activations of the rule units across the columns for each category output node, i.e., there is a *row* of rule units for each category output node. For the "combined" response, the activation of the output units of the Kohonen network is linearly combined with the activation values from the output nodes of the rule network. The greatest combined activation value determines the model's response.

Simulations

Stimuli
Stimuli were represented as an input vector with ten elements (or 'features'). Each feature may be thought of as some real-valued property. All stimuli had two high-valued elements (i.e., features that are present) and eight low-valued elements (i.e., features that are absent). These values differed for each stimuli, but, for example, Category A stimuli always had high values on features 7 and 8 and low values elsewhere. Specifically, each high-

valued feature could take a pre-normalisation value in the range 0.6 to 1, while low-valued features varied between 0 and 0.1. All stimuli were normalised. The stimuli were divided into three categories, A, B, and C, as shown in Figure 5. Categories A and B had an overlapping (and thus non diagnostic) feature: 8. Each category was defined by at least one *sufficient* feature.

We trained the model on the three categories of stimuli and then tested it on a novel, but atypical stimulus. This test item was a stimulus that, because of the presence of a diagnostic feature (10), belonged to category C, but also had perceptual overlap with stimuli from categories A and B because of its (non diagnostic) feature (8).

Method
The model was trained by presenting 200 exemplars from each of the three categories. The weights of the Kohonen network and the rule network were updated on every stimulus presentation. After training, the combined network was presented with an exemplar from each of the three categories to ensure that it classified novel elements of each category correctly (it did). Then, to demonstrate that the network's acquisition of rules actually made a difference in its classification behavior, we tested it on an "atypical" test stimulus. This was a stimulus that contained at least one diagnostic feature that meant that it belonged to a certain category, but also included other "distracter" features that were irrelevant for categorisation. The idea was that, once the network had learned the rule associating that diagnostic feature with a particular category, it would ignore the distracter feature(s) and produce a correct classification. On the other hand, the Kohonen network alone would be misled by the distracters and would misclassify the stimulus.

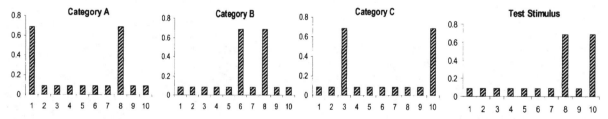

Figure 5. The value of each element in the input vector is shown for a prototypical item from Categories A, B and C, and for the Test Stimulus. Stimulus input vectors are normalised. Note that feature 8 is shared by both Categories A and B and is thus not a diagnostic feature. The test stimulus includes one diagnostic feature (10) for Category C as well as feature (8), which belongs to both Categories A and B.

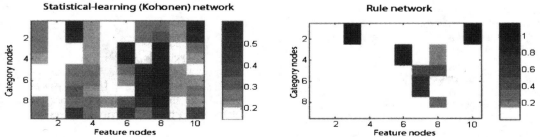

Figure 6. Left: Weight values of the Kohonen network trained on stimuli from categories A, B and C. Right: the rule network has discovered that feature 8 is far less relevant than features 3, 6, 7 and 10 for category determination

Results

As training progressed, exemplars from each of the three categories began to activate consistently the same region of the output layer of the Kohonen network. The diagrams in Figure 6 represent the weight values – from feature nodes to category nodes – of the Kohonen network (on the left) and the rule network (on the right). The pattern of weight values of the Kohonen network shows that Category A items (features 7 and 8 active) are represented by output units 5, 6 and 7), that Category B items (features 6 and 8 active) are represented by output units 3 and 4; and Category C items (features 3 and 10 active) are represented by output units 1 and 2.

Of paramount importance is what happens to feature node 8, a non diagnostic feature shared by items in both Categories A and B. In the Kohonen network, the weights produce — as they should — the activation of category units 3 through 8, the units corresponding to Categories A and B. But when we look at the column of weights for this feature in the rule network, we see that the weights are all low-valued. This has arisen because of the mutual inhibitory competition from the large number of strong feature-to-category weights associated with feature 8 in the Kohonen network. Feature 8 has effectively dropped out of consideration as a diagnostic feature.

The novel test stimulus (Figure 5) has an active feature 10 that makes it a Category C item and also has an active "distracter" feature 8. When this stimulus is presented to the system, the Kohonen network alone classifies it as belonging to Category A, while the rule network alone, as well as the combined rule-and-Kohonen network, classify it correctly as a Category C item.

Conclusion

We have presented a dual-network connectionist model of unsupervised categorisation using two interacting networks: a Kohonen network for extracting statistical information from the input and a competitive-learning network that extracts rule information from the Kohonen network. The addition of the rule network allows the system to correctly categorise novel, but unusual, items that the Kohonen network alone misclassifies.

In addition, preliminary simulations indicate that the model is also able to perform supervised category learning, which leads to an interesting observation. While the model can perform categorisation *with* feedback for stimulus categories with no clustering in stimulus space (e.g. the separable but not clustered categories of Erickson and Kruschke 1998), it can only perform categorisation *without* feedback if the stimuli cluster naturally into categories. This pattern surely echoes human behaviour: in an unsupervised version of Erickson and Kruschke's categorisation task, subjects would not have spontaneously categorised the stimuli according to the experimenter-imposed boundary. Category learning in a natural context generally proceeds with little or no feedback, but, happily, tends to involve categories that are perceptually clustered, at least for living things, making the unsupervised task much easier. This highlights a potentially fundamental difference between artificially constructed, supervised, categorisation tasks, in which categories are not clustered in stimulus space, and the type of category learning behaviour that is exhibited in a natural environment.

Acknowledgments

We acknowledge EC FP6 NEST Grant. 516542. We also thank Denis Mareschal for insightful comments on this work.

References

Ashby, F. G., Alfonso-Reese, L. A., Turken, A. U., & Waldron, E. M. (1998). A neuropsychological theory of multiple systems in category learning.. *Psych. Rev., 105,* 442-481.

Chalmers, D. (1990). Syntactic transformations on distributed representations. *Connection Sci.,* 2, 53-62.

Erickson, M. A. & Kruschke, J. K. (1998). Rules and Exemplars in Category Learning. *JEP:G,* 127, 107-140.

French, R. M., Mareschal, D., Mermillod, M. & Quinn, P. (2004) The role of bottom-up processing in perceptual categorization by 3- to 4-month old infants: Simulations and data. *JEP:G,* 133, 382-397.

Kohonen (1993). Physiological interpretation of the self-organizing map algorithm. *Neural Networks, 6,* 895-905.

Kohonen, T. (1982). Self-organized formation of topologically correct feature maps. *Biological Cybernetics, 43,* 59-69.

Kruschke, J. K. (1992). ALCOVE: An exemplar-based connectionist model of category learning. *Psych. Rev.,* 99, 22-44.

Marcus, G. F., Vijayan, S., Bandi Rao, S., and Vishton, P. M. (1999). Rule-learning in seven-month-old infants. *Science,* 283, 77-80.

Mareschal, D., Quinn, P. C., & French, R. M. (2002) Asymmetric interference in 3- to 4-month-olds' sequential category learning. *Cog. Sci.,* 26, 377-389.

Nosofsky, R. M. (1988). Exemplar-based accounts of relations between classification, recognition and typicality. *JEP:LMC,* 14(4):700–708

Pinker, S. & Prince, A. (1988) On language and connectionism: Analysis of a parallel distributed processing model of language acquisition. *Cognition, 28,* 73-193.

Posner, M.I. (1986). Empirical studies of prototypes. In Craig, C. (ed.) *Noun Classes and Categorization.* John Benjamins, Philadelphia, 53-61

Reber, A. S., (1967) Implicit learning of artificial grammars. *Journal of Verbal Learning and Verbal Behavior,* 6, 855-863.

Rosch, E. 1978 'Principles of categorization', in Rosch & Lloyd (eds) *Cognition and Categorization,* NY: Wiley.

Seidenberg, M.S., & McClelland, J.L. (1989). A distributed developmental model of word recognition and naming. *Psychological Review, 96,* 523-568.

Thomas E., Van Hulle M. & Vogels R. (2000). Encoding of categories by non-category specific neurons in the inferior temporal cortex. *J. Cog. Neuro,* 13:190-200.

Wittgenstein, L. (1951). *Philosophical Investigations.* Translation by G.E.M. Anscombe, Oxford: Blackwell, 1963

Behavioural priors:
Learning to search efficiently in action planning

Aapo Hyvärinen
Dept of Computer Science and HIIT
University of Helsinki, Finland

Abstract

We propose that an important part of planning (model-based reinforcement learning) in a biological agent is to use information on the statistical structure of near-optimal action sequences. Such statistical information can be collected simply by observing the action sequences that the agent has actually performed, assuming that the agent only performs action sequences that are the most optimal ones in a search set. Learning such a prior model for behaviour can be used to direct the search of action sequence to the most relevant parts of the action sequence space, and thus enables more efficient planning. The resulting "behavioural priors" are the behavioural counterpart of perceptual priors that are widely used in Bayesian models of perception.

Introduction

An agent must continuously decide which action to take. Actions move the agent to new states, and the states bring rewards (or punishments, which are considered negative rewards here). The agent is supposed to choose its actions so as to maximize the sum of obtained rewards.

A frequently used framework for learning to act based on rewards is reinforcement learning (RL). A well-known problem with the basic formulation of (model-free) RL is that the reinforcement function is assumed to remain constant as a function of time. This may be quite unrealistic for an agent since the locations of food, water, sexual partners and other reinforcing stimuli do change; in fact, they are often consumed and thus disappear from the environment. In particular, it can be argued that the reinforcements change *more quickly* than other parts of the environment, including the set of possible states and actions and the transition rules from one state to another (Foster and Dayan, 2002; Engel and Mannor, 2001). Basic model-free RL methods need to learn the new policy from scratch if the states where reinforcements are received change.

An alternative approach for action selection an agent is based on planning, or model-based reinforcement learning. Here, it is assumed that the agent has a model of the world and its interaction with the world. In a basic approach, the agent considers a number of different action sequences that it might take in the present state. The agent then predicts the consequences of those actions, and evaluates the reinforcement signals associated with each action sequence considered, finally choosing the action sequence with the highest (expected) reward.

Planning is a classical problem in artificial intelligence, although it is usually formulated by defining a single goal state instead of a reward function. The fundamental problem in planning is that the number of possible action sequences grows exponentially as a function of the number of future time steps considered, and thus planning many action steps in advance is computationally impossible. Modern neuroscience models emphasize dynamic programming, i.e. iterative computation of the future "value" of all states, as proposed in model-based reinforcement learning literature.

However, in the case of a biological agent or "animat", the planning problem might be actually much easier because the agent is often faced with similar action selection problems many times over its lifetime, and thus its action sequences have strong regularities. Thus, the agent could learn from its experience, as well as from its evolutionary history. This is in stark contrast to classical planning problems where the environment may be unique for each planning problem to be solved. For example, some work in RL has proposed methods for improving the performance of an agent by learning chunks of actions, called macroactions (Iba, 1989; McGovern, 2002), options (Sutton et al., 1999), or skills (Thrun and Schwartz, 1995).

Here we propose a simple framework for *learning to plan future actions* more efficiently. The agent observes the sequences that it has previously chosen, and learns a statistical model of the sequences — a *behavioural prior* model. Using statistical models for learning of environmental regularities has been a very succesful approach in perception (Knill and Richards, 1996; Olshausen and Field, 1996; Hyvärinen and Hoyer, 2000), and enables the application of the highly sophisticated machinery of Bayesian inference, which is the main motivation for our work. The effect of learning is then to bias the search towards sequences that have the same statistical regularities as the previously chosen ones. This enables the planning system to concentrate on more meaningful action sequences, thus searching the space of possible action sequences more efficiently, and eventually increasing the length of planned sequences to look further ahead. We suggest that this enables the agent to obtain larger average rewards. The framework includes learning of macroactions as a special case, and it can be incorporated in schemes that use a value function approximated by methods related to dynamic programming.

Basic Setting

At every time point $t = 1, 2, \ldots$, the agent finds itself in a state $s(t)$ which belongs to the discrete state space $S = \{s_1, s_2, \ldots, s_n\}$, and has the choice of a number of actions $a(i), i = 1, \ldots, I$ chosen from the set of actions A. Every action changes the state in a deterministic way. (For simplicity, we don't consider random state changes, but they would not change the basic idea.). Every action gives a reward which depends on the combination of the present state and the action taken therein. The agent attempts to obtain maximum reward.

The agent has a perfect model of the environmental dynamics, i.e. what is the next state and the obtained reward when taking a given action in a give state. In principle, it could then compute the values of all states, or the Q-values [1] of all state-action pairs, but it is assumed that the rewards change too fast for this to be computationally useful. Thus, the agent uses explicit planning to choose actions.

The agent has a planning system that searches the space of action sequences or plans $(a(i_1), a(i_2), \ldots, a(i_n))$ of length n. It is assumed that the agent needs to plan its actions a relatively large number of time steps ahead in order to find meaningful action sequences. This means that n is fixed to a relatively large value so that an exhaustive search of the plan space A^n is not possible due to excessive computational requirements. Long plans are necessary, for example, if rewards are *sparse*, that is, the reward is zero for most states, regardless of action taken. We assume this in the following.

Since exhaustive search is not possible, the agent uses a stochastic search strategy that consists of sampling a number of candidate plans from the space A^n of plans of length n. In the basic case, the agent simply samples plans so that each plan in the space A^n has equal probability. For the sampled plans, the agent evaluates the reward to be obtained by following them. The plan leading to the largest reward is then executed. The agent then finds itself in a new state, and starts a new planning process. See, for example, (Kearns et al., 1999) for a related approach.

Learning to Find Better Plans

Learning statistics of executed plans

We propose here that the planning system can learn from experience to constrain the search to a smaller set of plans that are likely to be better than others. This is based on the assumption that *good plans have statistical regularities* in the sense that any action $a(i)$ is typically followed by certain actions and not others. That is, we can use preceding actions *in a good plan* to predict the following actions. A "good" plan means, loosely, a plan that gives an above-average reward.

Thus, we learn to associate a probability to each plan in the plan space A^n: It is the probability that the plan is "good". How do we learn the probability that a plan is

good? Since the agent considers many plans before executing the best among them, we assume that all executed plans are good. Thus, the probabilities are learned by building a statistical model of the executed plans. This learning is possible in an unsupervised way. In Bayesian terminology, these probabilities can be called *behavioural priors*.

Improving planning

The statistical model of executed plans, which is based on experience, is then used in planning of future actions in the following way. All candidate plans are sampled from the space of possible plans *according to the probabilities given by the statistical model*. Thus, the system considers only plans which follow the same statistical regularities as the plans that were previously found best. This speeds up planning because it constrains the search to useful parts of the plan space. This learning is domain-independent and can be applied on any kinds of actions.

If the model is such that it can be naturally extended from n-dimensional to m-dimensional sequences, the computational saving due to learning can be used to extend the time horizon of the planning.

Markov models

A simple and useful concrete model that we can use is Markov models. Markov models are simple to estimate (at least for low model orders) and sampling of new plans is very easy, at least if the action space is discrete. Let us denote by $a(t)$ the action taken at time step t.

The k-order Markov model basically predicts the current action $a(t)$ given preceding actions $a(t-1), a(t-2), \ldots, a(t-k)$. The parameters of the model consists of the probabilities $P(a(t)|a(t-1), \ldots, a(t-k))$. Typically, Markov models are first-order, i.e. $a(t)$ is predicted simply by its predecessor $a(t-1)$.

The probabilities can be simply learned by just counting how often an action is followed by another action (in the first-order case) or a sequence of k preceding actions (in the general case). The Markov model also needs the initial probabilities. For a k-order model, we need a probability distribution of the k initial actions taken. Again, such probabilities can be learned by just counting the occurrences of different initial action sequences.

Sampling (generation) of data from the model is straighforward: first, pick up a sequence of k initial actions from the distribution of initial sequences, and set $a(1), \ldots, a(k)$ equal to the obtained sequence. Set $t = k + 1$. Recursively, pick up a new action from the conditional distribution $P(a(t)|a(t-1), \ldots, a(t-k))$, increase t by one, and repeat until the action sequence is as long as desired.[2]

Macro-actions (Iba, 1989; McGovern, 2002) can be easily incorporated in the framework. They correspond

---

[1]That is, expected discounted future reinforcement when performing a given action in a given state and following the optimal policy thereafter (Sutton and Barto, 1998)

[2]Alternatively, the k first actions could be sampled by using lower-order Markov models, so that first $a(1)$ is picked randomly form the distribution of initial sequences, then $a(2)$ is sampled using a 1st-order Markov model, and so on.

to a statistical model of plans that is based on recoding certain typical sequences as new actions by including them in the action space A. After such recoding, we can build a Markov model for the new, extended set of actions.

Combination with Dynamic Programming

Although in the preceding section we proposed learning behavioural priors in a basic framework where planning is done by sampling from a distribution over action sequences, the same idea carries over to the setting where more sophisticated planning methods are used. In particular, methods based on dynamic programming and value iteration can be easily combined with behavioural priors.

One of the key ideas in dynamic programming, and many RL methods, is that the agent only needs to consider actions one step ahead, since the value function contains all relevant information about the effect of later actions. However, this is only true if the value function is known exactly, which is not true during learning or if the reward structure changes — which was one of our motivations in the first place. As soon as we assume that the values assigned by the agent to different states are not necessarily correct, it is useful to combine planning with RL methods (Daw et al., 2005), and behavioural priors become useful.

In fact, the situation where the value functions are only known approximatively is formally closely related to the present case. The computed value function can be used as reinforcement in the framework described above (where only the reinforcement in the final state of the sequence is obtained). If the agent plans how to get to states having the maximum value, it will move towards the goal, approximately. Learning behavioural priors can be performed in the same way as above, and they will give meaningful sequences to evaluate.

There are many different reasons why the computed values could be far from the true values of the state (for the optimal policy). One case is where some reinforcement learning has been performed, but the value iteration has been carried out incompletely due to computational restrictions. Another possibility is that the reinforcements may have changed without the agent knowing it. Also, if the states are not discrete but points in a multidimensional real space, some function approximation scheme needs to be used to approximate the value function, and errors are likely to occur in the approximation. In all these case, the computed value function gives unreliable information on which action is the best to take. Combining the information they contain with the information given by behavioural priors would be very useful.

In the case of approximately known value function, using behavioural priors has a very similar function to perceptual priors in Bayesian theories in perception: since the sensory input is noisy and incomplete (corresponding to inexact value function), prior information can help infer the real values.

Deterministic planner	32.1
Random stochastic planner	53.7
Bayesian 1st-order planner	84.1
Bayesian 2nd-order planner	84.4

Table 1: Percentage of cases where each planner was the best in the first simulation. There were many ties so the percentages don't add to 100%.

Simulations

Planning by simple forward search

We made simulations in a very basic gridworld of 20×20 states. The state of the agent consists of x and y coordinates of integer values, and the actions are "left", "right", "up" and "down". Rewards are dependent on the states only: the reward values for each state are obtained by taking a random variable uniformly distributed in $[0, 1]$ and raising it to the 10th power. This gives very sparse rewards which are practically zero for most states. Reward was only given at the state where the action sequence terminated.

The simulations can be thought in terms of foraging where the agent moves in a 2D environment, and then implicitly performs an "eat" action at the end of every sequence. The agent tries to eat as much as possible.

First, we used deterministic full search in the action space. The depth of planning was fixed to 4 time steps (actions). Starting from a random initial point, all possible $4^4 = 256$ plans were considered and the best was chosen for execution. This was repeated 10,000 times, each time from a random initial position (state).

Both a first-order and second-order Markov models were learned from the sequences chosen by the deterministic planner. These were used as behavioural priors. Random planning based on sampling from the priors was then performed. Here, the action sequence length was fixed to 8, which gave a large space of 65536 action sequences to choose from. The sampler only considered a small number of choices. The number of considered candidate plans was fixed to 256 which was equal to the deterministic planning case to allow a fair comparison. The same 10,000 initial states as with the deterministic planner were used.

As another baseline comparison we considered the case where the planner takes 256 completely random sequences (uniform initial probabilities and transition probabilities from action to another) of length 8 and chooses the best one. This means planning parameters were similar to those one used with behavioural priors, but the statistical structure of typical action sequences was not used.

We computed the percentage of cases where each of the planners performed the best in terms of obtained reward. The results are shown in Table 1.

We see that the best performance was clearly obtained by the Bayesian planners. Going to a 2nd order Markov model did not really improve the performance.

What is the structure learned by the 1st-order Markov

model? The transition matrix $P(a(t)|a(t-1))$, when the actions are in the order ("left", "right", "up", "down") has the following form:

$$\begin{bmatrix} 0.62 & 0 & 0.19 & 0.19 \\ 0 & 0.60 & 0.20 & 0.20 \\ 0.19 & 0.22 & 0.59 & 0 \\ 0.20 & 0.20 & 0 & 0.60 \end{bmatrix}$$

This shows two kinds of structure. First, a very simple and intuitive structure: after going up, one should not go down and vice versa, after going right one should not go left and vice versa. Second, there is a strong tendency to *repeat* the same action in a sequence. This is not intuitively so obvious, but it is due to the fact that by repeating the movement in the same direction, the agent can go farther. Otherwise, it could take sequences such as "left","up", "right", "up" which does not really get the agent any further than two "up" actions, but consumes two more actions.

Planning combined with dynamic programming

In the second simulation, we combined simple search with dynamic programming techniques. The motivation was that the dynamic programming was incomplete and provided only approximations of the true values as discussed above, and thus it was useful to plan many steps ahead (Daw et al., 2005).

The setting was the same kind of gridworld as in the preceding simulation. Now, there was one goal state (in the middle, which bounced the agent to a new random initial position) and the agent performed 10,000 steps of Q-learning. The Q-values were initialized as small random values which provided a limited exploration mechanism in the initial stage of the learning, but the agent always chose the action greedily with no randomness. The step size was 0.5 and the the discount factor 0.9.

The obtained approximation of the optimal value function is given in Fig. 1. Clearly, the learning did not find a very good approximation of the optimal value function due to a limited number of steps, as well as the very primitive learning method that included no proper exploration or such sophisticated mechanims as eligibility traces.

Now, we consider an agent which is only given this rough approximation of the optimal value function. (The value of the goal state is further defined to be infinite). Initially, the agent is place in a random position on the grid. The agent plans a few steps ahead (just as in the previous section) to reach a state of maximum value function, and then executes that plan. This is repeated a maximum of ten times, starting from the state where the agent ended up due to execution of the previous plan, or until the agent reaches the goal state. After ten plans, or after reaching the goal state, a new random initial state is chosen, because often the agent gets stuck and does not move anywhere. The performance is assessed by counting how many times the agent reached the goal.

We used the same four planners as in the preceding section for this planning problem. First, we used the de-

Deterministic planner	2,422
Random stochastic planner	3,952
Bayesian 1st-order planner	4,961
Bayesian 2nd-order planner	4,733

Table 2: Number of times the agent reached the goal for different planning methods in the second simulation.

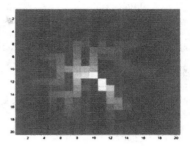

Figure 1: The approximation of the optimal value function, given in greyscale values, used in the second simulation. The approximation is rather bad, which is why it is useful to plan several steps ahead.

terministic one and learned the behavioural priors from the sequences chosen for action by that planner.[3]

The results are given in Table 2. We see that again, the best results were obtained using behavioural priors, modelled as a first-order Markov chain. The learned priors (not shown) were essentially the same as in the preceding section. Interestingly, the 2nd-order Markov model had a performance inferior to the 1st-order model.

Discussion

Related work

Learning motor synergies (Tresch et al., 2006) is closely related to our framework. Obviously, the planning activities can happen on the level of motor control as well. An important difference to our work is that the synergies in (Tresch et al., 2006) considered postures in each time point separately, whereas we emphasize the temporal aspect of planning. However, these two aspects are both easily combined in the framework of behavioural priors. If the action space is a n-dimensional real space, the behavioural priors can be defined on sequences of n-dimensional vectors.

In addition to macroactions already discussed above, researchers in RL have proposed another framework for learning temporally extended actions called options (Sutton et al., 1999). Options are not merely fixed sequences of actions but action selection subsystems that are activated based on some initial conditions, and include a stopping criterion. Options can therefore pro-

---

[3]In these simulations, there were also many cases where the planner was not able to find a better plan than to stay in the same place. Plans which ended in the initial state were excluded from the plans used in learning priors.

duce arbitrarily long action sequences. A probabilistic interpretation of options, which integrates them in our framework, is an important question for future research.

Case-based planning (Hammond, 1990) provides another closely related framework, together with related work in robotics (Haigh and Veloso, 2000) and AI (Perez and Carbonel, 1994). Our work is different from that framework in that the priors are in the behavioural space only and do not depend on the states; furthermore, we provide a probabilistic framework.

Related work using probabilistic (Bayesian) methods for planning include (Dearden et al., 1999; Attias, 2003). In particular, the methods in (Dearden et al., 1999), as well as (Daw et al., 2005) give estimates of the uncertainty of the value function approximation, and these could possibly be used for determining the optimal depth of planning in a manner similar to (Daw et al., 2005).

Another application of priors on actions or behaviour is in observation of action sequences of other agents in a multi-agent environment (Antonini et al., 2006). This is also an essential subtask in imitation learning. Also, perception of agency (Wegner, 2002) or may also be based on a statistical model of typical action sequences.

Assumption of world models

Planning requires a model of the environment. This may be a drawback with respect to some model-free reinforcement learning methods such as Q-learning (Sutton and Barto, 1998). However, one can argue that it is not unreasonable to assume that many animals have such an internal model, and many relevant computational neuroscience models are based on a world model (Dayan and Abbott, 2001). In fact, one of the functions of consciousness might be to enable model-based planning in a kind of virtual reality (Revonsuo, 1995).

Conclusion

We have proposed a framework for action planning based on importing the concept of priors from Bayesian theories of perception. The idea is that *action sequences have statistical regularities*, and these regularities can be learned. The regularities can be used to improve planning in a planner that samples possible action sequences from the distribution given by the prior. Thus, the system learns to bias the search towards useful sequences and to plan more efficiently.

References

Antonini, G., Venegas, S., Bierlaire, M., and Thiran, J. (2006). Behavioral priors for detection and tracking of pedestrians in video sequences. *International Journal of Computer Vision*, 69:159–180.

Attias, H. (2003). Planning by probabilistic inference. In *Proc. 9th International Conference on Artificial Intelligence and Statistics*, Key West, Florida.

Daw, N. D., Niv, Y., and Dayan, P. (2005). Uncertainty-based competition between prefrontal and dorsolateral striatal systems for behavioral control. *Nature Neuroscience*, 8:1704–1711.

Dayan, P. and Abbott, L. F. (2001). *Theoretical Neuroscience*. MIT Press.

Dearden, R., Friedman, N., and Andre, D. (1999). Model-based bayesian exploration. In *Proc. 15th Conf. on Uncertainty in Artificial Intelligence (UAI)*.

Engel, Y. and Mannor, S. (2001). Learning embedded maps of markov processes. In *Proc. Int. Conf. on Machine Learning (ICML)*, pages 138–145.

Foster, D. and Dayan, P. (2002). Structure in the space of value functions. *Machine Learning*, 49:325–346.

Haigh, K. Z. and Veloso, M. M. (2000). Learning situation-dependent costs: Improving planning from probabilistic robot execution. In *Proc. Second Int. Conf. on Autonomous Agents*, pages 231–238, Minneapolis, MN.

Hammond, K. J. (1990). Case-based planning: A framework for planning from experience. *Cognitive Science*, 14:385–443.

Hyvärinen, A. and Hoyer, P. O. (2000). Emergence of phase and shift invariant features by decomposition of natural images into independent feature subspaces. *Neural Computation*, 12(7):1705–1720.

Iba, G. (1989). A heuristic approach to the discovery of macro-operators. *Machine Learning*, 3:285–317.

Kearns, M., Mansour, Y., and Ng, A. (1999). A sparse sampling algorithm for near-optimal planning in large markov decision processes. In *Proc. 16th Int. Joint Conf. on Artificial Intelligence*, pages 1324–1331.

Knill, D. C. and Richards, W., editors (1996). *Perception as Bayesian Inference*. Cambridge University Press.

McGovern, A. (2002). *Autonomous Discovery of Temporal Abstractions from Interaction with an Environment*. PhD thesis, Univ. of Massachusetts.

Olshausen, B. A. and Field, D. J. (1996). Emergence of simple-cell receptive field properties by learning a sparse code for natural images. *Nature*, 381:607–609.

Perez, M. A. and Carbonel, J. (1994). Control knowledge to improve plan quality. In *Proc. Second Int. Conf. on AI Planning Systems*, pages 323–328, Chicago, IL.

Revonsuo, A. (1995). Consciousness, dreams, and virtual realities. *Philosophical Psychology*, 8:35–58.

Sutton, R. and Barto, A. (1998). *Reinforcement Learning: An Introduction*. MIT Press.

Sutton, R., Precup, D., and Singh, S. (1999). Between MDPs and semi-MDPs: A framework for temporal abstraction in reinforcement learning. *Artificial Intelligence*, 112:181–211.

Thrun, S. and Schwartz, A. (1995). Finding structure in reinforcement learning. In Tesauro, G., Touretzky, D., and Leen, T., editors, *Advances in Neural Information Processing Systems (NIPS) 7*, Cambridge, MA. MIT Press.

Tresch, M. C., Cheung, V. C., and d'Avella, A. (2006). Matrix factorization algorithms for the identification of muscle synergies: evaluation on simulated and experimental data sets. *J. of Neurophysiology*, 95(4):2199–212.

Wegner, D. M. (2002). *The Illusion of Conscious Will*. The MIT Press.

Evidencing Implicit Sequence Learning through the Process Dissociation Procedure: A Case against Previous Conclusions

Serban C. Musca (serbancmusca@gmail.com)
Laboratorio de Psicología del Aprendizaje, Departamento de Psicología, Universidad de Deusto,
Apartado 1, 48080 Bilbao, Spain

Julien Barra (jbarra@upmf-grenoble.fr)
Psychology and NeuroCognition Lab - CNRS UMR 5105, University Pierre Mendès France (Grenoble 2),
1251 avenue Centrale, BP 47, 38040 Grenoble cedex 9, France

Martial Mermillod (mermillod@univ-bpclermont.fr)
Laboratoire de Psychologie Sociale et Cognitive - CNRS UMR 6024, Université Blaise Pascal,
34, avenue Carnot, 63037 Clermont-Ferrand Cedex, France

Thierry Atzeni (thierry.atzeni@univ-savoie.fr)
Laboratoire de Psychologie et NeuroCognition, Université de Savoie,
Campus de Jacob-Bellecombette, rue du Sergent Revel, 73000 Chambery, France

Abstract

The seminal paper of Destrebecqz & Cleeremans (2001) brought a solution allowing for evidencing implicit learning without having recourse to null hypothesis testing. While the methodological contribution made by these authors is acknowledged here, two experiments are presented to make the case against the conclusion of implicit learning they reached. Experiment 1 shows that the baseline used by Destrebecqz & Cleeremans in order to determine whether learning was implicit is inappropriate. Experiment 2 is a replication of the condition of their experiment that yielded implicit learning. Since it is suspected that the conclusion of implicit learning arises partly because some participants did not learn the training sequence and acted haphazardly in the subsequent phase used to establish implicitness of learning, Experiment 2 includes changes aimed at removing noise during the learning phase. Taken together, these results show that learning is explicit. The conclusion discusses the importance of this result and of the verifications proposed here in order to convincingly prove implicit learning.

Implicit learning has been studied through many paradigms, among which the most influential are the control of complex system (e.g. Berry & Broadbent, 1995; Buchner, Funke & Berry, 1995), learning of artificial grammars (e.g. Perruchet, 1994; Perruchet & Pacteau, 1990; Reber, 1967; Vokey & Brooks, 1992) and serial reaction time (e.g. Destrebecqz & Cleeremans, 2001; Lewicki, Czyzewska & Hoffman, 1987; Nissen & Bullemer, 1987; Perruchet & Amorim, 1992; Perruchet, Bigand & Benoit-Gonin, 1997; Reed & Johnson, 1994; Shanks & Johnstone, 1998). In all these studies the demonstration of learning without awareness has relied on the dissociation paradigm (Erdelyi, 1986), a paradigm wherein separate indices of learning and awareness are used in the attempt to find circumstances in which exposure to a set of stimuli leads to detectable learning unaccompanied by reliable degree of awareness.

The Dissociation Paradigm: Problems and Solutions

While in theory the dissociation paradigm seems capable of leading to unequivocal evidence of implicit learning, in practice it has been plagued by numerous problems related to the awareness test. These problems have been discussed at length by Shanks & St. John (1994). They proposed that in order to avoid false positive conclusions, the condition of realization of experiments using a dissociation paradigm should be further constrained by two criteria that they proposed, the information criterion and the sensitivity criterion. After a close examination of the existing body of evidence in favour of implicit learning, these authors conclude their meta-analysis by asserting that unconscious learning has not yet been satisfactorily established.

In our view, the major concern with the dissociation paradigm should be that the task that checks for awareness has virtually always been designed in such a way that it implements a test of a null hypothesis with designs where the statistical power was (very) low — because of the small number of test stimuli. Indeed, implicitness of learning is based on the lack of difference (generally in an old/new recognition task) between participants' scores to trained stimuli vs. to new stimuli. The problem is obviously that null sensitivity (i.e. a lack of difference in performance on trained vs. new stimuli) is meaningless, as any lack of difference obtained in a condition of low statistical power. Proofs based on the null hypothesis lack of convincing power.

Destrebecqz and Cleeremans (2001) contributed the field a solution whereby implicit learning would be associated to a difference between participants' performance and a chance level performance. Based on Shanks & St. John's (1994) suggestion of building a task based on Jacoby's (1991) process dissociation procedure, the procedure uses a twofold generation task. Upon completion of 15 training blocks — composed each of 8 repetitions of a 12-element second order conditional (*SOC*) sequence — in a four-alternative serial reaction time (*SRT*) task, the participants were informed that a sequence was used and were to complete a generation task, under two conditions. First, they were to generate a sequence that would resemble as much as possible the training sequence (*Inclusion* condition). Immediately after, they were to generate a sequence as random as possible, and were told that avoiding reproducing the (parts of the) training sequence would help them in being more random (*Exclusion* condition). Inclusion condition implements a facilitation paradigm, because both explicit and implicit knowledge would help performing correctly with regard to the task (i.e. generate the training sequence).

Exclusion condition implements an interference paradigm, because explicit knowledge of the training sequence would help performing the task (by allowing the participant to avoid generating the training sequence and therefore being more random) but implicit knowledge would hinder the performance by creating intrusions of the training sequence into the "random" sequence a participant has to generate.

In line with Jacoby (1991), Destrebecqz and Cleeremans equate control with consciousness, that is, consider that control can only be exerted on conscious knowledge. Under this assumption, in the generation task performed under the Exclusion condition, one straightforward prediction emerges: If knowledge about the sequence is explicit, participants should be able to avoid generating more of the training sequence than the chance level, whereas if this knowledge is implicit participants are expected to generate significantly more parts of the training sequence than the chance level.

Implicitness of learning in Destrebecqz & Cleeremans (2001)

In a condition where during training the next stimulus appeared immediately after the previous response of the participant (*no RSI* condition, since the response-to-stimulus interval was null), participants in Destrebecqz & Cleeremans (2001) could not refrain at test from generating the training sequence above chance level in the generation task under Exclusion instructions. This was taken as evidence that learning was implicit.

Some concerns

First, this demonstration of implicit learning in the *no RSI* condition obviously depends on the chance level that is considered. Destrebecqz and Cleeremans considered a chance level of 33.33% since on each generation trial a participant could use any of the four possible keys except the one he/she has just used in the previous trial, that is, one among three. While this is theoretically correct, it will be shown in Experiment 1 that participants that do not receive

any training before generating a random sequence (with the same constraint of not pressing a key twice in a row) generate chunks of the sequences used by Destrebecqz and Cleeremans significantly above the theoretical chance level of 33.33%. According to the above-mentioned theoretical criterion, these naïve participants (i.e. that did not undergo any training with any sequence) would be qualified as people who learned implicitly about a sequence. This, of course, is problematic.

A sounder alternative would be to consider that the theoretical chance level of 33.33% is inappropriate and to consider the performance of naïve participants as a baseline for the comparison with the generation performance in the Exclusion condition. The reasoning to evidence implicit learning would be the same, only replacing the theoretical chance level of 33.33% by an experimental baseline established on naïve participants.

Now, when considering the experimental baseline established on naïve participants in the Experiment 1 presented here, the participants in the no RSI condition of Destrebecqz & Cleeremans (2001) do not generate significantly more parts of the training sequence and thus their learning cannot be called implicit anymore.

A second concern is closely related to the first one. The percent of training sequence chunks generated by the trained participants of Destrebecqz & Cleeremans (2001) in the Inclusion condition is not different from the experimental baseline established on naïve participants in our Experiment 1. This is a problematic finding, since it means that the participants in the no RSI condition of Destrebecqz & Cleeremans (2001) did not learn the training sequence[1].

A third concern stems from the possible interaction between the design of the training phase (i.e. the serial reaction time task) and the instructions that participants received for the Inclusion generation task. In order to show that the participants have learned the sequence, training block 13 used a different, transfer, sequence; as expected, reaction times increased significantly with respect to the previous training block[2].

The use of a second training sequence during block 13 may have introduced some noise and may have confused the participants. Indeed, while there were *two* different sequences during training, participants were told before the test phase that the training material followed *a* sequence and during the generation task under Inclusion instructions they

---

[1] This finding could also mean that the measure taken during the generation task is less sensitive than the one taken during training (i.e. mean reaction times). However, as a significant difference exists in the RSI condition between the percent of training sequence chunks generated by the trained participants in the Inclusion condition and the experimentally established baseline, we can exclude this possibility.

[2] Because only group mean reaction times were given (as opposed to the performance of every participant) and that error rates were not reported, these results do not convincingly prove sequence learning occurred.

were asked to generate *the* sequence (into the singular) they saw during training.

Experiments

As outlined above, our Experiment 1 tests whether the theoretical chance level of 33.33% considered as a baseline by Destrebecqz & Cleeremans (2001) is appropriate. Experiment 2 was designed and data from it will be analyzed in order to address the other aforementioned concerns.

Experiment 1

Humans are pretty bad at producing randomness (see Nickerson, 2002 for a review). What would be the consequence of departing from randomness in the Exclusion task? Could it be that participants generate more chunks of the training sequence than the theoretical chance level of 33.33% just because of production biases?

To answer these questions, naïve participants performed a generation task in conditions close to those used in the generation task of Destrebecqz & Cleeremans (2001).

Method

Participants: 19 psychology students (13 from Grenoble 2 University, and 6 from Deusto University) participated for course credit.

Stimuli: Stimuli were presented by a computer running E-Prime scripts. The display consisted of a black background and of four white dots of a diameter of one millimetre arranged in a horizontal line on the computer's screen and separated by intervals of 30 millimetres. To each screen position corresponded a key on the computer's keyboard (keys locations were fully compatible with the screen positions). The stimulus was a small white disc of 3.5 millimetres in diameter that appeared 10 millimetres above one of the four dots.

Design and procedure: Immediately after a 20-trials warm-up, participants were to generate a sequence as random as possible but with the constraint of not pressing the same key in a row. As in the original experiment, they were not informed about the length of the sequence they were to generate. Unlike in that experiment, where the procedure stopped after 96 trials, here it stopped after 200 trials. On the first trial the stimulus appeared in a random location. On a key press, the stimulus disappeared from its current location and immediately appeared in the location corresponding to the key that has just been pressed (thus the RSI was null, as in the generation tasks that followed training in the *no RSI* condition of Destrebecqz and Cleeremans).

Results

The sequences used by Destrebecqz & Cleeremans (2001) are particular because each stimulus is followed by any of the remaining three with equal probability, but two successive stimuli determine at 100% where the following one will occur (*SOC* sequences; see Reed & Johnson, 1994).

Because of their particular nature, one can count how many sequence chunks corresponding to a particular SOC are included in the production of a naïve participant: at any time during a free generation task, two elements in a row are followed by another one and this latter is either the one "expected" following the SOC or not.

The percentage of SOC chunks was computed both for the first 96 trials and for the whole 200 trials, for the two SOCs (SOC1: 121432413423; SOC2: 124314213234) used by Destrebecqz & Cleeremans (2001) as well as for the remaining 22 possible SOCs (121342314324, 1231342143-24, 123142132434, 123143242134, 123143421324, 12324-1342143, 123413214243, 123413243142, 123421324314, 123421413243, 123421431324, 123424132143, 12413214-2343, 124134232143, 124134321423, 124143213423, 124-231432134, 124314234132, 124321314234, 124321341423, 124321423413, and 124323142134).

It was first checked that the distributions were normal and the means were not unduly influenced by any extreme value(s). This was indeed the case, as the absolute value of all the studentized deleted residuals (*SDR*) from a regression of the empirical data against the *z*-scores from equivalent quantiles was always less than two for every SOC considered — a SDR value of at least 2.6 would be a reason to doubt of the representativeness of the mean (McClelland, 2000). In other words, the results showed in Figure 1 are representative and trustworthy.

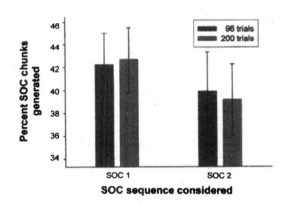

Figure 1: Percent SOC chunks generated by naïve participants as a function of the SOC sequence considered (SOC1 and SOC2 sequences from Destrebecqz & Cleeremans, 2001). Error bars stand for .95 confidence intervals. (See main text for details)

As can be seen from Figure 1, the percentage of SOC chunks generated by naïve participants is always significantly higher than the theoretical chance level of 33.33% considered as baseline by Destrebecqz & Cleeremans (2001). This is true whatever the SOC considered, be it SOC1, SOC2, or any other of the remaining 22 possible SOCs — no .95 confidence interval includes the value of 33.33%. This result was obtained whether only the first 96 trials or all 200 trials were considered — when considering all 24 possible SOCs, the interaction between SOC and number of trials is not significant [$F(23, 414) = 0.65$, $MS_E = 9.88187$, $p = .89$]. Also, the variance affecting the mean is higher for 96 trials than for 200 trials [$p < .0001$].

Dramatically, naïve participants generate more SOC1 chunks than expected at theoretical chance level [for 96 trials: mean = 42.23%, $SD = 2.84$, $t(18) = 13.67$, $p < .0001$; for 200 trials: mean = 42.68%, $SD = 2.86$, $t(18) = 14.25$, $p < .0001$]. The same is true for SOC2 chunks [for 96 trials: mean = 39.92%, $SD = 3.41$, $t(18) = 8.43$, $p < .0001$; for 200 trials: mean = 39.17%, $SD = 3.08$, $t(18) = 8.26$, $p < .0001$].

This result indicates that, in the Exclusion part of the generation task, a generation score significantly higher than the theoretical chance level of 33.33% considered by Destrebecqz and Cleeremans can arise be mere chance, because of production biases. Interpreting such a result as a proof of implicit learning seems as sensible as arguing that naïve participants who were never trained on a repeating sequence cannot refrain from generating it.

Experiment 2

This experiment replicates the *no RSI* condition of Destrebecqz & Cleeremans (2001) with some minor changes that aim addressing the concerns discussed before. First, in order to maximize the probability that learning occurs in all participants, the repeating SOC was presented 12 times per training block (instead of 8), for a total of 1440 training trials.

To avoid confusing the participants, only one SOC was used throughout the SRT phase, that is, there was no transfer block (i.e. no SOC change during a block). This raises the question of whether participants only learn to press the correct key more rapidly but without learning anything about the underlying SOC, or whether they also learn something about the regularities present in the sequence. To answer this question, the Inclusion scores will be considered, with the following reasoning: If a participant generates significantly more training SOC chunks in the Inclusion task than the baseline established in Experiment 1, than it can be considered that he/she had learned something about the regularities present in the training sequence, either explicitly or implicitly; otherwise, it will be considered that the participant has not learned anything about the training SOC.

A supplementary change concerns the generation tasks. Though no difference was found between scores based on 96 trials and those based on 200 trials in Experiment 1, the variance affecting the mean was higher in the former case. Therefore, it was decided to have the participants generate 200 trials under each generation instructions.

Method

Participants: 24 psychology students from Grenoble 2 University participating for course credit were randomly assigned to SOC1 or SOC2 condition.

Stimuli: The experimental apparatus was the same as in Experiment 1.

Design and procedure: During the first, SRT phase, participants were to react as fast and as accurately possible to the apparition of the stimulus by pressing the key corresponding to the screen location where the stimulus appeared. On a key press, the stimulus disappeared from its current position and appeared on its next position without any delay. The position where the next stimulus appeared was determined by the underlying SOC, no matter whether the correct or an incorrect key has been pressed; however, if an incorrect key has been pressed an 80 Hz tone signalled to the participant that he/she committed an error. The SRT phase included 12 training blocks separated by participant-paced pauses.

Upon completion of the first phase, participants were informed that the stimuli did not appear randomly but following a complex and repeating sequence and moved on to the generation tasks. They were to generate first under Inclusion instructions, then under Exclusion instructions. Generation instructions were the same as in Destrebecqz & Cleeremans (2001).

Results

Serial reaction times task: Mean reaction times and mean percent correct per training block and per training SOC are given for reference in Figure 2. Though mean reaction times decrease with practice, a possible speed-accuracy trade-off appears when taking into account the mean accuracy data.

However, as discussed above, these indexes do not speak to the matter of what is learned. Indeed, without a transfer block it is possible that the observed learning be due to other reasons than learning of the SOC structure present in the training material.

Generation tasks: The results of the generation task, under Inclusion and under Exclusion instructions, are given in Table 1.

SOC1			SOC2		
Participant	Inclusion	Exclusion	Participant	Inclusion	Exclusion
b	48.47	65.82	a	35.35	28.79
c	47.15	36.89	d	43.3	39.25
f	44.44	34.85	e	55.15	17.01
h	54.08	45.83	g	44.85	28.28
k	42.93	25.93	i	49.48	37.23
m	77.78	44.62	j	45.35	32.96
n	26.26	53.44*	l	30.89	24.23
o	41.92	44.09	q	43.94	34.36
p	61.02	58.95	r	38.92	31.77
s	34.34	51.06*	t	40.53	28.26
u	39.39	47.37*	v	42.27	32.14
x	47.4	34.69	w	76.28	37.63

Table 1: Mean percent SOC chunks generated, per participant and per SOC previously trained. Bold characters indicate that SOC learning occurred, italicized that learning was implicit, and an asterisk indicates an atypical result pattern. (See text for details)

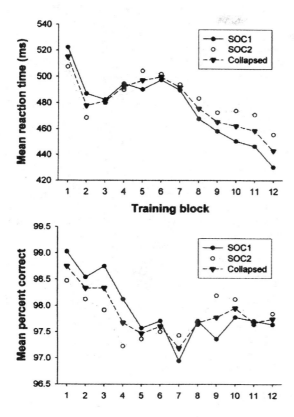

Figure 2: Mean reaction times and mean percent correct per training block and per training SOC used.

Considering the Inclusion results, one can see that 9 out of 12 participants trained on SOC1 and 10 out of 12 trained on SOC2 have learned the training sequence. Indeed, the remaining 3 (2) from SOC1 (SOC2) group generated a percentage of SOC1 (SOC2) chunks that was not superior to 45.54% (42.26%), the upper bound of the .95 confidence interval build from naïve participants data.

Considering the Exclusion results, it appears that no participant trained on SOC2 learned implicitly. Implicit learning occurred in one participant trained on SOC1. Also, one may see that participants *n*, *s*, and *u* trained on SOC1 display an atypical pattern of results, that is, they do not exhibit sequence learning (Inclusion task) but cannot refrain from generating more chunks of the training SOC under Exclusion instructions.

An analysis of generation data from the Exclusion condition that considers the two SOC conditions as a counterbalancing variable (i.e. that does not check for differences in the Exclusion scores as a function of the SOC used during training; this was the way Destrebecqz and Cleeremans analyzed data) is presented first. This analysis shows that participants generated significantly less SOC

chunks of their respective training SOC than control naïve participants [t(60) = 2.09, p < .05].

Next, complementary analyses of Exclusion data are presented, separately for each training SOC, because in this experiment the two SOC training conditions did give rise to different Exclusion scores [$t(22) = 2.97$, $p < .01$]. For participants trained with SOC1, whether including or not those participants who do not exhibit SOC learning, the group result is the same: the mean number of SOC1 chunks generated is not different from that generated by the control naïve participants [$p > .99$]. This result, in line with the previous subject-by-subject analysis, does not support the conclusion of implicit learning.

For participants trained with SOC2, whether including or not those participants who do not exhibit SOC learning, the group result is the same: participants generated significantly *less* SOC2 chunks than control naïve participants [when considering all 12 participants: $t(29) = 3.56$, $p < .005$; only for participants who have learned the sequence: $t(27) = 2.95$, $p < .01$].

In conclusion, data does not support the hypothesis of implicit learning. Instead, the overall pattern of results supports the opposite conclusion, that is, that participants can refrain from generating chunks of the SOC they have been trained on. In the methodological and theoretical framework delineated by Jacoby (1991) and further adapted to the sequence learning paradigm by Destrebecqz & Cleeremans (2001), this ability of control of one on his/her performance indicates explicit learning.

Discussion

The two experiments presented here asked whether participants could learn *implicitly* something on the structure of the sequence that determined the location where stimuli appeared in a serial reaction time (SRT) task. Destrebecqz & Cleeremans (2001) have answered by the positive in a condition where the response-to-stimulus interval during the SRT task was null (*no RSI* condition).

It was discussed here that the conclusion of implicit learning drawn by these authors rests entirely on the choice of a baseline, and it was shown that in practice that baseline was inappropriate (Experiment 1). Except for some changes whose importance and aim were discussed, Experiment 2 is a replication of the *no RSI* condition. Its results show that learning in this situation is not implicit, but rather explicit: when learning occurs, participants have control on what they have learned and can refrain from making use of this newly acquired knowledge when asked to do so.

Taken together the results presented here tend to invalidate the previous conclusion that implicit learning occurs in a sequence learning paradigm when the response-to-stimulus interval during the SRT task is null. Manipulating RSI does not suffice to induce reliable implicit learning.

In the following, some methodological issues and suggestions are discussed. First, this work emphasizes the importance of using a control group for the generation tasks in the paradigm proposed by Destrebecqz & Cleeremans (2001) and urges future researchers not do disregard the use of a control group.

A second methodological matter concerns the use of a transfer block in the SRT task. It is shown here that the paradigm proposed by Destrebecqz & Cleeremans can do without a transfer block: Learning of the training sequence can be reliably evidenced in the generation task under Inclusion instructions. This task has proven to be sensitive enough and has the supplementary advantage that the performance of each participant has to be assessed. Indeed, it prevents from the possibility that learning be "demonstrated" in the group because some participants have learned quite well the SOC while others did not. This is an important advantage because in our view some participants failing to learn the SOC and acting haphazardly in the generation tasks coupled to an inappropriate baseline can result in an erroneous conclusion of implicit learning.

Last but not least, it is important that the non-replication of the results of Destrebecqz & Cleeremans (2001) and the fact that we support another conclusion on the implicitness of learning do not be detrimental to the methodology proposed by these authors. We profoundly agree on the advantages of applying Jacoby's (1991) process dissociation procedure to generation tasks in a sequence learning paradigm and acknowledge its usefulness. Indeed, to our best knowledge, it is the only methodology available where implicitness on learning does not rest on a null hypothesis.

Acknowledgments

The authors thank Arnaud Destrebecqz for facilitating the data from Destrebecqz & Cleeremans (2001). We express our gratitude to Stéphane Rousset for various thought-provoking discussions, to Sandrine Thomé for her help with collecting data, and to Helena Matute and Miguel Ángel Vadillo for helpful comments on a previous draft.

References

Berry, D. C., & Broadbent, D. E. (1995). Implicit learning in the control of complex systems. In P. A. Frensch & J. Funke Eds., *Complex problem solving: The European perspective* (pp. 131-150). Hillsdale, NJ: Erlbaum.

Buchner, A., Funke, J., & Berry, D. 1995. Negative correlations between control performance and verbalizable knowledge: Indicators for implicit learning in process control tasks? *Quarterly Journal of Experimental Psychology, 48A,* 166-187.

Destrebecqz, A., & Cleeremans, A. (2001). Can sequence learning be implicit? New evidence with the process dissociation procedure. *Psychonomic Bulletin & Review, 8(2),* 343-350.

Erdelyi, M. (1986). Experimental indeterminacies in the dissociation paradigm. *Behavioural and Brain Science, 9,* 30-31.

Jacoby, L. L., (1991). A process dissociation framework: Separating automatic from intentional uses of memory. *Journal of Memory & Language, 30,* 513-541.

Lewicki, P., Czyzewska, M., & Hoffman, H. (1987). Unconscious acquisition of complex procedural knowledge. *Journal of Experimental Psychology: Learning, Memory, and Cognition, 13,* 523-530.

McClelland, G. H. (2000). Nasty data: Unruly, ill-mannered observations can ruin your analysis. In H. T. Reis & C. M. Judd (Eds.), *Handbook of Research Methods in Social Psychology* (pp. 393-411). Cambridge, UK: Cambridge University Press.

Nickerson, R. S. (2002). The production and perception of randomness. *Psychological Review, 109,* 330-357.

Nissen, M. J., & Bullemer, P. (1987). Attentional requirement of learning: Evidence from performance measures. *Cognitive Psychology, 19,* 1-32.

Perruchet, P. (1994). Learning from complex rule-governed environments: On the proper functions of nonconscious and conscious processes. In C. Umilta & M. Moscovitch Eds., *Attention and Performance XV: Conscious and nonconscious information processing* (pp. 811-835). Cambridge, MA: MIT Press.

Perruchet, P., & Amorim, M. A. (1992). Conscious knowledge and changes in performance in sequence learning: Evidence against dissociation. *Journal of Experimental Psychology: Learning, Memory & Cognition, 18,* 785-800.

Perruchet, P., Bigand, E., & Benoit-Gonin, F. (1997). The emergence of explicit knowledge during the early phase of learning in sequential reaction time. *Psychological Research, 60,* 4-14.

Perruchet, P., & Pacteau, C. (1990). Synthetic grammar learning: Implicit rule abstraction or explicit fragmentary knowledge? *Journal of Experimental Psychology: General, 119,* 264-275.

Reber, A.S. (1967). Implicit learning of artificial grammars. *Journal of Verbal Learning and Verbal Behavior, 6,* 855-863.

Reed, J., & Johnson, P. (1994). Assessing implicit learning with indirect tests: Determining what is learned about sequence structure. *Journal of Experimental Psychology: Learning, Memory & Cognition, 20,* 585-594.

Shanks, D. R., & Johnstone, T. (1998). Implicit knowledge in sequential learning tasks. In M. A. Stadler & P. A. Frensch (Eds.), *Handbook of implicit learning* (pp. 533-572). Sage Publications.

Shanks, D. R., & St. John, M. F. (1994). Characteristics of dissociable human learning systems. *Behavioral and Brain Sciences, 17,* 367-447.

Vokey, J. R., & Brooks, L. R. (1992). Salience of item knowledge in learning artificial grammars. *Journal of Experimental Psychology: Learning, Memory, and Cognition, 18,* 328-344.

Understanding Surprise:
Can Less Likely Events Be Less Surprising?

Rebecca Maguire (rebecca.maguire@dbs.edu)
Department of Psychology, Dublin Business School
Dublin 2, Ireland.

Phil Maguire (pmaguire@cs.nuim.ie)
Department of Computer Science, NUI Maynooth
Co. Kildare, Ireland.

Mark T. Keane (mark.keane@ucd.ie)
School of Computer Science and Informatics, University College Dublin
Belfield, Dublin 4, Ireland.

Abstract

Surprise is often thought of as an experience that is elicited following an *unexpected* event. However, it may also be the case that surprise stems from an event that is simply difficult to *explain*. In this paper, we investigate the latter view. Specifically, we question why the provision of an enabling factor can mitigate perceived surprise for an unexpected event despite lowering the overall probability of that event. One possibility is that surprise occurs when a person cannot rationalise an outcome event in the context of the scenario representation. A second possibility is that people can generate plausible explanations for unexpected events but that surprise is experienced when those explanations are uncertain. We explored these hypotheses in an experiment where a first group of participants rated surprise for a number of scenario outcomes and a second group rated surprise after generating a plausible explanation for those outcomes. Finally, a third group of participants rated surprise for the both the original outcomes *and* the reasons generated for those outcomes by the second group. Our results suggest that people *can* come up with plausible explanations for unexpected events but that surprise results when these explanations are uncertain.

Keywords: Surprise, expectation, representation, discourse.

Introduction

In day-to-day life, people have a remarkable ability to make sense of their surroundings and can effortlessly infer connections between events in order to create a rich and detailed representation of any given situation. Nevertheless, this coherent representation of the world can sometimes break down. More specifically, it is known that certain events have the potential to *surprise* us. Far from being an isolated occurrence, surprise is actually quite a common experience. Because of its prevalence, this phenomenon has received a great degree of research attention in cognitive science and psychology. Historically, Darwin (1879) was the first to classify it as one of the most basic emotions, a claim that has been adopted by many subsequent theorists. As well as being associated with a distinct subjective and physiological response, surprise is known to have some important cognitive manifestations. For example, the perception of a surprising event will usually cause a person to cease what they are currently doing and focus their attention on the event in question (Meyer, Reisenzein & Schützwohl, 1997). The purpose of such a reaction is to discover *why* the surprising event transpired, so that a similar event can be anticipated in future circumstances.

In this paper, we explore why people find certain events surprising and other events unsurprising. Specifically, we investigate why presenting an enabling condition for an unexpected event mitigates the level of surprise elicited by that event.

Surprise as unexpectedness

The most intuitive way of describing a surprising event is to say that it was *unexpected*. Likewise, it makes sense to assume that any expected event would be unsurprising if it were to occur. However, this account can be problematic, mainly due to the disagreement surrounding what it means to expect something. For instance, if we relate expectations to probabilities, then every low probability event should be extremely surprising, and vice versa. Evidently however, this is not always the case. For instance, while the outcome of a lottery draw always has an extremely low probability, it is rarely surprising

In light of this, Teigen and Keren (2003) suggested that surprise at a given event might be more accurately explained in terms of its subsequent comparison with an alternative outcome. Investigating this hypothesis, they carried out an experiment which described Erik, an athlete competing in a 5,000m race. In one condition, participants were informed that Erik was in second place behind a lead runner, while in another condition they were told that all the athletes, including Erik, had formed a large group as they approached the finish line. When asked to indicate how surprised they would be if Erik won the race, participants in the first condition (where Erik was in second place) gave slightly higher surprise ratings than those in the second condition (where all the athletes had formed one group), despite the fact that participants correctly rated Erik's *probability* of winning the race as higher in the first condition. One explanation for this result is that the first scenario induces an expectation (that the lead runner will win the race) which is disconfirmed by Erik winning. On the other hand, when all the athletes have an equal chance of winning the race, no expectation is contradicted if Erik wins. This finding can be said to support an *Expectation-Disconfirmation* hypothesis of surprise (see also Meyer et al, 1997).

Despite the intuitive plausibility of this hypothesis however, it may not always be the case that disconfirmed expectations lead to such a high level of surprise. Maguire and Keane (2006) proposed that surprise may be better thought of in terms of *Representation-Fit*. They pointed out that while disconfirmed expectations may frequently lead to perceived surprise, this may not always be the case. For instance, if a person can account for *why* an expectation was disconfirmed, then they might not be so surprised by it.

Surprise as representation-fit

Zwaan and Radvansky (1998) have shown that during reading, people routinely construct situation models, or rich representations, of the depicted events in a discourse. These consist of a number of complex inferences about the central characters, their goals and actions, as well as more general information about the story's temporal and spatial context. As the reader encounters new events, this representation must be continually updated, a process motivated by the need on the part of the reader to achieve coherence among the text constituents (Graesser, Singer & Trabasso, 1994). Accordingly, each new event in a text must be coherently integrated into the existing discourse representation for successful comprehension to result.

Based on this premise, Grimes-Maguire and Keane (2005b) devised a theory of representation-fit for surprise (see also Maguire & Keane, 2006). In short, this theory predicts that the more difficult it is for an individual to coherently integrate a new event into their discourse representation, the more surprising that event will appear. As well as being an intuitive view, the underlying principles of this theory rest on many well supported models of comprehension (e.g. *Constructivist theory*, Graesser et al, 1994; *Landscape model*, Linderholm, Virtue, van den Broek & Tzeng, 2004; *Situation models*, Zwaan & Radvansky, 1998). The main way in which this account differs from existing theories of surprise is that it does not view the process as being dependent on expectation. Instead surprise is considered as a retrospective judgement relating to how well a given event can be connected with those that have preceded it, like trying to fit a piece into a jigsaw puzzle. Consider a scenario, for instance, where you walk out your front door only to find that your car is no longer in the driveway. This is obviously an unexpected, or schema-discrepant, event. However, if this triggers your memory that the car is currently being serviced, you will no longer be surprised since a satisfactory explanation for the unexpected event has been identified. Conversely, there are other situations where you might not experience any surprise until the point where you realise that an event

cannot be easily explained. Consider, for example, meeting someone on the street but only later realising that they were supposed to be away on holiday.

A study conducted by Grimes-Maguire and Keane (2005a) offered substantive empirical evidence for these ideas. They found that when participants were asked to indicate their level of surprise for the end event in a scenario, they were extremely adept at detecting subtle differences in how strongly that event could be supported by prior events. They also observed that surprise ratings were *not* correlated with on-line expectations, or forward inferences, arguing against the claim that these two variables are linearly related.

Scenario body
Anna has a very important job interview in the morning. She has to get up far earlier than usual, so she makes sure to set her alarm clock radio for 7am.

	How surprised would you be if....?
1	The alarm clock woke her up at 7am *(Expectation Confirmed)*
2	The alarm clock failed to ring at 7am *(Expectation Disconfirmed)*
3	There was a power-cut during the night and the alarm clock failed to ring at 7am *(Expectation Disconfirmed+Enabling Event)*
4	She had a quiet, good night's sleep and the alarm clock failed to ring at 7am *(Expectation Disconfirmed+Control event)*

Table 1: Sample scenario alongside four experimental conditions examined by Maguire and Keane (2006)

More recently, Maguire and Keane (2006) explored whether Representation-Fit is a better explanation for perceived surprise than the Expectation-Disconfirmation hypothesis. They presented participants with simple everyday scenarios, such as that in Table 1, and asked them to rate surprise for one of four hypothetical endings. In the first condition, the ending was directly in line with the expected outcome. In the second condition, this ending disconfirmed the expectation (e.g. the alarm clock failing to ring at 7am goes against the content of the scenario body). In the critical third condition, participants were asked to rate their surprise for the same unexpected ending as in the preceding condition, alongside a potential enabling factor for that event. The fourth condition acted as a control whereby the same unexpected event was coupled with an irrelevant event that bore no causal relationship to it.

The resulting surprise ratings revealed that participants were significantly *less* surprised by the events in the third condition (i.e. 'Expectation Disconfirmed with Enabling Event') than in the second condition (i.e. 'Expectation Disconfirmed' alone). This suggests that surprise ratings were based on the ease with which the events could be connected with the previous scenario representation, rather than on the mere unexpectedness or probability of those events. Indeed, events in the third condition were *less* probable than those in the second condition, as a conjunction of two events is always logically less likely than one of those events on its own. Subsequent experiments ruled out the possibility that participants were interpreting the enabling condition as a 'given' in the scenarios (Maguire & Keane, 2006). Also, interestingly, the enabling events in isolation were rated as more surprising than when they formed part of the conjunction.

These results support the Theory of Representation-Fit. However, while they demonstrate that the provision of an enabling condition lowers the surprise for a scenario, it is not clear *why* this should be the case. In the following experiment we investigate this matter in more detail.

Experiment

One intuitive explanation for Maguire and Keane's (2006) findings is that participants became surprised in the Expectation Disconfirmed condition because they did not generate a plausible explanation for the unexpected event (e.g. they could not understand *why* the alarm clock failed to ring at 7am). According to this view, the Expectation Disconfirmed + Enabling Event condition appeared less surprising because an explanation was suggested (e.g. a power-cut during the night), thereby offering participants a means of integrating the unexpected event into their representation. If this was indeed the reason for the observed effect, it is important to establish whether participants were actually incapable of explaining the events in question or whether they simply did not generate such inferences spontaneously. An alternative and more intriguing possibility is that participants *were* able to generate plausible explanations, but that this did not mitigate the overall level of surprise. Surprise instead could be due to the *uncertainty* of the actual explanation.

In the following experiment, we differentiate between these two conflicting hypotheses using three between-participant conditions. Firstly, a *Control* group of participants were asked to rate surprise for the Expectation Disconfirmed (hereafter D) and Expectation Confirmed (hereafter C) scenarios used by Maguire and Keane (2006). A second *Generative* group carried out the same task but were first asked to generate a plausible reason for why they thought these events occurred (e.g. *"why do you think the alarm clock failed to ring at 7am?"*). A third *Conjunction* group of participants were asked to indicate how surprised they would be by the occurrence of the same events *in conjunction* with the reasons generated by the second group.

If participants cannot generate convincing explanations for the D scenarios, then we would expect no difference in surprise ratings between the Control and Generative groups, but higher ratings for the Conjunction group (reflecting the unsatisfactory reasons generated). However, if participants do not spontaneously generate enabling conditions for unexpected events but are able to do so when explicitly requested, then surprise ratings should be lower for the Generative and Conjunction groups relative to the Control group. Another possibility is that a greater level of surprise

is elicited when the enabling condition is *uncertain*. Thus, for example, participants may hypothesise that a power-failure caused the alarm clock to stop working, but the outcome event may still seem surprising because they cannot be certain of this explanation. If this is the case, then participants in the Conjunction group should give lower surprise ratings relative to the Control and Generative groups, since they are provided with enabling conditions as part of the outcome event, while participants in the other groups are required to hypothesise the enabling conditions.

Method

Participants A total of 100 undergraduate students from UCD took part in this experiment for partial course credit. Data from five participants were discarded due to a failure to complete the experiment.

Materials The same 16 scenarios as used by Maguire and Keane (2006) were employed for this experiment. Only the conditions of C (Expectation confirming scenarios) and D (Expectation disconfirming scenarios) were examined. For the Conjunction group, these conditions were paired with participant-generated enabling events, as described below.

Design The experiment had two stages. In the first stage, one group of participants (the *Control group*) were asked to read each scenario and indicate how surprising they found the final event, while another group of participants (the *Generative group*) were asked to write an explanation for this final event before rating it for surprise. Each participant in these two groups was randomly assigned to read six D and six C scenarios. The second stage of the experiment involved one group of participants (the *Conjunction group*) being assigned to read the same D and C scenarios as the other two groups, along with the dominant enabling event generated by the Generative group. In sum, this was a 3 (Group) x 2 (Scenario Type) design, where Group was a between-participants factor and Scenario Type was a within-participants factor.

Procedure For the first stage of the experiment, participants were randomly assigned to one of the two experimental groups as outlined above (Control or Generative). Participants in the Control group were told that they would be presented with a number of short stories and asked to indicate how surprising they found the final event on a scale of 1 – 7. Participants in the Generative group were also told that they would be presented with a number of stories, but were asked to write down a plausible reason for *why* the final event in the story occurred. Thus, for example, in the D scenario above, they were asked to indicate why they thought the alarm clock failed to ring at 7am. Following this, participants indicated how surprising they found this final event (as opposed to how surprising they found their generated explanation for the event). Each scenario was presented on a separate page and in a different random order for each participant.

Prior to the second stage of the experiment, the responses from the Generative group were analysed and the dominant rationalisation for each of the scenarios was identified. In order to do this, each participant's response to each scenario was categorised in terms of a distinct theme and the most common of these was identified (e.g. for the alarm clock scenario, responses fell into the theme of "battery-failure" or of "setting the alarm clock incorrectly"). It should be noted that there was great uniformity in the reasons generated. That is, the majority of participants generated the *same* potential reasons for the unexpected events. Inter-rater reliability for the categorization process was high (above 95%) and any disagreement was resolved by discussion. The dominant enabling event for each scenario was then presented alongside the original D or C outcome. So, for example, the most commonly generated response for the disconfirming scenario in Table 1 was *"the batteries in the alarm clock ran out"* and this was added to the original outcome to become *"The batteries in the alarm clock ran out and the alarm clock failed to ring at 7am"*. The Conjunction group were then presented with the original scenarios and asked to give surprise ratings for the conjoined outcomes.

Results and Discussion

While there was no difference in the surprise ratings between the Generative and the Control groups, the Conjunction group gave significantly lower surprise ratings for the scenario outcomes. These results can be seen in Figure 1. A 2 x 3 mixed ANOVA on the surprise ratings revealed a significant main effect of Condition, $F_1(1,92) = 827.543$, $p < 0.0001$, $MS_e = .408$; $F_2(1,45) = 923.080$, $p < 0.0001$, $MS_e = .190$, whereby the surprise ratings for the confirming scenarios ($M = 1.91$, $SD = 1.29$) were rated as reliably lower than those for the disconfirming scenarios ($M = 4.69$, $SD = 1.6$). There was also a significant main effect of Group, $F_1(2,92) = 7.582$, $p = 0.001$, $MS_e = .788$; $F_2(2,45) = 5.587$, $p = 0.007$, $MS_e = .608$. Post-hoc analysis using Bonferroni adjustments showed that the Conjunction group ($M = 2.88$, $SD = 1.89$) gave significantly lower surprise ratings on average than both the Control ($M = 3.52$, $SD = 2.07$) and the Generative groups ($M = 3.35$, $SD = 1.99$, $ps < 0.01$). The interaction between Group and Condition was also significant, $F_1(2,92) = 7.441$, $p = 0.001$, $MS_e = .408$; $F_2(2,45) = 9.664$, $p < 0.0001$, $MS_e = .190$, illustrating that the Group effect was greater in the disconfirming scenarios than in the confirming scenarios.

These results are interesting for several reasons. Firstly, they demonstrate that participants were capable of generating convincing reasons for unexpected outcomes (as evidenced by the lower surprise for the Conjunction group). However, even when they did this, participants in the Generative group did not find the outcomes less surprising than participants in the Control group. Therefore, the lower ratings for the Conjunction group cannot be explained by participants' inability or disinclination to generate appropriate explanations for those events.

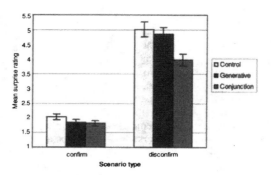

Figure 1: Surprise ratings across experimental conditions

The results leave open the possibility that, even though only one group of participants were explicitly asked to think of a reason for the unexpected events, participants in *both* the Control and the Generative group were attempting to do this. In other words, when they read the outcome *"The alarm clock failed to go off at 7am"* they tried to link this with the scenario body by means of some 'causal search' of their knowledge. This assumption is in line with most theories of discourse comprehension, which hold that people are motivated to coherently link all the events in a piece of text together using inferences (cf. Graesser et al., 1994).

Our results reveal that the reduction of surprise reported by Maguire and Keane (2006) was only manifested for the Conjunction group and not for the other two groups. At first this result seems counter-intuitive. Surely if people can think of an explanation for why something unexpected occurred, then they should not be so surprised by it? If a reader can somehow connect two events together (e.g., by hypothesising that the batteries in the alarm clock have gone flat), then they should be facilitating representational integration and thus lowering surprise. The reasons provided by the Generative group were certainly convincing, given they had the effect of lowering surprise for the Conjunction group. Consequently, the difference in surprise ratings between these groups is unusual, seeing as participants in both had access to the same information.

One explanation for this pattern of results is that hypothetical reasons are processed differently to those that are presented as part of the proposition to be evaluated. While people can easily generate a reason for an unexpected event, they may not be certain about that reason, and this may make the event seem more surprising. For any unexpected event, there will always be a number of different reasons for why that event occurred. In the alarm clock scenario for instance, an alarm clock failing to ring at 7am could be due to a power-cut, a failure of batteries, the person setting it incorrectly, or even something more bizarre like a sabotage effort. When people attempt to rationalise an event, they will be aware that multiple explanations are possible. Even if one of those explanations seems quite reasonable, it is potential that the actual sequence of events is *more* surprising than the most reasonable explanation. In other words, the less certain a given explanation is for an outcome event, the more surprising that event should be in the scenario context.

This kind of effect is evident in the way people reason about everyday events. For example, imagine you had arranged to meet someone in a city location. Ten minutes pass and they have not yet arrived – a fact that seems surprising. You imagine that perhaps they are stuck in traffic but, alternatively, you are aware that this may not be the case (e.g. they may have been involved in a car accident, which would also render them late). Eventually, when the person arrives, they explain that they *were* actually held up in traffic. Your level of surprise subsequently decreases, despite the fact that the actual reason for the delay is one that you have already considered.

It is important to note that an effect of this nature does not necessitate the generation of multiple hypotheses. On the contrary, models of hypothetical thinking maintain that people entertain only one hypothesis at a time (e.g. Evans, Over & Handley 2003). Consequently, the influence of uncertainty is likely to stem from a reduced confidence in the hypothesis rather than from the generation and consideration of alternatives. For example, in speculating why someone is late, you might feel somewhat uncertain about the *held up in traffic* explanation without having explicitly entertained any other alternatives. Thus, participants in the Generative group need not have generated more than one explanation for uncertainty to have had an effect.

General Discussion

The results of this experiment have revealed a number of interesting issues regarding the nature of surprise. Most importantly, they suggest that higher levels of uncertainty lead to higher levels of surprise. This finding is compatible with Maguire and Keane's (2006) theory of Representation-Fit which claims that surprise is based on the extent to which an event fits with a person's representation. Figure 2 illustrates this using a pair of diagrams. The first represents the Conjunction condition. Here, the explanation for the event is explicitly suggested and so surprise is based on the 'goodness of fit' between it and the existing representation. The second diagram represents the Generative condition. Here, multiple explanations are possible but since surprise is a retrospective judgement, people are aware that only one sequence of events can be correct. Given that only one of the routes linking the event to the representation can apply, the goodness of fit of each route is diluted. Although the existence of multiple explanations *increases* likelihood according to probability theory, it also serves to decrease the perceived level of fit and increase the level of surprise.

An example of this effect is a defence lawyer presenting an alibi for a defendant. Even though providing multiple possible alibis should increase the probability that the defendant is innocent, lawyers tend to present only the single strongest alibi. Because the jury is aware that only one alibi is applicable, presenting multiple explanations

would actually weaken the case (Kuhn, Weinstock & Flaton, 1994). In the same way, considering multiple possible reasons for an event makes it seem more surprising than considering only the least surprising reason on its own.

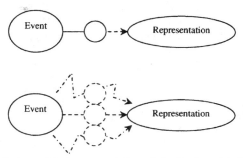

Figure 2: A graphical representation of the Conjunction (C) and the Generative (G) conditions

Surprise versus probability

Several studies have revealed a strong association between judgements of surprise and judgements of likelihood (e.g. Fisk, 2002). However, from a probability point of view, the above reasoning is clearly fallacious: a conjunction cannot be more likely than either of its constituents. For example, the conjunctive proposition of a power cut and an alarm clock failing to go off is evidently less likely than the occurrence of the latter event on its own, since this includes the possibility that the alarm clock failed to go off for other reasons. In this case, is it paradoxical that the less likely proposition should be rated as less surprising?

Given that surprise is not the same thing as probability, there is no reason why these concepts should correspond with each other. Probability takes into account the many different ways in which an event *might* occur. Thus, the more possible ways that something could happen, the more probable it will be. In contrast, surprise is a retrospective judgement concerning an event that has already occurred. Because this event can only have happened in one way, high levels of uncertainty will actually increase the potential for surprise. Accordingly, less likely events (e.g. a power cut and alarm clock failure) can actually appear less surprising than more likely events (e.g. alarm clock failure) because they minimize the potential for more surprising explanations (e.g. somebody maliciously turned off the alarm clock).

At first glance, the results of our experiments bear much resemblance to Tversky and Kahneman's (1983) study on the conjunction fallacy, raising the question of whether this might be related to surprise. In a series of experiments, Tversky and Kahneman found a pair of events was sometimes rated as more likely than the singular events on their own. For example when participants where presented with a short scenario description of a woman called Linda (who was described as an outspoken philosophy student, concerned with human rights etc), people frequently thought it was more probable that *Linda was a feminist <u>and</u> a bank teller* than that *Linda was a bank teller* in isolation. This occurs despite the fact that the latter option is evidently less probable than the former (i.e., since the second option covers both of the possibilities that Linda either is or is not a feminist). Discounting the possible influence of surprise, Tverksy and Kahneman (1983) explained this by virtue of a *representativeness heuristic* where people are likely to overestimate representative examples. However, recent work by Fisk (2002) has argued that this judgement fallacy is best explained in terms of Shackle's (1969) *potential surprise* theory. According to this theory, individuals' ratings of subjective probability are often influenced by the potential of that event to elicit surprise. Fisk (2002) argued that people use the potential surprise heuristic rather than Tversky and Kahneman's representativeness heuristic. In other words, people think that Linda is more likely to be a bank teller and a feminist because it is the least *surprising* possibility.

In the real world, probabilities and frequencies for particular events are rarely available. As a result, people are more likely to rely on 'gut feelings' rather than logical mathematical rules in assessing probability. It may be the case that in estimating likelihood, people often rely on judgements of how surprising an event would be were it to occur. The use of this strategy may be as a result of the singularity principle (Evans et al., 2003) which maintains that people are incapable of considering multiple hypothetical situations at the same time. Thus, the effect observed in our experiment may be of a similar nature to that observed by Tversky and Kahneman (1983). The possibility that *Linda is a bank teller and a feminist* is less surprising as an outcome than *Linda is a bank teller* because the latter includes the possibility that Linda is not a feminist. According to the singularity principle, people cannot appreciate the concept of Linda being both a feminist and not a feminist: she has to be one or the other and thus including both possibilities actually *increases* the potential for surprise. This idea can successfully explain why people tend to gravitate towards the representative sample, as reported by Tversky and Kahneman. If people base their likelihood judgements on a single hypothetical scenario then they are effectively thinking in terms of surprise rather than in terms of probability. In such cases, the most representative scenario will always be the least surprising.

Conclusion

In sum, this paper has investigated why the provision of an enabling condition decreases surprise for an unexpected event, while also decreasing probability. We found that even when participants were explicitly required to generate explanations for unexpected events, this had no significant effect on surprise ratings. Yet, when the same reasons were presented to another group, surprise was lowered. Thus, it appears that although people have the ability to infer plausible explanations for events, surprise remains high when those explanations are uncertain. In this way, a less likely event can actually be rated as less surprising than a more likely event. This effect is successfully accounted for by Maguire and Keane's (2006) Theory of Representation-Fit. Given the link between this effect and the conjunction fallacy, future study should investigate the extent to which people rely on potential surprise judgements in estimating likelihood.

Acknowledgments

This research was partially supported by the Irish Research Council for Science, Engineering and Technology.

References

Darwin, C. (1872). *The Expression of Emotion in Man and Animals*. London: J. Murray.

Evans, J.St.B.T., Over, D.E., & Handley, S.H. (2003). A theory of hypothetical thinking. In D. Hardman & L. Maachi (Eds.), *Thinking: Psychological Perspectives on Reasoning, Judgement and Fecision Making*. Chichester: Wiley.

Fisk, J.E. (2002). Judgements under uncertainty: Representativeness or potential surprise? *British Journal of Psychology, 93*, 431-449.

Graesser, A.C., Singer, M., & Trabasso, T. (1994). Constructing inferences during narrative text comprehension. *Psychological Review, 101*, 371-395.

Grimes-Maguire, R. & Keane, M.T. (2005a). Expecting a surprise? The effect of expectations in perceived surprise in stories. *Proceedings of the 27th Annual Conference of the Cognitive Science Society*. Hillsdale, NJ: Erlbaum.

Grimes-Maguire, R. & Keane, M.T. (2005b). A cognitive model of surprise in narrative. *Kogwis: Proceedings of the Seventh Biannual Meeting of the German Cognitive Science Society*.

Kuhn, D., Weinstock, M. & Flaton, R. (1994). How well do jurors reason? Competence dimensions of individual variation in a juror reasoning task. *Psychological Science, 5*, 289-296.

Linderholm, T., Virtue, S., van den Broek, P., & Tzeng, Y. (2004). Fluctuations in the availability of information during reading: Capturing cognitive processes using the landscape model. *Discourse Processes, 37(2)*, 165-186.

Maguire, R., & Keane, M.T. (2006). Surprise: Disconfirmed expectations or representation fit. *Proceedings of the 28th Annual Conference of the Cognitive Science Society*. Hillsdale, NJ: Erlbaum.

Meyer, W.U., Reisenzein, R. & Schützwohl, A. (1997). Towards a process analysis of emotions: The case of surprise. *Motivation and Emotion, 21(3)*, 251-274.

Shackle, G.L.S (1969). *Decisions, Order and Time in Human Affairs*. Cambridge: Cambridge University Press.

Teigen, K.H., & Keren, G. (2003). Surprises: Low probabilities or high contrasts? *Cognition, 87*, 55-71.

Tversky, A., & Kahneman, D. (1983). Extensional vs. intuitive reasoning: The conjunction fallacy in probability judgement. *Psychological Review, 90 (4)*, 293-315.

Zwaan, R.A. & Radvansky, G.A. (1998). Situation Models in Language Comprehension and Memory. *Psychological Bulletin, 123 (2)*, 162-185.

Either greedy or well informed:
The reward maximization – unbiased evaluation trade-off

Helena Matute (matute@fice.deusto.es)
Miguel A. Vadillo (mvadillo@fice.deusto.es)
Fernando Blanco (fblanco@fice.deusto.es)
Serban C. Musca (serbancmusca@gmail.com)

Departamento de Psicología, Universidad de Deusto
Apartado 1, 48080 Bilbao, SPAIN

Abstract

People often believe that they exert control on uncontrollable outcomes, a phenomenon that has been called illusion of control. Psychologists tend to attribute this illusion to personality variables. However, we present simulations showing that the illusion of control can be explained at a simpler level of analysis. In brief, if a person desires an outcome and tends to act as often as possible in order to get it, this person will never be able to know that the outcome could have occurred with the same probability if he/she had done nothing. Our simulations show that a very high probability of action is usually the best possible strategy if one wants to maximize the likelihood of occurrence of a desired event, but the choice of this strategy gives rise to illusion of control.

Introduction

The illusion of control has been observed in many different laboratory experiments since the initial studies by Langer (1975). It consists of people believing that they have control over desired outcomes that are uncontrollable but occur frequently. As a real life example, let us think of the way ancient tribes danced for rain, or the way many people, still today, believe in magical rituals rather than in scientific medicine as the best means to improve their health. These examples should give us an idea of the prevalence and importance of this problem in relation to human welfare.

Most explanations for this effect have been framed in terms of personality and self-esteem protection (e.g., Alloy & Abramson, 1982). However, and without discussing the importance of personality variables, what we would like to argue is that the basic tendency towards an illusion of control is present in all of us, as it is just a consequence of the way we interact with the world when we want to influence the occurrence of events. We will make use of simulations to illustrate our point.

The basic idea is a very simple one. Imagine a person who is trying to obtain an outcome that is of crucial importance for survival. Quite probably, this person will tend to act at every opportunity in order to obtain it. If the outcome is uncontrollable but occurs frequently, if this person is responding as often as possible, the occurrence of the outcome will surely coincide with the person's action most of the time. Thus, it is not strange that under such conditions, this person will develop an illusion of control. In order to be able to realize that the outcome would have occurred with the same probability regardless of responding, this person should adopt a much more scientific strategy: he or she should test not only what happens when a response is performed but also what happens when a response is not performed. That is, they should respond only in 50% of the trials so that they can equally sample both cases. However, are people ready to test what happens in the absence of a magical ritual when they believe that the ritual is responsible for a very important outcome?

The many studies that have been published showing that laboratory participants are indeed able to detect when outcomes are uncontrollable (e.g., Shanks & Dickinson, 1987; Wasserman, 1990) would make us believe that people do naturally behave in the scientific way described above and naturally detect response-outcome contingencies. However, those laboratory studies instruct their subjects very explicitly on how to behave and what to look for. If we manipulate the instructions that participants receive in an uncontrollable situation, participants who are simply instructed to obtain the outcomes tend to respond at every opportunity (and therefore, to develop an illusion of control as well); on the other hand, those participants who are instructed to adopt the scientific strategy, are the ones who are able to realize that the task is uncontrollable (Matute, 1996). In other words, people do have the cognitive capacity to detect the absence of control, but this does not necessarily mean that they will use it by default, in naturalistic settings. Indeed, Matute's (1996) studies suggested that, unless there is a special motivation to detect the degree of control that one has over the outcome, people will tend to respond as much as possible, rather than in 50% of the trials. In the present research we will show that even for an artificial system, responding as much as possible is the best possible strategy when its aim is to obtain an outcome that is controllable; but the counterpart of behaving this way is that the system will be more prone to develop an illusion of control when faced with uncontrollable situations.

Simulations

Procedure

Our simulations are based on the Rescorla-Wagner model (Rescorla & Wagner, 1972) model, which is one of the most widely used in the area of learning research to simulate how people learn to associate potential causes and effects (like, for example, responses and outcomes). This model is formally equivalent to the delta rule (Widrow & Hoff, 1960) used to train two-layer distributed neural networks through a gradient descent learning procedure. In the Rescorla-Wagner model the change (ΔV_R^n) in the strength of the association between a potential cause (in our case, the system's response, R) and a potential effect (a desired outcome) after each learning trial, takes place according to the following equation:

$$\Delta V_R^n = k \cdot (\lambda - V_t^{n-1}) \quad (1)$$

where k is a learning rate parameter that reflect the associability of the cause, α, and that of the effect, β, ($K = \alpha \cdot \beta$ in the original Rescorla & Wagner model); λ reflects the asymptote of the curve (which is assumed to be 1 in trials in which the outcome is present and 0 otherwise), and V_t^{n-1} is the strength with which the effect can be predicted by the sum of the strengths that all the possible causes that are present in the current trial had in trial $n-1$. For example, in a simulation of the illusion of control, there should be at least two possible causes for the occurrence of the outcome: one is the system's response, R, the other one is the context in which the response takes place (see, e.g., Shanks & Dickinson, 1987). Thus, for instance, when the outcome occurs but there is no response, the occurrence of the outcome will be attributed to other, background or contextual, potential causes. By the same reasoning, when the outcome occurs after a response has been given, the outcome will be attributed to both the response and the context, as a function of their respective associability. The task of the learner will be to learn how much is due to his or her own response, how much is due to other, unspecified potential causes. In general, contexts are assumed to be of low associability, thus, in all the simulations that we will report, k will be 0.10 for the context and 0.30 for the response. Also, it is often the case in many published simulations of this model that k takes different values as a function of whether the outcome occurs or as a function of age-related or species-related differences in sensitivity to the outcome. However, for the sake of simplicity we have preferred to ignore these additional parameters in our simulations. Thus, the value of k, for both the context and the response, will be kept constant, regardless of whether the outcome occurs or not. For each simulation, 100 learning trials and 500 iterations will be run.

In all simulations, the probability that the outcome occurs when the system makes a response, p(O|R), will be 0.75. The probability that the outcome occurs when there is no response, p(O|noR), will be 0.75 in some simulations and 0 in others. When those two probabilities are identical (e.g., both of them are 0.75), the outcome is said to be noncontingent on the response, or, in other words, *uncontrollable*. In this case, the actual contingency is 0 (i.e., 0.75 – 0.75). When these two probabilities are different (i.e., 0.75 and 0, respectively), then the outcome is controllable

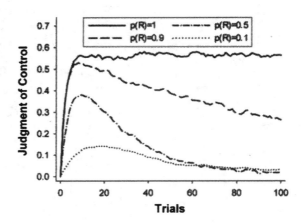

Figure 1: In Simulation 1 outcomes occur with a probability of 0.75 and are uncontrollable (i.e., they occur regardless of whether the system responds or not). The judgment of control is shown to depend on the probability of responding. (See main text for simulation details.)

(i.e., there is a positive contingency of 0.75). Thus, we will test both controllable and uncontrollable conditions. The reason why we are using a high probability of the outcome's occurrence (i.e., 0.75) both in controllable and uncontrollable conditions is that the illusion of control is more readily observed in uncontrollable conditions when the outcome occurs frequently (e.g., Alloy & Abramson, 1979; Matute, 1995).

The strength of the association between the response and the outcome is taken as an index of the strength of the response-outcome causal relation perceived by the system (i.e., the judgment of control). Thus, an illusion of control will be observed anytime when the strength of the association between the response and the outcome becomes higher than zero in a noncontingent situation.

Across simulations we will manipulate the probability that the system responds in each trial, p(R). In the first set of simulations we will compare the effect of different probabilities of responding, ranging from 0.1 to 1.0. In the second set of simulations, probabilities of responding will not be fixed, as they will change with experience.

Results

Simulations using a fixed p(R) Simulation 1 considers a noncontingent situation where the outcome occurs in 75% of the trials, regardless of whether there is a response or not. The results of this simulation, presented in Figure 1, show that the illusion of control is dependent on the probability of responding: As the probability of acting approaches 1, the illusion of control becomes stronger and more persistent over trials.

Now, if responding with a very high probability produces such illusions, why do people tend to respond so much? Wouldn't it make more sense to be less active so that the

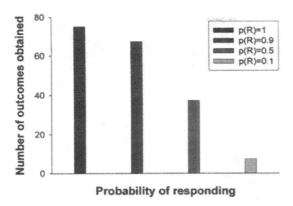

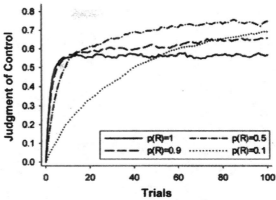

Figure 2. In Simulation 2 the outcome is said to be controllable because it occurs in 75% of the occasions in which the system responds and never in its absence. Simulation 2 shows that the number of outcomes that is obtained after 100 trials is considerably reduced as the probability of responding departs from 1.

Figure 3. Simulation 3 uses the same controllable condition as Simulation 2 (i.e., the outcome occurs in 75% of the occasions in which the subject responds and never in the absence of responding), but here the dependent variable is the judgment of control (associative strength). Simulation 3 shows that, even in contingent conditions, the high p(R) strategy is not the best one with respect to contingency detection.

actual contingency could be accurately detected? If a system is trying to find out how much control is available over an uncontrollable outcome, this system should, as shown in Simulation 1, be quite passive. A low probability of responding will certainly allow the system to correctly detect the uncontrollability of the outcome and would not affect the amount of the outcomes obtained, since in uncontrollable situations responding with a high or low probability does not affect the amount of outcomes that can be obtained.

However, let us now imagine a situation in which the outcome effectively depends on the subject's behavior. Thus, in Simulation 2, the outcome *is* controllable. Assume, for example, that the outcome occurs in 75% of the occasions in which the system responds, and it never occurs when the system does not respond. This case is shown in Figure 2: A system that acts with a probability of 1 will be able to obtain more outcomes than a system responding with at a lower probability. As the probability of responding drops down from 1, the percentage of desired outcomes obtained is reduced. This, of course, is true for any positive contingency situation (and the opposite is true for negative contingency). Thus, for any condition that depends on our performing a given action, the best thing we can do in order to maximize reward is to perform the action just in all occasions (Simulation 2). The bad news is that this strategy will produce an illusion of control when the outcome is uncontrollable (Simulation 1).

It is clear that the best strategy to maximize the number of outcomes are not optimal when the goal is to know how much control one has over the outcome. If the outcome happens to be uncontrollable, the high p(R) strategy will provide the user with data that is too noisy and incomplete to accurately calculate the actual contingency, thus giving

rise to illusion of control. But, is the high p(R) strategy problematic only in noncontingent situations?

Simulation 3 compares the detection of contingency that can take place in a contingent situation when the probability of responding is 1 as compared to when it is reduced (up to 0.1). Simulation 3 was conducted in the same conditions as Simulation 2, but the dependent variable is now the strength of the association (or judgment of control) rather than the number of outcomes obtained. Thus, it considers a contingent relation in which the outcome occurs in 75% of the trials in which the subject responds and never when there is no response. As can be seen in Figure 3, even when the outcome is contingent on responding – and therefore, the best thing one can do to maximize reward is to respond in all occasions (cf. Simulation 2) – the high p(R) strategy prevents the accurate detection of the contingency. In this case, the actual contingency is 0.75. Even a subject responding with a very low probability (0.1) will be able to produce a much better judgment of control than one who responds always. In this later case, there is no illusion in our high p(R) system because the outcome is contingent on responding, but the contingency that this system perceives between the response and the outcome is lower than the one that is actually present.

This may seem surprising at first. However, as was the case in the noncontingent conditions shown in Simulation 1, if the system responds in every single trial, it cannot know what happens when there is no response. In this case, the subject is just exposed to what happens when the response is given in a given context. And, according to Equation 1, the increment in the strength of the association that can be accrued in a given trial depends not only on the strength of the association between the response and the outcome in the

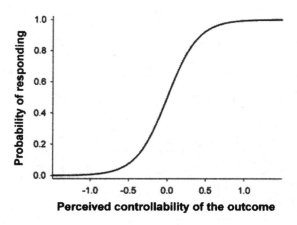

Figure 4. Sigmoid function for the probability of responding based on the perceived controllability of the outcome (i.e., on the strength of the response-outcome association).

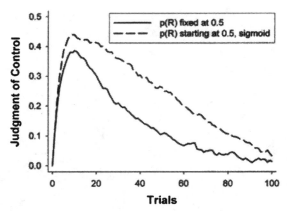

Figure 5. In Simulation 4 uncontrollable outcomes occur with a probability of 0.75. The illusion of control is more intense and persistent when the system's p(R) varies according to the strength of the response than when this probability is fixed.

previous trial, but also on the strength with which the other cues that are present (e.g., the context) are already associated with the outcome. This means that the associative strength that could be accrued by the response in a given trial will be shared by the response and the context (as a function of their relative associability; k in the equation, and their associative strength in the previous trial; V_t^{n-1} in the equation). By the same reasoning, the trials in which the response does not occur (in systems in which the p(R) is different from 1), can only affect the strength of the context. And, because in the contingent situation we are testing in Simulation 3, the outcome does not occur when there is no response, these no-response trials will reduce the strength of the context alone. Moreover, the reduction of the strength of the context will in turn have the (indirect) effect of increasing the strength of the response. This is because, after the context strength has been reduced, when a response is given in a subsequent trial, the competition that the context can exert for associative strength will be lower. In this way the response will get a larger proportion of the available strength in all systems responding with a p(R) lower than 1 in Simulation 3 (see Equation 1). However, a system that responds with a p(R) of 1 does not have information on what happens when the response is absent and just the context is present. In other words, there are no context-alone trials that will help the system discard the potential causal role of the context. If this is so, then the associative strength accrued by the response *and* the context in each trial (appreciate that they always occur in compound in this system) are shared between the two of them as a function of their respective ks. This is why it is impossible for a subject responding at every opportunity to accurately detect contingencies, not only in uncontrollable situations but also in controllable ones. As shown in Simulation 3, a subject responding with a probability of 0.9, or even 0.1 will be much more accurate in the detection of the actual

contingency than a subject responding all the time, even when the outcome is controllable. Still, one has to keep in mind that these would not be good strategies if what we want is to maximize reward.

Simulations using a modifiable p(R) One could argue that our previous simulations use artificial conditions, in that living organisms do not keep a fixed probability of responding regardless of what they learn; by contrast, they vary their probability of responding as a function of how strongly they believe that the response is the cause of the outcome. Thus, let us now suppose that if a response is very strongly associated to the outcome (in other words, the system believes the response is the cause of the outcome), the probability of responding will be stronger.

Simulation 4 (see Figure 5) is similar to the previous ones, but here the probability of responding is increased or reduced as a function of the strength of the association that is being learned. To this end, we use a simple sigmoid function that increases the probability of responding when the association increases and reduces it otherwise:

$$p(R) = 1/(1 + e^{-\theta \cdot V_R^{n-1}}) \ (2)$$

For the present purposes, the parameter describing the slope of the sigmoid function, θ, was set to 5. Figure 4 depicts the different values that p(R) can receive depending on the strength of the response-outcome association. As there can be seen, a system acting according to this equation will simply tend to respond with a very high probability when the response is apparently causing the outcome. If the perceived contingency between the response and the outcome is negative (that is, if the system believes that the response actually prevents the occurrence of the outcome), the probability of responding would be near 0. Finally, when the associative strength is near 0 and, therefore, the system believes that the outcomes are uncontrollable, the probability of response is intermediate.

Note that in Equation 2 the probability of responding is dependent on the strength of the association. This implies that for the first trial the probability of responding is to some extent arbitrary, because for the first trial there is no prior associative strength upon which to compute the probability of responding. In Simulation 4, the probability of responding for the first trial was set to the intermediate value of 0.50.

Thus, Simulation 4 corresponds to a more natural condition than the previous ones, in that cognitive systems generally vary their probability of responding according to the strength of the association that they have formed between the response and the outcome (or, in other words, the strength that they attribute to their own response as a cause of the outcome). As can be seen in Figure 5, the illusion of control that is developed in this way is even more intense and persistent than the one produced by a fixed p(R), as that used in Simulation 1.

But let us now suppose that not only do subjects vary their probability of responding as a function of what they learn, but also that different subjects probably start up from different backgrounds, beliefs, strategies... and personalities. This should at least produce some initial biases. These differences in the initial conditions, even though they are subsequently subject to a common learning function that will tend to make them similar to each other at asymptote, could perhaps produce important differences in the speed and slope of learning.

Simulation 5 tests whether the apparently innocuous little biases that many people may have during the initial stages of a new task (e.g. being more of less active), can have a profound effect on the strength and the durability of the illusion of control. This simulation is very similar to Simulation 4, but here two systems that are sensitive to the strength of the association (i.e., that use a sigmoid function, as in Simulation 4) are compared. The probability of making a response in the very first trial is what we manipulated here. The difference between the two systems is that the probability of responding in the first trial is 0.1 for one of them and 0.9 for the other. In all remaining trials, the probability of responding in both systems is computed according to Equation 2.

The results are presented in Figure 6. The initial bias – that represent the tendency to respond more or less due to previous history, background, beliefs, or personality – though implemented only in the very first trial still has an effect after 100 trials.

Discussion

The illusion of control is at the roots of many real world problems, like the reluctance of many people to believe in scientific medicine and the proliferation in today's world of so many magical and pseudoscientific remedies for almost everything. It is generally believed to be part of naïve

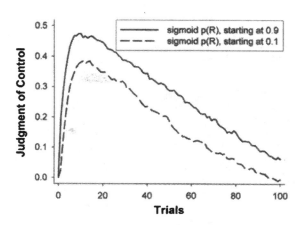

Figure 6. In Simulation 5 uncontrollable outcomes occur with a probability of 0.75 regardless of whether the system responds or not, as in Simulation 4. The two systems here considered do vary their probability of responding according to the strength of the association between the response and the outcome, but one of them starts with a stronger bias to act in the very first trial. This initial, first trial bias still has an effect on performance after 100 trials.

personalities, but we have shown that it is potentially a much more prevalent problem that can occur in all cognitive systems. Indeed, it is a logical consequence of how we interact with the world. Even though personality variables can also have an important influence and can surely be responsible for individual differences among people, they are not the only variables that are responsible, nor the only ones that should be taken into account when trying to set therapies and policies to eradicate this illusion. As shown in our simulations, the main problem has to do with what the goal of the system is. If our goal in the world is to maximize the number of rewards (and this is an important goal for survival that can certainly have been favored by evolution as an adequate strategy for many occasions), then the system will try to respond as much as possible in order to obtain those outcomes. As shown in Simulation 2, only those subjects responding in all possible occasions will get the majority of the available rewards when the situation is controllable (of course, this would be irrelevant if the situation were noncontingent). Thus it would not be strange that a default strategy in many people and even in animals would be to respond as much as possible. What is clear from our simulations is that this strategy, while optimal when one wants to maximize reward, is quite a bad one in the occasions in which the goal of the system is not to obtain the outcome, but to analyze to what degree it is controllable. Therefore, it is to some extent contradictory trying to maximize control over the environment and, at the same time, trying to make accurate inferences about the world. This means that, if a given outcome is important enough for people, the attempts they make to control it will surely interfere with the ability to accurately assess the degree of control they actually have.

In sum, imagine that twenty people were suddenly infected with an unknown mortal disease and that, for some reason, you suspect that medicine X might cure them. Would you be ready to test this medicine just in one half of your patients so as to check that the medicine is actually working? This is actually the difference between scientific reasoning and every day reasoning. As we have shown, none of these strategies can be said to be better than the other one; it is only a matter of choosing the right one at the right time. Thus if we would like people to apply more scientific reasoning to their everyday life, perhaps we should start by trying to convince them to test passive responding in situations in which the outcome is unimportant for them. In this way, they will be able to learn what they need about skepticism so that the next time they face a serious problem they will be able to actively chose the p(R) strategy that best complies with their own goals.

Acknowledgments

Support for this research was provided by Grant SEJ406 from Junta de Andalucía. Fernando Blanco was supported by a F.P.I. fellowship from Gobierno Vasco (Ref.: BFI04.484). We would like to thank Cristina Orgaz for valuable discussions on these points. Correspondence concerning this article should be addressed to Helena Matute, Departamento de Psicología, Universidad de Deusto, Apartado 1, 48080 Bilbao, Spain. E-mail: matute@fice.deusto.es.

References

Alloy, L. B., & Abramson, L. Y. (1979). Judgment of contingency in depressed and nondepressed students: Sadder but wiser? *Journal of Experimental Psychology: General, 108,* 441-485.

Alloy, L. B., & Abramson, L. Y. (1982). Learned helplessness, depression, and the illusion of control. *Journal of Personality and Social Psychology, 42,* 1114-1126.

Langer, E. J. (1975). The illusion of control. *Journal of Personality and Social Psychology, 32,* 311-328.

Matute, H. (1995). Human reactions to uncontrollable outcomes: Further evidence for superstitions rather than helplessness. *Quarterly Journal of Experimental Psychology, 48B,* 142-157

Matute, H. (1996). Illusion of control: Detecting response-outcome independence in analytic but not in naturalistic conditions. *Psychological Science, 7,* 289-293.

Rescorla, R. A., & Wagner, A. R. (1972). A theory of Pavlovian conditioning: Variations in the effectiveness of reinforcement and nonreinforcement. In A. H. Black & W. F. Prokasy (Eds.), *Classical conditioning II: Current research and theory* (pp. 64-99). New York: Appelton-Century-Crofts.

Shanks, D. R., & Dickinson, A. (1987). Associative accounts of causality judgment. In G. H. Bower (Ed.), *The psychology of learning and motivation, Vol. 21* (pp. 229-261). San Diego, CA: Academic Press.

Wasserman, E. A. (1990). Detecting response-outcome relations: Toward an understanding of the causal texture of the environment. In G. H. Bower (Ed.), *The psychology of learning and motivation, Vol. 26* (pp. 27-82). San Diego, CA: Academic Press.

Widrow, B., & Hoff, M. E. (1960). Adaptive switching circuits. *1960 IRE WESCON Convention Record* (pp. 96-104). New York: IRE.

Individual Differences in How Much People are Affected by Irrelevant and Misleading Information

Magne Jørgensen (magnej@simula.no)
Simula Research Laboratory, Box 134, NO-1325 Norway

Abstract

People differ in how much they update their beliefs based on new information. According to a recently proposed theory, individual differences in belief updating are, to some extent, determined by neurological differences, i.e., differences in the organization of the brain. The same neurological differences that affect belief updating may also affect handedness. In particular, more mixed-handed people may have a lower threshold for updating beliefs than strongly right-handed people. On the basis of the proposed theory, we hypothesize that mixed-handed software engineers will be more affected by irrelevant and misleading information when providing expert judgments. This hypothesis is tested in five experiments conducted in software engineering contexts. All five experiments supported the hypothesis and suggest that a low threshold for updating beliefs, as measured by degree of mixed-handedness correlates with inaccurate judgment in situations that contain irrelevant or misleading information. On the basis of the results, we argue that software engineering decisions, problem solving and estimation processes should take into account differences in individuals' threshold for updating belief and not be based on the assumption that one "process fits all".

Background

In a recent study of professional software engineers estimating the effort of software development tasks, we found that adding to a software specification information that was clearly irrelevant strongly increased the estimates of the required effort to develop the software (Grimstad and Jørgensen 2006). Similarly, Kemmelmeier (2004) found that increased awareness that certain information was irrelevant did not lessen that information's impact. He summarizes his finding as follows: "*This produced the somewhat ironic pattern that participants told the experimenter which information was useless, but then went on to use this information in their judgments.*"

Misleading information, relevant or not, may have an even stronger unwanted impact on expert judgment (see for example the studies on anchoring (Abdel-Hamid, Sengupta et al. 1993; Mussweiler and Strack 2001).) Unfortunately, the solution may not be as easy as removing or avoiding it. Crasswell (2006) examined the issue of misleading information from a legal perspective and found: "*In practice, though, eliminating misrepresentation often involves more subtle costs. For example, if we require defendants to say less, in order to eliminate statements that might mislead parties, some of those prohibited statements may also convey truthful and useful information, which will be lost if the statements are prohibited.*"

Empirical studies, e.g., (Long and Prat 2002), and common sense, suggest that there are large individual differences with respect to the degree to which irrelevant and misleading information affects performance. Cann and Katz (2005) summarize results from many studies and find that individuals more affected by irrelevant and misleading information have:

- Poorer memory.
- Higher degree of dissociation, defined as the lack of the normal integration of thoughts, feelings, and experiences into the stream of consciousness and memory.
- A higher disposition towards absorption, defined as the disposition for having episodes of total attention that fully engage one's representational resources.
- Higher level of depression.
- Stronger emotional self-focus, measured as greater fear of negative evaluation or higher self-esteem.
- A tendency to be more easily bored, and consequently less willing to sustain focused attention.
- A more external locus of control, e.g., they are more prone to believe that their successes are caused by environmental and situational factors (external reasons) rather than their own control and performance (internal reasons).
- Better imagery vividness, e.g., they are better able to create vivid visualizations of events.

A recent theory proposes that individual differences in the updating of beliefs are caused, to some extent, by neurological, i.e., brain organization-related, differences (Niebauer, Christman et al. 2004; Niebauer and Garvey 2004). This theory also hypothesizes that a higher threshold for updating belief is associated with a higher degree of communication between the left and the right hemispheres of the brain (larger *corpus callosum*) and can be measured by handedness.

Handedness is determined by the distribution of fine motor skill between the left and the right hands. A person is categorized as mixed-handed, relative to a set of task requiring fine motor skills, if he or she does not have one strongly dominating hand. A person is categorized as strong-handed if he or she has a strongly dominant hand for a set of tasks, e.g., always holds the spoon or the pencil in the right hand. A summary of studies leading to and supporting this theory and the relation between belief updating and handedness can be found in (Jasper and Christman 2005).

This paper tests the following **hypothesis** derived from this theory: *Mixed-handed software engineers are more* *affected by irrelevant and misleading information than strong-handed ones.*

This hypothesis is correlational and based on the belief that handedness and affectability are both, to some extent, caused by the same neurological differences. As we will discuss later on, we are not able to test this belief directly and there may be other reasons for observed correlations.

We tested the hypothesis through five experiments where we presented irrelevant and misleading information to software engineers, either software professionals or students, and asked for their judgments. Then, we analysed the connection between handedness and degree of effect from the irrelevant or misleading information. Although our hypothesis may seem to be a natural consequence of the theory, we found only one study relevant for the testing of it, i.e., (Jasper and Christman 2005). That study contained three experiments, not on software engineers, the results of which were mixed. Clearly, there are many factors and processes involved, and many different types of irrelevant and misleading information, i.e., the scope and validity of the theory is far from settled. In this paper, we focus on testing the theory in a software engineering context. Our long-term goal is to understand individual differences in the effect of irrelevant and misleading information sufficiently well to enable people to improve their processes of making decisions and judgments.

The remainder of this paper is organised as follows. Section 2 describes the design and results of the five experiments conducted to test the hypothesis. Section 3 briefly discusses the results and possible implications for software engineering processes. Section 4 concludes and suggests further work.

The Experiments

All participants completed Oldfield's test of handedness (Oldfield 1971) as part of the experiments. Oldfield's test of handedness provides a participant with a handedness value from -1 (perfectly left-handed) to +1 (perfectly right-handed) based on answers on ten questions. In the following analysis we categorize all participants with the value +1 as strong-handers, and all others as mixed-handed. None of the participants in the experiments had the value -1, i.e., the reported results may be due to right-handedness rather than strong-handedness.

The estimates and judgments produced by the respondents vary much and are typically not normally distributed. For this reason, we apply the more outlier robust median value instead of the mean as a measure of the central value. A combination of a high variation and relatively low number of participants, which is the case in several of the reported studies, means that the statistical power is low and not all of the reported differences are statistically significant. In our case, we argue, it is the set of results from five different studies that is our evidence. Replication of similar, even statistically non-significant, results in differently designed studies with different sets of participants is at least, we believe, just as valid evidence as highly significant results from one study. The graphs illustrating the distributions, effect sizes, and more information about the variation of

within-group responses, are not included of space limitation reasons.

Study 1: Anchoring Experiment

Participants: 93 computer science students at the University of Oslo.

Study design: The students were divided randomly divided into four groups:

Group A participants were presented with the following two questions: *1) Do you think you will use more than 5 minutes to read and answer your email tomorrow? 2) How much time do you think you will spend on reading and answering email tomorrow?*

Groups B, C and D were asked the same two questions but with different anchoring values, i.e., Group B received the high anchor value *4 hours*, Group B the very high value *10 hours*, and Group C the absurd value of *22 hours*.

Results: Table 1 shows that the mixed-handers were more impacted by the anchors, particularly by the by most absurd anchor (22 hours), i.e., they had lower estimates in Group A and higher estimates in all the other groups. Interestingly, the strong-handers did not seem to be much impacted by the anchors at all. The difference in response between mixed-handers and strong-handers in Group D is particularly interesting. While the mixed-handers seem to have increased the estimate as a reaction the absurd question "*Do you think you will use more than 22 hours to read and answer your mail tomorrow?*", the strong-handers had the opposite reaction. Possibly, the strong-handers have reacted defensively on the attempt to manipulate their judgment and decreased the estimate to compensate for the attempted manipulation.

Table 1: Median Estimated Time

Group	Mixed-handed	Strong-handed
A (5 min)	7,5 min (n=12)	10 min (n=12)
B (4 h)	15 min (n=17)	10 min (n=8)
C (10 h)	15 min (n=13)	10 min (n=8)
D (22 h)	30 min (n=14)	7,5 min (n=8)

We asked all participants about how much they felt they had been impacted by the anchor (on a scale from "not at all" to "very strong"). The strong-handers felt slightly more impacted than the mixed-handers, but only five mixed-handers and four strong-handers felt that the anchor had had much impact ("strong" or "very strong" impact) on the provided estimate.

Study 2: Hindsight Bias

Participants: Forty-four software professionals at a software process improvement seminar.

Study design: The software professionals were divided randomly into two groups.

Group A participants were presented the following text: *A large insurance company had ten software systems that registered customers and products. The company decided three years ago to replace these systems with one large system that should enable better and more efficient customer care. One important benefit would be that data* about the customer was registered and stored only one place. The plan was to develop the system in two years. After three years (today) the company has abandoned the project and still uses the old systems.

Group B participants were presented with the following text: *A large insurance company has ten software systems that register customers and products. The company considers replacement of these systems with one large system, that should enable better and more efficient customer care. One important benefit would be that data about the customer is registered and stored only one place. The plan is to develop the new system in two years from today.*

As can be seen, the important difference between Groups A and B is that Group A participants know the negative outcome, while Group B participants are given a description of a project that is about to start. Participants in Groups A and B were then asked to answer the same questions: *Considering what you believe and know about previous software projects, how frequently [in %] do you think this type of project fails in developing a useful system.*

The example of one failed project received by Group A participants should, rationally speaking, be close to irrelevant for assessing the overall frequency of failed projects of this type.

Results: Table 2 shows that the mixed-handers estimated on average twice as high failure rates in the Group A situation (with misleading information) as in the Group B situation. There was no such difference among the strong-handers.. The estimates of the mixed-handers were lower than those of the strong-handers in the situation without irrelevant information (the Group B situation), i.e., the judgmental processes may be different in the "normal" situation, as well as in the irrelevant information situation.

Table 2: Median Estimated Frequency

Group	Mixed-handed	Strong-handed
A	30% (n=11)	20% (n=11)
B	15% (n=11)	20% (n=11)

Later, we replicated this experiment in a context with 34 software programmers participating at a seminar on cost estimation. The results were similar to those of the previous experiment, see Table 3. The main difference was that the strong-handers were affected, too, although not as much as the mixed-handers. Again, the mixed-handers had the lower estimates of the failure rate in the situation without irrelevant information.

Table 3: Median Estimated Frequency

Group	Mixed-handed	Strong-handed
A	42% (n=10)	30% (n=7)
B	15% (n=10)	20% (n=7)

Study 3: Wishful Thinking

Participants: The same 34 software programmers participated as those in the replicated experiment in Study 2.
Study design: The participants were divided randomly into two groups. Group A participants were presented with

information that we believed would induce "wishful thinking", i.e., a situation where the wish to use little effort makes the estimator believe that little effort will be used. Group B were presented with a situation that was more neutral with respect to wishful thinking. All participants estimated the effort that they believed their company would need to develop software based on the same requirement specification, i.e., a specification describing an extension to an existing software system for purchasing football match tickets.

The information designed to induce wishful thinking that was presented to Group A participants was as follows:
"Moss FK [a Norwegian football club] has invited many providers (more than 10) to implement these extensions and will use the providers' performance on this project as important input in the selection of a provider for the development of the new ticketing system (which is a much larger and more important contract). An independent expert will evaluate the quality, effort and time used by each provider of this project. With sufficiently high quality of the delivered extension of the existing ticketing system, the provider that spends least effort and time will have a better chance of being selected as provider for the development of the new ticketing system. Assume that your company wants to be selected as the provider for the new project and that you are the one to complete the extensions (you represent your company). Estimate the work effort you think you MOST LIKELY will use to complete the described extension to the existing ticketing system. The estimate will not be presented to Moss FK and should be the effort you most likely will need."

Results: Again, the mixed-handers were more affected by irrelevant information, this time by the wishful thinking inducing information presented to Group A estimators. Similarly to Study 1, the mixed-handers had different (higher) estimates in the situation without misleading information, i.e., in the Group B situation. The results are displayed in Table 4.

Table 4: Median Effort Estimates

Group	Mixed-handers	Strong-handers
A	15 hours (n=10)	20 hours (n=7)
B	42 hours (n=10)	30 hours (n=7)

Study 4: Sequence Impact

Participants: Forty-two computer science students at University of Oslo (different from those in Study 1).
Design: The participants were divided randomly into two groups.

Group A participants were asked to estimate the effort required to develop software based on a reduced version of a software requirement specification. Then, they were presented with additional requirements and asked to update the estimate to cover the full specification. In other words, they first estimated a reduced version of the software and then the complete version.

Group B participants were only asked to estimate the effort required to develop the complete version.

The specified software was similar to software they had developed earlier as part of their university course, i.e., they had previous experience on development of this type of software. The estimation of the reduced version by the Group A participants should be irrelevant for the estimate of the full specification. However, in two previous studies, i.e., (Jørgensen and Carelius 2004) and (Jørgensen 2006), we observed that participants in Group A situations are likely to produce higher estimates than those in Group B situations. This study examines whether the previously observed difference between Group A and Group B participants was due principally to the mixed-handed estimators' responses.

Results: The results in Table 5 support our belief that the difference in estimates of the Group A and B situation was to a large extent caused by the mixed-handers' and not so much the strong-handers' responses. Similarly to the results in Study 3, the mixed-handers had the highest estimates in the situation without manipulative elements, i.e., the Group B situation. If higher estimates are more likely to be more realistic, this result indicates that mixed-handers are more realistic than strong-handers in situations with little irrelevant and misleading information.

Table 5: Median Effort Estimates

Group	Mixed-handers	Strong-handers
A	360 hours (n=11)	180 hours (n=11)
B	240 hours (n=9)	180 hours (n=11)

Study 5: Misleading Information

Participants: The same 44 software professionals as in Study 2.

Design: The participants were randomly divided into two groups.

Group A participants were provided with a fictive example of a successful risk-averse programmer (Linus Torvalds, Linux) and a fictive study from one company in Canada claiming that risk-accepting programmers (defined as those who agreed to the statement "I like to find my own, innovative ways of solving problems.") were less efficient and had code with lower quality than those who were more risk averse. The participants were asked to provide one likely reason for the finding in the Canadian study.

Group B participants were provided with a fictive example of a successful risk-accepting programmer (Bill Gates, Microsoft) and a fictive study from one company in Canada claiming that risk-accepting programmers were more efficient and did not have lower quality of code. The participants were asked to provide one likely reason for the finding in the Canadian study.

When the first part was finished, all participants were asked the following question: *The example and study from Canada clearly do not represent all situations. Which of the statements below do you think is, in general, most correct?*

I believe that the risk-accepting programmers are:

   a) *always better*
   b) *nearly always better*
   c) *most of the time better*
   d) *better in somewhat more than half of the situations*
   e) *better in half of the situations (no difference)*
   f) *worse in somewhat more than half of the situations*
   g) *most of the time worse*
   h) *nearly always worse*
   i) *always worse*

Results: Table 6 shows that both the mixed-handers and the strong-handers were strongly affected by the misleading information, i.e., the Group A participants thought the risk-accepting programmers were better and the Group B participants the opposite. This means that we may have increased the believability and perceived relevance of the information to a level higher than the belief updating threshold of many strong-handers, too. As before, however, the mixed-handers were more affected, e.g., they have slightly higher frequencies of g and h&i in Group A and of c and d in Group B. The difference is, however, not large.

Table 6: Belief in Risk-Accepting Programmers

Group	a&b	c	d	e	f	g	h&i
A (mixed)	0	0	1	0	2	6	2
A (strong)	1	0	0	1	5	4	0
B (strong)	0	6	3	1	1	0	0
B (mixed)	0	7	4	0	0	0	0

When the participants had provided their assessment, we informed them that the example and the Canadian study were invented for the purpose of manipulating their responses. Then, we asked them to update their beliefs, taking into account this information about the misleading information. Table 7 shows the number of adjustment steps made by the participants. Changing an answer from c to e is, for example, an adjustment of 2 steps.

Table 7: Adjustment Steps

Group	0	1	2	3	4
Mixed-handers	7	7	5	2	1
Strong-handers	11	8	0	1	2

Mixed-handers updated their judgments more (although not much more) than the strong-handers, e.g., while eight mixed-handers updated their beliefs with two or more steps, only three strong-handers did the same. One may argue that a stronger willingness to update belief by the mixed-handers was caused by the stronger need to update. However, an analysis of the answers showed that those who updated made similar initial judgments to those who did not update in both Groups A and B, i.e., it was probably not the *need* for updating that drove the actual updating of beliefs. This is, in our opinion, not surprising. The participants have no obvious way of knowing how much they had been affected by the misleading information.

Even after the corrective information was provided, as many as 60% of those in group A and only 23% of those in Group B believed that the risk-accepting programmers did worse in most situations. It is thus evident that the initial misleading information continued to have a strong impact even after the participants had been told that the information was misleading. It seems, consequently, to be difficult to return to an unaffected state of mind.

Discussion

Limitations

Handedness, as measured by Oldfield's test, is likely to be a far from perfect measure of the cognitive phenomenon we want to measure, i.e., the phenomenon termed "threshold for updating beliefs". Indeed, it is possible that handedness and impact from irrelevant information are not related at all, and that the test of handedness we apply measures something else, e.g., that a test of handedness also measure people's level of confidence in which hand they use for various seldom performed tasks, which again may be correlated to belief updating. This imperfection of the handedness measure may have, at least, two different consequences: i) The real connection between "threshold for updating of beliefs" and the effect of irrelevant and misleading information is stronger that measured by handedness, or ii) The underlying cognitive phenomenon indicated by handedness is not "threshold for updating beliefs", but something else, also connected to handedness, e.g., a difference in use of intuition and analysis-based mental processes. If ii) is correct, the observed connection between threshold for updating beliefs and handedness is accidental. This problem is accentuated by the problems of knowing to which degree belief updating actually takes place in the judgmental tasks of our studies. As long as we do not have a good understanding of the cognitive processes involved in updating beliefs, we should be careful about interpreting the results as more than possibly suggesting a correlation between handedness, as measured by Oldfield's test, and susceptibility to bias on some judgmental tasks. More studies are needed.

Our studies are experiments conducted under laboratory conditions. The experiments provide evidence for the presence of relationships, e.g., that mixed-handed software engineers are sometimes more easily affected by irrelevant and misleading information, but are not well suited to show the size of this effect in real-life situations. It is, for example, possible that many organizations somehow avoid unwanted effects by review of the judgments or by well-designed processes. On the other hand, the effects caused by irrelevant and misleading information are unconscious and a good defence may consequently be hard to develop.

The number of subjects in several of the studies is low and the individual study results may not be very robust. However, the observation that five different tasks with different populations gave similar results should, we believe, enable us to have some confidence in the robustness of the results.

Is a Low Threshold for Updating Beliefs Good or Bad?

Our five studies suggest that mixed-handers are more vulnerable to the effects of irrelevant and misleading information. However, our results also suggest that the mixed-handed participants who did not receive irrelevant and misleading information provided judgments different from the strong-handers. They provided, for example, higher (and, considering the typical tendency towards over-

optimism, possibly more realistic) effort estimates. This may indicate that the mixed-handers and the strong-handers were affected differently by both the relevant and the irrelevant information. It may, for example, be the case that a lower threshold for updating beliefs also means that relevant information affects judgment more easily.

The observation that mixed-handers sometimes perform better is consistent with a series of studies in several fields, e.g., (Propper, Christman et al. 2005) reports that mixed-handers seem to have better episodic memory and be less subject to false memories. In (Niebauer, Christman et al. 2004), for example, it is reported that mixed-handers were more willing to use scientific evidence and believed in Darwin's theory of evolution instead of creationism more frequently than the strong-handers.

Drake and colleges (Drake 1983; Drake and Bingham 1988) found that the left hemisphere plays the main role in belief persistence, while the right hemisphere (which is believed to be more active in judgmental tasks by people not strongly right-handed) is more important in changing one's belief. He pointed out that we need a certain degree of stability in our beliefs to benefit from our past experience, but that a degree of flexibility (belief updating) is required to benefit from new experiences, i.e., there is a fine balance between being consistent and being flexible. This balance is, we believe, related to finding the optimal threshold for updating beliefs.

In short, our studies do not show that software organizations should avoid strongly mixed-handed software engineers. The results do however provide some evidence that in situations with irrelevant or misleading information, mixed-handers seem to be easier to manipulate.

What Are the Practical Consequences?

Our results suggest that there are large individual differences in how much software engineers are affected by irrelevant and misleading information and that this may be connected to neuropsychological processes that can be measured by tests of handedness. Possible practical consequences our results include the following:

Software engineers asked to offer judgment in situations in which a great deal of irrelevant or misleading information is provided should be selected carefully with respect to threshold for updating belief. Possibly, software engineering specific tests of how much an individual is affected by irrelevant and misleading information in particular contexts should be developed. The software engineering specific tests may benefit from a comparison of scores with scores from tests of handedness. A high correlation between scores of the tests would suggest that the software engineering specific tests are connected to the underlying, presumably rather stable, neuropsychological processes of the individual, while still being specific enough to be good predictors for the performance of particular types of software engineering tasks.

Software engineers who know that they are easily affected, e.g., by previous experience or tests of threshold for updating beliefs, should learn to take precautions. When, for example, a manager with a low threshold for updating beliefs is in the process of hiring a new employee, he or she may benefit from a carefully structured process for evaluating candidates that leaves as little as possible to unconscious, intuition-based processes. This may, of course, be useful for all managers, but a person with a low threshold for updating beliefs should be especially careful.

The high impact of irrelevant and misleading information on some individuals should lead software organizations and researchers to design improved processes, i.e., processes that reduce the unwanted effects of irrelevant and misleading information. One example of a simple, yet effective, improvement is to remove irrelevant information from a text with a black permanent marker (Kemmelmeier 2004). While people following this process were not affected by the so-called dilution effect, i.e., the tendency to regress the judgment towards the midpoint of the scale with the inclusion of irrelevant information, people just marking the relevant text with a highlighter marker were significantly affected by the irrelevant information.

Conclusion and Further Work

There has, as far as we know, been only one previous study that examines the relation between differences in handedness, as a measure of differences in cognitive processes, and the effects of irrelevant and misleading information on the updating of beliefs. That study, i.e., (Jasper and Christman 2005), examined the effect of misleading anchors and was not conclusive about the relation between the effect of anchoring and handedness. All our five studies found that the mixed-handers were affected more by irrelevant and misleading information. This is, in our opinion, the result we should expect to happen in most situations, given the theory of threshold for updating beliefs and the neurological differences between mixed-handers and strong-handers.

Our results support the view that there are stable, neurological patterns that account for important aspects of how much a person, e.g., a software engineer, is affected by irrelevant and misleading information. We plan to design and evaluate processes that prevent unwanted effects of irrelevant and misleading information particularly designed for those with low thresholds for updating beliefs.

Acknowledge: Thanks to Stein Grimstad at Simula Resarch Laboratory for the useful input to the design of Study 1 and other useful input to this paper.

References

Abdel-Hamid, T. K., Sengupta, K. and Ronan, D. (1993). Software project control: An experimental investigation of judgment with fallible information. *IEEE Transactions on Software Engineering. 19(6),* 603-612.

Cann, D. R. and Katz, A. N. (2005). Habitual acceptance of misinformation: Examination of individual differences and source attributions. *Memory & Cognition. 33(3)*, 405-417.

Craswell, R. (2006). Taking information seriously: Misrepresentation and nondisclosure in contract law and elsewhere. *Virginia Law Review. 92(4)*, 565-632.

Drake, R. A. (1983). Toward a synthesis of some behavioral and physiological antecedents of belief perseverance. *Bulletin of the Psychonomic Society. 26(4)*, 313-315.

Drake, R. A. and Bingham, B. R. (1988). Cognitive style induced by hemispheric priming: consistent versus inconsistent self-report. *Bulletin of the psychonomic society. 26(4)*, 83-94.

Grimstad, S. and Jørgensen, M. (2006). The impact of irrelevant information on estimates of software development effort. Accepted for publication in *Journal of Systems and Software*.

Jasper, J. D. and Christman, S. D. (2005). A neuropsychological dimension for anchoring effects. *Journal of Behavioral Decision Making. 18*, 343-369.

Jørgensen, M. (2006). The Effects of the Format of Software Project Bidding Processes. *International Journal of Project Management. 6(24)*, 522-528.

Jørgensen, M. and Carelius, G. 2004. An Empirical Study of Software Project Bidding. *IEEE Transactions on Software Engineering. 30(12)*, 953-969.

Kemmelmeier, M. (2004). Separating the wheat from the chaff: does discriminating between diagnostic and nondiagnostic information eliminate the dilution effect? *Journal of Behavioral Decision Making. 17(3)*, 231-243.

Long, D. L. and Prat, C. S. (2002). Working memory and Stroop interference: An individual differences investigation. *Memory & Cognition. 30(2)*, 294-301.

Mussweiler, T. and Strack, F. (2001). The semantics of anchoring. *Organizational Behaviour and Human Decision Processes. 86(2)*, 234-255.

Niebauer, C. L., Christman, S. D., Scott, A. R. and Garvey, K. J. (2004). Interhemispheric interaction and beliefs in our origin: degree of handedness predicts belief in creationism versus evolution. *Laterality. 9(4)*, 433-447.

Niebauer, C. L. and Garvey, K. J. (2004). Gödel, Escher, and degree of handedness: differences in interhemispheric interaction predict differences in understanding self-reference. *Laterality. 9(1)*, 19-34.

Oldfield, R. L. (1971). The assessment of handedness: the Edinburgh inventory. *Neuropsychologia. 9*, 97-113.

Propper, R. E., Christman, S. D. and Phaneuf, K. A. (2005). A mixed-handed advantage in episodic memory: a possible role of interhemispheric interaction. *Memory & Cognition. 33*, 751-757.

Estimating the Probability of Negative Events

Adam Harris (harrisaj@cardiff.ac.uk)
Department of Psychology, Cardiff University
Tower Building, Park Place
Cardiff CF10 3AT

Adam Corner (corneraj@cardiff.ac.uk)
Department of Psychology, Cardiff University
Tower Building, Park Place
Cardiff CF10 3AT

Ulrike Hahn (hahnu@cardiff.ac.uk)
Department of Psychology, Cardiff University
Tower Building, Park Place
Cardiff CF10 3AT

Abstract

How well we are attuned to the statistics of our environment is a fundamental question in understanding human behaviour. It seems particularly important to be able to provide accurate assessments of the probability with which negative events occur so as to guide rational choice of preventative actions. One question that arises here is whether or not our probability estimates for negative events are systematically biased by their severity. In a minimal experimental context involving an unambiguous, objective representation of probability we found that participants nevertheless judged an event as more likely to occur when its utility was extremely negative than when it was just moderately negative.

Introduction

Decision theory (Pratt, Raiffa, & Schlaifer, 1995) posits that when selecting between alternative courses of action, an individual should select the alternative with the greatest expected benefit – that is, individuals should seek to maximise the *subjective expected utility* (SEU) of their choice. The normative principles of decision theory dictate that the assessment of an outcome's expected utility should be based on how probable that outcome is perceived to be (the expectancy component), and the subjective value attached to that outcome (the utility component). Our decision about whether or not to carry an umbrella should be based, therefore, on how likely we think it is that it will rain and how bad it would be if we were to get wet, as compared to the irritation of carrying an umbrella with us unnecessarily if, in fact, it did not rain.

This presupposes that probabilities and utilities are assessed independently. Intuitively, one might not expect an individual's estimate of the chance of rain to be based on their judgment of how bad it would be if they got caught without an umbrella. However, there is a long history of research querying whether probabilities and utilities *are* in fact assessed independently.

Estimating Probabilities

Early research on decision-making (Crandall, Solomon & Kellaway, 1955; Edwards, 1953, 1962; Irwin, 1953; Marks, 1951) gave some grounds for believing that people's estimates of an event's probability seem to be influenced, to some extent, by the event's utility, especially when that event is extremely positive or extremely negative (e.g. Irwin, 1953). However, these initial studies typically used choice paradigms, and thus assessed probabilistic judgments only indirectly. Given that choice is governed by both probability and utility, and that both of these factors can simultaneously and subjectively vary, it is very hard to isolate either factor using such an approach.

In examining choice data, there is no *direct* test of the hypothesis that probabilities and utilities are independent, rather their putative relationship must be inferred – and this inferential step is compromised by the degrees of freedom associated with the underlying estimates of both probability and utility. As such, the results from studies utilising decision-making paradigms could generally be explained in terms of non-linear utility functions. Consequently, Edwards (1962) concluded that these early studies failed to find any compelling evidence for the non-independence of probability and utility.

The same interpretative difficulties arise when trying to evaluate the substantial body of work by Kahneman & Tversky (see, e.g., Kahneman & Tversky, 1979) on risky decisions as evidence of probability-utility interdependence. They argued that "losses loom large" in the decision making process – i.e. people seem to be unduly influenced by the threat of negative potential consequences when assessing the best course of action. This led them to replace probabilities with decision weights in their formulation of Prospect Theory as a descriptive account of human decision-making. These weights can deviate systematically from probabilities (specifically they are in general lower than the corresponding probabilities, except in the low probability range), whilst actual estimates of probabilities can be assumed to remain intact. An alternative possibility would be to assume that subjective probabilities themselves are systematically distorted. What is really required to support this latter interpretation, however, is a direct test.

The remaining evidence for the existence of a dependency between probability judgments and outcome severity is also indirect in nature, and typically comes from empirical studies whose primary focus was elsewhere.

Some support for the idea that utilities influence probability estimates could be taken from research on the subjective interpretation of probability words (e.g. Weber & Hilton, 1990). The concept of probability is inherently numerical, yet we often communicate probabilities through verbal descriptors such as "unlikely", "possible" and "probable". Several empirical studies have attempted to investigate how such verbal statements are selected and interpreted. An example is provided by Wallsten, Fillenbaum, and Cox (1986, p. 574, italics added) whereby participants were instructed to respond with either a single probability or a probability range:

'You have a wart removed from your hand. The doctor tells you it is *possible* it will grow back again within 3 months. What is the probability it will grow back again within 3 months?_____'

People's numerical interpretations of verbal probabilities were found to depend on the outcome that was being estimated – suggesting that the interpretation of probabilistic information is context bound (see also Beyth-Marom, 1982; Brun & Teigen, 1988).

A key influence on people's interpretations is the base rate of the event under discussion (e.g. Wallsten, Fillenbaum, et al., 1986). However, within the study of context effects, there is also somewhat weak and conflicting evidence of the influence of outcome utility on subjective judgments of outcome probability. Weber and Hilton (1990) (see also Verplanken, 1997) found that verbal probability expressions were assigned higher numerical probabilities when they referred to a severe (i.e. very negative) event as opposed to a more neutral event. Opposite findings, whereby probability expressions referring to more severe events are given *lower* numerical values than those referring to more neutral events, have also been reported (Fischer & Jungermann, 1996; Merz, Druzdzel, & Mazur, 1991).

Crucially, however, there is nothing in this literature to suggest that these effects are governed by anything other than the pragmatics of language use (see, e.g. Grice, 2001). Context effects on the interpretation and selection of vague terms are ubiquitous. There exist, for example, studies demonstrating the effect of context on people's interpretations of verbal expressions of quantity. Borges and Sawyers (1974) and Cohen, Dearnley, and Hansel (1958), demonstrated that when participants were asked to select "a few", "some", or "several" marbles from a tray, the absolute number of marbles selected was dependent upon the total number of marbles in the tray. Our interpretation of the exact numerical meaning of such quantifiers depends to some extent on what they are referring to.

Hence, the most parsimonious interpretation of any potential influence of severity on the interpretation of probability expressions is that it serves a communicative intent. One cannot infer from contextually bound variation in the numerical interpretation of verbal probability statements that people's actual probability estimates are distorted by the utility of the outcome.

A further source that might suggest that people's utilities systematically bias their probability estimates is research on people's estimates of personal risk for negative life events. A sizeable literature reports that people are prone to "unrealistic optimism" (Kirscht, Haefner, Kegeles & Rosenstock, 1966; Weinstein, 1980, 1982, 1984). Individuals frequently regard their own personal risk to be less than that of the average person, displaying a kind of "invulnerability bias". On the assumption that one's own illnesses are subjectively more negative events than another's illnesses (in particular, if the "other" is simply the 'average person') this would suggest that the increased severity of an event leads to a (protective) depression of estimated probability (in contrast to the relationship between these variables posited by Weber & Hilton, 1990). As the range of negative life events included in these studies typically varies, examinations of correlations between the degree of unrealistic optimism and severity of event can test this interpretation more directly. It turns out that there is no evidence for such a relationship once other relevant variables are controlled for (Eiser, Eiser & Pauwels, 1993; Heine & Lehman, 1995; van der Velde, Hooykas & van Pligt, 1992; van der Velde, van der Pligt & Hooykas, 1994; Weinstein, 1982, 1987, Weinstein, Sandman & Roberts, 1990)[1].

Another reason to believe that the severity of negative events might influence estimates of probability stems from the fact that some research has suggested that *positive* events give rise to systematic distortions (e.g. Babad & Katz, 1991; Price, 2000). Attempts to find evidence that people rate the probability of desirable outcomes to be higher than less desirable outcomes under controlled, laboratory conditions, however, have been less successful, leading some researchers to speak of the "elusive wishful thinking effect" (Bar-Hillel & Budescu, 1995).

Finally, there is reason to believe that peoples' information accumulation can be affected by utilities (e.g., Slovic, 1966). Gordon, Franklin and Beck (2005), for

---

[1] The only exception is an experimental study by Taylor and Shepperd (1998) who led participants to believe they were being tested for a medical condition with either severe or non-severe consequences. An effect of severity was found such that when participants were told that test results were imminent, optimism was *eliminated* in the severe condition. This effect, seems down to a desire to 'not jinx' things. No effect of severity was found in participants who did not expect feedback.

example, found evidence that people misremembering the source of predictions had a tendency to attribute more desirable predictions to the more reliable source. Such influences on information accumulation could give rise to severity-related distortions of probability estimates; however, this leaves open the question of the generality of such influences, in particular, the question of whether or not severity influences probability estimates even in circumstances where all relevant information is readily available.

In summary, despite a long history of research potentially suggesting an influence of outcome utility on probability judgments for outcomes of both positive and negative valence, to the best of our knowledge there exists no clear demonstration of the *direct* effect of outcome severity on perceived outcome probability. Consequently, we sought to investigate estimates of negative events using a novel paradigm that allowed us to provide a direct test of the independence of probability judgments.

A Direct Test of Severity Influence

Are severe outcomes perceived as more probable, or less probable, than neutral outcomes? In attempting to answer this fundamental question, it seems necessary to dispose of as many potential confounds as possible, and avoid the ambiguities that trouble the interpretation of verbal probability expressions. We therefore wanted a task in which participants provided numerical estimates. The main difficulty in choosing appropriate materials for such estimates is that severity and probability are confounded in the real world (see also, e.g., Weber & Hilton, 1990), such that 'really bad' things are less frequent than 'moderately bad' or neutral ones. Simply comparing estimates across events of different severity would consequently be uninformative in respect of establishing a bias. What is minimally required is an objective measure of the probabilities involved. As such measures are difficult to obtain, and because differences in knowledge between people could furthermore give rise to rational deviations from these objective probabilities, we chose to develop fictitious scenarios. Crucial to our experimental design is the fact that participants are supplied with an objective basis for their subjective estimates and that this objective basis is *identical* across the severity manipulations. Any systematic difference that arises in participants' estimates of probability across conditions is consequently directly attributable to the influence of severity.

Experiment 1

The purpose of the first experiment was to provide a direct demonstration of the effect of extreme negative outcome utility (outcome severity) on estimates of outcome probability using a paradigm in which these estimates are anchored to an objective probability to which all participants have equal access. Specifically, the relevant probabilities were provided in a visual display. The use of visual displays as a means of supplying probability information to participants has considerable precedent in the literature (e.g., Bar-Hillel & Budescu, 1995; Cohen & Wallsten, 1991; Wallsten, Budescu, Rapoport, Zwick, & Forsyth, 1986), but has not been used to directly investigate the relationship between outcome severity and probability. Participants saw cell matrices in which different colored cells represented different outcomes. To make the interpretation of these matrices more natural, the cover story was chosen such that the spatial arrangement of the cells had a straightforward real-world correspondence. Specifically, the cells were presented as a graphical representation of a large apple orchard. Yellow cells corresponded to apple trees that had been treated with a pesticide; black cells corresponded to untreated apple trees. The matrix was made sufficiently large that counting the number of cells would have been unduly tedious, thus ensuring that participants would be giving *estimates* even though they were being presented with an objective probability. The cover story associated with the display varied the significance of the treated apples such that they were either fatally poisonous (the severe outcome) or tasted unpleasant (the neutral outcome). Participants were allocated to either the severe or the neutral cover story and asked to provide a probability estimate for the event in question. Crucially, however, all participants saw exactly the same visual displays. The paradigm therefore provided a direct test of the hypothesis that outcome utility may alter the subjective probability of that event occurring.

Method

Participants
One hundred participants took part in Experiment 1. The experiment was conducted remotely using an internet host (**iPsychExpts**). Fifty-five female and forty-five male participants with a mean age of 30 completed the experiment, in an average time of 2.54 minutes. Fifty participants provided probability estimates of severe outcomes, and fifty provided probability estimates of neutral outcomes.

Design
Experiment 1 was designed to test the hypothesis that probability estimates of severe outcomes are overestimated relative to the probability of neutral events. This hypothesis was tested using visual response matrices containing varying proportions of black and yellow cells. Outcome-severity was manipulated between-participants, such that the yellow cells in the display matrices corresponded to outcomes of either extremely negative or neutral utility. The number of yellow cells in the display matrices was manipulated within-participants, such that everyone gave three estimates of probability (low/medium/high outcome probability).

Materials and Procedure

A visual display containing 2236 square cells with a random distribution of black and yellow squares was constructed with a simple JAVA program designed specifically for the experiment (see Fig 1). Three different variants of the display were created, corresponding to the three levels of outcome probability manipulated in the experiment. In the low probability condition of the experiment, the randomly distributed yellow cells were constrained to occupy less than 5% of the display. In the medium probability condition, 50% of the cells in the display were yellow. In the high probability condition, more than 95% of the cells in the display were yellow.

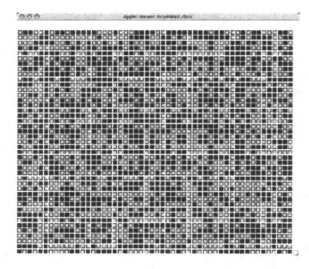

Figure 1: An example cell matrix (from the medium probability level).

Depending on the outcome-severity condition participants were randomly assigned to, they read one of the following cover stories:

Severe Outcome: A farmer has just bought an orchard that contains over 1000 apple trees. The picture below shows the layout of the orchard, with each coloured circle representing an apple tree. Trees that are coloured BLACK bear fruit that is tasty, and delicious to eat. Trees that are coloured YELLOW have been sprayed with a particularly potent type of pesticide, and bear fruit that is **fatally poisonous** to humans. The farmer's young daughter is always playing in the orchard, and despite her father's warnings, she often picks apples to eat from the trees in the orchard.

Unfortunately, however, there is no way of knowing whether an apple tree bears edible or inedible fruit without trying an apple from the tree (the colours black and yellow simply represent the different types of apple). The safety of his daughter is extremely important to the farmer, who is very concerned that she might eat a poisonous apple by mistake.

Neutral Outcome: A farmer has just bought an orchard that contains over 1000 apple trees. The picture below shows the layout of the orchard, with each coloured circle representing an apple tree. Trees that are coloured BLACK bear fruit that is tasty, and delicious to eat. Trees that are coloured YELLOW bear fruit that is sour, and unsuitable for eating. Unfortunately, however, there is no way of knowing whether an apple tree bears edible or inedible fruit without trying an apple from the tree (the colours black and yellow simply represent the different types of apple).

In the severe outcome condition, participants were asked by the farmer to "estimate the chance of his daughter choosing an apple from a tree that bears fatally poisonous fruit (BLACK), if she were to randomly pick an apple from any of the trees in the orchard". In the neutral outcome condition, participants were asked to estimate the chance of the daughter picking a sour and inedible apple. Probability estimates were made on a numerical scale from 0% (Absolutely Impossible) to 100% (Absolutely Certain) with 5 point increments. Participants responded by clicking on a radio button.

Results

As the experiment was conducted remotely using an internet experiment host, we followed Birnbaum (2004) and performed several basic checks prior to data analysis. All participants under the age of 18 were excluded (in line with the ethical guidelines of the British Psychological Society), data from the same Internet Protocol (IP) address were excluded (in order to guard against multiple entries from the same individual), and participants with demographic details that aroused suspicion of fabrication (e.g. an age entry of 99) were eliminated from subsequent analysis. In addition, we excluded participants who had obviously failed to understand the instructions in that they had provided estimates of the three, clearly distinct, levels of probability that deviated from their basic rank order. Participants who took longer then 15 minutes to complete such a basic task were also excluded, to ensure that people were *estimating,* and not *counting* the squares. Following these exclusions, 76 participants were included in the analysis, 43 in the severe outcome condition, and 33 in the neutral outcome condition.

A preliminary analysis was conducted to establish that the probability manipulation (i.e. the proportion of yellow cells in the display matrices) had in fact produced differentiated probability estimates. Collapsing across both outcome severity conditions, a significant main effect of probability in the expected direction was observed; $F_{(2, 148)} = 1003.6$, $p < .001$. More importantly, Figure 2 displays these probability estimates, but split by outcome severity condition. At each level of the probability manipulation, the estimated proportion of yellow cells in the display matrices was higher in the severe outcome condition, producing an overall main effect of outcome severity, $F_{(1, 74)} = 9.88$, $p < .01$. The probability x severity interaction was non significant, $F_{(2, 148)} = 1.606$, $p > .05$.

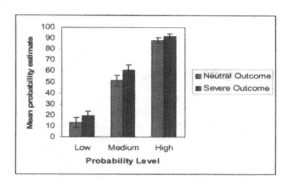

Figure 2: The effect of outcome utility on probability judgments. Error bars represent 95% confidence intervals.

Experiment 2

Finding a statistically significant effect of outcome severity on judgments of probability in such a minimal paradigm with a patently fictitious story of no personal relevance to participants was sufficiently surprising that we sought to replicate this result. Experiment 2 is a direct replication of Experiment 1 with a different set of participants.

Method

Participants

One hundred participants took part in Experiment 2. The experiment was conducted remotely using an internet host (**iPsychExpts**). Fifty-two female and forty-eight male participants with a mean age of 26 completed the experiment, in an average time of 2.56 minutes.

Design, Materials and Procedure

Experiment 2 was an exact methodological replication of Experiment 1.

Results

The same basic checks were undertaken prior to analysis as were performed in Experiment 1. On this occasion however, data collection continued until there were 50 participants suitable for analysis, after exclusions, in each experimental group.

The results obtained were very similar to those obtained in Experiment 1. A main effect of probability, $F(2, 196) = 1656.08$, $p< .001$, indicated that the within-participants probability manipulation had been successful. Once again, the estimated proportion of yellow cells in the display matrices was higher in the severe outcome condition at all levels of the probability manipulation, producing an overall main effect of severity $F(1, 98) = 4.07$, $p< .05$. The probability x severity interaction was, again, non significant, $F(2, 196) = .004$, $p>.05$.

Discussion

Our results provide direct empirical evidence that event severity influences probability judgments. In a minimal experimental paradigm, we found that participants judged the probability of a negative outcome to be higher than that of a directly matched neutral outcome. The fact that both groups of participants in our experiments were presented with identical visual representations of the underlying probabilities, and differed only in the severity manipulation included in the cover story, enables us to infer with confidence that the differences in their probability estimates were attributable to that severity manipulation.

That estimates of outcome severity and probability might interact is an idea with a long research history. However, this is, to our knowledge, the first direct test of this idea. The actual nature of the effect is also at odds with at least some of the potential evidence for severity-probability interactions that could be drawn from past research. In particular, the fact that negative outcomes give rise to higher estimates across the probability scale is incompatible with an alternative explanation of Kahneman and Tversky's (1979) findings that "losses loom large" in terms of distorted probability estimates, as their findings would imply increased estimates only at low levels of probability, with *lower* estimates at all other levels.

The most notable aspect of our results, however, must be that a systematic influence of severity on perceived probability could occur under such simple, well-defined conditions. In particular, participants have no personal stake in the probabilities they are providing, given that the story involves entirely fictitious third parties. Furthermore, there is a clear objective probability that is made available to participants. If a reliable and replicable effect of outcome utility on estimates of probability can be observed in such a reduced paradigm, there is reason to believe that influences of outcome severity on estimates of probability are pervasive and that they are likely to be considerably larger under conditions of emotional involvement as we might experience in day to day life. The immediate, practical importance of such effects mean that further investigations under more real-world circumstances are desirable. Given the fundamental importance of accurate probability judgment to our lives, such investigations should also include potential strategies to overcome this bias.

References

Babad, E., & Katz, Y. (1991). Wishful thinking – against all odds. *Journal of Applied Social Psychology 21, 1921-1938.*

Bar-Hillel, M., & Budescu, D. (1995). The Elusive Wishful Thinking Effect. *Thinking and Reasoning 1 (1) 71-103.*

Beyth-Marom, R. (1982). How probable is probable? a numerical translation of verbal probability expressions. *Journal of Forecasting, 1,* 257-269.

Birnbaum, M. H. (2004). Human research and data collection via the internet. *Annual Review of Psychology, 55,* 803-832.

Borges, M. A., & Sawyers, B. K. (1974). Common verbal quantifiers: usage and interpretation. *Journal of Experimental Psychology, 102,* 335-338.

Brun, W., & Teigen, K. H. (1988). Verbal probabilities: ambiguous, context-dependent, or both? *Organizational Behavior and Human Decision Processes, 41,* 390-404.

Cohen, B. L., & Wallsten, T. S. (1991). The effect of outcome desirability on comparisons of numerical and linguistic probabilities. *Journal of Behavioral Decision Making, 5,* 53-72.

Cohen, J., Dearnley, E. J., & Hansel, C. E. M. (1958). A quantitative study of meaning. *British Journal of Educational Psychology, 28,* 141-148.

Crandall, V.J., Solomon, D. & Kellaway, R. (1955). Expectancy statements and decision themes as functions of objective probabilities and reinforcement values. *Journal of Personality 24, p192-203.*

Edwards, W. (1953). Probability preferences in gambling. *American Journal of Psychology 66, 349-364.*

Edwards, W. (1962). Utility, subjective probability, their interaction, and variance preferences. *Journal of Conflict resolution, 6,* 42-51.

Eiser, J.R., Eiser, C., & Pauwels, P. (1993). Skin cancer: Assessing perceived risk and behavioural attitudes. *Psychology and Health,* 8, 393-404.

Fischer, K., & Jungermann, H. (1996). Rarely occurring headaches and rarely occurring blindness: Is rarely = rarely? Meaning of verbal frequentistic labels in specific medical contexts. *Journal of Behavioral Decision Making, 9,* 153-172.

Gordon, R., Franklin, N., & Beck, J. (2005) Wishful thinking and source monitoring. *Memory & Cognition,* 33, 418-429.

Grice, H.P. (2001). *Aspects of Reason.* Clarendon Press: Oxford.

Heine, S.J., & Lehman, D.R. (1995). Cultural variation in unrealistic optimism: Does the West feel more invulnerable than the East? *Journal of Personality and Social Psychology,* 68, 595-607.

Irwin, F. W. (1953). Stated expectations as functions of probability and desirability of outcomes. *Journal of Personality, 21,* 329-335.

Kahneman, D., & Tversky, A. (1979). Prospect theory: an analysis of decision under risk. *Econometrica, 47,* 263-291.

Kirscht, J.F., Haefner, D.P., Kegeles, S.S., & Rosenstock, I.M. (1966). A national study of health beliefs. *Journal of Health & Human Behaviour, 7,* 248-254.

Marks, R.W. (1951). The effect of probability, desirability and 'privilege' on the stated expectations of children. *Journal of Personality 19, 332-351.*

Merz, J. F., Druzdzel, M. J., & Mazur, D. J. (1991). Verbal expressions of probability in informed consent litigation. *Medical Decision Making, 11,* 273-281.

Pratt. J, Raiffa.H, & Schlaifer, R. (1995). *Introduction to Statistical Decision Theory.* Massachusetts: MIT Press.

Price, P.C. (2000). Wishful thinking in the prediction of competitive outcomes. *Thinking & Reasoning 6 (2) 161-172.*

Slovic, P. (1966). Value as a determiner of subjective probability. *IEEE Transactions on Human Factors in Electronics, HFE-7,* 22-28.

Taylor, K.M., & Shepperd, J.A. (1998). Bracing for the worst: Severity, testing and feedback as moderators of optimistic bias. *Personality and Social Psychology Bulletin,* 24, 9115-926.

van der Velde, F.W. , Hooykas, C., & van der Pligt, J. (1992). Risk perception and behaviour. Pessimism, realism and optimism about AIDS-related health behaviour. *Psychology and Health,* 6, 23-38.

van der Velde, F.W., van der Pligt & Hooykas, C. (1994). Perceiving AIDS related risk: Accuracy as a function of differences in actual risk. *Health Psychology,* 13, 25-33.

Verplanken, B. (1997). The effect of catastrophe potential on the interpretation of numerical probabilities of the occurrence of hazards. *Journal of Applied Social Psychology, 27,* 1453-1467.

Wallsten, T. S., Budescu, D. V., Rapoport, A., Zwick, R., & Forsyth, B. (1986). Measuring the vague meanings of probability terms. *Journal of Experimental Psychology: General, 115,* 348-365.

Wallsten, T. S., Fillenbaum, S., & Cox, J. A. (1986). Base-rate effects on the interpretations of probability words: perceived base rate and severity of events. *Journal of Memory and Language, 25,* 571-587.

Weber, E. U., & Hilton, D. J. (1990). Contextual effects in the interpretations of probability words: perceived base rate and severity of events. *Journal of Experimental Psychology: Human Perception and Performance, 16,* 781-789.

Weinstein, N.D. (1980). Unrealistic optimism about future life events. *Journal of Personality & Social Psychology, 39,* 806-820.

Weinstein, N.D. (1982). Unrealistic optimism about susceptibility to health problems. *Journal of Behavioural Medicine, 5,* 441-460.

Weinstein, N.D. (1984). Why it won't happen to me: Perceptions of risk factors and susceptibility. *Health Psychology, 3,* 431-457.

Weinstein, N.D. (1987) Unrealistic optimism about susceptibility to health problems: Conclusions from a community-wide sample. *Journal of Behavioral Medicine,* 10, 481-500.

Weinstein, N.D., Sandman, P.M., & Roberts, N.E. (1990). Determinants of self-protective behaviour: Home radon testing. *Journal of Applied Social Psychology,* 20, 783-801.

Testing a Causal Attribution account of the Conjunction Fallacy

Fintan J. Costello (fintan.costello@ucd.ie)
Department of Computer Science, University College Dublin
Belfield, Dublin 6, Ireland

Abstract

The conjunction fallacy occurs when people rate a conjunctive statement X-and-Y as more probable than a constituent X, contrary to the law of probability that $P(X \wedge Y)$ cannot exceed $P(X)$ or $P(Y)$. This fallacy occurs reliably in people's judgments of event probability, and also occurs in people's judgments of causal attribution (the assignment of causes to events). The conjunction fallacy is seen in causal attribution when people are asked to assign causes to events and reliably rate some conjunctive causes $X \wedge Y$ for events as more likely than single causes X or Y for the same events. This paper uses an experiment to test two accounts of the conjunction fallacy in causal attribution; one based on people's use of 'explanatory mechanisms' in forming causal attributions, and the other based on the mathematics of standard probability theory. The experimental results argue against the explanatory mechanisms account of the conjunction fallacy, but support the mathematical account.

Introduction

To what extent are human thought processes rational? How closely do people's mental operations correspond to consistent and logical rules? In a influential paper Tversky & Kahnemann (1983) addressed this question by looking at how people carried out the operation of conjunction (the AND operation) for judgements of likelihood. Standard logic and probability theory requires that the likelihood of a conjunction must always be less than the likelihood of both constituents of that conjunction: a conjunction cannot be more probable than one of its constituents. In most cases people follow this requirement when assessing conjunctive probability. Tversky and Kahnemann showed, however, that for some conjunctions people reliably deviate from this rule, judging a conjunction to be more likely than one or other of its constituents. The best-known of Tversky and Kahnemann's conjunction fallacy examples concerns Linda:

Linda is 31 years old, single, outspoken, and very bright. She majored in philosophy. As a student, she was deeply concerned with issues of discrimination and social justice, and participated in anti-nuclear demonstrations.

Participants in Tversky & Kahneman's study read this story and were asked to rank various statements "by their probability". Two of these statements were:

(B) Linda is a bank teller,

(B ∧ A) Linda is a bank teller and active in the feminist movement.

Tversky and Kahneman found that more than 85% of participants ranked $B \wedge A$ as more probable than B, committing the conjunction fallacy. The occurrence of the conjunction fallacy in people's judgments of probability has been confirmed in a number of subsequent studies.

Tversky & Kahnemann's studies focused on the conjunction fallacy in people's judgments of event probability. The conjunction fallacy has also been studied in another domain: that of causal attribution. In Leddo, Ableson & Gross's (1984) study of how people attribute or assign causes to events, people reliably rated some conjunctive explanations for events as more likely than single explanations for the same events. For example, participants in Leddo et al.'s study were given a story about John's decision to attend Dartmouth College. They were asked to rate the likelihood of various explanations for this decision, such as:

(A) John wanted to attend a prestigious college,

(B) Dartmouth offered a good course for John's major,

(A ∧ B) John wanted to attend a prestigious college and Dartmouth offered a good course for John's major.

From probability theory it is clear that the probability of a conjunctive explanation $A \wedge B$ being true can never exceed the probability of one or other of its constituent single explanations A or B being true. Participants in Leddo et al.'s study, however, regularly rated conjunctive explanations as more likely than their constituent single explanations, producing the conjunction fallacy.

The occurrence of the conjunction fallacy in causal attribution is important because it reveals something of the mechanism by which people understand and conceptualise causality, particularly in cases where there are multiple potential causes for an event. In this paper I investigate two accounts of the conjunction fallacy in causal attribution, a procedural account based on people's use

[1] This research was supported by the FP6 NEST Programme of the European Commission (ANALOGY: Humans the Analogy-Making Species: STREP Contr. No 029088)

of explanatory mechanisms (Ahn, Kalish, Medin & Gelman, 1995; Ahn & Bailenson, 1996), and a mathematical account derived from standard probability theory. I first describe these two accounts, then use a recent experiment (Costello, submitted) to test their competing predictions. To foreshadow the results, this experiment provides evidence against Ahn et al.'s 'explanatory mechanism' account of the conjunction fallacy, but supports the account derived from standard probability theory.

An 'explanatory mechanism' account

How do people attribute and assign causes to events? Traditionally, the principle of covariation has been proposed as the fundamental rule underlying causal attribution. This principle states that 'an effect is attributed to that condition which is present when the effect is present and which is absent when the effect is absent'. According to the principle of covariation, for example, people will attribute a driver's drinking alcohol as the cause of a car crash, because when many drivers drink alcohol, car crashes are more frequent, but when fewer drivers drink alcohol, car crashes are less frequent.

While the principle of covariation has been dominant in theoretical accounts of causal attribution, it has been criticised on a number of points. One criticism arises because the principle of covariation does not explain how conditions cause effects: the principle of covariation does not say anything about the explanatory mechanism which links a given condition and an effect. In the car crash example, for instance, covariation does not provide any causal mechanism through which drink-driving and car crashes might be associated (i.e. does not explain that alcohol impairs drivers reaction times and so increases the likelihood of a crash).

Ahn and her colleagues (Ahn, Kalish, Medin & Gelman, 1995; Ahn & Bailenson, 1996) propose an alternative approach to causal attribution, which is based on the use of explanatory processes rather than covariation. According to this proposal, when seeking to attribute a cause to an event, people primarily attempt to discover the processes underlying the link between the causing condition and the resulting event. According to this account, people judge that there is a causal link between drivers' drinking alcohol and car crashes not because the cause and effect covary, but instead because they can explain how drinking alcohol causes car crashes. Ahn et al.'s account is dependent on theoretical entities which represent peoples' models of causal processes: these are referred to as 'mechanisms'.

This 'explanatory mechanisms' account of causal attribution makes an interesting prediction about the occurrence of the conjunction fallacy in causal attribution: it predicts that the conjunction fallacy should occur when the two constituent elements of a conjunctive explanation are linked by a coherent underlying mechanism or story to the event being explained. In a series of studies, Ahn and her colleagues (Ahn, Kalish, Medin & Gelman, 1995; Ahn & Bailenson, 1996) compared this 'explanatory mechanisms' prediction about the conjunction fallacy with the prediction from the principle of covariance

that the conjunction fallacy will be most likely to occur when the two constituent elements of a conjunctive explanation covary with the event being explained. In the 'John attending Dartmouth' example described previously, according to the explanatory mechanisms account the occurrence of the conjunction fallacy for the conjunctive explanation 'John wanted to attend a prestigious college and Dartmouth offered a good course for John's major' would arise because there is a coherent story linking both constituents of that conjunctive explanation with John's decision to attend Dartmouth. According to the covariation account, however, the conjunction fallacy would arise because the conjunctive explanation covaries across students with their decision to attend Dartmouth. Ahn's studies found that the conjunction fallacy in causal attribution was much more likely when there was an underlying mechanism linking a conjunctive explanation to the event to be explained than when there was simply a covariational link between the conjunction and that event, supporting the explanatory mechanism account of causality.

In the explanatory mechanism account, the causal attribution process involves using mechanism information to construct a coherent story about how a given condition can cause a given effect. Ahn and her colleagues do not commit themselves to any representational account of how these stories are constructed, and leave the way open for various different representational implementations of their approach. In the next section I describe an alternative account for the conjunction fallacy which does make use of a precise, mathematical representation for conjunctive judgments, derived from standard probability theory.

A mathematical account

According to probability theory, if two statements or events X and Y are independent we can compute the probability a conjunction $Y \wedge X$ using the multiplicative rule:

$$P(Y \wedge X) = P(Y) \times P(X). \qquad (1)$$

If X and Y are not independent, this probability is

$$P(Y \wedge X) = P(Y) \times P(X|Y), \qquad (2)$$

which can be re-written as

$$
\begin{aligned}
P(Y \wedge X) &= P(Y) \times P(X) + P(Y) \times P(X|Y) \\
&\quad - P(Y) \times P(X) \qquad (3) \\
P(Y \wedge X) &= P(Y) \times P(X) + \\
&\quad P(Y) \times (P(X|Y) - P(X)). \qquad (4)
\end{aligned}
$$

Notice that Equation 4 here has two terms; the first representing multiplicative probability as in Equation 1, the second representing an increase or decrease in that probability proportional to the degree of association between the two events. (We will use this fact later.)

Do people use these probability theory rules when computing conjunctive probabilities? A strong argument in favour of these rules is that they are objectively correct, and presumably being able to reason correctly about conjunction would significantly aid human decision-making. A problem with these rules, however, is that they require the multiplication of real numbers rather than integers (a fairly complex mathematical task). For this reason it is difficult to see people consciously and explictly using these rules for computing conjunctive probabilities.

One way to resolve this problem is to assume that people obtain conjunctive probabilities by translating constituent probability judgments into inputs for a cognitive mechanism which directly implements these multiplicative rules. The output returned by that mechanism is then translated back into the required conjunctive probability. Since multiplication is simply the re-scaling of one value proportional to another, this multiplicative mechanism could be similar to other cognitive mechanisms which involve re-scaling (for example, the mechanisms which allow the rescaling of images of different sizes to recognise similarities between those images, or the mechanisms which rescale auditory inputs to recognise similarities between sounds;see e.g. Shepard & Cooper, 1982).

If people use the rules of probability theory in this way to compute conjunctive probabilities, will they ever produce conjunctive fallacy responses (responses where $P(Y \land X) > P(X)$)? Some readers, perhaps especially those used to analysing probabilities, will answer no. However, this answer depends on an implicit assumption that the inputs to the multiplication mechanism (that is, the constituent probabilities $P(X)$ and $P(Y)$) fall in the range 0 to 1. If these inputs are between 0 and 1, multiplication will produce a conjunctive probability that is less than or equal to both constituent probabilities. However, if one or both inputs are greater than 1, multiplication will produce a conjunctive probability greater than one or both constituent probabilities. Even when the logically correct multiplicative mechanism is used to compute conjunctive probabilities, if the inputs to this mechanism are sometimes erroneously translated so that they fall above the 'boundary' of 1, the conjunction fallacy will result.

Note that the argument here is not that the conjunction fallacy arises when people mistakenly judge that some constituent probability has a value greater than 1. Clearly, people are aware that event probability has a fixed range and that the likelihood of an event cannot exceed 100% (cannot exceed the probablity of 1). Instead, the argument is that people compute conjunctive probability by translating their constituent probability judgments into inputs to a cognitive mechanism implementing the multiplicative rules for conjunction, and that sometimes errors in this translation produce inputs which fall above the boundary of 1. These translation errors produce the conjunction fallacy.

This account can extend to cases where there constituent events X and Y are not independent (as in Equation 4, above). If the association between events X and Y is neutral or positive (if $P(X|Y) >= P(X)$; that is, if the probability of X given Y is higher than the basic probability of X), Equation 4 produces conjunctive prob-

abilities that are equal to or greater than those produced by the multiplicative rule in Equation 1, and so will produce conjunction fallacy responses whenever Equation 1 produces those responses. Only if the association between X and Y is negative (if $P(X|Y) < P(X)$) will Equation 4 be less than Equation 1, and so may not produce conjunction fallacy responses. In other words, among conjunctions for which the conjunction fallacy is likely (conjunctions with a high-probability constituent) the fallacy should be less frequent when there is no link between the two constituents of a conjunction (because this lack of a link reduces conjunctive probability and so reduces the chances of the conjunction fallacy). As before, the conjunction fallacy will not occur for conjunctions where neither constituent has high probability, irrespective of the degree of support between those constituents.

Experiment

This experiment uses a betting paradigm to test the competing predictions of the 'explanatory mechanism' and 'boundary' accounts of the conjunction fallacy. This paradigm is designed (as in e.g. Sides, Osherson, Bonini & Viale, 2002; Tentori, Bonini & Osherson, 2004) to eliminate explanations of the conjunction fallacy in terms of the pragmatics of conversation: explanations where participants prefer statement $B \land A$ to statement B because $B \land A$ is more informative than B, or where participants implicitly interpret B as meaning $B \land not A$ (Dulany & Hilton, 1991; Politzer & Noveck, 1991). Further, as the pragmatics of communication plays no role in betting, a betting paradigm minimises this pragmatic influence. Because the betting paradigm requires no mention of the word 'probability' it also avoids problems due to the ambiguity of that word (Hertwig & Gigerenzer, 1999). Finally, the betting paradigm also provides a realistic setting in which to make judgements about probability.

The explanatory mechanism account predicts that the conjunction fallacy will occur when there is an underlying causal mechanism or explanation linking a cause and an effect; the boundary account predicts that the conjunction fallacy will occur when the cause has a high probability. To test these accounts, in this experiment participants were shown simple statements X and conjunctive statements $Y \land X$, each describing events that could happen some months after the experiment was finished, and were asked to bet on one or other statement. Participants were told that an independent adjudicator would be shown the statements they had bet on, and that they could win a certain amount of money (25 euros) if the adjudicator decided that the event they had bet on had actually occurred. In the experiment each simple statement could be paired with 4 different conjunctive statements. These varied in the probability of the Y component of the conjunction, with Y either having high or low probability (PH versus PL conditions). These statements also varied in the degree of causal support the new Y component gives for the X component of the conjunction, with Y either giving high or low support

Table 1: The four possible $Y \wedge X$ conjunctive statements for the X statement 'In September medical figures produced at UCD will show a 10% decline in smoking in the 12 to 18 age range in Ireland.'

	SH (Y gives high support for X)	SL (Y gives low support for X)
PH (Y has high probability)	In early summer the government will announce an increase in cigarette prices aimed at discouraging smoking, and in September medical figures produced at UCD will show a 10% decline in smoking in the 12 − 18 age range in Ireland.	In early summer a number of pubs in Dublin will provide street furniture and table service for smokers outside pub doors, and in September medical figures produced at UCD will show a 10% decline in smoking in the 12 − 18 age range in Ireland.
PL (Y has low probability)	In June the government will announce a special police force whose sole purpose will be to confiscate cigarettes from underage smokers, and in September medical figures produced at UCD will show a 10% decline in smoking in the 12-18 age range in Ireland.	In July medical researchers at UCD will announce the discovery of an effective treatment for smoking-related lung cancer, and in September medical figures produced at UCD will show a 10% decline in smoking in the 12-18 age range in Ireland.

for X (SH versus SL conditions). The simple statement X was selected to have a medium degree of probability. High causal support between events in these materials was based on explanatory mechanisms linking cause and effect. For example, for the simple statement

(X) In September medical figures produced at UCD will show a 10% decline in smoking in the 12 − 18 age range in Ireland.

the four possible $Y \wedge X$ conjunctive statements were as shown in Table 1. The two high support conjunctions in Table 1 provide easily accessible explanatory mechanisms (increases in cigarette prices, or strict police enforcment of anti-smoking laws, causing a decline in the number of smokers) while the two low-support conjunctions do not provide any easily accessible explanatory mechanism linking constituents of those conjunctions.

Eight sets of the form shown in Table 1, each consisting of a simple statement plus four alternative conjunctive statements, were constructed. The results were analysed to see whether the conjunction fallacy occurred for SH but not SL conjunctions or for PH but not PL conjunctions. A materials pre-test was first used to ensure that there was a reliable difference between high versus low probability and high versus low support groupings, and no confound between probability and support.

Pre-test

Participants in this pre-test were 13 college students, all but 1 from UCD (University College Dublin). These participants were first asked to rate the probability of all X and Y statements (with each statement presented separately, not as part of a conjunction). Probability was rated on a 0 to 10 scale, and statements were presented in random order. Participants were then asked to assess the degree to which the different Y statements supported

X statements (with participants shown each X statement paired with 4 corresponding Y statements, and for each pair asked to rate the extent to which Y increases or decreases the probability of X). Support was rated on a -5 to +5 scale, where the '+' side of the scale represented positive support (Y increases the likelihood of X) and the '-' side negative support (Y decreases the likelihood of X). Pairs were presented in random order.

Table 2 shows the average rated probability for X and Y statements. Probability ratings for Y statements were analysed in a 2 (probability) × 2 (support) × 8 (item set) repeated-measures anova. This showed a significant difference between probability ratings for high-probability and low-probability items ($F(1, 12) = 91.77, p < .0001$), confirming the expected distinction. There was no significant difference between probability ratings for high-support and low-support items ($F(1, 12) = 2.79, p > .1$). There was no significant interaction between support and probability.

Table 3 shows the average rated degree of support which statement Y gave to statement X. These support ratings were analysed in a 2 (probability) × 2 (support) × 8 (item set) repeated-measures anova. This showed a significant difference between support ratings for high-support and low-support items ($F(1, 12) = 299.18, p < 0.0001$), confirming the required distinction, but no significant difference between support ratings for high probability and low probability items ($F(1, 12) = 0.36, p > .1$), indicating no confound. There was no significant interaction between support and probability.

Main test

In this experiment 8 different statement sets of the form in Table 1 were used, along with 6 filler sets (each consisting of two unrelated statements), to construct eight different electronic booklets. Each page in a booklet con-

Table 2: Average rated probability for the 4 different versions of statement Y (using a 0 to 10 scale).

	SH	SL	Average
PH	5.83	6.23	6.03
PL	2.40	2.68	2.54
Average	4.12	4.46	

Table 3: Average rated degree of support which statement Y gives to statement X (using a -5 to +5 scale)

	SH	SL	Average
PH	3.33	-.27	1.53
PL	3.02	-0.25	1.38
Average	3.17	-0.26	

tained a simple statement and a conjunctive statement from one of the 8 statement sets (or containing a pair of statements from a filler set). On each page participants were asked to select one or other statement to bet on, and were reminded that they could win if the event they bet on took place. Booklets were constructed so that, for each set, each of the four different possible pairings of simple statement and conjunctive statement occurred in two booklets, and so that each booklet contained two occurrences of each type of pairing. Thirty-two participants took part in the experiment, which was conducted electronically and run in two groups. All participants were computer science students at UCD. Each participant was randomly assigned one of the eight possible electronic booklets to complete, and given instructions explaining the task. The instructions stressed that the adjudicator would only see the statements they had bet on, and would not see the other statements. The instructions explained that the procedure for winning the money would involve the adjudicator selecting one participant at random, and selecting one of that participant's bets at random, and if the event bet on had actually occurred that participant would win the money (this was also the procedure used in Sides et al.'s earlier betting-paradigm studies of the conjunction fallacy). Materials in the booklets were presented in a different random order for each participant. Participants' email addresses were gathered for contact purposes.

Results and Discussion

On average the experiment took between a quarter and a half an hour to complete. The impression while running the experiment was that participants were motivated by the betting task and paid careful attention to the materials. When the adjudicator selected a participant's response for assessment, the event they had bet on had not occurred and so no money was won. There were 256 responses of interest in the experiment (32 participants, each responding to 8 different X versus $Y \wedge X$ bets). In total 98 out of those 256 responses (38%) were conjunction fallacy responses, where participants bet on a conjunctive statement rather than a single statement. The average number of conjunction fallacy responses per participant was $3.06 (SD = 1.44)$. Every participant committed the conjunction fallacy at least once.

Table 4 shows the number and percentage of conjunction fallacy responses for each type of $Y \wedge X$ conjunctive statement. This table suggests that the conjunction fallacy is mainly influenced by the probability of constituent statements, but not by the degree of causal support given by one constituent to the other. The fallacy occurs equally rarely, for example, for PL-SH conjunctions (high support but low probability) and for PL-SL conjunctions (low support and low probability). To assess the influence of support and probability on the conjunction fallacy, a by-participants analysis was carried out comparing fallacy rates for PL-SH statements and PH-SL statements. In total, 21 out of 32 participants produced more fallacy responses for PH-SL statements than for PL-SH statements, while only 3 participants produced more fallacy responses for PL-SH (Sign Test, $n+ = 21, n- = 3, p < .001$). The remaining 8 participants produced an equal number of fallacy responses for both PL-SH and PH-SL statements.

These results support the boundary account of the conjunction fallacy (which expects the conjunction fallacy to occur frequently when constituent probability is high, and rarely when constituent probability is low). The results go against the 'explanatory mechanism' account in two ways. First, the explanatory mechanism account would expect the conjunction fallacy to occur frequently when there is an explanatory mechanism linking the two constituents of a conjunction, even if the probability of one or other constituent is low. In other words, the explanatory mechanism account would predict overextension to be frequent for PL-SH conjunctions. Similarly, the the explanatory mechanism account would expect the conjunction fallacy to occur rarely when there is no explanatory mechanism linking the constituents of a conjunction, even if the probability of one constituent is high; in other words, the explanatory mechanism account would predict overextension to be rare for PH-SL conjunctions. The results, however, show just the opposite pattern, with overextension being frequent for PH-SL conjunctions but rare for PL-SH ones.

Table 4 shows that the observed difference between occurrences of the conjunction fallacy for SH and SL statements is entirely due to the fact that the conjunction fallacy is less frequent for PH-SL statements than for

Table 4: Conjunction fallacy responses for each type of Y ∧ X statement (total number and as a percentage of responses for each type of statement).

	SH	SL	Across cells
PH	44 (69%)	33 (52%)	77 (60%)
PL	10 (16%)	11 (17%)	21 (16%)
Across cells	54 (42%)	44 (34%)	98 (38%)

PH-SH statements. This is consistent with the boundary account's prediction that among conjunctions where the conjunction fallacy is likely (PH conjunctions) the fallacy should be less frequent when there is negative support between the two constituents of a conjunction than otherwise.

A comparison between the average number of fallacy responses produced for the conjunctions used in the experiment and the average rated probability of statement Y in those conjunctions, as obtained in the Pre-Test, showed a significant positive correlation ($r = 0.80, p < .0001$), backing the predictions of the boundary account. There was no reliable correlation between average number of fallacy responses and average rated degree of support which statement Y gave to statement X ($r=0.16$). Again, this supports the boundary account of the conjunction fallacy.

Conclusions

This paper used the results of a recent experiment (Costello, submitted) to test Ahn's 'explanatory mechanism' account of the conjunction fallacy in causal attribution and compare that account with an alternative 'boundary' account based on the equations of standard probability theory. The explanatory mechanism account predicts that the conjunction fallacy will occur when there is an underlying causal mechanism or story linking the constituents of a conjunction, while the boundary account predicts that the conjunction fallacy will occur when one constituent event of a conjunction has a probability close to the maximum probability boundary of 1. In the experiment the occurrence of the conjunction fallacy was controlled by constituent probability rather than by the existence of an explanatory mechanism linking events: the fallacy occurs frequently for conjunctions with high-probability constituents even when there is no causal mechanism linking those constituents, and does *not* occur frequently for conjunctions with low-probability constituents even where there is a causal mechanism linking those constituents. This goes against an explanatory mechanism account of the conjunction fallacy in causal attribution.

This conclusion does not mean that Ahn's explanatory mechanisms play no part in causal attribution; far from it. The original studies by Ahn and her colleagues have demonstrated the importance of explanatory mechanisms in causal attribution in various different ways. How can we reconcile those earlier findings with the current results? One way of reconciling these differences is to propose a two-stage process for causal attribution with multiple causes. In the first stage, explanatory mechanisms as proposed by Ahn and colleagues would be used to estimate the probability of individual constituent events as causes. In the second stage, those individual probabilities would be combined using the equations from standard probability theory as in the 'boundary' account, to produce an overall assessment of the degree to which a given conjunctive explanation is seen as causing a given event. This two-stage process would resolve the conflict between the results reported here and Ahn et al.'s earlier findings, and give a general account for the conjunction fallacy in causal attribution.

References

Ahn, W. K. , & Bailenson, J. (1996). Causal attribution as a search for underlying mechanisms: An explanation of the conjunction fallacy and the discounting principle. *Cognitive Psychology,* **31(1)**, 82-123.

Ahn, W., Kalish, C. W., Medin, D. L., & Gelman, S. A. (1995). The role of covariation versus mechanism iformation in causal attribution. *Cognition,* **54**, 299-352.

Costello, F. C. (submitted). Probability, Support, and the Conjunction Fallacy.

Dulany, D. E, & Hilton, D. J. (1991). Conversational implicature, conscious representation, and the conjunction fallacy. *Social Cognition,* **9**, 85-110.

Hertwig, R. & Gigerenzer, G (1999). The 'conjunction fallacy' revisited: How intelligent inference might look like reasoning errors. *Journal of Behavioural Decision Making,* **12**, 275-305.

Leddo, J, Abelson, P. H. & Gross, P. H. (1984). Conjunctive explanations: When two reasons are better than one. *Journal of Personality and Social Psychology,* **47**, 933-943.

Politzer, G., & Noveck, I. A. (1991) Are conjunction rule violations the result of conversational rule violations? *Journal of Psycholinguistic Research,* **20**, 83-103.

Sides, A., Osherson, D., Bonini, N., & Viale, R. (2002). On the reality of the conjunction fallacy. *Memory & Cognition,* **30**, 191-198.

Shepard, R. N., & Cooper, L. A. (1982). Mental images and their transformations. Cambridge, MA: MIT Press/Bradford Books.

Tentori, K., Bonini, N., & Osherson, D. (2004). The conjunction fallacy: a misunderstanding about conjunction? *Cognitive Science,* **20**, 467-477.

Tversky, A. and Kahneman, D. (1983). Extension versus intuititve reasoning: The conjunction fallacy in probability judgment. *Psychological Review* **90** 293-315.

Does Attentional Modulation of Early Vision Entail the Cognitive Penetrability of Perception?

Athanasios Raftopoulos (raftop@ucy.ac.cy)
Department of Psychology, University of Cyprus, P.O. BOX 20537
NICOSIA, 1678 CYPRUS

Abstract

It is argued that findings showing the early modulation of visual processing by endogenous cognitively driven attention provide evidence for the cognitive penetrability of perception. In this paper, I distinguish two stages of visual processing, early vision or perception and late vision. The former is cognitively impenetrable whereas the latter is penetrated top-down by cognitive information. Since I have argued for that thesis elsewhere, here I merely present its broad outline. Then, I examine the nature and timing of the attentional modulation of striate and extrastriate cortex that allegedly constitutes evidence for the cognitive penetrability of perception and argue that, contrary to the above claim, these studies provide ample justification for the opposite thesis, namely the cognitive impenetrability of perception.

Introduction

It is widely held that cognitively driven attention modulates visual processing very early and its effects can be found even in the striate cortex. Lamme (2003) and Lamme and Roelfsema (2000), for instance, who distinguish between an early unconscious stage of visual processing and a late conscious stage, claim that attention intervenes at the sites of unconscious processing and affects it. Attentional modulation is used as evidence that cognitive top-down information penetrates vision in all its stages and, thus, that there is no part of vision that is cognitively encapsulated. Against this view, I examine the nature and timing of the attentional modulation of striate and extrastriate cortex that allegedly constitutes evidence for the cognitive penetrability of perception and argue that, contrary to the above claim, these studies provide ample justification for the opposite thesis, namely the cognitive impenetrability of perception.

Stages of Visual Processing

Drawing from and elaborating on the work of Lamme, Roelfsema (Lamme, 2003; Lamme & Roelfsema, 2000), I have argued (Raftopoulos, 2006; Raftopoulos and Muller, 2006) that one can distinguish three stages in visual processing. The feedforward sweep (*FFS*), local recurrent processing (*LRP*), which is restricted within visual circuits and "full" or "global" recurrent processing (*GLP*) involving higher cognitive and mnemonic centers. According to Lamme activation from the retina cells reaches *V1* at a latency of about 40 ms. Multiple stimuli are all represented at this stage. Then this information is fed forward to the extrastriate areas, parietal, and temporal areas of the brain.

By 80 ms after stimulus onset most visual areas are activated. At this stage there are no attentional effects, a thesis that is further evidenced by findings that the first *ERP* wave subcomponent *C1*, which is registered at about 50-60 ms after stimulus onset and which represents the initial stimulus-evoked response in area *V1* is unaffected both by spatial and object-centered attention (Hopfinger, Luck, & Hillyard, 2004). This means that the initial feedforward sweep from *LGN* to the striate cortex leaves the *V1* neurons' responses unaffected by spatial attention. The highest levels of visual cortical processing hierarchy in the ventral stream are reached within 100 ms, and at about 120 ms activation is found in the motor cortex as well, although activation reaches the motor cortex at this latency only through the dorsal system, the activation through the ventral system arriving with a longer latency (Lamme & Roelfsema, 2000). 100 to 150 ms after stimulus onset the first signs of recurrent processing are found, which however are restricted within early vision and thus exclude top-down signals from either memory of other cognitive centers. At that stage, phenomenal awareness may arise. At 200 ms after stimulus onset, recurrent interactions with areas outside the visual stream make storage in visual short memory possible and allow eventually the emergence of access or report awareness, since they render the content of those perceptual states transparent to bearer of those states.

Lamme and Roelfsema (2000, 572) argue that response latencies at any hierarchical level are about 10 ms longer than those at a lower level. "Thus, because 10 ms is in the range of the minimal interspike interval, a typical cortical neuron can fire at most a single spike before the next hierarchical level is activated, leaving no time for lateral connections and no time for feedback connections to exert their effect. Therefore, the ensemble of neurons that participate in the first sweep of activity through the hierarchy of visual areas is primarily determined by the pattern of feedforward connections."

The unconscious processing in *FFS* is capable of generating increasingly complex receptive field tuning properties and thus extracting high-level information that could lead to categorization. Thus, the *FFS* determines the classical receptive field of the neurons and their basic tuning properties. *FFS* culminates at about 100 ms after stimulus onset and results in some initial feature detection. At about 100 ms, local recurrent processing starts, and this allow further binding and segregation to occur. This results in some form of perceptual organization of the stimuli.

Attentional Modulation of Visual Cortex

Since the *FFS* terminates at about 100 ms after stimulus onset, visual tasks (such as visual search for a target) that result in longer delays it is plausible to assume that they involve recurrent processing. Moreover, delays around that time interval indicate the result of lateral effects. These imply that the neurons in early visual pathways involved in such tasks should receive lateral and top-down signals (reentry signals) from other areas in the visual system and other cognitive centers higher in the brain. It is natural to assume that the attentional modulation of the visual pathways takes place through such reentrant top-down connections.

Various findings substantiate this assumption. Recordings (Roelfsema et al., 1998) from the visual cortex of monkeys who perform a texture segregation task show that *V1* cells select for orientation of textures at about 55 ms after stimulus onset. These cells are selective for the boundary between figure and ground at about 80 ms, and show an enhanced response when their receptive fields cover the figure surface compared to the background surface at about 100ms. This is clearly an effect of reentry signals that seem to originate at *V4* area of the brain.

Neurophysiological studies (Roelfsema's et al., 1998; Lamme and Roelfsema, 2000) with monkeys that were trained to perform a curve-tracing task in which the target curve started with a marker of a given color that the monkey had been cued before the presentation of the stimulus, show two things regarding the modulation of early visual processes by attention. First, *V1* cells representing the cued color enhance their response 159 ms after stimulus onset, an enhancement caused by a color-selective feedback signal from higher visual areas and reflecting the effect of object-centered (feature-based to be precise) attention. Second, object-centered attention enhances the responses of *V1* cells that respond to the target curve as opposed to the distractor curve 235 ms after stimulus onset. Roelfsema et al., (1998) trained macaques to select one of two equally salient curves and then they implanted 40-50 multiunit electrodes to various sites in *V1* cortex. Manipulating the experimental conditions they made certain that the enhancement of the neuronal activity in *V1* was due to object-centered attention and that it was not a simple sensory effect. However, the finding that the activity of cells in the primary visual cortex is enhanced by object-centered attention, and thus that attention modulates the primary visual cortex as well, does not undermine the thesis that attentional effects occur after the *FFS* and *LRP*, since the attentional effects enhance the responses of *V1* cells 235 ms after stimulus onset, a time by which both *FFS* and local *RP* have terminated.

Dipole studies (Martinez et al., 2001; DiRusso et al., 2003), using high spatial resolution *fMRI*, also show a delayed modulation of *V1* activity during spatial attention that starts about 130-160 ms after stimulus onset. Combined with evidence, which I discuss in the next section, showing that the first effects of spatial-attention occur about 70-100 ms after stimulus onset originating from in or near V3/V3a areas in the mid-occipital regions, these findings make plausible the hypothesis that selection of stimuli at the attended location first occurs at extrastriate cortical areas and it is a delayed feedback from these areas that modulates top-down the activity in primary visual cortex *V1*.

Aine et al., (1995) using visual evoked magnetic fields also report that the activity in striate cortex may be modulated by spatial attention. However, this occurs at long latencies (130-160 ms). The long latency indicates, in agreement with the interpretation of the results from the aforementioned dipole studies, that the activity is probably due to the reactivation of striate cortex as a result of recurrent signals from higher centers rather than in the modulation of the initial processing in the striate cortex.

Zipser et al., (1996) argue that a long latency component in the neuronal responses in striate cortex to a texture patch covering the receptive field of the relevant neurons is under certain conditions enhanced, which suggest that the activity of *V1* neurons can be modulated by activity that originates from extrastriate visual areas. Again here, the effect has a long latency. Furthermore, the response of *V1* cells is enhanced if the texture surrounding the central patch is made perceptually distinct from the central patch because of differences in illumination, orientation, color, or disparity. This means that the effect is stimulus driven by bottom-up spread of activation and it does not reflect top-down attentional modulation but exogenous attention; in this sense it is attributed to a preattentive mechanism (Roelfsema et al., 1998). Thus, it is due to contextual effects within the visual system and not to top-down signals.

These results concerning the modulation of *V1* area by attention contrast with other research that shows marginal modulation of attentional effects on the primary visual cortex. Studies that examine the modulatory effects of task instructions regarding some particular feature or the location that subjects are instructed to attend before stimulus presentation on visual areas from *V1* (Haenny and Schiller, 1998; Luck et al., 1997) through extrastriate areas *V2* and *V4* (Luck et al., 1997; Luck and Hillyard, 2000), to *MT* (Treue et al., 1996), suggest that the modulation is more pronounced in areas far removed from *V1*. Attentional effects on *V1* are marginal if at all observed (Hillyard et al., 1998). Processing in *V3/V3a* neurons is modulated by attentional effects in 70-90ms and in *V4* in 100-200 ms after stimulus onset, again after *FFS*. Thus, the attentional effects are associated more with enhanced activity in cells in extrastriate areas, when attention is directed to an image location to which these cells respond, rather than with activity in striate areas.

The Effects of Spatial Attention

In the previous section, I discussed evidence pertaining to the sites of attentional modulation in the striate and extrastriate visual cortex. One notices, first, that the effects of object-centered attention into striate cortex by being delayed (about 270ms after stimulus onset) do not affect early perceptual processing, to wit *FFS* and *LRP* that have ended by about 150 ms after stimulus onset. Second, the modulation of striate cortex by spatial attention is also delayed (100-130 ms). However, the modulation of extrastriate cortex by visuo-spatial attention seems to occur much earlier, 70-80 ms after stimulus onset, and thus it is well within the time set of *FFS* to affect it. This is certainly evidence that spatial attention modulates early visual processing. So let us examine that evidence in detail.

Studies of the effects of spatial attention on perceptual processing show two kinds of modulation. The first regards the attentional modulation of spontaneous activity (Freiwald and Kanwisher, 2004) and refers to the enhancement of the baseline activity of neurons that are tuned to a location that is cued and thus attracts, as it were, attention before the onset of any stimuli. Attending to a location may enhance the base-line activation, that is, the spontaneous firing rates, of the neuronal assemblies tuned to the attended location in specialized extrastriate areas *V2*, *V3/V3a*, *V4*, and in parietal regions (Freiwald and Kanwisher 2004; Hopfinger et al., 2004; Kastner and Ungerleider, 2000) and perhaps in striate cortex *V1* (Kastner et al., 1999), before the presentation of the stimulus. This phenomenon is referred to as the *attentional modulation of spontaneous activity*. The cue-related base response is similar for pattern-present and pattern-absent trials and exhibits the signature of spatial attention; it depends on task difficulty and selects retinotopically, that is, it is evident only in the subregion of visual cortex the neurons of which have receptive fields that fall within the attended location.

The attentional modulation of spontaneous activity is better described as an effect of attentional control rather than an effect of spatial attention on target processing. *ERP* studies (Hopfinger et al., 2004) reveal two components in areas contralateral to the attended hemispherical hemifield. An early, directing attention, negativity (*EDAN*) registered in posterior parietal areas with an onset of 200-400 ms and a late directing attention positivity (*LDAP*) over occipital scalp sites with an onset of 500-700 ms after cue presentation. The *LDAP* reflects a biasing of neural activity that may be responsible for the later selective processing of stimuli occurring at attended locations.

Spatial attention enhances the sensitivity of the neurons tuned to the attended spatial location before stimulus presentation by improving the signal-to-noise ratio of the neurons tuned to the attended location over the neurons with receptive fields outside the attended location that contribute only noise; this is done by elevating baseline activations of the neurons tuned to the attended locations. However, this effect does not determine what subjects perceive in that location because by enhancing the responses of all neurons tuned to the attended location independent of the neurons' preferred stimuli it keeps the differential responses of the neurons' unaltered and thus does not affect what it is perceived at that location. In other words, the relevant neurons' responses increase without affecting neural selectivity. What is perceived, the percept, depends on the

relative activity of appropriate assembles of neurons that selectively code the features of the stimulus compared to the activity of assemblies that do not code the features of the stimulus and thus contribute noise. Since the percept depends on the differential response of these assemblies, this very early effect of spatial attention by not evoking differential responses leaves the percept unchanged; it makes detection of the objects and their features in the scene easier but it does not determine what the observer perceives.

The second kind of visuospatial attentional effects concerns the modulation of perceptual processing by spatial attention itself and not by attentional control mechanisms of the type discussed above. Clark and Hillyard (1996) using visual evoked potentials (*VEP*) conducted studies on subjects who were presented with patterned flashes to the left and right visual fields, while the subjects maintained central fixation and attended to one visual field at a time. The flashes to attended locations elicited potentials with enhanced amplitude of the *P1* and *N1 ERP* subcomponents compared with the potentials elicited by unattended stimuli. These components were stable with changes in eye position and thus are insensitive to the position of the eyes; they are only affected by the direction of attention not by the shifts in eye position. Hillyard et al., (1998) report studies using *ERP* and event-related-magnetic fields (*ERF*) that show a similar enhancement of the *P1* and *N1* subcomponents.

The *P1* component was elicited at a latency of 80-100 ms in Clark and Hillyard (1996) and at a latency of 75-130 ms in Hillyard et al., (1998), which suggests that attentional selectivity and, thus, amplification of activation of stimulus information incoming from attended locations begins in extrastriate cortex at about 80 ms after stimulus onset. Since the enhancement of *P1* component is not accompanied by changes in its timing waveform or in its scalp voltage topography, it is likely that attention acts as a sensory gain control mechanism that modulates the flow of information from striate to extrastriate areas by improving the signal-to-noise ratio of the inputs at the attended location. Thus, attention modulates neural responses in multiplicative ways. It seems, therefore, to constitute a "gain-control mechanism that enhances the excitability of visual cortical neurons coding the attended regions of space" (Hopfinger et al., 2004, 570). The larger ratio means that more relevant information can be extracted from the input. The *N1* component was elicited at a latency of 120-200 ms (Clark and Hillyard, 1996), or 150-190 ms (Hillyard et al., 1998), which shows that the modulation of processing by spatial attention continues until 200 ms after stimulus onset.

Other studies on spatial attention (Luck and Hillyard, 2000; Luck et al., 1997) were conducted with subjects who were instructed to attend to the left visual field in some trial blocks and to attend to the right visual field in other trial blocks. The subjects were asked to respond when they detect an infrequent target stimulus among the nontarget stimuli at the attended location. The *P1* wave is larger in amplitude for stimuli presented at the attended location than for stimuli presented at the unattended location. Since the difference is due to the attended location, it is reasonable to assume that the amplitude of the *P1* wave is modulated by spatial attention. The effect begins 70 to 90 ms after stimulus onset, which means that it is clearly an early perceptual and not a postperceptual effect. The effect is sensitive to stimulus factors such as contrast and position. It occurs before the identification of the stimuli and is insensitive to the identity of the stimuli. It is independent of the task–relevance of the stimulus, since it is observed for both targets and nontargets, and it is independent of the nature of the task, since it is observed for a variety of tasks ranging from passive viewing to active searching locations (Hopfinger et al., 2004). The effect is also insensitive to the cognitive states of the observers (expectations, desires, beliefs etc.) In that sense, *P1* is thought to be an exogenous sensory component elicited by the onset of a stimulus at the attended location (Evans et al., 2000).

P1 shows in studies examining the effects of attention on the preconscious analysis of global structure (Han et al., 2000; Koivisto and Revonsuo, 2004). There is evidence that global and local levels of stimuli are processed in parallel at preconscious processing stages, although global stimuli are analyzed at that stage more than local stimuli. Han et al., (2000) showed that under focused-attention conditions the early *P1* component of spatial attention (recall that this component is detected at 70-80 ms after stimulus onset), as well as later components, show shorter latencies for global rather than local targets, which means that the processing of global features has been differentiated from that of local features at that early stage of visual processing. This effect is thought to reflect differential spatial attention to the area containing the global or local stimuli.

ERP recordings in general reveal various waveform components that are involved in the modulation of visual processing by attention. The first component that is modulated by attention, the *P1* waveform, consists of two components. The initial phase (at 80-100 ms) of *P1* originates from areas near or in *V3/V3a* and the later phase (at 100-130 ms) of *P1* originates from *V4* or near it. These imply that spatial attention influences first visual processing in extrastriate areas of the visual cortex. The initial sensory processing in the primary visual cortex *V1*, the *C1* component that is elicited about 50ms after stimulus onset, seems to be unaffected by attention (Luck and Hillyard, 2000). Thus, the *P1* component may represent the earliest stage of visual processing that is modulated by voluntary spatial attention (Mangun et al., 2000). However, the stage at which attentional selection will intervene depends on the conditions in which processing takes place (Mangun et al., 2000). Spatial attention seems to play two roles at the early stages of perceptual processing. It resolves ambiguous neural coding by suppressing competing input sources, and it improves signal to–noise–ratios by enhancing in a multiplicative gain control way the activation of neurons encoding attended locations. Indeed, there is evidence that attention selects both by enhancing relevant items (that is, those that are in the attended locations) and inhibiting irrelevant items (those in the unattended locations) (for a discussion see Treisman, 2004).

N1, the second waveform subcomponent of spatial attention, arises from multiple generators in posterior parietal areas (an early phase at 140-160 ms) and in ventral occipital-temporal areas (late phase at 160-200 ms). Unlike the *P1* that was found suppressed at the unattended locations and thus was considerably larger at the attended locations but did not show an enhancement at the attended locations, the *N1* was enhanced at the attended locations but it was not suppressed at the unattended locations. It seems that *P1* inhibits attended information from unattended locations, whereas N1 facilitates information from attended locations (Hopfinger et al., 2004).

N1 is considered to be an index of the orientation of spatial attention to task-relevant objects, that is, objects that are related to the task at hand and are found at the attended locations (Evans et al., 2000). Task-relevant objects are distinguished from target irrelevant objects at about 140-200 ms after stimulus onset. This agrees with Chelazzi et al. (1993) and Schall and Bichot (1998) findings that target (task-relevant)/nontarget (task irrelevant) discrimination occurs at about 150-200 and 120-200 respectively after stimulus onset. Moreover, experiments examining the precedence of global over local processing show that under certain conditions (difficult tasks in which the distractors are difficult to dissociate from the targets and attention is not easily allocated) both global and local information are processed in parallel at early stages and the asymmetry in their processing shows at latencies that coincide with the elicitation of *N2* (Evans et al., 2000). Unlike *P1* that is enhanced both in exogenous and endogenous attention, *N1* is enhanced only in endogenous or voluntary attention, that is, it is elicited only when subjects view a scene and decide where to attend, and do not just when they passively view the scene. This reflects the role of *N1* in target/nontarget discrimination. However, *N1* is insensitive to the type of the target and occurs long before the identification of the target.

The third waveform subcomponent observed in *ERP*'s is the *N2* component that is elicited about 200-300 ms after stimulus onset and whose site is in monkeys and, perhaps, humans the area *V4* and the inferotemporal cortex. Research (Chelazzi et al., 1993; Luck et al., 1997) suggests that *N2* reflects the allocation of attention to a location and/or object and is influenced by the type of the target and the density of the distractors. It is also sensitive to stimulus classification and evaluation. Its occurrence in local vs global processing tasks, for instance, may signify the process by which information is classified as having a global or local source (Evans et al., 2000). For this reason *N2* is considered to be an endogenous attentional component. The timing of *N2* is in line with the evidence discussed above that identification and classification of stimuli starts about 200 ms after stimulus onset.

The discussion about the modulation of visual processing by spatial attention shows that although the voluntary endogenous control of spatial attention is driven by cognitive and task–demands, its early effects, to wit *P1* and *N1*, are modulated by the nature of the stimuli and the nature of the stimuli and its relevance to the task respectively and not by the identity and or classificatory type of the stimulus. One would argue at this point that it is certainly cognitive factors that determine the nature of the task and that, thus, cognition affects through *N1* early visual processing. The rejoinder in defence of the cognitive impenetrability of perception is twofold. First, *N1*'s onset (about 150 ms after stimulus presentation) is delayed to affect *FFS*. Furthermore, the P1 component that does affect *FFS* is clearly an exogenous component that does not index any cognitive top-down transmission of information to early visual stages. Finally, *N1* is elicited after much of *LRP* has taken place. This means that for about 150 ms perceptual processing is unaffected from any kind of cognitive effects, despite its early modulation by spatial attention. Furthermore, *N1* is insensitive to the classification and identification of the stimulus. Second, the cognitive factors do not have an immediate effect on early visual processing; it is only by determining the nature of the task that they influence perception. Hence they modulate perception only indirectly. I have argued (Raftopoulos 2006) that this is evidence that cognitive factors affect perception only in an indirect way and that this indirect modulation of perception by cognition does not support any claims as to the cognitive-penetrability of perception.

Conclusion

I have examined several studies regarding the modulation of perception spatial and object-centered attention. Here is the overall picture that emerges when subjects perform cognitive tasks that require endogenously driven attentional search. When a visual scene is being presented, the feedforward sweep reaches *V1* at a latency of about 40 ms. Information is fed forward to the extrastriate areas, parietal, and temporal areas of the brain. The first *ERP* component, *C1*, is elicited at about 50 ms after stimulus onset and is unaffected by attention, be it spatial or object-centered. By 70-80 ms after stimulus onset most visual areas are activated. The preattentional *FFS* culminates within 100 or 120 ms after stimulus onset. 70 to 90 ms after the stimulus onset, spatial attention by modulating the *P1* waveform enhances visual processing in a voluntary task–driven search at the salient locations. However, *P1* is sensitive only to the characteristics of the stimulus. 100 ms after the presentation of the stimuli at those locations an extensive part of our brain responds to the physical characteristics of the visual array. 150 ms after the stimulus these features fuse to a single form or structural description of the objects in a visual scene by means of *LRP*. At 150 ms the onset of *N1* indexes the beginning of the registration of differences between targets and distractors and, in general, differences between task-relevant and task-irrelevant items in the visual scene. About 200-300 ms after stimulus presentation, a voluntary task-driven search is registered in the same areas that process the visual features in *FFS* and *LRP* enhancing

neuronal activation of the salient objects and/or locations. These attentional effects are indexed by the onset of *N2*, which also signifies the onset of the biasing of processing by object-centered attention. Thus, the top-down effects of attention to features and objects are delayed in time and involve the same anatomical areas as *FFS* and *LRP*, except that attention amplifies the recordings in these areas. Finally, about 250 ms after the stimulus, some of the same areas participate in the cognitive/semantic processing of the input. *GRP* takes place and objects are classified and recognized, a process that is indexed by the onset of *P3*. In sum, the active attention studies suggest that when top-down processes occur, the activation of some groups of neurons in early perceptual areas is enhanced and the source of this amplification is higher areas in the brain, although which sites are exactly involved in which component of attention is still debatable (see Treisman, 2004).

To put things into focus, consider the argument for the cognitive penetrability of perception. We know that there are many neural connections devoted to bringing information back to the sensory systems from higher cognitive centers. This allegedly constitutes evidence for the mediation of the output of the perceptual modules by information from higher cognitive states through the mediation of attention. It is important at this juncture to be explicit about the modes of attention involved (spatial-attention or object-centered attention). The attentional modulation of spontaneous activity, in which spatial attention enhances activity of neurons tuned to the attended location before stimulus presentation, is the earliest attentional effect. There are two interrelated reasons that claims regarding the cognitive impenetrability of perception are not threatened by the modulation of the baseline activation of neurons in early visual areas. The first is that this is clearly a preperceptual effect and, thus, does not affect the course of perceptual processing itself. The second is that, as I remarked above, this enhancement "does not evoke a percept, however, because percepts depend on a differential response, and the attentional boost does not evoke a differential response" (Heeger and Ress 2004, 339).

Things differ with respect to other kinds of visuo-spatial attentional, since these effects occur early and do affect perceptual processing. But the only effects that occur early enough to be within not only the *FFS* but the *LRP* as well, are those reflected in the *P1* and, at the limit, *N1* subcomponent waveform. However, these components are thought to be an exogenous sensory component elicited by the presentation of an object in the visual scene (*P1*) and a semi-exogenous component that indexes the orientation of attention to a task-relevant object but that otherwise depends on the characteristics of the stimulus (*N1*). Thus, *P1* is not the result of cognitive reentrant signals and *N1* modulates perception indirectly through the specification of the task.

Finally, object-centered attentional effects do not undermine the cognitive impenetrability of perception either. Early instruction cues regarding object features activate in working memory those cells that respond to the features of the cue. When the visual scene is presented to the subject, bottom-up activation spreads in parallel in the visual stream(s) activating the cells in the visual areas that are selective of the characteristics of all the objects in the visual field. The cells in working memory that have already been activated by the instruction cue enhance in a top-down manner the activation of the cells in the visual stream that are tuned to the features of the cued object, allowing it thus to win the competition for further processing. However, this top-down effect of working memory on visual processing, which reflects the effects of object-centered attention is delayed (170-300 ms after stimulus onset) and, thus, does not affect the *FFS* processing.

References

Aine, C. J., Supek, S., & George, J. S. (1995). Temporal dynamics of visual-evoked neuromagnetic sources: Effects of stimulus parameters and selective attention. *International Journal of Neuroscience, 80*, 79-104.

Chelazzi, L., Miller, E., Duncan, J., & Desimone, R. (1993). A neural basis for visual search in inferior temporal cortex. *Nature, 363*, 345-347.

Clark, V. & Hillyard, S. A. (1996). Spatial selective attention affects early extrastriate but not striate components of the visual evoked potentials. *Journal of Cognitive Neuroscience, 8(5),* 387-402.

DiRusso, F., Martinez, A., & Hillyard, S. A. (2003). Source analysis of event-related cortical activity during visuo-spatial attention. *Cerebral Cortex, 13,* 486-499.

Evans, M. A., Shedden , J. M., Hevenor, S. J., & Hahn, M. C. (2000). The effect of variability of unattended information on global and local processing: Evidence from lateralization at early stages of processing. *Neurophysiologia, 38,* 225-239.

Freiwald, W. A., & Kanwisher, N. G. (2004). Visual selective attention. In M.S. Gazzaniga (ed.), *The Cognitive neuroscience* (third edition). Cambridge, MA: The MIT Press.

Haenny, P. E., & Schiller, P. H. (1998). State dependent activity in monkey visual cortex. I. Single cells activity in V1 and V4 on visual tasks. *Experimental Brain Research, 69,* 225-244.

Han, S., Liu, W., Yund, E. W., & Woods, D. L. (2000). Interactions between spatial attention and global/local feature selection. *Neuroreport, 11,* 2753-2758.

Heeger, D. J., & Ress, D. (2004). Neuronal correlates of visual attention and perception. In M.S. Gazzaniga (ed.), *The Cognitive neuroscience* (third edition). Cambridge, MA: The MIT Press.

Hillyard, S. A., Teder-Salejarvi, W. A., & Munte, T. F. (1998). Temporal dynamics of early perceptual processing. *Current Opinion in Neurobiology, 8,* 202-210.

Hopfinger, J. B., Luck, S. J., & Hillyard, S. A. (2004). Selective attention. In M.S. Gazzaniga (ed.), *The Cognitive neuroscience* (third edition). Cambridge, MA: The MIT Press.

Kastner, S., Pinsk, M. A., De Weerd, P., Desimone, R., & Ungerleider, L. (1999). Increased activity in human visual cortex during directed attention in the absence of visual stimulation. *Neuron, 22,* 751-761.

Kastner, S & Ungerleider, L. G. (2000). Mechanisms of visual attention in the human cortex. *Annual Review of Neuroscience*, 23, 315-341.

Koivisto, M., & Revonsuo, A. (2004). Preconscious analysis of global structure: evidence from masked priming. *Visual Cognition, 11 (1),* 105-127.

Lamme, V. A. F. (2003). Why visual attention and awareness are different. *Trends in Cognitive Sciences, 7 (1),* 12-18.

Lamme, V. A. F, & Roelfsema, P. R. (2000). The distinct modes of vision offered by feedforward and recurrent processing. *Trends in Neuroscience, 23,* 571-579.

Luck, S. J., Chelazzi, L., Hillyard, S. A., & Desimone, R. (1997). Neural mechanisms of spatial selective attention in areas V1, V2, and V4 of macaque visual cortex. *Journal of Neurophysiology, 77,* 24-42.

Luck, S. J. & Hillyard, S.A. (2000). The operation of selective attention at multiple stages of processing: Evidence from human and monkey electrophysiology. In M. S. Gazzaniga (ed.), *The New Cognitive Neurosciences*, second edition. Cambridge, MA: The MIT Press.

Mangun, G.R., Amishi J.P., Hopfinger J.B., & Handy, C. T. (2000). The temporal dynamics and functional architecture of attentional processes in human extrastriate cortex. In M. S. Gazzaniga (ed.), *The new cognitive neurosciences*, second edition. Cambridge, MA: The MIT Press.

Martinez, A. F., DiRusso, F., Annlo-Vento, L., Sereno, M. I., Buxton, R. B., & Hillyard, S. A. (2001). Putting spatial attention on the map: Timing and localization of stimulus selection processes in striate and extrastriate visual areas. *Vision Research, 41,* 1437-1457.

Raftopoulos, A. (2006). Defending realism on the proper ground. *Philosophical Psychology, 19 (1),* 1-31.

Raftopoulos, A., & Muller, V. (2006). Deictic codes, object files, and demonstrative reference. Forthcoming in *Philosophical and Phenomenological Research, 72 (2).*

Roelfsema, P. R., Lamme, V. A. F., & Spekreijse, H. (1998). Object-based attention in the primary visual cortex of the macaque monkey. *Nature, 395,* 376-381.

Schall, J. D., & Bichot, N. P. (1998). Neural correlates of visual and motor decision processes. *Current Opinions in Neurobiology, 76,* 2841-2852.

Treisman, A. (2004). Psychological issues in selective attention. In M.S. Gazzaniga (ed.), *The Cognitive neuroscience* (third edition). Cambridge, MA: The MIT Press.

Treue, S., & Maunsell, J. H. R. (1996). Attentional modulation of visual motion processing in cortical areas MT and MST. *Nature, 382,* 539-541.

Zipser, K., Lamme, V. A. F., & Schiller, P. H. (1996). Contextual modulation in primary visual cortex. *Journal of Neuroscience, 16,* 7376-7389.

Biological Movements Are Detected Faster Than Artificial Ones

Christelle Aymoz (aymoz@pse.unige.ch)
Faculty of Psychology and Educational Science, University of Geneva, 40, Bd du Pont d'Arve, 1205 Geneva, Switzerland

Paolo Viviani (viviani@pse.unige.ch)
Faculty of Psychology and Educational Science, University of Geneva, 40, Bd du Pont d'Arve, 1205 Geneva, Switzerland
and
Faculty of Psychology, University Vita-Salute San Raffaele, 58 via Olgettina, 20132 Milan, Italy

Abstract

It has been suggested that different attributes of a visual scene are processed by dedicated functional modules. The hypothesis was supported by previous studies showing that colour, form and movement attributes of artificial stimuli are processed asynchronously. This asynchrony must be taken into account when addressing the so-called binding problem. Two experiments using realistic representations of a fetching movement investigated the hypothesis that one binding factor is the biological nature of the movement. The rate of processing of movement onset is compared with that of colour (Experiment 1) and form (Experiment 2) changes. By using a temporal order judgement task, we show that the large delay with which movement is perceived when using artificial stimuli is significantly reduced when the movement results from the intervention of a human agent.

Introduction

The visual brain consists of different visual areas that are functionally specialized to process distinct attributes of the visual scene (Livingstone & Hubel, 1988, Zeki, 1993, Bullier, 2001; Zeki, 2005). The results of these modular processes must than be made available to a mechanism (a "binding mechanism") that groups the perceptual attributes into a coherent percept.

The notion that the global perceptual process is distributed over independent and parallel channels of analysis entails an obvious prediction: if the rate of processing of the independent modules were to differ, simultaneous changes of distinct attributes in a visual scene should be perceived to occur at different times. Indeed, a number of psychophysical experiments demonstrated that simultaneous changes colour, form and movement are not perceived synchronously (Moutoussis & Zeki, 1997; Arnold, Clifford, & Wenderoth, 2001; Viviani & Aymoz, 2001; Nishida & Johnston, 2002; Aymoz & Viviani, 2004; Arnold, 2005). In fact, these asynchronies have been cited as supporting evidence for a modular view of consciousness (Zeki, 2003). Although the interpretation of the asynchronies in terms of processing rates has been questioned (Nishida & Johnston, 2002), their very presence, confirmed under diverse experimental conditions, is puzzling on two counts. On the one side, the fact that movement is perceived later than both colour and form changes seems to be inconsistent with the belief that the visual system processes motion information very quickly through rapid mylenated pathways to areas specialized for motion processing (Livingstone & Hubel, 1987; Britten, Shadlen, Newsome, & Movshon, 1992). On the other side, it is intriguing that the effect seems to be perceptually conspicuous only under laboratory conditions. One may wonder why asynchronies as large as those originally reported by Moutoussis and Zeki (1997) (about 80 ms) do not seem to be noticed under most real life conditions. As for the first problem, it has been argued that the inconsistency emerges only insofar as one equates conduction velocity along the afferent pathways with processing rate (Zeki & Bartels, 1999). As for the second point, one explanation may be attempted within the hierarchical model evoked by Zeki (2003), according to which unified consciousness results from binding the different microconsciousnesses distributed in time and space that arise from the activity of specialized neural mechanisms. Specifically, the hypothesis is that only certain laboratory conditions permit one to tap the states of microconsciousness, whereas the asynchronies are compensated for during the subsequent binding of these states. If so, the question is how temporal realignment is obtained.

This paper explores a hypothesis that calls into play the notion of motor-perceptual interaction. Specifically, we examine the possibility that the relevant states of microconsciousness are set into a correct temporal register by a motor representation of the perceived gesture triggered by the so called "mirror matching system" (Gallese, Fadiga, Fogassi & Rizzolatti, 2002). Based on the available extensive evidence for a special perceptual status of human gestures (for a review, Viviani, 2002), two experiments were designed to test whether the considerable lag with which movement onset is perceived relative to colour and form changes when the motion has no overt cause - as in all computer-generated stimuli used thus far - disappears when the movement is realistic, and results from the intervention of a real biological agent.

Experiment 1

This experiment concentrates on the comparison between the processing rate of colour and movement. By using video clips of a realistic scene in which a human hand fetches a ball, we manipulated the position in time when the colour of the ball changes relative to the instant when the ball leaves the support surface. The experiment adopts a temporal judgment paradigm in which participants are asked to whether colour change or movement onset occurred first.

Method

Participants. Twenty adults (13 female and 7 male; age range: 21-31 years) reported normal or corrected-to-normal acuity and had no known deficiency in colour perception.

Apparatus and Stimulus. Participants were seated in a quite room kept in dim light at a distance of about 50 cm from the computer monitor. We recorded with a digital camera a video clip of a hand gesture (Figure 1).

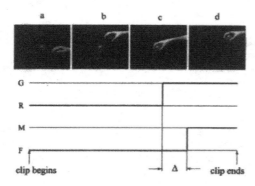

Figure 1: An excerpt from the video clip.

At the beginning of the clip, the sequence represented a ball placed at the centre of the screen. Then, the hand moved, seized the ball with the natural five-finger grip, and lifted outside the scene. The entire sequence lasted 2 s. The average velocity of the hand during the lifting was approximately 20 deg/s. The hue of the ball had been changed with a standard software. We generated 36 stimulus sequences: in half of them the ball was red (CIE coordinates X = 25.42, Y = 14.76, Z = 4.08) at the beginning of the clip and became green (CIE coordinates X = 7.87, Y = 14.95, Z = 3.24) in the course of the sequence; in the other half, the colour switched in the opposite direction. In both cases, the ball remained globally isoluminant. Each sequence within the two

subgroups of 18 was characterized by the rank order K of the frame in which the ball began to move. In 9 sequences, the colour switched before (K = +8, +7, …,+1) or at (K = 0) movement onset. In the remaining 9 the switch occurred after (K = -1, -2,…,-8) or at (K = 0) movement onset. At the recording speed of 25 frames/s, the asynchrony, Δ, between the switching of the Colour (C: Green/Red) and Movement (M: Fixed/Moving) attributes ranged between -320 and +320 ms in steps of 40 ms. By convention, the sign of the SOA (Δ) was set as negative when the ball left the ground before the change of colour and positive in the complementary case.

Experimental conditions, procedure and task. Trials began with a fixation point lasting 1 s at the centre of a uniform gray background. Immediately afterward, one video clip was displayed at the centre of the screen. At the end, the screen was filled with the background and remained so until the participant initiated a new trial by entering the response. The task was to indicate (forced-choice) which attribute had changed first, i.e. whether the colour of the ball had changed before (answer C), or after (answer M) the ball had started moving. Responses were entered by using two keys in the upper row of the keyboard. Each of the 72 different sequences was presented 10 times for a total of 720 trials. Sequences with Δ = 0 occurred twice. Thus, the sample size for computing individual response frequencies was 40 for $\Delta \neq 0$ and 80 for Δ = 0. The selection of sequence was randomised for each participant. An experimental session lasted approximately one hour.

Results

The results are presented in the form of a psychometric describing the relationship between the SOA (Δ), and the relative probability P(Colour) with which colour switching was perceived before movement onset. The lower panel in Figure 2 shows the psychometric function obtained by averaging the relative probabilities over all participants.

For all participants, the response probabilities P(Colour) increased monotonously toward as a function of the SOA, levelling at a value close to 1. Individual differences were estimated by three parameters of the psychometric function: $P_{\Delta=0}$, $\Delta_{P=0.5}$ and the Just-Noticeable-Difference (JND). There was some variability in $P_{\Delta=0}$, which was based on just one measure. By contrast, individual estimates of $\Delta_{P=0.5}$ and of the JND were quite homogeneous, and their population averages were very close to the corresponding values computed from the average psychometric function. Moreover, $\Delta_{P=0.5}$ did not differ significantly from 0 (two-tailed t-test, $t_{(19)}$ = 0.479).

The average psychometric function (lower panel in Figure 2) was used to estimate the distribution of the duration of the perceptual processing with the method devised in our previous studies (Viviani & Aymoz, 2001; Aymoz & Viviani, 2004). The results (upper panel of Figure 2) show that the processing times for colour and movement are indeed almost identical as suggested also by the individual data.

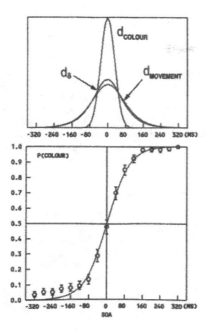

Figure 2: Upper panel: Probability density function (pdf) of the total processing times for Colour and Movement, and pdf of the difference between the total processing times (d_δ). Lower panel: Response probabilities as a function of the SOA between the change of colour and movement attributes.

Experiment 2

This experiment investigates the relative timing with which participants perceive that an object fetched by a hand starts moving, and changes its shape. This experiment adopts the Temporal Order Judgment paradigm already used in Experiment 1. Specifically, we manipulated the position in time when the shape of the object changes relative to the instant when the object leaves the support surface. Participants have to judge which of the two events has occurred first.

Method

Participants. Twenty students of the University of Geneva (15 female and 5 male; age range: 24-48 years) volunteered for the study. Participants reported normal or corrected-to-normal acuity.

Apparatus and Stimulus. The general conditions were as in Experiment 1. Stimuli were video clips of a hand gesture (Figure 3) recorded with a high speed (250 frames/s) digital camera (HotShot 1280, NAC Image Techonologies).

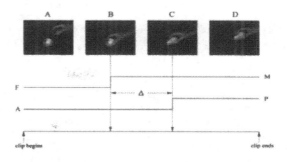

Figure 3: Four sample images from the video clip used as stimulus. The second image corresponds to movement onset. The third image corresponds to the time of transition from one form to another. The objective asynchrony between these two images (Δ) is varied between -160 ms to +160 ms.

At the beginning, the clip represented a fruit, either an apple or a pear, placed at the centre of the scene, on a horizontal surface. Immediately after, a hand entered the scene from the upper right corner, seized the fruit with the natural five-finger grip, and lifted it outside the scene. The lifting movement began approximately halfway through the sequence, which lasted 2 s.

The average velocity of the hand during the lifting was 20 deg/s approximately. We generated 20 different blends of the original sequences. In half of them, the fruit was an apple at the beginning of the clip and became a pear in the course of the sequence. In the other half, the initial fruit was a pear. Each sequence within the two groups of 10 was characterized by the rank order K of the frame at which the fruit changed with respect to frame at which the fruit began to move. In 5 sequences, the fruit changed before (K = +40, +30, +20, +10) or at (K = 0) movement onset. In the remaining 5 sequences the change occurred after (K = -10, -20, -30, -40) or at (K = 0) movement onset. At the recording speed of 250 frames/s, the asynchrony (SOA) Δ between the switching of the Form (F: Apple/Pear) and Movement (M: Fixed/Moving) attributes ranged between -160 and +160 ms in steps of 40 ms. By convention the sign of the SOA was set as negative when the fruit left the ground before the change of form and positive in the opposite case. By crossing the two original sequences with all combinations of attributes and SOA, we obtained 40 different stimuli.

Experimental procedure and task. Aside from the nature of the stimuli, and the fact that we tested only the Form/Movement comparison, the procedure was the same as in Experiment 1. The participant's task was to indicate (forced-choice) whether the fruit had changed before (answer F), or after (answer M) it had started moving. Each of the 40 sequences was presented 10 times for a total of 400 trials (sequences with $\Delta = 0$ were presented twice). Thus, the sample size for computing individual response frequencies was 40 for $\Delta \neq 0$ and 80 for $\Delta = 0$. The order of presentation of the sequences was randomised for each participant.

Results

The results were summarized by the relationship between the SOA (Δ) and the relative frequency P(Form) with which form switching was perceived before movement onset (psychometric function). For all participants, P(Form) increased as a function of Δ. However, even at the extreme values of (±160 ms) most participants were occasionally wrong. The lower panel in Figure 4 shows the psychometric function obtained by averaging the relative frequencies over all participants.

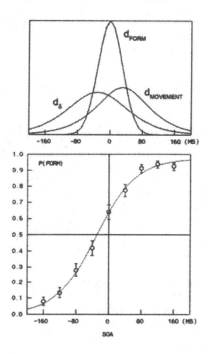

Figure 4: Upper panel: Probability density function (pdf) of the total processing times for Form and Movement, and pdf of the difference between the total processing times (d_δ). Lower panel: Response probabilities as a function of the SOA between the change of form and movement attributes.

The average psychometric function is very nearly a cumulative Gaussian distribution (lower panel of Figure 4). However, both the answer probability at $\Delta = 0$ ($P_{\Delta=0}$) and the median ($\Delta_{P=0.5}$) show that the function is not symmetric with respect to the values of the SOA. The asymmetry was present in 19 participants. The individual values of $P_{\Delta=0}$, $\Delta_{P=0.5}$ and of the differential limen (JND)

were estimated by logistic interpolations of the response frequencies. Statistical analysis showed that $P_{\Delta=0}$ differed significantly from 0.5 (one-sample 2-tailed t-test, $t_{(19)} = 5.613$, $p < .001$), and that $\Delta_{P=0.5}$ differed significantly from 0 (one-sample 2-tailed t-test, $t_{(19)} = -5.094$, $p < .001$). This suggests that, on average, form change is processed faster than movement onset.

The average psychometric function (lower panel in Figure 4) was used to estimate the distribution of the duration of the perceptual processing with the method devised in our previous studies (Viviani & Aymoz, 2001; Aymoz & Viviani, 2004). The analysis confirmed and extended the results of the individual performances by indicating that the processing of movement onset takes about 30 ms longer than the processing of form, and that its variability is considerably larger.

Discussion

Previous experiments with computer-generated displays in which a moving object changes in colour or form (Moutoussis & Zeki, 1997; Viviani & Aymoz, 2001; Clifford, Pearson, & Arnold, 2002; Bedell, Chung, Ogmen, & Patel, 2003; Aymoz & Viviani, 2004) have shown that the perception of movement onset is delayed with respect to the perception of both colour and form changes. The main point of this paper emerges when the results here are contrasted with those of a previous experiment (Viviani & Aymoz, 2001) in which changes in colour and shape occurred in artificial geometrical stimuli (squares and circles), and movement occurred without the intervention of a visible agent. Viviani and Aymoz (2001) adopted the same Temporal Order Judgment Task used here, so that the results can be compared directly. Figure 5 and Figure 6 report the psychometric functions obtained in the earlier study for the Colour/Movement and Form/Movement contrasts, respectively.

In all cases, perceptual asynchronies were estimated in two ways, namely by the probability $P_{\Delta=0}$ of perceiving either colour or form before movement when the changes are actually simultaneous, and by the median of the psychometric function $\Delta_{P=0.5}$ indicating how long in advance movement onset must occur in order for it to be perceived as simultaneous with form and colour changes. In the case of geometrical artificial stimuli (Viviani & Aymoz, 2001), the results were as follows:

	$P_{\Delta=0}$	$\Delta_{P=0.5}$
Colour/Movement	.884	-56 ms
Form/Movement	.891	-60 ms

In the case of a fetching gesture the corresponding values are:

	$P_{\Delta=0}$	$\Delta_{P=0.5}$
Colour/Movement	.517	-4 ms
Form/Movement	.663	-31 ms

The differences between the results for the two types of stimuli were highly significant:

	$P_{\Delta=0}$	$\Delta_{P=0.5}$
Colour/Movement	$t_{(38)} = -6.724$	$t_{(38)} = 4.625$
	$p < .001$	$p < .001$
Form/Movement	$t_{(38)} = -6.207$	$t_{(38)} = 3.334$
	$p < .001$	$p = .002$

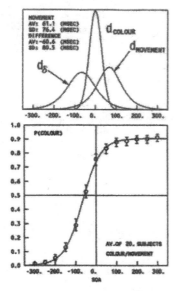

Figure 5: Results with artificial stimuli. Same format as Figure 4 (modified from Viviani & Aymoz, 2001).

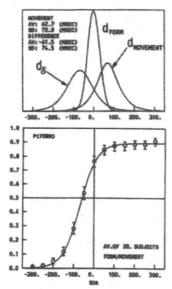

Figure 6: Results with artificial stimuli. Same format as Figure 4 (modified from Viviani & Aymoz, 2001).

Thus, perceptual asynchronies between movement and both colour and form changes are reduced significantly when the display is a video clip of a fetching gesture in which a real object is displaced by a human agent. It should be stressed that artificial and biological movements can be compared because in the two studies the trajectories of the moving object were the same. In particular, in both studies the movement began at the centre of the display, and continued toward the upper right corner at an average speed of 20 deg/s. Moreover, also the size of the objects was similar.

The reduction of the perceptual asynchrony induced by the intervention of the moving hand may be explained by invoking visual factors only. Watching the hand during the approach phase may permit the participant to anticipate the time of movement onset. By contrast, the display provides no clue about the time when colour or form change. Thus, the expected time of onset may replace the actual onset in generating the corresponding temporal marker. In other words, expectation would set the movement time marker earlier than the end of the duty cycle of the channel that processes the true onset of the movement. Alternatively, expectation may have a priming affect, by enhancing the dynamics on the movement channel.

A different explanation of the role of the moving hand calls into play the interaction between visual and motor factors. As noted in the introduction, neurons in the monkey ventral premotor cortex are activated both when it performs a hand gesture, and when it watches the same action being performed by someone else. It has been speculated (Gallese, Fadiga, Fogassi, & Rizzolatti, 2002) that these neurons are part of a network matching action observation and execution. A number of studies (Grèzes, Costes, & Decety, 1998; Hari, Forss, Avikainen, Kirverskari, Salenius, & Rizzolatti, 1998) strongly suggest that such a "mirror matching system" exists also in humans, where its primary function would be to allow us to understand the behaviour of others via an internal simulation of what we would do to emulate that behaviour. If so, the main difference between the present naturalistic stimuli and the computer-generated stimuli used in our previous experiment (Viviani & Aymoz, 2001) – would be that only the former, but not the latter activate the mirror matching system. Then, one can speculate that the reduction of the movement delay is the by-product of this activation. More specifically, if we assume that the hand fetching gesture activates covertly the same motor structures involved in their actual execution, it could be that this internal simulation of the ongoing action being displayed provides anticipatory clues as to when the object will begin to move. In the case of Experiment 1 the anticipation would reduce the processing time within the movement channel to an extent that is sufficient to make movement onset and colour change perceptually simultaneous. In the case of Experiment 2, an asynchrony of about 30 ms would instead persist with respect to form change, because form changes are processed faster than colour changes (Viviani & Aymoz, 2001; Aymoz & Viviani, 2004).

It should be stressed that the involvement of the "mirror matching system" in supporting a reliable motor simulation of the displayed human action is highly speculative. Indeed, other cortical areas are known to be activated selectively by the perception of biological motion (Oram & Perrett, 1994; Grossman et al., 2000), and may well provide alternative inputs to an internal simulation of the perceived action. Whatever its origin, however, the fact that such a simulation may in principle be used to anticipate the future course of the action suggests a solution to the problem of setting the dynamic attributes of the visual scene into time register with the other attributes before reaching consciousness.

Acknowledgments

This work was partly supported by research funds from the Vita-Salute San Raffaele University and from the University of Geneva.

References

Arnold, D.H. (2005). Perceptual pairing of colour and motion. *Vision Research, 45*, 3015-3026.

Arnold, D.H., Clifford, C.W.G., & Wenderoth, P. (2001). Asynchronous processing in vision: Color leads motion. *Current Biology, 11*, 596-600.

Aymoz, C. & Viviani, P. (2004). Perceptual asynchronies for biological and non-biological visual events. *Vision Research, 44*, 1547-1563.

Bedell, H.E., Chung, S.T.L., Ogmen, H., & Patel, S.S. (2003). Color and motion: Which is the tortoise and which is the hare? *Vision Research, 43*, 2403-2412.

Britten, K.H., Shadlen, M.N., Newsome, W.T., & Movshon, J.A. (1992). The analysis of visual motion: A comparison of neural and psychophysical performance. *The Journal of Neuroscience, 12*, 4745-4765.

Bullier, J. (2001). Feedback connections and conscious vision. *Trends in Cognitive Science, 5*, 369-370.

Clifford, C.W.G., Pearson, J., & Arnold, D.H. (2002). Asynchronous binding of colour and orientation. *Perception, 31*, 107.

Gallese, V., Fadiga, L., Fogassi, L., & Rizzolatti, G. (2002). Action representation and the inferior parietal lobule. IN W. Prinz & B. Hommel (Eds.), *Common mechanisms in perception and action: Attention and performance* (pp. 247-266). Oxford: Oxford University Press.

Grèzes, J., Costes, N., & Decety, J. (1998). Top-down effect of strategy on the perception of human biological motion: A PET investigation. *Cognitive Neuropsychology, 15*, 553-582.

Grossman, E., Donnelly, M., Price, R., Pickens, D., Morgan, V., Neighbor, G., & Blake, R. (2000). Brain areas involved in perception of biological motion. *Journal of Cognitive Neuroscience, 12 (5)*, 711-720.

Hari, R., Forss, N., Avikainen, S., Kirveskari, E., Salenius, S., & Rizzolatti, G. (1998). Activation of human primary motor cortex during action observation: A neuromagnetic study. *Proceedings of the National Academic Science of the USA, 95*, 15061-15065.

Livingstone, M.S. & Hubel, D.H. (1987). Psychological evidence for separate channels for the perception of form, color, movement, and depth. *The Journal of Neuroscience, 7*, 3416-3468.

Livingstone, M.S. & Hubel, D.H. (1988). Segregation of form, color, movement, and depth: Anatomy, physiology, and perception. *Science, 240*, 740-749.

Moutoussis, K. & Zeki, S. (1997). A direct demonstration of perceptual asynchrony in vision. *Proceedings of the Royal Society of London, Serie B, 264*, 393-399.

Nishida, S. & Johnston, A. (2002). Marker correspondence not processing latency determines temporal binding of visual attributes. *Current Biology, 12*, 359-368.

Oram, M.W. & Perrett, D.I. (1994). Responses of anterior superior temporal polysensory (STPa) neurons to "biological motion" stimuli. *Journal of Cognitive Neuroscience, 6*, 99-116.

Viviani, P. (2002). Motor competence in the perception of dynamic event. In W. Prinz & B. Hommel (Eds.), *Common mechanisms in perception and action: Attention and performance* (pp. 406-442). Oxford: Oxford University Press.

Viviani, P. & Aymoz, C. (2001). Colour, form, and movement are not perceived simultaneously. *Vision Research, 41*, 2909-2918.

Zeki, S. (1993). *A Vision of the brain*. London: Blackwell.

Zeki, S. (2003). The disunity of consciousness. *Trends in Cognitive Sciences, 7*, 214-218.

Zeki, S. (2005). The Ferrier Lecture 1995 Behind the seen: The functional specialization of the brain in space and time. *Philosophical Transactions of the Royal Scociety of London, Serie B, 360*, 1145-1183.

Zeki, S. & Bartels, A. (1999). Toward a theory of visual consciousness. *Consciousness and Cognition, 8*, 225-259.

Perceptual Learning vs. Context-Sensitive Retrieval:
Why do people judge green lines to be shorter/longer than red lines of the same length? Do they perceive them differently or do they retrieve a biased set of alternatives in their comparison set?

Penka Hristova (phristova@cogs.nbu.bg)
Boicho Kokinov (bkokinov@nbu.bg)

Central and East European Center for Cognitive Science, Department of Cognitive Science and Psychology,
New Bulgarian University, 21 Montevideo Street
Sofia 1618, Bulgaria

Abstract

The mechanisms of perceptual learning and contextually sensitive retrieval were recently suggested as possible explanations of the effect of irrelevant information on judgment: the judgment of the same stimulus was reported to depend on its irrelevant characteristics. The reported experiments test the chances for a perceptual learning explanation of the effect. Experiment 1 successfully induces the effect of irrelevant dimension in judgment of line lengths, while Experiment 2, performed immediately after the first experiment, tests the possibility that the perceptual learning mechanisms have led to a "rerepresentation" of the line length depending on its color and thus the participants will actually *see* the red lines as shorter/longer then the red ones. Since Experiment 2 failed to demonstrate any significant difference in perception of the stimulus length depending on its color, the possibility that perceptual learning mechanisms underlie the effect of irrelevant dimension was not empirically supported for the moment.

Introduction

Does irrelevant information influence judgment on a scale? The traditional answer to this question is *NO*, i.e. information that is not required by the target task is considered irrelevant and is neglected by the cognitive processes according to most theories of judgment, including the ones focusing on context sensitivity.

The effect of the irrelevant dimension represents a relatively new research tendency to demonstrate contextual effects on human judgment. Unlike most of the research on context sensitive judgment, the context within this micro-domain was manipulated through the irrelevant-to-the-task stimulus dimension. Suppose that you should judge how tall a person is. You probably do not expect that your judgment may depend on a completely irrelevant stimulus characteristic like the color of the eyes of the target person. Empirical results in this domain, however, suggest that this could be the case, at least under some circumstances.

This paper focuses on the possible mechanism that may underlie the effect of irrelevant information on human judgment and hopefully, to rule out some of the mechanisms that usually were suggested to underlie the effect of interest.

Empirical data on the effect of the irrelevant stimulus dimension

Probably for the first time such an effect of the irrelevant dimension was reported by Marks (1988). Participants in his experiment were asked to rate loudness of tones differing in frequency. To be more precise, the 500Hz tones were low in loudness and the 2 500Hz tones were high in one of the experimental conditions, while in the other - the pairing was reversed. The irrelevant dimension distinguishes the set of stimuli into two subgroups that differ in range, i.e. low and high. As a result, a 500 Hz tone at 70 dB was judged as loud as a 2500 Hz tone at 73 dB. On the contrary, when the 2500 Hz tones were relatively louder to the 500 Hz ones, a 500 Hz sound signal at 70 dB was judged as loud as a 2500Hz tone at 57 dB. These effects were called ´differential context effects´ (DCEs). In essence, DCEs represent a significant contrast effect, i.e. judgments of the same stimuli are shifted away from the context induced by the irrelevant dimension. If the irrelevant dimension joins the stimulus to a set of lower magnitudes, the target stimulus receives a greater rating compared to a situation, where the target stimulus is included in a set of higher magnitudes.

The same direction of the effect of the irrelevant-to-the-task dimension was observed in a series of experiments on judgments of line lengths (Kokinov at all, 2004; Hristova, 2005; Hristova et al., 2005; Hristova and Kokinov, 2006). The context was manipulated through the color of the lines, whose length participants were supposed to judge. Stimulus material comprised a set of 14 lines of different length that were presented either in green or red. Each of the line lengths were presented an equal number of times (7 or 14 times each, depending on the experiment). The frequency of the stimulus presentation was manipulated in such a manner that stimuli sharing the same color form a positively or negatively skewed distribution. As a result, participants´ ratings on a 7-point scale were influenced by the color of the lines and were systematically shifted in the expected direction, i.e. the same lines were overrated when their color was the color of the positively skewed set and underrated, when their color was the color of the negatively skewed set. This effect was called the effect of irrelevant-to-the-task-information and was constantly demonstrated in a number of experiments on judgments of line length that varied the time for stimulus presentation (Hristova & Kokinov, 2006) and the range of stimulus distributions with respect to the color of lines (Hristova, 2005). The same effect was demonstrated in judgment of age, depending on the color of the digits, representing the target's age (Hristova & Kokinov, 2006) and price judgments (Hristova et al., 2005). Overall, the effect was robustly found for the middle-range stimuli (Hristova & Kokinov, 2006; Hristova, 2005) and under some circumstances was successfully found to spread over the whole range of stimulus magnitudes (Hristova, 2005; Hristova et al., 2005). Most of these experiments varied only the skew of the distribution with respect to the irrelevant stimulus color and obtain small though significant effect of irrelevant-to-the-task dimension on judgment of the middle-range stimuli only. However, when irrelevant-to-the task information indicated not only the frequency but also the range of the stimulus distribution, the effect was successfully reproduced over the whole stimulus range. This finding reasonably conform to the Range-Frequency theory, which states that when the range and the frequency principles work together the effect of the stimulus distribution is larger (Parducci, A. 1965, 1974).

Finally, the effect of the irrelevant stimulus dimension was also reported by Goldstone (1995) regarding judgment of the object's color. Participants were asked to reproduce the color of the object on the screen and were influenced by the irrelevant-to-the-task shape of the objects. Basically, their color judgments were assimilated toward the prototype of the category to which the objects belong, depending on their shape. For example, if the object's shape belongs to the category of redder objects, the reproduced color was redder than the reproduced color of an identically colored object that belongs to a different shape, and hence, color category.

In sum, there is a sufficient amount of empirical data, which demonstrates that human judgments depend on the irrelevant stimulus dimension. Unfortunately, these data contradict to each other with respect to the direction of the observed contextual effect and differ on the scale on which the effect was measured. On one hand, Marks and colleagues (Marks, 1988, 1992, 1994, Marks & Warner, 1991; Arieh & Marks, 2002) and Goldstone (1995) used continuous scales to measure contextual effects on judgment, but demonstrated opposite shifts in judgment, i.e. Marks and colleagues always reported contrast, while Goldstone an assimilation effect due to the irrelevant information. On the other hand, Hristova and colleagues (Kokinov et al., 2004; Hristova, 2005; Hristova et al., 2005; Hristova & Kokinov, 2006) used the subjective scale from 1 to 7 in all their experiments and constantly observed a contrast effect from the context of the irrelevant information just like Marks and his colleagues but unlike Goldstone.

One possible explanation of these incompatible results may be hidden in the underlying mechanisms, since different demonstrations of the effect of irrelevant information suggest different cognitive mechanisms to be responsible for the phenomenon of interest. In this paper we will focus on testing the mechanisms that may be responsible for the effect of irrelevant stimulus dimension. More precisely, the study will try to shed light on the question whether a perceptual learning mechanism or a contextually sensitive retrieval mechanism underlies the effect of interest.

The mechanisms that may underlie the effect of irrelevant information

Usually the effect of the irrelevant stimulus dimension is related to perception. For example, Arieh and Marks (2002) argued that the irrelevant stimulus dimension "induce perceptual systems to "recalibrate their relative suprathreshold responsiveness". They demonstrated that visual length perception appeared to be specific to the eye and to the retinal region in which the context was induced. Thus, according to Arieh and Marks (2002) this confirms the hypothesis for early local changes in sensitivity due to the information conveyed by the irrelevant to the task stimulus dimension.

Goldstone (1995, 1998) also assumes that irrelevant information influences the judgment process relatively early in information processing and discusses the possibility for this effect to be a form of perceptual learning phenomena. Goldstone (1998) argues that contextual manipulation of the irrelevant stimulus dimension may cause on-line detectors to be build up, responsible for the effect of interest. Therefore, the same stimulus could be processed from different detectors depending on its irrelevant information. As a consequence the stimulus could be encoded in a different way depending on the detector that had processed it. For example, if the task requires judgment of line lengths and green lines form a positively skewed distribution, while red lines – a negatively skewed one, then according to the perceptual learning hypothesis, the lines would be processed through different detectors depending on their color. The green lines would be perceived through the detector that holds the information about the distribution of all green lines that were seen during the experiment, while the red lines would be perceived through the detector that holds the information about the skew of the red lines. As a consequence, it may happen that the same line length will be judged differently depending on its color because it has been processed through different detectors and thus represented differently (shifted in a particular direction). Overall, the assumption is that detectors change the way stimuli are encoded or "represented" during early perceptual processing of the input information (Goldstone, 1998). According to Goldstone (1998), once such detectors are formed, they may stay the same, at least until similar information is frequently processed, or may disappear with time.

In sum, both the "perceptual recalibration" of Marks and colegues (Marks, 1988, 1992, 1994, Marks & Warner, 1991; Arieh & Marks, 2002) and the perceptual learning mechanism suggested by Goldstone (1998) assume that the effect of the irrelevant dimension results from low-level perceptual "re-representation" of stimuli with respect to their irrelevant characteristic.

Entirely different mechanism for explaining the effect of irrelevant dimension was suggested by the computational model, called JUDGEMAP (Kokinov et al, 2004; Petkov, 2006a; 2006b). JUDGEMAP is based on the cognitive architecture DUAL (Kokinov, 1994). It uses mechanisms basic for analogy-making, like mapping and memory retrieval in modeling of contextual sensitive judgment.

The most important aspect of the JUDGEMAP Model with respect to the current discussion is that the effect of the irrelevant dimension is actually among the model's predictions. JUDGEMAP states that judgment of any particular stimulus is made within a comparison set of other stimuli. This set includes the some recently judged stimuli, some familiar exemplars of the target category and – very important – exemplars which are most *similar* to the target on all dimensions (both relevant and irrelevant to the task). The mechanism underlying this process in JUDGEMAP is spreading activation. As a result, the irrelevant target stimulus information may cause some exemplars to be retrieved in working memory and become part of the comparison set, against which the target stimulus would be judged. Thus, this irrelevant information will indirectly influence the judgment of the target.

Research Aims

This study aims to differentiate between the two mechanisms proposed as underlying the effect of the irrelevant stimulus dimension, i.e. perceptual learning vs. contextually sensitive retrieval. As was already mentioned, if some perceptual learning mechanism was responsible for the effect of irrelevant information, then it should be possible to demonstrate some sort of a "re-representation" of the stimulus magnitude depending on its irrelevant dimension, at least immediately after the judgment task. For example, if during the judgment of line length some detectors for green and red lines were formed, then these detectors should be still there and should be able to "re-represent" the length of green and red lines immediately after the judgment task. In other words, if such detectors were formed during the judgment task, then it should be possible to demonstrate that people saw green and red lines with the same physical length as different. We test this prediction in the following way. Experiment 1 induces the effect of the irrelevant dimension by the frequency of the stimuli that possess a particular color. We replicate the same design, used in a series of previous experiments on judgment of line length (Kokinov, et al., 2004, Hristova & Kokinov, 2006). Experiment 2 was conducted *immediately* after Experiment 1 with the same participants. This experiment was designed to test the prediction of the perceptual learning hypothesis, namely that, stimuli, which already have pushed perceptual system to form particular detectors in order to be able to process them, are "re-represented" by these detectors and hence, are seen in a different way. Experiment 2 applies the procedure of two-alternative forced choice. Participants were shown a pair of green and red lines on each trial and were asked to judge which one is shorter. The critical pair was formed by green and red lines of equal length. It was expected that if people perceive the two lines as equal then their judgments should be divided into 50/50. If their judgments, however, were divided unequally and were biased toward a particular line color, then we could conclude that people "see" the line of a particular color as a shorter one.

In short, this sequence of two experiments was designed to check whether lines with the same length but colored in red or green are perceived by participants as equal in length after the judgment task, where the effect of the irrelevant dimension is usually observed.

Experiment 1

Design

The color of the lines was a within-subject independent variable (varying at 2 levels – green and red). The experimental design was counterbalanced so that the positively and the negatively skewed stimuli to be presented were either in green or in red. The dependent variable was the mean rating of line lengths on a 7-point scale.

Stimuli

14 color lines that vary from 180 pixels to 505 pixels with an increment of 25 pixels were presented 8 times each forming a basic set of 112 trials. Each line was presented either in red or in green. The frequency distribution of green lines in the first experimental group was positively skewed, while that of the red lines – negatively skewed. In the second experimental group the presentation of lines was just the opposite, i.e., red lines formed a positively skewed distribution and green lines formed a negatively skewed one. The frequency of positively and negatively skewed lines is presented in Table 1.

Table 1. Frequency and color of the lines for a block of 112 trials, where the distribution of the lines of color*P* was positively skewed and of the lines of color*N* was negatively skewed.

Lines	*Length in pixels*	Number of lines of color P	Number of lines of *color N*
1;2	180;205	7	1
3;4	230;255	6	2
5;6	280;305	5	3
7;8	330;355	4	4
9;10	380;405	3	5
11;12	430;455	2	6
13;14	480;505	1	7

Procedure

Each line was presented horizontally on a grey background in a *random position* on the screen.

Each participant was instructed to judge the length of each line presented on the screen on a seven-point scale: 1- "it is not long at all", …, 7 - "it is very long". The experimenter pressed the button corresponding to the participant's answer and the next line appeared on the screen. No time restrictions have been imposed on the participants.

The experiment was conducted in sound-proof booths and lasted about 15 minutes for each participant.

Participants

24 students (16 female and 8 male) from New Bulgarian University from 19 to 35 years participated in the experiment in order to satisfy a course requirement. There were 12 students in each group.

Results and Discussion

The data was averaged by length (14 lengths) and color (color P and color N). In this manner we obtained 28 mean judgments (14 lines * 2 colors) for every participant. The color was analyzed as a within-subject factor, while the group was a between-subject factor. The Repeated Measurement Analyses showed a non-significant main effect of the group: $F (1, 22) = 0.665$, $p= 0.424$ which means that it does not matter whether the red color or the green one is positively skewed. Thus the results from the two groups are accumulated and we will use *color P* to indicate a positively skewed distribution and *color N* to indicate a negatively skewed distribution in all further analyses.

The main effect of the irrelevant dimension (color P vs. color N) on rating of the two middle lines was significant, as estimated with the Repeated Measurement Analysis: $F (1, 22) =6.095$, $p=0.022$, the effect size (ES) = 0.217. The difference between the mean judgments of positively skewed lines (5.276) and of negatively skewed middle lines (5.141) was 0.135. As in previous experiments (Hristova & Kokinov, 2006; Hristova, 2005), positively skewed middle-length lines were rated higher than negatively skewed middle-length lines despite the fact that they were equal in length (Figure 1).

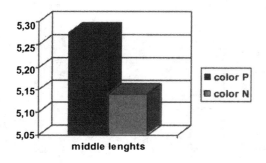

Figure 1. Mean ratings of the *middle line* lengths (line7&8) for each color. The black bar stands for ratings of the positively skewed lines, while the grey-textured bar – for ratings of negatively skewed lines with respect to their color.

The same effect reached marginal significance for the 4 middle lengths, i.e. lines 6, 7, 8 and 9: $F (1, 22)=4.009$, $p=0.058$, $ES=0.154$. The difference between mean judgments of the positively (5.236) and of the negatively (5.152) skewed lines was again in the expected direction, namely, a contrast from the context of the irrelevant to the task color of the lines. Like in most of the previous experiments (Hristova & Kokinov, 2006; Hristova et al., 2005), the effect of the irrelevant dimension was non-significant for all line lengths: $F (1, 22) =0.025$, $p=0.875$.

These results are in line with our previous findings demonstrated by experiments following the same design, procedure and stimulus material (Hristova & Kokinov, 2006; Hristova, 2005; Hristova et al., 2005; Kokinov et al., 2004). Therefore, the effect of the irrelevant dimension could be considered as being robust and reliable. Most importantly, however, these results allow us to test the possibility that once the effect of the irrelevant dimension is induced people "see" rather than "judge" line lengths differently.

Experiment2

This experiment was designed to test the prediction of the perceptual learning hypothesis applied to the effect of the irrelevant dimension in judgment of length, namely that once specific detectors for processing particular stimuli are created during a specific task, they, most probably, will re-represent the same stimuli in a subsequent task. To be more precise, if our green and red lines are judged differently because they have been "seen" differently in Experiment 1, then in a subsequent task (Experiment 2) that involves the same lines, they should be re-represented in the same manner as in the first task. We applied the procedure of two-alternative forced choice *before* the judgment task in order to find out whether lines are perceived as being different in length depending on their red or green color and we didn't found any indication for perceptual illusion (Kokinov et al., 2004). Thus, the effect of the irrelevant dimension could not be due to a perceptual illusion of the line lengths depending on their color but most probably to the specific manipulation of the skew of the line's distributions with a specific color. We haven't tried so far, however, to test whether such perceptual illusion is present *after* judgment of line lengths, where lines were presented with particular frequency depending on their irrelevant color. If we find some indications for perceptual illusion *after* the judgment task, then the effect of the irrelevant dimension may be explained by the perceptual learning mechanism that re-represents the length of the lines of a specific color, rather than to a contextually sensitive retrieval.

Design

In the second part of the experiment we use the procedure of the two-alternative forced choice. The independent variable was the difference in the lengths of the left and the right stimulus with 7 levels.

The dependent variable was the number of the left choices made by the participants, i.e. how many times the left line was chosen as the smaller one.

Stimuli

A set of 14 pairs of lines was designed. In each pair, one of the lines was always 270 pixels long[1]. The other varied within the 7 levels of the length - the smallest one was 252 pixels, the largest one was 288 pixels and the increment was 6 pixels (table 2).

---

[1] The stimuli in both experiments were projected on a 15 inch. Mac computer screen with a resolution 800*600 inches.

Table 2. Stimulus materials used for the two-alternative forced choice procedure.

Intervals		Difference: $\Delta I = I(l) - I(r)$
line4; green; 270pixels	Line3; red; 276pixels	1
line4; green; 270pixels	Line2; red; 282 pixels	2
line4; green; 270pixels	Line3; red; 288 pixels	3
line4; green; 270pixels	Line4; red; 270 -pixels	0
line4; green; 270pixels	Line5; Red; 264 pixels	-1
line4; green; 270pixels	Line6; red; 258 pixels	-2
line4; green; 270pixels	Line7; red; 252 pixels	-3

The constant line (270 pixels) was shown half of the times on the left and half of the times on the right. The whole set of 14 pairs was presented 7 times. All 98 pairs were randomly shown to the participants.

Procedure

The two-alternative forced choice procedure was used. Lines were presented on a computer screen in pairs (probes with two intervals). One of the lines in the pairs was always green and didn't vary in length from trial to trial (see Table 2). It was projected on the screen once on the right and once on the left for each pair (14 pairs). The other line in the pair was always red but varied in length. Each pair has ΔI (I (l) – I(r)) that represent the difference in the lengths of the lines that comprise it. All 14 pairs were shown 7 times on a gray background. The whole set of 98 pairs was randomly presented to the participants.

Participants were asked to answer, which is the shorter line– the left one or the right one, even when they find it difficult to reply.

Participants

The same 24 participants were tested immediately after the completion of Experiment 1.

Results and discussion

All choices were divided into 2 groups depending on the skew of green and red lines that participants judged in Experiment 1 and depending on the left line in each trial.

On one hand, if the left line was green and green lines were positively skewed in Experiment 1 or the left line was red and red lines were positively skewed in Experiment 1, the data was coded as belonging to the group "assimilation". Then if participants in group "assimilation" chose predominantly the left line as being the shorter line, their answers could be considered to be biased toward the lines that were positively skewed in Experiment 1, i.e. participants "see" lines of the color of positively skewed lines as smaller than the same lines that possess the color of the negatively skewed set. If we found such results, they could be interpreted in line with Goldstone's hypothesis (1998), that the context of irrelevant information pushes perceptual system to form detectors that assimilate stimulus "representation" toward the "prototype" of the stimuli that share the same irrelevant information.

On other hand, if the left line was green and the green lines were negatively skewed in Experiment 1 or if the left line was red and the red lines were negatively skewed in Experiment 1, the data would be coded as belonging to the group "contrast". If participants choose predominantly the left line as the shorter line in this group, then it will appear that lines of the color of the negatively skewed set in experiment1 are re-represented as smaller than lines of the same length but possessing the color of the positively skewed set. Since such "re-representation" should result in a contrast effect in judgment of line lengths, this group of observations was coded as "contrast" group. Such sort of "re-representation" was suggested by Arien and Marks (2002).

Probit analysis was applied separately on the data of group "assimilation" and group "contrast". In this way we obtained the interception points for every participant in each group, i.e. which is the difference between the left and the right line (ΔI) for every participant such that he/she chooses equally often the left or the right line as being the shorter one. If participants choose 50 times the left line as the shorter one and 50 times the right line as the shorter line when the two lines were equal in length ($\Delta I = 0$), then there will be no indication for perceptual illusion. On the other hand, if this result is obtained when ΔI is not equal to 0, then it would be reasonable to assume a perceptual length illusion with respect to a particular line color.

The ratio between the intercept for each participant and the intercept's standard error was compared between the "assimilation" and "contrast" groups by the Paired Samples T-Test. This Statistics doesn't reveal a significant difference between the choices made in the two groups: $t(23) = 0.426$, $p = 0.674$. The mean difference between the two groups was 0.389, Std.Deviation = 4.481 and the 95% Confidence Interval of this difference was [-1.5027; 2.2815]. This result does not support the claim that the perceptual learning mechanism underlies the effect of the irrelevant dimension since we didn't find any indication for perceptual length illusion after the judgment task, where, as usual, the discussed effect was found.

We wanted, however, to process our data further in order to be able to say what was the scope of the proposed "re-representation" in pixels that was found, though non-significantly, in our data. That is why, the lower and the upper bound of the received 95% Confidence Interval were multiplied by the mean standard error of the intercepts in both groups (0.03792) and then by the smallest difference between the left and right line in pixels (i.e., 4 pixels, see table 2). In this manner, we've got a 95% Confidence Interval of difference between group "assimilation" and group "contrast" in pixels: [-0.2279; 0.3440]. This additional transformation of the results allows us to say that whatever change in the line "representation" takes place after the effect of the irrelevant dimension was induced, it is between 0 and 0.34 pixels. Thus, even if we assume that some sort of stimulus "re-representation" exists, it seems too small to explain the effect of the irrelevant dimension on judgment.

Conclusion

The reported research focused on the cognitive mechanisms that were recently suggested as underlying the effect of the irrelevant dimension on judgment, namely the perceptual learning mechanism vs. the context-sensitive retrieval. The reported experiments do not find any evidence in favor of the perceptual learning mechanism explanation of the effect of the irrelevant-to-the-task information, since it failed to demonstrate a significant change in a stimulus "representation" with respect to its irrelevant dimension. Thus, up to now, it seems more reasonable to assume that the effect of interest results from context-sensitive retrieval, rather than perceptual learning mechanism, since the former mechanism does not require any sort of temporal or long lasting "re-representation" of stimuli that share the same irrelevant dimension. It should be mentioned, however, that although we didn't find a significant perceptual illusion of line length due to its color, someone might be able to demonstrate it using another methodology. Therefore this possibility cannot be completely ruled out. Moreover, it's quite possible that the type of scale (subjective or objective) may mater. Both Marks and colleges and Goldstone use continuous scale and although they received effects in opposite direction they both argue for a kind of perceptual learning mechanism as possibly underplaying the phenomenon of interest. Thus it seems reasonable to test the same hypothesis about stimulus "re-representation" after judgment on a continuous scale.

In conclusion, this study once again demonstrates the effect of the irrelevant dimension in judgment of line length on a subjective scale. Moreover, the dynamic formation of the comparison set postulated by the JUDGEMAP model and the spreading activation mechanism responsible for it, seems for the moment the best candidate for providing an account of this contextual effect of irrelevant information.

Acknowledgments

This research was supported financially by the ANALOGY project (NEST program, contract 29088) funded by the EC. We would like to thank Georgi Petkov and Alexander Gerganov for many useful comments.

References

Arieh & Marks, L., (2002) Context effects in visual length perception. Role of ocular, retinal, and spatial location. *Perception & Psychophysics*, vol. 64 (3), 478-492

Goldstone, R. (1995) Effects of Categorization on Color Perception. *Psychological Science*, vol. 6 (5), 298-304

Goldstone, R. (1998).Perceptual Learning. *Annual Review of Psychology*, 49, 585-612.

Hristova, P. (2005) The Mechanisms of Contextual Change in Judgment. *In: Proceedings of the Balkan Conference of Young Scientists*, 427-432

Hristova, P., Petkov, G., Kokinov, B. (2005). Influence of Irrelevant Information on Price Judgment. *In: Proceedings of the International Conference on Cognitive Economics*. NBU Press., 95-104

Hristova & Kokinov (2006) A Common Mechanism Is Possibly Underlying the Shift in Perceptual and Conceptual Judgment Produced by Irrelevant Information, *In: Proceedings of the 28th Annual Conference of the Cognitive Science Society, Erlbaum, Hillsdale, NJ., 1529-1534*

Kokinov, B. (1994). The context-sensitive cognitive architecture DUAL. *Proceedings of the Sixteenth Annual Conference of the Cognitive Science Society*. Hillsdale, NJ: Lawrence Erlbaum Associates.

Kokinov, B., Hristova, P., Petkov, G. (2004) Does Irrelevant Information Play a Role in Judgment? In: *Proceedings of the 26th Annual Conference of the Cognitive Science Society*, Erlbaum, Hillsdale, NJ., *72-726*

Marks, L. (1988) Magnitude estimation and sensory matching. *Perception and Psychophysics*, vol. 43, 511-525

Marks, L. (1992), The slippery context effect in psychophysics: Intensive, extensive, and qualitative continua. *Perception and Psychophysics*, 51, 187-198.

Marks (1994) "Recalibrating" the auditory system: The perception of loudness, *Journal of Experimental Psychology: Human Perception and Performance*, 20, 382-396.

Marks & Warner (1991), Slippery context effect and critical bands, *Journal of Experimental Psychology: Human Perception and Performance*, 17, 986-996

Parducci, A. (1965), Category Judgment: A Range-Frequency model, *Psychological Review*, 72(6), 407-418.

Parducci, A. (1974), Contextual Effects: A Range-Frequency Analysis, *Handbook of Perception*, vol.2, NY: Academic Press, 127-141.

Petkov, G. (2006a). Modeling Analogy-Making, Judgment, and Choice with Same Basic Mechanisms. *In: Proceedings of the Seventh International Conference on Cognitive Modeling*. Eds: Fum, D., Missier, F., Stocco, A., Edizioni Goliardiche, 220-225.

Petkov, G. (2006b) JUDGEMAP–Integration of Analogy-Making, Judgment, and Choice. *In: Proceedings of the 28 Annual Conference of the Cognitive Science Society,* 1950-1955.

Rankin & Marks (1991), Differential context effects in taste perception. *Chemical Senses*, 16, 617-629.

Rankin & Marks (1992)Effects of context on sweet and bitter tastes:Unrelated to sensitivity to PRO (6-n-propylthiouracil), *Perception and Psychophysics*, 52, 479-486.

Rankin & Marks, L., (2000), Differential context effects in chemosensation: Role of perceptual similarity and neural communality. *Chemical Senses*, 25, 747-759.

A Neural Model of Global Visual Saliency

Frank van der Velde (vdvelde@fsw.leidenuniv.nl)
Leiden Institute for Brain and Cognition,
Cognitive Psychology, Wassenaarseweg 52, 2333 AK Leiden, The Netherlands

Marc de Kamps (dekamps@comp.leeds.ac.uk)
Biosystems Group, School of computing,
University of Leeds, Leeds LS2 9JT, UK

Abstract

Global saliency refers to the saliency of one object (singleton) among a number of distracter objects. It differs from local saliency, which refers to the saliency of an object with respect to its immediate background. On the basis of the biased competition model of attention, we show that the neural activation of the distracter (identity) dominates the neural activation of the singleton (identity). Then, we present a neural model in which saliency results from an interaction between identity (object-based) processing and spatial processing. This interaction produces the saliency of the singleton. Finally, we show that the model predicts a gradual saliency effect, in which a minority set of objects is more salient. We discuss an experiment that investigated the gradual saliency effect.

Introduction

Visual saliency refers to the way in which an object stands out from its environment. For example, an object on a uniform background, such as a red ball on a green lawn, is highly conspicuous (or salient). This form of saliency can be referred as "local" saliency, because it depends on the contrast that the object makes with its immediate surround.

The basis for local saliency can be found in the early stages of visual processing. For example, neurons with center-surround receptive fields respond vigorously to a local discontinuity given by a contour or change in color or shading (e.g., Coren et al, 1999). Center-surround selectivity is tuned to boundaries or contrast, such as the boundary between light and shading, or the boundary between two colors. These neurons would be strongly activated when their receptive field covers the border between the red ball and the green lawn, but their activity is strongly reduced when their receptive field is entirely covered by the green lawn or by the red ball.

In perceptual terms, a locally salient object "pops-out" from its background and attracts attention. Local saliency has been modeled in terms of direct (bottom-up) processing, in which the local activity induced by the object dominates an inhibitory competition in a retinotopic "saliency" map (e.g., Itty and Koch, 2000). Li (2002) suggested that the primary visual cortex (V1) acts as a saliency map of this kind, in line with the observation that the response of a V1 neuron to a stimulus in its receptive field is affected by the contrast of that stimulus with other stimuli in the visual field.

However, the effect of contrast in V1 seems to be very local, as demonstrated by Rossi et al. (2001). Furthermore, Hedgé and Felleman (2003) showed that the response of V1 or V2 neurons was the same for stimuli that produce pop-out, such as line orientations or colors, and stimuli that do not produce pop-out, such as conjunctions of line orientations and colors. Thus, V1 and V2 neurons respond to local discontinuities, whether or not they result in pop-out.

The results of Rossi et al. (2001) and Hedgé and Felleman (2003) suggest a difference between local saliency and "global" saliency. An example of the latter is a display of single red ball (singleton) and a number of blue balls (distracters) on a green lawn. In this display, each ball is locally salient with respect to the lawn (its immediate background), and one can expect increased activity in V1 neurons for each ball (red and blue alike), in line with the observations of Rossi et al. and Hedgé and Felleman. But the red ball also stands out as among the blue balls. So, besides the local saliency of each ball with respect to its local background, there is also a saliency of the red ball (singleton) among the blue balls (distracters).

The saliency of the red ball (singleton) among the blue balls (distracters) can be seen as a form of global saliency because the singleton is salient with respect to the entire visual scene. Hochstein and Ahissar (2002) argued that global saliency (i.e., pop-out of a singleton among distracters) originates from feature categories represented at higher-level visual areas. Hedgé and Felleman (2003) also argued that global saliency results from processing in a distributed network, of which V1 is only a part.

Biased Competition

The saliency of the singleton entails that it attracts attention (pops out) among the distracters. In terms of the biased competition model (Desimone and Duncan, 1995), the singleton must somehow win the competition with the distracters.

The biased competition model is based on two assumptions. First, multiple stimuli activate populations of neurons that automatically compete. Second, the competition between the populations is biased by attention. Reynolds et al. (1999) investigated the competition between objects in the visual cortex. They showed that a combination of stimuli affects neuronal responses. For example, when a preferred stimulus of a neuron is combined with a non-preferred stimulus, the response of the neuron is reduced. The combined response is about the average of the response to the preferred stimulus presented alone and the response to the non-preferred stimulus presented alone.

Britten and Heuer (1999) found that the combined neuronal response (R) could be described with a generalized nonlinear summation model (scaled power-law summation):

$$R = a[(r_1)^n + (r_2)^n]^{1/n} + b$$

Here, r_1 and r_2 represent the neuronal responses to the stimuli presented alone. The scale factor a and the exponent n can be chosen to fit the response of a given neuron (b can be ignored for this discussion). In this way, the expression accounts for a broad range of possible neuronal responses. For most neurons, R could be determined by freely varying a and n (on average, a = 0.745, n = 2.72).

Scaled power-law summation also accounts for the competition between a preferred and a non-preferred stimulus. For example, when the response to the non-preferred stimulus, r, is about a third of the response to the preferred object, $3r$, (e.g., Reynolds et al., 1999, fig. 6), the combined response R is:

$$R_s = a[(3r)^n + r^n]^{1/n} = ar[3^n + 1]^{1/n}$$

With $a = 0.745$ and $n = 2.72$, the combined response $R \approx 2.3r$, which is about the average of the responses to the preferred and non-preferred stimuli presented alone.

Thus, scaled power-summation gives an adequate description of how neuronal responses are influenced by the competition between stimuli, when they are presented simultaneously in the receptive field of the neurons. Furthermore, Reynolds et al. (1999) showed that the neuronal response changes when one of the stimulus is attended. When the preferred stimulus is attended, the neuronal response is dominated by the preferred stimulus. But when the non-preferred stimulus is attended, the neuronal response reduces to that of the non-preferred response. Hence, attention biases the competition in favor of the attended stimulus, in line with the second assumption of the biased competition model.

However, in the Reynolds et al. (1999) experiments, an external source of attention was used in the form of a spatial cue. But in case of a singleton-distracter display, attention is drawn to the singleton without the use of an external source. The question arises whether the competition between the singleton and the distracters can account for this fact. This would be the case if the response of a neuron for which the singleton is the preferred stimulus and the distracter is the non-preferred stimulus (the "singleton neuron") would dominate the response of a neuron for which the distracter is the preferred stimulus and the singleton is the non-preferred stimulus (the "distracter neuron"), so that the singleton neuron (population) would win the competition with the distracter neuron (population).

A straightforward extension of scaled power-law summation can be used to estimate the behavior of the singleton neuron and the distracter neuron in case of a singleton-distracter display. We assume that the response to a preferred stimulus and a non-preferred stimulus is the same for both neurons, i.e., if the response to a non-preferred stimulus is r, the response to a preferred stimulus is kr, with $k > 1$.

The response of the singleton neuron (R_S) can be determined as follows. Its response to the singleton is given by kr, and its response to each distracter is given by r. The combined response for a singleton and N distracters is then given by:

$$R_s = a[Nr^n + (kr)^n]^{1/n} = ar[N + k^n]^{1/n}$$

The response of the distracter neuron (R_d) to each distracter is given by kr, and its response to the singleton is given by r. The combined response for a singleton and N distracters is then given by:

$$R_d = a[N(kr)^n + r^n]^{1/n} = ar[Nk^n + 1]^{1/n}$$

The competition between the singleton neuron (population) and the distracter neuron (population) is determined by the difference between R_S and R_d. This difference can be investigated by looking at the ratio R_d/R_S:

$$\frac{R_d}{R_s} = \frac{ar[Nk^n + 1]^{1/n}}{ar[N + k^n]^{1/n}} = \frac{[Nk^n + 1]^{1/n}}{[N + k^n]^{1/n}}$$

Clearly, when $N = 1$, $R_d/R_S = 1$. When N increases, the ratio increases as well. When N is (very) large, the numerator is dominated by Nk^n and the denominator is dominated by N. The ratio then reduces to:

$$\frac{R_d}{R_s} \approx \frac{[Nk^n]^{1/n}}{[N]^{1/n}} = k$$

Thus, when N is large, the ratio R_d/R_S approaches the ratio between the response to the preferred stimulus and the response to the non-preferred stimulus when they are presented alone. It is important to note that this behavior of the ratio R_d/R_S is not determined by any of the free parameters a or n in the expression of scaled power-law summation. Thus, the limit behavior of R_d/R_S holds for a very wide range of response functions.

The ratio R_d/R_S clearly indicates that the response of the distracter neuron dominates the response of the singleton neuron. So, the biased competition model would predict that the distracter neuron wins the competition and attention would be drawn to the distracter. Yet, this is not what happens. Attention is drawn to the singleton, even though the selective response to the singleton is dominated by the selective response to the distracter. The model presented below accounts for this fact.

Modeling Global Saliency

Figure 1 presents an outline of the model. The model is based on the architecture of combinatorial (compositional) processing in visual cognition, presented by Van der Velde and De Kamps (2001, 2006).

In this architecture, a display of objects is processed by a different pathways. The "ventral pathway" of the architecture is based on Van der Velde and De Kamps (2001). It processes the identity of objects in an object display (e.g., their shape or color) in an (initially) feedforward manner. When an object is selected in AIT (e.g., due to biased competition, or by using a cue), it initiates feedback processing in the pathway. Due to the interaction between feedforward (stimulus-based) activity and feedback activity, the location of that object is selected in the retinotopic areas of the ventral pathway. The selection of spatial information based on processing in the ventral pathway is summarized in a single "ventral" spatial map in figure 1.

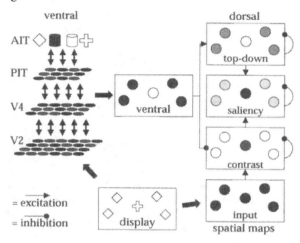

Figure 1: Outline of the model

An object display also activates a number of spatial maps in the "dorsal pathway" of the model. The first of these is an "input" map that is directly activated by the objects in the visual display (e.g., through V1 or V2). The neurons in the input map are not sensitive to the identity of an object, but only to the presence of visual information at a certain location in the visual field.

The input map activates a "contrast" spatial map in a retinotopic (point to point) manner. The contrast map is thus (initially) a copy of the input map. However, the ventral map inhibits the contrast map in a retinotopic manner. In this way, location information about the object selected in the ventral pathway is inhibited in the contrast map. The effect of this inhibition is a selection of location information about those objects that are not selected in the ventral pathway (hence the name "contrast" for this map). Furthermore, an inhibitory competition occurs within the contrast map. The effect of this competition is that spatial information in the contrast map is reduced when it derives from multiple locations.

The ventral map activates a "top-down" map in a retinotopic manner. The top-down map is thus (initially) a copy of the ventral map. However, an inhibitory competition occurs within the top-down map. The effect of this competition is that spatial information derived from the

ventral pathway is reduced when multiple object locations are selected in the ventral pathway. In this way, the top-down map forms a pre-selection of the spatial information derived from the ventral pathway (hence the name "top-down" for this map), in favor of a single object location.

The top-down map and the contrast map activate a "saliency" map in a retinotopic manner. The top-down map represents the spatial information selected in the ventral pathway, whereas the contrast map represents the spatial information not selected in the ventral pathway. Both forms of information interact in the saliency map due to an inhibitory competition within this map.

The architecture of spatial selection presented in figure 1 is tuned to select the location of the singleton object (the cross in figure 1). Figure 1 shows what happens when the identity of the distracter (diamond) is selected in AIT, due to biased competition. The locations of the diamonds are selected in the ventral map, and thus in the top-down map. But due to inhibitory competition, distracter representations are reduced in the top-down map. The contrast map represents the location of the singleton (cross), because the distracter locations are inhibited by the ventral map. As a result, the location of the singleton (cross) is most strongly activated in the saliency map. Therefore, it wins the competition in the saliency map, so that the location of the singleton is selected.

In turn, the spatial selection of the singleton acts like an "intrinsic" spatial attentional cue. In line with the biased competition model, this attentional cue biases the neuronal responses (in the ventral pathway) in favor of the singleton. In this way, the singleton attracts attention (pops-out).

Simulations of the Model

The simulation of the process illustrated in figure 1 proceeded as follows. Each of the spatial maps (ventral, top-down, saliency, contrast, and input) was modeled as a 31 x 31 matrix of (excitatory) neuron populations, with the population dynamics as used in Van der Velde and De Kamps (2001). The objects (a singleton and four distracters) were represented as disks in the each of the spatial maps.

The location of a disk was represented with 12 neuron populations in each of the spatial maps. Input to the dorsal pathway was represented as an external current injected at the location of each object in the input map. The effect of selection in the ventral map (simulated in Van der Velde and De Kamps, 2001) was represented as an external current injected at the location of each selected object in the ventral map. Inhibitory competition in each spatial map resulted from an inhibitory population that was activated by all (excitatory) populations in that map.

Figure 2 presents the simulations of the model when the distracter is selected in AIT, due to biased competition. Even though the distracter neuron dominates the response in AIT, the singleton is selected in the saliency map, and the activity of the distracter is low in the saliency map. When the distracter is selected in AIT, the activity of the singleton in the contrast map is stronger than the activity of the distracter in the top-down map. This activity difference in favor of the singleton determines the selection of the singleton in the saliency map, as illustrated in figure 1.

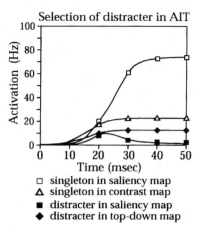

Figure 2: Simulation of singleton saliency

The process illustrated in figure 1 and simulated in figure 2 is in line with an effect of global saliency in the posterior parietal cortex (area 7a), observed by Constantinidis and Steinmetz (2005). In their experiment, neurons in areas 7a responded selectively to the location of a singleton. Initially, singleton activity in this area was similar to distracter activity, but after some 180 msec a difference in activity developed in favor of the singleton. This delay in response selectivity, as observed by Constantinidis and Steinmetz, is in line with the process illustrated in figure 1. The selection of the singleton in the saliency map is due to the effect of the selection of the distracters in the ventral map. This selection, in turn, depends on the interaction in the ventral pathway, which develops over time.

The model presented in figure 1 also produces the saliency of the singleton when the singleton's identity is selected in AIT, due to a cue stimulus presented earlier. In this case, the activity of the singleton in the top-down map is stronger than the activity of the distracter in contrast map. This activity difference in favor of the singleton again determines the selection of the singleton in the saliency map.

Gradual Saliency

Figure 3 illustrates the (final) activity in the saliency map that the model in figure 1 produces for displays with varying ratio's of two types of objects (e.g., crosses and diamonds). The number of objects in the displays is always the same (8), but the ratio between the two types of objects varies from 1/7 to 7/1. In one condition (the dashed line in the figure), the ratio is 8/0 ("all distracter display").

The displays with the ratio's 1/7 and 7/1 show the saliency of the singleton among 7 distracters, in line with figures 1 and 2. In the cases 2/6 and 6/2, two objects of one type are more salient than 6 objects of the other type, although less salient than a singleton. A similar but reduced situation occurs with the ratio's 3/5 and 5/3. This suggests that saliency is not an all-or-nothing phenomenon, but a gradual one. Thus, the model in figure 1 has a preference for a singleton object, but the dynamics involved also produce a form of "gradual" saliency.

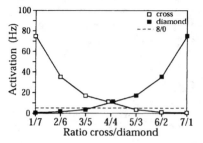

Figure 3: Simulation of gradual saliency

Figure 3 also shows that the activity in the saliency map for a display with 8 objects (all distracter display) is higher than the activity of the distracter in the saliency map for displays with 7 distracters and a singleton. This result is in line with an observation of neural activity in posterior parietal cortex (area 7a) by Constantinidis and Steinmetz (2005). They measured the activity of neurons responsive to a distracter in an all distracter display. The activity of these neurons was reduced when one of the other distracters (outside their receptive fields) was replaced by a singleton.

Experiment

Figure 4 illustrates an experiment that investigated the effect of gradual saliency (Van der Voort van der Kleij, 2006).

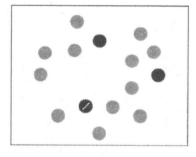

Figure 4: Gradual saliency experiment

Subjects first focused on a fixation point in the center of the screen. Then, a display of 15 colored disks was presented, which were located randomly on two imaginary circles around the point of fixation. The disks were either blue or green, in different ratio's. The blue-green ratio's used were 1/14, 3/12 (as in figure 4), 5/10, 7/8, 8/7, 10/5, 12/3 and 14/1. In one condition (15/0), all disk were in the same color (all distracter display). One of the disks contained an (black) line (target) in one of two orientations (left or right diagonal). The task of the subjects was to detect the orientation of the target as fast as possible.

Figure 5 presents the results of the experiment. The response times (in msec) are plotted in terms of the number of disks in the same-colored (sub)set in which the target appeared (e.g., 3 in figure 4). From 1 to 7, the target thus appeared in the "minority" set (the smallest subset of same-colored disks). From 8 to 14, the target appeared in the "majority" set (the largest subset of same-colored disks). With 15, the target appeared in the all distracter display. The results show a steady increase of response time from 1 to 7, thus when the target is in the minority set. From 8-14, when the target is in the majority set, the response time does not increase, and it drops even when the target is in the all distracter display.

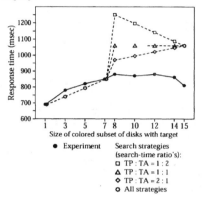

Figure 5: Response time for target

The increase in response time with the increasing number of items in the minority set suggest a serial search strategy, in which the subjects search for the target in the minority set first, before they search for it in the majority set. Three of these search strategies are presented in figure 5 (dashed lines). Each strategy begins with a search of the target in the minority set. When the target appears in the minority set, the response time is the same for all strategies, based on the average increase in response time of about 25 msec for each additional item in the minority set. When the target appears in the majority set (from 8 onwards), the response time in each search strategy results from first searching the target in the minority set, followed by searching the target in the majority set. In the all distracter display, the target is searched as in a minority set with 15 items.

The three search strategies in figure 5 differ in the ratio between TP (search time for each additional item when the target is present) and TA (search time for each additional item when the target is absent). TP is given by the average increase in response time in the experiment when the target is in the minority set (about 25 msec per item), so that TA can be calculated for each of the search strategies. The most likely ratio is TP:TA = 1:2, which is frequently found in

visual search experiments (Wolfe & Horowitz, 2004). It occurs when each item in a set is searched only once. In that case, it takes on average a search of half of the items in the set to find the target when it is present, but all items have to be searched when the target is absent. The ratio TP:TA = 1:1 and, in particular, the ratio TP:TA = 2:1 are less likely, but they are included to explore a wide range of search possibilities. None of the search strategies match the data when the target is in the majority set. With the ratio TP:TA = 1:2, the response times in fact decline with larger majority sets, because shifting an item from the minority set to the majority set reduces the response time with this ratio.

Thus, search strategies that begin with searching the target in the minority set do not provide an explanation of the data this experiment. Instead, the identification of the target seems to benefit from the saliency of the disks when the target is in a minority set (or even in the all distracter display). We investigate this saliency explanation below.

Effect of gradual saliency

The fact that the response time for the target in the minority set (figure 5) is lower than for the target in the majority set is in line with the suggestion that the identification of the target benefits from the saliency of the disks in the minority set. The increase in response time with the increasing number of items in the minority set (from 1 to 7) is also in line with this suggestion, because the saliency of the items in the minority set reduces when the number of items in the set increases, as in the simulations presented in figure 3. The drop in response time in the all distracter set could also be the result of (gradual) saliency, because the all distracter set in figure 3 was more salient than the distracters in a singleton-distracter display.

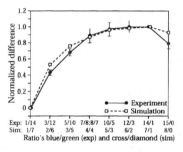

Figure 6: A comparison of simulation and experiment

Figure 6 presents a normalized comparison between the simulation of gradual saliency (figure 3) and the experimental results (figure 5). For the normalization of the experimental data, a simple change in presentation is needed. In figure 5, the data are presented in terms of the number of items in the (sub)set of colored disks in which the target appears. But they could also have been presented in terms of (say) the blue-green ratio's (1/14, 3/12, 5/10, 7/8, 8/7, 10/5, 12/3, 14/1, and 15/0), with the target always presented in a blue disk. The 1/14 and 14/1 ratio's are the singleton-distracter displays. The difference between them is that the target appears in the singleton in the 1/14 display and in one of the distracters in the 14/1 display. So, the two singleton-distracter displays represent the extreme ends of the saliency difference between the minority and majority sets. Therefore, we use the increase in response time between the 1/14 and 14/1 ratio's as a standard (unity), to normalize the increase in response time between the 1/14 ratio and the other blue/green ratio's (dividing each increase in response time by the increase between 1/14 and 14/1). These normalized increases (differences) in response time are plotted in figure 6 (with the average of the 7/8 and 8/7 ratio's, for the reason explained below). In all, we performed 5 experiments (3 without a cue, one with a color cue, one with a word cue). Figure 6 presents the average and root mean square of the experimental results.

For the normalization of the gradual saliency simulations (figure 3), the same procedure was used, based on the activity of the cross. The singleton-distracter displays in this case are the 1/7 and the 7/1 cross-diamond ratio's. In the first singleton-distracter display the cross is the singleton. In the second singleton-distracter display the cross is the distracter. The decrease in cross activity between the 1/7 and 7/1 ratio's was used to normalize the decrease in cross activity between the 1/7 ratio and the other cross/diamond ratio's. These normalized decreases (differences) in (cross) activity are also plotted in figure 6.

The singleton-distracter ratio's can be used to compare the simulations with the experimental data. Thus, the 1/7 and 7/1 ratio's in the simulations are matched with the 1/14 and 14/1 ratio's in the experiment. A similar match can be found for the 4/4 ratio in the simulation and the average of the 7/8 and 8/7 ratio's in the experiment, because these ratio's represent the displays in which the two different kinds of objects are (about) equal in number. Furthermore, the increasing minority ratio's 2/6 and 3/5 in the simulations can be matched with the increasing minority ratio's 3/12 and 5/10 in the experiment, and the increasing majority ratio's 5/3 and 6/2 in the simulations can be matched with the increasing majority ratio's 5/10 and 12/3 in the experiment. Finally, the all distracter display (8/0) in the simulations can be matched with the all distracter display (15/0) in the experiment.

The normalized response times and the normalized simulations in figure 6 follow a similar pattern: an initial increase (decrease) for the minority sets, which levels off for the majority sets, followed by a decrease (increase) for the all distracter display. Of course, the comparison between the simulations and experimental data is a qualitative one. But it shows that the pattern of activity in the saliency map matches the pattern of response times in the experiment. This supports the suggestion that the identification of the target benefits from the (relative) saliency of the disks in the minority sets (and in the all distracter display). The relative saliency of the disks in the minority set is produced by the interactive process illustrated in figure 1.

The results of the simulations and experiment presented here emphasize the importance of combinatorial processing in (visual) cognition (Van der Velde& De Kamps, 2006).

Acknowledgments

We thank Pascal Haazebroek and Gwendid van der Voort van der Kleij for their assistance in a pilot study of the model presented here.

References

Britten, K. H. & Heuer, H. W. (1999). Spatial summation in the receptive fields of MT neurons. *Journal of Neuroscience, 19*, 5074-5084.

Constantinidis, C. & Steinmetz, M. A. (2005). Posterior parietal cortex automatically encodes the location of salient stimuli. *Journal of Neuroscience, 25*, 233-238.

Coren, S., Ward, L. M., & Enns, J. T. (1999). *Sensation and perception*. Wiley.

Desimone, R. & Duncan, J. (1995). Neural mechanisms of selective visual attention. *Annual Review of Neuroscience, 18*, 193-222.

Hedgé, J. & Felleman, D. J. (2003). How selective are V1 cells for pop-out stimuli? Journal of Neuroscience, 23, 9968-9980.

Hochstein, S., & Ahissar, M. (2002). View from the top: Hierarchies and reverse hierarchies in the visual system. *Neuron, 36,* 791-804.

Itty, L. & Koch, C. (2000). A saliency-based search mechanism for overt and covert shifts of visual attention. *Vision Research, 40*, 1489-1506.

Li, Z. (2002). A saliency map in primary visual cortex. *Trends in Cognitive Sciences,* 6, 9-16.

Reynolds, J. H. & Chelazzi, L. & Desimone, R. (1999). Competitive mechanisms subserve attention in macaque areas V2 and V4. *Journal of Neuroscience, 19*, 1736-1753.

Rossi, A. F., Desimone, R. & Ungerleider, L. G. (2001). Contextual modulation in primary visual cortex of macaques. *Journal of Neuroscience, 21*, 1698-1709.

Van der Velde, F., & de Kamps, M. (2001). From knowing what to knowing where: Modeling object-based attention with feedback disinhibition of activation. *Journal of Cognitive Neuroscience, 13*, 479-491.

Van der Velde, F., & de Kamps, M. (2006). Neural blackboard architectures of combinatorial structures in cognition. *Behavioral and Brain Sciences, 29*, 37-108.

Van der Velde, F., de Kamps, M., & van der Voort van der Kleij, G. T. (2004). CLAM: Closed-loop attention model for visual search. *Neurocomputing, 58-60*, 607-612.

Van der Voort van der Kleij, G. T. (2006). *To be selected or not to be selected: A modeling and behavioral study of the mechanisms underlying stimulus-driven and top-down visual attention.* Doctoral dissertation, Cognitive Psychology, Leiden University, Leiden.

Wolfe, J. M. & Horowitz, T. S. (2004). What attributes guide the deployment of visual attention and how do they do it? *Nature Reviews Neuroscience, 5*, 1-7.

Investigating the Factors that Influence the Temporal Perception of Complex Audiovisual Events

Argiro Vatakis (argiro.vatakis@psy.ox.ac.uk)
&
Charles Spence (charles.spence@psy.ox.ac.uk)
Crossmodal Research Group, Department of Experimental Psychology
9 South Parks Road, Oxford, OX1 3UD UK

Abstract

We investigated the perception of synchrony for complex audiovisual events. In Experiment 1, music, speech, and object action video clips were presented while participants made unspeeded temporal order judgments (TOJs) regarding which stream (either the auditory or visual) appeared to have been presented first. The sensitivity of temporal discrimination performance was significantly higher for the object action than for the speech video clips, and both were significantly higher than for the music clips. In a second experiment, we investigated whether or not these differences in performance were driven by differences in stimulus complexity and/or stimulus type by presenting brief speech and music video clips. No effect of stimulus type was obtained. Audiovisual temporal discrimination sensitivity was, however, higher for stimuli of lower complexity as compared to stimuli having continuously time-varying properties.

Introduction

How do we perceive a proximal audiovisual event to be synchronized, when the auditory signal is processed faster than the visual signal (at the neuronal level)? How can we achieve an optimal television viewing experience if there are differences in the transmission rates between signals in the auditory and visual channels? Questions such as these highlight the importance of temporal perception in both the theoretical and applied domains (e.g., King, 2005; Rihs, 1995; Spence & Squire, 2003; Vatakis & Spence, 2006-a, -b).

The majority of previous research in this area has tended to focus on simple transitory stimuli (such as brief noise bursts and light flashes; e.g., Fendrich & Corballis, 2001; Vroomen & Keetels, 2006; Zampini, Shore, & Spence, 2003). However, in order to better understand the perception of realistic events we need to move toward the use of more ecologically-valid stimuli (de Gelder & Bertelson, 2003). To date, this move has primarily focused on the use of audiovisual speech stimuli (e.g. Dixon & Spitz, 1980; Grant & Greenberg, 2001), and only recently on other kinds of complex non-speech stimuli (such as musical and object action stimuli; e.g., Arrighi, Alais, & Burr, 2006; Dixon & Spitz, 1980; Vatakis & Spence, 2006-a).

One of the first studies to investigate the perception of synchrony for complex audiovisual events was reported by Dixon and Spitz (1980). Participants in this study had to monitor videos of continuous speech and repetitive object actions (i.e., a hammer being used to hit a peg repeatedly). These events were initially presented in synchrony and were gradually desynchronized at a rate of 51 ms/s (up to a maximum asynchrony of 500 ms) with either the auditory or visual stream leading. The participants had to respond as soon as they detected an asynchrony in the videos. Dixon and Spitz found that for speech, the auditory stream had to lag by an average of 258 ms or lead by 131 ms before the asynchrony was detected. These values were significantly different from those observed in the object action videos, where an auditory lag of 188 ms or a lead of 75 ms was required for the detection of asynchrony. These results were taken to suggest that participants are simply more sensitive to the presence of asynchrony in the object action videos than in the speech videos (see also Hollier & Rimell, 1998; Vatakis & Spence, 2006-a).

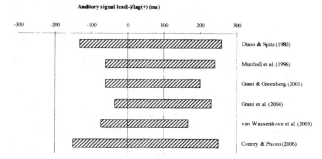

Figure 1: Variability in the temporal window of multisensory integration (PSS±JND) observed in previous studies using audiovisual speech stimuli.

The majority of the subsequent research that has also looked at audiovisual synchrony perception has tended to focus solely on the perception of speech stimuli (see Arrighi et al., 2006; Vatakis & Spence, 2006-a, -b, for recent exceptions). It should, however, be noted that the results reported in these studies that have used speech stimuli are highly variable. For example, Grant, van Wassenhove, and Poeppel (2004) reported that participants only noticed the asynchrony in a continuous stream of audiovisual speech when the speech sounds led the visual lip-movements by at least 50 ms or else lagged by 220 ms or more (see also Hollier & Rimell, 1998). These values are quite different from those reported in Dixon and Spitz's study, thus leading to the question of "what drives this variability?"

The inconsistency between the various different audiovisual asynchronies reported in previous studies (Figure 1) might be driven by a number of methodological factors. For example, in both Dixon and Spitz (1980) and Grant et al.'s (2004) studies, the auditory stream was presented over headphones while the visual stream was presented from in front of the participant on a monitor. Research has shown that the integration of multisensory stimuli can be facilitated by their spatial coincidence (e.g., see Calvert, Spence, & Stein, 2004). These previous studies may therefore have provided an erroneous estimate of people's sensitivity to asynchrony by providing additional spatial cues to help resolve temporal asynchrony. It is also unclear whether the gradual desynchronization of the videotapes in Dixon and Spitz's study might also inadvertently have presented their participants with subtle auditory pitch-shifting cues (see Reeves & Voelker, 1993). Finally, the lack of any catch trials in Dixon and Spitz's study means that one cannot rule out the possibility that criterion shifts may have influenced participants' performance.

In addition to the inconsistency of the previous results, the use of speech as the only stimulus to examine audiovisual temporal perception represents something of a concern. This concern stems from the fact that speech is a highly-practiced event and some have even argued that it represents a special type of stimulus (e.g., Tuomainen et al., 2005). Hence, any conclusions based solely on speech stimuli might not be representative and cannot necessarily be generalized to the audiovisual temporal perception of other complex non-speech stimuli.

The limited number of studies that have used non-speech stimuli, the inconsistencies between the results that have been reported to date, and the methodological limitations identified above, led us to conduct the present study. In our first experiment, we utilized a series of naturalistic audiovisual events in a short video clip format in order to assess the limits on the perception of synchrony using a temporal order judgment (TOJ; whereby, participants have to report which modality stream, either auditory or visual, they perceived to have been presented first) task. The stimuli were composed of audiovisual speech, music, and object action events that were presented with a wide range of auditory/visual stimulus onset asynchronies (SOAs) using the method of constant stimuli. This experimental design enabled us to examine how the effects observed in speech stimuli relate to those observed for these other kinds of complex non-speech stimuli, while at the same time eliminating the limitations that have been identified for previous research in this area.

Experiment 1

28 participants (14 female; mean age of 24 years) took part in the experiment. All were naïve as to the purpose of the study. All of the participants reported normal hearing and normal or corrected-to-normal visual acuity. 5 of the participants reported having had extensive prior musical experience (preliminary analysis showed no performance differences for music experienced versus naïve participants).

Methods

The visual stimuli were presented on a computer monitor, placed 68 cm in front of the participant, and the auditory stimuli were presented by means of two loudspeaker cones, one placed 25.4 cm to either side of the centre of the monitor. This placement ensured the spatial coincidence of the auditory and visual streams. The audiovisual stimuli consisted of video clips of the following: (a) a British male uttering the sentence "We go back a long way, how does it fit in vis-à-vis dad?" (duration of 5900 ms); and (b) the sentence "Keep up the good work" (1900 ms); (c) a male smashing a television with a hammer (5900 ms); (d) a female hitting a soda can with a block of wood (5900 ms); (e) a male playing a piece of music on a classical guitar (5900 and 6900 ms, respectively); and (f) on a piano (900 and 1900 ms, respectively). At the beginning and end of each video clip, a still image and cross-fading were utilized to ensure a smooth video transition and to avoid inadvertently cuing the participants as to the nature of the stream delay that they were being presented with (see Vatakis & Spence, 2006-a, for more details). The participants responded by pressing one of two response keys to indicate 'vision-first' or 'sound-first' responses.

Design

9 SOAs between the auditory and visual streams were used: ±400, ±300, ±200, ±100, and 0 ms (negative values indicate an auditory lead). The participants completed one block of 8 practice trials. The main experimental session consisted of 5 random blocks of 144 experimental trials (2 presentations of each condition per block) or of 8 fixed blocks of 90 experimental trials.

Procedure

The video clips were presented in a random order for 20 of the participants, while each of the 8 different video clips was presented in a separate block of trials for the remaining 8 participants (who were informed at the beginning of each block as to which type of video clip they would be presented with next).

Results and discussion

The proportion of 'vision-first' responses was converted to its equivalent z-score, under the assumption of a cumulative normal distribution (Finney, 1964). The data from the 9 SOAs were used to calculate the best-fitting straight lines for each participant and condition. In turn, these best-fitting lines were used to derive slope and intercept values. These values allowed us to calculate the Just Noticeable Difference (JND=0.675/slope; since ±0.675 represents the 75% and 25% point on the cumulative normal distribution) and the Point of Subjective Simultaneity (PSS=-intercept/slope) values (see Coren, Ward, & Enns, 2004, for further details). The JND provides a standardized measure of the sensitivity with which participants could judge the temporal order of the auditory and visual streams. The PSS indicates the amount of time by which one stream had to lead the other in order for participants to make the 'sound-first' and 'vision-first' responses equally often.

Collapsing the data from each stimulus pair gave rise to four conditions: speech, piano and guitar music, and object actions. A between-participants analysis of variance (ANOVA) on the JND data was performed with the between-participants factor of Stimulus Presentation (blocked or fixed) and the within-participants factor of Stimulus Type. This analysis gave rise to a significant main effect of Stimulus Type [$F_{(3,78)}$=6.16, p<.01] with higher sensitivity (i.e., lower JNDs) being reported for the object action video clips (M=126 ms) than for the speech (M=154 ms), guitar (M=257 ms), or piano playing video clips (M=258 ms) [p=.04, p=.02, and p<.01, respectively]. In addition, significantly higher sensitivity to temporal order was obtained for the speech video clips than for the guitar or piano playing clips (p<.05 for both comparisons). The higher temporal discrimination sensitivity for the speech stimuli as compared to the musical stimuli might be due to the increased capture of participants' attention during exposure to an audiovisual speech event (e.g., Soto-Faraco et al., 2004; Theeuwes & Van der Stigchel, in press). There was no significant main effect of Stimulus Presentation [$F_{(1,26)}$<1, n.s.], nor any interaction between Stimulus Presentation and Stimulus Type [$F_{(3,78)}$<1, n.s.] (Figure 2A).

A similar analysis of the PSS data revealed a significant main effect of Stimulus Type [$F_{(3,78)}$=8.78, p<.01], with the visual stream having to lead the auditory stream in the object action and guitar video clips (63 ms and 65 ms, respectively), as opposed to the auditory leads reported in the speech and piano playing video clips (36 ms and 84 ms, respectively) [p<.01, for all comparisons]. There was no main effect of Stimulus Presentation [$F_{(1,26)}$<1, n.s.], nor any interaction between Stimulus Presentation and Stimulus Type [$F_{(3,78)}$<1, n.s.] (Figure 2B).

Overall, the results of Experiment 1 provide evidence regarding the limits on the perception of synchrony for speech and object action events. Our results are consistent with Dixon and Spitz's (1980) previous results, with both studies showing that people find it easier to detect the temporal asynchrony present in desynchronized audiovisual object action video clips than in speech clips. Our study extends these findings to the temporal perception of audiovisual musical video clips, showing that people are less sensitive to asynchrony in musical video clips than in either speech or object action video clips.

The PSS values reported in Experiment 1 are smaller than the estimated values derived from the data reported in Dixon and Spitz's (1980) previous study, where the visual stream would have had to lead by approximately 120 ms and 103 ms for the PSS to be reached in the speech and object action video clips, respectively. The same holds true when comparing the speech results obtained here to those from Grant et al.'s (2004) study, in which the speech sounds had to lag behind the visual lip-movements by approximately 220 ms for the PSS to be reached. The smaller PSS values

obtained in our study as compared to previous studies might be due to the type of stimuli used and/or to the elimination of the methodological limitations identified earlier.

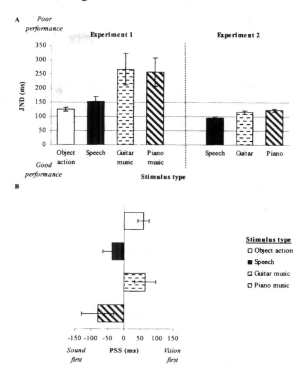

Figure 2: (A) JNDs for the conditions tested in Experiments 1 and 2. (B) Mean PSS values reported in Experiment 1. The error bars represent the standard errors of the mean.

The large JND values observed in the guitar and piano playing video clips (note also the large SE bars in Figure 2A) are difficult to explain given the limited number of studies dealing with the perception of musical events (Baader, Kazennikov, & Wiesendanger, 2005; see Arrighi et al., 2006; Vatakis & Spence, 2006-a, -b, for exceptions). We thought it possible that one explanation for the poor TOJ performance seen in our experiment might have been related to the difficulty that participants may have had in trying to divide their attention between the two different, fast, and spatially separated hand movements involved in playing the guitar and piano as seen in the particular video clips utilized in Experiment 1. Another explanation for these results might be related to the fact that the guitar strings and piano keys were not as distinctive (or discriminable) as was, for example, the single action of a soda can being crushed, thus potentially increasing the difficulty of the musical TOJ task. Finally, the fact that the fingers in close proximity to the finger plucking a string or depressing a key tend to move and pause together (a phenomenon known as enslaving) may have rendered it more difficult for our participants to pinpoint the exact moment in time at which the appropriate finger plucked the string (Baader et al., 2005) or else tapped the key.

Taken together, the results of Experiment 1 for the music, speech, and object action video clips would appear to highlight the existence of large differences in the acuity of our temporal perception relating to different types of naturalistic audiovisual stimuli. We thought it possible that the high complexity of the various naturalistic stimuli utilized (e.g., music pieces) in both the present and previous studies (e.g., Dixon & Spitz, 1980; Grant et al., 2004), might have been one reason for the large differences and variability observed between and within speech and music stimuli. The complexity of the stimulus is attributed here to the continuously time-varying pattern of the sentences or the music pieces and the physical differences involved (e.g., a segment of speech would be considered to be more 'visual' if it contained a large number of bilabial than alveolar consonants). In our second experiment, we therefore examined whether the stimulus complexity and/or the physical differences present in a particular stimulus could have driven the differences observed in our previous experiment. In Experiment 2, we utilized short video clips of audiovisual speech and music (guitar and piano) stimuli with varying levels of complexity (phonemes and single music notes, syllables and double musical notes).

Experiment 2

21 participants (11 female; mean age of 24 years) took part in the experiment (no musical experience was reported). The apparatus, stimuli, design, and procedure were exactly the same as for Experiment 1 with the sole exception that the audiovisual stimuli now consisted of (a) a British male saying /a/ and /p/ (both videos were 967 ms long); and (b) the syllables /lo/ and /me/ (833 ms); (c) a male playing the musical notes "a" and "d" (1700 ms); and (d) the note combinations "db" and "eg" on a classical guitar (2200 ms); (e) a female playing the notes "a" and "d" (1700 ms); and (f) the note combinations "ce" and "fd" on the piano (2200 ms).

Results and discussion

Preliminary analysis of the data revealed no differences in performance within each Category (e.g., for the speech stimuli, no differences were obtained for /a/, /p/, /lo/, and /me/), thus the data were averaged over Category and we compared performance as a function of the Stimulus Type (e.g., speech, guitar, and piano music). A one-way ANOVA revealed a significant main effect of Stimulus Type [$F(2,251)=8.33$, $p<.01$], with the accuracy of participants' temporal discrimination responses being significantly higher for speech stimuli than for either the guitar or piano music stimuli [$p \leq .01$ for both comparisons]. This result replicates the findings obtained in Experiment 1 (Figure 2A).

Analysis of the PSS data revealed a significant main effect of Category for the speech stimuli [$F(3,83)=7.69$, $p < .01$], but not for the guitar or piano music. The mean PSS values for the guitar and piano music were -7 ms and +41 ms, respectively. For the speech category, the /a/ stimulus

required an auditory lead of 66 ms for the PSS to be achieved. This value was significantly different from the auditory lead of 8 ms required for the /p/ stimulus, or the visual leads of 19 ms and 27 ms required for the syllables /lo/ and /me/, respectively [$p=.05$, $p<.01$, and $p<.01$, respectively] (Figure 3).

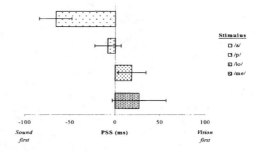

Figure 3: Mean PSS values for the various speech stimuli used in Experiment 2. The error bars represent the standard errors of the mean.

The PSS data revealed greater variability in the modality lead/lag for the speech video clips than for the musical video clips. For example, while the auditory stream had to lead by 66 ms for the /a/ stimulus, the visual stream had to lead by 27 ms for the /me/ stimulus. This difference may reflect the fact that the phonetic and physical properties involved in the production of speech sounds vary as a function of the particular speech sound being uttered (Kent, 1997). So, for example, the production of the vowel /a/ depends on the position of the jaw, tongue, and lips and for the bilabial, nasal consonant /m/ closure of the oral cavity is required, while uttering /ma/ requires the rapid combination of those movements. In addition, bilabial stimuli have a higher visibility, since the visual articulations are more pronounced as compared to the often ambiguous (i.e., less visible) articulation of vowels (Mattys, Bernstein, & Auer, 2002). These differences in the nature of the production and articulation of different speech sounds may explain the variations in the auditory or visual delays/leads required for the successful perception of synchrony for audiovisual speech (cf. van Wassenhove, Grant, & Poeppel, 2005). They may also help to account for the decreased sensitivity to continuous speech reported in previous studies, where the PSS will presumably have varied continuously as a function of the particular speech sound being uttered at any particular moment in the stream.

The results of Experiment 2 show, once again, that people were better able to detect the temporal asynchrony present in the desynchronized audiovisual speech video clips than in either the guitar or piano music video clips. The JND and PSS values reported for the brief speech stimuli were much smaller than those observed in previous studies of asynchrony detection using continuous speech stimuli (e.g., Dixon & Spitz, 1980; Grant et al., 2004), thus showing once again that the complexity and type of stimuli used can modulate temporal perception. In addition, even for a given type of stimulus, the physical differences that are present will also promote differences in the temporal perception of the particular event. This was shown here for the speech stimuli, where highly visible stimuli (e.g., the stop /p/) required less of a visual lead for the PSS to be achieved as compared to the less visible stimuli (e.g., the vowel /a/).

General discussion

Overall, the results of the two experiments reported in the present study provide robust empirical evidence concerning how stimulus type and stimulus complexity conjointly affect people's sensitivity to asynchrony for audiovisual stimuli. Additionally, our results also provide more convincing data concerning the limits on the perception of synchrony for speech, musical, and object action events, by eliminating the potential limitations inherent in previous studies (e.g., the lack of spatial coincidence, the potential presence of pitch-shifting cues, and the possibility of criterion shifts).

The results of Experiment 1 are consistent with those obtained by Dixon and Spitz (1980), in that people found it easier to detect temporal asynchrony in desynchronized audiovisual object action video clips than in speech video clips. We also extended these findings to the case of the perception of temporal order for audiovisual musical clips, suggesting that people are less sensitive to asynchrony in musical video clips (Vatakis & Spence, 2006-a) than in either speech or object action video clips. However, the results of Experiment 2 provided a better-controlled measure of participants' temporal perception of complex audiovisual stimuli (since all of the stimuli were matched in complexity). Under such conditions, no difference in the sensitivity of participants' temporal discrimination performance was observed between the speech and musical stimuli. The results of Experiment 2 also showed how physical differences between stimuli can affect temporal perception, given the differential PSS values obtained for the various speech sounds (phonemes and syllables) tested. Hence, our results clearly show that variations in stimulus properties modulate audiovisual temporal perception.

Comparison of the results of the two experiments reported here with previous studies suggest that people find it easier to discriminate the temporal order of stimuli that are of shorter duration and which are less complex (i.e., where the stimulus properties remain constant) than stimuli that are longer in duration and/or higher in complexity (e.g., as when we compared temporal perception for sentences as opposed to syllables). Specifically, the JND values reported for the speech, musical, and object action stimuli in Experiment 1 were noticeably higher than those reported in Experiment 2 where syllables and single notes were used and in previous studies that have utilized simple sound-light pairs as experimental stimuli (Hirsh & Sherrick, 1961).

The sensitivity differences observed between simple and complex audiovisual stimuli suggest that the perception of synchrony may be affected by the complexity of the particular stimuli that have to be judged. One possibility here is that stimulus complexity may promote the perception of synchrony (even for objectively slightly asynchronous stimuli) due to the increased low-level spatiotemporal correlations between the component stimuli that may facilitate binding in a bottom-up (i.e., stimulus-driven)

manner (cf. Vatakis & Spence, in press-a). Alternatively, however, increased stimulus complexity may also promote the perception of synchrony due to the increased likelihood of binding due to the influence of the unity assumption (whereby, if auditory and visual inputs are perceived as being consistent then an observer will be more likely to treat them as referring to a unified audiovisual event; cf. Vatakis & Spence, in press-a; though see also Vatakis & Spence, in press-b).

The focus of the present study on musical stimuli was driven by the fact that some researchers have argued that speech and music share a number of important properties. For instance, they are both composed of perceptually discrete basic elements (such as phonemes and notes) that can be organized into syntax-governed sequences (such as phrases and sentences). Interestingly, however, the results reported here revealed higher temporal discrimination sensitivity for speech stimuli than for musical stimuli. This might be due to the greater experience that people have with speech thus making the speech stimuli more perceptually salient than the musical stimuli. It could also be related to the possible special nature of the processes that some have argued to underlie speech perception (e.g., see Tuomainen et al., 2005). An alternative account for these findings may relate to differences in the temporal profile of the two stimuli (i.e., the rise times for speech and musical stimuli may be different which might also affect TOJ performance; cf. Jaśkowski, 1993).

Over the last few years, neuroimaging and electrophysiological studies involving both simple audiovisual stimuli and speech stimuli have started to investigate the neural circuitry underpinning multisensory temporal perception in humans (e.g., Bergmann et al., 2006; Noesselt et al., 2005). The results of these studies show that temporal processing occurs at an early level in cortical processing and is mediated via subcortical pathways (e.g., insular, regions of the prefrontal and parietal cortex; Bushara, Grafman, & Hallett, 2001; Macaluso et al., 2004). Although many differences exist between speech and music, it will be interesting in future research to examine whether the same pathways are involved in the temporal processing of musical stimuli as have been shown to be involved in the perception of speech stimuli. The future combination of psychophysical and neuroimaging studies should therefore help to further our understanding of the mechanisms involved in the multisensory perception of synchrony for complex realistic stimuli (cf. Navarra et al., 2005).

Acknowledgments

A.V. was supported by a Newton Abraham Studentship from the Medical Sciences Division, University of Oxford.

References

Arrighi, R., Alais, D., & Burr, D. (2006). Perceptual synchrony of audiovisual streams for natural and artificial motion sequences. *Journal of Vision*, 6, 260-268.

Baader, A. P., Kazennikov, O., & Wiesendanger, M. (2005). Coordination of bowing and fingering in violin playing. *Cognitive Brain Research, 23*, 436-443.

Bergmann, D., Spence, C., Heinze, H.-J., & Noesselt, T. (2006). Neural correlates of synchrony perception using audio-visual speech-stimuli. Poster presented at the 7th IMRF Meeting, 18-21 June, Trinity College, Dublin.

Bushara, K. O., Grafman, J., & Hallett, M. (2001). Neural correlates of auditory-visual stimulus onset asynchrony detection. *Journal of Neuroscience, 21*, 300-304.

Calvert, G. A., Spence, C., & Stein, B. E. (Eds.). (2004). *The handbook of multisensory processing.* Cambridge, MA: MIT Press.

Conrey, B., & Pisoni, D. B. (2006). Auditory-visual speech perception and synchrony detection for speech and nonspeech signals. *Journal of the Acoustical Society of America, 119*, 4065-4073.

Coren, S., Ward, L. M., & Enns, J. T. (2004). *Sensation and perception* (6th ed.). Harcourt Brace: Fort Worth.

de Gelder, B., & Bertelson, P. (2003). Multisensory integration, perception and ecological validity. *Trends in Cognitive Sciences, 7*, 460-467.

Dixon, N. F., & Spitz, L. (1980). The detection of auditory visual desynchrony. *Perception, 9*, 719-721.

Fendrich, R., & Corballis, P. M. (2001). The temporal cross-capture of audition and vision. *Perception & Psychophysics, 63*, 719-725.

Finney, D. J. (1964). *Probit analysis: Statistical treatment of the sigmoid response curve.* Cambridge University Press, London: UK.

Grant, K. W., & Greenberg, S. (2001). Speech intelligibility derived from asynchronous processing of auditory–visual speech information. *Proceedings of AVSP 2001 International Conference of Auditory–visual Speech Processing*, Scheelsminde, Denmark (pp. 132-137).

Grant, K. W., van Wassenhove, V., & Poeppel, D. (2004). Detection of auditory (cross-spectral) and auditory–visual (cross-modal) synchrony. *Journal of the Acoustical Society of America, 108*, 1197-1208.

Hirsh, I. J., & Sherrick, Jr., C. E. (1961). Perceived order in different sense modalities. *Journal of Experimental Psychology, 62*, 424-432.

Hollier, M. P., & Rimell, A. N. (1998). An experimental investigation into multi-modal synchronisation sensitivity for perceptual model development. *105th AES Convention*, Preprint No. 4790.

Jaskowski, P. (1993). Temporal-order judgments and reaction time to stimuli of different rise times. *Perception, 22*, 963-970.

Kent, R. D. (1997). *The speech sciences.* Singular: San Diego, USA.

King, A. J. (2005). Multisensory integration: Strategies for synchronization. *Current Biology, 15*, R339-R341.

Macaluso, E., George, N., Dolan, R., Spence, C., & Driver, J. (2004). Spatial and temporal factors during processing of audiovisual speech: A PET study. *NeuroImage, 21*, 725-732.

Mattys, S. L., Bernstein, L. E., & Auer, Jr., E. T. (2002). Stimulus-based lexical distinctiveness as a general word-recognition mechanism. *Perception & Psychophysics, 64*, 667-679.

Munhall, K. G., Gribble, P., Sacco, L., & Ward, M. (1996). Temporal constraints on the McGurk effect. *Perception & Psychophysics, 58*, 351-362.

Navarra, J., Vatakis, A., Zampini, M., Humphreys, W., Soto-Faraco, S., & Spence, C. (2005). Exposure to asynchronous audiovisual speech extends the temporal window for audiovisual integration. *Cognitive Brain Research, 25*, 499-507.

Noesselt, T., Fendrich, R., Bonath, B., Tyll, S., & Heinze, H. J. (2005). Closer in time when farther in space: Spatial factors in audiovisual temporal integration. *Cognitive Brain Research, 25*, 443-458.

Reeves, B., & Voelker, D. (1993). *Effects of audio-video asynchrony on viewer's memory, evaluation of content and detection ability.* Research Report Prepared for Pixel Instruments, Los Gatos: USA.

Rihs, S. (1995). The influence of audio on perceived picture quality and subjective audio-visual delay tolerance. In R. Hamberg & H. de Ridder (Eds.), *Proceedings of the MOSAIC workshop: Advanced methods for the evaluation of television picture quality*, pp. 133-137, Eindhoven, 18–19 September 1995.

Soto-Faraco, S., Navarra, J., & Alsius, A. (2004). Assessing automaticity in audiovisual speech integration: Evidence from the speeded classification task. *Cognition, 92*, 13-23.

Spence, C., & Squire, S. B. (2003). Multisensory integration: Maintaining the perception of synchrony. *Current Biology, 13*, R519-R521.

Theeuwes, J., & Van der Stigchel, S. (in press). Faces capture attention: Evidence from inhibition-of-return. *Visual Cognition.*

Tuomainen, J., Andersen, T. S., Tiippana, K., & Sams, M. (2005). Audio-visual speech perception is special. *Cognition, 96*, 13-22.

van Wassenhove, V., Grant, K. W., & Poeppel, D. (2005). Visual speech speeds up the neural processing of auditory speech. *Proceedings of the National Academy of Sciences, 102*, 1181-1186.

Vatakis, A., & Spence, C. (2006-a). Audiovisual synchrony perception for speech and music using a temporal order judgment task. *Neuroscience Letters, 393*, 40-44.

Vatakis, A., & Spence, C. (2006-b). Evaluating the influence of frame rate on the temporal aspects of audiovisual speech perception. *Neuroscience Letters, 405*, 132-136.

Vatakis, A., & Spence, C. (in press-a). Crossmodal binding: Evaluating the 'unity assumption' using audiovisual speech. *Perception & Psychophysics.*

Vatakis, A., & Spence, C. (in press-b). Evaluating the influence of the 'unity assumption' for the temporal perception of realistic audiovisual stimuli. *Acta Psychologica.*

Vroomen, J., & Keetels, M. (2006). The spatial constraint in intersensory pairing: No role in temporal ventriloquism. *Journal of Experimental Psychology: Human Perception & Performance, 32*, 1063-1071.

Zampini, M., Shore, D. I., & Spence, C. (2003). Multisensory temporal order judgements: The role of hemispheric redundancy. *International Journal of Psychophysiology, 50*, 165-180.

Modeling Top-Down Perception and Analogical Transfer with Single Anticipatory Mechanism

Georgi Petkov (gpetkov@mail.nbu.bg)
Kiril Kiryazov (kiryazov@cogs.nbu.bg)
Maurice Grinberg (mgrinberg@nbu.bg)
Boicho Kokinov (bkokinov@nbu.bg)
Central and East European Center for Cognitive Science, Department of Cognitive Science and Psychology,
New Bulgarian University, 21 Montevideo Street, Sofia 1618, Bulgaria

Abstract

A new approach to anticipations is proposed – anticipation by analogy. Firstly, the role of selective attention was explored both with simulation data and psychological experiment. After that, the AMBR model for analogy-making has been extended with a simple anticipatory mechanism and is demonstrated how top-down perception and analogical transfer can both be based on one and the same anticipatory mechanism. Finally, attention and action mechanisms were added to the model and AMBR was implemented in a real robot that behaves in a natural environment.

The Importance of Anticipations

Humans are anticipatory agents. They always have expectations about the world they live in (sometimes correct, sometimes wrong). Our everyday behavior is based on the implicit employment of predictive models. If, for example, we are looking for a certain book in an unknown room, we try to imagine where it could possibly be and then we go to look at this place. This is an example of anticipatory behavior as opposed to simple reactive behavior when we first see the object and then move towards it.

There are few attempts to implement anticipatory behavior in computational models or in real robots. Typically, the researchers from the neural network approach use learning as a main mechanism for generating implicit or explicit models of the environment. The learned network weights represent these models and the result could be considered an anticipatory system. Examples for this type of anticipations are the ALVIN model (Pomerleau, 1989), which learns not only to respond to the environment but also to predict the observations to be seen in the next step and the Anticipatory Learning Classifier Systems (Stolzmann, 1998, Butz at al, 2002), which combine online reinforcement learning and model learning methods and can learn several reward maps. The combination of online generalizing model learning and reinforcement learning allows the investigation of diverse anticipatory mechanisms including multi-objective goals integrating different motivations.

Another approach towards building anticipatory capacities is based on the DYNA-PI systems (Sutton, 1990). These systems are based on reinforcement learning systems that plan on the basis of a model of the world. Recently these models have been used to implement a neural network planner (Baldassarre, 2002) that is capable of finding efficient start – goal paths, and deciding to re-plan if

"unexpected" states are encountered. Planning iteratively generates "chains of predictions" starting from the current state and using the model of the environment. This model is a neural network trained to predict the next input when an action is executed.

Anticipation by Analogy

The learning techniques based on generalization described above are based on the assumption that there is regularity in the input-output coupling. However, in some tasks, for example when searching for a hidden object, there will be no regularity. This paper describes an alternative approach towards anticipation based on analogical reasoning. The main idea is to generate predictions by analogy with a single episode from the past experience. We modeled anticipatory mechanisms and we tested them with simulations in environment that consists of rooms; some geometrical objects – cubes, pyramids, etc; one robot; and a bone-toy, which can be hidden behind a certain object. We used a simulated (Webots software) and real - Sony AIBO robot (ERS-7). The simplest scenarios we are working on involves the robot searching for a bone hidden somewhere behind some object in one of the rooms of a house. In some cases two episodes might be very close analogies, e.g. the bone is hidden behind the same object in another room, or behind the same "pattern of objects", however, in other cases the robot may need to build a more abstract analogy, e.g. the bone was behind the object with unique color, but now all objects have the same color and therefore the object might be behind the object with unique form.

Analogy-making is a very basic human ability that allows a novel situation to be seen as another already known one (Hofstadter, 1995). There are a number of cognitive models developed of this process or various parts of it. One of the first such models is the SMT developed by Dedre Gentner and her colleagues (Gentner, 1983). SMT assumes that analogy is transfer of a system of relations from one situation to another. It assumes that attributes are not important and thus are ignored in mapping. It also assumes that the two situations should share the *same* relations. Thus the above case of analogy between unique color and unique form relations is not possible in SMT unless a re-representation is performed (Yan, Forbus and Gentner, 2003), however, it is not clear how such a re-representation could be computed in this particular case. Other models of analogy-making such as ACME (Holyoak, Thagard, 1989), LISA (Hummel, Holyoak, 1997), and AMBR (Kokinov,

1994a) allow for mapping of relations with different names. Comparing these models we decided to use AMBR since ACME is psychologically unrealistic for making all possible pairing of possible correspondences and is based on a fixed thesaurus for finding synonyms, and LISA is still not capable of comparing complex enough structures that will be needed in the real-world applications of the robot scenarios. AMBR has also the advantage of integrating mapping and retrieval processes of analogy-making. However, none of these models has ever been used for anticipation; neither has been applied in robot scenarios.

Implementing Anticipations in the AMBR Model of Analogy-Making

AMBR is a decentralized model in which computations emerge from the interactions among numerous micro-agents (Kokinov, 1994a, 1994b, Kokinov & Petrov, 2001). All the micro-agents run in parallel and interact with each other and the macro-behavior of the system emerges from the local interactions and micro-behavior of the individual agents. These micro-agents run at individual speed each and this speed is dynamically computed depending on the relevance of this micro-agent to the context (Petrov & Kokinov, 1999, Kokinov & Petrov, 2001). Each of these micro-agents is hybrid – it has a symbolic part that represents the specific piece of knowledge that the agent is responsible for, and it has a connectionist part that computes the activation level which reflects the relevance of the agent to the context.

Thus in AMBR there are no separate steps in the analogy-making process: retrieval and mapping overlap and interact with each other. This allows for the structural constraint, which is important for the mapping process, to influence also on the retrieval process and thus it is possible remote and abstract analogies to be constructed.

AMBR does not separate semantic from episodic memory. Instead, the memory episodes are represented with a coalition of interconnected instance-agents that point to their respective concept-agents. The representation of the target situation and the representation of the environment serve as sources of activation that spreads to the relevant concepts, their super-classes and close associations, and then back to some instances from memory situations. Thus the Working Memory of the model is not a separate part but is defined as the part of the Long-Term Memory that consists of relevant enough items.

Each instance-agent that enters in the Working Memory emits a marker that spreads up-wards in the conceptual class-hierarchy. When two markers meet somewhere a hypothesis for correspondence between their origins is created. It represents the fact that there is something in common between the respective marker-origins, namely, they are both instances of a same class. Several mechanisms for structural correspondence create new hypotheses on the basis of existing ones – if two relations are analogous, their respective arguments should also be analogous; if two instances are analogous, their respective concepts should be analogous, etc.

Thus, gradually, many hypotheses for correspondence emerge and form a constraint satisfaction network that is interconnected with the main one. The final answer of the system emerges from the relaxation of this constraint satisfaction network.

Simulation Results

In the first series of simulations we used only the simulated version of the robot and the environment, thus excluding perception and exploring only the role of selective attention. The robot faces several objects in the room and has to build their representation in its mind. Then the task of the robot is to predict behind which object would the bone be and then finally to go to the chosen object and check behind it.

Thus there is a representation building part of the model, which target representation is then used for recalling an old episode which could be used as a base for analogy, a mapping between the base and the target is built, and the place of the hidden object in this old episode is used for predicting the place of the hidden bone in the current situation. Finally, a command to go to the chosen object is send. It is important to emphasize that all these processes emerge from the local interactions of the micro-agents, i.e. there is no central mechanism that calculates the mapping or retrieves the best matching base from memory.

In the simulations described here the AIBO robot had four specific past episodes encoded in its memory, presented in Figure 1. In all four cases the robot saw three balls and the bone was behind one of them. The episodes vary in terms of the colors of the balls involved and the position of the bone.

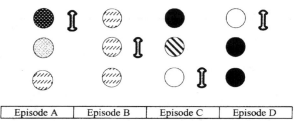

| Episode A | Episode B | Episode C | Episode D |

Figure 1: Old episodes in the memory of the robot (different colors are represented with different textures).

The robot was then confronted with eight different new situations in which it had to predict where the bone might be and to go and check whether the prediction was correct (Figure 2). The situations differ in terms of colors and shapes of the objects involved.

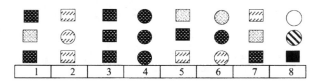

| 1 | 2 | 3 | 4 | 5 | 6 | 7 | 8 |

Figure 2: New tasks that the robot faces.

In Figure 3 one can see the representation of the target situations that is extracted from the description of the simulated environment. Representation building for perceived real environment is described in the next section.

For the first series of simulations, however, the representation involves relations known to the robot such as **color-of (object-1-sit001, red1), same-color (object-1-sit001, object-3-sit001), unique-color (object-2-sit001), right-of (object-2-sit001, object-1-sit001), instance-of (object-1-sit001, cube),** etc. (see Figure 3 for some examples). The relations are in turn interconnected in a semantic network. For example, **same-color** and **same-form** are both sub-classes of the higher-order relation **same**.

In the simulations described above the attention of the robot was simulated by connecting only some of these descriptions to the input list which results that even though all relations, properties, and objects will be present in the Working Memory (WM) of the robot, only some of them will receive external activation and thus will be considered as more relevant. Thus different simulations with the same situation, but focusing the attention of the robot towards different aspects of the given situation, could result in different outcomes.

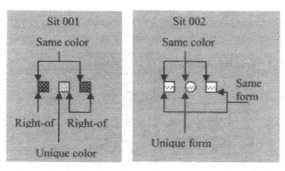

Figure 3: Representation of the target situations 1 and 2.

In each case there could be various solutions: different analogical bases could be used on different grounds and in some cases for the same base several different mappings could be established that will lead to different predictions (See Fugure 4 and Figure 5 for the specific mappings established and the predictions made).

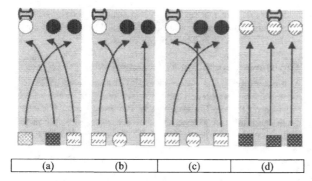

| (a) | (b) | (c) | (d) |

Figure 4: Examples of mappings established with changing the attention from form (a) and (b) to color (c) and (d).

In Figure 4 the mappings that the system has established for several situations are depicted: (a) Mapping established between target situation 1 and base D: unique colour goes to unique colour and the bone is predicted to be behind it. (b) and (c) Two different mappings established between situation 2 and base D: in (b) the focus of attention has been on the form of the objects and the mapping goes from unique form in the target to unique colour in the base, same form in the target to same colour in the base and the bone is predicted to be behind the object with unique form (namely behind the ball), in (c) the focus of attention is on the colours and therefore any mapping between the objects is possible, in this particular case the bone is predicted to be behind the right-most object. Finally, (d) presents the mapping between target situation 3 and base B where the focus of attention is on the colours: three objects of the same colour in both cases, independently of the difference in the form; the bone is predicted to be behind the middle object.

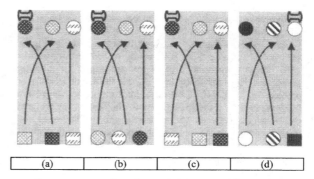

| (a) | (b) | (c) | (d) |

Figure 5: Examples of mappings based on the superficial color relations

The mappings that the system has established for several other target situations are shown on Figure.5. These are more superficial analogies where the color is dominating and where it is mapped on the same color in the old episode, i.e. if the bone was behind the red ball before then the robot would predict in these cases that the bone will be again behind the red object.

By varying the focus of attention on various aspects of the target situation one can get various results, thus figure 4b and 4c show two different mappings and therefore two different predictions will be generated by the system: 4b makes more sense, however, also humans do not produce always this specific mapping.

Evidently, situations 5, 6, 7, 8 (Figure.2) are more straightforward – they require a rather superficial mapping of the specific colors. Situations 1, 2, 3, 4 are more interesting because they invite less obvious mappings. Thus in Figure 4a the mapping is between two objects having same color in the target and two objects (although different in form) having the same color in the base, although the colors themselves are different (red goes to black, and yellow to white). The most interesting case is 4b where a rather abstract mapping has been established: the two objects in the target which have the same form (cube) are mapped onto the two objects in the base with the same color. Thus same-form goes to same-color as well as unique-form goes to unique-color. This mapping would be impossible with many other models of analogy-making (SMT maps only identical relations, ACME and LISA could not do it for different reasons – the pressure for mapping same-color onto same-color will be high). In AMBR this is possible because of the general knowledge that same-color and same-form are both special cases of the "sameness" relation and the markers starting from both episodes will cross in "same". In addition, focusing the attention on same-form would greatly help to find this mapping as demonstrated in the simulation.

Comparison with Human Data

After running the first series of simulations several times varying only the focus of attention to see whether the mapping changes; we conducted a psychological experiment. We showed the bases to the participants, changing the AIBO robot and the bone with a cover story about a child who has lost its bear-toy. We asked the participants to predict where the bear-toy would be in the given new situation.

The data from the human experiment are given in Figure 6a. As one can see there is a variety of answers for almost each target situation. Still there are some dominating responses. In order to be able to test the robot's behavior against the human data, 50 different knowledge bases have been created by a random generator that varies the weights of the links between the concepts and instances in the model. After that the simulation has been run with each of these knowledge bases in the "mind" of the robot. Figure 6b reflects the results. They show that the model has a behavior which is quite close to that of the participating human subjects in terms of the dominating response. The only major difference is in situation 2 where human subjects are "smarter" than AMBR: they choose an analogy with situation D (same-form goes onto same-color) much more often than AMBR. Still AMBR has produced this result in 25% of the cases. This means that AMBR is in principle able to produce this result, but it would requite some tuning of the model in order to obtain exactly the same proportion of such responses.

Using Anticipation Mechanisms for Modeling Top-Down Perception and Analogical Transfer

The main disadvantage of the version described above is that AMBR lacked completely any perceptive mechanisms except for manual coding of a presented situation (target) and additionally perceived objects. In order to overcome this limitation we developed new mechanisms modeling top-down perception and attention. In addition, we used some modules of the IKAROS platform (http://www.ikaros-project.org/) to manage with the difficult task of bottom-up visual perception and object recognition. Thus we enriched our model AMBR with perception abilities. It gives us the possibility to extract the representations from real physical environment and not coding them manually inside the model. Thus, we tested AMBR with a real AIBO robot in a real environment. The newly built mechanism for

anticipation-creation is described briefly in the next subsections, as well as its usage both for top-down perception and for analogical transfer.

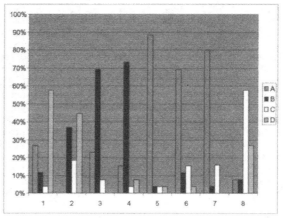

(a) Human data

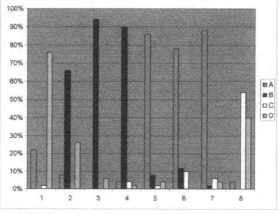

(b) AMBR simulation data

Figure 6: Comparing human and simulation data: which base has been used for analogy with each target situation and how many times.

Top-Down Perception as Anticipation

At the beginning, the robot is looking at a scene. In order for the model to "perceive" the scene, or parts of it, the scene must be represented as an episode, composed out of several agents standing for objects or relations, attached to the input or goal nodes of the architecture. It is assumed that the construction of such a representation is initially very poor. Usually, symbolic representations of only the objects from the scene without any descriptions are attached to the input of the model (for example, **cube-1, cube-2,** and **cube-3**). The representation of the goal is attached on the goal node (usually **find-t, Aibo-t,** and **bone-t**). During the run of the system, via the mechanisms of analogical mapping some initial correspondence hypotheses between the input (target) elements and some elements of previously memorized episodes (bases) emerge. The connected elements from the bases activate the relations in which they are included. If it happens all arguments of a certain relation from a base episode to be mapped to elements from the target, than the respective relation is transferred from the base to the target. However, the new relation is considered as anticipation. Later on, the perceptual system should check whether it is really present in the environment or not. This dynamic *perceptual mechanism* creates anticipations about the existence of such relations between the corresponding objects in the scene. For example, suppose that **cube-T** from the scene representation has been mapped onto **cube-11** in a certain memorized situation. The activation retrieval mechanism adds to working memory some additional knowledge about **cube-11** – e.g. that it is yellow and is positioned to the left of **cube-22**, etc. The same relations become anticipated in the scene situation, i.e. the system anticipates that **cube-T** is may be also yellow and could be to the left of the element, which corresponds to **cube-22** (if any), etc. Thus, various anticipation-agents emerge during the run of the system.

Attention

The *attention* mechanism deals with the anticipations *generated by the dynamic perceptual mechanism*, described above. With a pre-specified frequency, the attention mechanism chooses the most active anticipation-agents and asks the low-level perceptual system to check whether the anticipation is correct (e.g. corresponds to an actual relation between the objects in the scene). The low-level perceptual system (based on IKAROS) receives requests from AMBR and simply returns an answer based on the available information from the scene. This information is received from the IKAROS system which extracts symbolic visual information from the real environment. There are three possible answers: 'Yes', 'No', or 'Unknown'. The answer 'Unknown' is returned very often because typically AMBR asks for a variety of relations. In addition to colors ('color-of' relations), spatial relations, positions, etc., it generates also anticipations like **"the bone is behind 'object-1'"**, or **"if I move to 'object-3', I will find the bone"**. Those relations play a very important role for the next mechanism – the *transfer of the solution* (i.e. making a prediction on which an action will be based) – as explained below.

After receiving the answers, AMBR manipulates the respective agent. If the answer is 'Yes', it transforms the anticipation-agent into instance-agent (i.e. *token*). In this way the representation of the scene is successfully extended with a new element, for which the system tries to establish correspondences with memorized episodes elements. If the answer is 'No', AMBR removes the respective anticipation-agent together with some connected to it additional anticipations. Finally, if the answer is 'Unknown', the respective agent remains anticipation-agent but behaves just like a real instance, waiting to be rejected or accepted in the future. In other words, the system behaves in the same way if the respective anticipation is true. However, the perceptual system or the transfer mechanism (see below)

can remove this anticipation. In this way AMBR gradually builds the representation of the scene.

Transfer of the Solution

The representation of the scene emerges dynamically, based on top-down processes of analogical mapping and associative retrieval and on the visual information from the environment. The system creates many hypotheses for correspondence that self-organize in a constraint-satisfaction network. Some hypotheses become winners as a result of the relaxation of that network and in this moment the next mechanism – the *transfer of the solution* is triggered. In fact, the transfer mechanism does not create the agents, which represent the solution. Actually, the perceptual mechanism has already transferred many possible relations but now the task is to remove most of them and to choose the best solution. For example, suppose the target situation consists of three red cylinders and let the task of the AIBO robot is to find the bone. Because of various mappings with different past situations the anticipation mechanism would create many anticipation-agents with the form: **"The bone is behind the left cylinder"** because in a certain old situation A the bone was behind the left cube and now the left cylinder and the left cube are analogically paired. Because of the analogy with another situation B, for example, the anticipation that **"the bone is behind the middle cylinder"** could be independently created. For a third reason, the right cylinder may also be considered as a candidate for searching the bone. Thus many alternative anticipation-agents co-exist. When some hypotheses win, it is time to disentangle the situation.

The winner-hypotheses take care to propagate their winning status to the consistent anticipation-agents. In addition, the inconsistent ones are removed. In the example above, suppose that situation A happens to be the best candidate for analogy. Thus, the hypothesis **left-cylinder<--**>**left-cube** would become a winner. The relation 'behind' from situation A would receive this information and take care to remove the anticipations that the bone can be behind the middle or behind the right cylinder.

As a final result of the transfer mechanism, some complex causal anticipation-relations like **"if I move to the object-3, this will cause finding the bone"** become connected to the respective cause-relations in the bases via winner-hypotheses.

Action Executing

In order to finish the whole cycle from perception to action and to test all mechanisms with a real robot, *sending an action command* has been modeled. The cause-relations that are close to the GOAL node trigger it. The node GOAL sends a special message to the agents that are attached to it, which is in turn propagated to all cause-relations. Thus, at certain moment, the established cause-relation **"if I move to object-3, this will cause finding the bone"** will receive such a message and when one of its hypotheses becomes winner, it will search in its antecedents for an action-agents. The final step is to request the respective action and this is done by sending a message to the action execution module of the system. This module navigates the robot to the target object. The information for his/her position is updated from the IKAROS system. After arriving at the requested position the robot uncovers the object and takes his/her bone if it is there or stops.

Conclusions

This paper presents a new approach – we suggested that the analogy with previously experienced situations may be used for anticipation. Our attempt was to model these analogy-based anticipations with the AMBR model and to extend it with top-down perceptual and analogical transfer mechanisms. Finally, we used real AIBO robot to test the model in a natural environment.

Firstly, we explored the role of selective attention in the simulation and in a psychological experiment. After that, we implemented a simple anticipation mechanism in AMBR, namely transferring a relation from a memorized episode to the current situation if all arguments of the respective relation have been mapped. Thus, we actually extended AMBR both with top-down perceptual and with analogical transfer mechanisms, thus showing that may be one and the same basic mechanism underlie these seeming unrelated phenomena.

Finally, we added additional attention and action mechanisms in AMBR, and implemented it into a real AIBO robot that behaves in a natural environment.

However, this is just a small step in a larger project. We used the IKAROS system for bottom-up perception and for recognition of the objects. Further investigation and modeling of these processes should be made in order to achieve integrated active vision.

Now all the visual information for the environment is received from a global camera above the scene. The attention mechanism should be connected with the robot camera and particularly, with its gaze. Thus, both the salience maps from the environment and the top-down reasoning will influence the head-movement of the robot, and in turn, the order of checking of various anticipations.

This paper is an attempt to integrate high-level analogical reasoning with active attention and vision in a single model, based on a few main principles and in addition, to test this model with a robot in a real environment.

Acknowledgments

This work is supported by the Project **ANALOGY: Humans – the Analogy-Making Species**, financed by the FP6 NEST Programme of the European Commission. (STREP Contr. No 029088)

References

Baldassarre G. (2002). Planning with Neural Networks and Reinforcement Learning. PhD Thesis. Colchester - UK: Computer Science Department, University of Essex.

Butz, M. V., Goldberg, D. E., & Stolzmann, W. (2002). The anticipatory classifier system and genetic generalization. *Natural Computing*, 1, pp. 427-467.

Gentner, D. (1983). Structure-mapping: A theoretical framework for analogy. *Cognitive Science*, 7, 155-170.

Hofstadter, D. R. (1995). Fluid Concepts and Creative Analogies: Computer Models of the Fundamental Mechanisms of Thought, NY: Basic Books.

Holyoak K. & Thagard P. (1989). Analogical mapping by constraint satisfaction. *Cognitive Science*, 13, 295-355.

Hummel, J. & Holyoak, K. (1997). Distributed representation of structure: A theory of analogical access and mapping. *Psychological Review*, 104, 427-466.

Kokinov, B. (1994a). A hybrid model of reasoning by analogy. In: K. Holyoak & J. Barnden (Eds.), *Advances in connectionist and neural computation theory: Vol. 2. Analogical connections* (pp. 247-318). Norwood, NJ: Ablex

Kokinov, B. (1994b). The DUAL cognitive architecture: A hybrid multi-agent approach. In: *Proceedings of the Eleventh European Conference of Artificial Intelligence (ECAI-94).* London: John Wiley & Sons, Ltd.

Kokinov, B., Petrov, A. (2001). Integration of Memory and Reasoning in Analogy-Making: The AMBR Model. In: Gentner, D., Holyoak, K., Kokinov, B. (eds.) *The Analogical Mind: Perspectives from Cognitive Science*, Cambridge, MA: MIT Press

Petrov, A. & Kokinov, B. (1999). Processing symbols at variable speed in DUAL: Connectionist activation as power supply. In: *Proceedings of the Sixteenth International Joint Conference on Artificial Intelligence (IJCAI-99).* San Francisco, CA: Morgan Kaufman, p. 846-851.

Pomerleau, D. (1989). "ALVINN: An Autonomous Land Vehicle In a Neural Network", *Advances in Neural Information Processing Systems 1*, Morgan Kaufmann

Stolzmann, W. (1998). Anticipatory classifier systems. *Genetic Programming 1998: Proceedings of the Third Annual Conference*, 658-664.

Sutton, R.S. (1990). Integrated architectures for learning, planning, and reacting based on approximating dynamic programming. In: *Proceeding of the Seventh International Conference on Machine Learning*, San Mateo, Ca.: Morgan Kaufmann, pp. 216-224.

Yan, J., Forbus, K., and Gentner, D. (2003). A theory of rerepresentation in analogical matching. In R. Alterman & D. Kirsch (Eds.), *Proceedings of the Twenty-Fifth Annual Conference of the Cognitive Science Society.* Mahwah, NJ: Lawrence Erlbaum Associates, Inc., pp. 1265–1270

Relational Similarity in Identity Relation: The Role of Language

Stella Christie (christie@northwestern.edu)
Department of Psychology, Northwestern University
2029 Sheridan Rd., Evanston, IL 60201

Dedre Gentner (gentner@northwestern.edu)
Department of Psychology, Northwestern University
2029 Sheridan Rd., Evanston, IL 60201

Abstract

We investigated the development of the ability to perceive relational similarity. With a view to cross-species comparison, the relational matches employed in this study were identity relations, which have been widely used in research with nonhuman animals (Thompson & Oden, 2000) . Experiment 1 was a similarity judgment task wherein relational similarity was pitted against object similarity. 4.5-, 8.5-year-olds, and adults were shown triads in which the standard depicted an identity relation (e.g. two squares); they chose between a relational match (e.g. two triangles) or an object match (e.g. a square and a circle, one shape in common with the standard). 4.5-year-olds strongly preferred the object match, whereas adults preferred the relational match. In Experiment 2, we asked whether language could serve as a cognitive tool promoting relational insight. The same stimuli were used as in Experiment 1, but participants heard a novel word applied to the standard. Results provide evidence for a language benefit, as 4.5-, 8.5-year-olds and even adults showed a significant increase in relational responding after hearing the novel label.

Introduction

Relational concepts are critical to higher-order cognition. The ability to perceive relational similarities underlies a number of fundamental cognitive processes such as analogy (Gentner, 1983, 2003; Kokinov & French, 2003), categorization (Ramscar and Pain, 1996), and inductive inferencing (Holland, Holyoak, Nisbett, and Thagard, 1986). One speculation is that humans' exceptional relational ability is the major contributor to our high intelligence as a species (Gentner, 2003).

What is the ontogeny of relational concepts? Studies of comparative cognition in humans and animals have found marked differences in relational ability across species. Much of this work has focused on whether animals can perceive the relation of identity between two elements—perhaps the simplest possible relation, and the one most likely to be perceived across species. Many animals can succeed in a direct object-matching task, as in figure. 1.1. But the ability to succeed in a relation-matching task, even with the basic relation of identity (figure 1.2) is quite uncommon (Premack, 1983).

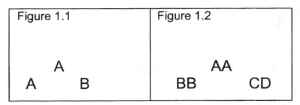

Figure 1. Matching-to-sample task over objects (1.1) and over relations (1.2)

Premack (1988) found in research with chimpanzees that animals who were taught specific symbols for *same* and for *different* were subsequently able to succeed on the relational match-to-sample task such as in Figure 1.2. Likewise, a study by Pepperberg and Brezinsky (1991) reported that an African gray parrot with significant amount of language training could indicate whether two objects were the same size and whether one object was larger or smaller than a comparison object. There is also evidence suggesting that a dolphin who received language training more readily generalized same/different concepts than a naïve dolphin (Herman, Kuczaj, & Holder, 1993). Most recently, Thompson, Oden and Boysen (1997) have confirmed that chimpanzees who were previously trained with *same* and *different* token training (e.g. given AA, then choose a heart shape), were successful in relational matching tasks, whereas a naïve chimpanzee in the same experiment failed. Gentner and Rattermann (1991) hypothesized that learning different symbols for *same* and *different* allowed the animals to use internal symbols that aided them in the relational matching task.

The results from animal studies suggest that relational concepts are non-obvious and elusive, and that quite possibly, symbolic training or language enculturation is needed to make the relational concept more explicitly available. What is the status of relational knowledge in human development? Although relational concepts are used extensively in human cognition—from everyday words like *mother* and *gift* to concepts such as *limit* in mathematics—

relational concepts are not easily accessible to young children (Gentner & Rattermann, 1991). Previous work has shown that children's appreciation of relational similarity in comprehension of metaphor and analogy develops very gradually (Gentner, 1988; Vosniadou, 1987; Vosniadou 1995). Relatedly, young children initially interpret a relational noun like "uncle" as a kindly man with a pipe, and refuse to call their father's adolescent brother an uncle (Keil, 1989). Similarly, in a word naming study, Hall and Waxman (1993) found that 3.5-year-olds were unable to map a novel word meaning to its intended relational meaning of "passenger", even when they were explicitly told the relational meaning of the word (e.g. this is a "murvil" because it's riding in a car).

There is considerable evidence that objects are more cognitively and perceptually salient than relations in the structure of the perceived world (Gentner, 1982; Gentner & Boroditsky, 2001). Thus a key question in the development of relational thinking concerns when children become able to perceive relational similarity in the presence of a competing object similarity. Many studies have found that when relational similarity is pitted against object similarity, younger children are more influenced by object matches, and less able to attend to relational matches (Gentner & Toupin, 1986; Gentner & Rattermann, 1991; Rattermann & Gentner, 1998a; Rattermann & Gentner, 1998b, Richland, Morrison, & Holyoak, 2006). The term *relational shift* (Gentner, 1988; Halford, 1993) has been used to capture this phenomenon: there is a shift from focus on object similarity to focus on relational similarity. This shift seems to occur at different ages in different domains (e.g., Brown, Kane, & Echols, 1986; Gentner & Toupin, 1986; Goswami, 1989; Smith, 1984; Uttal, Schreiber, & DeLoache, 1995; Vosniadou, 1987), suggesting that it is driven at least in part by domain knowledge (Gentner & Rattermann, 1991).

How do young children develop from strongly preferring object similarity to being able to appreciate relational similarity? We investigate this question in two ways. First, we ask whether there is a basic context allowing young children to spontaneously perceive relational similarity. Second, we ask what factors in development support the development of relational thinking. We propose that language is one such candidate factor. In Experiment 1, by measuring relational performance with a basic relation and simple objects, we gain insight to the initial state of relational knowledge. We then compare this initial performance with children's performance when given a linguistic label (Experiment 2) in order to determine the role of language in the development of relational thinking.

In investigating children's early relational abilities, we wanted to avoid relations for which the child simply lacks the requisite world knowledge. Therefore we used a simple, arguably basic relation – that of identity between two things. The identity relation is chosen as it has been attested as one conceptual relation that is available among varieties of (symbolically trained) species, as discussed previously. By using the identity relation in our research with humans, we

aimed to partly equate the difficulty level of the relational matching task, making the results more comparable to the results from animal research. Further, Smith (1984) found that using "follow-the-leader" task, 2-year-old children were highly accurate at copying an identity relation, as compared to same-attribute or same-dimension relations. We also used simple objects to create an easy environment, motivated by prior evidence that rich object matches compete strongly with relational matches, whereas simple object matches are relatively easy to overcome (Gentner & Rattermann, 1991; Paik and Mix, 2005).

The second question that we investigate is whether the use of linguistic symbols aids the ability to think relationally. As discussed above, symbolic training has been shown to improve relational performance in animal research. According to Vygotsky (1962), language provides a form of cultural scaffolding that contributes to children's learning. Gentner (2003) hypothesized that this support may be especially important in learning abstract relational concepts. Therefore, in our second study, we tested the hypothesis that language promotes the ability to perceive relational commonalities

Experiment 1

Method

Participants 18 4.5-year-olds (M = 55 months, range = 52-60 months); 16 8.5-year-olds (M = 99 months, range = 96-102 months); and 28 adults (college students) participated in the experiment.

Materials There were eight triads of simple geometric shapes. Each triad consisted of a standard and a pair of choices: an object similarity choice (object match), and a relational similarity choice (relational match) (Figure 2). Standards, object matches and relational matches were always composed of two geometric shapes. All eight standards were composed of two identical shapes (e.g. two circles) – hence depicting the identity relation. Within a triad, the object match was composed of one shape identical to the standard and another shape (e.g. a circle and a triangle). The relational match was composed of two identical shapes, not shared by either the standard or the object match (e.g. two squares). Hence, the relational match depicted an identity relation as in the standard, but did not share object similarity with the standard. Left and right placement of the object match and the relational match was counterbalanced.

Procedure Children were seated across from the experimenter. For each trial, the experimenter showed the standard while saying, "I am going to show you a picture, see this one?!" The child was given a few seconds to observe the standard. With the standard still at view, the experimenter next placed both the relational match and the object match below the standard and asked the child to make a similarity judgment, "Which one of these two pictures is more like the top picture?" The child indicated his or her choice by pointing at one of the two matches. No feedback was given beyond general encouragement. There were 8 trials in total, with different configurations of geometric shapes, all testing the identity relation. The procedure for adults was identical except that they wrote down their choices on an answer sheet instead of directly pointing to the picture. The two choices were labeled as right and left, and participant wrote down R or L on their answer sheet. We adopted this procedure so that the experimenter would not know the participant's answer during the testing session.

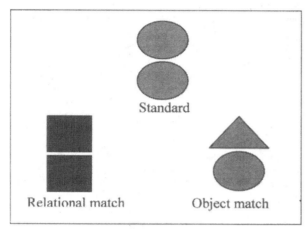

Figure 1. Sample triad: standard, relational match, and object match

Results

A T-test against chance (.50) showed that 4.5-year-olds strongly preferred the object match (M_{object} =.83, SD = .38), $t(17)$ = 3.68, $p < 0.005$). In contrast, adults significantly preferred the relational matches ($M_{relational}$ = .69, SD = .33), $t(27)$ = 3.03, $p < 0.05$. 8.5-year olds did not have any significant preference for either the object match or the relational match $(M_{object}$ = .66, SD =.42; $M_{relational}$ = .34, SD =. 42). A one-way ANOVA revealed significant differences of proportion of relational choices among the three age groups, $F(2, 61)$ = 11.81, $p < 0.001$. Using a criterion of 7 out of 8 trials ($p\ binomial$ = .013), we found that 15 out of 18 (83%) of the 4.5-year-olds chose the object match, whereas 8 out of 16 (50%) 8.5-year-olds did so, and only 3 out of 28 adults (10%) did so.

Discussion

Even with a very simple relational match, young children failed to show a preference for relational similarity. With object similarity pitted against relational similarity, 4.5-year-olds strongly preferred the object match, even though the relation tested was the basic identity relation and the competing object match was extremely simple. Furthermore, a trend towards preference for object similarity was also observed among the 8.5-year-olds.

Overall, the results suggest that object similarity is very salient among young children, and that the attraction towards object similarity may persist for a rather extensive period in development.

If easy context alone does not support learning beyond surface similarity, how do children eventually acquire relational knowledge? In Experiment 2, we investigated the hypothesis that for the same age groups where we saw strong preference for object similarity, hearing a novel linguistic label would reduce salience of object matches, and increase preference for relational similarity.

A number of studies have found a beneficial effect of relational labels in children's performance of relational mapping. Rattermann and Gentner (1998a) gave children relational labels that conveyed the relational system of *monotonic change in size* (e.g. Daddy/Mommy/Baby). They found that the use of relational labels improved young children's ability to carry out relational mapping, despite the lure of common objects. Likewise, Hermer-Vasquez, Moffet, & Munkholm (2001) found that children's performance in a retrieval task was correlated with their ability to use the spatial language relevant to the task. The use of spatial relational language can also improve children's performance in spatial mapping tasks (Loewenstein and Gentner, 2005).

In all these cases, the relational labels were familiar to the children. Thus the labels could have operated in two different ways: (1) by conveying a specific known relation; and (2) by inviting children to compare the two configurations that had the same labels. This second possibility stems from prior evidence suggesting that hearing a common label invites children to compare the two things, and this in turn highlights relational commonalities (Gentner and Namy, 1999; Namy and Gentner, 2002).

Evaluating the second possibility requires testing whether labels are helpful even without a prior associated meaning. Therefore, we used novel labels instead of familiar relational labels. In prior studies with similar stimuli, we have found that giving children an informative label (such as "double" for the standard with its identity relation) can improve children's performance (Christie & Gentner, 2005). The question is whether a *novel* label will promote relational responding.

Experiment 2

Method

Participants The same age groups as in Experiment 1 were tested: 16 4.5-year-olds (M = 55 months, range = 52-60 months); 16 8.5-year-olds (M = 98 months, range = 96-102 months); and 28 adults (college students).

Material and Procedure Same stimuli and procedure as in Experiment 1 was used, with the additional use of a novel label. The experimenter labeled the standards with a novel word, "Look, this is a truffet," and asked, "which one of these is also a truffet?" As in Experiment 1, children notified their choices by pointing, and adults wrote their answer in an answer sheet.

Results

4.5-year-olds' preference for relational match approached significance ($M_{relational}$ = .68, SD = .38), $t(15)$ = 1.9, p = 0.07. Adults, just like in Experiment 1, significantly preferred relational match ($M_{relational}$ = .91, SD = .29), $t(27)$ = 7.34, $p < 0.001$; similarly, 8.5-year olds also significantly preferred relational match ($M_{relational}$ = .84, SD = .33, $t(15)$ = 4.1, $p < 0.05$. One-way ANOVA revealed no significant differences of relational choices across age groups, $F(2, 59)$ = 2.39, ns.

We compared the proportions of relational choices across Experiments 1 and 2 for each age group. 4.5-year-olds in Experiment 2 chose relational matches significantly more than those in Experiment 1, $F(1,33)$ = 15.33, $p < 0.001$. Likewise, a significant increase in relational responding after hearing a novel label was observed among 8.5-year-olds, $F(1,31)$ = 14.33, $p < 0.005$ and even adults, $F(1, 55)$ = 6.74, $p < 0.05$.

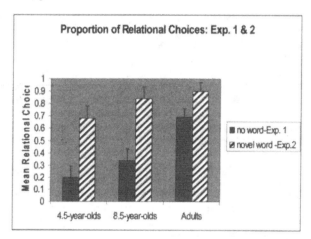

Figure 3. Results of Experiments 1 and 2.

Discussion

The results of Experiment 2 suggest that the presence of linguistic labels strongly supports children's perception of relational similarity. Upon hearing a novel label applied to the standards, 4.5-, and 8.5-year-olds were far more likely to choose the relational match than when they were given the same task without a label in Experiment 1. Rather surprisingly, even adults' preference for relational similarity was aided by the presence of a novel label.

General Discussion

The studies presented here were designed to explore the development of the perception of relational commonalities. In particular we asked whether young children would respond to relational similarity in a highly simplified choice task, using the identity relation depicted by simple objects. Even under these circumstances, 4.5-year-olds strongly preferred object matches over relational matches. However, performance shifted dramatically when the standard was given a novel label. These findings both underline the difficulty of focusing on relational similarity when competing object matches are present and suggest that learning language may exert a powerful effect on relational thinking.

It is rather surprising that even with simple objects and basic identity relations, 4.5-year-olds still found object similarity to be extremely compelling, and virtually ignored the relational matches. Even 8.5 year-olds responded relationally only about a third of the time. Would children show more relational responding if they were given richer objects? This is probably unlikely considering Rattermann & Gentner's (1998a) results: children in the rich object condition gave significantly fewer correct relational responses than those who were in the simple object condition.

Our finding that relational responding is low even with basic identity relations and simple objects highlights the elusiveness of relational concepts. This echoes the findings that perception of relational similarity is slow to develop. We are not suggesting that children lack the cognitive capacity to perceive relational similarities. However, the current result poses a question as to how children eventually arrive at spontaneous perception of relational commonality.

The role of language

How do children acquire the ability to notice and use relational commonalities? Although there may be a number of factors that aid in arriving at relational perception, we suggest that language may be one powerful tool by which humans gain relational insight (Gentner, 2003). Our results from Experiment 2 show that hearing novel labels dramatically increases 4.5- and 8.5-year-olds' relational responding.

These findings are consistent with prior findings that word learning facilitates acquisition of deep conceptual categories (Gelman & Markman, 1986; Golinkoff et al., 1992; Markman, 1989; Waxman & Gelman, 1986; Waxman & Kosowski, 1990). Evidence that common labels can highlight relational commonalities comes from studies by Namy and Gentner (2002), who found that the use of labels is important in encouraging children to compare and attend to relational commonalities. They presented children with two perceptually similar exemplars (e.g. a bicycle and a tricycle) that shared relational commonalties (both can be ridden, etc.). The exemplars were either given a unifying label or contrasting labels. Children then had to choose between a relational category match (a skateboard) and a perceptual match (a pair of glasses). Children in the unifying word condition chose the relational category match more often than those in the contrasting label condition.

What is the mechanism whereby labels invite relational

thinking? As discussed above, we suggest that one path lies through comparison; that is, common labels invite comparison (Gentner & Namy, 1999) and comparison tends to highlight relational commonalities (Gentner & Markman, 1997). Common labels have also been shown to heighten comparison effects over a direct comparison question in a similarity task judgment (Anggoro, Gentner, & Klibanoff, 2005). On this account, when children in our study heard the question "Which one of these two is a *truffet*?" they were likely to compare the standard *truffet* with each of the alternatives, thus highlighting common relations (identity) shared between the standard and the relational choice.

A second way in which the labels could have improved children's performance is that they may have helped in binding the two components of the standard into a unified whole. For example, in Fig. 2, it is possible that without the label, children simply compared one part of the standard (one green oval) with various parts of the alternatives. When the label was applied, children may have been more likely to consider the two green ovals of the standard as belonging to coherent whole. (However, the fact that adults also showed more relational responding when novel labels were used perhaps argues against this explanation, as it seems unlikely that adults would fail to understand that the standard was meant to be considered as a whole.)

One remarkable feature of these results is that the effects of language were immediate in children: we found no difference between performance on the first three trials and performance on the last three trials. This is all the more striking given that participants never received training on the novel word; after hearing it applied to the standard for the first time, they were immediately asked to extend the novel word.

Further Questions

To return to the theme of comparative cognition, we can compare these results with the findings from animal studies. Our findings suggest that the perception of relational similarity is difficult for human children, as for nonhuman animals. However, we note that the children in our study faced a harder task than that given to chimpanzees and other nonhuman animals. In the animal studies, the question is whether relational similarity can be perceived against an unrelated alternative; whereas our subjects had to choose relational similarity from a strongly competing alternative (the object match).

Thus, another important cross-species comparison would involve presenting human children with triads in which there is no competing object match. We are currently carrying out such studies. Our preliminary results suggest that even without a competing object match, 4- and 5-year-olds still do not perform above chance levels in choosing the relational match (Christie & Gentner, in preparation).

Another difference between our studies and the typical animal study is that our children did not receive any prior training on the relation of identity. In future studies, we will investigate this factor as well.

Summary

Our results suggest that even with a highly simplified task, the perception of relational similarity is not immediate in children. However, our results also suggest that language may provide an important route by which children can acquire relational insight. In this way, language appears to be an important contributor to human intelligence.

Acknowledgement

This research was supported by NSF-ROLE Award REC-0337360 and NSF SLC Grant SBE-0541957, the Spatial Intelligence and Learning Center (SILC). We thank Jennifer Hellige, Robin Rios, and Kathleen Braun their help in data collection, and Bartłomiej Czech for his help in editing the paper.

References

Anggoro, F., Gentner, D., & Klibanoff, R. (2005). How to go from nest to home: Children's learning of relational categories. *Proceedings of the Twenty-seventh Annual Meeting of the Cognitive Science Society*, 133-138

Brown, A. L., Kane, M. J., & Echols, C. H. (1986).Young children's mental models determine analogical transfer across problems with a common goal structure, *Cognitive Development, 1,* 103-121.

Christie, S., & Gentner, D. (2005) *Language highlights relational structure.* Poster presented at the biennial meeting of the Cognitive Development Society, San Jose, CA.

Gelman, S. A., & Markman, E. M. (1986). Categories and induction in young children. *Cognition, 23,* 183-209

Gentner, D., & Boroditsky, L. (2001). Individuation, relational relativity and early word learning. In M. Bowerman & S. Levinson (Eds.), *Language acquisition and conceptual development.* Cambridge, England: Cambridge University Press.

Gentner, D. (1983). Structure-mapping: A theoretical framework for analogy. *Cognitive Science, 7,* 155-170

Gentner, D. (1988). Metaphor as structure mapping: The relational shift. *Child Development, 59,* 47-59

Gentner, D. (2003). Why we're so smart. In D. Gentner and S. Goldin-Meadow (Eds.), *Language in mind: Advances in the study of language and thought.* Cambridge, MA: MIT Press

Gentner, D., & Markman, A. B. (1997). Structure mapping in analogy and similarity. *American Psychologist, 52,* 45-56.

Gentner, D., & Toupin, C. (1986). Systematicity and surface similarity in the development of analogy . *Cognitive Science, 10,* 277-300.

Gentner, D., & Rattermann, M. J. (1991). Language and the career of similarity. In Gelman, S. A. & Byrnes, J. P. (Eds.), *Perspectives on thought and language: Interrelations in development.* London: Cambridge University Press.

Golinkoff, R. M., Hirsh-Pasek, K., Bailey, L. M., & Wenger, N. R. (1992). Young children and adults use lexical principles to learn new nouns. *Developmental Psychology, 28*, 99-108.

Goswami, U. (1989), Relational complexity and the development of analogical reasoning. *Cognitive Development, 4*, 251-268.

Halford, G. S. (1993). *Children's understanding: The development of mental models.* Hillsdale, NJ: Erlbaum.

Hall, D. G., and Waxman, S. R. (1993). Assumptions about word meaning: Individuation and basic-level kinds. *Child Development, 64*, 1550-1570

Herman, L. M., Kuczaj, S. A., 2nd, & Holder, M. D. (1993). Responses to anomalous gestural sequences by a language-trained dolphin: Evidence for processing of semantic relations and syntactic information. *Journal of Experimental Psychology: General, 122*, 184–194.

Hermer-Vasquez, L., Moffet, A., & Munkholm, P. (2001). Language, space, and the development of cognitive flexibility in humans: The case of two spatial memory tasks. *Cognition, 79*, 263–299.

Holland, J. H., Holyoak, K. F., Nisbett, R. E., & Thagard, P. R. (1986). *Induction: Processes of inference, learning, and discovery.* Cambridge, MA: MIT Press.

Keil, F. (1989). *Concepts, Kinds and Cognitive Development, In Data and Knowledge Engineering.* The MIT Press

Kokinov, B., & French, R. M. (2002). Computational models of analogy-making. In L. Nadel (Ed.), *Encyclopedia of cognitive science.* London: Macmillan.

Kotovsky, L, & Gentner, D. (1996). Comparison and categorization in the development of relational similarity. *Child Development, 67*, 2797-2822.

Loewenstein, J., & Gentner, D. (2005). Relational Language and the Development of Relational Mapping. *Cognitive Psychology, 50*, 315-353.

Markman, E. M. (1989). *Categorization aid naming in children: Problems of induction.* Cambridge, MA: MIT Press.

Namy, L. L,. & Gentner, D. (2002). Making a silk purse out of two sow's ears: Young children's use of comparison in category learning . *Journal of Experimental Psychology: General, 131*, 5-15.

Paik, J. H., & Mix, K. S. (2005, April). *Preschoolers' similarity judgments: Taking context into account.* Paper presented at the biennial meeting of the Society for Research in Child Development, Atlanta, GA.

Pepperberg, I.M., & Brezinsky, M. V. (1991). Acquisition of relative class concept by African Grey parrot (Psittacus erithacus): Studies on a nonhuman, nonprimate, nonmammalian subject. In H.L. Roitblat, L.M. Herman, and P.E. Nachtigall (Eds.), *Language and communication: Comparative perspectives.* Hillsdale, NJ: Erlbaum.

Premack, D. Animal cognition. (1983) *Annual Review of Psychology, 34*, 351 -362

Premack, D. (1988). Minds with and without language. In L. Weiskrantz (Ed.), *Thought without language. A Fyssen Foundation symposium* (pp. 46-65). New York, NY, US: Clarendon Press/Oxford University Press

Rattermann, M. J., & Gentner, D. (1998a). More evidence for a relational shift in the development of analogy: Children's performance on a causal-mapping task. *Cognitive Development, 13,* 453–478.

Rattermann, M. J., & Gentner, D. (1998b). The effect of language on similarity: The use of relational labels improves young children's performance in a mapping task. In K. Holyoak, D. Gentner, & B. Kokinov (Eds.), *Advances in analogy research: Integration of theory & data from the cognitive, computational, and neural sciences.* Sophia: New Bulgarian University.

Ramscar, M. & Pain, H. (1996) Can a real distinction be made between cognitive theories of analogy and categorisation? In *Proceedings of the Eighteenth Annual Conference of the Cognitive Science Society.* 346 – 351

Richland, L.E., Morrison, R.G., & Holyoak, K.J. (2006) Children's development of analogical reasoning: Insights from scene analogy problems. *Journal of Experimental Child Psychology, 94*, 249-273

Smith, L. B, (1984). Young children's understanding of attributes and dimensions: A comparison of conceptual and linguistic measures. *Child Development, 55*, 363-380.

Thompson, R. K. R., Oden, D. L., (2000). Categorical perception and conceptual judgments by nonhuman primates: The paleological monkey and the analogical ape. *Cognitive Science, 24*, 363-396

Thompson, R. K. R., Oden, D. L., & Boysen, S. T. (1997). Language-naive chimpanzees (Pan troglodytes) judge relations between relations in a conceptual matching-to-sample task. *Journal of Experimental Psychology: Animal Behavior Processes, 23*, 31-43.

Uttal, D. H., Schreiber, J. C., & DeLoache, J. S. (1995). Waiting to use a symbol: The effects of delay on children's use of models. *Child Development, 66*, 1875-1889.

Waxman, S. R., & Gelman, R. (1986). Preschoolers' use of superordinate level relations in classification and language. *Cognitive Development, 1*, 139-156.

Waxman, S. R., & Kosowski, T. (1990). Nouns mark category relations: Toddlers' and preschoolers' word-learning biases. *Child Development, 61*, 1461-1473.

Vosniadou, S. (1987). Children and metaphors. *Child Development, 58*, 870-885.

Vosniadou S. (1995). Analogical Reasoning in Cognitive Development. *Metaphor and Symbolic Activity, 10,* 297-308.

Vygotsky, L.S., 1962. *Thought and language* (E. Hanfmann and G. Vakar, Trans.), MIT Press, Cambridge, MA.

Does the Family Analogy Help Young Children To Do Relational Mapping?

Milena Mutafchieva (mmutafchieva@nbu.bg)
Boicho Kokinov (bkokinov@nbu.bg)

Central and East European Center for Cognitive Science, Department of Cognitive Science and Psychology,
New Bulgarian University, 21 Montevideo Street
Sofia 1618, Bulgaria

Abstract

The experiment described in this paper tests the hypothesis that since the *family* is very familiar relational structure to even young children, the relational mapping between sets of objects will be significantly enhanced if children are invited to make an analogy with the family. This research is based on Gentner and Rattermann's, and Goswami's work in the same direction and tries to further extend it. The results present for the first time experimental support of Halford's hypothesis that the family analogy can help 4 years old children to manage the transitive mapping task. They can manage it even with non-monotonically displayed objects.

Introduction

In this paper we explore young children's ability to make transitive relational mapping, i.e. to map two sets of linearly ordered relations (A>B>C and X>Y>Z). Why is this task important? It is of some interest because it is related to transitive inference (A>B; B>C, therefore A>C) and our ultimate goal to test whether transitive inference may benefit from analogy with a more familiar domain. The specific subgoal that is pursued in this paper is to find out whether analogy-making with a third set of objects may help children to accomplish the transitive mapping task. Let us now unfold our theoretical motivation.

Piaget argues that transitive inference is a concrete operation being a simple version of a deductive task that is closely related to the concrete set of objects and is a smooth transaction towards more abstract formal deductive reasoning operations. Thus according to Piaget an understanding of transitivity emerges around 6-7 years of age (Inhelder & Piaget, 1958, 1964, Piaget, 1971). Many researchers have questioned this belief. They demonstrated in various ways that the initial experiments by Piaget failed to demonstrate children's ability to make transitive inference before 6-7 years of age, mainly due to the heavy memory load of the task and when this load is reduced or eliminated they do demonstrate transitive inference abilities (Bryant & Trabasso, 1971; Halford, 1984; Pears & Bryant, 1990).

Halford (1993) proposed a new theory about logical development. He linked transitivity directly to the development of relational mapping in children. He proposed that the ability to map binary relations (relations that link two objects) or to make relational mapping occurs approximately at the age of two, and that mapping of ternary relations (relations that link three items) or system mapping is available at the age of 5. Since, according to him, the ability for system mapping is closely related to the ability to make transitive inferences, the development of the transitive inference capacity is due to the development of the processing capacity of children, such as the ability to map complex relations.

Contrary to Piaget and his collaborators (Piaget, 1971; Inhelder & Piaget, 1958, Piaget) currently most researchers believe that analogy-making is a very basic ability and is present from early infancy (Gentner, 1989, Goswami, 1991, 1996, 2001; Halford, 1993). Thus an interesting hypothesis put forward by Halford (1993) is that logical development is analogical in it's nature and children solve transitive inference problems by making analogies to an ordering schema that represent ternary relations between objects in the real world. And since the "family" domain is very familiar to young children it can serve as an excellent source of analogy for solving various tasks, including transitive reasoning tasks, class inclusion problems, etc. Gentner and Rattermann (1991), Goswami (1995), Rattermann and Gentner (1998), Goswami and Pauen (2005), Loewenstein & Gentner (2005) have empirically explored various aspects of this hypothesis and the current paper tries to shed further light on this possibility. More specifically we will explore the role the analogy with the family can play in the transitive mapping task.

Previous Experimental Studies

There are two lines of studies related to our research in this paper. Gentner and her colleagues (Rattermann & Gentner, 1991, Gentner & Rattermann, 1998, Loewenstein & Gentner, 2005) have studied *the role of language*, and more specifically the use of relational labels (relational words), in the development of relational mapping capacity. Goswami (1995) has studies *the potential role analogy* may play in the development of transitive mapping. We are trying to combine the two approaches and further extend them.

In the first line of studies Rattermann and Gentner (1991, 1998) examined young children's ability to spontaneously notice relational mapping and whether the use of relational labels would draw children's attention towards relations. They were not specifically interested in whether the analogy can play a role in that process.

They modified an experimental paradigm used by DeLoache (1989) where children would have to find an object hidden in the room that would analogically correspond to the place in the room model. Rattermann and Gentner used two sets of stimuli – one for the child and one for the experimenter. Each of the sets consists of 3 objects (clay pots or blue plastic boxes) which are linearly ordered, i.e. increase in size (or decrease in size) monotonically. The experimenter points to one of her objects and the child would have to find the corresponding object in his/her set. The experimenter and the child play a game in which the experimenter hides a sticker under one of her objects and the child has to find her sticker under the corresponding objects of her. The stimulus set is designed to form cross-mappings, i.e. there is an object in the child's set that is exactly the same as the pointed object in the experimenter's set, and another one which is in the same relative position, although it is different in absolute size (and in some experiments also in its category). Thus superficial mapping was pitted against relational mapping. If the child chooses the corresponding relative size object (large, medium, or small) then her response is based on the relational similarity between the sets, but if she chooses the object with the same absolute size, then she relies on object similarity. In order to study the effects of object similarity, Rattermann and Gentner manipulate the degree of similarity between objects by varying the richness and distinctiveness of the stimulus (in the rich condition superficial similarity is based not only on size, but also on category – house, car, cup).

The results show that both age groups – 3- and 4-years-old find relational mapping quite difficult (only 47% of the responses are relational). There is an effect of the richness of the stimuli; children perform better in the simple set of the stimuli (54% relational responses for the 3-year-olds and 62% relational responses for the 4-year-olds) than in the rich set of the stimuli (32% relational responses for the 3-year-olds and 38% relational responses for the 4-year-old children). Thus spontaneous focusing on relations is not very common.

In a following up study Rattermann and Gentner explored if relational labels can direct children's attention to relations. They used labels like "Daddy", "Mummy" and "Baby" or "big", "small", and "tiny" for both stimulus sets, naming the objects on each trial. The assumption is that children at 3 are very familiar with these words.

The results show significant difference between the children's performance with and without labels. Rattermann and Gentner conclude that using familiar language labels can improve children's performance in transitive mapping task. Thus children and adults are possibly using the same similarity comparison processes and there is a change in the domain representation rather than a change in the cognitive competence. Thus the acquisition of language, specifically relational language, is an important contributor to this development.

There was no difference between the labels "Daddy, Mummy, Baby" and "Big, Small, Tiny" – 89-90% relational choices in 3 years old children. The assumption is that both have the same properties: ternary ordering relations which are well-known to the children. Loewenstein and Gentner (2005) performed a new series of experiments in which they explored various spatial relational labels, such as "on, in, under" and "top, bottom, and under". They found that "top, bottom, and under" has a much better effect. They explain the difference by the arity of the relations: "on", "in", and

"under" are examples of binary relations (they have two arguments), while "top, middle, bottom" is a ternary relation and thus contributes to the system mapping required for the transitive relational mapping.

There are a number of issues which are still problematic after these studies. The main issue is whether children can use some short-cut heuristics bypassing the transitive relational mapping and still get the same results. One such possibility is to use the location of the objects and respond with the "same location" regardless of the size of the objects. This strategy is possible because of the monotonically increasing size of the objects. Rattermann and Gentner argue that since the two sets are not exposed on parallel lines, but rather diagonally, this strategy cannot be used. On the other hand, they believe that monotonically increasing size of the objects is important because the transitive relation is one of linear order and if we present the objects in a random way children will be lost. Another potential weak point of the methodology is that naming the two sets by "Daddy", "Mummy" and "Baby" we give a chance to children to map the labels, instead of the objects. Thus they do not need to consider the rest of the objects in the set, they just need to remember who the "Mummy" was in this trial. A contra argument would be that still the children themselves decided who the "Daddy", "Mummy" and "Baby" are in their set and therefore they were able to do the mapping.

Goswami (1995) decided to test these possibilities and conducted three experiments, which examine young children's ability to map transitive size relations when both the spatial positions of the corresponding objects and the absolute size of the stimuli were systematically varied. In addition, in the naming condition, only the experimenter named her objects "Daddy", "Mummy" and "Baby", but not the child, thus precluding the possibility of mapping the labels. In addition, she was explicitly interested whether an analogy with a familiar domain may help children in the transitive mapping.

She used again two identical of size sets of plastic colored stacking cups and the sizes of the corresponding cups in the two arrays were different in every trial. The cup color per se cannot be used to find the correct solution.

The child was told that the experimenter was going to choose one cup from her array and that to play this game he/she had to select the same cup from his/her array. The analogy was provided by the story about the "Goldilocks and the Three bears" in order to support the mapping task.

The results showed that children found the mapping task easy, because the mapping performance was extremely good, averaging around 80-90% correct in most of the manipulations. Changing the absolute size (and the color) of the cups caused a slight drop in the performance (around 10-15%), and so did the varying spatial positions of the corresponding cups. The results of this experiment showed that there is no significant influence of the analogy on the performance of the children in this kind of mapping task.

The second and third experiment in this study were designed to answer if the young children mapping performance would be so successful if the transitive size relations were represented by two different sets of objects that differ in different dimensions (size in one set and proportion in the other) and if the relations between objects are mental, rather than directly observable. In order to answer the first question, Experiment 2 used two different types of stimuli – stacking cups and pictures of different proportions – for example one-half of a circle and one-fourth of a pica. The results showed that 3-year-old children found the cross-representational mapping task more difficult than 4-year-old children. The older children were less affected by changes in the spatial positions as well. The performance was significantly above chance – the lowest result was 54% for the 3-year-old children in Different Spatial Position Group.

In Experiment 3, the children were told a story of being in the Three bears' house and were told to imagine a different things they could find there. A number of different perceptual dimensions were also included in the context of the story about Three bears – for example loudness (of footsteps), pitch (of voice) and est. The results showed that 4-year-old children were successful in mapping transitive size relations onto various dimension (such as loudness, pitch, etc.), although they found some of the dimensions easier then the others. The majority of the responses of 3-year-olds were not relational.

Goswami concludes that children as young as 3 and 4 years of age can make transitive relational mappings based on size even when the size of the objects do not increase monotonically and the relative spatial position of the corresponding objects in the two sets differ. Four-years-old children are successful even when the presented transitive relations are rather abstract and represented mentally rather than directly observable. In contrast, 3-year-old children can only reliably coordinate and map relations when they are visually presented.

The three experiments examined the same children, so, there could be a training effect that was not measured, and it is not clear if the children would obtain the same results in the absence of prior experience.

To summarize the results from the previous studies it is clear that contrary to Piaget assumptions and even Halford's predictions 3 and 4 years old children are able to accomplish complex transitive relational mapping when they are supported by the use of relational language. As Rattermann and Gentner write relational terms invite the representation and use of relations.

A major still unresolved problem is the lack of support for the postulated by Halford role of analogy in transitive mapping. Rattermann and Gentner's results do not differentiate between "Daddy", "Mummy" and "Baby" on one side, and "big", "small", and "tiny" on the other. The first set of labels invites an analogy with the family domain, while the second does not, but the results were equivalent. Thus it seems that it is not the analogy, but rather the use of ternary relational terms that matters. Goswami's attempt to demonstrate the role of analogy by providing the Goldilocks story also failed – there was no difference between the analogy and non-analogy groups. Thus we decided to further explore the possible role of analogy using a similar experimental paradigm.

Experiment

The goal of our study was to find out whether the family domain makes any difference in a transitive relational mapping using relational labels, i.e. to explore the analogy effect. This will be tested under the severe conditions when the objects in the two sets have different spatial positions and do not increase monotonically.

Hypothesis

Our hypothesis was that 4 years old children will succeed in transitive relational mapping significantly better when the relational terms "Daddy, Mummy and Baby" are used than when the relational terms "Big, Medium, Small" are used, i.e. that in addition to the naming effect (the use of relational terms) there will be also an analogy effect because the relational terms "Daddy, Mummy and Baby" activate their knowledge about the family domain, while "Big, Medium, Small" does not.

Design

The experiment has a between group design and the factor is presence or absence of the family analogy:

- *Analogy condition*: the five mapping trials were presented by naming the objects in the experimenter set a *"family"* and the individual objects were called *"Daddy", Mummy", and "Baby"* (the instruction is described in the section Procedure).
- *Control condition*: the five mapping trials were presented with naming the objects in the experimenter set *"Big", "Medium",* and *"Small"* without calling them a "family" (the instruction is described in the section Procedure).

The dependent variable was the number of relational responses.

Stimuli

In each trial one set of animals was used which consists of 6 animals of the same type: 6 foxes, 6 bears, 6 owls, etc. All animals in the same set were of different size except two who were the same size. Three of the animals formed the experimenter's set, and three – the child's set. In every set there was big, middle and small animal and there was a difference in the absolute size of the corresponding animals in the experimenter's and the child's set. One element of the child's set was exactly the same size as one of the animals in the experimenter's set (See Figure 1). Different sets of stimuli with different sizes and spatial positions as well as different animals were presented in every task.

Five transitive relational mapping tasks were presented to every child plus two in the training session. The five transitive relational trials were designed to fulfill some criteria: 1) to vary the spatial configuration of the stimuli sets (e.g. the Biggest – left, vs. right, vs. middle); 2) to vary the spatial position of the relational response and the object with the same absolute size (surface similarity) in every trial and in the two sets.

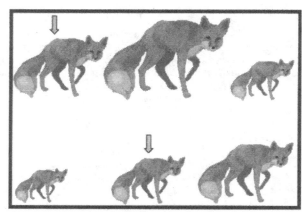

Figure 1. An example of the stimulus material for one trial.

Procedure

In each trial the child saw two triads of objects, both arranged in a random way (not always in monotonically increasing or decreasing order of size). The child watched the experimenter to hide a sticker under one of the objects in the experimenter's set. The child was told that he/she could find his/her own sticker *"in the same place"* in the child's triad. The correct response was arranged always to be at the relational similarity place: thus, in order to pick it up, the child had to choose the object with the same relative size, but not the same absolute size (object similarity) or the same relative position (because the spatial positions in the two sets varied in every trial). The children were always given a feedback by showing the correct response (and receiving the sticker) after their guess.

Each child participated in a single experimental session.

The experiment included two training trials and five test trials as described above. In the training trials the experimenter gave the child an explanation about the instruction and the question that she asked.

The test trial began with the following instruction for the Control Group:

*"We are going to play a game of hiding and finding stickers. I have three foxes and you have three foxes. From my foxes this is the big fox, this is the medium one, and this is the small one. Please, tell me from your foxes which is the **big fox**, and the **medium one**, and the **small one**? Now, I am going to hide my sticker under my medium fox, where do you think your sticker is hidden?"*

The instruction for the Analogy Group was the following:

*"We are going to play a game of hiding and finding stickers. I have a family of foxes and you have a **family of** foxes. From my family the biggest fox is **Daddy fox**, the medium one is **Mummy fox**, and the smallest one is **Baby fox**. Please, tell me from your family which is Daddy fox, which is Mummy fox, and which is Baby fox? Now, I am going to hide my sticker under my Mummy fox, where do you thing your sticker is hidden?"*

Participants

Forty children were studied in this experiment; the average age of children was 4 years and 4 months, ranging from 4 years to 5 years. Nineteen from children formed the Control Group, and 21 formed the Analogy Group.

Results

Data shown in Table 1 show the group statistics and Figure 2 and 3 show the difference between the groups. The mean for Control Group is 2,79 correct responses out of 5, and the mean for the Experimental Group is 4,10 correct responses out of 5. Both groups perform at a level much higher than the chance level (for the control group the difference is significant T(18)=3,627, p=0,002) thus replicating the results of Rattermann and Gentner (1998) and Goswami (1995) that the use of relational labels improves the performance of young children. In addition, however, we obtain a significant difference between the control group and the experimental group (T(38)=2.844, p=0.007) therefore demonstrating that the family labels are better facilitators than the size relational labels.

GROUP	N	Mean	Std. Deviation
Control	19	2,79	1,357
Experimental	21	4,10	1,546

Table1.Group Statistics.

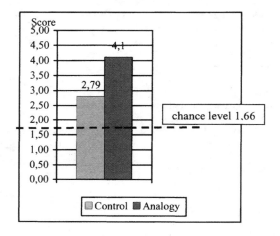

Figure 2. Score means for the two experimental groups.
T(38)=-2.844, p=0.007
The percentage of relational choices are 55,8% for the control group and 82% for the analogy group (chance level 33%). The Analogy group is comparable to Goswami's results in a similar condition: 71% of relational responses (Goswami, 1995).

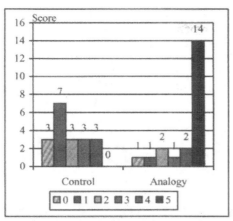

Figure 3. Number of children with each raw score in both groups.

The comparison of the two groups is even more evident if we consider the number of children with each raw score in both groups (Figure 3). As one can see in the figure, in the analogy group 14 out of 21 children responded always relationally, while 7 out of 19 children in the control group responded relationally only 2 times out of 5.

Group	Relational responses	Object-similarity responses	Other responses
Analogy	82%	8%	10%
Control	54%	20%	26%

Table 2. Percentage of the relational answers in the control and the analogy groups.

A more detailed description of the data can be seen in Table 2: 69,5% from all children's answers were relational responses, and only 13% from all answers were based on the surface similarity. In the Control Group 54% of all responses were based on relational similarity versus 82% for the Analogy Group; 20% from all responses in the Control Group were based on the surface similarity versus 8% from all responses in the Experimental Group. 26% from the responses in Control Group were based on strategies different from relational and surface similarity versus 10% for responses in the Analogy Group.

Discussion

The results clearly demonstrate that the children in the Analogy group performed better than in the Control group. Thus the main hypothesis of this study was confirmed: Analogy does facilitate transitive relational mapping. Since both conditions (control and analogy) used ternary relational terms the difference is not due to the structure of these relations (which is the same) but is due to the content. While in the case of "big", "medium", and "small" only the abstact terms are used (i.e. only the language effect is present), in the case of "Daddy", "Mummy", and "Baby" the family domain is invited and used as a base for analogy in addition to the language effect. This results supports Halford's claim about the effect of family analogy.

Our data showed also that monotonic increase of size is not a necessary condition for relational labels to improve performance on the transitive mapping task. Thus this finding extends the results obtained by (Gentner & Loewenstein, 2002).

Acknowledgments

This research was supported financially by the ANALOGY project (NEST program, contract 29088) funded by the EC. We would like to thank Olimpia, Elisaveta, Margarita, and Irina for their help in collecting the data.

References

Bryant, P.E., & Trabasso, T. (1971). Transitive inferences and memory in young children. *Nature*, 232, 456-458.

DeLoache, J. S. (1989). Young children's understanding of the correspondence between a scale model and a larger space. *Cognitive Development*, 4, 121-139.

Gentner, D. (1983). Structure–mapping: A theoretical framework for analogy. *Cognitive Science, 7, 155-170.*

Gentner, D., & Toupin, C. (1986). Systematicity and surface similarity in the development of analogy. *Cognitive Science, 10, 277-300.*

Gentner, D. (1989). Mechanisms of analogical learning. *In S. Vosniadou and A. Ortony, (Eds.), Similarity and Analogical Reasoning, 199-241. London: Cambridge University Press.*

Gentner, D., & Rattermann, M. J. (1991). Language and the career of similarity. In S. A. Gelman &. J. P. Byrnes (Eds.), Perspectives on thought and language: Interrelations in development (pp. 225-277). London: Cambridge University Press.

Gentner, D., Rattermann, M.J., Markman, A., & Kotovsky, L. (1995). Two forces in the development of relational similarity. *In G. Halford & T.Simon, Developing Cognitive Competence: New Approaches to Process Modeling (Eds.). Hillsdale: Erlbaum.*

Gentner, D., & Loewenstein, J. (2002). Relational language and relational thought. *In Amsel, E. (Ed); Byrnes, J.P. (Ed). Language, literacy, and cognitive development. The development and consequences of symbolic communication, pp. 87-120.*

Goswami, U., & Brown, A.L. (1990). Higher-order structure and relational reasoning: Contrasting analogical and thematic relations. *Cognition, 36, 207-226.*

Goswami, U. (1991). Analogical reasoning: What develops? A Review of Research and Theory. *Child Development, 62, 1-22.*

Goswami, U. (1995). Transitive relational mappings in 3- and 4-year-olds: The analogy of Goldilocks and the Three Bears. *Child Development, 66, 877-892.*

Goswami, U. (1996). Analogical reasoning and cognitive development. *In H.Reese (Ed.). Advances in Child Development and Behavior, 92-135. San Diego. CA: Academic Press.*

Goswami, U., Pauen, S. (2005). The effects of family analogy on class inclusion reasoning in young children. *Swiss Journal of Psychology, vol. 64, n 2, pp. 115-124*

Halford, G.S. (1984). Can young children integrate premises in transitivity and serial order tasks? Cognitive Psychology, 16, 65-93

Halford, G. (1993). Children's understanding: The development of mental models. *Lawrence Erlbaum Associates, Publishers, Hillsdale, New Jersey.*

Halford, G. (1998). Relational processing in higher cognition: Implications for analogy, capacity and cognitive development. *In K. Holyoak, D. Gentner, B. Kokinov (Eds.) Advances in Analogy Research: Integration of Theory and Data form the Cognitive, Computational, and Neural Sciences.New Bulgarian University, Sofia.*

Halford, G. (1998). Processing capacity defined by relational complexity: Implications for comparative, developmental, and cognitive psychology. *Behavioral and Brain Sciences, 21, 803-864.*

Inhelder, B. and J. Piaget (1958). The Growth of Logical Thinking from Childhood to Adolescence. New York: Basic Books.

Inhelder, B. and Piaget, J. (1964). The Early Growth of Logic in the Child: Classification and Seriation. London: Routledge and Kegan Paul.

Loewenstein, J. & Gentner, D., (2005). Relational language and the development of relational mapping. *Cognitive Psychology, vol. 50, pp. 315-353.*

Pears, R., & Bryant, P. E. (1990). Transitive inferences by young children about spatial position. *British Journal of Psychology,* 81, 497-510.

Piaget, J. (1971). Biology and knowledge. Edinburgh: Edinburgh University Press

Rattermann, M.J., & Gentner, D. (1998). The effect of language in similarity: The use of relational labels improves young children's performance in a mapping task. *In K. Holyoak, D. Gentner, & B. Kokinov. Advances in Analogy Research: Integration of Theory and Data from the Cognitive, Computational, and Neural Sciences. New Bulgarian University, Sofia.*

Analogy and Cognitive Style in the History of Invention: Inventor Independence and Closeness of Compared Domains

Lillian Hoddeson (hoddeson@uiuc.edu)
Department of History, 810 S. Wright Street
Urbana, IL 61801 USA

Abstract

Close study of the role of analogy in the history of technology has yet to be attempted. Drawing on the cognitive modeling of analogy by Dedre Gentner and others, in which analogy is conceived as a mapping of structures across the boundaries of different domains (the "target" and "source"), this paper presents early progress in a study that explores stylistic difference in the way inventors use analogy in their creative work. The two case studies outlined here focus on the different ways that John Bardeen and Stanford R. Ovshinsky used analogy in developing electronic control mechanisms. The domains compared in each case have notably different degrees of separation. In his inventing of the transistor, Bardeen compared structures in neighboring scientific areas. In contrast, Ovshinky, while inventing his amorphous solid threshold switch, compared widely separated domains on different levels (living vs. inanimate, macroscopic vs. molecular). This stylistic distinction in the way Bardeen and Ovshinsky used analogy in their creative work correlates with their different degrees of independence from the professional authorizing institutions of their day. Throughout his career Bardeen worked within his academic specialty. Ovshinsky, however, like the great inventors of the late nineteenth century, stood proudly apart from any discipline. The full explanation of the different ways that inventors use analogy likely extends well beyond purely cognitive approaches encompassing not only social positioning but aspects of their family backgrounds, values, and personal identity. This study points to a potentially fertile area for interdisciplinary study, one that might be referred to as "inventive cognitive style."

Introduction

Cognitive psychologists and historians of science have long been interested in the question of human creativity. Over the last decade, many workers in this field (e.g., Boden, 1996; Csikszentmihalyi, 1996; Feist and Gorman, 1998; Howe, 1999; Simonton, 1999; Sternberg, 1999; Sulloway, 1996; Ward, 1999; Weisberg, 1999) have examined features that creative people often share, such as their child-like focus on how the world works (Gardner, 1993), their ``intrinsic motivation" (Amabile, 1996), or their extensive use of analogy (e.g., Dunbar, 2001, Gentner, 1989, Hesse, 1963, Hofstadter, 1995). The emerging picture is enhanced by the useful description put forth by Herbert Simon and his collaborators and followers of solving problems by searching through a problem space (e.g.: Langley, Simon, Bradshaw, & Zytkow, 1987). To an historian of science it is natural to inquire how such features of creative work relate to the full range of human, social, and contextual factors.

In exploring issues of this kind, the methods of humanists and scientists each have advantages and disadvantages. For example, experiments allow controls and the possibility of varying parameters, but the opportunity to perform them with the most creative individuals is rare. Nor can experiments typically run over the long time periods that are usual for major creative work. Surveys and interviews allow people to be questioned about details, but the results are often unreliable and biased, and well as limited. Videorecording of research in the making offers the researcher a ringside seat at the moment of creativity, but the time during which one is able to record is so short that it is unlikely to include the most creative discoveries. While computer simulations offer the capability of analyzing a large variety of parameters, the possibilities for handling the relevant social or non-rational aspects (like values) is limited. Among the many social dimensions of creativity that computers assess poorly is the environmental setting in which creative work is carried out.

A rich, if extremely heterogeneous, set of data on creative problem-solving can be found in biographical studies that document the work over many years of some of the most creative people in the world. Useful biographical studies of creative people have been conducted by scholars with interests that straddle cognitive science and the humanities (e.g., Brem et al., 1997; Nersessian, 1984; Tweney, 1985; Gruber, 1981; Simonton 1999; Sulloway, 1983). Unfortunately, progress in this promising mode has been halting, perhaps because the opportunities for humanists and cognitive scientists to interact in common work are rare. This paper invites cognitive scientists to join historians of science and technology in an interdisciplinary effort to explore cognitive inventive style.

The history of technology provides a rich field for studying how analogy has been used in invention; its case studies offer the substantial advantage of being well documented, partly for patent reasons. Little attention has yet been paid to the way in which analogy has powered the history of technology. The few historians of technology who have addressed analogy as a motor of invention include George Basalla, who in 1985 offered a thought provoking, speculative account of the history of technology as an evolving chain of artifacts that follow from each other analogically (Bassala, 1988). More recently, Thomas P.

Hughes emphasized the use of analogy in cases of invention, especially those featuring great American inventors of the period 1875-1915. He tells, for example, how Elmer Sperry, the father of cybernetic or feedback-control engineering, compared machines with beasts, how Thomas Edison compared electrical and water systems in his invention of the telegraph, how Orville and Wilbur Wright developed the analogy between human and bird flight into viable flying machines, and how Lee de Forest, the inventor of the triode vacuum tube, compared the flow of electrical charge with tiny ferryboats, each "laden with its little electric charge, unloading their etheric cargo at the opposite electrode" (Hughes, 1989). Similarly, Evan Schwartz explained how Philo Farnsworth developed the concept for his invention of television by pondering Albert Einstein's photoelectric theory while plowing the parallel furrows of potatoes fields on his family's Idaho farm (Schwartz, 2002; Schwartz, 2004). These are interesting beginnings in studying the role of analogy in the history of technology but they are too general to lead to a theoretical framework.

As a first step toward a more detailed understanding of analogy in the history of invention, this paper examines the relationship between the social positioning of the inventor and the degree of separation of the domains he or she compared using analogy. Both Hughes and Schwartz point to the importance of an inventor's social isolation. Hughes underscores how "retreat from society" helped many of the great independent American inventors of the late 19th and early 20th century find the "solitude" needed to invent creatively. In withdrawing from the main currents of discussion, Hughes writes, these "inventors were like avant-garde artists resorting to the atelier or the alternative life-style of a historic Montmartre, Schwabing, or Greenwich Village." Working in "spaces of their own choice or design," they could develop their unorthodox ideas without interference "from the constraining influences of the status quo," while their isolation "sheltered them from the hostility or ridicule of those whose established views and institutions the inventors' new ideas would undermine" (Hughes, 1989).

Drawing part of the framework developed by cognitive psychologists of analogy into this historical analysis, we might argue that retreat from traditional social positions allowed inventors to muster the courage to cross the boundaries of well-separated domains and employ the structures and ideas from one of these domains in the other in their analogy-making. This formulation raises sharply defined research questions: If talented inventors retreat socially to private spaces that stand psychologically and physically apart from the mainstream, are they more likely to be able to bridge separated areas in their analogical thinking? Is there a correlation between the degree of separation between the domains that inventors compare and the degree of their institutional isolation or independence? We can begin to explore such questions by studying specific cases of invention. In this paper we examine two mid-twentieth-century electronic control devices that resulted from making analogies: the transistor by John Bardeen (and collaborators) and the amorphous material threshold switch by Stanford R. Ovshinsky. While the domains Bardeen compared in inventing the transistor were neighboring areas of mid-twentieth century electronics, Ovshinsky's invention grew out of a series of analogies across a number of domains spanning the gulf between inanimate and animate matter.

Bridging the Gap Between the Vacuum Tube and Semiconductor Amplifier

Analogy was a standard approach in the problem-solving toolkit of John Bardeen, the only person ever to win two Nobel-prizes in physics. (Hoddeson, 1981; Hoddeson & Riordan, 1997; Hoddeson & Daitch, 2002).[1] In his work leading to the transistor, Bardeen compared the triode vacuum-tube, which as an electrical engineer he was very familiar with, to the behavior of the semiconductor amplifier that he and his partner Walter Brattain were trying to invent. When their informed tinkering with semiconductors and other materials finally yielded a promising signal, Bardeen and Brattain worked to explain the amplifying properties of their new semiconductor amplifier, which in time became known as the transistor, by drawing on their knowledge of the structural elements of the vacuum tube amplifier. Bardeen's handwritten notes on December 24, 1947 clearly indicate that, in his effort to explain the amplification that he and Brattain saw in the novel point-contact semiconductor system they had accidentally constructed, Bardeen imported into this target domain a set of relationships between terms as they were understood in the base domain of vacuum tube physics. In particular, in seeking to relate the regions he called A and B in the semiconductor system in the same way that the corresponding analogous regions related to each other in triode vacuum-tube systems, in which a signal applied to the grid circuit appears amplified in the plate circuit, he wrote:

> Thus A acts as a cathode and B as a plate in the analogous vacuum tube circuit. The ground corresponds to the grid, as the action is similar to that of a grounded grid. The signal is introduced between the (sic) A (the cathode) and ground (grounded grid). The output is between B (the plate) and ground (Bardeen, 1947).

By making this analogy, Bardeen set the stage for developing a new theoretical picture for understanding transistor action, for the analogy brought the two men to recognize that in the semiconductor amplifier the analog of the grid in the vacuum tube was a set of ghostly "holes" in the semiconductor, i.e., unfilled electron states that behave

---

[1] Bardeen's approaches also included problem decomposition, interdisciplinary collaboration, the use of bridging principles, and library work (Hoddeson & Daitch, 2002).

electrically like positively charged particles. It is important to note that in making this extremely productive analogy Bardeen was comparing neighboring domains within the field of electronics.

Inventing a Threshold Switch by Analogy With a Human Nerve Cell

Unlike Bardeen, who preferred to compartmentalize the activities in his life, and for whom analogy was but one of many tools for solving problems within condensed matter physics (Hoddeson & Daitch, 2002), Ovshinsky routinely combined family, friendships, and all his work projects; in doing so he also drew on analogy repeatedly in his efforts to understand and relate the varied experiences in his life. (Ovshinsky, S. & Ovshinsky, I., 2006). As an analogy-maker Ovshinsky also differed from Bardeen in that he never hesitated to compare structures in widely separated domains, sometimes on different levels (macroscopic and microscopic, social and mechanical, or living and inanimate).

Ovshinsky's first major invention, which he made when he worked as a toolmaker during the 1940s, was an intelligent lathe he called the Benjamin Center Drive. The invention, which held the tool being worked on at its center while the ends were being machined, grew out of Ovshinsky's attempt to replicate mechanically some of the human roles he observed as a toolmaker in various machine shops in Ohio, Arizona, and Michigan. Ovshinsky went on to design many other machines for use in the tool or automotive industries.

During the early fifties, Ovshinsky worked on the physical basis of intelligence. He pursued, among other things, the neuronal basis of how humans learn. This effort proved a stepping-stone for Ovshinsky's inventive work starting in the late 1950s on electronic control devices. Recognizing that human learning is in part a function of cell plasticity, he argued that the neuronal seat of human intelligence must lie in sites located on the surface of the nerve cell's membrane. He gained wide recognition for this research when between 1957 and 1959 he applied what he learned about brain physiology to the medical problems of explaining epilepsy and schizophrenia. Schizophrenia was of great current interest at that time. One writer complained, "these days the average reader runs across the word *schizophrenia* in nearly every novel or play" (Turner, 1995, p. 354). Ovshinsky decided to mechanically model the biological process of plasticity by creating a thin film of disordered amorphous material as the analog of the cell membrane. In this way, by following analogically from the base domain of plasticity in living cells, Ovshinsky ventured into a completely new domain of science that of amorphous disordered materials; the area had not yet been worked to any extent by academic scientists, whose gaze in this two post-transistor decades was fixed on crystalline materials.

Drawing like an artist on the palate of elements in the periodic table, Ovshinsky began to design samples of the new amorphous materials, initially quite crudely by combining ground powders of elements and pressing them together in thin films. Seeking to imitate mechanically the behavior of the nerve cell's membrane he create a class of non-crystalline chalcogenides that demonstrated a property resembling the plasticity of neural cells. He then used this mechanical analog to create a device he called his threshold switch, a device that switched its state in response to electro-ionic surface impedance control, as in the human nerve cell. The new device was far more reliable than existing semiconductor devices in both switching and modulation of high-voltage alternating current circuits with small applied signals. Ovshinsky's public disclosure of this switch in July 1959 in New York's Waldorf Astoria Hotel, was he wrote, "inspired in part by a theoretic study of the electrochemical dynamics of the human nervous system." His disclosure briefly described the analogy he had used in making the invention:

> For, according to all modern theory of the metabolism and function of the neuron, this highly efficient and ultra reliable "control component" is surrounded by a semi-permeable membrane which is charged positively on the outside and negatively on the inside. When a stimulus reaches the surface of this membrane, its permeability to certain ions increases with a corresponding decrease in resistance—and its surface becomes activated by a spreading wave of potential. This change in permeability during passage of an impulse is accompanied by impedance changes on the membrane—thus effectively controlling the "output" of the large energy potential (Ovshinsky, S. & Ovshinsky, H., 1959).

Over the next forty years, Ovshinsky further developed the basic idea of adding energy to the switch in a percolation path causing the switch to change state like a nerve cell does when its threshold is reached. He and his co-workers have recently extended the concept into the design of a computer that is far more powerful than any existing device. Thus while Bardeen used analogy primarily to extend existing paradigms, crossing only the boundaries that lay between neighboring domains of the physics of electronics, Ovshinsky more often took adventurous analogical leaps between heterogeneous domains, in the process sometimes inventing new domains.

Analogy and Cognitive Style in the History of Invention

Comparing Bardeen's and Ovshinsky's different use of analogy in inventing their important electronic control switches suggests that it might be productive for humanists and scientists to collaborate in exploring the cognitive styles of inventors. Their cognitive differences appear to relate not only to their professional positioning, but also to their personal backgrounds (Zuckerman, 1977). For the half-century of his remarkably productive career in physics and engineering Bardeen stood firmly within the academic boundaries of his disciplinary area of condensed-matter physics, contributing importantly to solving a large number of major problems over the course of his career. But all the problems he worked on were in his own field of condensed matter physics. In contrast, during a comparable period of time, in his careers as machinist, toolmaker, neuroscientist, inventor, labor organizer, entrepreneur, and family man, Ovshinsky invented a vast arsenal of energy and information devices, some already in wide use today (e.g., rewritable CD and DVD computer memory disks, flat screen monitors, and the nickel-metal-hydride batteries found in most cell-phones), by repeatedly drawing structures analogically between widely separated domains—not only biological, material, atomic and subatomic, but personal and social as well.

And while Bardeen's period as an inventor of electronic devices was a well-circumscribed phase within the bounds of his otherwise academic career as a physicist, Ovshinsky's very identity was invested in inventing devices that could improve society (Howard, 2006). Even today, Ovshinsky, who is now in his mid-eighties, is hard at work bringing his cluster of energy and information inventions (e.g., solar panels, hydrogen fuel cells, electronic switches and amplifiers, nickel-non-polluting batteries and computer memories) to bear on creating an ecologically balanced energy economy, which he hopes will free society of its need to burn fossil fuels.

The explanation behind the different cognitive styles of inventing also reflects the educational and family backgrounds that shaped the lives of these inventors. Bardeen's progressive academic family stressed learning, diligence, and the joy that comes from working toward social betterment Bardeen's father was the Dean of the medical school at Wisconsin; his mother was a scholar of Asian art. Their well-to-do economic position made it possible for Bardeen to attend the best available schools and universities. Both parents applauded Bardeen's early tendency to "hang on" to problems stubbrnly. His father exemplified the academic scientist who is dedicated to solving problems in the public interest (Hoddeson, 2002).

Ovshinsky, on the other hand, emerged from a poor working-class immigrant family. His childhood was spent in a poor ethnic neighborhood of Akron where his father collected scrap metal and his mother had earlier worked in a rubber factory. He never even considered attending schools beyond high school to gain formal education in a particular area, although he did from a young age devour books and articles on many subjects, a practice he continued throughout his life. This background led him to work in small shops during his formative years, and to a set of experiences resembling those of many of the earlier great American inventors (Hughes, 1989). His life-long interest in the social issues of workers helped him and his wife and research partner Iris Ovshinsky create a novel invention laboratory in a Detroit storefront, an institution that evolved into a research and invention village reminiscent of Edison's Menlo Park. The strong liberal social values of Ovshinsky's family, based in large part on the ideology of the Workmen's Circle, an association of working-class immigrants committed to social justice, Yiddish culture, and making the world better, helped turn the focus of Ovshinsky's inventing toward establishing technologies and industries aimed at the social good.

While drawing freely and extensively on the fruits of twentieth-century sciences, including atomic and molecular physics, quantum mechanics, and molecular biology, Ovshinsky managed to work and prosper as an inventor outside the social networks of industry and academia, working in a kind of isolation that allowed him to draw his analogies out of a wider base of experience. Had Ovshinsky had the opportunities that Bardeen enjoyed, for example, to attend the best engineering schools or graduate physics programs of his day, he would perhaps have been less likely to question the received view that only crystalline materials could be used effectively in electronics. He might not have made his important inventions based on amorphous solids, whose irregular structure allows them to be employed in radical technologies. Just as Einstein, during his great period of creative work in physics, felt free in the secluded patent office to ask the kinds of questions that typically only children feel able to ask about space and time, by working in relative isolation Ovshinsky was able to position himself socially to be able to pose questions about machines, atoms, and society that were not part of the discourse of the academic science and engineering institutions of his time.

Acknowledgments

I am grateful to: the Madden Initiative in Technology, Arts, and Culture at the University of Illinois for a 2006-07 fellowship to study the work of Ovshinky; the Beckman Institute of the University of Illinois for seed support to explore analogies between neural and social systems; and Energy Conversion Devices, Inc. for generous support of my interviews with Stanford and Iris Ovshinsky.

References

Albert, R. S., & Runco, M. A. (1999). A history of research on creativity. In Sternberg, R. J., (Ed.) (1999). *Handbook of creativity* (pp. 16-31). Cambridge, UK, Cambridge.

Amabile, T.M. (1996). *Creativity in context*. New York: Westview.

Bardeen, J. (1947). Bell Laboratories Notebook, 20780, December 24, AT&T Archives, Warren, NJ.

Bassala, G. (1988). *The evolution of technology*. Cambridge, U.K.: Cambridge.

Boden, M. A. (Ed.) (1996). *Dimensions of Creativity*. Cambridge, Mass.:MIT.

Bradshaw, G. (1992). The airplane and logic of invention. In Giere, R. N. (Ed.), *Cognitive models of science*. Minneapolis, MN: University of Minnesota

Brem, S., Ferguson, R.W., Forbus, K. D., Gentner, D., Levidow, B. B., Markman, A. B., and Wolff, P. (1997). Analogical reasoning and conceptual change: A case study of Johannes Kepler, *Journal of the Learning Sciences,* Vol. 6, No. 1 (Conceptual Change), 3-40.

Csikszentmihalyi, M. (1996). *Creativity: Flow and the psychology of discovery and invention.* New York: HarperCollins.

Dunbar, K. (1997). How scientists think: On-line creativity and conceptual change in science. In Ward, T. B., Smith, S. M., & Vaid, J. (Eds.) *Creative thought: An investigation of conceptual structures and processes* (pp. 461-494). Washington, DC: American Psychological Association..

Dunbar, K. & Blanchette, I. (2001). The in vivo/in vitro approach to cognition: The case of analogy. *TRENDS in Cognitive Science, 5,* 334-339.

Gardner, H. (1993). *Creating minds: An anatomy of creativity seen through the lives of Freud, Einstein, Picasso, Stravinsky, Eliot, Graham, and Gandhi.* New York: Basic Books.

Gentner, D. (1989). Mechanisms of analogical learning. In S. Vosniadou & A. Ortony (Eds.*), Similarity and analogical reasoning* (pp. 199-24). New York: Cambridge.

Gentner, D., Holyoak, K.J., & Kokinov, B.N. (Eds.) (2001). *The analogical mind: Perspectives from cognitive science.* Cambridge, MA: MIT.

Giere, R. N. (E.d.) (1992). *Cognitive models of science. Minnesota Studies in the Philosophy of Science.* Minneapolis: Univ. of Minnesota..

Gruber, H.. (1981). *Darwin on man: A psychological study of scientific creativity.* Chicago: University of Chicago.

Hesse, M. B. (1963). *Models and analogies in science.* London & New York: Sheed & Ward.

Hoddeson, L. (1981). The discovery of the point-contact transistor. *Historical Studies in the Physical Sciences, 12,* 41-76.

Hoddeson, L. (2001). Modeling invention and discovery based on historical study: The transistor and the theory of superconductivity. *Model-based reasoning: Scientific discovery, technological innovation,* [Proceedings of conference in Pavia, Italy, May 17].

Hoddeson, L. & Riordan, M. (1997). *Crystal fire: The birth of the information age.* New York: W.W. Norton..

Hoddeson, L. & Daitch, V. (2002). *True genius: The life and science of John Bardeen,* Washington, D.C.: National Academy.

Hofstadter, D.R. (1995). *Fluid concepts and creative analogies: Computer models of the fundamental mechanisms of thought.* New York, NY: Basic Books.

Hofstadter, D.R. (2001). Epilogue: Analogy as the core of cognition. In Gentner et al. (Eds.), *The analogical mind: Perspectives from cognitive science.* Cambridge, MA: MIT.

Howard, G.S. (2006). *Stan Ovshinsky and the hydrogen economy: Creating a better world.* Notre Dame, IN: Academic Publications.

Howe, M. J. A. (1999). *Genius explained.* Cambridge, UK: Cambridge.

Hughes, T.P. (1989). *American genesis: A century of invention and technological enthusiasm,* New York, NY: Viking Penguin.

Kulkarni, D. & Simon, H.A. (1988). The processes of scientific discovery: The strategies of experimentation, *Cognitive Science 12,* 139-175.

Langley, P., Simon, H., Bradshaw, G., & Zytkow, J.. (1987). *Scientific discovery: computational explorations of the creative processes.* Cambridge, MA: MIT.

Nersessian, N..J.. (Ed.) (1986). *The process of science: Contemporary philosophical approaches to understanding scientific practice.* Dordrecht: Martinus Nijhoff.

Nersessian, N. J. (1984). *Faraday to Einstein: constructing meaning in scientific theories,* Martinus Nijhoff, Dordrecht.

Newell, A. & Simon, H. (1972). *Human problem-solvin.g* Englewood Cliffs, N.J.: Prentice-Hall.

Ovshinsky, S. & Ovshinsky, H. (1959). Public disclosure of An important new concept of static control in which the basic nerve cell phenomena of electro-ionic surface impedance changes are analogously applied to achieve ultra reliably in switching and modulating high wattage ac circuits by small signal means. The Waldorf-Astoria Hotel, NY, July 8.

Ovshinsky, S. & Ovshinsky, I. (2006). Interviews by L. Hoddeson, January 4-6, July 19-21, and August 16.

Perkins, D. (1981). *The mind's best work.* Boston: Harvard.

Runco, M.A. & Albert R. S. (Eds.) (1990). *Theories of creativiy.* Newberry Park, CA: Sage Publications.

Schwartz, E. (2002). *The last lone inventor: A tale of genius, deceit, and the birth of television.* New York, NY: Harper Collins.

Schwartz, E. (2004). *Juice: The creative fuel that drives world-class inventors.* Cambridge, MA: Harvard Business School.

Simonton, D. (1988). *Scientific genius: A psychology of science.* Cambridge, UK: Cambridge.

Simon, H. A. (1978). Information-processing theory of human problem solving. In W. K. Estes (Ed) *Handbook of Learning and Cognitive Process,* Vol. 5 (pp. 271-295) Hillsdale, H.J.: Eribaum.

Sternberg, R. J. (Ed.) (1999). *Handbook of creativity.* Cambridge, UK, Cambridge.

Sternberg, R.J. & Davidson, J. (Eds.) (1995). *The nature of insight.* Cambridge, MA: MIT.

Sulloway, F. J. (1983). *Freud: Biologist of the mind.* New York: Basic Books.

Turner, T. (1995). Schizophrenia. In Berrios, G. E. & Porter, R. (Eds.) A history of clinical psychiatry (pp. 348-359) London: Athlone.

Tweney, R.D., Doherty, M.E. & Mynat, C.R. (Eds.) (1981). *On scientific thinking* New York: Columbia.

Tweney, R. D. (1985). Faraday's discovery of induction: A cognitive approach. In *Faraday rediscovered: Essays on the life and work of Michael Faraday: 1791-1867*

Gooding, D. & James, F. (Eds). New York: Stockton Press.

Ward, T. B., Smith, S. M., & Finke, R. A. (1999). *Creative cognition.* In Sternberg, R. J. (Ed.) (1999). *Handbook of creativity* (pp. 189-212). Cambridge, UK, Cambridge.

Weisberg, R.W. (1993). *Creativity: Beyond the myth of genius.* (New York: W. H. Freeman

Weisberg, R. W. (1999). Creativity and knowledge: A challenge to theories. In Sternberg, R. J. (Ed.) (1999). *Handbook of creativity* (pp. 226-250). Cambridge, UK, Cambridge.

Zuckerman, H. (1977). *Scientific elite: Nobel Laureates in the United States.* New York: Free Press.

A Corpus Analysis of Conceptual Combination

Phil Maguire (pmaguire@cs.nuim.ie)
Department of Computer Science, NUI Maynooth
Co.Kildare, Ireland

Edward J. Wisniewski (edw@uncg.edu)
Department of Psychology,
University of North Carolina at Greensboro, USA

Gert Storms (gert.storms@psy.kuleuven.ac.be)
Department of Psychology,
University of Leuven, Belgium

Abstract

Although various theories of conceptual combination have been proposed in the past, these have addressed interpretation issues rather than the circumstances in which combinations are used. As a result, existing theories make no explicit predictions about the types of nouns that will combine most frequently. We address this issue by conducting two separate studies designed to reveal patterns in compounding. In the first, we categorize combinations in the BNC according to 25 different noun types. In the second, we investigate whether similar concepts tend to combine with similar constituents. The results of both studies reveal that conceptual content has a large influence in determining how a noun is used in combination. We discuss the significance of our findings for theories of conceptual combination.

Keywords: Conceptual combination; noun-noun compounds; BNC; WordNet similarity; web as a corpus.

Introduction

The combination of two words is a technique commonly adopted by speakers in order to refer to novel concepts and ideas (e.g. *holiday tension*, *picnic bee*). Although people have a well developed means of understanding these novel compounds, the associated comprehension process is not trivial, requiring many levels of understanding. Accordingly, the study of conceptual combination is important, both because it is intimately associated with the generativity and comprehension of natural language and because it is important for understanding how people represent concepts. In English, a language in which compounding is particularly productive, combinations consist of a modifier followed by a head noun. Usually, the head noun denotes the main category while the modifier implies a relevant subcategory or a modification of that set's typical members. In this way, a *kitchen chair* is interpreted as a particular type of chair, and more precisely as the type that is located in kitchens.

Traditionally, theories of conceptual combination have centered on explaining how combinations are interpreted. In contrast, little focus has been directed towards understanding the circumstances in which combinations are used. Slot-filling theories (e.g. Wisniewski, 1997) propose that a combination is interpreted by filling the modifier concept into an appropriate slot of the head schema (e.g. the combination *kitchen chair* is interpreted by filling the concept *kitchen* into the <located> slot of *chair*). According to this view, combination use for a head should therefore be influenced by the set of available slots associated with that concept. Similarly, combination use for a modifier should be influenced by its capacity to act as a filler. The slot-filling view implies that similar nouns will combine in similar ways since they will have many slots in common. For example, *stew* will combine in a similar way to *soup* since both are dishes and are hence associated with a slot relating to ingredients. Also, *plastic* will combine in a similar way to *metal* since both are substances and thus have the ability to fill the <made of> slot for a wide variety of object concepts.

Gagné and Shoben's (1997) Competition Among Relations Among Nominals (CARIN) theory suggests the opposite. This theory proposes that there is a fixed, relatively small taxonomy of standard relations that can be used to link the concepts in a combination. According to Gagné and Shoben, the most available standard relation is the one most frequently used to interpret other compounds containing that same modifier. For instance, the modifier *mountain* is most often associated with the <located> relation, thus making the combination *mountain stream* easier to interpret than *mountain magazine*, which uses the <about> relation. Gagné and Shoben's theory proposes that people store statistical knowledge about now often each relation has been used with a modifier concept in the past. The assumption that separate distributions must be stored with every noun implies that trends in combination use cannot be inferred from a noun's conceptual content. If similar nouns combined in similar ways (e.g. *stew* and *soup*) then storing individual relation frequency distributions for them would be unnecessary.

In the following sections we present a series of corpus-based studies of the English language which examine if combination use is affected by conceptual content. The first classifies the combinations in the British National Corpus

(BNC) into different categories while the second considers a sample of 50 common concepts and examines whether their similarity is correlated with that of their most frequent combining nouns. The findings of these experiments are used to differentiate between the slot-filling and relation-based views.

Study 1

The idea of this study was to extract a large sample of combinations and to separate these into different categories based on the conceptual content of the constituent nouns. Previous efforts have attempted to label combinations by hand but the scalability of this approach is limited by the sheer effort involved. In the following section we describe a novel automated approach for categorizing a large number of combinations.

Method

In order to obtain a sufficient number of combinations, we availed of the British National Corpus (BNC), a tagged, annotated corpus containing over 100 million words. The BNC is designed to represent a wide cross-section of modern English and therefore includes a comprehensive sample of both written and spoken language. In order to increase the accuracy of compound noun identification, we obtained a version that had been parsed using the Charniak parser and extracted all compound noun phrases consisting of two nouns. Additional filtering was used to remove acronyms, misspellings, common nouns and errors (see Maguire, Wisniewski & Storms, 2006 for a more detailed description). This process yielded a total of 252,127 different combination types, involving 16,878 (57%) of the 29,617 nouns appearing in the BNC.

In order to analyse the data, we required some way of classifying nouns into a limited number of broad types. The WordNet online lexicon contains definitions for all common nouns in the English language. These nouns happen to be arranged into 25 separate "lexicographer files" corresponding to such general categories as animal, plant, time period etc. The main obstacle to using this classification was that many nouns have multiple senses, with entries in multiple lexicographer files. For example, if we consider the noun *dog*, the most intuitive sense is that of the animal. However, in addition to this, we find alternative definitions in WordNet, inter alia "a dull unattractive woman", "a smooth textured sausage", and "a metal support for logs in a fireplace". Consequently, we cannot assume that the noun *dog* will always refer to the animal sense when used in combination.

In order to circumvent this issue, we constrained our sample to combinations whose constituents were diagnostic of one particular lexicographer file. For instance, some nouns such as *aardvark* have only a single sense while others such as *vest* have multiple senses which all come from the same lexicographer file (i.e. "a sleeveless garment worn underneath a coat" or "a collarless undergarment"). However, discarding all multi-sense nouns would have potentially biased our sample. In light of this, we selected an arbitrary threshold for diagnosticity which allowed a reasonable balance between accuracy and ecological validity. Any noun was included where the dominant sense accounted for at least 90% of the occurrences of that noun, as determined by the Senseval sense frequencies provided in WordNet. For example, we were able to include the canine sense of *dog* since the Senseval frequency for this sense is 42 while the combined frequency of all other senses is 0. Applying this diagnosticity constraint yielded a total of 12,960 diagnostic nouns, or 76.8% of all nouns appearing in combination in the BNC.

Some errors in classification arose due to WordNet anomalies while others were caused by unrepresentative Senseval frequencies. For example, *builder* has three senses, two of which are "a person who creates a business" and "someone who supervises construction". However, both of these have a Senseval frequency of 0 while the sense of "a substance added to soaps or detergents to increase their cleansing action" has a frequency of 11. The combination *yacht builder* was therefore classified as artifact-substance. In contrast, *notepad* has a single sense in WordNet, but is classified as a paper 'substance' rather than as an artefact. As a result, the combination *desk notepad* was classified as artifact- substance.

We analysed a random sample of 100 diagnostic combinations in order to ascertain the reliability of the classifications. Of these, 3 were not genuine combinations, namely *mother rose*, *word hippodrome* and *suspicion falls*. The inclusion of these phrases was a result of parsing errors by the Charniak parser and the fact that the verbs *falls* and *rose* are also included as nouns in WordNet. Of the remaining 97 combinations, only 4 included nouns that were incorrectly classified. The head *colours* in *rose colours* was categorised as an artefact because this plural form has a WordNet entry relating to "an emblem". Similarly, the plural head *hearts* in *leftist hearts* has a WordNet entry relating to "a form of whist". The head *acoustic* in *stereo acoustic* was categorised as artefact because the only sense in WordNet is that of "a remedy for hearing loss". Finally, the head *court* in *practice court* was incorrectly classified using the justice sense, since this has a Senseval frequency of 831, compared to 36 for the appropriate sports sense. Based on this analysis, we concluded that the level of accuracy was sufficient for identifying patterns of combination between the various noun types contained in the sample.

Results

We report our results in terms of combination types and tokens. A combination type is one particular pairing of a modifier and head (e.g. *kitchen chair* constitutes a single combinational type*)* while the token count reflects the total number of occurrences. In our first analysis, we considered the use of our diagnostic nouns in combination throughout the BNC. One marked trend was that these nouns appeared more frequently as modifiers than as heads. While there are obviously the same number of modifiers and heads in the BNC, our nouns appeared as modifiers 479,440 times but only 383,210 times as heads (123,221 versus 95,970 types respectively). Maguire et al. (2006) found that specific concepts are more likely to appear in the modifier role. Due to our selection process, whereby only the least ambiguous nouns were included, our diagnostic sample may have contained more concepts of this type. In general, abstract concepts are more likely to have multiple senses and are therefore less likely to be diagnostic of one lexicographer file (e.g. *security*). On the other hand, specific concepts are more likely to have a single sense (e.g. *turtle*), therefore explaining why they might have appeared more frequently in our sample.

We obtained the ratio between modifier type frequency and head type frequency for each of the 25 noun categories. The types of noun which appeared most frequently as a modifier were time periods and substances (82% and 79% respectively) while the types of noun appearing most frequently as a head were cognition and shape (e.g. *classroom strategy*, *cathedral square*, 66% and 61% respectively). These results support Maguire et al.'s (2006) finding that less specific concepts prefer the head role. Nouns from the cognition and shape categories are relatively abstract while time periods and substances are of a more precise nature. The productivity of time periods and substances as modifiers corresponds with their potential to participate in the <during> and <made of> roles.

We also expressed the frequency of each diagnostic noun appearing in combination as a percentage of that noun's occurrence in the BNC as a whole. The types of noun most likely to appear as part of a combination were substances, possessions and plants (49%, 41% and 39% of all occurrences respectively). In contrast, the type of noun least frequently used in combination were attributes, shapes and feelings (10%, 9% and 5% respectively). Again, this is consistent with Maguire et al.'s (2006) finding that abstract concepts appear less frequently in combination. These are less likely to interact with other concepts (modifier productivity) and are less likely to have identifiable subclasses (head productivity).

In our second analysis we filtered our sample of combinations down to those consisting of two diagnostic nouns, yielding a total of 72,510 (28.8% of the total). We then separated these into 625 different categories based on the 25 possible permutations of modifier and head type. In order to verify that the reduced sample was still representative of overall combination patterns in the BNC, we compared the modifier and head productivity for the different noun categories. The correlations between number of modifier and head types of the reduced sample and the complete BNC sample were both .986. The correlation between the modifier/head frequency ratio of both samples was .794 (all *p*s < .01). These statistics indicate that combination patterns for the various noun types was not biased by our restriction of the sample to combinations consisting of two diagnostic nouns.

Of the 625 possible combination categories, the most productive by types were artefact-artefact (7.0%, *bicycle shed*), person-person (3.4%, *peasant soldier*), artefact-act (2.8%, *guitar tuning*), artefact-person (2.8%, *clarinet teacher*), and substance-artefact (2.3%, *steel pipe*). Subsequently, we examined patterns of combination use for each type of noun as a modifier and as a head. In both cases, distinctive patterns were evident for different types of noun. Regarding modifier token use, the most peaked patterns were observed for substance, food, and plant nouns. For substance modifiers, the only two types of head with an incidence greater than 10% were artefacts (34%, *plastic robot*) and other substances (27%, *wax paste*). These types of head are likely to be associated with some consistency, which substance modifiers can indicate. In contrast, heads not typically associated with a consistency obtained far lower proportions (e.g. plant 1%, animal 1%, location 1%, event, feeling and time 0%). Food modifiers combined primarily with two categories of head noun, namely artefacts (40%, *egg spoon*) and other food heads (14%, *custard pie*). These two categories correspond with the <for> and <has as ingredients> relations. Plant modifiers combined primarily with two categories of head, namely artefact (29%, *cedar staircase*) and plant (20%, *flower seed*), reflecting the <made of>, <is> and <has> relations.

Regarding head noun use by tokens, the most distinctive patterns were observed for time, substance, phenomenon and artefact nouns. Time periods as head nouns combined with three types of modifier with an incidence greater than 5%, namely act (22%, *camping holiday*), artefact (20%, *firework night*), and time (23%, *autumn afternoon*). All three of these modifier types can elaborate on a time period, describing what occurs or when it occurs. In contrast, modifier types which were not easily associated with a time period were far less frequent (e.g. substance, 2%). Substance heads combined most frequently with other substances, (51%, *wax paste*), and body parts (13%, *blood protein*). Again, modifier types with no obvious relationship to substances scored far lower (e.g. feeling 0%). Phenomenon heads combined with time modifiers, (31%, *autumn sunlight*) and artefact modifiers (21%, *pipe smoke*), reflecting the <during> and <caused by> relations. Finally, artefact heads combined with artefact modifiers (35%, *gun ammunition*), act modifiers (12%, *gardening hat*) and substance modifiers (10%, *plastic robot*). In summary, these results provide converging evidence that the way in which nouns tend to be used in combination reflects the interaction of their conceptual content.

For the above analyses, the incidence of combinations involving the different noun types was strongly influenced by the frequency of that noun type in the corpus. For example, artefacts and acts constituted 20% and 13% of the 12,960 diagnostic nouns in our sample while animals and plants made up only 1% each. Consequently, combinations involving artefacts and acts were by far the most common. In order to control for this variance in noun type frequency, we conducted a further analysis. For each of the 625 different categories of combination, we computed the ratio of the number of tokens observed versus the number that would have been expected given the frequency of the modifier and head noun types. We then extracted the top ten of these ratios in cases where that category included at least 20 different types.

Of all the categories, plant-plant combinations had the highest ratio, being 27.5 times more common than the frequency of plant nouns would imply (*elm tree*, *flower bud*, *bramble leaf*). Food-food combinations had the next highest ratio, being 11.6 times more common than expected (*hamburger bun*, *kebab sauce*, *dessert beer*). These categories were followed by substance-substance combinations with 8.8 (*lithium metal*, *powder ice*, *wax paste*), animal-body with t 8.6 (*giraffe neck*, *lamb leg*, *rabbit teeth*), animal-animal with 8.1 (*terrier dog*, *rat flea*, *hen bird*), body-state with 6.9 (*eye trauma*, *kidney disease*, *muscle tension*), finance-finance with 6.7 (*pension money*, *tax profits*, *cash wage*), time-phenomenon with 6.6 (*autumn sunlight*, *dawn wind*, *winter mist*), body-body with 6.5 (*chest muscle*, *ankle tendon*, *jaw tooth*) and finally area-animal with 6.1 (*mountain cattle*, *ocean plankton*, *river bird*). In general, combinations with the same type of modifier and head were far more common than expected, demonstrating that nouns tend to combine with others from within the same domain. Many of the most productive categories were those associated with some specific relation. For example, area-animal combinations were more common than expected because of the fact that geographic areas are often used to reference the habitat of animal species.

In order to reinforce the intuitive observation that different noun types did not combine randomly, we performed a series of analyses. First, taking the log of each of the ratios, we tested the data for normality using a Wilks-Shapiro analysis and found that it was not normally distributed ($p > .05$). Instead, there were several very high ratios for the more productive patterns but far more lower ratios, indicating that noun types have strong preferences for combining with a small selection of other noun types. We also correlated the modifier and head ratios with each other in order to demonstrate the intuitive interaction between conceptual content and role. This correlation was not significant, $r = .04$, $p > .05$, showing that nouns combine differently depending on whether they are used as a modifier or a head. This result reveals a clear distinction between the two roles and demonstrates that the influence of conceptual content is manifested differently in each case. Finally, we physically divided our corpus of diagnostic combinations into two equal random halves. We recomputed separate ratios based on each of these sets and then compared them, obtaining a significant correlation of $r = .75$, $p < .01$. Given that both halves of the sample exhibited similar tendencies, this rules out the possibility that such trends arose randomly. Instead, our results indicate that nouns of the same type will tend to combine in predictable patterns.

Discussion

The principal finding of this experiment is that separating nouns into a small number of broad categories yields distinctive patterns in noun use as both modifiers and heads. Not only does this undermine Gagné and Shoben's (1997) proposal that the modifier is the only reliable indicator of combination use, it also undermines their assumption that every modifier will combine in a unique fashion, independent of its conceptual content. Using a large sample of combinations, we have observed that nouns of the same general type tend to combine in similar ways. In addition, the more productive pairings of noun types were those where the conceptual content of the constituents supported some specific relation. Given the association between semantics and combination use, there appears to be little motivation for storing a separate set of statistics with every concept. In the following study we explored the same issue using specific nouns as opposed to generalized noun types.

Study 2

In this study we analyzed the use of a sample set of 50 common concepts in combination. The objective was to ascertain whether similar concepts combine more frequently with the same constituents.

Method

In order to guarantee a broad sample of concepts, we consulted Battig and Montague's (1969) category norms. From this database, we selected 50 nouns that occurred at least 50 times as both a modifier and a head within the BNC. In order to ensure a broad selection, these nouns were taken from the following categories: body part, dwelling, furniture, insect, kitchen utensil, mammal, natural earth formation, profession, tool, vegetable, weapon, food, vehicle, weather and plants.

We employed two different methods for computing a 2-dimensional similarity matrix between the 50 nouns, one automatic and one participant-generated. The computational method was based on Resnik's Information Content metric as applied to the WordNet hierarchy. WordNet groups English words into sets of synonyms, as organized in a hierarchy. For example, *cat* and *dog* are hyponyms of the synset *mammal*, which itself is a hyponym of the synset *animal*. According to Resnik (1995), similarity can be determined by the amount of information two concepts have in common, as given by the most specific common abstraction that subsumes both concepts. If one does not exist, then the two concepts are maximally dissimilar. For example *dog* is similar to *cat*, because both are animals and only a small proportion of nouns contained in WordNet are animals. On the other hand, *dog* is very dissimilar to *rain* since the most specific common abstraction for these nouns is the *entity* node in WordNet, of which every entry is an example. Accordingly, the similarity ratings we derived for *dog* and *cat* (0.6) and *dog* and *rain* (0.0) reflect the inverse log of the proportion of WordNet synsets subsumed by their more specific common abstraction.

In order to verify the accuracy of these automated similarity ratings, four participants were asked to make the same judgments. Each participant rated the similarity of all 2,450 pairs of concepts and these values were averaged for each comparison. As participants were native Dutch speakers, concepts were therefore presented in Dutch. The estimated reliability of the resulting similarity values was .73. The correlation between the WordNet similarity metric and the participant ratings was .63, rising to .74 following correction for the unreliability of the latter ($p < .01$). These statistics show that WordNet similarities can be relied on to approximate human judgments. For each of 50 concepts, we selected the 10 most frequent combination types involving that noun as a modifier and as a head in the BNC (e.g. *train journey, train service, train station* for *train* as a modifier). In cases of a tie in frequency, the remaining types were selected randomly. In the following section we describe a series of analyses which investigated whether the similarity of the concepts was related to the similarity of the nouns they combined with.

Similarity of Combining Nouns

In this analysis we computed a two-dimensional matrix reflecting the degree of overlap between the top combining nouns for our 50 concepts. Given that the analysis was based on the 10 most frequent combination types for each concept, the maximum overlap was 10. For example, the modifiers *cat* and *dog* had an overlap of three, because they had *owner, food* and *show* in common. However, their seven other most frequent combining nouns were different. In fact, no two concepts had an overlap of greater than three and over 90% of entries in both the modifier and head overlap matrices were zero. We computed the correlation between the overlap and similarity matrices. The correlation involving the 50 nouns as modifiers was 0.31 while that involving the 50 nouns as heads was 0.19. Using the participant ratings in place of the WordNet similarities, these correlations rose to .35 and .20 respectively (all ps < .01). These results demonstrate that similar concepts are more likely to combine with the same noun, although the strengths of our correlations were relatively weak. The main problem with the above analysis was the low number of shared nouns, meaning that the overlap measure was not very informative. Furthermore, in cases where two words were very similar though not identical, no overlap was registered. For example, *dog dirt* and *cat faeces* were among the most common combination types for *dog* and *cat* respectively, yet the overlap for these was still zero.

Taking into account these issues, we ran a further analysis based on the level of similarity between the sets of combining nouns for a pair of concepts. In order to obtain similarity ratings we again made use of Resnik's metric. This time, in comparing *dog* and *cat*, we considered each of *dog*'s combining nouns and computed its maximum similarity with any of *cat*'s combining nouns (e.g. *faeces* and *dirt* had a similarity of 0.36). These ten values were then averaged to obtain the overall similarity between both

sets. Using this technique, we obtained pairwise similarity values for all 500 of the modifier and head combining nouns, involving a total of half a million comparisons. In order to compensate for contamination resulting from false positives, we squared all the values so that those that were relatively high (indicating very similar concepts) would have a greater influence than the lower ones. The correlation between the similarity of the 50 concepts and their set of associated combining nouns as modifiers was 0.29. The same correlation involving the 50 concepts as head nouns was 0.28. These correlations rose to .30 and .31 using the participant-generated frequencies (all ps < .01). Again, these correlations demonstrate that similar concepts tend to combine with similar constituents.

Although the correlations were significant, they were not as strong as we expected. One reason for this may have been the unreliability of the similarity ratings produced. Some of these were unrealistic due to peculiarities in the arrangement of the WordNet hierarchy. For example, *shop* is classified as a hyponym of the *structure* synset, yielding unrealistically high similarities with nouns such as *bridge, wall* and *door* (all .36). Nevertheless, we suspected that even had perfect ratings been available, the correlations would not have been much higher. The inherent problem with the above analyses is that they are based only on the top 10 most frequent combining nouns for a given concept. Because a noun can plausibly combine with thousands of other nouns, there is no guarantee that the 10 most frequent of these will provide a representative sample. Often, the most common combination types are idiosyncratic and unsuitable for comparison. For example, *tabby cat, pussy cat* and *tom cat* were among the most common types for *cat* as a head. Because these combination types are lexicalised and hence specific to *cat*, they are unlikely to be used with any other head concepts. Another problem associated with using a limited sample of combinations is that a certain type may not feature, even though it is highly plausible. For example, although *dog basket* is not among the most frequent combination types for *dog*, it is far more acceptable than a combination such as *ladder basket*, a fact which cannot be reflected by the current paradigm. In the following section we present an alternative method of comparison which avoids over-generalizing based on a limited sample of combination types.

Determining Frequency using Web Counts

The internet is being increasingly used as a data source in a wide range of natural language processing tasks. Given that it represents a corpus of some 100 billion words, we were able to obtain frequencies for combinations which would have been too unusual to be represented in a smaller corpus such as a BNC. We created novel combinations by taking the top 10 combination types for a given concept and substituting the 49 other concepts in its place. For example, performing this substitution for *cat breeder* yielded combinations of the form *dog breeder, ladder breeder, wind breeder* etc. Subsequently, the Google search engine was used in order to obtain frequency counts for the 490 artificial compounds generated for each concept. We computed the log of the number of hits for each compound and normalized this value according to the frequency of the nouns involved. The purpose of the normalization process was to control for the fact that some words are more common than others and therefore more likely to take part in a greater number of combinations as well as yielding more false positives. In order to obtain an overall 'interchangability' score for each entry in our two dimensional matrix, we averaged the values for each of the ten novel combinations produced. Thus, the value of 0.5 between *dog* and *cat* reflects the fact that substituting the modifier *cat* in place of *dog* yielded combinations with relatively high frequencies in Google (e.g. *cat owner, cat food, cat breeder*). The main problem with the use of the web as a corpus is the level of noise associated with the data. The Google search engine ignores punctuation and capitalization, leading to false positives whenever the paraphrase match crosses a sentence boundary (e.g "...he called his dog. Rain had started to fall..."). Matches are also likely to include links, web addresses, names and other non-textual data. Furthermore, web data is not tagged with part of speech information, meaning that a significant portion of hits for noun-noun compounds will inevitably involve the use of the constituent nouns as verbs or adjectives (e.g. "she watched the cat hunt the mouse").

The two-dimensional interchangability matrix was correlated with the original similarity matrix. Using the WordNet similarity values, the correlation between these two matrices for the 50 concepts as modifiers was .49 while that involving the 50 concepts as heads was .40. Using the participant-generated similarity ratings, these correlations rose to .53 and .47 respectively or .63 and .55 assuming perfectly reliable ratings (all *ps* < .01). Given the unreliability of Google frequencies, these results are particularly impressive and demonstrate that conceptual content has a strong bearing in determining how nouns are used in combination.

Discussion

Our results highlight a relationship between conceptual content and the way that nouns tend to combine as both modifiers and heads. This association was observed both in comparing the top ten most frequent combining types for a pair of concepts and in obtaining web counts for combinations in which one concept was substituted with another. These results offer converging evidence that similar nouns combine in similar ways and that the more similar they are, the more likely they are to combine with the same nouns.

The difference between the modifier and head correlations for the overlap and web count analyses was significant using both the participant generated and WordNet similarities (all *ps* < .01 using two-tailed *z*-tests). However, this discrepancy may simply be an artifact of our sample. The 50 nouns we selected were not particularly representative since many denote superordinate categories for which many subtypes exist (e.g. *grass, rice, cat*). As a result of this, many of the most frequent combination types for these nouns as heads were of a sub-type super-type nature (e.g. *marram grass, pilau rice, tabby cat*). Such modifiers are unlikely to overlap with any others and substitutions of the head concept are unlikely to result in sensible combinations (e.g. *marram tree, pilau potato, tabby dog*). As a result, the difference in the correlations for the modifier and head matrices cannot be interpreted as evidence that conceptual content is a better predictor of modifier use. On the contrary, our results reveal that the semantics of a noun influence its use as both a modifier and a head.

General Discussion

In recent years, many theories of conceptual combination have been proposed, yet no large-scale analysis of combination use had hitherto been conducted. We have addressed this issue, providing converging evidence that conceptual content strongly influences how a noun will be used in combination.

Our results can be interpreted as supporting the slot-filling view. On the other hand, they contradict the main principles of the CARIN theory. First, both modifiers and head nouns revealed distinctive patterns of combination, undermining the notion of modifier primacy. Second, if different nouns of the same type exhibit similar trends in combination then there should be no need to store separate statistical distributions for each. The CARIN theory fails to acknowledge the intuitive link between relation frequency and noun properties, a link which we has been consistently reinforced throughout our study. As a result, the statistics on which the theory bases itself may be measured at the wrong level of abstraction and relation frequency may actually be an epiphenomenon of conceptual content.

References

Battig, W.G., & Montague, W.E. (1969).Category norms for verbal items in 56 categories: A replication and extension of the Connecticut category norms. *Journal of Experimental Psychology Monograph, 80,* 1-127.

Gagné, C. L. & Shoben, E. J. (1997). Influence of thematic relations on the comprehension of modifier-noun combinations. *Journal of Experimental Psychology: Learning, Memory and Cognition, 23,* 71-87.

Maguire, P., Wisniewski, E. J. & Storms, G. (2006). An Investigation of the Productivity of Abstract and Concrete Nouns in Combination. In *Proceedings of the Twenty-Eighth Annual Conference of the Cognitive Science Society*, Vancouver, Canada.

Resnik, P. (1995). Semantic similarity in a taxonomy. An information based measure and its application to problems of ambiguity in natural language. *Journal of Artificial Intelligence Research, 11,* 95-130.

Wisniewski, E. J. (1997). When concepts combine. *Psychonomic Bulletin & Review, 4,* 167-183.

A Computational Usage-Based Model
for Learning General Properties of Semantic Roles

Afra Alishahi and **Suzanne Stevenson**
Department of Computer Science
University of Toronto
{afra,suzanne}@cs.toronto.edu

Abstract

We present a Bayesian model of early verb learning that acquires a general conception of the semantic roles of predicates based only on exposure to individual verb usages. The model forms probabilistic associations between the semantic properties of arguments, their syntactic positions, and the semantic primitives of verbs. Because of the model's Bayesian formulation, the roles naturally shift from verb-specific to highly general properties. The acquired role properties are a good intuitive match to various roles, and are useful in guiding comprehension in the face of ambiguity.

Learning and Use of Semantic Roles

Semantic roles, such as Agent, Theme, and Recipient in (1) and (2) below, are a critical aspect of linguistic knowledge because they indicate the relations of the participants in an event to the main predicate.[1]

(1) Mom$_{Agent}$ gave this$_{Theme}$ to her$_{Recipient}$.
(2) Mom$_{Agent}$ gave her$_{Recipient}$ this$_{Theme}$.

Moreover, it is known that people use the associations between roles and their syntactic positions to help guide on-line interpretation (e.g., Trueswell et al., 1994). How children acquire this kind of complex relational knowledge, which links predicate-argument structure to syntactic expression, is still not well understood. Fundamental questions remain concerning how semantic roles are learned, and how associations are established between roles and the grammatical positions the role-bearing arguments appear in.

Early theories suggested that roles are drawn from a pre-defined inventory of semantic symbols or relations, and that innate "linking rules" that map roles to sentence structure enable children to infer associations between role properties and syntactic positions (e.g., Pinker, 1989). However, numerous questions have been raised concerning the plausibility of innate linking rules for language acquisition (e.g., Fisher, 1996; Kako, 2006).

An alternative, usage-based view is that children acquire roles gradually from the input they receive, by generalizing over individually learned verb usages (e.g., Lieven et al., 1997; Tomasello, 2000). For instance, Tomasello (2000) claims that, initially, there are no general labels such as Agent and Theme, but rather verb-specific concepts such as 'hitter' and 'hittee,' or 'sitter' and 'thing sat upon.' Recent experimental evidence

---

[1] Such elements are also termed participant, thematic, or case roles, and more or less fine-grained semantic distinctions are attributed to them. We use the widely accepted labels such as Agent and Theme for ease of exposition.

confirms that access to general notions like Agent and Theme is age-dependent (Shayan, 2006). It remains unexplained, though, precisely how verb-specific roles metamorphose to general semantic roles. Moreover, experiments with children have revealed the use of verb-specific biases in argument interpretation (Nation et al., 2003), as well as of strong associations between general roles and syntactic positions (e.g., Fisher, 1996, and related work). However, specific computational models of such processes have been lacking.

We have proposed a usage-based computational model of early verb learning that uses Bayesian clustering and prediction to model language acquisition and use. Our previous experiments demonstrated that the model learns basic syntactic constructions such as the transitive and intransitive, and exhibits patterns of errors and recovery in their use, similar to those of children (Alishahi and Stevenson, 2005a,b). A shortcoming of the model was that roles were explicit labels, such as Agent, which were assumed to be "perceptible" to the child from the scene. In this paper, we have extended our model to directly address the learning and use of semantic roles.

Our Bayesian model associates each argument of a predicate with a probability distribution over a set of semantic properties—a *semantic profile*. We show that initially the semantic profiles of an argument position yield verb-specific conceptualizations of the role associated with that position. As the model is exposed to more input, these verb-based roles gradually transform into more abstract representations that reflect the general properties of arguments across the observed verbs.

The semantic profiles that we use are drawn from a standard lexical resource (WordNet; Miller, 1990), so that our results are not biased toward any theory of semantic roles. One limitation of this approach is that the profiles fail to reflect any event-specific properties that an argument might have. Such properties (like "causally affected") are almost certainly required in an accurate representation of roles, as in Dowty (1991). Despite their absence, we are able to show that intuitive profiles can be learned for each role from examples of its use. We further establish that such representations can be useful in guiding the argument interpretation of ambiguous input, an ability experimentally demonstrated in children in recent work (Nation et al., 2003).

Related Computational Work

A number of computational approaches for learning the selectional preferences of a verb first initialize WordNet concepts with their frequency of use as the particular argument of a verb, and then find the appropriate level in the WordNet hierarchy for capturing the verb's restrictions on that argument (e.g., Resnik, 1996; Clark and Weir, 2002). However, none of these models generalize their acquired verb-based knowledge to a higher level, yielding constraints on the arguments of general constructions such as the transitive or intransitive.

Many computational systems model human learning of the assignment of general roles to sentence constituents, using a multi-feature representation of the semantic properties of arguments (e.g., McClelland and Kawamoto, 1986; Allen, 1997). Others learn only verb-specific roles that are not generalized (e.g., Chang, 2004). As in our earlier work, these models require explicit labelling of the arguments that receive the same role in order to learn the association of the roles to semantic properties and/or syntactic positions. In the work presented here, we show that our extended model can learn general semantic profiles of arguments, without the need for role-annotated training data.

Our Bayesian Model

Our model learns the argument structure frames for each verb, and their grouping across verbs into constructions. An argument structure frame is the pairing of a syntactic form (a particular word order of a verb and its arguments) with the meaning of the expression (the semantic primitives of the predicate and the semantic properties of the arguments). A construction is a grouping of individual frames which probabilistically share form-meaning associations; these groupings typically correspond to general constructions in the language such as transitive, intransitive, and ditransitive.

Most importantly for this paper, the model forms probabilistic associations between syntactic positions of arguments, their semantic properties, and the semantic primitives of the predicate. These associations are generalized (through the constructions) to form more abstract notions of role semantics, dependent on argument position and verb primitives. The following sections review basic properties of the model from Alishahi and Stevenson (2005a,b), and introduce extensions that support the learning and use of semantic profiles.

The Input and Frame Extraction

The input to the learning process is a set of scene-utterance pairs that link a relevant aspect of an observed scene (what the child perceives) to the utterance that describes it (what the child hears). From each input pair, our model extracts the corresponding argument structure frame, which is a set of form and meaning features.

Figure 1 shows that we use a simple logical form for representing the semantics of an observed scene, while an utterance simply specifies a sequence of words in root form. In the extracted frame, verbs and prepositions are represented as predicates (e.g., **Make**, **On**) that can take a number of arguments. Each predicate has a set of semantic primitives which describes the event characteristics (e.g., [cause, become]). Each argument can be an entity (e.g., TIM, CAKE) or a predicate structure itself

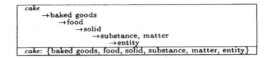

Scene-Utterance Input Pair	
Scene: **Make**[cause, become](TIM, CAKE)	
Utterance: *Tim made cake*	
Extracted Frame	
head verb	*make*
semantic primitives of verb	[cause, become]
arguments	⟨Tim, cake⟩
syntactic pattern	arg1 verb arg2

Figure 1: An input pair and its corresponding frame.

```
cake
    →baked goods
      →food
        →solid
          →substance, matter
            →entity
cake: {baked goods, food, solid, substance, matter, entity}
```

Figure 2: Semantic properties for *cake* from WordNet

(e.g., **On**(TABLE)). The syntactic pattern in the frame indicates word order of the predicate and arguments.

In a frame, each word for an entity has a link to the lexical entry that contains its semantic properties, which are extracted from WordNet (version 2.0) as follows. We hand-pick the intended sense of the word, extract all the hypernyms (ancestors) for that sense, and add all the words in the hypernym synsets to the list of the semantic properties. Figure 2 shows an example of the hypernyms for *cake*, and its resulting set of semantic properties.[2]

Learning as Bayesian Clustering

Each extracted frame is input to an incremental Bayesian clustering process that groups the new frame together with an existing group of frames—a construction—that probabilistically has the most similar properties to it. If none of the existing constructions has sufficiently high probability for the new frame, then a new construction is created, containing only that frame. We use a modified version of Alishahi and Stevenson's (2005a,b) probabilistic model, which is itself an adaptation of a Bayesian model of human categorization proposed by Anderson (1991). It is important to note that the categories (i.e., constructions) are not predefined, but rather are created according to the patterns of similarity over observed frames.

Grouping a frame F with other frames participating in construction k is formulated as finding the k with the maximum probability given F:

$$\textbf{BestConstruction}(F) = \underset{k}{\text{argmax}}\ P(k|F) \qquad (1)$$

where k ranges over the indices of all constructions, with index 0 representing recognition of a new construction.

Using Bayes rule, and dropping $P(F)$ which is constant for all k:

$$P(k|F) = \frac{P(k)P(F|k)}{P(F)} \sim P(k)P(F|k) \qquad (2)$$

The prior probability, $P(k)$, indicates the degree of entrenchment of construction k, and is given by the relative frequency of its frames over all observed frames. The posterior probability of a frame F is expressed in terms of

---

[2] We do not remove alternate spellings of a term in WordNet; this will be seen in the profiles in the results section.

the individual probabilities of its features, which we assume are independent, thus yielding a simple product of feature probabilities:

$$P(F|k) = \prod_{i \in FrameFeatures} P_i(j|k) \qquad (3)$$

where j is the value of the ith feature of F, and $P_i(j|k)$ is the probability of displaying value j on feature i within construction k. Given the focus here on semantic profiles, we return to the calculation of the probabilities of semantic properties below.

Language Use as Bayesian Prediction

In our model, language use (production and comprehension) is a prediction process in which unobserved features in a frame are set to the most probable values given the observed features. For example, sentence production predicts the most likely syntactic pattern for expressing intended meaning components, which may include semantic properties of the arguments and/or semantic primitives of the predicate. In comprehension, these semantic elements may be inferred from a word sequence.

The value of an unobserved feature is predicted based on the match between the given partial set of observed features and the learned constructions:

$$\textbf{BestValue}_i(F) = \underset{j}{\text{argmax}} \; P_i(j|F) \qquad (4)$$

$$= \underset{j}{\text{argmax}} \sum_k P_i(j|k) P(k|F)$$

$$= \underset{j}{\text{argmax}} \sum_k P_i(j|k) P(k) P(F|k)$$

Here, F is a partial frame, i is an unobserved (missing) feature, j ranges over the possible values of feature i, and k ranges over all constructions. The conditional probabilities, $P(F|k)$ and $P_i(j|k)$, are determined as in our learning module. The prior probability of a construction, $P(k)$, takes into account two important factors: its relative entrenchment, and the (smoothed) frequency with which the verb of F participates in it.

All predictions of the model are mediated by construction knowledge. For a well-entrenched usage of a verb, predictions are guided by the construction that the usage is a member of. For a novel verb, or a novel use of a known verb, predictions arise from constructions that are the best match to the observed partial frame.

Probabilities of Semantic Properties

In both learning and prediction, the probability of value j for feature i in construction k is estimated using a smoothed version of this maximum likelihood formula:

$$P_i(j|k) = \frac{\textbf{count}_i^k(j)}{n_k} \qquad (5)$$

where n_k is the number of frames participating in construction k, and $\textbf{count}_i^k(j)$ is the number of those with value j for feature i.

For most features, $\textbf{count}_i^k(j)$ is calculated by simply counting those members of construction k whose value for feature i exactly matches j. However, for the semantic properties of words, counting only the number of exact matches between the sets is too strict, since even highly

similar words very rarely have the exact same set of properties. We instead compare the set of semantic properties of a particular argument in the observed frame, S_1, and the set of semantic properties of the same argument in a member frame of a construction, S_2, using the Jaccard similarity score:[3]

$$\textbf{sem\_score}(S_1, S_2) = \frac{|S_1 \cap S_2|}{|S_1 \cup S_2|} \qquad (6)$$

For example, assume that the new frame represents the verb usage *John ate cake*, and one of the members of the construction that we are considering represents *Mom got water*. We must compare the semantic properties of the corresponding arguments *cake* and *water*:

cake: {baked goods,food,solid,substance,matter,entity}
water: {liquid,fluid,food,nutrient,substance,matter,entity}

The intersection of the two sets is {food, substance, matter, entity}, therefore the **sem_score** for these sets is $\frac{4}{9}$.

In general, to calculate the conditional probability for the set of semantic properties, we set $\textbf{count}_i^k(j)$ in equation (5) to the sum of the **sem_score**'s for the new frame and every member of construction k, and normalize the resulting probability over all possible sets of semantic properties in our lexicon.

Representation of Semantic Profiles

Recall that a semantic profile is a probability distribution over the semantic properties of an argument position. This requires looking at the probability of all the individual properties, j_p, rather than the probability of the full set, j. We use a modified version of equation (5) in which $\textbf{count}_i^k(j_p)$ is the number of frames in construction k that include property j_p for the argument whose set of semantic properties is the ith feature of the frame. The resulting probabilities over all j_p form the semantic profile of that argument.

A semantic profile contains all the semantic properties ever observed in an argument position. As learning proceeds, a profile may include a large number of properties with very low probability. In order to display the profiles we obtain in our results section below, we create truncated profiles which list the properties with the highest probabilities, in decreasing order of probability value. To avoid an arbitrary threshold, we cut the ordered list of properties at the widest gap between two consecutive probabilities across the entire list.

Experimental Results

The Input Corpora

Large scale corpora of utterances paired with meaning representations, such as required by our model, do not currently exist. The corpora for our experimental simulations are generated from an extended version of the input-generation lexicon used in our earlier work. The lexicon is created to reflect distributional characteristics of the data children are exposed to. We extracted 13 of the most frequent verbs in mother's speech to each of

---

[3]The selected semantic properties and the corresponding similarity score are not fundamental to the model, and could in the future be replaced with an approach that is deemed more appropriate to child language acquisition.

Adam (2;3–4;10), Eve (1;6–2;3), and Sarah (2;3–5;1) in the CHILDES database (MacWhinney, 1995). We entered each verb into the lexicon along with its total frequency across the three children, as well as its (manually compiled) set of possible argument structure frames and their associated frequencies. We also randomly selected 100 sentences containing each verb; from these, we extracted a list of head nouns and prepositions that appear in each argument position of each frame, and added these to the lexicon.

For each simulation in our set of experiments, an input corpus of scene-utterance pairs is automatically randomly generated using the frequencies in the input-generation lexicon to determine the probability of selecting a particular verb and argument structure. Arguments of verbs are also probabilistically generated based on the word usage information for the selected frame of the verb. Our generated corpora are further processed to simulate both incomplete and noisy data: 20% of the input pairs have a missing (syntactic or semantic) feature; another 20% of the pairs have a feature removed and replaced by the value predicted for the feature at that point in learning. The latter input pairs are noisy, especially in the initial stages of learning. Other types of noise (such as incomplete sentences) are not currently modelled in the input.

Formation of Semantic Profiles for Roles

Psycholinguistic experiments have shown that children are sensitive at an early age to the association between grammatical positions, such as subject and object, and the properties of the roles that are typically associated with those positions (Fisher and others; e.g., Fisher, 1996). Here we show that for each argument position in a construction, our model learns a general semantic profile from instances of verb usage. For some common constructions, we study the semantic profile of the arguments through prediction of the most probable semantic properties for that position, as detailed above. Although these semantic profiles do not include any event-specific knowledge, they can be considered as a weak form of the semantic roles that the corresponding arguments receive in that construction.

We train our model on 200 randomly generated input pairs,[4] and then present it with a test input pair containing a novel verb *gorp* appearing in a familiar construction, with unknown nouns appearing as its arguments. As an example, a test pair for a novel verb appearing in a transitive construction looks as follows:

$\textbf{Gorp}_{[cause,become]}(\mathsf{X},\mathsf{Y})$
x gorp y

We then have the prediction model produce a semantic profile for each of the unknown arguments, to reveal what the model has learned about the likely semantic properties for that position in the corresponding construction. We average the obtained probabilities over 5 simulations on different random input corpora.

Our model learns semantic profiles for argument positions in a range of constructions. Here, due to lack of space, we focus only on a few such profiles corresponding to roles that have received much attention in the literature. Figure 3 shows the predicted semantic profiles for the arguments in the subject and object positions of a transitive construction (corresponding to X and Y in the *gorp* test input above), and the subject position in an intransitive construction. Even though we use semantic properties from WordNet, which lack any event-specific features, the emerging semantic profile for each argument position demonstrates the intuitive properties that the role received by that argument should possess.

Transitive Subject	*Transitive Object*	*Intransitive Subject*
entity	entity	entity
object	object	object
physical object	physical object	physical object
being	artifact	being
organism	artefact	organism
living thing	whole	living thing
animate thing	whole thing	animate thing
causal agent	unit	causal agent
cause		cause
causal agency		causal agency
person		person
individual		individual
someone		someone
somebody		somebody
mortal		mortal
human		human
soul		soul

Figure 3: Semantic profiles of argument positions.

For example, the semantic profile for an argument that appears in the subject position in a transitive construction (the left box of Figure 3) demonstrates the properties of an animate entity, most likely a human. In contrast, the semantic profile for an argument in the object position (the middle box of Figure 3) most likely corresponds to a physical entity. These results are consistent with Kako (2006), who finds that, given unknown verbs and nouns in the transitive, adults attribute more Agent-like semantic properties to subjects, and more Patient-like properties to objects (specifically, a variation on Dowty's (1991) proto-properties). Kako (2006) also reports similar results using a *known* verb in an incompatible construction. To simulate this, we gave our model a transitive input like the *gorp* pair above, but with an intransitive-only verb *dance*. We found a similar profile for the noun in object position as in Figure 3. Since *dance* has never been seen with an object, this profile must come from the model's learned associations over existing verbs in the transitive construction.

The right box of Figure 3 shows the semantic profile for the subject of an intransitive. This argument can receive an Agent role (*John went*) or a Theme role (*the ball fell*). We think that the semantic profile represents more Agent-like characteristics because, in our input data, the probability of an Agent in that position is much higher than a Theme. We explore this issue next.

Multiple Possible Roles for a Position

Our model's failure to distinguish different roles assigned to the intransitive subject position might simply be a consequence of the bias of the input corpora. Alternatively, it might be due to an inherent deficiency of the model when faced with input that lacks explicit role labels—i.e., an inability of the model to distinguish the

[4]In most experiments, receiving additional input after 200 pairs ceases to make any significant difference in the output.

arguments of different types of verbs when those arguments occur in the same syntactic position.

To test this, we created an input corpus with an artificially increased frequency of *fall*, the only intransitive verb in our lexicon that can have a Theme (rather than an Agent) in the subject position, so that the model would be given sufficient examples of such a usage. We then tested the model with two kinds of novel verbs: one with semantic primitives [*act,move*] (associated with agentive intransitives like *come* and *go*), and one with semantic primitives [*move,direction,vertical*] (like the Theme-assigning verb *fall*). In response to the former (*go*-type) input, the model still predicts a semantic profile very similar to the one shown in the right box of Figure 3. In contrast, for the latter (*fall*-type) input, the predicted semantic profile contains {*artifact, artefact, whole, whole thing, unit*} in addition to the Agent-like properties, yielding a profile that overlaps that of the transitive object, shown in the middle box of Figure 3.

This experiment is crucial in showing that the model does not simply associate a single semantic profile with a particular argument position. If this were the case, the model would never be able to distinguish, e.g., transitive verbs that assign Agent and Theme, from those that assign Experiencer and Stimulus. This experiment demonstrates that the model forms a complex association among a syntactic pattern, an argument position, and the semantic primitives of the verb, allowing it to make a distinction between different roles assigned to the same position in the same syntactic pattern.

Verb-Based vs. General Semantic Profiles

Tomasello (2000) (among others) has proposed that children initially learn verb-specific roles such as 'hitter' and 'hittee,' and only later move to more general roles. Moreover, Shayan (2006) shows that general notions like Agent and Patient develop over time. Our model illustrates how such role generalization might come about. Although the semantic profiles of our model reflect the general properties that a particular role-bearing argument must have, they are formed from input that contains only argument properties for specific verb usages. The generalization occurs as more and more semantic properties are associated with an argument position, and only the most general ones are seen sufficiently frequently to have high probability.

We tracked the generalization process for each semantic profile, to see how it moves from a verb-based profile to a more general one. Figure 4 (left box) shows the semantic profile for the argument in the object position right after the first transitive usage. In this particular simulation, the first transitive verb in the corpus is *eat*, and its second argument in that input pair is *pie*. The semantic profile thus reflects the properties of a pie, and not the general properties of that argument position. The profile becomes more general after processing 50 and 100 input pairs, shown in the middle and right boxes of Figure 4, respectively. (Recall that Figure 3 shows a profile for transitive object after 200 inputs.)

To observe the trend of moving from a more specific to a more general semantic profile for each argument posi-

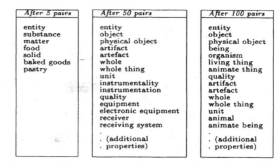

Figure 4: The evolution of the transitive object role.

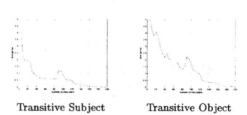

Transitive Subject   Transitive Object

Figure 5: Learning curves for semantic profiles. The x-axis is time (#inputs), and the y-axis is divergence from the profile that the model eventually converges to.

tion, we used relative entropy to measure the divergence between the semantic profile for an argument position at a given point in learning, and the profile for that position that the model eventually converges to at the end of each simulation.[5] We measured the profile divergence for subject and object positions of a transitive construction after every 5 input pairs over a total of 200 pairs, averaged over 5 simulations. Figure 5 shows that the profile for the subject position (i.e., the Agent) is learned faster than the profile for the object position (i.e., the Theme), which is a much less constrained role. The curves show that the model stabilizes on the final profiles at around 150 input pairs, when receiving more inputs ceases to make any significant difference in the profiles.

Using Semantic Profiles in Comprehension

Semantic roles are helpful in on-line ambiguity resolution, by guiding adults to the interpretation that best matches the role expectations of a verb for a given position (e.g., Trueswell et al., 1994). Nation et al. (2003) have shown that young children also draw on verb-specific biases in on-line argument interpretation.[6] Here we demonstrate the ability of our model to use its acquired semantic profiles to predict the best interpretation of an ambiguous partial input.

We consider cases using the verb *give*, in which an utterance beginning *you give ⟨noun⟩* can continue with

---

[5] $RelativeEntropy(P||Q) = \sum_i P(i) \log \frac{P(i)}{Q(i)}$, where P and Q are probability distributions.

[6] This work complements that of Fisher (1996) and others, who demonstrate that children use associations between argument properties and syntactic positions to choose the interpretation of an unknown verb in a full sentence.

either a second object (*you give ⟨noun⟩ something*) or a prepositional phrase (*you give ⟨noun⟩ to someone*). In the first case, ⟨noun⟩ is the Recipient of the action, and in the second case, it is the Theme (the thing given). We vary ⟨noun⟩ to be either *her*, which is a likely Recipient, or *this*, which is a likely Theme. We then observe in each case which interpretation our model prefers.

We set up the experiment as one where we compare the probability of the following two input pairs:

her as Recipient	$\mathbf{Give}_{[cause,possess]}(\mathrm{YOU}, \mathrm{X}, \mathrm{HER})$ *you give her x*
her as Theme	$\mathbf{Give}_{[cause,possess]}(\mathrm{YOU}, \mathrm{HER}, \mathrm{X})$ *you give her x*

We give each of these inputs to the model, have it extract the corresponding frame F, and then have it calculate $match\_score(F) = \max_k P(k)P(F|k)$, from the prediction model. The $match\_score$ corresponds to how well the model thinks the given input pair matches an existing construction. Having a higher $match\_score$ for the first pair means that the model has recognized *her* as the Recipient, while a higher score for the second pair means that the model has recognized *her* as the Theme.

We also compared analogous inputs pairs, using *this* instead of *her*. Since the only difference in these two sets of inputs is the use of *her* vs. *this*, differences in interpretation of the first object noun (as Recipient or Theme) depend only on the match of the noun's semantic properties to the semantic profiles of that argument position.

Table 1 shows the results after processing 20 and 200 input pairs, averaged over 5 simulations; a higher number (lower absolute value) indicates the preferred interpretation. After processing 20 pairs, the model displays a strong preference towards treating the first object as the Theme, for both *her* and *this*. This occurs because *give* is the only verb in our lexicon that appears in a ditransitive (Recipient-first) construction, whereas many high frequency verbs (e.g., *put* and *get*) appear in the competing (Theme-first) prepositional construction. Thus, at the early stages of learning, the ditransitive construction is relatively weak. However, after processing 200 input pairs, the model shows a preference for the "correct" interpretation in both cases. (The difference between the two frames for *you gave this x* is small, but consistently indicates a Theme preference across all simulations.)

The model is thus able to use its learned associations between semantic properties and argument positions to appropriately guide interpretation of an ambiguity. These results predict that very early on, children (like our model) would experience some difficulty in this type of task, when drawing on the knowledge of a less commonly observed construction.

Conclusions

We have shown that our Bayesian model for early verb learning, extended to include sets of semantic properties for arguments, can acquire associations between those properties, the syntactic positions of the arguments, and the semantic primitives of verbs. These probabilistic associations enable the model to learn general conceptions of roles, based only on exposure to individual verb us-

Table 1: log($match\_score$) for Recipient-first and Theme-first frames after processing 20 and 200 input pairs.

Utterance	20 Pairs		200 Pairs	
	Recipient	Theme	Recipient	Theme
You gave her x	-23.08	-20.47	-15.06	-19.89
You gave this x	-24.23	-20.78	-16.68	-16.55

ages, and without requiring explicit labelling of the roles in the input. Because of the model's Bayesian formulation, the roles naturally metamorphose from verb-specific to highly general properties. The acquired role properties are a good intuitive match to the expected properties of various roles, and are useful in guiding comprehension in the model to the most likely interpretation in the face of ambiguity.

References

Alishahi, A. and Stevenson, S. (2005a). The acquisition and use of argument structure constructions: A Bayesian model. In *Proc. of the 2nd Wkshp on Psycho-computational Models of Human Lang. Acqn.*, pages 82–90.

Alishahi, A. and Stevenson, S. (2005b). A probabilistic model of early argument structure acquisition. In *Proceedings of the 27th Annual Conf. of the Cognitive Science Society*.

Allen, J. (1997). Probabilistic constraints in acquisition. In Sorace, A., Heycock, C., and Shillcock, R., editors, *Proceedings of the GALA97 Conference*, pages 300–305.

Anderson, J. R. (1991). The adaptive nature of human categorization. *Psychological Review*, 98(3):409–429.

Chang, N. (2004). A computational model of comprehension-based construction acquisition. Child Lang. Res. Forum.

Clark, S. and Weir, D. (2002). Class-based probability estimation using a semantic hierarchy. *Computational Linguistics*, 28(2):187–206.

Dowty, D. (1991). Thematic proto-roles and argument selection. *Language*, 67(3):547–619.

Fisher, C. (1996). Structural limits on verb mapping: The role of analogy in children's interpretations of sentences. *Cognitive Psychology*, 31(1):41–81.

Kako, E. (2006). Thematic role properties of subjects and objects. *Cognition*, 101:1–42.

Lieven, E. V. M., Pine, J. M., and Baldwin, G. (1997). Lexically-based learning and early grammatical development. *Journal of Child Language*, 24:187–219.

MacWhinney, B. (1995). *The CHILDES project: Tools for analyzing talk*. Lawrence Erlbaum.

McClelland, J. L. and Kawamoto, A. H. (1986). *Mechanisms of sentence processing: assigning roles to constituents of sentences*, pages 272–325. MIT Press.

Miller, G. (1990). Wordnet: An on-line lexical database. *International Journal of Lexicography*, 17(3).

Nation, K., Marshall, C. M., and Altmann, G. T. M. (2003). Investigating individual differences in children's real-time sentence comprehension using language-mediated eye movements. *J. of Exp. Child Psych.*, 86:314–329.

Pinker, S. (1989). *Learnability and Cognition*. MIT Press.

Resnik, P. (1996). Selectional constraints: An information-theoretic model and its computational realization. *Cognition*, 61:127–199.

Shayan, S. (2006). How do children learn Agent and Patient roles? Submitted.

Tomasello, M. (2000). Do young children have adult syntactic competence? *Cognition*, 74:209–253.

Trueswell, J. C., Tanenhaus, M. K., and Garnsey, S. M. (1994). Semantic influences on parsing: Use of thematic role information in syntactic ambiguity resolution. *Journal of Memory and Language*, 33(3):285–318.

"Is There Any Coffee Left, Boss?" Face and Utility Concerns in the Interpretation of Ambiguous Questions/Requests

Virginie Demeure and Jean-François Bonnefon and Éric Raufaste
{demeure, bonnefon, raufaste}@univ-tlse2.fr
Université de Toulouse (CLLE; CNRS, UTM, EPHE)
5 allées Antonio Machado 31058 Toulouse cedex 9, FRANCE

Abstract

Requests are often made in an indirect manner, and phrased in such a way that they can also be construed as questions. E.g., the sentence "Is there any coffee left?" can be construed either as a question about coffee or as a request for coffee. This paper offers a combined test of some key predictions of two approaches to the disambiguation of question/request statements: (a) The face management approach, which gives a prominent role to variables such as status and potential face-loss; (b) and the utilitarian relevance approach, which gives a prominent role to the goals pursued by the speaker at the time she issued the statement. Ambiguous questions/requests statements provide a natural test-bed for the latter approach in particular. A board game paradigm is developed to allow for a clean, orthogonal manipulation of all variables. Results wholly support the utilitarian relevance approach and offer new perspectives on the face-management approach.

All of us, everyday, make all sorts of requests—but most of us often choose to make them indirectly. Rather than straightforwardly telling a colleague "Give me another cup of coffee," we tend to ask "Is there any coffee left?" The issue then arises of how people around us decide whether we simply need an answer to that question, or whether we do want a cup of coffee. In the first part of this article, we review the different answers to that question that have been put forward to date, and the data that support them. Alongside to the politeness-based, face management answer, we outline two relevance-based answers (i.e., post-Gricean, and utilitarian variants). We note that data are scarce about the post-Gricean variant, and almost nonexistent about the utilitarian variant.

We then report two experiments using a board game paradigm, which allows us to test in combination some untested key predictions of the utilitarian and face-management approaches. More precisely, when a statement can be construed either as a direct question or an indirect request, these approaches expect that: (a) The question interpretation is comparatively more frequent when the answer to that question would be highly useful to the speaker; (b) The request interpretation is comparatively more frequent when the fulfilment of that request would be highly useful to the speaker; (c) The request interpretation is comparatively more frequent when the listener's status is higher than the speaker's status; and (d) The request interpretation is comparatively more frequent when the listener has a special distaste for impositions.

Face Management

The face-management account of indirect requests derives from Brown and Levinson's (1978/1987) Politeness Theory, which posits that indirectness is a politeness strategy, and indeed the most polite communicative strategy of all. Requests threaten what Brown and Levinson (1978/1987) call the *negative face* of the listener, that is, the want of every competent adult member of a society that his actions be unimpeded by others (see also Goffman, 1967). Boldly asking the listener "Give me another cup of coffee" implies an imposition onto him,[1] which threatens his negative face. In contrast, using an indirect form such as "Is there any coffee left?" reduces this imposition by leaving it to the listener to interpret the sentence as a question or as a request. The listener is then free to answer the direct question rather than to fulfill the indirect request.

This conception of indirectness as politeness has straightforward consequences for the interpretation of ambiguous statements: The knowledge that speakers generally use indirectness to prevent a potential face-loss should orient the listener towards the most face-threatening interpretation of an ambiguous statement (Holtgraves, 1998, 1999; Holtgraves & Yang, 1990, 1992; Slugoski, 1995).

This suggests that listeners, when confronted with an ambiguous statement, select the interpretation that is the most threatening for their own face. Now, requests usually threaten the negative face of a listener, while questions do not (or, at least, less so). Thus, all other things being equal, listeners should show some tendency to interpret a statement like "Is there any coffee left?" as an indirect request rather than a direct question. Still, contextual factors might complicate this simple scheme. In particular, some aspects of the situation might increase the extent to which a request would be face-threatening, as compared to a question. For example, consider the situation where the listener has greater power/status than the speaker, compared to the situation where speaker and listener are of equal social status. According to Brown and Levinson (1978/1987), the need for politeness is greater, all other things being equal, when the listener has greater power than the speaker. Consequently, ambiguous statements of low-

---

[1] For clarity of exposition, we will use the feminine for the speaker and the masculine for the listener throughout this article, rather than alternate the two genders.

status speaker should be interpreted as indirect requests when they are addressed to high-status listeners, more so than when they are addressed to low-status listeners. We will return to this prediction after we have introduced the Relevance accounts of the interpretation of indirect requests.

Relevance

The Post-Gricean Relevance Theory

The Gricean approach to the interpretation of indirect requests (Grice, 1975) has not been conclusively supported, most notably the crucial assumption that the indirect interpretation of a statement will only be constructed when the literal interpretation has been judged unsatisfactory (Gibbs, 1983; Holtgraves, 1999). This approach has been reconsidered in the post-Gricean approach of Sperber and Wilson (1986/1995), which collapses the various aspects of the Cooperative Principle into one central principle of Relevance: All statements come with a presumption of optimal relevance, in that sense that the speaker is assumed to have maximized the cognitive effects of her statement on the listener, while minimizing the cognitive effort needed to process the message. Interpreting a statement then amounts to following a path of least effort, starting with the least demanding interpretation, and stopping as soon as the cognitive effects of that interpretation are deemed sufficient.

While this framework has been successfully applied to a variety of communicative situations, it does not as easily apply to the problem of question/request disambiguation. Note that the assessment of cognitive effects is quite simple in the case of assertions. Cognitive effects have been defined, e.g., as "a genuine improvement in knowledge" (Wilson & Sperber, 2002, p. 602). Thus, the cognitive effects of an assertion can be assessed by considering how much information it brings to the listener's attention, to what extent it reduce his uncertainty about the world, etc. In that sense, while it would be easy to assess the cognitive effect of a *reply,* it is quite difficult to assess the cognitive effects of a *question.*

Likewise, to characterize a speaker's request only in terms of what information it brings to the attention of the listener seems to miss the point. What seems crucial in the interpretation of a request is how it relates to the interests of the speaker, rather than to the information state of the listener. Relevance Theory has recently evolved on this problematic point. In their new version of the principle of optimal relevance, Henst and Sperber (2004) specify that the listener will take into account the preferences of the speaker, and keep in mind that the speaker certainly does not mean something that would go against her preferences.

This modification to Relevance Theory introduces the idea that the goals or preferences of the speaker can passively *eliminate* some possible interpretations of her statement. Taking one step further, we might expect that the goals and preferences of the speaker will actively *drive* the interpretation of her statement. This idea is at the core of the utilitarian reformulations of relevance.

The Utilitarian Reformulations

Utilitarian reformulations of the notion of relevance have independently emerged in recent years. What they have in common is to define the relevance of a statement in relation to the goals that the speaker is pursuing, more than to its epistemic effects on the listener. The central idea here is that the listener will attend to the goals of the speaker, and select the interpretation of her statement that is the most likely to help her achieve these goals.

This idea has been put forward in several fields by a number of authors. It is at the core of the Conversational Action Planning model of Hilton, Kemmelmeier, and Bonnefon (2005). It forms the basis of the semantics of deontic rules defined in Over, Manktelow, and Hadjichristidis (2004). It is the justification for the "utilitarian heuristic" that Raufaste, Longin, and Bonnefon (in press) have argued to be at work in the interpretation of a variety of speech acts. And finally, it has been formalized by Rooy (2001) in a theory of communicative relevance inspired by game theory.

According to Rooy (2001), to communicate is to attempt to influence others, and each statement is a move towards achieving the speaker's goals. The "relevance" of an interpretation is defined here as the expected utility for the speaker that her statement is interpreted that way. From that perspective, it becomes easy to compare the relevance of the two possible interpretations of a question/request statement such as "Is there any coffee left?" The relevance of the question interpretation is the average (epistemic) utility for the speaker of the different answers to that question, and the relevance of the request interpretation is the average utility of the actions the listener may take in response. The interpretation with the greater relevance, defined that way, is then selected.

Objectives

Our first objective is to test the key predictions of the utilitarian approach to the interpretation of ambiguous question/request statements. More precisely: (a) The question interpretation is comparatively more frequent when the answer to that question would be highly useful to the speaker; and (b) The request interpretation is comparatively more frequent when the fulfilment of that request would be highly useful to the speaker.

Testing these two predictions requires a systematic and orthogonal manipulation of the speaker's utilities. To that end, we developed a board game paradigm that allows a rigorously controlled manipulation of these two variables. This paradigm opens up a number of experimental possibilities, and its development is indeed a contribution of its own.

Furthermore, we wish to investigate an untested prediction of the face-management approach: The request interpretation is comparatively more frequent when the listener has higher status than the speaker. Our board game paradigm will allow us to manipulate the status of the speaker and the listener, orthogonally to the manipulation of the speaker's utilities.

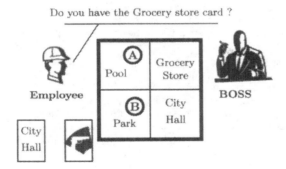

Do you have the Grocery store card ?

Employee   BOSS

Figure 1: Example of a game situation. Partner status is *higher*, utility of the swap is *low*, and utility of the information is *low*.

Experiment 1

Methods

Participants were 60 volunteer students at the University of Toulouse le Mirail (half men, half women, all in their early 20s). Participants read the rules of a simple board game, which provided a cover story for the experiment. They were told to imagine that this game was played at a corporate seminar, to foster interactions between employees of a firm.

> **Rules of the game.** The board shows four locations in a fictitious city, and the goal of the game is to take control of 3 of these 4 locations. The game is played by two teams of two male players.[2] Each player has two cards in hand, hidden from all other players. The whole deck includes 17 cards: 8 cards bearing the names of the locations (2 cards for each location); 8 gun cards; and one police card. To capture (or recapture) a location, a player must play simultaneously a gun card and the card of this location. The police card is used to definitively block a location: once this card is put on an uncontrolled location, this location cannot be captured for the rest of the game. When it is the turn of a player to play, he first has an opportunity to ask his partner whether he has a given card in hand, or whether he is willing to exchange a given card from his hand for one of the active player's cards. Once the information or the card is obtained, the player can choose to play or pass.

Once they had familiarized themselves with the rules of the game by studying an example, participants were presented with 8 game situations, according to a $2 \times 2 \times 2$ within-subject design (the entire procedure lasted for some 15 minutes). In all situations, a player of Team A (an employee) was asking his partner: "Do you have the grocery store card?" The board always showed that Team A was in control of the Park, that Team B was in control of the Swimming Pool, and that neither team was in control of the Grocery Store or the City Hall (see Figure 1).

---

[2]For this reason, we will not use the feminine for the speaker in this experimental section.

The three independent variables were the *Partner Status* (higher vs. equal), the *Utility of the Swap* (high vs. low), and the *Utility of the Information* (high vs. low). Partner status was higher when the partner was identified as a boss, equal when the partner was identified as another employee. Utility of the swap was high when the player could not capture any location with his current cards, but would be able to capture the Grocery Store if he could obtain this card. It was low if the player could already capture a location with his current cards. Utility of the information was low if knowing the answer to his question was irrelevant to the player's decision about which action to take. It was high when knowing the answer to his question could help decide which action the player should take.

Utility of the swap and of the information were manipulated by changing the cards of the active player:

1. **City Hall & Gun.** With these cards, the player can already capture a location: *utility of the swap is low*. Furthermore, knowing whether the partner is in possession of the Grocery Store card bears no consequence on the decision what to do: *utility of the information is low*.

2. **Gun & Gun.** Player cannot capture a location, but could do so by exchanging a Gun card for a Grocery Store card: *utility of the swap is high*. Again, knowing whether the partner is in possession of the Grocery Store card bears no consequence on the decision what to do: *utility of the information is low*.

3. **Grocery Store & Gun.** Player can already capture the Grocery Store: *utility of the swap is low*. On the contrary, knowing whether the partner has the second Grocery Store card from the deck can help to decide whether to capture this location now, as there would then be no risk that it will be recaptured by the other team: *utility of the information is high*.

4. **Police & Gun.** Player cannot capture a location, but could do so by exchanging the Police card for a Grocery Store card: *utility of the swap is high*. However, the mere knowledge that partner does not have the grocery store card can help to make a decision, namely, to use the police card to block the Grocery Store: *utility of the information is high*.

Once they had considered a game situation, participants judged whether the player was asking for a swap (a request) or simply asking for information (a question). They answered the question *According to you, what does this player want?* by checking one of 5 possible response options: I am sure he wants to swap (coded -2), He probably wants to swap, more so than he wants the information (-1), I cannot make up my mind (0), He probably wants the information, more so than he wants to swap ($+1$), I am sure he wants the information ($+2$).

Manipulation check

An independent manipulation check was conducted on 15 students, who judged for each of the four card combi-

Table 1: Interpretation of the statement in Experiment 1. Negative scores indicate interpretation as a request, positive scores indicate interpretation as a question.

	Partner status	
	Equal	Higher
Utility of information: Low		
Utility of swap: Low	+0.3 (1.5)	+0.6 (1.3)
Utility of swap: High	−1.1 (1.3)	−0.8 (1.6)
Utility of information: High		
Utility of swap: Low	+0.8 (1.2)	+1.0 (1.2)
Utility of swap: High	−0.6 (1.5)	−0.3 (1.5)

nations whether it was useful, interesting, and advantageous to the speaker to swap, or rather to obtain the information without swapping. Judgements were expressed on three separate 5-point scales. A 2 × 2 within-group analysis of variance was conducted on the average score across the three scales. The manipulation had the expected effect, $F(1, 14) = 8.1$, $p < .05$ for the manipulation of utility of swap; and $F(1, 14) = 6.1$, $p < .05$ for the manipulation of utility of information.

Results and Discussion

Results were analyzed by means of a 2 × 2 × 2 within-group analysis of variance. Table 1 displays the average answers of participants for each combination of the three manipulated factors. The analysis of variance revealed three main effects and no detectable interaction effect. (The analysis did not detect any gender effect.)

The key predictions of the utilitarian approach are well supported by the data. Participants tended to choose the interpretation that served the speaker best. High utility of the swap encouraged participants to interpret the statement as a request, $F(1, 59) = 47.9$, $p < .001$, $\eta^2 = .35$ (we report *semi partial* η^2, which are more appropriate and more conservative when using within-subject ANOVA). Average interpretation was −0.7 ($SD=1.0$) when utility of the swap was high, and +0.7 ($SD=0.8$) when utility of the swap was low. High utility of the information encouraged participants to interpret the statement as a question, $F(1, 59) = 10.0$, $p = .002$, $\eta^2 = .08$. Average interpretation was +0.2 ($SD=0.7$) when utility of the information was high, and only −0.3 ($SD=0.8$) when utility of the information was low. In plain contradiction with the face management prediction, higher partner status encouraged participants to interpret the statement as a question, $F(1, 59) = 4.6$, $p < .05$, $\eta^2 = .03$. Average interpretation was +0.1 ($SD=0.7$) when the partner was of higher status, and only −0.2 ($SD=0.7$) when the partner was of equal status.

Two explanations might be advanced for this surprising result. First, it might be that when the partner is of higher status, a request would be too face-threatening, even if it was made indirectly. As a consequence, participants would not find it conceivable that the speaker made a request, indirectly or otherwise.

Second, it might be that lower-status speaker are perceived as generally more likely to ask questions to their superiors, rather than make requests, and that this base-rate was factored in the judgments of participants. Indeed, Holtgraves (1994) found that the request interpretation was more frequent when the *speaker* was of higher status, and provided a similar base rate explanation for this effect.

Experiment 2 was designed to test these two explanations. In Experiment 2, we manipulated the face-threat to the listener by manipulating his personality orthogonally to his status. Consider the case of a high-status listener who is also a control-freak known to have a special distaste for impositions. According to the first explanation, an ambiguous question/request statement addressed to this listener would be extremely unlikely to be interpreted as a request: If the status of this listener already renders a request too face-threatening, his personality only makes things worse. Now, according to the second explanation, the status of the listener and his personality will have *opposing* influences: The status, through a base-rate effect, encourages a question interpretation; but the personality, in line with the face-management approach, encourages a request interpretation. Indeed, in order to make a request to someone who dislikes receiving orders, one has to be especially polite, because the face of one who dislikes directives is especially threatened by requests, compared with one who does not mind receiving directives. Consequently, ambiguous statements should be more likely to be interpreted as indirect requests when addressed to a listener with a special distaste for impositions.

Experiment 2

Method

Participants were 60 volunteer students at the Champollion University of Albi. They were 17 men and 43 women, all native French speakers, whose ages ranged from 18 to 27 (mean = 20.3, $SD = 2.1$).

Material and procedure were almost the same as in Experiment 1. The board, the rules of the game, and the statement under consideration did not change. Participants were presented with 8 game situations, according to a 2 × 2 × 2 full factorial design. The *Partner Status* (higher vs. equal) and *Partner Personality* (rigid vs. flexible) were visually and verbally manipulated, by presenting participants with a cartoon depicting the partner, together with a description of this partner's status and personality (see Figure 2).

Finally, as a control, two different game situations were used in the experiment. In the first one, both the utility of the swap and of the information were high (i.e., the active player's cards were Police and Gun); in the second one, both the utility of the swap and of the information were low (i.e., cards were City Hall and Gun). Just as in Experiment 1, after participants had considered each game situation, they judged whether the player was requesting a swap or simply asking for information.

Figure 2: Cartoons and descriptions used in Experiment 2 to manipulate the Partner Personality variable. From left to right: flexible employee, rigid employee, flexible boss and rigid boss (descriptions are translated from French).

An open-minded **employee**, who listens to others, cares about their opinions and ideas.

A very touchy **employee** who dislikes receiving orders. He likes to be in control and to impose his point of view.

An open-minded **boss**, who listens to others, cares about their opinions and ideas.

A very touchy **boss** who dislikes receiving orders. He likes to be in control and to impose his point of view.

Manipulation check

A manipulation check was independently conducted on 23 other students, who were told about the rules of the game and judged for each of the game partner depicted in Figure 2, on six separate 4-point scales, whether this person would find a request for a swap displeasing, hurtful, and offensive; and whether this person would find a question about his cards displeasing, hurtful, and offensive. An index of face-threat was computed by averaging the three ratings for displeasure, hurtfulness, and offensiveness. Both for questions and for requests, this index was higher when partner status was higher ($F(1,22) = 21.2$, $p < .01$); and it was higher when partner had a rigid personality ($F(1,22) = 49.3$, $p < .01$). No other effect was detected.

Results and Discussion

Results were analyzed by means of a $2 \times 2 \times 2$ within-group analysis of variance. Table 2 displays the average answers of participants for each combination of the three manipulated factors. The analysis of variance revealed three main effects and no detectable interaction effect. (The analysis did not detect any gender effect.)

In line with the face management approach (and the base-rate explanation of the effect of status), rigid partner personality encouraged participants to interpret the statement as a request, $F(1,59) = 8.62$, $p = .005$, $\eta^2 = .08$. Average interpretation was $+0.2$ ($SD=0.6$) when partner was flexible, and only -0.3 ($SD=0.8$) when partner was rigid. Conversely, and just as in Experiment 1, higher partner status encouraged participants to interpret the statement as a question, $F(1,59) = 3.7$, $p = .058$ $\eta^2 = .03$. Average interpretation was 0.0 ($SD=0.7$) when partner was of higher status, and only -0.2 ($SD=0.6$) when partner was of equal status. Finally, participants tended to interpret the statement as a request when both the utilities of the swap and of the information were high, $F(1,59) = 16.7$, $p < .001$, $\eta^2 = .17$. Average interpretation was $+0.3$ ($SD=1.0$) when both utilities were low, and -0.5 ($SD=0.7$) when

Table 2: Interpretation of the statement in Experiment 2. Negative scores indicate interpretation as a request, positive scores indicate interpretation as a question.

	Partner status	
	Equal	Higher
Utilities in Conflict: Low		
Flexible Partner	+0.3 (1.3)	+0.6 (1.3)
Rigid Partner	+0.1 (1.5)	+0.3 (1.5)
Utilities in Conflict: High		
Flexible Partner	−0.3 (1.4)	−0.0 (1.3)
Rigid Partner	−0.9 (1.2)	−0.8 (1.2)

both utilities were high.

We do not wish to extrapolate too much from the unexpected effect of the values of utility in conflict. More likely than not, this effect is simply due to some noise in the manipulation of the utility (e.g., the useless request might be perceived as even less useful than the useless question.)

Conclusion

The interpretation of indirect statements in general, and of ambiguous question/answer in particular, is a notoriously difficult problem. In two experiments, we have found support for key untested predictions of the utilitarian and face-management approaches.

1. In line with the utilitarian reformulation of relevance, the question interpretation is comparatively more frequent when the answer to that question would be highly useful to the speaker

2. In line with the utilitarian reformulation of relevance, the request interpretation is comparatively more frequent when the fulfilment of that request would be highly useful to the speaker;

3. In line with the face-management approach, the request interpretation is comparatively more frequent when the listener has a special distaste for impositions;

4. Unexpectedly to the face management approach, but in line with previous findings (Holtgraves, 1994), the question interpretation is more frequent when the listener has higher status than the speaker.

As both the face management approach and the utilitarian approach were shown in this paper to contribute decisively to the issue of ambiguous question/request statements, a natural next step would be to combine these two approaches into an integrated account. This integration was recently taken up by Rooy (2003) at the theoretical level—but everything has still to be done at the experimental level.

One possibility in particular is to integrate politeness considerations in the computation of the expected utility of a statement. Whilst it might be useful for the speaker that the listener complies with her request, the probability of the listener doing so might decrease in the absence of a politeness strategy. Put bluntly, people do not comply to rude requests. As a consequence, the *expected utility of a request interpretation* (i.e., the utility of the request being fulfilled, multiplied by the probability that the listener will fulfill the request) should be a function of the politeness strategy deployed by the speaker, and of its appropriateness to the context and to the listener.

References

Brown, P., & Levinson, S. C. (1987). *Politeness: Some universals in language usage.* Cambridge: Cambridge University Press. (Original work published 1978)

Gibbs, R. (1983). Do people always process the literal meaning of indirect requests? *Journal of Experimental Psychology: Learning, Memory, and Cognition, 9*(3), 524–533.

Goffman, E. (1967). *Interaction ritual: essays on face to face behavior.* Garden City, New York.

Grice, H. (1975). Logic and conversation. In P. Cole & J. Morgan (Eds.), *Syntax and semantics 3: Speech acts* (pp. 41–58). New York: Academic Press.

Henst, J.-B. Van der, & Sperber, D. (2004). Testing the principle of relevance. In I. Noveck & D. Sperber (Eds.), *Experimental pragmatics* (pp. 229–280). Basingstoke: Palgrave Macmillan.

Hilton, D. J., Kemmelmeier, M., & Bonnefon, J. F. (2005). Putting ifs to work: Goal-based relevance in conversational action planning. *Journal of Experimental Psychology: General, 135,* 388–405.

Holtgraves, T. (1994). Communication in context: effects of speaker status on the comprehension of indirect requests. *Journal of Experimental Psychology: Learning, Memory, and Cognition, 20*(5), 1205-1218.

Holtgraves, T. (1998). Interpreting indirect replies. *Cognitive Psychology, 37*(1), 1-27.

Holtgraves, T. (1999). Comprehending indirect replies: When and how are their conveyed meaning activated? *Journal of Memory and Language, 41,* 519–540.

Holtgraves, T., & Yang, J. (1990). Politeness as universal: Cross-cultural perceptions of request strategies and inferences based on their use. *Journal of Personality and Social Psychology, 59*(4), 719–729.

Holtgraves, T., & Yang, J. (1992). Interpersonal underpinnings of request strategies: General principles and differences due to culture and gender. *Journal of Personality and Social Psychology, 62*(2), 246–256.

Over, D., Manktelow, K., & Hadjichristidis, C. (2004). Condition for the acceptance of deontic conditionals. *Canadian Journal of Experimental Psychology, 52*(2), 96–105.

Raufaste, E., Longin, D., & Bonnefon, J. (in press). Utilitarisme pragmatique et reconnaissance d'intention dans les actes de langage indirects. *Psychologie de l'Interaction.*

Rooy, R. van. (2001). Relevance of communicative acts. In J. van Benthem (Ed.), *Proceedings of the 8th conference on theoretical aspects of rationality and knowledge (TARK-2001)* (pp. 83–96). Los Altos: Morgan Kaufmann.

Rooy, R. van. (2003). Being polite is a handicap: towards a game theoretical analysis of polite linguistic behavior. In J. Y. Halpern & M. Tennenholtz (Eds.), *Proceedings of the 9th conference on theoretical aspects of rationality and knowledge (TARK-2003)* (pp. 45–58). New York: ACM Press.

Slugoski, B. (1995). Mindless processing of requests? don't ask twice. *British Journal of Social Psychology, 34,* 335–350.

Sperber, D., & Wilson, D. (1995). *Relevance: Communication and cognition.* Oxford: Blackwell. (Original work published 1986)

Wilson, D., & Sperber, D. (2002). Truthfulness and relevance. *Mind, 111*(443), 583–632.

Time Flew By: Reading about Movement of Different Speeds Distorts People's Perceptions of Time

Louise Connell (louise.connell@manchester.ac.uk)
School of Psychological Sciences, University of Manchester, Oxford Road, Manchester M13 9PL, UK

Lucy Rayne (lucy.rayne@northumbria.ac.uk)
Dermot Lynott (dermot.lynott@northumbria.ac.uk)
Cognition & Communication Research Centre, Division of Psychology, Northumbria University
Newcastle upon Tyne NE1 8ST, UK

Abstract

How humans conceive of abstract domains such as time is a fundamental question in the cognitive sciences. Many theorists hold that we ground the abstract in the concrete, and understand time through the domain of space. Just as we can move through time quickly or slowly, we can move through space quickly or slowly: this study aims to examine to what extent our perception of time is dependent on space. Participants read a story that described slow movement (e.g., *strolled*), fast movement (e.g., *raced*) or movement without reference to speed (e.g., *travelled*) and were asked to provide a prospective time estimation of how long they had spent reading. Estimated reading times for fast stories were significantly shorter than those for neutral and slow stories. This finding indicates that even low-level judgements of temporal duration depend on spatial mappings, and suggesting that people simulate the attentional allocation of the protagonist during language comprehension.

Introduction

"Not only do we measure time by movement, but movement by time, because they define each other" (Aristotle, *Physics* IV:12).

A major question that has interested thinkers and philosophers for millennia is how we as humans conceive of the abstract. How do we think about things as diverse and intangible as postmodernism, metaphor, and integral calculus? How do we even understand a fundamental abstract domain such as time? Many researchers have suggested that abstract domains are grounded to some extent in more familiar concrete domains that we develop through sensorimotor experience (e.g., Barsalou & Wiemer-Hastings, 2005; Clarke, 1973; Gibbs, 1994; Lakoff & Johnson, 1999). Time, for example, can be understood through the domain of space, as reflected in our use of language: speakers of English may talk of looking *forward* to a party for a *long* time, or of regrets *after* partying *through* the night.

Moving Through Time and Space

We can move through time as we move through space, and this ego-moving perspective is the default view of time for approximately half the population (Gentner & Imai, 1992; McGlone & Harding, 1998), with the other half adopting the time-moving perspective (where time flows past us while we stand still).

Such perspectives on time are not fixed, however. Consciously moving through physical space influences how people think about time. When asked the question "Next Wednesday's meeting has been moved forward two days. What day is the meeting now that it has been rescheduled?", there are two possible responses: the ego-moving perspective (where you and the meeting move through time to Friday) and the time-moving perspective (where time and the meeting moves towards you to Monday). In normal circumstances, these responses are split around 50:50 (Gentner & Imai, 1992; McGlone & Harding, 1998). Ask the same question of people starting or ending a train journey, or travelling through an airport, and more respondents tend to adopt the ego-moving "Friday" perspective (Boroditsky & Ramscar, 2002). Indeed, one's own physical movement is not necessary to alter views of time: Boroditsky and Ramscar also found that ego-moving responses increased when people were betting on horseraces and were therefore focussed on the horses' forward movement.

There is also evidence to suggest that the effect of spatial movement on time is not limited to real, physical movement but also extends to imagined movement. The "Wednesday's meeting" paradigm was also used by Matlock, Ramscar and Boroditsky (2005), who first asked participants to draw a picture of either a static spatial description (e.g., "The highway is next to the coast") or a fictive motion description of the same scene (e.g., "The highway runs along the coast"). Matlock et al. found that fictive motion, where verbs of motion are used but no movement actually takes place (i.e., the highway does not literally run), influenced people's view of time in the same way as actual physical movement. Most people adopted the ego-moving perspective of time after reading about ego-moving fictive motion: imagining a highway "running" through space made people more likely to think of themselves as moving through time. This finding is consistent with other work showing that people mentally simulate movement during language comprehension (Zwaan et al., 2004), and represent spatial information from the perspective of the protagonist (Bryant, Tversky & Franklin, 1992; Zwaan & Radvansky, 1998).

Prospective Time Estimation

The research discussed above shows that our abstract thinking about time leans on our thinking about space.

However, the task of rescheduling a future meeting is relatively high-level. It could be argued that a temporal judgement about the movement of hypothetical events is relatively dependent on mapping to concrete space and thus is quite susceptible to manipulations of spatial movement. Does the same dependency exist for lower-level temporal judgements?

One such low-level temporal judgement is prospective time estimation, where people are aware in advance that they must make explicit judgements as to how much time they believe has elapsed. These judgements are influenced by the attentional demands of the concurrent task: the more difficult the required task, the less attention is available to monitor temporal information and the shorter the perceived duration (see Block & Zakay, 1997, for review). For example, sorting a deck of cards according to three criteria (a difficult task) seemed to take less time than sorting the deck according to a single criterion (a simple task), even when participants were interrupted after the same length of time (Hicks, Miller & Kinsbourne, 1976). Similarly, interesting stories engage our attention, and time estimates for listening to interesting stories were correspondingly shorter than those for dull stories of equivalent length (Hawkins & Tedford, 1976).

The Current Study

If we move through time as we move through space, then is our perception of temporal progress dependent on our representation of spatial progress? Just as time can seem to pass quickly or slowly, we can cover spatial distance quickly or slowly. Our thinking about time and space are inextricably interlinked through our thinking about speed.

The study reported in this paper examines to what extent our perception of time is dependent on space. Will time estimation be influenced by reading about movement of different speeds? Such a finding would lend support to the idea that we think about time in terms of space even for low-level tasks such as time estimation, and that language comprehension involves simulating not only motion but also the attentional allocation of the protagonist.

Experiment

This experiment presented participants with three brief stories describing different scenarios: one describing slow movement, one describing neutral movement without particular indication of speed, and one describing fast movement. For example, the same movement in one base story was described by the verb "strolled" (slow), "travelled" (neutral) or "raced" (fast). Participants were asked to read each story at a normal pace and then estimate how long they thought they had spent reading (i.e., prospective time estimation).

Moving at different speeds across the same space involves encountering the same number of attentional markers (visual or other landmarks that capture our attention and act as reference points in mental representation of space: e.g., Sadalla, Burroughs & Staplin, 1980) with varying intervals: slow movement results in long intervals while fast movement results in short intervals. If readers adopt the perspective of the protagonist in a story and simulate the corresponding movement (Bryant et al., 1992; Matlock, 2004; Zwaan et al., 2004), then their mental representation of the story may also simulate the attentional allocation of the protagonist: reading about slow movement will seem to encounter long intervals between markers (making time pass more slowly) and reading about fast movement will seem to encounter short intervals between markers (making time pass more quickly). This would lead to the prediction that estimated reading times should decrease as story speed increases (i.e., slow > neutral > fast).

On the other hand, psychophysical studies of time estimation may lead to different predictions. When people are asked to estimate how long a dot has spent moving a fixed distance onscreen, they generally estimate longer durations for fast movement than for slow movement (Brown, 1995), arguably because faster speeds represent more perceived changes in a given interval than slower speeds (see also Poynter, 1989), although some studies have failed to find this effect (e.g., Casasanto & Boroditsky, 2003). If perceived onscreen movement corresponds to simulated described movement, then one would predict that estimated reading times should increase as story speed increases (i.e., slow < neutral < fast).

Regarding actual reading times, there is some evidence to suggest that speed of described movement may also affect the speed of language comprehension. Zwaan (1996) found that participants reading brief narratives took longer to process sentences that started "an hour later" than sentences starting with "a moment later", arguing that such time shifts took longer for people to integrate into their situation models of the text. Similarly, it is possible that stories about slow movement (where there are long intervals between attentional markers) will take people longer to process than stories about fast movement (where there are short intervals between attentional markers). This view would predict that actual reading times may decrease as story speed increases (i.e., slow > neutral > fast).

Finally, since people tend to underestimate duration in prospective time judgements, especially for longer durations (Block & Zakay, 1997), we would expect estimated reading times to be overall shorter than actual reading times across speed conditions.

Method

Materials. Nine stories were used in this experiment, consisting of a 3x3 cross of base and speed: three base stories were created, and each base story was then manipulated to give rise to three speed versions (slow, neutral, fast). Stories had an average length of 133 words (range 131-137), designed to represent a moderate duration for the time estimation task (defined by Block & Zakay, 1997, as a range of 15-60 seconds). Sample stories can be seen in Table 1.

The speed manipulation of each base story was carefully controlled to ensure equivalence in factors important to reading times. Every sentence in each base story had at least one word altered to imply different speeds of movement. An average of 21.7 words per base story was

Table 1: Slow, neutral and fast versions of a sample base story used in this experiment.

Speed	Story
Slow	It was a cold morning but the sun was shining. Tom was waiting for the next bus, as a man in a red hat strolled passed with his dog, and a weary cat went slouching by. Tom drifted off of the pavement and onto the bus. He looked out of the window as the bus trudged off and overtook the man in the hat sitting with his dog in the nearby park. Tom noticed a milk cart rambling across the road, and a walker following sluggishly behind. The ticket inspector was crawling up and down the bus, looking annoyed with his job. Tom realized the next stop was his, and edged towards the front of the bus very slowly. As he slumped off the bus, he accepted that today was going to be a fairly quiet day.
Neutral	It was a cold morning but the sun was shining. Tom was walking for the next bus, as a man in a red hat travelled passed with his dog, and a ginger cat went passing by. Tom stepped off of the pavement and onto the bus. He looked out of the window as the bus drove off and overtook the man in the hat wandering with his dog in the nearby park. Tom noticed a hire van moving across the road, and a jogger following casually behind. The ticket inspector was moving up and down the bus, looking annoyed with his job. Tom realized the next stop was his, and headed towards the front of the bus very easily. As he got off the bus, he accepted that today was going to be a fairly average day.
Fast	It was a cold morning but the sun was shining. Tom was running for the next bus, as a man in a red hat raced passed with his dog, and a lively cat went dashing by. Tom jumped off of the pavement and onto the bus. He looked out of the window as the bus zoomed off and overtook the man in the hat sprinting with his dog in the nearby park. Tom noticed a sports car speeding across the road, and a cyclist following rapidly behind. The ticket inspector was rushing up and down the bus, looking annoyed with his job. Tom realized the next stop was his, and dashed towards the front of the bus very promptly. As he leaped off the bus, he accepted that today was going to be a fairly busy day.

manipulated, representing a 16.3% lexical difference between speed versions. Slow, neutral and fast words were equivalent in both orthographic length and number of syllables (both $Fs < 1$). In addition, there was no significant difference between slow, neutral and fast word frequencies using Kucera and Francis (1967) norms, $F(2, 192) = 1.46$, $p = .235$.

Design. Stories were divided into three lists to ensure participants read only one version (slow, neutral or fast) of each base story. Participants were randomly allocated to one of the lists, and stories were presented in a random order for each participant. Thus, the experiment was a 2 (time measure: actual, estimated) × 3 (speed: slow, neutral, fast) × 3 (list) design, with time measure and speed as within-participants variables and list manipulated between-participants.

Participants. Forty-five native speakers of English from Northumbria University volunteered to take part in this experiment. All participants had normal or corrected-to-normal vision and had no known reading impairments.

Procedure. Testing took place individually on portable computers running SuperLab software. Prior to the experiment, participants were asked to remove their wristwatches and place them face-down on a nearby table, and to switch off mobile phones and any other electronic devices with clock displays. Participants read instructions describing the experiment and instructing them to read each story normally and to estimate (in seconds) how long they thought they had spent reading. Participants were also asked to summarise the story in one sentence to ensure they were attending to the task.

Each trial began with a prompt to press any key to begin reading a story. Stories were displayed onscreen as 11 left-aligned lines of text (with line breaks located in the same place for each speed version of a base story). Response times (i.e., actual reading times) were measured from the display of the story until participants pressed the space bar to indicate they had finished reading. Following story presentation, a prompt was displayed asking participants to estimate their reading times, and then to provide a brief summary of the story.

Results & Discussion

One participant was excluded for using consistently incorrect keystrokes, and a further five were excluded for having mean actual reading times that were more than two standard deviations slower than the grand mean. All participants provided meaningful summaries for each story and no responses were excluded by this criterion.

Figure 1 shows actual and estimated reading times for the three speed conditions. Of 117 responses, 54% were overestimates of reading time ($M_{diff} = 30.7$ secs) and 46% were underestimates ($M_{diff} = -13.4$ secs). This led to analyses of variance showing a main effect of time measure with mean estimated reading times longer than actual reading times [$F(1, 36) = 4.60$, $MSE = 1200$, $p = .039$]. Planned pairwise comparisons showed that people estimated they had spent longer reading than they actually had in both the neutral ($p = .032$) and slow ($p = .048$) conditions, but the difference was only marginal in the fast condition ($p = .093$)

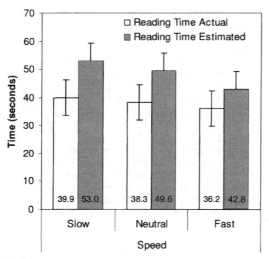

Figure 1: Actual and estimated readings times across the three speed conditions (means at base of bars). Error bars represent 95% confidence intervals for multifactor within-participant designs (Masson & Loftus, 2003).

(see Figure 1). The direction of this effect is against the general trend observed by Block and Zakay's (1997) meta-analysis (although there is some variability in the literature). One possible explanation is simply that participants did not find the stories particularly interesting, and hence experienced subjectively slower time (Hawkins & Tedford, 1976). There was also an overall main effect of speed [$F(2, 72)=3.76$, $MSE=229$, $p=.028$] but no reliable interaction between time measure and speed [$F(2, 72)=1.94$, $MSE=98.7$, $p=.179$]. However, since there were different predictions for estimated and actual reading times, the influence of story speed is explored further below in separate analyses. In this and all further analyses, the effect and interactions of the list variable were non-significant.

For estimated reading times, speed conditions differed significantly [$F(2, 72)=3.68$, $MSE=253$, $p=0.030$]. People thought they had spent less time reading the fast stories compared to the neutral (planned comparison $p=.046$) or slow ($p=.024$) stories. There was no difference between estimates of the neutral and slow stories ($p=.357$). This finding provides some support for the idea that we think about time in terms of space even for low-level tasks such as time estimation, and that language comprehension may involve simulating the attentional allocation of the protagonist. Reading about fast movement involves simulating short intervals between attentional markers (making time pass more quickly), while reading about slow and neutral movement involves simulating longer intervals between attentional markers (making time pass more slowly). The lack of significant difference between slow and neutral estimates suggests that the simulated speed of neutral stories was similar to that of slow stories in this materials set: for example, a ticket inspector *moving* up and down a bus (neutral) may be closer in speed to him *crawling* (slow) than *rushing* (fast).

For actual reading times, there was no significant effect of story speed [$F(2, 72)=1.66$, $MSE=75.6$, $p=0.197$]. Planned comparisons showed that the fast stories were marginally quicker to read than the slow stories ($p=.063$), although neither the slow nor fast stories were different in reading time to the neutral stories ($ps>.3$). This finding provides some support for the idea that closely-spaced events are easier to integrate into the reader's situation model of the narrative (Zwaan, 1996). Stories about fast movement (where there are short intervals between attentional markers) may be slightly quicker to process for this reason than stories about slow movement (where there are long intervals between attentional markers), although the 3.7 second difference between conditions in the current study is only marginal.

General Discussion

This work shows that people's perception of temporal progress is affected by their representation of spatial progress. Reading about fast movement caused people to make shorter estimates of temporal duration than for neutral or slow movement. Reading about slow movement, on the other hand, resulted in estimates similar to neutral movement.

So what does this study tell us about our understanding of time and space? It suggests that even low-level judgements of temporal duration are dependent on mapping to concrete space and are susceptible to influences of spatial movement. Fast movement in the real world causes landmarks, markers, and other objects that catch our attention to zoom by with relatively short temporal intervals between them. When participants read and simulate stories about fast movement, the short simulated intervals are reflected in short time estimates. It could be argued that time estimation is not a low-level task when compared, for example, to perception, but our use of the term is relative: the task of rescheduling hypothetical future events requires higher-level cognitive processing than making a short duration estimate. We can think about moving through time as we move through space not only at the relatively high level of moving events around like objects (Boroditsky & Ramscar, 2002), but also at the low-level perception of temporal duration.

These results are also consistent with the view that people represent the attentional allocation of the protagonist during narrative comprehension. Previous research showed that when participants read stories about movement, they simulated the implied motion (Zwaan et al., 2004) and speed (Matlock, 2004). This study further suggests that people simulate such stories using flexible temporal intervals: fast movement leads to short simulated intervals and short times estimates, while slow movement leads to long simulated intervals and long time estimates. An alternative possibility from psychophysical research (Brown, 1995; Poynter, 1989), suggesting that people may simulate the story using fixed temporal intervals, was not supported. Fast movement did not lead to long time estimates due to more perceived changes in a given interval, and slow movement did not lead to short time estimates due to fewer perceived changes in a given interval. The present finding underscores the difference between movement simulated during language comprehension and movement visually observed. Readers of text are free to simulate varying temporal intervals to fit the events in the narrative (see Zwaan & Radvansky, 1998), while viewers of onscreen movement must experience the temporal interval set by the experimenter.

Is there another explanation for the results? Prospective time estimations are shorter when more of a person's attentional resources must be allocated to processing a concurrent task instead of processing temporal information (Block & Zakay, 1997). It could be argued that readers in this study are not simulating the attentional allocation of the protagonist, but rather that the shorter estimates for stories about fast movement result from fast movement being more difficult to process. However, this explanation is not consistent with the findings reported here. Actual reading times for fast stories were marginally faster than those for slow stories, indicating that fast stories were not more difficult to process than slow stories. Indeed, this result suggests that fast stories may be slightly *easier* to process than slow stories, perhaps due to closely-spaced events being easier to integrate into the story simulation (Zwaan, 1996). Further research will investigate the influence of protagonist viewpoint, such as whether the effects reported here are dependent on having a protagonist on a clear trajectory, or whether they will still hold if multiple protagonists move in multiple directions.

As Aristotle argued, we measure and define time by movement through space. What this study shows is that it is not only real movement but imagined movement, as represented during language comprehension, that has the power to influence how we measure and define time.

Acknowledgments

This work was partly funded by the Division of Psychology in Northumbria University.

References

Barsalou, L.W., & Wiemer-Hastings, K. (2005). Situating abstract concepts. In D. Pecher and R. Zwaan (Eds.), *Grounding cognition: The role of perception and action in memory, language, and thought.* Cambridge: Cambridge University Press.

Block R. A, & Zakay, D. (1997). Prospective and retrospective duration judgments: A meta-analytic review. *Psychonomic Bulletin and Review, 4* (2), 184-197.

Boroditsky, L., & Ramscar, M. (2002). The roles of body and mind in abstract thought. *Psychological Science, 13,* 185–189.

Brown, S. W. (1995). Time, change, and motion: The effects of stimulus movement on temporal perception. *Perception & Psychophysics, 57* (1), 105-116.

Bryant, D. J., Tversky, B., & Franklin, N. (1992). Internal and external spatial frameworks for representing described scenes. *Journal of Memory and Language, 31,* 74-98.

Casasanto, D. & Boroditsky, L. (2003) Do we think about time in terms of space? *Proceedings of the 25th Annual Meeting of the Cognitive Science Society* (pp. 216-221).

Clark, H. (1973) Space, time, semantics, and the child. In T. Moore (Ed.), *Cognitive development and the acquisition of language.* New York: Academic Press.

Gentner, D., & Imai, M. (1992). Is the future always ahead? Evidence for system-mappings in understanding space-time metaphors. *Proceedings of the 14th Annual Meeting of the Cognitive Science Society* (pp. 510-515).

Gibbs, R. W. (1994). *The poetics of mind: Figurative thought, language, and understanding.* Cambridge: Cambridge University Press.

Hawkins, M. F., & Tedford, A. H. (1976). Effects of interest and relatedness on estimated duration of verbal material. *Bulletin of the Psychonomic Society, 8,* 301-302.

Hicks, R. E., Miller, G. W., & Kinsbourne, M.(1976). Prospective and retrospective judgments of time as a function of amount of information processed. *American Journal of Psychology, 89,* 719-730.

Kucera, H., & Francis, W. N. (1967). *Computational Analysis of Present-Day American English.* Providence, RI: Brown University Press.

Lakoff, G., & Johnson, M. (1999). *Philosophy in the flesh: The embodied mind and its challenge to Western thought.* New York: Basic Books.

Masson, M. E. J., & Loftus, G. R. (2003). Using confidence intervals for graphically based data interpretation. *Canadian Journal of Experimental Psychology, 57*(3), 203-220.

Matlock, T. (2004). Fictive motion as cognitive simulation. *Memory & Cognition, 32* (8), 1389-1400.

Matlock, T., Ramscar, M., & Boroditsky, L. (2005). The experiential link between spatial and temporal language. *Cognitive Science, 29,* 655-664.

McGlone, M., & Harding, J. (1998). Back (or forward?) to the future: The role of perspective in temporal language comprehension. *Journal of Experimental Psychology: Learning, Memory, and Cognition, 24,* 1211–1223.

Poynter, W. D. (1989). Judging the duration of time intervals: A process of remembering segments of experience. I. Levin & D. Zakay (Eds.), *Time and human cognition: A life-span perspective.* Amsterdam: North-Holland.

Sadalla, E.K., Burroughs, W.J., & Staplin, L.J. (1980). Reference points in spatial cognition. *Journal of Experimental Psychology: Human Learning and Memory, 6,* 516-528.

Zwaan, R. A. (1996). Processing narrative time shifts. *Journal of Experimental Psychology: Learning, Memory, and Cognition, 22,* 1196-1207.

Zwaan, R. A., Madden, C. J., Yaxley, R. H., & Aveyard, M. E. (2004). Moving words: Dynamic mental representations in language comprehension. *Cognitive Science, 28,* 611–619.

Zwaan, R. A., & Radvansky, G. A. (1998). Situation models in language comprehension and memory. *Psychological Bulletin, 123* (2), 162-185.

A Recurrent Connectionist Model of Retrospective Cue Interaction in Humans

Frank Van Overwalle (Frank.VanOverwalle@vub.ac.be)
Department of Psycholog y, Pleinlaan 2
B-1050 Brussel, Belgium

Abstract

Retrospective revaluation is now a well-established empirical phenomenon in associative learning, although existing associative revisions of the Rescorla-Wagner (1972) model generally fail to generate three benchmark retrospective findings including (a) backward blocking, (b) higher-order backward blocking and (c) the crucial role of (the retrieval of) cue compounds in backward revaluation. This paper proposes a modified recurrent network—very close to the original Rescorla-Wagner model—incorporating a mechanism for *retrospective contrast activation* when a cue is unexpectedly missing, that is capable of producing these three benchmark predictions, as well as many other basic cue interaction effects not only in a first-order backward order, but also in higher-order backward learning.

Introduction

Inspired by similarities with animal conditioning, associative theorists claim that human causal judgments are based on primitive associative processes that also underlie animal learning (e.g., Di ckinson, Shanks & Evenden, 1984). The most well -known computational model i n the associative field, developed b y Rescorla and Wagner (1972), postulates that learning of cue -outcome relationships is based on associations that are formed between the representations of a cue (or conditioned stimulus) and an outcome (or unconditioned stimulus) that are presented together.

Evidence in favor of this associative perspective has been harvested when animals and humans are faced with multiple cues. It has been typically found that one of them is selected as the most probable cue or cause, while the others are ignored as less relevant. This phenomenon is termed *cue competition* or *blocking* in the associative literature (Rescorla & Wagner, 1972) and *discounting* by social psychologists (Kelley, 1971).

In a typical blocking procedure, once an a lternative cause A sufficiently explains an effect in Phase 1, and when presented in compound with another target cause T in Phase 2, the additional cause T will acquire little associative strength and is judged as causally irrelevant. This sequence of events is typically abbreviated as A+ AT+, where A and T represent causes (or more generally, cues), and + the presence of the outcome (and − its absence) .

The crucial assumption in explaining c ue competition and other types of cue interaction is that the st rength of the target association does not only depend on the pairings of the target cue with the outcome, but also on the *summed association strength* of all other cues that are presented in compound. That is, as soon as the association of A becomes suffici ently strong to predict the outcome alone (after an A+ training), the addition of T (in an AT+ training) contributes little to the total associative strength in predicting the outcome.

However, one major stumbling block for the Rescorla - Wagner model is th at it fails to explain backward or retrospective training procedures. In these backward procedures, the typical ordering of learning is reversed. For instance, in backward blocking (denoted as AT+ A+) , the alternative cue A exerts its influence only in Pha se 2, after the AT compound has been presented in Phase 1. Although some studies failed to detect reliable backward blocking, an increasing number of studies now report this effect in humans (Aitken, Larkin & Dickinson, 2001; Dickinson & Burke, 1996; Larki n, Aitken & Dickinson, 1998; Le Pelley & McLaren, 200 1; Van Overwalle & Timmermans, 2005; Wasserman & Berglan, 1998). Hence, backward blocking is now established as a reliable empirical phenomenon.

Earlier Revisions and their Failures

This shortcoming of the Rescorla-Wagner approach has spurred a number of revisions to explain retrospective revaluation. They all attempt to address the observation that when cue T is absent during the (second) retrospective revaluation phase, it nevertheless modifies its ass ociative strength. The original Rescorla -Wagner model allows a cue to change strength only when present during training.

To resolve this limitation, some associative researchers (Van Hamme & Wasserman, 1994) suggested that an absent cue expected to be pr esent, should take on a negative activation value, to emphasize that its absence is unusual. This negative activation then leads to the decrease in associative strength. Dickinson and Burke (1996) further elaborated on this idea, and proposed that the init ial expectation that a cue should be present (but fails to be so) depends on the connections between cues that make up the compound: "Only the omission of an expected cue should generate a … negative activation … it is the formation of within-compound conn ections during the first stage of training that provides the basis for this expectation" (Dickinson & Burke, 1996, p. 63).

Applied to backward blocking, this implies that when two cues A and T of a compound are positively associated, then when A alone is present during the revaluation phase, the presence of the other cue T is also expected. However, when cue T is actually absent, this results in a large negative activation of T (leading to decreased strength or blocking). Conversely, when the two cues are unrelated, the absence of one of them should not come as a surprise, so that it receives no activation (which has no consequences on its associative strength). Note that this differs from forward competition, which Dickinson and Burke (1996) predict to occur regardless of the connection between cues —in line with the original predictions of the Rescorla -Wagner model and the delta learning algorithm.

By manipulating the association between cues, Dickinson and Burke (1996) and subsequent researchers found that retrospective effects were stronger when the compounds presented earlier were stronger and better remembered (Aitken, Larkin & Dickinson, 2001; Dickinson & Burke, 1996; Larkin, Aitken & Dickinson, 1998; Le Pelley & McLaren, 2001; Melchers, Lachnit & Shanks, 2004; Wasserman & Berglan, 1998). This attests to the essential role of within-compound associations in retrospective revaluation.

Later research demonstrated that retrospective competition is also possible for higher -order conditioning, that is, further backwards in time. For example, in a second -order design, the compounds AT1+ and T1T2+ are learned, and then the single alternative cue A+ is presented. It has been generally found not only that T1 is blocked, but also that T2 is increased retrospectively (De Houwer & Beckers, 2002, Melchers, Lachnit & Shanks, 2004). Moreover, it was shown that the retrieval of within -compound associations facilitates these higher -order learning effects (Melchers et al., 2004).

Recently, a number of revisions of the Rescorla-Wagner model have been put forward (see references in Table 1). However, to provide a viable account of retrospective revaluation, these proposals should pass a minimal number of benchmark predictions that have been clearly confirmed by empirical findings. I consider the following three findings as essential criteria that revised models must possess: They must predict (1) backward blocking, (2) higher-order blocking, and (3) the crucial role of within -compound association in backward, but not forward, designs.

To my best knowledge, however, none of the existing models fulfill all these three criteria or are silent with respect to them (see Table 1). In contrast, the model to be presented here provides an associative account that not only meets the three benchmark criteria, but also makes predictions on similar cue interaction effects that researchers only recently began to explore.

Table 1: Predictions by Revised Models.

Benchmark Criterium	(1)	(2)	(3)
Van Hamme & Wasserman (1994)	yes	no	no
Ghirlanda (2005)	yes	?	no
APECS (Le Pelley & McLaren, 2001)	no	?	yes
MSOP (Aitken & Dickinson, 2005)	no	no	yes
Graham (1999)	yes	no	yes
Comparator (Denniston et al., 2001)	yes	yes	no

A Recurrent Model of Retrospective Revaluation

The revision proposed here picks up elements of earlier proposals, but implements and extends them in a different manner. It is cast in a *recurrent* or *auto-associative* network

(McClelland & Rumelhart, 1988) which is well-known in the connectionist literature and that was used earlier in the revised model by Graham (1999). Essentially, the network is made up of all connections between as well as within cues and the outcome, in all possible directions. That is, the network contains not only cue →outcome connections, but also cue→cue and outcome →cue connections. This allows the network to represent within -compound associations.

In next section, I briefly introduce the key elements of the revised model in informal terms, and then in more mathematical terms. After that, I briefly describe a number of simulations that defy the Rescorla -Wagner model, and that the proposed recurrent model can account for.

Retrospective Contrast Activation

To incorporate the role of with -compound associations in the activation of absent cues, I follow the suggestion by Dickinson and Burke (1996). This modification recognizes absent but expected cues as missing and provides them with an opposite activation from connected units. This contrasts with the standard procedure in a recurrent model where an absent stimulus *m* will generally be "filled up" or assimilated by similar activation received from connected units.

This leads to two types of contrasts. In line with Dickinson and Burke (1996), if the cues of a compound AT are positively associated, then upon the presence of cue A, the expectation is that cue T should be present, that is, have a positive activation. Importantly, to emphasize the unexpected absence of cue T, its actual activation is contrasted away from the expected activation and is in fact reversed, and so results in greater negative activation of T. This mechanism can explain backward blocking.

To explain backward higher -order blocking, this mechanism is extended to negative expectations. This is exactly the opposite as explained above for positive expectations. That is, if the cues of a compound AT are negatively associated, then upon the presence of cue A, the expectation is that the T should have an opposite or negative activation. To emphasize the unexpected absence of cue T, its activation is again contrasted way from the expected activation, this time resulting in a positive activation of T. This mechanism for both positive and negative expectations, which I term retrospective contrast activation, has some intuitive parallels in real life. To give an example, if a zero Celsius temperature is below expectations, it is contrastively experienced as "colder" than when the same temperature is above expectations, and hence is contrastively experienced as "warmer".

The role of retrospective contrast activation and of within -compound connections is illustrated in Figure 1, for positive and negative expectations. In the figure, *external* activation reflects the cue's presence (+1) or absence (0) and is denoted below the units; *internal* activation reflects the activation received from other units and is denoted within the units; and *missing* activation is denoted within the gray units with dotted circles; Positive within -compound connections are denoted by → and negative connections by —•; Blocked arrows (in gray) denote the direction of weight change. The left panels reflect the standard model, the right panels the inclusion of the activation reversal mechanism .

In summary, the retrospective contrast activation may not only follow after absent cues tha t are expected to be present (i.e., positive within -compound connections) as proposed by Dickinson and Burke (1996), but also after absent cues that are expected to reveal an "opposite" presence (i.e., negative within-compound connections). After having in troduced the model in informal terms, I now turn to a more formal and mathematical description.

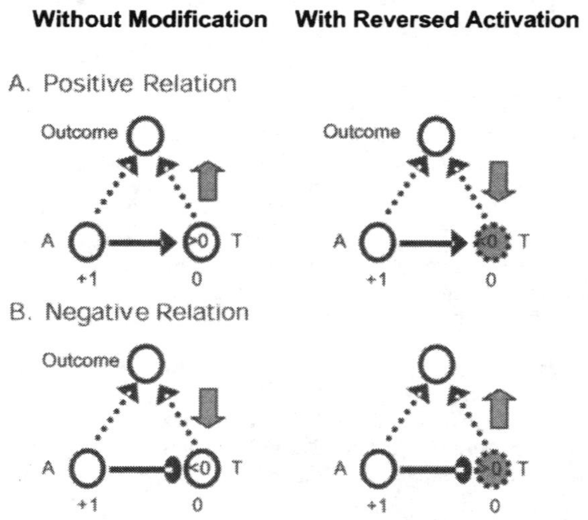

Without Modification   With Reversed Activation

A. Positive Relation

B. Negative Relation

Figure 1: Reversing the activation of missing units .

Implementation

The standard recurrent model poses problems because it predicts that an absent cue T receives from connected cues a positive activation, which results in enhanced conditioning of the absent cue T rather than blocking in retrospective revaluation. To explain backward blocking and similar cue interactions, it is necessary to incorporate the retrospective contrast activation mechanism. Mathematically, this is accomplished as follows. Each time the activation received from a connected unit i exceeds some missing threshold (denoted by μ), then the missing stimulus m accrues internal activation that is now termed *missing activation*. Specifically, for any unit m with zero external activation ($ext_m = 0$), the missing activation is accumulated in a standard manner as follows :

$$\text{If } |ext_i * weight_{im}| > \mu$$
$$\text{then } miss_m = \Sigma \, (ext_i * weight_{im}). \qquad (1)$$

where ext_i denotes the external activation from the other cues i. The missing acti vation in cue j is received in proportion to the weight of the $i \rightarrow m$ connections and then summed

In the simulations to discuss shortly, obtainin g substantial higher-order revaluation required a retrospective contrast

activation that is stronger for a negative missing activation than for a positive missing activation. It seems int uitive ly plausible to assume that a negative expectation has stronger consequences on retrospective revaluation, than the mere expectation that a cue should be present (positive). This idea is incorporated by providing twice as much missing activation in Equation 1 when the absent cue is expected to be negatively, rather th an positively activated.

Now we reach the critical modification of the standard recurrent network. Rather than summing the external activation received from other cues i to compute the final activation (as in the standard auto -associative model), the missing activation of an absent cue m is subtracted, effectively resulting in a retrospective contrast activation. In mathematical terms, if $ext_m = 0$ and given that the missing threshold of an absent cue m is exceeded, then

$$activation_m = - \, miss_m. \qquad (2)$$

Simulations of Cue Interaction

I now briefl y present the results of a series of simulations of cue interactions with the modified recurrent network . Due to space restrictions, I discuss only the first two benchmark criteria set out earlier.

Classic Cue Interac tion Effects

The modified recurrent model predict s the correct estimates for some basic cue interaction effects of blocking, conditioned inhibition, superconditioning and reduced overshadowing, both in a forward and backward order . To review briefly, apar t from blocking, the other cue interaction effects are:

- *Conditioned inhibition* is learning that a given cue inhibits the likelihood o f an outcome. Trials in which cue A produces the outcome are followed or preceded by trials in which cue A and T (the inten ded inhibitor y cue) do not produce the outcome . This procedure gives cue A an excitatory value and cue T an inhibitor y value.
- *Supercond itioning* results when a cue T gains more strength when it produces the outcome in the presence of a conditioned inhibito r A than wh en cue T produces the outcome alone, because for T to success fully produce the outcome it must gain additional strength to overcome the inhibitor y effect of A.
- *Overshadowing* is defined by a diminished strength of T when T and A both produce the outcome b ecause A and T compete for connection strength with each other . *Reduced overshadowing* or *unovershadowing* results when cue A alone does not produce the outcome, so that T gains strength.

Thus, blocking and conditioned inhibition lead to a decrease in cue T, while superconditioning and reduced overshadowin g lead to an increase in cue T, and these predictions were also made by the proposed model , in a forward and backward order .

Higher-Order Cue Interaction

As noted earlier, higher-order backward blo cking can be schematically described as follows. After an AT1+ and

T1T2+ training, and given a final A+ training, we tend to decrease our estimates of T1 (first-order blocking) and increase our estimates of T2 (second-order unovershadowing). If we extend this analysis further backward in time, we expect that an additional T2T3+ training in turn would reduce T3 ratings (third-order blocking). In sum, each time we go one step further forth or back in time, cues that were paired in a compound are alternatingly blocked or unovershadowed.

The modified recurrent model reproduces this effect as follows. Because A and T1 develop a positive connection, (first-order) backward blocking of T1 should occur. In contrast, because A and T2 are never trained in compound but share the common T1, they develop a negative connection so that (after contrast activation) T2 receives a positive activation and an increase (i.e., unovershadowing) of T2 takes place. Finally, given that they do not share a common cue, A and T3 develop a positive connection so that (after contrast activation) T3 receives a negative activation and (third-order) blocking of T3 results.

Simulations demonstrate that the predictions of the modified recurrent model for second-order cue interaction effects (mentioned in the previous section) are robust and typically stronger than for third-order backward interaction. Problematic in the third-order are reduced overshadowing and unovershadowing were the simulated effect is marginal and for superconditioning where it predicts a reverse effect. This latter failure is due the fact that cue A in the inhibitory C+/AC- pretraining acquires sufficient negative strength only after about the first half of the trials, so that it initially functions more as a blocking cue (like A+ in backward blocking) rather than a conditioned inhibitor as it should.

Conclusion

The proposed revision of the Rescorla-Wagner model generates predictions on retrospective revaluation that are consistent with current empirical findings, and that earlier revisions were unable to generate. In particular, it makes the correct predictions on classic cue interaction effects (including blocking, overshadowing, conditioned inhibition and superconditioning) not only in a forward order, but also in a backward order, and in second-order as well as third-order interaction. These cue interaction effects have not only implications for associative theory and its clinical applications, but also in other domains of theory such as social psychology, where these effects are known as discounting and augmentation (Kelley, 1971).

References

Aitken, M. R. F. & Dickinson, A. (2005) Simulations of a modified SOP model applied to retrospective revaluation of human causal learning. *Learning and Behavior, 33*, 147-159.

McClelland, J. L. & Rumelhart, D. E. (1988). Explorations in parallel distributed processing: *A handbook of models, programs and exercises*. Cambridge, MA: Bradford.

Aitken, M. R. F., Larkin, M. J. W. & Dickinson, A. (2001) Re-examination of the role of within-compound associations in the retrospective revaluation of causal judgments. *Quarterly Journal of Experimental Psychology, 54B*, 27—51.

De Houwer, J. & Beckers, T. (2002). Higher-order retrospective revaluation in human causal learning. The *Quarterly Journal of Experimental Psychology, 55B*, 137—151.

Denniston, J. C., Savastano, H. I., & Miller, R. R. (2001). The extended comparator hypothesis: Learning by contiguity, responding by relative strength. In Mowrer, R. & Klein, S. (Eds.). *Handbook of contemporary learning theories* (pp. 65—117). Hillsdale, NJ: Erlbaum.

Dickinson, A. & Burke, J. (1996). Within-compound associations mediate the retrospective revaluation of causality judgments. *Quarterly Journal of Experimental Psychology, 49B*, 60-80.

Dickinson, A., Shanks, & Evenden, J. (1984). Judgement of act—outcome contingency: The role of selective attribution. *Quarterly Journal of Experimental Psychology, 36A*, 29–50.

Ghirlanda, S. (2005). Retrospective revaluation as simple associative learning. *Journal of Experimental Psychology: Animal Behavior Processes, 31*, 107—111.

Graham, S. (1999). Retrospective revaluation and inhibitory associations: Does perceptual learning modulate our perceptions of the contingencies between events? *Quarterly Journal of Experimental Psychology, 52B*, 159-185.

Kelley, H. H. (1971). Attribution in social interaction. In E. E. Jones, D. E. Kanouse, H. H. Kelley, R. E. Nisbett, S. Valins & B. Weiner (Eds.) *Attribution: Perceiving the causes of behavior* (pp. 1—26). Morristown, NJ: General Learning Press.

Larkin, M. J. W., Aitken, M. R. F., Dickinson, A. (1998). Retrospective revaluation of causal judgments under positive and negative contingencies. *Journal of Experimental Psychology, Learning, Memory, and Cognition, 24*, 1331—1352.

Le Pelley, M. E. & McLaren, I. P. L. (2001). Retrospective revaluation in humans: Learning or memory? *Quarterly Journal of Experimental Psychology, 54B*, 311—352.

Melchers, K. G., Lachnit, H., & Shanks, D. R. (2004). Within-compound associations in retrospective revaluation and in direct learning: A challenge for comparator theory. *Quarterly Journal of Experimental Psychology, 57B*, 25—53.

Rescorla, R. A. & Wagner, A. R. (1972). A theory of Pavlovian conditioning: Variations in the effectiveness of reinforcement and nonreinforcement. In A. H. Black & W. F. Prokasy (Eds.) *Classical conditioning II: Current research and theory* (pp. 64–98). New York: Appleton-Century-Crofts.

Van Hamme & Wasserman (1994). Cue competition in causality judgments: The role of nonpresentation of compound stimulus elements. *Learning and Motivation, 25*, 127—151.

Van Overwalle, F. & Timmermans, B. (2005) Discounting and the Role of the Relation between Causes. *European Journal of Social Psychology, 35*, 199—224.

Simplifying the Development and the Analysis of Cognitive Models

Marcus Heinath, Jeronimo Dzaack, Andre Wiesner ({mhe, jdz, awi}@zmms.tu-berlin.de)
Center of Human-Machine-Systems - Technische Universität Berlin
Franklinstraße 28-29, FR 2-7/2, 10587 Berlin, Germany

Leon Urbas (leon.urbas@tu-dresden.de)
Institute of Automation - Technische Universität Dresden
01062 Dresden, Germany

Abstract

Usability of complex dynamic human computer interfaces can be evaluated by cognitive modeling to investigate cognitive processes and their underlying structures. Even though the prediction of human behavior can help to detect errors in the interaction design and cognitive demands of the future user the method is not widely applied. The time-consuming transformation of a problem "in the world" into a "computational model" and the lack of fine-grained analysis of simulation data are mainly responsible for this. Having realized these drawbacks we developed HTAmap and SimTrA to simplify the development and analysis of cognitive models. HTAmap, a high-level framework for cognitive modeling, aims to reduce the modeling effort. Within HTAmap the process of building cognitive models is transformed into a pattern-oriented task, based on "cognitive activity patterns". SimTrA supports the analysis of cognitive model data on an overall and microstructure level and enables the user to automatically compare simulated data with empirical data. This paper describes both concepts and first implementations. The practicability of both tools is shown using an example in the domain of process control.

Introduction

Recent introductions of new information technologies in the range of dynamic human-machine systems (e.g. process control systems in the chemical industry or airplane cockpits) have led to increasing cognitive requirements caused by a shift from manual processes of operation to the management of complex automated processes. This leads to user interfaces which are characterized by a high complexity and a high degree of dynamics. Because of the integrated functionality and the complex data structures, these interfaces require more cognitive information processing. The aim is to design systems which support the cognitive demands of users. Cognitive modeling seems to be a good candidate for this purpose because it allows to gain insight into cognitive aspects of human behavior in a more specific way than empirical or heuristic methods. But despite the promising potential, this method is still rarely used in industrial research departments. The main obstacles are time and cost efforts for building and analyzing cognitive models, caused by a lack of support tools and by sophisticated knowledge in both cognitive psychology as well as artificial intelligence programming (Heffernan, Koedinger & Aleven, 2003). Having realized this drawback we present *HTAmap* (Hierarchical Task Mapper) and

SimTrA (Simulation Trace Analyzer), two new approaches to simplify the development and analysis of cognitive models and thereby reducing costs and time. HTAmap provides two key features: firstly, it uses a plain high-level description based on appropriate task analysis methods. Secondly, it supports the reuse of cognitive model components based on cognitive activity pattern. SimTrA provides applications to extract and process cognitive model data on an overall and microstructure level. It allows to analyze cognitive model data and to compare the data with empirical data afterwards. Both are part of a series of software tools within an integrated modeling environment for cognitive models.

Potentials and Constraints of Cognitive Modeling as Method for System Evaluation

Cognitive architectures incorporate psychological theories (e.g. visual information processing, decision making, motor commands) and empirically based representations about aspects of human cognition. There is general agreement that these cognitive aspects are relatively constant over time and relatively task-independent (Howes & Young, 1997). Therefore, cognitive architectures present these aspects in a software framework to explain and predict human behavior in a detailed manner. In this context, a cognitive model can be seen as an application of a cognitive architecture to a specific problem domain with a particular knowledge set. Building a cognitive model, the modeler must describe cognitive mechanisms in a highly-detailed and human-like way. Two levels of cognitive architectures can be differentiated: High-level architectures (e.g. GOMS, CTT, HTA, see Limbourg & Vanderdonckt, 2004 for an overview) describe behavior on a basic level and define interactions as a static sequence of human actions. Low-level architectures (e.g. ACT-R, SOAR or EPIC, see Byrne, 2003 for an overview) describe human behavior on an atomic level. They allow a more detailed insight into cognitive processes than high-level architectures. Most low-level architectures use production systems to simulate human processing and cognition. The use of independent production rules allows cognitive models to react on external stimuli (bottom-up processes) and to model interruption and resumption of cognitive processes in contrast to high-level architectures which are usually controlled top-down. The research presented in this paper uses the cognitive architecture ACT-R (Anderson et al., 2004).

Determining Factors for Practical Application

In a practical application cognitive models can be used to evaluate the usability of prototypes. This helps to detect errors in the interaction design of interfaces and gives indications about the cognitive demands of the future user. Cognitive models extend classical usability methods and expand the repertoire by cognitive aspects. However, this method is seldom employed in usability research and development because of a lack of support tools for creating and analyzing cognitive models.

Development Effort for Cognitive Models

Various authors (Heffernan, Koedinger & Aleven, 2003; Crossman et al., 2004; Tollinger et al., 2005) analyzed the cognitive modeling process in detail, together with the necessary subtasks and requirements. Transformation of task knowledge into the computational description of the cognitive architecture is challenging and requires extensive programming experience. The resulting high cost/benefit ratio is an important constraint on the practical application. The real bottleneck lies in the transformation-gap after the preliminary task analysis process (see Figure 1) and is caused by the different levels of task decomposition and formalization. Task analysis methods formalize knowledge about cognitive processes with a greater degree of abstraction and less formalization compared to low-level modeling approaches such as ACT-R. For example, "read button" which is atomic at the level of task analysis corresponds to a complex sequence of production rules in ACT-R (e.g. retrieve-position, find-position, attend-position, read and store results) and a set of data elements for flow control and internal representation. It is up to the cognitive modeler to fill this gap between the high-level task description and the low-level implementation by the means of a cognitive architecture. A current topic in the cognitive research community is to minimize this gap with the development of high-level languages to model human cognition based on low-level cognitive architectures (for an overview of current approaches see Ritter et al., 2006). The main objectives are to simplify the model-building process and to improve concepts for sharing and reusing model components (Crossman et al., 2004).

Analyzing Effort for Simulation Data

Most low-level simulation experiments use global information to analyze the model and its fit to empirical data (e.g. errors or times). A problems is connected with this procedure. In order to validate that a current cognitive model acts like a human, not only the behavior of a cognitive model and the human have to be the highly comparable, but also the kind of computations and sub-processes to achieve the results have to be equivalent. With the psychological theories implemented in low-level cognitive architectures a more detailed analysis of cognitive model data is possible to enrich the explanatory power of cognitive models. This makes it possible to analyze the computations that lead to the cognitive model behavior and thereby to determine the level of correctness of the implemented cognitive model. For this purpose fine-grained patterns can be detected in the simulation data to enrich the

explanatory power of cognitive models (e.g. sequence of actions). For example, the arrangement and the appearance of elements of an interface can be evaluated with respect to theories of eye-movement or signal detection. Nevertheless using cognitive models reveals some problems. Cognitive architectures and models are incomplete and describe only a small part of the processes that make up human cognition. Reasons for this are the partial knowledge of internal cognitive processes in cognitive science and the insufficient implementation of all cognitive aspects that are needed to handle a task. Aspects like esthetics, boredom, fun or personal preferences which can be observed in empirical settings are not implemented (Byrne, 2003). When analyzing and comparing cognitive model data with empirical data, these differences have to be taken into account. So far, no tools exist for the extraction of fine-grained information from model data for the evaluation of user interfaces.

Integrated Environment for Cognitive Modeling and Analysis

To reduce the effort for developing cognitive models in ACT-R and to support the analysis of simulation and empirical data in a systematic way, *HTAmap* (Hierarchical Task Mapper) and *SimTrA* (Simulation Trace Analyzer) were developed. The placement of HTAmap and SimTrA within the general cognitive modeling process (consisting of the four steps: task analysis, empirical data collection, model implementation and validation) is shown in Figure 1. On the following pages the concepts, paradigms and first implementations of HTAmap and SimTrA are described in detail.

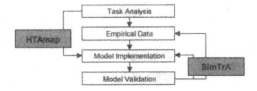

Figure 1: Placement of HTAmap and SimTrA within the general cognitive modeling process.

HTAmap

Building cognitive models is not easy and involves a strong process of synthesis, i.e. building a new solution by putting parts together in a logical way. For developing cognitive models in ACT-R this implies programming in a "cognitive assembly language". Behavior is expressed in terms of production-rules that manipulate knowledge expressed in declarative memory elements. To open cognitive modeling for a wider user group and make the developing task easier and more accessible, HTAmap addresses (1) a structured formalization method to minimize the "transformation-gap" between high-level task analysis and low-level approaches of cognitive modeling, and (2) programming paradigms with more immediate results. These can be achieved by model reuse and domain-oriented paradigms.

Pattern-oriented Cognitive Modeling

A number of task analysis methods have been developed for different purposes (see Limbourg & Vanderdonckt, 2004; for an overview), not many of them being a good starting point for cognitive modeling at all. To be suitable as base for a pattern oriented model engineering approach a task analysis method needs at least a minimal formal structure, clear rules for reuse and an appropriate level of detail. This is true for Ormerod & Shepherd's (2004) "sub-goal template" (SGT) method. The SGT method extends the "hierarchical task analysis" (HTA) method (Shepherd, 2001) by providing a nomenclature for stereotypical operator tasks and defining four essential steps (see Figure 2): the (1) initial task/subtask decomposition to the point where (2) "information-handling operations" (IHO) are recognized, followed by the (3) strategic decomposition and the (4) redescription in terms of sub-goal templates. Information handling operations are divided into three classes: receiving (IHO_R), evaluating (IHO_E) and acting on information (IHO_A). The identified IHOs are redescribed as operator tasks regarding one of the four sub-goal templates: (A)ct, (E)xchange, (N)avigate and (M)onitor. In addition, the SGT method defines a plan in which IHOs are sequenced relative to each other (i.e. fixed, free, parallel or contingent sequence). It specifies information requirements needed by an operator to carry out tasks during operation of a technical system.

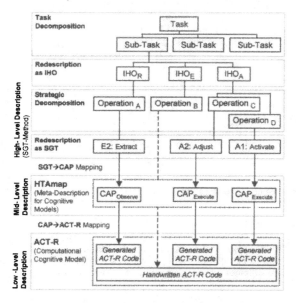

Figure 2: The mapping process from SGT to HTAmap and ACT-R code/models.

The redescription to the level of SGTs is the starting point for the HTAmap approach (see Figure 2). "Cognitive activity patterns" (CAP) are used to solve the high to low level mapping-problem. Within HTAmap, CAPs add a layer between a higher-level behavior specification in terms of SGTs and the lower-level behavior specification in terms of

the target architecture. Compound CAPs (cCAP) are composed by setting relations between elementary CAPs (eCAP). In general, the presented CAP approach allows the transition of IHOs into the less abstract level of the target architecture. In detail, a CAP comprises the necessary templates to generate declarative and procedural structures. While the general structure of the templates may be suitable for an arbitrary production system, the internals are highly specific for the target architecture (in our case ACT-R), because they need to be parameterized towards various control strategies, task environments and tasks. Table 1 shows a couple of implemented CAPs.

Table 1: Selection of CAPs and their definition.

CAP	Definition (after Hollnagel, 1998)
scan	Quick review of displays [...] to obtain a general but preferably complete impression of the state of a system or sub-system.
observe	Look for or read one or more specific measurement values or system indications.
monitor	Follow the development of one or of a set of specific parameters [...] over time.
execute	Perform a previously specified action.

Formalization and Implementation of the Cognitive Activity Pattern and the HTAmap-Model

The CAPs are implemented using a specific schema based on the "Extensible Markup Language" (XML) standard. The notation specifies semantic information about the pattern, descriptions of functionality in terms of ACT-R primitives, the relations to other CAPs and a structured documentation. The CAP's implementation concept provides reusable and task independent components, i.e. generic cognitive behavior blocks in the form of associated production rules and the specification of domain dependent components within one structure. The latter offers possibilities to parameterize the CAPs regarding particular task situations.

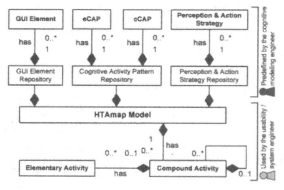

Figure 3: UML-diagram of the components of the HTAmap-model.

The HTAmap-model represents the meta-description of an ACT-R model concerning its associated high-level task model defined by elementary and compound cognitive activity patterns (eCAP/cCAP), a description of the used tasks interface elements (GUI element) and required strategies that handle the perception and action of models (see Figure 3). To build a cognitive model within HTAmap, the modeler selects one of the predefined CAPs stored in the CAP repository. In addition, compound CAPs are composed of their associated elementary CAPs and their relations to each other (e.g., sequencing information). Afterwards, the CAPs are parameterized on the basis of the predefined GUI elements and their associated strategies using the AGImap framework (Urbas & Leuchter, 2005). The high-level task is now specified as HTAmap-model in terms of the low-level cognitive architecture ACT-R relating to a specific task environment. The resulting HTAmap-model is transformed into specific ACT-R constructs and is executable within the cognitive framework.

SimTrA

To analyze cognitive model data for the evaluation of human computer interaction the simulation data has to be preprocessed and provided conveniently. For this reason the *Sim*ulation *Tr*ace *A*nalyzer (SimTrA) was developed. SimTrA is independent of the cognitive model and allows to process simulated and empirical data. For the analysis the data is transferred into a general-purpose format for complex, hierarchically structured data (XML). This forms the basis for a general algorithm-based analysis of the interaction processes. Two levels of abstraction have to be observed in order to analyze the model's performance on the basis of the integrated psychological theories (e.g. visual perception and processing): the global structure and the microstructure level to identify the underlying processes (Gray, 2006). For the global structure, aspects of the model's overall performance are analyzed (e.g. times, errors, and transition-matrices of areas of interest). The microstructure can be characterized by the sub-processes of the cognitive model, i.e. repeated short sequences of action such as control-loops, or scanpaths. For the automated simulation data analysis, algorithms are implemented and integrated into SimTrA. The results are plotted as in classical usability-evaluation methods.

Analyzing Cognitive Model Data

The important role of eye-movement studies in psychological and cognitive research shows that eye movement data is able to give an insight into human behavior and its underlying cognitive processes (Just & Carpenter, 1984; Rayner, 1990; Rötting, 2001). Cognitive models with ACT-R can process visual information, providing spatial and temporal information of the simulated eye movement as in empirical studies. The extraction of this information provides a way to analyze and compare cognitive model data with empirical data on an global (e.g., number of fixations) and microstructure level (e.g., scanpaths). That is the reason for the implementation of SimTrA for eye-movement data (empirical and simulated). The implemented process is divided into three components: the (1) preprocessing of the raw data, the (2) analysis of the preprocessed data and the (3) comparison with further models or empirical data (see Figure 4). This allows the

independent development of each module and an easy extension of its functionality in the future. SimTrA enables the user to apply basal applications regarding the process of analyzing and comparing. After each step the processed data is stored in a general-purpose format and can be processed by external tools (e.g. MatLab, R, SPSS). It is possible to import empirical data into SimTrA for comparison with cognitive model data.

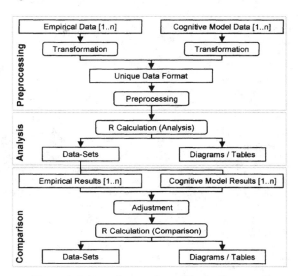

Figure 4: Schematic overview of the implementation concept of SimTrA.

Preprocessing

For the preprocessing of the raw data the empirical data and the cognitive model data are transferred into a general-purpose format (see Figure 4). The transformation allows processing of the data with different quality and origin (e.g. different cognitive architectures, empirical study) with the same algorithms afterwards. While preprocessing each dataset, the stored data is augmented by information on the origin of the data (e.g. cognitive model or empirical data), the subject and the trial identification (i.e. data-Id, subject-Id and trial-Id). In this component, the data of different origins can be scaled to a similar resolution by the user to ensure that the data is comparable. Each kind of information can be altered by the user in the preprocessing component of SimTrA. In this step the data is scaled to a similar resolution to ensure that it is comparable. After the transformation, the data is enriched by additional information that is needed for the analysis. The preprocessing of the raw data is finished by choosing the desired analysis methods.

Analysis

This component enables the analysis of the preprocessed data (see Figure 4). The algorithms for the analysis are implemented in R, a free tool for statistical computing. The results are saved in tables and as graphical plots. In this step algorithms are implemented to analyze the transition frequencies, the fixations on AOIs, the spatial density, the statistical dependency in visual scanning, the local scanpaths and a mean for each of these algorithms (for an overview see Rötting, 2001). In the result tables the data is distinguished by the data-Id, subject-Id and the trial-Id. The absolute and the cumulative number of fixations, fixation durations and general information are stored in a general table. Each algorithm accesses the general table and processes the information needed for the calculation of the respective parameter. To support the user, plots are generated for each analysis. All input-files (i.e. empirical and cognitive model data), results, general information and the distribution of eye movement data are stored in either tables or plots.

Comparison

This component enables the comparison between the analyzed data from cognitive models or empirical studies (see Figure 4). This allows the rating of the simulation experiment and the simulated behavior with respect to empirical findings and psychological theories. This last step enables the iterative adjustment of cognitive models (see Figure 1). Therefore the analyzed data is revised by the user in the provided interface (e.g. missing data, insufficient data points) and compared by algorithms implemented in the software R. To this point of the development of SimTrA the comparison is done by descriptive methods (e.g. mean, standard error and standard deviation) because today's cognitive model data do not have a high variance and statistical inference methods are not applicable.

Practical Application: Process Control System

The use of HTAmap and SimTrA can be illustrated by considering a user's interaction with a complex dynamic interface of a process control system (see Figure 5). The aim is to stabilize the level of liquid in a container which is moderated by inflow, outflow and evaporation. The level can be regulated by adjusting a valve and a heater. For the model based investigation we developed an ACT-R 6.0 model representing the internal knowledge of an experienced user who is familiar with the technical process (as found in a survey of experts). It also describes the graphical user interface (GUI) in terms of AGImap (Urbas & Leuchter, 2005), an interaction abstraction layer above the low-level ACT-R graphical interface (AGI).

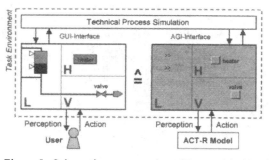

Figure 5: Schematic representation of the empirical study and the simulation experiment with the areas of interest (AOIs) for the human and the models interface.

Pattern Based Modeling of the Task

In dynamic human-machine systems, the human-machine dialogue is normally based on different levels of manual and supervisory control actions. Using the SGT method the regulation task is broken down into the IHOs: get a general idea of the system state (IHO_R), evaluate the system state (especially the level of the container) (IHO_E) and, as necessary, make adjustments to control the level (IHO_A). The identified IHO_R is mapped within the HTAmap-model to the compound CAP "scan" (see Table 1). The compound CAP "scan" environment is composed of a sequence of elementary "observe" CAPs, executed in turn (see Figure 6 left). Required task information for the "observe" CAPs are the interface elements and their values. Within the HTAmap-model the predefined "observe" CAPs are parameterized in the task environment by choosing the relevant GUI elements (i.e. valve, heater and level) and their associated perception strategies (i.e. read-button and read-level) from the particular repositories (see Figure 3). With the compound CAP "scan" two types of sequencing the "observe" CAPs have been implemented: a predefined order (fixed sequence: state-based/top-down control) and a non-defined order (free sequence: reactive/bottom-up control).

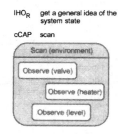 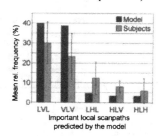

Figure 6: Schematic representation of the cCAP "scan" (right) and relative frequencies of the 5 important scanpaths for model and subject with one standard deviation (left).

Analysis of the Simulation Trace

After simulating the user behavior with the constructed model the simulation data was analyzed by the tool SimTrA. The aim of this analysis was to show that SimTrA is able to provide data that helps to classify the model and its fit to empirical data on a microstructure level. To analyze the microstructure behavior, the local scanpaths (consistent patterns of consecutive fixations; Groner et al., 1984) of actual perceptions were analyzed. They represent stimuli-driven bottom-up processes. Therefore the stimuli were divided in suitable areas of interest (AOI) in the first step (preprocessing) - heater: H, valve: V and level: L (see Figure 5). All theoretical triples of AOIs were determined by the algorithm in the second step (analysis) whereas any sequence of fixations falling into the same AOI is treated as a single gaze fixation and the number of occurrences in the whole sequence of AOIs is assigned to them (e.g. AOIs: 1, 2 - Sequence: 2122112 - triple: 121: 1, 212: 2). Ordering these by frequency shows the most important local scanpaths. Comparing the results with empirical data of a previous experiment in the last step (comparison) reveals that the important local scanpaths in model and empirical data are almost congruent (Dzaack & Urbas, 2006). Therefore local scanpaths with a frequency of 3% were excluded and the remaining five important scanpaths that cover 90% of the model data were used for the comparison human – model (see Figure 6 right). These scanpaths are found to be important for the subjects as well (all five scanpaths cover 80% of the subject's data) and the rank order of the first 3 empirical and predicted scanpaths is the same. The mean relative frequencies of 3 model's scanpaths are within one standard deviation of the subject's data. The mean deviation between the frequency of all scanpaths in the model and human data is about 4%. The comparative analysis of cognitive model data and the empirical data with SimTrA shows that SimTrA is able to process cognitive model data.

Outlook

We designed HTAmap, a pattern-oriented approach for high-level description of cognitive models. Within this approach the cognitive activity patterns (CAP) are the central elements that specify a generic solution for a stereotypical operator task on the description level of ACT-R. Currently, only a selection of CAPs is specified. To transfer more "associated" production rules into CAPs, further work on verification and validation is required. An editor for building HTAmap-models is being implemented and an usability evaluation will be conducted. Further work is needed on the extension of the analysis tool SimTrA. It has to be evaluated which additional usability related analysis algorithms can be integrated for this purpose. Subsequently a second experiment is planned where different interface designs for the task described above are tested with humans and with a cognitive model. We believe that building cognitive models with the help of HTAmap makes the modeling process more accessible for a wider user group, simplifies the reuse of model fragments and improves the model communication. SimTrA enables the comparison of cognitive model behavior with human behavior on a global and a microstructure level. Both together could lead to an increased application of cognitive models in the usability evaluation.

Acknowledgments

This project has been funded by Deutsche Forschungs-gemeinschaft (Research Training Group 1013 prometei) and VolkswagenStiftung.

References

Anderson, J. R., Bothell, D., Byrne, M. D., Douglass, S., Lebiere, C., & Qin, Y. (2004). An integrated theory of the mind. *Psychological Review, 111*, 1036-1060.

Byrne, M. D. (2003). Cognitive Architectures. In J. Jacko, & A. Sears (Eds.), *Handbook of Human-Computer Interaction.* Hillsdale, NJ: Lawrence Erlbaum Associates.

Crossman, J., Wray, R. E., Jones, R. M., & Lebiere C. A (2004) High Level Symbolic Representation for Behaviour Modeling. *Proc. Conference on Behavior Representation.* Arlington, VA.

Limbourg, Q., & Vanderconckt, J. (2004). Comparing Task Models for User Interface Design. In D. Diaper & N. Stanton (Eds.), *The Handbook of Task Analysis for Human-Computer Interaction.* NJ: LEA.

Dzaack. J., & Urbas, L. (2006). Kognitive Modelle zur Evaluation der Gebrauchstauglichkeit von Mensch-Maschine Systemen. In M. Grandt & A. Bauch (Eds.), *Cognitive Systems Engineering in der Fahrzeug- und Prozessführung.* Bonn: DGLR.

Ellis, S.R., & Smith, J.D. (1985). Patterns of Statistical Dependency in Visual Scanning. In R. Groner, G.W. McConkie & C. Menz (Eds.). *Eye Movement and Human Information Processing.* Amsterdam: Elsevier.

Gray, W. D., Sims, C. R., & Schoelles, M. J. (2006). Musings on Models of Integrated Cognition: What Are They? What Do They Tell Us that Simpler Approaches Cannot? How Do We Evaluate Them? *Proc. of the 7th ICCM* (pp. 12-13). NJ: LEA.

Groner, R., Walder, F., & Groner, M. (1984). Looking at faces: local and global aspects of scanpaths. In A. G. Gale & F. Johnson (Eds.), *Theoretical and Applied Aspects of Eye Movement Research.* North-Holland: Elsevier.

Heffernan, N. T., Koedinger, K. R., & Aleven, V. A. (2003). Tools Towards Reducing the Costs of Designing, Building, and Testing Cognitive Models. *Proc. BRIMS.*

Hollnagel, E. (1998). *Cognitive Reliability and Error Analysis Method (CREAM).* Oxford: Elsevier.

Howes, A., & Young, R. M. (1997). The role of cognitive architecture in modeling the user: Soar's learning mechanism. *Human-Computer Interaction 12,* 4, 311-343.

Just, M.A., & Carpenter, P.A. (1984). Using eye fixations to study reading comprehension: Individual differences in working memory. *Psychological Review 99,* 122-149.

Ormerod, T. C., & Shepherd, A. (2004). Using Task Analysis for Information Requirements Specification: The Sub-Goal Template (SGT) Method. In D. Diaper, & N., A. Stanton, (Eds.), *The handbook of task analysis for human-computer interaction.* Mahwah, NJ: LEA.

Rayner, K. (1999). Do eye movements reflect higher order processes in reading? In R. Groner, G. d'Ydewalle & R. Parham (Eds.), *From Eye to Mind: Information Acquisition in Perception, Search, and Reading.* NY: Elsevier.

Ritter, F. R., Haynes, S. R., Cohen, M., Howes, A., John, B., Best, B., et al. (2006). High-level Behavior Representation Languages Revisited. *Proc. ICCM '06* (pp. 404-407). Edizioni Goliardiche.

Rötting, M. (2001): *Parametersystematik der Augen- und Blickbewegungen für arbeitswissenschaftliche Untersuchungen.* Shaker, Aachen

Shepherd, A. (2001). *Hierarchical task analysis.* New York: Taylor & friends.

Tollinger, I., Lewis, R. L., McCurdy, M., Tollinger, P., Vera, A., Howes, A., et al. (2005). Supporting efficient development of cognitive models at multiple skill levels: exploring recent advances in constraint-based modeling. *Proc. CHI '05* (pp. 411-420). ACM Press.

Urbas, L., & Leuchter, S. (2005). Model Based Analysis and Design of Human-Machine Dialogues through Displays. *KI – Künstliche Intelligenz, 4,* 45-51.

Emotion Elicitation in an Empathic Virtual Dialog Agent

Magalie Ochs (magalie.ochs@orange-ftgroup.com)
France Telecom, R&D Division, Technology Center, France
LINC Lab., IUT of Montreuil, Université Paris VIII, France

Catherine Pelachaud (c.pelachaud@iut.univ-paris8.fr)
LINC Lab., IUT of Montreuil, Université Paris VIII, France

David Sadek (david.sadek@orange-ftgroup.com)
France Telecom, R&D Division, Technology Center, France

Abstract

Recent research has shown that a virtual agent able to express empathic emotions enhances human-machine interaction. To identify under which circumstances a virtual agent should express such emotions, we analyze the conditions of users' expression of emotion during their interaction with a virtual dialog agent. We have developed a new method of annotation based both on the psychological theory of emotion elicitation and on the philosophical speech act theory. Moreover, the tags of the coding scheme have been specifically designed to be easily integrated in a virtual dialog agent. A human-machine dialog corpus has been annotated with the scheme. The method of annotation and the results of the analysis of annotated dialogs are presented in this paper. Hypotheses as to the appropriate conditions of emotion elicitation for an empathic virtual dialog agent are set out.

Introduction

A growing interest in using virtual agents as interfaces to computational systems has been observed in recent years. This is motivated by an attempt to enhance human-machine interaction. Humanoid-like agents are generally used to embody some roles typically performed by humans, as for example a tutor (Johnson, Rickel & Lester, 2000) or an actor (André, Klesen, Gebhard et al., 2001). The expression of emotions can increase their believability by creating an *illusion of life* (Bates, 1994). Recent researches have shown that virtual agent's expressions of empathic emotions enhance users' satisfaction, engagement, perception of the virtual agents, and performance in task achievement (Brave, Nass & Hutchinson, 2005; Klein, Moon & Picard, 1999; Partala & Surakka, 2004; Prendinger, Mori & Ishizaka, 2005).

In our research, we are particularly interested in the use of virtual dialog agents as information systems. Users interact in natural language to find out information on a specific domain. We aim to give such agents the capability of expressing empathic emotions towards users during dialog, and thus to improve interaction(Klein, Moon & Picard, 1999; Prendinger, Mori & Ishizuka, 2005).

Empathy can be defined as the capacity to "put yourself in someone else's shoes". Through the empathic process, someone may feel the same emotion as another person because the former thinks that the latter feels (or could or should feel) this emotion (Poggi, 2004).

Introducing empathy into a virtual dialog agent means to give it the ability to identify emotions potentially felt by a user during interaction. This requires that the virtual dialog agent knows the circumstances under which a user may feel an emotion during the interaction. To identify them, we study, in light of the psychological theory of emotion elicitation and the philosophical speech act theory, real human-machine dialogs that lead a user to express emotions.

In this paper, we first introduce theoretical foundations that guide us in the design of our corpora-based method. We then set out a coding scheme that enables us to highlight the circumstances of emotions elicitation in human-machine dialogs. Finally, we present hypotheses on the conditions of users' emotion elicitation that we have identified through the analysis of dialogs annotated with our scheme.

Emotion Elicitation in Dialog: Theoretical Foundations

An empathic virtual agent should be able to identify the emotional meaning of a situation to determine emotions potentially felt by its interlocutors.

The Appraisal Theory of Emotion. To highlight characteristics of emotion-elicited situations, *the Appraisal Theory of Emotion* (Scherer, 2000), which aims to explain how human emotions are triggered, can be used. According to this theory, emotions are elicited by the evaluation of an event. This evaluation depends mostly on a person's beliefs and goals. Indeed, an event may trigger an emotion only if the person thinks that it affects one of her goals (Lazarus, 1991). The *consequence of the event* on the individual goal determines the elicited emotion. For instance, fear is triggered when a survival goal is threatened. Generally, failed goals elicit negative emotions whereas achieved goals trigger positive ones. Emotions depend on the *causes of the event* (another person for example). For instance, a goal failure caused by another agent may trigger anger.

The Speech Act Theory. To be able to identify a user's potentially felt emotions, a virtual dialog agent has to know, first, the user's goals and beliefs during the dialog. Researchers in philosophy have observed that language is not only used to describe something or to give some statement but also to do something with intention, *i.e.* to act (Austin, 1962; Searle, 1969). Then, a *communicative act* (or *speech act*) is defined as the basic unit of language used to express an intention. Based on the *Speech Acts Theory* (Austin, 1962; Searle, 1969), we suppose that users' goal during human-machine dialog is to achieve the *perlocutory effects* of the performed communicative act. The *perlocutory effects* describe the intention that the user wants to see achieved through the performed communicative act. For instance, the *perlocutory effect* of the act to inform agent j of proposition p is that agent j knows proposition p. In addition, we suppose that the user has the intention that her interlocutor knows her intention to produce the *perlocutory effects* of the performed communicative act. This intention corresponds to the *intentional effect* of the act (Sadek, 1991). For instance, the *intentional effect* of the act to ask agent j some information p, is that agent j knows that the speaker has the intention to know information p. The achievement of *intentional effect* of an act represents a precondition for the feasibility of the act's *perlocutory effects*.

In the context of dialog, an event corresponds to a *communicative act*. Consequently, according to the appraisal theory of emotion (Scherer, 2000), a communicative act may trigger a user's emotion if it affects one of her goals. The elicited emotion depends on consequences of the communicative act on her goal and its causes. Before modeling an empathic dialog agent, we have to answer several questions. During human-machine dialog, how can communicative acts affect a user's goals? What are the consequences on a user's goals that can lead her to feel emotions? Do the causes have an impact on a user's emotion elicitation?

To answer these questions, we aim to extract the proprieties to drive the emotion elicitation of a dialog agent by analyzing real human-machine dialogs that have triggered users's emotions.

A Coding Scheme for Annotating Conditions of Emotion Elicitation

In order to identify what triggers users' emotions, we annotate real human-machine dialogs to emphasize the characteristics of the situations that lead users to express emotions.

The Coding Scheme

An emotion may be elicited when a communicative act affects a user's goal. The consequences and causes of the communicative act on the user's goal determine the elicited emotion. Therefore, the annotation has to highlight impacts of communicative acts on users' goals and their causes.

We have manually analyzed 10 real human-machine dialogs (that corresponds approximately to 1000 dialog turns) during which users interact with a virtual dialog agent to find a specific restaurant in Paris or to obtain information on stock exchange. During theses dialogs,

users express emotions. We have studied them in order to identify the different impacts of communicative acts on users' goals and their causes which can occur in human-machine interaction.

From this analysis, we have identified the following consequences and causes of communicative acts that appear most often. Let's u be the user, a the agent, e an event, and g a goal.

- **Consequences of an event on a user's goal.** Event e is annotated by this tag if:
  - *Goal achievement* tag $goal\_achieve_u(e, g)$ event e has enabled u to achieve goal g, that she thought to produce by e.
  - *Goal failure* tag: $goal\_failure_u(e, g)$ event e has not enabled u to achieve goal g, that she thought to produce by e.

- **Causes of an event that lead to goal failure.** Event e is annotated by this tag if it is caused by the fact that:
  - *Unfeasibility tag* $unfeasibility_u(e, a, g)$ a does not have the capacity to achieve goal g of u.
  - *Belief conflict tag*: $belief\_conflict_u(e, a, g\_a)$ a believes that u has another goal g_a other than her own one.
  - *Goal conflict tag*: $goal\_conflict_u(e, a, g)$ a had a goal g that u thought that it was already achieved.

These tags constitute the coding scheme that enables us to annotate human-machine dialog corpora.

To use this coding scheme, beliefs and goals of the users (and of the virtual dialog agent) have to be known. Based on the Speech Act Theory (introduced previously), we suppose that if the user (or the virtual dialog agent) performs a communicative act, it means that:

- she has the *goals* to achieve the *intentional and perlocutory effects* of the act

- she *believes* that she can achieve the *intentional and perlocutory effects* of the act that she expresses.

For instance, a communicative act e performed by user u is annotated by the tag $goal\_failure_u(e, g)$ if the expression of act e has not allowed u to achieve the *intentional or perlocutory effect* g of act e.

Keeping in mind that we aim at using results of the annotation to create an empathic virtual dialog agent, we have represented such tags in a computational way. In the next section, after introducing the concept of a rational dialog agent used to create virtual dialog agents, we present our computational tag representation.

A computational representation of the coding scheme

The concept of a rational dialog agent To create a virtual dialog agent, we use a model of a rational agent based on a formal theory of interaction (called *Rational Interaction Theory*) (Sadek, 1991). This model uses a BDI-like approach (Rao & Georgeff, 1991; Cohen & Levesque, 1990). An implementation of this theory produced the rational dialog agent technology (named *Artimis*) that provides a generic framework to instantiate intelligent agents able to engage in a rich interaction with both human interlocutors and artificial agents (Sadek, 1997). The *mental state* of a rational agent is composed of two mental attitudes: *belief* and *intention*. They are formalized with the modal operators B and I (p being a closed formula denoting a proposition): $B_i p$ means "agent i thinks that p is true". $I_i p$ means "agent i intents to bring about p". Based on its mental state, a rational agent acts to achieve its intentions. Several others operators have been introduced to formalize the occurred actions, the agent who has achieved it, and the temporal relations. For instance, the formula $Done(e, p)$ means that event e has just taken place and p was true before e occurred. For more details see (Sadek, 1991; Sadek, Bretier & Panaget, 1997).

The computational tags representation   To easily integrate the results of the annotation in such rational dialog agents, we describe the tags of the coding scheme in terms of beliefs and intentions. Examples of tags follow:

- *Goal failure tag* can be described by the following combination of mental attitudes:

$$goal\_failure_u(e, g) =_{def}$$
$$B_u(Done(e, I_u(g) \wedge B_u(Done(e) => g))$$
$$\wedge B_u(\neg g)$$

This formula means: "agent u believes that event e has just taken place ($B_u(Done(e))$). Before the occurrence of event e, agent u had the intention g ($I_u(g)$), and believed that e would enable the achievement of g ($B_u(Done(e) => g)$). After the occurrence of e, agent u does not believe that g has been achieved ($B_u(\neg g)$)".

- *Belief conflict tag* can be described by the following combination of mental attitudes:

$$belief\_conflict_u(e, a, g\_a) =_{def}$$
$$B_u(Done(e, \neg I_u(g\_a) \wedge B_a(I_u(g\_a))))$$

This formula means: "agent u believes that event e has just taken place" ($B_u(Done(e))$). Before the occurrence of event e, agent u did not have the intention g_a ($\neg I_u(g\_a)$), and believed that agent a thought that u had this intention ($B_a(I_u(g\_a))$)".

The Conditions of User's Emotion Elicitation in Human-Machine Dialogs

In order to study the user's conditions of emotion elicitation, we have annotated human-machine dialogs with the tags described in the previous section. After introducing the copora we use, we present an example of annotated dialog.

Annotation of Human-Machine Dialog Corpora

Description of the Corpora   To construct the corpora, we collected 20 real vocal human-machine dialogs which lead users to express emotions. The corpora we use are derived from two vocal applications developed at France Telecom R&D: *PlanResto* and *Dialogue Bourse*. *PlanResto* is a restaurant guide for Paris. Users interact using natural language with a rational dialog agent to find a restaurant (for more details see Ancé, Bretier, Breton et al. ,2004). *Dialogue Bourse* is a stock exchange application that allows a user to consult her accounts, to find rates and to perform transactions by interacting with a rational dialog agent by phone. The dialogs are composed of 86 dialog turns on average. The user's utterances are generally short, averaging 4 words per utterance.

The dialogs have been annotated with two labels of emotions (positive and negative) by two annotators. However, only negative labels of emotion have been used by the two annotators (no agreement is appeared between the two annotators' annotations of positive emotion). The annotations were made based on vocal and semantic cues of users' emotions. In the dialogs transcribed into text, these tags represent the moment where a user expresses her emotion.

An example of annotated dialog   extracted from the corpora (translated from French) is below. Annotations based on the coding scheme described above are in bold in the dialog:

Agent: Welcome to PlanResto. PlanResto enables you to look for a restaurant according to its speciality, its localization and your budget. What are you looking for?
User: The Hippopotamus restaurant hmmm in the 14th urban district
Agent: A restaurant in the 14th urban district. I have found more than a hundred. You can specify a speciality, for example specific type of food. You can speak now. *(event e1)*
goal_failure$_{user}$(e1, the agent knows the user's intention is to have information on the Hippopotamus Restaurant)
User: hmmm
Agent: A Greek restaurant *(event e2)*
goal_failure$_{user}$(e2, the agent knows the user's intention is to have information on the Hippopotamus Restaurant)
belief_conflict$_{user}$(e2, agent, to have information on Greek restaurant)
User: no, grill food
Agent: I now have 8 restaurants. You can ask for them to be listed. What price range are you looking for? *(event e3)*
goal_achieve$_{user}$(e3, the agent knows the user's intention to find a grill restaurant)
User: hmmm more than fifteen euros
Agent: I have not understood you *(event e4)*

goal_failure$_{user}$(e4, **the agent knows the user's intention to find a restaurant with a price superior to 15 euros**)

[...]

A user's Expression of Negative Emotion

Results of the Annotation

From the 20 dialogs annotated with the coding scheme presented, 47 dialogical situations that lead a user to express negative emotions have been studied manually. These situations are sequences of communicative acts that occurred just before an emotional expression.

First of all, we have observed that negative emotions appeared generally after *goal failures*. In 45 situations, the user expresses a negative emotion after a sequence of communicative acts lead to the failure of one of her goals (Table 1). In the corpora studied, the most frequent situation is the failure of the goal to achieve the intentional effect of the performed communicative act. In other words, the goal failure is mainly due to the fact that the agent does not understand the user's request.

Table 1: The situations leading to a user's expression of emotion

Type of Situation	Number of Situations Observed
Goal Failure	45
Belief Conflict	2
Goal Conflict	3

We have observed that in some cases the expression of a negative emotion seems to be triggered by a *belief conflict* or a *goal conflict*, or by a *belief conflict* and a *goal conflict*. In two situations, the user expressed a negative emotion when it appeared that the virtual dialog agent tried to achieve a goal different from the user's one (*belief conflict*). In three situations, the user's expression of negative emotion appeared when the virtual agent tried to achieve a goal that the user knew had already been achieved and thus it is no more a user's active goal (*goal conflict*) (Table 1). *Goal failure*, *belief conflict* and *goal conflict* can appear in a single dialogical situation. For instance, in some cases, the virtual agent believed that the user had a goal different from her own one (*belief conflict*) and the user thought that this goal had already been achieved (*goal conflict*). A *belief conflict* or a *goal conflict* can also lead to a *goal failure*.

We have studied more precisely the situations of goal failures that lead a user to express emotion. We have observed that the causes of these goal failures are *belief conflicts* and *goal conflicts*. In the dialogs leading to a user's expression of emotion, the user's goals failed in the majority of observed situations (30 situations out of 45) because the virtual agent thought that the user had a goal different from her own one (*belief conflict*). In one situation, a goal failure led to a negative emotion due to the fact that the agent tried to achieve a goal that had already been achieved (*goal conflict*). However,

the goal failures caused by the *unfeasibility* of the agent to achieve the user's goal do not seem to elicit an expression of a negative emotion (Table 2). In the other goal failure situations, our coding scheme has not enabled us to highlight their causes. It's why we are able to identify the causes of only 31 out of 45 goal failures

Table 2: The causes of goal failures

Causes of Goal Failure	Number of Situations Observed
Belief Conflict	30
Goal Conflict	1
Unfeasibility	0

The expressions of a negative emotion are generally elicited after several successive failures to complete a goal. On average, three to four goal failures led a user to express a negative emotion (Table 3).

We have also studied the influence of an emotion, already expressed during the dialog, on the elicitation of a new emotion. Less goal failures are required to trigger a negative emotion expression when a negative emotion has already been expressed during the dialog. Indeed, the first negative emotion is triggered after the occurrence of 3 or 4 goal failures successively while the second negative emotion will be triggered after 2 goal failures (see Table 3). A negative emotion seems to be triggered more rapidly when the user has already expressed another negative emotion since the beginning of the dialog.

Table 3: The average number of goal failures that lead to a user's expression of emotion

Situation	Number of Goal Failures
General Case	3-4
2nd Emotion Expressed	2

Discussion

Hypotheses on users' conditions of emotion elicitation

According to the results of the annotation, negative emotions seem to be triggered after *goal failures* or after *belief* or *goal conflicts*. From these results, we introduce 2 definitions:

Primary conflicting mental state. A *goal failure* can be described as a conflict between a user belief before and after the goal failure: before the goal failure, the user believes that her goal is going to be achieved and after the goal failure she realizes that it is not. We introduce the concept of *primary conflicting mental state*. A user has this mental state when one of her beliefs about her environment is different from the reality that she has just observed. The reality observed is then in conflict with her beliefs. The *goal failure* is a *primary conflicting mental state*.

Secondary conflicting mental state. A *belief or goal conflict* corresponds to a conflict between a user's and the virtual agent's beliefs. Indeed, in the case of a *belief conflict*, the virtual agent thinks that the user has a goal that the user does not have. In a *goal conflict*, the user thinks a goal has already been achieved whereas the virtual agent does not. To describe these conflicting mental states, we use the term *secondary conflicting mental state*. A user has this mental state when one of her beliefs about her environment is different from her belief about the mental state of another agent. For instance, let's *p* be a user's belief on her environment. The user has a secondary conflicting mental state if she thinks that the agent thinks (not *p*). The beliefs of the user about her environment are in conflict with her beliefs on the mental state of another agent. The *belief conflict* and the *goal conflict* are *secondary conflicting mental states*.

Given the definitions just introduced and the results of the annotation, we venture the following hypotheses:

Hypothesis 1. A negative emotion may be elicited by *primary conflicting mental states*. A negative emotion can also be triggered by a *secondary conflicting mental state*.

We have observed that goal failures leading to a user's expression of emotion are caused by a belief or a goal conflict, which let us make the following hypothesis:

Hypothesis 2. The *primary conflicting mental states* that elicit emotions are caused by a *secondary conflicting mental state*.

In the dialogs observed, several goal failures are required to elicit a user's expression of emotion. The number of goal failures depends on the dialogic situation (see Table 3). We can suppose that this number informs us of the intensity of the emotion. Indeed, all the emotions felt are not expressed. More precisely, emotions with low intensity are generally not perceptible. Only emotions with an intensity reaching a certain threshold are expressed. We can presume that an emotion with low intensity requires more goal failures to be expressed. On the other hand, an emotion with high intensity is expressed after few goal failures. We have observed in the dialog corpora that less goal failures are necessary to elicit an emotional expression if an emotion has already been expressed during the dialog. This leads us to our third hypothesis:

Hypothesis 3. The intensity of an elicited emotion depends on the emotions already triggered during the dialog.

This influence may be explained by the fact that the intensity of the first elicited emotion is not null when the second one is triggered (since the dialogs we have studied are relatively short). Then, the intensity of the first emotion is added to the second one. The intensity are cumulative.

Future Works

According to psychological theories on emotion elicitation, other variables may influence the intensity of emotion. For instance, the *effort invested* to complete a goal influences the intensity of an emotion elicited by a goal failure (Ortony, Clore & Collins, 1988). If one fails to achieve something after trying very hard to achieve it, the triggered negative emotion is likely to be of greater intensity than if one fails after trying less hard. In the context of dialog, the effort can be represented by the number of communicative acts performed to achieve a goal. Our analysis of the corpora has not enabled us to show the influence of this variable on the intensity of emotion. This may be due to the few amount of dialogs studied. Others variables, such as the *importance for the agent to achieve its goal* or the *unexpectedness of an event that occurs*, can significantly influence the intensity of the elicited emotion. However, the current coding scheme does not highlight such variables.

Given the corpus used in this work, some affective information has not been taken into account, such as the influence of a user's personality and mood in the emotion elicitation. The emotional tags (positive and negative) do not enable us to study the elicitation of different kinds of emotion (such as anger, satisfaction, joy, relief, disappointment, etc) and their intensity. This work is, of course, not sufficient to model a user's emotions but enables us to provide to a virtual agent with some information on the dialogical situations that *may* trigger a user's emotions and thus enables us to model an empathic dialog agent.

Conclusion

An empathic virtual agent should express emotions in the situations that may potentially elicit a user's emotion. To identify these emotional situations, we have annotated human-machine dialogs that lead users to express negative emotions. We have constructed a particular coding scheme based on a theoretical and empirical approach. Each tag is described in terms of mental attitudes of beliefs and intentions. This semantically grounded formal representation will enable us to easily integrate the results of the analysis of the annotated corpora in a rational agent system. Dialogs that have been annotated with this coding scheme enable us to emphasize some features of emotional human-machine dialogs. A user's negative emotions seem to be elicited by particular *conflicting mental states*. The intensity of these emotions depends on if another emotion has already been triggered during the dialog or not.

The number of dialog situations that have been analyzed and that lead to a user's expression of emotions is not sufficient to draw conclusions on the user's conditions of emotion elicitation during human-machine dialogs.

The work presented in this paper represents a first step towards the creation of an empathic virtual dialog agent. We are currently implementing them in a rational dialog agent. A subjective evaluation will be performed to verify the believability of the conditions of the agent's empathic emotions expressions.

Acknowledgments

We thank Emilie Chanoni for her valuable comments on the concept of conflicting mental states.

References

Ancé, C., Bretier, P., Breton, G., Damnati, G., Moudenc, T., Pape, J.-P., Pele, D., Panaget, F., & Sadek, D. (2004). Find a restaurant with the 3d embodied conversational agent nestor. *Proceedings of the 5th Workshop on Discourse and Dialogue (SigDIAL)*, Boston, USA.

André, E., Klesen, P., Gebhard, P., Allen, S., & Rist, T. (2001). Integrating models of personality and emotions into lifelike characters. In A. Paiva (Eds), *Affective interactions: towards a new generation of computer interfaces*. New York: Springer-Verlag.

Austin, J. (1962). *How to do things with words*. London: Oxford University Press.

Bates, J. (1994). The role of emotion in believable agents. *Communications of the ACM, 37*, 122–125.

Brave, S., Nass, C., & Hutchinson, K. (2005). Computers that care: Investigating the effects of orientation of emotion exhibited by an embodied computer agent. *International Journal of Human-Computer Studies, 62*, 161–178.

Cohen, P., & Levesque, H. (1990). Intention is choice with commitment. *Artificial Intelligence, 42(2-3)*, 213–232.

Johnson, W., Rickel, J., & Lester, J. (2000). Animated pedagogical agents: Face to- face interaction in interactive learning environments. *International Journal of Artificial Intelligence in Education, 11*, 47–78.

Klein, J., Moon, Y., & Picard, R. (1999). This computer responds to user frustration. *Proceedings of the Conference on Human Factors in Computing Systems*, (pp. 242–243). New York: ACM Press.

Lazarus, R. S. (1991). *Emotion and adaptation*. New York: Oxford University Press.

Ortony, A., Clore, G., & Collins, A. (1988). *The cognitive structure of emotions*. United Kingdom: Cambridge University Press.

Partala, T., & Surakka, V. (2004). The effects of affective interventions in human-computer interaction. *Interacting with computers, 16*, 295–309.

Poggi, I. (2004). Emotions from mind to mind. *Proceedings of the Workshop on Empathic Agents AAMAS*, (pp. 11–17).

Prendinger, H., Mori, J., & Ishizuka, M. (2005). Using human physiology to evaluate subtle expressivity of a virtual quizmaster in a mathematical game. *International Journal of Human- Computer Studies, 62*, 231–245.

Rao, A. S. & Georgeff, M. (1991). Modeling rational agents within a bdiarchitecture.*Proceedings of the International Conference on Principles of Knowledge Representation and Reasoning (KR)* (pp. 473–484). Allen, J., Fikes, R., and Sandewall, E., editors, San Mateo: Morgan Kaufmann.

Sadek, D. (1991). *Attitudes mentales et interaction rationnelle: vers une théorie formelle de la communication*. Doctoral dissertation, Department of Computer Science, University of Rennes I., Rennes.

Sadek, D., Bretier, P., & Panaget, F. (1997). Artimis: Natural dialogue meets rational agency. *Proceedings of the 15th International Joint Conference on Artificial Intelligence (IJCAI 97)* (pp. 1030–1035), Nagoya, Japon.

Scherer, K. (2000). Emotion. In M. Hewstone, & W. Stroebe (Eds), *Introduction to Social Psychology: A European perspective*. Oxford: Oxford Blackwell Publishers.

Searle, J. (1969). *Speech Acts*. United Kingdom: Cambridge.

Motivated, Emotional Agents in the MicroPsi Framework

Joscha Bach (jbach@uos.de)
Institute for Cognitive Science, University of Osnabrück
49069 Osnabrück, Germany

Abstract

MicroPsi is a cognitive architecture based on the Psi theory of D. Dörner. The framework provides a neurosymbolic model that integrates emotion and motivation. Here, emotion is mainly discussed as modulatory states that can be interpreted as *configurations of cognition*. Motivation is clearly distinct from emotion, and based on a finite set of cognitive and motivational drives. We describe Dörner's model of emotion and motivation and how it is implemented in MicroPsi agents.

Introduction

The Psi theory (Dörner 1999, 2002) describes the regulation of high-level action in a cognitive agent. Psi agents have a memory and perceptual apparatus that might best be characterized as a perceptual symbol system (Barsalou 1999). Representations in the Psi theory are hierarchical spreading activation networks (Bach 2005, Bach and Vuine 2003), their lowest level being made up of sensors and actuators. The Psi theory puts its main focus on understanding the role of motivation and affect *within* a cognitive system, that is, motivation and emotion are not seen as an external modules communicating with a cognitive "problem solving machine". Rather, the Psi theory offers a *functional* explanation of emotion and motivation. This marks an important difference to other symbolic cognitive architectures, such as Soar (Laird, Newell, Rosenbloom 1987) and ACT-R (Anderson and Lebiere 1998), even though it shows several similarities to the CLARION architecture (Sun 2005).

Its unique properties have lead the author to implement the Psi theory as an agent architecture and to supply a framework for cognitive modeling, called MicroPsi. While our architecture has been the subject of several earlier publications (see for instance Bach 2003, Bach and Vuine 2006), we have found that the underlying theory should be made available to a greater audience. The following sections classify and describe Dörner's approach to modelling emotion and motivation, and briefly explain their implementation in MicroPsi model.

Models of Emotion

The growing number of models of emotion is arguably one of the most interesting developments in AI and cognitive science within the last two decades. Partly, this is due to the growing demand for solid research in the design and control of *believable agents* for character animation or behavior simulation in computer games and movies, and for animated avatars and/or dialogue systems (André and Rist 2001) that provide a human-like, *affective* interface to technical devices. These demands have given rise to *affective computing* (Picard 1997). Next to the creation of believable emotional expression, capturing the role of emotion in decision making may increase the accuracy of models of human social behavior (von Scheve 2000; Castelfranchi 1998; Cacioppo et al. 2002; Schmidt 2000). Emotional states, which range from momentary reactions and *affects*, over undirected and persistent *moods* towards *emotional dispositions*, also influence perception, planning, task execution and memory and are therefore incorporated in models of task performance (Belavkin, Ritter and Elliman 1999; Oatley and Jenkins 1996; Gratch and Marsella, 2001). Many individual differences in behavior are due to variances in emotional range, intensity and coping strategies, especially when comparing the behavior of adults and children (Belavkin et al., 1999). On the side of neurobiology, *affective neuroscience* (Damasio 1994; Panksepp 1998; Rolls 1999; Lane and Nadel 2000) has started to lend a physiological foundation to understanding emotion. Reflecting the growing recognition of the importance of emotion for understanding human behavior, a vast number of emotional architectures for different applications, and with very different methodologies, has been proposed during the last two decades. (For reviews, see Hudlicka and Fellous 1996; Picard 1997; Ritter et al. 2002; Gratch and Marsella 2005.)

Putting emotion into agent architectures may also have technical benefits: adopting emotional modes of information processing could possibly improve the performance of robots and software agents. Whenever environments get more complex and open, it becomes harder to define rules that are applicable and efficient in all interaction contexts that might arise. Thus, adaptive heuristics are called for, which control how information is acquired, processed and stored and which methods are used for decision making and action. Emotional architectures are good candidates for such heuristics, as emotions are fulfilling similar roles in biological organisms. (See, for instance, Sloman 1992, Pfeifer 1988.) Obviously, the majority of the immense number of decisions biological systems have to face in every given moment are not settled by rational reasoning but rather by more simple, reactive means, mainly because complex cognitive processes tend to be slow and require more mental resources. The same is true for decisions that apply to the organisation of mental processes. The way humans focus their deliberation on individual aspects of objects, for instance during perception, memorizing or planning, is highly variable and demands control mechanisms just as much as the organisation of physical resources. Emotions may also allow for fast and efficient evaluation of objects, events or the potential outcomes of actions with regard to their impact on the well-being of the agent, and impairments in emotional control systems have grave impacts on our ability to reason, to react to environmental stimuli and to behave socially adequate (Damasio 2003). Sometimes it is argued that artificial intelligence will *necessarily* have to incorporate artificial emotion, because emotions provide indispensable functionality to mental functioning (Toda 1982, Lisetti and Gmytrasiewicz 2002, Minsky 2006).

Classes of models

Architectures that represent implementations of artificial emotions can be classified in several ways, for instance by looking at the way emotions are embedded within the cognitive system. There are architectures, where

- Emotions act, in conjuction with the motivational system, as main control structures of the agent. Action control and behavior execution depends on the states of the emotional component, and deliberative processes are only consulted when the need arises. (This is the approach taken in the Psi theory.)
- Emotions are parts or descriptors of individual sub-agents that compete within the architecture for the control of behaviours and actions. (This is the organizational principle of *Cathéxis* by Velásquez (1997) and Cañamero's *Abbotts* (1997). Thus, the emotional agent itself is implemented as a multi-agent system, which makes it easy to model the co-occurrence of multiple emotions.
- Emotions are a module within the cognitive architecture that offers results to other, coexisting modules. Control is either distributed among these components or subordinated to a central execution or deliberation component (an approach that has been taken, for instance, in the *PECS* agents: Schmidt 2000).
- Emotions act only as an interface for communication with human users and as a guise for behavior strategies that bear no similarity to emotional processing. They might either model emotional states of the communication partner and help to respond accordingly, or they might just aid in creating believable communication (for instance, in an electronic shopping system).

A second possible way of classifying emotional architectures expands on the *method of modelling*. Common approaches consist in:

- Modelling emotions as explicit states. Thus, the emotional agent has a number of states it can be in, possibly with varying intensity, and a set of state transition functions. These states parameterise the modules of behaviour, perception, deliberation and so on.
- Modelling emotions by connecting them directly to stimuli, assessments or urges (like hunger or social needs) of the agent. (Appraisal models, suggested for instance by Frijda 1986, Scherer 1984, Roseman et al. 1996.)
- Modelling emotions as results of the co-occurrence of basic emotions. Suggestions for suitable sets of primary emotions and/or emotion determinants have been made by emotion psychologists (for instance Plutchik, 1980).
- Modelling emotions implicitly by identifying the parameters that modify the agent's behaviour and are thus

the correlates of the emotions. The manipulation of these parameters will modify the emotional setting of the agent. This way, the emotions are not part of the implementation but rather an emergent phenomenon.

Emotions in Dörner's Psi agents are implemented in the latter way: Instead of realizing them as distinct entities, the agents are modulated by parameters that are not emotions themselves. Emotions become an emergent phenomenon: they appear on a different descriptional level, as the particular way cognitive processing is carried out. For example, *anger* is, according to the Psi theory, initiated by the failure to attain a goal in the face of an obstacle and is characterized by a low resolution level, which leads to a limited problem solving capacity and neglect for details. Also, the failure increases the sense of urgency, which in turn amplifies the activation level, leading to more impulsive action, and a narrower examination of the environment. 'Anger' is the label that we use for this particular, typical configuration, as we observe it in humans – and Dörner (1999, p. 561) argues: if we agree, this set of conditions were indeed what we mean by 'anger', then it is reasonable to apply the same label to the same configuration in an artificial agent.

Emotion in the Psi Theory

The Psi theory does not explain emotions as a link between stimulus and behavior, but as a modulation of cognition. This idea has gained more ground in cognitive science in recent years, as other researchers focus on cognitive modulation, often also called *behavior moderation* (Hudlicka 1997) or *moderation of cognition* (Gluck, Gunzelmann, et al. 2006) and is also supported by findings in neuroscience (Erk, Kiefer et al. 2003). The view that the cognitive modulation through internal, subconscious measures of success and failure, represented in more detail as *competence* and *uncertainty* in the Dörner model, plays a role in problem solving, is for instance taken by Ritter and Belavkin (2000), and can be found in at least two other, independently developed models (Andreae 1998; Scherer 1993).

The emotion model of the Psi theory spans a six-dimensional continuous space: K. Hille (1998) describes it with the following proto-emotional dimensions: *arousal* (which corresponds to the physiological *unspecific sympaticus syndrome*), *resolution level*, *dominance* of the leading motive (usually called *selection threshold*), the level of *background checks* (the rate of the securing behavior), and the level of *goal-directed behavior*. (The sixth dimension is the *valence*, i.e. the signals supplied by the pleasure/displeasure system.)

Anger, for instance, is characterized by high arousal, low resolution, strong motive dominance (high selection threshold), few background checks and strong goal-orientedness; sadness by low arousal, high resolution, strong dominance, few background-checks and low goal-orientedness. The dimensions are not completely orthogonal to each other (resolution is mainly inversely related to arousal, and goal orientedness is partially dependent on arousal as well).

This way, the emotional dimensions are not just classified, but also explained as result of particular demands of the individual. The states of the modulators (the proto-emotional parameters) are a function of the urgency and importance of motives, and of the ability to cope with the environment and the tasks that have to be fulfilled to satisfy the motives.

As seen in figure 1, a high *urgency* of the leading motive will decrease resolution and increase goal orientation and selection threshold (motive dominance), while less time is spent checking for changes in the background; while a high *importance* of the leading motive will increase the resolution level. Uncertainty and lack of experience (*task specific competence*) increase the rate of securing behavior. A high level of confidence (*general competence*) increases the selection threshold, and the arousal is proportional to the general demand situation (urgency and importance of all motives). Uncertainty is measured by comparing expectations with events as they happen, competence depends on the rate of success while attempting to execute goal-directed behavior; the demands for uncertainty reduction and acquisition of competence are *urges* and parts of the motivational system (both can be motives on their own).

At all times, some motives are active, and one is selected to be the *dominant motive*, depending on its strength (importance), the time left to satisfy it (urgency), the current selection threshold and the expected chance to satisfy it (*task specific competence*). Thus, motive importances and urgencies are supplied by the *motivational system* (see below).

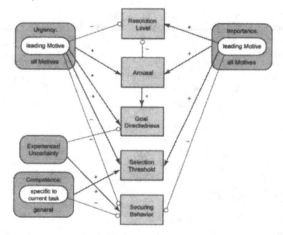

Figure 1: Dimensions of emotion according to the Psi theory

While the theory specifies the basic relationships between the regulatory parameters of the emotional system, it does not constrain the exact values. Implementations usually simply assume linear proportions, with multipliers that are chosen by the programmer to reflect individual variance. Also, the six-dimensional model is not exhaustive; especially when looking at social emotions, at least the demands for *affiliation* (external legitimacy signals) and 'honor' (internal legitimacy, ethical conformance), which are *motivational dimensions* like *competence* and *uncertainty reduction*, would need to be added.

Modeling Motivation

The notion of motivation is central to understanding and capturing the concept of autonomy in an agent architecture. In the Psi theory, the difference between emotion and motivation is very pronounced: "Motivation determines what has to be done, emotion determines how it has to be done." (Hille 1998)

Emotions can not be explained with cognitive modulation alone – without incorporating a cognitive content, an object of the affect, it is impossible to discern emotions like jealousy and envy. Both are negatively valenced affects that may create a high arousal, increase the selection threshold, reduce the resolution level, frustrate the competence urge and so on – but their real difference lies in the *object of the affect*. In Psi agents, this content is supplied by the motivational system. Motivational relevance binds affects to objects, episodes and events.

Dörner's motivational system is based on a finite number of urges (or drives):
1. Physiological urges (like energy and physical integrity)
2. Cognitive urges (competence and uncertainty reduction)
3. Social urges (affiliation).

Similar categories of drives have been suggested by Tyrell (1993) and Sun (2003), and by Knoll (2005). In the Tyrell-Sun model, the physiological urges are called *low level primary drives*, the social urges *high level primary drives*. Knoll, who gives a neurobiological basis to the assumptions of his model, calls the physiological urges *innate drives* and distinguishes between
- survival drives: homeostasis; avoidance of displeasure and danger; water and food
- reproductive drives: copulation; nurturing of offspring
(The Psi theory does contain homeostasis as an *implicit* principle and omits reproduction, but only because it is not part of the current agent worlds.)

Sun and Knoll assume a third category of drives, which are acquired, such as the drives of a collector, of a chess-player, a hunter, a mathematician. In the Psi theory, there is no such notion: every goal-directed action has to serve, directly or indirectly, a 'hardwired' drive. This is not necessarily a problem, because the Psi theory attempts to explain the behavior of the mathematician and the collector by their existing cognitive urges – because the urges may have arbitrary content as their object, as long as new strategies or refinements for handling this content can be learned (competence) and new avenues can be explored (uncertainty reduction). Even 'procrastinating' behavior can be explained this way, by avoidance of frustration of the competence urge in the face of cognitive difficulties.

In the area of modeling sociality, the notion of two urges for *legitimacy* (Dörner 2002) promises to have big explanatory power. Dörner differentiates between external legitimacy, which is also called *affiliation urge*; this urge is satisfied by signals of positive social acceptance by other agents ('l-signal') and frustrated by negative social signals ('anti-l-signals'). The agents may also generate legitimacy signals for themselves, called 'internal legitimacy'. These explain the satisfaction generated by the conformance to the agent's own, internalized ethical and social standards, and frustration and suffering, when the agent has to act against them. Social behaviour may be directed by *supplicative* signals, which are used by agents to get others to help them. Supplicative signals are, roughly speaking, a promise for (external and internal) legitimacy, and they express that an agent is unable to solve a problem it is facing on its own. If an agent sends a supplicative signal, then an urge to help is created by frustrating the affiliation urge of the receiver – a supplicative signal also is an *anti-l-signal*; it is unpleasant to perceive someone in distress (unless one wishes him ill). The 'plea' mechanism enabled by supplicative signals allows for altruistic group strategies that are beneficial for the population as a whole (Dörner and Gerdes 2005).[1]

A *motive* consists of an urge (that is, a need indicating a demand) and a goal related to this urge. The goal is a situation schema characterized by an action or event that has successfully reduced the urge in the past, and the goal situation tends to be the end element of a behavior program (see discussion of protocols above). The situations leading to the goal situation – that is, earlier stages in the connected occurrence schema or behavior program – might become intermediate goals. To turn this sequence into an instance that may initiate a behavior, orient it towards a goal and keep it active, we need a connection to the pleasure/displeasure system. The result is a *motivator* and consists of:

- a *demand sensor*, connected to the pleasure/displeasure system in such a way, that an increase in the deviation of the demand from the target value creates a displeasure signal, and a decrease results in a pleasure signal. The pleasure/displeasure signal should be proportional to the strength of the increment or decrement.
- optionally, a *feedback loop* that attempts to normalize the demand automatically
- an *urge indicator* that becomes active if there is no way of automatically getting the demand to its target value. The urge should be proportional to the demand.
- an *associator* (part of the *pleasure/displeasure* system) that creates a connection between the urge indicator and an episodic schema/behavior program, specifically to the aversive or appetitive goal situation. The strength of the connection should be proportional to the pleasure/displeasure signal.

Usually, an urge gets connected with more than one goal situation over time, since there are often many ways to satisfy or increase a particular urge.

Appetence and aversion

The actions of the Psi agent are directed and evaluated according to a set of "physiological" or "cognitive" urges. These urges stem from demands (e.g. for fuel and water) that have been hard-wired into the cognitive model. In order for an urge to have an effect on the behavior on the agent, it does not matter whether it *really* has an effect on its (physical or simulated) body, but that it is represented in the

proper way within the cognitive system. Whenever the agent performs an action or is subjected to an event that reduces one of its urges, a signal with a strength that is proportional to this reduction is created by the agent's "pleasure center". The name refers to the fact that – like in humans – its purpose lies in signaling the reflexive evaluation of positive or harmful effects according to physiological, cognitive or social demands.

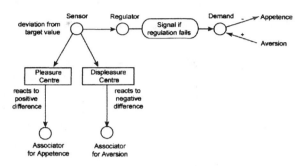

Figure 2: Appetence and aversion

Motive selection

When a motive becomes active, it is not always selected immediately; sometimes it will not be selected at all, because it conflicts with a stronger motive or the chances of success when pursuing the motive are too low. In the terminology of *Belief-Desire-Intention agents* (Bratman 1987), motives amount to *desires*, selected motives give rise to goals and thus are *intentions*. The selection of a motive takes place according to a *value* by *success probability* principle, where the value of a motive is given by its importance (indicated by the respective urge), and the success probability depends on the competence of the agent to reach the particular goal. The *motive strength* to satisfy a demand d is calculated as $urge_d \cdot (generalCompetence + competence_d)$, i.e. the product of the strength of the urge and the combined competence.

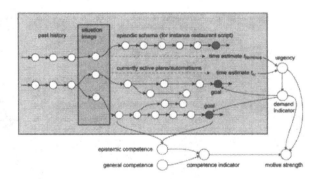

Figure 3: The structure of a motive

For a more sophisticated selection of goals that have to be fulfilled at a certain point in time (because there is a limited window of opportunity), the motive strength should be

---

[1] It may also explain the role of *crying*. Crying is mainly an expression of *perceived helplessness* (Miceli and Castelfranchi 2003), and, in a social context, a strong supplicative signal (Dörner 1999, p. 333). That is also the reason why crying is only perceived as 'sincere' if it is involuntary.

enhanced with a third factor: *urgency*. The rationale behind urgency lies in the aversive goal created by the anticipated failure of meeting the deadline.

Because only one motive is selected for the execution of its related behavior program, there is a competition between motives – and the winner takes it all. To avoid oscillations between motives, the switching between motives is taxed with an additional cost: the *selection threshold* (see above). The selection threshold is a bonus that is added to the strength of the currently selected motive, thus making it harder to another motive to overcome it. The value of the selection threshold can be varied according to circumstances, rendering the agent 'opportunistic' or 'stubborn'. By letting the activation of motives spread into the connected goals, behavior programs and episodic schemas, it is possible to pre-activate a suitable context for perception and planning. If the inhibition supplied by the selection threshold is allowed to spread too, it might suppress memory content not related to the pursuit of the currently selected motive and thus *focus* the agent on its current task.

Implementing the Psi Theory

Our group has created a toolkit for the design of cognitive agents, called MicroPsi.[2] Within MicroPsi, we use Dörner's motivational and emotional system to direct agents in their exploration of simulation worlds.

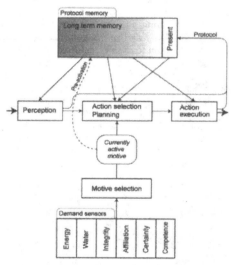

Figure 4: Psi agent model (modulators omitted)

MicroPsi agents are made up of spreading activation networks, capable of neural learning and script execution. Specific units within the net may include arbitrary functionality, so complex algorithms may be integrated with neural representations and semantic networks (see Bach 2005). MicroPsi agents are made up of a motivational system, capabilities for hierarchical perception and for action execu-

tion and learning (see figure 4). Emotional modulation aids in controlling the spreading of activation, and emotional states may be expressed using an animated avatar.

The emotional regulation of the MicroPsi agent calculates the emotional parameters from urges, relevant signals and values within a step-based simulation. The module maintains the following internal states: *competence*, *arousal*, *certainty*, resolution level (*resLevel*) and selection threshold (*selThreshold*). Any subsystem of the agent that is subject to emotional regulation is linked to the outputs of emotional regulation, receiving the current modulator parameters spreading activation.

At every time step t the regulation system performs the following calculations:

$$comp_t = \max\left(\min\left(comp_{t-1} + in_t^{efficiencyS}, 0\right), l^{comp}\right)$$
$$certainty_t = \max\left(\min\left(certainty_{t-1} + in_t^{certaintyS}, 0\right), l^{certainty}\right)$$

(l^{comp} and $l^{certainty}$ are constants to keep the values in range)

$$efficiencyU_t = target^{competence} - comp_t$$
$$certaintyU_t = target^{certainty} - certainty_t$$

($target^{certainty}$ and $target^{certainty}$ are target values representing the optimal level of competence and certainty for the agent.)

Applications

This work has been implemented within an AI architecture, which represents an artificial life scenario. Although it is difficult to compare to human performance, Dörner's group has attempted to match the performance of different, partial implementations against human performance in problem solving experiments (Dörner 2002). The MicroPsi architecture represents a more complete implementation and is made available for cognitive modelers outside our group. It represents ongoing research and is currently used as a robot control architecture at the University of Osnabrück and for cognitive modeling in industrial applications.

References

Anderson, J.R., Lebiere, C. (1998): The atomic components of thought. Mahwah, NJ: Erlbaum

André, E., Rist, T. (2001): Presenting through performing: on the use of multiple lifelike characters in knowledge-based presentation systems. *Knowledge Based Systems*, 14, 3-13

Andreae, J. H. (1998): Associative Learning for a Robot Intelligence. Imperial College Press

Bach, J. (2003): The MicroPsi Agent Architecture, *Proceedings of ICCM-5*, Germany, 15-20

Bach, J. and Vuine, R. (2003): Designing Agents with MicroPsi Node Nets, in *Proc. of KI 2003*, LNAI 2821, Springer, 164-178

Bach, J. (2005): Representations for a Complex World: Combining Distributed and Localist Representations for Learning and Planning. in S. Wermter, G. Palm., and M. Elshaw, (eds.), *Biomimetic Neural Learning for Intelligent Robots*. LNAI 3575, Springer, 265-280

Bach, J., and Vuine, R. (2006): MicroPsi Tutorial. *Proceedings of ICCM 2006*, Trieste, Italy

---

[2] See *http://www.cognitive-agents.org* for the MicroPsi homepage.

Barsalou, L. W. (1999): Perceptual Symbol Systems, in *Behavioral and Brain Sciences*, 22,4: 577-660

Belavkin, R. V., Ritter, F. E. (2000): Adding a theory of motivation to ACT-R. In *Proc. of the 7th Annual ACT-R Workshop. 133-139*. Pittsburgh, PA

Belavkin, R. V., Ritter, F. E., Elliman, D. G. (1999): Towards including simple emotions in a cognitive architecture in order to fit children's behaviour better. In *Proc. of CogSci 1999* (p. 784). Mahwah, NJ: Erlbaum

Bratman, M. (1987): Intentions, Plans and Practical Reason. Harvard University Press

Cacioppo, J. T., Gerntson, G. G. Adolphs, R., Carter, C. S., Davidson, R. J., McClintock, M. K., McEwen, B. S., Meaney, M. J., Schacter, D. L., Sternberg, E. M., Suomi, S. S., Taylor, S. E. (2002): Foundations in Social Neuroscience. Cambridge, MA, MIT Press

Cañamero, D. (1997): Modelling motivations and emotions as a basis for intelligent behavior. *Proceedings of Agents '97*. ACM

Castelfranchi, C. (1998): Modelling social action for AI agents, *Artificial Intelligence* 103: 157–182

Dörner, D. (1999). Bauplan für eine Seele. Reinbeck: Rowohlt

Dörner, D., Bartl, C., Detje, F., Gerdes, J., Halcour, D., Schaub, H., and Starker, U. (2002): Die Mechanik des Seelenwagens. Eine neuronale Theorie der Handlungsregulation. Verlag Hans Huber, Bern

Dörner, D., Gerdes, J. (2005): The Mice' War and Peace – Simulation of Social Emotions. *7. Fachtagung d. Gesellschaft für Kognitionswissenschaft*, Basel, Switzerland

Damasio, A. R. (1994): Descartes' Error. Emotion, Reason and the Human Brain. Avon Books

Damasio, A. R. (2003): Looking for Spinoza: Joy, Sorrow, and the Feeling Brain, Harcourt

Erk, S., Kiefer, M., Grothe, J., Wunderlich, A.P., Spitzer, M., Walter, H. (2003): Emotional context modulates subsequent memory effect. *NeuroImage* 18(439-47)

Frijda, N. H. (1986); The emotions. Cambridge University Press

Gluck, K., Gunzelmann, G., Gratch, J., Hudlicka, E., Ritter, F. E. (2006): Modeling the Impact of Cognitive Moderators on Human Cognition and Performance. *Symposium at CogSci 06*, Vancouver, Canada

Gratch, J., Marsella, S. (2001); Modeling emotions in the Mission Rehearsal Exercise. In *Proc. of the 10th Computer Generated Forces and Behavioural Representation Conference (10TH—CG-057)*. Orlando, FL

Gratch, J., Marsella, S. (2004): A framework for modeling emotion. *Cognitive Systems Research* 5 (4): 269-306

Hille, K. (1998); A theory of emotion. Memorandum Universität Bamberg, available online at www.uni-bamberg.de/ppp/insttheopsy/dokumente/ Hille_A_theory_of_emotion.pdf

Hudlicka, E. (1997): Modeling behavior moderators in military human performance models (Tech. Report 9716). Psychometrix. Lincoln, MA

Hudlicka, E., Fellous, J.-M. (1996): Review of computational models of emotion (Technical Report No. 9612). Psychometrix. Arlington, MA

Knoll, J. (2005): The Brain and its Self. Springer

Laird, J.E., Newell, A., and Rosenbloom, P. J. (1987): Soar: An architecture for general intelligence. *Artificial Intelligence*, 33(1), 1-64

Lane, R.D., Nadel, L. (eds.) (2000): Cognitive neuroscience of emotion. Oxford, Oxford University Press

Lisetti, C., Gmytrasiewicz, P. (2002): Can a rational agent afford to be affectless? *Applied AI*, 16, 577-609

Miceli, M., Castelfranchi, C. (2003): Crying: Discussing its basic reasons and uses. *New Ideas in Psychology*, Vol. 21(3), p. 247-273

Minsky, M. (2006): The Emotion Machine. New York, Elsevier

Oatley, K., Jenkins, J. M. (1996): Understanding Emotions. Blackwell

Panksepp, J. (1998): Affective Neuroscience: The Foundations of Human and Animal Emotions. Oxford University Press

Pfeifer, R. (1988): Artificial intelligence models of emotion. In: V. Hamilton, G. Bower, & N. Frijda (eds.). Cognitive perspectives on emotion and motivation. *Proc. of the NATO Advanced Research Workshop*. Dordrecht, Kluwer.

Picard, R. (1997): Affective Computing. Cambridge, MA: MIT Press

Plutchik, R. (1994): The Psychology and Biology of Emotion. New York: Harper Collins

Ritter, F. E., Shadbolt, N. R., Elliman, D., Young, R. M., Gobet, F., Baxter, G. D. (2002): Techniques for Modeling Human Performance in Synthetic Environments. Human Systems Information Analysis Center, State of the Art Report, Wright-Patterson AFB, Ohio, June 2002

Rolls, E.T. (1999). The Brain and Emotion. Oxford University Press

Roseman, I.J., Antoniou, A.A., Jose, P.A. (1996): Appraisal Determinants of Emotions: Constructing a More Accurate and Comprehensive Theory. In: *Cognition and Emotion*, 10 (3): 241-277

Scherer, K. (1984): On the nature and function of emotion. In K.R. Scherer, and P. Ekman (eds.). *Approaches to emotion*. Hillsdale, N.J., Erlbaum

Scherer, K. (1993): Studying the Emotion-Antecedent Appraisal Process: An Expert System Approach. In: *Cognition and Emotion*, 7 (3/4): 325-355

von Scheve, C. (2000): Emotionale Agenten - Eine explorative Annäherung aus soziologischer Perspektive. Diplomarbeit, Universität Hamburg, Institut für Soziologie

Schmidt, B. (2000). PECS. Die Modellierung menschlichen Verhaltens. SCS-Europe Publishing House, Ghent

Sloman, A. (2001). Beyond shallow models of emotion. *Cognitive Processing: International Quarterly of Cognitive Science*, 2(1): 177–198

Sun, R. (2003): A tutorial on Clarion 5.0, available online at http://www.cogsci.rpi.edu/~rsun/sun.tutorial.pdf

Sun, R. (2005): Cognition and Multi-Agent Interaction, Cambridge University Press, 79-103

Toda, M. (1982): Man, robot, and society. The Hague, Nijhoff

Tyrell, T. (1993): Computational Mechanism for Action Selection, PhD Thesis, University of Edinburgh

Velásquez, J. (1997). Modeling Emotions and Other Motivations in Synthetic Agents. *Proc. AAAI-9*. MIT Press

Updating Episodic Memories: A Special Role of Spatial Context

Almut Hupbach (ahupbach@u.arizona.edu)
Department of Psychology, The University of Arizona
Tucson, AZ 85721 USA

Rebecca Gomez (rgomez@u.arizona.edu)
Department of Psychology, The University of Arizona
Tucson, AZ 85721 USA

Oliver Hardt (oliver.hardt@mac.com)
Department of Psychology, McGill University
Montreal, QC H3A 1B1 Canada

Lynn Nadel (nadel@u.arizona.edu)
Department of Psychology, The University of Arizona
Tucson, AZ 85721 USA

Abstract

The traditional view in neurobiology holds that consolidated memories are resistant to change. This view has been challenged by recent animal studies showing that consolidated memories re-enter a labile state at the time they are reactivated. During this time, memories can be modified and subsequently require reconsolidation. Recently, Hupbach et al. (2007) demonstrated reconsolidation effects in human episodic memory: Memory for a list of objects was modified by the presentation of a new list, if, and only if participants were reminded of the first learning episode before learning the new list. The reminder was comprised of three different components: the experimenter, a reminder question, and the spatial context. The present study evaluates the contribution of each of these components, and shows that the spatial context carries the reminder effect. This finding supports models that treat spatial context as more than just one among many other retrieval cues. It also has important practical implications, for instance when it comes to minimizing memory distortions of eyewitness accounts.

Introduction

The traditional view in neurobiology holds that memories are labile only during a limited time period after encoding. With time, memories become consolidated and resistant to future modification (e.g., McGaugh, 2000). This view has been challenged by studies showing that reactivation destabilizes memories such that they can be modified and subsequently require another round of consolidation, so-called reconsolidation (e.g., Nader, 2003). Most of these studies have been carried out in animals.

Walker, Brakefield, Hobson, and Stickgold (2003) were the first to demonstrate reconsolidation effects in humans. Participants were trained on a procedural motor-skill task that involved finger-tapping a simple sequence (e.g., 4-1-3-2). Twenty-four hours later they briefly rehearsed the sequence (reactivating it), and learned a second sequence (e.g., 2-3-1-4). When tested on Day 3, accuracy performance for Sequence 1 was significantly impaired in comparison to a group of participants who did not rehearse Sequence 1 before learning Sequence 2. This shows that the reactivation of the memory for Sequence 1 on Day 2 destabilized it such that a competing motor pattern could interfere.

We recently asked whether reconsolidation effects are confined to procedural memory, a form of implicit memory that does not require conscious recollection, or whether reconsolidation also applies to episodic memory, a form of memory that allows for the conscious recollection of events (Hupbach, Gomez, Hardt, & Nadel, 2007). In our study, college students learned a list of objects on Day 1. On Day 2, they received a reminder or not, and then learned a second list. Memory for List 1 was tested on Day 3. The results show that although the reminder did not moderate the number of items recalled from List 1, subjects who received a reminder incorrectly incorporated items from the second list when recalling List 1. We interpreted this effect as showing that a reminder re-opens memory for List 1 such that new information can be incorporated. The reminder effect does not manifest itself immediately and thus is time-dependent as predicted by the reconsolidation account. Our study is the first demonstration of reconsolidation effects in human episodic memory, and it underlines the crucial role of reminders for the modification of episodic memory. In contrast to previous reconsolidation findings, the study shows that reconsolidation is also a constructive process, one that supports the incorporation of new information in memory.

The reminder we used in the study we just described was multidimensional, with spatial context, an experimenter, and a reminder question all contributing. In contrast to the reminder group, the no-reminder group was tested in a different spatial context, was not asked a reminder question and met a different experimenter. The present study is part of a larger study on the effects of spatial context on memory updating/reconsolidation (Hupbach, Gomez, Hardt, Nadel, submitted) and aimed to evaluate the contribution of each of the following three reminder components to the reminder effect observed by Hupbach et al. (2007).

(1) *Spatial context.* Participants in the reminder group learned the second list on Day 2 in the same room in which they had learned List 1 on Day 1. Thus, the spatial context could have served as a reminder reactivating List 1. Participants in the no-reminder group learned List 2 in a different room.

(2) *Experimenter.* For participants in the reminder group, the experimenter was the same on Day 1 and 2. Therefore, the experimenter herself could have served as a reminder. For participants in the no-reminder group, a different experimenter administered the procedure on Day 2.

(3) *Reminder question.* Participants in the reminder group were asked to describe the experimental procedure of Day 1 right before learning the second list. They were also shown a distinctive blue basket, which Day 1's objects were sorted in. For participants in the no-reminder group, the experimenter did not ask what had happened on Day 1 nor did they see the basket again.

Experiment 1: Stable Spatial Context

In the first experiment, we followed a "reductionist" approach in that we successively eliminated reminder components from the three-component reminder used in our previous study (Hupbach et al., 2007). In both Exp. 1A and 1B the Day 2 procedure took place in the same room as the Day 1 procedure.

Experiment 1A: Context plus experimenter

In Experiment 1A, we eliminated the reminder question. Thus, the reminder consisted only of the spatial context and the experimenter. If these two components are sufficient to reactivate the memory for List 1, we should replicate the reminder effect, i.e., participants should intermix items from List 2 in their recall of List 1. In contrast, if the reminder question is a crucial reminder component, the reminder effect should be diminished.

Methods

Subjects. Twelve undergraduate students from the University of Arizona participated in the experiment. They received course credit for their participation. The number of participants was based on the following power analysis (*G-Power*, Erdfelder, Faul, & Buchner, 1996). First, we calculated the effect size of the difference in the number of

intrusions between the reminder and the no-reminder group in Hupbach et al. (2007), which resulted in an effect size of 1.68. Second, we calculated the number of subjects needed to detect such an effect, given error probabilities α and β = .05. The analysis showed that 11 subjects would be needed. This calculation applies to all experiments reported in this paper. To keep the number of subjects consistent with our previous study (Hupbach et al., 2007), we included 12 participants in all experiments.

Materials. List 1 and List 2 materials each consisted of 20 unrelated objects. List 1 contained the following objects: balloon, bow, calculator, toy car, crayon, cup, dice, feather, flashlight, flower, glue, key, sock, sponge, spoon, sunglasses, teabag, tennis ball, toothbrush, whistle. List 2 contained the following objects: apple, band-aid, battery, book, cassette tape, cellular phone, comb, dollar bill, elephant, envelope, paper clip, toy pot, puzzle piece, rock, straw, thread, tissue, watch, shovel, zipper.

Procedure. The three sessions took place on Monday, Wednesday, and Friday of the same week. Students participated one at a time. *On Day 1,* the experimenter pulled out one item at a time from a bag and placed it in a distinctive blue basket. Participants were asked to name each item. After all 20 items were placed into the basket the experimenter hid the basket and asked the participants to remember as many items as possible. This procedure was repeated until the participants remembered at least 17 of the 20 objects or for a maximum of four learning trials. *On Day 2, the experimenter from Day 1* asked the participants to learn a second list of twenty objects (List 2) *in the same room as on Day 1.* All objects were placed in front of the participants, who were asked to name each of the objects, and were given 30 seconds to study them. The experimenter then removed the objects, and asked the participants to recall as many of the objects as possible. If participants recalled less than 17 objects, the procedure was repeated until participants recalled at least 17 objects, or for a maximum of four learning trials. *On Day 3,* the experimenter from Day 1 asked the participants to recall as many objects as possible from Day 1 in the same room as on Days 1 and 2. The recall test was repeated for a total of four consecutive recall trials in order to test reliability of recall.

Results

The mean percent of items recalled from List 1 (averaged over all four recall trials) and the mean percent of items falsely recalled from List 2 (intrusions, averaged over all four recall trials) are displayed in Figure 1. The number of learning trials on Day 1 was not significantly correlated with the number of recalled objects on Day 3 (r=.33, p=.29). This is true for all the reported experiments. Both the number of recalled objects and intrusions observed in Exp. 1A were compared with the corresponding values observed in the reminder group in Hupbach et al. (2007) with independent-sample t-tests. There were no differences both in the number of recalled objects ($t<1$) and the number of intrusions [$t(22)=1.34$ $p=.20$].

Discussion

Experiment 1A shows that eliminating the reminder question from the compound reminder did not diminish the reminder effect. Participants were as likely to intermix items from List 2 in their recall of List 1 as when the reminder question was part of the reminding procedure. Thus, Exp. 1A shows that the spatial context and the experimenter were sufficient in reactivating memory for List 1 such that new objects could be incorporated. However, what are the individual roles of the experimenter and the context? In Exp. 1B, we studied whether the spatial context alone would lead to similar results.

Experiment 1B: Context only

As a next step in our "reductionist" approach, we eliminated an additional component of the three-component reminder used by Hupbach et al. (2007), namely the possible contribution of the experimenter to the reminder effect. Thus, the *spatial context* was the only reminder in Exp. 1B.

Methods

Subjects. Twelve undergraduate students from the University of Arizona who had not participated in Exp. 1A participated in Exp. 1B. They received course credit for their participation.

Materials. We used the exact same materials as in Exp. 1A.

Procedure. The procedure was the same as in Exp. 1A with the exception that the Day 2 procedure was administered by a different experimenter.

Results

The results are depicted in Figure 1. A comparison (one-way ANOVA) between Exp. 1A, Exp. 1B, and the reminder group from Hupbach et al. (2007) revealed no differences in the number of objects recalled from List 1 ($F<1$) and the number of intrusions from List 2 ($F<1$).

Discussion

Experiment 1A und B suggest that the spatial context itself is a sufficient reminder. Eliminating the two other reminder components used by Hupbach et al. (2007), i.e., the reminder question and the experimenter did not diminish the reminder effect, or in other words, the experimenter and the reminder question did not add significantly to the reminder effect. However, Exp. 1A and B do not tell us whether the reminder question and/or the experimenter would

sufficiently reactivate the memory for List 1 in the absence of the spatial context. This was studied in Experiment 2.

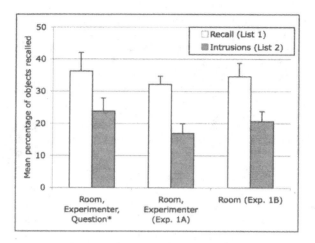

Figure 1: Mean percentage of objects correctly and falsely recalled in the different reminder groups of Exp. 1. All groups were tested in the same room on Day 1 and 2. (Error bars represent standard errors of means.) *Data from Hupbach et al. (2007).

Experiment 2: Different spatial context

Experiment 1 suggests a special role of the spatial context for the reactivation of episodic memories. However, we have yet to explore the role of the question and the experimenter in the absence of the spatial context. In Experiment 2, we chose the no-reminder group of Hupbach et al. (2007) as our reference and evaluated whether the reminder question (Exp. 2A) or the reminder question plus experimenter (Exp. 2B) would cause an increase in intrusions (i.e., a reminder effect).

Experiment 2A: Reminder question

The only reminder component given on Day 2 was the reminder question. Participants were asked to describe the experimental procedure of Day 1 before learning List 2.

Methods

Subjects. Twelve undergraduate students from the University of Arizona who had not participated in Exp. 1 participated in the experiment. They received course credit for their participation.

Materials. We used the exact same materials as in Exp. 1.

Procedure. The procedure was similar to Exp. 1. The only difference concerned Day 2: Participants learned List 2 in a *different room* than List 1, and *the experimenter was a* *different person.* Before learning of List 2, the participants were asked the reminder question (see above).

Results

The results are depicted in Figure 2. Both the number of recalled objects and intrusions observed in Exp. 2A were compared with the corresponding values observed in the no-reminder group in Hupbach et al.'s (2007) study with independent-sample t-tests. Participants in Exp. 2A recalled slightly fewer objects than the no-reminder group of Hupbach et al.'s (2007) study [$t(22)$=1.97, p=.06]. There was no significant difference in the number of intrusions ($t<1$).

Discussion

The question itself seems to be insufficient for reactivating memory for List 1 and inducing reconsolidation effects: When a different experimenter asked the reminder question in a different room, intrusions from List 2 into List 1 were low, and not different from those observed in the no-reminder group of Hupbach et al. (2007). Would we find different results if the same experimenter asked the reminder question, i.e., is the reminder question simply not powerful enough to reactivate memory for List 1? Exp. 2B tested this hypothesis.

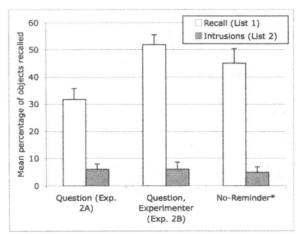

Figure 2: Mean percentage of objects correctly and falsely recalled in the different reminder groups of Exp. 2. *All groups were tested in a different on Day 2.* (Error bars represent standard errors of means.) *Data from Hupbach et al. (2007).

Experiment 2B: Reminder question plus experimenter

As in Exp. 2A the reminder was administered in a *different room* and the reminder question proceeded learning of List 2. However, in Exp. 2B, we "added" the experimenter to

the reminder, i.e. the *same experimenter* who administered the learning procedure on Day 1 asked the reminder question and administered the learning procedure on Day 2.

Methods

Subjects. Twelve undergraduate students from the University of Arizona who had not participated in any of the previous experiments participated in the Exp. 2B. They received course credit for their participation.

Materials. We used the exact same materials as in the previous experiments.

Procedure. The procedure was identical to Exp. 2A with one exception: The experimenter on Day 2 was the *same experimenter* who had administered Day 1's learning procedure.

Results and Discussion

The results are depicted in Figure 2. A comparison (one-way ANOVA) between Exp. 2A, Exp. 2B, and the no-reminder group of Hupbach et al.'s study revealed significant differences in the number of objects recalled from List 1 [$F(2, 35)$=5.31, p=.01]. Post-hoc comparisons (Scheffe) showed that participants in Exp. 2A recalled significant less items from List 1 than participants in Exp 2B. Most importantly, however, the number of intrusions from List 2 did not differ between the three groups ($F<1$).

Experiment 2B shows that adding the experimenter had no significant influence on the number of intrusions. Intrusions were still very low and not different from the no-reminder group in Hupbach et al.'s (2007) study.

Taken together, Exp. 2 shows that the experimenter and reminder question do not act as reminders in a different spatial context. Because the interpretation of the individual experiments is largely based on null effects, we additionally analyzed a subset of the data with a 2 (context: same room vs. different room) x 2 (same experimenter & reminder question vs. different experimenter & no reminder question) ANOVA. The different experimental groups are depicted in Table 1.

		Spatial Context	
		Same Room	Different Room
Same Experimenter & Reminder Question	Yes	Reminder Hupbach et al.	Exp. 2B
	No	Exp. 1B	No-Reminder Hupbach et al.

Table 1: Experimental groups that entered the 2-way ANOVA.

Both the analysis of List 1 recall and of the List 2 intrusions revealed significant main effects of spatial context [$F(1, 44)$=7.32, p=.01 (for List 1 recall); $F(1, 44)$=30.75), p<.01 (for List 2 intrusions); all other $F<1$]. Thus, the combined analysis largely confirms the findings of the individual experiments: The spatial context carries the reminder effect. Because of added power in the combined analysis we found that the same spatial context does not only cause a high number of List 2 intrusions into List 1 recall, but also a reduced recall of List 1 items.

General Discussion

We recently demonstrated reconsolidation effects in episodic memory (Hupbach et al., 2007). The present study which is part of a larger study (Hupbach et al., submitted) is a follow-up that aimed to estimate the individual and combined contributions of the three components that constituted the reminder in Hupbach et al.'s (2007) study: the experimenter, the reminder question, and the spatial context. The present study clearly shows that the spatial context is a necessary and sufficient reminder: Eliminating the reminder question (Exp. 1A) or the reminder question *and* the experimenter (Exp. 1B) from the three-compound reminder did not diminish the reminder effect. When the spatial context changed (Exp. 2), no reminder effects were observed, even when the same experimenter who had been present on Day 1 asked the reminder question (Exp. 2B).

How can the special role of the spatial context for reactivating episodic memories be explained? Our findings cannot be readily explained by theoretical frameworks that treat spatial context merely as one of many other retrieval cues (e.g., external cues such as modality in which material is presented or internal cues such as mood), or as one of many components contributing to feature overlap positively affecting retrieval (e.g., encoding specificity principle, Tulving & Thompson, 1973; transfer-appropriate processing, Morris, Bransford, & Franks, 1977; memory models such as SAM, Raaijmakers & Shiffrin, 1981). In contrast, Nadel and colleagues (Nadel & Willner, 1980; Nadel, Willner, & Kurz, 1985) have long argued that the spatial context is more than a simple cue or part of a memory representation. The spatial context provides a "map" or "scaffold" to which experiences are bound. Recent demonstrations that spatial context itself does not undergo reconsolidation after reactivation (Biedenkapp & Rudy, 2004) further underlines the special role of spatial context as a stable scaffold for events. When the context itself changes sufficiently, it becomes the scaffold for an entirely different experience. Following this argument, participants who learned List 2 in a different spatial context mapped the experience onto a different scaffold, and thus did not update the memory for List 1.

What are the practical implications of our findings? Context-dependent memory updating can be important in clinical and educational settings. For instance, keeping the spatial context constant helps incorporating new information into old memory traces, and thus, could improve learning in students. However, in some situations memory updating might not be desired. For instance, revisiting the scene of a witnessed event can lead to memory distortions in eyewitnesses. Future research is needed to explore in detail the boundary conditions for context-dependent memory reconsolidation.

References

Biedenkapp, J. C., & Rudy, J. W. (2004). Context memories and reactivation: Constraints on the reconsolidation hypothesis. *Behavioral Neuroscience, 118,* 956-964.

Erdfelder, E., Faul, F., & Buchner, A. (1996). GPOWER: A general power analysis program. *Behavior Research Methods, Instruments, & Computers, 28,* 1-11.

Hupbach, A., Gomez, R., Hardt, O., & Nadel, L. (2007). Reconsolidation of episodic memories: A subtle reminder triggers integration of new information. *Learning & Memory, 14,* 47-53.

Hupbach, A., Hardt, O., Gomez, R., & Nadel, L. (submitted). The dynamics of memory: Context-dependent updating.

McGaugh, J. L. (2000). Memory--a century of consolidation. *Science, 287,* 248-251.

Morris, C.D., Bransford, J.D., & Franks, J.J. (1977). Levels of processing versus transfer-appropriale processing. *Journal of Verbal Learning and Verbal Behavior, 16,* 519-533.

Nadel, L. & Willner, J. (1980). Context and conditioning: A place for space. *Physiological Psychology, 8,* 218-228.

Nadel, L., Willner, J., & Kurz, E.M. (1985). Cognitive maps and environmental context. In P. Balsam and A. Tomie (Eds.) *Context and learning.* Hillsdale, NJ: Lawrence Erlbaum Associates.

Nader, K. (2003). Memory traces unbound. *Trends in Neurosciences, 26,* 65-72.

Raaijmakers, J, G. W. & Shiffrin, R. M. (1981). Search of associative memory. *Psychological Review, 88,* 93-134.

Tulving, E. & Thomson, D.M. (1973). Encoding specificity and retrieval processes in episodic memory. *Psychological Review, 80,* 352-373.

Walker, M. P., Brakefield, T., Hobson, J. A., & Stickgold, R. (2003). Dissociable stages of human memory consolidation and reconsolidation. *Nature, 425,* 616-20.

The Role of Working Memory in the Use of Numerosity Judgment Strategies

Koen Luwel (Koen.Luwel@ped.kuleuven.be)
Department of Educational Sciences, University of Leuven
Vesaliusstraat 2, B-3000 Leuven, Belgium

Valérie Camos (valerie.camos@u-bourgogne.fr)
LEAD-CNRS, Université de Bourgogne
Pôle AAFE - Esplanade Erasme, BP 26513 – 21065 Dijon, France

Lieven Verschaffel (Lieven.Verschaffel@ped.kuleuven.be)
Department of Educational Sciences, University of Leuven
Vesaliusstraat 2, B-3000 Leuven, Belgium

Abstract

The present study investigated the role of working memory (WM) load on the strategic performance in the context of a numerosity judgment task. Participants solved the same set of items under single and dual task conditions. WM was loaded by having participants memorize and reproduce 5-letter strings in each trial. In both WM-load conditions we applied the choice/no-choice method (Siegler & Lemaire, 1997) to obtain measures of strategy efficiency and adaptiveness that were free of selection effects. Results show that WM load affected the frequency of strategy use, the efficiency of strategy execution and the adaptiveness of strategy choices and that these effects interacted with the difficulty level of the strategies. An account of these results is provided in the discussion section.

Theoretical Background

Working memory (WM) plays a crucial role in our daily life functioning in general and our performance in a variety of cognitive tasks in particular. Indeed, the accomplishment of complex cognitive tasks requires a good organization of processes and information sources. The resource used to organize these mental activities is referred to as *working memory*. Miyake and Shah (1999, p. 450) define WM as "those mechanisms or processes that are involved in the control, regulation, and active maintenance of task-relevant information in the service of complex cognition".

There exist several prominent WM models that vary on a number of dimensions (Miyake & Shah, 1999). One important distinction is whether WM is considered as a unitary system that is primarily involved in attentional control (e.g., Cowan, 1999) or that it is a multicomponent system of specialized subsystems for handling different kinds of information (e.g., Baddeley & Hitch, 1974). Probably the most influential model of WM is the multicomponent model proposed by Baddeley (Baddeley, 1986; Baddeley & Hitch, 1974).

Baddeley's WM model comprises four interdependent systems: a central executive, a phonological loop, a visuo-spatial sketchpad, and an episodic buffer. The central executive is responsible for planning and sequencing activities and allocates attentional resources to the various processes and subsystems. The central executive directs the activities of three subsystems. The phonological loop and the visuo-spatial sketchpad store and rehearse specific kinds of information. Speech-based information is stored in the phonological loop, whereas visual and spatial information is maintained in the visuo-spatial sketchpad. The episodic buffer is a storage system that integrates information from the phonological loop and the visuo-spatial sketchpad. This last subsystem has only recently been added to Baddeley's WM model (Baddeley, 2000) and its functioning remains to be empirically tested.

The bulk of the studies that investigated the role of WM in mathematical cognition relied on Baddeley's multicomponent model, the major reason being that this model lends itself to specific predictions. Indeed, if the same system subserves all cognitive tasks, and if its attentional capacity is limited, one might expect to observe impairments in an individual's performance when a given component is overloaded. This reasoning underlies the dual task methodology, which is often used to study the involvement of WM in mathematical tasks. In dual task studies participants perform a criterion task or primary task (e.g., making additions) in combination with a secondary task that involves storing or processing some other information. Depending on the type of secondary task that is being performed, one distinguishes between two kinds of dual tasks. In *concurrent dual tasks* primary and secondary tasks are done simultaneously. The nature of the secondary task is dependent on which specific working memory component this particular task is assumed to load (e.g., random letter generation is used to tax the central executive, whereas articulatory suppression loads the phonological loop). In *memory-load dual tasks*, participants are given some items to remember (e.g., a string of five letters), next solve a specific primary task, and then reproduce these items. In this paradigm, no specific assumptions are made regarding which subcomponents of WM are being loaded. In both dual task approaches, performance when the primary task and secondary tasks are combined is compared to performance when the tasks are done alone. If primary and secondary dual tasks use overlapping resources, the performance on the primary task will get worse as the secondary task becomes more demanding. This degrading of performance in the primary task is considered as evidence for the involvement of WM processing.

Most studies on WM and mathematical cognition have focused on the involvement of the different WM components in simple and complex mental arithmetic performance by using a concurrent dual task paradigm (see DeStefano & LeFevre, 2004, for a review). However, although people use several strategies to accomplish many mathematical tasks (Siegler, 1996), the issue of WM involvement in the selection and execution of strategies in mathematical tasks has scarcely been investigated. To the best of our knowledge, the few exceptions are the studies by Hecht (2002), Imbo, Duverne, and Lemaire (in press), Imbo and Vandierendonck (in press), Seyler, Kirk, and Ashcraft (2003), and Tronsky (2005).

The most relevant finding of the studies by Hecht (2002), Seyler et al. (2003), and Tronsky (2005) was that procedural strategies were more strongly affected by WM load than the retrieval strategy. However, these three studies have one important shortcoming: they studied strategy use under a choice condition only. As convincingly argued by Siegler and Lemaire (1997), this method bears the risk of confounding strategy selection and execution. Most probably, participants did not use the same strategies with the same frequency and/or on the same problems in single- and dual-task conditions. This makes it impossible to compare strategy selection and execution across both load conditions and to conclude whether impaired performance under WM load was due to changes in strategy selection only, or to changes in both strategy selection and execution. To circumvent this problem one needs to apply the choice/no-choice method (Siegler & Lemaire, 1997), which involves a number of no-choice conditions next to the choice condition. In these no-choice conditions, participants are required to apply one specific strategy on all trials of the task, which allows obtaining unbiased measures of strategy performance that are free from selection effects. Furthermore, the comparison of choice and no-choice data allows investigating whether participants selected their strategies adaptively. This latter strategy parameter was left largely unexplored in the studies by Hecht, Seyler et al., and Tronsky.

Imbo et al. (in press) and Imbo and Vandierendonck (in press) were the first to apply the choice/no-choice methodology to unambiguously assess the effect of WM load on strategy selection and strategy execution. In Imbo et al.'s study on computational estimation, participants were either involved in a choice condition (in which they could freely choose between a rounding-up or a rounding-down strategy to solve a set of computational estimation problems), or in one of two no-choice conditions in which they either had to use round up or round down on all items of the task. Each participant performed this task under single and dual-task conditions. These authors found that

WM load affected: (a) relative strategy frequencies in the sense that under dual-task conditions participants relied more on the easier round down strategy, (b) strategy execution, since both strategies were slower and less accurate under WM-load conditions, and (c) strategy adaptiveness because participants made less adaptive strategy choices under dual-task conditions.

Imbo and Vandierendonck (in press) examined the effect of executive and phonological load on simple arithmetic strategy use in a choice/no-choice design. They found that WM load had no effect on the relative frequencies of strategy use. However, executive load impaired strategy efficiency and this effect was stronger for non-retrieval than for retrieval strategies. Moreover, phonological load only affected counting strategies. Finally, executive load had a detrimental effect on strategy adaptiveness, whereas phonological load did not affect the quality of strategy choices.

As far as we know, the dual task methodology in combination with the choice/no-choice method has only been applied to the task domain of arithmetic by using a concurrent dual task paradigm. With the present study, we wanted to apply this combined methodology in another area of mathematical cognition (i.e., numerosity judgment) and with a memory-load paradigm).

The Present Study

The aim of the present study was to investigate the effect of WM load on strategy selection and execution while participants were judging different numerosities of colored blocks that were presented in a grid. As previous studies have demonstrated (e.g., Luwel, et al., 2003a), this task allows for two main strategies: (a) an *addition strategy* in which the different (subgroups of) green blocks are counted and added together and (b) a *subtraction strategy* in which the number of empty squares is subtracted from the total number of squares in the grid. Both strategies have a specific range of application: the addition strategy will especially be applied on trials with few blocks and many empty squares, whereas the subtraction strategy will preferentially be used on items with many blocks and few empty squares. Furthermore, since the subtraction strategy involves at least one additional processing step than the addition strategy (i.e., subtracting the number of empty squares from the total after having them determined first), it is considered as requiring more processing resources than the addition strategy.

In the present study, participants solved this numerosity judgement task under single and dual-task conditions. WM was loaded by letting them remember a 5-letter string. Under both WM-load conditions, the task was solved in a choice session, where participants were free to use either the addition or the subtraction strategy, and in two no-choice sessions in which they were required to respectively apply the addition and the subtraction strategy on all items of the task. This design allowed us to investigate the effect of WM load on each of the four parameters of strategic competence:

(a) the *repertoire* of strategies, (b) the relative *frequency* of strategy use (c) the *efficiency* of strategy execution, and (d) the *adaptiveness* of strategy choices (Lemaire & Siegler, 1995).

Given the differences in cognitive resources required by both strategies, the following predictions were formulated. First, we did not expect an effect of WM load on the strategic repertoire since application of the subtraction strategy on the highest numerosities under additional cognitive load will still result in considerable time gains as opposed to the addition strategy. Second, we expected that WM load would result in a less frequent use of the cognitively more demanding subtraction strategy. Third, WM load was expected to have a detrimental effect on the efficiency of both strategies. We predicted that both strategies would be executed slower and less accurately under dual than under single-task conditions and that this effect would be stronger for the subtraction than for the addition strategy. Finally, we expected a negative effect of WM load on the adaptiveness of strategy choices, since participants would have less resources left for choosing their strategies appropriately.

Method

Participants

Twenty-five psychology students of the University of Leuven (Belgium) participated in this study. Their mean age was 21.5 yrs (range: 18-25 yrs.). Both sexes were about equally represented in this sample.

Materials

Stimuli of the primary task (i.e., numerosity judgment) were 7 x 7 square grids that were presented on a black background. Each cell in the grid had a size of 1 x 1 cm and could either be filled (i.e., colored green) or remain empty (i.e., colored black). The colored blocks were placed randomly in the grid. The different cells were separated from each other by a red line of 1 pixel. The grid was surrounded by a red border of 4 pixels. All grids that contained between 20 and 40 green blocks were presented in all sessions. We used these numerosities since previous studies (e.g., Luwel, Lemaire, and Verschaffel, 2005) had found that the switch from the addition towards the subtraction strategy was typically made in this range. To avoid learning effects through which participants would retrieve the numerosity by merely seeing the stimulus, we created four different versions of each stimulus while controlling for the number of subgroups of blocks and the number of blocks within each subgroup, by simply rotating each grid 0°, 90°, 180° and 270°. Since participants ran six sessions, they were presented two versions of each stimulus once, whereas two other versions were presented twice.

Stimuli of the secondary task (i.e., letter recall) consisted of 78 randomly selected and ordered 5-letter strings (e.g., i-b-j-p-d). The letters were colored white and were presented in a 200 point Courier New font on a black background, at a rate of 1 s per letter. Special care was taken that each letter string did not correspond to a word or an abbreviation with a specific meaning in Dutch. The letter sequences were the same for all participants but their presentation order was randomized across participants and sessions.

The experiment was run on a PC with a 15" monitor set to a resolution of 800 x 600 pixels. The presentation of the different stimuli and the registration of participants' RTs, responses and strategy use were controlled by E-prime software (Schneider, Eschman, & Zuccoloto, 2002).

Design and Procedure

Each participant was tested individually in a quiet room and was seated at about 50 cm from the computer screen. All participants solved the numerosity judgment task under two conditions: one without and one with WM load. Both no-load and load conditions consisted of three sessions: a choice session and two no-choice sessions.

In order to obtain single-task data about letter recall, all participants were first presented 15 five-letter strings and were instructed to recall each letter string in the correct order at the end of each trial. Subsequently, half of the participants went over to the no-load choice session, followed by the WM-load choice session, whereas this order was reversed for the other half of participants. Both choice sessions were presented first to avoid carry-over effects from no-choice sessions on the strategy choices in the choice sessions. Then, the four no-choice sessions were administered following a Latin square design.

A no-load trial started with a fixation point appearing for 500 ms. Then a grid appeared on the screen containing a particular number of blocks. The grid remained visible until participants had made a numerosity judgment. As soon as a participant started to state his answer, the experimenter pressed a key which blanked the screen and stopped the computer timer. Then the experimenter entered participant's response and strategy into the computer, after which a new trial started. WM-load trials had the same sequence of events, except that participants were presented a 5-letter string after the fixation point, which they had to recall in the correct order after they had made their numerosity judgment.

In the choice session, participants were instructed to determine the number of green blocks as quickly and accurately as possible by either using the addition or subtraction strategy. In both no-choice sessions participants received the same instruction but they were required to use one specific strategy to solve all items in the sessions. In no-choice/addition they had to use the addition strategy, whereas in no-choice/subtraction they had to apply the subtraction strategy. During each trial, participants had to indicate on the screen which units (i.e., green blocks/empty squares) they were counting. This enabled a valid strategy identification in the choice sessions, and ensured that participants applied the required strategy in the no-choice sessions.

Results

Results were based on the data of 24 out of 25 participants. One participant was excluded from the analyses since he did not comply with the no-choice instructions.

Strategy Repertoire

Choice data revealed that, in line with our predictions, all participants used the addition and the subtraction strategy under both WM-load conditions.

Frequency of Strategy Use

A paired t-test on the percentage of subtraction strategy use in the choice sessions of both WM-load conditions indicated that, as expected, participants applied this strategy significantly more frequently in the no-load ($M = 64\%$) than in the WM-load ($M = 56\%$) condition, $t(23) = 2.88$, $p = .009$. Thus, additional WM load seems to decrease the use of the cognitively most demanding strategy.

Strategy Efficiency

Efficiency of strategy execution was analyzed on the basis of no-choice data. As outlined before, only no-choice sessions can provide measures of strategy performance that are free from selection effects. Strategy efficiency was measured in terms of strategy speed (i.e., RTs) as well as in terms of strategy accuracy (i.e., % correct responses).

Strategy Speed. A 2 (condition: no-load vs. WM-load) x 2 (strategy: addition vs. subtraction) repeated ANOVA was conducted on the RTs of the items that were solved correctly. As expected, this analysis revealed a main effect of condition, $F(1, 23) = 18.88$, $p = .0002$, indicating that items were solved quicker in the no-load ($M = 10.56$ s) than in the WM-load condition ($M = 12.66$ s). Moreover, we observed a main effect of strategy, $F(1, 23) = 41.98$, $p < .0001$, which showed that items were solved quicker with the subtraction ($M = 10.50$ s) than with the addition strategy ($M = 12.72$ s)[1]. We also observed a marginally significant condition x strategy interaction, $F(1, 23) = 3.50$, $p = .07$, which suggested that the disruptive effect of WM load was, as predicted, stronger for the subtraction ($M = 2.49$ s) than for the addition strategy ($M = 1.71$ s).

Percentage Correct Responses. A similar ANOVA as for RTs was conducted on the percentage of correct responses. This analysis revealed a significant main effect of condition, $F(1, 23) = 5.12$, $p = .03$, indicating that more items were correctly solved in the no-load ($M = 91\%$) than in the WM-load condition ($M = 87\%$). No other significant effects were observed, suggesting that the detrimental effect of WM load was the same for both strategies.

Adaptiveness of Strategy Choices

Two different methods for examining the adaptiveness of strategy choices were applied. A first measure was based on a comparison of the numerosity on which participants switched from the addition towards the subtraction strategy in the choice session (i.e., the actual change point) with the ideal numerosity to switch strategies as derived from the no-choice data (i.e., the optimal change point) (see Luwel, et al., 2003b for a detailed description of this analytic method). The second measure is based on a comparison of the overall performance in the choice condition with a simulation of what this performance would have looked like if participants would have chosen their strategies randomly or put differently, totally inadaptively (Siegler & Lemaire, 1997).

Comparison of the actual and the optimal change point. The *actual* change point can be defined as the numerosity on which participants switch from the addition towards the subtraction strategy in the choice sessions. Since people are not absolutely systematic in their strategy choices, this change point cannot always be determined unambiguously. Therefore, we applied the same criterion as Luwel, et al. (2005): the first numerosity on which participants started to use the subtraction strategy and do so for at least three consecutive numerosities. The *optimal* change point is determined by fitting a linear regression on the individual RT patterns of the correctly solved trials from both the no-choice/addition and no-choice/subtraction sessions (see Figure 1). The numerosity on which both regression lines intersect each other is considered as the optimal change point, since from this trial on, the subtraction strategy is executed faster than the addition strategy without a loss of accuracy.

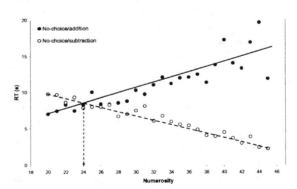

Figure 1: Example of two individual RT patterns from a no choice/addition and a no-choice/subtraction session with their corresponding linear regression lines. The arrow indicates the optimal change point.

---

[1] Since the subtraction strategy is cognitively more demanding compared to the addition strategy, this finding seems to be counter-intuitive. However, it is important to note that 76% of the items included a grid that was more than half filled with green blocks. It is especially on these large-numerosity items that the subtraction strategy becomes faster than the addition strategy.

Since the optimal change point indicates for each individual the numerosity on which it would be most adaptive to exchange the addition strategy for the subtraction strategy, the absolute difference in location between the actual and the optimal change point can be conceived as a measure of adaptiveness: the smaller this difference, the better an individual's strategy choices are calibrated to his/her strategy performance.

The mean actual change point was located on 25 in the no-load and on 30 in the WM-load condition, whereas the optimal change points were respectively located on 27 and 28. A paired t-test on the difference scores between both types of change points under both load conditions did not reveal a significant difference between the no-load and the WM-load condition. On the contrary, we observed a trend in the opposite direction, indicating a smaller difference between both change points in the WM-load ($M = 3.17$) than in the no-load condition ($M = 4.08$). This suggests that participants tended to make more instead of less adaptive choices when put under a heavier WM load.

Effects of having a choice on performance. A second way to measure adaptiveness is by comparing the performance in the choice session with a simulation of what this performance would look like if participants selected their strategies purely randomly. The underlying rationale here is that, if participants are free to choose their strategies and if they select their strategies adaptively, they will be much faster and/or accurate than when they select their strategies in a purely randomized fashion. This assumption can be tested by comparing the overall RT in the choice session (i.e. the actual RT) with the overall RT in both no-choice sessions, being statistically corrected for the frequency of strategy use in the choice session (i.e., the simulated RT). Take, for instance, a participant who applied the addition strategy on 60% of the trials and the subtraction strategy on 40% of the trials in the choice session; then his simulated RT will be .60(mean RT of no-choice/addition) + .40(mean RT of no-choice/subtraction). Thus, the more adaptive the strategy choices in the choice session, the larger the differences between the actual and the simulated RTs.

A paired t-test on the difference scores between both types of RTs in both WM-load conditions indicated that this difference was significantly larger in the WM-load ($M = 2.15$ s) than in the no-load condition ($M = 0.68$ s), $t(23) = 2.74$, $p = .01$. A similar analysis on the difference scores for the percentage of correctly solved items yielded the same result: participants were significantly more adaptive in the WM-load condition ($M = 0.40\%$) than in the no-load condition ($M = -4.40\%$), $t(23) = 2.30$, $p = .03$.

In sum, just like the results for the first adaptiveness measure, those for the second adaptiveness measure led to the surprising conclusion that participants made more adaptive choices in the WM-load than in the control condition.

Secondary Task Performance

In a final analysis, we investigated whether there was a difference in secondary task performance depending on the type of session. A one-way repeated measures ANOVA with session type (secondary task alone, primary + secondary task in choice, primary + secondary task in no-choice/addition, and primary + secondary task in no-choice/subtraction) as the sole factor was carried out on the number of letters recalled in correct order. This analysis revealed a significant effect of type of session, $F(3, 69) = 51.54$, $p < .0001$. A posteriori Tukey tests revealed that there were significantly more letters recalled in the correct order in the session with the secondary task alone ($M = 4.15$) than in the sessions in which the secondary task was solved together with the primary task (Ms: 2.07, 2.59, 2.69 for respectively the choice, no-choice/addition and no-choice/subtraction sessions). Furthermore, secondary task performance was significantly better in both no-choice sessions than in the choice session, while there was no difference between both no-choice sessions. These results show that, with limited WM resources, performance tended to be impaired not only in the primary but also in the secondary task (Hegarty, Shah, & Miyake, 2000). Furthermore, the mere fact of having to make a choice led to a reduction of secondary task performance in comparison with sessions without choice. This finding suggests that making (adaptive) choices consumes extra WM resources.

Discussion

The present study enabled us to assess the effect of WM load on the different dimensions of strategic performance by means of the choice/no-choice method. First, WM load had an effect on the frequency of strategy use: individuals relied less frequently on the cognitively most demanding strategy when being put under heavier WM load. This result confirms earlier findings by Imbo et al. (in press) in computational estimation. Second, it was shown that WM load had a negative effect on the speed as well as the accuracy of strategy execution, whereby the speed of the more demanding strategy tended to be affected more strongly than the speed of the cognitive easier strategy. This finding, which also parallels previous findings by Imbo et al. (in press) in computational estimation and Imbo and Vandierendonck (in press) in simple arithmetic, may explain why participants relied less frequently on the subtraction strategy when their WM resources were reduced.

The most striking result, however, was that all adaptiveness measures indicated that an increase in WM load resulted in more instead of less adaptive choices. This result is in contrast with previous findings showing that increased WM load impaired strategy adaptiveness (e.g., Imbo et al., in press; Imbo & Vandierendonck, in press). Similarly, Schunn and Reder (2001) found a positive relationship between WM capacity and strategy adaptiveness in the context of an air traffic control task. Other studies, using less complex tasks, seem, however, to suggest that WM is not involved in making adaptive strategy choices. (e.g., Camos, 2004 in the context of a counting task and Schunn, Lovett, & Reder, 2001 with a building sticks task). But, to the best of our knowledge, there is no study that previously reported a *positive* effect of WM load on the adaptiveness of people's strategy choices.

A possible interpretation for this unexpected finding is that participants were performing at a suboptimal level in the no-load condition (e.g., because they perceived the task as too easy and insufficiently challenging) and that the increased WM load in the dual-task condition forced them to perform at their full potential and, thus, at a maximum level of adaptiveness. Only by doing so they could save the cognitive resources needed to comply with the requirements of both the primary and secondary task.

Future studies should examine the extent to which the different components of Baddeley's WM model play a role in each of these aspects by using a concurrent dual task approach instead of a memory load approach. Furthermore, the positive effect of WM load on strategy adaptiveness should be assessed in greater detail by systematically varying the level of difficulty of the primary task.

Acknowledgments

Koen Luwel is Postdoctoral Fellow of the Fund for Scientific Research-Flanders (Belgium). This study is funded by the GOA grant 2006/1 from the Research Fund K.U. Leuven, Belgium to the CIP&T. The authors would like to thank Hélène Winandy for her help in collecting the data.

References

Baddeley, A. D. (1986). *Working memory*. New York: Clarendon Press.

Baddeley, A. D. (2000). The episodic buffer: A new component of working memory? *Trends in Cognitive Sciences, 4*, 417-423.

Baddeley, A. D., & Hitch, G. J. (1974). Working memory. In G. H. Bower (Ed.), *The psychology of learning and motivation*. New York: Academic Press.

Camos, V. (2004, August). Working memory capacity affects the use and choice of strategies but not the selection process in adults. Paper presented at the *Second International Conference on Working Memory*, Kyoto, Japan.

Cowan, N. (1999). An embedded-processes model of working memory. In A. Miyake & P. Shah (Eds.), *Models of working memory: Mechanisms of active maintenance and executive control*. Cambridge: Cambridge University Press.

DeStefano, D., & LeFevre, J-A. (2004). The role of working memory in mental arithmetic. *European Journal of Cognitive Psychology, 16*, 353-386.

Hecht, S. A. (2002). Counting on working memory in simple arithmetic when counting is used for problem solving. *Memory & Cognition, 30*, 447-455.

Hegarty, M., Shah, P., & Miyake, A. (2000). Constraints on using dual-task methodology to specify the degree of central executive involvement in cognitive tasks. *Memory & Cognition, 28*, 376-385.

Imbo, I., Duverne, S., & Lemaire, P. (in press). Working memory, strategy execution, and strategy selection in mental arithmetic. *Quarterly Journal of Experimental Psychology*.

Imbo, I., & Vandierendonck, A. (in press). The role of phonological and executive working-memory resources in simple arithmetic strategies. *European Journal of Cognitive Psychology*.

Lemaire, P., & Siegler, R. S. (1995). Four aspects of strategic change: Contributions to children's learning of multiplication. *Journal of Experimental Psychology: General, 124*, 83-97.

Luwel, K., Lemaire, P., & Verschaffel, L. (2005). Children's strategies in numerosity judgment. *Cognitive Development, 20*, 448-471.

Luwel, K., Verschaffel, L., Onghena, P., & De Corte, E. (2003a). Strategic aspects of numerosity judgment: The effect of task characteristics. *Experimental Psychology, 50*, 63-75.

Luwel, K., Verschaffel, L., Onghena, P., & De Corte, E. (2003b). Analyzing the adaptiveness of strategy choices using the choice/no-choice method: The case of numerosity judgement. *European Journal of Cognitive Psychology, 15*, 511-537.

Miyake, A., & Shah, P. (1999). Toward unified theories of working memory: Emerging general consensus, unresolved theoretical issues, and future research directions. In A. Miyake & P. Shah (Eds.), *Models of working memory: Mechanisms of active maintenance and executive control*. Cambridge: Cambridge University Press.

Schneider, W., Eschman, A., & Zuccolotto, A. (2002). *E-Prime User's Guide*. Pittsburgh: Psychology Software Tools Inc.

Seyler, D. J., Kirk, E. P., & Ashcraft, M. H. (2003). Elementary subtraction. *Journal of Experimental Psychology: Learning, Memory, and Cognition, 29*, 1339-1352.

Schunn, C. D., Lovett, M. C., & Reder, L. M. (2001). Awareness and working memory in strategy adaptivity. *Memory & Cognition, 29*, 254-266.

Schunn, C. D., & Reder, L. M. (2000). Another source of individual differences: Strategy adaptivity to changing rates of success. *Journal of Experimental Psychology: General, 130*, 59-76.

Siegler, R. S. (1996). *Emerging minds: the process of change in children's thinking*. Oxford: Oxford University Press.

Siegler, R. S., & Lemaire, P. (1997). Older and younger adult's strategy choices in multiplication: Testing predictions of ASCM using the choice/no choice method. *Journal of Experimental Psychology: General, 126*, 71-92.

Tronsky, L. N. (2005). Strategy use, the development of automaticiy, and working memory involvement in complex multiplication. *Memory & Cognition, 33*, 927-940.

A Memory Account of Children's Failure to Generalize Novel Names to Novel Instances and Novel Scenes

Thibaut, Jean-Pierre (jean-pierre.thibaut@univ-poitiers.fr)
University of Poitiers
LMDC, CNRS UMR 6215, 99 avenue du recteur Pineau
86000 Poitiers France

Abstract

When they learn novel names, young children are thought to perfectly segregate an object from its environment and to associate it with its name no matter the scene in which the object is included and, in a post-test, to designate the correct object in novel scenes or contexts and to generalize the association to new instances that might differ from the original object according to various dimensions. We show, in two experiments, that children aged three do not always generalize new names across contexts and across instances even when instances are categorized in the same set as the learning stimuli. These results suggest that novel name generalization is, to some extent, independent of conceptual generalization. These results are interpreted in terms of general mechanisms of memory: it is argued that a failure to generalize novel words to novel stimuli or to new contexts might result from a lack of retrieval cues.

Young children are supposed to be proficient learners of novel names. Each day, young children learn new lexemes (Fenson, L., Dale, P., Reznick, S., Bates, E., Thal, D., Pethick, S., 1994). One important dimension of the task is to associate each novel word with the appropriate referent in the world and to be able to use this association for future namings. Creating the association is an instance of a general and fundamental learning mechanism (Siegler, 1997). Children can learn a novel category name from hearing its name only once (Smith, 1999). This ability is well captured by the notion of fast mapping. Children can grasp aspects of the meaning of a new word on the basis of a small number of incidental exposures, without any explicit training or feedback (Carey & Bartlett, 1978; Bloom, 2000 for an overview). Carey and Bartlett (1978) showed that many young children who had learned the novel word "chromium", still remembered part of its meaning six weeks later. Markson and Bloom (1997) showed that, in a pointing task, three- and four-year-old children performed well above chance after a month delay.

One important notion regarding lexical learning and generalization is that young children are thought to be perfectly able to segregate a target referent from the scene it is embedded in and to associate it with its name. For example, the concept of fast mapping implies that children grasp an object (for instance) and associate it with a word, no matter the scene, the spatial context, in which the object is included. Later, the child is supposed to be able to recognize, name or designate the correct referent in novel contexts. It is also generally recognized that children are

able to generalize the new word to new instances that differ from the original object according to various dimensions (Clark, 1993; Mervis, 1987; Smith, 1999) (even though there is much debate regarding the dimensions according to which children will spontaneously generalize). This view of novel name learning and generalization predicts that the name of an object should be recovered later despite variations in the characteristics of the referents and of the scenes in which it was embedded in the learning phase.

The following experiments have several purposes. First, we assess the stability of performance across delays (immediate post-test, compared with a two-week delay). Following Markson and Bloom (1997), Bartlett and Carey (1978), we hypothesize that performance should be stable across delays. However, their results were obtained for a comprehension (pointing) task. In the same way, Childers and Tomasello (2002) assessed comprehension and naming at various intervals after training (immediate, one day and one week later) and found no effect of delay on both types of scores.

A second purpose of the present experiments, is to study generalization of novel names, as a function of superficial characteristics, such as the scene in which the stimulus was embedded during the learning phase and its congruence (see methods) with the scene in which the stimulus is embedded at test, or such as perceptual differences between the training referent and novel instances introduced later. More generally, our central question is whether the context in which the association between a novel name (e.g. the word "tapir") and a referent (the tapir) was "inserted" will influence future generalization tasks such as naming or pointing tasks. More specifically, we want to introduce memory factors in the question of novel word generalization. During lexical learning and generalization, children encounter objects belonging to the same category in various contexts. For example, a child plays with a new toy (e.g., a crane) and learns its name ("crane") in one room and, later, might play with a *new* crane in another room or another house. The same is true for pictures of objects: children can see a cat in a book and learn its name, while being confronted with a different cat later in another book.

Most lexical learning theories would assume that children spontaneously generalize a novel name to novel instances of the original referent, displayed in a new spatial setting if (i.e., a novel scene) (e.g., Mervis, 1987). In the same way, they do not consider the "delay" component of a lexical learning task as a central issue: in most experiments, one tests generalization immediately after a novel referent has been associated with a novel name and in situations in which the *learning object* remains *in view* (Mervis & Bertrand, 1994; Samuelson & Smith, 2000). Given the above evidence regarding delays (e.g., Childers & Tomasello, 2002) and the notion of fast mapping, memory factors do not seem to play any central role in lexical generalization. In other words, the implicit general hypothesis is that "context" parameters do not influence the encoding of the association between the word and the object and, thus, its later retrieval.

By contrast, our contention is that memory factors might interact with generalization of novel names to novel instances especially when they are displayed in new scenes. Our reasoning is based on the encoding specificity hypothesis (Tulving & Thomson, 1973), according to which an event is stored in memory together with the spatial and temporal information associated with the target stimulus during encoding (e.g., the scene a stimulus is embedded in). Later recovery is facilitated when the cues encoded during learning are available at test in the sense that properties of effective retrieval cues are determined by the specific encoding operations performed by the system on the input (see Baddeley, 1997; Balsam & Tomie, 1985).

In a lexical learning task, this view can be translated in the following terms: a child always learns a novel word for a particular instance of a category in a particular scene, which results in the encoding of retrieval cues that are specific to this learning setting. Later presentations of novel instances of the same category in new scenes should elicit, by definition, poorer retrieval cues than the retrieval cues provided by the original instance displayed in its original scene. This should result in a poorer recall of the stimulus name association. By contrast, if, as mentioned above, a novel word is spontaneously generalized to new instances of the same category even when they are displayed on new scenes, one should not predict any influence of these differences between training and recall situations.

Note that our view has important consequences on the notion of undergeneralization which is quite common in early lexical learning. It is defined as a lexical use in which children extend a novel word to a subset of the referents to which the adults extend the same word (e.g., the word "dog" used for small dogs only). The common explanation of these undergeneralizations is conceptual: preschool children fail to extend novel words because they do not understand that the novel entities belong to the same category as the referents to which they already extend the word. Within our memory hypothesis, we want to suggest that some undergeneralizations might not be conceptual but might result from poorer retrieval cues available when novel referents and/or novel scene settings are introduced, compared with the retrieval cues available when old stimuli and scenes are displayed.

In order to show that undergeneralization is not conceptually-based, one has to show that children extend novel words less well to referents they have never seen

before than to the learning referents; while, at the same time, they give independent evidence that they *understand* that these novel stimuli belong to the same category as the learning stimuli. In our first experiment we compared performance for old referents (i.e., the ones shown in the training phase) and new referents displayed on their novel training scenes or on new test scenes at two delays: immediate and two weeks after training.

Experiment 1

Methods

Subjects: Fifty-two three-year-old children (mean age= 42 months, range: 36 to 47 months, 25 boys and 27 girls) participated in this study. They were normally developing, had no hearing impairments, and were acquiring French as their native language. Informed consent was obtained from their parents.

Materials

In the learning phase, four pictures of unfamiliar basic level categories (two categories of mammals – tapir and ibex -, and two categories of tools – plane and trowel) were used. Each referent was displayed on a different background scene (see Figure 1 for the two categories of mammals). In the transfer phase, participants were shown two referents from two categories of the learning phase (e.g., the old tapir and the old plane) (same instance condition) and two new instances of the remaining two categories (e.g., a new ibex and a new trowel) (different instance condition). To this purpose, a new instance of the four training categories was also selected (in books or on the Web). To summarize, there were two instances for each of the four categories, one used as training stimulus (the old instance), and the other as the novel instance. Each stimulus was displayed on a scene, selected in a set of eight different scenes, each scene being associated with one stimulus only. The scenes for tools (e.g., an indoor scene such as a table) were not the same as the ones used for mammals (e.g., a wood). For each tool and each mammal, two versions were constructed: each referent was associated (pasted on) with two different scenes. The stimuli were constructed with the Photoshop© software. In the training phase, one instance of each of the four basic level categories was selected randomly, that is embedded in one of the two scenes each referent was associated with. The four test stimuli were selected according to the scene condition in which a child participated: in the same scene condition, all the scenes were the scenes shown in the training phase, two scenes associated with two training instances, and two scenes associated with two novel instances of the two remaining categories. In the novel scene condition, two novel scenes were associated with two old instances and the two remaining novel scenes were associated with a novel instance of each of the two remaining categories. We also constructed another version of the material, with referents pasted on a white background. This version was used to check children's knowledge of the real name of the referents, prior to the training phase itself. Four novel words (non-words) were used as labels of the referents throughout the experiment: moupa, duban, togon, kéni. For a given child, each name was randomly associated with one of the four referents.

Procedure

Each child was tested individually at school, in a quiet room. The experiment was composed of two phases: a learning phase, and a testing phase, the latter being composed of two posttests, immediate, and after two-week delay.

Learning phase. Prior to the learning phase, the experimenter introduced the stimuli pasted on the white background and asked the child to give the name of the referents. There was no case in which the child knew the correct name. The learning phase itself was composed of four trials, so that all the children saw the referents and heard their names the same number of times. The task was

introduced as a novel name learning task. The novel names were introduced as basic level names: "I'm going to show you animals and tools, and you will have to learn their name. Listen carefully because you will have to tell me their names, after". In each trial, the experimenter first showed one of the four stimuli and produced one of the four novel words: "this is a ....". Then, the child had to repeat the novel word, in order to assess his/her capacity to repeat it. When the child failed to repeat the name, the experimenter repeated it, until the child was able to repeat it correctly. The experimenter stopped these repetitions after four failures (which never happened since most children could repeat the word after the first presentation). The experimenter introduced the second stimulus in the same way, and so on with the third and fourth stimuli. Then, he introduced the four stimuli in a row and gave the name of the corresponding referent. Last, he showed the stimuli one at a time in a random order and asked the referent name. He

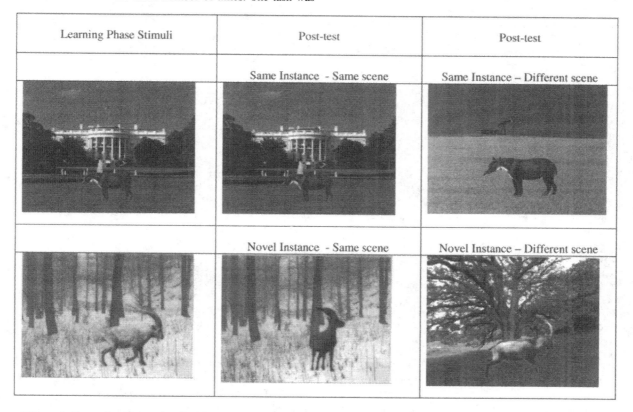

Learning Phase Stimuli	Post-test	Post-test
	Same Instance - Same scene	Same Instance – Different scene
	Novel Instance - Same scene	Novel Instance – Different scene

Figure 1: Examples of the stimuli and scenes used in Experiment 1: The left column displays training stimuli with the scene they were embedded in. The middle column and the rightmost columns display test stimuli.

gave a feedback for each production of the child (e.g., "yes, it is... ", "no, it's a ... ". This sequence composed a trial. There were four such trials.

Test phase. There were two post-tests: an immediate posttest which took place one minute after the last learning

trial, and a second post-test two weeks after the learning phase. Each post-test was composed of a naming phase in which the four stimuli were introduced one by one, in a random order ("do you remember the name of this one?"). The naming task was followed by a pointing task in which the four stimuli were interspersed with three new stimuli that were never shown during the previous stages of the experiment and that acted as fillers. The child had to point to each stimulus corresponding to the name given by the experimenter ("could you show me the *duban*?"). The two conditions defining the variable instance (old vs. novel referents) differed by the referents introduced in the posttests: in the "old" condition, the experimenter showed the same instances as in the learning phase, whereas in the "novel" condition, novel instances were shown to the children (e.g., a tapir not introduced during the previous stages of the experiment).

At the end of the second post-test, participants were shown all the referents, that is to say, the "old" items and their "novel" counterparts. The experimenter showed the training stimuli and asked children to put the test stimuli with the corresponding training stimuli. This was done in order to verify that children were able to classify the novel instances in the same category as the old instances. This was necessary since we wanted to avoid, in the novel condition, naming or pointing failures that would be due to children's (conceptual) misunderstandings that novel instances were belonging to the same category as their learning counterparts.

Experimental Design

The variables Instance (old vs. novel), Task (pointing vs. naming) and Post-test (immediate vs. 2 weeks later) were within variables, while the variable Scene (same vs. different) was a between factor.

Results

Eight children were removed from the sample because they failed to correctly classify *all* the novel referents with their "old" counterparts. Children's performance was calculated in the following way. In the naming task, a correct word pronounced correctly and correctly associated with its referent was given 1 point. However, sometimes children productions were only partly correct. In that case, we calculated the number of correct phonemes in a given word. Each correct phoneme in the correct location in the word was rated .25 (e.g., "keno" for "kéni" would give a score of .75). This was necessary because the mean number of entire words correctly pronounced was very low. In the pointing task, each correct association between a name and a referent was scored 1.

We conducted two separate mixed three-way ANOVAs on the data for the naming task and the pointing task, with the variable scene (same vs. different) as a between factor, and the variables post-tests (immediate vs. 2 weeks later) and instances (old vs. novel) as within factors. Since there were only two old instances and two novel instances, the maximum score was 2 for each cell of the experimental design. The 2 x 2 x 2 analysis on the naming scores revealed a significant effect of the post-test variable, $F_{(1,42)} = 6.22$, $p < 0.05$, with better performance for the immediate post-test (M = .35) than for the delayed post-test (M = .19). More importantly, there was a significant main effect of instance,

$F_{(1,42)} = 4.82$, $p < 0.05$, with better performance for the old instances (M = .35) than for novel instances (M = .17). No other effect or interaction reached significance.

The parallel ANOVA on the pointing scores also revealed a significant effect of instance, $F_{(1,42)} = 20.23$ et $p < 0.001$, with better performance in the Old condition (M = 1.19) than in the Novel condition (M = 0.81). There was also a significant post-test x scene interaction, $F_{(1,42)} = 8.83$ et $p < 0.005$, showing that the difference between the same scene and the different scene condition, in favour of the same scene condition, was important in the second post-test, not in the immediate post-test (see Figure 2).

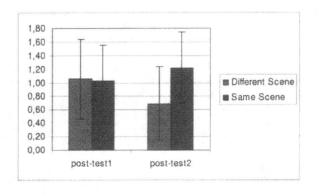

Figure 2: Scene x Post-test interaction in the pointing task

Discussion

In both the naming and the pointing tasks, performance was better in the old condition than in the novel instance condition. This result (which can be described as undergeneralization, that is a failure to apply a novel name to instances to which it could be applied) cannot be explained by conceptual factors since all the children kept in the analysis understood that the novel instances were to be classified with the corresponding old instances. Another interesting result was obtained for the variable scene, in the post-test x scene interaction, showing that participants' performance was weaker for the different scene condition and was not influenced by the scene congruence in the immediate test. Both results (on the variables scene and instances) are consistent with our retrieval cue hypothesis.

Note that we did not obtain a significant effect of scene in the naming task. This might be due to the very low scores or to the important variance in the results. A scene effect is particularly interesting because it reflects a lack of generalization of a novel which is certainly not due to conceptual factors, especially if the learning stimuli are the same in the training and the transfer phase. In the following experiment, we compared three conditions of scene congruence or incongruence between the training and the transfer phases, with the same instances used in both phases.

Experiment 2
Methods

Participants

A total of 113 french-speaking children participated in the study, (mean age = 52 months, range: 42 to 59 months). Children were tested in their school. (Note that the children were younger in this experiment than in the first one. In fact, Experiment 2 was conducted before Experiment 1, for which we decided to test younger children.) French was their native language. Informed consent was obtained from their parents.

Materials

Training phase stimuli. There were four experimental pictures representing real entities. Stimuli were coloured images (15 x 21 cm) of four unfamiliar animals or four unfamiliar musical instruments. Each stimulus was included in a scene. Four scenes highly contrasted were used for each category of stimuli. Animals were associated with a desert, snow, a park, or a house. Musical instruments were associated with a desk, in a room, on a seat, or in the street. A stimulus was pasted on a scene with the Photoshop$^{©}$ software. The four target stimuli of a category gave rise to several sets of stimuli, each set resulting from a different association between each of the four novel stimuli and a particular scene with the additional constrain that, in a given set, two stimuli could not be associated with the same scene.

Test phase stimuli. Three conditions were devised: same scene, mixed scene, new scene. In the *same* scene condition, a stimulus was associated with the same scene in the learning and the test phase. In the *mixed* scene condition, each stimulus swapped the scene it was associated with in the learning phase with the scene of one of the three remaining learning stimuli. In the *new* scene condition, eight new scenes were created for the test phase, four for the animals and four for musical instruments. In this condition, each learning stimulus was associated with one of the four new scenes.

Procedure

The training phase was similar to the training phase in Experiment 1 except that there were 5 trials instead of 4. Note that a child had to learn the name of four stimuli from the same category, either the four animals or the musical instruments. At the time of the experiment, we preferred to use two types of categories for the sake of generality. We also decided to separate the two types of categories in order to keep the conceptual heterogeneity of the stimuli for each child as low as possible. We agree that mixing the two types of stimuli would have been a possible strategy.

The test phase was composed of three post-tests. The first one took place one minute after the end of the learning phase, the second, two days later, and the third 2 weeks after the end of the learning phase. There were 3 post-tests here instead of 2 in the first experiment because, as mentioned above, this experiment was performed before Experiment 1 and at that time we had no idea of the effect of the length of the delay. In each post-test, the child had to perform the same naming and pointing tasks as in Experiment 1.

Results

We decided to split the group of participants into two subgroups of children, younger and older ones. The idea was to check whether potential scene effects would be equivalent in both age groups. Indeed, it is interesting to study whether younger children would be more influenced by irrelevant cues than older ones. Two separate analyses were performed on the naming and the pointing tasks. The analyses were mixed three-way-analyses of variance (ANOVA) 2 (Age: under 50 months vs. over 50 months) x 3 (Type of scene: same vs. mixed vs. new) x 3 (Time of post-test: immediate vs. 2 days vs. 2 weeks) with repeated measure on the factor Post-test variable.

For the naming task, the analysis of variance showed a significant effect of the variable Age, with older children obtaining better results than young children, $F(1, 107) = 6.36$, $p < 0.05$. Interestingly, there was a significant effect of the scene, $F(2, 107) = 3.479$, $p < 0.05$. A posteriori test (Tukey HSD) revealed that the "same scene" condition was only marginally significantly higher than the other two scenes (same scene, mean = 1.24, mixed scene, mean = .88, new scene, mean = .88). The post-test variable was significant, $F(2, 214) = 6.670$; $p < 0.01$. A posteriori test (Tukey HSD) showed that the first post-test was significantly lower than the other post-tests ($p < .05$; mean, first post-test = .81, second post-test = 1.06, third post-test = 1.13).

For the pointing task, there was also a significant effect of scene, $F(2, 107) = 8.351$; $p < 0.001$. The condition "same scene" was significantly higher than the two other conditions (Tukey HSD, $p < .05$) (same scene, mean = 2.96, mixed scene = 2.07, new scene = 2.40). No other effect reached significance.

Discussion

This experiment confirmed the role of the scene already demonstrated in the first experiment. The effect was present in both tasks and revealed better results for the "same scene" condition compared with the two other conditions, which is totally consistent with our retrieval cues hypothesis and is not compatible with a conceptual view of undergeneralization, since the stimuli were the same in the learning and the test phases. Note also the effect of age in the naming task, not in the pointing task. This interesting result suggests that the association between the name and the referent was equivalent in the two age groups. The difference in the naming task might reflect differences at the level of the production system and/or in the ability to retrieve the word when memory cues are poorer or a combination of these two variables.

General Discussion

Our purpose was to show that children might fail to generalize a novel word to new situations for non-conceptual reasons. The differences obtained between novel instances and old instances, in Experiment 1 the one hand, and between *same* scene and *new* scene in both experiments are important because they suggest that children did not use novel word for memory reasons. More precisely, when children did not use a novel word-referent association, this was not due to a failure to learn the association, or because they did not understand that the stimuli in the test phase belonged to the same category as the training stimuli. Our interpretation is that in a number of cases they encoded the word-referent association in terms of specific cues that were no longer or less available in the test phase.

Interestingly, our results suggest that a number of undergeneralizations described in previous contributions, especially those observed in natural communication situations, and that have been described as conceptually-based failures to generalize were probably due to the memory factors underlined here. Obviously, our claim is not that conceptual undergeneralizations do not exist: there are many cases in which children did not grasp the right dimensions leading to a correct generalization of the corresponding term in the adult language. Our claim is that, before assuming a conceptual undergeneralization, one should verify that children did not mention or understand that the novel stimuli did not belong to the same category as the corresponding learning stimulus. Moreover, it is quite clear that the scene effects observed in Experiment 2 cannot be described in conceptual terms.

More generally, in the lexical development literature, different views have been proposed. To summarize, on the one hand, authors have claimed that lexical learning depends on mechanisms that are specific to this task, either because these mechanisms are innately dedicated to lexical learning (Markman, 1989) or because children have learned productive regularities regarding lexemes in the course of their development (Smith, 1999). On the other hand, other authors view lexical learning as the product of general learning mechanisms, not specific to language, such as memory mechanisms or more conceptual mechanisms associated with the emergence of a theory of mind (Bloom, 2000). Our results, we think, are more consistent with this general mechanisms view of lexical learning. Indeed, our memory hypothesis is directly connected with the encoding specificity hypothesis (Tulving & Thomson, 1973) that has been applied to a wide number of encoding situations outside the language domain. Generally speaking, this view is consistent with the negative influence of non-congruent scenes observed in the present experiment.

Acknowledgments

This research also benefited from a grant from the "Fonds spéciaux de la recherche" of the University of Liège. We would like to thank Johanne Gregoire, Agnes Sadzot for assistance for data collection and analysis.

References

Baddeley, A.D. (1997). *Human Memory: Theory and Practice*. Psychology Press.

Balsam, P.D. & Tomie, A. (1985). Context and learning. Hillsdale, NJ. Lawrence Erlbaum Associates.

Bloom, P. (2000). *How children learn the meanings of words*. Cambridge: MA, MIT Press.

Carey, S. & Bartlett, E. (1978). Acquiring a single new word. *Papers and reports on child langage development, 15*, 17-29.

Childers, J. & Tomasello, M. (2002). Two-year-olds learn novel nouns, verbs, and conventional actions from massed or distributed exposures. *Developmental Psychology, 38*, 967-978.

Clark, E.V. (1993). *The lexicon in acquisition*. Cambridge : Cambridge University Press.

Fenson, L., Dale, P., Reznick, S., Bates, E., Thal, D., Pethick, S. (1994). Variability in early communicative development. *Monographs of the Society for Research in Child Development, 59,* (no. 242).

Markman, E.M. (1989). Categorization and naming in children. Problems of induction. Cambridge, MA. Cambridge University Press.

Markson, L. and Bloom, P. (1997). Evidence against a dedicated system for word learning in children. *Nature 385*, 813-815.

Mervis, CB (1987). Child-basic object categories and early lexical development. IN U. Neisser (Ed.), Concepts and conceptual development. Cambridge: Cambridge University Press.

Mervis, C.B., & Bertrand, J. (1994). Acquisition of the Novel Name-Nameless Category (N3C) Principle *Child Development*, 65, 1646-1662.

Siegler, R.S. (1998). *Children's thinking*. Englewood Cliffs, NJ: Prentice Hall.

Smith (1999). Children's noun learning: How general learning processes make specialized learning mechanisms. In B. MacWhinney (Ed.). *The emergence of language* (pp. 277-303).

Tulving, E. & Thomson, D.W. (1973). Encoding specificity and retrieval processes in episodic memory. *Psychological review, 80*, 352-73,

The Impact of Inhibition Control on Working Memory in Children with SLI

Klara Marton (kmarton@brooklyn.cuny.edu)
Department of Speech Communication Arts & Sciences, Brooklyn College, CUNY, 2900 Bedford Ave.,
Brooklyn, NY 11210 & Eotvos Lorand University, Barczi Gusztav Faculty of Special Education,
1097 Budapest, Ecseri ut 3.

Lyudmyla Kelmenson (Kelmenson_Lyudmyla@hotmail.com)
Department of Speech Communication Arts & Sciences, Brooklyn College, CUNY,
2900 Bedford Ave., Brooklyn, NY 11210

Abstract

This study examined the "inefficient inhibition" hypothesis (IIH; Bjorklund & Harnishfeger, 1990; Wilson & Kipp, 1998). The IIH suggests that individuals with efficient inhibition skills perform well on working memory tasks because they are able to keep out irrelevant information from working memory. To test this theory, we selected a group of children with specific language impairment (SLI) and 2 control groups (age-matched and language-matched). Children with SLI are known for their working memory capacity limitations. The question was whether this limitation is influenced by inhibition problems. The results revealed that children with SLI produce more inhibition errors than their peers across various tasks. Thus, an association between working memory and inhibition control was found, but the direction of causality was not clear.

Introduction

The aim of the present study was to examine the relationship between inhibition control and working memory. Specifically, this study evaluated the "inefficient inhibition hypothesis" (IIH; Bjorklund & Harnishfeger, 1990; Wilson & Kipp, 1998). The IIH suggests that individuals with better inhibition skills have more processing capacity than people who are less efficient in inhibition control. Thus, individuals with efficient inhibition skills perform better on various working memory tasks because they are able to keep out irrelevant information from working memory. There is a general consensus in the literature that children with specific language impairment (SLI) have processing capacity limitations. Thus, children with SLI are a great target group for testing the IIH. If these children show more difficulty in inhibition control than typically developing children (TLD), then, according to the IIH, their processing capacity limitation may be influenced by their poor inhibition control.

Inhibition control involves temporal delays in response and resistance to interference (Barkley, 1997, Friedman & Miyake, 2004). It can prevent perseveration in task performance through the suppression of irrelevant information. The frequency of perseveration may be affected by task complexity, experimental conditions, and response modality (Stedron, Sahni, & Munakata, 2005). During task performance, when there is a delay in response,

the contents of working memory have to be protected from external interfering stimuli that can distort or disrupt them. In addition to external stimuli, internal sources may also interfere with relevant information. These internal stimuli can be traces of information from previous actions, memory intrusions from previously relevant material.

Based on previous studies, it is a strong hypothesis that SLI children's working memory difficulties (e.g., in listening span tasks) are highly influenced by a weakness in inhibition. These children exhibited larger suffix effects (Gillam, Cowan, & Day, 1995) and showed diminished primacy and recency effects in linguistic span tasks (Ellis Weismer, Evans, & Hesketh, 1999; Marton & Schwartz, 2003, Marton, Schwartz, Farkas, & Katsnelson, 2006). The difference in recall accuracy across word positions (list-initial, -middle, and -final items) was diminished in children with SLI. These children were not able to process the old and the new information simultaneously. Children with SLI also differed from their peers in the coordination of information storage and retrieval in different modalities (Hoffmann & Gillam, 2004). As the amount of information increased, resource coordination decreased. In working memory tasks, children with SLI often show perseveration (Marton & Schwartz, 2003, Marton, et al., 2006); they repeat previous answers or other parts of the task. Inhibition control may play a crucial role behind these deficits.

To test the IIH, we performed a detailed error analysis of children's working memory performance. It was hypothesized that children with more limited working memory capacity indicate more difficulty in suppressing irrelevant information than children with better processing capacity and phonological working memory. Further, it was predicted that an increase in set size –the number of stimuli to remember- results in a decrease in working memory performance accuracy and in an increase in inhibition errors.

Methods

Participants

Three groups of children (15 children with SLI, 15 age-matched peers, and 15 language-matched controls) participated in this study. All participants attended elementary school and used English as their primary language. The first group consisted of children with SLI (age-range: 7;8 -10;1 years) who had been diagnosed by a speech-language pathologist as having specific language impairment. All children in this group were enrolled in speech-language treatment at the time of the study. Their language performance was at least 1.25 SD below the age appropriate level as measured by the Clinical Evaluation of Language Fundamentals-4 (CELF-4) language test (Semel, Wiig, & Secord, 2003). All participants in this group showed typical (>90) nonverbal intelligence on the Test of Nonverbal Intelligence (TONI-3, Brown, Sherbenon, Johnsen, 1997).

The second group included chronological age-matched (within 3 months) typically developing children (AM), ranging in age between 7;9 and 10;3 years. Interviews with parents and teachers ensured that all children in this group followed a typical developmental pattern. These participants passed a language screening (CELF-3 Screening Test; Semel, Wiig, &Secord, 1995) and showed typical nonverbal IQ.

The third group consisted of language-matched typically developing children who were younger than the participants in the previous 2 groups. Each child in this group was matched to 1 of the children with SLI within 3 raw scores on the Peabody Picture Vocabulary Test-III (Dunn & Dunn, 1997). Similar to the age-matched participants, these children passed a language screening (CELF-3 Screening Test) and exhibited typical nonverbal IQ.

There were 2 girls and 13 boys in each group. All participants passed a pure-tone audiometric screening of both ears at 20 dB HL (at 500, 1000, 2000, and 4000 Hz). None of the children demonstrated articulatory errors, motor, emotional, or physical handicaps.

Stimuli

Nonword Repetition
Participants' phonological working memory was tested with a nonword repetition task. There were 48 nonwords (3-and 4-syllable long). The stress pattern of all the nonwords followed the trochaic pattern of English (see more details in Marton & Schwartz, 2003).

Listening Span Task
This task included 2 lists of sentences (3 sets of 2 sentences per set, 3 sets of 3 sentences per set, 3 sets of 4 sentences per set, and 3 sets of 5 sentences per set in each list; total of 84 sentences). There was a question targeting sentence content in each set. Participants listened to the sentences, answered the question following sentence presentation, and then repeated the sentence-final word. The sentences were short including 10 or fewer syllables. The sentence-final words were high frequency words that children typically acquire during their preschool years. These words had been controlled for their phonological features. This task was designed to test processing capacity.

Data Analysis
Performance in the nonword repetition task was evaluated segment by segment. Any segment substitution, addition, deletion, cluster simplification were scored as incorrect. Other errors included incorrect stress pattern, or changes in segment order. Nonword repetition errors were categorized as single or multiple. An error was considered as single if the child produced only one segmental substitution or deletion, etc. The multiple errors category referred to nonwords that contained several errors.

In the listening span task, an answer was considered as an inhibition error if it was a target of a previous list or a non sentence-final word. Inhibition errors were categorized as immediate (from the current set) or delayed (from a previous set). They were either contextual distractions or perseverations. Contextual distractions were errors where the child recalled a non-target word from the current set (e.g., a word from the middle of the sentence), whereas perseverations included errors where the child repeated either a previously recalled sentence-final word or the answer to the question.

Results
First we compared children's phonological working memory performance in the nonword repetition task. A one-way ANOVA indicated significant group differences between the children with SLI and the two control groups (F (2, 41) = 23.93, $p < 0.001$), the effect sizes were large (SLI-AM: d: 2.53; SLI-LM: d: 2.03); the two groups of typically developing children performed similarly (AM-LM: d: 0.37). To further analyze working memory capacity performance, we examined the complexity of children's errors. Factorial ANOVA was performed to compare single versus multiple errors of nonword repetition across groups. The analysis yielded a significant main effect for group (F (2, 84) = 15.5, $p < 0.001$, SLI-AM: d: 1.8; SLI-LM: d: 1.46; AM-LM: d: 0.52) with more error productions in children with SLI than in the control groups. Another main effect was indicated for error type (single – multiple; F (1, 84) = 7.99, $p < 0.01$), and there was an interaction between error type and group (F (2, 84) = 6.34, $p < 0.01$). A post hoc Tukey test revealed that children with SLI made more multiple errors than the controls, but there was no difference across groups in the amount of single error production. A difference was yielded in the proportion of single versus multiple errors between the groups. Both control groups produced more single than multiple errors, whereas children with SLI produced more multiple than single errors. Thus, children with SLI not only produced more nonword repetition errors than their peers, their errors were more complex (see Figure 1).

Based on previous findings, we predicted larger listening span in the AM and LM groups than in the group of children with SLI. Listening span was defined as the set length at which participants recalled the sentence-final word correctly in 2 out of 3 occasions. The group effect was tested with a one-way ANOVA (F (2, 40) = 7.46, $p < 0.01$; SLI-AM: d: 1.5, SLI-LM: d: 0.87; AM-LM: 0.52).

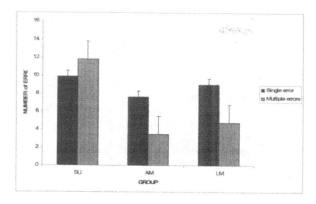

Figure 1. Nonword repetition errors

Further, it was predicted that an increase in set size (2-3-4-5 sentences per set) results in a decrease in performance accuracy –number of sentence-final words recalled correctly- in all groups. Factorial ANOVA was used to test group differences and to examine the effect of set size on working memory performance accuracy. There was a main effect for group (F (2, 168) = 28.19, p < 0.01; SLI-AM: d: 1.22, SLI-LM: d: 0.37, AM-LM: 0.72) and a main effect for set size (3, 168) = 25.39, p < 0.001). There was no group x set size interaction (F (6, 168) = 0.55, p = 0.77). All children's performance accuracy was negatively affected by an increase in set size (see Figure 2).

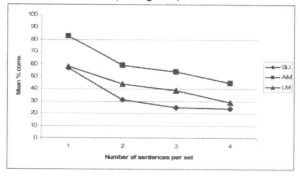

Figure 2. The effect of increased working memory load on performance accuracy.

To test the IIH, we examined whether children with SLI, who have limited working memory capacity, produce more inhibition errors than children with better working memory (AM; LM). A one-way ANOVA was performed to test overall inhibition errors (F (2, 42) = 10.64, p < 0.001, SLI-AM: d: 1.15; SLI-LM: d: 1.2, AM-LM: d: 0.1). Children with SLI produced significantly more inhibition errors than the typically developing children. Participants of the AM and LM groups did not differ in the number of inhibition errors. To provide further evidence for the IIH, we performed a correlation analysis of working memory span and overall inhibition errors in all participants. The results show a negative relationship (r (43) = -0.39, p < 0.05). Thus

children, who produced fewer inhibition errors, showed larger working memory capacity, as predicted by the IIH.

Factorial ANOVA was used to evaluate whether the groups differed in inhibition error types (immediate distraction versus delayed intrusion). A main effect was found for both independent variables and there was a group x error type interaction (group effect: F (2, 84) = 8.63, p < 0.001; inhibition type: F (1, 84) = 75.58, p < 0.001; interaction: F (2, 84) = 5.97, p < 0.01). Post hoc. Tukey tests indicated that all children produced more immediate than delayed errors (immediate-delayed errors within the SLI group: d: 2.18, within the AM group: d: 1.29, within the LM group: d: 2.13). Participants in the SLI group differed from the AM and LM groups in the amount of immediate errors. These children produced more immediate inhibition errors than the typically developing children (SLI-AM: d: 1.15, SLI-LM: d: 1.07). The age-matched and language-matched controls did not differ in the number of immediate inhibition errors (AM-LM: d: 0.21). There was no difference across groups in the number of delayed inhibition errors (see Figure 3).

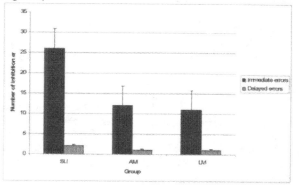

Figure 3. Inhibition errors

Inhibition errors were further categorized whether they reflected contextual distraction or perseveration. The results of factorial ANOVA showed a main effect for group (F (2, 83) = 11.01, p < 0.001) and a main effect for error type (F (1, 83) = 4.33, p < 0.05. There was no group x error type interaction (F (2, 83) = 0.15, p = 0.85. Children with SLI produced more errors in both categories than the typically developing children (SLI-AM contextual distraction: d: 0.9, SLI-LM: d: 0.88, SLI-AM perseveration: d: 0.83, SLI-LM: d: 1.23). The two typically developing groups showed similar performance (AM-LM contextual distraction: d: 0.11, AM-LM perseveration: d: 0.08). All participants produced more contextual distraction errors than perseverations.

The last analysis was performed to examine the effect of set size on the number of inhibition errors. There was a main effect for group (F (2, 168) = 18.52), but the increase in working memory load (set size) did not result in an increase in inhibition errors (F (3, 168) = 2.35, p = 0.075). There seems to be a tendency, but this result did not reach significance. There was no group x set size interaction ($F(3, 168) = 0.54$, $p = 0.9$).

Discussion

The aim of this study was to test the "inefficient inhibition hypothesis" (IIH, Bjorklund & Harnishfeger, 1990; Wilson & Kipp, 1998) in a group of children with limited working memory capacity and in their peers. Children with SLI are generally known for their limitations in working memory capacity. The IIH suggests that participants with inefficient inhibition skills perform more poorly on various working memory tasks because they are not able to keep out irrelevant information from working memory. Individuals who are able to expel previously relevant, but currently irrelevant information from working memory have less material to process. Thus, these persons need less processing space and capacity. This theory suggests that working memory capacity can be enhanced by increasing the efficiency of inhibition control.

The results of the nonword repetition and the listening span tasks are in line with previous findings. Children with SLI performed more poorly than their age-matched and language-matched peers in both tasks under various conditions. There was an age-effect between the age-matched and the language-matched groups because the language matched children were younger than the participants in the other 2 groups. This was only a quantitative difference because the 2 control groups showed very similar performance patterns in terms of error types. In nonword repetition, children with SLI differed from the control groups in both the number of errors they produced and in the proportion of single and multiple errors. These children showed more complex errors than the typically developing children. Children with SLI produced more multiple errors than single errors, whereas children in the 2 control groups performed with fewer multiple errors than single errors. The majority of their error words included single segment substitutions or deletions. This result is a replication of our previous findings (Marton & Schwartz, 2003, Marton et al., 2006).

The overall results in inhibition control support the IIH. The data show that children with SLI –with more limited working memory capacity- produce more inhibition errors than their peers, particularly more immediate errors. These children showed difficulty with both contextual distractions and perseverations. They seem to have difficulty with expelling previously activated information from working memory when that information is not relevant anymore.

Our findings are in agreement with the results of previous research that examined inhibition in children with autism and used the children with SLI as a control group (Bishop & Norbury, 2005; Liss, Fein, Allen, Dunn, Feinstein, Morris, Waterhouse, & Rapin, 2001). These authors found poor inhibition in children with SLI compared to typically developing children on different complex neuropsychological tests.

Inhibition efficiency may be affected by various components, such as testing conditions, stimulus type, etc. This study examined the effect of memory load (an increase in set size) on performance accuracy and on the number of inhibition errors. Increased set size had a negative effect on all children's performance accuracy. All participants made more errors in recall as the number of sentences increased. The effect of memory load on the number of inhibition errors is less clear. Typically developing children produced only a small number of inhibition errors; most of their errors were omissions, similar to other reported findings (McCormack, Brown, & Vousden, 2000). Children with SLI showed a tendency for an increased number of inhibition errors with an increase in memory load, but that result did not reach significance. Further examination of this question is needed.

The results of this study show an association between inhibition control and working memory capacity, however, these data do not indicate the direction of causality. More direct examinations of various inhibition functions should be performed in future research. Inhibition control is not limited to the suppression of irrelevant information. The evaluation of resistance to interference in children with SLI may help to clarify the relations between inhibition and working memory capacity. If resistance to interference works efficiently, irrelevant items are not encoded into working memory. The present study focused only on items that had been encoded previously. Thus, these data show that children with SLI, who have working memory capacity limitations, also have difficulty with suppressing information that is not relevant anymore. They show problems with expelling unnecessary material from working memory. The findings support the IIH, but more research is needed to understand the impact of inhibition functions on working memory performance in children with SLI. Future studies may examine whether these children are less susceptible to retroactive interference than their peers. Using a retroactive interference paradigm would provide us with further information regarding the relationship between inhibition control and working memory.

Acknowledgments

This study was supported by a research grant from the National Institute on Deafness and Other Communication Disorders (Working memory capacity in children with SLI, R03DC41449), by a sabbatical year fellowship for the first author from Brooklyn College. We thank Sabina Ajani for her help in data coding and analysis. Special thanks to Michael Bergen for his continuous support in recruiting participants and for providing testing space in the Speech and Hearing Center of Brooklyn College.

References

Barkley, R. A. (1997). Behavioral inhibition, sustained attention, and executive functions. Constructing a unifying theory of ADHD. *Psychological Bulletin, 121*, 65-94.

Bishop, D. V. M. & Norbury, C. F. (2005). Executive functions in children with communication impairments, in relation to autistic symptomatology 2: Response inhibition. *Autism, 9 (1)*, 29-43.

Bjorklund, D. F., & Harnishfeger, K. K. (1990). The resources construct in cognitive development: Diverse sources of evidence and a theory of inefficient inhibition. *Developmental Review, 10*, 48-71.

Brown, L., Sherbenon, R., Johnsen, S. K. (1997). *Test of nonverbal intelligence*. Third edition. (TONI-3). Austin, Texas: pro-ed.

Dunn, L. M. & Dunn, L. M. (1997). *Peabody Picture Vocabulary Test-III*. American Guidance Service, Circle Pines, MN.

Ellis Weismer, S., Evans, J., & Hesketh, L. J. (1999). An examination of verbal working memory capacity in children with specific language impairment. *Journal of Speech, Language, and Hearing Research, 42*, 1249-1260.

Friedman, N. P. & Miyake, A. (2004). The relations among inhibition and interference control functions: A latent variable analysis. *Journal of Experimental Psychology: General, 133*, 101-135.

Gillam, R. B., Cowan, N., & Day, L. S. (1995). Sequential memory in children with and without language impairment. *Journal of Speech and Hearing Research, 38*, 393–402.

Hoffman, L. M. & Gillam, R. B. (2004). Verbal and spatial information processing constraints in children with specific language impairment. *Journal of Speech, Language, and Hearing Research, 47*, 114-125.

Liss, M., Fein, D., Allen, D., Dunn, M., Feinstein, C., Morris, R., Waterhouse, L., & Rapin, I. (2001). Executive functioning in high-functioning children with autism. *The Journal of Child Psychology and Psychiatry and Allied Disciplines, 42*, 261-270.

Marton, K. & Schwartz, R. G. (2003). Working memory capacity limitations and language processes in children with specific language impairment. *Journal of Speech, Language, and Hearing Research, 46*, 1138-1153.

Marton, K., Schwartz, R. G., Farkas, L., & Katsnelson, V. (2006). Effect of sentence length and complexity on working memory performance in Hungarian children with specific language impairment (SLI): A cross-linguistic comparison. *International Journal of Language and Communication Disorders, 41 (6)*, 653-673.

McCormack, T., Brown, G. D. A., & Vousden, J. I. (2000). Children's serial recall errors: Implications for theories of short-term memory development. *Journal of Experimental Child Psychology, 76*, 222-252.

Semel, E., Wiig, E. H., & Secord, W. A. (1995). *Clinical Evaluation of Language Fundamentals: CELF-3 Screening Test*. San Antonio, TX: The Psychological Corporation.

Semel, E., Wiig, E. H., & Secord, W. A. (2003). *Clinical Evaluation of Language Fundamentals*. Fourth edition. (CELF-4). The Psychological Corporation.

Stedron, J. M., Sahni, S. D., and Munakata, Y. (2005). Common mechanisms for working memory and attention: The case of perseveration with visible solutions. *Journal of Cognitive Neuroscience, 17*, 623-631.

Wilson, S. P. & Kipp, K. (1998). The development of efficient inhibition: Evidence from directed forgetting tasks. *Developmental Review, 18*, 86-123.

Inattentional Blindness: An Investigation into the Effects of Working Memory Capacity and Processing Speed - An Individual Differences Approach

Emily M. Hannon (e.hannon@psychology.bbk.ac.uk)
Department of Psychology, Birkbeck College, University of London, Malet St.
London WC1E 7HX
Anne Richards (a.richards@bbk.ac.uk)
Department of Psychology, Birkbeck College, University of London, Malet St.
London WC1E 7HX

Abstract

Inattentional Blindness (IB) refers to an inability to notice highly salient though task-irrelevant stimuli in front of one's eyes when engaged in an attentionally demanding task. While previous research has investigated which factors attenuate or exacerbate the occurrence of IB, none has investigated whether some individuals are more prone to this or why. Using an individual differences approach, we have found that those who are IB are more likely to have a lower working memory capacity (WMC) and have demonstrated a slower processing speed across a variety of reaction time tasks, even when speed of responding was not an issue. Furthermore, in a visual search task where distractors were present/absent, those who were IB showed no difference in RTs but those who were not inattentionally blind (NIB) displayed reduced response time latencies in the presence of distractors. This is in line with research showing that high WMC individuals can adopt a more flexible attentional style and have a greater ability to inhibit task irrelevant stimuli in interference rich environments. It seems likely that IB in the general population is as a result of a reduced WMC together with the adoption of a slower processing style, in order to fulfil task demands.

Introduction

Inattentional Blindness describes a phenomenon whereby, when participants are engaged in a resource-consuming task, unexpected items that we may be looking at directly, will nonetheless fail to capture our attention. Results from both static and dynamic selective attention paradigms (e.g. Mack & Rock 1998; Simons & Chabris (1999) suggest IB may be a pervasive aspect of visual perception where the appearance of a new object does not automatically capture attention. While it is a common belief that unexpected yet important events will automatically draw our attention away from current goals, results from IB research suggests that the occurrence of IB is far more commonplace and remains a frequent cause of human errors, often leading to accidents.

According to Mack, Pappas, Silverman et al. (2002) 'we see what interests us, what we are looking for, or what we are expecting'. Therefore in some situations we do not see what we are not expecting. People are not only unaware of great amounts of visual information but they are also unaware of the extent to which they may be unaware of visual information. As Varakin and Levin (2004) state, such a metacognitive failure can go some way towards explaining why human/computer interaction can lead to 'cognitive tunnelling' and therefore be error prone.

While previous research has investigated which stimulus-driven properties have the greatest impact on levels of IB (Newby & Rock, 1998), attentional capture by sudden onsets appears to *reliably* occur only when observers are unsure where their target will appear, but these same sudden onsets will not capture attention when observers know the target location (Yantis & Jonides, 1990). Therefore, when given a task where the goals and targets are prespecified, IB may occur for unexpected events or stimuli.

Other factors such as conspicuity, attentional set, confirmation bias and perceptual load have also been identified as impacting on levels of IB (Gibson & Peterson, 2001; Most, Scholl, & Clifford, 2005; Cartwright-Finch & Lavie, 2006). However, even when manipulating a task so that there is the greatest likelihood of noticing unexpected stimuli, in research such as that conducted by Mack and Rock (1998), a minimum of 25% and sometimes as many as 80% of participants tested remained blind to an unexpected though highly salient object or event.

Given that all participants are presented with the same task under the same conditions, it seems likely that individual differences research will go some way towards providing a fuller explanation of this phenomenon. It may be that IB individuals are extremely task focussed and goal oriented so that any task irrelevant stimuli will not be processed or attended to.

Other mechanistic factors may be involved. It may be the case that IB occurs as a result of successful inhibition of the irrelevant stimulus. This ability to inhibit irrelevant information is very useful as it allows the system to deal with the main task in an uninterrupted manner and prevents 'information overload'. As Tipper and Baylis (1987) state: "the ability of all but the lowest animals to successfully attend to one, or few, objects whilst ignoring other distracting objects is crucial. Such a selection process is a fundamental component of most goal-directed behaviours". The problem occurs, however, when the ostensibly irrelevant stimulus is actually highly significant, as may be the case when a rogue aircraft crosses the screen of an air traffic controller.

Another proposal is that, rather than being actively inhibited, the irrelevant stimulus it is simply not processed. The IB individual may have limited resources and simply fails to process the irrelevant stimulus. If it is the case that people with IB need to use their available resources to maintain attentional focus on the primary task, then this is an efficient use of their available resources. There is evidence that high working memory capacity is associated with greater ability to inhibit distractors (Conway & Engle, 1994; Kane & Engle, 2003) and that increases in perceptual load is also associated with reduced ability to inhibit irrelevant information (Lavie, 1995; Lavie & Fox, 2000; Cartwright-Finch & Lavie, 2006).

The main difficulty attendant upon IB research is the lack of test-retest possibilities. Once asked 'did you see anything else' the individual becomes aware of the possibility of other stimuli or events and subsequently adopts a wider or more divided attentional set. With such a dichotomous variable, it becomes necessary to find other means in which hypotheses such as those described above can be investigated. Here we used a variety of reaction time and visual search tasks together with investigations into inhibitory differences using a negative priming Stroop task and a measurement of WMC using the Operation Span (OSPAN) task of Turner and Engle (1989). Initial experimental designs were simple Posner cueing experiments with Experiments 3-4 concentrating on inhibitory factors.

Experiment 1:

Method
One hundred and forty participants (mean age, 26, 52 females) completed a simple cueing task (a prime of M predicted a target MMM and a prime of Z predicted a target ZZZ) using a typical 80/20 cue/target validity ratio, to test whether those who are IB become over-focussed on targets predicted by primes as a result of heightened goal directed behaviour, with a resultant increase in response latencies to invalid cues. Four blocks, 100 trials each, were presented. Cues and targets were presented centrally with a 300ms SOA. Participants were told to be as fast and accurate as possible. All participants completed the OSPAN task. This requires participants to solve simple mathematical equations whilst memorising unrelated words, with word lists varying between 2 and 5 words in length. For example:

'does $(2 \times 4) + 1 = 9$? cave
'does $(6 \div 2) + 3 = 4$? bread

Three sets of each list length are presented (from two to five operations and words), in apparent random order, (but fixed across participants). List length in each set is unknown to participants until the cue '???' appears, when they write down the words they can remember from that set, in the exact order they appeared. Scoring the OSPAN task consists of summing the recalled words for only those sets recalled completely and in the correct word order. Scores can therefore range between 0 and 42.

Group differences in IB were measured using an IB task devised by Most, Simons, Scholl, and Chabris (2000). Four black and four white Ls and Ts move haphazardly around the screen, frequently 'bouncing' off the display's edges. Participants are asked to focus their attention on the white letters whilst ignoring the black letters with the task being to count the number of times the white letters bounce off the frame. During this 17-second task, a red plus sign traverses the screen for 7 seconds, (appearing 5 seconds after task onset). Those who are IB fail to notice this red cross.

Results & Discussion
Forty-seven per cent of participants were IB. More surprisingly, WMC, as measured by OSPAN was lower for IB than NIB participants. Consistent with Kane and Engle (2003) OSPAN scores between 12 and 17 were excluded (to maintain power, this is slightly less stringent than their cut-off points). Independent t-tests revealed that IB individuals have lower OSPAN than NIB participants $t(114) = 1.6$, $p = .057$ with means of 14 (SD 8.6) and 17 (SD 10.7) respectively. This goes against a possible inhibition account of IB as research has found that those with high WMC can more successfully inhibit task irrelevant stimuli. Age was also a significant factor such that older participants were more likely to be IB, $t(114) = 2.37$, $p = .02$, with IB mean age of 28.38 (SD 7.37) and NIB mean 25.28 (SD 6.71). While both groups had high levels of accuracy across trial type, IB participants were consistently slower than NIB participants in the cueing task, $F(1,114) = 686$, $p = .01$.

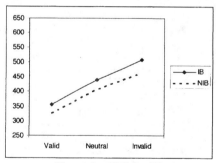

Figure 1: validity x IB

Experiment 2

It is possible that IB participants were overly relying on automatic processes in Experiment 1 rather than attentional control. To control for this possibility, the RT task was made slightly more difficult, such that a prime of E predicted a target MMM and a prime of H predicted a target ZZZ using the same 80/20 validity ratio. The design remained otherwise unchanged.

Method, Results and Discussion

Seventy participants (mean age 27, 40 females) completed the IB, OSPAN and RT tasks as described. 36% of participants were IB. As with Experiment 1, OSPAN data were filtered, yielding a sample size of 46, (30% IB). Independent t-tests revealed that IB participants have lower OSPAN than NIBs, $t(44) = 1.83$, $p = .037$ with means of 12.29 (SD7.01), and 17.01 (SD8.31) respectively. Age was again significant, $t(44) = 3.6$, $p = .001$, with IB mean age 33.50 (10.9), NIB mean age 24.47 (5.99). Between group differences in reaction times on the cueing task again approached significance $F(1,44) = 3.8$, $p = .057$ with the IB participant slower across trial type. While age related slowing may have some effect, it is more likely that those who are IB tend to experience this phenomenon more regularly as they get older. Combining the results from both experiments and holding age at 30 or under, (N = 130), 35% of participants were IB. The results from these initial experiments therefore suggest that IB may be as a result of lower WMC together with slower processing speed. However, we cannot draw such firm conclusions without investigating the inhibition hypothesis.

Experiment 3

Seventy-four participants (mean age 31, 36 female) took part. IB and OSPAN were tested as before. Additionally, as the OSPAN task is thought to measure executive functioning of working memory, to investigate the possibility that IB occurs as a result of greater limitations in visual working memory (VWM) rather than executive functioning per se, a visual working memory task was presented. This was adapted from Luck and Vogel (1997) with coloured squares presented in arrays varying between four and twelve squares. There were 160 trials, presented in 4 blocks, each comprising 40 samples with five x each set size per block each block with 20 correct and incorrect trials. Each trial was presented for 100ms followed by a 900ms interval. This was then followed by a test array that remained onscreen for 2,000ms with the task being to determine whether there was a difference between prime and test arrays. It was expected that a linear relationship would be found in accuracy levels such that the greater the number of squares the poorer would be the accuracy rates. With a 2,000ms test array presentation, only accuracy was stressed and therefore there was no possibility of a speed/accuracy tradeoff occurring. If between groups differences are as a result of deficits in visual working memory, we would expect IB participants to be less accurate than NIB participants, with this more apparent for larger arrays.

To also test for inhibition effects, a negative priming Stroop task was presented. Tipper (1985) and Tipper and Cranston (1985) developed this model of selective attention which investigated the possibility that, in order to maintain task goals, active inhibition of ignored objects must take place in order to make correct responses to the target. The classic Stroop task has been assumed to reveal impairments in inhibitory processes. It involves naming the ink colour that a word is printed in whilst ignoring the word. RT differences are measured between a control condition of naming the colour of a series of XXX's, a congruent condition where both the ink colour and word match e.g. the word 'red' printed in the ink colour red, and an incongruent condition e.g. the word 'red' printed in the ink colour blue with the task to respond 'blue'. It is thought that deficits in inhibitory processes are revealed due to increased interference experienced by individuals unable to suppress the distracting word in the incongruent condition. However the Stroop task does not clearly provide evidence for an inhibitory explanation with other theoretical accounts of selective attention in the Stroop task including excitatory, inhibitory and other relevant components such as cognitive units that represent task demands (Cohen, Dunbar, & McClelland, 1990). Interference effects could theoretically be due to impairment in excitatory processes or difficulty in maintaining task goals. However, in the negative priming Stroop task, an additional 'ignored repeated' condition is incorporated. Rather than the word/colour being incongruent, in the ignored repeated condition, the colour of the ink matches the word on the previous trial so that, having suppressed e.g. 'red' in order to name the colour 'blue' the individual is now faced with a word in the colour red. Having just suppressed the word red, retrieval of this word can lead to increased reaction times as a consequence of being more resource demanding and effortful. Engle, Conway, Tuholski, et al. (1995) argue that the process critical to negative priming relies heavily on attentional resources. Our task was adapted from Vitkovitch, Bishop, Dancey, et al. (2002) with control, congruent, incongruent and ignored repeated conditions, each with 30 trials, comprising colour words black, red, yellow, green, purple, blue with the control condition being a series of XXXs.

Results and Discussion

Forty-nine per cent of participants were IB. No age differences were found between groups. Mean OSPAN results, (filtered as before, N = 58, IB 43%) were IB 15.12 (SD 9.15), NIB 19.39 (SD 8.55). This was significant $t(56) = 1.8$ $p = .036$,. The VWM task showed no differences between groups with respect to accuracy. However, despite stressing that only accuracy was important, IB participants were again slower to make decisions regarding same/different responses with this difference increasing as array size increased. An independent t-test of overall RTs revealed significant differences $t(56) = 1.8$, $p = .039$. A 2 x 2 ANOVA was run with IB (IB,NIB) as between subjects factor and change (change, no change) as within subjects factor. This was marginally significant, $F(1,56) = 3.63$, $p = .062$ with a significant IB x change interaction $F(1,56) = 4.75$, $p = .034$. Independent t-tests were run for change' and 'no change' responses. While the no change responses approached significance, $t(56) = 1.40$, $p = .08$, the IB x change response was significant, $t(56) = 2.10$, $p = .02$. However the most parsimonious explanation seems one of simple RT differences.

Results from the negative priming Stroop task showed that, again, IB participants had slower RTs across trial type. (See Table 1) with RT differences increasing for the more controlled attention conditions of incongruent and ignored repeated. It seems likely that where more controlled processing is necessary, due to their lower WMC, they are slower in order to maintain task demands.

Table 1: Descriptive statistics x negative priming Stroop.

	Control	Congruent	Incongruent	Ignored repeated
IB	619.73 (122.64)	554.13 (109.00)	743.64 (170.88)	749.15 (199.31
NIB	564.58 (112.42)	505.26 (85.53)	660.76 (110.94)	684.79 (110.44)

A 2 x 4 mixed ANOVA revealed a significant effect of condition $F(3,168) = 60.15$, $p < .001$ and a significant between subjects effect $F(1,56) = 5.15$, $p = .027$. To investigate the a-priori prediction that greater inhibition effects would occur for the NIBs, related t-tests between incongruent and ignored repeated conditions were run. This approached significance for the NIB group, $t(32) = . 1.78$, $p = .085$ but was non significant for the IB group.

Experiment 4

When faced with competing task demands and/or complex stimulus arrays, the attentional trade-off may be that we employ strategies we have learned to cope with the task, depending on the limits, or otherwise of our own attentional system. Eriksen and St James (1986) suggest that under focused attention there is no measurable interference from distractors. The cost of such focused attention however is that it covers only a small area of the visual field. Participants who can quickly zoom their attention onto targets can avoid interference associated with distraction that is spatially separated from targets.

Bacon and Egeth (1994) and Lamy and Tsal (1999) argue that top down processes can override stimulus driven attentional capture. Indeed, Folk, Remington and Johnston (1992) suggest that exogenous signals capture attention only when the individual has adopted an attentional set for singleton detection. Bacon and Egeth (1994) suggest that goal-directed or top-down selection occurs when knowledge about the task can determine what is selected in the visual field. Therefore, if one is in a singleton detection mode, a broad attentional style may be adopted whereby irrelevant distractors would be detected. However, where there is prior knowledge of both task and target, then a feature search mode (parallel search) would mean that a narrower attentional set would be adopted so that the target but not the irrelevant distractor would be selected. This experiment was designed to further investigate attentional control and inhibition together with the hypothesis that differences in IB are as a result of differential deployment of exogenous and endogenous attentional control modes. 'Exogenous shifts of attention can arise from several sources, such as sudden

intense stimuli, an unexpected development or a personally meaningful object or event grabbing one's attention. Endogenous shifts and sustained attention result not from external stimulus changes but from motivational shifts in on line working memory processing.' (Faw, 2003). For this experiment we used the negative priming Stroop task as before, together with OSPAN and IB tasks. Additionally we used an adaptation of Bacon and Egeth's (1994) visual search task.

Method

Seventy-three participants, (mean age 27, 44 female) took part. IB, OSPAN, and negative priming Stroop tasks together with the visual search task of Bacon and Egeth (1994) were counterbalanced across participants.

In the visual search task, stimulus arrays consisted of five, seven or nine shapes (either diamond or circle), presented equally spaced around the circumference of an imaginary circle. Target shapes were circles within which was either a horizontal or vertical line. Non target shapes were diamonds, presented in the same blue colour as the target circles, which also contained either horizontal or vertical lines. In the distractor condition, one of the non-target diamonds was presented in green. Using a response box, participants had to indicate the orientation of the line (horizontal or vertical) contained within target circles.

Presentation of arrays was presented in eight blocks of 36 trials, (total = 288) with four blocks containing no distractor and four blocks containing the distractor. Presentation of blocks was alternated and counterbalanced between participants so that 50% of participants were presented with a no-distractor block first and 50% with a distractor block first. In each block there were equal numbers of trials at each of the display sizes (5, 7, 9) and equal numbers of horizontal and vertical targets. Additionally, up to three targets appeared per trial, with each target circle containing a line segment of the same orientation.

Results and Discussion

With OSPAN filtered as before, (N = 60), forty per cent were IB. OSPAN differences were again significant with larger scores for NIB participants $t(58) = 1.77$, $p = .04$. As with Experiment 3, age was not significant with means for IB and NIB being 27 and 26 respectively.

Negative Priming Stroop results show the same slower RT pattern for IB participants with a 2 x 4 mixed ANOVA revealing a significant main effect of condition $F(3,174) = 86$, $p < .001$ and a significant IB x condition interaction, $F(3,174) = 4.10$, $p = .008$. Unpacking this interaction, independent t-tests reveal a significant trend between groups for the congruent $(t(58) = 1.32$, $p = .09$ and incongruent condition $t(58) = 1.42$, $p = .08$. Although mean difference between incongruent and ignored repeated conditions was 16ms for NIB participants and 4ms for IB participants, related t-tests show this as non significant.

Table 2: Descriptive statistics x negative priming Stroop.

	Control	Congruent	Incongruent	Ignored repeated
IB	579.11 (111.37)	535.12 (118.48)	705.78 (122.73)	712.00 (137.29
NIB	580.76 (71.55)	571.51 (94.80)	670.12 (72.28)	686.17 (101.61

To lend power to the negative priming Stroop results, Experiments 3 and 4 were combined. With OSPAN filtered as before, this yielded a sample of 118, 41% IB. Slower RT patterns IB participants across trial type were as before. A 2 x 4 mixed ANOVA yielded a main effect of condition $F_{(3,348)} = 133.74$, $p < .001$, an IB x condition interaction $F_{(3,348)} = 2.72$, $p = .044$ and a between groups trend $F_{(1,116)} = 3.60$, $p = .06$. Descriptive statistics show negative priming effects for the NIB group with a mean difference between incongruent and ignored repeated of 20 ms with this being 6ms for the IB group. Unpacking the interaction, independent t-tests reveal significant differences between groups for both incongruent and ignored repeated conditions – t, (116) = 2.66, $p = .004$ and t(116) = 1.80, p= .038 respectively. Importantly, related t-tests between incongruent and ignored repeated conditions were significant for the NIB group t (68) = 2.01, $p = .049$ but not for the IB group t(48) = .37, $p = .71$.

In the visual search task, IB participants were slower across target number and condition (distractor/no distractor), although both groups could make use of target redundancy to improve performance. (See figures 2 & 3).

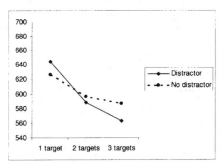

Figure 2: distractor x target interaction x NIB participants

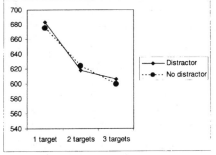

Figure 3: distractor x target interaction x IB participants

However, the IB participants ignored the salient distractor stimulus, as evidenced by their RTs under both distractor present/absent conditions. The NIB participants were however able to make use of the distractor information to perform the task more efficiently by flagging the salient distractor as a 'non target' thereby effectively reducing the visual display by one item. The IBs showed that whilst they were not distracted by the salient distractor (i.e. their RTs were not slower when the salient distractor was present), they failed to make use of the information inherent in the distractor. A related t-test between distractor and no distractor condition (3 targets) for the NIB participants was significant, t(35) = 4.37, p <.001 but was not significant for IB participants. This suggests IBs use a more endogenous processing style whereas the NIBs appear to make more use of the information provided by the stimulus display. This suggests they use a more flexible processing style, using an exogenous style when this is more appropriate.

General Discussion

We tested two hypotheses regarding possible predictors of IB. One proposal was that those who are IB are more goal directed and therefore actively inhibit task irrelevant stimuli. A further hypothesis was that rather than being actively inhibited, the irrelevant yet highly salient stimulus was simply not processed and that IB participants, faced with attentionally demanding and focused tasks simply use up all available resources with capacity for processing irrelevant stimuli being exhausted. Experiments 1 and 2 found evidence that IB participants have significantly lower WMC than NIB participants. Furthermore, whilst both IB and NIBs can perform their tasks equally well, those who are IB have significantly slower reaction times, indicating a slower overall processing speed. This is likely due to their reduced capacity to process information online, relative to higher WMC individuals. These findings suggest IB may therefore be capacity related rather than as a result of perceptual load, as suggested by Cartwright-Finch and Lavie (2006).

While this seems the most parsimonious explanation, it was necessary to rule out an inhibition account of IB. Experiments 3 and 4 investigated this possibility and found converging evidence that WMC is higher in NIBs than IB individuals. Using a negative priming Stroop task further evidence was found for slower reaction times, together with evidence of inhibition effects for the NIB participants only. These RT differences were also found in a visual working memory task. Furthermore, in Experiment 4, using a visual search task where salient distractors were present or absent, (allowing us to investigate IB with a more powerful research task), we again found all participants could perform the tasks equally well but that NIB participants were faster on all conditions. Also, in the presence of a distractor the NIB participants appeared to be actively inhibiting the salient distractor in order to improve performance.

To conclude, this research has repeatedly shown slower RTs for IB individuals across a variety of tasks with no evidence to suggest that IB is as a result of less discriminative inhibition. IB participants did not display enhanced inhibition in the negative priming Stroop task of Experiments 3 and 4. Contrary to an inhibition hypothesis of IB, only NIB participants showed such evidence in the presence of a distractor in the visual search task of Experiment 4 together with inhibitory evidence on the negative priming task. This evidence for active inhibition for NIB participants only is in line with the robust findings of their higher WMC, relative to IB participants. Accompanying this was the finding that IBs responded consistently slower across a variety of RT tasks. However, further research is necessary to complete the picture.

References

Bacon, W F., & Egeth, H. E. (1994). Overriding stimulus-driven attentional capture. *Perception and Psychophysics* 55, 485-496.

Cartwright-Finch, U., & Lavie, N. (2007). The role of perceptual load in inattentional blindness. *Cognition* 102 (3) 321-340.

Cohen, J D., Dunbar, K. & McClelland J. L. (1990). On the control of automatic processes: a parallel distributed processing account of the Stroop effect. *Psychological Review* 97, 332-361.

Conway, A. R. A. & Engle, R. W. (1994). Working memory and retrieval: a resource-dependent inhibition model. *Journal of Experimental Psychology: General* 123. 354-373.

Engle, R. W., Conway, A. R. A., Tuholski, S. W. & Shisler, R. J. (1995). A resource account of inhibition. *Psychological Science, 6*, 122-125.

Eriksen, C. W., & St. James, J. D. (1986). Visual attention within and around the field of focal attention: A zoom-lens model. *Perception and Psychophysics, 40*, 225-240.

Faw, B. (2003). Pre-frontal executive committee for perception, working memory, motor control, and thinking: A tutorial review. *Consciousness and Cognition, 12*, 83-139.

Folk, C. L., Remington, R. W. & Johnston, J. C. (1992). Involuntary covert orienting is contingent on attentional control settings. *Journal of Experimental Psychology: Human Perception and Performance* 18, 1030-1044.

Gibson, B. S. & Peterson, M. A. (2001) Attention Capture, Orienting and Awareness. In Folk, & Gibson .(Eds) *Attraction, Distraction and Action: Multiple Perspectives on Attentional Capture* Elsevier Science B.

Kane, M. J. & Engle, R. W. (2003). Working memory capacity and the control of attention. The contributions of goal neglect, response competition and task set to Stroop interference. *Journal of Experimental Psychology: General, 132*, 47-70.

Lamy, D., & Tsal, Y. (1999). A salient distractor does not disrupt conjunction search. *Psychonomic Bulletin and Review* 6 (1), 93-98.

Lavie, N. (1995). Perceptual load as a necessary condition for selective attention. *Journal of Experimental Psychology: Human Perception and Performance, 21*, 451-468.

Lavie, N., & Fox, E. (2000). The role of perceptual load in negative priming. *Journal of Experimental Psychology: Human Perception and Performance, 26*, 1038-1052.

Luck, S. J., & Vogel, E. K. (1997). The capacity of visual working memory for features and conjunctions. *Nature* 390, 279-281.

Mack, A., & Rock, I. (1998) Inattentional Blindness. Cambridge, MA: MIT Press.

Mack, A, Pappas, Z., Silverman, M, & Gay, R (2002). What we see: Inattention and the capture of attention by meaning. *Consciousness and Cognition* 11 (4), 488-506.

Most, S. B., Scholl, B. J. & Clifford, E. R. (2005). What you see is what you set: Sustained Inattentional Blindness and the capture of awareness. *Psychological Review* 112 (1), 217-242.

Most, S. B., Simons, D. J., Scholl, B .J., & Chabris, C. F. (2000). Sustained Inattentional Blindness: The role of location in the detection of unexpected dynamic events. *Psyche: An Interdisciplinary Journal of Research on Consciousness* 6(14).

Newby, E. A., & Rock, I (1998). Inattentional blindness as a function of proximity to the focus of attention. *Perception* 27, 1025-1040.

Posner, M. I. (1980). Orienting of attention. *Quarterly Journal of Experimental Psychology, 32*, 3-25.

Simons, D. J., & Chabris, C. F. (1999) Gorillas in our midst: sustained inattentional blindness for dynamic events. *Perception, 28*, 1059-1074.

Stroop, J. R. (1935). Studies of interference in serial verbal reactions. *Journal of Experimental Psychology, 18*, 643-662.

Tipper, S. P. (1985). The negative priming effect: Inhibitory priming by ignored objects. *Quarterly Journal of Experimental Psychology: Human Experimental Psychology, 37*, 571-590.

Tipper, S. P. & Baylis, G. C. (1987). Individual differences in selective attention: The relation of priming and interference to cognitive failure. *Personality and Individual Differences* 8 (5), 667-675.

Tipper, S. P. & Cranston, M. (1985). Selective attention and priming: Inhibitory and facilitatory effects of ignored primes. *Quarterly Journal of Experimental Psychology: Human Experimental Psychology.* 37, 591-611.

Turner, M. L., & Engle, R. W (1989). Is working memory capacity task dependent? *Journal of Memory and Language* 28 (2), 127-154.

Varakin, D. A., & Levin, D. T. (2004). Unseen and Unaware: Implications of recent research on failures of visual awareness for human-computer interface design. *Human-Computer Interaction, 19*, 389-422.

Vitkovitch, M., Bishop, S., Dancey, C, & Richards, A. (2002). Stroop interference and negative priming in patients with multiple sclerosis. *Neuropsychologia* 40, 1570-1576.

Yantis, S & Jonides, J (1990). Abrupt visual onsets and selective attention: Voluntary versus automatic allocation. *Journal of Experimental Psychology: Human Perception and Performance, 16*, 121-134.

Amodal Perception: Access or Visualization?

Bence Nanay (nanay@syr.edu)
Syracuse University, Department of Philosophy, 535 Hall of Languages
Syracuse, NY 13244 USA

Abstract

We are aware of the occluded parts of perceived objects. The question is how we represent them: this is the problem of amodal perception. I will consider three possible accounts: (a) we see them, (b) we have non-perceptual beliefs about them and (c) we have immediate perceptual access to them and point out that all of these views face both empirical and conceptual objections. I suggest a fourth account, according to which we visualize the occluded parts of perceived objects: amodal perception is in fact a species of visualization.

Introduction

Do we see the occluded parts of objects? Suppose that I am looking at a cat behind a picket fence, but the cat's tail is not visible, because it is occluded by one of the pickets. The question is how I represent the cat's tail? Do I see it? Do I have a non-perceptual belief about it?

This problem is sometimes referred to as the problem of amodal perception and sometimes it is called the puzzle of perceptual presence. I will consider three possible solutions, point out that they all face serious objections and then propose an alternative that may fare better than the rival theories. Maybe surprisingly, my claim is that we *visualize* the cat's tail.

Before I turn to the possible ways of explaining this phenomenon, I need to make it clear what I am not trying to explain. I am not trying to solve the old philosophical puzzle about what the object of our perception is. A question that is often raised in connection with objects occluding one another, such as the cat's tail behind the fence is about the object of our perception: what is it that we perceive (Clarke, 1965; Strawson, 1979; Noë, 2004, p. 76). Do we perceive the entire cat? Or those parts of the cat that are visible, that is, a tailless cat? I do not intend to answer any of these questions here. My question is not about what we perceive but about the way in which we represent those parts of objects that are not visible to us.

Also, I need to emphasize that amodal perception is not a weird but rare subcase of our everyday awareness of the world. Almost all episodes of perception include an amodal component. For example, typically, only three sides of a non-transparent cube are visible. The other three are not visible – we are aware of them 'amodally'. The same goes for houses or for any ordinary objects. We perceive the back side of any (non-transparent) object only amodally. It is very difficult to come up with a scenario, where one perceives, but does not perceive amodally. Thus, it is not

possible to fully understand perception itself without understanding amodal perception.

The perception-account

There are two straightforward answers to the question I posed. The first is that we do perceive the cat's tail and the second is that we do not see it, but only infer that it is there: we have a non-perceptual belief about it (Gibson, 1972).

The perceptual view may sound puzzling. The cat's tail does not project onto our retina. We receive no sensory stimulation from it. The necessary and sufficient conditions for perceiving an object have been notoriously difficult to pin down, but the only non-controversial necessary condition for perception is the presence of sensory stimulation. If I receive no sensory stimulation from an object, then I can't perceive it.[1]

Suppose that I receive no sensory stimulation from an object – I have no image of it on my retina. If we counted this case as perception, then having hallucinations would count as perception. Closing one's eyes and visualizing a chair would also count as perceiving a chair, but hallucination and visualization are exactly those mental events that are supposed not to be covered by the definition of perception.

Thus, amodal perception is not perception at all. But then what is it?

The belief-account

The second relatively straightforward view about amodal perception is that there is nothing perceptual about it. We see those bits of the cat that are visible – that are not occluded – and we infer, on the basis of perceiving the visible parts of the animal (as well as on the basis of our familiarity with cat tails) that the occluded parts have such and such properties. In other words, we do not see the cat's

---

[1] One may wonder about the blind spot. When we are looking at objects with one eye (and keep our eye fixated), we do not receive any sensory stimulation from objects that are projected onto the part of the retina where the blind spot is. Does this mean that we do not see them? The short answer is that we may 'fill in' part of objects that are projected onto our blind spot if the rest of the object is visible to us (this phenomenon itself is thought to be a version of the amodal perception problem by some), but we are not aware of those objects that project onto our blind spot entirely. Thus, it does not sound wrong to say that we do not perceive these objects at all.

tail at all, we just come to have a (non-perceptual) belief about it.

There are various problems with this suggestion (see Noë, 2004, pp. 62-64 for a couple of them). I would like to raise a new objection to the belief account. Amodal completion of occluded contours has been examined by psychologists for a long time. One of the most important findings from our perspective is that we use the simplest possible shape for completing the occluded part of a contour.

Figure 1: Amodal completion

In the example above (figure 1), for instance, when we see the image in the middle, we tend to complete it in the way shown on the left and not the way shown on the right. More importantly, even if we have some firm beliefs about how we should complete the contour, we cannot help completing it in the simplest way possible. Take the following example (figure 2):

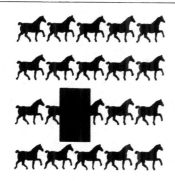

Figure 2: The horse illusion

Because of all the other horse contours, we do know that we should complete the occluded part of the picture with the front half of the horse on the left and the back of the half horse on the right. Still, we cannot help seeing one extremely long horse.

If the belief-account of amodal completion were correct, then this would mean that we infer on the basis of our background beliefs as well as the visible parts of the horses that the occluded shape is such and such. Thus, we form a non-perceptual belief that the occluded shape is such and such. But, as we have seen, we come to represent the occluded shape to be a long horse, in spite of the fact that we have firm beliefs that it is supposed to be completed as two normal size horses. The way we complete this shape is insensitive to our other beliefs. But a belief cannot be insensitive to our other beliefs, at least not too often and not

for too long.[2] Even worse, my belief that is said to represent the occluded long horse is supposed to be inferred from my background beliefs about the shape of (short) horse contours. Even if a belief could at least sometimes be insensitive to some of our other beliefs, it certainly cannot be insensitive to those of our beliefs it is supposed to be inferred from. Thus, the representation of the occluded shape is very unlikely to be a belief.

The access-account

It has been suggested recently that what makes us visually aware of the cat's tail is that we have perceptual access to it. I do not see the cat's tail now, but if I moved my head, I would see it. Thus, I have immediate perceptual access to the very fine-grained properties of this object right now – even if it is occluded from me at the moment (Pessoa et al., 1998; Noë, 2002; Noë, 2004; Noë, in press). This suggestion is an interesting alternative to the perceptual- and the belief-view, but I will argue that it will fail to provide a coherent account of amodal perception, for the following three reasons.

First, it is important to emphasize that amodal perception relies heavily on our background knowledge of how the occluded parts of the object (may) look. If I have never seen a cat, I will have difficulties attributing properties to its tail behind the fence. If I am familiar with cats, however, then this would not be a problem. Our perceptual presence of the cat's tail will be very different if we know how cat tails look and if we do not. And here we get a conflict with the access account. I would have the same perceptual access to the cat's tail whether or not I know how cat tails look. Thus, the access account cannot allow for the difference between our awareness of the cat's tail in these two cases.

Second, suppose that the cat has just disappeared behind the corner of the house. I hear it meow, and I can localize where it is. If I know the cat well enough, its tail can be as perceptually present to me as it was when the tail was occluded by the picket fence. It seems that the transition between being aware of the partly occluded cat's tail behind the fence and of the fully occluded cat's tail is a gradual one.

However, an immediate consequence of the access account is that immediate perceptual access does not come in degrees. I may have immediate perceptual access to the partly occluded cat's tail, but I certainly do not have immediate perceptual access to the tail of the cat in the next room. According to the access account, what constitutes amodal perception is that I have immediate perceptual access to the very fine-grained properties of the occluded object right now – even if it is not visible to me at the moment. We can never have a similar kind of access to anything in the next room. We could have some kind of

---

[2] See Harman, 1984 for a classical analysis of the topic of contradicting beliefs.

access to the cat in the next room, but not *immediate perceptual* access.

Thus, it follows from the access account that if the cat disappears entirely behind the fence, my way of representing it must change radically. So far, I had perceptual access to the cat's occluded parts – if I had moved my head, I could have seen them. Now, however, no matter, how I move my head, I cannot see the cat's tail. This is a very problematic consequence of the access account, especially given that in some cases I can localize the cat's tail in my egocentric space (almost) as well as I could when I saw it occluded by the picket fence and I may have almost as vivid an awareness of it in the two cases.

It is not clear what is supposed to constitute the difference between our access to the cat's tail behind the fence and in the next room, according to the access account. After all, I do have some kind of access to the cat's tail in the next room: I could walk over and have a look. The advocates of the access account tried to clarify the distinction between these two cases in several different ways. As Alva Noë points out in his latest attempt to do so, the big difference between our access to the cat's tail behind the picket fence and in the next room is the following. Our sensory stimulation varies as *we* move around in both cases (but in different degrees: I would move my head more in the second case), but in the second case, our sensory stimulation does not vary as the *object* moves. If the cat behind the picket fence wags its tail, this brings about a change in my sensory stimulation. If it does so in the next room, it does not (Noë, 2004, pp. 64-65). My main point is that regardless of the way we draw this distinction, the very existence of such a distinction is problematic.

One would expect that the advocates of the access-account would deny the intuition that there is a gradual transition between these two cases, which would be a valid move and it would weaken this objection significantly. Interestingly, they acknowledge this gradual transition and explicitly state that this is an important feature of amodal perception (Noë, 2002, p. 11, footnote 14; Noë, 2004, p. 65). The problem is that the access-account in general and Noë's way of drawing the distinction (Noë, 2004, pp. 64-65) in particular do not allow for such gradual transition. Thus, as it stands, the access account is inconsistent.

A third argument. Some of the most famous examples of amodal perception are examples of two dimensional figures, like the two pictures above. It is unclear what the access account would say in the case of amodal completion of the occluded parts of two dimensional figures, since there is no head- or eye-movement that would give us perceptual access to the momentarily invisible part of the curve in the first figure above. Thus, we do not have any perceptual access to the occluded parts of the circle.[3] Still, we are visually aware of them.[4]

The visualization-account

My suggestion is very simple: we visualize the cat's tail.

By visualization I mean roughly what Stephen Kosslyn means by visual imagery (Kosslyn, 1980). A paradigmatic case of visualization would be closing one's eyes and imagining seeing an apple 'in the mind's eye' (see also Ryle, 1949, chapter 8.6; Currie & Ravenscroft, 2002).

The proposal the we visualize the occluded parts of perceived objects does not face the problem that I posed in the case of the access-view. I can visualize a cat in the next room or even thousands of miles away from here. I will not be as accurate in doing so as I would be if I visualized the occluded parts of a cat I am looking at right now. For example, if I visualize the occluded parts of the cat I am looking at, I can use the highly specific properties of the color of the cat's visible parts as a basis for my visualization of the color of the occluded parts. If I visualize the cat in the next room, I cannot help myself to this – the cat's tail will be less accurately visualized. Nevertheless, I can still visualize it. The way I represent the cat's tail in the next room and the way I represent the occluded tail of the cat I am looking at are of the same kind – the difference between them is a difference in degree. As we have seen, the access view needs to say that they are different ways of representing the cat's tail – one is by means of our perceptual access, the other is not.

I pointed out earlier that amodal perception relies heavily on our background knowledge of how the occluded parts of the object (may) look. If I have never seen a cat, I will have difficulties representing its occluded tail behind the fence. The same is true for visualization. In order to visualize a chair, I need to know how chairs look. This is yet another indication of the similarity between amodal perception and visualization.

Some empirical support

Take the following image, which is considered to be an example of not amodal, but modal completion (figure 3).

Figure 3: The Kanizsa triangle

of 'immediate perceptual access' vacuous, as we could also have expectations about how a cat in the next room would look if we were to look, but the access account, rightly, wants to deny that we have immediate perceptual access to these objects.

[4] The proponents of the access account often use these examples of amodal perception when outlining their view. See Pessoa et al., 1998, pp. 729-730; Noë, 2002, p. 9; Noë, 2004, p. 61, p. 70.

---

[3] One could try to block this argument by saying that we do have expectations about how the occluded shape would look were we to look behind the occluding surface, even if I will never look behind the occluding surface. This move, however, would make the notion

Modal and amodal completion are different.[5] The standard way of drawing this distinction is the following. In the case of the amodal perception, we are aware of objects behind an occluder, whereas in the case of modal completion, we are visually aware of an object in front of inducers, such as the three circles in the figure above.[6]

There are, however, very important similarities. In the case of both modal and amodal completion we are perceptually aware of shapes or objects we do not see. In both cases, we experience contours that are not there. It is generally assumed that the early stages of the mental processes responsible for modal and amodal completion are the same. It has been argued that the neural mechanisms responsible for modal and amodal perception are the same in early vision and they only come apart in a very late stage of visual processing (Kellman & Shipley, 1991; Ramachandran, 1995; see also Driver et al., 2001). As a result, many early vision researchers as well as philosophers do not even make this distinction (Grossberg & Mingolla, 1985; Noë, 2002; Noë, 2004; Noë, in print).

Thus, in what follows, I assume that what is true for the early neural mechanisms responsible for our awareness of the nonexisting sides of the Kanizsa triangle and of the occluded contour of the horse above are the same. Thus, the empirical study of our awareness of the sides of the Kanizsa triangle may give us some important results about amodal perception.

The perception of Kanizsa triangle has been thoroughly examined experimentally. It turns out that although there is no activation of the cells in the retina that would correspond to the sides of the triangle, we do find such corresponding activation patterns in the primary visual cortex, which is the earliest stage of visual processing (Lee & Nguyen, 2001; see also Kamatsu, 2006). Incidentally, this is also where cells are activated when we visualize objects with our eyes closed (see e.g., Kosslyn et al., 1995). I take this result to be indicative that I am on the right track, but I will not argue that this confirms my suggestion. I do want to argue, however, that these empirical results help us to disqualify the other candidates we have been considering.

It would follow from the perceptual view that the cells of the retina are active when we are looking at the Kanizsa triangle. This turns out not to be the case. The belief-view would predict that there is no cell-activation in the early stages of visual processing. But, it turns out, there is. Thus, both the perceptual and the belief view seem to contradict these empirical results. Also, as we have seen in the last section, it is unclear how the amodal perception of two dimensional contours could even be explained by the access view.

Thus, it seems that the alternatives to my suggestion face some serious objections, both conceptual and empirical ones. Let us see whether similar objections could be raised in the case of my suggestion.

First objection

One possible worry about my suggestion is that this view implies that we visualize objects all the time, since we perceive partially occluded objects all the time. However, this sounds intuitively implausible. When I'm walking down the street, looking at one house occluding another one, it does not appear to me as if I visualized anything.

In order to answer this worry, it needs to be pointed out that attention plays a very important role in our everyday perception, thus, we should not be surprised if it played an equally important role in amodal perception. The inattentional blindness experiments demonstrated that we can be shockingly blind to those features of our surroundings that we are not paying attention to. Probably the most famous inattentional blindness experiment is the following (Simmons & Chabris, 1999). We are shown a short video-clip of two teams of three, dressed in white and black, passing a ball around. We are asked to count how many times the white team passes the ball around. On first viewing, most of the observers come up with an answer to this not very interesting question. On second viewing, however, when there is no counting task to be completed, they notice that a man dressed in gorilla costume walks right in the middle of the passing game, makes funny gestures and then leaves. The gorilla spends nine seconds in the frame and most viewers do not notice it when attending to the passing around of the ball.[7]

To move to a less radical example for the importance of attention in our everyday perception, I have no idea what color my office telephone is. I must have seen it millions of times, but this was not a property that I have been paying attention to. Properties of objects we are not attending to usually go unnoticed in our everyday perception.

Given the similarities between perception and visualization (see Kosslyn, 1980; Laeng & Teodorescu, 2002; O'Craven & Kanwisher, 2000), it is hardly surprising that the same is true for the way we visualize objects. If I visualize the house I grew up in as seen from the front, I am unlikely to be aware of whether there is light in the left window on the first floor. But if I attend to this specific feature of the visualized image, I can be aware of this.

Finally, if visualizing in general depends on our attention, then it the same argument can be run in the case of visualizing partially occluded objects. Most of the time, the shape, size or color of occluded object-parts go unnoticed, because we pay no attention to them. If, however, we do attend to them – if, for example, we wonder, what color an occluded part of the building is – then we do visualize them.

To sum up, the worry was that we do not seem to be consciously visualizing every occluded part of every object that surrounds us. But neither do we consciously perceive of

---

[5] See Singh, 2004 for a good overview of the differences between modal and amodal completion.

[6] See, for example, Tse, 1999, pp. 37-38. The terms originally come from Michotte et al., 1964.

[7] For more inattentional blindness experiments see Mack & Rock, 1998.

every part (or property) of every object that surrounds us. We only perceive those parts (or properties) of objects consciously that we attend to. Similarly, we only visualize those parts of objects consciously that we attend to. The worry turned out to be unjustified.

Second objection

One may also object to my view for the following reason. Visualization is something we usually do with our eyes closed. Our current perceptual experience plays no part in what we are visualizing and the way we do so. If amodal perception is visualization, then some instances of visualization are not like this. In amodal perception our current perceptual experience does play a very significant role in determining what we are visualizing and the way we do so. Thus, if my suggestion is right, we need to discard some intuitively obvious features of our everyday notion of visualization.

As in the previous objection, an analogy with everyday perception may help here. When we see objects, we usually also locate them in our egocentric space. If I see an apple, I do attribute a specific egocentric spatial location to this apple. If I do see it, I also know which direction I should move my hand towards in order to grab it.[8]

But there is an entirely different way of perceiving, which never allows us to localize the perceived object in our egocentric space. More specifically, there is a way of seeing – when we see objects in pictures – when we do see objects, but we do not locate them in our egocentric space. We can and do often locate them in some kind of space, presumably in the space of the picture, but not in our egocentric space. If you asked me to touch or point at this object, I could not do it. I could touch or point at the two dimensional representation of the object, but not the object itself.

To sum up, there are two ways of seeing. One localizes the perceived object in our egocentric space, whereas the other does not.

The same goes for visualization. We localize the visualized objects in our egocentric space in the case of amodal perception. We do know how to reach for or point at the occluded tail of the cat. Sometimes, however, we visualize objects without localizing them in our egocentric space. When I close my eyes and visualize a slice of apple

pie, I do not localize the pie in my egocentric space. I would not know how to reach for it.

These two ways of visualizing, then, correspond to the two ways of seeing objects. In the perception case, perception that provides egocentric spatial information about the perceived object seems to be the more elementary and more basic kind of perception. After all, some animals and small children are incapable of seeing objects in pictures, but they can perceive objects located in their egocentric space.

The same may be true for visualization. Animals and small children are capable of amodal perception (see, for example, Nieder, 2002). They are visually aware of occluded parts of objects they are looking at. It is unclear, however, whether they can visualize scenes with their eyes closed. Amodal perception may be more basic both phylogenetically and ontogenetically than visualizing with one's eyes closed.[9] Thus, we get a parallel claim as the one about the two kinds of perception: visualizing that provides egocentric spatial information about the perceived object seems to be the more elementary and more basic kind of visualization than the one that does not.

But one could argue that just because amodal perception is a similar but more elementary mental process than visualizing with our eyes closed, it does not follows that we are entitled to call it visualization. One can define visualizing any way one pleases – under some of these conceptions, it will exclude amodal perception. Although it is pointless to argue over terminology, it is important to point out that it is extremely difficult to draw a sharp distinction between visualizing and amodal perception. If we get up in a familiar but pitch dark room, we visualize the furniture, or rather, the obstacles in the room in such a way that provides egocentric information. Thus, localization in one's egocentric space or the lack thereof cannot be what keeps amodal perception and visualization apart. But we can also visualize object with our eyes wide open: we can visualize a chair while looking at the Pacific Ocean. Thus,

---

[8] It is very difficult to come up with examples where this is not the case. One such example may be the following. Suppose that I am in the middle of a very complex mirror-labyrinth, which makes me very disoriented: everything I see is a reflection of a reflection of a reflection. Suppose that I set eyes on an apple. Given that I have no idea how many mirrors are involved in bringing about this impression, I do not know where this apple is: I cannot locate it in my egocentric space. If I had to reach for it, I would have no idea how to do that. It needs to be added that there is some discussion in the literature whether we are entitled to call our awareness of the apple in this example perception at all. See, for example, Currie, 1995, esp. p. 70; Walton, 1997, esp. p. 70; Carroll, 1995, p. 71.

[9] This suggestion may also help us to explain why we came to have such a complex mental capacity as visualizing a scene with out eyes closed. It is unclear whether visualizing with one's eyes closed has significant selective advantage. Action planning does have some selective advantage, but action planning may happen in an entirely non-visual manner. If visualization has an evolutionary explanation, it is likely to lie elsewhere. Notice, however, that being aware of, and being able to localize, things that are (partly) occluded from us has huge selective advantage. Being able to localize the unseen parts of an animal hiding in a bush is an extremely survival-enhancing skill (Ramachandran, 1987 makes a similar suggestion). Thus, in the same way as the kind of perception that makes it possible to localize objects in one's egocentric space was more basic evolutionarily than the kind that does not allow us to localize anything, we can make a parallel claim about visualization. We can say that the kind of visualization that makes it possible for us to localize objects in one's egocentric space was evolutionarily more basic than the kind that does not allow us to localize anything. Like pictorial seeing, visualizing with one's eyes closed may also be an evolutionary exaptation.

whether or not we keep our eyes open or closed is also unlikely to provide a sharp divide between amodal perception and visualization. One could, of course, claim that amodal perception is *per definitionem* not visualization, whereas every other way of being aware of objects that are not perceptually present is, but this way of setting up such a strict boundary between visualizing and amodal perception would be not only question-begging, but also quite unmotivated.

Acknowledgments

I am grateful for the comments of Alva Noë and Robert Van Gulick as well as the members of my PhD seminar on Imagination at Syracuse University.

References

Carroll, Noël (1995). Towards an Ontology of the Moving Image. In: Cynthia A. Freeland and Thomas E. Wartenberg (Eds.), *Philosophy and Film*. New York: Routledge.

Clarke, Thompson (1965). Seeing surfaces and physical objects. In: M. Black (Ed.), *Philosophy in America*. Ithaca, NY: Cornell University Press, pp. 98-114.

Currie, Gregory (1995). *Image and Mind: Film, Philosophy and Cognitive Science*. Cambridge: Cambridge University Press.

Currie Gregory and Ian Ravenscroft (2002). *Recreative Minds: Imagination in Philosophy and Psychology*. Oxford: Oxford University Press.

Driver, Jon, Greg Davis, Charlotte Russell, Massimo Turatto and Elliot Freeman (2001). Segmentation, attention and phenomenal visual objects. *Cognition*, 10, 61-95.

Gibson, J. J. (1972). A theory of direct visual perception. In: J. R. Royce and W. W. Rozeboom (Eds.), The Psychology of Knowing. New York: Gordon and Breach, pp. 215-240.

Grossberg, Stephen and Mignolla, Ennio (1985). Neural Dynamics of Form Perception: Boundary Completion, Illusory Figures, and Neon Color Spreading. *Psychological Review*, 92, 173-211.

Harman, Gilbert (1984). Logic and Reasoning. *Synthese*, 60, 107-127.

Lee, Tai Sing – Nguyen, My (2001). Dynamics of subjective contour formation in the early visual cortex. *Proceedings of the National Academy of Sciences*, 98, 1907-1911.

Kellman, P. J. and T. F. Shipley (1991). A theory of visual interpolation in object perception. *Cognitive Psychology*, 23, 141-221.

Komatsu, Hidehiko (2006). The neural mechanisms of perceptual filling-in. *Nature Review Neuroscience*, 7, 220-231

Kosslyn, Stephen M. (1980). *Image and Mind*. Cambridge, MA: Harvard University Press.

Kosslyn, Stephen M., William L. Thompson, Irene J. Kim and Nathaniel M. Alpert (1995). Topographical representations of mental images in primary visual cortex. *Nature, 378*, 496-498.

Laeng, B. and Teodorescu, D-S (2002). Eye scanpaths during visual imagery re-enact those of perception of the same visual scene. *Cognitive Science, 26*, 207-231.

Mack A. and Rock, I. (1998). *Inattentional Blindness*. Cambridge, MA: MIT Press.

Michotte, A., Thinés, G., & Crabbé, G. (1964). Les complements amodaux des structures perceptives. In: G. Thinés, A. Costall, & G. Butterworth (Eds.), *Michotte's experimental phenomenology of perception*. Hillsdale, NJ: Erlbaum.

Nieder, A. (2002). Seeing more than meets the eye: processing of illusory contours in animals. *Journal of Comparative Physiology, A* 188, 294-260.

Noë, Alva (2002). Is the Visual World a Grand Illusion? *Journal of Consciousness Studies*, 9, no. 5-6, 1-12.

Noë, Alva (2004). *Action in Perception*. Cambridge, MA: The MIT Press.

Noë, Alva (in press). Real Presence.

O'Craven, K. M. and N. Kanwisher (2000). Mental Imagery of Faces and Places Activates Corresponding Stimulus-Specific Brain Regions. *Journal of Cognitive Neuroscience, 12*, 1013-1023.

Pessoa, Luiz, Evan Thompson and Alva Noë (1998). Finding out about filling-in: A guide to perceptual completion for visual science and the philosophy of perception. *Behavioral and Brain Sciences, 21*, 723-802.

Ramachandran, V. S. (1987). Visual perception of surfaces: a biological theory. In: Petry S. Meyer (Ed.), *The perception of illusory contours*. Berlin: Springler, pp. 93-108.

Ramachandran V. S. 1995 Filling in the gaps in logic: reply to Durgin at al. *Perception, 24*, 841-843.

Simmons, Daniel J. and Chabris, Christopher F. (1999). 'Gorillas in our Midst: sustained inattentional blindness for dynamic events,' *Perception, 28*, 1059-1074.

Singh, Manish (2004). Modal and amodal completion generate different shapes. *Psychological Science, 15*, 454-459.

Strawson, P. F. (1979). Perception and its objects. In: G. F. MacDonald (Ed.), Perception and Identity: Essays Presented to A. J. Ayer with His Replies. Ithaca, NY: Cornell University Press, pp. 41-60.

Tse, Peter Ulric (1999). Volume Completion. *Cognitive Psychology, 39*, 37-68.

Walton, Kendall (1997). On Pictures and Photographs. Objections Answered. In: Richard Allen and Murray Smith (Eds.), *Film Theory and Philosophy*. Oxford: Oxford University Press, pp. 60-75.

Internal Models and Transfer of Learning in Pursuit Tracking Task

Satoshi Kobori (kobori@rins.ryukoku.ac.jp)
Department of Electronics and Informatics, Ryukoku University
Seta, Otsu 520-2194, Japan

Patrick Haggard (p.haggard@ucl.ac.uk)
Institute of Cognitive Neuroscience, University College London
17 Queen Square, London, WC1N 3AR, UK

Abstract

Visuomotor manual tracking is a well-established method for studying the neural processes and computations underlying skilled action. Human subjects quickly and efficiently learn to track a target moving at constant velocity. Here, we measure tracking performance in two separate groups of participants while either the target or the manual cursor was suppressed for a brief period during each tracking trial. Subjects learned to maintain accurate tracking through periods of target or cursor suppression. During the suppressed period, feedback-error-driven mechanisms cannot be used, and tracking performance therefore relies on prediction alone. We used this manipulation to show that motor learning involves acquiring predictive models of the target motion and also of one's own hand movement. We also used a transfer of learning design to investigate whether acquiring models of target motion and of one's own hand motion involved linked or independent neural modules. We found clear positive transfer from learning to predict one's own manual action to learning target motions, and no evidence for transfer in the reverse direction. This asymmetric pattern suggests specific predictive neural mechanisms for learning to control one's own action, as opposed to general prediction of external events. We suggest that learning internal representations of one's own motor systems may play an important role in learning about the perceptual world.

Introduction

Motor learning is a fundamental feature of all motor performance. Pursuit tracking is well-established experimental paradigm for studying motor learning (Poulton, 1974). In pursuit tracking, the subject moves a manual lever to ensure that a visual cursor tracks a moving visual target on a screen. Early studies of tracking distinguished two components of the tracking motor response. First, subjects may make rapid movements to reposition their cursor on the target, typically catching up with the target, and then falling behind again. Such movements are intermittent, often with a frequency of around 1-2 Hz (Miall et al., 1993; Netick & Klapp, 1994). Tracking becomes more intermittent when the target moves unpredictably. Therefore, this component of the tracking response is assumed to involve visual feedback-error-driven correction. The subject sees a visual discrepancy between target position and cursor position, and moves the cursor to reduce this error to zero, only for the error to increase again.

Several lines of evidence suggest, however, that tracking is not purely feedback-driven, but also involves prediction. For example, motor output during tracking can be smooth rather than intermittent, and can sometimes lead the target rather than lag behind it. Moreover, tracking performance is typically better when the target moves in a predictable fashion (e.g., at constant velocity), than when it moves less predictably (Poulton, 1974). Finally, subjects can track accurately even when absence of either the target or the cursor signal makes error-detection impossible (Beppu et al., 1987).

The predictive element of tracking is often attributed to learning of internal models. Several studies have suggested the existence of internal models in addition to sensory feedback mechanisms. For example, functional imaging studies have separated specific neural activity related to acquisition of internal models from other neural activity associated with error correction (Imamizu et al., 2000). However, it is unclear precisely what is represented by such models, and how many separate models are involved. In computational terms, successful tracking requires a representation of current target position and of current hand/cursor position. Models which estimate the current output of a system given its inputs are termed 'forward models'. Thus, tracking performance could potentially involve two separate internal forward models. One model would estimate or predict the current position of the target based on its previous kinematic history. Another would estimate or predict the current position of the hand-cursor, based on the current motor command and any available proprioceptive feedback. We will call these putative models the target forward model and motor forward model respectively.

Learning is a key feature of all internal models. In manual tracking, the goal is to make the output of the motor forward model equal to the output of the target forward model. Clearly, internal models are useful for tracking only if their predictions are correct. According to one computational theory, visual feedback error provides an important learning signal which can be used to update the internal models (Kawato & Gomi, 1992).

Relatively few studies have investigated whether skilled tracking involves the learning and use of two dissociable models for target and for motor output, respectively. Evidence for predictive mechanisms in tracking is consistent with either a target forward model, or a motor forward model, or both. Recent computational studies have demonstrated efficiency and robustness of modular architectures for model learning. For example, multiple motor models may be learned, with one model corresponding to each task performed or object used (Wolpert & Kawato, 1998; Wolpert et al., 1998). However, in those architectures, the brain is assumed to learn multiple instances of the same general type of model. In pursuit tracking, however, the putative target model and motor model would use qualitatively different types of information. They perform dissociable information-processing functions, rather than being parallel instances of a single function. For example, the motor model refers to effects of the subject's voluntary motor commands on hand position, while the target model refers only to visual objects in external space.

One promising method for investigating the possible dissociation of target and motor models in tracking involves comparing the effects of target suppression and cursor suppression (Beppu et al., 1987). In target suppression, subjects track a predictably moving target. The target disappears at some point during the track, while the cursor remains visible. In cursor suppression, the cursor disappears but the target remains visible. Subjects continue to track for some interval, and the target or cursor display is then restored. No visual error signal is present during target-suppressed and cursor-suppressed tracking. Target and cursor are not simultaneously visible, so their discrepancy cannot be computed.

Thus, tracking performance during suppression reflects only the contributions of internal models, but the involvement of these models depends on what is suppressed. When the target is suppressed, the only representation of the tracking target comes from a putative target model which predicts the current target position from its previous motion. Therefore, poor tracking during target suppression can be attributed to an incorrect target model. Conversely, when the cursor is suppressed, the only representation of the current cursor position comes from the putative motor model. This model predicts the current cursor position from current motor commands and proprioceptive information. Therefore, poor tracking during cursor suppression can be attributed to an incorrect motor model.

If the target reappears after a period of target suppression, or if the cursor reappears after a period of cursor suppression, a visual feedback error signal is again available. This error signal can be used to update the target model in the case of target suppression, or the motor model in the case of cursor suppression. Learning and updating of these models would lead to improved tracking performance during the suppression period of subsequent trials.

We have used the target and cursor suppression approach to investigate the internal models used during tracking, and their updating during motor learning. We have focused on identifying differences in tracking behavior between target and cursor suppression conditions. If target-suppressed and cursor-suppressed conditions show differences in either short-term performance, or in longer-term learning, then this would provide strong evidence for the existence of separate and dissociable internal models for these two components of skilled action. We therefore measured tracking error during both target and cursor suppression, and described the learning curve in each condition. We assumed that

suppression tracking involves a number of dissociable processes. First, when the target or cursor disappears and suppressed tracking begins, the subject must rely on internal model-based tracking. Second, when the target or cursor reappears, a second, visual feedback process will detect any error, and issue a feedback-driven motor correction. We wanted to distinguish between these two processes, and obtain separate psychophysiological measures of learning-related changes in each of them. Finally, we investigated whether tracking involves learning just one internal model, or involves separate target and motor models using a learning transfer approach. We reasoned that asymmetric transfer of between target suppression and cursor suppression conditions would imply separable learning processes under these conditions, and thus distinct internal models in each case.

Methods

Apparatus

The experimental apparatus consisted of a joystick and computer display for tracking measurement system (Kobori & Haggard, 2003). The apparatus is shown in Figure 1.

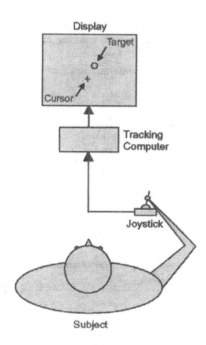

Figure 1: Experimental apparatus.

Tracking

Subjects observed a circular target (diameter 13 mm) moving at constant tangential velocity along a clockwise circular trajectory (diameter 148 mm) on a computer screen. The target cycle was 5 sec. The viewing distance was 66 cm. Each trial lasted 20 sec. Subjects held a modified joystick in their right hand, and moved it so that a visual cross hair cursor (width 13 mm) tracked the target as closely as possible. 1 degree of joystick movement produced a cursor movement of 0.39 degrees of visual angle. Target and cursor positions were digitized and stored on the computer at 30 Hz. Unsigned tracking error was calculated in subsequent analysis.

Tracking trials were of 2 types, normal and suppressed tracking. In normal trials, the movements of the joystick produced congruent movements of the subject's cursor on the screen. In suppressed tracking, we blanked out either the target or the cursor during the trial. The disappearance occurred at an unpredictable time between 5 and 7 sec. Then, the target or cursor reappeared at a random time between 11 and 13 sec.

Tracking error data from suppressed trials were aligned either to the time of disappearance, or reappearance of target/cursor as appropriate. An epoch from 4 sec before until 4 sec after was selected for display. Tracking error traces were then made for each subject in each block of the experiment. Analyses of normal trials used the average time of disappearance and reappearance across all suppressed trials (6 sec and 12 sec from trial onset) as the fictitious "event" for defining analysis epochs.

Experimental design

All experimental blocks consisted of 5 trials. Before the experiment, we explained the tracking task to the subject, and familiarized them with the equipment and apparatus. Then the experiment began with a pretest block of normal tracking trials.

Next, subjects performed 6 learning blocks of target or cursor suppressed trials each. Then, subjects performed a posttest block of normal trials similar to the pretest block. The experiment ended with 2 transfer blocks of the other kind of suppressed trials which was not performed in the learning phase.

Subjects took a break of a few minutes halfway through the experiment, between blocks 3 and 4 of the learning phase. The subjects were instructed to continue tracking as accurately as possible when target or cursor disappeared. The procedures were approved by the local ethical committee.

20 subjects were recruited from among the students of Ryukoku University. Subjects' ages ranged between 19 and 24 years. 10 subjects were male, and 10 were female. None had any known neurological abnormality, and all were naive to the purposes of the experiment.

We divided the subjects into 2 groups. Each group included 5 males and 5 females. The target suppression group performed target-suppressed trials in the learning blocks and cursor-suppressed trials in transfer blocks. The cursor suppression group performed cursor-suppressed trials in learning blocks and target-suppressed trials in transfer blocks.

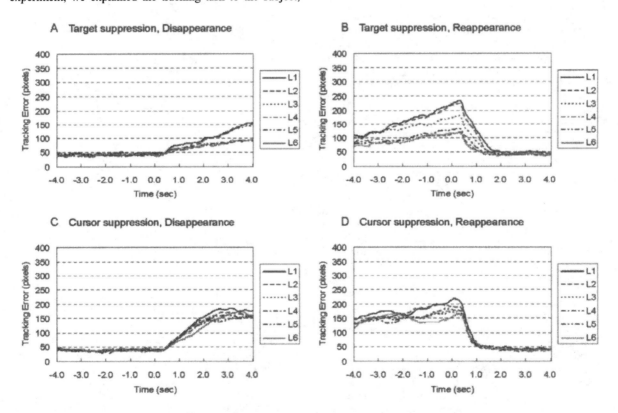

Figure 2: Grand average tracking error waveforms arranged by learning block.

Results

Tracking data

The grand average traces of unsigned tracking error for each learning block are shown in Figure 2. Data from suppressed trials are aligned either to the time of disappearance, or the time of reappearance as appropriate. The upper row shows the performance of the target suppression group at the point of target disappearance (panel A), and reappearance (panel B). The data for the cursor suppression group is shown in the lower row (C, D). L1 refers to learning block 1.

Figure 2 shows that tracking error is low prior to disappearance in both groups, and was comparable to pretest and posttest normal tracking trials (not shown). Second, tracking error increases gradually and monotonically after disappearance, and continues until just after the reappearance of the target or cursor. The initial increase in tracking error is more abrupt for the cursor suppression group than for the target suppression group. Error then decreases quickly and returns to the level before disappearance. Third, and most importantly for our purpose, the error during the suppression period varies across the learning blocks. In the target suppression group, tracking error is clearly higher for blocks 1-3 than blocks 4-6. The cursor suppression group also shows differences between blocks, but these are somewhat smaller than in the target suppression group.

The improvement across blocks in tracking during the suppression period arises from learning an internal model of either the target movement (target suppression group) or the subject's own movement (cursor suppression group). We therefore calculated mean tracking error on each trial during an epoch from the time of disappearance to 2 sec after reappearance. We compared the tracking error in the first and last learning blocks, using a mixed ANOVA with factors of group (between-subjects) and block (within-subjects). This showed a significant effect of block [$F(1,18) = 11.514$, $p = .003$] with lower tracking error in block 6 than in block 1, as predicted. There was no significant effect of group [$F(1,18) = 3.701$, $p = .070$] and no interaction [$F(1,18) = 1.859$, $p = .190$]. We also compared the tracking error in the first and last learning blocks in each group separately. The results showed significant effects of learning in target suppression group [$t(18) = 2.722$, $p = .0007$] and also in cursor suppression group [$t(18) = 1.923$, $p = .0035$]. Thus, subjects learned to track during the suppression period.

Transfer of Learning

We investigated transfer of internal-model learning by comparing tracking performance on the two transfer blocks with tracking performance on the first two learning blocks (Adams, 1987). A hypothesis of no transfer between one suppression condition and the other would predict that tracking error during the suppression period on the transfer task would be no better than at the very start of learning: subjects would need to learn the new suppression condition de novo. Conversely, if learning during one suppression condition transferred to the other condition, then performance on the transfer blocks should be better than the initial learning blocks. If no transfer between the two suppression conditions were observed, we would conclude that learning an internal model of the target and learning an internal model of the manual action were quite different processes, which involved separate internal models. However, if perfect transfer were found, we would conclude that a single, common learning process underlay both suppression conditions.

However, transfer between two tasks may also be asymmetric, and the direction of asymmetry gives important information about the underlying cognitive operations that are learned. In this experiment, for the group who learned target suppression, positive transfer to the subsequent cursor suppression test would suggest that learning an internal model of the target is sufficient for learning about the actions to track it. For the group who learned cursor suppression, positive transfer to the subsequent target suppression test would imply that learning an internal model of one's own action is sufficient for learning trajectories of external visual objects.

We therefore subjected the tracking error data to a mixed ANOVA model with factors of learning group (target suppression, cursor suppression) and learning phase (learning, transfer). The results showed a non-significant effect of group [$F(1,18) = 4.188$, $p = .056$], with those initially learning cursor suppression showing slightly better performance overall. There was a significant effect of learning phase [$F(1,18) = .401$, $p = .021$], due to an overall positive transfer effect. That is, performance in the transfer blocks was significantly better than initial learning. Most importantly, there was a significant interaction [$F(1,18) = 11.341$, $p = .003$]. Follow-up simple effects testing was used to investigate the source of this interaction. The results are shown in Figure 3. The group who initially learned with target suppression, showed a non-significant negative transfer to subsequent testing with cursor suppression [$t(18) = .001$, n.s.]. In contrast, the group who initially learned with cursor suppression showed significant positive transfer to subsequent testing with target suppression [$t(18) = 2.460$, $p = .024$].

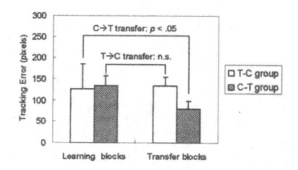

Figure 3: Transfer of learning.

Discussion

Predictive models in visuomotor learning

This paper has used a conventional pursuit tracking task with suppression of the tracking target or of the subject's own movement cursor as a method to investigate two kinds of predictive learning involved in visuomotor control. Suppressing either the target or the cursor removes the possibility of visual feedback-driven error corrections, and requires the subject to continue tracking based on purely predictive representations. In target suppression, the subject must predict the current position of the target, yet the cursor continues to give visual information about hand position. In cursor suppression, the subject must estimate or predict the current position of the cursor corresponding to their own hand position, although they continue to see the visual target. We found clear evidence for learning in both situations, based on a reduction in tracking error during the suppression period. Since feedback-error-driven correction cannot occur during either target or cursor suppression, improvements in suppressed tracking during the course of the experiment suggest that subjects must learn internal representations of the target movement, and also of their own movement. Many studies of tracking behavior agree that the motor learning underlying tracking performance is predictive in nature (Craik, 1947). Improvements in tracking performance may therefore occur because prediction improves with practice: subjects learn to predict. For example, the intermittent corrections associated with sampling methods of tracking control decreased over 5 days of learning (Miall & Jackson, 2006).

Learning about cursors or about targets

However, few tracking studies explicitly distinguished between prediction of the target trajectory, and prediction of one's own motor output. Beppu et al. (1987) reported tracking performance during periods of cursor suppression and target suppression in healthy volunteers, and cerebellar patients. They found that suppressing either signal prevented intermittent visual feedback-driven corrections, but they did not distinguish between target and cursor suppression. Haggard et al. (1995) distinguished between two error-correction processes in pursuit tracking, based on visual feedback-driven corrections and internal model estimates of current target and hand positions respectively. They found that both cursor suppression and target suppression had slight effects on normal subjects' tracking, but dramatically reduced intermittent feedback-driven corrections in cerebellar patients. More interestingly, cursor suppression, but not target suppression, produced a strongly cumulating pattern of error in the patients, where tracking movements became effectively open-loop. They interpreted this result in terms of an internal forward model of current hand position, which contributed to tracking performance both during normal and suppressed tracking. Cerebellar damage, however, impaired output of this model, making effective control of movement impossible.

Studies of model learning

Many recent studies have compared brain activity before and after tracking learning, and interpreted the observed differences as the result of learning an internal model. Many of these studies have focused on learning novel sensorimotor transformations (Imamizu et al., 1998, 2000). For example, Imamizu et al. (2000)'s subjects learned to move a computer mouse in a condition involving rotated visual feedback. After controlling for changes in brain activity related to tracking error, a further learning-related process was identified in the cerebellum. As this area was more active in rotated than in direct tracking, it was interpreted as an internal forward model of the sensorimotor transformation between the subject's movement and the on-screen cursor movement. However, their design cannot separate the operation of the internal model from the visual feedback from the cursor, in the same way that cursor-suppressed tracking does.

Study of target prediction

Grafton et al. (2001) studied the process of learning to predict target motions. Subjects tracked a target which alternated between a random and a predictable sequence. An implicit learning paradigm showed that subjects learned the predictable target sequences, with corresponding reduction in tracking error. Data from a similar PET experiment showed that this target learning was associated with increased activity in contralateral sensorimotor cortex, and decreased activity in ipsilateral cerebellum. However, these changes could reflect either changes in error signals or changes associated with learning a model of the target motion.

Transfer of learning

The suppression technique allows learning about the target to be clearly separated from learning about one's own movement. An important question is whether we learn two separate internal models; one for the target motion and a second for their own manual movement, or whether there is a single visuomotor learning process which generalizes across these two components. We used a classical transfer of learning design to investigate this issue. Our results showed a clear positive transfer from learning about one's own manual movement to learning about target motion, but not in the other direction. This finding has two important implications. First, learning internal models for motor control involves a distinct process from general prediction of external events. Second, our results suggest a hierarchical organization of visuomotor control. When subjects track in the cursor suppression condition, they learn an internal motor model. Acquisition of this motor model also implies learning about purely perceptual events in the external world, since those subjects then perform well on target-suppressed trials which require them to have an internal model of the target motion. Conversely, when subjects track in the target suppression condition, they learn an internal model which supports perceptual prediction of the target motion. However, acquisition of the target model does not assist in learning about one's own motor control, because those subjects subsequently perform badly on cursor-suppressed trials which require an internal motor model. From the point of view of underlying internal models, motor learning includes, or at least generalizes to, external perceptual learning. In contrast, external perceptual learning is quite distinct from motor learning. Our result implies an internal-external gradient of learning. Psychological theories have shifted from emphasis on passive perception to emphasis on interactive perception over recent decades (Goodale & Milner, 1992; Wexler & van Boxtel, 2005). We suggest that learning internal representations of our own action systems may play an important role in learning about our perceptual world.

Acknowledgments

This work was supported in part by a grant from High-tech Research Center of Ryukoku University to Satoshi Kobori. This paper was written at Institute of Cognitive Neuroscience, University College London, thanks to the Research Abroad Program of Ryukoku University.

References

Adams, J. A. (1987). Historical review and appraisal of research on the learning, retention, and transfer of human motor skills. *Psychological Bulletin*, 101, 41-74.

Beppu, H., Nagaoka, M., & Tanaka, R. (1987). Analysis of cerebellar motor disorders by visually guided elbow tracking movement, 2. Contribution of the visual cues on slow ramp pursuit. *Brain*, 110, 1-18.

Craik, K. J. W. (1947). Theory of the human operator in control systems: I. The operator as an engineering system. *British Journal of Psychology*, 38, 56-61.

Grafton, S. T., Salidis, J., & Willingham, D. B. (2001). Motor learning of compatible and incompatible visuomotor maps. *Journal of Cognitive Neuroscience*, 13, 217-231.

Goodale, M. A., & Milner, A. D. (1992). Separate visual pathways for perception and action. *Trends in Neurosciences*, 15, 20-25.

Haggard, P., Miall, R. C., Wade, D., Fowler, S., Richardson, A., Anslow, P., & Stein, J. (1995). Damage to cerebellocortical pathways after closed head injury: a behavioural and magnetic resonance imaging study. *Journal of Neurology, Neurosurgery and Psychiatry*, 58, 433-438.

Imamizu, H., Uno, Y., & Kawato, M. (1998). Adaptive internal model of intrinsic kinematics involved in learning an aiming task. *Journal of Experimental Psychology: Human Perception and Performance*, 24, 812-29.

Imamizu, H., Miyauchi, S., Tamada, T., Sakaki, Y., Takino, R., Puetz, B., Yoshioka, T., & Kawato, M. (2000). Human cerebellar activity reflecting an acquired internal model of a new tool. *Nature*, 403, 192-195.

Kawato, M., & Gomi, H. (1992). A computational model of four regions of the cerebellum based on feedback-error-learning. *Biological Cybernetics*, 68, 95-103.

Kobori, S., & Haggard, P. (2003). Cognitive Load during Learning of Tracking Task, *Proceedings of the European Cognitive Science Conference 2003* (pp.119-204). Mahwah, NJ: Lawrence Erlbaum Associates.

Miall, R. C., Weir, D. J., & Stein, J. F. (1993). Intermittency in human manual tracking tasks. *Journal of Motor Behavior*, 25, 53-63.

Miall, R. C., & Jackson, J. K. (2006). Adaptation to visual feedback delays in manual tracking: evidence against the Smith Predictor model of human visually guided action. *Experimental Brain Research*, [Online], 1-8.

Netick, A., & Klapp, S. T. (1994). Hesitations in manual tracking: A single-channel limit in response programming. *Journal of Experimental Psychology: Human Perception and Performance*, 20, 766-782.

Poulton, E. C. (1974). *Tracking skill and manual control.* New York, Academic Press.

Wexler, M., & van Boxtel, J. J. A. (2005). Depth perception by the active observer. *Trends in Cognitive Sciences*, 9, 431-438.

Wolpert, D. M., & Kawato, M. (1998). Multiple paired forward and inverse models for motor control, *Neural Networks*, 11, 1317-1329.

Wolpert, D. M., Miall, R. C., & Kawato, M. (1998). Internal models in the cerebellum, *Trends in Cognitive Sciences*, 2, 338-347.

Path choice heuristics for navigation related to mental representations of a building

Simon J. Büchner (buechner@cognition.uni-freiburg.de)
Christoph Hölscher (hoelsch@cognition.uni-freiburg.de)
Gerhard Strube (strube@cognition.uni-freiburg.de)
University of Freiburg
Center for Cognitive Science; Friedrichstr. 50
79098 Freiburg, Germany

Abstract

The paper investigates mental representations and path choice strategies in a multi-level building. Wayfinding tasks were conducted in a vertical grid-like setting. Path choice options were equal with respect to distance, time and complexity. A structure mapping task is introduced in order to analyze the structure of participants' mental representation of the building. It showed that participants spontaneously divided the building into regions that were inherent to the structure of the building. This representation was the basis for a hierarchical planning process. Trajectory choice was directly related to the representation of the building. Participants' movement patterns and the structure of their representations indicate that they followed a regionalization strategy that has also been observed in an earlier study (Hölscher et al., 2006b).

Introduction

Wayfinding in built environments is an everyday task that is often difficult, although it is performed frequently. For example, people prevalently consult external sources such as signs and maps for support in order to find their target. At the same time wayfinding is constrained by the structure of the environment. In order to change floors in a building, for example, it is necessary to move to a location that allows vertical movement such as a staircase. Cognitively speaking wayfinding is an instance of spatial problem solving. It requires knowledge about one's own position and the location of the goal. In a familiar environment this knowledge is partly available through a spatial representation of it, e.g. in the form of a cognitive map (Downs & Stea, 1977), but even in familiar environments people have rarely complete knowledge about it. In addition to pre-existing knowledge they always have to rely on currently available sensory information.

Wayfinding further requires a decision which path (out of multiple options) to take and subsequent locomotion toward the goal (Passini, 1992). When choosing a path people apply different heuristics in order to make a quick and efficient decision. Golledge (1995) identified a ranking of path choice heuristics that people apply when planning a trip on a map or in a real environment. He found that people chose a path through a university campus by the following criteria: shortest route, least time, proceeding in the direction of the goal, fewest turns. This shows that people try to optimize the path (either by time, distance, or number of turns). When paths are equal with respect to these criteria, other heuristics have to be applied.

Spatial Strategies

Christenfeld (1995) found people to defer turns in situations with three path choice options that were equal with respect to distance, time, and number of turns when crossing a street or parking lot. He speculates that the reduction of cognitive effort is the underlying principle. These results can also be explained by the Least-Angle Strategy (Hochmair & Frank, 2002; Conroy Dalton, 2003). This heuristic states that people choose the path that is closest (in terms of angularity) to a direct line between their current position and the goal. Bailenson, Shum, and Uttal (2000) found that people focus disproportionately on the initial segment of a route (rather than considering the path as a whole) and prefer routes that are initially long and have few turns. They proposed the Initial Segment Strategy (ISS) as a heuristic for path selection. Hochmair and Karlsson (2004) directly compared ISS and the Least-Angle Strategy (LAS) in a Virtual Reality (VR) setting by systematically varying length and angle of the initial path segment. They found a preference for the path that deviated the least from a direct line between start and goal when the initial segments of a path were equally long.

A second line of research describes heuristics derived from hierarchical representations of space. Stevens and Coupe (1978) demonstrated that people construe spatial representations that are geared to existing structures in the environment. They asked participants about the relative location of cities in two different states (e.g. What city is further east: San Diego or Reno?). Direction judgments were distorted by the superordinate structure of the states, i.e. Reno (Nevada) was usually judged being further east than San Diego (California). Wiener, Schnee, and Mallot (2004) conducted a study in a VR setting in which they found that people performed better in a search task when target landmarks were grouped by color than when they were not. Chown, Kaplan, and Kortenkamp (1995) integrated the process of regionalization in a computational model of route planning (PLAN). They report major advantages when adding regional maps to a predominantly scene-based model. When the system was able to plan hierarchically, it became more robust against breakdowns (when single path connections where cut) and made better judgments about the efficiency of a route. These studies indicate that people do mentally divide space into regions and that regionalized environments and respective representations can facilitate wayfinding, resulting in better performance.

Vertical Space

All of the aforementioned studies have been conducted in the horizontal plane. Only few studies have considered navigation in the vertical dimension. In buildings, vertical movement usually occurs when using staircases, elevators, or escalators. Vertical travel can disturb spatial cognition, often resulting in disorientation (Soeda, Kushiyama & Ohno, 1997). Dividing a building mentally into regions (i.e., chunk locations and areas by spatial principles) reduces cognitive effort and allows hierarchical planning. In most buildings, the floors provide a salient structure to regionalize the building. Dividing the three-dimensional structure of the building in a set of two-dimensional representations of each floor may help to overcome the problems observed in navigation through buildings. Hölscher, Meilinger, Vrachliotis, Brösamle, and Knauff (2006b) have conducted a wayfinding study in a complex conference center, showing that floor levels can serve as a structural pattern to mentally subdivide the building in different regions and that people indeed apply hierarchical planning when moving across different floors. Since that building was rather complex and very difficult to navigate this strategy was mainly applied by people who were familiar with the building. Hölscher, Büchner, Meilinger, and Strube (2006a) conducted a study in a complex multi-level university building in which they were again able to show that people do apply hierarchical floor and direction strategies. Strategy selection was adapted to the different tasks rather than being an idiosyncratic choice. In addition, the authors compared two different kinds of instructions about the location of the goal: visual and propositional. In the visual condition, people were shown the target location from outside the building, in the propositional condition they were told the room number. The room number was a 4-digit string providing the actual number of the room, the floor level and the building part. The results showed that in the visual condition people preferred the direction based strategy, in the propositional condition they preferred the floor strategy. In the visual condition participants saw the goal, memorized its relative location and followed the geometrically most direct path. In contrast, the preference for the floor strategy in the propositional condition was due to a hierarchical planning process. After initial movement to the correct floor, participants subsequently searched for the target room number within the floor. Since participants had only incomplete knowledge about the exact location of the room, they had to select a heuristic based on the information provided with the task instruction.

In the current study we want to show that the building structure alone, without supporting instructional information, can also lead to a regionalized representation and a selection of the associated floor strategy. We will introduce a structure mapping task that was used to analyze the structure of the participants' representation of the setting. In contrast to Hölscher et al. (2006a) the current study was conducted in a less complex, very regular, setting (Fig. 1). Participants were familiarized with the building and learned the exact location of landmarks. Thus, the uncertainty about the location of the goal was highly reduced.

The following four tasks were conducted: 1 floor-change changing 2 staircases (e.g. in Fig. 1 from the pipe to the shell), 1 floor-change changing 1 staircase (e.g. from the pipe to the apple), 2 floor-changes changing 2 staircases (e.g. from the pipe to the mug) and 2 floor-changes changing 1 staircase (e.g. from the pipe to the bell). The angles between starting point and goal were 3° for the 1 floor/2 stairs task, 7° for the 1 stair and 2 floors/2 stairs tasks and 17° for the 2 floors/1 stair task.

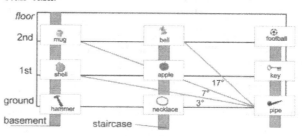

Figure 1: Schematic cross-section view of the building with landmarks and angles between starting point and different goals. For example, a task with 2 floor-changes changing one staircase would be moving from the pipe to the bell.

Based on the literature discussed above different expectations were derived. (1) People do not choose their path randomly. (2) An explicit regionalization of the building by floors should result in an initial vertical movement to the correct floor and a subsequent search for the target landmark within the floor (e.g. in Fig. 1 from the pipe to the mug one would pass the football). (3) An explicit regionalization of the building by staircases should result in an initial horizontal movement to the correct staircase and a subsequent search for the target landmark within the staircase (e.g. from the pipe to the mug one would pass the hammer). (4) A pure Least-Angle Strategy should result in initial horizontal movement in all tasks since the horizontal angle in all tasks is smaller than the vertical one.

Method

Participants

33 participants (17 of them female) between the ages of 20 and 53 (m = 25.6, SD = 6.3) were acquired through postings on campus. The majority of them were students from a variety of subjects. None of them were familiar with the building before the study. Participants were

either paid or received course credit for their participation.

Material

The study was conducted in a building of the University of Freiburg. One part of the building was chosen since it provided the required spatial structure of three corridors on top of each other, connected by three staircases, one at each end of the building and one in the middle forming a vertical grid-like structure. The drawings of nine different objects with their names written below them served as landmarks. The drawings had a size of about 20cm x 20cm and were placed at each intersection of a staircase and a floor level (cf. Fig 1), all facing the same direction. They showed common objects of similar size from different semantic categories. Their names were two syllables long (in German) and all started with different letters. These criteria were applied in order to prevent participants from chunking landmarks by other principles than spatial. Figure 1 shows a cross-section view of the building with the landmarks. Note that participants, of course, never saw the setting from this cross-section perspective or a map; they were led through the building and learned the location of the landmarks when they passed them on a particular path.

Procedure

Learning Phase Participants were welcomed at the lab of the Center for Cognitive Science and familiarized with the objects that later served as landmarks. The participants were presented a stack of cards in random order, each showing one object. They were told to memorize them. After three minutes they were asked to verbally recall the names of the objects. Order did not play a role. If they did not recall all nine objects correctly the procedure was repeated. All participants recalled the nine objects correctly after the second trial, at the latest. Participants were then brought to the building and were told that the objects they had learned before were placed at different locations within the building, though they did not know that the building had a grid-like structure. They received two tours through the building (Fig. 2) and were told to memorize the landmarks' spatial configuration. Half of the participants learned the location of the landmarks starting the first tour in the horizontal direction and the second one in the vertical direction. For the other half it was vice versa. The trajectory of the tour was chosen in a way that made it difficult for participants to solely rely on route knowledge (i.e. simply remember the order of the landmarks along the route). Multiple turns and moving back and forth between floors forced them to build up an integrated representation of the landmarks' configuration. At the same time it supported participants in constructing an integrated representation by showing the same space from multiple perspectives.

After the tour a structure mapping task (cf. Downs & Stea, 1977) was conducted. The purpose of this task was two-fold: (1) analyze the structure of participants' spatial representation; (2) check if the participants remembered the configuration of the objects correctly. The

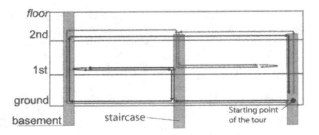

Figure 2: The tour participants got in the learning phase. Half of the participants were first led along the black line and then along the grey line. For the other half it was vice versa.

randomized stack of cards with the nine objects was handed to the participants again. They were asked to lay out the cards in the same configuration as they were located in the building from a cross-section point of view. Note that participants had never seen the building from a cross-section view. They structured the objects solely on the basis of the spatial representation they had acquired during the tour through the building. If they did not get the configuration correct in the first try, they were told the correct configuration, cards were re-shuffled and participants were asked to lay out the cards again. All participants got the configuration correct after the third attempt, at the latest. Out of the 33 participants 28 recognized the grid-like structure in the first attempt and laid out the cards accordingly. The remaining five participants laid out the cards in different structures though they realized the correct structure after receiving feedback. The structure of the laid out cards in each trial was photographed for later analysis.

Test Phase Participants were brought to the starting point of the test phase on the ground floor. Half of them started in the lower right corner, the other half started in the center of the ground floor. They were asked to find the way to the first destination (one of the landmarks). The investigator followed the participant at a distance of about two meters and recorded the participant's trajectory on a prepared data record sheet. The destination point of one task served as the starting point for the following task. The participants had to perform the four tasks described above. Each task was conducted twice, once going upstairs and once going downstairs resulting in eight tasks in total. Half of the participants performed the task in reverse order. After the last task the participants were brought back to the lab and had to complete two questionnaires. The study lasted about 75 min in total.

Results

The pictures from the structure mapping task were rated by three independent raters on a 5-point scale with respect to the way the cards were grouped (1 indicating definitive grouping by rows, 3 indicating no apparent grouping, 5 indicating definitive grouping by columns).

The inter rater reliability for multiple raters according to Fleiss (1971) was calculated as described in Bortz and Lienert (1998): $\kappa_m = .61$, p > .001. Means of the ratings for each participant were calculated. The ratings showed that most participants grouped landmarks either in rows or columns, some did not group the landmarks. Grouping the cards in columns reflects a representation regionalized by staircases. Grouping by rows reflects a representation regionalized by floors. A sample configuration of the structure mapping task is shown in Fig. 3.

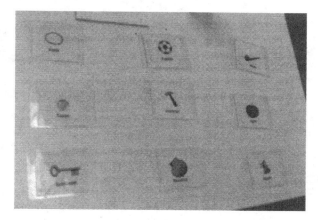

Figure 3: Example: landmarks grouped by columns

In a second step the ratings were dichotomized so that values larger than 3 were classified as column representations (N = 20), values lower than 3 were classified as row representations (N = 10). Participants with an exact rating of 3 were excluded from analyses that included the variable "representation" since their representation could not be assigned clearly to one of the two categories (N = 3).

Neither "gender", "learning direction" nor "starting point" had a significant effect on the representation ($\chi^2(1, N = 30) = 1.67$, p = .20; $\chi^2(1, N = 30) = 2.40$, p = .12 and $\chi^2(1, N = 66) = .27$, p = .61, respectively). Thus, in the following analyses these factors were not considered further.

The trajectories were classified in four categories: [1] *vertical* (initial vertical movement along one staircase to the appropriate floor, then horizontal movement to the goal), [2] *horizontal* (initial horizontal movement within the current floor to the appropriate staircase, then vertical movement to the goal), [3] *zigzag* (any combinations of vertical and horizontal movement except for [1] and [2]) and [4] *detour* (not moving along one of the shortest paths between starting point and goal).

Table 1 shows absolute (total number = number of tasks × number of participants) and relative frequencies of the four different trajectories. There was an overall preference for initial horizontal movement over vertical movement. The zigzag trajectory was rarely chosen indicating that people indeed tried to reduce the number of turns in the path. In only very few trials participants walked a detour. It shows that participants learned the configuration of the landmarks well and were able to determine the shortest path.

Table 1: Frequencies of path choices

Trajectory	Absolute	Relative
Vertical	93	35%
Horizontal	135	51%
Zigzag	26	10%
Detour	10	4%

A random choice of the shortest path between starting point and goal would result in the distribution shown in table 2. A pure Least-Angle Strategy predicts that people always choose the smaller of two angles. In all tasks the smaller angle is the horizontal one. Thus, according to a pure Least-Angle-Strategy, participants should choose the horizontal trajectory in all tasks. According to a pure floor strategy, participants should move to the appropriate floor first and only then move horizontally to the target landmark. Thus, according to a pure floor strategy participants should choose the vertical trajectory in all tasks.

Table 2: Relative frequencies of initial path choices: predicted by chance (upper panel) and observed (lower panel)

Task	Vertical	Horizontal	zigzag
(1) 2 stairs, 2 floors	25%	25%	50%
(2) 2 stairs, 1 floor	50%	25%	25%
(3) 1 stair, 2 floors	25%	50%	25%
(4) 1 stair, 1 floor	50%	50%	0%
(1) 2 stairs, 2 floors	19%	59%	22%
(2) 2 stairs, 1 floor	16%	76%	8%
(3) 1 stair, 2 floors	46%	43%	11%
(4) 1 stair, 1 floor	66%	34%	0%

The distribution of the observed relative frequencies of trajectories clearly shows that path choices are not made randomly. χ^2-statistics have been calculated for each task separately: all $\chi^2(2, N = 66) > 16.7$ (task 1-3), p < .001; $\chi^2(1, N = 66) = 6.5$, p = .01 (task 4). There is also no clear pattern of an exclusive movement neither vertically nor horizontally. Thus, neither the Least-Angle Strategy nor one of the regionalization strategies alone were sufficient to explain the observed data pattern.

Since we expect trajectory choices to be based on the representation of the building, trajectories in the wayfinding task should be related to our measure of representation. According to hierarchical planning people with a column representation should first go to the appropriate staircase and then move toward the goal vertically. Thus, they should move horizontally first. The correlation between the representation and the frequency of choosing the horizontal trajectory was $r(28) = .39$, p $< .04$ confirming our hypothesis that people who organized landmarks by staircases tended to choose the horizontal strategy. Additional evidence for the representation influencing trajectory choice is shown in Figure 4. Participants with a representation organized by rows more frequently choose the vertical trajectory, participants with a representation organized by columns prefer the horizontal trajectory ($\chi^2(1, N = 208) = 8.99$, p $<$ .01). [1] Figure 5 shows the relative frequencies of vertical trajectory choice. Participants with a row representation preferred the vertical trajectory over the horizontal one in all three task types.

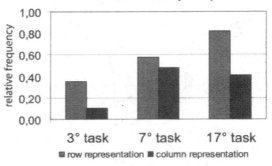

Figure 5: In all three kinds of tasks the vertical trajectory was most frequently chosen by participants with a row representation.

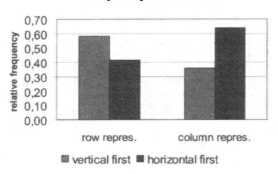

Figure 4: Relative frequencies of path choice grouped by representation.

The two tasks with 2 floor changes passing 2 staircases and 1 floor change passing 1 staircase were aggregated since they involved the same angle between starting point and goal. A loglinear analysis [2] of trajectory with factors task and representation showed that both factors act independently. The relationship between task and trajectory yielded a partial $\chi^2(2, N = 208) = 21.31$, p $< .001$; the relationship between representation and trajectory yielded a partial $\chi^2(1, N = 208) = 9.43$, p = .002. [3] The interaction between task and representation was not significant (partial $\chi^2(2, N = 208) = .54$, p = .762). Both factors, task and representation, independently have a significant influence on path choice. There was no interaction.

---

[1]Since one third of the participants didn't solve the structure mapping task in the first attempt we did the same analysis separately for those participants who solved the task in one attempt and those who received feedback. The pattern of results remained the same: feedback didn't modulate the effect of the incidental organization of the representation on trajectory choice.

[2]Loglinear Analysis was used since the dependent variable was not only categorical rather than quantitative but in addition categories were mutually exclusive.

[3]The above partial χ^2 statistics correspond to main effects in an ANOVA.

Discussion

Heuristics

With respect to heuristics, we can state that neither of the strategies alone is sufficient to explain the observed pattern of results. The LAS as well as a pure regionalization by staircases predicted horizontal movement in all tasks. This was clearly not the case. Only hierarchical planning on a floor wise representation can explain the choice of the vertical trajectory observed in more than a third of the trials. In the other two thirds of the trials, participants selected an initially horizontal trajectory. This choice can be explained by both heuristics, LAS and regionalization by staircases. However, the structure mapping task provides strong evidence that people regionalized the building by salient structures and followed a hierarchical planning strategy of first moving to the target region (either floor or staircase) and then searching for the goal. They did so even though they knew the exact location of the goal. Thus, the findings of Hölscher et al. (2006a) were not limited to the type of instructional information. The current study shows that the choice of one of the two trajectories was clearly related to the way participants regionalized the building. Participants who structured the building by staircases tended to follow a horizontal trajectory, those who structured the building by floors tended to follow a vertical trajectory.

The loglinear analysis of the trajectory choices showed that the kind of task and the representation have an independent influence on the trajectory choice. Thus, we conclude that the representation partly determines the trajectory choice. However, since the building has larger horizontal than vertical extension there is a general bias to move horizontally. This bias might be reflected by combining hierarchical planning with either the Least-Angle Strategy or the ISS.

Mental Representation

The analysis of the participants' mental representations showed that people can chunk landmarks by spatial principles. For most of the participants the configuration of the cards in the structure mapping task corresponded to one of the two salient structures in the building: floors and staircases. Contrary to Hölscher et al. (2006a) participants had to exclusively rely on their mental representation of the building they had acquired during the learning phase. Still, they spontaneously chunked the landmarks according to the structure of the building. The structure mapping task has proven to be a useful tool to analyze peoples' mental representations. However, it has to be tested further with spatial structures other than cross-sectional and rectangular arrangements.

Overall, the participants learned the configuration of the landmarks well: in only 4% of the trials they walked a detour instead of one of the shortest paths. As expected, and in line with Golledge's (1995) observation, participants selected a path with only one turn in the majority of the trials. In only 10% of the trials, participants chose a zigzag path. This observation of choosing the least complex path is consistent with the rationality principle. A majority of the participants chose the horizontal trajectory over the vertical one. It shows that there is a general bias to move horizontally first. This is probably directly related to the structure of the building, which is about 60m long and about 22m high.

Conclusion

We have shown that people structure their mental representation according to salient structures in the environment. So far this has been repeatedly shown for the horizontal plane. We extended this notion to built structures in the vertical plane. There is evidence that people base their path choice on the regionalized representation of a building in form of a hierarchical search, though they may use other strategies in addition. Future research will include a built structure with a larger vertical than horizontal extension, such as a high rise building. In this case there should be no bias toward horizontal movement but rather toward vertical movement. In addition we plan to investigate if it is possible to induce a particular representational structure by different learning conditions.

Acknowledgments

This research has been supported by the German Research Foundation (DFG) in the Transregional Collaborative Research Center "Spatial Cognition" (SFB/TR-8). The authors would like to thank Gregor Wilbertz, Henrike Sprenger and Christopher Kalff for their support in data collection and analysis. They also thank Monica Rivera-Malpica for proofreading the manuscript.

References

Bailenson, J. N., Shum, M. S., and Uttal, D. H. (2000). The initial segment strategy: A heuristic for route selection. *Memory & Cognition*, 28(2):306–318.

Bortz, J. and Lienert, G. (1998). *Kurzgefasste Statistik für die klinische Forschung*. Springer, Berlin.

Chown, E., Kaplan, S., and Kortenkamp, D. (1995). Prototypes, location, and associative networks (PLAN): Towards a unified theory of cognitive mapping. *Cognitive Science*, 19(1):1–51.

Christenfeld, N. (1995). Choices from identical options. *Psychological Science*, 6:50–55.

Conroy Dalton, R. (2003). The secret is to follow your nose: Route path selection and angularity. *Environment and Behavior*, 35(1):107–131.

Downs, R. M. and Stea, D. (1977). *Maps in minds: reflections on cognitive mapping*. Harper & Row, New York.

Fleiss, J. L. (1971). Measuring nominal scale agreement among many raters. *Psychological Bulletin*, 76(5):378–382.

Golledge, R. (1995). Path selection and route preference in human navigation: A progress report. In Frank, A. and Kuhn, W., editors, *Conference on Spatial Information Theory - Lecture Notes in Computer Science*, volume 988, Semmering, Austria.

Hochmair, H. and Frank, A. U. (2002). Influence of estimation errors on wayfinding decisions in unknown street networks - analyzing the least-angle strategy. *Spatial Cognition and Computation*, 2(4):283–313.

Hochmair, H. H. and Karlsson, V. (2004). Investigation of preference between the least-angle strategy and the initial segment strategy for route selection in unknown environments. *Spatial Cognition*, pages 79–97.

Hölscher, C., Büchner, S. J., Meilinger, T., and Strube, G. (2006a). Map use and wayfinding strategies in a multi-building ensemble. In *Spatial Cognition*, Bremen, Germany. Springer.

Hölscher, C., Meilinger, T., Vrachliotis, G., Brösamle, M., and Knauff, M. (2006b). Up the down staircase: Wayfinding strategies and multi-level buildings. *Journal of Environmental Psychology*, 26(4):284–299.

Passini, R. (1992). *Wayfinding in architecture*. Van Nostrand Reinhold Company, New York, 2nd edition.

Soeda, M., Kushiyama, N., and Ohno, R. (1997). Wayfinding in cases with vertical motion. In *Proceedings of MERA 97: International Conference on Environment-Behavior Studies for 21st Century*, pages 559–564, Tokyo, Japan.

Stevens, A. and Coupe, P. (1978). Distortions in judged spatial relations. *Cognitive Psychology*, 10(4):422–437.

Wiener, J. M., Schnee, A., and Mallot, H. A. (2004). Use and interaction of navigation strategies in regionalized environments. *Journal of Environmental Psychology*, 24(4):475–493.

Characteristics of diagrammatic reasoning

Catherine Recanati (catherine.recanati@lipn.univ-paris13.fr)
L.I.P.N., UMR 7030 of the CNRS, Paris 13 University,
av. J.B. Clément, 93430, Villetaneuse, FRANCE

Abstract

Diagrammatic, analogical or iconic representations are often contrasted with linguistic or logical representations, in which the shape of the symbols is arbitrary. We list here the main characteristics of diagrammatic inferential systems. This review reveals that diagrammatic and logico-linguistic representations have dual and complementary properties. This makes their combination in heterogeneous inferential systems including both linguistic and diagrammatic representations particularly attractive and promising for cognitive modeling and reasoning. We end this paper by an example of hybrid reasoning in a Master Mind game.

Introduction

With the advent of printing, textual transmission became dominant in communication. Today, partly because of the development of technologies to create, reproduce and transmit images, figures are again in the spotlight. But their increased use in communication is also due to the relatively recent discovery that graphical representations also can convey abstract meanings, by means of visual metaphors. Indeed the use of space makes it possible to capitalize on the considerable human abilities to make spatial inferences.

Although commonly used in Science (as in Physics, Mathematics and Logic) diagrammatic representations have long suffered from their reputation as mere tools in the search for solutions, as mere support for intuition. This general prejudice against diagrams has been strongly denounced in the 90's by Barwise and Etchemendy, who defended the idea that a general theory of valid inferences can be developed independently of the modes of representations (as implicit in Peirce). In fact, diagrams can also be considered as structured syntactic objects, which can be used for correct reasoning in a formal perspective. Their work yields to the rigorous demonstration, done by Sun-Joo Shin in her PhD thesis, that diagrammatic systems can be formally proved as being sound and complete[1] (Shin, 1994).

Historically, the use of circles to illustrate relations between classes has often been attributed to Euler (1768), but he was in fact preceded by others (as by Leibniz), one century earlier. But these circles were unable to express all the relations between two classes on the same diagram, and this reduced considerably their expressive and deductive power. In the nineteenth century, Venn found a way of correcting this lack. Twenty years later, Peirce added to his

---

[1] The only preceding attempt in this direction is due to J. Sowa in 1984 (Sowa, 1984).

system the possibility to express existential assertions (marked by a cross) and disjunctions (by means of lines joining crosses and small circles) – small circles being used to indicate the negation of existence in empty areas, instead of hatching as in Venn diagrams (Peirce, 1933)

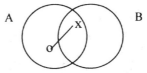

Figure 1: All A are B or some A are B (Peirce)

The idea of transformation rules on diagrams is also due to Peirce. But the question of the validity of these rules required a supplementary proof, which S. Shin provided. To do so, Shin provided graphical systems with a syntax (defining the primitive graphical objects and the well-formed diagrams) and a semantics (here representing sets of objects with areas) as in modern logic systems. Her two systems, based on Venn-Peirce diagrams, allow the resolution of syllogisms constituted by assertions on sets by means of transformation rules on diagrams (using the notion of equivalence between diagrams, and allowing the derivation of one diagram from others, with deletion and unification graphic rules).

Properties of diagrammatic systems

We list here the main characteristics of diagrammatic systems discussed in the literature. Note that these are neither necessary nor sufficient. For details, see (Recanati, 2005).

A structural homomorphism

Diagrammatic and linguistic representation systems may have several degrees of homomorphism between their representations and the situation they represent. Barwise and Etchemendy have emphasized that the main properties of diagrammatic systems are derived from the existence of a syntactical homomorphism such that, usually:

1. Objects are typically represented by icon tokens. It is often the case that each object is represented by a unique icon token and distinct tokens represent distinct objects.

2. There is a mapping ϕ from icon types to properties of objects.

3. The mapping ϕ preserves structure. For example, one would expect that:

a) If one icon type is a subtype of another (as in the case of shaded squares and squares, for example), then there is a corresponding subproperty relation among properties they represent.

b) If two icon types are incompatible (say squares and circles), then the properties they represent should be incompatible.

c) The converses of (a) and (b) frequently hold as well.

4. Certain relations among objects are represented by relations among icon tokens, with the same kinds of conditions as in (3a)-(3c).

5. Higher-order properties of relations among objects (like transitivity, reflexivity and the like) are reflected by the same properties of relations among icon tokens.

6. Every possibility (involving represented objects, properties, and relations) is representable. That is, there are no possible situations that are represented as impossible.

7. Every representation indicates a genuine possibility. (Barwise & Etchemendy, 1995)

But in many cases, diagrammatic system properties seem to be derived from the property of closure under constraints.

Closure under constraints

This is the most paradigmatic property of diagrammatic systems (first isolated by B&E). In such systems, the representations exhibit most of the previously cited characteristics. We reformulate this property as follows:

A diagrammatic system of representation is *closed under constraints* if, and only if, there exists a syntactical homomorphism requiring that all logical consequences of the represented situation be explicit in the representation.

Suppose you have to seat three people, Loana, Thierry and Claire, on aligned chairs. Knowing that Thierry is on the left of Loana, and Loana on the left of Claire, you can represent this situation diagrammatically by using three symbolic letters that you will place in accordance with these two hypotheses as in:

T   L   C

Conversely, in a linguistic representation system, you will write:

T on-the-left-of L
L on-the-left-of C

The consequence of these two hypotheses, namely, that T is on the left of C, is explicit in the diagrammatic case, while it requires an inference mechanism (and a rule of transitivity) to be derived in the linguistic one.

Duality of linguistic and diagrammatic reasoning The preceding example illustrates the deep duality between linguistic and diagrammatic modes of reasoning. Linguistic (or traditional logical) reasoning requires (1) the representation of initial facts, (2) an explicit representation of abstract properties (or relations between dimensions) of the objects, and (3) a computational mechanism linking the two sources of information to establish the validity of a non-

explicit consequence. To the opposite, diagrammatic reasoning (in closed under constraints systems) do not require the explicit representation of abstract properties, because *these properties are automatically taken into account by syntactic constraints on the representation itself.* They merely need the representation of facts, and to establish the validity of a consequence, the representations have only to be inspected to check whether the new fact is or not represented there. This makes these systems computationally very efficient[2].

Easy treatment of conjunction As just mentioned, the facts are then simply added within a (global) representation and their consequences automatically follow.

Difficulties with disjunction Diagrammatic representations lead frequently to consideration of alternatives, because self-contradictory situations cannot be represented on the same diagram[3].

Contradictions cannot be represented and each representation corresponds to a genuine situation To illustrate the last points let's take an example from B&E: « You are to seat four people, A, B, C and D in a row of five chairs. A and C are to flank the empty chair. C must be closer to the center than D, who is to sit next to B. From this information, show that the empty chair is not in the middle or on either end. Can you tell who is to be seated on the two ends? » (Barwise et Etchemendy, 1990).

A diagrammatic representation of a situation may consist in aligned letters (as in our first example), a cross to indicate the empty chair, and dashes for non-attributed chairs. Then, the first hypothesis requires distinguishing between three disjunctive cases:

1. A x C − −   2. − A x C −   3. − − A x C

The second hypothesis eliminates case 3, and the third (D next to B) case 2. (These cases are suppressed because B or D cannot be added to the representation).Then, case 1 yields to the two final possibilities :

1.1. A x C B D   1.2. A x C D B

Specificity and limited abstraction

Keith Stenning and Jon Oberlander (S&O) (1995) have introduced three classes of representational systems: the MARS (Minimal Abstraction Representational Systems), the LARS (Limited Abstraction Representational Systems) and the UARS (Unlimited Abstraction Representational

---

[2] Insofar as the inspection procedures are not too costly.

[3] We have seen that Peirce diagrams enabled the representation of disjunctive cases on the same diagram. Nevertheless, the efficiency may be partly lost with disjunction or second order relation (as with implication). This is the case with the Venn-II diagrams system developed by Shin, which supports disjunctions but requires more complex diagrams. In this system, the simple inspection of a representation to check a property is not always possible, and it may require extra (graphical) computation, as in the linguistic case.

Systems). They argue that this hierarchy of representational systems is analogous to that of languages isolated by Chomsky, and they claim that most diagrammatic representation systems are LARS.

MARS, LARS and UARS A MARS is a system in which a representation corresponds to a unique model of the world under the considered interpretation. For instance, a table of 0 and 1, representing the values of unary predicates of objects in a world W, will be a minimal abstraction representation, if each cell of the table is occupied by 0 or 1, and nothing else. MARS have no abstraction capacity and each new dimension brings as much alternative worlds as the number of possible values in this dimension.

But you can augment the number of models captured by a MARS by introducing new symbols that allow abstracting on a certain dimension of the representation. For instance, in the preceding table, you can allow empty cells. Such systems can quantify massively on possible models, but cannot specify arbitrarily complex dependences between the specified dimensions. This is why S&O called them LARS. The abstraction is performed over models that differ on the values of objects among their dimensions, but not on the nature of relations or constraints that may exist between these dimensions. Only linguistic symbols, added to a representation, could allow the description of arbitrarily fine dependences between dimensions. Thus, for S&O, a system is a UARS, if it expresses dependences, inside a representation, with equations or others, or outside a representation, with linguistic assertions on the «keys» defining the representation itself. *Diagrammatic representations thus differ from linguistic ones by a limited abstraction power, which augment their computational efficiency.*

Determined character and specificity S&O identify the restricted capacity of diagrammatic systems with a property called *specificity*, which requires information of a certain kind to be specified in all interpretable representation. Perry and Macken have opposed to this too strong notion (= the mandatory specification of values of properties other than the one you try to represent) the notion of determined character (in the sense of Berkeley) – only what is really necessary for diagrammatic representations (Perry & Macken, 1996).

Berkeley's notion of a determined character is derived from the fact that it is not possible to represent an object as having a certain property, without representing at the same time a specified value for this property. Thus, I cannot represent a triangle on a mathematical figure, without ending with a particular triangle. As well, it is not possible to represent a colored object on a drawing without specifying its color, but I can perfectly say, « this object has an interesting color », without specifying which one[4]. But

for P&M, the closure under constraints of B&E does not require the specificity of S&O, but another property, which they call *localization*.

Localization and perceptual inferences

J. Larkin and H. Simon have identified three advantages of diagrams on verbal descriptions for solving problems:

- Diagrams can group together all information that is used together, thus avoiding large amounts of search for the elements needed to make a problem-solving inference.
- Diagrams typically use location to group information about a single element, avoiding the need to match symbolic labels.
- Diagrams automatically support a large number of perceptual inferences, which are extremely easy for humans. (Larkin & Simon, 1987)

The first two properties are not clearly distinguished in the second point of L&S. The first is about what we call logical localization, and (2) refers both to logical localization and to what seems more distinctive of diagrammatic systems, and that we prefer to call spatial localization.

(Logical) localization (or *unique token constraint*) is the property of using only one token of a symbol to represent an object. This property disappears generally when you use a typed system. The omnipresence of representation of the same type designating the same object is thus observed in human language, where references to an object can be spread out everywhere in a document, so that information is not « localized » (Perry et Macken, 1996). For P&M, this additional character is the one required to give diagrammatic systems the closure under constraints property, when combined with iconicity and a constraint and systematic homomorphism.

Spatial localization consists in using « places » or « loci» of a geometrically structured space (usually of dimension 2), to encode several features (as color, texture, forms, etc, are in images). The abundance of visual interferences of these encoded dimensions allows defining relations between crossing dimensions, which can be detected for free by our perceptual abilities[5].

Reducing the number of dimensions The encoding evoked here may lead to a reduction in the number of dimensions, and similar techniques (using maps or charts) are exploited today for this purpose in data mining.

Symmetrical arguments The frequency of symmetrical arguments in diagrammatic reasoning, which has been noted in the literature, may obviously come from spatial localization (for instance, there was an implicit symmetrical argument in our chairs problem). But we believe this is not a

---

[4] The analogical/digital distinction is also based for Dretske on a notion of specificity (Dretske, 1981, p.137). For him, every signal transmitting information necessarily carries this information under two aspects: an analogical form and a digital form. The analogical

form always contains an additional specificity relative to the information properly conveyed by the digital form.

[5] The logician Jean Nicod, who developed cognitive models of euclidian spaces based on similarity relations, has analyzed these cognitive mechanisms with great subtlety.

specific feature of diagrammatic reasoning, since these arguments also appear in linguistic cases.

Iconicity

For Macken, Perry, and Cathy Hass (Macken et alii, 1993), this fundamental property allows representations with *Richly Grounded Meaning* (RGM). A RGM is a meaning whose relation to form is not arbitrary. This may come from several factors binding the form of the symbol to its meaning. An iconic sign may have a *Readily Inferable Meaning* (RIM), an *Easily Remembered Meaning* (ERM), or an *Internally Modifiable Meaning* (IMM). Road signs provide numerous examples of ERM and RIM (for instance, signposting bends). There also are in musical scores many examples of symbols having a RIM coming from their analogical character (as a crescendo situated under the stave).

Iconicity has been only very partially analyzed until now. We are convinced that it must be related to syntactical homomorphism because we believe that the main distinction between linguistic (or symbolic) representation systems and analogical representation systems (as diagrammatic systems) must be characterized in terms of the power of the meta-language required to provide the semantics of the system. In the analogical case, the meta-language involves reference to the syntactical properties of the object language, while in the symbolic case, this is not obligatory. Let's take the example of Thierry, Claire and Loana, who are represented as « ordered » in the diagrammatic case. A minimal difference, but an essential one, between the two types of representations is the following:

(I) left-of (a, b) & left-of (b, c)

and (II) ordered ([a, b, c]) (or just [a, b, c])

There is an additional syntactical complexity for (II) which prevents its meaning, contrary to that of (I), from being described as a function of one argument of its predicate's meaning. Indeed, you can easily assign a meaning to the semantic equation:

$$[\![\,\text{left-of}\,(\,a,\,b)\,]\!] = [\![\,\text{left-of}\,]\!]\,([\![\,a\,]\!],\,[\![\,b\,]\!])$$

while you cannot write anything else but:

$$[\![\,\text{ordered}\,([a,\,b,\,c])\,]\!] = [\![\,\text{ordered}\,]\!]\,(\,[\![\,[a,\,b,\,c]\,]\!]\,)$$

which implies giving meaning, *at the meta-language level*, to a *configuration* of terms (the list figuring between simple square brackets). Therefore, the semantic descriptive meta-language must *offer possibilities of syntactical structuring of data similar to the ones figuring in the representation language*, because it will sometimes be necessary to assign them a meaning. This is not to say that all syntactical nuances of the representational system must be reflected in the interpretation system, because not all iconic representation features are interpreted in a diagrammatic representation. As well, syntactical structuring is not always necessary for an iconic feature of a symbol to be exploited (as with the use of bold to indicate the focus on one element). Nevertheless, this shows that semantic compositionality relies on syntactic considerations, which leads to this interesting question: which syntax do we need (at the meta-language level) to describe human language?

Heterogeneous systems

The preceding section underlined what diagrammatic reasoning is good for computationally and what it is not, and the request of a unique syntactical homomorphism and a limited power of abstraction are obviously restricting. This review acts as a critique of current approaches, which tend to emphasize one mode, diagrammatic or logico-linguistic. These approaches are set up in opposition to the other mode (e.g. the mental logic vs mental models debate). We defend the idea that these modes are complementary at the representational and algorithmic level and that the shortcomings of both systems can be eliminated in heterogeneous representation systems (HRS) – which can benefit of the dual and opposite properties of logical and analogical systems.

Computational perspectives

Against all expectations, HRS may lead to amazing results in the domain of computational complexity. Diagrammatic systems have the fantastic property of bypassing computation, and the possibility of switching from one system to another opens up new research perspectives. The paradox is that a given demonstration may be limited by a minimal cost in *any* two systems, and still be *less costly* in a hybrid system binding the two. There is nothing sophistic here, because a heterogeneous system doesn't need a global language to bind its subsystems.

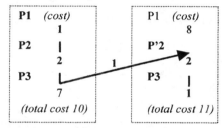

Figure 2: Minimal cost (*total 7*) of a diagonal proof

No doubt the supporters of traditional logic are ready to concede that deductive properties can be extended to non-linguistic representations in an HRS, but they may still be convinced that the final articulation of these subsystems requires a traditional intermediate language, in which any operation would have a cost, to be correctly based. But the articulation of different subsystems of representation in a complex representational system may be based simply on *the fact that they denote the same objects in the world*. Thus, two subsystems may denote different properties of objects, and what can be expressed in one subsystem need not be expressed in another; some information may nevertheless be transferred from one system to another, on the basis of safe correspondences, thus endowing the global system with superior inferential capacities. For instance the theoretical justification of the algorithms of *Hyperproof*[6] is

---

[6] Hyperproof is an interactive software, designed by B&E to teach logic; a world of simple geometrical forms of various sizes,

based on purely mathematical grounds, without using any intermediate language, lacking from the hybrid system.

Cognitive modeling

Logical formalisms are in many respects unsuited for the description of human inferential capacities. On top of their computational properties, HRS seem really better suited for this task. This thesis is reinforced for time and space by the abundance of schemas found in most contemporary semantic works in linguistic. Even though this fact is not a proof of the existence of diagrams in our mind, if they can explain the successes and failures of human inferences, they are of great significance.

Hybrid reasoning in a MasterMind game

We would like to end this paper by a new illustrative example. The game of MasterMind[7] is well suited to the study of human reasoning, because it constrains the player to logical reasoning, not such a frequent occasion in everyday life. In (Recanati, 2004) we highlighted the hybrid character of the reasoning carried out in this game, the geometry of the grid supporting the pawns encouraging the players to develop diagrammatic representations. We have insufficient room here to report our observations, but we will give the flavor of them.

For most beginners, the reasoning is fragmented and opportunistic, and consists in partial deductions using several types of representations. In fact, most of the deductions are performed graphically while the model under construction is frequently described linguistically. Each attempt played on a row generates new interpretation schemas and new information, but these cannot always be combined with the preceding. Nevertheless, mental projections of new assumptions are regularly propagated from one row to another, to check whether or not the considered hypotheses are contradictory.

Experienced players develop properly graphical strategies of resolution, and project on the grid several types of geometrical representations. The use of graphic representations mitigates limitations in the cognitive capacities of the player, anchoring reasoning on inexpensive visual capacities, thus relieving verbal memory. But in return, the visual capacities being also restricted, the form of the diagrams used and the ordering of hypotheses are biased. For instance, the left-to-right order of pins and

pawns, and the ease of visual translations, influence the choice of hypotheses to be considered first (as shown on Figure 3).

The grid ensures the memorizing of preceding attempts, but is also used as geometrical support for organizing proofs and backtracking. The reasoning begins with partial facts discovered on some attempt, but ends up being based on an interpretation of the first row. One frequently notes an ordering of global reasoning based on the vertical order of the rows, which helps the player in backtracking.

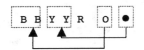

Figure 3: A favourite interpretation schema

The strategy of experienced players is based on the progressive construction of a model (very similar to the "mental models" of Johnson-Laird) by covering a tree of self-inclusive ordered models. They usually separate the play in two parts: determining first the colors, and then determining their places. In both phases of the game, they use representations (specific arrangement of pawns), which can be qualified as mental models. The interesting fact is that these models, which also correspond to the LARS of S&O, are constructed both *by increasing order of specificity and decreasing order of probability of appearance*. This makes backtracking easier and allows to converge quickly towards the solution. To illustrate this in a prototypical example, let's analyze the first four rows of Figure 4:

4.	R G R Y G	o o o ● ●
3.	R R R G G	o o o ●
2.	O O B B B	
1.	B B Y Y R	o ●

Figure 4: The grid at the middle of a game

The player begins on row 1 with a configuration, which is revealed to be statistically more informative than others. Given the answer on the right side, he considers first the interpretation of Figure 3, i.e. that one blue is correctly placed, one yellow misplaced, and that there is no red. (He might take in his hand a blue and a yellow pawn to help memorize, and note mentally that the three colors are exhausted). We will note this "mental model" by [1B] [1Y] (and no red) – using square brackets for the notion of exhaustivity defined by Johnson-Laird (1983). Then, he plays the second row, trying new places for blue (in anticipation of a future reasoning on places) and introducing a new color (orange). By luck he obtains that both orange and blue are missing. He then switches to a new model based on a new interpretation of the first row: namely [1 Y] 1R, (and neither blue, nor orange). The third row is played both to try new places for red and to add a new color. Getting 4 pins as a result, the player concludes that the colors of the solution must be yellow, red and green; then,

---

represented on the square of a checkerboard, is depicted using two formats: a logic language, and some visual representations on the checkerboard. The user can check the validity of new sentences, given these descriptions in both formats, by making « hybrid » proofs.

[7] The game consists in discovering a hidden row of five colored pawns. One player (the leader) hides a configuration of pawns. The second player can then dispose on a grid a tentative configuration of pawns, and the leader confirms by posting pins (on the right) indicating how many pawn have been discovered. A white pin means a good position and color, and a black one a misplaced color. The rows remain visible during the game, and the player has to find out the solution in a limited number of attempts.

given that there is only one yellow, he considers [1Y] [2R] [2G] (which seems more likely than [1Y] [3R] [1G]). He then begins to reason on places and supposes that on the first row, the first yellow pawn on the left is well placed (noted [– – Y – –]). Therefore, the red in the middle of the third row must be misplaced and the two greens must be correctly placed, with one of the two remaining reds as well (see the diagrammatic reasoning in Figure 5). He then concludes that the solution in this case necessarily is [R R Y G G]; but this is found to contradict the answer on row 3, which would then have four white pins.

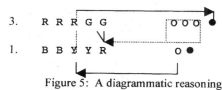

Figure 5: A diagrammatic reasoning

So the player is led to backtrack and reconsider the place of the yellow pawn on row 1: [– – – Y –]. A graphic reasoning very similar to the preceding reveals that the first green pawn is misplaced but that the second one is correct ([– – –Y G], with two of the reds at the beginning). The player then tries a fourth plausible configuration, but is unlucky. Nevertheless, [1Y] [2R] [2G] is confirmed and he knows by experience that getting 3 white pins and 2 black ones means that two pawns have to be exchanged to get the solution. Note that this automatic inference is directly activated by the pattern of pins, and the conclusion directly expressed on the representation. He then makes another attempt [G R R Y G] but is unlucky again. However, a graphic comparison of common parts of rows 3, 4, and 5, leads him to the conclusion that the two framed pawns (R and G) on the right have to be mapped onto either two white pins, or onto a white and a black one (see Figure 6). This strategy is anchored on operations of pattern matching between lines. (The strategy carried out can thus again be called graphic or visual).

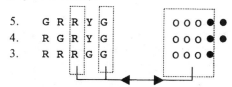

Figure 6: The mapping of common parts

The first hypothesis yields [– – R Y G], which is excluded by the last rows. Since a red can't be in the last position (due to the hypothesis on the first row), the green occupying the last position must be correctly placed, and the red in the middle misplaced, yielding [R R G Y G], which is revealed to be the solution.

Conclusion

The distinction between iconic and linguistic representations has been (partially) analyzed in the literature of the nineties.

The demonstration that iconic representations may be taken as syntactical objects in valid inferential systems (based on graphical rules of transformation) has been made. Furthermore, in most diagrammatic systems, the consequences of initials facts are included *de facto* in the representation and do not require extra computation. Diagrammatic representations seem to differ mainly from linguistic ones by having a more limited power of abstraction but a greater computational efficiency. This study also reveals that diagrammatic and logico-linguistic representations have distinct properties, frequently dual and complementary. This makes their combination in hybrid systems particularly attractive and promising both at algorithmic and representational levels. The study and use of such systems opens new research perspectives in the domains of cognitive science and natural language semantics, as well as in artificial intelligence.

References

Barwise, J. and Etchemendy, J. (1990). Visual Information and Valid Reasoning. In *Visualization in Mathematics*, Zimmerman, W., ed., Mathematical Association of America, Washington DC.

Barwise, J. and Etchemendy, J. (1995). Heterogenous Logic. In Glasgow J., and alii (Eds). *Diagrammatic reasoning: cognitive and computational perspective*. Cambridge, MA and London: AAAI Press/MIT Press.

Dretske, F. (1981). *Knowledge and the flow of information*. Oxford: Blackwell.

Euler, L. (1768-1772). Lettres à une princesse d'Allemagne sur quelques sujets de physique et de philosophie in Speiser A., Trost E. and Blanc C. (Eds.), 1960, *Œuvres Complètes d'Euler*, Orell Füssl., Zurich.

Johnson-Laird P.N., 1983, *Mental Models: towards a cognitive science of language, inference, and consciousness*, Cambridge University Press, Cambridge.

Larkin, J. and Simon, H. (1987). Why a Diagram Is (Sometimes) Worth Ten Thousand Words. *Cognitive Science*, vol 11.

Macken, E., Perry, J. and Hass, C. (1993). Richly Grounding Symbols in ASL, CSLI Report no. 93-180, Sep. 1993 (also in *Sign Language Studies*, dec. 93).

Peirce, C. S. (1933). *Collected Papers*. vol. 4, Hartshorne, C. & Weiss, P. (Eds.), Cambridge, MA: Harvard University Press.

Recanati, C. (2005). Raisonner avec des diagrammes : perspectives cognitives et computationnelles, *Intellectica* n° 40, pp. 9-42, Paris, 2005.

Recanati C. (2004). Diagrammes pour résoudre le problème d'Einstein et celui d'un joueur de MasterMind, rapport LIPN, Université Paris13.

Shin, S-J. (1994). *The logical status of Diagrams*. Cambridge University Press.

Sowa, J. (1984). *Conceptual Structure: Information Processing in Mind and Machine*, Reading, MA: Addison-Wesley.

Stenning, K. and Oberlander, I. (1995). A Cognitive Theory of Graphical and Linguistic Reasoning: Logic and Implementation. *Cognitive Science*, vol. 19 (1).

Imagery and the Interpretation of Ambiguous Noun-Noun Combinations

James A. Hampton (hampton@city.ac.uk)

Dyonne Francis and George Robson
Department of Psychology, City University, Northampton Squre
London, EC1V OHB, UK

Abstract

Novel ambiguous N-N combinations were created that had both a thematic relation and a property mapping interpretation (e.g., a cheetah truck = a fast truck vs. a truck for transporting cheetahs). Experiment 1 asked people to generate their own interpretations, which were then classified as involving thematic relations, property mapping or other. Experiment 2 asked people to choose which of the two interpretations was most plausible. Both Experiments showed that instructions to work rapidly through the task led to more thematic relational interpretations, whereas instructions to visualize and reflect more deeply on the problem led to more property mapping. Implications for models of conceptual combination are discussed.

N-N Combination

A number of languages, such as English, Dutch and German, include a mechanism for constructing novel noun phrases by concatenating bare nouns. There already exist many such NN combinations in the language (for example *fire truck* or *steam train*), but the mechanism is also productive allowing construction of indefinitely many novel noun phrases (for example *steam truck* or *fire train*). The mechanisms by which such phrases can be allocated an interpretation have been extensively studied in recent years. For example, Wisniewski (1996, 1997) collected a large database of people's free interpretations of novel combinations. From a qualitative analysis of the data, three main categories of interpretation emerged, each with parallels among more familiar noun phrases. Relation-linking, or thematic relation interpretations as they are also termed, involve the interposition of a semantic relation between the two nouns. The second noun is taken as the head noun (that is it determines the broad referential class of the combination) and the first noun modifies that class through some additional semantic constraint. For example a *robin snake* could be interpreted as a snake that primarily feeds on robins. Here the semantic relation "feeds on" has to be added to the two simple concepts in order to provide the interpretation. Note that there may be indefinitely many such relations that could be found in different cases.

The second category of interpretation described by Wisniewski involved property mapping, by which a salient property of the first (modifier) noun is taken as modifying the second (head) noun. In the case of a *robin snake* an alternative interpretation using property mapping would take a salient feature of robins – such as their red breasts – and map this to the head noun concept snake, thus giving the interpretation of a snake with a red patch on its breast. The success of such interpretations has been shown to depend on two important factors. First the modifier noun should have a well-known and distinctive property – robins should be known for having red breasts. Second, the head noun should have a dimension that can be readily modified by this property. In the case of snakes, this could be problematic since it is not clear in what sense a snake has a breast (Costello & Keane, 2001; Estes & Glucksberg, 2000).

The third kind of interpretation, that will not concern us in this paper is hybridization – where a novel concept is created that belongs (at least to some extent) in both categories. This type of interpretation was generally quite rare in Wisniewski's database.

Models of N-N Combination

Several distinct models have emerged for the explanation of N-N combinations (Gagné, 2000; Murphy, 1990; Wisniewski & Love, 1998). Gagné's CARIN model proposes a single process that incorporates both the relation and the property forms of combination. CARIN proposes that there are a limited number of fairly general semantic relations that are used in the large majority of cases – relations such as USED FOR, MADE OF or FOUND IN. Selection of the appropriate relation is driven by the past history of combinations using the particular modifier involved. Thus people are fastest to generate interpretations that use a relation that is of high frequency for the modifier (Gagné & Shoben, 1997). Should any such relation prove hard to find (as may occur with some novel combinations) then a relation IS SIMILAR TO may be employed, together with the retrieval of a suitable property that can be mapped from the modifier to the head noun. The model therefore predicts that property mapping will be used relatively infrequently, and should take longer to generate, predictions borne out by Gagné (2002).

The major competitor to CARIN is a proposal by

Wisniewski and Love (1998) for a dual processing system. According to this proposal, relations and properties are two independent strategies that may be employed for interpreting NN combinations. In support of this idea, Wisniewski and Love showed that the interpretation of ambiguous combinations such as *spear chisel* or *ant vegetable* could be influenced by priming with 10 combinations that could only be interpreted with either one or the other strategy. They therefore argued that both interpretation strategies are available, and that consequently there may be two independent ways in which an interpretation is sought for a novel combination (for priming of interpretations see also Estes, 2003; Gagné & Shoben, 2002).

Current aims of the research

The aim of our studies was to examine the two interpretation strategies in the light of processing demands. If, as CARIN would predict, property interpretations are used only as a "last resort" when no other thematic interpretation suggests itself, then whenever a reasonable thematic interpretation is available, it should be the preferred interpretation. It should not matter whether participants are working with or without time pressure – the thematic interpretation should normally be preferred.

On the other hand, if there are two processes of interpretation involved, manipulation of the cognitive load may influence which interpretation is arrived at. Specifically if (as is suggested by previous research, Gagné, 2002) relational interpretations are quicker and easier to generate whereas property interpretations take longer, then requiring participants to answer as quickly as possible should favor the relational interpretation of an ambiguous combination. On the other hand, instructions to retrieve and visualize the meanings of the nouns and to reflect carefully on the best interpretation may bias the interpretation in the direction of property interpretations (Wisniewski & Middleton, 2002).

Visualization may be particularly important for the generation of property interpretations because individual information about each concept needs to be retrieved. A thematic relation can be fairly unconstrained by the meaning of the modifier (e.g., a chocolate box, a horse box and a pencil box may all use the CONTAINS relation, regardless of the large semantic differences between chocolate horses and pencils). On the other hand a property relation requires that the salient property of the modifier become available, which will only happen if the distinctive meaning of the modifier is first retrieved.

Accordingly we conducted two studies in which ambiguous NN combinations were given to people to interpret, either under time pressure, or with instructions to respond carefully and after due reflection and visualization of the concepts involved. We argue that CARIN should predict no effect of this manipulation on the level of relation versus property interpretations generated, since if a relational interpretation is available it should always be selected first.

The dual process model would agree with the prediction that relation interpretations will be more likely to be generated when under time pressure, since property interpretations require more detailed retrieval of meanings. For the slow visualization condition however, the dual process model makes no clear prediction, although it would be easier to accommodate a switch in preference with condition within the dual process framework.

Experiment 1

In the first study, participants were presented with N-N pairs and asked to generate their own interpretations. Half performed the task under time pressure, and half were asked to imagine the object first. Proportions of relation and property interpretations were then calculated.

Method

Participants. Forty undergraduate students at City University, London participated for credit. All had English as a first language.

Materials. Property interpretations require a salient modifier property that is relevant to the head noun (Estes & Glucksberg, 2000). In order to generate suitable materials, 30 dimensional adjectives were used in an analogy task that was given to 10 participants to complete. For example participants had to complete phrases such as "*as strong as a _____*". The resulting responses were combined with head nouns in order construct ambiguous N-N combinations such as *ox rope*, which has either the interpretation "a strong rope" or "a rope for use with oxen". Other materials were selected from previous research to generate a total of 25 N-N pairs. The Appendix lists the materials used.

Design and Procedure. Participants were randomly allocated to one of two conditions (20 per condition), and instructions were manipulated between the two. For the Fast condition, the following instructions were given:

"On the following pages you will find pairs of words. Please think of the first meaning for the phrase that comes to mind. Work as fast as you can through the list. Some phrases may be ambiguous but it is the first meaning you think of that you should give. Please write this meaning in the space next to each pair."

For the Slow condition, the instructions were instead:

"On the following pages you will find pairs of words. Please read each word very carefully and try to form an image of what kind of thing it may be referring to. Then write a meaning in the space provided that best explains the phrase. Some phrases may be ambiguous but it is the meaning that on consideration you believe best that you should give."

In order to encourage participants to switch interpretation strategies, four unambiguous NN combinations were used as warm-up items at the start of the list, two with unambiguous property interpretations (e.g., *razor insult*), and two with unambiguous relation interpretations (e.g., *grocery bicycle)*. Two different random list orders were used.

Results and Discussion

Responses were judged by two independent judges, one of whom was blind to the aims of the study. Each response was categorized as Relation, Property or Other. Judges agreed on the classification of 85% of all responses, and disagreements were resolved by discussion. Responses categorized as Other were removed from further analysis. Table 1 shows the mean (and standard deviation) number of interpretations (out of 25) that were categorized as Property or Relation in each condition. (Because 18-29% of responses were rejected as Other, the number of interpretations of each type was free to vary independently).

Table 1: Interpretations generated in Experiment 1

Interpretation	Condition	
	Fast	Slow
Relation	12.6 (5.3)	3.4 (4.0)
Property	8.0 (3.6)	14.4 (4.5)

Table 1 shows a clear cross-over interaction in the preference for a relation or property interpretation as a function of condition. In the Fast condition, relations were used more often that properties, whereas in the Slow condition the pattern was reversed.

ANOVA was run with condition and interpretation type as factors, and with either participants or items as random effects. Neither main effect was significant across both analyses, but the interaction was highly significant (Min $F'(1,56) = 31.1$, $p < .001$).

As expected by CARIN, relations were the preferred interpretation in the Fast condition, consistent with a strategy that considers relations first. However CARIN would not predict the switch to property interpretation in the Slow condition. While not predicting the cross-over interaction, the dual process approach could accommodate this result. It would have to propose that in the slow visualization condition the property interpretation generates a more satisfying interpretation than the relational interpretation. Because the meaning of the modifier is retrieved more fully and a fit found to a dimension of the head, it may be that participants found

the resulting interpretation pragmatically more relevant than the more general relation interpretation.

In order to confirm the generality of our results, Experiment 2 used a different dependent measure, and extended the number of conditions to include a neutral control condition, to test the role of imagery in our instructions.

Experiment 2

Experiment 1 asked participants to generate their own responses. In Experiment 2 we instead presented people with two alternative interpretations and asked them to choose the one that they thought the more plausible. It is unclear why a single process model such as CARIN would predict any difference in the selection of a property or a relation interpretation as more plausible as a function of time pressure. On the other hand, if understanding property interpretations is more cognitively demanding, we expect that time pressure will lead to people preferring the relational interpretations, whereas without time pressure they may show no preference. If in addition the instruction to form images leads to discovery of the salient property of the modifier noun, then in the Imagery condition a preference should be expressed for the property interpretation being more plausible.

Method

Participants. Forty-eight students at universities in London participated without reward. Four were discarded because they failed to comply with instructions. One additional participant was recruited in order to rebalance the design.

Materials. A new set of materials was constructed using the same method as before. In addition, 3 different modifier nouns were selected for each head noun, all with the same property and relation interpretations. For example red colored wallpaper, or wallpaper with a pattern depicting a fruit was represented with the three pairs *Cherry wallpaper, Raspberry wallpaper* and *Strawberry wallpaper*. One of each of these pairs was allocated to each of the three conditions, so that three lists of 22 items each were created. A full list of materials is shown in the Appendix.

Design and Procedure. Three conditions were used, varying only in the instructions provided at the start. All participants contributed to each condition. Booklets were constructed with three sections, each with a different instructional condition. Each section contained one of the lists of NN combinations, so that for example section A would contain *cherry wallpaper,* section B *raspberry wallpaper,* and section C *strawberry wallpaper*. Allocation of list to the three conditions was fully rotated across booklets. Order of the three conditions within booklets was also balanced. Each section of the booklet began with an instruction sheet as follows:

Fast condition: "Please read and complete as fast as you can, you have 4 minutes in total"

Control condition: "There is no time limit, please read and choose the most plausible interpretation"

Imagery condition: "Please take your time and form an image of each noun before you choose the most plausible interpretation. For example for encyclopedia writer imagine an encyclopedia and imagine a writer and then select your answer."

Each section of the booklet contained the list of 22 items with a 1- 5 scale for recording judgments. The scale was printed underneath two interpretations, one on the left and one to the right. One interpretation was a relation and one was based on a property. The scale ratings 1-2 and 4-5 were used to indicate that either the left or the right interpretation was more plausible or most plausible, with the middle value of 3 reserved for a judgment that the two interpretations were equally plausible. Half the property interpretations were placed on the left and half on the right, and order was randomized within each list. There was no time restriction in any condition.

Results

Participants preferred one or other of the interpretations (rather than selecting the middle value of 3) on 86% of trials, and this value did not change significantly with condition. Mean scale values were calculated for each participant and each item under each of the three instructional conditions. A preference for the plausibility of the relation interpretation was scored as a low number and a preference for the property interpretation was scored as a higher number while 3 was the centre of the scale. Means (and SD) were 2.86 (.59) for the Fast condition, 2.96 (.52) for the Control condition, and 3.31 (.50) for the Deep condition.

Neither the Fast nor the Control conditions showed any significant preference for the relation or the property interpretations (means not significantly different from 3), and nor did they differ significantly from each other. However the Imagery condition showed a significant preference for the property interpretation ($t(44) = 4.1$, $p < .001$). Repeated measures ANOVA by subjects and by items was conducted with one factor of condition. The main effect of condition was significant (Min F' $(2, 131) = 6.81$, $p < .005$), and post hoc comparisons confirmed that the mean rating for the Imagery condition was significantly greater than that for the other two conditions, which did not differ. Overall, 19 of the 22 sets, and 32 of the 45 participants had the highest mean rating in the Imagery condition.

When data just from the first condition presented were analyzed as a between-participants design, the interaction of condition and response was significant ($F(2,42) = 17.7$, $p < .001$), and the control condition differed significantly from both the others. Respectively, the Imagery condition had 11.4 property interpretations and 7.5 thematic, the Control 9.3 and 9.5, and the Fast condition 6.4 property and 13.1 thematic interpretations. It is therefore possible that the difference between the Fast and Control conditions in the main ANOVA was masked by carry-over strategy effects affecting the second and third conditions presented.

Discussion

Experiment 2 tested the generality of the findings from Experiment 1 by asking participants to select one of two interpretations for an ambiguous N-N phrase, rather than to generate their own. The results were broadly in line with the earlier effect. When asked to form images of the concepts involved there was a greater preference for the property interpretations, compared with either a speeded judgment or a standard condition with neutral instructions. It would appear therefore that both time pressure and imagery instructions were responsible for the effect observed in Experiment 1. It is notable that the preference for property interpretations was found even when cognitive load was reduced (comprehension rather than production), and when the instructions to imagine each concept in turn may have encouraged people to visualise relations between the items, rather than properties that could be transferred.

The preference for relation interpretation in the Fast condition was not significant overall, although it did appear when the Fast condition was presented first. Given that the relation interpretations were all plausible (pig house = a house for pigs), CARIN would have predicted that they would be the interpretation that was most easily arrived at. Note however that the materials for Experiment 2 were different from those in the earlier experiment. Note also that when the interpretations are *given* to the participant to read then different processes are most likely invoked in judging which is to be preferred. We hypothesize that the two interpretations were well balanced in the default case of the Control and Fast conditions, but that instructions to visualize the concepts led to a bias towards the property interpretation for reasons similar to the preference for generating property interpretations in Experiment 1.

It was particularly notable that the size of the effect in Experiment 2 was much smaller than in the first experiment. When participants had to generate their own interpretations, there was a much larger effect of instruction. This difference could be expected, given that a production task is likely to place a heavier cognitive load on the participant, and so be more sensitive to instructions.

General Discussion

Two accounts of conceptual combination for N-N combinations have been compared. The CARIN model

(Gagné, 2002) argues for a single process based on the retrieval and confirmation of an appropriate thematic relation. Only in the case that such a relation fails to be retrieved may people then turn to property interpretations, under the general relation of IS LIKE. Alternatively, Wisniewski and others have argued that property interpretations are generated by a separate independent process.

The results of our experiments favor the second of these two accounts. Given that under time pressure people are able to generate and choose relational interpretations just as readily as property interpretations, it is not clear why they should then show a marked preference for generating and selecting property interpretations rather than relation interpretations in the Deep/Imagery conditions.

Generating and comprehending property interpretations for NN combinations appears to be a more effortful process. Whereas the relations involved in interpretation are often quite general (for example CARIN proposes a limited set of 15 such relations), the property interpretations require more detailed information to be retrieved about the modifier category. Experiment 1 clearly indicated that where a relation interpretation exists, then the "first meaning that comes to mind" is more often a relation. However when given the time to consider the meaning of each noun in a more reflective mode, a strong preference was shown for generating a property relation.

Our results place new constraints on models of how N-N phrases are interpreted. They strongly suggest that there are strategic effects involved (in keeping with earlier demonstrations of priming effects on interpretation, Wisniewski & Love, 1998), and that a single process account is unlikely to capture the full range of observable phenomena.

Acknowledgments

The authors thank Zachary Estes, Christina Gagné, Gregory Murphy, and Edward Wisniewski, and members of the Cognitive Workshop at City University, London for discussion.

References

Costello, F. J., & Keane, M. T. (2001). Testing two theories of conceptual combination: Alignment versus diagnosticity in the comprehension and production of combined concepts. *Journal of Experimental Psychology: Learning, Memory, and Cognition, 27*, 255–271.

Estes, Z. (2003) Attributive and relational processes in nominal combination. *Journal of Memory and Language, 48*, 304-319.

Estes, Z., & Glucksberg, S. (2000). Interactive property attribution in concept combination. *Memory & Cognition, 28*, 28-34.

Gagné, C.L. (2000). Relation-based combinations versus property-based combinations: A test of the CARIN theory and the dual-process theory of conceptual combination. *Journal of Memory and Language, 42,* 365-389.

Gagné, C.L. (2002). The competition-among-relations-in-nominals theory of conceptual combination: implications for stimulus class formation and class expansion. *Journal of Experimental Analysis of Behavior, 78,* 551-565.

Gagné, C.L., & Shoben, E.J. (1997). Influence of thematic relations on the comprehension of modifier-noun combinations. *Journal of Experimental Psychology: Learning, Memory and Cognition, 23,* 71-87.

Gagné, C.L., & Shoben, E.J. (2002). Priming relations in ambiguous noun-noun combinations. *Memory & Cognition, 30,* 637-646.

Murphy, G.L. (1990). Noun phrase interpretation and conceptual combination. *Journal of Memory and Language, 29,* 259-288.

Wisniewski, E.J. (1996). Construal and similarity in conceptual combination. *Journal of Memory and Language, 35,* 434-453.

Wisniewski, E.J. (1997). When concepts combine. *Psychonomic Bulletin and Review, 4,* 167-183.

Wisniewski, E.J., & Love, B.C. (1998). Relations versus properties in conceptual combination. *Journal of Memory and Language, 38,* 177-202.

Wisniewski, E. J., & Middleton, E. L. (2002). Of bucket bowls and coffee cup bowls: Spatial alignment in conceptual combination. Journal of Memory and Language, 46, 1–23.

Appendix

1) Materials used in Experiment 1

Unambiguous Fillers

Butcher Surgeon	Grocery Bicycle
Razor Insult	Adultery Sermon

Ambiguous Targets

Cheetah Train	House Truck	Spider Chair	Porcupine Cushion
Skyscraper Plant	Fossil Book	Book Magazine	Rock Head
Ox Rope	Sheet Space	Strawberry Box	Ice Foot
Fox Puzzle	Snail Cart	Mule Manager	Butterfly Girl
Mouse Teacher	Feather Purse	Ant Vegetable	Elephant Boat
Oven Room	Pig Socks	Doughnut Table	Skunk Perfume
		Zebra Jeep	

2) Materials used in Experiment 2

Modifier 1	Modifier 2	Modifier 3	Head noun	Relation Interpretation	Property Interpretation
dung	skunk	trash	perfume	perfume used to cover dung odor	stinky perfume
tower	giraffe	skyscraper	tree	tree that looks like a tower	tall tree
frost	ice	snow	toe	toe covered by frost	cold toe
stick	sheet	paper	space	space for sticks	thin space
stove	fire	oven	room	room that the stove is in	hot room
pin	razor	knife	beak	bird's beak shaped like a pin	sharp beak
kitten	baby	child	shelf	shelf holding kitten ornaments	weak shelf
iron	rock	steel	doughnut	iron shaped like a doughnut	hard doughnut
mouse	rabbit	hare	teacher	person who teaches mice to perform at the circus	timid teacher
leopard	zebra	tiger	socks	therapeutic socks used on leopards	yellow and black spotted socks
quill	feather	cotton	purse	purse that holds quills	light purse
cherry	strawberry	raspberry	wallpaper	wallpaper with a cherry pattern	red wallpaper
cheetah	rocket	bullet	truck	special truck for transporting cheetahs	fast truck
snail	sloth	turtle	train	a line of snails marching closely	slow train
fox	dingo	wolf	holiday	holiday watching wild foxes	wild holiday
book	block	slab	magazine	magazine about books	thick magazine
octopus	arachnid	spider	table	table serving octopus	table with eight legs
dinosaur	antique	fossil	scientist	scientist who studies dinosaurs	very old scientist
hedgehog	cactus	porcupine	cushion	cushion with hedgehog design	prickly cushion
mule	bull	donkey	manager	person who is in charge of mules at a zoo/fair	stubborn manager
peacock	flower	butterfly	dress	dress with peacocks on it	pretty dress
pig	sow	hog	house	house for pigs	dirty house

Do Implicit Learning Abilities depend on the Type of Material to be processed? A Study on Children with and without Dyslexia

Aurélie Simoës (simoes@univ-tlse2.fr)
Laboratoire PDPS E.A. 1687, Université Toulouse le Mirail
5 allées Antonio-Machado, F-31000 Toulouse, FRANCE

Pierre Largy (largy@univ-tlse2.fr)
Laboratoire PDPS E.A. 1687, Université Toulouse le Mirail
5 allées Antonio-Machado, F-31000 Toulouse, FRANCE

Abstract

The aim of the present study was to examine the material's impact on implicit sequence learning abilities assessed by a Serial Reaction Time task (SRTt). In this study, we developed an SRTt in which the target varied in its linguistic characteristics. In a first experiment, 78 children, 8- and 10-year-old, all normal readers, were tested to assess the sequential learning variations according to the level of reading expertise. Our results show that implicit sequence learning is efficient in normal readers regardless of the type of target being tracked. Our results also show that, implicit learning aside, reaction-time performances during testing are influenced by the nature of the material being tracked by the younger children (i.e. 8-year olds). In the second experiment, we compared performance in the same SRTt of 12 dyslexic children and 39 reading age-matched controls. We wished to show that the nature of the target to be tracked affected implicit learning skills in dyslexic subjects. Our results don't allow us to confirm our hypothesis, as we show the dyslexics' inefficiency in implicit sequence learning regardless of the target-item type. Nevertheless, we emphasize the latter's differentiated treatment of the item, resulting in shorter reaction times while tracking a linguistic item.

Introduction

For about forty years, the research on implicit learning has developed in a lot of fields (sound effect, native language, reading, writing, motor skills...). However, whatever the field, implicit learning always presents two essential characteristics: the subjects are unaware of being in a learning situation; the knowledge is not fully accessible to consciousness, in that subjects cannot provide a verbal account of what they have learned (Seger, 1994).

Implicit Learning Tasks

Developing the artificial grammar task, Reber (1967, 1976) was a forerunner of these reflections. This paradigm has shown that, after having been confronted with strings of letters generated by an artificial grammar, participants were able to correctly identify new strings as grammatical. Thus the participants managed to judge the grammaticality of the string, in spite of the fact that they were not able to describe the rules of the grammar. Four paradigms of implicit learning have been created as a result of the first

publications of Reber (1967): artificial grammar learning (Reber, 1967, 1976), control of dynamic systems (Berry & Broadbent, 1984), covariation learning (Lewicki, Hill & Czyzewska, 1992) and SRTt (Nissen & Bullemer, 1987).

Currently, the SRT paradigm is the most used. In the experiment of Nissen and Bullemer (1987), two groups had to respond to a series of stimuli which appears at one of four localisations on a screen. As quickly as possible, the subjects had to press one of four keys which correspond to the position of stimulus. Once the response is given, the stimulus reappears in another location, and the subject's task is to respond again with the key assigned to the new location. One group tracked a series of stimuli appearing randomly, and a second group tracked a repeated pattern of stimuli. The results showed that reaction times in the second group (repeated sequences) declined faster than those of the first group (random sequences). The subjects in the second group learned a series of locations without being instructed to do so.

Implicit learning abilities have been investigated in numerous psychological or neuropsychological perspectives. For example, some studies examine Parkinson's disease (Siegert, Taylor, Weatherall, & Abernethy, 2006), Alzheimer's disease (Bozoki, Grossman, & Smith, 2006), amnesia (Meulemans & Van der Linden, 2003; Vandenberghe, Schmidt, Fery & Cleeremans, 2006) or schizophrenia (Exner, Boucsein, Degner, & Irle, 2006). In the same way, some research investigates linguistic disorders (Howard, Howard, Japikse & Eden, 2006; Kelly, Griffiths & Frith, 2002; Stoodley, Harrison & Stein, 2006; Vicari et al., 2003, 2005; Waber et al., 2003).

Studies on SRTt ascribe no little importance to the target to be tracked. This entails questioning whether implicit learning is a general process, regardless of the material involved, or whether it is sensitive to the nature of this material. In other words, in the SRTt, is implicit learning founded exclusively on the target's perceptual dimension or do its linguistic characteristics interfere with the process itself? A current debate concerns the nature of learning in an SRTt. According to some authors, implicit sequence learning is largely perceptive (e.g. Dennis, Howard & Howard, 2006; Howard, Mutter & Howard, 1992), for others it is essentially motor (e.g. Lungu et al., 2004). We propose to study the eventual impact of another type of process that would be of a linguistic order. Hence, we propose two means of testing this hypothesis: firstly with children from every walk, but having different levels of experience with the written word, and secondly, by comparing the performances of children who are normal readers with those of dyslexic children.

Implicit Sequence Learning and Development

Few studies on implicit learning have taken an interest in the child. However, the majority of them tend to confirm the postulate made by Reber (1993) according to whom the implicit learning process is unrelated to the subjects' age. This is the case of work done by Meulemans, Van der Linden and Perruchet (1998) that showed no age-related differences in implicit knowledge in 6- and 10-year-old children or by Thomas and Nelson (2001) who adapted this paradigm to 4-year-old children.

Implicit learning olds an important place in the child's acquisition of reading skills. The child is confronted by written language very early on. However, it's around age six, on entering first grade, that the child begins to acquire the rules governing this complex system. Acquisition of this skill requires the establishment of two types or learning: (1) formal learning, dispensed by an academic institution and which allows the child to interate the rules necessary for reading, such as the mastery of the alphabet system or the grapheme-phoneme conversion rules; (2) implicit learning that corresponds to language regularities acquired by the child even before entering school thanks to repeated encounters with the written system. Thus, even before learning to read, the child is able to distinguish a word from a non-word. The works of Pacton, Perruchet, Fayol and Cleeremans (2001) in this field have shown that from the very beginning of first grade, the child is sensitive to certain regularities in French spelling. These learning types (formal and implicit) are indispensable to the acquisition of written language. While the majority of children manage to acquire language regularities, a certain number of them have great difficulties when faced with the written word. These children are qualified as dyslexic.

Implicit Sequence Learning and Dyslexia

According to general consensus, developmental dyslexia is a linguistic disorder observed in children with normal or above average intelligence, normal visual and hearing acuity, normal and regular education, no neurological disorder and no socioeconomical problem. The prevalence varies across countries and languages.

Several causal hypotheses have attempted to explain this difficulty attaining fluent, rapid reading skills. Among them, the hypothesis of a visual deficit tends to consider why these subjects have difficulty when dealing with stimuli presenting a high temporal frequency but a low spatial frequency (Stein, 2003; Stein & Talcott, 1999; Stein, Talcott & Walsh, 2000; Stein & Walsh, 1997). It would also explain their difficulties in focusing their visual attention while reading (Cornelissen et al., 1998) and therefore, all the errors of the letter inversion type.

A second hypothesis concerns a cerebellum deficit in acquiring cognitive and motor skills (Nicolson & Fawcett, 1990). Dyslexics would be deficient in automation of cognitive and motor processes. Indeed, automation is essential to becoming an expert reader. Another hypothesis concerns a phonological deficit in dyslexics. Phonological processing is essential for reading development, and some authors suggest that a phonological deficit is present in all dyslexic cases (Ramus et al., 2003). It considers the existence of a deficit at the level of speech sound perception. This deficit would not concern non-linguistic stimuli.

Dyslexia is often approached from an explicit learning point of view (school learning). In this point of view, difficulties are akin to a phonological deficit in linguistic awareness. However, we know that a sensitivity to the morphology of oral words exists before the actual learning to read (Gombert, 2003).

Few studies using SRTt have been interested in implicit learning efficiency in developmental dyslexia. Moreover, these studies bring to light controversial results. Some of them show efficient implicit sequence learning in dyslexia (Kelly et al., 2002; Waber et al., 2003). Others do not (Howard et al., 2006; Stoodley et al., 2006; Vicari et al., 2003). In view of these studies, it is impossible to ascertain whether or not implicit sequence learning is efficient in subjects with reading disabilities. The discrepancies in results could be attributed to the following: (1) the nature of the populations studied (dyslexic children and adolescents, dyslexic adults or children who are poor readers), (2) the way in which matching was done (matching of dyslexics/non-dyslexics according to reading or chronological age) and (3) the nature of the items to be tracked (asterisk, different colored circles, image of a dog, etc.).

In our first experiment, we submit normal readers, having a two-year difference in experience with the written word (8-year olds [3rd year elementary] and 10-year olds [5th year elementary]), to an SRT paradigm by varying the more or less linguistic nature of the items to be tracked. The SRTt used in this experiment is an adaptation of the standard protocol (Nissen & Bullemer, 1987), in which random series and sequenced series are counterbalanced all through the testing. We wish to study, on the one hand, whether implicit sequence learning differ in function of the more or less linguistic nature of the items to be tracked and on the other hand, whether this eventual difference evolves with the two-year difference in experience with the written word. Confirming the results of Meulemans et al. (1998), we take as our hypothesis that implicit sequence learning is efficient in children regardless of age and level of experience with the written word (3rd and 5th year elementary). We wish to see whether implicit sequence learning varies jointly in function of the nature of the item to be tracked and the level of written-word experience.

In our second experiment, we compare the performances

of the two groups (dyslexics and normal readers) in the same SRTt. In doing so, we wish to contribute to the current debate on the efficiency or inefficiency of implicit sequence learning in dyslexics, and in addition, to characterize their sensibility to the more or less linguistic nature of the item to be tracked by comparing it with that of subjects who present no learning disabilities concerning the written word. In dyslexics, we take as our hypothesis that implicit sequence learning will be inefficient for non-linguistic items, thus confirming the work of Howard et al. (2006), Stoodley et al. (2005) and Vicari et al. (2003). We wish to observe what the situation with this population is concerning the case of linguistic type items.

Method

Participants

Experiment 1 Seventy-eight children participated in the experiment. Thirty-nine children (mean age: 8.4 years; 19 girls and 20 boys) were in the third year of elementary school and 39 children (mean age 10.6; 17 girls and 22 boys) were in fifth year elementary. All pupils were recruited from two different schools in Toulouse (France). Children were included in the study if the following criteria were met: (1) Satisfactory reading age (L'Alouette, Lefavrais, 1967), (2) Normal orthographic level (dictation of regular words, irregular words and non-words, Jacquier-Roux, Valdois & Zorman, 2002) and, (3) no evidence of visuo-attentional impairment (Test des cloches, Gauthier, Dehaut & Joanette, 1989).

Experiment 2 Twelve dyslexics participated in the experiment. All were right-handed and were French native speakers. The 12 dyslexic participants were recruited by the same speech therapy clinic at the Purpan hospital of Toulouse. Dyslexics were compared with 39 reading age-matched controls (Lefavrais, 1967). Background information on the subjects is presented in Table 2.

Design Four items were chosen according to their more or less linguistic nature : word "ami" [friend] ; non word "uco" ; letters "eee" and symbols "###". The entire protocol was broken down into 4 parts. Each part corresponded to an "item type". In each part, the child received 40 blocks of stimuli (in the form of 8 blocks repeated 5 times, with a pause of a few seconds between each series of 8 blocks). The series of 8 blocks was composed of an alternation of randomized blocks (R) and sequenced blocks (S): 6S + 6R + 6S + 6R + 6S + 6R + 6S + 6R. A randomized block corresponds to 6 successive appearances of the target item, but in a random pattern within the four squares. A sequenced block corresponds to 6 successive appearances of the target item but following a predefined order and answering to two criteria: (1) the stimulus cannot appear twice in the same square and (2) there are as many right-hand responses as there are left-hand ones.

Four types of sequenced series were constructed according to the same criteria and counterbalanced in function of the children on the four item types.

Table 1. Information on the subjects of experiment 2

	Dyslexic group	Control group	F
Chronological age (month)	124	100	7,5 *
Reading age (month)	96	98	4,4 ns

*= p<.001
ns= non significant

Protocol The child is seated facing the computer. He/she is asked to place his/her index and middle finger of each hand on the « response » keys and to leave them in position until the testing is completed. A first phase composed of 50 appearances of the target « ooo » precedes the experiment to familiarize the subject. The signal « Prêt? » [Ready?] appears on the screen at the beginning of the experiment, then before starting each series of 8 blocks. The target appears 250 ms after a key is pressed. The reaction time between the appearance of the target and the child's motor response on the keyboard is automatically recorded.

Results

Experiment 1

Our dependant variable is the reaction time (RT) per subject and per experimental condition, averaged within each of the 20 blocks. This data was analyzed via an ANOVA of 2 (group: 3rd year elementary; 5th year elementary) x 2 (condition: randomized; sequenced) x 4 (item: symbols [###]; letters [eee]; non word [uco]; word [ami]) x 20 (block) with repeating measures in the last 3 factors.

Three simple effects are significant, that of Group, $F(1, 6080)=814.63$, $p<0.001$ of Block $F(19, 6080)=2.21$, $p<0.002$, and of Item, $F(3, 6080)=4.05$, $p=0.007$. These factors being involved in various interactions, their effects will be described within this framework.

In concordance with the results of Meulemans et al. (1998), the interaction Group x Condition does not appear, $F<1$, ns. The Condition factor effect does not seem to make itself felt any differently in the 3rd year than in the 5th year elementary children. Similarly, the evolution of reaction times in the two groups of children does not significantly differ as testing proceeds: Group x Bloc, $F<1$, ns.

However, we observed an interaction between Condition and Block, $F(19, 6080) = 2.32$, $p<0.001$ (Figure 1). Classically, this result is interpreted as translating the presence of implicit sequence learning in the subjects.

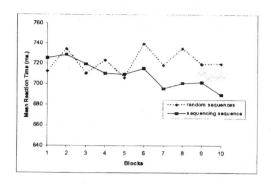

Figure 1. Mean reaction time as a function of block and condition (Block 1= block 1 and 2; Block 2 = block 3 and 4; Block 3 = block 5 and 6.).

The interaction Block x Item is significant, $F(57, 6080)=1.60$, $p<0.003$. As envisaged, the RTs evolve differently during testing according to the nature of the item to be tracked. This interaction proves to be also implicated in the double interaction Group x Block x Item, $F(57, 6080)=1.37$, $p<0.04$. This leads us, from now on, to pursue the analysis group by group; knowing that no other interaction reaches the conventional threshold of significance at .05 in the general analysis.

With the 3rd year elementary school children, the interaction Block x Item is significant, $F(57, 6080)=1.71$, $p<0.001$. As is seen in the straight-line regressions in Figure 2, the reaction times tend to decrease as testing proceeds for all the items, but this decrease appears to be more or less pronounced according to the nature of the item being tracked. An item by item analysis reveals that the Block factor effect is significant for the items « letters », $F(19,1520)=1.75$, $p<0.03$, « non word », $F(19,1520)=1.95$, $p=0.007$ and « word », $F(19,1520)=1.66$, $p<0.04$, but not for the item « symbols » $F<1$, ns. No other effect is significant concerning the analysis in 3rd-year elementary, $Fs<1$, ns.

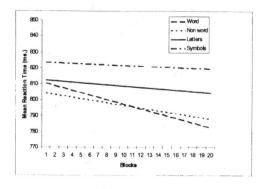

Figure 2. Straight-line regression per Item for 3rd grade primary school children

In 5th year elementary school children, the absence of interaction Block x Item, $F<1$, ns. would seem to indicate that the decreasing RTs as testing proceeds do not vary in function of the target item's nature. However, we observe a simple effect of the item, $F(3,6080)=8.93$, $p<0.001$, which shows that the reaction times are globally shorter with the items « word » 618 ms and « non word » 623 ms than with the items « symbol » 631 ms and « letters » 655 ms.

Experiment 2

We used a 2 (group: dyslexics; controls) x 2 (condition: random; sequencing) x 4 (item: word; non word; letters; symbols) x 20 (bock: 1-20) mixed design ANOVAs with repeated measures on the last three factors.

The analyse showed 2 single effects: Group, $F(1, 2081) = 12.75$, $p<0.001$ indicating dyslexics were faster than controls, and Item, $F(3, 2081) = 2.70$, p=0.044 indicating the serial reaction times moved around differently according to the item to track. There is no interaction between Group and Condition, $F<1$, ns.

We observed an interaction between Group and Item, $F(1, 2081) = 5.97$, $p<0.001$. This interaction showed reaction time differences between dyslexics and controls according to the item. This difference is explained when we made a group by group analysis. The effect of Group is attested by the reaction times that are globally shorter in dyslexic subjects (754 ms) than in control subjects (798 ms). However, the interaction shows that the observed differences in RTs between the two populations vary according to the nature of the item to be tracked (cf. Figure 3). Tested two by two, these differences only show up significantly for the items « letters », $t(2118)=8.81$, $p<0.01$ and « word », $t(2118)=4.55$, $p<0.001$.

In order to answer the question of whether or not implicit sequence learning exists in dyslexic subjects, we have pursued the analysis, focusing on this single population from this point on. To this end, we used a 2 (condition: random; sequenced) x 4 (item: symbols; letters; non word; word) x 20 (block: 1-20) ANOVA, with completely repeated measures.

No interaction reaches the conventional threshold of significance during this analysis. Only 2 simple effects proved significant, that of Block $F(19, 2081)=1.82$, $p<0.02$, and that of Item, $F(3, 2081)=9.1$, $p<0.001$. The effect of the Block factor on dyslexics translates a decrease in performances as testing proceeds, as manifested by a lengthening of reaction times. The Item factor effect reveals that the shortest reaction times are obtained with the item « word » (694 ms) and the longest with the item « symbols » (796 ms), the items « letters » (756 ms) and « non word » (772 ms) occupy an intermediary position (cf. Figure 3). The analysis on normal readers was already carried out in experiment 1.

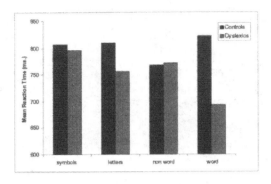

Figure 3. Mean Reaction Time per item and per group.

Discussion

Our study aimed to observe whether implicit sequence learning is sensitive to the linguistic nature of the material to be tracked in an SRTt. In order to reveal this sensitivity, two dimensions were retained: experience with the written word and learning disabilities.

In accordance with the results of Meulemans et al. (1998), our first experiment shows efficient implicit sequence learning in both 3rd- and 5th-year elementary children.

However, results don't allow us to conclude that this implicit sequence learning is manifested differently in function of the item type to be tracked, since the Block x Condition x Item interaction is not significant. The latter does not allow us to conclude that this learning is more particularly sensitive to the item type to be tracked in one of our two populations. Nevertheless, our data reveals that in an SRTt, the variation in RT during 20 successive blocks is sensitive to the interaction between the target's nature and the number of years of experience with the written word. In effect, our two groups differ as to their sensitivity to the type of item being tracked. As testing proceeded, only the children in 3rd year elementary presented an evolution in their RT which was sensitive to the nature of the target item. However, it is possible that this difference is not solely due to differences in reading expertise, since other maturational factors could also explain this difference. A new experiment with children of the same chronological age but with different reading expertise will be needed.

Our second experiment confirms the results of Vicari et al. (2003) showing the inefficiency of the implicit sequence learning in dyslexics. The originality of our second experiment resides in its demonstration that the absence of implicit sequence learning exists in this population, regardless of the nature of the item being tracked.

With the control group, the decrease in RT from block to block is particularly marked for the items « word », « non word », and « letters », but is not significant for the item « symbols ». This is not the case for the dyslexics, since the RT evolution is not sensitive to the more or less linguistic nature of the item being tracked. This result could be explained by the qualitative differences between our two groups, such as, a motor dysfunction in the dyslexics. If this were the case, we would have globally identical RT in this population, regardless of the nature of the item being tracked. In fact, we observe a general sensitivity to the item. It appears as significantly shorter RT when the item to be tracked is a word (all the more when familiar) than when symbols, letters or non words are involved. Even if these first results require confirmation, it seems difficult henceforth to study implicit sequence learning without questioning ourselves more precisely concerning the nature of the item to be tracked.

References

Berry, D.C. & Broadbent, D.E. (1984). On the relationship between task performance and associated verbalizable knowledge. *Quarterly Journal of Experimental Psychology, 36,* 209-231.

Bozoki, A., Grossman, M., & Smith, E.E. (2006). Can patients with Alzheimer's disease learn a category implicitly? *Neuropsychologia, 44*(5), 816-827.

Cornelissen, P. L., Hansen, P.C., Huitton, J.L., Evangelinou, U., Stein, J. F. (1998). Magnocellular Visual Function and Children's Single Word Reading. *Vision Research, 38*(3), 471-482.

Dennis, N. A., Howard, J.H., & Howard, D.V. (2006). Implicit sequence learning without motor sequencing in young and old adults. *Experimental Brain Research, 175,* 153-164.

Exner, C., Boucsein, K., Degner, D., & Irle, E. (2006). State-dependent implicit learning deficit in schizophrenia: Evidence from 20-month follow-up. *Psychiatry Research, 142*(1), 39-52.

Gauthier L., Dehaut F., Joanette Y. (1989). The bell test: a quantitative and qualitative test for visual neglect, *International Journal of Clinical Neuropsychology, 2,* 49-54.

Gombert, J-E. (2003). Implicit and Explicit Learning to Read: Implication as for Subtypes of Dyslexia. *Current Psychology Letters: Behaviour; Brain; and Cognition, 10.*

Howard, J.H., Howard, D.V., Japikse, K.C., Eden, G.F. (2006). Dyslexics are impaired on implicit higher-order sequence learning, but not on implicit spatial context learning. *Neuropsychologia, 44,* 1131-1144.

Howard, J. H., Mutter, S.A., & Howard D.V. (1992). Serial pattern learning by event observation. *Journal of Experimental Psychology: Learning, Memory, and Cognition, 18,* 1029-1039.

Jacquier-Roux, M., Vadois, S., Zorman, M. (2002). *ODEDYS.* IUFM, Académie de Grenoble.

Lefavrais, P. (1967). *Test de l'Alouette de P. Lefavrais.* Les Editions du Centre de Psychologie Appliquée, Paris.

Kelly, S. W., Griffiths, S., & Frith, U. (2002). Evidence for Implicit Sequence Learning in Dyslexia. *Dyslexia, 8*(1), 43-52.

Lewicki, P., Hill, T., & Czyzewska, M. (1997). Hidden covariation detection: A fundamental and ubiquitous phenomenon. *American Psychological Association, 23* (1), 221-228.

Lungu, O. V., Wachter, T., Liu, T., Willingham D.T., & Ashe, J. (2004). Probability detection mechanisms and motor learning. *Experimental Brain Research, 159*, 135-150.

Meulemans, T., & Van der Linden, M. (2003). Implicit learning of complex information in amnesia. *Brain and Cognition, 52*(2), 250-257

Meulemans, T., Van der Linden, M., & Perruchet, P. (1998). Implicit sequence learning in children. *Journal of experimental child psychology, 69*, 199-221.

Nicolson, R. I., & Fawcett, A.J. (1990). Automaticity: A new framework for dyslexia research? *Cognition, 35*(2), 159-182.

Nissen, M. J., & Bullemer, P. (1987). Attentional requirements of learning: Evidence from performance measures. *Cognitive Psychology, 19*, 1-32.

Pacton, S., Perruchet, P., Fayol, M., & Cleeremans, A. (2001). Implicit learning out of the lab: The case of orthographic regularities. *Journal of Experimental Psychology: General, 130*, 401-426.

Ramus, F., Rosen, S., Dakin, S. C., Day, B. L., Castellote, J. M., White, S., & Frith, U. (2003). Theories of developmental dyslexia: Insights from a multiple case study of dyslexic adults. *Brain, 126*, 841-865.

Reber, A. S. (1967). Implicit learning of artificial grammars. *Journal of Verbal Learning and Verbal Behaviour, 6*, 855-863.

Reber, A. S. (1976). Implicit learning of synthetic languages. *Journal of Experimental Psychology: Human Learning and Memory, 2*, 88-94.

Reber, A. S. (1993). *Implicit learning and tacit knowledge: an essay on the cognitive unconscious.* New York, NY, USA: Oxford University Press.

Seger, C. A. (1994). Implicit learning. *Psychological Bulletin, 115*, 163-196.

Siegert, R. J., Taylor, K. D., Weatherall, M., & Abernethy, D. A. (2006). Is Implicit Sequence Learning Impaired in Parkinson's Disease? A Meta-Analysis. *Neuropsychology, 20*(4).

Stein, J. (2003). Visual motion sensitivity and reading. *Neuropsychologia, 41*, 1785-1793.

Stein, J., & Talcott, J. (1999). Impaired neuronal timing in developmental dyslexia – the magnocellular hypothesis. *Dyslexia, 5*, 59-77.

Stein, J., Talcott, J., & Walsh, V. (2000). Controversy about the visual magnocellular deficit in developmental dyslexics. *Trends in Cognitive Sciences, 4*(6), 209-211.

Stein, J. F., & Walsh, V. (1997). To see but not to read; the magnocellular theory of dyslexia. *Trends in Neurosciences, 20*(4), 147-152.

Stoodley, C.J., Fawcett, A.J., Nicolson, R.I., Stein, J.F. (2005). Impaired balancing ability in dyslexic children. *Experimental Brain Research, 167*, 370-380.

Thomas, K. M., & Nelson, C. A. (2001). Serial reaction time learning in preschool- and school-age children.

Journal of Experimental Child Psychology, 79, 364–387.

Vandenberghe, M., Schmidt, N., Fery, P. & Cleeremans, A. (2006). Can amnesic patients learn without awareness? *Neuropsychologia, 44*(10), 1629-1641

Vicari, S., Marotta, L., Menghini, D., Molinari, M. & Petrosini, L. (2003). Implicit learning deficit in children with developmental dyslexia. *Neuropsychologia, 41*, 108-114.

Vicari, S., Finzi, A., Menghini, D., Marotta, L., Baldi, S., & Petrosini, L. (2005). Do children with developmental dyslexia have an implicit learning deficit? *Journal of neurology, neurosurgery and psychiatry, 76*, 1392-1397.

Waber, D. P., Marcus, D. J., Forbes, P. W., Bellinger, D. C., Weiler, M. D., Sorensen, L. G., & Curran, T. (2003). Motor sequence learning and reading ability: Is poor reading associated with sequencing deficits? *Journal of Experimental Child Psychology, 84*(4), 338-354.

Effects of Depression on Neurocognitive Performance in Different Stages of Parkinson's Disease.

Lambros Messinis (lambros@hellasnet.gr)
Epameinondas Lyros
Panagiotis Papathanasopoulos
Department of Neurology, Neuropsychology Unit, University of Patras Medical School

Abstract

Studies examining neurocognitive functions in Parkinson's disease have reported deficits mainly in explicit memory and executive functions due to dysfunctional frontal – striatal circuitry. The results concerning cognitive deficits observed in PD patients may, however, be influenced by affective changes such as depression, which appears to be the most frequent affective disorder in PD. The issue of the association between depression and neurocognitive functions is of special interest due to the strong relation between primary depressive symptoms and cognitive impairments, but this relationship in PD is far from clear at present. In the present study, the influence of depression on cognitive and speech performance in various stages of PD is examined. Our aim was to compare performance of PD patients with and without depression on cognitive and speech tasks and to assess possible effects of depression on cognitive and speech tasks in different stages of PD. In summary, the present results indicate that depressed mood may exacerbate cognitive and speech impairments and affective variables should be an integral part in the treatment of PD in all stages of the disease process, but especially in the later stages.

Keywords: Parkinson's disease (PD), depression, cognitive functions, memory, executive functions

Introduction

Parkinson's disease (PD) is a progressive neurological disorder characterized by tremor, rigidity, and slowness of movements, and is associated with progressive neuronal loss of the substantia nigra and other brain structures (Tolosa, Wenning & Poewe, 2006; Rektorova et al., 2005). Non-motor features, such as cognitive deficits and dementia, dysautonomia and other behavioural disturbances occur frequently, especially in advanced stages of the disease (Tolosa et al., 2006). The incidence and prevalence of associated dementia in PD depends on the method of investigation (Mindham & Hughes, 1993; Taylor & Saint-Cyr, 1991, 1995).

Several cognitive deficits can also be observed in non-demented patients with Parkinson's disease, even at the early stage of the disease, if appropriate and sensitive neuropsychological tests are used. These mainly include defective use of memory stores and executive functions in the form of a dysexecutive syndrome (Dubois & Pillion, 1997; Owen, 2004; Rektorova et al., 2005). In contrast, a more global impairment is less frequent and, in this latter case, the role of histological changes of cortical neurons, e.g., neurofibrillary tangles, is a matter of ongoing debate (Dubois & Pillion, 1997; Messinis & Antoniadis, 2001). Regarding the specific cognitive changes in PD, there is considerable evidence of visuospatial dysfunction, even when premorbid intelligence efficiency is preserved and the tests used require few motor components (Hovestadt, De Jong & Meerwaldt, 1987; Messinis & Antoniadis, 2001). The evidence as regards visuospatial dysfunctions relates these deficits to high cognitive demands e.g., set-shifting or forward planning capacity rather than actual visuospatial abilities (Dubois & Pillion, 1997; Messinis & Antoniadis, 2001). As regards memory functions, the storing and consolidation processes that are under the control of the temporal lobes appear to be preserved (Pillon et al., 1996). In contrast, explicit memory i.e. tasks that require temporal ordering or conditional associative learning is impaired (Dubois & Pillion, 1997; Messinis & Antoniadis, 2001). Executive functions, which are processes involved in the planning and allocation of attentional resources to ensure that goal-directed behaviour is initiated, maintained and monitored adequately to achieve goals are also significantly impaired (Owen, 2004). Several aspects of executive dysfunction have been shown to be extremely sensitive to the effects of controlled L-Dopa withdrawal, suggesting a predominantly dopaminergic substrate for the deficits observed (Owen, 2004).

Studies have also indicated that approximately 75-80% of PD patients have difficulties with speech and / or swallowing functions (Logeman, et al., 1978; Streifler & Hofman, 1984; Messinis & Antoniadis, 2001). The incidence and severity of speech problems (Hypokinetic Dysarthria) increases with PD disease progression (Johnson, 1990; Scott, 1995). Although the majority of studies have indicated impairments in all aspects of speech production, the most common impairments are observed in the areas of prosody, phonation and articulation (Logeman et al., 1978). More specifically, the clinical picture of hypokinetic dysarthria in PD involves: monotony of pitch and volume of voice, short rushes of speech, difficulty initiating speech, imprecise consonant production, disturbed respiratory support of speech, and typical pauses in speech production (Logeman et al., 1978; Scott, 1995).

Previous studies have further indicated that cognitive impairments are related to stage of disease progression in PD (Starkstein, 1989; Levin, 1989; Troster, 1995, Messinis & Antoniadis, 2001) and that these impairments may be associated with depression (Troster, 1995, Starkstein, 1990). Depression is accepted to be a frequent concomittant of PD and to occur with greater frequency in PD than in other chronic illnesses involving significant physical limitations (Troster et al., 1995). The influence of depression on cognitive functions in PD remains controversial, with several studies reporting greater severity of impairment in depressed than non depressed PD patients (Starkstein et al., 1990; Troster et al., 1995; Messinis & Antoniadis, 2001;

1

Uekermann et al., 2003), others have not (Biielauskas & Glantz, 1989; Taylor et al., 1988).

In the present study, the influence of depression on cognitive performance in various stages of PD is examined. Our aim is to compare performance of PD patients with and without depression on cognitive and speech tasks and to assess possible effects of depression on cognitive and speech tasks in different stages of PD. We also aim to determine whether cognitive and speech impairments in PD are related to the progression of the disease. These issues are of critical importance as depression seems to be associated with a faster progress of the disease progress in PD (Uekermann et al., 2003).

Methods

Participants

Forty four patients with PD were recruited from the outpatient neurology departments of the General Hospital of Larissa and the University Hospital of Patras in Greece. Patients were recruited from the above named institutions during a 12-month period preceding the presentation of this study. These patients were being evaluated and treated for PD. Diagnosis of PD was made by neurologists consulting at the above institutes based on a) the presence of an akineto-rigid syndrome and/ or resting tremor with asymmetric onset b) the exclusion of parkinsonian syndromes resulting from the chronic administration of neuroleptics, hydrocephalus, cerebrovascular disease and other neurodegenerative disorders e.g. progressive supranuclear palsy, dementia with Lewy bodies. Due to the varying definitions of diagnostic criteria in PD, neurologists in this study in an effort to minimize diagnostic inaccuracies, further made use of the clinical diagnostic criteria proposed by the UK Parkinson's Disease Society Brain Bunk (PDSBB) (Gobb, 1988; Soukoup et al., 1996) The above criteria have been shown to improve diagnostic accuracy by 82% (Soukoup et al., 1996). All patients satisfied the PDSBB criteria. Dementia was ruled out in all patients on the basis of the clinical neurological examination and the results of the Mini – Mental State Examination (MMSE, which were above 24/30 in every case) (Folstein et al., 1975). In order to achieve the objectives of the study, these patients were then divided into six groups, based on severity of PD symptoms and presence of depression. Stage of disease severity was determined using the Hoehn – Yahr Rating Scale. This scale has been used extensively in PD research to assess stage of severity (Soukoup et al., 1996; Starkstein, 1989). The scale grades severity of PD, using a five-stage classification, which reflects progressive levels of disability manifested during the course of the disease. In the present study, stage I and II, patients were considered as having minimal or mild functional impairments. i.e. symptomatic but not functionally disabled. Patients in stage III were considered moderately impaired and showed initial signs of significant progressive disability. Patients in stage IV had fully

developed clinical symptomatology i.e. rigidity and bradykinesia with tremor fluctuations. Stage V patients manifested severe impairments which adversely interfered with their motility and overall quality of life i.e. cachectic, wheel chair bound. Participants in Hoehn &Yahr stages 1 and 2 were considered as early stage PD patients, in stage 3 as middle stage PD patients and in stages 4 and 5 as late stage PD patients. Presence and severity of depression was established using the BDI (Beck Depression Inventory and the (HDRS) Hamilton Depression Rating Scale. DSM IV diagnostic criteria for major depressive disorder (major depression) and dysthymia -excluding the 2-year duration criteria (minor depression) were also utilized. The allocation of PD patients in to depressed and non-depressed groups from early, middle, and late stages was based on the BDI with a cut – off score < 10 (Leentjens, 2000), which has been demonstrated to be a valid diagnostic score for depression in PD. However, use of DSM - IV diagnostic criteria for depression, was still considered necessary in assessing depression in PD. The Hamilton Depression Rating Scale (HDRS) was further used with DSM - IV criteria to assess severity of depression in the patients (Hamilton, 1960). All patients were being treated for their parkinsonian symptoms with standard medications.

Measures

Beck Depression Inventory (BDI)

The BDI is a widely used and easily administered self-report psychometric instrument for assessing depression in various populations and settings. The full scale consists of 21 items, (scored from 0-3) making a maximum total score of 63. Studies of internal consistency and stability of the instrument indicate a high degree of reliability. Use of several reliability-testing paradigms (test re-test, split half and coefficient alpha) showed acceptable reliability (0.90, 0.84, and 0.91 respectively), for both clinical and nonclinical groups (Beck, 1987). The BDI has been used previously in assessing depression in PD patients (Troster, 1995). A Greek adapted version was utilized in this study.

Dysarthria Examination Battery (DEB)

Speech was assessed using the DEB. The DEB Yields, both quantitative and qualitative scores for dysarthric impairments in phonation, resonance, articulation, prosody and respiration. The DEB is composed of 23 tasks. These tasks provide 36 different measures - 21 measures allow for extraction of quantitative values and the remaining 15 utilize rating scales for response coding. The DEB has been used previously in assessing dysarthric impairments in PD patients (Drummond, 1993)

Halstead-Reitan Neuropsychological Battery (HRNB)

The HRNB has been used previously in the evaluation of patients with PD (Soukup & Adams, 1996). This battery has been demonstrated to be useful cross-culturally and appears to be able to identify cognitive impairments, without being affected by socio-cultural factors (Golden, Roraback & Pray, 1977; Faglioni, Saetti, & Botti, 2000). The battery is composed of various tests that assess performance across a wide spectrum of cognitive functions. The tests utilized for this study were: the category test (*concept function, abstraction, visual acuity*) the tactual performance test (*dexterity, tactual discrimination, spatial memory*) speech sounds perception test (*auditory discrimination, phonetic skills*) the finger – tapping test (*dexterity, motor speed*) trail making test (*visual motor perception, motor speed*).

Ravens Progressive Matrices

Ravens Progressive Matrices is a non-verbal assessment measure of the "eductive" component of general intelligence i.e. it measures fluid intelligence. It correlates highly with scores on other intelligence tests e.g. the Weschler scales (from 0.54 to 0.88). It is composed of 60 items, presented in 5 sets of twelve items of increasing difficulty. Reliability of the test has been established cross-culturally. It has been used previously to measure intelligence functioning level in PD patients (Raven & John, 1989)

Procedures

On initial recruitment all patients were assessed with the MMSE to exclude for dementia. The participants were assessed consecutively with the measures already mentioned above after written informed consent and a detailed explanation of the procedure. More specifically, the authors with the assistance of two clinical neuropsychologists and a speech pathologist assessed each patient on consecutive days with the neuropsychological test battery and the dysarthria examination battery. The tests were performed according to standardized published instructions. Patients were given time to rest when deemed necessary, but with at least 10-15 min. rest period between tests. All sessions were supervised by a physician - neurologist to ensure the general well being of the participants.

RESULTS

In the present study, a cross – sectional design was utilized. Data were analyzed using chi-square (X^2) tests and analysis of variance (ANOVA). Overall cognitive and speech performance were evaluated using multivariate analysis of variance (MANOVA) and post-hoc t-tests if a significant main effect was found

Comparison of Demographic characteristics

No significant differences were observed between the 6 groups with respect to gender distribution, ($X^2 = 2.25$, p= ns; mean age, p=ns; and mean education; p=ns. Significant between group differences were observed only as regards duration of illness F=8.09, p<. 001 (see Table 1)

Table 1: Demographic Characteristics for depressed and nondepressed groups in early, middle and late stages of Parkinson's disease (PD)

Variable	Early stage PD		Middle stage PD		Late stage PD	
	ED	END	MD	MND	LD	LND
Sex, Male (%)	54	56	52	49	57	48
Age (yrs)	65.5 (8.8)	60.3 (9.2)	67.1 (7.8)	66.2 (9.6)	65.5 (8.5)	69.4 (9.1)
*Illness duration (yrs)	5.95 (2.9)	5.10 (4.2)	10.4 (4.5)	7.55 (4.7)	12.9 (5.8)	12.5 (4.1)
Education	9.0 (2.0)	8.5 (1.8)	8.0 (1.15)	9.0 (0.95)	7.5 (1.32)	8.0 (2.5)

* p<. 05

ED= Early stage depressed group (*n* = 8); END= Early stage non-depressed group (*n* = 7); MD = Middle stage depressed group (*n* = 6); MND = Middle stage non-depressed group (*n* = 8); LD = Late stage depressed group (*n* = 8); LND = Late stage non- depressed group (*n* = 7)

Comparison of Cognitive Test Performance in Depressed and Non Depressed Groups across PD stages

The mean BDI score of the depressed groups in all stages was significantly higher than that of the non-depressed groups (p<. 05). The distribution of patients with minor and major depression between the groups did not differ significantly, (p<. 01). Patients in depressed groups showed significantly greater cognitive impairments than patients in non-depressed groups (p<. 05). Participants in late stage PD showed significantly more cognitive impairments compared to patients in Early and Middle stage PD (p<. 05) (see Table 2)

3

Comparison of Speech Performance using the Dysarthria Examination Battery (DEB)

Prosodic impairments were most profound in the late stage depressed PD group compared to the early and middle stage PD groups. Speech intelligibility impairments are most profound in late stage PD patients compared to middle and early stages, irrespective of the presence of depression. Phonetic impairments were most profound across all stages compared to articulatory and prosodic impairments (see Table 3)

Table 2: Mean Scores and Standard Deviations (in Parentheses) for depressed and nondepressed groups in early, middle and late stages of Parkinson's disease (PD) for the Halstead – Reitan Battery of Neuropsychological tests, Raven's Progressive Matrices, Beck Depression Inventory and the Hamilton Rating Scale

Test	Early stage PD		Middle stage PD		Late stage PD	
	ED	END	MD	MND	LD	LND
RPM	24.65 (1.42)	26.55 (1.92)	24.60 (1.78)	26.65 (1.94)	22.65 (1.14)	24.85 (1.68)
*BDI	21.0 (3.5)	9.5 (2.2)	18.0 (2.8)	8.0 (1.48)	26.0 (2.8)	8.5 (1.34)
*HDRS#	15.4 (3.7)	4.0 (1.3)	9.8 (2.40)	3.0 (1.1)	14.9 (2.0)	4.5 (2.4)
**Category # Test	90.8 (4.6)	85.3 (2.3)	91.6 (1.08)	83.7 (3.01)	97.2 (1.05)	93.4 (1.89)
*TPT Location #	2.8 (2.1)	3.2 (1.44)	2.4 (1.42)	3.6 (1.28)	1.5 (0.98)	2.2 (1.12)
*TPT Memory #	4.9 (1.15)	5.2 (1.06)	4.4 (1.48)	5.0 (0.85)	3.8 (1.7)	4.2 (1.41)
Speech Sounds Perception#	6.2 (2.6)	6.4 (2.2)	5.8 (1.12)	6.1 (1.15)	4.3 (2.13)	4.7 (1.42)
*Trails A (Sec) #	35.7 (2.89)	31.6 (2.54)	39.0 (4.24)	34.9 (3.8)	48.5 (4.7)	39.8 (5.1)
**Trails B (Sec) #	125.9 (8.23)	128.2 (6.21)	170.3 (8.60)	185.6 (8.30)	205.5 (2.37)	194.3 (3.85)

* p<.001; ** p<.05;

Note: # = Halstead – Reitan Battery of Neuropsychological Tests; RPM = Raven's Progressive Matrices; BDI = Beck Depression Inventory ; HDRS = Hamilton Depressive Rating Scale

ED= Early stage depressed group (n = 8); END= Early stage non-depressed group (n = 7); MD = Middle stage depressed group (n = 6); MND = Middle stage non-depressed group (n = 8); LD = Late stage depressed group (n = 8); LND = Late stage non- depressed group (n = 7)

Table 3: Mean Scores and Standard Deviations (in Parentheses) for the early, middle and late stages of Parkinson's disease (PD) groups on the Dysarthria Examination Battery (DEB)

Test	Early stage PD		Middle stage PD		Late stage PD	
	ED	END	MD	MND	LD	LND
Phonation *Pitch Range (Hz) F/M	150 /120	154 /131	142 /115	139 /113	138 /113	128 /110
Vocal Quality	3.9 (0.40)	3.88 (0.32)	3.6 (0.23)	3.7 (0.32)	3.1 (0.06)	3.7 (0.11)
Max. Phonation time:/ a/ (sec) F/M	32.5 (53.1)	37.8 (56.2)	29.9 (50.1)	33.2 (53.1)	27.6 (35.7)	29.1 (36.6)
Resonation Nasality (max 5)	4.9 (0.35)	4.8 (0.28)	4.3 (0.48)	4.1 (0.31)	3.9 (0.22)	3.0 (0.36)
Articulation Speech intelligibility %	89 (0.88)	86 (0.80)	80 (0.90)	78 (0.63)	64 (0.26)	68 (0.3)
Labial Movements (max 5)	4.6 (0.62)	4.4 (0.31)	4.5 (0.81)	4.2 (0.64)	4.0 (0.44)	4.3 (0.46)
Lingual movements: Non - Speech (max5)	4.0 (0.56)	4.3 (0.41)	3.8 (0.08)	4.2 (0.13)	3.3 (0.69)	3.8 (0.12)
Lingual movements: Speech (max5)	4.2 (0.78)	4.1 (0.17)	4.0 (0.61)	4.3 (0.58)	3.6 (0.24)	4.0 (0.37)
Prosody Stress and Intonation (Perception)	4.3 (0.79)	4.7 (0.81)	3.9 (0.44)	4.6 (0.51)	3.0 (0.19)	3.3 (0.13)

ED= Early stage depressed group (*n* = 8); END= Early stage non-depressed group (*n* = 7); MD = Middle stage depressed group (*n* = 6); MND = Middle stage non-depressed group (*n* = 8); LD = Late stage depressed group (*n* = 8); LND = Late stage non-depressed group (*n* = 7)

* Due to the differences in pitch ranges between Females and Males means for both are included

Discussion

Studies examining neurocognitive functions in Parkinson's disease have reported deficits mainly in explicit memory and executive functions due to dysfunctional frontal – striatal circuitry. The results concerning cognitive deficits observed in PD patients may, however, be influenced by affective changes such as depression, which appears to be the most frequent affective disorder in PD. The issue of the association between depression and neurocognitive functions is of special interest due to the strong relation between primary depressive symptoms and cognitive impairments, but this relationship in PD is far from clear at present.

Findings in the present study indicated that the frequency and severity of depression was higher in the early and late stages of disease, as compared to the middle stages. Participants with major depression showed significant cognitive impairments particularly in frontal lobe related executive functions and memory tasks as compared to participants with minor depression. In comparison, however, to non-depressed PD patients, patients with minor depression did not exhibit clinically significant cognitive deficits in memory related tasks. The finding that memory and executive dysfunctions are more profound in PD patients with depression compared to those without depression is consistent with findings of several prior studies (Rektorova, 1995; Starkstein, 1989; YoungJohn, 1992; Leentjens, 2004).

The above findings suggest that depression has an important effect on cognitive impairment particularly in the late stages of PD, implicating a probable interaction between the progression of PD and the effect of depression on cognitive functions. Depression probably affects severity, rather than pattern of cognitive impairment in PD.

Speech impairments were most profound in PD patients at the late stages of the disease, who were significantly inferior in their performance, compared to PD patients in the early stages, in tasks that assessed the prosodic, articulatory and phonatory aspects of speech.

The current findings have clinical implications for the management of PD patients. Specifically, they support the necessity for assessment of affective variables as an integral part in the treatment of PD in all stages of the disease process, but especially in the later stages.

REFERENCES

Beck, A.T. (1987). Beck *Depression Inventory*. San Antonio, TX: Psychological Corporation.

Drummond, S.S. (1993). *Dysarthria Exam Battery*. Tucson Arizona, Communication Skill Builders

Darley, F.L., Aronson, A.E., & Brown, J. R. (1975). *Motor Speech Disorders. Philadelphi*a: W.B. Saunders.

Dubois, B., & Pillion, B. (1997). Cognitive deficits in Parkinson's disease, *Journal of Neurology, 244*, 2-8.

Faglioni, P., Saetti, M.C., Botti, C (2000). Verbal learning Strategies in Parkinson's Disease, *Neuropsychology, 14*, 456-470.

Folstein, M.S., Folstein, S.E., & McHugh, P.R (1975). Mini-mental state: A practical method for grading the cognitive status of patients for the clinician, *Journal of Psychiatric Research, 12*,189-198

Golden, C.J., Roraback,J., Pray, S. (1977). Neuropsychological Evaluation in Remedial Education for the American Indian. *Journal of American Indian Education*, 16, (3).

Hamilton, M.A. (1960). A rating Scale for Depression. *Journal of Neurology, Neurosurgery and Psychiatry*, 23, 56-62.

Hovestadt, A., De Jong, G.J & Meerwaldt, J.D. (1987). Spatial disorientation as an early symptom of Parkinson's disease, *Neurology, 37*, 485-487.

Johnson, J.A., & Pring, T.R. (1990). Speech therapy and Parkinson's disease: A review and further data, *British Journal of Disorders of Communication, 25*, 183-194.

Leentjens, A.F.G., Verhey, F.R.J., Luigckx, G.J (2000). The validity of the Beck Depression Inventory as a screening and diagnostic instrument for depression in patients with Parkinson's disease, *Movement Disorders, 15*, 6,1221-1224.

Leentjens, A.F.G. (2004). Depression in Parkinsons Disease: Conceptual Issues and Clinical Challenges, *Journal of Geriatric Psychiatry and Neurology, 17*, 120-126.

Levin, B.E., Llabre, M,M., Weiner, W.J. (1989). Cognitive impairments associated with early Parkinson's disease. *Neurology, 39*, 557-561.

Levin, B.E., Tomer, R., & Rey, G. (1992). Cognitive impairments in Parkinson's disease, *Neurologic Clinics, 10*, (2) 471-485.

Logemann, J.A., Fisher, H.B., Boshes, B., & Blonsky, E.R. (1978). Frequency and co occurrence of vocal tract dysfunction in the speech of a large sample of Parkinson's patients, *Journal of Speech and Hearing Disorders, 43*, 47-57.

Ludlow, C.L., & Bassich, C.J. (1984). Relationships between perceptual ratings and acoustic measures of hypokinetic speech. In M.R. McNeil, J.C. Rosenbek & A.E. Aronson (Eds.), The *Dysarthrias: Psychology, acoustics, perception, management*, San Diego: College Hill Press.

Messinis, L & Antoniadis, G (2001). Cognitive and Speech impairments in different stages of Parkinson's disease. *International Symposium on Mental and Behavioral dysfunction in Movement Disorders*, Montreal, Canada.

5

Owen, A.M. (2004). Cognitive dysfunction in Parkinson's Disease: The Role of Frontostriatal Circuitry, *The Neuroscientist, 10*, 525-537.

Pillon, B., Ertle, S., Deweer, B., Sarazin, M., Agid, Y., Dubois, B. (1996). Memory for spatial location is affected in Parkinsons disease, *Neuropsychologia, 34*, 77-85.

Raven, J.C. & John, H. (1989). *Manual for Raven's Progressive Matrices and Vocabulary Scales: Research Supplement No.4*. London: H.K. Lewis.

Reitan, R.M., & Wolfson, D. (1985). *The Halstead Reitan Neuropsychological Test Battery*. Tuckson, A.Z: Neuropsychology Press

Reitan, R.M., & Wolfson, D. (1993). *The Halstead – Reitan Neuropsychological Test Battery* (2nd ed.). Tuckson, AZ: Neuropsychology Press.

Rektorova, I., Rektor, M., Bares, V., Dostal, E., Ehler, E., Fanfrdlova, Z., Fiedler, J., Klajblova, H., Kulistak, P.,

Ressner, P., Svatova, J., Urbanek, K., & Veliskova, J. (2005). Cognitive Performance in people with Parkinsons disease and mild or moderate depression: effects of dopamine agonists in an add-on to L-dopa therapy, *European Journal of Neurology, 12*, 9-15.

Scott, S., Caird, F.I., & Williams, B.O. (1995). *Communication in Parkinson's disease*. London: Groom Helm.

Soukup, V.M., & Adams, R.L (1996). Parkinson's Disease. In Russel L. Adams, Oscar A Parsons, Jan L. Culbertson, & Sara Jo Nixon (Eds). *Neuropsychology for Clinical Practice: Etiology, Assessment, and Treatment of Common Neurological Disorders*. American Psychological Association. Washington, D.C

Streifler, M., Hofman, S. (1984). Disorders of verbal expression in Parkinsonism. In R.G. Hassel & J.F. Christ (Eds). *Advances in Neurology, 40*, 385-393.

Starkstein, S.E., Bolduc, P, L., Preziosi, T.J., Robinson, R.G. (1989). Cognitive impairments in different stages of Parkinson's disease, *Journal of Neuropsychiatry and Clinical Neurosciences, 1*, 243-248.

Starkstein, S.E., Bethier, M.L., Bolduc, P.L Preziosi, T.J, Robinson, R.G. (1989). Depression in patients with early versus late Parkinson's disease, *Neurology, 39*, 1141-1445.

Starkstein, S.E., Bolduc, P.L., Mayberg, H.S., Preziosi, T.J, Robinson, R.G. (1990). Cognitive impairments and depression in Parkinson's disease: A follow – up study. *Journal of Neurology, Neurosurgery and Psychiatry, 53*, 597-602.

Taylor, A.E., Saint-Cyr, J.A. (1995). The Neuropsychology of Parkinson's Disease. *Brain and Cognition, 28*, 281-296.

Taylor, A.E., Saint-Cyr, J.A. (1991). Executive function. In S. Huber & J. Cummings (Eds.). *Parkinson's disease: Neurobehavioral aspects*. New York: Oxford University Press.

Tolosa, E., Wenning, G., & Poewe, W. (2006). The diagnosis of Parkinsons disease, *Lancet Neurology, 5*, 75-86.

Troster, A.L., Paolo, A.M., Lyons, K.E., Glatt, S.L., Hubble, J.P., Koller, W.C. (1995). The influence of depression on cognition in Parkinson's disease: a pattern of impairment distinguishing from Alzheimer's disease. *Neurology, 45*, 672-676.

Uekerman, J., Daum, I., Peters, S., Wiebel, B., Przuntek, H., Muller, T. (2003). Depressed Mood and executive dysfunction in early Parkinson's disease, *Acta Neurologica Scandanavia, 107*, 341-348.

Youngjohn, J.R., Beck, J., Jogerst, G., Caine, C. (1992). Neuropsychological impairment, depression, and Parkinson's disease, *Neuropsychology, 6*, 149-158

Consequences of genetically induced changes in neuronal morphology for information processing at the single neuron level

Nikos Green (Nikos.Green@gmail.com)
University of Amsterdam, Institute for interdisciplinary Studies, Track Cognitive Science
Amsterdam, The Netherlands

Ger J.A. Ramakers (G.Ramakers@nin.knaw.nl)
Neurons and Networks, Netherlands Institute for Neurosciences, Meibergdreef 33
1105 AZ Amsterdam ZO, The Netherlands

Abstract

To investigate how cognition arises from the brain, we make use of the causal relationship between mental retardation genes and IQ. Here we test the hypothesis that structural neuronal abnormalities in mental retardation cause deficient information processing. Quantitative morphological data from CA1 neurons in a genetic mouse model of mental retardation were used in the Neuron simulator to point out the consequences for information processing at the single neuron level. Several functional parameters were indeed changed, indicating the usefulness of computational approaches to better understand the relation between neuronal structure and cognition.

Genes and Cognition

Establishing the relationship between brain and cognition is one of the major challenges in modern day science. Clearly, the brain provides the infrastructure for cognitive behavior, but how does cognition arise from the neuronal circuitry of areas like cerebral cortex and hippocampus? Both IQ and brain structure are dependent on the interaction of genetic and environmental factors during development of the neuronal network. Or, as stated by Quartz and Sejnowski (1997): "The representational features of the cortex and the cognitive abilities are built from the dynamic interaction between neural growth mechanisms and environmentally derived neural activity".

To investigate the link between the neural level and cognition, we make use of genes that result in non-syndromic mental retardation when mutated. Non-syndromic mental retardation is characterized by a significantly lowered IQ (< 70) and problems in coping with every day life but without any non-cognitive 'side-effects'. The causal link between these genes and cognition establishes them as true cognition genes and the functions of the encoded proteins can be used to study the neurobiological basis of cognition. Clinical genetic research has revealed some 50 X-linked genes that can cause mental retardation (Ropers & Hamel, 2005; Raymond, 2005). A large number of these genes play a key role in the development of neuronal morphology and network connectivity (Ramakers, 2002; Dierssen & Ramakers, 2006). This is in agreement with the observation that many forms of MR are associated with structural brain abnormalities that will result in aberrant neuronal connectivity: reduced numbers of neurons, abnormal layering of the cerebral cortex and more subtle changes in dendritic complexity and altered spine morphology and densities (Kaufmann & Moser, 2000). Based on these findings a structural neuronal network hypothesis of MR was proposed, which states that all forms of MR are primarily due to abnormal neuronal connectivity, which subsequently results in deficient information processing Ramakers, 2002; Van Galen & Ramakers, 2005). This hypothesis specifically rules out physiological deficiencies as primary cause of MR, such as altered neurotransmission or action potential (AP) conductance.

One of the non-syndromic MR genes is ARHGEF6, which encodes the αPix protein. αPix shows a direct interaction with Rac1 and Cdc42, two members of the Rho GTPase family of signal transduction proteins (for details see Van Galen & Ramakers, 2005). Rho GTPases act as molecular switches that integrate a large range of extracellular and intracellular signals to subsequently coordinate the dynamics of the actin cytoskeleton (Luo, 2002). By modulating the actin cytoskeleton Rho GTPases control the outgrowth and branching of axons and dendrites and the formation of dendritic spines in response to a large range of extracellular messengers as well as electric activity. In this way Rho GTPases act as central regulators of neuronal morphogenesis and connectivity. It is not surprising therefore that mutations in genes that alter signaling through the Rho GTPase system are likely to change neuronal network formation (Ramakers, 2002). At least four MR genes encode proteins that are directly involved in Rho signaling, indicating the importance of this cellular signaling system for cognition. ARHGEF6 is one of these. Although it is not known if and how mutations in MR genes alter neuronal connectivity in humans, we have found that deletion of ARHGEF6 in mice leads to significant alterations in neuronal morphology and connectivity in area CA1 of the hippocampus Van Galen et al., in preparation). Deletion of αPix produces longer apical and basal dendrites (+30%), mainly because of increased branching, and a minor contribution of increased elongation. In addition, the density of adult type spines on the apical dendrites is increased by about 50%. Loss of αPix does not alter the number of pyramidal neurons in CA1. Since spine synapses represent the majority of excitatory synapses in hippocampus, area CA1 is characterized by a considerable overabundance of mature excitatory connections. As these spines are innervated by synaptic terminals of the Schaffer collaterals coming from area CA2, an 'overconnectivity' between the Schaffer collaterals and CA1 pyramidal neurons is clearly suggested in the αPix knock-out (KO) mouse.

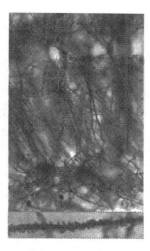

Figure 1: Reconstructed neuron with dendritic spines.

To test for functional consequences of the loss of αPix, Schaffer collaterals were stimulated at a high frequency to induce long-term potentiation (LTP). LTP is characterized by a long-lasting increase in synaptic efficacy, and is regarded as a physiological correlate of learning at the synaptic level. Whereas wild type (WT) mice showed an increase in synaptic efficacy of more than 100%, this rise was only half in the KO mouse. This indicates a considerable decrease in synaptic plasticity in the αPix KO mouse.

The reduced synaptic plasticity would predict that also learning performance, at least in paradigms dependent on hippocampus, should be impaired. This notion was tested in various behavioural tasks, including the Morris water maze and contextual fear conditioning. These tests measure spatial and contextual learning, which are both highly dependent on intact hippocampal function. Basal motor activity and anxiety were normal in the αPix KO mouse, whereas the acquisition phase in the water maze showed mild impairment. When the submerged platform in the water maze was relocated, it was found that the KO mice were less flexible in changing search strategy (impaired reversal learning). Contextual fear conditioning was also impaired, while auditory cued conditioning, which is in many ways similar to context conditioning, but independent of the hippocampus, was not altered. A cognitive flexibility task and a working memory task, which are dependent on prefrontal cortex, were not affected by the mutation, suggesting the learning impairments to be more or less specific for the hippocampus. In summary, loss of expression of αPix in mice results in excitatory

overconnectivity and reduced synaptic plasticity in area CA1 of the hippocampus and impaired hippocampus dependent learning, in particular learning that involves mental flexibility.

How are these phenomena related? A large body of evidence has led to the idea that LTP is the result of the insertion of excitatory AMPA receptors into the plasma membrane of the synaptic spine, which thereby becomes more efficient in generating postsynaptic currents. Insertion of AMPA receptors is associated with enlargement of the spine head. In this way induction of LTP leads to morphological and functional maturation of spines. Whereas immature spines are rather instable, but quite susceptible to LTP-induction, mature spines are stable and less responsive to LTP-induction. As loss of αPix resulted in a higher proportion of mature spines, induction of LTP was reduced. Evidence also supports the idea that mature spines represent stored memory traces, while immature spines represent structures ready for the acquisition of new memories. Our findings in the αPix KO mouse of reduced hippocampal learning, and in particular paradigms that require flexibility, are consistent with this view. The combined alterations in network connectivity and impaired learning are in support of our Structural Network Hypothesis of mental retardation (Ramakers, 2002, Van Galen & Ramakers, 2005). They show moreover that not only reduced connectivity, but also synaptic overconnectivity can result in cognitive impairment, at least in the mouse.

What are the functional consequences of the structural alterations in dendrites and spines observed in the αPix KO mouse? Since spine synapses are estimated to represent 80% of all excitatory synapses and are considered to be focal points of synaptic plasticity, it is likely that alterations in spine shape and number will affect interneuronal communication, synaptic plasticity and information processing. Given the complexity of just one synapse or one neuron, it seems impossible to answer these questions by experimental methods only.

Computational modeling may provide a useful solution to tackle the complexities of network structure and function, provided it is based on quantitative empirical data. Since neurodevelopmental disorders provide "atypical settings of (initial) neurocomputational parameters affecting the representational end-states that can be reached" (Karmiloff-Smith, Scerif & Thomas, 2002) the combined approach may be very productive. Computational studies have shown that alterations in dendritic geometry, in the absence of changes in membrane properties, can lead to considerable changes in single neuron firing patterns, indicating altered dendritic integration of inputs and single neuron information processing (Mainen & Senowski, 1996). Similarly, topological alterations (i.e. changes in dendritic branching pattern) also induce altered firing patterns (Van Ooyen et al., 2002).

In a first attempt to establish how structural alterations in neuronal networks may alter information processing, we focused on the effects of morphological changes for information processing at the single neuron level. Since neural network function relies on (synaptic) interactions between neurons with specific electrophysiological and morphological characteristics, we investigated to what extent deletion of the ARHGEF6 gene influences the functional abilities of single pyramidal neurons of the hippocampal area CA1. Our research question focuses on the functional difference between WT- and αPix KO cells. The simulations were performed in the NEURON simulator (Hines & Carnevale, 2001) to investigate synaptic integration and firing patterns. Simulations were based on previous studies (Mainen & Sejnowski, 1996; Graham, 2001; Senselab Database) with reconstructed CA1 pyramidal cells (N = 22, aged 12 weeks) from both animal (WT vs. KO) groups.

Results

Simulation 1

The first simulation analysed firing rate. A qualitative difference in firing type was not found. This result is as expected since the neurons are of the same cell class (CA1) and have a similar topological structure.

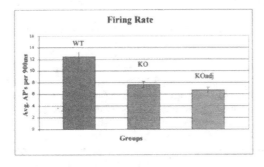

Figure 2: Firing Frequency.

Further analysis (Figure 2) revealed a significant quantitative difference in averaged mean firing rate between WT- and αPix-neurons (p = 0.045); for WT neurons it is considerably higher than for KO neurons. When the surface was adjusted for the increased number of spines reconstructed in the αPix neurons, the difference between WT neurons and αPix neurons increased (p = 0.018). The mean of action potentials was reduced in KO cells because a higher surface area (as found in KO- in contrast to WT neurons) leads to a higher signal decays at the soma (Koch & Segev, 1998). A correlation analysis revealed a negative correlation between surface area and average number of Action Potentials (r=-.912, p=0.01, 2 tailed).

Simulation 2

The second simulation tested the ability of neurons to integrate synaptic input from synapses located in the stratum radiatum, an area covering large proximal parts of the dendritic structure. Synapses were explicitly modelled in this simulation based on spine distribution estimations from the reconstruction of the used cells. Synapses were randomly distributed across the apical dendrites, activated with synchronous Action Potential and somatic Excitatory Post Synaptic Potentials (EPSP - depolarization of the soma and speed of depolarization) were measured (Figures 3 and 4).

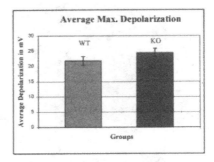

Figure 3: Avg. Max. Depolarization based on reconstructed spine numbers.

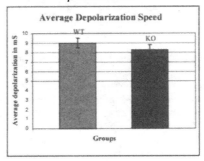

Figure 4: Depolarization speed based on reconstructed spine numbers.

When using the reconstructed number of spines for each group specifically average depolarization maxima and speeds are not significantly different in WT and KO neurons (Figure 3 and 4). However, our sample size is small and we also measured different spine distributions in other reconstructed neurons. Therefore we used equal numbers of synapses in a further simulation to highlight the effect of gross morphology. Results indicate a difference between WT and KO neurons. Both neuron groups follow similar patterns (Figure 5). The more synapses are activated the higher the peak of the somatic EPSP. However, both groups differ significantly in their peak depolarization amplitude. The αPix somatic EPSP's are lower than the WT somatic EPSP's due to a larger electrotonic length (spread of electrical signal constrained by attenuation). The speed of the somatic EPSP's shows that WT neurons are slower in reaching their peak compared to KO neurons (p=. 001). An interesting result is that the pattern for each group is different. In the αPix group the maximum amplitude is reached at later stages the more synapses are activated. The WT group only shows this pattern for the first two conditions (100 and 200 synapses). For 300 synapses the speed was reduced. The speed of the somatic EPSP's revealed that WT neurons were slower in reaching their peak (p=. 001). In this case (same number of synapses) the difference is due to the difference in gross morphology that results in distinct passive properties.

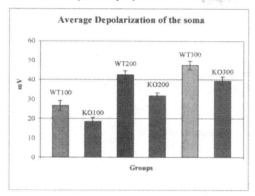

Figure 5: Depolarization maxima with equal #spines.

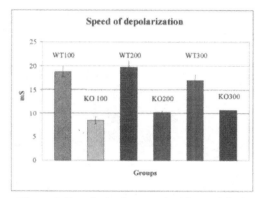

Figure 6: Depolarization speed with equal #spines.

Conclusion

Studying the relationship between network structure, connectivity and information processing at the network level is a vast enterprise that may be extremely difficult to accomplish by experimental methods. In the end, computational approaches, based on quantitative data taken from the same biological model system, may be te only way to resolve this issue. As shown by several authors, morphological parameters can strongly affect signal transfer in dendrites (Mainen & Sejnowski, 1996); Koch &Segev, 1998). Here, we studied the effects of genetically induced altered morphology on information processing in single cells, using fairly simple computational models. The purpose of these modeling attempts was to assess whether WT and KO neurons differ also functionally as a consequence of the morphological alterations. The results show that gross neuronal morphology (length, branching,

surface area) has considerable impact on firing frequency. Our results let us conclude that input is processed differently in WT cells than in KO cells. This is expressed as differences in magnitude and timing of electrical events for the cell groups using the same simulation conditions. Although our findings are at the single cell level, they provide support for the Structural Network hypothesis. Obviously, a large gap remains between single neuron findings and cognition at the organismal level. However, insertion of findings at the single neuron level into higher level network models (e.g. Talamini et al., 2005; Samsonovich & Ascoli, 2005), that simulate information processes such as memory consolidation and spatial navigation, would be a natural step to further bridge this gap. A third simulation that tests the effect of dendritic morphology on backpropagation is in progress and tetrode recordings from single neurons in area CA1 of behaving mice are planned. If our Network hypothesis of MR is true, than counteracting or preventing cognitive impairment in MR would require altering (correcting) the neuronal circuitry itself. To enable such interventions a thorough understanding of the relationship between cause, neural architecture and information processing would be a necessity. In addition, we would have to know more about the developmental trajectory and its deviations in MR. As such information is very difficult to come by, at least at the cellular and network level in humans, we will have to rely on findings in animal models and their extrapolation to humans. Understanding the neurobiological basis of MR will also contribute to our understanding of the neurodevelopmental processes that shape cognition in the normal population.

Acknowledgments

We would like to thank the Neurons and Networks Group and the Institute for Interdisciplinary Studies in Amsterdam, Elly van Galen, Anne Doggenaar, Michiel Remme, Joop van Heerikhuize and Koos de Vos for their help.

References

Carnevale N.T. & Hines M.L. The NEURON Book, *Prepublished version obtained form the Neuron Workshop*

Dierssen M. & Ramakers G.J. (2006). Dendritic pathology in mental retardation: from molecular genetics to neurobiology. *Genes Brain Behav. 5 Suppl. 2.* 48-60.

van Galen E. J. & Ramakers G. J. (2005). Rho proteins, mental retardation and the neurobiological basis of Intelligence. *Prog. Brain Res., 147,* 295-317.

Graham B.P. (2001). Pattern recognition in a compartmental model of a CA1 pyramidal neuron. *Network. 12(4),*473-92

Hines M. L. & Carnevale N. T. (2001). NEURON: a tool for neuroscientists. *Neuroscientist. 7 (2),* 123-35.

Karmiloff-Smith A. & Scerif G. & Thomas M. (2002). Different approaches to relating genotype to phenotype in developmental disorders. *Dev. Psychobiol. Apr., 40(3),* 311-22.

Karmiloff-Smith A. & Thomas M. (2003). What can developmental disorders tell us about the neurocomputational constraints that shape development? The case of Williams syndrome. *Dev. Psychopathol. 15(4)*, 969-90.

Kaufmann W.E. & Moser H. W. (2000). Dendritic anomalies in disorders associated with mental retardation. *Cereb. Cortex, 10(10)*, 981-91.

Koch C. & Segev I (1998). Methods in Neuronal Modeling: From Ions to Networks, 2-nd edition. *MIT Press, Cambridge, MA.*

Luo L. (2002). Actin cytoskeleton regulation in neuronal morphogenesis and structural plasticity. *Annu. Rev. Cell. Dev. Biol. 18*, 601-35.

Mainen Z. F. & Sejnowski T. J. (1996). Influence of dendritic structure on firing pattern in model neocortical neurons. *Nature. 382(6589)*, 363-6.

van Ooyen A. & Duijnhouwer J. & Remme M. W. & van Pelt J. (2002). The effect of dendritic topology on firing patterns in model neurons. *Network, 13(3)*, 311-25.

Poirazi P. & Brannon T. & Mel B.W. (2003) Arithmetic of subthreshold synaptic summation in a model CA1 pyramidal cell. *Neuron. 37(6)*, 977-87.

Quartz S. R. & Sejnowski T. J. (1997). The neural basis of cognitive development: a constructivist manifesto. *Behav Brain Sci.*, 20(4), 537-56, discussion 556-96.

Ramakers G. J. (2002). Rho proteins, mental retardation and the cellular basis of cognition. *Trends Neurosci., 25(4)*, 191-9.

Raymond F.L. (2006). X linked mental retardation: a clinical guide. *Journal Med. Genet.43(3)*, 193-200.

Ropers H.H, & Hamel B.C. (2005). X-linked mental retardation. *Nat. Rev. Genet. 6(1)*. 46-57.

Samsonovich A.V. & Ascoli G.A.(2005) A simple neural network model of the hippocampus suggesting its pathfinding role in episodic memory retrieval. *Learn Mem. 12(2)*, 193-208.

Scerif G. & Karmiloff-Smith A.(2005). The dawn of cognitive genetics? Crucial developmental caveats. *Trends in Cognitive Science,* 9(3),126-35.

Senselab Database *http://senselab.med.yale.edu/senselab/*

Talamini L.M. & Meeter M. & Elvevag B. & Murre J.M. & Goldberg T.E. (2005). Reduced parahippocampal connectivity produces schizophrenia-like memory deficits in simulated neural circuits with reduced parahippocampal connectivity. *Arch Gen Psychiatry 62(5)*, 485-93.

Brain Correlates of Syllable and Non-Syllable-Based Word Parsing

Javier S. Sainz (JSAINZ@Psi.Ucm.Es)
Psycholinguistic Research Unit, Department of Cognitive Processes,
Universidad Complutense de Madrid, Madrid 28223, Spain
Rubén García-Zurdo (RGARCIA-ZURDO@Psi.Ucm.Es)
Department of Psychology
Cardenal Cisneros University College, Madrid 28006, Spain

Summary

A simulation of the orthotactic structure of Spanish is run by using a RNN. Stimuli are selected according to this simulation and two ERP experiments are carried out to test the role played by syllable- and non-syllable-based word parsing. Readers have to decide on whether a letter string contains a word (1st Experiment) or whether a letter string constitutes a word (2nd Experiment). According to the hypothesis that assigns no role to syllable units, readers are expected to base their lexical decisions exclusively upon letter sequence probabilities, regardless of whether or not the sequence constitutes a legal syllable. Results show processing of letter sequence probabilities much earlier than of syllable units, but syllables seem to play a role when, with enough attention, letter sequences have access to lexical entry cues.

Competing mechanisms of word parsing

What role does orthotactic regularity play in word reading? In transparent languages, of which Spanish is considered an example, are syllable-based regularities the only key to lexical access? The identification of a word entry is the result of a forced selection process, which by default selects the entry that best matches the available cues. This probabilistic approach means that the lexical selection of an entry depends on cues which distinguish it from competing lexical entries. Is syllable parsing required for word identification?

Recent studies using the forward masking paradigm have shed light on the role of the syllable in word reading in English and Dutch (Schiller, 2000; 2004), in French (Ferrand, Segui, & Grainger, 1996; Ferrand, Segui, & Humphreys, 1997) and in Spanish (Carreiras, Vergara, & Barber, 2005). In Levelt's speech production model (Cholin, Schiller, & Levelt, 2004), it is assumed that syllables are the basic components of articulation. Using different phonosyllabic structures, Cholin et al. (2004) provide evidence that Dutch speakers use the syllable as a processing unit, facilitating speech production.

No matter how strong the evidence may seem for a syllabic priming effect on words, there is data to support the idea that the priming effect is not exclusively syllable-based. For the syllable to be treated as the key linguistic processing unit, we need to confirm that syllabic segmentation is mandatory and reject other theoretical alternatives.

Neither theoretical analysis nor empirical data entirely support a strong version of the hypothesis: the syllable as a mandatory, unique linguistic processing unit. Three kinds of evidence call into question the syllable's role in the process: a) cross-linguistic evidence which reveals that the syllable does not constitute a language processing unit in some languages; the syllable may be a processing unit for languages whose structure features "clearly defined syllable boundaries", such that syllables act as "functional sublexical units of visual word recognition" (Barber, Vergara, & Carreiras, 2004, p. 547). The syllable may or may not coexist with other units of segmentation. These features need not be primitives, and may be phonological/orthographic -e.g. syllable and mora in Japanese- or morphonological -e.g. in Chinese script, where each syllable corresponds to a morpheme, or in modern Korean orthography (Perfetti, 2003). The syllable may be an articulatory motor unit and not strictly speaking have a unique representational status in word segmentation. b) The evidence from non-syllabic priming which reveals that other units of segmentation may serve as efficient primers of a lexical sequence. Pollatsek, Perea, & Carreiras (2005) provide evidence of a phonological priming effect associated with Stimulus Onset Asynchrony (SOA) of 66ms. but not 50ms., with the phonological realization of the same phoneme in both prime and primed word, i.e. cinal-CANAL vs. Conal-CANAL in lexical decision tasks. This piece of empirical data suggests a similarity to the syllabic priming effect. Other alternative units of segmentation such as the syllable head and coda, or the onset and rhyme seem to play an undisputable role in the processing of other languages, though their effect is not the same in all of them (Perfetti, 2003). c) The evidence from non-segmental non-syllabic priming which reveals that priming does not always occur between parsed units and lexical entries; e.g. in the pseudohomophone effect we can observe non-segmental phonological priming of a lexical entry by a pseudoword which evokes the same acoustic image with a different spelling; in the priming effect on presentation of a lexical sequence where the original letter order was transposed from the lexical entry it primes for (Perea & Lupker, 2004); in the effect of recombining letters in anagrams which involves a lexical conflict between the word evoked by the prime and other entries sharing the same letters in a different order (Sainz, 2006).

The syllable may be a primitive, basic processing unit which later comes into conflict with processing units from different levels of linguistic composition, but it is not clear that this constitutes an early, unique and mandatory linguistic processing mechanism. Carreiras et al. (2005) report two experiments in Spanish taking evoked potentials, which add weight to the idea that the syllable is a syllabic processing unit in low frequency words but not in high frequency words. The high frequency words access the lexicon without any need for syllabic breakdown. This effect is observed in an early component (P200) -the time window when the stimulus is classified previous to the observation of later N400 lexical effects. Whilst the data in Spanish raise some doubt about the role of the syllable at an early stage, other studies show that the syllable may not be a mandatory processing unit. The syllabic segmentation of a word may be the result of an optional process (Carreiras et al., 2005), an adaptive, flexible process (Goswami, Ziegler, Dalton, & Schneider, 2003), may compete with other units of processing during access, or not compete (Carreiras et al, 2005), and/or may be the result of some strategic or attentional process (Brand, Rey, & Peereman, 2003; Schiller, 2000; 2004). Evidence for syllabic units in spoken word recognition is more easily obtained in syllable-timed languages such as French than in stress-timed languages such as English or Dutch. The strength of the lexical effects in phonological processing can be modulated by attention (Norris, McQueen, & Cutler, 2000). The allocation of attentional resources is not homogeneous for all stimulus tasks and situations; Rees and Lavie (deFockert, Rees, Frith, & Lavie, 2004) indicate that the processing of irrelevant stimuli depends on whether the relevant task leaves attentional resources free, and on the structural similarity between target and potential distracter. Norris et al. (2000) have suggested that the absence of a role for attention is the true Achilles' heel of the interactive word recognition model.

Three experiments were carried out in French by Brand et al. (2003), systematically replicating the studies of Ferrand et al. (1996, 1997). In the word BALANCE, the syllable boundary falls neither clearly before nor clearly after the L because this intervocalic consonant is permissible in both word-initial and word-final positions. In Ferrand, et al.' studies, CVC and CV primes were equally effective, and these results were thus compatible with the Syllable Hypothesis. Brand et al. (2003), however, failed to replicate these findings in French, finding no trace of a significant interaction between Target Type and Syllabic Priming Type. Schiller' masked priming studies (2000; 2004) failed to show the critical syllable priming effect in both Dutch and English. Interestingly, Schiller has found that CVC primes always yielded shorter naming latencies than CV primes, whatever the syllabic structure of the target word -an overlap effect.

The role of pattern similarity in syllabic priming

At a purely conceptual level, studies aiming to test the hypothesis that the syllable is a linguistic processing unit manipulate the similarity between patterns. Analyzing the similarity between two patterns, a syllable and the word it primes for, should help to find an explanation for the empirical research that favors the role of the syllable as processing unit and the empirical research that seems to question this. On its own the similarity hypothesis would not explain why Ferrand et al. found a syllabic priming effect in French, using exactly the same materials with which Brand, Rey, & Peereman (2003) found no effect, but it may resolve much of the contradictory evidence and pinpoint the role of attention in the process.

The evidence against the role of the syllable is congruent with Seidenberg's hypothesis (Seidenberg, 1987) that the syllabic priming effect in alphabetic languages is a special case of the associative frequency of series of letters. The syllable effect may result from the similarity between the pattern processed and the structure of the patterns it evokes in the lexicon. This is the hypothesis in the present study. The ability of the participant to discern the segmental composition of the candidate lexical patterns depends on the frequency of combination of its letters in the lexicon and the attentional resources required to discriminate between a lexical entry and its competing candidates.The stimulus material is carefully constructed by computing first letter transition probability. The transition probability of letter sequences is simulated with a RNN. The material is later constructed generating patterns that satisfy the requirements of the design. The methodological control of the experimental material plays a decisive role in this study.

In the following experiments, readers have to decide on whether a letter string contains a word (1st Experiment) or whether a letter string constitutes a word (2nd Experiment). We would expect that, wherever possible, readers would base their decisions exclusively upon letter sequence probabilities, regardless of whether or not the sequence constitutes a legal syllable. According to this hypothesis it should be expected that the higher letter sequence probability prevails over the lower letter sequence probability, with no role for syllable-based parsing of words. The role of attention in the process is studied by registering electrical brain activity while performing the task.

Recurrent Neural Network Simulation

Artificial neural networks (ANN) are computational models of the human brain which are eventually capable of simulating cognitive processing (Rumelhart & McClelland, 1986). Figure 1 depicts Elman's (1990) RNN, an ANN endowed with internal memory: it features a connection between the hidden layer and context layer that keeps track of past events; hidden layer information backpropagates to the context layer, actually a part of the input layer.

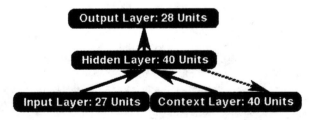

Fig.1: A Recurrent Neural Network: Structural parameters.

A simple recurrent neural network can simulate the lexical selection process in reading by taking into account solely orthotactic regularities present in the lexicon. During training, a word is presented to the RNN one letter at a time; the hidden layer accumulates knowledge about sequences of letters from a lexical corpus. The letter following the current input letter is the current successor, which the network should predict, giving this as its output. A training error is defined as the difference between the desired and the current output activation for each neuron. This error is used by the training algorithm to adjust connection weights. The RNN's ability to simulate lexical selection in word recognition derives from the way it reproduces the structural similarity of lexical entries. In this study, a RNN is being used to control for letter-by-letter transition probability, and to shed light on how the reader recognizes a word embedded in a letter string (Experiment I) or when two letter strings are to be blended to spark lexical access (Experiment II).

Modelling orthotactic structure with RNNs

Learning orthotactics means learning symbol order. An Elman's RNN with BPTT was trained to predict structural graphemic regularities of Spanish at the output layer using the LEXESP corpus (Sebastián, Cuetos, Martí, & Carreiras, 2000), well-suited to the purpose of this study, comprising 2,000,000 words and 90,000 different lexical entries.

The words were presented to the network, one letter at a time. All characters were orthogonally encoded in a vector of length 27 plus the end-of-word character '#'. The vectors are encoded with value 0 at all positions except that of the character's place in the alphabet, which is set to 1. The learning process was organized in epochs. In each epoch, all words from a block were presented to the network. 270,000 random trials of the LEXESP corpus's 90,000 words were presented to the RNN. Every word in the lexicon is randomly presented to the RNN but the frequency of a word's appearance in an epoch is proportional to the logarithm of its frequency in the lexicon. The linguistic corpus was first cleaned up to remove foreign words, since they do not reflect typical Spanish orthotactics. The simulation was aimed at selecting appropriate stimuli for the following experiments.

If training words are presented to the network in order of frequency, the more frequent initial symbol sequences are heavily weighted. To avoid primacy effects on the initial segments and balance every position, each sequence is weighted according to its position as suggested by Moscoso del Prado Martin, Schreuder, & Baayen (2004). LENS software (Rohde, 1999) was used to run all simulations. The following network parameters, Learning Rate: 0.1; Moment: 0.9; Weight Decay: 0; and Cross Entropy, were adopted.

To measure how well a trained RNN learnt the orthotactics of Spanish, the likelihood that any symbol follows in the current context was assessed according to word length, word frequency, neighborhood-lexical-density –number of lexical neighbors differing in one letter from a given target- and word-string lexical status. These variables were taken to measure the sensitivity of a RNN to represent orthotactic regularities of the Spanish lexicon. Samples of 100 words and pseudowords per condition were constructed to test for these effects.

Results and Discussion

The Pearson correlation between input and output patterns reveals significant differences for lexical status: word (.94), pseudoword (.93), and nonword (.90) (F(1,99)= 90.434. p< 0.001, MSe = 0.002); and for string length: long (.96), short (.89) (F(1,99)= 811.375, p< 0.001, MSe= 0.000). Neighborhood Density (N) and Frequency (F) Effects are also significant. The correlation between output and input patterns for High N is .93 and for Low N is .95, (F(1,99) = 143.006, p< 0.001, MSe=0.000). The correlation between output and input patterns for both High F (.94) and Low F approaches (.92), is significant (F(1,99) = 6.835, p< 0.005, MSe=0.001). These small differences are still significant due to the number of words presented. All these significant correlations express the ability of a RNN to distinguish between legal and non-legal lexical entries, and among those lexical entries that differ each other according to the main properties that configure a language. These results endorse the use of a RNN to select stimuli according to letter sequence transition probabilities as predicted by a RNN after training (see also Moscoso del Prado Martin, et als., 2004).

I Experiment

If Spanish were an entirely syllable-based lexical system, no letter sequence information other than syllables should affect recognition of a word when embedded in a nonword string. To compute word similarity, it seems the two parsing mechanisms (syllable- and non-syllable-based) cannot be mutually exclusive. Here we are testing whether syllable-based word subunits are the sole information needed to compute lexical similarity in Spanish.

Methodology

Using SuperLab software (Cedrus Corporation, 2006), 18 Spanish-native readers (11 women; 7 men of 21,6 years-old in average) were serially presented with two postmasked word fragments: a legal syllable primer (i.e. "dis") and a letter-string containing that primer (i.e "plomo" –lead). The entire letter sequence was always a pseudoword (i.e. "displomo"), which in only half the trials contained a word. These words were embedded in longer patterns with sequences controlled for letter transition probability (i.e. "s-p"). While their brain activity was recorded using a 32 electrode cap and a BrainVision Recording System endowed of 32 electrodes, readers were asked to make a lexical decision on whether a word was embedded in a letter string. Syllable primers and words were generated from the LEXESP corpus and selected, after blending both fragments, according to letter transition probability (LTP: sequential probability of the combination of the last letter of the prime and initial letter of the word candidate as predicted by the simulation) and Syllable Transition Probability (STP: syllable primer frequency, according to LEXESP). Words (W) were drawn from the LEXESP corpus; Pseudowords (P) were constructed by changing a letter in the selected words.

Cross-trial average ERPs elicited by the stimuli were computed for each participant, and then averaged across subjects for every combination of Letter Transition Probability, Syllable Transition Probability, and Lexical

Status (W, P). Word Frequency and Neighborhood Lexical Density were also controlled. The average amplitude in the 300 ms preprobe interval was used as the baseline, the interval in which no stimulus is being presented before a new trial. The averaged brain activity across all the electrodes was taken as reference. The time epoch extended from 300 ms prior to the probe onset to the end of the response interval, 600 ms after probe onset. ERPs elicited by the probes were computed for each of 6 latency peaks (70, 100, 150, 200, 250, 300, 400) by averaging amplitudes over the latency interval peak (-25, +25 ms), once DC and vertical and horizontal ocular artifacts were removed. Since error rate was very low, all trials were used. Impedances were kept below 2k-ohms. Baseline reference is computed across all the electrodes in the scalp.

Repeated-measures ANOVAs were conducted for each time interval and for every major brain area in the relevant variables, by averaging amplitudes of the electrodes in the area, in each hemisphere (RO, LO, LP, RP, LT, RT, LF, RF).

Results and Discussion

This design sought to study how letter-transition (LT) and syllable transition (ST) probabilities contribute to a lexical decision on a masked word. According to a factorial design, High/Low LT probabilities are combined with High/Low ST probabilities. It is hypothesized that nonword parsing costs to locate a hidden word are primarily related to LT probabilities (LTPs), and that syllable-based parsing (ST) is secondary to LTPs.

Letter Transition Probability Effects.

An early Frequency effect at N70 is found to be significant ($F(1,17)=5.466$, $p< 0.05$. MSe=0.130) showing that word Frequency (F) puts a constraint on the entire task: searching within a letter string is easier if it contains a high frequency word because this is perceived as a unitary pattern.

Table 1: Mean P100 amplitudes for F, ND and LTP.

	High Frequency		Low Frequency	
	H-LTP	L-LTP	H-LTP	L-LTP
HND	0.220	0.244	0.162	0.189
LND	0.175	0.157	0.140	0.210

Table 2: Mean P150 amplitudes for ND, L/R H and LTP.

	HND	LND		H-LTP	L-LTP
LH	.418	.409	HND	.377	.349
RH	.308	.245	LND	.300	.355

As seen in Table 1, an early Neighborhood Density (ND) x Frequency (F) x Letter Transition Probability (LTP) interaction ($F(1,17)=4.475$, $p< 0.05$ MSe=0.03) emerges significant in the 100ms. latency interval. The usual F-ND interaction is being modulated by LTP. Low-LTP requires

greater brain activity on average. An early P170 (identifying categorizing operations) emerges for LTP showing subjects' sensitivity to orthotactic regularities.

Neighborhood Density effects are displayed in Table 2. The significant P150 main effect for ND ($F(1,17)=5.539$, $p< 0.05$, MSe=0.01) shows the different roles played by Left and Right Hemispheres. A significant Neighborhood Density (ND)-Letter Transition Probability (LTP) interaction ($F(1,17)=8.472$, $p< 0.05$, MSe=0.01) emerges: ND and LTP are inversely related during the selection of a lexical entry.

Table 3: Mean P200 amplitudes for STP and ND.

	Frontal		Temporal		Parietal		Occipital	
	HST	LST	HST	LST	HST	LST	HST	LST
HND	0.04	0.05	0.49	0.48	0.50	0.48	1.76	1.69
LND	0.11	0.09	0.47	0.46	0.43	0.51	1.60	1.76

Syllable Transition Probability Effects.

A Neighborhood Density (ND) x Syllable Transition Probability (STP) interaction becomes significant ($F(1,17)= 4.353$, $p=.05$, MSe=0.035): ND and STP are inversely related (Table 3) as were ND and LTP (Table 2). The significant STP-F interaction ($F(1,17)=4.409$, $p=.05$, MSe=0.099) that emerges at P250 might be related to Low-Syllable Transition Probability as shown in Figure 1 (red arrows in Upper Panel). At P250, lexical entries are accessed according to their frequency. H-STP takes the former role played by F.

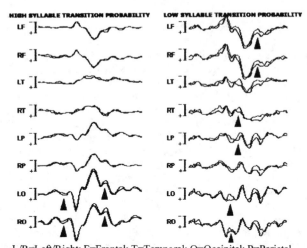

L/R=Left/Right; F=Frontal; T=Temporal; O=Occipital; P=Parietal

Figure 2: ERP time waweforms for high syllable transition probability (left), and low syllable transition probability for words (black), and pseudowords (red).

As seen in Figure 2, a different brain activity pattern emerges for pseudowords and words according to STP in P200, N250, and P400 windows. L-STP requires less brain activity at O and P sites and more at F and T sites than H-

STP, which displays just the opposite pattern. Selection conflicts emerge for words when preceded by a letter of Low STP and for pseudowords when preceded by a letter of High STP. H-STP is resolved in dorsal circuits, while L-STP requires additional attentional resources as seen by a P350-400 effect. This effect is congruent with top-down processing. A significant P400 main effect for STP (F(1,17)= 7.502, p< 0.05, MSe=0.001) confirms it.

II Experiment

If Spanish is a syllable-based lexical system, blending costs of word fragments should be different depending on whether readers have to blend word strings with unbroken or broken syllables while LTPs involved are kept constant. Both LTPs and STPs as well as whole-word lexical selection cues are presumably involved in modulating feedback from lexical entries to the letter sequence formed by blending two letter strings. All stimuli were made by using the RNN simulation on LEXESP.

Methodology

20 Spanish-native readers (13 women; 7 men of 21,2 years-old in average) were serially presented with two postmasked word fragments, and then required to blend them and decide whether the resulting string was a word or not. The procedure was identical to that of the 1st Experiment.

This design was aimed at testing whether letter-transition (LT) and syllable-transition (ST) probabilities contribute to a lexical decision after word string blending. Blending costs are assumed to be primarily dependent on LTPs, and to a lesser extent on STPs. Although both variables LTP and STP are independently manipulated, both points to the same evidence: the combinatorial likelihood of two letters in a sequence. As in the 1st experiment, LTP refers to letter combination regardless of whether it constitutes a syllable. STP does not express the same letter sequence transition as that of the 1st Experiment. It expresses the same transition as LTP but with an additional constraint: STP specifies whether a particular letter sequence constitutes a legal syllable. The variable STP is digitized on two levels: Broken (BS) and Unbroken Syllables (US).

Results and Discussion

An N70 Frequency (F) effect, as found previously, is significant but seems to interact with Neighborhood Density (ND) and is different across hemispheres (F(1,19)= 4,827, p< 0.05, MSe=0.187). Frequency and Neighborhood Density constrain the reader's ability to decide on a blended pattern.

An early STP x LTP interaction (F(1,19)=4.957, p< 0.05, MSe=0.945) reaches significance at P100 interval (Table 4). Under High-LTP, a word is expected regardless whether syllabic structure is preserved. Under Low-LTP, though, a broken syllable is expected. A significant interaction STP x ND at P150, (F(1,19)=4.250, p=0.05, MSe=0.651) shows more brain activity for High-ND at every site except at F,

where H-ND changes directions (Table 5: BS under Low-ND). ND is usually resolved by ventral —occipito-temporal- and dorsal —temporo-parietal- circuits, but enhanced brain activity at F and T sites reveals that BS L-ND targets require additional attentional resources allocation. Real BS L-ND words must be re-checked.

Table 4: Mean P100 amplitudes for STP and LTP

	High-LTP	Low-LTP
Broken Syllable	0.642	0.311
Unbroken Syllable	0.537	0.689

Table 5: Mean P150 amplitudes for STP and ND

P150	Frontal		Temporal		Parietal		Occipital	
	BS	US	BS	US	BS	US	BS	US
HND	0.12	0.10	1.26	1.08	1.67	1.71	2.20	2.21
LND	0.38	-.03	0.97	1.10	1.50	1.48	1.93	2.19

Table 6: Mean P200 amplitudes for STP and ND

P200	Frontal		Temporal		Parietal		Occipital	
	BS	US	BS	US	BS	US	BS	US
HND	0.48	0.54	1.22	0.94	1.45	1.54	2.15	2.08
LND	0.68	0.34	0.84	1.03	1.43	1.24	1.84	1.89

Table 7: Mean P300 amplitudes for STP and ND

P300	Frontal		Temporal		Parietal		Occipital	
	BS	US	BS	US	BS	US	BS	US
HND	2.18	1.99	1.55	1.54	0.87	1.20	0.35	0.86
LND	2.56	2.33	1.74	1.78	1.23	1.12	0.78	0.86

The same pattern is found at P200 in Table 6 (STP x ND: F(1,19)=6.539. p< 0.05. MSe=1,342) and, at P300 in Table 7 (STP x ND: F(1,19)=8.470, p< 0.01, MSe=0,302). Changes are mainly related to an emergent enhanced brain activity in F and T.

Table 8: Mean P400 amplitudes for F x ND x STP

High Frequency				Low Frequency			
H-ND		L-ND		H-ND		L-ND	
BS	US	BS	US	BS	US	BS	US
1.07	1.44	1.48	1.16	1.23	0.60	1.25	1.43

An interaction between Frequency, Neighborhood Density and Syllable Transition Probability becomes significant at P400 (F(1,19)= 5.062, p< 0.05, MSe= 9.046) indicating that when word fragments are blended, Frequency and Neighborhood Density are inversely related. L-ND targets require more attentional resources under pressure from broken and unbroken syllables of HF; conversely, under pressure from unbroken syllables of LF, the reader's ability to select a lexical entry depends on it having few neighbors. After an early computation of Letter Transition Probability, Syllable Transition Probability takes the lead according to Neighborhood Density at the point where the two word fragments become blended.

General Discussion

Consistent LTP and STP effects are obtained in both experiments, but LTP effects appear to be earlier than STP as predicted. In the first experiment, where the STP variable is defined as syllabic prime frequency, consistent P100 LTP effects emerge earlier than STP effects. In the second experiment, the STP variable is re-defined as a refinement of LTP, a syllabic transition between the two letter segments to be blended. In this second experiment, earlier P100 effects are obtained for LTP and STP overall. In the same latency windows (150, 200, 300 ms) where no LTP effect is observed, significant STP effects take place. In this instance STP represents the way readers manage to blend two fragments by combining letters which form broken and unbroken syllables. In these experiments, in every significant interaction, a clear Neighborhood Density effect emerges. ND seems to be the backbone of a lexical decision mechanism that takes whole-word and letter-sequence cues as decisional criteria. As we work toward a lexical decision, the allocation of attentional resources becomes increasingly important, as shown by repeated brain activity in Frontal and Parietal sites. Whether Syllable effects could become a residual effect of Letter Transition Probabilities when letter sequences come into contact with phonological and articulatory representations merits additional research.

References

Barber, H. C. A., Vergara, M., & Carreiras, M. (2004). Sylllable-frequency effects in visual word recognition: evidence from ERPs. *Neuroreport, 15*(3), 545-548.

Brand, M., Rey, A., & Peereman, R. (2003). Where is the syllable priming effect in visual word recognition? *Journal of Memory and Language, 48*, 435-443.

Carreiras, M., Vergara, M., & Barber, H. (2005). Early Event-related Potential Effects of Syllabic Processing during Visual Word Recognition. *Journal of Cognitive Neuroscience, 17*, 1803-1817.

Cedrus Corporation (2006). *Stimulus Presentation Software SuperLab 4.0.* Pedro, CA: Cedrus Corporation.

Cholin, J., Schiller, N. O., & Levelt, W. J. M. (2004). The preparation of syllables in speech production. *Journal of Memory and Language, 50*, 47-61.

deFockert J., Rees, G., Frith, C. D., & Lavie, N. (2004). Neural correlates of attentional capture. *Journal of Cognitive Neuroscience, 16*, 751-759.

Elman, J. (1990). Finding Structure in Time. *Cognitive Science, 14*, 179-211.

Ferrand, L., Segui, J., & Grainger, J. (1996). Masked priming of word and picture naming: the role of syllabic units. *Journal of Memory and Language, 35*, 708-723.

Ferrand, L., Segui, J., & Humphreys, G. W. (1997). The syllables role in word naming. *Memory and Cognition, 35*, 458-470.

Goswami, U., Ziegler, J. C., Dalton, L., & Schneider, W. (2003). Nonword reading across orthographies: How flexible is the choice of reading units? *Applied Psycholinguistics, 24*(2), 235-249.

Moscoso del Prado Martin, F., Schreuder, R., & Baayen, R. H. (2004). Using the structure found in time: Building real-scale orthographic and phonetic representations by accumulation of expectations. In Bowman, H. and Labiouse, C. (eds), *Connectionist Models of Cognition, Perception and Emotion.* Singapore: World Scientific.

Norris, D., McQueen, J. M., & Cutler, A. (2000). Merging information in speech recognition: Feedback is never necessary. *Behavioral & Brain Sciences, 23*(3), 299-370.

Perea, M., & Lupker, S. J. (2004). Can CANISO activate CASINO? Transposed-letter similarity effects with nonadjacent letter positions. *Journal of Memory and Language, 51*, 231-246.

Perfetti, C. A. (2003). The universal grammar of reading. *Scientific Studies of Reading, 7*, 3-24.

Plaut, D. C., McClelland, J. L., Seidenberg, M. S., & Patterson, K. (1996). Understanding normal and impaired word reading: Computational principles in quasi-regular domains. *Psychological Review, 103*, 56-115.

Pollatsek, A., Perea, M., & Carreiras, M. (2005). Does conal prime CANAL more than cinal? Masked phonological priming effects in Spanish with the lexical decision task. *Memory and Cognition, 33*, 3, 557-565.

Rohde, D. L. T. (1999). *LENS: The light, efficient network simulator* (Tech. Rep. CMU-CS-99-164). Pittsburgh, PA: Carnegie Mellon University, Department of Computer Science.

Rumelhart, D. E., & McClelland, J. A. (1986). (Eds). *Paralell Distributed Processing Explorations in the Microstructure of Cognition. Vol 1. Foundations.* Cambridge, MA: The MIT Press,

Sainz, J. S. (2006). Literacy acquisition in Spanish. In M. Joshi, & P.G. Aaron (Eds.), *Handbook of Orthography and Literacy.* Hillsdale, NJ: Lawrence Erlbaum Associates.

Schiller, N. O. (2000). Single word production in English: the role of subsyllabic units during phonological encoding. *Journal of Experimental Psychology: Learning, Memory and Cognition, 26*, 512-528.

Schiller, N. O. (2004). The onset effect in word naming. *Journal of Memory and Language, 50*, 477-490.

Sebastián, N., Cuetos, F., Martí, M. A., & Carreiras, M. (2000). *LEXESP. Léxico informatizado del español* [Lexesp: A Spanish Computerized Lexical DataBase] Barcelona: UB.

Seidenberg, M. (1997). Language acquisition and use: Learning and applying probabilistic constraints. *Science 275*, 1599-1603.

Is sidedness influenced by action directionality?

Alessia Tessari (alessia.tessari@unibo.it)
Department of Psychology, 5 Viale Berti Pichat
Bologna, 40135 Italy

Giovanni Ottoboni (giovanni.ottoboni@uniurb.it)
Institute of Psychology, 15 Via Saffi,
Urbino, 61029, Italy

Valentina Bazzarin (valentina_bazzarin@hotmail.com)
Department of Psychology, 5 Viale Berti Pichat
Bologna, 40135 Italy

Abstract

In this work we investigate whether the dynamic information that can be extracted by static hands can interact with the sidedness effect previously described in Ottoboni, Tessari, Cubelli, and Umiltà (2005). In two experiments, we tested the sidedness effect for hands showed in both a frontal view and rotated along their vertical axes in order to investigate any possible effect due to attribution of action intentionality. Results only showed a classical sidedness effect suggesting that hands are automatically linked to a mental body image and this is the only spatial information they seem to convey.

Introduction

For many years, the cognitive mechanism for hand recognition has been only studied in its overt components and was suggested to results in the observer superimposing his/her own imagined corresponding hand over the showed one in order to recognize it as a right or a left hand (e.g., Parsons, 1994). On the basis of the high accuracy of the handedness judgements and the constancy in the reaction times' pattern, it has been supposed that the overlapping movement is based on an automatic coding process of the hand stimulus. In other words, observers should have already coded the hand stimulus handedness before beginning the mental overlapping movement (Parsons, 1994).

The automatic processing of handedness was studied for the first time by Ottoboni, et al. (2005). The authors used a modified Simon paradigm. This paradigm allows exploring how some stimulus features (e.g., shape, position or colour) are coded by the observer even when this is not required by the instructions. These features, indeed, are mandatory processed and tune participants' behaviour by modifying the response velocity to the task-relevant features (For a review on the Simon Effect see, Rubichi, Nicoletti, Iani, & Umiltà, 1997). In particular, the non-relevant spatial position of the stimulus seems to be automatically coded and interact with the spatial code generated by the position of the response.

Because the responses are lateralized, when stimulus is in the same position of the corresponding response (compatibility condition), reaction times are faster than in the case the two positions do not correspond.

Ottoboni et al. (2005) modified the classical Simon paradigm by presenting hand pictures in the centre of a computer screen. The stimuli were both right and left palm and back views of a hand. A red or blue circle was superimposed in the middle of the stimulus. Participants were instructed to press one of two keys on the left and the right of their midline according to the colour of the circles. When considering the correspondence between the handedness of the hand and the hand of response, a classical Simon effect was found for the back view and a reverse for the palm view. The authors suggested that the observers did not automatically code handedness but the position the stimulus assumes with reference to an envisioned or real body of reference: A right hand seen from the back generates a right code, because it lies at the right side of a body envisioned from the back, whereas, a right hand seen from the palm view generates a left code, as it lies at the left side of a body envisioned facing the observer. These right and left codes were observer-centred. For these reasons, the authors named the effect Sidedness Effect. The sidedness effect was found to be very robust, despite many stimulus manipulations (Ottoboni, Cubelli, & Umiltà, 2005) and it only disappears when hands are presented without their forearms. Indeed, the forearm seems to be crucial to connect the hand to the body of reference, and to allow the effect to emerge.

The stimuli use so far were static hand in a frontal canonical view (Cooper & Shepard, 1975), but what might happen with stimuli appearing as "being-going-to-act"? indeed, some studies reported that static photograph of the human body might convey information about implied motion. Freyd (1983) have demonstrated that the motion implied in static photographs allows us to anticipate the future position of the actor. It has been suggested that observers can extract this kind of dynamic information by extrapolating the future position from the motion implied in a static photograph. Kourtzi and Kanwisher (2000) have shown an involvement of the medial temporal/medial superior temporal cortex, i.e. brain areas involved in the visual analysis of motion, during observation of static photographs with implied motion compared to static photographs without implied motion.

Those findings lead us to hypothesize that static photographs of an oriented hand might suggest a direction, which an action can be performed along. If direction of the "intended" movement were actually processed, the sidedness effect might disappear as a "spatial compatibility effect" might emerge according to the final position of the intended-action (e.g., a right back hand looking like going to act from the right side toward the left one should orient observer's attention toward that side) or, even, the two codes, the one generated by Sidedness and that from the action direction, might contrast each other and give a resulting null effect (For a review on direction and SRC effect see Bosbach, Prinz and Kerzel, 2005).

In the first experiment, we tried to replicate previous results using hands in a frontal view (Ottoboni, et al., 2005). This Experiment worked as a control condition. In the second Experiment, hands were rotated along their vertical axes from a canonical starting position canonical view (e.g., Cooper & Shepard, 1975).

Experiment 1

Method

Participants

Ten students of the University of Bologna took part in the experiment. All of them were right handed, according to the Edinburgh Inventory Test (Oldfield, 1971), with a normal or corrected - to normal vision, and naïve to the purpose of the experiment.

Apparatus and procedures

The stimuli were photographs of hands in back and palm views with the forearm, with the fingers grouped together, presented in according to the canonical posture (Cooper & Shepard, 1975) (See Figure 1). The hands were open with the fingers grouped together and straight forearm. The dimensions of the picture were of 23° X 9° visible angle.

A red or blue circle was superimposed in the middle of the hand. The experiment was run using a Pentium III, 512 Mb, connected to a 15" screen. The experiment was controlled by E-Prime 1.1 (SP3) software (Psychology Software Tools Inc.). The stimuli were 120 for both the back and palm conditions and lasted on the screen for 100 ms, each. The next stimulus appeared after participant's response and no longer than 1000 ms after. Participants were required to respond according to the colour of the circle by pressing one of two keyboard keys ("X" and "."), respectively on the left and the right side. Feedbacks about reaction times, errors and omissions were given after each response (it last for 1500 ms).

The response conditions were counterbalanced between subjects.

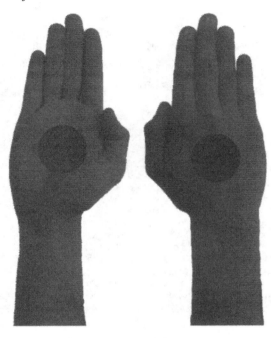

Figure 1: Hand stimuli used in Experiment 1: Examples for both the palm and the back views are shown.

Results

Data were analyzed in a two-way Analysis of Variance (ANOVA). View (Palm and Back) and Correspondence (corresponding and non-corresponding pairings). None of them was significant ($F(1,9) = 0.08$, MS = 26.91, p >.05, $F(1,9) = 1.82$, MS = 75.48, p >.05, respectively) but their interaction was ($F(1,9) = 11.53$, MS = 1844.56, p <.05). Paired-samples T-test with Bonferroni correction was carried out for the Correspondence factor for the back and palm view separately. The factor was significant for both the back and the palm view ($t(9) = 3.09$, p <.05, $t(9) = 3.07$, p <.05, respectively). The corresponding pairings between the stimulus hand and the response hand were faster in the back view condition, whereas reaction times presented the reversed patterns in the palm view condition (See Figure 2 and Table 1).

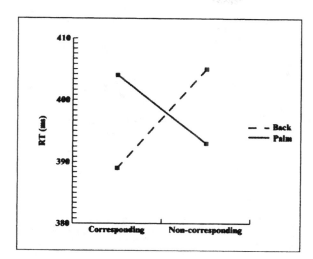

Figure 2: Mean reaction times (RTs; in milliseconds) for corresponding and non-corresponding pairings as a function of handedness of hand and side of response.

The errors were analysed with a 2 X 2 ANOVA. Overall errors were 4.42% of which 4.21% were left-right errors and 0.21% were omission errors. Error percentages were treated with a two-way ANOVA for repeated measures. Two main factors were analysed: View and Correspondence. Both factors did not reached significance (F(1,9) = 0.25, MS = 0.22, p >.05, F(1,9) = 0.11, MS = 0.02, p >.05, respectively), whereas their interaction was significant (F(1,9) = 5.55, MS = 5.62, p <.05).

Table 1: Mean reaction times (RTs; millisecond) and mean of errors (each paired with its standard deviation - in brackets) as a function of conditions (hand views) and pairings between stimulus handedness and side of response.

Pairings	Back View	Palm View
	Reaction Time	
Corresponding	389 (31)	404 (30)
Non- Corresponding	405 (33)	393 (29)
	Errors	
Corresponding	1.00 (1.03)	1.65 (1.03)
Non- Corresponding	1.65 (1.08)	0.75 (0.80)

Discussion

Results indicate a clear Sidedness effect: the Rts for hands seen from the back view are faster when the handedness of the hand stimulus corresponds to the side of the response; on the contrary, the Rts produced by hands seen from the palm view are faster when the handedness of the hand stimulus does not correspond to the side of the response.

Experiment 2

In this experiment we tried to understand whether the intention-to-act conveyed by the posture of the hand might be a more important feature compared to sidedness. Were the former more important than the latter feature, a Simon effect should emerge according to the final position of the action (e.g., a right back hand looking like going to act from the right side toward the left one should orient observer's attention toward that side). Another alternative result pattern might be that the two codes, generated by sidedness and action direction, might contrast each other and give a resulting null effect

Method

Participants

Ten students of the University of Bologna participated in this experiment. All of them were right handed, according to the Edinburgh Inventory Test (Oldfield, 1971), with a normal or corrected - to normal vision, and naive to the purpose of the experiment.

Apparatus and procedures

The stimuli were photographs of hands in back and palm views with the forearm.
The hands held a posture little inclined (slightly 30°) along their vertical axes (See Figure 3). The dimensions of the picture were the same of the previous experiment. A red or blue circle was superimposed in the middle of the hand. The experiment was run using the same apparatus and procedure previously described.

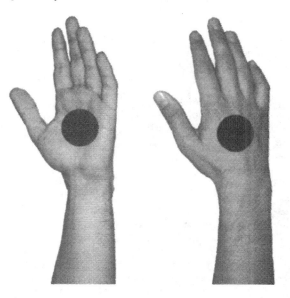

Figure 3: Hand stimuli used in Experiment 2: examples for both the palm and the back views are shown.

Results

Data were analysed by using a two-way Analysis of Variance (ANOVA), as main factors View and Correspondence. None of them was significant (F(1,9) = 2.10, MS = 1031.41, p >.05, F(1,9) = 1.76, MS = 347.31, p >.05, respectively) but their interaction was (F(1,9) = 11.33, MS = 5705.74, p <.01).

Therefore, we performed a paired sample T-test with Bonferroni correction for the Correspondence factor for the back and palm view separately. The factor was significant for both the back and the palm view (t(9) = 3.03, p <.05, t(9) = 2,73, p <.05, respectively). The corresponding pairings between the stimulus hand and the hand of response were faster in the back view condition, whereas in the palm view condition, the Rts presented reversed patterns (See Figure 4 and Table 2).

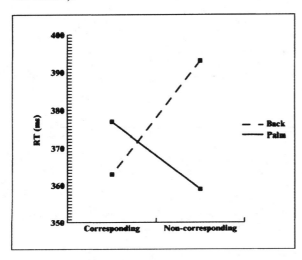

Figure 4: Mean reaction times (RTs; in milliseconds) for corresponding and non-corresponding pairings as a function of handedness of hand and side of response

The errors were analysed with a 2 X 2 ANOVA. Overall errors were 9.79% of which 8.79% were left-right errors and 1.00% were omission errors. Error percentages were treated with a two-way ANOVA for repeated measures. Two main factors were analysed: View and Correspondence. Both factors reached significance (F(1,9) = 5.97, MS = 6.01, p <.05, F(1,9) = 8.48, MS = 11.56, p <.05, respectively), and also their interaction was significant (F(1,9) = 22.22, MS = 18.90, p <.005). In order to further investigate the interaction, we performed on a Paired Sample T-test for back and palm separately (one-tailed paired samples t-test, t(9) = 4.63, p <.005, and t(9) = 0.77, p >.05, respectively). Percentages of errors are reported in Table 2: there were less errors in corresponding pairings than in non-corresponding ones for the back view, but no differences were found for the palm view.

Table 2: Mean reaction times (RTs; millisecond) and mean of errors (each paired with its standard deviation - in brackets) as a function of conditions (hand views) and pairings between stimulus handedness and side of response.

Pairings	Back View	Palm View
	Reaction Time	
Corresponding	363 (55)	393 (61)
Non- Corresponding	377 (68)	359 (54)
	Errors	
Corresponding	1.8 (2.24)	2.4 (2.28)
Non- Corresponding	4.25 (2.43)	2.1 (1.54)

Discussion

The results showed the same pattern as in Experiment 1: For hands seen from the back view, corresponding pairings were faster than the non-corresponding ones; For hands seen from the palm view, non-corresponding pairings showed faster RTs than the corresponding ones. These results are congruent with the notion that coding of the spatial position of a hand does happen on the sidedness relation with respect to the image of a body to which the hand is connected.

No effect of the directionality of the hand emerges. Indeed, this were the case, the opposite results pattern should have emerged, because each acting hand should have triggered the observer attention toward the opposite side with respect to their sidedness (e.g., a right palm view hand oriented toward the midline, that activates a left sidedness, should have appear as a hand going to act toward the opposite side, that is the right one, resulting in faster reaction time for right hand response).

General discussion

Previous studies (Freyd, 1983; Kourtzi & Kanwisher, 2000) have been demonstrated that the brain seems to be inclined to perceive motion even in static stimuli. Observers seem to be able to extract dynamic information from static stimuli by using the stored internal representation of dynamic information. This information is used to recall past movement and anticipate future movements from partial visual information (Blakemore & Decety, 2001). These results have also been interpreted in the light of theory of mind and understanding of intentions (See Blakemore, Sarfati, Bazin, and Decety (2003), for a review) and the brain has been seen as a machine able to detect biological motion in order to extract intentions from the motion and to predict the future actions on another individuals. In this study, we investigated whether passive observation of static photograph of oriented hands might bring dynamic information about the direction of the intended action and whether this information might generate a spatial code able to contrast or interact with that of sidedness. Results of both Experiment 1 and 2 indicate that the sidedness effect emerges either for frontal and rotated hands: we found a regular Simon effect for the back view and a reverse one for the palm view. No effect emerged for the directionality of the hand in Experiment 2. Therefore, the hypothesis on the potential effect of the orientation of the hand as a cue for the intention to act toward to opposite space has to be put a part. We propose that observers automatically referred the hand to an imaginary body, regardless of its left or right nature. In the case of the back view, the imaginary body should face away from the observer; in the case of the palm view, the imagined body should face toward the observer. Ottoboni, et al. (2005) proposed that participants mentally align his or her midline with the midline of the imaginary body, and, in this configuration, a left hand viewed from its back is in the participant-aligned left visual space, whereas a right hand viewed from the back is in the participant aligned right visual space. Likewise, when the hand faces the observer (the palm view), the imaginary body too faces the observer. In this condition, after a mental alignment of the body midline, a left palm is in the observer's right visual space, and a right palm is in the observer's left visual space (see figure 5).

Figure 5: A schematic representation of the sidedness effect according to the mental alignment between observer's body and the imaginary body.

It has been suggested that hand and forearm together activate the system of structural description of the body and its parts, that defines the local relations between the body parts in a perceptual format and is body-centred (Buxbaum & Coslet, 2001; Sirigu, Grafman, Bressler, & Sunderland, 1991).

However, another possible interpretation for the emerging of the sidedness effect might be proposed in light of embodied cognition. Indeed, embodied cognition theorists claim that cognition depends on the kinds of experiences that the particular perceptual and motor capacities of our body allow us to link within memory, emotion, language, and all other cognitive aspects (Thelen, Schoner, Scheier, & Smith 2001). The representation we have of our body and of its parts arises from the bodily interactions with the world. Interacting bodily with the environment human beings can develop the ability to code the sidedness of their own and others' specific body parts. Indeed, learning to control our own movements and perform some actions, we might develop a knowledge about human body and the spatial relation among its parts.

References

Blakemore, S. J., & Decety, J. (2001). From the perception of action to the understanding of intention. *Nature Reviews Neuroscience*, 2, 561-567.

Blakemore, S. J., Sarfati, Y., Bazin, N., & Decety, J. (2003). The detection of intentional contingencies in simple animations in patients with delusions of persecution. *Psychological Medicine*, 33(8), 1433-41.

Buxbaum, L. J., & Coslet, H. B. (2001). Specialized structural description for human body parts: evidence from autotopagnosia. *Cognitive Neuropsychology*, 18, 289-306.

Cooper, L. A., & Shepard, R. N. (1975). Mental transformations in the identification of left and right hands. *Journal of Experimental Psychology: Human Perception and Performance*, 104(1), 48-56.

Freyd, J. J. (1983). The mental representation of movement when static stimuli are viewed. *Percept Psychophys*, 33(6), 575-81.

Kourtzi, Z., & Kanwisher, N. (2000). Activation in human MT/MST by static images with implied motion. *Journal of Cognitive Neuroscience*, 12(1), 48-55.

Oldfield, R. C. (1971). The assessment and analysis of handedness: the Edinburgh inventory. *Neuropsychologia*, 9(1), 97-113.

Ottoboni, G., Cubelli, R., & Umilta', C. (2005). Preattentive spatial coding in hand recognition. In E. S. for Cognitive Psychology (Ed.), *Proceedings of the XIVth Meeting of the European Society for Cognitive Psychology* (p. 109).

Ottoboni, G., Tessari, A., Cubelli, R., & Umiltà, C. (2005). Is handedness recognition automatic? A study using a Simon-like paradigm. *Journal of Experimental Psychology: Human Perception and Performance*, 31(4), 778-89.

Parsons, L. M. (1994). Temporal and kinematic properties of motor behavior reflected in mentally simulated action. *Journal of Experimental Psychology: Human Perception and Performance*, 20(4), 709-30.

Rubichi, S., Nicoletti, R., Iani, C., & Umiltà, C. (1997). The Simon effect occurs relative to the direction of an attention shift. *Journal of Experimental Psychology: Human Perception and Performance*, 23(5), 1353-64.

Sirigu, A., Grafman, J., Bressler, K., & Sunderland, T. (1991). Multiple representations contribute to body knowledge processing. Evidence from a case of autotopagnosia. *Brain*, 114 (Pt 1B), 629-42.

Thelen, E., Schoner, G., Scheier, C., and Smith, L.B. (2001). "The Dynamics of Embodiment: A Field Theory of Infant Perservative Reaching." *Behavioral and Brain Sciences*, 24, 1-86.

Papers Presented as Posters

Proportional Reasoning as a Heuristic-Based Process: In Search for Evidence in Students' Reaction Times

Ellen Gillard (ellen.gillard@ped.kuleuven.be)
Centre for Instructional Psychology and Technology, Vesaliusstraat 2
B-3000 Leuven, Belgium

Wim Van Dooren (wim.vandooren@ped.kuleuven.be)
Centre for Instructional Psychology and Technology, Vesaliusstraat 2
B-3000 Leuven, Belgium

Walter Schaeken (walter.schaeken@psy.kuleuven.be)
Laboratory of Experimental Psychology, Tiensestraat 102
B-3000 Leuven, Belgium

Lieven Verschaffel (lieven.verschaffel@ped.kuleuven.be)
Centre for Instructional Psychology and Technology, Vesaliusstraat 2
B-3000 Leuven, Belgium

Abstract

Research has demonstrated that students often over-use proportional strategies. The present paper tries to interpret this phenomenon from a dual process framework. Current dual process theories claim that analytic operations involve time-consuming executive processing, whereas the heuristic system would operate fast and automatically. We set up an experiment to test the claim that proportional reasoning relies on heuristic-based processing, by experimentally manipulating students' time to solve proportional and non-proportional word problems. Results did not fully confirm our expectations, but there were indications that proportional reasoning is indeed heuristic-based.

Introduction

Over-use of Proportionality

Proportional reasoning is a major tool for human beings to interpret phenomena in everyday life. Because of the usefulness of proportional strategies for solving a variety of problems in mathematics and science, it is also a key concept in primary and secondary education, where it is often trained with missing-value word problems (in which three numbers are given, and a fourth has to be found by calculating the value of x in the equation $a/b = c/x$). In the long run, students' growing familiarity with and competence in proportional strategies, together with the intrinsic simplicity and self-evident character of the proportional idea, causes a deeply entrenched tendency to apply proportional solution methods also in situations where this is inadequate. This phenomenon has been demonstrated in different domains of mathematics education, such as elementary arithmetic, geometry and probability (De Bock, Van Dooren, Verschaffel, & Janssens, 2002; Van Dooren, De Bock, Depaepe, Janssens, & Verschaffel, 2003). For example, most sixth graders erroneously give the answer

"90" to the following non-proportional arithmetic problem (see Van Dooren, De Bock, Hessels, Janssens, & Verschaffel, 2005):

> *Ellen and Kim are running around a track. They run equally fast but Ellen started later. When Ellen has run 5 laps, Kim has run 15 laps. When Ellen has run 30 laps, how many has Kim run?*

In the present study we attempt to apply a dual process framework, which is one of the most influential current frameworks in the psychology of reasoning and thinking, to the over-use of proportionality in mathematical word problem solving.

Dual Process Framework

One of the main themes of the cognitive reasoning research over the past decades is that human reasoning frequently violates traditional normative standards. An impressive body of research has demonstrated that in a wide range of reasoning tasks most educated adults fail to provide the response that is correct according to logic or probability theory (Evans, 2002; Kahneman, Slovic, & Tversky, 1982). Dual process theorists (e.g., Epstein, 1994; Evans & Over, 1996; Goel, 1995; Kahneman, 2000; Sloman, 1996; Stanovich, 1999) have tried to account for this gap between normative standards and actual performances by claiming the existence of two distinct cognitive reasoning systems. There are several dual process theories, but, in general, the *first system* (also called the *heuristic system*) is characterized as automatic, associative, unconscious and undemanding of computational working memory capacity, whereas the *second system* (also called the *analytic system*) is characterized as consciously controlled, deliberate and effortful. The heuristic system is assumed to operate fast, and to generate answers based on similarity to stored prototypes (Sloman, 1996). Analytic processing is assumed to operate on 'decontextualized' representations, to be serial and time-consuming. The fast and preconscious heuristics often provide correct responses, but sometimes they can also bias reasoning in situations that require more elaborate, analytic processing. That is, the two systems will sometimes conflict and cue different responses. In these cases, the analytic system needs to override the responses generated by the heuristic system to obtain correct responses. Hence, a failure to provide the normatively correct answer may be attributed to the pervasiveness of the heuristic system, and the failure of the analytic system to intervene.

The dual process framework makes two important processing claims. First, it is assumed that there is a differential involvement of executive, working memory resources in heuristic and analytic processing: Heuristic operations are automatic, hence undemanding of executive resources, whereas analytic operations heavily draw on the executive resources. Otherwise stated, with more resources available, it is more likely that the analytic system will be successfully engaged and that the correct response will be provided. Second, the heuristic system is assumed to operate faster than the analytic system. Otherwise stated, heuristic responses require less processing time than analytic responses. Both processing claims are strongly interrelated and have been successfully demonstrated for the most paradigmatic examples in the dual process literature, like the 'Wason selection task' and the 'Linda problem' (see De Neys, 2006).

Over-use of Proportionality Interpreted from a Dual Process Account

Recently (e.g., Leron & Hazzan, 2006), attempts were made to interpret (errors in) mathematical problem solving from a dual process account. It is our opinion that such an account also can be used to interpret students' over-use of proportionality. We suggest that, due to the usefulness of proportionality and to the extensive classroom exercising of proportional methods, a 'proportional heuristic' is created as part of the heuristic system, which is triggered by contextual features of word problems, like the missing-value format. The proportional heuristic provides students with correct responses to proportional missing-value word problems in a fast and almost effortless way. However, when solving non-proportional word problems with the same contextual features, the analytic system will need to override the proportional response generated by the heuristic system and apply the right non-proportional strategy to the problem in order to provide the correct response. We want to stress that we assume that preconscious heuristics determine the *selection* of the mathematical solution method, while thereafter, the *computation* of the actual answer may of course also rely on analytic processing.

When translating the two above-mentioned processing claims of the dual process framework to word problem solving, we expect that limiting students' resources, by putting them under working memory load or by limiting their response time, will result in an increase in the choice of heuristic-based proportional strategies. As these are correct for proportional word problems, we expect no effect of working memory load or limited response time when students solve proportional problems. For non-proportional problems, however, we expect an increase in the inadequate choice of proportional strategies (and hence a decrease of correct answers).

Previous Work

As we already mentioned, the first processing claim – related to the role of working memory – was already successfully demonstrated (e.g., for the 'Wason selection task' and the 'Linda problem', see De Neys, 2006), by using a dual task methodology (the dot memory task, Miyake, Friedman, Rettinger, Shah, & Hegarty, 2001), in which subjects' executive resources are experimentally burdened with an attention demanding secondary task that needs to be accomplished simultaneously.

In a previous experiment (Gillard, Van Dooren, Schaeken, & Verschaffel, 2006), we investigated whether this methodology can also be applied to the over-use of proportionality when solving word problems: An experimentally burdened working memory could be expected to elicit an increase of proportional answers to non-proportional word problems, and make no difference in the answers to proportional word problems. In this experiment, sixth grade students were presented with proportional and non-proportional (in this case: additive) word problems, each time together with a possible solution (either a proportional or an additive one), which they needed to accept or reject. A (correct) additive solution to, for example, the word problem in the introduction would be: *To go from 5 to 15, you do + 10, so you also do 30 + 10, which is 40.* An (incorrect) proportional solution would be: *To go from 5 to 15, you do × 3, so you also do 30 × 3, which is 90.* Half of the students' executive resources were burdened using the dot memory task (Miyake et al., 2001), whereas for the other students there was no secondary task.

The results showed that working memory load had no effect on accuracy for the proportional word problems (the acceptance of the proportional solution remained equally high, and there was only a slight increase for the rejection of the additive solution), but contrary to our expectation, the amount of correct answers to the non-proportional word problems (i.e., both the acceptance of the additive solution and the rejection of the proportional solution) increased rather than decreased under working memory load.

A plausible interpretation for this unexpected result was that when confronted with a less familiar problem the additional working memory task causes students to start to merely guess, rather than to reason in a truly heuristic manner. This would explain the increase in accuracy on the non-proportional problems, while the accuracy on the proportional problems is not affected. In these young subjects, it seemed problematic to combine the dual task methodology – or at least this secondary task – with our primary task: Word problems are quite different from other primary tasks in the literature that were already combined with the dot memory task. Therefore, we decided to conduct an experiment that didn't need the use of dual task methodology, by focussing on the second processing claim of the dual process framework in relation to the over-use of proportionality.

Present Experiment

This experiment directly tests the claim that proportional reasoning is part of the automatic-heuristic system. Participants had to solve a series of proportional and non-proportional (additive) word problems which are known to elicit proportional answers (Gillard et al., 2006; Van Dooren et al., 2005). Crucial in this experiment was the manipulation of the available time for solving the word problems. In the long (L) condition, participants had a long time available to solve the word problem, while in the short (S) condition the available solution time was drastically reduced. Assuming that the automatic-heuristic system operates faster than the executive-analytic system (Evans & Over, 1996; Sloman, 1996; Stanovich & West, 2000), inadequate proportional answers to non-proportional word problems should be provided faster than correct answers. If proportional answers to non-proportional word problems are heuristic responses (which need to be overridden by the analytic system to arrive at the correct answer), we expect an increase in heuristic proportional responses to non-proportional word problems when there is no time for the analytic system to intervene. More specifically, we expect a differential effect of time constraint for proportional and non-proportional word problems: For non-proportional additive word problems, there should be an increase of the frequency of proportional answers under time constraint – resulting in a decrease of the frequency of correct answers – whereas for proportional word problems no significant effect is expected.

Method

Participants Participants were 111 sixth graders from two randomly chosen Flemish elementary schools.

Materials and Design Participants were presented with 12 missing-value word problems in random order. Six of them were proportional (i.e., a proportional strategy must be applied to find the correct answer) and six were non-proportional, additive word problems (i.e., an additive strategy must be applied to find the correct answer). The proportional and non-proportional word problems were formulated as similarly as possible, and were controlled for length, amount of syllables and technical reading complexity (reading index 72-77, Visser, Van Laerhoven, & Ter Beek, 1998). They can also be considered as parallel in terms of computational difficulty.

All word problems were presented on the screen together with two response alternatives – a proportional and an additive solution – and students were asked to choose the correct one. For example:

Proportional problem
Erik and Tom buy boxes of pencils in the shop. All boxes are equally expensive, but Erik buys fewer boxes. Erik buys 4 boxes of pencils, while Tom buys 8 boxes. Knowing that Erik has to pay 24 euros, how much does Tom have to pay?

1. To go from 4 to 24, you do × 6, so you also do 8 × 6, which is 48.
2. To go from 4 to 24, you do + 20, so you also do 8 + 20, which is 28.

Non-proportional problem:
Ellen and Kim are running around a track. They run equally fast but Ellen started later. When Ellen has run 5 laps, Kim has run 15 laps. When Ellen has run 30 laps, how many has Kim run?

1. To go from 5 to 15, you do + 10, so you also do 30 + 10, which is 40.
2. To go from 5 to 15, you do × 3, so you also do 30 × 3, which is 90.

The available time to read the word problem and choose an answer was experimentally manipulated as a between participant variable. We wanted the participants in the S condition to have sufficient time to respond but to experience severe time pressure, whereas we wanted participants in the L condition to have sufficient time to respond thoughtfully. Participants in the short (S) condition had 25 seconds, while participants in the long (L) condition had 90 seconds[1]. The bottom of the screen showed a bar indicating elapsed and remaining time. Time started running as soon as the word problem and the answers appeared on the screen.

Procedure Participants were randomly assigned to the control or time limit group (55 were assigned to the L condition and 56 were assigned to the S condition). They were tested in small groups in an empty classroom, where each participant worked on an individual laptop.

Participants were first briefly instructed by the researcher about the task and response format, using two word problems that were unrelated to the experimental problems. The time constraint was explained as well, and participants could experience the time available to respond. The individual task started with one extra practice item, again unrelated to the experimental items. Then participants received the 12 experimental word problems in a randomised order, along with the two response alternatives, appearing in random order on the screen. Participants responded by pressing '1' or '2' on the keyboard. After that, the problem disappeared, and students could press the space bar to continue to the next problem.

Results

Data Treatment Trials where no response was given within the time limit were removed from the analysis. This resulted

---

[1] The 25 second limit in the S condition was determined in a pilot study where students worked without any time constraint. It was the median time of students choosing proportional answers to additive problems. In contrast, we didn't want the participants in the L condition to feel under any time pressure to respond. The 90 second limit in the L condition was the longest response time observed in that pilot study.

Table 1: Mean accuracy rates for Type of word problem by Time condition.

| Time | Type of word problem | | | |
| | Proportional | | Non-proportional | |
	Mean	n	Mean	n
Long	.82 (.04)	148	.29 (.05)	91
Short	.73 (.02)	325	.24 (.02)	331
Long ≤25000	.95 (.02)	182	.19 (.02)	239

Note. Standard deviations in parentheses.

in an elimination of 2.4 % of the data in the S condition, while in the L condition no data were removed for this reason. In the L condition, data were removed from the analysis if the response was given *before* the time limit of the S condition, thus if the response had an associated reaction time of 25 seconds or smaller. After all, it can be argued that when students in the L condition used less time to respond than was available in the S condition, these responses would be based on heuristic processes as well. In those cases, the operationalisation in the L condition may not have reached its goal. Hereafter, only 35.6% of the data in the L condition remained in the analysis. An analysis of the eliminated responses (see Table 1) supports this assumption: These eliminated responses showed the highest number of proportional answers to both types of word problems, indicating that these responses were based on heuristic processes.

Analysis We ran an ANOVA with Type of word problem and Time condition as factors and proportion of correct answers as dependent variable. As expected, we observed a main effect of Type of word problem: The accuracy for proportional word problems was significantly higher than for non-proportional word problems, $F(1, 891) = 234.50$, $p = .00$. Under time pressure, we observed a decrease of the frequency of correct responses, but, contrary to our expectations, this was the case both for the proportional and the non-proportional word problems (see Table 1). So, there was a main effect of Time condition, $F(1, 891) = 4.37$, $p = .04$, but no interaction effect between Time condition and Type of word problem, $F(1, 891) = .74$, $p = .39$.

During the data collection, however, the suspicion has arisen that there were considerable differences between the class groups with respect to their engagement in the experiment. Therefore the data were separated for each of the class groups. As shown in Table 2, the expected pattern emerged for three out of six class groups (i.e., 1, 2, and 5): There was a decrease of the accuracy for non-proportional answers, whereas the accuracy for proportional answers remained intact under time pressure. In two other class groups (i.e., 3 and 4), there already was a floor effect on the non-proportional problems in the L condition, so a decrease under time pressure could hardly occur. In a last class group (class 6), there also was a floor effect in the L condition, and under time pressure the accuracy went to about 50% for both the proportional and the non-proportional word problems.

Conclusions and Discussion

First of all, the large difference in accuracy on the proportional and non-proportional problems again confirmed the very strong tendency in students to over-use proportional methods. Second, and more importantly, our results generally did not confirm our expectation: Under time pressure, the accuracy on both the proportional and the non-proportional word problems decreased moderately. However, when looking separately at the data for the different class groups, evidence arose that proportional reasoning is indeed heuristic-based: In half of the class groups the expected pattern of results emerged. In the other class groups, the L condition showed a floor effect: The accuracy to the non-proportional word problems was

Table 2: Mean accuracy rates (and number of trials) for Type of word problem by Time condition separated for Class group.

| Class group | Time | Type of word problem | | | |
| | | Proportional | | Non-proportional | |
		Mean	n	Mean	n
1	Long	.67 (.08)	30	.43 (.09)	23
	Short	.84 (.06)	45	.13 (.06)	46
2	Long	.76 (.10)	17	.33 (.14)	9
	Short	.79 (.06)	48	.09 (.06)	47
3	Long	.95 (.09)	20	.10 (.13)	10
	Short	.75 (.05)	75	.18 (.05)	77
4	Long	.81 (.06)	42	.21 (.08)	28
	Short	.74 (.07)	34	.23 (.07)	35
5	Long	.91 (.09)	22	.42 (.12)	12
	Short	.77 (.07)	39	.12 (.06)	42
6	Long	.94 (.10)	17	.11 (.14)	9
	Short	.58 (.05)	84	.52 (.05)	84

Note. Standard deviations in parentheses.

already so low that a decrease under time pressure could hardly be obtained. Hence in those class groups the experimental manipulation of response time did not function as intended. In one of those class groups, moreover, accuracy in the S condition went to about 50% for the proportional and the non-proportional word problems, which strongly suggests that for these students, the time pressure lead to mere guessing behaviour (perhaps because they perceived the available time as too short to give a reasonable answer) instead of truly heuristic reasoning.

The overall conclusion of our study seems to be that if students – in normal circumstances, i.e., when not working under time pressure – do not perform at a floor level on non-proportional word problems, time pressure causes a decrease in the accuracy on the non-proportional word problems, while the accuracy on the proportional problems remains the same. When students – even without time pressure – already perform at floor level on non-proportional problems, this may remain the same under time pressure, or students may start guessing.

We are aware that we did not find convincing evidence for our claim that proportional reasoning is heuristic-based. Future research will need to confirm the above-made interpretations. If our hypothesis is correct that proportional responses are fast and heuristic-based, particular methodological measures might be taken to provide more convincing evidence for it. It is worthwhile, in future studies, to try to avoid floor effects in accuracy to non-proportional word problems. This could be done either by stimulating reflectivity in all students participating in the study (which would be effective in the L condition but not in the S condition because of the limited response time). Another possibility is to continue the research with older subjects. Working with older subjects has several advantages. First, there is less variability in reading and arithmetic ability, so an imposed time limit would approximately have the same effect for all subjects. Second, it might be possible to offer the experimental items in an open-answer format (instead of a forced-choice format as in the current study). This would allow to eliminate the suspicion that under time pressure, subjects are merely guessing instead of reasoning in a heuristic manner. Third, research has shown (see Van Dooren, et al. 2005) that fifth and sixth grade students are at the peak of applying proportional strategies to non-proportional word problems. Hence, we assume that students at that age are affected by a very strongly developed proportional heuristic, and that it is very hard for them to inhibit it. This is also demonstrated by the fact that in the present study, floor effects were found on the non-proportional problems in three classes in the L condition, and about two-thirds of the trials in the L condition had a response time smaller than the time limit of the S condition. So, for this age group, manipulations (like working memory load or limiting response time) that try to stimulate heuristic processes can be expected to have little effect. It is assumed, however, that older students still have a tendency toward inadequate proportional reasoning, but are able to suppress this tendency. But, even in older students, inadequate proportional reasoning could re-emerge in situations where heuristic processing is stimulated, so manipulations that make it hard for the analytic system to intervene – like working under time or working memory constraints – might appear more useful in these older students, and thus show the heuristic character of proportional reasoning.

References

De Bock, D., Van Dooren, W., Janssens, D., & Verschaffel, L. (2002). Improper use of linear reasoning: An in-depth study of the nature and the irresistibility of secondary school students' errors. *Educational Studies in Mathematics, 50,* 311-334.

De Neys, W. (2006). Automatic–heuristic and executive–analytic processing during reasoning: Chronometric and dual-task considerations. *The Quarterly Journal of Experimental Psychology, 59,* 1070-1100.

Epstein, S. (1994). Integration of the cognitive and psychodynamic unconscious. *American Psychologist, 49,* 709-724.

Evans, J. St. B. T. (2002). Logic and human reasoning: An assessment of the deduction paradigm. *Psychological Bulletin, 128,* 978-996.

Evans, J. St. B. T., & Over, D. E. (1996). *Rationality and reasoning.* Hove, UK: Psychology Press.

Gillard, E., Van Dooren, W., Schaeken, W., & Verschaffel, L. (2006). Proportionality as a conceptual obstacle: Considerations from a dual-process framework. *Proceedings of the 5th Symposium of the EARLI Special Interest Group on Conceptual Change* (pp. 17-18). Stockholm: Stockholm University.

Goel, V. (1995). *Sketches of thought.* Cambridge, MA: MIT Press.

Kahneman, D. (2000). A psychological point of view: Violations of rational rules as a diagnostic of mental processes. *Behavioral and Brain Sciences, 23,* 681-683.

Kahneman, D., Slovic, P., & Tversky, A. (1982). *Judgement under uncertainty: Heuristics and biases.* Cambridge, MA: Cambridge University Press.

Leron, U., & Hazzan, O. (2006). The Rationality Debate: Application of cognitive psychology to mathematics education. *Educational Studies in Mathematics, 62,* 105-126.

Miyake, A., Friedman, N. P., Rettinger, D. A., Shah, P., & Hegarty, M. (2001). How are visuospatial working memory, executive functioning, and spatial abilities related? A latent-variable analysis. *Journal of Experimental Psychology: General, 130,* 621-640.

Sloman, S. A. (1996). The empirical case for two systems of reasoning. *Psychological Bulletin, 119,* 3-22.

Stanovich, K. E. (1999). *Who is rational? Studies of individual differences in reasoning.* Mahwah, NJ: Erlbaum.

Stanovich, K. E., & West, R. F. (2000). Individual differences in reasoning: Implications for the rationality debate. *Behavioral and Brain Sciences, 23,* 645-726.

Van Dooren, W., De Bock, D., Depaepe, F., Janssens, D., & Verschaffel, L. (2003). The illusion of linearity: Expanding the evidence towards probabilistic reasoning. *Educational Studies in Mathematics, 53,* 113-138.

Van Dooren, W., De Bock, D., Hessels, A., Janssens, D., & Verschaffel, L. (2005). Not everything is proportional: effects of age and problem type on propensities for overgeneralization. *Cognition and Instruction, 23*, 57-86.

Visser, J., Van Laerhoven, A., & Ter Beek, A. (1998). *AVI toetspakket (handleiding)* [*AVI testing package (manual)*]. 's Hertogenbosch, The Netherlands: KPC Groep.

Inhibition of Intuitive Interference by Cognitive Conflict Training: The Case of Geometrical Shapes

Ruth Stavy (ruth@post.tau.ac.il)
Reuven Babai (reuvenb@post.tau.ac.il)
Dina Tirosh (dina@post.tau.ac.il)
Hanna Zilber (zilber2@netvision.net.il)
Department of Science Education, The Constantiner School of Education, Tel Aviv University
Tel Aviv 69978, Israel

Abstract

The current study focuses on comparison of perimeters of geometrical shapes in the framework of the intuitive rule *more A -- more B*. Our previous findings suggested that conflict training could lead to improvement in students' performance. Here we used such training and compared accuracy of responses and reaction times before and after training. Two test conditions were examined, congruent: in which correct responses are in line with the intuitive rule, and incongruent: in which correct responses run counter to the rule leading to lower rate of success. Two eighth's grade classes took part in the study. One class, the experimental group, received cognitive conflict training while the other, the control group, did not. The post-test results showed that in terms of accuracy the experimental group benefited from the intervention as compared with the control group. In terms of reaction times, the control group had shorter reaction times in the post-test as compared with the pre-test and the experimental group had longer reaction times compared to the pre-test. It seems that raising students' awareness by cognitive conflict to the possible interference of the intuitive rule activates effortful and time-consuming control mechanisms that help them overcome the interference of the intuitive rule. Research in science and mathematics education could benefit from applying cognitive psychology techniques, as done in the current study. Using such methodologies could lead to a deeper understanding of students' difficulties and reasoning processes, and to the development of improved instructional strategies.

Introduction

The present study evolves from the intuitive rules research program developed by Stavy and Tirosh (2000). This program examines students' reasoning in the context of science and mathematics. Stavy and Tirosh (2000) observed that students react in similar ways to a wide variety of tasks that share some common, external features. They proposed that specific, salient features of a given task be it mathematical, scientific, or logical, will induce students to rely on a particular type of rule, which is domain general. So far, four types of responses were identified and, accordingly, four intuitive rules were defined: two relate to comparison tasks (*more A -- more B* and *same A -- same B*), and two to subdivision tasks (*everything comes to an end* and *everything can be divided endlessly*). Here we focus on the intuitive rule: *more A -- more B*.

Stavy and Tirosh (2000) suggested several teaching strategies that aim to help students overcome the effects of the intuitive rules, one of which is creating a cognitive conflict between intuitive and formal/logical reasoning. However, the impact of these strategies needs to be further examined. The purpose of this study is to investigate the effects of a cognitive conflict teaching strategy in the context of comparison of perimeters of geometrical shapes on accuracy of responses and reaction times.

The Intuitive Rule *More A -- more B*

We start by presenting a comparison-of-perimeter task, demonstrating the intuitive rule *more A -- more B*. Then we describe this intuitive rule in more general terms.

Children in grades 1, 3, 5, 7 and 9 (20 from each grade level) were presented with the following rectangle and polygon task, related to the comparison of perimeters (Azhari, 1998):

Two identical rectangles are presented. A small square is removed from the corner of one rectangle (e.g., from the upper right corner of the rectangle depicted on the right hand side of the figure) to form a polygon (see Figure 1).

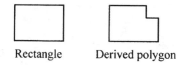

Rectangle   Derived polygon

Figure 1: A rectangle and a derived polygon.

The area of the rectangle is larger than that of the polygon, but their perimeters are equal. Participants are asked to compare the perimeters of the two shapes.

Azhari (1998) found that in each of these grade levels, at least 70% of the students incorrectly claimed that the perimeter of the rectangle is larger than that of the derived polygon because "the rectangle has more area", "a corner was not taken away" etc. These high percentages of *more A* (area or size of rectangle) -- *more B* (length of perimeter) responses at all grade levels suggest that this rule has a very strong effect on students' reasoning.

Responses of the type *more A -- more B* are observed in many scientific and mathematical tasks, including classic Piagetian conservation tasks and tasks related to intensive quantities. In all these tasks, relationships between two objects that differ in a salient quantity A are presented or described ($A_1 > A_2$). The participant is then asked to compare the two objects with respect to another quantity B (B_1 is not bigger than B_2 namely, $B_1 = B_2$ or $B_1 < B_2$). In all the cases examined, a substantial number of participants responded incorrectly according to the rule *more A* (the salient quantity) -- *more B* (the quantity in question), claiming that $B_1 > B_2$ (Babai & Alon, 2004; Stavy & Tirosh, 1996; Zazkis, 1999). We have suggested that students' responses are largely determined by the specific, irrelevant salient feature of the task (A), which trigger the intuitive rule *more A -- more B*, and not necessarily by their ideas about the task-specific content.

Responses in line with this intuitive rule are often correct as everyday life offers many opportunities in which a perceptual difference in one quantity (A) serves as a criterion for comparing another quantity (B), i.e., the more money you have the more you can buy. However, this rule, in many cases, is at variance with science, mathematics and logic and therefore leads to incorrect judgments as exemplified in students' responses to the comparison-of-perimeter task. These responses are regarded as intuitive because they are immediate, and are given with high confidence (Fischbein, 1987).

Recently, we have attempted to study the reasoning processes involved in intuitive responses of the type *more A -- more B*. For this purpose we used the comparison-of-perimeter task, employing reaction time technique. Babai, Levyadun, Stavy, and Tirosh (2006) presented 22 11th and 12th grade students with the following conditions:

1) Congruent - in which the correct response is in line with the intuitive rule. Namely, the polygon (created by adding a small square to the rectangle) has a larger area and a longer perimeter as compared to the rectangle (See Figure 2.A).

2) Incongruent - in which the correct response runs counter to the intuitive rule (see Figure 2.B). Namely, the polygon has larger area, but its perimeter is not longer than that of the rectangle (either shorter, i.e., incongruent-inverse, or equal, i.e., incongruent-equal).

These conditions are described in Figure 2.

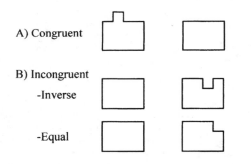

A) Congruent

B) Incongruent

-Inverse

-Equal

Figure 2: Congruent and incongruent task conditions.

As expected, almost all students provided correct responses to the comparison-of-area task in all conditions (Babai, et al., 2006). Similarly, almost all students correctly responded to the comparison-of-perimeter, congruent task. The reaction times for these tasks were relatively short (about 1300 ms). About 99% and 54% provided correct responses to the incongruent-inverse and incongruent-equal comparison-of-perimeter task, respectively, with relatively longer reaction times (1634 ms and 1785 ms, respectively). Clearly, reaction times of responses that are in line with the intuitive rule are shorter than the reaction times of responses that run counter to the intuitive rule.

These results can be explained as follows:

In this task the reasoning about perimeter is interfered by intuitive reasoning about area. The comparison of the areas of the two shapes is probably automatically processed since it is the salient feature in this task. This processing goes in parallel to that of the comparison of perimeter, about which the participants are asked. When the processing of area and perimeter result in the same conclusion (e.g., in-line with intuitive rule: larger area and larger perimeter) as it happens in the congruent condition, this is de facto the end of the processing and the participant correctly responds. If the result is two different conclusions (e.g., counter-intuitive: larger area - smaller perimeter, or larger area - equal perimeter) as it happens in the incongruent conditions, the created conflict has to be resolved either by overcoming (or inhibiting) the irrelevant component of the processing stream or by giving incorrect response relying on the area input. Resolution of the conflict is a time consuming process as it involves the activation of control mechanisms, and is reflected in longer reaction times and often also in lower accuracy. It is noteworthy that the interference of the intuitive rule in the incongruent-equal condition was larger than that of incongruent-inverse one. The incongruent-equal condition involves comparison of equal perimeters while the incongruent-inverse condition involves unequal perimeters. Judging equalities is known to be more demanding than inequalities (Vigotsky, 1962; Fias, Dupont, Reynvoet, & Orban, 2002).

A recent fMRI brain imaging study that used the same task supports our explanation related to the mechanism of resolving the conflict between intuitive and formal/logical reasoning in the incongruent condition (Stavy, Goel, Critchley, & Dolan, 2006). Activation of bilateral orbital frontal cortex, known for its executive inhibitory control over other brain regions, was evident when participants overcome the interference in the comparison-of-perimeter task in the incongruent condition and correctly completed the task. This finding suggests that the reasoning processes underlying correct responses to the incongruent problems involve activation of control mechanisms that overcome the conflict by inhibiting the irrelevant task feature (area).

The experiments described above suggest the importance of control mechanisms in overcoming the conflict between intuitive and formal/logical reasoning. In addition, Houde and colleagues (Houde & Guichart, 2001; Moutier, Angeard, & Houde, 2002; Moutier & Houde, 2003) and Dempster (Dempster & Corkil, 1999) suggested that reasoning biases are due to the failure of control mechanisms in the reasoning process and not necessarily to a lack of relevant logical components. They also showed that inhibition-training helped participants overcome these biases pointing again to the possibility of improving students' performance by strengthening their control mechanisms.

In the present study we used cognitive conflict training, in which students were confronted with a conflict between their intuitive incorrect responses (based on the salient feature, area) and the correct response. We compared accuracy of responses and reaction times before and after training. It is predicted that accuracy of responses to the comparison-of-perimeter incongruent conditions will increase as a result of the cognitive conflict training. With respect to reaction times, if the training effect is to strengthen control mechanisms it is predicted that reaction times will increase as students will be more aware of the conflict and will devote more effort to overcome it.

Methods

Participants

Forty seven students in Grade 8th from two classes in the Sharon area in Israel (middle class population) participated in the study. These students comprised all the students in these classes. One class was defined as the experimental group (N=24) and the other as the control group (N=23).

Instruments

In this study we used the comparison-of-area and comparison-of-perimeter test that was used in our previous study (Babai et al., 2006). The test consists of 48 trials, divided evenly into three types (congruent, incongruent-inverse and incongruent-equal). In each trial two polygons, were presented, one shape was the basic shape and the other was derived from it by adding or removing a small square. In half of the trials the basic shape was presented on the right-hand side whereas in the other half the basic shape was presented on the left-hand side.

The trials were prepared using Microsoft PowerPoint software and were presented on a computer screen by a computer program written in Microsoft Visual Basic 6.0, running under Microsoft Windows 2000. Each trial was presented on the screen until the subject responded by pressing one of the following keyboard keys: "a", ":" or space bar, each key was marked on the keyboard (corresponding to left is bigger, right is bigger or both are equal, respectively). The computer program measured the reaction time (from presentation of the trial to response) and type of response ("a", ":" or space). The trials were presented in a pseudo-random order, with an inter-stimulus interval of 500 ms, with the following constrains: 1) the same type of response (right shape is larger, left shape is larger, the two shapes are equal) did not appear on more than two consecutive trials; 2) the same type of task (congruent, incongruent-inverse, incongruent-equal) did not appear on more than two consecutive trials.

Procedure

Each participant was twice presented with the entire test, first as a pre-test and, after a month, as a post-test. In both occasions the participants were tested individually, in two sessions (the comparison-of-area part and the comparison-of-perimeter part) on two different days seven days apart. Half of the participants were asked to perform the comparison-of-perimeter part in the first session and the comparison-of-area part in the second, while the other half performed the tasks in reversed order. The trials that were presented in the comparison-of-perimeter part and in the comparison-of-area part were identical, and were shown in the same order. Moreover, the instructions in each session were similar: "Please determine if the left shape has a larger area/perimeter (click "a"), the right shape has a larger area/perimeter (click ":") or the areas/perimeters of both shapes are equal (click space bar). Try to answer correctly and as fast as you can".

At the start of each session, participants were presented with 14 training trials, randomly selected from the experimental trials, for practicing with the task and the experimental setting. Accuracy of responses and reaction times were recorded.

Cognitive Conflict Training

Step 1: Individual Work- Comparison of Perimeters
Each student received three opaque bags each containing two cardboard shapes (S1 and S2; see Figure 3): Bag A (contained shapes which represent the congruent condition), Bag B (contained shapes which represent the incongruent-inverse condition) and Bag C (contained shapes which represent the incongruent-equal condition). They were asked to sequentially open each bag, to compare the perimeters of the two shapes in each bag and to write their decisions and their explanations. The cardboard shapes were different from those that were included in the comparison-of-area and comparison-of-perimeter test.

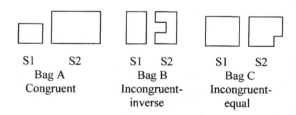

Figure 3: Schematic description of problems in Step 1 of the training.

Step 2: Creating Cognitive Conflict Students were asked to volunteer to present their solutions on the board and to explain them to the entire class. Many students wanted to present their solution to the congruent problem in Bag A. One student was invited. He correctly argued that both the area and the perimeter of Shape 2 are larger than those of Shape 1. All students agreed with him. The student then argued in respect to the incongruent-inverse problem in Bag B that Shape 1 has larger area and larger perimeter than

Shape 2. About half of the students agreed with him. Three students argued, correctly that this answer is wrong; they stated that although the area of Shape1 is larger than that of Shape 2 its perimeter is smaller. Many students became involved in this discussion. The conflict was resolved only after putting Shape 2 on Shape 1 and showing visually that the areas and the perimeters of the two shapes do not go "hand in hand": The area of Shape 1 is larger, but its perimeter is smaller. Many students then changed their reactions to the incongruent-equal problem in Bag C stating correctly that the area of Shape 1 is larger, but its perimeter is equal to that of Shape 2. Still, some students argued that Shape 1 has larger area and larger perimeter than Shape 2. The dispute was resolved when the students who correctly responded to the task used the strategy of overlapping the shapes and visually showing the decrease in area in Shape 2 and the equivalence in the perimeters of the two shapes.

Step 3: Individual Work - Consolidation Exercises
Students were given 10 additional problems (congruent, incongruent-inverse and incongruent-equal) each presenting two shapes (the basic shape was a square). Each student worked individually on this assignment. Practically all students correctly responded to these problems. The few incorrect responses were corrected by the teacher.

Results

Pretest

Table 1 shows the results obtained in the pre-test.

Table 1: Mean accuracy (N=47) and reaction times (RT) of correct responses (N=22) in the pre-test.

Condition	Area Task		Perimeter Task	
	Accuracy [%] (SEM)	RT [ms] (SEM)	Accuracy [%] (SEM)	RT [ms] (SEM)
Con-gruent	90.3 (1.8)	1068 (73)	93.2 (1.4)	1602 (176)
Incon-gruent-inverse	90.4 (2.9)	1229 (95)	55.6 (6.4)	2517 (478)
Incon-gruent-equal	93.8 (1.9)	1062 (72)	22.9 (4.2)	2888 (867)

The pattern of behavior of the students in this study is similar to that reported by Babai et al. (2006). More than 90% of the students provided correct responses to the comparison-of-area task in all conditions and the reaction times were shorter than those of the comparison-of-perimeter task (See Table 1). Similarly, almost all students (93%) provided correct responses to the comparison-of-perimeter congruent condition. The percentages of correct responses to the two comparison-of-perimeter incongruent conditions are smaller than those provided to the congruent condition. These differences are significant between congruent and incongruent-inverse ($t(46)=6.137$; $p<0.001$), and also the between congruent and incongruent-equal ($t(46)=16.883$; $p<0.001$). The percentages of correct responses to the incongruent-inverse condition are larger than those of the incongruent-equal condition and these differences are significant ($t(46)=6.426$; $p<0.001$). Regarding reaction times, the differences between the comparison-of-perimeter conditions are significant ($F(20)=4.11$; $p=0.032$).

The percentages of correct responses to the comparison-of-perimeter task in the two incongruent conditions are somewhat smaller than those reported by Babai et al. (2006) and the related reaction times are somewhat longer. These differences could result from the difference in ages between the two populations (8th graders in the current study, 11-12 graders in Babai et al.) and/or from the fact that the students in Babai et al. study were all majoring in mathematics (5 points, the most advanced level) whereas the students in the current study are in grade eight and thus they are not yet grouped by level of mathematics achievements. Once again these results support our previous assertion that area is the salient feature in this task and that responses that are in line with the intuitive rule *more A -- more B* are more accurate and are provided in a shorter time than responses that run counter to the intuitive rule.

Effect of Cognitive Conflict Training

As mentioned above, our intervention aimed at improving students responses to the incongruent comparison-of-perimeter task. Therefore in examining the effect of the intervention we focus on students who initially provided correct responses to less than 50% of the comparison-of-perimeter incongruent trials (13 students in the experimental group and 7 in the control group).

Table 2: Mean accuracy in the incongruent comparison-of-perimeter conditions before and after intervention.

Condition	Experimental (N=13)		Control (N=7)	
	Pre-test [%] (SEM)	Post-test [%] (SEM)	Pre-test [%] (SEM)	Post-test [%] (SEM)
Incon-gruent-inverse	3 (0.26)	88 (0.48)	15 (0.36)	65 (0.65)
Incon-gruent-equal	2 (0.17)	45 (0.69)	10 (0.23)	12 (0.94)

Accuracy As can be seen from Table 2 the intervention was instrumental in increasing the accuracy of responses of the students in the experimental group to both incongruent conditions. These differences are significant for the incongruent-inverse and incongruent-equal conditions ($t(12)=16.4$; $p<0.001$ and $t(12)= -5.123$; $p<0.001$ respectively). The accuracy of responses of the experimental group to the incongruent-inverse condition is significantly higher than to the incongruent-equal condition (t(12)=5.477; $p<0.001$).

Interestingly, the accuracy of responses to the incongruent-inverse condition of students in the control group, who only repeated the task, significantly increased from pre-test to post-test (t(6)=5.7767; $p<0.001$). Yet, in this group no improvement was observed in the incongruent-equal condition from pre-test to post-test.

Reaction Time In addition to examining the impact of intervention on accuracy of responses we also examined its impact on reaction times to correct responses before and after the intervention. The comparison is made in reference to the congruent, area and perimeter tasks before and after intervention (these are the only tasks that were answered correctly by most participants both before and after intervention).

In both groups, reaction times to the comparison-of-area task decreased in the post-test. In the experimental group the reaction time decreased from 1317 ms to 1000 ms (t(12)= 2.15; $p=0.052$). In the control group the reaction time decreased from 1405 ms to 912 ms (t(6)= 2.455; $p<0.05$).

Reaction times to the comparison-of-perimeter task showed a different pattern. In the experimental group the reaction time increased from 1245 ms to 1467 ms, while in the control group it decreased from 1416 ms to 1075 ms. The interaction: group (experimental, control) x time (pre-test, post-test) was obtained with significance level of $p=0.07$ (F(18)=3.487).

Discussion

Our aim in this study was to examine the impact of a cognitive conflict training on students' responses to comparison-of-perimeter task. We predicted that a cognitive conflict training, consisting of confronting students with a discrepancy between their intuitive incorrect responses and the correct response, will result in increment in accuracy of responses to comparison-of-perimeter incongruent trials. Our data show that indeed, the cognitive conflict training used in this study resulted in increment in the accuracy of responses to both incongruent conditions.

A careful examination of the data reveals that the increment in the accuracy of responses of the experimental group to the incongruent-inverse condition is significantly higher than to the incongruent-equal one. This suggests that the incongruent-equal condition is more demanding than the incongruent-inverse. The finding that in the control group the accuracy of responses to the incongruent-inverse condition significantly increased by mere repetition whereas the accuracy of responses to the incongruent-equal condition did not, also implies that the incongruent-equal condition is indeed more demanding than the incongruent-inverse.

The results are in line with our previous findings that the accuracy of responses of 11th grade, mathematics major students to the incongruent-inverse perimeter trials is higher than that given to the incongruent-equal ones (Babai, et al., 2006). The data of the current study provide further support to our assertion that the interference of the area in the incongruent-equal condition is larger than that in the incongruent-inverse one. Again we realize that judging equalities is more demanding than judging inequalities (Vigotsky, 1962; Fias, Dupont, Reynvoet, & Orban, 2002). These differences have a substantial effect not only on responses to tasks but also on the learning related to them.

The situation is more complex regarding reaction times. The reaction times for both congruent comparison-of-area and congruent comparison-of-perimeter trials in the control group were significantly shorter in the post-test. This suggests that mere repetition increases participants' efficiency in solving the task. However, in the experimental group, while the reaction time to the congruent comparison-of-perimeter task increased, the reaction time to the congruent comparison-of-area task decreased from pre-test to post-test. It seems that raising students' awareness by cognitive conflict training to the possible interference of the intuitive rule: *more A* (area) -- *more B* (perimeter) resulted in an increment in reaction time to the congruent perimeter task. This suggests that such awareness activates effortful and time consuming control mechanisms. It may very well be that the activation of control mechanisms is general in the sense that it implies to all comparison-of-perimeter task conditions: congruent as well as incongruent. Thus, activation of control mechanisms results in increment in accuracy of responses (to the incongruent condition), yet trials that were solved correctly and fast before the intervention (congruent) will still be correctly solved but not as fast as prior to the intervention.

We believe that research in science and mathematics education would benefit from applying cognitive psychology techniques, as done in the current study. Using such methodologies could lead to a deeper understanding of students' difficulties and reasoning processes, and to the development of improved instructional strategies.

References

Azhari, N. (1998). *Using the intuitive rule "Same A – same B" in conservation tasks.* Unpublished manuscript (in Hebrew).

Babai, R. & Alon, T. (2004). *Intuitive thinking, cognitive level or grade level: What predict students' incorrect responses in science and mathematics?* Paper presented at the National Association of Research in Science Teaching, NARST - Annual Conference. Vancouver, Canada

Babai, R., Levyadun, T., Stavy, R., & Tirosh, D. (2006) Intuitive rules in science and mathematics: A preliminary reaction time study. *International Journal of Mathematics Education in Science and Technology* (in press).

Dempster, F. N. & Corkil, A. J. (1999). Interference and inhibition in cognition and behavior: Unifying themes for educational psychology. *Educational Psychology Review, 11,* 1-88.

Fias, W., Dupont, P., Reynvoet, B., & Orban G. A. (2002). The quantitative nature of a visual task differentiates between ventral and dorsal stream. *Journal of Cognitive Neuroscience, 14,* 646-658.

Fischbein, E. (1987). *Intuition in science and mathematics.* Dordrecht, The Netherlands: Reidel.

Houde, O. & Guichart, E. (2001). Negative priming effect after inhibition of number/length interference in a Piaget-like task. *Developmental Science, 4*, 119-123.

Moutier, S., Angeard, N., & Houde, O. (2002) Deductive reasoning and matching-bias inhibition training: Evidence from a debiasing paradigm. *Thinking and Reasoning, 8*, 205-224.

Moutier, S. & Houde, O. (2003). Judgement under uncertainty and conjunction fallacy inhibition training. *Thinking and Reasoning, 9*, 185-201.

Stavy, R., Goel, V., Critchley, H., & Dolan, R. (2006) Intuitive interference in quantitative reasoning. *Brain Research, 1073-1074*, 383-388.

Stavy, R. & Tirosh, D. (1996). Intuitive rules in science and mathematics: The case of 'more of A – more of B". *International Journal of Science Education, 18*, 653-667.

Stavy, R. & Tirosh, D. (2000) *How students (mis-)understand science and mathematics*. New York: Teachers College Press.

Vygotsky, L. S. (1962). *Thought and language*. Cambridge, MA: MIT press.

Zazkis, R. (1999). Intuitive rules in number theory: Example of 'the more of A, the more of B' rule implementation. *Educational Studies in Mathematics, 40*, 197-209.

Neuro-Mathematics Education: Report on an International Emerging Sub-discipline

Anthony E. Kelly (akelly@nsf.gov)
National Science Foundation, 4201 Wilson Blvd.
Arlington, VA 22030 USA

Abstract

A decade has passed since the publication of Bruer's (1997) critique of the value of cognitive neuroscience studies for education. Since that time, important strides have been made in the development of brain-imaging technologies. Further, the design of stimulus tasks to better understand the correlates of brain activity with learning behaviors has advanced. This presentation will report on international efforts to foster a new subdiscipline at the intersection of cognitive neuroscience and mathematics education research. The findings of three interdisciplinary conferences in 2006 (Learning Lab Denmark, Copenhagen; George Mason University, USA, and Vanderbilt University, USA) and one at NSF in 2007 will be summarized and future implications drawn.

History of International Efforts - OECD

Bruer wrote an influential article that questioned the value of pursuing linkages between neuroscience and education (Bruer, 1997). Based on a review of the literature at that time, it appeared to Bruer that the gulf between the two fields was, "a bridge too far." However, by 2005, the US National Science Foundation extended its educational research program announcement to consider how these linkages might be bridged over time in the Research on Learning and Education (ROLE) program, noting that:

> The effort to understand the relationships among learning, intelligence, and the human brain is one of the most fundamental and profound journeys of basic science. . . Fundamental aspects of visual and spatial cognition, language, and mathematics are beginning to be understood in terms of neural processes and biological context. Discoveries in these and other areas are influencing our understanding of behavior, cognition, and the nature of human learning.

The inaugural award funded by the ROLE program to the Organization for Economic Cooperation and Development (OECD) in 1999. The project, "Learning Sciences and Brain Research" tackled Bruer's challenged directly. The project's synthesis document was turned into an OECD publication entitled: "Understanding the Brain: Towards a New Learning Science." A second award from the NSF to the OECD attracted additional international financial support from the British Ministry of Education (DfES), the Lifelong Learning Foundation (UK), RIKEN Brain Sciences Institute, and the Japanese Ministry of Education, Culture, Sports, Science, and Technology (MEXT).

Three networks, each composed of a dozen scientists, educational researchers and policy makers, coordinated by a leading scientific institute, formed innovative groups to seek synergistic points of contact between current domains of research in cognitive and brain science on the one hand, and education practice and policy on the other. The networks were in numeracy, literacy, and life-long learning. The literacy and numeracy networks are closely related, not only methodologically (both involve quite similar experimental designs and tools such as neuroimaging, developmental paradigms, or rehabilitation software), but also in the terms of their subject matter. Advanced numeracy, for instance word problem solving or elementary algebra, depends on reading and writing skills. Furthermore, the same mechanisms of learning, reasoning, and working memory are likely to be at work in both domains. Finally, both domains are often (though not always) jointly affected in children who suffer from both dyscalculia and dyslexia. Although dyslexia research is much more advanced that dyscalculia research, the latter can benefit considerably from the theories and experimental designs which, in the last 15 years, have lead to considerable advances in dyslexia research. A second OECD publication, summarizing the second phase of NSF funding, is expected in 2007.

A Focus on Mathematics Learning

Mathematics is an attractive focus for cognitive neuroscience because: (a) its concepts can be expressed using multiple representations; (b) these representations can be related to specific brain areas in many cases; and (c) there is growing evidence that some brain areas appear to be "hard wired" for mathematics learning. Furthermore, mathematics problems are well suited to the simplified task design that allows for powerful use of brain-imaging technologies.

Brain-imaging research has begun to reveal which areas of the brain are most relevant to number processing. The parietal lobe appears to be important, particularly a small region deep inside the intraparietal sulcus (for reviews see S. Dehaene, Molko, Cohen, & Wilson, 2004; S. Dehaene, Piazza, Pinel, & Cohen, 2002). This region is systematically activated whenever we calculate or think about numbers. It is present in both hemispheres. This region appears to be involved in the representation and manipulation of numerical quantities (whether as numbers presented as

Arabic digits, spoken or written words, or even as sets of dots), and is thus a good candidate for a brain area involved in our developing "number sense" (Dehaene, 1997). An emerging body of literature suggests that there may be anatomical and functional deficits of the intraparietal sulcus at the precise coordinates where activation is observed in normal subjects during arithmetic (e.g., in severe infant prematurity, Isaacs et al. , 2001; genetic diseases such as Turner syndrome or fragile X).

Human beings appear to be born with a simple "number sense" that seems to precede facility with language. From a very early age, infants "mathematize" the world and do not start with a "blank slate" (for a review, see Feigenson, Dehaene, & Spelke, 2004). They can see the difference between 2 and 3 objects, or even between much larger quantities such as 8 versus 16 dots (Xu, 2003). They are also sensitive to number in the auditory modality, for instance discriminating 2 and 3 sounds, and might even recognize the common number concept behind "two" sounds and "two" objects (Starkey, Spelke, & Gelman, 1990). There is also evidence that infants can operate with numbers abstractly. For instance, when one object, then another, is hidden behind a screen, they expect to see two objects when the screen drops (Wynn, 1992). They also expect 5 objects plus 5 objects to make about 10 objects (McCrink & Wynn, 2004).

Regrettably, some children (perhaps 3-5% of the population) suffer from a weakness in a hypothesized quantity system in a manner similar to children who suffer from dyslexia (e.g., Butterworth, 1999). This condition, known as dyscalculia, severely hampers mathematics learning and typically involves related emotional difficulties that can distract children from focusing on their mathematics learning.

Most importantly, we are learning that brain-based deficits are not a "death sentence" for learning. The brain shows remarkable plasticity, and we believe that concerted cognitive neuroscience effort in the area of mathematics education can be begin to find ways to take advantage of this plasticity. Learning gains due to extensive computer-based training have already been shown in dyslexia (e.g., McCandliss, Beck, Sandak & Perfetti, 2003; Temple, Deutsch, Poldrack, Miller, Tallal, Merzenich & Gabrieli, 2003).

At more advanced levels of learning mathematics, Qin, Carter, Silk, Stenger, Fissell, Goode and Anderson (2004) found that the same regions are active in children solving algebra equations as are active in experienced adults solving equations. For both children and adults, practice in symbol manipulation produced a reduced activation in the prefrontal cortex area. However, practice for children seemed also to produce a decreased activity in a parietal area that may be thought of as holding an image of the equation. These results are integrated in a cognitive model that predicts both the behavioral and brain-imaging results.

Affective and Attentional Processes. It has been known for some time that mathematics performance can be lowered by related emotional difficulties, e.g., "mathematics anxiety" (Ashcraft & Ridley, 2005; Hembree, 1990). The drastic effect of emotion on the learning of mathematics by dyscalculic children is clear from the work of Butterworth, and colleagues (e.g., Butterworth, 2005).

Work by McCandliss, and colleagues has explored a linkage between attentional processes and learning (e.g., Tamm, et al., in press; Fan et al., 2002). At the cognitive and brain levels, Bush, Luu and Posner (2000) examined attentional disruptions within healthy adults performing simple cognitive tasks, and found distinct brain regions associated with attentional disruptions caused by emotional vs. cognitive factors.

Neuro-mathematics Education: The Latest Phase

Growing out of the OECD initiatives, a related international project was begun in 2006, also with NSF support (Kelly; REC-0107008). This project has co-funded three interdisciplinary conferences: one in Copenhagen in cooperation with the Learning Lab, Denmark; one near Washington, DC, in cooperation with George Mason University; and one in Nashville, TN, in cooperation with Vanderbilt University, Sackler Institute for Developmental Psychobiology, Weill Cornell Medical College, and George Mason University. The National Science Foundation is supporting a conference on neuron-mathematics education in May 2007. These last two meetings, which will be described in greater detail during the presentation, narrowed the focus to mathematics learning and cognitive neuroscience.

The Importance of Task Design. An analysis of successful interdisciplinary work in Phases I and II of the OECD projects showed that progress at the intersection of learning and neuroscience occurs when researchers cooperate in designing diagnostic tasks for brain-imaging technology. These tasks must be simple enough to be used in a brain-imaging study, yet powerful enough to assess deep knowledge in the content area. The classic example is the use of rhyming and non-rhyming nonsense words as a simple, yet illuminating, test for dyslexia (for the specificity of task design, see Shaywitz, et al., 1998). Similarly, in mathematics education, varying stimuli even by a simple feature, advances powerful brain-imaging analyses.

Once suitable tasks are identified, and whose solution is known to have certain brain activity correlates, work can begin on the design of related instructional assessments and interventions. The efficacy of these instructional interventions on promoting learning can then be tested in a brain-imaging context. One classic example here is the work of Temple, et al. (2003) who showed that specifically-designed reading interventions can lead to the recruitment of brain regions for dyslexics that were typically only recruited by fluent readers. In other words, instruction was shown to be effective, not only behaviorally, but also at the level of brain processing.

Task Design in Neuro-Mathematics Education. The first two meetings of interested international researchers in cognitive neuroscience and mathematics education were devoted to establishing cordial and trusting relationships, which form the backbone of interdisciplinary study. The third meeting, at Vanderbilt University, focused specifically on the design of stimulus tasks for use in fMRI and EEG studies. The presentation at EuroCogSci 07 will detail the themes and deliberations, particularly those taking place between November 2006 (the date of the most recent meeting) and May 2007. The guiding questions for the meeting were:

(a) What are the major milestones of achievement and the major obstacles to success that define the developmental path to mathematical competence and mathematical expertise? What is the evidence that supports the conclusions that we can draw about these milestones and obstacles?

(b) How can achievement of these milestones and overcoming of these obstacles be measured? What kinds of tasks, problems, and testing situations provide the best measures? Which of these tasks, problems, and situations are compatible with cognitive-neuroscience methodology and hence could be used in studies of brain function?

(c) How can functional imaging techniques – fMRI, PET, ERP, MEG, TMS -- be applied to illuminating the nature of these milestones and obstacles as well as the changes that result from educational and instructional experiences and interactions, using the kinds of tasks, problems, and situations that provide the best measurements?

Acknowledgments

This work was sponsored in part by NSF award, REC-0107008. Opinions expressed are those of the author and do not necessarily reflect the opinions of the National Science Foundation.

References

Ashcraft, M. H., & Ridley, K. S. (2005). Cognitive consequences of math anxiety: A tutorial review. In J. I. D. Campbell (Ed.), *Handbook of Mathematical Cognition* (pp. 315-327). New York: Psychology Press.

Bruer, J. T. (1999), Education and the brain: A bridge too far. *Educational Researcher*, 26(8), 4-16.

Bush, G., Luu, P., & Posner, M. I. (2000, June), Cognitive and emotional influences in the anterior cingulate cortex, *Trends in Cognitive Sciences*, 4(6).

Butterworth, B. (1999). *The mathematical brain*, London: Macmillan.

Butterworth, B. (2005). Developmental dyscalculia. In Campbell,, J.I.D. (Ed.) *Handbook of Mathematical Cognition*. Hove: Psychology Press, 455-467.

Dehaene, S. (1997). *The number sense*. New York: Oxford University Press.

Dehaene, S., Molko, N., Cohen, L. & Wilson, A. J. (2004). Arithmetic and the brain. *Current Opinion in Neurobiology*, 14, 218-224.

Dehaene, S., Piazza, M., Pinel, P., & Cohen, L. (2002). "Three parietal circuits for number processing". *Cognitive Neuropsychology*, 20:(3), 487-506.

Fan, J.I., McCandliss, B. D., Somer, T., Raz, A., and Posner, M.I. (2002). Testing the efficiency and independence of attentional networks. *Journal of Cognitive Neuroscience*, 14, 340-347.

Feigenson, L., Dehaene, S., & Spelke, E. (2004). Core systems of number. *Trends in Cognitive Science*, 8(7), 307-314.

Hembree, R. (1990). The nature, effects and relief of mathematics anxiety. *Journal for Research in Mathematics Education*, 21(1), 33–46.

McCandliss, B.D., Beck, I., Sandak, R., & Perfetti, C. (2003). Focusing attention on decoding for children with poor reading skills: A study of the Word Building intervention. *Scientific Studies of Reading*.7(1),75-105.

McCrink, K., & Wynn, K. (2004). Large-number addition and subtraction by 9-month-old infants. *Psychological Science*, 15(11), 776-781.

Shaywitz, S. E., Shaywitz, B. A., Pugh, K. R., Fulbright, K. R., Constable, R. T., Einar Mencl, W., Shankweiler, D. P., Liberman, A. M., Skudlarski, P., Fletcher, J. M., Katz, L., Marchione, K. E., Lacadie, C., Gatenby, C. & Gore, J. C. (1998). *Proceedings of the National Academy of Sciences*, Vol. 95, Issue 5, 2636-2641

Starkey, P., Spelke, E. S., & Gelman, R. (1990). Numerical abstraction by human infants. *Cognition*, 36, 97-127.

Tamm, L., *McCandliss, B. D.*, Liang, B. A., Wigal, T. L., Posner, M. I., & Swanson, J. M. (in press). Can attention itself be trained? Attention training for children at-risk for ADHD. In K. McBurnett (Ed.), *Attention Deficit/Hyperactivity Disorder: A 21st Century Perspective*. New York: Marcel Dekker.

Temple, E., Deutsch, G. K., Poldrack, R. A., Miller, S. L., Tallal, P., Merzenich, M. M., & Gabrieli, J.D.E. (2003). Neural deficits in children with dyslexia ameliorated by behavioral remediation: Evidence from functional MRI. *Proceedings of the National Academy of Sciences*, 100(5), 2860-2865.

Qin, Y., Carter, C. S., Silk, E., Stenger, V. A., Fissell, K., Goode, A. & Anderson, J.R. (2004). The change of the brain activation patterns as children learn algebra equation solving. *Proceedings of National Academy of Sciences*,101(15), 5686-5691.

Wynn, K. (1992b) Addition and subtraction by human infants. *Nature* 358, 749–750

Xu, F. and Spelke, E.S. (2000) Large number discrimination in 6-month old infants. *Cognition* 74, B1–B11

Students' Appraisals and Emotions for Interpersonal Relationships with Teachers

Georgia Stephanou (gstephanou@uowm.gr, egoky1@otenet.gr)
University of Western Macedonia
Florina, 53100 Greece

Abstract

This research examined (a) students' (N = 216, 5th - 6th grades) attributions and emotions for the perceived quality of their interpersonal relationships with their teachers, (b) the association of attributions and intuitive appraisal of the relationships with the emotions, and (c) the association of appraisals and emotions with academic performance. The results showed that: (a) students attributed satisfactory interpersonal relationships to their own self and communication with teachers, and the negative relationships to teachers, (b) they experienced positive and negative emotions (mainly, outcome-) for positive and negative relationships, respectively, (c) attributions, and, particularly, intuitive appraisal had significant effect on emotions, and (d) emotions and, mainly, intuitive appraisal was positively related to academic performance.

Introduction

While teacher - student interaction is related to students' academic and behavioral outcomes, little research has examined children's own perceptions of their relationships with their teachers (Brok, Bergen, Stahl, & Brekelmans, 2004; Pianta, 1999; Pintrich & Schunk, 2002; Wang, Haertel, & Walberg, 1997; Stephanou, 2004, 2005a). Similarly, although students' emotions have important implications for their emotional well being and academic achievement, little research has investigated students' emotions for their interpersonal relationships with their teachers (Diener, 2000; Jarvenoja, & Jarvela, 2005; Pekrun, 2000; Pekrun, Goetz, Titz, & Perry, 2002; Stephanou, 2004; 2005b; Valeski & Stipek, 2001). Also, a limited number of investigations have studied the association of students' perceptions of such relationships, and emotions, with their academic performance in upper elementary school, although the high importance of this period in students' future academic development (Birch & Ladd, 1998; Furrer & Skinner, 2003; Hamre & Pianta, 2001; Harter, 1999; Lynch & Cicchetti, 1997; Skinner, 1998).

In sum, previous findings support that children, who have a close and secure relationship with the teacher, are more emotionally and behaviourally engaged in academic work, and, usually, succeed (Skinner & Belmont, 1993; Stephanou, 2005a; Wubbels & Brekelmans, 1998). Similarly, children's satisfaction with school is positively related to their own perceptions of teachers' support (Baker, 1999). Also, positive emotions, such as enjoyment and pride, enhance motivation, facilitate learning and increase performance (Meyer & Turner, 2002, Pekrun et al., 2002; Stephanou, 2004).

While the antecedents of emotions for an interpersonal relationship are extent and various, attributional appraisal is a major source of them (Fletcher, 2002; Pintrich & Schunk, 2002; Weiner, 2002). However, the correlation among attributions and the mentioned factors has limitedly studied.

This research is based on Weiner's (1992, 2001, 2002) theory of attributions which has been used in studying interpersonal relationships (see Argyle, 2001; Fletcher, 2002; Hewstone & Antaki, 2001).

Attributions and Emotions for Interpersonal Relationships

Although, an interpersonal relationship could be attributed to infinite number of attributions, self, other person, situation, environment, self – other person interaction, and relationship itself are the most prominent causes in describing positive and negative relationships (Argyle, 2001; Erber & Gilmour, 1995; Planalp & Rivers, 1996). Attributions are categorized into causal dimensions of locus of causality (internal / external), stability (stable / unstable over time) and controllability (personal and external controllable / uncontrollable), which have psychological and behavioral consequences.

Individuals tend to attribute the positive interpersonal relationships to themselves (internal, stable, personal controllable, and the external uncontrollable), and the negative relationships to the other person and situational factors (Weiner, 2001, 2002). Furthermore, the more negative the interpersonal relationship the more the attributions to the other person's constant negative properties (Argyle, 2001; Hewstone & Antaki, 2001) -

According to attribution theory of emotions, there are 'outcome- dependent' (e.g., happiness, pleasure, sadness) emotions, that are probably the initial and strongest reaction to perceived interpersonal relationship, and 'attribution – dependent' (e.g., gratefulness, hope) emotions, that are influenced by the causal explanation for the relationship (Oatley & Jenkins, 1998; Weiner, 1992). Locus of causality, stability and controllability mainly influence the self-esteem (pride)- expectancy (hope)- and social (shame, anger, gratitude)- related affects, respectively.

The belief that a student has about the causes of his / her interpersonal relationship with his / her teacher influences his / her feelings for the teacher, and expectations for the quality of the relationship in the future (Fletcher, 2002; Fletcher & Thomas, 1996; Stephanou, 2001; Weiner, 2001). Then, emotions and expectancy influence students' actual behavior toward the teacher and the relationship between them (Fletcher & Clark, 2002, Weiner, 2001).

Aim of this Study

This research aimed to examine (a) students' attributions and emotions for the perceived quality of their interpersonal relationships with their teachers, (b) the association of the attributional and intuitive appraisals of relationships with the subsequent emotions, and academic performance, and (c) the correlation of emotions with academic performance.

Hypotheses

1. (a) Students would attribute the perceived interpersonal relationships with their teachers to various factors (among them, teacher, self, teacher - student interaction and environment). (b) Positive relationships would be attributed to internal, stable, personal controllable and external uncontrollable (e.g., self properties) causes, while negative interpersonal relationships would be ascribed to external, unstable, external controllable, and personal uncontrollable (e.g., teacher- related) causes. (c) Locus of causality would be the strongest dimension in discriminating the two groups of students.
2. Students would experience positive and negative emotions (mainly, outcome- dependent) for the positive and negative interpersonal relationships, respectively.
3. (a) Each attributional dimension would be mainly related to specific kind of emotions, as suggested in attributional theories. (b) The intuitive appraisal and the reflective appraisal, compared the one to other, would be better associated with the outcome- and attribution- dependent emotions, respectively.
4. The intuitive appraisal of the interpersonal relationships and the emotions (particularly, achievement- related) for the same relationships would be associated with academic performance.

Methodology

Participants

A total of 216 elementary school students, both gender, fifth and sixth grades, and a total of 18 teachers participated in this research. The participants came from eighteen different schools from Greece. Teachers and students came from the same classes, with twelve students participating form each class. 130 and 86 pupils perceived that they had positive and negative interpersonal relationships with their teachers, respectively.

Measurements

Students' emotions for the perceived interpersonal relationships with their teachers were assessed by mentioning the extent to which they experienced 11 emotions (happiness, satisfaction, pleasure, pride, encouragement, love, hope, not angry – angry, cheerfulness, not irritated – irritated, gratefulness) (e.g., happy 7 6 5 4 3 2 1 unhappy). The consistency of the affect scale based on literature for interpersonal relationships, Feelings About School (FAS; Valeski & Stipek, 2001) measure, and findings from a pilot research. Alpha value was .81.

Students' attributions for the perceived interpersonal relationships with their teachers were examined via the modified Causal Dimension Scale II (CDSII, McAuley, Duncan, & Russell, 1992; Stephanou, 2001, 2005a). The scale allowed the students to indicate the most important factor which, according to their opinion, influenced the quality of their interpersonal relationships with their teachers, how much this factor contributed to the given interpersonal relationship, and then to classify that cause along the causal dimensions of locus of causality, stability, personal controllability and external controllability. Each subscale consists of three items, ranging form 1 (not at all stable) to 9 (totally stable). Alpha values were .83, .80, .76, and .81 for locus of causality, personal controllability, stability, and external controllability, respectively.

Students' perceptions of the quality of their interpersonal relationships with their teachers were estimated by responding to a seven- point four items ("I am satisfied for my relationship with my teacher"; "I have good relationship with my teacher") scale. This scale based on Student Teacher Relationship Scale (STRS; Pianta, 1999), and similar research (Hamre & Pianta, 2001; Stephanou, 2004). Alpha value was .72.

Students themselves defined their *interpersonal relationships with their teachers* as positive or negative. Students completed twice the interpersonal relationship scale. They, first, filled it for the current relationship, and, then, mentioned the lowest value in each item over which their relationship with the teacher would be positive. The mean score of the latter scale that was lower and equal / or above the mean score of the former scale was perceived as unsatisfactory and satisfactory relationships, respectively.

Teachers rated students' academic performance by responding to question 'Please rate the student's average academic performance this school year', very poor 1 2 3 4 5 6 7 8 9 10 excellence.

All questionnaires were in Greek Language.

Procedure

In order to ensure that the students had good time to form an impression about their interpersonal relationships with their teachers, they completed the scales at the middle of a school year. Similarly, they filled out first the emotions scale and then the attribution scale, to ensure that any relationship between attributions and emotions was not due to procedure used. Teachers completed the academic performance scale about each participating child in their classes.

Results

Attributions for the Interpersonal Relationships

Examination of the open – ended responses to attribution scale suggested that these could be categorized into the general categories presented in Table 1. The reliability of this coding scheme was evaluated by asking two judges, who were familiar with attribution theory, to place each of the open – ended responses into one of these categories.

There was a total agreement of 87% of the responses. Thus, Hypothesis 1a was confirmed.

Hypothesis 1b and 1c were in main confirmed.

Analysis of frequencies of attributions revealed significant effects. More precisely, the students attributed their positive interpersonal relationships with their teachers mainly to personal abilities (15.40%), effective communication with their teachers (23.10 %), teachers' understanding of their needs (13.80%) and teachers' care for them (11.50%), $x^2(8, N = 130) = 34.60$, $p < .01$, whereas they attributed their negative interpersonal relationships with their teachers mainly to teachers' bad behavior (21.20.%), teachers' lack of care for them (17.60%), ineffective communication with their teachers (15.30%) and teachers' lack of understanding their needs (11.80), $x^2(9, N = 86) = 29.00$, $p < .01$. In addition, the students, who estimated their interpersonal relationship with the teachers as positive, compared to students, who estimated these relationships as negative, mentioned often personal abilities, $x^2(1, N = 24) = 10.67$, $p < .01$, communication $x^2(1, N = 43) = 6.80$, and discussion, $x^2(1, N = 16) = 4.20$, $p < .05$.

Table 1: Frequency of students' attributions for their interpersonal relationships with their teachers

Attribution elements	Positive relationships		Negative relationships	
	f	%	f	%
Personal abilities	20	15.40	4	4.70
Communication	30	23.10	13	15.30
Teachers' care for students	17	11.50	16	17.60
Understand students' needs	18	13.80	10	11.80
Teaching methods	8	6.20	7	8.20
Discussion – conversation	12	9.20	4	4.70
Teachers' behavior	14	12.30	18	21.20
Criticism by teachers	--		6	7.10
Academic subjects	7	5.40	5	5.90
Other causes (e.g., friends, classmates, parents)	4	3.10	3	3.50

Regarding the findings for the attributional dimensions, one-way MANOVA analysis, with the perceived interpersonal relationship as independent variable and the attributional dimensions as dependent variables, showed a significant effect ($F(4, 211) = 44.60$, $p < 0.01$). Subsequent Discriminant Function analysis, with stepwise method, (Table 2) indicated that the students attributed their positive interpersonal relationship with their teachers to internal, personal controllable and stable factors, whereas they ascribed their negative relationships with their teachers to external, personal uncontrollable and unstable factors. However, there was not significant difference between the students with the positive relationships and the students with the negative relationships with respect to external controllable attributions. In addition, the locus of causality (.85) was the strongest dimension in discriminating the one

group of students from the other group, followed by personal controllability (.56), and stability (.37).

Table 2: Descriptive statistics and results from Discriminant analysis for students' attributional dimensions for their interpersonal relationships with their teachers

Attributional dimensions	Positive relationships		Negative relationships		Power	F*
	Mean	SD	Mean	SD		
Locus	18.90	5.00	13.50	5.90	.85	77.20
Personal con.	19.30	4.30	14.20	6.70	.56	68.30
Stability	18.60	5.75	14.80	5.80	.37	40.00
External con.	15.40	6.95	15.20	6.90	--	--

Note: *: $F(1, 215) \geq 40.00$, $p. < .01$; $-- = $ F- values $p > .05$.

Emotions for the Interpersonal Relationships

MANOVA analysis revealed significant effect of the perceived interpersonal relationship on students' emotions ($F(11, 204) = 51.65$, $p < 0.01$). More precisely, univariate analysis (Table, 3) showed that the students who perceived that they had good interpersonal relationships with their teachers experienced the intense positive emotions of happiness, pleasure, satisfaction, cheerfulness, pride, encouragement, hope, not irritated, love, gratefulness and no angry, whereas the students, who perceived that they had negative relationships with their teachers experienced the intense negative emotions of unhappiness, displeasure, dissatisfaction, sadness, irritation, shame, discouragement, hopelessness, not love, not gratefulness and angry. In addition, Discriminant Function analysis, with stepwise method, showed that the feeling of happiness (.85) was the strongest in discriminating the one from the other group of students, followed by the feelings of gratefulness (.71), pleasure (.68), hope (.65), satisfaction (.61), cheerfulness (.59), love (.53) and anger (.51), while the emotions of not irritation irritated, pride and encouragement had not significant effect. Part confirmation of Hypothesis 2

Table 3: Descriptive statistics and findings from t- tests for students' emotions for their relationships with their teachers

Emotions	Positive relationships		Negative relationships		t
	Mean	SD	Mean	SD	
Happiness	5.60	1.20	3.50	1.40	10.20
Satisfaction	5.50	1.20	3.60	1.60	8.90
Pleasure	5.65	1.40	3.70	1.70	9.20
Pride	4.90	1.50	4.00	1.50	6.50
Encouragement	5.00	1.40	4.00	1.60	6.55
Hope	5.80	1.30	3.85	1.70	9.00
Love	4.10	1.25	2.80	1.90	7.05
Anger-No anger	5.00	1.40	3.20	1.75	8.90
Cheerfulness	5.20	1.80	3.50	1.50	8.60
Not-irritated	4.80	1.35	3.00	1.60	8.75
Gratefulness	5.65	1.05	3.60	1.30	9.70

Note: *: All $t(1, 215)$- values are significant at $p < .01$ level.

Correlations among Intuitive and Attributional Appraisals of Student-Teacher Interpersonal Relationship, Emotions and Performance

The results from correlations coefficients analyses (Table 4), partly in agreement with Hypothesis 3a and 3b, showed: (a) the more positive relationship a student has with his / her teacher the more intense the positive emotions, mainly love and satisfaction, (b) the more negative relationship a student has with his / her teacher, the more intense the negative emotions, mainly unhappiness, sadness and dissatisfaction, (c) by attributing the positive interpersonal relationships to personal controllable, external uncontrollable, stable and internal factors, students felt intense positive emotions, particularly, happiness, satisfaction, pleasure and love, (d) by attributing the negative relationships to external, personal uncontrollable, unstable and external controllable factors, students experienced less intense negative emotions, particularly, angry, dissatisfaction and displeasure, (e) external controllability, followed by locus of causality, evidenced the strongest association with most of the emotions in negative interpersonal relationships, while stability, along with locus of causality, was most closely related to majority of emotions in positive relationships, (f) general (satisfaction / sadness), self (pride /shame)-, expectancy (hope, encouragement / hopelessness)- and other social (not anger, gratefulness / anger, not gratefulness, irritation)- related emotions were more strongly correlated to locus of causality, personal controllability, stability and external controllability dimension in positive / negative teacher-student interpersonal relationships, (g) attributions were more closely associated with general (happiness, love, sadness, dissatisfaction)- than attribution dependent- emotions (h) emotions were more strongly related to perceived teacher-student relationship than attributions, expect for hope in the positive relationships.

The results from the correlation analyses (Table 4), confirming Hypotheses 4a and 4b, showed that: (a) the more positive relationship a student has with his / her teacher the higher was his / her academic performance, (b) emotions (particularly, not angry / angry, encouragement / discouragement, hope / hopelessness, cheerfulness / sadness) were positively related to academic performance in the group of students with the positive and, mainly, with the negative interpersonal relationships with their teachers, and (c) the perceived teacher – student interpersonal relationships rather than the subsequent emotions were associated with academic performance.

Discussion and Conclusions

The observed attributional pattern for the teacher - student interpersonal relationships is, in main, consistent with our predictions. The elementary school children attributed their interpersonal relationships with their teachers to various causes, reflecting the high importance of such relationships in their life (Argyle, 2001; Hascher, 2003; Stephanou, 2005a). Furthermore, by attributing the positive relationships to personal properties, along with teacher-related factors, and external controllable causes, the students enhanced themselves, multiplied the chances of good relationship in the future, and indicated the crucial role of teacher in forming a supportive classroom climate (Furrer & Skinner, 2003; Durlak, 1998; Hofman, Hofman, & Guidemond, 2001; Jarvenoja, & Jarvela, 2005). By attributing the negative relationships to teachers' bad behavior and lack of care for students, pupils, on one hand, protected themselves, and, on the other hand, expressed their need for teachers' 'care for them' (Stephanou, 2005b; Wener, 2001). However, it should be mentioned that considering the other person as responsible for the negative interpersonal relationship does not facilitate future positive relationship (Mason, 2001; Weiner, 2001). Similarly, attributing the negative relationship to constant and external controllable negative factors (e.g., teacher's constant bad behavior) minimizes the chances for positive relationship in the future (Fletcher, 2002; Planalp & Rivers, 1996).

Students mentioned communication for their relationships with their teachers. This finding supports the interactive nature of the relationship, and the necessity of development students' and teachers' effective communicative skills.

The high importance of the positive student–teacher relationship for the students proved a significant source of their emotions (mainly, general) for the current quality of their interpersonal relationships with their teachers. Also, the students, being at the specific age and educational level, might have expected and needed positive relationships with their teachers (Meyer & Turner, 2002; Pianta, 1999; Pintrich & Schunk, 2002). Thus, non confirmation of students' expectations leaded to intense negative affects, while confirmation of them produced intense positive affects. However, research is needed to valid such correlations.

In sum, the correlations among emotions, attributions and intuitive appraisal of the teacher – student relationship are mainly in agreement with our predictions. For example, the fact that attributions were more closely related to emotions in negative than positive relationships supports the notion that individuals search for explanations of their negative than positive experiences (Weiner, 2002). Also, the pattern of correlations between attributions and emotions supports that each attributional dimension is related to specific kind of emotions. However, unexpectedly, external controllable attributions played a significant role in students' emotions, particularly, for negative relationships, hinting the children's sensitivity to classroom surroundings (Baker, 1999; Birch & Ladd, 1998; Hidi & Harackiewicz, 2002). Also, in contrast to our hypothesis, the intuitive appraisal rather than the attributional appraisal of the teacher- student interpersonal relationship was associated to students' attribution- dependent emotions, proposing the high importance of the relationship itself in students' emotional experience.

The present study also reveals that students' perceived quality of their relationship with their teachers, and emotions for this relationship correspond to their academic performance. It seems, in line with similar research (e.g.,

Table 4: Correlations among intuitive and attributional appraisals of student-teacher interpersonal relationship, subsequent emotions and academic performance

	Perceived relationship	Locus of Causality	Personal controllability	Stability	External Controllability	Academic performance
	Positive interpersonal relationships (N = 130)					
Happiness	.50	.40	.35	.42	-.32	--
Satisfaction	.52	.43	.34	.40	-.42	.18
Pleasure	.48	.38	.34	.30	-.34	.26
Pride	.28	.28	.30	.26	--	.29
Encouragement	.16	.19	--	.30	--	.35
Hope	.35	.34	.22	.40	-.18	.33
Love	.57	.40	.35	.42	-.45	--
Not Angry	.34	--	.25	.25	-.38	.37
Cheerfulness	.45	.34	.40	.32	-.32	.30
Not Irritated	.44	.19	.32	.32	--	--
Gratefulness	.46	.38	.32	.30	-.40	--
Perceived relationship						.45
	Negative interpersonal relationships (N = 86)					
Unhappiness	.64	-.35	-.30	-.36	.45	--
Dissatisfaction	.66	-.40	-.28	-.32	.52	.26
Displeasure	.60	-.38	-.35	-.25	.46	.32
Shame	.30	-.35	-.38	---	.25	.22
Discouragement	.50	-.22	--	-.20	.25	.40
Hopelessness	.58	-.32	-.20	-.40	.34	.38
Hate	.38	--	--	--	.25	--
Angry	.54	-.38	-.32	-.38	.45	.37
Sadness	.65	-.35	--	-.27	.30	.42
Irritated	.32	--	--	--	.28	.21
Not grateful	.46	--	--	-.30	.34	.36
Perceived relationship						.65

Notes *: r (130) ≥ .25, p < .01, r (130) < .25, p < .05, r (86) ≥ .28, p < .01, r (86) < .28, p < .05, -- = values are not significant at the .05 level of significance.

Valeski & Stipek, 2001; Stephanou, 2004, 2005a), that the students who perform relatively poorly in school are disadvantaged, and they perceive their relationship with their teachers as negative.

Overall, the findings reveal association among students' relationships with the teachers, attributions, emotions, and performance. Thus, teachers should concern about all aspects of students' experience in school. Attributional retraining helps students to change maladaptive attributional patterns. Research is needed to examine the effect of socio-cognitive factors, such as self-efficacy and perceived teachers' support, on the observed association.

References

Argyle, M. (2001). Social relationships. In M. Hewstone, W. Stroebe, J. P. Codol, & G. M. Stepheson (Eds.), *Introduction to social psychology*. Oxford: Blackwell.

Baker, J. (1999). Teacher – student interaction in urban at-risk classrooms: Differential behavior, relationship quality, and student satisfaction with school. *The Elementary School Journal, 100*, 57 – 70.

Birch, S., & Ladd, G. (1998). Children's interpersonal behaviours and the teacher - child relationship. *Developmental Psychology, 34*, 934 – 946.

Brok, P. den, Bergen, T., Stahl, R. J., & Brekelmans, M. (2004). Students' perceptions of teacher control behaviours. *Learning and Instruction, 14*, 425 – 443.

Diener, E. (2000). Subjective well-being. The science of happiness and a proposal for national index. *American Psychologist, 55*(1), 34 – 43.

Durlak, J. A. (1998). Common risk and protective factors in successful prevention programs. *American Journal of Orthopsychiatry, 68*, 512 – 520.

Erber, R., & Gilmour, R (1995). *Theoretical frameworks for personalrelationships*. Hillsdale, N.J.: Lawrence Erlbaum.

Fletcher, G. J. O. (2002). *The new science of intimate relationships*. Oxford: Basil Blackwell.

Fletcher, G. J. O., & Clark, M. S. (2002). *Handbook of social psychology: Interpersonal processes*. Oxford: Basil Blackwell.

Fletcher, G. J. O., & Thomas, G. (1996). Close relationship lay theories: Their structure and function. In G. J. O. Fletcher & J. Fitness (Eds.), *Knowledge structures in close relationships: A social psychological approach*. New Jersey: Lawrence Erlbaum.

Furrer, C., & Skinner, E. (2003). Sense of relatedness as a factor children's academic engagement and performance. *Journal of Educational Psychology, 95*(1), 148 – 163.

Hamre, B. K., & Pianta, R. C. (2001). Early teacher-child relationships and the trajectory of children's school outcomes through eighth grade. *Child Development, 72*(2), 625 – 638.

Harter, S. (1999). *The construction of the self: A developmental perspective.* New York: Guilford.

Hascher, T. (2003). Well-being in school – why students need social support. In Ph. Mayring, & Ch. V. Rhoneck (Eds.), *Learning emotions. The influence of affective factors on classroom learning* (pp. 127 – 142). NY: Lang.

Hidi, S., & Harackiewicz, J. M. (2002). Motivating the academically unmotivated: A critical issue for the 21st century. *Review of Educational Research, 70*(2), 151-179.

Hewstone, M., & Antaki, M. (2001). Attribution theory and social explanations. In M. Hewstone, W. Stroebe, J. P. Codol, & G. M. Stepheson (Eds.), *Introduction to social psychology.* Oxford: Basil Blackwell.

Hofman, H. R., Hofman, A., & Guidemond, H. (2001). Social context, effects on pupils' perception of school. *Learning and Instruction, 11*(3), 171 – 194.

Jarvenoja, H., & Jarvela, S. (2005). How students describe the sources of their emotional and motivational experiences during the learning process: A qualitative approach. *Learning and Instruction, 15*, 465 480.

Lynch, M., & Cicchetti, D. (1997). Children's relationships with adults and peers: An examination of elementary and junior high school students. *Journal of School Psychology, 35*, 81 – 89.

Mason, L. (2001). Response to anomalous data on controversial topics and theory change. *Learning and Instruction,* 11, 453 - 483.

McAuley, E., Duncan, T. E., & Russell, D. W. (1992). Measuring causal attributions: The revised Causal Dimension Scale (CDSII). *Personality and Social Psychology Bulletin, 18*, 566 – 573.

Meyer, D. K., & Turner, J. C. (2002). Discovering emotion in classroom motivation research. *Educational Psychologist, 37*(2), 107 – 114.

Pekrun, R. (2000). A social- cognitive, control - value theory of achievement emotions. In J. Heckhausen (Ed.), *Motivational psychology of human development.* Oxford: Elsevier.

Pekrun, R., Goetz, T., Titz, W., & Perry, R. P. (2002). Academic emotions in students' self-regulated learning and achievement: Program of qualitative and quantitative research. *Educational Psychologist, 82*(1), 33- 40.

Pianta, R. (1999). *Enhancing relationships between children and teachers.* Washington: Psychological Association.

Pintrich, P. R. (2003). A motivational science perspective on the role of student motivation in learning and teaching contexts. *Journal of Educational Psychology, 95*(4), 667-686.

Pintrich, P. R., & Schunk, D. (2002). *Motivation in education: Theory, research, and applications* (2nd ed.). Upper Saddle River, NJ: Prentice Hall.

Planalp, S., & Rivers, M. (1996). Changes in knowledge of personal relationships. In G. J. O. Fletcher & J. Fitness (Eds.), *Knowledge structures in close relationships: A social psychological approach.* NJ: Lawrence Erlbaum.

Skinner, E. A. (1998). Commentary: Strategies for studying Social Influences on Motivation. In J. Heckhausen & C. S. Dweck (Eds.), *Motivation and self – regulation across the life – span.* New York: Cambridge University Press.

Skinner, E. A., & Belmont, M. J. (1993). Motivation in the classroom: Reciprocal effects of teacher behaviour and student engagement across the school year. *Journal of Educational Psychology, 85*, 571-581.

Stephanou, G. (2001). Attributions and emotions for the interpersonal relationship between students and teachers. In L. Beze (Ed.), *Proceeding of the 8[ov] Hellenic Congress of the Psychological Research* (CD form). Greece: Publisher.

Stephanou, G. (2004). School learning and achievement as social activities: The role of the interper-sonal relationships and the subsequent emotions in academic achievement. In N. P. Terzis (Ed.), *Proceedings of the 5th International Congress of Balkan Society for Pedagogy and Education: Quality in Education in the Balkans* (pp. 195 – 203). Thessaloniki: Kyriakidis Brothers s.a.

Stephanou, G. (2005a). Academic performance and interpersonal relationships. In F. Vlachos, F. Bonoti, P. Metallidou, I. Dermitzaki, & A. Efklides (Eds.), Human behavior and learning. *Scientific Annals of the Psychological Society of Northern Greece*, Vol. 3 (pp. 201 - 228). Athens: Ellinika Grammata

Stephanou, G. (2005b, June). Kindergarten pupils' cognitive style: Effects on their preferences for teacher characteristics, interpersonal relationships and academic emotions. *Proceeding of the 10th Annual Conference of the European Learning Styles Information Network* (CD Form). University of Surrey, UK.

Valeski, T. N., & Stipek, D. J. (2001). Young Children's Feelings about School. *Child Development, 72*(4). 1198 - 1213.

Wang, M. C., Haertel, G. D., & Walberg, H. J. (1997). Learning influences. In H. J. Walberg & G. D. Haertel (Eds.), *Psychology and educational practice.* Berkeley, CA: McCatchan.

Weiner, B. (1992). *Human motivation: Metaphors, theories and research.* London: Sage.

Weiner, B. (2001). Intrapersonal and interpersonal theories of motivation from an attribution perspective. In S. Farideh & C. Chi-yue (Eds.), *Student motivation: The culture and context of learning.* Dordrecht, Netherlands: Kluwer Academic Publishers.

Weiner, B. (2002). *Social emotions and personality inferences: A Scaffold for a new direction in the study of achievement motivation.* Key Speech at the 8th WATM & Motivation and Emotion Conference, Moskow, Russia.

Wubbels, T., & Brekelmans, M. (1998). The teacher factor in the social climate of the class. In B. J. Fraser, & K. G. Tobin (Eds.), *International handbook of science education.* London: Kluwere Academic publishers.

Learning Difficulties of Language and Cultural Minority Children: An Evaluative Approach

Maria Tzouriadou (tzour@nured.auth.gr)
Department of Psychology and Special Education
School of Preschool Education Sciences,
Aristotle University of Thessaloniki
54124 Thessaloniki Greece

Giorgos Barbas (gbarbas@nured.auth.gr)
Department of Psychology and Special Education
School of Preschool Education Sciences,
Aristotle University of Thessaloniki
54124 Thessaloniki Greece

Eleni Anagnostopoulou
Department of Psychology and Special Education
School of Preschool Education Sciences,
Aristotle University of Thessaloniki
54124 Thessaloniki Greece

**Zoi Anagnostou, Kiriaki Antifakou, Sofia Koupidou,
Sofia Papadopoulou, Paraskeyi Roumen, Sofia Chatzigeorgiadou**
Department of Psychology and Special Education
School of Preschool Education Sciences,
Aristotle University of Thessaloniki,
54124 Thessaloniki Greece

Abstract

In the recent years there has been a considerable increase in the number of language and cultural minority children into Greece many of which demonstrate learning difficulties. Teachers tend to attribute these difficulties to problems of adjustment to the language of the host country, to cultural differences between the school and the family environment, as well as to adverse sociocultural living conditions. The cognitive-learning characteristics of the minority children are downgraded or ignored. The aim of this research study was to investigate these cognitive-learning characteristics of language and cultural minority children and to assess the suitability of the educational frame they are placed in. The research sample consisted of 70 fourth, fifth and sixth graders with learning difficulties who were assessed on DTLA-4. Additionally, evidence was collected about the learning behaviour of the children in the sample through semi-structured interviews with their teachers. Research findings verify the view that if children's low achievement is related only to socio-cultural factors and their cognitive – learning characteristics are ignored then children run the risk of inappropriate placement in unsuitable provisions.

Introduction

In the recent years there has been an influx of economic immigrants into Greece, the result of which was a rapid increase in the number of language and cultural minority children in the Greek school and a consequent change in the composition of the school population (Damanakis, 1998). Although minority children were a new reality for the Greek educational system, worldwide they had been studied since the early 60´s and various pedagogical approaches had been implemented to cope with them. Both in the U.S. and in Europe, during the 60´s and the 70´s, language and cultural minority children were considered a "special population" of low achievement and ability (Modgil et al., 1997).The evaluation criteria used ignored children's language and cultural differences (Tomlinson, 1997). Therefore, most of the minority children were directed to special education settings, as they had been assessed to be mentally retarded or language and learning disordered (Cummins &Swain, 1989).

This evaluation approach proved biased and so new, culture-free assessment criteria were developed, while the education systems of the U.S. (Mattes & Omark, 1987) and European countries made provisions to reinforce the acquisition of the host country language. As a result, emphasis moved to the socioeconomic and cultural background of the children because it was believed to affect school learning (Cummins, 1984). Sociocultural background refers to the living conditions and to the status of the minority family, which are reckoned to have a major impact not only on the language and learning abilities of the children but also on their motivation for school learning (Tzouriadou et al., 2000).

In Greece, in 1994, immersion classes for language and cultural minority children were set up and in 1996 the law for intercultural education was enacted, which adopted the socioeconomic and cultural differences approach. Under this law, intercultural schools were established all over the country. In practice, teachers still associate sociocultural factors with the poor support from the family environment. Relevant research studies have shown that immigrant parents care the least about their children's education, that they are unable to help them with their homework, while they constantly reinforce children's "difference" by using their native language at home rather than Greek (Bezirtzoglou, 2002, Filippardou, 1997, Psalti, 2000).The approach actually downgrades students' abilities and weaknesses and attributes their learning difficulties to arbitrary generalizations, without any prior overall and systematic evaluation. Therefore, the widely accepted belief that environmental and inherent factors interact during the learning process is in fact refuted.

School achievement is the resultant of a number of factors that concur in the learning process, the most important of which are the education system, the sociocultural status and the cognitive and emotional characteristics of the child (Obiakor & Utley, 2004). Therefore either students who have not yet acquired proficiency in the Greek language or students who cannot cope with the school requirements, because of adverse educational and family conditions, are likely to be characterized as poor learners. Or again, students who are not able to actively participate in the learning process because of their cognitive deficits. Each of these categories needs different pedagogical support within the proper educational framework. Most particularly, minority children who lack proficiency in Greek should be placed in immerse classes or in intercultural schools. Students with learning difficulties caused mainly by sociocultural factors should receive support teaching in a regular school, while students with cognitive deficits would rather be placed in resource rooms, a setting of special education.

However, minority children with learning difficulties are arbitrarily placed in any of the above settings, without overall evaluation but only on the grounds of their low school achievement. This is so, either because the cognitive characteristics are not *evaluated* (taken into account) or because teachers have an ambiguous idea about the function of each supportive setting

The hypothesis of this research study formulated on the above analysis was that if teachers attribute minority children's low achievement only to sociocultural factors and ignore their cognitive – learning characteristics, then children run the risk of being inappropriately placed and of receiving unsuitable school provisions.

Methodology

To verify the above hypothesis, the cognitive-learning characteristics of minority students and the type of the school setting they had been placed in were assessed.

For the needs of the research study, students with serious learning difficulties were chosen (underachievers), who had been placed either in various support settings (resource rooms, supportive teaching, immersion classes) or in an ordinary class without any support. According to the international practice, students two years behind their class level of achievement and behind their chronological age aptitude are classified as underachievers (Lerner, 1993).

In order to determine the sample, primary school teachers of minority students were interviewed. They proposed 98 minority low achievers who had been living in Greece for at least 3 years, sufficient enough time in the host country to have acquired relatively fluent, peer-appropriate communicative command of the Greek language (Cummins, 1984). The choice was made among fourth, fifth and sixth graders because it is at this age that learning difficulties become more evident (Markovitis & Tzouriadou, 1991

For the choice of the final sample, two screening tools were constructed across the context of the second, third and fourth grade curriculum, in order to detect underachievers: one for reading comprehension, grammar and syntax and one for mathematical operations and problem solving. Assessment data resulted from the written and oral testing.

The final sample therefore consisted of 70 students who had been scored below the lower class level on both tools (62 students) or on one of the two tools (8 students). 30 of the students were fourth graders, 23 were fifth and 17 were sixth graders. 48 students were of Albanian origin, 21 were children of immigrants from the ex-Soviet Union Republics, while one of them was of Turkish origin. 15 were in resource rooms, 20 received supportive teaching, 9 were in an immersion class for language assistance and 26 were not given any additional assistance whatsoever.

To test the cognitive- learning characteristics of the children we used the DTLA-4 battery (Hammill & Bryant, 1992), which is appropriate for individuals between 6 and 17 years of age. DTLA-4 is a culture-free diagnostic battery that enables differential assessment. In Greece it has been linguistically reviewed and adapted by staff members of the Department and has already been used in a previous research study (Barbas, Toutounzi & Pappa, 2006). The battery consists of 10 subjects that measure specific learning abilities relating to language function, visual, and auditory memory skills, attention span, fine motor ability, visual-motor abilities, design reproduction and non-verbal reasoning. The 10 subtests can be combined in such a way as to constitute composites grouped in 4 sets. These composites are the best estimates of a person's higher level of performance and allow comparisons across domains of aptitude.

The first basic composite is the General Mental Ability Composite. It does not only reflect the general developed ability-competence of the child for school learning but also its basic mental ability. It is probably the best estimate of Spearman's *g* factor as it reflects status on a wide range of developed abilities, such as reading, writing, spelling, professional success, etc (Hammill & Bryant, 1992). This criterion includes 3 pairs of dichotomous-contrasting composites, from which, according to the battery designers, the linguistic domain composites are of primary importance for the detection of learning disabilities. For this reason we used only one pair of composites in the present research, which is the following:

a) Verbal Composite: Children who do well on this composite display an uncommon facility in understanding, integrating and using spoken language. They also have good vocabularies and use correct grammar and syntax. This verbal composite may also be a strong predictor of their written ability as it correlates with reading and writing. Low scorers possess weak vocabularies and have difficulty in recalling oral instruction or organizing verbal ideas into logical sequences.

b) Non-Verbal Composite: Children who do well on this composite have unusual ability for spatial relationships and nonverbal symbolic reasoning. They have the ability to recall objects and letters and to draw figures accurately from memory. Low scorers, on the other hand, show trouble remembering non-verbal information, perceiving or organizing visual data.

According to the battery, composite quotients are classified into 7 ratings of learning ability: above 130 - very superior, 121-130 – superior, 111-120 - above average, 90-110 - average, 80-89 - below average, 70-79 – poor, below 70 - very poor. Additionally, children who score above 90 on one of the linguistic composites and below 90 on the other with significant difference between the two scores are strongly predicted to have learning disabilities. Battery designers have provided a formula to help determine how large a difference score must be to be considered significant. The formula reads: "Difference Score $> SD \cdot z_a \cdot \sqrt{(2-r_v-r_{nv})}$", where SD = standard deviation (value 15); z_a = statistical significance level (value 1.96, represented on the z distribution table as statistical significance 0.05); r_v, r_{nv} = reliability of the verbal and non-verbal quotient (Anastasi & Urbina, 1997).

A student who scores below 90 on General Mental Ability Quotient (GMAQ) is expected to display generalized difficulties in school learning that correlate closely with mental deficits and adverse environmental factors. The lower the GMAQ, the more likely it is that the child is mentally retardarde. For research purposes the battery designers set the quotient basis to 80 for GMAQ (rating between below average and poor ability). If, however GMAQ is **above 89**, then environmental factors are probably the cause for difficulties at school.

Based on the above analysis, the students in the sample were classified in four categories of cognitive-learning ability, according to DTLA-4. One category was that of learning disabilities according to the criteria of the battery. All the other students fell into the other three categories according to their GMAQ: poor (below 80), below average (80-85) and average (above 90) learning ability.

Apart from DTLA-4, semi-structured interviews were used to record class and support class teachers' opinions on each one of the students in the sample on the following: characteristics of the learning difficulties, degree of participation in the learning process, interpretation of the difficulties and suitability of the school setting. These data went under qualitative analysis and were compared to the DTLA-4 categories.

Findings –Comments

Reliability test on the 3 DTLA-4 quotients (General Mental Ability Quotient, Verbal and non-Verbal quotient) showed Cronbach's alpha 0.86, 0.85 and 0.89 respectively. These scores represent a satisfactory reliability level (Bryman & Cramer, 1997).

Table 1: Cognitive-Learning categories on the DTLA-4

Cognitive-learning categories	percentage (%) (n = 70)
poor	65.7
below average	18.6
learning disability	10.0
average	5.7
total	100.0

To detect the category of learning disability with DTLA-4, it was necessary to determine the value beyond which the difference between verbal and non-verbal composites became significant. On the "Difference Score" formula the value found was 15. On this basis students in the sample were allocated in the 4 categories that DTLA-4 measures, as follows.

Most of the students in the sample were classified as "poor learners" (46 students, 65.7% of the sample). More specifically, 7 of these students had scored below 80 on General Mental Ability Quotient (GMAQ), and showed significant individual differences. (Difference score >15). This is the profile of a student with organic mild mental retardation, as becomes clear from the large discrepancy in the profile (Scott, 1994). 35 of them had scored below 80 on GMAQ, and had no significant individual differences. This profile indicates either border line mental retardation or mild mental retardation, depending on the general quotient. The remaining 4 students had scored below 40 on GMAQ and showed significant differences between verbal, non–verbal quotients, with one rating very close to 90, a profile which can be considered indicative of learning disabilities. All the students in the "poor learning" category had serious difficulty in performing both tools of the screening test.

13 of the students in the sample (18.6%) were classified as "below average". They did not show significant difference score, and were considered borderline mentally retarded. Their achievement on the screening tools was low, without any differentiations (Scott, 1994).

7 students were classified in the "learning disabilities" category (10% of the sample), according to the criteria of the battery (difference score >15; one of the two ratings above 90). The students in this category had great difficulty in performing the screening tools, mostly reading comprehension, grammar and syntax tasks, a fact that verifies the profile of learning disabilities (Deisinger, 2004).

Finally, 4 students were classified as "average" (5,7% of the sample) with GMAQ between 90 and 99, without any significant difference score. This is the profile of average normal intelligence. They achieved better than the previous group in the screening tools but had considerable difficulty to do the morphosyntactical tasks. This finding fosters the approach, that grammar and syntax feature the core properties that govern the deep and surface **language (linguistic)** structures, which can hardly change through education and therefore consists a serious difficulty for language and culture minority students (Chomsky,1981, pp 7).

Findings analysis showed that 75.7 % of the sample had some sort of inherent deficits (65.7 % poor learners, 10.0 %

learning disabled), which were expected to affect school learning. At this point, it is necessary to mention that below average students are not always able to cope with the academic demands of the cognition-centred school. Such students usually fail to do well on composite tasks that request the use of relevant methods and strategies not fostered by traditional teaching procedures (Paraskevopoulos, 1982). Therefore, below average students need additional supportive teaching. In this respect, we may claim that the difficulties 18.6 % of the sample had were not only due to sociocultural factors but also to the gap between academic demands and the children's learning ability.

Table 2: Distribution of cognitive-learning categories across school settings

percentage (%) (n = 70)	Cognitive-Learning categories on the DTLA-4				total
	poor	below average	learning disabil.	average	
school settings resource room	18.6	2.8	0	0	21.4
supportive teaching	15.7	7.2	4.3	1.4	28.6
immersion class	10.0	1.4	1.4	0	12.8
regular class	21.4	7.2	4.3	4.3	37.2
total	65.7	18.6	10.0	5.7	100.0

Table 2 shows how minority students were distributed across the different types of school settings according to their cognitive-learning characteristics. Data analysis showed the following:

a) Most of the 21.4 % of the students in the sample who were in resource rooms (i.e. 15 students) displayed poor learning abilities (18.6 %). More specifically, all but one of these students had very poor learning ability (below 70), which was highly indicative of mental retardation. It is worth mentioning, that only 6 of the students had been referred to Centres for Diagnosis, Assessment and Support. The remaining 9 students had been placed in a resource room after the class teacher's suggestion and parents' consent. The above finding indicates that the resource room seemed a suitable placement as it offered supportive assistance to pupils with cognitive deficits.

b) Statistical criterion x^2 showed that children were distributed to the different placement options on the classification of their cognitive-learning characteristics according to DTLA-4 ($x^2 = 7.75$, df = 9, p = 0.56). More specifically, it was found that almost half of the students with poor or below average cognitive-learning ability attended a setting that helped them cope with their learning difficulties (resource room or supportive teaching). The other half were not given any support. This important finding, along with the confusion about supportive options teachers had, (e.g. there were immersion classes where they did supportive teaching in maths or resource rooms in the role of supportive teaching) led to the assumption that whether a language and cultural minority child would be placed in such setting or not had

nothing to do with the category of the cognitive-learning characteristics he probably had. According to what class teachers said in the interviews, children were referred for placement in one or another supportive option on: a) the provisions the school could offer, b) the availability of options c) teachers' opinion of the support class teacher, d) their opinion about the effectiveness of the job done in these classes. Placement was much less made on the assessment of their cognitive - learning difficulties. Teachers made an exception though when they referred children with very poor learning ability for placement in a resource room. This incident supported the belief that teachers are usually able to recognize learning difficulties associated with mental retardation (Barbas, et al., 2006, Tzouriadou, et al., 2002).

During the interviews, teachers and support class teachers were asked to interpret the school difficulties of minority students. The former answered for 47 and the latter for 27 students in the sample. In both cases, finding analysis pointed out 3 basic issues in their answers: a) the role of parents (insufficient support of children with their homework), b) characteristics of the family and cultural environment (particular emphasis was given to which language they used at home and to their social habits) and c) inherent causes (mental retardation and learning disability).

In their view these issues could coexist in all possible combinations. Class teachers claimed that insufficient support at home was one of the reasons that accounted for the learning difficulties of 76.6 % of the students; the cultural characteristic of the family and the social environment for the difficulties of 31.9 % of the students while inherent causes accounted for the difficulties of 25.5 % of the students. On the other hand, support setting teachers believed that insufficient assistance of children at home caused learning difficulties to 17 out of 22 students; the cultural background of the family and the social environment were the causal factor for 6 students, while inherent causes for 16 students. The use of the statistical criterion x^2 showed that students distribution across the categories of DTLA-4 was irrelevant of how the class teachers' interpreted their difficulties ($x^2 = 1.67$, df = 3, p = 0.64 for parents' role, $x^2 = 4.85$, df = 3, p = 0.18 for cultural factor, $x^2 = 2.48$, df = 3, p = 0.48 for inherent causes). Similar were the findings of the support setting teachers' interpretation of the minority students' problems ($x^2 = 1.51$, df = 3, p = 0.68 for parents' role, $x^2 = 0.32$, df = 3, p = 0.96 for cultural factor). However they claimed that the learning difficulties of students placed in resource rooms were accounted mainly to inherent deficits ($x^2 = 9.97$, df = 3, p < 0.05). This last finding supports the previous finding, that most teachers were usually able to recognize mental retardation. This was proved by the fact that 13 out of the 16 students to which teachers rendered inherent causes, had been placed in resource rooms and had very poor learning abilities (below 70). Summarizing the findings about how teachers interpret the minority children's learning difficulties we feel that the initial hypothesis was fostered. More particularly, it was found that irrelevant of the characteristics or problems a minority student might have, teachers tended to render the causes of their learning difficulties to family and cultural factors.

Teachers and support class teachers were also asked to assess minority students learning behaviour. The former answered for 58 students and the latter for 26 students. In both cases, teachers claimed that a high percentage of the sample did not manifest any behavioural problems and participated actively in the learning procedure (39.7 % i.e. 23 students, according to class teachers; 38.5 %, i.e. 10 students, according to support teachers). However, class teachers thought indifference and deprived motivation to be a very serious problem for 55.2 % (32) of the students while support teachers for 46.2 % (12 students). 2 students showed aggressive or delinquent behaviour and 4 students were said to be indifferent and isolated. It is worth mentioning that support teachers primarily tended to account children's indifference and deprived motivation to whether parents used to help them sufficiently with their homework or not.

As for how class teachers and support class teachers assessed the suitability of the sample's placement, when interviewed the former answered for 53 students and the latter for 22 students. Support teachers seemed to agree with the placement of 17 students (12 in a resource room, 5 in support setting) but disagreed with the placement of 5 students (1 in a resource room, 4 in support class). On the other hand, the class teachers seemed to agree with the placement of 27 of the students (50.9 %) but disagreed with the placement of 26 of the students (49 %) (Table 3).

The use of the statistical criterion x^2 showed that class teachers' agreement or disagreement depended on the kind of placement options ($x^2 = 16.2$, df = 3, p < 0.01). According to the adjusted residual, this dependency resulted from the fact that agreement mostly concerned students placed in resource rooms or in supportive teaching classes, while disagreement concerned either students placed in immersion classes or students not receiving any kind of support. They made alternative suggestions for the cases they disagreed with (for 24 students out of 26).

Table 3: Class teachers' views on placement distribution

percentage (0%) (n=53)		class teachers' views		total
		agreement	disagreement	
school placement	resource room	5.7	0	5.7
	adjusted residual	1.7	-1.7	
	supportive teaching	28.3	7.5	35.8
	adjusted residual	3.0	-3.0	
	immersion class	0	9.4	9.4
	adjusted residual	-2.4	2.4	
	class	16.9	32.2	49.1
	adjusted residual	-2.3	2.3	
	total	50.9	49.1	100.0

For two of the students they suggested placement in a special setting and for 22 students placement in support classes. It is worth mentioning that with their suggestions teachers put emphasis on the need for specialized intervention regardless of whether minority children were placed in resource rooms or in support classes. The above findings suggested that teachers' opinions were compatible with the

type of learning difficulties the sample children had according to the cognitive-learning classification on DTLA-4. The above assumption seemed to differ from the previous finding where teachers rendered students' learning difficulties to external factors. Most probably these controversies relate to the fragmentary pedagogical opinions of the teachers and in all cases need to be further investigated.

Concluding, the research hypothesis was verified. Findings have shown that low achievement is mainly associated with sociocultural factors and placement in a special setting is made regardless the minority children's cognitive-learning characteristics. It is made evident that the pedagogical support offered does not answer to the cognitive-learning characteristics of each child and thus placement becomes precarious. The educational approach to learning difficulties therefore needs to be reconsidered. This means that prior to placement in one of the support settings overall evaluation of the student is necessary, which will take into account the sociocultural factors along with the cognitive-learning characteristics of each individual child.

References

Anastasi, A., & Urbina, S. (1997). *Psychological testing* (7th ed.) Upper Saddle River, NJ: Prentice- Hall.

Barbas, G., Toutountzi, E., & Pappa, M. (2006). Assessment criteria for learning difficulties of primary school students. *Mentoras*, 9, 60-77.

Bezirtzoglou, M. (2002). School effectiveness and underachievement of ethnic minority children. In E. Tressou & S. Mitakidou (Eds.), *The teaching of language and mathematics. The education of language minority students*. Thessaloniki: Paratiritis.

Bryman, A., & Cramer, D. (1997). *Quantitative Data Analysis with SPSS for Windows: A guide for social Sciences*. London: Routledge.

Chomsky, N. (1965). *Aspects of the theory of syntax*. Cambridge, Massachusetts: MIT Press.

Cummins, G., & Swain, M. (1989). *Bilingualism in Education*. New York: Longman

Cummins, J. (1984). *Bilingualism and special education: Issues in assessment and pedagogy, Multilingual Matters*. Clevedon: Avon

Damanakis, M. (1998). *The education of return emigrants and foreign students in Greece: an intercultural approach*. Athens: Gutenberg, Intercultural Education.

Deisinger, J. (2004). Conceptualizations of Learning Disabilities: beyond the ability – achievement discrepancy. In S. Burkhardt, F. Obiakor & A. Rotatori (Eds.) *Current Perspectives on Learning Disabilities: The ability achievement discrepancy*. Amsterdam: Elsevier.

Filippardou, C. (1997). Teachers' views on primary school bilingual students in the city of Rodes. In E.Scourtou (Ed.), *Bilingualism and Education*. Athens: Nisos.

Hall, D. (1995). *Assessing the Needs of Bilingual Pupils*. London: David Fulton Publishers, Ltd.

Hammill, D.D., & Bryant R.B. (2000). *Learning Disabilities Diagnostic Inventory, A method to help identify intrinsic processing disorders in children and adolescents, Examiner's Manual*. Austin, Texas: ed. Pro.ed.

Lerner, J. (1993). *Learning Disabilities, theories, diagnosis and teaching strategies.* Boston: Houghton Mifflin Company.

Markovitis, M., & Tzouriadou, M. (1991). *Learning disabilities, theory and practice.* Thessaloniki: Promithefs.

Mattes, L., & Omark, D.R. (1987). *Speech and Language Assessment for the Bilingual Handicapped.* Boston: College-Hill Publications.

Modgil, S., Verma, G., Mallick, K., & Modgil, C.(1997). Multicultural education, The inderminable debate. In S. Modgil, G. Verma, K. Mallick & C. Modgil (Eds.), *Multicultural education, The inderminable debate* (in greek). Athens: Ellinika Grammata.

Obiakor, F. & Utley, C. (2004). Multicultural learners with learning disabilities: beyond Eurocentric perspectives. In S. Burkhardt, F. Obiakor & A. Rotatori (Eds.) *Current Perspectives on Learning Disabilities: The ability achievement discrepancy.* Amsterdam: Elsevier.

Paraskevopoulos, I. (1982). *Educating the mentally retarded.* Athens: O.E.D.B.

Psalti, A. (2000). *Students from the ex-Soviet Union and Albania in Greek schools. Attitudes, needs and expectations.* Dissertation in the Department of Psychology, Thessaloniki: AUTH.

Scott, S. (1994). Mental Retardation. In M. Rutter, E. Taylor & L. Hersov (Eds.), *Child and adolescent psychiatry, Modern approaches.* Oxford: Blackwell Scientific Publications.

Tomlinson, S. (1997). Ethnic Identity and School Success. In S. Modgil, G. Verma, K. Mallick & C. Modgil (Eds.), *Multicultural education, The inderminable debate* (in greek). Athens: Ellinika Grammata.

Tzouriadou, M., Barbas, G., Ziakaki, M., Kaltsera, K., Pappa, M., Papastergiou, O., & Tripopoulou, O. (2002). Detecting learning difficulties in the primary school. *Proceedings of the 4th Psychological Conference in Cyprous* (pp. 190-199). Nicosia.

Tzouriadou, M., Koutsou, S., Kidoniatou, E., Stagiopoulos, P., & Tzelepi, T. (2000). Language minority children: inferior or different? *Proceedings of Special Education Conference* (pp. 557-565). Rethymno: Kavathia Brothers.

Construction of semiopictorial knowledge and communicational skills during picture book interactive readings in preschool: An interdisciplinary study

Christine Gamba (christine.gamba@pse.unige.ch)
Faculty of Psychology and Educational Sciences, 40 Bvd du Pont d'Arve
CH-1204 Genève 11

Anne-Christel Grau (anne-christel.grau@pse.unige.ch)
Faculty of Psychology and Educational Sciences, 40 Bvd du Pont d'Arve
CH-1204 Genève 11

Abstract

This contribution deals with picture-based narrative comprehension (semiopictorial knowledge) examined during interactive reading sessions and aims at familiarizing preschool teachers in day-care environments with this practice. A group of three year-old children are asked to infer on the meaning and the outcome of the story while reading a wordless picture book together with their teacher, thus eliciting causal relations, which refer to the narrative structure. The purpose of this paper is to study how semiopictorial knowledge is built *during the interaction itself* and how this construction depends on communicational skills allowing interactants to achieve a zone of common meaning. A double construction thus occurs during the interaction and involves a double analytical approach: on the one hand, a microgenetic analysis will examine the construction of semiopictorial knowledge and how it depends on an adjustment of interactants' meanings. On the other hand, an interactional analysis of communicational disruptions will study how children develop their communicational skills necessary to adjust or re-adjust one to another. The data collected is in process, but results so far show that the construction of semiopictorial knowledge depends, on the one hand, on the children's development of social skills relevant to the interactive reading setting and rely on the teacher's management of attention. On the other hand, the teachers - familiarised in the analysis of the formal narrative cues of the wordless picture books prior to the reading - guide the children to attend to narrative cues in both directive and open ways, thus pointing out the significant cues all the while, allowing children to build their own meanings on the latter.

Introduction

Previous studies in emergent literacy have shown the impact of interactive reading practices on the development of oral and written language (Sénéchal, 2000; Massey, 2004; Whitehurst, Epstein, Angell, Payne, Crone & Fischel, 1994). Moreover, it allows preschool children to develop narrative comprehension as they are requested to infer on the meaning and the outcomes of the story (Saada-Robert, 2003) and to establish causal relations (Makdissi & Boisclair, 2004). Following studies on picture-based

narrative comprehension (Paris & Paris, 2003), the main question addressed in this study is thus how do children elaborate meaning from pictures in a picture book together with a teacher in day-care, before they infer meaning from textual cues?

More precisely, this paper will analyse how picture-based narrative comprehension (hence semiopictorial knowledge) is built throughout the interaction jointly by a group of preschool children and their teacher while reading a wordless picture book, which refers to everyday life, and highlight how this co-construction depends on the joint construction of meaning, i.e. how partners adjust their significations and understand each other. In order to achieve this, preschool children must develop and strengthen their communicative skills. Therefore, two complementary analytical procedures are involved in this study: A didactic microgenetic analysis will focus on the co-construction of knowledge and of meaning during the interaction itself, while an interactional analysis will study the occurrence, the role and effect of communicational disruptions on the process of adjustment in the interaction.

Theoretical framework
Narrative comprehension

Narrative comprehension evolves during shared readings of picture books and involves the capacity to build schemas concerning narrative structure (Fayol, 2004) and thus to infer the outcomes of the story (Saada-Robert, 2003), more specifically, to develop chronological causal inferences (Makdissi & Boisclair, 2004). Moreover, the same comprehension processes are involved in settings using wordless narrative picture books for preschool children before they develop decoding skills in reading (Paris & Paris, 2003).

Makdissi & Boisclair (2004) show through their developmental grid of narrative comprehension how children develop causal relations, shifting from attending to minute descriptive cues to more narrative ones. This grid highlights how children use implicit information from the text and pictures as well as everyday knowledge to build the general frame of the story. As the reading progresses, the story frame is constantly reorganised while causal relations are built progressively and hierarchised through transitive operations allowing children to link actions to an initial aim or difficulty encountered by the main characters and to the final resolution ending the story.

Didactic microgenesis

As Makdissi and Boisclair's grid was elaborated from data collected during children's recall of the story, this paper focuses on how semiopictorial knowledge is built during the interaction itself. Thus, as "the study of on line processes of knowledge acquisition, in a short time and a specific situation" (Nguyen-Xuan, 1990, p. 197), didactic migrogenesis refers to studies on situated cognition and situated learning (Allal, 2001) and dialogic analysis of children-adult interactions in the classroom (Grossen, 1999; Trognon, 1999). It analyses the situated ongoing process of knowledge co-construction between teacher and learners and how this depends on a process of adjustment of the interactants' own meanings about the story in order to achieve a zone of common meaning (Martinet, Balslev & Saada-Robert, 2006). A distinction is thus made between knowledge (such as defined in different academic subjects) and to-be-built meanings during the interaction.

The specific questions concerning this analytical procedure are the following:

- Which components of semiopictorial knowledge do children and their teacher address during the reading?
- How does semiopictorial knowledge progress during the reading session?
- How do the teacher and the children adjust to each other's meanings in order to achieve a zone of common meaning?

Interactional analysis

The interactional side of this project is aimed to study the moments of communicational disruptions in the interaction, which can appear at the level of meanings or behaviours. It will point out how, why and when they appear, and how the teacher manages the situation in order to continue the activity and to maintain the group cohesion. The ventured hypothesis is namely that disruptions have a real impact on the child's social and linguistic development, that is that they allow him to construct his communicative competence. This study will follow a linguistic approach, the interactional analysis, according to Kerbrat-Orecchioni's theory (1990/2006) on interactionism:

- Each speech is a co-construction by speakers. Indeed, teacher and children are supposed to construct meaning and knowledge together, within an interaction;
- Disruptions are thus defined as reactions to the interaction, that is to the teacher, to the peers and/or to the context; however, they are interactions and couldn't exist without the main interaction;
- Children haven't yet acquired a complete communicative competence. In opposition to Chomsky's grammatical competence, which only

allows to build correct sentences, this notion considers the child's capacity to master conversational rules (e.g. speech turns, politeness, relevance, etc.). Communicational disruptions occur indeed when this communicative competence isn't mastered. So, the more children interact, the more they develop this competence. At the same time, the interaction improves in quality, and so does the construction of semiopictorial knowledge.

The methodological implications of these three basic items are thus the following:

First, priority is given to dialogal discursive forms, considering that interactions are composed of dialogues, and not as appended monologues.

Priority is also given to oral forms and to natural and authentic data. Namely, oral language wasn't considered as noteworthy, because it contains many language "mistakes". Nowadays, it is considered that oral conversations are real and worth to be studied. Traditionally, data was chosen out of literary corpuses, or invented in order to imitate reality. If one chooses to study oral forms however, and even if these forms are transcribed, one can't accept to invent written data, which would be pure fiction and couldn't help research about human beings. Interactions are thus transcribed in complete and continuous verbatims: complete because nothing is to be put aside, everything can be relevant either for the microgenetic or the linguistic study, and continuous because disruptions are very significant issues.

Third, oral communication is considered as a multi-code construction. Interactants don't only speak thanks to verbal language, but also thanks to gesture and sounds. This aspect is particularly relevant for young children who don't yet manage grammar and vocabulary very well.

Finally, interactional analysis ought to be thought as a complement to psycho-sociological studies. This presentation is representative of such a stand: a same corpus of data opens two different types of studies which contribute one to another.

Methodological procedure

Common procedure

Data was collected from four day-care centers in low SES urban zones in Switzerland. In two day-care centers(DDC1 & DDC2), the teachers involved in the study were familiarised with the formal pictorial cues pointed out (group A teachers), prior to the reading, by a semiological analysis (Grau, 2005) of the two selected picture books [1]. In the remaining day-care centers, an informal discussion on the books took place with the two teachers (group B teachers). Per day-care, four interactive reading sessions involved two separate groups of children (ages 3 and 4), in two month intervals between September 2005 and March

---

[1] *Der fliegende Hut*, by Rotraut Susanne Berner (book 1, session 1 and 3), and *Un géant vraiment très chic*, by Julia Donaldson & Axel Scheffler (book 2, session 2 and 4). For both books, color copies were made in order to eliminate text, namely on book 2.

2006. Each book was used twice, alternatively. Book 1, used for the first interactive reading session (an extract of which is shone on table 2 below), has a narrative structure with repetitive sequences. The main narrative feature is a hat being blown off a boy's head and which falls into different hands until it comes back to its initial owner.

Data is actually being processed and this paper presents the results analysed so far according to the different methodological steps involved in didactic microgenesis and to the interactional analysis applied specifically to the study of communicational disruptions. Therefore, we have chosen to present these approaches through examples out of two already organised verbatims of session 1, in the pictures' formal cues familiarised DCC.

Table 1: Research design, repeated 4 times in each day-care center

Discussion researcher-teacher	1 hour	Preparation
Comprehension tests (initial-intermediate-final)	1 day	Children Groups 1 & 2
Interactive reading	1st week 2nd week	Group 1 Group 2
Recall	Following day 1st week 2nd week	Group 1 Group 2

Through a dual deductive and inductive approach and following the first methodological principle of didactic microgenesis, complete verbatims are first segmented into *units of meaning* according to the content of knowledge being addressed and to modalities of speech revealing underlying intentions of the utterances (i.e. reformulations, validations, etc.)

A deductive procedure thus allows to define the components of knowledge that could be potentially activated during the interaction according to a conceptual framework while an inductive analysis requires a «full immersion» attitude of researcher allowing meanings being built effectively during the interaction to emerge from the data itself (Martinet, Balslev & Saada-Robert, 2006).

Table 2 below shows how an extract of verbatim is segmented into units of meaning. The principle of the first analytical steps of didactic microgenesis is illustrated on the basis of this extract. Concerning the interactional analysis, the same verbatim will serve to define the methodological principles adapted for the study of communicational disruptions.

The story corresponding to the picture being "read" in this extract involves a dog with a hat on its mouth taking it to its mistress away from a duck which had it on his head on the previous page.

Didactic microgenesis

The first question in this approach concerns which components of knowledge are effectively addressed during this extract of interaction. The following components appear:

- As the teacher turns the page, the children immediately mention the hat (OBJPRIN).
- As the teacher asks what they can see (passes floor Passcontr), she is concerned with the progression of activity (PROGACT) and refers to a general semantic content when asking "what is happening?" (SEMANT). A child then imitates the posture of the duck flapping its wings (ACTPRIN/DESC), thus grasping the main event spontaneously. Following the teacher's validation (Valid+) and her request to elaborate more (Rel) on this, the child imitates its cross facial expression, and posture. The teacher then asks her to infer on the meaning of this gesture, to put the child's action into words (INFER1). For an answer, the child refers to the hat, the main narrative feature, and lets out a cry of complaint, thus explicating the cause of the duck's emotional state (INFER2). The teacher then would like to go further with this (Rel) and asks what the dog is doing but the children then interact on a different content of knowledge, referring to life context (CONTVIE) as they imitate a dog barking in a contagious way.

This extract allows thus to point out two separate sequences defined according to a dominant unit of meaning, revealing the progression of semiopictorial knowledge (corresponding to the second question concerning didactic microgenesis): the first one involves the description and inferences concerning the main action (the dog taking the hat away from the duck) while the second one contains the interaction on life context.

Finally, the third question concerning the adjustment of interactants' meanings may be answered through the modalities of speech revealed in this extract. The following modalities are significant cues of a reciprocal adjustment: the teacher's questions (Passcontr) aiming at explicating children's meanings, her validations (Val+), the way she encourages the children to put gestures into words and the fact she encourages to push their reasoning further (Rel). On the children's side, the expected degree of their answers (RA/RNA) is interpreted according to the teacher's question and to the content she is trying to elaborate on (hence the cause of the duck's irritation). The degree of freedom of child's utterance is also interpreted according to the degree of "openness" within the teacher's question (questions allowing yes/no answers are the less open ones). Thus, this extract allows us to see that both expected and unexpected answers are considered by the teacher who leans more specifically on those that refer to narrative cues as a basis to elaborate more on this level.

So far, the data of the first reading session of two DCC (involving group A teachers) have been analysed. Results concerning DCC1 show that, prior to building semiopictorial knowledge, children need to understand the purpose of the activity and develop social skills involved in it as the interactional analysis points out. Thus, attention management by the teacher was a big issue in DCC1. As this was not the case in the second one, this finding highlights how reading practices and children's degree of familiarity with the latter differ between different daycare environments. Despite this difference, in both DCC, children prefer to describe minute cues (OBJPRIN and PERPRIN mainly) and/or events (ACTPRIN/DESC) within each picture, and both teachers accept to attend to these cues. Both ask open questions (Passcontr) to help children explicit their meanings of the story while helping them to shift their attention to narrative cues (INFER1 and 2). But, being both inexperienced in interactive reading and perhaps due to children's age and to this being their first interactive reading session with an unfamiliar picture book, the two teachers tended to be directive by informing children (Appinfo), or repeating the utterances of the latter without pushing them forward (low frequency of modalities named Rel) and by inducing answers (Induc), especially in DCC2. Nonetheless, in both environments children engaged in inferential activity in a spontaneous way, as revealed by a high degree of unexpected interventions. The analysis of contents, especially in DCC2, shows that children and their teacher attend to the same cues in a more or less equal proportion, which thus gives us a first insight into how a construction of a common zone of meaning is achieved.

Interestingly, despite more frequent communicational disruptions in DCC1, a certain degree of adjustment of meanings was achieved as children engaged in inferential activity as well, thanks to the teacher's open questions (Passcontr). Moreover, this finding suggests that the narrative cues in the picture book used in this session may be significant enough for children to grasp easily the narrative structure concerning the transportation of the hat, as children refer to it in a descriptive way (OBJPRIN) as well as inferring on its future transportations as children turn pages to look for it.

Interactional analysis

As we can observe in the organised verbatims, the modalities present in this type of interaction are limited and quite regular. Moreover, 3-year children don't use a very complex language (Rondal, Esperet, Gombert, Thibaut & Comblain, 1999): sentences are simple, often constructed with a deictic and a noun/verb. Considering these points, the analysis concentrates on disruptions, because they break this regularity and can be interesting in order to show how children do develop their communicative competence throughout difficulties. Let's see an example (table 2 below), which will then allow to develop some research questions:

The disruption begins with a non-expected answer (RNA) by Bri, who shows a duck and says : "birds" (67). The teacher is expecting something else and tries to focus the child on a specific aspect of the picture (68-69). Bri remains however concentrated on the duck and imitates it by sounds and by gesture (70): she describes what the duck is doing, but not why it's doing so.

Because the activity is aimed at letting the children *tell* a story and explain what they see on the pictures, the teacher tries to ask the child more precisely, in order to let her build an explanation (73) and shows by mirroring her facial expression that she doesn't understand Bri's action. Bri is then more precise by mentioning the hat and lamenting (74): she infers that it has been stolen from the duck, who is angry.

During this interaction focused on Bri, the two other children remain alone and begin to quarrel (75). They may unconsciously try to capture the teacher's attention. Anyway, a new rupture occurs and the teacher has to deal with it. The issue isn't to precise the activity anymore, but to rebuild the group cohesion (75a-b), and she eventually achieve this. The first disruption does however still influence the interaction: children don't explicit what they see but imitate a dog's barking (INA) (80, 81, 83-85).

Disruptions appear thus when the child doesn't act in an expected way. In this case, the teacher and the children aren't adjusted anymore, the interaction about the ongoing activity is partly broken and continues in a new interaction trying to solve the rupture. Such an example is quite common in the first analysed data (session 1, out of the two DCC where the teacher is familiarised with the formal pictorial cues pointed out prior to the reading). However, disruptions of this type appear more frequently in DCC1, where the children are not very used to communicational and institutional rules. Moreover, contents and modalities relevant for the activity are much more frequent in the other day-care center. This point seems to confirm the following hypothesis: the better the communicative competence is mastered, the better the narrative competence can be constructed, as the interaction is of better quality. In order to verify this, six questions are then asked, aimed to allow a comparative study of all the interactive reading sessions:

1. What types of communicational disruptions can be found in the observed data?
2. When and how do communicational disruptions occur? Through which verbal or non-verbal communicative channel? Is there a regularity in the way it appears? Do children improve their communicative competence between the observation sessions and, if yes, are the disruptions less frequent?
3. What provokes these disruptions (context, book, peers, teacher,…)?
4. How do interactants react directly /indirectly?
5. How do disruptions affect the interaction and the ongoing activity?
6. How does the teacher manage the situation in order to continue the activity and to maintain the group cohesion?

As this part of the research is at its beginning, no relevant analysis model has been constructed yet allowing to investigate these disruptions deeper. It will have to be modulated from other studies on disruptions of all kinds, on language in institutions and on discourse analysis. Then, it will be adapted to this particular data. This research is aimed to contribute to the analysis of the semiopictorial competence.

Perspectives

As this paper focuses on a dual approach, the contributive domains cast two different lights on the same object, i.e. the construction of semiopictorial knowledge *during interaction*. We assume that our interdisciplinary research contributes, in the field of education as well as language studies, to improve our understanding of the micro processes of knowledge construction and of the communicational skills allowing the latter to take place. On the one hand, this study highlights how interactive readings help children to explicit causal relations concerning narrative structure and underlines the importance of children developing comprehension of implicit relations, which appear to determine later academic success. On the other hand, this contribution shows the relevance of familiarizing day-care teachers in interactive reading practices. In order to achieve this, our research shows that teachers need first to help children develop communicational skills in the day-care environment allowing these reading activities to take place. Moreover, our research points out that preschool teachers also need to have more insight into the issues involved in narrative comprehension and to understand how picture books elicit implicit relations by helping them analyze the narrative cues of the latter.

Acknowledgments

Research granted by the Swiss National Research Fund (n° 10013-108509/1) and the Swiss Institute for Youth and Media.

References

Allal, L. (2001). Situated cognition and learning : From conceptual frameworks to classroom investigations, *Revue suisse des sciences de l'éducation, 23,* 407-422.

Alles-Jardel, M., Bernard, V., Meyer N. & Touzet, V. (1997). Analyse du langage d'enfants de maternelle selon le contexte et l'interlocuteur. *Calap n°14* (pp. 11-37). CNRS Paris X.

Balslev, K., Martinet, C., & Saada-Robert, M. (2006). La lecture interactive d'albums de littérature enfantine à 4 ans en classe. Etude microgénétique. Les Dossiers des sciences de l'éducation (15).

Coulthard M. (1983). An introduction to Discourse Analysis. Essex: Longman.

Fayol, M. (2004), Comprendre et produire des textes écrits: l'exemple du récit, dans M.KAIL & M. FAYOL, *L'acquisition du langage. Le langage en développement au-delà de trois ans,* Paris, Ed. Puf, Coll. Psychologie et Sciences de la Pensée, 183-213.

Grau, A.-C. (2005). Analyse sémiologique du livre d'images pour enfants *Der fliegende Hut* de Rotraut Susanne Berner. Document interne au projet FNRS 10013-108509/1.

Grossen, M. (1999). Approche dialogique des processus de transmission-acquisition de savoirs. Une brève introduction. *Actualités Psychologiques*, 7, 1-32.

Hudelot, C. (1989). «Circulation et restructuration de la référence dans un dialogue adulte-enfant. *Calap n°6* (pp. 79-91). CNRS Paris X.

Kerbrat-Orecchioni, C. (2006). Les interactions verbales. Paris : Armand Colin [1990].

Makdissi, H. & Boisclair, A. (2004). La lecture interactive : un lieu d'expansion de l'expression des relations causales chez l'enfant d'âge préscolaire. Rapport de recherche soumis au Programme de partenariats en développement social, Développement des ressources humaines, Canada.

Martinet, C., Balslev, K. & Saada-Robert, M. (2006). The implemented knowledge transformed in the classroom, regarding the curriculum offered and the student's outcomes. A microgenetic analysis. Paper presented at the European Conference on Educational Research, Geneva 2006, Transforming Knowledge, September 2006, Université de Genève.

Massey, S. L. (2004). « Teacher-child conversation in the Preschool Classroom », *Early Childhood Education Journal*, vol. 31, n° 4, pp. 227-231.

Paris, A.H. & Paris, G.S. (2003). Assessing narrative comprehension in young children. Reading Research Quarterly, vol.1, n°3 (pp. 36-76).

Nguyen-Xuan, A. (1990). Apprentissage et développement. In J. F. Richard, C. Bonnet, & R. Ghiglione (Eds.), *Traité de psychologie cognitive 2. Le traitement de l'information symbolique.* (pp. 196-206). Paris : Dunod.

Saada-Robert, M. (2003). Early emergent literacy. In T. Nunes & P. Bryant (Eds.), *Handbook of literacy. (*pp575-598*).* Dordrecht: Kluwer.Academic Publishers.

Saada-Robert, M et al. : (2003). Ecrire pour lire dès 4 ans. Didactique de l'entrée dans l'écrit. Genève: FPSE, Cahiers de la section des Sciences de l'Education

Sénéchal, M. (2000), Examen du lien entre la lecture de livres et le développement du vocabulaire chez l'enfant préscolaire, *Enfance,* n° 2, 169-186.

Trognon, A. (1999). Eléments d'analyse interlocutoire. In M. Gilly, J. P. Roux & A. Trognon (Eds.), *Apprendre dans l'interaction* (pp. 69-94). Nancy : Presses Universitaires de Nancy ; Aix-En-Provence : Publications de l'université de Provence.

Whitehurst, G. J., Epstein, J. N., Angell, A. L., Payne, A. C., Crone, D. A., & Fischel, J. E. (1994). Outcomes of an emergent literacy intervention in Head Start. *Journal of Educational Psychology, 86*(4), 542–555.

Table 2: Example of verbatim

Comp. ACTPRIN/DESC and INFER1: description of main action and inference of its cause						
0.03.00						
	64a	(nods head)			INFER 2	Valid+

UM n° within speech turns		Teacher's and children's speech turns in 2 separate columns			Content of UM	Speech modality
	64b	(EDU turns page, p.3)			PRAGM	Appinfo
	65		Gr	the hat (4sec)	OBJPRIN	I/NAsusc
	66	///what can you see here on the picture?/// (brings book closer to children)			PROGACT	Passcontr
	67		Bri	birds (6sec)	PERSEC	R/Asusc
	68	/// and there, what is there?			PROGACT	Reorient
			Gr	…		
	69	(looks at the page on the right) what is happening here?			ACTPRIN/DESC	Passcontr
	70		Bri	it's doing ouh ouh (Bri imitates duck flapping its wings)	ACTPRIN/DESC	R/NAsusc
	71a	yes/			ACTPRIN/DESC	Valid+
	71b	what is the duck doing ?			ACTPRIN/DESC	ReformCom
	72		Bri	(imitates ducks posture : pulls a cross face, wrists clenched on her hips)	ACTPRIN/DESC	R/Asusc
	73	(looks at Bri imitating facial expression) what does it mean to do that ? (7sec)			INFER1	Rel
	74		Bri	the hat/(then lets out a cry of complaint)	INFER2	R/Ainv
	75			Ulr and Eri squabble	ENGA -	
	76a	Ulr look here//			PROGACT	Inj
	76b	what is happening here?// Ulr what happened?			SEMANT	Passcontr
	76c	look///			PROGACT	Inj
	77		Ulr	a ginnaf (9sec)	PERSEC	R/NAsusc
	78	///yes			PERSEC	Valid+
0.04.00	79		Ulr	a ginnaf	PERSEC	ReformRep
Teacher misses attempt to engage all children on inference mentioned before. Children refer to life context CONTVIE						
	80	///what more ?/ what did the dog do?			INFER2	Reorient
	81		Ulr	ouh ouh (imitates a dog barking)	CONTVIE	R/NAsusc
	82		Eri	ouh ouh	CONTVIE	ReformRep
	83a	yes			CONTVIE	Valid+
	83b	but here on the picture/what is the dog doing (points the dog)			ACTPRIN/DESC	Reorient
	84		Eri	ouh ouh ouh ou	CONTVIE	R/NAsusc
	85		Ulr	noooo/// ouh ouh ouh ouh	CONTVIE	ReformRep
	86		Eri	ouh ouh ouh ou	CONTVIE	ReformRep

UM n° within speech turns   Teacher's and children's speech turns in 2 separate columns   Content of UM   Speech modality

Insight Problem Solving, Fluid Intelligence, and Executive Control: A Structural Equation Modeling Approach

Bysław Paulewicz (boraxp@interia.pl)
Institute of Psychology, Jagiellonian University
3 Al. Mickiewicza, 31-120 Cracow, Poland

Adam Chuderski (achud@emapa.pl)
Institute of Psychology, Jagiellonian University
3 Al. Mickiewicza, 31-120 Cracow, Poland

Edward Nęcka(ednecka@ apple.phils.uj.edu.pl)
Institute of Psychology, Jagiellonian University
3 Al. Mickiewicza, 31-120 Cracow, Poland

Abstract

As there exist individual differences in the ability to solve insight problems, the aim of our study was to examine whether these differences correlate with measures of general fluid intelligence (*Gf*) and of executive functioning (*EF*). It was shown that insight problem solving ability strongly correlates with both *Gf* and *EF*. Structural equation modeling (SEM) revealed that it is *Gf* latent variable that underlies insight problem solving and executive control. This result, obtained with enhanced methodology in comparison with previous studies on cognitive basis of insight problem solving, suggests that insight is not a 'special' ability, but a phenomenon strongly linked to abstract reasoning.

Introduction

The phenomenon of insight always fascinated experimental psychologists. According to the Gestalt tradition (e.g., Wertheimer, 1959/1945), insight consists in restructuring, that is, changing the mental representation of the problem at hand. The idea of restructuring has survived and can be found in modern conceptions of insight as well (e.g., Ohlsson, 1984). A problem may be very difficult, or even impossible to solve, unless a person changes the way in which he or she looks at it. As soon as such a change happens, a formerly difficult problem becomes quite easy or even trivial. Therefore, insight should be viewed as a pivotal moment in the process of thinking an problem solving.

It seems that cognitive scientists did not pay enough attention to the phenomenon of insight, although the studies of thinking and problem solving are quite popular in the field. However, the cognitive science approach to thinking and problem solving has been influenced by the seminal work by Newell and Simon (1972). The authors used very special kind of problems in their research, namely, the problems that can be solved through gradual increment of knowledge and careful application of a valid problem solving strategy. A well-known example is cryptarithmetics (Newell and Simon, 1972). There are, however, other types of problems that people solve both in cognitive psychology

labs and real-life. They are called insight problems, and they are typically characterized by the fact that neither gradual increment of knowledge, nor proper strategy, are sufficient conditions of a good solution. We believe that cognitive science needs more research about such problems: how they are solved, is there a special psychological ability to deal with them, and whether such an ability is in any relation to the general mental ability (i.e., fluid intelligence), on one hand, and the cognitive control processes (i.e., executive functions), on the other hand. Therefore, we designed a study which refers to three domains of research: cognitive science proper, differential psychology (or psychometrics), and the experimental cognitive psychology.

A well-known example of an insight problem is a so called 'candle problem' invented by Duncker (1945). A subject has to imagine a closed door, a candle, and a box full of pins. The goal is to fit vertically the candle to the door without opening it. Some incorrect solutions involve building a small shelf out of pins (it is impossible in reality), opening the door and putting the candle on its top (the door should remain closed), etc. A correct solution involves changing a function of the box: it should be emptied out of the pins and used as a horizontal shelf. Thus, a crucial step in solving the candle problem is to see in an insight that the box can be used in a new, non-obvious function. Before this idea comes to mind the problem seems difficult, but afterwards the solution seems obvious.

Two main groups of theories and models were proposed in order to explain insight problem solving: the 'special process' versus 'nothing special' theoretical proposals (Davidson, 1995). The former (e.g., Dominowski & Dallob, 1995) ascribe a crucial role to some qualitatively different process that causes a sudden change in the whole problem space representation. Some well known evidence in favor for the discontinuity of the insight solving process was presented by Metcalfe (1986), who showed that people do not have apt metacognitions indicating how close they are to solving insight problems even just before finding the correct solution, while they can easily estimate such a distance in case of algebra problems.

The latter theories explain the solving of insight problems in terms of ordinary cognitive processes of gradual activation and combination of knowledge (Weisberg & Alba, 1987; Yaniv & Meyer, 1987). The subjective effect of insight comes from the fact that the combined or retrieved representation reaches in some moment an activation threshold, above which it becomes conscious and impacts the process of thinking.

There has been some experimental work (e.g., Kershaw & Ohlsson, 2004) and computational modeling (e.g., Kaplan & Simon, 1990) aimed at discovering processes underlying insight problem solving. A different approach to studying insight is psychometric (Davidson, 1995): it focusses on observing how people differ in their ability to solve insight problems. While some people easily invoke insights and can flexibly generate non-obvious but correct problem solutions, others find overcoming impasses very hard and rarely come to the right answers. If we could find strong correlations between efficiency of insight problem solving and measures of performance in other tasks that are believed to grasp relatively well defined parameters of human cognitive architecture, we could speculate which cognitive resources and processes might be involved in insight problem solving.

Davidson (1995) examined whether a result in insight problem test that contained 48 problems correlated with general fluid intelligence measures. She found a strong and significant correlation ranging from 0.49 to 0.61. However, such strong correlation could reflect similarity between insight problem solving test and intelligence test, rather then between the processes involved both in abstract reasoning (strongly associated with Gf) and insight ability.

Murray and Byrne (2005) were interested whether eight insight problems' test score correlated with attention switching, selective visual attention, and working memory capacity (WMC). To measure the attention switching ability two tasks were used. In the first one, participants had to follow in their imagination an elevator journey represented on a test card. The elevator moved up and down by a certain number of floors. Subjects had to switch between counting down and counting up. Accuracy and latency measures were collected. The second task required adding the number three to one column of 30 random two-digit numbers, then subtracting number three from another such column, and finally continuously alternating between adding and subtracting three from the last column. The cost of switching was calculated as a difference between the time to process the last column and the mean time of processing the first and the second one. Switching scores obtained from tasks correlated significantly ($r = 0.51$) with the test score.

Two WMC measures used by authors (i.e., backward digit span and reading span tasks) also correlated significantly with the insight test score ($r = 0.39$, $r = 0.51$, respectively). Neither attention selectivity measure derived from map search task nor attentional inhibition of response correlated significantly with insight test score.

In our opinion, the previous research on cognitive basis of insight ability has had at least three methodological flaws. First, we believe that a insight problem test should rely on some theoretical basis for gaining high probability that problems used in the test are really insight problems (what may be doubted in case of Davidson's study). For example, Weisberg (1995) proposed a taxonomy that differentiates 'pure' and 'hybrid' insight problems. Only pure insight problems cannot be solved without overcoming an impasse. Weisberg indicated also four domains of insight problems: geometric, mathematical, word, and object. Following his proposal we developed an insight test including only 'pure' problems covering all four problem domains.

Second, when single measures (so called *manifest variables*) of two psychological constructs are used (as in Davidson's, and Murray and Byrne's studies), these measures reflect each construct only in part. This so-called *task impurity problem* can result in considerable underestimation of the correlation coefficients. The problem can be dealt with by means of *latent variable* analysis. For each construct, at least two measures are used, which differ as much as possible in all aspects (in order to minimize common task variance) other then those closely associated with the measured construct. The construct is thus reflected by a common variance between the measures, and is modeled as a latent variable. We used two measures of an insight ability and two measures of a fluid ability. We used five tasks measuring diverse executive functions.

Third, it is worth to analyze not only correlation or regression patterns among variables (done in previous studies), but also the underlying hidden structure modeled as a set of relations between latent variables. Structural equation modeling is one of the ways this can be achieved. The goodness of fit indices of alternative models can be compared and different hypotheses concerning the latent variables can be tested. Such models will be presented.

The goal of the presented study was to replicate previous studies with a corrected methodology escaping below mentioned flaws. Our aim was to verify the finding that Gf is strongly linked to insight ability (discovered in Davidson's study) and to estimate the strength of this link. As working memory storage and processing capacity share large proportion of variance with Gf (probably up to 75%; Oberauer, Schulze, Wilhelm, & Süß, 2005), we assumed that a positive test of strong relation between Gf and insight ability will be consistent with significant correlation between the latter construct and WMC, found by Murray and Byrne. We also wanted to explore relationships between executive functions of working memory that lie beyond storage and processing (Miyake, Friedman, Emerson, & Witzki, 2000). In the presented study, not only task switching and response inhibition (as in Murray and Byrne's study), but also memory updating, goal monitoring and dual-tasking were included. The finding that people differ in insight problem ablility, and what other abilities it depends on, may tell us much about possible cognitive basis of insight, and will help to define the proper assumptions for computational models of insight problem solving.

Method

112 participants (m = 22.6, sd = 3.5, 64 women) were recruited from colleges in Łódź, Poland. In order to include subjects representing a wide range of abilities, only private-owned colleges, in which selection procedures are not particularly strict, were covered. Each subject was paid 10€. Two *Gf* tests, five computerized WM tests, and two insight ability tests were administered to each participant in two six-hour sessions, during two consecutive days. Before each test written instructions were presented. Each computerized task was preceded by several training trials. There were also four visual attention tasks administered, but due to both the limited space as well as insignificant correlations between attention and insight problems' tests, the results are omitted.

General fluid intelligence tests

We used two paper-and-pencil tests. Raven's Advanced Progressive Matrices test (Raven, Court, & Raven, 1983) consists of 36 items, which difficulty increases from the start to the end of the test. Each item is a 3 × 3 matrix of figural stimuli that are organized according to latent rules. A subject's aim is to discover proper rules and to choose one correct answer from eight possible ones. The second test was Figural Analogy Test (Orzechowski & Chuderski, personal communication), which consists of 24 figural analogies in form 'A is to B as C is to X', where X has to be chosen from four alternatives. Figural analogies are believed to highly load *Gf* factor (Sternberg, 1985). The test was administered in two versions: easy and hard ones. The score in the easy version of the test was a time to complete the test plus 90 seconds penalty for each error. The score in the hard version was a number of analogies solved correctly.

Executive function tasks

Five tasks represented five executive functions commonly attributed to working memory. These were four functions proposed by Miyake et al. (2001): inhibition, updating, switching, and dual task coordination, and a monitoring function proposed by Duncan, Emslie, and Wilson (1996).

Response inhibition This task required inhibition of prepotent response. Subjects were required to categorize digits onto odd or even by pressing the proper of two buttons. In a training phase they had to categorize 30 stimuli. In an experimental phase, participants were asked to continue categorization with the same category-button associations, except for stimuli which appeared surrounded by a border. In that case subjects were required to emit opposite response. A total number of errors in the 'border' condition was taken as a dependent variable.

Memory updating Modified n-back task (McErlee, 2001) was used, that required memory updating of four most recent stimuli presented in a random length stream of several two-digit numbers. Each stimulus was presented for 2000 ms, followed by a 500 ms mask. A subject was expected to press a space button during presentation of a stimulus (or a mask following it), if she or he recognized that this stimulus (always last one in a stream) was repeated.

Two task versions were used. In an inclusive version, a target on any of four possible positions (1-, 2-, 3-, or 4-back) could be repeated. In an exclusive version of the task, subjects were required to press a button only when a number on exact position (2-, 3-, or 4-back, depending on a trial) was repeated. Repetitions on other positions should be ignored. There were 96 trials in the inclusive and 144 trials in the exclusive version of the task. A total number of omission errors was taken as a dependent variable.

Task switching Two versions of a switching test were used. In alternating runs version (Rogers & Monsell, 1995), fixed length sequence of three letters (from set of eight possible ones) were presented in each block. Depending on presented cues, one of two tasks should be performed. Task alternated predictably from block to block. In the first task, subjects were to categorize stimuli onto vowels or consonants. In the other task, subjects were to press one button if a letter contained angles (A, E, K, N) and another if it did not (C, O, S, U). The task cueing version (Meiran, 1996) of switching test consisted on presenting a cue informing (unpredictably) which task should be performed before presenting a digit stimulus. The tasks could be: (1) categorizing digits onto higher or less than 5, or (2) categorizing them onto even or odd. There were 144 stimuli presented in the former version of the test, and another 144 stimuli presented in the latter. In both tests, computer program waited for 3000 ms for response after a stimulus appearance. A total number of errors was taken as a dependent variable.

Dual task coordination In this task subjects were presented a 2 × 2 matrix of stimuli, with two digits on one (random) diagonal, and two letters on the opposite diagonal. Subjects were required first to compare the digits, checking if they both are odd. If they were, a subject should press a left button with the left hand. Then, a subject had to check, whether both letters are identical. If so, she or he should press a right button with the right hand. There were four conditions: (1) 'press nothing' when one or two digits were even and letters differed, (2) 'press a left button' – both digits were odd but letters differed, (3) 'press a right button' – one or two digits were even but letters were identical, and (4) 'press both buttons' when both digits were even and letter were identical. Stimuli were presented for 4 sec. followed by a 500 ms mask. 80 trials of each condition were presented (320 total) on random. A total number of errors was taken as a dependent variable.

Goal monitoring We designed a version of Duncan et al. (1996) task for monitoring goal change. We continuously presented pairs of figures. The task consisted on categorization of a figure on left or on right, depending on a cue, onto triangles or polygons. A symbol (a cue) presented between figures every several figures reminded which side is the relevant one. The cue could inform subjects directly showing the side ('<' or '>' symbols), or it could remind the relevant side indirectly ('=' indicated 'stay on the same side', '+' indicated 'change sides'). Subjects were expected to continuously monitor and change the goals. Duncan et al. used analogous task to show that some subjects reveal 'goal neglect', i.e. they are not able to change a goal after seeing the indirect symbol, while they have no problems in following the direct symbols. Thus, a total number of errors in indirect condition was taken as a dependent variable.

Insight tests

Two paper-and-pencil tests specially designed for the study were administered. First one consisted of ten insight problems: nine pure insight problems taken from Weisberg's taxonomy, and a ping-pong ball problem, which has full characteristic of a pure problem, taken from Murray and Byrne (2005). Problems from all four categories proposed by Weisberg were covered: i.e., word riddles ('animals in pens', 'checker games', and 'lazy policeman' problems), object manipulation ('ping-pong ball', 'candle', and 'two strings' problems), geometrical ('matchsticks' problem), and mathematical problems ('horse trading', 'socks', and 'water lilies' problems).

The second test consisted of 24 tribonds: three word sets in Polish that formed remote semantic association (e.g., 'cake', 'children', 'taxes'). Subjects were asked to search for a fourth word that captures an association among the former three (e.g., all three objects from the example 'get bigger'). Finding remote associates is believed to require insight (Bowers, Regher, Balthazard, & Parker, 1990).

Results and Discussion

Test scores and correlations

Table 1 presents descriptive statistics for ability tests used in the study. Table 2 presents correlations between test scores and numbers of errors in five computerized tasks. Analysis of correlation matrix clearly shows that all correlations are significant, except for correlation between a number of insight problems solved and a number of errors in dual-task coordination test (which anyway is marginally significant: $p = .082$). The correlation between both tests of fluid ability is high ($r = .738$), as well as the one between both tests of insight ability ($r = .498$). The correlation ($r = .651$) between insight problems test and Raven PM exactly matches the value reported by Davidson (1995). As all tests and tasks correlate positively, and tests correlate negatively with tasks (the higher tests score the less errors in a task), the correlation matrix does not yield any meaningful pattern of data. Thus we turn to analysis on the latent variable level.

Table 1: Test scores statistics.

Test	Min.	Max.	Mean	St. Dev.
Raven PM	10	36	24.8	6.1
Analogy	4	23	16.6	4.1
Problems	0	10	4.6	2.3
Remote Associates	0	20	8.7	4.4

Latent variables and structural equation models

Structural Equation Modeling was used in order to answer the research questions. Thanks to this approach the hypotheses were more directly tested than is possible with simpler, standard statistical methods, such as those based on general linear model. Structural models can be thought of as a compromise between simplicity and interpretability of conventional statistical models, and sophistication and explanatory power of elaborate, full blown algorithmic models. Since more detailed, mathematical models of insight are not readily available, the SEM approach to understanding the nature of insight seems justified.

All the analyses were conducted in the R software environment (version 2.4.0). Structural models were fit using John Fox's sem library (version 0.9-5). In the confirmatory stage three theoretically plausible models were fit, but only one appeared to be in a good agreement with the data. In an attempt to explore some other possibilities, one additional model was analyzed, which also fit well, but seemed somewhat unnecessary, based on the parameter values. In what follows, results concerning all four models will be described, treated as a formal test of alternative hypotheses about the relationship between three latent variables: GF (representing common variance among three fluid intelligence tests), EF (representing common variance among five computerized measures of executive functioning), and IA (insight ability reflected by a common variance between insight problems test and remote associates test), as measured in the present study.

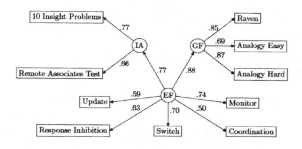

Figure 1: Structure and standardized coefficients of the paths in Model 1.

The Model 1, shown in Figure 1, represents a rather simple hypothesis associating the three latent variables. EF is treated here as a low level construct, underlying both GF and IA. Even though all the free parameters were highly significant ($p < .001$), the overall fit was not acceptable ($\chi2(33) = 73.13$; $p < .001$; $GFI = .88$; $AGFI = .80$; $BIC = -82.58$; $RMSEA = .10$), so the path coefficients cannot be interpreted aptly.

Structural part of Model 2 combined two directional paths, one from EF to IA, and other one from GF to IA variables, making IA dependent on both latent variables. The model was not acceptable being the worst fitting one among all three models ($\chi2(33) = 103.36$; $p < .001$; $GFI = .86$; $AGFI = .77$; $BIC = -52.35$; $RMSEA = .14$), so neither the parameter values nor the measurement part is shown.

Table 2: Matrix of correlations between all pairs of tests/tasks used in the study (* - p < .05, ** - p < .01, *** - p <.001)

	1. Insight problems	2. Remote associates	3. Raven matrices	4. Figural analogies	5. Memory updating	6. Task switching	7. Response inhibition	8. Dual tasking	9. Goal monitoring
1	1	.498***	.651***	.584***	-.348***	-.296**	-.304**	-.167	-.371***
2		1	.461***	.530***	-.230*	-.378***	-.280**	-.281**	-.265**
3			1	.738***	-.427***	-.450***	-.440***	-.308**	-.518***
4				1	-.454***	-.480***	-.483***	-.389***	-.539***
5					1	.358***	.426***	.231*	.476***
6						1	.515***	.418***	.627***
7							1	.374***	.440***
8								1	.367***

The last model (Model 3) tested in the confirmatory stage is depicted in Figure 2. Here GF variable is treated as a common source of variance for IA and EF variables. Again all the parameters were significant ($p < .001$), but this time the fit was acceptable ($\chi2(33) = 43.62$; $p = .102$; $GFI = .92$; $AGFI = .87$; $BIC = -112.09$; $RMSEA = .05$), i.e. the $\chi2$ statistic appeared to be not significant, what indicates that both observed and predicted patterns of data did not differ significantly. The best way to compare all three models is by means of BIC index, as it is based both on the amount of 'variance explained' and a model complexity. A difference in BIC values of about 10 is usually considered conclusive evidence in favor of the model with lower BIC (Raftery, 1993). The difference in BIC values for the third and the first model was about 24, and about 50 for the third and the second one, leaving the third model the most supported one.

The path coefficients, which this time can are fully interpretable, are very high. Gf factor loads the insight ability on the level of $r = .87$, which means that more than 75% percent of variance in the insight ability is predicted by fluid abilities. Gf also appear to load executive functioning highly, explaining nearly 58% of variance in the ability of executive control.

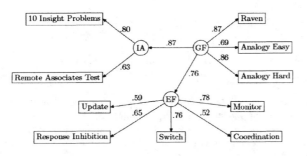

Figure 2: Structure and standardized coefficients of the paths in Model 3.

In a more exploratory stage of analysis directional path leading from EF to IA variable was added to the Model 3. This model also fitted the data quite well ($\chi2(33) = 41.38$; $p = .124$; $GFI = .93$; $AGFI = .88$; $BIC = -109.09$; $RMSEA = .05$), but the BIC value was a bit lower then for the Model 3, and the standardized parameter estimate for the path connecting GF to IA was equal to 1.09, forcing us to conclude that there was some redundancy in the parametrization, and such a model should be discarded.

Summary and Conclusions

The research question investigated in this study was whether executive functioning, fluid intelligence, and ability to solve insight problems are related. New methodology for studying insight phenomena was used, based on measurement of hypothesized constructs with latent variables derived from at least two different manifest measures, and the analysis of a hidden structure of relations underlying measured constructs by means of alternative structural equation models selection

As it is disputed in the literature on WM and fluid abilities, whether efficient WM underlies high Gf (or g), or it is high Gf (or g) that makes highly intelligent people efficient in WM tasks (e.g., Colom et al., 2004), we tested the model where latent variable reflecting WM executive functioning underlies variables reflecting both fluid and insight abilities, as well as the model, where it is Gf which is considered as the low-level construct that underlies both abilities of insight and executive functioning. The latter model appeared to be better supported by the observed data. It was also the only model that predicted the pattern of data that did not differ significantly from the observations. Four main conclusions can be drawn from these results.

First of all, both tests of insight ability appeared to aptly measure what they were in fact designed to be measuring. The loadings of IA latent variable were high (.80 and .63 for problems and associates tests, respectively), and similar in value to the loadings of GF variable on fluid ability tests.

Second, results obtained in Davidson's (1995) study were replicated and extended. With corrected methodology, the link between intelligence and insight ability constructs appeared to be even stronger, the former construct predicted three fourth of variance in the latter construct.

Third, modeling results show that it is the Gf factor (which is strongly correlated with WM capacity) rather than the efficiency of executive control that underlies insight ability. This result corroborates in part Murray and Byrne's (2005) findings concerning the strong link between insight ability and WMC, but does not support the correlations between insight ability and scores in attention switching tests (which might be an artifact due to high loadings of task switching tests, used by Murray and Byrne, on WMC). The result suggests that insight is not a kind of 'special' ability, but a phenomenon strongly linked to abstract reasoning.

Finally, as far as we know, the present work is the first SEM study that relates executive functioning, as measured directly with a battery of executive tests, to the fluid abilities. Some theories of cognitive basis of *Gf* postulate some aspects of controlled processing being crucial for abstract reasoning (e.g., attention control; Engle et. al, 1999; goal management; Carpenter, Just & Shell, 1990; Duncan et al. 1995), but relations between fluid abilities and executive control, measured with the battery of diverse tests, were not examined up till now. The link is quite strong (SEM model shows more than a half of common variance) and, at least in the present study, it leads from *Gf*, treated as an underlying ability, to the level of efficiency of executive control, treated as a consequence of a level of *Gf* ability.

Correlational studies do not allow for drawing conclusions about the nature of casual links, so processes involved in insight problem solving and executive functioning should be studied further with central methods of cognitive science: experimentation and computational modeling. However, the present study sheds the light on cognitive basis of this processes (i.e., *Gf*) and shows that proper models of both insight problem solving and executive control should account for individual differences in these abilities, observed among people.

References

Bowers, K. S., Regher, G., Balthazard, C., & Parker, K. (1990). Intuition in the context of discovery. *Cognitive Psychology, 22*, 72-110.

Carpenter, P. A., Just, M. A., & Shell, P. (1990). What one intelligence test measures: A theoretical account of the processing in the Raven Progressive Matrices test. *Psychological Review, 97*, 404-431.

Colom, R., Rebollo I., Palacios, A., Juan-Espinosa, M., & Kyllonen, P. (2004). Working memory is (almost) predicted by g. *Intelligence, 32*, 277-296.

Davidson, J. E. (1995). The suddennes of insight. In R. J. Sternberg & J. E. Davidson (Eds.), *The nature of insight* (pp. 125-155). Cambridge, MA: MIT Press.

Dominowski, R. L., & Dallob P. (1995). Insight and problem solving. In R. J. Sternberg & J. E. Davidson (Eds.), *The nature of insight* (pp. 125-155). Cambridge, MA: MIT Press.

Duncan, J., Emslie, H., & Williams, P. (1996). Intelligence and the frontal lobe: The organization of goal-directed behavior. *Cognitive Psychology 30*, 257-303.

Duncker, K. (1945). On problem solving. *Psychological Monographs, 58* (Whole No. 270).

Kaplan, C. A., & Simon, H. A. (1990). In search of insight. *Cognitive Psychology, 22*, 374-419.

Kershaw, T. C., & Ohlsson S. (2004). Multiple causes of difficulty in insight: The case of the nine-dot problem.

Journal of Experimental Psychology: Learning, Memory, and Cognition, 30, 3-13.

McErlee, B. (2001). Working memory and focal attention. *Journal of Experimental Psychology: Learning, Memory, and Cognition, 27*, 817-835.

Meiran, N. (1996). Reconfiguration of processing mode prior to task performance. *Journal of Experimental Psychology: Learning, Memory, and Cognition, 22*, 1423-1442.

Metcalfe, J. (1986). Feeling of knowing in memory and problem solving. *Journal of Experimental Psychology: Learning, Memory, and Cognition, 12*, 288-294.

Miyake, A., Friedman, N. P., Emerson, M. J., Witzki, A. H., & Howerter, A. (2000). The unity and diversity of executive functions and their contributions to complex "frontal lobe" tasks: A latent variable analysis. *Cognitive Psychology 41*, 49-100.

Murray, M. A., & Byrne, R. M. J. (2005). Attention and working memory in insight problem-solving. In B. Bara, L. Barsalou, & M. Bucciareli (Eds.), *Proceedings of 27th Annual Meeting of Cognitive Science Society*, (pp. 1571-1576) Mahwah, NJ: Erlbaum.

Newell, A., & Simon, H. A. (1972). Human problem solving. Englewood Cliffs, NJ: Prentice-Hall.

Oberauer, K., Schulze, R., Wilhelm, O., & Süß, H-M. (2005). Working memory, intelligence–their correlation and their relation: Comment on Ackerman, Beier, & Boile (2005). *Psychological Bulletin, 131*, 61-65.

Ohlsson, S. (1984). Restructuring revisited: Summary and critique of the gestalt theory of problem solving. *Scandinavian Journal of Psychology, 25*, 65-78.

Raftery, A., E. (1993). Bayesian Model Selection in Structural Equation Models. [in:] K. A. Bollen & J. S. Long (Eds.). *Testing Structural Equation Models*, (pp. 163-180). Newbury Park CA: Sage.

Raven, J. C., Court, J. H., & Raven J. (1983). Manual for Raven's Progressive Matrices and vocabulary scales (Section 4: Advanced Progressive Matrices). London: H. K. Lewis.

Rogers, R. D., & Monsell, S. (1995). Costs of a predictable switch between simple cognitive tasks. *Journal of Experimental Psychology: General 124*, 207-231.

Sternberg, R. J. (1985). *Beyond IQ: A triarchic theory of human intelligence*. Cambridge: Cambridge Univ. Press.

Weisberg, R. W. (1995). Prolegomena to theories of insight in problem solving: a taxonomy of problems. In R. J. Sternberg & J. E. Davidson (Eds.), *The nature of insight* (pp. 157-196). Cambridge, MA: MIT Press.

Weisberg, R. W., & Alba J. W. (1981). An examination of the alleged role of "fixation" in the solution of several "insight" problems. *Journal of Experimental Psychology: General, 110*, 169-192.

Wertheimer, M. (1959). *Productive thinking*. New York: Harper and Row (originally published in 1945).

Yaniv, I., & Meyer, D. E. (1987). Activation and metacognition of inaccessible stored information: Potential bases for incubation effects in problem solving. *Journal of Experimental Psychology: Learning, Memory, and Cognition, 13*, 187-205.

An Exploratory Study of High-Order Thinking Skills in Chemistry-Based Discourse

Selva Ranee Subramaniam
Universiti Malaya

Abstract

Malaysia, being a developing country has undergone multiple phases of reforms in Science teaching which ranged from the early dissemination of facts to the recent constructivist approach. Teacher trainers have placed emphasis on teacher's questioning as an approach to stimulate high-order thinking amongst students. However, the student generated questions and statements were often side-tracked. This component of students' statements and questions are initiators in adopting a constructivist approach and should be dwelled to further promote thinking. This study takes the form of an action research which aims to explore the high-order thinking skills of Form Four(Grade 10) students in the study of Chemistry. The study was conducted in the central region of Malaysia. The qualitative method of data collection enabled the researcher to investigate the real time verbal discourse among the students during chemistry laboratory activities. The observation was validated with the students' document of the learning process. In the first teaching cycle, students were given structured activities which required them to follow instructions and obtain results which was a mere verification of facts. These activities did not pose a challenge to teachers and students alike as there was minimum opportunity for further discussion. Everything seemed to work in a tight framework to satisfy standardized examination demands. In designing the implementation of the second cycle of this action research, the practitioner and the researcher discussed (dialogue reflection) and analysed critically the first teaching cycle. A plan of action was developed to implement strategies with the ultimate goal of providing opportunities for students to interact verbally and intellectually. Analysis of data from the study showed that there were distinctive differences in the type of students' questions and statements used during verbal discourse. The different positions of the learners in the verbal interplay scaffold learning among individuals of mixed ability. Student generated questions triggered further thinking in the content-related discipline. Students' discourse could be utilized by the teacher in facilitating the development of high-order thinking skills. This pedagogical strategy would be a useful tool to catalyse a student-centered learning environment.

Background and Significance

Science learning in school occurs in a dynamic environment incorporating the acquisition and use of science process skills. Scientific knowledge is organized, constructed and reconstructed through scientific methods. This inquiry process is a systematic and creative application of scientific methods to seek answers and solve problems. Through inquiry experiences, students not only learn about science, but also learn skills that help them to think logically, ask reasonable questions, seek appropriate answers, and solve daily problems. The teacher's questioning skill was always in the forefront and given utmost importance. Discussion of activities was predominantly "going through" instructions for the activity, getting feedback on whether the students' understood the instruction, what they should look for, what they need to complete at the end of the activity and emphasis on getting the "right" answer.

There is tendency to be confused about dialogue and conversation. According to Bakhtin (1981) dialogue possesses a greater degree of structure and is differentiated from conversation by the purposeful use of questioning in the pursuit of inquiry. Wells (1999) draws on the twin sources of Leont'ev's activity theory and Halliday's systemic functional linguistics to formulate the concept of dialogic inquiry, in which knowledge is co-constructed by teacher and students as they engage in joint activities. Bringing together insights from the two theoretical traditions, discourse was defined as the collaborative behaviour of two or more participants as they use the potential of a shared language to mediate the establishment and achievement of their goals in social action. Through discussions, ideas can be refined and clarified, in a process which Bereiter (1994) termed as "progressive discourse" in which contributions refer to and build upon what has gone before (by agreeing, disagreeing, adding, qualifying etc.).

The study of classroom discourse is essential as different modes of interaction place students in different positions as learners (Nystrand 1997). Sometimes this tentative probing sharing of ideas was better facilitated by the absence of the teacher than by their presence. The ultimate outcome for effective pedagogical instruction is the quality of student learning which is associated closely with the quality of classroom talk viz. student-student talk. This dialogue is concerned with the verbal interplay pattern of student-student interaction aimed at maximizing active student participation as a strategy in enhancing content understanding. In a constructivist viewpoint, learning is not a separate entity from the intellectual and social component of the learner thus leading to dialogic literacy which is the ability to engage productively in discourse thereby generating new knowledge and understanding (Bereiter & Scardamalia 2005). This form of literacy is fundamental for a knowledge-based society and reforms in educational policy should address this as a prime objective.

Objectives

The present study is an action research which will explore the high-order thinking skills in a specific content-related chemistry discourse. The discourse analysis will focus on the type of tasks, questions posed by students and category of questions used to attain the expected goals of the activity.

Research Questions

Specifically, this study aims to study the following:
(i) To investigate the type of tasks addressed in the co-construction of knowledge?
(ii) To investigate the type of questions posed by students during the verbal interplay?
(iii) To investigate the category of questions used in the verbal interplay during the chemistry activities?

Methodology

The participants in this research were twelve From Four students (three groups comprising of four students each) in a chemistry classroom. Purposive sampling was done to secure a rich and saturated data as the participants were considered as "key informants" and not subjects in this research (Spindler 1985). Non-participant observation was used to record the verbal discourse of the subjects during group discussion. This type of observation has enabled the researcher to differentiate herself from the happenings of the environment, thus facilitating the real and authentic learning process to continue uninterrupted (Hammersley & Atkinson 1993). The "focused" observation encompassed the individual student's utterances from the perspective of thoughtful thinking. For purposes of accuracy and reliability, the transcriptions were reviewed by both the researcher and the respondent until there was agreement. The lessons chosen are of experimental nature. As this is an action research, observation was carried out during the initial and successive teaching cycles. In the third action research teaching cycle, the practitioner and the researcher has re-designed the experimental activities which are pertinent for understanding chemistry and non-experimental activities which are interrelated.

Analysis of Data

The observation data were recorded and transcribed. The individual utterances and the extended exchanges were analysed. Each aspect of the verbal discourse was examined with reference to four questions: In what ways is the talk collaborative? What aspects of the task are addressed in the participant's talk? What aspects of learning are being enabled in the talk? How are the participants responsive to each other? The individual utterances were analysed in terms of the thinking processes involved in planning, cognitive strategies and evaluation involved in co-construction of new knowledge.

Results and Discussion

In the first action research cycle, the practitioner carried out activities as stipulated in the standardized laboratory book which is used by all students and teachers. The design of the science activities was rigid and structured. There was minimum provision for students to rationalise, debate, argue or even to suggest alternative laboratory procedures. Self-generated questioning on the part of the students was minimum, comprising mostly from the laboratory book, if any. This is not only limited to experimental procedures, but also the way the results should be presented and provided in the laboratory book. In other words, it is rigidly guided. In the second action research cycle, the practitioner used the same laboratory book as a guide and instructed students to present the results and conclusion in a way they felt appropriate. However, the Dialogue was limited to questions like "How to change...?". "This is suitable, we use the same as written in the book....?". Do you all agree...? As to the tasks of planning, everything was sequentially structured. The only planning that was done was allocation of tasks among group members. The observations did not differ much from the first action research cycle, as the students followed presentation of results as in the laboratory book and evaluation was merely a process of determining whether the correct results were obtained. In the third action research cycle, the laboratory activities were re-designed to provide room for dialogue and tapped on the students' prerequisite knowledge. The topics selected and activities re-designed are critical in understanding the basics of chemistry. An excerpt of the activity is as follows:

Scenario 1: Open-Ended Laboratory Activity

In the first stage of the laboratory activity, teacher instructed students (role played as chemists) to discuss in groups how to conduct an experiment to investigate the reactions of three unknown substance X, Y and Z with air, oxygen and chlorine. The teacher showed that the reagent bottles containing the unknown substances which were stored in paraffin oil to the students. The teacher also cautioned the students on the reactivity of the elements in water, oxygen and chlorine. Students were reminded to take into consideration this fact in planning for the experiment. The type of tasks, type of questions and category of questions during the verbal interplay are presented in Table 1.

The findings of the study indicated that the students were able to compare and contrast the alternative use of apparatus. As mentioned by the student, coded as S1 on the use of test tube for this experiment received opposition by other students, coded S3. Student S1 questioned student S3 by a inquiry question "Why?...cannot". In the choice of alternative apparatus, students S1 and S3 were able to analyse the properties of the unknown element X which will be entered into a suitable container to be used for the reaction. The test tube which was suggested was not suitable because a student coded, S4 was of the opinion that "explosion....glass.......like a bomb...... cannot stand active reactions" (Observation Class 1, 4E1). This showed that there was construction of new knowledge by the students as a result of verbal discourse. Another student in the group, student coded as S4 suggested an alternative use of a big beaker. The discussion in evaluating the appropriate use of a suitable apparatus resulted finally in reaching a solution of using a plastic basin. The statement made by the student was a clear indication of the construction of new knowledge as a result of collaborative thinking. Students are able to evaluate the choices generated by the groups members if the opportunity is given for exploratory and inquiry investigations.

The analysis of the observation of the individual utterances during the laboratory activity showed that that the students interacted among themselves using high-order thinking questions. Students used critical thinking questions which included why, if use this method....can or not? in thinking what needs to be done. In the first stage, students need to identify the issue which is to plan the procedure for the experiment. Using the information given as a precaution to reason, the students generated alternative ways which could be used to carry out the experiment. Students, during the discussion voiced their rational for the choice of the procedures to be used by comparing and contrasting the alternative solutions before selecting the most appropriate procedures in conducting the experiment in a safe manner. In making a decision on the most appropriate procedure to conduct the experiment, the students evaluated the strengths and weakness of each of the choice.

In accumulating the ideas on how the experiment could be carried out, students are able to sequence the procedures in carrying out the experiment. Students are able to reason and sequence the steps in the experimental procedures. Students are aware that the aim of the experiment and work towards achieving the goal. Each group presented the experimental procedure they proposed. After each group presented, the teacher demonstrated the experiment to the class. Students recorded the observations and discussed with the students on the conclusions of the reactivity of the unknown elements X, Y and Z.

In stage 2, students are to record all observations during the demonstration of the experiment by the teacher. Students discussed in groups and made conclusions on the reactivity series based on the observations. The analysis of the data showed that students planned and chose alternatives to demonstrate in a systematic way to facilitate drawing conclusions. In making conclusions, students analysed observations by comparing and contrasting all observations for the reactions for elements X, Y and Z, comparing the reactions of the element X, Y and Z, classifying the reactions in terms of reactivity, and sequencing the elements in order of reactivity. Students explored for reasons, explained the reasons and justified the reasons prior to making decisions of the reactivity order. Students had to undergo the process of making decisions and exhibited the summary of the experiment in the form of a flow chart which showed the significant physical and chemical properties of the unknown elements of X, Y and Z. Students coded as S1, S2, S3 and S4 discussed the best appropriate graphic representation in demonstrating the results and conclusion of the experiment.

Table 1: Type of Cognitive Tasks, Questions and Category of Questions During the Verbal Interplay.

Cognitive Thinking Tasks	Type of Questions	Category of questions
Planning	How ...?, Can use...? Why ?...cannot...? Can you recall...? How to explain...?	High-order questions
Cognitive strategies	Why...? What...? What if...? How would you...? How to classify...? How to identify...? Which statement supports...? Can you explain...? What other way...? Why do you think...? What proof...? What changes to make...? Can be done this way...?	High-order questions
Evaluating	What if...? Suppose I use...? Can I do like this...? How about this...? Is it correct...? How if...? Is it better.../ Why...? What choice...? What is your opinion...? Do you agree...?	High-order questions

Discussion

The current science textbooks in Malaysia design activities which are fully guided. The verbal interaction among the students were minimum and there was minimum inquiry opportunities in the activities. The practitioner and the researcher for seeing this as a setback in instilling high-order thinking skills among the students re-designed the activities thereby providing room for dialogue among the students. The action research model adopted   Students had to plan, devise their own cognitive strategies in the process of rationalising, arguing, debating and evaluating options. The verbal interplay among the students in accomplishing the activities portrayed a landscape of thoughtful words which can be classified as high-order thinking. The pattern of thoughtful words among others frequently used was Why..?, What if..., How can..?., What is...? . In presenting the different scenarios, the different ways in which students engage in dialogic inquiry is demonstrated. The importance of peer assistance became very apparent as we reviewed the recordings made, both of the small group practical work and of the whole class discussion. Learning thus was not unidimensional i.e. from teacher to students but rather every member made a significant contribution that led to the expected learning outcome. Every member in the group has the potential in one way or other that can assist the others and everyone could learn and benefit from one another's input and response. Classroom practice is always in authentic context and is shaped by immediate demands and constraints at that particular point of time. The individual student utterances showed that the students are able to trigger high-order thinking among their peers if the activity designed provides the necessary opportunities. The thoughtful words used in the verbal interplay showed that given the learning opportunities, students are capable to explore, investigate issues and provide alternative solutions.. In the discussion, the students not only talked about the design of the experiments/activities, but also used and explained terms like density, physical properties, chemical properties etc. This scientific language came not from teacher's formal lessons but from the practical experiences and the experiments that the students were engaged in. In this way, they are reconstructing the used of scientific terminology and explanations hat were developed as tools to assist them in the activity of doing science. The participants jointly resolved problems and constructed solutions as evident in students generated questions activities. Hence, there is a critical need for educators to revisit this pedagogical strategy as an intervention for inculcating high-order thinking skills among students. Educators can use this as a way of assessing formatively the construction and understanding of knowledge.

References

Bakhtin, M..M. (1981). The dialogic imagination: Four essays (C. Emerson & M. Holquist, Trans.). Austin, Texas: University of Texas Press.

Bereiter, C. (1994). Implications of postmodernism for science, or , science as progressive discourse. Educational Psychologist, 29(1): 3-12.

Bereiter, C. & Scardamalia, M. Technologies and Literacies: From Print Literacy to Dialogic Literacy, Ontario institute for Studies in Education of the University of Toronto, accessed, July 2005, at http://ikit.org/fulltext/TechandLit.htm.

Brown, A.L., & Campione, J.C. (1994). Guided discovery in a community of learners. In K. McGilly (Ed.). Integrating cognitive theory and classroom practice: Classroom lessons (pp. 229 – 272). Cambridge, MA: MIT Press/ Bradford Books.

Hammersley, M. & Atkinson, P. 1993. Ethnography: Principles in practice. London:Routledge.

Lave, J., & Wenger, E. (1991). Situated learning: Legitimate peripheral participation. New York: Cambridge University Press.

Nystrand, M. (1997). Opening Dialogue: Understanding the Dynamics of Language and Learning in the English Classroom. New York: Teachers College Press.

Spindler, G. (Ed.). (1982). Doing ethnography of schooling: Educational ethnography in action. New York: Holt, Reinhart & Winston.

Wells, G. & Chang- Wells, G.L. (1996). The literate potential of collaborative talk. In B. Power & R. Hubbard (Eds.) Language development: A reader for teachers (pp. 155-167). Englewoods Cliffs, NJ: Prentice-Hall.

Wells,G. (1999). Dialogic Inquiry: towards a Sociocultural Practice and theory of Education. Cambridge: Cambridge University Press.

Reading about Computer Cache Memory: The Effects of Text Structure in Science Learning

Evangelos Kanidis (vkanidis@di.uoa.gr)
Interdisciplinary Program of Graduate Studies in Basic and Applied Cognitive Science
University of Athens, Panepistimioupolis, Ilisia 157 71, Athens- GREECE

Maria Grigoriadou (gregor@di,uoa.gr)
Department of Informatics and Telecommunications
University of Athens, Panepistimioupolis, Ilisia 157 71, Athens-GREECE

Abstract

In the current paper, we present some aspects about the influence that a scientific text structure has on students understanding. The research was conducted in the Department of Informatics and Telecommunications of the University of Athens on a text referring to the structure and operation of computer cache memory. Previous research results revealed that students have difficulties in understanding notions referring to time and causal relationships of the cache memory operations, the placement operation, as well as the concept of word and block address in main and cache memory. In the present study we use three forms of text. The first text (form A) is based on books written by Hennessy and Patterson (1996;1999). The second text (form B) is a re-organized form of the text form A according to text comprehension theories of Kintsch (1988) and Denhiere & Baudet (1992). The third text (form C) is based on the form B with additional refutations. The results of the study showed that students who read a text organized according to the text comprehension theories or a refutational text have a better understanding about the computer cache memory as opposed to students who read the text form A.

The influence of a text form to students' understanding

Despite the promise of new technologies and other educational media, it is quite clear that textbooks still dominate the classrooms and are a ubiquitous part of education (Woodward, 1993; Otero, León, Graesser, 2002). Text has been and continues to be a primary medium of learning. More importantly, the ability to acquire information from text determines the extent to which an individual can engage in independent, life-long learning (Diakidoy, 1999; Diakidoy, Kendeou, & Ioannides, 2003). As Glaser (1991) notes, the schoolbook constitutes the vehicle for learning and its form should help students develop their own information models. It is generally accepted that text comprehension is a more profound process than mere reading. In order for students to comprehend a text, they should not only retain the basic information of a text, but also understand in depth the issues presented and be able to actually use the knowledge they have gained (Graves, 1991).

Many early studies on text comprehension have focused their interest on sentence structure presented in the text (Brown & Day, 1983, Stevens, 1988, Williams, 1986). This approach assumes that text structure itself could be organized on the basis of hierarchy which determines its basic points. On the contrary, Afflerbach (1990) questions this hierarchical text structure, because it presupposes that different readers construct the text in the same way and therefore have the same main ideas for the same text and this has been experimentally proved that is not true. Moreover, Reynolds and Shirey (1988) have concluded in their research that the elements that readers characterize as important depend on the interaction of external factors, such as text form as well as the purpose of reading, with internal factors such as preexisting knowledge and students' interests.

In approaching the scientific text comprehension, many researchers are examining issues that are focusing on ways to assist comprehension and learning through the design of the text form. These efforts assume that readers build mental representations of information contained in the text. Mental representations capture elements of the surface text, of the referential meaning of the text, and of the interpretation of the referential meaning constructing a microworld of characters, objects, spatial settings, actions, events, feelings, etc (Goldman & Bisanz 2002).

Britton, Gulgoz & Glynn (1993) mention that the best evidence they found in their research is that rewriting improves learning from textbooks. They refer to 18 studies that fit the following two criteria: (a) Textbook materials were rewritten, and (b) The original textbook material was then tested against the rewritten version. Of the 18 studies, 16 succeeded in significantly improving learning from the texts. The rewriting techniques included (a) reordering ideas, (b) signaling the structure of the content, (c) incorporating preview sentences, (d) adding logical connectives and other structural information, (e) changing or removing details, and (f) explicitly stating main ideas and examples. Also the same researchers found that texts can also be improved by adding linguistic or paralinguistic elements to them without rewriting or otherwise changing the texts. Elements used in this way included headings, logical connectives, preview sentences, underlining, summaries, numbering of listings, and typographical emphasizers such as capitalization, italics, type size, and typeface.

Another text structure that has also been found to be particularly effective in students understanding is the *refutational* text. A refutational text first presents common misconceptions and then directly refutes them before presenting the accurate version of the content. Studies revealed that refutational texts were more effective in dispelling prior misconceptions than non-refutational texts (Hynd & Alvermann, 1986; Maria, 1987; Maria & MacGinitie, 1981; Guzzetti, Williams, Skeels, & Wu, 1997; Diakidoy, Kendeou, & Ioannides, 2003). Alvermann and Hynd (1989) examined text structure and activation of prior knowledge obtained before reading and their findings suggest that merely activating prior knowledge is not as effective as activating existing misconceptions and then explicitly directing students to attend to ideas that may be in conflict with their own. Also Scopeliti and Vosniadou (2006) found that the use of a refutational text can be an effective way of promoting conceptual change on children's ideas about the Earth.

The cognitive psychological approach supports that the internal variables of the reader such as his/her personal goals, interests and preexisting knowledge, hold a primary role in text comprehension, (Eysenck & Keane, 2000). However, cognitive science does not ignore the influence of text form, in which factors such as text cohesion and logical coherence of facts presented have been proved to be significant elements that facilitate its comprehension All these variables play a major role in the construction of mental representation and processing of a text.

It is widely accepted that especially the content of scientific texts have multiple levels of representation, but two are the most important: the shallow and the deep knowledge. Shallow knowledge consists of explicitly mentioned ideas in a text that refer to: lists of concepts, a handful of simple facts or properties of each concept, simple definitions of key terms, and major steps in a procedure (not the detailed steps). Deep knowledge consists of coherent explanations of the material that fortify the learner to generate inferences, solve problems, make decisions, integrate ideas, synthesize new ideas, decompose ideas into subparts, forecast future occurrences in a system, and apply knowledge to practical situations (Otero, León, Graesser, 2003; van der Broek, 2003; León & Penalba, 2003)

Models of text comprehension

Some researchers develop text comprehension models that have explicit assumptions about representations and cognitive processes that readers go through during text comprehension. We present two of these models.

One of the basic units of text analysis within the Kintsch and van Dijk (1978) model is the *proposition* which is the smallest unit meaning to which we can assign a true value. The proposion has the form *predicate(arguments)*. The text according to the model, is processed by the reader to form structures at two main levels:

- The micro-structure at which the propositions extracted from the text are formed into a connected structure.
- The macro-structure at which an edited version of the micro-structure is formed.

The macro-structure combines schematic information with an abbreviated version of the micro-structure propositions according to specific rules such as deletion, generalization and construction. Kintsch (1988;1998) put forward the construction–integration model that developed and extended his previous model. The new model provides more information about the way in which inferences are formed and stored knowledge interacts with textual information to form the macro structure.

Kintsch (1998) claims that the comprehension process produces a mental representation of a text in memory as a unitary structure, but for analytic purposes it is useful to distinguish two components: the *textbase* model and the *situation* model. The textbase model is simpler and consists of those elements and relations that are directly derived from the text itself. The situation model is a more coherent and complete structure that interprets the information in terms of the reader's prior knowledge, and intergrates it with the reader's personal storage of knowledge and experience. Developing a situation model, enables the student to gain information from a text and not just remember and recall a text.

In the model of text comprehension by Denhiere & Baudet (1992) the primary role is held by the conceptual categories *state*, *event* and *action*. The term *state* is static and describes a state in which no change occurs in the course of time. The term *event* refers to an action that causes changes but is not originated by man. The *event* can be coincidental or caused by a non-human action e.g. by a machine. An *action* is an effect that causes changes, but is originated by man.

Deniere & Baudet (1992) expressed the opinion that in order to examine the representation constructed by students during the comprehension process of a text, text analysis in relation to the conceptual categories of state, event and action is not enough. The organization and structure of cognitive representation that students construct during the comprehension process should be examined in both micro-level and macro-level. The person who reads a text gradually constructs the microstructure of text representation, i.e. the situations, facts and compound actions of the world described in the text as well as the time and causal relationships that interlock those structures. In the macro-level, the development of macrostructure by the reader is achieved through reconstruction of microstructure and the establishment of a hierarchical structure according to the system type the text refers to and contains compound static situations, relations of part-total, time and causal relations of facts' sequence and relations of cause and side-cause.

Denhiere & Baudet (1992) hold that a person who wants to explain the operation of a technical system has to construct a representation of "natural flow of things", where every new event should be causally explained by the conditions of events already occurred. A technical system that has at its disposal a sum of interrelating units defined by hierarchical relations of the part-total type and could be organized in a tree of causes and side-causes is called operating system. The creation of such a text that allows for a precise description of a technical system and facilitates the reader in constructing its macrostructure is called analysis of a technical subject in a operating system.

The operating system analysis of a technical subject contains three aspects: causality, description of facts sequence and teleology. In particular, the text to be used has to allow for descriptions that involve:

- The description of units that constitute the system based on the causal relationship that unites them.
- The description of facts sequence taking place in these units with respect to the causal relationships as well as the changes they bring to the situation of the system.

The present study

The subject of computer memory is an important issue because all programs spend much of their time accessing memory. The cache memory is a small and fast memory that holds the most recently accessed code or data and its role is to increase the computer performance by facilitating the communication between processor and main memory.

In our previous researches we found that students face difficulties in understanding the organization and operation of computer cache memory (Grigoriadou, Toula & Kanidis, 2003; Grigoriadou & Kanidis, 2001 ; 2003). More specifically, the students describe a cache memory operation as:

(a) only a part of this operation (e.g. the identification operation as the address bit partitioning).

(b) another operation (e.g. the placement operation as the identification operation).

(c) a part of another operation (e.g. the placement operation as the mapping techniques).

Also the students believe that

(a) the write operation takes place without a prior need to perform the identification operation, followed by a placement or replacement operation in case of a cache miss

(b) the placement operation rather than the replacement operation is performed, when the result of the identification operation is a cache miss caused by the block tag field while the valid bit is set.

The main purpose of the present study is to examine how the form of a scientific text about the organization and operations of cache memory influences students' comprehension. More specifically, we hypothesize that students who read a text organized according to the text comprehension theories have a better understanding about the computer cache memory as opposed to students who read a simple text. Also, we hypothesize that students who read the refutational text have a better comprehension as opposed to students who read the one organized according to the text comprehension theories.

Method

Participants

Our sample consisted of 60 students, all students of Informatics and Telecommunications Department of the University of Athens. All the students took part in "Computer Architecture II" course. The students were randomly divided in three groups of twenty people each.

Materials

In this study we use three forms of text. The first text (form A) is based on two of the most famous books written by Hennessy and Patterson (Hennessy & Patterson, 1996; Patterson & Hennessy, 1999) that are used as reference books in many Universities worldwide. The second text (form B) is a re-organized form of the text form A according to text comprehension theories of Kintsch (1988) and Denhiere & Baudet (1992). Form B has 22,2% more text information than text form A. This increase occurs not only by adding more information but because the whole textbook material is reorganized to be more coherent and more precisely related to causality and temporal sequences of the various cache memory operations. The third text (form C) is based on form B with 12,7% additional refutations. In specific points we present students' common misconceptions, that we have recorded in our previous research, and immediately refute them. Some examples follow.

Where can a block be placed in a cache?

The restrictions on where a block is placed create three categories of cache organization:

If each block has only one place it can appear in the cache, the cache is said to be *direct mapped*....

If a block can be placed anywhere in the cache, the cache is said to be *fully associative*.

If a block can be placed in a restricted set of places in the cache, the cache memory is said to be *set associative*...

Figure 1: The mapping techniques as described in text form A.

In Figure 1 we can see an example of text form A. In this text we observe that:

- Under the title "Where can a block be placed in a cache" the text describes the mapping techniques. The analysis of students' difficulties in relation to the educational material that the students use, shows that the difficulty of the substitution of the mapping techniques, which is part of the identification operation, with placement operation is due to the use of the verb "place" instead of the right one: "map". The placement operation is partly described in text form A through an example.

- The starting conditions of the placement operation, the causal and temporal relationships between this operation with the other operations of the cache memory and the result of this operation are not described.

- The execution steps of the placement operation with causal and temporal relationships are not described either.

In text form B, we present the mapping techniques separately and before the analytical presentation of the cache memory operations. Moreover, in order to present the "natural flow of things" the identification operation is described before the placement operation.

In Figure 2, we can see a part of the re-organized text form B which describes the placement operation.

Placement operation after a read CPU command

The placement operation starts when the result of the identification operation of a block in cache memory is a miss (cache miss) due the fact that the valid bit is zero.

The placement operation is implemented through the following steps:

- The main memory block containing the desired address is transferred to cache memory.
- Moreover, at the same time the main memory block tag field that is mapped to the cache memory updates the tag field of the cache memory block, and the valid bit is set to 1.

The block of cache memory, where the main memory block will be mapped, depends on the cache memory organization and the corresponding mapping techniques....

Figure 2: The placement operation as described in text form B.

Placement operation after a read CPU command

Students often confuse the mapping techniques with the placement operation. The placement operation aims to transfer a data block from main memory to a correspondent block in cache memory. The mapping techniques is a part of the identification operation and aims to find in which block of cache memory the main memory block will be mapped. The result depends on the cache memory organization and the corresponding mapping techniques.

The placement operation starts when the result of the identification operation of a block in cache memory is a miss (cache miss)....

Figure 3: The placement operation as described in text form C.

In Figure 3, we can see a part of the refutational text form C. In the first paragraph, we present students' common misconception that the placement operation is the same as the mapping techniques and immediately refute this and present the accurate version.

Procedure

The study was conducted in three phases. In phase one, the students were given a pretest which they did in a classroom situation. They have two hours time to answer the questions. In phase two, during the following two weeks, instruction of the concept of cache memory was carried in the classroom. In the third phase, the students were randomly given one of the three text versions and the posttest, also in a classroom situation. They were instructed to study the text normally and to answer the questions in the posttest. There was no time limit, but it took approximately two and a half hours to read the text and do the assignments.

The same four open-ended questions were included in both the pretest and the posttest. In more detail, the students were asked:
- to explain the necessary conditions for starting
  A1. the identification operation and
  A2. the write operation.
- B. to compare the execution steps of the placement operation after a read C.P.U command against the execution steps after a write C.P.U command
- C1. to describe the cache memory state before and after a sequence of three events taking place during cache memory operations.
  C2. also to find the missing intermediate event.
- D. to design the cache memory contents after a sequence of five processor requests to main memory addresses.

The measures used in the pre- and post test were exactly the same. Questions A1 and A2 were scored 0-3 each, question B was scored 0-6, questions C1 and C2 were scored 0-3 each and exercise D was scored 0-6.

After analyzing the written answers, six students were asked to be interviewed in order to further investigate their answers.

Results

A t-test was performed for every text versions and the results show that there were no statistical differences in the prior knowledge between treatment groups in the pretest.

Students responses to questions along with the corresponding means (M) and standard deviations (SD) are presented in Table 1 and performance on test are presented in Table 2:

A one-way ANOVA was performed within subjects factor for each text form. The test showed significant differences between text A and text B, $F(1,38)=28,566$, $p<0,001$ and also between text A and text C, $F(1,38)=33,640$, $p<0,001$. On the contrary differences between text B and text C were not significant $F(1,38)=0,08$ n.s. It is interesting to note that the performance of the students who had read the text form B and C was almost the same without any significant differences. However, on the interview students who had read text form C seemed to have a better explanation frame than the students who had read text form B. For example, both students find the missing event in question C2 but only the student who had read the text form C explained the role of the valid bit in a cache miss.

Table 1: students' responses

Questions	Text A		Text B		Text C	
	pre	post	pre	post	pre	post
Questions A1 and A2	M=0,8 SD=0,9	M=3,4 SD=1,0	M=0,8 SD=0,9	M=4,9 SD=1,1	M=0,7 SD=0,9	M=5,0 SD=1,1
Question B	M=0,5 SD=0,8	M=3,5 SD=1,1	M=0,3 SD=0,6	M=4,8 SD=1,1	M=0,5 SD=0,9	M=4,7 SD=1,0
Questions C1 and C2	M=0,5 SD=0,7	M=3,3 SD=1,3	M=0,4 SD=0,6	M=4,5 SD=1,3	M=0,5 SD=0,8	M=4,6 SD=1,2
Exercise D	M=0,1 SD=0,2	M=3,6 SD=1,1	M=0,1 SD=0,2	M=3,9 SD=1,0	M=0,0 SD=0,0	M=3,8 SD=1,0
Total Means	M=0,44	3,26	M=0,38	M=4,63	M=0,41	M=4,69

Table 2: Performance on test

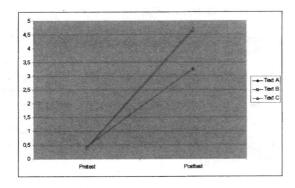

Discussion

The results of the present study confirmed our main hypothesis that the students who read a text organized according to the text comprehension theories have a better understanding about the computer cache memory organization and operations as opposed to students who read a simple text. These findings are in agreement with previous research examining the contribution of re-organized text according to text comprehension theories. Moreover, in this study we found that the performance of students who read the refutational text outperformed students who read the simple test but the performance of these students was not significantly different from the performance of students who read the text which was created according to text comprehension theories.

Further research is needed to establish the depth of understanding and the extent of conceptual structuring that can be achieved through exposure to these two text structures. However, we consider the findings of this

research, as well as those of the research about the effects of text form, important from an educational perspective.

Also, it must be noted that more pronounced effects have been obtained when a reorganized text according to text comprehension theories was combined with some type of supportive activity and a simulation program (Grigoriadou, Kanidis, Gogolou, 2006).

References

Afflerbach, P. P. (1990). The influence of prior knowledge on expert readers' main idea construction strategies. *Reading Research Quarterly.* 25(1), 31-46.

Alvermann, D. E. & Hague, S. A. (1989). Comprehension of counterintuitive science text: Effects of prior knowledge and text structure. *Journal of Educational Research*, 82 (4), 197-202.

Alvermann, D. E. & Hynd, C. R. (1989). Effects of prior knowledge activation modes and text structure on nonscience majors' comprehension of physics. *Journal of Educational Research*, 8 (2), 97-102.

Britton, B. K., Gulgoz, S. & Glynn, S. M. (1993). Impact of good and poor writing on learners: Research and theory. In B. K. Britton, A. Woodward, & M. Binkley (Eds.), *Learning from textbooks*. Hillsdale, NJ: Erlbaum.

Brown, A.L., & Day, J.D., (1983), Macrorules for summarizing texts: The development of expertise. *Journal of Verbal Learning and Verbal Behavior*, 22, 1–14.

Denhiere G. & Baudet S., (1992), *Lecture, comprehension de texte et science cognitive*. P.U.F,

Diakidoy, I. N., Kendeou P. & Ioannides C. (2003). Reading about energy: The effects of text structure in science learning and conceptual change. *Contemporary Educational Psychology, 28*(3), 335-356

Diakidoy, I. N. (1999). Comprehension and learning from scientific text. In A. Gagatsis (Ed.), *A multidimensional approach to learning in mathematics and science* (pp. 361-389). Thessaloniki, GR.

Eysenck, M. W., & Keane, M. T. (2000). *Cognitive psychology: A student's handbook* (4th ed.). Philadelphia: Psychology Press/Taylor and Francis

Glaser R. (1991), The maturing of the Relationship between the Science of learning and Cognition and Educational Practices. *Learning and Instruction*, t 1, 129-144.

Goldman, S. R. & Bisanz, G. (2002). Toward a functional analysis of scientific genres: Implications for understanding and learning processes". In J. Otero, J. A. León, & A. C. Graesser (Eds.), *The psychology of science text comprehension*. 19-50. Mahwah, NJ: Erlbaum.

Graves, F. M. (1991). Fostering High Levels of Reading and Learning in Secondary Students, Available on line at 2002 from http://www.readingonline.org/articles/graves1/main.html

Grigoriadou, M. & Kanidis, E. (2001), "Students Approaches to the Computer Cache Memory and their Exploitation in the Development of a Web-based

Learning Environment", *Proceedings of 8th Pan Hellenic Conference in Informatics*, Cyprus, 472-481

Grigoriadou, M. & Kanidis, E. (2003). Cognitive aspects in teaching the computer cache memory with learning activities based on a coherent technical text and a simulation program. *Proceedings of the 6th Hellenic European Research on Computer Mathematics and its applications Conference (HERCMA 2003)*, Athens, 429-435

Grigoriadou, M., Toula, M. & Kanidis, E., (2003), Design and Evaluation of a Cache Memory Simulation Program," in *Proc. of the 3rd IEEE International Conference on Advanced Learning Technologies*, 170-174.

Grigoriadoy M., Kanidis E. & Gogoulou A. (2005), A Web-Based Educational Environment for Teaching the Computer Cache Memory, *IEEE Transactions on Education, Vol 49, 1,* 147-156

Guzzetti, B. J., Williams, W.O., Skeels, S. A. & Wu, S. M. (1997). Influence of text structure on learning counterintuitive physics concepts. *Journal of Research inScience Teaching, 34,* 701-719.

Hennessy, L. J. & Patterson, A. D. (1996). *Computer Architecture - A quantitative approach*, Second edition, Morgan Kaufman Publishers inc, 1996.

Hynd, C. R., & Alvermann, D. E. (1986). Prior knowledge activation in refutation and non-refutation text. In J. A. Niles & R. V. Lalik (Eds.), *Solving problems in literacy: Learners, teachers, and researchers, Thirty-fifth Yearbook of the National Reading Conference,* 55-60. Rochester, NY: National Reading Conference.

Kintsch, W. & van Dijk. T. A. (1978). Towards a model of text comprehension and production, *Psychological Review,* 85, 363-394.

Kintsch, W. (1988). The use of knowledge in discourse processing: A construction-integration model. *Psychological Review, 95,* 163-182.

Kintsch, W. (1998). *Comprehension: A Paradigm for Cognition.* Cambridge University Press.

León, J. A. & Peñalba, G. (2002). Understanding causality and temporal sequence in scientific discourse. In J.C. Otero, J.A. León, A. C Graesser (Eds.), The Psychology of the scientific text (pp. 155-178) Mahwah, New Jersey: Lawrence Erlbaum Associates.

Maria, K. (1987). Overcoming misconceptions in science: A replication study at the fifth grade level. Paper presented at the annual meeting of the National Reading Conference, St. Petersburg Beach, FL.

Maria, K. & MacGinitie, W. H. (1981). Congruence of prior knowledge and text information as a factor in the reading comprehension of middle-grade children (Technical Report #16). Washington, DC: Office of Special Education and Rehabilitative Services (ED). (ERIC Document Reproduction Service No. ED 220 803.

Otero, J., León, A. & Graesser, C. A. (2003). *The Psychology of Science Text Comprehension* (19-50). Mahwah, NJ: Erlbaum.

Patterson, A. D. & Hennessy, L. J. (1999). *Computer Organization & Design,* Second edition, Morgan Kaufman Publishers inc.

Reynolds, R. E., & Shirey, L. L. (1988). The role of attention in studying and learning. In E.T. Goetz, C.E. Weinstein, & P.A. Alexander (Eds.), *Learning and study strategies: Issues in assessment, instruction, and evaluation,* 77–100. Washington, dc: Academic Press.

Skopeliti, I. & Vosniadou, S. (2006). The Influence of Refutational Text on Children's Ideas about the Earth. Poster submitted for publication in the *Proceedings of the 28th Annual Conference of the Cognitive Society,* Vancouver, BC Canada.

Stevens, R. J. (1988). Effects of strategy training on the identification of the main idea of ex-positorypassages. *Journal of Educational Psychology,* 80, 21–26.

Van den Broek, P., Virtue, S. E., Tzeng, M. G, & Sung, Y. (2002). Comprehension and memory of science Texts: Inferential processes and Construction of a mental Representation. In J. Otero, J. A. León, A. C. Graesser (Eds.), *The Psychology of science text comprehension,* 131-154. Mahwah, NJ: Lawrence Erlbaum Associates, Inc

Van Dijk, T. A., & Kintsch, W. (1983), *Strategies of discourse comprehension.* New York: Academic Press.

Williams, J. P. (1986). Research and instructional development on main idea skills. In J.F. Baumann (Ed.), *Teaching main idea comprehension,* 73–79. Newark, de: International Reading Association.

Woodward A. (1993). Introduction: Learning from Textbooks, in Britton K.B.,Woodward A., Binkley M.,(Ed), *Learning from Textbooks, Theory and Practice,* Lawrence Erlbaum, New Jersey

Towards a Unified Model of Language Acquisition

Fernand Gobet (fernand.gobet@brunel.ac.uk)
Centre for the Study of Expertise, Brunel University
Uxbridge, UB8 3PH, UK
Julian M. Pine (julian.pine@liverpool.ac.uk)
Daniel Freudenthal (d.freudenthal@liverpool.ac.uk)
School of Psychology, University of Liverpool
Liverpool, L69 7ZA, UK

Abstract

In this theoretical paper, we first review and rebut standard criticisms against distributional approaches to language acquisition. We then present two closely-related models that use distributional analysis. The first deals with the acquisition of vocabulary, the second with grammatical development. We show how these two models can be combined with a semantic network grown using Hebbian learning, and briefly illustrate the advantages of this combination. An important feature of this hybrid system is that it combines two different types of distributional learning, the first based on order, and the second based on co-occurrences within a context.

Introduction

Distributional approaches to language learning have a long history in psychology and linguistics. Moreover, recent research has demonstrated that an enormous amount of information is present in the statistical distribution of words contained in large text-based and conversation-based corpora (e.g. Brent & Cartwright, 1996; Finch & Chater, 1992; Landauer & Dumais, 1997). However, distributional models of language learning have traditionally faced two specific kinds of criticism.

The first of these is based on a set of logical arguments against the possibility of successful distributional learning derived from learnability theory. While such arguments are useful in illustrating the scale of the problem facing a distributional approach to language learning, they derive much of their power from the way in which they conceptualise language acquisition as a single logical problem rather than as a complex developmental process. Once one accepts the possibility that distributional learning procedures may interact in complex ways with cognitive and developmental constraints, the issue of whether it is possible to build a successful distributional learning model of language acquisition becomes an empirical rather than a logical question.

The second kind of criticism reflects the idea that distributional-learning accounts make unrealistic assumptions about the child's processing abilities. However, this kind of criticism, while valid for the specific models at which it has been aimed (e.g. Maratsos & Chalkley, 1980), does not generalise to all distributional analysers. For example, we have recently built computational models of grammatical

development (Croker, Pine & Gobet, 2000; Freudenthal, Pine, & Gobet, 2006) and the acquisition of vocabulary (Jones, Gobet & Pine, 2005) based on the EPAM/CHREST architecture (Feigenbaum & Simon, 1984; Gobet et al., 2001). These models are capable of extracting a great deal of linguistic information from realistic input samples using a relatively simple performance-limited distributional learning mechanism. Moreover, one of the interesting features of these simulations is the extent to which the performance limitations built into the distributional learning mechanism are actually responsible for the similarity between the child's and the model's output (see below).

Distributional approaches have traditionally focused either on syntax (e.g. Finch & Chater, 1992), or on phonology (e.g. Brent & Cartwright, 1996), or on semantics (e.g. Landauer & Dumais, 1997). However, it would obviously be of scientific interest to have a single computational model that covered these three aspects of language, taking as input naturalistic data (i.e. corpora of mothers' child-directed speech). The aim of this theoretical paper is not to present detailed simulations of a particular phenomenon but to show (a) how different aspects of language (phonology and syntax) can be modelled using what is essentially the same system; (b) how a semantic network can be grown incrementally; and (c) how these different sub-models can be brought together into a single unified model. We first briefly present the EPAM/CHREST architecture, and then our models of the acquisition of syntax and vocabulary. We then describe a model that incrementally builds up a semantic network. Next, we show how this semantic network can be connected to our models of syntax and vocabulary acquisition, and provide some examples of the behaviour of this composite system.

The EPAM/CHREST Architecture

The EPAM theory (Feigenbaum & Simon, 1984) is the computational framework behind our models of syntax and vocabulary acquisition. EPAM has a long history of successful simulation of human cognition, including verbal learning behaviour, expert behaviour, and concept formation (see Gobet et al., 2001, for a review).

EPAM is a self-organising system that models learning as the construction of a discrimination net (see Figure 1a). The nodes in the discrimination net are LTM symbols, having arbitrary subparts and properties, that can be used as processing units, and the links contain tests that must be satisfied in order to reach the next node. The basic mechanisms are as follows. During perception, an object is sorted through a sequence of tests, each relating to some feature of the object. When the description of the object mismatches the internal representation (the *image*) it has been sorted to, a new test-link, which relates to the mismatched feature, is added. When the object is sorted to an internal representation that under-represents it, new features are added to the image by chunking.

Figure 1: (a) A simple discrimination net, as used in the EPAM models. (b) A discrimination net with lateral links, as used in the CHREST models. Lateral links can be used to connect nodes which share several features, or to create productions, one node serving as the condition, and the other as the action.

Until recently, EPAM has been explored mainly as a theory modelling access to long-term memory (LTM). Simon (1989) has proposed that EPAM nets constitute an index to procedural and declarative memories, but has not given any details about how this should be implemented in a working computational model. CHREST (Gobet & Simon, 2000; Gobet et al., 2001), an extension to EPAM, aims to tackle this question by showing how procedural and declarative knowledge can be created by connecting nodes of the discrimination net by 'lateral' links (see Figure 1b).

MOSAIC

A major aim of our research has been to build a computational model of syntax acquisition in children (MOSAIC), based on the CHREST framework. The basic assumptions are that (a) syntactic categories are actively constructed by the child, using distributional learning abilities; and (b) cognitive constraints in learning rate and memory capacity limit these learning abilities. The major addition to EPAM, as just mentioned, is the presence of lateral links that connect nodes in the discrimination net as a function of similarity in the test links occurring immediately below.

Description

The input given to MOSAIC consists of a set of maternal utterances, taken from the Manchester corpus of the CHILDES database. MOSAIC learns by scanning each utterance in turn, and by adding information to the net using the mechanisms described above. In addition, when a node is accessed by recognition, it is compared with other recently recognised nodes with respect to both preceding and

following words. When the overlap is larger than a preset parameter, a lateral link is added that connects the relevant nodes (see Figure 2).

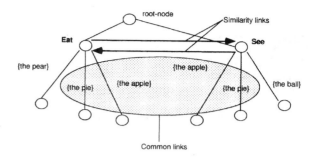

Figure 2: Creation of lateral links in MOSAIC. As the links below 'Eat' and 'See' have sufficient overlap, lateral (or similarity) links are created between them. These links can be used to generate utterances, such as 'Eat the ball'. (Only a subset of the network and only the following context to compute overlap are shown).

Production of utterances can occur in two ways. First, the program can follow a path down using only test links. This will generate utterances that were already in the input. We call this production mechanism *rote output*. Second, in addition to test links, the program can also follow lateral links. This will produce new utterances that were not present in the training input. We call this production mechanism *generation*. Generation can rapidly produce a very large number of new sentences (Jones, Gobet & Pine, 2000).

The performance of MOSAIC has been tested in detail on different sets of phenomena in early syntactic development, of which we describe two here (a) 'Verb-Island' phenomena (i.e. the verb-specific nature of children's early use of word order patterns; Tomasello, 1992) and (b) Optional-Infinitive phenomena (i.e. children's tendency to use finite and non-finite verb forms interchangeably in contexts where a finite verb form is obligatory) (Wexler, 1994).

Verb-Island Phenomena

One of the most important recent constructivist models of early grammatical development is Tomasello's (1992) Verb-Island hypothesis. According to this view, children's early grammars consist of inventories of lexically-specific predicate structures (or 'Verb Islands'). The Verb-Island hypothesis can account for a number of phenomena in children's early multi-word speech. For example, it can explain the lexically-specific patterning of children's early verb use, i.e. the fact that in the early stages of grammatical development, children's ability to generate longer sentences builds up piecemeal around particular verbs, and fails to generalise to new verbs. It can also explain differences in the flexibility with which children use nouns and verbs in their early multi-word speech. For example, young children will readily slot novel nouns into familiar verb structures but tend to restrict their use of novel verbs to the structures in which they have heard those same verbs modelled in the input (e.g. Akhtar & Tomasello, 1997). However, one problem for a strict version of the Verb-Island hypothesis is the fact that, in addition to verb- or predicate-islands, young children also appear to be acquiring structures based around high-frequency items that would not normally be considered predicates such as proper nouns and case-marked pronouns (Pine, Lieven & Rowland, 1998)

MOSAIC is able to simulate the basic Verb-Island phenomenon as the product of a performance-limited distributional analysis of real child-directed speech (Jones et al., 2000). That is to say, it acquires generative structures based around particular lexical items by linking together high frequency words that behave in similar ways in the input. Since such words are more likely to be verbs than nouns, verbs tend to function as structuring items in the model's output whereas nouns tend to function as slot-fillers. Interestingly, however, MOSAIC also acquires structures based around high-frequency words other than nouns (e.g. proper nouns such as 'Mummy' and the child's own name and case-marked pronouns such as 'I' and 'You'). It is therefore also able to simulate the kind of 'other-island' effects reported by Pine, Lieven & Rowland (1998). Moreover, the performance limitations built into MOSAIC's distributional learning mechanism result in MOSAIC generating output which is more similar to the speech of the target child than it is to the speech of the mother on which it has been trained.

Optional-Infinitive Phenomena

One of the most influential recent nativist models of early grammatical development is Wexler's (1994) Optional Infinitive hypothesis. According to this view, by the time that children begin to produce multi-word utterances they have already correctly set all the basic inflectional/clause structure parameters of their language. However, there is an initial stage — the Optional-Infinitive stage — during which they lack the knowledge that tense and agreement are obligatory in finite clauses.

The Optional-Infinitive hypothesis makes very clear predictions about what children in the OI stage will and will not say. Thus, it predicts, first, that children will use tensed and untensed forms interchangeably in contexts where tensed forms are obligatory (e.g. producing 'she going' and 'she go' as well as 'she's going' and 'she goes'); second, that children will make various kinds of case-marking errors (e.g. producing 'her go' and 'her did' instead of 'she goes' and 'she did'); and third, that children will not make case-marking or agreement errors with agreeing forms (e.g. 'him goes' instead of 'he goes' or 'he are' instead of 'he is').

MOSAIC is able to simulate the basic Optional-Infinitive phenomenon by learning sequences such as 'he going' and 'he go' from questions such as 'Is he going?' and 'Does he go?' and then acquiring generative patterns such as 'he + untensed verb' by forming lateral links between pronouns (Croker et al., 2000; Freudenthal et al., 2006). It is also able to reproduce the basic pattern of errors seen in young children. This includes the occurrence of case-marking errors such as 'her go' and 'her did', but also the occurrence of other low frequency errors (e.g. 'him goes' and 'he are') that are problematic for a strict version of the Optional-Infinitive hypothesis. Although some of these errors are produced by rote learning (e.g. by learning sequences such as 'her go' from 'let her go'), most of them are produced by generating across lateral links. This includes errors for which there is no direct model in the input (e.g. 'her goes') and errors for which there is such a model (e.g. 'her go'). Note that some of the simulations on the Optional-Infinitive phenomenon have been done in four languages (English, Dutch, German, and Spanish).

EPAM-VOC

There has recently been a great deal of interest in vocabulary acquisition, with Baddeley and Hitch's working-memory model being adapted to account for vocabulary learning (e.g. Gathercole & Baddeley, 1989). Gathercole and Baddeley claim that the phonological loop part of the model is a critical mechanism for learning new words. The phonological loop has two linked components: the phonological short-term store, and the sub-vocal rehearsal mechanism.

A key experimental task for investigating Gathercole & Baddeley's model is the nonword repetition test. This test involves two sets of nonwords, one with single consonants (e.g. 'rubid') and one with clustered consonants (e.g. 'glistow'). Several studies using these types of nonwords have found that repetition accuracy decreases as the number of syllables in the nonword increases, excepting one-syllable nonwords (e.g. Gathercole & Adams, 1993), and that accuracy decreases for clustered consonant nonwords. Performance on this test correlates strongly with vocabulary knowledge.

Vocabulary acquisition is another domain to which we have applied EPAM/CHREST (Jones et al., 2005). As with syntax acquisition, learning is seen as the development of a discrimination network. The model (EPAM-VOC) also makes assumptions about verbal working memory.

Description

We give as input to the model utterances from mothers' child-directed speech so that it can learn phonemes and combinations of phonemes. The mothers' utterances are converted into a sequence of phonemes before being used as input. This is done using the CMU Lexicon database which cross-references words with their phonemic representations. The use of phonemic input assumes that some form of phonemic feature primitives already exist to distinguish one phoneme from another.

EPAM-VOC begins with an empty root node. When it sees an input (a sequence of phonemes), new nodes and links are created. At first, most of the new nodes and links are just for single phonemes. As learning progresses, the information at nodes will become sequences of phonemes and therefore segments of speech (e.g. specific words) rather than just individual phonemes.

The model offers a specification of the phonological loop and a method by which the loop interacts with long-term memory. The storage part of the phonological loop is a decay-based store which allows items to remain in the store for about 2000 ms (i.e. consistent with the phonological loop estimates). The input is cut-off as soon as the time limit is reached, because there is no rehearsal to refresh the input representations.

The cumulative time required to encode the input provides a theory of how the amount of information in the phonological store is mediated by long-term memory. When an input is heard, long-term memory (the EPAM-VOC network) is accessed and the input is represented using the minimum number of nodes possible. Rather than the actual input being placed in the phonological store, the nodes which capture the input are used. The length of time taken to represent the input is therefore calculated on the number of nodes that are required to represent the input. The time allocations are based on estimates from Zhang and Simon (1985), who estimate about 400 ms to match each node, and about 84 ms to match each syllable in a node except the first (which takes 0 ms).

Simulations

When trained on speech addressed to 2-3 year old children (4,000 maternal utterances), EPAM-VOC provides a good approximation to the performance of 2-3 year olds on the nonword repetition test (Jones et al., 2005). However, attempts to simulate the performance of 4-5 year olds simply by increasing the size of the input sample (to 25,000 maternal utterances) result in a much poorer fit to the data, with the model seriously underestimating children's level of performance on 3- and 4-syllable non-words. Interestingly, however, when the model is trained on a smaller but more varied input sample (consisting of 5,000 words selected at random from the CMU lexicon), its performance improves beyond that of 4-5 year old children so that it now performs at ceiling on 3-syllable non-words. These results illustrate the critical role that input characteristics play in determining the model's level of performance, and suggest that non-word repetition performance may be highly sensitive to the lexical diversity of the input which different children receive.

Combining EPAM-VOC with MOSAIC and Adding a Semantic Network

In order to keep the analysis of our simulations relatively simple, we have so far treated MOSAIC and EPAM-VOC as separate models. However, it is worth noting that the two models are conceptually very similar. Moreover since EPAM-VOC can take phonemically coded utterances and use them to learn both lexical items and strings of lexical items (which is basically what MOSAIC is doing), it is possible to collapse EPAM-VOC and MOSAIC into a single model, MOSAIC-VOC, that is capable of learning both vocabulary and syntactic structure in the same way.

Even so, when compared with children, MOSAIC-VOC lacks access to several important kinds of linguistic information (in particular, semantic, pragmatic and communicative information). We now consider how semantic knowledge (or more accurately, an approximation to semantic knowledge) can be added to MOSAIC-VOC.

Approximating Semantics

A fully-fledged model of semantics would require a theory of how semantic information is linked to perceptual, motor and proprioceptive information. Although research with autonomous robots is making impressive progress (e.g. Roy & Pentland, 2002), we are far from even approximating how semantics is derived from these types of information. We will therefore have to settle for a lesser goal and use an approximation to semantics.

As noted above, recent work has shown that large text-based corpora contain a vast amount of syntactic and semantic information that can be extracted with surprisingly simple techniques. In their ground-breaking article, Landauer and Dumais (1997) propose a method for extracting semantic information from such texts. Latent Semantic Analysis (LSA) is a mathematical method for extracting the similarity of meanings of words and passages from the analysis of large text-based corpora. Using a general form of factor analysis known as singular-value decomposition, LSA reduces large matrices of word-by-context data into 100-500 dimensions.

The central rationale is that the contexts in which a given word does and does not appear powerfully constrain and determine the similarity of word meanings and sets of word meanings to each other. As indicated by the term "Latent Semantic Analysis," the similarity values estimated by LSA are not simply based upon co-occurrence frequencies, but depend on a deeper statistical analysis.

What LSA is doing is computing correlations between words within different contexts. The method represents an efficient solution, but there are other ways of achieving this goal as well. The method we use here is to dynamically create a semantic network capturing correlations between words belonging to the same context (utterance) using Hebbian learning. We first describe how the semantic network is created, and then how its creation is combined with MOSAIC-VOC.

Creating a Hebbian Semantic Network

The semantic network is made up of a set of units with sparse connections. As in the previous simulations, utterances from a mother speaking to her child are used as input. At the beginning of learning, the semantic network is empty. When words unknown to the network are presented, units are created for each of these words. Connections are also created between units denoting words belonging to the same utterance (context). When words appear again in the same context, the connections between them are updated using a simple Hebbian learning rule. Thus, this method creates connections only for words that have co-occurred in the same context.

Units have a default activation of 0. Spreading activation within the semantic network occurs as follows. The words in the input set have an activation of 1. Activation then spreads from one unit to another by multiplying the activation of the unit by the weight of the connection. For each unit, the difference in activation is the sum of all weight/activation products. The final activation of the unit is 'squashed' using a sigmoid function.

Linking the Syntactic and Semantic Networks

The learning of the MOSAIC network[1] and of the semantic network occur in parallel, with, in addition, the creation of links joining the nodes of the former with the units of the latter (see Figure 3). When an utterance is presented to MOSAIC, the nodes traversed during sorting are activated. At the same time, units in the semantic network that refer to words mentioned in the utterance are activated. Interlinks are created between activated nodes and units, fully connecting them, and later on, updated using Hebbian learning. When activation is spread from the semantic network, the activation of a node in MOSAIC is computed as follows. First, for each node, the products of the connected units by their interlink weights are summed. Second, this sum is squashed using a sigmoid function. Third, this squashed sum is multiplied with the (squashed) size of the image associated with that node. During the production of utterances (either by rote or by generation), activation is used to bias the choice of words or sequences of words.

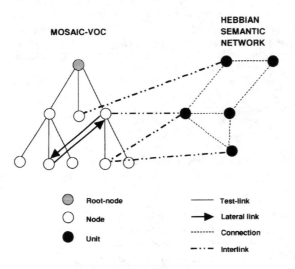

Figure 3. How MOSAIC-VOC is connected to a sparse Hebbian semantic network in the system described in the paper. Hebbian learning operates on connections and interlinks. (Only a subset of interlinks are shown.)

Generating Output

At the end of the learning stage (actually, at any time during learning), we have an EPAM-like discrimination network linked to a semantic neural network. There are several ways

---

[1] To keep the presentation simple, we focus here on the connections between the semantic network and MOSAIC.

this hybrid system can be used: (a) the semantic network can be used to spread activation to MOSAIC and generate sentences; (b) MOSAIC can be used to parse an utterance and to propagate the activation to the semantic network, thus approximating the "understanding" of a verbal utterance; (c) finally, two hybrid networks can interact together, combining the operations outlined above. An utterance produced by the first network is parsed by the second network, and its semantic memory is activated accordingly. This activation leads to the generation of a new utterance through the MOSAIC network of the second network.

An Example: Using the Semantic Network to Generate Sentences

A corpus of 21,329 utterances was used as input, taken from a mother interacting with her child. Each utterance in the corpus was learned by the method described above.

To generate an utterance, we activated one or several node(s) in the semantic network, spread activation through the semantic network, spread activation to MOSAIC, and used MOSAIC to produce a sentence. When outputting an utterance, MOSAIC was biased in favour of nodes having a high activation, and nodes with activation below a threshold cannot be used.

At the end of one pass through the corpus, MOSAIC contained 49,640 nodes and 367 lateral links. 2,797 units were created in the semantic network, with an average of 22 connections within the semantic network (minimum = 0; maximum=1,182). 261,100 interlinks were created (average 93 per unit; minimum=0; maximum=7,213).

In general, the semantic network proves itself useful in filtering out the utterances generated by MOSAIC. For example, MOSAIC generates about 20 times less utterances when the semantic network is used.

The semantic network allows some semantic generalisation. For example, when activating 'DADDY', the model may produce utterances containing 'MUMMY' or 'BABY'. Or, activating 'CAT' may yield utterances with 'DOG', 'COW', or even 'ZOO'. The semantic network also allows some 'weak-contextualized' generalisation. For example, activating the set {ME EAT DRINK} produces utterances like 'ME PLEASE' or 'ME NOW'. However, not all utterances can be categorised as semantic generalisation or as weak-contextualized' generalisation. Finally, some fairly sophisticated utterances can be generated by the model, such as 'I NEARLY TORE IT' or 'I DRYED IT FOR ME'. In general, the same results apply when MOSAIC produces rote outputs.

In spite of these positive features, the Verb-Island and Optional-Infinitive phenomena we have described above are still present in the model's output.

Conclusion

The most original feature of our approach to the study of vocabulary and syntax acquisition is our attempt to use computational modelling based on unsupervised learning with naturalistic input data and to carry out detailed comparison of the model's output with children's data. Until now, we have randomly selected utterances produced by MOSAIC, with the difficulty that some of them may be semantically anomalous. We are confident that the addition of the semantic network will alleviate this problem and that the hybrid system may turn out to be useful for selecting utterances during simulations. Two characteristics of our approach—use of naturalistic data as input and detailed comparison with children's data—single it out from other attempts to develop computational models addressing both syntax and semantics, such as the neural net used by Hadley and Hayward (1995). Such models are typically limited to small artificial grammars.

While systematic evaluation is obviously needed, we speculate that this hybrid system, which scales up well in preliminary simulations, may obtain interesting results because it combines two different types of distributional learning, the first based on order, and the second based on co-occurrences within a context. We plan to test the plausibility of this hypothesis by looking at the extent to which patterns of semantic activation can be used to constrain MOSAIC's performance and thereby reduce the frequency of certain kinds of errors which, although present in children's speech, occur less often than they do in the model's output.

While our main interest is in simulating in detail language development in children, it is also worth pointing out that this hybrid system may have wider relevance, to the study of language in general. For example, a similar approach could be used in the field of human-computer interaction. Alternatively, it could be used in the study of text understanding. The way the semantic network is created is consistent with the type of networks used by one of the prominent theories in this field, the construction-integration model (Kintsch, 1998), and seems psychologically more plausible than LSA. In addition, the MOSAIC module could be extended to act as an adult syntactic parser — something that currently requires hand coding in the construction-integration model.

References

Akhtar, N. & Tomasello, M. (1997). Young children's productivity with word order and verb morphology. *Developmental Psychology, 33*, 952-965.

Brent, M.R. & Cartwright, T.A. (1996). Distributional regularity and phonotactic constraints are useful for segmentation. *Cognition, 61*, 93-125.

Croker, S., Pine, J. & Gobet, F. (2000). Modelling optional infinitive phenomena: A computational account of tense optionality in children's speech. *Proc. of the 3rd International Conference on Cognitive Modelling* (pp. 78-85). Veenendaal (NL): Universal Press.

Feigenbaum, E.A. & Simon, H.A. (1984). EPAM-like models of recognition and learning. *Cognitive Science, 8*, 305-336.

Finch, S. & Chater, N. (1992). Bootstrapping syntactic categories. *Proc. of the 14th Annual Conference of the Cognitive Science Society* (820–825). Hillsdale, NJ: Erlbaum.

Freudenthal, D., Pine, J., & Gobet , F. (2006). Modelling the development of children's use of optional infinitives in English and Dutch using MOSAIC. *Cognitive Science, 30*, 277-310.

Gathercole, S.E. & Adams, A.M. (1993). Phonological working memory in very young children. *Developmental Psychology, 29*, 770-778.

Gathercole, S.E. & Baddeley, A.D. (1989). Evaluation of the role of phonological STM in the development of vocabulary in children: A longitudinal study. Journal of *Memory and Language, 28*, 200-213.

Gobet, F., Lane, P.C.R., Croker, S., Cheng, P.C.H., Jones, G., Oliver, I., & Pine, J.M. (2001). Chunking mechanisms in human learning. *Trends in Cognitive Sciences, 5*, 236-243.

Gobet, F. & Simon, H.A. (2000). Five seconds or sixty? Presentation time in expert memory. *Cognitive Science, 24*, 651-682.

Hadley, R.F. & Hayward, M.B. (1995). Strong semantic systematicity from unsupervised connectionist learning. *Proc. of the 17h Annual Meeting of the Cognitive Science Society*, pp. 358-363. Hillsdale, NJ: Erlbaum.

Jones, G., Gobet, F. & Pine, J.M. (2000). A process model of children's early verb use. *Proc. of the 22nd Annual Meeting of the Cognitive Science Society*. Mahwah, NJ: Erlbaum

Jones, G., Gobet, F., & Pine, J. M. (2005). Modelling vocabulary acquisition: An explanation of the link between the phonological loop and long-term memory. *Journal of Artificial Intelligence and Simulation of Behaviour, 1*, 509-522.

Kintsch, W. (1998). *Comprehension. A paradigm for cognition.* Cambridge: CUP.

Landauer, T.K. & Dumais, S.T. (1997). A solution to Plato's problem: The latent semantic analysis theory of acquisition, induction, and representation of knowledge. *Psychological Review, 104*, 211-240.

Maratsos, M.P. & Chalkley, M.A. (1980). The internal language of children's syntax: The ontogenesis and representation of syntactic categories. In K.E. Nelson (Ed.), *Children's Language.* (Vol. II). NY: Gardner.

Pine, J.M., Lieven, E.V.M. & Rowland, C.F. (1998). Comparing different models of the development of the English verb category. *Linguistics, 36*, 807-830.

Roy, D., & Pentland, A. (2002). Learning words from sights and sounds: A computational model. *Cognitive Science, 26*, 113-146.

Simon, H.A. (1989). *Models of thought.* (Vol. II). New Haven: Yale University Press.

Tomasello, M. (1992). *First verbs.* Cambridge: CUP.

Wexler, K. (1994). Optional infinitives, head movement and the economy of derivations in child grammar. In D. Lightfoot & N. Hornstein (Eds.) *Verb movement.* Cambridge, MA: CUP.

Zhang, G. & Simon, H.A. (1985). STM capacity for Chinese words and idioms: Chunking and acoustical loop hypotheses. *Memory and Cognition, 13*, 193-201.

Two CV syllables for one pointing gesture as an optimal ratio for jaw-arm coordination in a deictic task: a preliminary study

Amélie Rochet-Capellan (amelie.rochet-capellan@icp.inpg.fr)
Jean-Luc Schwartz (jean-luc.schwartz@ic.inpg.fr)
Institut de la Communication Parlée
INPG / Université Stendhal/ CNRS UMR 5009 - INP Grenoble 46, avenue Félix Viallet 38031 GRENOBLE CEDEX 1, France

Rafael Laboissiere (laboissiere@cbs.mpg.de)
Arturo Galvan (galvan@cbs.mpg.de)
Max Planck Institute for Psychological Research Amalienstrasse 33 80799 Munich

Abstract

According to the "Vocalize-to-Localize" framework (Abry et al., 2004), the association of oral and brachiomanual gestures in the deictic function could be the root of the first words emergence in both ontogeny and phylogeny. This association may require a close coordination between the two gestural systems, possibly anchored in a 2:1 harmonic ratio between the natural oscillatory frequencies of the *Speech frame* (open-close jaw cycle) and the Sign frame (arm-hand-finger pointing cycle). This could explain why both languages and first words favor bi-syllabic forms (Ducey-Kaufman et al., 2005). The present study used a new paradigm to test this 2:1 ratio in adult on-line productions. The results provide first evidence that supports the 2:1 ratio and suggest new arguments for a substance-based approach of language evolution.

Introduction

Language and Action

In the last 25 years, language and action have been more and more considered as connected systems. A major evidence for this assumption is the coordination of speech and gestures in on-line face-to-face interactions (McNeill, 1981). Moreover, this coordination appears to be motor rather than purely perceptual. For example, gestures are as well involved in linguistic communication between blind people (Iverson and Goldin-Meadow, 1998). In addition, the link begins early in development, inside the corporal "babbling" of speech and hands (Iverson and Thelen, 1999) and then with the association of words and pointing gestures in the passage from one- to two-words production (Pizzuto et al., 2005; Volterra et al. 2005). The neuroimagery data also lead to a cortical neuroanatomy in which language, perception and action share a same temporo-parieto-frontal circuit (Pulvermüller, 2005, for a review). The Broca's area itself, considered as a "pure language area" for a long time, has been shown to be involved in perception, action understanding and imitation (Nishitani et al. 2005, for a review). Moreover, overlapping brain areas subtend oral and sign languages (Emmorey et al, 2002, MacSweeney et al., 2002) leading to suspect that some characteristics of language are modality-free (San José-Robertson et al., 2004). All this background favors the assumption of a close

link between orofacial and brachiomanual actions in the emergence of language.

Deriving language from gestures

Corballis (2003) proposed that language could have first emerged as a manual communication system and then, progressively evolved towards mouth and speech in the course of phylogeny. On the contrary, the "Frame then Content" (FC) theory (MacNeilage, 1998) links the emergence of speech and language to the orofacial motor control system, considering ingestive mechanisms as a primary step towards oral communication. This theory further relates universals in adult languages and infant babbling to an evolutionary-developmental scenario (MacNeilage and Davis, 2000) in which jaw motor cyclicities (*the frame*) would have been primary. Then the independent and coordinated control of the tongue and the lips would have been mastered (*the content*). In this "frame-then-content" sequence experimentally displayed in the course of ontogeny (Munhall and Jones, 1998; Green et al., 2002), the jaw is considered as the carrier of speech gestures. This "frame dominance" would explain the preference for Consonant-Vowel syllable forms in both human languages and infant babbling. However, these "mono-modal" scenarios about language origins gave rise to criticisms (Abry et al., 2004; Arbib, 2005) that let appear a consensus: the two motor systems might have in fact evolved conjointly towards an elaborated communication system involving both brachiomanual and orofacial gestures. Coming back to McNeill, the evolutionary process would have selected the capacity to associate speech and gestures in a coherent communicative process.

Deriving language from deixis

In this evolutionary process, the deictic function might have played a pivotal role. Indeed, the deictic gesture has been considered as the primary indexical sign in both phylogeny and ontogeny (Haviland, 2000). Furthermore, according to Abry et al. (2004) the association of voice and hand in a deictic function is a key step of both the phylogenetic and ontogenetic development of language. They assumed that language would provide a new deictic tool enabling humans to "vocalize to localize". In this "Vocalize to Localize" framework, the baby's – and by extend, the humanity's - first words would be the product of a developmental "rendez-vous" between the motor control mastery of arm-hand-finger pointing (the *Sign Frame*) and the jaw opening-closing gestures that subtend babbling (the *Speech Frame*, referring to the FC theory). This "rendez-vous" requires the coordination of the two systems, constrained and shaped by the physical and motor properties of the speech and the arm-hand systems. Indeed, Ducey-Kaufmann et al. (2005) displayed a 2:1 harmonic ratio between the *Speech Frame* and the *Sign Frame* for 6 French children between 6- and 18-months old. In other words, the babies tend to utter two CV syllables (associated to two jaw cycles) inside one pointing gesture. According to Ducey-Kaufmann et al., since the first words would emerge from the rendez-vous between the *Speech Frame* and the *Sign Frame*, the 2:1 ratio could explain why both infants' first words and human languages favor two-syllables words (Rousset, 2004). In this "Vocalize to Localize" framework, the goal of this paper is to provide a new experimental evidence for the 2:1 ratio in adult deictic tasks.

Evaluating the 2:1 hypothesis in adults

Previous studies showed a coordination between speech and pointing gestures, mainly resulting from a speech adaptation (Levelt et al., 1985 Feyreisen, 1997). Other studies displayed preferential synergies between speech and finger taping motion (Kelso et al. 1983, Treffner et Peter, 2002). Jaw preferential oscillatory frequency has also been estimated through dynamics studies (Nelson et al., 1984). Yet, no study has tried to establish the favored ratio between the *Speech Frame* and the *Sign Frame* in adult. Here, we propose an original experimental paradigm testing the 2:1 hypothesis for arm-jaw coupling in a deictic task involving utterances with 1, 2, 3 or 4 CV syllables. The basic assumption is that at most two jaw cycles can be contained inside one pointing cycle. Considering that one CV syllable requires one jaw cycle, the pointing cycle should stay constant for 1- and 2- CV syllables utterances. It should then increase for 3-syllables and remain the same for 3- and 4-syllables utterances. This portrait (1=2<3=4) is the focus of the present experiment. In order to measure the period of the arm-finger pointing cycle while avoiding rhythmic tasks and keeping a relatively natural deictic gesture, the task was to show a target while naming it (with 1-, 2-, 3- or 4- CV syllable(s) logatoms) twice in rapid succession.

Method

Procedure

The subjects were 9 native Brazilian female speakers, all right-handed and without any speech or hearing problems. As in the princeps study by Levelt et al. (1985), the experiment involved a gesture + speech pointing task. The subject was seated at a table. A target (red smiley ☺ icon) together with the logatom to pronounce were projected in front of her on a board during 2.5 sec +/- a random delay (with a 1-sec mean and a 0.15-sec standard deviation). The target appeared in the right visual field, either at a near or a far position. The logatom was projected at the same time in the middle of the visual field, as displayed on Figure 1. The logatom could be either /pa/, /papa/, /papapa/ or /papapapa/. It was introduced as a person's name and the target-smiley as a symbolic representation of that person. The instruction was to name and show "the person" two successive times as soon as the icon color changed (go-signal). The subject was invited to put her finger on a black square mark on the table before and after each trial. For, example, for a /pa/ item, the speaker showed the target a first time saying /pa/, put her finger back on the black square and immediately showed the target again saying /pa/. As some subjects tended to confuse /papapa/ with /papapapa/, the experimenter read the logatom aloud in order to remove the ambiguity. This methodology problem will be discussed here after. Before starting, the subject was asked to show objects in the room while naming them in order to link the task with real-world pointing situations. The experimental phase was divided into four blocks separated by a 30-sec pause. Each block started with 4 practice trials followed by 40 experimental ones, five for each of the eight experimental conditions (number of syllables) * (target position). The order of the trials was differently randomized for each block and each speaker.

Data recording

Jaw and hand motions were recorded using an optotrack system at a 100 Hz sample frequency. Two sensors were pasted on the subject's right forefinger, one on the middle of the nail and the other on the left part next to the nail. This allowed keeping the finger in the visible optotrack field when the finger turned towards the right during the pointing gesture. A third sensor was pasted between the top of the chin

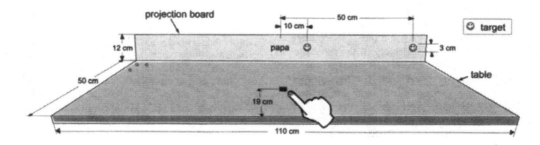

Figure 1: Experimental apparatus (inspired from Levelt et al. (1985))

and the lower lip on the speaker's face. It tracked a flesh point rather than the jaw itself, but in light of the phonetic material used here, with only opening-closing movements between a stop labial consonant and an open /a/, this sensor was considered as a good indicator of jaw motion. For simplification, it is now referred as the jaw sensor. Three fixed sensors on the table and three others maintained on the subject's head provided two referentials, respectively for the finger and jaw moving sensors. The sound was recorded at a 16 kHz sampling frequency with a computer connected to a microphone. Synchronization between acoustic and optotrack signals was achieved by a beep generated on the second sound channel when the optotrack record started.

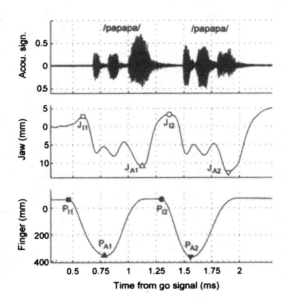

Figure 2: Acoustic signal (top) and trajectories of jaw (middle) and finger (bottom) for a /papapa/ trial. The points marked on the trajectories curves are the initiations and the arrivals of motions labeled for the jaw (J_{I1}, J_{A1}, J_{I2} and J_{A2}) and for the finger (P_{I1}, P_{A1}, P_{I2} and P_{A2}), see text for detail.

Data processing

After the experiment, each trial was checked in order to detect speech errors (e.g. non respect of the required number of syllables) and gesture errors (e.g. departure before the go signal). Then, finger, head and jaw sensors coordinates were projected into the table referential and then, jaw coordinates into the head referential. The trajectory of the three sensors against time was estimated running a Principal Component Analysis on x-y-z sensors coordinates. The first component explained most of the variance for all subjects (from 92% for the jaw to 98% for both finger sensors) and so, was used as the estimator of sensors trajectories against time. These signals were lowpass filtered by a Butterworth filter with a cutting frequency at 15 Hz. On these valid trials signals, onset and offset events were positioned on finger and jaw

trajectories (respectively for speed increasing above or decreasing under a threshold, set at 10% of the maximum speed on the corresponding stroke). Thus, P_{I1}, P_{I2} and P_{A1}, P_{A2} are, respectively, the initiation (onset) and the apex (offset) times from the go signal for the first and the second finger pointing gesture (Figure 2, bottom). Similarly, J_{I1} and J_{I2} are the initiation (onset) events of the jaw opening motion for the first syllable of the two utterances. Finally, J_{A1} and J_{A2} are the apex (offset) events of the jaw opening gesture for the last syllable of the two utterances (Figure 2, middle). Automatic labels were checked in order to correct errors and to detect trials for which one sensor was partially hidden in the optotrack. For the finger, the rule was to take the trajectory of the left sensor if the middle one was masked (the mean correlations between the two finger sensors were above .99 for each of the x-y-z coordinates).

Experimental design and hypothesis

The experiment manipulated two within-subject factors: the number of syllables (1 vs. 2 vs. 3 vs. 4) and the target position (near vs. far). As explained in the introduction, a (1=2<3=4) portrait should be observed for the period of pointing cycle. This period was computed for each trial as the duration between the apex of the two finger gestures. It will be referred as P_T:

$$P_T = P_{A2} - P_{A1}$$

Hence, the main hypothesis was that P_T should stay stable from the 1- to the 2- syllable(s) condition. It should then increase from the 2- to the 3- syllables condition and stay stable from the 3- to the 4- syllables condition. Two main questions would remain regarding the (1=2<3=4) portrait: (1) If actually displayed, does it resists to the increase of the pointing motion amplitude from the near- to the far- target position? (2) How is it achieved considering the different phases of pointing motion, that are the onset-to-apex duration and the post-apex phase? In order to give first element of answer to this question, the onset-to-apex pointing durations P_{D1} and P_{D2} were computed respectively for the first and second pointing gestures:

$$P_{D1} = P_{A1} - P_{I1} \qquad P_{D2} = P_{A2} - P_{I2}$$

These durations were compared with the total jaw motion duration necessary to produce the utterance, referred as J_{D1} and J_{D2} respectively for the first and second utterances:

$$J_{D1} = J_{A1} - J_{I1} \qquad J_{D2} = J_{A2} - J_{I2}$$

Results

Factor effects on dependent variables were tested using within-subject ANOVAs. As the number of syllables has more than two levels, sphericity was systematically tested (indicated only when it could not be assumed). Comparisons between 1- and 2- (C1), 2- and 3- (C2) and 3- and 4- (C3) syllables conditions were achieved using paired t-tests with Dunn-Sidák alpha-level adjustment in the case of a priori comparisons and with Bonferroni corrections in the case of post-hoc comparisons. Non-significant tests correspond to p-value greater than .05.

Apex-to-apex pointing duration (P_T)

Figure 3 displays P_T means and standard deviations for each experimental condition. Mauchly' sphericity test being significant for the number of syllables (Greenhouse-Geisser: Epsilon = .47. p < .05), ddl and p-values are given after Greenhouse-Geisser correction (which explains the non-integer values given for ddl). P_T mean is 961 ms for both 1- and 2- syllable(s) conditions while it increases to 1025 ms for the 3- and to 1056 ms for the 4- syllables conditions (F(1.4, 11.2) = 9.3, p < .01). Results of the three planned comparisons are: t(8) = 0.05, p = .96, for C1; t(8) = 3.1, p = 0.015, for C2 and t(8) = 2.5, p = .04, for C3. The Dunn-Sidák method shows that C3 is significant (p < (1 - (1 - 0.05)$^{1/3}$)) but not C2 (p > (1 - (1 - 0.05)$^{1/2}$)). This agrees with the (1=2<3=4) expected portrait. In addition, P_T is significantly longer in the far- (1022 ms) than in the near- (979 ms) target condition (F(1, 8) = 13.9, p < .01). Yet, the interaction with the number of syllables effect is not significant (F(2, 15.8) = 1.7). Hence, the +43 ms increase from the near to the far- target condition might be too small to affect the (1=2<3=4) clustering. The analysis will now investigate if this portrait is also observed for the onset-to-apex pointing duration.

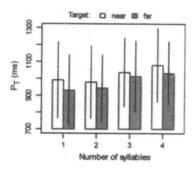

Figure 3: Means and standard deviations of the elapsed time between the apex of the two pointing gestures (P_T) according to the number of syllables and to the target position.

Onset-to-apex pointing duration (P_D)

Figure 4 displays P_D means and standard deviations for each experimental condition and respectively for the first (P_{D1}) and the second (P_{D2}) gesture. In the analysis, the gesture (first vs. second) was introduced as a third factor in a 3-within factors ANOVA (number of syllables * target position * gesture). The results show that durations for the first (364 ms) and the second (365 ms) gestures are very close to each other and do not significantly differ (F(1, 8) = 0.02). Then, gesture durations tend to be longer in the far- (P_{D1} = 375 ms, P_{D2} = 379 ms) than in the near- target condition (P_{D1} = 352 ms, P_{D2} = 350 ms). This target effect is significant (F(1, 8) = 11.4, p < .01) and does no significantly interact with gesture position (F(1, 8) = 2.4). Furthermore, P_D mean is about 356 ms for both the 1- and the 2- syllable(s) conditions, and increases to 369 ms in the 3- and to 376 ms in the 4-syllables conditions. The number-of-syllables effect is significant (F(3, 24) = 4.4, p < 0.05). However, C2 (+13 ms)

and C3 (+7 ms) comparisons fail to reach significance. All other interactions are not significant.

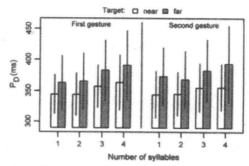

Figure 4: Means and standard deviations of the onset-to-apex pointing duration (P_D) according to the number of syllables and to the target position for the first (P_{D1}, left) and the second (P_{D2}, right) gestures

Comparison of jaw (J_D) and pointing (P_D) durations

Figure 5 displays the means of jaw motions durations (J_D) and standard deviations for each experimental condition and respectively for the first (J_{D1}) and the second (J_{D2}) utterance. As for P_D, the utterance (first vs. second) was introduced as a third factor for the ANOVA. The results show that jaw motion duration increases with the number of syllables. From the 1- to the 4- conditions, J_D is, respectively, 187, 390, 522 and 637 ms (F(3, 24) = 566, p < .0001). C1 (+203 ms), C2 (+132 ms), and C3 (+115 ms) are all significant ((t8) > 16, p < .0001). On the contrary, the target effect is not significant (near: 432 ms, far: 436 ms, F(1, 8) = 3.6).

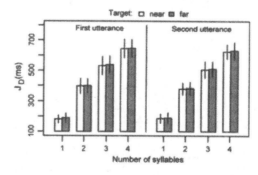

Figure 5: Means and standard deviations of jaw motion duration (J_D, see text for detail) according to the number of syllables and to the target position for the first (J_{D1}, left) and the second (J_{D2}, right) utterances.

The global comparison of J_D with P_D shows that the 365 ms mean observed for P_D is closer to the 390 ms mean observed for J_D in the 2- syllables condition than in the three other syllables conditions. The analysis of ($J_D - P_D$) shows that the mean of the ($J_D - P_D$) difference is -169, 34, 153 and 261 ms respectively from the 1- to the 4- syllable(s) conditions. These values significantly differ from zero at post-hoc t-tests (Bonferroni Correction) for the 1-, the 3- and the 4-

syllables condition (t(8) > 9, p_BF < .0001) but not for the 2-syllables one (t(8) = 2.2). Hence, the trend is that the duration of the pointing gesture corresponds rather closely with the duration of a sequence of two jaw cycles necessary for uttering a two-syllables component.

Discussion

Overall, the present findings agree with the 2:1 hypothesis. However, their interpretation has to be discussed in regard to a possible methodological problem: the eventuality of a higher processing load for /papapa/ and /papapapa/ than for /pa/ and /papa/.

Processing load

It could be suspected that the 1-2 vs. 3-4 clustering observed for P_T is due, at least partly, to a processing load higher for the motor programming of 3- vs. 4- syllables utterances. Indeed, the visual presentation of the items on the screen induced a trend to produce much confusion between these two kinds of sequences, while it was not the case for 1- and 2-syllable(s). In order to solve this problem, the experimenter gave a help to the subject by reading aloud the logatom, which avoided utterance errors. The impact of this intervention was reduced by the fact that the task is an "off-line" one: the subject waits for the go-signal to answer (e.g. Levelt et al. (1985)). However, this could have resulted in artificially clustering pointing durations at a high value, similar for the two kinds of sequences. If this was the case, the onset of pointing (P_{II}) and jaw (J_{II}) motions for the 3-4-syllables conditions might occur later than for the 1-2-syllable(s) conditions.

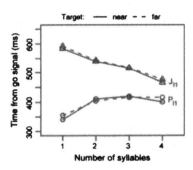

Figure 6: Means of elapsed time from the go signal to the pointing onset (P_{II}) and to the onset of jaw opening gesture for the first vowel (J_{II}) according to the number of syllables and to the target position.

Figure 6 displays the means of P_{II} and J_{II} according to the target position and to the number of syllables. The P_{II} mean is 348, 408, 418 and 408 ms, respectively for the 1-, 2-, 3- and 4- syllables conditions. A 2-within-factors ANOVA shows that the effect of the number of syllables is significant (F(3, 24) = 7.6, p < 0.001) while the target effect is not significant (F(1, 8) = 0.3). Moreover C1 is significant (t(8) = 3.1, p_BF < 0.05) while neither C2 (t(8) = 0.7) nor C3 (t(8) = 0.8) are significant. Similarly, the number of syllables significantly affects J_{II} (F(3, 24) = 10.6, p < 0.001) while it is

not the case for the target position (F(1, 8) = 1.4). J_{II} tends to decrease with the increase of the number of syllables: 588, 542, 516 and 471 ms, respectively for the 1-, 2-, 3- and 4-syllables conditions. However, C1 (t(8) = 1.5), C2 (t(8) = 1.3) and C3 (t(8) = 2.8) are not significant (p_BF > .05). Altogether, these patterns are not in favor of the "processing load" effect.

Arguments for the 2:1 hypothesis

The present study provides interesting results for the 2:1 hypothesis assumed in the Vocalize-to-Localize framework. Firstly, the oscillatory period of pointing motion is the same for 1- and 2- syllable(s) while it increases for 3- and 4-syllables. On the contrary, the onset-to-apex pointing duration is rather stable for a given target position. Yet, in agreement with the 2:1 ratio, the duration of this gesture corresponds rather well with the total duration of jaw motions for the realization of two CV syllables utterances. Hence, the (1=2<3=4) clustering observed for the whole pointing cycle may mainly result from the arm-hand-finger waiting for the jaw during the post-apex period in the 3- and 4- syllables conditions. In addition, because of the lack of gesture-alone condition in this preliminary experiment, we do not know if for the 1- and 2- syllables conditions, the arm-hand-finger system keeps its natural frequency. Nevertheless, previous data by Levelt et al. (1985) suggest that the duration of finger pointing motion with a 1- syllable utterance is close to the duration in a gesture-alone condition. Hence, two syllables might be the maximum number of syllables that could be realized on one finger pointing motion without affecting the duration of the pointing period. The lack of difference between the 3- and 4- syllables conditions and the proximity of values of jaw and pointing motion durations in the 2-syllables condition strengthen this assumption.

The 2:1 ratio as a new piece in language embodiment theories

Altogether, this preliminary experiment supports the assumption that the 2:1 ratio between speech and pointing observed in developmental studies (Ducey-Kaufmann et al., 2005) also tends to appear for adult productions. This adds new evidence for a close motor link between speech and hand gestures. Moreover, considering the importance of deixis in language acquisition and especially in first-words emergence and vocabulary expansion, it seems not so "astonishing" (Ducey-Kaufmann et al., 2005) to propose that this relationship between the durations of pointing and jaw gestures could have played a role in the course of phylogeny and may still play a role in the preference for bi-syllabic forms both in infants' first words and adults' lexicons (Rousset, 2004). Hence, we suggest that the 2:1 ratio assumption should be introduced as a new piece in computational models that attempt to derive phonology from substantial constraints (Lindblom, 1990, Steels, 2003, Schwartz et al., 2006). This integration might provide a basis for explaining the preference for bi-syllabic forms in human languages.

Conclusion

The present study leads to assume that two jaw cycles is the maximum number of cycles that could be realized inside a pointing cycle without affecting the pointing duration. Moreover, it provides a new paradigm for the investigation of the coordination between the *Speech frame* and the *Sign frame*. Of course, more investigations are needed, particularly concerning the lack of pure vocal and gestural conditions, and further assessment of the processing load problem. This is why this study is presented as a preliminary investigation. In any case, further investigations about coordination between articulatory motion and hand gestures should provide new elements for a better understanding of the relationships between oral and sign communication, and of the real nature of human language.

Acknowledgments

This work is part of the "Patipapa" project funded by the French Ministry of Research (Action Concertée Incitative "Systèmes Complexes en Sciences Humaines et Sociales"). It benefited from inspiring discussions with Christian Abry.

References

Abry, C., Vilain A. and Schwartz J.L. (2004). Introduction: Vocalize to Localize? A call for better crosstalk between auditory and visual communication systems researchers: From meerkats to humans. In Abry C., Vilain, A. and Schwartz, J.L., editors, *Vocalize to Localize*, 313–325.

Arbib, M. A. (2005). Interweaving protosign and protospeech: Further developments beyond mirror. In C. Abry, A. Vilain & J.-L. Schwartz (Eds.) *Special issue: "Vocalize to Localize II". Interaction Studies. Social Behaviour and Communication in Biological and Artificial Systems, 6 (2)*, 145-171.

Corballis, M.C. (2003). From mouth to hand : Gesture, speech and the evolution of right-handedness. *Behavioral and Brain Sciences*, 26, 199-260.

Ducey-Kaufmann, V., Abry, C. & Vilain, C. (2005). When the Speech Frame meets the Sign Frame in a developmental framework. In *Proceedings of Emergence of Language Abilities: Ontogeny and phylogeny*, Lyon.

Emmory, K., Damasio, H., McCullogh, S., Grabowski, T., Ponto, L.L.B., Hichwa, R.D. and Bellugi, U. (2002). Neural Systems underlying spatial language in American Sign Language, *Neuroimage*, 17:812-24.

Feyereisen, P. (1997). The competition between gesture and speech production in dual-task paradigms. *Journal of Memory and Language*, 36(1):13-33.

Green, J.R., Moore, C.A., & Reilly, K.J. (2002). The sequential development of jaw and lip control for speech. *Journal of Speech, Language, and Hearing Research*, 45, 66-79.

Haviland, JB. (2000). Pointing, gesture spaces, and mental maps. In McNeill, D., editor, *Language and gesture*, 13–46.

Iverson, J.M. and Goldin-Meadow, S. (1998), 'Why people gesture when they speak', *Nature*, 396, p.228.

Iverson, J.M. and Thelen, E. (1999). Hand, mouth, and brain: The dynamic emergence of speech and gesture. Journal of Consciousness Studies, 6:19-40.

Kelso, J., Tuller, B. & Harris, K. (1983). A "Dynamic Pattern" perspective on the control and coordination of movement. In: *The production of speech*, MacNeilage, P.F. (ed.), Springer Verlag: New York, pp. 137–173.

Levelt, W. J. M., Richardson, G. and La Heij, W. Pointing and voicing in deictic expressions. *Journal of Memory and Language*, 24:133-164, 1985.

Lindblom, B. (1990). *Explaining Phonetic Variation, A Sketch of the H H Theory*, pages 403-439. Academic Publishers.

MacNeilage, P.F. (1998).The frame/content theory of evolution of speech production. *Behavioral and Brain Sciences.*, 21:499-511.

MacNeilage, P.F. and Davis B.L. (2000). On the origins of internal structure of word forms. *Science*, 288:527-531.

McNeill, D. (1981). Action, thought and language. *Cognition* 10: 201-208

MacSweeney. M., Woll, B., Campbell, C., McGuire, P.K., Calvert, G.A., David, A.S., Williams, S.C.R. and Brammer, M.J. (2002). Neural systems underlying British Sign Language sentence comprehension. *Brain*, 125:1583-93.

Munhall K.G. and Jones J.A. (1998). Articulatory evidence for syllabic structure. *Behavioral and Brain Sciences*, 21:524-525.

Nelson, W.L., Perkell, J.L. and Westbury, J.R. (1984). Mandibule movements during increasingly rapid articulations of single syllables : Preliminary observations. *J. Acoust. Soc. Am.*, 75(3):945-951.

Nishitani N, Schurmann M, Amunts K, Hari R. (2005). Broca's region: from action to language. Physiology (Bethesda), Feb;20:60-9. Review.

Pizzuto, E., Capobianco, M., & Devescovi, A. (2005). Gestural-vocal deixis and representational skills in early language development. In C. Abry, A. Vilain & J.-L. Schwartz (Eds.) *Special issue: "Vocalize to Localize II". Interaction Studies. Social Behaviour and Communication in Biological and Artificial Systems, 6 (2)*, 223-252.

Pulvermuller. F. (2005). Brain mechanisms linking language and action. Natural Review of Neuroscience, 6(7):576-82.

Rousset, I. (2004). *Structures syllabiques et lexicales des langues du monde. Données typologiques, tendances universelles et contraintes substantielles*. Thèse en Sciences du Langage, Université Grenoble III.

San Jose-Robertson L, Corina DP, Ackerman D, Guillemin A, Braun AR. (2004) Neural systems for sign language production: Mechanisms supporting lexical selection, phonological encoding, and articulation, Human Brain Mapping 23(3), 156.

Schwartz, J.L., ., Boë, L.J., & Abry, C. (2006). Linking the Dispersion-Focalization Theory (DFT) and the Maximum Utilization of the Available Distinctive Features (MUAF) principle in a Perception-for-Action-Control Theory (PACT). In M.J. Solé, P. Beddor & M. Ohala (eds.) Experimental Approaches to Phonology. OUP (to appear).

Steels, L. (2003) Evolving grounded communication for robots. *Trends in Cognitive Sciences*, 7(7):308-312.

Treffner, P. and Peter, M. (2002). Intentional and attentional dynamics of speech-hand coordination. Human Movement Science, 21(5-6):641-97, 2002.

Volterra, V. , Caselli, M. C. , Capirci,O. , Pizzuto, E. (2005). Gesture and the emergence and development of language. In M. Tomasello and D. Slobin, (Eds.). *Beyond nature-nurture – Essays in honor of Elizabeth Bates*. Mahwah, N. J. : Lawrence Erlbaum Associates, pp. 3-40.

Semantic priming between words and iconic gestures

Paolo Bernardis (bernardis@psico.units.it)
Scuola Superiore di Studi Umanistici
Bologna, Italy

Nicoletta Caramelli (nicoletta.caramelli@unibo.it)
Dipartimento di Psicologia
Bologna, Italy

Abstract

The interaction between words and gesture meanings was highlighted in two experiments with a priming paradigm. The results converge in showing the peculiarities of the two meaning systems, thus supporting the Information Packaging Hypothesis (Kita, 2000) against the Lexical Retrieval Hypothesis (Butterworth & Hadar, 1989).

Introduction

Since the pioneering studies of Bellugi and Brown (1964) and Kendon, (1982), the variety of the dimensions underlying the complex structure of gesture has provided a rich taxonomy according to which each type of gesture is characterized by specific properties depending on the function it accomplishes.

The present research deals with a particular type of gesture, the so-called 'iconic gesture' (McNeill, 1992), or, better, 'pantomime' (Kendon, 1982) and, more generally, 'representational gesture'. This type of gesture is produced when people move their arms and hands to produce a dynamic visual representation of the properties of the objects or events they want to communicate. Thus, for instance, when somebody raises his/her right arm bringing his/her closed hand, eventually with the thumb and the little finger protracted in opposite direction, close to his/her ear, we understand that s/he is referring to something about a telephone call. While shared knowledge and contextual cues aid the unambiguous identification of the entire message (e.g., 'I'll call you' or 'Call me up, please'), this gesture unambiguously refers to a telephone call in absence of speech.

Iconic gestures can be produced both with and without speech and can vary in their degree of conventionality, nonetheless they are straightforwardly understood. The transparency of the meaning of iconic gestures raises the problem of their relationship with language with which they often co-occur. Even if the language and the gesture systems greatly differ, because speech is segmented and linear while gestures convey information all at once as they rest on the visuo-spatial medium instead of the verbal one, they share the function of conveying meaning. Since McNeill's (1992) idea that iconic gestures undergo semantic processing by listeners, as both language and gesture provide complementary meanings, much supportive evidence has been provided that has developed his view mainly in two complementary directions. One, pragmatically oriented, holds that gesture reflects the variations in speech acts (Kendon, 2000) and that the gestural and the linguistic systems interact in a flexible manner depending on the communicational intent of the speaker (Holler, & Beattie, 2003). The other, instead, holds that language and gesture dynamically interact in shaping thought, expanding on McNeill's (1992) suggestion that gesture reflects the imagistic mental representation activated at the moment of speaking. Gestures are no more conceived of as a mere communication device subservient the production and comprehension of language. Gesture, instead, has been acknowledged to help modulating cognition as shown by the fact that, for example, it can highlight stages of learning (Alibali, & DiRusso, 1999; Church & Goldin-Meadow, 1986; Perry, & Elder, 1996; Pine, Lufkin, & Messer, 2004), problem solving strategies (Alibali, Bassok, Solomon, Syc, & Goldin-Meadow, 1999), and how attention is directed (Goodwin, 2000). Thus, recent research has focused on the deep interplay between gesture and cognitive activity stressing the pervasive influence of gesture on cognition and thought, overcoming the Lexical Retrieval Hypothesis. According to this hypothesis, iconic gestures do not carry meaning by their own, but derive it from the lexicon (Butterworth & Hadar, 1989) or simply facilitate accessing lexical entries that incorporate syntactic and semantic information (Krauss, Chen, & Chawla, 1996). Instead, in the Information Packaging Hypothesis (Kita, 2000), gesture helps speakers package spatial information into units appropriate for verbalization and, thus, plays a relevant role in the conceptual planning of the message to be verbalized (Alibali, Kita, & Young, 2000; Hostetter, Alibali, & Kita, (2006). Stressing the interaction between language and gesture in shaping thought, this view grants gesture's meaning a greater autonomy than that offered by the Lexical Retrieval Hypothesis, according to which gestures play a direct role only in the process of speaking as they simply embody spatially encoded knowledge. In the Information Packaging Hypothesis, gestures convey meanings that can be independent of those conveyed by language, as shown by the finding that incongruent concurrent gestures can negatively affect the processing of speech (Kelly, Kravitz, & Hopkins, 2004). Moreover, studying the effects of representational gestures on memory, Feyereisen (2006) has highlighted that it is the meaningfulness of gesture that is responsible for memory improvement and not gesture by itself, as gestures that are incongruent with the sentence meaning, do not facilitate recall.

The studies reported thus far, however, have considered gestures produced, or understood, concomitantly with language production, or understanding. They did not consider gesture's meaning outside a linguistic context where gestures assume the burden of expressing meaning by themselves. As Golding-Meadow (2005) has pointed out, gesture changes its function and form when it is produced as a complement to language or on its own. As she has remarked, in this last case gesture takes on the discrete and segmented form characteristic of all linguistic systems becoming 'language-like' as she puts it. That is, gestures have a different structure depending on the linguistic functions they stand for.

Aim of the present research is precisely to assess on line the interaction between the meaning of gesture and that of language. If the meaning of words can prime that of gestures the Information Packaging Hypothesis, with its emphasis on the cognitive planning of the content to be expressed by the two systems, will be verified. Otherwise, if the meaning of gesture can prime that of words, the Lexical Retrieval Hypothesis will be verified. In fact, if an effect of priming can be obtained between words and gestures outside any communicative context, this means that the language and the gesture systems are characterized by two independent meaning systems that can match or mismatch depending on the situation. Thus, the complex and articulated messages, which characterize the communicative settings, can be conceived of as the result of the deep interaction of the language and the gesture systems at the conceptual level in planning the meanings to be conveyed by the two modalities.

Moreover, studying deaf children, Goldin-Meadow, Butcher, Mylander, & Dodge (1994) have identified different types of iconic gestures corresponding to the different functional roles of words such as the referential function of nouns and the predicative and commenting function of verbs. Thus, it is also possible to suppose that these same functional roles of words can affect the priming effect in both words and gestures differently.

In order to verify these hypotheses, two experiments were carried out. The first was aimed at verifying whether words with four different functional roles could prime gestures having the same meaning as words. The second was aimed at verifying whether gestures could prime words with four different functional roles having the same meaning as gestures. The words' functional roles considered were: simple reference to an object (e.g., eye glasses), reference to an object usually used to accomplish an action (e.g., glass), a simple action (e.g., to knock), and an action to be performed with a tool (e.g., to cut). Thus, the words in the two first functional roles were nouns, while the ones in the second two functional roles were verbs.

Experiment 1

The hypotheses of Experiment 1 were:
- If the language and the gesture systems share meaning at the cognitive level, then words should prime the recognition of the meaning of pantomimes.

- If the gesture system, when used without language, shares the functional roles of linguistic categories, such as those expressed by nouns and verbs, with that of language, then different types of reference (reference to a simple object, to an object usually used to accomplish an action, to a simple action and to an action to be performed with a tool) should interact whit the priming of pantomimes.

In order to verify whether words can prime pantomimes, apt materials had to be checked and selected from the materials that were devised by the experimenters only on intuitive grounds. Thus, two different pre-tests were performed. The first pre-test was performed on gestures and the second on words.

Gesture Assessment The experimenters identified 50 pantomimes representing both objects and actions according to the referential function of nouns and verbs. Four types of referential functions where devised: to simple objects, like "tie" (13 pantomimes), to objects strictly linked to an action, like "guitar" (12 pantomimes), to actions to be performed directly on objects, like "to knock" (13 pantomimes), and to actions requiring a tool to be performed, like "to write" (12 pantomimes). For each of the 50 pantomimes a short video-clip was prepared in which the half body of an actor appeared while gesturing with both arms and hands. The face of the actor was blurred so that the participants could focus only on the pantomime. The duration of each pantomime, i.e., of each video-clip, varied from a minimum of 2320 ms to a maximum of 4680 ms. Each video-clip started with the actor with his hands placed on a table in a fixed position, and beginning the movement after 280 ms (7 frames). The actor ended the pantomime with his arms and hands in the same position as at the beginning. The video-clips were projected on a 19" monitor with cathodic ray tube filling the entire surface.

Twenty students at the University of Trieste volunteered for their participation in this pre-test. They were presented with the video clips one at a time, while sitting on a chair 80 cm distant from the monitor. From this distance, the vertical dimension of the actor's half-body was approximately 15 degrees of visual angle. Their task was to watch the video-clip and to name the pantomimes presented while one of the experimenters recorded the words used to name them. From the set of the 50 video-clips presented, 40 pantomimes (10 for each type) were retained to be used in the following experiments as all the participants labeled them with the same noun or verb.

In order to better assess the results of the following experiments, a baseline of the selected gestures recognition time was collected. Twenty more students at the University of Trieste volunteered for their participation in this assessment. They were presented with the 40 video-clips of pantomimes (10 for each type) that were retained from the naming task to use in the following experiments. The description of the apparatus for pantomime presentation and response collection is the same as that described in the procedure section of Experiment 1. This time participants were asked to name the pantomime on the video-clip as soon as they could recognize it. The mean pantomime recognition time was 2339 ms (sd = 462 ms). Two ANOVAs were performed one with subjects and the other with material as random factors, the results of which will be presented together. The ANOVA main factor was the referential function of the pantomime at four levels (reference to a simple object, to an object usually used to accomplish an action, to a simple action and to an action to be performed with a tool). The analysis showed a significant difference between the four referential functions (F_{part} (3,57) = 49.583, Mse = 1.305, p < 0.0001; F_{mat} (3,36) = 3.144, Mse = 0.591, p < 0.0369). Pantomimes representing simple objects were the slowest to recognize (mean = 2645 ms; sd = 291 ms), while those representing objects usually used to accomplish an action was the fastest to recognize (mean = 2024 ms; sd = 230 ms). The recognition time for the pantomimes of the two other referential functions, i.e., simple action and action to be performed with a tool was 2305 ms (sd = 265 ms), and 2380 ms (sd = 327 ms) respectively.

As the video-clips of the 40 pantomimes varied in length, a regression analysis between the pantomimes' duration and their recognition time was performed in order to prevent any possible bias. The results did not show any correlation between these two factors (t = 1.63, p = 0.11).

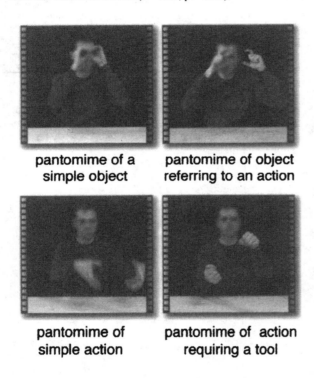

pantomime of a simple object

pantomime of object referring to an action

pantomime of simple action

pantomime of action requiring a tool

Fig. 1: Examples of the four different types of pantomimes.

Word Assessment. In addition to the 40 words used to name the pantomimes by all the participants in the Gesture Assessments, 40 other words were added (10 for each referential function) that were unrelated to those used to name the gestures. Two independent groups of fifteen students each, who did not take part in any other part of the research, were presented with the list of the 80 words thus obtained. The first group was asked to rate each word on a 7-point Likert scale for concreteness and the other group for familiarity.

The mean concreteness value for the words naming the pantomimes was 5.33 (± 0.78) and for the unrelated words was 4.96 (± 0.82). The mean familiarity value for the words naming the pantomimes was 4.57 (± 1.14), and for the unrelated words 5.06 (± 0.91). The mean syllable length for the words naming the pantomimes was 3.1 (± 0.2) and for the unrelated words 3.3 (± 0.1).

In order to better assess the results of the following experiments, a baseline of the reading times of the 80 words (20 for each referential function) used in the following experiments, was collected. Twenty more students at the University of Trieste volunteered for their participation in this assessment. Each of them sat in front of a computer screen on which each word appeared one at a time. Participants were asked to read the word aloud. The reading times were collected from the onset of the word to the beginning of its reading. Two ANOVAs were performed on the words' reading times, one with subject and the other with items as random factors. No significant difference between the four conditions of the factor referential function was found. Mean words' reading times were 461 ms (sd = 49 ms), 465 ms (sd = 56 ms), 449 ms (sd = 45 ms), and 460 ms (sd = 40 ms) for reference to a simple object, to an object usually used to accomplish an action, to a simple action and to an action to be performed with a tool respectively.

Method

Participants Twenty students at the University of Trieste volunteered for their participation in the experiment receiving course credit for their participation. All of them were fluent Italian speakers (12 female; mean age = 23 years) and did not take part in any of the others studies.

Materials The materials were the 40 (10 for each referential function) video-clips of the pantomimes selected in the pre-test to be used as targets and the 80 words (20 for each referential function, 10 out of which naming the pantomimes and 10 unrelated to them) already checked for familiarity, concreteness and length to be used as primes.

Procedure Each participant, sat in front of a computer screen, was asked to attend to the screen, to read the word and to name the following pantomime as soon as possible. On the screen, a central fixation cross (500 ms) preceded the word used as prime (500 ms) and a beep-sound (200 ms), used as trigger for the following analyses, signaled the starting of the pantomime video-clip (average duration 3627 ms). The inter-trial interval was 1000 ms.

The randomization and the presentation of the stimuli were controlled automatically by a routine written with Matlab Software (The MathWorks, Inc.) A headset microphone plugged into a PC recorded both the beep sound and the voice of the participants. Each of the 40 video-clips was paired to 2 words, one naming the pantomime and the other unrelated. The pairs of word and video-clip were arranged in a balanced way so that participants were presented with all the video-clips in the two conditions (same vs. different meaning). A practice trial (four items) was run to familiarize participants with the equipment and materials before the experimental session.

Data analysis and results

The dependent variable analyzed was response time. Response times were calculated as the difference between the onset of the video-clip and the beginning of the response recorded by the emission of the voice. These computations were made manually using the Praat Open Source Software (www.praat.org). In a follow up recall test on 80 words, 40 of which belonging to the experimental materials, the average percent correct response was 82% (t (79) = 7.60; p < 0.0001).

Overall, the mean gesture recognition times for prime related gestures was 1973 ms, while for unrelated gestures was 2143 ms. Two ANOVAs were performed on the mean response times, one with participants and the other with materials as random factors (that will be presented together). In both the analyses the main factors were the relation between the word and the pantomime at two levels (same/different meaning) and the different referential functions at four levels (reference to a simple object, to an object usually used to accomplish an action, to a simple action and to an action to be performed with a tool).

experiment 1

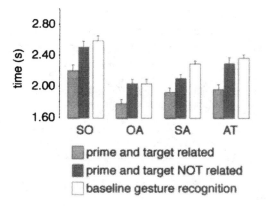

Fig.2: Average recognition time. SO means pantomimes representing simple objects; OA means pantomimes representing objects strictly linked to an action; SA means pantomimes representing actions to be performed directly on objects; AT means pantomimes representing actions requiring a tool to be performed. Error bars are 1 standard error.

The analyses showed a significant effect of the main factor relation between word and pantomime (F_{part} (1,19) = 21.052,

Mse = 2.994, p = 0.0002; F_{mat} (1,72) = 10.89, Mse = 1.618, p = 0.0015). On average, the recognition of the pantomime was 168 ms faster when the word had the same meaning than when it had a different meaning. Also the other main factor, referential function, was significant (F_{part} (3,57) = 41.954, Mse = 1.566, p < 0.0001; F_{mat} (3,72) =5.153, Mse = 0.766, p = 0.003). The referential function of simple objects was the slowest to recognize (mean = 2360 ms; sd = 726 ms), while that of objects usually used to accomplish an action was the fastest to recognize (mean = 1917 ms; sd = 540 ms). In the analyses on both participants and material Neumann-Keuls *post hoc* test (p level at .01) showed that the time required to recognize the referential function of simple objects (mean = 2360 ms; sd = 726 ms) was significantly slower than that of both objects usually used to accomplish an action (mean = 1917; sd = 540 ms) and simple actions (mean = 2023 ms; sd = 524 ms). In the analysis on participants there was also a difference between actions to be performed with a tool (mean = 2131 ms; sd = 698 ms), which took longer to be recognized than the 3 other referential functions.

As the participants had to name the recognized gestures, the percentage of nouns and verbs used was calculated. The referential function of simple objects was named with nouns in 78% of the responses, the referential function of objects usually used to accomplish an action was named with verbs in 67% of the responses while both the referential functions of simple actions and actions to be performed with a tool were named with verbs in 100% of the responses.

The eventual effect of the video-clips different lengths was ruled out performing an Analysis of Covariance with the presentation times of the video-clips as covariate (Relation factor: F (1,19) = 16.059, Mse = 14.46, p = 0.0008).

Discussion

As predicted by the Information Packaging Hypothesis, according to which the language and the gesture systems activate meaning at the cognitive level, the words sharing meaning with the pantomimes facilitated their recognition to a greater extent (1973 ms) than unrelated words did (2141 ms). The comparison with the mean baseline recognition times of pantomimes (2339 ms) clearly shows that the priming word had a positive effect on gesture recognition even when it was unrelated in meaning to the pantomime (198 ms) perhaps due to the overall activation of the meaning system. However, when both words and pantomimes shared meaning, the advantage was significantly greater (366 ms; t (78) = 3.86; p = 0.0002). Moreover, the effect of the different types of reference (to a simple object, to an object usually used to accomplish an action, to a simple action and to an action to be performed with a tool) affected the recognition of pantomimes. In fact, while the referential function of simple objects was the slowest to recognize, that of objects usually used to accomplish an action was the fastest, with those of both simple actions and actions to be performed with a tool in between. The slower recognition time of pantomimes referring to objects can be explained with the contrasting static character of objects and the dynamic character of gestures, which are best suited to convey actions and events.

This is shown by the fastest recognition times of objects usually used to accomplish an action, which are simpler than the pantomimes of events as expressed by verbs. In fact, in naming the pantomimes of objects usually used to accomplish an action participants used verbs instead of nouns. Thus, it can be concluded that while words generally prompt the activation of the meaning system of gesture, when there is semantic priming as that produced by the same meaning, gesture recognition is significantly enhanced.

Regarding the second hypothesis, the lack of interaction between the factor relation and the factor functional role of the categories contrasts the Lexical Retrieval Hypothesis according to which gestures do not carry meaning by their own.

Experiment 2

In this experiment the reversed condition was studied as pantomimes were used as primes and words as targets. Accordingly, the hypotheses were the following:

- If the language and the gesture systems share meaning at the cognitive level, then pantomimes should prime the recognition of same meaning word. Moreover, if the Lexical Retrieval Hypothesis holds, the activation of words' meaning should be faster than in the baseline condition as gestures help accessing the lexicon. Instead, if the Information Packaging Hypothesis holds, the activation of words' meaning should not differ from the baseline.

- If it is the gesture system that shares the functional roles of linguistic items with that of language, when used without language, then no difference should be found in accessing the meanings of words differing in the type of reference. In fact, reference is the specific function of words.

Method

Participants Twenty students at the University of Trieste volunteered for their participation in the experiment receiving course credit for their participation. All of them were fluent Italian speakers (14 female; mean age = 23 years) and did not take part in any of the others studies in this research.

Materials The sets of gestures and words used was the same as in Experiment 1.

Procedure The apparatus and settings for presenting the materials and collecting the responses were the same as described in Experiment 1. Only the order of the presentation of the materials was reversed. Participants were presented with the pantomimes used as prime after a central fixation cross (500 ms). A beep-sound (200 ms), used as trigger for the analysis, signaled the presentation of the word (500 ms). The inter-trial interval was 1000 ms. The task of the participants was to pay attention to the gesture and to name the word as soon as possible. The time recorded was from the onset of the word to the beginning of naming.

Data analysis and results

Two ANOVAs were performed on the mean reading times, one with subjects and the other with materials as random factors, the results of which will be presented together. In both the analyses the main factors were the relation between the pantomimes and the words at two levels (same/different meaning) and the different referential functions of pantomimes at four levels (reference to a simple object, to an object usually used to accomplish an action, to a simple action and to an action to be performed with a tool). A significant effect of the main factor relation in meaning between the pantomimes and the words was found (F_{part} (1,19) = 47.174, Mse = 0.064, p < 0.001; F_{mat} (1,72) = 19.201, Mse = 0.032, p = 0.00004). On average, the naming time was 470 ms (sd = 26 ms) in the same meaning condition, and 509 ms (sd = 22 ms) in the different meaning condition. The other main factor, i.e., the different referential functions of pantomimes did not reach significance in any of the analyses.

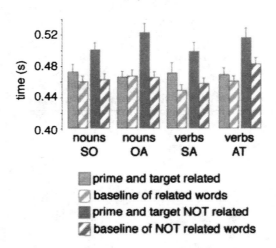

Fig.3: Average naming time. SO means nouns referring to simple objects; OA means nouns referring to objects strictly linked to an action; SA means verbs referring to actions to be performed directly on objects; AT means verbs referring to actions requiring a tool to be performed. Error bars are 1 standard error.

Discussion

When gestures and words match in meaning, gestures do not prime naming words as words naming times (470 ms) do not differ from the baseline (459 ms; t = 1.499, p = .138), even if they are faster than in the mismatching condition. When gestures and words mismatch in meaning, there is an interference effect. In fact, words naming times takes longer than the baseline. These results, while supported by the Information Packaging Hypothesis, disprove the prediction allowed by the Lexical Retrieval Hypothesis. As expected, the different referential functions of pantomimes do not affect word-naming time.

Conclusion

As suggested by recent research on the effects of gesture on cognitive processes, the meanings of the gesture system do not depend on the meanings of the linguistic system. Even if they jointly co-operate in shaping the complex meanings that characterize the communicative settings in everyday social interaction, nonetheless both the systems preserve their specificity with the gesture meaning system assuming linguistic-like features when replacing the linguistic one (Experiment 1). However, the meaning system of gesture is independent from the linguistic one (Experiment 2) as it is grounded in sensori-motor experience and gesture production may be an overt way of accessing embodied knowledge (Schwartz & Black, 1999). It is from this last that it draws the visuo-spatial knowledge necessary to integrate the abstract knowledge of language.

Acknowledgments

We would like to thank Isabella Poggi for insightful discussions on the relationship between language and gesture. This research was supported by the Scuola Superiore di Studi Umanistici at Alma Mater Studiorum-University of Bologna with a postdoctoral fellowship (Bando n. 1723) to the first author.

References

Alibali, M. W., Bassok, M., Solomon, K. O., Syc, S. E., & Goldin-Meadow, S. (1999). Illuminating mental representations through speech and gesture. *Psychological Science, 10*, 327–33.

Alibali, M. W. & DiRusso, A. A. (1999). The function of gesture in learning to count: More than keeping track. *Cognitive Development, 14*, 37-56.

Alibali, M. W., Kita, S., & Young, A. J. (2000). Gesture and the process of speech production: We think, therefore we gesture. *Language and Cognitive Processes, 15*, 593–613.

Bellugi, U., & Brown, R. W. (1964). *The acquisition of language*. Chicago and London: University of Chicago Press.

Butterworth, B. & Hadar, U. (1989). Gesture, speech, and computational stages: A reply to McNeill. *Psychological Review, 96*, 168–74.

Church, R. B. & Goldin-Meadow, S. (1986). The mismatch between gesture and speech as an index of transitional knowledge. *Cognition, 23*(1), 43-71.

Feyereisen, P. (2006). Further investigation on the mnemonic effect of gestures: Their meaning matters. *European Journal of Cognitive Psychology, 18*(2), 185-205.

Goldin-Meadow, S., Butcher, C., Mylander, C., & Dodge, M. (1994). Nouns and verbs in a self-styled gesture system: what's in a name? *Cognitive Psychology, 27*(3), 259-319.

Goldin-Meadow, S. & Wagner, S. M. (2005). How our hands help us learn. *Trends in Cognitive Sciences, 9*(5), 234-41.

Goodwin, C. (2000). Action and embodiment within situated human interaction. *Journal of Pragmatics, 32*, 1489–522.

Holler, J. & Beattie, G. (2003). How iconic gestures and speech interact in the representation of meaning: Are both aspects really integral to the process? *Semiotica, 146*, 81–116.

Hostetter, A. B., Alibali, M. W., & Kita, S. (2006). I see it in my hands' eye: Representational gestures reflect conceptual demands. *Language and Cognitive Processes, 21*. DOI: 10.1080/01690960600632812.

Kelly, S. D., Kravitz, C., & Hopkins, M. (2004). Neural correlates of bimodal speech and gesture comprehension. *Brain and Language, 89*, 243–60.

Kendon, A. (1982). The study of gesture: some observations on its history. *Recherches Semiotique/Semiotic Inquiry, 2*(1), 25-62.

Kendon, A. (2000). Language and gesture: Unity or duality?. In D. McNeil (Ed.), *Language and gesture.* (pp. 47–62). Cambridge, UK: Cambridge University Press.

Kita, S. (2000). How representational gestures help speaking. In D. McNeill (Ed.), *Language and gesture.* (pp. 162–85). Cambridge, UK: Cambridge University Press.

Krauss, R. M., Chen, Y., & Chawla, P. (1996). Nonverbal behavior and nonverbal communication: What do conversational hand gestures tell us? *Advances in Experimental Social Psychology, 28*, 389–450.

McNeill, D. (1992). *Hand and Mind: What Gestures Reveal about Thought.* Chicago: University of Chicago Press.

Perry, M. & Elder, A. D. (1996). Knowledge in transition: Adults' developing understanding of a principle of physical causality. *Cognitive Development, 12*, 131–57.

Pine, K. J., Lufkin, N., & Messer, D. (2004). More gestures than answers: Children learning about balance. *Developmental Psychology, 40*, 2059–67.

Schwartz, D. L. & Black, T. (1999). Inferences through imagined actions: knowing by simulated doing. *Journal of Experimental Psychology: Learning, Memory, and Cognition, 25*, 116-36.

L2 Lexical Activation in the Bilingual Mental Lexicon: an Experimental Study

Yuliya Leshchenko (naps1976@mail.ru)
Perm State Pedagogical University, 24 Sybirskaya Street
Perm, 614070, Russia

Abstract

The present study aims at analyzing the peculiar properties of an L2 word processing in the mental lexicon of low-level, intermediate-level and advanced-level bilinguals with an unequal command of the two languages. Two longitude free association experiments with the Russian-speaking University students studying English as a foreign language were conducted. Results showed that an L2 stimulus can be processed differently at different levels of the L2 proficiency. The general tendency of the changes occurring lies in the direction from "language-specific" to "language-independent" lexical activation, as well as from the surface (formal) level of the mental lexicon to the deep-laid (semantic) one.

Although our knowledge of the mental lexicon structure and functioning has grown considerably in recent years, certain key questions are still discussed, the main of them being the question of how a foreign word is acquired, retained and retrieved in the process of L2 acquisition. A lot of research are being carried out to find out how a lexical item, belonging to a different language, is introduced into the mental lexicon of an individual; what links unite lexical items of the mother and foreign tongues; in what way - shared or separately - the L1 and L2 representations are stored; what kind of interaction occurs between the items of the two languages etc. (Grosjean 1982; Paradis 1985; Имедадзе 1979; Леонтьев 1986, 1999; Cook 1992; Bialystok & Hakuta 1994; Groot & Hoeks 1995; Elliot & Adepoju 1997; Colomé 2001 and others).

The bilingual mental lexicon is generally represented as a network from which words are accessed through spreading activation (Myers-Scotton 1992; de Bot 1992; Poulisse & Bongaerts 1994). The question that is yet to be answered concerns the extent of the activation process: researchers have argued whether a word spreads activation to a group of related words only within the given language ("language-specific" activation) or it is able to activate the lexical systems of both languages, known to the individual ("language-independent" activation).

It is assumed that the mental lexicon structure of highly fluent bilinguals is characterized by equally strong associative links, connecting the native language and the foreign language lexical items, what can be said about people with an unequal command of the two languages? In most studies of the so-called "artificial" bilingualism (a case when a foreign language is acquired intentionally, in class conditions) it is pointed out that the L2 system is constructed fully on the basis of the already existing native tongue system (Выготский 1956; Негневицкая, Шахнарович 1981). This is especially the case in a situation when the latter has already been built and fully realized by the moment of the start in L2 acquisition. Therefore we come across extensive transfer from one language into the other: the transfer of certain strategies, skills and knowledge formed during the process of the L acquiring. Such transfer concerns all levels of the linguistic system (phonological, morphological, lexical and syntactical) and logically determines that the L2 elements are to a great extent linked to and made similar with the corresponding L1 elements.

In the case of the L2 lexical system acquisition this compels us to anticipate that the L2 lexical items will be primarily linked with the semantically related to them L1 words, whereas the within- (L2) language links will be weak or absent at all. The predominance of between-language links will determine the situation when an L2 stimulus activates not another L2 word, but a word belonging to the L1 lexical system. Later in the text we will refer to this type as "between-language" activation. The "between-language" activation obviously implies the impossibility of the direct access to the L2 lexical system: in order to retrieve a certain L2 word the individual will have to access the corresponding L1 word first which, in its turn, will activate the target one. In other words the L2 lexical access will always be mediated by the L1 one which will make the process of L2 speech production rather slow and complicated, to say nothing of all the possible word combination errors necessarily to arise via direct transfer from the native language. On the other hand, it can be supposed that to accomplish L2 speech production successfully an individual should be able to retrieve L2 words fast enough as well as to combine them according to the L2 lexical compatibility rules. That requires the existence of relatively strong within-language links which will make the direct "within-language" activation possible.

The aim of our research is to prove experimentally what kind of lexical activation takes place when an individual with an unequal command of the two languages processes an L2 word. The question we seek to answer is whether in this case the activation type will be restricted to either the between-language or the within-language one (which will prove the "language-specific" hypothesis) or, similar with the case of fluent bilinguals, both lexical systems will be able to be activated simultaneously (the "language-independent" hypothesis). We also seek to discover whether the activation type formed at the beginning of L2 studying will remain stable and invariable, or whether certain changes will occur along with the increase in L2 proficiency.

Two experiments were conducted to test the validity of either of the hypotheses. The free association technique was chosen as it is considered to be one of the most reliable means to gain important insights into the mental lexicon structure. Since in the course of such experiment only the reaction that occurs to the participant first is fixed, the strongest link of the given stimulus in the mental lexicon is revealed. The associative reactions produced by the participants provide an extensive account of diverse and polytypic links connecting the items in the mental lexicon and objectively existing in the consciousness of a speaker.

Experiment 1

Participants: 55 students of the Perm Pedagogical University, Economic department, aged from 17 to 23, who have never studied English before (at school they were taught either German or French). The course of studies lasts 2 years; the students are taught to perform minimum communication in English as well as to read and understand authentic texts on their specialty (Economics). By the end of studies the students are expected to possess elementary knowledge of spoken English and intermediate knowledge in profile reading and understanding. In general over the whole period of studies this group of participants is considered as having a low level of the L2 proficiency.

Materials: 50 English words, selected according to the frequency criterion, the selection method being a variation of directed verbal-associative line reproduction (Агибалов 1995) with the elements of psychometric scaling (Фрумкина 1971). Five teachers of the Economic department were asked to make up a list of English words, used at the lessons most frequently. The majority of the stimuli (about 80%) turned out to be high frequent for the native speakers of English as well (according to the data of the British National Corpus 2003).

Design: Each participant was given an experimental form with the stimuli words printed in column; spaces for the answers were left on the right of each stimulus. The task ran as follows: "Respond to each stimulus with the first word that occurs to you". The participants were instructed to react quickly, without much thinking over each word; the language code of the reaction word was not restricted. The experiment was conducted four times with the same group of participants during the whole period of their studies (2 years). The first experiment was carried out after the first two months of studies, the next ones followed with an interval of four months each. Such prolonged design enabled us to observe the dynamics of the L2 lexicon construction: the process of a foreign word entry into the existing mental lexicon system, various associative links formation and their further restructuring.

Results: All the associations received from our participants were grouped into two categories according to their language encoding: the within-language and the between-language reactions. The first group includes cases when an English stimulus evokes a reaction in Russian (girl → девушка, old → молодой, street → машина); the second one is the case when an English word stimulates a reaction also in English (girl → beautiful, old → young, street → car). The proportion of between- and within-language reactions at the four stages of Experiment 1 is represented in Figure 1.

Figure 1. Between-language and within-language reactions (in percentages): Experiment 1

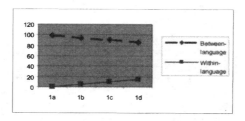

Our data demonstrate a significant discrepancy in the intensity of between- and within-language links in the student's mental lexicon. The lexicon structure at the beginning stage of acquiring English as a foreign language (Experiment 1a) is characterized by the overwhelming majority (99,5%) of between-language links: L2 stimuli activate predominantly L1 lexical items related to the former semantically or otherwise. Further on the number of within-language reactions gradually increases; undoubtedly the progress in studies is followed by within-language links' strengthening (in Experiment 1d they are activated in 14,1% of cases, compared to 0,5% in Experiment 1a). Nevertheless the "language-specific" activation directed from the L2 to the L1 lexical system undoubtedly prevails over the whole period of studies.

The analysis of within-language reactions reveals that the changes occurring are not only quantitative (the augmentation of their number) but also qualitative (their type change). Thus at the first stage of our experiment (Experiment 1a) an L2 word is most often processed by the participants on the surface level of the mental lexicon, and the so-called "formal" associations are produced (son → sun, polite → police, place → face, think → pink). In this case the phonological/graphic characteristics of the stimulus turn to be its most striking features and, as a result, a similar pronounced/written word is activated. The extent of the phonological/graphic overlap can be different: from some letters/phonemes, common for both words (answer → were, suppose → position) up to their maximum overlap, when only one phoneme/letter difference in the stimulus → reaction pair exists (work → word, red → read, son → soon). Along with the increase in the L2 proficiency and, therefore, with the expansion of the vocabulary, the access to the deep-laid semantic level of the lexicon occurs and the so-called "semantic" reactions begin to appear much more frequently. These associations reproduce combinatory patterns of the English language, such as "action → its object" (read → book, translate → word, open → door) and "quality → object" (happy → child, large → family, beautiful → girl).

The proportion of the "formal" and "semantic" reactions at the four stages of Experiment 1 is summarized in Table 1.

Table 1. "Formal" and "semantic" reactions (in percentages): Experiment 1

	1a	1b	1c	1d
Formal	77,3	62,1	27,6	19,2
Semantic	22,7	37,9	72,4	80,8

Experiment 2

Participants: 52 students of the Perm Pedagogical University, the department of foreign languages, aged from 17 to 26. All have been taught English before entering the University and by the first years of studying possess intermediate-level skills in oral and written English. The course of studies lasts 5 years after which the students are expected to have mastered the language well enough to become teachers of English at schools and Universities. Although the last year students are highly advanced in the four aspects of speech production and perception (speaking, listening, reading and writing), their command of the English language is worse than that of the native one, as the former is used much more seldom, only at the lessons and rarely - in real communication. In general the 1st — 3rd year students are considered to have an intermediate L2 proficiency level, whereas the 4th — 5th year students are highly advanced.

Materials and Design: identical to the previous experiment with the only difference in trials' quantity and the intervals between them. All in all five experiments were conducted, each in the middle of the academic year.

Results: Alike with the previous experiment's results, our participants produced both within-language and between-language associative reactions. Their proportion (in percentages) at the five stages of the experiment is presented in Figure 2.

Figure 2. Between-language and within-language reactions (in percentages): Experiment 2

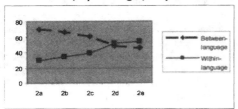

As was the case in Experiment 1, we can observe a steady growth of the within-language associations along with the increase in the L2 proficiency. Moreover, at the last stages of our experiment (Experiments 2d and 2e) the intensity of within-language links begins to prevail over the between-language ones, although this predominance is not significant enough (it does not exceed 10%). It appears, though, that this tendency begins to slacken by the final stage of the experiment: we can not observe a steady progress of one type of reactions with respect to the other any more, both seem to be equalized and to be activated approximately parallel. The general discrepancy between the ratios of the Russian and English reactions tends to decrease gradually from one experiment stage to another until the gap between them becomes almost insignificant.

As for the within-language associations in particular, we observe that number of "formal" reactions has reduced considerably, whereas the "semantic" reactions become much more numerous and diverse (see Table 2).

Table 2. "Formal" and "semantic" reactions (in percentages): Experiment 2

	2a	2b	2c	2d	2e
Semantic	90,4	91,5	90,3	96,8	97,4
Formal	9,6	8,5	9,7	3,2	2,6

Moreover, the semantic associative field of an L2 word expands greatly and the combinatory patterns activated are getting more various. Among the latter are the following: "object → quality" (tea → herbal, mint, hot, grey; picture → funny, perfect, abstract, expensive; book → boring, exciting, new, popular; street → wide, green, overcrowded, central), "quality → object" (funny → clown, guy, boy, girl, picture, story, turn, face, joke; proud → woman, parent, mother, father, teacher, people; red → face, dress, hair, hat, car, shirt, jeans; young → child, girl, man, woman, actress), "action → object" (meet → people, me, them, us, parents, friends, robbers; open → letter, book, window, door, box, case; have → money, fun, dinner, meals, rest, car; tell → stories, fortune, tails, secrets), "action → quality" (work → hard, a lot, better; open → quickly, eagerly, slowly).

General discussion

It has been proved in a number of research works that the mental lexicon of highly fluent bilinguals (those having studied the L2 in childhood, almost parallel with the L1, and in the natural surroundings) is characterized by equally strong associative links, connecting the L1 and the L2 items, which determines the "language-independent" activation. The L2 system formation, begun by the moment when the native tongue system has been fully constructed and entirely realized, implies that the latter will, to a great extent, determine the accomplishment of the former. This will logically stipulate the L2 elements' linking to the corresponding L1 elements; in the case of the lexical system acquisition it will cause the between-language lexical activation development. The proposed assumption will prove to be correct if in our experimental conditions an English stimulus will first of all spread activation to a Russian word.

The analysis of the experimental data demonstrated that to some extent our assumption turned out to be true. A considerable number of between-language reactions received at each stage of the two experiments prove extensive interrelation and interaction of the two lexical systems in the direction from the L2 to the L1. It shows that in our participants' mental lexicons the between-language links very often prove to be stronger than the within-language ones; this fact determines the between-language activation occurrence. On the other hand even the initial stage of the L2 acquisition (Experiment 1a) does not exclude the stimulus' spreading activation within the L2 lexical system and retrieving another L2 word related to the former semantically or otherwise. Along with the increase in the L2 proficiency we can observe a considerable strengthening and expansion of the within-language links which makes within-language activation possible. By the final stage of our research (Experiments 2d and 2e with the advanced-level participants) the number of within-language associations begins to prevail over the between-language ones, although the latter are by no means fully substituted or replaced by the former.

Thus having studied a considerable period of the L2 class acquisition we come to the conclusion that the L2 lexical activation is a complicated dynamic process changing along with the progress in studies. The type of the former to a great extent depends on the language proficiency level of an individual: low proficiency level mostly implies "language-specific" activation in the direction from the L2 to the L1. The increase in the proficiency level leads to a gradual switch over to the "language-independent" activation - a case when an L2 stimulus is able to spread activation to both lexical systems known to the individual and, therefore, to retrieve either an L1 or an L2 reaction with a relatively equal probability. This fact argues that both link types become, so to say, competitive: obviously the between-language and the within-language links of foreign words within the limits of the unified lexical network are able to exist parallel and do not prove to be mutually exclusive. Therefore the general tendency of the L2 lexical activation formation proceeds in the direction from the "language-specific" (L2 lexical item → L1 lexical item) to the "language-independent" one (L2 lexical item → L1/L2 lexical item).

We have also discovered certain peculiar features of the L2 word associative structure formation. The participants' associative reactions demonstrate that this structure is formed by stages, in which process both quantitative and qualitative changes occur. On the one hand, along with the progress in the L2 studies we observe numerical growth and expansion of the L2 word associative field (the number of various association to one and the same stimulus increases

considerably); on the other hand, the associations' types change noticeably. Thus the initial stage of the L2 acquisition implies a great majority of the so-called "formal" reactions which prove that the L2 lexical item is processed at the surface (phonetic-phonological) level of the mental lexicon. In this case the phonetic/graphic characteristics of the word turn out to be most significant for its introducing and securing in the mental lexicon system. The following stages are characterized by the stimuli more frequent processing at the deep-laid semantic level of the mental lexicon, when an L2 word meaning becomes the basis for its linking. By the intermediate L2 proficiency level (Experiments 2a — 2c) the "semantic" reactions prevail considerably over the "formal" ones; by the advanced level (Experiments 2d — 2e) the latter are almost fully expelled.

The main conclusion we have come to is, therefore, that an L2 word can be processed differently at different levels of the individual's L2 proficiency. The general tendency of the changes occurring lies in the direction from "language-specific" to "language-independent" lexical activation as well as from the surface (formal) level of the mental lexicon to the deep-laid (semantic) one.

Bibliography

Агибалов, А.К. (1995): Вероятностная организация внутреннего лексикона человека. Санкт-Петербург.

Выготский, Л. С.(1956): Мышление и речь. Москва: Наука.

Залевская, А. А.(1990): Слово в лексиконе человека: психолингвистическое исследование. Воронеж: Издательство Воронежского гос. ун-та.

Залевская, А.А. (2005): Психолингвистические исследования. Слово. Текст: Избранные труды. Москва: Гнозис.

Имедадзе, Н.В. (1979): Экспериментально-психологические исследования овладения и владения вторым языком. Тбилиси: Мецниереба.

Леонтьев, А. А. (1986): Психолингвистические и социолингвистические проблемы билингвизма в свете методики обучения неродному языку. В: Зимняя, И. А. (ред): Психология билингвизма. Москва, 25-31.

Леонтьев, А. А. (1999): Основы психолингвистики. Москва: Смысл.

Негневицкая, Е. И. & Шахнарович, А. М. (1981): Язык и дети. Москва: Наука.

Фрумкина, Р. М. (1971): Вероятность элементов текста и речевое поведение. Москва: Наука.

Bialystok, E. & Hakuta, K. (1994): In other words: The Science and Psychology of Second Language Acquisition. Oxford: Basic Books.

Bot, K. de (1992): A Bilingual Production Model: Levelt's "speaking" model adopted. In: Applied linguistics, vol.13/1, 1-24.

Colomé, A. (2001): Lexical Activation in Bilinguals' Speech Production: Language- Specific or Language-

Independent? In: Journal of memory and Language, vol. 45, 721-736

Cook, V.(1992): Evidence for Multicompetence. In: Language Learning, vol. 42, 557- 591.

Elliot, R & Adepoju, A. (1997): First Language Words as Extra-stimulus Prompts in Learning Second Language Vocabulary. In: Nickel, Gerhard & Pottier, Bernard (eds): International Review of Applied Linguistics in Language Teaching, vol.35, 237-250.

Groot, A. de & Hoeks, J. (1995): The Development of Bilingual Memory: Evidence from Word Translation by Trilinguals. In: Language Learning, vol. 45/4, 683-724.

Grosjean, F. (1982): Life with Two Languages. An introduction to bilingualism. Harvard: Harvard University Press.

Myers-Scotton, C. (1992): A Lexically-based Production Model of Codeswitcing. In: L. Milroy, G. Ludi & P. Muysken (eds): One Speaker, Two Languages; Cross-Disciplinary perspectives on Codeswitching. European Science Foundation.

Paradis, M. (1985): On the Representation of Two Languages in One Brain. In: Language sciences, vol. 61/7, 1-40.

Poulisse, N. & Bongaerts, T. (1994): First Language Use in Second Language Production. In: Applied Linguistics, vol.15/1, 36 - 57.

On the Implementation of Concept Structures in Fuzzy Logic

Stephan van der Waart van Gulik (Stephan.vanderWaartvanGulik@UGent.be)
Center for Logic and Philosophy of Science, Ghent University
Blandijnberg 2, 9000 Ghent, Belgium

Abstract

A procedure is presented which can modify a large number of fuzzy logics in such a way that the result integrates a logically meaningful representation of the family resemblance structure of fuzzy concepts. The most important aspect of this modification is the implementation of so-called 'concept matrices'. The interpretation and construction of these new formal objects is based upon Fintan Costello's 'Diagnostic Evidence Model' (2000), a contemporary cognitive scientific model of concept structure and concept combination. As a result, it becomes possible to formalize, explain and simulate new logical aspects of cognitive fuzziness such as meaning transformations by means of non-scalar hedges, and interpretational and inferential operations over non-intersective concept combinations.

Introduction

The disciplines of fuzzy logic (Hájek, 1998; Zadeh, 1965) and fuzzy concept theory (Rosch, 1973) often referred to each other, c.f. (Rosch & Mervis, 1975) and (Zadeh, 1982). However, the similarities between the formal machinery in fuzzy logic and models of fuzzy concepts in cognitive science are, generally speaking, rather superficial, and indeed often problematic (Osherson & Smith, 1981). Principles like graded extensions and connectives which function over a set of ordered truth-degrees in the truth-functional semantics of contemporary fuzzy logics such as Petr Hájek's $BL\forall$ (1998), can only be interpreted as indirect references to the fuzzy structure of concepts. There are no principles or objects integrated in these formalisms which simulate for instance the well known family resemblance structure of fuzzy concepts. However, a modification procedure can be defined which allows us to enrich a large number of fuzzy logics in such a way that the result integrates a logically meaningful formal representation of family resemblance structure. The most important aspect of this modification is the integration of so-called 'concept matrices' (CM). The interpretation and construction of these new formal objects is based upon Fintan Costello's Diagnostic Evidence Model (DEM)(2000), a contemporary cognitive scientific model for the modeling of concept structure and concept combination. As a result it becomes possible to formalize, explain and simulate new logical aspects of cognitive fuzziness. In what follows, I will first discuss this modification procedure. Given that

this procedure can be applied to a large class of FL, I will use 'FL' as the generic name for the basic fuzzy logic of choice, and 'FL_c' for the corresponding modified result. Next, I will give two examples of new aspects of cognitive fuzziness which can be explained by means of FL_c.

Implementing Concept Structures in Fuzzy Logic

Since Rosch's seminal work in prototype theory, it is a classic idea in cognitive science that many fuzzy concepts have a family resemblance structure, cf. (1975) in particular. It has become quite common to interpret a fuzzy concept C as a conglomerate of associated concepts $\{F_1,..., F_n\}$ of which some are indicative for the presence of C only to a certain degree. As it is also natural in cognitive linguistics and lexical semantic models to understand concepts as the mental representations of meaning or 'intension', we can interpret the meaning of most lexical terms denoting fuzzy concepts as a conglomerate of associated concepts. In correspondence to this interpretation, the cognitive linguist George Lakoff (1973) defines fuzzy concepts as sets of 'meaning components' (themselves again being conceived as concepts).

As already mentioned in the introduction, the most important aspect of the modification of a FL into its FL_c-variant, is the integration of CM's. Formally speaking, a CM incorporates ordered sets of meaning components and relates each of these n-tuples to a unique element of a specific subset of predicates of the FL_h-language schema. These predicates are named 'complex (unary) predicates' (thereby functioning in FL_c as lexical items denoting complex fuzzy concepts). Semantically, these CM's are used to calculate the continuous membership values of instances for the extensions of complex predicates. Proof-theoretically, CM's are treated as part of a special premise called a 'matrix-set' which can be consulted during any inferential action involving formulas using complex predicates.

As already mentioned, the extra-logical construction of CM's is based upon Costello's DEM (2000). The model resolves around the notion 'diagnosticity'. Informally speaking, the diagnosticity of a concept D for a concept C is the output of a function which quantifies the extend to which D is indicative for the presence of C. I have chosen DEM as the model for the basis of the

CM's as DEM also predicts very well the dynamics of different types of concept combinations which are relevant in example 2 under. Of course, for the basic set-up of FL_c, there are also other valid options like standard 'cue-validity'. After having defined the set of meaning components $\{F_1,..., F_n\}$ of each complex concept C by means of this function, the components are ordered in function of their respective diagnosticity values for C. The result is an n-tuple of meaning components forming a row in a CM which is linked uniquely to C.

Apart from the construction demands above, the CM's used in FL_c need to meet some extra conditions in order to keep the semantics of FL_c recursive and realistic. For example, there cannot be any auto-definition for complex predicates. In other words, there cannot be any complex predicate π_i for which some (again possibly complex) meaning component denoted by a predicate π_j, ultimately comprises the meaning component denoted by π_i.

Example 1: Non-Scalar Hedges

A first example of how FL_c can be used to explicate new aspects of cognitive fuzziness deals with the logical usage and interpretation of so-called 'non-scalar hedges'. Examples of non-scalar hedged sentences are "Technically speaking, *it's a bird*" or "Loosely speaking, *it's a game*". This type of hedge can only operate over complex predicates and is used to narrow down, loosen, or even shift the concept of a predicate. In other words, non-scalar hedges transform meaning. In (1973), Lakoff constructs a innovating theory concerning this type of hedges. For this, he mainly uses linguistic analysis of non-scalar hedged sentences. Lakoff explains what needs to be assumed with respect to fuzzy concepts if their corresponding predicates are equipped with non-scalar hedges. Basically, a fuzzy concept should be conceived as 'an ordered set of sets of meaning components'. Given this general theory, Lakoff also presents a formal semantic account of the non-scalar hedges *technically*, *strictly speaking*, and *loosely speaking*.

Though Lakoff's ideas are very powerful and inspiring, it is problematic that his formal semantic account of these hedges remains only an onset. No complete semantics, nor any actual pure logical analysis of valid reasoning with non-scalar hedges is developed. However, when some small extra modification of the CM's is carried through and some extra semantic definitions are integrated in the semantics of FL_c, it is possible to develop a variation named FL_h, in which these hedges and their semantics can be easily implemented. As mentioned above, Lakoff explains that, in the context of non-scalar hedges, every complex fuzzy concept needs to be conceived as an ordered set of sets of meaning components. More specifically, Lakoff defines 3 different sets of meaning components which are needed for the semantics of *technically*, *strictly speaking*, and *loosely speaking*. Translated in terms of Costello's DEM, these sets consist out of respectively those meaning components with definitional or absolute diagnosticity, medium diagnosticity and relatively low diagnosticity. Recall that the CM's defined above already consist of ordered sets of meaning components corresponding to a unique complex predicate. Also recall that each meaning component's place in an ordering depends on its the level of diagnosticity. In order to get the 3 sets needed according to Lakoff, a k-means cluster algorithm can be applied to the respective diagnosticity values of the initial ordered set. Next, Lakoff's semantic definitions of *technically*, *strictly speaking*, and *loosely speaking* using these newly obtained sets of ordered sets in the CM's can be integrated easily in the semantics.

Developing a complete formal logical account of Lakoff's theory such as FL_h brings along many advantages. For example, FL_h makes it possible to generate several interesting theorems concerning the inferential relation between hedged formulas and their non-hedged variant. These type of theorems, only possible in a fully developed logic, turn out to confirm our linguistic intuitions concerning *technically*, *strictly speaking*, and *loosely speaking* and the way in which they transform meaning. Finally, it is important to realize that CM's are critical for the development of FL_h. Consequentially, it is safe to say that the implementation of a formal variant of family resemblance structure in a FL has enabled us to get more precise insights in the logical dynamics of (a set of typical) non-scalar hedges.

Example 2: Non-intersective Concept Combination

Daniel Osherson and Edward Smith (1981) have presented a series of problems that arise when simulating concept combinations suing prototype theory formalized by means of fuzzy set theory. One of these problems is a sort of 'extension shift' (also historically referred to by some authors as the 'guppy-effect'). Consider the following example. Let the concepts *Apple*, *Striped*, and *Striped-Apple* be denoted respectively by the predicates A, S and SA. Let μ_π be the function characterizing the extension of a predicate π. Now imagine an apple a in front of you which is perfectly striped. Of course, in this case, a is more a typical *Striped-Apple* than it is an *Apple*, as a typical *Apple* is not *Striped*. Consequentially, (1) $\mu_{SA}(a) > \mu_A(a)$ should hold. Given an instance the standard fuzzy operators defined by Zadeh (1965), it is clear that also (2) $\mu_{SA} = min(\mu_A(a), \mu_S(a))$ necessarily holds. From (2), $\mu_{SA}(a) \leq \mu_A(a)$ follows, thereby clearly contradicting (1). Osherson and Smith conclude that, because of this contradiction, formalizations of prototype theory using fuzzy set theory are not compatible with strong intuitions concerning the combinations of concepts. In the following decades, many researchers accepted Osherson and Smith's conclusion and, generally speaking, FL was no longer considered an option for the formalization of fuzzy common sense reasoning.

However, the already used contemporary DEM is a powerful model. By means of an alternative diagnosticity function using a different contrast class than in the case of single concepts, DEM also predicts very well the cognitive dynamics active in different types of non-intersective concept combinations like property concept combinations and hybrid combinations. In property concept combinations a meaning component of one concept also holds for the other (e.g. 'cactus fish'). In the case of a hybrid concept combinations, each constitutive concept's ordered set of meaning components is modified by the semantic influence of the other (e.g. 'pet fish'). By now, it should not come as a surprise that it is possible to develop an extra pair of CM's simulating the meaning component sets of these two types of non-intersective combinations for all possible combinations of complex concepts present in the language of the logic under consideration. More specifically, in order to extend FL_c into a logic which can deal with these types of non-intersective concept combinations in an intuitively clear and logically valid manner, only two things have to be done. First the two extra CM's are integrated in a completely similar way as was done for the initial CM's of FL_c. Next, the semantics of FL_c is extended in such a way that when interpreting a specific type of combination the correct type of meaning components are consulted. The result is generically named FL_{nicc}.

A great advantage of FL_{nicc} is that, despite the fact that FL_{nicc} deals with predicates denoting non-intersective concept combinations, contradictions of the type described by Osherson and Smith are excluded. Moreover, it is even possible to generate many nuanced inference rules for formulas using complex predicates denoting property and hybrid combinations combinations. The scope and precision of these inference rules is also larger compared to other known, contemporary strategies, e.g. the supervaluationist strategy suggested Hans Kamp and Barbara Partee (1995) which uses a recalibration function which only deals with property combinations of a very specific kind. As a result, we can safely conclude that, also in this case, the implementation of a rich concept structure by means of CM's is an interesting and promising technique both for logic and cognitive science.

Acknowledgments

Research for this paper was funded by the Special Research Fund of the Ghent University.

References

Costello, F. (2000). An exemplar model of classification in simple and combined categories. *Proceedings of the Twenty-Second Annual Conference of the Cognitive Science Society* (pp. 95–100). Hillsdale, NJ: Lawrence Erlbaum Associates.

Hájek, P. (1998). *Metamathematics of fuzzy logic.* Dordrecht: Kluwer Academic Publishers.

Kamp, H., & Partee, B. (1995). Prototype theory and compositionality. *Cognition, 57,* 129–191.

Lakoff, G. (1973). Hedges: A study in meaning criteria and the logic of fuzzy concepts. *Journal of Philosophical Logic, 7,* 458–508.

Osherson, D.N., & Smith, E.E. (1981). On the adequacy of prototype theory as a theory of concepts. *Cognition, 11,* 237–262.

Rosch, E. H. (1973). On the internal structure of perceptual and semantic categories. In T. E. Moore (Ed.), *Cognitive Development and the acquisition of language.* New York: Academic Press

Rosch, E. H., & Mervis, C. (1975). Family resemblances: Studies in the internal structure of categories. *Cognitive Psychology, 7,* 573–605.

Zadeh, L. A. (1965). Fuzzy sets. *Information and Control, 8,* 338–353.

Zadeh, L. A. (1982). A note on prototype theory and fuzzy sets. *Information and Control, 12,* 291–297.

Human Conditional Reasoning Explained by Non-Monotonicity and Probability: An Evolutionary Account.

Gerhard Schurz (gerhard.schurz@phil-fak.uni-duesseldorf.de)
Department of Philosophy, University of Duesseldorf
Universitaetsstrasse 1, Geb. 32.21, 40225 Duesseldorf, Germany

Abstract

Intuitive conditional reasoning of humans deviates from the rules of deductive logic. Based on the results of an experimental study as well as on evolution-theoretic considerations it is argued that this fact can be explained by assuming that humans interpret conditionals as *high conditional probability* assertions (*normic* conditionals) which admit of exceptions, and their reasoning follows certain rules of *non-monotonic reasoning* which can be shown to be *probabilistically reliable*. However, this holds only for reasoning with *descriptive* conditionals, while human *normative* reasoning with conditional obligations follows deductive rules for strict conditionals, because they are needed to detect *rule-breakings*.

Introduction

It is well-known that human reasoning, in particular conditional reasoning (i.e., reasoning from conditionals) seems to violate central the laws of deductive logic (cf. Evans 1982, ch. 8-9). Similarly, it seems that human reasoning with probabilities does not match certain laws of probability (Kahneman et al. 1982; but cf. Gigerenzer 2000, ch. 12). As a result of these findings, we have today at least three divergent paradigms on the nature of humans' (intuitive) reasoning. According to the paradigm of *general rationality*, human reasoning is governed by general (not content-specific) mechanisms which are logically rational and involve certain additional features, for example Grice's maxims of relevance (cf. Grice 1975). These mechanisms may be described as mental rules (cf. Rips 1994) or as mental models (cf. Johnson-Laeird & Byrne 1991). An important alternative is the paradigm of *modular rationality*, according to which humans reasoning obeys function- and content-specific mechanisms, which are rational only in certain domains of application in which they have been selected in evolution (Barkow et al. 1992; Gigerenzer 2000). Finally, adherents of the *cognitive illusion* paradigm think that to a large extent, human reasoning is illusionary and in this sense irrational (cf. Kahneman 1982). Based on theoretical considerations as well as on an experimental study, the following paper argues for a certain *combination* of the paradigm of general rationality with that of modular rationality.

Theory

Non-monotonic Reasoning from Normic Conditionals

Normic conditionals are uncertain conditionals of the form "if A, then normally B", which admit of *exceptions*. These normic conditionals entail qualitative *high conditional pro-bability assertions* of the form "most As are Bs" (or P(B|A) = 1−ε, for ε a small number). An example is "if something is a bird, it can fly" or "birds can fly". I represent these conditionals formally as "A ⇒ B". The basic feature of non-monotonic reasoning from normic conditionals (NMR for short) is that new factual information can *defeat* a hitherto correct inference. Assume the premises contain the conditional information "Bird ⇒ CanFly" and the factual information "Bird(a)" (where 'a' denotes a particular individual; so "Bird (a)" stands for "a is a bird"). From these two premises, one may infer by default "CanFly(a)" as long as no contradictory information is available, as for example "Penguin(a)" and "Penguin ⇒ not-CanFly". The point here is the rule of monotonicity, which holds for strict conditionals (from "A → B" infer "A∧C → B" for arbitrary C) *does not hold* for normic conditionals ("A ⇒ B" does not entail "A∧C ⇒ B"); and therefore, the factual premises need not only contain *some* known facts about the individual a, but must contain *all* known and relevant facts about a.

Pelletier & Elio (2001) have argued that NMR doesn't have external *standards of soundness*, in contrast to deductive logic whose standard is strict truth-preservation. In this paper I argue to the contrary, that the standard of NMR is *high probability preservation* according to the *core* rules of the *system P* (although Pelletier & Elio are presumably right about complicated extensions of NMR systems). The rules of the system P allow to derive a *conditional conclusion* from a *set of conditional premises*. Most of the existing non-monotonic logics obey the rules of the system P (cf. Gabbay 1994). The connection between the rules of the system P and reasoning from conditional + factual premises to factual conclusions is established by the *principle of total evidence* which says the following: a premise set of conditionals together with a factual information F(a) (= F_1(a)&F_2(a)&...) entails a conclusion C(a) in the system P iff the conditional F ⇒ C (*if* factual information, *then* conclusion) follows from the premise conditionals by the rules of the system P.

Based on the pioneer work of Adams (1975), it has been proved that the rules of the system P are *sound* with respect to the following *probability semantics* (cf. Schurz 1998; Gilio 2002): if a *factual conclusion* C(a) follows in the system P from factual premise F(a) and a set conditional premises, then the *uncertainty* of the factual conclusion, given the factual premise, is not greater than the *sum of the uncertainties* of the conditional premises; where the conditional uncertainty of X given Y is defined as 1 minus the conditional probability P(X|Y). This means that if the conditionals involved in the reasoning are not too many and express high probabilities, then the probability of the factual conclusion given the factual premises will still be high.

The Proposed Account: Two Theses

Thesis 1. Conditional reasoning in humans is based on some cognitively deep-rooted rules of non-monotonic reasoning with normic conditionals. These rules correspond to certain core rules of the system P and are probabilistically sound. These rules are performed *unconsciously*, which means that a conditional, either of the (explicit) form "if A, then B" or of the (implicit) form "As are Bs", will automatically be processed as a high conditional probability assertion which may have exceptions, unless told otherwise. Since the core rules of probabilistic NMR are *weaker* that those of deductive reasoning with strict (exceptionless) conditionals, this explains why human reasoning deviates from classical logic. One famous example is the rule of *Modus Tollens* (or, denial of the consequence: from $A \Rightarrow B$ and not-B infer not-A), which is deductively valid, but not mastered by the majority of test persons – in fact, this rule is not generally probabilistically sound for uncertain conditionals. Since the core rules of probabilistic NMR are only probabilistically sound but *not* complete, thesis 1 is compatible with the fact that humans perform badly in other probability tasks which are not covered by these rules (cf. Kahneman et al. 1982).

Theoretical support for my thesis 1 is provided by the evolution-theoretic account in Schurz (2001). The natural and social environment of human beings mainly consists of *'evolutionary systems'*. Evolutionary systems, such as organisms, social institutions, etc., are *self-regulatory* systems with certain functional capacities which are needed for their survival and have been gradually selected under 'normal' circumstances – those circumstances which made up their selective environment – but they may dysfunction under exceptional circumstances. Therefore, evolutionary systems are not governed by strict conditionals, but by *normic* conditionals of the form "if A, then normally B", which entail high conditional probability assertions of the form "most As are Bs" (or $P(B|A)$ = high). Almost all conditionals of common sense knowledge, such as birds can fly, rives contain fish, or parents take care of their kids, have this normic structure. It is no wonder, therefore, that humans' conditional reasoning is well adapted to reasoning with uncertain and implicitly probabilistic conditionals.

Empirical support of my thesis 1 is provided by my experimental study which is described in the section "Experiment". So far, only a few studies have been performed on NMR. Pelletier & Elio (2003) and in particular Ford & Billington (2000) have found only small correlations between intuitive human reasoning and the rules of existing NMR-systems. In contrast, the experiment which I have performed shows that to a high degree, humans *do* reason according to rules of the core system P. The reason for the difference between my findings and the findings of Pelletier & Elio and Ford & Billington will be explained below. Independent empirical support for thesis 1 is reported by the experiment of Pfeifer & Kleiter (2005), but with respect to other rules of the system P. Further support for thesis 1 is provided by the experiments of Evans, Handley & Over (2003) and of Oberauer and Wilhelm (2003): both studies (in particular, the second one) indicate that humans understand conditionals in the sense of high conditional probability assertions.

Thesis 2. Thesis 1 holds only for *descriptive* reasoning – conditional reasoning about the probable behaviour of the things in our natural or social environment. It is very different in *normative* reasoning – e.g., reasoning from *conditional permissions* of the form "a person is allowed to do such-and-such only if (s)he satisfies these-and-these conditions". Cosmides & Tooby (1992) and other authors have convincingly argued that in this domain evolution has shaped our human's skills to detect cheaters, i.e. rule-breakers. This hypothesis explains the remarkable experimental finding of Cosmides and Tooby (1992) that in this domain human reasoning obeys the logical rules for *strict conditionals*, especially the rule of *Modus Tollens*: from "if someone is allowed to do A, (s)he must satisfy B" infer "if someone does not satisfy B, then (s)he isn't allowed to do A". Modus Tollens is needed in order to detect rule-breakers.

The results of Cosmides & Tooby (1992) have been discussed controversially (for an overview cf. Over 2003), but their basic empirical findings seem to be profound. It has been concluded from these findings that in general, humans' reasoning capabilities are *modular*, i.e. adequate only in certain *domains of application* in which they have been selection through evolutionary history (cf. Gigerenzer 2000; ch. IV.). I propose to interpret these results in a different way: it is indeed true that we find a modular structure of strict conditional reasoning in the domain of normative reasoning, which has an evolutionary explanation in terms of the selection of humans' abilities to detect rule-breakers, but this does not mean that the general structure of human reasoning from descriptive conditionals does not follow any rational pattern at all; it follows the weaker pattern of probabilistic reasoning, which, too, has an evolutionary explanation in terms of humans' adaptation to an environment which is governed by normic laws.

Experiment

Method

In my study I presented examples of arguments with two opposite conclusions to the test persons. For each of the two possible conclusions, the test persons should tell whether the conclusion follows or not. The answers were classified on a 5 point ordinal scale and they were numerically scored according to their fit with the system P (4 means fully in accord with system P, 0 means the opposite). Table 1 gives an example.

Table 1: Default Modus Ponens.

y for yes (follows), + for tend to yes, ? for cannot decide, – for tend to no, n for no

If something has wings, it can fly.
This animal has wings.

This animal can fly.	(4) y	+	?	–	n	(0)
This animal cannot fly.	(0) y	+	?	–	n	(4)

Experimental result:
Mean score m: 3.33 / 3.34 (1st answer / 2nd answer)
Standard deviation s: 1.22 / 1.09 (-"- / -"-)

In this example, the NMR-hypothesis (thesis 1) predicts "yes" for the first and "no" for the second conclusion. The method of presenting 'opposite conclusions' (cf. Evans 1982, 123ff) is especially adequate for non-monotonic inferences, on the following reason: although in most cases the obtained answers to the two opposite conclusion were in accord with each other and the obtained mean scores were approximately equal, there are also special examples of arguments for which test persons frequently give either *inconsistent* answers ("yes" for both conclusions) and *skeptical* answers ("no" for both conclusions").

My sample consisted of 114 students of different faculties which did *not* have special training in *deductive* logic (e.g., they have not visited a logic course). The test persons were carefully *instructed* by a tutoring person. Because the experiment was about *intuitive* reasoning, the test persons were asked to answer the question after a relatively short time of consideration, not more than 30 seconds per questions in the average.

I presented 22 test questions (arguments) which were divided into structurally similar groups (for example, default Modus Ponens, strict specificity, etc.). In what follows, I present the results to some typical questions for each of these groups. The results were evaluated with SPSS 9.0. Since many test persons tend to answer cautiously and prefer "+" (3 points) instead of "yes" (4 points), an obtained mean value of 3 or more is a clear indicator for the intuitive recognition of the argument as valid. The standard deviations varied between 1.0 and 1.5; this value is quite natural in tests of this sort and fits with the literature. Part of the standard deviation may be caused by random mistakes such as superficial readings at the side of the test persons.

Results and Discussion

The argument pattern of default Modus Ponens cannot *discriminate* between the deductive-monotonic reasoning hypothesis (*DMR* for short) and the non-monotonic reasoning hypothesis (*NMR*). The most important argument pattern of NMR which can discriminate is the pattern of *specificity*, which has the following premises:

(1) two conditionals with an inconsistent consequent: $A \Rightarrow B$ and $C \Rightarrow$ not-B;

(2) the so-called *specificity*-conditional, which says that the Cs included in the As ($C \Rightarrow A$), i.e. being a C is a more specific information than being an A, and

(3) the factual premises that the given individual a is an A as well as a C.

In this case, NMR predicts that the conditional with the more specific information will *fire*; hence not-B(a) but not B(a) will be inferred. In the system P, this follows from the so-called rule of cautious monotonicity which implies that from the conditionals $A \Rightarrow B$, $C \Rightarrow$ not-B, $C \Rightarrow A$, the conditional $A \wedge C \Rightarrow$ not-B can be inferred, but not $A \wedge C \Rightarrow B$. This implies, by the explained principle of total evidence, that from these conditionals plus the factual premises A(a)&C(a), not-B(a) can be inferred. If C is a logical streng-

thening of A, e.g. C = A&D, we speak of *logical specificity*; in this case the specificity conditional need not be mentioned in the premises. If the specificity-conditional is a strict conditional ($C \rightarrow A$), we speak of *strict specificity*; if it is merely normic ($C \Rightarrow A$), we speak of *weak specificity*. We have introduced a further differentiation in our test examples for specificity: the exception conditional, i.e. the conditional with the more specific antecedent ($C \Rightarrow$ not-B), may either be explicitly contained in the premises, or the example is chosen in a way where the exception law is implicitly known by the test person. Here are most typical examples of my test questions to these specificity patterns and the experimental results:

Table 2: Strict specificity with explicit exception-conditional.

All ravens are black. All glacier-ravens are white. Al glacier-ravens are ravens. In front of my window there is a glacier-raven.						
It is black.	(0) y	+	?	−	n	(4)
It is white.	(4) y	+	?	−	n	(0)
m: 3.50 / 3.36 (s: 1.05 / 1.24)						

The results to test question (table 2) and to structurally analogous test questions show that humans follow the pattern of strict specificity to a high degree. This result *cannot be explained* by the rivaling DMR hypothesis. For if the test persons would understand the conditional as strict, then they would reason from logically inconsistent premises. However, for premises sets which are *recognized* as inconsistent, humans tend to conclude nothing, i.e. they reason *skeptically*. We have verified this by the following test question which involves an argument with obviously inconsistent premises:

Table 3: Inconsistent premise set (scored according to classical deductive logic).

Peter and Paul have the same nationality (are compatriots) Peter is a Frenchman. Paul is an Italian.						
Peter is an Italian.	(4) y	+	?	−	n	(0)
Paul is a Frenchman.	(4) y	+	?	−	n	(0)
m: 0.96 / 1.05 (s: 1.29 / 1.38)						
(hence m: 3.04 / 2.95 for skeptical reasoning)						

To be sure, skeptical reasoning is *not* in fit with classical logic, because classically, everything is entailed by an inconsistent premise set, i.e. both conclusions follow (in fact, 12% have reasoned inconsistently). That people tend to reason skeptically from inconsistent premises may be explained in terms of (ir)relevance considerations of the Gricean sort (cf. Schurz 1991). What is important for us is that the strikingly different result of (table 2) as compared with (table 3) is strong evidence for the NMR-hypothesis and counterevidence for the DMR-hypothesis. We have tested strict specificity by several structurally similar examples, and all of them have yielded similar results.

When the exception conditional is only implicit, the tendency to reason according to the specificity rule is weaker but still clearly present. Test question (table 4) is an example in which the known degree of exceptionality is very strong (salt instead of sugar), which explains the high mean scores in this examples.

Table 4: Strict specificity without explicit exception conditional, logical specificity.

Chocolate tastes sweet. By mistake this chocolate cake has been baked with salt instead of sugar.					
This chocolate cake tastes sweet.	(0) y	+	?	−	n (4)
This chocolate cake does not taste sweet.	(4) y	+	?	−	n (0)
m: 3.26 / 3.18 (s: 1.18 / 1.30)					

We tested this kind of pattern at hand of many other examples. Depending on the known degree of exceptionality the obtained mean scores were between 2.5 and 3.5; so the tendency to reason according to the NMR hypothesis was stronger or weaker, but always clearly present.

An important part of thesis 1 which is supported by our data is that NMR in humans is *implicit*. Independent of different linguistic formulation of a conditional, such as

> Bird can fly,
> All birds can fly,
> If something is a bird, it can fly

as long as it is a descriptive conditional (as opposed to a conditional *norm*), humans treat it in a non-monotonic fashion. These linguistic variations of our test questions did not produce significant differences in the obtained data.

We also obtained the effect that if we explicitly add a phrase saying that the conditional is uncertain, such as in

> Normally, birds can fly,
> Most birds can fly,

then the tendency to draw an inference from this conditional *decreases* – here is an example:

Table 5: Default Modus Ponens with explicit mentioning of uncertainty.

Most tigers are dangerous. Here is a tiger.					
It is dangerous.	(4) y	+	?	−	n (0)
It is not dangerous.	(0) y	+	?	−	n (4)
m: 2.76 / 2.82 (s: 1.18 / 1.13)					

Also this result can be explained by one aspect of Gricean relevance, on which the literature on Gricean maxims broadly agrees (cf. Sperber & Wilson 1986; Levinson 2001): humans tend to assume automatically – as a kind of conversational implicature – that the information which is explicitly mentioned as a premise is or should somehow be relevant for the conclusion, because it is assumed that the 'speaker' is cooperative and does not mention this information without a good reason. The addition of the qualifier "most" explicitly draws the test persons' attention to the uncertainty of the conditional and makes them more uncertain as to whether or not one should apply default Modus Ponens. We obtained a similar effect by adding "normally" to the conditional premises.

The following argument instantiates an example of weak specificity:

Table 6: Weak specificity with explicit exception conditional.

Students are normally unemployed. Adults are normally employed. Students are normally Adults Mary is a student.					
Mary is employed.	(0) y	+	?	−	n (4)
Mary is unemployed.	(4) y	+	?	−	n (0)
m: 2.51 / 2.53 (s: 1.31 /1.28)					

Weak specificity is followed by human reasoning to a lower but nevertheless a significantly positive degree. (Given a standard dispersion between 1.0 and 1.5, a difference of means between about 0.4and 0.5 is significant at the 5%-level.) Because of the Gricean effect explained above it is plausible that the explicit mentioning of "normally" in (table 6) lowered the obtained mean score.

Gricean effects may also explain the differences between our results and that of two other studies on NMR. Pelletier and Elio (2003) have investigated the effect of irrelevant versus relevant information. They found that test persons tend to consider irrelevant information as relevant, which seems to stand in conflict with principles of NMR. But according to the Gricean principles, humans assume that every information contained in the premises is or should be relevant for the conclusion; and this effect may be the explanation of some of Pelletier's results. The major divergence of Ford & Billington's results (2003), as compared to the results of my study, was their low result on the performance of strict specificity patterns. One reason for this may lie in the fact that Ford & Billington explicitly mention the phrase "usually" in their formulation of conditionals which, according to Gricean principles, hence weakens the tendency to draw non-monotonic inferences. A second explanation of Ford & Billington's results may lie in the fact that Ford & Billington did not choose natural language predicates such as 'birds' or 'can-fly,' but fictitious predicates such as "Hittas" or "Jukks", which are introduced as alien species of a foreign planet. This complicates the complexity of the cognitive tasks and prevents the application of intuitive NMR-principles.

In a separate test with students which had a course in classical logic, we found that such a training slightly increases the tendency to reason deductive-monotonically und thus increases the obtained mean scores; but only in a few examples the difference was significant. Apart from that, we did not find influences of other external variables, such as age or sex.

We inserted questions into our test which were not characteristic instances of NMR-reasoning but served to compare the our results with standard results in the literature. Of particular importance are the results for the four basic types of conditional reasoning:

Table 7: Basic pattern of conditional reasoning.

Modus Ponens MP:	Denial Antec. DA	Affirmat. Cons. AC	Modus Tollens MT:
If A, then B A	If A, then B not-A	If A, then B B	If A, then B not-B
Therefore B	Therefore not-B	Therefore A	Therefore not-B

Only MP and MT are deductively valid, while DA and AC are not. Evans (1982, 128ff) reports various results from the literature whose variations are listed below (in percentages of test persons who consider the argument as valid). For comparison we add our results to these arguments, by transforming our ordinal scale into a simple *yes-no-undecided* scale (we added the yes- and plus-results and divided through the number of test persons). Unfortunately we had no question testing DA.

Table 8: % of yes-answers ('conclusion follows').

	MP	DA	AC	MT
Data reported by Evans lie between:	89-99	52-82	57-84	63-87
Our results (scale-transformed: 'y' and '+' put together)	89	–	47	73

In conclusion, the results of our study are in agreement with the other literature results, which deviate from each other by about 10 to 15%.

In the literature, the results on MP, AC, DC and MT are usually regarded as evidence for the deviation of human conditional reasoning from the rational rules of logic (this deviation is even more extreme in Wason's famous selection task). However, as we will explain in the next section, this is not so if we assume that humans' conditional reasoning is implicitly probabilistic and non-monotonic. For probabilistically, only default-MP is valid (i.e., high-probability preserving). MT is valid only under certain additional probabilistic assumptions. But the same is true also for the deductively invalid arguments AC and DA. This changes the interpretations of the experimental results in (table 8) completely and gives additional evidence for the NMR hypothesis.

The Effect of Negations in Conditional Reasoning

It is a well-known fact that the use of negated predicates leads to remarkable changes in the frequencies in which of conditional reasoning patterns are recognized as valid. Evans (1982, 128ff) presents the following data:

Table 9: % of yes-answers ('conclusion follows').

	MP	DA	AC	MT
If p then q	100	69	75	75
If p then not-q	100	12	31	56
If not-p then q	100	50	81	12
If not-p then not-q	100	19	81	25

The simple negation hypothesis according to which negated predicates are more difficult to process cannot explain these results (cf. Evans 1982, 133): for example, it cannot explain why AC in the case of a negated antecedent predicate is found to be correct by a *higher* (instead of a lower) percentage of test persons. According to our evolutionary hypothesis, an inference should be the more strongly entrenched in human cognition, the more probable its conclusion is. The crucial probabilistic consideration which may explain these results according to our evolutionary hypothesis is the following: a *negated predicate* (such as *not*-being-a bird) is normally much *more unspecific* and, hence, has a much *greater prior probability* than a positive predicate (such as being-a-bird). Based on this observation, a simple probabilistic calculation yields a weak probabilistic justification of the results concerning the effects of negation. A similar argument has been outlined in Oaksford & Chater (1994) in application to Wason's selection task, but by much more complicated Bayesian calculations, while we try to explain these results here in a simpler way. Recall that the uncertainty of a predicate Fx is 1 minus its probability, $U(Fx) = 1-P(Fx)$, and that the conditional probability $P(Fx|Gx)$ is defined as $P(Fx\&Gx)/P(Gx)$.

Concerning Modus Tollens: From A => B infer not-B => not-A.

Calculation yields: $U(\text{not-A}|\text{not-B}) = P(A|\text{not-B}) = P(\text{not-B}|A)\cdot P(A)/P(\text{not-B}) = U(B|A)\cdot P(A)/U(B)$.

MT is justified (probabilistically successful) iff $U(\text{not-A}|\text{not-B})$ is not (significantly) greater than $U(B|A)$, which (by the calculation) *is the case if $P(A) \leq U(B)$.* This explains, first, why the tendency for MT-inferences is high when both predicates are positive, for then $P(A)$, $P(B)$ will (usually) be much smaller than $1/2$, and hence $P(A) \leq U(B) = 1-P(B)$ will hold. Second, it explains why the tendency to draw a MT-inference sinks drastically in case of the argument "if not-p then q", because here the prior probability of not-p (=A) is high and may well be higher than the uncertainty of q (=B). In the case of "if p then not-q", the prior probability of p (A) is small, but also the uncertainty of not-q (B) is small, which again makes MT unsafe. Finally in the fourth case, the prior probability of not-p (A) is great and the uncertainty of not-q (B) is small, which speaks against MT.

Concerning AC: From A => B infer B => A.

Calculation yields: $P(A|B) = P(B|A)\cdot P(A)/P(B)$.

AC is justified (probabilistically successful) iff $P(A|B) \geq P(B|A)$, which (by the calculation) *is the case if $P(B) \leq P(A)$.* This consideration explains why the frequency of drawing an AC-inference strongly *decreases* if the consequent predicate is negated (P(B) becomes large as compared to P(A)), and also why this frequency *increases* if the antecedent predicate A is negated (P(A) gets great as compared to P(B)). The frequency-increase in the case where both predicates are negated is, however, not explained by the NMR-hypothesis.

Concerning DA: From A => B infer not-A =>not -B:
Calculation yields: $P(B|not\text{-}A) \cdot U(A) = P(B\&not\text{-}A) = P(B) - P(B\&A)$, thus

$U(not\text{-}B|not\text{-}A) = P(B)/U(A) - P(B\&A)/U(A) =$
$= P(B)/U(A) - P(A)/U(A) + U(B|A) \cdot P(A)/U(A) =$
$= U(B|A) \cdot P(A)/U(A) + (P(B)-P(A))/U(A).$

DA is justified (probabilistically successful) iff U(not-B/not-A) $\leq$ U(B/A), which (by the calculation) *is the case if (a) P(A) is sufficiently small and/or (b) if P(B) $\leq$ P(A)* (this condition is more complicated than the above ones). This explains, first, why the frequency of inferring DA sinks if B occurs negated (not-q), for this increases B's probability, against condition (b). It also explains why this frequency sinks only slightly if the antecedent is negated because this goes against condition (a) (it makes A's prior probability high) but speaks in favor of condition (b). Finally, the low frequency of DA in the case where both A and B are negated predicates is explained because here condition (a) is violated while condition (b) is untouched.

Conclusion

The effects of negation on the data concerning the four standard patterns of conditional reasoning are in good (though not perfect) accord with the probabilistic analysis of conditional reasoning according to the NMR-hypothesis. The NMR-hypothesis was independently confirmed by our experimental study, and receives additional support from other studies. The NMR-hypothesis has an evolution-theoretic explanation: the natural and social environment of human beings is full of evolutionary systems, whose behaviour is governed by normic laws (expressing high conditional probabilities), and evolutionary selection has shaped humans' intuitive reasoning as to satisfy basic and probabilistically sound rules of non-monotonic reasoning from normic conditionals. However, the NMR-hypothesis holds only for reasoning with *descriptive* conditionals, in tasks such as prediction, diagnosis or explanation. In contrast, humans' *normative* reasoning with conditional obligations follows certain deductive rules for strict conditionals. Also this fact has an evolutionary explanation in terms of the evolutionary selection of humans' ability to detect rule-breakers (cheaters), which requires mastership of Modus Tollens and other rules of the deductive rules with strict conditionals.

Acknowledgment

The experimental part of this work has been supported by the special research grant SFB F012 at the University of Salzburg, Austria.

References

Adams, E. W. (1975). *The Logic of conditionals*. Dordrecht: Reidel.

Barkow, J., Cosmides, L. & Tooby, J. (1992, Eds.). *The adapted mind: evolutionary psychology and the generation of culture*. New York: Oxford Univ. Press.

Cosmides, L. & Tooby, J. (1992). Cognitive adaptations for social exchange. In Barkow et al. (1992, Eds.).

Evans, J. St. (1982). *The psychology of deductive reasoning*. London: Routledge & Kegan Paul.

Evans, J. St., Simon, J. H., & Over, D.E. (2003): Conditionals and conditional probability. *Journal of Experimental Psychology: Learning. Memory, and Cognition* 29/2, 321-335.

Ford, M., & Billington, D. (2000). Strategies in Human Nonmonotonic Reasoning. *Computational Intelligence* 16/3, 446 - 467.

Gabbay, D. M. et al.:(1994, Eds.). *Handbook of logic in Artificial Intelligence Vol. 3*. Oxford: Clarendon Press.

Gigerenzer, G. (2000). *Adaptive thinking*. Oxford: Oxford Univ. Press.

Gilio, A. (2002). Probabilistic reasoning under coherence in system P. *Annals of Mathematics and Artificial Intelligence* 34, 5-34.

Grice, P. (1975). Logic and conversation. In P. Cole & J. Morgan (Eds.), *Syntax and Semantics Vol. 3*. New York.

Johnson-Laeird, P.N., & Byrne, R. M. (1991). *Deduction*. East Sussex: Lawrence Erlbaum Associates.

Kahneman, D., Slovic, P., and Tversky, A. (1982, Eds.): *Judgement under uncertainty: heuristics and biases*. Cambridge: Cambridge Univ. Press.

Levinson, S. C. (2001). *Presumptive meanings*. Cambridge/Mass: MIT Press.

Oaksford, M., & Chater, N. (1994). A rational analysis of the selection task as optimal data selection. *Psychological Review* 101/4, 608-631.

Oberauer, K., & Wilhelm, O. (2003): The meaning(s) of conditionals: conditional probabilities, mental models, and personal utiliti*es*. *Journal of Experimental Psychology: Learning. Memory, and Cognition* 29/4, 680-693.

Over, D.E. (Ed.) (2003). *Evolution and the psychology of thinking: The debate*. Hove, UK: Psychology Press.

Pelletier, F. J., & Elio, R. (2001). Logic and computation: human performance in default reasoning. In P. Gaerdenfors et al. (Eds.), *Logic, Methodology and Philosophy of Science*. Kluwer: Dordrecht.

Pfeifer, N., & Kleiter, G. (2005). Coherence and non-monotonicity in human reasoning. *Synthese* 146/1-2, 93-109.

Rips, L .J. (1994). *The psychology of proof*. Cambridge/Mass.: MIT Press.

Schurz, G. (1991): Relevant deduction. *Erkenntnis* 35, 391 – 437.

Schurz, G. (1998): Probabilistic semantics for Delgrande's conditional logic. *Artificial Intelligence* 102/1, 81-95.

Schurz, G. (2001): What is 'normal'? An evolution-theoretic foundation of normic laws. *Philosophy of Science* 28, 476-97.

Schurz, G. (2005): Non-monotonic reasoning from an evolutionary viewpoint. *Synthese* 146/1-2, 37-51.

Sperber, D. & Wilson, D (1986). *Relevance, communication and cognition*. Oxford: B. Blackwell.

Between browsing and search, a new model for navigating through large documents

Thibault Mondary, Amanda Bouffier Adeline Nazarenko
(firstname.name@lipn.univ-paris13.fr)
Computer Science Lab of the Paris 13 University (CNRS UMR 7030)
99, avenue J.-B. Clément, F-93430 Villetaneuse, France

Abstract

This paper proposes a new model for document access, which combines the search and browsing approaches. We define a good navigation as a navigation which is as quick and direct as possible and which offers good precision and recall rates in finding the text segments that are relevant for the user's information need. Our navigation model relies on recent advances in natural language processing and it is based on two traditional cognitive principles that are inherited from works on the visualization of information. This model is implemented in a navigation prototype which is designed for physicians who want to consult official recommendations to take medical decisions. Even if this model has not been really evaluated yet, we show the dynamicity and the efficiency of our approach on few detailled examples.

Introduction

Developing methods and tools that help users to get access to the content of documents is a challenging task as the volume and heterogeneity of accessible information are constantly increasing. In this paper we are considering a specific medical task. Medical organizations such as HAS or AFSSAPS[1] are producing recommendations to help physicians in their diagnosis and treatment tasks. These recommendations take the form of 10 to 50 pages documents. A sample of the diabetes care guideline is given below.

I. Diabetes Care

I.1. Lifestyle modification

In a first step, patients should receive individual advice on nutrition. Whenever possible, they should be referred to a dietitian who will assess their current intake and nutrition needs.

Figure 1: Extract from of a diabete care guideline

Unfortunately, these recommendations are seldom used: it takes too much time to refer to such a large and complex document to find a precise piece of information dealing with a specific patient case.

---

[1]Haute Autorité de Santé and Agence Française de Sécurité Sanitaire des Produits de Santé.

In this paper we present a navigation model that has been designed to facilitate the consultation of these medical recommendations by physicians. Specific constraints have been taken into consideration. Navigation *quickness* is important as the physicians must be able to refer to recommendations during their consultations. The navigation tool must guide the user towards all the text segments that are relevant to his/her information need (*relevance* and *exhaustivity*). The tool must be *reliable* as it supports medical decisions: any short paragraph dealing with a specific drug interaction or a rare complication of a given disease may be important.

Traditional information access tools fall into two different categories, which focus either on search or browsing. We argue that recent advances in natural language processing (NLP) now make it possible to combine these two information access means into a unique navigation tool that offers a better compromise between quickness, relevance, exhaustivity and reliability.

The first section presents the various methods that have been proposed to give access to document content. The second and third sections describe our navigation method and the prototype in which it has been implemented. The last section shows the navigation process through the detailed analysis of few medical queries.

Methods for textual information access

Many tools have been designed to facilitate the document access, over the last two decades. Our own approach stems in three different research domains: robust text mining, information visualization and natural language processing.

Text mining

Text mining tools differ along two main axes.

The first one deals with the size of the document base and consequently the granularity of the information needs addressed. Search engines are designed to cope with numerous and usually heterogeneous collections of documents [Baeza-Yates and Ribeiro-Neto, 1999]. General purpose web search engines rely on a very simple representation of the document content and allow any kind of keyword queries. They may also take into account the hypertextual structure of the document collection which is the web. Such engine support only one part of the information access process. The user still has 1) to select some documents out of the list of returned documents and 2) to read or browse them. On the opposite side, traditional devices like tables of contents or back-of-the book indexes help the reader to find out interesting segments in a single document. Some indexing tools are designed to give such a content-based access to digital documents [Chi et al., 2004, Zargayouna et al., 2006]. Between these extremes, one can find various solutions, ranging from domain specific or intranet search engines to web site or multidocument indexes [Anick, 2001].

The second axis is more important from a cognitive point of view. It deals with the diversity of the users' information needs [O'Hara, 1996]. Search tools help users to find rapidly an answer but they must be able to word their information need in the form of a question or a keyword query. Beyond search engines, question-answering systems aim at giving a precise answer to the user's question (*e.g.* "Roma" for the question "In which city is the Coliseo?") [Burger and al, 2002]. Browsing is less focused. Browsing tools are designed for users that are interested in a document but without any precise information need in mind. They help users to locate interesting segments or to get a general view of what the document is about. Hypertextual links are a typically designed for browsing documents. Abstracts, tables of contents, explicit indexes are alternative means to get an overview of the document content.

Search favors the quickness and relevance of information access but the user has to blindly rely on the system selection. Browsing gives a broader access to information, let the users make their own choices and favours information serendipity, with the risk for the users to get lost (cognitive disorientation [Conklin, 1987]) or to spend too much time wandering around the interesting segments.

Search and browsing should not be opposed, however. Except for very specific information needs which can be easily and unambiguously answered by the document, search must be complemented with browsing. The search engine user usually has to browse the list of returned documents, which is sometimes only used as a starting point for hypertextual navigating through the collection. Most question-answering systems deliver an answer together with the document passage from which it has been extracted so that the user can interpret the answer in its context.

Visualizing information

Over the last few years, the search model based on a low-level preprocessing of the documents has become the standard approach, even for small collections or single document access. In parallel, text mining tools have often been augmented with visualization techniques, which ensure the browsing functionalities [Hearst, 1999].

Many visualization devices and visual metaphors have been proposed to help users to get an overall picture of the document content and to categorize it. Three simple but interesting principles have emerged from this past experience. The contrast between relevant and irrelevant information must be visually evident (various underlying

or size variation means have been used). It is also important that the user can easily pan and zoom the document content. To avoid disorientation, one must have a global view of the document in mind even while focusing on a specific segment. The local and global views are often presented concomitantly and interlinked to guide the browsing. The third important aspect is categorization as it helps the user to distinguish between different types of documents and/or textual segments.

Our approach is based on the same principles.

Natural language processing (NLP)

Even if innovation in text mining has mainly came from visualization techniques in the last decade, we argue that recent advances in specialized language processing can enhance domain specific document access.

Thanks to the development of computational terminology, it is possible to identify the technical vocabulary of a document and the terminological collocations which are often highly semantically relevant in a specialized domain (example "Hypoalphalipoproteinemia"). Terminological analysis can contribute to a more specialized indexing of documents. It has been used to produce explicit indexes of document or collections [Wacholder et al., 2001, Anick, 2001, Nazarenko and Aït El Mekki, 2005].

Current research also focuses on the textual structure of the document. It has been shown that information retrieval can benefit from the exploitation of the structure of the documents (usually represented as an XML markup) [Vittaut and Gallinari, 2006]. It is also clear that extracting a text segment or a specific piece of information must take the context into account: an introduction, a definition or a figure legend do not have the same informational status. It is therefore important to make explicit the structure of the documents [Marcu, 2000, Schilder, 2002].

Finally, the development of methods for corpus-based ontology building [Després and Szulman, 2006] facilitates the creation of ontologies, in which the ontological knowledge is connected with the linguistic one and which can be used for the semantic annotation of documents. The semantic metadata associated with documents can in turn be exploited in text mining, for instance for document categorisation [Pratt et al., 1999].

Navigation model

Relying on our previous work in document annotation [Derivière et al., 2006] and terminological analysis [Aubin and Hamon, 2006], we argue that it is possible to develop new tools for accessing document content, which better addresses the complexity and heterogeneity of users' information needs. We have designed a new model of navigation and a corresponding navigation tool that help the consultation of the medical recommendations by physicians.

As shown above, searching and browsing models to document access both have their own advantages and limitations. Our navigation model aims at taking the best of the two worlds. From usual browsing tools, we keep the idea that information must always be related to its context. From the standard searching approach, we learn the fact that discriminating between relevant and irrelevant document passages is important. We argue that, compared with traditional approaches, our navigation model proposes a better compromise between quickness, relevance, exhaustivity and reliability.

Evaluating the quality of a navigation

Let $N = (s_{a,1}, s_{b,2}, ..., s_{i,n})$ be a navigation composed of n steps in which the user successively reads the textual segments S_a, S_b.... Some of these segments may be relevant for the user but some others may not. The same segment can be visited twice as the navigation may have cycles or backward steps. A navigation tail is the subsequence of navigation steps that are visited after the last relevant segment has been consulted. The quality of a given navigation is measured according to the following metrics:

- The navigation *precision* is the proportion of relevant segments in the navigation: $precision(N) = r/n$, where r is the number of relevant segments in N.

- The navigation *recall* is the proportion of relevant segments that are retrieved by the system: $recall(N) = r/R$ where R is the total number of relevant segments present in the document.

- The navigation *efficiency* is the proportion of steps that are useful to find relevant textual segments in N: $Eff(N) = (n - rep - tail)/n$, where rep is the number of segment repetitions, and *tail* the length of the navigation tail.

In an optimal navigation, $recall(N) = precision(N) = Eff(N) = 1$, and $Eff(N)$ is redundant with $recall(N) = 1$. In other cases, however, efficiency distinguishes the case where the user navigates straight to the relevant information ($Eff(N) = 1$) and the case where he/she wanders around (cycles, feedbacks) and/or keep on browsing whereas he/she has found the available information (tail) ($Eff(N) < 1$).

Presenting information in context

According to the visualization principles, we consider that a textual segment must be contextualized, as the context guides its interpretation. Two different localization systems (maps) are proposed to the reader.

The first one is the overall structure of the document (document map), usually represented by its table of contents. It is traditionally explicitly designed by the author of the document to help the reader to locate information. In technical documents such as the medical recommendations, the author's table of contents is often too coarse-grained. NLP document segmentation methods help to identify fine-grained structures in documents. In any case, we suppose that we have an explicit hierarchy of segments, which can be labeled[2] and presented in the

---

[2]When the segment is an explicit document section, its label is its title. When the segment is smaller such as a

form of a tree. The document map is not sufficient however. A document may have several types of readers, whereas the table of contents is designed for a specific reader's profile.

One of the originality of our navigation model is to offer a second localization system (domain conceptual map). It is based on a conceptual model of the domain of the document and oriented by the readers' profile. This conceptual map requires of course that the textual segments are indexed according to the domain conceptual model. In that perspective, the conceptual model can be considered as a segment categorization where a single segment can be attached to different categories. This second map functions as an alternative to the first one. It presents a new organization of the document content. In that perspective, it is similar to a back-of-the book index, which offers a second way to access document, which is complementary to the table of contents. The difference is that the conceptual map is based on the domain model of the document rather than its terminology.

These two maps play an important role in our navigation model. They give a direct access to the textual segments and therefore reduce the navigation length. Compared with full reading or random navigation, they increase both the precision and efficiency.

Discriminating relevant information

The second important feature of our navigation model is the discrimination between relevant and irrelevant textual segments. If the reader is able to express his/her information need in the form of a query, the entire navigation model is parameterized according to that query.

This relevance is based on a terminological analysis of the document which computes a set of variant terms $t_1, t_2, ...t_i$, supposedly semantically equivalent to the user's initial query term t. For instance, if the initial request is "elderly", we consider that a textual segment dealing with "aged patient" is relevant.

For sake of simplicity, lets consider a query q composed of a single term t. We consider the following relevance definitions:

- A textual segment is relevant with respect to q if it contains an occurrence of t or of a variant t' of t. We consider that a segment that contains a relevant segment is not relevant as such but that it nevertheless helps to localize segments.

- A conceptual category is relevant with respect to a query q if one or several of its attached segments are relevant with respect to q.

Once a query has been expressed, the reader is able to discriminate in the document and conceptual maps where are the relevant segments. The segments can be gathered in a single section or scattered all over the document. They can also be clustered under a single cat-

---

discursive frame, its label is given by a "Frame introducer" which is a detached adverbial. Figure 1 shows a frame example introduced by "In a first step".

egory in the conceptual model. This increases the precision/recall of the navigation. The maps help the user to glance at the various contexts in which he/she should look for information. This is important as the navigation must go on until all relevant segments have been read (to augment recall) but should stop as soon as they have been read (to increase efficiency). Our hypothesis is that the maps increase the reliability of the system (which appears as an increased efficiency).

Navigation prototype

Our prototype is currently developed in C++ with the graphical toolkit Qt 4.2. It is fast and portable.

User interface

Four areas are present in our interface, as shown on Figure 2: the keyword input area (area 0), two maps of the document, and the document itself.

The *conceptual map* (area 1) locates the results of the request in a conceptual model. The conceptual model is a hierarchy in which every category used to describe a section of the document is kept. The *document map* (area 2) locates the results of the request in a table of contents. This view gives the user an overview of the structure of the document, such as it was designed by its author. The *document view* (area 3) locates into the document structure the results of the query or the sections which have been selected by the user in one of the other views.

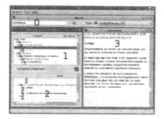

Figure 2: Main window of the user interface

Foreground colors are used to discriminate relevant segments, categories or sections. For instance, a section is light gray if it has no occurrence of the query terms. It is black if it is directly relevant to the query and it is dark gray if the section has a relevant section as subsection. For categories if the conceptual map, the colors are the same but refer to the ratio $prop = rc/tc$ with rc the number of relevant sections attached to the category c and tc the total number of sections attached to c. If $prop < 1/3$ we use light gray, if $prop \geq 1/3$ and $prop < 2/3$ we use gray, and black otherwise. In the document, occurrences of the query terms are highlighted with a yellow background.

Views are linked together. If the user types a keyword, the other views become active: the maps are filled with categories and sections, and the document view shows the entire document. When the user selects one or more categories in the conceptual view, the others are affected: relevant sections are highlighted in the document map

and shown in the document view. If the user selects more than one category, the selection depends of the state of the check box named "categories conjunction". If it is enabled, only sections relevant for every selected categories are highlighted. Otherwise, sections relevant for at least one of the selected categories are highlighted. When the user selects some sections in the document map, they are simply shown in the document view. Finally, when the user clicks on the document view, the current section is automatically located in the document map.

Behind the interface

The system is composed of three subsystems. The *user subsystem* relies on the search engine, which locates the occurrences of the query terms in the documents, and computes the relevance of each section. To improve the accuracy, the search engine exploits a terminology which contains a list of terms and their synonyms. A tree deployment module chooses dynamically how the hierarchies of conceptual and document maps are deployed, expanding relevant nodes, and to collapsing others. The *knowledge management subsystem* contains a tagged corpus, a domain model used to type the corpus and a set of terminological relations. The *administrator subsystem* is composed of NLP tools used for knowledge acquisition. Our prototype relies on four types of tools for terminology acquisition[3], corpus-based ontology building [Després and Szulman, 2006], corpus preparation (conversion, segmentation) and corpus annotation.

Navigation scenarii

The user can choose to navigate with the conceptual map, with the document map, through the document itself or by mixing different views. The selection of categories can be viewed as a semantic query expansion. For example, if the initial request is "dietetic" and the selected category is "young people" then the user wants to view every part of the text dealing with young people and containing the keyword 'dietetic' (or one of its variations). When the user chooses more than one category, it could be a conjunction or a disjunction of each, depending of the state of the check box described above.

Using the document map, the user may have a direct access to any section identified as relevant for the query. It is useful when information is scattered or to vizualize the repartition of a specific term (*e.g.* a molecule name) through the document.

The document view shows the graphical aspect of the document, or its length. Since each section is coloured with respect of the relevance, the user has indications to navigate in the document with the scroll bar.

The recommended navigation strategy exploits the different views. The user enters a keyword, then select some categories to expand its request, uses the document map to jump in relevant sections and read them in the document view.

---

[3]The current version of the protype is based on YaTeA [Aubin and Hamon, 2006] and Faster [Jacquemin, 1995].

Discussion: search *vs.* navigation

Our navigation prototype has not been evaluated yet. This section presents detailed examples of navigation, which show that the navigation model seems to be more efficient than the classical search method. The end of the section also present the evaluation protocol that we plan to set up to validate the proposed approach.

We have defined with medicine experts (LIM&BIO, Paris 13) a sample of queries which are relevant for a physician in consultation. One of those is the following: "What treatment should I prescribe to my elderly patient who has no cardiovascular disease history and who has been on a diet with no success ?" We compare how the user can find the relevant textual segments using either our navigation prototype or a classical search engine. If we suppose that the physician chooses the keyword "elderly" in order to formulate his query (currently our system only handles single keyword queries), both systems return the same 20 textual segments (those containing the keyword) but the results are presented in different ways as shown on Figures 3 and 4.

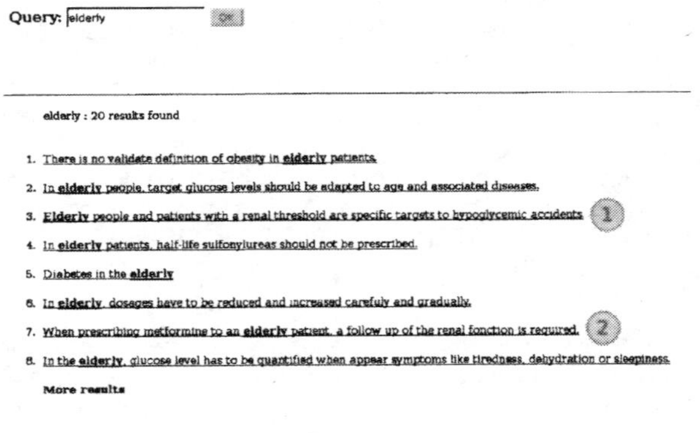

Query: elderly

---

elderly : 20 results found

1. There is no validate definition of obesity in **elderly** patients.
2. In **elderly** people, target glucose levels should be adapted to age and associated diseases.
3. **Elderly** people and patients with a renal threshold are specific targets to hypoglycemic accidents ①
4. In **elderly** patients, half-life sulfonylureas should not be prescribed.
5. Diabetes in the **elderly**
6. In **elderly** dosages have to be reduced and increased carefuly and gradually.
7. When prescribing metformine to an **elderly** patient, a follow up of the renal function is required. ②
8. In the **elderly**, glucose level has to be quantified when appear symptoms like tiredness, dehydration or sleepiness.

More results

Figure 3: Result presentation (classical search method)

Figure 4: Result presentation (navigation model)

The search method presents the result list, with the sentences containing the keyword occurrences, whereas the navigation method presents the results with respect to the document and the conceptual maps[4]. In our

---

[4]Only one map is presented on Figure 4 for sake of lisibil-

approach, categories associated to one or more result (like "follow-up" or "side effects") are coloured differently from categories which are not associated with any result (like "bitherapy" or "physical activity"). We want to show how these different result presentations affect the navigation quality with respect to our three criteria: precision, recall and efficiency.

Example 1 Let's consider the following result (number 1 in the two figures):

- elderly *people and patients with a renal threshold are a specific target to hypoglycemic accidents*

In the search method, the meaning of this result cannot be fully captured because the sentence is not a sufficient context. If we read a larger segment, we understand that these accidents are side effects of a drug class which specifically affects elderly patients. The navigation model gives more contextual information. The keyword (*i.e.* "elderly") is presented in a larger textual segment than the sentence, which facilitates the comprehension. The result is also localized on the conceptual map, where it falls under the category "Side effects". This givee the context required to get the whole meaning of the result and consequently increases the user ability to quickly discriminate relevant results from irrelevant ones.

Example 2 Let's now consider the two following results (numbers 1 and 2 in the figures):

- elderly *people and patients with a renal threshold are a specific target to hypoglycemic accidents*
- *where prescribing metformine to an* elderly *patient, a follow-up of the renal function is necessary*

With the list presentation of a traditional search engine, the two results are disconnected whereas they both deal with drugs side effects that specifically affect elderly people. In contrast, in the navigation model, these two results are linked together because they fall under the same category "Side effects". We argue that the navigation model facilitates the user understanding and thus increases the navigation precision and efficiency.

Example 3 With the search method, if the users want to be sure that they have got all the results needed, they have to browse all the items until the last one even if they have already got all the relevant ones. The navigation model is designed to avoid this useless browsing by showing a global, synthetic and well-comprehensive view on the results through the conceptual map.

For instance, a physician will be able to quickly discriminate on the map the relevant categories like "Elderly people", "Pharmacological treatment" and "Side effects" and the irrelevant ones like "Follow up" (because he/she is interested in first treatments, for instance) or "Cardiovascular disease history" (because

---

ity.

his/her patient has no history of that type). So, after he/she has read the results in the relevant categories, he/she can stop browsing without reading the remaining results. In that way also, the navigation model increases physician's efficiency.

These three examples show that the navigation model offers to physicians a better control of the research process and therefore increases the navigation efficiency.

Evaluation protocol Even if this navigation model is based on commonsense principles and if it seems to perform properly on some navigation examples, it must be more thoroughly evaluated.

To analyze the advantages and drawbacks of our navigation model, we plan to compare it with other traditional methods used to get access to the document content, as shown in the examples above (manual browsing, traditional information retrieval and search assisted by a table of content or a back of the book index). The various methods will be compared on formal grounds. We are currently defining a unified language L to describe the different document access methods in the form of a list of the browsed titles and segments.

We have defined a query test set with our physician partners. For the first evaluation, few physicians will be asked to answer the test queries using the different document access methods, while an independent observer will codify their various operations in L. The various methods will be then compared on the basis of their resulting document access traces (length of the navigation trace, presence of cycles, length of tails, etc.).

Conclusion

We have presented a new navigation model that combines the search and the browsing techniques to give to the user a comprehensive and flexible tool for accessing document content. Our approach relies on a terminological relevance calculus and on two different maps, which help the user to localize any textual segment(s) in the whole document and with respect to the conceptual model of the domain. The dynamicity of our system ensures that the coloration of the maps and the document is automatically updated according to any new user's query. The user sees what is relevant but remains free to navigate as he/she wants.

The analysis of a small set of navigation log confirms our initial intuitions but our model and prototype must be more thoroughly evaluated. We plan to compare our navigation model with other existing models (manual browsing, traditional information retrieval and search assisted by a table of content or a back of the book index).

References

Anick, P. G. (2001). The automatic construction of faceted terminological feedback for interactive document retrieval. In Bourgault, D. *et al.* editors, *Recent Advances in Computational Terminology*, pp. 29–52. John Benjamins, Amsterdam.

Aubin, S. and Hamon, T. (2006). Improving Term Extraction with terminological resources. In Salakoski, T. *et al.* editors. *Advances in Natural Language Processing*, LNAI 4139, pp. 380–387. Springer.

Baeza-Yates, R. and Ribeiro-Neto, B., editors (1999). *Modern Information Retrieval*. Addison-Wesley Longman Publishing Company, Wokingham, UK.

Burger, J. and al (2002). Issues, tasks and program structures to roadmap research in question & answering (q&a). Technical report, DARPA.

Chi, E., Hong, L., Heiser, J., and Card, S. (2004). ebooks with indexes that reorganize conceptually. In *Proc. of the Human Factors in Computing Systems Conf.*, pp. 1223–1226, Vienna. ACM Press.

Conklin, J. (1987). Hypertext: An introduction and survey. *IEEE Computer*, 20(9):17–41.

Derivière, J., Hamon, T., and Nazarenko, A. (2006). A scalable and distributed NLP architecture for Web document annotation. In Salakoski, T. *et al.* editors, *Advances in Natural Language Processing*, LNAI 4139, pp. 56–67. Springer.

Després, S. and Szulman, S. (2006). Terminae method and integration process for legal ontology building. In *Advances in Applied Artificial Intelligence*, pp. 1014–1023. Springer Berlin/Heidelberg.

Hearst, M. A. (1999). *Modern Information Retrieval*, chapter User Interfaces and Visualization. Addison-Wesley Longman Publishing Co., Wokingham, UK.

Jacquemin, C. (1995). A symbolic and surgical acquisition of terms through variation. In *Learning for Natural Language Processing*, Lecture Notes in Computer Science, pp. 425–438.

Marcu, D. (2000). The rhetorical parsing of unrestricted texts: a surface-based approach. *Computational Linguistics*, 26(3):395–448.

Nazarenko, A. and Aït El Mekki, T. (2005). Building back-of-the-book indexes. *Terminology*, 11(1):193–218.

O'Hara, K. (1996). Towards a typology of reading goals. Tech. Report EPC-1997-107, RXRC/Cambridge Lab., Cambridge, UK.

Pratt, W., Hearst, M. A., and Fagan, L. M. (1999). A knowledge-based approach to organizing retrieved documents. In *Proc. of the 16th Nat. Conf. on Artificial Intelligence*, pp. 80–85.

Schilder, F. (2002). Robust discourse parsing via discourse markers, topicality and position. *Natural Language Engineering*, 8(3):235–255.

Vittaut, J.-N. and Gallinari, P. (2006). Machine learning ranking for structured information retrieval. In *Proc. of the European Conf. on Information Retrieval*, pp. 338–349.

Wacholder, N., Evans, D., and Klavans, J. (2001). Automatic identification and organization of index terms for interactive browsing. In *Proc. of First ACM/IEEE-CS Joint Conf. on Digital Libraries*, pp. 126–134, Roanoke, VA.

Zargayouna, H., Aït El Mekki, T., Audibert, L., and Nazarenko, A. (2006). IndDoc: An aid for the back-of-the-book indexer. *The Indexer*, 25(2):122–125.

An Approach to the Semantics of Analogical Relations[1]

Helmar Gust, Ulf Krumnack, Kai-Uwe Kühnberger, Angela Schwering
University of Osnabrück
Institute of Cognitive Science
{hgust, krumnack, kkuehnbe, aschweri}@uos.de

Abstract

Whereas approaches for deductive and inductive reason-ing are well-examined for decades, analogical reasoning seems to be a hard problem for machine intelligence. Although several models for computing analogies have been proposed, there is no uncontroversial theory of the semantics of analogies. In this paper, we will investigate semantic issues of analogical relations, in particular, we will specify a model theory of analogical transfers. The presented approach is based on Heuristic-Driven The-ory Projection (HDTP) a framework that computes an analogical relation between logical theories describing a source and a target domain. HDTP establishes the anal-ogy by an abstraction process in which formulas from both domains are generalized creating a theory that syn-tactically subsumes the original theories. We will show that this syntactic process can be given a sensible in-terpretation on the semantic level. In particular, given models of the source and the target domains, we will examine the construction of models for the generalized theory of source and target. Furthermore, we will spec-ify some properties of both, the corresponding models and the underlying analogical relation.

Introduction

Human cognitive reasoning capacities include not only abilities like drawing inferences from given facts (deduc-tions), generalizing rules from given examples (induc-tion), or finding appropriate premises for certain rules (abduction). Humans are also able to conceptualize new situations *in analogy to* experiences in the past. These analogical transfers play an important role in explaining human creativity, productivity, and adaptivity (Hoft-stadter & The Fluid Analogies Research Group, 1995; Indurkhya, 1992).

Research in analogical reasoning has been taken place in an interdisciplinary environment in which methods from cognitive science, psychology, computer science, and AI were applied. Analogical reasoning was discussed in areas such as proportional analogies in string domains (Hofstatder *et al.* 1995) and between geometric fig-ures (Dastani, 1998). Further discussions were centered around the relation between analogies and metaphors (Gentner, Bowdle, Wolff & Boronat, 2001) and ana-logical problem solving (Anderson & Thompson, 1989).

Methods used for modeling analogies range from al-gebraic accounts (Dastani, Scha & Indurkhya, 1997; Indurkhya, 1992) to graph-based approaches (Falken-hainer, Forbus & Gentner, 1989) and similarity-based approaches (Gentner, 1989). Although the mentioned models for analogical reasoning show non-trivial differ-ences there seems to be a non-controversial core inter-pretation of analogies: Analogical relations can be es-tablished between a well-known domain (source domain) and a formerly unknown domain (target domain) with-out taking much input data (examples) into account. Rather it is the case that a conceptualization of the source domain is sufficient to generate knowledge about the target domain. This can be achieved by associating attributes and relations of the source domain and the target domain. Moreover, a projection of attributes and relations from source to target can productively intro-duce new concepts on the target domain.

Although a variety of syntactic and algorithmic core mechanisms for analogy making were proposed, no sim-ilar mechanisms has been developed to provide a model theoretic semantics of analogical relations. Clearly it is possible to formulate a denotational semantics based on term algebras for algebra inspired approaches of analog-ical reasoning (Indurkhya, 1992; Dastani, 1998) or for models using pattern matching methods (Falkenhainer, Forbus & Gentner, 1989). Even if such ideas had been explicitly developed, it would remain unclear how the semantic meaning of dynamically established analogi-cal relations can emerge from these approaches. This paper tries to bridge the gap between algorithmic ap-proaches for analogical reasoning and the denotational semantics underlying these algorithms. The framework used here is Heuristic-Driven Theory Projection (HDTP, Gust, Kühnberger & Schmid, 2006) a mathematically sound theory for analogy making. The core algorithm HDTP-A_h is implemented in Prolog (Gust, Kühnberger & Schmid, 2003) and has been applied to a variety of domains.

The paper has the following structure: In the next sec-tion, we roughly summarize basic ideas of HDTP with respect to the underlying syntax and describe the con-cept of generalization using the well-known Rutherford analogy as an example. The semantics of the analogical relation is discussed in the main section of this paper: We introduce model theoretic notions in the context of an analogical scenario and present a way to interpret the

[1] The work has been supported by the German Research Foundation (DFG) through the project "Modeling of predic-tive analogies by Heuristic-Driven Theory Projection" (grant KU 1949/2-1). The publication was supported by the Uni-versitätsgesellschaft Osnabrück.

syntactic analogical relation on a semantic level. Furthermore we propose two construction methods (a quotient construction and a product construction) for the generalized model of HDTP which is left open in Gust *et al.* (2006). Last but not least some model theoretic properties of HDTP are discussed. The last section concludes with final remarks.

HDTP – A Theory for Analogy Making

We will roughly sketch some ideas of HDTP and refer to Gust *et al.* (2006) for a complete description of the theory. The notions introduced will be exemplified by the famous Rutherford analogy, in which an analogical relation is established between the solar system (source domain) and the inner structure of an atom (target domain).[2] Based on such a relation, analogical inferences can be drawn, i.e. knowledge from the source domain can be transferred to the target to gain an intuition and state a hypothesis about that domain. Although HDTP addresses the whole process of analogy making, for the concerns of this paper it is sufficient to concentrate on the first step, i.e. the establishment of an analogical relation.

Syntactic Properties

HDTP is syntactically based on a many-sorted first-order language. As analogy involves two domains which do not have to be connected in any way prior to the estabishment of an analogical relation, both domains can be formalized independently. That is, each formalization can introduce its own signature and axioms. However, if the same symbol occurs in both domains it has to be used in the same way: it should have same type and argument structure (in case it is a function symbol) and the same meaning. We refer to this as the unique name assumption and discuss it in some more detail in the section on semantics below.

In figure 1 a possible formalization of the solar system domain is given. It contains two constants representing the sun and a planet. The functions are observable values as the *mass* of the objects and for a given point in time their *distance* as well as the *gravity* and *centrifugal* force between two of them (here attracting forces will be positive while repelling forces will have a negative sign). Knowledge is encoded by logical formulas, divided into rules and facts. The facts state that the mass of the sun is larger than the mass of the planet and that the distance between them is always positive. Also there is an attracting gravitational force between them. Finally it is claimed that the planet revolves around the sun. The laws are included to give an explanation for the last fact: the first law states that if two objects are attracting each other but keep a positive distance, then

---

[2]Although Rutherfords atom model was falsified by physicists and soon superseded by Bohrs model, it is still of interest from a cognitive perspective. It demonstrates how known patterns can be used to structure new domains via analogy and thereby boost the learning process. This may be a reason why this model, despite its inaccuracy, is still taught in high school.

types
  real, *object*, *time*

constants
  sun : *object*, *planet* : *object*

functions
  $mass : object \rightarrow real \times \{kg\}$
  $dist : object \times object \times time \rightarrow real \times \{m\}$
  $gravity : object \times object \times time \rightarrow real \times \{N\}$
  $centrifugal : object \times object \times time \rightarrow real \times \{N\}$

facts
  $mass(sun) > mass(planet)$
  $\forall t : time : gravity(planet, sun, t) > 0$
  $\forall t : time : dist(planet, sun, t) > 0$
  $revolves\_around(planet, sun)$

laws

(i) $\forall t : time, o_1 : object, o_2 : object :$
  $dist(o_1, o_2, t) > 0 \wedge gravity(o_1, o_2, t) > 0$
  $\rightarrow \exists force : force(o_1, o_2, t) < 0 \wedge$
  $force(o_1, o_2, t) = centrifugal(o_1, o_2, t)$

(ii) $\forall t : time, o_1 : object, o_2 : object :$
  $dist(o_1, o_2, t) > 0 \wedge mass(o_1) < mass(o_2) \wedge$
  $centrifugal(o_1, o_2, t) < 0$
  $\rightarrow revolves\_around(o_1, o_2)$

Figure 1: Formalization of solar system domain.

there must be a counterforce, that equals to the centrifugal force. The second law says that in this case the less massive object revolves around the heavier one.

A similar formalization of the atom is given in figure 2. Here two constants for the nucleus and an electron are introduced. It is known that the nucleus is heavier than the electron and that they have opposite electrical charge causing an attracting coulomb force. Further it has been observed that nucleus and electrons are spatially seperated. By analogical inference one now might suggest that the electron revolves around the nucleus.

Generalization

A basic idea of HDTP is to see analogy as an abstraction process. Common structures of source and target domain are identified and made explicit. The syntactical tool applied is an extended version of anti-unification (Plotkin, 1970). The idea of anti-unification can be illustrated by the following example: take the term $mass(sun)$ from the source domain and $mass(nucleus)$ from the target domain. A syntactical more general term is $mass(X)$ as the original terms can be regained by sub-

types
   real, object, time

constants
   nucleus : object, electron : object

functions
   $mass : object \rightarrow real \times \{kg\}$
   $dist : object \times object \times time \rightarrow real \times \{m\}$
   $electric\_charge : object \rightarrow real \times \{eV\}$
   $coulomb : object \times object \times time \rightarrow real \times \{N\}$

facts
   $mass(nucleus) > mass(electron)$
   $electric\_charge(electron) < 0$
   $electric\_charge(nucleus) > 0$
   $\forall t : time : coulomb(electron, nucleus, t) > 0$
   $\forall t : time : dist(electron, nucleus, t) > 0$

Figure 2: Formalization of Rutherford atom model.

stituting the variable X by *sun* or *nucleus* respectively.

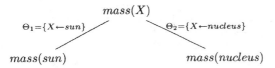

Anti-unification is the process of finding a common generalization and substitutions for a given set of terms. In general there are several possibilities to anti-unify two given terms t_1 and t_2. Therefore the concept of an anti-instance is introduced as the most specific common generalization.

Definition 1 *A term t together with two substitutions Θ_1 and Θ_2 is called an anti-instance of two terms t_1 and t_2 iff t, Θ_1, and Θ_2 is a common generalization of t_1 and t_2 and for every other common generalization t', Θ'_1 and Θ'_2 it holds: there exist a substitution σ such that $t'\sigma = t$.*

It was shown in Plotkin (1970) that anti-instances exist and are uniquely defined (up to renaming of variables). However, this classical form of anti-unification has some shortcomings as it is not flexible enough to reflect all possible commonalities within a pair of terms. Therefore HDTP extends the idea of anti-unification:

- An equational theory E is added to the system. For example, an equation describing the symmetry of the distance function, $dist(X, Y) =_E dist(Y, X)$ would introduce new ways to anti-unify the terms $dist(sun, planet)$ and $dist(electron, nucleus)$. By equational theories the uniqueness of the anti-instance is lost but greater flexible is gained in finding appropriate anti-instances.

- Higher-order anti-unification is allowed, i.e. not only terms but also functions and relations can be anti-unified resulting in the introduction of second-order

types
   real, object, time

constants
   $X : object, Y : object$

functions
   $mass : object \rightarrow real \times \{kg\}$
   $dist : object \times object \times time \rightarrow real \times \{m\}$
   $F : object \times object \times time \rightarrow real \times \{N\}$

facts
   $mass(X) > mass(Y)$
   $\forall t : time : F(X, Y, t) > 0$
   $\forall t : time : dist(X, Y, t) > 0$

Figure 3: Generalized theory for the Rutherford analogy.

variables for functions and relations. In our example, such a variable could be used to introduce a generalization for the *gravity* and *coulomb* functions. It is also possible to realign arguments of functions to get more specific generalizations for functions with different argument structure.

- Whole first-order formulas can be anti-unified. Also anti-unification is allowed to be established modulo logical equivalence, so formulas can be transformed into a normal form prior to the generalization process.

Due to these extensions Gust *et al.* (2006) introduced the term *generalization* instead of anti-instance of two first-order formulas. They also provided the algorithm HDTP-A_h that can anti-unify two given first order theories, controlled by different heuristics. This algorithm delivers as output a generalized version of the input theories as well as the substitutions which are used to align symbols from the different domains. An example of a generalized theory for the Rutherford analogy is illustrated in 3. The substitutions introduced in this case are

$$
\begin{aligned}
X &\leftarrow sun/nucleus \\
Y &\leftarrow planet/electron \\
F &\leftarrow gravity/coulomb
\end{aligned}
$$

These data establish a syntactical analogical relation R between the formalization of the solar system and that of the Rutherford atom model. It might be used to draw analogical inferences by transferring formulas from the source to the target side as described in Gust *et al.* (2006).

Semantic Properties of HDTP

Having defined a syntactic analogical relation as a mapping of symbols, terms and formulas, this construction will now be analyzed from a semantical point of view. An intuitive idea of the semantics of an analogy is the establishment of an analogical relation between source and

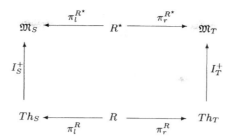

Figure 4: Diagrammatic representation of an analogical relation R between two theories Th_S and Th_T and the induced relation $R^\star$ on the model theoretic level.

target corresponding to a (psychologically) preferred interpretation of the analogy.[3] Such a relation should be compatible with the structure of the logical language. In this section we will develop a model-oriented approach towards the semantics to support this intuition.

Foundations

Recall that an interpretation for a many-sorted first-order language is given by a pair $\mathfrak{M} = \langle D, I \rangle$ where I is a function that assigns a set $D_s \subseteq D$ to every sort symbol s. Constants are mapped to elements of the set corresponding to their sort and function symbols to functions with appropriate argument structure. Predicate symbols are mapped to relations. On this basis validity of formulas can be defined as usual.

Definition 2 *Given an interpretation* $\mathfrak{M} = \langle D, I \rangle$, *truth of formulas is defined:*[4]

$$
\begin{array}{lll}
\mathfrak{M} \models t = s & \textit{iff} & I^+(t) = I^+(s) \\
\mathfrak{M} \models P(t_1, \ldots t_n) & \textit{iff} & \langle I^+(t_1), \ldots, I^+(t_n) \rangle \in I(P) \\
\mathfrak{M} \models \alpha \wedge \beta & \textit{iff} & \mathfrak{M} \models \alpha \textit{ and } \mathfrak{M} \models \beta \\
\mathfrak{M} \models \alpha \vee \beta & \textit{iff} & \mathfrak{M} \models \alpha \textit{ or } \mathfrak{M} \models \beta \\
\mathfrak{M} \models \phi \rightarrow \psi & \textit{iff} & \mathfrak{M} \not\models \phi \textit{ or } \mathfrak{M} \models \psi \\
\mathfrak{M} \models \forall s : x\phi & \textit{iff} & \textit{for all } m \in D_s : \mathfrak{M} \models \phi(m) \\
\mathfrak{M} \models \exists s : x\phi & \textit{iff} & \textit{for some } m \in D_s : \mathfrak{M} \models \phi(m)
\end{array}
$$

$\mathfrak{M}$ *is called a model for a (consistent) set of formulas* Ax, *if it makes every formula* $\varphi \in Ax$ *true.*

As we are dealing with two domains, we will consider pairs of models $\langle \mathfrak{M}_S, \mathfrak{M}_T \rangle$. These have to be consistent according to the unique name assumption. There are at least two possible versions of this statement: the hard version will force identical sorts to be mapped on the same set and the interpretation of constants, function and predicate symbols have to be literally the same. The weak version allows different sets for the same sort, which may intersect. It then is required that identical constants lie within the intersecting parts and functions and relations agree on that parts. In what follows, the weaker version is sufficient.

---

[3]Clearly the interpretation of an analogy cannot be true of false. Rather it is the case that certain interpretations are psychologically more of less preferred. Empirical evidence for such preferred interpretations in case of metaphors can be found in Kokinov & Petrov (2001).

[4]I^+ denotes the homomorphic extension of I to terms.

Induced Analogical Relation for Models

Regarding model theoretic aspects it should be mentioned that there are in general infinitely many models $\mathfrak{M}_T$ and $\mathfrak{M}_S$ for Th_T and Th_S respectively, provided the underlying axioms are consistent. An analogical relation reflects these ideas: based on the association of facts and laws of the two domains, it is required that for every model making facts and laws true on the source side, there is a model of the target domain making the corresponding theory true. Given two models $\mathfrak{M}_S$ and $\mathfrak{M}_T$ a syntactical analogical relation R induces a relation $R^\star \subseteq \mathfrak{M}_S \times \mathfrak{M}_T$ between this models by

$$
\langle I_S^+(s), I_T^+(t) \rangle \in R^\star \textit{ iff } \langle s, t \rangle \in R.
$$

This definition respects functions and so the interpretation functions I_S^+ and I_T^+ shift the syntactic association to the semantic level, namely to the relation $R^\star$ between two models. These ideas are represented in figure 4.

Constructing Generalized Models

The algorithm HDTP-A_h generates as a byproduct a set of (syntactically) generalized axioms inducing a generalized theory Th_G of the source and the target. We claim that there are canonical ways to construct a model $\mathfrak{M}_G$ for every pair of given models $\mathfrak{M}_S$ and $\mathfrak{M}_T$ which are related by the induced relation $R^\star$. The idea is to construct $\mathfrak{M}_G$ in a way such that precisely the associated terms and formulas of source and target that are related by the relation $R^\star$ are covered. This resulting model $\mathfrak{M}_G$ can be interpreted as the explicit model theoretic meaning of an analogical relation R.

This idea is illustrated in figure 5. The generalized theory Th_G is computed from the given source and target theories Th_S and Th_T respectively and related to them via appropriate substitutions. Models for source and target are given with their interpretations I_S and I_T. The intuitive understanding of a model $\mathfrak{M}_G$ for the generalized theory Th_G would be an interpretation that contains common elements from $\mathfrak{M}_S$ and $\mathfrak{M}_T$. In the case of the Rutherford analogy, this could be the concept of a central force system, consisting of a massive body attracting a lightweight sattelite. An appropriate interpretation I_G has to be defined that maps terms and formulas of Th_G to that construction. Also it would be

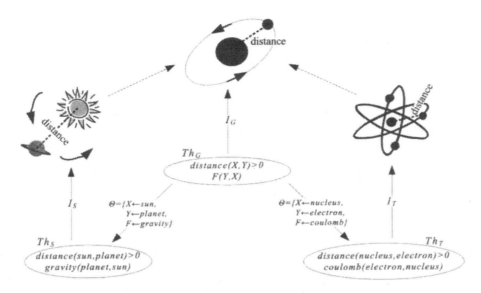

Figure 5: Generalized model for the generalized theory.

nice to relate elements from this generalized model to the models of source and target domain.

The main issue is the understanding of the new variables which are introduced by the generalization process of HDTP-A_h. These variables replace domain specific terms, functions, and predicates. So one can find an interpretation for those variables by looking at the interpretation of the specialization in the domains. This suggests to read the variables introduced in the generalization process as existentially quantified.

The following definition specifies the first construction method of the generalized model based on a quotient operation.

Definition 3 *Assume two models* $\mathfrak{M}_S = \langle D_S, I_S \rangle$ *and* $\mathfrak{M}_T = \langle D_T, I_T \rangle$ *of the source and the target domain are given. The generalized model* $\mathfrak{M}_G = \langle D_G, I_G \rangle$ *is defined via the equivalence relation* $\tilde{R}^\star$ *on* $D_S \cup D_T$ *generated by* $R^\star$ *(i.e. the reflexive, symmetric and transitive hull) such that the following two conditions hold:*

(i) $D_G := (D_S \cup D_T)/\tilde{R}^\star$

(ii) $I_G(t) := \begin{cases} I_S(t) & \text{if } t\Theta_1 \in Term_S \\ I_T(t) & \text{if } t\Theta_2 \in Term_T \end{cases}$

The recursive extension of I_G *to formulas is defined as usual.*

Obviously Definition 3 is well-defined since terms from $Term_S \cap Term_T$ are interpreted identically by I_S and I_T according to the unique name assumption.

The presented construction of a generalized model collapses distinct interpretations of terms t_1, t_2 of one domain if they are analogically related by R to the same term s of the other domain. In other words, equivalence classes are built making such distinct terms indiscernible in the object language. We do not oversee, whether this

is desirable in all settings, although for classical examples of analogy making, e.g. from the domain of physics, this seems to be reasonable. However, in cases where this doesn't seem appropriate, one might choose a different construction method based on products.

Definition 4 *Assume two models* $\mathfrak{M}_S = \langle D_S, I_S \rangle$ *and* $\mathfrak{M}_T = \langle D_T, I_T \rangle$ *of the source and the target domain are given. The generalized model* $\mathfrak{M}'_G = \langle D'_G, I'_G \rangle$ *is defined as follows:*

(i) $D'_G \subseteq D_S \times D_T$

(ii) $I'_G(t) := \langle I_S(t\Theta_1), I_G(t\Theta_2) \rangle$

The recursive extension of I'_G *to formulas is defined as usual.*

The first model construction in Definition 3 is induced by the analogical relation $R^\star$, whereas the second model construction in Definition 4 is induced directly by R, i.e. the syntactically computed substitutions Θ_1 and Θ_2 are used to construct the generalized model.

Some Semantic Properties of HDTP

The application of the algorithm HDTP-A_h to given source and target theories Th_S and Th_T computes a generalized theory Th_G. The generalized theory is based on a language including variables, constants, and predicates from both theories Th_S and Th_T provided they occur in Th_S and Th_T. Furthermore existentially quantified first-order or second-order variables are added to the language for generalizations. Provided we restrict Th_G to the first-order case, the source and target theories result from the generalized theory Th_G by extending the language of Th_G with constants, functions, and predicates. On the other hand, if a source theory Th_S is restricted to the language of Th_G, then every expression derivable from Th_S is also derivable from Th_G. Therefore the following fact can be stated.

Fact 5 *Assume two input theories Th_S and Th_T are given and Th_G is the generalized theory computed by the algorithm HDTP-A_h such that second-order variables do not occur. Then, both theories Th_S and Th_T are conservative extensions of Th_G.*

Notice that in the general case, Th_G allows to quantify over predicate variables, i.e. Th_G is a second-order variant of the first-order theories of the source and target domain. Therefore, from $Th_G \vdash \phi$ it does not follow in general that $Th_S \vdash \phi$.

Concerning the underlying models, we first restrict our considerations again to the first-order case. Given two models $\mathfrak{M}_S$ and $\mathfrak{M}_T$ of the source and the target domain, the following fact is a direct consequence of the Definitions 3 and 4.

Fact 6 *Assume two models $\mathfrak{M}_S$ and $\mathfrak{M}_T$ of the source and the target domain are given. Provided the generalized models $\mathfrak{M}_G = \langle D_G, I_G \rangle$ and $\mathfrak{M}'_G = \langle D'_G, I'_G \rangle$ defined according to Definitions 3 and 4 are first-order models, then $\mathfrak{M}_G$ and $\mathfrak{M}'_G$ can be embedded into $\mathfrak{M}_S$ and $\mathfrak{M}_T$, i.e. the generalized models are substructures of $\mathfrak{M}_S$ and $\mathfrak{M}_T$.*

Whereas $\mathfrak{M}_G$ allows to build equivalence classes of two terms t_1 and t_2 in the source domain that are associated to one term in the target via $R^\star$, t_1 and t_2 remain distinguishable in the construction of $\mathfrak{M}'_G$. Therefore the following fact holds.

Fact 7 *Given generalized models $\mathfrak{M}_G$ and $\mathfrak{M}'_G$ relative to models $\mathfrak{M}_S$ and $\mathfrak{M}_T$ it holds:*

$$\mathfrak{M}_G \models \phi \qquad \Longrightarrow \qquad \mathfrak{M}'_G \models \phi$$

It is possible to loose information of the involved input domains if we compute the quotient construction of Definition 3. It is a question of the particular modeling whether distinct elements of one domain should be kept distinct in all cases or whether we allow to collapse different elements to one equivalence class if they are associated to one element in the other domain.

Final Remarks

HDTP is a theory that allows to compute structural descriptions for first-order theories using a generalization process in order to compute analogical relations. We presented important details of the semantics of HDTP. We continued by adding two construction methods for the generalized model $\mathfrak{M}_G$, one by using a quotient construction and a second one by a product construction. Finally we presented results concerning the underlying model theory of HDTP.

It was shown that the generalized theory and the analogical relation that are established by HDTP-A_h on a purely syntactic basis can be related to model theoretic operations on the semantic level in a coherent manner. Not only the syntactical analogical relation induces a relation between given models for the source and target theory but it is also possible to construct a model for the generalized theory in a canonical way. This general

model in fact reflects the common substructures of the original domain models.

We think that the analysis of the model theoretic semantics of analogical relations will be helpful for developing and improving computational models for analogical reasoning. A better understanding of this type of reasoning can help to model certain types of creativity and to understand and explain certain cognitive capacities of humans.

References

Anderson, J., & Thomson, R. (1989). Use of analogy in a production system architecture. In Vosniadou and Ortony (eds.): *Similarity and analogical reasoning*, pages 267–297, Cambridge, MA.

Dastani, M. (1998). *Languages of Perception*. ILLC Dissertation Series 1998-05, available on the www: http://www.illc.uva.nl/Publications/Dissertations/DS-1998-05.text.ps.gz.

Dastani, M., Scha, R., & Indurkhya, B. (1997). An algebraic method for solving proportional analogy problems involving sequential patterns. In *Mind II: Computational Models of Creative Cognition* Dublin, pp. 1-15.

Falkenhainer, B., Forbus, K., & Gentner, D. (1989). The structure-mapping engine: Algorithm and example. *Artificial Intelligence*, 41(1):1–63.

Gentner, D. (1989). The mechanisms of analogy learning. In Vosniadou and Ortony (eds.): *Similarity and Analogical Reasoning*, pages 199–237, New York, Cambridge University Press.

Gentner, D., Bowdle, B., Wolff, P., & Boronat, C. (2001). Metaphor is like analogy. In Gentner, Holyoak, Kokinov (eds.): *The analogical mind: Perspectives from cognitive science*, pages 199–253, Cambridge, MA.

Gust, H., Kühnberger, K.-U., & Schmid, U. (2003). *Anti-unification of axiomatic systems.*. Available on the www: http://www.cogsci.uni-osnabrueck.de/~helmar/analogy/.

Gust, H. & Kühnberger, K.-U., & Schmid, U. (2006). Metaphors and heuristic-driven theory projection (HDTP). *Theoretical Computer Science*, 354(1):98–117.

Hofstadter, D., & The Fluid Analogies Research Group (1995). *Fluid concepts and creative analogies*. New York.

Indurkhya. B. (1992). *Metaphor and Cognition*. Dordrecht, The Netherlands, Kluver.

Kokinov, B., & Petrov, A. (2001). Integrating memory and reasoning in analogy-making. In Gentner, Holyoak, Kokinov (eds.): *The analogical mind: Perspectives from cognitive science*, pages 59–124, Cambridge, MA.

Plotkin, G. (1970). A note on inductive generalization. *Machine Intelligence*, 5:153–163.

An Attempt to Rebuild Claude Bernard's Scientific Steps

Jean-Gabriel Ganascia (Jean-Gabriel.Ganascia@lip6.fr)

Laboratoire d'informatique de Paris 6; University Pierre and Marie Curie (Paris VI)

104, avenue du Président Kennedy, 75016 Paris FRANCE

Abstract

Our aim is to reconstruct Claude Bernard's empirical investigations with a computational model. We suppose that Claude Bernard had in mind what we call "kernel models" that contain the basic physiological concepts upon which Claude Bernard builds his general physiological theory. The "kernel models" provide a simplified view of physiology, where the internal environment – the so-called "milieu intérieur" –, mainly the blood, plays an essential role. According to this perspective, we assume that the "kernel models" allow Claude Bernard to make some hypotheses and to draw out their logical consequences.

We shall show how those "kernel models" can be specified using both description logics and multi-agent systems. Then, the paper will explain how it is possible to build, on these "kernel models", a virtual experiment laboratory, which lets us construct and conduct virtual experiments that play a role similar to the role of thought experiments. More generally, the paper constitutes an attempt to correlate Claude Bernard's experiments, achieved to corroborate or refute some of his working hypotheses, to virtual experiments emulated on "kernel models".

The CYBERNARD Project

Claude Bernard (1813–1878) was one of the most eminent 19th century physiologists. He was a pioneer in many respects. He introduced the concept of internal environment (the "Milieu intérieur") (Grmek, 1997), which corresponds to today's principle of "homeostasis". He investigated and enlightened many physiological mechanisms, e.g. the glycogenic liver function (Prochiantz, 1990), effects of carbon monoxide, (Bernard, 1864; Grmek, 1973), effects of curare (Bernard, 1857; Bernard, 1864), etc.

But, Claude Bernard was not only a great physiologist; he was also a theoretician who generalized his experimental method in his famous book, "Experimental Medicine" (Bernard, 1927), which is nowadays a classic that all young students in medicine are supposed to have read.

However, there is debate in the epistemology community about the importance of the book. Some think that Claude Bernard revolutionized the physiology while others consider that he is only a great physician who successfully tried to vulgarize his scientific works. In a way, the structure of the book makes this debate possible since the first part exposes abstract principles on which relies a general experimental method, while the second exemplifies the application of the method on discoveries that are mainly derived from Claude Bernard's own work. Therefore, it could be possible to interpret the experimental method as an introduction to the description of Claude Bernard's personal scientific contribution. On the other hand, some philosophers think that the "Experimental Medicine" (Bernard, 1927) played the same role for the 19th and 20th century physiology that the Descartes "Discourse on Method" for the 17th century physical sciences. In modern terms, it originated a "change of paradigm" in experimental medicine. Even if the knowledge of physiological mechanisms is far more detailed today than it was at the Claude Bernard's time and if the statistical techniques make the analysis of experimental data more rigorous, the principles on which relies the methodology of clinical experimentations are based on the same theoretical foundations. It is the argument of those who promote the "Experimental Medicine" as a key contribution for the modern medicine.

The CYBERNARD project aims at contributing to this debate by the achievement of a computer model and by a computer assisted diachronic analysis of Claude Bernard's texts. More precisely, the goal of the CYBERNARD project is twofold. The first is to clarify and to generalize the experimental method by formalizing it with artificial intelligence techniques and by simulating it on computers. It will then be possible to understand in what respect this method is general and can be applied to contemporaneous clinical medicine. Once this first goal will be achieved, we shall attempt synchronous reconstructions of some of the Claude Bernard's scientific discoveries, i.e. reconstructions of the discoveries that he has described at the end of his life, in his large audience papers. The second goal is then to confront the original Claude Bernard's scientific texts – i.e. his personal notes, scientific papers, etc. — to the reconstruction of his own work he made when he wrote the "Experimental Medicine" (Bernard, 1927). Our aim is to understand the effective status of the method described in the "Experimental Medicine": does it correspond to the actual method that Claude Bernard used or to an ideal reconstruction of what it should have been This confrontation can be called a diachronic reconstruction, since it is to compare the own Claude Bernard's latest reconstruction of his work to its effective ideas as they were expressed in his papers and published articles at the time of discovery. Three teams participate to the CYBERNARD project, which is highly interdisciplinary: an artificial intelligence group headed by Jean-Gabriel Ganascia, the ACASA team, belonging to the LIP6 computer science laboratory, the epistemology department of the École Normale Supérieure directed by Claude Debru and the linguistic team of the ITEM laboratory that is specialized in genetic criticism.

This paper relates a preliminary work of the ACASA team that is to build and simulate on computers "kernel models". Within this work, our aim is to reconstruct Claude Bernard's empirical investigation with a computational model that simulates his experimental method. We are mainly interested in his investigations of carbon monoxide and curare effects. To start, we shall refer to two of Claude Bernard's texts, (1857; 1864), where he rationalizes his own discoveries. In parallel, with the help of epistemologists and philologists, we shall confront Claude Bernard's computer reconstruction with his former reasoning as it appeared in his writings. However, this paper focuses only on the first point.

The first part recalls the Claude Bernard's experimental method. The second is dedicated to the description of a two level model build to simulate the experimental method. The third formalizes the Bernard's medical ontology. The fourth describes the notion of "kernel model"; the fifth, the virtual laboratory on the top of which virtual experiments may be done. A sixth section presents the hypothesis generation module. The final and last part envisages possible generalizations of the experimental method and of its simulation to multi-scale "kernel models".

The Experimental Method

According to Claude Bernard's views, scientific investigation cannot be reduced to the sole observation of facts nor to the construction of theories that have not been previously confirmed by empirical evidence. In other words, Claude Bernard is neither an inductivist who reduces the scientific activity to the pure induction of general rules from particulars, nor an idealist – or a neo-Platonist – who thinks that ideal, pure and perfect theories are given before any experimentation. The experimental method he promotes begins with an initial theory, which is usually built from passive observations or preconceived ideas. When the phenomenon is unknown, some experiments "to see" are done.

For instance, when Claude Bernard investigated the effects of the curare, he began with some general experiments in order to see what happened and to provide a first idea. Claude Bernard does not detail the way the first idea or the initial theory is built. It corresponds to an intuition or to what he called a feeling that has to be validated and refined or adjusted according to empirical results generated by relevant experiments. The experimental method starts there.

More precisely, the experimental method described by Claude Bernard is an iterative procedure of theory refinement that proceeds in three steps, each step involving a specific scientific function:

Experimentation: an hypothesis that has to be validated is given. It is called an idea or a theory. For the sake of clarity, we shall refer to it as the *current theory*. The first step is to design an experimental apparatus able to generate observations that can be compared to expectations derived from the current theory. In other words, the experimentation is designed to test the hypothesis under investigation, i.e. the current theory.

Observation: the second step consists in collecting observations from the designed experiments. It is not only a receptive step, since the experimenter may interpret observations and note unexpected details.

Analysis : this third step is the most crucial an original. It is to confront the current theory predictions to the observations and to generate plausible hypotheses that may transform the current theory when its predictions are not in accordance with the experimental observation.

The key question concerns the analysis and, consequently, the hypothesis generation: how, from a set of observations that invalidates a set of theories, would it be possible to generate new theories that will then be evaluated and refined until experiments will fully validate them? That step plays a crucial role in the experimental method. One has to clarify and to generalize it if we want to model and to simulate the method. In other words, designing an experiment to validate or invalidate a theory is a very complicated task that requires intuition, skill and imagination. It is out of the scope of our project to automatize such a design.

On the other hand, the observation is mainly a matter of patience. Nowadays, it may appear that censors and computers could both help looking out and gathering data. Therefore, it is not central to the experimental method that mainly has to analyze observational data and then to generate new theories. Our point is to automate the analysis of experimental results and the hypothesis generation process that corresponds to the most crucial step. We focus on it in this paper. We assume that abduction plays an important role here, since it is to explain experimental results by modifying the current theory.

Abductive reasoning makes generally use of background knowledge on the top of which hypothesis are formulated. Considering all Claude Bernard's hypotheses and revisions, it appears that they had some resemblance; they were formulated using the same words; they seemed to be generated from the same "ontology". In the late reconstruction of his discoveries, Claude Bernard elicited the "ontology" he had in mind. The next section describes it.

The Claude Bernard's Ontology

To have a clear understanding of the Claude Bernard's ontology and of its originality, one has first to cast a glance at previous medical conceptions. Let us first recall that the old theory of fluids introduced by Galen (131–201), during the 2nd century, and very much developed by Santorio Sanctorius (1561–1636) in the early 1600's was prevalent in the 17th and 18th century European medical schools. According to this theory, the body is made of solid tissues and fluids, which naturally tend to become corrupted without excretions and perspiration. As a consequence, most of the diseases and of the body dysfunctions are due to fluid corruption. At the end of the 18th century, inspired by the physics and the chemistry, François–Xavier Bichat (1771–1802) and François Magendie (1783–1855), who was the Claude Bernard's professor, studied the body anatomy and the organs. The physiology was then viewed as a physical interaction between organs. As a consequence, the causes of body dysfunctions and diseases were attributed to organ damages. Post-mortem dissection could then help to diagnose the organs responsible of the diseases. Claude Bernard opposed to this reduction of organs to physical bodies; he thought that organs are not only inert solid tissues, but that each of them has its autonomy and its own functions, which have to be investigated. More precisely, in his writings (cf. (Bernard, 1864; Grmek, 1973)), Claude Bernard presumes that organisms are composed of organs, themselves analogous to organisms since each of them has its own aliments, poisons, excitations, actions etc. Organs are categorized into three classes – skeleton, tissues (e.g. epithelium, glandular tissue or mucous membrane) and fibers (i.e. muscles and nerves) – that are recursively subcategorized into subclasses, sub-subclasses etc. Each class and subclass has its own characteristics, which can easily be formulated, according to Claude Bernard's explanations.

The internal environment – i.e. the "milieu intérieur" –, mainly the blood, carries organ poisons and aliments, while the organ actions may have different effects on other organs and, consequently, on the whole organism. More precisely, for Claude Bernard, the life is synonymous of exchanges. The organisms exchange through the external medium that is the air for outside animals or the water for fish. The external medium may also carry aliments, poisons etc. Similarly, organs can be viewed as some sorts of organisms living in the body and participating to its life. Their life is also governed by exchanges; but the medium that supports exchanges is not air or water; it is the so-called "milieu intérieur", which mainly corresponds to blood. The Claude Bernard's ontology may easily be derived from these considerations. It is then easy to formulate it in an ontology description language.

For instance, below are some of the previous assertions expressed with description logics.

The organs belong to the class Organ and are all parts of the organism:

$$Organ \sqsubseteq \exists PART.Organism \qquad (1)$$

The organs are tissues, skeleton or fibers:

$$Organ \equiv Tissue \sqcup Skeleton \sqcup Fiber \qquad (2)$$

$$Tissue \sqcap Fiber = \perp \qquad (3)$$

$$Tissue \sqcap Skeleton = \perp \qquad (4)$$

$$Fiber \sqcap Skeleton = \perp \qquad (5)$$

Fibers may be nerves or muscles:

$$Fiber \equiv Nerve \sqcup Muscle \qquad (6)$$

Nerves may be sensitive or motor:

$$Nerve \equiv Sensitive\_Nerve \sqcup Motor\_Nerve \qquad (7)$$

Epithelium, glandular tissue, mucous membrane etc. are tissues:

$$Tissue \sqsupseteq Epithelium \sqcup Glandular\_Tissue$$
$$\sqcup Mucous\_Membrane \sqcup \cdots \qquad (8)$$

Each organ can be viewed as some sort of organism that has its own nutriments, its own poisons, its own actions, etc.

$$Organ \sqsubseteq \exists Aliment \qquad (9)$$

$$Organ \sqsubseteq \exists Poison \qquad (10)$$

$$Organ \sqsubseteq \exists Action \qquad (11)$$

$$etc. \qquad (12)$$

The physiological ontology plays a crucial role in the way Claude Bernard erected new hypotheses. It can be considered as a clue for the discovery process. All scientific hypotheses obviously depend on the concepts with which they may be expressed. On the one hand, when a concept is lacking, one may miss some efficient hypotheses; on the other hand, the presence of some useless concepts leads to formulate misleading and confusing explanations. For instance, the old fluid theory precluded the observation of correlations between the evolution of the scurvy disease and the presence of fruit and vegetable in nutriments. Claude Bernard himself was unable to precisely locate the effects of curare, despite his relentless work during more than twenty years; one explanation could be that the concept of motor nerve ending did not belong to his ontology.

The question is how the ontologies are originated? What is their relevancy? And how do they evolve? Up to now, we don't yet feel able to provide fully convincing answers; but our goal within this work is to contribute to get a better understanding of those ontology evolution processes. In the case of Claude Bernard, the ontology here described corresponds to the one he gave at the end of his scientific life, in his large audience papers (e.g. (Bernard, 1864) or (Bernard, 1857)) and books (Bernard, 1927). There is no doubt that it appears naive and wrong with respect to the modern medical knowledge. Nevertheless, the main question for us does not concern its today relevance, but its evolution during Claude Bernard's scientific career.

This paper is focused on the rational reconstruction of Claude Bernard's own discoveries that he achieved by himself when he was famous. Our ultimate goal is to go further and to confront this late and personal reconstruction of Claude Bernard's scientific discoveries to the actual Claude Bernard's discovery process as it appears through informal notes, laboratory books, scientific papers etc.

Two-level Model

As previously stated, abduction played a crucial role in Claude Bernard's investigations. More precisely, he always considered an initial hypothesis, which he called an idea or a theory. He then tried to test it by designing in vivo experiments. According to the observational results of his experiments, he changed his hypotheses, until he reached a satisfying theoretical explanation of empirical phenomena.

"Kernel Models"

To design a computational model that simulates the intellectual pathway leading Claude Bernard to his discovery, we have supposed that he had in mind what we call "kernel models" that contain basic physiological concepts — such as internal environment, organ names etc. — upon which he builds his theories. More precisely, theories correspond to hypothetical organ functions that Claude Bernard want to elucidate, while "kernel models" describe the physical architecture of the organism.

The "kernel models" enable Claude Bernard to hypothesize tentative assumptions and draw out their logical consequences. These "kernel models" constitute the core on which the reasoning process is based; they correspond to putative architectures of the organisms. Depending on the question under investigation, they may be more or less simplified. For instance, if one want to investigate the hart function, it is not necessary to detail the precise role of all muscles. Our aim is to build and to simulate those "Kernel models" using multi-agent architectures. Such simulations have to show, on a simplified view, both the normal behavior of the organism and the consequences of an organ dysfunction.

Working Hypotheses Management

The second level of the considered model manages hypotheses relative to the function of different organs. Each working hypothesis is evaluated through empirical experiments. Claude Bernard assumes that one can use toxic substances as tools of investigation — he evokes the idea of "chemical scalpel" — to dissociate and identify the functions of different organs. He presupposes, as an underlying principle, that each toxic substance neutralizes one organ first. When a toxic substance affects an organ, the anatomy of death shows how the organism behaves without the poisoned organ. Nevertheless, even when laying down such a presupposition, the investigation puzzles lot physiologists, because it is a double entry enigma: they have to elucidate both the organs corrupted by toxic substances and the function of affected organs.

Two questions need to be solved when we want to rationally reconstruct the discovery process: how are working hypotheses generated and how are validating experiments designed? In order to answer these questions, we add to the "kernel model" a working hypothesis management module that has both to guide working hypothesis generation and to design experiments. Once an hypothesis is made, virtual experiments have to simulate, on the top of the "kernel model", the probable observable consequences of this hypothesis, which helps designing real experiments. Such virtual experiments play a role analogous to thought experiments in traditional physics: they are required as a preliminary step to any empirical experiment. For the sake of clarity, let us recall that though experiments are experiences that scientists do not conduct in the outside world, but only in their head. One may attempt to describe some of those though experiments with computer models that can be simulated on computers.

In case of Claude Bernard, we have found in his writings personal notes describing ideas of experiments. Some of them correspond to experiments that have been achieved, while most of them remain imaginary. Our aim is to simulate those ideas of experiments with "kernel models" and to understand the place of those experiments in the discovery process with the hypothesis management module.

"Kernel Model" Simulation

The "kernel models" contain organs and connections between organs through the internal environment, mainly the blood, and direct connections. Both organs — e.g. muscles, hart, lung, nerves etc. — and connections between organs are represented using automata, i.e. entities characterized by their inputs, their outputs and their internal state. A "kernel model" may then be viewed as a network of automata. Each organ corresponds to an automaton with an internal environment plus external or internal excitations as inputs, organ actions and modified internal environment as outputs and a symbol characterizing the state. It is possible, for the internal environment, to lose or gain some substance, for instance oxygen, and some pressure when passing by an organ. In the usual case, e.g. for muscles, the input internal environment corresponds to arterial blood while the output corresponds to venous blood. Most of the connections correspond just to transmitters that associate the outputs of some organs to the inputs of others. Nevertheless, connections may also act as crossing points, for instance, as an artery splitting or as a vein join that divide or concentrate the flow.

From a computational point of view, each organ is viewed as an agent (Russel & Norvig, 1995) that communicates with other organs and evolves in the "milieu intérieur" viewed as the internal environment. As a consequence, the organism is modeled as a synchronous multi-agent system, where each agent has its own inputs, transfer function and states. The organ activation cycle follows the blood circulation. The time is supposed to be discrete and after each period of time, the states of the different automata belonging to the "kernel model" and their outputs are modified.

A first implementation was programmed in JAVA using object oriented programming techniques. It helped both to simulate the "kernel model" evolutions and to conduct virtual experimentations (see next section) on those "kernel models", which fully validates our first ideas concerning the viability of the notion of "kernel model". Within this implementation, organs and connections between organs are associated to objects. The instantiation and inheritance mechanisms facilitate the programming task. However, since our ultimate goal is to simulate the hypothesis generation and especially the abuctive reasoning on which relies the discovery process, we are currently rebuilding "kernel models" using logic programming techniques on which it is easy to simulate logical inferences, whatever they are, either deductive or abductive.

The logic programming implementation of the "kernel model" is programmed in SWI Prolog[1]. It makes use of modules to emulate object oriented programing techniques, i.e. mainly the instantiation, inheritance and message sending mechanisms. The resulting program looks like a collection of modules similar to the one given in figure ??. Each of those modules describes a class of organs, e.g. muscles. Finally, on the top of the inheritance hierarchy of modules, there is a conjunction of literals corresponding to a virtual organism expressed as a network of connected organs. Once an initial condition and some ulterior events are given, it is possible to make the organism evolve by itself and to print states characterizing this evolution.

Virtual "Thought Experiments"

Once the "kernel model" is built, it is not only possible to simulate normal organism behavior, but also to introduce pathologies (i.e. organ deficiencies) in the multi-agent system that models the organism and then emulate its evolution. In a way, these abnormal behavior simulations can be viewed as virtual experiments, or as "thought experiments": they help to draw consequences of virtual situations under a working hypothesis, i.e. a supposition concerning both the effect of a substance on some organs and the function of the implied organs. In order to complete the range of virtual experiments, we introduce, according to Claude Bernard's practices, some virtual experimental operators, such as injection and ingestion of substances, application of tourniquet on members, excitations, etc.

For instance, if one wants to understand the effects of a substance A, one can hypothesize that its concentration in the blood may affect such or such organ subclass that has such or such function in the organism. Under these hypotheses, it is possible with the "kernel model" simulation to predict the consequences of a direct injection of A combined with any combination of experimental operations (applying a tourniquet on a member and/or exciting another part of the organism before or after injecting the substance A etc.). In other words, it is possible to specify virtual experiments and to anticipate the subsequent model behavior under a working hypothesis.

For the sake of clarity, let us consider the experimental device described by Claude Bernard in (1864) with the help of figure 1. In this experiment, Claude Bernard mentioned that curare has been introduced on I while a tourniquet was applied on N. Let us now suppose that one lay down, as a tentative hypothesis, that curare only

[1]See http://www.swi-prolog.org/ for more details

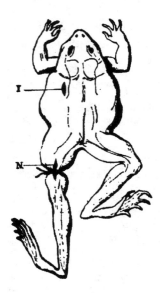

Figure 1: This schema was published by Claude Bernard in (Bernard 1864).

affects the muscles — that corresponds to one of the Claude Bernard hypotheses — but neither the sensitive nerves, nor the motor nerves, then the frog perceives excitations while the muscles belonging to all the organism are unable to move, except those on the right leg, because the tourniquet protects them from the curare effect. Let us now imagine that we excite the right leg on a "kernel model" built to model this experiment. It has to provoke a reaction on the left leg of the "kernel model", while other virtual limbs are not able to move because of the curare effect. This can be deduced from the current hypothesis. The role of the virtual experiment is to automatically generate such evolutions from an adequate "kernel model". One can also envisage to browse all the hypotheses, i.e. all the organ dysfunctions, which could generate the same behaviors. The virtual experiment may then prove the viability of the experiment.

Abduction

The previous section presented the virtual experiment laboratory built over the "kernel model". However, as suggested, the virtual experiments are achieved under working hypotheses that assume, for instance, that a substance A affects such or such a function of such or such an organ class. Being given a toxic substance, one has to explore all the possible hypotheses and, suggest, for each, experiments that could corroborate or refute them by showing observable consequences. It is the role of the working hypothesis management module to investigate all these hypotheses. Nevertheless, the goal is neither to achieve, nor to generate experiments, as would be the case with a robot scientist (see for instance (King & al. 2005)); it is just to reconstruct the scientific steps of Claude Bernard by simulating hypothesis exploration and by providing, for each hypothesis, the key experiments carried out by Claude Bernard.

More precisely, the computer reconstruction of "kernel models" shows that tentative explanations are built on three levels. The first corresponds to the ontological level. As previously said, it is out of the scope of the present study to automatically create new concepts. In a way, the ontology transformation may be assimilated to some kind of paradigm shift. In the future, it may be a very exciting challenge to tackle this problem, but up to now it appears to be premature.

The second level covers hypothetical function of organs. The aim of scientific discovery would undoubtedly be to elucidate the organ function. The study of toxic substance effects may be viewed as a mean to investigate those organ functions. However, today it seems too difficult to automate the generation of those functions. Therefore, we do not focus our study on this point.

Our present goal is more modest: being given a physiological ontology and explicit theories about organ functions, it is to find out the effect of toxic substances. That corresponds to the third level of investigation. More precisely, the computer has to browse all the possible effects of a toxic substance, i.e. all the organs that may be affected by the substance of which we investigate the effects. Under each of the plausible hypotheses, experiments are formulated with "kernel models" that may be simulated on a computer and then confronted to empirical observations. It is then possible either to invalidate or to confirm each of the plausible explanations. Both explorations of all the tentative explanations and attempts to confirm or disconfirm plausible explanations belong to abductive inference processes. Let us note that one can test the consistency of our model, i.e. that one can check that it is in accordance with the empirical evidences as they are mentioned by scientists. Moreover, anotations containing original experiments and observations are associated to each of the plausible hypotheses. It may help epistemologists and historians of science to understand the way scientific investigations were conducted.

Conclusion

A first version of both the "kernel model" and the virtual laboratory are programmed in Java. They allowed us to build virtual experiments associated with different working hypotheses about the toxic effects of carbon monoxide and curare. It was then possible to correlate those virtual experiments to actual experiments done by Claude Bernard, and then to corroborate or refute working hypotheses according to the observations. As a consequence, we are able to computationally reconstruct part of Claude Bernard's intellectual pathway. A second implementation using logic programming techniques is now under construction. The reason is that is seems easier to model abductive reasoning using logic programming than traditional object oriented programming languages. We hope to reproduce the different steps of the Claude Bernard's toxic substance investigations, mainly carbon monoxide and curare.

However, this work relies on a fixed ontology, which biases the investigation and may prevent discovery. For instance, Claude Bernard's study of curare's toxic effect was precluded by the absence of the motor nerve ending concept. Our further research will concern the way the "kernel models" evolved in Claude Bernard's research, especially the way both the Claude Bernard's ontology and the hypotheses concerning the different organ functions were transformed during Claude Bernard's scientific life. The detailed study of Claude Bernard's personal writings and scientific papers with genetic criticism techniques will help us in such an investigation.

We also investigate the possibility to build multi-scale "kernel models" in which physiological behaviors can be studied at different scales — organ, cell, molecule etc. —. It should open new perspectives to modern clinical medicine. As a matter of fact, principles on which lay down Claude Bernard empirical method are always valid, even if the "kernel models" considerably changed with time. Today, the effect of new substances is usually studied at the cell or molecule scale, while the organ scale was dominant at Claude Bernard's epoch. A model that could help to simulate the consequences of physiological dysfunctions at different levels would be of great help to determine the effects of new substances by recording different experiments and by ensuring that all the plausible hypotheses that have already been explored.

Acknowledgments

I wish to thank Claude Debru and Jean-Louis Lebrave who helped me in my attempts to understand Claude Bernard's scientific work.

References

Bernard, C. (1927), *An Introduction to the Study of Experimental Medicine*, First English translation by Henry Copley Greene, Macmillan & Co., Ltd.

Bernard, C. (1864), *Études physiologiques sur quelques poisons américains*, Revue des deux mondes, *Vol. 53*, 164–190.

Bernard, C. (1857), *Leçon sur les effets des substances toxiques et médicamenteuses*, Cours de médecine du collège de France, J.-B. Baillière et Fils.

King, R., Whelan, K., Jones, F., Reiser, P., Bryant, C. & Muggleton, S. (2005), *Functional genomic hypothesis generation and experimentation by a robot scientist*, Nature, Vol. 427, 247–252.

Grmek, M. (1991), *Claude Bernard et La méthode Expérimentale*, Paris, Payot.

Grmek, M. (1997), *Le legs de Claude Bernard*, Fayard.

Grmek, M. (1973), *Raisonnement expérimental et recherches toxicologiques chez Claude Bernard*, Genève, Droz.

Russel, S. & Norvig, P. (1995), *Artificial Intelligence a Modern approach*, Series in Artificial Intelligence, Prentice Hall.

Prochiantz, A. (1990), *Claude Bernard: la révolution physiologique*, Paris, Presses Universitaires de France.

Analogical Reasoning with SMT and HDTP

Angela Schwering, Ulf Krumnack, Kai-Uwe Kühnberger, Helmar Gust
{aschweri | krumnack | kkuehnbe | hgust}@uos.de
Institute of Cognitive Science University of Osnabrück; Albrechtstr. 28
49076 Osnabrück, Germany

Abstract

Analogical reasoning is one of the most important inference mechanisms humans use for creating new knowledge and for learning. This paper introduces two approaches for analogical reasoning: the structure mapping theory (SMT) as a graph-based analogy model and the Heuristic-Driven Theory Projection (HDTP) as a symbolic model. We describe both approaches, outline their commonalities and differences and discuss their impact on analogy making and analogical reasoning.

Introduction and Motivation

Analogical thinking and reasoning has often been identified as the core cognitive process for creativity, discovery and invention. "Analogy is indeed an indispensable and inevitable tool for scientific progress" [Oppenheimer, 1956].

Besides classical methods for logical inferences - deduction, induction and abduction - analogies function as the main driver for creating new knowledge and for learning. In analogical reasoning, two cases - a source and a target - are compared and commonalities are identified. New knowledge is created via transferring additional knowledge about the source case to the target case. Figure 1 illustrates the formal structure of the different types of reasoning. While a deductive inference is truth-preserving, inductive, abductive and analogical inferences are not. But the likeliness of inductive inferences increases with the number of valid cases. Therefore the set of cases must be sufficiently large to draw sound conclusions. However, analogical reasoning requires only two cases: the likeliness of analogical inferences increases with the number of analogical matches between the source and the target [Ujomov, 1967]. In principle, φ can be any kind of formula. However, since analogies are characterized via structural commonalities [Gentner and Markman, 1997], φ stands typically for structural relations and laws.

This paper represents two analogy models: Gentner's structure mapping theory (SMT) and the Heuristic-Driven Theory Projection (HDTP). We describe both methods for analogical reasoning and outline their commonalities and differences. Our comparison was motivated by the paper by [Ifukor, 2005] who compares both approaches and concludes by proposing a combination of both.

Deduction	Abduction	Induction	Analogical Inference	
$p \rightarrow q$	$p \rightarrow q$	$\varphi(case_1)$	source:	$\varphi_1,...,\varphi_n, \varphi_{n+1}$
p	q	$\vdots$ $\varphi(case_n)$	target:	$\varphi_1,...,\varphi_n$
q	p	$\forall x: \varphi(x)$	target:	φ_{n+1}

Figure 1: Reasoning types.

The remainder of the paper is organized as follows: in the second section we review SMT and analyze the different phases it runs through to map the analogy. The third section introduces HDTP, a mathematically sound framework for analogy identification and analogical reasoning. Afterwards we point out the commonalities and differences of HDTP and SMT. We use the Rutherford analogy between the solar system and the atom model as running example. The last section summarizes the results.

Structure Mapping Theory

Gentner's Structure Mapping Theory [Gentner, 1983, Gentner, 1989, Falkenhainer et al., 1989] is probably the best known analogy model and had great formative influence on analogy research. SMT claims that analogies between domains are characterized by structural and relational commonalities, while superficial attribute similarity is of no or minor importance.

SMT uses graph structures to describe domains and supports four different representational elements: Entities are individuals in the domain, functions map entities to some value, attributes are unary predicates describing properties of an entity and relations are n-ary predicates describing the relationship of its arguments.

The analogy identification process follows three principles: The *one-to-one mapping* allows one element in the target to map maximally to one single element in the source and vice versa. *Parallel connectivity* states that the arguments of two aligning relations or functions in the source and target domain have to align as well to guarantee structural consistency. The *systematicity principle* states that an element belonging "to a mappable system of mutually interconnecting relationships is more likely to be imported into the target than is an isolated predicate" [Gentner, 1983, p. 163]. SMT supports analogies which comprise a hierarchically deep match, because this indicates a structural system of in-

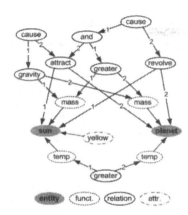

Figure 2: SMT formalization of the solar system domain (1 indicates the first and 2 the second argument of relations).

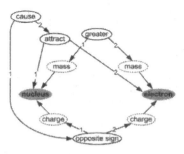

Figure 3: SMT formalization of the Rutherford atom domain.

terconnected knowledge.

Identification of Analogies. The identification of analogies in SMT is a stepwise process: *local match construction* identifies all pairwise matching elements. Entities are matched indirectly "on the basis of their roles in the predicate structure" [Falkenhainer et al., 1989, p. 15]. While entities and functions can be aligned without matching literally, the alignment of attributes and relations requires identical labels. The alignment of elements is a parallel process and results in a set of potentially matching items (called match hypotheses). Afterwards, local matches are combined in one coherent composition: the *partial match* builds partial mappings which consists of a local match hypotheses and all other match hypotheses structurally implied by the parallel connectivity. The *global match construction* composes gradually larger mappings which combine consistent match hypotheses to construct the best inter-domain mapping. In figure 2, the relation "and" implies the lower-order relations "attract" and "greater", because they are its arguments and higher-order relation "cause", because "and" is itself an argument of "cause". There may exit several, competing analogies with different cognitive plausibili-

types
　　real, *object*, *time*

entities
　　sun : *object*, *planet* : *object*

functions
　　mass : *object* × *time* → *real* × {*kg*}
　　dist : *object* × *object* × *time* → *real* × {*m*}
　　gravity : *object* × *object* × *time* → *real* × {*N*}
　　centrifugal : *object* × *object* × *time* → *real* × {*N*}

facts
　　$mass(sun) > mass(planet)$
　　$\forall t : time : gravity(planet, sun, t) > 0$
　　$\forall t : time : dist(planet, sun, t) > 0$
　　$revolves\_around(planet, sun)$

laws

　　$\forall t : time, o_1 : object, o_2 : object :$
　　$dist(o_1, o_2, t) > 0 \wedge gravity(o_1, o_2, t) > 0$
　　$\rightarrow \exists force : force(o_1, o_2, t) < 0 \wedge$
　　$force(o_1, o_2, t) = centrifugal((o_1, o_2, t)$
　　$\forall t : time, o_1 : object, o_2 : object :$
　　$dist(o_1, o_2, t) > 0 \wedge centrifugal(o_1, o_2, t) < 0$
　　$\rightarrow revolves\_around(o_1, o_2)$

Figure 4: HDTP formalization of solar system domain.

ties.

Analogical Reasoning. Analogies are typically drawn between two domains, where a lot of information is available about the source while many relational and attributive properties are still unknown in the target domain. New knowledge about the target domain is created based on the analogy to the source domain. The representation of the source domain is therefore richer than the representation of the target domain. Analogical reasoning in SMT denotes the process of transferring the information which does not exist in the target domain. All those relations or functions in the source domain which have not been aligned are possible inferences. SMT proposes relations or functions as analogical inferences and carries them over to the target domain, if they satisfy parallel connectivity and one-to-one mapping and if they are structurally grounded within the analogy (the inference must intersect the global mapping). Constants are mapped directly.

Heuristic-Driven Theory Projection

Heuristic-Driven Theory Projection [Gust et al., 2006] is a mathematically sound model for processing analogies. The source and target domain are described by theories based on full first-order logic. Analogous expressions in both domains are aligned via a common, general theory: this general theory is the result of the anti-unification of source and target theory. While the above described Structure Mapping Theory is a psychologically motivated graph-based approach for analogy making, HDTP is a formal logic-based symbolic approach.

In HDTP, the representation of source and target domain consists of a set of formulas. The representation comprises the following elements (figure 4): constants

types
    real, object, time

entities
    nucleus : object, electron : object

functions
    $mass : object \times time \rightarrow real \times \{kg\}$
    $dist : object \times object \times time \rightarrow real \times \{m\}$
    $electric\_charge : object \times real \rightarrow real \times \{eV\}$
    $coulomb : object \times object \times time \rightarrow real \times \{N\}$

facts
    $mass(nucleus) > mass(electron)$
    $electric\_charge(electron) < 0$
    $electric\_charge(nucleus) > 0$
    $\forall t : time : coulomb(electron, nucleus, t) > 0$
    $\forall t : time : dist(electron, nucleus, t) > 0$

Figure 5: HDTP formalization of Rutherford atom model.

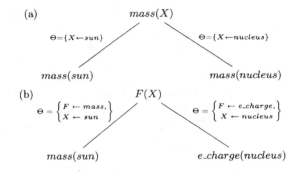

Figure 6: Anti-Unification of terms.

describe entities in the domain. Each constant is of a certain type, e.g. sun of type entity and the mass of the sun of the type real. Variables are placeholders for entities and occur in laws. Function symbols represent functions that map entities or variables to other entities. Predicates express relations between entities: unary predicates correspond to attributes in SMT and n-ary correspond to relations. Logical operators and the quantifiers $\exists$ and $\forall$ are available to construct complex facts and laws.

A theory Th describing a domain is a consistent and finite set of well-formed formulas - either facts or laws. Facts are variable-free literals, called axioms; laws are quantified formulas. Figure 4 shows Th_S, the specification of the solar system domain, and figure 5 shows Th_T, the specification of the Rutherford atom. HDTP identifies analogies via comparing formulas of Th_T to formulas of Th_S to find a common, general formula for two corresponding formulas. The theory of anti-unification is used for generalizing two formulas.

Anti-Unification for Generalization. Anti-unification [Plotkin, 1970] is a theory for determining the most specific generalization for two terms and is used to generate a general structural description of the commonalities between both domains. HDTP uses an extension of anti-unification [Gust et al., 2003]:

- First-order anti-unification: two formulas $p(a)$ and $p(b)$ are anti-unified by $p(X)$, where the variable X is substituted by a respectively b.

- Second-order anti-unification: two formulas $p_1(a)$ and $p_2(a)$ are anti-unified by $P(a)$, where the general predicate P is substituted by p_1 respectively p_2.

Figure 6 illustrates some examples for anti-unification from the Rutherford analogy. The axiom $mass(nucleus)$ can be aligned to $mass(sun)$ and generalized to $mass(X)$. If $e\_charge(nucleus)$ is aligned to $mass(sun)$, the anti-instance $F(X)$ is very general, because there are not many commonalities. Therefore HDTP prefers generalization (a) to (b). The anti-unification can be ap-

plied to laws as well: atomic formulas are anti-unified as shown above and logical symbols are maintained. We transform all formulas in a normal form to avoid that compatible formulas cannot be matched because of syntactic differences.

Identification of Analogies. The identification of analogies in HDTP is an iterative process: the algorithm goes through all axioms in one domain and searches for corresponding formulas in the other domain to anti-unify both formulas. These general formulas form together the axioms for a generalized theory Th_G which represents the commonalities of source and target at an abstract level. Like in SMT, there may be competing alignments of axioms in HDTP which may lead to different analogies. The alignment process in HDTP follows several heuristics analogous to the "three principles" of SMT: Logical consistency with other axioms in the generalized theory is a necessary condition for two axioms being aligned and their generalization being added to Th_G. HDTP does not require one-to-one mapping, however it always aims at the most specific generalization which best reflects the structure of both specific axioms. In most cases this will be a one-to-one mapping. An example for a reasonable one-to-many mapping in the Rutherford analogy is the alignment of the gravity force between sun and planet with the two forces gravity and coulomb between the nucleus and the electron: gravity as well as coulomb are both attracting forces. Since the coulomb force between nucleus and electrons is much stronger than the gravity force between them (and therefore the coulomb force is the main reason for holding together the atom), it is important to include the coulomb force in the analogy.

To find the most reasonable analogy between both domains, HDTP has to evaluate the quality of the alignment. This process is driven by several heuristics: Since the alignment process in HDTP is sequential, there is a heuristic for determining the order in which axioms are chosen to find an alignable match. Another heuristic determines the generalization to a least general anti-instance. Those generalizations are preferred that conserve as much information and structure as possible, because every generalization implies information loss. Moreover, the substitutions required to transform a generalized to a specific axiom shall be as simple as possible, because the complexity of substitutions indicates the degree of structural divergence. Moreover, second-order substitutions shall be avoided. In SMT, only identical attributes and relations are aligned. HDTP allows also the alignment of distinct predicates, however the alignment of identical predicates (i.e. first-order substitution) is preferred. Furthermore, axioms that maximize the number of shared terms with already generalized axioms are preferred, because they show a strong alignment with the already identified part of the analogy.

Analogical Inference and Reasoning. In general, analogical reasoning means transferring additional knowledge about the source to the target domain: in HDTP this means transfer of formulas. The specification of the source domain is typically richer than the one of the target domain: additional knowledge about the source is represented by those formulas which have not been aligned to formulas in the target and which are therefore not part of the generalized theory. The transfer of formulas underlies several restrictions:

- Formulas can be transferred, if they have not been aligned so far, however, the existing generalizations guide the transfer. Formulas must be connected to the generalized theory (e.g. an argument of the predicate is already generalized) and the generalization of this formula must be logically consistent with the existing generalized theory.

- Transferred formulas are proven for logical consistency within the target domain (and if exists, also with background knowledge). Inconsistent formulas cannot be transferred.

- The strength of HDTP is its ability to transfer laws. In our example we know from the source domain, that there must exist some counter-force, if two attracting objects have a positive distance. Laws can be transferred, if the premise (in this case $\forall t : time, o_1 : object, o_2 : object : dist(o_1, o_2, t) > 0 \land gravity(o_1, o_2, t) > 0$) can be proven as true also in the target domain.

- Besides logical consistency, transferred knowledge can also be tested within experiments. Based on the set of possible inferences experiments are generated in order to test whether analogical transfers yield experimentally valid results. One of these experiments is essentially an abstract representation of the Rutherford experiment, i.e. an experiment that shows that electrons and nucleus have a distance from each other greater than 0.

If inference candidates meet all these requirements, they are transferred and added to the target domain.

Commonalities and Differences

Structure mapping theory and Heuristic-Driven Theory Projection are two theories for analogy making and analogical reasoning. There are many parallels between both theories. They both identify potential analogies, which are characterized by structural commonalities of two domains: a source and the target domain. While lot of knowledge is available about the source domain, only little knowledge is available about the target domain. Once a potential mapping is identified, additional knowledge from the source can be transferred to the target domain as analogical inference. However, the approaches differ as well with respect to their motivation, the knowledge representation formalism, the alignment and the analogical reasoning.

Motivation. The Structure Mapping Theory is a psychologically motivated approach and reflects the cognitive processes during analogy making. The cognitive adequacy was tested in many experiments. HDTP is a mathematically sound model. It is based on a logical language in the tradition of artificial intelligence. Both approaches consider abstraction to play a central role in human analogy making: SMT uses abstraction implicitly in the graph comparison process. HDTP accounts explicitly for the generalization process and constructs a generalized theory. Th_G is the generalized theory describing the common structures of the source and the target domain. It can be interpreted separately from the source and target: in the Rutherford analogy the generalized theory of the solar system and the atom can be interpreted as a central force system [Gust et al., 2007].

Representation. SMT uses finite graphs to represent domain knowledge. Concrete and abstract entities of the domain, as well as relations, are represented as nodes of a graph. This formalization is appropriate to represent given situations in accordance with psychological findings. HDTP is based on formal logic and reasoning techniques, that are standard in artificial intelligence applications and theoretically well-founded. Besides entities, functions and predicates, which are also available in SMT, knowledge can be specified using variables, logical operators and quantifiers. As a benefit, HDTP can not only represent a certain situation, but it can apply general laws like *every two bodies with positive mass will attract each other*. It might be possible to simulate one representation formalism within the other. E.g. it is easy to encode finite graphs in first-order logic. However, it is an open task to examine how such a simulation can be extended to the rest of the analogy engine.

Identification of Analogies. The alignment process in SMT is mainly driven by common relations and functions, while attributes are neglected. HDTP includes all formulas in the analogy identification process.

SMT aligns relations only if they match literally. Functions can be aligned to other functions independently of their label. HDTP matches functions and predicates with same and different labels, but anti-instances for identical functions and predicates are more specific than for different ones (see figure 6 (a) for identical and (b) for different ones). The same holds for structural differences: in SMT only elements with the same structure align (or they require re-representation, see below). HDTP matches also formulas with different structure, which might end up in a very generic anti-instance. In general, SMT tends to align too few elements, because the requirement of having identical relation names is very strict. Lately research in SMT has identified, that non-identical, but semantically overlapping relations are also relevant for analogy making [Gentner and Kurtz, 2006]. SMT could apply ontological knowledge to ease the restrictions for alignment and allow also similar relations to align. On the other hand, HDTP tends to align too many formulas. To avoid nonsense alignments and compensate the weak restrictions, HDTP introduces additional constraints such as including the type information in the mapping: only entities of the same type may align.

The alignment process has different restrictions: SMT alignment follows the three principles one-to-one mapping, parallel connectivity and systematicity. HDTP supports the idea of one-to-one mapping in the heuristic, but does not reject alignable formulas which violate the one-to-one mapping criteria. The major restriction of HDTP alignment is logical consistency: an alignment is only accepted, if the generalized formula is consistent with the rest of the generalized theory.

SMT as well as HDTP identify competing analogies and try to evaluate which one is the best. The main criteria in SMT is systematicity. Higher-order relations indicate a better analogy. In HDTP, the criteria depend mainly on the heuristics applied. It is possible to imitate SMT's systematicity principle in the heuristic.

Alignment in SMT is a stepwise process: first, the elementary elements are aligned and afterwards they are combined to partial and global mappings. HDTP anti-unifies not only axioms, but whole theories, i.e. axioms of the target theory are mapped on expressions which are either explicit axioms in the source theory or inferred from it. This process is called re-representation: differences due to different representations are handled by the system via converting formulas in logically equivalent and structurally matching formulas. The importance of automatic re-representation can be illustrated within the Rutherford analogy: We assume that the gravity force between sun and planets is not given explicitly in the source domain, but only a general law stating that there exists an attracting force between two solids with positive mass. On the target side, the nucleus is described as having a positive electric charge, the electron having a negative electric charge and a general law states that two elements with an opposite charge attract each other. SMT uses finite graphs to represent domain knowledge and has no elaborated framework that allows for restructuring graphs. It might be possible to introduce such general laws as nodes into an SMT style graph and state *the sun attracts the planet because of the law of gravitation*. But such statements have to be coded explicitly when setting up the domain representations and there is no way to deduce them when they are missing. Opposing to this, HDTP can apply rules to deduce new formulas from the axioms. That is, it can make implicit knowledge explicit when it is needed during the process of analogy making. HDTP can automatically deduce on both sides, that there exists an attracting force - the gravity force on the source and the coulomb force on the target side. This ability equips HDTP in a rather nat-

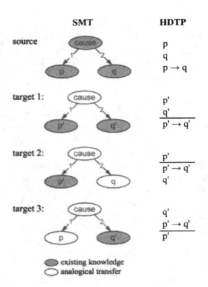

Figure 7: Inferences in SMT and corresponding inferences in HDTP.

ural way with the ability to do re-representation, namely the deduction of appropriate formulas, whenever they are required. SMT may be able to overcome structural differences to a certain extend, but SMT itself cannot prove the logical equivalence: an additional component such as a theorem prover is required.

Analogical Inference and Reasoning. The analogical inference is not an inference in the classical sense: analogical inference means the transfer of knowledge from a source domain to a new domain. SMT and HDTP both support analogical inferences. SMT transfers knowledge, which is "connected" to the analogy (i.e. the transfer must be related to the existing alignment) and is structurally consistent (according to the three principles). HDTP transfers formulas, if they are connected with the analogy (the generalized theory) and if they are logically consistent with the generalized theory, the target theory and the background knowledge.

The transfer of laws is one of the major differences of the system: figure 7 illustrates possible inferences in SMT and corresponding inferences in HDTP. In SMT, rules are modeled as a cause relations between the premise and the conclusion which are treated as two equal arguments. In our example, SMT specifies the source domain by the elements p and q and a cause relation between them. In HDTP, p and q are facts and the relation between them is logically specified as the law $p \rightarrow q$. The following three cases show three different target domain specifications with different analogical inferences:

1. Transfer of rule: the target domain contains p' and q'. In SMT, the cause relation is transferred to the target domain. The same is done in HDTP: p and p' are anti-unified as well as q and q'. The law $p \rightarrow q$ is

transferred and the analogous law $p' \rightarrow q'$ is added to the target domain specification.

2. Deduction by analogy: the target domain contains p'. When p is aligned with p', SMT transfers the cause relation and the second argument q to the target domain. In HDTP, p is anti-unified with p'. The law can be transferred, because the premise is logically consistent in the target domain. Having the analogous law $p' \rightarrow q'$ on the target side, the new axiom q' can either be inferred via deduction or analogical transfer.

3. Abduction by analogy: in SMT, the target domain does only contain q'. Like before, SMT transfers the cause relation and p regardless of the fact that cause relation actually holds only from the premise to the conclusion. In HDTP, the target domain is specified as q' and the law $p' \rightarrow q'$. q' and the law can be anti-unified. HDTP proposes to transfer p', but does check the consistency of p'. If the target domain contains a fact $\neg p'$ there will be no transfer in HDTP. SMT could not detect such logical inconsistency.

Since cause is a binary relation and SMT does not support variables as placeholders, it is impossible to have a cause relation with only one argument - e.g. only the premise - and transferring only the conclusion. SMT can model only instantiated laws, i.e. cause relations between concrete entities. However, HDTP can specify laws without making a statement about the truth of premise or conclusion. As the example showed, SMT can model different types of inferences, however it cannot explicitly distinguish between these different types, neither check consistency with other formula. This difference between SMT and HDTP becomes obvious in the third case of our example.

Summary

SMT and HDTP are two models for analogical reasoning. SMT uses a graph-based representation and identifies analogies via graph comparison and matching. HDTP represents the source and target domain via first-order logic theories. Analogies are identified via comparing both theories and constructing a common, general theory. Therefore domain representations in SMT are less expressive than in HDTP. SMT follows as well a rather restrictive alignment process and therefore the analogy making process has a comparatively low complexity and is very efficient. First-order logic theories in HDTP allow for a greater expressivity than graphs in SMT, because it allows for variables and logical symbols. Using the extended anti-unification to construct the generalized theory and identify the analogy is more flexible than SMT, e.g. also relations with different labels and different structure can be aligned and anti-unified. The analogical inference mechanisms differ as well: While SMT constrains the transfer of non-aligned subgraphs based on structural consistency, HDTP distinguishes different forms of inferences and requires logical consistency of transferred formulas. We think that the optimal solution for analogy making is a trade-off between efficiency and expressivity.

Acknowledgement
We thank the four anonymous reviewers for their valuable comments. The work has been supported by the German Research Foundation (DFG) through the project "Modeling of predictive analogies by Heuristic-Driven Theory Projection" (grant KU1949/2-1). The publication was supported by the Universitätsgesellschaft Osnabrück.

References

[Falkenhainer et al., 1989] Falkenhainer, B., Forbus, K. D., and Gentner, D. (1989). The structure-mapping engine: Algorithm and examples. *Artificial Intelligence*, 41(1):1–63.

[Gentner, 1983] Gentner, D. (1983). Structure-mapping: A theoretical framework for analogy. *Cognitive Science*, 7(2):155–170.

[Gentner, 1989] Gentner, D. (1989). The mechanism of analogical learning. In Vosniadou, S. and Ortony, A., editors, *Similarity and analogical reasoning*, pages 199–241. Cambridge University Press, New York, USA.

[Gentner and Kurtz, 2006] Gentner, D. and Kurtz, K. J. (2006). Relations, object, and the composition of analogies. *Cognitive Science*, 30:1–34.

[Gentner and Markman, 1997] Gentner, D. and Markman, A. B. (1997). Structure mapping in analogy and similarity. *American Psychologist*, 52(1):45–56.

[Gust et al., 2007] Gust, H., Krumnack, U., Kühnberger, K.-U., and Schwering, A. (2007). An approach to the semantics of analogical relations. In *2nd European Cognitive Science Conference*, Delphi, Greece.

[Gust et al., 2003] Gust, H., Kühnberger, K.-U., and Schmid, U. (2003). Anti-unification of axiomatic systems. Technical report, Institute for Cognitive Science, University of Osnabrück.

[Gust et al., 2006] Gust, H., Kühnberger, K.-U., and Schmid, U. (2006). Metaphors and heuristic-driven theory projection (HDTP). *Theoretical Computer Science*, 354(1):98–117.

[Ifukor, 2005] Ifukor, P. A. (2005). Modelling the mapping mechanism in metaphors. *Journal of Cognitive Science*, 6(1):21–44.

[Oppenheimer, 1956] Oppenheimer (1956). Analogy in science. *American Psychologist*, 11:127–135.

[Plotkin, 1970] Plotkin, G. D. (1970). A note on inductive gneralization. *Machine Intelligence*, 5:153–163.

[Ujomov, 1967] Ujomov, A. I. (1967). Die Hauptformen und -regeln der Analogieschlüsse. In Ruzavin, G. I., editor, *Studien zur Logik der wissenschaftlichen Erkenntnis*, pages 307–360. Akademie-Verlag, Berlin.

Unsupervised learning of an embodied representation for action selection

Aapo Hyvärinen

Dept of Computer Science and HIIT
University of Helsinki, Finland

Abstract

We propose a principle on how a computational agent can learn the structure of a classic discrete state space. The idea is to do a kind of principal component analysis on a matrix describing transitions from one state to another. This transforms the space of discrete, completely separate, states into a dimensional representation in a Euclidean space. The representation supports action selection, ideally turning action selection into a trivial problem: the route to a goal state can be directly obtained from the representation. Thus, the computations typically performed by dynamic programming and reinforcement learning are largely replaced by learning the representation. This has the benefit that the representation is not dependent on which state happens to be the goal state; thus, change of goal does not necessitate re-learning, which is in stark contrast to classic reinforcement learning theory.

Introduction

How to find the best course of action? This is the fundamental computational question in embodied cognitive science. Typically, the problem is considered in the framework of reinforcement learning (Sutton and Barto, 1998; Dayan and Abbott, 2001). In the basic setting, the agent finds itself in a state, in which it has a number of actions available. The agent selects an action, and depending on which one it selected, it receives a reward, a punishment, or none. The action taken also determines the new state in which the agent finds itself in the next time step. In the simplest case, a reward is obtained only in a single state, the goal state. For example, a rat might be running around in a maze, and a small portion of cheese is found in a particular location.

Planning and dynamic programming are the two basic approaches to selecting the optimal action. These are closely related to the distinction between model-based and model-free reinforcement learning. If a model of the world is available, one can simply simulate the effects of different actions according to that model, and choose the one that leads to the reward or goal. The problem here, as already realized in classic artificial intelligence, is that the simulation may have to be many steps long before any reward is obtained (it takes some running to get to the cheese), and the number of action sequences to be simulated grows exponentially as a function of the number of steps. Thus, various kinds of partial search strategies have to be developed. The model-free alternative is

to compute only the "values" of states[1] or state-action pairs, based on the principle of dynamic programming. The drawback is that such learning tends to be very slow, presumably because it attempts to operate with minimum knowledge of the structure of the world.

We propose here to approach action selection from the viewpoint of finding a suitable representation of the world, i.e. the set of states. This is is stark contrast to the classic theory of reinforcement learning, in which the question of representation is rather much reglected (though see (Dayan, 1993)). In the classic theory, the world is represented as a finite set of different states which are separate and unconnected from each other; or, a representation is given *a priori*, such that the values are computed as linear functions.

We propose a computational theory in which the agent learns a continuous-valued representation of the discrete-state world, and this representation enables a very simple model-based action selection mechanism. More specifically, the learned representation tells the agent which states are "close" to each other in the sense that the states can be reached from each other in a small number of steps. This solves most of the problem of "How to get to state j from state i". Planning is reduced to simply always choosing that action, among the alternatives immediately available, which leads to the new state with minimum distance from the goal. Thus, the exponential explosion in planning is completely avoided.

Learning in our system is unsupervised in the sense that it does not use any kind of reinforcement signal: only observations of state-action sequences. Thus, the learned representation is not bound to any single goal; in general it does not depend on which action in which state gives reward or punishment. This is again in stark contrast to classic (model-free) reinforcement learning, in which the goal is fixed once and for all (but see (Daw et al., 2005)). Thus, if the goal is changed (e.g. the cheese is given in another part of the maze), the learned value functions become useless, and learning has to be started all over again. In our learning system, as long as the state-action structure does not change (e.g. the maze does not change), no re-learning is needed, which gives it great flexibility. Our framework is also applicable to any problem domain, in contrast to some related work which consider navigation only.

---

[1]i.e. expected reinforcements when starting from that state and following an optimal policy

Learning the Representation

Basic principle

Consider a simple graphical representation of the world as a graph (see Fig. 1 a), where each state corresponds to a node, and each possible transition from one state to another, by a single action, is represented as an arc connecting those two nodes. The agent finds itself in one of the nodes, and selects an action by a method to be specified. The agent then moves along one of the arcs, and finds itself in that new node at the next time point. The agent knows a priori the immediate results of its actions, i.e. to which node it will move after a given action at a given state. What the agent observes is the number (or some other label) of the state in which it is: the states are numbered according to some arbitrary way. There is a single goal state: when the agent moves to that state, it receives a reward.

The agent knows which state is the goal. However, as is typical in reinforcement learning, the agent does not know how to get to that state. From an intuitive viewpoint, the computational problem is that the agent does not have any way of knowing how to get "closer" to the goal because it has no notion of distance.

The first part of our proposal is that it is possible to learn a notion of distance in this setting. The basic principle is that the agent observes that it is now in state j and that it was, in the previous time step, in state i. Thus, it can observe which states are "close" to each other in the sense that it is possible to move from state i to state j in a single step. Observing many state-to-state transitions, the agent could in principle just use the minimum number of steps required to move from state i to state j as a measure of distance between states i and j. The second part of our proposal is a computational scheme which learns something like this but with computational advantages.

Once the agent knows how to compute such a distance, action selection becomes rather trivial. First, the agent computes the distance to the goal state from all states to which the agent can go in one step. Second, the agent chooses the action which leads to the state minimizing that distance. (In practice, it may be necessary to introduce some randomness in this choice because the distance is learned only approximately.) Thus, the action of the agent typically reduces the distance at each step and eventually the agent will reach the goal.

Such computation of distance could, in principle, be achieved by classic shortest-path algorithms. However, it would demand a lot of computation, and possibly memory as well, to actually compute such distances for all the candidate states to which the agent might want to move. Thus, we propose to learn a dimensional representation for the points, i.e. to associate each state with a point in an n-dimensional real space. The distance between two points can then be simply computed as the Euclidean distance (sum of the differences of squares) of those representational points. Such a distance can be very quickly computed when needed, and the system only needs to store the n coordinates for each state; n is typically rather small, perhaps even one or two.

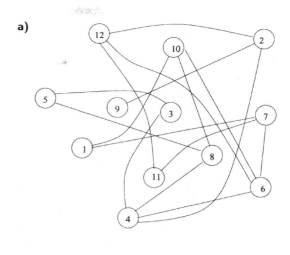

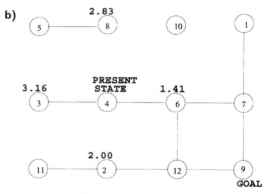

Figure 1: Representing states properly can make action selection trivial. a) A graph which represents the world so that each state is a node and each arc between two nodes means that there is an action which takes the agent from one state to the other. For simplicity of illustration, it is assumed in this figure that actions are reversible, so the arc can be travelled in both direction. (This representation does not show which action corresponds to which arc.) b) If the states can be arranged on a two-dimensional plane (or any other simple part of an n-dimensional real space), one can compute the distance of two nodes in that representation and use that as a guide to action selection. In particular, if the goal node is number 9 (bottom right-hand corner), and the present state is number 4, the Euclidean distances computed for the nodes to which one can move from the present node (shown next to those nodes) indicate that the agent should move down or right (the Euclidean distance favours "right" here but this is not the case for all distances).

Intuitively, it is clear how much the problem is simplified if instead of a general graph, the states can be arranged as grid of points on a two-dimensional plane (Fig. 1 b) so that the actions correspond to moving up, down, left or right. In fact, the graph in Fig. 1 a) can be arranged so. The agent can now use some notion of distance which is closely related to the conventional distance of the nodes on the graph on this graph.

Learning algorithm

Now we describe our learning algorithm. It can be considered a variant of classic principal component analysis (PCA) which has been used in many different situations for learning a low-dimensional representation. It is also very closely related to spectral methods as used in clustering and seriation (Shi and Malik, 2000; Ng et al., 2002; Atkins et al., 1998).

We assume that the agent chooses completely random actions during an initial learning period. During this period, the agent collects information on the transition probabilities, i.e. what is the probability of going from each state to any other state, when the actions are completely random. These probabilities essentially contain the information on which arcs are present in the graph[2] in Fig. 1.

Let us denote by p_{ij} the probability of going from state i to j, and by k the total number of states. The probabilities can be collected in a matrix with k rows and columns, denoted by $\mathbf{P}$:

$$\mathbf{P} = \begin{pmatrix} p_{11} & p_{12} & \cdots & p_{1k} \\ p_{21} & p_{22} & \cdots & p_{2k} \\ \cdots & & & \\ p_{k1} & p_{k2} & \cdots & p_{kk} \end{pmatrix} \quad (1)$$

Now, we want to find n vectors which represent most of the "variation" in this matrix. A precise formulation of such variation can be obtained using the theory of singular value decomposition. Different variants are possible here; we proceed as follows.

First, we add an identity matrix $\mathbf{I}$ to $\mathbf{P}$, i.e. we add one to all the diagonal elements of the matrix; this does not change the eigenvectors but makes sure that their real parts are all non-negative, which avoids cumbersome absolute value computations. Denote the new matrix by $\tilde{\mathbf{P}} = \mathbf{P} + \mathbf{I}$. We compute the eigenvectors corresponding to the $n + 1$ eigenvalues with the largest real parts, ignoring their imaginary parts. Note that all eigenvalues in this paper are right eigenvectors instead of left. The eigenvalues are related to the amount of variation each eigenvector explains. Now, with any transition probability matrix, the largest eigenvalue is equal to 1, and corresponds to an eigenvector which has all constant entries.[3] We discard this degenerate eigenvector. We then take the n eigenvectors which correspond to the n next

eigenvalues with largest real parts. These vectors form our representation.

A complication with this kind of eigenvectors computations is that since the transition matrix need not be symmetric, the eigenvalues and vectors can be complex-valued. Some mathematical analysis which is outside of the scope of this paper shows that the interesting eigenvectors and eigenvalues are, under some theoretical assumptions, all real-valued. This justifies considering only the real parts of the eigenvalues. In practice, the eigenvalues might be complex-valued due to violations of those theoretical assumptions, but we avoid this problem by using an eigenvector calculation method, the power method, which does not give complex values if it is initialized with real values.

Each of those obtained n eigenvectors of $\tilde{\mathbf{P}}$, denote them by $\mathbf{v}_q, q = 1, \ldots, n$, associates a real number with each state: the i-th entry in an eigenvector, $\mathbf{v}_q(i)$, gives one of the coordinates of that state in our representation. Altogether, we obtain n such coordinates, one for each eigenvector, so we associate to each state n real coordinates. This is our representation.

The actual computation of the eigenvectors can be done by classic methods. The situation is quite simple if the agent actually computes and stores all the transition probabilities. The computation of the probabilities is very simple: the agent just has to count how many times it went from state i to state j, and divide this frequency by the total number of times it found itself in state i. It could be argued that the storage of the probabilities is a major problem because the number of states k can be very large, and the number of probabilities to be stored (i.e. the number of entries in the matrix $\mathbf{P}$) is equal to the square of k. However, this need not be a problem because the matrix is typically very sparse: most states are accessible from only a few other states, so most of the entries p_{ij} are zero, and one needs to store only those which are non-zero. This can radically reduce the amount of memory needed by the agent. If the matrix $\mathbf{P}$ is stored in the memory of the agent, a number of classic methods for computing the eigenvectors can be used. We used the power method (Golub and van Loan, 1996) in our simulations, since it has the additional benefit of constraining the search to real values if it is initialized with real values. The off-line learning algorithm which results from this choice is described in Table 1.

If one wants to investigate the neurobiological plausibility of such learning, a simple on-line algorithm may be more interesting. Using the classic theory of on-line learning, based on stochastic approximation, we have developed a simple online algorithm for learning this representation. This algorithm does not store the transition probabilities in memory but uses each observed transition immediately for learning. The algorithm is adapted from previously proposed online methods for PCA (Oja,

---

[2]Actually, the probabilities contain more information because probabilities is not simply binary, 0/1. Moreover, the probability from going from state i to state j might not be equal to the probability of going from j to i, so the arcs would actually be directed in the general case.

[3]This holds for the largest right eigenvector; the corresponding *left* eigenvector gives the stationary probabilities of the Markov chain, i.e. the probabilities of being in each state when the chain is run an infinite number of times. The eigenvectors we use are not related to this left eigenvector.

1982; Hyvärinen et al., 2001). Our algorithm does, however, need to store the total probabilities of being in each of the states in the memory. This algorithm is described in Table 1 as well.

Simulations

Simple grid-world

As an archetype of a reinforcement learning problem, consider a grid of states on a two-dimensional plane. At each time step the agent finds itself in one of these states, and can decide to move up, down, left or right. The agent then moves in the chosen direction, and finds itself in that new state at the next time point (unless it tried to move into the walls marking the boundaries of the grid, in which case the agent does not move at all). The size of the grid was 25×25.

There was first a learning period in which the agent randomly took actions in order to learn the structure of the world. There were a total of 2,500 trials; the goal state was randomly chosen, independently in each trial. The agent took 250 steps in each trial. Since the actions were random, the agent rarely found the goal, but the performance in this initial period provides a baseline against which we can measure the performance of the learning.

At the end of the learning phase, a two-dimensional representation was learned using the off-line version of our algorithm. The learned representation is shown in Fig. 2 a), b). The vectors $\mathbf{v}_1$ and $\mathbf{v}_2$ are shown in grey-scale: black is negative, and the lighter the grey, the larger the value of $\mathbf{v}_q(i)$, white being positive. Fig. 2 c) shows, for one randomly selected goal state, the value of the distance function as grey-scale One can see that the learned distance is computed in a meaningful way. The individual coordinates correspond quite well to the two coordinate axes of the world. They are slightly rotated version of the horizontal and vertical axis, but this has no significance, because such a rotation does not change the Euclidean distances.

In the test phase, we ran another 2500 trials, again with a maximum of 250 steps for each trial. Now, the action selection was done according to the learned representation. We computed the distances to the goal from each of the (typically four) states which are accessible from the present state. We then chose the next action so that the probability of going to the state was larger for those states with smaller distance from the goal. Specifically, we normalized the distances of the immediately accessible states to be between 0 and 1 by subtracting the smallest distance and dividing by the largest distance. Then, we computed the probabilities of going to those states according to the Boltzmann distribution $p(j|i) \propto \exp(-a_{ij}/T)$ where a_{ij} are the normalized distances, and T is a temperature parameter, chosen to equal 0.2 in our simulations.

To show that our method was effective in action selection, we computed the proportion of trials in which the agent was able to find the goal, see Fig. 5. As a baseline, we show how often the agent found the goal by moving randomly as in the learning phase. The success rate for

---

Off-line algorithm for learning representation

1. Initialize representational vectors $\mathbf{v}_q(i)$, $q = 1, \ldots, n$ and $i = 1, \ldots, k$ to random values, where n is the dimension of the representational space, and k is the number of states.

2. Initialize state transition counters of f_{ij}, $i, j = 1, \ldots, k$ to zero.

3. Repeat at each time step of learning phase

   (a) Take random action. Denote by i the state at previous time step, and by j the current state.

   (b) Update frequency counters: $f_{ij} \leftarrow f_{ij} + 1$

4. Compute transition probabilities:
   $p_{ij} \leftarrow f_{ij} / \sum_{j'} f_{ij'}$ for all $i, j = 1, \ldots, k$.

5. Repeat until convergence

   (a) Repeat for each $q = 1, \ldots, n$
      i. Power iteration in matrix multiplication formulation: $\mathbf{v}_q \leftarrow \mathbf{P}\,\mathbf{v}_q$
      ii. Subtract mean: $\mathbf{v}_q(h) \leftarrow \mathbf{v}_q(h) - \frac{1}{k}\sum_{h'} \mathbf{v}_q(h')$ for all $h = 1, \ldots, k$.

   (b) Orthogonalize vectors $\mathbf{v}_q$. (A number of methods is available for this operation (Golub and van Loan, 1996; Hyvärinen et al., 2001).)

On-line algorithm for learning representation

1. Initialize representational vectors $\mathbf{v}_q(i)$ as above.

2. Initialize state frequency counters of f_i, $i = 1, \ldots, k$ to zero.

3. Repeat at each time step

   (a) Take random action. Denote by i the state at previous time step, and by j the current state.

   (b) Update frequency counters: $f_i \leftarrow f_i + 1$

   (c) Compute state probabilities:
   $p_i \leftarrow f_i / \sum_{i'} f_{i'}$

   (d) Repeat for each $q = 1, \ldots, n$:
      • Main update step:
      $\mathbf{v}_q(i) \leftarrow \mathbf{v}_q(i) + \mu\,\mathbf{v}_q(j)/p_i$,
      where μ is a small step size constant.

   (e) Subtract means: $\mathbf{v}_q(h) \leftarrow \mathbf{v}_q(h) - \frac{1}{k}\sum_{h'} \mathbf{v}_q(h')$ for all q and h.

   (f) Orthogonalize vectors $\mathbf{v}_q$. (See (Hyvärinen et al., 2001) for on-line methods for orthogonalization.)

Table 1: The off-line and on-line versions of our learning algorithm. The subtraction of the mean of each vector is equivalent to discarding the degenerate eigenvector with eigenvalue 1.

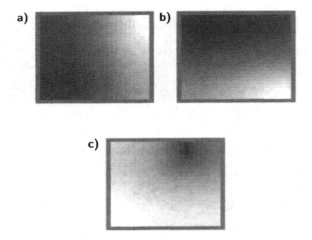

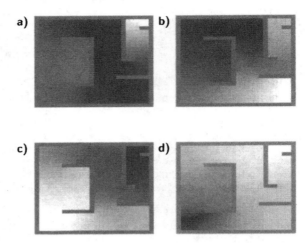

Figure 2: Simulation of a world where the states form a simple two-dimensional grid surrounded by a wall. Our algorithm is able to learn that underlying structure. a) First coordinate in the representation, shown as grey-scale. b) Second coordinate in the representation. c) The distance function from a random goal state, shown as grey-scale.

Figure 3: Simulation of a world in which there are obstacle (inaccessible) states among the states forming the grid. Our algorithm is able to learn that underlying structure. a-c) The three coordinates in the representation, shown as grey-scale. Obstacles are shown in grey as well. d) The distance function from a random goal state, shown as grey-scale.

the case 100% ("no obstacles"). In the baseline trial, the success rates were around 15%. Thus, learning the representation was very efficient in action selection.

Grid world with obstacles

In the next set of simulations, obstacles are added: These are pieces of wall which again prevent movement into or through them. Figure 3 shows the results with such obstacles, which are shown in medium grey in Fig. 3 a)-d). Now, we learned three coordinate axes instead of two to account for the increase in the complexity of the world, shown in Fig. 3 a), b), c). Again, the learned distance, shown for a randomly chosen goal state, is shown in Fig. 3 d). The learned coordinates show that the fundamental thing the system learned is that the dead ends in the "maze" are far way from the rest. This is logical because it takes many steps to get anywhere from those dead ends.

The improvement in action selection is again shown in Fig. 5: success rate was 93% after learning whereas it was around 15% without learning (random case).

Tower of Hanoi

Finally, we used our method in a rather different kind of world: the Tower of Hanoi with 3 disks and 3 pegs. Due to the simplicity of the problem, the number of steps in each trial was reduced to 12. The learned representation is shown in Fig. 4. Action selection was tested by assigning completely random initial and goal states: success rate was 99.8% after learning this representation, and 25% without learning (Figure 5).

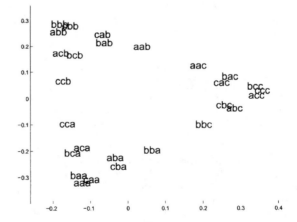

Figure 4: The two-dimensional representation learned in the Tower of Hanoi world. The pegs are denoted by the letters a, b, c and the states are represented as triplets of such letters, so that the first letter tells the location of the first disk and so on. The states form a triangle whose corners (aaa,bbb, and ccc) correspond to states where all the disks are in the same peg.

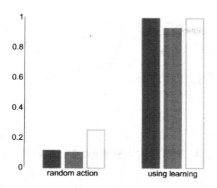

Figure 5: Success rates of finding the goal using the learned representation and the baseline of random actions, in the case of the basic grid world with no obstacles (black bar on the left), the grid with obstacles (red or grey bar on the middle), and the Tower of Hanoi domain (white bar on the right)

Discussion

Our method was originally inspired by the successor representation (Dayan, 1993). However, here we emphasize the low dimensionality of the representation, whereas the successor representation does not reduce the dimension at all, which may be computationally very demanding. Another closely related method was proposed by (Engel and Mannor, 2001). Instead of PCA, they used a more complicated learning method. However, the their goal and philosophy were very similar to ours.

Our learning principle could be interpreted as trying to find a representation which changes as slowly as possible. In a random representation (where each state is a random point is the n-dimensional space), the point that represents the agent's present state jumps randomly from one place to another when the agent takes actions. In contrast, in the representation learned by our method, the point moves slowly, since two points which are accessible from each other tend to be close to each other in the representation. Thus, our method is closely related to models which try to maximize temporal coherence or stability of a representation (Földiák, 1991; Hurri and Hyvärinen, 2003).

Here, we considered the theoretical setting widely used in machine learning where the world is given as a set of discrete states and transitions between them. In other words, we assumed that the perceptual system classifies the state into a discrete set efficiently and unambiguosly. Future work will address how this method could be adapted to the case where the information about the state comes in the form of high-dimensional sensory input. Related work can be found in robotics (Thrun, 2002) and in computational neuroscience (Trullier and Meyer, 2000), but these are usually very different from our approach in that they are constrained to navigation, or 2D environments, whereas we consider completely general problem domains.

To conclude, we proposed a computational model for learning a dimensional representation of a discrete-state world, with the goal of facilitating action selection. The basic principle is to do a kind of principal component analysis on the matrix of transition probabilities between the states. Then, action selection and planning can become quite simple. Similar to model-based reinforcement learning, or planning, adaptation to changing goals is straightforward and re-learning is not needed. However, the exponential explosion of computation, which is inherent in planning, is avoided. Thus, our method seems to combine some of the advantages of model-based and model-free reinforcement learning.

References

Atkins, J. E., Boman, E. G., and Hendrickson, B. (1998). A spectral algorithm for seriation and the consecutive ones problem. *SIAM J. on Computing*, 28(1):297–310.

Daw, N. D., Niv, Y., and Dayan, P. (2005). Uncertainty-based competition between prefrontal and dorsolateral striatal systems for behavioral control. *Nature Neuroscience*, 8:1704–1711.

Dayan, P. (1993). Improving generalisation for temporal difference learning: The successor representation. *Neural Computation*, 5:613–624.

Dayan, P. and Abbott, L. F. (2001). *Theoretical Neuroscience*. MIT Press.

Engel, Y. and Mannor, S. (2001). Learning embedded maps of markov processes. In *Proc. Int. Conf. on Machine Learning (ICML)*, pages 138–145.

Földiák, P. (1991). Learning invariance from transformation sequences. *Neural Computation*, 3:194–200.

Golub, G. and van Loan, C. (1996). *Matrix Computations*. The Johns Hopkins University Press, 3rd edition.

Hurri, J. and Hyvärinen, A. (2003). Simple-cell-like receptive fields maximize temporal coherence in natural video. *Neural Computation*, 15(3):663–691.

Hyvärinen, A., Karhunen, J., and Oja, E. (2001). *Independent Component Analysis*. Wiley Interscience.

Ng, A. Y., Jordan, M. I., and Weiss, Y. (2002). On spectral clustering: Analysis and an algorithm. In *Advances in Neural Information Processing Systems 14*. MIT Press.

Oja, E. (1982). A simplified neuron model as a principal component analyzer. *J. of Mathematical Biology*, 15:267–273.

Shi, J. and Malik, J. (2000). Normalized cuts and image segmentation. *IEEE Transactions on Pattern Analysis and Machine Intelligence*, 22(8):888–905.

Sutton, R. and Barto, A. (1998). *Reinforcement Learning: An Introduction*. MIT Press.

Thrun, S. (2002). Robotic mapping: A survey. In Lakemeyer, G. and Nebel, B., editors, *Exploring Artificial Intelligence in the New Millenium*. Morgan Kaufmann.

Trullier, O. and Meyer, J.-A. (2000). Animat navigation using a cognitive graph. *Biological Cybernetics*, 83:271–285.

A Traffic Forecast Neurocomputational Behavioural Model

Spyridon Revithis (revithiss@cse.unsw.edu.au)
Artificial Intelligence Group, School of Computer Science and Engineering
University of New South Wales, UNSW-Sydney, NSW 2052 Australia

Abstract

In this work we introduce a neurocomputational model of human behaviour applied in the domain of traffic forecast. A multiagent system, consisting of artificial agents, uses a Kohonen self-organizing traffic behavioural model in order to coordinate a human multiagent system situated in a metropolitan road network. The result of our analysis establishes the proposed model as theoretically and computationally valid, and it demonstrates its applicability potential in real-life domains; also, and most importantly, it supports existing claims and follows up our previous work that link cognitive modeling of behaviour and the Hebbian neural self-organization approach.

Introduction

The study of human behaviour cognitive models spawns a wide range of applications, and has significant implications in related fields of study including artificial intelligence, computer science, cognitive science, and computational neuroscience (Sun & Ling, 1997; Polk & Seifert, 2002; Shultz, 2003; Sun, Coward, & Zenzen 2005). The incentive for this work was to introduce a computational tool that could contribute towards cataloguing and classifying the vast repertoire of human cognitive behaviour in a particular family of activities. The focus here is on tasks that contain a significant spatial-reasoning and planning component; specifically, driving behaviour.

In this study we present a *cooperative multiagent system* that can be used as a coordination framework for an *antagonistic multiagent system* in a specific domain. The former system consists of *artificial agents*, whereas the latter one of *human agents*. Since coordination between humans can be very challenging we incorporate connectionist machine learning capabilities to the former system; to that effect, we employ a form of *behavioural modeling* of the human agents in order to predict their domain-specific behaviour. The human behavioural model described in this work is a Hebbian type (Hebb, 1949) *neurocomputational model* that belongs to the class of Kohonen self-organizing maps (Kohonen, 1982, 1984).

We present our work in three parts. The first one contains a description of the problem domain, and an analysis of the proposed solution from an engineering and cognitive science perspective. The second part provides particular implementation details and technical aspects of our design. In the last part we discuss performance issues, cognitive modeling implications of the proposed model, and future work.

The T-MAS and MAS-TFC Systems

Description of the Domain

Our engineering goal was to design a system that would be capable of efficiently regulating heavy traffic in geographical areas with dense road networks, most characteristically metropolitan areas.

We expect that in an uncomplicated road network with light traffic there is no call for any additional type of traffic control beyond the application of the code of road traffic behaviour and its supporting technologies. Rather, traffic problems systematically arise in metropolitan areas, where the road network is complicated and the traffic is frequently heavy. In such cases, there is a need for dynamic adjustments in the traffic that will prevent bottlenecks and other major traffic problems, and maximize the capacity of the road network. This calls for a system that maintains traffic load uniformity.

This domain can be regarded as a multiagent system (Weiss, 1999; Wooldridge 2002) consisting of "indifferent" human agents; we call it *T-MAS* (Traffic Multi-Agent System). Each agent's driving goal in T-MAS is to reach a certain destination with minimum traffic overhead, via the road network, with no respect to any other agent's goal. However, since all T-MAS agents use the same road network, they need to be coordinated with each other in order to achieve their goal and avoid traffic problems. In this coordination scenario there is a trade-off between minimizing the traffic for every agent's itinerary and achieving traffic load uniformity. The human agents in T-MAS need to negotiate over their individual driving goals by compromising on the degree of traffic load within their itinerary. Consequently, we can view T-MAS as an antagonistic multiagent system having a global goal, which can be described as the *coordination of the individual goals of the human agents* within it (Huhns & Stephens, 1999).

General Description of MAS-TFC

In this section we introduce a multiagent system, consisting of artificial agents, which can be used to achieve T-MAS' global goal; we call this system *MAS-TFC* (Multi-Agent System for Traffic Forecast and Control).

Unlike T-MAS, MAS-TFC is a cooperative multiagent system (Huhns & Stephens, 1999), in which agents work together. The system's global goal is to produce a *traffic forecast*, which can be used to inform T-MAS agents on the likelihood of future traffic problems within their vicinity and elsewhere within the road network. The human agents can then voluntarily adjust their itinerary by avoiding those parts of the road network listed by the MAS-TFC as most likely to readily develop heavy traffic; since an adjustment of this type will help them reach their driving goal, it is expected that will be followed by most, if not all, agents in T-MAS.

Human agents potentially exhibit any behaviour that will lead them to success according to their intentions; techniques employed for this cause include misleading, pretending, and cheating (Falcone & Firozabadi, 1999; Castelfranchi & Yao-Hua Tan, 2001; Hexmoor, Venkata & Hayes, 2006). Voluntary type of coordination schemes, as in our case, should have provision for such behavioural techniques. In MAS-TFC isolated human agent behaviour that deviates from the norm (i.e. an outlier) has no effect in the coordination efficacy since the system is sensitive only to behavioural patterns that represent collective behaviours.

Analysis of MAS-TFC

In our implementation of MAS-TFC, we employ 25 artificial agents[1], which we call *T-Agents* (Traffic Agents), to cover the entire road network. Each T-Agent monitors a specific segment of the road network, and systematically records the local traffic, over a universally-fixed period of time, in the form of a *traffic report* volume (e.g. average number of vehicles). The concatenation of the entirety of traffic reports produced by the T-Agents at each such period of time yields a *traffic report grid* that depicts the traffic situation of the entire road network. Figure 1 depicts this scheme.

| A road network example (The numbers represent T-Agents) | A traffic report grid example (Trafic report numbers have been converted into grayscales) |

Figure 1: T-MAS monitoring by T-Agents.

T-Agents produce traffic reports on a timely basis; in our implementation, every half-hour[2]. This results in 48 traffic reports daily, approximately 17,520 traffic reports annually, per T-Agent. Although the resulting amount of data is particularly large (close to half a million traffic reports

---

[1] Various implementation values (e.g. number of T-Agents, traffic report intervals) were chosen in order to analyze the system under specific parameters; they do not imply a particular property or an inherent constraint in our design.

[2] See previous footnote.

annually even for our modest-scale segmentation of 25 traffic regions per road network), it is nevertheless vital in order for MAS-TFC to be capable of producing a reliable traffic forecast and enable dynamic traffic adjustments.

The core component of MAS-TFC is a machine learning subsystem, we call *T-SOM* (Traffic Self-Organizing Map), which can be considered as a behavioural model of the human agents in T-MAS. As the name suggests it is a Kohonen *self-organizing neural network* (Kohonen, 1982, 1984), which is configured to form a complete *map* of the driving behaviour of the T-MAS agents. In Figure 2 we present a diagrammatic relationship of the systems involved in the proposed design.

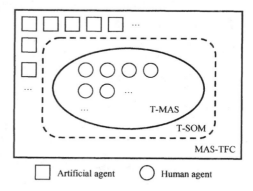

Figure 2: Functional hierarchy of MAS-TFC and T-MAS.

Each T-Agent not only gathers traffic data from its segment but also transmits *notifications* to T-MAS agents about future traffic load on its segment on a timely basis (specifically, in half-hour intervals, as compared to the rate of producing traffic reports). Such notifications do not necessarily require additional IT device installations per T-MAS agent as they can be projected on large electronic road signs across the road network.

Within MAS-TFC, T-Agents interact with a *Q-Agent* (Query Agent) responsible of compiling queries from the traffic reports; every half-hour such a query contains the current traffic status of the road network represented by the traffic report grid. The Q-Agent utilizes the behavioural map of T-SOM and, based on the current query data, extracts a traffic forecast for the entire road network. Based on the latter, the Q-Agent will send a customized traffic forecast to each T-Agent containing the traffic load trend for the corresponding segment of the road network. In this way, T-Agents are provided with up-to-date individualized future traffic information for each traffic report they communicate to the Q-Agent; it is, then, their responsibility to post a traffic forecast notification within their segment. This coordination mechanism is shown in a conceptual diagram in Figure 3.

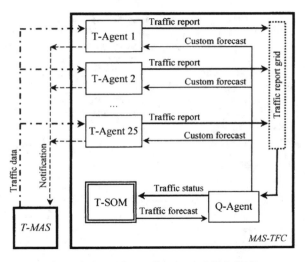

Figure 3: T-MAS coordination in MAS-TFC.

The T-SOM Behavioural Model

There is an open issue in the analysis presented in the previous section. The Q-Agent can make successful queries to T-SOM provided that the latter represents the behavioural traffic model of the T-MAS agents. Since T-SOM is a learning subsystem of MAS-TFC, a method must be in place to enable T-SOM knowledge acquisition of the traffic behaviour of T-MAS agents. T-SOM is an instance of the Kohonen neural model, and uses a Hebbian type developmental self-organizing form of unsupervised learning to extract environmental regularities based on its training set (Munakata & Pfaffly, 2004; Johnson & Munakata, 2005). It is a biologically inspired computational method capable of data compression, and although resists formal analysis it has been empirically shown to be reliable and efficient; Cottrell, Fort, & Pagès (1998), and Haykin (1999) offer a detailed account on SOM's technical aspects and features. Such a learning subsystem needs appropriate temporal input from its environment in order to function correctly. The information contained in the Q-Agents' queries is not sufficient since the T-SOM learning architecture requires input that is statistically sufficient to allow for successful generalizations.

According to the Kohonen learning algorithm (Haykin, 1999), acquiring the T-MAS behavioural traffic model in T-SOM translates into the formation of a map that compresses the vast input space of traffic report grids in a statistically valid manner. The principal idea behind this type of human behaviour modeling is that human agents tend to form certain behavioural patterns over time, especially in environmentally constrained tasks such as driving a vehicle; given enough time, such patterns of behaviour can be observed. In MAS-TFC, we employ a dedicated L-Agent (Learning Agent) that trains the T-SOM subsystem using a statistically large number of traffic reports.

In our implementation, the T-SOM's training set consists of the traffic reports produced over the period of one year. Using the latter set as input, T-SOM initiates an unsupervised training session that concludes with the formation of a map in the form of a 10×10 lattice of neural nodes; each node contains one learned behavioural traffic pattern in the form of a traffic report grid (represented internally as an ordered vector of 25 numbers, in accordance with the analysis of MAS-TFC discussed in the previous section). Each traffic report grid in the lattice represents a family of traffic report grids; as the Kohonen learning model suggests, this can be viewed as compressing the whole family into a feature unit. If we consider the annual traffic report training set as representative of the entire input space of traffic behaviours in the specific road network at the time then the resulting T-SOM map is a good approximation of that space; it is a valid traffic behavioural model.

By moving across the T-SOM lattice we observe a smooth transition among neighboring nodes in the sense that *topological* distance implies *temporal* distance. This means that neighboring traffic report grids are also neighboring in a temporal manner: if any traffic report grid G in the T-SOM map is observed in the actual road network then the next traffic report grid reported by the T-Agents is expected to be one of the immediate neighboring traffic report grids of G (or G itself) in the map as illustrated in Figure 4.

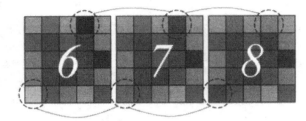

An example of three (6, 7, and 8) neighboring T-SOM trained nodes; smooth transition between traffic report grid patterns demonstrates topological and temporal relationship, and facilitates traffic forecasting.

Figure 4: Spatiotemporal ordering in T-SOM.

Claiming that a traffic report grid F of the road network matches with one of the traffic report grids, lets call K, in the T-SOM map, implies that F belongs to the family of traffic report grids that K represents; since a traffic report grid is internally represented as a vector, equality between traffic report grids translates to some vector similarity criterion such as the Euclidean distance.

Another important property of the T-SOM map, inherited by the Kohonen model, is that it maintains the *density distribution* of the input space. Thus, if a certain family of traffic report grids is dominant or relatively large –in a statistical sense– in the annual traffic report then it will remain so in the resulting behavioural map. If, on the contrary, there is an extremely small number of related traffic report grids or near-single instances scattered within the annual traffic report, then no node in the map is expected to be allocated for their representation.

Once the annual traffic report is provided to the T-SOM by the L-Agent, and the map is formed, the T-SOM can be used for traffic forecasting by the Q-Agent. The procedure is straightforward and can be regarded as a map lookup for a node that best matches the Q-Agents' current traffic status. Since both the Q-Agents' current traffic status and the nodes in the map are in the form of traffic report grids (ordered vectors), finding a match is simply a matter of applying a Euclidean distance similarity criterion. After finding the best match, the Q-Agent can take advantage of the topological ordering within the map to foresee the most highly probable traffic report grids in the immediate future; these are the immediate neighbors of the matching node in the map. Since the T-SOM map is two-dimensional the maximum number of neighboring traffic report grids is eight (i.e. an interior node) and the minimum three (i.e. a corner-node), plus the case where the traffic status will remain unchanged (i.e. thus, counting the matching node as well). After evaluating the forecast information the Q-Agent can send the appropriate traffic report grids to the T-Agents on a need-to-know basis (i.e. each T-Agent receives forecast information regarding its designated segment only); based on the later information the T-Agents can, in turn, perform some formatting manipulation on the received information and post it in the form of traffic notifications.

After the first T-SOM training has occurred, forecasting and subsequent training can be performed in parallel. While the Q-Agent uses the T-SOM subsystem, the dedicated L-Agent keeps gathering traffic reports in the form of traffic report grids as they are produced by the T-Agents. With each completed annual traffic report set the T-SOM becomes subject to a new training session by the L-Agent in order to update its behavioural knowledge base. In this way, the T-SOM model approximates on-going learning, and becomes sensitive to changes in the traffic behavioural pattern of the T-MAS agents.

Implementation of MAS-TFC

MAS-TFC Algorithms

In this section we provide some high-level algorithms that describe the roles of the agents and their interactions in MAS-TFC. We have decomposed the algorithms in an object-oriented fashion: each algorithm links to an agent class. These algorithms follow directly from the previous discussion, and are used to clarify the concepts and processes that have been presented in this work.

```
T-Agent (i)
   LOOP FOR One Year EVERY Half-Hour
      COMPUTE Current Traffic Report
      SEND Current Traffic Report TO L-Agent
   END-FOR-LOOP
   LOOP EVERY Half-Hour
      COMPUTE Current Traffic Report
```

```
      SEND Current Traffic Report TO L-Agent
      SEND Current Traffic Report TO Q-Agent
      RECEIVE Traffic Notification FROM Q-Agent
      FORMAT AND POST Traffic Notification
         ACROSS Road Segment i
   END-LOOP
END
```

Note in the above algorithm the existence of an initial one-time loop, which corresponds to the first year of the system. No forecast is possible during that time since T-SOM has yet to learn its first traffic behavioural pattern of the T-MAS agents. The sole goal of T-Agents during that period is to gather the first training set for the L-Agent.

```
Q-Agent
   LOOP
      LOOP WHILE i < 26
         RECEIVE Current Traffic Report FROM T-Agent(i)
      LOOP-NEXT i
      FORM Traffic Report Grid f
      FIND Traffic Report Grid g IN T-SOM: ||g–f|| IS MIN
      FOR EACH Traffic Report Grid d IN T-SOM DO
         IF d IS AN IMMEDIATE NEIGHBOR OF g
            THEN GET d FROM T-SOM
            ADD d IN D
         END-IF
      LOOP-NEXT d
      FORM Custom Traffic Forecasts FROM D
      FOR EACH T-Agent(t) DO
         SEND Custom Traffic Forecast TO T-Agent(t)
      LOOP-NEXT t
      DISCARD D
   END-LOOP
END
```

The Q-Agent uses f to represent the current traffic status of the road network, whereas g is the traffic behavioural pattern in the T-SOM map that f belongs to. Furthermore, D is the T-SOM forecast, which the Q-Agent uses to form customized traffic forecasts for each of the T-Agents.

```
L-Agent
   LOOP
      LOOP FOR One Year
         LOOP WHILE i < 26
            RECEIVE Current Traffic Report
               FROM T-Agent(i)
            ADD Current Traffic Report IN R
         LOOP-NEXT i
      END-FOR-LOOP
      TRAIN T-SOM* USING R
      REPLACE T-SOM WITH T-SOM*
      DISCARD T-SOM*
      DISCARD R
   END -LOOP
END
```

There is a counter intuitive mechanism in the L-Agent algorithm. The L-Agent never trains T-SOM directly; instead, it trains another backup T-SOM* which only takes the place of the outdated T-SOM after the training of the T-SOM* has been completed. This is a synchronization strategy since both training (learning) and using T-SOM (forecasting) are performed simultaneously. In this way the Q-Agent can query T-SOM while the L-Agent supervises the training session of T-SOM*. At the conclusion of the latter session T-SOM can be updated by acquiring T-SOM* without the Q-Agent ever noticing anything more than an insignificant response delay. In the next section we present a detailed discussion of the T-SOM training algorithm.

Technical Aspects of T-SOM

The most sophisticated task of MAS-TFC is the realization of its learning subsystem, T-SOM. Although MAS-TFC cannot be evaluated using artificial data, due to the nature of its input space, we have argued in favour of its theoretical and computational properties. Furthermore, in this section we establish its mathematical aspects, incorporating the L-Agent in T-SOM, based on the design parameters introduced. The mathematical and algorithmic form of the SOM neural network used is according to Haykin (1999), and consistent with our ANSI C implementation. For the sake of accuracy in our technical description we use, for the remainder of this section, the terminology of the Kohonen neural model to describe the mathematical structure and algorithm of T-SOM.

Competition, cooperation, and synaptic adaptation are sequenced within a loop that constitutes the T-SOM main training loop. Competition among neurons within the network lattice occurs every time a new feature (i.e. input vector) is introduced to the neural network. The winning neuron i with lattice index $i(x)$ of each competition satisfies the Euclidean minimization equation

$$i(x) = \arg \min_{j} \| x - w_j \|, \quad j = 1, 2, ..., l$$

where x is the feature vector, w is the weight vector of the winning neuron, and l is the total number of neurons.

Each time a winning neuron has been determined the training goes through the cooperation part, in which the neighbourhood of that neuron is specified and all neurons within it are considered excited. The topological neighbourhood of the winning neuron i is specified by the translation invariant Gaussian function

$$h_{j,i(x)}(n) = \exp(-\frac{d_{j,i(x)}^2}{2 \cdot \sigma^2(n)}), \quad n = 0, 1, 2, ..., t$$

where j denotes an excited neuron, and n refers to the current iteration of the main training loop. The neighbourhood function h is based on the lateral distance d between the winning neuron i and an excited neuron j, which is expressed by the equation

$$d_{j,i}^2 = \| r_j - r_i \|^2$$

where vector r defines the position of j and i neuron, respectively. The width σ of the neighbourhood function h

is a temporal function with exponential decay, which is specified by the equation

$$\sigma(n) = \sigma_0 \cdot \exp(-\frac{n}{\tau_1}), \quad n = 0, 1, 2, ..., t$$

where σ_0 is the initial width of h, and τ_1 is a temporal constant. The latter was set according to the formula

$$\tau_1 = \frac{t}{\log \sigma_0} .$$

In the last part of the main training loop the network goes through a synaptic adaptation process, in which the synaptic weights of the neurons within the neighbourhood of the winning neuron are updated in relation to the feature vector. The updated weight vector w $(n + 1)$ of each excited neuron j is computed by the equation

$$w_j(n + 1) = w_j(n) + \eta(n) \cdot h_{j,i(x)}(n) \cdot (x - w_j(n))$$

where x is the feature vector, and $w(n)$ denotes the old weight vector. T-SOM uses stochastic approximation, which is realized by the time-varying learning rate η with exponential decay as depicted in the equation

$$\eta(n) = \eta_o \cdot \exp(-\frac{n}{\tau_2}), \quad n = 0, 1, 2, ..., t$$

where η_0 denotes the initial learning rate, and τ_2 is a temporal constant.

The main training loop is executed until the network converges to a stable state at a rate largely dictated by the parameter values presented in this section.

Algorithmic Analysis

The complexity of the algorithm, as implemented in our ANSI C code, can be easily realized by the following analysis that follows standard notation (Cormen, Leiserson, & Rivest, 1990). Let m be the cardinality (size) of the training set. This translates into $m \approx 17,520$ assuming that each feature is regarded as one input element. Similarly, let n be the size of the network's neuron lattice. In our implementation we decided a lattice size of 10×10 to reserve enough representational space in the resulting T-SOM map. Accordingly, this yields $n = 100$. If k denotes the number of iterations of the self-organizing and convergence part of the self-organizing feature map algorithm, then the complexity of the algorithm is $\Theta(m \cdot n \cdot k)$ in general. In our case we have a fixed relationship between m and n, which is defined as $m \approx n^{4.2435}$. Then, for different values of k we can distinguish the following three cases:

1st case: $m > n > k$. The number of iterations is less than the size of the neuron lattice. Then, the training algorithm has complexity $\Theta(m \cdot n \cdot k)$ which is the lowest possible bound for this algorithm.

2nd case: $m > k > n$. The number of iterations stands between the size of the neuron lattice and that of the training set. In this case the algorithm's bound increases to $\Omega(m \cdot n^2)$.

3rd case: $k > m > n$. The number of iterations exceeds both m and n quantities. Then, the algorithm has the worst-case complexity of $\Omega(m^2 \cdot n)$; if k becomes arbitrarily large then the algorithm's running time bound becomes looser at $\omega(m^2 \cdot n)$.

MAS-TFC as a Cognitive Model

Scope of the Proposed Design and Future Work

There have been numerous enginnering approaches to traffic forecast in the literature based on various metrics and methods (Dougherty, 1997; Han & Song, 2003; Chrobok, Kaumann, Wahle & Schreckenberg, 2004). Our model is an alternative that carries a number of attractive features including ease of implementation, straightforward design, feasibility, and being open to merging into hybrid subsequent models.

Nevertheless, our principal aim was not to construct a better traffic forecast method but to examine the characteristics and nature of our design as a domain-specific instance of a cognitive model of behaviour, if valid. Due to its effectiveness, in representing the particular domain-specific instinctive and strategic cognitive behaviour via enabling human-agent traffic forecasting, we consider it valid. This work is part of an investigation on the role of neural-based self-organization in psychological behaviour from a cognitive modeling standpoint via the use of behavioural outcome models (Sun & Ling, 1997).

Future work includes empirical assessment, based on real-life data, in order to accurately measure the model's efficiency. In subsequent work we are planning to use it, together with findings from similar models (Revithis, 2001, 2003, 2006), in order to investigate the existence of domain-general neurocomputational parameters that could be characterized as the "source of power" (Sun & Ling, 1997) in our specific approach to cognitive modeling.

Acknowledgments

The author would like to thank Dr. William Wilson, Dr. Nadine Marcus (University of New South Wales, Australia), and Dr. George Tagalakis (University College Dublin, Ireland) for reviewing this paper.

References

Castelfranchi, C. & Yao-Hua Tan (Eds.) (2001). *Trust and deception in virtual societies*. Springer.

Chrobok, R., Kaumann, O., Wahle, J., & Schreckenberg M. (2004). Different methods of traffic forecast based on real data. *European Journal of Operational Research, 155,* 558-568.

Cormen, T. H., Leiserson, C. E., & Rivest, R. L. (1990). *Introduction to Algorithms*. Cambridge, MA: MIT Press.

Cottrell, M., Fort, J. C., & Pagès, G. (1998). Theoretical aspects of the SOM algorithm. *Neurocomputing, 21,* 119-138.

Dougherty, M. (1997). A review of neural networks applied to transport. *Transportation Research C, 3,* 247-260.

Falcone, R., & Firozabadi, B. S. (1999). The challenge of trust, The Autonomous Agents '98 Workshop on Deception, Fraud and Trust in Agent Societies. *The Knowledge Engineering Review, 14,* 81-89.

Han, C., & Song, S. (2003). A review of some main models for traffic flow forecasting. *Proceedings of the 2003 IEEE International Conference on Intelligent Transportation Systems* (pp. 216-219).

Haykin, S. (1999). *Neural networks – A comprehensive foundation*. Upper Saddle River, NJ: Prentice-Hall.

Hebb, D. O. (1949). *The organization of behaviour*. New York: Willey.

Hexmoor, H., Venkata, S. G., & Hayes, D. (2006). Modelling social norms in multiagent systems. *Journal of Experimental Artificial Intelligence, 18,* 49-71.

Huhns, M. N., & Stephens, L. M., (1999). Multiagent systems and societies of agents. In G. Weiss (Ed.), *Multiagent systems: a modern approach to distributed artificial intelligence*. MIT Press.

Johnson, M. H., & Munakata, Y. (2005). Processes of change in brain and cognitive development. *Trends in Cognitive Science, 9,* 152-158.

Kohonen, T. (1982). Self-organized formation of topologically correct feature maps. *Biological Cybernetics, 53,* 59-69.

Kohonen, T. (1984). *Self-organization and associative memory*. New York: Springer-Verlag.

Munakata, Y., & Pfaffly, J. (2004). Hebbian learning and development. *Developmental Science, 7,* 141-148.

Polk, T. A., & Seifert, C. M. (Eds.) (2002). *Cognitive modeling*. Cambridge, MA: The MIT Press.

Revithis, S. (2001). *A Case of Modeling Human Behavior in Learning Environments*, MS Thesis, Computer Engineering and Computer Science Department, University of Missouri, Columbia, MO.

Revithis, S. (2003). *Modeling Aspects of Political Thought in Democratic Political Systems: A Connectionist Approach Overview*. Hamilton Institute for Policy Research.

Revithis, S., Wilson, W. H., & Marcus, N. (2006). IPSOM: A Self-Organizing Map Spatial Model of How Humans Complete Interlocking Puzzles. In A. Sattar & B. H. Kang (Eds.), *AI 2006, Lecture Notes in Artificial Intelligence, LNCS Vol. 4304*. Heidelberg Berlin: Springer-Verlag.

Shultz, T. R. (2003). *Computational developmental psychology*. Cambridge, MA: The MIT Press.

Sun, R., & Ling, C. (1997). Computational cognitive modeling, the source of power and other related issues. *AI Magazine, 19,* 113-120.

Sun, R., Coward, L. A., & Zenzen, M. J. (2005). On levels of cognitive modeling. *Philosophical Psychology, 18,* 613-637.

Wooldridge, M. (2002). *Introduction to multiagent systems*. John Wiley & Sons.

A Neural Network Model for Explaining the Asymmetries between Linguistic Production and Linguistic Comprehension

Marco Mirolli (marco.mirolli@istc.cnr.it)
Institute of Cognitive Sciences and Technologies, CNR,
44 Via S. Martino della Battaglia, 00185, Roma, Italy

Federico Cecconi (federico.cecconi@istc.cnr.it)
Institute of Cognitive Sciences and Technologies, CNR,
Via S. Martino della Battaglia 44, 00185, Roma, Italy

Domenico Parisi (domenico.parisi@istc.cnr.it)
Institute of Cognitive Sciences and Technologies, CNR,
Via S. Martino della Battaglia 44, 00185, Roma, Italy

Abstract

Several kinds of empirical evidence point to the existence of an asymmetry between linguistic production and linguistic comprehension: in general, understanding words seems to be easier than producing them. In this contribution we propose a neural model of the relationships between the semantic and the lexical systems. Our model explains the asymmetry between language comprehension and production as an effect of the difference between the dimensions of the brain areas which process semantic and lexical information. In fact, the model's performance in lexical recall is worse than the performance in semantic recall due to the fact that the semantic network is constituted of more computational units (neurons) then the lexical network.

Introduction

A considerable number of empirical evidences of various kind point to the presence of an asymmetry between linguistic production and linguistic comprehension. In general, comprehension seems to be easier than production.

This asymmetry takes several forms. First, the asymmetry is well documented in developmental linguistics: it is in fact a very well known fact that children learn to understand words far earlier than to produce them (see, for example, Bates, Thal, Finlay, & Clancy, 2002).

Another field in which the asymmetry is well documented is the psychology of aging. As people get older, in fact, it gets more and more difficult to retrieve known words (the so called 'tip of the tongue' or TOT phenomenon). On the other hand, there seems to be no decrease in the language understanding capacity whatsoever (see, for example, Burke & MacKay, 1997; Burke, MacKay, & James, 2000).

Furthermore, the fact that word production is more difficult than word comprehension seems to hold in the whole lifetime, and not only in elderliness. In fact, everyone experiences sometimes the tip of the tongue state, and empirical evidences confirm that such a phenomenon just increases with age, but is present also in all normal adults (see, for example, Brown, 1991; Heine, Ober, & Shenaut, 1999).

Finally, there seems to be also some spare evidence that the asymmetry between language production and comprehension exists even in neuropathologies. In this case, the asymmetry takes the form of a larger number of patients with linguistic production deficits than patients with linguistic comprehension ones. For example, it seems that *all* the various kinds of aphasias imply some deficit in word production (anomia), while a dysfunction in linguistic production is not necessarily correlated with comprehension problems (see Bates & Goodman, 1997; Dick, Bates, Wulfeck, Utman, & Dronkers, 2001).

Notwithstanding the fact that all the above mentioned empirical evidences regard very different phenomena, the phenomenon of an asymmetry between linguistic production and linguistic comprehension is common. This suggest that it could have a common cause. In this paper we model the relationships between semantics and the lexicon as the coupling (bi-directional connection) between two associative, Hopfield-like (Hopfield, 1982) networks. With our model we try to explain the asymmetry between production and comprehension of language – in particular, the fact that linguistic production is more difficult than linguistic comprehension – as an effect of the quantitative difference in size of the computational spaces which are devoted to the processing of semantics (word meanings) and the lexicon (word forms), respectively. In particular, our model assumes that the parts of the brain which are devoted to the processing of word forms are smaller, in terms of the number of recruited neurons, than the parts of the brain which are devoted to the processing of word meanings. Our hypothesis is that the production-comprehension asymmetry is determined by this difference in size between the semantical and the lexical areas.

The rest of the paper is structured as follows. In the next section we describe the model which we have used for modelling the semantic and the lexical systems, that is, Hopfield networks, and then we describe the details of our simulations. In the following section we describe the principal results of the simulations, and finally, in the final section, we discuss the strengths and weaknesses of the proposed model together with possible future work.

The Model

We model the linguistic system as the coupling (reciprocal connection) between two auto-associative neural networks, that is, two Hopfield networks (Hopfield, 1982; Rolls & Treves, 1998): the semantic networks and the lexical network.

Hopfield Networks

An Hopfield network is a neural network constituted by a single group of reciprocally connected processing units (neurons). Neuron's activation is bipolar, that is can be either -1 or $+1$. Every neuron is connected with all the others but not with itself, and connections are symmetrical: in other words, the weight of the connection which links neuron i to neuron j is equal to the weight which links neuron j to neuron i. This symmetry in connection weights is guaranteed by the learning rule which is used for training the network, which is a simple Hebbian rule (Hebb, 1949). Basically, the Hebb rule is such that connections which link neurons with correlated activation (that is, which are usually either both active or both inactive) increase their strength, while connections which link neurons whose activation is uncorrelated decrease their strength. Formally, the Hebb rule is expressed by the following formula:

$$\Delta w_{ij} = r\, a_i\, a_j$$

where Δw_{ij} is the change to the weights connecting unit i to unit j, a_x is the activation of unit x, and r is a constant, called the learning rate.

The network learns to memorize in its connection weights a certain number of activation patterns across its units, with a pattern consisting in a vector of N bipolar (-1 or $+1$) values, where N is the number of network's nodes. In our case, patterns of activation stand either for internal representations of words' meaningsor for internal representations of words' forms, in the cases of the semantic and lexical networks, respectively.

Weights learning happens in the following way. At the beginning, weights are all set to zero. Then, for each activation pattern, network's nodes are all activated to the bipolar values of that pattern, and weights are modified according to the Hebb rule.

After this kind of training, Hopfield networks have an interesting property. If we present any, even random, pattern as the network's input, and we let the network re-calculate the activation of each node as a consequence of the input coming from other nodes through the connection weights, after a certain number of cycles (usually less than 15), the network converges to a stable state, called an attractor, which doesn't change any more.

To understand Hopfield network's functioning, the activation state of its neurons can be conceived as a surface in a multi-dimensional space, with $N + 1$ dimensions: one dimension for each neuron, plus one dimension representing network's *energy* (Figure 1). Each point of the surface is a possible state of the network, and the local minima of energy (the valleys) are the network's attractors: given any given pattern the network will tend to follow the energy gradient until it reaches one of its valleys, where it will stop indefinitely unless external interference is applied.

The property of having attractors is guaranteed just by the network's rules of connectivity: that connection weights are symmetrical and that there are no self-connections. The role of the above mentioned Hebbian learning procedure is that of shaping the network's activation space so that the patterns on which the network is trained become its attractors. Hence, after successful training, if we present to the network one of the learned patterns, it will be indefinitely maintained. Furthermore, if we present a *partial* pattern, that is a learned pattern in which some percentage of the nodes are set to 0, in a few activation cycles the network is able to perfectly reconstruct the learned pattern, which will be maintained constant in the following cycles.

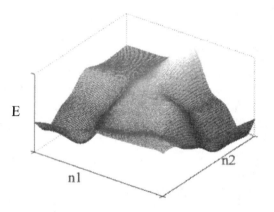

E

n1   n2

Figure 1: Hypothetical activation space of an Hopfield with just two neurons (n1 and n2). The third dimension (vertical axis) represents the energy (E) of the point which stands for the corresponding state of the network. Valleys represent network's stable states (attractors), towards which the activity of the network converges.

The choice of modeling the semantical and the lexical system through Hopfield networks is due to the fact that this kind of networks represent (reasonably) good models of the functioning of single brain areas (Rolls & Treves, 1998). In fact, beyond possessing all those bio-mimetic properties which are shared by all kinds of parallel-distributed-processing neural networks (Plaut & Shallice, 1993; Rumelhart, McClelland & the PDP Research Group, 1986), such as robustness to noise, graceful degradation, and pattern completion, Hopfield networks have at least two other properties which make them biologically plausible. First, the Hebbian learning rule, of which the neural implementation has been found in the phenomena of synaptic long term potentiation and lond term depression (Kelso, Ganong & Brown, 1986; Stanton, & Sejnowski, 1989). Second, connections' recurrencies, that is the fact that neurons within the same group are reciprocally interconnected, represents an important anatomic characteristic of the brain. Furthermore, it is the presence of these recurrencies that makes it possible for the network to show temporal dynamics which permits to model important empirical phenomena like semantic priming or, more generally, differences in reaction times (see, for example, Masson, 1995; Sharkey & Sharkey, 1992).

The Semantic and the Lexical Networks

Our model consists in two Hopfield networks which represent, respectively, the semantic and the lexical systems. The two networks function in just the same way. The only difference between the two lies in their dimensionality. In fact, the semantic network is constituted by 2500 nodes, while the lexical network is constituted by 500 nodes. This difference correspond to the assumption that the parts of the brain which are devoted to the processing of word forms are much smaller than the parts of the brain which are devoted to the processing of word meanings. The two networks are coupled, that is mutually interconnected (Figure 2). But while nodes which belong to the same network are fully connected between each other, the probability p for two nodes belonging to different networks is very low (in between 0.02 and 0.001, see below).

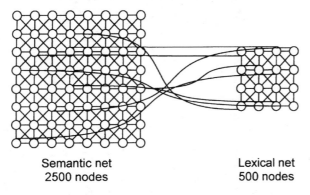

Semantic net   Lexical net
2500 nodes   500 nodes

Figure 2: Schematic representation of the model. Circles represent nodes (neurons), while lines represent bidirectional connection between nodes. Within the same network neurons are fully interconnected, while the connectivity between the two networks is much lower. See text for details.

Each sub-network is trained with 50 different patterns: the semantic network learns to memorize 50 patterns of 2500 values, which each pattern representing a 'meaning'. The

lexical network learns to memorize 50 patterns of 500 values, with each pattern representing a 'word' (form). All patterns are generated randomly, with a uniform probability, for each node, to be either in the active (1) or inactive (−1) state.

Each word form is associated with one word meaning, and the whole network, formed by the two semantical and lexical networks, learns such association in the following way. For each word form-word meaning pair, the corresponding word form pattern is presented to the lexical network, while, simultaneously, the corresponding word meaning pattern is presented to the semantic network. Connection weights which link the nodes of the two sub-networks are learned through the Hebb rule described above, in a way which is completely analogous to the learning of the intra-network connection weights.

Results

In our model (correct) linguistic production consists in activating the pattern in the lexical network (the word form) which corresponds to the pattern which is present in the semantic network (the word meaning). Viceversa, linguistic comprehension consists in activating, the semantic network, the meaning which corresponds to the word form which is present in the lexical network.

We have network's performance under two conditions: lexical recall and semantic recall. The lexical recall test, which is meant to test linguistic production, is done in the following way. For each pattern representing a meaning, that pattern is presented to the semantic network while the activations of all the nodes of the lexical network are set to zero. The whole network is then let relax, that is, nodes' activations are updated until the net has reached an attractor. At this point, we verify whether the pattern which is present in the lexical network is the correct one, that is, the pattern representing the word forms which corresponds to the given meaning. The semantic recall test, which is meant to test linguistic comprehension, is done in an analogous way: given a word form as the input to the lexical network, we check whether the recalled semantic pattern is the correct one.

In order to check for the presence of an asymmetry between linguistic production and linguistic comprehension in our model we have studied the behavior of the whole network with various levels of connectivity between the two sub-networks: in particular, with inter-networks connectivity in between 0.020 and 0.001.

For both conditions of semantic and lexical recall, and for each connectivity degree, we take two measures: (a) the percentage of correctly recalled patterns, and (b) the average recall time of the correctly recalled patterns (this is measured as the number of cycles which are necessary for the network to reach a stable point).

Figure 3 shows the percentage of correctly recalled patterns in the two experimental conditions as a function of the inter-networks connectivity, while Figure 4 shows average recall time. Reported data of both figures represent average results of 10 replications of each test with different random values.

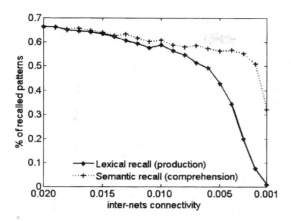

Figure 3: Percentage of correctly recalled patterns in both the lexical and the semantic recall tests as a function of inter-networks connectivity.

Generally speaking, the results show a clear asymmetry between production and comprehension, with a pattern simular to that which is found in reality: in fact, word production results to be more difficult than word comprehension, both in terms of number of correctly recalled patterns (Figure 3) and in terms of recall times (Figure 4).

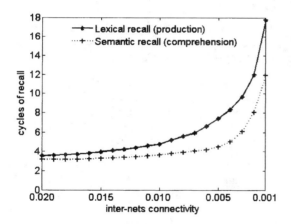

Figure 4: Average recall times of correctly recalled patterns in both the lexical and the semantic recall tests as a function of inter-networks connectivity.

Let's compare, for example, the results of the two conditions with a inter-nets connectivity degree of 0.002. In this case, while given a word form the correct meaning is recalled in about 50% of cases, given a meaning the probability of recalling the corresponding word form is just about 8%. Furthermore, with the same connectivity degree, while the average recall time in the semantic recall test is about 8 activation cycles, the average recall time in the lexical recall test is about 12 cycles.

Another interesting result of our simulations regards the different pattern which is shown by the production and comprehension curves as inter-nets connectivity decreases. In fact, the differences between lexical and semantic recall seem to increase as the connectivity degree decreases. This is in line with the fact, mentioned in the introduction, that while the asymmetry between linguistic production and linguistic comprehension is present during the whole lifetime, the asymmetry sharpens with aging, with a progressive impairment of linguistic production capabilities paralleled by an apparent preservation of linguistic comprehension capabilities. Our model suggests that this sharpening of the production-comprehension asymmetry could be due to the progressive decrease in the connectivity between the semantic and the lexical systems due to degenerative mechanisms related to aging.

Discussion and Conclusion

The model we have proposed in this paper represents an attempt to explain the asymmetry between production and comprehension of language which seems to take various forms: several different lines of evidence point to the fact that producing words is more difficult than understanding them, either for children, for normal adults, for elders, and, probably, also for patients with cerebral lesions. All these lines of evidence regard quite different phenomena and it is very likely that the various forms of production-comprehension asymmetries depend, in part, on different factors. Just to make an example, some degree of asymmetry between production and comprehension in child linguistic development is certainly due to the fact that words are socially learned. In fact, the capacity of comprehending a word, that is the ability to understand in which context that word is correctly applied, is of course a pre-requisite for the ability to produce it correctly, that is in the appropriate context. In other words, you cannot appropriately produce words which you do not understand. Hence, it seems inevitable that the number of understood words represent the superior limit with respect to the number of produced ones, and that linguistic production follow chronologically linguistic comprehension.

Notwithstanding the different factors which may underly the various forms which the production-comprehension asymmetry can take, it is also possible that these various forms have also a common cause.

In this contribution we proposed a neural model of the relationships between the semantic and the lexical systems which explains the greater difficulty in producing words than in comprehending them as a an effect of the size difference between the computational spaces which are devoted to the processing of word forms and word meanings, respectively. In fact, by just assuming that the brain regions devoted to semantic processing are considerably bigger (in terms of number of neurons involved) than those devoted to lexical processing, we have shown that lexical recall is more difficult than semantic recall, and that a decrease in the connections between the two areas leads to a decrease in lexical recall, while semantic recall remains more stable.

Obviously, our model suffer several limitations. A first limitation lies in the fact that in our model the asymmetry can be observed only when the network is able to recall, in both directions, only about 70% of the word forms or the word meanings of its repertoire. In reality, the asymmetry can be observed earlier: for example, elderly people begin to suffer word-finding problems when they are still able to comprehend all the words that they know. We are currently experimenting various ways in which this limitation might be overcome: for example, one possibility is to increase the size difference between the semantic and the lexical networks; another one is to decrease intra-networks connectivity (in our model, as in standard Hopfield networks, there is a full intra-net connectivity, but in the real brain the connectivity is certainly lower); still another possibility consists in abandoning the requirement of symmetrical connections which holds for standard Hopfield networks (in other words, a possibility is to make it possible for a neuron i to be connected with a neuron j without requiring that neuron j be connected to i: this is another change which would render the model more biologically realistic).

There are also more general limitations of our model. For example, in the current model the semantic system has no internal structure whatsoever. Meanings are represented, as it is common in neural network research, as patterns of activation distributed on a single group of neurons, which stands for the 'semantic system'. We already know that this is a strong oversimplification. For example, we know that different kinds of words, like names and verbs, are represented, in the real brain, in distinct groups of neurons (see, for example, Caramazza & Hillis, 1991). And even words of the same kind seem to be processed, at least partially, in different parts of the brain depending on their meaning (Martin, Wiggs, Ungerleider & Haxby, 1996; Plaut, 2002; Pulvermüller, 1999; Tettamanti, Buccino, Saccuman, Gallese, Danna, Scifo, Fazio, Rizzolatti & Cappa, 2005). Furthermore, the connectivity between different sub-groups of neurons devoted to processing different kinds of words it is certainly not uniform: not every group is connected to every other, or, at least, the connectivity degree between different pairs of groups is certainly different. As our model have already shown that the connectivity between groups influences inter-networks dynamics, an important way to improve the model is to consider this kind of empirical constrains. This possible line of future research might also allow us to explain other important phenomena, like the various forms of double-dissociations which are found language neuropsychology (see, for example, Caramazza & Mahon, 2005).

Another, even more general, limitation of our model consists in the fact that semantic representations (and also linguistic ones) are provided by us, the researchers, instead of being learnt (developed) by the network itself, as happens both in reality and in many other connectionist simulations. In order to solve this kind of limitation the model needs to be modified considerably, in that Hopfield networks, being constituted of a single group of neurons, cannot develop internal representations by themselves which would mediate between network's input and output, as happens in layered networks. Consequently, Hopfield networks require that memorized patterns be generated and provided directly by the researcher.

Notwithstanding the limitations we have just discussed, we claim that our model represents an important first attempt to find an explanation to the very well documented asymmetry between linguistic production and linguistic comprehension. In this respect, still another line of possible future research consists in trying to give a more detailed model of the various forms which the asymmetry can take. For example, we could differentiate between two possible different causes (beyond the size difference between the semantic and the lexical systems) which might underly the Tip-Of-the-Tongue phenomenon in young and elder adults. The first cause, common to both young and elder people, would be the presence of noise in neural transmission, which we know to be largely present in real brains and which could be easily simulated in various ways, for example by adding some noise in the information transfer between simulated neurons and/or in neurons' activation function. The second cause, which might underly the progressive deterioration of linguistic production in elderly people would lie, as already shown in our current model, in the decrease of connectivity both within and between the semantic and the lexical networks due to neuro-degenerative processes associated with aging.

Acknowledgments

The research presented in this paper has been supported by the ECAGENTS project founded by the Future and Emerging Technologies program (IST-FET) of the European Community under EU R&D contract IST-2003-1940. The information provided is the sole responsibility of the authors and does not reflect the Community's opinion. The Community is not responsible for any use that may be made of data appearing in this publication.

References

Bates, E., & Goodman, J.C. (1997). On the inseparability of grammar and the lexicon: Evidence from acquisition, aphasia, and real-time processing. *Language and Cognitive Processes*, 12(5-6), 507-584.

Bates, E., Thal, D., Finlay, B.L., & Clancy, B. (2002). Early language development and its neural correlates. In I. Rapin, & S. Segalowitz (eds.), *Handbook of neuropsychology*, Vol. 7: Child neurology. Amsterdam: Elsevier.

Brown, A.S. (1991). A review of the tip-of-the-tongue experience. *Psychological Bulletin*, 109(2), 204-223.

Burke, D.M., & MacKay, D.G. (1997). Memory, language and ageing. *Philosophical Transactions of the Royal Society: Biological Sciences*, 352, 1845-1856.

Burke, D.M., MacKay, D.G., & James, L.E. (2000). Theoretical approaches to language and aging. In T. Perfect, & E. Maylor (Eds.), *Models of cognitive aging*. Oxford: Oxford University Press.

Caramazza, A.H., & Hillis, A.E. (1991). Lexical organization of nouns and verbs in the brain. *Nature*, 349, 788-790.

Caramazza, A., & Mahon, B. (2005). The organisation of conceptual knowledge in the brain: the future's past and some future directions. *Cognitive Neuropsychology*, 22, 1-25.

Dick, F., Bates, E., Wulfeck, B., Utman, J., & Dronkers, N. (2001). Language deficits, localization, and grammar: Evidence for a distributive model of language breakdown in aphasics and normals. *Psychological Review*, 108 (4), 759-788.

Hebb, D. O. (1949). *The Organization of Behavior*. New York: John Wiley.

Heine, M., Ober, B., & Shenaut, G. (1999). Naturally occurring and experimentally induced tip-of-the-tongue experiences in three adult age groups. *Psychology and Aging*, 14(3), 445-457.

Hopfield, J. J. (1982). Neural networks and physical systems with emergent collective computational abilities. *Proceedings of the National Academy of Sciences*, 9, 2554–2558.

Kelso, S., Ganong, A., & Brown, T. (1986). Hebbian synapses in hippocampus. *Proceedings of the National Academy of sciences of the USA*, 83, 5326-5330.

Plaut, D.C. (2002). Graded modality-specific specialization in semantics: A computational account of optic aphasia. *Cognitive Neuropsychology*, 19(7), 603-639.

Plaut, D.C., & Shallice, T. (1993) Deep dyslexia: A case study of connectionist neuropsychology, *Cognitive Neuropsychology*, 10(5), 377-500.

Rolls, E. T., & Treves, A. (1998). *Neural Networks and Brain Function*. Oxford: Oxford University Press.

Rumelhart, D., McClelland, J. & the PDP Research Group (1986), *Parallel Distributed Processing: Explorations in the Microstructure of Cognition*, Vol. 1 & 2, Cambridge, MA: MIT Press.

Sharkey, A.J.C., & Sharkey, N.E. (1992) Weak contextual constraints in text and word priming. *Journal of Memory and Language*, 31, 543-572.

Stanton, P., & Sejnowski, T. (1989). Associative long-term depression in the hippocampus induced by hebbian covariance, *Nature*, 339(6221), 215-218.

Martin, A., Wiggs, C., Ungerleider, L., & Haxby, J. (1996). Neural correlates of category-specific knowledge. *Nature*, 379(6566), 649-52.

Pulvermüller, F. (1999). Words in the Brain's Language. *Behavioral and Brain Sciences*, 22, 253-279.

Tettamanti, M., Buccino, G., Saccuman, M., Gallese, V., Danna, M., Scifo, P., Fazio, F., Rizzolatti, G., & Cappa, S.P. (2005). Listening to action-related sentences activates fronto-parietal motor circuits. *Journal of Cognitive Neuroscience*, 17, 273-281.

A Sampling Explanation of Stereotype Formation

Jing Qian (qian@mpib-berlin.mpg.de)
Center for Adaptive Behavior and Cognition, Max Planck Institute for Human Development, Lentzeallee 94,
14195 Berlin, Germany

Rocio Garcia-Retamero (rretamer@mpib-berlin.mpg.de)
Center for Adaptive Behavior and Cognition, Max Planck Institute for Human Development, Lentzeallee 94,
14195 Berlin, Germany

Abstract

Previous studies on the process of stereotype formation have typically focused on the perception of correlation between group membership and certain behaviors or traits (Schaller & O'Brien, 1992), the effect of information loss (Fiedler, 1991), or pseudocontingencies (Fiedler & Freytag, 2004). We aim to provide an alternative explanation for the formation of social stereotypes using a sampling approach. We hypothesize that when the sample size is relatively small, after repeated sampling from a population where the proportional base rates of two groups differ greatly there will be a larger variance in the impressions formed of the underrepresented group, on average, than of the overrepresented group. We further assume that decision makers who are generally risk averse will prefer groups with low variance when they are faced with a choice between the two groups. Thus, on the one hand, risk aversion will lead decision makers to make a biased choice, but on the other hand, individuals are likely to adapt to the difference in opportunities by internalizing stereotypic beliefs associated with their roles. These stereotypes are difficult to modify due to a confirmatory bias (i.e., further sampling is likely to support existing stereotypes; Denrell, 2005).

Theoretical Approaches to the Formation of Stereotypes

To understand relations between groups in social cognition, we need to investigate how individuals come to perceive and learn about their own and other groups. A frequent topic in recent discussions about this issue is how social stereotypes are formed. Social stereotypes can be defined as perceived contingencies between social groups and certain behaviors or traits (Meiser & Hewstone, 2004).

One of the first theoretical attempts to address the question of how stereotypes are formed was proposed by Hamilton and Gifford (1976). They focused on the formation of distorted negative stereotypes about minorities. Specifically, they assumed that stereotypes can be explained by a consistent and erroneous association of minority group membership with a distinctive type of behavior. That is, people perceive relations between group membership and certain behaviors when no such relationship exists, an effect termed illusory correlation.

According to Hamilton and Gifford (1976), the cognitive process underlying the illusory correlation effect is that the co-occurrence of two relatively infrequent phenomena (i.e., being part of a minority group and having a particularly distinctive behavior) is especially noticeable. As a consequence, it automatically triggers the observer's attention. These jointly infrequent events are hence better encoded and more accessible for retrieval. Evidence for the illusory correlation effect in stereotype formation is abundant (see McGarty & de la Haye, 1997 for a review). However, in recent years a number of new explanations about how stereotypes are formed have been developed.

Schaller and O'Brien (1992) proposed that group memberships are perceived to correlate with certain behaviors, but such correlation is often spurious in nature because both group membership and behavior correlate with additional confounding factors (e.g., situational constraints such as town of residence). Therefore, accurate group inferences require that people recognize and control for the different confounding factors by using reasoning analogous to a statistical analysis of covariance. Schaller and O'Brien (1992) suggested that people often fail to engage in such reasoning and, consequently, form erroneous group impressions as a result of an incomplete statistical reasoning process. Schaller (1994) proposed a twofold explanation for the incomplete reasoning process: On the one hand, confounding factors may be overlooked or their correlations with group membership and the behavior may go unnoticed. On the other hand, people may perceive the correlations with confounding factors but fail to use this knowledge in judgment formation because of cognitive constraints on engaging in complex reasoning strategies. In either case, group impressions that result from incomplete reasoning should mirror the spurious correlation between group membership and behavior.

A departure from these approaches about stereotype formation was proposed by Fiedler (1991). His main thesis was that illusory correlation rested not so much on the detection and encoding of correlations, but emerged instead from the loss of information and regressive judgments, which are ubiquitous features of the social environment. This explanation forms the theoretical basis of Fiedler's (1996) BIAS model. According to the model, erroneous stereotypes typically arise from regressive effects in the presence of information loss for samples of small groups. That is, regressive effects apply to both small and large groups, but impressions based on small groups will suffer more distortion due to random information loss and regressive effects than those based on large groups.

Fiedler and Freytag (2004) provided another explanation for the formation of erroneous stereotypes by means of pseudocontingencies. The term pseudocontingency denotes the inference of correlation between group membership and a certain behavior on the basis of their marginal frequency distributions or their pairwise correlations with a third confounding factor. That is, if two variables (i.e., group membership and behavior) are positively correlated with a third factor and only little information is available about the correlation between the two variables, individuals may conclude that the two variables must show a positive correlation.

A wide range of research has tested the predictions of these theoretical explanations of stereotype formation. For instance, the incomplete statistical reasoning account gained support from studies that demonstrated that the judgment bias could be eliminated by interventions that counteract simplistic information processing. Specifically, providing explicit cues to take the confounding context variable into account (Schaller & O'Brien, 1992) and training in statistical reasoning with confounding factors led to less biased group judgments. More recent research has revealed, however, that simplistic information processing can occur even if people are aware of the correlation of group membership and a behavior with a confounding variable. For example, Fiedler, Walther, Freytag, and Nickel (2003) demonstrated that participants were sensitive to correlations with a confounding variable but they nonetheless fell prey to spurious correlations.

Meisser and Hewstone (2004) tested the predictions from the three recent competing theoretical accounts of stereotype formation mentioned above: the incomplete statistical reasoning account (Schaller & O'Brien, 1992), the BIAS model (Fiedler, 1996), and the pseudocontingency approach (Fiedler & Freytag, 2004). In three studies, a biased group stereotype was found together with sensitivity to covariation with a confounding factor. Furthermore, the relation between stereotype formation and learning of the covariation with the confounding factor was even stronger if participants' attention was focused on the confounding factor. These results support the assumptions of the pseudocontingency view that perceived pairwise correlation with a confounding factor is taken as the basis for inferring a contingency between group membership and a behavior and that this inferential process is strengthened by increased salience of the confounding factor.

In sum, these theoretical approaches to understanding the cognitive processes that cause biased group impressions have focused on the case of misleading covariation of group membership and certain traits or behaviors. The empirical evidence supports an explanation of biased group judgments by pseudocontingencies. However, in these accounts, behaviors and traits are typically considered as dichotomous variables; that is, group members either do or do not exhibit a particular trait or behavior. Yet there is evidence that frequently the traits and behaviors involved in people's stereotypic beliefs are not dichotomous. For instance, several studies on gender stereotypes have demonstrated that women are thought to be more communal (selfless and concerned with others) and less agentic (self-assertive and motivated to lead) than men (Eagly, 1987; Garcia-Retamero & Lopez-Zafra, in press). Although these studies identify stereotypic beliefs as continuous variables, there is no theoretical explanation of how these stereotypes are formed. In the following, we attempt to assess the formation of stereotypes in a quantitative manner. Specifically, we present a sampling process to explain the formation of biased group impressions.

An Alternative Explanation of Stereotype Formation: A Sampling Approach

Social stereotypes refer to the behaviors of individuals who belong to different groups. Information about group membership and behavior is sampled by observers from their environment. Sampling here can refer to direct sampling from the environment or to sampling from memory. Impressions of members of a group can be formed after sampling at each point in time. An overall impression of a group can be extracted over repeated sampling. Sampling never stops.

How can sampling contribute to the formation of stereotypes? Different stereotypes can be associated with groups that essentially share the same behavioral traits. People sample naturally from the environment, but if the members of different groups are represented with very different frequencies in the population, then biased impressions of the groups may arise even if the sampling process itself is not biased (see Kruschke, 1996, for a similar argument about category learning). For illustration, let us assume that a continuous behavioral trait is being assessed for members belonging to two different groups. If an observer samples more members from one group than the other at each sampling time stamp, the proportional base rates for the two groups will differ. For instance, in particularly male-congenial industries, it is very common for more men to be sampled than women. In female-congenial industries, more women are sampled than men. In the rest of this paper, we will illustrate with a male-congenial environment only. For the larger sample, the mean of the sample at each sampling time stamp is closer to the true population mean (according to the law of large numbers). In contrast, the mean of the smaller group is likely to be more variably distributed around the population mean. Over repeated sampling, different frequencies within each sample due to different base rates will result in the observer having a fairly clear impression of the overrepresented group, and a rather ambiguous one of the underrepresented group.

The size of a sample drawn from a population also has an effect on the distribution of the sample means. If the sample size is small, the means of the two groups are more variably distributed around the true population mean value, compared with the means calculated from a larger sample size. This statistical fact, however, is not easily grasped, as shown in Sedlmeier & Gigerenzer's (2000) experiments. The effect of sample size could have an impact on impressions. Specifically, if the sample sizes for both men and women are small, over repeated sampling, the variability of sample means (for men and women, respectively) will be larger compared with those derived from larger samples.

The impact of sample size on social stereotypes has been considered before (see Fiedler, 1991, 2000). However, the focus of previous studies has been on illusory *correlations* between group size and behavior. We will argue, as well as demonstrate with the results of a simulation study, that even if the means of two groups (e.g., mean intelligence for men and women) calculated for different sample sizes are not different, the variance for these means will differ as a result of sampling with different relative frequencies. We will further argue from the choice behavior point of view how groups with different variabilities are processed. Generally, risk-averse decision makers will prefer groups with low variance, thus resulting in biased choice. Finally, our conclusion that a biased choice may be internally justified by the decision maker and externally imposed on the members of each group to adopt social stereotypes.

We will illustrate our theory of stereotype formation using a simplified case about gender stereotypes. We restrict our focus to the beliefs about gender in the workplace because they are better documented by research and theoretical discussions than other stereotypic impressions (Eagly, 1987; Garcia-Retamero & Lopez-Zafra, 2006). In industrialized societies, women have entered the workforce in steadily increasing numbers. However, the percentage of women in many companies is still lower than that of men, especially in top positions and in male-congenial environments (Human Development Report, 2003). Therefore across different professions, men and women are unequally distributed in the paid workforce. For the sake of clear illustration, we further simplify the various gender stereotypes by focusing on a continuous trait of employability (analogously illustrated by IQ score), which is of a normal distribution. In the following paragraphs, we demonstrate that through disproportional sampling of the two gender subgroups within a population due to unequal distribution, favorable and unfavorable stereotypes concerning employability may emerge.

Imagine that there is a job opening for a position in a typical company and a personnel manager is engaged in an active sampling of potential employees. Following our argument, let us assume that there are more men than women applying for such positions, which is a consequence of the unequal distribution of men and women in the paid workforce. The manager will make the hiring decision based on the assessed employability of the candidates, which can be summarized in a holistic and intuitive impression about their suitability. For the purpose of exposing the logic behind this argument, we will use the well-known case of IQ scores to represent the general one-dimensional impression of employability. IQ scores are normally distributed with a mean of 100 and a standard deviation of 10. In this paper, we present the sampling argument by applying the central limit theorem[1] in two specific ways to illustrate the formation of gender stereotypes. First, we hypothesize that the more extreme the difference in the proportional base rates of the underrepresented and overrepresented groups, the larger the difference in the variance of the impressions formed for each subgroup. Second, we also hypothesize that the smaller the size of the samples, the larger the difference in the variance of the impressions for the two subgroups. Following our example, across repeated sampling, it might be the case that the variance of the impressions that the personnel manager forms for male candidates will be relatively small compared with the variance of the impressions of the female candidates. We tested these two hypotheses with a computer simulation. Following the simulation results we will show in more detail the effect of sample variance on the formation and reinforcement of social stereotypes.

Simulation

Method

In a series of computer simulations, we manipulated the process of sampling from a population where there was an underrepresented subgroup (women) and an overrepresented subgroup (men). We varied the proportional base rates of these two gender subgroups with six levels (i.e., males constituted 95%, 90%, 80%, 70%, 60%, and 50% of the candidates). We also manipulated the size of the samples drawn from the population with six levels (i.e., 15, 25, 50, 100, 200, and 1000 individuals). In sum, the design has three factors: 2 (gender) × 6 (sample size) × 6 (base rate), thus creating 36 combinations for each gender group.

For each combination of sample sizes and base rates, 1000 samples were drawn from a normally distributed

---

[1] The central limit theorem is a factual statement about the distribution of means. It states that given a population with mean μ and variance σ^2, the distribution of sample means will have a mean equal to μ and a variance equal to σ^2/N, as the sample size increases (Howell, 1997).

population of IQ scores. We then used a biased coin procedure to decide which subgroup the IQ scores belonged to. For example, if the base rate for males was 95%, a random number from a uniform distribution was generated, and if this number was larger than .95, we assigned the IQ score to a female, otherwise to a male.

In each sample, we computed the average IQ score in the male and female subgroups. For each gender group and combination of sample sizes and base rates, we then calculated the variance of the mean IQ score, and the maximum and minimum means.

Results

In general, we found the difference in variance of the mean IQ scores was negatively related to the size of the samples. Thus when the proportional base rate was held constant, smaller sample sizes led to larger variances of the mean score. This result applies to both gender groups. Contrasting the two gender groups, when the sample size was held constant, the larger the proportional base rate, the larger the variance of the mean score for the underrepresented group.

Figure 1 shows the average IQ scores of the female candidates across the 1000 simulated samples for the different sample sizes and base rate levels (i.e., 36 conditions altogether). In line with our hypothesis, in the female group, the smaller the sample size, the larger the variance of the mean. For instance, across all base rate levels the average variance of the mean IQ scores is 37.8 for a sample size of 15 and 0.7 for a sample size of 1000. The mean IQ score for the female group is 99.97.

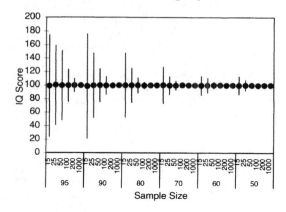

Figure 1: The means and the variances of the mean IQ scores for female candidates for different sample sizes and base rates. The filled circles represent the overall mean for each condition and the vertical lines represent the variance of the sample means.

Likewise, Figure 2 shows the average IQ scores of the male candidates across the 1000 simulated samples. Also in line with our hypothesis, in the male group, the smaller the sample size, the larger the variance of the mean. For

instance, across all base rate levels the average variance of the mean IQ scores is 9.8 for a sample size of 15, and 0.1 for a sample size of 1000. The mean IQ score for the male group is 100.

The effect of different base rates is shown by contrasting Figure 1 with Figure 2. For the most extreme base rate (i.e., 95%), the average variance of the mean IQ scores for the female group was 33.6, and for the male group 2.6, summed over all sample sizes. This is where the variance between two gender groups is largest. However, when the base rate for both males and females was 50%, the average variance of the mean IQ scores for both the male and female candidate groups was 4.99.

We can also see from Figures 1 and 2 that the mean IQ scores across all conditions do not vary noticeably. The sample means are usually a sufficient and unbiased estimator of the population mean, when scores in a population are normally distributed. Subgroups (samples) have equal average IQ scores in the population.

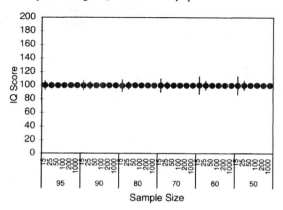

Figure 2: The means and the variances of the mean IQ scores for male candidates for different sample sizes and base rates. The filled circles represent the overall mean for each condition and the vertical lines represent the variance of the sample means.

Discussion

The main conclusion from our simulation results is that when the proportional base rates of two subgroups differ greatly, the scores for the underrepresented group have a wider distribution than those held by the relatively overrepresented group. As a consequence, a more variable impression about the underrepresented group would be formed. This is especially the case when small samples are drawn from the population.

Why does large variability of an impression pose a disadvantage for the subgroup carrying that impression? We will proceed by outlining several related studies that focus on (1) the process of associating favorable and unfavorable categorical impressions with groups of different sizes (Kruschke, 1996); (2) the outcome of typical versus atypical behavior associated with groups of different variability (Park & Hastie, 1987); and (3) the reinforcement of biased impressions, and the difficulty of correcting negative stereotypes (Denrell, 2005). Furthermore, we will present ways of correcting biased stereotypes and argue for the importance of adopting measures of positive discrimination in correcting negative stereotypes of underrepresented groups. We will conclude by arguing that our sampling approach offers an alternative way (using variance between different social subgroups rather than the correlations of means) to explain, at least theoretically, the formation of stereotypes. Our argument is natural and intuitive: It confirms our belief that the more we sample, especially about a relatively foreign group, the less biased view we will have of that group.

Now let us trace back to review the link between stereotype formation and the perception of variability of different social groups. For categorically dichotomous social groups (such as gender groups), when a particular trait is associated with one of the two subgroups, it is plausible and almost logical to infer the other group bears the opposite trait, especially when there is not sufficient information to refute the assumption. This argument is mentioned in a study on the effect of base rate and category learning (Kruschke, 1996), where the author showed that (under natural sampling) high-frequency categories are learned before low-frequency categories. Therefore, when people learn about low-frequency categories, they learn them in light of what they already know about the high-frequency categories, which are more commonly encountered. As a consequence, frequent categories are encoded by their typical features, whereas rare categories are encoded by their distinctive features. These effects of base rate on category learning tend to bias a decision maker to choose the more frequent categories when making a subsequent judgment. Thus, following Kruschke's argument, a typical trait such as good employability is more readily associated with the more frequently sampled group (assuming most candidates selected are fairly good in their performance). In our simulation the mean impression of employability formed for men and women did not differ much. However, it is still reasonable to assume that if such a favorable impression was associated with a particular group, that group is more likely, on average, to be the male group.

Park and Hastie (1987) provided a similar argument to Kruschke's, but from the point of view of variability within groups rather than different relative sample sizes. In two experimental studies, they manipulated the variability of the traits for members belonging to two groups, and they showed that participants were sensitive to the variability information and were more likely to associate a typical trait with the less variable group, and an atypical trait with the more variable group.

Our sampling approach used a continuous variable rather than dichotomous traits, thus we can assess the impact of sample size and proportional base rate on the strength of impressions formed about the two groups. Following our argument, individuals can form a more consistent stereotype about a majority group than about a minority group due to the number of observations sampled for each group. In situations where people do not have a consistent or strong belief about stereotypes formed by their individual observations, they often exchange information socially. Although not elaborated in the current theory, the psychological process of stereotype formation is most certainly also a result of social communication, especially when individual learning is costly. In such cases, people may adopt a heuristic approach in forming their own stereotypes about minority groups, and such a process often involves adopting the existing stereotypes held by an authoritative voice or by the majority of their community (Hastie & Kameda, 2005). Furthermore, our approach to stereotype formation does not assume a cognitive process that correlates particular behaviors or traits with a particular group but rather uses the results of choice behavior to show the establishment and reinforcement of social stereotypes.

Despite individual differences, there is abundant evidence arguing for a general risk-averse attitude toward choices involving risk and uncertainty (e.g., ambiguity aversion in decision making under uncertainty; Ellsberg, 1961). Typically, people prefer less risky over more risky options in the domain of potential gains. This phenomenon is referred to as the certainty effect. For instance, when choosing between a riskless option (e.g., earning $3 for sure) versus a risky option (e.g., an 80% chance of earning $4 or otherwise nothing), people tend to choose the risk-free option although the expected value for the risky option is higher. In other words, people tend to avoid taking an option that has more variance than a safer option. Following the example we presented earlier, when selecting a candidate for an open position, a personnel manager will be influenced by the certainty effect, thus picking the male candidate because it is a less risky option. Under such reinforcement, risk aversion and differences in variance of the impressions formed about the subgroups will lead to biased choices.

Men and women will adapt to differences in job opportunities by internalizing stereotypes associated with their gender roles and acquiring role-related skills. That is, women might think that they tend to occupy positions of lower power and control fewer resources than men. Possibly, the acquisition of role-related skills congruent with gender stereotypes will help men and women maximize their outcomes within the constraints of the societal structure.

Stereotype is often used as a simplified code that ultimately influences organization decisions (e.g., whether to hire a person from a particular social group) or social decisions (e.g., whether to interact with a person from a social group; Denrell, 2005). It is most likely that individuals with stereotypic beliefs about a certain group will sample less information about the members of such groups and in such a way as to strengthen the stereotypic beliefs. For instance, when a positive impression about employability about male candidates is formed, an employer is likely to sample more men than women. This kind of selective sampling can occur when people seek to confirm a hypothesis they are already holding (Klayman & Ha, 1989). This biased sampling process and the even more asymmetric gender distributions in the society will lead to an even more variable impression about the underrepresented group in the population, which, ultimately, will support people's risk perceptions and confirm their stereotypic beliefs (i.e., employing men might be perceived as an even wiser choice).

That is, in the case of using gender stereotype as a cue to decide which candidate to hire in the future, a personnel manager will be more prone to select a male candidate over a female candidate. As a consequence, the stereotypic beliefs will maintain differences in gender distributions in the society.

References

Denrell, J. (2005). Why most people disapprove of me: Experience sampling in impression formation. *Psychological Review, 112,* 951–978.

Eagly, A. H. (1987). *Sex differences in social behavior: A social-role interpretation.* Hillsdale, NJ: Lawrence Erlbaum.

Ellsberg, D. (1961). Risk, ambiguity, and the Savage axioms. *Quarterly Journal of Economics, 75,* 643–669.

Fiedler, K. (1991). The tricky nature of skewed frequency tables: An information loss account of distinctiveness-based illusory correlations. *Journal of Personality and Social Psychology, 60,* 24–36.

Fiedler, K. (1996). Explaining and simulating judgment biases as an aggregation phenomenon in probabilistic, multiple-cue environments. *Psychological Review, 103,* 193–214.

Fiedler, K., & Freytag, P. (2004). Pseudocontingencies. *Journal of Personality and Social Psychology, 87,* 453–467.

Fiedler, K., Walther, E., Freytag, P., & Nickel, S. (2003). Inductive reasoning and judgment interference: Experiments on Simpson's paradox. *Personality and Social Psychology Bulletin, 29,* 14–27.

Garcia-Retamero, R., & Lopez-Zafra, E. (2006). Prejudice against women in male-congenial environments: Perceptions of gender role congruity in leadership. *Sex Roles, 55,* 51-61.

Hamilton, D. L., & Gifford, R. K. (1976). Illusory correlation in interpersonal perception: A cognitive basis of stereotypic judgments. *Journal of Experimental Social Psychology, 12,* 392–407.

Hastie, R., & Kameda, T. (2005). The robust beauty of majority rules in group decisions. *Psychological Review, 112,* 494-508.

Howell, D. C. (1997). *Statistical methods for psychology* (4th ed.). Belmont, CA: Duxbury Press.

Human Development Report. (2003). *Millennium development goals: A compact among nation to end human poverty.* Retrieved August 4, 2006, from http://hdr.undp.org/reports/global/2003/pdf/hdr03_complete.pdf.

Klayman, J., & Ha, Y-W. (1987). Confirmation, disconformation and information in hypothesis testing. *Psychological Review, 94,* 211-228.

Kruschke, J. (1996). Base rates in category learning. *Journal of Experimental Psychology: Learning, Memory and Cognition, 22,* 3–26.

McGarty, C., & de la Haye, A. M. (1997). Stereotype formation: Beyond illusory correlation. In R. Spears, P. J. Oakes, N. Ellemers, & S. A. Haslam (Eds.), *The social psychology of stereotyping and group life.* Oxford: Blackwell.

Meisser, T., & Hewstone, M. (2004). Cognitive processes in stereotype formation: The role of correct contingency learning for biased group judgments. *Journal of Personality and Social Psychology, 87,* 599–614.

Park, B., & Hastie, R. (1987). Perception of variability in category development: Instance- versus abstraction-based stereotypes. *Journal of Personality and Social Psychology, 53,* 621-635.

Schaller, M. (1994). The role of statistical reasoning in the formation, preservation and prevention of group stereotypes. *British Journal of Social Psychology, 33,* 47–61.

Schaller, M., & O'Brien, M. (1992). "Intuitive analysis of covariance" and group stereotype formation. *Personality and Social Psychology Bulletin, 18,* 776–785.

Sedlmeier, P., & Gigerenzer, G., (2000). Was Bernoulli wrong? On intuitions about sample size. *Journal of Behavioral Decision Making, 13,* 133-139.

Level of representation and semantic distance:
Rating author personality from texts

Alastair J. Gill (A.Gill@ed.ac.uk)
LEAD-CNRS UMR 5022, University of Burgundy
Dijon 21000, France

Robert M. French (robert.french@u-bourgogne.fr)
LEAD-CNRS UMR 5022, University of Burgundy
Dijon 21000, France

Abstract

Increasingly our perception of others is based on short samples of written text, for example, in e-mail or chat rooms. In this paper we will examine the extent to which text co-occurrence techniques, such as LSA, HAL, and PMI-IR, can be successfully applied to human personality perception based on short written texts. In particular, we compare two approaches: The first compares a "surface similarity" judgment of the text being rated to a description by the author of the text of his/her personality (Simulation 1). The second relies on extracting a very simple representation of author personality from extreme texts and judging the experimental texts on the basis of this representation (Simulation 2). Both of these approaches fail to distinguish personality type. We conclude that co-occurrence techniques, at least used in a relatively canonical way to assess personality from small text samples, are not only inadequate but, most probably, are not doing this in a way that is similar to how we humans rate personality from short text samples.

Introduction

In daily life we may open up our e-mail inbox to discover a message from an unknown individual. We may read through the message and notice that the text's author mentions *parties*, *people*, and *socializing* very frequently. How do we then make a judgment about the author's personality on the basis of these few 'key terms' extracted from the text?

Personality traits are relatively stable over time and relate to an individual's "core qualities". Therefore, judging an individual's personality involves trying to predict future behaviour on the basis of their current or observed behaviour. In this paper we focus on the two traits central to personality theories, Extraversion and Neuroticism (Kline, 1991). Key adjectives that characterize these two traits were taken from Goldberg's five-factor model (FFM; Goldberg, 1992) and used to conceptualise personality in Simulation 1 (see Table 1).

Studies of personality perception show remarkable levels of consensus for these two traits (especially for Extraversion), even in text-only computer-mediated communication (CMC) environments, such as e-mail, chatrooms, and personal websites (Gill, Oberlander & Austin, 2006; Markey & Wells, 2002; Vazire & Gosling, 2004). Furthermore, both Extraversion and Neuroticism influence language at the level of both content and grammar (Oberlander & Gill, 2006; Pennebaker & King, 1999), a fact

that has been successfully applied to the task of author personality classification from text (Argamon, Sushant, Koppel, & Pennebaker, 2005; Oberlander & Nowson, 2006).

Although there are models of human processes of personality judgment and perception (cf. Realistic Accuracy Model, Funder, 1995; Weighted-Average Model, Kenny, 1991), these models do not address how representations of personality types – such as those described in the Five-Factor Model (FFM; Goldberg, 1992) – are actually used to determine real world behavior.

In what follows we present two possible explanations of how this might be done. We then test these explanations using three well-known text co-occurrence programs (LSA, HAL, PMI-IR). The first possible explanation, explored in Simulation 1, is that people are simply doing a (largely unconscious) comparison of the overall semantic distance of a number of key terms in the written text directly to the words representing the personality concept: We refer to this as a "surface similarity" judgment. In this case, for example, we would make a rapid mental calculation of the overall semantic similarity between *parties*, *people*, *socializing* (words taken from the text under consideration) and *active*, *enthusiastic*, *talkative*, words that we know (cf. Goldberg, 1992) to be indicative of extraversion. In Simulation 2, we explore an arguably more realistic, stronger method. How do individual raters use abstract personality concept information (e.g., *active*, *enthusiastic*, *talkative*) to develop a higher-level representation of an extravert, from which they can then form a shared meaning system (Kenny, 1991; French, 1995). In text rating situations, such a meaning system may give rise to concepts like *parties*, *fun*, and *exciting* which would be expected to be in extravert writing. This "representative extravert text" would then be compared – in terms of its semantic similarity – to the key terms derived from the text written by the unknown author in order to determine the extent to which he/she seems to be an extravert. Note that the former strategy does not require the building of a higher-level structural representation of the personality of the text's author. Therefore, it would be computationally less intensive and, in a world of constant competition for cognitive resources, it would be the preferred assessment strategy, assuming it was sufficient for accurate personality ratings.

To explore the two means of evaluating a short written text in order to determine the personality of its author, we adopt statistical text co-occurrence measures of semantic space. These programs are able to compare texts in terms of their general meaning level which make them more suitable for the exploration of human behavior compared to traditional machine learning techniques which search for particular words or types (e.g., Argamon, Sushant, Koppel, & Pennebaker, 2005; Oberlander & Nowson, 2006). The driving idea behind co-occurrence programs, such as, HAL (Lund, Burgess & Atchley, 1995), LSA (Landauer and Dumais, 1997), and PMI-IR (Turney, 2002), is that they can determine the semantics (or, at least, some of the semantics) of a word by analyzing "the company it keeps" in a large corpus of text (Firth, 1957). In short, the average degree of physical proximity over a large number of texts of two words is a measure of their semantic proximity. The size of the *semantic neighbourhood* varies across the different approaches. For example in HAL, it is limited to a few words, whereas for LSA it is the entire document in which the word is found. Although the statistical methods employed to determine co-occurrence vary across the programs, they have demonstrated human-like ability and performance in tasks such as English language learner synonym tasks (e.g., Landauer & Dumais, 1997), classifying the semantic orientation (good vs bad, etc.) of individual words and movie reviews (Turney, 2002; Turney & Littman, 2003), analogical retrieval, (Ramscar & Yarlett, 2003), and even in visual fixations (Huettig et al, 2006; cf. Bullinaria & Levy, in press).

However, critics of co-occurrence techniques as models of human semantic processing argue that to have a truly human understanding of meaning requires human world knowledge and human experience (Glenberg & Robertson, 2000; French & Labiouse, 2002): To correctly judge semantic distances between words, for example, to know how good *John* is as the name of a child's mother, one needs world knowledge, in this case, that mothers are always female, and that John is a male name (French & Labiouse, 2002). Indeed, Bullinaria & Levy (in press) observe that "obviously, co-occurrence statistics *on their own* [original emphasis] will not be sufficient to build complete and reliable lexical representations".

In this paper, we examine the abilities HAL, LSA, and PMI-IR in measuring the semantic similarity between the language of texts actually written by Extravert authors, and words representing Extraverts (such as those used to describe Extraverts, e.g., *enthusiastic*, *talkative* in Simulation 1; or those derived from highly Extravert authors, e.g., *parties, fun, exciting*, in Simulation 2).

Simulation 1

Method

Procedure Here we infer high/low personality orientation for Extraversion and Neuroticism on the basis of direct semantic associations between words in the target texts and "personality trait words" considered to characterize these two traits, taken from Goldberg's Five-Factor Model. The personality orientation of a given word is calculated from the strength of associations with the set of high personality trait words (i.e., words that "define" the trait) minus the

strength of its association with a set of low personality trait words (cf. Turney, 2002 and Turney and Litttman, 2003). The precise formula used for this calculation can be found in Turney (2002).

Calculation of Semantic Space
The following programs and parameters were used for the calculation of semantic association:

- **HAL** was implemented using the British National Corpus (BNC), using a rectangular window of 7 words and distance between vectors calculated using cosine, as reported in Huettig et al. (2006).[1]
- **LSA** (Landauer, & Dumais, 1997) uses the University of Colorado at Boulder website[2] using the default semantic space derived from the 'General Reading up to 1st year of college' TASA corpus, and the maximum number of factors available (300). The comparison type used was 'term to term'.
- **PMI-IR** uses the Waterloo MultiText System (WMTS) corpus of around 5×10^{10} English words (due to changes in the functioning of AltaVista; cf. Turney, 2002).[3]

Extraversion		Neuroticism	
High	Low	High	Low
talkative	silent	emotional	calm
bold	timid	nervous	relaxed
assertive	compliant	subjective	objective
spontan-eous	inhibited	worrying	placid
active	passive	volatile	peaceful
energetic	lethargic	insecure	independ-ent
enthusi-astic	apathetic	fearful	inhibited

Table 1: Matched pairs of words associated with high/low Extraversion or Neuroticism (from Goldberg, 1992). These were the words used in Simulation 1 to determine how well the personality traits they characterized were related to the key words taken from the experimental texts.

Derivation of Personality Trait Words
Goldberg's (1992) five-factor model of personality (FFM) provided adjectives to describe the high/low extremes of the Extraversion and Neuroticism personality traits used in Simulation 1 (cf. prose descriptions of EPQ-R; Eysenck &

---

[1] A local version of this software was made available by Scott McDonald; an online version is available at: http://www.cogsci.ed.ac.uk/~scottm/semantic_space_model.html.
[2] Available from: http://lsa.colorado.edu.
[3] The Perl scripts used for the calculation of PMI-IR were modified from original versions kindly supplied by Peter Turney who also arranged for access to WMTS. An alternative version using Google can be found at: http://www.d.umn.edu/~tpederse.

Eysenck, 1991). Duplicates and multi-word phrases were removed, as were any words that did not appear in the 100 million-word British National Corpus (BNC). Seven matched high-low pairs for Extraversion (e.g., talkative-silent) and Neuroticism (e.g., emotional-calm) were selected in order of their strength in rating the trait, as in Goldberg's original study (cf. Goldberg, 1992, p. 33, Table 2). These matched pairs can be found in Table 1.

Selection of Personality Texts

All experimental texts (a corpus of around 65,000 words) were collected as part of previous experimentation (Gill et al. 2006; Oberlander & Gill, 2006): This consisted of e-mail texts collected from 105 current or recently graduated university students each of whom completed the Eysenck Personality Questionnaire (Revised form, EPQ-R; Eysenck & Eysenck, 1991), thereby providing self-report information for Extraversion and Neuroticism. Thus, for each of the texts we have a self-report by its author of his/her degree of Extraversion and Neuroticism. We did not do co-occurrence analyses of all words in each text, but rather extracted the following key words from the texts:

- The 10 most frequent open-class words, since these represent contentful language at its most general level. These were selected following the removal of the 363 most commonly occurring closed-class words (e.g. prepositions, determiners, conjunctions, and pronouns);
- The 10 most frequent adjectives and;
- The 10 most frequent adverbs.

The adjectives and adverbs were extracted from the texts after automatic tagging for parts of speech (Oberlander & Gill, 2006). We chose these classes of words since they have been used previously for semantic orientation (cf. Turney, 2002).

Relating Semantic Space and Author Personality

HAL, LSA, and PMI-IR were used to derive distances of semantic association for each experimental text with the high/low personality description adjectives for Extraversion and Neuroticism. The semantic orientation value for each of the 105 experimental texts (in the form of top 10 Open-class words, top 10 adjective, and top 10 adverb groups) was then correlated with author self-ratings derived using the EPQ-R (Eysenck & Eysenck, 1991).

Results and Discussion

There was only one significant – but *inverse* – correlation between the ten most frequent open-class words, the ten most frequent adjectives and the ten most frequent adverbs taken from the sample texts and the personality-defining words (see Table 1) from Goldberg's Five-Factor Model (1992). This was the correlation identified by PMI-IR between 10 Adjectives extracted from texts and the high-low Neuroticism trait-defining words from Table 1 ($r=-.25$; $p<.05$). No other significant correlation was found by any of the programs.

The surprising result of this simulation is that the most frequently occurring words (open-class, adjectives and adverbs) taken from short texts written by authors who provided self-ratings of their personality are simply not in the proximal co-occurrence neighborhoods of the trait-defining words established by Goldberg (1992). The difficulty lies perhaps in the fact that Extraverts may not actually write texts which includes language fitting an abstract description of themselves and their behavior. Indeed, this is a particularly important consideration for traits such as Neuroticism, which are often characterized more by internal behavior, rather than outward, expressive behaviors towards others, including, in this case, any description of one's own Neuroticism.

In any event, these results show that personality-appraisal techniques relying on semantic similarities between the most frequently used words in a text and words providing an abstract characterization of a particular trait do not work. It therefore appears likely that human personality raters do not rely on cues from the most frequently used words, but rather know ahead of time the sorts of words to look for. In order to do this, he/she must already have at least a simple *model* (i.e., a more complex internal representation) of an extravert or a neurotic person. This intuition is the basis of the second simulation.

Simulation 2

Method

Procedure In Simulation 1, we have shown that a direct co-occurrence comparison of personality-defining concepts (see Table 1) with a pre-selected set of text words does not seem to be enough to enable accurate personality judgments from short textual data. We have proposed that a human judge may use personality information at a conceptual level to create a simple representation of an imagined author of such a short text message and derive personality conclusions based on that. For example, by inferring that an Extraverted individual may write texts that talk about *parties, people,* and *socializing*, the judge would then be able to assess how closely the text in front of him or her matched such a schema. In Simulation 2, we consider one simple means of developing a "high-level" representation of personality, and, once again, examine the results using standard co-occurrence programs as in Simulation 1.

Calculation of Semantic Space

The same programs (HAL, LSA, and PMI-IR) with parameters as in Simulation 1 were used for the calculation of semantic space.

Derivation of Personality Trait Words The authors of the short texts used in this study rated themselves in terms of Extraversion and Neuroticism facets of their overall personality. We were therefore able to identify authors in our e-mail corpus who scored greater than 1 standard deviation from the mean for the personality traits under investigation (cf. Oberlander & Gill, 2006). This gave us four groups of individuals: High Extraversion, Low Extraversion, High Neuroticism and Low Neuroticism. These four groups contained the e-mails texts of 11, 4, 6, 9

Trait	Top 7 Open-class words extracted from e-mail texts		Top 7 adjectives extracted from e-mail texts		Top 7 adverbs extracted from e-mail texts	
	Extraversion	**Neuroticism**	**Extraversion**	**Neuroticism**	**Extraversion**	**Neuroticism**
High	back	people	other	many	hopefully	even
	nice	going	long	local	as	though
	also	film	cool	big	still	better
	Christmas	write	more	awful	anyway	away
	too	try	great	total	out	actually
	come	home	big	short	however	out
	long	want	busy	positive	better	only
Low	play	know	second	sure	much	still
	much	day	same	same	fairly	rather
	first	come	hard	least	especially	here
	actually	plan	funny	flat	down	ever
	know	year	fresh	usual	recently	down
	give	too	least	long	sure	forward
	down	new	full	exciting	often	long

Table 2: Simulation 2 exemplars derived from High/Low e-mail texts

authors respectively. These texts were then concatenated so as to form one large text for each of the four groups. After removing the most frequent closed-class words, we then selected the seven most frequent Open-class words, Adjectives and Adverbs for each of the four personality groups as in Simulation 1. These empirically derived personality-trait words can be found in Table 2.

Selection of Personality Texts

The same experimental texts were used as in Simulation 1. However, after excluding the texts of the 15 most extreme High Neurotic, Low Neurotic, High Extravert, Low Extravert authors, whose texts were used to derive the "personality representation" words, we used the remaining 90 texts for co-occurrence testing (rather than all of the original 105 texts).

Relating Semantic Space and Author Personality

As in Simulation 1 we attempt to infer high/low personality orientation for Extraversion and Neuroticism on the basis of semantic associations, again using HAL, LSA, and PMI-IR. The only difference is that that personality-trait words were not derived, as they were in Simulation 1, from an abstract model of personality discrimination -- in this case, the Goldberg's Five-Factor Model (Goldberg, 1992) -- but rather were derived directly from the texts written by authors whose personality self-ratings placed them at the extremes of the High-Low continuum for Neuroticism and Extraversion. We considered that these latter sets of words, derived directly from participants' texts, constituted a simple "representation" of the written texts by the strongest representatives of each of the four classes, namely, High Extraversion, Low Extraversion, High Neuroticism, and Low Neuroticism. In short, we felt that this technique would provide an even better chance for LSA, HAL, and PMI-IR

to succeed in correctly classifying the remaining 90 texts correctly as to the personalities of their authors.

In all other respects this simulation was identical in methodology to Simulation 1.

Results and Discussion

Quite surprisingly, the results of the co-occurrence analyses using exemplars derived from high/low Extravert and Neurotic authors (Table 3) once again showed that all correlations were less than 0.20 and none of them were significant at the $p<.05$ level. The results from the co-occurrence analyses are not even close to those to the personality perception abilites of human judges for the same material, for example, Gill et al. (2006) found that target-judges agreement of $r=0.89$ ($p<0.05$) for ratings of Extraversion using the e-mail texts of the present study. Markey & Wells (2002) found agreement in ratings of Extraversion following one-on-one CMC chat of $r=.32$ ($p<0.05$), with other forms of CMC, such as personal websites (Vazire & Gosling, 2004) giving self-observer agreement of $r=.26$ and $r=.21$ for Extraversion and Neuroticism (both $p<0.05$), although we note that these were not necessarily text-only. We discuss possible reasons for this disparity in the General Discussion, below.

General Discussion

Humans are able to form, to a significant level of agreement, impressions of each other via short written texts, such as e-mail or chat rooms. However little is known about this process. In this paper we proposed two possible methods of such judgment processes, and implemented them using three widely-used co-occurrence techniques.

First, we explore the possibility, and note the benefits of, a 'fast and frugal' method of personality text classification, which simply assesses, at a surface level, 'how Extraverted' the words in the texts appear (cf. Friedrich, 1993; French, 1995). We simulate this model by calculating co-occurrence associations between our experimental texts and personality trait adjectives taken from a standard model of personality-trait judgment (Goldberg, 1992) and which describe high/low Extraversion and high/low Neuroticism (Simulation 1).

Second, in contrast to this first, simple comparative technique where personality trait words are directly compared to the experimental texts, we propose a more structural approach in which a set of words is derived from the texts written by authors with the (self-evaluated) strongest personalities along the two trait dimensions. We reasoned that these texts would be the best representatives of texts written by authors from the four categories of personality traits. We extracted the key words from these texts and then used these words to judge the remaining texts. Even under these conditions, we still observe no useful correlations obtained by any of the three co-occurrence programs that would allow them to be able to reliably extract a personality judgment from any given text sample.

These results are somewhat surprising in light of the clear success of co-occurrence programs in areas such as synonym matching and assessing opinions from text (Landauer & Dumais, 1997; Lund et al. 1995; Turney, 2002; Turney & Littman, 2003). In our view, this argues for the intrinsic difficulty of the task of personality perception. In other words, it is reasonable to assume that, had there been *some* significant co-occurrence correlations between either standard personality-trait words and words used in short texts (Simulation 1) or frequently used words derived from texts that are arguably representative of texts written by authors at the extremes of the personality traits under consideration (Simulation 2), LSA, HAL, or PMI-IR would have noticed these correlations. However, this was not the case and one must assume, therefore, that these correlations do not exist, at least, for the sets of words that we chose to characterize the texts and the personality traits. This was, presumably, why the performance of all three co-occurrences programs was not even close to human-like performance on this task.

Humans, it turns out, are able to accurately rate short written texts in terms of the personality of their authors (e.g., Gill, et al. 2006; Markey & Wells, 2002). So, why, when given the input, at first blush, reasonable, described in our simulations, do co-occurrence programs fail so completely on this task? The answer almost certainly lies with the selection of the data. We have characterized texts by looking at the most frequently used closed-class words, adjectives and adverbs. This is necessary to provide concise textual representations for the computationally intensive semantic space calculations by the co-occurrence programs. Human raters, in contrast, have access to the full texts (cf. Gill, et al. 2006) and can, therefore, build a far richer representation, aided by years of experience and world knowledge about how various kinds of people write, of the text's author. We have characterized the various personalities by a set of words taken from Golberg's FFM personality judgment model or from texts written by authors

at the ends of each personality-trait continuum. Clearly, both the representations of our sample texts on the basis of their top-ten closed-class words, adjectives, and adverbs and these personality-trait representations are insufficient. It is not that LSA, HAL, or PMI-IR are "not working correctly". Presumably, they are working fine. They simply are not doing what humans are doing in performing this task because they lack the extra-text information that people have at their disposal and that has been gathered from years of experience with correlating people behavior with their writing styles. We would argue that humans, on the basis of several words in the text, can build a rich and complex representation – unlike the skeletal representations that we were able to derive from simple analysis of "paradigmatic" texts – of the potential author of the short text message they are considering. This representation is grounded in a lifetime of experience judging people based on what they say and write and, therefore, people are able to intuit far more accurately the personality of the author of the text they are reading than a co-occurrence program that is given only scant textual information on which to make its judgment.

These results would appear to suggest that, in order to do reliable extraction of personality-trait information from short texts, it is necessary to have a representation-building capacity that is, at present, beyond the reach of standard co-occurrence programs.

Conclusion

In this paper we have explored the possibility of using well-known co-occurrence programs (LSA, HAL, and PMI-IR) to perform personality judgments based on short, written texts. We first examined an approach based on a surface similarity judgment of the text being compared to words taken from a standard, abstract personality-trait model (Goldberg, 1992). None of the co-occurrence programs using this approach were able to reliably extract any personality-trait information from the texts. Next we attempted to use words taken from paradigmatic examples of texts written by authors who identified themselves as high/low Extravert or Neurotic via the EPQ-R self-rating personality questionnaire. Here again, all co-occurrence programs failed to find any reliable correlation between key words taken from these paradigmatic texts and a sample of 90 short written texts, for each of which we had a personality self-rating by the text's author.

This leads us to the conclusion that, at the present time, co-occurrence programs are not appropriate tools for this kind of evaluation. We suggest, however, that this is because they cannot presently develop the high-level representations of personality that we humans can. Once they begin to acquire this ability, we believe their ability to judge personality from short texts will gradually come in line with that of humans. Finally, this work suggests the somewhat unsuspected difficulty of automatic personality assessment. It would seem that humans, in order to perform this task, rely on information garnered from years of experience correlating people's behavior with their writing styles and this information is simply not present in an analysis of even a relatively large sample of texts (over a hundred).

Acknowledgments

This work was supported in part by a Région de Bourgogne FABER Post-Doctoral Fellowship (05512AA06S2469) and by European Commission Sixth Framework grant NEST 516542 (second author). Thanks to Jon Oberlander, Matthias Mehl, Jim Friedrich and our anonymous reviewers for their helpful comments on earlier versions of this paper. We gratefully acknowledge the generosity of Scott McDonald and Peter Turney for making their software available and for their assistance in responding to questions.

References

Agamon, S., Sushant, D., Koppel, M. & Pennebaker, J. (2005). Lexical predictors of personality type. In *Proceedings of the 2005 Joint Annual Meeting of the Interface and Classification Society of North America*.

Bullinaria, J.A. & Levy, J.P. (in press). Extracting Semantic Representations from Word Co-occurrence Statistics: A Computational Study. *Behavior Research Methods*, 38.

Eysenck, H. & Eysenck, S. B. G. (1991). *The Eysenck Personality Questionnaire-Revised*. Hodder & Stoughton, Sevenoaks.

Firth, J.R. (1957). A synopsis of linguistic theory 1930-1955. In *Studies in Linguistic Analysis*, pp. 1-32. Oxford: Philological Society; reprinted in Palmer, F., (ed. 1968), Selected Papers of J. R. Firth, Longman, Harlow.

French, R.M. (1995). *The Subtlety of Sameness*. Cambridge: MIT Press.

French, R. M. & Labiouse, C. (2002). Four Problems with Extracting Human Semantics from Large Text Corpora. *Proceedings of the 24th Annual Conference of the Cognitive Science Society*. NJ:LEA.

Friedrich, J. (1993), Primary Error Detection and Minimization (PEDMIN) Strategies in Social Cognition: A Reinterpretation of Confirmation Bias Phenomena, *Psychological Review*, 100 (2), 298-319.

Funder, D.C. (1995). On the accuracy of personality judgment: A realistic approach. *Psychological Review*, 102, 652-670.

Gill, A.,J. Oberlander, J. & Austin, E. 2006. Rating e-mail personality at zero acquaintance. *Personality and Individual Differences*, 40:497–507.

Goldberg, L. (1992). Development of markers for the Big-Five factor structure. *Psychological Assessment*, 4, 26-42.

Huettig, F., Quinlan, P. T., McDonald, S. A. & Altmann, G. T. M. (2006). Models of high-dimensional semantic space predict language-mediated eye movements in the visual world. *Acta Psychologica*, 121, 65-80.

Landauer, T.K., & Dumais, S.T. (1997). A solution to Plato's problem: The latent semantic analysis theory of the acquisition, induction, and representation of knowledge. *Psychological Review*, 104(2):211–240.

Lund, K., Burgess, C., & Atchley, R.A. (1995). Semantic and associative priming in high-dimensional semantic space. In *Proceedings of the 17th Annual Conference of the Cognitive Science Society*, pages 660-665.

Markey, P. and Wells, S. (2002). Interpersonal perception in internet chat rooms. *Journal of Research in Personality*, 36:134–146.

Oberlander, J. & Gill, A.J. (2006). Language with character: A stratified corpus comparison of individual differences in e-mail communication. *Discourse Processes*, 42, 239–270.

Oberlander, J. and Nowson, S. (2006). Whose thumb is it anyway? Classifying author personality from weblog text. In *Proceedings 44th Annual Meeting of the Association for Computational Linguistics, Sydney, Australia*.

Pennebaker, J.W. & King, L. (1999). Linguistic styles: Language use as an individual difference. *Journal of Personality and Social Psychology*, 77, 1296–1312.

Ramscar M.J.A. and Yarlett D.G. (2003). Semantic Grounding in Analogical Processing: An Environmental Approach, *Cognitive Science*, 27, 41-71.

Turney, P.D. (2002), Thumbs up or thumbs down? Semantic orientation applied to unsupervised classification of reviews, Proceedings of the 40th Annual Meeting of the Association for Computational Linguistics (ACL'02), Philadelphia, Pennsylvania, pp. 417-424.

Turney, P.D., & Littman, M.L. (2003). Measuring praise and criticism: Inference of semantic orientation from association, *ACM Transactions on Information Systems (TOIS)*, 21(4), 315-346.

Vazire, S., & Gosling, S. D. (2004). E-perceptions: Personality impressions based on personal web sites. *Journal of Personality and Social Psychology*, 87, 123–132.

Cognitive Reconstruction of Reversed Speech in Normal and Dyslexic Adults

Claire Grataloup (claire.grataloup@univ-lyon2.fr)
Laboratoire Dynamique du Langage. UMR 5596 CNRS - Université Lyon2.
Institut des Sciences de l'Homme. Lyon – France

Michel Hoen (michel.hoen@phonak.com)
Phonak AG Laubisruetistrasse, 28 CH-8712 Staefa - Switzerland

Fanny Meunier (fanny.meunier@univ-lyon2.fr)
& Francois Pellegrino (françois.pellegrino@univ-lyon2.fr)
Laboratoire Dynamique du Langage. UMR 5596 CNRS - Université Lyon2.
Institut des Sciences de l'Homme. Lyon - FRANCE

Evelyne Veuillet (evelyne.veuillet@chu-lyon.fr)
& Lionel Collet (lionel.collet@chu-lyon.fr)
Neurosciences & Systèmes Sensoriels. UMR 5020. CNRS - Université Claude Bernard Lyon 1
Lyon - FRANCE

Abstract

In the present study we explore the implication of high and low level mechanisms in degraded (time-reversed) speech comprehension in dyslexic adults and controls. In experiment 1 we compared the loss of intelligibility due to the increasing size of reversion windows in both words and pseudowords. Results showed that words are generally reconstructed better than pseudowords in both groups, suggesting the existence of a lexical benefit in degraded speech restoration. Overall the normal group performed better than dyslexic group in particular, performances of dyslexics did not show any word-property effect. In the normal group, there was greater variability between individuals when reconstructing pseudowords than words. In experiment 2, we demonstrated that this interindividual variability in normal subjects correlated with theirs medial olivocochlear bundle functionality. Auditory measurements on dyslexics are in progress. These experiments highlight the importance of low-level auditory mechanisms in degraded speech restoration in non dyslexic participants. Together, these results put forward the existence of major interindividual variability in the capacity to reconstruct degraded speech, which correlates with the physiological properties of the auditory system. In addition, our results also suggest the existence of multiple higher-level strategies that can compensate on-line for the lack of information caused by speech degradation.

Keywords: Developmental dyslexia, High and low levels processes, Intelligibility, Medial OlivoCochlear Bundle, Reversed speech.

Introduction

Developmental dyslexia is a disorder of reading acquisition. It is widely accepted that developmental dyslexia results from some sort of phonological deficit (Vellutino, 1979, Snowling, 2000, Ramus, 2001). According to the phonological theory of dyslexia this disorder results from a specific impairment of phonological representations and processes. This phonological deficit occurs difficulties in several cognitive tasks such as speech perception and production. In non dyslexics adults understanding speech is fast and automatic; this process is a daily task achieved without any difficulty although it involves cognitive functions which are both numerous and complex. The intelligibility of speech depends both on the quality of the emitted signal and on the ability of the cognitive system to process this signal. To understand spoken messages requires the complementary engagement of low-level (auditory) and high-level mechanisms (e.g., lexical knowledge, contextual integration).

At the sensory level, the human auditory system may be described throw two types of pathway: "ascending" and "descending" auditory pathways. Ascending pathways carry the auditory message from receptive hair cells in the cochlea to the primary auditory cortex. Descending pathways extending from the auditory cortex to the periphery through the superior olivary complex constitute a sort of inhibitory filter (Khalfa & Collet, 1996) which may play a role in degraded speech comprehension. The existence of a central influence on the sensory level by means of efferent feedback pathways has been highlighted with the investigation of the medial olivocochlear bundle (MOCB). It is possible to explore the MOCB in a simple and non invasive way through contralateral suppression of otoacoustic emissions (OAEs), sounds produced by the outer hair cells of the cochlea (Collet, Kemp, Veuillet, Duclaux, Moulin & Morgnon, 1990). Important interindividual variability in normal hearing subjects was also observed by the same authors when assessing the functionality of the MOCB. Though the precise functional role of the MOCB remains unclear, several studies have suggested its involvement in speech intelligibility in degraded conditions. A correlation between the functionality of MOCB and the detection threshold of pure tones present in noise was first reported by

Micheyl and Collet (1996). Giraud, Garnier, Micheyl, Lina, Chays and Chéry-Croze (1997), also reported that MOCB activation via contralateral noise stimulation improved speech-in-noise intelligibility in normal hearing subjects. More recently Kumar and Vanaja (2004) suggested a correlation between the contralateral suppression of evoked OAEs and speech identification scores at certain signal/noise ratios.

However speech comprehension is likely to benefit during auditory sentence comprehension from higher level knowledge such as lexical knowledge stored in the mental lexicon or contextual information. Interactive theories of speech perception postulate that several sources interact during perceptual analysis (McClelland & Elman, 1986).

The aim of our study was to characterize involvement of high and low-level processes during the comprehension of speech in degraded conditions. To study these mechanisms we manipulated the intelligibility of speech signals by applying temporal reversions on different-sized windows (i.e., flipping the signal on its horizontal axis). Reversed speech has the particularity that it maintains the physical characteristics of speech such as the distribution frequency of sounds, their global amplitude and, to some extent, their temporal and rhythmic characteristics. The main difference between speech and reversed speech lies in the coarticulations which are totally distorted in the reversed signal. Thus, reversed speech is unpronounceable though to some extent it remains understandable. Saberi and Perrott (1999) demonstrated that it is possible to reconstruct locally reversed English speech (for comparable results see Greenberg & Araï, 2001 and Meunier, Cenier, Barkat & Magrin-Chagnolleau, 2002, for results on French). All these studies applied time reversions according to arbitrarily augmenting time-windows (20 ms, 40 ms, 60 ms, etc.) For the present work, in order to carefully control our linguistic material, we chose to use bisyllabic words and pseudowords and to base the degradation on the syllable unit as it has been identified as a privileged unit for lexical access in French (Content, Dumay & Frauenfelder, 2000). It has never been done to test reversed speech reconstruction in dyslexics. Comparing performances of dyslexics and non-dyslexics could lead to better understand cognitive mechanisms associated to such language deficits. In experiment 1, we measured the accuracy in restoring single words and pseudowords to quantify the lexical effects during this process in dyslexics and in non dyslexic adults and to compare performances of both groups of subjects. In experiment 2 auditory measurements on non dyslexics were made to test the implication of auditory pathways in the reconstruction phenomenon.

Experiment 1: Behavioural measures

Materials and methods

Stimuli Word stimuli consisted of 120 French nouns. All were common disyllabic words. They were selected according to two main criteria: their frequency (High or Low) and their number of phonological neighbours (Many or Few). (*Lexique* database, New, Palier, Ferrand & Matos, 2001). For example the word /ballon/ (balloon) is a high frequency noun (f=4.39) that has many phonological neighbours (20) (e.g., /vallon/, /baron/, /baton/...). We crossed Frequency and Neighbour factors in order to create 4 categories of 30 experimental nouns each. For each category Table 1 gives the mean and the standard deviation of each factor (frequency and number of phonological neighbours).

Table 1: The four categories of experimental words.

Category	Frequency (log2)	Neighbours
Low-Few	M=0.51; SD=0.87	M=3.79; SD=1.96
Low-Many	M= 1.16; SD=1.2	M= 17.73; SD=4.12
High-Few	M= 4.4; SD=1.53	M=3.63; SD=1.87
High-Many	M=4.65; SD=1.51	M=19.37; SD=5.66

We also constructed 120 experimental disyllabic pseudowords (e.g.: *lantin*) using the same syllables contained in the 120 experimental words. These pseudowords satisfied the constraints observed in French phonotactics. All 240 items were recorded in a soundproof room by a native French speaker. We applied five kinds of reversion to the items:

- Condition R_0: no reversion applied.
- Condition $R_{0.5}$: first half syllable reversed.
- Condition R_1: first syllable reversed.
- Condition $R_{1.5}$: first syllable and a half reversed.
- Condition R_2: whole item reversed.

The half syllable was defined as the half in terms of the duration of a syllable.

Experimental procedure Participants faced a computer screen (PC type) and heard the stimuli delivered binaurally via headphones at a comfortable level of hearing (more than 50dB). The presentation order of the 240 stimuli was randomized across subjects. Dyslexic participants repeated what they had understood and the experimenter transcribed the response on a computer keyboard. Controls had to type responses on the computer keyboard on their own.

Participants 31 French dyslexic adults and 50 French control adults participated in this study. They were all volunteers and were paid 7.5 € for their participation.

Results and Discussion

Results were obtained by comparing the subjects' transcriptions to the original words or pseudowords and were expressed as percentages of correctly reported syllables. Repeated measures analyses of variance (ANOVA) were performed with % of reconstruction as independent variable. $F1$ corresponds to analyse by subjects and $F2$ analyse by items.

Dyslexic group Taken as a whole, the percentage of intelligibility decreased with increasing distortion. The average reconstruction score was 90.93% for condition R_0; 68.48% for $R_{0.5}$; 44.29% for R_1; 3.02% for $R_{1.5}$ and 1.81% for R_2. Figure 1 shows intelligibility rates for words and pseudowords as a function of the reversion size in dyslexic participants.

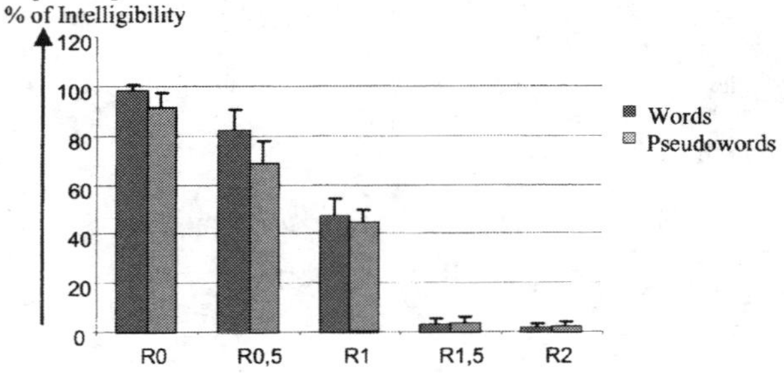

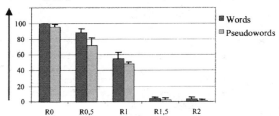

Figure 1: Rate of intelligibility for words and pseudowords plotted against the size of the reversion in dyslexics.

Dyslexics performed better overall with words than with pseudowords ($F1(1,30)=28.7$; $p<.0001$, $F2(1,238)=37.73$; $p<.0001$).

Normal group Normal participants performed also better overall with words than with pseudowords ($F1(1,49)=158.5$; $p<.0001$, $F2(1,238)=72.08$; $p<.0001$). The average reconstruction score was 97.3% for condition R_0; 79.65% for $R_{0.5}$; 51.15% for R_1; 2.85% for $R_{1.5}$ and 1.81% for R_2. Figure 2 shows intelligibility rates for words and pseudowords as a function of the reversion size in normal group.

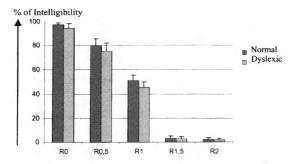

Figure 2: Rate of intelligibility for words and pseudowords plotted against the size of the reversion in normal group.

Comparison between the two groups Overall percentages of intelligibility were higher (from 0% to 7.26% in average depending on the condition considered) in normal than in dyslexic group ($F1(1,79)=27.1$; $p<.0001$, $F2(1,238)=69.25$; $p<.0001$). Figure 3 shows intelligibility rates and standard deviation for the whole items as a function of the reversion size in both groups.

Figure 3: Rate of intelligibility plotted against the size of the reversion in dyslexic and normal groups.

For both categories of stimuli the degradation of the first half syllable ($R_{0.5}$) gave high scores of restoration (average 68.48% for dyslexic group and 79.65% for normal group). When a little part of the first syllable is degraded the cognitive system is able to reconstruct the signal. Results are lower for dyslexics meaning that the short distortion disturbed them stronger than normal adults. The second syllable is almost always reported by dyslexics whereas the first one (which is only partly damaged) is only sometimes reported.

When only the first syllable is degraded scores were below 50% for dyslexics (44.29%) and turned around 50% for normals as the second syllable was quite well identified. However, the degradation of one syllable and a half ($R_{1.5}$) gave disastrous reconstruction scores (below 4% for both categories of participants). When the distortion is longer than the syllable the system seems to be unable to reconstruct neither the first syllable nor the second one which is only partly damaged in both categories of participants. This tends to confirm the main role of the syllable as a unit in French comprehension processes both in dyslexic and normal cognitive systems.

Comparing words and pseudowords in condition R_1 (first syllable degraded) in dyslexics, results show that the first syllable is almost never reported neither in words (46.91% of reconstruction) nor in pseudowords (44.29%) moreover the degradation disturbs the well understanding of the second syllable (though it is intact). At the opposite, in the normal group we observed that the first syllable is sometimes reconstructed but only in words (so the whole word is found): 54.8% of words are reconstructed. In pseudowords the first syllable is almost never reconstructed (47.5% of reconstruction) such as dyslexics' performances.

In addition we observed that for pseudowords restitution participants sometimes answer a real word phonologically similar to the target instead of the right pseudoword. In average participants answer by a word for 3.65% (SD= 3.76) of the 120 pseudowords. For example the word "*parfum*" was frequently given as an answer of the target stimulus "*rafin*". This result shows the robustness of lexical effects in a non lexical task such as pseudowords restoration.

Furthermore we observed opposite lexical effects for dyslexics and normals: for words reconstruction, dyslexics did not show any frequency effect ($F1(1,30)=9.38$; n.s, $F2(1,118)=3.97$; n.s) nor phonological neighbours effect ($F1(1,30)=1.96$; ns, $F2(1,118)=2.04$; n.s)

At the opposite for the normal group we found both a frequency effect by participants ($F1(1,49)=17.12$; p=.0001; $F2(1,118)=3.05$; n.s) and a neighbour effect by participants ($F1(1,49)=20.15$; p<.0001, $F2(1,118)=3.17$; n.s) on word reconstruction. The most frequent words were better reconstructed whatever the inversion degree was and words with fewer neighbours were also better reconstructed. The interaction between Frequency and Neighbour was significant only for condition R_1. This interaction indicates that when the first syllable is distorted the number of neighbours is the first criterion that could modify the reconstruction process in normal group. A high frequency could thus help the reconstruction but only for words with few phonological competitors. However the most intriguing result is that dyslexics seem to be insensitive to lexical properties of words. This result is coherent with the ERP study of Johannes, Mangun, Kussmaul and Münte (1995) on developmental dyslexia that show differential word frequency effects between dyslexics and non dyslexics.

The fact that pseudowords were more difficult to reconstruct than words for both categories of participants seems coherent because pseudowords do not have any representation stored in the mental lexicon. Consequently, they do not benefit as much from lexical help. Looking at pseudowords results we can observe that performances are very heterogeneous in dyslexics for every condition. This is not the same in normal group. Overall performances for pseudowords were very homogenous over normal participants for most conditions. However, the condition $R_{0.5}$ showed a large interindividual variability only for these participants (see Figure 4). In this condition, some controls were undisturbed by the inversion whereas others were deeply perturbed and failed the reconstruction task: performances ranged from 47.9% to 91.7% of correct reconstruction (M=71.2%, SD=10.4).

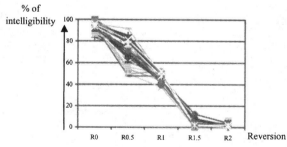

Figure 4: Reversed pseudowords reconstruction in normal group. Each curve represents the results of one subject.

Interestingly, this important variability was not observed in normal group for word reconstruction (% of reconstruction varied from 72.9% to 97.9%; M= 88.2%

SD=5.67). Moreover, non dyslexic participants who had difficulties in reconstructing pseudowords in condition $R_{0.5}$ (63.2% of reconstruction for the 25 lowest and 78.5% for the 25 highest performing participants) had no trouble in reconstructing words in the same reversed condition (89.4% of words were reconstructed against 86.6% for higher score participants). The correlation between the performance for word and pseudoword reconstruction was not significant. This intriguing result suggests that lexical help can to some extent compensate poor performance on pseudoword reconstruction.

Pseudowords are considered as speech and thus general phonotactics apply (giving cues to the identity of the contiguous phonemes) but they do not have any representation stored in the mental lexicon. Consequently, reversed pseudoword reconstruction is primarily based on auditory information. So why did the subjects of the normal group present such varied performances? Given that descending auditory pathways could interfere in speech perception and that their contribution is unequal among normal hearing subjects, we can formulate the hypothesis that the MOCB functionality may be responsible for the behavioural results we observed in normal group. In order to answer this question we compared the results obtained for pseudoword reconstruction in normal group and auditory performance in each participant.

Experiment 2: Auditory measurements

Two groups of 10 persons each were then formed from the subjects of the normal group in experiment 1 according to their performance for pseudowords reconstruction in condition $R_{0.5}$ (i.e., the condition showing the largest variability). The HP group (High Performance) was composed of the 10 persons from the normal group who showed the best performances (M=83.3%). The LP group (Low Performance) was composed of the 10 subjects from the normal group who showed the lowest performances (M=50%). We measured the functionality of the MOCB of these selected subjects (uncrossed pathway) in a soundproof room. OAEs were recorded according to the method of Bray and Kemp using the Otodynamics ILO88 measuring device. A miniaturized microphone placed in the external ear canal delivered acoustic stimulations (clicks) and recorded responses. For each participant we recorded OAEs for 20 ms after clicks delivery with and without a broadband noise (30dBSL) applied in the contralateral ear. We calculated the contralateral suppression of OAEs in each ear and the corresponding lateralization (for details see Veuillet, Collet & Bazin, 1999). The tests lasted one hour.

Participants The 20 participants selected from the normal group of the experiment 1 were all volunteers. They all had normal peripheral hearing (thresholds better than 20 dB HL between 250 Hz and 8000 Hz) and a normal tympanometry (stapedian reflex greater than 65 dB HL). The subjects had no history of otological or neurological disorders and all were right handed (more than 80% according to the Edinburgh test).

Results and Discussion

Results are clear cut: the HP group showed better contralateral suppressions in both ears than did the LP group. Table 2 shows the mean and the standard deviation of contralateral suppressions of OAEs in the right and left ears respectively, for each group of subjects. The last column indicates the lateralization (Contralateral suppression of OAEs on right ear minus left ear).

Table 2: Contralateral suppressions of OAEs.

	Right ear	Left ear	Lateralization
HP Group	- 4.2 (1.1)	-2.7 (1.8)	-1.5 (2)
LP Group	-1.4 (2)	-1.8 (1.3)	0.4 (1.6)

The ANOVA analysis ran on lateralisation showed a significant effect of the Group factor ($F(1,9)=7.64$; $p=.022$ see Figure 5): HP group was more lateralized on the right ear than LP group.

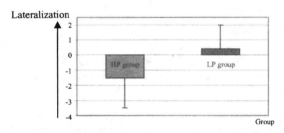

Figure 5: Lateralization for the two groups of normal subjects.

Indeed auditory areas are asymmetric and the peripheral auditory system reflects this asymmetry. An efficient MOCB is characterised by a large inhibitory power and by the lateralization (for right handed people, the more negative the lateralization the more efficient the MOCB).

Auditory measurements demonstrated clearly that the HP group had a better MOCB and was more right lateralized than the LP group. We found a correlation between behavioural performances and the lateralization of the subjects ($r=0.7$; $p<.001$). It suggests that the stronger the asymmetry of the auditory system the better the behavioural performances in non dyslexic participants. This demonstrates the link between the MOCB and the cognitive processes of reversed speech restoration. The role of the MOCB could be to filter the damaged signal in order to highlight perception of those elements which are pertinent. The MOCB would be a sort of adapting mechanism of the ear to situations in which the signal is perceived.

Taken together, experiments 1 and 2 throw light on the participation of high and low-level mechanisms in reversed speech restoration in normal subjects. To get complementary information about these processes in language impairment subjects, auditory measurements in dyslexic participants are in progress. It would be interesting to test the functionality of the MOCB of dyslexics and to look for a correlation with reconstruction performances. A deficit of these auditory pathways could be responsible of the lower performances observed in dyslexics.

General discussion

The aim of the study was to understand the respective influence of high and low-level mechanisms that underlie the cognitive reconstruction of degraded speech in normal and dyslexic subjects. Our results about normal adults suggest that descending auditory pathways may intervene significantly during this process: more precisely, activity in MOCB may be one of the neurophysiologic mechanisms participating in restoration process in non dyslexic subjects. In addition, high-level knowledge is activated to help the reconstruction; we observed such results in both dyslexics and non dyslexic participants. Speech comprehension is the result of an interaction between low-level mechanisms and elaborated knowledge stored in the mental lexicon. In experiment 1 we saw that the system was able to reconstruct speech signal to some extent. However reversed words and pseudowords are not reconstructed in the same way. For words both high and low-level mechanisms intervene, often resulting in successful comprehension. Both phonological neighbours and the frequency of noun effects in the normal group suggest the implication of high-level mechanisms (lexical search) in word reconstruction. These mechanisms may not interfere in the case of dyslexia as we did not observe any lexical effect in dyslexic participants. These results are consistent with previous study showing deficits in processing low frequency words and irregular words by dyslexics. However, in non dyslexic subjects such lexical mechanisms may either improve the signal reconstruction in a top-down scheme or more probably compensate for the lack of information if the low-level mechanisms fail to reconstruct the signal.

Pseudowords are not listed in the mental lexicon however; high-level mechanisms are still involved as demonstrated by the restitution of real words phonologically similar to pseudowords. In addition, our results showed a syllable effect. As long as the damaged information is shorter or equal to one syllable subjects still understand, even if the target item exhibits numerous phonological neighbours. When the distortion gets larger than one syllable, the reconstruction becomes more difficult. These results are consistent with the hypothesis that the syllable could be a perceptual unit in French.

Another interesting finding is the large variability observed between normal adults for pseudowords reconstruction. For the reversion of the first half syllable some of the participants had no trouble in reconstructing pseudowords whereas others largely failed. Moreover, behavioural results and MOCB functionality of the subjects correlate significantly (experiment 2). This suggests implication of the efferent auditory pathways in reversed speech reconstruction. Reversed speech intelligibility seems to be linked with functioning MOCBs. The MOCB seems to modify the properties of auditory fibres in order to improve the ability of the auditory system to focus on pertinent information included in the percept. However, we did not find any correlation between auditory measurements and word reconstruction. The variability may fade during word reconstruction because of the intervention of lexical strategies which leads us to speculate on the importance of lexical strategies as a consequence of poor functionality of the MOCB. Further investigations are needed to shed some light on theories that assume that an auditory deficit may be the cause of the phonological deficit in dyslexics. It would also be interesting to test whether lexical strategies are more important to people with hearing impairments.

Conclusion & Perspectives

Speech reconstruction is the result of rapid, efficient activation of several complex mechanisms. Our experiments show that the respective involvements of the high and low-level mechanisms depend on the nature of the stimuli: pseudoword stimuli highlight the major role of the MOCB while word stimuli emphasize lexical strategies in non dyslexic adults. Further experiments will be necessary to precisely determine the role of each mechanism. More particularly the extension of hearing measures to dyslexic adults is in progress. In the long term it could lead to improve speech therapy methods.

Acknowledgments

This study was supported by an ACI (n° 67068) of the French *Ministère de l'Enseignement Supérieur et de la Recherche* attributed to Fanny Meunier.

References

Collet, L., Kemp, D. T., Veuillet, E., Duclaux, R., Moulin, A., & Morgnon, A. (1990). Effect of contralateral auditory stimuli on active cochlear micro-mechanical properties in human subjects. *Hearing Research. 43*, 251-262.

Content, A., Dumay, N., & Frauenfelder, U.H. (2000). The role of syllable structure in lexical segmentation in French. *In Proceedings of the Workshop on Spoken Word Access Processes, 29-31st May 2000*, Max-Planck Institute for Psycholinguistics, Nijmegen, The Netherlands.

Giraud A.L., Garnier S, Micheyl C., Lina-Granade G, Chays A. & Chery-Croze S. (1997). Medial Olivocochlear Efferent Involved In Speech In Noise Intelligibility. *Neuroreport, 8*, pp. 1779-1783.

Greenberg, S. & Arai, T. (2001). The relation between speech intelligibility and the complex modulation spectrum, *Proceedings of the 7th Eurospeech Conference on Speech Communication and Technology (Eurospeech-2001)*, pp. 473-476.

Johannes, S., Mangun, G. R., Kussmaul, C.L., and Münte, T. F. (1995) Brain potentials in developmental dyslexia: differential effects of word frequency in human subjects. *Neuroscience letters 195(3)*, 183-186

Khalfa, S. & Collet, L. (1996). Functional asymmetry of medial olivocochlear system in humans. Towards a peripheral auditory lateralization. *NeuroReport 7*, 993-996.

Kumar, U. A. & Vanaja, C. S. (2004). Functioning of olivocochlear bundle and speech perception in noise. *Ear and Hearing. 25*(2):142-6.

McClelland, J.L. & Elman, J.L. (1986) The TRACE model of speech perception. *Cognitive Psychology 18*:1-86.

Meunier, F., Cenier, T., Barkat, M. & Magrin-Chagnolleau, I. (2002). Mesure d'intelligibilité de segments de parole à l'envers en français, *Actes des 24ème Journées d'étude sur la parole (JEP)*, p.117-120, Nancy, France.

New, B., Pallier, C., Ferrand, L., & Matos, R. (2001). Une base de données lexicales du français contemporain sur internet : LEXIQUE. *L'Année Psychologique, 101*, 447-462.

Ramus, F. (2001). Outstanding questions about phonological processing in dyslexia. *Dyslexia, 7*, 197-216. Copyright 2001 John Wiley & Sons Ltd.

Saberi, K. & Perrott, D. R. (1999). Cognitive restoration of reversed speech. *Nature, 398*, 760.

Snowling, M.J. (2000) Dyslexia, 2nd edition. Blackwell: Oxford.

Vellutino, F.R. (1979) Dyslexia: Research and Theory. MIT Press: Cambridge, MA.

Veuillet E., Collet L. & Bazin F. (1999). Objective evidence of peripheral auditory disorders in learning-impaired children. *Journal of Audiological Medicine, 8*(1): 18-29.

Investigating the Emergence of Speech Communication –
A Study on Infants' Ability to Predict Phonetic Information

Klintfors Eeva (eevak@ling.su.se)
Department of Linguistics, Universitetsvägen 10C,
106 91 Stockholm, Sweden

Lacerda Francisco (frasse@ling.su.se)
Department of Linguistics, Universitetsvägen 10C,
106 91 Stockholm, Sweden

Marklund Ellen (ellen@ling.su.se)
Department of Linguistics, Universitetsvägen 10C,
106 91 Stockholm, Sweden

Abstract

The introduction of this paper provides an overview of infants' prediction skills of action goals, as well as their ability to predict perceptual acoustic information. Prediction skills' neurological correlates in general are discussed. A central hypothesis under investigation is that there are commonalities between the development of speech and manipulation. The current research is focused on the communication mode investigating infants' ability to associate images of familiar objects with auditory-stimuli presented both as whole words in intact form and as disrupted (partly noise-replaced) spoken words. The looking behaviour of the infants' was measured with the Tobii eye-tracking device. The results suggested that 11 to 16 month-old infants recognize the target object when the word referring to it was intact, i.e. when the name of the object was presented in its entirety. However, the infants did not seem to recognize the target object when the word referring to it was partially masked so that only its initial phonetic information was presented. These results indicate that young infants are sensitive to the phonetic information of the words and may need more extensive linguistic experience in order to derive full lexical forms from partially masked words. The paper concludes with suggestions for future demonstrations of infant anticipation of speech.

Introduction

Prediction of Other People's Action Goals

Recent research indicates that one-year-old infants are able to predict other people's action goals (Falck-Ytter et al., 2006). In these experiments, proactive goal-directed eye-movements of adults were compared with 6-month-old and 12-month-old infants' gaze behaviour. The subjects were exposed to video presentations showing trials in which toys were moved by an actor's hand into a bucket. The results showed that adults, as well as 12-month-old infants directed their gaze towards the bucket before the toy had reached it, while 6-month-old infants seemed to fail anticipating the goal of the action. The younger infants' inability to predict the actor's intention was suggested to indicate that predictive action perception in children develops simul-

taneously with other social competences such as imitation, "theory of mind" and communication. Such gestural and linguistic competencies are assumed to emerge typically by about 8-12 months of age. The authors also speculated on the possibility that the 6-month-old infants' inability to predict the actor's action goal could originate from their general inability to predict future events with their gaze. However this assumption was rejected as it conflicts with the results from earlier experiments demonstrating that 6-month-olds could indeed predict the reappearance of temporarily occluded objects.

Falck-Ytter et al.'s (2006) study also suggested that successful goal prediction relies on observing the interaction between the hand of the agent and the object. Indeed, the results from another experimental condition where the objects moved along the same paths while the actor's hand was not visible showed that predictive eye movements were not activated for any of the subject groups (adults, 12-month-old, or 6-month-old infants), suggesting that self-propelled objects are not perceived as performing goal-directed actions.

Neurological Coding System of Mirror-Neurons

The recent discovery of mirror-neurons presents a powerful neurological correlate of predictive perceptual behaviour. Activation of the mirror-neuron system (MNS) was first found in the ventral premotor cortex (area F5) of macaque monkeys (Rizzolatti & Arbib, 1998; Keysers et al., 2003) when a macaque observed another individual (human or monkey) performing an action that could be related to observer's own repertoire of actions. An important aspect is that MNS was only activated when the goal of the action was clear to the animal. In fact, mimicking the gestures of goal-directed actions, without actually using the objects typically involved in the actions (like when pretending to peal an invisible banana) did not lead to activation of the MNS. The behavioural study by Falck-Ytter et al. (2006) is well in line with this assumption, indicating that the absence of an actor impairs the observer's predictive perception of goal-oriented actions.

Furthermore, data from neuro-physiological and brain-imaging experiments indicates that MNS also exists in humans (Fadiga et al., 1995; Grafton et al., 1996) and it has been suggested that it may constitute a neurological base for coding empathy, social understanding and the ability for human communication (Rizzolatti & Craighero, 2004) .

Mirror-Neuron System and Communication

Mirror neurons may account for coding of object-directed actions in which the gestural meaning is intrinsic to the gesture itself, but the question of whether the same system may be able to mediate abstract symbolic representations that are typically involved in human communication must also be addressed. In line with this, a relevant finding by Ferrari et al. (Ferrari et al., 2003) indicated that mirror-neurons of F5 may also code *mouth*-actions. Most of these "mouth mirror-neurons" were observed to become active both during the execution and observation of mouth-actions related to ingestive functions (e.g. grasping, sucking or breaking food) but some of the mirror neurons responded particularly to *communicative* mouth gestures (e.g. lip smacking). Therefore these findings extend the scope of MNS from hand-actions to mouth-actions suggesting that area F5, considered to be the homologue of human Broca´s area, is also involved in communicative behaviour.

From an evolutionary perspective, Ferrari et al. (Ferrari et al., 2003), suggested that understanding words related to mouth-actions may have evolved via activation of *audio-visual* mirror neurons. Mirror neurons initially responding to ingestive behaviour, may have led to a further development in which a set of F5 audio-visual mirror neurons eventually became responsive to the *sound* associated with the original actions, like hearing the sound of ripping a piece of paper without actually seeing the action (Kohler et al., 2002). Pursuing this evolutionary perspective Rizzolatti & Craighero (Rizzolatti & Craighero, 2004) speculated that the human individuals' improved imitation capacities may have enabled the generation of onomatopoetic sounds without actually performing the action that originally generated the sounds. Hence, this capacity might have led to the acquisition of an *auditory* mirror system on the top of the original audio-visual one, progressively independent of it (see also (MacNeilage & Davis, 2000)).

Prediction of Phonetic Information

Earlier research (Samuel, 1996; Warren, 1970; Warren & Obusek, 1971; Warren & Warren, 1970) has shown that adults are able to interpret and reconstruct disrupted speech signals. In these studies adult listeners could identify both words disrupted by noise (Warren, 1970), as well as words disrupted by silence (Warren & Obusek, 1971). In the noise-disrupted case subjects reported that the disrupted words sounded intact. This phenomenon suggests that listeners perceive the word to continue behind the noise and "restore" missing phonemes – a phenomenon known as "phoneme restoration". In the silence-disrupted case, subjects did not perceive the word as intact even though they were able to identify the word.

To examine school children's perceptual ability in noisy environments, Newman (Newman, 2004) studied 5.5 year-old children's ability to use partial phonetic information to identify familiar words. The results of this study showed that children's perceptual ability, just like adults', was better when speech signals were disrupted by noise as opposed to silence. However, compared to adults, children were overall more affected by signal disruptions, suggesting that young children are more dependent on the speech signal, particularly in noisy environments. These results are in agreement with Walley's (Walley, 1988) who showed that children's phoneme restoration demands more phonetic information than adults' (i.e. children need to listen to longer portions of the disrupted word).

A study by Fernald, Swingley, & Pinto (Fernald et al., 2001) suggests that 18 and 21 months-old children are able to recognize words without access to complete acoustic speech signals. In this study the subjects associated pictures with auditory-stimuli presented both as whole words in intact form and as disrupted words in which only the initial 300 ms of the word was heard. Their results showed that children from both age groups could recognize whole words, as well as disrupted words. There were no differences in the two age-groups reaction times to these two types of stimuli. Instead their study indicated that children's word processing ability was related to their lexical development – the children with greater productive vocabularies were more accurate in their recognition, a conclusion that departs somewhat from earlier findings by Fernald, Pinto, Swingley, Wineberg & McRoberts (Fernald et al., 1998) indicating an age dependence on the ability to identify partial words for infants in the age range 15 to 24 months.

The Nature of Infants' Lexical Representations

There is an ongoing discussion on whether infants' lexical representations are of a holistic or of a more specific nature. As an example, the fact that younger infants were not so accurate in identifying partial words was taken as an indication of lacking segmental structure in their lexical representations of words (Fernald et al., 1998). On the other hand, studies concerning language-specific tuning of vowels have shown that 11-12 months-old infants are sensitive to the detailed sound structure of the ambient language, as opposed to a structure of a non-native language (Kuhl et al., 1992; Polka & Werker, 1994). This indicated, according to the authors, that infants have a rather detailed representation of native segments. However, these studies were not aimed at studying word processing explicitly, so there is a possibility that infants do have detailed lexical representations of words, but they do not process words incrementally, i.e. they do not make use of the acoustic information before the offset of a word to the extent that adults do.

Modular or General Perceptual Restoration

There is evidence that the perceptual restoration phenomenon is not restricted to speech, to the modality of spoken language, or to the human species. Indeed, top-down processing has been demonstrated in musical perception (DeWitt & Samuel, 2006), in the interpretation of American Sign Language (Schultz-Westre, 1985) as well as in the perception of starlings' birdsong (Braaten & Leary, 1999).

Yet, due to psychoacoustic and methodological factors, some potential restrictions to the generality of the perceptual restoration phenomenon should be taken into consideration. As an example, for the perceptual restoration effect to take place, the class of the phoneme being masked and the nature of the masker (e.g. type of noise) as well as the amplitude of the masker have to be sufficiently similar (Newman, 2004). Originally a cough was used as a masker of the phoneme /s/ so that both the masker and the phoneme to be masked contained energy at several frequencies (Warren, 1970). Also the type of laboratory task facing subjects may differ in number of ways from e.g. everyday listening to speech in noisy environments. In the study by Newman (Newman, 2004), adults and school children were to detect interruptions presented at high rate (at slowest 2 per second). The interruptions also occurred at constant rate and were accordingly easily predictable by the subjects. Further, the stimuli in the experiment were presented over headphones and the adults were asked to type into a keyboard what they thought they heard, while the children were to repeat the sentences into a microphone. These recordings were later transcribed by an experimenter. In sum, the cognitive load intrinsic to the procedure of typing or repeating might have been rather demanding for the subjects. On contrary, an analysis of infants' looking behaviour like in the studies by Fernald et al. (Fernald et al., 1998; Fernald et al., 2001) makes use of the infants' spontaneous tendency to look at images of objects while hearing names corresponding to them.

Rationale for the Current Study

Although several studies have shown that adults and children possess the ability to identify words from partial phonetic information, less is known about the corresponding restoration ability in young infants. The aim of the present study was to investigate 11-16 months-old infants' ability to identify spoken words on the basis of their initial sounds. The theoretical motivation for this study is inspired by analogue experiments performed on infant's ability to predict other people's action goals interpreted as a foundation of empathy and social understanding. The current study is further designed to investigate whether infants' ability to predict phonetic events might be related to their age or to their productive vocabulary size. Therefore the youngest infants in the current study were chosen as representatives of subjects essentially lacking productive vocabularies.

As opposed to heavy-cognitive-load procedures, the current eye-tracking method (Tobii, http://www.tobii.com), just like the method used in the studies by Fernald et al. (Fernald et al., 1998; Fernald et al., 2001), takes advantage of the infants' spontaneous tendency to look at images of objects while hearing names corresponding to them.

Method

The infants' eye-movements were recorded as the subjects watched short video sequences displaying images of four familiar objects (a watch, a car, a ball and a teddy-bear). The objects were first introduced one at the time, along with a speaker voice presenting the Swedish names (target-nouns) of the objects embedded in carrier phrases. After these presentations, all the four objects were displayed simultaneously, one object per quadrant, while the speaker asked for *one* of the objects.

Subjects

A total of 17 infants participated in this study. Data from two infants were excluded due to interrupted recoding (failure to complete test session), resulting in 15 subjects (8 girls and 7 boys, age range 11.6-16.2 months, mean age 13.7 months). The infants were divided in two age groups, separated by the global median age – one group ranging from 11.6-13.5 months and the other from 13.5-16.2 months. All the subjects were primarily exposed to Swedish in their families. According to parental reports, none of the subjects had hearing abnormalities as revealed by BOEL-distraction test ("Blicken Orienterar Efter Ljud") routinely used by Swedish Child health centres to screen all infants 7-10 months of age. The subjects' receptive vocabularies were assumed to include the target-nouns used in the tests but nevertheless these target-nouns were explicitly presented in the video materials of this study. The infants were not expected to have these target-nouns in their productive vocabularies, although this may not be the case for some of the older infants.

Speech Materials

The target-nouns were selected from SECDI (Swedish Early Communicative Development Inventories) (Eriksson & Berglund, 1996) language assessment data base, which is a Swedish version of the MacArthur Communicative Development Inventories (CDI) based on parental reports. In order to assess age-appropriate test words, the "words and gestures" version of the database designed for children 8-16 months of age was used. In addition, only disyllabic target-nouns were selected and the words to be used in the test had to be matched regarding their initial phonemes. The target-nouns selected were:
- /klok:an/ (Watch)
- /nal:en/ (Teddy-bear)
- /bi:len/ (Car) (occurred only in manipulated version)
- /bol:en/ (Ball) (occurred only in manipulated version)

The disrupted target-nouns were prepared as follows: the first sound of /bi:len/ was extracted and concatenated with brown noise, the first sound of /bol:en/ was extracted and concatenated with brown noise, the first *two* sounds of /bil:en/ were extracted and concatenated with brown noise and the first *two* sounds of /bol:en/ were extracted and concatenated with brown noise resulting in:
- /b(i)/+NOISE (the /b/ carrying traces of /i/)
- /b(o)/+NOISE (the /b/ carrying traces of /o/)
- /bi/+NOISE
- /bo/+NOISE

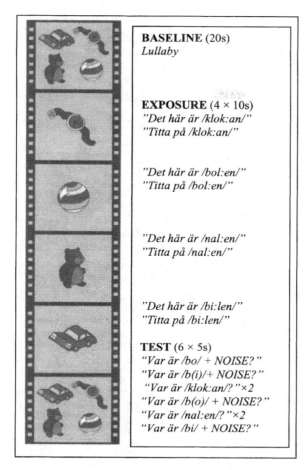

BASELINE (20s)
Lullaby

EXPOSURE (4 × 10s)
"Det här är /klok:an/"
"Titta på /klok:an/"

"Det här är /bol:en/"
"Titta på /bol:en/"

"Det här är /nal:en/"
"Titta på /nal:en/"

"Det här är /bi:len/"
"Titta på /bi:len/"

TEST (6 × 5s)
"Var är /bo/ + NOISE?"
"Var är /b(i)/+ NOISE?"
"Var är /klok:an/?"×2
"Var är /b(o)/ + NOISE?"
"Var är /nal:en/?"×2
"Var är /bi/ + NOISE?"

Figure 1: An illustration of the type of familiar objects and audio materials presented in the video materials.

Video Materials

The video materials (1min 30s) consisted of a BASELINE, an EXPOSURE, and a TEST phase, as follows (Figure 1):

- BASELINE (20s): The four objects were displayed to measure infants' spontaneous preference before EXPOSURE. The audio played a lullaby to catch the infants' attention towards the screen.
- EXPOSURE (4 × 10s): Each object was presented one at the time. A recorded female voice named the objects in carries phrases, uttered in Infant-Directed Speech style – *"This is a X"* or *"Look at the X"* (where *X* represents the actual target-noun).
- TEST (6 × 5s): Subsequently a split screen of the four objects was presented again. The voice asked for one of the objects – *"Where is the X?"* The target-nouns /klok:an/ (Watch) and /nal:en/ (Teddy-bear) were presented intact and repeated twice (TEST1 & TEST2). The other two target-nouns occurred only in their manipulated versions (TEST /bi/ + NOISE, TEST /b(i)/ + NOISE, TEST /bo/ + NOISE, TEST /b(o)/ + NOISE).

There were four counterbalanced versions of the video materials in which the presentation order of the objects (during EXPOSURE) and questions (during TEST) was systematically varied to control for possible memory effects.

Procedure and Instrumentation

A Tobii 1750 eye-tracker integrated with a 17" TFT monitor was used in the measurements. For each subject the system was calibrated at the beginning of each session. The infant was seated facing the monitor at a distance of approximately 60 cm. The care-giver, listening to masking music through sealed head-phones with active noise reduction, sat by the infant, slightly behind, out of the infant's visual field.

The equipment uses infrared light to generate gaze measurements sampled at 50 Hz and its average nominal accuracy of gaze estimation is 0.5 degrees. The ClearView 2.2.0 software was used to store gaze data. The data collected was exported from ClearView to Matematica 5.2 and SPSS 14.0 for statistical analysis.

Results

The distribution of the looking times during the BASELINE showed a slight, non-significant, preference for Teddy-bear.

The data was assessed in terms of departures from the BASELINE to TEST expressed in looking times towards each object shown in the split screen. Figures 2-5 show detailed results for each of the target words pooled for all the infants. The results indicate that intact target nouns were recognized in a much more accurate way than the partially masked words. Significant departures/tendencies according to paired samples test (2-tailed) from BASELINE to TEST are shown in Table 1.

Additional phonetic information (i.e. partially masked words represented by their first two sounds as opposed to by one sound only) did not seem to improve the infant's ability to predict the target word.

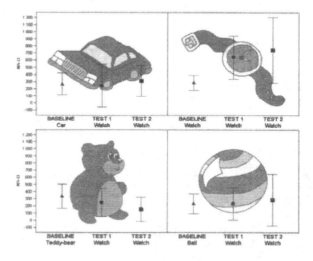

Figure 2: **Target Watch**. CI (95%) from left to right indicate looking time (ms) during BASELINE, TEST 1 (1st rep. of /klok:an/), and TEST 2 (2nd rep. of /klok:an/).

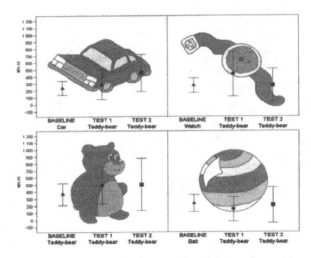
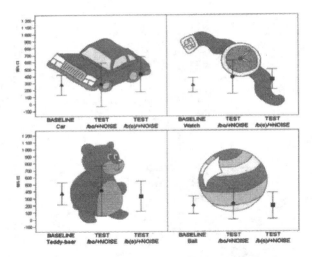

Figure 3: **Target Teddy-bear**. CI (95%) from left to right indicate looking time (ms) during BASELINE, TEST 1 (1st rep. of /nal:en/), and TEST 2 (2nd rep. of /nal:en/).

Figure 5: **Target Ball**. CI (95%) from left to right indicate looking time (ms) during BASELINE, TEST (/bo/+NOISE), and TEST (/b(o)/+NOISE).

The two age groups (11.6 to 13.5 and 13.5 to 16.2 months) behaved in about the same way, although there was a slight advantage for the older group in responding to intact words.

Summary and Discussion

Infants seem to possess prediction skills for anticipation of other people's goal-directed behaviour already by the age of 12 months (Falck-Ytter et al., 2006). The mirror-neuron system (MNS) coding for learning to do an action from seeing it done, and functioning as the neurological correlate of these and similar results, is suggested to exist both in monkeys (area F5) (Rizzolatti & Arbib, 1998) and humans (Broca's area) (Fadiga et al., 1995). As an extension, the MNS hypothesis of social cognition (Rizzolatti & Craighero, 2004) proposes this system to constitute a neurological base for coding social understanding and language abilities. Evolutionarily, the coding of hand-actions is progressively assumed to be transferred to mouth-actions in general and further through ingestive behaviour (such as breaking food) to communicative mouth-actions (such as lip smacking) in particular. Accordingly, the original function of *audio-visual* mirror neurons might have transferred to respond to sound only, leading to a separate *auditory* mirror system on the top of the original audio-visual one (Rizzolatti & Craighero, 2004).

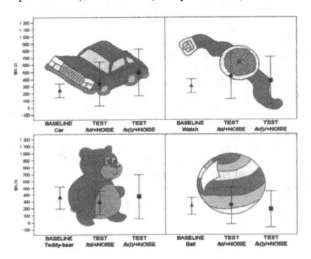

Figure 4: **Target Car**. CI (95%) from left to right indicate looking time (ms) during BASELINE, TEST (/bi/+NOISE), and TEST (/b(i)/+NOISE).

Table 1: Paired samples test (2-tailed). Significant departures/tendencies from BASELINE to TEST for intact and interrupted target nouns are shown in grey.

Intact target nouns		Interrupted target nouns	
TEST 1 /klok:an/ (Watch)	t(13)=2.482, p<0.027	/bi/+NOISE (Car)	t(13)=0.161, p<0.874
TEST 2 /klok:an/ (Watch)	t(12)=2.102, p<0.057	/b(i)/+NOISE (Car)	t(13)=1.814, p<0.093
TEST 1 /nal:en/ (Teddy-bear)	t(14)=2.057, p<0.059	/bo/+NOISE (Ball)	t(13)=-0.011, p<0.991
TEST 2 /nal:en/ (Teddy-bear)	t(12)=0.974, p<0.349	/b(o)/+NOISE (Ball)	t(13)=0.401, p<0.695

Experimental evidence points at commonalities between the development of prediction skills of action goals for motor and speech events. Infants, as young as 18-21 months-old, seem to be able to predict partial acoustic information (Fernald et al., 2001). In addition, these results suggested that recognition of non-complete acoustic speech signals is related to infants' lexical development (productive vocabulary sizes) and/or to their age (Fernald et al., 1998). Further, the "perceptual restoration" phenomena – which comprises that the observer perceives the word/song/signing to continue behind the noise and restore what ever is missing – is suggested to function in a domain- and species-general manner (e.g. to exist also in music, sign-language, and in birdsong).

The current study was set up to investigate young infants' (age range 11-16 months) ability to use partial phonetic information. The choice of age-continuum and the youngest infants' supposedly non-existing productive vocabularies were a result of the endeavour to bring light on the discussion of whether infants' ability to predict acoustic information is correlated to productive vocabulary size and/or age. Caution has been taken concerning potential methodological pitfalls regarding the class of phonemes to be masked and the energy levels of the masker at different frequencies, as well as regarding the type of laboratory task facing the infants. The brown noise used (containing energy at all the frequencies) was simply added – as opposed to superimposed on the phonemes to be masked – to the first phoneme/phonemes after excising the last phonemes of the signal. In this way the masker was prepared to function effectively assuring the perceptual restoration effect to be able to take place. In addition, the interrupted signals were not presented in a predictable or in a cognitively demanding manner. The infants' spontaneous tendency to look at objects while hearing names referring to them was used.

To test the perceptual restoration effect's modularity to speech processing versus it's generality as a part of auditory behaviour, studies on infant's restoration of *non-linguistic stimuli*, as well as studies on *non-human mammals'* restoration of linguistic stimuli, are to be performed in future experiments.

Acknowledgments

Research supported by The Swedish Research Council, The Bank of Sweden Tercentenary Foundation, European Commission, and Birgit and Gad Rausing's Foundation. The authors are grateful to a group of speech-therapist students (Logopedprogrammet 2005) for performing the subject running.

References

Braaten, R. F. & Leary, J. C. (1999). Temporal induction of missing birdsong segments in European starlings. *Psychological Science, 10,* 162-166.

DeWitt, L. A. & Samuel, A. G. (2006). The role of knowledgebased expectations in music perception: Evidence from musical restoration. *Journal of Experimental Psychology, 119,* 123-144.

Eriksson, M. & Berglund, E. (1996). Swedish Early Communicative Development Inventory -- words and gestures. *First Language, 19,* 55-90.

Fadiga, L., Fogassi, L., Pavesi, G., & Rizzolatti, G. (1995). Motor Facilitation During Action Observation - A Magnetic Stimulation Study. *Journal of Neurophysiology, 73,* 2608-2611.

Falck-Ytter, T., Gredebäck, G., & von Hofsten, C. (2006). Infants predict other people's action goals. *Nature Neurosci., 9,* 878-879.

Fernald, A., Pinto, J. P., Swingley, D., Wineberg, A., & McRoberts, G. W. (1998). Rapid games in speed of verbal processing by infants in second year. *Psychological Science, 9,* 228-231.

Fernald, A., Swingley, D., & Pinto, J. P. (2001). When half a word is enough: infants can recognize spoken words using partial phonetic information. *Child Dev., 72,* 1003-1015.

Ferrari, P. F., Gallese, V., Rizzolatti, G., & Fogassi, L. (2003). Mirror neurons responding to the observation of ingestive and communicative mouth actions in the monkey ventral premotor cortex. *European Journal of Neuroscience, 17,* 1703-1714.

Grafton, S. T., Arbib, M. A., Fadiga, L., & Rizzolatti, G. (1996). Localization of grasp representations in humans by positron emission tomography .2. Observation compared with imagination. *Experimental Brain Research, 112,* 103-111.

Keysers, C., Kohler, E., Umilta, M. A., Nanetti, L., Fogassi, L., & Gallese, V. (2003). Audiovisual mirror neurons and action recognition. *Experimental Brain Research, 4,* 628-636.

Kohler, E., Keysers, C., Umilta, M. A., Fogassi, L., Gallese, V., & Rizzolatti, G. (2002). Hearing sounds, understanding actions: action representation in mirror neurons. *Science, 297,* 846-848.

Kuhl, P., Williams, K., Lacerda, F., Stevens, K. N., & Lindblom, B. (1992). Linguistic experience alters phonetic perception in infants by 6 months of age. *Science, 255,* 606-608.

MacNeilage, P. & Davis, B. L. (2000). Deriving speech from nonspeech: a view from ontogeny. *Phonetica, 57(2-4),* 284-296.

Newman, R. S. (2004). Perceptual restoration in children versus adults. *Applied Psycholinguistics, 5,* 481-493.

Polka, L. & Werker, J. F. (1994). Developmental changes in perception of nonnative vowel contrasts. *J.Exp.Psychol.Hum.Percept.Perform., 20,* 421-435.

Rizzolatti, G. & Arbib, M. A. (1998). Language within our grasp. *Trends in Neurosciences, 21,* 188-194.

Rizzolatti, G. & Craighero, L. (2004). The Mirror-Neuron System. *Annual Review of Neuroscience, 27,* 169-192.

Samuel, A. (1996). Phoneme restoration. *Language and Cognitive Processes, 11,* 647-654.

Schultz-Westre, C. (1985). A visual analogue of phonemic restoration: Sign restoration in American Sign Language. *Milwaukee, WI: University of Wisconsin-Milwaukee.*

Walley, A. C. (1988). Spoken word recognition by young children and adults. *Cognitive Development, 3,* 137-165.

Warren, R. M. (1970). Perceptual Restoration of Missing Speech Sounds. *Science, 167,* 392-393.

Warren, R. M. & Obusek, C. J. (1971). Speech perception and phonemic restorations. *Perception and Psychophysics, 9,* 358-362.

Warren, R. M. & Warren, R. P. (1970). Auditory Illusions and confusions. *Scientific American, 223,* 30-36.

Simon Effect with Central Stimuli: A Time-Course Analysis

Antonio Pellicano (apellica@dsc.unibo.it)
Luisa Lugli (lugli@dsc.unibo.it)
Giulia Baroni (baroni@dsc.unibo.it)
Roberto Nicoletti (nicoletti@dsc.unibo.it)

Dipartimento di Discipline della Comunicazione
Via Azzo Gardino 23 - 40122 Bologna (Italy)

Abstract

In three experiments, the Simon effect was investigated with centrally presented stimuli that conveyed a left/right spatial information through iconic-symbolic (Experiment 1) and semantic (Experiments 2 and 3) codes.
Experiment 1 provided clear evidence of a Simon effect produced by left/right pointing arrows while Experiments 2 and 3 suggested that extra time for stimulus coding is needed to allow for a Simon effect to show up with "LEFT"/"RIGHT" spatial words. The time-course investigation of the Simon effects showed that the effects increased in magnitude with increasing reaction times, suggesting that a more time-consuming activation of a cognitive spatial code was responsible for the Simon effects to emerge.

Introduction

In a two-choice reaction time tasks, when stimuli are presented in the left and right locations performance is better when stimulus location corresponds to response location (corresponding S-R pairings) than when it does not (non-corresponding S-R pairings), even when location is irrelevant and participants are instructed to respond to a non-location feature of the stimulus (e.g. stimulus colour). This phenomenon is called the Simon effect (see Kornblum, Hasbroucq & Osman, 1990; Lu & Proctor, 1995; Simon, 1990).

Craft and Simon (1970) provided the first demonstration of the Simon effect with visual stimuli by modifying a stereoscope to divide the visual field into left and right halves. In one condition, the stimulus was presented monocularly, that is, a red or green light was presented in the left visual field to the left eye or in the right visual field to the right eye. Subjects were instructed to respond with a left-hand keypress to a green light and with a right-hand keypress to a red light, or vice versa. Responses were faster when the right stimulus (e.g., red light) was presented to the right eye rather than to the left eye and when the left stimulus (e.g., green light) was presented to the left eye rather than to the right eye. The Simon effect for lateralized visual stimuli has since been replicated many times with colour as the relevant stimulus dimension (e.g., Wühr, 2006) and with a variety of other relevant stimulus dimensions, such as geometric forms (Nicoletti & Umiltà, 1989) and

letters (Proctor & Lu, 1994).

It is widely assumed that in the Simon task a spatial code is generated for the stimulus location attribute that cannot be ignored even if it is irrelevant to the task. Moreover, the Simon effect is thought to be located at a response selection stage (e.g., see reviews in Lu & Proctor, 1995; Umiltà & Nicoletti, 1990). The so called dual-route models have been proposed to account for the Simon effect (e.g., De Jong, Liang, & Lauber, 1994; Kornblum, Hasbroucq & Osman, 1990). In general, these models maintain that, on its identification, the imperative stimulus (i.e. the colour or geometric form) activates the correct response via a conditional (controlled) route. In addition, and independent of stimulus identification, the spatial attribute of the stimulus (i.e. right or left position), is thought to activate the corresponding response via an unconditional (direct) route. If the conditional and the unconditional route activate the same response, the correct response is quickly executed. If the two routes activate different responses, the incorrect response must be aborted in favour of the correct one, so that execution of the correct response requires extra time. A number of studies provided further investigation of the effects of irrelevant spatial stimulus dimension on response selection processes in Simon tasks with lateralized stimuli. In these studies the distributional analysis of reaction times (RTs) (Ratcliff, 1979) has been employed to study more in depth the functionality of the dual-route models. On the one hand, De Jong et al. (1994) demonstrated that activation of responses along the unconditional and conditional routes has different time courses. According to their findings, the activation of the unconditional effect is time locked to stimulus onset. The locational stimulus code, which gives rise to the automatic process, is formed faster than the nonspatial stimulus code, on which the controlled process is based. So, the automatic process begins earlier than the controlled process. Moreover, the task-irrelevant stimulus location code tends to decay across time, resulting in a smaller Simon effect when the response to the relevant stimulus dimension is slowed down (see also Hommel, 1993; Roswarski & Proctor, 1996; Rubichi & Pellicano, 2004). The activation of the conditional route is instead time locked to the response and largely independent of relative response speed. On the other hand, Ansorge (2003) showed an opposite time course of the Simon effect across bins, when centrally presented stimuli were employed. The Simon effect increased in magnitude with increasing RT and was only significant among the slowest responses. That is, activation of the automatic response along the unconditional route was slow and unable to affect performance before longer time intervals. However, the interpretation of the RT bin distribution analyses for Simon tasks is not undisputed. For example, Roswarski and Proctor (2003) have recently questioned the validity of the distributional analysis of RTs by stressing its post-hoc character. One has to agree with Roswarski and Proctor (2003) that the shape of the effect function is related to RTs variance. That is, a decreasing effect function is obtained whenever the RTs variance is larger for the corresponding than for the noncorresponding condition, whereas an increasing effect function is related to more variance in the noncorresponding condition (see also Zhang & Kornblum, 1997). However, it has to be pointed out that, in contrast to Roswarski and Proctor's (2003) critique, other authors do not dismiss the possibility of distinguishing between processes based on RT distributions (see Balota & Spieler, 1999; Mewhort, Braun & Heathcote, 1992; Wiegand & Wascher, 2005; Zhang & Kornblum, 1997).

In a number of studies, the Simon effect was also obtained with stimuli whose spatial information was not conveyed by their physical location in space but through iconic-symbolic or semantic codes. For example, in Masaki, Takasawa and Yamazaki (2000) participants were instructed to respond by lifting the right or left middle finger to the colour of a red or blue arrow pointing to the left or to the right direction and presented at the centre of the screen. A significant Simon effect was obtained, that is, RTs were 120 ms faster when the pointing orientation of the arrows corresponded to the position of the responding hand than when they did not. Also Proctor, Marble and Vu (2000) employed centrally presented left/right pointing arrows intermixed with "LEFT"/"RIGHT" words, both varying in colour. In their Experiment 2, location-relevant and location-irrelevant trials were presented. When the stimulus (arrow or word) was red or green the response was to be selected on the basis of the colour (location-irrelevant trials). When the stimulus was white, the response was to be selected on the basis of stimulus location (location-relevant trials) with an incompatible mapping. The authors provided indirect evidence of a Simon effect with both arrows and words even though they were presented in the centre of the screen. Moreover, Lu and Proctor (2001, Experiment 3) observed a significant Simon effect when participants had to respond by pressing a left or right key to the colour of a frame that was presented centrally and simultaneously around to a spatial word (i.e. "RIGHT" and "LEFT"). Ansorge (2003) and Zorzi, Mapelli, Rusconi and Umiltà (2003) investigated the presence of a Simon effect when stimuli were centrally presented cartoon faces and the spatial value was conveyed by the direction of their gaze. Participants had to respond to the colour of the irises while ignoring the gaze direction. Responses were faster when the response position and the gaze direction corresponded than when they were opposite.

Although Simon effects obtained with arrow directions and spatial word stimuli have been investigated more than the Simon effect obtained with face stimuli, no time-course investigation of the effect have been conducted on such stimuli.

In the present study the time-course of the Simon effect was investigated with arrows and spatial words which shared the same central spatial location as the face stimuli employed by Ansorge (2003). Therefore, evidence of an increasing magnitude of the effect with increasing RT were expected as a function of the central position of the stimuli. If a pattern of results similar to the one obtained by Ansorge (2003), that is, slow activation process along the unconditional route, we can conclude that such a pattern of activation and time-course are not stimulus specific but can be representative of central stimuli other than eyes.

Recently, it has been proposed that two dissociable mechanisms are responsible of the time-course differences in Simon effect. On the one hand, a Simon effect decreasing in magnitude with increasing RT, is supposed to be produced by a visuomotor facilitation for S-R corresponding pairings. On the other hand, a Simon effect increasing in magnitude with increasing RT is supposed to be generated by a cognitive interference of higher-level spatial codes (Wiegand & Wascher, 2005). More interestingly, these authors suggested that the locus of these two different mechanisms may be the dorsal and the ventral streams, respectively (see also Rossetti & Pisella, 2002).

Clearly, the presence of a temporally sustained, instead of a transient, Simon effect with central arrow and spatial word stimuli would suggest that a kind of cognitive interference, rather than a visuomotor facilitation mechanism, was critically involved and maybe located the ventral stream.

Experiment 1

Method

Participants Fourteen volunteer students of the University of Bologna participated. They were all right-handed, had normal or corrected-to-normal vision, and were not aware of the purpose of the experiment.

Apparatus and stimuli The experiment took place in a dimly lit and noiseless room. Subjects were seated facing a 17" cathode-ray tube screen driven by a 700 MHz computer. The subject's head was positioned in a adjustable head-and-chin rest. Stimulus selection, response timing, and data collection were controlled by the E-Prime 1.1 software. A fixation cross ($0.95° \times 0.95°$ of visual angle) was presented at the beginning of each trial. The stimuli were blue or red arrow pointing to the left or to the right, presented at the centre of a white screen and at a viewing distance of 42 cm. The arrow was $5.45°$ wide $\times 2.72°$ high. Responses were made by pressing either the "3" or the "9" key on the computer keyboard with left or right index finger, respectively.

Procedure Each trial began with the fixation cross presented in the centre of the screen for 1000 ms. The fixation was replaced by a blank of 500 ms in duration. After that the stimulus appeared and remained on the screen for 150 ms. At the disappearance of the stimulus, subjects had 400 ms to respond, after which the word "ERROR" or "DELAY" appeared on the screen for incorrect and delayed response, respectively.

Participants were tested individually in a single session, which comprised 40 practice trials, followed by 240 trials (60 for each stimulus) split into two blocks of 120 trials. Subjects took a short break between the first and second block.

Participants were instructed to respond to the colour of the stimulus (half the participants responded to the red stimulus by pressing the right key and to the blue stimulus by pressing the left key, whereas the other half had the reverse assignment). Stimulus presentation occurred according to a random sequence. The instructions stressed the speed and accuracy of response.

Results and discussion

For each participant RTs faster than overall mean minus 2 standard deviations (0.6%) and slower than overall mean plus 2 standard deviations (3.4%) and omissions (2.2%) were excluded from analyses. In order to measure the Simon effect, responses were coded as corresponding (the response key corresponded to the direction of the arrow) and noncorresponding (the response key did not correspond to the direction of the arrow).

RTs for corresponding and non-corresponding S-R pairings were portioned into quintiles (5 bins) for each participant. Mean correct RTs were submitted to a repeated-measures ANOVA with Bin (1st to 5th) and Simon (corresponding vs. non-corresponding S-R pairings) as the within-subjects factors. Note that, considering the way data were grouped, the Bin main effect turned out to be significant in all analyses. Therefore, it will not be reported and discussed here or in the following experiments.

Arcsin-transformed percentage of wrong responses (ERs) was submitted to an ANOVA with the only Simon as the within-subjects factor. Therefore, errors x bin interactions were not included in the analyses. For a better comprehension we reported actual ERs.

For RT, the main effect of Simon was significant, $F(1,11) = 22.85$, $p < .001$. RTs were faster for the corresponding than for the non-corresponding responses (324 vs. 350 ms). In addition, the interaction between Simon and Bin was significant, $F(1,11) = 7.73$, $p < .001$. Paired Samples T-test showed that the Simon factor was significant for all the five bins. A second ANOVA was performed on the Simon effect (1st to 5th) within-subject factor that was significant $F(1,11) = 7.73$, $p < .001$. Contrasts displayed that the magnitude of the Simon effect increased significantly from the first to the fourth bin (14, 21, 28, 34 ms respectively), $Fs(1,11) = 4.77$, $p = .048$ (bin 1st vs. bin 2nd); 7.37, $p = .018$ (bin 2nd vs. bin 3rd); 8.24, $p = .013$ (bin 3rd vs. bin 4th) and decreased from the

fourth to the fifth (34, 32 ms), $F(1,11) = 9.89$, $p = .008$.

For ERs the main effect of Simon was significant, $F(1,11) = 12.2$, $p = .004$. The ER was higher for non-corresponding than for corresponding responses (7.3% vs. 1.9%).

Results of Experiment 1 showed a clear 26-ms Simon effect. This confirms the presence of the effect with centrally presented stimuli as in the previous experiments where the spatial value was conveyed by the iconic-symbolic information contained in the arrows (Masaki, Takasawa & Yamazaki, 2000). More interestingly, the time course of the effect is similar to the one found by Ansorge (2003). In our data, the Simon increased in magnitude from the 1st to the 4th and then slightly decreased from the 4th to the 5th bin.

In Experiment 2 we presented the word "Right" and "Left" as imperative stimulus. If the effects of spatial information conveyed by centrally presented arrows are also present with spatial meaning words, the presence of a significant Simon effect with a magnitude and a time course similar to the one displayed in Experiment 1 would suggest that spatial words can be considered spatial indicators as effective as the arrows.

Experiment 2

Method

Eighteen new students from the same subject pool as in previous experiment participated.

Apparatus and procedure were the same as in Experiment 1. The stimuli were presented at the centre of the screen and consisted of a blue or red Italian word: "DESTRA" (right) or "SINISTRA" (left). The word was written in capital letters and was 5.45° wide X 0.95° high (DESTRA), while SINISTRA was 7.23° wide X 0.95° high.

Results and discussion

As for Experiment 1, for each participant RTs faster than overall mean minus 2 standard deviations (0.4%) and slower than overall mean plus 2 standard deviations (5%) and omissions (3%) were excluded from analyses. ANOVAs with the same factors as those in Experiment 1 were performed. For RT, the main effect of Simon was not significant (314 vs. 313 ms for corresponding and noncorresponding condition, respectively), $F(1,17) = .699$, $p = .415$, as for the interaction between Simon and Bin, $F(1,17) = .157$, $p = .959$. The magnitude of the nonsignificant Simon effect was 0, -1, -1, -2, -2 ms from bin 1st to bin 5th, respectively. For ERs the main effect of correspondence approached significance (4.8% vs. 7.1%) $F(1,17) = 3.70$, $p = .072$.

Results of Experiment 2 showed no Simon effect when the spatial information of the central stimulus was conveyed by the meaning of the words. Moreover, the effect was absent in all the five bins showing no relation between the effects of semantic spatial coding of stimuli and response speed. These results suggest that spatial word did not act as spatial indicators, being unable to elicit automatic activation of a spatial code which interacted with response selection processes. However, it is possible that the time needed to extract spatial information from spatial words is longer than the time needed for arrows. As a consequence, for spatial word only, the response to colour could have been executed before the automatic response to the irrelevant spatial attribute being activated. Consistently, significant Simon effects were obtained by Proctor, Marble and Vu (2000) and Lu and Proctor (2001, Experiment 3) with longer time intervals available for response execution. In order to verify this possibility, in Experiment 3 we employed the same stimuli as Experiment 2 increasing their exposition time until response.

Experiment 3

Method

Ten new students, selected as before, participated.
Apparatus, stimuli and procedure of this experiment were the same as Experiment 2, except for the fact that the stimulus remained on the screen until a response was made. Therefore, the feedback consisted only by the word "ERROR" for incorrect responses.

Results and discussion

As for the previous experiments, for each participant RTs slower than overall mean plus 2 standard deviations (4.1%) were excluded from analyses. No omissions and RTs faster than overall mean minus 2 standard deviations were observed. ANOVAs with the same factors as those in Experiment 2 were performed.
For RT, the main effect of Simon was significant, $F(1,9) = 10.21$, $p = .011$. RTs were faster for corresponding (446 ms) than for non-corresponding (472 ms) condition. The interaction between Simon and Bin was also significant, $F(1,9) = 12.92$, $p < .001$. Paired-Sample T-tests showed that the Simon factor was significant for the last three bins. A second ANOVA was performed on the Simon effect, with Bin (1st to 5th) as a within-subject factor which resulted significant $F(1,9) = 12.92$, $p < .001$. The Simon effect was 7, 10, 21, 33 and 62 ms from bin 1st to 5th respectively. Contrasts displayed that the magnitude of the Simon effect increased significantly from the 3rd to the 5th bin, $Fs(1,9) = 5.78$, $p = .040$ (bin 2nd vs. bin 3rd), 7.85, $p = .021$ (bin 3rd vs. bin 4th), 18.01, $p = .002$ (bin 4th vs. bin 5th).
For ERs, the main effect of Simon was significant, $F(1,9) = 10.32$, $p = .011$. Responses were less accurate for non-corresponding than for corresponding condition (3.3% vs. 0.42%).
The results of Experiment 3 showed that longer exposition time of spatial words led to a clear 26 ms and 2.9% Simon effect for both RT and ER measures. The time course of the effect was very similar to the one found by Ansorge (2003). The Simon effect was not significant in the fastest bins (bin 1st and 2nd), it reached significance in bin 3rd and then increased in magnitude from the 3rd to the 5th bin.

General discussion

In the most common version of the Simon task, that is when the stimuli are presented to the left or to the right of a central fixation point, the spatial value of the stimulus is given by its spatial position. In this work, we studied the Simon effect in three experiments with centrally presented stimuli which conveyed spatial information through iconic-symbolic (Experiment 1) and semantic (Experiments 2 and 3) codes. Experiment 1 provided clear evidence of a Simon effect produced by left/right pointing arrows as in Masaki et al.'s work (Masaki, Takasawa & Yamazaki, 2000), while evidence from Experiments 2 and 3 suggested that extra time for response execution must be provided to allow for a Simon effect to show up with LEFT/RIGHT spatial words. In both Experiments 1 and 3, the magnitude of the effect was 26 ms, even if activation of corresponding response was faster for arrow than for spatial word stimuli. This value is congruent with the expected magnitude, which, with lateralized stimuli, typically ranges between 20 and 30 msec (see Lu & Proctor, 1995).
It is well known that the time course analysis of performance in lateralized Simon tasks showed a Simon effect that decreased in magnitude with increasing RTs, suggesting that activation is very fast and tends to decay rapidly across time (Hommel, 1993; Roswarski & Proctor, 1996; Rubichi & Pellicano, 2004). On the contrary, the time course analysis of a Simon effect produced by the direction of the gaze in centrally presented faces, showed a Simon effect of increasing magnitude with increasing RTs (Ansorge, 2003).
For this reason, the time course of the Simon effects we obtained was investigated through the distributional analysis of RTs, to show the temporal dynamics of response activation. Although Roswarski and Proctor (2003) claimed that significant interactions with bins are only a meaningless secondary phenomenon, which derive from differences in variances of RTs for the two corresponding and noncorresponding conditions, other authors did not exclude the possibility for this technique to discriminate between processes based on RT distributions (Zhang & Kornblum, 1997). Furthermore, similar results were obtained with different techniques such as psychophysiological measures of the Simon effect (Wiegand & Wascher, 2005).
In summary, our results clearly suggest that, in dual-route models such a delayed pattern of activation of the automatic response along the unconditional route was not stimulus specific, but can be considered the product of those stimuli whose spatial information is not given by their physical location in space.
Recently, Wiegand and Wascher (2005) proposed that two dissociable mechanisms are involved in generating the Simon effect: a visuomotor facilitation of same side responses, which leads to a transient Simon effect and a more cognitive process of interference leading to a sustained Simon effect. Moreover, they suggest that the locus of the visuomotor facilitation and the cognitive interference mechanisms may be the dorsal and the ventral streams, respectively (see also Rossetti & Pisella, 2002).

This study supports the notion that the first mechanism, that is, the dorsal pathway, is active only when stimuli and responses are horizontally displaced and the responding effectors are in anatomical position (i.e., the left hand presses a left button and the right hand presses a right button). For all the other different stimulus-response displacements and in crossed-hand conditions, a more time consuming activation of a cognitive spatial code (which operates along the ventral pathway) is responsible for the Simon effect to emerge. Our results support this notion, suggesting that Simon effect for centrally presented stimuli was generated by the slower activation of a cognitive spatial code. From a broader point of view, the present investigation increased our knowledge of the way the spatial features of the environmental objects is coded and processed by humans.

Acknowledgments

Thanks to Valentina Bazzarin, Anna Borghi, Cristina Iani, Sandro Rubichi and Alessia Tessari, for helpful comments on this contribution.

References

Ansorge, U. (2003). Spatial Simon effects and compatibility effects induced by observed gaze direction. *Visual Cognition, 10*, 363–383.

Balota, D. A., & Spieler, D. H. (1999). Word frequency, repetition, and lexicality effects in word recognition tasks: Beyond measures of central tendency. *Journal of Experimental Psychology: General, 128*, 32–55.

Craft, J. L., & Simon, J. R. (1970). Processing symbolic information from a visual display: Interference from an irrelevant directional cue. *Journal of Experimental Psychology, 83*, 415–420.

De Jong, R., Liang, C-C., & Lauber, E. (1994). Conditional and unconditional automaticity: A dual-process model of effects of spatial stimulus-response correspondence. *Journal of Experimental Psychology: Human Perception and Performance, 20*, 731–750.

Hommel, B. (1993). The relationship between stimulus processing and response selection in the Simon task: Evidence for temporal overlap. *Psychological Research, 55*, 280–290.

Kornblum, S., Hasbroucq, T., & Osman, A. (1990). Dimensional overlap: Cognitive basis for stimulus-response compatibility–A model and taxonomy. *Psychological Review, 97*, 253–270.

Lu, C.-H., & Proctor, R.W. (1995). The influence of irrelevant location information on performance: A review of the Simon and spatial Stroop effects. *Psychonomic Bulletin & Review, 2*, 174–207.

Lu, C.-H., & Proctor, R. W. (2001). Influence of irrelevant information on human performance: Effects of S-R associations strength and relative timing. *Quarterly Journal of Experimental Psychology, 54A*, 95–136.

Masaki, H., Takasawa, N., & Yamazaki, K. (2000). An electrophysiological study of the locus of the interference effect in a stimulus-response compatibility paradigm. *Psychophysiology. 37*, 464–472.

Mewhort, D. J., Braun, J. G., & Heathcote, A. (1992). Response time distributions and the Stroop task: A test of the Cohen, Dunbar, and McClelland (1990) model. *Journal of Experimental Psychology: Human Perception and Performance, 18*, 872–882.

Nicoletti, R. & Umilta, C. (1989). Splitting visual space with attention. *Journal-of-Experimental-Psychology:-Human-Perception-and-Performance, 15*, 164–169.

Proctor, R. W., Marble, J. G., & Vu, K.-P. L. (2000). Mixing incompatibly mapped location-relevant trials with location-irrelevant trials: Effects of stimulus mode on the reverse Simon effect. *Psychological Research, 64*, 11–24.

Proctor, R. W., & Lu, C.-H. (1994). Referential coding and attention shifting accounts of the Simon effect. *Psychological Research, 56*, 185–195.

Ratcliff, R. (1979). Group reaction time distributions and an analysis of distribution statistics. *Psychological Bulletin, 86*, 446–461.

Roswarski, T. E., & Proctor, R. W. (1996). Multiple Spatial codes and temporal overlap in choicereaction tasks. *Psychological Research, 59*, 196–211.

Roswarski, T. E., & Proctor, R. W. (2003). Intrahemispherical activation, visuomotor transmission, and the Simon effect: Comment on Wascher et al. (2001). *Journal of Experimental Psychology: Human Perception and Performance, 29*, 152–158.

Rossetti, Y., & Pisella, L. (2002). Several 'vision for action' systems: A guide to dissociating and integrating dorsal and ventral functions. In W. Prinz & B. Hommel (Eds.), *Common mechanisms in perception and action. Attention and performance, Vol.11*. Oxford, England: Oxford University Press.

Rubichi, S. & Pellicano A. (2004). Does the Simon effect affect movement execution? *European Journal of Cognitive Psychology, 16*, 825–840.

Simon, J.R. (1990). The effects of an irrelevant directional cue on human information processing. In R.W. Proctor & T.G. Reeve (Eds.), *Stimulus–response compatibility: An integrated perspective*. Amsterdam: North-Holland.

Umiltà, C., & Nicoletti, R. (1990). Spatial stimulus-response compatibility. In R. W. Proctor & T. G. Reeve (Eds.), *Stimulus-response compatibility: An integrated perspective*. Amsterdam:North-Holland.

Wiegand, K. & Wascher, E. (2005). Dynamic Aspects of Stimulus-Response Correspondence: Evidence for Two Mechanisms Involved in the Simon Effect. *Journal-of-Experimental-Psychology:-Human-Perception-and-Performance, 31*, 453–464.

Wühr, P. (2006). Response preparation modulates interference from irrelevant spatial information. *Acta Psychologica, 122*, 206–220.

Zorzi, M., Mapelli, D., Rusconi, E., & Umiltà, C. (2003). Automatic spatial coding of perceived gaze direction is revealed by the Simon effect. *Psychonomic Bulletin &Review, 10*, 423–429.

Integrating Cognitive and Emotional Parameters into Designing Adaptive Hypermedia Environments

Zacharias Lekkas, Nikos Tsianos, Panagiotis Germanakos, Kostas Mourlas

Faculty of Communication and Media Studies, National & Kapodistrian University of Athens, 5 Stadiou Str, GR 105-62, Athens, Hellas

ntsianos@media.uoa.gr, pgerman@media.uoa.gr, mourlas@media.uoa.gr

Abstract

This paper introduces a "new" user profiling model in the field of adaptive hypermedia, which integrates cognitive and emotional parameters, in particular (but not exclusively) when information perception and processing are involved in a Web-based learning environment. The proposed model combines theories from the field of cognitive psychology, applying them on Web-based interactions, in order to improve learning performance and, most importantly, to personalize Web-content to users' needs and preferences, eradicating known difficulties that occur in a "one size fits all" approach.

The specific article emphasizes on the emotional aspect of our model, since it presents results of our efforts to measure and include Emotional Control parameters, by re-constructing a theory that addresses emotion and is feasible in Web- learning environments.

Introduction

One of the main challenges in Adaptive Hypermedia research is alleviating users' orientation difficulties, as well as making appropriate selection of knowledge resources, since the vastness of the hyperspace has made information retrieval a rather complicated task (De Bra, Aroyo, Chepegin, 2004).

Adaptivity is a particular functionality that distinguishes between interactions of different users within the information space (Eklund, & Sinclair, 2000; Brusilovsky & Nejdl,, 2004). Adaptive Hypermedia Systems employ adaptivity by manipulating the link structure or by altering the presentation of information, on the basis of a dynamic understanding of the individual user, represented in an explicit user model (Brusilovsky, 2001; 1996).

A system can be classified as an Adaptive Hypermedia System if it is based on hypermedia, has an explicit user model representing certain characteristics of the user, has a domain model which is a set of relationships between knowledge elements in the information space, and is capable of modifying some visible or functional parts of the system, based on the information maintained in the user model (Brusilovsky, 2001; 1996; Brusilovsky & Nejdl, 2004).

In further support of the aforementioned concept of adaptivity, when referring to information retrieval and processing, one cannot disregard the top-down individual cognitive processes (Eysenck & Keane, 2005), that significantly affect users' interactions within the hyperspace, especially when such interactions involve educational or learning, in general, goals.

Consequently, besides "traditional" demographic characteristics that commonly comprise the user model in hypermedia environments, we believe that a user model that incorporates individual cognitive characteristics and triggers corresponding mechanisms of adaptivity, increases the effectiveness of Web- applications that involve learning processes.

The goal of our research in general is to integrate individual cognitive and emotional characteristics as main parameters in an adaptive system we have already developed. Our system focuses on educational purposes, and its personalization mechanism relies on mapping the provided content on each user's preferences and inclinations.

This paper focuses on emotional factors that we hypothesize to be proven significant in defining usability and aesthetics aspects, taking into consideration psychometric challenges, as well as the complicated matter of quantifying and subsequently mapping emotions on a hypermedia environment.

At a first level, we have experimented with two variables that we expect to correlate with each other, anxiety and Emotional Control. Our main hypothesis is that the moderating role of Emotional Control reduces the negative effect of high levels of anxiety, and should be taken into account in an adaptive e-learning process.

User Perceptual Preference Characteristics

This is the new component / dimension of the user profiling defined above. It contains visual attention and cognitive processes (including emotional parameters) that could be described as user "perceptual preferences", aiming to enhance information learning efficacy.

User Perceptual Preferences could be described as a continuous mental process, which starts with the perception of an object in the user's attentional visual field, and involves a number of cognitive, learning and emotional processes that lead to the actual response to that stimulus.

This model's primary parameters formulate a three-dimensional approach to the problem. The first dimension investigates the visual and cognitive processing of the user,

The project is co-funded by the European Social Fund and National Resources (EPEAEK II) PYTHAGORAS the second his / her learning style, while the third captures his / her emotionality during the interaction process with the information space.

Visual & Cognitive Processing

Special emphasis is given to visual attention, in the sense of tracking user's eye movements, and in particular scanning his / her eye gaze on the information environment (Gulliver & Ghinea, 2004).

It is composed of two serial phases: the pre-attentive and the limited-capacity stage. The pre-attentive stage of vision subconsciously defines objects from visual primitives, such as lines, curvature, orientation, color and motion and allows definition of objects in the visual field. When items pass from the pre-attentive stage to the limited-capacity stage, these items are considered as selected. Interpretation of eye movement data is based on the empirically validated assumption that when a person is performing a cognitive task, while watching a display, the location of his / her gaze corresponds to the symbol currently being processed in working memory and, moreover, that the eye naturally focuses on areas that are most likely to be informative.

Cognitive Processing parameters could be primarily summarised in (i) control of processing (refers to the processes that identify and register goal-relevant information and block out dominant or appealing but actually irrelevant information), (ii) speed of processing (refers to the maximum speed at which a given mental act may be efficiently executed), and (iii) working memory (refers to the processes that enable a person to hold information in an active state while integrating it with other information until the current problem is solved).

Many researchers (Demetriou et al., 1993; Demetriou & Kazi, 2001) have identified that the speed of cognitive processing and control of its processing is directly related to human age, as well as to continuous exercise and experience, with the former to be the primary indicator. Therefore, the processing development speed decreases non-linearly at the ages between 0 – 15 (1500 msec), it is further stabilized at the ages between 15 - 55-60 (500 msec) and increases from that age on (1500 msec). However, it should be stated that the actual cognitive processing speed efficiency is yielded from the difference (maximum value 0.8 msec) between the peak value of the speed of processing and the peak value of control of processing.

Learning Styles

Learning styles represent a particular set of strengths and preferences that an individual or group of people exhibit when they perceive and process information. By taking into account these preferences and defining specific learning strategies (in our case by mechanisms of adaptation), empirical research has shown that more effective learning can be achieved (Boyle et al., 2003), and that learning styles correlate with academic achievement in an e-learning web-based environment [Wang et al., 2006].

A selection of the most appropriate and technologically feasible learning styles (those that can be projected on the processes of selection and presentation of Web-content and the tailoring of navigational tools) has been studied in order to identify how users transforms information into knowledge (constructing new cognitive frames):

- Riding's Cognitive Style Analysis [Verbal-Imager and Wholistic-Analytical] (2001).
- Felder / Silverman Index of Learning Styles [4 scales: Active vs Reflective, Sensing vs Intuitive, visual vs Verbal and Global vs Sequential] (Felder & Silverman, 1988).
- Witkin's Field Dependency [Field-Dependent vs Field-Independent] (Witkin et al., 1977).
- Kolb's Learning Styles [Converger, Diverger, Accommodator and Assimilator] (Kolb & Kolb, 2005).

We consider that Riding's CSA and Felder / Silverman's ILS implications can be mapped on the information space more precisely, since they are consisted of distinct scales that respond to different aspects of the Web.

Learning style theories that define specific types of learners, as Kolb's Experiential Learning Theory, have far more complex implications, since they relate strongly with personality theories, and therefore cannot be adequately quantified and correlated easily with Web objects and structures.

As part of our research, we did find significant correlation between academic performance and adaptation on specific learning style (Tsianos et al, 2005), though we now work on implementing Riding's typology implications in hypermedia applications, rather than Felder's that we first used.

Emotionality

An effort to construct a model that predicts the role of emotion, in general, is beyond the scope of our research, due to the complexity and the numerous confounding variables that would make such an attempt rather impossible. However, there is a considerable amount of references concerning the role of emotion and its implications on academic performance (or achievement), in terms of efficient learning (Kort & Reilly, 2002). Emotional Intelligence seems to be a possible predictor of the aforementioned concepts, and is a grounded enough construct, already supported by academic literature.

On the basis of the research conducted by Goleman (1995), as well as Salovey & Mayer (1990), who have introduced the term, we are in the process of developing an EQ questionnaire that examines the 3 out of 5 scales that comprise the Emotional Intelligence construct (according to Goleman), since factors that deal with human to human interaction (like empathy) are not present in our Web-applications - at least for the time being.

As a result, our variation of the EQ construct, which we refer to as Emotional Control, consists of:

- The Self- Awareness scale

- The Emotional Management scale
- The Self- Motivation scale

While our sample is still growing, Cronbach's alpha, which indicates scale reliability, is currently 0.756. Revisions on the questionnaire are expected to increase reliability.

Still, there is a question about the role of primary / secondary emotions, and their cognitive and / or neurophysiologic intrinsic origins (Damasio, 1994). Emotions influence the cognitive processes of the individual, and therefore have certain effect in any educational setting. Again, bibliographic research has shown that anxiety is often correlated with academic performance (Cassady, 2004), as well with performance in computer mediated learning procedures (Smith & Caputi, 2005; Chang, 2005). Subsequently, different levels of anxiety should have also a significant effect in cognitive functions.

We believe that combining the level of anxiety of an individual with the moderating role of Emotional Control, it is possible to clarify, at some extent, how affectional responses of the individual hamper or promote learning procedures. Thus, by personalizing on this concept of emotionality the educational content that our already developed adaptive system provides, we can avoid stressful instances and take full advantage of his / hers cognitive capacity at any time.

At a practical level, we assume that users with high anxiety levels lacking the moderating role of Emotional Control are in a greater need of enhancing the aesthetic aspects of our system, while users with low anxiety levels focus more on usability issues.

This is why we are interested in clarifying the relationship between the construct of Emotional Control and anxiety, and if a typology could be extracted.

There are two ways to measure anxiety. Firstly, with anxiety questionnaires, many of them dealing with anxiety at educational settings, providing information about how an individual reacts when is obliged to learn or to go through exams (cognitive test anxiety).

Still, since we are interested also in his emotional state during the Web-based learning procedures, real- time monitoring of anxiety levels would also provide us useful indications. That can be done by a self-reporting instrument (e.g. by giving the user the possibility to define his anxiety level on a bar shown on the computer screen), and / or by specially designed gadgets that measure heart rate, sweat and other physical evidence.

We intend to use all these methods of measurement, as the main direction of our future work, controlling at the same time confounding or correlated variables like verbal ability (or IQ), in an effort to ground our hypothesis that personalizing web content according to the participants

emotional characteristics (an individual's capability or incapability to control his / hers emotions and use anxiety in a constructing way), is of high significance in optimizing computer mediated learning processes.

Incorporating Emotional Intelligence and Anxiety in User Modeling

At the time being, we used a battery of questionnaires to clarify and shape the aforementioned typologies, intending to enhance our adaptive educational hypermedia environment by incorporating all aspects of the proposed user model. In terms of emotionality, the instruments we have used are a standardized (in greek) version of Cassady & Johnson's Cognitive Test Anxiety Scale (2002), and the Emotional Control questionnaire which consists of the three sub-scales we mentioned above.

These questionnaires, as all tests involved in our proposed method of user profiling, are taken on-line within the context of our adaptive web system. The reason that we use questionnaires relates strongly to the very nature of Web environments, where psychometric instruments are bound to be presented verbally or graphically and have to be answered in the form of multiple choices, allowing the system to quantify the collected data.

In order to manipulate the parameters of our adaptive system according to user characteristics, our research has to go through the stage of extracting quantified elements that represent deeper psychological and emotional abilities. The latter cannot be directly used in a Web environment, but a numerical equivalent can define a personalization parameter.

After the construction and standardization of our instruments we are currently trying to find the weighting, the importance and the implications of Emotional Control and anxiety, the two basic terms that comprise our emotionality factor. Our main hypothesis is that Emotional Control and anxiety are negatively correlated. It is proposed that an individual with high emotional control will have low anxiety levels because of his ability to control and organize his emotions. The procedure that we followed as a part of the standardization process and our first statistical analyses is the following:

Method

Sampling and data collection: The study was carried out within the University of Athens. All participants are students. They were given a battery of questionnaires and tests covering our three dimensional proposed model. A total of 108 questionnaires were filled and 88 could be used. Twenty of them were half completed or had inadequate answers and were omitted from the sample. Participants varied from the age of 18 to the age of 25, with a mean age of 20. 30% of the respondents were male and 70% were female.

Procedure

The participants were asked to fill in the questionnaires that could be found in the adaptive hypermedia webpage. The results were kept in a database for easier access and retrieval.

Questionnaires

The study used two questionnaires to collect quantitative data. The Emotional Control Questionnaire included three measures, emotional Self-Awareness, Emotional Management and Self-Motivation, and a total of 28 items. The Cognitive Test Anxiety Scale included 26 items. Participants received two questionnaires with 54 questions total and scales from 1 to 5 for all items.

Design

Internal consistency was assessed by computing Cronbach alphas for the two questionnaires. Although there are no standard guidelines available on appropriate magnitude for the coefficient, in practice, an alpha greater than 0.60 is considered reasonable in non-clinical research. After the inspection of the alpha's coefficients it was decided that item 13 from the Emotional Control Questionnaire and items 8, 17, 20 from the Cognitive Test Anxiety Questionnaire if removed from the scale could lead to an improved alpha coefficient. Consequently the above items were removed from each scale (see Table 1).

Table 1: Scale reliabilities for psychometric scales

Variable	Coefficient α
Emotional Control	0.756
Cognitive Test Anxiety Scale	0.684

Descriptive statistics for the study sample as a whole are provided in Table 2.

Table 2: Means, standard deviation and scale range for Emotional Control and Cognitive Test Anxiety variables

Variable	Mean	S.D.	Range Scale
Emotional Control	3.39	0.38	1-5
Cognitive Test Anxiety	2.88	0.37	1-5

Results

Correlation Analyses (Pearson's r): For the purposes of the study correlation analyses were performed in order to indicate the relationships between the variables of the study. For the comparisons between scores Pearson's r coefficient analyses were used. Table 3 presents the main correlations between the scale emotional control and cognitive test anxiety. The analyses indicated that Emotional Control negatively correlated with Cognitive Test Anxiety (r=-0.261, p<0.05). This finding indicates that as scores in Emotional Control rise, scores in anxiety decrease. High

emotional control means lower anxiety levels. This seems to support our hypothesis, although at moderate levels.

Table 3: Correlation analysis for the variables (Pearson's r)

Variables	Emotional Control.	Cognitive Test Anxiety
Emotional Control	-	-.261*
Cognitive Test Anxiety	-.261*	-

*p<0.05 - Correlation is significant at the 0.05 level (one-tailed).

Discussion

More than a technologically driven determinism, adaptive hypermedia provide a very flexible platform for individual differences to be taken into account, and to assess their importance and role in cognitive processes.

Still, there is the issue of which users' characteristics are to comprise the basis of personalization, since it is not yet clarified which cognitive science theories apply to human-computer interaction.

Knowing that, we intend to continue conducting experiments involving the aforementioned three-dimensional model, in order to optimize and refine it. We have already built a Web-platform that supports personalizing techniques, and have designed corresponding educational material.

The content itself presents a number of challenges, since it must be written as fine-grained as possible, and it must address all possible learning (or cognitive) styles. Our experience has shown that the match/ mismatch factor of teaching and learning style is of importance.

The issue of Emotionality is under research, since its role and effect on academic performance is yet to be proven. We have some indications that Emotional Control and Anxiety correlate as we hypothesized- still, safe conclusions can be drawn only after we have conducted further experiments within the actual learning environment. The same applies for the Visual Attention and Cognitive Parameters.

Nevertheless, our intention is to fine-tune our proposed model, and its equivalent Web- architecture, in order to cover numerous approaches in the field of cognitive studies, always in terms of applicable in hyperspace theories.

References

Boyle, E. A., Duffy, T. & Dunleavy, K. (2003). Learning styles and academic outcome: The validity and utility of Vermunt's Inventory of Learning Styles in a British higher education setting, *British Journal of Educational Psychology*, 73, 267–290.

Brusilovsky, P. (1996). Adaptive Hypermedia: an attempt to analyse and generalize, In Brusilovsky, Kommers, & Streitz (Eds.), *Multimedia, Hypermedia, and Virtual Reality*. Berlin: Springer-Verlag.

Brusilovsky, P. (2001). Adaptive Hypermedia, *User Modeling and User-Adapted Interaction,* 11, 87-110.

Brusilovsky, P. & Nejdl, W. (2004). *Adaptive Hypermedia and Adaptive Web.* CSC Press LLC.

Cassady J. C., Jonhson, R. E. (2002). Cognitive Test Anxiety and Academic Performance. *Contemporary Educational Psychology,* 27, 270-295.

Cassady, J. C. (2004). The influence of cognitive test anxiety across the learning–testing cycle, *Learning and Instruction,* 14, 569–592.

Damasio, A. R. (1994). *Descartes' error: Emotion, reason, and the human brain.* New York: Putnam Publishing Group.

De Bra, P., Aroyo L. & Chepegin, V. (2004). The Next Big Thing: Adaptive Web-Based Systems, *Journal of Digital Information,* Volume 5, Issue 1, Article No 247.

Demetriou, A., Efklides, A. & Platsidou, M. (1993). The architecture and dynamics of developing mind: Experiential structuralism as a frame for unifying cognitive development theories. *Monographs of the Society for Research in Child Development,* 58 (Serial No. 234), 5-6.

Demetriou, A. & Kazi, S. (2001). *Unity and modularity in the mind and the self: Studies on the relationships between self-awareness, personality, and intellectual development from childhood to adolescence.* London: Routdledge.

Eklund, J. & Sinclair, K. (2000). An empirical appraisal of the effectiveness of adaptive interfaces of instructional systems. *Educational Technology and Society,* 3 (4), ISSN 1436-4522.

Eysenck, M. W. & Keane, M. T. (2005), *Cognitive Phychology.* Psychology Press.

Felder, R. M. & Silverman, L. K. (1988). Learning and Teaching Styles in Engineering Education, *Engineering Education,* 78, 674-681.

Felder R. & Spurlin J. (2005). Application, reliability and validity of the Index of Learning Styles, *International Journal of Engineering Education,* Vol. 21, No. 1, 103-112.

Goleman, D. (1995). *Emotional Intelligence: why it can matter more than IQ.* New York: Bantam Books.

Gulliver, S. R. & Ghinea, G. (2004). Stars in their Eyes: What Eye-Tracking Reveals about Multimedia Perceptual Quality, *IEEE Transactions on Systems, Man and Cybernetics,* Part A, 34(4), 472-482.

Kolb, A. Y. & Kolb, D. A. (2005). *The Kolb Learning Style Inventory – Version 3.1 2005 Technical Specifications,* Experience Based Learning Systems.

Kort, B. & Reilly, R. (2002). Analytical Models of Emotions, Learning and Relationships: Towards an Affect-Sensitive Cognitive Machine. *Conference on Virtual Worlds and Simulation (VWSim 2002),* http://affect.media.mit.edu/projectpages/lc/vworlds.pdf.

Riding R. (2001). *Cognitive Style Analysis – Research Administration.* Learning and Training Technology.

Salovey, P. & Mayer, J. D. (1990). Emotional intelligence, *Imagination, Cognition, and Personality,* 9, 185-211.

Smith, B. & Caputi, P. (2005). Cognitive interference model of computer anxiety: Implications for computer-based assessment, *Computers in Human Behavior,* 21, 713-728.

Tsianos N., Germanakos P. & Mourlas C. (2006). Assessing the Importance of Cognitive Learning Styles over Performance in Multimedia Educational Environments, *Proceedings of the 2nd International Conference on Interdisciplinarity in Education (ICIE2006),* Athens, May 11-13, 2006.

Vosniadou, S., 2004. *Cognitive Science: The New Science of the Mind.* Athens: Gutenberg (Greek).

Wang, J. & Lin, J. (2002). Are Personalization Systems Really Personal? – Effects of Conformity in Reducing Information Overload. *Proceedings of the 36th Hawaii International Conference on Systems Sciences (HICSS'03),* 0-7695-1874-5/03.

Wang, K.H., Wang T.H, Wang W.L. & Huang S.C. (2006). Learning Styles and Formative Assessment Strategy: Enhancing Student Achievement in Web-based Learning. *Journal of Computer Assisted Learning* 22 (3), 207–217

Witkin H., Moore C., Gooddenough D. & Cox P. (1977). Field- dependent and field- independent cognitive styles and their educational implications, *Review of Educational Research,* 47, 1-64.

Dimension and Quality Concepts in Synaesthetic Metaphors

Hakan Beşeoğlu (beseoglu@phil.uni-duesseldorf.de)
Jens Fleischhauer (fleischhauer@phil.uni-duesseldorf.de)
Department of Philosophy, Heinrich-Heine University Düsseldorf
Universitätsstr. 1, 40225 Düsseldorf, Germany

Abstract

A (strongly) synaesthetic metaphor (e.g. *loud yellow*) is a metaphor that results from a combination of a modifier and a head, where both express perceptual qualities. Not all synaesthetic metaphors are cognitively equally accessible. In this paper a modification of classical directionality claims will be suggested. Semantical and empirical evidence will be shown to support a differentiation concerning the concepts of each sense modality. In the end these evidences could lead to a new interpretation of the directionality claim itself.

Introduction

In the context of metaphors, especially synaesthetic metaphors, there is a debate about the claim, that there is a directionality concerning the metaphorical mapping. According to our definition (Werning, Fleischhauer and Beşeoğlu 2006, p.2365f.) a metaphor is a synaestethic one if and only if its source domain is perceptual. A metaphor is strongly synaesthetic if its target domain, too, is perceptual. An example for a weakly synaesthetic metaphor is (1), while (2) is an example for a strongly synaesthetic metaphor.

(1) "cold heart"

(2) "cold smell"

Regarding synaesthetic metaphors the directionality thesis claims that there is a hierarchy in respect of order the sense modalities. This means that there is a order in which the different sense modalities can be used in a synaesthetic metahpor. Those metaphors according to this order or hierarchy seem to be more accessible than metaphors which contradict it. In literature several hierarchies were postulated ((cf. Ullmann 1967), Williams (1976), Shen 1997)). Werning, Fleischhauer and Beşeoğlu did an empirical investigation to answer the question if there is such a hierarchy just in lyrics or if it is possible to confirm a form of hierarchy empirically in spoken language. For that reason, in short, a number of adjective-noun pairs representing strongly synaesthetic metaphors were created Subjects then voted these metaphors as accessible or not. The result of this study was that there is an ordering of the sense modalities in deed but in a different way than suggested by Ullmann, Williams or Shen. Figure 1 shows the ordering of the sense modalities according to our study.

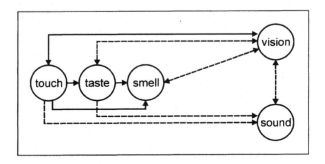

Figure 1: Directionalities of synaesthetic metaphors according to Werning, Fleischhauer and Beşeoğlu 2006. Black arrows show directions significantly rated as accessible, while dotted lines represent not significantly impeded directions. Where there is no arrow this direction is significantly rated as inaccessible.

But not only the hierarchy of sense modalities seems to influence the accessibility of synaesthetic metaphors, also the frequency and morphological status of the adjectival concepts used in the source domain. The more frequent the word used as modifier is, the more the participants voted the metaphor as accessible in this study. If the adjective was derived by productive morphological rules from a noun or verb, the accessibility was decreased, compared with not derived adjectives.[1]

But some questions remain open after this study. In classical directionality claims by Ullmann or Williams the sense domain of vision is the worst source domain in synaesthetic metaphors. Our results of the visual sense modality as a source domain according to this first study is shown in table 1. Since we assigned the value +1 to 'accessible' and −1 to 'not accessible', a mean value of 0 should be expected if there was no directionality (null hypothesis). But nearly all mean values are not significant and near around zero. The direction vision → touch is even significantly enhanced.

---

[1] For a more detailed account of this study cf. Werning, Fleischhauer and Beşeoğlu (2006).

Table 1: Former results of modality vision (first study)

	vision → smell	vision → taste	vision → sound	vision → touch
N	184	180	173	147
mean value	0,08	-0,13	0,02	0,20*

Table 3: Dimension concepts as source domain (first study

	vision → smell	vision → taste	vision → sound	vision → touch
N	93	67	86	106
mean value	0,29*	0,07	0,35*	0,45**

But these results hide the extreme heterogenic answers in accessibility to metaphors of these equal directions. This is the reason for such an indifferent mean value. For example the metaphors

(3) *"gelbe Ruhe"* (*"yellow silence"*)

(4) *"blasser Klang"* (*"pale sound"*)

were judged as accessible to a different degree. All subjects assessed the first metaphor 'not accessible', but for 93% the second metaphor was accessible. It is unsatisfactory for an explanation of these constraints if some metaphors follow and some do not. Is there really no directionality in the end or is there still a systematic in those different answers? here could still be other factors relevant in metaphor comprehension but which? In this first study we did not differentiate between concepts that denote definite qualities like colours and those that denote such qualities as darkness or brightness. But this could be one of these relevant factors in explaining the asymmetry between the different accessibility rates for both of these mentioned metaphors. As we will show, these are concepts out of semantically totally different categories, and criteria for distinguishing will be formulated.

If there is such a difference in concepts, it has to be shown in the first study as well. So it is a reasonable to ask if it is possible to find a difference between quality concepts and dimension concepts in this first study. This would be a first indication that it would be useful to follow this line of investigation. So the same data of the former visual sense modality as source domain was divided in the two categories mentioned, namely quality and dimension by criteria that will be explained in the next section. After this reinterpretation the results are much more different than shown in table 1. This new interpretation is shown in table 2 for quality concepts and in table 3 for dimension concepts.

Table 2: Quality concepts as source domain (first study)

	vision → smell	Vision → taste	vision → sound	vision → touch
N	114	90	87	41
mean value	-0,05	-0,40**	-0,31*	-0,46*

For now all directions concerning a source domain used genuine quality concepts are no longer good modifiers. Indeed some of them (vision → touch, vision → sound) are now significantly impeded. At least the direction vision → taste is even highly significantly impeded. The direction vision → smell is still not significant in either direction, but it changes its sign from plus to minus.

In regard of this reinterpretation of the data from the early study a different empirical study was designed. The new criteria for the distinction of the concepts of the modalities in quality and dimension concepts were used in this study. On concentration on these categories of concepts the claim was to clarify if this differentiation can be shown again in spoken language or if it was a relict of the first study. Exemplarily just the former sense modality of vision was tested.

For that it will be the task of this paper to advocate for such a distinction within the sense modalities. It will conclude in a claim, that there is not only semantically but also empirically evidence for the view that the classical sense modality concepts are heterogenic classes that have to be divided. But before we present this new empirical investigation to support this claim, we first have to present semantic arguments in favour of dividing concepts denoting colours and concepts denoting such qualities as 'brightness' and 'darkness'. The first type we will call *quality concepts* and the second type we call *dimension concepts*. After establishing linguistic criteria we will show, that theses concept types do differ in accessibility in synaesthetic metaphors. In the end new possibilities to interpret the understanding of synaethetical metaphors will be suggested.

Linguistic Criteria

A differentiation of concepts out of the sense modalities in 'dimension concepts' and 'quality concepts' can be founded on linguistic criteria, at least for German. (For the use of the criteria see: Kaiser (1979)) Both concept-types show different characteristics in language use. There is no syntactic difference between them, they both can be used predicatively (7 and 8) and attributively (9 and 10):

(7) *"Das Auto ist rot"* (*"The car is red"*)

(8) *"Das Auto ist hell"* (*"The car is bright"*)

(9) *"Das Auto hat eine rote Farbe"* / *"Das rote Auto ist schnell"* (*"The car has a red colour"* / *"The car is fast"*.)

(10) *"Das Auto hat eine helle Farbe" / "Das helle Auto ist schnell"* (*"The car has a bright colour" / "The bright car is fast"*)

But there are differences in respect of the comparative forms and the use of comparison classes. There is no problem to use the comparative in connection with dimension concepts

(11) *"Diese Farbe ist heller als jene Farbe"* (*"This colour is brighter than that colour"*)

The comparative form in (11) has the following interpretation: One given colour is brighter than a second given colour in respect on a brightness scale. In connection with quality concepts the comparative form is possible but achieves a different interpretation:

(12) *"Diese Farbe ist röter als jene Farbe"* (*"This colour is more red than that colour"*)

The interpretation of the comparative form used in (12) does not mean that two colours are compared on a colour scale and that one of the colours reaches a higher value than the other colour on that scale. Rather it means that two colours are compared in respect to a focal colour (here 'red') and that one of these colours is more similar to the focal red than the other colour. This is a comparison within the colours' spectrum and one colour is said to be more similar with a colour mentioned in the context. But this does not mean that one of these colours in comparison is really red.

In the case of comparison classes the same pattern emerges. The use of comparison classes is possible for dimension concepts:

(13) *"Diese Farbe ist hell im Vergleich zu einer anderen Farbe"* (*"This colour is bright in comparison to another colour"*)

But this appears not possible for quality concepts:

(14) *"Diese Farbe ist rot im Vergleich zu einer anderen Farbe"* (*"This colour is red in comparison to another colour"*)

Example (14) can just be interpreted, that a certain colour is more similar to focal red than another colour. In contrast (13) means that a certain colour is bright in respect of the whole colours' spectrum. The colour mentioned in (13) reaches a high value on the brightness scale compared to any other colour.

The use of the comparative form has the following effect. If an adjective is scalar then it is monotone. (cf. Löbner: 1990) This means if t is for example bright / as bright as k / brighter than k / bright enough / the brightest and t' is brighter than t, then t' is also bright / as bright as k and so on. But what should it mean that t is red and t' is more red than t? This does not mean that t' is red to a higher degree

then t, but this would be the meaning of the comparative form. So there is no monotone increase concerning colour concepts and a different interpretation of the comparative form in both types of concepts.

Thus two semantic criteria can be used to differentiate quality concepts and dimension concepts, namely the interpretation of comparative classes and the interpretation of the comparative forms. Our point of view is rather similar to Lehrer & Lehrer's view concerning colour concepts: '*A is more red than B* indicates not a single dimensional color scale but rather the existence of a focal point for each color' (Lehrer & Lehrer 1982: 495). While the meaning of a sentence like '*A is brighter than B*' indicates a single brightness scale (cf. Löbner 1985, 1990).

A further point is that dimension concepts form antonym pairs, while quality concepts are not antonymic. The antonym, the opposite extreme, of *bright* is *dark*, but what is the antonym of *red*? Is the antonym a certain colour or the whole colour spectrum? Is every other colour the antonym of *red*? In our view there is no opposite extreme of a certain colour or quality. (for antonyms and dimension concepts see: Bierwisch (1987), Löbner (1990), (2002)).

The distinction between these two types of concepts is that quality concepts establish a similarity relation between the qualities which are denoted by the concepts and a focal colour. Dimension concepts establish a relation between their referents on a certain scale. This is at least valid for their connection with the comparative form and comparison classes. Some further argument in favour of this view will be presented by results of our empirical studies done in the last times.

Experiment

Method

Subjects 85 students from Düsseldorf at an age from 20 to 33 (mean 23.612) participated in the study. 52 of them were female and 33 were male. All but 14 were native speakers; the others still were competent in German.

Design

From the sample of German adjectives which express a concept from the domain of visual sense modality, we choose 12 adjectives (see Appendix I . These adjectives were chosen for their easy distinction in quality concepts and dimension concepts. So we used just clear examples, according to the criteria mentioned before. Each of these adjectives was combined which three different nouns (see Appendix II) to form adjective-noun pairs, which express strongly synaesthetic metaphors. Each of these three nouns belongs to a different sense modality (smell, taste and sound).

To accomplish a broad range of metaphors, we randomly divided the subjects into two groups with an average size of 42.5. Each group was presented a list of just 18 synaesthetic metaphors. So, altogether 36 different metaphors were tested. To ensure a constant degree of concentration we did not want to present the whole list of 36 metaphors to one subject.

Subjects were asked to assess the intuitive accessibility of each metaphor. Possible values were -1 for 'not accessible' and +1 for 'accessible'. Gender, age, and mother tongue of the subjects were also recorded.

We just used adjective-noun pairs where the adjectival concept represents the source domain and the noun concept represents the target domain of the metaphor. Syntactically the adjective functions as the modifier of the noun. In the case of the attributive use of adjectives the syntactic function of the modifier and the semantic function of the source domain coincide.

Corpus Analysis To consider additional variables that could affect the subjects' answers we analyzed the frequencies of the adopted adjectives and nouns. The frequencies were determined from the German version of the CELEX corpus (Baayen, Piepenbrock, & Gulikers, 1995). This corpus consists of about six million words taken from written and spoken sources representative for contemporary German. The nouns were chosen for a nearly equipartition of frequency, but there was a greater variance in the frequency of the adjectives.

Morphological Analysis As a further variable we considered the morphological derivation status of the modifier adjectives. In German some adjectives are genuine adjectives, e.g., *warm ('warm')*, while others are derived from verbs or nouns by productive morphological rules, e.g., *riechen – riechend ('smell' – 'smelling'), Aroma – aromatisch ('aroma' – 'aromatic')*. We just used genuine (not derived) adjectives and one derived adjetive (*glänzend – glossy*, which is derived from the noun *Glanz – gloss*).

Results

In this second study gender, age, and mother tongue did not significantly correlate with the judgements of accessibility. In the case of mother tongue we could not establish a significant difference between German native speakers and not native speakers, but it would be an interesting issue to extend the focus on such effects.

The frequency and morphological derivation of the adjectives showed no effect in this study. But the concept type did.

Like in the first study one might expected a mean value of 0, if there be no directionality (null hypothesis). The results are shown in table 4 and 5.

Table 4: Quality concepts as source domain (second study)

	vision → smell	vision → taste	vision → sound	vision → touch
N	209	212	216	-
mean value	-0,59**	-0,47**	-0,69**	

Table 5: Dimension concepts as source domain (second study)

	dimension → smell	dimension → taste	dimension → sound	dimension → touch
N	214	211	208	-
mean value	-0,07	0,15	0,43**	

The data show a clear difference between accessibility of metaphors either using quality or dimension concepts. The results are now much more significant. All directions for *quality concepts* as source domain are now highly significantly impeded. On the other hand the *dimension concepts* used as a source domain has shown no impeded significance or in the case of dimension→sound even a highly significant enhancement (The direction dimension→touch was not regarded). According to these results a new edited directionality thesis can be made as shown in fig 2. Please note that the editions only concern the clearer division of the visual sense modality which is now called "colour", other modalities were not changed in the same way. The concepts of dimension are not presented in the figure. It appears to be unclear how to integrate the dimension concepts in connection with the sense modalities. They can be seen as subclasses of each sense modality or as a modality by itself.

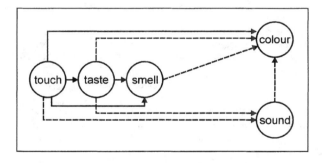

Figure 2: Edited directionalities. Black arrows show significant enhancement, while dotted lines represent not significantly impeded directions.

Discussion

It seems to be shown, that the claim dividing the *sense modalities* in quality and dimension concepts is semantically reasonable and there is indeed empirical evidence to do so, too. This is not a solution in explaining directionalities but it can be seen as an indication for directionality to be more complex than described in literature so far. Nevertheless these new variables, namely quality and dimension concepts, leads us to some new problems and there are a lot of questions arising with these results.

While in the first of our studies the frequency and the morphological derivation status of the adjective appeared to influence to cognitive accessibility of synaesthetic metaphors, at least the frequency do not show any influence in the second study (morphological influences where not tested, see section Experiment for details). If the task is to explain how metaphors are understood one has to investigate whether or not frequency and morphological derivation have minor effects in the background of metaphor comprehension. It seems plausible that a more frequent adjective can be better used in metaphors, because it appears in more contexts and has a wider distribution in language. Also it seems plausible that a morphological less complex adjective is easier to comprehend in metaphors than a more complex one. But as the results of our second study indicate, the semantic of the adjectives is much more important than the other two mentioned factors. This does not mean that they are unimportant, but that they just have minor influence. Some additional work regarding the mentioned factors influencing the accessibility of synaesthetic metaphors need to be done.

A further question is why semantic effects show up. At the moment we can not explain this, but we would like to raise some speculations. One can analyze the concepts of the adjectives in the *frame format* used by Barsalou (1992) and Barsalou & Hale (1993) in cognitive psychology. Frames are a universal format for describing the structure of mental concepts. The mental concepts are described by a set of attributes, like 'form' or 'function'. One attribute of the concept colour might be for example "brightness" with the possible values 'low' and 'high'. The interpretation of 'low' and 'high' is 'bright' and 'dark' respectively.

Dimension concepts can be analyzed in a generalized format called *phase quantification* (cf. Löbner 1985, 1990). According to this format every dimension concept assigns their referent to a phase of a scale. The underlying scale is separated in phases. So the brightness scale for example is separated in the two phases 'bright' and 'dark'. The use of an adjective like 'bright' assigns the referent of the modified noun in the phase denoted "bright" on the underlying scale. (For details see: Löbner 1990)

The case is different for quality concepts. Quality concepts can not be analyzed in the same format then dimension concepts. They do not form antonym pairs and do not assign their referents onto a scale. These differences between dimension and quality concepts show up in the frame analysis of the concept types. This would explain the differences between both concept types in synaesthetic metaphors. Some structures of attributes with dimension concepts as values in a frame are alike. This is not the case for quality concepts. For example the adjective "loud" modifies the attribute "intensity" of the concept colour in the following metaphor:

(15) *"loud colour"*

The meaning of 'loud' is *high value of auditory input*. In its metaphorical use 'loud' has still the same meaning but modifies the attribute "intensity" in a different domain, namely the domain of vision.

In some cases there is no or just a very little understanding of a synaesthetic metaphor consisting of a dimension concept and a noun. One of those examples taken from our results which was judged as nearly inaccessible is:

(16) *"dunkler Geruch"* (*"dark smell"*)

At the moment we are not able to explain such a case in detail, whether it depends on the structure of the dimension concept (adjective) or on the used noun. But it might be explained by the fact that not all attributes in the frame of the nouns are comparable. Maybe there are different classes of attributes which require different types of values (e.g. different types of underlying scales) or the values themselve can just match with certain attributes. Which semantic restrictions there might exist is one additonal question for future work.

Quality concepts like 'red' on the other side modify the attribute "hue", but there is no attribute like this in concepts of the sense domain of sound, for example. In other words there is no attribute to which a value like 'red' can match in concepts out of a different sense domain than colour. We believe that the frame theory can help to explain why both concept types behave in a different way in synaesthetic metaphors.

An open question concerns the transferability of our results to other languages. It would be very interesting to see how dimension and quality concepts, if there are any, behave in synaesthetic metaphors in other languages than German. There is a lot of work regarding perception concepts in different languages. One branch is a discussion about the extension of perception concepts (e.g. 'see', 'hear', 'smell') in other sense or cognitive domains, for example using perception concepts to describe knowledge in sentences like "*I see what you mean*" (cf. Viberg 1984, Evans & Wilkins 2000). The connection between these works and the presented one is not fully established yet, but it would be interesting to connect both research fields in a stronger way. Primarily Viberg and Evans & Wilkins are also talking of a hierarchy of the sense modalities, but not explicitly in connection with synaesthetic metaphors. A more general account on the structure of perception concepts could be established in connecting the mentioned research fields.

An open question remains what falls under the concept of a sense modality. It seems to be very plausible to identify quality concepts with the classical view of genuine sense modalities (cf. Keeley 2002 for a discussion of the concept of sense modalities). In the classical view there are five separated sense modalities: touch, taste, smell, sound and vision. Each sense modality is independent of the others and can be uniquely individuated. But what is the connection between dimension concepts and sense modalities? Are they really part of the certain sense modality? Or do these concepts represent an independent and separated modality by their own? We do not want to answer this question at the moment, but we believe that it is reasonable to be in doubt about the classical view of the sense modalities unless it is not clear if the dimension concepts build up an own modality. In respect of their semantics they do fall in one class and this class is more separated from quality concepts than from many other dimension concepts regardless their semantically connection to the senses.

At the end the presented study is just a refinement of our first study and shows that the phenomenon of directionality of synaesthetic metaphors is more complex than we first guessed. There is a deep connection to semantic factors, at least in German. We guess that the frame theory can help us to explain the semantic factors influencing the accessibility of synaesthetic metaphors. To get clearer of this phenomenon one has to study more languages, too. It seems for us possible and reasonably to extend our work to other languages and to go into more detail in the German language.

Acknowledgments

We would like to thank Gerhard Schurz, Axel Bühler Wiebke Peterson and Marc Breuer for inspiring discussions, also Robert Forster and Stephanie Korsten. Research for this paper was made possible by the grant FOR 600 of the German Research Foundation.

References

Baayen, R., Piepenbrock, R., & Gulikers, L. (1995). *The CELEX lexical database (release 2)*. Philadelphia, PA: Linguistic Data Consortium, University of Pennsylvania. (CD-ROM)

Barsalou, L.W., & Hale, C.R. (1993). Components of conceptual representation: From feature lists to recursive frames. In I. Van Mechelen, J. Hampton, R. Michalski, & P. Theuns (Eds.), *Categories and concepts: Theoretical views and inductive data analysis* (97-144). San Diego, CA: Academic Press.

Barsalou, L.W. (1992). Frames, concepts, and conceptual fields. In E. Kittay & A. Lehrer (Eds.), *Frames, fields, and contrasts: New essays in semantic and lexical organization* (pp. 21-74). Hillsdale, NJ: Lawrence Erlbaum Associates.

Bierwisch, M. (1987). Semantik der Graduierung. In: M. Bierwisch & E. Lang (Eds.), *Grammatische und konzeptuelle Aspekte von Dimensionsadjektiven*. (1987)

Evans, N., & Wilkins, D. (2000). In the Mind's Ear: The Semantic Extension of Perception Verbs in Australian Languages. Language, 76(3), 546-592

Kaiser, G. (1979). Hoch und gut – Überlegungen zur Semantik polarer Adjektive. *Linguistische Berichte, 59/79, 1-26*.

Kelley, B. (2002). Making Sense of the Senses: Individuating Modalities in Humans and other Animals. *The Journal of Philosophy, 99(1), 5-28*.

Lehrer, A., & Lehrer, K. (1982). Antonymy. *Linguistics and Philosophy, 5, 483-501*.

Löbner, S. (1985). Natürlichsprachliche Quantoren: Zur Verallgemeinerung des Begriffs der Quantifikation. *Studium Linguistik, 17/18, 79-113*.

Löbner, S. (1990). *Wahr neben Falsch*. Tübingen, Max Niemeyer Verlag.

Löbner, S. (2002). *Understanding Semantics*. London, Arnold.

Shen, Y. (1997). Cognitive constraints on poetic figures. *Cognitive Linguistics, 8-1. 33-71*.

Ullmann, S. (1967). *The principles of Semantics*. Blackwell, Oxford.

Viberg, A. (1984). The verbs of perception: A typological study. In B.Butterworth, B. Comrie, & Ö.Dahl (Eds.), Explanations for language universals. (pp. 123-162). Berlin: Morton de Gruyter.

Werning, M., Fleischhauer, J., & Beseoglu, H. (2006). The cognitive accessibility of synaesthetic metaphors. In R. Sun & N. Miyake (Eds.), *Proceedings of the Twenty-eighth Annual Conference of the Cognitive Science Society* (pp. 2365-70). London: Lawrence Erlbaum Associates.

Williams, J.M. (1976). Synesthetic adjectives: A possible law of semantic change. *Language, 52(2), 461-478*.

Appendix

Appendix I: List of used adjectives

quality concepts	dimension concepts
matt ('*dull*')	braun ('*brown*')
glänzend ('*glossy*')	weiß ('*white*')
blass ('*pale*')	grau ('*grey*')
dunkel ('*dark*')	rot ('*red*')
hell ('*bright*')	schwarz ('*black*')
finster ('*gloomy*')	blau ('*blue*')

Appendix II: List of used nouns

noun	sense modality
Geschmack ('*taste*')	taste
Geruch ('*smell*')	smell
Geräusch ('*sound*')	sound

Toward more general models on relative clause processing

Claire Delle Luche (Claire.DelleLuche@univ-lyon2.fr)

Fréderique Gayraud (Frederique.Gayraud@univ-lyon2.fr)

Bruno Martinie (B.Martinie@wanadoo.fr)

Fanny Meunier (Fanny.Meunier@univ-lyon2.fr)
Laboratoire Dynamique du Langage
14, avenue Berthelot
69 007 Lyon, France

Abstract

An important issue in psycholinguistic studies is the processing of relative clauses. Numerous theories have demonstrated that object relative clauses are more difficult than subject ones (Bever, 1970; Gibson, 1998, 2000; Sheldon, 1974). However, these theories, by considering only two syntactic functions, cannot propose a general explanation on relative clause processing. In this article, the authors investigated a wider range of relative clauses regarding the Accessibility Hierarchy proposed by Keenan and Hawkins (1987) and extended predictions from some psycholinguistic theories. Two self-paced reading experiments demonstrate that, instead of an ascending processing difficulty, there is a dichotomy between a simple subject relative clause and all the other types, where both canonical word order and parallel functions are lost.

Introduction

Theories on relative clause processing

Some sentences are more complex than others. A large body of literature considered the complexity induced by relativization: object relative clauses (henceforth object RCs) like (2) are more difficult to process than subject RCs (1).

(1) L'escroc qui venge le truand vole les bijoux (The crook that avenged the gangster stole the jewellery).

(2) L'escroc que le truand venge vole les bijoux (The crook that the gangster avenged stole the jewellery).

RCs in French differ from their corresponding independent clauses because of a structural gap (for a recent survey of relativisation in French, see Creissels, 2006). Subject RCs raise a specific problem for a gap analysis: given the French canonical SVO order and the initial position of relativisers in RCs, it could be argued that, when relativising the subject, the relativiser *qui* holds the function of subject, without any structural gap, hence an analysis such as (1a). For all the other relativisable functions in French, the initial position of the relativiser induces the loss of the canonical SVO order, making the presence of a structural gap obvious (2a). This suggests that the correct structure for subject RCs is in fact (1b).

(1a) L'escroc [qui venge le truand] vole les bijoux.

(1b) L'escroc [qui — venge le truand] vole les bijoux.

(2a) L'escroc que le truand venge —] vole les bijoux.

The function of the RC is a complexity factor and several explanations were proposed, focusing exclusively on subject and object RCs. For example, the Canonical Word Order hypothesis (Bever, 1970) assumes that object RCs are more difficult because of the non-canonical word order in the RC.

According to the Parallel Function hypothesis (Sheldon, 1974), the difficulty in object RCs (2) is caused by the non parallel function of the first NP (*escroc*), that is subject of the main clause but object of the RC. King and Just (1991) proposed a similar argument: the first NP in a subject RC assumes the role of agent both in the RC and the main clause. In an object RC, it assumes a double thematic role, agent in the main clause and patient in the RC, which is more difficult.

Most theories agree that more processing will tax more working memory resources, but Gibson's theory, the Dependency Locality Theory (DLT, Gibson, 1998; 2000), goes into deeper details by proposing a computational account of the demands on working memory resources required for processing sentences containing RCs. This theory relies on two processing costs: storage and integration. When the comprehender starts reading a sentence, he/she develops expectations about future word categories. For example, after reading the determiner *L'* in (1), one would expect a NP, then a verb and possibly a verb complement. The memory cost increases with respect to the distance between the prediction of a word category and its fulfilment.

The integration cost (Figure 1) reflects the integration of one word onto the syntactic structure currently processed. Some integrations are costless, as is the integration of the NP to its determiner, but most are not. In an object RC (2), the integration cost of the RC verb (*venge*) is (+1+2). First, *venge* has to be integrated as the verb and thus linked to its subject. As one constituent has been processed since the subject was integrated (the very word *venge*), there is a (+1) integration cost. A similar cost is found for the RC verb in a subject RC (1). The verb has also to be linked to its preverbal object (*que*) and a (+2) integration cost is added because two constituents, the subject and the verb, have been processed since the object processing. Overall, the DLT predicts high integration costs on the main clause verbs, and the highest difficulty for object RCs located on the RC verb, compared to subject RCs.

---

(1) L'escroc qui venge le truand vole les bijoux.
        (+1)   (+1)   (+3)   (+1)
(The crook that avenged the gangster stole the jewellery)

(2) L'escroc que le truand venge vole les bijoux.
            (+1+2) (+3)   (+1)
(The crook that the gangster avenged stole the jewellery)

Figure 1: Integration costs for subject (1) and object (2) RCs (Gibson, 1998, 2000).

As stated above, these two processing costs tax working memory resources. A superior processing cost will affect reading times (Gayraud, & Meunier, submitted; Gibson, 1998; Gibson et al., 2005; King, & Just, 1991; Traxler, Morris, & Seely, 2002).

The Accessibility Hierarchy

A general theory on RC processing should not be restricted to subject and object RCs only. For example, various RCs are available in English and can be displayed on the Accessibility Hierarchy (AH, Keenan, & Comrie, 1987), a typological scale presenting the different relativisable syntactic functions (Figure 2).

---

subject < object < indirect object < oblique < genitive < comparative

---

Figure 2: The Accessibility Hierarchy (Keenan, & Comrie, 1987).

The AH presents an accurate description of RC production in numerous languages, either qualitatively, that is, across languages (Keenan, & Comrie, 1987), or quantitatively, with a corpus analysis (Keenan, 1987). The AH should also apply on comprehension (Depth of Embedding hypothesis, see Hawkins, 2004). Keenan and Hawkins (1987) investigated this aspect with an experiment using a repetition task. Their results confirmed the AH. However, the methodology employed here casts some doubts about the results, mostly because of the material used (e.g. lack of control of the number of animate nouns).

Generalising the theories

The initial goal of this article is to present more controlled experiments testing the AH, but also to investigate whether the predictions formulated by some psycholinguistic theories on subject and object RCs would match the behavioural data observed on other type of relatives, such as Centre-embedded RCs.

The first step in our work is to extend their predictions on lower levels of the AH, thus providing us with a proper difficulty scale for each theory. Centre-embedded RCs in French are considered in the present paper.

The Canonical Word Order hypothesis According to Bever (1970), it is the non-canonical word order that will lead to additional difficulties of processing. The movement induced by relativisation generates a non-canonical word order for all the syntactic functions but the subject one. As a consequence, this hypothesis predicts a dichotomy between the subject function on the one hand and all the other functions on the other hand.

The Parallel Function hypothesis The Parallel Function hypothesis (Sheldon, 1974), like the former, would predict a dichotomy between the subject function and the lower ones. Indeed, if there is a difficulty when the first NP does not have the same function in both clauses. All functions but the subject one have lost this parallelism.

These two theories predict a global difficulty, which can be measured on the error rate on comprehension questions or the global reading times, provided that the sentences have the same length.

The Dependency Locality theory The two processing costs proposed in the DLT (Gibson, 1998; 2000) provide us with more refined, word-located predictions which can be observed on the reading times for each word.

If we consider a syntactic function that is lower on the AH than the subject and object one, like object genitive, the DLT makes the following integration costs' predictions (see Figure 3):

- On the RC verb (*venge* in 3), the integration cost is (+1) because only one constituent has been integrated since the subject has been processed.

- On the object of the RC (*crime*), the processing cost should be higher than it was in (2): on account of a link between that constituent and the first one (*escroc*).

- The main verb (*vole*) should require more processing resources than in (1) or (2), simply because there is an additive constituent between this verb and its subject (*le crime*, that is, the object in the RC).

---

(3) L'escroc dont le truand venge le crime vole les bijoux.
           (+1)   (+1+2) (+4)   (+1)
(The crook whose crime the gangster avenges steals the jewellery)

Figure 3: Integration costs for object genitive RCs.

Globally, an object genitive RC should be more difficult to process. This will induce longer reading times on the main verb and object of the RC, compared to subject (main verb and object of the RC) and object RCs (main verb only).

Summary of the predictions

From all these theories, two types of hierarchy emerge: a dichotomy on the one hand (Canonical Word Order, Parallel Function hypotheses) and on the other hand a scale similar to the AH (Keenan and Comrie's predictions and DLT).

The theories introduced above make predictions for relative difficulties in the processing of sentences containing RCs. The most convenient test is to measure the reader's comprehension of such sentences, namely the errors on comprehension questions.

The DLT, however, is the only one to provide sufficiently detailed predictions on the reading times which will be discussed only regarding this theory. Indeed, the other theories make predictions on the global reading times, but comparing the latter across RC types is not possible as there is more content words in object genitive RCs.

Experiment 1: Comparison of subject, object and object genitive RCs

The goal of Experiment 1 was to conduct an experiment presenting subject and object RCs, along with a function lower on the AH like object relative RCs, thus providing a test of the different predictions.

Method

Participants Thirty students (mean age 21.2 years) from the Lumière Lyon 2 University participated in the experiment and were awarded a course credit. All were native speakers of French and had normal or corrected to normal vision.

Stimuli Experiment 1 presents only one factor with 36 sentences in three conditions:

- Subject RC: L'escroc qui venge le truand vole les bijoux. (The crook that avenged the gangster stole the jewellery)
- Object RC: L'escroc que le truand venge vole les bijoux. (The crook that the gangster avenged stole the jewellery)
- Object genitive RC: L'escroc dont le truand venge le crime vole les bijoux. (The crook whose crime the gangster avenges steals the jewellery)

In order to provide a more controlled material than in Keenan and Hawkins (1987)'s experiment, the sentences contain only two animate nouns. If the object of the object relative RC is also animate, longer reading times may be attributed to the additive difficulty of processing three animate nouns. This factor may be the reason why Keenan and Hawkins (19987) observed more difficulties for functions low in the AH, as systematically contained additive animate nouns. The nouns (escroc and truand, examples 1 to 3) were matched for length (+/-1 character), number of syllables and frequency of use (Lexique data base). Care was taken that both characters were good agents of the main and the RC verbs.

Procedure The participants were seated in a dimly lit room.

Sessions were collective but participants were isolated from one another. Instructions were given orally and individually.

The experiment was run with DMDX (Forster, & Forster, 2000), using a non-cumulative self-paced reading paradigm (Just, Carpenter, & Wooley, 1982; King, & Just, 1991). Each trial started with a set of dashes symbolizing the size of the sentence and its words. Words were successively revealed as the participant pushed a button on his joystick. At the end of the sentence, a screen centered yes-no question appeared (e.g. *C'est le truand qui venge l'escroc?*, *Is it the gangster who avenged the crook?*), to which the participant answered by pressing either the right (Yes) or left (No) button.

The 36 sets of 3 target conditions were distributed across three lists to which 36 additional fillers were added. The 72 sentences of each list were shuffled.

Results

Analyses were conducted on the accuracy of comprehension questions and reading times. When reading times were higher than 9s on one word, the whole sentence was discarded from the analyses. Deviant reading times (inferior to 100ms or superior to the mean plus 2.5 standard deviations) were also discarded (8.4 % of trials).

We conducted a series of repeated-measure analyses of variance (ANOVA) and applied the Greenhouse-Geisser correction (Greenhouse, & Geisser, 1959) whenever all repeated measures had more than one degree of freedom. The analyses were carried by Subjects (F1) and by Item (F2). The critical p-values in the post-hoc analyses were adjusted using the Bonferroni method.

Accuracy on comprehension question As specified in the introduction, the prediction of the Word Order, Parallel Function and AH hypotheses deal with the accuracy on comprehension questions (Table 1).

Table 1: Mean error rate (%) on comprehension questions.

Relative clause type	Error rate
Subject	18.1
Object	28.1
Object genitive	25.6

We found a significant main effect of RC type ($F1(2, 29) = 6.1$; $p = .005$; $F2(2, 35) = 9.2$; $p = .004$). Post-hoc tests reveal that questions on subject RCs are better answered than on object ($p = .006$) and object genitive RCs ($p = .009$). The two latter, however, do not show any significant difference (n.s.).

Subject RCs are easier to comprehend than object and object genitive RCs which do not differ in processing difficulty.

Reading time analysis According to the DLT, we would expect differences on words where the number of integrations increases, namely the clause verbs and objects in the RCs.

We will first compare the reading times on the object of the RC in subject an object RCs (Table 2). Even though the mean reading time on the object of the subject RC is longer (615 ms) than in its object genitive counterpart (557 ms). This difference is not significant either by Subject ($F1(1, 29)$ = 1.8; n.s.) or by Item ($F2(1,35)$ = 1.6; n.s.).

Let us now consider the RC verb. As exemplified above, we expect the shortest reading times for subject RCs and no difference between object and object genitive RCs. Results are presented in Table 2.

Table 2: Mean reading times (ms) on the verbs and object of the RC verb.

Relative clause type	Object of RC verb	RC verb	Main verb
Subject	612.2	522.3	590.7
Object	n.a.	620.0	627.1
Object genitive	556.8	630.8	615.4

The analysis by Subject shows a marginally significant effect of RC type ($F1(2,29)$ = 3.0; p = .07), whereas the analyses by Item reveal a significant effect ($F2(2,35)$ = 6.6; p = .003); post-hoc analyses confirm that the verb in subject RCs is easier to process than in object (p = .005) but not easier than object genitive RCs (n.s.). Object and object genitive RCs do not differ significantly (n.s.).

Finally, the results on the main clause verb show slightly longer reading times for object RCs (627.1 ms) than for object genitive (615 ms) or subject RCs (591). There is, however, no significant main effect of RC type ($F1$ < 1; n.s.; $F2$ < 1; n.s.).

Discussion

The pattern emerging from the comprehension questions results tends to show a dichotomy between subject RCs, on the one hand and the two other types, on the other hand. Such a dichotomy was predicted by the Canonical Word Order and the Parallel Function hypotheses, but not by the AH. Contrary to Keenan and Hawkins (1987)' claim, there is no exact mapping between their typology scale and the comprehension of RCs.

If we now turn to the reading time measures, few predicted differences were actually observed. If we consider the reading on the object of the RC in subject and object genitive RCs, Gibson's integration cost should induce longer reading times for the object genitive RCs, which was not the case. It is likely that this lack of difference is due to a differing animacy. In subject RCs, the object is animate whereas in object genitive RCs the object is inanimate. Inanimate entities are more likely patients and therefore might be less difficult to integrate as object and patient than animate entities. The comparison between two animate objects would have been more comfortable, but we intentionally avoided the inclusion of a third one in object genitive RC. Indeed, if we refer to the material used by Keenan and Hawkins (1987) in their repetition experiment, the gap found between simple RCs (high on the AH) and

more complex ones can be explained by the fact that there was systematically one additive animate noun in the latter ones.

The reading times hierarchy exhibited on the RC verb are not quite as expected by the integration cost. While we confirm previous findings that object RCs are more difficult than subject RCs (Ford, 1983; Gayraud, & Meunier, submitted; King, & Just, 1991; Traxler, Morris, & Seely, 2002), the reading times on the object genitive RC verb is not faster than the object RC verb, contrary to what was predicted. One possible explanation is that the ambiguity caused by the relativiser *dont* that could refer to more than one syntactic function (object genitive or indirect object), whereas *qui* and *que* refer to subject and object functions exclusively. However, the reader has already processed the subject of the RC when reaching the RC verb and it is not very likely that the superior reading times on the object genitive RC verb is a spillover from the relativiser region. We suggest that the longer reading time may be due to the tentative integration of *dont* and the RC verb, even though the object has not been read yet.

The integration costs on the main clause verb should have induced a lack of difference between subject and object RCs, and a higher cost for object genitive RCs, which the results fail to reproduce. The most likely explanation is that the difference between (+3) and (+4) is not big enough to be captured by the reading times.

Experiment 1 compared the two highest levels of the AH with the lowest one available in French, object genitive. The structures of the sentences cast also some doubts about the comparison of some regions of interest. If we compare the RC verb, it is either preceded by the relativiser (subject) or by the subject (object and object genitive). Preceding content words may lenghten the reading times. A similar problem is also found on the main clause verb: the object RC verb is following the RC verb and a spillover effect may occur.

The solution we envisioned was to test another level of the AH with indirect object RCs (Figure 4). Its structure is similar to the object RC one. The integration of the reflexive pronoun *se* is considered costless. Therefore, the processing costs of the RC and main verbs should be equal to those in the object RCs.

(3) L'escroc dont le truand se venge vole les bijoux.
        (+1+2)   (+3)   (+1)
(The crook on which the gangster took revenge stole the jewellery)

Figure 4: Integration costs for indirect object RCs.

The comparisons we are most interested in are located on the RC verb, for object, indirect object and object genitive RCs : an object genitive RC verb should be read faster than object or indirect object RCs. On the main clause verb, we will compare subject and object genitive RCs (subject faster are than object genitive) and also the object and indirect object RCs (no difference).

According to the Canonical Word Order and Parallel Function hypotheses, we should replicated the dichotomy found in Experiment 1, while the AH still predicts a hierarchy.

Experiment 2: Comparison of subject, object, indirect object and object genitive RCs

Method

Participants Forty students (mean age 20.7 years) from the same population as the previous experiment participated. None had taken part to Experiment 1.

Stimuli Forty-eight sentence quadruplets were generated as follows:

- Subject RC: L'escroc qui venge le truand vole les bijoux.
- Object RC: L'escroc que le truand venge vole les bijoux.
- Indirect object RC: L'escroc dont le truand se venge vole les bijoux.
- Object genitive: L'escroc dont le truand venge le crime vole les bijoux. (The crook on which the gangster took revenge stole the jewellery)

The material was controlled with constraints similar to those used in Experiment 1. Eighty filler sentences were also presented.

Procedure The procedure was identical to the previous experiment.

Results

The analyses were carried on the same regions of interest, accuracy rate, and the main and RC verbs. Reading times outside the time limits were discarded from the data analysed (8.9 % of trials).

Accuracy on comprehension question Like in Experiment 1, subject RCs appear to be easier to understand (21.3 %) than the other types (28.5, 32.9, and 31.0%, Table 3). This is confirmed by the ANOVAs ($F1(3,39) = 4.9$; $p = .005$; $F2(3,47) = 6.3$; $p = .001$) and post-hoc tests (subject-object, $p = .07$; subject-indirect object, $p = .006$; subject-object genitive, $p = .01$, no other significant difference).

Table 3: Mean error rate (%) on comprehension questions.

Relative clause type	Error rate
Subject	21.3
Object	28.5
Indirect object	32.9
Object genitive	31.0

Reading time analysis As stated before, we will first compare the reading times on the RC verb of object, indirect object and object genitive RCs (Table 4). We find a significant main effect of the RC type ($F1(3,39) = 8.9$; $p <$

.0001; $F2(3,47) = 7.9$; $p < .0001$). A post-hoc analysis reveals that it is only the subject condition that contributed to the significance and no significant difference was found between object, indirect object and object genitive RCs. Once more, it seems that it is the non-canonical word order (lost in all the conditions but the subject one) that caused the superior reading times.

Table 4: Mean reading times (ms) on the verbs and object of the RC verb.

Relative clause type	RC verb	Main verb
Subject	333.4	511.2
Object	418.2	633.2
Indirect object	416.9	563.6
Object genitive	409.8	588.8

The ANOVAs conducted on the main clause verb fail to show any significant main effect of the RC type ($F1 < 1$; $F2 < 1$). Where we expected a difference between subject and object genitive RCs, none was found. As predicted, no difference was found between the main verbs in object and indirect object RCs.

Discussion

The error rates confirm once more the existence of a dichotomy between subject RCs and the other syntactic functions. This is what was predicted by the Canonical Word Order and Parallel Function hypotheses, but not by the AH. Subject RCs are easier to process than any lower level of the AH.

The comparisons we conducted on the reading times failed to reveal any significant difference where it was expected. On the RC verb, it looks as if the reader tries to integrate the genitive to the verb and thus spends more time processing the RC verb. This may contribute to the lack of difference.

Subject and object genitive main verbs do not differ, contrary to what was expected. The inanimate object in the RC does not seem to induce a much higher processing cost, although the comprehension is less accurate.

General discussion

On the whole, Experiment 2 confirms the results found in Experiment 1 regarding the reading times. Subject RCs are the easiest to process, as observed on question accuracy and reading times on the RC verb. RC verbs are read faster in Object genitive RCs than in Object RCs. The syntactic processing model proposed by Gibson (1998, 2000) may need to consider the effect of semantic factor such as animacy. Indeed, an inanimate noun is less difficult to integrate than an animate noun and the integration cost on the object genitive verb is not higher than in the other RCs.

Obviously, one cannot draw conclusions from a lack of difference. Moreover, a lack of difference does not mean that the mean reading times are equal. Still, the fact that similar result patterns were reproduced in these two experiments allows us to establish that the lack of difference is reproductible. It will be possible to draw stronger conclusions once we have investigated sentences where the structures vary even less. This is possible if we compare subject and object RCs (5, 6), and sentences like (7, 8).

- (5) L'escroc qui *venge le truand* vole les bijoux.

- (6) L'escroc que *le truand venge* vole les bijoux.

- (7) L'escroc qui *se venge du truand* vole les bijoux. (The crook who avenged himself from the gangster stole the jewellery)

- (8) L'escroc dont *le truand se venge* vole les bijoux.

The regions in italic should differ two by two. If a difference is found between (7) and (8), this will demonstrate that the overall difficulty is not due to the syntactic functions in the RC but due to the syntactic function born by the relativiser.

If we consider now the results on the accuracy rate, the two experiments confirm the predictions formulated by the Bever (1970) and Sheldon (1974) as long as the canonical word order or the parallel functions are lost, the comprehension is less accurate. The argument that the AH could map onto comprehension as accurately as it does on production (Keenan, & Hawkins, 1987) can be rejected. Other experimental contributions confirm our results. Diessel (2004; Diessel, & Tomasello, 2005) investigated the development of the comprehension of various RCs with a repetition paradigm and failed in reproducing a hierarchy like the AH, just as we did.

If the Canonical Word Order and the Parallel Function hypotheses make accurate predictions, it is impossible to tell them apart. One way of doing so would be to include right-branched RCs (9, 12). With this kind of sentences, we would be able to manipulate the canonical word order and the parallel functions independently.

- (9) L'homme qui regarde la femme promène le chien. (canonical word order and parallel functions are preserved, The man that is looking at the woman is walking the dog)

- (10) L'homme que la femme regarde promène le chien. (both are lost, The man that the woman is looking at is walking the dog)

- (11) L'homme regarde le chien que la femme promène. (parallel functions preserved; The man is looking at the dog that the woman is walking)

- (12) L'homme regarde la femme qui promène le chien (canonical word order preserved, The man is looking at the woman that is walking the dog).

References

Bever, T. G. (1970). The cognitive basis for linguistic structures. In J. R. Hayes (Ed.), *Cognition and the development of language*. New York: Wiley.

Creissels, D. (2006). *Syntaxe générale, une introduction typologique*. Hermès Paris.

Diessel, H. (2004). *The acquisition of complex sentences*. Cambridge: Cambridge University Press.

Diessel, H., & Tomasello, M. (2005). A new look at the acquisition of relative clauses. *Language, 81*, p. 882-906.

Ford, M. (1983). A method for obtaining measures of local parsing complexity throughout sentences. *Journal of Verbal Learning and Verbal Behavior, 22*, 203-218.

Forster, K. I., & Forster, J. C. (2000). DMDX version 2. Retrieved 12/2000, from the World Wide Web: http://www.u.arizona.edu/~jforster/dmdx.htm

Gayraud, F. A., & Meunier, F. E. (submitted). Respective roles of function and branching in the processing of French relative clauses. *Cognition*.

Gibson, E. (1998). Linguistic complexity: Locality of syntactic dependencies. *Cognition, 68*, 1-76.

Gibson, E. (2000). The dependency locality theory: A distance-based theory of linguistic complexity. In A. Marantz (Ed.), *Image, language, brain: Papers from the first Mind Articulation Project symposium*. Cambridge, MA: MIT Press.

Gibson, E., Desmet, T., Watson, D., Grodner, D., & Ko, K. (2005). Reading relative clauses in English. *Cognitive Linguistics, 16*, 313-353.

Greenhouse, S. W., & Geisser, S. (1959). On the methods in the analysis of profile data. *Psychometrika, 24*, 95-112.

Hawkins, J. A. (2004). *Efficiency and complexity in grammars*. Oxford: Oxford University Press.

Just, M. A., Carpenter, P. A., & Wooley, J. D. (1982). Paradigms and processes in reading comprehension. *Journal of Experimental Psychology: General, 111*, 228-238.

Keenan, E. L. (1987). Variation in Universal Grammar. In E. L. Keenan (Ed.), *Universal Grammar: 15 essays*. London: Croom Helm.

Keenan, E. L., & Hawkins, S. (1987). The psychological validity of the Accessibility Hierarchy. In E. L. Keenan (Ed.), *Universal Grammar: 15 essays*. London: Croom Helm.

Keenan, E. L., & Comrie, B. (1987). Noun phrase accessibility and Universal Grammar. In E. L. Keenan (Ed.), *Universal Grammar: 15 essays*. London: Croom Helm.

King, J. W., & Just, M. A. (1991). Individual differences in syntactic processing: The role of working memory. *Journal of Memory and Language, 30*, 580-602.

Sheldon, A. (1974). On the role of parallel function in the acquisition of relative clauses in English. *Journal of Verbal Learning and Verbal Behavior, 13*, 272-281.

Traxler, M. J., Morris, R. K., & Seely, R. E. (2002). Processing subject and object relative clauses: Evidence from eye-movements. *Journal of Memory and Language, 47*, 69-90.

Construction-Driven Language Processing

Jerry T. Ball (jerry.ball@mesa.afmc.af.mil)
Air Force Research Laboratory
6030 S. Kent St., Mesa, AZ 85212

Abstract

Construction Grammar is an emerging linguistic theory based on the notion of *constructions*—linguistic representations of form, function and meaning. The key insights of Construction Grammar are beginning to have a significant impact on other linguistic formalisms. However, to date, Construction Grammar has had little impact on research in language processing. This paper describes an approach to language processing during comprehension based on the *activation*, *selection*, and *integration* of *constructions* corresponding to the linguistic input. Whereas activation is based on parallel spreading activation, selection and integration rely on serial processing combined with a mechanism of *context accommodation*—a cognitively plausible alternative to algorithmic backtracking.

In considering the use of constructions as the basis for language representation and processing, it becomes clear that fully integrated representations may not in principle be possible. Instead, representations are likely to be integrated just to the extent supported by the constructions activated by the input and selected for integration, with different constructions often representing different tiers or dimensions of meaning that are not fully integratable.

Construction Grammar

Construction Grammar (Fillmore, 1988; Fillmore and Kay, 1993; Goldberg, 1995) is an emerging linguistic theory based on the notion of *constructions*. "Constructions are stored pairings of form and function, including morphemes, words, idioms, partially lexically filled and fully general linguistic patterns…any linguistic pattern is recognized as a construction as long as some aspect of its form and function is not strictly predictable from its component parts" and even fully predictable constructions may be stored "as long as they occur with sufficient frequency" (Goldberg, 2003:219). A classic example of a construction is the *transitive verb clause* consisting of a *subject, transitive verb* and *object* as exemplified by "the man$_{subject}$ hit$_{trans-verb}$ the ball$_{object}$". A less common construction is the *caused-motion* construction as exemplified by "she$_{subject}$ sneezed$_{intrans-verb}$ the napkin$_{object}$ off the table$_{direction}$" (Goldberg, 1995). The caused-motion construction is interesting in that a verb which is normally *intransitive* as exemplified by "she sneezed" occurs with an object "the napkin" and directional prepositional phrase "off the table". Many normally intransitive verbs can occur in this construction. (An alternative viewpoint is that the caused-motion construction is integrated with a distinct intransitive verb construction in this example.) Although Construction Grammar began with the exploration of many unusual constructions (e.g. the "let alone" construction in Fillmore, Kay and O'Connor, 1988), it has come to be recognized that the basic principles of Construction Grammar apply to common constructions as well. In fact, a basic claim of Construction Grammar is that "the network of constructions captures our knowledge of language *in toto* – in other words, it's constructions all the way down" (Goldberg, 2003).

The key insights of Construction Grammar are beginning to have a significant impact on other linguistic formalisms including Cognitive Grammar (Langacker, 1987, 1991; Talmy 2000; Lakoff, 1987), HPSG (Sag and Wasow, 1999; Sag, 1997) and even Generative Grammar as reformulated by Culicover and Jackendoff (2005). However, to date, Construction Grammar has had little impact on research in language processing (exceptions include Bergen & Chang, 2005; Steels & De Beule, 2006).

Phrase and Clause Level Constructions

Constructions are learned chunks of linguistic knowledge that tie subordinate linguistic elements together. The elements of phrase and clause level constructions may be specific lexical items (e.g. "is", "was"), lexemes (e.g. "be") or linguistic categories. Fully lexicalized constructions containing multiple words are called *multiword expressions*. The more general a construction, the more likely it is to contain categories as elements rather than specific lexical items. Categories may be *form-based* or *functional*, although the focus of this paper is on functional categories. For example, the [subject predicator object]$_{clause}$ construction (where predicator roughly corresponds to *verb group*—i.e. verb + tense, aspect, modality, and polarity) describes a sequence of three functional categories, whereas the [subject *hit*$_{predicator}$ object]$_{clause}$ construction is specific to the verb "hit". For the most part, constructions are sequence specific, although the possibility of constructions whose elements are not sequence specific is not precluded.

The following notation is used for the representation of constructions:

$$[A_{sub}\ B\ C_{sup}]_D$$

In this representation, square brackets enclose the construction, which consists of an ordered list of elements A, B and C. The elements in a construction may be specific lexical items, lexemes (i.e. abstracted dictionary forms) or functional categories (i.e. functionally typed variables). A subscript, $_{sub}$ or $_{sup}$, on an element may be used to indicate a functional subcategory or super type (and conceivably a form-based category). The functional category of the construction is indicated by the subscripted $_D$ to the right of the construction. Lexical items are italicized to distinguish them from lexemes.

Over the course of a lifetime, humans acquire a large knowledge base of constructions at multiple levels of abstraction and generalization. For language comprehension, the most lexically specific constructions matching the input are likely to activated, selected and integrated, and language comprehension can be viewed as lexically driven within the context of constructions. For example, the [subject (kicked the bucket)predicate]clause construction (where predicate roughly corresponds to *tensed VP*) will be preferred over the [subject kickpredicator object]clause construction where both are activated by the input, since the former is more lexically specific. In addition, constructions which match the largest chunks of input are likely to be preferred (cf. Grossberg and Myers, 1999). Thus, [subject atepredicator object]clause will be preferred over [subject atepredicate]clause given the input "she ate the sandwich".

It should be noted that constructions may contain actual and ambiguous lexical items. For example, the construction [(take a hike)predicate]imperative-clause contains the ambiguous lexical items "take", "a" and "hike", although the construction as a whole unambiguously means "go away" in its idiomatic interpretation.

Construction-Driven Language Processing

A processing mechanism based on the *activation, selection* and *integration* of constructions is proposed. Constructions are activated in memory by a parallel, automatic *spreading activation process* to the extent that they match the current input and prior context. The most highly activated constructions are selected for integration by a (largely) serial *control process*. Selected constructions with categorical elements and as yet unrealized lexical items establish expectations which drive the processing mechanism. Category expectations in constructions can function to establish the category of the prior input or to set the context for processing the subsequent input and also determine how inputs are integrated. For example, the [subject hitpredicator object]clause construction, activated by the word "hit", establishes the expectations that the prior input is functioning as a subject and the subsequent input is functioning as an object. A prior input capable of functioning as a subject and a subsequent input capable of functioning as an object can be integrated into this construction. Of course, expectations may be violated and when they are, the violations must be accommodated. Possible mechanisms of *accommodation* include the selection and integration of a different construction (in the context of the expectation violation and not via algorithmic backtracking), modification of the selected construction (Ball, 2004), or construal of the *to be integrated* element as being of the required functional type (Langacker, 2000)—as in construal of the infinitive phrase "to be integrated" as a nominal head modifier in this sentence. For example, in the context of the construction

[the head]nominal, activated by the processing of the word "the" within the expression "the hit", the word "hit" can subsequently be integrated as the head. The [subject hitpredicator object]clause construction which is also activated by "hit" may or may not be selected for integration during processing. Note that instantiating "hit", a type of action, as the head of a nominal construction involves construing the action that the nominal refers to as though it were an object. This is a common form of construal in English—especially for words describing actions which occur instantaneously and are easily objectified.

A construction-driven language processing system is likely to lead to messier representations than those typically posited in other computational linguistic or cognitive science approaches. Although constructions can be integrated to some extent, there is no guarantee that this integration will lead to anything like a well-formed tree, let alone a binary branching tree (Kayne, 1994). In fact, to the extent that constructions are independent of each other, they can only be integrated via the lexical items and categories they share. Further, it is likely that constructions will often conflict with each other, leading to representations that are in part inconsistent (in the sense that they assign different, often competing, representations to the same input). Issues in determining the basic structure of clauses—is it SVO or Subject-Predicate—are a reflection of this inconsistency. The subject has a saliency in the Subject-Predicate construction that it does not have in the more symmetric SVO construction. Both constructions are likely to be available in the inventory of constructions available to fluent comprehenders of English. Which one gets activated and selected (or perhaps both) is likely to vary from utterance to utterance depending on the prior context and variability in the manner and form of expression of the current utterance. For example, in

John hit (pause) and Sue kicked (pause) the door

the Subject-Predicate construction is unlikely to be selected given the grammatical separation of the subject and verb from the object which would normally form part of the predicate (combining with the verb). Similarly, in

He's hitting the ball

the cliticization of "is" with "he" argues against selection of a Subject-Predicate construction (assuming the auxiliary verb is normally part of the *predicate*). In fact, there is very likely to be a specialized [he's predication]clause construction (where predication roughly corresponds to *untensed VP*) that gets activated and selected. Finally, question forms argue against the necessary activation and selection of a Subject-Predicate construction. Consider

Where is he going?

which suggests a specialized construction like [where be subject predication]wh-clause.

In general, there are a number of different constructions which come in to play in the processing of clausal heads. These constructions overlap in various respects, but all of them can be motivated by different linguistic expressions—especially expressions involving conjunction:

(he's) **kicking the ball** and **throwing the rock** →
$[V_{head} \; obj_{comp}]_{predication}$
(he) **is kicking** and **was hitting** (the ball) →
$[be_{spec} \; V\text{-}ing_{head}]_{predicator}$
(he) **kicked the ball** and **threw the rock** →
$[V\text{-}ed_{spec/head} \; obj_{comp}]_{predicate}$
(why did) **he kick the ball** and **she throw the rock** →
$[subj_{comp} \; kick_{head} \; obj_{comp}]_{proposition}$

The term *predication* is used to describe a construction consisting of an untensed clausal head along with its non-subject complements. The term *predicator* is used to describe a construction consisting of a clausal head along with its tense specification, but without the non-subject complements. Note that the head of a predication or predicator need not be a verb, nor is an object required in a predication. In "he is *running*", the verb "running" is the head, in "he is *sad*", the adjective "sad" is the head, and in "he is *there*", the adverb "there" is the head—and there is no object in these examples (Ball, 2005). The functional categories *predicator* and *predication* generalize over these alternative phrasal forms. The term *predicate* is used to describe a construction consisting of a clausal head along with its tense specification and non-subject complements. The term *proposition* is used to describe a construction consisting of an untensed clausal head along with its complements (including the subject).

A Processing Example

During the processing of the sentence

He is kicking the ball

the following constructions are likely to be activated:

he → $[he_{3\text{-}sing\text{-}male\text{-}human\text{-}pron}]_{nominal}$
is → $[be_{3\text{-}pres\text{-}sing}]_{verb}$
he is → $[ref\text{-}pt_{comp} \; be_{spec} \; predn_{head}]_{clause}$
kicking → $[kick_{v\text{-}ing}]_{verb}$
kicking →
$[subj_{comp} \; kick_{head} \; obj_{comp}]_{proposition}$
kicking → $[V_{head} \; obj_{comp}]_{predication}$
is kicking → $[be_{spec} \; V\text{-}ing_{head}]_{predicator}$
is kicking → $[be_{spec} \; V\text{-}ing_{head} \; obj_{comp}]_{predicate}$
the → $[the_{spec} \; head]_{nominal}$
the ball → $[the_{spec} \; ball_{head}]_{nominal}$

The $[he_{3\text{-}sing\text{-}male\text{-}human\text{-}pron}]_{nominal}$ construction encodes the knowledge that pronouns like "he" (3rd person, singular, male, human) can function as full nominals, encoding both a *referential specifier* function and an *objective head* function (Ball, 2005). The $[be_{3\text{-}pres\text{-}sing}]_{verb}$ construction encodes the status of "is" as the 3rd person,

present tense, singular form of the verb "be". The $[ref\text{-}pt_{comp} \; be_{spec} \; predn_{head}]_{clause}$ construction captures the use of a *reference point* complement (Taylor, 2000) and a referential specifier (be_{spec}) to tie a predication functioning as head of a clause to the larger discourse situation via the reference point and referential specifier. The $[kick_{v\text{-}ing}]_{verb}$ construction captures the "V-ing" verb form of "kicking". The $[subj_{comp} \; kick_{head} \; obj_{comp}]_{proposition}$ construction captures the basic relational meaning of the verb "kick" which combines with a subject and object complement to form a *proposition*. This construction is closely related to the basic SVO form of a clause. The $[V_{head} \; obj_{comp}]_{predication}$ construction captures the combining of a tenseless verb head with an object complement to form a *predication* that functions as the head of the $[ref\text{-}pt_{comp} \; be_{spec} \; predn_{head}]_{clause}$ construction. The $[be_{spec} \; V\text{-}ing_{head}]_{predicator}$ construction captures the combining of the auxiliary verb "be" functioning as a specifier with the progressive form of a verb functioning as the head in forming a *predicator*. The $[be_{spec} \; V\text{-}ing_{head} \; obj_{comp}]_{predicate}$ construction captures the combining of the auxiliary verb "be" functioning as a specifier with the progressive form of a verb functioning as the head and an object complement in forming a *predicate*. The $[the_{spec} \; head]_{nominal}$ construction captures the encoding of a referential specifier and objective head to form a nominal. The $[the_{spec} \; ball_{head}]_{nominal}$ construction captures the encoding of "ball" as the head of the $[the_{spec} \; head]_{nominal}$ construction.

The actual processing of this utterance is likely to proceed as follows:

he →

Nominal
|
$[he_{3\text{-}sing\text{-}male\text{-}human}]_{pron}$
|
he

The word "he" activates a *nominal* construction which is capable of referring to some object independently of any larger linguistic unit in which it may participate.

he is →

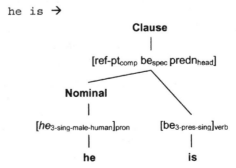

The word "is" following "he" activates a *clause* construction. The assumption here is that the nominal "he" and auxiliary verb "is" are immediately integrated into the [ref-pt_comp be_spec predn_head]_clause construction. In general, delaying integration of linguistic elements into constructions is likely to lead to processing difficulties since the need to retain separate linguistic units in memory will run up against limits on the number of unintegrated linguistic elements which can be separately retained in *working memory*.

he is kicking →

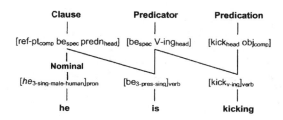

Two additional constructions—*predicator* and *predication*—are activated by "kicking" and immediately integrated to the extent possible. It is assumed that the *predicate* and *proposition* constructions are not selected for integration in this example, even though they are activated. Time constraints and selection competition are likely to preclude integration of all activated constructions and the *predicate* and *proposition* constructions are not likely to be as strongly activated as the *predicator* and *predication* constructions in this example. Note the implication that neither the basic SVO nor the basic Subject-Predicate clause construction is integrated into this representation!

the →

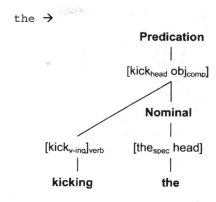

The word "the" activates a *nominal* construction and integrates "the" as the specifier. This nominal construction is integrated as the object of the *predication* construction even before the head of the nominal construction is processed and integrated into the nominal!

the ball →

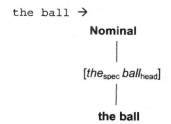

The noun "ball" is integrated as the head of the nominal "the ball". After processing, the linguistic representation for the utterance "he is kicking the ball" is shown below:

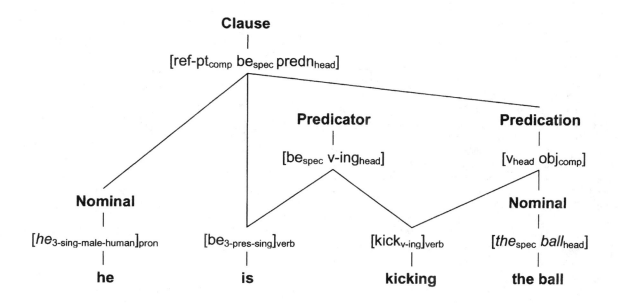

— 725 —

In this example, it is assumed that a single clause level construction [ref-pt$_{comp}$ be$_{spec}$ predn$_{head}$]$_{clause}$ was selected for integration. However, two "predicate" level constructions [be$_{spec}$ V-ing$_{head}$]$_{predicator}$ and [V$_{head}$ obj$_{comp}$]$_{predication}$ were selected for integration. One way of viewing such representations is as having multiple tiers corresponding to different grammatical dimensions of meaning encoded via constructions. These different tiers of meaning get integrated just to the extent that selected constructions have overlapping lexical items and functional categories. Such an approach opens up the possibility of having additional tiers to capture meaning distinctions conveyed by topic-focus and given-new contrasts, among others. A tiered approach to representing different grammatical dimensions of meaning is in alignment with current tiered theories of phonology (cf. Kaye, 1989) and (to some extent) with lexical semantic approaches which assume a multidimensional space for representing the meaning of words (Landauer & Dumais, 1997).

Activation, Selection and Integration

Activation is a *parallel* process that biases or constrains the selection and integration of corresponding declarative memory (DM) elements into a linguistic representation. The activation mechanism is based on the spreading activation mechanism of the ACT-R cognitive architecture (Anderson et al. 2004). A computational cognitive model intended to validate the processing mechanism is being implemented in this architecture (Ball, Heiberg & Silber, in preparation). Based on the input and prior context, a collection of DM elements is activated in parallel.

The selection mechanism is based on the *serial* retrieval mechanism of ACT-R—an alternative to the parallel *competitive inhibition* mechanism typical of connectionist models (cf. Vosse & Kempen, 2000). Retrieval occurs as a result of selection and execution of a production—only one production can be executed at a time—whose right-hand side provides a retrieval template that specifies which type of DM chunk is eligible to be retrieved. The single, most highly activated DM chunk matching the retrieval template—subject to random noise—is retrieved. The retrieval template varies in its level of specificity in accord with the production selected for execution. For example, when a production that retrieves a DM chunk of type *word* executes, the retrieval template may specify the form of the input (e.g. "airspeed") in addition to the DM type *word*. When a production that retrieves a DM chunk of type *part of speech* (POS) executes, the retrieval template may specify the word without specifying the POS—allowing the biasing mechanism to constrain POS determination.

The retrieved DM chunk is matched on the left-hand side of another production which, if selected and executed, determines how to integrate the retrieved DM chunk into the representation of the preceding input. Production selection is driven by the matching of the left-hand side of the production against a collection of buffers (e.g. goal, retrieval, context, short-term working memory) which

reflect the current goal, current input and previous context. The production with the highest utility—learned on the basis of prior experience—which matches the input and prior context, is selected for execution—subject to random noise. A default production which simply adds the retrieved DM chunk to a short-term working memory (ST-WM) stack executes if no other production matches. The ST-WM stack—which is limited to four linguistic elements—constitutes part of the context for production selection and execution.

Context Accommodation

A key element of the integration process is a mechanism of *context accommodation* which provides for *serial processing without backtracking*. According to Crocker (1999), there are three basic mechanisms of language processing: 1) serial processing with backtracking, 2) parallel processing, and 3) deterministic processing. Context accommodation is an alternative non-backtracking, serial processing mechanism. The basic idea behind this mechanism is that when the current input is inconsistent with the preceding context, the context is modified to accommodate the current input without backtracking. This mechanism is demonstrated using the example "no airspeed or altitude restrictions". The processing of the word "no" leads to retrieval of a nominal construction containing the following functional elements: specifier, modifier, head, post-head modifier (an extension of the earlier example):

[specifier modifier head post-mod]$_{nominal}$

"No" is integrated as the specifier in this nominal construction and expectations are established for the occurrence of the remaining functional elements.

[no$_{spec}$ mod head post-mod]$_{nominal}$

This nominal construction is made available in the ST-WM stack to support subsequent processing. The processing of the noun "airspeed" leads to its integration as the head of the nominal construction, since nouns typically function as heads of nominals.

[no$_{spec}$ mod airspeed$_{head}$ post-mod]$_{nominal}$

The processing of the conjunction (or disjunction) "or" leads to its addition to the ST-WM stack since the category of the first conjunct of a conjunction cannot be effectively determined until the linguistic element after the conjunction is processed—due to rampant ambiguity associated with conjunctions. Note that delaying determination of the category of the first conjunct until after processing of the linguistic element following the conjunction provides a form of deterministic processing reminiscent of Marcus's deterministic parser (1980). The processing of the noun "altitude" in the context of the conjunction "or" and the nominal "no airspeed" with head noun "airspeed" results in the accommodation of "altitude" such that the head of the nominal construction is modified to reflect the disjunction of the nouns "airspeed" and "altitude".

$[no_{spec}\ \text{mod}\ (airspeed\ or\ altitude)_{head}$
$\text{post-mod}]_{nominal}$

The processing of "restrictions" in the context of the nominal "no airspeed or altitude" results in the accommodation of "restrictions" such that the current head "airspeed or altitude" becomes the pre-head modifier and "restrictions" becomes the head. The final representation has the form:

$[no_{spec}\ (airspeed\ or\ altitude)_{mod}$
$restrictions_{head}\ \text{post-mod}]_{nominal}$

This representation was arrived at using a serial processing mechanism without backtracking, despite the rampant local ambiguity of the utterance!

Context accommodation is a powerful serial processing mechanism which overcomes the limitations and cognitive implausibility of serial processing mechanisms which rely on backtracking, without sacrificing the advantages of serial processing over parallel and deterministic processing. It is unrealistic to expect a parallel processing mechanism to carry forward more than a few possible representations at once, which means a mechanism like context accommodation is needed in any case, and deterministic mechanisms require delaying integration of linguistic elements for indeterminate periods—requiring their separate representation—which is likely to exceed the limited capacity of ST-WM if used extensively.

Summary

This paper presents an approach to language comprehension based on the *activation*, *selection* and *integration* of *constructions* corresponding to the linguistic input. Multiple, often conflicting, constructions are likely to be activated by each lexical item in the input. The resulting linguistic representations depend crucially on which activated constructions are selected for integration, and the degree to which selected constructions are integratable. Whereas activation is based on a parallel spreading activation mechanism, selection and integration rely on a serial processing mechanism combined with a mechanism of *context accommodation*—a cognitively plausible alternative to algorithmic backtracking.

References

Anderson, J. R., Bothell, D., Byrne, M. D., Douglass, S, Lebiere, C, and Qin, Y. (2004). An Integrated Theory of the Mind. *Psychological Review* 111, (4). 1036-1060

Ball, J. (2004). A Cognitively Plausible Model of Language Comprehension. In *Proceedings of the 13th Conference on Behavior Representation in Modeling and Simulation*, 305-316. ISBN: 1-930638-35-3

Ball, J. (2005). A Bi-Polar Theory of Nominal and Clause Structure and Function. In *Proceedings of the 2005 Cognitive Science Conference*. Sheridan Printing.

Ball, J., Heiberg, A. & Silber, R. (in preparation). Toward a large-scale, functional model of language comprehension in ACT-R 6.

Bergen, B. & Chang, N. (2005). Embodied construction grammar. In J. Östman and M. Fried, eds., *Construction Grammars: Cognitive Grounding and Theoretical Extensions*. Amsterdam: John Benjamins

Crocker, M. (1999). Mechanisms for Sentence Processing. In Garrod, S. & Pickering, M. (eds), *Language Processing*, London: Psychology Press.

Culicover, P. & Jackendoff, R. (2005). *Simpler Syntax*. Oxford: Oxford University Press.

Fillmore, C. (1988). The Mechanisms of Construction Grammar. *BLS* 14: 35-55.

Fillmore, C. and Kay, P. (1993). *Construction Grammar Coursebook*. Berkeley, CA: Copy Central.

Fillmore, C., Kay, P. and O'Connor, M. (1988). Regularity and Idiomaticity in Grammatical Constructions: The Case of let alone, *Language*, Vol. 64, Number 3, 501-538

Goldberg, A. (1995). *A Construction Grammar Approach to Argument Structure*. Chicago: The University of Chicago Press.

Goldberg, A. (2003). Constructions: a new theoretical approach to language. *TRENDS in Cognitive Sciences*. Vol. 7, No. 5, pp. 219-224.

Grossberg, S. & Myers C. (1999). The Resonant Dynamics of Speech Perception: Interword Integration and Duration-Dependent Backward Effects. Technical Report CAS/CNS-TR-99-001. Boston, MA: Boston University.

Kaye, J. (1989) *Phonology, a cognitive view*. Hillsdale, NJ: LEA.

Kayne, R. (1994). *The Antisymmetry of Syntax*. Cambridge, MA: The MIT Press.

Lakoff, G. (1987). *Women, Fire and Dangerous Things*. Chicago: The University of Chicago Press.

Landauer, T. & Dumais, S. (1997). A solution to Plato's problem: the Latent Semantic Analysis theory of acquisition, induction and representation of knowledge. *Psychological Review, 104(2)*, 211-240.

Langacker, R. (1987, 1991). *Foundations of Cognitive Grammar*, Volumes 1 & 2. Stanford, CA: Stanford University Press.

Langacker, R. (2000). Why a mind is necessary: Conceptualization, grammar and linguistic semantics. In Albertazzi, L. (ed.), *Meaning and Cognition*. Amsterdam: John Benjamins, 25–38.

Marcus, M. (1980). *A Theory of Syntactic Recognition for Natural Language*. Cambridge, MA: The MIT Press.

Sag, I. (1997). English Relative Clause Constructions. *Journal of Linguistics* . 33.2: 431-484.

Sag, I. & Wasow, T. (1999). *Syntactic Theory, A Formal Introduction*. Stanford: CSLI Publications.

Steels, L. & De Beule, J. (2006). A (very) Brief Introduction to Fluid Construction Grammar. In *Proceedings of the Third International Workshop on Scalable Natural Language Understanding*.

Talmy, L. (2000). Toward a Cognitive Semantics, Vols I and II. Cambridge, MA: The MIT Press

Taylor, J. (2000). Possessives in English, An Exploration in Cognitive Grammar. Oxford: Oxford University Press.

Vosse, T. & Kempen, G. (2000). Syntactic structure assembly in human parsing. *Cognition*, 75, 105-143.

In Search of the Frog's Tail:
Investigating the Time Course of Conceptual Knowledge Activation

Phil Maguire (phil.maguire@ucd.ie)
Department of Computer Science, NUI Maynooth
Co.Kildare, Ireland

Rebecca Maguire (rebecca.maguire@dbs.edu)
Department of Psychology, Dublin Business School
Dublin 2, Ireland.

Arthur. W.S. Cater (arthur.cater@ucd.ie)
School of Computer Science and Informatics,
University College Dublin, Dublin 4, Ireland.

Abstract

Slot-filling theories of conceptual combination assume that both constituent concepts are activated before they are combined. However, these theories have difficulty in explaining why combined phrase features are sometimes more available than the features of the constituent nouns. In this study, we investigate the time course of conceptual knowledge activation. Using three verification tasks of varying complexity we demonstrate that basic taxonomic knowledge is retrieved more quickly than modal specific conceptual features. Applying this finding to conceptual combination, we demonstrate that participants take longer to reject combinations requiring the activation of instance specific features (e.g. *frog tail*) than those that can be rejected based on more generalized taxonomic knowledge (e.g. *daffodil tail*). These findings provide convergent evidence that conceptual knowledge is activated dynamically and selectively rather than all at once. We discuss the implications for existing theories.

Keywords: Conceptual combination; noun-noun compounds; knowledge representation; knowledge activation.

Introduction

The combination of two words is a technique commonly adopted by speakers in order to refer to novel concepts and ideas (e.g. *holiday tension, picnic bee*). Although people have a well developed means of understanding these novel compounds, the associated comprehension process is not trivial, requiring many levels of understanding. Accordingly, the study of conceptual combination is important, both because it is intimately associated with the generativity and comprehension of natural language and because it is important for understanding how people represent concepts. In English, a language in which compounding is particularly productive, combinations consist of a modifier followed by a head noun. Usually, the head noun denotes the main category while the modifier implies a relevant subcategory or a modification of that set's typical members. In this way, *kitchen chair* is interpreted as a particular type of chair, and more precisely as the type that is located in kitchens.

Thus far, theories of conceptual combination have generally assumed that the comprehension of a compound phrase is dependent on both concepts being fully activated. For example, the Concept Specialization model (Murphy, 1988) assumes a schema structure for concepts, consisting of a series of slots. This theory proposes that during the combination process the modifying concept fills one or more of the slots in the head noun concept. First, the appropriate slot is selected based on world knowledge about the constituent concepts and subsequently this combined concept is elaborated (e.g. realizing that a *car magazine* is likely to have a picture of a car on the front cover).

According to the slot-filling view, an identical set of features is activated whenever a particular concept is used in combination, regardless of the noun it is paired with. Clearly though, people cannot retrieve all associated knowledge about a concept every time it is encountered. Much of that information would be irrelevant and would impair rather than aid comprehension. A more economical approach would be for conceptual information to be activated selectively, thereby avoiding the need for additional processes to suppress irrelevant information. However, current theories of conceptual combination offer no clue as to how a selective activation process might operate.

The inadequacy of slot-filling theories is highlighted by their inability to explain key observations relating to knowledge availability. Springer and Murphy (1992) compared the time taken to verify a property that was true of the head versus a property that was true of the phrase. For instance, the feature *green* applies to both *celery* and *boiled celery* (noun feature). In contrast, the feature *soft* is only valid for *boiled celery* (phrase feature). Based on the idea that concepts must be fully activated before being combined, Springer and Murphy expected that the noun property would be verified more quickly than the phrase property. However, the opposite findings emerged, with participants being quicker to verify the phrase property (i.e.

that boiled celery is soft). According to Springer and Murphy, these findings are paradoxical because they suggest that emergent features of the combined concept are activated before the features of the constituent concepts.

One possible explanation for this result is that people become aware of a compound phrase structure before activating the constituent nouns and are therefore in a position to activate only the conceptual knowledge that is relevant to the combination. The idea that word meanings emerge gradually rather than all at once is well supported. For example, Till, Mross & Kintsch (1988) identified clear stages in word comprehension, with sense selection occurring around 400ms and further semantic inferences following around 1,000ms. Eye-tracking measures show that eye fixations last on average 200ms during the reading of linguistic text (Rayner, 1988), suggesting that people will be able to retrieve preferentially those features that are relevant to the combination. In this case, the instantiation of the concept *boiled celery* should proceed in much the same way as if it was referenced by a single label, in that the properties of ordinary celery that are not pertinent to boiled celery should not be activated.

The enabling condition for selective activation is that knowledge retrieval is a gradual incremental process rather than an all at once phenomenon. The existence of a distinction between different levels of conceptual detail is well supported by neurological evidence. For example, Warrington (1975) described a patient with a dementing illness who had lost subordinate attribute information (e.g. knowing that a cabbage was green) yet retained superordinate classification information (e.g. knowing that a cabbage was a plant). Also, several distinct event-related brain potentials have been identified that occur at different time intervals during concept activation (Kumar & Debruille, 2004). These have been linked to various different stages of the knowledge activation process, specifically phonological matching, activation of syntactic word category information, semantic processing, evaluation and finally representation construction.

In light of this, we propose that knowledge activation is a dynamic process and that this phenomenon can successfully explain how phrase features for conceptual combinations can be more available than noun features. In this paper we present two experiments which investigate this possibility. In the first we compare response times for three verification tasks of differing complexity. In the second we apply these findings to conceptual combination and investigate the time taken to reject phrases requiring the activation of different levels of conceptual detail.

Experiment 1

The aim of this experiment was to present participants with a series of words and to analyze the time taken to verify different conceptual features. We wished to ascertain whether the more general taxonomic knowledge about a concept becomes available prior to the retrieval of detailed features. For example, do people realize that a *dog* is a thing before they realize that it is an animal? Do they realize it is an animal before they know what it looks like?

We required a set of verification tasks that would test the availability of different conceptual features. Three tasks were selected, one requiring word-level information (does it name a thing?), a second requiring the activation of basic conceptual knowledge (is this thing alive?) and a third requiring the activation of a specific perceptual feature (is this organism hairy?). In the latter task, the hairiness attribute was selected because this information is not accurately reflected by the conceptual hierarchy (e.g. although many mammals have hair, hippos and rhinos do not). Importantly, for all three tasks, the concepts did not need to be situated within a context in order to verify the relevant property. Given our hypothesis that the activation of conceptual knowledge proceeds from the basic to the more detailed, we predicted the following trend in response times: Object < Animate < Feature.

Method

Participants Twenty-seven first year undergraduate students from University College Dublin participated in the experiment for partial course credit.

Design The experiment used a within-participants design, with three conditions corresponding to the three verification tasks, namely Object, Animate and Feature. In order to facilitate a within-participants design it was necessary to use a separate list of words for each condition. Had the same list been used for all three tasks, then the equal partitioning of true and false responses would not have been possible. Each participant saw the same set of 180 stimuli, comprising the three conditions of 60 items each.

This design improves on that of previous verification tasks (e.g. McElree & Murphy, 2006) involving the introduction of an additional concept (e.g. *boiled celery* is soft). In our experiment, the words under consideration are presented on their own. Participants are already aware of the feature to be verified so they are not required to activate information about other concepts in order to respond. In addition, participants apply the same verification task to a broad variety of words, therefore providing a more reliable measure of feature availability.

Materials We compiled separate lists of 60 different nouns for each of the three conditions. In each we included 30 items which were representative of the feature being verified and 30 items which were not. In the Object condition, half of the items were nouns (e.g. *vase, couch*) while the other half were connectives and other parts of speech (e.g. *because, when*). In the Animate condition, half of the items were organisms (e.g. *mouse, tulip*) while half were artifacts (e.g. *shed, pebble*). In the Feature condition, half of the items were haired creatures (e.g. *leopard, panda*) while the other half were hairless (e.g. *whale, rhinoceros*). All sets of words were controlled for length and familiarity. Analysis revealed no significant differences in average word length between the three conditions (5.2, 5.1 and 5.5 for the Object, Animate and Feature conditions respectively, $F(2, 177) = 1.5$, $p = .22$). There were also no significant differences between average word lengths for the representative and non-representative items in the Object condition (5.3 and 5.0 respectively, $t(58) = .83$, $p = .41$), the Animate condition (5.1 and 5.2, $t(58) = -.22$, $p = .83$) and the Feature condition (5.4 and 5.6, $t(58) = -.57$, $p = .84$). The familiarity of the nouns in the various conditions was compared by taking the log of their BNC frequency. This revealed no significant differences in frequency for the representative items (3.0, 2.8 and 2.9 for the Object, Animate and Feature conditions respectively, $F(2, 87) = .69$, $p = .50$). Furthermore, there was also no significant difference in the log of the frequency for the representative and non-representative items in the Animate (2.8 and 3.0, $t(58) = -1.01$, $p = .32$) and the Feature conditions (2.9 and 2.8, $t(58) = .87$, $p = .39$). We did not include the frequencies of the non-nouns in our analyses, as a comparison of this nature would have been misleading. The relationship between familiarity and frequency of use is not consistent when comparing nouns with other parts of speech. All of the nouns included in our experiment were associated with tangible manifestations (e.g. artifacts and plants), meaning that even those with a relatively low frequency were recognizable (e.g. *walrus* occurs only 64 times in the BNC). In contrast, non-nouns can occur more frequently yet be unfamiliar due to their abstractness (e.g. *trenchant* has a BNC frequency of 74). In order that all of the words in our Object condition be comparatively familiar, the frequency of our non-nouns was necessarily higher (4.5).

Procedure Participants sat in front of a computer screen and placed the index finger of their left hand on the F key of the computer keyboard and the index finger of their right hand on the J key. They were informed that a series of words would be displayed on the screen and that the objective was to decide whether the words were representative of the feature in question, pressing J for 'yes' and F for 'no'. For the Object condition, the task presented to participants was to verify whether the word in question referred to a thing or not. For the Animate condition, the task was to decide if the item in question was alive or not. For the Feature condition, the task was to decide if the animal in question was covered in hair. Prior to the start of the experiment, participants were provided with several worked examples in order to demonstrate the nature of the verification task. During the experiment, words appeared in the middle of the screen and participants had to make a decision by pressing the appropriate key. Trials were separated by a blank screen lasting for one second.

Each condition began with 10 practice trials which did not form part of the experiment. The purpose of these trials was to allow participants to adjust to the task, although they were not aware that the trials in question would not be included. Subsequently, the 60 experimental stimuli followed seamlessly. In each condition, the words were

presented in a random order to each participant. Furthermore, the three conditions were randomized so that participants performed the tasks in a different order.

Results and Discussion

A total of 6.5% of the data were omitted from the analysis. 3.7% of responses were incorrect and hence these trials were not considered. Additionally, response times deemed unreasonably fast (< 400ms, 0.1%) or unreasonably slow (> 4000, 0.6%) were also excluded. After this initial elimination process, any remaining response times which were more than three standard deviations outside each participant's mean for that condition were also excluded. This eliminated a further 2.0% of trials.

The mean response times were 738, 802 and 884 ms for the Object, Animate and Feature conditions respectively. Further analysis revealed that the mean response times for the representative items in the three conditions were 727, 768 and 873 ms while the mean response times for the non-representative items were 749, 837 and 897 ms respectively. These data are illustrated below.

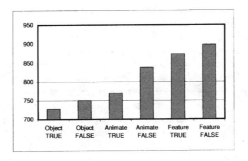

Figure 1. Mean positive and negative response times (ms)

We conducted a series of ANOVAs in order to examine the differences between the various conditions. For the by-participants analysis we computed a two-way repeated measures ANOVA, with three levels corresponding to the different tasks and two levels corresponding to the appropriate response type, all within-participants. For the by-items analysis we computed a non-repeated measures ANOVA with two fixed factors. There was no significant interaction between task and response, $F_1(2, 52) = 2.48$, $p = .09$, MSE = 3652.76; $F_2(2, 174) = 1.28$, $p = .28$, MSE = 6816.40. However, there was a significant main effect of task, $F_1(2, 52) = 21.89$, $p < .001$, MSE = 16321.42; $F_2(2, 174) = 54.32$, $p < .001$, MSE = 370306.12. A Page's L trend analysis revealed a significant increasing trend in response times according to Object < Animate < Feature, $L(2) = 364$, $p < 0.01$. In other words, participants were able to verify that a word was a thing before they were able to verify that it was alive or that it had hair. This pattern of results supports our view of knowledge activation as constituting a dynamic, incremental process.

There was also a significant main effect of response, F_1 (1, 26) = 23.20, $p < .001$, MSE = 3987.85; F_2 (1, 174) = 13.78, $p < .001$, MSE = 93960.26. Thus, across all three conditions, participants were quicker at verifying word features than they were at discounting them. This pattern of results suggests that property verification involves some kind of active search process which terminates as soon as confirming information is identified but which otherwise continues until a certain threshold of certainty is reached. This challenges the notion that people store information about concepts in a propositional format, as assumed by the schema-structures used in slot-filling models. For example, if the knowledge as to whether an animal is hairy or not is explicitly stored with that concept then there should be no difference between the time needed to confirm or discount the feature. The fact that we observed a difference suggests that the verification process involves more than simply accessing propositional knowledge.

The idea of a gradual knowledge activation process may explain some features of conceptual combination which could not be accounted for by schema-based theories, such as the fact that phrase features can be verified more quickly than noun features. If the most basic knowledge about concepts is activated first, then this provides a means by which more detailed information can be activated selectively (i.e. only the combined concept itself need be simulated). In the following experiment we investigate whether dynamic knowledge activation can contribute to the understanding of how concepts are combined.

Experiment 2

The aim of this experiment was to investigate whether dynamic knowledge activation can explain some of the counterintuitive effects observed involving conceptual combination (e.g. Springer and Murphy, 1992). Specifically, we wished to ascertain whether the combination process begins before the constituent concepts have been fully activated. In order to do this, we created two conditions of implausible combinations, one where explicit featural knowledge was required in order to reject the combination (e.g. *frog tail*), and another where more basic taxonomic knowledge was sufficient (e.g. *daffodil tail*). Our hypothesis was that participants would reject combinations from the Basic condition more quickly than those from the Detailed condition, based on the differences in time taken to activate the requisite knowledge.

Existing theories of conceptual combination have difficulties in explaining how combinations can be rejected as implausible. The Competition Among Relations in Nominals (CARIN) theory (Gagné & Shoben, 1997) proposes that combinations are interpreted by applying one of a small set of possible relations to the constituent nouns. The theory therefore implies that combinations can only be rejected when every single possible relation has been applied and none result in a satisfactory interpretation. People cannot know if a relation will be successful or not until they apply it, meaning that they have to option but to

apply them all. According to the CARIN theory then, there should be no difference in the time taken to reject combinations from either condition. Slot-filling theories suggest that the modifier fills a slot in the head noun and that this process is guided by general knowledge about the two concepts. These theories assume that both concepts are completely activated prior to their combination (e.g. Murphy, 1988). If people have retrieved the concepts *frog* and *tail* before attempting to combine them, then they will be aware that *tail* cannot fill the <has as body part> slot in *frog* since frogs do not have tails. On the other hand, the link between *daffodil* with *tail* is less obvious, suggesting that a more extensive search for plausible relationships will be required before this combination can be ruled out. Thus, the slot-filling view predicts that *frog tail* should be easier to dismiss as the appropriate slot and filler are clear yet obviously incompatible.

According to our dynamic activation view, the combination process will begin *before* both nouns have been fully activated. *Daffodil tail* can be rejected as soon as the basic semantic categories of the constituent concepts becomes available since the pairing <plant-body part> does not match a productive pattern. On the other hand, *frog tail* matches a very productive pattern and can only be rejected when the precise knowledge that frogs do not have tails becomes available. We propose that this detailed knowledge about frogs will only be activated when people attempt to visualize the combined concept and fail. Accordingly, we propose that combinations in the Detailed condition will take longer to reject than those in the Basic condition.

Method

Participants Twenty-six first year undergraduate students from University College Dublin participated in the experiment for partial course credit.

Design A within-participants design was used for the experimental manipulation of condition. Each participant saw the same set of 80 stimuli, comprising the two conditions of 20 items each and the 40 sensible fillers.

Materials Twenty combinations were generated for each of the conditions. For the Detailed condition, this set constituted a series of combinations that were exemplars of a productive pattern of combination (e.g. <animal-body part>). However, all happened to be implausible by virtue of some instance-specific detail of one of the constituents. For example, *frog tail* is an implausible combination since frogs do not have tails, yet many other reptiles and animals do. *Raspberry peel* is implausible since raspberries cannot be peeled, yet many other fruits can. Also, *train tyres* are implausible because trains do not have tyres, yet many other vehicles have tyres. In the Basic condition we created a matching set of combinations which substituted the concept for which detailed knowledge was required. This substituted concept was too far removed in the conceptual hierarchy to yield a sensible combination. For example, both daffodil and frog are organisms. However, *daffodil* is a plant and the lowest common abstraction of entities that tend to have tails is *animal*. Our hypothesis was that *daffodil tail* would be rejected before *frog tail* because the knowledge that daffodils are not animals would be activated before the knowledge that frogs do not have tails. In other examples, *raspberry peel* was paired with *doughnut peel* and *train tyres* was paired with *vase tyres*.

The combinations were controlled for length and also for familiarity. The average number of letters in the Detailed and Basic conditions was not significantly different (both 10.75). The average number of syllables between these conditions was not significantly different (both 3.25). The log of the average BNC frequency of the words used in the Detailed and Basic conditions was not significantly different (6.1 and 6.3 respectively, $t(19) = -.99$, $p = .33$). Finally, the log of the Google frequency of the combinations used in both conditions was not significantly different (2.7 and 2.3 respectively, $t(19) = 1.81$, $p = .09$), which was to be expected given that none of the combinations were intended to be sensible.

As well as the 40 implausible stimuli we also included 40 sensible filler items in order to balance the sample (e.g. *tomato sandwich*). We avoided including overtly lexicalized items, in order that participants would be required to actively combine the constituent concepts.

Procedure Participants sat in front of a computer screen and placed the index finger of their left hand on the F key of the computer keyboard and the index finger of their right hand on the J key. They were informed that a series of noun-noun compounds would be displayed on the screen for which they would have to make plausibility judgments, pressing J for plausible and F for implausible. Each trial was separated by a blank screen lasting for one second. The combination then appeared in the middle of the screen and participants had to make a decision by pressing the appropriate key.

Participants were initially given a short practice session where feedback was given regarding their judgments. The aim of this practice session was to familiarize them with the process of making quick plausibility judgments and also to set a reliable threshold for plausibility. After completing the practice session, participants were instructed that they were now beginning the experiment. The stimuli were then presented in a random order to each participant.

Results and Discussion

A total of 14.5% of the data were omitted from the analysis. We eliminated any positive responses to the implausible stimuli (12.5%). Additionally, response times deemed unreasonably fast (< 400ms, 0.1%) or unreasonably slow (> 4000, 1.6%) were also excluded. After this initial elimination process, any remaining response times which were more than three standard deviations outside each participant's mean for that condition were also excluded. This eliminated a further 0.3% of trials.

The average response time for the Detailed condition was 1,503ms while that for the Basic condition was 1,333ms. Repeated measures ANOVAs revealed that this difference was significant both by-items and by-participants, $F_1(1,25) = 27.89$, $p < .001$, MSE = 12360.01; $F_2(1,19) = 9.53$, $p < .01$, MSE = 48560.09. The difference in accuracy for the Detailed and Basic conditions (93% and 78% respectively) was also significant both by-items and by participants, $F_1(1,25) = 17.47$, $p < .001$, MSE = 6.36; $F_2(1,19) = 15.80$, $p < .001$, MSE = 9.14. Only two of the stimuli were incorrectly judged by the majority of participants (both Detailed), namely *liquid ice* (13 correct responses) and *evening sunrise* (9 correct responses).

These results demonstrate that participants were quicker and more accurate in dismissing the Basic combinations than the Detailed combinations. This finding provides converging evidence that knowledge activation is not an all at once phenomenon, therefore providing a means by which conceptual information might be activated selectively in combination. Importantly, the difference in response times between both conditions indicates that the combination process begins *before* all knowledge relevant to the constituent nouns has been activated. Had the participants in our experiment activated both concepts first, then the items in the Detailed condition would certainly have been rejected first: a full representation of *frog* and *tail* would have permitted the speedy realization that the concepts were incompatible.

This experiment has demonstrated that implausible combinations can be quickly and reliably rejected without the need for a long search for potential interpretations. Yet, how could participants be confident that a combination was not sensible before trying every single possibility? Clearly, they must have been relying on some kind of heuristic in order to guide the combination process, or else the more ambiguous items in the Basic condition would have taken longer to reject. Given the finding of Experiment 1 that basic taxonomic knowledge is the first to be activated, we propose that people rely on this information in order to constrain the interpretation process, and that more detailed information is applied selectively, thereby 'homing in' on the precise meaning of the combination. For example, knowing that *frog* is an animal and that *tail* is a body part is enough to strongly suggest the <has> relation, thereby greatly reducing the range of possible interpretations which must be considered. Similarly, the knowledge that daffodil is a plant is sufficient for dismissing *daffodil tail* since the pattern <plant-body part> is highly irregular. In sum, we propose that people are sensitive to how different types of concept tend to interact in combination and that they use this heuristic in order to activate conceptual detail selectively. This guided selective activation process might explain how people can interpret potentially ambiguous combinations so quickly and so reliably, an issue which previous theories have failed to explain satisfactorily.

General Discussion

We have provided evidence that conceptual knowledge is activated dynamically, with detailed features being less available than more basic taxonomic knowledge. One reason for this effect might be that the latter is represented amodally while the verification of specific features requires the manipulation of a representation. Most interpretations of property verification tasks have assumed that participants make use of amodal representations, accessing data structures such as semantic networks, feature lists or schemas in order to find the required information. In contrast, our results have suggested that conceptual knowledge is not stored in this way.

Much evidence has been garnered supporting the idea that a significant part of conceptual knowledge is modality-specific. Barsalou (2005) maintains that during property verification, people scan mental simulations in order to evaluate whether test properties can be perceived. This view is supported by numerous studies showing that variables such as occlusion, size, shape and orientation affect conceptual processing. For example, Solomon and Barsalou (2004) analyzed response times for a property verification task and found that as features became larger, they took longer to verify, suggesting that people must attend to particular regions of a simulation in order to perceive a feature. Supporting this stance, many of our participants reported using visual imagery in order to discriminate between hairy and non-hairy animals, particularly in cases where this information could not be deduced from the conceptual hierarchy. The idea that people instantiate concepts visually in order to verify visual features would explain the differences in response time between our conditions. For example, it may be the case that participants had to instantiate a visual representation of a rhinoceros before being able to tell whether it was hairy or not, thus lengthening the response time for this task. The greater the level of representational manipulation required, the longer the time taken to verify the feature.

Barsalou (2005) proposed that rather than being regarded as a general description of a category, a concept can be more accurately described as the productive ability to generate many different situated conceptualizations. For example, traditional models involving conceptual knowledge view the concept *dog* as a detached collection of amodal facts that becomes active as a whole every time the category is processed. However, this idea cannot provide for the specialized inferences needed in particular situations (e.g. a growling guard-dog as opposed to a playful pup). An understanding of the concept entails the ability to produce a wide variety of situated conceptualizations that support goal achievement in specific contexts. In light of this, the concept for *dog* cannot simply be a detached global description of a fixed set of propositional features.

This view is compatible with the findings of our experiments. Basic taxonomic knowledge is likely to be stored propositionally in order to facilitate conceptualization (e.g. knowing whether a word refers to a thing, or whether that thing is an artefact or an organism). However, for reasons of economy, the number of features stored in this way is likely to be relatively small. More obscure properties are likely to be verified by scrutinizing a modal-specific simulation. However, if basic taxonomic knowledge is sufficient for indicating how the constituent nouns of a combination are related, then this can be used to inform the activation process so that only the combined concept need be simulated.

Conclusion

We have shown that conceptual knowledge is activated dynamically, with generalized taxonomic information being more available than specific features. Our findings are compatible with previous findings in neuroscience (e.g. Kumar & Debruille, 2004; Warrington, 1975) and psycholinguistics (e.g. Solomon & Barsalou, 2004) and suggest a distinction in how people represent different types of information. We have shown that the phenomenon of dynamic knowledge activation may be crucial to the understanding of how concepts are combined. The idea of a selective activation process can successfully explain how people avoid accessing conceptual information that is not relevant to a combination. Future work should investigate in more detail how conceptual knowledge is represented in memory and further analysis of the processes involved in conceptual combination may prove revealing in this regard.

References

Barsalou, L.W. (2005). Situated conceptualization. In H. Cohen & C. Lefebvre (Eds.), *Handbook of categorization in cognitive science* (pp. 619-650). St. Louis: Elsevier.

Gagné, C.L. & Shoben, E. J. (1997). Influence of thematic relations on the comprehension of modifier-noun combinations. *Journal of Experimental Psychology: Learning, Memory and Cognition, 23,* 71-87.

Kumar, N. & Debruille, J.B. (2004). Semantics and N400: Insights for schizophrenia. *Journal of Psychiatry and Neuroscience, 29,* 89-98.

McElree, B. & Murphy, G.L. (2006). Time course of retrieving conceptual information. A speed-accuracy trade off study. *Psychonomic Bulletin and Review, 13,* 848-853.

Murphy, G.L. (1988). Comprehending complex concepts. *Cognitive Science, 12,* 529-562.

Rayner, K. (1998). Eye movements in reading and information processing: 20 years of research. *Psychological Bulletin, 124,* 372-422.

Solomon, K.O. & Barsalou, L.W. (2004). Perceptual simulation in property verification. *Memory and Cognition, 32,* 244-259.

Springer, K., & Murphy, G.L. (1992). Feature availability in conceptual combination. *Psych. Science, 3,* 111-117.

Till, R.E., Mross, E.F., & Kintsch, W. (1988). Time course of priming for associate and inference words in a discourse context. *Memory and Cognition, 16,* 283-298.

Warrington, E.K. (1975). The selective impairment of semantic memory. *Quarterly Journal of Experimental Psychology, 27,* 635-657.

What triggers early decomposition of morphologically complex words?

Delphine Fabre (delphine.fabre@univ-lyon2.fr)
Institut des Sciences de l'Homme, 14 av Berthelot
69363 Lyon cedex 07, France

Liliane Schoot (liliane.schoot@univ-lyon2.fr)
Institut des Sciences de l'Homme, 14 av Berthelot
69363 Lyon cedex 07, France

Fanny Meunier (fanny.meunier@ish-lyon.cnrs.fr)
Institut des Sciences de l'Homme, 14 av Berthelot
69363 Lyon cedex 07, France

Abstract

Recent results using the masked priming paradigm have shed light on the importance of surface morphological structure in early word processing and the morphological decomposition procedure (e.g., Rastle et al., 2000; Longtin, Segui & Hallé 2003; Rastle & Davis 2004 among other). The two experiments reported in this paper examine if only one component between the stem and the suffix can spark off the decompositional procedure rather than the surface morphological structure. In Experiments 1 and 2, prime words are either pseudo-derived words as *baguette* "breadstick" that, at a surface level, can be parsed into the stem *bague* and the suffix *-ette*, words composed of a stem plus a non suffixal ending (*brin-gue*, "binge"), or words composed of a string of letters that do not matched with a stem and a suffix ending (*chand-ail*, "pullover"). Prime and target words share their initial sequence of letters, and targets are simple words in Experiment 1 while consist into morphologically derived word in Experiment 2. The target recognition time analyses showed that the sole presence of a suffix ending can trigger the decomposition procedure.

Introduction

Often in natural languages many words can be analyzed as two or more morphemic units. For example the French word *lunaire* "lunar" contains the stem *lune* "moon" and the adjectival suffix *-aire*. In French about 75% of the words contained in the lexicon are morphologically complex (Rey-Debove, 1984). Since Taft and Forster's (1975) seminal article, research on the role of morphological units in lexical access and their representation in the mental lexicon has received an increasing amount of attention and many evidences showing the implication of morphological structure have been found. The theoretical implications of these evidences are far from consensual and many models have been proposed to explain how morphological structure influences complex word processing; they contrast on their assumptions about how morphologically complex words are processed and stored in the brain. Initially Butterworth (1983) and Manelis and Tharp (1977) have proposed that all morphologically complex words are listed in the mental lexicon, while Taft and Forster (1975) suggested that only morphemic units and their combinatorial information are stored, without any whole-word representations. More recent models allow the coexistence of whole-word and morpheme representations. This has been done in different ways. Some authors proposed to add a morphemic level of representation distinct from the lexical level that features the whole-word representations. This morphemic level has been postulated as prelexical or as supralexical. In the former a morphologically complex word like *lunaire* is decomposed into *lune* and *-aire* prior to the activation of its full lexical representation (Colé, Segui, & Taft, 1997; Taft, 1994; 2003; 2005); in the latter it is only when the whole word representation *lunaire* has been activated that the morphemic units *lune* and *-aire* are accessed (Giraudo & Grainger, 2000; 2001; 2003). Two route models have also been postulated, proposing that morphemes and whole-word representations are accessed in parallel (Caramazza, Laudanna, & Romani, 1988; Frauenfelder & Schreuder, 1992; Schreuder & Baayen, 1995). In these models, morphologically complex words can be accessed via two routes: a direct route that is using the whole-word representations, and a decompositional route, using the morphemic units. Whether it is the direct or the decompositional route that lead to identification depends on the linguistic and distributional properties of the word, such as frequency, formal and semantic transparency, morpheme productivity, lexicality, etc. (see Schreuder & Baayen, 1995).

Recently, many authors have published results which pose challenges for a number of models. Indeed results obtained with a masked priming paradigm suggest that the morphological effect emerge prelexically in visual word processing (e.g. Diependaele, Sandra, & Grainger, 2005; Feldman, 2000; Forster & Azuma, 2000; Frost et al., 1997; Giraudo & Grainger, 2000; 2001; Grainger et al., 1991; Pastizzo & Feldman, 2002; Rastle et al., 2000; Rastle & Davis, 2003). Visual masked priming technique consists of presenting a prime on a screen for a very short duration (typically for less than 50 ms) and to mask it by the subsequent presentation of the target. Masked priming was first used to avoid episodic effects associated with the unmasked priming paradigm, and to avoid strategies in the lexical decision process (see Forster & Davis, 1984; Forster, 1998). It is assumed that the observed masked priming effects reflect the early stages of word processing, and reveal what properties of words are extracted before they are consciously perceived. Recent studies on morphological processing conducted using this priming paradigm have shown that prelexical decomposition was achieved on every letter string that can be fully parsed into existing morphemes, including real derived words like *gardener*, pseudo-derived words like *corner*, or derived pseudowords like *quickify* (Longtin & Meunier, 2005; Longtin, Segui, & Hallé, 2003; Rastle et al., 2000; Rastle & Davis, 2003; Rastle, Davis, & New, 2005). These conclusions were drawn from visual masked priming experiments (with a 47 ms prime duration) showing facilitation effects on the pseudo-stem whenever the prime is morphologically decomposable at the surface level. For instance at the surface level, *gardener* and *corner* are both decomposable into a stem + -er. However, in fact, only *gardener* is truly derived from its stem. Nevertheless, in masked priming paradigm, *gardener* primes *garden* as much as *corner* primes *corn*. By contrast, words containing an embedded pseudo-stem but no suffix, such as *brothel*, does not prime their embedded words, in this case *broth* (Diependaele, Sandra, & Grainger, 2005; Longtin et al., 2003; Rastle, Davis, Tyler, & Marlsen-Wilson, 2000; Rastle & Davis, 2003; Rastle, Davis, & New, 2004). Longtin and Meunier (2005) further showed that this morphological priming effect can be obtained even with morphologically complex pseudowords, such as *quickify* and *sportation*. In this masked priming study, French morphologically structured pseudowords produced a facilitation effect for their stems equivalent to that shown by existing derived words: for instance, the pseudoword *rapidifier* "quick + ify" primed *rapide* "quick" with the same magnitude as the existing derived word *rapidement* "quickly". However, no priming effect was found with non-morphological pseudowords (such as *rapiduit*, made of the stem *rapid-* and the non-morphological French ending -*uit*), demonstrating that the mere occurrence of the target at the beginning of the pseudoword prime is not sufficient to produce any priming. Overall, these masked priming results suggest that there is a blind morphological decomposition process very early on during visual word recognition, applied to every item that looks morphologically complex, irrespective of its lexicality and whether its morphological structure is linguistically motivated or not. An issue that still unclear is the unit that triggered the morphological decomposition. Previous experiments demonstrated that the stem on its own is not sufficient to observe priming effect. The word *brothel* does not prime *broth* because -*el* is not a suffix in English. However, it is still unanswered if the decomposition is due to the presence of the combination of a potential stem + a potential suffix or if the suffix on its own is sufficient to produce decomposition and therefore a priming effect. We ran two masked priming experiments in order to answer this

question and identify the unit(s) that triggered morphological decomposition.

Experiment 1

In order to test the role of the suffix on morphological decomposition, we ran a first experiment in which we manipulated the surface construction of the word-prime: is it fully decomposable in morpheme-like units? Is there a stem? Is there a suffix? In a first condition we used as primes, words that finished with a pseudo-suffix but in which the first part is not a stem. For example *ourlet*, contained the French suffix -*et* (as in *muret* "small wall"), but *ourl-* is not a stem. As a target we used a monomorphemic word that started orthographically as the prime such as *ours* "bear". The observation of a priming effect on the target recognition would indicate the isolation of this sequence during prime processing and therefore that a decomposition procedure has been engaged. Two other conditions were also tested: one condition with primes consisting of pseudo-derived words and the other condition with primes consisting of word composed with a stem and an ending that do not match with a suffix in French (as in *abricot* in which *abri-* is a stem but -*cot* is not a suffix). In these cases targets were the pseudo-stems.

Method

Participants Thirty seven students of the Institut des Sciences Politiques at the Université Lyon 2 participated in the experiment. They were all native speakers of French with no language disturbance and had normal or corrected to-normal vision.

Stimuli We selected 24 French prime-target pairs for each of the three following experimental conditions: Pseudoderived, Stem and Suffix. In the Pseudo-derived condition, the prime is a monomorphemic word, which can nevertheless be parsed into existing morphemes but is actually neither synchronically nor diachronically composed of them. For instance the word *baguette* is composed of *bague*, meaning "ring" and the suffix -*ette*, which in French added the meaning of 'small' to the base it's attached to (as in *maisonette* meaning "small housse" or *fillette* meaning "femal little child"…). However regarding the word *baguette* its meaning is not "small ring" but "breadstick"; hence the meaning of the surface form is unrelated to the meaning of its components. *Baguette* is therefore what we call a pseudo-derived word. In the Stem condition, the prime word is composed of an existing stem in French and an ending which do not correspond to a suffix. For instance, the word *bringue*, "binge" in English, is composed of *brin* and of the ending -*gue*. *Brin-* matched with a French stem that means "blade" and that is found for example in the word *brindille* "thin blade", while the ending -*gue* do not correspond to a French suffix. In this condition, the target word is the pseudo-stem (*BRIN* in the example given). Finally, in the Suffix condition prime words are composed of a string of letters and a suffix ending. For instance the words *ourlet* "hemline" is composed of *ourl-* that do not match with a French stem, and the suffix *-et* which is a French suffix that generally added the meaning of "small" to the stem it is added to, as in *garçonnet* "small boy" derived from the French word *garcon* "boy" . In this condition the target word consist into a word that share its initial letters with those of the prime word, as *OURS* "bear" for the example given (*ourlet*).

Moreover, for each of the 24 target-words of the three conditions described above, 24 other prime words are attributed to set up the control condition. These prime words are unrelated to target-words regarding their initial component, although their internal structure is similar to the ones used for related primes. Moreover 72 prime target pairs have been selected as filers in order to reduce the proportion of related pairs to 33 %. Thus each list contained 214 target words, and consequently an equal number of non-word targets have been constructed in order to balance "word" and "nonword" answers.

Conditions	Prime	Target
Pseudo-derived	baguette 'breadstick'	BAGUE 'RING'
Stem	bringue 'binge'	BRIN 'SHALTER'
Suffix	ourlet 'hemline'	OURS 'BEAR'

Table 1: Sample of stimuli used in Experiment 1.

Design

Procedure We used a masked priming procedure as in Forster and Davis (1984). Each trial began with a pre-mask of hashmarks (# # # # # # #) which appeared in the middle of the screen for 500 ms, immediately followed by the prime, in lower case, displayed for 47 ms and then immediately masked by the target, in upper case. The stimulus remained on the screen until the participant responded or when a 2000 ms deadline was reached, whichever came first. The experiment was run on PC-compatible computer using DMDX software (Foster & Foster, 2000). Participants were instructed to respond as quickly and accurately as possible whether the letter string in upper case is a French word or not. We did not mention the presence of the prime. Participants responded "yes" if the item displayed is a word by pressing one of the two response buttons and "no" by pressing the other response button if the item is not a word. Prior to the experiment proper, participants completed a series of 15 warm-up trials that were similar to the experimental trials.

Results

Only reaction times for correct "yes" responses shorter than 1100 ms and longer than 300 ms were retained for reaction time (RT) analyses (outliers corresponded to 2.5 % of the data). The error rate is 5.4%. Regarding this low rate, no analysis has been conducted on errors. Priming effects are displayed in Figure 1.

Overall analysis on RTs show an effect of the link shared between the prime and the target on response latencies [$F(1,36) = 7.68$, $p < .01$], an effect of the experimental condition [$F(2,72) = 8.27$, $p < .001$], and an interaction of these two factors [$F(2,72) = 10.63$, $p < .0001$]. Planned comparisons show that participants responded to 26 ms more rapidly when target words are preceded by a pseudo-derived word than when preceded by unrelated primes. This effect is highly significant [$F(1,36) = 20.38$, $p < .0001$]. No priming effect is observed in the Stem condition [$F < 1$]. Finally, participants responded to 12 ms less rapidly in the Suffix condition regarding to the unrelated one. This inhibitory priming effect is marginally significant [$F(1,36) = 3.36$, $p = .07$].

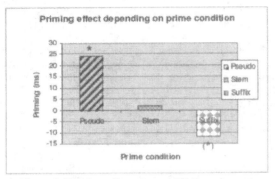

Figure 1: Priming effect observed in Experiment 1

Discussion

This experiment replicates the finding observed in Longtin et al. (2003) regarding the Pseudo-derived condition. Indeed, we observed that a morphologically simple word is recognized faster if preceded by a pseudo-derived related word than if preceded by an unrelated one. According to the principle of the priming effect, it comes into sight that words with surface morphological structure are decomposed during their early processing, leading to the isolation of morphemes, that if presented as targets are identified more rapidly. The aim of the two other conditions (Stem and Suffix) is to clarify if one of the two components which shape a surface morphological structure, namely stem or suffix, is sufficient to trigger the decompositional processing.

The Stem condition shows no priming effect at all. Hence, it appears that the sole presence of a stem in a word is not sufficient to induce the decompositional processing.

In the Suffix condition we observed a trend for an inhibitory priming effect. We interpreted this tendency as indicating that a decomposition procedure has been engaged, leading to the isolation a string of letters (e.g., *ourl* in the prime word *ourlet*) which does not entirely overlap with the target word (*ours*). Hence an orthographic competition could be engaged which lead to an inhibitory process on the target word recognition, while in the Pseudo-derived condition, the decomposition procedure leads to the isolation of a string of letters (e.g., *bague* in the prime word *baguette*) which entirely overlaps with the target word (e.g., *bague*) leading for a facilitative priming effect.

We ran a second experiment to investigate if a facilitative priming effect could be obtained in the Suffix condition if a better control of the orthographic overlap is done between the prime word and the target word. To this aim, we used in this second experiment prime words which have the same characteristics than the ones used in Experiment 1, only target characteristics are different and instead of pseudo-stem they were suffixed words. This allowed a more consistent orthographic overlap through the three experimental conditions, especially if we assume that the suffix target word is decomposed when processed. It has to be notice that in English one of the striking results reported on morphology is a lack of priming between two suffixed words derived from the same stem while all other morphological links between prime and target do produce priming effect (Marslen-Wilson, Tyler, Waksler & Older, 1994), however Meunier and Segui (2002) did find clear facilitation in that case in French.

Experiment 2

This second experiment aim to clarify the result observed in the first experiment, especially regarding the Suffix condition. To this end, we ran a second masked priming experiment. The primes have the same characteristics than the ones used in Experiment 1, only target characteristics are different; in this experiment target words are suffixed words. This allowed a more consistent orthographic overlap through the three experimental conditions.

Method

Participants Thirty four students of the Institut des Sciences Politiques at the Université Lyon 2 who have not participated to the previous experiment participated to this one. They were all native speakers of French with no language disturbance and had normal or corrected-to-normal vision.

Stimuli The 3 x 24 French prime-target pairs in this experiment that constitute the Pseudo-derived, Stem and Suffix conditions have been selected following the same criterion than in Experiment 1, except the nature of target words (morphologically complex). The 3 x 24 control prime words were selected in the same manner than those of the previous Pseudo-derived, Stem and Suffix but unrelated to the target words regarding their initial letter sequence. 72 prime-target pairs have been selected as filers in order to reduce the proportion of related pairs to 33 %. Because each list thus contained 214 target words, an equal number of non-word targets have been constructed associated to word primes.

Conditions	Prime	Target
Pseudo-derived	laiton 'brass'	LAITERIE 'DAIRY'
Stem	article 'article'	ARTÈRE 'ARTERY'
Suffix	bouquet 'bouquet'	BOUQUIN 'BOOK'

Table 2: Sample of stimuli used in Experiment 2.

Procedure The priming design is the same than in Experiment 1.

Results

Only reaction times for correct 'word' responses shorter than 1100 ms and longer than 300 ms were retained for RT analyses (outliers corresponded to 4.2 % of the data). The error rate is 6.12 %, regarding this low rate, no analysis has been conducted on errors. Priming effects are displayed in Figure 2.

Overall analysis on RTs show an effect of the experimental condition [$F(1,33) = 5.29$, $p < .01$], an effect of the link share between the prime and the target (related vs. unrelated) [$F(2,33) = 9.01$, $p < .005$], and a marginally significant interaction of these two factors (condition * link) [$F(2,66) = 2.46$, $p = .09$]. Planned comparisons show that participants responded to 20 ms more rapidly when target words are preceded by a pseudo-derived word than when preceded by unrelated primes. This effect is significant [$F(1,33) = 5.68$, $p = .02$]. No priming effect is observed in the Stem condition [$F < 1$]. Finally, participants responded to 28 ms more rapidly in the Suffix condition regarding to the unrelated one. This facilitative priming effect is significant [$F(1,33) = 9.66$, $p = .003$].

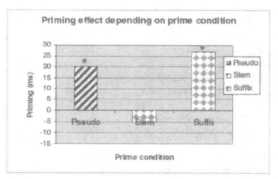

Figure 2: Priming effect observed in Experiment 2

General Discussion

The presented study aims at identifying what triggers the decompositional procedure engaged during the processing of morphologically complex words. More precisely, recent experiments using masked priming paradigm and manipulating the linguistics' features of the prime have demonstrated that words or pseudo-words with a surface morphologically complex form are decomposed prelexically (e.g., *gardener primes garden, corner primes corn and quickify primes quick*) while words or pseudo-words that only embedded a potential stem are not (*brothel* does not prime *broth*, or *rapiduit*[1] does not prime *rapid 'quick'*) (e.g., Longtin et al., 2003; Rastle, & al., 2000; Longtin & Meunier, 2005). Then, it seems that the sole presence of a potential stem is not sufficient to trigger the decompositional procedure. The remaining question was to understand whether the combination of potential stem + suffix triggers the decompositional procedure or the sole presence of a suffix is sufficient.

To answer this question we proposed first a masked priming experiment with three prime types: i) combining a potential stem + a suffix (the Pseudo-derived condition), ii) combining a potential stem and an ending which does not match with a French suffix (the Stem condition), iii) combining a suffix and an initial sequence of letters which does not match with a potential stem in French (the Suffix condition). The target word checks with the potential stem in the Pseudo-derived and Stem conditions (*baguette-bague* and *bringue-brin*), and overlap orthographically with the initial sequence of letters in the Suffix condition (e.g., *ourlet-ours*). The results obtained show a priming effect in the first condition and a trend for an inhibitory effect in the third one. No influence on the response time to recognize the target word is observed in the second condition (Stem). These results corroborate with previous experiments described above. Words with a surface morphologically complex form are decomposed prelexically (priming effect) while words with only an embedded stem do not. Now, regarding words with only an embedded suffix, we suggest that the inhibitory effect may be due to a competition between the representation made of the initial prime's sequence of letters -which suggest then that a decomposition have taken place-and the target word representation, as this two components do not entirely overlap regarding their orthographic features.

The second experiment clarifies this view, using prime and target with better orthographic overlap in the Suffix condition. To this end we used the same type of prime word than in Experiment 1, but morphologically complex word as target. The results obtained in this second experiment show once again a priming effect in the Pseudo-derived condition and no effect in the Stem condition. Regarding the Suffix condition a facilitative priming effect is obtained, *bouquet* primes *bouquin* (Suffix condition) as *laiton* primes *laiterie* (Pseudo-derived condition).

Overall, the results obtained in this study corroborate the early decompositional hypothesis, and further imply the critical role play by the suffix to initiate the decompositional procedure.

---

[1] The ending *-uit* is not a suffix in French.

Acknowledgments

The work reported here was supported by a Grant given by the Ministère délégué à l'Enseignement supérieur et à la Recherche (ACI 11523) to Fanny Meunier.

References

Butterworth, B. (1983). Lexical representation. In B. Butterworth (Ed.) Language Production (pp. 257-294). London : Academic Press.

Caramazza, A., Laudanna, A. & Romani, C. (1988). Lexical access and in ectional morphology, *Cognition, 28*, 297-332.

Colé P., Segui J. & Taft M. (1997). Words and morphemes as units for lexical access. *Journal of Memory and Language, 37*, 312-330.

Diependaele, K., Sandra, D. & Grainger, J. (2005). Masked crossmodal morphological priming: Unravelling morphoorthographic and morpho-semantic influences in early word recognition. *Language and Cognitive Processes, 20*, 75 114.

Forster, K. (1998). The Pros and Cons of Masked Priming. *Journal of Psycholinguistic Research, 27*(2), 203-233.

Forster, K. & Azuma, T. (2000). Masked priming for prefixed words with bound stems : Does submit prime permit ? *Language and Cognitive Processes , 15*, 539-561.

Forster, K. & Davis, C. (1984). Repetition priming and frequency attenuation in lexical access. *Journal of Experimental Psychology: Learning, Memory, and Cognition, 10*, 680-698.

Frauenfelder, U. H. & Schreuder, R. (1992). Constraining psycholinguistic models of morpho-logical processing and representation : The role of productivity. In G. E. Booij et J. Van Marle (Eds.), Yearbook of Morphology 1991 (pp. 165-183). The Netherlands : Kluwer Academic Publi-shers.

Frost, R., Forster, K.I., & Deutsch, A. (1997). What can we learn from the morphology of Hebrew: a masked priming investigation of morphological representation. *Journal of Experimental Psychology: Learning Memory, & Cognition, 23*, 829-856.

Giraudo. H., & Grainger, J. (2000). Effects of prime word frequency and cumulative root fre-quency in masked morphological priming. *Language and Cognitive Process, 15*(4/5), 421-444.

Giraudo, H. & Grainger, J. (2001). Priming complex words: Evidence for supralexical representation of morphology. *Psychonomic Bulletin & Review, 8*, 127-131.

Giraudo, H. (2005). Un modèle supralexical de représentation de la morphologie dérivationnelle en Français. *L'Année Psychologique, 105*(1), 171-195.

Grainger, J., Colé, P., & Segui, J. (1991). Masked morphological priming in visual word recognition. *Journal of Memory and Language, 30*, 370-384.

Grainger, J. & Jacobs, A.M. (1996). Orthographic processing in visual word recognition: A multiple read-out model. *Psychological Review, 103*, 518-565.

Longtin, C-M., Segui, J. & Hallé, P. (2003). Morphological priming without morphological relationship in French.*Language and Cognitive Processes.18*, 313-334.

Longtin, C. M. & Meunier, F. (2005). Morphological decomposition in early visual word processing. *Journal of Memory and Language, 53*:1, pp. 26-41.

Pastizzo, M. J., and Feldman, L. B. (2002). Discrepancies between orthographic and unrelated baselines in masked priming undermine a decompositional account of morphological facilitation. *Journal of Experimental Psychology: Learning, Memory and Cognition, 28,* 244-249.

Rastle, K., Davis, M. H., Marslen-Wilson, W. D. & Tyler, L. K. (2000). Morphological and semantic effects in visual word recognition : A time course study. *Language and Cognitive Processes, 15*(4-5), 507-537.

Rastle, K., Davis, M. H. & New, B. (2004). The broth in my brothers brothel : Morpho-orthographic segmentation in visual word recognition. *Psychonomic Bulletin Review, 11*(6), 1090-1098.

Rastle, K., & Davis, M. [H.] (2003). Reading morphologically complex words: Some thoughts from masked priming. In S. Kinoshita & S. J. Lupker (Eds.), Masked priming: State of the art (pp. 279-305). New York: Psychology Press

Rastle, K., Davis, M., New, B. (2005) Morpho-orthographic segmentation in visual word recognition. *Psychonomic Bulletin & Review, 11*(6), 1090-1098.

Rey-Debove, J. (1984). Le domaine de la morphologie lexicale. *Cahier de lexicologie 45,* 3-19.

Schreuder, R. &. Baayen, R. H. (1995). Modeling morphological processing, dans L.B. Feld-man, Morphological Aspects of Language Processing, Hillsdale (New-Jersey), Lawrence Erlbaum,

Taft, M. & Forster, K. I. (1975). Lexical storage and retrieval of prefixed words. *Journal of Verbal Learning and Verbal Behavior, 14,* 638-647.

Taft, M., (2003). Morphological representation as a correlation between form and meaning. In E. Assink D. Sandra (Eds.), Reading complex words. Amsterdam : Kluwer.

Taft, M. (1994). Interactive-activation as a framework for understanding morphological processing. *Language and Cognitive Processes 9*(3), 271-294.

The cognitive mechanisms that underlie the centre of Piraeus, Greece, or which are the elements of an old city that construct its mental map?

Eirini Rafailaki (irenerafl@yahoo.com)
Bartlett School of Graduate Studies, University College of London,
1-19 Torrington Place WC1E 6BT, London, UK

Abstract

This paper aims to explore the cognitive mechanisms which govern the individual behaviours of the pedestrians of Piraeus, Port of Athens, by examining the relationship between the spatial syntax of mental representations and the spatial syntax of the environment. The superimposed urban grids of the core of the city create a "palimpsest" on which the mental spatial models of the users are constructed. An experiment that involves the construction of mental maps of the city was conducted in the main pedestrian street, Sotiros Dios St. The configurational, geographical and topological characteristics of the peninsula provide rather an ambiguous sense of the ease or difficulty of the cognitive understanding of the site. Using tools of a quantitative analytical methodology (space syntax) and descriptive statistics, it is highlighted that the spatial representations of maps' data, provide insights in city's spatial properties underlying the knowledge structures (mental schemes) of the pedestrians of Piraeus. It is concluded that the cognitive knowledge of the formers, is created, transmitted and applied by the geometrical forms of the city, the morphology of the local visual field – which involves issues of configuration and scale of a space layout – and by topological relations.

Introduction

Human navigation and *wayfinding* in general and in built environments in particular have been studied extensively in the past in architectural design (Gärling, Lindberg & Mäntylä, 1983) in Artificial Intelligence (Kuipers, 1978; McDermott & Davis, 1984; Leiser & Zilbershatz, 1989) and in Cognitive Science (Siegel & White, 1975, Golledge, 1992, Hirtle & Heidron, 1993).

This paper explores the relationship between the spatial configuration of the physical environment of the centre of Piraeus, the port of Athens, Greece and the spatial cognition of its users; the latter are the *Locals (L)*, the *Regional Locals (RL)* (those who live around Piraeus and they visit it frequently) and the *Visitors (V)*. The paper initially presents a brief theoretical review related to how people cognise the built environment while navigating through it and what kind of knowledge they may retrieve and use in a wayfinding performance. Then, the experiment and a description of the survey procedure are presented. The methodology of the research and data analysis is explained. Finally, the conclusion of this research is discussed.

Literature review

City's "Palimpsest"

The city of Piraeus or *Peiraeus* has a history of many centuries and has, in fact, been inhabited since about 2,600 B.C. Since 5th century B.C., Piraeus was established as the major naval and commercial port, and it was planned by *Hippodamus* of Miletus, the most famous Greek urban theorist and city planner.

This fully informational through history environment is constructed in multidimensional terms. As each city is a "mosaic of social worlds" (Park, 1952), the behavioural settings (Lawson, 2001) comprise both the physical and the social environment. In this way, the urban environment of Piraeus could be characterised as a "*palimpsest*" of urban grids, a multi-layered record of streets, squares and passages that are being explored by the everyday walkers – both *inhabitants* and *visitors*. Everybody, while *walking in the City* read it "as a *text* but, crucially they also write it" (De Certeau, 1984). When people navigate through this "palimpsest", they create and simultaneously receive multiple cues that use for updating their spatial position and orientation.

Spatial Cognition, Wayfinding Performance and Cognitive Maps

To *find the way* from one place to another is a task that involves the act of travelling from origin to destination plus the act of spatial problem solving. Therefore, the task encompasses a person's cognition of his/her environment; cognition of the different spatial components of the "palimpsest", in order to use them for updating his/her spatial position and orientation.

Spatial cognition concerns "the study of knowledge and beliefs about spatial properties of objects and events in the world. Cognition is about knowledge: its acquisition, storage and retrieval, manipulation and use" (Montello, 2001). Spatial knowledge changes over time, through processes of learning and development. The acquisition, the development and the application of knowledge establish different movement behaviour, and therefore discrete approach in a *wayfinding* task, i.e. in the act of travelling to a destination by a continuous, recursive process of making route-choices whilst evaluating previous spatial decisions against constant cognition of the environment." (Conroy-Dalton, 2001). The human reasoning and decision-making involved in spatial behaviour has gained insight from the work of *Kevin Lynch,* who is attributed to be the first who used the definition of wayfinding, as "a consistent use and organisation of definite sensory cues from the external environment" (Lynch, 1960).

The *spatial syntax* of the environment consists of properties that include location, size, distance, direction, separation and connection, shape, pattern, and movement. Using the *spatial syntax*, people form their own "texts" of a place, *mental representations* of the spaces whether from navigation or from maps or from descriptions or from a combination, that allow them to arrive at their destinations and to give directions to others with some success. Coined by Tolman (Tolman, 1948), these internal representations are called *cognitive maps*. The latter term has been extendedly studied and analysed. One definition that seems to satisfy all aspect of the task is the following: A cognitive map: "... is a process composed of a series of psychological transformations by which an individual acquires, codes, stores, recalls and decodes information about the relative locations and attributes of phenomena in his/her everyday spatial environment" (Downs & Stea, 1973).

Although many cognitive theories of space influential in the built environment emphasise the *position of the subject* at the centre of the map, in the cognitive neuro-science the distinction between *allocentric* (object to object) and *ego-centred* (body to object) models of cognition is a crucial matter. The *allocentric navigation* enables humans and animals to generate an internal representational system based on the Cartesian or Polar coordinates of the environment. (Klatzky 1998). The egocentric navigation implies using other available information such as internal cues, motor input, vestibular and directional information.

The experiment was conducted within an *allocentric* frame of reference. The process of knowledge development over time differs for each group and individuals vary in the extent and accuracy of the spatial knowledge that they acquire from direct experience (*continuous* framework, Montello, 1998), as the degree of familiarity with the place they were walking is different. Following Hart and Moore (1976) who refined the concepts from an interpretation of earlier work by Piaget and Inhelder (1967), it could be argued that the spatial knowledge of the pedestrians of Piraeus varies remarkably; the Visitors have the most basic form of knowledge, *the landmark knowledge,* which is developed by acquiring information about discrete features in the environment, so as to be able to identify a place. Going further, Regional Locals' spatial abilities are mostly rely on *route knowledge,* which is based on travel routines that connect ordered sequences of landmarks. Last, the *Locals,* being fully familiar with the environment, they use *survey knowledge,* knowledge of two dimensional layouts that includes the simultaneous interrelations of locations; survey knowledge would support detouring and shortcutting. For this research, both the *dominant* framework (progression from landmark to survey knowledge, Siegel & White, 1975) and the *continuous* framework (Montello, 1998) have been taken into account; however, none of them do full justice to the significant qualitative as well as quantitative nature of large individual variations[1].

The Experiment

The experiment was conducted *in Sotiros Dios Street* with a sample of 76 people (17 L, 19 RL, 15 V). It concerns the construction of mental maps and it is an *allocentric* type of representation. The participants were given a diagrammatic map of the centre (on which no elements were indicated) and they were asked to draw a sketch map of the spatial layout of the city, including every kind of element such as streets, buildings, areas and open spaces. As through the experiment the frequency of the occurrence of the city elements was substantial to be measured, no instructions or guidance was provided. A wide range of competence in drawing maps was found among the participants. Figure 1 shows Piraeus map. Figures 2, 3&4 show a poorly drawn and two relatively well drawn sketch maps.

Figure 1: Map of the centre of Piraeus.

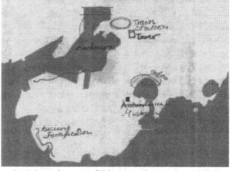

Figure 1 : Mental map of Piraeus, drawn by a Visitor.

---

[1] The continuous framework appears to be a developmental theory for people with a good sense-of direction (Ishikawa & Montello, 2006). As we will show in the research, this framework is apparently correct in positing that metric knowledge (distances&directions) of layout begins to be acquired more or less immediately, upon first exposure to a new place. However, this occurs only for some participants.

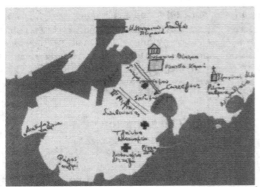

Figure 2 : Mental map of Piraeus, drawn by a Local.

Figure 3 : Mental map of Piraeus drawn by a Regional Local.

Data analysis/Observations

From the analysis of the maps, it was found that there are a number of typical errors, including incompleteness, variations in scale across the area, roads being drawn too wide, possible straightening of roads and use of single lines to represent streets. Another issue is the variation of the shape and position of symbols representing the spatial features of objects and the arrangement of their components (Cheng, 1996). The maps are also sometimes very simple, highly selective, distorted, and augmented. These typical errors are valuable in this study because they may allow us to understand the syntactic characteristics of sketch maps that reflect how people perceive and represent the real environment.

In this part of the research, three techniques are used to elicit cognitive information from the maps. First, a conventional analysis is performed by disaggregating depicted elements. The *Lynch-defined environmental components (landmarks, paths, edges, nodes and districts)* are invoked in order to classify the elements of Piraeus. The number of times each element was drawn is counted. Figure 5 illustrates the number of participants that represented the city Elements in their maps. The Landmarks tend to be

depicted more often in the maps – 237 times – while Districts were represented 144 times, Edges 34 times, Paths 30 times and Nodes 20 times. This result suggests that the *visual descriptor* of Landmark (Conroy Dalton & Bafna, 2003) plays the primary role in the acquisition and transmission of knowledge of the environment (and not the *visual descriptor* of Edge). Additionally, the *spatial descriptor* of District (the other two are the Nodes and the Paths) is utilised as anchor for location in the process of wayfinding.

The hierarchical difference between the *spatial* and *visual* elements has been demonstrated by recent studies in wayfinding, such in the research of Benjamin's Kuipers (Kuipers, 1996). According to Kuipers, the mental maps are primary structured by the spatial elements ("first order elements"), which then may be elaborated, or fine-tuned by the addition of visual elements ("second order elements"). However, in the mental maps that the pedestrians of Piraeus drawn, the inverse finding seems to be observed; the visual elements seem to play a more crucial role than the spatial ones.

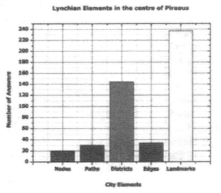

Figure 4 : The Lynchian Elements in the centre of Piraeus depicted by the subjects.

Further Analysis

In further analysis, Space syntax analysis is applied and an axial break–up (longest and fewest lines of access) that contains all the axial lines which enclose, or are adjacent to, the aforementioned elements was drawn. Therefore, the resultant "set" of the axial lines is held, in statistical terms, to be a "population". This population consists of *963 axial lines*. Furthermore, the ten most frequently occurring elements are chosen and in statistical terms these are held to be a *"sample"* of the wider *"population"*. The sample consists of *91 axial lines* (1 line is common for "Main Harbour" and "Train Station" and one line is common for "Municipal Theatre" and "Korai Sq."*)*. Table 1 illustrates the percentages of the most often represented elements that indicate the "sample".

Table 1 : Most frequent in occurrence elements.

	Elements	Classification	Perc. of occur. (%)	No of subjects
1	Main Harbour	District	7.96	37
2	Mun.Theatre	Landmark	4.52	21
3	Passalimani	District	4.09	19
4	Mikrolimano	District	4.09	19
5	Sotiros D. St.	Path	3.01	14
6	Train Station	Landmark	2.80	13
7	Arch. Museum	Landmark	2.58	12
8	Peraiki Coast	Edge	2.37	11
9	*My House*	*Landmark*	*2.15*	*10*
10	Korai Sq.	District	1.94	9
11	Ag. Nikolaos	Landmark	1.94	9

Table 2 : Averages of syntactic values (Global Integration, Local Integration R3, Connectivity).

City Elements	No of axial lines	Av. Global Integration	Av.Local Integration R3	Av.Con.
Main Harbour	28	1.5837	0.5885	0.2015
Mun.Theatre	4	0.801	0.8348	0.4345
Passalimani	10	0.5207	2.5276	0.0976
Mikrolimano	6	1.0535	0.3677	0.0793
Sotiros Dios St.	1	2.3881	3.7086	28
Train Station	4	0.6318	0.7403	0.2916
Arch.Museum	4	0.6665	0.8265	18.5
Peraiki Coast	28	0.1968	0.3809	0.0697
Korai Sq.	4	0.8043	0.8326	19.25
Ag. Nikolaos	4	0.6008	0.7795	0.3511
Total	93	1.5602		

Through the analysis the characteristics of the configuration of spaces and features could be quantified and the syntactic values of the lines that describe the elements could be measured. Not only were the values of global integration[2] calculated, but the connectivity[3] values for each element as well (Table 2). On the maps, the location of the participants' residents *("My House")* is frequently depicted, at 5.74%. Although this observation is included in the statistical analysis, for the purpose of this study is excluded from the "sample", as the location of "My house" cannot be considered as a specific one. (Table 1).

---

[2] *Global Integration* is a measure of the axial map analysis showing the degree to which each line is closer to every other line in the network under the logic of the simplest route - min changes of directions (Hillier&Hanson, 1984). A version of integration called *local integration R3* restricts the measurement of routes from any line to only those that are up to two steps away from it.
[3] The *Connectivity* of a space measures the number of immediate neighbors that are directly connected to a space.

Descriptive Statistics - Central Limit Theorem & Z-Test

As one of the main objectives of the research is to investigate the association between configurational features and cognitive representations and thus throw light on how configurational aspects of the built environment may affect the cognitive knowledge, descriptive statistics were again applied. Using a couple of statistical tests, the central limit theorem and the z-test, it is possible to compare the sample of the selected axial lines to its population and determine how likely it is that the sample was drawn at random from that population.

Using the statistical method of z-test, we tested the initial hypothesis which assumed that the pedestrians of Piraeus *don't* randomly select the 10 aforementioned elements to represent in their mental maps. The test requires stating a hypothesised mean difference, which in the hypothesis has a value of 0.7031. A confidence level is also required for this test and the standard 95% confidence level has been used. Essentially, if the resultant value of z is less than a specified value (listed on a statistical look-up table), then the sample (the most often depicted elements) *could have been drawn at random* from the population. If the value of z is larger, then it implies that participants were not depicting certain elements randomly.

The two tests were made three times. In the first case *(Case 1)* the values of all lines of the sample were calculated. In the second case *(Case 2)* the three elements that consist of the greatest number of lines were excluded (Main Harbour, Passalimani and Peraiki Coast), as the difference in terms of number of lines between them and the rest elements is highly significant. However, those lines were *not* excluded from the total number of lines of the Sample (remained 91 lines). In the third case *(Case 3)* not only the three aforementioned elements were excluded but their lines as well (the Sample consists of 26 lines). The results of the two tests, (z-test and central limit theorem) for the three cases are presented in the following Table 3.

Table 3: Z-Test&Central Limit Theorem for 3 Cases

	Sample Av.	Sample Standard Dev.	Sample Variance	" Z " from c. l t.	" Z " from Z-test
Case1	1.5602	0.5255	0.2762	-22.8363	0.00001
Case2	1.8647	0.5295	0.2804	-41.5767	0.00001
Case3	1.8647	0.5295	0.2804	-77.7825	0.00001

	Measure	No of lines - Sample	Pop.Av.	Pop.Stand.Dev.	Pop. Variance
Case1	InRn	91	1.5579	0.3080	0.0949
Case2	InRn	91	1.5579	0.3080	0.0949
Case3	InRn	26	1.5579	0.3080	0.0949

According to the results of the z-tests, z_1, z_2 and z_3 have a value of 0.00001, with z_1 from c.l.t. being $|22.8363|$, z_2 $|41.5767|$ and z_3 $|77.7825|$. The fact that it is less than a specified value (1.65 for a one-tailed distribution and 1.96 for a two-tailed distribution), implies that in all cases the sample of the elements was *not* drawn randomly from the population and especially the third value (z_3 | 77.7825 | – which is the highest –) indicates that the 26 selected lines have been selected for certain reasons.

The table of results also indicates that the average value of global Integration for the sample of 91 lines is 1.5602, lower than the average of the sample of 26 lines which is 1.8647, while both of the averages are higher than the average value of the population (1.5579). This result shows that the cognitive model of Piraeus is constructed in relation to the closeness or accessibility of spaces from all others – in other words the measure of integration.

Furthermore, the values of Standard Deviation for the two samples are quite similar. For the sample of 91 lines is 0.5255 and for the sample of 26 lines is 0.5295 and they are both higher than the value of the population (which is 0.3080). This result indicates that the second sample that includes the most integrated lines also contains lines of greater range in integration.

Analysing the syntactic properties of the population with a respect to the syntactic variables of the spaces represented in the maps using axial-analysis methods, it could be suggested that not all the depicted elements are located in areas of high connectivity or high integration. Figure 6 shows Global Integration of the "population" and the locations of the "sample" (91 lines).

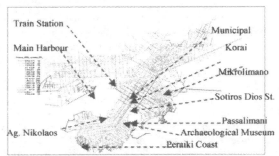

Figure 6: Global Integration Rn of axial analysis of the "population" and the locations of the "sample" (91 lines).

In order to construct a picture of the ease or difficulty with which we come to understand the shape of this complex space by seeing a part of it at a time through movement within it, the concept of *"intelligibility"* (Hillier, 1996a) is built on this relation. The scattergram demonstrating the systematic relation between grid structure and movement, namely the correlation between the connectivity and integration values of the lines making up the axial map of the grid (intelligibility), reveals that the "sample" has an ambiguous performance within the whole system. The adjusted r-square value 0.5066 (Figure 7) implies that the sample is oscillating between intelligibility and unintelligibility. The ten lines that seem to have the best performance (marked in a red dotted ellipse) are those that "grasp" the three grids of the city and especially the oldest of all grids; that of the centre (Figure 8).

This analysis reveals two outlier groups, one in the upper right part, marked in a red dotted ellipse, and another in the lower left, marked in a blue dotted ellipse (Figure 7). The first outlier group consists of spaces that enclose Landmarks and the Path and the second group consists of spaces that are mostly Districts and Edges. The Landmarks have high global integration values, and indeed these spaces are the most frequently represented on the mental maps (Figure 5). However, considering the ten most often in occurrence, it is certain Districts that play the crucial role in the cognitive knowledge of the pedestrians (21.3% for the Main Harbour, 10.9% for Passalimani and 10.9% for Mikrolimano).

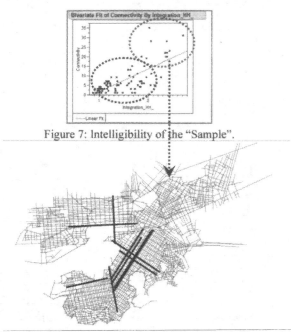

Figure 7: Intelligibility of the "Sample".

Figure 8: Axial Map of the selected "Population". The most intelligible lines of the "sample" are highlighted.

Conclusions

From the research above, it can be concluded that there is a clear pattern of association between the syntactic properties of the real environment and those of the mental maps, suggesting that the measure of global integration is a good predictor of cognitive representations of spatial configuration. In the *cognitive maps*, the depicted features appeared not to be randomly made, revealing that most of the participants clearly know more than the identities of landmarks, and do not simply locate points on paper randomly or based on crude heuristic rules. These subjective structures that encode the spatial relations "confirmed" the identity of Piraeus as being the "Main Port" with the *three natural harbours* (Passalimani and Mikfrolimano on the East and Main Harbour on the West). It cannot be discounted that all pedestrians started constructing their maps in relation to the distinguishing geomorphology of the three harbours. It has been already suggested that the depicted features appeared not to be randomly made. It can be further suggested that there is not only a close relationship between the spatial configuration in the real world and its representation in spatial cognition (as that can be elicited through cognitive mapping), but also between the spatial component and its significance as part of the "common sense spatial knowledge" which is the knowledge base for most people. This could explain why the frequency with which elements are identified on the cognitive maps is not necessarily highly correlated with all the syntactic measures. Therefore, the mental maps provide insights in city's spatial properties depicting the mental schemes of the pedestrians; cognitive mechanisms rely on local and global configurational features of the environment, on spatial knowledge that is acquired and interpreted as a system of topological spatial relations and on various cues that may affect spatial reasoning and visuo-spatial representations.

Last but not least, it can be argued that the most ancient grid although it contains the elements that have shaped the city's contemporary urban space, are not easily recognisable by "strangers"; they are mostly found in *"inhabitants'"* mental representations. The elements from the neoclassical and the modern period of Piraeus are more frequently cited. As the latter two grids contain features that have still a crucial role in the city's social activities (Train Station, Municipal Theatre, Town Hall), they appear to be better situated and framed in the cognitive models of Piraeus' pedestrians.

Acknowledgments

My deepest gratitude goes to my supervisor, Dr Ruth Conroy-Dalton, for her invaluable support and guidance and to Professor Bill Hillier for his advice and his indispensable comments. I would also like to thank P. Karaiskos and H. Koumantarea (Statistical Survey of Greece) and the participants–habitants of Piraeus and those who visit it–whose enthusiastic participation was invaluable.

References

Conroy Dalton, R. (2001). *Spatial navigation in immersive virtual environments.* Doctoral dissertation, Bartlett, UCL (University College London).

Conroy Dalton, R. & Bafna, S. (2003) *The syntactical image of the city: a reciprocal definition of spatial elements and spatial syntaxes.* In: 4th International Space Syntax Symposium, 17-19 June 2003, London, UK.

Downs, R. M. & Stea D. (1973). *Image and Environment: Cognitive Mapping and Spatial Behavior.* Chicago, Aldine Publishing Company.

De Certeau, M., (1984). *The Practice of Everyday Life,* University of California Press: Berkeley.

Gärling, T., Lindberg, E., & Mäntylä, T. (1983). Orientation in buildings: Effects of familiarity, visual access, and orientation aids. *Journal of Applied Psychology, 68,* 177-186.

Golledge, R. (1992). Place recognition and wayfinding: Making sense of space. *Geoforum, Vol. 23(2),* 199-214.

Hart R.A. & Moore. G.T. (1976). *The development of spatial cognition: A review. Ittelson,* Proshansky, and Rivlin (Eds.). In

Environmental Psychology: People and Their Physical Settings. New York: Holt, Rinehart and Winston, 2nd Edition.

Hillier, B. &Hanson, J. (1984). *The social logic of space,* Cambridge University Press.

Hillier, B., (1996a), *Space is the Machine,* Cambridge, Cambridge University Press.

Hirtle S. &Heidron. B. (1993). The structure of cognitive maps: Representations and processes. In T. Grling &R. Golledge, editors, *Behavior and Environment: Psychological and Geographical Aspects.* Elsevier Science Publishers.

Ishikawa, T., & Montello, D. R. (2006). Spatial knowledge acquisition from direct experience in the environment: Individual differences in the development of metric knowledge and the integration of separately learned places. *Cognitive Psychology, 52,* 93-129.

Klatzky, R. L. (1998). Allocentric and egocentric spatial representations: Definitions, distinctions, and interconnections. In C. Freksa, C. Habel, & K. F. Wender (Eds.), *Spatial cognition - An interdisciplinary approach to representation and processing of spatial knowledge* (Lecture Notes in Artificial Intelligence 1404) Berlin: Springer-Verlag. 1-17.

Kuipers, B. (1996). *A Hierarchy of Qualitative Representations for Space,* Tenth International Workshop on Qualitive Reasoning about Physcial Systems, QR-96, Menlo Park CA, AAAI Press.

Kuipers. B. (1978). Modeling spatial knowledge. *Cognitive Science, Vol. 2* 129–154.

Lawson B. (2001). *The language of space.* Publisher: Architectural Press.

Leiser D. & Zilbershatz A. (1989). The traveler - a computational model for spatial network learning. *Environment and Behavior, Vol. 21(3)* 435–463.

Lynch, K. (1960). *The image of the city,* Cambridge: MIT Press.

McDermott D.& Davis E. (1984). Planning routes through uncertain territory. *Artificial Intelligence, Vol. 22(1)* 551–560.

Miller, G.A. (1956). The magical number seven, plus or minus two: Some limits on our capacity for processing information. *Psychological Review, 63,* 81-97.

Montello, D. R. (2001). Spatial cognition. In N. J. Smelser &P. B. Baltes (Eds.), *International Encyclopedia of the Social & Behavioral Sciences.* Oxford: Pergamon Press. 14771-14775.

Montello, D. R. (1998). A new framework for understanding the acquisition of spatial knowledge in large-scale environments. In M. J. Egenhofer & R. G. Golledge (Eds.), *Spatial and temporal reasoning in geographic information systems* (pp. 143–154). New York: Oxford University Press.

Norman, D. (1988). *The Design of Everyday Things.* New York: Doubleday.

Park R., (1952). *Human Communities: the City and Human Ecology.* Glencoe, Ill: Free Press.

Piaget J. &Inhelder B. (1967). The Child's Conception of Space. W. W. Norton, New York, USA.

Siegel & White S.. (1975). *The development of spatial representations of large-scale environments, volume 10.* Academic Press. 9–55.

Tolman E. C. (1948). Cognitive maps in rats and men. *Psychological Review,* 55: 189-208.

Turner, A., Doxa, M. O'Sullivan, D. &Penn, A. (2001) From isovists to visibility graphs: a methodology for the analysis of architectural space. *Environment and Planning B: Planning and Design, 28* 103-121.

Tversky, B. *Remembering spaces.* (2000b). In E. Tulving & F. I. M. Craik (Eds.), Handbook of Memory, ch.23. New York: Oxford University Press. 363-378.

Advancing the Understanding of Spatial Cognition by Considering Control

Holger Schultheis (schulth@sfbtr8.uni-bremen.de)
SFB/TR 8 Spatial Cognition, Universität Bremen, 28334 Bremen, Germany

Abstract

The ability to process spatial information is crucial for various tasks as diverse as, navigation, planning layouts, and managing abstract concepts. Accordingly, considerable effort has been spent on understanding how spatial cognition is realized in the human mind. These endeavors have, however, so far virtually neglected one important aspect of spatial cognition, namely control. In this contribution we show that neglecting control constitutes a serious lack in understanding spatial cognition. Moreover, we propose conceptions for computational cognitive models including control for two particular spatial cognition tasks. Besides constituting first approaches to integrating control and spatial cognition these models potentially allow giving a more detailed account of the respective spatial cognition phenomena than currently available theories.

Control in Spatial Cognition

The ability to process spatial information, reason about space, and communicate about it is crucial in various domains of human endeavor. Without this ability people would not be able to, for instance, navigate their environment, exchange knowledge about dangerous or attractive places, plan vacations, execute directed movements, etc. Apart from these domains spatial cognition has furthermore been shown to be essential for managing abstract concepts (e.g., Torralbo, Santiago, & Lupianez, 2006) and gaining scientific insight (Machamer, Darden, & Carver, 2000). Thus, spatial cognition plays an important role in virtually all human activity.

According to this importance there has been considerable effort to unravel how spatial information is processed in the human mind. For example, abundant experimental data exists on human performance in tasks like perspective taking (e.g., Avraamides & Kelly, 2005), navigation (e.g., Golledge, 1995), and architectural design (e.g., Verstijnen, Leeuwen, Goldschmidt, Hamel, & Hennessey, 1998). Such data has usually been analyzed and interpreted with respect to the types of representations and / or operations defined on these representations used during spatial cognition. By taking such a focus on representations and (corresponding) operations, researchers, so far, mostly (see Allen, 1999, for an exception) seem to have neglected a third aspect essential for understanding spatial cognition, namely control.

The necessity for taking control into account is nicely exhibited by work done in the philosophy of science. There it is a general observation that proper explanations of scientific phenomena need to include—though sometimes named differently—control aspects. For instance, in terms of the mechanisms approach to scientific explanation proposed by Machamer et al. (2000), to be able to understand a phenomenon it is not enough to consider only the entities and activities involved in the scientific phenomenon. As Bechtel (2005) remarks, "The secret (...) is to organize components appropriately so that their operations are orchestrated to produce something beyond what the components can do." In addition to illustrating that control should be part of a proper explanatory description, Bechtel's remark highlights the fact that control (which he terms "organize", and "orchestrated") might in some cases even be an indispensable aspect for arriving at a satisfactory explanation of some phenomenon.

Consequently, neglecting control in trying to understand spatial cognition and, thus, an essential part of human behavior, seems to be insufficient. It is not alone the (type of) representations and their associated processes which constitute the basis for human spatial cognition, but also how these representations and operations are organized. To the best of our knowledge, however, detailed accounts of control in spatial cognition are missing so far. This is not to say that existing models of human spatial knowledge processing (e.g., Gunzelmann, Anderson, & Douglas, 2004; Barkowsky, 2001) are realized without involving control mechanisms. Any computational model necessarily has some form of control mechanisms implemented, because otherwise it would not lead to reasonable results. However, these control mechanisms have been realized more as the result of this necessity than as the result of a careful consideration of the specifics of human control mechanisms in the respective tasks. Put differently, available control conceptions are rather unelaborate by-products of developing models which mainly focus on representations and operations.

In this contribution we will show that explicitly considering control in spatial cognition is directly relevant to gain a satisfactory understanding of spatial cognition and, thus, the available approaches are insufficient. Furthermore, we will propose conceptions for two computational models including control for two spatial cognition tasks. Since control has been virtually neglected so far in spatial cognition research, these models are the first to integrate aspects of both cognitive control and spatial cognition. In addition, the models potentially allow giving more detailed accounts of the modeled spatial cognition phenomena than previously proposed theories for these phenomena.

The remainder of this article is structured as follows: In the next section the phenomena observed in human imaginal perspective taking, existing explanatory approaches for this task, how considering control might improve the explanatory power of existing approaches, and first steps towards a computational cognitive model for imaginal perspective taking will be detailed. The subsequent section will comprise the same aspects, but for a different spatial cognition task, namely the apprehension of spatial terms. Finally, issues for future work will be highlighted in the conclusions.

Control in Imaginal Perspective Taking

As Rieser (1989) remarks, planning and executing actions when moving through an environment requires judging spatial relations in this environment from certain locations and / or orientations before the moving body actually is at the corresponding locations / orientations. Likewise, for example tele-operating a vehicle, giving and understanding route directions, or considering whether changing one's location will improve one's view on some audio-visual display may call for judging spatial relations from certain perspectives without moving the body into this perspective. Common to all these situations is that (a) one is inside the environment for which the spatial relations have to be identified and (b) the sensory information about the environment available is just the egocentric visual and auditory impression (i.e., in particular, a map-like bird's eye view is not available). The task of judging spatial relations in such situations from a different perspective than the bodily one has been termed *imaginal perspective taking* (*IPT* see May, 2004).

As illustrated by the above examples, IPT is essential for everyday life. Thus, IPT mirrors the importance of spatial cognition in general for human behavior (see above) and, accordingly, in order to understand how this ability is realized in the human mind numerous experiments have been conducted. The general setup of such experiments and their main results will be described in the next section.

Investigation of Imaginal Perspective Taking

Growing interest in understanding IPT has resulted in an abundant number of experiments (see e.g., Avraamides & Kelly, 2005; May, 2004; Farrell & Robertson, 1998; Easton & Sholl, 1995; Presson & Montello, 1994; Rieser, 1989). Although they differ with respect to the precise factors they are investigating, the general design is usually the same in these experiments.

A typical IPT experiment consists of two phases. In the first phase subjects are placed at a certain location with a certain orientation in an environment. Besides the participants there are a number of objects in the environment which surround the subject (see Figure 1; the location of the person is at the origin of the two arrows, her orientation is indicated by the solid arrow). The participants are told to memorize the locations of the objects. After the subjects have sufficiently learned the spatial arrangement the second phase begins[1]. In the second phase they are placed in the same environment and usually at the same location and orientation as in the first phase. This time, however, they are deprived of any visual or auditory information (e.g., by blindfolding and putting on headphones). The subjects are then asked to judge a number of orientation relations between themselves and the surrounding objects. Importantly, they often have to judge this relation

---

[1]Sometimes the participants are tested in environments they already know from everyday life. The first phase is obsolete then.

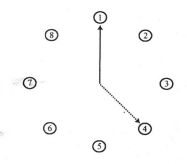

Figure 1: Prototypical experimental arrangement used in IPT studies.

as if they would be located or oriented differently than they actually are. For example, considering the setup shown in Figure 1 the subject might be asked to judge the relation of object 6 to herself as if she would be oriented to object 4 (the pretended orientation is indicated by the dashed arrow). The measures commonly used in such experiments are the times participants need to indicate and the accuracy (determined as degrees of angular deviation) with which they can indicate the asked for orientation.

Based on this general framework several factors have been varied in the particular experiments to elucidate the representations and processes used by humans during IPT. Studies differ, for instance, whether (a) they use irregularly or regularly arranged objects, (b) they test in small scale (e.g., a room) or large scale environments (e.g., a campus), (c) they test in familiar or unfamiliar (i.e., newly learned) environments, (d) a virtual or real environment is used, or (e) the participants have to indicate the asked for orientation verbally or by pointing. Regardless of such specifics, however, there are some general results occurring under virtually every experimental condition. First, judging relations from an imaginal perspective is harder, that is, takes more time and is less accurate, than judging relations from the actual perspective. This is true for both imaginal perspectives resulting from a change in orientation (the subject has to imagine facing in a different direction than he actually is) or a change in location (the subject has to imagine being in a different location than he actually is). Second, imaginal orientation changes seem to be more difficult than imaginal location changes. Third, the decline in performance observed with imaginal changes in orientation is linearly proportional to the angular difference between the actual and the imaginal orientation. Some studies, like the one by Easton and Sholl (1995), also point at a proportional relation between the performance in imaginal change of location and the distance between the actual and the imagined location. Yet, this relation seems to hold only under certain environmental / experimental conditions (cf. May, 2004; Rieser, 1989).

Existing Explanations

The prevalent explanation for the experimental results described in the previous section has been in terms of analogical rotation and translation processes (e.g., Sholl, 2001; Farrell & Robertson, 1998). Simply speaking, the general assumption is that humans are able to mentally rotate and / or translate themselves into the position requested for the current task and then can judge spatial relations from this (mentally taken) position. To give a more detailed account on how such mental rotation of oneself might be realized, several types of representation structures and processes have been proposed.

Sholl (2000), for example, has suggested that the human IPT ability relies on a set of separate allo- and ego-centric representation structures. The former mainly represents the object-to-object relations of the objects in the environment. The latter constitutes a viewpoint-dependent self-centered coordinate system which is superimposed / based on the allocentric representation. This ego-centric coordinate system can be viewed as some kind of filter or mediator between the allo-centric representation and the ego-centric representation of space: By superimposing the ego-centric coordinate system over the allo-centric representation the object-to-object relations can be transformed into self-referenced coordinates (e.g., some object is in front of oneself).

Normally this ego-centric representation coincides with the actual bodily position in the environment, that is, objects in the environment which are in front of one's body will be represented as being in front of oneself. Importantly, however, Sholl (2000) assumes that it is also possible to dissociate the ego-centric coordinate system from the bodily position. In doing so, humans are able to transform the allo-centrically represented spatial information into an ego-centric representation assuming a position and / or orientation of oneself which is different from the bodily held position. According to Sholl it is precisely this ability to dissociate the self-centered coordinate system from the body which allows IPT. When asked to judge the relation between an object as if oneself would have a position and / or orientation which differs from the bodily one, humans need only rotate and / or translate their ego-centered coordinate system to the requested position and can then read off the spatial relation between themselves and the target object. Yet, rotating and translating the ego-centric coordinate system is not without cost. Similar to the conception of the mental rotation of objects proposed by Shepard and Metzler (1971), it is assumed that mentally rotating / translating the self-reference system is analog to rotating / translating one's body. This implies that the time needed to take an imaginal perspective is proportional to the angular disparity between actual and imagined perspective or the distance between actual and imagined position for rotation and translation, respectively.

These implications are supported regarding rotations, where the time needed to take the imaginal perspective grows proportionally with increasing disparity (see above). Yet, the empirical evidence regarding translations is ambiguous. Only some of the studies investigating translations (e.g., Easton & Sholl, 1995) have found a relation between distance and mental translation times, while other experiments could not replicate this finding (e.g., Rieser, 1989).

As the work by May (2004) (see also May, 2000, 1996) suggests these ambiguous results regarding translation tasks stem from a misconception of analogical transformation theories of IPT. Instead of positing that people mentally rotate or translate themselves, he assumes that the performance patterns observed in IPT studies are better explained by conflicts between incompatible action vectors. More precisely, in his conception the ego-centric pointing direction defined by the actual body position and orientation interferes with the requested (imaginal) pointing position and thus hampers judging spatial relations from the imaginal perspective. May assumes that the conflict is so much more severe the greater the angular difference between the actual and the imagined direction is. Several things are noteworthy with respect to this account. First, the conflict is assumed to occur at the level of action selection. Second, the difficulty of imaginal translations should depend only on the discrepancy of pointing directions between actual and imaginal perspective and not on the distance between actual and imagined position—a claim which has been supported by the experiments of May (2004). Third, May's conception can also easily account for the proportionally increasing difficulty of imaginal rotations with increasing rotation angle, since the angular disparity between actual and imagined pointing direction increases with rotational angle. Consequently, this conflict theory does not only reconcile contradictory experimental results, but also gives a more parsimonious account for IPT. Thus, May's theory seems to be superior to the analogical transformation approaches.

Nevertheless, on closer inspection of the theory, two things become apparent. For one, May's conception is still far from constituting a satisfactory explanation of human IPT. Besides positing that conflicts underlie the performance deficits in IPT the theory does not provide much detail on complementary aspects necessary to give a full account of human IPT. In addition, control seems to be crucial for explaining the human behavior in IPT tasks.

In the next section we will elaborate why and how control is essential for explaining IPT. Doing this will not only substantiate and corroborate our initial claim of the importance of considering control in spatial cognition, but at the same time result in a first conception for a computational model of IPT.

Including Control

The importance of control for explaining IPT becomes clear when considering research on task switching. *Task switching* (see Monsell, 2003, for an overview) refers to the ability of humans to change the task currently worked on and still perform the involved tasks quite accurately even if the stimuli and motor responses involved in the tasks are quite similar or even identical (called *bivalent* stimuli and responses). Since task switching requires the organized reconfiguration of mental resources, it is generally assumed that successful task switching heavily involves the control faculties of the human mind. Due to this relation task switching has been studied extensively (e.g., Allport, Styles, & Hsieh, 1994) to gain insight into human control mechanisms. In the light of the current discussion the following three results which have emerged from the studies are of major importance:

- Task execution is slower and more error prone just after a task switch. This decrement in task performance after switching is called *switch cost*.

- Switch cost can be reduced if the participants are allowed to prepare for a change in tasks before performing the (just changed to) task.

- Preparation for a switch does not eliminate switch cost completely. This has been interpreted such that a complete switch of tasks can only be executed after the stimuli to be processed in the scope of the task have been presented.

In the light of these three effects reconsideration of typical IPT tasks as described above reveals several similarities of IPT to task switching. To see this assume (a) that the case in which the imagined perspective coincides with the bodily perspective corresponds to the condition where the task is not switched and (b) that the case in which actual and imagined perspective do not coincide corresponds to the condition where the task has to be switched. Given these correspondences the similarities between IPT and task switching are the following: First, IPT uses bivalent stimuli and responses, because both the stimuli (i.e., the target objects) and the responses (indicating the direction to the target object) are used for all perspectives. Second, taking an imagined perspective (as task switching) is costly. Third, as shown by Sohn and Carlson (2003) the costs for taking an imagined perspectives can be reduced by a suitable preparation time. Fourth, preparation time does not completely abolish the cost for taking an imagined perspective (May, 2004; Sohn & Carlson, 2003; Sholl, 2001). Importantly, as the experiments by (May, 2004) exhibit the requested perspective can only be taken completely after the stimulus for the task (namely the target object) has been presented.

Given this correspondence between task switching and IPT as well as the fact that task switching is generally assumed to rely on control mechanisms implies that considering control is crucial for understanding human IPT behavior. Moreover, it allows drawing on already existing results from task switching research when developing accounts of IPT processes. Meiran (2000), for instance, proposed a computational model of task switching which is able to explain several of the empirically observed effects. Interestingly, in reproducing the effects the model explains task switching difficulties as mainly arising from a response conflict between the response for the previous task and the response for the current (i.e., just switched to) task. Transferred to the perspective switching domain this means that IPT difficulties mainly arise from the conflict between the response when the imagined and the bodily perspective are alike ("no switch") and the response when the two perspectives are not alike ("switch"). Not only does this correspond nicely to May's original conception, but also a study by Wang (2004) has recently supported this idea. It is because of this correspondence regarding the locus of conflict that the approach of Meiran (2000) seems especially suited as a starting point for developing a control model of IPT.

Of course, it is not possible to import the model of Meiran (2000) one-to-one into the IPT domain. For example, the representation format for stimuli and responses needs to be modified to account for the particularities of the IPT task. Furthermore, it is not immediately clear whether response repetition effects (i.e., the increased performance during task switching if the response is the same in two subsequent trials) and, thus, the corresponding model behavior also holds for IPT. Nevertheless, main parts of Meiran's model like the task dependent—and dynamically changing—weighting of the task sets and the computations used to select the final re-

sponse seem well suited to model IPT. As a result, the presented analysis of IPT shows the relevance of control for understanding IPT. What is more, the analysis leads to a first detailed conception of a computational model for IPT[2].

Control in Spatial Term Apprehension

Another highly researched area of human spatial cognition is how people use language to communicate about spatial situations. Although the use of language in spatial cognition has many more facets (e.g., Tversky & Lee, 1998; Levinson, 1996), we will concentrate on the apprehension of spatial terms such as "above", "right", etc. More precisely, we will focus on the computational framework for spatial term use developed by Logan and colleagues (see, e.g., Carlson & Logan, 2001; Logan & Sadler, 1996). Although such a focus might seem restrictive given the multitude of approaches to spatial term apprehension, for this contribution such focusing seems necessary / expedient for at least three reasons. First, due to space limitations it is not possible to discuss more than one approach and its relation to control. Second, the considered computational framework has been proven to be a valuable framework for analyzing and accounting for empirical data. Third, the framework particularly nicely allows pointing out the relevance of control for understanding the processes involved in spatial term apprehension.

Based on a number of experiments the computational framework proposes that apprehending spatial terms comprises at least (a) spatially indexing (i.e., identifying) the relevant objects, (b) imposing a frame of reference (FoR) on one of the objects, and (c) based on this FoR determine the relation between the two objects. To illustrate this account, consider the following example: You are asked to verify the assertion "The fly is above the table" given a depiction containing a fly and a table (see Figure 2). According to Logan's account, to verify the statement you first need to find the table and the fly in the depiction. Once you found them you now need to judge the relation between them. To do this, Logan and Sadler (1996) posit, you superimpose a FoR on the table (indicated with dashed arrows in Figure 2). The FoR is superimposed on the table, because the fly has to be located with respect / reference to the table. Furthermore, FoRs are assumed to be coordinate system-like representations which can be anchored in objects and which structure the space on which they are imposed. Thus, by imposing a reference frame on the table the space surrounding the table is structured and objects populating this surrounding space can be assigned a spatial relation with respect to the table. In the scope of the example this means that once you have imposed the FoR on the table you can determine the spatial relation of the fly to the table and, as a result, verify the given statement.

Given this conception the need for and importance of control for understanding the use of spatial terms stems from the fact that there are situations in which more than one (type

---

[2]At first sight it may seem that this is not a first detailed conception, since Hiatt, Trafton, Harrison, and Schultz (2004) and Gunzelmann et al. (2004) have already proposed computational models of perspective taking. Yet, the former seems to be more a cognitively inspired technical solution than a cognitive model and the latter does model a task which differs regarding important aspects from IPT (e.g., a map-like view of the environment is continuously visually available).

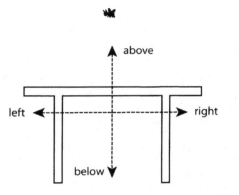

Figure 2: An example situation for assigning / verifying spatial terms.

of) FoR can be superimposed on the reference object. Considering again the above example at least three FoRs—which correspond to the three FoRs proposed by Levinson (1996)—could be employed to verify the assertion: First, one could use the intrinsic reference frame of the table where the above-below axis runs parallel to the legs of the table. Second, one could also use a relative FoR where the above-below axis coincides with the spine. Finally, a third alternative would be to use an absolute reference frame. In an absolute FoR the above-below axis coincides with gravity or cardinal directions. As a result, if several FoRs are potentially available, the selection of one of the FoRs becomes an essential aspect of the apprehension of spatial terms. In particular, as Carlson (1999) has shown (see also Carlson-Radvansky & Irwin, 1994; Carlson-Radvansky & Jiang, 1998) this selection exhibits the following properties:

- When using spatial propositions, initially, several FoRs are activated simultaneously.

- The activation of the different FoRs is automatic in the sense that people do not seem to be able to deliberately avoid activation of separate FoRs.

- Final selection of one of the rivaling FoRs seems to be realized by inhibiting the other (not selected) FoRs.

This pattern of properties of the processes involved in the selection of FoRs strongly suggests the relevance of control to the use of spatial terms, since it parallels observations in tasks usually assumed to largely involve control mechanisms. The Stroop task, for instance, has been shown (see, e.g., Cohen & Huston, 1994) to exhibit nearly identical patterns of properties as those outlined above: Representations for word meaning and word color are activated simultaneously; activation of word meaning cannot deliberately be avoided; and final selection of one of the representations is realized by inhibiting the other. Following a similar argument as in the case of IPT this shows that considering control is crucial to obtain a complete and satisfactory understanding of the use of spatial terms. What is more, this correspondence also opens up possible approaches for developing a detailed account of one crucial aspect of human spatial term apprehension.

Due to the nature of the selection process winner-takes-all networks (i.e., networks in which the nodes inhibit each other and activate themselves through reflexive connections, cf. Hagan, Demuth, & Beale, 1996) seem to be especially suited for realizing a detailed account of the involved control mechanisms (see Schultheis, under review, for a more thorough argument regarding the appropriateness of winner-takes-all networks). As with IPT this first conception of a computational account will probably need to be adapted to the specifics of the use of spatial terms. Nevertheless, even this first conception of adapting existing computational principles constitutes a more detailed explanation of the mechanisms involved in the selection of FoRs during spatial term apprehension than those currently available.

Conclusions

Previous research in spatial cognition has mainly concentrated on identifying representations and processes but virtually neglected control. In this article it is shown that rather than investigating spatial cognition in isolation from control these two aspects of human cognition need to be considered together. A close analysis of two well researched spatial cognition tasks, namely imaginal perspective taking and apprehension of spatial terms, revealed that in both tasks control processes can be assumed to play an important role. As a result, trying to understand human spatial cognition without considering control seems to be unreasonable.

In response to these observations we conceptualized two computational models for the two spatial cognition tasks. Importantly, these two models take into account control aspects and thus realize first detailed accounts integrating control and spatial cognition. Besides being integrated the two proposed models also potentially allow a more thorough explanation of human performance in both spatial cognition tasks than previous theories.

One major issue for future work is to further investigate to what extent the control mechanisms for particular spatial tasks differ from each other. Judging from the above analysis it would seem that the control mechanisms involved in spatial cognition might differ considerably for different spatial tasks. Yet, it seems premature to take a definite decision on this question at the moment—further investigations will have to show whether the control mechanisms in the different tasks are distinct or can be reconciled with each other or maybe reduced to a common basis. In exploring this issues, we plan to (a) refine the two proposed models, (b) extend the general ideas exhibited by the models to other areas of spatial cognition, and (c) identify further control principles which might be important for understanding spatial cognition.

Acknowledgments

In this paper work done in the project R1-[ImageSpace] of the Transregional Collaborative Research Center SFB/TR 8 Spatial Cognition is presented. Funding by the German Research Foundation (DFG) is gratefully acknowledged. We also thank the reviewers for their helpful suggestions.

References

Allen, G. L. (1999). Children's control of reference systems in spatial tasks: Foundations of spatial cognitive skill?

Spatial Cognition and Computation, 1(4), 413 - 429.

Allport, A., Styles, E. A., & Hsieh, S. (1994). Shifting intentional set: Exploring the dynamic control of tasks. In C. Umilta & M. Moscovitch (Eds.), *Attention and Performance XV*. Cambridge, MA: MIT Press.

Avraamides, M. N., & Kelly, J. W. (2005). Imagined perspective changing within and across novel environments. In C. Freksa, M. Knauff, B. Krieg-Brückner, B. Nebel, & T. Barkowsky (Eds.), *Spatial cognition IV*.

Barkowsky, T. (2001). Mental processing of geographic knowledge. In D. R. Montello (Ed.), *Spatial information theory (COSIT 2001)*. Berlin: Springer-Verlag.

Bechtel, W. (2005). The challenge of characterizing operations in the mechanisms underlying behavior. *Journal of the experimental analysis of behavior, 84*(3), 313 - 325.

Carlson, L. A. (1999). Selecting a reference frame. *Spatial Cognition and Computation, 1*(4), 365 - 379.

Carlson, L. A., & Logan, G. D. (2001). Using spatial terms to select an object. *Memory & Cognition, 29*(6), 883 - 892.

Carlson-Radvansky, L. A., & Irwin, D. E. (1994). Reference frame activation during spatial term assignment. *Journal of Memory and Language, 33*, 646 - 671.

Carlson-Radvansky, L. A., & Jiang, Y. (1998). Inhibition accompanies reference-frame selection. *Psychological Science, 9*(5), 386 - 391.

Cohen, J. D., & Huston, T. A. (1994). Progress in the use of interactive models for understanding attention and performance. In C. Umilta & M. Moscovitch (Eds.), *Attention and Performance XV*. Cambridge, MA: MIT Press.

Easton, R. D., & Sholl, M. J. (1995). Object-array structure, frames of reference, and retrieval of spatial knowledge. *Journal of Experimental Psychology: Learning, Memory, and Cognition, 21*(2), 483 - 500.

Farrell, M. J., & Robertson, I. H. (1998). Mental rotation and the automatic updating of body-centered spatial relationships. *Journal of Experimental Psychology: Learning, Memory, and Cognition, 24*(1), 227 - 233.

Golledge, R. G. (1995). Path selection and route preference in human navigation: A progress report. In *Proceedings of the conference on spatial information theory*.

Gunzelmann, G., Anderson, J. R., & Douglas, S. (2004). Orientation tasks with multiple views of space: strategies and performance. *Spatial Cognition and Computation, 4*(3).

Hagan, M. T., Demuth, H. B., & Beale, M. (1996). *Neural network design*. Boston: PWS Publishing.

Hiatt, L., Trafton, J., Harrison, A., & Schultz, A. (2004). A cognitive model for spatial perspective taking. In M. Lovett, C. Schunn, C. Lebiere, & P. Munro (Eds.), *Proceedings of the 6th ICCM*. Mahwah, NJ: LEA.

Levinson, S. (1996). Frames of reference and molyneux's question: Cross-linguistic evidence. In P. Bloom,

M. Peterson, L. Nadel, & M. Garrett (Eds.), *Language and space*.

Logan, G. D., & Sadler, D. D. (1996). A computational analysis of the apprehension of spatial relations. In P. Bloom, M. Peterson, M. Garrett, & L. Nadel (Eds.), *Language and space* (chap. 13). MA: M.I.T Press.

Machamer, P., Darden, L., & Carver, C. F. (2000). Thinking about mechanisms. *Philosophy of Science, 67*, 1 - 25.

May, M. (1996). Cognitive and embodied modes of spatial imagery. *Psychologische Beiträge, 38*, 418 - 434.

May, M. (2000). *Kognition im Umraum*. Wiesbaden: Deutscher Universitäts-Verlag.

May, M. (2004). Imaginal perspective switches in remembered environments: transformation versus interference accounts. *Cognitive Psychology, 48*, 163-206.

Meiran, N. (2000). Modeling cognitive control in task switching. *Psychological Research, 63*, 234 - 249.

Monsell, S. (2003). Task switching. *TRENDS in Cognitive Sciences, 7*(3), 134 - 140.

Presson, C. C., & Montello, D. R. (1994). Updating after rotational and translational body movements: coordinate structure of perspective space. *Perception, 23*, 1447 - 1455.

Rieser, J. J. (1989). Access to knowledge of spatial structure at novel points of observation. *Journal of Experimental Psychology: Learning, Memory, and Cognition, 15*(6), 1157 - 1165.

Schultheis, H. (under review). A computational model of control mechanisms in spatial term use.

Shepard, R. N., & Metzler, J. (1971). Mental rotation of three-dimensional objects. *Science*(171), 701–703.

Sholl, M. J. (2000). The functional separability of self-reference and object-to-object systems in spatial memory. In S. Ó Nualláin (Ed.), *Spatial cognition*.

Sholl, M. J. (2001). The role of a self-reference system in spatial navigation. In D. R. Montello (Ed.), *Spatial information theory (COSIT 2001)*. Berlin: Springer.

Sohn, M.-H., & Carlson, R. A. (2003). Viewpoint alignment and response conflict during spatial judgement. *Psychonomic Bulletin & Review, 10*(4), 907 - 916.

Torralbo, A., Santiago, J., & Lupianez, J. (2006). Flexible conceptual projection of time onto spatial frames of reference. *Cognitive Science, 30*(4), 745 - 757.

Tversky, B., & Lee, P. (1998). How space structures language. In C. Freksa, C. Habel, & K. F. Wender (Eds.), *Spatial cognition. an interdisciplinary approach to representing and processing spatial knowledge*.

Verstijnen, I. M., Leeuwen, C. van, Goldschmidt, G., Hamel, R., & Hennessey, J. M. (1998). Creative discovery in imagery and perception: Combining is relatively easy, restructuring takes a sketch. *Acta Psychologica, 99*, 177–200.

Wang, R. F. (2004). Action, verbal response and spatial reasoning. *Cognition, 94*(2), 185 - 192.

Functionalism, Computational Complexity and Design Stance

Francesco Gagliardi (francesco.gagliardi@libero.it)
Department of Physical Sciences — University of Naples "*Federico II*"
Via Cintia — I-80126 Napoli, Italy

Abstract

In this paper we present some considerations concerning links between functionalism and computational complexity in the field of cognitive models of human mind. The computational complexity theory allows us to relate the problem of the *fungibility* of internal implementation of a function with its computational tractability and therefore we propose the design of the heuristic as a key aspect of the explanatory power of a model. These considerations allow us to introduce the *mesoscopic functionalism* as a functionalism for which internal implementation is not negligible but that permits multiple realization only for the implementation of the heuristic. This kind of functionalism overcomes underdetermination of traditional functionalistic models and, at the same time, avoids a shift toward hyperdetermination. The word *mesoscopic*, borrowed from the statistical physics, is meant as the intermediate level between the macroscopic one of the system behaviour and microscopic one of its implementation. Moreover, the need for a mesoscopic descriptive level is related with some explanatory strategies proposed by Dennett such as the intentional and the design stance. The latter is the one we propose as the most adequate.

Keywords: Functionalism; Computational Complexity; Intractability; Heuristic; Design Stance; Intentional Stance; Artificial Intelligence; Mesoscopic Functionalism.

Introduction

Functionalism was introduced in the philosophy of mind as a critical position of reductionist materialism in the mind-body problem, by H. Putnam in her seminal article *Minds and machines* (1960). Putnam introduced the idea that the mental states can be studied not by referring them directly to brain states, but on the basis of their functional organization.

The functionalistic models are based on the reproduction of the macroscopic properties of the system behaviour by means of the specifications of the stimulus-response relations. Therefore, the functionalism allows a function to have the multiple realizability, given the input-output relation.

A possible criticism to this types of models is their *underdetermination* (e.g. Verschure et al., 1995) which can be faced considering how the internal structure of a model can have a explanatory role.

Then we start analysing the link between function and structure on the base of the computational complexity of the function under study.

Functionalism and Computational Complexity

Theory of Computational Complexity

Theory of computational complexity (Papadimitriou 1994) is part of the theory of computation dealing with the resources required during computation to perform a given task.

Complexity theory differs from computability theory, which deals with whether a problem can be solved at all, regardless of the resources required.

The most common considered resource is time. The time complexity of a problem is the number of steps that it takes to solve an instance of the problem as a function of its size, independently of implementation.

There are two main complexity classes belonging to tractability of function. The class P (*Polynomial*) is the set of problems that can be solved by a deterministic machine in polynomial time.

The class NP (*Non deterministic Polynomial*) consists of all those problems whose solutions can be verified in polynomial time given the right information, or equivalently, whose solution can be found in polynomial time on a non-deterministic machine. Roughly speaking, a problem is called NP if the time required to solve problem instances grows at least exponentially with the size of the instances and the problems in this class have the property that their solutions can be checked in a efficient manner.

This class contains many combinatorial problems that people would like to be able to solve effectively, including the boolean satisfiability problem, the travelling salesman problem, max-cut graph problem and Thagard's foundational formalization of coherence-based cognitive problems (Thagard, 2000; Thagard & Verbeurgt, 1998).

Tractable and Intractable Problems

Problems solvable in theory, but which cannot be solved in practice, are called intractable. What can be solved "in practice" is open to debate, but in general only problems which have polynomial-time solutions are solvable for more than the smallest inputs.

Indeed a problem with at least exponential-time solution are not usable in practice, because exponential growth means that even moderate-sized instances cannot be solved in any reasonable time, for an actual example its computation would take much longer than the current age of the universe.

Then the P class corresponds to an intuitive idea of the problems which can be effectively solved in the worst cases, and NP class corresponds to intractable problems.

We can also argue that the NP class corresponds to our own real-world experience of the problems that are hard to solve, but whose solutions are easy to verify.

Heuristics

The *designer* of systems facing to intractable problems, as the *natural selection* does for biological systems, should strive to find smart way to bypass these problems.

A heuristic is any aid to reduce problem-solving effort, a rule of thumb, but may be unproved or incapable of proof.

Computationally, a heuristic is a procedure which usually finds good solutions and runs quickly, but with no absolute assurances.

The most known heuristic techniques are neural networks, Boltzman machines, genetic algorithms, hill climbing, tabu search, simulated annealing, swarm computing, ant colony optimisation, and other (Kumar, 1992; Reeves, 1993). Many of these techniques are bio-inspired and they are widely used or created within bio-inspired AI research.

More formally, in combinatorial optimisation (Cook et al., 1997), a heuristic is a technique designed to solve a problem that ignores whether the output can be proven to be correct, but which usually produces a good result. It is intended to gain computational performance or conceptual simplicity at the cost of accuracy or precision. The aim is to achieve a *good enough* output rather than exact output but this is rewarded with a great computational performance able to turn intractable problems into tractable ones.

Experimental evidence shows that heuristics work well under many circumstances, but in certain cases lead to very poor performances. One can find specially crafted problem instances where the heuristic will produce very bad results or run very slowly.

Functionalism and Tractability

We observe that canonical functionalism, concerning tractable problems, is well posed and poorly exposed to criticisms, in fact these functions can be considered *structure independent* entities.

We consider, for instance, the simple task of putting elements of a list in a certain order (e.g. sorting phrase list in lexicographical order). This is a tractable problem and there are many well-known algorithms to solve it in polynomial time (e.g. Quick sort, Merge sort, Heap sort, Shell sort, Insertion sort, Bubble sort, Selection sort, and many more). Notwithstanding the spectrum of solution techniques is extremely wide, many typical sorting algorithms have all quite similar time performances: average time complexity is $O(n \log n)$ and is upper bounded by $O(n^2)$ for the worst case, where n denotes the size of the given input (Cormen et al., 2001). Obviously we exclude intentionally computationally expensive dummy algorithms.

Then the input-output function specification is well posed and the used specific algorithm is entirely negligible

because this choice weakly biases only the execution time (see Table 1).

So we can argue there is not a *function-structure coupling* for tractable functions. A system designed to perform these tasks can be rightly modelled at functional macroscopic level as black-box with well-know stimulus-response behaviour (see Figure 1, on top). Then the *mesoscopic* level of solution techniques between macroscopic functional specification and microscopic implementative details can be neglected.

In other words, the resolving algorithm (the internal realization) is an exchangeable, *fungible* part of the computational system, then we have the correctness of multiple-realizability and we can consider tractable functions as *structure-free* entities without underdetermination.

Table 1: Influence of internal realization on functions.

	Function		
	Tractable	**Intractable**	
		Without Heuristic	**With Heuristic**
System Behaviour (I/O)	The same	The same (It is *de facto* incomputable)	Variable
System Execution Time	Weakly Variable	Variable	Variable

Functionalism and Intractability

All computable functions, in principle, are defined by an effective input-output relation, but intractable ones are *de facto* incomputable for almost all not trivial inputs.

A computational inexpensive strategy must be pursued by means of heuristic computations and due to this, the systems output becomes dependent from specific selected heuristic and also from its internal parameters. The concrete realized function is different from the exact intractable function because the choice of heuristic influences the carried out output in addition to execution time (see Table 1).

So the heuristic, between macroscopic functionality and microscopic implementation, is the real responsible of the arising input output relationship of systems.

Due to this we can argue there is a coupling between functional and executional aspects of a system, this implies a *function-structure coupling* for intractable functions.

Contrarily to tractable function, intractable ones are not structure-independent entities: the internal realization is the *core* of the function because it is absolutely not an exchangeable, fungible part of the computational system.

We observe that the multiple realizability for computationally intractable functions is not realizable at all because if we choose an exact fungible algorithm, the function becomes *de facto* incomputable and if we adopt a heuristic, the input-output behaviour is not more unambiguously defined. The multiple realizability produces a kind of "multiple behaviour" (more formally, we have a collection of heuristic functions, everyone with univocal output) (see Figure 1).

For a heuristically computed intractable function, the mesoscopic level of heuristic, or more precisely its design (that is a functional specification), is the essential aspect of the system because it defines unambiguously the input-output relation.

Obviously, also for intractable functions, the microscopic level of specific implementation can be neglected because it is uninfluential on system behaviour. Then multiple realizability can be allowed only underneath the mesoscopic level at the microscopic one.

Concluding, we remark that a macroscopic functionalist model is more than simply underdetermined, it is even unsuitable for intractable functions.

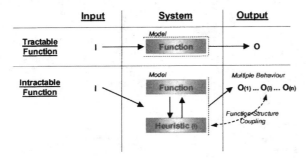

Figure 1: Function-Structure Relationship.

Cognitive Relevance of Heuristics and Computational Intractability

Experimental Evidences

In psychology the heuristics were proposed to explain how people make decisions, come to judgments and solve problems, typically when facing complex or incomplete information problems (e.g. Gigerenzer et al., 1999).

In real-world problems there are too many uncertainties and conflicts for having any hope to obtain a best solution for an optimisation function which perhaps could be indeterminate. The alternative approach to maximizing is *satisficing*, an alternative to optimisation for cases in which one gives up the idea of obtaining the *best* solution.

Satisficing is a concept due to Herbert Simon (1957, chap. 14, 15; see also Slote, (1989)) who identifies the decision making process whereby one chooses an option that is, while perhaps not the best, good enough. In this context of bounded rationality, humans search for good enough solutions by using heuristics.

Heuristic works well under many circumstances, but in certain cases leads to systematic cognitive poor performances. Tversky and Kahneman are two key figures in the discovery of human heuristics (Tversky & Kahneman;

1974) which lead to cognitive bias or irrational behaviour (e.g. availability heuristic, clustering illusion, and others).

Notably, they originated the *prospect theory* (Kahneman & Tversky; 1979) to explain irrational economic behaviour, these researches climaxed with the Nobel's prize at 2002.

Hence we observe how the impossibility of obtaining the best solution in condition of bounded rationality, forces to content with good enough solutions to be found by means of heuristics and how these sometime bring instead to the irrational behaviour.

In both cases is the heuristic internal implementation of the cognitive function to be responsible for the macroscopic behaviour.

Foundational Aspects

The *Cognitive Naturalism* is a computational conceptual framework for human mind understanding. It was proposed by Thagard (2000) and it is well-rooted on concepts related to computational complexity.

In fact the cognitive naturalism is based on the foundational computational formalization of the coherence as a combinatorial problem. This problem is proved to be computationally intractable and it is often efficiently faced with heuristics (see Thagard & Verbeurgt (1998) for a benchmarking among connectionist and other techniques).

According to the cognitive naturalism much of the human thinking is naturally understood as heuristic-based solution to combinatorial problems, in domains as diverse as social impression formation, scientific-theory, choice, discourse comprehension, visual perception, and decision making (see Thagard (2000) and Thagard & Verbeurgt (1998) for a panorama and related bibliography).

Thus, because of both experimental evidence and foundational aspects of the cognitive science, the theory of computational complexity, the combinatorial optimisation and the natural and computational heuristics become all theoretically interleaved key concepts to mind understanding.

The Mesoscopic Level of Functionalism

As we have shown above classical functionalism is well posed only for simply tractable functions because they can be considered structure independent entities.

In fact, the macroscopic descriptive level for the system behaviour is exhaustive respect to whole system (the internal realization is a fungible part of the system). However, this type of tractable functions are not much interesting for the cognitive modelling.

For the intractable functions, which are of great cognitive interest, the descriptive level for explaining and predicting the macroscopic behaviour is the mesoscopic level of the computational heuristic. In fact, in accordance with the theoretical considerations of the computational complexity and the experimental evidences with the human beings, it is not possible to predict the system behaviour without considering the used specific heuristic.

Then, functionalism neglecting the mesoscopic level of internal realization is unsuitable for human mind modelling. So we need to shift descriptive level of models from the macroscopic one to the mesoscopic one, taking into account subject-explicit heuristics as well as implicit unconscious heuristics.

A computational cognitive model has to realize the particular considered function through the same heuristic used by the human mind.

According to concept of the "fine-grain correspondence" proposed by Pylyshyn (1984; p. 121) the explanatory abilities of mesoscopic models is guaranteed from the equivalence between the heuristic internally used (both psychological ones and biological ones) and the heuristic realized by the natural systems.

In this mesoscopic models we are able to describe the heuristic in a functional way, because the internal realization of the heuristic at the lower microscopic-implementative level is absolutely irrelevant for the system behaviour.

Mesoscopic models are functional and structural models at the same time. They are *functional* models of computational heuristics because they neglect theirs internal microscopic implementation and from a another viewpoint they are *structural* models of macroscopic functionality because they resolve underdetermination of macroscopic level (see Figure 2).

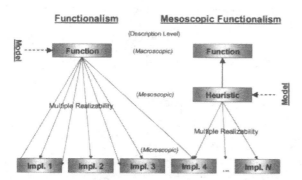

Figure 2: Functionalism and Mesoscopic Functionalism

We call this modelling approach *mesoscopic functionalism* because it shifts underdetermination only under the mesoscopic level, and then it allows multiple realizability only at microscopic level and not elsewhere.

Mesoscopic Functionalism and Artificial Intelligence

We can roughly divide artificial intelligence (AI) research field (Russel and Norvig; 2002) in two main schools of thought: *Classical* AI and *Nouvelle* AI.

Mesoscopic functionalism is utilized, more or less explicitly, both from the classical and nouvelle AI oriented to the cognitive modelling.

Some systems of classical AI are not pure functional models because the intractability of combinatorial explosion

for these systems is faced with heuristics. For instance, one of the early AI systems, General Problem Solver (GPS) (Newell & Simon, 1961), was designed from the beginning to carry out a heuristic computation, employing the same heuristic used by humans in some simple problems. The system used the heuristic of *means-ends analysis* realizing in this way a simple cognitive system. Within the limited class of puzzles it can handle, it turned out that the order in which the system considers subgoals and possible actions is similar to the way humans approach the same problems.

Also the nouvelle AI follows this mesoscopic approach if we observe that many of the bio-inspired techniques used, such as the connectionism and genetic algorithms, are widely used as heuristic in intractable computational problems also independently from their explicative role for the cognitive science.

The nouvelle AI, following the methodology of the bio-plausibility (e.g. PDP - Parallel Distributed Processing in Rumelhart et al. (1986) and McClelland et al., 1986), tacitly identified a descriptive mesoscopic level, which allows to reproduce the functionalities of the biological structures (e.g. the heuristic of the neural networks or the evolutionary algorithms of natural selection) and to neglect the physical-chemical microscopic details. So nouvelle AI reutilises the heuristic solution "designed" by nature to deal with intractable combinatorial problems.

Summarizing, the mesoscopic level has been tacitly selected from some bio-inspired nouvelle AI interested to structural bio-plausible models and also it has been taken into account explicitly from some cognitive oriented classical AI (e.g. IPP – Information Processing Psychology by Newell and Simon (1972)).

The cognitive explanatory power of all these mesoscopic models, both classical and nouvelle, is assured from constraints addressing correspondence of heuristics between human mind processing and internal artificial system processing, and this constraints are a requirement for the achievement of *thinking humanly* artificial systems.

In fact wholly according to Cordeschi (2002, Ch. 7) the prevalent attempt to line up functional versus structural model, with classical AI versus nouvelle AI is without real foundations (see also Cordeschi 2006a; 2006b).

Design Stance and Mesoscopic Functionalism

Daniel Dennett (1987) analysed three predictive explanatory strategies used by humans in order to understand the systems behaviour: the *intentional stance*, the *design stance* and the *physical stance*.

When we adopt the intentional stance regarding an entity, we try to explain its behaviour considering it as a rational agent whose actions are governed by its own desires and opinions. Instead, when we make predictions using the design stance, we assume the considered entity behaves such as it has been designed. We use the physical stance just for a not designed system and which we expect behaves according to the "laws of nature".

Table 2: Synthetic scheme of some ideas discussed in the text.

Complexity Class	Computation	Optimal Design	Solution	System Behaviour	Theories of Human Behaviour	Stances
Tractable	Exact	Yes	The best	Rational (Übermensch)	Classical	Intentional Stance
Intractable	Heuristic	No	Good Enough	Bounded Rational	Satisficing Theory (Simon)	Design Stance
			Poor	Irrational	Prospect Theory (Kahneman-Tversky)	

Following Dennett, the best strategy to be adopted to explain the human behaviour is the intentional stance. This hypothesis is based on a strong adaptationistic view of the natural selection (see Dennett, 1995), that assumes the optimality of the design of the human functionalities.

In fact, an optimal design enables us to neglect the internal realization of the considered functionalities and to adopt the intentional stance, while the design stance is to be used for those systems that are not optimally designed.

An objection to the use of the intentional stance comes from the computational complexity and from the finiteness of the resources, because in case of intractable functions, the optimal design would imply the use of the exact solution for the internal realization. But this is, *de facto*, incomputable and as matter of fact, we observe experimentally the effects of a "design" which is necessarily sub-optimal: in the best cases, a human behaviour characterized by a bounded rationality and in the worst cases, by an evident irrationality (see Table 2).

The computational limitations impose some limitations to human intentionality, as Brian Cantwell Smith (2002) argues:

> "Taken together, these [...] results (finite, embodied participatory creatures, subject to **massively strong computability limits**) radically undermine the classical image of a rational, all-knowing, übermensch. In its place we get an increasingly deep sense of a world of finite, embodied creatures, struggling to make their way around in —and struggling to make sense of— the world around them, **using partial, flawed, perspectival, incomplete, knowledge and skill**. [...] It is a humbling image."[1]

For "finite, embodied, participatory" entities such as human beings, the intentional stance is not able to explain the behaviour which in general cannot be assumed rational.

On the other hand, the design stance enables us to consider in which way a given cognitive functionality is internally realized (using "partial, flawed, perspectival, incomplete" heuristic knowledge and ability) and hence design stance allows us to explain the not rational behaviour (both bounded rational and irrational) taking into account the mesoscopic level of heuristics.

At most, the intentional stance can explain only, and just approximately, the bounded rational behaviour, but not the whole heuristic thinking (see last column of table 2).

In fact, for the good enough solutions, it is possible a description of the overall intent of the system, but only if we are not interested in explaining the specific good enough solution, obtained by the system through a heuristic computation.

Then we can state for entities that embody intractable functions, the necessity to adopt the design stance coincides with the construction of models based on that we called mesoscopic functionalism.

Concluding Remarks

The mesoscopic functionalism, here presented, enables us to overcome the contraposition between functional and structural models, being able to identify an intermediate descriptive level which resolves the under-determination of functionalistic models, avoiding the risk of hyperdetermination due to an *"asymptotic"* (see. Rosenblueth & Wiener; 1945) regression to the microscopic level of the structural models pushed up to synthetic bio-chemical or physical recreation (see Harnad, 1994).

Therefore mesoscopic functionalism, with its theoretic foundation on theory of computational complexity and its cognitive explicative role of heuristics, is the right *epistemological trade-off*, about model building, between full recreation of internal realization and explanatory power.

Also this methodological point of view is congruous with design stance which, according to computational limits of human intentionality, is more adequate than intentional stance to understand the human mind.

---

[1] Bold style is not in the original.

Acknowledgments

I wish to thank Prof. V. Cordeschi and Prof. G. Trautteur for the fruitful comments on an earlier version of this paper.

Heartedly thanks are due to Dr. A. Brindisi for her support.

References

Brian Cantwell Smith (2002) *God, approximately.* in Mark Richardson, W., Russell, R.J., Clayton, P., Wegter-McNelly, K. (Eds) (2002) *Science and the Spiritual Quest: New Essays by Leading Scientists.* Ed. Routledge; pp. 207-228. (ISBN: 0415257662) (http://www.ageofsignificance.org/people/bcsmith/print/smith-godapprox4.pdf)

Cook, W. J., Cunningham, W. H., Pulleyblank, W. R & Schrijver, A. (1997) *Combinatorial Optimization.* John Wiley & Sons

Cordeschi, R. (2002), *The Discovery of the Artificial: Behavior, Mind and Machines Before and Beyond Cybernetics*, Kluwer Academic Publishers, Dordrecht

Cordeschi, R. (2006a). Steps towards the synthetic method. Symbolic information processing and selforganizing systems in early Artificial Intelligence modeling. In M. Wheeler, P. Husbands, & O. Holland (Eds.), *The Mechanisation of mind in history.* Cambridge, MA: MIT Press (Forthcoming).

Cordeschi, R. (2006b). AI turns fifty: revisiting its origins. *Applied Artificial Intelligence*, Special Issue (Forthcoming).

Cormen, T. H., Leiserson, C. E., Rivest, R.L., & Stein, C. (2001) *Introduction to Algorithms, Second Edition.* MIT Press and McGraw-Hill.

Dennett, D. (1987). *The Intentional Stance.* The MIT Press.

Dennett, D. (1995). *Darwin's Dangerous Idea: Evolution and the Meanings of Life.* Simon and Schuster, New York.

Gigerenzer, G. & Todd, P.M. & the ABC Research Group (1999), *Simple Heuristics That Make Us Smart*, Oxford University Press

Harnad, S. (1994), Levels of functional equivalence in reverse bioengineering, *Artificial Life*, 1, pp. 293-301.

Kahneman D. e Tversky A. (1979). Prospect theory: An analysis of decision under risk. Econometrica, 47, 263-291

Kumar, V. (1992) *Algorithms for Constraint Satisfaction Problems: A Survey.* AI Magazine 13(1): 32-44.

McClelland, J.L., D.E. Rumelhart and the PDP Research Group (1986). *Parallel Distributed Processing: Explorations in the Microstructure of Cognition. Volume 2: Psychological and Biological Models*, Cambridge, MA: MIT Press

Newell, A. & Simon, H. A. (1961). GPS, a program that simulates human thought. In Billing, H., (Ed.), *Lernende Automaten*, pp. 109-124. R. Oldenbourg, Munich, Germany.

Newell, A., & Simon, H. A. (1972). *Human problem solving.* Englewood Cliffs, NJ: Prentice-Hall.

Papadimitriou, C.H. (1994) *Computational Complexity* Addison-Wesley.

Putnam, H. (1960). Minds and machines. In Hook, S., (Ed.) *Dimensions of Mind*, pp.138-164. Macmillan, London.

Pylyshyn, Z.W. (1984), *Computation and Cognition: Toward a Foundation for Cognitive Science*, MIT Press, Cambridge, MA.

Reeves, C. R. (Ed.) (1993) *Modern Heuristic Techniques for Combinatorial Problems.* John Wiley & Sons, Inc. New York, NY, USA

Rosenblueth, A. & Wiener, N. (1945) The role of Models in Sciences. *Phil. Sci.* Vol. 12, pp. 316-321

Rumelhart, D.E., J.L. McClelland and the PDP Research Group (1986). *Parallel Distributed Processing: Explorations in the Microstructure of Cognition. Volume 1: Foundations*, Cambridge, MA: MIT Press

Russell S. J., Norvig P. (2002), *Artificial Intelligence. A Modern Approach* (2nd ed.) Prentice Hall.

Simon, H. (1957) *Models of Man.* New York, John Wiley and Sons.

Slote, M. (1989) *Beyond Optimizing.* Cambridge, Mass., Harvard University Press.

Thagard, P. (2000). *Coherence in thought and action.* Cambridge, MA: MIT Press.

Thagard, P. & Verbeurgt, K. (1998). Coherence as constraint satisfaction. *Cognitive Science*, 22: 1-24.

Tversky, A. & Kahneman, D. (1974) Judgment Under Uncertainty: Heuristics and Biases. *Science* 185: 1124-1131.

Verschure, P.F.M.J., Wray, J., Sporns, O., Tononi, T. & Edelman, G.M. (1995), Multilevel analysis of classical conditioning in a behaving real world artifact, *Robotics and Autonomous Systems*, 16, pp. 247-265.

Extending ACT-R's Memory Capabilities

Holger Schultheis (schulth@sfbtr8.uni-bremen.de)
SFB/TR 8 Spatial Cognition, Universität Bremen, Enrique-Schmidt-Str. 5, 28359 Bremen, Germany

Shane Lile (slile@alumni.calpoly.edu)
Department of Computer Science, California Polytechnic State University, San Luis Obispo CA 93407, USA

Thomas Barkowsky (barkowsky@sfbtr8.uni-bremen.de)
SFB/TR 8 Spatial Cognition, Universität Bremen, Enrique-Schmidt-Str. 5, 28359 Bremen, Germany

Abstract

To resolve several problems of ACT-R's *declarative memory* (DM), Schultheis, Barkowsky, and Bertel (2006) developed a new long-term memory (LTM) component, called LTM^C. In this paper we present two ACT-R interfaces which integrate LTM^C into ACT-R. This integration of LTM^C makes it easily accessible to ACT-R modelers and allows to more thoroughly evaluate it in its interplay with other components of a cognitive architecture. By considering four different memory phenomena we show that ACT-R with LTM^C is superior to ACT-R employing only DM and, thus, (a) LTM^C's benefits are not impaired when integrating it into a cognitive architecture and (b) using the newly developed interfaces improves ACT-R. In particular, integrating LTM^C into ACT-R allows computationally exploring memory conceptions which cannot be modeled with ACT-R utilizing only DM.

Introduction

As a cognitive architecture ACT-R (Anderson et al., 2004) aims at constituting a computational model of all human cognition. And indeed a wide variety of psychological phenomena have successfully been modeled using ACT-R. Despite this success, concerns have recently been raised by Rutledge-Taylor (2005) and by Schultheis et al. (2006) regarding the suitability of ACT-R's *declarative memory* (DM) component as a model of human long-term memory (LTM). In response to these concerns Schultheis et al. (2006) have developed a new LTM component called LTM^C.

As shown in Schultheis et al. (2006) this new LTM component is able to solve the problems currently associated with ACT-R's DM. However, so far LTM^C was only available as a stand-alone component which is disadvantageous for at least two reasons. First, one might argue that it is not possible to thoroughly judge the suitability of an LTM component without considering it in its interplay with other components of a cognitive architecture. Put differently, it would be possible that shortcomings associated with LTM^C would only become obvious when utilized in the framework of generally accepted assumptions about human cognition. Second, as a stand-alone component, LTM^C would be inaccessible for most cognitive modelers, because considerable programming expertise would be necessary to employ LTM^C. To eliminate these problems we developed two interfaces, *LTM-DM* and *LTM-Buffer*, to integrate LTM^C into ACT-R. This integration not only allows further evaluating LTM^C in the scope of generally accepted assumptions about the functioning of the human information processing apparatus, but also makes LTM^C and its advantages easily accessible for ACT-R modelers.

LTM-Buffer and LTM-DM constitute two mutually exclusive approaches to integrate LTM^C into ACT-R and lead to different overall memory conceptions in ACT-R. Since evaluation (see below) suggests that both approaches are valid, we will present both interfaces in the following. Before describing the interfaces and their application we will give a short recap of ACT-R's existing memory structure and its problems as well as the structure and processes of LTM^C and how it is able to solve these problems. Subsequently, the ways LTM-Buffer and LTM-DM integrate LTM^C into ACT-R are explicated and evaluated. In concluding, issues for future work are highlighted.

ACT-R and its Limitations

In ACT-R's DM knowledge is represented by *chunks*. Chunks are data structures that contain one or more *slots*, which may contain values or other chunks. The slots a chunk contains are determined by its chunk type. Chunk types are declared separately for each model and are assumed to be fixed, that is, cannot and will not change during model runs. Thus, the chunk type specifications impose an unalterable structure on declarative knowledge. In particular, the imposed structure is assumed to be identical for knowledge currently being processed and knowledge stored in LTM (see Anderson et al., 2004, for a more detailed description of DM).

This means of representing knowledge is inappropriate to model human LTM, since the way chunks and chunk types structure knowledge renders knowledge situation-specific. Whereas this is unproblematic for knowledge currently being processed, a situation-specific representation of knowledge in LTM—which supposedly is the source of human knowledge in all situations—seems implausible.

Concretizing this general concern, Schultheis et al. (2006) identified the following three problems with ACT-R's knowledge representation: first, chunk types are too specific to their models. Every model defines its own chunk type(s). Consequently, at the moment it is uncertain (a) whether chunk types working well when considered in isolation still do so when considered together or (b) whether one could create a unified chunk structure which both represents all knowledge used in ACT-R models so far and still gives adequate modeling results. Second, the fact that chunk types cannot be altered during model runs makes the knowledge representation rather inflexible: Information retrieved together (i.e., in a chunk) from LTM in one context will be retrieved together in all contexts, an idea that is contrary to the common finding of context dependence of memory access (cf. Godden & Baddeley, 1975).

Finally, several studies (e.g., Erickson & Mattson, 1981; Park & Reder, 2004) have shown that humans in certain situations retrieve information from LTM which only partially matches the information originally requested. Yet, in ACT-R this effect does not arise from the basic architectural mechanisms. Instead, it is necessary to specify the degree to which partial matching is to occur between two chunks by hand.

An Outline[1] of LTM^C

Structure

In LTM^C knowledge is represented as a network of nodes. Every node comprises a name and a unique identifier. The name of a node is a string signifying which entity in the world this node stands for. The unique identifier is an alphanumeric sequence allowing to unambiguously identify and address each node[2]. In addition to its name and identifier, every node contains links to other nodes in LTM. These links represent associations between different entities—if two entities are associated with each other their corresponding nodes are mutually linked.

One noteworthy property of LTM^C is that the links between the nodes generally bear no meaning apart from indicating that the connected nodes are associated. In particular, links do not stand for relations, but relations are also represented as nodes. Thus, the fact that London is north of Paris would be represented by three nodes (London, north-of, and Paris) associatively linked to each other.

Besides knowledge about concrete entities such as "north-of", LTM^C also contains knowledge about categories of entities such as "direction relation" and knowledge about respective subsumption relations such as "north-of" "is a" "direction relation". Different from all other relations, however, subsumption relations are represented as links, since representing them as nodes would lead to infinite regress. By organizing the knowledge in a hierarchy (i.e., an ontology) the knowledge representation in LTM^C roughly takes the form of a tree with the most general entity as the root and concrete instances as the leaves.

This structure bears some resemblance to the knowledge representation proposed by Kokinov (2003) and Kokinov and Petrov (2001). However, due to the dissimilar processes at work in LTM^C, the overall functioning of LTM^C differs from the system proposed by Kokinov and colleagues. These processes will be described in the next section.

Processes

The processes employed to realize retrieval of knowledge from LTM^C are activation-based. Each node has an activation value that determines which nodes are retrieved on a certain request. This activation value is calculated on every new retrieval request as the sum of the node's base-level activation,

the activation spread to that node, and some randomly varying activation (i.e., noise). Base-level activation, like in ACT-R, reflects the recency and frequency of a node's retrieval: the more frequently and recently a node has been retrieved previously the higher is its base-level activation.

The activation spread to a node, on the contrary, does not depend on events of the past, but on the current context (i.e., entities in working memory or the environment) in which the retrieval takes place. If, for example, a person is asked which direction relation holds between London and Paris the activation of the corresponding nodes "direction relation", "London", and "Paris" will be increased. Importantly, the nodes receiving some activation directly from the context will spread activation to nodes with which they are associated. Nodes receiving activation from other nodes will again spread activation to the nodes they are associated with and so on. This activation spreading is subject to four constraints: first, only a fraction of the activation just received is spread to other nodes. Second, activation is not spread back to that node from which the to be spread activation has been received. Third, the amount of activation which will be spread to associated nodes will be equally distributed to these nodes. Fourth, the received activation will only be spread if it is high enough (i.e., above a certain threshold).

Once spreading has stopped, the amount of activation accumulated in a node during spreading is added to its base-level activation. By furthermore adding noise—computed as in DM (see Anderson et al., 2004)—the final activation of each node is computed. On the basis of these final activation values the nodes to be retrieved are determined: only those nodes having an activation which is higher than the average activation of nodes in LTM will be retrieved.

This spreading process requires setting four parameters when using LTM^C: The amount of activation a node receives from the context at the beginning of the spreading (cA), the fraction of activation to be distributed to associated nodes (f), the threshold to terminate spreading (t), and the strength of the noise (n). The latter three were set to $f = 0.6$, $t = 0.01667$, and $n = 0.1$ for all simulations reported below, whereas cA was allowed to vary across the different models.

Given its structure and processes, LTM^C can easily account for basic human memory phenomena such as context and time dependence of knowledge availability or the fan effect (cf. Anderson, 1974). More importantly, as Schultheis et al. (2006) have shown LTM^C solves the problems which have been identified with ACT-R's LTM (see above): due to its more flexible structure LTM^C is better able to model the context-dependent grouping of knowledge in the scope of a retrieval. In addition, LTM^C allows modeling the effect of partial matching (cf. Park & Reder, 2004) more plausibly and parsimoniously. Accordingly, LTM^C keeps the advantages of ACT-R's LTM (i.e., being able to account for basic human memory effects) while at the same time avoiding some of its weaknesses.

Interfacing LTM^C and ACT-R

One main aim in developing the two interfaces LTM-DM and LTM-Buffer—besides making LTM^C available in ACT-R—was to check whether these advantages persist for LTM^C as a part of a general cognitive architecture. Both ways of inter-

---

[1] A more detailed description of the structure and processes of LTM^C can be found in Schultheis et al. (2006)

[2] Using strings and alpha-numeric sequences for identifying nodes are arbitrary representational conventions. The strings are meant to help the modeler to quickly see what is represented by a node. The alphanumerical sequences are just one way of assigning a unique key to each node which is necessary to realize a working implementation. Thus, using strings and alphanumeric sequences is not meant to suggest that conceptual knowledge is language based.

facing and their evaluation will be explicated in the following sections. The first module, called LTM-DM, is an extension to ACT-R's existing DM module. The second is called LTM-Buffer and is intended to be an ACT-R module to be used independently of DM. The two modules are intended to be used exclusively of one another and represent two different approaches to accessing knowledge from LTM^C and using it in ACT-R. In describing the interfaces we will first explicate those aspects of using LTM^C in ACT-R which both interfaces have in common and then go into more detail on the particulars of LTM-DM and LTM-Buffer, respectively.

Retrieving Knowledge from LTM^C

As argued above, the advantages of LTM^C compared to DM mainly arise from LTM^C's more flexible representation structure. Instead of imposing a fixed grouping of information onto the contents of LTM, the node network employed in LTM^C allows for a context-dependent and context-appropriate grouping of information. Put differently, the improvements realized by LTM^C are achieved mainly by avoiding the use of chunks and chunk types for representing long-term knowledge. Nothing, however, speaks against using chunks as a representation for the knowledge currently being processed (see above). Accordingly, the use of chunks for representing declarative knowledge in ACT-R is only problematic regarding LTM and thus the best way to integrate LTM^C into ACT-R seems to be to keep chunks as representations for processing while using LTM^C instead of DM as the LTM component.

Taking this approach the result of a retrieval request to LTM^C cannot directly be processed by the other ACT-R components, since a retrieval result is given in the form of a subnet of the overall net representing long-term knowledge and not in the form of chunks. Consequently, to interface LTM^C with ACT-R, retrieved subnets have to be recast as chunks. To achieve this we introduced a new construct called *mapping* which accompanies chunk type definitions. A mapping specifies how the slots of a chunk type relate to the nodes in LTM^C. If the newly developed LTM modules are employed in ACT-R, support for mapping definitions is automatically enabled. On a retrieval request the resulting subnet will be recast as chunks according to the defined mappings. This approach has the following advantages: first, ACT-R modelers can still use any types of chunks they like, that is, using LTM-DM or LTM-Buffer does not restrict the freedom of modelers to define and use particular chunk types. Second, by means of the mapping definitions chunk types are anchored in the general ontological structure of LTM^C. This potentially allows to compare and relate the knowledge used in different ACT-R models and thus alleviates one of the above identified problems of ACT-R's DM, namely the model specificity of chunks and chunk types.

By using the mapping mechanism retrieving knowledge from LTM^C is very similar to the process of obtaining chunks from DM. Figure 1 outlines the retrieval process. The first step of a retrieval is to issue a normal ACT-R request to the buffer of the corresponding module. The ACT-R LTM modules are able to use—employing the mapping—such an ACT-R request to activate nodes in LTM^C and spread that activation to those nodes' neighbors. Once this is complete, the

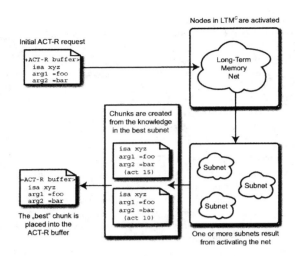

Figure 1: Retrieval process for LTM^C in ACT-R

nodes with an activation smaller than the average activation of the entire semantic net are discarded to create one or more disjoint subnets. The modules find the best subnet (i.e., the subnet with the highest total activation) and—again relying on the mapping—use it to create chunks of the requested type for ACT-R to use. The chunk with the highest activation is selected and placed in the buffer that requested the knowledge. The retrieval time is computed from the activation of the chunk finally put into the buffer using the same formula as in ACT-R.

Apart from this common procedure employed to retrieve information from LTM^C, the two interfaces differ with respect to certain aspects. Most notably, the overall memory conception realized in ACT-R changes depending on whether LTM-DM or LTM-Buffer is employed. The next two sections illustrate the differences between the two interfaces.

LTM-DM

LTM-DM is an extension to the existing DM in ACT-R. It offers the capabilities of LTM^C as an additional source of information, but if information is already present in DM then this may be used instead. Chunks retrieved from LTM^C are given a base-activation equal to their activation in LTM^C and then placed directly in DM to allow it to determine which chunk to place in its buffer. This might include any subsymbolic processes (e.g., spreading activation, noise, etc.) of DM. Thus, using LTM-DM establishes a two-component memory structure with a strict separation between the two components.

At first sight, using both DM and LTM^C might seem unreasonable, since—in light of the usual interpretation of DM as LTM—this might look like creating a system with two distinct LTM stores. Yet, as stated above, there are strong arguments for the stance that DM with its chunk structure is insufficient as a model of human LTM and is better viewed as holding the knowledge in a representation format used for the information currently processed. Thus, the memory structure resulting in ACT-R when using LTM-DM can be taken to implement not two types of LTM, but one long-term store

(LTM^C) and one store transiently holding the knowledge which is currently (or has recently been) processed (DM).

Seen this way LTM-DM is nicely in accord with a number of recent suggestions regarding the nature of the human memory system. For example, Baddeley (2000) proposed the *episodic buffer* as that part of working memory which (a) is a multi-dimensional store, that is, a store combining information from different modalities and sources, (b) can hold information for a longer duration than other parts of working memory, and (c) mediates between working memory and LTM. Since DM as used in LTM-DM also has these three features, it can be viewed as instantiating the episodic buffer instead of a second LTM.

Other areas of research that parallel LTM-DM are the sensory-perceptual episodic memory proposed by Conway (2001). In the case of Conway's research, LTM^C takes the place of autobiographical memory, "a type of memory that persists over weeks, months, years, decades, and lifetimes," and "retains knowledge at different levels of abstraction." Accessing the memories in LTM^C follows Conway's description of access to autobiographical memory. Conway describes these memories as "patterns of activation over the indices of autobiographical memory knowledge structures." His explanations of autobiographical memory describe a system not unlike LTM^C's semantic net, in which specific cues stimulate specific memories and spread activation throughout memory in order to retrieve larger collections of memories. DM is Conway's episodic memory. These structures "keep track of progress on active goals as plans are executed." Importantly, Conway (2001) describes episodic memory as having its own retrieval process, which is consistent with the strict separation of LTM^C and DM kept by LTM-DM.

Thus, LTM-DM allows modeling these and similar working memory conceptions; an advantage which will be explored in more detail below.

LTM-Buffer

The second module for interfacing LTM^C with ACT-R, LTM-Buffer, was implemented as a complete alternative to using DM. As such, LTM-Buffer is a complete stand-alone ACT-R module and has its own buffer, *pretrieval*, which needs to be used to access LTM^C. Instead of passing chunks to DM after traversing the knowledge in LTM^C, LTM-Buffer handles selecting which chunk to place in its buffer. This means that the activation of the chunk put into the pretrieval-buffer stems directly from the processes working in LTM^C and is not influenced by subsymbolic computations in ACT-R.

Where LTM-DM suggests separate stores for long-term and working memory, LTM-Buffer's approach follows the view that working memory is not a separate memory store, but rather that it is highly-activated portions of LTM (see, e.g., Cowan, 1999). Thus, the memory structure realized in ACT-R when using LTM-Buffer is the same as in ACT-R proper. The only differences is that LTM is implemented by LTM^C instead of DM.

Evaluation

To evaluate the suitability of LTM^C in the scope of generally accepted assumptions about the functioning of the human information processing apparatus, we modeled several memory phenomena with ACT-R using only DM, ACT-R using LTM-DM, and ACT-R using LTM-Buffer. In doing so we had three aims: The first was to check the cognitive plausibility of LTM^C as part of a cognitive architecture. Second, we compared the performance of LTM-DM and LTM-Buffer to that of ACT-R using only DM to investigate possible advantages or disadvantages of using LTM^C in ACT-R. In particular, comparing the modeling abilities of ACT-R employing only DM and ACT-R using LTM-Buffer allowed attributing any differences between model performances directly to the respective LTM component employed. Put differently, any differences in model performance cannot be due to other parts of the architecture, since ACT-R using DM and ACT-R using LTM-Buffer differed only in the LTM component utilized. Finally, since the theoretical conceptions of memory underlying the two interfaces are quite different, it seemed interesting to compare LTM-DM and LTM-Buffer to determine which of the two might be more suitable as a model of human LTM.

In order to achieve these aims we considered four memory phenomena which seemed to be most informative regarding the above evaluation questions. The first two, namely the fan effect (Anderson, 1974) and a phenomenon related to the hierarchical structure of the knowledge representation in LTM (Sharifian & Samani, 1997), illustrate properties of human LTM for which established ACT-R models already exist. If our interfaces can perform at least as good as the ACT-R models this constitutes a proof of their cognitive plausibility, since the ACT-R models we used are generally thought to realize fine models of the two phenomena. The second two phenomena we considered were the *Moses Illusion* (Erickson & Mattson, 1981) and a case study reported in Baddeley (2000). These effects were chosen because they were assumed to illustrate more clearly possible difference between the two interfaces and ACT-R proper as well as between the two interfaces as such.

Model Setup

As just mentioned, established models were used for simulation of ACT-R proper whenever they were available. More precisely, for the fan effect and the hierarchical memory effect we employed the models presented in tutorial 5 and tutorial 1, respectively, of the ACT-R 6 distribution (see http://act-r.psy.cmu.edu/actr6/). For the Moses Illusion we wrote a new model which basically retrieves chunks using the partial matching mechanism of ACT-R, where the similarity values were set by hand to obtain optimal results. Importantly, for all of the standard ACT-R models DM consists of precisely those chunks needed for the task. In the models for ACT-R extended by LTM^C, on the contrary, DM was not equipped with any prior chunks. Any knowledge used during the task had to be retrieved from LTM^C. The information for the fan effect was represented by, for example, the nodes "hippie" and "park" which are associated with a node "in". For the hierarchy experiment the relevant knowledge was represented by pairs of subsumptions relations connecting three nodes as, for instance, "rose" isa "flower" isa "plant". For the Moses Illusion the represented knowledge consisted of facts about the involved objects as, e.g., "Moses" isa "Person", "Noah" isa "Person", "Noah" and "Ark" are both linked to "sailed", etc. In particular, LTM^C also contained the knowledge neces-

Table 1: Results for modeling Anderson's fan experiment ("Fan"), the Sharifian experiment ("Hierarchy") and the Moses Illusion experiment of Erickson and Mattson (1981). The values shown are correlations of model and experimental data.

Module	Fan	Hierarchy	Illusion
DM	0.864	0.948	0.988
LTM-Buffer	0.869	0.999	0.992
LTM-DM	0.817	0.999	0.980

sary for the fan effect and the hierarchy effect when modeling the Moses Illusion and vice versa, that is, was not taylored specifically for each modeled phenomenon.

All models together with the newly developed interfaces are available online[3]. The memory phenomena together with modeling results are reported in more detail below.

In the Realm of ACT-R ...

The Fan Experiment. The fan experiment of Anderson (1974) explored the hypothesis that the more knowledge a person has regarding a target concept, the longer it will take them to retrieve specific corresponding knowledge from LTM. In the experiment, participants had to memorize several facts such as "a hippie is in the park" and "a captain is in the cave." Knowing more facts about a specific person or place (e.g., the hippie is in the park and cave, versus the captain who is only in the cave) increased the time it took to recognize whether or not a target sentence was a known fact. Participants were also given foil sentences, in which a known person and place were paired up in a way the participant had not seen previously (e.g., the hippie is in the church; participants knew facts about the hippie and the church, but were never told "the hippie is in the church"), and were expected to respond that they did not recognize the target sentence. In accord with the hypothesis the main dependent measure in the experiment was the time the participants needed to verify the target sentences and, thus, in modeling this experiment we also concentrated on reaction times.

The column "Fan" in Table 1 shows how the response times of the ACT-R models using the different modules correlate to participants' response times in the actual experiment. As can be seen from the table, the data from the model runs employing LTM-Buffer and the model run employing LTM-DM strongly correlate to the experimental results, and are very close to the results obtained when using ACT-R's DM to model the effect.

The Hierarchical Spreading Experiment. The second memory effect we considered is related to the hierarchical organization of knowledge in LTM, illustrated by, for example, the results of Sharifian and Samani (1997). In their experiment the authors presented subjects with pairs of words, such as "flower" and "plant", asking them to identify whether or not the pairs were related. These pairs of words were based off of triads of words where the first and second words were directly related and the second and third words were directly

related, thus making the first and third words indirectly related via the second word. For example, one such triad used in the experiment of Sharifian and Samani (1997) was plant-flower-rose. Sharifian and colleagues measured the time it took for subjects to correctly identify whether or not two words presented in a pair were related. Since, again, response times are the major focus of the original experiment, we used those as the dependent measure to evaluate our models.

As can be seen from column "Hierarchy" in Table 1, all three ACT-R modules show a very high correlation to the experimental results found by Sharifian and Samani (1997). In particular, the two newly defined interfaces are again as good as the available ACT-R model.

... and Beyond

Moses Illusion. If people are asked "How many animals of each kind did Moses take on the ark?" most of them will answer "two", although the correct answer would be "none": it was not Moses who sailed the ark, but Noah. This effect is called Moses Illusion and appears in a number of situations similar to the Moses Question. As Park and Reder (2004) show, this effect is most likely the result of partial matching processes working on LTM. Erickson and Mattson (1981) were the first to investigate this effect. They presented their participants with the Moses question and three additional questions of the same kind. The dependent measure was the relative frequency with which the participants answered the questions as if they were correct.

In ACT-R proper the only way of modeling partial matching and, thus, the Moses Illusion is by (a) enabling a special feature and (b) specifying similarity values between those concepts which are supposed to partially match (e.g., "Moses" and "Noah" in the above example)[4]. Consequently, our model for ACT-R proper realizes the Moses Illusion by using partial matching.

On the contrary, when using LTM-Buffer or LTM-DM, it is not necessary to specify any special retrieval mode or hand-picked similarity values. By relying on LTM^C the two interfaces can account for partial matching in human LTM employing the same memory structure and processes as in modeling the other memory effects (see Schultheis et al., 2006).

Column three of Table 1 shows the modeling results for the three modules. Like with the above memory phenomena the model accuracies are quite similar across the different modules. However, their more parsimonious approach to modeling this effect makes LTM-Buffer and LTM-DM superior to the model using only DM.

Episodic Buffer and Related Conceptions. As already explained when describing LTM-DM, this interface establishes a new overall memory conception in the ACT-R architecture. In particular, by creating such a memory LTM-DM allows modeling memory phenomena completely out of the

---

[3]http://www.sfbtr8.uni-bremen.de/project/r1/models/

---

[4]The ACT-R model presented in Budiu and Anderson (2004) realizes the Moses Illusion without using the partial matching mechanism of ACT-R. However, this is achieved by (a) using retrieval processes not available in the standard ACT-R distribution and (b) also relying on similarity values defined between different concepts. Thus, the Moses Illusion effect is essentially reduced to similarity values without explaining from which structures or processes these similarities might arise.

scope of ACT-R using only DM. Consider, for example, the memory performance of patient PV as reported by Baddeley (2000): PV showed normal LTM performance while at the same time having a reduced word (one item) and sentence span (5 items). Using standard ACT-R it is not possible to model such a pattern of memory performances since it is not possible to change short-term memory capabilities without affecting LTM capabilities, since both are instantiated by DM. Employing LTM-DM, on the contrary, easily allows modeling also such memory performance patterns as PV exhibits: LTM^C would serve as the (intact) LTM and DM could be modified, such that it implements the reduced short-term capabilities of PV.

Evaluation Summary

By considering the discussions and model results from the above sections it is possible to answer the three evaluation questions posed at the beginning. First, the suitability of LTM^C as a model of human LTM has been corroborated. LTM^C yields accurate modeling results of human LTM effects not only as a stand-alone component, but also when integrated into a general cognitive architecture: The correlations of model data and empirical data are very high for each modeled phenomenon (the lowest correlation was 0.817), and, in particular, the two LTM^C modules are at least as good as the standard ACT-R model in every of the modeled tasks. Second, LTM-Buffer and LTM-DM are superior to ACT-R using only DM, because they allow modeling memory phenomena with the same accuracy, but more parsimoniously than standard ACT-R. LTM-DM furthermore enables modeling memory conceptions and related phenomena previously not available in ACT-R. Third, LTM-DM seems to be slightly superior to LTM-Buffer. Besides modeling several memory phenomena as accurately as LTM-Buffer it additionally allows to model memory phenomena out of the scope of LTM-Buffer.

Conclusions

This paper presents two new interfaces for the ACT-R architecture, called LTM-DM and LTM-Buffer which integrate the LTM component LTM^C developed by Schultheis et al. (2006) into ACT-R. One major aim of integrating LTM^C into ACT-R was to more thoroughly validate its advantages by employing LTM^C as one part of a general cognitive architecture. Through modeling several memory phenomena we evaluated LTM^C as part of ACT-R and compared ACT-R using LTM-DM and LTM-Buffer with ACT-R using only DM. The results of this evaluation clearly show that LTM-Buffer and LTM-DM are at least as good as DM and in some cases considerably better in modeling human LTM. Particularly powerful seems the LTM-DM module, since it opens up a completely new field of memory phenomena to model with ACT-R.

Thus, our future work will concentrate on further exploring the possibilities and the power of LTM-DM as an extension to ACT-R. In addition, to complete the integration of LTM^C we will devise mechanisms for storing knowledge in LTM^C based on the mappings described above. If a mapping exists for every chunk type used in ACT-R, correspondence between any chunk and the knowledge stored in LTM^C can be established. Roughly speaking this allows transforming any chunk to a node and integrating it into the ontology given by LTM^C.

Acknowledgments

In this paper work done in the project R1-[ImageSpace] of the Transregional Collaborative Research Center SFB/TR 8 Spatial Cognition is presented. Funding by the German Research Foundation (DFG) is gratefully acknowledged. We also thank Eduard Krieger for his help with the implementation and the anonymous reviewers for their valuable suggestions.

References

Anderson, J. R. (1974). Retrieval of propositional information from long-term memory. *Cognitive Psychology, 6*, 451 - 474.

Anderson, J. R., Bothell, D., Byrne, M. D., Douglass, S., Lebiere, C., & Qin, Y. (2004). An integrated theory of the mind. *Psychological Review, 111*(4), 1036 - 1060.

Baddeley, A. (2000). The episodic buffer: a new component of working memory? *Trends in Cognitive Science, 4*, 417-423.

Budiu, R., & Anderson, J. R. (2004). Interpretation-based processing: a unified theory of semantic sentence comprehension. *Cognitive Science, 28*, 1 - 44.

Conway, M. (2001). Sensory-perceptual episodic memory and its context: autobiographical memory. In *Episodic memory*. Oxford University Press.

Cowan, N. (1999). An embedded-process model of working memory. In P. Shah & A. Miyake (Eds.), *Models of working memory: Mechanisms of active maintenance and executive control*. Cambridge University Press.

Erickson, T. D., & Mattson, M. E. (1981). From words to meaning: a semantic illusion. *Journal of Verbal Learning and Verbal Behavior, 20*, 540 - 551.

Godden, D. R., & Baddeley, A. D. (1975). Context-dependent memory in two natural environments: On land and under water. *British Journal of Psychology, 66*, 325 - 331.

Kokinov, B. (2003). The mechanisms of episode construction and blending in DUAL and AMBR: Interaction between memory and analogy. In B. Kokinov & W. Hirst (Eds.), *Constructive memory*. NBU Press.

Kokinov, B., & Petrov, A. (2001). Integration of memory and reasoning in analogy-making: The AMBR model. In D. Gentner, K. Holyoak, & B. Kokinov (Eds.), *The analogical mind: Perspectives from cognitive science*. Cambridge, MA: MIT Press.

Park, H., & Reder, L. M. (2004). Moses illusion: Implication for human cognition. In R. F. Pohl (Ed.), *Cognitive illusions*. Hove: Psychology Press.

Rutledge-Taylor, M. (2005). Can ACT-R realize "Newell's dream"? In *Proceedings of the 27th annual meeting of the Cognitive Science Society*.

Schultheis, H., Barkowsky, T., & Bertel, S. (2006). LTM^c — an improved long-term memory for cognitive architectures. In *Proceedings of the 7th international conference on cognitive modeling, 2006, Trieste*.

Sharifian, F., & Samani, R. (1997). Hierarchical spreading of activation. *Proc. of the Conference on Language, Cognition, and Interpretation*.

Attitudes and Content
The Non-Conceptual but Cognitive Content of Attitudes

Manuel Liz (manuliz@ull.es)
Faculty of Philosophy, Univ. of La Laguna
La Laguna. Canary Islands. SPAIN

Abstract

I will assume that intentional mental states are constituted by certain psychological attitudes directed toward some intentional contents, and that intentional contents can be described as having a conceptual, or propositional, structure and an inferential articulation giving to them a cognitive character. But I will distinguish between intentional contents and the contents of the intentional states themselves, arguing that intentional mental states themselves bear a non-conceptual and non-propositional content that can have an inferential articulation and a very relevant cognitive character beyond the inferential articulation and cognitive character coming from the intentional contents involved. I will maintain that the attitudinal component of the intentional mental states always originates such a non-conceptual, but yet cognitive, content. That thesis would entail a serious reconsideration of some of the issues involved in the recent debates on conceptual and non-conceptual content. In particular, it would suggest new perspectives in order to connect intentional mental states with other kinds of non-intentional, qualitative mental states.

Introduction

Are the contents of our intentional mental states something *exhausted* by the contents present in the concepts and propositions employed in describing the things we are thinking about? Are the contents of our mental states something reducible to the intentional contents *contained* in our intentional mental states? And how could the contents of the intentional mental states themselves be related with the contents of other kinds of non-intentional mental states, for instance qualitative ones? These are the questions I want to address here.

As an introduction to the way I will face those questions, let consider the content expressed by "?", in the context of a written question. Does "?" express a non-conceptual, but yet inferentially relevant, and therefore cognitive, content? I think that the answer would have to be affirmative. But to make questions would be only one example of a very wide field of both linguistic and mental phenomena. All sorts of linguistic indicators of illocutionary force and all sorts of spoken or written devices to make emphasis would express differences in the psychological or mental attitudes of the subjects towards the intentional contents of their thoughts. Those indicators of illocutionary force, and the other devices to make emphasis, appear to be uneliminable from our discursive practices. And in an analogous sense, the attitudes expressed by them appear to be uneliminable

constitutive parts of the intentional mental states involved[1]. Moreover, those attitudes display a very relevant role in relation to our real inferential practices. Our inferences are orientated and bounded by them. In that sense, something like "?" would express an important non-conceptual, but yet inferentially articulated and therefore cognitive, content.

I want to note from the beginning that what I will say is intended to be largely independent on any substantive claim about the qualitative or phenomenal features of our subjective experience, about how to understand concept possession and conceptual abilities, and about how to analyse the nature of things like representations, informational content, or propositions. The rule in the literature on conceptual and non-conceptual content has been to focus on those topics[2]. However, as I am going to argue, the existence of a non-conceptual, but in many cases cognitive, content in our mental states, even in our intentional mental states, could be found in other much more unproblematic and obvious place. And that place would be the one occupied by psychological attitudes.

Intentional Mental States and Their Contents

Intentional mental states are constituted by certain psychological attitudes (believing, desiring, etc.) directed toward some intentional contents (what is believed, desired, etc.). But, it would be necessary to distinguish here between intentional contents and the contents of the intentional mental states *themselves*. In other words, the notion of mental content would not be exhausted by the notion of intentional content. Really, the word "of" in the expression "the content of an intentional mental state" is ambiguous. There would be two very different ways in which we can speak about the *content* of an intentional mental state:

1. we can be referring to the content *contained* in the intentional mental state in question, in the sense that there would be a content we could find in it, or
2. we can be referring to the content *of the state* itself, i.e. to the mental content of the state as a whole.

First, let us focus on the contents contained in our intentional mental states. We can say that these intentional contents can be described with the help of certain *propositions*. In the attributions of intentional mental states

---

[1] The sense would be only analogous because of the conventional ingredient present in the "expression" of attitudes. We will not discuss here this point.

[2] See, for instance, Bermúdez, J. (2003) and Stalnaker, R. (1997).

to others, and in the self descriptions of our intentional mental states, we use propositions as a way to *identify* the things we are thinking about, i.e., the intentional contents of our thoughts[3]. To have intentional mental states is to have mental states intentionally directed to something that can be identified through certain propositions.

But, what are propositions? Propositions are very peculiar objects and there are many theories about what propositions can be. I will not discuss them[4]. However, and only for the sake of the argument, let us consider the following three features: 1) propositions are essentially connected with truth conditions, 2) they have an inferential articulation, and 3) they have a conceptual structure.

Intentional mental states as beliefs, or speech acts as assertions, also can be seen as being in some way connected with truth conditions. More in general, intentional mental states and speech acts would be connected with satisfaction conditions. And I will argue that they can be seen also as having an inferential articulation. But, could they also can have a conceptual structure? The answer would be negative. And the main reason for that negative answer is very important. To have a conceptual structure is a property of (certain) abstract objects. Mathematical and logical objects, propositions, meanings, etc., may have a conceptual structure. However, intentional mental states and speech acts would not be abstract objects of that kind, but facts of the world. Even though perhaps they get to involve relationships with abstract objects (for instance, propositions), they are facts of the world. And, as facts of the world, they only can have a conceptual structure as a feature derived of the way we employ certain abstract objects (for instance, propositions) in making descriptions of those facts.

We said that to have intentional mental states is to have mental states involving something that can be identified through certain propositions. Now, two options are open. It is possible to argue that propositions are only *a way to identify* the things we are thinking about. Or it is also possible to argue that those things can be *identified with* propositions. In that second case, and assuming a fine-grained conception of propositions according to which propositions would be made of concepts, the things we are thinking about would always have a conceptual structure. To have intentional mental states would entail to be intimately connected with an abstract world of concepts. Moreover, perhaps also to have perceptual states, feelings and the like, would entail to be connected with such a conceptual world. This would be the position recently held

by McDowell[5]. In the first case (propositions as only a way to identify intentional contents), the door would remains open to consider that the things we are thinking about, and not only for instance the things we are able to perceive or feel, have by themselves a non-conceptual structure. That would be the position recently held by Stalnaker[6].

We can adopt any of those radical options, or we can adopt more moderate ones. In any case, there is an important point worthy of attention. Intentional mental states involve more than the things we are thinking about. They are not only constituted by their intentional contents. Intentional mental states are also constituted by certain psychological *attitudes*. And attitudes are able of giving to intentional states themselves a kind of inferential articulation which is not conceptual.

The Non-Conceptual Inferential Articulation of Intentional Mental States

Intentional mental states are constituted by certain intentional contents and certain psychological attitudes directed toward those intentional contents. The relationships between both components can be more or less intricate and difficult to analyze, but we are conscious of our attitudes at least in the same obvious sense in which we are conscious of the things we are thinking about. Attitudes are not less epistemically accessible that intentional contents.

Moreover, it has full sense to say that not only intentional contents but also intentional mental states themselves are inferentially articulated and that, because of that, they can have a quite peculiar cognitive content. To have a cognitive content in that sense would be to have a direct relevance in relation to the inferences we can do.

Between our inferential practices and the logical relations among propositions there are very important parallelisms. However, our inferential practices do not consist only in propositional relationships. Our inferential practices are certain thinkings and doings and, therefore, they are facts of the world. The inferences we really do have to stop at certain points and not at other ones, they involve criteria of relevance and opportunity, they need heuristics, etc. In other words, the inferences we really do are orientated and bounded by our attitudes.

We can say that intentional mental states are inferentially articulated both in relation to their intentional contents and in relation to the attitudes involved. On the one hand, intentional contents are inferentially articulated because they are identified with, or at least they are identified by means of, propositions, and propositions are inferentially articulated. On the other hand, attitudes give to intentional mental states another inferential articulation making pressure over certain inferential moves and not over other ones. In a nutshell, propositions would be like a "map" and

---

[3] We could use here the expression "representational content" as equivalent to "intentional content". It is very common to have a representational conception of the intentional contents of intentional mental states. Propositions would serve to identify that representational content.

[4] Very relevant discussions about propositions, concepts and intentional contents can be found in Fodor, J. (1998), Richard, M. (1990), and Stalnaker, R. (1999).

[5] See, for instance, McDowell, J. (1994). According to him, content would be conceptual "all the way down".

[6] See, for instance, Stalnaker, R. (1997). According to him, and in clear contrast with McDowell, content would be non-conceptual (not qualitative or phenomenal, but of an informational kind) "all the way up".

attitudes would be like "forces" moving us in one direction or other.

Of course, intentional contents are cognitive contents. But attitudes give other kind of cognitive content to the mental contents involved in the intentional states themselves. The contents coming from attitudes would be like inferential "forces". They would be facts of the world that, even being cognitively relevant, cannot have a conceptual structure.

According to what we have said, it can have a clear sense to speak of the cognitive content of the intentional states themselves. And even though those states get to involve propositions and conceptual contents in the more radical sense, if we assume that those intentional states are facts of the world, then they have to be considered as having, or as also having, a cognitive content which is non-conceptual.

Because having an intentional mental state is a fact of the world, not an abstract object, the characteristic cognitive content of an intentional mental state cannot have a conceptual structure. Or it only can have such a conceptual structure in a derived sense. Even though that cognitive content were to involve close connections with an abstract world of propositions and concepts, the state itself would not have a conceptual structure by itself. Exactly in the same sense in which the worldly fact that a is F can be closely connected with the conceptual fact that to be F is to be G or to be H without having, the former fact, any conceptual structure.[7]

The intentional contents contained in the intentional states could be always cognitive. And we can consider that they are conceptual contents, or we can consider that they are of a non-conceptual kind. But with independence of the option chosen here, the contents of the intentional mental states themselves would be always non-conceptual. The attitudinal component of the intentional mental states always originates a non-conceptual, but in many cases cognitive, content not exhausted by the intentional contents involved in the intentional mental states, nor reducible either to any intentional contents that can be contained in other possible intentional mental states.

In order to better show that intentional states themselves always have some sort of non-conceptual content, let us represent different intentional mental states using the standard terminology for symbolizing different kinds of illocutionary acts. And let us take p as the proposition that I will bring you a glass of water. Further, let us suppose that p is the intentional content of some of your intentional mental states. You can be, for instance, in the following intentional mental states:

1. $\vdash p$
2. $!p$
3. $?p$

---

[7] If the fact that a is F were to have a conceptual structure because there are certain conceptual relations between to be F and to be G or to be H, then all the facts of the world would have conceptual structure. Indeed, this would be very close to some theses maintained by McDowell (but surely his reasons to maintain them are not of that simple sort).

Here, we would have to distinguish not only the proposition that I will bring you a glass of water (i.e., proposition p) from the proposition that you are believing that I will bring you a glass of water (i.e., the proposition that $\vdash p$), but, also, we would have to distinguish the last proposition from the intentional mental state 1, an (let us say) assertive intentional mental state we can describe saying "You are believing that I will bring you a glass of water". And the same can be said of the proposition that $!p$, in relation to the (let us say) demanding intentional mental state 2 we can describe saying "You are requiring that I will bring you a glass of water"; and of the proposition that $?p$ in relation to the (let us say) asking intentional mental state 3 we can describe saying "You are asking whether I will bring you a glass of water".

That I will bring you a glass of water (i.e., proposition p) is something that can be true or false. Also, it can be true or false that you are believing, demanding, asking, etc., that p (i.e., the propositions that $\vdash p$, that $!p$, and that $?p$). And your believing, demanding, asking, etc., have satisfaction conditions, and can be satisfied or not satisfied. However, your believing, demanding, asking, etc., that p are not properly the sorts of things that can be said to be true or false. And this is so even in the case of your believing. If p is true and you believe that p, then you have a true belief, and it is also true that you believe it, and you believing it has satisfaction conditions (the truth of what you believe), but your believing p is not something that can be true or false. Believing, demanding, asking, etc., are not propositions but thinkings (related with certain doings, with certain speech acts). And these thinkings are facts that happen in the world, facts that (as all facts of the world) do not have any conceptual or propositional structure.[8]

This entails that intentional mental states like 1, 2, and 3 cannot have by themselves any conceptual structure. Even though they involve intentional contents with propositional and conceptual structure, they do not have any such structure by themselves.

But if we consider that inferential relevance is the crucial feature in order to have cognitive content, we would have to conclude that 1, 2, and 3 have a content of a cognitive kind. 1, 2, and 3 have a non-conceptual but yet cognitive content.

The inferential relevance of 1, 2, and 3 is clear if we think, for instance, that even though we assume *Modus Ponens* as a logical (propositional-conceptual) truth, and you have the belief that if p, then q (for some q), the more probable intentional mental states you will arrive at would

---

[8] $\vdash p$ and that $\vdash p$ would be very different entities. The first one would be something happening in the world (a certain doing in the case of speech acts, a certain thinking in the case of intentional states), the second one would be an abstract object (a proposition). In its more direct form, my argument for the existence of a non-conceptual content in the intentional mental states would be supported by that difference, and by the assumption that facts of the world (including here our doings and thinkings) do not have by themselves a conceptual structure. The cognitive character of those non-conceptual contents would be originated by the role they are able to play in our actual inferential practices.

be quite different depending on your being in the intentional mental states 1, 2, or 3. With 1, you will probably arrive quite directly to $\vdash q$, but not with 2 nor with 3.

Actual inferences are oriented and bounded by our intentional mental states in a way that goes *beyond* the conceptual structure and propositional character that can be assumed for their respective intentional contents. Even though intentional contents are identified with propositions having a conceptual structure, the attitudes linked to those intentional contents give to the intentional mental states themselves a non-conceptual, but yet cognitive, character.[9]

Next sections are devoted to extract some consequences of the above theses in relation to the recent debates on conceptual and non-conceptual content, particularly in relation to the relationships between intentional mental states and other kinds of non-intentional mental states.

The Conceptual/Non-Conceptual Divide

The distinction between conceptual and non-conceptual content would make crucial reference to conceptual capacities. In contrast with conceptual content, non-conceptual content would not be linked to the conceptual capacities of the subject. Conceptualists would defend that the way a subject represent the world is determined by the subject's conceptual capacities. Non-conceptualists would defend the existence of ways of representing the world which are not determined by the subject's conceptual capacities. Non-conceptualists focus mainly on three representational domains where their claim appears to be quite plausible: 1) perceptual states, 2) subpersonal or subdoxastic representational states, and 3) representational states of non-human animals, preverbal children, etc.[10] I will say something about these three domains. But now, let us consider more closely the conceptualist thesis.

According to Bermúdez, conceptualism would adopt what he calls "The conceptual constraint"[11]:

(CC) Specifications of the content of a sentence or propositional attitude state must not employ concepts that are not possessed by the utterer or thinker.

And the plausibility of CC would follow from two ideas:

1. In specifying what a thinker believes, what a perceiver perceives or what a speaker is saying by uttering a certain sentence, in a particular context one has to be as faithful as possible to the way in which

that thinker, perceiver or speaker apprehends the world.

2. The way in which a speaker, perceiver or thinker apprehends the world in speaking about it or having beliefs about it is a function of the concepts he possesses.

The question I want to ask is: Does CC entail that mental states only can have conceptual contents? My answer would be negative. It is possible to argue that even if the way in which the subjects apprehend the world is a function of the concepts possessed by the subjects, and even if specifications of the contents contained in their intentional mental states must not employ concepts that are not possessed by the subjects, the peculiar ways in which the world is apprehended through the intentional mental states always go beyond the conceptual capacities of the subjects. And this would be so because of the great variety of different psychological attitudes that the subjects can adopt with respect to the same intentional contents.

Three Domains for Non-Conceptual Content

As we have noted, non-conceptualism usually focus on three representational domains where the existence of a non-conceptual content appears to be quite plausible: 1) perceptual states, 2) subpersonal or subdoxastic representational states, and 3) representational states of non-human animals, preverbal children, etc. We have argued that with independence of these issues, non-conceptual content can be found in the intentional mental states themselves. Even when the intentional mental contents of those states is propositionally characterized and conceptually structured, the attitudes towards those intentional contents introduce important non-conceptual, but yet cognitive, ingredients.

The representational domains 1, 2, and 3 are usually analyzed without making relevant differences in relation to the attitudes present in them. We have distinguished between the content contained in the intentional mental state, i.e., the intentional content of the state, and the content of the intentional mental state itself, i.e., the mental content of the state in the full sense. Also, we have distinguished between cognitive and conceptual content (more precisely, between cognitive and non-cognitive content, and between conceptual and non-conceptual content). All of that would offer us a wide range of descriptive recourses to deal with the above domains 1, 2, and 3. In particular, there would be an important difference to be made between domains 1 and 2, on the one hand, and domain 3, on the other:

–   To begin with, some of the intentional mental states of adult humans could be characterized as involving intentional contents of a conceptual and cognitive kind, but as having themselves, or having also, a non-conceptual but cognitive content.
–   Now, it may be that perceptual states and subpersonal or subdoxastic representational states (domains 1 and 2) also can be characterized as involving intentional contents of a conceptual and cognitive kind. But, even though they involve intentional contents of a non-conceptual kind, if these contents can have a

---

[9] That point would have stronger consequences if we adopt a "fusion" theory concerning the relationships between attitudes and contents. In that case, even intentional contents propositionally and conceptually characterized would have a non-conceptual content. However, we do not need to take that step in order to argue that intentional states themselves have a non-conceptual but cognitive content.

[10] See, for instance, Bermúdez (2003).

[11] Bermúdez, J. (2003) includes a very important discussion of that constraint.

cognitive relevance in our inferential practices, then they would have to be considered as having a cognitive character. And the same could be said of the non-conceptual contentfull attitudes linked to them.

- Representational states of non-human animals, preverbal children, etc. (domain 3), could be considered intentional mental states or non-intentional ones. In the second case, there would not be attitudes, and we could not make any distinction between the intentional content contained in the state and the content of the state itself. There would be only one single content. And if the subject has not conceptual capacities, that content would be non-conceptual and non-cognitive[12]. In the first case, we could distinguish between the intentional content and the content of the state itself. But the lack of conceptual capacities makes very difficult to see that intentional content as having a conceptual or cognitive character, and also to see the content of the intentional state itself as having any cognitive character. The content of the state would be non-conceptual and non-cognitive.

There would be another important point to be made in relation to domain 3. The attitudes potentially involved in domain 3 could be very similar to the attitudes one could find in other intentional mental states containing intentional contents with a conceptual character. And this would offer a very interesting clue in order to see continuities and differences among all these mental states.

From Non-Intentional Mental States to Intentional Contents with a Conceptual Character

The role of attitudes in the transition from non-intentional, qualitative mental states to intentional states containing intentional contents full of conceptual structure has not received too much attention in the literature. The emphasis has been placed in the relationships between intentional contents of a non-conceptual kind and intentional contents of a conceptual kind. But attitudes would be in a very good position to bridge the *gap* between non-intentional mental states and intentional states containing intentional contents with conceptual structure.

Let us see how that gap could be bridged. On the one hand, consider non-intentional mental states with a non-conceptual and non-cognitive content. On the other hand, consider intentional mental states including both attitudes generating a non-conceptual content and certain intentional contents which, in principle, could be non-conceptual or conceptual. If these intentional contents are conceptual, then they are able to have a direct cognitive character. But, even if they are non-conceptual, the contents generated by the attitudes could give a cognitive character to the intentional

states themselves[13]. This suggests that we could begin with something which is non-conceptual and non-cognitive obtaining at the end something which is conceptual and cognitive, having in the middle something that being non-conceptual can be cognitive.

We could describe a possible transition from the non-conceptual and non-cognitive to the conceptual and cognitive. And it would have two main steps. In the first one, we could go from a non-intentional mental state, with a non-conceptual and non-cognitive content, to an intentional mental state that, thanks to its attitudinal component, has a content which can be cognitive but non-conceptual. In the second one, we could go from that intentional state to something cognitive and conceptual as its peculiar intentional content.

Attitudes originate the possibility of having intentional contents with a conceptual character. And therefore, there is a sense in which attitudes are very close to the conceptual world displayed in our intentional contents conceptually structured. But attitudes, even when they have a cognitive content, always have by themselves a non-conceptual content. In that sense, they would be also very close to the non-conceptual and non-cognitive world of our more basic non-intentional, qualitative mental states. Because of these two-faced character, attitudes would be in a very good position to bridge both worlds.[14]

At the beginning of the paper, I made explicit my independence with respect to (among other things) claims about concept possession. However, I cannot resist now the temptation to say something about that topic. By themselves, all attitudes would lack conceptual content. But attitudes lacking cognitive content could play quite a special role in relation to the acquisition of intentional contents of a conceptual kind. Perhaps there can be intentional contents without a conceptual character, but there cannot be intentional contents without attitudes. Even when intentional contents are intended to be non-conceptual, attitudes are needed in order to have intentional states. And even in these cases, attitudes could originate a content with a cognitive character. That cognitive character will be dependent on the relevance these attitudes can have in relation to the inferential practices of the subject. This suggests the following very important question: How could these attitudes be related with other attitudes and intentional contents full of cognitive character in a way that they can achieve a cognitive character?

Here is a tentative answer. We have said that attitudes with a cognitive content are those able to be relevant in relation to our inferential practices. They orientate and bound the inferences we in fact do. But things also can go

---

[12] Even if we can find here an informational content, that content could not have any inferential relevance and, therefore, it cannot have any cognitive character.

[13] More precisely, they could originate a cognitive character in relation to other intentional states of the subject.

[14] If we subtract from the non-conceptual but cognitive content of "yes!" the conceptual content of "yes", then we would obtain something like a pure non-conceptual content. That content would be, let us say, the content expressed by "!". That would be a content that we can find in some drawings and icons, and that we can also find in many sorts of non-intentional, qualitative mental states.

the other way around. Those attitudes can be *sensitive* to the conceptual structure of the intentional contents. Attitudes have always a non-conceptual content. In some cases, mainly when their intentional contents are conceptual, they can have a clear cognitive character. And, without ceasing to have a non-conceptual content, they also can become *sensitive* to conceptual structures. According to these ideas, we can propose the following very interesting hypothesis:

(H) The fact that intentional contents can be identified through, or even be identified with, some propositions is reducible to the fact that attitudes are sensitive to certain conceptual, abstract structures.

To Become Engaged in the Space of Reasons

We have argued that intentional mental states always have by themselves some kind of non-conceptual, but yet cognitive, content. This would have very important consequences in relation to the notion of "the space of reasons".

By different ways, Brandom and McDowell have made use of Sellars's notion of "the space of reasons", as contrasted with "the space of facts", in order to reject non-conceptual content[15]. The space of reasons would be the realm of spontaneity, the only realm where our peculiar human nature may flourish, and it would be only through conceptual content that we get to be engaged in that space of reasons.

The distinction we have made between conceptual content and cognitive content suggests a direct reformulation of the last claim. The only way to be engaged in the space of reasons is through our psychological attitudes (attitudes of asserting, questioning, asking, demanding, and so on). And as we have seen, even when we adopt psychological attitudes towards intentional contents conceptually structured, and therefore our attitudes get to achieve a direct cognitive relevance, these attitudes always originate a certain non-conceptual content. We cannot become engaged in the space of reasons but through certain non-conceptual contents.

Non-conceptual content is always necessary to make real inferences, both theoretical and practical. One of the more conclusive arguments showing the need to assume that would come from the so called "frame problem" in Artificial Intelligence. Situated conversational skills, for instance, only can be implemented with the help of heuristic rules able to give criteria of relevance and opportunity which cannot be conceptualized by means of other rules. Heuristic rules try to orientate and bound the propositional contents of the system, conceptually structured, in a very similar way to the way our attitudes orientate and bound the propositional contents, conceptually structured, of our intentional states. Without heuristic rules, the system cannot make situated real inferences (decisions, etc., both theoretical and practical). And without the non-conceptual, but yet cognitive, content introduced by our attitudes, we cannot either. Only a non-conceptual but cognitive content

would prevent us from inferring irrelevant or trivial consequences of our thoughts.

From that point of view, the realm of spontaneity would have more to do with attitudes than with intentional contents propositionally characterized and conceptually structured. The space of reason would be only a "map", the conceptual map or rationality. But, to use that map entails moving from one place to another ones. We cannot initiate any moving without something beyond the map. What move us is the "force" of our attitudes. And to use the map is to be sensitive to rational relations. Because of that, our attitudes can have a cognitive character. But attitudes give to our intentional states a content that cannot be, or that cannot be only, conceptual.[16]

Acknowledgments

This paper is part of the Research Project HUM2005-03848/FISIO, Ministry of Education and Science (Spain).

References

Bermúdez, J. (2003). *Thinking without Words*. New York: Oxford Univ. Press.

Brandom, R. (1994). *Making it Explicit. Representing and Discursive Commitment*. Cambridge: Harvard Univ. Press.

Fodor, J. (1998) *Concepts. Where Cognitive Science Went Wrong*. Oxford, Clarendon Press.

McDowell, J. (1994). *Mind and World*. Cambridge: Harvard Univ. Press.

Richard, M. (1990) *Propositional Attitudes*, Cambridge, Cambridge Univ. Press.

Stalnaker, R. (1997). What Might Non-conceptual Content Be? Paper presented at the *SOFIA Conference (Barcelona, June 1997)*.

---------- (1999) *Context and Content*, Oxford, Oxford Univ. Press.

---

[15] See, for instance, Brandom, R. (1994), and McDowell, J. (1994).

[16] This would be "implicit" (but only implicit!) in Brandom's supposition of a background of inferential practices, full of doxastic compromises and other attitudinal ingredients. On the other side, I think that McDowell is not at all clear in the way he makes use of the Kantian notion of "judgment". As in real trials (and this is the Kantian model), cognitive judgments would not be possible without the non-cognitive forces of certain attitudes towards what is offered as "evidences", or as "the given". Here (and not, or not only, in the pure logical space of reasons!) is where our "spontaneity" would have a crucial role to play.

Some Humean Doubts about the Cognitive/Non-Cognitive Divide
Kant, Pragmatism, Sellars, Brandom, and McDowell

Manuel Liz (manuliz@ull.es)
Faculty of Philosophy, Univ. of La Laguna
La Laguna. Canary Islands. SPAIN

Abstract

My aim is to explore the possibility to take a fully Humean stance with respect to the way Kant, Pragmatism, Sellars, Brandom, and McDowell have articulated the distinction between the cognitive and the non-cognitive. I will focus on two problems we can find in all those authors: the problem of circularity and the problem of the metatheoretical lack of justification. I will argue that it would be possible to give an adequate answer to those problems from a fully Humean reinterpretation of Sellars'rejection of the "Myth of the Given".

Introduction: From Hume to Hume

In this paper, I want to explore the possibility to take a fully Humean stance with respect to the way Kant, Pragmatism, Sellars, Brandom, and McDowell have articulated the distinction between the cognitive and the non-cognitive.

There is a strong connection between Sellars' criticism of the Myth of the Given[1] and Hume's thesis about the impossibility of deriving any normative "ought" from any factual "is". But there are also crucial differences between them concerning the extension and limits of those realms. For Hume, all our intentional life related with our experiences and factual beliefs would be inside the realm of the "is", and it cannot have any cognitive value involving a normativity having to do with rationality, epistemic justification, etc.. This would be the source of many of Hume's sceptical positions. In particular, that scepticism also would make very difficult to have any epistemological theory with that kind of cognitive value.

Sellars shares with Kant and with Pragmatism the aim to enlarge the realm of the normative "ought", making room for the cognitive value of experiences and empirical beliefs and, also, for the possibility of an epistemological theory with cognitive value. However, the routes followed are quite different.

On the one hand, Kant maintains a constitutive approach based on transcendental considerations, and his approach would entail an important problem of circularity. In the end, the cognitive outcomes are in serious danger to be simply the cognitive incomes. On the other hand, Pragmatism and Sellars want to maintain a non-transcendentalist approach based on some non-cognitive, buy yet normative, features of

our practices as agents and speakers[2]. The problem of circularity is intended to be solved in that approach. However, this time we would be faced with another problem of metatheoretical lack of justification quite similar to a certain persistent problem we can find in Hume, a problem in relation to the possibility of having an epistemological theory with cognitive value. If the distinction between cognitive value and non-cognitive value, a distinction made by our epistemological theory, has to have itself a cognitive sense, then our epistemological theory would have to have a cognitive value much more *robust* than the one we can obtain merely claiming that certain *prima facie* non-cognitive, but yet normative, facts really are cognitive facts.

Brandom[3] has offered new developments of the line of research initiated by Pragmatism and Sellars. And he pretends to avoid the problem of circularity giving no role to experience in our empirical thinking. In any case, his "expressivist" stance has not solved the problem of the metatheoretical lack of justification.

Trying to preserve a role for experience in empirical thinking, McDowell[4] has tried a more Kantian solution. He reject transcendentalism in favour of a "second nature" naturalism. But he goes on maintaining with respect to experience and empirical beliefs a constitutive approach. As we will see, what we obtain is only a substitution of "inextricability" for transcendentalism. Moreover, his approach would not be enough to solve the problem of circularity.

It is at this point that it seems to me that perhaps it would be better to go back to Hume. Indeed, it would be possible to interpret in a fully Humean sense Sellars' rejection of the Myth of the Given, making room for some non-cognitive, even non-normative, ingredients in concrete tokenings of experiences and empirical beliefs (in general, in concrete tokenings of all of our mental states). And if it is possible such interpretation, then we could have in those concrete tokens of experiences and empirical beliefs certain blends of non-normative (and, therefore, non-cognitive) facts, normative but non-cognitive facts, and cognitive (and, therefore, normative) facts. And, perhaps, these blends

---

[1] See Sellars (1997).

[2] On the pragmatist side, that idea would be specially clear in Dewey and James. See the account of the development of American pragmatism given by Murphy (1990).

[3] Mainly in Brandom (1994).

[4] McDowell (1994).

would be able to bridge Hume's gap between the "is" and the "ought".

Tokens of experiences and tokens of empirical beliefs would be always something between a purely factual "is" and a purely cognitive "ought". In concrete tokens of experiences and concrete tokens of empirical beliefs we would always have something factual making pressure over some cognitive initiatives. I will argue that from that perspective it would be also possible to give an adequate answer to the problem of circularity and to the problem of the metatheoretical lack of justification.

Sellars and Hume: The Factual "Is" and the Cognitive "Ought"

There is a strong *connection* between Sellars' criticism of the Myth of the Given and Hume's thesis about the impossibility of deriving any normative "ought" from a factual "is". Both of them assume that there is no way to derive something normative from something non-normative. In other terms, we could say that we would be always making some kind of "naturalistic fallacy". In the final section, I will distinguish two different ways to take that claim, but for the moment it would be enough that formulation.

However, there are also crucial *differences* between Hume and Sellars concerning the extension and limits of those realms. For Hume, all our intentional life related with our experiences and factual beliefs would be inside the realm of a bare and contingent "is". Perceptions and empirical beliefs would arise through a natural process of copy (or "impression") of non-normative facts[5], and they would not have any cognitive value. They only can have an emotive (or expressive) value. They would be simply the result of our habits and customs[6].

By *"cognitive"*, let us understand in this context simply being able to be a reason for or against a certain claim. So, to have "cognitive value" would be being able to offer reasons for or against certain claims. Here, the key notion would be *rationality*. There would be normative "oughts" of a cognitive kind, and many other ones of a non-cognitive kind. And the impossibility of deriving any normative "ought" from a factual "is" would entail the impossibility of deriving any cognitive "ought" from a factual "is".

As we have said, perceptions and empirical beliefs would be placed, for Hume, only in the space of a bare and contingent factual "is". We are faced with them without being able to *rationally* decide among them[7]. They are

decided only by habit and custom. They arise purely as the result of custom and habit, and reason can neither assist nor oppose that process. Indeed, this would be the source of many of Hume's sceptical positions[8]. Any way, what I want to note is that Hume's perspective would make also very difficult to have any *epistemological theory* with cognitive value. In a strict sense, Hume's approach cannot be presented as an epistemological theory with a cognitive value. That supposed epistemological theory would be also the result of habit and custom.

It appears, however, as if it were possible to make a further move. Even though it cannot be represented as an epistemological theory, certain let us say *Humean facts* could constitute our very "human condition". In other words, it can be argued that there would be no contradiction in maintaining at the same time:

1. It can be true that *p*.
2. It is not possible to claim (with some kind of reasons, or justification, in the context of a theory) that *p* is true

When I say 1, I am claiming that it is possible that *p* is true. But I am not claiming that it is possible to claim (with some kind of justificatory reasons in the context of a theory) that *p* is true. I simply claim that *p* can be true. Hence, there would not be any contradiction in the conjunction of claims 1 and 2.

However, we could reply, to say 1 would not be enough in order to say something with cognitive value. In order to say something with cognitive value when we say 1, it is necessary to reject 2. If what we say in saying 1 has to have a *cognitive* value, then we have to be able to give some answers to questions like "Why are you claiming that it is possible that P?", or "Which reasons do you have to claim that p?" So, it would be contradictory to maintain 1 with cognitive value and, at the same time, to maintain 2. In consequence, no appeal to certain *Humean facts*, facts beyond the reach of our epistemological theories, could have any cognitive value.

Things are very different for Sellars. Here, all intentional phenomena would be inside the realm of a normative "ought" of a cognitive kind. Sellars argues that all intentional events are full of normative features, and this would entail that there is no possible way to bridge the gap

---

[5] I will use the term "fact" in a very liberal sense. That use intends to be neutral with respect to theses like, for instance, Sellars' thesis that sensation deals with particulars whereas perception, belief, and knowledge deal with facts.

[6] We can read in Hume, for instance, the following: "... belief is more properly an act of the sensitive, than of the cogitative part of our natures". (*Teatrise*, Book I, part iv, sec. ii).

[7] "All probable reasoning is nothing but a species of sensation. [...] When I am convinced of any principle, this is only an idea, which strikes more strongly upon me. When I give preference to one set of arguments above

another, I do nothing but decide from my feeling concerning the superiority of their influence". Hume (*Teatrise*, Book I, part iii, sec. viii).

[8] Beyond the classical areas for such Humean scepticism (induction, causality, the self, morality, religion, etc.), there would be two other possible areas: non-empirical beliefs (beliefs involving relations among "ideas"), regulated by the principle of non-contradiction, and the peculiar force attributed to habit and custom. These two areas are in the core of Hume's project. But, on the one hand, particular tokens of non-empirical beliefs would be so contingent as any other particular fact, and, on the other hand, the claim about the peculiar force attributed to habit and custom is a claim derived from an induction (it would be odd to say that it is a non-empirical claim). Could it be coherently maintained an extension of Humean scepticism to those two areas? This would be a very important problems that I cannot discuss here.

between non-intentional facts, of any kind, and intentional ones. Moreover, those normative features would be fully *cognitive*. All intentional events would live in the cognitive "space of reasons". Even apparently bare perceptive experiences would be full of cognitive ingredients. They would be mediated by our thoughts about the world and the authority we allow each other over various kinds of reports.

With respect to the possibility of an epistemological theory, we do not find in Sellars the sort of problem we have found in Hume. Hand to hand with the rest of our beliefs and theories, our epistemological theory would live *also* in the normative and cognitive "space of reasons".

Transcendentalism and Two Open Problems: Circularity and Metatheoretical Lack of Justification

Sellars shares with Kant and with Pragmatism the aim to enlarge the realm of the "ought", making room for the cognitive value of perceptive experiences and empirical beliefs and, also, for the possibility of an epistemological theory with cognitive value. However, the route followed by both Pragmatism and Sellars is quite *different* from the route followed by Kant.

Kant maintains a *constitutive* approach based on *transcendental* considerations. Experiences and empirical beliefs would have a cognitive value because they are constitutively structured by something having just that kind of cognitive value, having the epistemological theory describing those facts a transcendental character.

Against Hume, Kant maintains the transcendental need to understand perceptive experiences and empirical beliefs in terms of constitutive rules and organizing principles that are normative and *cognitive*, and not in terms of any kind of "copy" of certain non-normative facts given in experience. Perceptive experiences and empirical beliefs would be, for Kant, full of cognitive ingredients all the way down. So, they can have a robust cognitive value. And it would be *also* possible to have an epistemological theory. That epistemological theory, however, would be of a very special kind. It would be a *transcendental* theory establishing the conditions of possibility of certain phenomena.

Really, it is a hard problem to assure the cognitive value of a transcendental epistemological theory. That cognitive value cannot have an empirical source, nor having a mere logical character either. Any way, I want to note another sort of problem. The Kantian approach would entail an important *problem of circularity*. The cognitive outcomes obtained in perceptive experiences and empirical beliefs are in serious danger to be no more than the cognitive incomes received from the subject.

The Kantian transcendental route has been followed by some continental philosophies, for instance by Phenomenology. But both Pragmatism and Sellars reject it. Instead of an transcendental constitution internal to the subject of the cognitive contents of perception and belief, what we have here are some *external, prima facie non-cognitive, but yet normative, facts* from which those

cognitive contents can be obtained. Pragmatism and Sellars want to maintain a non-transcendentalist approach[9] based on some features of our practices as agents and speakers. Experiences and empirical beliefs would have a cognitive value coming from other *prima facie* non-cognitive, but yet normative, facts. Our epistemological theory would argue for the identification of these facts with something having the intended cognitive value.

The problem of circularity appears to be solved in that approach. However, this time we would have another *problem of metatheoretical lack of justification* quite close to the one we have detected in Hume. According to this epistemological theory, there would not be more cognitive value in our perceptive experiences and empirical beliefs than the cognitive value we can find in some *prima facie* non-cognitive, but yet normative, facts. But if the distinction between cognitive value and non-cognitive value has to have any cognitive sense, then the epistemological theory would have to have a cognitive value much more *robust* than the cognitive value we can obtain merely claiming that those *prima facie* non-cognitive, but yet normative, facts really are cognitive facts.

Pragmatism, Brandom, and McDowell

Some classical pragmatist theses would illustrate perfectly the relationships between the problem of circularity and the problem of the metatheoretical lack of justification. And those relationships would serve to introduce the recent proposals of Brandom and McDowell.

There is a crucial, let us say, *problem of identification* in classical pragmatism about the key notion of practical success ("success in action", "to work satisfactorily", and the like). The problem is to answer the following question: How can we identify a practical success having some cognitive value (in the sense we are using that term)?

There would be two different ways to try to give an answer to that question:

1. Theoretical answer: A practical success with cognitive value never is something given. It is always identified in the *context* of our concepts, beliefs, theories, general conceptions about the life, etc.

2. Metatheoretical answer: As something given, we are able to identify a practical success with certain *prima facie* non-cognitive, but yet normative, features, and we attribute to that practical success a cognitive value through a certain *epistemological* theory.

Usually, these two kinds of answers are *not* very well distinguished. But they are very different. In James, for instance, we can find the view that to work satisfactorily has to be understood in the broadest sense of the word, involving in the end our whole conception of the life.

---

[9] To say here "a naturalistic approach" would force us to define the sort of naturalism involved and, surely, we would find important differences between classical pragmatists and Sellars. In any case, what is clearly shared by both, classical pragmatists and Sellars, is their rejection of transcendentalism.

Sometimes, Dewey also gives an answer to the problem of identification in such contextualist terms. These would be theoretical answers of the first kind. But we can also find metatheoretical answers. James' view of practical success as having a normative force that would have to be identified with truth is of that second kind. Peirce account of truth as what processes of enquiry would tend to accept if pursued to an ideal limit would be too a sort of metatheoretical answer to the problem of identification and, also, the idea of Dewey that selection natural has made of us cognitive creatures because our beliefs can have practical success.

Now, it is easy to see that the theoretical answer is directly faced with a *problem of circularity* quite similar to the Kantian one. Our concepts, beliefs, theories, general conceptions, etc., make possible the identification of something as a practical success with cognitive value. But, we can ask, where do the cognitive value of those concepts, beliefs, theories, general conceptions, etc., come from? The cognitive outcomes of our perceptive experiences and empirical beliefs are in danger of being no more than the cognitive incomes provided by the subjects.

As we have noted in relation to Sellars, to give a metatheoretical answer to the problem of identification would make us able to avoid the problem of circularity. However, we would be involved in the *problem of the metatheoretical lack of justification* we have found both in Sellars and Hume. How to understand the epistemological theories proposed? All of these theories would claim that cognitive value can be identified with certain *prima facie* non-cognitive, but yet normative, features. But, if there is a cognitively relevant *distinction* between the cognitive and the non-cognitive, then those epistemological theories would have to offer a cognitive value more *robust* than the one present in those *prima facie* non-cognitive, but yet normative, facts. In other words, if it is possible a robust, not merely "*emotivist*" or "*expressivist*", epistemological theory claiming, for instance, that truth is reducible to practical success, then that epistemological theory itself has to have a truth not reducible to practical success

In other words, the reasons for those epistemological theories reducing cognitive value to other *prima facie* non-cognitive, but yet normative, facts *cannot be reduced* to what we can find in these *prima facie* non-cognitive, but yet normative, facts. If it is claimed that they can be so reduced, then this would entail that there is *no cognitively relevant distinction* between the cognitive and the non-cognitive. And in that case, just as in the case of Hume, there would be no point in formulate any of those epistemological theories. They could not have *any* cognitive value.

There are in Sellars many of the ideas we can find in classical Pragmatism. Sellars' insistence in the role of concepts and beliefs in perception, as something opposed to mere sensation, places him very close to the *theoretical* answer of Pragmatism to the problem of identification. And there is also in Sellars an appeal to the limit of "the scientific image of the world" very close to Pragmatist *metatheoretical* answers.

Brandom[10] has offered new developments of the line of research initiated by Pragmatism and Sellars. And, in fact, he gets to avoid the problem of circularity adopting some sort of *radical* metatheoretical answer. He takes as something given certain *prima facie* non-cognitive, but yet normative, facts having to do with our ability to be involved in certain *linguistic practices*. And he adopts the strategy to give no role to experience in our empirical thinking. In any case, that radical metatheoretical answer has not solved the *problem of the metatheoretical lack of justification*. Moreover, "expressivism" would be a name for that very problem.

Brandom's epistemological theory would be expressivist. Its main aim is to make *explicit* what we implicitly do when we are engaged in certain cognitive practices. And according to Brandom, making something explicit would be *saying* it, putting it into a form in which it *can* be given as a reason (or reasons can be commanded for it). The epistemological theory would say what we do when we are involved in cognitive practices.

Now, the problem would be that in order to give reasons, it is not enough to say something that *can* be given as a reason. There is a crucial difference between, on the one hand, to say something that *can* be a reason and, on the other hand, to *be* a reason. But the *expressivist* epistemological theory of Brandom only can offer things of the first kind. And in order to offer things of the second kind we would have to *abandon* expressivism. We would have to elaborate more *robust* epistemological theories.[11]

Trying to preserve a role for experience in empirical thinking, McDowell[12] has tried a more *Kantian* solution. As we have said, he reject transcendentalism in favor of a "second nature" naturalism. And he goes on maintaining with respect to experience and empirical beliefs a *constitutive* approach. But, what we obtain is only a substitution of "inextricability" for transcendentalism, and this would not be enough to solve the *problem of circularity*.

McDowell claims that perceptive experiences should be regarded as combining receptivity and spontaneity in an "*inextricable*" way. The subject is made receptive (responsive to reality) by the fact that his conceptual spontaneity is already operative in perceptive experience.

---

[10] See Brandom (1994). Brandom (2000) would offer an easy introduction to the complexities of his approach.

[11] Consider, for instance, the following text of Brandom (1994): "To express something is to make it *explicit*. What is explicit in the fundamental sense has a *propositional* content –the content of a claim, judgment, or belief (claimable, judgeable, believable contents). That is, making something explicit is *saying* it: putting it into a form in which it can be given as a reason, and reasons demanded for it. Putting something forward in the explicit form of a claim is the basic move of giving and asking for reasons". The important point would be that to make explicit a claim does not entail to make another claim. It only entails *to say* what the claim is. Hence, an expressivist epistemology theory would be of a "Humean sort". In a strict sense, it cannot *make* any claim. More precisely, it only can *say* what our claims are.

[12] See McDowell (1994). In order to assess the relationships between McDowell and Kant, see also McDowell (1998).

But we cannot look at the features of perceptive experience and divide out those which come from the side of receptivity and those which come from the side of spontaneity. McDowell works within the Kantian picture in which conceptual, cognitive capacities are not exercised "on" what receptivity delivers, but instead they are exercised "in" receptivity. Receptivity and spontaneity make a "not even notionally" separable contribution.[13]

We can accept that one can maintain that thesis of inextricability *without* assuming the transcendentalism of Kant. And I think that this can be done adopting something like McDowell's "second nature" naturalism. However, this would not be enough in order to give an answer to the problem of circularity. To give an answer to that problem requires to *distinguish* contents of perceptive experiences from contents of empirical beliefs. And this seems to entail a rejection of the inextricability thesis. Moreover, in an analogous way to what happens in the case of Brandom, "inextricability" appears here as a mere name of that very problem of circularity.

Hume vs. Sellars: Cognitive Tokens

At this point, I want to argue that perhaps it would be more useful to go back to Hume. Indeed, it would be always possible to interpret in a fully *Humean* sense Sellars' rejection of the Myth of the Given. The extension of the realm of the "ought" could be *not so wide* as it is intended to be by Sellars, Pragmatism, and Kant.

As we have said, the key notion involved in the concept of a cognitive value would be the notion of rationality. And exactly in the same way in which we can speak in other fields of a *"bounded rationality"*, in opposition to an "ideal rationality", we could maintain here that the realm of the factual "is" puts severe limits to every *concrete* tokening or exemplification of a cognitive value in our perceptual experiences and empirical beliefs

Hume's rejection of the cognitive value of perceptive experiences and empirical beliefs is based on the *contingent* character of every concrete token in the space of facts. But, by such concrete tokens we would not have to think only on the intentional objects of our perceptive experiences and empirical beliefs. The *having* of perceptive experiences and empirical beliefs would be also concrete tokens, particular facts or events. Moreover, in these concrete tokens we would necessarily have certain blends of non-normative (and, therefore non-cognitive) facts, normative but non-cognitive facts, and cognitive (and, therefore, normative) facts. Now, we can ask, would these blends be able to bridge Hume's gap between the "is" and the "ought"?

The thesis about the impossibility of deriving any normative "ought" from an "is" can be interpreted in *two* very different ways:

1. as saying that no "ought" can be derived from anything else, or
2. as saying that no bare "is" can entail any "ought".

---

[13] "We must not suppose that receptivity makes an even notionally separable contribution to its co-operation with spontaneity" McDowell (1994: 41).

The important point is that the first interpretation would be *too much strong*. Not only because the realm of the "ought" appears to be here something autonomous and self-sufficient, but because it makes also very difficult to derive any particular "ought" from *other ones*.

Even if we admit the existence of certain *relevant kinds* of interrelated normative facts, according to the first interpretation we could not derive normative facts of one kind from normative facts of *other kinds*. That would be also fallacious. Each kind of normativity would be peculiar, autonomous and self-sufficient. But this is what would happen in the project of deriving cognitive facts from other *prima facie* non-cognitive, but yet normative, facts. In analogy with the expression "naturalistic fallacy", this other fallacy could be called a *"normative fallacy"*. Unless we consider that all those normative facts are *fully cognitive* all the way down, i.e., that there are not relevant differences between perceptive experiences and all the other kinds of cognitive facts (conceptual contents, beliefs, theories, etc.), to make room for that entailment would force the adoption of the *second interpretation* of the thesis.

Here, it is important to note that to consider that those normative facts are fully cognitive all the way down would entail to be directly faced with the Kantian problem of circularity. As we have said, McDowell would follow that approach.

Now, what I am going to argue is that if we try to avoid that peculiar version of the problem of circularity through an *epistemological* theory, like the ones we can find in Sellars or in Pragmatism, or if we try to avoid that problem through a more radical strategy like that of Brandom (an extreme reinterpretation of some of the ideas we can find in Sellars and Pragmatism), then we will arrive to a position from which, if we adopt the second interpretation of the impossibility of deriving an "ought" from an "is", then perhaps we could be able both to bridge in some way the Humean gap, between the "is" and the "ought", and also to go out of the problems of circularity and of the metatheoretical lack of justification.

Under the second interpretation of the thesis about the impossibility of deriving any normative "ought" from an "is", it would be possible to derive an "ought" from something that is not a *bare* "is". And this would be what we would necessarily have in every concrete tokening or exemplification of our perceptive experiences and empirical beliefs. *Tokens* of perceptive experiences and *tokens* of empirical beliefs would be always something between a *bare* factual "is" and an *ideal* cognitive "ought".

Moreover, in concrete tokens of perceptive experiences and concrete tokens of empirical beliefs, we would always have *something factual making pressure over some cognitive initiatives*. The pure cognitive value of these initiatives would be appreciated adopting an *ideal* point of view. But, when those cognitive initiatives are *tokened*, they loose that ideal character. They become something cognitive (and, therefore, normative) placed in the "space of non-normative facts".

An useful *picture* of the relationships that the non-normative and the cognitive would be able to maintain in concrete tokens of perceptive experiences and concrete tokens of empirical beliefs would consist in a series of cognitive possibilities following an *orthogonal* series of non-normative facts. The superposition of all those cognitive possibilities would constitute the Sellarsian "cognitive space of reasons". However, *only some* of those cognitive possibilities would be linked to each concrete factual tokening of our perceptive experiences and empirical beliefs, and in that sense the non-normative would be making certain kinds of *pressures* over the cognitive.[14]

Would this proposal be able to give an adequate answer to the problem of circularity and to the problem of the metatheoretical lack of justification? What is needed in order to go out of the *problem of circularity* is a way to establish relevant differences between perceptive experiences and all the other kinds of cognitive facts (conceptual contents, beliefs, theories, etc.). A suggesting hypothesis would be that this could be done through some differences in the *kinds of pressures* involved in the tokenings of perceptive experiences with respect to the tokening of all the other cognitive facts.

It would be much more easy to give an answer to the *problem of the metatheoretical lack of justification*. As we have said, tokens of beliefs (of any kind) and other intentional states would be always a *blend* of non-normative (and, therefore, non-cognitive) facts, normative but non-cognitive facts, and cognitive (and, therefore, normative) facts. So, all of our beliefs could have a *robust* cognitive value. This would make possible to have an epistemological theory full of cognitive value and, at the same time, free of the problem of the metatheoretical lack of justification.

Acknowledgments

This paper is part of the Research Project HUM2005-03848/FISIO, Ministry of Education and Science (Spain).

References

Brandom, R. (1994). *Making it Explicit. Representing and Discursive Commitment*. Cambridge: Harvard Univ. Press.

Brandom, R. (2000). *Articulating Reasons. An Introduction to Inferentialism*. Cambridge: Harvard Univ. Press.

McDowell, J. (1994). *Mind and World*. Cambridge: Harvard Univ. Press.

McDowell, J. (1998). Having the World in view: Sellars, Kant, and Intentionality (The Woodbridge Lectures 1997). *The Journal of Philosophy*, vol. XCV, n° 9, 431-491.

Murphy, J. (1990) *Pragmatism: From Peirce to Davidson*. Boulder: Westview Press.

Sellars, W. (1997). *Empiricism and the Philosophy of Mind (with an introduction by Richard Rorty and a study guide by Robert Brandom*. Cambridge: Harvard Univ. Press [originally published in *Minnesota Studies in the Philosophy of Science*, vol. 1, ed. Herbert Feigl and Michael Scriven, Minneapolis: Univ. of Minnesota Press, 1956].

---

[14] We could say similar things with respect to the relationships between the cognitive and the normative but non-cognitive, and also with respect to the relationships between the normative but non-cognitive and the non-normative. Of course, this would make our picture much more complex.

Grounding a Cognitive Modelling Approach for Criminal Behaviour

Tibor Bosse (tbosse@few.vu.nl)   **Charlotte Gerritsen (cg@few.vu.nl)**   **Jan Treur (treur@few.vu.nl)**

Vrije Universiteit Amsterdam, Department of Artificial Intelligence
De Boelelaan 1081, 1081 HV, Amsterdam, The Netherlands

Abstract

This article presents a cognitive modelling approach for criminal behaviour, which is illustrated by a case study for the behaviour of three types of violent criminals as known from literature within the area of Criminology. The model can show each of their behaviours, depending on the characteristics set and inputs in terms of stimuli from the environment. Based on literature in Criminology about motivations and opportunities and their underlying factors, it is shown by a formal mapping how the model can be related to a biological grounding. This formal mapping covers ontology elements for states and dynamic properties for processes, and thus shows how the cognitive model can be biologically grounded.

Introduction

The field of Criminology, which addresses the analysis of criminal behaviour, is a multi-disciplinary area with a high societal relevance; e.g., (Cohen and Felson, 1979; Cornish and Clarke, 1986; Gottfredson and Hirschi, 1990; Raine, 1993; Towl and Crighton, 1996; Turvey, 1999). Criminal behaviour, which is shown by a minority of the overall population, typically comes in many types and variations, often related to specific individual characteristics. Not many contributions in the literature can be found that address formalisation and computational modelling of criminal behaviour; e.g., (Baal, 2004; Brantingham and Brantingham, 2004; Melo, Belchior, and Furtado, 2005; Liu, Wang, Eck, and Liang, 2005).

This paper first discusses a modelling approach at the cognitive level for different types of violent criminal behaviour. The cognitive model involves motivations (in particular desires and intentions) and beliefs in opportunities; e.g., (Georgeff and Lansky, 1987; Rao and Georgeff, 1991). Dynamical models were incorporated, addressing psychological factors relating to desires, such as levels of anxiety and excitement arousal, empathy or theory of mind (TOM), impulsiveness, and aggressiveness; e.g. (Raine, 1993; Moir and Jessel, 1995; Delfos, 2004). For example, certain types of criminal actions are more likely to be performed by persons that have a high impulsiveness, or a lack of empathy. Another part of the cognitive model addresses the generation of beliefs in opportunities, formalising the well-known Routine Activity Theory within Criminology; e.g., (Cohen and Felson, 1979). This (informal) theory assumes a certain motivation of the criminal and covers opportunities based on the perceived presence of targets (e.g., potential victims) and social control (e.g., guardians). The resulting cognitive model covers eight categories of aspects that play a role in criminal behaviour, and dynamical system models for these aspects.

To show how this cognitive model can be grounded in biological states and processes, a formal mapping was defined. This mapping relates ontology elements describing cognitive states to ontology elements describing biological states. Moreover, it relates temporal relationships between cognitive states, specified in the form of dynamic properties, to corresponding relationships between biological states. This mapping, covering both states and processes shows how the cognitive model can be grounded in the biological area.

To formalise the overall model, the language LEADSTO (Bosse, Jonker, Meij, and Treur, 2005) has been used. In LEADSTO direct temporal dependencies between two state properties in successive states are modelled by *executable dynamic properties*. The format of such dynamic properties is defined as follows. Let α and β be state properties of the form 'conjunction of ground atoms or negations of ground atoms'. In this language the notation $\alpha \twoheadrightarrow_{e, f, g, h} \beta$, means:

If state property α holds for a certain time interval with duration g, then after some delay (between e and f) state property β will hold for a certain time interval of length h.

Here atomic state properties can have either a qualitative, logical format, such as an expression desire(d) (expressing that desire d occurs), or a quantitative, numerical format, such as an expression has_value(x, v) (which expresses that variable x has value v). For more details of the language LEADSTO, see (Bosse, Jonker, Meij, and Treur, 2005).

The cognitive model as presented involves a variety of cognitive characteristics and states that affect the motivational states and hence the behaviour. A relevant, but nontrivial question is how these characteristics and states can be grounded. In (Bosse, Jonker and Treur, 2006) three ways of grounding of a cognitive state are considered: (1) by its functional role, (2) by its representation relations, (3) by its physical realisation. For the various cognitive states in the model, these types of grounding are addressed in the current paper. In the first place, the functional roles of the cognitive states are specified in a formal manner that is also used as a basis for the simulation model. Second, representation relations (Kim, 1996) can be obtained by a transitive closure of such functional role descriptions. Finally, for each of the cognitive states it is shown how it can be mapped onto a biological state that plays the role of realiser of this cognitive state; cf. (Nagel, 1961; Kim, 1996). This mapping between states has been formally defined, and extended to dynamic properties, as a variant of the concept of interpretation mapping in Logic.

Three Types of Criminals

The case study made in this paper focuses on three types of violent offenders: the violent psychopath, the offender with an antisocial personality disorder (APD), and the offender who suffers from an intermittent explosive disorder (IED). Below, these types of criminals are briefly introduced and differences between them are discussed, based on (Raine, 1993; Moir and Jessel, 1995; Delfos, 2004):

- Violent psychopaths do not have feelings like the rest of us. They lack the normal mechanisms of anxiety arousal, which ring alarm bells of fear in most people. Their kind of violence is similar to predatory aggression, which is accompanied by minimal sympathetic arousal, and is purposeful and without emotion. Moreover, they like to exert power and have unrestricted dominance over others, ignoring their needs and justifying the use of whatever they feel compelling to achieve their goals. They do not have the slightest sense of regret.
- Persons with APD have characteristics that are similar to the psychopath. However, they may experience some emotions towards other persons, but these emotions are mainly negative: they are very hostile and intolerant.
- Persons with IED, in contrast, appear to function normally in their daily life. However, during some short periods (which will be referred to as *episodes* from now on), their brain generates some form of miniature epileptic fit. As a result, some very aggressive impulses are released and expressed in serious assault or destruction of property. After these episodes, IED persons have no recollection of their actions and show feelings of remorse.

These three types of criminals can be distinguished by taking a number of aspects into account (which are all incorporated in the model):

Anxiety Threshold: this is a threshold that needs to be passed by certain stimuli, in order to make a person anxious. Thus, when a person's anxiety threshold is high, it is very difficult for this person to become anxious (and as a result, (s)he hardly knows any fear). This is the case for the violent psychopath and the person with APD: in these persons, a notion of fear is almost completely lacking. In contrast, persons with IED have a medium anxiety threshold. Nevertheless, in some special circumstances (i.e., during episodes) the anxiety threshold of a person with IED suddenly becomes much higher.

Excitement Threshold: this is a threshold that needs to be passed by certain stimuli, in order to make a person excited. Thus, when a person's excitement threshold is high, it is very difficult for this person to become excited (and as a result, (s)he is often bored). This is the case for the violent psychopath and for persons with APD. Persons with IED have a medium excitement threshold, but under certain circumstances (during episodes) their excitement threshold becomes high, and they get bored very easily. Consequently, they will generate the desire to perform certain actions that provide strong stimuli (which are often criminal actions).

Theory of mind: the notion of theory of mind (e.g., Humphrey, 1984; Dennett, 1987; Baron-Cohen, 1995)

covers two concepts: 1) having the understanding that others (also) have minds, which can be described by separate mental concepts, such as the person's own beliefs, desires, and intentions, and 2) being able to form theories as to how those mental concepts play a role in the person's behaviour. The violent psychopath has a theory of mind that is specialised in aspects that can contribute to his own goals. He is able to form theories about another person's beliefs, desires and intentions and may use these theories (e.g., to manipulate this person), but just does not care about these states. A person with APD has a less developed theory of mind. Persons with IED mostly have a normal theory of mind and can make the distinction between themselves and others, but during episode, their theory of mind decreases.

Emotional attitudes towards others: these concepts express the extent to which a person may have positive or negative feelings with respect to other persons' wellbeing. For the violent psychopath, both attitudes are low: these persons hardly show any emotion concerning other persons, so for them, both the positive and the negative emotional attitude towards others are low. For the criminal with APD, the situation is slightly different. Like the violent psychopaths, these persons do not have many positive feelings towards others, but they may have some negative feeling towards others. Finally, criminals with IED usually have a normal (medium) positive and negative emotional attitude towards others, but during episodes, all their positive feelings disappear, and substantial additional negative feelings arise.

Aggressiveness: since this paper focuses on violent criminals, by definition all considered types of criminals are aggressive. However, the criminals with IED only become highly aggressive during episodes, whereas the other two types are always aggressive.

Impulsiveness: when someone acts impulsive, this means that the action was not planned. All types of violent criminals mentioned in this paper are impulsive, but they differ in the type of impulsive action they perform. While the APD offender may lash out in disproportionate overreaction, the psychopath, with his emotional detachment, will impulsively take whatever course of action will supply him with the necessary gratification. Persons with IED normally have a medium impulsiveness but during episodes they become highly impulsive.

Sensitivity to alcohol: For psychopaths and persons with APD, a small amount of alcohol or drugs can result in violent behaviour. For persons with IED, episodes can be triggered by small amounts of alcohol.

The Simulation Model

In this section the simulation model that has been developed is described in more detail[1]. It has been built by composing three submodels:

---

[1] Appendix A in www.cs.vu.nl/~tbosse/crim/sim-model.pdf shows a complete overview of the model (both in textual and in visual representation) and some simulation traces.

1. a model to determine actions based on beliefs, desires and intentions (*BDI-model*)
2. a model *to determine desires* used as input by the BDI-model
3. a model *to determine beliefs in an opportunity* as input for the BDI-model

The BDI-model bases actions on motivational states. It describes how desires lead to intentions and how intentions lead to actions, when the appropriate opportunities are there. It needs as input desires and beliefs in opportunities, generated by the other two submodels.

The BDI-submodel

Part of the model for criminal behaviour is based on the BDI-model, a model that bases the preparation and performing of actions on beliefs, desires and intentions (e.g., Georgeff and Lansky, 1987; Rao and Georgeff, 1991; Jonker, Treur, and Wijngaards, 2003). This model shows a long tradition in the literature, going back to Aristotle's analysis of how humans (and animals) can come to actions. In this model an action is performed when the subject has the intention to do this action and it has the belief that the opportunity to do the action is there. Beliefs are created on the basis of stimuli that are sensed or observed. The intention to do a specific type of action is created if there is a certain desire, and there is the belief that in the given world state, performing this action will fulfil this desire:

desire(d) ∧ belief(satisfies(a, d))   ⟶ intention(a)
intention(a) ∧ belief(opportunity_for(a))   ⟶ is_performed(a)

Assuming that beliefs about how to satisfy desires are internally available, what remains to be generated in this model are the desires and the beliefs in opportunities. Generation of desires often depends on domain-specific knowledge, which also seems to be the case for criminal behaviour. Beliefs in opportunities are based on the Routine Activity Theory by (Cohen and Felson, 1979).

The Submodel to Determine Desires

To determine desires, a rather complex submodel is used incorporating various aspects. To model these, both causal and logical relations (as in qualitative modelling) and numerical relations (as in differential equations) have been integrated in one modelling framework. This integration was accomplished, using the LEADSTO language as a modelling language. A variety of aspects, which were found relevant in the literature (such as Raine, 1993; Moir and Jessel, 1995; Bartol, 2002; Delfos, 2004) are taken into account in this submodel. These aspects can be grouped as: (a) use of a *theory of mind* (e.g., understanding others), (b) desires for *aggressiveness* (e.g., using violence), (c) desires to *act* (no matter which type of action) and (d) to *act safely* (e.g., avoiding risk), (e) desires for *actions with strong stimuli* (e.g., thrill seeking), (f) desires for *impulsiveness* (e.g., unplanned action), and (g) social-emotional *attitudes with respect to others* (e.g., feel pity for someone). Note that these aspects are derived on the basis of (but not exactly equal to) the eight characteristics as described in the previous section. Different combinations of such elements lead to different types of (composed) desires, for example:

- the desire to perform an exciting planned nonaggressive nonrisky action that harms somebody else (e.g., a pick pocket action in a large crowd),
- the desire to perform an exciting impulsive aggressive risky action that harms somebody else (e.g., killing somebody in a violent manner in front of the police department)

The following LEADSTO property (LP) is used to generate a composed desire out of the different ingredients covered by (a) to (g) above; here the x_1, x_2, x_3, x_4, x_5, x_6, x_7, x_8 are qualitative labels (e.g., high, medium, low) or numerical values (integer or real numbers):

LP24 A combination of values for theory of mind, desire for aggressiveness, desire to act, desire to act safely, desire for actions with strong stimuli, desire for impulsiveness, emotional attitude towards others(pos) and emotional attitude towards others(neg) will lead to a specific composed desire, represented as $d(x_1, x_2, x_3, x_4, x_5, x_6, x_7, x_8)$.

∀x1,x2,x3,x4,x5,x6,x7,x8:SCALE
theory_of_mind(x1) ∧ desire_for_aggressiveness(x2) ∧ desire_to_act(x3) ∧ desire_to_act_safely(x4) ∧ desire_for_actions_with_strong_stimuli(x5) ∧ desire_for_impulsiveness(x6) ∧ emotional_attitude_towards_others(pos,x7) ∧ emotional_attitude_towards_others(neg,x8)
⟶ desire(d(x1, x2, x3, x4, x5, x6, x7, x8))

Due to space limitations, the parts of the submodel to determine each of the ingredients (a) to (g) cannot be described in detail. To give an impression, a rough sketch of part of this submodel is given. Stimuli are labeled with two aspects, indicating the strength with respect to anxiety (risk), and with respect to excitement (thrill), respectively. For both aspects, thresholds represent characteristics of the person considered. The excitement threshold depends on other aspects in the model, such as sensitivity for (and use of) drugs and alcohol, and basic sensitivity to stimuli. A stimulus with excitement strength below the excitement threshold leads to being bored, and being bored leads to a desire for actions with strong(er) stimuli (which are often criminal actions). In contrast, a stimulus with anxiety strength above the anxiety threshold leads to internal alarm bells, which (depending on another characteristic, the tendency to look for safety) leads to the desire to perform only 'safe' actions (which are usually not criminal actions).

The Submodel to Determine Opportunities

Beliefs in opportunities are based on two of the three criteria as indicated in the Routine Activity Theory by (Cohen and Felson, 1979), namely the *presence of a suitable target*, and the *absence of social control* (guardians). The third criterion of the Routine Activity Theory, the *presence of a motivated offender*, is indicated by the intention in the BDI-model. This way, the presence of the three criteria together leads to the action to perform a criminal act, in accordance with (Cohen and Felson, 1979). This was specified by the following property in LEADSTO format:

LP34 When a suitable target for a certain action is observed, and no suitable guardian is observed, then a belief is created that there is an opportunity to perform this action.

∀a:ACTION
observes(suitable_target_for(a)) ∧ not observes(suitable_guardian_for(a))
⟶ belief(opportunity(a))

An Example Simulation Trace

The model described in the previous section has been used to generate a number of simulation traces for the different types of violent criminals addressed. In Figure 1, an example simulation trace is depicted, addressing the case of the criminal with APD. Here, time is on the horizontal axis; state properties are on the vertical axis. A dark box on top of the line indicates that the property is true during that time period, a lighter box below the line indicates that it is false.

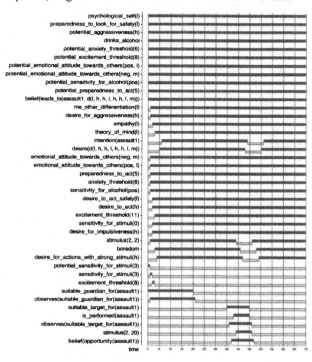

Figure 1: Example simulation trace.

The initial state properties that have been set to model the person with APD are (see time point 0): low psychological self, low preparedness to look for safety, high potential aggressiveness, rather high potential anxiety and excitement threshold (resp. value 6 and 8), potentially a low positive and a medium negative emotional attitude towards others, a low potential sensitivity for stimuli (value 3), and (s)he drinks alcohol and is sensitive for it. These initial characteristics, combined certain world stimuli, eventually lead to a specific composed desire d(l, h, h, l, h, h, l, m) (see time point 5), characterised by the following ingredients: low theory of mind, high aggressiveness, high desire to act, low desire to act safely, high desire for actions with strong stimuli, high impulsiveness, low positive and medium negative emotional attitude towards others. As a result, the criminal generates an intention to perform a specific type of assault (denoted by assault1), and, as soon as the opportunity is there, actually performs the assault. As a result, the stimuli increase, which satisfies the desires of the criminal.

Mapping Cognitive to Biological States

The psychological concepts used within Criminology to describe criminal behaviour are often complex concepts for which it is not always easy to give a precise definition. It may even be argued that for some of these concepts, there is a risk of circularity. For example, the internal state of aggressiveness may be related to aggressive or violent behaviour[2]. To clarify such issues, it may be worthwhile to have some reflection on how these concepts are embedded in reality. In (Bosse, Jonker and Treur, 2006) three perspectives are put forward: (1) specification of functional roles, (2) specification of representation relations, cf. (Kim, 1996), and (3) specification of realisation relations. Here (1) is already covered by the LEADSTO properties of the simulation model. Moreover, (2) can be obtained from these functional role specifications by determining their transitive closure. For the third way of grounding of the cognitive model, a mapping from this model to biological concepts has been established; this maps cognitive states to anatomical, neurophysiological and biochemical states, and cognitive dynamics onto biological dynamics. In this section it is discussed how a conceptualisation based on cognitive state properties can formally be mapped onto a conceptualisation based on biological states properties. In the following section this basic mapping is extended to a mapping of dynamics based on traces, executable (LEADSTO) properties and more complex dynamic properties.

In literature within Criminology, often relationships between cognitive states and biological (anatomical, neurological, biochemical) states are discussed; e.g., (Raine, 1993; Moir and Jessel, 1995). A mapping from the cognitive to a biological conceptualisation of the case study is shown in Table 1. Here a state property a in the left hand side column corresponds to the state property $\varphi(a)$ as indicated in the right hand side column; for example,

$$\varphi(\text{desire\_for\_aggressiveness}(v)) = \text{chemical\_state}(\text{testosterone}, v).$$

The assumption behind the mapping is that if $b = \varphi(a)$, then b is true if and only if a is true.

In the literature on reduction in Philosophy of Mind or Philosophy of Science, this mapping is called a biconditional bridge principle, sometimes denoted by $a \leftrightarrow b$; e.g., (Kim, 1996; Nagel, 1961). Based on this mapping of state properties, cognitive states as a whole can be mapped onto biological states. A state S over state ontology Ont is characterised by an assignment of truth values S: At(Ont) → {true, false}. Each cognitive state S can be mapped onto a biological state $\varphi(S)$ by $\varphi(S)(\varphi(a)) = S(a)$ for any cognitive ground atom a (with $\varphi(a)$ the corresponding biological atom). In other words, the truth value of any mapped ground atom $\varphi(a)$ in the mapped state $\varphi(S)$ is the truth value of the original atom in the original state. The next question to be addressed is whether this mapping of state properties preserves temporal relations. This will be done in a number of ways in the next section.

---

[2] A similar example is: "Opium puts people to sleep, because it contains a *dormative principle*" (Bateson, 1979).

Table 1: Mapping cognitive to biological state properties.

Cognitive Conceptualisation	Biological Conceptualisation
potential_anxiety_threshold(v)	brain_configuration_for_anxiety_threshold(v)
potential_sensitivity_for_alcohol(s)	brain_configuration_for_sensitivity_for_alcohol(s)
potential_excitement_threshold(v)	brain_configuration_for_excitement_threshold(v)
potential_emotional_attitude_towards_others(s,v)	brain_configuration_for_emotional_attitude_towards_others(s, v)
potential_aggressiveness(v)	tendency_for_chemical_state(testosterone, v)
potential_sensitivity_for_stimuli(v)	tendency_for_chemical_state(serotonin, v)
potential_preparedness_to_act(v)	tendency_for_chemical_state(adrenalin, v)
psychological_self(v)	biological_self(v)
sensitivity_for_alcohol(s)	brain_state_for_sensitivity_for_alcohol(s)
anxiety_threshold(v)	brain_state_for_anxiety_threshold(v)
excitement_threshold(v)	brain_state_for_excitement_threshold(v)
sensitivity_for_stimuli(v)	chemical_state(serotonin, v)
preparedness_to_act(v)	chemical_state(adrenalin, v)
preparedness_to_look_for_safety(v)	chemical_state(oxytocine, v)
theory_of_mind(v)	brain_state_for_theory_of_mind(v)
emotional_attitude_towards_others(s, v)	brain_state_for_emotional_attitude_towards_others(s, v)
desire_for_actions_with_strong_stimuli(v)	brain_state_for_stimulation(w) and is_opposite(v,w)
desire_for_aggressiveness(v)	chemical_state(testosterone, v)
desire_to_act(v)	chemical_state(adrenalin, v)
desire_to_act_safely(v)	chemical_state(oxytocine, v)
desire_for_impulsiveness(v)	chemical_state(bloodsugar, v)
desire(d(v1, v2, v3, v4, v5, v6, v7, v8))	biological_state(v1, v2, v3, v4, v5, v6, v7, v8)

The Extended Mapping for Dynamic Properties

Above it was shown how the basic interpretation mapping can be defined as a mapping between state properties. The next question is how this mapping preserves temporal relationships, for example, in the following sense:

- if α holds at time point t in a trace γ, then also $\varphi(\alpha)$ holds at t in a corresponding trace
- if a temporal relationship $\alpha \twoheadrightarrow \beta$ holds, then also the temporal relationship $\varphi(\alpha) \twoheadrightarrow \varphi(\beta)$ holds
- if a more complex temporal relationship holds, expressed in the logical language TTL (Bosse, Jonker, Meij, Sharpanskykh, and Treur, 2006), then also this relationship holds between the mapped states

First it is addressed how a cognitive trace can be mapped onto a biological trace. This can be done as follows, based on the mapping of states defined above: a trace over state ontology Ont is a time-indexed sequence of states over Ont and is characterised by an assignment of states over Ont to time points: γ: TIME $\rightarrow$ STATES(Ont). Each cognitive trace γ can be mapped onto a biological trace $\varphi(\gamma)$ by $\varphi(\gamma)(t) = \varphi(\gamma(t))$ for any time point t. In other words, the state at t in the mapped trace $\varphi(\gamma)$ is the mapped state of γ at t.

The above mapping shows one answer to the question how temporal relationships are preserved. Another answer addresses temporal LEADSTO relationships. The mapping between state properties can be extended to a mapping between local dynamic properties in LEADSTO format as follows, where α and β are conjunctions of literals:

$$\varphi(\alpha \twoheadrightarrow \beta) = \varphi(\alpha) \twoheadrightarrow \varphi(\beta)$$
$$\varphi(\alpha1 \wedge \alpha2) = \varphi(\alpha1) \wedge \varphi(\alpha2)$$
$$\varphi(\neg \alpha) = \neg \varphi(\alpha)$$

and when α is an atom that is not an internal state property (e.g., an inequality relation or observation state)

$$\varphi(\alpha) = \alpha$$

Using this mapping, combined with the basic mapping of the state ontology elements described above, mappings between the dynamic LEADSTO properties of the case study can be found. For example:

$\varphi(anxiety\_threshold(y) \wedge observes\_stimulus(x1, x2) \wedge x1>y$
$\quad\quad \twoheadrightarrow$ preparedness_to_act(w))
$= \varphi(anxiety\_threshold(y) \wedge observes\_stimulus(x1, x2) \wedge x1>y)$
$\quad\quad \twoheadrightarrow \varphi(preparedness\_to\_act(w))$
$= \varphi(anxiety\_threshold(y)) \wedge \varphi(observes\_stimulus(x1, x2)) \wedge \varphi(x1>y)$
$\quad\quad \twoheadrightarrow \varphi(preparedness\_to\_act(w))$
$= brain\_state\_for\_anxiety\_threshold(y) \wedge observes\_stimulus(x1, x2) \wedge x1>y$
$\quad\quad \twoheadrightarrow$ chemical_state(adrenalin, w)

The mapping of traces shows that the syntactic mapping between local properties preserves semantics: if the cognitive relationship $\alpha \twoheadrightarrow \beta$ holds in cognitive trace γ, then the corresponding biological relationship $\varphi(\alpha \twoheadrightarrow \beta)$ holds in the corresponding trace $\varphi(\gamma)$.

In addition, it is possible to extend the mapping to the wider class of temporal relationships expressed in the dynamic modelling language TTL (Bosse, Jonker, Meij, Sharpanskykh, and Treur, 2006). TTL expressions are predicate logical formulae, built on atoms of the form state(γ, t) |= p, which indicates that state property p is true in trace γ at time point t. By the basic mapping the cognitive state property p can be mapped onto $\varphi(p)$ in the biological conceptualisation, and cognitive trace γ can be mapped onto the corresponding biological trace $\varphi(\gamma)$. Then the extended interpretation mapping for state(γ, t) |= p is defined by $\varphi(state(\gamma, t) |= p) = state(\varphi(\gamma), t) |= \varphi(p)$. After these TTL-atoms have been mapped, TTL expressions as a whole can be mapped in a straightforward compositional manner:

$$\varphi(A \& B) = \varphi(A) \& \varphi(B) \quad\quad \varphi(A \vee B) = \varphi(A) \vee \varphi(B)$$
$$\varphi(\neg A) = \neg \varphi(A) \quad\quad \varphi(A \Rightarrow B) = \varphi(A) \Rightarrow \varphi(B)$$
$$\varphi(\forall v\, A(v)) = \forall v'\, \varphi(A(v')) \quad\quad \varphi(\exists v\, A(v)) = \exists v'\, \varphi(A(v'))$$

Discussion

In this paper, a method to analyse criminal behaviour based on cognitive modelling has been proposed and applied, in a case study, to three types of violent criminals: violent psychopaths, criminals with an antisocial personality disorder (APD), and criminals who suffer from an intermittent explosive disorder (IED). A cognitive model has been developed that indeed can show the behaviour as known for the three types of criminals. Within the model, various psychological aspects as found in the literature are taken into account; e.g., (Raine, 1993; Moir and Jessel, 1995; Delfos, 2004). By means of this model, it was shown how the internal process within the criminal subjects can be conceptualised and formalised from a cognitive perspective. However, as a main contribution, it was also shown how this model can be biologically grounded. To this end it was shown how an ontological mapping from the cognitive model to a biological formalisation can be formally defined. For example, the fact that under certain circumstances states of impulsiveness and aggressiveness that play a role in the cognitive model, may lead to an impulsive, violent crime can be described in terms of biological states concerning high testosterone and low blood sugar. It has been shown in detail how ontology elements for such psychological states can be formally mapped onto ontology elements for biological states. Moreover, this formal ontology mapping has been extended to a formal mapping of temporal dynamic properties. Thus it is shown how the process description at the cognitive level relates to a process description at the biological level. Having a mapping as described above allows one on the one hand to explain behaviour in terms of psychological concepts, but on the other hand to relate it to a biological grounding.

In principle, validation can address both the dynamics of the cognitive model and the dynamics of the underlying biological model. Moreover, the mapping between the cognitive and the underlying biological model can be validated. All of these have been validated positively against literature on the specific types of criminals addressed. Here one remark can be made on validation of the mapping. For some of the cognitive states used in the cognitive model, it is not clear how they would be defined without reference to underlying biological states. Within literature on reduction, such as (Nagel, 1961; Kim, 1996) such reduction relations are called definitional, in contrast to those that are empirical.

Concerning related work, only a handful of other papers address computational modelling of criminal behaviour. However, most of the existing papers concentrate more on social and environmental aspects (e.g., Baal, 2004; Bosse, Gerritsen, and Treur, 2007b), whereas the current article focuses on cognitive aspects and their relation to biology. Cognitive models for criminal behaviour as presented in this paper are very useful for case analysis, i.e., given a certain crime case, to find out which type of person has performed this crime. For more information about this topic, see (Bosse, Gerritsen, and Treur, 2007a).

References

Baal, P.H.M. van (2004). *Computer Simulations of Criminal Deterence: from Public Policy to Local Interaction to Individual Behaviour*. Ph.D. Thesis, Erasmus University Rotterdam. Boom Juridische Uitgevers.

Baron-Cohen, S. (1995). *Mindblindness*. MIT Press.

Bartol, C.R. (2002). *Criminal Behavior: a Psychosocial Approach*. Sixth edition. Prentice Hall, New Jersey.

Bateson, G. (1979). *Mind and Nature: A Necessary Unity*. E. P. Dutton, New York.

Bosse, T., Gerritsen, C., and Treur, J. (2007a). Case Analysis of Criminal Behaviour. In: *Proceedings of the 20th International Conference on Industrial, Engineering & Other Applications of Applied Intelligent Systems, IEA/AIE'07*. LNCS, Springer Verlag, 2007, in press.

Bosse, T., Gerritsen, C., and Treur, J. (2007b). Cognitive and Social Simulation of Criminal Behaviour: the Intermittent Explosive Disorder Case. In: *Proceedings of the Sixth International Joint Conference on Autonomous Agents and Multi-Agent Systems, AAMAS'07*. ACM Press, 2007, in press.

Bosse, T., Jonker, C.M., Meij, L. van der, Sharpanskykh, A., and Treur, J. (2006). Specification and Verification of Dynamics in Cognitive Agent Models. In: Nishida, T. et al (eds.), *Proc. of the 6th Int. Conf. on Intelligent Agent Technology, IAT'06*. IEEE Computer Society Press, 2006, pp.247-254.

Bosse, T., Jonker, C.M., and Treur, J. (2006). Developing Higher-Level Cognitive Theories by Reduction. In: R. Sun, N. Miyake (eds.), *Proc. of the 28th Annual Conference of the Cognitive Science Society, CogSci'06*, 2006, pp. 1032-1037.

Bosse, T., Jonker, C.M., Meij, L. van der, and Treur, J. (2005). LEADSTO: a Language and Environment for Analysis of Dynamics by SimulaTiOn. In: Eymann, T. et al. (eds.), *Proc. of the 3rd German Conf. on Multi-Agent System Technologies, MATES'05*. Springer LNAI, vol. 3550, 2005, pp. 165-178. Extended version to appear in *Int. Journal of Artificial Intelligence Tools*, 2007.

Brantingham, P. L., & Brantingham, P. J. (2004). Computer Simulation as a Tool for Environmental Criminologists. *Security Journal*, 17(1), 21-30.

Cohen, L.E. and Felson, M. (1979). Social change and crime rate trends: a routine activity approach. *American Sociological Review*, vol. 44, pp. 588-608.

Cornish, D.B., and Clarke, R.V. (1986). *The Reasoning Criminal: Rational Choice Perspectives on Offending*. Springer Verlag.

Delfos, M.F. (2004). *Children and Behavioural Problems: Anxiety, Aggression, Depression and ADHD; A Biopsychological Model with Guidelines for Diagnostics and Treatment*. Harcourt book publishers, Amsterdam.

Dennett, D.C. (1987). *The Intentional Stance*. MIT Press. Cambridge Mass.

Georgeff, M. P., and Lansky, A. L. (1987). Reactive Reasoning and Planning. In: *Proceedings of the Sixth National Conference on Artificial Intelligence, AAAI'87*. Menlo Park, California. American Association for AI, 1987, pp. 677-682.

Gottfredson, M., and Hirschi, T. (1990). *A General Theory of Crime*. Stanford University Press.

Humphrey, N. (1984). *Consciousness Regained*. Oxford University Press.

Jonker, C.M., Treur, J., and Wijngaards, W.C.A., (2003). A Temporal Modelling Environment for Internally Grounded Beliefs, Desires and Intentions. *Cognitive Systems Research Journal*, vol. 4(3), 2003, pp. 191-210.

Kim, J. (1996). *Philosophy of Mind*, Westview Press.

Liu, L., Wang, X., Eck, J., & Liang, J. (2005). Simulating Crime Events and Crime Patterns in RA/CA Model. In F. Wang (ed.), *Geographic Information Systems and Crime Analysis*. Singapore: Idea Group, pp. 197-213

Melo, A., Belchior, M., and Furtado, V. (2005). Analyzing Police Patrol Routes by Simulating the Physical Reorganisation of Agents. In: Sichman, J.S., and Antunes, L. (eds.), *Proceedings of the Sixth International Workshop on Multi-Agent-Based Simulation, MABS'05*. Lecture Notes in Artificial Intelligence, vol. 3891, Springer Verlag, 2006, pp 99-114.

Moir, A., and Jessel, D. (1995). A Mind to Crime: the controversial link between the mind and criminal behaviour. London: Michael Joseph Ltd; Penguin.

Nagel, E. (1961). The Structure of Science. London: Routledge & Kegan Paul.

Raine, A. (1993). *The Psychopathology of Crime: Criminal Behaviors as a Clinical Disorder*. New York, NY: Guilford Publications.

Rao, A.S. & Georgeff, M.P. (1991). Modelling Rational Agents within a BDI-architecture. In: Allen, J., Fikes, R. and Sandewall, E. (eds.), *Proceedings of the Second International Conference on Principles of Knowledge Representation and Reasoning, (KR'91)*. Morgan Kaufmann, pp. 473-484.

Towl, G.J., and Crighton, D.A. (1996). *The Handbook of Psychology for Forensic Practitioners*. Routledge, London, New York.

Turvey, B. (1999). *Criminal Profiling: an Introduction to Behavioral Evidence Analysis*. Academic Press.

Commitment to Explicitly Reported Choices:
Evidence in Decision Making under Uncertainty

Giovanni Pezzulo (giovanni.pezzulo@istc.cnr.it)
Institute of Cognitive Sciences and Technologies - CNR
Via S. Martino della Battaglia, 44 - 00185 Roma, Italy

Abstract

We present some experimental evidence about the different roles and values of information in belief building and decision making under uncertainty. We adopt the *Two Cards Gambling Game* experimental paradigm and we present to the participants choice situations in which multiple sources of information, having different reliability, are available, in different experimental conditions: one or more sources, presented either together or at different times. Our results show that decisions depend on the availability and quality of their sources are are biased by commitment to explicitly reported choices as well as by the (subjectively felt) need for information.

Keywords: decision making, uncertainty, belief revision, commitment

Introduction

In several related fields a distinction between two kinds of knowledge exists, the former being more related to "inert' knowledge and the latter being more related to knowledge either used for action (such as decision making), or under attentive control, etc.

In philosophy and AI (Dennett, 1987; Dummett, 1991) there is a distinction between *implicit* and *explicit* knowledge; even if these terms can assume different meanings, one of the main claims is that we have direct access to explicit knowledge and we can express it in a linguistic format (Dummett, 1991). Humans have a great amount of potentially available knowledge (which can be inferred when required (Dennett, 1987)) as well as some *tacit* knowledge which is exploited but not represented at all (Chomsky, 1965). Only some knowledge is explicitly available, typically in a declarative format; heuristics such as *availability* (Kahneman, 2003) testify that knowledge can be more or less ready to be used.

In decision making (Kahneman, 2003) there is a related distinction between *preferences* and *choices*. Even if they can influence behavior, preferences can be revised or negotiated before a choice. On the contrary choices are explicitly reported, are considered definitive, imply a certain commitment and have a resistance to be modified; some phenomena such as *cognitive dissonance* (Festinger, 1957) testify that we are able to revise post-hoc our preferences in order to explain our choices.

A similar distinction between *information, beliefs* and *acceptances* appears in the field of belief revision (Castelfranchi, 1997; Paglieri, 2006). Information basically means data having a source and supported by reasons, stimuli, evidence, etc. A belief instead is an "internalized' information, i.e. information which has undergone a cognitive process of evaluation (e.g. against previously known information) and selection (e.g. on the basis of a lack of information). These operations can be either deliberated or automatic (Castelfranchi, 1997). Typically a cognitive agent firstly builds its belief structure depending on its information and their

sources, and then decides on the basis of its beliefs. However, it is only by using a certain belief for action (e.g. for a decision) that it assumes the role of an *acceptance*. It is not strictly necessary that something is believed to be used as a basis for deciding (i.e. as an acceptance), even if this typically the case of rational agents. It is not the case that all the information or the beliefs are used for deciding, too: this is why cognitive agents typically exploit sophisticated cognitive operations (such as selecting the best sources, negotiating contradictions, etc.) before deciding, having the goal to make the belief structure supporting decision very strong. However, after deliberation a cognitive agent either acts or intends to act according to its decision; in this case it is typically *committed* to its decision. As (Cohen & Levesque, 1990) puts it, *intention is choice with commitment*. Consequently, we claim that this is a side-effect of the operations for strengthening the belief structure: choices are *accepted* and involve a certain degree of commitment since they have been integrated in the belief system and it is costly to revise them.

The aim of this paper is twofold. (1) We present some experimental evidence about commitment to explicitly reported choices which depends on the reliability of the sources of information. In the discussion we propose that these data can be due to different strategies for accepting or rejecting information in the different cases. (2) In order to better frame these findings, we then introduce the *Multiple Source Evaluation Model (MSEM)*, which predicts that individuals adopt different cognitive strategies for dealing with uncertain and ambiguous situations depending on contextual parameters such as the kinds and levels of ambiguity, uncertainty, ignorance, etc. In particular, the MSEM indicates that before deciding individuals adopt *epistemic actions* (Kirsh & Maglio, 1994) (i.e. actions aiming to modify its belief structure, either by accepting new information or by modifying/rejecting beliefs). Epistemic actions have the effect to strengthen the initial beliefs supporting decision making, and are thus candidates for explaining the commitment effect we have found.

The Experiments

The inspiration for the experiments presented here comes from our past work. In Pezzulo (2006); Pezzulo and Couyoumdjian (2006) we investigated how humans deal with multiple sources of information, either in accord or in disaccord, in the field of decision making under uncertainty. The experiments were conducted by using the *Two Cards Gambling Game* experimental paradigm, which we use also for the experiments we present here. In the TCGG the participant is shown a movie representing two cards, one red and one black. The cards are then turned over (the backs are identical) and shuffled (at different velocities, depending on the experiment). The participant is instructed to look at the movie and bet on the placement of the red card. In some experiments participants were also presented with information about how one or two Gamblers (depending on the experiment) had bet; in these cases it was also shown the competence of the Gamblers, either "novice" or 'expert' (the Gamblers are simulated; their bets are biased: experts bet better). In deciding the participant has to bet as quickly and accurately as possible; he has an initial pool of 50 Euros. The participant has 5 choices: 'bet 5 Euros on right card'; 'bet 5 euros on left card'; 'bet 10 euros on right card'; 'bet 10 euros on left card'; 'do not bet'. After the bet, the outcome is shown: if the participant gave the correct response, he gains the bet, otherwise he loses the same amount of money. The TCGG experimental paradigm permits to manipulate the number of sources and the levels of ambiguity, and to study how the difficulty of a decision making task varies depending on the levels of ambiguity, the degree of accord between the sources and their reliability.

Review of former experiments The first experiment we have conducted with the TCGG paradigm aims at investigating role of multiple sources of evidence in the decision process. The experiment is split into three cases: case 1A investigates the only perceptual source; case 1B investigates also the contribution of an external source (one Gambler); case 1C investigates also the contribution of two external sources (two Gamblers). Participants thus deal with ambiguous situations: for example, the opinion of the participant can contrast with the opinion of the Gamblers; or two Gamblers can bet differently.

Our findings indicate that individuals base their decision on available information; however, different strategies for integrating them can be adopted. In particular participants integrating two different sources of evidence (case 1B) have less Ignorance and are facilitated in the task, thus they bet significantly more and take significantly less time. We have interpreted these findings according to the MSEM (introduced later on), indicating that specific cognitive operations, the *epistemic actions*, are adopted for reducing ambiguity before deciding, especially in the case of disaccord between two sources (this explains certain patterns in response time).

In case 1C, by introducing two external sources of evidence (two Gamblers), the participants' performance worsens. Our findings indicate that this is mainly due to the case of disaccord between the external sources; again, we have interpreted these findings according to the MSEM, which indicates that the cause is an higher level of Uncertainty. Thus it is not the case that 'more information is better', but on the contrary an optimal trade-off between amount of information and coherence is required in order to decide accurately and fast. Gigerenzer and Todd (1999) presents similar evidence of 'less is more effect': choosing only the most relevant cues is better for deciding in environments having a non compensatory information structure, and if extra information is added on it can worsen the performance. An alternative explanation is the use of the *anchoring* heuristic (Kahneman, 2003): participants remain committed to their perceptual source, because the external sources are in disaccord and thus are unreliable.

Explicit vs. Implicit knowledge It has to be noted that the kind of contradiction found in case 1C has a peculiarity: it is *explicit*, i.e. it involves already established/accepted beliefs of other agents (their *choices* and not simply *preferences*).

Consider in fact that during the decision process contradiction very often arise, due to contrasting evidence (e.g. perceptual vs. external source). During the process, however, this is likely a contrast of preferences, in the sense that their values are assumed to be tentative, defeasible and not definitive; the participant is not yet committed to any choice. The point is that this kind of contradiction can be negotiated and reduced by many kinds of epistemic actions (e.g. by strengthening or lowering some factors). Instead, once contradictory information is explicitly reported as in case 1C, it can not be reduced except by a selection of the sources, and by selectively accept or reject incoming information, i.e. choose one or another Gambler; and this is a costly epistemic operation.

How information is integrated before or after a choice In order to further investigate the 'explicit vs. implicit' issue, here we present two experiments using the TCGG experimental paradigm. The former is condition B of the already introduced experiment, with one external source of information (one Gambler). In the latter the same materials are used, but subjects report their choice before looking at the bet of the external source; they can decide whether or not to revise it after looking at the external source's bet. Two sets of fifteen undergraduate students at the University of Rome 'La Sapienza' participated in each condition of the experiments. Participants were presented with a set of 40 short movies showing shuffling cards, balanced between 'easy' and 'difficult', in random order. Items were presented the center of a computer screen. We are interested in comparing the strategies for integrating information in the two different cases: information is the same in both studies, but while in the former it is available before any choice, in the latter part of it is only available after a choice has been explicitly reported.

Experiment 1: Perceptual Source plus One Gambler

In experiment 1 participants, before betting, see the bet of another Gambler. It serves to investigate the combination of two different source of information, the former perceptual and the latter external (one Gambler). Sixty movies varying in difficulty (thirty easy and thirty difficult) were presented, together with information about how a Gambler (either expert or novice) has bet. The main hypothesis is that in difficult tasks, in which uncertainty (in the perceptual source) is higher, the role of the external source is more relevant. However, our main aim here is investigating the mean 'percentage of accord' between the participants bets and the Gamblers bets, i.e. the cases of the same bet between the two[1]; this is done in order to compare this experiment with the next one.

Method and Results The experimental conditions resulted from a factorial combination of difficulty of the task (easy vs. difficult) and competence of the Gambler (novice vs. expert). An analysis of variance (ANOVA) has been conducted with the mean 'percentage of accord' (between the participants bets and the Gamblers bets) as dependent variable. Difficulty of task and competence of the Gambler were the within-subjects factors. The main hypothesis is that there is more accord with the most reliable external source, experts.

The main effect of competence is significant,

---

[1] It don't indicate if the perceptual and the external source are concordant, but if the subject and the Gambler bet on the same card.

F(1,14)=47,29; p<,00001: participants are more in accord with expert Gamblers that with novices. Difficulty of the task is not significant, F(1,14)=,46; p<,5080; interactions are not significant, too, F(1,14)=,54; p<,4730.

Results are shown in Table 1.

MOVIE	ACC.	GAMBLER	ACC.
difficult	,606	expert	,679
easy	,615	novice	,541
(a) Difficulty		(b) Competence	

Table 1: Mean Percentage of Accord in Experiment 1

Percentage of Accord and Reaction Time In order to better understand the cases of accord and disaccord, we also analyzed the reaction times in accord an disaccord: an analysis of variance (ANOVA) has been conducted with reaction time as variable. Competence of the Gambler (novice or expert) and Accord between participant and Gambler (accord or disaccord) were the within-subjects factors. We want to investigate if the accord influences the cognitive load of the participant before decision. The main hypothesis is that in the case of accord reaction time is lower.

The main effect of accord is significant, F(1,14)=17,43; p<,0009; participants bet faster when they are in accord with the Gambler. There is also significant interaction between competence and accord, F(1,14)=6,50; p<,0232. From a posteriori analysis (Duncan Test) it emerges that participants bet faster when they are in accord (vs. disaccord) both with novices (p<,0076) and experts (p<,00007).

Results are shown in Table 2.

ACCORD	TIME		GAMB.	ACC.	TIME
accord	4,190		expert	accord	4,05
disaccord	5,118		expert	disaccord	5,317
			novice	accord	4,330
			novice	disaccord	4,918
(a) Accord			(b) Interactions		

Table 2: Mean Percentage of Accord and Reaction Time in Experiment 1

Discussion Participants are in accord with expert Gamblers more than with novice ones in both easy and difficult tasks. Moreover, reaction times are significantly lower in the case of accord with an expert, indicating that there is no 'epistemic conflict' to resolve and thus the level of uncertainty is low. The case we are more interested in is that of a conflict between the perceptual and the external source; in this case, in fact, the external evidence can be either accepted (revising a belief), or rejected (we can call those operations *epistemic actions*). Different strategies can be used: for example, a dubious perceptual evidence could be challenged by evidence provided by a reliable expert Gambler, but not by a novice one. We have also analyzed our results by introducing another factor, correct or uncorrect responses. It is interesting to note that the higher reaction time (7,23 seconds) is in the cases of 'accord with an expert, uncorrect response' (significant with all the other times). It seems to be the case of a high 'computational cost' of revising a previously correct and strong belief, formed on the basis of perceptual evidence, relying upon an expert. This example indicates that belief revision do not rely on a generic rule for information negotiation, otherwise there would have been no difference in time. On the contrary, it is possible that depending on the strength of the initial belief, the reliability of the sources and the level of uncertainty specific strategies are adopted for deciding which information or belief to accept as a basis for deciding, and which to discard. The next experiment, about belief revision, further investigates this point.

Experiment 2: Effects of Revision

Experiment 2 is about belief revision; the materials are the same of experiment 1 but now there are two phases, called *Before* and *After*. In the first phase (Before) the participant bets only seeing the cards shuffling. In the second phase (After) after the bet he sees the bet of one Gambler and can choose either to confirm the bet or to change it. Since participants can decide to change their bet after assuming new information, this is a case of belief revision; our main hypothesis is that expert Gamblers will lead to more belief revision. Since the decision process has as a precondition a solid belief structure, we assume that it is more difficult for successive information to influence it. Our main hypothesis is that the degree of accord in this case is lower than what happens in experiment 1, in which both sources are presented together. In facts, by explicitly expressing a preference the player both explicitly reports a belief and commits to it; so, there is an additional cost in changing opinion.

Method The experimental conditions resulted from a factorial combination of difficulty of the task (easy vs. difficult) and expertise of the Gambler (novice vs. expert). Analysis of variance (ANOVA) has been conducted with mean percentage of accord with the Gambler and mean amount of bet as dependent variables. Phases of the experiment (Before or After) and competence of the Gambler (Novice or Expert) were the within-subjects factors.

Percentage of Accord The main effect of the phase is significant, F(1,14)=13,78; p<,0023. In the After phase participants are more accord with the Gambler. An important note: since in the Before phase participants do not see any Gambler, we only calculated the 'hypothetical accord' in order to match it with the After phase, in order to see if their choice is influenced by the Gambler (i.e. if their accord grows).

There is significant interaction between the competence of the Gambler and percentage of accord, F(1,14)=5,14; p<,0397. From post hoc analysis (Duncan Test) it emerges that with expert Gamblers participants are more in accord in the After than in the Before phase (p<,000732); this does not happen with novice Gamblers (p<,29456).

Results are shown in Table 3.

Amount of Bet The main effect of phase is significant, F(1,14)=5,75; p<,0310. In the After phase participants bet more. There is significant interaction between competence of the Gambler and amount of bet (F(1,14)=18,45; p<,0007).

PHASE	ACC.		GAMBLER	PHASE	ACC.
Before	,528		Expert	Before	,517
After	,561		Expert	After	,567
			Novice	Before	,540
			Novice	After	,555
(a) Accord			(b) Interactions		

Table 3: Mean Percentage of Accord in Experiment 2

EXP.	ACCORD		GAMB.	EXP.	ACCORD
2	,561		Expert	2	,567
1B	,61		Expert	1B	,679
			Novice	2	,555
			Novice	1B	,540
(a) Accord			(b) Interactions		

Table 5: Mean Percentage of Accord, comparing Experiments 1B and 2

From post hoc analysis (Duncan Test) it emerges that with an Expert participants bet more in the After than in the Before phase (p<,000302); this does not happen with a Novice. Moreover, while in the first phase (before) there is not significant difference, in the After phase participants bet more with an Expert than with a Novice (p<,000108).

Results are shown in Table 4.

PHASE	BET		GAMBLER	PHASE	BET
Before	7,260		Expert	Before	7,261
After	7,526		Expert	After	7,906
			Novice	Before	7,260
			Novice	After	7,147
(a) Bet			(b) Interactions		

Table 4: Mean Amount of Bet in Experiment 2

Discussion We can see that when there is an Expert the participants modify significantly their bet; also the percentage of accord before and after changes significantly; moreover, they modify in a significant way the amount of bet. On the contrary in presence of a Novice data are not significant. This means that only Experts are able to produce an appropriate change in the strength of beliefs, while the (late) influence of Novices is too weak. These findings indicate that participants commit to their explicitly reported choices, which are thus more difficult to revise. Later on we compare this experiment with the previous one and, as we will see, a more marked commitment effect emerges.

Comparison between Experiments 1B and 2.

Analysis of variance (ANOVA) has been conducted with mean percentage of accord with the Gambler as dependent variable. Experiment (1B and 2-After) and competence of the Gamblers (Novice or Expert) were the factors (the former between-subjects, the latter within-subjects).

The main effect of experiment is significant, $F(1,28)=4,34$; p<,0465. Participants in Experiment 2 (phase After) are less in accord with Gamblers than participants of Experiment 1B.

Significant interaction was found, too, $F(1,28)=5,44$; p<,0270. From post hoc analysis (Duncan Test) it emerges that participants in Experiment 1B are more in accord with expert Gamblers than those of Experiment 2 (p<,007003); this does not happen with novice Gamblers (p<,706332)[2].

Results are shown in Table 5.

---

[2] A control experiment with successive phases but without ex-

Discussion We can see that there is less accord with the Gambler in the After phase of Experiment 2 than in Experiment 1. This means that there is a tendency of participants in Experiment 2 to maintain their choices which are explicitly reported. Even if they assume new information, they are less prone to revise: we call it a *commitment effect*. Our data can be interpreted on the basis of the *anchoring heuristic* (Kahneman, 2003): we are better at relative than absolute thinking, so we try to adjust judgments starting from a familiar position or assumption. In this case, participants have a more stable opinion in experiment 2 since they already start from a reported (and stable) choice.

However, this is only part of the answer. Our findings indicate that beliefs can be maintained or revised depending on their strength (i.e. how much evidence they account for), and that under different conditions new information which contrasts with previous knowledge can be integrated or rejected. We therefore introduce the Multiple Source Evaluation Model (MSEM), which describes the belief formation and revision process during decision making, and use it for interpreting the results of our experiments. For a complete description of the MSEM we refer to (Pezzulo, 2006; Pezzulo & Couyoumdjian, 2006). Here we only describe its main components and focus on the role of epistemic actions in different contexts.

The Multiple Source Evaluation Model

The *Multiple Source Evaluation Model (MSEM)* focuses on (1) how information coming from different evidential sources, either converging or diverging, is integrated and (2) how Ignorance, Uncertainty and Contradiction are evaluated and reduced before deciding in ambiguous domains. We argue that these operations involve an unique satisficing strategy, *ambiguity-reduction*: *individuals tend to select the epistemic action resulting in a more stable basis for deciding in order to reduce ambiguity to an acceptable degree*. This criterium needs a limited amount of knowledge and processing time, without pre-calculating them, according to the desiderata of the 'bounded rationality' research program (Gigerenzer & Todd, 1999). Consistently, we also claim that many coarse-grained heuristics such as representativeness and availability (Kahneman, 2003) emerge from this more fine-grained strategy, depending on contextual factors.

The fundamental claim of the MSEM is that the result of a decision depends on the supporting epistemic structure, composed of: (1) beliefs *in* the domain of decision (base beliefs

---

plicitly reporting the choice (no significant differences) has been conducted, too, showing no significant results.

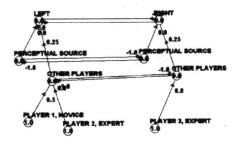

Figure 1: The Balance with Two Plates

about information sources and their reliability); (2) beliefs *about* the domain of decision (the meta-beliefs: evaluation of ambiguity in the current decision); (3) declarative and procedural expertise in the domain of decision.

The Base Beliefs The knowledge structure of a participant can be described as a network of beliefs, whose edges are 'sustain/activation' or 'contrast/inhibition' relationships. Beliefs have a certain *strength*, i.e. the degree of confidence of reliability people assign them (Castelfranchi, 1997). We consider many kinds of beliefs and sources, including *inside* evidence, focused on the contingent situation (e.g. perceptual data) and *outside* evidence, focused on categorical knowledge (e.g. previous similar situations, statistical information, etc.); this distinction is also presented in (Kahneman, 2003). A good analogy is a *Balance with two Plates* where evidence are 'put on the plate', each one weighted with its 'relevance', which is proportional to the reliability of the evidential source. Fig. 1 shows a sample network realizing this model with nodes for evidence and (weighted) edges for their influence; it calculates the strength values for 'left' and 'right' by integrating information from perception as well as from other Gamblers; vertical and horizontal edges represent 'sustain' and 'contrast' relations. The Balance shares some resemblances with the Leaky, Competing Accumulator Model (LCAM, Usher and McClelland (2001)).

The Meta Beliefs People not only use information about the problem (e.g. 'I have seen that the left card is red') but also what we call meta-beliefs, i.e. beliefs about the domain, that are an evaluation of their metacognitive state (e.g. 'I still do not have enough information'). In several studies 'lack of information' as well as uncertainty and ambiguity have been shown to affect the decision process; for example ambiguity aversion in subjects has been identified (see Camerer and Weber (1992) for a review). In particular, in the MSEM three meta beliefs, *Ignorance, Uncertainty and Contradiction*, are claimed to have a crucial role in decision making. According to the MSEM, before deciding the subject tries to minimize (under domain-specific thresholds) the values of these three meta-beliefs. For doing so, he performs one or more *epistemic actions*, such as 'ask for more information', or 'reject information from an unreliable source', until the levels of ambiguity are considered acceptable.

Declarative and Procedural Expertise The model also describes *declarative and procedural expertise* for dealing with

uncertain situations. Here we focus mainly on procedural expertise, consisting of applying a set of rules, the *epistemic actions*, which aim mainly at strengthening a belief structure before deciding, for example by reducing uncertainty and ignorance. Some good examples of epistemic actions are the fast and frugal heuristics such as 'Take The Best' introduced by Gigerenzer and Todd (1999), but also strategies such as 'ask for new information' or 'revise reliability of a source'.

The model introduces three kinds of *epistemic actions* for accepting, integrating and revising beliefs in presence of specific kinds of ambiguity: (1) epistemic actions for integrating new knowledge: they decide whether or not to assume knowledge, etc. (2) epistemic actions for assessing the epistemic structure during decision: searching new evidence, reinforcing lateral inhibitions, etc. (3) epistemic actions for revising knowledge: raising or lowering the reliability of sources or epistemic actions, etc.

In order to interpret the results of the experiments presented here, we focus only on the former kind of epistemic actions. In fact, while the Balance describes a standard, compensatory (Payne, Bettman, & Johnson, 1988) way to integrate new information, either in accord or disaccord with previous information, individuals can employ various cognitive strategies for this integration. New knowledge is not in fact merely added to the Balance, but must be *accepted*, i.e. integrated into the preexisting epistemic structure. In a similar way Boutilier, Friedman, and Halpern (1998) argues that information (e.g. incoming data, sensori stimuli, etc.) is only *accepted* under certain conditions such as being consistent with existing knowledge or, in the case of disagreement, being more likely than previous knowledge.

Integration of evidence is highly contextual and depends on many factors: possible conflicts, the amount of information already available, etc. There are many possible situations in which new information cannot simply be accepted by default, such as conflicts with strong previous knowledge; in these cases, specific epistemic actions are utilized for filtering new knowledge. For example, if new evidence conflicts with one priorly assumed, depending on the context (e.g. new sources are reliable or unreliable; agents ignorance is high or low) it can be accepted or rejected.

As an example, some of the epistemic actions used in the MSEM are presented here. The format is close to fuzzy logic[3], which is also the language which has been used for implementing the model (see Pezzulo (2006) for details and for comparison with experimental data). All these epistemic action are of type (1): they serve to decide if accepting or rejecting new information.

```
(reliability: ,92)
IF new_evidence_conflicts_with_assumed_knowledge
AND source is reliable
THEN accept_new_evidence
EXPECT uncertainty is low
```

---

[3]Epistemic actions are fuzzy rules having 1) a context for applying the rule (the IF part); 2) an operation (the THEN part) which describes the procedure to be applied ; 3) an expectation (the EXPECT part) indicating the expected value of one or more meta-beliefs if the rule is applied in the given context ; 4) a degree of reliability indicating how much the EXPECT part is reliably produced when the rule is applied, and serving for rule selection.

```
(reliability: ,90)
IF new_evidence_conflicts_with_assumed_knowledge
AND source is unreliable
OR uncertainty is very_low
THEN reject_new_evidence
EXPECT uncertainty is low
```

As a consequence of the process of strengthening the belief structure before a choice, it is much more difficult to revise a belief structure after than a choice. This means that when a participant is asked to report explicitly a choice, in order to do so he firstly builds a 'solid enough' belief structure. This structure is now much more resistant to revisions. Our claim has some resemblances with the literature about *cognitive dissonance* (Festinger, 1957), that is a post-hoc revision in order to explain our choices. The difference in our interpretation is that most of the work or reinforcing the reasons to believe (i.e. the belief structure) is done *before* choosing and *in order to* choose. According to the MSEM, in facts, individuals try not to decide until uncertainty is considered acceptable.

Conclusions

We have found evidence that the levels of reliability of the sources influences the levels of uncertainty in decision making (Exp. 1); and that a *commitment effect* occurs after explicitly reporting beliefs (Exp. 2). In order to understand these phenomena we have proposed to look at which epistemic actions are adopted for accepting or rejecting information in different contexts, and we have introduced the MSEM.

The results of Exp. 1 can be explained in the MSEM as the 'computational cost' in reducing uncertainty, by means of successive epistemic actions, in the different conditions. The commitment effect of Exp. 2 can be explained in the MSEM by considering that before deciding the belief structure serving as support has to be strengthened in order to obtain tolerable levels of uncertainty, and this happens by applying specific epistemic actions. After an explicitly reported choice it is much more difficult to revise the belief structure. In particular, epistemic actions for accepting or rejecting new information have to be used; information has to be selected and it is no more possible to simply negotiate or adjust information or to simply use compensatory heuristics. It is worth noting that, differently from Festinger (1957), we do not interpret this phenomenon as a post-hoc revision, but as a side-effect of uncertainty-reduction occurring *before* choice.

There is a related aspect which influences the selection of information: the 'need for information'. In (Pezzulo & Couyoumdjian, 2006; Pezzulo, 2006) we presented an experiment using the TCGG paradigm in which participants are not shown the bet of other gamblers, but can explicitly ask to see it (by paying 0,1 Euro each). Our results show that in that case participants are significantly more in accord with gamblers than in the experiments here presented: *explicitly requested data are more useful, since they resolve a need for information* (reducing Perceived Ignorance). According to the MSEM model, epistemic structures are organized in a network of relationships; epistemic actions are conducted in order to solidify the structures before deciding, so people only search for information that is required to fill in the gaps in the structure.

We think that our results can support the distinctions between different kinds of knowledge which exist in many literatures, and in particular between many *roles* that the same knowledge assumes before, during and after a choice, e.g. as evidence, as belief (integrated in a belief structure) or as acceptance (used for deciding). We have also shown that the order of presentation of information, and the cognitive strategies adopted for integrating or rejecting them, can influence decision making -and this aspect is often underestimated.

References

Boutilier, C., Friedman, N., & Halpern, J. Y. (1998). Belief revision with unreliable observations. In *Proceedings of AAAI/IAAI 1998* (p. 127-134).

Camerer, C., & Weber, M. (1992). Recent developments in modeling preferences: Uncertainty and ambiguity. *J. Risk Uncertainty, 5*, 325–370.

Castelfranchi, C. (1997). Representation and integration of multiple knowledge sources: issues and questions. In S. e. T. Cantoni Di Gesu' (Ed.), *Human and machine perception: Information fusion*. Plenum Press.

Chomsky, N. (1965). *Aspects of the theory of syntax*. Cambridge, MA: MIT Press.

Cohen, P. R., & Levesque, H. J. (1990). Intention is choice with commitment. *Artificial Intelligence, 42*, 213–261.

Dennett, D. (1987). *The intentional stance*. MIT Press.

Dummett, M. (1991). *The logical basis of metaphysics*. Cambridge, MA: HarvardUniversity Press.

Festinger, L. (1957). *A theory of cognitive dissonance*. Stanford University Press.

Gigerenzer, G., & Todd, P. M. (1999). *Simple heuristics that make us smart*. New York: Oxford University Press.

Kahneman, D. (2003). A perspective on judgment and choice: Mapping bounded rationality. *American Psychologist, 58*, 697-720.

Kirsh, D., & Maglio, P. (1994). On distinguishing epistemic from pragmatic action. *Cognitive Science, 18*, 513-549.

Paglieri, F. (2006). *Belief dynamics: From formal models to cognitive architectures, and back again*. Unpublished doctoral dissertation, University of Siena.

Payne, J. W., Bettman, J. R., & Johnson, E. J. (1988). Adaptive strategy selection in decision making. *Journal of Experimental Psychology: Learning, Memory and Cognition, 14*, 534–552.

Pezzulo, G. (2006). *Into the gambler's frame of mind: Decision making under uncertainty in the two cards gambling game*. Unpublished doctoral dissertation, University of Rome "La Sapienza".

Pezzulo, G., & Couyoumdjian, A. (2006). Ambiguity-reduction: a satisficing criterion for decision making. In *Proceedings of Cogsci 2006* (pp. 669–674).

Usher, M., & McClelland, J. L. (2001). On the time course of perceptual choice: The leaky, competing accumulator model. *Psychological Review, 108(3)*, 550–592.

Cognitive, Emotional, and Physiological Components of Emotional Stroop using Associative Conditioning

Anne Richards (a.richards@bbk.ac.uk)
School of Psychology, Birkbeck College, University of London, Malet St.
London, UK, WC1E 7HX

Isabelle Blanchette (isabelle.blanchette@manchester.ac.uk)
School of Psychological Sciences, University of Manchester, Oxford Road
Manchester, UK, M13 9PL

Victoria Hamilton (v.hamilton@bbk.ac.uk)
School of Psychology, Birkbeck College, University of London, Malet St.
London, UK, WC1E 7HX

Anastasia Lavda (anastasia.lavda@manchester.ac.uk)
School of Psychological Sciences, University of Manchester, Oxford Road
Manchester, UK, M13 9PL

Abstract

In two studies we independently manipulated the emotional connotations of non-words by using a simple associative conditioning paradigm. These conditioned stimuli were then used in an emotional Stroop paradigm in which electrodermal activity was simultaneously recorded. In the first experiment, the predicted emotional Stroop effect using unmasked stimuli was observed, showing that conditioned emotional connotations transferred to the Stroop task. Skin conductance responses (SCR) failed to predict Stroop interference, but state anxiety predicted both Stroop interference and SCR. The second experiment found that stimuli conditioned at a conscious (unmasked) level did not transfer to a non-conscious attentional task (masked) Stroop task. However, state anxiety and awareness predicted electrodermal activity during the Stroop task. Affective ratings did not predict Stroop interference in Experiment 1. In Experiment 2, however, affective ratings of unmasked, but not masked, stimuli reflected the emotional connotations of those stimuli.

Experiment 1

Emotion has a powerful influence on attentional processes, with threat-related stimuli attended to more than neutral stimuli. This effect is particularly pronounced in high anxiety, as anxious people show both a selective bias for threat (e.g., MacLeod, Mathews, & Tata, 1986; Yiend & Mathews, 2001) and an inability to disengage from such stimuli (Fox, Russo, Bowles, & Dutton, 2001). Although attempts are made to equate negative and neutral verbal stimuli in terms of word length, category membership, word frequency, etc, the best control for potential extraneous characteristics is to condition the emotional value of neutral stimuli using, for example, a series of negative, positive, or neutral pictures. Blanchette and Richards (2004) have developed a simple associative classical conditioning technique in which a series of neutral words were repeatedly paired with negative or neutral images (see Cacioppo, Marshall-Goodell, Tassinary, & Petty, 1992; Montoya, Larbig, Pulvermueller, & Flor, 1996). Here, neutral words and non-words were conditioned using negative and neutral pictures selected from the International Affective Picture System (IAPS; Lang, Bradley & Cuthbert, 1995). Any effects could not be due to semantic or other associated features of the stimuli, as the non-words were negatively conditioned for some participants and neutrally conditioned for others, with all participants being exposed to both negative and neutral conditioning in the same experiment. Richards and Blanchette (2004) extended this technique to examine the effects of emotion on attention by presenting conditioned stimuli in an emotional Stroop paradigm. The emotional Stroop task has been extensively used with clinical and normal populations to show that both clinical anxiety and high-trait anxiety are associated with an increase in the time taken to identify the colour of threat-related stimuli (for a review, see Williams, Mathews, & MacLeod, 1996). However, these effects could be due to differences in word frequency. It is plausible that anxious individuals take longer to identify the colour of threat-related stimuli simply because such stimuli are encountered more frequently in their everyday lives. Richards and Blanchette (2004) found that high-trait individuals took longer to identify the colour of negatively conditioned non-words thereby ruling out word frequency, etc, as possible explanations.

The experiments reported here take the research further by exploring the relationships and possible distinctions between explicit and implicit contributions to attentional bias in anxiety. Explicit measures evaluate the results of processes that are made available to conscious awareness, whereas implicit measures assess those processes that are inaccessible to consciousness as they operate outside of conscious awareness. Lang (1985) proposes three separate response systems: behavioural, physiological and cognitive. These systems are all responsive to anxiety, but there is a high degree of discordance between them. We are interested in the relationships between different components of anxiety. If negative connotations become attached to neutral items, are these connotations accessible to different systems? We examined the evaluation of such stimuli by using both implicit and explicit measures. In two experiments we conditioned meaningless non-words with pictures using unmasked presentation. These conditioned stimuli were then used in an unmasked (Experiment 1) or masked (Experiment 2) emotional Stroop paradigm. During the Stroop task, electrodermal activity was simultaneously recorded as it is a known marker of physiological arousal (e.g., van den Hout, et al., 2000) and represents an implicit measure of emotional processing. At the end of the session, explicit affective ratings of the conditioned non-words were taken and these represent an explicit measure of emotional awareness. The predictive value of these implicit and explicit measures for Stroop interference was explored. We predicted that SCR would a better predictor than the affective ratings of the level of interference from negative stimuli in the Stroop task. Experiment 2 presented masked Stroop stimuli in an attempt to investigate potential dissociations between conscious and non-conscious processes in relation to the transfer of acquired emotional significance, i.e., would the emotional connotations acquired consciously transfer to both conscious and non-conscious processes?

Method

Participants Sixty participants took part in the experiment, but two were excluded for having outlying Stroop RTs or SCR responses. Participants scoring above the median score on the trait form of the Spielberger State-Trait Anxiety Inventory (STAI: Spielberger, Gorsuch, Lushene, Vagg, & Jacobs, 1983) were assigned to the high-anxiety group, and the rest to the low-anxiety group. The group had a mean age of 21.17 years (28 males).

Apparatus A Dell computer, Optiplex GX620 with a colour monitor, Ïyama Vision Master, Pro 454, was used for the presentation of stimuli using E-Prime software (Schneider, Eschman & Zuccolotto, 2002). A PST Serial response box (type #200A; Psychology Software Tools, Pittsburgh, PA) was attached to the PC to collect manual RTs. SCR was measured using a Biopac Systems Inc., Model MP 150A, attached to a second Dell Dimension 8200 computer. SCRs were collected using computer software AcqKnowledge III for MP150WS (version 3.8.1). Ag-AgCl electrodes were used with isotonic paste as electrolyte (0.5% NaCl/100ml H_2O). The two Dell computers were linked to synchronize the presentation of stimuli with SCR collection. Stimulus presentation was synchronized with the vertical retrace of the Ïyama monitor.

Design Twenty non-words were created, ten of which were assigned to Set A and ten to Set B. One of these sets was conditioned to the negative photographs and the other set to the neutral photographs. A total of 50 negative and 50 neutral photographs were selected from the International Affective Picture System (Lang, Bradley & Cuthbert, 1999). Each block involved 50 non-word/picture pairings where each non-word was presented 5 times, each time with a different photograph of the same emotional valence.

Procedure The experiment comprised four phases.
Phase 1 - Conditioning: Participants were presented with a neutral block of picture/non-word pairings followed by a negative block, or vice versa. For each trial the picture appeared on the screen for 2000 ms. After 500 ms, the non-word, written in white on a small black rectangle, appeared in the middle of the image for the remaining 1500 ms. There was a 500 ms blank before the next trial. Participants were instructed to look at the pictures and the non-words.
Phase 2 - Stroop Interference: There were two experimental blocks, each with 40 trials of the same conditioned emotional valence. The ten non-words in each set were presented four times, once in each of the four colours (red, green, yellow and blue). The order of the blocks was determined randomly for each participant. Each trial began with a fixation cross for 500 ms, followed by the presentation of the stimulus in the centre of the screen. The stimulus remained on the screen until the participants identified its colour by pressing the appropriate colour-coded key on the keyboard. There was then a blank screen for 1500 ms before the next trial began.
Phase 3 - Affective ratings: Each of the non-words was presented on the screen for rating using a 9-point scale (*1 = very negative and 9 = very positive*). Each stimulus remained on the screen until a manual response was made.
Phase 4 – Picture/non-word association test: To check that participants were not simply remembering which non-word had been presented with which picture type, and therefore making judgements on the basis of this memory rather than on the emotional quality of stimuli, a picture/non-word association test was performed. Pairs of images were presented, one negative and one neutral, on the screen. A non-word, previously presented with either negative or neutral images, appeared above the two images, and the participant indicated which of the two pictures was associated with the non-word.
Skin conductance response: SCR was recorded for 8 minutes before the conditioning phase, as a baseline. Participants were instructed to relax during this period. SCRs were recorded during the conditioning phases. The two blocks of Stroop trials were presented and SCRs recorded. Between the two blocks, there was a rest period of 3 minutes. At the end of the Stroop task, the electrodes were removed from the participant prior to the rating task.

Results

Stroop interference: A 2 (anxiety group: high- vs. low-trait anxious) x 2 (valence of conditioning: negatively- vs. neutrally-conditioned) ANOVA was performed on the mean Stroop RTs. Anxiety group interacted with valence of conditioning in the predicted direction ($F(1,56) = 5.95$, $p = .018$, $\eta^2_p = .10$). The low-trait group responded slower to neutrally than negatively conditioned non-words ($F(1,29) = 6.87$, $p = .014$, $\eta^2_p = .19$), and the high-trait group showed a non-significant trend in the opposite direction ($F(1,27) = 1.63$, $p = .21$; see Figure 1).

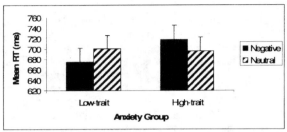

Figure 1: Mean Stroop RTs to negatively and neutrally conditioned non-words for high- and low-trait anxious groups in Experiment 1 (Negative = negative conditioning, Neutral = neutral conditioning).

In order to examine the relative contributions of state and trait anxiety to Stroop interference, an index was created as the DV (mean RT to neutrally conditioned Stroop minus the RT to negatively conditioned Stroop). State and trait anxiety scores were entered as the IVs. Only state anxiety was a significant predictor ($t = 2.18$, $\beta = .30$, $p = .034$).

Skin Conductance Response: We recorded *area* (defined as the total *area* between the waveform and the straight line that is drawn between the two endpoints, measured in microSiemens) for negatively and neutrally conditioned Stroop stimuli. An ANOVA performed using the factors outlined above failed to reveal any significant effects. However, a multiple regression on the difference in *areas* between the negatively and neutrally conditioned Stroop non-words as the DV, and state and trait anxiety as the IVs, revealed that state anxiety was a significant predictor of the index ($t = 2.14$, $\beta = -.29$, $p = .037$).

Affective Ratings: An ANOVA using the same factors as above failed to show any significant effects.

Picture/non-word association test: Using a series of binomial tests, we found that only one participant successfully linked the non-words to the appropriate type of image (negative vs. neutral), suggesting that participants were not performing the tasks on the basis of conscious memory of the corresponding images associated with the non-words in the conditioning phase of the study.

Predicting Stroop Interference: In order to examine the relative contributions of state, trait anxiety, SCR and explicit ratings, difference indices were created for *area*, ratings and Stroop, by calculating the difference in RTs for

the negatively- and neutrally-conditioned stimuli. The Stroop difference index was entered as the DV and the remaining indices were entered as IVs. Only state anxiety was a significant predictor ($t = 2.01$, $\beta = .29$, $p = .05$).

Discussion

This experiment successfully manipulated emotional connotations of neutral stimuli using a simple associative conditioning paradigm. Predicted effects in the Stroop task were observed, and these were related to self-reported state anxiety levels. In addition, although the electrodermal activity was non-significant in the ANOVA, the more powerful multiple regression analysis revealed that state anxiety was significant predictor of the difference in the value of *area* of neutrally versus negatively conditioned stimuli, thereby reflecting the Stroop findings. This analysis revealed that electrodermal activity was a marker for the processing of conditioned emotional stimuli, and this processing was differentially related to self-report levels of state anxiety. However, neither the explicit measures of non-word rating nor the implicit physiological measure were significant predictors of Stroop performance. The perceived emotional state of the participant was related to both electrodermal activity and emotional Stroop performance.

To examine these effects further, a second experiment was performed in which the Stroop task was presented in a masked form. In addition to the unmasked rating task that was presented in Experiment 1, participants also completed a masked rating task. This experiment will also allow us to explore the transfer of emotional significance from conscious to non-conscious processes.

Experiment 2

There is evidence that an emotional response can be invoked without a corresponding conscious appraisal of the stimulus (e.g., Esteves & Öhman, 1993; Lim & Kim, 2005; Mogg, Bradley, Williams & Mathews, 1994; Richards & Blanchette, 2004; Winkielman & Berridge, 2004) although some effects of emotion have been shown to be reduced or to disappear under masked as compared to unmasked conditions (Van den Hout, De Jong, & Kindt, 2000; Wikström, Lundh, Westerlund & Högman, 2004). Richards and Blanchette (2004) observed masked Stroop interference for stimuli that had been conditioned using a conditioning paradigm in which the images were presented in unmasked format but the non-words, presented along with the images, were in a masked format. In the later Stroop task, some of the Stroop non-words were presented in masked format (mirroring the earlier conditioning phase) whereas other Stroop non-words were presented in an unmasked format. More robust interference was observed for the masked stimuli compared to the unmasked stimuli, suggesting that the mode of conditioning was important in the transfer of emotional connotation. The current experiment extended this by examining for possible transfer of emotional connotation from an unmasked conditioning paradigm (in which both picture and non-words are presented in full view) to a masked emotional Stroop paradigm. Electrodermal activity was again measured to see if there were dissociations between behavioural and physiological measures.

Method

Participants Seventy participants took part in the experiment, but four were excluded for having outlying Stroop RTs or SCR responses. Participants scoring above the median score on the trait form of the STAI were assigned to the high-anxiety group, and the rest to the low-anxiety group. The group had a mean age of 29.20 years (30 males).

Design The same design was used as for Experiment 1, but stimuli in the Stroop phase were sandwiched between a forward and a backward mask, created separately from a series of symbols (e.g. ℿↂⅉⅈ⊖⌂⅏). At the end of the study, participants performed an awareness test in which masked non-words or blanks were presented and the participant was instructed to decide (or guess if necessary) if a non-word or a blank had been presented between the two pattern masks. Participants completed a second awareness check where non-words had to be distinguished from words. The non-words were then presented in masked format and rated for affect. Finally, this affective rating task was repeated, but the stimuli were presented in unmasked format.

Procedure The procedure was identical to that of Experiment 1, but with the following modifications. The Stroop stimuli were masked, so that each trial began with a fixation for 500 ms. A pattern mask was presented for 150 ms. This was replaced by the conditioned non-word for 16.67 ms. A second, different, pattern mask was then presented on the screen for 50 ms. Participants were required to identify the briefly presented colour as quickly and accurately as possible. At the end of the Stroop task, participants completed the awareness checks, gave affective ratings to masked and unmasked non-words, and finally performed the picture/non-word association task.

Results

Awareness check: A chi-square was calculated for each participant on their data from the non-word/blank awareness check (where 50% of the trials contained a non-word sandwiched between two pattern masks, and the other 50% contained a blank between the two masks) to determine whether they could significantly differentiate the two types of trials. The results from the word/non-word awareness check produced similar results to those of the non-word/blank test, but the analysis focuses on the former test as this is the more stringent test.

Stroop interference: A 2 (group: high- vs. low-trait anxious) x 2 (valence of conditioning: negatively- vs. neutrally-conditioned) x 2 (aware vs. non-aware) ANOVA performed on the mean RTs to Stroop stimuli failed to produce any significant effects.

Skin Conductance Responses: An ANOVA was performed on the *area* values using the same factors as outlined above during the negatively and neutrally conditioned Stroop trials. Valence of conditioning interacted with awareness, $F(1,62) = 6.58$. $p = .013$, $\eta^2_p = .10$. However, of more interest here was the interaction between these two variables and anxiety group, $F(1,62) = 4.24$, $p = .044$, $\eta^2_p = .06$. Two partial interaction analyses were performed. The first revealed that those participants (irrespective of anxiety level) who showed awareness of the subliminal stimuli also had larger *area* values for the negatively compared to the neutrally conditioned stimuli (means of .087 and .068 microSiemens, respectively; $F(1, 38) = 8.95$, $p =.005$, $\eta^2_p = .19$). However, the second analysis revealed that for those individuals who were unaware of the subliminal non-words in the awareness test, there was an interaction between anxiety group and valence of conditioning, showing that the high-trait group showed physiological reactivity to the subliminal Stroop stimuli, $F(1,24) = 5.11$, $p =.033$, $\eta^2_p = .18$, see Figure 2.

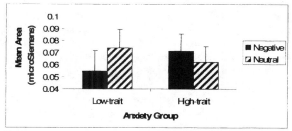

Figure 2. Mean *area* values for the high- and low-trait anxious groups *who were unaware in awareness check* for the Stroop phase of Experiment 2 (Negative = negative conditioning, Neutral = neutral conditioning).

To be consistent with Experiment 1, a multiple regression on the difference in *areas* between the negatively and neutrally-conditioned Stroop non-words as the DV, and state, trait anxiety and awareness as the IVs was performed. This revealed that awareness ($t = 2.60$, $\beta = .32$, $p =.012$, two-tailed) and state anxiety were also a significant predictors ($t = 1.79$, $\beta = .263$, $p =.038$, one-tailed) were significant predictors of physiological responses to Stroop stimuli. Trait anxiety, again, was not relevant ($t < 1$).

Affective Ratings: The affective rating data were analysed with a 2 (group: high- vs. low-trait anxiety) x 2 (aware: aware vs. unaware) x 2 (presentation: masked vs. unmasked) x 2 (valence of conditioning: negative vs. neutral). Negatively-conditioned non-words were rated as more negative than neutrally-conditioned ones (means of 4.77 and 4.94, respectively; $F(1,62) = 7.03$, $p <.01$, $\eta^2_p = .10$), and masked non-words were rated as more negative than unmasked ones (means of 4.66 and 5.05, respectively; $F(1,62) = 11.93$, $p <.001$, $\eta^2_p = .16$). However, of greater importance was the interaction between valence of conditioning and masking, with masked negatively and neutrally conditioned stimuli having non-significantly different ratings ($F = 1.2$) but ratings of the unmasked non-words showed negatively conditioned stimuli were rated as more negative than neutrally conditioned ones ($F(1,62) = 20.58$, $p < .001$, $\eta^2_p = .25$; see Figure 3).

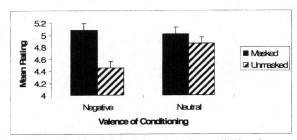

Figure 3. Mean affective ratings for masked and unmasked negatively and neutrally conditioned non-words for Experiment 2.

Picture/non-word association test: Again, only one participant successfully linked the non-words to the appropriate type of image (negative vs. neutral), suggesting that participants were not performing the tasks on the basis of conscious memory of the corresponding images associated with the non-words in the conditioning phase of the study.

Discussion

Experiment 2 has not shown an emotional Stroop effect for masked stimuli, suggesting that emotional significance did not transfer from a conscious cognitive task (conditioning) to a non-conscious cognitive task (masked Stroop). However, electrodermal activity appeared to be sensitive to emotional connotation. All participants who showed some awareness of the masked stimuli (as determined by the awareness check at the end of the session) showed electrodermal reactivity consistent with the emotional connotations of the non-words. State anxiety was also a significant predictor of this differential electrodermal activity observed during the Stroop task. Of particular interest is the sensitivity of the high-trait individuals, who failed to show awareness during the awareness check, to the emotional significance of the conditioned non-words. These high-trait individuals showed physiological sensitivity to the stimuli, whilst not responding differentially to them during the Stroop task. Moreover, this group's explicit affective ratings of the masked non-words did not differentiate negatively- from neutrally-conditioned stimuli.

All participants' explicit affective ratings, irrespective of their anxiety, showed sensitivity to the emotional connotations of the unmasked non-words. It appears that when rating the masked stimuli, participants were not accessing the emotional connotations of the non-words, as the ratings for both the negatively- and neutrally-conditioned non-words were the same as the unmasked neutrally-conditioned non-words. It therefore appears that the masked non-words were rated as if they were simply

neutral stimuli. One explanation for the differential ratings of the unmasked non-words is that participants were simply retrieving the picture/non-word pairings from the conditioning phase rather then responding to the emotional valence of the non-words themselves. However, the picture/non-word association task showed that only one out of sixty-six participants was able to identify above chance level which type of image the two sets of non-words were associated with. This suggests that the affective ratings were not the result of conscious retrieval of the picture/non-word pairings.

General Discussion

In two experiments, we successfully manipulated the emotional connotations of neutral non-words by using a simple associative conditioning paradigm. The first experiment found the predicted anxiety-related emotional Stroop interference and the size of this interference was related to state anxiety. The difference in the SCR data for negatively- and neutrally-conditioned Stroop stimuli was also related to state anxiety, but neither the affective ratings nor SCR responses predicted the size of the Stroop interference effect. Williams, Mathews and MacLeod (1996) cite studies in which state anxiety and/or trait anxiety have been implicated in Stroop interference, and although trait anxiety is often of primary importance, state anxiety is also influential. The second experiment failed to show an emotional Stroop effect, but the electrodermal activity and affective ratings showed sensitivity to the emotional connotations of the non-words. Consistent with Experiment 1, Experiment 2 found that state anxiety was a significant predictor of electrodermal activity during the Stroop task. Showing some awareness during the awareness check at the end of the study also predicted differential electrodermal activity during the Stroop task.

When the mode of conditioning matched the mode of Stroop presentation, i.e., when they were both presented in unmasked format, the predicted pattern of RTs was evident. However, when there was a mismatch, that is, when the non-words were presented in unmasked format during the conditioning phase, but presented in masked format for the Stroop phase, the predicted pattern of RTs was not observed, and this supports our previous work (Richards & Blanchette, 2004, 2006). Richards and Blanchette found Stroop interference effects when conditioning and Stroop presentation were both masked or both unmasked. However, when conditioning was masked and Stroop unmasked, we found no transfer effects.

Electrodermal activity, however, appears to be sensitive to the emotional connotations created during conditioning, even when there was a mismatch between the conditioning task and the Stroop task, and therefore such an indirect measure may be useful for future research. Activation of the emotional connotations produced Stroop interference in Experiment 1 and evidence of differential electrodermal activity whereas the activation in Experiment 2 produced differential electrodermal activity but no Stroop interference. Further research is needed to untangle these effects. It is interesting that there was only electrodermal sensitivity in low-trait participants when these individuals showed some awareness of the masked stimuli. However, the high-trait participants showed sensitivity to the emotional significance of the masked Stroop non-words irrespective of their awareness level, despite not showing any Stroop RT differences, and not giving lower affective ratings to the stimuli. Overall, the size of this differential activation was related to state anxiety in both experiments.

The finding that all participants gave the non-words lower affective ratings when they were rated in unmasked format, but not masked format, suggests that the conditioning was successful. These ratings may be the result of some indirect access to a memory of the earlier picture/non-word pairing, although there was no evidence from the picture/non-word pairing task that individuals had conscious access to this information.

The data from these two experiments suggest that there are complex dissociations between the various implicit and explicit components of emotional processing, and further research is required to understand how they interact in emotional and attentional processing.

Acknowledgments

This research was supported by a Bursary for Scientific Research awarded to the first two authors from the BIAL Foundation (Award 78/04).

References

Blanchette, I. & Richards, A. (2004). Reasoning about emotional and neutral materials: Is logic affected by emotion? *Psychological Science, 15,* 745-752.

Bradley, B. P., Mogg, K., Millar, N., & White, J. (1995). Selective processing of negative information: Effects of clinical anxiety, concurrent depression, and awareness. *Journal of Abnormal Psychology, 104,* 532–536.

Cacioppo, J. T., Marshall-Goodell, B. S., Tassinary, L. G., & Petty, R. E. (1992). Rudimentary determinants of attitudes: Classical conditioning is more effective when prior knowledge about the attitude stimulus is low than high. *Journal of Experimental Social Psychology, 28,* 207–233.

Esteves, F. & Öhman, A. (1993). Masking the face: recognition of emotional facial expressions as a function of the parameters of backward masking. *Scandinavian Journal of Psychology, 34,* 1-18.

Fox, E., Russo, R., Bowles, R. J., & Dutton, K. (2001). Do threatening stimuli draw or hold visual attention in sub-clinical anxiety? *Journal of Experimental Psychology: General, 16,* 355-379.

Lang, P. L. (1985). The cognitive psychophysiology of emotion: Fear and anxiety. In A. H. Tuma & J. Maser (Eds.), *Anxiety and the anxiety disorders* (pp. 131-170). Hillsdale, NJ: Erlbaum.

Lang, P. L., Bradley, M. M., & Cuthbert, B. N. (1995). International Affective Picture System (IAPS): Technical Manual and Affective Ratings, The Center for Research in Psychophysiology, University of Florida, Gainesville, FL).

Lim, S. L., & Kim, J. H. (2005). Cognitive processing of emotional information in depression, panic, and somatoform disorder. *Journal of Abnormal Psychology, 114,* 50-61.

Lundh, L.-G., Wikström, J., Westerlund, J. & Öst, L.-G. (1999). Preattentive bias for emotional information in panic disorder with agoraphobia. *Journal of Abnormal Psychology, 108,* 222–232.

MacLeod, C., Mathews, A., & Tata, P. (1986). Attentional biases in emotional disorders. *Journal of Abnormal Psychology,* **95,** 15-20.

Mogg, K., Bradley, B. P., Williams, R., & Mathews, A. (1993). Subliminal processing of emotional information in anxiety and depression. *Journal of Abnormal Psychology, 102,* 304-311.

Montoya, P., Larbig, W., Pulvermueller, F., & Flor, H. (1996). Cortical correlates of semantic classical conditioning. *Psychophysiology, 33,* 644–649.

Richards, A., & Blanchette, I. (2004). Independent manipulation of emotion in an emotional Stroop task using classical conditioning. *Emotion, 4,* 275-281.

Richards, A., & Blanchette, I. (2006). Affect and cognition: Associative conditioning and anxiety. Submitted for publication.

Schneider, W., Eschman, A., & Zuccolotto, A. (2002). *E-Prime User's Guide.* Pittsburgh: Psychology Software Tools Inc.

Spielberger, C. D., Gorsuch, R. L., Lushene, R., Vagg, P. R., & Jacobs, G. A. (1983). *Manual for the State–Trait Anxiety Inventory (Form Y).* Palo Alto, CA: Consulting Psychologists Press.

Van Honk, J., Tuiten, A., van den Hout, M., Putman, P., de Haan, E. & Stam, H. (2001). Selective attention to unmasked and masked threatening words: relationships to trait anger and anxiety. *Personality and Individual Differences, 30,* 711–720.

van den Hout, M. A., de Jong, P., & Kindt, M. (2000). Masked fear words produce increased SCRs: An anomaly for Ohman's theory of pre-attentive processing in anxiety. *Psychophysiology, 37,* 283-288.

Williams, J. M. G., Mathews, A., & MacLeod, C. (1996). The emotional Stroop task and psychopathology. *Psychological Bulletin, 120,* 3–24.

Wikström, J., Lundh, L-G., Westerlund, J., & Högman, L. (2004). Preattentive bias for snake words in snake phobia? *Behaviour Research and Therapy, 42,* 949-970.

Winkielman, P. & Berridge, K. C. (2004). Unconscious emotion. *Current Directions in Psychological Science, 13,* 120-123.

Yiend, J. & Mathews, A. (2001). Anxiety and attention to threatening pictures. *Quarterly Journal of Experimental Psychology: Human Experimental Psychology, 54,* 665-681.

Does The Face Fit The Facts? Testing Three Accounts Of Age Of Acquisition Effects

James H. Smith-Spark (Smithspj@Lsbu.Ac.Uk)
Department of Psychology, London South Bank University, 103 Borough Road,
London, SE1 0AA, UK

Viv Moore (V.Moore@Gold.Ac.Uk)
Department of Psychology, Goldsmiths College, University of London, New Cross,
London, SE14 6NW, UK

Tim Valentine (T.Valentine@Gold.Ac.Uk)
Department of Psychology, Goldsmiths College, University of London, New Cross,
London, SE14 6NW, UK

Abstract

Naming and perception tasks show robust effects of age of acquisition (AoA), with faster processing of stimuli learnt earlier in life compared to stimuli acquired later. That AoA effects prove to be more elusive on semantic processing tasks is of importance in attempting to determine the mechanism and locus (or loci) of AoA effects. Three accounts of AoA effects were tested empirically using perceptual familiarity decision tasks to record response latency and accuracy to the faces and names of famous people, with the quantity of semantic knowledge being manipulated. The results do not support the semantic 'hub' network or arbitrary mapping explanations of AoA but are consistent with the Set-up of a Specialized Processing System hypothesis.

Introduction

The ability to recognize and name objects, words, and faces is fundamentally important to our understanding of, and ability to interact with, the environment. However, the ubiquity, ease, and speed of such processing contrasts with the complexity of the cognitive processes involved. In addressing these complexities, it has been common to select a set of variables and to decide which variable from this set has the most influential effect on processing. Age of acquisition (AoA) has been found to be one such important predictor of processing speed. Using tasks that require responses to the names and faces of well known figures in popular culture, the differences between three accounts of the AoA phenomenon are examined in this paper, namely the arbitrary mapping hypothesis (Ellis & Lambon Ralph, 2000), the semantic 'hub' network model (Steyvers & Tenenbaum, 2005), and the Set-up of a Specialised Processing System hypothesis (SSPS; e.g., Moore, 2003).

All things being equal, individuals are faster to process items that are learnt earlier in life than items acquired later. This processing advantage for early-acquired stimuli, the AoA effect, has been reported across many tasks and domains (e.g., Brysbaert, Lange, & van Wijnendaele, 2000; Moore, Smith-Spark, & Valentine, 2004; Morrison & Ellis, 1995). Early theories attributed AoA effects to a single locus, the phonological output lexicon (e.g., Brown & Watson, 1987), arguing that the phonological representations of early-acquired words are stored in a more complete form than those of words acquired later. The advantage for early-acquired items was thus proposed to result from the phonological reassembly of late-acquired items for production. Morrison and Ellis attributed AoA effects on lexical decision tasks to the automatic activation of phonology in the output lexicon. A locus at speech output suggests that the AoA effect arises during spoken language acquisition. However, children learn to read long after they have learnt to speak so this account cannot readily explain AoA effects on the decoding of *written* words.

Reports of AoA effects on proper name and face processing (Moore & Valentine, 1998, 1999) are also problematic for the phonological output lexicon explanation, because early-acquired items in this domain are acquired subsequent to any period of critical language development. Furthermore, evidence indicates that names are not automatically activated when seeing a face; firstly, the difficulty of naming familiar faces argues against any automatic process (e.g., Brédart, 1996) and, secondly, no direct links from face perception to naming have been found to exist (Valentine, Hollis, & Moore, 1998). Performance on face familiarity decision tasks has been argued to be based on activation of PINs (Person Identity Nodes, which act as a gateway to semantic information) rather than phonology (Burton, Bruce, & Johnson, 1990). As a consequence, Moore and Valentine (1998, 1999; also Brysbaert, van Wijnendaele, & De Deyne, 2000) propose that because knowledge of famous people is acquired after the language learning period, AoA effects reflect the *order of acquiring* information in a specific stimulus domain rather than the *age* at which items were acquired.

Originally devised to explain the empirical effects of preserved memory in organic amnesia (Mayes, Poole, & Gooding, 1991), the SSPS hypothesis can account for empirically reported AoA effects on lexical, object, and face processing tasks, as well as second language learning (e.g., Moore, 2003; Moore & Valentine, 1999). Under this account, exposure to novel exemplars will instantiate a new system (or reconfigure an existing one) to process them. The *interaction* between novel exemplars and a lack of mediation from the semantic system will stimulate a physiological orienting response (Lang, Bradley, & Cuthbert, 1997). This bi-directional influence would create a vehicle for greater attention to be given to subsequent, similar examples. Such a situation would effectively initiate an SSPS by pegging out, or 'hard clamping', the parameters of distinction between the earliest observed examples. Thus, a different pattern of activity between representations would create a discrete state space for that type of information, producing a gateway into the semantic system for processing. Moore argues that learning at this stage is explicit and effortful. Once a gateway is created, a more automatised form of processing takes over to facilitate the learning of similar exemplars (Langer, 2000). The performance of any perceptual or motor task for which specialised representations are established should therefore be influenced by AoA. Moore proposed that only this can explain the empirically measured effects of AoA on face processing. Children can process faces from a very early age (e.g., Barrera & Maurer, 1981), but ratings taken from adults show that individuals typically start to become aware of celebrity status at around 6 years of age (Moore & Valentine, 1999). This awareness requires the recruitment of a new processing strategy or the reconfiguration of the specific state-space to process similar items.

Historically, connectionist back-propagation models were considered to be unable to implement AoA effects (e.g., Morrison & Ellis, 1995) due to catastrophic interference. However, it has since been demonstrated that AoA is, in fact, a natural and emergent property of such networks (Anderson & Cottrell, 2001; Ellis & Lambon Ralph, 2000). Models trained on interleaved early- and late-learned patterns produced a processing advantage for items introduced in earlier training epochs, thereby replicating human empirical data. Ellis and Lambon Ralph attributed the effect to a gradual reduction in network plasticity, with neural plasticity being hard clamped by exposure to early exemplars. Accordingly, AoA effects should occur in the binary mappings between two sets of representations and especially in the case of arbitrary mappings, such as those between the name or face of a person and semantic knowledge about that individual (also Zevin & Seidenberg, 2002). One of the major differences between object and person processing lies in the fact that recognition of an individual requires a *unique identifier*. Naming a face requires the identification of a unique concept (unlike in the case of a ball or a chair). Very strong physical similarities exist between identical twins, but they are still distinguishable to people who know them. Equally, there are many people with the name "John Smith' (both first and family names are highly frequent in the UK), but each John Smith is a unique individual and uniquely separable from all of the other John Smiths in the world. According to various connectionist (and, indeed, many cognitive) models,

the distinction between pictures and labels (or written words) is that text follows certain rules. Therefore, input and output have a 'linear' relationship. On the other hand, input and output for pictorial information is much more arbitrary. For example, a linear relationship between the label 'balloon' and the image of a balloon is not evident.

To date, there is no compelling evidence in favour of an unambiguous effect of AoA on semantic processing tasks. An initial report by Rubin (1980) argued that semantic classifications were significantly affected by AoA. However, more recent research (Moore, 2003) has failed to uncover any effects of AoA on a battery of semantic processing tasks, despite robust AoA effects on perceptual and naming tasks involving the same stimuli. Other reports of AoA influencing semantic processing (e.g., Lewis, 1999) may be premature, as complications exist with tasks and stimuli (see Moore, Valentine, & Turner, 1999). In those studies, participants were typically aged between 18 and 25 years, so there was only a short age distance between early- and late-acquired stimuli. Early-acquired stimuli were classed as those learnt before the age of 12 and late-acquired stimuli were considered to be those learnt after 18 years old. To obviate this criticism, the present study was conducted on adults aged over 40 years.

The SSPS view is that it *should* be possible to elicit AoA effects on semantic face processing tasks. However, Moore (2003) has argued that such effects may be elusive since the processing framework would be clamped by the *individual's* exposure to novel items. Whilst words and objects learnt early in vocabulary development are likely to be shared by children within the same culture and educational system, a child's early exposure to the individual as a celebrity will be highly dependent on parental interests (be they in film, sport, music, politics, etc.). Thus, selecting a set of stimuli that share universal semantic properties is far more difficult than finding stimuli for other types of experiments that manipulate AoA.

Brysbaert and Ghyselinck (2006) state that when frequency is controlled in lexical processing, there is no speed advantage for early-acquired words on either naming or classification tasks, but there is a significant influence of AoA on object processing. Brysbaert and Ghyselinck argue that this dual-AoA effect is caused by letter strings being *yoked* to frequency, whereas picture formats are frequency-independent (see also Lambon Ralph & Ehsan, 2006). They relate their findings to the Steyvers and Tenenbaum (2005) semantic 'hub' network model. From this perspective, the organisation of the semantic system can explain AoA effects; as a novel concept is perceived, it becomes represented in the semantic system and interconnects with pre-established concepts. Early-acquired concepts form a central hub with a far richer interconnectivity than later-acquired concepts, resulting in more efficient retrieval. According to this account, AoA can be equated with (if not be superseded by) the richness of interconnections between concepts. However, it cannot account for robust AoA effects on naming and familiarity tasks in the absence of a semantic effect for identical stimuli (Moore, 2003).

Brédart, Valentine, Calder, and Gassi (1995) found that participants were faster to name celebrity faces about whom many pieces of semantic information were known than those belonging to celebrities about whom little was known. However, their stimuli were controlled for familiarity, but not for AoA. This paper adopts a similar approach but incorporates AoA into the experimental design and probes familiarity decisions rather than naming responses.

The theories outlined above allow distinguishable predictions to be made about the outcome of the experiment. The work of Ellis and Lambon Ralph (2000) would suggest that there will be an AoA effect based on arbitrary mappings, such that there will be an early-acquired processing advantage in classifying both pictures of faces and printed names of the same celebrities. However, an interaction between AoA and format of presentation (faces or names) should occur. The magnitude of the AoA effect will not be so strong in the case of the responses to written names as it will be in response to faces. The arbitrary mapping hypothesis predicts that early-acquired faces should receive a greater processing advantage than names of the same celebrities, as a consequence of the more arbitrary connection between a face and an individual rather than between a name and the same individual. The semantic 'hub' network model (Steyvers & Tenenbaum, 2005) would predict that faster processing will occur for items possessing the most semantic connections. That is to say, there will be faster and more efficient processing of celebrities about whom many pieces of semantic information are known than for those about whom relatively little information is known. Furthermore, while an AoA effect is predicted by the model, the effects will be secondary to the processing advantage conferred by the rich interconnectivity of nodes for celebrities about whom many facts are known. Finally, the SSPS model (Moore, 2003) makes the prediction that there will be faster processing of early-acquired items regardless of the amount of information known about each celebrity. Furthermore, the *magnitude* of the difference will be the same for *both* the printed names and the faces.

Method

Participants

Forty-eight adults (32 female, 16 male) took part in the experiment (mean age = 66.92 years, SD = 8.59). All the participants had lived their whole lives in the UK. They were randomly allocated to one of two conditions, such that half were presented with faces (15 female, 9 male; mean age = 69.38 years, SD = 8.59) and half saw names (17 female, 7 male; mean age = 64.46 years, SD = 6.71).

Materials

Participants (N =105, mean age = 60.44 years, SD = 11.80) wrote down all the facts they knew about highly familiar celebrities (previously rated by 182 participants, see Smith-

Spark, Moore, Valentine, & Sherman, 2006). Participants were informed of the type of factual information required: nationality, family details (e.g., marital status, famous parents, siblings, or children), the titles of films or television programmes in which s/he had appeared, and any other information (such as anecdotes) known to them (see Brédart et al., 1995). The responses were cross-checked for their veracity using several internet-based biographical sources.

From the above data, 40 famous people were selected on the basis of having either few or many facts known about them. These stimuli had been rated as either early- or late-acquired (Smith-Spark et al., 2006) and were chosen as being amongst those most easily recognised by participants aged over 40 years. It is difficult to remove all individual differences in 'world knowledge' from the experimental design, but a priori and post hoc ratings were employed to ensure that the stimuli were very well known to the participants[1]. The stimulus selection procedure allowed AoA and the number of facts known (NoF) to be manipulated orthogonally, creating four stimulus groups of 10 items. The groups were i) early-AoA, few-NoF, ii) early-AoA, many-NoF, iii) late-AoA, few-NoF, and iv) late-AoA, many-NoF. The groups were matched for familiarity, facial distinctiveness, and the number of syllables in the celebrities' names (see Smith-Spark et al.). The critical items were subjected to one-way ANOVAs (see Table 1) to verify that there were significant differences between the levels of the independent variables and that there were no differences across the control variables (e.g., familiarity).

Table 1: Means and *p*-values for each stimulus grouping.

NoF	Early-acquired		Late-acquired		
	Few	Many	Few	Many	*p*
Syll.	3.30	4.20	4.10	3.90	.196
Gen.	69.10	69.30	71.40	76.30	.941
AP Fam.	4.37	4.66	4.48	4.65	.421
AP Dist.	4.51	4.46	4.27	4.58	.667
AP AoA	3.31	3.59	6.03	6.31	< .001
AP Facts	3.14	5.45	2.97	6.15	< .001
PH Fam.	4.30	4.51	4.32	4.55	.583
PH Dist.	4.28	4.32	4.15	4.32	.898
PH AoA	3.58	3.93	6.57	6.69	< .001
PH Facts	3.88	5.71	3.19	5.36	< .001

Key: AP = a priori ratings; PH = post hoc ratings; Syll. = number of syllables in the name; Gen. = number of times a name was generated; Fam. = rated familiarity (7-point scale); Dist. = rated distinctiveness (7-point scale); AoA = rated AoA (10-point scale); Facts = NoF.

The celebrity stimuli were supplemented with 40 unfamiliar faces and names. Unfamiliar faces were selected from a collection of photographs of university staff and students and faces from the Psychological Image Collection at Stirling (PICS) database. The unfamiliar names were

---

[1] Space constraints mean it is not possible to list the stimuli and indicate areas of fame; this information is available on request.

constructed by recombining the first and family names of other famous people recorded by Smith-Spark et al. (2006); for example, Rosemary West and Stephen Hawking produced 'Stephen West' and 'Rosemary Hawking'.

Testing was conducted using an IBM-compatible computer running the E-Prime experiment generator package (Psychology Software Tools, Inc.). The faces were presented as 256x256 pixel 16-bit greyscale images and the names were presented in reverse video 12-point Courier New font. A two-button response box connected to the PC was used to log reaction time (RT) and accuracy.

Design

A 2x2x2 mixed-measures ANOVA design was employed. Stimulus format (faces vs. names) was the between-subjects factor. The two within-subjects factors were AoA (early vs. late) and NoF (few vs. many). Since the same celebrities were used in the names and faces conditions, it was not possible to perform a purely repeated measures design without priming participants' responses and increasing the impact of individual differences in world knowledge. Participant group was taken as the random factor. This provides an appropriate test because stimuli have been matched on other variables, making an analysis with items as the random factor unnecessary (Raaijmakers, 2003). The dependent variables were RT and percent accuracy. Responses were deemed to be correct when participants correctly identified famous people as being familiar or when unfamiliar stimuli were correctly identified as unfamiliar.

Procedure

A 12-item practice session preceded the main experiment. Each trial began with a central fixation point appearing on the VDU for 700ms, followed by a warning tone (2000 Hz for 250 ms). The stimulus then immediately appeared on the screen and remained until the participant made a response by pressing the 'YES' button on the response box if the stimulus was familiar to them or the 'NO' button if it was unfamiliar. This response extinguished the display and the next trial was initiated. The participants were asked to respond as quickly and accurately as possible.

Post hoc ratings The participants were then requested to rate the critical items for their familiarity, facial distinctiveness, and AoA, using Moore and Valentine's (1998) method. Rating scores are also shown in Table 1.

Post hoc NoF scores Finally, the participants were asked to report verbally all the facts they knew about each celebrity (Brédart et al., 1995). These reports were again checked with internet biographical sources (see Table 1).

Results

The mean response rate to unfamiliar items was 1291 ms (SD = 452.96). Distractor names were responded to at a mean latency of 1502 ms (SD = 476.36), whilst the mean

RT to distractor faces was 1079 ms (SD = 314.57). A mean percentage accuracy of response was also derived for the distractor items (mean = 93.70, SD = 6.50). The participants were less accurate in their responses to names (mean = 90.94, SD = 6.83) than to faces (mean = 96.46, SD = 4.89).

Analysis of the post hoc ratings indicated that there were no significant differences between the groups of critical items in their familiarity and facial distinctiveness, indicating that the items were well matched on these variables. Post hoc AoA and NoF scores differed significantly, thereby confirming the a priori allocation of items to the 4 stimulus groupings. The results of the post hoc ratings analyses are shown in Table 1. Having thus ensured the validity of the groupings, mixed-measures ANOVAs were carried out on RT and percent accuracy.

There was a significant main effect of AoA on RT, with the participants responding significantly faster to early-acquired stimuli, $F(1, 46) = 45.52$, $MSE = 7114.393$, $p < .001$. The mean RTs were 1061ms ($SE = 29.32$) to early-acquired and 1143ms ($SE = 32.35$) to late-acquired stimuli.

There was also a significant main effect of NoF, $F(1, 46) = 13.22$, $MSE = 3107.127$, $p = .001$. Participants were faster to respond to many-NoF (mean = 1087ms, $SE = 30.24$) than to few-NoF stimuli (mean = 1117ms, $SE = 30.82$).

Presentation format had no significant effect, $F(1, 46) = 1.73$, $MSE = 175871.120$, $p = .195$. Mean RTs were 1062ms ($SE = 42.80$) to faces and 1142ms ($SE = 42.80$) to names.

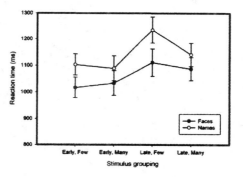

Figure 1: Mean RT

There was no significant interaction between AoA and presentation format, $F(1, 46) < 1$, $MSE = 7114.393$, $p = .457$. However, there was a significant NoF x presentation format interaction, $F(1, 46) = 10.21$, $MSE = 3107.127$, $p = .003$. Non-significant trends suggested that both early-acquired, $t(46) = 1.56$, $p = .127$, and late-acquired few-facts faces $t(46) = 1.73$, $p = .090$, were responded to faster than their few-fact name counterparts. There was also a significant interaction between AoA and NoF, $F(1, 46) = 4.30$, $MSE = 10378.203$, $p = .044$. A related-samples t-test indicated that there was a significant difference between responses to late-few and late-many facts stimuli, $t(47) = 31.93$, $p < .001$. The mean RTs for each stimulus grouping are shown in Figure 1. There was no evidence of a significant AoA x NoF x presentation format interaction, $F(1, 46) = 0.474$, $MSE = 10378.203$, $p = .494$.

The percentage accuracy data also indicated that there was a significant main effect of AoA on performance, $F(1, 46) = 4.38$, $MSE = 93.252$, $p = .042$. Participants produced more accurate responses to early-acquired celebrities (mean = 92.40%, $SE = 0.99$) than to those that were late-acquired (mean = 89.48%, $SE = 1.17$).

However, there was no significant effect of NoF on response accuracy, $F(1, 46) = 2.87$, $MSE = 58.832$, $p = .097$. The mean accuracy scores were 90.00 ($SE = 1.06$) for low-NoF and 91.88 ($SE = 0.93$) for high-NoF groupings.

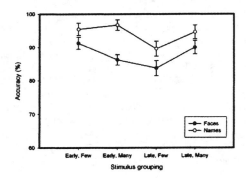

Figure 2: Mean percent accuracy

Format of presentation significantly affected accuracy, $F(1, 46) = 14.13$, $MSE = 132.745$, $p < .001$. More accurate responses were produced to names (mean = 94.06, $SE = 1.18$) than to faces (mean = 87.81, $SE = 1.18$).

A significant interaction between AoA and NoF was also found, $F(1, 46) = 8.86$, $MSE = 76.223$, $p = .005$. Differences lay between early-few and late-few, $t(47) = 3.40$, $p = .001$, early-many and late-few, $t(47) = 2.68$, $p = .010$, and between late-few and late-many items, $t(47) = -2.92$, $p = .005$. There were no further significant interactions (AoA x presentation format, $F(1, 46) = 0.56$, $MSE = 93.252$, $p = .459$; NoF x presentation format, $F(1, 46) = 1.28$, $MSE = 58.832$, $p = .265$; AoA group x NoF group x presentation format, $F(1, 46) = 2.21$, $MSE = 76.223$, $p = .144$). Figure 2 shows the percent mean accuracy scores for each grouping.

Discussion

Adults were tested on perceptual familiarity decision tasks requiring classification responses to names or faces. The participants were faster to respond to familiar stimuli than to unfamiliar items. Distractor faces were rejected more rapidly and more accurately than were unfamiliar names. As predicted, there was a significant main effect of AoA, with participants responding faster and more accurately to early-acquired than late-acquired items. In addition, the participants made significantly more rapid and accurate responses to many-NoF celebrities than to few-NoF

celebrities. A significant AoA x NoF interaction revealed that knowing more facts about a celebrity reduced response latencies to late-acquired items, but not to early-acquired stimuli. A similar pattern of results was found for the accuracy data, confirming that no speed-accuracy trade-off had occurred. The data will now be discussed in relation to the three theoretical approaches set out in the Introduction.

The arbitrary mapping hypothesis (Ellis & Lambon Ralph, 2000) predicted that items presented pictorially would result in the strongest effect of AoA. However, this was not borne out by the data. There was no significant effect of presentation format on RT, even though faces were indeed responded to faster than names. In fact, the magnitude of the AoA effect on RT was very similar for faces (7%) and names (8%). The absence of an AoA x format interaction is thus problematic for this hypothesis.

According to the semantic 'hub' network model (Steyvers & Tenenbaum, 2005), any effect of AoA should be overridden by enhanced processing of the more richly interconnected 'many facts' hubs. Faster responses did occur to celebrities about whom many facts were known, but the significant AoA x NoF interaction demonstrated that this effect only influenced the processing of late-acquired items. In the case of early-acquired stimuli, neither RT nor accuracy were significantly influenced by the richness of semantic information known about a person. Furthermore, all groups were matched on a priori and post hoc familiarity ratings. If it were to be argued that these ratings represented a stronger indication of interconnectivity, no significant AoA effect should have occurred. Thus, the data do not support the predictions derived from the 'hub' model.

The results are, however, consistent with earlier research (e.g., Moore & Valentine, 1999) in suggesting that multiple loci of AoA effects exist; that is, at perceptual recognition (as reported here) and at motor output, such as in naming.

Only the predictions derived from the SSPS hypothesis were fully supported. The AoA x NoF interaction revealed that the amount of semantic information known did not influence the speed with which early-acquired celebrities were processed, with there being a 1ms difference between the mean RTs of the two NoF groupings (few-NoF = 1060ms vs. many-NoF = 1061ms). However, knowing many facts did facilitate responses to late-acquired stimuli, with a 60ms advantage in the processing of celebrities about whom much was known (few-NoF = 1173ms vs. many-NoF = 1113ms). The second SSPS prediction, that the magnitude of the AoA effect would be the same for both names and faces, was also supported by the lack of an AoA x presentation format interaction. The results thus support research on object processing (Brysbaert & Ghyselinck, 2006). While a picture and a letter string represent the same person or object, the pattern of recognition is defined by the associated physical properties from the pictorial format. Reading and writing printed letter strings would be acquired in a later order than the representations of the physical properties (Funnell, Hughes, & Woodcock, 2006), because the child has already learnt to identify the picture or object before learning to read the name. The same may be said for processing celebrities- knowledge of who they are and what they are famous for will usually be acquired before reading about them. If not, one would simply be reading about an unfamiliar person!

Acknowledgements

This research was supported by an Economic and Social Research Council (UK) grant (R000 23 9009) to Viv Moore.

References

Anderson, K. L., & Cottrell, G. W. (2001). Age of acquisition in connectionist networks. In J. D. Moore & K. Stenning (Eds.), *Proceedings of the twenty-third annual conference of the Cognitive Science Society.* Mahwah, NJ: Erlbaum.

Barrera, M. E., & Maurer, D. (1981). Discrimination of strangers by the three-month-old. *Child Development, 52,* 559-563.

Brédart, S. (1996). Person familiarity and name-retrieval failures: How are they related? *Current Psychology of Cognition, 15,* 113-120.

Brédart, S., Valentine, T., Calder, A., & Gassi, G. (1995). An interactive activation model of face naming. *Quarterly Journal of Experimental Psychology, 48A,* 466-486.

Brown, G. D. A., & Watson, F. L. (1987). First in, first out: Word learning age and spoken word frequency as predictors of word familiarity and word naming latency. *Memory & Cognition, 15*(3), 208-216.

Brysbaert, M., & Ghyselinck, M. (2006). The effect of age of acquisition: Partly frequency related, partly frequency independent. *Visual Cognition, 13*(7/8), 992-1011.

Brysbaert, M., Lange, M., & van Wijnendaele, I. (2000). The effects of age of acquisition and frequency of occurrence in visual word recognition: Further evidence from the Dutch language. *European Journal of Cognitive Psychology, 12,* 65-85.

Brysbaert, M., van Wijnendaele, I., & De Deyne, S. (2000). Age-of-acquisition effects in semantic processing tasks. *Acta Psychologica, 104,* 215-226.

Ellis, A. W., & Lambon Ralph, M. A. (2000). Age of acquisition effects in adult lexical processing reflect loss of plasticity in maturing systems: Insights from connectionist networks. *Journal of Experimental Psychology: Learning, Memory and Cognition, 26,* 1103-1123.

Funnell, E., Hughes, D., & Woodcock, J. (2006). Age of acquisition for naming and knowing: A new hypothesis. *Quarterly Journal of Experimental Psychology, 59*(2), 268-295.

Lambon Ralph, M. A., & Ehsan, S. (2006). Age of acquisition effects depend on the mapping between representations and the frequency of occurrence: Empirical and computational evidence. *Visual Cognition, 13*(7/8), 928-948.

Lang, P. J., Bradley, M. M., & Cuthbert, B. N. (1997). Motivated attention: Affect, activation and action. In P. J. Lang, R. F. Simons, & M. T. Balaban (Eds.), *Attention and orienting: Sensory and motivational processes.* Hillsdale, NJ: Erlbaum.

Langer, E. J. (2000). Mindful learning. *Current Directions in Psychological Science, 9*(6), 220 223.

Lewis, M. B. (1999). Age of acquisition in face categorisation: Is there an instance-based account? *Cognition, 71,* B23-B39.

Mayes A. R., Poole, V. M., & Gooding, T. (1991). Increased reading speed for words and pronounceable non-words: Evidence of preserved priming in amnesics. *Cortex, 27,* 403-415.

Moore, V. (2003). An alternative account for the effects of age of acquisition. In P. Bonin (Ed.), *Mental lexicon: Some words to talk about words.* New York: Nova Science Publications.

Moore, V., Smith-Spark, J. H., & Valentine, T. (2004). The effects of age of acquisition on object recognition. *European Journal of Cognitive Psychology, 16*(3), 417-439.

Moore, V., & Valentine, T. (1998). Naming faces: The effect of age of acquisition on speed and accuracy of naming famous faces. *Quarterly Journal of Psychology, 51,* 485-513.

Moore, V., & Valentine, T. (1999). The effects of age of acquisition in processing famous faces and names: Exploring the locus and proposing a mechanism. In M. Hahn & S. C. Stoness (Eds.), *Proceedings of the twenty-first annual conference of the Cognitive Science Society.* Mahwah, NJ: Erlbaum.

Moore, V., Valentine, T., & Turner, J. (1999). Age of acquisition and cumulative frequency have independent effects. *Cognition, 72,* 305-309.

Morrison, C. M., & Ellis, A. W. (1995). The roles of word frequency and age of acquisition in word naming and lexical decision. *Journal of Experimental Psychology: Learning, Memory & Cognition, 21,* 116-133.

Raaijmakers, J. G. W. (2003). A further look at the "Language-as-Fixed-Effect Fallacy". *Canadian Journal of Experimental Psychology, 57*(3), 141-151.

Rubin, D. C. (1980). 51 properties of 125 words: A unit analysis of verbal behavior. *Journal of Verbal Learning and Verbal Behavior, 19,* 736-755.

Smith-Spark, J. H., Moore, V., Valentine, T., & Sherman, S. M. (2006). Stimulus generation, ratings, phoneme counts, and group classifications for 696 famous people by British adults aged over 40 years. *Behavior Research Methods, 38*(4), 590-597.

Steyvers, M., & Tenenbaum, J. B. (2005). The large scale structure of semantic networks Statistical analyses and a model of semantic growth. *Cognitive Science, 22,* 41-78.

Valentine, T., Brennen, T., & Brédart, S. (1996). *The cognitive psychology of proper names. On the importance of being Ernest.* London: Routledge.

Valentine, T., Hollis, J., & Moore, V. (1998). On the relationship between reading, listening and speaking: It's different for people's names. *Memory & Cognition, 26,* 740-753.

Zevin, J. D., & Seidenberg, M. S. (2002). Age of acquisition effects in word reading and other tasks. *Journal of Memory and Language, 47,* 1-29.

Visual guidance and the impact of interruption during problem solving: Interface issues embedded in Cognitive Load Theory

Christof van Nimwegen (christof@cs.uu.nl)
Herre van Oostendorp (herre@cs.uu.nl)

Center for Content and Knowledge Engineering, Utrecht University
Padualaan 14, De Uithof, 3584CH, Utrecht, The Netherlands

Abstract

It is assumed that performance on problem solving tasks improves when task-related information is *externalized* on the interface. Without this visual guidance information must be *internalized*, stored in the user's memory. We expect the latter to instigate better planning, efficiency and understanding. We embed these concepts in Cognitive Load Theory. In an experiment we show that when users have to *internalize* themselves, task execution was not affected by a severe interruption (a system crash), in contrast to when information was *externalized*. We see better survival of the interruption as a consequence of more solid imprinting provoked by internalizing information oneself. When understanding of what underlies a task, and when stable task execution is required, designers should beware of giving users (too) much assistance.

Introduction

A tendency in software development is to take the user by the hand by limiting choices and providing feedback (Van Oostendorp & De Mul, 1999). Examples are wizards, help-options and graying-out menu-items that don't permit using them thus offering a context-sensitive interface with just "possible" actions (see figure 1). For example in Word, you cannot select "paste" from the "edit"-tab in the menu, when nothing is copied first. "Paste" shown in gray color indicates its presence, but using it is impossible.

Figure1: Externalized information in Windows.

It is argued that guided support from an interface during problem solving makes interactions easier and performance better. Relevant task information is displayed, which makes recall unnecessary. It could relieve working memory (WM), and is referred to as *externalization*. Zhang (1997) used various problem solving tasks as material and showed that externalizing information *can* be useful for cognitive tasks, depending on retrieval strategy and the way information was encoded. The more information was externalized, the easier it can be to solve the problem. However, the externalization of information might not necessarily instigate planning, understanding and knowledge acquisition from the user.

When information is *not* externalized, certain task information is less directly available and needs to be *internalized*, i.e. inferred and stored in memory before it can be used. In our research we question and investigate whether externalization of information really has beneficial effects in terms of performance on tasks or acquired knowledge. Furthermore, we wonder whether WM really can be said to be relieved in the first place because one could argue that the information offered to the user also has to be perceived and processed, and can have a distracting influence, or even make the user less proactive. In our research project we have studied the influence of internalization/externalization in the context of various criteria: correctness, the time needed, task efficiency, knowledge, and transfer of skills. As will be elaborated on in this paper, in our research so far no positive effects of externalization were found. Externalizing led to strong reliance on the visually displayed information, and is thought to *discourage* planning. It provoked more shallow thinking, resulting in less efficient solutions by users, which is not desirable when the goal is better performance and transferable task knowledge.

In the current study we will investigate these interface styles once more, but focus on the effect of a severe interruption, meant to disrupt the user. We study this issue to see whether it contributes to the theory that the nature of problem solving instigated by internalization is more resistant against interruption. If this is the case, it can in turn be useful for interface design when learning is the aim, or when having solid knowledge of what underlies a situation is important. The issue also deserves attention in the context of mobile device interaction paradigms. Devices are more mobile than ever before and during interactions with them a wide range of interruptions and distractions are commonplace (Nagata, 2006). Depending on the task, it could be preferable that users resume interacting on the basis of solid internalized plans and knowledge, rather than catching up on the basis of an assisting interface.

We will lay out the theoretical framework of our research and describe former results by us and others. After that we elaborate on the current experiment and its conclusions.

Theoretical framework: cognitive load theory

Few people would disagree with the notion that WM is limited and can only process a limited amount of information at a time (Baddeley, 1986). Also from a multimedia context it has been stated that the demands by interactive media may exceed the capacity of the cognitive system and prevent learning (Mayer & Moreno, 2003). We chose to embed our concepts in cognitive load theory (CLT), which has become a fundamental theory used to describe cognitive processes in learning with new technologies, such as multimedia environments. It is originally an instructional theory with the basic premise that learning is hindered if the instructional material overwhelms learners' cognitive resources. The theory differentiates between intrinsic, germane, and extraneous cognitive load (Sweller, van Merrienboer & Paas, 1998). Intrinsic cognitive load (ICL) is the load imposed by the task and refers to the complexity of a concept itself. The numbers of interacting elements and their relationships have to be kept active in WM and this reflects the difficulty of learning (figure 2). Extraneous cognitive load (ECL) results from the design of the instructional material, and refers to the *unnecessary* load caused by inefficient instructional design. Germane cognitive load (GCL) refers to the degree of effort involved in the processing, construction and automation of schemas. GCL is the load that is *effective* for learning and is also associated with motivation and interest. ICL is seen as unchangeable from the outside, whereas designers are thought to be able to influence ECL and GCL by *triggering* learner activity via instructional designs. Various augmentations to the theory have been proposed. Rikers, van Gerven and Schmidt (2004) stated that the theory cannot account for the importance of the role of learner's expertise. Gerjets and Scheiter (2003) suggested augmentations to the model to account for learner's goal and task configurations. Still CLT proves to be a valuable framework also for HCI research, e.g. in information retrieval (Back & Oppenheim, 2001) or web based instruction (Feinberg & Murphy, 2000).

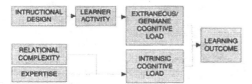

Figure 2: Cognitive load theory.

While our research issues are not related to *instruction* per se, we will map them to the assumptions of CLT (figure 3), which also state that a good portion of WM should be devoted to effortful cognitive processes. We questioned whether externalization implemented to relieve cognitive load, is beneficial. In our human computer interaction (HCI) context we position both internalization and externalization on the dimension of extraneous cognitive load. So far we concluded that experiencing *high* cognitive load (caused by internalization) resulted in more efficient task solutions and better knowledge afterwards, presumably because of a better *plan* or more elaborated strategies. Externalization makes recall of certain knowledge elements unnecessary, and is supposed to relieve WM. Since users make *less* plans and mental effort and devote fewer resources to problem solving, one could regard the effect of externalization as cognitive load of a *different type*. After all, the externalized information takes attention and *also* has to be perceived and processed, regardless whether it is feedback or other pointers, cues or information. We see the processing of this

externalized information, subsequently accompanied by shallow processing, as corresponding with high ECL. High ECL is ineffective, and takes resources away from the task. When ECL is high, fewer resources are left for germane cognitive load (Sweller et al., 1998). GCL will consequently be low and leads users to engage in activities *not* directed at schema acquisition or automation (figure 3).

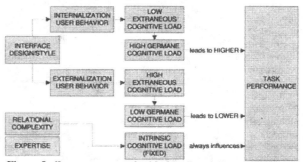

Figure 3: Our concepts embedded in Cognitive Load Theory

We see internalization as corresponding with *low* extraneous cognitive load. When ECL is low, resources can be devoted to mindful cognitive processes that are associated with *germane cognitive load* (relevant processes such as schema construction). The consequence of increased germane cognitive load is comparable with "provoking plan based behavior" as we attempted with internalization. Increased GCL is associated with motivation and interest, and results in a high degree of mindful effort involved in processing and construction of schemas or plans (Sweller et al., 1998).

Former findings

The notion that learning is more effective when people experiment and actively discover for themselves is not new. Carroll (1990) for example, propagated minimalism in design and instructions. Making a system "harder to use", or "incomplete" on purpose causes users to explore the system actively. Kerr and Payne (1994) pondered why active learning *with* a target system would be more effective than with reading instructions. Is it because the user is free to set his own goals, or to use their own words, "*is it that the learner has to attempt to solve problems himself, actively choosing or inferring the next command, rather than merely reading and applying potted solutions?*". Perhaps *more difficult* conditions instigate a deeper level of cognitive processing, resulting in more effective learning.

Van Nimwegen, van Oostendorp and Tabachneck-Schijf (2004) performed various experiments involving the effects of internalization and externalization. They used an abstract version of "Missionaries and Cannibals" called Balls & Boxes (B&B) in two interface versions: externalization and internalization. Externalization was realized by graying out inapplicable (momentarily unavailable) buttons needed to perform operations, informing the user of rules and constraints. In the internalization version this support was absent. The subjects solved puzzles, and performance, rule knowledge, and transfer were measured. Surprisingly, not on any measure did externalization subjects perform better. The internalization subjects had better knowledge of the rules and solution of the problem. After 6 tasks there was a pause, in which subjects received a distraction-task. Internalization subjects were expected to perform better on resumption of the tasks. The idea behind it is that internalization causes low ECL, allowing high GCL which leads to better internalized knowledge-elements and a more elaborated plan (figure 3). Internalization indeed caused smarter behavior and less deviation from solution paths after the pause, although the difference was not significant at a conventional level. After a re-run with the *same* subjects 8 months later, internalization subjects *still* had better knowledge and now also better performance, also on a transfer task. This suggests that internalization caused more solid encoding and imprinting of strategies. In a follow up study using the same task, Van Nimwegen et al. (2005) tried to *externally* influence the mental effort (corresponding with germane cognitive load) subjects would invest. Subjects were either encouraged to do the tasks fast, errors did not matter (low-planning) or to plan carefully and work as efficiently as possible (high-planning). Of the internalization and externalization groups, one half received the low-planning instruction and one half received the high-planning instruction. Externalization subjects showed no difference in performance after the different instructions and ignored or forgot the planning instruction altogether. However, when *internalization* subjects were instructed high-planning, they made twice as little illegal moves and less unnecessary moves, compared to those with low-planning instruction. The internalization version allowed subjects to be positively influenced by planning instruction (leading to high GCL, see figure 3), whereas the guidance of the externalization version took all the attention of the users.

Van Nimwegen, Oostendorp, Schijf and Burgos (2006) investigated whether their assumptions also held with a more realistic life-like task. They created an application called "Conference Planner" in which speakers with their constraints have to be scheduled in conference rooms with their own facilities by drag-and-drop movements (figure 4). It is a constraint-satisfaction problem in which one has to uncover heuristics of problem solving. Externalization was implemented by highlighting legal slots where persons can be placed. In the internalization version this feedback was absent. The problem can be approached in various ways, but the most useful heuristic is to start with speakers with the most constraints, or to start identifying slots in the conference rooms that are hardest to fill. Strategies involving less effort and planning (e.g. trial-and-error) are less smart in the end. Without planning, scheduling will be suboptimal and extra moves will be needed. Again the reasoning behind this setup is that internalization causes low ECL, which allows high GCL. High CGL, associated with motivation and interest causes a high degree of mindful effort in processing and schema construction, or in this case, strategy (figure 3). This in turn leads to better performance. Subjects' cognitive style was measured using NFC (need for cognition). It refers to the tendency to engage in and enjoy effortful cognitive tasks (Cacioppo, Petty & Kao, 1984). However, NFC did not have significant effects on behaviour and performance. The results showed positive effects of *internalization*. It led to

more plan-based behavior, smarter solution paths, better declarative knowledge, and less feeling lost. Externalization led to less efficient solutions and less thinking before moves.

This is reminiscent of a study by Schnotz and Rasch (2005) investigating the conditions under which animated pictures enhance comprehension and learning. They found that the facilitating quality that animations can have, were not always beneficial. The external support made processing unnecessarily easy: students invested less cognitive effort in learning. From the perspective of CLT, animation can thus result in an (unintended) decrease of germane cognitive load.

The above findings suggest that the design of problem-solving environments should put the facilitation of high GCL in focus and *not discourage* planning. Externalizing information may not be beneficial when the goal is to achieve better and transferable task performance and knowledge and might even lead to high ECL. Designers should beware of giving a user (too) much assistance.

The current experiment: interruption and CLT

In this experiment (again using Conference Planner) we investigate how solid internalized information is by introducing an interruption. We assume that resumption after interruption is easier if one mindfully plans moves (internalization) than when working in a shallower manner (externalization). Interruptions can be *computer-initiated*, e.g. by GUI-events, proactive systems, or software agents. Coordination and management of interruptions is interesting in multitasking contexts where the right moment to interrupt is important. But interruptions can also be *externally induced*, such as phone calls, people entering, or mobile contexts such as a subway door opening while using a PDA.

Bailey, Konstan and Carlis (2002) measured the disruptive effects of computer-initiated interruptions by looking at the resumption of tasks after interruption. They interrupted subjects doing web based tasks at inopportune moments. Interrupted tasks took subjects more time than other tasks that were not. Also performance on tasks with greater memory load was more affected by interruptions.

We did not study interruptions yet as such, but earlier we found that a pause with a distracter task resulted in a slight advantage for internalization subjects, indicating better insight. Our 8-month interval can hardly be called an interruption, but retesting of the same persons also resulted in an advantage for the internalization group. However, these intermezzos did not come as unexpectedly as interruptions mostly do, but were announced. It took place *after* a task or a long interval, not at an inopportune moment, making it less disrupting. Nevertheless, we take the results of these two types of pauses as indicators that internalization indeed leads to more solid encoding and imprinting of strategies. We have put internalization on the ECL dimension as (relatively) low, allowing high germane cognitive load. This in turn results in more efficient and more planful behavior, because an adequate portion of WM can be devoted to effort involved in processing and construction of schemas or plans. According to CLT, high GCL leads to better encoded schemas. This corresponds to how we expect internalization to lead to more processing effort. Consequently, we expect internalization to "survive" interruptions better. In the context of how CLT conceives encoding in memory, it is interesting to look at the assumptions of short-term working memory (STWM) and long-term working memory (LTWM). This theory (Ericsson & Kintsch, 1995) sees LTWM as an intermediate memory which is part of the classic "long term memory". Information can be encoded in LTWM into organized systems retrieval structures. STWM is a capacity and time limited store that updates and manipulates representations, and can contain pointers to structures in LTWM. Oulasvirta and Saariluoma (2006) connected their work on interruptions to LTWM, and state that if one is to survive an interruption task, representations must be stored so that they can be later accessed rapidly and in an error-free manner. They call this outcome of cognitive task processing "safeguarding of task representations". A suggestion for interface design to support interruption tolerance is to actively support and facilitate the development of memory skills. This is in accordance with the beneficial effects we expect from requiring to internalize information and consequently allowing high GCL (figure 3).

Our interruption was severe and occurs at an inopportune moment as in real working situations. We mimicked a power failure, which besides interrupting is also upsetting: the power went of, and the computer screen turned black. Also the experimenter "suffered" this power failure and acted surprised, to make it more credible. Our main hypothesis is that users of the externalization version are affected by the interruption more because they work in a shallower manner. The internalization group is less (or not) affected by the interruption; they work on the basis of a more solid plan.

Method

Design, subjects and measures

The experiment was conducted in the Usability lab of the Center for Content and Knowledge Engineering, Utrecht University. The 46 participants were all students and received a €6 reward. The independent variable is interface version (internalization vs. externalization) and the dependent variables we focus on are time and path measures.

Material: The Conference Planner Application

Conference speakers with different demands have to be scheduled into one of three rooms, each with its facilities and availability (figure 4). The task is not *very* difficult but if the entire situation is *not* taken into account, one gets stuck later because speakers will not fit in the remaining slots. Then speakers must be replaced to make room, making the solution less efficient. To move a speaker from the left to a slot on the right, the icon in front of a speaker's name had to be picked up and dragged to its destination and dropped. Some timeslots were never available, indicated with gray. Available timeslots were shown in white, and already occupied slots displayed the speaker's name. Externalization was implemented by highlighting legal slots where a person can be placed (figure 4). When clicking on a speaker, "legal" slots (meeting the constraints) in the timetable turned green. Note that it does not show the *best* slot, only *possible* slots.

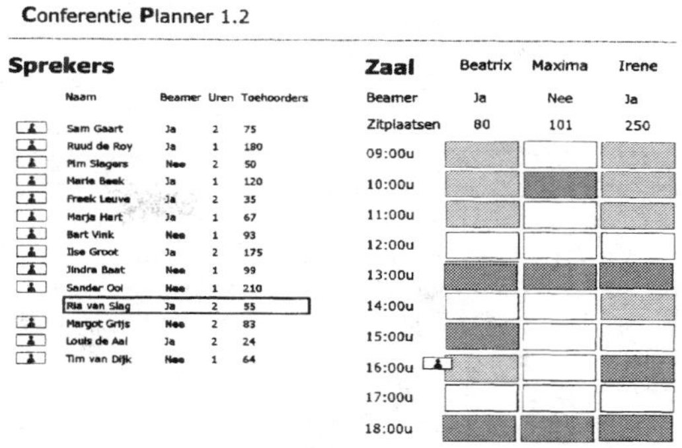

Figure 4: Conference Planner: externalization version

The internalization version lacked feedback, and users have to look up information and constraints themselves (figure 5).

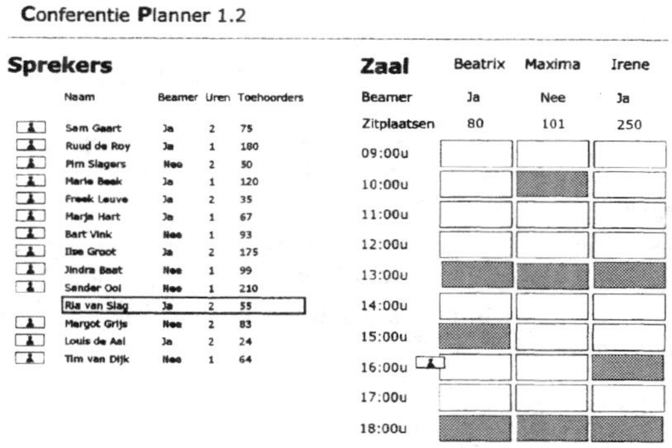

Figure 5: Conference Planner: internalization version

The speakers, listed on the left, had constraints next to them:
- Projector (beamer) is needed (yes/no, in Dutch: ja/nee)
- Number of speaking hours (1 or 2, in Dutch: uren)
- Number of expected listeners (in Dutch: toehoorders)

Participants performed 5 tasks in which the rooms, the speakers, and constraints varied (a solution always existed).

Procedure and Instruction

The experiment took 45 minutes. Subjects performed the tasks, and during the 4th task after placing the 5th speaker the system "crashed". The experimenter mimicked surprise:
"Oh...my PC crashed also; something seems to have gone wrong. I'll look into it. For now, do the next task on another computer, while I try to fix the problem here".
Subjects were brought to a PC out of sight, which *did* work and were given a questionnaire (unrelated to the tasks). After 3 minutes they were called back and were told:
"I fixed the problem. The state at which it crashed has been recovered, so you can continue where you were".

Results

The data were analyzed with SPSS (repeated measures ANOVA analysis). The 5 tasks were all solved correctly by all the subjects. Several findings from earlier experimentation (van Nimwegen et al., 2006) were reconfirmed. We will only briefly mention these here.

As before, interface style (internalization - externalization) had no effect on the *total time overall* subjects needed. Once more there were several indications that internalization subjects worked in a more careful and plan based manner. Several time measures for example, showed that the internalization subjects generally think longer *before doing moves*. The finding that there was no time difference *overall* is explained by the fact that although internalization subjects think longer before moves, they also make significantly fewer moves (reflecting higher efficiency). The findings concerning time were general. Also in task 4 where the interruption took place and subjects had a 3 minute "break" from the task. The interruption in task 4 did not result longer solving times than other tasks (after subtracting 3 minutes).

Efficiency: Path measures

We expected that the internalization interface would lead to low ECL and high GCL. We consequently expected higher effort and better motivation, resulting in smarter and better imprinted strategies leading to more efficient solutions (figure 3). A measure that informs us about efficiency is the solution path. The 5 problems have a shortest path solution (an optimal amount of moves, speakers dragged from left to right to solve them). In the problems we used there was always a list with 14 speakers, so the optimal solution would be 14 moves (placing all speakers at once, not making any unnecessary move). Superfluous moves are all the extra unnecessary actions apart from this shortest path.

As before (van Nimwegen et al., 2006) there was a main effect for interface version F $(1,43)=8.63$, $p < 0.05$. Subjects that worked with the externalization version made more superfluous moves than internalization subjects (M=8.77, SD=8.49 vs. M=2.90, SD=1.52). Furthermore, there was an interaction effect, F$(4,43)=2.34$, $p < 0.05$. Post hoc analysis showed that the difference in superfluous moves between the two versions was always significant, except for task 3. The interaction effect concerns two things. Firstly the difference in superfluous moves decreased fast. In figure 6 it is visible how in the beginning the externalization subjects perform many more actions than internalization subjects. In task 2, this difference is already smaller and in task 3 the difference is not significant anymore, externalization subjects improved their performance. The second issue concerns the main focus of the experiment, the interruption in the 4th task. After placing the 5th speaker the PC "crashed". This indeed had a different effect on the externalization subjects than on the internalization subjects. On task resumption, externalization subjects fell back dramatically, again making many more superfluous moves than before, while internalization subjects calmly went on, with fewer superfluous moves. The measure "superfluous moves" refers to not only all the *performed* moves, but also *attempted* moves that were illegal. We also looked at the amount of *legal moves* in the problem space that *actually were performed*. The pattern was similar to figure 6. First a learning effect in task 1 and 2, in task 3 no difference any more followed by the fallback in task 4 and 5.

We also asked subjects how they perceived their own efficiency. Internalization subjects rated their own efficiency higher than externalization subjects on a 7-item likert-scale T$(44)=2.10$, $p < 0.05$. The internalization version made people feel they performed the task better, as has been shown by the data already (M=5.2, SD=1.1 vs. M=4.4, SD=1.3).

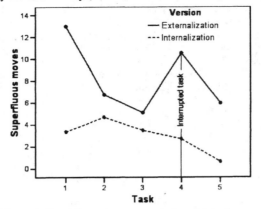

Figure 6: Superfluous moves per task and interface version

Conclusion & Discussion

As in earlier research (van Nimwegen et al., 2006), interface guidance was counter effective and yielded no advantages. It was reconfirmed that externalization causes more superfluous moves, reflecting worse efficiency. Although they make more moves, they think shorter before making them (indicating less contemplation) and therefore there was no *overall* time difference between the versions. In certain tasks, efficiency is crucial, e.g. when learning is the *aim* or when errors generate a high cost. Examples are medical tasks, or process operating tasks in a power plant. Process control software can assist, and prevent errors with actions that need a certain order (opening valves, closing circuits). But if the system breaks down and the job must be done "manually", would one still know what underlies the task, or is one *too* used to feedback from the interface, and get stuck?

The main focus of this experiment was an interruption of which we believed it would be disrupting. Our main measure was efficiency in terms of superfluous moves. Our hypothesis that externalization subjects suffer negative impact from the interruption was supported. In the course of the experiment, performance of internalization and externalization subjects converged; externalization subjects improved their performance by task 3, making less superfluous moves than before. However, right after the interruption externalization subjects fell back significantly, again making a lot more superfluous moves. The fact that they were more affected indicates that the externalization subjects had worse insight in how to resume the task. We interpret this as stemming from less solid plans and worse strategies and knowledge imprinted in memory.

One could argue that in the externalization version, the problem space is reduced because items *not* turning green can be discarded. Still, central to solving these problems efficiently, is to plan first, and then act. Externalization subjects get the feeling the work is carried out for them, and this, rather than making use of using the reduction of the search space, seems to make users lazier and makes them behave more shallowly. This is paradoxical, because if a well instructed problem solver would do the task and start with proactive thinking and applying a smart strategy, the green feedback *could* be useful, because it saves time in studying the grid. But exactly this issue, choosing the right strategy is being obstructed by offering assisting feedback.

Our findings strengthen our idea that externalization as we implemented it does provoke behavior that is *not* directed at developing schemas and strategies. This is corresponding to what happens when ECL is high, as mentioned in Cognitive Load Theory. Furthermore, it can hold that internalization resulting in low ECL can correspond with high GLC, allowing mindful effort and better motivation to look for what underlies the tasks. We think that adopting CLT as we attempted is a promising approach. An important reason is that models known from information processing theory do not sufficiently acknowledge effort and motivational factors, whereas CLT does incorporate these (Sweller et al,. 1998). Lastly, in the internalization version the subjects (correctly) judge their own efficiency higher. The fact that the feeling of better performance is justified, is another positive consequence of internalization.

Future Research

Since we theorize about *where* users look and use terms as "distracting", "attention" and "perceiving information", in a follow-up experiment eye tracking data will be collected to backup our assumptions. We expect externalization to cause more eye movements and activity directed at the feedback areas. This can be considered as high, ineffective ECL. Cognitive load is central in our research, where overt behavior (efficiency) was analyzed. Various studies showed that pupil size is indicative for cognitive load, although one has to be careful (Schultheis & Jameson, 2004) because pupil size also responds to other influences. Also the type of externalization deserves attention. We externalized the underlying rules, the legal actions with the object at hand, and concluded that it discourages deeper contemplation. We are interested to see which kind of externalization *does* instigate contemplation and plan based behavior.

References

Back, J. & Oppenheim, C. (2001). A model of cognitive load for IR: implications for user relevance feedback interaction. *Information Research, 6*(2).

Baddeley, A.D. (1986). *Working Memory.* Oxford, UK: Oxford University Press.

Bailey, B., Konstan, J., & Carlis, J. (2000). Measuring the effects of interruptions on task performance in the user interface. *Proceedings IEEE Conference on Systems, Man, and Cybernetics* (pp.757-762). Piscataway, NJ: IEEE Press.

Cacioppo, J.T., Petty, R.E. & Kao, C.E. (1984). The efficient assessment of need for cognition. *Journal of Personality Assessment, 48* (1984), 306-307.

Carroll, J.M. (1990). *The Nurnberg Funnel: Designing Minimalist Instruction for Practical Computer Skill.* Cambridge, MA: MIT Press.

Feinberg, S., & Murphy, M. (2000). Applying cognitive load theory to the design of web-based instruction. *Proceedings of the 18th Annual ACM International Conference on Computer Documentation: Technology and Teamwork* (pp. 353-360). Piscataway, NJ: IEEE Press.

Gerjets, P., & Scheiter, K. (2003). Goal configurations and processing strategies as mediators between instructional design and cognitive load: Evidence from hypertext-based instruction. *Educational Psychologist, 38*, 33-41.

Ericsson, K. A., & Kintsch, W. (1995). Long-term working memory. *Psychological Review, 102*, 211-245.

Kerr, M.P. & Payne, S.J. (1994). Learning to use a spreadsheet by doing and watching. *Interacting with Computers, 6*, 3–22.

Mayer, R.E., & Moreno, R. (2003). Nine Ways to Reduce Cognitive Load in Multimedia Learning. *Educational Psychologist, 38*(1), 43-52.

Nagata, S. (2006). *User Assistance with Interruptions on a Mobile Device.* Doctoral Dissertation Utrecht University, The Netherlands.

Nimwegen, C. van, Oostendorp, H. van, & Tabachneck-Schijf, H.J.M. (2004). Can more help be worse? The over-assisting interface. *Proceedings of the conference on Dutch directions in HCI ACM International Conference Proceeding Series.* New York, NY: ACM Press.

Nimwegen, C. van, Burgos, D., Oostendorp, H. van, & Schijf, H.J.M. (2006). The Paradox of the Assisted User: Guidance can be Counterproductive. *Proceedings of the SIGCHI Conference on Human Factors in Computing Systems* (pp. 917-926). New York, NY: ACM Press.

Nimwegen, C., van, Oostendorp, H. van, & Tabachneck-Schijf, H.J.M. (2005). The role of interface style in planning during problem solving. *Proceedings of the 27th Annual Cognitive Science Conference* (pp. 2271-2276). Mahwah, NJ: Lawrence Erlbaum.

Oostendorp, H. van & De Mul, S. (1999). Learning by exploration: Thinking aloud while exploring an information system. *Instructional Science, 27*, 269-284.

Oulasvirta, A., & Saariluoma, P. (2006). Surviving task interruptions: Investigating the implications of long-term working memory theory. *International Journal of Human-Computer Studies, 64*(10), 941-961.

Rikers, R.M.J.P., Gerven, P.W.M. van, & Schmidt, H.G. (2004). Cognitive load theory as a tool for expertise development. *Instructional Science, 32*, 173-182.

Schnotz, W. & Rasch, T. (2005). Enabling, Facilitating, and Inhibiting Effects of Animations in Multimedia Learning: Why Reduction of Cognitive Load Can Have Negative Effects on Learning. *Educational Technology Research and Development, 53*(3), 47-58.

Schultheis, H., & Jameson, A. (2004). Assessing cognitive load in adaptive hypermedia systems: Physiological and behavioral methods. *Proceedings of the 3rd International Conference on Adaptive Hypermedia and Web-Based Systems.* (pp. 225–234). Heidelberg: Springer-Verlag.

Sweller, J., Merrienboer, J. van & Paas, F. (1998). Cognitive architecture and instructional design. *Educational. Psychology Review, 10*, 251-296.

Zhang, J. (1997). The nature of external representations in problem solving. *Cognitive Science, 21*(2), 179-217.

Managing Cognitive Load in Instructional Simulations

Slava Kalyuga (s.kalyuga@unsw.edu.au)
School of Education, University of New South Wales,
Sydney, NSW 2052 Australia

Jan Plass (jan.plass@nyu.edu)
Steinhardt School of Education, New York University,
239 Greene Street, Suite 300,
New York, NY 10003-6674 USA

Abstract

High levels of working memory load could be responsible for instructional failures of many simulations. The paper analyzes representational formats for input parameters and levels of instructional guidance as important factors that may differentially influence effectiveness of simulations for learners with various levels of prior knowledge. Traditional symbolic representational formats were compared with iconic versions that contained additional "situated" graphics to represent the various elements of the physical environment (e.g. flames to represent temperature, weights to represent pressure, etc.). Empirical data from studies comparing different formats of simulations for learning gas laws in high-school chemistry is used to support the theoretical model.

Introduction

Increased use of simulations in education (especially in science education) has not yet produced an expected strong contribution to improving students' academic performance. Recent research suggests that although interactive visualizations can enhance learning under some conditions (Schnotz & Rasch, 2005; Tversky, Morrison, & Betrancourt, 2002), static images may result in better learning outcomes under different conditions (Schnotz, Böckler, & Grzondziel, 1999). This paper addresses the questions of why, under what conditions, and for whom are instructional simulations effective based on the assumption that a major reason for lower than expected instructional effectiveness of simulations is that they are not always consistent with the nature of human cognitive architecture and limitations of our cognitive system.

Processing limitations of human cognitive system is a major factor influencing learning processes. Limited working memory capacity could be easily overloaded if more than a few chunks of unfamiliar information are processed simultaneously (e.g., Baddeley, 1986; Miller, 1956). *Cognitive Load Theory* describes the capacity limitations of the human cognitive architecture in processing multimedia information (Sweller, 1999; 2003; Van Merriënboer & Sweller, 2005) and could, therefore, be a promising theoretical framework for studying higher-level cognitive processes of image comprehension and the design of visual displays for computer simulations.

Organized knowledge structures held in long-term memory may significantly reduce or eliminate working memory limitations by chunking many elements of information into a single, higher-level element (Chi, Glaser, & Rees, 1982). Therefore, long-term memory knowledge base is the most significant factor influencing learning processes that alter significantly with the development of learners' expertise in a domain. As a consequence, instructional designs should be tailored to changing levels of learner expertise in a particular task area.

The specific approach used in this study is based on a) optimizing cognitive load imposed by visual representations and b) considering the impact of learner expertise. In contrast to verbal information that consists of discreet symbolic representations that are usually processed sequentially, visual information is relational in nature and its elements can be encoded simultaneously. According to some recent studies (e.g., Carlson, Chandler, & Sweller, 2003), pictorial (iconic) representations may reduce cognitive load imposed by intrinsically complex materials (with high levels of element interactivity) compared to the written (symbolic) information, freeing cognitive resources and allowing students to solve complex tasks.

This study was designed to investigate cognitive load effects of adding iconic representations to symbolic information in instructional simulations. Even though such redundant information representations would obviously require some additional processing resources, we hypothesized that iconic representations would eliminate or reduce resources needed for interpreting and storing meanings of symbolic information in working memory, thus delivering overall cognitive benefits (Lee, Plass, & Homer, in press).

Cognitive load generated by processing visual representations depends not only on characteristics of the visual displays, but also on cognitive characteristics of particular learners, first of all, their domain specific prior knowledge base that has been found to be one of the strongest predictors for learning outcomes and has recently been described in terms of an Expertise Reversal Effect (e.g., Kalyuga, 2005; 2006; Kalyuga, Ayres, Chandler, & Sweller, 2003). In accordance with general cognitive studies of expert-novice differences (e.g., Chase & Simon, 1973;

De Groot, 1965), these studies have demonstrated that many instructional design techniques that were highly effective with less knowledgeable learners could lose their effectiveness and even have negative consequences when used with more experienced learners and vice versa. An important implication of these findings is that instructional techniques and media formats need to be tailored to levels of learner knowledge in a domain.

Cognitive load in interactive visual displays

Two specific factors contributing to cognitive load in interactive visual displays were investigated in this study. The first factor is related to how the semantic content of the visual information is represented and how well this representation supports relevant cognitive processes and assists in managing visual cognitive load. A simulation for exploring the relationships between main characteristics of an idealized gas by controlling pressure, volume, and the temperature of the gas by moving sliders (with one parameter locked) was used in this study. Figure 1 represents a screenshot of a modified version of the simulation.

In addition to the word "temperature" next to the slider (a symbolic representation of the concept of temperature), there is a representation of the temperature in the form of burners below the gas container that change in number as the value of the temperature changes. Pressure is represented in the form of weights that are displayed on top of the cylinder containing the gas, and volume is represented by the position of the indicator connected to the piston and volume slider. Buttons for fixing (locking) parameter values were also represented as locks in open (green) or closed (red) states. In a symbolic-only version all these iconic representations were absent and locking facilities were simple radio-buttons.

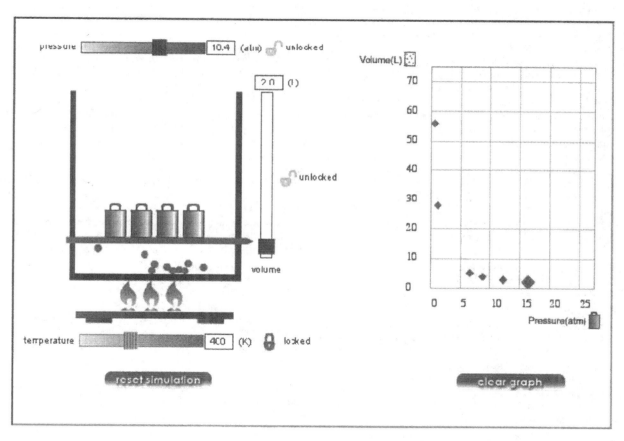

Figure 1: A screenshot of a gas laws simulation.

The burners, weights, and the size of the container below the piston are iconic representations that have a close direct association with the concept of temperature, pressure, and volume respectively. Although adding redundant iconic information would lead to a visually more complex display, it is nevertheless expected to induce less extraneous load because the added representations externally represent information that the learner would otherwise have to hold internally in working memory. In other words, we argue that a display with a higher visual complexity and redundant representations can be less difficult to understand than one with a lower complexity because the added information enables learners to better relate the new information to their prior knowledge.

The second factor is related to the level of prior knowledge in a domain. In accordance with the expertise reversal effect, instructional effectiveness of suggested iconic additions to simulations may be effective for novice learners but could become less effective as learner level of expertise increases. A number of studies of individual differences in learning from text and visual displays (e.g., Hegarty & Just, 1989; Lowe, 1993; Schnotz, 2002; Schnotz, Picard, & Hron, 1993) have demonstrated that the instructional advantages of diagrams depend on student domain-specific knowledge and experience. Less knowledgeable learners may have difficulty processing visual information because the limited capacity of WM. For example, cognitive load could be increased because the learner has to infer meaning of symbolic representations.

Acquiring sufficient prior knowledge in the domain could reduce WM overload associated with processing visual representations and thus enhance learning. As experience increases, limited duration and capacity of WM become less important because many relevant schematic representations may already be held in LTM. The available knowledge structures may require integration with displayed redundant graphics thus imposing an extraneous cognitive load for more experienced learners and eliminating or even reversing the learning effect. Therefore, we hypothesized that learners with lower levels of prior knowledge (Experiment 1) will benefit more from simulations with added iconic representations of visual information than from symbolic-only representations, but there will be no differences between formats for learners with higher levels of prior knowledge (Experiment 2).

Experiment 1

Method

Participants. Thirty 11-12 grades (age range 16-18) students from New York City public high school science classes participated in this experiment. Pre-test scores indicated that participants' prior knowledge of gas laws area of chemistry was low (mean total score 4.45 out of 16, SD = 2.17). The study was conducted in the school computer lab during regular class hours in intact classes. Instructional treatments were delivered online with all the performance data collected on a remote server.

Materials and Procedure Instructional materials included two versions of simulations. All of them were designed using Flash MX software and delivered online through desktop PCs. Treatment 1 (15 students) contained a simulation with symbolic-only representations of input parameters. Treatment 2 (15 students) contained the same simulation with added iconic representations for temperature, pressure, and volume. The experimental procedure included an initial pre-test of learners' knowledge, an instructional session, and a final post-test.

Pre-test of prior knowledge consisted of 9 items. Three short-answer questions tested general knowledge of situations that involve gas features. Prior knowledge of relations between gas characteristics was assessed using 6 multiple-choice questions.

Instructional phase. Students were instructed to manipulate the temperature, volume, and pressure of the gas, and observe the resulting change of the other properties of the gas. Before they started to explore, students had been advised to do some exercises with changing different variables by moving sliders. General guidelines for exploring the system were also provided. For example, when exploring a system with many variables, a good strategy is to change only one variable to observe its effects on another variable. Students were advised to lock one of the variables and explore how changing one of the remaining variable would affect the other unlocked variable. For example, exploring the following questions was suggested: *How the gas pressure changes when you change the volume with constant temperature? How will it change if you double the volume?* In both versions of the simulation, students were advised to take all the time they needed to study the material and not to proceed to the test before they had studied (or explored) the simulations thoroughly.

Post-test included 16 items. 10 multiple-choice questions composed a comprehension test which included 2 questions on knowledge of basics of kinetic theory, 3 questions on qualitative relations between pressure, volume, and temperature, 3 questions on quantitative relationships, and 2 questions that tested knowledge of graphical representations of relationships. Transfer test consisted of 6 short-answer questions that required explaining different phenomena and real life situations using the learned gas laws. Two of these were questions on applying knowledge to explain real-life phenomena, 2 questions required applying knowledge to predict phenomena, and 2 questions required applying knowledge to suggest solutions to some real-life problems.

In both pre- and post-tests, scoring procedures for multiple-choice questions allocated a score 1 for a correct answer; short-answer questions were scored independently by two graders according to the specified scales (for most questions, the scores were 0 for no answer or completely incorrect answer, 1 for some elements of a correct answer indicated, 2 for most elements of a correct answer indicated, and 3 for a complete correct answer).

Results

The independent variable was the type of representation of visual information (iconic vs. symbolic). The dependent variables under analysis were differences between the final and initial test z-scores (calculated separately for multiple-choice and short-answer scores) as indicators of the relative gains in learners' knowledge due to the instructional session. (Because pre- and post- tests were structurally different, standardized z-scores were used as indicators of students' relative standing and changes in performance).

Table 1 Means and standard deviations for Experiment 1.

	symbolic N=15	iconic N=15
short answers M SD	-.10 1.55	.15 .97
multiple-choice M SD	.09 1.17	.00 1.09

Although there were no statistically significant differences between the treatments, the effect size of 0.29 (using a pooled standard deviation value) for the short-answer questions indicated a possible small-to-medium effect favoring the iconic format over the symbolic format for transfer tasks. Thus, adding iconic representations to simulations could have possible positive effect on transfer performance for novice learners.

Experiment 2

Experiment 2 was conducted with relatively more knowledgeable learners (pre-test mean total score 8.03 out of 16, SD = 3.02; in comparison with Experiment 1, the total pre-test score almost doubled).

Method

Participants Sixty two 11-12 grades (age range 16-18) students from another New York City public high school participated in this experiment. By the time of the experiment, students had studied some material related to gas laws and, therefore, were relatively more knowledgeable in the topic. The study was conducted in the school's computer lab during regular class hours in intact classes. All instructional treatments were delivered online with all the performance data collected on the remote server. Due to a technical glitch in allocating students to instructional treatments, the numbers of students in experimental groups were not equal (27 and 35).

Materials and Procedure The experimental procedure was identical to that used in Experiment 1.

Results

The independent and dependent variables were the same as in Experiment 1.

Table 2 Means and standard deviations for Experiment 2.

	symbolic N=35	iconic N=27
short answers M SD	.06 .93	-.08 1.24
multiple-choice M SD	-.02 .92	.02 .78

There were no significant differences between the treatments. For short-answer questions, results showed a possible reversed tendency for means (effect size .14) to that obtained in Experiment 1: iconic group performed relatively worse than symbolic group. This possibility needs to be corroborated by further studies with more expert learners (for example, university science students). Thus, in accordance with a prediction within a cognitive load framework, adding iconic representations did not seem to influence performance scores for relatively more knowledgeable learners (with a possible reversed tendency for transfer tasks).

Experiment 3

Rather weak results obtained in Experiment 1 could be related to a general inefficiency of purely exploratory simulations for novice learners. According to cognitive load theory, exploratory learning environments may impose excessive levels of cognitive load for these learners. In Experiment 3, in addition to highly interactive exploratory simulations that required learners to generate and test hypotheses, a less interactive, direct instruction version was also used. It was based on a worked-out simulation as a series of static frames demonstrating step-by-step procedures of actual hypothesis testing. In this instructional format, the learner interactions with the learning environment were limited to selecting sequential procedural steps to study. Within a cognitive load framework, it could be expected that worked-out instructional formats could reduce cognitive overload for less experienced learners and enhance learning outcomes. Adding iconic representations could have stronger learning effects when used with worked-out simulations.

Method

Participants Sixty six students in 11-12 grades (age range 16-18) from Texas public schools participated in this experiment. Students had not studied any materials related to gas laws by the time of the experiment, and, therefore, were novices to the topic. The study was conducted in the school computer lab during regular class hours in intact classes. Students were assigned to one of the four treatment groups. All instructional treatments were delivered online with all the performance data collected on a remote server.

Materials and Procedure Instructional materials included four versions of simulations, all designed using Flash MX software and delivered on a web page that was viewed using desktop PCs. Treatment 1 (15 students) contained the worked-out simulation with symbolic-only representations of input parameters. Treatment 2 (16 students) contained the same worked-out simulation with added iconic representations for temperature, pressure, and volume. Treatments 3 and 4 (17 and 18 students accordingly) contained exploratory simulations with, correspondingly, symbolic and added iconic representations identical to those used in Experiments 1 and 2. The experimental procedure included an initial pre-test of learners' knowledge, an instructional session, and a final post-test. Pre- and post-tests were similar to those used in the previous experiments.

Results

The independent variables were the type of representation of visual information (iconic vs. symbolic) and the degree of interactivity (worked-out vs. exploratory). As before, the dependent variables under analysis were differences between the final and initial test z-scores.

Means and standard deviations are displayed in Table 3. The students' novice status in the gas laws area of chemistry was supported by relatively low pre-test scores. Means and standard deviations were correspondingly 2.97 (SD = 1.54) out of the maximum possible value of 10 for short-answer questions; and 2.17 (SD = 1.20) out of 6 for multiple-choice questions.

Table 3 Means and standard deviations for Experiment 3.

	symbolic worked-out (1) N=15	iconic worked-out (2) N=16	symbolic exploratory (3) N=17	iconic exploratory (4) N=18
short answers M SD	.13 .78	.30 .57	-.15 1.00	-.23 1.05
multiple-choice M SD	-.22 1.12	.32 .92	-.22 1.23	.11 1.39

Since we had a specific cognitive load theory-generated directional hypotheses about the expected pattern of means prior to running this experiment, one-tailed planned-comparisons tests of the hypotheses were applied. Two hypotheses for this experiment (dealing with novice learners) were that worked-out simulations would be more beneficial than exploratory simulations; and that simulations using added iconic representations would be more beneficial than symbolic-only representations. The results for corresponding contrasts for testing these hypotheses were:

- overall difference between worked-out and exploratory simulations indicated significant results favoring worked-out simulations for short-answer questions, t = 1.86, p = 0.03; there were no statistically significant differences for multiple-choice questions, although the effect size .2 indicated a possible small effect favoring the worked-out format;

- overall difference between iconic and symbolic representations indicated marginally significant results favoring iconic representations for multiple-choice questions, t = 1.51, p = 0.07;

- difference between iconic and symbolic representations for worked-out simulations indicated marginally significant results favoring iconic representations for multiple-choice questions, t = 1.44, p = 0.08; there were no statistically significant differences for short-answer questions, although the effect size of 0.25 indicated a possible small-to-medium effect favoring the iconic format;

- difference between iconic and symbolic representations for exploratory simulations indicated no statistically significant results, although for multiple-choice tasks, the effect size of 0.25 indicated a possible small-to-medium effect favoring the iconic format;

- difference between worked-out and exploratory simulations using symbolic representations indicated no statistically significant results, although for transfer tasks, the effect size of 0.31 indicated a possible small-to-medium effect favoring the worked-out format;

- difference between worked-out and exploratory simulations using iconic representations indicated significant results favoring worked-out simulations for transfer tasks, t = 1.86, p = 0.04: for multiple-choice tasks, the effect size of 0.17 indicated a possible small effect favoring the worked-out format.

Discussion

Overall conclusion from this study is that for novice learners, worked-out simulations and simulations using added iconic representations represent preferable instructional options, especially when these two features are combined together. No difference between iconic and symbolic representations in exploratory simulations was found for more knowledgeable learners (with an indication of a possible reversed tendency). Based on the expertise reversal effect (see Kalyuga 2005; 2006 for recent overviews), exploratory simulations without added iconic representations could be appropriate formats for learners who are relatively more experienced in a domain.

In an independently conducted evaluation of levels of cognitive load imposed by different formats of simulations, concurrent verbal reports with audio and video tracking were used (Plass & Kalyuga, manuscript in preparation). The generated qualitative verbal data was analyzed as reflecting different types of cognitive load expressed through the participants' own language (e.g., *too difficult to understand, it is annoying, it is changing too fast, plenty of new things, need to jump across the screen, too much to remember,* etc.). For each potential source of load, sample keywords and phrases served as a coding scheme for classifying participants' remarks. The results were in line with the cognitive load hypothesis: more instructionally effective formats imposed relatively lower levels of load.

General implications for the design of simulations are: 1) formats of simulations need to be tailored to levels of learner prior knowledge in a specific domain; 2) for novice learners, worked-out simulations and simulations with added iconic representations need to be used; 3) when designing simulations in the absence of information about levels of expertise of intended learners, elements of worked-out simulations and iconic representations should be incorporated in order to provide optional instructional support (e.g. hints on exploratory strategies). Eventually, cognitively optimized adaptive procedures for simulation-based learning environments need to be developed.

Further studies should establish if the results could be replicated in laboratory and authentic educational settings with other materials, including both more and less difficult subject areas, and with learners with more differentiated levels of prior knowledge. Quantitative measures of mental effort (e.g., subjective rating scales or dual-task techniques) need to be used for supporting cognitive load hypotheses.

The reported study tested hypotheses generated within the cognitive load framework to manage cognitive load in instructional simulations. The data indicated that the application of suggested methods for reducing cognitive load resulted in increased learning of gas laws. The results support the assertions that the optimal use of instructional simulations needs to be consistent with human learning processes, and that the selection of an appropriate format of interactive dynamic visual representations of scientific phenomena should take into account levels of learner knowledge.

Acknowledgments

The authors would like to thank Juan Barrientos for his assistance with data collection. The research was supported in part by the Institute of Education Sciences (IES), U.S. Department of Education through Grant R305K050140 to Jan L. Plass (PI), Bruce D. Homer, Catherine Milne, and Trace Jordan (Co-PIs) at New York University.

References

Baddeley, A. D. (1986). *Working memory*. New York: Oxford University Press.

Carlson, R., Chandler, P., & Sweller, J. (2003). Learning and understanding science instructional material. *Journal of Educational Psychology, 95*, 629-640.

Chase, W. G., & Simon, H. A. (1973). Perception in chess. *Cognitive Psychology, 4,* 55-81.

Chi, M., Glaser, R., & Rees, E. (1982). Expertise in problem solving. In R. Sternberg (Ed.), *Advances in the psychology of human intelligence* (pp. 7-75). Hillsdale, NJ: Erlbaum.

de Groot, A. D. (1965). *Thought and choice in chess*. The Hague: Mouton.

Hegarty, M., & Just, M. A. (1989). Understanding machines from text and diagrams. In H. Mandl & J. Levin (Eds.), *Knowledge acquisition from text and picture* (pp. 171-194). Amsterdam: North Holland.

Kalyuga, S. (2005). Prior knowledge principle. In R. Mayer (Ed.), *Cambridge Handbook of Multimedia Learning* (pp. 325-337). New York: Cambridge University Press.

Kalyuga, S. (2006). Instructing and testing advanced learners: A cognitive load approach. Hauppauge, New York: Nova Science Publishers.

Kalyuga, S., Ayres, P., Chandler, P., & Sweller, J. (2003). Expertise reversal effect. *Educational Psychologist, 38,* 23-31.

Lowe, R.K. (1993). Constructing a mental representation from an abstract technical diagram. *Learning and Instruction, 3,* 157-179.

Miller, G. A. (1956). The magical number seven, plus or minus two: Some limits on our capacity for processing information. *Psychological Review, 63,* 81-97.

Lee, H., Plass, J.L., & Homer, B.D. (in press). Optimizing cognitive load for learning from computer-based science simulations. *Journal of Educational Psychology*.

Plass, J., & Kalyuga, S. (in preparation). Evaluation of learner cognitive load in interactive learning environments using concurrent verbal protocols.

Schnotz, W., Böckler, J., & Grzondziel, H. (1999). Individual and co-operative learning with interactive animated pictures. *European Journal of Psychology of Education, 14,* 245-265.

Schnotz, W., Picard, E., & Hron, A. (1993). How do successful and unsuccessful learners use text and graphics? *Learning and Instruction, 3,* 181-199.

Schnotz, W., & Rasch, T. (2005). Enabling, Facilitating, and Inhibiting Effects of Animations in Multimedia Learning: Why Reduction of Cognitive Load Can Have Negative Results on Learning. *Educational Technology Research and Development, 53*(3), 47–58.

Sweller, J. (1999). *Instructional design in technical areas*. Camberwell, Australia: ACER Press.

Sweller, J. (2003). Evolution of human cognitive architecture. In B. Ross (Ed.), *The psychology of learning and motivation, Vol. 43* (pp. 215-2.

Tversky, B., Morrison, J.B., & Betrancourt, M. (2002). Animation: Can it facilitate? *International Journal of Human Computer Studies, 57,* 247-262

Van Merriënboer, J. & Sweller, J. (2005). Cognitive load theory and complex learning: Recent developments and future directions. *Educational Psychology Review, 17,* 147-177.

Influence of Activity in Episodic Memory, Use of Virtual Environment

Gaën Plancher (gaen.plancher@univ-paris5.fr)
Valérie Gyselinck (valerie.gyselinck@univ-paris5.fr)
Serge Nicolas (serge.nicolas@univ-paris5.fr)
Pascale Piolino (pascale.piolino@univ-paris5.fr)
Laboratoire de Psychologie et de Neurosciences Cognitives, Université Paris Descartes, CNRS
71, avenue Edouard Vaillant 92774 Boulogne-Billancourt
Cedex FRANCE

Abstract

Two experiments were conducted in a virtual town in order to investigate the influence of participating actively or passively in an episodic memory task. In both experiments, the active participants drove a car through a virtual town whereas passive participants were only passengers. In the first experiment, the active participants were better at recalling the elements that composed the town and to recall the spatial location of an event (a car accident). The passive participants were better at localizing the town elements and had a higher global episodic score than the active participants. In the second experiment, we controlled the attentional bias that may have occurred during driving. We found an advantage of the passive condition on the spatial and temporal recalls. Nevertheless significant interactions were found between the sex and the active/passive effect. Men had higher scores in the passive condition than in the active condition, whereas the reverse was observed for women. These results suggest that the active condition improves memory of women. The absence of enhancement for men was discussed.

Introduction

The majority of memory studies use very minimalist experimental conditions, for example learning and recalling a list of words. This kind of experiment is far from what we experience in daily life. For studying episodic memory a rich context is needed in order to assess the memories of what, when and where which are essential components of episodic memory. Virtual reality (VR) can provide fully controlled experimental situations with a rich context. In addition, in daily life motor activity is present in whatever situation we experiment. In the present study, we assessed the effect of sensory-motor implication on the components of the episodic memory with a virtual environment.

According to Tulving (2002), episodic memory allows conscious recollection of personal events, together with their phenomenological and spatio-temporal encoding contexts. It involves mental "time travel" accompanied by personal subjective experience of remembering. Episodic memory involves true memories but also false memories. False memory occurs when people think they lived an event that did not happen (Schacter & Curran, 2000).

Everyday, all our senses are stimulated. A number of theorists have emphasised the importance of differentiation or trace distinctiveness in memory (Nelson, 1979). It was shown that when the visual stimuli are images, the memory is better than when the stimuli are words (Paivio, 1991). There are fewer false memories when the stimuli to learn are images compared to words (Dodson, Koutstaal & Schacter, 2000). The authors argued that this reduction of false memories after picture presentation occurs because trying to remember the information demands access to pictorial information as a basis for judging items as previously studied. Absence of memory for this distinctive information indicates that the item is new. By contrast, participants who studied only words would not expect detailed recollections about studied items and therefore, would not base recognition decisions on the presence or absence of memory for distinctive information. Thus, the more complex the information, the more the memory trace is distinctive and the better the memory.

In the same way, a situation that allows the accessibility of proprioceptive stimulation will enhance memories compared to a situation without proprioceptive stimulation. Motor information is critical to memory (Engelkamp, Zimmer, Mohr & Sellen, 1994; Engelkamp & Zimmer, 1997). In the Subject Performed Tasks (SPTs), participants typically learn the action described in a brief verbal phrase and have to perform it (for instance: peel a banana). In the passive condition, they only learn the phrase. Then they perform a verbal recall test. Recall of SPTs is superior to recall of verbal phrases. This SPT effect is usually attributed to the good item-specific information provided by enactment. In active situations, conceptual, visual, sensory and motor components were involved. In these studies, however, the visual and motor modalities are confounded. It is necessary to understand the effect of proprioceptive stimulation alone on episodic memory.

Virtual reality is an interesting tool for assessing the effect of proprioception in a complex environment. During the past decade, the use of VR has become increasingly widespread in fields as diverse as medicine, engineering, design, architecture, learning and transfer to reality, etc. Techniques for the use of VR in neuropsychology (Marié, Chemin, Lebreton & Klinger, 2005; Marié, Klinger, Chemin & Josset, 2003; Parslow, Morris, Fleminger, Rahman, Abrahams & Recce, 2005) and cognitive psychology (Gaggioli, 2003) are under development. Indeed, the advent of virtual environments has given a new kind of tool for studying cognition. This tool provides the possibility of creating more complex environments, active interactions and it opens up the possibility of simulating any environment. In the framework of memory research, VR has been essentially used to investigate spatial memory and navigation (e.g. Aguirre & D'Esposito, 1997; Morris, Parslow, Fleminger, Brooks, Brammer & Rose, 2002; Tlauka, Keage & Clark, 2005). Other components of episodic memory have been studied in virtual environments essentially by one group of authors (Burgess, 2002; Burgess, Maguire & O'Keefe, 2002; Burgess, Maguire, Spiers & O'Keefe, 2001; King, Hartley, Spiers, Maguire & Burgess, 2005). In their experiments the subjects were active; they followed a route with a joystick along which they repeatedly encountered a number of people in a number of locations. Memory for the objects, for where and from whom they were received was then assessed. These authors investigated the neural substrates associated with episodic memory and they were not interested in the effect of active versus passive participation on memory.

Brooks, Attree, Rose, Clifford & Leadbetter (1999) investigated the nature of the motor information exploited in SPTs with VR. They compared an active and a passive condition in a virtual environment on the recall of a spatial layout, of objects and of their locations. In this study, active participants had to find a route through the rooms and at the same time they had to study the objects seen "en route". Passive participants saw the record of active participants who got around in this environment. The only thing that differed between the two conditions was the requirement of action. The results show that the active participants recall the spatial layout better than the passive participants. However, no difference was found between participants for both recall and recognition of objects and their locations. This study suggests that active participation enhances only spatial memory.

The majority of studies made in the virtual reality had assessed only one component of the episodic memory, the spatial component, and had measured only the true memories. No study has assessed the effect of an active versus passive situation on all components of episodic memory neither for true nor for false memories. Consequently, the present study proposes to investigate episodic memory in virtual reality by distinguishing the effect of sensory-motor implication on the retrieval of true and false memories. In the active condition, the subject drove a virtual car by manipulating a steering wheel, a gas pedal and a brake pedal. Like Brooks et al. (1999) we predicted an advantage of active over passive condition on spatial memory, but also on the other components of the episodic memory: what, when and context. This means that true memories will increase and false memories will decrease when participants act in the virtual environment compared to participants who do not act.

Experiment 1

Method

Participants

In this preliminary study, 20 female undergraduate psychology students from the Paris Descartes University participated voluntarily in exchange for course credit. The participants ranged in age from 19 to 25 ($M =20.95$, $SD =1.71$). Participants were randomly assigned to two groups, one active group with 10 subjects and one passive group with 10 subjects. Inclusion of subjects was based on absence of neurological or psychiatric medical history and signs of depression (Beck depression inventory). No medication known to impair memory was allowed. The groups did not differ on verbal abilities according to the 44-item Mill Hill test (French translation by Deltour, 1993). All participants have experience with video games. Finally, every participant possessed a driving licence.

Materials

The Virtual Apparatus The virtual apparatus was composed of a computer generated 3-D model of a created environment. The environment was built with Virtools Dev 3.0 software (www.virtools.com). The environment was run on a PC laptop computer and explored using a steering wheel, a gas pedal and a brake pedal. It was projected with a video projector onto a screen (85 cm high and 110 cm long).

The virtual environment We built a town that was based on photos of Paris, France (figure 1). In the town there was one possible route with nine turns. Eight *specific areas* with their *context* composed the town's elements. The interconnected *specific areas* were: a park, an area of tall buildings, a crowd, a town hall, an accident, a train station, a parking lot, a big square with an arcade building (figure 2). In one of these areas, a specific event occured, a car accident in which two cars crashed into one another, a horn was heard and black smoke appeared. Buildings connected each area with another. People, garbage containers, barriers, trees, billboards and motionless cars were the *context* of the town. Participants saw the interior of the car (see figure 1).

Figure 1. Example of a view of the town

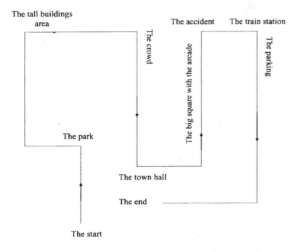

Figure 2. Map of the town

Design

Sensory-motor implication (active, passive) was the main factor; it was a between-subjects factor. We measured true and false memory.

Procedure

Participants were tested individually. They were seated on a comfortable chair. The virtual environment was projected on the wall, 150cm ahead of subjects. In order to match the visual stimulation between active and passive participants, we recorded the navigation of all active participants. Each passive participant saw the record of one active participant. In addition, encoding was incidental: we did not tell subjects they had to remember what they perceived. The subjects were told to drive through the virtual town and pay attention to the town, as if they had just arrived to live there. The conditions varied as a function of the experimental condition.

Active condition The participants manipulated a steering wheel, a gas pedal and a brake pedal to move around in the virtual town. Before the immersion within the town, the participants trained in an empty environment until they were comfortable. Participants were free to navigate anywhere on the track. We notified the subjects that they did not have to drive too fast. Only one trip was possible, the participants could not stop and could not turn back. Navigation stopped at the end of the route. Driving in this town lasted approximately two minutes.

Passive condition In the passive condition, the experimenter told subjects to imagine that a friend was driving them around in their new town. We said to subjects they were sitting on the passenger side. The passive participants saw the recorded route of the active participants.

Both conditions

The free recall test After navigation, all participants carried out episodic memory tests. First, they had to recall the elements of the areas they remembered, the spatial component, the temporal component and the context associated with these elements. For example, they had to recall "the train station" and they had to report where it occurred, "it was in front of us", when, "at the beginning of the town" and all other contextual aspects they remembered, "people beside the town hall". The recall was scored out of a possible 24 points (8 elements with 3 recalls for each element: spatial recall, temporal recall and contextual recall). Then, subjects were informed that they had to recall all their memories about the accident. This recall was scored on a maximum of 4-points, respectively one point by recall: where, when, the circumstances and the context. After that, subjects had to draw the map of the town and put the elements they remembered. It was scored with the number of correct turns recalled (maximum score was 9) and with the number of correct locations of various elements of the town on this map (the maximum score was 8).

The recognition test A recognition test was presented after the recall. Seven questions about the town, most of them about the accident, were presented. The subjects had to choose the item presented in the town out of three different items. Recognition performance was scored out of a possible 7 points.

The total episodic memory score A total episodic memory score was calculated which summed up the correct recalls and the correct recognitions.

The DRM Paradigm In order to correlate true and false memories in our virtual environment and standard measures of episodic memory, participants then took a DRM test (Deese, 1959; Roediger and McDermott, 1995). Subjects studied word lists with semantic associations (for instance:

thread, pin, eye, sewing, sharp, point, pricked, thimble, haystack, pain, hurt and injection), then, recall and recognition tests were performed. Six lists of 15 semantically related words were presented; the participants had to recall all the words they remembered after each list. Then, they performed a recognition test composed of 6 related non-presented items, 17 presented items and 24 unrelated non-presented items.

Results

The Wald-Wolfowitz Test was used for analysing the data recorded in the episodic memory tasks. Analyses showed a main effect of sensory-motor implication. The participants of the passive condition were significantly better at remembering locations of elements on the map than the active participants [$Z= -2.45$, $p<0.05$]. They had also a higher total episodic memory score [$Z= 2.03$, $p<0.05$]. The memory of the location of the accident on the map was marginally significantly higher in the active condition than in the passive condition [$Z= 1.93$, $p=0.05$]. The recall of specific areas of the town (for example: the train station, the crowd, etc.) was also better in the active situation [$Z= -1.91$, $p=0.05$].

There was no sensory-motor effect either on the recall of the where (spatial recall), on the when (temporal recall), on the recall of context, on the recall of turns or on the recognition test. Moreover, we did not find any correlation between true recognitions of the town and true recognitions of the DRM paradigm, nor between the false recognitions.

Discussion

The aim of this experiment was to test the effect of sensory-motor implication on episodic memory. We saw on the one hand, that the active condition enhanced the recall of the town's elements and the recall of the accident's location. These results appear not to be completely in accordance with those of Brooks et al. (1999). These authors did not find differences on memory of objects and object locations. We found that an active situation improves memory, thus proprioceptive stimulations associated with the elements which have to be memorised allows better memory. This is consistent with the idea that the richer sensory information, the better memory (Paivio, 1991, Engelkamp et al., 1994).

On the other hand, we saw that the passive condition enhanced the recall of the locations of the elements on the map and the total episodic memory score. Brooks et al. (1999) showed that an active participation enhanced spatial memory. In our study, we found that spatial memory could be improved in the active condition (spatial location of the accident) and in the passive condition (spatial location for other elements). In our virtual experiment, the active and the passive conditions were probably not equivalent in terms of difficulty. Driving and observing required some division of attention. It has been shown that divided attention during encoding has been associated with large reductions in memory (Craik, Govoni, Naveh-Benjamin, & Anderson, 1996). We can suppose that this divided attention had a positive influence in the passive condition on the memory performance.

We need to improve our experimental situation in order to match the difficulty of the active and the passive conditions. In the second experiment, we told passive subjects to pay attention to the driving and to the itinerary of the driver. Thus, the second experiment assessed the sensory-motor effect controlling the bias of attention. Moreover, we decided to test the influence of encoding on memory performance and the interaction of encoding with the sensory-motor effect. First, we suppose that in the first study, the encoding was not incidental because the participants could guess that their memory would be assessed. We prefered thus control this aspect. Second, we know that the depth of processing influences memory performance (Craik & Tulving, 1975). Maybe the difference between active and passive conditions will change in an intentional encoding task which is more explicit. We suppose that proprioceptive knowledge is not used explicitly to enhance memory. Thus in an intentional memorisation, where subjects can use a strategy to help the memorisation, the advantage of sensory-motor implication, i.e. proprioception, should decrease.

Experiment 2

Method

Participants

90 participants (66 female and 24 male) were assigned to one of the four conditions. Each condition resulted from the crossing of the sensory-motor implication factor and the encoding. Participants ranged in age from 18 to 30 ($M = 21.87$; $SD = 2.87$). The participants were under the same medical and psychological verifications as in the first experiment.

Material and Design

The material was exactly the same as in the first experiment. The sensory-motor implication (active, passive) was the first factor manipulated. The second factor was the type of encoding; it could be intentional or non-intentional. Both factors were between-subjects factors. The same measurements of memory as in the first experiment were made.

Procedure

The procedure was the same as in the first experiment except that in the passive condition subjects were told to pay attention to the driving and to the itinerary. Moreover, in the intentional encoding, we asked participants to try to remember the most elements they saw in the town and the itinerary of the driver in order to recall them at the end of the presentation.

Results

Analyses of variance (ANOVA) were performed on the data recorded from the episodic memory tasks. Gender was included as a third factor in order to control its effect on memory tasks. A significant main effect of the sensory-motor implication on memory was obtained. The spatial recall [$F(1,82)=4.91$, $p<0.05$], the temporal recall [$F(1,82)=4.27$, $p<0.05$] and the recall of the location of the elements on a map [$F(1,82)=5.17$, $p<0.05$] were significantly better in the passive condition compared to the active condition. In addition, a main effect of the encoding was found, the intentional encoding lead to a better recall of the elements [$F(1,82)=8.85$, $p<0.01$], a better spatial recall (where) [$F(1,82)=11.15$, $p<0.001$], a better temporal recall (when) [$F(1,82)=10.79$, $p<0.001$], a better recall of localisation of the elements on a map [$F(1,82)=6.54$, $p<0.01$] and an higher score in the recognition test [$F(1,82)=15.98$, $p<0.0001$]. We found no interaction between sensory-motor implication and encoding on any score.

Nevertheless, interactions were found between sensory-motor implication and sex. Men were marginally significantly better at recalling the number of turns in the passive condition compared to the active condition but the women were better in the active condition compared to the passive condition [$F(1,82)=3.89$, $p=0.05$]. We found a significant interaction between sensory-motor implication and sex for the recall of the locations of the elements on the map [$F(1,82)=5.15$, $p<0.05$], the men showing more correct recalls in the passive condition compared to the active condition while the women were better in the active condition than in the passive condition. Moreover, the men showed more false recalls of the locations on the map in the active condition than in the passive condition and the women more in the passive condition than in the active condition [$F(1,82)=4.57$, $p<0.05$]. Last, we computed a verbal score with element, temporal, spatial and context recalls and we computed a spatial score with the map recall, the turns recall and the recall of the location of the elements on the map. We found that the men had a better verbal score in the passive condition than in the active condition while the women were better in the active situation compared to the passive condition [$F(1,82)=8.04$, $p<0.005$]. Moreover, the men had a better for the spatial score in the passive situation and the women were better in the active condition [$F(1,82)=4.99$, $p<0.05$].

Discussion

The results of the second experiment showed an advantage of the passive condition compared to the active condition on memory. These results contradict our predictions which proposed that active situation leads to better memories compared to passive situation. We can thus suppose that the accessibility of proprioception during a memory task does not enhance memory. Sensory-motor implication would even be detrimental for memory. Notwithstanding, we found some interactions between sensory-motor implication and sex. These interactions showed that the men were better in a passive situation than in an active one while the women were better in an active condition than in a passive one for true memories and false memories were lower respectively. Thus, the main effect of sensory-motor implication was skewed by sex. The results of the women confirmed our predictions: an active situation leads to better episodic memory. We could suppose that only the women benefited from the stimulations of the proprioception. A reason of this lack of benefit for men is maybe that they were more implicated in the driving than women. Their attention was more oriented to the driving than to the town, their memory was thus better when they did not drive.

A strong effect of the encoding was found showing that an intentional encoding lead to better memories. We were not surprised by this result which was found in many memory studies (Craik, 2002).

General Discussion

The aim of our studies was to investigate episodic memory in virtual reality by distinguishing the effect of sensory-motor implication on retrieval of true and false memories. In the first experiment, we saw that an active situation improved the recall of the town elements and the accident location. A passive advantage was found for the recall of the locations of the elements on the map and the total episodic memory score. In this experiment all the participants were women. We conducted a second experiment in order to control the attentional bias present in the active condition. The results of this second experiment indicated that the men were better in a passive situation and the women were better in an active condition for true and for false memories. We could suppose that the men's attention was more oriented to the driving than to the town, the memory was thus better when they did not drive, in the passive condition. Indeed, the experimenter noted that the men drove more quickly than the women and were more implicated in the driving. Indeed, we observed an active advantage on memory for women in the second experiment.

The results observed for women are consistent with the idea that the richer sensory information, the better memory (Paivio, 1991, Engelkamp et al., 1994). Consequently, in these studies we showed for the first time that proprioceptive knowledge associated with the event enhances the memory of this event. The motor activity would be integrated in the mnesic-trace of what we experience in life and would contribute to recollection. Moreover, virtual reality seems to be an interesting tool for assessing episodic memory.

Acknowledgements

We thank anonymous reviewers for helpful comments on the earlier version of this manuscript. We gratefully acknowledge the collaboration and help of Sylvain Haupert (sylvain.haupert@lip.bhdc.jussieu.fr) and Emmanuel Gueriero (emmanuel@guerriero.net) for the program and the design of the town. We also thank Thérèse Collins for her re-reading the manuscript.

References

Aguirre, G.K. & D'Esposito, M. (1997). Environmental knowledge is subserved by separable dorsal/ventral neural area. *Journal of Neuroscience, 17,* 2512-2518.

Brooks, B.M., Attree, E.A., Rose, F.D., Clifford, B.R., & Leadbetter, A.G. (1999). The specificity of memory enhancement during interaction with a virtual environment. *Memory, 7,* 65-78.

Burgess, N. (2002). The hippocampus, space, and viewpoints in episodic memory. *The Quarterly Journal of Experimental Psychology, 55 A,* 1057-1080.

Burgess, N., Maguire, E.A. & O'Keefe, J. (2002). The human hippocampus and spatial and episodic memory. *Neuron, 35,* 625-641. Review.

Burgess, N., Maguire, E.A., Spiers, H.J. & O'Keefe, J. (2001). A temporoparietal and prefrontal network for retrieving the spatial context of lifelike events. *Neuroimage; 14,* 439-453.

Craik, F.I.M., Govoni, R, Naveh-Benjamin, M., Anderson, N. D. (1996).The effects of divided attention on encoding and retrieval processes in human memory. *Journal of Experimental Psychology: General, 125,* 159-180.

Craik, F. I. M., & Tulving, E. (1975). Depth of processing and theretention of words in episodic memory. *Journal of ExperimentalPsychology: General, 104,* 268-294.

Craik, F.I.M. (2002). Levels of processing : past, present...and future ? *Memory, 10,* 305-318.

Deltour, J.J. (1993). Echelle de vocabulaire de Mill Hill de J.C. Raven : adaptation française et normes comparées du Mill Hill et du Standard progressive matrices (PM 38). Braine-le-Château, Belgique : Editions L'application des Techniques Modernes.

Deese, J. (1959). On the prediction of occurrence of particular verbal intrusions in immediate recall. *Journal of Experimental Psychology, 58,* 17-22.

Dodson, C. S., Koutstaal, W. & Schacter, D.L. (2000). Escape from illusion: reducing false memories. *Trends in Cognitive Science, 4,* 391-397.

Engelkamp, J., Zimmer, H.D., Mohr, G. & Sellen, O. (1994). Memory of self-performed tasks: self-performing during recognition. *Memory and Cognition, 22,* 34-39.

Engelkamp J. and Zimmer H.D. (1997). Sensory factors in memory for subject-performed tasks. *Acta Psychologica, 96,* 43-60.

Gaggioli, A. (2003). Using virtual reality in experimental psychology. In G. Riva & C. Galimberti, C. (Eds). *Towards Cyberpsychology: Mind, Cognition and Society in the Internet Age.* Amsterdam: IOS Press.

King, J.A., Hartley, T., Spiers, H.J., Maguire, E.A. & Burgess, N. (2005). Anterior prefrontal involvement in episodic retrieval reflects contextual interference. *Neuroimage, 15,* 256-267.

Marié, R.M., Chemin I., Lebreton, S. & Klinger, E. (2005). Cognitive planning assessment and virtual environment in Parkinson's disease. *Laval virtual 2005 proceedings,* 115-119.

Marié, R.M., Klinger, E., Chemin I., & Josset M. (2003). Cognitive planning assessed by virtual reality. *VRIC 2003 proceedings,* 119-125.

Morris, R.G., Parslow, D., Fleminger, S., Brooks, B., Brammer, M. & Rose, D. (2002). Functional magnetic resonance imagining investigation of allocentric spatial memory tested using virtual reality in patients with anoxic hippocampal damage. *Proceedings of the 4th international conference on disability, virtual reality and associated technologies, Hungary,* 87-92.

Nelson, D.L. (1979). Remembering pictures and words: Appearance, significance and name. In L.S. Cermak & F.I.M. Craik (Eds.), *Levels of processing in human memory.* Hillsdale, NJ: Lawrence Erlbaum Associates Inc.

Paivio, A. (1991). Dual coding theory : retrospect and current status. *Canadian journal of psychology, 45,* 255-287.

Parslow, D.M., Morris, R.G., Fleminger, S., Rahman, Q., Abrahams, S. & Recce, M. (2005). Allocentric spatial memory in humans with hippocampal lesions. *Acta Psychologica, 118,* 123-47.

Roediger, H.L. & McDermott, K.B. (1995). Creating false memories: remembering words not presented in lists. *Journal of Experimental Psychology, 21,* 803-814.

Schacter, D.L. & Curran T. (2000). Memory without remembering and remembering without memory: Implicit and false memories. In M.S Gazzaniga. (Ed.), *The New Cognitive Neurosciences.* (2nd Ed.). Cambridge: MIT Press.

Tlauka, M., Keage, H. & Clark, C.R. (2005). Viewing a map versus reading a description of a map: modality-specific encoding of spatial information. *Cognitive Science, 29,* 807-818.

Tulving, E. (2002). Episodic memory: from mind to brain. *Annual Review of Psychology, 53,* 1-25.

Cognitive heuristics in multitasking performance

Juergen Kiefer (juergen.kiefer@zmms.tu-berlin.de)
Research Training Group prometei,
Center of Human-Machine-Systems - Technische Universität Berlin
Franklinstraße 28-29, J2-7/2, 10623 Berlin, Germany

Michael Schulz (michael.schulz@zmms.tu-berlin.de)
Institute of Psychology
Department of General Psychology
Franklinstraße 28-29, J2-7/2, 10623 Berlin, Germany

Dirk Schulze-Kissing (dsk@zmms.tu-berlin.de)
Institute of Psychology and Ergonomics
Department of Work, Engineering & Organizational Psychology
Marchstr. 12, F 7
10587 Berlin

Leon Urbas (leon.urbas@mailbox.tu-dresden.de)
Institute of Automation - Technische Universität Dresden
01062 Dresden, Germany

Abstract

A cognitive approach towards the understanding of human multitasking is presented in this contribution. We provide four dual-task studies showing evidence for the development and application of cognitive strategies which we refer to as "heuristics": these fast and frugal *rules of thumb* help to adaptively use the information and structure of the environment to successfully perform two tasks concurrently. This work aims to show that heuristics not only arise unconsciously, but also change the selective visual attention by allowing different behavioral mechanisms (i.e., perception and action) to be performed in parallel. Interestingly, using the cognitive heuristics leads to an increase in performance. A short synthesis of two realistic studies in a driving simulator (study I and study II) and a third, systematically controlled and cognitively enriched tracking task in the laboratory (study III) support our perspective. The last study is of main interest in this paper. Throughout all studies, the results support our assumptions, namely that people use cognitive heuristics to manage human multitasking and encourage us to extend our research focus to other domains in the field of human machine interaction.

Multitasking

In the 1920s, early approaches in the context of *Gestalt Psychology* investigated task interruption and dual task situations (Ovsiankina, 1928; Telford, 1931). Half a century ago, Cherry (1953) referred to "human's natural ability to multitask". While in the last two decades, main interest was on the *psychological refractory period* (*PRP*-studies, see Pashler, 1994; Meyer & Kieras, 1997a, 1997b) or the *central bottleneck* – debate, the presented work is interested in the management of multiple goals within a real-life context. From a cognitive modeling perspective, multitasking can be considered as "the ability to integrate,

interleave, and perform multiple tasks and/or component subtasks of a larger complex task" (Salvucci, 2005). Lee & Taatgen (2002) understand multitasking as "the ability to handle the demands of multiple tasks simultaneously". Pew & Mavor (1998) refer to multitasking as "doing several things at once". Our approach does not strive for a precise definition of "multitasking". Moreover, we intend to reveal the cognitive processing when doing several task at the same time. One prominent domain is the daily use of technology such as mobile devices. Thus, the area of human-machine-interaction provides a perfect context for our investigations.

A taxonomic classification of dual task studies

Before we concretize the applied dual task scenario, it is necessary to classify dual-task-situations in general. With respect to realistic scenarios, Salvucci (2005) proposes four possible models that are worth introducing.

Models of discrete successive tasks

The first category specifies situations where we switch back and forth, from one task to another. In empirical investigations, usually this is applied in alternating trials of simple choice-reaction tasks. Main interest is on temporal costs for switching (Rogers & Monsell, 1995). Sometimes the time to resume a task is also referred to as resumption costs. This category does not contain a dynamic component and consequently does not fulfill our requirements.

Models of discrete concurrent tasks

PRP-studies (Pashler, 2000) belong to the second category. Offset by a short delay, a second task starts before the first one ends. This delay leads to a short overlapping of the two applied tasks. In the 1990s, many studies investigated the

PRP-phenomenon. Nevertheless we believe that these models do not represent an adequate candidate for our purpose.

Models of elementary continuous tasks

The third category allows one continuous task (e.g., an experimental scenario with tracking as main task). Short discrete tasks occasionally appear and initiate task concurrency.

Models of compound continuous tasks

If two or more simultaneous tasks appear, we talk about *models of compound continuous tasks*: each of the both tasks is an "ongoing continuous process" (Salvucci, 2005). The last category contains a high degree of ecological validity and reflects human behavior in typical real-life-situations. Especially in the context of human machine interaction, people often have to deal with the concurrency of two (sometimes even more) tasks. We consider our empirical studies to be part of this last category.

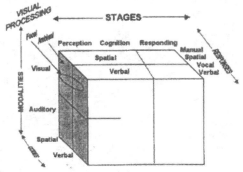

Figure 1: Multiple resource model (Wickens, 2002)

The boundedness of human cognitive resource

Doing several tasks at the same time leads us to the question of resource management. In contrast to assumptions about a single resource which is responsible for the management of human performance (Kahneman, 1992), the reference frame for our studies is the *four-dimensional multiple resource model* proposed by Wickens (2002, 2004): *processing stages* (perception, cognition, responding), *perceptual modalities* (auditory, visual), *visual channels* (focal, ambient), and *processing codes* (spatial, verbal) rely on different physiological mechanism (Fig. 1). Following this model, two tasks do not influence each other and can be executed in parallel if they use different resources. This is a core assumption in our studies: motor action, for instance, can be done in parallel with visual perception without interference provided sufficient training.

Summary of study I and study II

A closer description of the first two studies is given in Kiefer & Urbas (2006). Here, we summarize the core results to prepare for study III. In both study I and II, we applied a dual task scenario: main task was driving (simple tracking in a driving simulator), secondary task was the *D2-Drive* test (Fig. 2) based on the *D2 test of attention* developed by Brickenkamp (2001): this test measures the individual amount of visual attention, it can be interrupted and easily be learned. This makes it a perfect candidate to identify performance strategies under multitasking. We measured performance in both main task (derivation of lane) as well as secondary task (number of correctly performed patterns). Three levels of complexity (version a, b, and c) of *D2-Drive* were applied (see Kiefer & Urbas, 2006): subjects were ask to perform the pattern in the middle only (version A), the complete line (version B), or the complete line in combination with a memory task, i.e. to keep in mind which line to perform next (version C). In both studies, the experiment ended with a structured interview in which subjects were asked about their multitasking performance. Using eye-tracking data, we were able to reconstruct the visual attention.

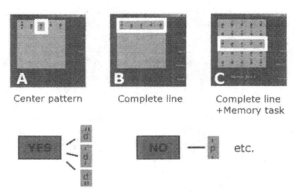

Figure 2: D2-Drive test (Kiefer & Urbas., 2006)

Study I: Identification of cognitive strategies

The main results of the first study are:
(1) Performance in main task is not influenced by the interruption via the secondary task.
(2) Relative performance (secondary task) increases under multitasking.
(3) A short period of training leads to error-free performance in both primary as well as secondary task.
(4) Performance in the secondary task highly depends on the version (structure) of the task.

The most essential result of the first study is the identification of cognitive strategies. Due to the fact that subjects do not necessarily have to be aware of their applied strategies, we hence refer to their processing as applying cognitive heuristics: in particular, this is true for version B (Fig. 2): here, the task configuration promotes the merging of several patterns. This approach is confirmed by the structured interviews and justifies a deeper analysis of the strategic processing.

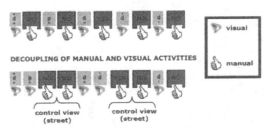

Figure 3: Development of a cognitive heuristic

"Blocking", an example of multitasking heuristics

Starting with the *D2-Drive* in single task condition, subjects performed pattern by pattern. This stepwise approach goes in line with people doing a task for the first time, as described by Taatgen (2005). Under dual task condition (and for some people, this is even true at the end of the single task condition), subjects intuitively understand that part of the secondary task (more precisely, the respond-action) does not require focal visual attention, but only manual action (Fig. 3). Manual and visual activities are decoupled: when entering the sequence of responses (from 2 up to 4 patterns), the visual channel is free. Consequently, during this time subjects are able to afford a control view at the street. This finding goes in line with the theoretical assumptions derived by the Wickens' *model of multiple resources* (Wickens, 2002). Please note that subjects do not necessarily have conscious access to the described cognitive strategies, as indicated by the structured interviews we did after the study. For this reason, we refer to them as "*cognitive heuristics*": heuristics are replicable methods often discovered in the field of complex problem solving or learning and provide a high efficiency in performance. In this article, the words "*strategy*" and "*heuristic*" are treated synonymously, even though the term "*heuristic*" captures a broader sense. To verify the use of *cognitive heuristics* such as the one example represented in Fig.3, we did a second study in the driving simulator.

Study II: The influence of experience

Study II was a replication of the first study. We aimed to confirm the results of the first study and questioned what might happen if subjects were given more training. We expected a more pronounced effect if subjects are more experienced in a specific multitasking situation.

Findings of Study II As in study I, performance increased under multitasking in study II as well, both for version A and B. Even in version C, there is no decrease in performance. For details and results, please have a look at Kiefer & Urbas (2006). Although observational data (eye tracking) as well as (structured) interviews support the proposed cognitive heuristics, we decided to formalize our hypotheses and thus make it revisable. To do so, we used the method of *cognitive modeling*.

Cognitive Modeling

Psychological research starts with a theory, for instance on human multitasking (see Salvucci, 2005). The derived hypotheses (*assumptions*) subsequently are tested (*empirical investigation*): *results* of the experiments support or reject the assumptions and thus the theory. Going one step further, the theory-based assumption can precisely be formalized in a cognitive model (Fig. 4). We used the ACT-R framework (Anderson, Bothell, Byrne, Douglass, Lebiere, & Qin, 2004). The model-based predictions are compared with the empirical results, and the degree of matching constitutes the value of the cognitive model.

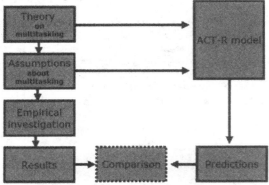

Figure 4: Cognitive modeling

In the first two studies, the same versions of *D2-Drive* were applied. While doing these tests, two different levels of performance can be highlighted: on a *micro-level* (i.e., reading a single pattern), participants' visual scan paths give insight into how one generous test element is treated. This process is similar to reading. For almost all participants, their "reading style" developed over time: whilst beginning as expected ("read" complete pattern, e.g. middle-upper-lower area), most people realize already after a short time that for *p*-patterns (i.e., patterns containing the letter *p*), it is sufficient to stop after checking the middle part. Such a processing is a reasonable *short-cut* to save important time. We call it "*micro-strategy*" and distinguish it from a stepwise processing on a *macro-level*: the sequential processing (i.e., visual orientation – read first pattern – react – read second pattern – look at street – etc.) is called "*macro-strategy*", the successfully repeated use of a concrete *macro-strategy* is treated as a *cognitive heuristic*.

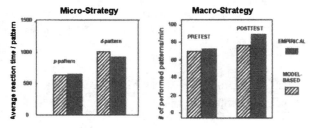

Figure 5: Empirical results vs. model-based predictions

Both *micro-* as well as *macro-strategies* were implemented in ACT-R (Anderson et al., 2004): a comparison between model(s) (simulation) and empirical results (experiments) in all cases highly support the claim that subjects use cognitive heuristics within the structure of the given task environment.

Study III: The impact of task configuration

The first two studies concentrated on the basic mechanisms of human multitasking in a realistic task scenario. Kiefer & Urbas (2006) showed how subjects succeeded in performing both tasks partially in parallel. Purpose of study III was twofold: on the one side, we aimed to enrich the primary task with a cognitive component (main task in study I and study II was *tracking*, i.e. keeping the lane). A second extension referred to a systematic variation of the degree of freedom in the secondary task (D2-Drive). One major objection deals with the complexity of the primary task: a high degree on ecological validity, however, often reveals a lack of systematic control. Whereas, one might wonder what happens in more complex situations. Study III incorporates this issue: we used the *lane change task* (*LCT*, Mattes, 2003) in a standardized PC-based version (Fig. 6): in this test, participants first see a sign (*perception*) which tells them to which position they must change the lane (e.g., to the right lane). In a second step, participants decide what to do and change the lane accordingly (*reaction*) which constitutes step three (i.e., the lane change maneuver). Finally, they have to *keep the "new" lane* until a next sign appears.

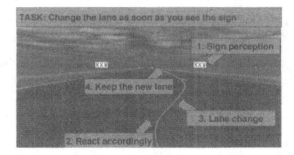

Figure 6: Lane change task, *LCT* (Mattes, 2003)

Task complexity in the primary task was obtained by applying the *LCT* (i.e., an additional cognitive component). The first two studies suggest that version B of the *D2-Drive* test is convenient for investigating multitasking heuristics due to its structure. We therefore created four different version (see Table 1) to testify whether a task' s degree of freedom generates the postulated strategic behavior. The four versions were tested before we started the experiment and turned out to systematically vary the way we expected und intended.

Table 1: Complexity of the secondary task

Version	Task description
D2-Drive-1	Performing complete line of five patterns (see version *D2-Drive-B* in study I and study II).
D2-Drive-2	Same as *D2-Drive-1* (performing from position 1 up to 5), but after each response, the complete row changes.
D2-Drive-3	Same as *D2-Drive-1*, but enhanced by additional marker to show current position.
D2-Drive-4	Combination of *D2-Drive-2* and *D2-Drive-3*: patterns dynamically change after each response, but current position is highlighted by visual marker.

Table 1 specifies the four different version in detail: *D2-Drive-1* and *D2-Drive-3* contain a fixed row of five patterns, in *D2-Drive-1* and *D2-Drive-3*, the row changes after each manual action and five new patterns are presented. Version *D2-Drive-1* and *D2-Drive-3* allow to anticipate the response behaviour and to merge together several patterns (as described in Fig. 3), whereas version *D2-Drive-2* and *D2-Drive-4* do not contain this option. *D2-Drive-3* and *D2-Drive-4* share as common feature a "visual eye", i.e. a marker that highlights the current position. This is a useful assistance when switching back to D2-Drive. *D2-Drive-1* and *D2-Drive-2* do not provide such a helping mechanism for visual orientation. We expected a higher amount of strategy use for *D2-Drive-1* and *D2-Drive-2*, but not for *D2-Drive-3* and *D2-Drive-4* due to forced focusing. We further assumed *D2-Drive-1* and *D2-Drive-3* to support the use of cognitive heuristics as a consequence of possible anticipating.

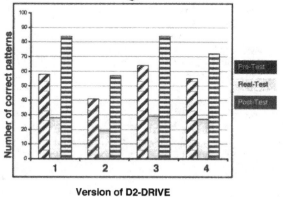

Figure 7: Empirical results vs. model-based predictions

Fig. 7 presents the performance in the secondary task for study III: over all 40 subjects participating the study, *D2-Drive-1* as well as *D2-Drive-3* win in terms of number of correct performed patterns, this was also confirmed by eye-tracking data as well as interviews after the study (22 out of 40 subjects reported to be supported by the "visual help", i.e. the additional marker). The results confirm our assumption that the task configuration highly influences and determines the development and the application of cognitive strategies as described in Fig. 3. Please keep in mind that *D2-Drive-1* and *D2-Drive-3* allow using of heuristics such as *"blocking"* only by their structure. Subjects were not given any instructions or recommendations of how to multitasking. This encourages us to continue our analyses and investigate eye tracking data recorded in this study to a deeper extend. However, this is still work in progress.

Conclusion

Four studies describe the current state of our effort to understand human behaviour in complex multitasking situations. We conclude the main results and discuss them subsequently.

Synopsis

In this contribution, we aimed to provide ample evidence for (1) the existence of cognitive heuristics. We hope to have shown that these heuristics emerge without instruction (2). Subjects are not necessarily aware of applying these *"rules of thumb"* in multitasking (3): some reports of the structured interviews support the assumptions, but even a lack conscious access does not exclude the adaptive use of cognitive heuristics, as supported by eye tracking data. The use of different multitasking scenarios supports our hypothesized domain independence (4). As we systematically investigated structure and complexity of the applied secondary task, we claim that task configuration is one of the main factors influencing time and frequency of strategy use (5).

Discussion

In various scenarios we applied, subjects seem to manage the demands of multiple concurrent tasks. The illustrated heuristic performance of subjects tremendously depends on a deeper analysis of *eye tracking data*. This is work to be done in future. However, in our eyes we already provide evidence for people using such heuristics both with as well as without conscious access. Another critical aspect is *domain dependency*: all reported studies take place in the context of driving which itself is multitasking per se. We therefore would like to extend the area of the primary task (e.g., how do people coordinate walking and concurrently using a mobile phone). Complexity of main task and secondary task has been systematically investigated. But what is further missing is an answer to the question what happens if *task priority* plays a role. For ecological reasons, driving in all studies was main task with main priority. But this assumption might be too artificial and too unrealistic. To conclude we think that the aspects *task domain* and *task priority* are key issues for the understanding how people multitask in real life.

Acknowledgments

This project is funded by Deutsche Forschungs-gemeinschaft (research training group 1013 prometei).

References

Anderson, J. R., Bothell, D., Byrne, M. D., Douglass, S., Lebiere, C., & Qin, Y. (2004). An integrated theory of the mind. *Psychological Review*, 111, 1036-1060.

Brickenkamp, R. (2001). Test D2, *Aufmerksamkeits-Belastungs-Test*. 9., überarbeitetet und neu normierte Auflage. Hogrefe Verlage. Bern, Schweiz.

Cherry, E.C. (1953). Some experiments on the recognition of speech, with one and with two ears. *Journal of the Acoustical Society of America*, 25(5):975-979.

Kahneman, D. (1992). *Attention and effort*. Englewood Cliffs, NJ: Prentice-Hall.

Kiefer, J. & Urbas, L. (2006): Multitasking-Strategien in der Mensch-Maschine-Interaktion. *MMI-Interaktiv*,11.

Lee, F.J. & Taatgen, N.A. (2002). Multitasking as Skill Acquisition. *Proceedings of the twenty-fourth annual conference of the cognitive science society* (pp. 572-577). Mahwah, NJ: Erlbaum. Fairfax, VA: August, 2002.

Mattes, S. (2003). The lane-change-task as a tool for driver distraction evaluation. *In Proceedings of IGfA*, 2003.

Meyer, D. E., & Kieras, D. E. (1997a). A computational theory of executive cogni-tive processes and multiple-task performance: Part 1. Basic mechanisms. *Psychological Review*, 104, 3-65.

Meyer, D. E., & Kieras, D. E. (1997b). A computational theory of executive cogni-tive processes and multiple-task performance: Part 2. Accounts of psychologi-cal refractory period phenomena. *Psychological Review*, 104, 749-791.

Ovsiankina M. (1928) Die Wiederaufnahme unterbrochener Handlungen. *Psychologische Forschung*, 11 (1), 302-379.

Pashler, H. (1994). Dual-task interference in simple tasks: Data and theory. *Psychological Bulletin*, 116, 220-244.

Pashler, H. (2000). Task switching and multitask performance. In Monsell, S., and Driver, J. (editors). *Attention and Performance XVIII: Control of mental processes*. Cambridge, MA: MIT Press.

Pew, R.W., and Mavor, A.S., eds. (1998). Modeling Human and Organizational Behavior: Application to Military Simulations. Washington, DC: National Academy Press.

Rogers, R., & Monsell, S. (1995). Costs of a predictable switch between simple cognitive tasks. *Journal of Experimental Psychology: General*, 124, 207-231.

Salvucci, D. D. (2005) A multitaksing general executive for compound continuous tasks. *Cognitive Science*, 29, 457-492.

Taatgen, N.A. (2005). Modeling parallelization and speed improvement in skill acquisition: from dual tasks to complex dynamic skills. *Cognitive Science*, 29, 421-455.

Telford, C. W. (1931). The refractory phase of voluntary and associative response. *Journal of Experimental Psychology*, 14, 1-35.

Wickens, C.D. (2002). Multiple resources and performance prediction. *Theoretical Issues in Ergonomics Science*, 3(2), 159-177.

Wickens, C.D. 2004. Multiple Resource Time Sharing Mode. In: *Handbook of Human Factors and Ergonomics Methods*, ed. Stanton, N., A. Hedge, K. Brook-huis, E. Salas and H.W. Hendrick. London, United Kingdom: CRC Press.

Temporal Factorisation and Realisation in Cognitive Dynamics and Beyond

Jan Treur (treur@cs.vu.nl)

Vrije Universiteit Amsterdam, Department of Artificial Intelligence
De Boelelaan 1081, NL-1081 HV, Amsterdam, The Netherlands   http://www.few.vu.nl/~treur

Abstract

Temporal factorisation is a principle underlying approaches to dynamics used within many disciplines. According to this principle any temporal relationship of the form 'past pattern implies future pattern' can be factorised into a relationship of the form 'past pattern implies present state' and a relationship of the form 'present state implies future pattern'. To enable this, the principle postulates the existence of certain mediating state properties in the present state. In this paper the question is addressed whether and how a postulated mediating state property relates to other state properties in the (present) state in which it occurs. This analyses provides a conceptual framework covering concepts and themes that usually are considered unrelated, such as, the notions of differential equations in Mathematics, of transition system and rule-based system in Computer Science, Cognitive Science and Artificial Intelligence, and of reduction and realisation of mental states in Cognitive Science and Philosophy of Science.

Introduction

In (Treur, 2006) the temporal factorisation principle was identified, formalised, and shown to play a crucial role for modelling dynamics in different disciplines such as Physics, Chemistry, Biology, Mathematics, Computer Science, and Cognitive Science. The temporal factorisation principle claims that if a certain (past) pattern of events leads to a certain (future) pattern of events, then there exists a state property p such that the past pattern leads to a (present) state where this property p holds, and any state where the state property p holds leads to the future pattern. This postulated state property p is called a mediating state property for the 'past pattern implies future pattern' relationship. For some of the foundational themes and approaches discussed in the literature in the cognitive domain, it has been shown in (Treur, 2006) how they can be generalised beyond the cognitive area, and incorporated in the more general conceptual framework based on temporal factorisation; in particular this has been addressed for the notion of mental state, and the notion of representational content of a mental state property. For another theme, namely, physical realisation of mental state properties, it is considered in the current paper, how it can be generalised beyond the cognitive domain and added to the framework based on the temporal factorisation principle. Thus the conceptual framework for dynamics based on 'temporal factorisation' as introduced in (Treur, 2006) will be extended to a conceptual framework based on 'temporal factorisation and realisation'.

To obtain this extension, the question of realism is addressed for the mediating state properties postulated in temporal factorisation. The corresponding type of question for the cognitive area, as addressed within Philosophy of Mind, namely the question of how real mental state properties are, will be a source of inspiration, in particular, the perspective of *physicalism* which aims at relating mental state properties in one way or the other to physical state properties; e.g., (Kim, 1996, pp. 9-13). By itself, the temporal factorisation principle does not give any suggestion on whether and how, within a state, a mediating state property relates to other state properties. It could have a purely synthetic nature, isolated from other, more genuine, state properties. Indeed, for a number of historical cases, the state properties obtained by temporal factorisation seem to have no relationship to other state properties in the same state whatsoever.

This holds, for example, for state properties within Physics in empty space such as velocity and momentum (inertia of motion). In other cases, such as the state property 'force' within Physics, such relationships to specific other state properties in the same state are assumed to exist (e.g., laws for specific types of forces, such as gravitational, electrical or magnetical forces), and they are often exploited in scientific practice. These relationships are not systematic, however, but differ from context to context, so they are rather heterogeneous, as, for example, pointed out by Nagel (1961), pp. 190-192.

For the cognitive domain, one of the advantages of a relation between mental state properties and physical state properties is that in such a case causation by a mental state property (mental causation; cf. Kim, 1996, pp. 125-154) can be explained as causation by the realising physical state property. For mediating state properties it can also be questioned how they can cause physical state properties in successive states. A one-to-one relationship of a postulated mediating state property with a more genuine physical state property may provide an explanation of causation by the mediating state property similar to the one in the case of mental causation by a realised mental state property. In this paper it is shown that for mediating state properties realisation is often but not always possible, and whenever it is possible it may concern multiple realisation.

The paper is structured as follows. First a brief introduction of the temporal factorisation principle and its formalisation is presented, adopted from (Treur, 2006). Next it is discussed how mediating state properties can co-occur with other state properties, and introduces the notion of (*multiple*) *realisation relation* for a mediating state property. Furthermore, it is shown how in quantitative mathematical dynamic modelling approaches based on continuous state properties within the area of calculus in Mathematics, realisation relations are expressed in the form of difference equations (discrete time) or differential equations (continuous time). In addition it is shown how for qualitative dynamic modelling approaches based on discrete state properties, such as transition systems in Computer Science or rule-based systems in Cognitive Science or Artificial Intelligence, a qualitative format is used to express realisation relations. Finally, it is discussed how within Physics realisation relations for the second-order mediating state property 'force' play an important role.

The Temporal Factorisation Principle

The temporal factorisation principle as introduced in Treur, 2006) is formulated in terms of temporal relationships between past patterns, present states, and future patterns. Here a *past pattern a* refers to a property of a series of states or events in the past, and a *future pattern b* refers to a property of a series of states or events in the future. The temporal factorisation principle states that any systematic temporal 'past pattern implies future pattern' relationship $a \rightarrow b$ between a past pattern a and a future pattern b can be factorised in the form of temporal relationships $a \rightarrow p$ and $p \rightarrow b$ for some state property p of the present world state. More specifically, the principle claims that for any 'past pattern implies future pattern' relationship $a \rightarrow b$ *there exists* a world state property p (expressed in the ontology for state properties) such that temporal relationships 'past pattern implies present state property' $a \rightarrow p$ and 'present state property implies future pattern' $p \rightarrow b$ hold.[1] In short:

$$a \rightarrow b \quad \Rightarrow \quad \exists p \; a \rightarrow p \; \& \; p \rightarrow b$$

Notice that the notation $\rightarrow$ is used here to indicate logical implication (between temporal properties). The postulated state property p is called a *mediating state property* for the given 'past pattern implies future pattern' relationship. The principle claims that the state ontology is (or can be chosen to be) sufficiently rich to express all the relevant information on the past in some condensed form in one state description, and the same with respect to the future. The principle can be viewed as a way to make temporal complexity of dynamics more manageable by relating it to state complexity, where an underlying assumption is that the state complexity needed can be kept limited.

As an example from Physics, temporal factorisation can be illustrated by the notion 'momentum' of a moving object in classical mechanics as a mediating state property. Different histories of the object can lead to the same momentum in the present state. The future of the object only (besides the object's current position) depends on this momentum in the present state, not on the specific history. This was the criterion by which the concept momentum was introduced in Physics in history (see Treur, 2005, for a more detailed historical case study). Therefore the state property momentum can be understood as a mediating state property for past and future patterns in (change of) position of an object; the temporal factorisation principle indicates the existence of this state property. For more details of this case within Physics, see Section 6.

Formalisation of the principle in the predicate logical temporal language TTL is given by:

$$\forall \gamma, t \; [\; \varphi(\gamma, t) \; \Rightarrow \; \psi(\gamma, t) \;] \; \Rightarrow$$
$$\exists p \; [\; \forall \gamma, t \; [\; \varphi(\gamma, t) \; \Rightarrow \; state(\gamma, t) \models p \;] \; \&$$
$$\forall \gamma, t \; [\; state(\gamma, t) \models p \; \Rightarrow \; \psi(\gamma, t) \;] \;]$$

where $\varphi(\gamma, t)$ is a past pattern specification and $\psi(\gamma, t)$ a future pattern specification in TTL. Moreover, γ ranges over traces, t over time and p over state properties, and $state(\gamma, t) \models p$ denotes that state property p holds in the state of trace γ at time t. For more details, and more extensive examples, also in the cognitive domain, see (Treur, 2006).

Realisation of Mediating State Properties

To embed mediating state properties more intensively in the states in which they occur, their relationship to other properties of these states is considered. If in states, a mediating state property p always co-occurs with a certain state property c (or combination of state properties), such a co-occurring property c is called a *realiser* (see also Figure 1; the vertical double arrow indicates the *realisation relation* between p and c).

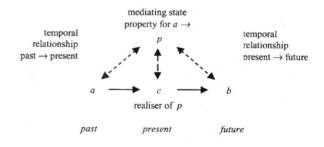

Figure 1. Realisation of a mediating state property

An example of the occurrence of realisers of mediating state properties are the following. An open a tap will lead to the presence of water in a glass in a next state, where the size of the opening determines how much water will be present at this next point in time. So the mediating state property between the past and the future (i.e., from opening the tap to water present in the glass) is in a sense hardwired in the physical configuration of the opened tap, which is described by state properties in the present state.

If a mediating state property has a realiser, it can be created or prevented by manipulating the state property that realises the mediating state property. For example, a mental

---

[1] Sometimes such relationships are simply called 'past to present', present to future', or 'past to future' relationships.

state property can be created or prevented by affecting its realiser by physical means (e.g., by using drugs). Similarly, for example, a mediating state property to fall can be created or prevented by either putting or keeping an object close to the earth, or by taking it far away.

A natural question arising in the context of realisation is whether a mediating state property, which co-occurs with some other state property, should be considered identical to this state property. This would solve the problem of how mediating state properties can be genuine state properties and how they can cause other state properties. Within physicalism, a mental state property is assumed to co-occur with its physical realiser; for mental state properties indeed such proposals to make identifications have been put forward in the form of different types of reductionism; e.g., (Kim, 1996, pp. 125-154, pp. 211-240; Bickle, 1998); see also (Bennett and Hacker, 2003; Bickle, 2003; Kim, 2005). One of the advantages of such a mental-physical state property identification is that for relationships between states at different points in time, the causation relation from Physics can describe, for example, how a mental state property such as an intention affects the world state. However, the phenomenon of multiple realisation obstructs a direct one-to-one identification.

The complicating issue of *multi-realisability* of mediating state properties is that there may sometimes be a co-occurrence with one other state property and sometimes with another one. Mental state properties usually have a large variety of realisers, for example in different animal species. Relating a mental state property in a biconditional manner to all of these mutually distinct (non-equivalent) realisers will lead to a contradiction: if p is equivalent to each of two realisers q_1 and q_2, then it follows that q_1 is equivalent to q_2, and thus they always co-occur. In a multiple realisation case where in different states sometimes one, sometimes another realiser co-occurs with p, this is a contradiction.

In the case of multiple realisers, the relation between mediating state property p and its realisers can be described by a supervenience relation (e.g., Kim, 1998).

> 'Mental properties supervene over physical properties in that for every mental property M that occurs at some point in time t, there exists some physical property P that also occurs at t, such that always if P occurs at some point in time t', also M occurs at t'.' (Kim, 1998, p. 9)

This can be formalised in TTL by

$\forall \gamma, t$ state(γ, t) |= M $\Rightarrow$ $\exists P$ physical(P) & state(γ, t) |= P & $\forall \gamma', t'$ [state(γ', t') |= P $\Rightarrow$ state(γ', t') |= M]

Following this line, the following can be defined (see also Kim, 1996, Ch. 9): A set Q of state properties (or combinations thereof) is a *complete set of realisers* of p if and only if: (1) if p occurs in a state then one of the q in Q occurs in this state, and (2) if one of the q in Q occurs in a state then p occurs in this state. The elements q of Q are called the (*non-unique*) realisers of p. The relations between p and the elements of Q are called (*multiple*) realisation relations. This can be formalised by

$\forall \gamma, t$ [state(γ, t) |= p $\Rightarrow$ $\exists q$ [in(q, Q) & state(γ, t) |= q] & $\forall \gamma', t', q$ [in(q, Q) & state(γ', t') |= q $\Rightarrow$ state(γ', t') |= p]]]

Supervenience applied to mediating state properties, expresses that mediating state properties are always realised in one way or the other. However, this can happen in a nonsystematic, ad hoc manner: for every situation a different realiser. Sometimes, variants are introduced for each context by context characterising assumptions: local reduction; cf. (Kim, 1996, pp. 211-240).

Realisation Relations in Quantitative Cases: Differential Equations

In this section it is shown how quantitative dynamic modelling methods from the area of calculus within Mathematics can be described by realisation relations. In Treur (2006, Section 7) it is discussed in which sense the derivative of a continuous variable at a certain time point can be viewed as a mediating state property for a past to future relationship in the form of a smoothness condition. In this section it is discussed in which form a realisation relation of such a mediating state property can occur. Let p be such a mediating state property (i.e., change rate) for variable x. How can this mediating state property be related to other state properties? As a special case, the relationship of (the value of) p to other state properties can focus on properties that can be expressed in terms of (the value of) x. A plain case of this idea is when a value v of p in a state is considered always to co-occur with this value v for some expression or function F in the value of x in the same state:

has_value(p, v) $\leftrightarrow$ $\exists w$ has_value(x, w) & $v = F(w)$

or

has_value(p, F(w)) $\leftrightarrow$ has_value(x, w)

This shows a bi-conditional form for the co-occurrence of the two properties in states, where the right hand side of the 'if and only if' is the realiser of the mediating state property at the left hand side (cf. Nagel, 1961, pp. 345-358; Kim, 1996, pp. 212-216). An alternative way to express the same biconditional relationship is:

$p(t) = F(x(t))$

Keeping in mind that the mediating state property p is the derivative of x, sometimes denoted by dx/dt the last way of expressing can be also written as

$dx/dt = F(x(t))$

This is the usual notation for a *differential equation*. These formats allow us to relate a mediating state property at time t to other state properties of the state at t. As an example, take the function F defined by:

$F(x) = \alpha x(1 - x/C)$

For this example, mediating state property p is related to another state property as follows:

has_value(p, $\alpha w(1 - w/C)$) $\leftrightarrow$ has_value(x, w)

Or, alternatively expressed:

$$p(t) = \alpha x(t)(1 - x(t)/C)$$

In the usual notation for a differential equation this is also formulated as

$$dx/dt = \alpha x(t)(1 - x(t)/C)$$

The differential equation based on this example function F describes (with the parameters α and C within a certain range; e.g., $\alpha = 0.5$ and $C = 10$) a logistic growth pattern with asymptotic value C (carrying capacity) and initial growth rate α.

It turns out that (first-order) differential equations can be understood from the conceptual framework based on 'temporal factorisation and realisation' as realisation relations for mediating state properties. The differential equation format

$$dx/dt = F(x(t))$$

expresses in a variety of cases how a mediating state property relates to another state property. Moreover, this can easily be extended to a system of differential equations, such as

$$dx/dt = F(x(t), y(t))$$
$$dy/dt = G(x(t), y(t))$$

where each of the mediating state properties dx/dt and dy/dt has a realisation relation to a combination of the state properties x and y, defined by F and G, respectively. In a discretised form a *difference equation* is obtained:

$$x(t') - x(t) \quad = \quad F(x(t))\,(t' - t)$$

or

$$\Delta x = F(x(t))\Delta t$$

with

$$\Delta x = x' - x \text{ and } \Delta t = t' - t$$

The patterns of relations used in the calculation based on this difference equation are depicted in Figure 2 (a picture similar to the one in Figure 1). Here, the lower line shows the successive states, with state properties indicating values for x by a_0, a_1, a_2 and a_3. Above each of these state properties, the mediating state property is depicted that is realised by it in the same state.

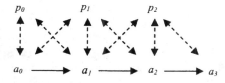

Figure 2 Mediating state properties realised in successive states

The vertical bi-arrow is exploited by calculating $F(a_i)$ from a_i. The arrow to the next state by adding the resulting mediating state property to the present a_i, thus obtaining, the state property a_{i+1} as a successor for a_i. In Section 5 it will be shown that a similar pattern of relations occurs in the context of qualitative dynamic modelling techniques such as transition systems, causal models, logical models and rule-based systems.

In summary, quantitative dynamic modelling approaches based on differential equations can be understood from the conceptual framework for dynamics based on temporal factorisation and realisation in the sense that they express realisation relations for mediating state properties. A characteristic of this area is that all state properties are based on variables and numerical values assigned to them. This excludes modelling approaches where dynamics is analysed based on qualitative state properties. In the next section such qualitative approaches are addressed.

Realisation Relations in Qualitative Cases: Causal, Rule-Based and Transition Systems

In this section qualitative dynamic modelling methods are considered. Examples of such methods are transition systems (e.g., Arnold, 1994), production or rule-based systems (e.g., Anderson, 1996; Buchanan and Shortliffe, 1984), causal models (e.g., Bosse et al., 2005), and executable temporal logic (e.g., Barringer et al., 1996; Fisher, 2005). These methods specify in a qualitative manner how a state in a system may change. These methods can be analysed from the perspective of temporal factorisation and realisation as described below. Viewed from an abstract perspective, the following format is used in such methods. In a rule[2] $c \twoheadrightarrow d$ with antecedent c and consequent d:

- the first description c indicates a combination of state properties for the current state
- the second description d indicates one or more state properties for the next state

As an illustration, a simple example scenario describes the following rules for preparing a cup of tea: getting hot water, getting a cup, getting a tea bag, and finally, by combining these, getting the tea.

$not\ hot\_water\_present \quad \twoheadrightarrow \quad hot\_water\_present$
$not\ cup\_present \quad \twoheadrightarrow \quad cup\_present$
$hot\_water\_present \wedge cup\_present \wedge not\ tea\_bag\_present$
$\quad \twoheadrightarrow \quad tea\_bag\_present$
$hot\_water\_present \wedge cup\_present \wedge tea\_bag\_present$
$\quad \twoheadrightarrow \quad tea\_present \wedge not\ tea\_bag\_present$

From the conceptual framework based on temporal factorisation and realisation such a rule can be understood as a relationship between mediating state properties and other state properties in the following manner. For example, for the second rule: if in a state *not cup_present* occurs, also a specific mediating state property $p1$ occurs in this state which anticipates on *cup_present*. Thus, any rule $c \twoheadrightarrow d$ can be interpreted as an implication $c \rightarrow p$, describing a logical relationship between state properties in a given state. In the current context, c can be considered a (single) realiser for p.

---

[2] So, what is called a rule here can have the form of a transition in a transition system, a production rule, a causal relation, or an executable temporal formula.

In the given specification this is the case because also the converse implication $p \rightarrow c$ holds (i.e., always if p occurs in a state, also c occurs). Thus the following biconditional realisation relations for mediating state properties $p1$ to $p5$ occur in the tea scenario:

$p1 \leftrightarrow$ not hot_water_present

$p2 \leftrightarrow$ not cup_present

$p3 \leftrightarrow$ hot_water_present ∧ cup_present ∧ not tea_bag_present

$p4 \leftrightarrow$ hot_water_present ∧ cup_present ∧ tea_bag_present

$p5 \leftrightarrow$ hot_water_present ∧ cup_present ∧ tea_bag_present

Here the mediating state properties $p1$ to $p5$ anticipate on respectively hot_water_present, cup_present, tea_bag_present, tea_present, not tea_bag_present. Some of the relationships as depicted in Figure 2 are for this case:

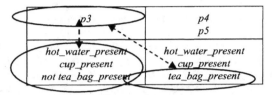

In a qualitative dynamic modelling approach, it is not always the case that all realisers are unique. For example, in the chosen specification, the mediating state property to have a tea bag present is based on the presence of hot water and cup. However, there may be alternative ways to achieve the presence of the tea bag, for example right at the start, based on the absence of a tea bag and absence of a cup; this would provide two multiple realisers for a mediating state property leading to the tea bag being present:

hot_water_present ∧ cup_present ∧ not tea_bag_present

and

not cup_present ∧ not tea_bag_present

Realisation Relations in Physics: Forces

In Section 2 the notion of momentum in Physics was mentioned as an example of a mediating state property for the notion of position. The state property momentum abstracts from the various histories that could have happened and would have resulted in the same mediating state property for the future. In the other time direction, no matter what future will arise, a momentum indicates from what pattern it originated, so it abstracts from futures. In some more detail, if for the variable x the position (on a line) of an object with mass m is taken, then the temporal factorisation of temporal relationships between positions before and after a certain time point t provides as a mediating state property the instantaneous velocity (or change rate of position) v of the object at time point t. Momentum of the object is obtained by $p = mv$, or by temporal factorisation of the quantity mx. In addition, Newton's second law $F = ma$ (with a the acceleration) can be fomulated as

$$m \, dv/dt = F \quad \text{or} \quad dp/dt = F$$

This shows how force can be obtained as a second-order mediating state property (the change rate of momentum, which itself is a first-order mediating state property).

A specific example, showing how a specific force can be realised, is the following. For the trajectory of an object in space, with mass m, approaching earth (with mass M), Newton's second law can be used in conjunction with his law of gravitation, for the interaction between the two objects involved (here x is the distance between the object and the earth, and c is a constant):

$$m \, d^2x/dt^2 = F$$
$$F = c \, mM/x^2$$

An assumption here is that no other interaction plays a role. In this case, the force-function identified is $F(x) = c \, mM/x^2$, as described by Newton's gravitation law. This provides a second-order differential equation for the distance x of the object to the earth, depending on time t:

$$m \, d^2x/dt^2 = c \, mM/x^2$$

Here, the left hand side provides the second-order mediating state property F and the right hand side is a realiser of this mediating state property: the equality guarantees that both properties will always co-occur in states. Note that in this case the (realised) second-order mediating state property leads to a not realised first-order mediating state property (a changed momentum) in a next state. In turn, this first-order mediating state property momentum leads to a next state in which the changed state property position occurs.

In Nagel (1961, pp. 186-192), the multiple realisation of the notion of force is discussed. In line with what was stated above, his analysis asserts that for various different situations specific force-functions, specifying how force relates to other properties of the state (and/or first-order mediating state properties) are needed. Forces can occur due to state properties involving, for example: the presence of an object pushing or pulling, deformation such as caused by collisions (e.g., billiard balls), the presence of objects with electrical charge, the presence of magnetic objects, the presence of other masses (gravitation), atmospheric pressures. For each of these circumstances, a different expression in terms of the world state ontology (a force-function) describes the force that occurs. Only if for a given situation such a force-function has been identified, something can be done using the laws of classical mechanics. In this sense, this case shows a heterogeneous situation, where past patterns and present states relating to a force mediating state property are described in some heterogeneous disjunctive form with at least, say, up to 5 to 10 essentially different contexts of the origin of the force. In this heterogeneous situation, in different contexts different force-functions (and hence realisers) are identified, which still allows succesful use of the notion of force in applications. This shows an example of an approach to multiple realisation, comparable to the notion of local or context-dependent reduction as described by Kim (1996), pp. 211-240.

Notice that an additive property for this mediating state property force holds in the following sense: the combined effect of any number of different contributions to the second-order mediating state property can be obtained by adding their values. So, any value w for this second-order mediating state property can be obtained as the combined effect from, for example, gravitation, electrical charge, and deformation by collision. For example, considering one dimension where all effects work along the same axis, this can occur in the form of an infinite number of possible sums $w = w_1 + w_2 + w_3$, where the terms are the contribution of one of the three effects (e.g., w_1 by gravitation, w_2 by electrical charge, w_3 by collision). This shows that the complete set of realisers Q can be infinite, and that in contexts can not always be separated.

Discussion

Mediating state properties obtained by temporal factorisation provide a quite general concept to describe dynamics. Special cases can be found, for example, in mental state properties in Cognitive Science and several concepts in Physics. In many (but not all) cases mediating state properties can be grounded in the (present) state in which they occur by relating them to realisers: other state properties or combinations thereof that co-occur with the mediating state property. These realisers often are useful in modelling and calculation of trajectories or traces over time, for example, by using diffferential equations to specify realisation relations. However, apart from this convenience, how necessary are these realisations?

On the one hand, a mediating state property may not be defined by relating it to another state property, but solely by its temporal relational specification. In this case, in principle mediating state properties can be left out as they do not add powers over and above the power of the direct 'past pattern implies future pattern' temporal relationships.

On the other hand, there is no harm in assuming them: what they are used for can also be done using temporal relationships without mediating state properties as state properties. So, a possible view is that the temporal relationships actually justify the postulation and use of mediating state properties as a convenient shorthand for more complex temporal specifications, in line with the position put forward in (Jonker, Treur and Wijngaards, 2002) that higher levels of conceptualisation often may pay off. If, in addition, realisation relations are known, then the mediating state property can become more than a convenient shorthand: a concept like any other concept, occurring in a network of relations to other concepts. In particular, this applies to mental state properties as a special case of mediating state properties.

Notice that the temporal factorisation principle is not a (first-order) law of nature. Due to its reference to and quantification over state properties it is a second-order principle. Therefore the temporal factorisation principle contributes another route in the direction of unification of cognition and nature, not based on common first-order laws, but on common second-order principles. Such second-order principles may play an important role in bridging the gap between different disciplines, as shown in this paper, but also within the discipline of Physics it turns out that they can play an important role, as Nagel (1961) has pointed out concerning Newton's laws (although there they sometimes mistakenly are called laws).

Acknowledgements
The author is grateful for feedback from and discussions with Mark Bickhard.

References

Anderson, J. R. (1996). ACT: A simple theory of complex cognition. *American Psychologist*, vol. 51, pp. 355-365.

Arnold, A. (1994). *Finite transition systems*. Semantics of communicating systems. Prentice-Hall, 1994.

Barringer, H., Fisher, M., Gabbay, D., Owens, R., and Reynolds, M., (1996). *The Imperative Future: Principles of Executable Temporal Logic*. Research Studies Press Ltd. and John Wiley & Sons.

Bennett, M. R., and Hacker, P. M. S. (2003). *Philosophical foundations of neuroscience*. Malden, MA: Blackwell.

Bickle, J. (1998). *Psychoneural Reduction: The New Wave*. MIT Press, Cambridge, Massachusetts.

Bickle, J. (2003). *Philosophy and Neuroscience: A Ruthless Reductive Account*. Kluwer Academic Publishers.

Bosse, T., Jonker, C.M., Meij, L. van der, and Treur, J., LEADSTO: a Language and Environment for Analysis of Dynamics by SimulaTiOn. In: Eymann, T., et al. (eds.), *Proc. of the Third German Conference on Multi-Agent System Technologies, MATES'05*. Lecture Notes in Artificial Intelligence, vol. 3550. Springer Verlag, 2005, pp. 165-178. Extended version to appear in *International Journal of Artificial Intelligence Tools*, 2007.

Buchanan, Bruce G. and Shortliffe, Edward H. (eds.) (1984). *Rule-Based Expert Systems*. MA: Addison-Wesley, 1984.

Davidson, D. (1993), Thinking Causes. In: J. Heil & A. Mele (eds.), *Mental Causation*. Clarendon Press, Oxford.

Jonker, C.M., Treur, J., and Wijngaards, W.C.A., (2002). Reductionist and Antireductionist Perspectives on Dynamics. *Philosophical Psychology Journal*, vol. 15, pp. 381-409.

Kim, J. (1996). *Philosophy of Mind*. Westview press.

Kim, J. (1998). *Mind in a Physical world: an Essay on the Mind-Body Problem and Mental Causation*. MIT Press, Cambridge, Mass.

Nagel, E. (1961). *The Structure of Science*. Routledge and Kegan Paul; Harcourt, Brace and World, London.

Treur, J., (2006). Temporal Factorisation and the Dynamics of Cognitive Agent States. In: R. Sun, N. Miyake (eds.), *Proc. of the 28th Annual Conference of the Cognitive Science Society, CogSci'06*, 2006, pp. 2275-2280. Extended version to apear in: *Cognitive Systems Research Journal*, 2007.

Sensitivity of primacy effect to interactions

Sylvie Huet (Sylvie.Huet@Cemagref.fr) and
Guillaume Deffuant (Guillaume.Deffuant@Cemagref.fr)
Cemagref, LISC,
BP 50085, 63172 AUBIERE CEDEX, France

Abstract

We propose an individual based model of attitude dynamics which, in some conditions, reproduces primacy effect behaviours. The primacy effect takes place when the attitude of an individual depends on the reception order of features describing an object. Typically, when receiving a strong negative feature first, the individual keeps a negative attitude whatever the number of moderate positive features it receives afterwards. We consider a population of individuals which receive the features from a media, and communicate with each other: in some cases, interactions increase the number of individuals exhibiting a primacy effect, in other cases they decrease this number. We study the sensitivity of this phenomenon to the interaction structure and to the part of the population with an initial negative attitude.

Introduction

"Attitude is a psychological tendency that is expressed by evaluating a particular entity with some degree of favour or disfavour". Attitudes have been postulated to motivate behaviour and to exert selective effects at various stages of information processing (Eagly and Chaiken 1998): information may be filtered by the individuals, i.e. they ignore it. Festinger in his theory of cognitive dissonance (1957) proposes some mechanisms for this selection: people seek out information that supports their attitudes and avoid information that challenges them, in order to minimise their cognitive dissonance. Following this theory, even if they assimilate information which contradicts their global attitude, people are reluctant to talk about it, because they avoid expressing their dissonance. Such selection mechanisms can imply sensitivity to the order of information delivery. Without making assumptions about selection mechanisms, Asch (1946), Miller and Campbell (1959) have shown one of the main known order effects: the primacy effect. The primacy effect occurs when somebody who encounters two opposing messages forms judgments more consistent with the first message.

Several researchers in social modelling include some effect of attitude on information transmission and vice-versa (Allport and Postman 1947; Lawson and Butts 2004; Galam 2003, Huet and Deffuant 2006; Tsimring and Huerta 2003). The bounded confidence models (see Urbig 2003 for a review) implement reception and emissions filters on attitudes or opinions. In the model of innovation diffusion of Deffuant et al. (2005), this opinion dynamics is coupled with a propagation of information. However, none of these models focuses specifically on the primacy effect and the interaction between individuals.

We propose a simple agent based model of individual primacy effect. We particularly focus on the following question: how an individual primacy effect is favoured or disfavoured by interactions in a population? The simple model we consider gives interesting tracks to explore. Indeed, in some cases, the number of agents showing primacy effect is significantly increased by interactions, and, in other cases, significantly decreased. This paper focuses on the impact on the primacy effect of various characteristics of the initial population with, or without interactions.

First, we describe the individual-based model. Using a simple example, we next present the primacy effect at the individual level and the influence of interactions on this effect. Then, we integrate these new results in a larger picture, including previous work (Huet and Deffuant 2006, 2007; Deffuant and Huet 2007, 2006). We finally study the primacy effect in populations with heterogeneous initial global attitudes.

A model of dynamics of attitudes exhibiting the primacy effect

We model the dynamics of attitude considering its links with information. Attitude formation and attitude change are linked to accumulation and organization of information about people, objects, situations and ideas.

The basis of our modelling consists of the dissonance theory (Festinger 1957) on the one hand, and on Allport's work on rumour diffusion (1947) on the other hand. We notice that individuals avoid incongruent information, and, keep only important information.

We consider a population of N individuals who discuss about an object. We define this object by a set of features $F = (1,2...,d)$, which are associated with positive or negative real values $(u_1,...,u_j,...,u_d)$ with $u_j \in \Re$. An individual can have a partial view of the object, in which case it has a real value for some features and nil for others. To simplify we use feature instead of feature value.

An individual i is characterised by:
- g: an initial attitude (suppose the same for all individuals in the following).
- L_i: a subset of F containing the features currently retained by the individual (empty at the beginning).

- $G_i = g + \sum_{j \in L_i} u_j$: global attitude about the object (related to information integration theory of Anderson (1971)),
- a neighbourhood corresponding to the subset of individuals with whom i can communicate.

The dynamics of the model have four main aspects:

1. **Exposure to feature values**: individuals are exposed to features diffused by the media or interaction between individuals.
2. **Selective retaining**: A feature is congruent when it has the same sign as the individual's global attitude to the object, incongruent otherwise: when $G_i u_j \geq 0$, feature j is said congruent for individual i, and incongruent otherwise. The dynamics of filtering are determined by a positive number, Θ the incongruence threshold. Being told about feature j, an individual will react as follows:
   ◊ If j is congruent → "retain the feature.
   ◊ If j is incongruent: if $|u_j| > \Theta$ → "retain the feature";
   otherwise "ignore the feature" .
   Here, "retain the feature" means that j is added to L_i (if L_i does not include j yet), "ignore the feature" means that the feature is filtered (not added to L_i).
3. **Selective emission**: individuals only talk about congruent features
4. **Computation of attitude**: an individual computes its global attitude each time it retains a new feature.

Moreover, we assume that a media delivers at each time step a randomly chosen feature to a fraction of the population called f.

In some cases, individuals are sensitive to order of feature reception and exhibit the primacy effect. We now describe when this phenomenon appears. We consider an individual with an initial attitude $g > 0$, and an object with at least one negative feature of absolute value higher than Θ, and positive features lower than Θ (the same reasoning can be done with inverted signs). In this case, the final attitude can depend on the reception order:

- If the individual receives the negative feature first, if g is low enough, it can change its global attitude, and the positive features become incongruent. As they are lower than Θ, they are not retained.
- If the individual receives the positive features first, these features are necessarily retained.

When the individual attitude is sensitive to the feature reception order, we can observe primacy effect: the individual's attitude sign is defined by the first few features it receives. This leads us to a more concrete example to help understand how the effect appears. We suppose that the initial attitude g is positive. Then we consider an object described by 5 features: two major negative ones, called U, such that $|U| > \Theta$, and three positive ones, called u, such that $u < \Theta$. We suppose that the object is globally neutral, that is: $3u + 2U = 0$. For instance, we choose $U = -6$ and $u = 4$, with $\Theta = 5$. Figures 1 show the evolution of a global

attitude, for a given reception order. Initially, our individual has an attitude $g = 6.5$. First, it receives a positive feature, which is retained because it is congruent, and its attitude increases to 10.5. Second, it receives a negative feature, which is incongruent, but is retained because its absolute value is higher than the threshold, and its attitude decreases to 4.5. Next, it receives the second negative feature, which is incongruent and also retained and its attitude decreases to -1.5. It is now going to be exposed to the fourth and the fifth positive features, which are incongruent with an absolute value below the threshold, and therefore they are not retained. Its attitude thus does not change anymore. It has finally a negative attitude although the object is globally neutral. The diagram on figure 2 shows the ten possible trajectories of attitude.

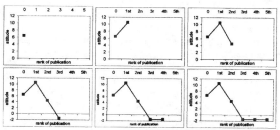

Figures 1. Example of temporal evolution of the attitude of an individual which receives features in order u, U, U, u, u

As all positive features are equal and all negative features are also equal, we just have to consider 10 different feature orders to describe all possible individual trajectories. Depending on the cases, the first, the two first, or at most, the three first features received determine the final sign of attitude: this is the primacy effect.

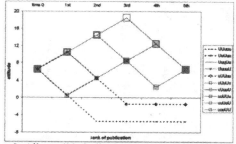

Figure 2. All possible individual trajectories in case $g = 6.5$, 5 features composed of 2 U and 3 u with $U = -6$ and $u = +4$

Individual primacy effect and population state: a particular interaction effect

With the help of the same simple example we have already used, we are now going to explain the particular effect of interaction on the final population state. This effect is pointed out by the comparison between the final state of a population of non-interacting individuals and the one of a population of interacting individuals. We will, afterward, synthesize all the knowledge we have about the conditions leading to this interaction effect.

The example for non-interacting individuals

A directly predictable global state. We consider now a population of isolated individuals, with the same initial attitude *g*. Each trajectory shown on figure 2 has the same probability of occurring. Thus we can read on figure 2 the final state of the population. Because we observe that 7 trajectories are finally positive, 70 % of population have a final positive attitude and, because we observe that 3 trajectories are finally positive, 30 % have a final negative attitude.

The major role of *g*, the initial attitude. We can observe on figure 3 (see dark bars) the final percentage of negative individuals for various values of the initial attitude, *g*. Horizontal axis represents the attitude intervals corresponding to one possible value of the effect defined as the percentage of final negative attitudes. Since we are on the zone of "primacy effect", from *g*>0 to *g*<|2*U*|, we observe its effect: from 80% to about 10% of individuals are finally negative. This takes place even though we have no negative individuals initially and a neutral global value for the object. This strong influence of the initial attitude *g* can be seen as the first primacy effect.

The example for individuals in interaction

We add interaction by a simple algorithm. We choose at random a couple (*i,j*) such as *j* is a neighbour of *i*. When the social network is all the population all *j≠i* is a neighbour of *i*. *i* tells *j* about one of its randomly chosen congruent features. The complete algorithm, containing exposure to the diffusion by media and exposure from interaction is:

For a population of *N* individuals, at each time step:
N times repeat:
- *Media diffusion.* choose individual *i* at random with probability *f*, choose feature *j* at random in the object, send feature *j* to individual *i*.
- *Interactions:* choose couple of individuals (*i,j*) at random; *i* tells *j* about one of its randomly chosen congruent features

Now, let see on our example how primacy effect can be amplified or decreased by the interactions. The population size is *N* = 5041.

Interactions can increase the number of primacy effects. Figure 3 shows a comparison of the number of final negative attitudes between the isolated and the interaction case. The isolated case is represented by black bars, and the interaction case is represented in grey bars (average results on 100 replications with minimum and maximum results).

We observe, on the left of the figure, that, for an initial attitude ranging from 0 to the absolute value of the most important incongruent feature (in this case -6), interactions induce more negative final attitudes than the isolated case. For example, for an initial attitude *g*=2.5 (0.5*u*<*g*<*u*), we obtain 83% of negative individuals with "interaction", but only 70% with the "isolated" case.

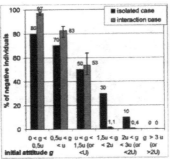

Figure 3. Final percentage of negative individuals for various values of *g* for both approaches: deduce from analysis and simulated with interaction

The interaction can decrease the effect of individual primacy effect. On the right of the figure 3, we note that for an initial attitude *g* = 8.5 (*g* between 2 and 3*u*), the isolated case yields 10% of negative individuals whereas the "interaction" yields only 0.4% of them (light bars). This is the "decrease" effect of interaction. This effect takes place for initial attitudes between *U* and 2*U*, which correspond to the values between the absolute value of the most negative feature *U* and the sum of the absolute values of positive features. This implies that this "decrease" interaction effect cannot be observed with object having only one negative feature.

We now have a look on the synthesis of all our previous results on this topic.

Interaction effect: synthesis of what we know

We have, in previous work, considered different variations of parameter values and dynamics. Deffuant and Huet, 2007; Huet and Deffuant, 2006, 2007 studied different ways to formulate the individual filters: based on constant attitudes, dynamic threshold value depending on current attitude value, individuals without emission filter. We considered a population of individuals divided in subscribers to media and non-subscribers (Huet and Deffuant, 2006). We better understand the effect of the initial attitude, studying the model with the help of an aggregated model (Deffuant and Huet 2006). For an object described by both negative and positive features, we considered various numbers of features, various global values of the object and various frequencies of diffusion features by media (Deffuant and Huet, 2007; Huet and Deffuant, 2007). We can do, from all of that, the following synthesis.

A primacy effect can appear when a proposed feature to an individual is differently treated by him, depending on its current attitude value or sign. It is observed when the object of diffusion is described by both negative and positive features, and when the features of one given sign (say negative) have a higher absolute value than the threshold Θ.

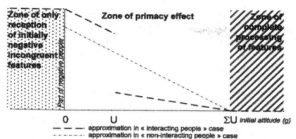

Figure 4. Final percentage of negative individuals for various values of initial attitudes when the object's description contains negative and positive features

When individuals interact, we can observe particular final states at the population level due to the difference between individuals and media in emission probability for each feature. In particular, as it is presented in the simple example applied to our model and summed-up in figure 4, interactions affect the number of individuals having finally a negative attitude due to the primacy effect:

1. This number increases when individuals have an initial attitude smaller than the absolute value of the most negative feature they are exposed to. This effect of interaction can be only explained by the existence of the individual reception filter. This occurs each time the object of discussion is described by more than two features.

2. This number decreases when individuals have an initial attitude value between the absolute value of the most negative feature and the absolute value of the sum of all negative features. This effect is due to the emission filter. This effect occurs only if the object of discussion is described by 5 or more features.

Increasing the number of features globally increases the interaction effect for a small value of initial attitude. Moreover, we have observed that the primacy effect still takes place on objects which are moderately negative or positive (i.e. not neutral).

Interaction effects persist for all values of diffusion frequency of features by media even if quantitative results are sensitive.

Minority and interaction structure effects on interaction effects

We now consider the sensitivity of interaction effect to various characteristics of the initial population, which is the main contribution of this paper. Firstly, we look at this effect for populations mixing negative and positive initial attitudes. Further on an individual with a negative (respectively positive) attitude is called "a negative" (respectively "a positive"). Then, we study the effect of interaction structures.

Impact of initially negatives randomly spatialized

Until now, we have considered a population of individuals having initially all the same attitude. Figure 5

shows the impact of introduction of negative individuals in the initial population. In case of "increase" interaction effect, we simply observe an additional increase of the final negative individual number. In case of "decrease" interaction effect, this is a little surprise to see that it is necessary to have much more than 30% of initial negative individuals (here 50% or 70%) to obtain more negative individuals than in the "no interaction" case.

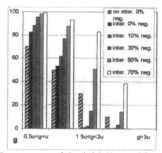

Figure 5. Percentage of the initially positive population which becomes negative for various initial parts of negative attitudes in the population

Indeed, initially negative individuals do not have a great effect because, even if they are negative they do not have, at the beginning, a negative feature and thus, they do not diffuse it. It is the reason why for example, even for 70% of initially negatives, only about 40 % of the initial 30% positives become negative during the simulation when g is comprised between $2u$ and $3u$.

Impact of initially negatives randomly spatialized and various interaction structures

We know three fundamental properties of large social interaction structures:

◊ the average path length is small; this means the number of people to link two randomly individuals of a population is quite small, about 5-6; this property implies information can easily quickly diffused in a network;

◊ the clustering coefficient is about 0.4, 0.5 on real networks (Watts and Strogatz, 1998); this means the probability of two of my friends to be also friends are quite important; on the contrary of the previous one, this property implies the diffusion is very slow because of the redundancy of links between individuals;

◊ the distribution of the number of neighbours for an individual follows a power law; this means few people know a large part of the population and many have a very small number of neighbours (Albert R. and Barabási A.-L., 2002).

Considering these three properties, we tested many possible values for each of them. We especially considered three different degree distributions (uniform, Poisson and scale free) with various average degrees; various values of clustering coefficient and average path length (various values of Beta on a Beta algorithm with a 2D lattice for substratum; random homogeneous and scale free networks);

We only present in the following figures the most relevant results.

Figures 6 and 7 show that the interaction structure has no significant impact on the "increase" and "decrease" interaction effects. Notice that we approximately observed the same result in case of average degree 3, 4, 6, 8 or 10. A very low average degree, like 1, can produce an effect but we can consider it as a particular case.

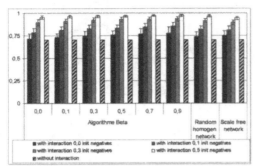

Figure 6. Part of the initially positive population becoming negative for g=2.5 (increase case), various networks, and various initial parts of negatives randomly located on the network (average degree 4)

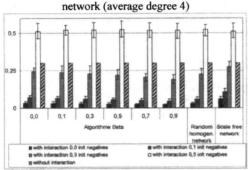

Figure 7. Part of the initially positive population which becomes negative for g=6.5 (decrease case), various networks, and various initial parts of negatives randomly located on the network (average degree 4)

Until now, we look at the effect of various interaction structures and parts of initially negatives which are randomly located in the network. We are now considering the case where initially negatives are all connected to each other.

Impact of initially negatives spatialized in clusters and various interaction structures

Practically, to initialise the population, we choose one individual at random and set it negative, then all its neighbours, and all neighbours of its neighbours and so on until we get the desired quantity of negatives. Figure 8 shows the results for the initially "clustered" negatives for

an average degree of 4 and a decrease PB situation. It appears that, the initial negatives have less effect when clustered than when randomly located. We particularly notice the quasi lack of sensitivity to clustered negatives when the structure is a regular lattice. We now study the specificity of each interaction structure to understand why.

The difference between clustered and random initial negatives is necessarily linked with the "geometry" of the initial boundary between positives and negatives. Indeed, only at this boundary negatives can send messages to positives, and thus can have an impact on the number of final negatives. Therefore, the larger this boundary, the higher is the effect of the initial negatives on the final result. Of course, the boundary is much smaller when the individuals are clustered, because then an important part of the initial negatives have their neighbours all negatives. When the negatives are randomly chosen, this part is much smaller. This explains why, in general, initially clustered negatives have a lower impact than when randomly distributed.

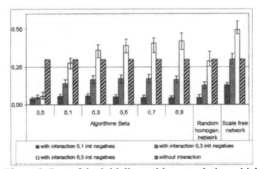

Figure 8. Part of the initially positive population which becomes negative for g=6.5 (decrease PB case), various networks, and various initial parts of negatives which are located in a unique cluster (average degree 4)

The reason for a particularly low effect of clustered negatives in a Von Neumann lattice is also related to the boundary: In such networks, the size of the boundary grows very slowly with the number of negatives (compared with the boundary size growth observed in random networks).

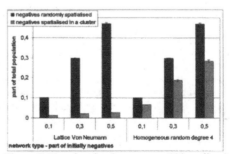

Figure 9. Frontier size (average on 100 replicas)

Figure 9 shows the size of the boundary, measured and averaged on 100 runs, for each considered network, each location condition and several initial parts of negatives. The boundary here comprises the negative individuals which have at least one positive neighbour. We notice, for a lattice, in the clustered case, that the size of frontier does not vary much with the part of initially negatives.

Conclusion and future research

We propose an individual based model of "information" filtering mainly based on the current attitude of an individual. Sensitive to the order of exposure to features of an object randomly diffused by media, the individual can exhibit the primacy effect. This takes place when the object includes features of one sign which are higher (in absolute value) than the filtering threshold, and features of the other sign which are lower (in absolute value) than this threshold. To fix the ideas, we suppose that negative features are higher (in absolute value) than the threshold, and positive features lower.

Interactions between individuals modify the proportion of individuals changing of attitude sign due to primacy effect: it is increased for individuals with an initial attitude lower than the absolute value of the negative major features; it is decreased for individuals with initial attitudes higher than the absolute value of the negative feature and lower than the absolute value of their sum.

These results have been established for a population having all the same features and a very simple way to discuss by pairs randomly chosen in the population. In this paper, we investigate further considering various initial state for the population (part of negatives/positives) and various properties of the interaction structures.

Our results show that the interaction structure does not significantly change the interaction effects. Introducing negative individuals in the initial population increases the final number of negatives. However, this increase is not as high as one can think, particularly in case of decrease primacy effect. Indeed, a negative individual has to receive a negative feature before diffusing it and the diffusion probability of negative features is thus not so high compared with the one of positive features.

Furthermore, we showed that, on a regular lattice, the initial number of negatives has no significant influence on the number of positives turning negatives.

We have found no social psychological references about of the effects of interactions on the "primacy effect". This theoretical work points out some potential properties of the primacy effect dynamics. However, before experimenting in laboratory on real individuals, further investigations should be done. Indeed, this work assumes the primacy effect is due to the individual current attitude. We know from Haugtvedt, C.P.; Wegener, D.T. (1994) that primacy effect appears especially in case of high relevance of the issue. In case of low relevance, recency effect appears. This conclusion can refute our results if we consider a high relevance of the issue implies a quite high attitude in

absolute value. This question has to be the object of further investigations.

References

Albert, R.; Barabasi, A.L. (2002). Statistical mechanics of complex networks. *Reviews Modern Physics*, 74-1, 47-97

Allport, G.W.; Postman; L. (1947). *The psychology of rumor*. Russel & Russell, Inc., 1947, 1965.

Asch, E.S. (1946). Forming Impressions of Personality. *J. of Abnormal and Social Psychology*, 41:258-290.

Deffuant, G.; Huet, S. and Amblard, F. (2005). An individual-based model of innovation diffusion mixing social value and individual payoff dynamics. *American Journal of Sociology*, 110-4, January, pp.1041-1069.

Deffuant, G. and Huet, S. (2007). Propagation effect of filtering incongruent information. *J. of Business Research*, 9 p., forthcoming.

Deffuant, G. and Huet, S., (2006). Collective Reinforcement of First Impression Bias. *Proceedings of the First World Congress on Social Simulation, Kyoto* (Japan), August.

Deffuant, G.; Weisbuch, G.; Amblard, F.; Faure, T. (2003). Simple is beautiful... and necessary. *JASSS*, 6(1).

Eagly, A.H.; Chaiken, S. (1993). *The psychology of attitudes*. Thomson/Wadsworth; 1993, 1998, 800 pages

Festinger, L. (1957) *A Theory of Cognitive Dissonance*. Stanford, CA: Stanford University Press.

Galam, S. (2003). Modelling rumors: the no plane Pentagon French hoax case. *Physica A*. Vol. 320., pp 571-580.

Haugtvedt, C.P.; Wegener, D.T. (1994). Message Order Effects in Persuasion: An Attitude Strength Perspective. *Journal of Consumer Research, 21:205-218*.

Huet, S. and Deffuant, G. (2006). Effets d'un filtre cognitif sur la diffusion d'information. *Proc. MOSIM* 2006, Rabat.

Huet, S. and Deffuant G. (2007). When do interactions increase or decrease primacy bias? Int. conference *Model To Model*, March 2007, Marseille, 19 p.

Lawson, G.; and Butts, C.T. (2004). "Information Transmission Through Human Informants: Simulation", *Proceedings of CASOS'04*.

Miller, N. and Campbell D. T. (1959). Recency and primacy in persuasion as a function of the timing of speeches and measurements. *J. Abnormal & Social Psychology*, 59, 1-9

Tsimring, L.S.; and Huerta, R. (2003). Modeling of Contact Tracing in Social Networks. *Physica A*, 325, pp. 33-39.

Urbig, D. (2003). Attitude Dynamics With Limited Verbalisation Capabilities. *Journal of Artificial Societies and Social Simulation* (JASSS). vol. 6 no. 1.

Watts D.J. and Strogatz S.H. (1998). Collective dynamics of Small-world networks. *Nature*, 393, 440-442.

False Memories in the DRM paradigm: Role of Suggestion and Context

Gaën Plancher (gaen.plancher@univ-paris5.fr)
Serge Nicolas (serge.nicolas@univ-paris5.fr)
Pascale Piolino (pascale.piolino@univ-paris5.fr)
Laboratoire de Psychologie et de Neurosciences Cognitives, Université Paris Descartes, CNRS
71, avenue Edouard Vaillant 92774 Boulogne-Billancourt
Cedex FRANCE

Abstract

Suggestion in the case of eyewitness memory often leads to false recall of this information. We hypothesized that varying the quantity of details associated with the material could modify the type of judgement associated to these false memories. We adapted the suggestion to the DRM paradigm (Deese, 1959; Roediger & McDermott, 1995) and to the Remember/Know paradigm (Tulving, 1983; 1985). At the same time we manipulated the level of visual details associated to the words. The experimenter suggested the existence of the non-presented word, either by simply inquiring as to its presence (moderate suggestion), or by affirming its presence (strong suggestion); a condition without suggestion was used as a control. False recognitions occurred at a greater rate when the suggestion was strong and were more associated with "know" than "remember" judgements. Moreover, false memories were more often associated with remember judgements under the condition without details.

Introduction

Bartlett (1932) observed that his subjects often created false memories and concluded that memory is a reconstruction of events rather than a reproduction. We know also that after a long retention interval, the memory of an event loses some details (Johnson, Hashtroudi & Lindsay, 1993). In addition, when items are without detail, false memories occur more frequently than with a detailed material (Dodson, Koutstaal & Schacter, 2000). Thus, the quality and the conscious experience associated with a memory both change over time. After a long retention interval, false memories become more a recollection than a simply feeling of familiarity (Roediger, Jacoby & McDermott, 1996; Frost, 2000). In fact, the delay causes the loss of detail. Therefore, we hypothesized that varying the quantity of details associated with the material to be learned could modify the state of consciousness associated with the memory of false information. The role of the enrichment of visual information in encoding is investigated here in the framework of false memory occurring after suggestion.

Koriat, Goldsmith and Pansky (2000) stress the fact that for some years human memory has principally been studied with methodologies oriented toward the quality such as the measurement of accuracy rather than quantity, which had been the focus of much traditional memory research. The quantity of articles published about false memories increases constantly but what is called false memory is not always clear (Pezdek & Lam, 2007). Schacter and Curran (2000) define false memory as the conscious recall of an event which never happened.

With the aim of isolating the factor to be studied, researchers tend to create a perfectly controlled and thus minimalist situation. To understand false memories, it was necessary to develop a paradigm which allowed frequent intrusion of false memories while limiting confounding variables. The first empirical study demonstrating false recalls in a list-learning paradigm was conducted by Deese (1959). This paradigm was subsequently modified by Roediger and McDermott (1995). Participants saw lists of words and were required to remember all the words on the list. All lists of items were semantically related to a single, non-presented item (referred to as the critical lure). For instance *hill, valley, climb, summit, top, molehill, peak, plain, glacier, goat, bike, climber, range, steep, ski* are all strongly semantically associated to the critical lure *Mountain*. When we asked participants to freely recall lists or to recognize items on the lists among distractor items, subjects often falsely reported that non-presented critical lures had been experienced in the earlier study lists.

Another way to create false memories is to suggest false information to the subject. According to Schacter (1999), suggestion causes the incorporation of information provided by others into one's own recall of events, is one of the seven sins of memory. Some experiments have shown that the way in which a question concerning the past is formulated can influence what a person claims to remember (McCloskey & Zaragoza, 1985; Loftus, 1975; 1979; Loftus, Miller & Burn, 1978). These authors studied the effect of misleading post-event information (MPI) on memory. In this MPI paradigm, participants are exposed to an event; they are later misinformed about some details, and are finally given a forced recognition test requiring a choice between the original and suggested details.

It is important to know if the phenomenological conscious experience associated to memory of misinformation is a feeling of recollection or a feeling of familiarity. In fact, if the phenomenology is more a familiarity than a recollection, the confidence of false memory should be lower. Thus false memory could disappear more easily than false memory with episodic details like in the case of recollection. This can be assessed with Tulving's remember/know paradigm (1983; 1985). Tulving proposed that there are two mind–brain systems, *episodic* and *semantic* memory, and that one of their distinguishing characteristics is that they give rise to two different kinds of consciousness: *autonoetic* and *noetic*. These two kinds of consciousness are, in turn, expressed in two kinds of subjective experiences: *remembering* and *knowing*. Remembering involves travelling back in time mentally to previous personal event and what was experienced at the time of its original occurrence, i.e. the context of encoding (see Tulving,

2002). Knowing does not entail any such experience but involves a more abstract awareness of personal events for which memory is experienced only in a factual way, without any awareness of mentally reliving those events. Later, some authors added the judgement "guess"(G) to the list including "know"(K) and "remember"(R) (Gardiner, Ramponi & Richardson-Klavehn, 1998). In recent years, the phenomenology associated with false memories has received increased attention. Without misinformation, the phenomenology associated with false memory is more R than K in the DRM paradigm (Roediger & McDermott, 1995), but the memory of misinformation was more likely to be associated with a K judgement than with a R judgement after a short retention interval (Roediger, Jacoby & McDermott, 1996). However, after a long retention interval, R judgements are more frequent (Frost, 2000).

Two complementary hypothesis have been proposed to explain the fact that the phenomenology changes with a delay: the source monitoring hypothesis (Johnson, Hashtroudi & Lindsay, 1993) and the distinctiveness heuristic (Dodson, Koutstaal & Schacter, 2000).

The source monitoring hypothesis claims our ability to distinguish our memories from our imagination depends on the recall of the source of information. This hypothesis predicts that misinformation is more likely remembered as the amount of perceptual detail associated with an event decreases. Thereby, as details decrease with delay, R judgments increase in the same time. We hypothesised that the presence of detailed visual information with semantic information in the encoding phase could disturb semantic categorization of the material and reinforce the control of the source and sense of remembering during recall and recognition. Moreover, if there is no detail, the critical item may not evoke a feeling of familiarity and as a result the source of this item, perception or imagination, may not be controlled. In this case, this critical lure will become more associated to R than K judgments without detail.

The second hypothesis, the distinctiveness heuristic refers to a decision rule whereby absence of memory for expected distinctive information is taken as evidence that an event is new, and thus not previously experienced (Dodson, Koutstaal & Schacter, 2000). It was shown that studying items accompanied by pictures, instead of as words alone, dramatically reduces false recognition rates (Schacter, Israel & Racine, 1999; Israel & Schacter, 1997). The authors argued that this reduction of false memories after picture presentation occurs because the participants use the distinctiveness heuristic. In fact, when the subject tries to remember the information, they demand access to pictorial information as a basis for judging items as previously studied. Absence of memory for this distinctive information indicates that the item is new. By contrast, participants who studied only words would not expect detailed recollections about studied items and therefore, would not base recognition decisions on the presence or absence of memory for distinctive information.

Thus, accompanying the stimuli likely to produce false memories with distinctive information, like visual information, could reinforce the control of the source and develop a distinctiveness heuristic that will reduce false memory. Bruce, Phillips, Conrad and Bona (2004)

presented words of the DRM paradigm with a context such as: an edge around each word (circle, rhombus, etc.), a variable police force, a small drawing on the left of the word (crab, dinosaur, engine or revolver), etc. This study showed that the false recognition rate was lower when there was context.

Therefore, in the present study, we associated for the first time the DRM paradigm (Deese, 1959; Roediger & McDermott, 1995) with suggestion and with the RKG paradigm (Tulving, 1983; 1985). In addition, we manipulated the enrichment of visual information associated to the words. Our first aim was to test the effect of suggestion in the DRM paradigm on the quantity of false recognition and on the phenomenology associated to false recognitions. We predicted that more suggestion will be strong, more false recognitions will occur and R judgments will decrease. Our second aim was to assess the effect of an enrichment of the visual information on false recall, false recognitions and phenomenology. We predicted that false memories and R judgements will be lower in a condition with enrichment than in a condition without enrichment.

Method

Participants

We recruited 133 undergraduate psychology students as participants from the University Paris Descartes, France. But we removed 13 subjects who presented extreme values, we kept thus 120 participants. Ages of the participants varied from 18 to 27 years old (M = 21.65). 32 participants were male and 88 were female. Students received course credit as a compensation for their participation. They were randomly assigned to one of the six conditions (each with 20 participants) which resulted from the crossing of the type of suggestion and the presence of enriched visual information. Participants were tested individually and did not know the aim of the experiment. They gave informed consent to the experimental procedure.

Materials

The present study was composed of six experimental conditions. The material common to all conditions was as follows: a succession of 12 lists of 15 words, each list connected semantically to the same topic, but the name of the topic itself was not presented in the list. The experiment was conducted in French, so the lists were in French. As an example, translating into English, the words *steps, go up, floor, go down, banister, lift, wood, spiral, building, height, weariness, fall, high, low* and *ladder* were in one list all related to the critical lure *stairway*.

For conditions without enrichment, words were written in lowercase, were presented in black on a light blue background and font of the words was 96 and Times New Roman. For conditions with enrichment, we added visual information to the lists of words. The enrichment consisted in variation along three different dimensions: the background colour, which could be red, blue, green, yellow or white; the font, which could be Castellar, Times New Roman, or Bauhaus 93; and finally, the case of the letters in the word, uppercase or lowercase. All of the settings on these three dimensions were crossed randomly. For example the word *"banister"* was accompanied with a blue colour, written in Castellar and in uppercase. Words were presented using PowerPoint software, using an automatic scheduler. Each word was presented for 1 second, and each list presentation lasted 15 seconds.

Design

We manipulated three types of suggestion: no suggestion, moderate suggestion (question) and strong suggestion (statement). The second factor manipulated was the enrichment of visual information and comprised two dimensions: either the words were enriched by visual information or they were presented without. This variable was between-subjects and was crossed with the factor suggestion. Each subject underwent only one of the conditions.

To compare the influence of the various dimensions of suggestion and enrichment, we evaluated subjects' performance in different ways. To estimate the effect of suggestion, we measured the number of critical lures falsely recognized and the percentage of judgements associated with the recognition: R,K,G. To test the effect of the enrichment, we measured the average number of critical items recalled, the average number of critical recognitions and the percentage of associated judgements.

Procedure

Participants were tested individually. They were told that they would see 12 lists of 15 words each in the screen of the computer. Then the experimenter said to the subjects that their memory would be tested by a free recall on a sheet of paper immediately after the presentation of each list, specifying that the recall would be limited to 45 seconds. The experiment could then take several forms according to the type of suggestion (see figure 1.).

For the condition without suggestion we did not intervene at any time. After the first list presentation the subject recalled the words he remembered, and then the second list was presented, the subject recalled, and so on until the recognition test.

For the conditions with suggestion, if the participant did not recall the critical lure, we suggested false memories, either with a question (moderate suggestion), or with a statement (strong suggestion). If the suggestion was a question, the experimenter said for example after the recall of the list: "Were *fall* and *stairway* in the list?". The words suggested were one non-recalled target word (ex: *fall*) and the list's critical lure (ex: *stairway*) if it was not recalled. If the suggestion was a statement, after the recall the experimenter said for example "There were also *fall* and *stairway*". In these both conditions, if the critical lure was falsely recalled, the experimenter suggested two non-recalled target words (ex: *fall* and *spiral*). We proceeded in this manner after each list. When the 12 lists were presented, we finished with a test of recognition (see figure 2.). The test was composed of 94 items: 12 critical items (not presented), 35 target items (presented), 47 false alarms (not presented) either slightly connected or not connected to the topic of the lists. The participants were asked to judge whether the word was old or new. If they chose "old", We asked the subject to report if he "remembered" that the word was in the list, if he simply "knew" that it was in the list or if he "supposed" it was in the list. On average the experiment took about 25 minutes.

		Type of suggestion		
		No	Moderate (question)	Strong (statement)
Presentation	Enrichment	Banister	Go up	BUILDING
	No enrichment	Spiral	Steps	Fall
Recall		yes	yes	yes
After the recall		Nothing	"Were *fall* and *stairway* in the list?"	"There were also *fall* and *stairway*"
Recognition		yes	yes	yes

Figure 1: Procedure according the experimental condition

	Old	New	Remember R	Know K	Guess G
Spiral					
Stairway					
Bird					
Love					

Figure 2: Example of the recognition test

Results

Mean of target recalls and recognitions, critical recalls and recognitions and last RKG judgements associates were computed for each participant and are given in Table 1 for each experimental condition. We wished to have homogeneous groups in the production of false recalls so that differences between subjects would not skew the influence of suggestion. We thus removed subjects with false recall rates more than 2 standard deviations away from the mean (13 subjects). Then an analyse of variance (ANOVA) showed no main effect of the suggestion on the false recalls [F(2, 114)=1.35, n.s.]. Consequently, we had a constant base of false recall.

We performed an ANOVA of the false recognitions data with three different suggestions and the presence of enrichment. There was a significant main effect of suggestion [F(2, 114)=14.19, p<0.001], indicating that the group with strong suggestion (statement) falsely recognized more critical lures than other groups [F(1, 114)=27.55, p<0.001]. But no difference was shown on the false recognitions between the moderate suggestion (question) and the none suggestion [F(1,114)=0.82, n.s.].

In addition, a main effect of suggestion was found on K judgements associated to false recognitions, indicating that the group with strong suggestion made more K judgements than the other groups [F(2, 114)=10.24, p<0.001]. On the other hand, a main effect of suggestion was found on G judgements, indicating that the group with no suggestion and moderate suggestion made more G judgements than the group with strong suggestion [F(2, 114)=5.40, p<0.006]. No difference between the suggestion groups was found for R judgements [F(2, 114)=1.42, n.s.]. No main effects of the enrichment of visual information appeared on false recalls [F(1, 118)=0.24, n.s.] or on false recognitions [F(1, 114)=1.47, n.s.]. But a significant main effect of enrichment appeared on R judgements [F(1, 114)=5.09, p=0.03]: with no enrichment conditions showed more R judgements than with enrichment conditions. Moreover, no effect was found on K and G judgements (for K, [F(1, 114)=1.04, n.s.], for G, [F(1, 114)=2.13, n.s.]. No significant interaction effects between suggestion and enrichment were found on any measure.

Table 1: Mean of false recall, false recognitions and memory judgements according to the experimental condition.

Suggestion	Context	False Recalls/12	False Recognitions/12	Memory judgement Percentages of R/K/G on the total of false recognition		
				Remember R	Know K	Guess G
No	*No*	2.55	8	.46	.23	.31
	Yes	2.85	8.65	.42	.24	.34
Question	*No*	2.05	8.6	.56	.17	.27
	Yes	2.4	6.95	.49	.23	.28
Statement	*No*	2.9	11.2	.54	.38	.08
	Yes	2.7	11.5	.32	.44	.24

Discussion

This paper examined the state of consciousness associated to false recognitions resulting from suggestion by comparing a situation where visual information was enriched and a condition without enrichment. To do so, we manipulated, for the first time, the type of suggestion and we combined two paradigms: the DRM paradigm (Deese, 1959; Roediger & McDermott, 1995) and the RKG paradigm (Tulving, 1983; 1985).

First, we found that the strong suggestion condition frequently induced false memories. In fact, the number of false recognitions was significantly higher when the suggestion was a statement rather than a question or when there was none. These results confirm previous findings observed with the misinformation paradigm (McCloskey & Zaragoza, 1985; Loftus, 1975; 1979a;

Loftus, Miller & Burn, 1978). Thus, firstly we can conclude that strong suggestion or misinformation leads to false recognitions in the DRM paradigm.

But our results showed that false recognitions occurred more under strong suggestion; moderate suggestion (question) did not lead to more false recognitions than no suggestion. Thus, simple exposure to false information is not more detrimental to memory than non-exposure. The effect of strong suggestion on memory may result from a reaction to the authority of the experimenter and not from the exposure itself. Many works in social psychology have focused on the effects of authority (Asch, 1956; Milgram, 1956; Blass, 1999). For instance, Asch (1956) showed that judgements of non-ambiguous object, such as the evaluation of the length of their segments can be influenced by suggestion from the majority or a leader. We can suppose that authority effects could occur in memory also and lead subjects to deform their memory under pressure from authority.

Second, we confirm also results showing that memory of misinformation was more likely to be associated with know rather than remember judgments in the situation with strong suggestion (Roediger, Jacoby & McDermott, 1996; Frost, 2000). In fact, we found that in the DRM paradigm, the group with strong suggestion made more K judgments associated to false recognitions than other groups. As previously, this effect found in the misinformation paradigm is replicated in the DRM paradigm.

Third, we found that visual enrichment decreased the frequency of R judgments, regardless of the type of suggestion. This is consistent with the idea that an unfulfilled expectation of detailed source memory leads to decrease confidence in evoked false memory traces. This could explain the reduction of false memory with image presentation compare to words (Dodson et al., 2000; Schacter et al., 1999; Israel & Schacter, 1997; Bruce et al., 2004). However, in our study the complexity of material did not decrease the probability of false recalls and recognitions, most likely because the enrichment of visual information was very poor and not linked to semantic information. This reason could also explain the absence of interaction between kind of suggestion and presence of enrichment.

Nevertheless the enrichment of visual information has an effect on recollection (R judgments) even if it is poor and unlinked. It would be interesting to test the state of consciousness associated to words with a linked enrichment, as in image presentation, to confirm this result.

In the daily life, these results suggest that to avoid confident recollection of false information, it would be better to present memory material in a detailed context rather than without distinctive information. Moreover, it should be helpful to tell people who want to learn something to pay attention to the context associated with central information in order to avoid forming false memories.

In conclusion, we showed that suggestion can cause false memories in the DRM paradigm, possibly because of an authority effect, and that these false memories are more associated with a feeling of familiarity than false memories that emerge without suggestion. In addition we showed that presentation of DRM words with an enrichment of visual information compared to words alone causes a reduction in the feeling of recollection. This reduction of confidence could explain the diminution of false memory in image presentation. Last, we suggest that a way to avoid false memory is to focus on detailed information that comes along with semantic information.

Acknowledgements

We thank anonymous reviewers for helpful comments on the earlier version of this manuscript. We thank also Paul Reeve and Sebastien Pacton for theirs re-readings.

Reference

Asch, S. (1956). Studies of independence and conformity in minority of one against an unanimous majority. *Psychological monographs, 70,* 416.

Bartlett, F.C. (1932). *Remembering: A study in experimental and social psychology.* Cambridge, England: Cambridge University Press.

Binet, A. (1900). *La suggestibilité.* Paris : Schleicher frères.

Blass, T. (1999). The Milgram paradigm after 35 years: Some things we now know about obedience to authority. *Journal of Applied Social Psychology, 29,* 955-978.

Bruce, D., Phillips-Grant, K., Conrad, N. & Bona, S.. (2004). Encoding context and false recognition memories. *Memory, 12,* 562-570.

Deese, J. (1959). On the prediction of occurrence of particular verbal intrusions in immediate recall. *Journal of Experimental Psychology, 58,* 17-22.

Dodson, C. S., Koutstaal, W. & Schacter, D.L. (2000). Escape from illusion: reducing false memories. *Trends in Cognitive Science, 4,* 391-397.

Gardiner, J. M., Ramponi, C. & Richardson-Klavehn, A. (1998). Experiences of remembering, knowing, and guessing. *Consciousness and Cognition, 7,* 103-7.

Johnson, M.K., Hashtroudi, S. & Lindsay, D.S. (1993). Source monitoring, *Psychological Bulletin, 114,* 3-28.

Johnson, M.K. (1997). Source monitoring and memory distortion. *Philosophical Transaction of the Royal Society of London. Series B. Biology Sciences, 352,* 1733-45.

Koriat, A., Goldsmith, M. & Pansky, A. (2000). Toward a psychology of memory accuracy. *Annual Review of Psychology, 51,* 481-537.

Loftus, E. F. (1975). Leading questions and the eyewitness report. *Cognitive Psychology, 7,* 560-572.

Loftus, E.F., Miller, D.G. & Burns, H.J. (1978). Semantic integration of verbal information into a visual memory. *Journal of Experimental Psychology, 4,* 19-31.

Loftus, E. F. (1979). Eyewitness testimony, Harvard University Press Cambridge, Mass.

Loftus, E.F. (2003). Our changeable memories: legal and practical implications. *Nature Review Neuroscience, 4,* 231-234.

McCloskey, M. & M. Zaragoza (1985). Misleading postevent information and memory for events: arguments and evidence against memory impairment hypotheses. *Journal of Experimental Psychology General, 114*(1): 1-16.

Milgram, S. (1956). Group pressure and action against a person. *Journal of Abnormal Social Psychology, 25*, 115-129.

Pezdek, K. & Lam, S. (2005). What research paradigms have cognitive psychologists used to study "False memory," and what are the implications of these choices? *Consciousness and Cognition, 16*, 2-17.

Roediger, H.L. & McDermott, K.B. (1995). Creating false memories: remembering words not presented in lists. *Journal of Experimental Psychology: Learning, Memory and Cognition, 21*, 803-814.

Roediger, H.L. & Gallo, D.A. (2004). Associative memory illusions. Chapter 17. In: R. Pohl (Ed.), *Cognitive illusions: Fallacies and biases in Judgement, Thinking, and Memory.* Oxford: Oxford University Press".

Schacter, D.L. (1999). The seven sins of memory: Insights from psychology and cognitive neuroscience. *American Psychologist, 54*, 182-203.

Schacter, D.L. & Curran T. (2000). Memory without remembering and remembering without memory: Implicit and false memories. In M.S Gazzaniga. (Ed.), *The New Cognitive Neurosciences.* (2nd Ed.). Cambridge: MIT Press.

Tulving, E. (1983). *Elements of episodic memory.* Oxford University Press New York.

Tulving, E. (1985). Memory and consciousness, *Canadian Psychology, 26*, 1-12.

Tulving, E. (2002). Episodic Memory: From Mind to Brain. *Annual Review of Psychology, 53*, 1-25.

Temporal Differentiation of Attentional Processes

Tibor Bosse[1] (tbosse@cs.vu.nl)
Peter-Paul van Maanen[1,2] (peter-paul.vanmaanen@tno.nl)
Jan Treur[1] (treur@cs.vu.nl)

[1]Vrije Universiteit Amsterdam, Department of Artificial Intelligence
De Boelelaan 1081a, 1081 HV Amsterdam, The Netherlands
[2]TNO Human Factors, P.O. Box 23, 3769 ZG, Soesterberg, The Netherlands

Abstract

In this paper an analysis of the notion of attention is described that comprises a differentiation according to five stages of an attentional process related to action selection and performance. The first stage deals with the allocation of attention to external and internal stimuli, the second with examination and analysis, the third with decision making and action selection, the fourth with action preparation and performance, and the fifth with action assessment. The analysis involves temporal formalisation and validation based on data from a human operator executing a warfare task.

Introduction

In the literature on attention, an assumption often implicitly made is that attention is a single, homogeneous concept (e.g., Itti and Koch, 2001; Theeuwes, 1994). However, in recent years, an increasing amount of work is aimed at identifying different subprocesses of attention. For example, many researchers distinguish at least two types of attention, i.e. perceptual and decisional attention (e.g., Pashler, 1998). Some others even propose a larger number of functionally different subprocesses of attention (e.g., Laberge, 2002; Parasuraman, 1998). However, most of these studies describe the different subprocesses of attention in an informal manner. In contrast, the current paper explores the possibility of describing different subprocesses of attention in more detail, using formal techniques from areas such as Artificial Intelligence. According to this perspective, the following research question is formulated (in the context of a situation where multiple objects exist and where actions have to be undertaken with respect to these objects):

Is it possible to formally define a temporal differentiation of a number of subprocesses within an attentional process?

A first answer to this question could be affirmative in the sense that, for example, attention to examine a number of options, attention to prepare for a selected action, and attention to assess the effects of an action performed, seem different types of attention. This results in the hypothesis that such a differentiating definition indeed is possible.

Being able to distinguish between different types of attentional processes can be beneficial for a number of reasons. First of all, on a theoretical level, the attempt can be used to enhance the understanding of the attentional processes. But on a more practical level it can be beneficial as well. For example, in the domain of naval warfare, a crucial but complex task is tactical picture compilation. In this task, the naval warfare officer has to compile a tactical picture of the situation in the field, based upon the information (s)he observes on a computer screen. Since the environment in these situations is often complex and dynamic, the warfare officer has to deal with a large number of tasks in parallel. Therefore, in practice (s)he is often supported by automation that takes over part of these tasks. However, a problem is how to determine an appropriate work division between human and system. Within a rapidly changing environment, such a work division cannot be fixed beforehand (Bainbridge, 1983; Campbell, Cannon-Bowers, Glenn, Zachary, Laughery, and Klein, 1997; Inagaki, 2003). A solution to this is to let the system determine such a task allocation at runtime: the system decides which of the tasks it takes over from the user, and which tasks it leaves to the user. This is a setting in which it can be very useful for the system to have information about the particular attentional state or process a user is in. For example, in case the user has just started to prepare for performing an action with respect to a certain track on the screen, it will be better to leave that track for him or her, whereas it is better to take over some of the tracks for which there is only attention of an examinational type or no attention at all.

To answer the above mentioned question on attentional process differentiation in a more systematic manner, in relation to a specific type of sense-reason-act cycle, in this paper five attentional subprocesses are distinguished and formally defined. These characterisations not only refer to state aspects, such as gaze directions, but also to temporal aspects for the time interval in which the state occurs. The temporal specifications identified have been validated in an empirical case study. This validation has been performed by representing the empirical data in a formal manner and by automatically checking the temporal specifications against this formally represented empirical data.

The structure of the paper reflects the research method used. First, at a conceptual level, different types of attentional processes were distinguished and an empirical case study was chosen. The empirical data were formally represented to enable automated analysis, and the different attentional processes were formalised in a temporal manner. Finally, validation of these specifications for the empirical material was performed in an automated manner using the TTL software environment (Bosse, Jonker, Meij, Sharpanskykh and Treur, 2006).

Distinguishing Attentional Processes

This section provides a (temporal) differentiation of an attentional process into a number of different types of subprocesses. The attentional process is considered in the context of a situation where multiple objects occur and where actions have to be undertaken with respect to (some of) these objects, for example as in the case study described below. To differentiate the process into subprocesses, a cycle *sense – examine – decide – prepare and execute action – assess action effect* is used. It will be discussed how different types of attention within these phases can be distinguished.

- *attention allocation*

This is a subprocess in which attention of a subject is drawn to an object by certain exogenous (stimuli from the environment) and endogenous (e.g., goals, expectations) factors, see, e.g., (Theeuwes, 1994). At the end of such an 'attention catching' process an attentional state for this object is reached in which gaze and internal focus are directed to this object. The informal temporal specification of this *attention allocation process* is as follows:

> From time t1 to t2 attention has been allocated object O iff
> at t1 a combination of external and internal triggers related to object O
> occurs, and at t2 the mind focus and gaze are just directed to object O.

Note that in this paper validation only takes place with respect to gaze and not to mind focus, as the empirical data used have no reference to internal states.

- *examinational attention*

Within this subprocess, attention is shared between or divided over a number of different objects. Attention allocation is switched between these objects, for example, visible in the changing gaze. The informal temporal specification of this *examinational attentional process* is as follows:

> During the time interval from t1 to t2 examinational attention occurs iff
> from t1 to t2 for a number of different objects attention is allocated
> alternatively to these objects.

- *decision making attention*

A next subprocess distinguished is one in which a decision is made on which object to select for an action on a certain object to be undertaken. Such a *decision making attentional process* may have a more inner-directed or introspective character, as the subject is concentrating on an internal mental process to reach a decision. Temporal specification of this attentional subprocess involves a criterion for the decision, which is based on the relevance of the choice made; it is informally defined as follows:

> During the time interval from t1 to t2 decision making attention occurs iff
> at t2 attention is allocated to an object, from which the relevance is higher
> than a certain threshold.

- *action preparation and execution attention*

Once a decision has been made for an action, an *action preparation and execution attentional process* occurs in which the subject concentrates on the object, but this time on the aspects relevant for action execution. The informal temporal specification is as follows:

> During the time interval from t1 to t2 attention on action preparation and
> execution occurs iff from t1 to t2 the mind focus and gaze is on an object
> O and at t2 an action a is performed for this object O.

- *action assessment attention*

Finally, after an action has been executed, a retrospective *action assessment attentional process* occurs in which the subject evaluates the outcome of the action. Here the subject focuses on aspects related to goal and effect of the action. For example, Wegner (2002) focuses on such a process in relation to the experience of conscious will and ownership of action. The informal temporal specification of this attentional process is as follows:

> During the time interval from t1 to t2 action assessment attention occurs
> iff at t1 an action a is performed for this an object O and from t1 to t2 the
> mind focus and gaze is on this object O and from t2 they are not on O.

Case Study

The characterisations of the different attentional processes as presented above have been validated in a case study. This case study is based on a human participant executing a warfare officer-like task (cf. Bosse, van Maanen, Treur, 2006). The software Multitask (Clamann, Wright & Kaber, 2002) was altered in order to have it output the proper data to validate or reject the hypothesis stated in the introduction of this paper. This study did not yet deal with altering levels of automation (as was the subject of study in Clamann et al.'s work), and the software environment was momentarily only used for providing relevant data. Multitask was originally meant to be a low fidelity air traffic control (ATC) simulation. In this study it is considered to be an abstraction of the cognitive tasks concerning the compilation of the tactical picture, i.e., warfare officer-like task. A snapshot of the task is shown in Figure 1.

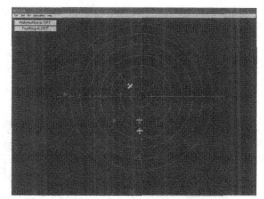

Figure 1: The interface of the used experimental environment based on MultiTask (Clamann et al., 2002).

In the case study, the participant (controller) had to manage an airspace by identifying aircrafts that all are approaching the centre of a radarscope. The centre contains a high value unit (HVU) and had to be protected. In order to do this, airplanes needed to be cleared and identified to be either hostile or friendly to the HVU. This task involves the following elements. Clearing involves six phases: (1) a *red* colour indicates that the identity of the aircraft is still unknown, (2) *flashing red* indicates that the warfare officer is establishing a connection link, (3) *yellow* indicates that the connection was established, (4) *flashing yellow* indicates that the aircraft is being cleared, (5) *green* indicates that either the aircraft was attacked when hostile or left alone when friendly or neutral, and finally (6) the target is *removed* from the radarscope when it reaches the centre. Each phase takes a certain amount of time. In order to go from phase 1 to 2 and from phase 3 to 4, the participant has to click on the left and the right mouse button, respectively. Within the conducted experiment three different aircraft types were used: *military*, *commercial*, and *private*. The type of aircraft was not related to hostility. The different types merely resulted in different intervals of speed of the aircrafts. All of the above were environmental stimuli that resulted in constant change of the participant's attention.

The data that were collected consist of all locations, distances from the centre, speeds, types, and states (i.e., colour). Additionally, data from a Tobii x50 eye-tracker[1] were extracted while the participant was executing the task. All data were retrieved several times per second (10-50 Hz).

Empirical Data Representation

In order to analyse the results of the experiment conducted based on the above mentioned case study, the retrieved empirical data have been converted to a formal representation based on *traces*. Traces are time-indexed sequences of states. Here a *state* S is described by a truth assignment to the set of basic *state properties* (ground atoms) expressed using a state ontology Ont; i.e., S: At(Ont) → {true, false}. A state ontology Ont is formally specified as a sets of sorts, objects in sort, and functions and relations over sorts. The set of all possible states for state ontology Ont is denoted by States(Ont). A trace γ is an assigment of states to time points; i.e., γ: TIME → States(Ont). To represent the empirical data of the case study, a state ontology based on the relations in Table 1 has been used.

Table 1: State ontology used to represent the data.

gaze(x:COORD, y:COORD)	The subject's gaze is currently directed at location (x,y)
is_at_location(i:TRACK_NR, x:COORD, y:COORD)	The track (aircraft) with number i is currently at location (x,y)
mouse_click(x:COORD, y:COORD)	The subject is clicking with the mouse on location (x,y)
has_status(i:TRACK_NR, v:INT)	Track i has status v; e.g., 'red'.[2]
has_distance(i:TRACK_NR, v:INT)	The distance between track i and the centre of the screen is v.[3]
has_type(i:TRACK_NR, v:INT)	Track i has type v; e.g., 'military'.[4]
has_speed(i:TRACK_NR, v:INT)	The speed of track i is v.[5]

---

[1] http://www.tobii.se.

[2] Here, 9 = "red", 8 = "yellow", 5 = "flashing red", 4 = "flashing yellow", 3 = "green", and 1 means that the track is currently not active.

[3] This v is calculated using the formula v=10-(d/550), where d (which is a number between 0 and 5500) is the actual distance in pixels from the centre of the screen; v=1 indicates that the track is currently not active.

[4] Here 8 = "military plane", 6 = "commercial plane", 4 = "private plane", and 1 means that the track is currently not active.

Note that in the last four relations in Table 1, v is an integer between 0 and 10. The idea is that, the higher the value of v, the more salient the corresponding track (aircraft) is for within this task. For example, a red track is more salient than a yellow track (since red tracks need to be clicked on more often before they are cleared), but a yellow track is assumed to be more salient than a flashing red track (since it is not possible to click on flashing tracks; one has to wait until they stop flashing). Based on the above state ontology, states are created by filling in the relevant values for the state atoms at a particular time point. Traces are built up as time-indexed sequences of these states. An example of (part of) a trace that resulted from the experiment is visualised in Figure 2. Each time unit in this figure corresponds to 100 ms in real time.

Formalisation of the Attentional Processes

In this section, the different attentional subprocesses, as earlier described informally, are formalised as dynamic properties in the Temporal Trace Language TTL (Bosse et al., 2006). This predicate logical temporal language supports formal specification and analysis of dynamic properties, covering both qualitative and quantitative aspects. TTL is built on atoms referring to *states*, *time points* and *traces*, which are defined as explained in the previous section. In addition, *dynamic properties* are temporal statements that can be formulated with respect to traces based on the state ontology Ont in the following manner. Given a trace γ over state ontology Ont, the state in γ at time point t is denoted by state(γ, t). These states can be related to state properties via the formally defined satisfaction relation denoted by the infix predicate $\models$, comparable to the Holds-predicate in the Situation Calculus: state(γ, t) $\models$ p denotes that state property p holds in trace γ at time t. Based on these statements, dynamic properties can be formulated in a formal manner in a sorted first-order predicate logic, using quantifiers over time and traces and the usual first-order logical connectives such as $\neg$, $\wedge$, $\vee$, $\Rightarrow$, $\forall$, $\exists$. A dedicated software environment has been developed for TTL, featuring both a Property Editor for building and editing TTL properties and a Checking Tool that enables formal verification of such properties against a set of (simulated or empirical) traces.

First, some useful predicates are defined that are used in the formalisation of the different attentional processes:

gaze_near_track(γ:TRACE, c:TRACK, t1:TIME) $\equiv$
$\exists$x1,y1,x2,y2:COORD
    state(γ, t1) $\models$ gaze(x1, y1) &
    state(γ, t1) $\models$ is_at_location(c, x2, y2) &
    |x2-x1| $\leq$ 1 & |y2-y1| $\leq$ 1
mouseclick_near_track(γ:TRACE, c:TRACK, t1:TIME) $\equiv$
$\exists$x1,y1,x2,y2:COORD
    state(γ, t1) $\models$ mouse_click(x1, y1) &
    state(γ, t1) $\models$ is_at_location(c, x2, y2) &
    |x2-x1| $\leq$ 1 & |y2-y1| $\leq$ 1

---

[5] The variable v is calculated using the formula v=s/100, where d (which is a number between 100 and 1000) is the actual speed (in pixels per second). Furthermore, v=1 indicates that the track is currently not active.

```
action_execution(γ:TRACE, c:TRACK, t2:TIME) ≡
    mouseclick_near_track(γ, c, t2) &
    ∃t1:TIME  t1 < t2 &
        ∀t3:TIME [t1 ≤ t3 ≤ t2 ⇒ gaze_near_track(γ, c, t3) ]
```

The reason for using gaze_near_track instead of something like gaze_at_track is that a certain error is allowed in order to handle noise in retrieved empirical data. Usually, the precise coordinates of the mouse clicks do not correspond exactly to the coordinates of the tracks and the gaze data. This is due to two reasons: 1) a certain degree of inaccuracy of the eye tracker, and 2) the fact that people often do not click exactly on the, for instance, centre of a track.

Based on these intermediate predicates, the five types of attentional (sub)processes as described earlier are presented below, both in semi-formal and in formal (TTL) notation:

A. Allocation of attention
From time t1 to t2 attention has been allocated to track c iff at t2 the gaze is directed to track c and between t1 and t2 the gaze has not been directed to any track.

```
has_attention_allocated_during(γ:TRACE, c:TRACK, t1, t2:TIME) ≡
    t1 < t2 & gaze_near_track(γ, c, t2) &
    ∀t3:TIME, c1 :TRACK
        [t1 ≤ t3 < t2 ⇒ ¬ gaze_near_track(γ, c1, t3) ]
```

B. Examinational attention
During the time interval from t1 to t2 examinational attention occurs iff at least two different tracks c1 and c2 exist to which attention is allocated during the interval from t1 to t2 (resp. between t3 to t4 and between t5 and t6).

```
has_examinational_attention_during(γ:TRACE, t1, t2:TIME) ≡
    ∃t3,t4,t5,t6:TIME ∃c1,c2:TRACK
        t1 ≤ t3 ≤ t2 & t1 ≤ t4 ≤ t2 & t1 ≤ t5 ≤ t2 & t1 ≤ t6 ≤ t2 &
        c1 ≠ c2 &
        has_attention_allocated_during(γ, c1, t3, t4) &
        has_attention_allocated_during(γ, c2, t5, t6)
```

C. Attention on decision making and action selection
During the time interval from t1 to t2 decision making attention for c occurs iff from t1 to t2 attention is allocated to a track c, for which the saliency at time point t1 (based on features type, distance, colour and speed) is higher than a certain threshold th.

```
has_attention_on_action_selection_during(γ:TRACE, c:TRACK,
t1, t2:TIME, th:INTEGER) ≡
    t1≤t2 &
    ∃p1,p2,p3,p4:VALUE ∀t3 [ t1≤t3≤t2 ⇒
    state(γ, t3) ⊨ has_type(c, p1) ∧ has_distance(c, p2) ∧
                     has_colour(c, p3) ∧ has_speed(c, p4) ] &
    (0.1*p1+0.5*p2+0.8*p3+0.5*p4)/1.9 > th &
    has_attention_allocated_during(γ, c, t1, t2)
```

D. Attention on action preparation and execution
During the time interval from t1 to t2 attention on action preparation and execution for c occurs iff from some t4 to t1 attention on decision making and action selection for c occurred and from some t3 to t2 attention on the execution of an action on c occurs.

```
has_attention_on_action_prep_and_execution_during(γ:TRACE,
c:TRACK, t1, t2:TIME, th:INTEGER) ≡
    t1≤ t2 &
    ∃t3:TIME [ t3 ≤ t1 &
```

```
    has_attention_on_action_selection_during (γ, c, t3, t1, th) ] &
    ∀t4:TIME [t1 ≤ t4 ≤ t2 ⇒ gaze_near_track(γ, c, t4) &
    action_execution(γ, c, t2)
```

E. Attention on action assessment
During the time interval from t1 to t2 action assessment attention for c occurs iff at t1 an action on c has been performed and from t1 to t2 the gaze is on c and at t2 the gaze is not at c anymore.

```
has_attention_on_action_assessment_during(γ:TRACE, c:TRACK,
t1,t2:TIME) ≡
    [ t1 ≤ t2 &
    action_execution(γ, c, t1) &
    ¬ gaze_near_track(γ, c, t2) &
    ∀t3:TIME [t1 ≤ t3 < t2 ⇒ gaze_near_track(γ, c, t3) ]
```

All the above TTL properties can be checked in the Checking Tool. An example of how one could check such a property for certain parameters is the following:

```
check_action_selection ≡
∀γ:TRACES
    ∃t1,t2:TIME ∃c:TRACK
    has_attention_on_action_selection_during (γ, c, t1, t2, 5)
```

This property states that the phase of decision making and action selection holds for track c, from time point t1 to time point t2, with a threshold of 5, for all loaded traces. This property either holds or does not. If so, the first instantiation of satisfying parameters are retrieved.

Validation

In order to check automatically whether (and when) the above properties are satisfied by the empirical traces, the TTL checker tool (Bosse et al., 2006) has been used. This software takes a set of traces and a TTL property as input, and checks whether the property holds for the traces. Using this tool, all properties as presented in the previous section indeed turned out to hold for the formal trace that was created on the basis of the empirical data. This confirms the hypothesis that a temporal differentiation of a number of attentional subprocesses can be found in empirical data, namely those that are defined in terms of the above properties.

In addition to stating whether TTL properties hold, the TTL checker also provides useful feedback about the exact instantiations of variables for which they hold. For example, suppose that the property check_action_selection holds for a certain trace, the checker will return specific values for time point t1 and t2 and for track c for which that property holds. This approach has been used to identify certain instances of attentional processes in the empirical trace that resulted from the experiment described earlier.

To illustrate, Figure 2 shows part of this trace.[6] For this trace, the five properties as mentioned earlier hold for the following parameter values:

- has_attention_allocated_during holds for track c=9, for time points t1=0 and t2=6

---

[6] Due to space limitations, in Figure 2 a mere selection of atoms has been made from the actual empirical trace, i.e., the time interval [65,85].

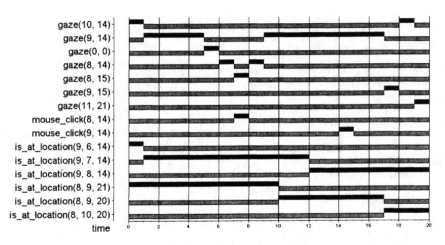

Figure 2: Visualisation of (part of) the empirical trace on the interval [65,85). The vertical axis depicts atoms that are either true or false. This is indicated, respectively, by dark or light boxes on the horizontal axis, in units of 10 ms.

- has_examinational_attention_during holds for tracks c1=8 and c2=9, for time points t1=0 and t2=19, because has_attention_allocated_during holds for track c=9, for time points t1=0 and t2=6 *and* for track c1=8, for time points t1=18 to t2=19 (note that for t=17 the gaze is still on track c=9)
- has_attention_on_action_selection_during holds for track c=9, for time points t1=1 and t2=6, and threshold value th=4. This is due to the fact that has_type(9, 4), has_distance(9, 3), has_colour(9, 5), and has_speed(9, 4), not shown in Figure 2, result in a combined saliency above th=4, for this time period
- has_attention_on_action_prep_and_execution_during holds for track c=9, for time points t1=6 and t2=7, because has_attention_on_action_selection_during holds for track c=9, for time points 1 to 6, and action_execution holds at t2=7, and the gaze is near track c=9 at time point 7
- has_attention_on_action_assessment_during holds for track c=9, for time points t1=7 and t2=9 (note that after t2=9 the gaze is not on c=9 anymore)

Furthermore, the TTL checker enables additional analyses, such as counting the number of times a property holds for a given trace, using a built-in operator for summation. Using this mechanism, one can calculate that the property has_attention_allocated_during holds three times for track 1, four times for track 7, one time for track 8, and two times for track 9, in the time interval [0,100) of the empirical trace. A similar calculation shows that has_attention_on_action_prep_and_execution_during holds only once, namely for track 9, for the same time interval. Comparison between such counts can be used to, for instance, indicate different task progresses or workload differences.

Discussion

In the literature on attention, various perspectives on the notion of attention can be found (e.g., Itti and Koch, 2001; Theeuwes, 1994). Although they identify various aspects that play a role in attentional processes, most authors still make the implicit assumption that attention is a single, homogeneous concept. However, this assumption makes it difficult to make distinctions between different types of attention that play a role in different phases in the attentional process (e.g., to distinguish between 'global' examinational attention that is aimed at several objects and 'local' focussed attention that is aimed at only one object). Therefore, the current paper addresses an analysis of the situation that occurs when this assumption is dropped, by explicitly involving the dynamics of attentional processes in the context of a situation where multiple objects occur and where actions have to be undertaken. Given this context, in this paper a number of attentional subprocesses have been identified within the process of attention, following the ideas of (Laberge, 2002; Parasuraman, 1998; Pashler, 1998). Each subprocess plays a specific role in the sense-reason-act cycle. These attentional subprocesses have first been described at a conceptual level, in an informal notation.

In order to obtain empirical data, an experiment has been conducted in which a human subject performs a warfare officer-like task in a simulated environment (cf. Bosse, van Maanen, and Treur, 2006). The data of the subject's performance were logged, together with the data of an eye tracker that monitored the subject's gaze during the experiment. After that, both types of data were represented in formal notation (based on a specific ontology), to obtain formalised traces of the empirical process.

Moreover, the semiformal specifications of each of the subprocesses have been formalised in the form of dynamic properties, using the temporal language TTL. Subsequently, these dynamic properties have been automatically checked against the formalised traces by means of the TTL checker (Bosse et al., 2006). The checks pointed out that the dynamic properties indeed held for the traces, which confirmed the existence of the predicted attentional subprocesses in the empirical data. Moreover, since the TTL checker allows the modeller to find out exactly for which time points the properties hold, the analysis method can also be used to indicate in detail which type of attentional subprocess occurs when. This has been done successfully for the data from the experiment.

As also indicated in the introduction, distinguishing between different types of attentional processes can be very useful, for example, in the domain of naval warfare. To determine (in a dynamical manner) an appropriate cooperation and work division between human and system, it has a high value for the quality of the interaction and cooperation between user and system if the system has information about the particular attentional state or process a user is in. For example, in case the user is already allocated to some task, it may be better to leave that task for him or her, and allocate tasks to the system for which there is less or no commitment from the user (yet).

Whereas the current paper is a first step towards a more precise definition of different attentional subprocesses, it is yet far from complete. For example, the attentional processes identified are all related to a certain object, whereas in principle it is also possible to have attention for an empty space (e.g., because one expects that a track will soon appear there). Moreover, the current model mainly addresses the exogenous aspect of attention (i.e., attention triggered by external stimuli), whereas it leaves the endogenous aspect (i.e., attention triggered by internal stimuli (Theeuwes, 1994), e.g. expectations) almost untouched. In future work, it will be explored whether such aspects of attention can be incorporated in the analysis method as well; e.g., (Castelfranchi and Lorini, 2003; Martinho and Paiva, 2006).

Another direction of future research is to validate the formal specification of attentional subprocesses against more data. This step would imply that more traces of attentional processes are acquired, and that the TTL properties mentioned earlier are checked against these traces. Since the TTL checker can take both empirical and computer (simulated) traces as input, it is also possible to check the properties against traces that result from simulation models. In this respect, an interesting challenge would be to generate traces using attention models in cognitive architectures such as ACT-R (Anderson, Matessa, and Lebiere, 1997) or EPIC (Kieras and Marshall, 2006) and compare them to the formal specification of attentional subprocesses being developed.

Acknowledgments

This research was partly funded by the Royal Netherlands Navy (program number V524). Moreover, the authors are grateful to the anonymous referees for their comments to an earlier version of this paper.

References

Anderson, J.R., Matessa, M., and Lebiere, C. (1997). ACT-R: A theory of higher level cognition and its relation to visual attention. *Human-Computer Interaction 12*, pp. 439-462.

Bainbridge, L., (1983). Ironies of automation. Automatica, 19, pp. 775-779.

Bosse, T., Jonker, C.M., Meij, L. van der, Sharpanskykh, A, and Treur, J. (2006) Specification and Verification of Dynamics in Cognitive Agent Models. In: *Proc. of the Sixth International Conference on Intelligent Agent Technology, IAT'06.* IEEE Computer Society Press, pp. 247-254.

Bosse, T., Maanen, P.-P. van, & and Treur, J. (2006), A Cognitive Model for Visual Attention and its Application, In: *Proc. of the Sixth International Conference on Intelligent Agent Technology, IAT'06.* IEEE Computer Society Press, pp. 255-262.

Campbell, G., Cannon-Bowers, J., Glenn, F., Zachary, W., Laughery, R., and Klein, G., (1997). *Dynamic function allocation in the SC-21 Manning Initiative Program.* Naval Air Warfare Center Training Systems Division, Orlando, SC-21/ONRS&T Manning Affordability Initiative.

Castelfranchi, C. and Lorini, E. (2003), Cognitive Anatomy and Functions of Expectations. In: R. Sun (ed.), *Proc. of IJCAI '03 Workshop on Cognitive modeling of agents and multi-agent interaction*, Acapulco.

Clamann, M. P., Wright, M. C. and Kaber, D. B. (2002), Comparison of performance effects of adaptive automation applied to various stages of human-machine system information processing. In: *Proc. of the 46th Ann. Meeting of the Human Factors and Ergonomics Soc.*, pp. 342-346.

Inagaki, T. (2003). Adaptive automation: Sharing and trading of control. *Handbook of Cognitive Task Design*, pp. 147–169.

Itti, L. and Koch, C. (2001). Computational Modeling of Visual Attention, *Nature Reviews Neuroscience*, vol. 2, pp. 194-203.

Kieras, S. and Marshall, S.P. (2006). Visual Availability and Fixation Memory in Modeling Visual Search using the EPIC Architecture. In: Sun, R. (ed.), *Proceedings of the 28th Annual Conference of the Cognitive Science Society, CogSci'06*, pp. 423-428.

LaBerge, D. (2002). Attentional control: brief and prolonged. *Psychological Research 66*, pp. 230-233.

Martinho, C., and Paiva, A. (2006). Using Anticipation to Create Believable Behaviour. In: *Proceedings of AAAI'06*, AAAI Press, pp. 175-180.

Pashler, H. (1998). *The psychology of attention.* Cambridge, MA: MIT Press.

Parasuraman, R. (1998). *The attentive brain.* Cambridge, MA: MIT Press.

Theeuwes, J., (1994). Endogenous and exogenous control of visual selection, *Perception*, 23, pp. 429-440.

Wegner, D.M. (2002). *The illusion of conscious will.* Cambridge, MA. MIT Press.

Lateralized Object Naming: Effects of Image Agreement, Name Agreement, Age of Acquisition and Animacy

Armina Janyan (ajanyan@cogs.nbu.bg)
Department of Cognitive Science and Psychology, New Bulgarian University
21 Montevideo St., 1618 Sofia, Bulgaria

Abstract

The present study explores lateralized picture naming processing and the impact of various characteristics of the picture and its name on visual field reaction time variance. The results of regression analysis showed a similar pattern of processing across two visual fields, in particular, the most powerful predictors of picture naming such as image agreement, name agreement, and age of word acquisition significantly contributed to the reaction time variance. The only difference was obtained in sensitivity to animacy semantic property: when animate objects were presented to the right visual field, they were named slower than the non-animate ones. This pattern was not obtained in the left visual field condition. The results are discussed in terms of property activation and linguistic systems distribution across hemispheres.

Introduction

The bulk of research is dedicated to investigation of the organizational structure of lexical (verbal) and conceptual (nonverbal) systems in the brain, to hemispheric abilities to process these types of information and to brain areas associated with this information. Neuroimaging research (based mostly on visual word recognition) has shown some contradictory results. For example, it was shown that highly imageable words are processed by both hemispheres (e.g., Wise et al., 2000) and that nouns highly associated with a visual sense are processed bilaterally in occipital areas (Pulvermüller, Lutzenberger & Preissl, 1999). On the other hand, it has been suggested that a semantic system common to abstract and concrete words is bilaterally distributed (West & Holcomb, 2000) or that both concrete and abstract words are processed solely by the left hemisphere (Fiebach & Friederici, 2003). Finally, a recent reaction time study by Janyan & Andonova (2003) has suggested that lateralized word naming activates non-verbal word properties in the right hemisphere and verbal, or lexical, properties in the left hemisphere.

The present study does not aim to resolve the contradictions. Its aim is rather an exploratory one. Working with a hemifield experimental paradigm which is usually used in research on hemispheric differences in lexical/semantic information access and processing, this study is an attempt to explore hemispheric potentials in the processing of different types of information that is carried by pictorial stimuli. Different types of information refer here to such conceptual, semantic, lexical and phonological information that is usually measured and analyzed in traditional picture naming experiments.

Picture naming is a complex production-like process influenced by many, usually interconnected, factors (Johnson, Paivio & Clark, 1996). Models of picture naming postulate at least three distinct stages – object identification, name activation, and response production (Johnson et al., 1996). In picture naming with a central presentation mode, the most powerful predictors of performance are name agreement and/or number of alternative names to a picture (measures of uncertainty), image agreement, word frequency and age of response word acquisition (AoA). Name agreement usually refers to the degree to which participants agree on the name of the picture measured by the percentage of people who produced a given name. The number of alternative names refers to the number of valid names given to a picture. Image agreement reflects the degree (subjectively rated) to which a mental image generated by participants in response to the name of the picture matches the picture. AoA, measures of uncertainty and image agreement have been shown to be strong predictors of picture naming reaction time (RT) in a number of studies (e.g., Barry et al., 1997; D'Amico et al., 2001; Bonin et al., 2002).

Most recent studies on picture naming with a central presentation mode use multivariate regression analysis to determine and discuss predictors of picture naming processing as picture naming is influenced by many factors that are sometimes difficult to control. In the area of divided visual field (VF) processing studies are devoted to a number of semantic memory systems, to peculiarities of perceptual processing in the two hemispheres and to the recognition capacities for different categories of each hemisphere. The results of these studies based on an analysis of variance indicate that the right hemisphere (RH) is as accurate as the left one in the categorization of pictorial stimuli (Nieto et al., 1990) and faster than the left hemisphere in object identification (McAuliffe & Knowlton, 2001). Zaidel (1994) found in a categorization task a left visual field (LVF) processing time advantage for typical over atypical members of a category and no RT difference between these exemplars in the right visual field (RVF). Zaidel (1994) suggests that the RH may be specialized in the processing of standard and/or stereotypical concepts. Somewhat contradictory to these results were findings by Laeng et al. (2003). The results of a picture-name verification task showed that pictures were identified faster in the RVF than in the LVF when basic-level labels followed the presentation of pictures and faster in the LVF when subordinate-level labels had to be matched. The authors suggest that two distinct systems underlie the two processes for object identification at different categorization levels with the left hemisphere (LH) being more specialized for basic-level members of a category and the RH – for subordinate, or exemplar members.

Thus, it is difficult to draw clear conclusions from the small number of lateralized context-free picture processing studies especially since none of them used an overt picture naming task examining the influence of picture and name characteristics on RT variance in the two visual fields (VFs). Such a study is important in that it potentially shows not only the applicability of multiple regression analyses to the hemifield experimental paradigm but it may also be helpful in teasing apart the importance of various factors that reflect different levels of response word structure and the degree of picture-name matching in the two VF processing RTs.

In addition to the commonly used predictor variables, the present study included subjectively rated animacy as a potential semantic predictor. Animacy is of special interest in the present study since the results of many neurological studies have demonstrated a category-specific deficit in the differential processing of living vs. non-living semantic categories (e.g., Gainotti et al., 1995; Caramazza & Shelton; 1998; Ilmberger et al., 2002). Studies have obtained contradictory findings. While an earlier review by Gainotti et al., (1995) showed that damage to the LH leads to impaired processing of non-living categories which is consistent with more recent research (e.g., Ilmberger, et al., 2002), other studies found impairment of non-living categories with RH damage (e.g., Turnbull & Laws, 2000). Impairment of the cognition of animate objects is associated with the left frontal and parietal lobes, with the left temporal lobe (Caramazza & Shelton; 1998) or with both temporal lobes (Luckhurs & Lloyd-Johnes, 2001).

Thus, the present experiment aims at obtaining additional information concerning the representation of and access to animacy semantic information with the use of lateralized picture presentation. More specifically, a significant contribution of subjectively rated animacy to visual field RT variance could indicate activation of or access to this semantic property in the corresponding hemisphere. The same concerns other potential predictors, too. The study uses several predictor variables that reflect various levels of picture and picture-related word structures such as picture visual complexity, uncertainty measures, image agreement, object familiarity, frequency and AoA of the response word, phonological length, etc. Research on picture naming suggests that visual complexity presumably affects an early stage of object recognition (Johnson et al., 1996; Bonin et al., 2002). Image agreement and object familiarity have an impact on the level of object identification/concept activation that is, the better the match between a pictured object and the object's representation in the brain and the more familiar the object is, the faster it would be processed (Bonin et al., 2002). Uncertainty affects picture naming at or around the object postidentification stage of name activation

(Johnson et al., 1996; Barry et al., 1997; Bonin et al., 2002) which implies that the effect is presumably lexico-semantic. Frequency and AoA may affect name activation at the phonological stage or between the semantic and phonological stages (Bock & Levelt, 1994; Johnson et al., 1996; Bonin et al., 2002). Word length affects name activation and/or response generation (Johnson et al., 1996). Thus, the significant contribution of a predictor to VF RT variance may indicate not only activation of / access to the property in the corresponding hemisphere but also approximately the processing stage(s) of picture naming. Finally, activation of a property and/or of a corresponding processing level can be seen as indication of activation of the corresponding conceptual, semantic, lexical, and phonological systems in the hemisphere.

The expectations in the present study are derived from recent neuropsychological, neuroimaging and computational evidence, the majority of which suggests that semantic systems are represented bilaterally, while lexico-phonological systems are represented only in the LH (e.g., Chiarello, 1991; Gainotti et al., 1995; Lambon Ralph et al., 2001; Martin, 2003). Thus, if any of the semantic variables make a significant contribution to RT variance, it should emerge in both VFs. However, lexical and phonological variables are expected to contribute only to the RVF RT variance.

Method

Participants 120 subjects (58 male and 62 female) participated in the experiment. They were university students with an average age of 22.0 years (age range 18 to 35 years), right-handed Bulgarian monolinguals. All of them had normal or corrected to normal vision. Participants received course credit or were paid for the participation.

Stimuli and Predictor Variables 140 stimuli were selected from the pictures in an on-line object naming task with 520 pictorial stimuli in Bulgarian (Bates et al., 2003). For more details on participants, procedures, and pictorial stimuli in the picture naming norming study, visit an on-line data base at http://www.crl.ucsd.edu/~aszekely/ipnp/.

All target names were subjected to six different tests aimed at obtaining separate subjective ratings for word frequency, object familiarity, image agreement, imageability (procedure adopted from Paivio, Yuille & Madigan, 1968), concreteness and animacy, all rated on a 1 to 7 scale, from lowest to highest. Five different groups composed of 40 university students each participated in the frequency, object familiarity, concreteness, animacy and imageability ratings. In addition, 20 students participated in the image agreement procedure. 30 students participated in an AoA rating task on a 1 to 7 scale where 7 referred to the earliest acquired items (under 2 years of age) and 1 – to the latest acquired items (over 13 years old). None of the participants in the rating tests participated in the on-line picture naming experiment. Target names were coded for word length measured in number of phonemes. Finally, subjective ratings of picture visual complexity (7-point scale, 7 – the most visually complex) were obtained from a test with the help of 30 Hungarian university students (Székely, unpublished).

The number of valid alternative names to a picture and name agreement for each VF separately were derived empirically after experimental data collection and included as predictor variables. All target names were grammatically unambiguous nouns, identical for each VF. Table 1 summarizes the descriptive statistics for each predictor.

Table 1: Pictorial and target word characteristics for each word class.

Predictors	Mean (SD)	Range
Name agreement (LVF)	88.4 (14.3)	23-100
Name agreement (RVF)	86.7 (15.7)	10-100
Alternative names (LVF)	2.7(2.0)	1-13
Alternative names (RVF)	2.8 (2.2)	1-15
Visual complexity	3.1 (1.2)	1.2-5.8
Image agreement	5.8 (0.4)	5.1-6.6
No of phonemes	5.5 (1.5)	3-11
Frequency	4.5 (1.0)	2.5-6.7
Imageability	6.2 (0.3)	5.6-6.8
Object familiarity	6.1 (0.3)	5.4-6.6
Concreteness	6.0 (0.5)	4.5-6.7
Animacy	3.1 (1.7)	1.5-6.2
AoA	5.3 (0.6)	3.6-6.5

Procedure Stimuli (black and white line drawings, 4.5 x 4.5 cm) were presented unilaterally, to the right or to the left of a fixation point (a cross; "+") in the center of the screen. The distance to the center of the stimuli subtended a horizontal visual angle of 4 degrees in relation to the subject. The visual angle from the fixation point to the nearest edge was 1.9 degrees. The distance between the participant's head and the screen was kept 60 cm.

Participants were tested in a sound-proof booth. Six pseudo-randomized orders were constructed such that stimuli did not appear in the same VF more than three consecutive times. The experimental session started with 8 practice trials. None of the practice pictures appeared in the experimental part. Appearance of the stimuli in each visual field was counterbalanced across subjects, i.e., half of the subjects saw a stimulus in one VF, and another half saw the stimulus in the other VF. Each stimulus was presented only once to each participant – either in the left or in the right visual field. Each stimulus was displayed for 200 msec. Immediately after stimulus disappearance a mask (ten variants of randomly distributed black lines and curves on a white background, which were arbitrarily chosen for each trial) was displayed at the same place as the stimulus for 200 msec. Participants were instructed to name pictures as fast and as accurately as possible without moving their gaze away from the fixation point. The importance of maintaining one's gaze on the fixation point was repeatedly stressed. The intertrial interval varied randomly between 1 and 2 sec. The response interval was set to 5 sec. Responses were recorded by the experimenter. Reaction time was measured from the offset of each stimulus. A Carnegie Mellon button box recorded voice onset RT and controlled stimuli presentation timing. A Power Macintosh 6400/200 equipped with the PsyScope software (Cohen et al., 1993) controlled order of presentation and size of the stimuli. The experiment lasted 15-20 min.

Results and Discussion

Trials on which no response was registered (2.3%) and trials with technical errors (0.6%) were excluded from the analyses. Response times lying more than 2.5 standard deviations from the mean were removed which resulted in the removal of 2.3% of overall responses. The data were averaged by items and VFs over subjects and a mean RT for each valid response was obtained. The number of alternative names to a picture (including target), name agreement (cf. Table 1) and target names for each picture in each VF were derived from these data. The target names obtained were identical in each VF. As a result, a total of 87.5% of the originally collected RT data were included in further analyses. 7.1% of data of non-target responses were disregarded. A one-way repeated measures ANOVA obtained no significant main effect ($F(1,139)=2.69$; $p=.1034$), i.e., no VF processing differences in the picture naming task were obtained in terms of overall naming speed (Mean [SD] RT in LVF=942 [137] ms; RVF=953 [159] ms).

Simultaneous regression analyses were performed separately for the two VFs examining the contribution of the 11 predictors on RTs. Results of the analyses are presented in Table 2[1]. The predictors together accounted for 69.3% of RVF RT variance and 59.3% of LVF RT variance.

Table 2: Simultaneous multiple regression analysis on RT separately for each VF.

	LVF			RVF		
	β	t	$p<$	β	t	$p<$
NA	-0.64	-9.22	0.00	-0.67	-11.25	0.00
AN	0.01	0.11	0.91	0.00	-0.02	0.98
VC	-0.12	-1.53	0.13	-0.12	-1.73	0.09
ImAgr	-0.12	-1.83	0.07	-0.12	-2.15	0.03
No Ph	0.00	-0.02	0.99	0.08	1.39	0.17
Freq	-0.10	-0.85	0.40	-0.04	-0.36	0.72
Image	-0.05	-0.59	0.56	-0.03	-0.45	0.66
Fam	-0.03	-0.24	0.81	-0.12	-1.16	0.25
Concr	0.03	0.48	0.64	-0.02	-0.47	0.64
Anim	0.12	1.41	0.16	0.20	2.55	0.01
AoA	-0.21	-2.24	0.03	-0.19	-2.37	0.02

Note. LVF – left VF, RVF – right VF, NA – name agreement, AN – number of alternative names, VC – visual complexity, ImAgr – image agreement, No Ph – number of phonemes,

---

[1] As one of the reviewers suggested, the regression was performed also on normalized variables; no difference was observed between the two analyses.

Freq – word frequency, Image – word imageability, Fam – familiarity, Concr – concreteness, Anim - animacy.

Four predictors made their significant contribution to RVF RT variance (Table 2). Image agreement, name agreement, animacy, and AoA influenced RT in RVF. The independent contributions of these predictors suggest different loci of their influence and, consequently, activation of different, though highly interrelated, systems. Image agreement influences picture naming at the early stage of object recognition (Barry et al., 1997), that is, the impact is on the conceptual level. As far as name agreement is concerned, it influences the early name competition stage, that is, the target pre-selection stage, and activates a lexico-semantic system. Animacy's contribution indicated activation of this semantic property, that is, LH made a difference between animate and inanimate objects. To test the observed difference, a repeated measures ANOVA[2] was conducted with binary coded animacy (animate vs. non-animate) and VF as independent variables. The analysis showed main effect of VF (F(1,138)=7.51; p<.01) with LVF overall advantage, main effect of Animacy (F(1,138)=7.03; p<.01) with non-animate object naming advantage, and a significant interaction (F(1,138)=5.92; p<.05). Figure 1 shows that animate objects were named significantly slower (p<0.01) than non-animate when presented to the RVF. LVF (RH) remained indifferent to the animacy property. Thus, ANOVA confirmed and strengthened the results of the regression analysis.

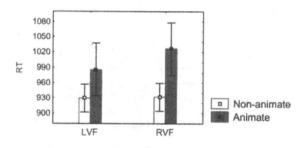

Figure 1. Animacy by VF interaction (vertical bars denote 0.95 confidence intervals).

As noted earlier, AoA influences name activation somewhere in between the semantic and phonological levels[3]. It may be suggested that AoA influences the target selection stage (lemma level) and the target post-selection

---

[2] I thank an anonymous reviewer for this suggestion.
[3] To determine the characteristics of AoA in the given set, all factors were subjected to a principal components factor analysis with varimax normalized. AoA loaded solely and heavily (loading >.8) on a factor containing imageability, familiarity and frequency (loadings >.7) and length in phonemes (loading >.5). Thus, AoA in the set reflects semantic, lexical, and, to a lesser extent, word-form properties.

stage or, in other words, it activates (lexico-)semantic and lexico-(phonological) systems. Although the review on AoA effects suggests uncertainty about the exact locus of AoA, it also suggests certainty about AoA influences on lexical and semantic processing (Juhasz, 2005). In addition, results of a study of repetition priming of picture naming (Barry et al., 2001) showed that AoA functions at the level of lexico-phonological retrieval (the lexeme level). It seems that the AoA characteristic combines semantic, lexical, and phonological properties which cannot be teased apart, at least, in the present study. Thus, it could be suggested that picture presentation to the right VF prompted activation of conceptual, lexico-semantic, semantic (animacy) and lexico-phonological systems. Two predictors made significant unique contributions to LVF RT (Table 2), namely, name agreement and AoA. That is, picture presentation to the LVF activated lexico-semantic and lexico-phonological systems. Image agreement just missed the significance level. It should be noted here, that failure of a variable to reach significance does not necessarily mean that the variable has no effect on processing. However, significant contribution of the variable suggests confidence in its influence (see D'Amico et al., 2001).

To summarize, the results on RVF RT are in agreement with most picture naming studies with a central presentation mode (e.g., Bonin et al., 2002; D'Amico et al., 2001) in the sense that the most robust predictors of picture naming emerged in the analysis across both VFs. The only significant difference between the two VF processing patterns was different VF sensitivity to the animacy property.

Conclusion

The primary purpose of this study was to examine the hemispheric activation of various types of language systems such as the semantic, lexical and phonological ones in context-free lateralized picture naming. For this purpose, a multiple regression analysis was used here for the first time with lateralized picture presentation. The initial assumption and logic for applying this methodology was based on the relationship between linguistic systems, processing stages in picture naming and the loci of impact of various factors representing different levels of picture and target name characteristics. It was expected that semantic systems would be activated bilaterally while lexical and phonological systems would be activated only in the LH. The expectations were not fulfilled, which shows the need for further research applying a variety of methodologies and experimental paradigms.

Regression analyses obtained similar patterns of activation induced in the two VFs, which provided information concerning the corresponding stages and systems of picture naming processing activated in each hemisphere. Picture presentation to the LVF (RH) prompted the activation of a lexico-semantic system in the RH at the early name identification stage where several picture name candidates compete with each other and where target lemma is selected, and the activation of lexico-phonological system (target post-selection stage). Some support for these findings comes from an MEG study of centrally presented picture naming (Levelt et al., 1998) in which time windows were identified for each of the picture naming stages and right parietal activation was found in the processing of lemma selection. Furthermore, in support of the right-hemispheric lexico-semantic and lexico-phonological systems are data that suggest that a route of concrete noun acquisition passes via temporal lobes (Wise et al., 2000) and that temporal lobes may be involved not only in lexical retrieval but also in visual/perceptual processing, that is, in some semantic activation (Damasio et al., 1996). Finally, recent data suggest that the right inferior frontal region and right supplementary motor area are involved in lexical word-form retrieval and phonological processing (Indefrey & Levelt, 2004).

Picture presentation to the RVF (LH) reflected object identification/concept activation stage(s), lexical competition and, finally, lexical access processing which is not at all surprising taking into account the overwhelming number of neural correlates in the left hemisphere found to be related to word production (Indefrey & Levelt, 2004). Furthermore, neuroimaging studies of centralized picture naming found major (e.g., Levelt et al., 1998) or unique (e.g., Ilmberger et al., 2001) involvement of LH in the processing. As far as an object recognition system is concerned, the present data are in accord with the suggestion that this system requires greater left than right hemisphere involvement (Goldstein et al., 2004).

The results showed sensitivity to the animacy semantic property in the RVF (LH) presentation. In particular, the results suggested disadvantage for living things in the LH. This result seemingly disagrees with a recent study (Pilgrim, Moss, & Tyler, 2005) that obtained the opposite pattern: disadvantage for nonliving things in terms of RT in both VFs. The study applied a semantic categorization task of laterally presented words. The authors suggested that since the task required concept identification, many shared properties of living things were activated and facilitated RTs. However, nonliving things have much fewer shared properties, hence, no processing facilitation obtained (Pilgrim et al., 2005). Furthermore, the authors assume that this observed advantage should disappear or be reversed in the case of a task that requires access to distinctive object properties such as picture naming. This is exactly what was obtained in the present study. However, another interpretation of living things' disadvantage is also possible. Since animate objects share many features among themselves, their production (picture naming) might generate a conflict or a competition between many lexical concepts that share these features and to impede the processing of object identification and name activation. Nonliving things have no such a wide range of shared properties, hence, no competition and processing inhibition is observed. The "competition" account may also explain the left hemispheric lateralization of the animacy effect. It is argued that RH activates semantic properties broadly and weakly while LH activates the properties strongly and more

focused (Pilgrim et al., 2005). That is, in the LH the competition between animate lexical concepts with shared features is strong enough to slow down the processing while in the RH it is much weaker. Since nonliving things do not have many shared features, their processing does not involve strong competition and is similar in both VFs.

To conclude, a combination of the results reported here and the results of a previous study (Janyan & Andonova, 2003) which showed that lateralized word naming activated a verbal system in the LH and a non-verbal one – in the RH, suggests that visual word and pictorial stimuli are processed via different access routes (Koivisto & Revonsuo, 2003) and/or access different types of information (Saffran, Coslett & Keener, 2003) and that presentation of words or pictures to one or another visual field may activate qualitatively different information sources in the two hemispheres. Overall, one possible interpretation is that both verbal and nonverbal systems may be bilaterally distributed and may have different within- and between-hemispheric weights that are sensitive to different pictorial and word characteristics and to different experimental conditions.

Acknowledgments

I thank Velina Balkanska for her help in gathering the data and Elena Andonova and three anonymous reviewers for useful comments and suggestions. This study was partially supported by a McDonnell foundation grant on "Cross-linguistics studies of aphasia."

References

Barry, C. & Hirsh, K.W., Johnston, R.A. & Williams, C.L. (2001). Age of acquisition, word frequency, and the locus of repetition priming of picture naming. *Journal of Memory and Language, 44,* 350-375.

Barry, C., Morrison, C.M. & Ellis, A.W. (1997). Naming the Snodgrass and Vanderwart pictures: Effects of age of acquisition, frequency, and name agreement. *The Quarterly Journal of Experimental Psychology, 50A(3),* 560-585.

Bates, E., D'Amico, S., Jacobsen, T., Székely, A., Andonova, E., Devescovi, A., Herron, D., Lu, C.-C., Pechmann, T., Pléh, C., Wicha, N., Federmeier, K., Gerdjikova, I., Gutierrez, G., Hung., D., Hsu, J., Iyer, G., Kohnert, K., Mehotcheva, T., Orozco-Figueroa, A., Tzeng, A., & Tzeng, O. (2003). Timed picture naming in seven languages. *Psychonomic Bulletin and Review, 10(2),* 344-380.

Bock, K. & Levelt, W. (1994). Language production. Grammatical encoding. In: M.A. Gernsbacher (Ed.), *Handbook of Psycholinguistics,* San Diego: Academic Press.

Bonin, P, Chalard, M., Méot, A., & Fayol, M. (2002). The determinants of spoken and written picture naming latencies. *British Journal of Psychology, 93,* 89-114.

Caramazza, A., & Shelton, J.R. (1998). Domain-specific knowledge systems in the brain: The animate-inanimate distinction. *Journal of Cognitive Neuroscience, 10(1)*, 1-34.

Chiarello, C. (1991). Interpretation of word meanings by the two cerebral hemispheres: One is not enough. In P. Schwanenflugel (Ed.), *The Psychology of Word Meanings* (pp. 251-278). Hillsdale, NJ: Erlbaum.

Cohen, J.D., MacWhinney, B., Flatt, M., & Provost, J. (1993). PsyScope: A new graphic interactive environment for designing psychology experiments. *Behavioral Research Methods, Instruments and Computers, 25(2)*, 257-271.

Damasio, H., Grabowski, T.J., Tranel, D., Hichwa, R.D., & Damasio, A.R. (1996). A neural basis for lexical retrieval. *Nature, 380(11)*, 499-505.

D'Amico, S., Devescovi, A., & Bates, E. (2001). Picture naming and lexical access in Italian children and adults. *Journal of Cognition and Development, 2(1)*, 71-105.

Fiebach, C.J., & Friederici, A.D. (2003). Processing concrete words: fMRI evidence against a specific right-hemisphere involvement. *Neuropsychologia, 42*, 62-70.

Gainotti, G., Silveri, C.M., Daniele, A., & Giustolisi, L. (1995). Neuroanatomical correlates of category-specific semantic disorders: a critical survey. *Memory, 3(3/4)*, 247-264.

Goldstein, B., Armstrong, C.L., Modestino, E., Ledakis, G., John, C., & Hunter, J.V. (2004). The impact of left and right intracranial tumors on picture and word recognition memory. *Brain and Cognition, 54*, 1-6.

Ilmberger, J., Eisner, W., Schmid, U., & Reulen, H.-J. (2001). Performance in picture naming and word comprehension: Evidence for common neuronal substrates from intraoperative language mapping. *Brain and Language, 76*, 111-118.

Ilmberger, J., Rau, S., Noachtar, S., Arnold, S., & Winkler, P. (2002). Naming tools and animals: Asymmetries observed during direct electrical cortical stimulation. *Neuropsychologia, 40*, 695-700.

Indefrey, P., & Levelt, W.J.M. (2004). The spatial and temporal signatures of word production components. *Cognition, 92*, 101-144.

Janyan, A. & Andonova, E. (2003). Visual field differences in word naming. *Proceedings of the European Cognitive Science Conference* (pp. 187-192), Mahwah, NJ: Lawrence Erlbaum Associates.

Johnson, C.J., Paivio, A., & Clark, J.M. (1996). Cognitive components of picture naming. *Psychological Bulletin, 120(1)*, 113-139.

Juhasz, B.J. (2005). Age-of-acquisition effects in word and picture identification. *Psychological Bulletin, 131(5)*, 684-712.

Koivisto, M., & Revonsuo, A. (2003). Interhemispheric categorization of pictures and words. *Brain and Cognition, 52*, 181-191.

Laeng, B., Zarrinpar, A., & Kosslyn, S.M. (2003). Do separate processes identify objects as exemplars versus members of basic-level categories? Evidence from hemispheric specialization. *Brain and Cognition, 53*, 15-27.

Lambon Ralph, M.A., McClelland, J.I., Patterson, K., Galton, C.J., & Hodges, J.R. (2001). No right to speak? The relationship between object naming and semantic impairment: Neuropsychological evidence and a computational model. *Journal of Cognitive Neuroscience, 13(3)*, 341-356.

Levelt, W.J.M., Praamstra, P., Meyer, A.S., Helenius, P., & Salmelin, R. (1998). An MEG study of picture naming. *Journal of Cognitive Neuroscience, 10(5)*, 553-567.

Luckhurst, L., & Lloyd-Johnes, T.J. (2001). A selective deficit for living things after temporal lobectomy for relief of epileptic seizures. *Brain and Language, 79*, 266-296.

Martin, R.C. (2003). Language processing: Functional organization and neuroanatomical basis. *Annual Review of Psychology, 54*, 55-89.

McAuliffe, S.P. & Knowlton, B.J. (2001). Hemispheric differences in object identification. *Brain and Cognition, 45*, 119-128.

Nieto, A., Hernández, S., Gonzales-Feria, L., & Baroso, J. (1990). Semantic capabilities of the left and right cerebral hemispheres in categorization tasks: Effects of verbal-pictorial presentation. *Neuropsychologia, 28(11)*, 1175-1186.

Paivio, A., Yuille, J.C., & Madigan, S. (1968). Concreteness, imagery, and meaningfulness value for 925 nouns. *Journal of Experimental Psychology Monograph Supplement, 76(1)*, Part 2, 1-25.

Pilgrim, L.K., Moss, H.E., & Tyler, L.K. (2005). Semantic processing of living and nonliving concepts across the cerebral hemispheres. *Brain and Language, 94*, 86-93.

Pulvermüller, F., Lutzenberger, W., & Preissl, H. (1999). Nouns and verbs in the intact brain: Evidence from event-related potentials and high-frequency cortical responses. *Cerebral Cortex, 9*, 497-506.

Saffran, E.M., Coslett, H.B., & Keener, M.T. (2003). Differences in word associations to pictures and words. *Neuropsychologia, 41*, 1541-1546.

Székely, A. (unpublished). Unpublished normative data in Hungarian language.

Turnbull, O., & Laws, K. (2000). Loss of stored knowledge of object structure: Implications for "category-specific" deficits. *Cognitive Neuropsychology, 17(4)*, 365-389.

West, W.C., & Holcomb, P.J. (2000). Imaginal, semantic, and surface-level processing of concrete and abstract words: An electrophysiological investigation. *Journal of Cognitive Neuroscience, 12(6)*, 1024-1037.

Wise, R.J.S., Howard, D., Mummery, C.J., Fletcher, P., Leff, A., Büchel, C., & Scott, S.K. (2000). Noun imageability and the temporal lobes. *Neuropsychologia, 38*, 985-994.

Zaidel, D.W. (1994). Worlds apart: Pictorial semantics in the left and right cerebral hemispheres. *Current Directions in Psychological Science, 3*, 5-8.

Acquisition of Literacy skills in children with Specific Language Impairment: A Longitudinal Investigation in French

Filio Zourou (Filio.Zourou@univ-lyon2.fr)
Laboratory EMC (EA 3082 CNRS), University Lyon 2, Institute of Psychology,
5, av. Mendes-France, 69676 Bron, Cedex, France

Jean Ecalle (Jean.Ecalle@univ-lyon2.fr)
Laboratory EMC (EA 3082 CNRS), University Lyon 2, Institute of Psychology,
5, av. Mendes-France, 69676 Bron, Cedex, France

Annie Magnan (Annie.Magnan@univ-lyon2.fr)
Laboratory EMC (EA 3082 CNRS), University Lyon 2, Institute of Psychology,
5, av. Mendes-France, 69676 Bron, Cedex, France

Abstract

This study examined the link between phonological development and literacy acquisition in the case of children with Specific Language Impairment (SLI). A sample of 20 beginning-reader French-speaking children with SLI participated in our longitudinal study. Their performances on phonological awareness were evaluated at three points in time over 2 ½ years, Time 1 (T1), Time 2 (T2) and Time 3 (T3). Their oral language was evaluated at T2 and T3, while at T3 we also evaluated their literacy skills. According to our results, at T3 none of the children showed any delay at phonological awareness, yet the literacy skills of the majority of them were significantly below average compared to normally developed children. At T3 our entire sample presented significant improvement in their utterances as well. We argue about the existence of a reciprocal influence between the early language deficit and the later literacy development of children with SLI. Children with SLI improve significantly their oral language outcomes due to explicit instruction of written language; however their phonological representations seem to remain flawed and this reflects on literacy tasks that demand a high level of phoneme manipulation.

Introduction

Specific language impairment (SLI) is commonly acknowledged when oral language lags behind other areas of development for no apparent reason (Leonard, 1998). By definition, the children in question have normal hearing and intelligence, suffer no neurological dysfunction and have sufficient opportunities to learn language, yet they learn to talk relatively late. Some of their basic linguistic characteristics are production of immature speech sounds, fewer utterances than expected for their age and intelligence, limited vocabularies and use of basic grammatical structures. In brief, children with SLI experience important difficulties in understanding and/or in producing spoken language and are usually impaired in one or more linguistic aspects (phonology, morphology, syntax). For the purposes of the present study, SLI was defined as impaired language (below 1SD from the mean) in the context of normal nonverbal abilities (a standard score of 80 or above).

At present there is considerable evidence that the term SLI does not refer to a homogenous group of children and as such should not be treated as a unitary construct. For over 40 years studies of children with SLI have been trying to determine the deficit nature of these children. However, its' causes are being still hotly debated, ranging from non-linguistic deficits in auditory perception and in general processing to high-level deficits in grammar. Recently, Ziegler et al. (2005), testing children with SLI under different conditions of stationary and fluctuating masking noise, found that their basic temporal and spectral capacities are relatively sparse· hence, concluded that the deficit must be due to an inefficient mapping of acoustic information onto phonetic features at a central (postcochlear) conversion stage.

Although children with SLI constitute a heterogeneous group, it has been made clear that phonology is among the areas of language adversely affected in many of them. Indeed, children with SLI exhibit significant difficulties in phonological processing and phonological awareness (Bortolini & Leonard, 2000). As for the grammatical deficits that are typical in SLI they are often considered to be the sequel of impaired speech perception rather than their cause. Joanisse and Seidenberg (2003) explored the hypothesis that this perceptual deficit specifically affects the use of phonological information in working memory, which in turns leads to poorer than expected syntactic comprehension.

The exact nature of the impairment as long as the extent to which it can explain the full range of language problems in children with SLI still remain the subject of considerable debate. However, the main bulk of research in recent literature contains evidence that due to their difficulties in oral language, children with SLI are at risk for literacy problems, the majority of them evolving as poor readers, even those who have overcome their oral language difficulties (Catts et al, 2002). Since most of the education is largely dependent on the ability to read, any difficulties in this area could cause a wider disruption. In our studies, we adopted the psycholinguistic perspective which provides an explanation on why children with SLI often have associated literacy problems evolving from poor readers to dyslexics (Stackhouse & Wells, 1997; 2001). As we already mentioned, children with SLI face difficulties in sound discrimination and categorization and in manipulating the phonemes of their language. Stackhouse and Wells, argue that impaired speech perception interferes with the development of phonological representations, which in turn affects spelling and reading abilities.

The essence of the psycholinguistic model is the assumption that children establish a speech processing system (input, lexicon and output) from implicitly manipulating oral language. However, this system is also the foundation for the subsequent literacy development. In the case of children with SLI, impaired speech perception will affect the construction of phonological representations, provoking boundaries to literacy development. The early and premature phonological representations are of great importance in the first stages of word recognition, when the stored orthographic representations are still very restricted. During this early stage, children rely massively on their phonological representations in order to decode words. If the phonological representations are vague and inaccurate, due to impaired speech perception, children are bound to face significant difficulties in the decoding procedure.

One of the most robust findings emerging from research across languages is the existence of a causal connection and of a reciprocal influence between a child's phonological awareness and his / her literacy development (Bishop & Snowling, 2004). A number of longitudinal studies, most of them conducted with English-speaking SLI children show that they are at high risk for reading difficulties, even if their oral language no longer seems to be deficient. Catts et al. (2002) conducted an epidemiological study involving 328 kindergartners with language impairments. At each time point, children were assessed on tests of phonological awareness, letter identification, word identification, word attack and reading comprehension. According to their results, approximately 50% of their sample was considered to have significant reading difficulties after 2 or 4 years of schooling.

Studies of the reading outcomes of children with SLI have also been trying to specify the factors that seem to differentiate those with good reading outcomes from those with poor. Bishop and Adams (1990) were the first to argue that the major factor related to reading outcomes was the persistence of the language impairment. In particular, they reported that 4-year-old children with SLI who continued to have language problems at 5 ½ years had poor reading achievement at 8 ½ years, whereas those who had resolved

their language problems did not. On the basis of these findings Bishop et al. proposed the 'critical age hypothesis', considering the age to which phonological problems persisted as an important factor. However, according to other studies, the relationship between oral and written language impairments is more complex than the results cited above. Scarborough & Dodrich (1990) argue that sometimes early recovery in language may be illusory and the language problems may resurface in elementary school years in children deemed to have outgrown these problems.

In contrast to the large amount of evidence about the reading skills of children with SLI, the development of spelling skills has attracted much less attention. Nevertheless, the development of spelling skills poses more of a challenge to children than learning to read, especially in an opaque orthography, such as French. We should note that French is an alphabetic language with simple syllabic structure and deep orthography, containing orthographic inconsistencies and complexities, multi-letter graphemes, context dependent rules, irregularities and morphological effects. In other words, the correspondences between phonemes and graphemes are not highly predictable in French. It is well established that children's ability to learn how to spell is influenced by a variety of skills, such as phonological awareness, knowledge of grapheme-phoneme correspondences and reading. It has also been acknowledged that phonological skills are critical to spelling and could be considered as a good predictor of later literacy development (Caravolas, Hulme & Snowling, 2001). Children with weak phonological skills will do poorly on tests of orthographic processing because they have failed to develop appropriate mappings between phonology and orthography.

The main objective of our study was the investigation of the language and literacy skills of children with SLI attending primary school. We, therefore, conducted a 2½ ys longitudinal study with French-speaking school-aged SLI children. The goal of this follow-up investigation was to study children with SLI as they develop their literacy skills, in order to examine 1) the role of explicit instruction of written language, through the development of phonological awareness, to the resolution of oral language difficulties and 2) the repercussions of the early language deficit on literacy acquisition.

Method

Participants

Participants were 20 French-speaking monolingual children (14 boys and 6 girls) diagnosed with SLI at the inter-disciplinary services of Hospitals Lyon-Sud and Debrousse, Reference Centers of the Rhone-Alps area in Lyon, France. The foremost criterion by which we selected our participants was that they had a history of expressive and/or receptive language delays (significant discrepancy between VIQ and PIQ, according to the Wechsler Scales), having neither hearing nor visual difficulties. Among them, only children who had a PIQ score (WPPSI-R or WISC-III scale) superior or equal to 80 were recruited (mean PIQ = 100.85, SD = 16.3) and only those who at T1 attended the appropriate to their chronological-age school class. Of the 20 children of our initial sample, 11 of them were seen three times and 9 of them two times[1].

From these 20 children we identified two subgroups, according to the class they followed at T1. These consisted of a subgroup A of children at kindergarten (n = 8, mean age 5;3, SD = 4.48) and of a subgroup B of children attending Grade 1 (n = 12, mean age 6;2, SD = 3.08). We should note that at T2 a child (ClG) of subgroup B had to repeat her G1 and at T3 the number of children who repeated a class increased to 4 (DL, JoL, BM and ClG).

At T1 and T2 we also recruited a control group (n = 20) matched at age, sex and PIQ in order to compare our samples phonological skills. At T3 both verbal and nonverbal skills were assessed by an extensive battery of standardized formal tests which provided us the possibility to compare our sample with a large control group.

Materials

Oral language development We administered a test of Grammatical Closure (TCGR-C, Deltour, 2002), which comprises a series of images, presented in couples. A target phrase is given for the first image that the participant is required to complete according to the second image. The test includes 52 items giving a maximum of 52 points. The obtained raw scores were converted to age of development (AD) equivalents.

Phonological awareness
Phoneme deletition: We used a forced-choice task in which the participants were required to delete the initial sound from the beginning of a spoken word and give the remaining sound sequence. At T1 and T2 the stimuli were 18 words presented in pictures and named by the examiner (ex. /boeuf/, [beef], /oeuf/, [egg]). The child is required to choose the target word designed in a picture, among three others, 2 phonological (ex. /banc/, [bench], /neuf/ [new, nine]) and 1 semantic distractor (ex. /viande/ [meat]). At T3 we used the standardized phoneme deletition subtest of ODEDY'S (Jacquier-Roux, Valdois & Zorman, 2002). The stimuli were 10 words given orally and the participants are required to pronounce the remaining word or non-word.
Phoneme blending: For this task administered only at T3 children were required to use the initial sounds from the beginning of two spoken words (e.g. /bonne/, /année/) to produce a syllable (/ba/). The stimuli are 10 pairs of words from the phoneme blending subtest of the ODEDY's. One point was awarded for each correct syllable produced, giving a maximum of 10 points.

---

[1] At T2 9 children were not seen due to lack of parental motivation. However, at T3 we were able to examine our entire sample.

Literacy Skills As a measure of the child's current reading attainment we administered two subtests of the K-ABC test (Kaufman & Kaufman, 1993), the reading/decoding (R/D) and the reading/understanding (R/U) subtest. The raw scores were converted to age of development (AD) equivalents.
Word Recognition: The R/D subtest of the K-ABC measures the participant's ability to accurately pronounce French printed words. The stimuli were 38 printed single words.
Comprehension: The K-ABC R/U subtest comprises a series of short phrases (1 to 20 words) that the child is required to read one by one (either aloud or silently) in order to perform the order given by the phrase presented (ex 'Eat', 'Show me how you drink a glass of milk').
Spelling: We administered the spelling subtest of the 'BREV' that comprises a series of 10 words and non-words. In this task, children were asked to spell single words and single non-words and a series of words presented in a sentence context. Table 1 displays the tests administered over the course of this investigation.

Table 1: Summary of the tasks administered.

Task	T1	T2	T3
Oral language			
Grammatical closure		x	x
Phoneme deletition	x	x	x
Phoneme blending			x
Literacy skills			
Reading/Decoding			x
Reading/Understanding			x
Spelling			x

Procedure

In all three times participants were assessed individually over a single session (~1 h) that took place at their home, including breaks so as to avoid fatigue. All measures had a small number of demonstration items in which the examiner provided feedback regarding the correctness of the participant's response.

Results
Oral language development
According to the results we obtained at T2 and T3, the sample of this study (n = 11) diminished significantly, z=-2.5, p=0.013 (Wilcoxon Signed-Rank Test) the discrepancy between their chronological age (CA) and their age of development (AD) at T3. In other words, their skills on oral language at T3 are much closer to the skills attended according to their CA than they are at T2. Only for a single participant (DL) the discrepancy has increased at T3. Figure 1 displays the discrepancy between CA and AD for each participant at T2 and T3. The results of this study are compatible to our hypothesis according to which explicit

instruction of written language has eventually a positive effect on oral language development as well. Further analyses indicated that 54.5% of our participants no longer seem to present SLI characteristics if we sustain oral language development as the single criterion (AC-AD < 6 months). On the contrary, 27% of our participants continue at T3 to show a significant discrepancy of more than 2 years between their CA and their AD.

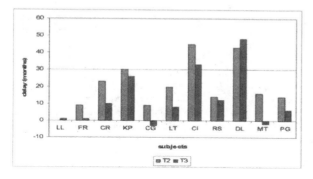

Figure 1: Delay at oral language development (AC-AD) at T2 and T3 for each of the participants.

Phonological awareness development in relation to literacy development

In order to assess our samples' ($n = 20$) deviancy from normal development on the tasks of phoneme deletion (Ph.D.), phoneme blending (Ph.B.) and spelling (S) we used a modified T-test (Crawford et al. 2004) based on the mean and SD of the controls and the control sample N (we used standardized measures). The scores that fell below $p < .05$, one tailed[2], were considered statistically significant and were taken as an indication that the participant has a deficit on the task in question. Table 2 displays the raw scores at T1 and T3 on Ph.D, Ph.B and S for each participant.

On the contrary, raw scores on reading tasks, R/D and R/U, and oral language (TCGR-C) were converted to AD equivalents, where only delay of more than 6 months was considered as significant. Figure 2 displays the prevalence of children showing delay on word recognition (R/D task), comprehension (R/U task) and oral language (TCGR-C task) at T3. We, then, compared the deviant scores on phonological tasks with the literacy skills for each participant. Our goal was to highlight plausible persistent deficits in phonological awareness and their effect on literacy acquisition. The results we obtained, lacking strict regularity, seem to underline by large the heterogeneity of SLI children.

---

2 We used one-tailed tests as it is the tool mostly recommended in single-case research; as Crawford et al. 2004 suggest 'they are more powerful and are legitimate given that the possibility of enhanced performance in the patient can be discount except in very rare and highly specific circumstances' (p. 754).

Table 2: Individual raw scores on phoneme deletion (Ph.D.), phoneme blending (Ph.B.) and spelling (S)

	Ph.D.(T1)	Ph.D. (T3)	Ph.B. (T3)	S. (T3)
RS	4*	4	8	5.5**
DL	3*	6	3	2***
JoL	2**	2	3	3***
MT	5	2	3	6,5
JL	4*	10	7	7,5
GM	6	7	2	7
FG	5	6	5	7,5
PG	6	7	6	4.5**
LL	5**	9	6	4**
AP	4**	6	7	3***
FR	4**	10	7	3.5**
NM	8	7	3*	4**
CR	4**	9	7	4**
CN	5**	7	7	5*
KP	2***	8	4	3***
CG	10	10	7	4.5**
GB	4**	7	10	5,5
BM	4**	4	6	3***
LT	11	6	10	5*
ClG	5**	5	0	4**

* $p < .05$; ** $p < .01$; *** $p = .001$.

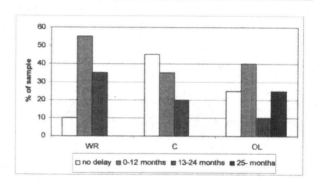

Figure 2: Prevalence of children showing delay on word recognition (WR), comprehension (C) and oral language (OL) at T3.

However, there seem to be two undeniable facts about T3. On the one hand, our entire sample presents non-deviant skills on phonological tasks and on the other hand 91% of it presents a significant difficulty on spelling, even children who no longer present any delay at phonological awareness. As far as reading skills are concerned, 35 % of our sample presents an important delay of 13 to 24 months in the R/D task. However, the R/U skills of our sample are better, with 45% of them presenting no delay. We could therefore, wonder if they use semantic access instead as it is often suggested being the path used by dyslexics. Finally, 35% of our sample continue to present an important delay of 13 to more than 25 months on their oral language, even after 2 (group A) or 3 (group B) years of schooling. Over all, our results corroborate with those obtained in Anglo-Saxon longitudinal studies of SLI children, according to which SLI children are at risk for literacy problems.

Discussion

The main findings of the present study can be summarized as follows. The first one, largely suggested by our data is that children with SLI eventually improve their utterances and develop their phonological skills through the acquisition of grapho-phonemic correspondences (GPC) and the development of literacy skills. According to our results, our entire sample after 2 or 3 years of schooling showed no delay compared to normally developed children on phonological awareness, being able to handle phonemes sufficiently on metaphonological tasks. Moreover, 91% of our sample decreased significantly the discrepancy between their AD and their CA at their utterances. However, according to our study 45% of our sample continues to exhibit a delay of more than 6 moths in oral language development (8 to 48 months).

The reason why we evaluated the level of phonological awareness using the deletion task is that such tasks rank highly among phonological awareness tasks in predicting reading achievement (Torgessen et al, 1994). At T3 we proposed a second phonological task to explore a bit further the metaphonological skills of our sample. Recent research has consistently shown that the acquisition of GPC improves the phonological skills of children, and consequently their level of phonological awareness. The acquisition of the alphabetical code contributes significantly to the sensitivity of children with SLI on the phonemic aspects of their language. However, it seems of great importance to highlight the fact that although our sample seems to have acquired over time a certain level of phonological awareness, their skills remained mostly task-specific. In other words, they seemed unable to generalize the use of this knowledge to tasks other than phoneme deletion and phoneme blending, such as reading and spelling that require a high level of phoneme manipulation.

The second most important finding of our study is related to the difficulties that children with SLI exhibit on reading (word identification and comprehension) and spelling. Recent literature provides evidence that certain children with a history of SLI in spite of a clear improvement of their language impairment have difficulties learning to read and tend to be rather poor readers. This type of results is awaited if we make the assumption that there is a causal connection between oral language development and literacy acquisition, independently of the direction of influence. Eventually, a certain number of SLI children after 2 or 3 years of normal schooling present a level of phonological skills close to the standard. Thus, we could expect literacy skills in line with their phonological skills since the second ones seem to be of great importance for the acquisition of reading· yet this is not the case.

To go further, one can also wonder about the potential of children with SLI to truly take advantage of the explicit instruction of written language as it is at present provided. The metaphonological skills that emerge due to explicit instruction will specify the representations stored in the lexicon· yet one does not find the attended repercussions in tasks requiring a spontaneous activation of the phonological representations such as spelling for example. We argue, that the early phonological representations developed due to oral language exposure do indeed become better specified during literacy acquisition. However, they somehow preserve the traces of the early deficit, and this is regularly documented in literacy tasks. In other words, although the phonological representations seem to have approached normal levels of specification, the manipulation of them remains overdrawn. We, therefore, conclude that although in some cases of SLI children the speech problem may seem to have resolved, yet the underlying phonological processing problem persists and interferes with later literacy development.

Conclusion

In the light of the above we would argue that reality is set between two positions: a minimum level of phonological awareness is important for the acquisition of literacy skills; literacy acquisition helps the child develop his phonological awareness. An efficient system of phonological coding, which allows good performances in all kinds of phonological tasks improves both oral and written language. Any default in the system of speech processing will have repercussions in the development of written language. As a consequence, children with a history of SLI are bound to develop less precise phonological representations, which is consequently reflected on literacy skills.

Our results have consistently shown that a history of SLI seems to be an important factor for literacy difficulties, agreeing with those obtained in Anglo-Saxon longitudinal studies. However, at the same time they raise a number of questions concerning the exact nature of the deficit and its repercussions that seek to be tested in future studies. It is important to highlight the issue of the heterogeneity SLI children which is present throughout our study. The variety of performances observed in our study in all five variables oral language, phonological awareness, reading, comprehension and spelling are attributable to the great heterogeneity of the disorder. Due to the relatively limited sample of participants of our study we did not take into consideration any inter-individual variables during the discussion of our results. Although our research has documented the relationship between language impairment and literacy difficulties, it has not clearly specified the exact nature of this association. Factors responsible for the lack of specificity include the relatively small size of participant sample and the limited consideration of subgroups of children with SLI.

The importance of factors such as the acquisition of the grammatico-syntactic rules and the expansion of the vocabulary has already been discussed in literature. As far as our study is concerned it would have been interesting to measure the vocabulary of our participants and to examine its role on language and literacy development. The pursue of longitudinal studies on SLI children beginning-readers will eventually define our comprehension of the nature of the early phonological deficit and its repercussions on literacy acquisition in order to eventually be able to propose effective means of instruction of literacy and phonological skills.

Acknowledgements

Thanks are extended to the neuropsychologist Monique Sanchez for finding the population and for collecting the raw data at T1, to the neurologist Sibylle Gonsalez, the psychologists Christelle Glissoux and Annie Ritz (Hospital Lyon-Sud) and the neuropsychologist Vania Herbillion (Hospital Debrousse) all for kindly letting us have access to the population, to Celine Castello-Lopez for collecting the raw data at T2 and to the families of all children.

References

Billard, C., Vol, S., Livet, M.O., Motte, J., Vallée, L., & Gillet, P. (2002). The BREV neuropsychological test: Part I. Results from 500 normally developing children. *Developmental Medecine and Child Neurology. 44,* 391-398

Bishop, D.V.M., & Adams, C. (1990). A prospective study of the relationship between specific language impairment, phonological disorders and reading retardation. *Journal of Child Psychology and Psychiatry, 31,* 1027-1050.

Bishop, D.V.M., & Snowling, M.J. (2004). Developmental dyslexia and specific language impairment: Same or Different. *Psychological Bulletin, 130(6),* 858-886.

Bortolini, U. & Leonard, L.B. (2000). Phonology and children with specific language impairment: Status of structural constraints in two languages. *Journal of Communication Disorders, 33,* 131-150.

Caravolas, M., Hulme, C., & Snowling, M.J. (2001). The foundations of spelling ability: evidence from a 3-year longitudinal study. *Journal of Memory and Language, 45,* 751-774.

Catts, H.W., Fey, M.E., Tomblin, J.B., & Zhang, X. (2002). A longitudinal investigation of reading outcomes in children with language impairments. *Journal of Speech, Language and Hearing Research, 45,* 1142-1157.

Crawford, J.R., Garthwaite, Ph., Howell, D.C. & Gray, C.D. (2004). Inferential methods for comparing a single-case with a control sample: modified *t*-tests versus Mycroft et al's (2002) modified *ANOVA. Cognitive Neuropsychology, 21(7),* 750-755.

Deltour, J.J. (2002). *Test de Closure Grammaticale* [Test of Grammtical Closure]. Paris : EAP.

Jacquier-Roux, M., Valdois, S., & Zorman, M. (2002). Outil de Depistage des Dyslexies, ODEDY's. [Tool for the depiction of Dyslexia]. Laboratoire Cogni-Sciences IUFM : Grenoble.

Joanisse, M.F. & Seidenberg, M.S. (2003). Phonology and syntax in specific language impairment: Evidence from a connectionist model. *Brain and language, 86,* 40-56.

Kaufman A.S. & Kaufman N.L. (1983). *Kaufman Assessment Battery for Children (K-ABC). American Guidance Service.* [Adaptation française: Batterie pour l'examen psychologique de l'enfant. 1993]. Paris : Editions CPA

Leonard, L.B. (1998) *Children with specific language impairment.* Cambridge, MA: MIT Press.

Scarborough, H.S., & Dodrich, W. (1990). Development of children with early language delay. *Journal of Speech and Hearing Research, 33,* 70-83.

Stackhouse, J., & Wells, (Eds) (1997). *Children's speech and literacy difficulties: a psycholinguistic framework.* London: Whurr Publishers.

Stackhouse, J., & Wells, (Eds) (2001). *Children's speech and literacy difficulties: identification and intervention.* London: Whurr Publishers.

Torgessen, J.K., Wagner, R.K., & Rashotte, C.A. (1994). Longitudinal studies of phonological processing and reading. *Journal of Learning Disabilities, 27,* 276-286.

Ziegler, J.C., Pech-Georgel, C., George, F., Alario, F-X., & Lorenzi, C., (2005). Deficits in speech perception predict language learning impairment. *PNAS, 102(39),* 14110-12115.

Mental Verbs and Memory Functioning in Children with Language Difficulties and Typically Developing Children: Structural Similarities and Differences

George Spanoudis (spanoud@ucy.ac.cy)
Department of Psychology, University of Cyprus, Kallipoleos 75, P.O Box 20537, 1678 Nicosia, Cyprus

Demetrios Natsopoulos (ednats@ucy.ac.cy)
Department of Psychology, University of Cyprus, Kallipoleos 75, P.O Box 20537, 1678 Nicosia, Cyprus and
The Philips College, 10, Lamia Str., Cyprus

Abstract
The memory function and mental verb acquisition was investigated in a group of 50 children with language learning impairment (LLI) in comparison with a group of 50 typically developing children (TDC) matched on age and nonverbal cognition. Verbal IQ of the two groups was different in favour of the latter group. The participants were tested on four memory and four mental verb measures. The results have shown that the children with LLI performed significantly lower than the group of TDC. The working and long-term memory tasks classified significantly the participants into two groups but a confirmatory factor analysis indicated that the pattern of the factor structure was qualitatively very similar, despite minor differences between the two groups.

Introduction

Children with LLI display diminished language skills despite having normal nonverbal intelligence and hearing, and no signs of neurological impairments, or behavioural or social disturbances (Tallal & Benasich, 2002). Two streams of work have been purporting to account for developmental language learning disorders. According to the first, the language impairments are directly linked with linguistic functioning, such as the morphosyntactic rules. With respect to the second, the language difficulties the children with LLI have lie out of modular boundaries of the linguistic 'system' and might also be associated with the cognitive system in general (Leonard, 1998).

Further, based on the second research line, three different approaches have been proposed: Tallal (2003) is the exponent of the first approach; she has argued that the problem of language difficulties in children with LLI lies in the acoustic-perceptual discrimination level. Unlike Tallal's view, Baddeley and his associates (Baddeley, 2003; Baddeley, Gathercole & Papagno, 1998) theorize that language impairments in children relate to memory dysfunction and especially to short-term and working memory. On the other hand, Miller, Kail, Leonard and Tomblin (2001) estimate that the slower speed of information processing by children with language disorders, in comparison with their peers, is the root cause of the difficulty they experience in language competence.

Of the three positions, Baddeley and his associates' approach has been the most influential and testable account of the possible cause linked with atypical language development in children. According to the theory, the short-term and working memory functioning constitute the phonological (articulatory) loop which with the visuo-spatial scratch pad component (both auxiliary) sub-serve the central executive representing the focus of the control of the cognitive system and determining how inputs should be dealt with and information retrieved from long-term store (see also Baddeley, 2003). Evidence suggests that inefficient functioning of short-term and working memory which may reflect possible impairment of the phonological store placed within the phonological loop (Baddeley et al., 1998) may also have as direct outcome an atypical lexical development and cause, in turn, disorders of grammatical and pragmatic development in children. Additional research data also indicate that difficulties in learning new words and sustaining sequence of words in short-term and working memory has often been observed in children with Specific Language Impairment (SLI) (Leonard, 1998; Miller et al., 2001; Montgomery, 2002).

The evidence accumulated so far relative to short-term and working memory functioning in children with SLI and/or language learning impairments resulted from performance on non-word repetition task, an experimental technique used extensively by Baddeley and his colleagues as an index of memory weakness. Indeed, the Baddeley's model seems to provide a satisfactory explanation of developmental language learning difficulties insofar as the link between phonological loop and atypical vocabulary acquisition is concerned. Some other data (Conti-Ramsden, 2003) also provide support that the non-word repetition task is a reliable phenotypic marker of developmental language impairment. Edwards and Lahey (1998) argue against the notion that non-word repetition engages only phonological store processes within the phonological loop; instead, they contend that the same test also measures some kind of long-term lexical knowledge. By the same token, the model does not seem to offer a satisfactory answer relative to how deficient vocabulary might determine the nature of language impairment.

Alternatively, on the face of this argument one may assume that the central executive as the locus of control of the cognitive system dealing with incoming information into phonological loop and retrieving knowledge from the long-term store, may also play a specific role in the emergence and consolidation of language disorders in children with learning difficulties as Marton and Schwartz (2003) and Montgomery (2002) incline to believe.

In a similar spirit, Adams and Gathercole (2000) stress the need for greater specificity of the fractionated working memory model in order to investigate how working memory deals with stored linguistic knowledge (lexicon and grammar) when processing verbal inputs over an interface trade off with the long-term memory. As yet, there are not comprehensive data about the role the long-term memory plays in the emergence of language learning difficulties in children. Also given that the group of children with LLI is particularly heterogeneous as the reviewed literature suggests, the role of each component of the memory faculty and cognition system, separately and in concert, may account for subgroups of children emerging with various profiles of language competence.

The aim of the present study was to extend the findings of prior research by accounting for the contribution of each memory sub-system to language learning difficulties using a number of language and memory ability measures. With regard to language measures we decided to include the class of mental verbs because we believe that the acquisition of verb, in general, and mental verbs specifically, plays a significant role in children's language development.

In particular, the verb system which is the most complex linguistically and conceptually part of the language, the course of its development is slower and goes beyond the school-age. This especially applies to the class of mental verbs (Naigles, 2000) which denote inner mental states (*think, know, remember, believe, regret, intend, forget, promise*) and are associated with interesting syntactic, semantic and pragmatic aspects. From the semantic point of view, mental verbs relate to the 'language of mind' (Astington & Jenkins, 1999) and to some theorists the mental verbs through syntax, namely complementation (de Villiers & Pyers, 2002), contribute to the understanding of Theory of Mind. Moreover, mental verbs have multiple pragmatic functions (Harris, de Rosnay, & Pons, 2005), such as marking the degree of certainty by which a statement is made. In this sense, the mental verbs constitute a bridge of direct connection of language with the development of cognition.

The present study addressed the following research questions: **1.** Do the group of LLI children and TDC differ in memory functioning and mental verb acquisition? **2.** If yes, which of the memory measures are the strongest marker for discriminating the two groups; or alternatively, which of the mental verb measures might have discriminated them? **3.** If the two groups are different in performance in memory and mental verb measures, to what extent these measures are quantitatively or qualitatively different?

Method

Participants

Two groups of children participated in this study; the experimental group consisted of 50 children and the control group of 50 typically developing children also. The experimental group included 33 males and 17 females and the control group 39 males and 11 females. All children attended primary school, had hearing and corrected vision within normal limits, and had no reported behavioural, emotional, or neurological problems. All the participants were Greek native speakers; their age range was 8;0-12;0 years. All children were recruited from 22 urban and suburban public schools in Nicosia, the capital city, Cyprus.

The recruitment of children with putative LLI was based on the following criteria: score on Verbal IQ at least 1 SD below the mean as measured by a standardised intelligence test (WISC-III, 1997); Performance IQ on WISC-III within the normal range; poor verbal scholastic performance on language ability assessed by their class teachers on a 5-point scale, ranging from 1 (poor) to 5 (excellent).

Table 1 displays scores on age, verbal and non-verbal intelligence, and verbal scholastic performance on the two groups. The two groups were matched on WISC-III Performance [t(88)=-1.63, p=.11] and on age [t(98)=1.47, p=.14]. In contrast, the two groups differed significantly on WISC-III Verbal Intelligence [t(65)=-17.97, p<.001] and verbal scholastic ability [(t(98)=-5.97, p<.001)].

Table 1: Age, verbal IQ (VIQ), non-verbal IQ (NVIQ), and verbal scholastic performance (VSP) of the LLI and TDC group

	LLI (N=50)			TDC (N=50)		
	M	SD	Range	M	SD	Range
Age	122.5	10.3	102-142	119.1	12.3	86-142
VIQ	82.2	3.7	71-86	107.1	9.1	92-136
NVIQ	101.7	9.7	90-122	104.4	6.8	90-117
VSP	1.5	.61	1-3	2.9	1.5	3-5

Tasks and Procedure

All the participants were seen in two sessions; in the first session the matching procedure took place with WISC-III and in the second, the main test procedure. The main test consisted of *four memory* and *four language ability* tasks.

Memory tasks

Two of the four memory tasks, a *nonword repetition (NWRT)* and a *real word repetition (WRT)* task, aimed to assess phonological short-term memory (PhS-TM). The third, the task of *sentence recall (SRT)* intended to estimate ability of verbal working memory (VWM). The fourth task, a *delayed story recall (DSRT), was* designed to measure the relationship between the two memory systems, namely the long-term (L-TM) and short-term and working memory.

More specifically, the nonword repetition task consisted of a set of 16 pairs of nonwords ranging from two to five syllables in length (i.e., 4 pairs of words for each word length). A sample of 58 undergraduate students of psychology aged 19-23 were used to judge the wordlikeness of 64 nonwords, on a scale ranging from 1 (very unlikely to be rated as a real Greek word) to 5 (very likely to be rated as a real Greek word). The nonwords with averaged wordlikeness ratings nearest to 2.5 were included in this test (Gathercole, 1998).

In turn, the nonword pairs were presented in a randomized sequence to all children. Instructions and test stimuli were recorded into WAV computer files by a male speaker at normal rate (160 wpm). The presentation to the children was performed by means of E-Prime software. The children had to hear carefully the stimuli, seating in front of two loudspeakers, and repeat the pairs of nonwords. The participants before proceeding to the main testing procedure had to practice by repeating two pairs of nonwords in order to become familiar with the task. For each nonword, the presentation time was 1500 msec for all types of word length. The inter-stimulus interval on each pair of nonwords was 750 msec. That is, the whole amount of time for each pair of nonwords was approximately 3750 msec. After the presentation of each pair of nonwords a prompt appeared on the screen of computer asking the participant to repeat accurately the pair of nonwords heard. The experimenter scored online the accuracy of the participant's response. Repetition responses were scored either as correct (score 1) or incorrect (score 0). The maximum correct score was 16 for each participant.

The structure of the real word repetition task was the same as the nonword one, having nouns of two to five syllables, whose frequency and concreteness was controlled. The administration and scoring procedure was also the same as the one with nonword task.

Relative to the structure of sentence recall task, it was similar to the homologous subtest of WPPSI-R (Wechsler, 1989). Namely, it consisted of twelve sentences of increasing length and syntactic complexity; 8 adjusted from WPPSI-R, five to twenty words in length, and 4 constructed by the authors, which were syntactically more complex, containing main and dependent relative clauses with different thematic roles. The participants before engaged in the main experiment procedure were presented with two practice examples to be acquainted with the requirement of the task. All sentences and practice stimuli were recorded into WAV files by a male speaker at normal rate. The presentation procedure was the same as in nonword task. The responses of each child were scored online according to the WPPSI-R manual. Specifically, if the recalling of sentence was completely accurate, without any word omission or substitution, the child was credited with 2 points. If there were word substitutions with synonyms, the child was credited with 1 point. In all the other cases, the scoring was 0. The maximum score was 24.

The task which aimed to assess long-term memory (L-TM) was a text taken from a children's story book. The text was a story familiar to school-age children and consisted of about 375 words. The whole story was divided into four parts of 6-10 sentences each. The four parts were written on four cards presented one at a time to the participants. Also four to six questions were constructed for each part of the story. These questions preserved main concepts which the participants had to infer and store in memory as they went through out the text. The children were instructed to read carefully each card and told that they had to answer a number of questions relative to the text they read it. The children were engaged in solving simple arithmetic problems for 15 minutes after finished the reading of the text. After 15 minutes the experimenter asked each child to answer the 4-6 questions relative to each text mentioned above.

Children were credited with 2 points for each correct answer. For a child, to be credited with a correct answer she had to answer in an adult-like manner i.e., in a detailed way. In that case the score was of 2. If the answer was less detailed the child was credited with 1 point. In all other cases the child was scored with 0. The maximum possible

score was 40. Two inter-raters agreement on the total correct score was 97%.

Language ability tasks

The first language task was a *mental verb definition task* (MVD) that consisted of 25 instances of mental verbs like: *compare, guess, decide, believe, agree, think* etc. aiming to measure knowledge of semantics linked with understanding and production of this class of verbs. In particular, the participants were provided with a single sentence followed by four mental verb instances out of which they should select the most appropriate verb to fit the meaning of the sentence, as the following example indicates: '*I can give an answer to my teacher's question*' (**reason, learn, know, think**).

All mental verbs used in the four language tasks were derived from grade appropriate reading text-books, due to lack of published norms of word frequency in Greek, after they were evaluated in a pilot study with 53 children of the same grades as those of the participants in the study. More specifically, to select the mental verbs all children were presented with a list of the verbs one at a time, and asked to give at least one synonym verb to the one presented. Accordingly, only verbs that were understood by more than 90% of the children in this sample were finally used for the current study.

The aim of the second language task was to assess the children's competence in taking advantage of preceding context which provided more communicative information compared to the previous language task. The task was a *mental verb story* task (MVS) and consisted of 35 mental verbs (25 also used in the first task and 10 new ones) for which an equivalent number of short stories (vignettes) dramatized simple everyday life episodes with 2 to 3 children as 'heroes' whose sex was balanced across the presentation. Accordingly, participants were asked to select the most appropriate mental verb out of four presented and fill in the blanks of sentences derived from the preceding context, like the following example shows: '*John and Mary went to the movies to see a film they liked very much. On the way to their house, Mary liked to see whether John kept in mind the name of hero and asked him to tell it. 'John ... (think, learn, recognize, remember) the name of hero*'. The rationale of using the same 25 mental verbs of the previous task stemmed from the assumption that performance might be differentiated by the two groups when more contextual restrictions, like those in the first task, would impose more demanding inferential processes compared with those in the second task. The children were told that they would read very short fictitious stories on the computer screen which some times might appear funny. They were instructed to read each story carefully and then complete the missing part of the following sentence, by choosing the word (verb) which fitted best the entire story.

The objective of the third task was to investigate possible differences in word organization in mental lexicon, relative to meaning and grammatical class. This task was a *mental verb association task* (MVAT) and consisted of 15 mental verbs. The children were instructed to produce as many similar words as they could, after they were exposed to two examples. They also were told to avoid repetitions of the same words, use unrelated words and phrases and the same words in negative form. A concordance criterion (94%-98%) based on inter-rater reliability between two blind research assistants was deployed for scoring.

The fourth task with factive (*know, remember, understand, learn, forget*) and nonfactive mental verbs (FV and NFV, respectively) was intended to measure children's ability to draw implications signified by the two previous classes of mental verbs that the event described in the complement clause (infinitival and/or nominal) is true, in comparison with nonfactive verbs [*promise, agree,*('commissives')] denoting an obligation or declaring intention; and *think, imagine, believe* ('expositives') stating reasons, arguments and communications, respectively. It was thought that typically developing children would be able to demonstrate higher command of making inferences relative to mental verbs, factive and nonfactive (Natsopoulos, 1987) in comparison with children who have language difficulties. Also, children were instructed to read carefully very short stories on the screen and select one of the three answers that would best fit in the meaning of the story.

Results

Group Differences on Memory and Language Tasks

A one-way MANOVA was used to assess group differences in four memory tasks with group as independent variable and the four memory measures as within variable (nonword repetition, word repetition, sentence recall, and delayed story recall). The analysis indicated that the controls were significantly higher in overall performance [$F(5,95) = 19.40$, $p < .001$, $\eta^2 = .45$] and F-univariate tests in comparison with the experimental group [$F(1,98) = 57.62$, $p < .001$, $\eta^2 = .37$; $F(1,98) = 5.96$, $p = .016$, $\eta^2 = .06$; $F(1,98) = 35.12$, $p < .001$, $\eta^2 = .26$; $F(1,98) = 45.47$, $p < .001$, $\eta^2 = .32$, respectively]. Also, to compare the two groups a MANOVA was conducted on four language ability tasks (mental verb definition, mental verb story, mental verb association, and factive and nonfactive verbs). The analysis showed that the TDC were significantly different in overall performance [$F(5,95) = 8.12$, $p < .001$, $\eta^2 = .25$] and F-univariate tests relative to the children with LLI [$F(1,98) = 28.31$, $p < .001$, $\eta^2 = .22$; $F(1,98) = 18.69$, $p < .001$, $\eta^2 = .16$; $F(1,98) = 17.85$, $p < .001$, $\eta^2 = .15$; $F(1,98) = 11.11$, $p < .001$, $\eta^2 = .10$, respectively]. Table 2 shows means and standard deviations on all memory and language measures (see hypothesis 1).

Table 2: Means, standard deviations and range on all memory and language tasks

	LLI (N=50)			TDC (N=50)		
	M	SD	Range	M	SD	Range
NWR	4.8	2.7	1-11	8.8	2.7	2-14
WOR	15.4	.73	14-16	15.7	.57	14-16
SER	12.9	4.2	3-22	17.8	3.9	9-24
DSR	14.9	6.5	2-29	23.7	6.5	6-38
MVA	6.66	4.4	0-18	11.5	6.87	0-33
MVD	13.4	4.8	4-22	18.2	4.19	5-25
FNFV	5.94	1.85	2-10	7.08	1.55	2-10
MVS	18.78	6.58	5-32	24.7	7.1	7-34

NWR=nonword repetition, WOR=word repetition, SER= Sentence recall, DSR= delayed story recall, MVA=mental verb association, MVD=mental verb definition, FNFV=factive & nonfactive verbs, MVS=mental verb story

Correlational analyses

Correlations between and within the two categories of tasks on both groups range from low positive significant to moderate (.29 - .63), except for the two language tasks where the correlations were strong positive (.74 - .77) in the group of TDC. Also, correlation of delayed story with nonword repetition task was not significant in the group of LLI in comparison with strong correlation of the two tasks in the group of TDC (.58).

Logistic regression analysis

A sequential logistic regression analysis was applied to assess prediction of membership in one of two groups (LLI children, TDC), first on the basis of four language tasks (mental verb definition, factive and nonfactive verbs, mental verb story, and mental verb association), and then after addition of four memory tasks (delayed story recall, nonword repetition, word repetition, and sentence recall). The analysis showed a good fit of data when based on the four language tasks alone [$\chi^2(4) = 29.03$, $p < .001$] but after the addition of the four memory tasks the fit of data to the model further improved [$\chi^2(8) = 58.49$, $p < .001$, Nagelkerte $R^2 = .59$ with a 95% confidence interval ranging from .41 to .68 (Steiger & Fouladi, 1992)]. Thus, the log-likelihood ratio for models with and without memory measures indicates the statistically significant improvement resulting from the addition of memory tasks [$\chi^2(4) = 29.47$, $p < .001$]. In particular, *delayed story recall* and *nonword repetition* contributed significantly to the model (Wald statistic = 7.13 and 8.94, respectively); of the remaining tasks no one contributed significantly to the same model (see hypothesis 2).

Table 3: Classification of participants into groups

	Predicted		Total
	LLI	TDC	
LLI	41	9	82%
TDC	12	38	76%
Overall			79%

According to Table 3, 41 (82%) and 38 (76%) of the participants were classified as LLI children (LLIc) and TDC (TDCc), respectively. Of the remaining, 12 (24%) of TDC group were misclassified as LLI children (TDCm), and 9 (18%) of LLI children were misclassified as TDC(LLIm), respectively. It should be noted that the discrimination of the participants into two main groups was significantly high (79% overall).

Groups of participants classified and misclassified

According to Table 3 there have been four groups of participants: The 12 TDCm present a profile very similar to that shown by LLIc children, and the 9 LLIm very similar to the TDCc. More specifically, the group of TDCm compared with the group of LLIc children on all memory and language tasks were not statistically different except for the nonword repetition [$t(51) = -2.56$, $p = .013$]. It should, however, be noted that the LLIc children were significantly older in age compared with the 12 TDCm [$t(51) = 2.62$, $p = .011$] and the latter group was significantly higher in VIQ [$t(51) = -11.48$, $p < .001$].

Comparison of the 9 LLIm children with TDCc group revealed significant differences only in delayed story recall [$t(45) = 3.72$, $p < .001$]; no significant differences were found in nonword and word repetition, and sentence recall task. In contrast, significant differences were resulted in all four language tasks [mental verb story, $t(45) = 2.57$, $p = .013$; mental verb definition, $t(45) = 2.55$, $p = .014$; factive and nonfactive verbs, $t(45) = 2.40$, $p = .021$; and mental verb association, $t(45) = 2.30$, $p = .026$]. It should be remarked that the two groups were not significantly different in age but the TDCc group had higher VIQ compared with LLIm children, [$t(45) = 9.30$, $p < .001$] in agreement with the originally designed procedure for recruitment of the participants.

Confirmatory factor analysis

Although different patterns of relationships can be hypothesized, there are only a few studies which examine the relationships of language and memory structures in children with LLI and TDC. Consequently, to test the hypothesis that the children with LLI may have similar structure of language and memory functioning capacity, despite statistical differences in language and memory measures deployed in the present study, a confirmatory factor analysis was applied. A two factor model was hypothesized could be performed on our test battery of eight tasks through EQS 6.1 (Bentler, 2003). The four language tasks served as indicators of language ability factor and the four memory tasks as the indicators of memory capacity factor. The two factors were hypothesized to covary with one another. Maximum likelihood estimation was applied to assess all models. The error term associated with each indicator and the variances of the latent factors were also free parameters in the model. Since in the present study there were data for two groups Confirmatory Factor Analysis (CFA) provided a powerful test for the equivalence of solution across the two groups. The following hierarchical ordering of models was used which facilitates comparison among the different models and provides evidence for differences and/or similarities between the two groups: (i) same pattern of fixed and free loadings for each group (configural invariance or baseline model); (ii) factor loadings invariant across groups (weak invariance); (iii) factor loadings and factor correlations invariant across groups; and (iv) totally invariant model with all parameters (factor loadings, factor correlations and uniquenesses).

Table 4: Differences in fit of alternative models

Model	χ^2	Df	CFI	RMSEA	$\Delta\chi^2$	Δdf	p
Baseline model	50.61	34	.94	.071	-	-	-
FL	62.92	40	.93	.076	12.3	6	NS
FL, FC	63.12	41	.93	.074	.2	1	NS
FL, FC, UN	69.26	45	.92	.074	6.14	4	NS

NS=nonsignificant, FL=factor loadings, FC=factor correlation, UN=uniquenesses

First, in the analysis we tested the efficacy of the model to fit the data on each group (children with LLI and TDC). Either solution provides a good fit to the data because all the goodness of fit indices were acceptable in relation to typical standard. That is, CFI for the group of children with LLI =.967, RMSEA= .079, and $\chi^2(16, N=50)=20.84$, p= .18; CFI for the group of TDC= .954, RMSEA= .09, and $\chi^2(19, N=50)=26.47$, p = .12. These data provide good support for the hypothesized model but do not address the issue of the invariance of the parameter estimates across the two groups. Because one of the objectives of the study was to investigate structural differences and similarities of mental verb acquisition and memory functioning between TDC and children with LLI we tested more specific hypothesis about the lack of measurement invariance (see hypothesis 3). To this aim, we pursued three more specific tests by imposing invariance constraints for a set of parameters (i.e., factor loadings, factor correlations, and error terms) across the two groups. In agreement with the hierarchy described earlier, we started with tests of the equality of factor loadings across the two groups followed by tests of factor correlations and error terms. Table 4 summarizes the results of invariance measurement analysis.

Main Conclusions

The group of children with LLI was outperformed by the group of TDC in all memory tasks (nonword and real word repetition, sentence recall, and delayed story recall), and in all mental verb language tasks (mental verb definition, mental verb story, mental verb association, and factive and nonfactive verbs) (see Table 2).

Correlations between memory and mental verb measures ranged from low positive significant to moderate for both groups. Correlations within memory measures were not significant on either group except strong correlation of nonword measure (phonological memory) with delayed story recall (long-term memory) in the group of TDC.

The logistic regression analysis indicated that phonological memory (nonword) and long-term memory measure (delayed story recall) contributed significantly to classification of the participants in the two groups, children with LLI (82%) and TDC (76%) and overall classification 79%. Twenty four percent (24%) of participants originally included into group of TDC were misclassified as children with LLI and 18% of participants originally classified as children with LLI, were misclassified as TDC.

To answer the question whether the distinction of the participants through the logistic regression is of a quantitative or qualitative nature, a confirmatory factor analysis was used. The analysis verifies that the structure of two factors, namely language and memory follows the same pattern, despite minor differences in factor loadings, in the two groups. The analysis offers a complementary interesting answer relative to misclassified children resulting from the logistic regression. That is, the misclassified TDC and children with LLI might still be in a turning point of development, because they are significantly younger than the main group of LLI and the TDC, while the misclassified children with LLI are developmentally closer to the main group of TDC than to the main group of the LLI as originally were recruited. A follow up study would offer a clearer answer as to the time the misclassified groups would finally consolidate their developmental affinity with one or the other group, respectively.

Overall, our data supports Baddeley's view that the phonological memory contributes to mental verb acquisition. In contrast with Baddeley's theory, our data indicate that long-term memory, in concert with short-term memory, also plays a significant role in contributing to mental verb acquisition. The two memory levels may not be considered as distinctly functioning as Baddeley and his colleagues posit. Also, the fact that the LLI children differed in all measures suggests that language ability to the extent it relates to cognitive level may provide the group of TDC, in comparison with LLI children, with an advantage of storing new linguistic information, a prerequisite for acquisition of various and more complex aspects of language ability such as mental verbs. Further, the fact that the two groups were matched on nonverbal ability and differed only in general verbal ability also attests to the argument that language ability level in synergy with memory functioning underlies the degree of language acquisition by the two groups (see Mainela-Arnold & Evans, 2005).

References

Adams, A.-M. and Gathercole, S. E. (2000). Limitations in working memory: implications for language development. *International Journal of Language and Communication Disorders, 35*, 95-116.

Astington, J. W. & Jenkins, J. M. (1999). A longitudinal study of the relation between language and theory-of-mind development. Development. *Developmental Psychology, 35*, 1311-1320.

Baddeley, A. (2003). Working memory and language: An overview. *Journal of Communication Disorders, 36*, 189-208.

Baddeley, A. D., Gathercole, S. E. and Papagno, C. (1998). The phonological loop as a language learning device. *Psychological Review, 105*, 158–173.

Bentler, P.M. (2003). *EQS 6: Structural Equation Program Manual. Encino*. CA: Multivariate Software

Conti-Ramsden, G. (2003). Processing and linguistic markers in young children with specific language impairment (SLI). *Journal of Speech, Language, and Hearing Research, 46*, 1029-1037.

de Villiers, J. G. and Pyers, J. E., 2002, Complements to cognition: a longitudinal study of the relationship between complex syntax and false-belief-understanding. *Cognitive Development, 17*, 1037-1060.

Edwards, J., & Lahey, M. (1998). Nonword repetitions of children with specific language impairment: Exploration of some explanations for their inaccuracies. *Applied Psycholinguistics, 19*, 278–309.

Gathercole, S. E. (1998). The development of memory. *Journal of Child Psychology and Psychiatry, 39*, 3-27.

Harris, P. L, de Rosnay, M. and Pons, F., (2005). Language and children's understanding of mental states. *Current Directions in Psychological Science, 14(2)*, 69-73.

Leonard, L. B. (1998). *Children with specific language impairment*. Cambridge, MA: MIT Press.

Mainela-Arnold, E. and Evans, J. L. (2005). Beyond capacity limitations: determinants of word recall performance on verbal working memory span tasks in children with SLI. *Journal of Speech, Language, and Hearing Research, 48*, 897-909.

Marton, K., & Schwartz, R. G. (2003). Working memory capacity and language processes in children with specific language impairment. *Journal of Speech, Language, and Hearing Research, 46*, 1138-1153.

Miller, C., Kail, R., Leonard, L., & Tomblin, B. (2001). Speed of processing in children with specific language impairment. *Journal of Speech and Hearing Research, 44*, 416-433.

Montgomery, J. W. (2002). Understanding the language difficulties of children with specific language impairments: Does verbal working memory matter? *American Journal of Speech-Language Pathology, 11*, 77-91.

Naigles, L. R. (2000). Manipulating the input: Studies in mental verb acquisition. In B. Landau, J. Sabini, J. Jonides and E. Newport (eds.), *Perception, Congition, and Language*, (pp. 245-274). Cambridge: MIT Press

Natsopoulos, D. (1987). Processing implications and Presuppositions by school children and adults: A developmental cross-linguistic comparison. *Journal of Psycholinguistic Research, 16(2)*, 133-164.

Steiger, J.H., & Fouladi, R.T. (1992). R2: A computer program for interval estimation, power calculation, and hypothesis testing for the squared multiple correlation. *Behavior Research Methods, Instruments, and Computers, 24*, 581-582.

Tallal, P. (2003). Language learning disabilities: integrating research approaches. *Current Directions in Psychological Science, 12*, 206-211.

Tallal, P. and Benasich, A.A. (2002). Developmetnal language learning impairments. *Development and Psychopathology, 14*, 559-579.

Wechsler D. (1997). *Wechsler Intelligence Scale for Children (WISC-III^{UK})*. (Standardized version in Greek). Athens: Ellinika Grammata Publishers.

Wechsler D. (1989) *Wechsler Preschool and Primary Scale of Intelligence–Revised*. London: Psychological Corporation.

Temporal Modified Speech Perception in Dyslexia

Caroline Jacquier (jacquier@isc.cnrs.fr)

Fanny Meunier (fanny.meunier@univ-lyon2.fr)
Laboratoire Dynamique Du Langage
14 avenue Berthelot
69007 Lyon, France

Abstract

The phonological or the auditory hypotheses are the two main views still debated to explain nature and origin of dyslexia. In the experiments presented we investigated the auditory temporal processing deficit in dyslexic adults. By time-compression of rapid acoustic cues, we explored their capacities of extraction and analyze of this acoustic features (voice onset-time and second formant transition). Moreover, we evaluated their abilities to reconstruct a degraded speech signal. Compared with controls, dyslexics exhibit deficit in time-compressed speech perception, the impairment is stronger for voicing feature than place of articulation. The temporal information would be inefficiently extracted and analyzed by dyslexics.

Keywords: Dyslexia, Speech Perception, Auditory Temporal Processing.

Introduction

Dyslexia is defined as learning and reading problems in spite of neurological or sensory deficits, education and social background and normal IQ. In spite of numerous researches, neurological and cognitive basis of dyslexia are still debated. There are two major competing theories of the cognitive deficit: the phonological (Snowling, 2000; Ramus, 2003) and the auditory hypothesis (Tallal, 1980). The first one underlines specific cognitive deficits to representation and processing of speech sounds: dyslexic individuals would have a degraded phoneme representation that is not efficient in the conversion into grapheme. This conversion is essential in the phonological pathway for reading and writing abilities (Mody, Studdert-Kennedy, & Brady, 1997). The second hypothesis highlights more precisely a more basic auditory deficit: it is the temporal resolution that would be deficient. Dyslexics exhibit deficiencies in perceiving some brief sounds and rapid transitions. What this means is that speech sounds like phonemes are poorly differentiated by subjects with dyslexia. The inabilities in auditory temporal processing would induce poor phonological code representation. Thus, it is postulated that dyslexics have a general auditory deficit in temporal processing (Tallal, Galaburda, Llinás, & von Euler, 1993). Indeed, two complementary studies have shown that an intensive training of language impaired children with temporally stretched speech improves their language ability (Merzenich, Jenkins, Johnston, Schreiner, Miller, & Tallal, 1996; Tallal, Miller, Bedi, Byma, Wang, Nagarajan, Schreiner, Jenkins, & Merzenich, 1996). However, this improvement has not been clearly demonstrated for dyslexic deficits. Otherwise, fast speech studies have underlined that artificially time-compressed speech was easier to process than naturally produced fast speech (Janse, 2003). One of the processing disadvantages of naturally produced fast speech is due to its changed timing, the temporal organisation of spoken language would be relatively unimportant at a normal rate, but that it may become more critical to comprehension, the more the speech rate is increased (Foulke, 1971). Thus, following this, we can hypothesis that an acceleration of the speech signal rate would change the speech perception and comprehension of dyslexic adults.

Our study investigated the auditory temporal processing of accelerated speech on dyslexic adults and adults without language impairments. Our hypothesis is that dyslexics would have more difficulties to process artificially time-compressed speech than controls. Moreover, we focused the time-compression on rapid transition and brief sound of the speech signal. In the present study, we focused on the temporal modulation of two acoustic cues: the Voice Onset-Time (VOT) and the second Formant Transition (FT2) mainly implicated in speech perception and comprehension. Indeed, the speech signal is a complex combination of a wide range of acoustic cues. All acoustic cues do not have the same effectiveness for speech restoration. Previous studies have underlined the importance of acoustic cues in speech perception (Kent, & Moll, 1969; Lisker, & Abramson, 1967; Serniclaes, 1987).

In one hand, VOT is one of the primary acoustic cues contrasting syllable-initial stop consonants across languages both in production and perception. According to Lisker and Abramson (1964), the VOT is defined as the time interval between the plosive release and the onset of low-frequency periodicity generated by rhythmic vocal cord vibration. If we assign a value of zero to the instant of stop release, unvoiced stops (/p/, /t/ and /k/) are then measured as a positive VOT, because there is a delay between the stop release and the voicing onset, whereas voiced stops (/b/, /d/ and /g/), with a laryngeal vibration that continues from closure up to the moment of release are measured as a negative VOT. Thus, VOT values correspond to the degree of voicing. In other hand, formant transition corresponds to the rapid changes in formant frequency which occurs at the moment of release of the stop constriction. Rapid changes in formant frequency are crucial in identifying sound segments. The transition of the second formant functions as a cue for determining the place of articulation of the plosive consonants. Ziegler, Pech-Georgel, George, Alario and Lorenzi (2005) investigated the perception of phonetic features such as voicing, manner and place of articulation in the presence of masking noise on specific language impairment (SLI) children. Their results showed that perception for all phonetic features were impaired and strongly for voicing. The extraction and analyze of the acoustic cues were inefficient. Our hypothesis is that dyslexics would show more or less specific impairment for each acoustic cue compared to controls. Moreover, we expected that our results would be in favor of the auditory hypothesis because of the nature of our task. Indeed, in the auditory non-word identification task, dyslexics should not use the phonological pathway. Their task should be at a very basic level of auditory and linguistic processing.

A huge problem in speech perception and comprehension is the variable nature of the acoustic patterns. Modulations of those acoustic details induce some variability in the speech comprehension. However, speech comprehension in normal hearing individuals is an impressively robust cognitive faculty that resists to the important variability existing in acoustical properties of speech signal. In this context, it has been demonstrated that speech remained identifiable and to some extent intelligible even after important physical manipulations as drastic filtering, spectral decompositions or time-reversions (see for example, Meunier, Cenier, Barkat, & Magrin-Chagnolleau, 2002; Warren, 1970). The cognitive system appears to be able to compensate and reconstruct even a corrupted speech signal. However, it appears that we are not all on an equal footing faced with the perception and comprehension of degraded speech. The necessary cognitive restoration seems to rely on individual abilities. Moreover, this reconstruction ability depends on the type of distortion and on its importance. In our study, we may expect that dyslexics would have quantitatively and qualitatively different cognitive restoration abilities than controls, i.e. their percentage of errors would be higher and it is likely that their nature would be different.

Our aim was to investigate the acceleration effect of rapid acoustic cues on both groups and to yield results in accordance with the phonological or auditory theories of dyslexia. Moreover, cognitive restoration mechanisms should be less efficient in dyslexic group. We used an auditory identification task with CVCV non-words which were time-compressed on the duration of VOT and FT2 then control and dyslexic group were compared.

Experimental Procedure

Participants

Experiment 1: Voice Onset-Time Compression Data were collected from thirty two adults with dyslexia and thirty two controls. The mean age was 23.3 (SD = 5.5, range = 16-35) for the dyslexics and 22.6 (SD = 5, range = 18-39) years for the controls. Each dyslexic participant was matched to one of the controls on age and gender (Table 1).

Experiment 2: Formant Transition Compression Two groups were investigated in this experiment: the same 32 dyslexic adults and thirty two controls. The mean age was 23.3 (SD = 5.5, range = 16-35) for the dyslexics and 22.6 (SD = 5, range = 19-39) years for the controls. Each dyslexic participant was matched to one of the controls on age and gender (Table 1).

The dyslexia of the present participants had been independently diagnosed by a psychologist or a speech pathologist recently or at least at their majority. This was first documented when recruiting the subjects and then verified with a French dyslexia detection test (ODEDYS created by Jacquier-Roux, Valdois, & Zorman, 2002) which is an analytic evaluation of the written language. This test is composed by the Alouette test (Lefavrais, 1965), reading, orthographic, metaphonological evaluations, a short term verbal memory task and a visual tasks. Control participants reported having no hearing problems and no history of speech problems whereas auditory thresholds were measured for each dyslexic participant and was at or better than 20 dB hearing level. All the participants were native speakers of French.

Table 1: Subject groups in experiment 1.

| | Experiment 1 | | Experiment 2 | |
	Control adults (N = 32)	Dyslexic adults (N = 32)	Control adults (N = 32)	Dyslexic adults (N = 32)
Mean Age (yrs)	22.6	23.3	22.6	23.3
Gender male	10	10	10	10
female	22	22	22	22

Material

The experiment consisted of an auditory identification non-word task. The participants were asked to identify 80 non-words. The material consisted of 64 disyllabic CVCV non-words and 16 VCV fillers. Four stop consonants (/b/, /d/, /p/ and /t/) and two vowels (/a/ and /i/) were combined to form each stimulus. Each consonant occurred with every other consonant in both syllable positions and with two different vowels (4C1 x 4C2 x 2V1 x 2V2 = 64 CVCV).

The stimuli were recorded by a native male French speaker in a sound-proof cabin. The files were saved as wave files and sampled at 22 kHz (stereo, 16 bits).

The duration of each acoustic cue (VOT and FT2) were manually measured for each item with Praat software

(Figure 1). Moreover, VOT was manually segmented from the onset of periodic oscillations and the onset of release of the consonant: VOT is positive for unvoiced stop and negative for voiced stop consonants. FT2 was delimited from the moment of rapid change of the direction of the second formant, during the transition between consonant and vowel, to the steady-state part of the vowel (formants parallels). In a first experiment, only the duration of VOT was accelerated (Experiment 1) and in a second experiment, only FT2 was time-compressed (Experiment 2). The duration of the acoustic cue was time-compressed according to four experimental conditions:

- 100%   = control condition
- 50%   = 50% of original duration
- 25%   = 25% of original duration
- 0%   = totally deleted

The time-compression is made using the Pitch-Synchronous Overlap Add (PSOLA) time scaling technique, used in the Praat software. Segmented parts of the waveform can be time-compressed, while the rest of the waveform remains unaffected. In this way, each syllable can be selectively time-compressed.

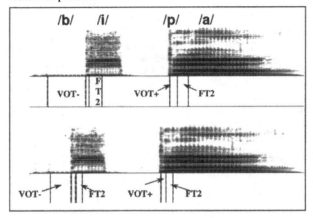

Figure 1: Spectrogram of non-word [bipa].
VOT of [b] is negative and VOT of [p] is positive. Control condition 100%_100% (in top) and time-compression condition 50%_50% (in bottom).

Procedure

The auditory identification non-words task was preceded by a practice session containing 12 spoken examples, which were meant to familiarize participants with the task. After this, 80 stimuli were presented to the participants once. The stimuli were randomized across subjects. Participants were seated in a silent room facing a computer monitor. The stimuli were delivered binaurally via headphones (Beyerdynamic DT 48, 200Ω). The material was presented at a comfortable listening level. The subjects were informed that a speech signal, though not necessarily a word, was to be emitted. Control participants then had to type on a computer keyboard whatever they heard whereas dyslexic

subjects had to repeat the stimuli. To avoid an additional stage of phonological processing, dyslexics were not ask to write down the stimuli. Indeed, we expected that dyslexics showed dysorthographical problems. Consequently, only the decoding-encoding auditory capacities would be evaluated. Each experiment took approximately 15 minutes to complete including the practice.

Results

In the next subsections, identification rates and errors' nature with accompanying statistics results are presented. We computed identification rates for stimuli across subjects, for consonants and for vowels.

Identification rates

Experiment 1: VOT Time-Compression We ran a 3-way ANOVA including as factors: Group (control, dyslexic), Position of consonant (attack, intervocalic) and Time-compression conditions (100, 50, 25, 0%). We observed a main effects of Group [$F(1,31) = 28.56$, $p < .001$], Position [$F(1,31) = 15.99$, $p < .001$] and Time-compression [$F(3,93) = 356.18$, $p < .001$]. Control group has a better identification rate (89.6%) than dyslexic group (83.6%) in this experiment. The identification rate of the intervocalic consonant (88.3%) is better than the attack consonant identification rate (84.9%). A post-hoc Newman-Keuls test showed that the identification rate is significantly lower at 25% and 0% of compression (90% and 65%) than at 100% and 50% (96.4% and 95%). In addition, we observed a significant interaction between Group and Position [$F(3,31) = 4.76$, $p < .05$]. A Position effect for the dyslexic group but not for the control group was obtained. For the dyslexic group, the intervocalic consonant is better identified than the attack consonant whereas there are no significant differences between both consonant positions for the control group. The interaction between Position and Time-compression was also significant [$F(3,93) = 4.48$, $p < .01$], this was mainly due to the effect of Position that is stronger for 100% and 50% compressions than for all the others compressions. Furthermore, we observed a Group effect at 100% and then for all conditions (Table 2) but the interaction between Group and Time-compression was not significant.

Table 2: Identification rates (%) for VOT and FT2 compression experiments for Control *vs.* Dyslexic groups.

		VOT compression		FT2 compression	
		Control adults	Dyslexic adults	Control adults	Dyslexic adults
C_1	100%	97.3	91.2	97.5	93.9
	50%	95.5	87.9	98.2	92.4
	25%	92.8	85.2	96.5	92
	0%	70.1	59.2	85.2	80.5
C_2	100%	99.6	97.5	99.6	98.2
	50%	99	97.7	99.4	98.4
	25%	94.7	87.3	99.6	97.3
	0%	67.8	62.9	95.7	95.3

A 2-way ANOVA including Group (control, dyslexic) and Phoneme (C_1, V_1, C_2, V_2, CVCV) showed main effects of Group [$F(1,31) = 27.50$, $p < .001$] and Phoneme [$F(4,124) = 417.42$, $p < .001$]. Table 3 displays the significant interaction between Group and Phoneme [$F(4,124) = 16.11$, $p < .001$], significant effects of Group for C1, C2 and CVCV.

Experiment 2: FT2 Time-Compression

A 3-way ANOVA including Group (control, dyslexic), Position of consonant (attack, intervocalic) and Time-compression conditions (100%, 50%, 25%, 0%) reported main effects of Group [$F(1,31) = 12.01$, $p < .01$], Position [$F(1,31) = 71.71$, $p < .001$] and Time-compression [$F(3,93) = 81.61$, $p < .001$]. Control group has a better identification rate (96.5%) than dyslexic group (93.5%) in this experiment. The identification rate of the intervocalic consonant (97.9%) is better than the attack consonant identification rate (92%). A post-hoc Newman-Keuls test showed that the identification rate is significantly lower at 0% (89.2%) than at 100%, 50% and 25% of compression (97.3%, 97.1% and 96.3%). The interaction between Group and Position [$F(1,31) = 6.97$, $p < .05$] and the interaction between Position and Time-compression also were significant [$F(3,93) = 35.30$, $p < .001$]. This was mainly due to the effect of the Group that is significant only for the attack consonant position ($p < .001$); the identification of the attack consonant is more difficult for dyslexics. In addition, we observed a group effect as 100% and then for all conditions (Table 2) but the interaction was not significant.

A 2-way ANOVA including Group (control, dyslexic) and Phoneme (C_1, V_1, C_2, V_2, CVCV) showed main effects of Group [$F(1,31) = 12.08$, $p < .01$] and Phoneme [$F(4,124) = 133.34$, $p < .001$]. Table 3 displays the significant interaction of the group and phoneme [$F(4,124) = 9.60$, $p < .001$], significant effect of group for C1 and CVCV.

Table 3: Identification rates (%) for VOT and FT2 compression experiments for Control *vs.* Dyslexic groups. 2-way ANOVA: * p < 0.05, ** p < 0.01, *** p < 0.001.

	VOT Compression			*FT2 Compression*		
	Control adults	Dyslexic adults	p	Control adults	Dyslexic adults	p
C_1	88.9	80.9	***	94.3	89.7	***
V_1	99.7	99.1	ns	99.9	99.9	ns
C_2	90.3	86.3	***	98.6	97.3	ns
V_2	99.8	99.3	ns	100	99.9	ns
CVCV	80.3	70.7	***	92.9	87.5	***

Errors' Nature

Experiment 1: VOT Time-Compression Observation of confusions made by participants showed qualitative and quantitative error differences between both groups. Indeed, overall dyslexics make more errors than controls. Moreover, confusion matrixes reveal, in both groups, different type of errors according to the consonant position (Table 4, left part). The attack consonant is most of the time confounded with the unvoiced corresponding consonant (/b/->/p/ or /d/->/t/) even at 100% (control condition) for dyslexics whereas the intervocalic consonant is more often confounded with the approximant liquid consonant /l/.

Experiment 2: FT2 Time-Compression Dyslexic adults made more errors than control adults. The observation of Table 4 (right part) displays a main type of confusion that is a place of articulation error for voiced consonants (/b/->/d/). This result is observed in both consonant positions for both groups but appears as from the control condition (100%) for dyslexics. It is noteworthy that dyslexic adults present significant auditory non-words identification deficit in the control condition in which the speech signal is intact.

Discussion

In this paper, we investigated the speech perception processing in dyslexia. The phonological and auditory theories are still discussed to explain cognitive deficits in dyslexia. We studied the effect of time-compression of rapid acoustic cues on speech intelligibility by dyslexic subjects compared to control participants with no history of reading deficit. We compressed either the voicing phonetic features (Experiment 1: Voice Onset-Time) or the place of articulation phonetic features (Experiment 2: second Formant Transition). We wonder if the artificially time-compressed speech, in opposition to the lengthened speech signal (Merzenich, Jenkins, Johnston, Schreiner, Miller, & Tallal, 1996; Tallal, Miller, Bedi, Byma, Wang, Nagarajan, Schreiner, Jenkins, & Merzenich, 1996), would be improve dyslexic's performance in an auditory non-word identification task.

Overall, the main results showed a group effect; indeed dyslexic adults exhibit more difficulties to identify the temporal modified speech for both phonetic features (voicing and place of articulation). The acceleration of these rapid acoustic cues would disturb the extraction and the analysis of these temporal segments needed in speech perception. The temporal organisation seems to play an important role for dyslexics. Moreover, results of experiment 1 demonstrated that dyslexics had a stronger deficit of integration for the VOT than for the second formant transition. Indeed, the difference between control and dyslexic groups in experiment 1 affected the attack and the intervocalic consonants whereas in experiment 2, only the attack consonant was sensible to a group effect. This result is in accordance with the strongly effect of voicing observed in Ziegler et al. study (2005). Thus, voicing feature might play a more important role in the discrimination between consonants in spite of the position consonant in non-word. And, place of articulation feature of the intervocalic consonant might be easy compensated by the signal redundancy.

Table 4: Confusion matrixes of plosive consonants.

Experiment 1 Dyslexic group – Attack consonant

		b	d	g	p	t	k	l	f	nul
100%	b	114	3	0	9	0	0	0	0	2
	d	3	117	1	0	6	0	0	0	1
	p	0	3	0	117	6	0	0	0	2
	t	0	2	0	5	119	2	0	0	0
50%	b	121	2	0	4	0	0	0	0	1
	d	2	119	0	0	6	0	0	0	1
	p	9	2	0	96	5	0	0	0	16
	t	0	1	0	8	114	0	0	0	5
25%	b	117	3	0	6	0	0	0	0	2
	d	1	120	0	1	5	0	0	0	1
	p	8	0	0	104	5	0	0	0	11
	t	2	10	0	10	95	0	0	1	10
0%	b	90	9	0	14	0	0	0	0	15
	d	4	108	0	2	14	0	0	0	0
	p	4	1	0	61	1	0	0	1	60
	t	5	12	0	23	43	0	1	0	44

Experiment 1 Control group – Attack consonant

		b	d	g	p	t	k	v	m	nul
100%	b	128	0	0	0	0	0	0	0	0
	d	0	124	0	0	4	0	0	0	0
	p	0	0	0	122	5	0	0	0	1
	t	0	1	0	1	124	2	0	0	0
50%	b	128	0	0	0	0	0	0	0	0
	d	0	124	1	0	2	0	0	0	1
	p	4	0	0	116	0	0	0	0	8
	t	0	1	0	4	121	0	0	0	2
25%	b	126	2	0	0	0	0	0	0	0
	d	0	123	0	0	5	0	0	0	0
	p	2	0	0	118	4	0	0	0	4
	t	0	4	0	12	108	0	0	0	4
0%	b	109	1	0	8	0	0	0	1	8
	d	0	118	0	0	10	0	0	0	0
	p	6	0	0	73	1	0	0	0	48
	t	4	12	0	17	59	0	0	0	36

Experiment 1 Dyslexic group – Intervocalic consonant

		b	d	p	t	l	r	f	v	m	nul
100%	b	120	3	4	0	0	0	0	0	1	0
	d	2	126	0	0	0	0	0	0	0	0
	p	0	0	128	0	0	0	0	0	0	0
	t	0	0	1	127	0	0	0	0	0	0
50%	b	127	0	1	0	0	0	0	0	0	0
	d	0	122	0	1	5	0	0	0	0	0
	p	1	0	125	1	0	0	1	0	0	0
	t	0	2	0	126	0	0	0	0	0	0
25%	b	95	9	2	0	14	2	0	1	0	5
	d	1	119	0	1	7	0	0	0	0	0
	p	1	0	126	1	0	0	0	0	0	0
	t	0	11	7	110	0	0	0	0	0	0
0%	b	42	17	4	1	42	3	0	0	0	19
	d	2	80	1	0	43	2	0	0	0	0
	p	3	0	121	0	0	0	0	0	0	4
	t	2	17	10	77	1	0	0	0	0	21

Experiment 1 Control group – Intervocalic consonant

		b	d	p	t	l	r	nul
100%	b	128	0	0	0	0	0	0
	d	0	126	0	1	0	0	1
	p	0	0	128	0	0	0	0
	t	0	0	0	128	0	0	0
50%	b	126	0	1	0	0	1	0
	d	1	126	0	1	0	0	0
	p	0	0	128	0	0	0	0
	t	0	0	1	127	0	0	0
25%	b	111	5	1	0	4	5	2
	d	0	127	0	0	0	1	0
	p	1	0	127	0	0	0	0
	t	0	3	4	120	0	0	1
0%	b	60	10	6	1	43	3	5
	d	0	86	1	3	30	7	1
	p	4	0	121	1	0	0	2
	t	0	24	11	80	0	0	13

Experiment 2 Dyslexic group – Attack consonant

		b	d	G	p	t	k	r	m	nul
100%	b	118	4	0	4	0	0	0	1	1
	d	6	115	0	0	7	0	0	0	0
	p	2	0	0	126	0	0	0	0	0
	t	1	1	0	3	122	1	0	0	0
50%	b	118	5	0	4	0	0	0	0	1
	d	7	117	0	0	4	0	0	0	0
	p	5	0	0	121	1	0	0	0	1
	t	1	3	0	4	117	1	0	0	2
25%	b	122	1	0	4	0	0	0	0	1
	d	12	109	1	0	4	0	0	0	2
	p	1	0	0	119	2	0	0	0	6
	t	0	2	0	3	121	0	0	0	2
0%	b	115	4	0	4	0	0	1	1	3
	d	37	78	0	1	8	0	0	0	4
	p	3	0	0	113	2	0	0	0	10
	t	0	2	0	10	107	0	0	0	9

Experiment 2 Control group – Attack consonant

		b	d	g	p	t	k	nul
100%	b	128	0	0	0	0	0	0
	d	0	126	0	0	2	0	0
	p	1	0	0	125	2	0	0
	t	0	1	0	6	120	1	0
50%	b	127	1	0	0	0	0	0
	d	2	123	0	0	3	0	0
	p	0	0	0	128	0	0	0
	t	0	1	0	2	125	0	0
25%	b	128	0	0	0	0	0	0
	d	9	118	1	0	0	0	0
	p	0	0	0	127	1	0	0
	t	0	2	0	2	121	1	2
0%	b	126	1	0	0	0	0	1
	d	45	80	1	0	1	0	1
	p	3	0	0	118	2	0	5
	t	0	1	0	4	112	0	11

Experiment 2 Dyslexic group –Intervocalic consonant

		b	d	p	t	nul
100%	b	125	0	2	1	0
	d	4	124	0	0	0
	p	0	0	126	2	0
	t	0	1	0	127	0
50%	b	123	3	2	0	0
	d	1	127	0	0	0
	p	1	0	127	0	0
	t	0	1	0	127	0
25%	b	124	3	1	0	0
	d	3	124	0	0	1
	p	0	0	126	0	2
	t	0	2	2	124	0
0%	b	127	1	0	0	0
	d	12	111	0	1	4
	p	1	0	127	0	0
	t	0	1	4	123	0

Experiment 2 Control group –Intervocalic consonant

		b	d	g	p	t	l	nul
100%	b	128	0	0	0	0	0	0
	d	2	126	0	0	0	0	0
	p	0	0	0	128	0	0	0
	t	0	0	0	0	128	0	0
50%	b	128	0	0	0	0	0	0
	d	2	126	0	0	0	0	0
	p	0	0	0	127	0	0	1
	t	0	0	0	0	128	0	0
25%	b	128	0	0	0	0	0	0
	d	1	127	0	0	0	0	0
	p	1	0	0	127	0	0	0
	t	0	0	0	0	128	0	0
0%	b	127	1	0	0	0	0	0
	d	7	114	1	1	0	1	4
	p	0	0	0	126	1	0	1
	t	0	0	0	3	123	0	2

Our results show a time-compressed non-word auditory identification deficit for dyslexic adults compared to control adults that would be in favour of the auditory hypothesis. Indeed, in our task, the phoneme-grapheme conversion stage of classic speech perception model is not necessary to succeed the repetition task for dyslexic group. It is likely that dyslexics only took part in a direct auditory pathway to repeat the stimuli: they only have to decode stimuli at the first acoustic stage (acoustic features extraction). None phonological codes are needed to the dyslexic group to accurately identify non-words so we hypothesis that dyslexics probably show an auditory deficit in temporal processing and particularly in time-compressed speech. Rosen (2003) have reported a variety of auditory tasks that demonstrated an auditory processing deficit with dyslexia: a modulation frequency as well as a masking condition. However, in opposition with Rosen's opinion who affirms that the impairment is not due to rapid auditory processing deficit, we argue that our dyslexic adults displayed in all time-compression conditions significant identification deficit compared to control adults. Consequently, the rapid auditory processing would be impaired with dyslexia.

Further statistic analysis on errors' nature and nature of confusions showed specific identification deficit on consonant even at normal rate for dyslexics and it is worst and worst with the speech degradation.

In addition of this temporal processing deficit, we assume that cognitive restoration capacities of dyslexics are also deficient. The descendant auditory pathway might be a cognitive feedback to modulate the temporal resolution. Further hearing tests in order to evaluate the central auditory system of dyslexic adults would inform us on their central auditory abilities.

Conclusion

To conclude, our temporal modification on two different acoustic cues induced a loss of intelligibility for dyslexic adults that is significantly larger than control subjects. Dyslexics exhibit a deficit of accelerated acoustic cues integration (VOT and FT2); in particular, the inefficiency of the extraction and the manipulation of phonetic features are stronger for voicing compared to place of articulation. Finally, our results would be in accordance with the auditory hypothesis of dyslexia.

Acknowledgments

This research has been funded by the EMERGENCE program of the French *Région Rhône-Alpes*.

References

Foulke, E. (1971). The perception of time-compressed speech. In D. L. Horton & J. J. Jenkins (Eds.), *The perception of language*. Columbus, Ohio: Charles E. Merrill publishing company.

Janse, E. (2003). *Production and perception of fast speech*. Doctoral dissertation, University of Utrecht.

Kent, R. D., & Moll, K. L. (1969). Vocal-tract characteristics of the stop cognates. *Journal of the Acoustical Society of America, 46(6)*, 1549-1555.

Lefavrais, P. (1965). *Test de l'Alouette*. Paris: E.C.P.A.

Lisker, L., & Abramson, A. S. (1964). A cross-language study of voicing in initial stops: acoustical measurements. *Word 20*, 384-422.

Lisker, L., & Abramson, A. S. (1967). Some effects of context on voice onset time in English stops. *Language and Speech, 10*, 1-28.

Merzenich, M. M., Jenkins, W. M., Johnston, P., Schreiner, C., Miller, S. L., & Tallal, P. (1996). Temporal processing deficits of language-learning impaired children ameliorated by training. *Science, 271*, 77-81.

Meunier, F., Cenier, T., Barkat, M., & Magrin-Chagnolleau, I. (2002). Mesure d'intelligibilité de segments de parole à l'envers en français. *Proceedings of the XXIVèmes Journées d'Etude sur la Parole* (pp. 117-120).

Mody, M., Studdert-Kennedy, M., & Brady, S. (1997). Speech perception deficits in poor readers: Auditory processing or phonological coding? *Journal of experimental child psychology, 64*, 199-231.

Ramus, F. (2003). Developmental dyslexia: specific phonological deficit or general sensorimotor dysfunction? *Current Opinion in Neurobiology, 13*, 212-218.

Rosen, S. (2003). Auditory processing in dyslexia and specific language impairment. Is there a deficit? What is its nature? Does it explain anything? *Journal of Phonetics, 31*, 509–527.

Serniclaes, W. (1987). *Etude expérimentale de la perception du trait de voisement des occlusives du Français*. Doctoral dissertation, Université Libre of Bruxelles.

Snowling, M. J. (2000). Dyslexia. 2nd ed. Oxford: Blackwell Publishers Ltd.

Tallal, P. (1980). Auditory temporal perception, phonics, and reading disabilities in children, *Brain and language, 9*, 182-198.

Tallal, P., Galaburda, A. M., Llinás, R. R. & von Euler, C. (Eds.) (1993). *Temporal information processing in the nervous system*. New York: New York Academy of Sciences.

Tallal, P., Miller, S. L., Bedi, G., Byma, G., Wang, X., Nagarajan, S. S., Schreiner, C., Jenkins, W. M., & Merzenich, M. M. (1996). Language comprehension in language-learning impaired children improved with acoustically modified speech. *Science, 271*, 81-84.

Jacquier-Roux, M., Valdois, S., & Zorman, M. (2002) Outils de dépistage des dyslexies. Académie de Grenoble: Laboratoire Cogni-Sciences et Laboratoire de Psychologie et Neuro-cognition.

Warren, R. M. (1970). Perceptual restoration of missing speech sounds. *Science, 167(917)*, 392–393.

Ziegler, J. C., Pech-Georgel, C., George, FX., Alario, F. & Lorenzi, C. (2005). Deficits in speech perception predict language learning impairment. *Proceedings of the National Academy of Sciences* (pp. 14110-14115).

Graphical Perception and Mental Imagery:
An Electrophysiological Examination.

Lisa A. Best (lbest@unbsj.ca)

Aren C. Hunter (aren.hunter@unb.ca)

Brandie M. Stewart (z1r77@unb.ca)

Department of Psychology
University of New Brunswick
P.O. Box 5050
Saint John, NB E2L 4L5, Canada

Abstract

Researchers in graphical perception and cognition often attribute the strength of a graph to its pictorial qualities and argue that, *a picture is worth 1000 words*. Preliminary studies on the physiological processing of graphs suggest interesting similarities and differences between pictures and graphs. The purpose of the current study was to examine the electrophysiological processing associated with scatterplot perception. Specifically, we were interested in determining if the mental image associated with an everyday object would be similar to those constructed when participants were presented with a statistical concept. Results suggest that people are able to construct a mental image of a statistical concept but that the event-related potentials of the mental image are different from those associated with perception.

Graphical cognition is defined as a progression that "occurs when a symbol system used to convey a message interacts with psychological processes active in the person who receives it" (Friel, Curcio & Bright, 2001, p. 226) and graphical comprehension refers to the graph reader's ability to derive the intended meaning from a display. Roth and Bowen (2003) indicated that a correct interpretation of a graph requires that all graphed elements graph be combined in a way that allows the intended meaning to be apparent. In general, researchers in this area focus on the ability of the brain to organise, store, and process the information contained in a visual display (Lohse, 1993).

Pinker's (1990) theory of graphical comprehension was based on the premise that the process of graphical cognition involves two processes: the formation of a visual description and the subsequent formulation of a graph schema. In the initial stages of graphical analysis, information contained in the graph is analyzed by the visual system and, during these processing stages, graphs are processed in the same way as other types of visual information. In the subsequent stages of visual cognition, the graph reader must construct a "structural description" of the graph wherein the graph elements and their interrelationships are identified, and the graph schema is activated. When the graph schema is activated, the reader draws on his or her graphical knowledge and selects, based in part on their personal graph schema, an appropriate interpretation.

Theories that integrate graph perception and cognition describe the process of graph comprehension as a series of perceptual and cognitive events that result in overall comprehension. Shah, Freedman, and Vekiri (2005) drew a distinction between perceptual and conceptual processes in graphical comprehension and described the perceptual processes as bottom-up encoding mechanisms focused on the visual features of the display (formation of the visual description) and the cognitive processes as top-down encoding mechanisms that influence interpretation (activation of the graph schema). Drawing on both perceptual and cognitive theories, Trickett and Trafton (2006) presented an integrative theory of graph comprehension to outline the sequence of events that occur when information is extracted from a graph. Initially, a graph reader is presented with a problem that requires the extraction of a specific piece of information. To answer specific questions, the reader examines the graph, their graph schema and Gestalt grouping processes are activated, and the salient features are encoded. Trickett and Trafton suggested that, at this point, the reader understands which cognitive strategies are appropriate and have formed a graph schema that allows them to identify important elements of the display. After these initial cognitive processes, the reader extracts relevant information from the graph in visual chunks and compares different sets of chunks. These comparisons allow for the extraction of the information necessary to accurately extract information from the graph.

Trickett and Trafton (2006) identified several different tasks required of a graph reader and argued that these tasks could involve either perceptual or spatial processing. Perceptual processing involves making direct or explicit comparisons of graph elements and requires simply reading values directly from the graph (for example, *is Bar A higher than Bar B?*). If a reader is asked to compare points that are separated by other elements or asked to compare between different graphs, a more complex strategy, involving the spatial transformation of graphed elements, is necessary. In this case, the reader must superimpose graph elements to new positions in order to create overlap with other elements. Superimposition involves spatial processing because during these types of tasks, graph elements must be mentally moved from one location to another.

The Electrophysiology of Graph Perception

Much of the graphical perception and cognition research has focused on the behavioural aspects of graphical readability. Thus far, researchers have assumed that graphs are a specific type of image and, as a result, are processed in the same manner as other images. Electrophysiological technology allows one to evaluate this claim by presenting participants with different graphs and recording patterns of activity in different brain sites. Posterior brain sites (T6 and T5) are generally accepted to reflect activity in the junction of the parietal and temporal lobes. Medial brain sites (T3 and T4) correspond to sites in the temporal lobes and anterior brain sites (F7 and F8) correspond to frontal lobe sites. Although ERP analysis does not allow one to make conclusions about the localisation of cognitive processes, this technique does provide excellent temporal resolution and, hence, it is possible to examine the time course of processing.

Using electroencephalograph recordings, Best, Adams, Jones, Hickman, Hunter, LeBlanc, Stewart and Woodland (2006a) presented participants with a series of everyday objects and graphs and extracted the event-related potentials (ERPs) associated with cognitive processing. Results indicated that, in posterior and medial brain sites, the processing of graphs and images was similar and no amplitude or time course differences were reported. In anterior brain sites, the time course of processing was similar but everyday images produced higher amplitudes. Research such as this supports Pinker's (1990) theory of graph cognition and provides physiological support for the idea that, at a basic perceptual level, graphs and images are processed similarly but, in higher brain centers, processing differs.

Best, Hunter, and Stewart (2006b) examined how scatterplots depicting different relationships were processed. In this study, scatterplots depicting different relationships (positive or negative, strong or weak) were presented and recordings were taken from the left and right temporal and frontal brain sites. It is interesting to note that in right and left hemisphere recording sites, the initial processing (from stimulus onset to 200msec) of positive and negative relationships was quite different. In both cases the early processing of negative relationships produced waveforms that were distinguishable from those of positive relationships. Between 200 and 400msec after stimulus onset the waveforms produced were quite similar. Between 400 and 800msec after stimulus onset the waveform associated with negative relationships remained higher than that associated with positive relationships. This is an interesting result, since behavioural graph perception research suggests that people make less accurate judgments when presented with negative relationships in comparison to positive relationships.

Best and her colleagues (2006b) also found that the amplitudes associated with the stronger relationships were lower than those associated with moderate or weak relationships. It is possible that these differences are due to the fact that moderate relationships ($r=.3$ and $r=.5$) are more difficult to judge than relationships that are very strong or very weak. The efficiency hypothesis explains these results nicely; it suggests that viewing a scatterplot depicting a very strong or very weak relationship requires less mental effort than viewing a scatterplot with a moderate relationship (Jausovec, 1996). When moderate relationships are presented, it is possible that participants were not sure what type of relationship they are examining, and thus, their mental effort increased.

Purpose of the Current Experiment

Trickett and Trafton (2006) suggested that one component of graph comprehension is the ability to perform tasks that involve the mental manipulation of graph elements. We were interested in further examining the spatial processes involved in comprehension and wanted to extend this research to determine if graph readers are able to form mental images of statistical concepts. Our goal is to answer the question, *If a participant is given a statistical term, such as $r=+.95$, are they able to form a mental image of a scatterplot depicting a strong, positive relationship?* To examine this issue, we examined the ERPs associated with two types of mental images: those formed when different types of statistical relationships were presented and those formed when one constructs a mental image of common objects.

Methods

Participants

Seven undergraduate psychology students were recruited to participate. All participants were enrolled in a fourth year cognitive neuroscience course and had completed two undergraduate courses in statistics. All participants understood the basic principles of correlation and regression and completed a brief tutorial explaining the basics of linear regression. Participants were instructed how to read a scatterplot and predict the value of the underlying relationship.

Materials

A Grass model 8-10 electroencephalograph (EEG) was used to record electrical activity near the surface of the brain. Using the standard 10-20 electrode placement system, each site is labelled with a letter (referring to the underlying brain area) and a number (odd=left side of brain and even=right side of brain). A 12-bit A/D converter sampled continuously at 200Hz, and continuous EEG was parsed, stored, and averaged using a statistical program.

Procedure

Recordings were taken from posterior (T6, T5), medial (T4, T3), and anterior (F8, F7) sites. These placement sites were selected based on our previous research; we wanted to compare ERPs associated with perceptual and imagery tasks. ECL electrode gel was spread over the electrotrode tips to increase conductivity and an ECL electro cap was placed on the scalp. Mild abrasion of the scalp ensured a conductivity level of less than 5 Kohms. Differential recordings were made possible by the use of a referential montage whereby an electrode was attached to both earlobes and used as a common reference point with impedances below 10Kohm. Eye blinks were recorded using a pair of electrodes placed just outside the canthus of the right eye and this allow us to correct for EEG activity due to eye blinks. Once prepared, the participants were led into a soundproof box and all instructions and experimental stimuli were presented to them on a computer screen.

Participants were presented with two sets of stimuli (statistical and control). The statistical stimuli were Pearson Product Moment Correlation Coefficients depicting increasing (r = +.9, +.5, +.1) and decreasing (r = -.9, -5, -.1) linear relationships. Participants were presented with a single *r*-value and instructed to form a mental image of a scatterplot representing that value. In the control condition, participants were presented with the names of common objects (apple, bottle, cup, desk, dog, house) and were instructed to form a mental image of the object. Participants were instructed to keep their eyes open while they formed their mental images. Each stimulus was presented for 1000msec. In total, participants were asked to make 240 mental images.

The signals were filtered between 0.1Hz and 35Hz, with a notch filter, and sampled continuously at 200Hz with 12-bit resolution for offline analysis. The EEG recordings were parsed into epochs from 100ms prior to stimulus onset through 800ms after stimulus onset. The sections of epochs contaminated by eye blink artefacts were eliminated by deleting all samples falling within a window of +/- 50ms of any EOG value in excess of +/- 100uV. Each stimulus was presented 20 times and average waveforms for each stimulus type were calculated. To correct for individual differences in baseline ERP recordings, the average activity for the 100msec prior to stimulus onset were calculated and subtracted from individual ERPs and the resulting data series were smoothed.

Results

A 3 (brain site) x 2 (side of brain) x 3 (strength of correlation) x 2 (direction of correlation) x 2 (imagery condition) repeated measures analysis of variance was conducted. Results indicated statistically significant main effects and interactions that will be discussed below.

Activity in Posterior, Medial, and Anterior Sites

Because posterior brain areas are generally assumed to be responsible for processing elementary visual information, we expected that object and graph imagery would be similar in these sites. Anterior areas are generally thought to be responsible for higher level cognitive processing and thus, we expected that activity in these sites would occur later. As can be seen in Figure 1, the processing of objects and scatterplots was similar in posterior sites. For both types of stimuli, a positive peak (P1) occurred approximately 180msec after stimulus onset and was followed by a negative peak (N1) at approximately 200msec. The latency of N1 was similar for object and scatterplot imagery but the deflection was greater when participants formed a mental image of a scatterplot.

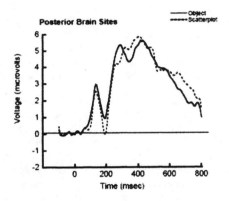

Figure 1a. Activity in posterior brain sites in response to object and scatterplot imagery.

Activity in medial and anterior sites produced similar activity from stimulus onset to approximately 200msec (although in anterior sites, scatterplot imagery led to a more pronounced N1). After 200msec, the amplitudes associated with scatterplot imagery were greater than those produced when objects were imagined. Differences in amplitude were especially evident in anterior sites and suggest that the cognitive load associated with producing mental images of scatterplots was greater than those associated with object imagery.

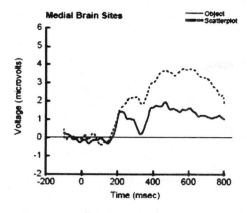

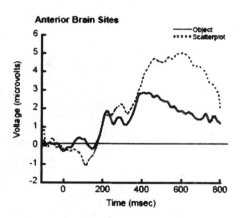

Figure 1b. Activity in medial and anterior brain sites in response to object and graph imagery.

Activity occurring after 400msec is considered to be indicative of endogenous (or top-down) processing, and, during this time period, activity tends to be higher when participants devote more effort to a task (suggestive of increased resource allocation). Given that research suggests that anterior and medial sites are responsible for categorization of stimuli and higher level cognitive processing, it was hypothesized that activity in the medial and anterior areas would be higher after 400msec. As can be seen in Figure 1, this hypothesis was confirmed—in posterior sites, the ERPs began to decrease approximately 400msec after stimulus onset but, in anterior sites, the decrease did not begin until approximately 600msec after stimulus onset.

Activity in Right and Left Brain Sites

A comparison of the activity in the right and left hemispheres indicates interesting differences. Because spatial processing is generally accepted to be under right hemisphere control and given the current emphasis on

importance of spatial processing on graph comprehension, it was hypothesized that the activity in the right and left electrode sites would be different. As can be seen in Figure 2, the time course of processing was similar for object and scatterplot imagery but there were amplitude differences. As presented in Figure 2, the greatest amplitudes resulted in right hemisphere sites when participants constructed a mental image of a scatterplot; supporting the theory that graph reading is, in part, a spatial cognition task. The differential processing in the right and left brain sites suggest that graph reading involves an integration of language and spatial processing (which support dual-coding models).

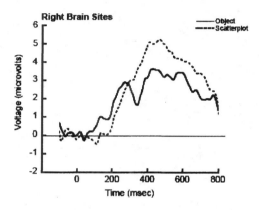

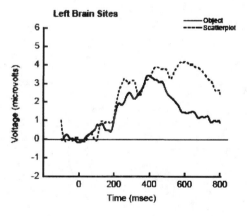

Figure 2. Activity in right and left hemisphere recording sites.

Graph Imagery and Relationship Type

Best and her colleagues (2006b) found the amplitudes associated with stronger relationships were lower than those of moderate or weak relationships and suggested that these differences are due to the fact that moderate relationships are more difficult to judge than relationships that are very strong or very weak. To examine differences between graph perception and imagery, we examined how the strength of a relationship affected imagery. Figure 3 presents the activity associated with strong (r = +/-0.9), moderate (r = +/-0.5) and weak (r = +/-0.1) relationships. As can be seen, activity associated with the different types of relationships was similar from stimulus onset to 400msec. After 400msec, although the time course of processing is similar, there are clear amplitude differences. Amplitudes were highest when scatterplots depicting strong relationships were presented and lowest when weak relationships were presented.

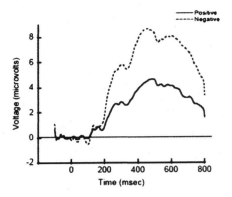

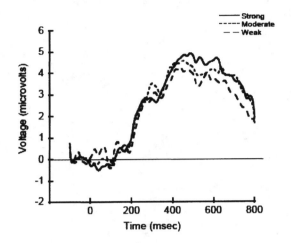

Figure 3. Overall activity associated with strong, moderate, and weak relationships. For this comparison, activity in all electrode sites was averaged.

Figure 4 presents the overall ERP waveforms associated with positive and negative relationships. As can be seen in the figure, the time course of processing was similar but the amplitudes associated with negative relationships were greater. This finding is similar to Best et al (2006) and is an interesting result, given that behavioural graph perception research suggests that people make less accurate judgments when presented with negative relationships in comparison to positive relationships. The higher amplitude, especially in later processing (after 400msec) is indicative of increased cognitive load that results in increased resource allocation. Thus, it appears that forming a mental image of a scatterplot depicting a negative relationship is more difficult than forming an images positive relationships.

Figure 4. The ERPs associated with positive and negative relationships. Activity in all electrode sites was averaged.

Discussion and Conclusions

One goal of the present study was examine how graphs are processed in the brain. We were specifically interested in whether people with statistical experience are able to construct a *mental* graph of a statistical concept. Results suggest that participants were able to construct mental images of statistical concepts. In posterior brain sites, the time course and amplitudes produced when participants constructed images of objects or graphs were quite similar. In medial and anterior brain sites, the amplitudes produced during scatterplot imagery were greater than those of object imagery. These findings lend support to Pinker's (1990) theory of graph perception—it appears that posterior regions code simple visual elements and, at this level, there was less differentiation between different image types. Because there was differential processing in right and left recording sites, the current results support Trickett and Trafton's (2006) argument that spatial cognition is central to graph comprehension.

It is generally accepted that mental imagery uses many of the same resources as perceptual processing (Ward, 2006). To examine possible links between the graphical perception and imagery, a comparison of the current data with that of Best et al. (2006b) was conducted. Figure 5 presents overall activity in perceptual (Best et al., 2006b) and imagery (current study) conditions (in each case activity for the recording sites was averaged and the overall pattern of activity is presented). As can be seen in the Figure, for the first 200msec after stimulus presentation, the activity associated with graph perception and graph imagery was similar. Between 200 and 400msec, a positive peak occurred when participants viewed a scatterplot. In the imagery condition, the corresponding amplitude was not as pronounced and latency of the peak was later. By 800msec after stimulus presentation, the waveform associated with perception had returned to baseline levels but the waveform in the imagery condition remained higher (although there was a decrease in amplitude). These results are interesting but comparisons must be made with caution, given that the participants in the studies were different (ERP comparisons are optimal when repeated measures designs are used).

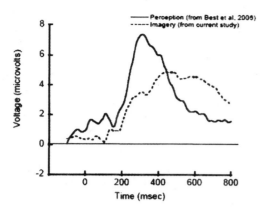

Figure 2. A comparison of activity due to perception and mental imagery. This figure presents a comparison of previous and current results.

The overall purpose of this study was to expand our understanding of how graphs are perceived and processed by the brain. One of our goals was to determine if graphs are processed in the same brain areas as other types of images. Preliminary evidence suggests that, in many ways, graphs and images are processed in the same way there are interesting processing differences. The current study was an attempt to extend our understanding of how graphs are processed and we wanted to determine if people are able to construct mental images of statistical constructs and if *graphical* imagery is similar to *object* imagery.

Limitations of the Current Study

There are several limitations to the current study that must be addressed. Firstly, in this study, participants were presented with a textual cue and asked to construct a visual image of a corresponding object. This design allowed for the comparison of object and graph imagery but the choice of control trials was less than optimal. Given that it is possible that the object imagery task involved less effort and attention than the graphical imagery task. In addition, in our follow-up studies, we will design control trials to closely match experimental trials; for example, on control trials participants could be asked to perform mathematical (but nongraphical) imagery tasks.

Given the possibility that graph comprehension and interpretation involves spatial cognition, future studies will include an evaluation of individual spatial ability. The inclusion of multiple tests of graph perception and cognition would allow for a better understanding of the overall process of graph comprehension.

Acknowledgments

The New Brunswick Innovation Fund Research Assistantship Initiative and the University of New Brunswick Faculty Research Fund funded this project. We would like to thank Elizabeth Hickman and Jennifer Woodland for their assistance with data collection.

References

Best, L. A., Adams, A., Jones, S, Hickman, E., Hunter, A. C., LeBlanc, A., Stewart, B., Woodland, J. (2006a, June). *Is a picture worth 1000 words?: An electrophysiological examination of graph perception.* Paper presented at the annual meeting of the Canadian Psychological Association annual meeting.

Best, L. A., Hunter, A.C., & Stewart, B. (2006b). Perceiving relationships: A physiological examination of the perception of scatterplots. In D. Barker-Plummer, R. Cox, and N. Swoboda (Eds), *Diagrammatic Representation and Inference (pp.244-257).* Berlin: Springer.

Culbertson, H. M., and Powers, R. D. (1959). A study of graph comprehension difficulties. *Audio-Visual Communication Review, 7,* 97-100.

Friel, S. N., Curcio, F and Bright, G. W. (2001). Making sense of graphs: Critical factors influencing comprehension and instructional implications. *Journal for Research in Mathematics Education, 32,* 124-158.

Jausovec, N. (1996). Differences in EEG alpha activity related to giftedness. *Intelligence, 23,* 159-173.

Kosslyn, S. M. (1994). *Elements of graph design.* New York: W. H. Freeman.

Lohse, G.L. (1993). A cognitive model for understanding graphical perception. *Human Computer Interaction, 8,* 353-388.

Pinker, S. (1990). A theory of graph comprehension. In R. Friedle, *Artificial intelligence and the future of testing.* Hillsdale, NJ: Erlbaum.

Roth, W.M. and Bowen, G. M. (2003). When are graphs worth ten thousand words? An expert/expert study. *Cognition and Instruction, 21,* 429–473.

Shah, P., Freedman, E., & Vekiri, I. (2005). The comprehension of quantitative information in graphical displays. In P. Shah and A. Miyake, (Eds.). *The Cambridge handbook of visuospatial thinking* (pp. 426-476). New York: Cambridge University Press.

Trickett, S., & Trafton, G. (2006). Toward a comprehensive model of graph comprehension: Making the case for spatial cognition. In D. Barker-Plummer, R. Cox, and N. Swoboda (Eds), *Diagrammatic Representation and Inference.* Berlin: Springer.

Ward, J. (2006). *The Student's Guide to Cognitive Neuroscience.* East Sussex. UK: Psychology Press.

Posters

Students' Difficulties with Algebraic Expressions Containing Literal Symbols

Konstantinos P. Christou (kochrist@phs.uoa.gr) & Stella Vosniadou (svosniad@phs.uoa.gr)
Cognitive Science Lab, Department of Philosophy and History of Science,
National and Kapodistrian University of Athens, Ano Ilissia, 15771, Greece

Introduction

In the present study we use the conceptual change approach as an explanatory framework for better understanding students' difficulties with algebraic expressions containing literal symbols. The conceptual change approach focuses on knowledge acquisition in specific domains and describes learning as a process that sometimes requires the significant reorganization of existing knowledge structures and not just their enrichment (Vosniadou, 2007).

Previous research has shown that many students tend to use their initial knowledge of natural numbers to interpret new mathematical concepts introduced in formal instruction (Gelman, 2000; Resnick et. al., 1989). This can be an important source of difficulty in the learning of the algebraic notation. We hypothesized that students' prior knowledge about numbers, in particular natural numbers, in the context of arithmetic would affect students interpreting literal symbols. More specifically, we hypothesized that students would tend to interpret literal symbols, which represent variables, as natural numbers only.

In a previous study, in order to test this hypothesis, we used two open-ended questionnaires where we asked the students to give numbers that could and could not be assigned to a set of given algebraic expressions (Christou & Vosniadou, 2005). However, it can be argued that when an open-ended questionnaire is used, students respond with the first answer that comes in mind, which is usually a natural number. This does not mean that the students are unwilling to accept non-natural numbers, such as rational or real numbers, as substitutes for the literal symbols.

In order to address this issue, a forced-choice questionnaire was used in the present study. The advantage of a forced-choice questionnaire is that it presents students with specific alternatives that include both natural and non-natural numbers. It can thus provide a more rigorous test of our hypothesis.

Method

Thirty-four 8th and 9th graders participated in this study. The students were asked to choose from a given set of numbers those they thought <u>could not</u> be assigned to the same algebraic expressions used in the previous study, i.e. a, -b, 4g, a/b, k+3. For each algebraic expression students were given a set of alternatives which consisted of positive and negative rational numbers, integers, and also the correct alternative, namely, that all numbers can be assigned to each algebraic expression. We asked the questions using the negative form because it is only in this condition that we can say with certainty that only the correct response applies.

Results

The results showed that only 18.6% of the students understood that all the given numbers could be possibly assigned to each algebraic expression. In one third of the students' responses (30.3%), numbers other than naturals, such as fractions or decimals, were not accepted as numbers that could be assigned to the literal symbols of the given expressions. In addition, in 25.4% of the students' responses, all negative numbers from the given set were not accepted as numbers that could be assigned to the positive-like algebraic expressions, such as for example the '4g' or the 'k+3'. In the case of '-b', however, because of the presence of the negative sign, about half of the students (52.9%) responded that positive numbers <u>could not</u> be assigned to it.

Discussion

The results from the present study provided further support to our hypothesis. This conclusion was based on two sources of evidence: First, because many students excluded the non-natural numbers of the given set, as numbers that could not be assigned to the literal symbols. Second, because many students tended to interpret the phenomenal sign of the algebraic expressions as the sign of the numbers it represents. In the context of arithmetic, a number with 'no sign' denotes 'positive value', whereas a number with 'negative sign' denotes 'negative value'. This is a characteristic of natural numbers which holds also for all positive numbers, but do not apply to variables. In order for students to accept that literal symbols can stand for any real number, they need to realize such differences.

References

Christou, K.P., & Vosniadou, S. (2005). How students interpret literal symbols in algebra: A conceptual change approach. In B.G. Bara, L. Barsalou, & M. Bucciarelli (Eds.) *Proceedings of the XXVII Annual Conference of the Cognitive Science Society*, pp. 453-458.

Gelman, R. (2000). The epigenesis of mathematical thinking, *Journal of Applied Developmental Psychology*, 21, 27-37.

Resnick, L.B., Nesher, P., Leonard, F., Magone, M., Omanson, S., & Peled, I. (1989). Conceptual bases of arithmetic errors: The case of decimal fractions. *Journal for Research in Mathematics Education*, 20, 8–27.

Vosniadou, S. (2007). The conceptual change approach and its reframing. In S. Vosniadou, A. Baltas, & X. Vamvakoussi, *Reframing the conceptual change approach in learning and instruction*. Oxford: Elsevier Press.

Aspects of students' rational number reasoning: A conceptual change perspective

Xenia Vamvakoussi (xenva@phs.uoa.gr)
Cognitive Science Laboratory, Department of History and Philosophy of Science, University of Athens
Ano Ilissia, 15771, Greece

Stella Vosniadou (svosniad@phs.uoa.gr)
Cognitive Science Laboratory, Department of History and Philosophy of Science, University of Athens
Ano Ilissia, 15771, Greece

Introduction

Rational numbers are difficult for students to understand and this fact has been demonstrated in numerous studies (Smith, Solomon, & Carey, 2005). An aspect of rational number reasoning that has not been extensively investigated so far is students' understanding about the dense structure of the rational number set. In this study we investigated the development of students' understanding of density from a conceptual change perspective. A key assumption of the particular theoretical framework that we adopted (Vosniadou, in press) is that children form initial explanatory frameworks about numbers, which are tied around their understanding of natural numbers. When new information about rational numbers comes in contrast with what is already known, the conceptual change framework predicts the formation of a specific type of misconceptions, called *synthetic models*, which reflect the assimilation of new information in prior, incompatible knowledge.

The set of natural numbers consists of discrete elements which share a similar form, in the sense that any natural number is represented as the combination of a finite number of digits. On the contrary, the set of rational numbers is dense and any rational number can be represented either as a fraction or as a decimal.

We assumed that the particular characteristics of the natural numbers set mentioned above are key elements of students' initial number concept and are bound to constrain students' understanding of the dense structure of rational numbers. Prior research has provided evidence that the idea of discreteness is indeed a barrier to the understanding of density (e.g. Merenluoto & Lehtinen, 2002). It is also documented that students have many difficulties moving flexibly and effectively among the various forms of rational numbers (e.g. Khoury & Zazkis, 1994). We claim that students draw on symbolic notation to treat decimals and fractions as different, unrelated sorts of numbers and this interferes with their understanding of density. We hypothesized that students form synthetic models of the structure of rational numbers intervals, reflecting the constraints associated with their initial explanatory frameworks about numbers, as well as the assimilation of new knowledge about rational numbers. This hypothesis was tested in an empirical study.

Method

The participants of the study were 164 9th and 137 11th graders, who were administered open-ended and forced-choice questionnaires, consisting of six questions. In both cases, students were asked about the number of numbers between two pseudo-successive rational numbers (like 0.005, 0.006 or 1/3, 2/3)

Results and Discussion

According to our results, students' accounts of the rational numbers intervals reflected the expected constraints. More specifically, our participants generated the following types of synthetic models: a) intervals that preserve the discrete structure of natural numbers, while the initial numbers were considered successive, b) intervals preserving the discrete structure of natural numbers, while the initial numbers were not considered successive, c) intervals containing "infinitely many" equivalent numbers d) intervals containing infinitely many numbers, when the initial numbers were decimals (or fractions) and intervals with a finite number of numbers, when the initial numbers were fractions (or decimals), and e) intervals containing infinitely many numbers of the same symbolic representation. We draw on our results to argue that the development of rational number reasoning cannot be accomplished by mere enrichment of students' initial explanatory frameworks of number.

References

Khoury, H.A., & Zazkis, R. (1994). On fractions and non-standard representations: Preservice teachers' concepts. *Educational Studies in Mathematics*, 27, 191–204.

Merenluoto, K., & Lehtinen, E. (2002). Conceptual change in mathematics: Understanding the real numbers. In Limon, M. & L. Mason (Eds.), *Reconsidering Conceptual Change: Issues in Theory and Practice* (pp.233-258). Dordrecht: Kluwer Academic Publishers.

Smith, C.L., Solomon, G.E.A., & Carey, S. (2005). Never getting to zero: Elementary school students' understanding of the infinite divisibility of number and matter. *Cognitive Psychology, 51*, 101–140.

Vosniadou, S. (in press). The conceptual change approach and its reframing. In S. Vosniadou, A. Baltas, & X. Vamvakoussi, *Reframing the conceptual change approach in learning and instruction*. Oxford: Elsevier Press.

Using animated interactive analogies for understanding the programming variable

Dimitrios Doukakis (doukakis@di.uoa.gr),
Interdisciplinary Program of Graduate Studies in Basic and Applied Cognitive Science
University of Athens, Greece

Maria Grigoriadou (gregor@di.uoa.gr), Grammatiki Tsaganou (gram@di.uoa.gr)
Department of Informatics and Telecommunications,
University of Athens, Greece

Introduction

Various studies of high school novice programmers have described difficulties and misconceptions in understanding the important concept of the programming variable. A powerful framework for explaining these difficulties and misconceptions concentrating on the role of students' prior knowledge is the framework of conceptual change (Vosniadou, 2007) that. Students' prior knowledge of the concept of variable comes from high school mathematics. The concept of the mathematical variable shares common features with the concept of the programming variable but also has a lot of important differences. Several of student's misconceptions about the concept of programming variable and the value assignment command related to it, can be explained by their prior knowledge about the concept of mathematical variable that acts as a barrier to the understanding of the concept of programming variable (Grigoriadou et al., in press).

The analogies usually used in instruction to help students understand the programming variable are the box analogy and the plate analogy. However, we decided to use a different analogy in this study, because these analogies were not very successful,. The analogy used in this study was a Learning Object (L.O.) consisting of a number of rotating cylinders with digits, characters, or Boolean values on them, depending on the type of the variable they represented (see fig. 1). The analogy presentation was strengthened using animation and interactivity. The performance of a group using a L.O. that included the analogy and a group using an L.O. without the analogy was compared.

Figure 1: Analogy used for the integer variable "Books_number" with current value 200178

Method

Participants

Thirty-three introductory programming students from the last three grades of a high school (aged 15-17 years) in the Athens area participated in this study. Twenty-one were placed in the analogy group and twelve in the control group.

Materials

An L.O. that included the interactive animated analogy and an L.O. that had the same interactivity that did not employ the animated analogy were used. A questionnaire for misconceptions detection based on questionnaires of previous studies was a also constructed.

Procedure

Both groups studied the learning objects without any time restriction. Then both groups answered the questionnaire.

Results

The differences in performance were in favor of the analogy group for all the 9 questions of the questionnaire but it was statistically significant for 4 of the questions $[t(31)=2.328, p<.05]$, $[t(31)=2.436, p<.05]$, $[t(31)=3.798, p<.05]$, $[t(31)=3.521, p<.05]$. Furthermore the analogy group students found the analogy "familiar" (83%), "very interesting" (38%) and "very much interesting" (62%). There was also an increase in favor of analogy group in the total time spent on parts containing the animated analogy $[t(31)=2.329, p<.05]$ and on number of students' visits on parts containing the animated analogy $[t(31)=3.826, p<.05]$.

Discussion

This pilot experiment revealed that the combined use of a properly selected analogy along with animation and interaction can help novice programmers deal with their misconceptions in the concept of programming variable. Its success also supported this technique as a fruitful approach that could be used in other cases of conceptual change. The experiment also indicated that students were familiar with the analog and interested on experimenting with it. Subsequent experiments are planned to measure the individual effects of the entangled factors (analogy, animation and interaction).

References

Grigoriadou, M. Kanidis, E. Doukakis, D. (in press) Students' beliefs on computer science concepts and the problem of conceptual change. *NOESIS (3)* Athens, Gutenberg: Typothito, (in Greek).

Vosniadou, S.(in press). The conceptual change approach and its reframing. In S. Vosniadou, A. Baltas, & X. Vamvakoussi (Eds.), *Reframing the Conceptual Change Approach in Learning and Instruction.* Oxford: Elsevier.

Conceptions and Practices of University Teachers in Various Disciplines

Louise Langevin (langevin.louise@uqam.ca)
Gilles Raîche (raiche.gilles@uqam.ca)
Diane Leduc (leduc.diane@uqam.ca)
Monik Bruneau (bruneau.monik@uqam.ca)
Catherine Gagnon (catherine.gagnon@perfocom.net)
Nadine Talbot (education@videotron.ca)
Ilia Essopos, (iliaessopos@sympatico.ca)
Département d'éducation et pédagogie, Université du Québec à Montréal,
Succ. 8888, Centre-Ville, Montréal (Québec), H3C 3P8, Canada

Context

Much research in applied cognitive sciences has focused on teaching through demonstrating the importance of different conceptions, or beliefs, and their influence on practices. These conceptions constitute stable frames of reference that orient teachers' actions and so must be considered in any teacher training. They (Kember, 1997) range from "teacher-centred education based on transmission of information" to "student-centred learning," with intermediate categories (Samuelowicz and Bain, 2001). Generally, approaches centred on the teacher and content predominate amongst professors (Kember & Kwan, 2000), due to the absence of pedagogical training, past student experience, and the influence of the institutional and disciplinary context. The disciplines, truly "tribal", socialize professors with regard to their educational approaches (Becher, 1994), both epistemologically (Donald, 2002) and culturally (Kekäle, 1999) and influence their educational intentions and ideas (Prosser & Trigwell, 1996) since it is within their disciplines that professors discover their own identity (Smeby, 1996). Donald (2002) defines the concept of "discipline" as follows: "A body of knowledge with a reasonably logical taxonomy, a specialized vocabulary, an accepted body of theory, a systematic research strategy, and techniques for replication and validation (p.8)."

Goal and method

Our research goal was to identify similarities and differences in teaching conceptions and practices of professors in various disciplines in three universities of varying size and type/location in Quebec (Canada). Our research strategy was multi-methodological, employing a hybrid design by means of an on-line questionnaire (with a 27% response rate, that is, 180 out of 659), interviews with 45 professors, and more than 270 hours of classroom observations. From this, we categorized five disciplines : pure sciences, applied sciences, business administration, humanities, and arts and letters.

Results

The findings from the questionnaire (Trigwell and Prosser, 2004) indicate that, in the applied sciences, a conception based on the professor and the transmission of information predominates significantly. Women, much more than men, are oriented towards students and their learning. Qualitative data indicate that professors see themselves as guides and transmitters of knowledge, except in arts and letters where the terms/verbs "awaken/arouse" and "develop sensitivity" prevail, and in applied sciences, where the relationship being forged is most frequently mentioned. Amongst the activities observed in class, the lecture is most common, followed by situation scenarios or practical exercises and contextualization. Pure sciences where PBL (problem-based learning) is applied in biology are notable for the frequency of these reflective activities. The 180 teachers also identified their *good practices* and expressed their difficulties and needs. From this data, often common across the disciplines, we conclude that pedagogical training could be designed for a broad-based clientele/addressed to everyone but that specific material and subsequent handouts or training sessions should be planned for each discipline.

References

Becher, T. (1994). The Significance of Disciplinary Differences. *Studies in Higher Education, 19(2): 151-161.*

Donald, J. (2002). *Learning to Think. Disciplinary Differences*. San Francisco: Jossey-Bass.

Kekäle, J. (1999). Preferred Patterns of Academic Leadership in Different Disciplinary (Sub)Cultures. *Higher Education,* 37, 217-238.

Kember, D. (1997). A Reconceptualisation of the Research into University Academics' Conceptions of Teaching. *Learning and Instruction, 7*(3), 255-275.

Kember, D., & Kwan, K., (2000). Lecturer's Approaches to Teaching and Their Relationship to Conceptions of Good Teaching. *Instructional Science*, 28, 469-490.

Samuelowicz, K., Bain, J.D. (1992). Conceptions of teaching held by academic teachers. *Higher Education* : 93-111

Smeby, J.C. (1996). Disciplinary Differences in University Teaching. *Studies in Higher Education*, 21(1), 69-79.

Trigwell, K., Prosser, M. (2004). Development and use of the Approaches to Teaching Inventory. *Educational Psychology review*, Vol.16, No 4, december : 409-424.

Catching eureka on the fly

Paulina (Paulina.Lindstrom@lucs.lu.se)
Lund University Cognitive Science, Sweden

Agneta.Gulz (Agneta.Gulz@lucs.lu.se)
Lund University Cognitive Science, Sweden

Eureka and its pedagogical potential

There is a growing interest within the domain of intelligent tutoring systems (ITS) to develop systems that are capable of detecting affective responses and states in students and to adapt teaching strategies and processes accordingly.

Our work focuses on the affective state of eureka – or insight experienced as *"Ah, now I get it!"* – and on the pedagogical potentials of an ITS that can identify this state.

It can easily be seen how the recognition of *confusion* or *frustration*, can be useful in guiding the pedagogical interventions of an intelligent tutoring system – or a teacher. But how could identification of the relatively brief and clearly positive emotion of eureka be useful? How could an ITS make use of such information?

First, the experience characterized by *"Alright, I've got it now"* or *"Oh now I really understand it"* can be useful in signaling that the student is now ready to proceed in the learning process. Such a functional communicative characteristic is a crucial point that might seem quite obvious but refers to the delicate balance between providing well-timed support and well-timed challenges to a student.

Second, and importantly, pedagogical adaptivity in a powerful ITS (as well as in a human teacher) involves *learnability* on the part of the teaching system. In order to *improve* ones teaching, an ability to analyze and identify the kinds of learning situations or activities that *precede* students' eureka experiences can be highly relevant. Not the least so with respect to material that is well known to be hard for students really to understand. Here an identification of eureka experiences can help to pinpoint the teaching strategies, the set of examples and tasks etc. that seem to work well in guiding students' towards an understanding of such material that is often difficult to get a grip of.

Attempting to study the erueka experience

Our study was set up in line with a suggestion by Craig et al. (2004) to aim at *more precise identifications* of *when* emotions occur during the learning process: in a sense, to try to catch emotions on the fly. In the study, 40 participants were asked to identify 26 stimuli consisting of pictures, which were pre-validated to yield an eureka-experience when identified: ambiguous pictures, incomplete pictures and mathematical logical problems; each picture accompanied by a written sentence to provide subjects with a context to interpret the stimulus within. Participants were asked to click the mouse button as soon as they identified the stimuli. The measurements consisted of a combination of a behavioral measure – eye movements – with two physiological measures: skin conductance and pupil dilation. It was predicted that participants identifying a stimulus would look more on critical areas of the stimulus picture, have larger pupil dilation and higher skin conductance compared to participants not identifying the stimulus.

Results and discussion

The result was in line with the predictions, and clearly so for the eye movement data (with a distinct peak occurring around 6 seconds before reporting identification of the stimulus by clicking the button.) The overall pattern on the physiological measures was, though, *less dramatic* than expected. This result though, points towards the important issue about *the span of eureka*. An eureka experience in the sense of *Newtonian insight* may be prototypical in our conceptions of eureka. Such intense moments or states are, however, probably quite rare. Our working hypothesis is that there are *less intense*, but still very similar experiences when something falls into place and is finally or suddenly clear or solved, that occur much more frequently in learning contexts.

The tasks and situation in the actual study are more likely to produce such affective states than Newtonian eruekas.

Our aim is to continue to explore the eureka phenomenon in its entire manifestation. In this quest the next step is to focus on more typical learning contexts and tasks and to continue to work on refinements of the measuring methods.

Acknowledgments

Thanks to K. Holmqvist, R. Andersson and J. van der Weijer at the Humanities laboratory, Lund University.

References

Lindström, P. & Holmqvist, K. (in preparation)

Craig, S. D., Graesser, A. C., Sullins, J., & Gholson, B. (2004). Affect and learning: an exploratory look into the role of affect in learning with AutoTutor. *Journal of Educational Media,* 29(3), 241-250.

Absence of Blocking in Cognitive Map Learning in Humans

Oliver Hardt (hardt@u.arizona.edu)
Psychology Department, The University of Arizona
1503 E University Blvd., Tucson, AZ 85721 USA

Lynn Nadel (nadel@u.arizona.edu)
Psychology Department, The University of Arizona
1503 E University Blvd., Tucson, AZ 85721 USA

Cognitive map theory (O'Keefe & Nadel, 1978) proposes that different learning mechanisms are used in the *locale* and the *taxon* systems. The locale system acquires cognitive maps, allocentric representations of the spatial environment, in a one-trial learning mechanism. The taxon systems use associative learning mechanisms to acquire egocentric spatial representations. In contrast to cognitive map theory, associative learning theories posit that *all* learning takes the same form, regardless of what is acquired.

These differential assumptions can easily be tested. While cognitive map theory predicts that specific associative learning phenomena should occur only in taxon, but not locale learning, associative learning theories predict these phenomena for both.

One such phenomenon is *blocking*. In a blocking experiment, subjects are first exposed to a contingency (e.g., $A \rightarrow B$), learning that A predicts B. After acquisition, another stimulus (C) is added, such that $(A + C) \rightarrow B$ (compound training). In this blocking paradigm subjects fail to acquire information about the relation between B and the newly added stimulus C because B was already fully predicted by A (e.g., Kamin, 1969).

Demonstrations of blocking effects in spatial learning have been taken to suggest that associative learning mechanisms are involved in the acquisition of cognitive maps (e.g., Biegler & Morris, 1999). This conclusion thus challenges a fundamental assumption of cognitive map theory. However, the central problem of these studies is that they failed to demonstrate that subjects indeed recruited the locale system for spatial learning. It remains possible that subjects used taxon strategies instead, and, if that was the case, the results confirm, not falsify, cognitive map theory.

Addressing this issue, we show in Experiment 1 that blocking is not observed in a computer-based version of the Morris water-maze task (cMWM) in which the locale system is indeed recruited and cognitive maps are created. Experiment 2 showed that a cognitive map is not created in the cMWM in which blocking in humans was reported (Hamilton & Sutherland, 1999): Subjects predominantly associated the target location with a small number of cues, such that their ability to find the target was compromised when these cues were removed. Such an effect would not be observed if a cognitive map guided behavior, as, by definition, a map permits navigation when any subset of distal cues is available.

These findings suggest that unless it is independently demonstrated whether taxon or locale strategies were recruited to produce spatial behavior, the implications of associative learning effects for cognitive map theory cannot be interpreted.

Furthermore, we identified two variables – concreteness of the distal cues and knowledge about the nature of the spatial task at hand – that moderate recruitment of the locale and the taxon systems. Experiment 3 and 4 showed that blocking is observed when the cues added to the enviroment show abstract (Chinese pictographs), but not when they show concrete objects. Finally, Experiment 5 showed that providing subjects with specific task knowledge eliminated blocking in the very task in which it was originally reported (Hamilton & Sutherland, 1999).

These results are consistent with cognitive map theory, but cannot readily be explained by associative learning theories. Neither the Rescorla-Wagner model, attentional theories, nor configural association theory can account for why the concreteness of cues and knowledge about the relation between the target location and distal cues moderates whether associative learning phenomena are observed. The obvious conclusion is that some forms of spatial learning do not follow the principles proposed in these accounts.

Acknowledgments

This report was part of the first author's dissertation at The University of Arizona, and was supported by grants to the Cognitive Neuroscience Center from the Flinn Foundation and the McDonnell-Pew Program.

References

Biegler, R., & Morris, R. G. M. (1999). Blocking in the spatial domain with arrays of discrete landmarks. *Journal of Experimental Psychology: Animal Behvioral Processes, 25*, 334–351.

Hamilton, D. A., & Sutherland, R. J. (1999). Blocking in human place learning: evidence from virtual navigation. *Psychobiology, 27*, 453–461.

Kamin, L. J. (1969). Predictability, surprise, attention, and conditioning. In B. A. Campbell & R. M. Church (Eds.), *Punishment and aversive behavior*. New York: Appleton-Century-Crofts.

O'Keefe, J., & Nadel, L. (1969). *The hippocampus as a cognitive map*. Oxford: Clarendon Press.

Synthetic Models in Finswimming

Maria Koulianou (mkoulian@phs.uoa.gr) & Stella Vosniadou (svosniad@phs.uoa.gr),
Cognitive Science Lab Department of Philosophy and History of Science,
National and Kapodistrian University of Athens, Ano Ilisia 157 71 Greece

Nickos Geladas (ngeladas@cc.uoa.gr) & Konstantinos Boudolos (nboudol@cc.uoa.gr)
Department of Sport Medicine and Biology of Physical Activity ·Faculty of Physical Education and Sport Science,
National and Kapodistrian University of Athens, Daphne, Greece

Introduction

The purpose of the present study was to compare the finswimming performance in two different samples: finswimmers (Fins) and finswimmers with prior experience in butterfly style (BFins). Finswimming (FS) is a sport of speed in which performance is based on whole–body symmetrical oscillations. When FS is practiced underwater for the first 15m it is called underwater undulatory swimming (UUS). This technique is utilized also by the swimmers in the butterfly events. In butterfly swimming (UUBS), the starting point for the underwater motion is the ankle, producing a whip-like action, whereas in finswimming (UUFinS) this motion starts from the hip level with the knee and the hip ankles in opposite phase producing symmetric oscillations.

The theoretical framework of the study is based on work in cognitive science (Vosniadou, in press), which shows that prior knowledge can stand in the way of acquiring new information, which is incompatible with it. In such cases the new information is often assimilated into prior but incompatible knowledge creating synthetic models.

In a previous study we investigated the hypothesis that the BFins swimmers would create a synthetic representation of the finswimming style in which the body propulsion would start at the ankle and not at the hip. This hypothesis was investigated using the methodology of a forced-choice questionnaire. The results confirmed the hypothesis that the BFin group would construct prior – knowledge - linked mistakes in their representation of the finswimming style (Koulianou & Vosniadou 2006).

In the present study we examine the hypothesis that synthetic models can also be found in the motor swimming performance of the BFins group. More specifically, we expected to find elements from both underwater swimming techniques (UUFinS versus UUBS) on the BFins group's motor performance but not in the performance of the Fins group. Thus, we hypothesized a higher vertical displacement of the hip and ankle joint for the BFinS group but not for the Fins group.

Method

Participants

Fifty-two finswimmers with mean age of 15 years and 9 months participated in the study. Twenty of them had a mean of 4 years of finswimming competition and no prior knowledge of butterfly swimming (Fins). Thirty-two had a mean of 2.5 years of finswimming competition with 5.5 years of prior experience in the butterfly swimming style (BFins).

Procedure

The measurement was carried out in a 25m pool. Both groups were instructed to perform a 1x15m underwater finswimming trial. The finswimmers equipped with joints markers (wrist, shoulder, hip, knee, ankle) were recorded (Sony DCR – TRV 730E 50Hz) in the sagittal plane. The position of these anatomical marks was digitized at 50 Hz. The 2D Logger Pro 3.3 software yielded vertical displacement and angular position.

Results & Discussion

The results showed symmetric oscillations of hip and ankle joints for the Fins group and a whip-like action for BFins group. An Independent-Samples T-Test analysis showed that the average difference of vertical displacement of the two joints was significantly higher for BFins group, $[t = -2.31, df = 50$, 2-tailed $p<.01]$ only at the upward phase compared to the Fins group. This variation can be explained by the different starting point in UUFinS and UUBS and the different oscillations that produced. The results support the hypothesis that the BFns group's performance had elements from both swimming techniques. These results are consistent with previous findings (Koulianou & Vosniadou, 2006).

References

Koulianou, M. & Vosniadou, S. (2006). Effects of incompatible prior knowledge in butterfly style on understanding finswimming style. In Sun, R. & Miyake, N., Proceedings of the 28th Annual Conference of the Cognitive Science Society (pp. 2539), Vancouver.

Vosniadou, S. (2003). Exploring the relationships between conceptual change and intentional learning. In G.M. Sinatra and P.R. Pintrich (Eds.) Intentional Conceptual Change. Mahwah, NJ: *Lawrence Erlbaum Associates*. 377- 406.

Vosniadou, S. (in press). The Conceptual change approach and its re-framing. In S. Vosniadou, A. Baltas, X. Vamvakousi (Eds), *Re-framing the conceptual change approach in learning and instruction*. Oxford Elsevier Press.

Children's Knowledge about Consciousness: A Developmental Perspective

Nikos Makris (nmakris@eled.duth.gr)
Department of Primary Education, Democritus University of Thrace
Nea Chili, Alexandroupolis, TK 68100, Greece

Dimitris Pnevmatikos (dpnevmat@uowm.gr)
Department of Primary Education, University of Western Macedonia, Florina,
3rd Km National Road Florina – Niki, Florina, GR-53100, Greece

Despite the vast body of research on the field of children's theory of mind (see Wellman, Cross, & Watson, 2001), we still know little about children's understanding of certain aspects of the human mind, such as consciousness. Flavell, Flavell, & Green, (1995) have shown that preschoolers have a limited understanding of consciousness. Specifically, they are not able to understand what James (1890/1983) had called the stream of consciousness or to infer the object of a person's thinking even in cases where clear evidence is available. However, these studies have focused on children's knowledge about consciousness regarding perceptual activities rather than higher cognitive activities such as problem solving. Moreover, they have investigated children's knowledge about primary consciousness, that is, awareness of thinking and its content, rather than reflective consciousness, that is, the existence of thoughts about thinking itself (Fathring, 1992).

Aim of the Study

The present study aims at providing an insight into the knowledge children have about primary and reflective consciousness from a developmental perspective.

Participants

Five groups of children and one group of young adults were tested: 13 5-year-olds, 17 6-year-olds, 15 7-year-olds, 14 9-year-olds, 15 11-year-olds, and 14 young adults. All participants came from middle class families.

Material and Procedure

Participants were tested individually with a battery consisted of seven illustrated stories. In each of these stories the protagonists were involved in the processing of a cognitive task demanding the activation of a general cognitive function (such as list memory, episodic memory, attention or understanding) or a specialized cognitive capacity, such as mathematical, verbal or imaginal capacity (Demetriou, Christou, Spanoudis, & Platsidou, 2002). Participants were asked a) to estimate whether the protagonist of the story is thinking (primary-consciousness activities), b) to determine the content of protagonist's thinking, c) to determine whether the protagonist know what she/he is thinking (reflective consciousness activities), and d) whether protagonist could change the content of her/his thinking.

Moreover, participants were asked to describe what the protagonist has to do for the effective processing of the task at hand.

Results and Discussion

The developmental milestones of the knowledge acquisition about consciousness vary across aspects of consciousness. Specifically, there were not any significant differences across the age groups regarding children's knowledge about reflective consciousness. However, children's ability to determine the content of one's mental experience seems to develop gradually during childhood. As for children's knowledge about primary consciousness and control of mental activity, the relevant data reflect an N and a U shape developmental pattern, respectively. Moreover, it was found that children made significantly more consciousness attributions in specialized capacity situations than in general cognitive function ones. As for participants' estimations regarding the ways that the protagonists would perform on the given tasks, it was found that children are able to specify accurately the mental functions and capacities required for the processing of the various tasks not until the age of 10. The results are discussed with reference to the literature regarding children's theory of mind as well as in relation to a 'person – time – condition' enacted conception of cognitive development.

References

Demetriou, A., Christou, C., Spanoudis, G., & Platsidou, M. (2002). The development of mental processing : Efficiency, working memory, and thinking. *Monographs of Society of Research in Child Development, 67*, Serial Number 268.

Farthing, G. W. (1992). *The psychology of consciousness.* NJ: Prentice-Hall.

Flavell, J. H., Flavell, E. R., & Green, F. L. (1995). Young children's knowledge about thinking. *Monographs of the Society for Research in child Development 60*, Serial number 243.

James, W. (1890/1983). *The principles of psychology.* New York: Dover Publications.

Wellman, H. M., Cross, D., & Watson, J. (2001). Meta – analysis of theory of mind development: The truth about false belief. *Child Development, 72*, 655-684.

Inference and Reference in Language Evolution

August Fenk (august.fenk@uni-klu.ac.at)
Department of Media and Communication Studies and Department of Psychology, Alps-Adriatic University of Klagenfurt

Gertraud Fenk-Oczlon (gertraud.fenk@uni-klu.ac.at)
Department of Linguistics and Computational Linguistics, Alps-Adriatic University of Klagenfurt
Universitaetsstrasse 65-67, 9020 Klagenfurt, Austria

Reference needs inference

Our cognitive apparatus functions as an inferential machinery extracting or constructing patterns and regularities. Such regularities are a precondition for an "indexical" interpretation of events with respect to possible causes and consequences. The extraction of domain-specific regularities by explorative and hypothesis-testing behaviour has most probably been our great strength long before the emergence of "language" in the narrow sense of the term. Such an inferential machinery is required for anticipating events and for "anticipating" what the other would already know or understand or intend, i.e. for efficient "mind-reading". Thus it is also required to infer the meaning of linguistic utterances (Sperber & Wilson 1986) and, moreover, for the development and acquisition of language and for the extraction and application of particular grammatical rules. Even more basic: "Sensitivity to the frequency with which different sounds follow each other in speech" helps us to break the speech record up into words (Zacks & Hasher 2002). Pattern recognition is inevitable for the identification of any form used as a symbol and/or icon. From all that follows that *indexicality* does not constitute a sign-specific function (Fenk 1998) but should be viewed as a fundamental cognitive principle pervading and transcending referential systems.

Reference "feeds" inference

Our advanced intelligence has "invented" language in order to disclose a new source of information: the experiences, the thoughts, i.e. the "knowledge" of our fellows. The situation-bound signalling system became more differentiated and moreover a medium for the communication and maintenance of "empirical" and "technical" knowledge. Reciprocal access to the thoughts of fellows offers a new basis for decision making and cooperative behaviour.

A second advantage of language was its use for "higher" cognitive activities. With the (respective) language we internalize its ways of structuring the world: its conceptualisations and categorisations as well as the rules appropriate for operating with the respective symbols. Maybe language is efficient in the sense of a corset, too (linguistic relativism); but it is at any rate or at least (Carruthers 2002) a necessary framework for the build up of more complex cognitive constructs.

Co-evolution of language and cognition?

Unlike Terrence Deacon's "brain-language co-evolution" or Susan Blackmore's "meme-gene coevolution" we place cognition as the co-evolutionary partner of language (Fenk-Oczlon & Fenk 2002), i.e. a second behavioural/functional system instead of a common neural, genetic, or otherwise physical substrate: Let us assume that both an efficient cognitive system and an efficient communication system are advantageous for the relevant population as well as for its individual members so that both systems are, more or less, permanently, under selective pressure ("drive 1"). These two systems are coupled: Each step forward in the evolution of language has to allow for the level of cognitive capabilities actually reached at least by the best "cognizers" of the population. This advanced language makes growing demands on the cognitive system, but has a double advantage – as a further developed communication tool and because of its use as a cognitive tool. This means an additional drive ("drive 2") which does not directly come from the environment in the usual sense but from a refined (cultural?) technique. Drive 2 will be doubly forceful because of the double advantage mentioned above. Thus, progress in language will stimulate progress in cognition and vice versa.

The dynamics of this co-evolution will dramatically increase a population's fitness for coping with rapid changing conditions and for conquering new habitats. And it will pull along genetic change and will favour the integration between those subsystems involved in the planning, analysing and control of sound patterns. The system thus evolving is not only able for rehearsal and for short-term retention of linguistic information in an articulatory code (as in Baddeley's phonological loop model). It becomes, moreover, functioning as a self-feeding, symbol-manipulating system. The emergence of our language-bound working memory?

References

Carruthers, P. (2002). The cognitive functions of language. *Brain and Behavioral Sciences, 25,* 657-726.

Fenk, A. (1998). Symbols and icons in diagrammatic representation. *Pragmatics & Cognition, 6, 1/2,* 301-334.

Fenk-Oczlon, G., & Fenk, A. (2002). The clausal structure of linguistic and pre-linguistic behavior. In T. Givón & B.F. Malle (Eds.), *The evolution of language out of pre-language.* Amsterdam: John Benjamins.

Sperber, D., & Wilson, D. (1986). *Relevance: communication and cognition.* Oxford: Blackwell.

Zacks, R.T., & Hasher, L. (2002). Frequency processing: A twenty-five year perspective. In P. Sedlmeier & T. Betsch (Eds.), *Etc. Frequency processing and cognition.* Oxford: Oxford University Press.

First Language Translations in New Language Learning

Asha H. Smith (Ashas@psych.stanford.edu)
Department of Psychology, Stanford University
450 Serra Mall, Jordan Hall, Building 420, Stanford, CA 94305 USA

Michael Ramscar (Michael@psych.stanford.edu)
Department of Psychology, Stanford University
450 Serra Mall, Jordan Hall, Building 420, Stanford, CA 94305 USA

Introduction

Experience may influence the approach used in vocabulary learning in a new language. For example, adults who have already learned a second language (L2) perform better in new language vocabulary learning than adults with no previous L2 learning experience (Keshavarz & Astaneh, 2002). One possible reason for this difference might be that the different groups are tending to employ different learning strategies.

Children rely less on learning L2 vocabulary through L1 translations than adults (factoring out reading-level) (Chen & Leung, 1989). Can the strategy used for first L2 learning experience influence the learning strategies used in acquiring vocabulary in subsequent languages?

Because extra L1 information is less relevant for a non-L1-mediated learning strategy, early L2 learners should be equally successful at learning new language names for items whether or not an L1 translation is easier to access. Later learners should be more successful at learning new language vocabulary when L1-translation are more accessible because the extra information may heighten the effectiveness of their more practiced strategy.

Methods

Thirty-four healthy native English speakers between the ages of 17 and 23-years-old took part in this study. The L2s of participants included French, Italian, Japanese, Malay, Mandarin, Cantonese, Tagalog, and Yoriba. Participants were separated into two groups: early and late L2 learners. Early learners had their first experience with new language learning before the age of 7. Late learners obtained this experience after 6-years-old. This age split was selected in accordance with relevant developmental changes that occur around this time period (see review in Bronson, 2000).

Participants were told that they would be taught new language names for a series of objects (12 familiar objects). The experimenter dictated the new language names. Items were presented on a screen long enough for participants to repeat the new name of each object. Using a between subjects design, early and late L2 learners were shown pictured objects either with or without an English label. After a filler task, they were given a comprehension and a free recall task. Proportion of accuracy in memory for the new object names was recorded for each task.

Results

There was a significant interaction between language learning group and object presentation (with versus without English label) for the comprehension portion of the task (p = .045). Early learners accurately identified more new language terms when the L1 word was not present (mean = .93; std. = .10; n = 7) than when it was present (mean = .76; std. = .12; n = 6). The later learners performed similarly when the object was presented with the L1 label (mean = .88; std. = .11; n = 12) and when it was not (mean = .85; std = .18; n = 11).

There was also a significant interaction in performance during the free recall portion of the task (p = .011). The later new language learners recalled more when the English word was presented (mean = .39; std. = .21) than when it was not (mean = .18; std. = .09). Early learners performed similarly when the English word was presented (mean = .37; std. = .23) and when it was not (mean = .25; std. = .12).

Discussion

Participants performed in line with our hypothesis during the free recall portion of the task. During the comprehension task, however, late learners seemed less influenced by the manipulation, while early learners were hindered by the presented translation. It may be that pushing early learners to translate interferes with their more practiced strategy. Follow-up studies must be done in order to better understand these findings and how they may influence proficiency in language learning.

References

Bronson, M.B. (2000). *Self-regulation in early childhood.* New York: The Guilford Press.

Chen, H-C. & Leung, Y-S. (1989). Patterns of lexical processing in a nonnative langauge. *Journal of Experimental Psychology: Learning, Memory, and Cognition, 15*(2), 316-325.

Keshavarz, M. H. & Astaneh, H. (2002). The impact of binguality on the learning of English vocabulary as a foreign language (L3). *Proceedings II Simposio Internacional Bilinguismo.*

Construction of Assisting Symbolic Models based on Novice Users Perception

David Leray (leray@limsi.fr)
LIMSI-CNRS BP 133 F-91403 Orsay Cedex France

Jean-Paul Sansonnet (jps@limsi.fr)
LIMSI-CNRS BP 133 F-91403 Orsay Cedex France

The need for new assisting tools

With the development of the new technologies and the Internet at home there is an exponential growth of the class of novice users. Consequently, there is a need for new assisting tools with two ideal features:

- The assisting content must be 'novice user'-oriented: instead of computer-oriented technical documentation which is incomprehensible for ordinary people, it must be expressed in their 'cognitive world'.
- The access to the assisting content must be as natural as possible.

In the InterViews and subsequent Daft projects we developed agent-mediated contextual help systems where the NLU and reasoning capabilities are at the core of the architecture. We made experiences with novice users in front of several simple assisted applications in an attempt to characterize novices' requests.

The first qualitative analysis of the Daft corpus showed that novices tend to express their problems with two strong characteristics:

- First, they refer to the application's entities via their perceptual features.
- Second, they express the problem in a declarative (their goals) rather than in a procedural form.

These two characteristics have the same cause: they categorize/reify entities (objects and behaviors) on the basis of their own perceptions. This can result in a dramatic 'cognitive drift' between their model and the programmer's model. This phenomenon opens an important scientific issue for the domain of assistance that will not be easily resolved.

A Perceptual Model Dedicated to Assistance

The first part of the poster presentation will be about the corpus we gathered through experimentations. The experiences with novice subjects resulted in the constitution of a corpus of ~8000 different requests acquired over 20 months. It provides a first coverage in French of the linguistic sublanguage of dialogical assistance (for an introduction, from a computational point of view, on linguistic domains Cf. (Kittrege 2003).

The second part of the poster will be about the description of a model dedicated to assistance: how we incorporate perceptual features useful to the assisting task. We show the language use for the model as well as a methodology to acquire such perceptual features through the use of a framework of application design named Kiwi (see figure 1).

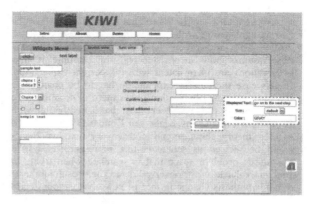

Figure 1: Screen shot of part of the web page for the building of simple web-oriented applications.

The final part of the poster shows how to use the environment so as to synthesize perceptual models that can then be used by an assisting agent to handle the class of requests that exemplify the cognitive drift.

References

Amalberti, R., Carbonell, N., Falzon, P. (1993). User representations of computer systems in human-computer speech interaction. International Journal of Man-Machine Studies, 38, 547- 566.

Capobianco A., Questioning the effectiveness of contextual online help: some alternative propositions HCI - INTERACT '03 M.Rauterberg et al. (Eds.), pp 65-72, IOS Press IFIP 2003

Capobianco, A., Carbonell, N. (2001). Contextual online help: elicitation of human experts' strategies. In Proceedings of HCI'01, New Orleans, August 2001, Lawrence Erlbaum, Vol. 3.

Sansonnet J.-P., Leray D., Martin J.-C., Architecture of a Framework for Generic Assisting Conversational Agents, IVA 2006, LNAI 4133, Marina Del Rey (CA), 2006

Sansonnet J-P., Martin J-C., Leguern K., A Software Engineering Approach Combining Rational and Conversational Agents for the Design of Assistance Applications, T. Panayiotopoulos et al. (Eds.): IVA 2005, LNAI 3661, 2005

Modeling diagnostic reasoning with fuzzy pattern classification

Franziska Bocklisch (franziska.bocklisch@phil.tu-chemnitz.de)
Martin R.K. Baumann (martin.baumann@phil.tu-chemnitz.de)
Josef F. Krems (krems@phil.tu-chemnitz.de
Department of Psychology
Chemnitz University of Technology
09107 Chemnitz, Germany

Reasoning with contradictory data

Diagnostic reasoning is a key component in many real world tasks, such as medical diagnosis or software debugging. We view diagnostic reasoning as a comprehension process by which observations are sequentially comprehended and integrated into a mental representation that represents the current explanation of the observations (Johnson & Krems, 2001). This integration is especially difficult if the observations show inconsistencies, for example if new observations are inconsistent with the current explanation. In this case the current explanation has to be changed to integrate the new observation given there is no alternative explanation for the new observation that is compatible with the current explanation. Klahr and Dunbar (1988) assumed in their theory about scientific discovery that hypotheses could be viewed as schemata that represent states in a hypothesis problem space that is searched when trying to find an explanation for observed data. Their results indicate that a hypothesis change in face of new observations seems to be easier if this change can be represented as a value change in the slots of the existing hypothesis schema than if the hypothesis change involves the creation of a new one. This assumption should be tested in this experiment on abductive reasoning.

Experiment

11 participants saw 3 – 4 observations per trial that consisted of symptoms, such as headache, skin rush, and so on, that were caused by one of 6 possible chemicals the hypothetical patient could have been in contact with. After each symptom the participants had to rate the plausibility of each chemical as a possible explanation of the symptoms seen so far. The 6 chemicals were grouped into 2 groups with 3 chemicals in each group, each chemical associated with 3 – 4 symptoms. There were specific symptoms caused only by the chemicals of one group thereby defining each group and unspecific symptoms caused by the chemicals of both groups. The participants had to solve 39 trials. 4 trials contained contradictory data. In these trials the third symptom contradicted the explanation for the first two ones. In two of these trials participants had to change the hypothesis within the chemical group, in the other two trials participants had to change between groups to solve the task.

Fuzzy pattern classification

The ratings were then modeled using fuzzy pattern classification. For that purpose normatively correct ratings after each symptom presentation were determined defining a class of ratings. For each participant's rating the degree of membership to this class was computed. The resulting membership value for each rating represents the similarity between the participant's rating and the normatively correct rating. These are values of truth therefore not probability or frequency based. This ensures the suitability to our small sample. If the participants followed the normative rating strategy these membership values would be high otherwise values would be medium or low. As the hypothesis change for those trials that involved a change within the current group should be easier we expected that the membership values should be higher for these trials and lower for the more difficult hypothesis change between groups.

Results and Discussion

Contrary to our prediction the results indicate that the hypothesis change was more difficult if the hypothesis had to be changed within the same group than between groups. The average membership value for ratings after the contradicting symptom was .67 for trials with a within group change and .82 for a between group change. This pattern of results might be due to the specificity of the contradictory symptom. In trials requiring a between group change the contradicting symptom had to be specific for the other group currently not considered. Participants seemed to use this information to completely abandon the current group and to change their focus of consideration to the other group supporting their search for the correct hypothesis in the new group. In trials requiring a within group hypothesis change the contradicting symptom had to be unspecific. It therefore did not allow participants to exclude a group on the whole. It seems that this lead to more hypotheses being considered as plausible than in the between change trials despite the fact that the number of plausible hypotheses after the contradicting symptom was the same in both types of trials. Hence, the specificity of symptoms seems to be of much more importance for facilitating or inhibiting the change of hypotheses after contradicting symptoms than the change within or between groups of hypotheses.

References

Johnson, T. & Krems, J.F. (2001). Use of current explanations in multicausal abductive reasoning. *Cognitive Science*, 25, 903 – 939.

Klahr, D. & Dunbar, K. (1988). Dual space search during scientific discovery. *Cognitive Science*, 12, 1 – 48.

Automatic Classification of Instantaneous Cognitive States

Rafael Ramirez (rafael@iua.upf.es)
Montserrat Puiggros (mpuiggros@iua.upf.es)
Music Technology Group, Pompeu Fabra University
Ocata 1, 08003 Barcelona, Spain

Introduction

The study of human brain functions has dramatically increased in recent years greatly due to the advent of Functional Magnetic Resonance Imaging (fMRI), a brain imaging technique that allows the observation of brain activity in human subjects. While fMRI has been used extensively to test hypothesis regarding the location of activation for different brain functions, the problem of automatically classifying cognitive states has been little explored (Mitchell, 2003). The study of this problem is important because it can provide a tool for detecting and tracking cognitive processes (i.e. sequences of cognitive states) in order to diagnose difficulties in performing a complex task. In this paper we apply and compare different machine learning techniques to the problem of classifying the instantaneous cognitive state of a person based on her functional Magnetic Resonance Imaging data. In particular, we present successful case studies of induced classifiers which accurately discriminates between cognitive states such as listening to melodic tonal stimuli versus listening to nonsense speech, listening to an auditory stimulus (melody or nonsense speech) versus mentally rehearsing the stimulus, listening to a pure tone versus listening to a band-passed noise burst, and listening to a low-frequency tone versus listening to a high-frequency tone.

Classifying Cognitive States

Given a person's observed instantaneous fMRI data at time t, we train a classifier in order to predict the cognitive state that gave rise to the observed data. The training data is a set of examples of fMRI. This is, we are interested in obtaining classifiers of the following form:

$$Classifier(fMRIdata(t)) \rightarrow CognState$$

where $fMRIdata(t)$ is an instantaneous fMRI image at time t and $CognState$ is a set of cognitive states to be discriminated. For each subject in the fMRI data sets we trained a separate classifier. We explored a number of classifier induction methods, including decision trees, support vector machines, artificial neural networks, lazy methods and ensemble methods.

Evaluation. We evaluated each induced classifier by performing the standard 10-fold cross validation in which 10% of the training set is held out in turn as test data while the remaining 90% is used as training data. When performing the 10-fold cross validation, In order to avoid optimistic estimates of the classifier performance, we explicitly remove from the training set all images occurring within 6 seconds of the hold out test image.

Case Studies

Melody, speech and rehearsal study. In this fMRI study (Hickok, 2003) twenty-one short unfamiliar piano melodies were recorded using a MIDI synthesizer. An equal number of nonsense sentences (nouns and verbs were replaced by pseudo words), were recorded and digitalized. Each trial in this experiment consisted of an initial stimulus presentation, followed by a rehearsal period, and ended with a period of rest. For the melody-versus-speech, audition-versus-rehearsal, and melody-versus-speech-versus-rehearsal classifiers the average accuracies obtained for the most successful trained classifier were 97.19%, 84.83%, and 69.44%, respectively. For these classifiers the best subject's accuracies were 100%, 98.57%, and 81.67%, respectively. The results are statistically significant which indicates that it is indeed feasible to train successful classifiers to distinguish these cognitive states.

Pure tones and band-passed noise. In this fMRI study (Wessinger, 2001) twelve subjects with normal hearing listened passively to one of six different stimulus sets. These sets consisted of either pure tones (PTs) with a frequency of 0.5, 2 or 8 kHz, or band-passed noise (BPN) bursts with the same logarithmically spaced center frequencies and a bandwidth of one octave. For the both PT-High versus PT-Low, and the PT versus BPN classifiers we obtained average accuracies of 100%. These results are clearly statistically significant.

Acknowledgments

This work is supported by the Spanish TIN project ProSeMus (TIN2006-14932-C02-01).

References

Mitchell, T., et al. (2003). Classifying Instantaneous Cognitive States from fMRI Data, American Medical Informatics Association Symposium.

Hickok, G., et al. (2003). Auditory-Motor Interaction Revealed by fMRI: Speech, Music and Working Memory in Area Spt. Journal of Cognitive Neuroscience, Vol. 15, Issue 5.

Wessinger, C.M., et al. (2001). Hierarchical organization of the human auditory cortex revealed by functional magnetic resonance imaging. J Cogn Neurosci.1;13(1).

Frequency trajectory effects in human and artificial neural systems with different input-output mappings

Martial Mermillod, Patrick Bonin, Sébastien Roux, Ludovic Ferrand & Alain Méot
LAPSCO/CNRS (UMR 6024) – 34 avenue Carnot, 63037 Clermont-Ferrand, FRANCE
Martial.Mermillod@univ-bpclermont.fr

Introduction

Words acquired early and more frequently in life are processed faster and more accurately than words acquired later and less frequently (for a review Johnston & Barry, 2006). The existence of an interaction between frequency of encounters and the age of acquisition (AoA) of the words has lead to some debate in the psycholinguistic literature (Barry, Morrison, & Ellis, 1997; Bonin, Barry, Méot & Chalard, 2004; Cuetos, Alvarez, Gonzales-Nosti, Méot, & Bonin, 2006). Connectionist models have recently explored the influence of the AoA and frequency of the items (Zevin & Seidenberg, 2002, Lambon Ralph & Ehsan, 2006). Recently, AoA effects have been explored with the use of frequency trajectory (FT) – which refers to changes in frequency of the words over long period of ages – instead of the classical AoA adult estimations because FT is thought to better index age limited learning effects (Bonin et al., 2004; Zevin & Seidenberg, 2002).

As shown by Zevin & Seidenberg (2002),, the influence of FT varies as a function of the kind of mappings between input and output units in a connectionist model of word recognition. Arbitrary mappings are involved object naming whereas quasi-systematic mappings are involved in word reading (Bonin et al., 2004). We explored this phenomenon in a **more general connectionist model** and in close connection with **empirical data**.

Simulations

Material and procedure

The connectionist network consists of a standard 3-layers back-propagation neural network similar to Lambon Ralph and Ehsan (2006). The connectionist architecture was a 100-50-100 backpropagation neural network identical to the connectionist architecture used by (Lambon Ralph & Ehsan, 2006). For arbitrary exemplars, input and output vectors were 100 binary vectors randomly generated. The first 33 vectors had an increasing frequency trajectory, the 34 next vectors were perfectly stable and the 33 last vectors had a decreasing frequency trajectory. A second simulation was run using another pattern of vectors having a systematic relationship between the input layer and output layer. These training vectors, reproduced from (Lambon Ralph & Ehsan, 2006) represent word reading task in empirical data.

Results

A reliable FT effect on Sum Squared Error (SSE) was found using arbitrary input/output mapping at the end of the training. Therefore, age limited learning effects were replicated by means of FT component in a general learning model in **line with picture naming reaction times data**. In simulation 2, we showed that more systematic relationships between input and output mappings suppressed the FT effect as observed in the Zevin & Seidenberg reading model and in **word reading times for empirical data** (Bonin et al., 2004).

Discussion

Using a general learning model (Lambon Ralph & Ehsan, 2006), FT effects were found only when the mappings between input/output items are arbitrary. As suggested by both Zevin & Seidenberg (2002) and Lambon Ralph & Ehsan (2006), the systematic relationship between input/output units is completely suppressing the effect showing a better encoding of decreasing frequency exemplars, in line with empirical data showing FT effects only in picture naming.

Acknowledgments

The authors wish to thank M. Lambon-Ralph for providing us helpful information about his connectionist simulations. This work was supported by the French CNRS and ANR.

References

Barry, C., Morrison, C. M., & Ellis, A. W. (1997). Naming the Snodgrass and Vanderwart pictures : Effects of age of acquisition, frequency, and name agreement. *Quarterly Journal of Experimental Psychology : Human Experimental Psychology, 50A,* 560-585.

Bonin, P., Barry, C., Méot, A., Chalard, M. (2004). The influence of age of acquisition in word reading and other tasks: A never ending story? *Journal of Memory and Language, 50,* 456-476.

Cuetos, F. Alvarez, B., Gonzales-Nosti, M., Méot, A., & Bonin, P. (2006). Determinants of lexical access in speech production: Role of word frequency and age of acquisition. *Memory & Cognition.*

Johnston, R. A., & Barry, C. (2006). Age of acquisition and lexical processing. *Visual Cognition, 13,* 789-845.

Lambon Ralph, M.A., Ehsan, S. (2006). Age of acquisition effects depend on the mapping between representations and the frequency of occurrence: Empirical and computational evidence. *Visual Cognition, 13,* 7-8.

Zevin, J.D., Seidenberg, M.S. (2002). Age of acquisition effects in word reading and other tasks. *Journal of Memory and Language, 47,* 1-29.

Semi-supervised category learning in an information integration task

Katleen Vandist (Katleen.Vandist@Ugent.be)
Maarten De Schryver (Maarten.DeSchryver@Ugent.be)
Yves Rosseel (Yves.Rosseel@Ugent.be)
Department of Data-Analysis,Ghent University
H. Dunantlaan 1, 9000 Gent, Belgium

In this poster, we introduce a new category learning paradigm called semi-supervised classification. In a standard supervised classification paradigm, stimuli are presented one at a time, participants make a classification, and feedback (containing the true category label) follows immediately. In this type of studies participants can learn complex category structures, including category structures that are used in the so called 'integration information task' (e.g., Ashby & Maddox, 1992; McKinley & Nosofsky, 1995). To obtain good performance in such tasks, a participant must combine the perceptual information of the underlying stimulus dimensions. This makes the task difficult because, measuring the dimensions in very different units, the optimal decision bound has no verbal analog. The supervised learning paradigm implies that in all category situations, our environment act as an omnipresent, totally reliable, item-by-item teacher. Even in the most scholastic forms of learning, this total-feedback constraint is unlikely. Perhaps even more unlikely is the unsupervised classification learning paradigm. The task is identical to the supervised paradigm except that participants never get feedback about their responses. Not surprisingly, empirical findings suggest that participants use one stimulus dimension only in this type of task (e.g., Ahn & Medin, 1992; Regehr & Brooks, 1995). The unsupervised paradigm implies that in all category situations in our lives, we never get a clue from anybody about the category structures in our environment. As a conclusion, nor the supervised nor the unsupervised classification learning paradigm is plausible. To us, it seems more likely that during category learning both supervised and unsupervised experiences occur and eventually interacts with each other. In this semi-supervised approach, we investigate what happens when feedback is given after a prespecified percentage of trials only. The issue is whether we have benefits from no feedback trials or not during the learning process. In Experiment 1, feedback was given in 100%, 50%, 25% and 0% of the trials respectively. Previous research reported by Ashby, Queller & Berretty (1999) indicated that in an information-integration task with two categories, perfect accuracy could be obtained in the supervised (100%) condition, but not in the unsupervised (0%) condition. The goal of Experiment 1 was to replicate the Ashby et al (1999) experiment (i.e. 100% and 0% feedback) and to extend the experiment with 50% and 25% semi-supervised conditions (i.e. feedback was given in 50% and 25% of the trials). There were two categories, using the same information-integration task as Ashby et al (1999). Stimuli varied continuously in two dimensions.

Our results show that in both the 100% and 50% conditions, participants were able to achieve (nearly) maximum accuracy. In the 0% and the 25% conditions, participants were not able to learn the task. Clearly the 50% condition indicates that participants do not need feedback after each trial to learn. However, giving only 25% of the trials feedback is too little to learn. In Experiment 2 we investigated the question whether the no feedback trials in the 50% favours the learning process or not. To find out, the 50% condition of Experiment 1 was adjusted, using unrelated filler trials instead of the no feedback trials. The learning process was similar: participants achieved perfect accuracy as quickly as in the 50% condition of Experiment 1. As a consequence, these results suggest that the no feedback trials have no or little impact on the learning process.

Acknowledgments

The first author is an assistant of the Department of Data-Analysis of Ghent University.

References

Ahn, W.K., & Medin, D.L. (1992). A two-Stage Model of Category Construction. *Cognitive Science, 16,* 81-121.

Ashby, F.G., & Maddox, W.T. (1992). Complex decision rules in categorization: Contrasting novice and experienced performance. *Journal of Experimental Psychology: Human Perception & Performance, 18,* 50-71.

Ashby, F.G., Queller, S. & Berretty, P.M. (1999). On the dominance of unidimensional rules in unsupervised categorization. *Perception & Psychophysics, 61(6),* 1178-1199.

McKinley, S.C., & Nosofsky, R.M. (1995). Investigations of exemplar and decision bound models in large-size, ill-defined category structure. *Journal of Experimental Psychology: Human Perception & Performance, 21,* 128-148.

Regehr, G., & Brooks, L. R. (1995). Category of organization in free classification: The organizing effect of an array of stimuli. *Journal of Experimental Psychology: Learning, Memory & Cognition, 21,* 347-363.

The Effects of Prior Knowledge on Perceptual Classification

Lewis Bott (Bottla@Cardiff.ac.uk)

Department of Psychology, Cardiff University, Tower Building, Park Place, Cardiff, CF10 3AT, UK

Prior knowledge is fundamental to the way in which we learn and use categories. For example, prior knowledge affects the speed with which a novel category is learned (e.g., Murphy & Allopenna, 1994), and the order of difficulty of learning category structures (e.g., Pazzani, 1991). Despite the wealth of evidence investigating how prior knowledge aids learning, however, there has been very little research conducted on how prior knowledge affects perceptual classification. The experiment presented here investigates the effects of prior knowledge after classification accuracy has reached asymptote.

Participants learned about two categories of artificial bugs, presented pictorially. Each category consisted of seven bugs, each of which varied on six binary dimensions. For each dimension, one of the features was an aggressive bug feature, and the other a passive bug feature. For example, the aggressive feature for the tail dimension was scorpion-like, whereas the passive feature was flat and wide. Participants in the *themed* condition learned about categories of bugs that were either aggressive or passive. In the aggressive bug category, each bug had a majority of aggressive features, whereas in the passive bug category, each bug had a majority of passive bug features. Participants in the *mixed* condition learned about bugs that had a mixture of aggressive and passive features. Each bug could not therefore be classified as aggressive or passive. Participants in the themed condition were also given a cover story highlighting the aggressive/passive nature of the bugs.

There were three phases to the experiment. In the *training* phase, participants classified each bug individually and received visual and auditory feedback on their responses. After successfully classifying all of the bugs, participants proceeded onto a *testing* phase in which they classified the same bugs for 24 blocks (24 by 14 exemplars = 336 trials), but received only auditory feedback. They then completed an *individual feature-testing* phase, in which they saw six blocks of bugs with only one feature (6 by 12 = 72 trials), and did not receive feedback. These bugs were constructed by using the body of the bug with only a single feature attached.

Participants in the themed condition required fewer learning blocks to reach criterion than those in the mixed condition, $M = 5.89$ ($SD = 2.88$) *vs.* $M = 14.53$ ($SD = 7.65$), $t(36) = 4.60$, $p < .001$. The reaction time results for the testing phase are shown in Figure 1. Participants in the themed condition responded more quickly than those in the mixed condition, $F(1,36) = 6.37$, $p < .05$, and there was a reliable interaction between block and presence of the theme, $F(23,828) = 1.77$, $p < 0.05$. Learning accuracy was at ceiling in both conditions. In the individual feature testing phase, participants in the themed condition were more accurate overall than those in the mixed condition, $F(1,36) = 15.22$, $p < .005$.

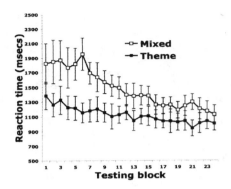

Figure 1. Response times to items presented in the testing phase.

The effects of knowledge, therefore, had a lasting effect on classification after the learning phase had been completed. Why might knowledge speed up classification? There are several possibilities. First, participants in the themed condition knew more dimensions than those in the mixed condition (as shown by the individual feature testing results). This could mean that sufficient evidence for a classification decision was achieved more quickly in the themed condition (see Lamberts, 2000). Another possibility is that participants in the mixed condition were applying several consecutive rules based on individual dimensions, whereas those in themed condition made a single, holistic judgment. Finally, knowledge of other aggressive and passive bugs may have strengthened links between the exemplars and the category labels (see Rehder & Murphy, 2003). Any or all of these explanations are possible, but it is clear that prior knowledge facilitates categorization beyond learning.

References

Lamberts, K. (2000). Information-accumulation theory of speeded categorization. *Psychological Review, 107*(2), 227-260.

Murphy, G. L., & Allopenna, P. D. (1994). The locus of knowledge effects in concept-learning. *Journal of Experimental Psychology Learning Memory and Cognition, 20*(4), 904-919.

Pazzani, M. J. (1991). The influence of prior knowledge on concept acquisition. *Journal of Experimental Psychology-Learning Memory and Cognition, 17,* 416-432.

Rehder, B., & Murphy, G. L. (2003). A knowledge-resonance (KRES) model of category learning. *Psychonomic Bulletin & Review, 10*(4), 759-784.

Categorization of Substances in Relation to Explanations of Changes in State of Matter

Ourania Gikopoulou (rgicop@phs.uoa.gr)   & Stella Vosniadou (svosniad@phs.uoa.gr)
Cognitive Science Lab, Department of Philosophy and History of Science,
National and Kapodistrian University of Athens, Ano Ilisia 157 71 Athens – Greece

Introduction

The purpose of the present study was to compare elementary school children's and university students' categorizations of substances in relation to their explanations about changes in state of matter. We argue that one of the main reasons why children have difficulty in understanding the scientific explanations of changes in state of matter is because they categorize substances based on their physical state (solid, liquid, gas) rather than on their chemical structure (pure substances, mixtures), and apply to them the properties of the corresponding physical state (i.e. solids are rigid, liquids are flexible, etc.).

Based on previous studies we hypothesized that elementary school children will categorize substances based on a physical theory of matter (Carey, 1991). Unlike previous studies in astronomy where we observed theory-based categorization shifts even in elementary school children (Vosniadou & Skopeliti, 2005), we hypothesized theory-based categorization shifts only in chemistry students' categorizations of substances. We also hypothesized a high correlation between participants' categorizations and their explanations about changes in the state of matter.

Method

Participants: The sample consisted of 84 elementary school children (42 2nd graders and 42 6th graders) and 36 university students (20 from the Chemistry Department and 16 from the Philosophy and History of Science Department (PHS) of the University of Athens).

Materials: The Categorization Task consisted of 12 objects which the participants were asked to categorize (peddle, coin, aluminium-foil, ice, water, salted water, alcohol, coffee, air, fumes, oxygen and water vapour). These objects could be categorized either based on their physical state or on their chemical structure. Four categorization questions were asked and each of them was followed by a justification question. At the Change of State Task participants were asked to explain the melting of ice and the evaporation of water.

Procedure: The elementary school children were interviewed individually in a separate classroom in their school by the experimenter, who kept detailed notes of children's responses. The university students completed a questionnaire. All the participants were given the Categorization Task and the Change of State of Matter Task.

Results

Participants' responses in the Categorization Task were marked as 3 when they categorized objects based on their chemical structure, 2 when they categorized them based on their physical state, 1 when they used other categories and 0 when there was no response. The total scores of the participants were analysed using a one way ANOVA which showed main effects for grade ($F_{(3)} = 76,398$, $p < .001$) in favour of the Chemistry students. Only the students from the chemistry department categorized substances based on their chemical structure. The non-chemistry majors and the 6th graders categorized substances based on their physical state. This was not the case for 2nd graders, who used mostly similarity in shape or in function to categorize substances.

With respect to the Change of State Task, the participants were assigned to an initial, alternative or scientific category, based on the explanations they provided concerning the composition of water, ice and vapour. None of the elementary school children provided scientific explanations of the changes in the state of matter. The non-chemistry majors also faced difficulties in explaining change of state. Only the students from the chemistry department were able to provide scientific explanations about the changes in the state of matter. The correlations between participants' categorizations and their explanations about the changes in the state of matter (water-ice and water-vapour) were statistically significant: $r_{(4)} = -0,556$; $p < .001$ and : $r_{(6)} = -0,628$; $p < .001$.

Discussion

The results supported our hypothesis that there are theory-based categorization shifts in the categorization of substances and that these will be observed only in the students studying Chemistry. High correlations were also obtained between the categorization of substances and the understanding of Change of State of Matter, supporting the idea that the shift from categorizing substances based on their physical state to categorizing them based on their chemical structure is related to the scientific understanding of the change of state of matter.

References

Carey, S. (1991) Knowledge Acquisition: Enrichment or Conceptual Change?, in S. Carey and R. Gelman (eds) *The Epigenesis of Mind: Essays on Biology and Cognition* (Hillsdale, New Jersey: Lawrence Erlbaum Associates), 257-292.

Kouka, A., Vosniadou, S., Tsarpalis, G., (submitted). Students' difficulties in the understanding of the concept of water as chemical compound, *Themes of Education*.

Vosniadou, S., Skopeliti, I. (2005). Developmental Shifts in Children's Categorization of the Earth, In B. Bara, L. Barsalou, & M. Bucciarelli (Eds.) *Proceedings of the XXVII Annual Conference of the Cognitive Science Society*, pp. 2325-2330.

Solving Systems of Equations: A Case Study in Analogical Problem Solving

Svetlana Polushkina (polushkina@mathematik.tu-darmstadt.de)
Graduate School "Feedback Based Quality Management in eLearning"
Technical University of Darmstadt, 64289 Darmstadt, Germany

Kai-Uwe Kühnberger(kkuehnbe@uos.de)
Institute of Cognitive Science, University of Osnabrück, 49078 Osnabrück, Germany

Helmar Gust (Helmar.Gust@uos.de)
Institute of Cognitive Science, University of Osnabrück, 49078 Osnabrück, Germany

Psychological and computational research in analogical reasoning has a long-standing tradition (for a review see e.g. O'Donoghue, 2004).

This work is a case study in analogical problem solving in the domain of higher-order polynomial equations in two variables. The framework of Heuristic-Driven Theory Projection (HDTP; Gust, Kühnberger, & Schmid, 2003), proposing a generalisation-based model for analogy, employing the anti-unification algorithm, was tested for its applicability to a special case of mathematical problem solving. The particular example used is depicted in Figure 1.

SOURCE (solution is given)	TARGET (solution is to be produced)
$4a^2 + 4ab + b^2 = 0 \;\&\&\; a - b = 6$	$9m^4 + 24m^2n + 16n^2 = 0 \;\&\&\; m^2 - n = 7$

Figure 1: The working example.

First, an experiment was carried out with 54 male and female students of the 8th grade of the gymnasium to test the influence of some particular kinds of additional information on the efficiency of analogical problem solving. The students were presented with the solution of the source example and asked to solve the target example problem. The material provided to the students included, or not, verbal explanations on the derivation of the source solution and hints on direct or generalisation-based mapping between the source and target systems of equations. Time consumption and solution correctness data were obtained and evaluated. Both kinds of mapping hints significantly reduced the time necessary to solve the target problem (t(50)=1.8183, p<.05). No advantage of either kind of hint could be detected. The results for time consumption are summarised in Table 1.

Table 1: Time consumption in minutes.

Factor group	All participants	Successful participants
Without Mapping Hint	M = 23.50; SD = 3.03	M = 23.64; SD = 3.20
With Mapping Hint	M = 21.94; SD = 2.89	M = 22.27; SD = 3.25
With Flat Mapping Hint	M = 21.71; SD = 3.14	M = 22.30; SD = 3.83
With Hierarchical Mapping Hint	M = 22.18; SD = 2.70	M = 22.20; SD = 1.48
Without Derivation Explanations	M = 23.00; SD = 2.93	M = 23.73; SD = 1.90
With Derivation Explanations	M = 22.00; SD = 3.05	M = 22.20; SD = 3.82

Furthermore, immediately before and after the problem solving, the students made similarity preference choices between systems of equations structurally or superficially similar to the source and target ones. Changes in such preferences were put in relation to the success of problem solving. Structural similarity was prefered much more often by the students, and especially by those, who solved the target problem correctly.

The outcomes of the experiment suggest the effectiveness of structure-preserving generalisation-based mapping and transfer in analogical problem solving, as predicted by the HDTP framework.

Second, a model of the analogical problem solver, based on the many-sorted higher-order anti-unification, was devised. The model allows for flexible mapping, obeying at the same time to the systematicity principle. It accounts for equivalence classes of algebraic expressions, allowing for problem re-representation, if necessary.

After providing the model with additional information, an equivalent to the experimental manipulation, the effects on the model's problem solving efficiency were investigated. The results of the computational modelling paralleled those of the experiment with human participants.

In sum, the results of the case study support the utility of anti-unification as a mechanism and a part of a model for analogical mapping and transfer. In this way, the study contributes to the understanding of the nature of analogical reasoning in general.

Acknowledgements

This work was carried out in preparation of the Master's Thesis of the first author. The studies of the first author were supported by the Studienstiftung des deutschen Volkes (German National Merit Foundation).

References

Gust, H., & Kühnberger, K.-U., & Schmid, U. (2003). Solving Predictive Analogy Tasks with Anti-Unification. In: *Proceedings of the Joint International Conference on Cognitive Science 2003 (AMCS / ICCS 2003)*, Sydney.

O'Donoghue, D. (2004). *Finding Novel Analogies*. PhD Thesis. Department of Computer Science, University College Dublin.

How many exemplars do we need? A replication of Nosofsky, Clark and Shin's (1989) "Rules and exemplars in categorization, identification and recognition"

Maarten De Schryver (Maarten.DeSchryver@Ugent.be)
Katleen Vandist (Katleen.Vandist@Ugent.be)
Yves Rosseel (Yves.Rosseel@Ugent.be)
Department of Data Analysis, Ghent University
Henri Dunantlaan 1, B-9000 Gent, Belgium

It is probably fair to say that in most empirical studies that have been reported in the categorization literature, the exemplar models have been extremely successful. Nevertheless, despite its success, the exemplar approach has been criticized by many authors (see for e.g. Minda & Smith, 2001). Many issues have been raised, but the one we will focus on in this poster is the following: is it really plausible that *all* exemplars are stored in memory? Do we really have a memory trace of every car we have seen? Or have we only stored some of them? In fact, our main objective in this poster is to test the following simple hypothesis: not all exemplars (that are presented during a training phase of a categorization experiment) are stored, but only a subset of these exemplars are stored and used to classify new stimuli according to exemplar theory principles. Our experiment is a replication of experiment 1 in Nosofsky, Clark & Shin (1989). The main reason for our replication is gathering individual data: despite some interesting results being reported for individual subjects in the originally paper, only aggregated data is available. The experiment ($N = 5$) consisted of four phases. In a first training phase, the three stimuli assigned to category A and the four stimuli assigned to category B were presented (see figure 1). In the first test phase, the 16 stimuli (seven old and nine new) were presented. A second training phase only served as a recapitulation of the first training phase. Finally, a second test phase was appended, whereby 324 stimuli were presented that spanned the whole stimulus-space. Two models were fit to the data: the Generalized context model (GCM) (Nosofsky, 1986) and the Rex Leopold I model (Rosseel,2002, submitted). According to the GCM, all the exemplars learned during the training phase, are stored. The Rex Leopold I model is designed to be identical to the GCM, except that the full set of exemplars can be replaced by a reduced set of exemplars. The remaining exemplars form a true subset of the full set. The results support the hypothesis that only a subset of exemplars is stored. Indeed, for all participants, better fits were obtained by the reduced exemplar model. Interestingly, different participants used different subsets. Our analysis based on the *individual* data gave us better insight in the psychological processes that have been used by the participants during the categorization task. The results of this experiment confirm the basic assumption of the 'Rex leopold I' model: namely, not all exemplars are stored, but only

a subset of exemplars is sufficient for category representation. Unfortunately, the model has no a priori idea which exemplars should be retained, and which should not.

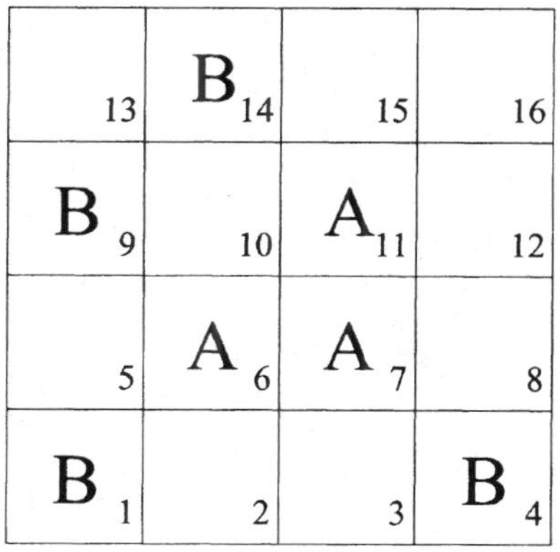

Figure 1: The category structure: 'A' refers to category A exemplars; 'B' refers to category 'B' exemplars.

Acknowledgments

The first author is an assistant of the Department of Data-Analysis of Ghent University.

References

Minda, J. P., & Smith, J. D. (2001). Prototypes in category learning: the effects of category Size, category structure, and stimulus complexity. *Journal of Experimental Psychology: Learning, Memory, & Cognition, 27,* 775–799.

Nosofsky, R. M. (1986). Attention, similarity, and the identification-categorization relationship. *Journal of Experimental Psychology: General, 115,* 39–57.

Nosofsky, R. M., Clark S. E., & Shin, H. J. (1989). Rules and exemplars in categorization, identification, and recognition. *Journal of Experimental Psychology: Learning, Memory, and Cognition, 15,* 282–304.

Rosseel, Y. (2002). Mixture models of categorization. *Journal of Mathematical Psychology, 46,* 178–210.

Rosseel, Y. (submitted). Reduced exemplar models of categorization.

Young children's recognition of commonalities between animals and plants: revisiting the role of human-based inference

Christelle Declercq (christelle.declercq@univ-reims.fr)
& Florence Labrell (florence.labrell@univ-reims.fr)

Laboratoire Accolade, Université de Reims Champagne-Ardenne
57 rue Pierre Taittinger, 51096 Reims Cedex, France, www.accolade-reims.org

Lots of research on conceptual development suggests that children as young as 4 years distinguish between living entities (animals and plants) and non-living ones. Young children seem to possess a naive theory of biology, a theory-like knowledge system that enables them to make predictions and explanations about living things.

Even if naive theory of biology can be seen as independent from naive theory of psychological phenomena, most authors assume that children knowledge on living entities is related to their knowledge on human beings (Inagaki & Hatano, 2006). Children possess rich knowledge about humans that can be applied to less familiar living entities such as animals and plants. Thus, children should draw analogically on their knowledge about humans to attribute properties to animals and to plants. This process may be useful because humans share biological properties with other living entities like animals. Inagaki and Hatano (1996) showed that 5-year-old children are able to grasp commonalities between animals and plants. For instance, in their second experiment, they used an induction paradigm in which children were presented human properties (growth, feeding, taking food/water and being ill). Children were then asked whether different plants, animals or artefacts would have these properties. Some of the children received the properties with a biological context including a vitalistic explanation that refers to a vital force taken from food and water. According to Inagaki and Hatano (1996), vitalism is a previous kind of understanding of living mechanisms for children who do not conceptualize the photosynthesis.

However, even if Gutheil, Vera and Keil (1998) obtained similar results confirming the influence of the context, several questions remain. First, context helps children as young as 5 years: they have a naive theory but they do not totally master the properties attribution. Thus, the abilities to attribute biological properties to animals and plants should still progress after this age, since children are known to master them around 8 years of age (Carey, 1985). Second, the analogy with human beings may be useful when a child does not perfectly understand the functioning of biological entities. However, it might interfere with a correct attribution of the properties with an older child who better understands biological entities. Last, the role of person analogy could vary according to living entities. For instance, drawing analogically on the knowledge about humans should be less useful when attributing properties to plants as they less look like humans than animals. Two experiments examined these questions. Experiment 1 aimed at replicating Inagaki and Hatano's data with older children.

Experiment 2 used their paradigm to study properties attribution to plants.

Experiment 1

The participants were 400 children aged from 4 (±3 months) to 8 (±3 months). They were presented pictures of target objects, three of each from animal, plant and non-living thing categories. The children were questioned about the properties used in Inagaki and Hatano's experiment. Two conditions were set up. The children in the no-context condition were told that a person had a given property without any explanation of its function. In the context condition, properties were given with an explanation that emphasized their features for humans. Results showed that property attribution increased from 4 to 8 and appeared earlier for animals than for plants. Context helped 4-year olds, interfered with attribution property in 5-year-olds, and ith had no effect with older children whereas.

Experiment 2

The participants were 425 children aged from 4 (±3 months) to 8 (±3 months). They were presented pictures of targets objects, four of each from flowers, plants (without flowers) and non-living thing categories. The procedure was the same as in experiment 1 except that children were questioned about two properties: growth and illness. Results showed that attribution property increased from 5 to 6 and then from 7 to 8. Context had no effect.

Thus, children might benefit from human-based inference to understand biological world. However, our data suggest that, when they begin to understand it, emphasizing the functioning of properties for human might interfere with property attribution.

References

Carey, S. (1985). *Conceptual change in childhood.* Cambridge, MA: MIT Press.

Gutheil, G., Vera, A., & Keil, F.C. (1998). Do houseflies think? Patterns of induction and biological beliefs in development. *Cognition,* 66, 33-49.

Inagaki, K., & Hatano, G. (1996). Young children's recognition of commonalities between animals and plants. *Child Development,* 67, 2823-2840.

Inagaki, K., & Hatano, G. (2006). Young children's conception of the biological world. *Current Directions on Psychological Science,* 15, 177-181.

Motor Memory: Movement- and Position-Specific Sequence Representations

Elena V. Bobrova (Bobrova@Pavlov.Infran.Ru)
Pavlov Institute of Physiology RAS, nab. Makarova 6
St Petersburg, 199034 Russia

Vsevolod A. Lyakhovetskii (V_la2002@Mail.Ru)
St Petersburg Electrotechnical University, ul. Prof. Popova 5
St Petersburg, 197376 Russia

Introduction

Studies of sequence acquisition revealed that the movements of dominant right hand activate cortical areas of the left hemisphere, while non-dominant left hand learning demonstrate recruitment of many additional brain areas in both hemispheres (Grafton e.a., 2002). These areas were supposed to be "associated with memory processes that provide an alternative representation of the sequence, one that is less closely tied with action system". We tested the hypothesis that motor memory uses two types of sequence representations: *movement-specific representation* that codes the sequence of the trajectories of movements and *position-specific representation* that codes the sequence of hand positions.

Method

The hand of the blindfolded volunteer was moved by experimenter through 7 different positions at a sheet of paper A4. The volunteer had to remember and immediately after that to reproduce by pen the sequence of positions. Each of 47 right-handed volunteers completed one run with right hand and one run with left hand. The errors of coding in the case of movement-specific representation (eM) were estimated as an angle between vectors connecting the successive positions of the hand, when it was moved by experimenter and by volunteer himself; the errors of coding in the case of position-specific representation (eP) were estimated as a distance between position of the hand, when it was moved by experimenter and by volunteer. To reveal the prevalence of movement- or position-specific representation, the average values eM_{aver} and eP_{aver} were calculated. Then the sign of difference between each value of eM_i and eM_{aver}; eP_i and eP_{aver} was estimated. The cases when $(eM_i-eM_{aver})<0$ and $(eP_i-eP_{aver})>0$ were supposed to demonstrate the prevalence of movement-specific representation, the cases when $(eM_i-eM_{aver})>0$ and $(eP_i-eP_{aver})<0$ - the prevalence of position-specific representation.

Results

Table 1 demonstrates the percentage of cases when the differences $(eM_i - eM_{aver})$ and $(eP_i -eP_{aver})$ have the same signs (1, 2) or different signs (3, 4). The quantity of cases (3) are lower than the quantity of cases (4) both for the right and for the left hand. According to our suggestion it means the prevalence of movement-specific representation during sequence acquisition. The differences between (3) and (4), estimated by sign test, are significant for the right hand ($p<0.001$) and are not significant for the left one ($p>0.05$). Thus the prevalence of movement-specific representation is significant for the right hand only.

Table 1.

	$(eM_i - eM_{aver})$	$(eP_i -eP_{aver})$	Right hand (%)	Left hand (%)
1.	< 0	<0	55.3	52.6
2.	> 0	>0	21.2	25.5
3.	< 0	>0	6.8	8.3
4.	> 0	<0	16.7	13.6

Discussion

It is supposed that the prevalence of the movement-specific representation in the case of the right hand corresponds to the role of the left hemisphere in sequence movement control, while position-specific representation is specifically connected with the right hemisphere role in spatial relations coding (Bradshaw, 2001; Jager, Postma, 2003). The absence of the significant prevalence of one or another type of representation during task performed by the left hand corresponds to the data on recruitment of both hemispheres in sequence acquisition by non-dominant left hand (Grafton e.a., 2002). Two types of sequence representation in motor memory, movement- and position-specific one, are supposed to reflect the hemispheric specialization in perception and motor control.

Acknowledgments

Supported by RFBR grants #06-04-49488 and #06-06-80152.

References

Bradshaw, J. L. (2001). Asymmetries in preparation for action. *TRENDS in Cognitive Science, 5,* 184–185.

Grafton, S. T., Hazeltine, E. & Ivry, R. B. (2002) Motor sequence learning with the nondominant left hand. A PET functional imaging study. *Exp. Brain Res., 146,* 369– 378.

Jager, G. & Postma, A. (2003). On the hemispheric specialization for categorical and coordinate spatial relations: a review of the current evidence. *Neuropsychologia, 41,* 504-515.

Perception of Action: Influence of the Presence or Absence of Goal in the Interference between Observed and Executed Movements.

Cédric A. Bouquet (cedric.bouquet@univ-poitiers.fr)
Université de Poitiers, Maison des Sciences de l'Homme et de la Société
99 av. Recteur Pineau, 86000 Poitiers, France

Thomas Shipley (tshipley@temple.edu)
Department of Psychology, Temple University, Weiss Hall
1701 N 13th Street, Philadelphia, PA 19122, USA

Introduction

The disturbance of observers/actors' movements by the observation of another human making different movements may rely on the activation of observer's motor and/or mirror system (Blakemore & Frith, 2005). This *interference effect* was obtained in humans observing non-goal directed movements. This contrasts with studies in the monkey indicating that mirror neurons are most responsive to goal-oriented actions (i.e. when the observed movement comes in contact with an object, as opposed to movements with no explicit goal) (Binkofski & Buccino, 2006). The present study sought to specify whether the interference effect varies with the presence or absence of visible goals in the observed movement. We had participants make arm movements while observing a video of another human making either similar or different movements, with or without visible goals (red dots that were reached for by the hand of the observed actor).

Methods

Participants (n = 21) made horizontal movements (Fig. 1A) from the arm while simultaneously observing a video. In the Congruent (CM) and Incongruent Movement (IM) conditions the participants observed a video of a model making horizontal and vertical movements, respectively (Figure 1A and C). In the Congruent Movement + Goal (CM+G) and Incongruent Movement + Goal (IM+G) conditions, they observed the same video as in the CM or IM conditions, but two dots were superimposed on each video sequence at the movement endpoints, so that the hand of the model moved from one dot to the other (Figure 1B and D); in the Congruent Goal (CG) and Incongruent Goal (IG) conditions they observed only the two still dots presented in the CM+G and IM+G video sequences, respectively. In a Control condition participants made movements while not observing anything.

Figure 1: Movements made (A) or observed (A, B, C, D) by participants.

Results

The variability in movement trajectory orthogonal to the horizontal axis was the same in all the congruent conditions (p>.05), which did not differ from that measured in the control condition (p>.05). In contrast, the variability measured in both the incongruent IM and IM+G conditions was larger than in the control condition (p<.01). The IG condition did not differ from the control condition (p>.05). Most importantly, the variability was larger in the IM+G condition than in the IM and IG conditions (p<.05 for both).

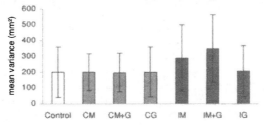

Figure 2: Mean variance in the different conditions (error bars indicate standard errors).

Discussion

Our results show that the interference between executed and observed movement is modulated by the presence or absence of visible goals in the observed movement. Such an interference effect would relate to mirror system activation in an observer's brain (Blakemore & Frith, 2005). In line with studies in the monkey (Binkofski & Buccino, 2006), our data suggest that mirror activity is more pronounced during observation of goal-directed action, leading to a larger interference effect. However, an interference effect was found also during observation of movements with no visible goal (though reduced compared with the IM+G condition). Overall, this may indicate that though attuned to goal-oriented action, the human mirror system responds to movements with or without explicit goal.

References

Binkofski, F., & Buccino, G. (2006). The role of ventral premotor cortex in action execution and action understanding. *Journal of Physiology-Paris*, 99, 396-405.
Blakemore, S.J., & Frith, C. (2005). The role of motor contagion in the prediction of action. *Neuropsychologia*, 43, 260-267.

Cognitive Structure of Phonological Processes and Sound Change Transitions

Ching-Pong Au (ching-pong.au@ish-lyon.cnrs.fr)
Dynamique Du Langage, CNRS - Université Lumière Lyon 2
Institut des Sciences de l'Homme, 14 avenue Berthelot, 69363 Lyon, CEDEX 07, France.

Introduction

The basic mechanism of sound change has been debated for many years. Neogrammarians believed that all words containing the same sound segment (e.g. [X] in fig. 1a) change gradually and simultaneously (e.g. from [X] to [Y]). Different from the Neogrammarian hypothesis, Wang proposed that a sound change should be initiated by some of the words (e.g. W_2 and W_5, in fig. 1b) and then the change diffuses to the remaining words containing the same sound segment (Wang, 1969). Since both hypotheses were supported by empirical data from on-going sound changes, the debate has still not been satisfactorily settled (see Labov, 1994).

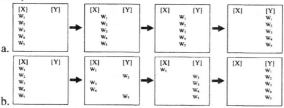

a.

b.

Figure 1: (a) Neogrammarian's pattern; (b) Lexical diffusion.

A computer simulation model was built in order to investigate the transition of sound changes (Au, 2005). In the simulated population of agents, young agents acquired the sound-meaning correspondence from their elder generation. The simulation repeated for a large number of runs. The main results can be generalized as in figure 2.

Simulation Results

Observing the changes in the cognitive systems of the simulated agents throughout the generations, both lexically regular and irregular changes happen under different conditions: (1) When the quality of sound segment of a group of words changes without involving other groups of words containing another sound segment (e.g. a shift), the transition pattern follows Neogrammarian hypothesis (fig. 2a); (2) When two groups of words merge into the same sound (i.e. a merger), the sound quality of the words changes irregularly (fig. 2b).

The cognitive structure of the agents in the model is based on recent cognitive and language acquisition studies. The sensitivity towards speech sounds is induced according to the distributional information of the speech sounds the infants listen to (Kuhl et al, 1992; Maye et al, 2002). We found that the appearance of the transitions is highly dependent on the perceptual patterns emerged during language acquisition. During a merger, the perceptual categories of the two neighboring sounds formed inconsistently from agent to agent when the acoustic

locations of the two categories become closer. Due to the inconsistent perception among speakers, the spoken form of each word may differ among agents and scatter irregularly across the two original acoustic locations of the sounds (i.e. the region r_2 in fig. 2b). On the contrary, in a shift, the perceptual category emerges without the influence of other nearby categories. Thus, the spoken forms of the words can be consistently located in a relatively smaller region (region r_1, in fig. 2a). With the slight changes of sound quality accumulated from generation to generation, the spoken forms change simultaneously and gradually as described in the Neogrammarian hypothesis.

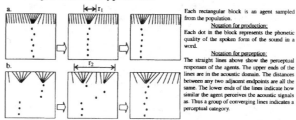

Figure 2: Simulation results (a) a shift; (b) a merger.

Discussions and Conclusion

The causes of the controversy seem to be some traditional concepts in phonology: (1) elimination of phonetic details in the phonological level and (2) symmetry of perception and production. In the cognitive structure of our model, phonetic details are stored in subsystems that are individually responsible for listening and speaking sides. Simulation results by this new cognitive structure with the algorithms based on recent psycholinguistic researches suggest that none of the two transition patterns are the basic mechanism of sound changes. Instead, both patterns are the consequence of the acquisition and interaction among of the people in a speech community.

References

Au, C.-P. (2005). Acquisition and Evolution of Phonological Systems. PhD Dissertation. City University of Hong Kong.

Kuhl, P. K., Williams, K. A., Lacerda, F., Stevens, K. N. & Lindblom, B. (1992). Linguistic Experience Alters Phonetic Perception in Infants by 6 Months of Age. *Science*, 255, 606-608.

Labov, W. (1994). *Principles of Linguistic Change, vol. 1: Internal Factors*. Oxford: Blackwell.

Maye, J., Werker, J.F., & Gerken, L. (2002). Infant Sensitivity to Distributional Information Can Effect Phonetic Discrimination. *Cognition*, 82(3), B101-B111.

Wang, W. S-Y. (1969). Competing Changes as a Cause of Residue. *Language*. 45:9-25.

Rapid Apprehension of Gist in Action Scenes

Reinhild Glanemann (r.glanemann@uni-muenster.de)
Jens Bölte (boelte@psy.uni-muenster.de)
Pienie Zwitserlood (zwitser@psy.uni-muenster.de)
Institute of Psychology, University of Münster
Fliednerstr. 21., 48149 Münster, Germany

Christian Dobel (cdobel@uni-muenster.de)
Institute for Biomagnetism and Biosignalanalysis, University of Münster
Malmedyweg 15, 48149 Münster, Germany

Introduction

The *gist* of a visual scene entails its 'general semantic interpretation' as well as 'some aspects of its global spatial layout' (Henderson & Ferreira, 2004). It has been shown repeatedly that the gist can be perceived within a single glance and that scene gist and scene components are processed interactively (e.g. Davenport & Potter, 2004).

Similar results have been obtained recently for action scenes. Thematic roles in two-participant actions can be recognized after only 150 ms of peripheral presentation (Glanemann, Dobel, Bölte, Kreysa, & Zwitserlood, subm.). Furthermore, viewers correctly name the two participants of an action, that was presented for 200 ms, in more than two thirds of the trials (Dobel, Gumnior, Bölte, & Zwitserlood; in press). Interestingly, agents are identified more frequently than recipients, and even better for coherent (= meaningful) than incoherent actions. In this study, coherence was disrupted by mirroring both actors such that they faced opposite directions.

The aim of the present study was to examine in more detail how viewers determine the coherence of visual action scenes when presentation times are not long enough for eye movements to be made. We manipulated coherence by varying body direction or exchanging the object of the action.

Methods

Stimuli were 20 photo-realistic two-participant action scenes (22.2° x 16.7°). In 10 actions, coherence was varied by exchanging the original object (e.g. 'comb' for hairdressing) with an inappropriate object ('soup ladle'). In the other 10 actions, coherence was varied by using four different body orientations of the two participants (face-to-face, agent facing the patient's back, patient facing the agent's back, back-to-back). Agent position (left/right) and coherence were balanced over trials.

The pictures were presented for 100 ms or 50 ms (masked) on a computer screen, following a pre-trial central fixation cross. In each duration condition, 16 participants judged coherence (yes/no) by pressing a button.

Results

We calculated d' for each condition. All were greater or less than zero. With 100 ms presentation, accuracy was above chance in both coherence conditions but d' was larger in the 'body orientation' condition (d' mean = 2.9) than in the 'object' condition (d' mean = 1.0). With 50 ms presentation, participants correctly judged coherence only in the 'body orientation' condition (d' mean = 1.4). The orientation of the agent played the most important role in the participants' decision. Scenes were judged as 'coherent' when the agent faced the patient and as 'incoherent' when the agent stood backwards to the patient, even when the action was actually coherent (e.g. 'to kick backwards at somebody'). This effect was less pronounced with 50 ms than with 100 ms.

Discussion

The rapid understanding of the meaningfulness of visual action scenes was driven more by body orientation of the participants than by the object used. This was the case even though the object was positioned centrally in the images. These results conform to the Reverse Hierarchy Theory (Hochstein & Ahissar, 2002) and emphasize earlier findings that rapid apprehension of scene gist ('high-level representation') is achieved via the spatial layout of the scene. The scene will only be perceived in more detail after this holistic analysis ('vision with scrutiny').

Acknowledgments

This research is supported by the 'Deutsche Forschungs-gemeinschaft' DO 711/4-1.

References

Davenport, J. L., & Potter, M.C. (2004). Scene consistency in object and background perception. *Psychological Science, 15*, 559-564.

Dobel, C., Gumnior, H., Bölte, J., Kreysa, H., & Zwitserlood, P. (in press). *Describing scenes hardly seen.* Acta Psychologica.

Glanemann, R., Dobel, C., Bölte, J., & Zwitserlood, P. (subm.). Event cognition in free view and at an eyeblink.

Henderson, J., & Ferreira, F. (2004). Scene perception for psycholinguists. In J. Henderson & F. Ferreira (Eds.), *The Interface of Language, Vision, and Action.* New York: Psychology Press.

Hochstein, S., & Ahissar, M. (2002). View from the top: hierarchies and reverse hierarchies in the visual system. *Neuron, 36*, 791–804.

Role of sensorimotor activity in spatial perception

Eve Dupierrix (eve.dupierrix@upmf-grenoble.fr)
Laboratoire de Psychologie et NeuroCognition, CNRS – UMR 5105/ Université Pierre Mendès-France, BP 47
38040 Grenoble cedex 09, France
ERT TREAT Vision, Service de Neurologie, Fondation Ophtalmologique A. de Rothschild
Paris, France

Théophile Ohlmann (theophile.ohlamnn@upmf-grenoble.fr)
Laboratoire de Psychologie et NeuroCognition, CNRS – UMR 5105/ Université Pierre Mendès-France, BP 47
38040 Grenoble cedex 09, France

Sylvie Chokron (Sylvie.chokron@upmf-grenoble.fr)
Laboratoire de Psychologie et NeuroCognition, CNRS – UMR 5105/ Université Pierre Mendès-France, BP 47
38040 Grenoble cedex 09, France
ERT TREAT Vision, Service de Neurologie, Fondation Ophtalmologique A. de Rothschild
Paris, France

Introduction and Methods

Research on healthy individuals and human lesion may suggest that sensorimotor experience influences space perception. Using bisection protocols, Chokron and De Agostini (1995) have demonstrated the role of reading habits in space perception. When the participant is asked to estimate the centre of a line, French participants (left-to-right readers) transected the line to the left of centre while Israeli participants (right-to-left readers) erred to the right of centre. Moroever recent studies on prism adaptation may even indicate that sensorimotor processes could induce change in cognitive spatial processing (Michel et al., 2003; Rossetti et al., 1998). All these findings raise the question of the role of lateralized sensorimotor activity in spatial biases exhibited by both neglect and healthy individuals. The present study aimed to show that a brief non-conflictual lateralized sensorimotor experience should induce spatial biases in normal individuals.

To reach this aim, twenty seven healthy volunteers were submitted to a proprioceptive straight ahead pointing (SAP) task and both visuomotor (VB) and perceptual (PB) versions of a bisection task before and after a short lateralized pointing task (toward targets displayed in the left hemispace for half of the participants and in the right hemispace for the remaining half). VB task consisted for participants to mark the centre of horizontal lines while PB task consisted to judge if cross-marked lines had been transected to the left or to the right of the true centre.

Results and Discussion

Results showed that the position of the egocentric reference (SAP) was not changed in the post-test compared to pre-test. However, findings indicate that subjective midpoint in both VB and PB tasks were deviated toward the hemispace investigated by the pointing task. In addition, these spatial biases varied as a function of the group pointing, spatial location, and length of lines.

These results clearly demonstrate that a short low-order lateralized sensorimotor training with no perceptual or motor conflict can affect bisection task even in a purely perceptual task involving high-level processing. This study support the view that acquired cultural factors may influence space organization (Chokron & De Agostini, 1995) and could argue in favour of the recent explanation of improvement in neglect patients using prim adaptation (Serino, Angeli, Frassinetti, & Ladavas, 2006). Finally, if this study does not allow us to explain neglect disease, it can suggest the role of the asymmetric spatial exploration and action in the poor recovery after left neglect.

Acknowledgments

This research was supported by the university Pierre Mendès France of Grenoble and the Centre National de la Recherche Scientifique. We wish to thank the Laboratory of Psychology & NeuroCognition for providing the support of this experiment.

References

Chokron, S., & De Agostini, M. (1995). Reading habits and line bisection: a developmental approach. *Brain Res Cogn Brain Res, 3*(1), 51-58.

Michel, C., Pisella, L., Halligan, P. W., Luauté, J., Rode, G., Boisson, D., et al. (2003). Simulating unilateral neglect in normals using prism adaptation: Implications for theory. *Neuropsychologia, 41*(1), 25-39.

Rossetti, Y., Rode, G., Pisella, L., Farné, A., Li, L., Boisson, D., et al. (1998). Prism adaptation to a rightward optical deviation rehabilitates left hemispatial neglect. *Nature, 395*, 166-169.

Serino, A., Angeli, V., Frassinetti, F., & Ladavas, E. (2006). Mechanisms underlying neglect recovery after prism adaptation. *Neuropsychologia, 44*(7), 1068-1078.

Activation Followed by Suppression in the Simon Task: Influence of an Accessory Peripheral Signal

Kathleen Maetens (kmaetens@vub.ac.be) and Eric Soetens (esoetens@vub.ac.be)
Department of Psychology and Educational Sciences, Vrije Universiteit Brussel
Pleinlaan 2, 1050 Elsene, Belgium

Introduction

In a Simon task subjects react to the identity (e.g. colour) of a stimulus, while ignoring the stimulus location. Even though stimulus location is irrelevant, responses are faster and more accurate when stimulus (S) and response (R) location correspond.

The Simon effect (SE) can be interpreted in terms of a dual-route model, where relevant information is processed by a controlled route and irrelevant information by an automatic route. Hommel (1993) suggested that the SE is the consequence of the overlap in time between these two processes (TOM = Temporal Overlap Model). Evidence for this idea was found by presenting the stimulus gradually so that the stimulus location is processed before the relevant information. The SE was reduced in comparison to an abrupt presentation. According to Hommel (1993) the decrease of the effect reflects spontaneous decay of the irrelevant spatial code.

Previous experiments with a central coloured stimulus and a peripheral go/nogo stimulus revealed a Simon effect, using a fixed stimulus-onset asynchrony of 0, 100 and 600 ms. To investigate the temporal characteristics of the Simon effect, we dissociated the processing of the relevant and irrelevant stimulus information by presenting both features at different points in time. An accessory signal was used so we could present the peripheral information before and after the response initiation was already started. In order to prevent anticipations, we used go and no-go trials.

Method

Subjects were instructed to respond to the colour of a central stimulus, presented during 100 ms. Instead of responding immediately, they had to postpone their response until a go stimulus appeared 600 ms later. At different intervals, an irrelevant peripheral stimulus could appear before, after or simultaneously with the go or no-go stimulus.

Results

We found an interaction between congruency and the time when the irrelevant information was presented. A SE was found when the irrelevant location information was shown 150 ms before (p=0.01), or together with, the go-signal (p=0.02). When the irrelevant signal was presented 150 ms after the go-signal started, we found a significant reversal of the SE (p=0.03). Presenting the irrelevant information more than 150 ms before or after the go-signal had no influence on RT (no SE).

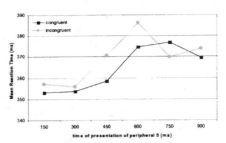

Figure 1: Mean RT for congruent and incongruent trials in function of time of presentation of the irrelevant information

Discussion

In support of the TOM and the decay hypothesis, the SE only shows up when the accessory peripheral signal is presented shortly before or simultaneously with the go signal. However, when the peripheral signal appears shortly after the go signal, the SE reverses, probably showing the presence of an active suppression mechanism that inhibits the activation caused by the irrelevant information, as suggested in the activation-suppression model of Ridderinkhof (2002).

Alternatively these results can be explained by S-R binding. At the start of the trial, colour and response code bind. When the go-signal appears, the response is initiated leading to an occupation of the response code. The slower responses on congruent trials, when the accessory signal appears shortly after the go signal, indicates that the code occupation interferes with the attempt to integrate the same code (of the accessory signal) during response initiation. This is supported by a study where relevant information is not given in advance and no reversed SE was found.

Acknowledgments

This research was funded by the Fund for Scientific Research of Flanders, Belgium.

References

Hommel, B. (1993). The relation between stimulus processing and response selection in the Simon task: Evidence for a temporal overlap. *Psychological Research, 55,* 280-290.

Ridderinkhof, R. (2002). Activation and suppression in conflict tasks: Empirical clarification through distributional analyses. In W. Prinz & B. Hommel (Eds.), *Attention and performance XIX: Common mechanisms in perception and action*, Oxford: Oxford University Press.

A Perceptual Adaptation Account of Preview Effects in the Eriksen Flanker Task

Eddy J. Davelaar (e.davelaar@bbk.ac.uk)
School of Psychology, Birkbeck, University of London
Malet Street, WC1E 7HX, London, UK

David E. Huber (dhuber@psy.ucsd.edu)
Department of Psychology, University of California, San Diego
9500 Gilman Drive, La Jolla, CA 92093, USA

In the Eriksen flanker paradigm, peripheral flankers can help or harm performance depending on whether they indicate the correct or incorrect response of a central target. With this paradigm it has been observed that immediate preview of the flankers reduces flanker effects (e.g., Flowers, 1990). We report four experiments that investigated this phenomenon, establishing the separate contributions of target priming and flanker preview at different preview durations.

Experiments

Participants were seated in front of a computer and were instructed to make a consonant-vowel judgment only to the middle letter of a five-letter string (Experiments 1, 2, and 3) or a single target letter (Experiments 1, 2, 4), as quickly and accurately as possible. Feedback was provided on every trial and between blocks. The letters in the experiments were B, K, A, and E and formed three types of flanker conditions: stimulus-congruent (CC: AAAAA), response-congruent (IC: EEAEE), or response-incongruent (II: BBABB). The participant saw a preview stimulus that was four-letter string with a space between the second and third letter and always contained four identical letters (e.g., AA AA). The duration of the preview stimulus was 100ms or 800ms with a blank interval of 0ms (Experiments 1, 3, and 4) or 100 ms (Experiments 2, 3, and 4) between the preview- and response-frame. Figure 1 reveals that at short preview duration, the response (difference between the II and the IC conditions) and identity (difference between the IC and the CC conditions) effects increase. At longer preview durations, the response interference disappears, but the identity effect remains when flankers are presented in the response frame and disappears when a target stimulus is presented without flankers.

Discussion

We explain these effects in terms of perceptual discounting that accrues over time as a function of preview durations. This theory is implemented in a model with dynamic neural accommodation (Huber & O'Reilly, 2003) within spatially specific identity detectors and spatially non-specific evidence accumulators (response units). In the model, short preview durations prime the activation of identity units, leading to faster accumulation of the corresponding response unit. However, adaptation causes the spatially-specific identity detectors to loose their ability to "jump-start" the response units, leading to decreased response and identity effects in the condition without flankers (thin lines). In the condition with flankers (thick lines), the adaptation eliminated the response interference earlier (800 ms) than the identity effect (900ms). In the model this is due to lateral inhibition eliminating residual activation of non-identical identity detectors. In sum, preview results in identity priming and increased response interference at short durations and a "repetition blindness" at long durations, which reduces flanker interference.

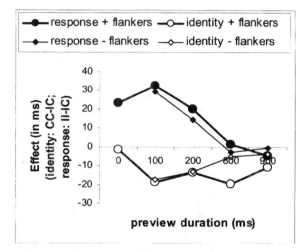

Figure 1: Response and identity effects as a function of preview duration. Combined data of four experiments.

Acknowledgments

This research is funded by a NIH grant # MH063993 to R. M. Shiffrin and D. E. Huber.

References

Flowers, J. H. (1990). Priming effects in perceptual classification. *Perception & Psychophysics, 47*, 135-148.

Huber, D. E., & O'Reilly, R. C. (2003). Persistence and accommodation in short-term priming and other perceptual paradigms: temporal segregation through synaptic depression. *Cognitive Science, 27*, 403-430.

Weighing-Up Perception-Action Dissociation:
Does Grasping Object Mass Rely On Perception?

Martin Gareth Edwards (m.edwards.1@bham.ac.uk)
School of Sport and Exercise Sciences, University of Birmingham
Edgbaston, Birmingham, B15 2TT. UK

Daniel Eastough (dan.eastough@googlemail.com)
School of Sport and Exercise Sciences, University of Birmingham
Edgbaston, Birmingham, B15 2TT. UK

In a recent paper, we reported that grasping objects of different physical mass resulted in an increased peak grasp aperture, a final finger and thumb placement on the object that more closely passed through the object centre of mass, increased lift delay and reduced peak lift velocity for actions to heavy compared to light objects (see Eastough and Edwards, 2007). From these data, we suggested that increased object mass influenced the grasp component movement kinematics prior to contact in preparation for a stable final grip placement on the object. Doing so would reduce the chances of object slippage from the grip or rotation around the grip points during object lift (especially for the heavier objects).

One consequence of the finding was that the data provided a challenge to the perception-action, ventral-dorsal stream dissociation model put forward by Milner and Goodale, and colleagues (see for example Goodale et al. 1991; Milner & Goodale 1995). In Eastough & Edwards (2007), the visual aspects of the light and heavy objects were identical (i.e., they were the same size and colour etc.). However, the trials were blocked by mass, with different sized objects randomized within each block. Therefore, even though the light and heavy objects were visually identical, as the object mass condition was ran in separate trial blocks, participants could predict the mass of the object that they were about to grasp. It seemed that the perceptual expectation of mass influenced action.

In the poster reported here, we report two follow-up experiments that tested whether manipulations to perceived object mass could further influence prehensile kinematics.

In Experiment 1, we set out to replicate recent data that showed action kinematics to be influenced by object labeling (see for example, Gentilucci et al., 2000; Glover & Dixon, 2002). In the experiment, the perceptual labels "SMALL" versus "LARGE" and "LIGHT" versus "HEAVY" were attached to one of four physically small or large and light or heavy objects. Ten right-handed participants (aged 19-31 years old) made reach, grasp and lift actions to one of the objects, and their actions were recorded using a three-dimensional motion tracker. The results showed no evidence that the labels had any influence on any of the movement kinematics measured. However, we did find that increased physical object mass caused a greater

peak grasp aperture, led to a grip placement on the object that closely passed through the object's centre of mass and increased the time needed to lift the object (replicating our original data; see Eastough & Edwards 2007).

In Experiment 2, we tested a more direct perceptual manipulation than Experiment 1, in which small and large, clear or painted glass jars were filled with light polystyrene or heavy lead (diving weight) balls. Therefore, in the clear jar conditions, the mass of the object could be recognized from the jar content. Ten right-handed participants (aged 18-30 years old) made reach, grasp and lift actions to one of the objects, and their actions were recorded using a three-dimensional motion tracker. As in the previous experiments, the different mass objects were conducted in a light and heavy trial block condition, but also this time, a randomized object mass trial block was also carried out. The aim was to determine whether participants would use recognition of the object's contents in the clear jar randomized condition to predict the object's mass. The results showed that only the blocked mass condition replicated our original mass effect findings (with no mass effects in the randomized trials).

In summary, these data show that manipulations of perceived mass had no influence on action. Yet, despite the null effects, the original finding was consistently replicated when trials were blocked by mass. The data are discussed in relation to the Perception-Action dissociation model.

References

Eastough D. & Edwards, M. G. (2007). Movement kinematics in prehension are affected by grasping objects of different mass. *Experimental Brain Research*, *176*, 193-198.

Gentilucci, M., Benuzzi, F., Bertolani, L., Daprati., E & Gangitano, M. (2000). Language and Motor Control. *Experimental Brain Research*, *133*, 468-490.

Glover, S. & Dixon, P. (2002). Semantics affect the planning but not control of grasping. *Experimental Brain Research, 146*, 383-387.

Goodale, M. A., Milner, A. D., Jakobson, L. S., & Carey, D. P. (1991). A neurological dissociation between perceiving objects and grasping them. *Nature, 349*, 154-56.

Milner, A. D., & Goodale, M. A. (1995). *The Visual Brain in Action.* Oxford University Press.

Seeing It Your Way:
Cognitive Processes Underlying Visual Perspective Taking

Dana Samson (D.Samson@bham.ac.uk)
School of Psychology, University of Birmingham
Edgbaston, Birmingham, B15 2TT UK

Ian A. Apperly (I.A.Apperly@bham.ac.uk)
School of Psychology, University of Birmingham
Edgbaston, Birmingham, B15 2TT UK

Jason J. Braithwaite (J.J.Braithwaite@bham.ac.uk)
School of Psychology, University of Birmingham
Edgbaston, Birmingham, B15 2TT UK

Benjamin J. Andrews (BJA080@bham.ac.uk)
School of Psychology, University of Birmingham
Edgbaston, Birmingham, B15 2TT UK

The task of inferring what someone else can or cannot see has often been used to assess how children or adults are able to disengage from their own perspective to take someone else's point of view (e.g., Michelon & Zacks, 2006; Vogeley, May, Ritzl, Falkai, Zilles, & Fink, 2004). In a series of experiments, we investigated the nature of the cognitive processes underlying this visual perspective taking ability.

Participants saw the picture of an avatar standing in a room with circles pinned on the wall (see Figure 1). They were asked to verify the number of circles seen either from their own perspective or from the avatar's perspective. On half of the trials, the two perspectives were congruent and, on the other half of the trials, the two perspectives were incongruent. In Experiment 1, we found that participants were significantly slower in verifying the avatar's perspective when their own perspective was incongruent. More surprisingly, participants were also significantly slower in verifying their own perspective when the avatar's perspective was incongruent. In Experiment 2, we found that the avatar's perspective intrusion effect persisted even when participants had to repeatedly verify their own perspective within the same block. In Experiment 3, we replaced the avatar by a bicolor stick and asked participants to verify the number of circles pinned either on all the three walls (global space equivalent to self-perspective in Experiments 1-2) or on the wall closest to the green side of the stick (local space equivalent to the avatar's perspective in Experiments 1-2, see Figure 1). Participants were significantly slower in verifying the number of circles in the local space when the global space was incongruent. But, interestingly, the congruency of the local space did not influence participants' response time when they verified the number of circles presented in the global space. In other words, when the local space was cued by the orientation of the avatar, local space did interfere on the global space;

however, when the local space was cued by the color of the stick, local space did not interfere on global space. The avatar's body orientation and gaze direction may have acted as powerful cues to the local space.

In sum, our own visual experience of the world modulates how we think other people see the world and this seems to be due to general spatial processing properties (global over local precedence). But perhaps more surprisingly, observing someone else also modulates our own visual experience of the world, suggesting that other people's gaze can cue us to be less egocentric.

Figure 1: Example of stimuli (Experiments 1 and 2 on the left, Experiment 3 on the right). On half of the trials, the local and global spaces were incongruent as shown here. Participants were asked to verify (yes or no response) the global space (e.g., "you – 2?" or "room – 2?") or the local space (e.g., "he – 1?" or "stick – 1?")

Acknowledgments

We thank Sarah Bodley Scott for her help in collecting the data and Luc Vennes for his help in creating the stimuli.

References

Michelon, P., & Zachs, J.M. (2006). Two kinds of visual perspective taking. *Perception & Psychophysics, 68,* 327-337.

Vogeley, K., May, M., Ritzl, A., Falkai, P., Zilles, K., Fink, G.R. (2004). Neural correlates of first-person perspective as one constituent of human self-consciousness. *Journal of Cognitive Neuroscience, 165,* 817-827.

Quantitative Estimation of illusionary band on the Muller-Lyer illusion

Shusaku Nomura (nomura@cis.shimane-u.ac.jp)
Department of Mathematics and Computer Science, Shimane University
1060 Nishikawatsu, Matsue, Shimane 6908504 JAPAN

Introduction

Muller-Lyer figure was well known as the illusionary figure and it has frequently used with various variations on the studies investigating human visual perception process and mechanisms (e.g., Franz et al., 2001). But few studies attempt to estimate quantitatively how much the difference in size between real and perceptual objects and/or how much the properties of the figure, such as the angle of arrows, affects on such illusionary perception. In this study, the blender-type Muller-Lyer figures were repetitively tested to subjects with changing its figure properties, and the amount of subjective illusionary perception was estimated statistically.

Experiments

We introduced the blender-type Muller-Lyer figures as shown in Figure 1. Subjects (Ten healthy students, ages from 21 to 31) were required repetitively adjusting a set of Muller-Lyer figures shown on the PC screen to the level in which both centerlines (denoted as "L1" and "L2" in Figure 1) of the figures were perceptually the same size. The set of the presented Muller-Lyer figures consisted of the 72 of figures in different angles of the arrows ranges from 20 to 180 degrees (denoted as theta in Figure 1) and the length of the centerline. Adjusting was easily handled by changing the L2 with the mouse device (L1 was fixed). In the experiment, the two way of adjusting direction were tested, one was the figures which L2 was perceptually clearly shorter than L1 (named as "PS"), thus subjects had to make L2 longer, and the other was the figure with perceptually longer L2 (named as "PL"). Then 144 types of the Muller-Lyer figures were randomly and repetitively presented on the PC's 17 inches liquid crystal display placed 50 cm from subjects. The figures were shown in the area of 600 × 600 within 1028 × 768 pixels of the display.

Result and Discussion

Although the large difference within individual, the amount of estimated illusionary difference between real and perceptual figures clearly shows parameters' dependent feature. Figure 2 shows the relation of the arrow angles and the amount of illusion. By statistical analysis like as *ANOVA*, we could assume that the amount of illusion was larger when the angle is smaller. That result is consistent with past studies though few studies assessed such a detailed-change of parameters.

On the other hand, the result focused on the adjusting direction was intriguing. As Figure 2 shows, the PS experiments marked greater illusionary effect than PL ($p<.05$ by t-test). This result suggests that some illusionary band could exist in the human perception of the Muller-Lyer illusion (as shown in Figure 3) and such an illusionary band could change accompanying with the arrow angle. This results might reflects some differences in the physiological process of recognition of illusionary figures, such as possible feedback in adjusting process, but much more systematic experiment would need for further discussion.

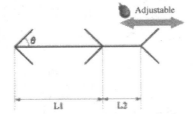

Figure 1: A set of Muller-Lyer figure.

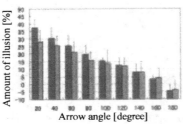

Figure 2: The arrow angle and the amount of illusion.

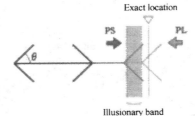

Figure 3: Possible illusionary band of Muller-Lyer figure.

References

Franz, V. H., Fahle, M., Bulthoff H. H., & Gegenfurtner, K. R. (2001). Effects of visual illusions on grasping. *Journal of Experimental Psychology. Human Perception and Performance*, 27(**5**), 1122-1144.

Visuo-Haptic Device – Telemaque – Increases Kindergarten Children's Handwriting Acquisition

Anne Hillairet de Boisferon (anne.hillairet@upmf-grenoble.fr)
Richard Palluel-Germain (germainr@einstein.edu)
Florence Bara (florence.bara@univ-savoie.fr)
Edouard Gentaz (edouard.gentaz@upmf-grenoble.fr)
Psychology and NeuroCognition Laboratory (CNRS UMR-5105),
Grenoble, France

Bernard Hennion (Bernard.hennion@orange-ft.com)
Philippe Gouagout (philippe.gouagout@orange-ft.com)
France Telecom Division Research Development, France

Introduction

Handwriting acquisition consists in acquiring visual representation of the letters and motor representation which is specific to each letter. This acquisition is slow and difficult. Children must automate the low-level processes of handwriting so that working memory resources are freed up for the high level constructive aspects of composing. Handwriting acquisition could be the consequence of a change from retroactive control of movement (based on sensorial feedback) to proactive control (based on an internal representation of the motor act) (cf. Zesiger, 1995). It is of a crucial interest to improve this handwriting acquisition. We developed an original ergonomic visuo-haptic device, named Telemaque, which used a force-feedback programmable pen (Hennion, Gentaz, Gouagout & Bara, 2005). This device is used to teach children how to reproduce a letter according to a standard that is not only static (correct shape) but also dynamic (rules of motor production). The main aim of the present study was to show that incorporating this visuo-haptic device in a classical training may increase the fluency of handwriting production in kindergarten children.

Method

Forty two 5 year-old children were assigned an intervention involving either Telemaque (Visuo-Haptic training; VH group) or not (control training; C group). An intervention consisted of one session, lasted 20 min, per week and per letter. Six cursive letters (*a,b,f,i,l,s*) were trained. The fluency of handwriting was tested 1 and 2 weeks before and after both interventions. Fluency was analysed by kinematics parameters: Average velocity, number of velocity peaks, and number of breaks during the production of the six cursive letters.

Results

Figure 1 shows that the fluency of handwriting production for all letters was higher after the VH training than after the C training: The movements were faster, exhibited less

velocity peaks and children lifted the pen less often during the letter production.

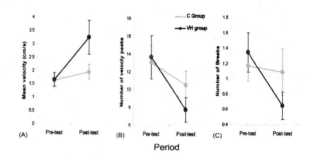

Figure 1: Mean Velocity (A), Number of velocity peaks (B), Number of breaks (C) according to the period (Pre-and Post-test) and the group (VH or C).

Discussion

The results show that the dynamic and the static rules generated by Telemaque may help children to improve their motor handwriting production. This confirms the previous results obtained with older children (Palluel-Germain, Bara, Hennion, Gouagout & Gentaz, 2006). The use of Telemaque may induce the motor system to incorporate the basic rules of motor production and therefore helps children to increase the proactive strategy to control handwriting movements.

References

Hennion, B., Gentaz, E., Gouagout, P. & Bara, F. (2005). Telemaque, a new visuo-haptic interface for remediation of dysgraphic children. *IEEE, WorldHaptic*, 410-419.

Palluel-Germain, R., Bara, F., Hennion, B., Gouagout, P. & Gentaz, E. (2006). Early handwriting acquisition: Evaluation of Telemaque, a new visuo-haptic interface. *IEEE, EuroHaptics*, 551-554.

Zesiger, P. (1995). *Ecrire: Approche cognitive, neuropsychologique et développementale.* Paris: PUF.

HOMER: A Design for the Development of Acoustical-Haptic Representations of Document Meta-Data for Use by Persons with Vision Loss

K. Ikospentaki (kikospe@phs.uoa.gr) & S. Vosniadou (svosniad@phs.uoa.gr)
Department of Philosophy and History of Science, University of Athens
Panepistimiopolis, GR157 71 Athens – Greece

D. Tsonos (ea02534@di.uoa.gr) & G. Kouroupetroglou (koupe@di.uoa.gr)
Department of Informatics and Telecommunications, University of Athens
Panepistimiopolis, GR157 71 Athens – Greece

The aim of the HOMER project is to study the accessibility of text formatting and text structure meta-data in structured and electronic documents through the acoustic (and complementally haptic) modality. Text formatting meta-data include the formation elements of the text, font elements (e.g., font type, size, color, etc.) and typesetting (e.g., bold, italics, underlined). Text structure meta-data specify the attribute of the part of the document, such as chapter, title, subtitle and header/footer. Almost all of the available Text-to-Speech systems do not incorporate a facility to associate specific meta-information of the source electronic documents with speech and audio representations.

Following a design-for-all approach, we investigate different acoustic (and haptically supplemented) representations of the above-mentioned document meta-data in order to find out which ones better communicate the relevant information to visually impaired individuals.

The project HOMER combines expertise from cognitive and computer science to investigate how document meta-data is represented in sighted and non-sighted individuals and which kinds of acoustic representations are more effective in conveying the semantics of information. After an in depth analysis of the users' needs, which is currently taking place, we will proceed with a series of cognitive tasks that enable us to select groups of sighted and visually impaired individuals with comparable cognitive skills.

The different acoustic–haptic representations of text formatting and text structure documents' meta-data will be investigated by conducting a number of psychoacoustic experiments. In these experiments the semantic representation of meta-data will be mapped to appropriate sonification parameters by changing the features of synthetic speech, using earcons or auditory icons, or a combination of them. Supplementary to the acoustic mapping the haptic modality will also be used. Based on the results of the above experiences we will propose the architecture of an appropriate information system that could operate as a real-time augmented learning environment. This system will be XML – based, and it will follow the accessibility guidelines of the World Wide Web Consortium (W3C). It will be multilingual and polyglot, device-independent, having the ability to process domain-free, context-free in both printed and electronic documents.

For the evaluation of the system we will use a scientific document, which will be projected, by making a simple projection of this document on a whiteboard to be read by the students under teacher guidance in a whiteboard. The same document will also be processed by the above-mentioned system, and will be presented acoustically, haptically and visually under teacher guidance. Two questionnaires will be given to the students (sighted and visually impaired), after each presentation. The first one will include specific questions, in order to measure: (1) whether the participants of the traditional instruction understood the utility, the semantics and the logic behind the use of the visual and the non-visual metadata in the document, and (2) whether the participants of the multi-modal presentation understood the utility, the semantics and the logic behind the use of the acoustic – haptic representation of visual and non-visual meta-data in the document and in the process. The second questionnaire will include questions to test whether the students understood the scientific information conveyed in the text.

This task is designed for the evaluation of the implemented system and at the same time for the evaluation of the appropriateness of its use in the classroom setting. The results may show that a multi-modal presentation of meta-data information in documents is more appropriate for congenitally blind children, in order to overcome their visual limitations. But a multi-modal presentation may be more appropriate for sighted children, in order to better understand some scientific explanations.

Acknowledgments

This research is co-funded by the European Social Fund and National Resources under the HOMER project of the Competitiveness Programme: PENED, Hellenic General Secretariat of Research and Technology.

References

Eysenck, W. M., & Keane, T. M. (2000). *Cognitive Psychology A Students Handbook.* Psychology Press Ltd, U.K.

Warren, H. D. (1994). *Blindness and Children: An Individual Differences Approach*, Cambridge University Press.

Xydas, G. & Kouroupetroglou, G. (2001). Text-to-Speech Scripting Interface for Appropriate Vocalisation of e-Texts. *Proceedings of EUROSPEECH 2001*, Sept. 3-7, Aalborg, Denmark, pp. 2247-2250.

Cognitive Style and Graphical Interpretation

Katherine P. McGuire (mcguire@unbsj.ca)
Amber D. Leblanc (s42sd@unbsj.ca)
Aren C. Hunter (t91hy@unbsj.ca)
Lisa A. Best (lbest@unbsj.ca)
Department of Psychology, University of New Brunswick
100 Tucker Park Road, P.O. Box 5050, Saint John, New Brunswick, Canada E2L 4L5

Graphical representations are often utilized in education to facilitate learning. However, students report having difficulty interpreting the information depicted in graphs (Shah & Hoeffner, 2002). Research has attempted to identify learner characteristics which may affect graph comprehension, such as prior knowledge of the topic depicted in the graph and visuospatial ability (Vekiri, 2002). However, to date, the possibility that cognitive style may affect graph comprehension has not been addressed.

Cognitive styles and learning styles are described as individual ways of processing information (Sternberg & Zhang, 2001). Riding (2001) indicated that a major dimension of these styles is the visualiser-verbaliser dimension. Individuals described as visualisers tend to understand information better if it is presented visually whereas semantic presentation leads to better understanding in individuals described as verbalisers. Based on these differences, the goal of this study was to investigate if level of graph comprehension will vary as a function of the visualiser-verbaliser dimension.

Method

Participants, consisting of 192 Introductory Psychology students from the University of New Brunswick, completed an informed consent, followed by a questionnaire package consisting of the Multimedia Learning Preference Questionnaire (MLPQ); the Santa Barbara Learning Style Questionnaire (SBLSQ); the Learning Style Inventory (LSI); the Vividness of Visual Imagery Questionnaire (VVIQ); and the Graphical Comprehension Scale (based on Trickett & Trafton, 2006). The survey results from the MLPQ, the SBLSQ, the LSI and the VVIQ were then correlated to measures of graph interpretation using the Graphical Comprehension Scale. Based on previous factor analytic research of the visualiser-verbaliser dimension (Mayer & Massa, 2003), it was expected that the LSI and the SBLSQ would be related. Also, based on Riding (2001), it was assumed that the visualiser—verbaliser dimension of these learning style scales would also be an indicator of the same dimension in cognitive style.

Results

As can be seen in Figure 1, visualisers and verbalisers were equally accurate in reading, referred to as "read off"

requiring the identification of a single data point ($F(20,167)$ =.78, p=.73); transforming ($F(20,167)$=.90, p=.59); and interpreting ($F(20,167)$=1.50, p=.09) graphical information. An unexpected finding was a lack of relationship between the LSI and SBLSQ.

These results have positive implications for graph comprehension in that the visualiser-verbaliser dimension does not appear to affect the accuracy of graph interpretation. In relation to cognitive style, further investigation of how to conceptualize and measure its dimensions is needed.

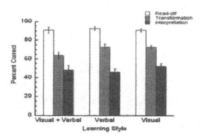

Figure 1: Graph comprehension for visualisers/verbalisers

References

Mayer, R. E., & Massa, L. J. (2003). Three facets of visual and verbal learners: Cognitive ability, cognitive style and learning preferences. *Journal of Educational Psychology, 95* (4), 833-846.

Riding, R. J. (2001). The nature and effects of cognitive style. In R. J. Sternberg & L. Zhang (Eds.) *Perspectives on thinking learning and cognitive styles*. Mahwah, NJ: Erlbaum.

Shah, P., & Hoeffner, J. (2002). Review of graph comprehension research: Implications for instruction. *Educational Psychology Review, 14* (1), 47-69.

Sternberg, R. J., & Zhang, L. (Eds.) (2001). *Perspectives on thinking learning and cognitive styles*. Mahwah, NJ: Erlbaum.

Trickett, S., & Trafton, G. (2006). Toward a comprehensive model of graph comprehension: Making the case for spatial cognition. In D. Barker-Plummer, R. Cox, & N. Swoboda (Eds.), *Diagrammatic representation and inference*. Berlin: Springer.

Vekiri, I. (2002). What is the value of graphical displays in learning? *Educational Psychology Review, 14* (3), 261-312.

Frequency and Interpretation of Figurative Language in Children's Literature: Match or Mismatch?

Sara Verbrugge (Sara.Verbrugge@psy.kuleuven.be)
Laboratory of Experimental Psychology, University of Leuven
Tiensestraat 102, Leuven, Belgium

Introduction

A study will be reported of frequencies of different kinds of figurative language used in children's literature and children's understanding of these instances of figurative language. For a good interpretation of children's literature there should be a match between the occurrence of particular kinds of figurative language and children's level of comprehension. Colston and Kuiper (2002) showed that there is a discrepancy between the materials that are used in figurative language comprehension studies and figurative language used in popular children's literature. By means of a comparison between a corpus study and a comprehension experiment, we will investigate the match or mismatch between use and comprehension of figurative language. In both studies, we discerned the following types of figurative language: metaphor (Me), personification (Pe), synesthesia (Sy), metonymy (My), saying (Sa), and simile (Si).

Corpus Study

Fourteen children's books were studied: seven books were awarded a prize by an adult jury; the other seven books were awarded a prize by a children's jury. The books covered the age span from below six to twelve. The frequencies of figurative language were described in terms of occurrence per 10000 words. Table 1 gives an overview of the relative frequency of all instances of figurative language taken together, compared for adult and children's jury and below and above 8 years as intended public. It shows that the relative frequency of figurative language is higher in books awarded a prize by an adult jury than by a children's jury (χ^2=30.48, df=1, p<.001). Also, books for younger children contain fewer instances of figurative language than books for older children (χ^2=15.76, df=1, p<.001). If we put the level of comprehension for the different types of figurative language on a scale, we observe two groups: similes, personifications, and sayings on the one hand (high relative frequency); and metonymy, synesthesia, and metaphor on the other hand (low relative frequency).

Table 1: Frequencies of instances of figurative language.

Age	Jury	Relative frequency
< 8	Adult	41.45
	Children	13.6
> 8	Adult	72.1
	Children	32.23

Experiment

78 children took part in an experiment testing their comprehension. There were two age groups (age 7 and age 9). Examples of each of the six categories discussed above were selected out of the books of the corpus study. Only the relevant sentences and no further context was given. The children were asked to explain what they thought the sentence meant. Answers were recorded on tape. The answers of the children were scored on a scale from 0 (no comprehension at all) to 5 (complete comprehension). An ANOVA-analysis with type of figurative language as within subjects variable and age as between subjects variable revealed a main effect of age (F(1,70)=40.70, p<.01) and a main effect of type of figurative language (F(5,350)=9,47, p<.0001). No interaction was observed (see Figure 1).

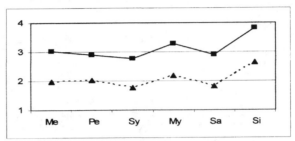

Figure 1: Comprehension levels per type of figurative language for age 7 (dotted line) and age 9 (straight line).

Conclusion

We can conclude that there is no mismatch between the occurrence of figurative language in children's books and children's understanding. Similes have the highest relative frequency and are also best understood by participants. This may be because a simile makes explicit the link between literal and figurative language (by means of *as, like*). Synesthesia has the lowest relative frequency and is poorly understood by participants. The other categories lie in between, but there is never an obvious discrepancy between frequency and comprehension. No big gap looms between the author's intentions and the children's understanding.

Acknowledgments

The research was carried out thanks to a grant for the author: Research Assistant of the Research Foundation Flanders. Special thanks to Lynn Nijs for collecting the data.

References

Colston, H.L., & Kuiper, M.S. (2002). Figurative language development research and popular children's literature: why we should know, "Where the wild things are". *Metaphor and Symbol, 17(1)*, 27-43.

Thematic difficulty causes processing cost for sentence comprehension

Satoru Yokoyama[1][2][*], Masatoshi Koizumi[3], Jungho Kim[3],
Noriaki Yusa[4], Kei Yoshimoto[1], Ryuta Kawashima[2]
(*yokoyama@idac.tohoku.ac.jp)
1. Graduate School of International Cultural Studies, Tohoku University, Kawauchi 41, Aoba-ku, Sendai, 980-8576 Japan.
2. Institute of Development Aging and Cancer, Tohoku University, Seiryo-cho 4-1, Aoba-ku, Sendai, 980-8575 Japan.
3. Department of Linguistics, Tohoku University, Kawauchi 27-1, Aoba-ku, Sendai, 980-8576 Japan.
4. Department of English, Miyagi Gakuin Women's University, Sakuragaoka 9-1-1, Aoba-ku, Sendai, 981-8557 Japan.

Introduction

Bornkessel et al. (2003) investigated whether thematic difficulty causes processing cost in sentence comprehension. However, to examine the issue, they used active verbs (e.g., *the priest followed the gardener*) and psych verbs (e.g., *the monk pleased the boy*) which have different involvement of action from each other. Although they showed a significant difference in the processing, the results can also be explained by the difference not only in thematic difficulty but also in a semantic difference.

In the present study, to overcome the above problem, we used pairs of *te-ageru* sentences such as (1) and *te-morau* sentences such as (2) in Japanese as experimental stimuli.
(1) John-ga   Mary-ni   hon-wo kashite-ageta.
  "John lent the book to Mary."
(2) Mary-ga   John-ni   hon-wo kashite-moratta.
  "Mary borrowed the book from John."
These two types of sentences have different assignment patterns of thematic roles onto nouns from each other but the identical case particle order, main verb (*kashite* (lend) in the above examples), and logically the same meaning. The former accords with an unmarked thematic role assignment. Thus, if we find different task performances between them, the results will indicate that not syntactic/semantic but thematic difficulty causes processing cost for on-line sentence comprehension.

Methods

Firstly, we confirmed that there was no difference between the two conditions in syntax by using a questionnaire method. In experiment 1, subjects were asked to perform a plausibility judgment task in a whole sentence presentation manner. In experiment 2, subjects were asked to perform a self-paced reading task in a phrase-by-phrase presentation manner. Each condition (i.e., *te-ageru* and *te-morau*) has 24 items. In each experiment, 24 Japanese native speakers participated. No one performed both experiment 1 and 2. For data analysis, ANOVA was used.

Results and Discussion

In a questionnaire method, there was no difference between the two conditions in syntax (p=.18). In experiment 1, there was a significant difference between the two conditions in both response times (F1 p<.05, F2 p<.001) and error rates (F1 p=.08, F2 p<.05). In experiment 2, a significant difference was observed between the two conditions in reading times at only phrase 7, which is the place where there is a difference between the two conditions in thematic role assignment (F1 p<.05, F2 p<.001). These results indicate that thematic, not syntactic, difficulty causes processing cost for on-line sentence comprehension. These results suggest that since assignment patterns of thematic roles are predicted before inputting their head, readers need to re-analyze thematic role assignment patterns for *te-morau* sentences but not for *te-ageru* counterparts.

Table 1: Results of mean reaction times in experiment 1.

	Ageru	Morau
Reaction	1923ms(SD=308)	2131ms(SD=353)
Error	0%(SD=0)	1.3%(SD=3.66)

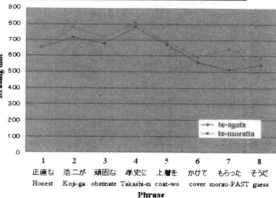

Figure 1: Results of reading times in experiment 2.

Acknowledgments

This study was supported by the 21st COE Program, entitled "A Strategic Research and Education Center for an Integrated Approach to Language and Cognition" (Tohoku University). "

References

Bornkessel, I., Schlesewsky, M., Friederici, A., (2003). Eliciting thematic reanalysis effects: the role of syntax-independent information during parsing. Language and Cognitive Processes 18, 269-298.

Conversational precedents and lexical ambiguity: When consistency is not enough

Edmundo Kronmüller (ekron001@ucr.edu) and Dale J. Barr (dale.barr@ucr.edu)
Department of Psychology, University of California, Riverside
900 University Avenue, Riverside, CA 92521 USA

Introduction

When interpreting referential expressions in a conversation, listeners expect speakers to follow conversational precedents—that is, they expect them to use the same linguistic expression to refer to the same referent. Listeners' expectation of consistency in referring is grounded in the fact that speakers in a conversation tend to stabilize the descriptions they give to the same objects across time, a phenomenon called *lexical entrainment*. Brennan and Clark (1996) explain lexical entrainment as the result of a conceptual pact, collaboratively reached between the participants in a conversation, that states how an object is to be conceptualized. Speakers' lexical choices, then, reflect that agreed-upon conceptualization. Because this pact is between specific interlocutors, listeners should consider the speaker's perspective when they interpret referential expressions. Multiple experiments have shown, however, that the benefit of precedent use to comprehension is speaker-independent: people interpret a referential expression faster and more accurately when a referent is described consistently with a conceptual pact, regardless of whether the speaker currently using the expression is the same one who originally established the pact, or a different speaker who is uninformed of the pact (Barr & Keysar, 2002; Metzing & Brennan, 2003; Kronmüller & Barr, 2006).

All the experiments showing this speaker-independence involve a referential domain that is structured to reward the expectance of consistency: in the set of possible referents there has been only one that matches with the expression previously used. Consequently, the precedent is a good anchor for comprehension, independently of the identity and knowledge of the current speaker. In the following experiment we created an ambiguous situation in which two referents could be named using the same conventional expression. We hypothesized that information about the speaker's perspective would be integrated in comprehension since it would be useful to solve the referential task.

The Experiment

Participants heard pre-recorded instructions from two different speakers (male and female) to select a target picture from an array of three pictures of conventional objects. They were told that the speakers could name these objects differently because there was no interaction between them when they recorded the instructions, and also that the speakers only could see two of the three pictures on the screen when they recorded the instructions. We introduced ambiguity by having in the set of objects two that could be named using the same word. For example, one display contained a flying mammal bat (the target), a baseball bat (the competitor) and a shoe (irrelevant), and the instruction was to "Click on the bat". Each critical trial was embedded in a block of 10 trials. Before the critical trial, the target was named twice (precedent condition) or never (no precedent condition). Also, the instruction in the critical trial was given by the same speaker who named the objects before (same speaker condition), or by a different one (different speaker condition).

We recorded participants' eye movements as they followed the instructions. Time course data, defined as the proportions of trials looking at the target at different moments, shows that in early moments of comprehension (between 180 and 600 ms) participants spent more time looking at the target object in the precedent condition compared to the no-precedent condition, independent of the speaker. At 600 ms, however, participants in the precedent-same speaker condition began looking more at the target than participants in the precedent-different speaker condition. This difference yields a significant interaction in the 1200 ms to 1500 ms window frame.

These results suggest that when relying on precedents does not yield a successful solution to the referential task (because of the presence of an ambiguity, for example), listeners make use of other information that potentially could be useful; in this case, information about the speaker's perspective (what the speaker does and doesn't know). The results, then, conflict with memory-based and multiple constraints approaches that argue that speakers' perspective is routinely integrated on comprehension along with other sources of information, and support a multiple process approach in which speakers' information is used and integrated on comprehension optionally, when other simple low-level heuristics fail.

Acknowledgments

We thank Shreya Bernejee, Kimberly Hazlewood and Danielle Pearson who assisted in collecting the data.

References

Barr, D.J., & Keysar, B. (2002). Anchoring comprehension in linguistic precedents. *Journal of Memory and Language, 46,* 391-418.

Brennan, S. & Clark, H.H. (1996). Conceptual pacts and lexical choice in conversation. *Journal of experimental Psychology: Learning, Memory annd cognition, 22,* 1482-1493.

Kronmüller, E., & Barr, D.J. (2006). Perspective-free pragmatics: Broken precedent and the recovery-from-preemption hyphothesis. *Journal of Memory and Language,* in press.

Metzing, C., & Brennan, S. E. (2003). When conceptual pacts are broken: Partner-specific effects on the comprehension of referring expressions. *Journal of Memory and Language, 49*(2), 201-213.

Multiple Word Meanings in the Strengthening of Semantic Operations

Christopher A. Was (CWAS@Kent.Edu)
Educational Foundations and Special Services, 405 White Hall
Kent, OH 44242

Introduction

Woltz and Was (2006) demonstrated an increased availability of long-term memory (ALTM) elements following attention-based processing in working memory (WM). Increased ALTM was measured using category comparison trials in which two category exemplars were simultaneously displayed and the goal of the task was to determine whether the displayed exemplars were from same or different categories. Increases in ALTM effects were found for exemplars of a category identified within the task and for a category not specifically identified, but only represented by exemplars as compared to exemplars of a category not present in the memory load. Woltz and Was (2006) concluded that the increased ALTM was due in part to strengthening of the specific memory operation demands of the category comparison trials.

The current study investigated the effects of the instantiation of the subordinate meaning of a homograph on the category comparison trials. Results indicated that the instantiation of the subordinate meaning of a homograph attenuated the increased availability related to the dominant meaning of that homograph.

Method

24 undergraduate students completed an experimental task adapted from the Woltz and Was (2006) ALTM task. The task consisted of four components: (1) four words presented in succession on a computer screen for 1500 ms each, comprised a memory load containing 2 biased homographs and 1 word related to the subordinate meaning of each homograph (homographs appeared before the related words) *arms...boxer...guns...poodle* (2) an instruction to remember a subset of the memory load based on the subordinate meaning of one homograph (focus homograph) designed to instantiate the subordinate meaning, *"Remember the words that mean weapons"* (3) recall of the selected subset and (4) a series of word meaning comparisons, required participants to determine if two simultaneously presented words were related. Following 2 warm-up comparison trials, 6 random trials were completed. Trials consisted of words related to the dominant meaning the focus homograph (FH: *foot/leg*) and the ignored homograph (IH: *beagle/hound/*), subordinate meaning of the FH (*missiles/bombs*) and the IH (*fighter/combatant*) or a homograph not presented (NP). For each type, there was one match and one non-match trial. 48 biased homographs were chosen from published norms. Dominant meanings of biased words had a mean probability of 0.70. Subordinate meanings had a mean probability of 0.21. One third of the homographs were used as the focused, ignored, and not-presented category counter balanced across subjects. Participants completed 16 trials.

Results

Figure 1 displays the mean speed for the comparisons trials of words related to the subordinate and dominant meanings of the FH, IH, and NP. Comparison trials related to the dominant meaning of the IH were significantly faster than those for the dominant meaning of the FH, $F (1,24) = 6.06$, $\underline{MSe} = 116.47$. The contrast between the dominant FH and NP comparison trials, was not significant. The contrast between the NP and the subordinate meaning of the FH comparison trials was significant, $F(1,24) = 7.16$, $\underline{MSe} = 88.61$. Contrast analysis completed with proportion correct data displayed the same pattern of results. All contrasts provided evidence that in the absence of context, access to the dominant meaning of a homograph is increased unless the subordinate meaning is subsequently instantiated.

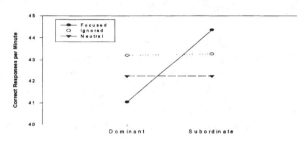

Figure 1: Mean correct responses for relatedness comparisons by category of memory load.

Discussion

The results provided evidence that the dominant meaning of a homograph, of which the subordinate meaning was instantiated, is no longer highly accessible. In the memory load, the dominant meanings of the FH and IH were represented an equal number of times (the homograph only), yet there was a significant difference in facilitation of the dominant meanings of these words as measured by response speed and proportion correct to related comparison trials. It was concluded that the "inhibition" effect is a reduction in the strength of the specific memory procedure.

References

Woltz, D. J., & Was, C. A. (2006). Activation in long-term memory before and after attention focus in working memory. *Memory and Cognition, 34*(3), 668-684.

Are Scalar Inferences Local Processes?

Bart Geurts (bart.geurts@phil.ru.nl)
Department of philosophy, University of Nijmegen
Postbox 9103, 6500 HD Nijmegen, The Netherlands

Nausicaa Pouscoulous (pouscoulous@isc.cnrs.fr)
Institut Jean Nicod
1bis, Avenue de Lowendal, 75007 Paris, France

It is widely agreed that (1) may give rise to the inference that (2) holds, as well, and that this scalar inference (SI) is not an ordinary entailment:

(1) Some of the goats are sick.

(2) Not all of the goats are sick.

According to classical Gricean account, (2) is a conversational implicature based on the proposition expressed by (1); i.e. results from a global process. According to the localist account which has been gaining support recently (e.g. Levinson, Landman, Chierchia), the "not all" inference is more or less directly associated with the word *some*, and is evaluated locally, even before the complete meaning of the sentence has been computed. The two accounts make different predictions about the interpretation of scalar expressions occurring in the scope of, e.g., quantifiers, modals, or attitude verbs. For example, while the localist account predicts that (3) should imply (4), the Gricean account predicts a weaker SI, namely (5):

(3) Every lawyer sent some of his clients a bill.

(4) No lawyer sent all of his clients a bill (i.e. every laywer did not send a bill to all of his clients).

(5) Not every lawyer sent all of his clients a bill.

The localist account also leads us to expect that the derivation of SIs should not be task-dependent, and that there should be no differences between scalar expressions (e.g. *some* vs. *or*).

We report on two pairs of experiments aimed at clarifying the nature of SIs. In the first two experiments, we employed an inference task: we asked participants, e.g., whether (2) and (4) follow from (1) and (3), respectively. Our results show that the rates at which SIs are derived fall dramatically if a scalar expression is embedded under an operator. For example, while 59% of our participants infer (2) from (1), only 34% infer (4)

from (3). Furthermore, the decrease is not constant across embeddings, which is not in accord with the localist view, either. Finally, we found that *some* is associated with higher rates of SIs than *or*.

Our second pair of experiments explored to what extent the derivation of SIs is task-dependent. In one experiment we compared the inference task with a verification task, in which participants had to judge whether a sentence is true in a given situation presented in a picture. For example, using a sentence like (6), the inference task would be to decide if this sentence implies that not all of the A's are in the box on the right, while in the verification task participants had to decide whether the sentence is true in a situation in which all the A's are in the box on the right.

(6) Some of the A's are in the box on the right.

The main result was that the verification task gives rise to significantly lower rates of SIs. Moreover, the difference between *or* and *some* was confirmed in both tasks.

Finally, we compared the inference task with a consistency-checking task, in which participants had to say whether (6) is consistent with the possibility that all the A's are in the box on the right. Here we found more or less the same pattern of results as in the previous experiment, except that the decrease in SI rates was less sharp.

Overall our results argue against a localist account of scalar inferences, while they are attuned with the gloablist view.

Word order and Type of relation effects in Conceptual Combination during the early school years

Sandra Jhean-Larose (jhean@paris.iufm.fr)
IUFM de Paris et Laboratoire Cognition & Usages
Université Paris VIII France
Guy Denhière (denhiere@up.univ-mrs.fr)
Laboratoire de Psychologie Cognitive
UMR 6146 au CNRS et Université de Provence France

The present research addresses how people interpret novel conceptual combinations. In understanding a novel combination « Noun-Noun », how do people determine the relation that links its constituents. In english compounds, the first word or Modifier attaches further meaning to the second word or Head noun, thus creating a reference to the intended concept. According to Gagné & Shoben's (1997) Competition Among Relations in Nominals (CARIN) theory, there is a fixed, relatively small taxonomy of standard relations (Levi, 1978) that can be used to link the modifier and head noun concepts. The most evidence for the CARIN model is the finding that the more frequently a relation is associated with the modifier noun, the easier it is to judge that the combination is sensible.

The first goal of this study was to investigate whether the alleged importance of the modifier in relation selection is due to the fact that it comes first or whether it can be attributed to the modifier's functional role. Accordingly, we conducted our study in French, language in which the order of the nouns is the reverse of English : the head noun precedes the modifier and we studied the effect of the order of presentation of combination's constituents on interpretation. The second goal of this research focuses in two types of conceptual combinations : property combinations and relational combinations. In a property combination, a property of the first word in the combination is selected to be carried over to the second word (« Elephant Garlic ») Property interpretations are thought to involve the construction of a new meaning (Wisniewski, 1997). A relational combination establishes some kind of unique relation between two words. Wisniewski's Dual Process theory creates a comprehensive model of conceptual combinations to explain both relational and property interpretation kinds (1997). So, a total of 24 conceptual combinations were used, 12 of which were property combinations and 12 were relational combinations. Finally, the effects of the order of presentation of the constituents and the type of combinations, property and relational, were studied with 3 groups of 6 ; 8 and 10 year-olds children.

Production Experiment

We carried out an experiment in which the participants (n=150) were asked to orally produce an interpretation to 2*12 combinations presented in the Modifier→ Head Noun order for half of the participants and in the reverse order for the other half.

Evidence of Word order, Type of conceptual combinations and Age effects

The results clearly contradict CARIN's principle that the Head Noun has little effect on the interpretation process (Maguire & Cater, 2005. The majority of the interpretations produced followed the Head noun → Modifier order and they were signficantly more numerous in the Head noun→ Modifier order (=17,8) than in the reverse order (m=13,2), F (1,144)= 92,861, p<.001. This effect increased as fuction as Age, F (2,144)= 6,348, p<.002. Participants responded mostly in establishing a relation between the 2 constituents, and this answer was more frequent for relational combinations than for property ones, F (1,144)= 20,553, p<.001. Interpretations consisting in tranferring a property significantly increased as function as Age for property combinations, F (2,144)= 4,03, p<.007. When the participants produced a relation, the nature of this relation was identical to the a priori relation induced by the experimentators (Part of, Localisation, Goal, Cause, Material and Made of) in more than 91,6%. For the property combinations, the «localization » and « look like » relations were the most frequent (65,0% and 8,2%, respectively).

References

Gagné, C. L. & Shoben, E. J. (1997). Influence of thematic relations on the comprehension of modifier-noun combinations. *Journal of Experimental Psychology : Learning, Memory and Cognition*, 23, 71-87.

Wisniewski, E. J. (1997). When concepts combine. *Psychonomic Bulletin and Review*, 4, 167-183.

Maguire, P. & Cater, A. (2005) Turnip Soup : Head Noun influence on the comprehension of Noun-Noun Combinations. *In Proceedings of the twenty seventh Annual Conference of the Cognitive Science Society* , Strese, Italy. Hillsdale, NJ :: Erlbaum.

Cognitive Modeling of Human Planning and Human Interaction

Alexandre Pauchet (LIPN - UMR 7030 , pauchet@lipn.univ-paris13.fr)
Nathalie Chaignaud (LITIS - EA 4051, chaignaud@insa-rouen.fr)
Amal El Fallah Seghrouchni (LIP6 - UMR 7606, Amal.ElFallah@lip6.fr)

We aim at developing a computational model of human planning and interaction. A psychological experiment was conducted, during which subjects had to solve a problem related to a travel-agency application. Each solving produces three experimental protocols (actions recorded by the software interface, emails exchanged and verbalization noted by an experimenter). A set of protocols were analyzed to design the cognitive models and the remaining protocols were used for the validation of these models. The analysis was conducted from two points of view: human planning and human interaction.

The cognitive models

The planning model.

The protocols were analyzed individually to construct a planning model which uses the notions of *phase* (the different situations during the problem-solving), *state of mind* (the problem constraints taken into account), *strategies* (the way plans are built), *tactics* (the different choices of actions to be performed), *observations* (that subjects can make about the current situation) and *personality* (the individual differences between subjects).

The interaction model

Each three protocols were merged and analyzed considering both the utterance level and the discourse level.

Messages were matched with a *performative*, either *descriptives*, *directives* or *commissives*, referring to the speech act theory [Searle, 1969]. A performative is applied to a mental state (a belief or a desire), the scope of which is a predicate: a *descriptive* is applied to a *belief*, a *directive* is applied to a *desire of the sender* and a *commissive* is applied to a *desire of the receiver*.

At the discourse level, the analysis is based on Vanderveken's work [Vanderveken, 2001]. The experimental protocols were divided into *exchanges* (a set of bounded messages). Each of these exchanges is guided by the initiator's discourse goal, according to the first performative he sent. The way exchanges end defines their satisfaction. Nevertheless, an exchange can be considered as finished by the interlocutors even without explicit emission of an ending performative. Time is important regarding to re-queries and to terminate exchanges. Therefore, timed automata [Alur and Dill, 1994] are used to model these message exchanges and the temporality. To represent the observed exchanges, a pair of automata (an automaton for each interlocutor) is designed for each type of exchange.

A semantics of the performatives has been designed, in terms of beliefs and desires. Using beliefs and desires in both the syntax and the semantics of a performative, links the utterance and the discourse levels in our human interaction model.

Simulation and validation

The cognitive models are implemented into an agent architecture called BDIGGY. A BDIGGY instance is an agent which imitates a subject's behavior. To simulate the travel-agency problem, three BDIGGY agents have been running simultaneously, generating new artificial protocols through the interface.

The validation is based on a Turing-like test: experts were asked to hand analyze a random set of mixed protocols (human or artificial) and to classify them according to their type. The main result is that experts are not able to reliably separate the two classes of protocols.

Conclusion

This study deals with three main issues: cognitive modeling, human cooperative planning and human interaction. It proposes a complete study, from the collection of the experimental protocols to the implementation of the simulation system and its validation. The architecture of the cooperative planning model is generic, only the domain specialists have to be re-implemented to support another problem. The interaction model is exhaustive concerning the information-search dialogs. It has to be extended to other kind of dialogs. More details about this research can be found in [Pauchet, 2006].

References

[Alur and Dill, 1994] Alur, R. and Dill, D. L. (1994). A theory of timed automata. *Theoretical computer science*, 126:183–235.

[Pauchet, 2006] Pauchet, A. (2006). *Modélisation cognitive d'interactions humaines dans un cadre de planification multi-agents*. PhD thesis, University of Paris 13, Villetaneuse.

[Searle, 1969] Searle, J. (1969). *Speech Acts – An Essay in the Philosophy of Language*. Cambridge Press.

[Vanderveken, 2001] Vanderveken, D. (2001). Illocutionary logic and discourse typology. *Revue Internationale de philosophie*, 55(216):243–255.

Path planning under spatial uncertainty

Matthieu Lafon, Jan M. Wiener, Alain Berthoz
({matthieu.lafon, jan.wiener, alain.berthoz}@college-de-france.fr)
LPPA, Collège de France / CNRS
11, place Marcelin Berthelot, 75005 Paris, France

Introduction

In this work we investigate human path planning and navigation behavior under spatial uncertainties. The experimental task is analogous to the following scenario: "As you leave work to go home you realize that you have forgotten your keys at home so you can not enter your house. You know, however, that your colleague, who has another set of keys, goes to a dinner in a restaurant at 6 pm and will visit one of the nearby bars afterwards. Obviously, the probability to still find your colleague in the restaurant depends on the time you are leaving work. Given different timings, what is the best path, i.e. in which order should you visit the restaurant and the different bars, to find your colleague, get the keys, and get home as quickly as possible". What is being described here is a path planning task with an intermediate target whose exact whereabouts is uncertain, but which can be described by a probability matrix over multiple places. This probability matrix varies with different timings. With advancing time, the probability to find your colleague in the restaurant decreases, while the probability to find your colleague in one of the bars increases. In order to solve the task described here, one not only has to minimize distance in order to visit the possible target places, but one also has to take into account the probability to find the target in the different places. Up to now, only few studies investigated path planning behavior (e.g. Gärling & Gärling, 1988; Wiener et al., 2004), and to our knowledge path planning under uncertainty has not yet been studied in humans. Special interest in this study concerned the decision strategies and heuristics applied when solving path planning tasks under spatial uncertainty, because humans could not compute all solutions in this task.

Task

14 Subjects participated in this experiment (7 males, 7 females). Subjects' task was to navigate the shortest possible path from the startpoint to find a target, hidden in one of 4 places (A,B,C,O), and to bring that target to the endpoint. Subjects were told that the target was at the origin (O) at the beginning of each trial, and that with a certain probability (jump probability), the target would jump to one of the remaining three target places (A,B,C). Thus, the probability to find the target was different for the 4 places (probability matrix). The jump probability varied between three conditions (10%,50%,90%). Given such uncertainties about the target's location, path planning becomes quite challenging. Rather than planning a single path, subjects had to generate, what we call meta-plans consisting of multiple path plans. For example, if the target was found in place A, subjects directly proceeded to the endpoint; if, however, the target was not found in place A, subjects had to proceed to the next place. The optimal meta-plan, rendering the shortest average path length if repeatedly applied, depends on the probability matrix. In each experiment, naïve subjects first received 30 training trials to learn the jump probability. In the test phase, they were asked to judge the jump probability and to navigate the optimal meta-plan for the current probability matrix.

Results and discussion

Subjects showed very good performance in the test phase (2.28 percent above optimal [PAO]). Performance systematically differed between the different jump probabilities (10%: 0.28 PAO, 50%: 5.23 PAO, 90%: 1.33 PAO and subjects judged the actual jump probabilities quite precisely (9.43%, 47.14%, 82.75%). Overall, the quality of the chosen paths in the test-phase demonstrates effective integration of the probability matrix during path planning. We present 2 simple planning heuristics that could account for subjects' navigation behavior as well as for systematic errors and performance differences between the three experiments: A *Cluster*-strategy, stating a clustering of space and predicting that subjects explore cluster by cluster, and a *Rich Target First*-strategy predicting that subjects first visit places with high probabilities to hold the target.

Conclusion

Subjects solved the path planning tasks fastly and efficiently. Obviously, rather than actually calculating and comparing all possible path alternatives, human navigators rely on strategies and heuristics allowing for the reduction of cognitive effort while resulting in reasonably short paths. This work allows for first insights into path planning strategies and heuristics under spatial uncertainties.

Acknowledgments

Matthieu Lafon benefits from a 3-year grant from EDF for his PhD. thesis.

References

Gärling, T. & Gärling, E. (1988). Distance minimization in downtown pedestrian shopping. *Environment and Planning A, 20*, 547–554.

Wiener, J. M., Schnee, A., & Mallot, H. A. (2004). Use and Interaction of Navigation Strategies in Regionalized Environments. *Journal of Environmental Psychology, 24*(4), 475 – 493.

Interactivist navigation

Jean-Luc Basille (basille@enseeiht.fr)
Jean-Christophe Buisson (buisson@enseeiht.fr)
Jean-Charles Quinton (quinton@enseeiht.fr)
Institut de Recherche en Informatique de Toulouse (IRIT-ENSEEIHT)
2, rue Charles Camichel, BP 7122 - F 31071 Toulouse Cedex 7 France

Introduction

Moving in any complex environment for a natural or artificial agent mostly requires understanding the changes caused by its own actions – saccades, limb movements – and external dynamics. It must also subordinate and regulate this behavior to more abstract tasks such as goal reaching. From local anticipations in the visual field to understanding context or determining location, navigation can be approached as a network of activities.

Classical approaches

In more classical approaches, segmentation is performed on a frame to identify and label all objects of interest. Apart from computational complexity, they are faced with the problem of matching objects from frame to frame, sometimes losing them because of perceptual noise. Without any sense of object permanency, occlusion is equivalent to disappearance. When using optical flow balance to stay far from obstacles, similar problems occur when objects come in and go out of the visual field.

Interactivist framework

In order to fully integrate the agent's actions, the world dynamics and their concomitant effects on sensors, we propose to use a network of regulative and anticipative interactions. The approach is based on the general framework of interactivism, developed by Bickhard, which find echoes in enaction and Piaget's constructivist theory. These interactive processes link eye and body movements to retinal projections of the environment elements of all sizes and levels of detail. For a car to stay on the road, regulating interactions in order to remain in a stable pattern of activity inside the network is sufficient and no precise recognition is necessary. This pattern is at the same time modulated by higher order processes, influencing factors such as speed, direction or risk taking.

Computer implementation

To illustrate this model in a more concrete way, we apply it to a car driving computer program using a custom made simulator. It allows us to vary the experimental situations at will, from road signs to lighting conditions, and reduce commands to steering, braking and accelerating. The agent is composed by a set of sensori-motor interactions, whose size depends on learning and targeted behavior complexity. Regulated actions and anticipations, present at every level, are cooperating directly or through the environment. To show that such a structure is already present in low level visual processes, we model MT-cells existing in visual cortex, which detect local motion and exhibit a proto-anticipatory behavior. Following a road then implies moving away from environment elements having anticipated trajectory towards the agent.

Problems addressed

This approach can be applied to other sensory modalities as we previously experimented with music recognition. In this navigation application we are dealing with common theoretical problems found in psychology and robotics, namely: symbol grounding problem, internal error criterion, perceptual constancy, object permanency, integrating the impact of action on perception, attention, motivation, skill learning and memory.

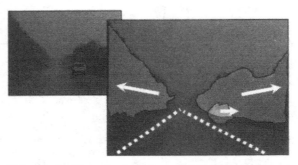

Figure 1: Anticipated trajectories and objects (dashes) based on local motion detectors in a noisy car driving scene.

References

Bickhard, M. H. (2004) The Dynamic Emergence of Representation. In H. Clapin, P. Staines, P. Slezak (Eds.) *Representation in Mind: New Approaches to Mental Representation.* (pp. 71-90). Elsevier.

Buisson, J-C. (2004) A rhythm recognition computer program to advocate interactivist perception. In Cognitive Science 28 (pp. 75-88). Elsevier.

Diaz, J., Ros, E., Mota, S., Rotella, G., Cañas, A. and Sabatini, S.P. (2003).Optical flow for cars overtaking monitor: the rear mirror blind spot problem, *10th. International Conference on Vision in Vehicles (VIV'2003), Granada (Spain).*

O'Regan, J.K., Noë, A. (2001) A sensorimotor account of vision and visual consciousness, In *Behavioral and Brain Sciences*, 24(5), (pp. 939-1011).

What's in a Mental Model? On Conceptual Imagery in Reasoning

Göran Hagert (goran.hagert@ts.mah.se)
School of Technology and Society, Malmö University School
SE 20506 Malmö, Sweden

The Mental Model Challenge

The nature of reasoning as performed by the mind is a well-researched phenomenon and various explanations (i.e., theories) have been exposed in the literature. It is a challenge in many ways. The study of reasoning is also a route to a deeper understanding of the cognitive architecture principles.

This paper reports on an ongoing project in modeling mental models. As the notion is used here, a *mental model* represents the phenomenon we want to understand and explain. Figure 1 shows the view taken in the project. The mental model is a major part of the task environment. It consists of three component structures of which the conceptual model is the generative mechanism as well as the semantics of the task domain at hand.

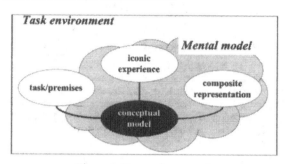

Figure 1: Processing overview

The work by Byrne and Johnson-Laird (Byrne & Johnson-Laird, 1989) and Goodwin and Johnson-Laird (Goodwin & Johnson-Laird, 2005) forms a solid empirical background for the theoretical work on "iconic reasoning".

Earlier work by Hagert (1985) and Rayner, Hugosson and Hagert (1988) provides a "Logic Modeling" (c.f., Hagert, 1985) framework for studying cognitive reasoning and qualities of a cognitive architecture.

Task environment: single vs. multiple "views"

A on right of B	B on right of A
C on left of B	C on left of B
D in front of C	D in front of C
E in front of A	E in front of A
Relation between D and E?	**Relation between D and E?**

Figure 2: Task examples

Reasoning about Spatial Relations

Figure 2 contains two examples of tasks used in the literature (Goodwin & Johnson-Laird, 2005). As can be verified the only difference between the two tasks hides in premise #1. In fact, if we try to sketch the layouts we will see that one has a single view whereas the other has two. What consequences does this indetermination have on cognitive reasoning?

Assuming a conceptual model containing the semantics of spatial concepts and relations, it is possible to experiment and simulate different inference paths. Figure 3 depicts a snap-shot during processing of two premises above.

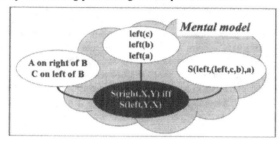

Figure 3: Knowledge state example

Summary

The main contribution to the cognitive reasoning area is the *component structure* of mental models. In fact, the theory very briefly outlined, assumes that a generative mechanism can explain the dual perspective on experience: sometimes iconic and sometimes abstract. The particular emphasis during reasoning is dependent on the task environment. Moreover, the feeling of "knowing" or "seeing" is dependent on the chosen interpretation driven by domain knowledge.

References

Byrne, M. J. & Johnson-Laird, P. N. (1989). Spatial Reasoning. *Journal of Memory and Language*, 28.

Goodwin, G. P. & Johnson-Laird, P. N. (2005). Reasoning about Relations. *Psychological Review*, 112.

Hagert, G. (1985). What's in a mental model? *On conceptual models in reasoning with spatial descriptions. Proceedings of the ninth International Joint Conference on Artificial Intelligence*, Los Angeles, USA, 274 – 277.

Rayner, M., Hugosson, Å. & Hagert, G. (1988). Using a logic grammar to learn a lexicon. *Proceedings of the 12th conference on Computational linguistics*, Budapest, Hungry, 524 – 529.

Causal, Counterfactual Reasoning and Type of Causal Chains

William Jimenez-Leal (W.Jimenez@warwick.ac.uk)
Department of Psychology, University of Warwick, Coventry, CV5 7AL, England, UK

Nick Chater (N.Chater@ucl.ac.uk)
Department of Psychology, University College of London, Gower Street - London - WC1E 6BT UK

Introduction

Mandel (2003) introduced the Judgement Dissociation Theory (JDT) to explain the apparent mismatch between factors identified in causal and counterfactual reasoning. According to JDT, causal reasoning identifies sufficient factors in the production of the effect, whereas counterfactual reasoning focuses on prevention by means of altering enabling conditions.

However, this dissociation seems to depend on factors external to the reasoning process, such as the type of causal chain. In the experiments that proved the dissociation, only cases of preemptive causation chains were used. In this type of chain many causes act in parallel, undermining the counterfactual dependence of the effects on their causes (Lewis, 2001). JDT has not been tested in the case of linear causal chains that relate more than two events.

Using different kinds of causal chains allows us to either extend the dissociation effect or test its limits. With this objective, the experiment reported here used two other causal chains (described in Hilton et al (2005)): unfolding and coincidental. In the former, the first event described is an enabling condition, whereas in the latter, all events hold the same causal status.

For causal judgments, JDT predicts that in both types of chain, people will focus on the most recent events previous to the effect, as they are sufficient to cause the effect. For counterfactual judgments, in the case of the unfolding chain people would focus on the enabling factor while there is no prediction for the coincidental chain as there is not a specific event acting as enabling condition.

However, these predictions are clearly at odds with causal order effects where the first element of a causal chain tends to be undone by counterfactual reasoning (Segura et al, 2002). Attribution of causality would also match this pattern, according to Segura et al (2002), where counterfactual alternatives are actually elicited by the initial causal representation of the situation. The following experiment tests JDT in presence of order effects.

Method

57 students answered causal and counterfactual attribution questions about the events of the two types of causal chains. Participants read a story for each causal chain and had to rate from 1 to 10 the causal importance of each of the elements presented and also the counterfactual efficacy of altering the elements in undoing the outcome. The order between the tasks was counterbalanced and the item presentation was randomized.

Results and Discussion

2(type of causal chain) X 2(position in chain) X 2(judgment type) repeated measures ANOVA was used to test if there was any difference in causal and counterfactual efficacy ratings depending on the kind of causal chain and the position of the event in it. Results are summarized in figure 1.

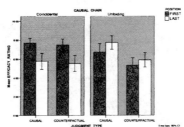

Fig 1. Mean efficacy ratings by causal chain and judgement type

There is a significant difference between the ratings according to the type of causal chain and the position in the sequence. $(F_{(6,56)}=10.1, p<.05)$. In the coincidental chain the first event was rated as both more effective in undoing the situation and more causally effective $(F_{(1,56)}=5.8, p<.05)$. In the unfolding chain there was no significant difference between the counterfactual efficacy between the events, and the first event was considered as causally effective as the last. $(F_{(2,56)}=1.8, p=.35)$, contrary to the prediction by JDT.

This result is not effectively explained by JDT and, contrary to what JDT proposes, it suggests that causal event representation is closely linked with its counterfactual possibility during reasoning, in at least some causal chains.

References

Hilton, D.J. McClure, J.L. & Slugoski, B.R. (2005). The course of events: Counterfactuals, causal sequences and explanation. In D. Mandel, D.J. Hilton & P. Catellani (Ed.).*The psychology of counterfactual thinking*. London: The Psychology Press.

Mandel, D. R. (2003). Judgment dissociation theory: An analysis of differences in causal, counterfactual, and covariational reasoning. *Journal of Experimental Psychology: General, 137*, 419-434.

Lewis, D. (1986): *Philosophical Papers: Volume II*. Oxford: OUP.

Segura, S., Fernandez-Berrocal, P., & Byrne, R. M. J. (2002). Temporal and causal order effects in thinking about what might have been. *Quarterly Journal of Experimental Psychology, 55A*, 1295-1305.

How Children reason about probabilities: the *Conjunction Fallacy* and the *Framing Effect*

Gabriella Passerini (gabriella.passerini@unimib.it)
Università degli Studi di Milano- Bicocca
Piazza dell'Ateneo Nuovo 1- 20123 Milano

Valentina Sala (valentina.sala@unimib.it)
Università degli Studi di Milano- Bicocca
Piazza dell'Ateneo Nuovo 1- 20123 Milano

Introduction

The vast majority of researches in decision making have been conducted with adults rather than children.

A question addressed by the present research with children is whether children commit the same errors of adults in two judgmental tasks: a conjunction task and a choice task modelled on the standard Asian Disease Problem (Tversky &Kahneman, 1981).

Conjunction Fallacy

While adults are known to exhibit biases when making conjunctive probability judgments, little is known about childhood competencies in this area.

The conjunction fallacy is a reasoning error in which the conjunction of two events (A & B) is judged more probable than one of its single constituent (e.g. A), violating the Conjunction Rule which states that the probability of the conjunction of two events is always less than or equal to the probability of each event on its own.

Fisk and Slattery (2005) found that children aged between 4 and 5 years, and 8 and 10 years committed the conjunction fallacy in probabilistic task in which the objective probability of the critical event was available.

We conducted a control task (Fisk & Slattery, 2005) and two experiments to explore whether children aged between seven and thirteen years commit the conjunction fallacy because they don't have the Logical Rule of Inclusion or because they adequate their answers to the structure of the task.

Findings and discussion

Under a specific construction of the text, which don't alter the structure of the original problem of Fisk and Slattery (2005), children of all age are able to reason in according to the Logical Rules without committing the Conjunction Fallacy.

Framing Effect

Judgment and choice under uncertainty are basic to everyday cognition and there has been much interest in the principles that guide them. Normatively, a rational decision-maker should always act so as to maximise Expected Value (EV), defined as the multiplicative conjunction of goal value and the likelihood of attaining it (von Neumann & Morgenstern, 1947).

The Framing Effect is the systematic tendency of risk aversion in the positively framed problem and of risk seeking in the negatively framed problem (Tversky & Kahneman, 1981).

Schlottman and Tring (2005) found that children's choices, like adults', show the framing effect.

We conduct two experiments to explore how children reason about wins and losses, framed positively or negatively. The task had the same structure of the original Asian Disease Problem (Tversky &Kahneman, 1981) but adequate to children's age (9 years old). In the experiment 1 the expected value was 0,33 and in the experiment 2 the expected value was 0,50.

Findings and discussion

In the two experiments children made risky choices both in win and in loss situations without confirming the *Framing Effect*. These findings can be explained by the fact that the stimuli used were visual and children have immediately access to the complementary alternatives of the choices presented even if it was not explicit. This explanation is in accord with Jou, Shanteau and Harris's study about *Framing Effect* in adults.

References

Fisk, J. E. & Slattery, R. (2005). Reasoning About Conjunctive Probabilistic Concepts in Childhood. *Canadian Journal of Experimental Psychology*, 59,168-178.

Jou, J., Shanteau, J. & Harris, R. J. (1996). An information processing view of framing effects: The role of causal schemas in decision making. *Memory & Cognition*, 24, 1-15

Schlottmann, A. & Tring, J. (2005). How children reason about gains and losses: framing effects in judgement and choice. *Swiss journal of psychology*, 64, 153-171

Tversky, A., & Kahneman, D. (1981). The framing of decisions and the psychology of choice. *Science, 211*, 453–458.

von Neumann, J. & Morgenstern, O. (1947). *Theoy games and economic behavior..* Princeton, N.J., Princeton University Press.

The Dilution Effect in Legal Judgments by Individuals

Valentina Sala (valentina.sala@unimib.it)
Department of Psychology
University of Milano Bicocca, ITALY

Gabriella Passerini (gabriella.passerini@unimib.it)
Department of Psychology
University of Milano Bicocca, ITALY

The Dilution Effect (DE) refers to a tendency to produce less extreme judgments, when diagnostic information is presented together with some pieces of non-diagnostic information (Nisbett, Zukier & Lemley, 1981).

Dilution in Legal Judgment

The influence of the DE upon judgment has been demonstrated also in jury contexts (Smith, Stasson & Hawkes, 1998), with the aim of verifying if its consequences could affect criminal trials. Smith et al. found results consistent with a DE, only when there was a 4-1 ratio of non-diagnostic information to diagnostic information.

We want to verify this claim, by maintaining the 4-1 ratio, with a particular kind of relevant information. We suppose that it could be not only the quantity of evidence (the 4-1 ratio), but also its quality (e.g. physical evidence vs. eyewitness) to influence judgment and that different types of evidence would lead to different judgments, diluted or not.

We decided to investigate the DE with a piece of physical evidence as diagnostic information, because it is usually looked at as a definite event, by naïf subjects.

The aim of the following experiment is to verify if 4 pieces of non-diagnostic information could "dilute" a guilty judgment that is based upon a piece of physical evidence, which assumes different diagnostic values.

Experimental Research

The study investigates the DE in a legal judgment task involving the case scenario of a crime taken from the Wagenaar et al. collection (1993). A manipulation of the pieces of evidence was made in order to obtain 4 pieces of diagnostic information and 8 pieces of non-diagnostic information. The irrelevance of non-diagnostic information was tested in a control task.

The 4 pieces of diagnostic information describe a physical evidence (traces of gunpowder): 2 of them have a High Diagnostic Value (Incriminating or Exonerating) while the others have a Slight Diagnostic Value (Incriminating or Exonerating). Evidence with a H.D.V. confirm a story and disconfirm the other, at the same time. Evidence with a S.D.V. only verifies one narrative, without falsifying the other.

Non-diagnostic information is neutral or irrelevant for the trial, but 4 have a Positive value for the defendant while the other 4 have a Negative value.

Eight case scenarios were prepared: 4 of them presented only 1 diagnostic piece of evidence; the others presented the diagnostic evidence together with 4 non-diagnostic pieces of evidence. Incriminating diagnostic information was paired with positive non-diagnostic information and vice-versa.

Subjects (160 non-law students) were presented with one of the case scenario (20 subjects for each one). They had to judge the defendant as guilty or not, to declare their rate of certainty for the judgment on a 10 points scale and to state which elements of the scenario had guided their decision.

A 2 (Value of Diagnostic information: High vs. Slight) x2 (added non-diagnostic information: presence vs. absence) log-linear analysis was conducted with the guilty judgment as dependant variable. Means of rates of certainty for the judgment were compared and a qualitative analysis of verbal protocols was carried out.

Findings and Discussion

We found no effect either for presence of non-diagnostic information or for the value of diagnostic information, with both incriminating and exonerating evidence.

Results seem to show that there is no DE: subjects based their judgment upon the diagnostic evidence and recognized non-diagnostic information as irrelevant. However, there is no difference between judgments based upon evidence with H.D.V. and evidence with a S.D.V. These data suggest that our subjects give a great importance at the physical nature of the proof, also when it is only confirming one story without falsifying the other.

A future proposal is to study different kinds of diagnostic evidence (e.g. eyewitnesses), in order to verify if the presence of DE can be due to the particular type of diagnostic evidence used in the scenario.

References

Nisbett, R.E., Zukier, H., & Lemley, R. (1981). The dilution effect: Nondiangostic information. *Cognitive Psychology, 13,* 248-277.

Smith, H.D., Stasson, M. F. & Hawkes, W. G. (1998-1999). Dilution in legal decision making: Effect of non-diagnostic information. *Current Psychology, 17 (4),* 333-345.

Wagenaar, W. A., van Koppen, P. J. & Crombag, H. F. M. (1993). *Anchored Narratives. The psychology of criminal evidence.* Hertfordshire, HP2 7EZ, England: Harvester Wheatsheaf.

Decisions from Experience under Comprehensive Sampling

Christoph Ungemach (C.Ungemach@Warwick.ac.uk)
Neil Stewart (Neil.Stewart@Warwick.ac.uk)
Department of Psychology, University of Warwick,
Coventry, CV4 7AL, UK

Nick Chater (N.Chater@ucl.ac.uk)
Department of Psychology, University College London,
Gower Street, London WC1E 6BT, UK

Introduction

Recent experiments in the domain of experienced-based decision making have revealed that people show a different choice behaviour when prior knowledge of the options's outcomes and probabilities are not available and have to instead be inferred from repeated choices or free exploration of the available options prior to the choice task (e.g. Hertwig, Barron, Weber & Erev, 2004; Weber, Shafir & Blais, 2004). Under these conditions people seem to make choices as if they underweight small probabilities. This stands in contrast to the findings in the literature on descriptive choice tasks where small probabilities are usually overweighted.

According to Hertwig et al. (2004) this behaviour is based on the combination of a reliance on small samples and overweighting of recently sampled information. The following two studies try to test if the described properties of the experiential choice task are in fact necessary conditions for the observation of this unusual choice pattern.

Method

In the first experiment 51 undergraduate students and members of staff from the University of Warwick had to choose from six pairs of lotteries with different expected values. The options within the pairs were presented in the form of two buttons on a computer screen. In an initial learning phase each button had to be explored 39 times. With every button click an outcome from the underlying payoff distribution of the button was sampled randomly and presented for one second. The order of the choice problems and their assignment to the two buttons was randomised. After the exploration of the options the participants had to indicate their preferred option within each pair.

In the second web-based experiment (n=197) the objective probabilities for each option were mapped onto a sequence of 40 samples per option to make the choice problems structurally more similar to the descriptive choice tasks.

Results and Discussion

In both experiments the percentages of maximizing choices for the six pairs were similar to the percentages found in the original decisions from experience experiment (r (4) = .81,

p=.049; r (4) = .90, p=.014). However, a comparison of the predictive power regarding the actual choice behaviour between the two halves of each sampling sequence did not confirm an overweighting of recently sampled outcomes.

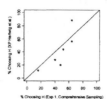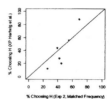

Figure 1: Similarity of percentages of maximizing choices.

These findings show that decision from experience can also be replicated when the participants are sampling more comprehensively and even when the experienced probabilities match the objective probabilities. The results therefore suggest that reliance on small samples and overweighting of recently sampled information are not necessary conditions for the underweighting of small probability events. To identify the properties responsible for the inversed choice behaviour future experiments should investigate the connection between decision from experience and frequency estimations which are widely assumed to be a crucial part of many cognitive processes (Hasher & Zacks, 1984).

Acknowledgments

This research is supported by the Economic and Social Research Council.

References

Hertwig, R., Barron, G., Weber, E. U., & Erev, I. (2004). Decisions from experience and the effect of rare events in risky choice. *Psychological Science, 15*(8), 534-539.

Weber, E. U., Shafir, S., & Blais, A. R. (2004). Predicting risk sensitivity in humans and lower animals: Risk as variance or coefficient of variation. *Psychological Review, 111*(2), 430-445.

Hasher, L., & Zacks, R.T. (1984). Automatic processing of fundamental information: The case of frequency of occurrence. *American Psychologist, 39*, 1372-1388.

The effect of spatial frequency on the perception of facial gender

Tim M Gale (t.gale@herts.ac.uk)
Samar Buchala (s.buchala@herts.ac.uk)
Neil Davey (n.davey@herts.ac.uk)
Ray Frank (r.j.frank@herts.ac.uk)

Department of Computer Science, University of Hertfordshire
College Lane, Hatfield, Herts, AL10 9AB, UK

Background

The human perceptual system is thought to decompose visual stimuli into different spatial frequencies (De Valois and De Valois, 1990). Images can be considered as a distribution of light intensities in 2 dimensions and, by using techniques like Fourier analysis, they can be represented by a set of sine waves of different frequencies and orientations at different phases. In face processing, it is thought that lower spatial frequencies are important for recognizing the more general characteristics of faces (e.g. sex, race), while higher spatial frequencies are more important for identifying specific individuals (Sergent, 1986). Recently Cellerino, Borghetti and Sartucci (2004) progressively quantized a series of human face images, such that higher-scale information was gradually reduced, and asked participants to identify the gender of the faces. A stimulus-gender by quantization-level interaction was reported with recognition accuracy for female faces decreasing proportionally as high-scale information was lost, whereas recognition accuracy for male faces remained relatively unimpaired. In other words, it seems that less information is required to classify a face as male. The corollary to this, which has not been explicitly tested, is that high scale information may be more important for classifying female faces. Previous work in this area has not examined higher-scale information independently of lower-scale information A test of this prediction would require a method of preserving high scale information while removing low-scale information. In the current study we compare the classification performance for male and female faces using Fourier-transformed variants of each face image to isolate high- and low-scale information respectively.

Method

The stimuli were 46 greyscale face images of 130x150 pixels (23 male, 23 female). Images were processed, using Fourier Transformation, such that they contained either lower spatial frequencies or higher spatial frequencies: low-pass filtering was applied to create images that contained frequencies below 10, 20, and 30 cycles/face, while high-pass filtering was applied to create images that contained frequencies above 10, 20, and 30 cycles/face. Thus for each of the 46 facial stimuli, 6 versions were created that varied in the level of high- and low-scale information present. The stimuli were presented in 6 different questionnaires. Each questionnaire contained one version of each face, with an equal proportion of male and female faces. Questionnaires included faces represented at different frequency cut-offs. 240 participants took part in a gender classification task (40 per questionnaire, 20 male, 20 female) and were asked to (i) state the gender of each face and (ii) state the level of confidence (1-5) attributed to their judgement.

Results & Conclusion

There was a main effect of stimulus gender with male faces being classified more accurately than female faces (means: 86% correct vs. 67% correct, $p < 0.0001$). This emphasizes the strength of the previously reported male bias. As expected, there was an effect of frequency cut-offs in the images: images displaying high spatial frequencies were classified more accurately than images displaying low spatial frequencies (for male faces, 90% vs. 81%, $p < 0.0001$; for female faces, 72% vs. 61%, $p < 0.0001$). Within each type of image (high vs. low frequency), there was a graded decline in accuracy as the number of included frequencies was reduced. Overall, there was a significant correlation between confidence and classification accuracy for male faces ($r = 0.5$, $p < 0.0001$). The correlation was considerably lower for female faces, though still significant ($r = 0.218$, $p < 0.0001$).

Acknowledgments

This study was supported by British Academy grant no. SG-42885.

References

Cellerino, A., Borghetti, D. and Sartucci, F. (2004). Sex differences in face gender recognition in humans. *Brain Research Bulletin, 63.* 443-449.

De Valois, R. L. and K. K. De Valois (1990). Spatial Vision. New York, Oxford University Press.

Sergent, J. (1986). Microgenesis of face perception. Aspects of face processing. H. D. Ellis, M. A. Jeeves, F. Newcombe and A. Young, Dordrecht: Martinus Nijhoff.

Meeting a Virtual Character: Effects of Characters' Emotional Expression on Eye Movements and Facial EMG of Human Observers

Franziska Schrammel (schrammel@applied-cognition.org)
Sven-Thomas Graupner (graupner@applied-cognition.org)
Sebastian Pannasch (pannasch@applied-cognition.org)
Boris M. Velichkovsky (velich@applied-cognition.org)
Institute of Psychology III, Unit of Engineering Psychology and Cognitive Ergonomics
Technische Universität Dresden, Helmholtzstrasse 10, Dresden, D-01069 Germany

Introduction

In social interaction, the human face is a complex source of information holding besides visible speech two crucial aspects for communication: gaze direction and facial expression. Both can be interpreted in terms of basal action dispositions like approach and avoidance (Adams & Kleck, 2003). Facial features are often investigated in static paradigms while their dynamic aspects are neglected. In a study by Schilbach et al. (2005), subjects watched short animated video sequences showing male and female virtual characters moving along the screen. The paradigm allowed the dynamic manipulation of gaze direction (towards observer vs. averted) and facial expression (socially relevant vs. arbitrary). After each video sequence the observer's task was to decide where the virtual character gazed and to evaluate the social relevance of the character's facial expression. These variables were found to have an influence on eye movements, facial muscle activity (Mojzisch et al., 2006), and the activation of different brain structures (Schilbach et al., 2005). The present study used the same paradigm but the characters showed facial expressions with different affective valences (happy, neutral, anger). Our aim was to investigate the influence of the characters' facial expression and gaze/ approach direction on the eye movements, facial expression and emotional experience of observers.

Methods

During the experiment 120 video clips were presented to 42 young adult subjects (21 females, 21 males). Each video clip began with the entrance of a virtual character on the screen (*walk in:* 0-1500 ms), followed by positioning either towards the observer or towards an imaginary third person located 30° to the left or to the right of the observer (*turn:* 1500-2500 ms). The character then displayed either a happy, an angry or a neutral facial expression with the apex at 3300 ms *(emotion:* 2500-5500 ms), turned away and walked out of the screen frame (5500-7500 ms).

Participants were instructed to be part of a virtual 3D scene standing between two other invisible agents. After each video clip subjects indicated whether the agent had looked at them directly or at a virtual other located aside. Furthermore they rated their experience of valence, arousal and dominance evoked by the character's facial expression on the Self-Assessment Manikin (SAM; Lang 1980). Eye movements and EMG activity (corrugator and zygomatic sites) were recorded during the experiment.

Results and Discussion

Analysis of the eyetracking data revealed significant effects of the agent's gender for both fixation duration during the *walk in* segment, $F(2,80) = 11.606, p < .001$, and pupil size, $F(1,40) = 14.567, p < .001$. Moreover, in the *turn* segment fixation duration was significantly longer if a virtual agent turned directly to the observer, $F(2,80) = 7.206, p = .001$. Fixations were also prolonged if the character displayed anger or a neutral facial expression compared to happiness $F(4,160) = 6.059, p < .001$. The EMG activity of corrugator and zygomatic muscles was reflective of the valence of the displayed emotional expression. Moreover, activity was significantly enhanced when observers were gazed at directly. Finally, the SAM ratings indicated that emotional experience was influenced both by displayed expression and, once again, by gaze direction.

We speculate that eye-to-eye contact amplifies and mediates sensory-motor and mental responses to facial expression, contributing in this way to such higher-order cognitive functions as constituting a theory of mind.

References

Adams, R.B., Jr., & Kleck, R.E. (2003). Perceived gaze direction and the processing of facial displays of emotion. *Psychological Science, 14*(6), 644-647.

Lang, P.J. (1980). Behavioral treatment and bio-behavioural assessment: Computer applications. In J. B. Sidowski, J. H. Johnson & T. A. Williams (Eds.), *Technology in mental health care delivery systems* (pp. 119-137). Norwood, NJ: Ablex.

Mojzisch, A., Schilbach, L., Helmert, J.R., Pannasch, S., Velichkovsky, B., & Vogeley, K. (2006). The effects of self-involvement on attention, arousal, and facial expression during social interaction with virtual others. *Social Neuroscience, 1*, 184-195.

Schilbach, L., Helmert, J.R., Mojzisch, A., Pannasch, S., Velichkovsky, B.M. & Vogeley, K. (2005). Neural correlates, visual attention and facial expression during social interaction with virtual others. *Proceedings of the First Workshop Toward Social Mechanisms of Android Science.* July 25-26, 2005, Stresa, Italy, pp. 74-86.

Political Semantic Concepts Investigated through Taylor's Paradigm

Mariangela Grimaudo (hyena@psicologia.unipa.it)
Department of Psychology, University of Palermo
viale delle Scienze ed. 15, 90128 Palermo Italy

Stefano Boca (shepherd@unipa.it)
Department of Psychology, University of Palermo
viale delle Scienze ed. 15, 90128 Palermo Italy

The spontaneous use of group types

Many studies have demonstrated that not all social groups are alike. First of all they differ in the extent to which they are perceived as coherent units (Campbell, 1958). Lickel et al. (2000) established that by using similarities and differences groups can be clustered into five different types.

Recently Sherman et al (2002) demonstrated, using Taylor's paradigm (1981), that this categorization of groups into group types is a spontaneous process. If the characteristics used to categorize groups into different typologies are automatically extracted, specific information about two groups that share the same group type (and therefore have similar defining characteristics) should be more likely to be confused.

Sherman's results showed that within-group-type errors were more likely than between-group-types errors.

Replicating this study in a political context, if the categorization of Italian political parties into political groups as "right", "left", and "centre" is a spontaneous process, we should expect to find the same results found by Sherman et al. (2002).

Experiment

Participants

Forty-nine participants, twenty-three males and twenty-six females.

Procedure

In the first phase of our experiment, participants saw 60 pictures (faces of Caucasians) on the screen. Below each picture there was label indicating a specific political party to which the person belonged. We chose the six political parties (two each for right, left and centre) that were the most representative of the three political concepts investigated.

In the first phase the participant's task was to look at the faces and to read aloud the labels. In the second one a recognition task was presented: the participants saw again the same pictures, this time without the label. Their task was to remember the political parties to which each person belonged, using six labeled keys on the computer keyboard.

Responses and their latencies were collected.

Results and discussion

We performed a 3 (type of group: right vs. left vs. centre) × 2 (direction of errors: within-group vs between-group) analysis of variance (ANOVA) as within-subject factors. We found a significant main effect for the direction of the errors. As predicted, within-group-type errors were more common than were between-group-types errors, $F(1,48) = 7,46$, $p<.01$ (see Figure 1). No other effect was significant. The results suggest that people spontaneously use the political concepts of "right", "left", and "centre" to organize the incoming information regarding political parties.

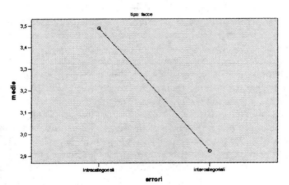

Figure 1: Main effect of the direction of errors.

References

Campbell, D. T. (1958). Common fate, similarity, and other indices of the status of aggregates of persons as social entities. *Behavioral Sciences, 3,* 14–25.

Lickel, B., Hamilton, D. L., Wieczorkowska, G., Lewis, A. C., Sherman, S. J., & Uhles, A. N. (2000). Varieties of groups and the perception of group entitativity. *Journal of Personality and Social Psychology, 78,* 223–246.

Sherman Steven J., Castelli Luigi, Hamilton David L.(2002). The Spontaneous Use of a Group Typology as an Organizing Principle in Memory. *Journal of Personality and Social Psychology, 82, 328-342*

Taylor, S. E. (1981). A categorization approach to stereotyping. In D. L. Hamilton (Ed.), *Cognitive processes in stereotyping and intergroup behavior.* Hillsdale, NJ: Erlbaum.

Categorical Perception of Emotions in Healthy People and Schizophrenics

Casati P. (Paola.Casati@pse.unige.ch)
Department of Psychology, 40 boulevard Pont-d'Arve
1211 Geneva, CH

Viviani P. (Paolo.Viviani@pse.unige.ch)
Department of Psychology, 40 boulevard Pont-d'Arve
1211 Geneva, CH

Introduction

Several studies (Etcoff & Magee, 1992; Calder et al. 1996; Viviani et al. 2007) suggested the presence of categorical perception (CP) for facial identity and facial expression of emotions. Schizophrenics suffer from disruptions of their emotional life, which may include an impaired recognition of facial expressions, particularly for negative emotions (Walker, 1981; Feinberg et al., 1986; Mandal, 1987; Kerr & Neal, 1993). We explored the possibility that one aspect of such impairment is a reduced ability to establish categorical boundaries between affective facial expressions.

Experiment

The aim of this experience is to compare the perception of facial expressions in controls and in schizophrenics, and to evaluate the extent to which CP is present in schizophrenic patients.

Method

Participants: Two groups have been tested. The experimental group included 10 schizophrenic patients aged from 19 to 30 years. The control group included 20 healthy subjects matched for age and sex.

Stimuli: High-quality colour pictures sampled from a morphing sequence transforming a neutral expression in the emotional expression of happiness or rage.

Procedure: Participants performed two tasks. In the identification task, for each image participants had to indicate (forced choice) whether the expression was closer to the neutral or to the emotional one. In the ABX discrimination task we presented sequentially three images $[S_A, S_B, S_X]$ from the morphing sequence between neutral and emotional expressions. S_A and S_B were at a fixed distance but varied in their position along the sequence. S_X was always equal S_A or S_B. Participants had to indicate which of the two possibilities had occurred.

Figure 1: Examples of stimuli.

Results

The identification task allowed us to estimate the point of subjective equality (PSE), and the discrimination power (JND) for the perception of facial expressions. Whenever CP occurs, the PSE corresponds to the boundary between categories. The results showed that schizophrenics perceive emotions later along the morphing sequence than controls. The shift of the PSE is larger for the negative emotion (rage) than for the positive one (happiness). For both emotions controls discriminate better than patients. Statistical analysis showed that, on both counts, the two groups differed significantly. The discrimination task investigated directly the CP issue by estimating the probability of a correct discrimination as a function of the position of the pair $[S_A, S_B]$ along the morphing sequence. CP occurs if this probability is higher when the pair $[S_A, S_B]$ straddles the PSE estimated by the identification task than in all other cases. Results show that such a local increase of the number of correct answers is statistically significant only in the control group for rage. In schizophrenics the number of correct answers was significantly lower than in controls. There was also a tendency toward CP for rage, which, however, failed to reach significance. No evidence of CP was found for happiness in either group.

References

Calder, A.J., Young, A.W., Perrett, D.I., Etcoff, N.L., & Rowland, D. (1996). Categorical perception of morphed facial expressions. *Visual Cognition, 3*, 81-117.

Etcoff, N.L., & Magee, J.J. (1992). Categorical perception of facial expressions. *Cognition, 44*, 227-240.

Feinberg, T.E., Rifkin, A., Schaffer, C., & Walker, E. (1986). Facial discrimination and emotional recognition in schizophrenia and affective disorders. *Archives of General Psychiatry, 43*, 276-279.

Kerr, S.L., & Neale, J.M. (1993). Emotion perception in schizophrenia: specific deficit or further evidence of generalized poor performance? *Journal of Abnormal Psychology, 102*, 312-318.

Mandal, M.(1987).Decoding the facial emotions in terms of expressiveness by schizophrenics.*Psychiatry,50*,371-376.

Viviani, P., Binda, P., & Borsato, T. (2007). Categorical perception of unfamiliar faces. *Visual cognition*, in press.

Walker, E. (1981). Emotion recognition in disturbed and normal children. *Journal of Child Psychology and Psychiatry, 22*, 263-269.

Deficits in Facial Affect Recognition in Bimodal Context in Greek Patients with Schizophrenia

Vasiliki Psarra (lilian4@otenet.gr)
Cognitive Science Lab, National and Kapodistrian University of Athens
Katerina Ligovanli (kaligova@phs.uoa.gr)
Cognitive Science Lab, National and Kapodistrian University of Athens
Nikolaos Dimopoulos (dmpnikos@yahoo.gr)
Mental Clinic « Asklipeion »
Athanase Tzavaras (atzavar@phs.uoa.gr)
Cognitive Science Lab, National and Kapodistrian University of Athens

Introduction

Deficits in the recognition of facial expressions of emotion in patients with schizophrenia are well known from several studies and across different cultures (Mandal et al, 1998). This deficit has been found to be more important for fear and sadness (Edwards et al, 2001). The underlying factors that may account for poorer emotion recognition are not well understood, however Sachs et al. (2004) propose that difficulties in emotion recognition in schizophrenia are associated with key cognitive deficits.

A study was performed in a Greek sample of patients with schizophrenia, in order to investigate possible deficits and the effects of bimodal context in the recognition of facial expressions.

Subjects

Six males and three females, with schizophrenia (paranoid subtype), aged between 31-49 years, participated in the study. The participants were either hospitalized in the 4th psychiatric department or residents of psychiatric hostels of psychiatric hospital of Attiki- "Dafni".

Materials

The visual stimuli consisted of eight photographs, one male and one female for each of the emotions of happiness, sadness, fear and surprise (Ekman & Friesen, 1976). The auditory stimuli were twelve verbal statements with neutral intonation, three for each of the four emotions, formulated and judged in a previous study with healthy participants to elicit these emotions e.g.: "You are promoted" for happines and "The house is on fire" for fear (Ligovanli & Vosniadou, 2006).

Procedure

"Bimodal scenes" were used, with congruent or incongruent emotional meaning of two variables (photograph-verbal statement). The result of the combination of the two variables was four congruent and four incongruent "bimodal contexts". The two stimuli were presented simultaneously for 2 seconds. The participants were instructed to attend to the facial expression and name the emotion in a total of 96 "bimodal scenes", choosing one out of four emotional terms: happiness, sadness, fear, surprise. The participants had to name the facial emotion in order to view the next "bimodal scene". There was no time limit for the response. The whole procedure was computerized and the type and time of response was recorded. The Positive and Negative Symptoms Scale was rated for all participants.

Results

Schizophrenia patients performed worse in the recognition of happiness, fear and surprise in both congruent and incongruent scenes compared to normal controls of a previous study (Ligovanli & Vosniadou, 2006). These deficits are statistically significant only concerning the recognition of surprise in both congruent [$p<.05$] and incongruent context [$p<.05$]. Patients with schizophrenia performed significantly better in the congruent context [$p<.05$].

Conclusion

Patients with schizophrenia present deficits in facial emotion recognition in both congruent and incongruent context. The modification of these deficits and the deterioration of the patients' performance in the incongruent context support the idea that a cognitive process underlies facial emotion recognition, which is probably impaired in patients with schizophrenia.

References

Edwards, J., Pattison, P. E., Jackson, J. E., Wales, R. J. (2001). Facial affect and affective prosody recognition in first-episode schizophrenia. *Schizophrenia Research*, 48, 235-253.

Ekman, P., & Friesen, W. V. (1976). Pictures of facial affect. Palo Alto, CA: Consulting Psychologists Press.

Ligovanli, K., Vosniadou, S. Context effects on facial emotion recognition. *Noisis*, 2, 75-103. In Greek.

Mandal, M., Pandey, R., Prasad, A. (1998). Facial expressions of emotion and schizophrenia-a review. *Schizophrenia Bulletin*, 24, 399-412.

Sachs, G., Steger-Wuchse, D., Kryspin-Exner, I, Gur, R. C., Katschning, H. (2004). Facial recognition deficits and cognition in schizophrenia. Schizophrenia Research, 68, 27-35.

Context Effects on Facial Emotion Attribution:
A replication of Kuleshov Experiment

**Katerina Ligovanli (kaligova@phs.uoa.gr), Athanase Tzavaras (atzavar@phs.uoa.gr),
Stella Vosniadou (svosniad@phs.uoa.gr)**
Cognitive Science Lab
157 71 University Campus, Athens, Greece

Introduction

In an anecdotal experiment conducted by the Russian director Lev Kuleshov in 1919, the audience tended to attribute emotions to neutral facial expressions preceded by unrelated shots (Kuleshov effect). Unimodal (Wallbott, 1988) and bimodal (Ligovanli & Vosniadou, 2006) context effects were also reported in the case of facial emotion recognition. The present study attempted to replicate the standard Kuleshov experiment. We also conducted a modified version, to investigate whether the Kuleshov effect modifies the perception of basic facial emotions, in addition to neutral expressions. We expected a significant reduction of accuracy in the recognition of facial expressions in juxtaposition conditions, as a result of the tendency to integrate the meaning of the independent shots with the meaning of the neutral or emotional facial expressions.

Method

Twenty-three Greek university students, 9 males and 14 females, aged between 18 and 43 years (mean age 25,48) participated in the experiments.

The procedure consisted of presenting to the participants the stimuli in four computerized experimental blocks: 1. trial test, 2. standard experiment, 3. modified version and 4. control conditions.

Fifty four videos -6 for the standard experiment and 48 for the modified version- with dynamic neutral or facial expressions of happiness, sadness, fear and surprise preceded by a contextual cue (baby, dead, soup) were the visual stimuli of the main experimental blocks. The two neutral and the sixteen emotional expressions used in the experimental conditions were the stimuli of the control conditions. The participants were instructed to name freely the facial expressions.

Results

In the case of standard Kuleshov experiment, only the dead context reduced the mean of correct recognition of neutral expressions. In the modified version of the Kuleshov experiment, the mean correct score of fear and surprise was reduced for each type of context. The means of correct responses for the happiness and sadness expressions were reduced in the soup context, but increased in the baby context. Dead context reduced correct recognition for the happiness, but increased the mean score of facial expressions for the sadness (Table 1).

Table 1: Mean of correct recognition for isolated facial expressions and expressions in context

	Out of context	Baby	Dead	Soup
Neutral	1,13	1,17	1,04	1,13
Happiness	3,96	3,96	3,87	3,70
Sadness	2,91	3,09	3,04	2,48
Fear	3,09	2,70*	2,57*	2,43*
Surprise	3,74	3,39	3,26	3,39

*$p<.05$

For both the standard and the modified version of the Kuleshov experiment, the only significant reduction of facial emotion recognition in context, compared to control conditions, was found for the recognition of fear expressions [Paired-samples T-test: a) Baby: $t(22)=2.398$, $p=.025$, b) Dead: $t(22)=2.958$, $p=.007$ and b) Soup Context: $t(22)=3.045$, $p=.006$].

Discussion

The results of the present study provided limited evidence in favour of the Kuleshov effect. One possible explanation for the limited effect of context is that the luck of clarity of the contextual source caused bias in favour of the facial stimuli (Ekman, et al. 1982). Currently we are investigating this issue by trying to control for the clarity of contextual sources.

Acknowledgments

The project is co-financed within Op. Education by the ESF (European Social Fund) and National Resources.

References

Ekman, P., Friesen, W. V., & Ellsworth, P. (1982). What are the relative contributions of facial behaviour and contextual information to the judgment of emotion? In P. Ekman (ed.). *Emotion in the Human Face* (pp. 111-127). New York: Cambridge University Press.

Ligovanli, K. & Vosniadou, S. (2006). Context effects on facial emotion recognition. Noisis, *2*, 75-103. (In greek).

Wallbott, H. (1988). In and out of context: Influences of facial expression and context information on emotion attributions. *British Journal of Social Psychology, 27*, 357-369.

1

The Expression but not Learning of Implicit Sequence Knowledge is enhanced by the Controlled Allocation of Attention

Natacha Deroost (nderoost@vub.ac.be)
Inge Zeeuws (inzeeuws@vub.ac.be)
Eric Soetens (esoetens@vub.ac.be)
Department of Cognitive and Biological Psychology, Vrije Universiteit Brussel
1050 Brussels, Belgium

In many of everyday tasks like handwriting, language production and car-driving, sequencing of information is involved. This indicates that learning sequence structure is a fundamental process that is involved in the acquisition of basic skills as well as complex cognition. Although the exact nature of sequence learning is still highly controversial, many authors assume that it occurs in an implicit fashion (see e.g. Cleeremans, Destrebecqz, & Boyer, 1998). This implies that learning takes place automatically.

In order to investigate the automatic nature of implicit sequence learning, we made use of an adapted version of the Serial Reaction Time task (SRT task) of Nissen and Bullemer (1987) In the SRT task, participants have to react to a target stimulus that appears in one of four locations. Unbeknown to the participants, the presentation of the target location follows a regular sequence. Typically, reaction times (RTs) decrease progressively with training and increase when the target suddenly appears in a random location. The RT disruption with the insertion of a random sequence indicates the presence of sequence learning. Because participants demonstrate sequence learning without being instructed to and often without being aware of it, SRT results are assumed to reflect the acquisition of implicit sequence knowledge.

In the present study, we examined the need for attentional processing in sequence learning by manipulating the automatic or controlled nature of visual search strategies within the SRT task. Based on a variation of the SRT paradigm developed by Remillard (2003, see also Deroost & Soetens, 2006) participants had to search for a target stimulus (XO or OX, the identity was irrelevant) that was surrounded with either similar distractor items (YQ or QY, at random) or dissimilar distractor items (NM or MN, at random). They were instructed to react to the location of the target that appeared in one of four locations on a row, by pressing one of four spatially compatible response keys. We assumed that in case of similar distractors, participants had to allocate their attention in a controlled or endogenous way in order to ignore the irrelevant information and select the target stimulus. In contrast, when the target was surrounded with dissimilar distractors, target identification could be based on the automatic or exogenous orienting of attention. The target location followed a probabilistic sequence in all of 15 blocks of 100 trials, except in Block 13, where the location changed at random. The results of Experiment 1 demonstrated that the RT disruption with the introduction of the random sequence in Block 13 was larger in the endogenous condition than in the exogenous condition. This suggests that sequence learning was enhanced by the controlled orienting of attention. Alternatively, it is possible that endogenous attention facilitated the expression of what was being learned, rather than improving the learning process itself.

To dissociate learning from the behavioral expression of learning, participants were trained under either endogenous or exogenous conditions (similar to Experiment 1) during Blocks 1-11 of Experiment 2. Subsequently, participants in both conditions were transferred to the same condition during Blocks 12-15. During these transfer blocks, the target was presented without surrounding distractor items. All training and transfer blocks followed the same probabilistic location sequence as in Experiment 1, except in transfer Block 13 where the location changed at random. The results showed that the RT increase in Block 13, and hence learning, was similar in the endogenous and exogenous condition. This demonstrates that the controlled orienting of attention enhanced the expression of what was being learned, but not the learning process itself. Accordingly, the present findings contribute to the growing evidence that implicit sequence learning runs independently of attentional processing.

Acknowledgments

This research was supported by the Research Council of the Vrije Universiteit Brussel – Grant OZR-1388.

References

Cleeremans, A., Destrebeqz, A., & Boyer, M. (1998). Implicit learning: news from the front. *Trends in Cognitive Sciences, 2*(10), 406-416.

Deroost, N., & Soetens, E. (2006). Spatial processing and perceptual sequence learning in SRT tasks. *Experimental Psychology, 53*(1), 16-30.

Nissen, M. J., & Bullemer, P. (1987). Attentional requirements of learning: evidence from performance measures. *Cognitive Psychology, 19*, 1-32.

Remillard, G. (2003). Pure perceptual-based sequence learning. *Journal of Experimental Psychology: Learning, Memory and Cognition, 29*, 518-597.

Attention Allocation in Learning an XOR Classification Task

James E. Corter (jec34@columbia.edu)
Department of Human Development, Teachers College, Columbia University
525 W. 120th St, New York, NY 10027 USA

Toshihiko Matsuka (toshihiko.matsuka@stevens.edu)
Howe School of Technology Management, Stevens Institute of Technology
Castle Point on Hudson, Hoboken, NJ 07030 USA

Arthur B. Markman (markman@psy.utexas.edu)
Department of Psychology, University of Texas
Box A8000, The University of Texas at Austin, Austin, TX 78712 USA

We studied how category learners allocated attention across stimulus dimensions in learning the classic "XOR" task of Medin, Altom, Edelson, and Freko (1982). This replication study used an "information-board" interface to study how learners directed attention to individual values of dimensions across blocks of training. Large individual differences were found in both final classification accuracy and in patterns of attention allocation.

Method

Twenty participants were trained on the stimulus structure of Medin et al. (1982), using a simulated medical diagnosis task (Table 1). Dimensions 1 and 2 were probabilistically diagnostic of the classification criterion, but Dimensions 3 and 4 can be used together to form a perfectly predictive XOR rule. Values of stimulus dimensions were instantiated as symptoms (e.g., "red throat" versus "scratchy throat").

Table 1: Category structure of training task.

patient	class	D1	D2	D3	D4
01	A	1	1	1	1
02	A	1	1	0	0
03	A	0	1	1	1
04	A	1	0	0	0
05	B	0	0	1	0
06	B	0	0	0	1
07	B	1	0	1	0
08	B	0	1	0	1

The information board interface used was that developed by Matsuka (2002). Category exemplars (i.e., fictitious patients) were presented in blocks of four, all four displayed simultaneously on the computer screen, with patients corresponding to rows of the displayed table and stimulus dimensions corresponding to columns. The table was initially blank, but participants could uncover the contents of a square by clicking on it with the mouse button. Once a participant had viewed all or part of a patient description, a diagnosis could be entered for that patient. Corrective feedback was then given.

The total time spent viewing individual features was summed by dimension to yield a measure of attention paid to that dimension. Detailed information on cell transitions was also collected but not reported here.

Results and Discussion

Analysis of the group data seemed to show gradually increasing attention to the XOR dimensions and a gradual increase in classification accuracy. However, the individual learning curves for classification accuracy and attention allocation gave a very different picture. These curves revealed a mix of classification strategies. XOR rule learning was exhibited by some subjects, as shown by a pattern in which classification accuracy quickly rose to 1 while attention to D1 and D2 rapidly dropped off to 0. Other participants showed effective exemplar learning, indicated by a pattern in which attention remained equally split among all four dimensions, but accuracy more gradually rose to 1. Other participants showed a failure to learn the task, usually accompanied by a roughly stable pattern of equal attention to all four dimensions. Some subjects showed evidence of suboptimal rules (using three dimensions), and some subjects exhibited switching of strategies.

The results may be seen as supporting multiple-systems accounts of categorization. It appears that humans are flexible learners, able to apply multiple strategies to accomplish even difficult or "unnatural" tasks.

References

Matsuka, T. (2002). Attention processes in computational models of category learning. Unpublished doctoral dissertation, Columbia University, New York, NY.

Medin, D. L., Altom, M. W., Edelson, S. M., & Freko, D. (1982). Correlated symptoms and simulated medical classification. *Journal of Experimental Psychology: Learning, Memory, and Cognition, 8,* 37-50.

Effects of Task Switching Policy on Interruption Handling in Text Editing

Boris B. Velitchkovsky (velitchk@mail.ru)
Maria S. Kapitsa (kapitsa@ru.ru)
Irina V. Blinnikova (blinnikova@ru.ru)
Faculty of Psychology, Moscow State University
Mokhovaya street 11/5, Moscow, 125009 Russian Federation

Task switching studies have a long history in psychology. However, most of the studies explored switching effects in the context of highly artificial tasks (e.g. Rubinstein, Meyer, & Evans, 2001). Important results were obtained, regarding the influence of factors like task complexity, priming, or switching procedure on switching cost. Presently, task switching and interruptions are also being studied in more natural settings (Kapitsa & Blinnikova, 2003; Czerwinski, Horwitz & Wilhite, 2004). Our study investigates these processes during the execution of a typical text editing task.

Method

25 subjects (aged 18-21, mostly female, having same amount of formal training in computer use) took part in the study. Two networked computers (one for the subject and another for the experimenter) were placed in separate rooms, connected by an intercom telephone. Messaging software ICQ was installed on both computers. The video signal of an observation camera was mixed with the video signal of the subject's screen and recorded. The main task consisted of editing a text in the MS Word text processor (correcting orthographical errors, repositioning text fragments and typing in a new fragment). Additional tasks were introduced either during typing a missing text block in or moving a text block with the help of the 'cut-and-paste' technique (Factor OPERATION). The requirement to switch came either through intercom or ICQ (Factor CHANNEL). The additional task could be either simple (calling a built-in text statistics function) or complex (bibliography search) (Factor COMPLEXITY). All factors were within-subject.

Results

The following data were obtained: the time to switch (measured from the command to switch to the beginning of additional task execution, TS), the duration of the additional task (TAT) and the time to switch back (from the end of the additional task to the resumption of the main task, TSB).

Factor CHANNEL showed no effects. There were main effects of COMPLEXITY and OPERATION on TAT and TSB. A OPERATION*TASK interaction was obtained for TS ($F(1,24) = 10.7$, $p<0.01$). For simple additional tasks, there was no difference in switching from typing and moving operation. For a complex additional task, the nature of interruption is important. Switching from typing takes less time and switching from moving takes more time than in the case of simple additional task. The same interaction is significant for TAT ($F(1,24) = 18.2$, $p<0.01$). The time to execute a simple additional task doesn't depend on the interrupted operation. For complex tasks previous typing hampers the execution of the subsequent task (mean TAT is almost twice as high). The same interaction for TSB was on the edge of significance ($F(1,24) = 2.8$, $p=0,106$).

Discussion and Conclusions

Our previous research (Kapista & Blinnikova, 2003) indicates that subjects employ different switching policies. In the present study, we addressed this question in more detail. Additionally, the channel of interruption was manipulated, affecting the degree of voluntary control.

To explain the present data, we suggest the existence of three switching policies. The N(ull)-policy involves no preparation to switching, and relies on simultaneous representation of both tasks in working memory. This results in short TS and TSB, but slows down the execution of the additional task. Subjects use the N-policy in switching from typing operations to complex additional tasks. S(hallow)-policy consists in some preparation, forming a "compressed" representation of the interrupted operation. The policy leads to longer TS and TSB, but imposes no cost on the execution of the additional task. This is the default policy for simple additional tasks. With the D(eep)-policy, the preparation is elaborated leading to a representation is formed that minimizes the memory load. In this case, TS and also TSB increase, because of the cost, associated with the access to the representation. No cost on the execution of the additional task arises. Subjects use the D-policy in switching from moving operations to complex tasks. Thus, the policy used is a function of the interrupted operation type and the complexity of the additional task.

Acknowledgments

This work was supported by Russian Foundation for Basic Research (RFFI, Grant No 05-06-80366).

References

Czerwinski, M., Horvitz, E., & Wilhite S. (2004). A diary study of task switching and interruptions. *Proceedings of CHI'04* (pp. 175-182). New York: ACM Press.

Kapitsa, M.S., & Blinnikova, I.V. (2003). Task performance under the influence of interruptions. In G.R J. Hockey, A.W.K. Gaillard & O. Burov (Eds.), *Operator functional state* (pp. 323-329). Amsterdam: IOS Press.

Rubinstein, J., Meyer, D. E., & Evans, J. E. (2001). Executive control of cognitive processes in task switching. Journal of Experimental Psychology: Human Perception and Performance, 27, 763-797.

Models for the Evaluation of Workload in a Multimodal Interaction Task: NASA-TLX *vs.* Workload Profile

Dominique Fréard[1], Eric Jamet[2], Gérard Poulain[1], Olivier Le Bohec[2], Valérie Botherel[1]
({dominique.freard, gerard.poulain, valerie.botherel} @orange-ftgroup.com,
{eric.jamet, olivier.lebohec} @uhb.fr)

[1] France Telecom, 2 av. Pierre Marzin
22307 Lannion cedex, France

[2] Université Rennes 2, place Recteur Henri Le Moal
35000 Rennes, France

As workload evaluation is a diagnostic aid for design, it can also help in understanding and predicting cognitive load. We compare two multidimensional subjective workload questionnaires to verify which underlying model best fits user effort. We aim at validating a model for cognitive load prediction.

Subjective workload measurement in HCI

NASA-TLX (Hart & Staveland, 1988) is the classical multidimensional instrument for workload measure in HCI. It includes six dimensions: mental, physical and temporal demands, effort, satisfaction and frustration. It is based on a mixed model of task-related and cognitive parameters.

Another measure, named Workload Profile (Tsang & Velasquez, 1996) includes eight dimensions: perceptive/central, response, visual, auditory, spatial, verbal processing; manual and verbal responses. This is based on a model of the subject's attention structure. We added two emotional scales inspired from Lazarus and Folkman's (1984) model of stress: frustration and loss of control feeling.

Rubio, Diaz, Martin and Puente (2004) showed that Workload Profile (WP) leads to a better discrimination of task conditions than NASA-TLX for experimental tasks. As a consequence, we hypothesized that WP should produce a richer and more informative description of users' effort compared to TLX.

Experiment

The experiment focused on modality allocation in a medical appointments system. We categorized three kinds of information in a dialogue turn: feedbacks, responses and openings. We associated feedbacks and openings as belonging to the interaction task whereas responses belong to the field task. A third task concerns the management of personal goals and knowledge. This analysis allowed us to propose four configurations: (1) entirely auditory, (2) interaction related information in auditory and field information in visual, (3) the opposite of (2), and (4) entirely visual. Two are mono modal and two are bimodal.

The protocol was a Wizard of Oz. The *configuration* was tested as a between-subjects factor. An ASR error was also introduced in one dialogue as a within-subject factor (*trial*). Eighty subjects participated in the experiment. Half rated NASA-TLX, while the other half rated the modified version of WP.

Results

A canonical discriminant analysis discriminated configurations with WP (*Lambda Wilk* = 0,207; $F_{(30,79)}$ = 1,88; $p < .02$). Principally, the visual configuration was more manual response demanding and the three other configurations were more auditory demanding. No discrimination was revealed with TLX (*Lambda Wilk* = 0,533; $F_{(18,88)} = 1,21$; $p = .26$).

The variance analyses revealed that TLX was only sensitive to trial while WP was sensitive to configuration and trial. Among dimensions, for TLX, mental demand, temporal demand and frustration increased in the trial with the error, while effort and satisfaction decreased. For WP, visual configuration was more demanding than the three others on visual processing, spatial processing and manual response. No equivalent effect appeared for auditory configuration. The perceptive/central processing was rated higher for visual configuration compared to the two bimodal configurations, and vocal configuration was in between. Stress and feeling of loss of control were rated higher in the trial with the error. Furthermore, WP permitted us to classify the two possible strategies for error recovery: cancellation was costlier than direct correction.

Conclusion

The results show that WP was more sensitive than TLX for the task studied. We find that, for cognitive load prediction in a multimodal interaction task, cognitive models of attention structure and stress are more appropriate than TLX mixed model of task related and cognitive integration parameters.

References

Hart, S. G., & Staveland, L. E. (1988). Development of nasa-tlx (task load index): Results of empirical and theoritical research. In P. A. Hancock & N. Meshkati (Eds.), *Human mental workload* (pp. 139-183). Amsterdam: North-Holland.

Rubio, S., Diaz, E., Martin, J., & Puente, J. M. (2004). Evaluation of subjective mental workload: A comparison of swat, nasa-tlx, and workload profile methods. *Applied Psychology, 53(1)*, 61-86.

Tsang, P. S., & Velasquez, V. L. (1996). Diagnosticity and multidimensional subjective workload ratings. *Ergonomics, 39(3)*, 358-381.

Head-Up Displays Reduce the Effects of Divided Visual Attention in Driving

Valentinos. Zachariou (vzachari@purdue.edu)
Marios N. Avraamides (mariosav@ucy.ac.cy)
Georgia Panayiotou (georgiap@ucy.ac.cy)
Department of Psychology, University of Cyprus
P.O.Box 20537, CY 1678, Nicosia Cyprus

Introduction

The allocation of attentional resources to multiple tasks is formally referred to as *divided attention* (DA). DA has been shown to impair performance in driving (Lengenfelder, Schultheis, Al-Shihabi, Mourant, & DeLeca, 2002). The extent by which DA is implicated in driving varies between extreme multitasking events such as browsing the menu of a cell phone while steering, to minor ones such as occasionally monitoring the car's own instrument board. We hypothesized that a significant amount of attention is shifted away from the road every time the driver inspects the car's instrument board for information such as current vehicle speed. If this is the case, then a potential solution to this problem is the introduction of *head up displays (HUD)* in vehicles. HUD's allow the driver to observe information, such as speed, as part of the external scene, thus eliminating the need to look away from the road. However, there is still much debate as to whether HUD displays benefit driving performance. Young-Ching and Ming-Hui, (2004) claim that drivers are faster to respond when a HUD system is used. Wolffsohn, McBrien, Edgar and Stout, (1998) provide evidence instead that HUD displays increase reaction times during driving. This study examines performance in a demanding virtual drive scenario which requires continuous monitoring of driving speed on a HUD versus a conventional HDD. The innovation of this study lies in the use of a drive simulator that allows levels of interactivity between the subject and the driving scene, immersion, and precise data collection that could not be achieved before. This close simulation of real driving conditions may help resolve how HUDs versus HDDs affect attention during driving.

Methods & Results

The driving simulator was designed with Valve's Source 3D graphics engine. Tracks were designed to be attention demanding and consisted of sharp curves, frequently changing speed limits and traffic lights that would randomly change to red. The task was to drive while closely obeying speed limits and stopping to all red traffic lights. Changing lanes, exiting the paved road, failing to follow speed limits and failing to stop in time on red lights were recorded as violations. *Reaction times* (RTs) to red lights were also recorded. The experiment followed a within subjects design with the HUD and the conventional HDD being the two conditions (Figure 1). Results revealed a statistically significant difference between a HUD and conventional HDD system in the RT to red traffic lights. Participants were faster at stopping to red lights, in the HUD conditions than in the HDD conditions. The two conditions did not differ on other measures.

Conclusion

Results from this experiment support the hypothesis that there is significant loss of visual attention when observing information on the conventional instrument panel of a vehicle. It appears that attentional resources are better utilized with a HUD system, which incorporates the extra visual information from the instrument panel in the areas of the visual field where attention is already focused. This fusion of the two sources of information decreases DA in comparison with HDDs. HDDs instead force the user to divide attention between the environment and the instrument displays, thus working against the areas of the visual field where the driver is already primed to attend.

Figure 1: HDD & HUD conditions.

References

Lengenfelder, J., Schultheis, T. M., Al-Shihabi, T., Mourant, T., & DeLuca, J. (2002). Divided attention and driving: A pilot study using virtual reality technology. *Journal of Head Trauma Rehabilitation*, 17(1), 26-37.

Wolffsohn, J. S., McBrien, N. A., Edgar, G. K., & Stout, T. (1998). The influence of cognition and age on accommodation, detection rate and response times when using a car head-up display (HUD), *Ophthalmic and Physiological Optics*, 18(3), 243-253.

Yung-Ching, L., & Ming-Hui, W. (2004). Comparison of head-up display (HUD) vs. head-down display (HDD): Driving performance of commercial vehicle operators in Taiwan, *International Journal of Human-Computer Studies*, 61(5), 679-697.

Vigilance decrement: boredom or cognitive fatigue?

Nathalie Pattyn (npattyn@vub.ac.be)
Department of Cognitive and Biological Psychology, Vrije Universiteit Brussel
Pleinlaan, 2; 1050 Brussel, BELGIUM
Department of Behavioral Sciences, Royal Military Academy
Renaissancelaan, 30; 1000 Belgium, BELGIUM

David Henderickx (david.henderickx@vub.ac.be); Eric Soetens (esoetens@vub.ac.be)
Department of Cognitive and Biological Psychology, Vrije Universiteit Brussel
Pleinlaan, 2; 1050 Brussel, BELGIUM

Introduction

Some authors (e.g. Stuss, 1995) state the vigilance decrement is a consequence of attentional withdrawal of the supervisory attentional system, due to underarousal caused by the insufficient workload inherent to typical vigilance tasks. Others (e.g. Warm & Dember, 1984) view the decrement as the result of a decreased attentional capacity and thus the impossibility to sustain mental effort. Fisk and Schneider (1981) demonstrated that controlled processing is the locus of the vigilance decrement, which has been mainly investigated through tasks tapping endogenous attentional control. This experiment aimed at answering two questions: 1° Do physiological measures of arousal provide evidence to support the underload vs overload hypothesis? 2° Is there a different effect for endogenous and exogenous attention?

Method

We used a conjunction search, where stimuli were preceded by a valid, invalid or neutral cue. For endogenous cueing (N=20), the cue consisted in a central arrow, whereas for exogenous cueing (N=21), it was a peripheral brightness increase. The experimental (210 trials, with RSI ranging from 7 s to 39 s) lasted for 1,5 hr, analyzed as three blocks of 30 min. ECG, respiration and thoracocardiography were recorded through the LifeShirt (VivoMetrics, Inc). Parasympathetic tone (PT) was inferred from Respiratory Sinus Arrhythmia (RSA), computed by the peak-valley method and sympathetic tone (ST) was inferred from normalized low frequency power (LF).

Results & Discussion

Cognitive results showed increased RTs with time-on-task, and a higher cost in RTs of invalid cues with time-on-task for the endogenous group only.

Physiological results clearly support the underload hypothesis to subtend the vigilance decrement. As shown in Figure 1, the overall decrease in arousal (increased PT, decreased ST) is more pronounced for the endogenous group. A repeated measures MANOVA revealed a significant effect of time [$F_{(2,117)}=27,8;p<0,0001$] and a significant interaction between time and group [$F_{(2,117)}=2,8;p=0,049$]. Subsequent analyses revealed the effect of time to be only significant for RRI and RSA, and the interaction for RSA.

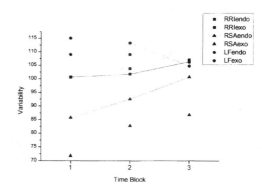

Figure 1: Variability in %, as normalized to baseline values, for heart period (RRI), RSA and LF for endogenous (full) and exogenous (dotted) groups.

Conclusion

Our results support the attentional withdrawal hypothesis as subtending the vigilance decrement over time. Furthermore, endogenous attentional control seems more vulnerable to time-on-task. This implies that the usual description of the vigilance decrement indexes boredom rather than cognitive fatigue.

Acknowledgements

Supported by the Dept of Defence grant ERM HF-10

References

Fisk, A. D. & Schneider W. (1981). Control and automatic processing during tasks requiring sustained attention: A new approach to vigilance. *Human Factors, 23,* 737-750.

Stuss, D. T. (1995). A Sensible Approach to Mild Traumatic Brain Injury. *Neurology, 45,* 1251-1252.

Warm, J. S. & Jerison, H. J. (1984). The psychophysics of vigilance. In J.S.Warm (Ed.), *Sustained attention in human performance.* Chichester,England: Wiley.

Cognitive stress and sleep quality

Gabriella Pravettoni (gabriella.pravettoni@unimi.it)
Department of Social Science, University of Milan
Via Conservatorio n.:7, 20122 Milano

Salvatore N. Leotta (leotta@dti.unimi.it)
Department of Social Science, University of Milan
Via Conservatorio n.:7, 20122 Milano

Claudio Lucchiari (claudio.lucchiari@unimi.it)
Department of Social Science, University of Milan
Via Conservatorio n.:7, 20122 Milano

Introduction

There are many conceptualizations of rumination. According to Martin and Tesser (1989), rumination is a generic term which covers a wide range of perseverative thinking. Such thinking, they argue, is characterized: (1) by its frequency, (2) as involving automatic and controlled processing, and (3) for hindering goal attainment.

There is much evidence to suggest that people tend to ruminate about symptoms of distress or their stressful situations (Lyubomirsky, Tucker, Caldwell, & Berg, 1999; Nolen-Hoeksema, McBride, & Larson, 1997). Alloy and colleagues have recently coined the term "stress-reactive rumination" to describe the type of thinking that occurs following the exposure to stressful life experiences (Robinson & Alloy, 2003).

Sleep is one of the most important recovery mechanisms available to humans, allowing for recovery from daily strains, and therefore a prerequisite for optimal daily functioning and health.

Our study was aimed at studying the relation between the condition of rumination and stress and the general sleep condition (quantity and quality) and test the influence of other subjective variables.

Since sleep seem to be closely related to cognitive stress (Hall et al., 1996), we expected to find stressed people to report a worse sleeping condition.

Methods

Participants: 186 subjects took part in the study. Their age ranged from 20 to 66 (mean: 37.1; s.d.: 10.06).

Materials: The questionnaire consisted of a personal information section, a rumination inventory, a self report stress scale, and the Pittsburg scale (Buysse et al., 1989).

Furthermore, subjects were asked to fill a questionnaire about their sleep quantity each morning.

We classified subjects into two cluster (two-step cluster analysis) using stress and rumination variables. In this way, we obtained a two level factor (low stress and high stress).

We then performed a multivariate analysis of variance of quality and quantity of sleeps.

Results and discussion

The MANOVA test showed that subjects classified in the high cluster reported a worse sleep condition (F =18.8; p<.000). In particular, the mean quality of sleep of subjects in the low cluster is significantly higher (M =46.6; SD = 0.7) than the one of subjects in the high cluster (M =38.5; SD= 1.1). At the opposite, the average amount of sleep per night was not different (M= 6.6 for the low cluster; M = 6.7 for the high cluster). Both gender and age showed not to affect the quality and the quantity of life.

In conclusion, our data suggest that cognitive stress as measured by standardized scales, may explain and important quote of sleep disturbances and their effects on health. Thus future researches will have to address the problem of stress management, to be considered a key issue to treat and understand the relation between sleep, cognitive performances and quality of life.

References

Buysse DJ, Reynolds CF 3rd, Monk TH, Berman SR, Kupfer DJ. (1989) The Pittsburgh Sleep Quality Index. *Psychiatry Research*; 28(2):193-213

Hall M., Buysse D., Reynolds C., Kupfer D., Baum A. (1996). Stress related intrusive thoughts disrupt sleep onset and continuity. *Sleep Research*.

Lyubomirsky, S., Tucker, K. L., Caldwell, N. D., & Berg, K. (1999). Why ruminators are poor problem solvers: Clues from the phenomenology of dysphoric rumination. *Journal of Personality and Social Psychology*, 77, 1041 – 1060.

Martin, L. L., & Tesser, A. (1989). Toward a motivational and structural theory of ruminative thought. In J. Uleman & J. A. Bargh (Eds.), *Unintended thought* (pp. 306 – 326). New York: Guilford Press.

Nolen-Hoeksema, S., McBride, A., & Larson, J. (1997). Rumination and psychological distress among bereaved partners. *Journal of Personality and Social Psychology*, 72, 855 – 862.

Robinson, M. S., & Alloy, L. B. (2003). Negative cognitive styles and stress-reactive rumination interact to predict depression: A prospective study. *Cognitive Therapy and Research*, 27, 275 – 291.

More Focal Attention on the Impossible:
An Eye Movement Study with Possible and Impossible Objects

Fiona B. Mulvey* (mulvey@applied-cognition.org)[1]
Stuart T. Smith (stuart.smith@ucd.ie)[2]
Aidan P. Moran (aidan.moran@ucd.ie)[2]
Boris M. Velichkovsky (velich@applied-cognition.org)[1]

[1]Applied Cognitive Research / Psychology III, Dresden University of Technology, D-01062 Dresden, Germany
[2]School of Psychology, University College Dublin, Belfield, D4, Ireland

*corresponding author

Introduction

Previous research has found that level of attentional processing can be explicated from eye movement parameters, as evidenced by different recognition scores for presumed ambiently and focally processed areas (Velichkovsky, Dornhoefer, Pannasch & Unema, 2001; Velichkovsky, Joos, Helmert, & Pannasch, 2005). The aim of this study was to investigate the levels of visual processing approach to eye movement analysis using two visually similar stimuli with differing cognitive demands. 50 closely matched possible and impossible objects were presented in a free view judgment task.

Method

Forty-six participants; 24 male and 22 female (M = 25.38 years, SD = 4.47, range 18-42) completed testing. Eye movements were recorded using the Eyegaze binocular remote tracking system from LC Technologies Inc. running NYAN analysis software from interactive-minds, Dresden. Images were presented on a 34 cm X 27 cm colour monitor extending to 31.6° of vision horizontally and 25.4° of vision vertically, with resolution of 1280 x 1024. Stimuli consisted of 50 objects (25 possible and 25 impossible) presented full screen, one at a time, in random order. Each impossible object was matched to a similar possible version of equal size, luminosity, and complexity. Participants were required to judge each object in turn and respond by pressing corresponding labeled keys on the keyboard. Key-press automatically ended view time.

Results and Discussion

Eye movements were analysed and classified according to levels of processing, number of fixations, fixation durations, percentage areas foveated and view time. Firstly, median fixation durations were calculated for each individual. A paired samples t-test revealed that impossible objects were associated with longer fixation durations than possible objects, $t(46)$ = 5.45, p < .001. The analysis also revealed that there was no difference in view time on impossible and possible objects, $t(46)$ = 1.45, p = .153, or between number of fixations on impossible and possible objects, $t(46)$ = 0.32, p = .743. Eye data were subsequently coded as follows; ambient processing was identified as fixations with durations less than 180 ms, followed by saccades of over five degrees of vision. Focal processing was defined as fixations with durations over 180 ms, followed by saccades less than five degrees of vision (Velichkovsky et al, 2005).

Rates of ambient and focal fixations were calculated for each participant for each image. Paired samples analysis revealed that impossible objects were associated with significantly higher rates of focal fixations than possible objects, $t(46)$ = 8.63, p < .001. Impossible objects were also found to have significantly lower rates of ambient fixations, $t(46)$ = -5.51, p < .001. Finally, the analysis showed that possible objects were associated with a larger area being foveated than impossible objects, $t(46)$ = 4.48, p < .001.

We found that impossible objects elicited more focal processing than possible objects, which, conversely, involved more ambient processing. Since focal processing is usually more conscious and explicit, this may also explain previous findings that encoding attributes of possible, but not impossible objects facilitates later implicit recognition (Cooper & Schacter, 1992). Overall, these results support the explication of levels of visual processing from eye movement parameters in a paradigm where stimuli with similar bottom up properties, but known differences in terms of representation, are contrasted. We suggest that comparing ambient and focal eye movements on stimuli with known encoding differences may be useful in the investigation of modes and levels of visual attention and the brain mechanisms behind them, in the first line, the dorsal and ventral streams of the visual system (Milner & Goodale, 1995).

References

Cooper, L.A. & Schacter, D.L. (1992). Dissociations between structural and episodic representations of visual objects. *Current Directions in Psychological Science, 1*(5), 141-146.

Milner, D. & Goodale, M. (1995). Visual brain in action. Oxford: Oxford University Press.

Velichkovsky, B.M., Dornhoefer, S.M., Pannasch, S. & Unema, P.J.A. (2001). Visual fixations and level of attentional processing. In A. Duhowski (Ed.), *Proceedings of the International Conference Eye Tracking Research & Applications*, Palm Beach Gardens, FL, ACM Press.

Velichkovsky, B.M., Joos, M., Helmert, J.R., & Pannasch, S. (2005). Two visual systems and their eye movements. In Bara, B. G., Barsalou, L., Bucciarelli, M. (Eds.), *Proceedings of the 27th Annual Conference of the Cognitive Science Society*, pp. 2283-2288. Mahwah, NJ: Erlbaum.

On the relationship of eye position and experienced focus of visual work under localisation, identification and categorisation tasks

Jens R. Helmert (helmert@applied-cognition.org)
Sebastian Pannasch (pannasch@applied-cognition.org)
Boris M. Velichkovsky (velich@applied-cognition.org)
Applied Cognitive Research / Psychology III,
Dresden University of Technology, D-01062 Dresden, Germany

Introduction

A large body of work investigated the temporal relation of eye movement planning and attention allocation using "fixate-and-jump" experiments (e.g. Posner, 1980, Deubel, Irwin, & Schneider, 1999). What is usually found is that shifts of visual attention are faster than the physical movement of the eyes. However, research in more natural settings has resulted in conflicting data, so that often the actual eye position was ahead of the experienced focus of visual work (e.g. Tatler, 2001; Helmert, Pannasch, & Velichkovsky, 2006; Velichkovsky, 1995). We present a new study allowing multi-saccade trials and a variation of three tasks: localization, identification and categorisation.

Methods

The participants included 32 male (n=9) and female (n=23) young adult persons. Eye movements were recorded at 250 Hz, using the SR Research Ltd. EyeLink eye-tracking system. Stimuli consisted of circular arrays each containing six circular pictograms with a radius of 1 degrees of visual angle. There were six categories each holding 24 different pictograms. In every trial six pictograms – one of each category – were randomly presented. Subjects' task was to view items clockwise starting at a randomly predefined position. After an unpredictable time the stimulus was removed. In *localisation* trials they had to indicate their eye position, whereas in *identification* tasks they were instructed to choose the pictogram they had dealt with at removal. In *categorisation* task they had to specify the category of the item. The algorithm used in the experiment allowed for fixation-based initiation of stimulus removal.

Results and Discussion

Based on fixation times on the item at removal, all trials were sorted into three viewing time groups; short, medium, and long. We analysed those trials in which subjects either chose the previous or the next pictogram, as picking the actual one fixated only indicates the overlap of eye position and the experienced focus of visual work. A repeated measures ANOVA on data from *previous* responses yielded significance for viewing time, $F(2,60) = 24.799$ $p < .001$, task, $F(2,60) = 14.980$ $p < .001$, and the interaction of both, $F(4,120) = 4.848$ $p = .001$. The same analysis on *next* responses revealed significant differences for viewing time, $F(2,60) = 5.007$ $p = .010$, task, $F(2,60) = 11.206$ $p < .001$, and their interaction, $F(4,120) = 3.250$ $p = .014$.

As expected on the basis of previous results (Helmert, Pannasch, & Velichkovsky, 2006), the choice of an item differed substantially depending on task and viewing time: When viewing time was short and the task at hand demanded identification or categorisation then the probability of choosing the previous item was highest. In localisation trials the situation was the opposite: probability of choosing the next position was highest when viewing time was long.

Though we did not find any difference in performance between identification and categorisation tasks, their reaction times differed strongly, by about 300 ms, $F(2,60) = 174.602$ $p < .001$. This suggests that both tasks have a similar perceptual basis, but categorisation additionally recruits some 'extra-perceptual' component, most probably related to verbal processing (e.g. Velichkovsky, Klemm, Dettmar & Volke, 1996). Overall, the data from the present study testify to the dependence of the relationship between experienced focus of visual work, visual attention and eye movements on the nature of task.

References

Deubel, H., & Schneider, W.X. (1996). Saccade target selection and object recognition: evidence for a common attentional mechanism. *Vision Research*, *36*(12), 1827-1837.

Helmert, J.R., Pannasch, S., & Velichkovsky B.M. (2006). 'Functional Fovea' revisited: On the temporal relationship of attentional shifts and eye movements. In B.M. Velichkovsky, T.W. Chernygovskaya, J.I. Alexandrow, & D.N. Achapkin (Eds.) *Proceedings of the Second Biennial Conference on Cognitive Science*, St. Petersburg/Russia, June 9-13, pp. 511-512.

Posner, M.I. (1980). Orienting of attention. *Quarterly Journal of Experimental Psychology, 32*, 3-25.

Tatler, B.W. (2001). Characterising the visual buffer: Real-world evidence for overwriting early in each fixation. *Perception, 30*(8), 993-1006.

Velichkovsky, B.M. (1995). Communicating attention: Gaze position transfer in cooperative problem solving. *Pragmatics and Cognition, 3*(2), 199-222.

Velichkovsky, B.M., Klemm, T., Dettmar, P. & Volke, H.-J. (1996). Evozierte Kohärenz des EEG: II. Kommunikation der Hirnareale und Verarbeitungstiefe. *Zeitschrift für Elekroenzephalographie, Elektromyographie und verwandte Gebiete, 27*, 111-119.

Training in Inconsistency Checking and Elaboration to Facilitate Verbal Insight Problem Solving

Afia Ahmed (Ahmed@cardiff.ac.uk)
John Patrick (PatrickJ@cardiff.ac.uk)
School of Psychology, Cardiff University,
Park Place, Cardiff, CF10 3AT, UK

Introduction

Verbal insight problems are difficult to solve because such problems trigger stereotypical assumptions that constrain problem solving (Ohlsson, 1992). An example of a verbal insight problem is the directory problem: 'There is a town in Northern Ontario where 5% of all the people living in the town have unlisted phone numbers. If you selected 100 names at random from the town's phone directory, on average, how many of these people selected would have unlisted phone numbers?' (Ansburg & Dominowski, 2000). Participants incorrectly assume that a calculation is required to solve this problem. According to Ohlsson (1992), elaboration of the problem information is required to alter this incorrect representation in order to arrive at the correct solution i.e., none will have *un*listed phone numbers because a phone directory contains listed numbers only.

Few training studies have successfully facilitated performance on verbal insight problems (e.g., Ansburg & Dominowski, 2000). Patrick, Grainger, Gregov, Halliday, Handley, James, and O'Reilly (1999) found that inconsistency checking could be used to trigger a change in representation in an applied problem solving context. This approach was used by Ahmed and Patrick (2006, Experiment 2) who found that generic training in identifying inconsistencies between the problem solver's representation and the problem specification increased performance from 21% to 40%. In the current experiment, a strategy was trained involving inconsistency checking combined with elaboration in order to facilitate performance on five 'elaboration' problems, as categorized by Ansburg and Dominowski (2000). The strategy encouraged participants to systematically work through a problem by considering whether every solution they generated was consistent with the problem specification. If a solution was inconsistent, problem solvers were encouraged to select a part of the problem, which they considered important and to use their general knowledge to elaborate this information.

Method

Forty-two undergraduate students from Cardiff University were randomly allocated to one of three training conditions. The practice condition completed three practice 'elaboration' problems, without receiving any experimenter support, whereas the strategy condition used the strategy to solve the same practice problems. A control, no training condition was also used. All participants first received 'think-aloud' training and completed five test problems, which were randomly presented. Four minutes were given for each test problem. Verbal protocols were collected to explore how participants' problem solving was influenced by training (Fleck & Weisberg, 2004).

Results and Discussion

A one-way analysis of variance revealed significant differences between training conditions, $F(2, 39) = 6.87$, $MSE = 0.431$, $p < 0.01$. The strategy condition (M = 0.61, SD = 0.23) was significantly better in solving problems than both the practice (M= 0.34, SD = 0.21), ($p < 0.05$) and the control conditions (M = 0.29, SD = 0.30), ($p < 0.01$), which were not significantly different. This suggests that practice without instruction is insufficient in facilitating problem solving. Verbal protocols revealed that participants in the control condition were influenced by implicit constraints triggered by the test problems and thus were more likely than the strategy condition to accept the first, often incorrect, hypothesis they generated. However, comments made by participants in the strategy condition such as 'It doesn't say in the problem...so the solution isn't consistent' and 'I'll go through the problem again' demonstrated that participants actively applied what they had learnt during strategy training. These results suggest that inconsistency checking can be used as a successful cue for elaboration, hence facilitating verbal insight problem solving.

References

Ahmed, A., & Patrick. J. (2006). Making implicit assumptions explicit in verbal insight problem solving. In *Proceedings of the Twenty-Eighth Annual Conference of the Cognitive Science Society* (pp. 956-960). Mahwah, NJ: LEA.

Ansburg, P. I., & Dominowski, R. L. (2000). Promoting insightful problem solving. *Journal of Creative Behavior, 34*(1), 30-60.

Fleck, J. I., & Weisberg, R. W. (2004). The use of verbal protocols as data: An analysis of insight in the candle problem. *Memory and Cognition, 32*(6), 990-1006.

Ohlsson, S. (1992). Information-processing explanations of insight and related phenomena. In M. T. Keane & K. J. Gilhooly (Eds.), *Advances in the psychology of thinking* (pp. 1-44). New York; London; Toronto; Sydney; Tokyo; Singapore: Harvester Wheatsheaf.

Patrick, J., Grainger, L., Gregov, A., Halliday, P., Handley, J., James, N., & O'Reilly, S. (1999). Training to break the barriers of habit in reasoning about unusual faults. *Journal of Experimental Psychology: Applied, 5*(3), 314-335.

The influence of the nature and the causal strength of contextual information on the temporal course of predictive inferences.

Sonia Galletti (sonia.galletti@univ-lyon2.fr)

University of Lyon 2 - Institute of psychology- Laboratory for the Study of Cognitive Mechanisms- U.M.R. 5596, CNRS
5, avenue Pierre Mendès-France, 69676 Bron cedex FRANCE

Isabelle Tapiero (isabelle.tapiero@univ-lyon2.fr)

University of Lyon 2 - Institute of psychology- Laboratory for the Study of Cognitive Mechanisms- U.M.R. 5596, CNRS
5, avenue Pierre Mendès-France, 69676 Bron cedex France

Causal Strength and context

Text comprehension requires the construction of a coherent memory representation. Such coherent representation results from a complex problem solving activity in which the readers infer relations among events described by the text and are able to draw different types of inferences based on the text. In two experiments, we focused our interest on predictive inferences defined as one particular kind of causal inferences. The properties of the focal event determine predictive inferences' specificity and their activation strength (van den Broek, 1990). The focal event is the specific part of the text that is actually treated being part of the focal attention. Moreover, sufficiency (i.e., causal constraint) has been shown to be a central criterion in generating predictions. Thus, there is no doubt that causality plays a crucial role in text comprehension. However, other dimensions such as emotion, in particular the protagonist's emotional states, are part of readers' mental representation and should be taken into account. The two following experiments were designed to further explore whether multidimensional information (causal and emotional) had an influence on the generation of predictive inference and on the causal strength of a focal event. We assumed that generating predictive inferences result in the convergence between contextual information and causal strength. First, causal elaboration should enhance the integration of predictive inference whereas emotional elaboration should disrupt it. Second, compared to causality, emotion should weaken the effect of causal strength. In both experiments, we used two contextual versions, one dealing with causal contextual information and the other one with emotional information. The contextual information was followed with the presentation of a focal event either high or low in causal sufficiency. Two critical sentences (emotional and causal) in relation with the contextual information ended each text. Subjects were probed during, and at the end of the reading of each text with two critical tests. The same procedure as in experiment 1 was used in experiment 2, the only difference between the two experiments was that in the latter, we reinforced the strength of emotional and causal contextual information.

Main results

ANOVA 's were performed on reading times for critical sentences and on response times to critical tests.

Reading times

Whereas for causal critical sentences, reading times were longer after high sufficient focal events than low sufficient focal events, the reverse was obtained for emotional critical sentences. In addition, after reinforcing the context (Exp. 2), reading times to emotional and causal critical sentences were shorter with emotional contextual information than with causal contextual information.

Response times to causal tests

We observed shorter response times for causal context than for emotional context. Also, our results showed a reliable interaction between Causal strength and Nature of contextual information. Indeed, we had shorter response times for the causal tests in the high sufficiency condition when the contextual information was causal $((F= 1, 78) = 10,04; p = .0022)$, whereas subjects had shorter response times for the causal tests in the low sufficient condition when the context was emotional. When the context was reinforced, we showed a significant interaction between the causal strength and the time course of comprehension: with low sufficiency, we had shorter response times to intermediate causal test, whereas final causal tests were processed faster with high sufficient information.

In sum, first we showed that predictive inferences are not activated in an all-or-none fashion. Second, emotional contextual information tends to influence the sufficiency of causal information and consequently the activation strength and the level of integration of predictive inferences. Follow-up studies will be conducted to investigate in more depth the time course of predictive inferences. Simulations with different nature of contextual information will be run with the Landscape Model.

Acknowledgments

This research is based on a doctoral dissertation and is supported by the EMC laboratory, France.

Main reference

van den Broek, P. (1990). Causal inferences and the comprehension of narrative texts. In Graesser, A.C., Bower, G.H. (Eds.), *Inferences and text comprehension*, (pp.175-196). London : Academic Press, inc.

Lexicality and Frequency Effects in Italian Developmental Dyslexia

Despina Paizi (despina.paizi@istc.cnr.it)
Institute for Cognitive Sciences and Technologies (ISTC-CNR) and Department of Psychology, University of Rome "La Sapienza"
Via S. Martino della Battaglia 44, 00185, Rome, Italy

Maria De Luca (maria.deluca@uniroma1.it)
Neuropsychological Unit, IRCCS Fondazione Santa Lucia, via Ardeatina 306, 00179, Rome, Italy

Pierluigi Zoccolotti (pierluigi.zoccolotti@uniroma1.it)
Department of Psychology, University of Rome "La Sapienza", via dei Marsi 78, 00176, Rome, Italy
and Neuropsychological Unit, IRCCS Fondazione Santa Lucia, via Ardeatina 306, 00179, Rome, Italy

Cristina Burani (cristina.burani@istc.cnr.it)
Institute for Cognitive Sciences and Technologies (ISTC-CNR). Via S. Martino della Battaglia 44, 00185, Rome, Italy

Introduction

Italian is a language with transparent orthography, characterised by an almost one-to-one grapheme-to-phoneme correspondence, yet it has been demonstrated that Italian proficient readers do employ lexical reading. Developmental dyslexics show a marked length effect, interpreted as over-reliance on the sub-lexical reading route. With four experiments on a group of 17 dyslexic children and a group of 17 normally developing readers, using both reading aloud and visual lexical decision tasks, we aim to challenge this view.

Lexicality (words read faster and more accurately than nonwords) and word frequency effects (high frequency words read faster and more accurately than low frequency words) for Italian developmental dyslexics would indicate that they have access to the mental lexicon similarly to proficient readers. The first two experiments investigate the effects of lexicality testing reading and lexical decision on high and low frequency short words and nonwords. In the third and fourth experiments, we manipulated word frequency and length in an orthogonal design in order to investigate the independence of frequency effects from length and assess whether and to what extent lexical reading is available to Italian developmental dyslexics.

The experiments

Following previous findings for Italian proficient readers, the results showed that both high and low frequency words were named faster and more accurately than nonwords by both participating groups. Similarly, words were decided faster and more accurately than nonwords and high frequency words faster than low frequency words by both controls and dyslexics. Lexicality effects for both high and low frequency words demonstrate that Italian developmental dyslexics employ lexical reading similarly to proficient readers.

The next set of experiments showed that the effect of frequency was present for both groups. High frequency words were named faster and more accurately than low frequency words by both groups. However, only the dyslexics showed a marked length effect. The effect of frequency was also present in the lexical decision task for both groups, but the effect of length was present for the dyslexics only.

Conclusions

The aim of our study was to investigate in a systematic way whether Italian developmental dyslexic readers rely prevalently on the nonlexical route. Even though the fact that dyslexic readers make use of the lexical route in reading does not necessarily mean that the sub-lexical route is completely inactive, the effects of lexicality and frequency point to lexical reading for Italian dyslexics, contrary to previous interpretations for over-reliance on the nonlexical reading procedure. In the lexical decision task the dyslexics showed a strong length effect, regardless of word frequency, that may indicate use of the sub-lexical route to access the lexicon. Yet, it could be hypothesised that there is an additional locus for the length effect, possibly on a visual-attentional component of processing prior to the activation of the two reading routes. Such an interpretation is supported by the fact that the length effect is also present in lexical decision, a task that does not require overt phonological output. It must be acknowledged that children with reading difficulty do no represent a homogeneous population. In particular, it is conceivable that length effects arise at different levels in different children. Based on inspection of individual experimental and clinical data, we were not able to detect any systematic individual pattern in this respect and this question remains open to future investigation.

Effects of Sentence Context on Lexical Ambiguity Resolution in Patients with Schizophrenia

Christina Andreou (chrandre@auth.gr)
1st Department of Psychiatry, Aristotle University of Thessaloniki
Al. Svolou 57, 54621 Thessaloniki, Greece
Kyrana Tsapkini (tsapkini@psy.auth.gr)
Department of Psychology, Aristotle University of Thessaloniki
54124 Thessaloniki, Greece
Athanasios Karavatos (karath@med.auth.gr)
1st Department of Psychiatry, Aristotle University of Thessaloniki
K. Palama 21, 55133 Thessaloniki, Greece

Introduction

It has been suggested that context information-processing failures may account for the variable clinical manifestations and cognitive impairments observed in schizophrenia (Servan-Schreiber, Cohen, & Steingard, 1996). In the domain of language, context processing in schizophrenia has been investigated mostly with single-word semantic priming paradigms (e.g. Moritz et al., 2001); however, natural language comprehension depends on more than semantic relations between words. So far, studies of sentence context effects on meaning activation in patients with schizophrenia have reached divergent conclusions (e.g. Bazin et al., 2000; Titone, Levy, & Holzman, 2000). The present study aimed to systematically assess context effects on lexical ambiguity resolution in patients with schizophrenia.

Method

A cross-modal primed lexical decision task was used. Primes were sentences biasing the dominant, subordinate or neither meaning of a sentence-final homonym; balanced homonyms were used in order to minimize effects of relative frequency. Control sentences were constructed by replacing the homonym in each sentence set with a control word, while keeping all other elements of the sentence identical. Targets were related either to the dominant (i.e. slightly more frequent) or to the subordinate meaning of the homonym.

Participants included 14 stable outpatients diagnosed with schizophrenia according to DSM-IV criteria and 14 normal controls matched to the patients on sex, age, education and parental education. Participants were tested in 6 sessions over 2-3 months, in order to minimize repetition effects.

A 4-way repeated measures ANOVA was carried out on priming effects across items, with Group, Sentence Context, Target Type and ISI (0 msec vs 750 msec) as dependent variables. Priming effects were calculated as the percentage decrease of RT in the related (i.e. homonym-bearing) sentence in comparison to the control sentence in each condition, in order to adjust for the slower overall reaction times of patients in comparison to control subjects.

Results

There was a significant main effect of Group, with schizophrenia patients exhibiting less priming than control subjects. Group significantly interacted with Sentence Context; planned pairwise comparisons of priming effects collapsed across Target Type and ISI showed that patients exhibited similar priming to control subjects following subordinate meaning-biased and unbiased contexts, but significantly less priming following dominant meaning-biased contexts.

Discussion

The use of sentence context for ambiguity resolution appeared impaired in patients with schizophrenia –but not uniformly, as the performance of patients was differentially affected according to the type of context bias. The most plausible explanation for our findings is that some aspect of dominant sentence contexts was particularly difficult to process by subjects with schizophrenia in this study; further analyses of the data are under way to clarify this point.

References

Bazin, N., Perruchet, P., Hardy-Bayle, M.C., & Feline, A. (2000). Context-dependent information processing in patients with schizophrenia. *Schizophrenia Research, 45,* 93-101.

Moritz, S., Mersmann, K., Kloss, M., Jacobsen, D., Andresen, B., Krausz, M., Pawlik, K., & Naber, D. (2001). Enhanced semantic priming in thought-disordered schizophrenic patients using a word pronunciation task. *Schizophrenia Research, 48,* 301-305.

Servan-Schreiber, D., Cohen, J.D., & Steingard, S. (1996). Schizophrenic deficits in the processing of context. *Archives of General Psychiatry, 55,* 186-188.

Titone, D., Levy, D.L., & Holzman, P.S. (2000). Contextual insensitivity in schizophrenic language processing: Evidence from lexical ambiguity. *Journal of Abnormal Psychology, 109,* 761-767.

Length effects on reaction times and ocular fixations in reading: A study on French dyslexic and skilled readers

Lallier Marie* (marie.lallier@upmf-grenoble.fr)
Lassus Delphine* (D.Lassus@chu-grenoble.fr)
Valdois Sylviane* (sylviane.valdois@upmf-grenoble.fr)
*Laboratoire de Psychologie et Neurocognition, Université Pierre Mendès France
BP 47, 38040 Grenoble Cedex 9, FRANCE

Introduction

Previous experimental studies showed that reaction times and number of ocular fixations in reading increased according to item length for pseudo-words but not for words in skilled readers and for both types of items in dyslexics (Juphard et al., 2001; De Luca et al., 2002).

Both dual route models (Coltheart et al., 2001) and the connectionist multi-trace model (Ans et al., 1998) assume the existence of two reading procedures (analytic and global) which could account for these length effects more straightforwardly than PDP connectionist models (Plaut, 1998). Indeed, length effects are viewed as resulting from the use of the analytic reading procedure through the sequential processing of grapheme-phoneme conversion rules in the dual route models, and through visual attentional recaptures in the multitrace model (Valdois et al., 2006). This latter model makes the particular assumption that syllable length effects should be observed regarding reaction times as well as number of fixations in reading. These effects should be stronger and should extend to familiar words in the context of developmental dyslexia.

Methods and results

In a first experiment, the naming reaction times of 12 French skilled readers and 12 dyslexic readers were analyzed according to the lexicality (words vs pseudo-words) and length (1, 2 or 3 syllables) of the items. The results showed syllable length effects for pseudo-words only in skilled readers whereas length effects were also found for words in the dyslexic participants (see fig.1). In a second experiment conducted on 21 skilled readers and 10 dyslexic adults, length effects on fixation number were obtained for both words and pseudo-words in skilled readers as in dyslexics. However, length effect on naming latencies was stronger for pseudo-words than for words in skilled readers only.

Discussion and conclusion

The current findings show that French dyslexic readers show syllable length effects in reading whatever the familiarity of the items to be processed. These results replicate those previously reported in other languages, like English, Italian or German. They suggest a preferential use of the analytic reading procedure in the context of

developmental dyslexia. In contrast, the absence of length effect on naming latencies in skilled readers and evidence for a stronger length effect on fixation number for pseudo-words than for words suggests that they rely on different analytic and global reading procedures according to the familiarity of the item to be read.

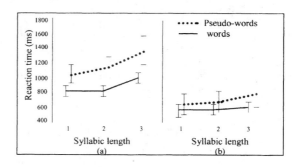

Figure 1: Length effects in dyslexics (a) and skilled readers (b) on naming reaction times

References

Ans, B., Carbonnel, S., & Valdois, S. (1998). A connectionist multiple-trace memory model for polysyllabic word reading. *Psychological Review, 105*, 678-723.

Coltheart, M., Rastle, K., Perry, C., Langdon, R., & Ziegler, J. (2001). DCR: A Dual Route Cascaded Model of Visual Word Recognition and Reading Aloud. *Psychological Review, 108*, 204-256.

De Luca, M., Borrelli, M., Judica, A., Spinelli, D. & Zoccolotti, P. (2002). Reading Words and Pseudowords: An Eye Movement Study of Developmental Dyslexia. *Brain and Language, 80*, 617-626.

Juphard, A., Carbonnel, S., & Valdois, S. (2004). Length effect in reading and lexical decision: Evidence from skilled readers and a developmental dyslexic participant, *Brain and Cognition, 55*, 332-340.

Plaut, D.C. (1998). A connectionist approach to word reading and acquired dyslexia: Extension to sequential processing. *Cognitive Science*, 23, 543-568.

Valdois, S., Juphard, A., Baciu, M., Ans, B., Peyrin, C., Segebarth, C. & Carbonnel, S. (2006). Differential length effect in reading and lexical decision: convergent evidence from behavioural data, connectionist simulations and functional MRI. *Brain Research*, 1085, 1, 149-162.

Event-related brain potentials elicited by verbal mood anomalies in Spanish

Josep Demestre & José E. García-Albea (josep.demestre@urv.net; jegarcia.albea@urv.net)
Departament de Psicologia, Universitat Rovira i Virgili
Ctra. de Valls, s/n, Tarragona, 43007, SPAIN

Brain Responses to Syntactic Anomalies

Over the last two decades the understanding of language mechanisms has been greatly improved following the application of event-related brain potentials (ERPs) to paradigms which have used different kinds of linguistic anomalies (semantic or syntactic ones) within sentences. In the syntactic domain, the study of violations (such as phrase-structure violations, gender and number agreement violations, subcategorization violations, and case violations) has provided valuable information concerning the time at which different sources of information exert their influence during language comprehension. There are two major syntax-related ERP components: (1) an (early) left anterior negativity, mostly associated with phrase-structure, word-category and morphosyntactic violations, and (2) a late centro-parietal positive component, called P600 or syntactic positive shift (SPS), observed in response to a greater variety of syntactic phenomena (including syntactic violations and garden-path sentences).

The Present Study

This study aimed to examine the responses elicited by mood anomalies in Spanish to further study the role of verb-specific information in the early stages of parsing. The information we studied is the mood constraints a matrix verb imposes on the subordinate verb. Since subcategorization for a subjunctive (or indicative) sentence complement (SC) is assumed to be a lexical property of verbs, the role of lexical information in parsing can be studied in a novel way by examining the (rapid or late) detection of mood anomalies.

The anomalies were created by using (1) verbs that subcategorize for a subjunctive-SC and verbs that subcategorize for an indicative-SC, and (2) by manipulating the mood (subjunctive/indicative) of the SC. Thus, in ungrammatical sentences the subordinate verb did not satisfy the mood constraints imposed by the matrix verb. Subjects read sentences such as those in (1). Whereas verbs such as "aconsejar" (to advise) in (1a-1b) obligatorily require the subjunctive in the SC, verbs such as "prometer" (to promise) in (1c-1d) obligatorily require the indicative. In (1a) and (1c) the subordinate verb is in the mood required by the matrix verb. In (1b) and (1d) the subordinate verb is not in the mood required by the matrix verb. In order to detect the anomalies the parser needs to access the mood constraints stored at the lexical entry of the matrix verb.

Since the anomalies we examined do not imply phrase-structure or word category violations, we expected to observe a P600 effect in response to verbs that did not satisfy the mood requirements of the matrix verb.

Method

Participants. 20 Psychology students.

Materials. 120 quartets of sentences were constructed.

(1a) María le ha aconsejado a Pedro$_i$ que (pro$_i$) llegue (subjunctive) antes de las diez
[Mary has advised Peter$_i$ that (pro$_i$) arrive (subjunctive) before ten o'clock]

(1b) * María le ha aconsejado a Pedro$_i$ que (pro$_i$) llegará (indicative) antes de las diez

(1c) María$_i$ le ha prometido a Pedro que (pro$_i$) llegará (indicative) antes de las diez
[Mary$_i$ has promised Peter that (pro$_i$) arrive (indicative) before ten o'clock]

(1d) * María$_i$ le ha prometido a Pedro que (pro$_i$) llegue (subjunctive) antes de las diez

Procedure and EEG recording. Sentences were presented word-by-word; words were presented for 400 ms with an ISI of 300 ms. The EEG was recorded from 11 scalp locations. Bandpass between 0.01 and 40 Hz.

Results

The results clearly showed that the ERPs elicited by the ungrammatical verbs were reliably distinct from the ones elicited by their grammatical counterparts. In both types of matrix verbs, ungrammatical subordinate verbs elicited a robust P600, starting at approximately 500 msec and with a peak amplitude at around 600 msec after the onset of the subordinate verb. The P600 was widely distributed over central and posteriors regions of both hemispheres.

Conclusion

The data show that the parser is sensitive to mood anomalies, and that the anomalies are detected at the first possible word (the subordinate verb). This indicates that (at the critical word) mood information is available to the processor, and that it is used to assess the mood of the critical verb. This finding is in accordance with the claim – made by lexicalist parsing models– that lexical information plays a crucial role in the early stages of parsing. The next question we will address is whether mood information becomes available as soon as the main verb is recognized.

Acknowledgments

The present research was partially supported by project grant (BSO2003-04854) from the Spanish Ministry of Science and Technology.

Semantic priming effects on event-related potentials for living and nonliving categories

Olga P. Marchenko (domains1@rambler.ru)
Institute of Psychology, Russian Academy of Sciences
13, Yaroslavskaya St., Moscow, 129366, Russia

Boris N. Bezdenezhnykh (bezbornik@psychol.ras.ru)
Institute of Psychology, Russian Academy of Sciences
13, Yaroslavskaya St., Moscow, 129366, Russia

Caramazza and Shelton hypothesized that the animate and inanimate conceptual categories represent evolutionarily adapted domain-specific knowledge systems that are subserved by distinct neural mechanisms (Caramazza & Shelton, 1998).

The aim of the study was to test whether or not there are differences in semantic priming effect for living and nonliving categories.

Method

Thirty right-handed undergraduate students participated in the experiment. Every trial consisted of two words (prime and target). Different living and nonliving categories were used. Name of living or nonliving category appeared as prime event in a random order. Names of different items of living or nonliving categories appeared as a target in a random order.

Subjects were asked to indicate if the target was of the category represented by the word prime. They were required to respond as fast and as accurately as possible. Words presented consecutively in the center of a monitor. Trials presented with SOA (stimulus onset asynchrony) of 700ms between prime and target. Prime words presented for 200ms. Event-related potentials (ERPs) were recorded while subjects performed the task.

Results

Results were analyzed using one-way ANOVA. Reaction times and error rates were different in situations, when target was of the semantic category represented by the prime and when it was of another category. Subjects responded more quickly and more accurately to related targets than to unrelated ($p < .0001$).

The amplitude of N200 was attenuated for related words. The amplitude of P300 was enhanced for related words. Latency of P300 was shorter for related targets than for unrelated ($p < .001$).

This effect was different for living and nonliving categories. Reactions to words from living categories were faster than to words from nonliving categories in positive condition ($p < .0001$). It was easer for subjects to perform task for living categories. They were less accurate in their responses to the targets of nonliving categories.

ERP patterns were different for living and nonliving categories. There were some differences in amplitudes of N200 and P300. Differences in amplitudes between positive and negative conditions were more evident for living categories than for nonliving. Behavioral priming effect for living categories was greater too ($p < .001$).

ERP patterns for primes of living and nonliving categories were also different.

It can be presupposed that living and nonliving domains are different in many aspects. For example knowledge of living domain is faster activated than knowledge of nonliving domain (Kiefer, 2005). These domains can have different morphological organization and different ontogenetical and phylogenetical history of development.

That is why certain differences in priming effects on living and nonliving domains are evident.

Acknowledgments

This research was supported by Russian Foundation for Humanities (grant 05-06-06055a, 06-06-00318a), by grant of the President of Russian Federation for research schools support № SS-4455.2006.6 and federal contract from 9.06.06 № 02. 445.11.7441

References

Anderson, J.E, Holcomb, P.J. (1995) Auditory and visual semantic priming using different stimulus onset asynchronies: an event-related brain potential study. *Psychophysiology, 32,* 177-90.

Caramazza, A. & Shelton, J.R. (1998) Domain specific knowledge systems in the brain: the animate-inanimate distinction. *Journal of Cognitive Neuroscience, 10,* 1–34.

Damasio, H., Tranel, D., Grabowski, T., Adolphs, R., Damasio, A. (2004) Neural systems behind word and concept retrieval. *Cognition, 92,* 179-229.

Kiefer, M. (2005) Repetition-priming modulates category-related effects on event-related potentials: further evidence for multiple cortical semantic systems. *Journal of Cognitive Neuroscience, 17,* 199-210.

Pulvermüller, F. (2005) Brain mechanisms linking language and action. *Nature, 6,* 576-581.

Wolff, P., Medin, D.L., Pankratz, C. (1999) Evolution and devolution of folkbiological knowledge. *Cognition, 73,* 177-204.

Differential cortical activity for visual stimuli at near and far space: a MEG study

Areti Tzelepi (areti@iccs.gr)
Styliani Xanthi (xanthigerman@in.gr)
Aggelos Amditis (a.amditis@iccs.gr)
I-sense group, ICCS, National Technical University of Athens
Polytechnic Campus - DECE, 15773, Athens, Greece
Stella Vosniadou (svosniad@phs.uoa.gr)
Cognitive Science and Educational Technol. Lab, Dept of Philosophy and History of Science,
University Campus 15771, Athens, Greece
Zoi Kapoula (zoi.kapoula@college-de-france.fr)
LPPA, CNRS-College de France
11, place Marcelin Berthelot, 75005 Paris, France

Introduction

Evidence from clinical, neuroimaging and psychophysical studies have supported a different functional significance for perception and action in far and near. Near, or peripersonal space encompasses the visual world within arm reach; far or extrapersonal space lies beyond this limit. Patients with neglect have demonstrated selective impairment in spatial tasks performed either at near, or far space. The overall pattern of results in these studies suggested that the ventral visual system in primarily involved in attending to and acting in far space, while the dorsal visual system is primarily involved in attending to and acting in near space. In this study, we examined the distribution of cortical activity when subjects performed a simple spatial detection task at a near (30 cm) and a far distance (90 cm). We compared this activity with the corresponding one when subjects viewed the same stimuli passively (i.e. without attending to a particular feature) at a near and a far distance. We used MEG (Magnetoencephalography) which offers temporal resolution at a millisecond scale and sufficient spatial resolution.

Methods

Nine healthy subjects participated in the study. The stimuli consisted of four circles, each one subtending $1.2°$, and placed at $10°$ on the left, right, up, and down from a central fixation cross. In the passive condition, the stimuli appeared in an on-off mode and subjects had to maintain fixation at the central fixation cross. In the active condition, one of the circles was replaced by a triangle and subjects had to locate it and make a saccade to that location after 1.9 sec. MEG activity was recorded with a whole head MEG system (151 sensors, CTF Canada). The anatomical MRI scan was acquired and 3-D reconstruction of the head and cortical surface was carried out for each subject. Each subject's cortical surface was separated into 46 distinct areas, according to the anatomical location of the gyri. For each cortical area an activation curve (ACV) was computed based on the maximum operator applied to the instantaneous

currents source estimates. Our results are based on the ACVs from the MEG trials averaged on stimulus onset.

Results and Discussion

Modulation of brain activity according to distance, near or far, was different when subjects viewed passively versus when subjects attended to the stimulus. In the passive condition occipital activity was higher for near than for far stimuli in 140-190 ms, and posterior temporal activity was higher for far than for near stimuli in 190-240 ms (Figure 1).

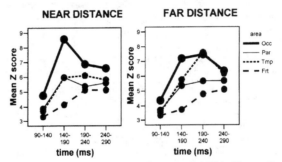

Figure 1: Mean Z scores of averaged ACVs (from all subjects) in time intervals of 50 ms (90-140, 140-190, 190-240, 240-290) over Occ (occipital), Par (Parietal), Tmp (Temporal), and Frt (Frontal) areas for Near and Far stimuli.

Brain activity in the attention condition was stronger than in the passive condition for both far and near stimuli, showing that attention modulated the responses, as expected. Moreover, attending to the stimulus appeared rather to diminish the differences of activity in occipital, and inferior temporal areas found in the passive condition.

Our results provide evidence of different visual processing related to presentation of stimuli at near and far when stimuli are presented passively without requiring any response from the subject. More research is required to elucidate the role of vergence in modulating the cortical activity and its possible interactions with different neural pathways.

The Effect of Feedback Type on Brain Activation: Individual Differences in Achievement Goals

Sung-il Kim (sungkim@korea.ac.kr)   **Su-Young Hwang (sueissun@korea.ac.kr)**

Department of Education, Korea University
Anam-Dong 5 Ga, Seongbuk-gu, Seoul 136-701, Korea

Corrective feedback providing specific information about learner's performance affects learner's motivation. If the corrective feedback plays a role of reinforcement such as monetary rewards, it can overcome the side effects of external rewards undermining the learner's intrinsic motivation. The goal of this study is to investigate how two types of feedback activate the specific brain regions known as reward-sensitive regions. In addition, the individual difference in neural activation was examined depending on the achievement goal orientation. Since the orbitofrontal cortex (OFC) and the ventral striatum have consistently been reported in the numerous functional neuroimaging studies on reward, these regions were selected as ROIs (region of interest) in this study.

Method

Ten healthy right-handed volunteers (6 males and 4 females) with a mean age of 22.3 ± 1.8 years (range 20-25) participated in the study. A bundle of red/blue 'H' and 'T' letters were presented visual screen during one second. The participants performed simple perceptual tasks and received one of the two types of feedback (confirmation feedback and corrective feedback) during scan. Their tasks were to decide whether the target letter 'T' was three or not (T detection task) and whether red stimuli were more than blue (color detection task). All data were preprocessed and performed second level analysis with SPM 99 ($p < .005$ uncorrected).

Results & Discussion

In behavioral data, there was a significant interaction effect on accuracy and reaction time between types of feedback and valence of feedback. The corrective feedback condition showed higher accuracy and faster reaction time than confirmation feedback only when they received negative feedback. The imaging data indicated that both reward-sensitive areas such as OFC and ventral striatum and executive function area such as the DLPFC were activated regardless of valence of feedback when corrective feedbacks were provided (Figure 1). However these areas were not activated with confirmation feedback. In addition, it was found that the activation of different brain regions was correlated with the achievement goal orientation scores. When negative corrective feedback was given, the positive correlation with the performance goal orientation scores was found in the putamen, whereas the positive correlation with the mastery goal orientation scores was found in the ACC

(Figure 2). These findings suggest that corrective feedback can function as reward even if it is a negative feedback, and particularly it might induce learners with mastery goal to monitor their current performance and make plans or strategies for next performance.

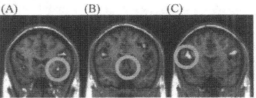

Figure 1: Brain activation of corrective feedback. Right OFC (A), NAcc (B), and DLPFC (C).

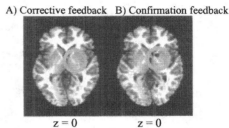
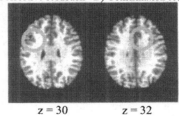

Figure 2: Brain regions related to performance (A & B) and mastery goal orientation (C & D) with negative feedback.

Acknowledgments

This research was supported as a Brain Neuroinformatics Research Program sponsored by Minister of Commerce, Industry and Energy and BK 21.

References

McClure, S. M., Laibson, D. I., Loewensterin, G., and Cohen, J. D. (2004). Separate neural systems value immediate and delayed monetary rewards. *Science*, 306, 503-507.

Top-down attentional modulation of visual neglect following right hemisphere stroke

Margarita Sarri (m.sarri@ucl.ac.uk)
Institute of Cognitive Neuroscience & Department of Psychology,
University College London, 17 Queen Square, London, WC1N 3AR, UK

Jon Driver (j.driver@ucl.ac.uk)
Institute of Cognitive Neuroscience & Department of Psychology,
University College London, 17 Queen Square, London, WC1N 3AR, UK

Visual neglect is a common neurological syndrome after right hemisphere stroke involving loss of awareness and reduced exploration towards the contralesional (left) side of space, even when all primary sensory and motor functions remain intact. Neglect does not invariably affect a fixed portion of space, but instead can be modulated by stimulation and task demands, including apparent attentional factors.

Cancellation tasks are often used in clinical practice to assess spatial exploratory behavior in such patients. Most often they are administered as paper and pencil tests and require patients to search visually for identifiable target items in an array and to mark these with a pen, without explicit time constraints. Different versions of clinical cancellation tasks can reveal different degrees of neglect in the same patient, possibly due to variations in the attentional demands, although different versions typically vary in both top-down and bottom-up ways (e.g. Aglioti, Smania, Barbieri & Corbetta 1997; Gauthier, Dehaut & Joanette, 1989; Husain & Kennard, 1997).

Here we describe three cancellation experiments using overall 16 patients in which we manipulated solely 'top-down' attentional factors in different versions of a cancellation-task, while always keeping visual displays identical across conditions. In each experiment, patients were asked to cancel target items (as defined by task goal) in a visual display. In Experiment 1, we show that the level of difficulty for the required target discrimination (judging overall shape [circle or cross] vs. a fine shape detail [presence or absence of a small gap]) for the same stimulus displays can dramatically modulate neglect performance (see Figure 1, E1). In Experiment 2, we show that increasing judgment difficulty for every item in the display (by now asking patients to point to each item in the display and make a shape or a gap/no-gap judgment for every single one) can increase the number of contralesional omissions, even when no target selection process is required (see Figure 1, E2); but neglect can be more severe when attention has to be selectively directed to specific targets among non-targets. Finally, in Experiment 3 we investigate the possible effects of shifting attention from a more 'global' to a more 'local' level of discrimination, which has been suggested to be a crucial factor in visual neglect (e.g. Halligan & Marshall, 1995). We show that while this may have some effect (by asking patients to selectively cancel targets based on colour vs. fine colour shade, therefore requiring judgments varying

in difficulty but involving the same spatial scale), it is not a necessary condition for neglect to be exacerbated by discrimination difficulty (see Figure 1, E3). Our results overall show that top-down, goal-defined attentional demands can have a major impact on neglect performance in cancellation, with increasing demands on visual attention adversely affecting exploration towards the contralesional side of space.

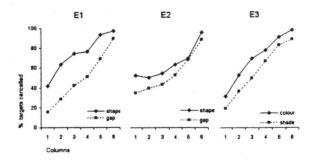

Figure 1: % of target items cancelled per condition and per column of cancellation page (1 being the leftmost and 6 being the rightmost) for each of experiments 1, 2 and 3.

Acknowledgments

This research was funded by a Wellcome Trust programme grant to JD, and a Wellcome Trust prize studentship to MS.

References

Aglioti, S., Smania, N., Barbieri, C., & Corbetta, M. (1997). Influence of stimulus salience and attentional demands on visual search patterns in hemispatial neglect. *Brain and Cognition, 34*(3), 388-403.

Gauthier, L., Dehaut, F., & Joanette, Y. (1989). The bells test, a quantitative and qualitative test for visual neglect. *International Journal of Clinical Neuropsychology, 11*, 49-54.

Husain, M., & Kennard, C. (1997). Distractor-dependent frontal neglect. *Neuropsychologia, 35*, 829±841.

Marshall, J. C., & Halligan, P. W. (1995). Seeing the forest but only half the trees? *Nature, 373*, 521-523.

Memory and ERP Effects of Distance in Semantic Space

Petter Kallioinen (petter.kallioinen@lucs.lu.se)
Lund University Cognitive Science
Kungshuset, Lundagrd, 222 22 Lund, SWEDEN

Sverker Sikstrm (sverker.sikstrom@lucs.lu.se)
Lund University Cognitive Science

Introduction

Pre-existing semantic relations and associations among items supposedly enhance memory. Closer semantic relatedness among common words than among rare words has been invoked as an explanation of word frequency effects in recall (e.g., Deese, 1957; Gregg, Montgomery, & Castao, 1980; Hulme, Stuart, Brown, & Morin, 2003.). Control of semantic relatedness and associations are difficult to achieve without extensive collection of association norms. Latent Semantic Analysis (LSA, see Landauer, & Dumais, 1997), may provide a tool to achieve semantic control of word-stimuli and could also be seen as a model of semantic memory. LSA creates a semantic space based on co-occurrence of words in a corpus. The dimensions of the original matrix of co-occurencies are reduced, with singular value decomposition, to a number that perform optimally on a synonym test. The result is a semantic space were distance is a measure of semantic relatedness. N400 is a negative central deflection in ERPs reflecting difficulty of semantic integration (Hinojosa, Martn-Loeches, & Rubia, 2001). If semantic control with LSA is successful N400 is expected to be larger for words with longer distances in LSA-space to the previous word. In this poster behavioral and electrophysiological effects of semantic relatedness, as measured with LSA, are presented.

Method

In the present experiment 29 students studied 42 sequences of 6 words and were tested with free recall after each list. ERPs were measured during encoding. There were three semantic conditions in the experiment, controlled high semantic relatedness (HS), controlled low semantic relatedness (LS) and not controlled semantic relatedness (NS). Nouns were extracted from Stockholm-Ume-Corpus (SUC), a balanced corpus of 1 million swedish words. Lists of semantically related words and lists of unrelated words were created based on distance in LSA-space measured as cosine between word vectors.

Results

Recall was superior for HS words and followed semantic relatedness in the expecetd pattern: HS>NS>LS. However the difference between HS and NS was larger than the difference between NS and LS. This dissociates behavioral and electrophysiological results: amplitude of N400 was similar for HS and NS but larger for LS.

Discussion

The results show that the three conditions, based on control with LSA, are dissociated behaviorally and eletrophysiologically in expected ways. LSA-space thus seem to reflect some relevant aspects of semantics or, if you will, model aspects of semantic memory. Both theoretical discussion (about among other things distributions in different semantic models) and this kind of empirical investigations are needed to evaluate LSA as a tool and a model in cognitive neuroscience.

References

Deese, J. (1959). Influence of inter-item associative strength upon immediate free recall., *Psychological Reports, 5,* 305–312.

Gregg, V. H., Montgomery, D. C., & Castao, D. (1980). Recall of common and uncommon words from pure and mixed lists. *Journal of Verbal Learning and Verbal Behavior, 19,* 240–245.

Hinojosa, J. A., Martn-Loeches, M., & Rubia, F. J. (2001). Event-related potentials and semantics: An overview and an integrative proposal. *Brain and Language, 78,, 6,* 128–139.

Hulme, C., Stuart, G., Brown, G. & Morin, C. (2003) High- and low-frequency words are recalled equally well in alternating lists: Evidence for associative effects in serial recall. *Journal of Memory and Language, 49,* 500–518.

Landauer, T. K. & Dumais, S. T. (1997), Solution to Plato's Problem: The Latent Semantic Analysis Theory of Acquisition, Induction and Representation of Knowledge. *JPsychological Review, 104 (2),* 211–240.

Pragmatic Understanding of Hyperbole Trough Interpreting Proverbs and Metonymies

Afroditi B. Papaioannou (afropapai@yahoo.com)

Department of Philosophy and History of Science, Graduate Program in Basic and Applied Cognitive Science, University of Athens, 15771, Athens, GREECE

Introduction

Present research investigated pragmatic competence of hyperbole performed through proverbs and metonymies in everyday Greek language. Research based on Lawal's theoretical model of pragmatics (1992), the one and only theoretical model related to our research on pragmatic competence and metaphorical speech.

Study 1

Method

In Study 1 were used 23 Greek metaphors (11 proverbs and 12 metonymies) selected from a two thousand proverbs and metonymies base of Greek culture. Their criteria of selection were: i) being hyperboles, ii) used in everyday Greeks' communication, iii) being 'diaphanous'. Its of them evaluated according to Lawal's theoretical model of pragmatics (1992), according to six pragmatic competencies: i) linguistic, ii) situational, iii) psychological, iv) social, v) sociological, vi) cosmological. Through them performed different types of illocutionary acts, direct and indirect.

Results

Evaluation and results revealed that six pragmatic competencies suggested by Lawal (1992) fit with Greeks' complex task of recall in order to understand, interpret, select and use effectively proverbs and metonymies in everyday communication, to identify, understand and use metaphorical language, in general. Furthermore, through them performed different types of illocutionary acts: (a) direct, with most frequent type 'claiming' (78.3%), (b) indirect, with most frequent type 'evaluating' (34.8%).

Study 2

Method

In Study 2 we aimed to research the correlation of different demographic factors ('sex', 'age', 'education') with understanding, interpreting, selecting and using metaphorical meaning. This study concluded two tests, the Proverb Test and the Metonymy Test: a) Proverb Test involved one hundred-eighty, 28-98 year-old Greeks (mean age 61.49, range 70.0). There were 78 men (43.3%) and 101 women (56.1%), residents to different places of Greece, with variances in age and education. Exclusion criteria included Greek as a second language and any history of neurological or psychiatric illness. We gave to the participants the Proverb Test which concluded 11 Greek proverbs from the metaphors we used at Study 1. Participants required to interpret given proverbs and their answers graded with 0-2 points ('0': participant's interpretation was literal or irrelevant with the meaning of the proverb, '1': it was incomplete, '2': it was complete) b) Metonymy Test involved ninety-eight, 18-91 year-old Greeks (mean age 47.99, range 73.0). There were 47 men (48.0%) and 51 women (52.0%), residents to different places of Greece, with variances in age and education. Exclusion criteria were common to those at Proverb Test. We gave to the participants the Metonymy Test which concluded 12 incomplete scripts. Every script could be right completed with a metonymy from those we used at Study 1. Participants required to complete these scripts by choosing one of the four answers given for each script. One of them was metonymy and the right end for the script, as well. Participant's answers categorized from 1-4 ('1': participant's selection was equivalent to 'literal', '2': to 'irrelevant-literal', '3': to 'relevant-metaphorical', '4': to 'metaphorical-right').

Results

Demographic factors don't seem to effect on understanding, interpreting, selecting and using hyperbole.

References

Colston, H.L., & O'Brien, J. (2000a). Contrast and pragmatics in figurative language: Anything understatement can do, irony can do better. *Journal of Pragmatics, 32*, 1557-1583.

Colston, H.L., & O'Brien, J. (2000b). Contrast of Kind Versus Contrast of Magnitude: The Pragmatic Accomplishments of Irony and Hyperbole. *Discourse Processes, 30*, 179-199.

Kreuz, R.J. *et al.* (1996). Figurative Language Occurrence and Co-occurrence in Contemporary Literature. In: Kreuz, R. J. & MacNealy, Mary Sue (ed.), *Empirical Approaches to Literature and Aesthetics.* Norwood, NJ: Ablex (pp. 83-97).

Lawal, R.A. (1992). English language and patriarchal view. *Savanna, 13 (2)*, 74-79.

Author Index